Features

Visit us on the Web at
http://www.census.gov/statab/www/

D1444161

Statistical Abstract of the United States: 2001

121st edition

The National Data Book

Issued November 2001

U.S. Department of Commerce
Donald L. Evans,
Secretary

Economics and Statistics
Administration
Kathleen B. Cooper,
Under Secretary for Economic Affairs

U.S. CENSUS BUREAU
William G. Barron, Jr.,
Acting Director

SUGGESTED CITATION

U.S. Census Bureau,
Statistical Abstract of the United States: 2001
(121st edition)
Washington, DC, 2001

Library of Congress
Card No. 4-18089

ECONOMICS
AND STATISTICS
ADMINISTRATION

**Economics
and Statistics
Administration**

Kathleen B. Cooper,
Under Secretary
for Economic Affairs

U.S. CENSUS BUREAU

William G. Barron, Jr.,
Acting Director

William G. Barron, Jr.,
Deputy Director

Nancy A. Potok,
Principal Associate Director
and Chief Financial Officer

Ted A. Johnson, Associate Director
for Finance and Administration

Walter C. Odom, Chief, Administrative
and Customer Services Division

Acknowledgments

Lars B. Johanson was responsible for the technical supervision and coordination of this volume under the general direction of **Glenn W. King,** Chief, Statistical Compendia Branch. Assisting in the research and analytical phases of assigned sections and in the developmental aspects of new tables were **Rosemary E. Clark, Edward C. Jagers, David J. Fleck,** and **Stacey M. Lowe. Catherine Lavender** and **Joyce Mori** provided primary editorial assistance. Other editorial assistance was rendered by **Kristen Iversen, Patricia S. Lancaster, Barbara Shugart,** and **Daphanie Smallwood.**

Barry Hill, Penny Heiston, Gloria Davis, Shirley Clark, Kevin Proctor, and **Arlene C. Butler** of the Administrative and Customer Services Division, **Walter C. Odom,** Chief, provided publications and printing management, graphics design and composition, and editorial review for print and electronic media. General direction and production management were provided by **Michael G. Garland,** Assistant Chief, and **Gary J. Lauffer,** Chief, Publications Services Branch.

The cooperation of many contributors to this volume is gratefully acknowledged. The source note below each table credits the various government and private agencies that have collaborated in furnishing information for the *Statistical Abstract*. In a few instances, contributors have requested that their data be designated as subject to copyright restrictions, as indicated in the source notes to the tables affected. Permission to use copyright material should be obtained directly from the copyright owner.

For sale by Superintendent of Documents, U.S. Government Printing Office
Internet: bookstore.gpo.gov; Phone: toll-free 1-866-512-1800;
DC area 202-512-1800; Fax: 202-512-2250; Mail: Stop SSOP
Washington, DC 20402-0001

For sale by the U.S. Government Printing Office
Superintendent of Documents, Mail Stop: SSOP, Washington, DC 20402-9328
ISBN 0-16-042805-X

Preface

The *Statistical Abstract of the United States,* published since 1878, is the standard summary of statistics on the social, political, and economic organization of the United States. It is designed to serve as a convenient volume for statistical reference and as a guide to other statistical publications and sources. The latter function is served by the introductory text to each section, the source note appearing below each table, and Appendix I, which comprises the Guide to Sources of Statistics, the Guide to State Statistical Abstracts, and the Guide to Foreign Statistical Abstracts.

This volume includes a selection of data from many statistical publications, both government and private. Publications cited as sources usually contain additional statistical detail and more comprehensive discussions of definitions and concepts than can be presented here. Data not available in publications issued by the contributing agency but obtained from unpublished records are identified in the source notes as unpublished data. More information on the subjects covered in the tables so noted may generally be obtained from the source.

Except as indicated, figures are for the United States as presently constituted. Although emphasis in the *Statistical Abstract* is primarily given to national data, many tables present data for regions and individual states and a smaller number for metropolitan areas and cities. Appendix II, Metropolitan Area Concepts and Components, presents explanatory text, a complete current listing and population data for metropolitan statistical areas (MSAs), the primary metropolitan statistical areas (PMSAs), and the consolidated metropolitan statistical areas (CMSAs) defined as of June 30, 1999. Table 31, in Section 1, presents selected population characteristics for MSAs with population of 250,000 or more. Statistics for the Commonwealth of Puerto Rico and for outlying areas of the United States are included in many state tables and are supplemented by information in Section 29. Additional information for states, cities, counties, metropolitan areas, and other small units, as well as more historical data are available in various supplements to the *Abstract* (see inside back cover).

Statistics in this edition are generally for the most recent year or period available by summer 2001. Each year over 1,400 tables and charts are reviewed and evaluated; new tables and charts of current interest are added, continuing series are updated, and less timely data are condensed or eliminated. Text notes and appendices are revised as appropriate.

USA Statistics in Brief, a pocket-size pamphlet highlighting many statistical series in the *Abstract,* is available separately. Single copies can be obtained free from U.S. Census Bureau, Customer Service, Call Center, Washington, DC 20233 (telephone 301-763-INFO(4636). We attempt to update the pamphlet several times during the year. The latest data can be found on our Web site: <http://www.census.gov/statab/www/brief.html>.

Changes in this edition—As frequent users of the *Statistical Abstract* will note, we have altered the presentation of the topical sections. The previous Section 7, Parks, Recreation, and Entertainment, has been eliminated with most of the material now being distributed into the two new sections on Information and Communications, or Arts, Entertainment, and Recreation. The previously separate Sections 21 and 22 on Land Transportation and Air and Water Transportation are now combined into one section on Transportation. Also a new section on Accommodation, Food Services, and Other Services has been developed. In addition, most of the 1997 Economic Census tables appearing in Section 32 of last year's *Abstract* have been distributed to their appropriate sections this year. These changes, along with the changes in the ordering of sections, were made to reflect the changes in collection of economic data from the Standard Industrial Classification (SIC) to the

v

North American Industry Classification System (NAICS). See text, Section 15, Business Enterprise for more information.

As usual we have designed new tables covering a wide range of subject matter. These include several in Sections 1 and 20 from the 2000 Census of Population and Housing; several tables in Section 15 present data form the 1997 Surveys of Minority- and Women-Owned Businesses. We have also greatly expanded the data we present from the *Service Annual Survey.* The topics of some other new tables include national health expenditures, advanced telecommunications in private schools, drivers stopped by police, water quality, temporary assistance for needy families, job search methods, pesticides, pharmaceutical preparations, and E-Commerce. For a complete list of new tables, see Appendix VI, p. 929.

Statistical Abstract on other media— The *Abstract* is available on the Internet and on CD-ROM, an enhanced version (except for a few copyrighted tables deleted by the request of source organizations). Our Internet site, <http://www. census.gov/statab/www>, contains this 2001 edition and earlier editions of the book, as well as summary items— Statistics in Brief, Frequently Requested Tables, and State Rankings, which will be updated as time allows.

The CD-ROM version of the *Abstract* is also available. Information for the CD-ROM is located in the inside back cover.

Statistics for counties and cities— Extensive data for counties can be found in the *County and City Data Book: 2000.* It features 191 data items covering everything from age and agriculture to water use and wholesale trade for all states and counties with U.S. totals for comparison. Also included are 103 data items for cities with population of 25,000 or more. The primary sources are Census 2000 and the 1997 Economic Census. Two tables present 11 data items from Census 2000 for all places and MCDs with a population of 2,500 or more.

This publication, as well as selected rankings will be available on our Internet site

at <http://www.census.gov/statab/ www/ccdb.html>. Some data items that appear in the book from private sources are not available on the Internet or CD-ROM versions because we did not receive copyright permission to release the data items in these formats. For a database with over 5,000 county items, check out USA Counties at <http://www. census.gov/statab/www/county.html>.

Statistics for states and metropolitan areas—Extensive data for the states and metropolitan areas of the United States can be found in the *State and Metropolitan Area Data Book: 1997-98.*

This publication minus some data items, as well as selected rankings of the states and metropolitan areas, is available on our Internet site at <http://www.census. gov/statab/www/smadb.html>. The CD-ROM version is also available. See the inside back cover for more information.

Limitations of the data—The contents of this volume were taken from many sources. All data from either censuses and surveys or from administrative records are subject to error arising from a number of factors: Sampling variability (for statistics based on samples), reporting errors in the data for individual units, incomplete coverage, nonresponse, imputations, and processing error. (See also Appendix III, pp. 903.) The Census Bureau cannot accept the responsibility for the accuracy or limitations of the data presented here, other than those for which it collects. The responsibility for selection of the material and for proper presentation, however, rests with the Census Bureau.

For additional information on data presented—Please consult the source publications available in local libraries or write to the agency indicated in the source notes. Write to the Census Bureau only if it is cited as the source.

Suggestions and comments—Users of the Statistical Abstract and its supplements (see inside back cover) are urged to make their data needs known for consideration in planning future editions. Suggestions and comments for improving coverage and presentation of data should be sent to the Director, U.S. Census Bureau, Washington, DC 20233.

Contents

[Numbers following subjects are page numbers]

U.S. Census Bureau, Statistical Abstract of the United States: 2001

Example of Table Structure

No. 313. Immigration and Naturalization Service Enforcement Activities: 1990 to 1998

[1,169.9 represents 1,169,900. **For fiscal years ending in year shown.** See text, Section 8, State and Local Government Finances and Employment]

Item	Unit	1990	1992	1993	1994	1995	1996	1997	1998
Deportable aliens located	1,000	1,169.9	1,258.5	1,327.3	1,094.7	1,394.6	1,650.0	1,536.5	1,679.4
Border Patrol	1,000	1,103.4	1,199.6	1,263.5	1,031.7	1,324.2	1,549.9	1,413.0	1,555.8
Southwestern border	1,000	(NA)	1,145.6	1,212.9	979.1	1,271.4	1,507.0	1,368.7	1,516.7
Mexican	1,000	1,054.8	1,168.9	1,230.1	999.9	1,293.5	1,523.1	1,387.7	1,522.9
Canadian	1,000	5.7	6.2	5.2	3.4	3.5	2.7	2.9	2.3
Other	1,000	42.8	24.4	28.1	28.4	27.2	24.0	22.4	30.5
Number of seizures by Border Patrol	Number	17,275	11,391	10,995	9,134	9,327	11,129	11,792	14,401
Value of seizures by Border Patrol	Mil. dol.	843.6	1,247.9	1,382.9	1,598.1	2,011.8	1,255.4	1,094.6	1,405.0
Narcotics	Mil. dol.	797.8	1,216.8	1,337.8	1,555.7	1,965.3	1,208.8	1,046.3	1,340.0
Aliens expelled:									
Formal removals [1]	1,000	30.0	43.7	42.5	45.6	50.9	69.6	114.3	172.5
Voluntary departures [2]	1,000	1,022.5	1,105.8	1,243.3	1,029.1	1,313.7	1,573.4	1,440.6	1,569.8

NA Not available.   [1] Include deportations, exclusions, and removals.   [2] Includes aliens under docket control required to depart and voluntary departures not under docket control.

Source: U.S. Immigration and Naturalization Service, *Statistical Yearbook,* annual; and unpublished data.

Headnotes immediately below table titles provide information important for correct interpretation or evaluation of the table as a whole or for a major segment of it.

Footnotes below the bottom rule of tables give information relating to specific items or figures within the table.

Unit indicators show the *specified quantities* in which data items are presented. They are used for two primary reasons. Sometimes data are not available in absolute form and are estimates (as in the case of many surveys). In other cases we round the numbers in order to save space to show more data, as in the case above.

EXAMPLES OF UNIT INDICATOR INTERPRETATION FROM TABLE

Year	Item	Unit Indicator	Number shown	Multiplier
1990	Deportable aliens located	Thousands	1,169.9	1,000
1990	Value of seizures by Border Patrol	$ Millions	843.6	1,000,000

To Determine the Figure It Is Necessary to Multiply the Number Shown by the Unit Indicator:
Deportable aliens located - 1,169.9 x 1,000 = 1,169,900 (over 1 million)
Value of seizures by Border Patrol - 843.6 x $1,000,000 - $843,600,000 (over $843 million).

When a table presents data with more than one unit indicator, they are found in the headnotes and column headings (Tables 2 and 4), spanner (Table 41), stub (Table 28), or unit column (shown above). When the data in a table are shown in the same unit indicator, it is shown in boldface as the first part of the headnote (Table 2). If no unit indicator is shown, data presented are in absolute form (Table 1).

Vertical rules are used to separate independent sections of a table, (Table 1), or in tables where the stub is continued into one or more additional columns (Table 2).

Averages—An average is a single number or value that is often used to represent the "typical value" of a group of numbers. It is regarded as a measure of "location" or "central tendency" of a group of numbers.

The *arithmetic mean* is the type of average used most frequently. It is derived by summing the individual item values of a particular group and dividing the total by the number of items. The arithmetic mean is often referred to as simply the "mean" or "average."

The *median* of a group of numbers is the middle number or value when each item in the group is arranged according to size (lowest to highest or visa versa); it generally has the same number of items above it as well as below it. If there is an even number if items in the group, the median is taken to be the average of the two middle numbers.

Per capita (or per person) quantities. A per capita figure represents an average computed for every person in a specified group (or population). It is derived by taking the total for an item (such as income, taxes, or retail sales) and dividing it by the number of persons in the specified population.

Index numbers—An index number is the measure of difference or change, usually expressed as a percent, relating one quantity (the variable) of a specified kind to another quantity of the same kind. Index numbers are widely used to express changes in prices over periods of time but may also be used to express differences between related subjects for a single point in time.

To compute a price index, a base year or period is selected. The base year price (of the commodity or service) is then designated as the base or reference price to which the prices for other years or periods are related. Many price indexes use the year 1982 as the base year; in tables this is shown as "1982=100." A method of expressing the price relationship is: The price of a set of one or more items for a related year (e.g. 1990) **divided by** the price of the same set of items for the base year (e.g. 1982). The result multiplied by 100 provides the index number. When 100 is subtracted from the index number, the result equals the percent change in price from the base year.

Average annual percent change—
Unless otherwise stated in the *Abstract* (as in Section 1, Population), average annual percent change is computed by use of a *compound interest formula.* This formula assumes that the rate of change is constant throughout a specified compounding period (1 year for average annual rates of change). The formula is similar to that used to compute the balance of a savings account which receives compound interest. According to this formula, at the end of a compounding period the amount of accrued change (e.g. school enrollment or bank interest) is added to the amount which existed at the beginning the period. As a result, over time (e.g., with each year or quarter), the same rate of change is applied to a larger and larger figure.

The *exponential formula,* which is based on continuous compounding, is often used to measure population change. It is preferred by population experts because they view population and population-related subjects as changing without interruption, ever ongoing. Both exponential and compound interest formulas assume a constant rate of change. The former, however, applies the amount of change continuously to the base rather than at the end of each compounding period. When the average annual rates are small (e.g., less than 5 percent) both formulas give virtually the same results. For an explanation of these two formulas as

they relate to population, see U.S. Census Bureau, *The Methods and Materials of Demography,* Vol. 2, 3d printing (rev.), 1975, pp. 372-381.

Current and constant dollars—
Statistics in some tables in a number of sections are expressed in both current and constant dollars (see, for example, Table 652 in Section 13, Income, Expenditures, and Wealth). Current dollar figures reflect actual prices or costs prevailing during the specified year(s). Constant dollar figures are estimates representing an effort to remove the effects of price changes from statistical series reported in dollar terms. In general, constant dollar series are derived by dividing current dollar estimates by the appropriate price index for the appropriate period (for example, the Consumer Price Index). The result is a series as it would presumably exist if prices were the same throughout, as in the base year—in other words as if the dollar had constant purchasing power. Any changes in this constant dollar series would reflect only changes in real volume of output, income, expenditures, or other measure.

Explanation of Symbols

The following symbols, used in the tables throughout this book, are explained in condensed form in footnotes to the tables where they appear:

- Represents zero or rounds to less than half the unit of measurement shown.

B Base figure too small to meet statistical standards for reliability of a derived figure.

D Figure withheld to avoid disclosure pertaining to a specific organization or individual.

NA Data not enumerated, tabulated, or otherwise available separately.

NS Percent change irrelevant or insignificant.

S Figure does not meet publication standards for reasons other than that covered by symbol B, above.

X Figure not applicable because column heading and stub line make entry impossible, absurd, or meaningless.

Z Entry would amount to less than half the unit of measurement shown.

In many tables, details will not add to the totals shown because of rounding.

x   Guide to Tabular Presentation

Telephone & Internet Contacts

To help *Abstract* users find more data and information about statistical publications, we are issuing this list of contacts for federal agencies with major statistical programs. The intent is to give a single, first-contact point-of-entry for users of statistics. These agencies will provide general information on their statistical programs and publications, as well as specific information on how to order their publications. We are also including the Internet (World Wide Web) addresses for many of these agencies. These URLs were current in September 2001.

Executive Office of the President
Office of Management and Budget
Administrator
Office of Information and Regulatory Affairs
Office of Management and Budget
725 17th Street, N.W.
Washington, DC 20503
Information: 202-395-3080
Internet address:
 http://www.whitehouse.gov/omb

Department of Agriculture
Economic Research Service
Information Center
U.S. Department of Agriculture
1800 M St. N.W., Rm. North 3050
Washington, DC 20036-5831
Information and Publications:
 202-694-5050
Internet address:
 http://www.ers.usda.gov/

National Agricultural Statistics Service
National Agricultural Statistics Service
U.S. Department of Agriculture
1400 Independence Ave., S.W.,
 Room 5829
Washington, DC 20250
Information hotline: 1-800-727-9540
Internet address:
 http://www.usda.gov/nass/

Department of Commerce
U.S. Census Bureau
Customer Services Branch
U.S. Census Bureau
U.S. Department of Commerce
Washington, DC 20233
Information and Publications:
 301-763-4636
Internet address:
 http://www.census.gov/

Bureau of Economic Analysis
Bureau of Economic Analysis
U.S. Department of Commerce
Washington, DC 20230
Information and Publications:
 202-606-9900
Internet address:
 http://www.bea.doc.gov/

Department of Commerce —Con.
International Trade Administration
Trade Statistics Division
Office of Trade and Economic Analysis
International Trade Administration
Room 2814 B
U.S. Department of Commerce
Washington, DC 20230
Information and Publications:
 202-482-2185
Internet address:
 http://www.ita.doc.gov/tradestats/

National Oceanic and Atmospheric Administration
National Oceanic and Atmospheric
 Administration Central Library
U.S. Department of Commerce
1315 East-West Highway
2nd Floor
Silver Spring MD 20910
Library: 301-713-2600
Internet address:
 http://www.lib.noaa.gov/

Department of Defense
Department of Defense
Office of the Assistant Secretary of
 Defense (Public Affairs)
Room 3A750
Attention: Directorate for Public
 Communications
1400 Defense Pentagon
Washington, DC 20301-1400
Information: 703-697-5737
Internet address:
 http://web1.whs.osd.mil/diorhome.htm

Department of Education
National Library of Education
U.S. Department of Education
400 Maryland Avenue, S.W.
Washington, DC 20202-5621
Education Information and Statistics
 1-800-424-1616
Education Publications 1-877-433-7827
Internet address: http://www.ed.gov/

Department of Energy

Energy Information Administration

National Energy Information Center
U.S. Department of Energy
1000 Independence Ave., S.W.
1E238-EI-30
Washington, DC 20585
Information and Publications:
202-586-8800
Internet address:
http://www.eia.doe.gov/

Department of Health and Human Services

Health Resources and Services Administration

HRSA Office of Communications
5600 Fishers Lane, Room 14-45
Rockville, MD 20857
Information Center: 301-443-3376
Internet address: http://www.hrsa.gov/

Substance Abuse Mental Health Services Administration

U.S. Department of Health and Human Services
5600 Fishers Lane
Room 12-105
Rockville, MD 20857
Information: 301-443-4795
Publications: 1-800-729-6686
Internet address:
http://www.samhsa.gov/

Centers for Disease Control and Prevention

Office of Public Affairs
1600 Clifton Road, N.E.
Atlanta, GA 30333
Public Inquiries: 1-800-311-3435
Internet address: http://www.cdc.gov/

Centers for Medicare and Medicaid Services (CMS)

Office of Public Affairs
U.S. Department of Health and Human Services
Room 303D, Humphrey Building
200 Independence Ave., S.W.
Washington, DC 20201
Media Relations: 202-690-6145
Internet address: http://www.cms.gov

National Center for Health Statistics

U.S. Department of Health and Human Services - Centers for Disease Control and Prevention
National Center for Health Statistics
Data Dissemination Branch
6525 Belcrest Rd., Rm. 1064
Hyattsville, MD 20782 301-458-INFO
Internet address:
http://www.cdc.gov/nchswww

U.S. Department of Housing and Urban Development

Office of the Assistant Secretary for Community Planning and Development

451 7th St., S.W.
Washington, DC 20410-0555
Information and Publications:
1-800-998-9999
Internet address: http://www.hud.gov/

Department of the Interior

Geological Survey

Earth Science Information Center
Geological Survey
U.S. Department of the Interior
507 National Center
Reston, VA 20192
Information and Publications:
1-888-275-8747
Internet address for minerals:
http://minerals.usgs.gov/
Internet address for other materials:
http://ask.usgs.gov/

Department of Justice

Bureau of Justice Statistics

Statistics Division
810 7th St., N.W. 2nd Floor
Washington, DC 20531
Information and Publications:
202-307-0765
Internet address:
http://www.ojp.usdoj.gov/bjs/

National Criminal Justice Reference Service

Box 6000
Rockville, MD 20849-6000
Information and Publications:
301-519-5500
Publications: 1-800-732-3277
Internet address: http://www.ncjrs.org/

Federal Bureau of Investigation

U.S. Department of Justice
J. Edgar Hoover FBI Building
935 Pennsylvania Ave., N.W.
Washington, DC 20535-0001
202-324-3000
Information and Publications:
202-324-3691
Research and Communications Unit:
202-324-5611
Internet address: http://www.fbi.gov/

Immigration and Naturalization Service

Statistics Branch
Immigration and Naturalization Service
U.S. Department of Justice
425 I St., NW, Rm. 4034
Washington, DC 20536
Information and Publications:
202-305-1613
Internet address:
http://www.ins.gov/graphics/ index.htm

Department of Labor

Bureau of Labor Statistics
Office of Publications and Special Studies
Services
Division of Information
Bureau of Labor Statistics
2 Mass. Ave., N.E., Room 2850
Washington, DC 20212
Information and Publications:
202-691-5200
Internet address: http://www.bls.gov/

Employment and Training Administration
Office of Public Affairs
Employment and Training Administration
U.S. Department of Labor
200 Constitution Ave., N.W.,
Room S4231
Washington, DC 20210
Information and Publications:
202-693-3900
Internet address: http://www.doleta.gov/

Department of Transportation

Federal Aviation Administration
U.S. Department of Transportation
800 Independence Ave., S.W.
Washington, DC 20591
Information and Publications:
202-267-3484
Internet address: http://www.faa.gov/

Bureau of Transportation Statistics
400 7th St., S.W. Room 3430
Washington, DC 20590
Products: 202-366-3282
Statistical Information:800-853-1351
Internet address: http://www.bts.gov/

Federal Highway Administration
Office of Public Affairs
Federal Highway Administration
U.S. Department of Transportation
400 7th St., S.W.
Washington, DC 20590
Information: 202-366-0660
Internet address:
http://www.fhwa.dot.gov/

*National Highway Traffic Safety
Administration*
Office of Public & Consumer Affairs
National Highway Traffic Safety
Administration
U.S. Department of Transportation
400 7th St., S.W.
Washington, DC 20590
Information: 202-366-4000
Publications: 202-366-8892
Internet address:
http://www.nhtsa.dot.gov/

Department of the Treasury

Internal Revenue Service
Statistics of Income Division
Internal Revenue Service
P.O. Box 2608
Washington, DC 20013-2608
Information and Publications:
202-874-0410
Internet address:
http://www.irs.ustreas.gov/cover.html

Department of Veterans Affairs

Office of Public Affairs
Department of Veterans Affairs
810 Vermont Ave., N.W.
Washington, DC 20420
Information: 202-273-5400
Internet address: http://www.va.gov/

Independent Agencies

Administrative Office of the U.S. Courts
Statistics Division
1 Columbus Circle, N.E.
Washington, DC 20544
Information: 202-502-1455
Internet address:
http://www.uscourts.gov/

Environmental Protection Agency
Information Resource Center, Rm. M2904
Environmental Protection Agency
1200 Pennsylvania Ave., N.W.
Mail Code 3201
Washington, DC 20460
Information: 202-260-9152
Internet address: http://www.epa.gov/

Federal Reserve Board
Division of Research and Statistics
Federal Reserve Board
Washington, DC 20551
Information: 202-452-3301
Publications: 202-452-3245
Internet address:
http://www.federalreserve.gov/

National Science Foundation
Office of Legislation and Public Affairs
National Science Foundation
4201 Wilson Boulevard
Arlington, Virginia 22230
Information: 703-292-5111
Publications: 703-292-8129
Internet address: http://www.nsf.gov/

Independent Agencies —Con.

Securities and Exchange Commission

Office of Public Affairs
Securities and Exchange Commission
450 5th St., N.W.
Room 2500
Mail Stop 0213
Washington, DC 20549
Information: 202-942-0020
Publications: 202-942-4040
Internet address: http://www.sec.gov/

Independent Agencies —Con.

Social Security Administation

6400 Security Blvd
Baltimore, MD 21235
Information and Publications:
1-800-772-1213
Internet Address: http://www.ssa.gov/

Section 1

Population

This section presents statistics on the growth, distribution, and characteristics of the U.S. population. The principal source of these data is the U.S. Census Bureau, which conducts a decennial census of population, a monthly population survey, a program of population estimates and projections, and a number of other periodic surveys relating to population characteristics. For a list of relevant publications, see the Guide to Sources of Statistics in Appendix I.

Decennial censuses—The U.S. Constitution provides for a census of the population every 10 years, primarily to establish a basis for apportionment of members of the House of Representatives among the states. For over a century after the first census in 1790, the census organization was a temporary one, created only for each decennial census. In 1902, the Census Bureau was established as a permanent federal agency, responsible for enumerating the population and also for compiling statistics on other population and housing characteristics.

Historically, the enumeration of the population has been a complete count. That is, an attempt is made to account for every person, for each person's residence, and for other characteristics (sex, age, family relationships, etc.). Since the 1940 census, in addition to the complete count information, some data have been obtained from representative samples of the population. In the 1990 and 2000 censuses, variable sampling rates were employed. For most of the country, 1 in every 6 households (about 17 percent) received the long form or sample questionnaire;
in governmental units estimated to have fewer than 2,500 inhabitants, every other household (50 percent) received the sample questionnaire to enhance the reliability of sample data for small areas. Exact agreement is not to be expected between sample data and the 100-percent count. Sample data may be used with confidence where large numbers are involved and assumed to indicate trends and relationships where small numbers are involved.

Census Bureau data presented here have not been adjusted for underenumeration. Results from the evaluation program for the 1990 census indicate that the overall national undercount was between 1 and 2 percent. The estimate from the Post Enumeration Survey (PES) was 1.6 percent, and the estimate from Demographic Analysis (DA) was 1.8 percent. Both the PES and DA estimates show disproportionately high undercounts for some demographic groups. For example, the PES estimates of percent net undercount for Blacks (4.4 percent), Hispanics (5.0 percent), and American Indians (4.5 percent) were higher than the estimated undercount of non-Hispanic Whites (0.7 percent). Historical DA estimates demonstrate that the overall undercount rate in the census has declined significantly over the past 50 years (from an estimated 5.4 percent in 1940 to 1.8 percent in 1990), yet the undercount of Blacks has remained disproportionately high.

Current Population Survey (CPS)—This is a monthly nationwide survey of a scientifically selected sample representing the noninstitutional civilian population. The sample is located in 754 areas comprising 2,121 counties, independent cities, and minor civil divisions with coverage in every state and the District of Columbia and is subject to sampling error. At the present time, about 50,000 occupied households are eligible for interview every month; of these between 4 and 5 percent are, for various reasons, unavailable for interview.

While the primary purpose of the CPS is to obtain monthly statistics on the labor force, it also serves as a vehicle for inquiries on other subjects. Using CPS data, the Bureau issues a series of publications

U.S. Census Bureau, Statistical Abstract of the United States: 2001

under the general title of *Current Population Reports,* which cover population characteristics (P20), consumer income (P60), special studies (P23), and other topics.

Estimates of population characteristics based on the CPS will not agree with the counts from the census because the CPS and the census use different procedures for collecting and processing the data for racial groups, the Hispanic population, and other topics. Caution should also be used when comparing estimates for various years because of the periodic introduction of changes into the CPS. Beginning in January 1994, a number of changes were introduced into the CPS that effect all data comparisons with prior years. These changes include the results of a major redesign of the survey questionnaire and collection methodology and the introduction of 1990 census population controls, adjusted for the estimated undercount. This change in population controls had relatively little impact on derived measures such as means, medians, and percent distribution, but did have a significant impact on levels.

Population estimates and projections—National population estimates start with decennial census data as benchmarks and add annual population component of change data. Component of change data come from various agencies, as follows: National Center for Health Statistics (births and deaths), Immigration and Naturalization Service (legal immigrants), Office of Refugee Resettlement (refugees), U.S. Census Bureau's International Programs Center (net movement between Puerto Rico and the U.S. mainland), Armed Forces, Department of Defense, and Office of Personnel Management (movement of military and civilian citizens abroad). Emigration and net undocumented immigration are projected based on research using census data. Estimates for states, counties, and smaller areas are based on the same component of change data and sources as the national estimates. School statistics from state departments of education and parochial school systems, federal income tax returns from the Internal Revenue Service, group quarters from the Federal-State Cooperative program and the Veterans

Administration, and medicare data from the Centers for Medicare and Midicaid Services are also included.

Data for the population by age for April 1, 1990 (shown in Tables 12, 16, and 17) are modified counts. The review of detailed 1990 information indicated that respondents tended to provide their age as of the date of completion of the questionnaire, not their age as of April 1, 1990. In addition, there may have been a tendency for respondents to round-up their age if they were close to having a birthday. A detailed explanation of the age modification procedure appears in 1990 Census of Population and Housing Data Paper Listing (CPH-L-74).

Population estimates and projections are published in the P25 Series of *Current Population Reports* as *Population Paper Listings* (PPLs), and on the Census Bureau Internet site <http://www.census.gov>. These estimates and projections are generally consistent with official decennial census figures and do not reflect the amount of estimated census underenumeration. However, these estimates and projections by race have been modified and are not comparable to the census race categories (see section below under "Race"). For details on methodology, see the sources cited below the individual tables.

Immigration—The principal source of immigration data is the *Statistical Yearbook of the Immigration and Naturalization Service,* published annually by the Immigration and Naturalization Service (INS), a unit of the Department of Justice. Immigration statistics are prepared from entry visas and change of immigration status forms. Immigrants are aliens admitted for legal permanent residence in the United States. The procedures for admission depend on whether the alien is residing inside or outside the United States at the time of application for permanent residence. Eligible aliens residing outside the United States are issued immigrant visas by the U.S. Department of State. Eligible aliens residing in the United States are allowed to change their status from temporary to permanent residence at INS district offices. The category, immigrant, includes persons who may have entered

2   Population

the United States as nonimmigrants or refugees, but who subsequently changed their status to that of a permanent resident. Nonresident aliens admitted to the United States for a temporary period are nonimmigrants (Table 1262). Refugees are considered nonimmigrants when initially admitted into the United States but are not included in nonimmigrant admission data. A refugee is an alien outside the United States who is unable or unwilling to return to his or her county of nationality because of persecution or a well-founded fear of persecution.

U.S. immigration law gives preferential immigration status to persons with a close family relationship with a U.S. citizen or legal permanent resident, persons with needed job skills, or persons who qualify as refugees. Immigration to the United States can be divided into two general categories: (1) those subject to the annual worldwide limitation and (2) those exempt from it. The Immigration Act of 1990 established major revisions in the numerical limits and preference system regulating legal immigration. The numerical limits are imposed on visas issued and not on admissions. The maximum number of visas allowed to be issued under the preference categories in 1998 was 366,000 – 226,000 for family-sponsored immigrants and 140,000 for employment-based immigrants. There are nine categories among which the family-sponsored and employment-based immigrant visas are distributed, beginning in fiscal year 1992. The family-sponsored preferences are based on the alien's relationship with a U.S. citizen or legal permanent resident (see Table 6). The employment-based preferences are (1) priority workers (persons of extraordinary ability, outstanding professors and researchers, and certain multinational executives and managers); (2) professionals with advanced degrees or aliens with exceptional ability; (3) skilled workers, professionals without advanced degrees, and needed unskilled workers; (4) special immigrants; and (5) employment creation immigrants (investors). Within the overall limitations the per-country limit for independent countries is set to 7 percent of the total family-sponsored and employment-based limits, while dependent areas are limited to 2 percent of the total. The 1998 limit

allowed no more than 25,620 preference visas for any independent country and 7,320 for any dependency. Those exempt from the worldwide limitation include immediate relatives of U.S. citizens, refugees and asylees adjusting to permanent residence, and other various classes of special immigrants (see Table 6).

The Refugee Act of 1980, effective April 1, 1980, provides for a uniform admission procedure for refugees of all countries, based on the United Nations' definition of refugees. Authorized admission ceilings are set annually by the President in consultation with Congress. After 1 year of residence in the United States, refugees are eligible for immigrant status. The Immigration Reform and Control Act of 1986 (IRCA) allows two groups of illegal aliens to become temporary and then permanent residents of the United States: aliens who have been in the United States unlawfully since January 1, 1982 (legalization applicants), and aliens who were employed in seasonal agricultural work for a minimum period of time (Special Agricultural Worker (SAW) applicants). The application period for temporary residency for legalization applicants began on May 5, 1987, and ended on May 4, 1988, while the application period for SAW applicants began on June 1, 1987, and ended on November 30, 1988. Legalization applicants became eligible for permanent residence beginning in fiscal year 1989. Beginning 1989 immigrant data include temporary residents who were granted permanent residence under the legalization program of IRCA.

Metropolitan Areas (MAs)—The general concept of a metropolitan area is one of a core area containing a large population nucleus, together with adjacent communities that have a high degree of social and economic integration with that core. Metropolitan statistical areas (MSAs), consolidated metropolitan statistical areas (CMSAs), and primary metropolitan statistical areas (PMSAs) are defined by the Office of Management and Budget (OMB) as a standard for federal agencies in the preparation and publication of statistics relating to metropolitan areas. The entire territory of the United States is classified as metropolitan (inside MSAs or CMSAs—

U.S. Census Bureau, Statistical Abstract of the United States: 2001

PMSAs are components of CMSAs) or non-metropolitan (outside MSAs or CMSAs). MSAs, CMSAs, and PMSAs are defined in terms of entire counties except in New England, where the definitions are in terms of cities and towns. The OMB also defines New England County Metropolitan Areas (NECMAs) which are county-based alternatives to the MSAs and CMSAs in the six New England states. Over time, new MAs are created and the boundaries of others change. The analysis of historical trends, therefore, must be made cautiously. For descriptive details and a listing of titles and components of MAs, see Appendix II.

Urban and rural—According to the 1990 census definition, the urban population comprises all persons living in (a) places of 2,500 or more inhabitants incorporated as cities, villages, boroughs (except in Alaska and New York), and towns (except in the New England states, New York, and Wisconsin), but excluding those persons living in the rural portions of extended cities (places with low population density in one or more large parts of their area); (b) census designated places (previously termed unincorporated) of 2,500 or more inhabitants; and (c) other territory, incorporated or unincorporated, included in urbanized areas. An urbanized area comprises one or more places and the adjacent densely settled surrounding territory that together have a minimum population of 50,000 persons. In all definitions, the population not classified as urban constitutes the rural population.

Residence—In determining residence, the Census Bureau counts each person as an inhabitant of a usual place of residence (i.e., the place where one usually lives and sleeps). While this place is not necessarily a person's legal residence or voting residence, the use of these different bases of classification would produce the same results in the vast majority of cases.

Race—For the 1990 census, the Census Bureau collected and published racial statistics as outlined in Statistical Policy Directive No. 15 issued by the U.S. Office of Management and Budget. This directive provided standards on ethnic and racial categories for statistical reporting to be used by all federal agencies. According to

the directive, the basic racial categories were American Indian or Alaska Native, Asian or Pacific Islander, Black, and White. (The directive identified Hispanic origin as an ethnicity.) The question on race for Census 2000 was different from the one for the 1990 census in several ways. Most significantly, respondents were given the option of selecting one or more race categories to indicate their racial identities. Because of these changes, the Census 2000 data on race are not directly comparable with data from the 1990 census or earlier censuses. Caution must be used when interpreting changes in the racial composition of the U.S. population over time. Census 2000 adheres to the federal standards for collecting and presenting data on race and Hispanic origin as established by the Office of Management and Budget (OMB) in October 1997. Starting with Census 2000, the OMB requires federal agencies to use a minimum of five race categories: White, Black or African American, American Indian or Alaska Native, Asian, and Native Hawaiian or Other Pacific Islander. For respondents unable to identify with any of these five race categories, OMB approved and included a sixth category—"Some other race"—on the Census 2000 questionnaire. The Census 2000 question on race included 15 separate response categories and three areas where respondents could write in a more specific race group. The response categories and write-in answers can be combined to create the five minimum OMB race categories plus "Some other race." People who responded to the question on race by indicating only one race are referred to as the race *alone* population, or the group that reported only one race category. Six categories make up this population: White *alone*; Black or African American *alone*; American Indian and Alaska Native *alone*; Asian *alone*; Native Hawaiian and Other Pacific Island *alone*; and Some other race *alone*. Individuals who chose more than one of the six race categories are referred to as the *Two or more races* population, or as the group that reported *more than one race*.

The concept of race the Census Bureau uses reflects self-identification by respondents; that is the individual's perception of his/her racial identity. The concept is not intended to reflect any biological or anthropological definition. Furthermore, the Census Bureau recognizes that the categories of the race item include both racial and national origin or sociocultural groups.

Data for the population by race for April 1, 1990 (shown in Tables 10 and 14 through 17) are modified counts and are not comparable to the 1990 census race categories. These numbers were computed using 1990 census data by race which had been modified to be consistent with the guidelines in Federal Statistical Policy Directive No. 15 issued by the Office of Management and Budget. A detailed explanation of the race modification procedure appears in 1990 Census of Population and Housing Data Paper Listing (CPH-L-74).

In the CPS and other household sample surveys in which data are obtained through personal interview, respondents are asked to classify their race as: (1) White; (2) Black; (3) American Indian, Aleut, or Eskimo; or (4) Asian or Pacific Islander. The procedures for classifying persons of mixed races who could not provide a single response to the race question are generally similar to those used in the census.

Hispanic population—The question on Hispanic origin for Census 2000 was similar to the 1990 census question, except for its placement on the questionnaire. For Census 2000, the question on Hispanic origin was asked directly before the question on race. For the 1990 census, the order was reversed—the question on race preceded questions on age and marital status, which were followed by the question on Hispanic origin. In the 1990 census, the Census Bureau collected data on the Hispanic origin population in the United States by using a self-identification question. Persons of Spanish/Hispanic origin are those who classified themselves in one of the specific Hispanic origin categories listed on the questionnaire/Mexican, Puerto Rican, Cuban, as well as those who indicated that they were of Other Spanish/Hispanic origin. Persons of Other Spanish/Hispanic origin are those whose origins are from Spain, the Spanish-speaking countries of Central

or South America, or the Dominican Republic. In 1980, 1990, and 2000, the Hispanic-origin question contained prelisted categories for the largest Hispanic-origin groups—Mexican, Puerto Rican, Cuban, and Other Spanish/Hispanic. The 1990 Hispanic-origin question differed from the 1980 question in that it contained a write-in line for the Other Spanish/Hispanic category. This was coded only for sample data. Another difference between the 1980 and 1990 Hispanic-origin question is that in 1980 the wording of the Hispanic-origin question read: "Is this person of Spanish/Hispanic origin or descent?" while in 1990 the word "descent" was dropped from the question. Persons of Hispanic origin may be of any race.

In the CPS information on Hispanic persons is gathered by using a self-identification question. Persons classify themselves in one of the Hispanic categories in response to the question: "What is the origin or descent of each person in this household?" Hispanic persons in the CPS are persons who report themselves as Mexican-American, Chicano, Mexican, Puerto Rican, Cuban, Central or South American (Spanish countries), or other Hispanic origin.

Nativity—The native population consists of all persons born in the United States, Puerto Rico, or an outlying area of the United States. It also includes persons born in a foreign country who had at least one parent who was a U.S. citizen. All other persons are classified as "foreign born."

Mobility status—The U.S. population is classified according to mobility status on the basis of a comparison between the place of residence of each individual at the time of the survey or census and the place of residence at a specified earlier date. Nonmovers are all persons who were living in the same house or apartment at the end of the period as at the beginning of the period. Movers are all persons who were living in a different house or apartment at the end of the period than at the beginning of the period. Movers are further classified as to whether they were living in the same or different county, state, or region or were

U.S. Census Bureau, Statistical Abstract of the United States: 2001

movers from abroad. Movers from abroad include all persons, either U.S. citizens or noncitizens, whose place of residence was outside the United States at the beginning of the period; that is, in Puerto Rico, an outlying area under the jurisdiction of the United States, or a foreign country.

Living arrangements—Living arrangements refer to residency in households or in group quarters. A "household" comprises all persons who occupy a "housing unit," that is, a house, an apartment or other group of rooms, or a single room that constitutes "separate living quarters." A household includes the related family members and all the unrelated persons, if any, such as lodgers, foster children, wards, or employees who share the housing unit. A person living alone or a group of unrelated persons sharing the same housing unit is also counted as a household. See text, Section 20, Construction and Housing, for definition of housing unit.

All persons not living in housing units are classified as living in group quarters. These individuals may be institutionalized, e.g., under care or custody in juvenile facilities, jails, correctional centers, hospitals, or nursing homes; or they may be residents in noninstitutional group quarters such as college dormitories, group homes, or military barracks.

Householder—The householder is the first adult household member listed on the questionnaire. The instructions call for listing first the person (or one of the persons) in whose name the home is owned or rented. If a home is owned or rented jointly by a married couple, either the husband or the wife may be listed first. Prior to 1980, the husband was always considered the household head (householder) in married-couple households.

Family—The term family refers to a group of two or more persons related by birth, marriage, or adoption and residing together in a household. A family includes among its members the householder.

Subfamily—A subfamily consists of a married couple and their children, if any, or one parent with one or more never-married children under 18 years old living in a household. Subfamilies are divided into "related" and "unrelated" subfamilies. A related subfamily is related to, but does not include, the householder. Members of a related subfamily are also members of the family with whom they live. The number of related subfamilies, therefore, is not included in the count of families. An unrelated subfamily may include persons such as guests, lodgers, or resident employees and their spouses and/or children; none of whom is related to the householder.

Married couple—A married couple is defined as a husband and wife living together in the same household, with or without children and other relatives.

Statistical reliability—For a discussion of statistical collection and estimation, sampling procedures, and measures of statistical reliability applicable to Census Bureau data, see Appendix III.

6 Population

Figure 1.1
Percent Population Change: 1990 to 2000

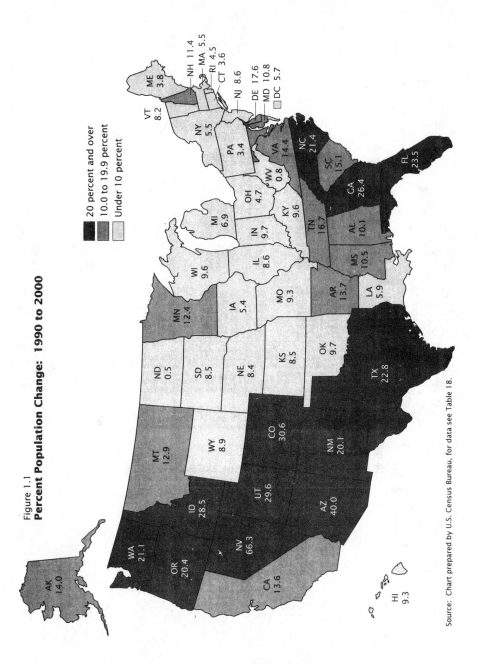

20 percent and over
10.0 to 19.9 percent
Under 10 percent

ME 3.8
VT 8.2
NH 11.4
MA 5.5
RI 4.5
CT 3.6
NY 5.5
NJ 8.6
PA 3.4
DE 17.6
MD 10.8
DC 5.7
VA 14.4
WV 0.8
OH 4.7
KY 9.6
NC 21.4
SC 15.1
GA 26.4
AL 10.1
TN 16.7
FL 23.5
MI 6.9
IN 9.7
WI 9.6
IL 8.6
MS 10.5
AR 13.7
LA 5.9
MN 12.4
IA 5.4
MO 9.3
OK 9.7
TX 22.8
ND 0.5
SD 8.5
NE 8.4
KS 8.5
MT 12.9
WY 8.9
CO 30.6
NM 20.1
UT 29.6
AZ 40.0
ID 28.5
WA 21.1
OR 20.4
NV 66.3
CA 13.6
AK 14.0
HI 9.3

Source: Chart prepared by U.S. Census Bureau, for data see Table 18.

No. 1. Population and Area: 1790 to 2000

[Area figures represent area on indicated date including in some cases considerable areas not then organized or settled, and not covered by the census. Total area figures for 1790 to 1970 have been recalculated on the basis of the remeasurement of states and counties for the 1980 census, but not on the basis of the 1990 census. The land and water area figures for past censuses have not been adjusted and are not strictly comparable with the total area data for comparable dates because the land areas were derived from different base data, and these values are known to have changed with the construction of reservoirs, draining of lakes, etc. Density figures are based on land area measurements as reported in earlier censuses]

Census date	Resident population				Area (square miles)		
	Number	Per square mile of land area	Increase over preceding census		Total	Land	Water
			Number	Percent			
CONTERMINOUS U.S. [1]							
1790 (Aug. 2)	3,929,214	4.5	(X)	(X)	891,364	864,746	24,065
1800 (Aug. 4)	5,308,483	6.1	1,379,269	35.1	891,364	864,746	24,065
1810 (Aug. 6)	7,239,881	4.3	1,931,398	36.4	1,722,685	1,681,828	34,175
1820 (Aug. 7)	9,638,453	5.5	2,398,572	33.1	1,792,552	1,749,462	38,544
1830 (June 1)	12,866,020	7.4	3,227,567	33.5	1,792,552	1,749,462	38,544
1840 (June 1)	17,069,453	9.8	4,203,433	32.7	1,792,552	1,749,462	38,544
1850 (June 1)	23,191,876	7.9	6,122,423	35.9	2,991,655	2,940,042	52,705
1860 (June 1)	31,443,321	10.6	8,251,445	35.6	3,021,295	2,969,640	52,747
1870 (June 1)	[2]39,818,449	[2]13.4	8,375,128	26.6	3,021,295	2,969,640	52,747
1880 (June 1)	50,155,783	16.9	10,337,334	26.0	3,021,295	2,969,640	52,747
1890 (June 1)	62,947,714	21.2	12,791,931	25.5	3,021,295	2,969,640	52,747
1900 (June 1)	75,994,575	25.6	13,046,861	20.7	3,021,295	2,969,834	52,553
1910 (Apr. 15)	91,972,266	31.0	15,977,691	21.0	3,021,295	2,969,565	52,822
1920 (Jan. 1)	105,710,620	35.6	13,738,354	14.9	3,021,295	2,969,451	52,936
1930 (Apr. 1)	122,775,046	41.2	17,064,426	16.1	3,021,295	2,977,128	45,259
1940 (Apr. 1)	131,669,275	44.2	8,894,229	7.2	3,021,295	2,977,128	45,259
1950 (Apr. 1)	150,697,361	50.7	19,028,086	14.5	3,021,295	2,974,726	47,661
1960 (Apr. 1)	178,464,236	60.1	27,766,875	18.4	3,021,295	2,968,054	54,207
UNITED STATES							
1950 (Apr. 1)	151,325,798	42.6	19,161,229	14.5	3,618,770	3,552,206	63,005
1960 (Apr. 1)	179,323,175	50.6	27,997,377	18.5	3,618,770	3,540,911	74,212
1970 (Apr. 1)	[3]203,302,031	[3]57.4	23,978,856	13.4	3,618,770	[3]3,540,023	[3]78,444
1980 (Apr. 1)	[4]226,542,199	64.0	23,240,168	11.4	3,618,770	3,539,289	79,481
1990 (Apr. 1)	[5]248,718,301	70.3	22,176,102	9.8	[6]3,717,796	[6]3,536,278	[6][7]181,518
2000 (Apr. 1)	281,421,906	79.6	32,703,605	13.1	(NA)	(NA)	(NA)

NA Not available.   X Not applicable.   [1] Excludes Alaska and Hawaii.   [2] Revised to include adjustments for underenumeration in southern states; unrevised number is 38,558,371 (13.0 per square mile).   [3] Figures corrected after 1970 final reports were issued.   [4] Total population count has been revised since the 1980 census publications. Numbers by age, race, Hispanic origin, and sex have not been corrected.   [5] The April 1, 1990, census count includes count question resolution corrections processed through December 1997, and does not include adjustments for census coverage errors.   [6] Data reflect corrections made after publication of the results.   [7] Comprises Great Lakes, inland, and coastal water. Data for prior years cover inland water only. For further explanation, see Table 343.

Source: U.S. Census Bureau, *1990 Census of Population and Housing, Population and Housing Unit Counts* (CPH-2); 1990 Census of Population and Housing Listing (1990 CPH-L-157); and "Table DP-1 Profile of General Demographic Characteristics for the United States"; published 15 May 2001; <http://www.census.gov/Press-Release/www/2001/cb01cn67.html>.

No. 2. Population: 1960 to 2000

[In thousands, except percent (180,671 represents 180,671,000). Estimates as of July 1. Total population includes Armed Forces abroad; civilian population excludes Armed Forces. For basis of estimates, see text of this section]

Year	Total		Resident population	Civilian population	Year	Total		Resident population	Civilian population
	Population	Percent change [1]				Population	Percent change [1]		
1960	180,671	1.60	179,979	178,140	1981	229,966	0.98	229,466	227,818
1961	183,691	1.67	182,992	181,143	1982	232,188	0.97	231,664	229,995
1962	186,538	1.55	185,771	183,677	1983	234,307	0.91	233,792	232,097
1963	189,242	1.45	188,483	186,493	1984	236,348	0.87	235,825	234,110
1964	191,889	1.40	191,141	189,141	1985	238,466	0.90	237,924	236,219
1965	194,303	1.26	193,526	191,605	1986	240,651	0.92	240,133	238,412
1966	196,560	1.16	195,576	193,420	1987	242,804	0.89	242,289	240,550
1967	198,712	1.09	197,457	195,264	1988	245,021	0.91	244,499	242,817
1968	200,706	1.00	199,399	197,113	1989	247,342	0.95	246,819	245,131
1969	202,677	0.98	201,385	199,145	1990	249,973	1.06	249,464	247,824
1970	205,052	1.17	203,984	201,895	1991	252,665	1.08	252,153	250,542
1971	207,661	1.27	206,827	204,866	1992	255,410	1.09	255,030	253,445
1972	209,896	1.08	209,284	207,511	1993	258,119	1.06	257,783	256,310
1973	211,909	0.96	211,357	209,600	1994	260,637	0.98	260,327	258,915
1974	213,854	0.92	213,342	211,636	1995	263,082	0.94	262,803	261,452
1975	215,973	0.99	215,465	213,789	1996	265,502	0.92	265,229	263,943
1976	218,035	0.95	217,563	215,894	1997	268,048	0.96	267,784	266,531
1977	220,239	1.01	219,760	218,106	1998	270,509	0.92	270,248	269,027
1978	222,585	1.06	222,095	220,467	1999	272,945	0.90	272,691	271,491
1979	225,055	1.11	224,567	222,969	2000 [2]	275,372	0.89	275,130	273,936
1980	227,726	1.19	227,225	225,621					

[1] Percent change from immediate preceding year.   [2] These 2000 figures do not reflect the results of the 2000 census.

Source: U.S. Census Bureau, *Current Population Reports*, P25-802 and P25-1095; and "Monthly estimates of the United States population: April 1, 1980, to July 1, 1999; with short-term projections to November 1, 2000"; published: 2 January 2001; <http://www.census.gov/population/estimates/nation/intfile1-1.txt>.

No. 3. Resident Population Projections: 2001 to 2100

[In thousands (277,803 represents 277,803,000). As of July 1. The projections are based on assumptions about future childbearing, mortality, and migration. The level of childbearing among women for the middle series is assumed to remain close to present levels, with differences by race and Hispanic origin diminishing over time. Mortality is assumed to decline gradually with less variation by race and Hispanic origin than at present. International migration is assumed to vary over time and decrease generally relative to the size of the population. Assumptions for the lowest and highest series are summarized in "Methodology and Assumptions for the Population Projections of the United States: 1999 to 2100, Working Paper No. 38"]

Year	Middle series [1]	Lowest series [2]	Highest series [3]	Zero international migration series [4]	Year	Middle series [1]	Lowest series [2]	Highest series [3]	Zero international migration series [4]
2001	277,803	276,879	278,869	275,279	2015	312,268	297,977	331,636	294,741
2002	280,306	278,801	282,087	276,709	2020	324,927	303,664	354,642	301,636
2003	282,798	280,624	285,422	278,112	2025	337,815	308,229	380,397	307,923
2004	285,266	282,352	288,841	279,493	2030	351,070	311,656	409,604	313,219
2005	287,716	284,000	292,339	280,859	2035	364,319	313,819	441,618	317,534
2006	290,153	285,581	295,911	282,219	2040	377,350	314,673	475,949	321,167
2007	292,583	287,106	299,557	283,579	2045	390,398	314,484	512,904	324,449
2008	295,009	288,583	303,274	284,945	2050	403,687	313,546	552,757	327,641
2009	297,436	290,018	307,060	286,322	2075	480,504	303,970	809,243	349,032
2010	299,862	291,413	310,910	287,710	2100	570,954	282,706	1,182,390	377,444

[1] Total fertility rate in 2050 = 2,219; life expectancy in 2050 = 83.9 years; and annual net immigration in 2050 = 984,000. These are middle level assumptions. For explanation of total fertility rate; see headnote, Table 73. [2] Total fertility rate in 2050 = 1,800; life expectancy in 2050 = 82.2 years; and annual net immigration in 2050 = 169,000. These are lowest level assumptions. [3] Total fertility rate in 2050 = 2,647; life expectancy in 2050 = 86.1 years; and annual net immigration in 2050 = 2,812,000. These are highest level assumptions. [4] Middle level assumptions for fertility and mortality; zero level assumption for international migration.
Source: U.S. Census Bureau, "Annual Projections of the Total Resident Population as of July 1: Middle, Lowest, Highest, and Zero International Migration Series, 2000 to 2100"; published: 14 February 2000; <http://www.census.gov/population/projections/nation/summary/np-t1.txt>.

No. 4. Components of Population Change, 1980 to 1999, and Projections, 2005 to 2050

[226,546 represents 226,546,000. Resident population. The estimates prior to 1990 are consistent with the original 1990 census count of 248,709,873. Starting with 1990, estimates reflect the revised April 1, 1990, estimates base count of 248,790,925 which includes count resolution corrections processed through August 1997. It generally does not include adjustments for census coverage errors. However, it includes adjustments estimated for the 1995 Test Census in various localities in California, New Jersey, and Louisiana, and the 1998 census dress rehearsals in localities in California and Wisconsin. These adjustments amounted to a total of 81,052 persons]

Year	Population as of Jan. 1 (1,000)	Net increase [1] Total (1,000)	Net increase [1] Per- cent [2]	Calendar year Births (1,000)	Calendar year Deaths (1,000)	Net migra- tion [3] (1,000)	Rate per 1,000 midyear population Net growth rate [1]	Rate per 1,000 midyear population Birth rate	Rate per 1,000 midyear population Death rate	Rate per 1,000 midyear population Net migration rate [3]
1980 [4]	226,546	1,900	0.8	2,743	1,463	724	11.1	16.0	8.6	4.2
1981	228,446	2,200	1.0	3,629	1,978	690	9.6	15.8	8.6	3.0
1982	230,645	2,157	0.9	3,681	1,975	595	9.3	15.9	8.5	2.6
1983	232,803	2,066	0.9	3,639	2,019	592	8.8	15.6	8.6	2.5
1984	234,868	2,070	0.9	3,669	2,039	589	8.8	15.6	8.6	2.5
1985	236,938	2,171	0.9	3,761	2,086	649	9.1	15.8	8.8	2.7
1986	239,109	2,158	0.9	3,757	2,105	661	9.0	15.6	8.8	2.8
1987	241,267	2,195	0.9	3,809	2,123	666	9.1	15.7	8.8	2.7
1988	243,462	2,243	0.9	3,910	2,168	662	9.2	16.0	8.9	2.7
1989	245,705	2,438	1.0	4,041	2,150	712	9.9	16.4	8.7	2.9
1990 [5]	248,143	2,535	1.0	4,148	2,155	[6]542	10.2	16.6	8.6	[6]2.2
1991	250,718	2,901	1.2	4,111	2,170	[6]960	11.5	16.3	8.6	[6]3.8
1992	253,620	2,896	1.1	4,065	2,176	1,007	11.4	15.9	8.5	3.9
1993	256,516	2,614	1.0	4,000	2,269	883	10.1	15.5	8.8	3.4
1994	259,131	2,485	1.0	3,953	2,279	811	9.5	15.2	8.8	3.1
1995	261,615	2,446	0.9	3,900	2,312	858	9.3	14.8	8.8	3.3
1996	264,061	2,513	1.0	3,891	2,315	937	9.5	14.7	8.7	3.5
1997	266,574	2,544	1.0	3,881	2,314	977	9.5	14.5	8.6	3.6
1998	269,118	2,466	0.9	3,944	2,338	860	9.1	14.6	8.7	3.2
1999	271,584	2,440	0.9	3,934	2,350	856	8.9	14.4	8.6	3.1
PROJECTIONS [7]										
2005	286,549	2,443	0.9	4,045	2,480	878	8.5	14.1	8.6	3.1
2010	298,710	2,425	0.8	4,283	2,578	720	8.1	14.3	8.6	2.4
2015	311,069	2,521	0.8	4,476	2,695	740	8.1	14.3	8.6	2.4
2020	323,724	2,530	0.8	4,613	2,840	757	7.8	14.2	8.7	2.3
2025	336,566	2,621	0.8	4,736	3,033	918	7.8	14.0	9.0	2.7
2030	349,789	2,688	0.8	4,878	3,257	1,067	7.7	13.9	9.3	3.0
2040	376,123	2,601	0.7	5,286	3,702	1,018	6.9	14.0	9.8	2.7
2050	402,420	2,699	0.7	5,661	3,952	990	6.7	14.0	9.8	2.5

[1] Prior to April 1, 1990, includes "error of closure" (the amount necessary to make the components of change add to the net change between censuses), for which figures are not shown separately. [2] Percent of population at beginning of period. [3] Covers net international migration and movement of Armed Forces, federally affiliated civilian citizens, and their dependents. [4] Data are for period April 1 to December 31. [5] Net change for 1990 excludes "error of closure" for the 3 months prior to the April 1 census date. Therefore, it may not equal the difference between the populations at the beginning of 1990 and 1991. [6] Data reflect movement of Armed Forces due to the Gulf War. [7] Based on middle series of assumptions. See footnote 1, Table 3.
Source: U.S. Census Bureau, Current Population Reports, P25-1095 and unpublished data; and "Population Projections of the Total Resident Population by Quarter: Middle Series, April 1, 1999, to January 1, 2101"; published 13 January 2000; <http://www.census.gov/population/projections/nation/summary/np-t2.txt>; and "Components of Change for the Total Resident Population: Middle Series, 1999 to 2100"; published 13 January 2000; <http://www.census.gov/population/projections/nation/summary/np-t6-a.txt> and <http://www.census.gov/population/projections/nation/summary/np-t6-b.txt>.

Population   9

No. 5. Immigration: 1901 to 1998

[In thousands, except rate (8,795 represents 8,795,000). For fiscal years ending in year shown; see text, Section 8, State and Local Government Finances and Employment. For definition of immigrants, see text of this section. Data represent immigrants admitted. Rates based on Census Bureau estimates as of July 1 for resident population through 1929 and for total population thereafter (excluding Alaska and Hawaii prior to 1959)]

Period	Number	Rate [1]	Year	Number	Rate [1]
1901 to 1910	8,795	10.4	1980	531	2.3
1911 to 1920	5,736	5.7	1990	1,536	6.1
1921 to 1930	4,107	3.5	1991	1,827	7.2
1931 to 1940	528	0.4	1992	974	3.8
1941 to 1950	1,035	0.7	1993	904	3.5
1951 to 1960	2,515	1.5	1994	804	3.1
1961 to 1970	3,322	1.7	1995	720	2.7
1971 to 1980	4,493	2.1	1996	916	3.4
1981 to 1990	7,338	3.1	1997	798	3.0
1991 to 1998	7,605	3.6	1998	660	2.4

[1] Annual rate per 1,000 U.S. population. Rate computed by dividing sum of annual immigration totals by sum of annual U.S. population totals for same number of years.

Source: U.S. Immigration and Naturalization Service, *Statistical Yearbook*, annual.

No. 6. Immigrants Admitted by Class of Admission: 1990 to 1998

[For fiscal year ending September 30. For definition of immigrants, see text of this section]

Class of admission	1990	1994	1995	1996	1997	1998
Immigrants, total	1,536,483	804,416	720,461	915,900	798,378	660,477
New arrivals	435,729	490,429	380,291	421,405	380,719	357,037
Adjustments	1,100,754	313,987	340,170	494,495	417,659	303,440
Preference immigrants, total	272,742	335,252	323,458	411,673	303,938	268,997
Family-sponsored immigrants, total	214,550	211,961	238,122	294,174	213,331	191,480
Unmarried sons/daughters of U.S. citizens and their children	15,861	13,181	15,182	20,909	22,536	17,717
Spouses, unmarried sons/daughters of alien residents, and their children	107,686	115,000	144,535	182,834	113,681	88,488
Married sons/daughters of U.S. citizens [1]	26,751	22,191	20,876	25,452	21,943	22,257
Brothers or sisters of U.S. citizens [1]	64,252	61,589	57,529	64,979	55,171	63,018
Employment-based immigrants, total	58,192	123,291	85,336	117,499	90,607	77,517
Priority workers [1]	(X)	21,053	17,339	27,501	21,810	21,408
Professionals with advanced degrees [1]	(X)	14,432	10,475	18,462	17,059	14,384
Skilled workers, professionals, unskilled workers [1]	(X)	76,956	50,245	62,756	42,596	34,317
Special immigrants [1]	4,463	10,406	6,737	7,844	7,781	6,584
Employment creation [1]	(X)	444	540	936	1,361	824
Professional or highly skilled immigrants [1][2]	26,546	(X)	(X)	(X)	(X)	(X)
Needed skilled or unskilled workers [1][2]	27,183	(X)	(X)	(X)	(X)	(X)
Immediate relatives	234,090	251,647	222,254	302,090	322,440	284,270
Spouses of U.S. citizens	125,426	145,247	123,238	169,760	170,263	151,172
Children of U.S. citizens	46,065	48,147	48,740	63,971	76,631	70,472
Orphans	7,088	8,200	9,384	11,316	12,596	14,867
Parents of U.S. citizens	60,189	56,370	48,382	66,699	74,114	61,724
Children born abroad to alien residents	2,410	1,883	1,894	1,660	1,432	902
Refugees and asylees	97,364	121,434	114,664	128,565	112,158	54,645
Refugee adjustments	92,427	115,451	106,827	118,528	102,052	44,645
Asylee adjustments	4,937	5,983	7,837	10,037	10,106	10,000
Other immigrants	932,287	96,085	60,085	73,572	59,842	52,565
Diversity Programs [3]	29,161	41,056	47,245	58,790	49,374	45,499
Amerasians (P.L. 100-202) [4]	13,059	2,822	939	956	738	346
Immigration Reform and Control Act of 1986 legalization adjustments	880,372	6,022	4,267*	4,635	2,548	955
Legalization dependents [5]	(X)	34,074	277	184	64	21
Other	9,695	12,109	7,357	9,007	7,118	5,744

X Not applicable.   [1] Includes spouses and children.   [2] Category was eliminated in 1992 by the Immigration Act of 1990.   [3] Includes categories of immigrants admitted under three laws intended to diversify immigration: P.L. 99-603, P.L. 100-658, and P.L. 101-649.   [4] Under Public Law 100-202, Amerasians are aliens born in Vietnam between January 1, 1962, and January 1, 1976, who were fathered by U.S. citizens.   [5] Spouses and children of persons granted permanent resident status under provisions of the Immigration Reform and Control Act of 1986.

Source: U.S. Immigration and Naturalization Service, *Statistical Yearbook*, annual.

No. 7. Immigrants by Country of Birth: 1981 to 1998

[In thousands (7,338.1 represents 7,338,100). For fiscal years ending Sept. 30. For definition of immigrants, see text of this section]

Country of birth	1981-90, total	1991-96, total	1997	1998	Country of birth	1981-90, total	1991-96, total	1997	1998
All countries	7,338.1	6,146.2	798.4	660.5	Taiwan	(4)	76.8	6.7	7.1
Europe [1]	705.6	875.6	119.9	90.8	Thailand	64.4	36.1	3.1	3.1
France	23.1	16.9	2.6	2.4	Turkey	20.9	15.7	3.1	2.7
Germany	70.1	43.7	5.7	5.5	Vietnam . . . . , . . .	401.4	317.8	38.5	17.6
Greece	29.1	10.0	1.0	0.9	North America [1]	3,125.0	2,740.7	307.5	253.0
Ireland	32.8	54.9	1.0	0.9	Canada	119.2	90.7	11.6	10.2
Italy	32.9	14.7	2.0	1.8	Mexico . . , ...	1,653.3	1,651.4	146.9	131.6
Poland	97.4	130.2	12.0	8.5	Caribbean [1]	892.7	655.4	105.3	75.5
Portugal	40.0	17.1	1.7	1.5	Cuba	159.2	94.9	33.6	17.4
Romania	38.9	34.3	5.5	5.1	Dominican				
Soviet Union, former [2] .	84.0	339.9	49.1	30.2	Republic	251.8	258.1	27.1	20.4
Armenia	(NA)	[3]20.8	2.1	1.1	Haiti	140.2	114.4	15.1	13.4
Azerbaijan	(NA)	[3]12.3	1.5	0.5	Jamaica	213.8	109.8	17.8	15.1
Belarus	(NA)	[3]21.4	3.1	1.0	Trinidad and				
Russia	(NA)	[3]70.4	16.6	11.5	Tobago . . . , ...	39.5	41.1	6.4	4.9
Ukraine	(NA)	[3]92.2	15.7	7.4	Central America [1]	458.7	342.8	43.7	35.7
Uzbekistan	(NA)	[3]16.1	3.3	0.6	El Salvador	214.6	147.7	18.0	14.6
United Kingdom	142.1	95.0	10.7	9.0	Guatemala	87.9	70.3	7.8	7.8
Yugoslavia	19.2	31.7	10.8	8.0	Honduras	49.5	41.9	7.6	6.5
Asia [1]	2,817.4	1,941.9	265.8	219.7	Nicaragua	44.1	50.4	6.3	3.5
Afghanistan	26.6	13.6	1.1	0.8	Panama	29.0	16.9	2.0	1.6
Bangladesh	15.2	35.4	8.7	8.6	South America [1]	455.9	344.0	52.9	45.4
Cambodia	116.6	11.9	1.6	1.4	Argentina	25.7	17.1	2.0	1.5
China	[4]388.8	268.7	41.1	36.9	Brazil	23.7	32.4	4.6	4.4
Hong Kong	63.0	52.9	5.6	5.3	Chile	23.4	11.4	1.4	1.2
India	261.9	236.5	38.1	36.5	Colombia	124.4	81.7	13.0	11.8
Iran	154.8	79.4	9.6	7.9	Ecuador	56.0	45.2	7.8	6.9
Iraq	19.6	26.8	3.2	2.2	Guyana	95.4	53.6	7.3	4.0
Israel	36.3	22.9	2.4	2.0	Peru	64.4	66.7	10.9	10.2
Japan	43.2	39.9	5.1	5.1	Venezuela	17.9	16.2	3.3	3.1
Jordan	32.6	25.1	4.2	3.3	Africa [1]	192.3	213.1	47.8	40.7
Korea	338.8	114.1	14.2	14.3	Egypt . . . . , ...	31.4	28.0	5.0	4.8
Laos	145.6	37.8	1.9	1.6	Ethiopia	27.2	30.9	5.9	4.2
Lebanon	41.6	29.9	3.6	3.3	Ghana	14.9	18.0	5.1	4.5
Pakistan	61.3	70.5	13.0	13.1	Nigeria	35.3	37.9	7.0	7.7
Philippines	495.3	348.5	49.1	34.5	South Africa	15.7	14.2	2.1	1.9
Syria	20.6	16.6	2.3	2.8	Other countries [5]	41.9	31.0	4.5	10.9

NA Not available. [1] Includes countries not shown separately. [2] Includes other republics and unknown republics, not shown separately. [3] Covers years 1992-1996. [4] Data for Taiwan included with China. [5] Includes unknown countries.

Source: U.S. Immigration and Naturalization Service, *Statistical Yearbook*, annual; and releases.

No. 8. Immigrants Admitted as Permanent Residents Under Refugee Acts by Country of Birth: 1981 to 1998

[For fiscal years ending September 30]

Country of birth	1981-90, total	1991-96, total	1997	1998	Country of birth	1981-90, total	1991-96, total	1997	1998
Total	1,013,620	748,122	112,158	54,645	Cambodia	114,064	6,088	163	62
Europe [1]	155,512	312,815	39,795	19,048	China	[4]7,928	5,079	692	898
Czechoslovakia,					India	(NA)	1,125	462	373
former	8,204	1,201	40	15	Iran	46,773	20,126	1,447	754
Hungary	4,942	1,231	24	14	Iraq	7,540	14,464	1,774	999
Poland	33,889	7,210	143	54	Laos	142,964	33,701	1,363	1,110
Romania	29,798	15,139	322	116	Thailand	30,259	19,323	1,112	1,134
Soviet Union,					Vietnam . . . . , . .	324,453	169,560	22,297	4,921
former [2]	72,306	264,187	30,880	13,200	North America [1] . . .	121,840	111,744	32,898	16,372
Armenia	(NA)	[3]1,546	213	158	Cuba	113,367	76,370	30,377	14,915
Azerbaijan . . .	(NA)	[3]10,049	1,000	196	El Salvador	1,383	3,623	198	129
Belarus	(NA)	[3]19,545	2,486	557	Haiti	(NA)	7,309	1,074	537
Georgia	(NA)	[3]1,834	425	100	Nicaragua . . . , .	5,590	21,252	666	316
Kazakhstan . . .	(NA)	[3]2,823	612	152	South America [1] . .	1,976	3,025	890	712
Moldova	(NA)	[3]9,300	1,043	272	Peru	(NA)	1,285	489	338
Russia	(NA)	[3]44,367	6,985	2,225	Africa [1]	22,149	34,224	7,651	4,225
Tajikistan	(NA)	[3]2,191	239	24	Ethiopia	18,542	15,849	1,056	507
Ukraine	(NA)	[3]81,263	12,137	3,641	Liberia	(NA)	2,712	505	225
Uzbekistan . . .	(NA)	[3]14,638	2,885	292	Somalia	(NA)	7,864	3,607	2,270
Yugoslavia	324	[3]13,271	7,597	5,312	Sudan	(NA)	3,422	1,119	287
Asia [1]	712,092	286,125	30,335	11,743	Other	51	189	89	2,545
Afghanistan	22,946	9,065	356	137					

NA Not available. [1] Includes other countries, not shown separately. [2] Includes other republics and unknown republics, not shown separately. [3] Covers years 1992-1996. [4] Includes Taiwan.

Source: U.S. Immigration and Naturalization Service, *Statistical Yearbook*, annual; and releases.

Population   11

No. 9. Immigrants Admitted by State and Leading Country of Birth: 1998

[For year ending September 30. For definition of immigrants, see text of this section]

State and other area	Total [1]	Mexico	China	India	Philippines	Dominican Republic	Vietnam	Cuba	Jamaica
Total	660,477	131,575	36,884	36,482	34,466	20,387	17,649	17,375	15,146
Alabama...........	1,608	178	117	165	85	2	51	29	15
Alaska	1,008	105	56	14	254	32	13	1	1
Arizona...........	6,211	3,209	253	230	220	7	96	7	7
Arkansas	914	305	46	59	42	2	38	3	-
California	170,126	62,113	12,582	7,177	16,202	72	6,519	289	186
Colorado..........	6,513	2,293	317	218	143	10	287	27	6
Connecticut........	7,780	272	304	478	181	186	145	43	856
Delaware	1,063	135	79	141	26	11	23	8	28
District of Columbia	2,377	42	112	36	80	46	111	4	83
Florida...........	59,965	2,788	628	1,079	837	1,483	437	14,265	4,795
Georgia	10,445	1,630	435	882	163	44	592	110	211
Hawaii	5,465	75	482	16	3,140	2	101	-	3
Idaho	1,504	984	63	29	25	4	37	1	-
Illinois	33,163	10,127	1,357	3,446	1,350	67	306	98	131
Indiana...........	3,981	904	208	375	117	9	78	20	25
Iowa	1,655	366	78	129	56	4	218	1	1
Kansas...........	3,184	1,357	91	184	78	4	279	8	6
Kentucky	2,017	141	72	119	50	5	195	243	7
Louisiana	2,193	132	94	129	70	32	201	83	4
Maine............	709	9	80	41	9	5	23	8	9
Maryland	15,561	364	697	1,108	625	137	251	44	545
Massachusetts........	15,869	105	1,355	958	179	1,138	443	40	340
Michigan..........	13,943	1,055	557	1,484	330	72	206	124	93
Minnesota.........	6,981	536	270	455	156	10	328	14	34
Mississippi	701	56	69	94	64	1	31	27	4
Missouri	3,588	491	197	271	139	7	184	23	16
Montana..........	299	21	42	8	17	-	6	-	-
Nebraska	1,267	542	52	88	36	2	71	3	1
Nevada	6,106	2,881	231	145	712	14	95	195	9
New Hampshire.......	1,010	28	73	91	56	28	39	3	8
New Jersey.........	35,091	772	1,318	4,284	1,648	2,478	271	437	1,037
New Mexico........	2,199	1,359	76	116	32	1	43	59	4
New York	96,559	1,616	8,850	4,017	1,490	10,719	646	322	5,874
North Carolina	6,415	880	318	618	151	33	310	78	40
North Dakota........	472	12	9	41	9	2	16	18	-
Ohio	7,697	311	493	900	221	32	263	18	51
Oklahoma..........	2,273	812	96	204	60	2	131	3	5
Oregon...........	5,909	1,879	411	239	165	1	365	81	8
Pennsylvania........	11,942	625	938	1,127	265	245	586	78	349
Rhode Island........	1,976	27	73	62	38	284	15	1	6
South Carolina.......	2,125	259	96	182	96	2	63	4	11
South Dakota	356	36	13	8	19	-	6	13	1
Tennessee	2,806	300	148	291	60	9	118	43	19
Texas............	44,428	22,956	1,159	2,663	851	97	1,576	218	108
Utah	3,360	1,035	120	101	72	5	133	17	6
Vermont	513	9	30	53	6	4	13	1	2
Virginia...........	15,686	541	523	910	921	31	686	60	117
Washington.........	16,920	4,129	843	599	1,159	5	940	47	27
West Virginia	375	10	23	65	20	-	2	5	4
Wisconsin..........	3,724	680	234	314	106	5	50	4	44
Wyoming	159	42	10	15	7	-	2	-	-
Guam	1,835	1	54	10	1,507	-	9	-	-
Northern Mariana Islands	103	-	10	1	76	-	-	-	-
Puerto Rico.........	3,251	39	36	1	1	2,647	1	147	-
Virgin Islands........	979	-	5	12	6	349	-	-	9
Armed Services posts ...	88	1	-	-	38	-	-	-	-
Other............	6,030	-	1	-	-	-	-	-	-

- Represents zero. [1] Includes other countries, not shown separately.

Source: U.S. Immigration and Naturalization Service, *Statistical Yearbook*, annual.

U.S. Census Bureau, Statistical Abstract of the United States: 2001

No. 10. Resident Population—Selected Characteristics, 1950 to 2000, and Projections, 2025 and 2050

[In thousands (75,187 represents 75,187,000)]

Date	Sex		Race				
	Male	Female	White	Black	American Indian, Eskimo, Aleut	Asian, Pacific Islander	Hispanic origin [1]
NUMBER							
1950 (Apr. 1)	75,187	76,139	135,150	15,045	(NA)	(NA)	(NA)
1960 (Apr. 1) [2]	88,331	90,992	158,832	18,872	(NA)	(NA)	(NA)
1970 (Apr. 1) [2]	98,926	104,309	178,098	22,581	(NA)	(NA)	(NA)
1980 (Apr. 1) [3][4] . . .	110,053	116,493	194,713	26,683	1,420	3,729	14,609
1990 (Apr. 1) [3][5] . . .	121,284	127,507	208,741	30,517	2,067	7,467	22,379
1991 (July 1) [6]	122,956	129,197	210,975	31,137	2,112	7,929	23,391
1992 (July 1) [6]	124,424	130,606	212,874	31,683	2,149	8,324	24,283
1993 (July 1) [6]	125,788	131,995	214,691	32,195	2,187	8,710	25,222
1994 (July 1) [6]	127,049	133,278	216,379	32,672	2,222	9,054	26,160
1995 (July 1) [6]	128,294	134,510	218,023	33,116	2,256	9,408	27,107
1996 (July 1) [6]	129,504	135,724	219,636	33,537	2,290	9,765	28,099
1997 (July 1) [6]	130,783	137,001	221,333	33,989	2,326	10,135	29,182
1998 (July 1) [6]	132,030	138,218	222,980	34,427	2,361	10,479	30,252
1999 (July 1) [6]	133,277	139,414	224,611	34,862	2,397	10,820	31,337
2000 (July 1) [6][7] . . .	134,511	140,619	226,232	35,307	2,434	11,157	32,440
2025 (July 1) [8]	165,009	172,806	265,306	47,089	3,399	22,020	61,433
2050 (July 1) [8]	197,047	206,640	302,453	59,239	4,405	37,589	98,229
PERCENT DISTRIBUTION							
1980 (Apr. 1) [3][4] . . .	48.6	51.4	85.9	11.8	0.6	1.6	6.4
1990 (Apr. 1) [3][5] . . .	48.7	51.3	83.9	12.3	0.8	3.0	9.0
2000 (July 1) [6][7] . . .	48.9	51.1	82.2	12.8	0.9	4.1	11.8
2025 (July 1) [8]	48.8	51.2	78.5	13.9	1.0	6.5	18.2
2050 (July 1) [8]	48.8	51.2	74.9	14.7	1.1	9.3	24.3

NA Not available. [1] Persons of Hispanic origin may be of any race. [2] The revised 1970 resident population count is 203,302,031; which incorporates changes due to errors found after tabulations were completed. The race and sex data shown here reflect the official 1970 census count. [3] The race data shown have been modified; see text of this section for explanation. [4] See footnote 4, Table 1. [5] The April 1, 1990, estimates base (248,790,925) includes count resolution corrections processed through August 1997. It generally does not include adjustments for censuc coverage errors. However, it includes adjustments estimated for the 1995 Test Census in various localities in California, New Jersey, and Louisiana; and the 1999 census dress rehearsals in localities in California and Wisconsin. These adjustments amounted to a total of 81,052 persons. [6] Estimated. [7] These 2000 figures do not reflect the results of the 2000 Census. [8] Middle series projection; for assumptions, see Table 3.

Source: U.S. Census Bureau, *U.S. Census of Population, 1950*, Vol. II, part 1; *1960*, Vol. I, Part 1; *1970*, Vol. I, Part B; *Current Population Reports*, P25-1095; "National Estimates, Annual Population Estimates by Sex, Race, and Hispanic Origin, Selected Years from 1990 to 2000"; published 26 May 2000; <http://www.census.gov/population/www/estimates/nation3.html>; and "National Population Projections-Summary Tables"; published 13 January 2000; <http://www.census.gov/population/www/projections/natsum-T3.html>.

No 11. Resident Population by Sex and Age Group: 1990 and 2000

[248,710 represents 248,710,000. As of April 1. 1990 data are uncorrected counts. Minus sign (-) indicates decrease]

Characteristic	Number (1,000)		Percent distribution		Percent change, 1990-2000
	1990	2000	1990	2000	
Total population	**248,710**	**281,422**	**100.0**	**100.0**	**13.2**
Male	121,239	138,054	48.7	49.1	13.9
Female.	127,470	143,368	51.3	50.9	12.5
Under 5 years	18,354	19,176	7.4	6.8	4.5
5 to 9 years.	18,099	20,550	7.3	7.3	13.5
10 to 14 years	17,114	20,528	6.9	7.3	19.9
15 to 19 years	17,754	20,220	7.1	7.2	13.9
20 to 24 years	19,020	18,964	7.6	6.7	-0.3
25 to 34 years	43,176	39,892	17.4	14.2	-7.6
35 to 44 years	37,579	45,149	15.1	16.0	20.1
45 to 54 years	25,223	37,678	10.1	13.4	49.4
55 to 59 years	10,532	13,469	4.2	4.8	27.9
60 to 64 years	10,616	10,805	4.3	3.8	1.8
65 to 74 years	18,107	18,391	7.3	6.5	1.6
75 to 84 years	10,055	12,361	4.0	4.4	22.9
85 years and over	3,080	4,240	1.2	1.5	37.6
Median age (years).	32.9	35.3	(X)	(X)	(X)
18 years and over	185,105	209,128	74.4	74.3	13.0
Male.	88,655	100,994	35.6	35.9	13.9
Female	96,450	108,134	38.8	38.4	12.1
65 years and over	31,242	34,992	12.6	12.4	12.0
Male.	12,565	14,410	5.1	5.1	14.7
Female	18,677	20,582	7.5	7.3	10.2

X Not applicable.

Source: U.S. Census Bureau, "Table DP-1 Profile of General Demographic Characteristics for the United States"; published 15 May 2001; <http://www.census.gov/Press-Release/www/2001/cb01cn67.html>.

Population 13

No. 12. Resident Population by Age and Sex: 1980 to 1999

[In thousands, except as indicated (226,546 represents 226,546,000). 1980 and 1990 data are enumerated population as of April 1; data for other years are estimated population as of July 1. Excludes Armed Forces overseas. For definition of median, see Guide to Tabular Presentation]

Year and sex	Total, all years	Under 5 years	5-9 years	10-14 years	15-19 years	20-24 years	25-29 years	30-34 years	35-39 years	40-44 years	45-49 years	50-54 years	55-59 years	60-64 years	65-74 years	75-84 years	85 years and over	5-13 years	14-17 years	18-24 years	Median age (yr.)
1980, total [1]	**226,546**	**16,348**	**16,700**	**18,242**	**21,168**	**21,319**	**19,521**	**17,561**	**13,965**	**11,669**	**11,090**	**11,710**	**11,615**	**10,088**	**15,581**	**7,729**	**2,240**	**31,159**	**16,247**	**30,022**	**30.0**
Male	110,053	8,362	8,539	9,316	10,755	10,663	9,705	8,677	6,862	5,708	5,388	5,621	5,482	4,670	6,757	2,867	682	15,923	8,298	15,054	28.8
Female	116,493	7,986	8,161	8,926	10,413	10,655	9,816	8,884	7,104	5,961	5,702	6,089	6,133	5,418	8,824	4,862	1,559	15,237	7,950	14,969	31.3
1981, total	229,466	16,893	16,060	18,300	20,541	21,663	20,169	18,731	14,366	12,028	10,985	11,595	11,554	10,359	15,890	7,982	2,349	30,711	15,609	30,245	30.3
1982, total	231,664	17,228	15,958	18,145	19,962	21,682	20,704	18,714	15,566	12,464	11,011	11,414	11,463	10,567	16,147	8,203	2,437	30,528	15,057	30,162	30.5
1983, total	233,792	17,547	16,053	17,869	19,388	21,632	21,141	19,067	16,117	13,150	11,201	11,155	11,457	10,655	16,414	8,429	2,518	30,279	14,740	29,922	30.8
1984, total	235,825	17,695	16,338	17,450	18,931	21,529	21,459	19,503	16,867	13,636	11,429	10,957	11,352	10,803	16,626	8,656	2,595	30,062	14,725	29,461	31.1
1985, total	237,924	17,842	16,665	17,027	18,727	21,265	21,671	20,025	17,604	14,087	11,606	10,854	11,229	10,906	16,858	8,890	2,667	29,893	14,888	28,902	31.4
1986, total	240,133	17,963	17,098	16,474	18,813	20,744	21,893	20,479	18,611	14,398	11,878	10,781	11,135	10,885	17,137	9,129	2,742	30,078	14,824	28,227	31.7
1987, total	242,289	18,052	17,430	16,377	18,698	20,192	21,857	20,984	18,619	15,068	12,294	10,802	10,968	10,783	17,426	9,376	2,823	30,502	14,502	27,694	32.0
1988, total	244,499	18,195	17,759	16,496	18,496	19,655	21,739	21,391	18,993	15,688	12,954	10,995	10,722	10,791	17,626	9,612	2,885	31,028	14,023	27,356	32.3
1989, total	246,819	18,508	17,917	16,797	18,133	19,258	21,560	21,676	19,455	16,960	13,421	11,212	10,534	10,707	17,864	9,850	2,968	31,413	13,536	27,156	32.6
1990, total [2]	**248,791**	**18,765**	**18,042**	**17,067**	**17,893**	**19,143**	**21,336**	**21,838**	**19,851**	**17,593**	**13,747**	**11,315**	**10,489**	**10,627**	**18,048**	**10,014**	**3,022**	**31,839**	**13,345**	**26,961**	**32.8**
Male	121,284	9,603	9,236	8,742	9,178	9,749	10,708	10,866	9,837	8,679	6,741	5,494	5,009	4,947	7,908	3,745	842	16,301	6,860	13,744	31.6
Female	127,507	9,162	8,806	8,325	8,714	9,394	10,629	10,973	10,014	8,914	7,006	5,821	5,480	5,679	10,140	6,268	2,180	15,538	6,485	13,217	34.0
1991, total	252,153	19,189	18,205	17,679	17,235	19,156	20,713	22,157	20,530	18,761	14,099	11,648	10,422	10,581	18,271	10,319	3,189	32,470	13,452	26,352	33.1
1992, total	255,030	19,492	18,293	18,102	17,180	19,047	20,140	22,240	21,098	18,807	15,359	12,055	10,483	10,438	18,442	10,538	3,315	32,943	13,703	25,976	33.4
1993, total	257,783	19,674	18,442	18,508	17,375	19,047	19,570	22,227	21,605	19,209	15,931	12,728	10,678	10,236	18,629	10,738	3,446	33,382	13,989	25,740	33.7
1994, total	260,327	19,700	18,752	18,716	17,743	18,785	19,107	22,133	21,978	19,716	16,678	13,195	10,931	10,077	18,703	10,946	3,562	33,713	14,492	25,397	34.1
1995, total	262,803	19,532	19,096	18,853	18,203	18,982	18,905	21,825	22,296	20,259	17,458	13,642	11,086	10,046	18,757	11,178	3,685	34,195	15,112	25,112	34.3
1996, total	265,229	19,292	19,439	19,004	18,708	17,982	18,933	21,313	22,553	20,812	18,430	13,928	11,206	9,997	18,690	11,446	3,800	34,604	15,243	24,843	34.7
1997, total	267,784	19,099	19,754	19,097	19,146	17,488	18,820	20,739	22,636	21,378	18,467	15,158	11,755	10,061	18,528	11,744	3,913	35,005	15,499	24,980	34.9
1998, total	270,248	19,099	19,929	19,242	19,542	17,678	18,575	20,168	22,615	21,378	18,853	15,722	12,403	10,263	18,390	11,947	4,050	35,005	15,518	25,476	35.2
1999, total	**272,691**	**18,942**	**19,947**	**19,548**	**19,748**	**18,026**	**18,279**	**19,727**	**22,545**	**22,268**	**19,356**	**16,446**	**12,875**	**10,514**	**18,218**	**12,147**	**4,175**	**35,603**	**15,654**	**26,011**	**35.5**
Male	133,277	9,683	10,208	10,012	10,151	9,183	9,055	9,771	11,216	11,039	9,501	7,998	6,183	4,968	8,199	4,871	1,241	18,223	8,055	13,276	34.3
Female	139,414	9,259	9,739	9,537	9,597	8,843	9,154	9,956	11,329	11,229	9,856	8,448	6,693	5,546	10,020	7,275	2,936	17,379	7,600	12,736	36.6
Percent:																					
1980 [1]	100.0	7.2	7.4	8.1	9.3	9.4	8.6	7.8	6.2	5.2	4.9	5.2	5.1	4.5	6.9	3.4	1.0	13.8	7.2	13.3	(X)
1990 [2]	100.0	7.5	7.3	6.9	7.2	7.7	8.6	8.8	8.0	7.1	5.5	4.5	4.7	4.3	7.3	4.0	1.2	12.8	5.4	10.8	(X)
1999	**100.0**	**6.9**	**7.3**	**7.2**	**7.2**	**6.6**	**6.7**	**7.2**	**8.3**	**8.2**	**7.1**	**6.0**	**4.7**	**3.9**	**6.7**	**4.5**	**1.5**	**13.1**	**5.7**	**9.5**	**(X)**
Male	100.0	7.3	7.7	7.5	7.6	6.9	6.8	7.3	8.4	8.3	7.1	6.0	4.6	3.7	6.2	3.7	0.9	13.7	6.0	10.0	(X)
Female	100.0	6.6	7.0	6.8	6.9	6.3	6.6	7.1	8.1	8.1	7.1	6.1	4.8	4.0	7.2	5.2	2.1	12.5	5.5	9.1	(X)

X Not applicable. [1] Total population count has been revised since the 1980 census counts. See text of this section for explanation. The April 1, 1990, estimates base (248,790,925) includes count resolution corrections processed through August 1997. It generally does not include adjustments for census coverage errors. However, it includes adjustments estimated for the 1995 Test Census in various localities in California, New Jersey, and Louisiana; and the 1998 census dress rehearsals in localities in California and Wisconsin. These adjustments amounted to a total of 81,052 persons. [2] The data shown have been modified from the official 1990 census count. Numbers by age, race, Hispanic origin, and sex have not been corrected.

Source: U.S. Census Bureau, Current Population Reports, P25-1095; and "Resident Population Estimates of the United States by Age and Sex: April 1, 1990, to July 1, 1999; with short-term projections to April 1, 2000"; published 24 May 2000; <http://www.census.gov/population/estimates/nation/intfile2-1.txt>.

No. 13. Resident Population Projections by Sex and Age: 2005 to 2050

[In thousands, except as indicated (287,716 represents 287,716,000). As of July. Data shown are for middle series; for assumptions, see Table 3]

Age	2005 Total	2005 Male	2005 Female	2010 Total	2010 Male	2010 Female	2015	2020	2025	2030	2035	2040	2045	2050	Pct 2005	Pct 2010	Pct 2015	Pct 2020	Pct 2025	Pct 2050
Total	287,716	140,698	147,018	299,862	146,679	153,183	312,268	324,927	337,815	351,070	364,319	377,350	390,398	403,687	100.0	100.0	100.0	100.0	100.0	100.0
Under 5 years	19,212	9,815	9,397	20,099	10,272	9,827	21,179	21,951	22,551	23,183	24,016	25,014	26,013	26,914	6.7	6.7	6.8	6.8	6.7	6.7
5 to 9 years	19,122	9,774	9,348	19,438	9,936	9,502	20,321	21,403	22,197	22,845	23,509	24,358	25,364	26,366	6.6	6.5	6.5	6.5	6.6	6.5
10 to 14 years	20,634	10,564	10,069	19,908	10,183	9,724	20,229	21,146	22,289	23,186	23,870	24,571	25,459	26,503	7.2	6.6	6.5	6.5	6.6	6.6
15 to 19 years	20,990	10,788	10,202	21,668	11,132	10,536	20,892	21,020	21,224	23,449	23,748	24,660	25,813	26,715	7.3	7.2	6.7	6.5	6.6	6.6
20 to 24 years	20,159	10,269	9,889	21,151	10,776	10,375	21,748	21,384	21,411	22,481	22,333	23,552	25,360	26,054	7.0	7.1	7.0	6.6	6.3	6.5
25 to 29 years	18,351	9,144	9,207	19,849	9,901	9,948	20,765	21,410	20,761	21,257	22,174	22,845	24,430	25,104	6.4	6.6	6.6	6.6	6.1	6.2
30 to 34 years	18,582	9,146	9,436	19,002	9,385	9,617	20,484	20,938	21,111	21,615	22,281	22,953	23,928	25,354	6.5	6.3	6.2	6.4	6.5	6.3
35 to 39 years	20,082	9,927	10,155	19,039	9,380	9,659	19,442	20,759	21,926	22,728	23,222	21,966	23,349	25,152	7.0	6.3	6.2	6.1	6.3	6.2
40 to 44 years	22,634	11,222	11,412	20,404	10,069	10,335	19,346	19,773	21,308	22,374	22,112	20,543	22,522	24,436	7.9	6.8	6.4	6.1	6.3	6.1
45 to 49 years	22,230	10,965	11,264	22,227	10,967	11,260	20,057	19,034	19,473	21,031	20,884	18,575	22,798	23,072	7.7	7.4	7.0	6.4	5.8	5.7
50 to 54 years	19,661	9,578	10,082	21,934	10,739	11,195	21,929	19,804	19,366	19,318	18,989	17,349	21,622	22,373	6.8	7.3	7.0	6.6	5.7	5.5
55 to 59 years	16,842	8,101	8,741	19,177	9,248	9,929	21,400	21,412	19,717	18,452	18,027	18,104	20,123	22,445	5.9	6.4	6.9	6.1	5.6	5.5
60 to 64 years	12,848	6,086	6,762	16,252	7,725	8,528	18,519	20,696	20,759	19,844	18,104	17,962	17,962	21,199	4.5	5.4	5.9	6.6	6.1	5.3
65 to 69 years	10,086	4,661	5,425	12,159	5,640	6,520	15,410	17,598	19,717	19,844	18,068	16,555	15,912	19,477	3.5	4.1	4.9	5.4	5.8	4.8
70 to 74 years	8,375	3,757	4,618	8,995	4,066	4,929	10,897	13,864	15,886	17,878	15,895	16,170	14,908	16,537	2.9	3.0	3.5	4.3	4.7	4.1
75 to 79 years	7,429	3,172	4,257	7,175	3,110	4,065	7,772	9,484	12,159	14,029	11,220	12,820	13,140	14,407	2.6	2.4	2.5	2.9	3.6	3.6
80 to 84 years	5,514	2,157	3,356	5,600	2,247	3,353	5,484	6,024	7,439	9,638	8,068	9,808	11,220	12,225	1.9	1.9	1.8	1.9	2.2	3.0
85 to 89 years	3,028	1,046	1,982	3,476	1,242	2,234	3,612	3,611	4,045	5,077	6,678	7,884	9,123	9,463	1.1	1.2	1.2	1.1	1.2	2.3
90 to 94 years	1,402	404	998	1,625	497	1,128	1,930	2,074	2,135	2,457	3,155	4,243	5,115	6,030	0.5	0.5	0.6	0.6	0.6	1.5
95 to 99 years	442	104	338	556	139	417	678	844	948	1,015	1,213	1,606	2,226	2,764	0.2	0.2	0.1	0.1	0.3	0.7
100 years and over	96	18	77	129	26	103	177	235	313	381	441	551	757	1,095	(Z)	(Z)	0.1	0.1	0.1	0.3
5 to 13 years	35,475	18,144	17,331	35,321	18,056	17,265	36,497	38,361	40,054	41,377	42,592	44,004	45,740	47,582	12.3	11.8	11.7	11.8	11.9	11.8
14 to 17 years	16,931	8,709	8,222	16,681	8,583	8,098	16,437	16,839	17,741	18,653	19,325	19,881	20,477	21,252	5.9	5.6	5.3	5.2	5.3	5.3
18 to 24 years	28,498	14,543	13,956	30,163	15,388	14,774	30,254	29,593	30,305	31,910	33,590	34,803	35,779	36,804	9.9	10.1	9.7	9.1	9.0	9.1
16 years and over	224,447	108,336	116,111	236,301	114,175	122,126	246,455	256,230	266,342	277,222	288,108	298,453	308,456	318,601	78.0	78.8	78.9	78.9	78.8	78.9
18 years and over	216,098	104,030	112,068	227,761	109,768	117,993	238,155	247,776	257,469	267,857	278,386	288,450	298,168	307,938	75.1	76.0	76.3	76.3	76.2	76.3
10 to 49 years	163,661	82,026	81,635	163,247	81,794	81,453	162,961	165,929	171,482	178,100	184,120	189,717	195,335	202,390	56.9	54.4	52.2	51.1	50.8	50.1
55 years and over	66,060	29,505	36,555	75,145	33,939	41,206	85,878	95,841	102,766	107,624	111,790	116,295	120,888	125,643	23.0	25.1	27.5	29.5	30.4	31.1
65 years and over	36,370	15,318	21,052	39,715	16,966	22,749	45,959	53,733	62,641	70,319	74,774	77,177	79,142	81,999	12.6	13.2	14.7	16.5	18.5	20.3
85 years and over	4,968	1,572	3,396	5,786	1,904	3,882	6,396	6,763	7,441	8,931	11,486	14,284	17,220	19,352	1.7	1.9	2.0	2.1	2.2	4.8
Median age (years)	36.7	35.4	37.9	37.4	36.0	38.8	37.6	38.1	38.5	38.9	39.1	39.0	38.8	38.8	(X)	(X)	(X)	(X)	(X)	(X)

X Not applicable. Z Less than 0.05 percent.

Source: U.S. Census Bureau, "National Population Projections-Summary Tables"; published 13 January 2000; <http://www.census.gov/population/www/projections/natsum-T3.html>.

No. 14. Resident Population by Race, 1980 to 2000, and Projections, 2005 to 2050

[In thousands, except as indicated (226,546 represents 226,546,000). As of July, except as indicated. These data are consistent with the 1980 and 1990 decennial enumerations and have been modified from the official census counts; see text of this section for explanation]

Year	Total	White	Black	American Indian, Eskimo, Aleut	Asian, Pacific Islander
1980 (April) [1]	226,546	194,713	26,683	1,420	3,729
1981	229,466	196,635	27,133	1,483	4,214
1982	231,664	198,037	27,508	1,537	4,581
1983	233,792	199,420	27,867	1,596	4,909
1984	235,825	200,708	28,212	1,656	5,249
1985	237,924	202,031	28,569	1,718	5,606
1986	240,133	203,430	28,942	1,783	5,978
1987	242,289	204,770	29,325	1,851	6,343
1988	244,499	206,129	29,723	1,923	6,724
1989	246,819	207,540	30,143	2,001	7,134
1990 (April) [2]	248,791	208,741	30,517	2,067	7,467
1991	252,153	210,975	31,137	2,112	7,929
1992	255,030	212,874	31,683	2,149	8,324
1993	257,783	214,691	32,195	2,187	8,710
1994	260,327	216,379	32,672	2,222	9,054
1995	262,803	218,023	33,116	2,256	9,408
1996	265,229	219,636	33,537	2,290	9,765
1997	267,784	221,333	33,989	2,326	10,135
1998	270,248	222,980	34,427	2,361	10,479
1999	272,691	224,611	34,862	2,397	10,820
2000 [3]	275,130	226,232	35,307	2,434	11,157
PROJECTIONS [4]					
2005	287,716	234,221	37,619	2,625	13,251
2010	299,862	241,770	39,982	2,821	15,289
2015	312,268	249,468	42,385	3,016	17,399
2020	324,927	257,394	44,736	3,207	19,589
2025	337,815	265,306	47,089	3,399	22,020
2030	351,070	273,079	49,535	3,599	24,858
2040	377,350	287,787	54,462	4,006	31,095
2050	403,687	302,453	59,239	4,405	37,589
Percent distribution:					
2005	100.0	81.4	13.1	0.9	4.6
2010	100.0	80.6	13.3	0.9	5.1
2015	100.0	79.9	13.6	1.0	5.6
2020	100.0	79.2	13.8	1.0	6.0
2025	100.0	78.5	13.9	1.0	6.5
2030	100.0	77.8	14.1	1.0	7.1
2040	100.0	76.3	14.4	1.1	8.2
2050	100.0	74.9	14.7	1.1	9.3
Percent change:					
2010-2020	8.5	6.5	12.7	14.9	31.3
2020-2030	8.4	6.5	11.9	13.7	28.1
2030-2040	8.2	6.3	11.1	12.7	26.6
2040-2050	8.0	6.1	10.7	12.2	26.9

[1] See footnote 4, Table 1.   [2] The April 1, 1990, estimates base (248,790,925) includes count resolution corrections processed through August 1997. It generally does not include adjustments for census coverage errors. However, it includes adjustments estimated for the 1995 Test Census in various localities in California, New Jersey, and Louisiana; and the 1999 census dress rehearsals in localities in California and Wisconsin. These adjustments amounted to a total of 81,052 persons.   [3] These 2000 figures do not reflect the results of the 2000 census.   [4] Based on middle series of assumptions. See footnote 1, Table 3.

Source: U.S. Census Bureau, *Current Population Reports*, P25-1095; "National Estimates, Annual Population Estimates by Sex, Race, and Hispanic Origin, Selected Years From 1990 to 2000"; published 26 May 2000; <http://www.census.gov/population/www/estimates/nation3.html>; and "(NP-T4) Projections of the Total Resident Population by 5-Year Age Groups, Race, and Hispanic Origin With Special Age Categories: Middle Series, 1999 to 2100"; published 13 January 2000; <http://www.census.gov/population/www/projections/natsum-T3.html>.

No. 15. Resident Population by Hispanic Origin Status, 1980 to 2000, and Projections, 2005 to 2050

[In thousands, except as indicated (226,546 represents 226,546,000). As of July, except as indicated. These data are consistent with the 1980 and 1990 decennial enumerations and have been modified from the official census counts; see text of this section for explanation]

Year	Total	Hispanic origin [1]	Not of Hispanic origin			
			White	Black	American Indian, Eskimo, Aleut	Asian, Pacific Islander
1980 (April) [2]	226,546	14,609	180,906	26,142	1,326	3,563
1981	229,466	15,560	181,974	26,532	1,377	4,022
1982	231,664	16,240	182,782	26,856	1,420	4,367
1983	233,792	16,935	183,561	27,159	1,466	4,671
1984	235,825	17,640	184,243	27,444	1,512	4,986
1985	237,924	18,368	184,945	27,738	1,558	5,315
1986	240,133	19,154	185,678	28,040	1,606	5,655
1987	242,289	19,946	186,353	28,351	1,654	5,985
1988	244,499	20,786	187,012	28,669	1,703	6,329
1989	246,819	21,648	187,713	29,005	1,755	6,698
1990 (April) [3]	248,791	22,379	188,315	29,304	1,797	6,996
1991	252,153	23,391	189,634	29,858	1,831	7,439
1992	255,030	24,283	190,726	30,346	1,858	7,817
1993	257,783	25,222	191,697	30,795	1,884	8,184
1994	260,327	26,160	192,538	31,210	1,909	8,511
1995	262,803	27,107	193,328	31,590	1,932	8,846
1996	265,229	28,099	194,037	31,951	1,956	9,186
1997	267,784	29,182	194,746	32,339	1,979	9,537
1998	270,248	30,252	195,414	32,718	2,002	9,863
1999	272,691	31,337	196,049	33,092	2,026	10,186
2000 [4]	275,130	32,440	196,659	33,476	2,050	10,504
PROJECTIONS [5]						
2005	287,716	38,189	199,414	35,446	2,171	12,497
2010	299,862	43,688	201,956	37,483	2,300	14,436
2015	312,268	49,255	204,590	39,551	2,428	16,444
2020	324,927	55,156	207,145	41,549	2,550	18,527
2025	337,815	61,433	209,340	43,528	2,668	20,846
2030	351,070	68,168	210,984	45,567	2,787	23,564
2040	377,350	82,692	212,475	49,618	3,023	29,543
2050	403,687	98,229	212,991	53,466	3,241	35,760
Percent distribution:						
2005	100.0	13.3	69.3	12.3	0.8	4.3
2010	100.0	14.6	67.3	12.5	0.8	4.8
2015	100.0	15.8	65.5	12.7	0.8	5.3
2020	100.0	17.0	63.8	12.8	0.8	5.7
2025	100.0	18.2	62.0	12.9	0.8	6.2
2030	100.0	19.4	60.1	13.0	0.8	6.7
2040	100.0	21.9	56.3	13.1	0.8	7.8
2050	100.0	24.3	52.8	13.2	0.8	8.9
Percent change:						
2010-2020	8.5	29.0	2.6	11.6	11.8	31.6
2020-2030	8.4	26.3	2.6	10.8	10.9	28.3
2030-2040	8.2	24.7	2.3	10.1	9.9	26.8
2040-2050	8.0	23.6	1.9	9.7	9.3	27.2

[1] Persons of Hispanic origin may be of any race.   [2] See footnote 4, Table 1.   [3] The April 1, 1990, estimates base (248,790,925) includes count resolution corrections processed through August 1997. It generally does not include adjustments for census coverage errors. However, it includes adjustments estimated for the 1995 Test Census in various localities in California, New Jersey, and Louisiana; and the 1999 census dress rehearsals in localities in California and Wisconsin. These adjustments amounted to a total of 81,052 persons.   [4] These 2000 figures do not reflect the results of the 2000 census.   [5] Based on middle series of assumptions. See footnote 1, Table 3.

Source: U.S. Census Bureau, Current Population Reports, P25-1095; "National Estimates, Annual Population Estimates by Sex, Race and Hispanic Origin, Selected Years From 1990 to 2000"; published 26 May 2000; <http://www.census.gov/population/www/estimates/nation3.html>; and "(NPT4) Projections of the Total Resident Population by 5-Year Age Groups, Race, and Hispanic Origin With Special Age Categories: Middle Series, 1999 to 2100"; published 13 January 2000; <http://www.census.gov/population/www/projections/natsum-T3.html>.

No. 16. Resident Population by Race and Age, 1990 to 2000, and Projections, 2005 and 2010

[In thousands (208,741 represents 208,741,000), except as indicated. As of July, except 1990 as of April. For definition of median, see Guide to Tabular Presentation. Projections are based on middle series of assumptions; see footnote 1, Table 3]

Age group	White					Black					American Indian, Eskimo, Aleut					Asian, Pacific Islander				
	1990	1995	2000[1]	2005, proj.	2010, proj.	1990	1995	2000[1]	2005, proj.	2010, proj.	1990	1995	2000[1]	2005, proj.	2010, proj.	1990	1995	2000[1]	2005, proj.	2010, proj.
Total	208,741	218,023	226,232	234,221	241,770	30,517	33,116	35,307	37,619	39,982	2,067	2,256	2,434	2,625	2,821	7,467	9,408	11,157	13,251	15,289
Under 5 years	14,963	15,452	15,020	15,041	15,609	2,943	3,039	2,792	2,907	3,103	221	204	206	222	240	639	837	917	1,042	1,147
5 to 9 years	14,505	15,137	15,566	15,074	15,127	2,715	3,017	3,086	2,829	2,953	210	228	212	212	232	613	715	904	1,006	1,126
10 to 14 years	13,672	14,993	15,621	16,077	15,506	2,633	2,872	3,172	3,246	2,977	197	234	254	238	237	565	753	851	1,073	1,187
15 to 19 years	14,357	14,481	15,744	15,965	16,804	2,718	2,831	3,053	3,370	3,444	191	204	239	259	242	627	688	844	957	1,178
20 to 24 years	15,644	14,369	14,706	15,965	16,524	2,658	2,654	2,782	3,000	3,303	179	189	201	236	255	662	771	784	958	1,068
25 to 29 years	18,192	15,302	14,151	14,490	15,586	2,783	2,596	2,586	2,661	2,915	188	182	192	207	240	723	823	888	944	1,109
30 to 34 years	18,654	17,939	15,738	14,642	14,891	2,720	2,825	2,654	2,744	2,775	181	187	184	195	208	745	875	971	1,084	1,127
35 to 39 years	16,654	18,476	18,200	16,049	14,894	2,362	2,791	2,898	2,931	2,744	157	179	185	183	193	678	850	976	1,107	1,207
40 to 44 years	15,003	16,945	18,683	18,354	16,247	1,884	2,393	2,815	2,741	2,775	132	157	177	184	182	575	764	931	1,072	1,199
45 to 49 years	11,828	14,855	16,619	18,447	18,095	1,415	1,855	2,324	2,270	2,855	100	126	148	168	175	405	622	801	967	1,102
50 to 54 years	9,746	11,724	14,686	16,429	18,119	1,178	1,382	1,809	1,749	2,676	79	94	118	140	159	312	442	646	650	980
55 to 59 years	9,132	9,534	11,448	14,334	16,041	1,042	1,139	1,330	1,274	2,194	64	72	86	109	130	252	341	451	472	813
60 to 64 years	9,381	8,718	9,161	11,022	13,824	972	990	941	1,042	1,676	53	58	66	80	101	220	281	354	365	652
65 to 69 years	8,985	8,155	8,155	8,621	10,393	860	922	757	780	1,230	43	47	51	59	71	179	237	281	279	465
70 to 74 years	7,192	7,912	7,722	7,270	7,724	639	698	562	621	872	30	38	41	45	52	121	183	227	209	346
75 to 79 years	5,519	6,047	6,660	6,563	6,237	484	513	341	383	648	22	25	33	36	39	80	115	164	134	251
80 to 84 years	3,567	4,076	4,459	4,972	4,976	288	320	184	202	428	12	17	20	26	28	42	66	92	66	168
85 to 89 years	1,858	2,148	2,462	2,746	3,131	150	165	92	105	230	6	9	12	14	18	20	30	47	31	96
90 to 94 years	690	916	1,061	1,257	1,453	50	83	37	42	118	2	4	6	9	10	6	13	20	10	44
95 to 99 years	184	239	317	386	485	17	24	9	13	49	1	1	3	4	5	2	3	7	3	16
100 years and over	29	41	54	78	105	6	6	1	6	17	-	-	1	2	3	1	1	1	3	4
5 to 13 years	25,561	27,150	28,103	27,827	27,494	4,844	5,315	5,651	5,391	5,334	369	415	415	400	421	1,065	1,314	1,583	1,858	2,072
14 to 17 years	10,665	11,770	12,411	13,160	12,940	2,059	2,306	2,422	2,747	2,593	151	176	198	212	194	470	575	686	812	955
18 to 24 years	21,951	20,060	21,115	22,532	23,527	3,821	3,754	4,020	4,309	4,750	257	263	292	333	351	932	1,036	1,114	1,324	1,534
18 years and over	162,943	169,436	176,919	184,689	192,336	21,717	23,586	25,645	27,936	30,313	1,401	1,543	1,713	1,898	2,065	5,533	6,955	8,312	9,925	11,587
16 years and over	157,552	163,651	170,690	178,193	185,727	20,671	22,456	24,442	26,575	28,952	1,326	1,460	1,615	1,791	1,967	5,293	6,681	7,970	9,539	11,115
16 to 64 years	134,920	139,337	146,030	152,796	157,833	19,223	20,855	22,723	24,749	26,720	1,285	1,402	1,546	1,703	1,837	5,083	6,307	7,473	8,828	10,196
55 years and over	46,536	48,350	51,498	57,249	64,369	4,508	4,859	5,335	6,210	7,462	233	272	319	383	459	923	1,269	1,643	2,218	2,855
65 years and over	28,023	30,099	30,889	31,893	34,504	2,494	2,731	2,922	3,187	3,592	116	142	167	194	228	450	648	839	1,097	1,391
85 years and over	2,761	3,344	3,894	4,467	5,174	223	278	321	361	414	9	15	22	29	37	29	48	75	110	161
Median age (yrs)	33.7	35.4	36.9	37.9	38.8	27.9	29.2	30.3	31.5	32.3	26.0	26.8	27.8	28.4	29.3	29.4	30.7	32.0	33.1	33.7

- Represents or rounds to zero. [1] These 2000 figures do not reflect the results of the 2000 census.

Source: U.S. Census Bureau, "Monthly Postcensal Resident Population, by Single Year of Age, Sex, Race and Hispanic Origin": <http://www.census.gov/population/www/estimates/nat_90s_1.html>; a,d "Projections of the Total Resident Population by 5-Year Age Groups, Race, and Hispanic Origin With Special Age Categories: Middle Series, 1999 to 2100"; published 13 January 2000; <http://www.census.gov/population/www/projections/natsum-T3.html>.

No. 17. Resident Population by Hispanic Origin Status and Age, 1990 to 2000, and Projections, 2005

[In thousands (22,379 represents 22,379,000), except as indicated. As of July 1, except 1990 as of April 1. For definition of median, see Guide to Tabular Presentation. Projections are based on middle series of assumptions: see footnote 1, Table 3]

Age group	Hispanic origin				Not of Hispanic origin — White				Black				American Indian, Eskimo, Aleut				Asian, Pacific Islander			
	1990	1995	2000[1]	2005, proj.	1990	1995	2000[1]	2005, proj.	1990	1995	2000[1]	2005, proj.	1990	1995	2000[1]	2005, proj.	1990	1995	2000[1]	2005, proj.
Total	22,379	27,107	32,440	38,189	188,315	193,328	196,659	199,414	29,304	31,590	33,476	35,446	1,797	1,932	2,050	2,171	6,996	8,846	10,504	12,497
Under 5 years	2,469	3,206	3,541	4,027	12,722	12,523	11,779	11,353	2,802	2,859	2,597	2,686	186	171	167	176	587	773	852	970
5 to 9 years	2,180	2,609	3,343	3,681	12,516	12,774	12,514	11,707	2,600	2,863	2,897	2,625	179	191	177	171	567	659	837	937
10 to 14 years	1,991	2,417	2,874	3,622	11,855	12,801	13,025	12,781	2,528	2,737	3,001	3,039	170	198	211	196	523	699	787	996
15 to 19 years	2,087	2,401	2,842	3,307	12,451	12,290	13,159	13,409	2,608	2,700	2,896	3,176	165	172	198	212	582	640	786	887
20 to 24 years	2,324	2,394	2,784	3,224	13,525	12,179	12,156	13,022	2,531	2,529	2,636	2,827	151	159	166	192	612	722	732	894
25 to 29 years	2,341	2,447	2,620	3,011	15,509	13,078	11,754	11,737	2,652	2,459	2,450	2,551	161	151	158	166	674	770	834	885
30 to 34 years	2,047	2,519	2,692	2,888	16,332	15,648	13,291	12,007	2,603	2,679	2,501	2,504	156	158	149	157	701	822	914	1,026
35 to 39 years	1,643	2,177	2,667	2,851	15,162	15,777	15,777	13,464	2,267	2,661	2,739	2,573	138	153	154	147	641	803	922	1,047
40 to 44 years	1,278	1,740	2,273	2,767	13,840	16,503	16,622	15,936	1,813	2,290	2,677	2,762	117	136	150	152	546	726	884	1,016
45 to 49 years	937	1,314	1,759	2,278	10,971	15,369	15,023	16,289	1,364	1,779	2,218	2,600	90	111	128	141	385	593	763	921
50 to 54 years	750	964	1,345	1,778	9,058	13,660	13,462	14,816	1,138	1,328	1,730	2,161	72	84	104	120	297	421	618	785
55 to 59 years	634	762	986	1,352	8,548	10,844	10,548	13,103	1,009	1,096	1,273	1,669	58	65	77	95	240	326	431	623
60 to 64 years	550	634	775	989	8,872	8,836	8,452	10,120	946	955	1,039	1,216	48	53	59	70	210	228	339	453
65 to 69 years	431	542	635	770	8,584	8,221	7,573	7,918	840	893	904	995	40	43	46	52	172	228	270	351
70 to 74 years	284	406	513	599	6,928	8,136	7,248	6,721	625	679	730	746	28	35	37	40	116	176	218	268
75 to 79 years	212	260	373	470	5,321	7,535	6,314	6,130	475	500	544	596	20	24	30	32	76	111	158	202
80 to 84 years	128	174	216	308	3,446	5,806	4,258	4,685	284	312	331	368	11	16	18	23	40	63	89	129
85 to 89 years	65	90	124	155	1,797	3,913	2,345	2,601	148	162	179	195	6	8	11	13	19	29	45	64
90 to 94 years	19	40	56	78	672	2,063	1,009	1,184	49	82	89	101	2	4	6	8	6	13	19	30
95 to 99 years	6	9	19	27	178	879	299	361	17	17	36	40	1	1	3	4	2	3	7	10
100 years and over	2	2	3	7	28	231	51	72	6	6	8	13	-	-	1	2	-	1	1	3
5 to 13 years	3,786	4,539	5,664	6,590	22,107	23,038	22,955	21,813	4,644	5,053	5,324	5,020	316	349	346	325	985	1,216	1,464	1,726
14 to 17 years	1,576	1,922	2,223	2,708	9,224	10,022	10,402	10,707	1,978	2,200	2,296	2,588	131	149	165	174	436	535	638	753
18 to 24 years	3,219	3,361	3,956	4,536	19,015	16,984	17,496	18,398	3,645	3,576	3,810	4,060	218	222	241	271	863	970	1,038	1,234
16 years and over	15,349	18,391	22,134	26,176	148,919	152,663	156,733	160,849	20,885	22,556	24,400	26,435	1,230	1,334	1,454	1,582	5,211	6,577	7,868	9,405
18 years and over	14,547	17,440	21,012	24,863	144,263	147,744	151,523	155,540	19,880	21,478	23,259	25,152	1,164	1,263	1,372	1,495	4,988	6,323	7,550	9,047
16 to 64 years	14,202	16,869	20,194	23,763	121,965	123,976	127,637	131,179	18,441	19,899	21,578	23,379	1,122	1,203	1,302	1,407	4,780	5,954	7,061	8,349
55 years and over	2,331	2,918	3,701	4,754	44,374	45,659	48,096	52,892	4,398	4,708	5,134	5,940	214	249	288	341	882	1,218	1,577	2,132
65 years and over	1,147	1,522	1,940	2,413	26,954	28,687	29,096	29,670	2,443	2,657	2,822	3,055	108	130	152	175	432	623	807	1,057
85 years and over	91	141	202	266	2,675	3,211	3,705	4,218	219	273	313	350	9	14	20	27	27	45	72	107
Median age (yrs)	25.3	26.1	26.6	27.0	34.8	36.6	38.5	40.1	28.0	29.4	30.5	31.7	26.5	27.4	28.5	29.2	29.7	31.0	32.3	33.4

- Represents or rounds to zero. [1] These 2000 figures do not reflect the results of the 2000 census.

Source: U.S. Census Bureau, "Monthly Postcensal Resident Population, by Single Year of Age, Sex, Race and Hispanic Origin"; <http://www.census.gov/population/www/estimates/nat_90s_1.html>; and "Projections of the Total Resident Population by 5-Year Age Groups, Race, and Hispanic Origin With Special Age Categories: Middle Series, 1999 to 2100"; published 13 January 2000; <http://www.census.gov/population/www/projections/natsum-T3.html>.

Figure 1.2
Center of Population: 1970 to 2000

[Prior to 1960, excludes Alaska and Hawaii. The median center is located at the intersection of two median lines, a north-south line constructed so that half of the nation's population lives east and half lives west of it, and an east-west line selected so that half of the nation's population lives north and half lives south of it. The mean center of population is that point at which an imaginary, flat, weightless, and rigid map of the United States would balance if weights of identical value were placed on it so that each weight represented the location of one person on the date of the census]

Year	Median center		Mean center		
	Latitude-N	Longitude	Latitude-N	Longitude-W	Approximate location
1790 (August 2)	(NA)	(NA)	39 16 30	76 11 12	In Kent County, MD, 23 miles E of Baltimore MD
1850 (June 1)..	(NA)	(NA)	38 59 00	81 19 00	In Wirt County, WV, 23 miles SE of Parkersburg, WV[1]
1900 (June 1)..	40 03 32	84 49 01	39 09 36	85 48 54	In Bartholomew County, IN, 6 miles SE of Columbus, IN
1950 (April 1)..	40 00 12	84 56 51	38 50 21	88 09 33	In Richland County, IL, 8 miles NNW of Olney, IL
1960 (April 1)..	39 56 25	85 16 60	38 35 58	89 12 35	In Clinton County, IL, 6.5 miles NW of Centralia, IL
1970 (April 1)..	39 47 43	85 31 43	38 27 47	89 42 22	In St. Clair County, IL, 5.3 miles ESE of Mascoutah, IL
1980 (April 1)..	39 18 60	86 08 15	38 08 13	90 34 26	In Jefferson County, MO, .25 mile W of DeSoto, MO
1990 (April 1)..	38 57 55	86 31 53	37 52 20	91 12 55	In Crawford County, MO, 10 miles SE of Steelville, MO
2000 (April 1)..	38 45 23	86 55 51	37 41 49	91 48 34	In Phelps County, MO, 3 miles E of Edgar Springs, MO

NA Not available.   [1]West Virginia was set off from Virginia, Dec. 31, 1862, and admitted as a state, June 19, 1863.

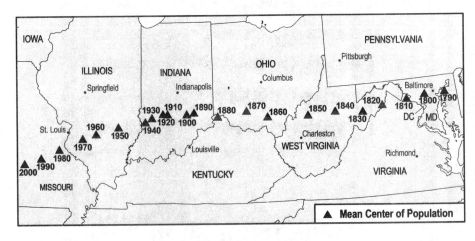

U.S. Census Bureau, Statistical Abstract of the United States: 2001

No. 18. Resident Population—States: 1980 to 2000

[226,546 represents 226,546,000. As of April 1. Insofar as possible, population shown for all years is that of present area of state. For area figures of states, see Table 343. Minus sign (-) indicates decrease]

State	Population (1,000)			Rank			Percent change		Population per sq. mile of land area [3]	
	1980 [1]	1990 [2]	2000	1980	1990	2000	1980-1990	1990-2000	1990	2000
United States..	**226,546**	**248,791**	**281,422**	(X)	(X)	(X)	9.8	13.1	70.4	79.6
Alabama	3,894	4,040	4,447	22	22	23	3.8	10.1	79.6	87.6
Alaska	402	550	627	50	49	48	36.9	14.0	1.0	1.1
Arizona	2,718	3,665	5,131	29	24	20	34.8	40.0	32.3	45.1
Arkansas.	2,286	2,351	2,673	33	33	33	2.8	13.7	45.1	51.3
California.	23,668	29,811	33,872	1	1	1	26.0	13.6	191.1	217.2
Colorado	2,890	3,294	4,301	28	26	24	14.0	30.6	31.8	41.5
Connecticut	3,108	3,287	3,406	25	27	29	5.8	3.6	678.5	702.9
Delaware.	594	666	784	47	46	45	12.1	17.6	340.8	400.8
Dist. of Columbia .	638	607	572	(X)	(X)	(X)	-4.9	-5.7	9,884.4	9,316.9
Florida	9,746	12,938	15,982	7	4	4	32.7	23.5	239.9	296.3
Georgia	5,463	6,478	8,186	13	11	10	18.6	26.4	111.8	141.3
Hawaii	965	1,108	1,212	39	41	42	14.9	9.3	172.5	188.6
Idaho	944	1,007	1,294	41	42	39	6.7	28.5	12.2	15.6
Illinois.	11,427	11,431	12,419	5	6	5	(Z)	8.6	205.6	223.4
Indiana	5,490	5,544	6,080	12	14	14	1.0	9.7	154.6	169.5
Iowa.	2,914	2,777	2,926	27	30	30	-4.7	5.4	49.7	52.4
Kansas	2,364	2,478	2,688	32	32	32	4.8	8.5	30.3	32.9
Kentucky.	3,661	3,687	4,042	23	23	25	0.7	9.6	92.8	101.7
Louisiana	4,206	4,222	4,469	19	21	22	0.4	5.9	96.9	102.6
Maine	1,125	1,228	1,275	38	38	40	9.2	3.8	39.8	41.3
Maryland.	4,217	4,781	5,296	18	19	19	13.4	10.8	489.1	541.8
Massachusetts . . .	5,737	6,016	6,349	11	13	13	4.9	5.5	767.6	810.0
Michigan	9,262	9,295	9,938	8	8	8	0.4	6.9	163.6	174.9
Minnesota	4,076	4,376	4,919	21	20	21	7.4	12.4	55.0	61.8
Mississippi.	2,521	2,575	2,845	31	31	31	2.2	10.5	54.9	60.6
Missouri	4,917	5,117	5,595	15	15	17	4.1	9.3	74.3	81.2
Montana	787	799	902	44	44	44	1.6	12.9	5.5	6.2
Nebraska	1,570	1,578	1,711	35	36	38	0.5	8.4	20.5	22.3
Nevada.	800	1,202	1,998	43	39	35	50.1	66.3	10.9	18.2
New Hampshire . .	921	1,109	1,236	42	40	41	20.5	11.4	123.7	137.8
New Jersey	7,365	7,748	8,414	9	9	9	5.2	8.6	1,044.3	1,134.2
New Mexico.	1,303	1,515	1,819	37	37	36	16.3	20.1	12.5	15.0
New York	17,558	17,991	18,976	2	2	3	2.5	5.5	381.0	401.8
North Carolina . . .	5,882	6,632	8,049	10	10	11	12.8	21.4	136.1	165.2
North Dakota	653	639	642	46	47	47	-2.1	0.5	9.3	9.3
Ohio.	10,798	10,847	11,353	6	7	7	0.5	4.7	264.9	277.2
Oklahoma	3,025	3,146	3,451	26	28	27	4.0	9.7	45.8	50.2
Oregon	2,633	2,842	3,421	30	29	28	7.9	20.4	29.6	35.6
Pennsylvania	11,864	11,883	12,281	4	5	6	0.2	3.4	265.1	274.0
Rhode Island	947	1,003	1,048	40	43	43	5.9	4.5	960.3	1,003.2
South Carolina . . .	3,122	3,486	4,012	24	25	26	11.7	15.1	115.8	133.2
South Dakota. . . .	691	696	755	45	45	46	0.8	8.5	9.2	9.9
Tennessee.	4,591	4,877	5,689	17	17	16	6.2	16.7	118.3	138.0
Texas	14,229	16,986	20,852	3	3	2	19.4	22.8	64.9	79.6
Utah.	1,461	1,723	2,233	36	35	34	17.9	29.6	21.0	27.2
Vermont	511	563	609	48	48	49	10.0	8.2	60.8	65.8
Virginia	5,347	6,189	7,079	14	12	12	15.8	14.4	156.3	178.8
Washington	4,132	4,867	5,894	20	18	15	17.8	21.1	73.1	88.5
West Virginia	1,950	1,793	1,808	34	34	37	-8.0	0.8	74.5	75.1
Wisconsin	4,706	4,892	5,364	16	16	18	4.0	9.6	90.1	98.8
Wyoming.	470	454	494	49	50	50	-3.4	8.9	4.7	5.1

X Not applicable.   Z Less than 0.05 percent.   [1] See footnote 4, Table 1.   [2] The April 1, 1990, census counts include corrections processed through August 1997, results of special censuses and test censuses, and do not include adjustments for census coverage errors.   [3] Persons per square mile were calculated on the basis of land area data from the 1990 census.

Source: U.S. Census Bureau, *1990 Census of Population and Housing, Population and Housing Unit Counts* (CPH-2); "ST-99-3 State Population Estimates: Annual Time Series, July 1, 1990, to July 1, 1999"; published 29 December 1999; <http://www.census.gov/population/estimates/state/st-99-3.txt>; and *Population Change and Distribution: 1990 to 2000, Census 2000 Brief*, (C2KBR/01-2), April 2001.

No. 19. Resident Population—States: 1991 to 1999

[In thousands (252,153 represents 252,153,000). As of July 1. Insofar as possible, population shown for all years is that of present area of state]

State	1991	1992	1993	1994	1995	1996	1997	1998	1999
United States. .	252,153	255,030	257,783	260,327	262,803	265,229	267,784	270,248	272,691
Alabama	4,091	4,139	4,193	4,233	4,263	4,290	4,320	4,351	4,370
Alaska	569	587	597	601	601	605	609	615	620
Arizona.	3,762	3,867	3,993	4,148	4,307	4,432	4,552	4,667	4,778
Arkansas.	2,371	2,394	2,424	2,451	2,480	2,505	2,524	2,538	2,551
California.	30,414	30,876	31,147	31,317	31,494	31,781	32,218	32,683	33,145
Colorado.	3,368	3,460	3,561	3,654	3,738	3,813	3,891	3,969	4,056
Connecticut	3,289	3,275	3,272	3,268	3,265	3,267	3,269	3,273	3,282
Delaware.	680	690	699	708	718	727	735	744	754
Dist. of Columbia .	593	584	576	565	551	538	529	521	519
Florida	13,289	13,505	13,714	13,962	14,185	14,427	14,683	14,908	15,111
Georgia	6,621	6,759	6,894	7,046	7,189	7,332	7,486	7,637	7,788
Hawaii	1,131	1,150	1,162	1,174	1,180	1,184	1,189	1,190	1,185
Idaho	1,039	1,066	1,101	1,135	1,165	1,188	1,211	1,231	1,252
Illinois.	11,536	11,635	11,726	11,805	11,885	11,953	12,012	12,070	12,128
Indiana	5,602	5,649	5,702	5,746	5,792	5,835	5,872	5,908	5,943
Iowa.	2,791	2,807	2,821	2,829	2,841	2,848	2,854	2,861	2,869
Kansas	2,495	2,526	2,548	2,569	2,587	2,598	2,616	2,639	2,654
Kentucky.	3,715	3,756	3,792	3,823	3,855	3,881	3,908	3,934	3,961
Louisiana	4,241	4,271	4,285	4,307	4,328	4,339	4,351	4,363	4,372
Maine	1,235	1,236	1,238	1,238	1,237	1,241	1,245	1,248	1,253
Maryland.	4,856	4,903	4,943	4,985	5,024	5,057	5,093	5,130	5,172
Massachusetts . . .	5,999	5,993	6,011	6,031	6,062	6,085	6,115	6,144	6,175
Michigan	9,395	9,470	9,529	9,584	9,660	9,739	9,785	9,820	9,864
Minnesota	4,427	4,472	4,522	4,566	4,605	4,648	4,688	4,726	4,776
Mississippi.	2,591	2,610	2,636	2,663	2,691	2,710	2,732	2,751	2,769
Missouri	5,158	5,194	5,238	5,281	5,325	5,368	5,407	5,438	5,468
Montana	808	822	840	855	869	877	879	880	883
Nebraska	1,591	1,602	1,612	1,622	1,635	1,648	1,656	1,661	1,666
Nevada.	1,285	1,331	1,380	1,456	1,526	1,596	1,676	1,744	1,809
New Hampshire . .	1,107	1,113	1,122	1,133	1,146	1,161	1,173	1,186	1,201
New Jersey	7,784	7,828	7,875	7,919	7,966	8,010	8,054	8,096	8,143
New Mexico.	1,547	1,581	1,615	1,653	1,682	1,706	1,723	1,734	1,740
New York	18,030	18,082	18,141	18,157	18,151	18,144	18,143	18,159	18,197
North Carolina . . .	6,748	6,832	6,947	7,061	7,185	7,308	7,429	7,546	7,651
North Dakota	634	635	637	640	642	643	641	638	634
Ohio.	10,934	11,008	11,070	11,111	11,155	11,187	11,212	11,238	11,257
Oklahoma	3,166	3,204	3,229	3,246	3,266	3,290	3,314	3,339	3,358
Oregon.	2,919	2,974	3,034	3,087	3,141	3,195	3,243	3,282	3,316
Pennsylvania	11,943	11,981	12,022	12,043	12,045	12,038	12,016	12,002	11,994
Rhode Island	1,004	1,001	998	993	989	988	987	988	991
South Carolina . . .	3,559	3,601	3,635	3,666	3,700	3,739	3,790	3,840	3,886
South Dakota. . . .	701	709	716	723	728	731	731	731	733
Tennessee.	4,947	5,014	5,086	5,163	5,241	5,314	5,378	5,433	5,484
Texas	17,340	17,650	17,997	18,338	18,680	19,006	19,355	19,712	20,044
Utah.	1,772	1,821	1,876	1,930	1,977	2,022	2,065	2,101	2,130
Vermont	567	570	574	579	583	586	589	591	594
Virginia	6,284	6,383	6,465	6,537	6,601	6,665	6,733	6,789	6,873
Washington	5,013	5,139	5,248	5,335	5,431	5,510	5,604	5,688	5,756
West Virginia	1,798	1,805	1,816	1,818	1,821	1,819	1,816	1,812	1,807
Wisconsin	4,953	5,005	5,055	5,096	5,137	5,174	5,200	5,222	5,250
Wyoming.	458	463	469	475	478	480	480	480	480

Source: U.S. Census Bureau, "ST-99-3 State Population Estimates: Annual Time Series, July 1, 1990, to July 1, 1999"; published 29 December 1999; <http://www.census.gov/population/estimates/state/st-99-3.txt>.

No. 20. Resident Population by Age and State: 2000

[In thousands, except percent (281,422 represents 281,422,000). As of April. Includes Armed Forces stationed in area]

State	Total	Under 5 years	5 to 17 years	18 to 24 years	25 to 34 years	35 to 44 years	45 to 54 years	55 to 64 years	65 to 74 years	75 to 84 years	85 years and over	Percent 65 years and over
U.S.	281,422	19,176	53,118	27,143	39,892	45,149	37,678	24,275	18,391	12,361	4,240	12.4
AL.	4,447	296	827	440	603	686	600	416	317	196	67	13.0
AK.	627	48	143	57	89	114	95	45	23	11	3	5.7
AZ.	5,131	382	985	514	743	769	628	442	364	235	69	13.0
AR.	2,673	182	499	262	353	398	350	257	198	129	46	14.0
CA.	33,872	2,487	6,763	3,366	5,229	5,485	4,332	2,614	1,888	1,282	426	10.6
CO	4,301	298	803	430	664	737	614	339	226	142	48	9.7
CT.	3,406	223	618	272	452	581	481	309	232	174	64	13.8
DE.	784	52	143	75	109	128	104	72	56	35	11	13.0
DC	572	33	82	73	102	88	75	50	36	25	9	12.2
FL.	15,982	946	2,701	1,331	2,084	2,485	2,069	1,559	1,452	1,024	331	17.6
GA	8,186	595	1,574	838	1,299	1,354	1,080	661	436	262	88	9.6
HI	1,212	78	218	115	171	191	171	107	85	58	18	13.3
ID	1,294	98	271	139	169	193	170	108	76	52	18	11.3
IL	12,419	877	2,369	1,211	1,812	1,984	1,627	1,041	772	536	192	12.1
IN	6,080	423	1,151	615	831	961	817	530	395	266	92	12.4
IA	2,926	188	545	298	363	445	393	257	212	159	65	14.9
KS.	2,688	189	524	276	349	420	354	220	176	129	52	13.3
KY.	4,042	266	729	402	568	643	557	373	274	173	58	12.5
LA	4,469	317	902	474	601	692	586	379	283	175	59	11.6
ME	1,275	71	231	104	158	213	193	123	96	64	23	14.4
MD	5,296	353	1,003	451	749	916	755	470	321	211	67	11.3
MA	6,349	397	1,103	579	927	1,063	873	546	428	316	117	13.5
MI	9,938	672	1,924	932	1,362	1,598	1,368	863	643	434	142	12.3
MN	4,919	330	957	470	673	824	666	405	296	213	86	12.1
MS	2,845	204	571	311	382	425	362	246	186	115	43	12.1
MO	5,595	370	1,058	536	739	888	742	507	393	264	99	13.5
MT	902	55	175	86	103	142	135	85	63	43	15	13.4
NE.	1,711	117	333	174	223	264	226	142	116	83	34	13.6
NV.	1,998	146	366	180	307	322	269	190	132	70	17	11.0
NH	1,236	76	234	103	160	221	184	110	78	51	18	12.0
NJ.	8,414	564	1,524	677	1,189	1,435	1,159	754	575	402	136	13.2
NM	1,819	131	378	178	234	282	246	159	118	71	23	11.7
NY.	18,976	1,239	3,451	1,765	2,757	3,074	2,553	1,688	1,276	861	311	12.9
NC	8,049	540	1,425	807	1,213	1,287	1,085	724	534	330	105	12.0
ND	642	39	121	73	77	98	85	53	46	34	15	14.7
OH	11,353	755	2,133	1,057	1,520	1,805	1,566	1,009	790	541	177	13.3
OK	3,451	236	656	357	452	524	454	316	242	156	57	13.2
OR	3,421	223	624	328	471	527	507	304	219	161	57	12.8
PA	12,281	728	2,194	1,094	1,560	1,948	1,705	1,132	969	712	238	15.6
RI	1,048	64	184	107	140	170	142	89	74	58	21	14.5
SC.	4,012	265	745	408	561	625	550	373	270	165	50	12.1
SD.	755	51	152	78	91	115	98	62	53	39	16	14.3
TN.	5,689	375	1,024	549	816	903	787	533	383	239	81	12.4
TX.	20,852	1,625	4,262	2,199	3,162	3,322	2,611	1,598	1,143	692	238	9.9
UT.	2,233	209	509	317	327	300	238	143	102	67	22	8.5
VT.	609	34	114	57	75	102	94	57	41	27	10	12.7
VA.	7,079	462	1,276	679	1,037	1,201	999	632	432	273	87	11.2
WA	5,894	394	1,120	559	841	975	846	497	337	241	84	11.2
WV	1,808	102	301	172	229	272	270	185	148	97	32	15.3
WI	5,364	342	1,026	521	706	876	732	458	355	252	96	13.1
WY	494	31	98	50	60	79	74	45	31	20	7	11.7

Source: U.S. Census Bureau, "Demographic Profiles: Census 2000"; <http://www.census.gov/Press-Release/www/2001/demoprofile.html>.

Population 23

No. 21. Resident Population by Sex, Age, and State: 2000

[In thousands (138,054 represents 138,054,000). **As of April.** Includes Armed Forces stationed in area]

State	Total population Male	Total population Female	Persons 65 years and over Male	Persons 65 years and over Female	State	Total population Male	Total population Female	Persons 65 years and over Male	Persons 65 years and over Female
U.S.	**138,054**	**143,368**	**14,410**	**20,582**	MO.	2,720	2,875	307	448
AL	2,147	2,301	231	348	MT	449	453	53	68
AK	324	303	17	19	NE	843	868	96	137
AZ	2,561	2,570	296	372	NV	1,018	980	102	117
AR	1,305	1,369	154	220	NH	608	628	62	86
CA	16,875	16,997	1,514	2,082					
					NJ	4,083	4,332	447	666
CO	2,166	2,135	177	240	NM	894	925	93	119
CT	1,649	1,756	190	280	NY	9,147	9,830	976	1,472
DE	381	403	43	59	NC	3,943	4,107	389	580
DC	269	303	27	43	ND	321	322	40	55
FL	7,798	8,185	1,217	1,591					
					OH	5,512	5,841	609	899
GA	4,027	4,159	311	474	OK	1,696	1,755	188	268
HI.	609	603	71	89	OR	1,697	1,725	186	252
ID.	649	645	64	82	PA	5,930	6,351	768	1,152
IL.	6,080	6,339	602	898	RI.	504	545	60	92
IN.	2,982	3,098	304	449					
					SC	1,949	2,063	197	289
IA.	1,436	1,491	177	259	SD	375	380	46	63
KS	1,328	1,360	146	211	TN	2,770	2,919	282	421
KY	1,975	2,066	204	301	TX	10,353	10,499	862	1,210
LA	2,163	2,306	208	309	UT	1,119	1,114	83	107
ME	620	655	76	107					
					VT	298	310	32	45
MD.	2,558	2,739	244	355	VA	3,472	3,607	323	470
MA.	3,059	3,290	342	519	WA	2,934	2,960	282	380
MI	4,873	5,065	501	718	WV	879	929	113	164
MN	2,436	2,484	247	347	WI	2,649	2,715	292	411
MS	1,374	1,471	136	208	WY	248	245	25	32

Source: U.S. Census Bureau, "Demographic Profiles: Census 2000"; <http://www.census.gov/Press-Release/www/2001/demoprofile.html>.

No. 22. Resident Population by Region, Race, and Hispanic Origin: 2000

[281,422 represents 281,422,000. **As of April.** For composition of regions, see map, inside front cover]

Race and Hispanic origin	Population (1,000) United States	Population (1,000) North- east	Population (1,000) Midwest	Population (1,000) South	Population (1,000) West	Percent distribution United States	Percent distribution North- east	Percent distribution Mid- west	Percent distribution South	Percent distribution West
Total population	**281,422**	**53,594**	**64,393**	**100,237**	**63,198**	**100.0**	**19.0**	**22.9**	**35.6**	**22.5**
One race	274,596	52,366	63,370	98,390	60,470	100.0	19.1	23.1	35.8	22.0
White	211,461	41,534	53,834	72,819	43,274	100.0	19.6	25.5	34.4	20.5
Black or African American ...	34,658	6,100	6,500	18,982	3,077	100.0	17.6	18.8	54.8	8.9
American Indian and Alaska Native	2,476	163	399	726	1,188	100.0	6.6	16.1	29.3	48.0
Asian	10,243	2,119	1,198	1,922	5,004	100.0	20.7	11.7	18.8	48.8
Asian Indian	1,679	554	293	441	391	100.0	33.0	17.5	26.3	23.3
Chinese	2,433	692	212	343	1,186	100.0	28.4	8.7	14.1	48.8
Filipino	1,850	202	151	245	1,253	100.0	10.9	8.2	13.2	67.7
Japanese	797	76	63	77	580	100.0	9.6	7.9	9.7	72.8
Korean	1,077	246	132	224	474	100.0	22.9	12.3	20.8	44.0
Vietnamese	1,123	115	107	336	564	100.0	10.3	9.5	29.9	50.3
Other Asian [1]	1,285	233	239	257	556	100.0	18.2	18.6	20.0	43.2
Native Hawaiian and Other Pacific Islander	399	21	22	51	304	100.0	5.2	5.6	12.8	76.3
Native Hawaiian	141	4	6	12	118	100.0	3.2	4.1	8.9	83.8
Guamanian or Chamorro ..	58	5	5	15	34	100.0	7.9	7.9	25.1	59.1
Samoan	91	4	5	9	73	100.0	4.2	5.6	9.7	80.5
Other Pacific Islander [2] ...	109	8	7	15	79	100.0	7.3	6.4	14.0	72.2
Some other race	15,359	2,430	1,417	3,889	7,623	100.0	15.8	9.2	25.3	49.6
Two or more races	6,826	1,228	1,022	1,847	2,728	100.0	18.0	15.0	27.1	40.0
Hispanic or Latino (of any race) .	35,306	5,254	3,125	11,587	15,341	100.0	14.9	8.8	32.8	43.5
Mexican	20,641	479	2,200	6,548	11,413	100.0	2.3	10.7	31.7	55.3
Puerto Rican.	3,406	2,075	325	759	247	100.0	60.9	9.6	22.3	7.2
Cuban	1,242	169	45	921	106	100.0	13.6	3.6	74.2	8.5
Other Hispanic or Latino	10,017	2,531	554	3,358	3,574	100.0	25.3	5.5	33.5	35.7
Not Hispanic or Latino	246,116	48,340	61,268	88,650	47,857	100.0	19.6	24.9	36.0	19.4
White alone	194,553	39,327	52,386	65,928	36,912	100.0	20.2	26.9	33.9	19.0

[1] Other Asian alone, or two or more Asian categories.   [2] Other Pacific Islander alone, or two or more Native Hawaiian and Other Pacific Islander categories.

Source: U.S. Census Bureau, "Demographic Profiles: Census 2000"; <http://www.census.gov/Press-Release/www/2001/demoprofile.html>.

No. 23. Resident Population by Hispanic or Latino Origin and State: 2000

[In thousands, except percent (281,422 represents 281,422,000). As of April. Persons of Hispanic or Latino origin may be of any race]

State	Hispanic or Latino							Not Hispanic or Latino	
	Total		Percent of total population	Mexican	Puerto Rican	Cuban	Other Hispanic or Latino	Total	White alone
	Total population	Number							
U.S.	281,422	35,306	12.5	20,641	3,406	1,242	10,017	246,116	194,553
AL.	4,447	76	1.7	45	6	2	23	4,371	3,126
AK.	627	26	4.1	13	3	1	9	601	424
AZ.	5,131	1,296	25.3	1,066	18	5	207	3,835	3,274
AR.	2,673	87	3.2	61	2	1	22	2,587	2,100
CA.	33,872	10,967	32.4	8,456	141	72	2,298	22,905	15,817
CO	4,301	736	17.1	451	13	4	268	3,566	3,203
CT.	3,406	320	9.4	23	194	7	95	3,085	2,639
DE.	784	37	4.8	13	14	1	9	746	568
DC	572	45	7.9	5	2	1	36	527	159
FL.	15,982	2,683	16.8	364	482	833	1,004	13,300	10,459
GA	8,186	435	5.3	275	36	13	112	7,751	5,129
HI	1,212	88	7.2	20	30	1	37	1,124	277
ID	1,294	102	7.9	79	2	(Z)	20	1,192	1,139
IL	12,419	1,530	12.3	1,144	158	18	210	10,889	8,424
IN	6,080	215	3.5	153	20	3	39	5,866	5,219
IA	2,926	82	2.8	61	3	1	18	2,844	2,710
KS.	2,688	188	7.0	148	5	2	33	2,500	2,234
KY.	4,042	60	1.5	31	6	4	19	3,982	3,608
LA.	4,469	108	2.4	32	8	8	59	4,361	2,794
ME	1,275	9	0.7	3	2	(Z)	4	1,266	1,230
MD	5,296	228	4.3	40	26	7	156	5,069	3,287
MA	6,349	429	6.8	22	199	9	198	5,920	5,198
MI	9,938	324	3.3	221	27	7	69	9,615	7,807
MN	4,919	143	2.9	96	7	3	39	4,776	4,337
MS	2,845	40	1.4	22	3	2	14	2,805	1,728
MO	5,595	119	2.1	78	7	3	31	5,477	4,686
MT	902	18	2.0	12	1	(Z)	5	884	808
NE.	1,711	94	5.5	71	2	1	21	1,617	1,494
NV.	1,998	394	19.7	286	10	11	86	1,604	1,303
NH	1,236	20	1.7	5	6	1	9	1,215	1,175
NJ.	8,414	1,117	13.3	103	367	77	570	7,297	5,557
NM	1,819	765	42.1	330	4	3	428	1,054	813
NY.	18,976	2,868	15.1	261	1,050	63	1,494	16,109	11,761
NC	8,049	379	4.7	247	31	7	94	7,670	5,647
ND	642	8	1.2	4	1	(Z)	3	634	589
OH	11,353	217	1.9	91	66	5	55	11,136	9,538
OK	3,451	179	5.2	133	8	2	37	3,271	2,556
OR	3,421	275	8.0	215	5	3	52	3,146	2,858
PA.	12,281	394	3.2	55	229	10	100	11,887	10,322
RI	1,048	91	8.7	6	25	1	58	957	858
SC.	4,012	95	2.4	53	12	3	27	3,917	2,652
SD.	755	11	1.4	6	1	(Z)	4	744	665
TN.	5,689	124	2.2	77	10	4	32	5,565	4,506
TX.	20,852	6,670	32.0	5,072	70	26	1,502	14,182	10,933
UT.	2,233	202	9.0	136	4	1	60	2,032	1,904
VT.	609	6	0.9	1	1	(Z)	3	603	585
VA	7,079	330	4.7	74	41	8	206	6,749	4,966
WA	5,894	442	7.5	330	16	5	91	5,453	4,652
WV	1,808	12	0.7	4	2	(Z)	6	1,796	1,710
WI	5,364	193	3.6	127	30	2	33	5,171	4,682
WY	494	32	6.4	20	1	(Z)	11	462	439

Z Less than 500.

Source: U.S. Census Bureau, Census 2000 Redistricting Data (P.L. 94-171) Summary File for states, Tables PL1 and PL2.

U.S. Census Bureau, Statistical Abstract of the United States: 2001

[281,422 represents 281,422,000. As of April]

State	Number (1,000)							
		One race						
	Total population	White	Black or African American	American Indian, Alaska Native	Asian	Native Hawaiian and Other Pacific Islander	Some other race	Two or more races
U.S. ..	281,422	211,461	34,658	2,476	10,243	399	15,359	6,826
AL.	4,447	3,163	1,156	22	31	1	29	44
AK.	627	435	22	98	25	3	10	34
AZ.	5,131	3,874	159	256	92	7	597	147
AR.	2,673	2,139	419	18	20	2	40	36
CA.	33,872	20,170	2,264	333	3,698	117	5,682	1,608
CO	4,301	3,560	165	44	95	5	310	122
CT.	3,406	2,780	310	10	82	1	147	75
DE.	784	585	151	3	16	(Z)	16	13
DC	572	176	343	2	15	(Z)	22	13
FL.	15,982	12,465	2,336	54	266	9	477	376
GA	8,186	5,327	2,350	22	173	4	196	114
HI	1,212	294	22	4	504	114	15	259
ID	1,294	1,177	5	18	12	1	55	26
IL	12,419	9,125	1,877	31	424	5	723	235
IN	6,080	5,320	510	16	59	2	98	76
IA	2,926	2,749	62	9	37	1	37	32
KS.	2,688	2,314	154	25	47	1	91	56
KY.	4,042	3,641	296	9	30	1	23	42
LA	4,469	2,856	1,452	25	55	1	31	48
ME	1,275	1,236	7	7	9	(Z)	3	13
MD	5,296	3,391	1,477	15	211	2	96	104
MA	6,349	5,367	343	15	238	2	237	146
MI	9,938	7,966	1,413	58	177	3	130	192
MN	4,919	4,400	172	55	142	2	66	83
MS	2,845	1,746	1,034	12	19	1	14	20
MO	5,595	4,748	629	25	62	3	46	82
MT	902	817	3	56	5	(Z)	5	16
NE.	1,711	1,533	69	15	22	1	48	24
NV.	1,998	1,502	135	26	90	8	159	76
NH	1,236	1,187	9	3	16	(Z)	7	13
NJ.	8,414	6,105	1,142	19	480	3	451	214
NM	1,819	1,214	34	173	19	2	310	66
NY.	18,976	12,894	3,014	82	1,045	9	1,342	590
NC	8,049	5,805	1,738	100	114	4	187	103
ND	642	593	4	31	4	(Z)	3	7
OH	11,353	9,645	1,301	24	133	3	89	158
OK	3,451	2,628	261	273	47	2	83	156
OR	3,421	2,962	56	45	101	8	145	105
PA	12,281	10,484	1,225	18	220	3	188	142
RI	1,048	891	47	5	24	1	53	28
SC.	4,012	2,696	1,185	14	36	2	40	40
SD.	755	669	5	62	4	(Z)	4	10
TN.	5,689	4,563	933	15	57	2	56	63
TX.	20,852	14,800	2,405	118	562	14	2,438	515
UT.	2,233	1,993	18	30	37	15	93	47
VT.	609	589	3	2	5	(Z)	1	7
VA.	7,079	5,120	1,390	21	261	4	139	143
WA	5,894	4,822	190	93	322	24	229	214
WV	1,808	1,719	57	4	9	(Z)	3	16
WI.	5,364	4,770	304	47	89	2	85	67
WY	494	455	4	11	3	(Z)	12	9

See footnote at end of table.

U.S. Census Bureau, Statistical Abstract of the United States: 2001

[281,422 represents 281,422,000. As of April]

State	Percent distribution						
	One race						
	White	Black or African American	American Indian, Alaska Native	Asian	Native Hawaiian and Other Pacific Islander	Some other race	Two or more races
U.S. ..	75.1	12.3	0.9	3.6	0.1	5.5	2.4
AL.......	71.1	26.0	0.5	0.7	(Z)	0.7	1.0
AK.......	69.3	3.5	15.6	4.0	0.5	1.6	5.4
AZ.......	75.5	3.1	5.0	1.8	0.1	11.6	2.9
AR.......	80.0	15.7	0.7	0.8	0.1	1.5	1.3
CA.......	59.5	6.7	1.0	10.9	0.3	16.8	4.7
CO.......	82.8	3.8	1.0	2.2	0.1	7.2	2.8
CT.......	81.6	9.1	0.3	2.4	(Z)	4.3	2.2
DE.......	74.6	19.2	0.3	2.1	(Z)	2.0	1.7
DC.......	30.8	60.0	0.3	2.7	0.1	3.8	2.4
FL.......	78.0	14.6	0.3	1.7	0.1	3.0	2.4
GA	65.1	28.7	0.3	2.1	0.1	2.4	1.4
HI	24.3	1.8	0.3	41.6	9.4	1.3	21.4
ID	91.0	0.4	1.4	0.9	0.1	4.2	2.0
IL	73.5	15.1	0.2	3.4	(Z)	5.8	1.9
IN	87.5	8.4	0.3	1.0	(Z)	1.6	1.2
IA	93.9	2.1	0.3	1.3	(Z)	1.3	1.1
KS.......	86.1	5.7	0.9	1.7	(Z)	3.4	2.1
KY.......	90.1	7.3	0.2	0.7	(Z)	0.6	1.1
LA.......	63.9	32.5	0.6	1.2	(Z)	0.7	1.1
ME	96.9	0.5	0.6	0.7	(Z)	0.2	1.0
MD	64.0	27.9	0.3	4.0	(Z)	1.8	2.0
MA	84.5	5.4	0.2	3.8	(Z)	3.7	2.3
MI.......	80.2	14.2	0.6	1.8	(Z)	1.3	1.9
MN	89.4	3.5	1.1	2.9	(Z)	1.3	1.7
MS	61.4	36.3	0.4	0.7	(Z)	0.5	0.7
MO	84.9	11.2	0.4	1.1	0.1	0.8	1.5
MT	90.6	0.3	6.2	0.5	0.1	0.6	1.7
NE.......	89.6	4.0	0.9	1.3	(Z)	2.8	1.4
NV.......	75.2	6.8	1.3	4.5	0.4	8.0	3.8
NH	96.0	0.7	0.2	1.3	(Z)	0.6	1.1
NJ.......	72.6	13.6	0.2	5.7	(Z)	5.4	2.5
NM	66.8	1.9	9.5	1.1	0.1	17.0	3.6
NY.......	67.9	15.9	0.4	5.5	(Z)	7.1	3.1
NC.......	72.1	21.6	1.2	1.4	(Z)	2.3	1.3
ND	92.4	0.6	4.9	0.6	(Z)	0.4	1.2
OH	85.0	11.5	0.2	1.2	(Z)	0.8	1.4
OK	76.2	7.6	7.9	1.4	0.1	2.4	4.5
OR	86.6	1.6	1.3	3.0	0.2	4.2	3.1
PA.......	85.4	10.0	0.1	1.8	(Z)	1.5	1.2
RI	85.0	4.5	0.5	2.3	0.1	5.0	2.7
SC.......	67.2	29.5	0.3	0.9	(Z)	1.0	1.0
SD.......	88.7	0.6	8.3	0.6	(Z)	0.5	1.3
TN.......	80.2	16.4	0.3	1.0	(Z)	1.0	1.1
TX.......	71.0	11.5	0.6	2.7	0.1	11.7	2.5
UT.......	89.2	0.8	1.3	1.7	0.7	4.2	2.1
VT.......	96.8	0.5	0.4	0.9	(Z)	0.2	1.2
VA.......	72.3	19.6	0.3	3.7	0.1	2.0	2.0
WA	81.8	3.2	1.6	5.5	0.4	3.9	3.6
WV.......	95.0	3.2	0.2	0.5	(Z)	0.2	0.9
WI.......	88.9	5.7	0.9	1.7	(Z)	1.6	1.2
WY	92.1	0.8	2.3	0.6	0.1	2.5	1.8

Z Less than 500 or 0.05 percent.

Source: U.S. Census Bureau, "Demographic Profiles: Census 2000"; <http://www.census.gov/Press-Release/www/2001/demoprofile.html>.

Population   27

No. 25. Annual Inmigration, Outmigration, and Net Migration for Regions: 1990 to 1999

[In thousands (346 represents 346,000). As of March. For persons 1 year old and over. Excludes members of the Armed Forces except those living off post or with their families on post. Based on Current Population Survey; see text of this section and Appendix III. For composition of regions, see map, inside front cover. Minus sign (-) indicates net outmigration]

Period	North-east	Mid-west	South	West	Period	North-east	Mid-west	South	West
1990-91: Immigrants.	346	782	1,421	835	Net internal migration . .	-203	120	230	-146
Outmigrants	932	797	987	668	Movers from abroad	247	170	416	370
Net internal migration . .	-585	-15	433	167	Net migration	44	290	646	224
Movers from abroad	209	208	351	617	**1998-99**:				
Net migration	-376	193	784	784	Total inmigrants	461	736	1,339	743
1995-96: Immigrants.	441	842	1,284	792	From Northeast	(X)	94	383	146
Outmigrants	675	775	1,134	775	From Midwest	98	(X)	556	253
Net internal migration . .	-234	68	150	16	From South	262	463	(X)	344
Movers from abroad	285	130	470	476	From West	101	178	400	(X)
Net migration	51	198	620	492	Total outmigrants	624	906	1,068	679
1996-97: Immigrants.	481	661	1,338	688	To Northeast	(X)	98	262	101
Outmigrants	600	814	947	806	To Midwest	94	(X)	463	178
Net internal migration . .	-119	-154	391	-118	To South	383	556	(X)	400
Movers from abroad	239	169	445	450	To West	146	253	344	(X)
Net migration	120	15	836	332	Net internal migration	-163	-171	270	63
1997-98. Immigrants.	504	873	1,335	660	Movers from abroad	198	221	544	466
Outmigrants	708	753	1,105	806	Net migration	35	50	814	529

X Not applicable.

No. 26. Mobility Status of the Population by Selected Characteristics: 1980 to 2000

[221,641 represents 221,641,000. As of March. For persons 1 year old and over. Excludes members of the Armed Forces except those living off post or with their families on post. Based on Current Population Survey; see text of this section and Appendix III. For composition of regions, see map, inside front cover]

Mobility period and characteristic	Total (1,000)	Non-movers	Percent distribution						Movers from abroad
			Movers (different house in United States)						
			Total	Same county	Different county				
					Total	Same state	Different state		
1980-81.	221,641	83	17	10	6	3	3	1
1985-86.	232,998	82	18	11	7	4	3	1
1990-91.	244,884	83	16	10	6	3	3	1
1995-96.	260,406	84	16	10	6	3	3	1
1999-2000, total	270,219	84	15	9	6	3	3	1
1 to 4 years old.	15,740	77	22	14	8	4	4	1
5 to 9 years old.	20,379	82	17	11	6	3	3	1
10 to 14 years old.	20,328	86	13	8	6	3	3	1
15 to 19 years old.	20,102	83	16	9	7	3	3	1
20 to 24 years old	18,441	65	34	20	13	7	6	2
25 to 29 years old	18,268	68	31	18	13	7	6	1
30 to 44 years old	64,323	83	16	10	7	3	3	1
45 to 64 years old	60,017	92	8	4	4	2	2	(Z)
65 to 74 years old	17,796	95	4	2	2	1	1	(Z)
75 to 84 years old	11,685	96	4	2	2	1	1	(Z)
85 years old and over	3,140	95	5	2	2	1	1	(Z)
Northeast.	51,364	88	12	7	5	3	2	1
Midwest.	62,618	85	15	8	6	3	3	(Z)
South	94,646	83	16	9	8	4	4	1
West.	61,592	81	18	12	6	3	3	1
Persons 16 years and over	209,845	84	15	9	6	3	3	1
Civilian labor force.	140,454	83	17	10	7	4	3	1
Employed.	134,338	83	17	10	7	4	3	1
Unemployed . . . . :	6,116	75	24	14	10	5	5	1
Armed Forces.	777	59	35	11	23	4	20	6
Not in labor force	68,613	89	11	6	5	2	3	1
Persons 15 years and over	213,773	84	15	9	6	3	3	1
Without income.	18,137	82	16	9	7	3	4	2
With income	195,636	85	15	9	6	3	3	(Z)
Less than $5,000.	26,138	84	15	8	6	3	3	1
$5,000 to $9,999.	26,254	84	15	9	6	3	3	1
$10,000 to $14,999	23,047	84	16	10	6	3	3	(Z)
$15,000 to $24,999	37,234	82	17	10	7	4	3	(Z)
$25,000 to $34,999	27,505	84	16	9	6	3	3	(Z)
$35,000 to $49,999	24,898	87	13	7	6	3	3	(Z)
$50,000 to $74,999	18,023	88	12	6	5	3	3	(Z)
$75,000 and over.	12,538	89	11	5	8	3	3	1
Tenure:								
Owner-occupied units	189,408	91	9	5	4	2	2	(Z)
Renter-occupied units	80,811	68	31	19	12	6	6	2

Z Less than 0.5 percent.

Source of Tables 25 and 26: U.S. Census Bureau, *Current Population Reports*, P20-538.

28   Population

No. 27. Mobility Status of Households by Household Income: 1999-2000

[104,711 represents 104,711,000. As of March. See headnote, Table 26]

Household income	Total (1,000)	Non-movers	Percent distribution						
			Movers (different house in United States)						Movers from abroad
			Total	Same county	Different county				
					Total	Same state	Different state		
Householders, 15 years and over...	104,711	85	15	9	6	3	3		(Z)
Less than $5,000	3,010	74	24	13	11	5	6		2
$5,000 to $9,999	6,646	81	19	12	7	4	3		1
$10,000 to $14,999	7,660	84	16	10	6	3	3		(Z)
$15,000 to $24,999	14,720	82	18	11	7	3	3		(Z)
$25,000 to $34,999	13,273	82	17	11	6	3	3		(Z)
$35,000 to $49,999	16,539	85	15	9	6	3	3		(Z)
$50,000 to $74,999	19,274	87	13	7	6	3	3		(Z)
$75,000 and over	23,589	89	10	5	5	3	2		(Z)

Z Less than 0.5 percent.

Source: U.S. Census Bureau, *Current Population Reports*, P20-538.

No. 28. Population in Coastal Counties: 1970 to 2000

[3,536 represents 3,536,000. Enumerated population as of April 1, except as indicated. Areas as defined by U.S. National Oceanic and Atmospheric Agency, 1992. Covers 673 counties and equivalent areas with at least 15 percent of their land area either in a coastal watershed (drainage area) or in a coastal cataloging unit (a coastal area between watersheds)]

Year	Total	Counties in coastal regions					Balance of United States
		Total	Atlantic	Gulf of Mexico	Great Lakes	Pacific	
Land area, 1990 (1,000 sq. mi.)	3,536	888	148	114	115	510	2,649
POPULATION							
1970 (mil.)........................	203.3	110.0	51.1	10.0	26.0	22.8	93.3
1980 (mil.)........................	226.5	119.8	53.7	13.1	26.0	27.0	106.7
1990 (mil.)........................	248.7	133.4	59.0	15.2	25.9	33.2	115.3
1995 (July 1) (mil.)	262.8	139.4	61.0	16.5	26.6	35.2	123.4
2000 (mil.)........................	281.4	148.3	65.2	18.0	27.3	37.8	133.1
1970 (percent)....................	100	54	25	5	13	11	46
1980 (percent)....................	100	53	24	6	11	12	47
1990 (percent)....................	100	54	24	6	10	13	46
1995 (July 1) (percent)	100	53	23	6	10	13	47
2000 (percent)....................	100	53	23	6	10	13	47

Source: U.S. Census Bureau, *U.S. Census of Population: 1970; 1980 Census of Population*, Vol. 1, Chapter A (PC80-1-A-1), *U.S. Summary; 1990 Census of Population and Housing* (CPH1); and unpublished data.

No. 29. Number and Population of Metropolitan Areas by Population Size of Area in 2000: 2000

[226.0 represents 226,000,000. As of April. Data exclude Puerto Rico. CMSA=consolidated metropolitan statistical area. MSA=metropolitan statistical area. PMSA=primary metropolitan statistical area. Areas are as defined by U.S. Office of Management and Budget, June 30, 1999. For area definitions, see Appendix II]

Population size of metropolitan area in 2000	CMSAs and MSAs			MSAs and PMSAs		
	Number	Population		Number	Population	
		Total (mil.)	Percent in each class		Total (mil.)	Percent in each class
Total, all metropolitan areas ...	276	226.0	100	331	226.0	100
1,000,000 or more	49	161.5	71	61	146.7	65
2,500,000 or more	19	117.4	52	18	79.8	35
1,000,000 to 2,499,999	30	44.1	20	43	66.9	30
250,000 to 999,999	95	45.1	20	121	56.7	25
500,000 to 999,999	32	22.1	10	42	28.3	13
250,000 to 499,999	63	22.9	10	79	28.4	13
100,000 to 249,999	112	17.7	8	129	20.8	9
Less than 100,000	20	1.7	1	20	1.7	1

Source: U.S. Census Bureau, unpublished data.

Population 29

No. 30. Metropolitan and Nonmetropolitan Area Population by State: 1980 to 2000

[177,505 represents 177,505,000. As of April. Metropolitan refers to 258 metropolitan statistical areas and 18 consolidated metropolitan statistical areas as defined by U.S. Office of Management and Budget, June 30, 1999; nonmetropolitan is the area outside metropolitan areas; see Appendix II. Minus sign (-) indicates decrease]

State	Metropolitan population						Nonmetropolitan population					
	Total (1,000)			Percent change, 1990-2000	Percent of state		Total (1,000)			Percent change, 1990-2000	Percent of state	
	1980	1990	2000	2000	1990	2000	1980	1990	2000	2000	1990	2000
U.S.	177,505	198,407	225,968	13.9	79.8	80.3	49,037	50,311	55,453	10.2	20.2	19.7
AL	2,636	2,797	3,109	11.2	69.2	69.9	1,258	1,244	1,338	7.6	30.8	30.1
AK	174	226	260	15.0	41.1	41.5	227	324	367	13.3	58.9	58.5
AZ	2,339	3,202	4,527	41.4	87.4	88.2	378	463	604	30.4	12.6	11.8
AR	1,026	1,109	1,321	19.1	47.2	49.4	1,260	1,242	1,352	8.9	52.8	50.6
CA	22,907	28,797	32,750	13.7	96.8	96.7	760	961	1,121	16.6	3.2	3.3
CO	2,408	2,779	3,608	29.8	84.4	83.9	482	515	694	34.7	15.6	16.1
CT	2,982	3,148	3,257	3.5	95.8	95.6	126	140	149	6.5	4.2	4.4
DE	496	553	627	13.4	83.0	80.0	98	113	157	38.3	17.0	20.0
DC	638	607	572	-5.7	100.0	100.0	(X)	(X)	(X)	(X)	(X)	(X)
FL.	9,039	12,024	14,837	23.4	92.9	92.8	708	915	1,145	25.2	7.1	7.2
GA	3,507	4,351	5,667	30.2	67.2	69.2	1,956	2,127	2,520	18.5	32.8	30.8
HI	763	836	876	4.8	75.5	72.3	202	272	335	23.3	24.5	27.7
ID	322	362	508	40.4	35.9	39.3	622	645	786	21.9	64.1	60.7
IL	9,461	9,574	10,542	10.1	83.8	84.9	1,967	1,857	1,878	1.1	16.2	15.1
IN	3,885	3,962	4,390	10.8	71.5	72.2	1,605	1,582	1,691	6.9	28.5	27.8
IA	1,198	1,200	1,326	10.5	43.2	45.3	1,716	1,577	1,600	1.5	56.8	54.7
KS	1,184	1,333	1,521	14.1	53.8	56.6	1,180	1,145	1,167	2.0	46.2	43.4
KY	1,735	1,780	1,973	10.9	48.3	48.8	1,925	1,907	2,069	8.5	51.7	51.2
LA	3,125	3,160	3,370	6.7	74.9	75.4	1,082	1,061	1,099	3.6	25.1	24.6
ME	405	443	467	5.4	36.1	36.6	721	785	808	3.0	63.9	63.4
MD	3,920	4,438	4,911	10.7	92.8	92.7	297	343	385	12.5	7.2	7.3
MA	5,530	5,788	6,088	5.2	96.2	95.9	207	229	261	14.1	3.8	4.1
MI	7,719	7,698	8,169	6.1	82.8	82.2	1,543	1,598	1,769	10.7	17.2	17.8
MN	2,674	3,011	3,463	15.0	68.8	70.4	1,402	1,364	1,456	6.7	31.2	29.6
MS	806	874	1,024	17.1	34.0	36.0	1,715	1,701	1,821	7.1	66.0	64.0
MO	3,314	3,491	3,795	8.7	68.2	67.8	1,603	1,626	1,800	10.7	31.8	32.2
MT	265	270	306	13.2	33.8	33.9	522	529	597	12.7	66.2	66.1
NE	728	787	900	14.3	49.9	52.6	842	791	811	2.6	50.1	47.4
NV	666	1,014	1,748	72.4	84.4	87.5	135	188	251	33.4	15.6	12.5
NH	535	659	740	12.3	59.4	59.9	386	450	496	10.1	40.6	40.1
NJ.	7,365	7,730	8,414	8.9	100.0	100.0	(X)	(X)	(X)	(X)	(X)	(X)
NM	675	842	1,035	23.0	55.6	56.9	628	673	784	16.4	44.4	43.1
NY	16,144	16,516	17,473	5.8	91.8	92.1	1,414	1,475	1,503	1.9	8.2	7.9
NC	3,749	4,380	5,437	24.1	66.0	67.5	2,131	2,253	2,612	16.0	34.0	32.5
ND	234	257	284	10.3	40.3	44.2	418	381	358	-6.1	59.7	55.8
OH	8,791	8,826	9,214	4.4	81.4	81.2	2,007	2,021	2,139	5.9	18.6	18.8
OK	1,724	1,870	2,098	12.2	59.4	60.8	1,301	1,276	1,352	6.0	40.6	39.2
OR	1,867	2,056	2,502	21.7	72.3	73.1	766	787	919	16.8	27.7	26.9
PA	10,067	10,084	10,392	3.0	84.9	84.6	1,798	1,799	1,890	5.1	15.1	15.4
RI.	886	938	986	5.1	93.5	94.1	61	65	62	-5.2	6.5	5.9
SC	2,114	2,422	2,807	15.9	69.5	70.0	1,006	1,064	1,205	13.2	30.5	30.0
SD	194	221	261	18.3	31.7	34.6	497	475	494	3.9	68.3	65.4
TN	3,058	3,311	3,862	16.7	67.9	67.9	1,533	1,567	1,827	16.6	32.1	32.1
TX	11,539	14,166	17,692	24.9	83.4	84.8	2,686	2,821	3,160	12.0	16.6	15.2
UT	1,132	1,341	1,708	27.4	77.8	76.5	329	382	525	37.4	22.2	23.5
VT	133	152	169	11.8	26.9	27.8	378	411	439	6.9	73.1	72.2
VA	3,966	4,775	5,528	15.8	77.2	78.1	1,381	1,414	1,550	9.6	22.8	21.9
WA	3,366	4,036	4,899	21.4	82.9	83.1	766	830	995	19.8	17.1	16.9
WV	796	748	766	2.3	41.7	42.3	1,155	1,045	1,043	-0.2	58.3	57.7
WI.	3,176	3,331	3,640	9.3	68.1	67.9	1,530	1,561	1,723	10.4	31.9	32.1
WY	141	134	148	10.2	29.6	30.0	329	319	346	8.3	70.4	70.0

X Not applicable.

Source: U.S. Census Bureau, *1990 Census of Population and Housing, Population and Housing Unit Counts* (CPH-2-1); and unpublished data.

No. 31. Large Metropolitan Areas—Population: 1980 to 2000

[In thousands, except percent (825 represents 825,000). As of April. Covers 18 consolidated metropolitan statistical areas (CMSAs), their 73 component primary metropolitan statistical areas (PMSAs), and the remaining 126 metropolitan statistical areas (MSAs) with 250,000 and over population in 2000 as defined by the U.S. Office of Management and Budget as of June 30, 1999. For definitions and components of all metropolitan areas and population of NECMAs (New England County metropolitan areas), see Appendix II. Minus sign (-) indicates decrease]

Metropolitan area	Number (1,000)			Rank		Net change, 1990-2000 (1,000)	Percent change	
	1980	1990 [1]	2000	1990	2000		1980-1990	1990-2000
Albany-Schenectady-Troy, NY MSA	825	862	876	49	56	14	4.5	1.6
Albuquerque, NM MSA	485	589	713	66	61	124	21.4	21.0
Allentown-Bethlehem-Easton, PA MSA	551	595	638	64	65	43	8.0	7.2
Anchorage, AK MSA	174	226	260	141	138	34	29.8	15.0
Appleton-Oshkosh-Neenah, WI MSA	291	315	358	113	115	43	8.2	13.7
Atlanta, GA MSA	2,233	2,960	4,112	13	11	1,153	32.5	38.9
Augusta-Aiken, GA-SC MSA	363	415	477	85	86	62	14.2	15.0
Austin-San Marcos, TX MSA	585	846	1,250	52	37	404	44.6	47.7
Bakersfield, CA MSA	403	545	662	70	64	117	35.2	21.4
Baton Rouge, LA MSA	494	528	603	71	69	75	6.9	14.1
Beaumont-Port Arthur, TX MSA	373	361	385	101	106	24	-3.2	6.6
Biloxi-Gulfport-Pascagoula, MS MSA	300	312	364	115	113	52	4.1	16.5
Binghamton, NY MSA	263	264	252	127	140	-12	0.4	-4.6
Birmingham, AL MSA	815	840	921	53	54	81	3.0	9.7
Boise City, ID MSA	257	296	432	117	96	136	15.2	46.1
Boston-Worcester-Lawrence, MA-NH-ME-CT CMSA	5,122	5,456	5,819	7	7	364	6.5	6.7
Boston, MA-NH PMSA	3,149	3,228	3,407	(X)	(X)	179	2.5	5.5
Brockton, MA PMSA	225	236	255	(X)	(X)	19	5.1	8.1
Fitchburg-Leominster, MA PMSA	125	138	142	(X)	(X)	4	10.6	2.9
Lawrence, MA-NH PMSA	298	354	396	(X)	(X)	43	18.5	12.0
Lowell, MA-NH PMSA	249	281	302	(X)	(X)	21	12.5	7.5
Manchester, NH PMSA	146	174	198	(X)	(X)	25	18.8	14.2
Nashua, NH PMSA	134	168	191	(X)	(X)	23	25.5	13.4
New Bedford, MA PMSA	167	176	175	(X)	(X)	(-Z)	5.4	-0.3
Portsmouth-Rochester, NH-ME PMSA	189	223	241	(X)	(X)	18	18.0	7.9
Worcester, MA-CT PMSA	439	478	511	(X)	(X)	33	8.8	7.0
Brownsville-Harlingen-San Benito, TX MSA	210	260	335	131	120	75	24.0	28.9
Buffalo-Niagara Falls, NY MSA	1,243	1,189	1,170	33	42	-19	-4.3	-1.6
Canton-Massillon, OH MSA	404	394	407	93	100	13	-2.6	3.3
Charleston-North Charleston, SC MSA	430	507	549	73	76	42	17.8	8.3
Charleston, WV MSA	270	250	252	136	141	1	-7.1	0.5
Charlotte-Gastonia-Rock Hill, NC-SC MSA	971	1,162	1,499	34	33	338	19.6	29.1
Chattanooga, TN-GA MSA	418	424	465	83	89	41	1.5	9.7
Chicago-Gary-Kenosha, IL-IN-WI CMSA	8,115	8,240	9,158	3	3	918	1.5	11.1
Chicago, IL PMSA	7,246	7,411	8,273	(X)	(X)	862	2.3	11.6
Gary, IN PMSA	643	605	631	(X)	(X)	27	-5.9	4.4
Kankakee, IL PMSA	103	96	104	(X)	(X)	8	-6.5	7.9
Kenosha, WI PMSA	123	128	150	(X)	(X)	21	4.1	16.7
Cincinnati-Hamilton, OH-KY-IN CMSA	1,726	1,818	1,979	22	23	162	5.3	8.9
Cincinnati, OH-KY-IN PMSA	1,468	1,526	1,646	(X)	(X)	120	4.0	7.9
Hamilton-Middletown, OH PMSA	259	291	333	(X)	(X)	41	12.6	14.2
Cleveland-Akron, OH CMSA	2,938	2,860	2,946	14	16	86	-2.7	3.0
Akron, OH PMSA	660	658	695	(X)	(X)	37	-0.4	5.7
Cleveland-Lorain-Elyria, OH PMSA	2,278	2,202	2,251	(X)	(X)	49	-3.3	2.2
Colorado Springs, CO MSA	309	397	517	91	80	120	28.3	30.2
Columbia, SC MSA	410	454	537	79	79	83	10.7	18.3
Columbus, GA-AL MSA	255	261	275	130	136	14	2.4	5.3
Columbus, OH MSA	1,214	1,345	1,540	29	32	195	10.8	14.5
Corpus Christi, TX MSA	326	350	381	104	108	31	7.3	8.8
Dallas-Fort Worth, TX CMSA	3,046	4,037	5,222	9	9	1,185	32.5	29.3
Dallas, TX PMSA	2,055	2,676	3,519	(X)	(X)	843	30.2	31.5
Fort Worth-Arlington, TX PMSA	991	1,361	1,703	(X)	(X)	342	37.4	25.1
Davenport-Moline-Rock Island, IA-IL MSA	385	351	359	103	114	8	-8.8	2.3
Dayton-Springfield, OH MSA	942	951	951	43	52	-1	1.0	-0.1
Daytona Beach, FL MSA	270	399	493	88	82	94	48.1	23.5
Denver-Boulder-Greeley, CO CMSA	1,742	1,980	2,582	21	19	601	13.7	30.4
Boulder-Longmont, CO PMSA	190	225	291	(X)	(X)	66	18.8	29.3
Denver, CO PMSA	1,429	1,623	2,109	(X)	(X)	486	13.6	30.0
Greeley, CO PMSA	123	132	181	(X)	(X)	49	6.8	37.3
Des Moines, IA MSA	368	393	456	94	90	63	6.9	16.1
Detroit-Ann Arbor-Flint, MI CMSA	5,293	5,187	5,456	8	8	269	-2.0	5.2
Ann Arbor, MI PMSA	455	490	579	(X)	(X)	89	7.7	18.1
Detroit, MI PMSA	4,388	4,267	4,442	(X)	(X)	175	-2.8	4.1
Flint, MI PMSA	450	430	436	(X)	(X)	6	-4.4	1.3
El Paso, TX MSA	480	592	680	65	63	88	23.3	14.9
Erie, PA MSA	280	276	281	125	135	5	-1.5	1.9
Eugene-Springfield, OR MSA	275	283	323	123	123	40	2.8	14.2
Evansville-Henderson, IN-KY MSA	276	279	296	124	131	17	1.0	6.2
Fayetteville, NC MSA	247	275	303	126	129	28	11.1	10.3
Fayetteville-Springdale-Rogers, AR MSA	179	211	311	148	128	100	18.1	47.5
Fort Collins-Loveland, CO MSA	149	186	251	158	142	65	24.8	35.1
Fort Myers-Cape Coral, FL MSA	205	335	441	110	94	106	63.3	31.6
Fort Pierce-Port St. Lucie, FL MSA	151	251	319	135	125	68	66.1	27.2
Fort Wayne, IN MSA	445	456	502	78	81	46	2.6	10.1
Fresno, CA MSA	578	756	923	56	53	167	30.8	22.1
Grand Rapids-Muskegon-Holland, MI MSA	841	938	1,089	45	47	151	11.5	16.1
Greensboro—Winston-Salem—High Point, NC MSA	951	1,050	1,252	39	36	201	10.5	19.2
Greenville-Spartanburg-Anderson, SC MSA	744	830	962	55	51	132	11.6	15.9

See footnotes at end of table.

Population 31

[See headnote, page 31]

Metropolitan area	Number (1,000)			Rank		Net change, 1990-2000 (1,000)	Percent change	
	1980	1990 [1]	2000	1990	2000		1980-1990	1990-2000
Harrisburg-Lebanon-Carlisle, PA MSA	556	588	629	68	66	41	5.7	7.0
Hartford, CT MSA	1,081	1,158	1,183	35	41	25	7.1	2.2
Hickory-Morganton, NC MSA	270	292	342	120	118	49	8.1	16.9
Honolulu, HI MSA	763	836	876	54	55	40	9.7	4.8
Houston-Galveston-Brazoria, TX CMSA	3,118	3,731	4,670	10	10	939	19.6	25.2
Brazoria, TX PMSA	170	192	242	(X)	(X)	50	13.0	26.1
Galveston-Texas City, TX PMSA	196	217	250	(X)	(X)	33	11.1	15.1
Houston, TX PMSA	2,753	3,322	4,178	(X)	(X)	856	20.7	25.8
Huntington-Ashland, WV-KY-OH MSA	336	313	316	114	126	3	-7.1	1.0
Huntsville, AL MSA	243	293	342	118	117	49	20.6	16.8
Indianapolis, IN MSA	1,306	1,380	1,607	28	28	227	5.7	16.4
Jackson, MS MSA	362	395	441	92	95	45	9.2	11.5
Jacksonville, FL MSA	722	907	1,100	46	45	194	25.5	21.4
Johnson City-Kingsport-Bristol, TN-VA MSA	434	436	480	80	84	44	0.6	10.1
Kalamazoo-Battle Creek, MI MSA	421	429	453	82	91	23	2.1	5.4
Kansas City, MO-KS MSA	1,449	1,583	1,776	25	25	193	9.2	12.2
Killeen-Temple, TX MSA	215	255	313	133	127	58	19.0	22.6
Knoxville, TN MSA	546	586	687	69	62	101	7.2	17.3
Lafayette, LA MSA	331	345	386	105	105	41	4.3	11.8
Lakeland-Winter Haven, FL MSA	322	405	484	87	83	79	26.0	19.4
Lancaster, PA MSA	362	423	471	84	88	48	16.7	11.3
Lansing-East Lansing, MI MSA	420	433	448	81	92	15	3.1	3.5
Las Vegas, NV-AZ MSA	528	853	1,563	51	31	711	61.5	83.3
Lexington, KY MSA	371	406	479	86	85	73	9.4	18.0
Lincoln, NE MSA	193	214	250	147	144	37	10.8	17.2
Little Rock-North Little Rock, AR MSA	474	513	584	72	73	71	8.1	13.8
Los Angeles-Riverside-Orange County, CA CMSA	11,498	14,532	16,374	2	2	1,842	26.4	12.7
Los Angeles-Long Beach, CA PMSA	7,477	8,863	9,519	(X)	(X)	656	18.5	7.4
Orange County, CA PMSA	1,933	2,411	2,846	(X)	(X)	436	24.7	18.1
Riverside-San Bernardino, CA PMSA	1,558	2,589	3,255	(X)	(X)	666	66.1	25.7
Ventura, CA PMSA	529	669	753	(X)	(X)	84	26.4	12.6
Louisville, KY-IN MSA	954	949	1,026	44	49	77	-0.5	8.1
Macon, GA MSA	273	291	323	122	124	31	6.6	10.8
Madison, WI MSA	324	367	427	99	97	59	13.5	16.2
McAllen-Edinburg-Mission, TX MSA	283	384	569	95	74	186	35.4	48.5
Melbourne-Titusville-Palm Bay, FL MSA	273	399	476	90	87	77	46.2	19.4
Memphis, TN-AR-MS MSA	939	1,007	1,136	40	43	128	7.3	12.7
Miami-Fort Lauderdale, FL CMSA	2,644	3,193	3,876	11	12	684	20.8	21.4
Fort Lauderdale, FL PMSA	1,018	1,256	1,623	(X)	(X)	367	23.3	29.3
Miami, FL PMSA	1,626	1,937	2,253	(X)	(X)	316	19.2	16.3
Milwaukee-Racine, WI CMSA	1,570	1,607	1,690	24	26	82	2.4	5.1
Milwaukee-Waukesha, WI PMSA	1,397	1,432	1,501	(X)	(X)	69	2.5	4.8
Racine, WI PMSA	173	175	189	(X)	(X)	14	1.1	7.9
Minneapolis-St. Paul, MN-WI MSA	2,198	2,539	2,969	15	15	430	15.5	16.9
Mobile, AL MSA	444	477	540	77	78	63	7.5	13.3
Modesto, CA MSA	266	371	447	97	93	76	39.3	20.6
Montgomery, AL MSA	273	293	333	119	121	41	7.3	13.9
Naples, FL MSA	86	152	251	177	143	99	76.9	65.3
Nashville, TN MSA	851	985	1,231	41	38	246	15.8	25.0
New London-Norwich, CT-RI MSA	273	292	294	121	132	2	7.0	0.6
New Orleans, LA MSA	1,304	1,285	1,338	31	34	52	-1.5	4.1
New York-Northern New Jersey-Long Island, NY-NJ-CT-PA CMSA	18,906	19,567	21,200	1	1	1,633	3.5	8.3
Bergen-Passaic, NJ PMSA	1,293	1,296	1,373	(X)	(X)	77	0.3	5.9
Bridgeport, CT PMSA	439	444	459	(X)	(X)	16	1.2	3.5
Danbury, CT PMSA	175	194	218	(X)	(X)	24	10.5	12.4
Dutchess County, NY PMSA	245	259	280	(X)	(X)	21	5.9	8.0
Jersey City, NJ PMSA	557	553	609	(X)	(X)	56	-0.7	10.1
Middlesex-Somerset-Hunterdon, NJ PMSA	886	1,020	1,170	(X)	(X)	150	15.1	14.7
Monmouth-Ocean, NJ PMSA	849	986	1,126	(X)	(X)	140	16.2	14.2
Nassau-Suffolk, NY PMSA	2,606	2,609	2,754	(X)	(X)	145	0.1	5.5
New Haven-Meriden, CT PMSA	500	530	542	(X)	(X)	12	5.9	2.3
New York, NY PMSA	8,275	8,547	9,314	(X)	(X)	767	3.3	9.0
Newark, NJ PMSA	1,964	1,916	2,033	(X)	(X)	117	-2.4	6.1
Newburgh, NY-PA PMSA	278	336	388	(X)	(X)	52	20.8	15.5
Stamford-Norwalk, CT PMSA	326	330	354	(X)	(X)	24	1.2	7.3
Trenton, NJ PMSA	308	326	351	(X)	(X)	25	5.8	7.7
Waterbury, CT PMSA	205	222	229	(X)	(X)	7	8.2	3.3
Norfolk-Virginia Beach-Newport News, VA-NC MSA	1,201	1,445	1,570	27	30	125	20.3	8.6
Ocala, FL MSA	122	195	259	149	139	64	59.1	32.9
Oklahoma City, OK MSA	861	959	1,083	42	48	125	11.4	13.0
Omaha, NE-IA MSA	605	640	717	60	60	77	5.6	12.1
Orlando, FL MSA	805	1,225	1,645	32	27	420	52.2	34.3
Pensacola, FL MSA	290	344	412	106	99	68	18.9	19.7
Peoria-Pekin, IL MSA	366	339	347	108	116	8	-7.3	2.4
Philadelphia-Wilmington-Atlantic City, PA-NJ-DE-MD CMSA	5,649	5,893	6,188	6	6	295	4.3	5.0
Atlantic-Cape May, NJ PMSA	276	319	355	(X)	(X)	35	15.6	11.1
Philadelphia, PA-NJ PMSA	4,781	4,922	5,101	(X)	(X)	179	2.9	3.6

See footnotes at end of table.

U.S. Census Bureau, Statistical Abstract of the United States: 2001

[See headnote, page 31]

Metropolitan area	Number (1,000)			Rank		Net change, 1990-2000 (1,000)	Percent change	
	1980	1990 [1]	2000	1990	2000		1980-1990	1990-2000
Vineland-Millville-Bridgeton, NJ PMSA	133	138	146	(X)	(X)	8	3.9	6.1
Wilmington-Newark, DE-MD PMSA	459	513	586	(X)	(X)	73	11.9	14.2
Phoenix-Mesa, AZ MSA	1,600	2,238	3,252	19	14	1,013	39.9	45.3
Pittsburgh, PA MSA	2,571	2,395	2,359	18	21	-36	-6.9	-1.5
Portland-Salem, OR-WA CMSA	1,584	1,793	2,265	23	22	472	13.3	26.3
Portland-Vancouver, OR-WA PMSA	1,334	1,515	1,918	(X)	(X)	403	13.6	26.6
Salem, OR PMSA.	250	278	347	(X)	(X)	69	11.3	24.9
Providence-Fall River-Warwick, RI-MA MSA	1,077	1,134	1,189	36	39	54	5.4	4.8
Provo-Orem, UT MSA.	218	264	369	129	111	105	20.9	39.8
Raleigh-Durham-Chapel Hill, NC MSA.	665	859	1,188	50	40	329	29.1	38.4
Reading, PA MSA	313	337	374	109	109	37	7.7	11.0
Reno, NV MSA	194	255	339	134	119	85	31.5	33.3
Richmond-Petersburg, VA MSA	761	866	997	47	50	131	13.7	15.1
Rochester, NY MSA	1,031	1,062	1,098	38	46	36	3.1	3.4
Rockford, IL MSA	326	330	371	111	110	42	1.2	12.6
Sacramento-Yolo, CA CMSA	1,100	1,507	1,797	26	24	290	37.0	19.3
Sacramento, CA PMSA	986	1,366	1,628	(X)	(X)	263	38.4	19.2
Yolo, CA PMSA	113	141	169	(X)	(X)	27	24.6	19.4
Saginaw-Bay City-Midland, MI MSA	422	399	403	89	101	4	-5.3	0.9
St. Louis, MO-IL MSA.	2,414	2,492	2,604	17	18	111	3.2	4.5
Salinas, CA MSA.	290	356	402	102	102	46	22.5	13.0
Salt Lake City-Ogden, UT MSA	910	1,072	1,334	37	35	262	17.8	24.4
San Antonio, TX MSA.	1,089	1,325	1,592	30	29	268	21.7	20.2
San Diego, CA MSA.	1,862	2,498	2,814	16	17	316	34.2	12.6
San Francisco-Oakland-San Jose, CA CMSA	5,368	6,278	7,039	5	5	762	16.9	12.1
Oakland, CA PMSA	1,762	2,108	2,393	(X)	(X)	284	19.7	13.5
San Francisco, CA PMSA	1,489	1,604	1,731	(X)	(X)	128	7.7	8.0
San Jose, CA PMSA.	1,295	1,498	1,683	(X)	(X)	185	15.6	12.4
Santa Cruz-Watsonville, CA PMSA	188	230	256	(X)	(X)	26	22.1	11.3
Santa Rosa, CA PMSA	300	388	459	(X)	(X)	70	29.5	18.1
Vallejo-Fairfield-Napa, CA PMSA.	334	450	519	(X)	(X)	69	34.6	15.2
Santa Barbara-Santa Maria-Lompoc, CA MSA	299	370	399	98	103	30	23.7	8.0
Sarasota-Bradenton, FL MSA.	351	489	590	74	72	100	39.6	20.5
Savannah, GA MSA	231	258	293	132	133	35	11.8	13.6
Scranton—Wilkes-Barre—Hazleton, PA MSA	659	639	625	61	67	-14	-3.2	-2.2
Seattle-Tacoma-Bremerton, WA CMSA	2,409	2,970	3,555	12	13	584	23.3	19.7
Bremerton, WA MSA.	147	190	232	(X)	(X)	42	28.9	22.3
Olympia, WA MSA	124	161	207	(X)	(X)	46	29.8	28.6
Seattle-Bellevue-Everett, WA PMSA.	1,652	2,033	2,415	(X)	(X)	381	23.1	18.8
Tacoma, WA PMSA	486	586	701	(X)	(X)	115	20.7	19.6
Shreveport-Bossier City, LA MSA	377	376	392	96	104	16	-0.1	4.2
South Bend, IN MSA	242	247	266	137	137	19	2.2	7.5
Spokane, WA MSA	342	361	418	100	98	57	5.7	15.7
Springfield, MO MSA	228	264	326	128	122	61	15.9	23.2
Springfield, MA MSA	570	588	592	67	71	4	3.2	0.7
Stockton-Lodi, CA MSA.	347	481	564	76	75	83	38.4	17.3
Syracuse, NY MSA	723	742	732	57	59	-10	2.7	-1.4
Tallahassee, FL MSA	190	234	285	140	134	51	22.7	21.8
Tampa-St. Petersburg-Clearwater, FL MSA.	1,614	2,068	2,396	20	20	328	28.2	15.9
Toledo, OH MSA.	617	614	618	62	68	4	-0.4	0.7
Tucson, AZ MSA	531	667	844	59	57	177	25.5	26.5
Tulsa, OK MSA	657	709	803	58	58	94	7.9	13.3
Utica-Rome, NY MSA.	320	317	300	112	130	-17	-1.1	-5.3
Visalia-Tulare-Porterville, CA MSA	246	312	368	116	112	56	26.9	18.0
Washington-Baltimore, DC-MD-VA-WV CMSA.	5,791	6,726	7,608	4	4	882	16.2	13.1
Baltimore, MD PMSA	2,199	2,382	2,553	(X)	(X)	171	8.3	7.2
Hagerstown, MD PMSA.	113	121	132	(X)	(X)	11	7.3	8.7
Washington, DC-MD-VA-WV PMSA.	3,478	4,223	4,923	(X)	(X)	700	21.4	16.6
West Palm Beach-Boca Raton, FL MSA.	577	864	1,131	48	44	268	49.7	31.0
Wichita, KS MSA	442	485	545	75	77	60	9.7	12.4
York, PA MSA	313	340	382	107	107	42	8.5	12.4
Youngstown-Warren, OH MSA	645	601	595	63	70	-6	-6.8	-1.0

X Not applicable.   Z Less than 500.   [1] Reflects revisions to an area's 1990 census population count that may occur as the result of (1) post-1990 census corrections of political boundaries or geographic misallocations or documented under-enumerations or over-enumerations and (2) geographic boundary updates made after the 1990 census, resulting from annexations, de-annexations, new incorporations, and governmental mergers. Includes revisions processed through January 1, 1998.

Source: U.S. Census Bureau, *1990 Census of Population and Housing, Supplementary Reports, Metropolitan Areas as Defined by the Office of Management and Budget, June 30, 1993* (CPH-S-1-1); "(MA-99-1) Metropolitan Area Population Estimates for July 1, 1999, and Population Change for April 1, 1990, to July 1, 1999 (includes April 1, 1990, Population Estimates Base)"; published: 20 October 2000; <http://www.census.gov/population/estimates/metro-city/ma99-01.txt>; and "Ranking Tables for Metropolitan Areas: 1990 and 2000 (PHC-T-3)"; published: 2 April 2001; <http://www.census.gov/population/www/cen2000/phc-t3.html>.

Population   33

No. 32. Incorporated Places by Population Size: 1970 to 2000

[131.9 represents 131,900,000]

Population size	Number of incorporated places				Population (mil.)				Percent of total			
	1970	1980	1990	2000	1970	1980	1990	2000	1970	1980	1990	2000
Total	18,666	19,097	19,262	19,452	131.9	140.3	152.9	173.5	100.0	100.0	100.0	100.0
1,000,000 or more. . .	6	6	8	9	18.8	17.5	20.0	22.9	14.2	12.5	13.0	13.2
500,000 to 999,999 . . .	20	16	15	20	13.0	10.9	10.1	12.9	9.8	7.8	6.6	7.4
250,000 to 499,999 . . .	30	33	41	37	10.5	11.8	14.2	13.3	7.9	8.4	9.3	7.7
100,000 to 249,999 . . .	97	114	131	172	13.9	16.6	19.1	25.5	10.5	11.8	12.5	14.7
50,000 to 99,999.	232	250	309	363	16.2	17.6	21.2	24.9	12.2	12.3	13.9	14.3
25,000 to 49,999.	455	526	567	644	15.7	18.4	20.0	22.6	11.9	13.1	13.0	13.0
10,000 to 24,999.	1,127	1,260	1,290	1,435	17.6	19.8	20.3	22.6	13.3	14.1	13.3	13.0
Under 10,000	16,699	16,892	16,901	16,772	26.4	28.0	28.2	28.7	20.0	20.0	18.4	16.6

Source: U.S. Census Bureau, *Census of Population: 1970* and *1980*, Vol. I; *1990 Census of Population and Housing, Population and Housing Unit Counts* (CPH-2-1); and *County and City Data Book 2000.*

No. 33. Households—Cities with 350,000 or More Population: 2000

[183.2 represents 183,200. As of April. For definitions of household and family, see text, this section]

City	Households (1,000)							
	Family households					Nonfamily households		
	Total [1]			Married couple				
	Total	Total	With own children under 18 years	Total	With own children under 18 years	Total	House-holder living alone	Average household size
Albuquerque, NM	183.2	112.6	55.4	79.9	35.5	70.6	55.8	2.40
Atlanta, GA	168.1	83.2	37.7	41.2	15.5	85.0	64.7	2.30
Austin, TX	265.6	141.6	71.3	101.1	49 1	124.1	87.0	2.40
Baltimore, MD	258.0	147.2	65.8	68.8	25 7	110.8	90.1	2.42
Boston, MA	239.5	115.1	54.3	65.7	28.2	124.4	88.9	2.31
Charlotte, NC	215.4	132.4	66.0	94.0	44.3	83.1	63.6	2.45
Chicago, IL	1,061.9	632.6	306.5	373.0	179.4	429.4	345.8	2.67
Cleveland, OH	190.6	112.0	57.1	54.2	23.2	78.6	67.2	2.44
Colorado Springs, CO. . .	141.5	93.0	48.1	72.8	34.9	48.5	38.2	2.50
Columbus, OH.	301.5	165.4	84.5	108.7	49.8	136.2	102.9	2.30
Dallas, TX.	451.8	266.8	136.9	175.3	87.8	185.0	148.9	2.58
Denver, CO.	239.2	119.3	55.6	83.0	35.9	119.9	94.0	2.27
Detroit, MI.	336.4	218.5	114.0	89.7	42.1	117.9	99.9	2.77
El Paso, TX.	182.1	141.1	77.2	99.4	54.1	41.0	35.0	3.07
Fort Worth, TX.	195.1	127.5	67.7	89.4	46.2	67.5	55.8	2.67
Fresno, CA	140.1	97.9	56.6	64.6	35.5	42.2	32.6	2.99
Honolulu, HI [2]	140.3	87.4	33.2	63.8	24.6	53.0	41.7	2.57
Houston, TX	717.9	457.5	237.7	310.1	159.3	260.4	212.7	2.67
Indianapolis, IN [3]	324.3	195.5	96.8	132.0	58.4	128.9	103.8	2.39
Jacksonville, FL.	284.5	190.5	96.4	132.8	61.8	94.0	74.5	2.53
Kansas City, MO	184.0	107.4	51.7	70.0	29.8	76.6	62.7	2.35
Las Vegas, NV	176.8	117.5	56.4	85.4	38.1	59.3	44.3	2.66
Long Beach, CA	163.1	99.7	57.1	64.0	35.2	63.4	48.2	2.77
Los Angeles, CA	1,275.4	798.7	427.3	535.0	288.8	476.7	363.5	2.83
Memphis, TN.	250.7	158.5	78.6	85.5	37.1	92.3	76.6	2.52
Mesa, AZ	146.6	99.9	48.9	77.3	35.2	46.8	35.5	2.68
Miami, FL.	134.2	83.3	35.3	49.1	19.7	50.9	40.8	2.61
Milwaukee, WI	232.2	135.2	70.9	74.8	33.3	97.0	77.8	2.50
Minneapolis, MN	162.4	73.9	36.7	47.0	20.8	88.4	65.5	2.25
Nashville-Davidson, TN [3].	237.4	138.1	63.3	94.8	39.2	99.3	79.2	2.30
New Orleans, LA	188.3	113.0	55.1	58.0	25.0	75.3	62.4	2.48
New York, NY	3,021.6	1,853.2	897.9	1,124.3	532.4	1,168.4	962.6	2.59
Oakland, CA	150.8	86.3	43.2	51.3	24.8	64.4	49.0	2.60
Oklahoma City, OK.	204.4	129.4	63.0	93.6	41.3	75.1	62.8	2.41
Omaha, NE.	156.7	94.9	47.1	68.6	31.3	61.8	50.1	2.42
Philadelphia, PA.	590.1	352.3	162.9	189.3	79.9	237.7	199.5	2.48
Phoenix, AZ	465.8	307.2	166.4	218.5	113.2	158.6	118.4	2.79
Portland, OR	223.7	118.4	54.7	85.3	36.2	105.3	77.3	2.30
Sacramento, CA.	154.6	91.1	46.7	59.3	28.1	63.4	49.5	2.57
San Antonio, TX.	405.5	280.8	145.6	194.9	97.7	124.6	101.6	2.77
San Diego, CA.	450.7	271.4	136.1	201.2	98.1	179.3	126.2	2.61
San Francisco, CA	329.7	145.2	54.7	104.3	40.3	184.5	127.4	2.30
San Jose, CA	276.6	203.7	105.9	155.0	82.7	72.9	50.9	3.20
Seattle, WA.	258.5	113.4	46.3	84.6	32.3	145.1	105.5	2.08
Tucson, AZ	192.9	112.5	56.0	76.5	34.5	80.4	62.3	2.42
Tulsa, OK	165.7	99.1	47.3	71.4	30.4	66.6	56.2	2.31
Virginia Beach, VA	154.5	111.0	59.9	86.0	44.2	43.5	31.4	2.70
Washington, DC	248.3	114.2	49.1	56.6	20.7	134.2	108.7	2.16

[1] Includes family householders with no spouse present, not shown separately. [2] The population shown in this table is for the census designated place (CDP). [3] Represents the portion of a consolidated city that is not within one or more separately incorporated places.

Source: U.S. Census Bureau, *2000 Census of Population and Housing, Profiles of General Demographic Characteristics.*

34 Population

No. 34. Incorporated Places With 100,000 or More Inhabitants in 2000—Population, 1970 to 2000, and Land Area, 2000

[Population: As of April 1 (90 represents 90,000). Data for 1990 and 2000 refer to boundaries in effect on January 1, 2000; data for 1970 and 1980 refer to boundaries in effect for those censuses. Minus sign (-) indicates decrease]

Incorporated place	1970, total population (1,000)	1980, total population (1,000)	1990, total population (1,000)	Population, 2000 Total (1,000)	Rank	Percent change, 1990-2000	Per square mile	Land area, 2000 (square miles)
Abilene, TX	90	98	107	116	193	8.4	1,103	105.1
Akron, OH	275	237	223	217	81	-2.7	3,497	62.1
Albuquerque, NM	245	332	387	449	35	15.9	2,483	180.6
Alexandria, VA	111	103	111	128	166	15.4	8,452	15.2
Allentown, PA	110	104	105	107	215	1.1	6,011	17.7
Amarillo, TX	127	149	158	174	118	10.0	1,932	89.9
Anaheim, CA	166	219	267	328	55	23.0	6,702	48.9
Anchorage, AK	48	174	226	260	65	15.0	153	1,697.2
Ann Arbor, MI	100	108	110	114	195	3.5	4,221	27.0
Arlington, TX	90	160	262	333	53	27.1	3,475	95.8
Arvada, CO	50	85	90	102	231	13.8	3,128	32.7
Athens-Clarke County, GA [1]	(NA)	(NA)	87	100	239	15.9	852	117.8
Atlanta, GA	495	425	394	416	39	5.8	3,161	131.7
Augusta-Richmond County, GA [1]	(NA)	(NA)	186	195	97	4.8	646	302.1
Aurora, CO	75	159	222	276	61	24.6	1,940	142.5
Aurora, IL	74	81	100	143	147	42.6	3,712	38.5
Austin, TX	254	346	494	657	16	32.8	2,610	251.5
Bakersfield, CA	70	106	184	247	69	34.3	2,184	113.1
Baltimore, MD	905	787	736	651	17	-11.5	8,058	80.8
Baton Rouge, LA	166	220	222	228	74	2.5	2,965	76.8
Beaumont, TX	118	118	114	114	196	-0.5	1,339	85.0
Bellevue, WA	61	74	99	110	206	11.1	3,564	30.7
Berkeley, CA	114	103	103	103	227	-0.1	9,823	10.5
Birmingham, AL	301	284	266	243	71	-8.7	1,620	149.9
Boise City, ID	75	102	135	186	105	37.5	2,913	63.8
Boston, MA	641	563	574	589	20	2.6	12,166	48.4
Bridgeport, CT	157	143	142	140	152	-1.4	8,721	16.0
Brownsville, TX	53	85	115	140	151	21.3	1,738	80.4
Buffalo, NY	463	358	328	293	58	-10.8	7,206	40.6
Burbank, CA	89	87	94	100	238	7.1	5,782	17.3
Cambridge, MA	96	95	96	101	233	5.7	15,766	6.4
Cape Coral, FL	[2]	32	75	102	230	36.1	972	105.2
Carrollton, TX	14	41	83	110	205	32.7	3,005	36.5
Cedar Rapids, IA	111	110	109	121	181	10.9	1,913	63.1
Chandler, AZ	14	30	91	177	114	94.7	3,051	57.9
Charlotte, NC	241	315	427	541	26	26.7	2,232	242.3
Chattanooga, TN	120	170	153	156	129	1.8	1,151	135.2
Chesapeake, VA	90	114	152	199	90	31.1	585	340.7
Chicago, IL	3,369	3,005	2,784	2,896	3	4.0	12,750	227.1
Chula Vista, CA	68	84	135	174	120	28.3	3,551	48.9
Cincinnati, OH	454	385	365	331	54	-9.1	4,249	78.0
Clarksville, TN	32	55	77	103	224	35.2	1,091	94.9
Clearwater, FL	52	85	97	109	208	11.9	4,302	25.3
Cleveland, OH	751	574	505	478	33	-5.4	6,167	77.6
Colorado Springs, CO	136	215	283	361	48	27.5	1,943	185.7
Columbia, SC	114	101	114	116	191	1.6	929	125.2
Columbus, GA [1]	155	169	179	186	106	4.0	860	216.1
Columbus, OH	540	565	636	711	15	11.8	3,384	210.3
Concord, CA	85	104	111	122	177	9.5	4,041	30.1
Coral Springs, FL	1	37	79	118	186	48.5	4,917	23.9
Corona, CA	28	38	76	125	170	64.0	3,556	35.1
Corpus Christi, TX	205	232	258	277	60	7.4	1,794	154.6
Costa Mesa, CA	73	83	97	109	209	12.3	6,954	15.6
Dallas, TX	844	905	1,007	1,189	8	18.1	3,470	342.5
Daly City, CA	67	79	92	104	223	12.4	13,704	7.6
Dayton, OH	243	194	182	166	123	-8.9	2,979	55.8
Denver, CO	515	493	468	555	24	18.6	3,617	153.4
Des Moines, IA	201	191	193	199	92	2.8	2,621	75.8
Detroit, MI	1,514	1,203	1,028	951	10	-7.5	6,855	138.8
Downey, CA	89	83	91	107	212	17.3	8,642	12.4
Durham, NC	95	101	148	187	103	26.0	1,976	94.6
El Monte, CA	70	79	106	116	192	9.2	12,139	9.6
El Paso, TX	322	425	516	564	22	9.3	2,263	249.1
Elizabeth, NJ	113	106	110	121	182	9.5	9,865	12.2
Erie, PA	129	119	109	104	222	-4.6	4,723	22.0
Escondido, CA	37	64	109	134	160	22.5	3,681	36.3
Eugene, OR	79	106	114	138	156	21.1	3,403	40.5
Evansville, IN	139	130	126	122	178	-3.6	2,987	40.7
Fayetteville, NC	54	60	113	121	180	7.4	2,059	58.8
Flint, MI	193	160	141	125	171	-11.6	3,715	33.6
Fontana, CA	21	37	88	129	163	46.7	3,570	36.1
Fort Collins, CO	43	65	89	119	185	33.5	2,549	46.5
Fort Lauderdale, FL	140	153	149	152	130	2.4	4,803	31.7
Fort Wayne, IN	178	172	203	206	84	1.3	2,606	79.0
Fort Worth, TX	393	385	448	535	27	19.3	1,828	292.5
Fremont, CA	101	132	173	203	85	17.3	2,652	76.7
Fresno, CA	166	217	355	428	37	20.3	4,098	104.4
Fullerton, CA	86	102	113	126	169	11.1	5,676	22.2
Garden Grove, CA	121	123	144	165	124	15.0	9,165	18.0
Garland, TX	81	139	181	216	82	19.3	3,778	57.1
Gary, IN	175	152	117	103	226	-11.9	2,046	50.2
Gilbert, AZ	2	6	30	110	204	265.6	2,554	43.0

See footnotes at end of table.

U.S. Census Bureau, Statistical Abstract of the United States: 2001

[Population: As of April 1 (90 represents 90,000). Data for 1990 and 2000 refer to boundaries in effect on January 1, 2000; data for 1970 and 1980 refer to boundaries in effect for those censuses. Minus sign (-) indicates decrease]

Incorporated place	1970, total population (1,000)	1980, total population (1,000)	1990, total population (1,000)	Population, 2000 Total (1,000)	Rank	Percent change, 1990-2000	Per square mile	Land area, 2000 (square miles)
Glendale, AZ	36	97	151	219	80	45.0	3,930	55.7
Glendale, CA	133	139	180	195	98	8.3	6,362	30.6
Grand Prairie, TX	51	71	99	127	168	28.1	1,785	71.4
Grand Rapids, MI	198	182	190	198	93	4.3	4,431	44.6
Green Bay, WI	88	88	97	102	229	5.8	2,332	43.9
Greensboro, NC	144	156	192	224	77	16.9	2,138	104.7
Hampton, VA	121	123	134	146	143	9.5	2,828	51.8
Hartford, CT	158	136	137	122	179	-11.4	7,025	17.3
Hayward, CA	93	94	115	140	150	22.1	3,159	44.3
Henderson, NV	16	24	65	175	116	169.4	2,201	79.7
Hialeah, FL	102	145	188	226	75	20.5	11,767	19.2
Hollywood, FL	107	121	123	139	153	13.5	5,097	27.3
Honolulu, HI [3]	325	365	377	372	46	-1.4	4,337	85.7
Houston, TX	1,234	1,595	1,698	1,954	4	15.1	3,372	579.4
Huntington Beach, CA	116	171	183	190	101	3.7	7,184	26.4
Huntsville, AL	139	143	160	158	127	-1.3	909	174.0
Independence, MO	112	112	112	113	198	0.8	1,446	78.3
Indianapolis, IN [1]	737	701	732	782	12	6.9	2,163	361.5
Inglewood, CA	90	94	110	113	200	1.9	12,323	9.1
Irvine, CA	(2)	62	111	143	146	28.4	3,098	46.2
Irving, TX	97	110	155	192	100	23.5	2,850	67.2
Jacksonville, FL	504	541	635	736	14	15.8	971	757.7
Jackson, MS	154	203	197	184	109	-6.3	1,756	104.9
Jersey City, NJ	260	224	228	240	72	5.1	16,094	14.9
Joliet, IL	79	78	79	106	217	35.2	2,791	38.1
Kansas City, KS	168	161	151	147	142	-3.0	1,182	124.3
Kansas City, MO	507	448	435	442	36	1.5	1,408	313.5
Knoxville, TN	175	175	173	174	117	0.4	1,877	92.7
Lafayette, LA	69	81	103	110	203	7.5	2,317	47.6
Lakewood, CO	93	114	126	144	144	14.2	3,465	41.6
Lancaster, CA	(2)	48	98	119	184	20.6	1,263	94.0
Lansing, MI	131	130	127	119	183	-6.1	3,399	35.0
Laredo, TX	69	91	125	177	115	41.2	2,251	78.5
Las Vegas, NV	126	165	260	478	32	84.1	4,223	113.3
Lexington-Fayette, KY	108	204	225	261	64	15.6	916	284.5
Lincoln, NE	150	172	193	226	76	17.0	3,022	74.6
Little Rock, AR	132	159	177	183	110	3.4	1,576	116.2
Livonia, MI	110	105	101	101	237	-0.3	2,815	35.7
Long Beach, CA	359	361	430	462	34	7.4	9,150	50.4
Los Angeles, CA	2,812	2,969	3,485	3,695	2	6.0	7,877	469.1
Louisville, KY	362	299	270	256	66	-5.0	4,125	62.1
Lowell, MA	94	92	103	105	218	1.7	7,636	13.8
Lubbock, TX	149	174	187	200	89	6.9	1,738	114.8
Madison, WI	172	171	191	208	83	9.0	3,030	68.7
Manchester, NH	88	91	99	107	214	7.9	3,241	33.0
McAllen, TX	38	66	86	106	216	24.3	2,315	46.0
Memphis, TN	624	646	619	650	18	5.0	2,327	279.3
Mesa, AZ	63	152	290	396	42	36.6	3,171	125.0
Mesquite, TX	55	67	102	125	172	22.4	2,868	43.4
Miami, FL	335	347	360	362	47	0.7	10,161	35.7
Milwaukee, WI	717	636	628	597	19	-5.0	6,214	96.1
Minneapolis, MN	434	371	368	383	45	3.9	6,970	54.9
Mobile, AL	190	200	198	199	91	0.3	1,687	117.9
Modesto, CA	62	107	166	189	102	13.5	5,277	35.8
Montgomery, AL	133	178	191	202	87	5.6	1,297	155.4
Moreno Valley, CA	(2)	(2)	119	142	148	19.9	2,779	51.2
Naperville, IL	23	43	87	128	165	47.6	3,628	35.4
Nashville-Davidson, TN [1]	426	456	488	546	25	11.7	1,153	473.3
New Haven, CT	138	126	130	124	175	-5.0	6,558	18.9
New Orleans, LA	593	558	497	485	31	-2.5	2,684	180.6
New York, NY	7,896	7,072	7,323	8,008	1	9.4	26,402	303.3
Newark, NJ	382	329	275	274	63	-0.6	11,495	23.8
Newport News, VA	138	145	171	180	113	5.1	2,638	68.3
Norfolk, VA	308	267	261	234	73	-10.3	4,363	53.7
North Las Vegas, NV	46	43	48	115	194	140.8	1,471	78.5
Norwalk, CA	94	85	94	103	225	9.7	10,667	9.7
Oakland, CA	362	339	400	399	41	-0.1	7,127	56.1
Oceanside, CA	40	77	129	161	125	25.2	3,967	40.6
Oklahoma City, OK	368	404	445	506	29	13.8	834	607.0
Omaha, NE	347	314	358	390	44	9.0	3,371	115.7
Ontario, CA	64	89	133	158	128	18.6	3,174	49.8
Orange, CA	77	91	111	129	164	16.4	5,506	23.4
Orlando, FL	99	128	163	186	104	13.8	1,989	93.5
Overland Park, KS	78	82	112	149	139	33.3	2,627	56.7
Oxnard, CA	71	108	142	170	122	19.6	6,730	25.3
Palmdale, CA	9	12	77	117	190	50.9	1,112	105.0
Pasadena, CA	113	118	132	142	149	7.5	3,208	44.2
Pasadena, TX	90	113	119	134	159	12.2	5,799	23.1
Paterson, NJ	145	138	158	149	138	-5.6	17,675	8.4
Pembroke Pines, FL	15	36	65	137	157	110.0	4,158	33.1
Peoria, AZ	5	12	51	108	210	111.8	784	138.2

See footnotes at end of table.

U.S. Census Bureau, Statistical Abstract of the United States: 2001

No. 34. Incorporated Places With 100,000 or More Inhabitants in 2000—Population, 1970 to 2000, and Land Area, 2000—Con.

[Population: As of April 1 (90 represents 90,000). Data for 1990 and 2000 refer to boundaries in effect on January 1, 2000; data for 1970 and 1980 refer to boundaries in effect for those censuses. Minus sign (-) indicates decrease]

Incorporated place	1970, total population (1,000)	1980, total population (1,000)	1990, total population (1,000)	Population, 2000 Total (1,000)	Population, 2000 Rank	Population, 2000 Percent change, 1990-2000	Population, 2000 Per square mile	Land area, 2000 (square miles)
Peoria, IL	127	124	114	113	199	-0.8	2,543	44.4
Philadelphia, PA.	1,949	1,688	1,586	1,518	5	-4.3	11,233	135.1
Phoenix, AZ	584	790	989	1,321	6	33.6	2,782	474.9
Pittsburgh, PA	520	424	370	335	52	-9.6	6,019	55.6
Plano, TX	18	72	129	222	78	72.8	3,102	71.6
Pomona, CA	87	93	132	149	137	13.0	6,544	22.8
Portland, OR	380	368	486	529	28	8.9	3,939	134.3
Portsmouth, VA	111	105	104	101	236	-3.2	3,033	33.2
Providence, RI	179	157	160	174	119	8.3	9,401	18.5
Provo, UT	53	74	87	105	219	20.7	2,653	39.6
Pueblo, CO.	98	102	99	102	232	3.1	2,266	45.1
Raleigh, NC	123	150	220	276	62	25.3	2,409	114.6
Rancho Cucamonga, CA	(2)	55	101	128	167	26.0	3,411	37.4
Reno, NV	73	101	135	180	112	33.9	2,611	69.1
Richmond, VA	249	219	203	198	94	-2.4	3,293	60.1
Riverside, CA	140	171	227	255	67	12.6	3,267	78.1
Rochester, NY	295	242	231	220	79	-4.8	6,133	35.8
Rockford, IL	147	140	144	150	136	4.3	2,680	56.0
Sacramento, CA.	257	276	395	407	40	3.0	4,189	97.2
Salem, OR	69	89	109	137	158	25.8	2,994	45.7
Salinas, CA.	59	80	109	151	134	38.8	7,948	19.0
Salt Lake City, UT	176	163	160	182	111	13.6	1,666	109.1
San Antonio, TX.	654	786	997	1,145	9	14.8	2,809	407.6
San Bernardino, CA	107	119	171	185	108	8.3	3,152	58.8
San Buenaventura (Ventura), CA .	58	74	94	101	235	7.8	4,791	21.1
San Diego, CA.	697	876	1,111	1,223	7	10.1	3,772	324.3
San Francisco, CA	716	679	724	777	13	7.3	16,634	46.7
San Jose, CA	460	629	783	895	11	14.2	5,118	174.9
Santa Ana, CA.	156	204	294	338	51	14.8	12,452	27.1
Santa Clara, CA.	86	88	93	102	228	9.7	5,566	18.4
Santa Clarita, CA.	(2)	(2)	124	151	133	22.2	3,159	47.8
Santa Rosa, CA	50	83	120	148	140	22.5	3,678	40.1
Savannah, GA.	118	142	138	132	162	-4.4	1,760	74.7
Scottsdale, AZ	68	89	130	203	86	55.8	1,100	184.2
Seattle, WA.	531	494	516	563	23	9.1	6,717	83.9
Shreveport, LA	182	206	198	200	88	0.9	1,941	103.1
Simi Valley, CA	60	78	100	111	202	11.0	2,842	39.2
Sioux Falls, SD	72	81	101	124	174	22.2	2,201	56.3
South Bend, IN	126	110	106	108	211	1.6	2,786	38.7
Spokane, WA	171	171	178	196	96	9.8	3,387	57.8
Springfield, IL	92	100	107	111	201	3.9	2,064	54.0
Springfield, MA	164	152	157	152	131	-3.1	4,738	32.1
Springfield, MO	120	133	141	152	132	7.4	2,072	73.2
Stamford, CT.	109	102	108	117	187	8.3	3,102	37.7
Sterling Heights, MI	61	109	118	124	173	5.7	3,397	36.6
Stockton, CA.	110	150	211	244	70	15.3	4,456	54.7
St. Louis, MO	622	453	397	348	49	-12.2	5,623	61.9
St. Paul, MN	310	270	272	287	59	5.5	5,442	52.8
St. Petersburg, FL	216	239	240	248	68	3.3	4,163	59.6
Sunnyvale, CA.	96	107	117	132	161	12.3	6,006	21.9
Syracuse, NY	197	170	164	147	141	-10.1	5,871	25.1
Tacoma, WA	154	159	177	194	99	9.1	3,865	50.1
Tallahassee, FL	73	82	125	151	135	20.1	1,574	95.7
Tampa, FL	278	272	281	303	57	8.1	2,708	112.1
Tempe, AZ	64	107	142	159	126	11.7	3,959	40.1
Thousand Oaks, CA	36	77	104	117	188	12.5	2,133	54.9
Toledo, OH	383	355	333	314	56	-5.8	3,890	80.6
Topeka, KS.	125	119	121	122	176	1.3	2,185	56.0
Torrance, CA.	135	130	133	138	155	3.5	6,716	20.5
Tucson, AZ	263	331	417	487	30	16.7	2,500	194.7
Tulsa, OK	330	361	367	393	43	7.0	2,152	182.6
Vallejo, CA	72	80	111	117	189	5.3	3,868	30.2
Vancouver, WA	42	43	105	144	145	37.3	3,355	42.8
Virginia Beach, VA	172	262	393	425	38	8.2	1,713	248.3
Waco, TX	95	101	104	114	197	9.4	1,351	84.2
Warren, MI	179	161	145	138	154	-4.7	4,032	34.3
Washington, DC.	757	638	607	572	21	-5.7	9,316	61.4
Waterbury, CT	108	103	108	107	213	-0.9	3,755	28.6
West Covina, CA	68	80	96	105	220	9.6	6,525	16.1
West Valley City, UT	(2)	(2)	87	109	207	25.2	3,076	35.4
Westminster, CO	20	50	74	101	234	36.1	3,204	31.5
Wichita Falls, TX	96	94	97	104	221	7.7	1,474	70.7
Wichita, KS.	277	280	309	344	50	11.5	2,536	135.8
Winston-Salem, NC	134	132	167	186	107	11.1	1,707	108.9
Worcester, MA.	177	162	170	173	121	1.8	4,597	37.6
Yonkers, NY	204	195	188	196	95	4.2	10,847	18.1

NA Not available. [1] Represents the portion of a consolidated city that is not within one or more separately incorporated places. [2] Not incorporated. [3] The population shown in this table is for the census designated place (CDP).

Source: U.S. Census Bureau, 1990 Census of Population and Housing, Population and Housing Unit Counts, (CPH-2); "Population Estimates for Cities with Populations of 10,000 and Greater (Sorted Within State by 1999 Population Size): July 1, 1999 (includes April 1, 1990 Population Estimates Base)"; published 20 October 2000; <http://www.census.gov/population/estimates/metro-city/SC10K-T3.txt>; 2000 Census of Population and Housing, Profiles of General Demographic Characteristics; and unpublished data.

No. 35. Cities With 250,000 or More Inhabitants in 2000—Selected Racial Groups: 2000

[In thousands (448.6 represents 448,600). As of April. Data refer to boundaries in effect on January 1, 2000]

City		One race						Two or more races
	Total population	White	Black or African American	American Indian, Alaska Native	Asian	Native Hawaiian and Other Pacific Islander	Some other race	
Albuquerque, NM	448.6	321.2	13.9	17.4	10.1	0.5	66.3	19.3
Anaheim, CA...........	328.0	179.6	8.7	3.0	39.3	1.4	79.4	16.5
Anchorage, AK	260.3	188.0	15.2	18.9	14.4	2.4	5.7	15.6
Arlington, TX..........	333.0	225.4	45.7	1.8	20.0	0.5	29.8	9.8
Atlanta, GA............	416.5	138.4	255.7	0.8	8.0	0.2	8.3	5.2
Aurora, CO	276.4	190.3	37.1	2.2	12.1	0.5	22.5	11.7
Austin, TX.............	656.6	429.1	66.0	3.9	31.0	0.5	106.5	19.7
Baltimore, MD	651.2	206.0	419.0	2.1	10.0	0.2	4.4	9.6
Boston, MA............	589.1	320.9	149.2	2.4	44.3	0.4	46.1	25.9
Buffalo, NY	292.6	159.3	109.0	2.3	4.1	0.1	10.8	7.2
Charlotte, NC	540.8	315.1	177.0	1.9	18.4	0.3	19.2	9.0
Chicago, IL	2,896.0	1,215.3	1,065.0	10.3	126.0	1.8	393.2	84.4
Cincinnati, OH..........	331.3	175.5	142.2	0.7	5.1	0.1	2.1	5.6
Cleveland, OH..........	478.4	198.5	243.9	1.5	6.4	0.2	17.2	10.7
Colorado Springs, CO......	360.9	291.1	23.7	3.2	10.2	0.8	18.1	13.9
Columbus, OH..........	711.5	483.3	174.1	2.1	24.5	0.4	8.3	18.8
Corpus Christi, TX	277.5	198.7	13.0	1.8	3.6	0.2	51.6	8.7
Dallas, TX.............	1,188.6	604.2	308.0	6.5	32.1	0.6	204.9	32.4
Denver, CO............	554.6	362.2	61.6	7.3	15.6	0.6	86.5	20.8
Detroit, MI.............	951.3	116.6	775.8	3.1	9.3	0.3	24.2	22.0
El Paso, TX............	563.7	413.1	17.6	4.6	6.3	0.6	102.3	19.2
Fort Worth, TX..........	534.7	319.2	108.3	3.1	14.1	0.3	75.1	14.5
Fresno, CA	427.7	214.6	35.8	6.8	48.0	0.6	99.9	22.1
Honolulu, HI [1]........	371.7	73.1	6.0	0.7	207.6	25.5	3.3	55.5
Houston, TX	1,953.6	962.6	494.5	8.6	103.7	1.2	321.6	61.5
Indianapolis, IN [2]	781.9	540.2	199.4	2.0	11.2	0.3	15.9	12.9
Jacksonville, FL.........	735.6	474.3	213.5	2.5	20.4	0.4	9.8	14.6
Kansas City, MO	441.5	267.9	137.9	2.1	8.2	0.5	14.2	10.8
Las Vegas, NV	478.4	334.2	49.6	3.6	22.9	2.1	46.6	19.4
Lexington-Fayette, KY......	260.5	211.1	35.1	0.5	6.4	0.1	3.2	4.1
Long Beach, CA	461.5	208.4	68.6	3.9	55.6	5.6	95.1	24.3
Los Angeles, CA	3,694.8	1,734.0	415.2	29.4	369.3	5.9	949.7	191.3
Louisville, KY...........	256.2	161.3	84.6	0.6	3.7	0.1	1.7	4.3
Memphis, TN...........	650.1	223.7	399.2	1.2	9.5	0.2	9.4	6.8
Mesa, AZ	396.4	323.7	10.0	6.6	5.9	0.9	38.3	11.1
Miami, FL..............	362.5	241.5	80.9	0.8	2.4	0.1	19.6	17.2
Milwaukee, WI..........	597.0	298.4	222.9	5.2	17.6	0.3	36.4	16.2
Minneapolis, MN	382.6	249.2	68.8	8.4	23.5	0.3	15.8	16.7
Nashville-Davidson, TN [2]....	545.5	359.6	146.2	1.6	13.0	0.4	13.7	11.0
New Orleans, LA	484.7	136.0	325.9	1.0	11.0	0.1	4.5	6.2
New York, NY	8,008.3	3,576.4	2,129.8	41.3	787.0	5.4	1,074.4	394.0
Newark, NJ	273.5	72.5	146.3	1.0	3.3	0.1	38.4	11.9
Oakland, CA	399.5	125.0	142.5	2.7	60.9	2.0	46.6	19.9
Oklahoma City, OK.......	506.1	346.2	77.8	17.7	17.6	0.4	26.7	19.7
Omaha, NE............	390.0	305.7	51.9	2.6	6.8	0.2	15.3	7.5
Philadelphia, PA.........	1,517.6	683.3	655.8	4.1	67.7	0.7	72.4	33.6
Phoenix, AZ	1,321.0	938.9	67.4	26.7	26.4	1.8	216.6	43.3
Pittsburgh, PA..........	334.6	226.3	90.8	0.6	9.2	0.1	2.2	5.4
Portland, OR	529.1	412.2	35.1	5.6	33.5	2.0	18.8	22.0
Raleigh, NC	276.1	174.8	76.8	1.0	9.3	0.1	8.9	5.2
Riverside, CA	255.2	151.4	18.9	2.8	14.5	1.0	53.6	13.0
Sacramento, CA.........	407.0	196.5	63.0	5.3	67.6	3.9	44.6	26.1
San Antonio, TX.........	1,144.6	774.7	78.1	9.6	17.9	1.1	221.4	41.9
San Diego, CA	1,223.4	736.2	96.2	7.5	167.0	5.9	151.5	59.1
San Francisco, CA	776.7	385.7	60.5	3.5	239.6	3.8	50.4	33.3
San Jose, CA	894.9	425.0	31.3	6.9	240.4	3.6	142.7	45.1
Santa Ana, CA..........	338.0	144.4	5.7	4.0	29.8	1.2	137.4	15.5
Seattle, WA............	563.4	394.4	47.5	5.7	73.9	2.8	13.4	25.1
St. Louis, MO	348.2	152.7	178.3	1.0	6.9	0.1	2.8	6.5
St. Paul, MN	287.2	192.4	33.6	3.3	35.5	0.2	11.0	11.1
Tampa, FL	303.4	194.9	79.1	1.2	6.5	0.3	12.6	8.8
Toledo, OH	313.6	220.3	73.9	1.0	3.2	0.1	7.2	8.1
Tucson, AZ	486.7	341.4	21.1	11.0	12.0	0.8	82.0	18.4
Tulsa, OK.............	393.0	275.5	60.8	18.6	7.2	0.2	13.6	17.3
Virginia Beach, VA	425.3	303.7	80.6	1.6	20.9	0.4	6.4	11.7
Washington, DC.........	572.1	176.1	343.3	1.7	15.2	0.3	22.0	13.4
Wichita, KS	344.3	258.9	39.3	4.0	13.6	0.2	17.6	10.7

[1] The population shown in this table is for the census designated place (CDP). [2] Represents the portion of a consolidated city that is not within one or more separately incorporated places.

Source: U.S. Census Bureau, 2000 Census of Population and Housing, Profiles of General Demographic Characteristics.

U.S. Census Bureau, Statistical Abstract of the United States: 2001

No. 36. Cities With 250,000 or More Inhabitants in 2000—Hispanic and Non-Hispanic Groups: 2000

[In thousands, except percent (448.6 represents 448,600). As of April. Data refer to boundaries in effect on January 1, 2000]

City	Hispanic or Latino — Total, Total population	Number	Percent of total population	Mexican	Puerto Rican	Cuban	Other Hispanic or Latino	Not Hispanic or Latino — Total	White alone
Albuquerque, NM	448.6	179.1	39.9	68.5	1.7	1.7	107.1	269.5	223.9
Anaheim, CA	328.0	153.4	46.8	126.0	1.3	0.9	25.2	174.6	117.6
Anchorage, AK	260.3	14.8	5.7	7.2	1.7	0.3	5.6	245.5	182.0
Arlington, TX	333.0	60.8	18.3	46.8	2.1	0.3	11.6	272.2	198.6
Atlanta, GA	416.5	18.7	4.5	12.7	1.1	0.9	4.0	397.8	130.2
Aurora, CO	276.4	54.8	19.8	38.3	1.6	0.3	14.6	221.6	163.6
Austin, TX	656.6	200.6	30.5	153.9	2.5	1.4	42.8	456.0	347.6
Baltimore, MD	651.2	11.1	1.7	3.0	2.2	0.5	5.3	640.1	201.6
Boston, MA	589.1	85.1	14.4	4.1	27.4	2.2	51.3	504.1	291.6
Buffalo, NY	292.6	22.1	7.5	1.0	17.3	0.4	3.4	270.6	151.5
Charlotte, NC	540.8	39.8	7.4	22.2	2.4	1.1	14.1	501.0	297.8
Chicago, IL	2,896.0	753.6	26.0	530.5	113.1	8.1	102.0	2,142.4	907.2
Cincinnati, OH	331.3	4.2	1.3	1.5	0.6	0.2	1.8	327.1	173.8
Cleveland, OH	478.4	34.7	7.3	3.0	25.4	0.5	5.9	443.7	185.6
Colorado Springs, CO	360.9	43.3	12.0	23.0	2.7	0.3	17.3	317.6	271.7
Columbus, OH	711.5	17.5	2.5	8.7	2.8	0.6	5.4	694.0	475.9
Corpus Christi, TX	277.5	150.7	54.3	98.1	0.7	0.3	51.5	126.7	106.9
Dallas, TX	1,188.6	422.6	35.6	350.5	2.4	2.3	67.4	766.0	410.8
Denver, CO	554.6	175.7	31.7	120.7	1.6	0.7	52.7	378.9	288.0
Detroit, MI	951.3	47.2	5.0	33.1	6.6	0.9	6.5	904.1	99.9
El Paso, TX	563.7	431.9	76.6	359.7	3.7	0.5	68.0	131.8	103.4
Fort Worth, TX	534.7	159.4	29.8	132.9	1.9	0.6	24.0	375.3	245.0
Fresno, CA	427.7	170.5	39.9	144.8	1.1	0.3	24.4	257.1	159.5
Honolulu, HI [1]	371.7	16.2	4.4	4.0	4.6	0.2	7.4	355.4	69.5
Houston, TX	1,953.6	730.9	37.4	527.4	6.9	5.0	191.5	1,222.8	601.9
Indianapolis, IN [2]	781.9	30.6	3.9	21.1	1.9	0.5	7.2	751.2	527.7
Jacksonville, FL	735.6	30.6	4.2	6.1	11.1	3.2	10.2	705.0	457.5
Kansas City, MO	441.5	30.6	6.9	24.0	0.7	0.8	5.0	410.9	254.5
Las Vegas, NV	478.4	113.0	23.6	83.5	2.9	3.4	23.2	365.5	277.7
Lexington-Fayette, KY	260.5	8.6	3.3	6.0	0.5	0.2	1.8	252.0	206.2
Long Beach, CA	461.5	165.1	35.8	127.1	2.3	1.1	34.6	296.4	152.9
Los Angeles, CA	3,694.8	1,719.1	46.5	1,091.7	13.4	12.4	601.5	1,975.7	1,099.2
Louisville, KY	256.2	4.8	1.9	1.6	0.4	1.5	1.3	251.5	158.7
Memphis, TN	650.1	19.3	3.0	14.1	0.7	0.5	4.0	630.8	216.2
Mesa, AZ	396.4	78.3	19.7	63.5	1.5	0.4	12.9	318.1	290.2
Miami, FL	362.5	238.4	65.8	3.7	10.3	123.8	100.7	124.1	42.9
Milwaukee, WI	597.0	71.6	12.0	43.3	19.6	0.6	8.1	525.3	271.0
Minneapolis, MN	382.6	29.2	7.6	19.8	1.2	0.5	7.6	353.4	239.1
Nashville-Davidson, TN [2]	545.5	25.8	4.7	16.1	1.9	0.8	7.0	519.8	349.1
New Orleans, LA	484.7	14.8	3.1	2.6	1.0	1.6	9.6	469.8	128.9
New York, NY	8,008.3	2,160.6	27.0	186.9	789.2	41.1	1,143.4	5,847.7	2,801.3
Newark, NJ	273.5	80.6	29.5	2.3	39.7	3.0	35.7	192.9	39.0
Oakland, CA	399.5	87.5	21.9	65.1	2.3	0.6	19.5	312.0	94.0
Oklahoma City, OK	506.1	51.4	10.1	41.0	1.2	0.4	8.8	454.8	327.2
Omaha, NE	390.0	29.4	7.5	23.3	0.6	0.3	5.2	360.6	293.9
Philadelphia, PA	1,517.6	128.9	8.5	6.2	91.5	2.7	28.5	1,388.6	644.4
Phoenix, AZ	1,321.0	450.0	34.1	375.1	5.1	2.0	67.8	871.1	736.8
Pittsburgh, PA	334.6	4.4	1.3	1.2	0.8	0.3	2.1	330.1	224.0
Portland, OR	529.1	36.1	6.8	25.1	1.0	1.3	8.6	493.1	399.4
Raleigh, NC	276.1	19.3	7.0	12.2	1.3	0.4	5.4	256.8	166.4
Riverside, CA	255.2	97.3	38.1	79.0	1.6	0.6	16.1	157.9	116.3
Sacramento, CA	407.0	88.0	21.6	70.8	2.1	0.5	14.7	319.0	165.0
San Antonio, TX	1,144.6	671.4	58.7	473.4	7.8	1.5	188.7	473.3	364.4
San Diego, CA	1,223.4	310.8	25.4	259.2	5.9	1.9	43.7	912.6	603.9
San Francisco, CA	776.7	109.5	14.1	48.9	3.8	1.6	55.2	667.2	338.9
San Jose, CA	894.9	270.0	30.2	221.1	4.1	1.0	43.8	625.0	322.5
Santa Ana, CA	338.0	257.1	76.1	222.7	0.7	0.6	33.1	80.9	42.0
Seattle, WA	563.4	29.7	5.3	17.9	1.5	0.8	9.6	533.7	382.5
St. Louis, MO	348.2	7.0	2.0	4.1	0.5	0.4	2.0	341.2	149.3
St. Paul, MN	287.2	22.7	7.9	16.6	1.0	0.4	4.8	264.4	183.9
Tampa, FL	303.4	58.5	19.3	6.3	17.5	14.7	20.0	244.9	154.9
Toledo, OH	313.6	17.1	5.5	13.3	0.7	0.2	2.9	296.5	212.7
Tucson, AZ	486.7	173.9	35.7	145.2	2.1	0.6	25.9	312.8	263.7
Tulsa, OK	393.0	28.1	7.2	21.1	1.1	0.3	5.5	364.9	263.8
Virginia Beach, VA	425.3	17.8	4.2	4.9	6.3	0.6	6.0	407.5	295.4
Washington, DC	572.1	45.0	7.9	5.1	2.3	1.1	36.4	527.1	159.2
Wichita, KS	344.3	33.1	9.6	27.0	0.8	0.3	5.1	311.2	246.9

[1] The population shown in this table is for the census designated place (CDP). [2] Represents the portion of a consolidated city that is not within one or more separately incorporated places.

Source: U.S. Census Bureau, *2000 Census of Population and Housing, Profiles of General Demographic Characteristics.*

Population   39

Demographic and Economic Profiles of Selected Racial and Hispanic Origin Populations

[211,461 represents 211,461,000. Hispanic persons may be of any race. Population data based on 2000 Census of Population. Other items except business ownership based on Current Population Survey, see text, this section]

Characteristic	White	Black	Asian	Native Hawaiian and Other Pacific Islander	American Indian, Alaskan Native	Hispanic
POPULATION, 2000						
Total persons (1,000).	211,461	34,658	10,243	399	2,476	35,306
Percent of total population.	75.1	12.3	3.6	0.1	0.9	12.5
Under 5 years old.	12,860	2,805	670	33	213	3,718
5-14 years old	28,268	6,327	1,365	72	485	6,787
15-44 years old	89,850	16,253	5,254	206	1,194	18,221
45-64 years old	50,078	6,451	2,153	66	445	4,847
65 years old and over	30,406	2,823	801	21	138	1,734
Five states with largest number of specified group [1]	CA (20.2) TX (14.8) NY (12.9) FL (12.5) PA (10.5)	NY (3.0) TX (2.4) GA (2.4) FL (2.3) CA (2.3)	CA (3.7) NY (1.0) TX (.6) HI (.5) NJ (.5)	CA (.117) HI (.114) WA (.024) UT (.015) TX (.014)	CA (.333) OK (.273) AZ (.256) NM (.173) TX (.118)	CA (11.0) TX (6.7) NY (2.9) FL (2.7) IL (1.5)
Five states with largest percent of specified group	ME (97%) VT (97%) NH (96%) WV (95%) IA (94%)	DC (60%) MS (36%) LA (33%) SC (30%) GA (29%)	HI (42%) CA (11%) NJ (6%) NY (6%) WA (6%)	HI (9.4%) UT (0.7%) AK (0.5%) WA (0.4%) NV (0.4%)	AK (16%) NM (10%) SD (8%) OK (8%) MT (6%)	NM (42%) CA (32%) TX (32%) AZ (25%) NV (20%)
EDUCATIONAL ATTAINMENT, 2000						
Persons 25 years old and over (1,000) . .	147,067	20,036	[2]6,667	([2])	(NA)	17,150
Percent high school graduate or more	84.9	78.5	[2]85.7	([2])	(NA)	57.0
Percent bachelor's degree or more	26.1	16.5	[2]43.9	([2])	(NA)	10.6
Percent with advanced degree	8.8	5.1	[2]15.3	([2])	(NA)	3.3
VOTING PARTICIPATION, 1998						
Percent reporting they registered	63.9	60.2	(NA)	(NA)	(NA)	33.7
Percent reporting they voted	43.3	39.6	(NA)	(NA)	(NA)	20.0
FAMILY INCOME IN 1999						
Total families (1,000)	60,256	8,664	[2]2,506	([2])	(NA)	7,561
Percent distribution—						
Less than $10,000	4.4	14.6	[2]6.6	([2])	(NA)	10.0
$10,000 to $14,999	4.2	9.1	[2]4.8	([2])	(NA)	8.9
$15,000 to $24,999	11.6	16.0	[2]9.0	([2])	(NA)	19.7
$25,000 to $34,999	11.8	13.6	[2]9.1	([2])	(NA)	15.9
$35,000 to $49,999	16.7	15.3	[2]14.8	([2])	(NA)	16.7
$50,000 to $74,999	22.1	15.8	[2]18.5	([2])	(NA)	15.9
$75,000 or more	29.3	15.6	[2]37.1	([2])	(NA)	12.8
Median income (dol.)	51,224	31,778	[2]56,316	([2])	(NA)	31,663
POVERTY, 1999						
Families below poverty level (percent)	7.3	21.9	[2]10.3	([2])	(NA)	20.2
Persons below poverty level (percent)	9.8	23.6	[2]10.7	([2])	(NA)	22.8
BUSINESSES OWNED BY SPECIFIED GROUP, 1997						
All firms:						
Number (1,000)	(NA)	823	[2]913	([2])	197	1,200
Sales and receipts (mil. dol.).	(NA)	71,215	[2]306,933	([2])	34,344	186,275
Firms with paid employees:						
Number (1,000)	(NA)	93	[2]290	([2])	33	212
Sales and receipts (mil. dol.).	(NA)	56,378	[2]278,294	([2])	29,226	158,675
Employees (1,000)	(NA)	718	[2]2,203	([2])	299	1,389
Payroll, annual (mil. dol.)	(NA)	14,322	[2]46,180	([2])	6,624	29,830

NA Not available.   [1] Number in parentheses in millions.   [2] Native Hawaiian and Other Pacific Islander included in data for Asian population.

Source: U.S. Census Bureau, 2000 Census of Population, Summary File 1, <http://www.census.gov/Press-Release/www/2001/sumfile1.html>; *Current Population Reports*, P20-523, P20-536, P60-209, and P60-210; and "1997 Economic Census, Minority- and Women-Owned Businesses, United States"; published 24 May 2001; <http://www.census.gov/epcd/mwb97/us/us.html>.

[134,687 represents 134,687,000. As of March, except labor force status, annual average. Excludes members of Armed Forces except those living off post or with their families on post. Data for 1990 are based on 1980 census population controls; 1995 and 2000 data based on 1990 census population controls. Based on Current Population Survey; see text, this section, and Appendix III]

Characteristic	Number (1,000)						Percent distribution			
	White			Black			White		Black	
	1990	1995	2000	1990	1995	2000	1990	2000	1990	2000
EDUCATIONAL ATTAINMENT										
Persons 25 years old and over	134,687	141,113	147,067	16,751	18,457	20,036	100.0	100.0	100.0	100.0
Elementary:										
0 to 8 years...........	14,131	11,101	10,035	2,701	1,800	1,417	10.5	6.8	16.1	7.1
High school:										
1 to 3 years...........	14,080	[1]12,882	[1]12,153	2,969	[1]3,041	[1]2,899	10.5	[1]8.3	17.7	[1]14.5
4 years..............	52,449	[2]47,986	[2]49,105	6,239	[2]6,686	[2]7,050	38.9	[2]33.4	37.2	[2]35.2
College:										
1 to 3 years...........	24,350	[3]35,321	[3]37,353	2,952	[3]4,486	[3]5,366	18.1	[3]25.4	17.6	[3]26.8
4 years or more	29,677	[4]33,824	[4]38,421	1,890	[4]2,444	[4]3,303	22.0	[4]26.1	11.3	[4]16.5
LABOR FORCE STATUS [5]										
Civilians 16 years old and over	160,625	166,914	174,428	21,477	23,246	25,218	100.0	100.0	100.0	100.0
Civilian labor force	107,447	111,950	117,574	13,740	14,817	16,603	66.9	67.4	64.0	65.8
Employed	102,261	106,490	113,475	12,175	13,279	15,334	63.7	65.1	56.7	60.8
Unemployed	5,186	5,459	4,099	1,565	1,538	1,269	3.2	2.3	7.3	5.0
Unemployment rate [6]	4.8	4.9	3.5	11.4	10.4	7.6	(X)	(X)	(X)	(X)
Not in labor force.........	53,178	54,965	56,854	7,737	8,429	8,615	33.1	32.6	36.0	34.2
FAMILY TYPE										
Total families	56,590	58,437	60,251	7,470	8,093	8,664	100.0	100.0	100.0	100.0
With own children [7] ...	26,718	27,951	28,107	4,378	4,682	4,782	47.2	46.6	58.6	55.2
Married couple	46,981	47,899	48,790	3,750	3,842	4,144	83.0	81.0	50.2	47.1
With own children [7]......	21,579	22,005	21,809	1,972	1,926	2,093	38.1	36.2	26.4	24.2
Female householder, no spouse present	7,306	8,031	8,380	3,275	3,716	3,814	12.9	13.9	43.8	45.1
With own children [7]......	4,199	4,841	4,869	2,232	2,489	2,409	7.4	8.1	29.9	27.8
Male householder, no spouse present	2,303	2,507	3,081	446	536	706	4.1	5.1	6.0	7.8
With own children [7]......	939	1,105	1,429	173	267	280	1.7	2.4	2.3	3.2
FAMILY INCOME IN PREVIOUS YEAR IN CONSTANT (1999) DOLLARS										
Total families [8]	56,590	58,444	60,256	7,470	8,093	8,664	100.0	100.0	100.0	100.0
Less than $5,000..........	(NA)	(NA)	1,083	(NA)	(NA)	543	1.8	1.8	7.2	6.3
$5,000 to $9,999.........	(NA)	(NA)	1,554	(NA)	(NA)	721	3.0	2.6	11.7	8.3
$10,000 to $14,999	(NA)	(NA)	2,514	(NA)	(NA)	793	4.6	4.2	9.7	9.1
$15,000 to $24,999	(NA)	(NA)	6,970	(NA)	(NA)	1,384	11.8	11.6	18.0	16.0
$25,000 to $34,999	(NA)	(NA)	7,090	(NA)	(NA)	1,176	12.6	11.8	13.3	13.6
$35,000 to $49,999	(NA)	(NA)	10,046	(NA)	(NA)	1,326	18.3	16.7	15.4	15.3
$50,000 or more	(NA)	(NA)	30,998	(NA)	(NA)	2,723	47.9	51.4	24.6	31.4
Median income (dol.) [9]	48,334	45,960	51,224	27,152	27,764	31,778	(X)	(X)	(X)	(X)
POVERTY										
Families below poverty level [10].	4,409	5,312	4,377	2,077	2,212	1,898	7.8	7.3	27.8	21.9
Persons below poverty level [10].	20,785	25,379	21,922	9,302	10,196	8,360	10.0	9.8	30.7	23.6
HOUSING TENURE										
Total occupied units	80,163	83,737	87,671	10,486	11,655	12,849	100.0	100.0	100.0	100.0
Owner-occupied	54,094	57,449	62,077	4,445	4,888	6,055	67.5	70.8	42.4	47.1
Renter-occupied	24,685	24,793	24,253	5,862	6,547	6,563	30.8	27.7	55.9	51.1
No cash rent............	1,384	1,494	1,340	178	220	231	1.7	1.5	1.7	1.8

NA Not available.   X Not applicable.   [1] Represents those who completed 9th to 12th grade, but have no high school diploma.   [2] High school graduate.   [3] Some college or associate degree.   [4] Bachelor's or advanced degree.   [5] Source: U.S. Bureau of Labor Statistics, *Employment and Earnings*, January issues. See footnote 2, Table 567.   [6] Total unemployment as percent of civilian labor force.   [7] Children under 18 years old.   [8] Includes families in group quarters.   [9] For definition of median, see Guide to Tabular Presentation.   [10] For explanation of poverty level, see text, Section 13, Income, Expenditures, and Wealth.

Source: Except as noted, U.S. Census Bureau, Black Population in the U.S.: March 2000, PPL-142; *Current Population Reports*, P60-209, P60-210, and earlier reports; and unpublished data.

No. 39. Social and Economic Characteristics of the Asian and Pacific Islander Population: 1990 and 2000

[6,679 represents 6,679,000. As of March. Excludes members of Armed Forces except those living off post or with their families on post. Data for 1990 are based on 1980 census population controls; 2000 data are based on 1990 census population controls. Based on Current Population Survey; see text, this section, and Appendix III]

Characteristic	Number (1,000)		Percent distribution	
	1990	2000	1990	2000
Total persons	**6,679**	**10,925**	**100.0**	**100.0**
LABOR FORCE STATUS [1]				
Civilians 16 years old and over.	**4,849**	**8,225**	**100.0**	**100.0**
Civilian labor force	3,216	5,458	66.3	66.4
Employed	3,079	5,246	63.5	63.8
Unemployed	136	212	2.8	2.6
Unemployment rate [2]	4.2	3.9	(X)	(X)
Not in labor force	1,634	2,767	33.7	33.6
FAMILY TYPE				
Total families	1,531	2,506	100.0	100.0
Married couple	1,256	1,996	82.1	79.6
Female householder, no spouse present	188	331	12.3	13.2
Male householder, no spouse present	86	179	5.6	7.1
HOUSING TENURE				
Total occupied units	1,988	3,337	100.0	100.0
Owner-occupied	977	1,766	49.1	52.9
Renter-occupied	982	1,526	49.4	45.7
No cash rent	30	46	1.5	1.4

X Not applicable.   [1] Data beginning 1994 not directly comparable with earlier years. See text, Section 12, Labor Force, Employment, and Earnings.   [2] Total unemployment as percent of civilian labor force.
Source: U.S. Census Bureau, *Current Population Reports*, P20-459, and "The Asian and Pacific Islander Population in the United States: March 2000 (Update)" (PPL-146).

No. 40. Persons 65 Years Old and Over—Characteristics by Sex: 1980 to 2000

[24.2 represents 24,200,000. As of March, except as noted. Covers civilian noninstitutional population. Excludes members of Armed Forces except those living off post or with their families on post. Data for 1980 and 1990 are based on 1980 census population controls; 1995 and 2000 data based on 1990 census population controls. Based on Current Population Survey; see text, this section, and Appendix III]

Characteristic	Total				Male				Female			
	1980	1990	1995	2000	1980	1990	1995	2000	1980	1990	1995	2000
Total (million)	**24.2**	**29.6**	**31.7**	**32.6**	**9.9**	**12.3**	**13.2**	**13.9**	**14.2**	**17.2**	**18.5**	**18.7**
PERCENT DISTRIBUTION												
Marital status:												
Never married	5.5	4.6	4.2	3.9	4.9	4.2	4.2	4.2	5.9	4.9	4.2	3.6
Married	55.4	56.1	56.9	57.2	78.0	76.5	77.0	75.2	39.5	41.4	42.5	43.8
Spouse present	53.6	54.1	54.7	54.6	76.1	74.2	74.5	72.6	37.9	39.7	40.6	41.3
Spouse absent	1.8	2.0	2.2	2.6	1.9	2.3	2.5	2.6	1.7	1.7	1.9	2.5
Widowed	35.7	34.2	33.2	32.1	13.5	14.2	13.5	14.4	51.2	48.6	47.3	45.3
Divorced	3.5	5.0	5.7	6.7	3.6	5.0	5.2	6.1	3.4	5.1	6.0	7.2
Family status:												
In families [1]	67.6	66.7	66.6	67.4	83.0	81.9	80.6	79.7	56.8	55.8	56.7	58.2
Nonfamily householders	31.2	31.9	32.4	31.1	15.7	16.6	18.4	18.2	42.0	42.8	42.4	40.7
Secondary individuals	1.2	1.4	1.0	1.5	1.3	1.5	1.0	2.1	1.1	1.4	0.9	1.1
Living arrangements:												
Living in household	99.8	99.7	99.9	100.0	99.9	99.9	100.0	100.0	99.7	99.5	99.9	100.0
Living alone	30.3	31.0	31.5	30.1	14.9	15.7	17.3	17.0	41.0	42.0	41.7	39.6
Spouse present	53.6	54.1	54.7	54.6	76.1	74.3	74.5	72.6	37.9	39.7	40.6	41.3
Living with someone else	15.9	14.6	13.7	15.3	8.9	9.9	8.1	10.4	20.8	17.8	17.6	19.1
Not in household [2]	0.2	0.3	0.1	0.1	0.1	0.1	-	0.1	0.3	0.5	0.1	0.1
Years of school completed:												
8 years or less	43.1	28.5	21.0	16.7	45.3	30.0	22.0	17.8	41.6	27.5	20.3	15.9
1 to 3 years of high school	16.2	16.1	[3]15.2	[3]13.8	15.5	15.7	[3]14.5	[3]12.7	16.7	16.4	[3]15.6	[3]14.7
4 years of high school	24.0	32.9	[4]33.8	[4]35.9	21.4	29.0	[4]29.2	[4]30.4	25.8	35.6	[4]37.1	[4]39.9
1 to 3 years of college	8.2	10.9	[5]17.1	[5]18.0	7.5	10.8	[5]17.1	[5]17.8	8.6	11.0	[5]17.0	[5]18.2
4 years or more of college	8.6	11.6	[6]13.0	[6]15.6	10.3	14.5	[6]17.2	[6]21.4	7.4	9.5	[6]9.9	[6]11.4
Labor force participation: [7]												
Employed	12.2	11.5	11.7	12.4	18.4	15.9	16.1	16.9	7.8	8.4	8.5	9.1
Unemployed	0.4	0.4	0.5	0.4	0.6	0.5	0.7	0.6	0.3	0.3	0.3	0.3
Not in labor force	87.5	88.1	87.9	87.2	81.0	83.6	83.2	82.5	91.9	91.3	91.2	90.6
Percent below poverty level [8]	15.2	11.4	11.7	9.7	11.1	7.8	7.2	6.9	17.9	13.9	14.9	11.8

- Represents zero.   [1] Excludes those living in unrelated subfamilies.   [2] In group quarters other than institutions.   [3] Represents those who completed 9th to 12th grade, but have no high school diploma.   [4] High school graduate.   [5] Some college or associate degree.   [6] Bachelor's or advanced degree.   [7] Annual averages of monthly figures. Source: U.S. Bureau of Labor Statistics, *Employment and Earnings*, January issues. See footnote 2, Table 567.   [8] Poverty status based on income in preceding year.
Source: Except as noted, U.S. Census Bureau, *Current Population Reports*, P20-537, and earlier reports; P60-210; and unpublished data.

42 Population

No. 41. Social and Economic Characteristics of the Hispanic Population: 2000

[32,804 represents 32,804,000. As of March, except labor force status, annual average. Excludes members of the Armed Forces except those living off post or with their families on post. Based on Current Population Survey; see text, this section, and Appendix III]

Characteristic	Number (1,000)						Percent distribution					
	His-panic, total	Mexi-can	Puerto Rican	Cuban	Central and South Ameri-can	Other His-panic	His-panic, total	Mexi-can	Puerto Rican	Cuban	Central and South Ameri-can	Other His-panic
Total persons	32,804	21,701	2,959	1,300	4,743	2,101	100.0	100.0	100.0	100.0	100.0	100.0
Under 5 years old	3,665	2,701	278	67	404	215	11.2	12.4	9.4	5.1	8.5	10.2
5 to 14 years old	6,346	4,453	571	129	788	405	19.3	20.5	19.3	9.9	16.6	19.3
15 to 44 years old	16,277	10,842	1,414	526	2,534	960	49.6	50.0	47.8	40.5	53.4	45.7
45 to 64 years old	4,764	2,769	518	305	794	377	14.5	12.8	17.5	23.4	16.7	18.0
65 years old and over	1,752	936	178	273	222	143	5.3	4.3	6.0	21.0	4.7	6.8
EDUCATIONAL ATTAINMENT												
Persons 25 years old and over	17,150	10,625	1,612	965	2,768	1,180	100.0	100.0	100.0	100.0	100.0	100.0
High school graduate or higher	9,783	5,416	1,037	705	1,781	845	57.0	51.0	64.3	73.0	64.3	71.6
Bachelor's degree or higher	1,821	738	209	222	481	171	10.6	6.9	13.0	23.0	17.4	14.5
LABOR FORCE STATUS [1]												
Civilians 16 years old and over	22,393	14,386	2,025	1,104	3,456	1,422	100.0	100.0	100.0	100.0	100.0	100.0
Civilian labor force	15,368	9,955	1,278	680	2,486	969	68.6	69.2	63.1	61.6	71.9	68.1
Employed	14,492	9,364	1,196	650	2,365	917	64.7	65.1	59.1	58.9	68.4	64.5
Unemployed	876	591	82	30	120	53	3.9	4.1	4.0	2.7	3.5	3.7
Unemployment rate [2]	5.7	5.9	6.4	4.4	4.8	5.5	(X)	(X)	(X)	(X)	(X)	(X)
Male	4.9	5.1	5.7	4.1	4.1	4.8	(X)	(X)	(X)	(X)	(X)	(X)
Female	6.7	7.2	7.1	4.7	5.8	6.3	(X)	(X)	(X)	(X)	(X)	(X)
Not in labor force	7,025	4,430	747	424	970	454	31.4	30.8	36.9	38.4	28.1	31.9
FAMILY TYPE												
Total families	7,561	4,794	770	385	1,109	504	100.0	100.0	100.0	100.0	100.0	100.0
Married couple	5,133	3,352	437	296	721	326	67.9	69.9	56.8	77.1	65.0	64.7
Female householder, no spouse present	1,769	1,013	275	70	272	138	23.4	21.1	35.8	18.3	24.6	27.4
Male householder, no spouse present	658	428	57	18	115	40	8.7	8.9	7.4	4.6	10.4	7.9
FAMILY INCOME IN 1999												
Total families [3]	7,561	4,794	770	385	1,109	504	100.0	100.0	100.0	100.0	100.0	100.0
Less than $5,000	323	187	53	14	47	21	4.3	3.9	6.9	3.6	4.3	4.2
$5,000 to $9,999	434	270	66	18	49	31	5.7	5.6	8.6	4.6	4.5	6.2
$10,000 to $14,999	674	425	72	43	86	48	8.9	8.9	9.4	11.2	7.7	9.5
$15,000 to $24,999	1,489	1,002	144	52	206	85	19.7	20.9	18.7	13.4	18.6	16.8
$25,000 to $34,999	1,202	775	102	60	199	67	15.9	16.2	13.2	15.6	17.9	13.3
$35,000 to $49,999	1,263	806	134	46	189	89	16.7	16.8	17.4	12.0	17.0	17.6
$50,000 or more	2,177	1,330	200	152	333	163	28.8	27.7	25.9	39.6	30.0	32.4
Median income (dol.) [4]	31,663	31,123	30,129	38,312	33,105	34,935	(X)	(X)	(X)	(X)	(X)	(X)
Families below poverty level [5]	1,525	1,018	177	58	181	91	20.2	21.2	23.0	15.0	16.3	18.1
Persons below poverty level [5]	7,439	5,214	760	224	789	452	22.8	24.1	25.8	17.3	16.7	21.6
HOUSING TENURE												
Total occupied units	9,319	5,733	1,004	523	1,372	687	100.0	100.0	100.0	100.0	100.0	100.0
Owner-occupied	4,243	2,739	352	307	515	330	45.5	47.8	35.0	58.7	37.6	48.0
Renter-occupied [6]	5,075	2,993	652	216	857	357	54.5	52.2	65.0	41.3	62.4	52.0

X Not applicable. [1] Source: U.S. Bureau of Labor Statistics, *Employment and Earnings*, January 2001. [2] Total unemployment as percent of civilian labor force. [3] Includes families in group quarters. [4] For definition of median, see Guide to Tabular Presentation. [5] For explanation of poverty level, see text, Section 13, Income, Expenditures, and Wealth. [6] Includes no cash rent.

Source: Except as noted, U.S. Census Bureau, *Current Population Reports*, P20-535.

No. 42. Native and Foreign-Born Population by Place of Birth: 1950 to 1990

[In thousands, except percent (150,216 represents 150,216,000). Data are based on a sample from the census; for details, see text, this section. See source for sampling variability]

Year	Total population	Native population						Foreign born	
		Total	Born in state of residence	Born in other states	State of birth not reported	Born in outlying areas [1]	Born abroad or at sea of American parents	Number	Percent of total population
1950	150,216	139,869	102,788	35,284	1,370	330	96	10,347	6.9
1960	178,467	168,806	118,802	44,264	4,526	817	397	9,661	5.4
1970	203,194	193,454	131,296	51,659	8,882	873	744	9,740	4.8
1980	226,546	212,466	144,871	65,452	(NA)	1,088	1,055	14,080	6.2
1990	248,710	228,943	153,685	72,011	(NA)	1,382	1,864	19,767	7.9

NA Not available.   [1] 1950, includes Alaska and Hawaii. Includes Puerto Rico.

Source: U.S. Census Bureau, *1970 Census of Population*, Vol. II, PC(2)-2A; and *1990 Census of Population Listing* (1990CPH-L-121).

No. 43. Native and Foreign-Born Populations by Age, Sex, Race, and Hispanic Origin: 1990 to 1999

[In thousands (228,945 represents 228,945,000), except as indicated. As of July, except 1990 as of April. Foreign-born residents are those people born outside the United States to noncitizen parents, while native residents are those people born inside the United States or born abroad to U.S. citizen parents. One notable difference between the two populations concern children. Any child born to foreign-born parents after entering the United States, by definition, becomes part of the native population. The foreign-born child population, therefore, is quite small, while the native child population (and the overall native population) are inflated by births to foreign-born parents after migrating to the United States. Data are consistent with the 1990 population estimates base]

Characteristic	Native population			Foreign-born population			Percent distribution, 1999	
	1990	1995	1999	1990	1995	1999	Native	Foreign born
Total	**228,945**	**239,826**	**246,859**	**19,846**	**22,978**	**25,831**	**100.0**	**100.0**
Under 5 years old.	18,495	19,372	18,766	270	160	176	7.6	1.4
5 to 9 years old	17,555	18,580	19,481	488	517	466	7.9	2.5
10 to 14 years old	16,334	18,001	18,645	733	852	904	7.6	3.7
15 to 19 years old	16,687	16,886	18,317	1,206	1,317	1,431	7.4	6.1
20 to 24 years old	17,260	16,146	16,077	1,883	1,837	1,949	6.5	9.5
25 to 29 years old	19,077	16,566	15,827	2,259	2,338	2,382	6.4	11.4
30 to 34 years old	19,583	19,103	16,832	2,255	2,723	2,895	6.8	11.4
35 to 39 years old	17,862	19,719	19,524	1,989	2,577	3,021	7.9	10.0
40 to 44 years old	15,865	18,031	19,554	1,729	2,229	2,714	7.9	8.7
45 to 49 years old	12,400	15,607	17,117	1,347	1,851	2,239	6.9	6.8
50 to 54 years old	10,166	12,207	14,614	1,150	1,435	1,832	5.9	5.8
55 to 59 years old	9,547	9,877	11,452	942	1,209	1,423	4.6	4.7
60 to 64 years old	9,763	9,059	9,320	864	988	1,194	3.8	4.4
65 to 69 years old	9,278	9,050	8,483	789	876	964	3.4	4.0
70 to 74 years old	7,452	8,095	7,975	529	736	796	3.2	2.7
75 to 79 years old	5,577	6,226	6,700	527	474	629	2.7	2.7
80 to 84 years old	3,479	4,082	4,463	431	396	354	1.8	2.2
85 to 89 years old	1,740	2,088	2,367	296	264	258	1.0	1.5
90 to 94 years old	628	869	1,007	121	148	140	0.4	0.6
95 to 99 years old	168	224	289	35	44	54	0.1	0.2
100 years old and over	30	39	48	6	9	11	-	-
5 to 13 years old	30,783	33,027	34,452	1,056	1,168	1,151	14.0	5.3
14 to 17 years old	12,557	13,898	14,657	788	930	997	5.9	4.0
18 to 24 years old	24,496	22,688	23,411	2,465	2,425	2,601	9.5	12.4
65 years old and over	28,351	30,672	31,334	2,733	2,947	3,206	12.7	13.8
85 years old and over	2,565	3,220	3,712	457	465	463	1.5	2.3
Female.	117,398	122,705	126,055	10,109	11,805	13,360	51.1	50.9
Male	111,547	117,121	120,805	9,737	11,173	12,472	48.9	49.1
White.	195,313	203,093	208,035	13,428	14,930	16,575	84.3	67.7
Black	28,812	30,999	32,346	1,705	2,117	2,517	13.1	8.6
American Indian, Eskimo, and Aleut	1,981	2,136	2,247	86	120	150	0.9	0.4
Asian and Pacific Islander . . .	2,840	3,597	4,231	4,627	5,811	6,589	1.7	23.3
Hispanic origin.	14,381	17,575	20,234	7,997	9,532	11,103	8.2	40.3
White, not Hispanic.	182,131	186,993	189,502	6,184	6,335	6,547	76.8	31.2
Black, not Hispanic.	28,096	30,096	31,288	1,208	1,494	1,805	12.7	6.1
American Indian, Eskimo, and Aleut, not Hispanic	1,771	1,897	1,982	26	35	43	0.8	0.1
Asian and Pacific Islander, not Hispanic	2,765	3,264	3,853	4,431	5,582	6,333	1.6	22.3

- Represents or rounds to zero.

Source: U.S. Census Bureau, "National Population Estimates by Nativity"; published 25 April 2000; <http://148.129.129.31:80/population/www/estimates/usnativity.html>.

No. 44. Native and Foreign-Born Populations by Selected Characteristics: 2000

[**In thousands (245,708 represents 245,708,000). As of March.** The foreign-born population includes some undocumented immigrants, refugees, and temporary residents such as students and temporary workers as well as legally-admitted immigrants. Based on Current Population Survey; see text, this section, and Appendix III]

Characteristic	Native population	Foreign-born population				
		Total	Year of entry			
			Before 1970	1970 to 1979	1980 to 1989	1990 to 2000
Total......................	245,708	28,379	4,547	4,605	8,022	11,206
Under 5 years old................	19,319	289	(X)	(X)	(X)	289
5 to 17 years old................	50,169	2,548	(X)	(X)	545	2,003
18 to 24 years old	23,384	3,148	(X)	148	891	2,110
25 to 29 years old	15,366	2,902	(X)	332	778	1,792
30 to 34 years old	16,284	3,233	85	407	1,224	1,517
35 to 44 years old	38,571	6,235	626	1,273	2,497	1,838
45 to 64 years old	53,108	6,910	1,910	2,065	1,640	1,295
65 years old and over............	29,507	3,115	1,926	381	446	362
Male	119,733	14,200	2,079	2,243	4,186	5,692
Female.......................	125,975	14,179	2,468	2,362	3,836	5,514
White........................	205,545	19,261	3,874	3,052	4,838	7,498
Black........................	33,288	2,221	217	396	752	856
American Indian/Eskimo/Aleut.........	2,656	191	26	36	55	75
Asian or Pacific Islander	4,218	6,706	430	1,121	2,377	2,778
Hispanic origin [1].................	19,962	12,841	1,448	2,057	3,809	5,527
EDUCATIONAL ATTAINMENT						
Persons 25 years old and over	152,836	22,394	4,547	4,457	6,586	6,804
Not high school graduate............	20,456	7,397	1,368	1,445	2,337	2,247
High school grad/some college........	93,312	9,219	2,087	1,813	2,733	2,586
Bachelor's degree................	26,225	3,615	562	778	979	1,297
Graduate or professional degree........	12,843	2,162	530	421	538	674
INCOME IN 1999						
Persons 16 years old and over	187,401	26,372	4,547	4,605	7,777	9,443
Without income	14,116	4,021	207	381	1,109	2,324
With income	173,285	22,351	4,340	4,224	6,668	7,119
$1 to $9,999 or loss	45,926	6,465	1,284	969	1,815	2,397
$10,000 to $19,999..............	36,876	6,097	1,020	938	1,877	2,263
$20,000 to $34,999..............	40,134	4,679	869	999	1,537	1,273
$35,000 to $49,999..............	22,749	2,150	394	548	693	514
$50,000 or more.................	27,600	2,960	773	770	746	672
POVERTY STATUS [2]						
In poverty......................	27,507	4,751	379	528	1,222	2,623
Not in poverty	217,638	23,597	4,168	4,077	6,797	8,555
HOMEOWNERSHIP						
In owner-occupied unit	177,393	14,224	3,568	3,053	4,128	3,475
In renter-occupied unit	68,315	14,155	978	1,552	3,893	7,731

X Not applicable.   [1] Persons of Hispanic origin may be of any race.   [2] Persons for whom poverty status is determined.

Source: U.S. Census Bureau, *Current Population Reports*, P20-534.

No. 45. Foreign-Born Population by Country of Origin and Citizenship Status: 2000

[**In thousands, except percent (28,379 represents 28,379,000).** See headnote, Table 44]

Country of origin	Foreign-born, total		Naturalized citizen		Not U.S. citizen	
	Number	Percent	Number	Percent	Number	Percent
All countries	28,379	100.0	10,622	100.0	17,758	100.0
Mexico............................	7,841	27.6	1,592	15.0	6,249	35.2
Cuba	952	3.4	552	5.2	400	2.3
Dominican Republic	692	2.4	234	2.2	458	2.6
El Salvador	765	2.7	151	1.4	614	3.5
Great Britain	613	2.2	273	2.6	341	1.9
China and Hong Kong.................	1,067	3.8	507	4.8	560	3.2
India..............................	1,007	3.5	362	3.4	644	3.6
Korea.............................	701	2.5	341	3.2	361	2.0
Philippines.........................	1,222	4.3	774	7.3	448	2.5
Vietnam...........................	863	3.0	411	3.9	453	2.5
Elsewhere.........................	12,655	44.6	5,424	51.1	7,230	40.7

Source: U.S. Census Bureau, *Current Population Reports*, P20-534.

Population 45

No. 46. Population by Selected Ancestry Group and Region: 1990

[1,119 represents 1,119,000. As of April 1. Covers persons who reported single and multiple ancestry groups. Persons who reported a multiple ancestry group may be included in more than one category. Major classifications of ancestry groups do not represent strict geographic or cultural definitions. Based on a sample and subject to sampling variability; see text, this section. For composition of regions, see map, inside front cover]

Ancestry group	Total (1,000)	Percent distribution by region				Ancestry group	Total (1,000)	Percent distribution by region			
		North-east	Mid-west	South	West			North-east	Mid-west	South	West
European: [1]						Central & South America [3]					
British.	1,119	17	18	39	26	and Spain:					
Czech	1,296	10	52	22	16	Hispanic [4]	1,113	13	6	31	50
Danish	1,635	9	34	12	45	Mexican	11,587	1	9	33	57
Dutch.	6,227	16	34	29	21	Puerto Rican . .	1,955	66	11	15	8
English	32,652	18	22	35	25	Spanish	2,024	16	8	30	45
French [2]	10,321	26	26	29	20						
German	57,947	17	39	25	19	Asia:					
Greek.	1,110	37	23	21	19	Chinese	1,505	25	8	12	55
Hungarian. . . .	1,582	36	32	17	16	Filipino	1,451	10	9	13	68
Irish	38,736	24	25	33	17	Japanese	1,005	9	8	11	72
Italian.	14,665	51	17	17	15						
Norwegian. . . .	3,869	6	52	10	33	North America:					
Polish.	9,366	37	37	15	11	Afro-American .	23,777	15	21	54	10
Portuguese . . .	1,153	49	3	8	41	American Indian	8,708	9	22	47	23
Russian	2,953	44	16	18	22	American	12,396	10	18	61	11
Scotch-Irish . . .	5,618	14	19	47	20	French Cana-					
Scottish	5,394	20	21	33	26	dian	2,167	45	20	20	15
Slovak	1,883	40	34	14	11	White	1,800	7	13	53	28
Swedish	4,681	14	40	14	32						
Swiss.	1,045	16	36	17	30						
Welsh.	2,034	22	24	27	27						

[1] Non-Hispanic groups.   [2] Excludes French Basque.   [3] Hispanic groups.   [4] A general type of response which may encompass several ancestry groups.

Source: U.S. Census Bureau, *1990 Census of Population, Supplementary Reports, Detailed Ancestry Groups for States* (1990 CP-S-1-2).

No. 47. Persons 5 Years Old and Over Speaking a Language Other Than English at Home by Language: 1990

[198,601 represent 198,601,000. As of April. Based on a sample and subject to sampling variability]

Language spoken at home	Persons who speak language (1,000)	Language spoken at home	Persons who speak language (1,000)
Speak only English	198,601	Portuguese	430
Spanish	17,339	Japanese	428
French	1,702	Greek.	388
German	1,547	Arabic.	355
Italian.	1,309	Hindi (Urdu).	331
Chinese	1,249	Russian	242
Tagalog.	843	Yiddish	213
Polish.	723	Thai (Laotian).	206
Korean	626	Persian	202
Vietnamese	507	French Creole	188

Source: U.S. Census Bureau, *1990 Census of Population and Housing Data Paper Listing* (CPH-L-133); and Summary Tape File 3C.

No. 48. Living Arrangements of Persons 15 Years Old and Over by Selected Characteristics: 2000

[In thousands (213,773 represents 213,773,000). As of March. Based on Current Population Survey which includes members of Armed Forces living off post or with families on post but excludes other Armed Forces; see text, this section, and Appendix III]

Living arrangement	Total	15 to 19 years old	20 to 24 years old	25 to 34 years old	35 to 44 years old	45 to 54 years old	55 to 64 years old	65 to 74 years old	75 years old and over
Total [1].	213,773	20,102	18,441	37,786	44,805	36,631	23,387	17,796	14,825
Alone	26,724	127	1,016	3,848	4,109	4,304	3,538	4,091	5,692
With spouse.	112,920	344	3,350	20,246	29,316	25,451	16,388	11,326	6,500
With other persons	74,129	19,631	14,075	13,692	11,380	6,876	3,461	2,379	2,633
White	177,581	15,843	14,671	30,320	36,915	30,790	20,163	15,528	13,352
Alone	22,307	91	770	2,959	3,291	3,500	2,942	3,542	5,212
With spouse.	99,191	315	2,994	17,479	25,318	22,246	14,583	10,248	6,009
With other persons	56,083	15,437	10,907	9,882	8,306	5,044	2,638	1,738	2,131
Black	25,855	3,057	2,762	5,163	5,699	4,103	2,316	1,624	1,130
Alone	3,605	25	176	628	680	691	526	461	418
With spouse.	8,392	14	215	1,620	2,518	1,885	1,136	671	333
With other persons	13,858	3,018	2,371	2,915	2,501	1,527	654	492	379
Hispanic origin [2]	22,793	2,889	2,755	5,660	4,974	3,019	1,745	1,132	621
Alone	1,296	12	73	246	215	207	184	211	147
With spouse.	11,189	103	774	3,269	3,212	1,909	1,042	609	270
With other persons	10,308	2,774	1,908	2,145	1,547	903	519	312	204

[1] Includes other races and persons not of Hispanic origin, not shown separately.   [2] Persons of Hispanic origin may be of any race.

Source: U.S. Census Bureau, unpublished data.

46 Population

No. 49. Marital Status of the Population by Sex, Race, and Hispanic Origin: 1980 to 2000

[In millions, except percent (159.5 represents 159,500,000). As of March. Persons 18 years old and over. Excludes members of Armed Forces except those living off post or with their families on post. Based on Current Population Survey, see text, this section, and Appendix III]

Marital status, race, and Hispanic origin	Total				Male				Female			
	1980	1990	1995	2000	1980	1990	1995	2000	1980	1990	1995	2000
Total [1]	159.5	181.8	191.6	201.8	75.7	86.9	92.0	96.9	83.8	95.0	99.6	104.9
Never married	32.3	40.4	43.9	48.2	18.0	22.4	24.6	26.1	14.3	17.9	19.3	22.1
Married	104.6	112.6	116.7	120.1	51.8	55.8	57.7	59.6	52.8	56.7	58.9	60.4
Widowed	12.7	13.8	13.4	13.7	2.0	2.3	2.3	2.6	10.8	11.5	11.1	11.1
Divorced	9.9	15.1	17.6	19.8	3.9	6.3	7.4	8.5	6.0	8.8	10.3	11.3
Percent of total	100.0	100.0	100.0	100.0	100.0	100.0	100.0	100.0	100.0	100.0	100.0	100.0
Never married	20.3	22.2	22.9	23.9	23.8	25.8	26.8	27.0	17.1	18.9	19.4	21.1
Married	65.5	61.9	60.9	59.5	68.4	64.3	62.7	61.5	63.0	59.7	59.2	57.6
Widowed	8.0	7.6	7.0	6.8	2.6	2.7	2.5	2.7	12.8	12.1	11.1	10.5
Divorced	6.2	8.3	9.2	9.8	5.2	7.2	8.0	8.8	7.1	9.3	10.3	10.8
White, total	139.5	155.5	161.3	168.1	66.7	74.8	78.1	81.6	72.8	80.6	83.2	86.6
Never married	26.4	31.6	33.2	36.0	15.0	18.0	19.2	20.3	11.4	13.6	14.0	15.7
Married	93.8	99.5	102.0	104.1	46.7	49.5	50.6	51.8	47.1	49.9	51.3	52.2
Widowed	10.9	11.7	11.3	11.5	1.6	1.9	1.9	2.2	9.3	9.8	9.4	9.3
Divorced	8.3	12.6	14.8	16.5	3.4	5.4	6.3	7.2	5.0	7.3	8.4	9.3
Percent of total	100.0	100.0	100.0	100.0	100.0	100.0	100.0	100.0	100.0	100.0	100.0	100.0
Never married	18.9	20.3	20.6	21.4	22.5	24.1	24.6	24.9	15.7	16.9	16.9	18.1
Married	67.2	64.0	63.2	62.0	70.0	66.2	64.9	63.5	64.7	61.9	61.7	60.2
Widowed	7.8	7.5	7.0	6.8	2.5	2.6	2.5	2.7	12.8	12.2	11.3	10.7
Divorced	6.0	8.1	9.1	9.8	5.0	7.2	8.1	8.8	6.8	9.0	10.1	10.7
Black, total	16.6	20.3	22.1	24.0	7.4	9.1	9.9	10.7	9.2	11.2	12.2	13.3
Never married	5.1	7.1	8.5	9.5	2.5	3.5	4.1	4.3	2.5	3.6	4.4	5.1
Married	8.5	9.3	9.6	10.1	4.1	4.5	4.6	5.0	4.5	4.8	4.9	5.1
Widowed	1.6	1.7	1.7	1.7	0.3	0.3	0.3	0.3	1.3	1.4	1.4	1.4
Divorced	1.4	2.1	2.4	2.8	0.5	0.8	0.8	1.1	0.9	1.3	1.5	1.7
Percent of total	100.0	100.0	100.0	100.0	100.0	100.0	100.0	100.0	100.0	100.0	100.0	100.0
Never married	30.5	35.1	38.4	39.6	34.3	38.4	41.7	40.2	27.4	32.5	35.8	38.3
Married	51.4	45.8	43.2	42.1	54.6	49.2	46.7	46.7	48.7	43.0	40.4	38.3
Widowed	9.8	8.5	7.6	7.1	4.2	3.7	3.1	2.8	14.3	12.4	11.3	10.5
Divorced	8.4	10.6	10.7	11.7	7.0	8.8	8.5	10.3	9.5	12.0	12.5	12.8
Hispanic, [2] total	7.9	13.6	17.6	21.1	3.8	6.7	8.8	10.4	4.1	6.8	8.8	10.7
Never married	1.9	3.7	5.0	5.9	1.0	2.2	3.0	3.4	0.9	1.5	2.1	2.5
Married	5.2	8.4	10.4	12.7	2.5	4.1	5.1	6.2	2.6	4.3	5.3	6.5
Widowed	0.4	0.5	0.7	0.9	0.1	0.1	0.2	0.2	0.3	0.4	0.6	0.7
Divorced	0.5	1.0	1.4	1.6	0.2	0.4	0.6	0.7	0.3	0.6	0.8	1.0
Percent of total	100.0	100.0	100.0	100.0	100.0	100.0	100.0	100.0	100.0	100.0	100.0	100.0
Never married	24.1	27.2	28.6	28.0	27.3	32.1	33.8	32.7	21.1	22.5	23.5	23.4
Married	65.6	61.7	59.3	60.2	67.1	60.9	57.9	59.6	64.3	62.4	60.7	60.7
Widowed	4.4	4.0	4.2	4.2	1.6	1.5	1.8	1.9	7.1	6.5	6.6	6.5
Divorced	5.8	7.0	7.9	7.6	4.0	5.5	6.6	6.7	7.6	8.5	9.2	9.3

[1] Includes persons of other races, not shown separately.   [2] Hispanic persons may be of any race.

Source: U.S. Census Bureau, *Current Population Reports*, P20-491, and earlier reports; and unpublished data.

No. 50. Married Couples of Same or Mixed Races and Origins: 1980 to 2000

[In thousands (49,714 represents 49,714,000). As of March. Persons 15 years old and over. Persons of Hispanic origin may be of any race. Except as noted, based on Current Population Survey; see headnote, Table 54]

Race and origin of spouses	1980	1990	1995	1999	2000
Married couples, total	49,714	53,256	54,937	55,849	56,497
RACE					
White/White	44,910	47,202	48,030	48,455	48,917
Black/Black	3,354	3,687	3,703	3,868	3,989
Black/White	167	211	328	364	363
Black husband/White wife	122	150	206	240	268
White husband/Black wife	45	61	122	124	95
White/other race [1]	450	720	988	1,086	1,051
Black/other race [1]	34	33	76	31	50
All other couples [1]	799	1,401	1,811	2,045	2,127
HISPANIC ORIGIN					
Hispanic/Hispanic	1,906	3,085	3,857	4,480	4,739
Hispanic/other origin (not Hispanic)	891	1,193	1,434	1,647	1,742
All other couples (not of Hispanic origin)	46,917	48,979	49,646	49,722	50,016

[1] Excluding White and Black.

Source: U.S. Census Bureau, *Current Population Reports*, P20-488, and earlier reports; and unpublished data.

Population   47

No. 51. Marital Status of the Population by Sex and Age: 2000

[96,900 represents 96,900,000. As of March. Persons 18 years old and over. Excludes members of Armed Forces except those living off post or with their families on post. Based on Current Population Survey; see text, this section, and Appendix III]

Sex and age	Number of persons (1,000)					Percent distribution				
	Total	Never married	Married	Wid-owed	Divorced	Total	Never married	Married	Wid-owed	Divorced
Male	**96,900**	**26,124**	**59,631**	**2,601**	**8,544**	**100.0**	**27.0**	**61.5**	**2.7**	**8.8**
18 to 19 years old	4,082	4,011	70	-	1	100.0	98.3	1.7	-	-
20 to 24 years old	9,208	7,710	1,397	-	101	100.0	83.7	15.2	-	1.1
25 to 29 years old	8,943	4,625	3,967	9	342	100.0	51.7	44.4	0.1	3.8
30 to 34 years old	9,621	2,899	5,996	15	712	100.0	30.0	62.3	0.2	7.4
35 to 39 years old	11,032	2,241	7,440	42	1,308	100.0	20.3	67.4	0.4	11.9
40 to 44 years old	11,103	1,740	7,842	54	1,467	100.0	15.7	70.6	0.5	13.2
45 to 54 years old	17,889	1,697	13,660	157	2,377	100.0	9.5	76.4	0.9	13.3
55 to 64 years old	11,137	612	8,809	329	1,387	100.0	5.5	79.1	3.0	12.5
65 to 74 years old	8,051	348	6,411	667	625	100.0	4.3	79.6	8.3	7.8
75 years old and over . . .	5,838	242	4,044	1,327	225	100.0	4.1	69.3	22.7	3.9
Female	**104,863**	**22,089**	**60,436**	**11,054**	**11,284**	**100.0**	**21.1**	**57.6**	**10.5**	**10.8**
18 to 19 years old	4,009	3,727	270	2	10	100.0	93.0	6.7	-	0.2
20 to 24 years old	9,232	6,720	2,333	11	168	100.0	72.8	25.3	0.1	1.8
25 to 29 years old	9,326	3,627	5,106	18	575	100.0	38.9	54.8	0.1	6.2
30 to 34 years old	9,897	2,172	6,758	63	904	100.0	21.9	68.3	0.6	9.1
35 to 39 years old	11,288	1,610	8,061	131	1,486	100.0	14.3	71.4	1.2	13.2
40 to 44 years old	11,382	1,341	8,163	172	1,706	100.0	11.8	71.7	1.5	15.0
45 to 54 years old	18,742	1,606	13,191	725	3,220	100.0	8.6	70.4	3.9	17.2
55 to 64 years old	12,251	606	8,333	1,441	1,871	100.0	4.9	68.0	11.8	15.3
65 to 74 years old	9,748	363	5,424	3,055	906	100.0	3.7	55.6	31.3	9.3
75 years old and over . . .	8,988	317	2,799	5,435	438	100.0	3.5	31.1	60.5	4.9

- Represents or rounds to zero.

Source: U.S. Census Bureau, unpublished data.

No. 52. Unmarried Couples by Selected Characteristics: 1980 to 1999

[In thousands (1,589 represents 1,589,000). As of March. An "unmarried couple" is two unrelated adults of the opposite sex sharing the same household. See headnote, Table 54]

Presence of children and age of householder	1980	1985	1990	1995	1999
Unmarried couples, total.	**1,589**	**1,983**	**2,856**	**3,668**	**4,486**
No children under 15 years old	1,159	1,380	1,966	2,349	2,981
Some children under 15 years old	431	603	891	1,319	1,505
Under 25 years old	411	425	596	742	824
25 to 44 years old	837	1,203	1,775	2,188	2,554
45 to 64 years old	221	239	358	558	888
65 years old and over	119	116	127	180	220

Source: U.S. Census Bureau, Current Population Reports, P20-491, and earlier reports; and unpublished data.

No. 53. Households, 1980 to 2000, and Persons in Households, 2000 by Type of Household

[80,776 represents 80,776,000. As of March. Based on Current Population Survey; see headnote, Table 54]

Type of household	Households					Persons in households, 2000		Persons per house-hold, 2000
	Number (1,000)			Percent distribution		Number (1,000)	Percent distribu-tion	
	1980	1990	2000	1990	2000			
Total households	**80,776**	**93,347**	**104,705**	**100**	**100**	**273,901**	**100**	**2.62**
Family households	59,550	66,090	72,025	71	69	233,115	85	3.24
Married couple family.	49,112	52,317	55,311	56	53	180,224	66	3.26
Male householder, no spouse present. . .	1,733	2,884	4,028	3	4	12,734	5	3.16
Female householder, no spouse present .	8,705	10,890	12,687	12	12	40,156	15	3.17
Nonfamily households	21,226	27,257	32,680	29	31	40,787	15	1.25
Living alone	18,296	22,999	26,724	25	26	26,724	10	1.00
Male householder	8,807	11,606	14,641	12	14	19,674	7	1.34
Living alone	6,966	9,049	11,181	10	11	11,181	4	1.00
Female householder	12,419	15,651	18,039	17	17	21,112	8	1.17
Living alone	11,330	13,950	15,543	15	15	15,543	6	1.00

Source: U.S. Census Bureau, Current Population Reports, P20-447, and earlier reports; and unpublished data.

No. 54. Households, Families, Subfamilies, and Married Couples: 1980 to 2000

[In thousands, except as indicated (80,776 represents 80,776,000). As of March. Based on Current Population Survey; includes members of Armed Forces living off post or with their families on post, but excludes all other members of Armed Forces; see text, this section, and Appendix III. For definition of terms, see text, this section. Minus sign (-) indicates decrease]

Type of unit	1980	1985	1990	1995	1997	1998	1999	2000	Percent change 1980-90	Percent change 1990-2000
Households	80,776	86,789	93,347	98,990	101,018	102,528	103,874	104,705	16	12
Average size	2.76	2.69	2.63	2.65	2.64	2.62	2.61	2.62	(X)	(X)
Family households	59,550	62,706	66,090	69,305	70,241	70,880	71,535	72,025	11	9
Married couple	49,112	50,350	52,317	53,858	53,604	54,317	54,770	55,311	7	6
Male householder [1]	1,733	2,228	2,884	3,226	3,847	3,911	3,976	4,028	66	40
Female householder [1]	8,705	10,129	10,890	12,220	12,790	12,652	12,789	12,687	25	17
Nonfamily households	21,226	24,082	27,257	29,686	30,777	31,648	32,339	32,680	28	20
Male householder	8,807	10,114	11,606	13,190	13,707	14,133	14,368	14,641	32	26
Female householder	12,419	13,968	15,651	16,496	17,070	17,516	17,971	18,039	26	15
One person	18,296	20,602	22,999	24,732	25,402	26,327	26,606	26,724	26	16
Families	59,550	62,706	66,090	69,305	70,241	70,880	71,535	72,025	11	9
Average size	3.29	3.23	3.17	3.19	3.19	3.18	3.18	3.17	(X)	(X)
With own children [2]	31,022	31,112	32,289	34,296	34,665	34,760	34,613	34,605	4	7
Without own children under [2]	28,528	31,594	33,801	35,009	35,575	36,120	36,922	37,420	18	11
Married couple	49,112	50,350	52,317	53,858	53,604	54,317	54,770	55,311	7	6
With own children [2]	24,961	24,210	24,537	25,241	25,083	25,269	25,066	25,248	-2	3
Without own children [2]	24,151	26,140	27,780	28,617	28,521	29,048	29,703	30,062	15	8
Male householder [1]	1,733	2,228	2,884	3,226	3,847	3,911	3,976	4,028	66	40
With own children [2]	616	896	1,153	1,440	1,709	1,798	1,706	1,786	87	55
Without own children [2]	1,117	1,332	1,731	1,786	2,138	2,113	2,270	2,242	55	30
Female householder [1]	8,705	10,129	10,890*	12,220	12,790	12,652	12,789	12,687	25	17
With own children [2]	5,445	6,006	6,599	7,615	7,874	7,693	7,841	7,571	21	15
Without own children [2]	3,261	4,123	4,290	4,606	4,916	4,960	4,948	5,116	32	19
Unrelated subfamilies	360	526	534	674	615	575	522	571	48	7
Married couple	20	46	68	64	50	41	50	37	(B)	(B)
Male reference persons [1]	36	85	45	59	77	72	64	57	(B)	(B)
Female reference persons [1]	304	395	421	550	487	463	408	477	39	13
Related subfamilies	1,150	2,228	2,403	2,878	2,907	2,870	2,901	2,984	109	24
Married couple	582	719	871	1,015	1,012	947	1,029	1,149	50	32
Father-child [1]	54	116	153	195	244	250	281	201	(B)	31
Mother-child [1]	512	1,392	1,378	1,668	1,651	1,673	1,591	1,634	169	19
Married couples	49,714	51,114	53,256	54,937	54,666	55,305	55,849	56,497	7	6
With own household	49,112	50,350	52,317	53,858	53,604	54,317	54,770	55,311	7	6
Without own household	602	764	939	1,079	1,062	988	1,079	1,186	56	26
Percent without	1.2	1.5	1.8	2.0	1.9	1.8	1.9	2.1	(X)	(X)

B Not shown; base less than 75,000.   X Not applicable.   [1] No spouse present.   [2] Under 18 years old.

Source: U.S. Census Bureau, *Current Population Reports*, P20-515, and unpublished data.

No. 55. Households by Age of Householder and Size of Household: 1980 to 2000

[In millions (80.8 represents 80,800,000). As of March. Based on Current Population Survey; see headnote, Table 54]

Age of householder and size of household	1980	1985	1990	1995	1999	2000 Total [1]	2000 White	2000 Black	2000 Hispanic [2]
Total	80.8	86.8	93.3	99.0	103.9	104.7	87.7	12.8	9.3
Age of householder:									
15 to 24 years old	6.6	5.4	5.1	5.4	5.9	5.9	4.5	1.0	0.9
25 to 29 years old	9.3	9.6	9.4	8.4	8.5	8.5	6.7	1.3	1.1
30 to 34 years old	9.3	10.4	11.0	11.1	10.3	10.1	8.1	1.4	1.3
35 to 44 years old	14.0	17.5	20.6	22.9	24.0	24.0	19.8	3.1	2.5
45 to 54 years old	12.7	12.6	14.5	17.6	20.2	20.9	17.5	2.6	1.5
55 to 64 years old	12.5	13.1	12.5	12.2	13.6	13.6	11.6	1.5	0.9
65 to 74 years old	10.1	10.9	11.7	11.8	11.4	11.3	9.9	1.1	0.6
75 years old and over	6.4	7.3	8.4	9.6	10.2	10.4	9.5	0.8	0.4
One person	18.3	20.6	23.0	24.7	26.6	26.7	22.3	3.6	1.3
Male	7.0	7.9	9.0	10.1	11.0	11.2	9.2	1.6	0.7
Female	11.3	12.7	14.0	14.6	15.6	15.5	13.1	2.0	0.6
Two persons	25.3	27.4	30.1	31.8	34.3	34.7	30.1	3.4	1.9
Three persons	14.1	15.5	16.1	16.8	17.4	17.2	13.8	2.5	1.8
Four persons	12.7	13.6	14.5	15.3	15.0	15.3	12.8	1.7	1.9
Five persons	6.1	6.1	6.2	6.6	7.0	7.0	5.7	0.9	1.3
Six persons	2.5	2.3	2.1	2.3	2.4	2.4	1.8	0.4	0.6
Seven persons or more	1.8	1.3	1.3	1.4	1.3	1.4	1.1	0.2	0.5

[1] Includes other races, not shown separately.   [2] Hispanic persons may be of any race.

Source: U.S. Census Bureau, *Current Population Reports*, P20-515, and earlier reports; and unpublished data.

Population   49

No. 56. Households—States: 2000

[105,480 represents 105,480,000. As of April. For definitions of household and family, see text, this section]

State	Households (1,000)									
	Family households							Nonfamily households		
	Total [1]			Married couple		Female family householder [2]			House-	Average
	Total	Total	With own children under 18 years	Total	With own children under 18 years	Total	With own children under 18 years	Total	holder living alone	household size
U.S.	**105,480**	**71,787**	**34,588**	**54,493**	**24,836**	**12,900**	**7,562**	**33,693**	**27,230**	**2.59**
AL	1,737	1,216	561	907	391	246	141	521	454	2.49
AK	222	152	88	116	63	24	17	69	52	2.74
AZ	1,901	1,287	608	986	429	211	130	614	472	2.64
AR	1,043	732	335	566	237	127	77	310	267	2.49
CA	11,503	7,920	4,117	5,877	2,990	1,449	835	3,583	2,708	2.87
CO	1,658	1,084	544	859	405	159	102	574	436	2.53
CT	1,302	881	419	676	307	157	91	421	344	2.53
DE	299	205	95	153	66	39	23	94	75	2.54
DC	248	114	49	57	21	47	25	134	109	2.16
FL	6,338	4,211	1,780	3,192	1,215	759	438	2,127	1,687	2.46
GA	3,006	2,112	1,051	1,549	733	435	258	895	711	2.65
HI	403	287	129	216	97	50	24	116	88	2.92
ID	470	336	170	277	132	41	27	134	105	2.69
IL	4,592	3,106	1,515	2,354	1,114	564	316	1,486	1,230	2.63
IN	2,336	1,603	768	1,251	556	259	160	734	605	2.53
IA	1,149	770	361	633	275	98	64	380	313	2.46
KS	1,038	702	345	568	261	97	63	336	280	2.51
KY	1,591	1,104	516	858	375	188	111	486	414	2.47
LA	1,656	1,156	572	809	374	275	162	500	419	2.62
ME	518	341	157	272	113	49	32	178	140	2.39
MD	1,981	1,359	662	995	461	280	159	622	495	2.61
MA	2,444	1,577	749	1,198	548	290	164	867	684	2.51
MI	3,786	2,576	1,237	1,948	873	474	284	1,210	994	2.56
MN	1,895	1,255	626	1,018	478	169	111	640	509	2.52
MS	1,046	747	363	521	234	181	106	299	258	2.63
MO	2,195	1,477	700	1,141	497	254	157	718	600	2.48
MT	359	237	112	192	82	32	21	121	98	2.45
NE	666	443	218	361	166	60	40	223	184	2.49
NV	751	498	239	373	166	83	51	253	187	2.62
NH	475	324	158	262	120	43	27	151	116	2.53
NJ	3,065	2,155	1,026	1,638	776	387	197	910	751	2.68
NM	678	467	235	342	158	90	56	211	172	2.63
NY	7,057	4,639	2,231	3,290	1,527	1,038	573	2,417	1,983	2.61
NC	3,132	2,159	996	1,645	708	390	227	973	795	2.49
ND	257	166	80	137	62	20	14	91	75	2.41
OH	4,446	2,993	1,410	2,286	996	537	323	1,453	1,216	2.49
OK	1,342	922	435	718	312	153	94	421	359	2.49
OR	1,334	878	411	693	296	131	83	456	348	2.51
PA	4,777	3,208	1,431	2,468	1,043	555	298	1,569	1,321	2.48
RI	408	265	125	197	86	53	32	143	117	2.47
SC	1,534	1,073	495	783	334	227	131	461	383	2.53
SD	290	194	95	157	71	26	18	96	80	2.50
TN	2,233	1,548	707	1,174	499	288	166	685	576	2.48
TX	7,393	5,248	2,723	3,990	2,002	938	564	2,146	1,752	2.74
UT	701	535	300	443	246	66	40	166	125	3.13
VT	241	158	76	126	56	22	15	83	63	2.44
VA	2,699	1,848	882	1,426	646	320	187	851	677	2.54
WA	2,271	1,499	742	1,182	542	225	147	772	594	2.53
WV	736	504	213	397	157	79	42	232	200	2.40
WI	2,085	1,387	665	1,109	494	200	129	698	558	2.50
WY	194	130	63	106	47	17	12	63	51	2.48

[1] Includes male family householders with no spouse present, not shown separately.   [2] No spouse present.

Source: U.S. Census Bureau, 2000 Census of Population and Housing, Profiles of General Demographic Characteristics.

No. 57. Family Groups With Children Under 18 Years Old by Race and Hispanic Origin: 1980 to 2000

[In thousands (32,150 represents 32,150,000). As of March. Family groups comprise family households, related subfamilies, and unrelated subfamilies. Excludes members of Armed Forces except those living off post or with their families on post. Based on Current Population Survey; see text, this section, and Appendix III]

Race and Hispanic origin of householder or reference person	1980	1990	1995	2000 Total	Family households	Subfamilies Total	Related	Unrelated
All races, total [1]	32,150	34,670	37,168	37,496	34,605	2,890	2,346	544
Two-parent family groups.	25,231	24,921	25,640	25,771	25,248	523	512	11
One-parent family groups.	6,920	9,749	11,528	11,725	9,357	2,368	1,834	534
Maintained by mother	6,230	8,398	9,834	9,681	7,571	2,110	1,633	477
Maintained by father	690	1,351	1,694	2,044	1,786	258	201	57
White, total	27,294	28,294	29,846	30,079	28,107	1,973	1,558	415
Two-parent family groups.	22,628	21,905	22,320	22,241	21,809	433	422	11
One-parent family groups.	4,664	6,389	7,525	7,838	6,298	1,540	1,136	404
Maintained by mother	4,122	5,310	6,239	6,216	4,869	1,347	995	352
Maintained by father	542	1,079	1,286	1,622	1,429	193	140	53
Black, total	4,074	5,087	5,491	5,530	4,782	748	642	106
Two-parent family groups.	1,961	2,006	1,962	2,135	2,093	41	41	- -
One-parent family groups.	2,114	3,081	3,529	3,396	2,689	706	600	106
Maintained by mother	1,984	2,860	3,197	3,060	2,409	651	550	101
Maintained by father	129	221	332	335	280	55	50	5
Hispanic, total [2]	2,194	3,429	4,527	5,503	4,814	688	596	92
Two-parent family groups.	1,626	2,289	2,879	3,625	3,423	203	194	9
One-parent family groups.	568	1,140	1,647	1,877	1,391	486	402	84
Maintained by mother	526	1,003	1,404	1,565	1,145	420	347	73
Maintained by father	42	138	243	313	246	66	55	11

- Represents or rounds to zero.   [1] Includes other races, not shown separately.   [2] Hispanic persons may be of any race.

Source: U.S. Census Bureau, *Current Population Reports*, P20-488, and earlier reports; and unpublished data.

No. 58. Families by Number of Own Children Under 18 Years Old: 1980 to 2000

[59,550 represents 59,550,000. As of March. Based on Current Population Survey; see headnote, Table 59]

Race, Hispanic origin, and year	Number of families (1,000) Total	No children	One child	Two children	Three or more children	Percent distribution Total	No children	One child	Two children	Three or more children
ALL FAMILIES [1]										
1980	59,550	28,528	12,443	11,470	7,109	100	48	21	19	12
1990	66,090	33,801	13,530	12,263	6,496	100	51	20	19	10
1995	69,305	35,009	14,088	13,213	6,995	100	51	20	19	10
2000	72,025	37,420	14,311	13,215	7,080	100	52	20	18	10
Married couple . . ;	55,311	30,062	9,402	10,274	5,572	100	54	17	19	10
Male householder [2] .;	4,028	2,242	1,131	483	171	100	56	28	12	4
Female householder [2]	12,687	5,116	3,777	2,458	1,336	100	40	30	19	11
WHITE FAMILIES										
1980	52,243	25,769	10,727	9,977	5,769	100	49	21	19	11
1990	56,590	29,872	11,186	10,342	5,191	100	53	20	18	9
1995	58,437	30,486	11,491	10,983	5,478	100	52	20	19	9
2000	60,251	32,144	11,496	10,918	5,693	100	53	19	18	9
Married couple . . ;	48,790	26,981	8,023	8,970	4,816	100	55	16	18	10
Male householder [2] .;	3,081	1,652	885	400	144	100	54	29	13	5
Female householder [2]	8,380	3,511	2,588	1,548	732	100	42	31	18	9
BLACK FAMILIES										
1980	6,184	2,364	1,449	1,235	1,136	100	38	23	20	18
1990	7,470	3,093	1,894	1,433	1,049	100	41	25	19	14
1995	8,093	3,411	1,971	1,593	1,117	100	42	24	20	14
2000	8,664	3,882	2,101	1,624	1,058	100	45	24	19	12
Married couple . . ;	4,144	2,050	838	754	501	100	49	20	18	12
Male householder [2] .;	706	427	196	62	21	100	60	28	9	3
Female householder [2]	3,814	1,405	1,066	807	536	100	37	28	21	14
HISPANIC FAMILIES [3]										
1980	3,029	946	680	698	706	100	31	22	23	23
1990	4,840	1,790	1,095	1,036	919	100	37	23	21	19
1995	6,200	2,216	1,408	1,406	1,171	100	36	23	23	19
2000	7,561	2,747	1,791	1,693	1,330	100	36	24	22	18
Married couple . . ;	5,133	1,710	1,139	1,276	1,008	100	33	22	25	20
Male householder [2] .;	658	412	141	68	38	100	63	21	10	6
Female householder [2]	1,769	625	511	350	284	100	35	29	20	16

[1] Includes other races, not shown separately.   [2] No spouse present.   [3] Hispanic persons may be of any race.

Source: U.S. Census Bureau, *Current Population Reports*, P20-488, and earlier reports; and unpublished data.

No. 59. Families by Size and Presence of Children: 1980 to 2000

[In thousands, except as indicated (59,550 represents 59,550,000). As of March. Excludes members of Armed Forces except those living off post or with their families on post. Based on Current Population Survey; see text, this section, and Appendix III. For definition of families, see text, this section]

Characteristic	Number					Percent distribution				
	1980	1985	1990	1995	2000	1980	1985	1990	1995	2000
Total..........	59,550	62,706	66,090	69,305	72,025	100	100	100	100	100
Size of family:										
Two persons.........	23,461	25,349	27,606	29,176	31,455	39	40	42	42	44
Three persons........	13,603	14,804	15,353	15,903	16,073	23	24	23	23	22
Four persons........	12,372	13,259	14,026	14,624	14,496	21	21	21	21	20
Five persons........	5,930	5,894	5,938	6,283	6,526	10	9	9	9	9
Six persons.........	2,461	2,175	1,997	2,106	2,226	4	4	3	3	3
Seven or more persons..	1,723	1,225	1,170	1,213	1,249	3	2	2	2	2
Average per family.....	3.29	3.23	3.17	3.19	3.17	(X)	(X)	(X)	(X)	(X)
Own children under age 18:										
None..............	28,528	31,594	33,801	35,009	37,420	48	50	51	51	52
One..............	12,443	13,108	13,530	14,088	14,311	21	21	20	20	20
Two..............	11,470	11,645	12,263	13,213	13,215	19	19	19	19	18
Three.............	4,674	4,486	4,650	5,044	5,063	8	7	7	7	7
Four or more.........	2,435	1,873	1,846	1,951	2,017	4	3	3	3	3
Own children under age 6:										
None..............	46,063	48,505	50,905	53,695	57,039	77	77	77	77	79
One..............	9,441	9,677	10,304	10,733	10,454	16	15	16	15	15
Two or more.........	4,047	4,525	4,882	4,876	4,533	7	7	7	7	6

X Not applicable.

Source: U.S. Census Bureau, Current Population Reports, P20-488, and earlier reports; and unpublished data.

No. 60. Families by Type, Race, and Hispanic Origin: 2000

[In thousands, except as indicated (72,025 represents 72,025,000). As of March. Excludes members of Armed Forces except those living off post or with their families on post. Based on Current Population Survey; see text of this section and Appendix III. For definition of families, see text of this section]

Characteristic	All families	Married couple families				Female family householder [3]				Male family house-holder, [3] all races
		All races [1]	White	Black	His-panic [2]	All races [1]	White	Black	His-panic [2]	
All families	72,025	55,311	48,790	4,144	5,133	12,687	8,380	3,814	1,769	4,028
Age of householder:										
Under 25 years old.......	3,353	1,450	1,298	93	315	1,342	770	502	213	560
25 to 34 years old	13,007	9,390	8,128	783	1,436	2,732	1,586	1,039	433	886
35 to 44 years old	18,706	14,104	12,271	1,194	1,534	3,499	2,455	918	512	1,102
45 to 54 years old	15,803	12,792	11,174	984	911	2,299	1,555	658	307	713
55 to 64 years old	9,569	8,138	7,269	554	509	1,080	701	323	158	351
65 to 74 years old	7,025	5,929	5,380	360	291	894	632	229	102	203
75 years old and over......	4,562	3,508	3,270	175	136	841	681	146	44	213
Without own children under 18..	37,420	30,062	26,981	2,050	1,710	5,116	3,511	1,405	625	2,242
With own children under 18....	34,605	25,248	21,809	2,093	3,423	7,571	4,869	2,409	1,145	1,786
One own child under 18 ..	14,311	9,402	8,023	838	1,139	3,777	2,588	1,066	511	1,131
Two own children under 18 ..	13,215	10,274	8,970	754	1,276	2,458	1,548	807	350	483
Three or more own children under 18.....	7,080	5,572	4,816	501	1,008	1,336	732	536	284	171
Average per family with own children under 18.....	1.87	1.94	1.93	1.99	2.14	1.75	1.66	1.91	1.95	1.50
Marital status of householder:										
Married, spouse present....	55,311	55,311	48,790	4,144	5,133	(X)	(X)	(X)	(X)	(X)
Married, spouse absent.....	2,434	(X)	(X)	(X)	(X)	1,878	1,210	567	404	555
Separated...........	1,757	(X)	(X)	(X)	(X)	1,426	908	463	301	331
Other..............	677	(X)	(X)	(X)	(X)	452	302	104	103	224
Widowed	2,797	(X)	(X)	(X)	(X)	2,371	1,764	522	252	426
Divorced.............	5,820	(X)	(X)	(X)	(X)	4,431	3,431	874	475	1,389
Never married.........	5,665	(X)	(X)	(X)	(X)	4,007	1,974	1,851	639	1,658

X Not applicable.   [1] Includes other races now shown separately.   [2] Persons of Hispanic origin may be of any race.   [3] No spouse present.

Source: U.S. Census Bureau, unpublished data.

No. 61. Family Households With Own Children Under Age 18 by Type of Family, 1980 to 2000, and by Age of Householder, 2000

[31,022 represents 31,022,000. As of March. Excludes members of Armed Forces except those living off post or with their families on post. Based on Current Population Survey; see text, this section, and Appendix III]

Family type	1980	1990	2000 Total	15 to 24 years old	25 to 34 years old	35 to 44 years old	45 to 54 years old	55 to 64 years old	65 years old and over
NUMBER (1,000)									
Family households with children...	31,022	32,289	34,605	2,000	9,886	15,104	6,617	865	133
Married couple	24,961	24,537	25,248	834	6,830	11,405	5,401	671	107
Male householder [1]	616	1,153	1,786	123	530	737	305	74	15
Female householder [1]	5,445	6,599	7,571	1,042	2,525	2,962	911	119	11
HOUSEHOLDS WITH CHILDREN, AS A PERCENT OF ALL FAMILY HOUSEHOLDS BY TYPE									
Family households with children, total	52	49	48	60	76	81	42	9	1
Married couple	51	47	46	58	73	81	42	8	1
Male householder [1]	36	40	44	22	60	67	43	21	4
Female householder [1]	63	61	60	78	92	85	40	11	1

[1] No spouse present.

Source: U.S. Census Bureau, Current Population Reports, P20-447, and earlier reports; and unpublished data.

No. 62. Nonfamily Households by Sex and Age of Householder: 2000

[In thousands (14,641 represents 14,641,000). As of March. See headnote, Table 59]

Item	Male householder					Female householder				
	Total	15 to 24 yr. old	25 to 44 yr. old	45 to 64 yr. old	65 yr. old and over	Total	15 to 24 yr. old	25 to 44 yr. old	45 to 64 yr. old	65 yr. old and over
Total	14,641	1,286	6,709	4,116	2,530	18,039	1,221	4,161	5,031	7,626
One person (living alone)..	11,181	556	4,848	3,422	2,355	15,543	588	3,108	4,420	7,427
Nonrelatives present	3,460	731	1,860	693	175	2,496	634	1,052	612	199
Never married..........	7,274	1,246	4,465	1,188	374	5,671	1,169	2,910	1,119	472
Married [1]	1,180	25	527	460	166	980	19	293	390	278
Widowed	1,684	-	36	269	1,380	7,018	5	73	1,047	5,894
Divorced	4,503	15	1,680	2,198	610	4,371	28	885	2,476	982

- Represents or rounds to zero.   [1] No spouse present.

Source: U.S. Census Bureau, unpublished data.

No. 63. Persons Living Alone by Sex and Age: 1980 to 2000

[18,296 represents 18,296,000). As of March. Based on Current Population Survey; see headnote, Table 59]

Sex and age	Number of persons (1,000)					Percent distribution				
	1980	1985	1990	1995	2000	1980	1985	1990	1995	2000
Both sexes	18,296	20,602	22,999	24,732	26,724	100	100	100	100	100
15 to 24 years old	1,726	1,324	1,210	1,196	1,144	9	6	5	5	4
25 to 34 years old	[1]4,729	3,905	3,972	3,653	3,848	[1]26	19	17	15	14
35 to 44 years old	(1)	2,322	3,138	3,663	4,109	(1)	11	14	15	15
45 to 64 years old	4,514	4,939	5,502	6,377	7,842	25	24	24	26	29
65 to 74 years old	3,851	4,130	4,350	4,374	4,091	21	20	19	18	15
75 years old and over.....	3,477	3,982	4,825	5,470	5,692	19	19	21	22	21
Male..............	6,966	7,922	9,049	10,140	11,181	38	39	39	41	42
15 to 24 years old	947	750	674	623	556	5	4	3	3	2
25 to 34 years old	[1]2,920	2,307	2,395	2,213	2,279	[1]16	11	10	9	9
35 to 44 years old	(1)	1,406	1,836	2,263	2,569	(1)	7	8	9	10
45 to 64 years old	1,613	1,845	2,203	2,787	3,422	9	9	10	11	13
65 to 74 years old	775	868	1,042	1,134	1,108	4	4	5	5	4
75 years old and over.....	711	746	901	1,120	1,247	4	4	4	5	5
Female..............	11,330	12,680	13,950	14,592	15,543	62	62	61	59	58
15 to 24 years old	779	573	536	572	588	4	3	2	2	2
25 to 34 years old	[1]1,809	1,598	1,578	1,440	1,568	[1]10	8	7	6	6
35 to 44 years old	(1)	916	1,303	1,399	1,540	(1)	4	6	6	6
45 to 64 years old	2,901	3,095	3,300	3,589	4,420	16	15	14	15	17
65 to 74 years old	3,076	3,262	3,309	3,240	2,983	17	16	14	13	11
75 years old and over.....	2,766	3,236	3,924	4,351	4,444	15	16	17	18	17

[1] Data for persons 35 to 44 years old included with persons 25 to 34 years old.

Source: U.S. Census Bureau, Current Population Reports, P20-491, and earlier reports; and unpublished data.

U.S. Census Bureau, Statistical Abstract of the United States: 2001

No. 64. Persons in Group Quarters—States: 2000

[As of April. For definitions of group quarters, see text, this section]

State	Group quarters population		Institutionalized population	Noninstitutionalized population
	Number	Percent of total population		
United States, total	7,778,633	2.8	4,059,039	3,719,594
Alabama.	114,720	2.6	65,363	49,357
Alaska	19,349	3.1	4,824	14,525
Arizona.	109,850	2.1	63,768	46,082
Arkansas	73,908	2.8	45,152	28,756
California	819,754	2.4	413,656	406,098
Colorado.	102,955	2.4	52,741	50,214
Connecticut.	107,939	3.2	55,256	52,683
Delaware	24,583	3.1	11,510	13,073
District of Columbia	35,562	6.2	7,964	27,598
Florida	388,945	2.4	248,350	140,595
Georgia	233,822	2.9	126,023	107,799
Hawaii	35,782	3.0	7,690	28,092
Idaho.	31,496	2.4	17,717	13,779
Illinois	321,781	2.6	174,727	147,054
Indiana.	178,154	2.9	90,885	87,269
Iowa	104,169	3.6	50,256	53,913
Kansas.	81,950	3.0	45,396	36,554
Kentucky	114,804	2.8	62,057	52,747
Louisiana	135,965	3.0	90,002	45,963
Maine.	34,912	2.7	13,091	21,821
Maryland	134,056	2.5	69,318	64,738
Massachusetts.	221,216	3.5	88,453	132,763
Michigan.	249,889	2.5	126,132	123,757
Minnesota.	135,883	2.8	63,058	72,825
Mississippi	95,414	3.4	50,826	44,588
Missouri	162,058	2.9	90,430	71,628
Montana.	24,762	2.7	12,068	12,694
Nebraska	50,818	3.0	26,011	24,807
Nevada	33,675	1.7	22,173	11,502
New Hampshire.	35,539	2.9	13,784	21,755
New Jersey.	194,821	2.3	110,169	84,652
New Mexico	36,307	2.0	19,178	17,129
New York	580,461	3.1	262,262	318,199
North Carolina.	253,881	3.2	106,659	147,222
North Dakota.	23,631	3.7	9,688	13,943
Ohio	299,121	2.6	172,368	126,753
Oklahoma.	112,375	3.3	66,746	45,629
Oregon.	77,491	2.3	37,901	39,590
Pennsylvania.	433,301	3.5	213,790	219,511
Rhode Island.	38,816	3.7	13,801	25,015
South Carolina.	135,037	3.4	60,533	74,504
South Dakota	28,418	3.8	14,387	14,031
Tennessee	147,946	2.6	83,397	64,549
Texas.	561,109	2.7	374,704	186,405
Utah	40,480	1.8	19,467	21,013
Vermont	20,760	3.4	5,663	15,097
Virginia.	231,398	3.3	111,484	119,914
Washington.	136,382	2.3	57,218	79,164
West Virginia.	43,147	2.4	24,009	19,138
Wisconsin.	155,958	2.9	79,073	76,885
Wyoming	14,083	2.9	7,861	6,222

Source: U.S. Census Bureau, *2000 Census of Population and Housing, Profiles of General Demographic Characteristics*.

No. 65. Religious Bodies—Selected Data

[Membership data: **2,500 represents 2,500,000.** Includes the self-reported membership of religious bodies with 65,000 or more as reported to the *Yearbook of American and Canadian Churches.* Groups may be excluded if they do not supply information. The data are not standardized so comparisons between groups are difficult. The definition of "church member" is determined by the religious body]

Religious body	Year reported	Churches reported	Membership (1,000)	Pastors serving parishes [1]
African Methodist Episcopal Church	1999	6,200	2,500	(NA)
African Methodist Episcopal Zion Church	1999	3,125	1,277	2,731
American Baptist Association, The	1998	1,760	275	1,740
American Baptist Churches in the U.S.A.	1999	5,775	1,454	4,895
Antiochian Orthodox Christian Archdiocese of North America, The	1999	227	65	290
Armenian Apostolic Church of America	1999	36	360	35
Armenian Apostolic Church, Diocese of America	1991	72	414	49
Assemblies of God	1999	12,055	2,575	18,159
Baptist Bible Fellowship International	1997	4,500	1,200	(NA)
Baptist General Conference	1999	880	143	(NA)
Baptist Missionary Association of America	1999	1,334	235	1,525
Buddhist [2]	1990	(NA)	401	(NA)
Christian and Missionary Alliance, The	1999	1,973	348	1,493
Christian Brethren (a.k.a. Plymouth Brethren)	1997	1,150	100	(NA)
Christian Church (Disciples of Christ)	1999	3,765	831	3,307
Christian Churches and Churches of Christ	1998	5,579	1,072	5,525
Christian Congregation, Inc., The	1999	1,438	118	1,436
Christian Methodist Episcopal Church	1999	3,069	784	2,058
Christian Reformed Church in North America	1999	732	198	675
Church Of God In Christ, The	1991	15,300	5,500	28,988
Church of God of Prophecy	1999	1,862	75	2,000
Church of God (Anderson, Indiana)	1998	2,353	234	3,034
Church of God (Cleveland, Tennessee)	1999	6,328	870	3,352
Church of Jesus Christ of Latter-day Saints, The	1999	11,315	5,113	33,945
Church of the Brethren	1997	1,095	141	827
Church of the Nazarene	1998	5,101	627	4,598
Churches of Christ	1999	15,000	1,500	14,500
Conservative Baptist Association of America	1998	1,200	200	(NA)
Coptic Orthodox Church	1992	85	180	65
Cumberland Presbyterian Church	1999	775	86	535
Episcopal Church	1998	7,390	2,318	(NA)
Evangelical Covenant Church, The	1999	636	99	607
Evangelical Free Church of America, The	1995	1,224	243	1,936
Evangelical Lutheran Church in America	1999	10,851	5,150	9,542
Free Methodist Church of North America	1999	971	71	(NA)
Full Gospel Fellowship of Churches and Ministers International	2000	896	325	2,070
General Association of General Baptists	1998	719	67	780
General Association of Regular Baptist Churches	1999	1,398	92	(NA)
General Conference of Mennonite Brethren Churches	1996	368	82	590
Greek Orthodox Archdiocese of America	1998	523	1,955	596
Hindu [2]	1990	(NA)	227	(NA)
International Church of the Foursquare Gospel	1999	1,836	253	4,802
International Council of Community Churches	1999	180	200	198
International Pentecostal Holiness Church	1999	1,771	185	1,609
Jehovah's Witnesses	1999	11,257	990	(NA)
Jewish [3]	1999	(NA)	6,061	(NA)
Lutheran Church— Missouri Synod (LCMS), The	1999	6,220	2,582	5,210
Mennonite Church [2]	1999	935	92	(NA)
Muslim / Islamic [2]	1990	(NA)	527	(NA)
National Association of Congregational Christian Churches	1999	426	66	506
National Association of Free Will Baptists	1999	2,476	217	2,800
National Baptist Convention of America, Inc.	1987	2,500	3,500	8,000
National Missionary Baptist Convention of America	1992	(NA)	2,500	(NA)
Old Order Amish Church	1993	898	81	3,592
Orthodox Church in America, The	1999	710	1,000	735
Pentecostal Assemblies of the World, Inc.	1998	1,750	1,500	4,500
Pentecostal Church of God	1999	1,237	105	(NA)
Presbyterian Church in America	1999	1,206	299	(NA)
Presbyterian Church (U.S.A.)	1999	11,216	3,561	9,292
Progressive National Baptist Convention, Inc.	1995	2,000	2,500	(NA)
Reformed Church in America	1999	901	293	880
Religious Society of Friends (Conservative)	1994	1,200	104	(NA)
Reorganized Church of Jesus Christ of Latter Day Saints	1999	1,236	137	(NA)
Roman Catholic Church, The	1999	19,627	62,391	(NA)
Salvation Army, The	1999	1,410	473	3,072
Serbian Orthodox Church in the U.S.A. and Canada	1986	68	67	60
Seventh-day Adventist Church	1999	4,421	862	2,501
Southern Baptist Convention	1998	40,870	15,729	(NA)
Unitarian Universalist Association of Congregations	1999	(NA)	217	(NA)
United Church of Christ	1999	5,961	1,402	4,264
United Methodist Church, The	1999	35,609	8,378	24,998
Wesleyan Church, The	1999	1,594	121	1,946
Wisconsin Evangelical Lutheran Synod	1999	1,239	723	1,230

NA Not available.   [1] Does not include retired clergy or clergy not working with congregations.   [2] Figures obtained from the National Survey of Religious Identification, a survey conducted by the City University of New York in 1990 and published in *One Nation Under God: Religion in Contemporary American Society,* by Barry Kosmin and Seymour Lachman (1993).   [3] Source: American Jewish Committee, New York, NY, *American Jewish Year Book* (copyright). See Table 67.

Source: Except as noted, National Council of the Churches of Christ in the USA, New York, NY, *2001 Yearbook of American and Canadian Churches,* annual (copyright). (For more info visit <www.ncccusa.org>.)

Population   55

No. 66. Religious Preference, Church Membership, and Attendance: 1980 to 2000

[In percent. Covers civilian noninstitutional population, 18 years old and over. Data represent averages of the combined results of several surveys during year or period indicated. Data are subject to sampling variability, see source]

Year	Religious preference							Church/ synagogue members	Persons attending church/ synagogue [1]
	Protes- tant	Catholic	Jewish	Ortho- dox	Mormon	Other specific	None		
1980	61	28	2	(NA)	(NA)	2	7	69	40
1985	57	28	2	(NA)	(NA)	4	9	71	42
1990	56	25	2	(NA)	(NA)	6	11	65	40
1995	56	27	2	1	1	5	[2]8	69	43
1996	58	25	3	1	1	3	[2]9	65	38
1997	58	26	2	1	1	4	[2]8	67	40
1998	59	27	2	2	1	4	[2]8	70	40
1999	55	28	2	1	2	2	[2]10	70	43
2000	56	27	2	1	1	5	[2]8	68	44

NA Not available.   [1] Persons who attended a church or synagogue in the last 7 days.   [2] Includes those respondents who did not designate.

Source: The Gallup Organization, Princeton, NJ, "Gallup Poll Releases-Easter Season Finds a Religious Nation"; published 13 April 2001; <http://www.gallup.com/poll/releases/pr010413.asp>.

No. 67. Christian Church Adherents, 1990, and Jewish Population, 1999—States

[Christian church adherents were defined as "all members, including full members, their children and the estimated number of other regular participants who are not considered as communicant, confirmed or full members." Data on Christian church adherents are based on reports of 133 church groupings and exclude 34 church bodies that reported more than 100,000 members to the Yearbook of American and Canadian Churches. The Jewish population includes Jews who define themselves as Jewish by religion as well as those who define themselves as Jewish in cultural terms. Data on Jewish population are based primarily on a compilation of individual estimates made by local Jewish federations. Additionally, most large communities have completed Jewish demographic surveys from which the Jewish population can be determined]

State	Christian adherents, 1990		Jewish population, 1999		State	Christian adherents, 1990		Jewish population, 1999	
	Number (1,000)	Percent of population [1]	Number (1,000)	Percent of population [1]		Number (1,000)	Percent of population [1]	Number (1,000)	Percent of population [1]
U.S.	131,084	52.7	6,061	2.2	MO	2,892	56.6	62	1.1
AL	2,858	70.7	9	0.2	MT	341	42.7	1	0.1
AK	175	31.8	4	0.6	NE	1,000	63.4	7	0.4
AZ	1,505	41.1	82	1.7	NV	366	29.6	58	3.2
AR	1,423	60.5	2	0.1	NH	431	38.9	10	0.8
CA	11,665	39.2	967	2.9	NJ	4,305	55.7	465	5.7
CO	1,244	37.8	68	1.7	NM	883	58.3	10	0.6
CT	1,933	58.9	101	3.1	NY	9,970	55.5	1,651	9.1
DE	297	44.6	14	1.8	NC	3,949	59.6	25	0.3
DC	349	57.5	25	4.9	ND	485	75.9	1	0.1
FL	5,106	39.5	637	4.2	OH	5,313	48.9	144	1.3
GA	3,659	56.5	88	1.1	OK	2,097	66.5	5	0.1
HI	391	35.3	7	0.6	OR	904	31.8	30	0.9
ID	507	50.4	1	0.1	PA	6,960	58.6	282	2.4
IL	6,579	57.5	270	2.2	RI	754	75.1	16	1.6
IN	2,615	47.1	18	0.3	SC	2,149	61.7	10	0.3
IA	1,674	60.3	6	0.2	SD	474	68.1	(Z)	0.1
KS	1,346	54.3	14	0.5	TN	2,968	60.8	18	0.3
KY	2,213	60.1	11	0.3	TX	10,788	63.5	124	0.6
LA	2,959	70.1	16	0.4	UT	1,371	79.6	4	0.2
ME	439	36.1	8	0.6	VT	233	40.4	6	1.0
MD	2,101	43.9	216	4.1	VA	2,898	46.8	76	1.1
MA	3,666	60.9	274	4.4	WA	1,579	32.4	35	0.6
MI	4,580	49.2	107	1.1	WV	740	41.3	2	0.1
MN	2,807	64.2	42	0.9	WI	3,125	63.9	28	0.5
MS	1,804	70.1	1	0.1	WY	216	47.6	(Z)	0.1

Z Fewer than 500.   [1] Based on U.S. Census Bureau data for resident population enumerated as of April 1, 1990, and estimated as of July 1, 1999.

Source: Christian church adherents—M. Bradley; N. Green, Jr.; D. Jones; M. Lynn; and L. McNeil; Churches and Church Membership in the United States 1990, Glenmary Research Center, Atlanta, GA, 1992 (copyright); Jewish population—American Jewish Committee, New York, NY, American Jewish Year Book (copyright).

Vital Statistics

This section presents vital statistics data on births, deaths, abortions, fetal deaths, fertility, life expectancy, marriages, and divorces. Vital statistics are compiled for the country as a whole by the National Center for Health Statistics (NCHS) and published in its annual report, *Vital Statistics of the United States,* in certain reports of the *Vital and Health Statistics* series, and in the *National Vital Statistics Reports* (formerly *Monthly Vital Statistics Report).* Reports in this field are also issued by the various state bureaus of vital statistics. Data on fertility, on age of persons at first marriage, and on marital status and marital history are compiled by the U.S. Census Bureau from its Current Population Survey (CPS; see text, Section 1) and published in *Current Population Reports,* P20 Series. Data on abortions are published by the Alan Guttmacher Institute, New York, NY, in selected issues of *Family Planning Perspectives.*

Registration of vital events—The registration of births, deaths, fetal deaths, and other vital events in the United States is primarily a state and local function. The civil laws of every state provide for a continuous and permanent birth- and death-registration system. Many states also provide for marriage- and divorce-registration systems. Vital events occurring to U.S. residents outside the United States are not included in the data.

Births and deaths—The live-birth, death, and fetal-death statistics prepared by NCHS are based on vital records filed in the registration offices of all states, of New York City, and of the District of Columbia. The annual collection of death statistics on a national basis began in 1900 with a national death-registration area of 10 states and the District of Columbia; a similar annual collection of birth statistics for a national birth-registration area began in 1915, also with 10 reporting states and the District of Columbia. Since 1933, the birth- and death-registration areas have comprised

the entire United States, including Alaska (beginning 1959) and Hawaii (beginning 1960). National statistics on fetal deaths were first compiled for 1918 and annually since 1922.

Prior to 1951, birth statistics came from a complete count of records received in the Public Health Service (now received in NCHS). From 1951 through 1971, they were based on a 50-percent sample of all registered births (except for a complete count in 1955 and a 20- to 50-percent sample in 1967). Beginning in 1972, they have been based on a complete count for states participating in the Vital Statistics Cooperative Program (VSCP) (for details, see the technical appendix in *Vital Statistics of the United States)* and on a 50-percent sample of all other areas. Beginning 1986, all reporting areas participated in the VSCP. Mortality data have been based on a complete count of records for each area (except for a 50-percent sample in 1972). Beginning in 1970, births to and deaths of nonresident aliens of the United States and U.S. citizens outside the United States have been excluded from the data. Fetal deaths and deaths among Armed Forces abroad are excluded. Data based on samples are subject to sampling error; for details, see annual issues of *Vital Statistics of the United States.*

Mortality statistics by cause of death are compiled in accordance with World Health Organization regulations according to the *International Classification of Diseases* (ICD). The ICD is revised approximately every 10 years. The ninth revision of the ICD was employed beginning in 1979. Deaths for prior years were classified according to the revision of the ICD in use at the time. Each revision of the ICD introduces a number of discontinuities in mortality statistics; for a discussion of those between the eighth and ninth revisions of the ICD, see *Monthly Vital Statistics Report* (renamed, *National Vital Statistics Report),* Vol. 28. No. 11, supplement.

Vital Statistics   57

Some of the tables present age-adjusted death rates in addition to crude death rates. Age-adjusted death rates shown in this section were prepared using the direct method, in which age-specific death rates for a population of interest are applied to a standard population distributed by age. Age adjustment eliminates the differences in observed rates between points in time or among compared population groups that result from age differences in population composition.

Fertility and life expectancy—The total fertility rate, defined as the number of births that 1,000 women would have in their lifetime if, at each year of age, they experienced the birth rates occurring in the specified year, is compiled and published by NCHS. Other data relating to social and medical factors which affect fertility rates, such as contraceptive use and birth expectations, are collected and made available by both NCHS and the Census Bureau. NCHS figures are based on information in birth and fetal death certificates and on the periodic National Surveys of Family Growth; Census Bureau data are based on decennial censuses and the CPS.

Data on life expectancy, the average remaining lifetime in years for persons who attain a given age, are computed and published by NCHS. For details, see the technical appendix in *Vital Statistics of the United States.*

Marriage and divorce—The compilation of nationwide statistics on marriages and divorces in the United States began in 1887-88 when the National Office of Vital Statistics prepared estimates for the years 1867-86. Although periodic updates took place after 1888, marriage and divorce statistics were not collected and published annually until 1944 by that office. In 1957 and 1958, respectively, the same office established marriage- and divorce-registration areas. Beginning in 1957, the marriage-registration area comprised 30 states, plus Alaska, Hawaii, Puerto Rico,

and the Virgin Islands; it currently includes 42 states and the District of Columbia. The divorce-registration area, starting in 1958 with 14 states, Alaska, Hawaii, and the Virgin Islands, it currently includes a total of 31 states and the Virgin Islands. Procedures for estimating the number of marriages and divorces in the registration states are discussed in *Vital Statistics of the United States,* Vol. III—Marriage and Divorce. Total counts of events for registration and nonregistration states are gathered by collecting already summarized data on marriages and divorces reported by state offices of vital statistics and by county offices of registration.

Vital statistics rates—Except as noted, vital statistics rates computed by NCHS are based on decennial census population figures as of April 1 for 1940, 1950, 1960, 1970, 1980, and 1990; and on mid-year population figures for other years, as estimated by the Census Bureau (see text, Section 1).

Race—Data by race for births, deaths, marriages, and divorces from NCHS are based on information contained in the certificates of registration. The Census Bureau's Current Population Survey obtains information on race by asking respondents to classify their race as (1) White, (2) Black, (3) American Indian, Eskimo, or Aleut, or (4) Asian or Pacific Islander.

Beginning with the 1989 data year, NCHS is tabulating its birth data primarily by race of the mother. In 1988 and prior years, births were tabulated by race of the child, which was determined from the race of the parents as entered on the birth certificate.

Trend data by race shown in this section are by race of mother beginning with the 1980 data. Hispanic origin of the mother is reported and tabulated independently of race. Thus persons of Hispanic origin maybe of any race. In 1994, 91 percent of women of Hispanic origin were reported as White.

No. 68. Live Births, Deaths, Marriages, and Divorces: 1950 to 1999

[3,632 represents 3,632,000. Prior to 1960, excludes Alaska and Hawaii. Beginning 1970, excludes births to and deaths of non-residents of the United States. See Appendix III]

Year	Number (1,000)					Rate per 1,000 population				
		Deaths		Mar-	Di-		Deaths		Mar-	Di-
	Births [1]	Total	Infant [2]	riages [3]	vorces [4]	Births [1]	Total	Infant [2]	riages [3]	vorces [4]
1950	3,632	1,452	104	1,667	385	24.1	9.6	29.2	11.1	2.6
1955	4,097	1,529	107	1,531	377	25.0	9.3	26.4	9.3	2.3
1957	4,300	1,633	112	1,518	381	25.3	9.6	26.3	8.9	2.2
1960	4,258	1,712	111	1,523	393	23.7	9.5	26.0	8.5	2.2
1965	3,760	1,828	93	1,800	479	19.4	9.4	24.7	9.3	2.5
1970	3,731	1,921	75	2,159	708	18.4	9.5	20.0	10.6	3.5
1971	3,556	1,928	68	2,190	773	17.2	9.3	19.1	10.6	3.7
1972	3,258	1,964	60	2,282	845	15.6	9.4	18.5	10.9	4.0
1973	3,137	1,973	56	2,284	915	14.8	9.3	17.7	10.8	4.3
1974	3,160	1,934	53	2,230	977	14.8	9.1	16.7	10.5	4.6
1975	3,144	1,893	51	2,153	1,036	14.6	8.8	16.1	10.0	4.8
1976	3,168	1,909	48	2,155	1,083	14.6	8.8	15.2	9.9	5.0
1977	3,327	1,900	47	2,178	1,091	15.1	8.6	14.1	9.9	5.0
1978	3,333	1,928	46	2,282	1,130	15.0	8.7	13.8	10.3	5.1
1979	3,494	1,914	46	2,331	1,181	15.6	8.5	13.1	10.4	5.3
1980	3,612	1,990	46	2,390	1,189	15.9	8.8	12.6	10.6	5.2
1981	3,629	1,978	43	2,422	1,213	15.8	8.6	11.9	10.6	5.3
1982	3,681	1,975	42	2,456	1,170	15.9	8.5	11.5	10.6	5.1
1983	3,639	2,019	41	2,446	1,158	15.6	8.6	11.2	10.5	5.0
1984	3,669	2,039	40	2,477	1,169	15.6	8.6	10.8	10.5	5.0
1985	3,761	2,086	40	2,413	1,190	15.8	8.8	10.6	10.1	5.0
1986	3,757	2,105	39	2,407	1,178	15.6	8.8	10.4	10.0	4.9
1987	3,809	2,123	38	2,403	1,166	15.7	8.8	10.1	9.9	4.8
1988	3,910	2,168	39	2,396	1,167	16.0	8.9	10.0	9.8	4.8
1989	4,041	2,150	40	2,403	1,157	16.4	8.7	9.8	9.7	4.7
1990	4,158	2,148	38	2,443	1,182	16.7	8.6	9.2	9.8	4.7
1991	4,111	2,170	37	2,371	1,187	16.3	8.6	8.9	9.4	4.7
1992	4,065	2,176	35	2,362	1,215	15.9	8.5	8.5	9.3	4.8
1993	4,000	2,269	33	2,334	1,187	15.5	8.8	8.4	9.0	4.6
1994	3,979	2,279	31	2,362	1,191	15.0	8.8	8.0	9.1	4.6
1995	3,900	2,312	30	2,336	973	14.8	8.8	7.6	7.6	4.1
1996	3,891	2,315	28	2,344	1,150	14.7	8.7	7.3	8.8	4.3
1997	3,881	2,314	28	(NA)	(NA)	14.5	8.6	7.2	(NA)	(NA)
1998	3,942	2,337	28	(NA)	(NA)	14.6	8.7	7.2	(NA)	(NA)
1999	3,959	(NA)	(NA)	(NA)	(NA)	14.5	(NA)	(NA)	(NA)	(NA)

NA Not available. [1] Prior to 1960, data adjusted for underregistration. [2] Infants under 1 year, excluding fetal deaths; rates per 1,000 registered live births. [3] Includes estimates for some states through 1965 and also for 1976 and 1977 and marriage licenses for some states for all years except 1973 and 1975. Beginning 1978, includes nonlicensed marriages in California. [4] Includes reported annulments and some estimated state figures for all years.

Source: U.S. National Center for Health Statistics, *Vital Statistics of the United States*, annual; and *National Vital Statistics Reports (NVSR)* (formerly *Monthly Vital Statistics Report*); and unpublished data.

No. 69. Live Births by Race and Type of Hispanic Origin—Selected Characteristics: 1990 and 1999

[4,158 represents 4,158,000. Represents registered births. Excludes births to nonresidents of the United States. Data are based on Hispanic origin of mother and race of mother. Hispanic origin data are available from only 48 states and the District of Columbia in 1990]

Race and Hispanic origin	Number of births (1,000)		Births to teen-age mothers, percent of total		Births to unmarried mothers, per-cent of total		Prenatal care beginning first trimester		Late or no prenatal care		Percent of births with low birth weight [1]	
	1990	1999	1990	1999	1990	1999	1990	1999	1990	1999	1990	1999
Total	4,158	3,959	12.8	12.3	26.6	33.0	74.2	83.2	6.0	3.8	7.0	7.6
White	3,290	3,133	10.9	10.9	16.9	26.8	77.7	85.1	4.9	3.2	5.7	6.6
Black	684	606	23.1	20.7	66.7	68.9	60.7	74.1	10.9	6.6	13.3	13.1
American Indian, Eskimo, Aleut	39	40	19.5	20.2	53.6	58.9	57.9	69.5	12.9	8.2	6.1	7.1
Asian and Pacific Islander [2]	142	181	5.7	5.1	(NA)	15.4	(NA)	83.7	(NA)	3.5	(NA)	7.4
Filipino	26	31	6.1	5.9	15.9	21.1	77.1	84.2	4.5	2.8	7.3	8.3
Chinese	23	29	1.2	0.9	5.0	6.9	81.3	88.5	3.4	2.0	4.7	5.2
Japanese	9	9	2.9	2.1	9.6	9.9	87.0	90.7	2.9	2.1	6.2	7.9
Hawaiian	6	6	18.4	18.2	45.0	50.4	65.8	79.6	8.7	4.0	7.2	7.7
Hispanic origin [3]	595	764	16.8	16.7	36.7	42.2	60.2	74.4	12.0	6.3	6.1	6.4
Mexican	386	541	17.7	17.4	33.3	40.1	57.8	73.1	13.2	6.7	5.5	5.9
Puerto Rico	59	57	21.7	21.1	55.9	59.6	63.5	77.7	10.6	5.0	9.0	9.3
Cuban	11	13	7.7	7.7	18.2	26.4	84.8	91.4	2.8	1.4	5.7	6.8
Central and South American	83	103	9.0	10.0	41.2	43.7	61.5	77.6	10.9	5.2	5.8	6.4
Other and unknown Hispanic	56	50	(NA)	19.5	(NA)	45.8	(NA)	74.8	(NA)	6.3	(NA)	7.6

NA Not available. [1] Births less than 2,500 grams (5 lb.-8 oz.). [2] Includes other races not shown separately. [3] Hispanic persons may be of any race. Includes other types, not shown separately.

Source: U.S. National Center for Health Statistics, *Vital Statistics of the United States*, annual; *National Vital Statistics Report (NVSR)* (formerly *Monthly Vital Statistics Report*); and unpublished data.

Vital Statistics 59

No. 70. Births and Birth Rates by Race, Sex, and Age: 1980 to 1999

[Births in thousands (3,612 represents 3,612,000). Births by race of mother. Excludes births to nonresidents of the United States. For population bases used to derive these data, see text this section, and Appendix III]

Item	1980	1985	1990	1992	1993	1994	1995	1996	1997	1998	1999
Live births [1]	3,612	3,761	4,158	4,065	4,000	3,953	3,900	3,891	3,881	3,942	3,959
White	2,936	3,038	3,290	3,202	3,150	3,121	3,099	3,093	3,073	3,119	3,133
Black	568	582	684	674	659	636	603	595	600	610	606
American Indian	29	34	39	39	39	38	37	38	39	40	40
Asian or Pacific Islander	74	105	142	150	153	158	160	166	170	173	181
Male	1,853	1,928	2,129	2,082	2,049	2,023	1,996	1,990	(NA)	2,016	2,027
Female	1,760	1,833	2,029	1,983	1,951	1,930	1,903	1,901	(NA)	1,925	1,933
Males per 100 females	105	105	105	105	105	105	105	105	(NA)	105	105
Age of mother:											
Under 20 years old	562	478	533	518	514	518	512	503	500	485	476
20 to 24 years old	1,226	1,141	1,094	1,070	1,038	1,001	966	945	946	965	982
25 to 29 years old	1,108	1,201	1,277	1,179	1,129	1,089	1,064	1,071	1,075	1,083	1,078
30 to 34 years old	550	696	886	895	901	906	905	898	888	889	892
35 to 39 years old	141	214	318	345	357	372	384	400	408	425	434
40 to 44 years old	(NA)	(NA)	(NA)	(NA)	(NA)	(NA)	(NA)	(NA)	(NA)	81	83
45 to 49 years old	(NA)	(NA)	(NA)	(NA)	(NA)	(NA)	(NA)	(NA)	(NA)	4	4
Birth rate per 1,000 population	15.9	15.8	16.7	15.9	15.5	15.2	14.8	14.7	14.5	14.6	14.5
White	15.1	15.0	15.8	15.0	14.7	14.4	14.2	14.1	13.9	14.0	13.9
Black	21.3	20.4	22.4	21.3	20.5	19.5	18.2	17.8	17.7	17.7	17.4
American Indian	20.7	19.8	18.9	18.4	17.8	17.1	16.6	16.6	16.6	17.1	16.8
Asian or Pacific Islander	19.9	18.7	19.0	18.0	17.7	17.5	17.3	17.0	16.9	16.4	16.7
Male	16.8	16.7	17.6	16.7	(NA)	(NA)	(NA)	(NA)	(NA)	(NA)	(NA)
Female	15.1	15.0	15.9	15.2	(NA)	(NA)	(NA)	(NA)	(NA)	(NA)	(NA)
Plural birth ratio [2]	19.3	21.0	23.3	24.4	25.2	25.7	26.1	27.4	28.6	30.0	30.7
White	18.5	20.4	22.9	24.0	24.9	25.5	26.0	27.5	28.7	30.2	30.9
Black	24.1	25.3	27.0	28.2	28.7	29.4	28.8	29.8	30.9	32.0	32.9
Fertility rate per 1,000 women [3]	68.4	66.2	70.9	68.9	67.6	66.7	65.6	65.3	65.0	65.6	65.9
White [3]	64.8	64.1	68.3	66.5	65.4	64.9	64.4	64.3	63.9	64.6	65.1
Black [3]	84.7	78.8	86.8	83.2	80.5	76.9	72.3	70.7	70.7	71.0	70.1
American Indian [3]	82.7	78.6	76.2	75.4	73.4	70.9	69.1	68.7	69.1	70.7	69.7
Asian or Pacific Islander [3]	73.2	68.4	69.6	67.2	66.7	66.8	66.4	65.9	66.3	64.0	65.6
Age of mother:											
10 to 14 years old	1.1	1.2	1.4	1.4	1.4	1.4	1.3	1.2	1.1	1.0	0.9
15 to 19 years old	53.0	51.0	59.9	60.7	59.6	58.9	56.8	54.4	52.3	51.1	49.6
20 to 24 years old	115.1	108.3	116.5	114.6	112.6	111.1	109.8	110.4	110.4	111.2	111.0
25 to 29 years old	112.9	111.0	120.2	117.4	115.5	113.9	111.2	113.1	113.8	115.9	117.8
30 to 34 years old	61.9	69.1	80.8	80.2	80.8	81.5	82.5	83.9	85.3	87.4	89.6
35 to 39 years old	19.8	24.0	31.7	32.5	32.9	33.7	34.3	35.3	36.1	37.4	38.3
40 to 44 years old	3.9	4.0	5.5	5.9	6.1	6.4	6.6	6.8	7.1	7.3	7.4
45 to 49 years old	0.2	0.2	0.2	0.3	0.3	0.3	0.3	0.3	0.4	0.4	0.4

NA Not available. [1] Includes other races not shown separately. [2] Number of multiple births per 1,000 live births. [3] Per 1,000 women, 15 to 44 years old in specified group. The rate for age of mother 45 to 49 years old computed by relating births to mothers 45 years old and over to women 45 to 49 years old.

Source: U.S. National Center for Health Statistics, *Vital Statistics of the United States*, annual; *National Vital Statistics Report (NVSR)* (formerly *Monthly Vital Statistics Report*); and unpublished data.

No. 71. Teenagers—Births and Birth Rates by Race and Sex: 1990 to 1999

[Birth rates per 1,000 women in specified group, see text, this section]

Item	1990	1991	1992	1993	1994	1995	1996	1997	1998	1999
NUMBER OF BIRTHS										
All races, total [1]	521,826	519,577	505,415	501,093	505,488	499,873	494,272	489,211	484,975	476,050
15-17 years	183,327	188,226	187,549	190,535	195,169	192,508	186,762	183,324	173,252	163,588
18-19 years	338,499	331,351	317,866	310,558	310,319	307,365	307,509	305,886	311,724	312,462
White	354,482	352,359	342,739	341,817	348,081	349,635	346,509	342,029	340,894	337,888
15-17 years	114,934	118,809	118,786	121,309	126,388	127,165	124,031	121,864	116,699	111,624
18-19 years	239,548	233,550	223,953	220,508	221,693	222,470	222,477	220,164	224,195	226,264
Black	151,613	150,956	146,800	143,153	140,968	133,694	131,059	130,401	126,865	121,166
15-17 years	62,881	63,571	63,000	63,156	62,563	59,112	56,218	54,883	50,062	45,919
18-19 years	88,732	87,385	83,798	79,997	78,405	74,582	74,841	75,518	76,803	75,247
BIRTH RATE										
All races, total [1]	59.9	62.1	60.7	59.6	58.9	56.8	54.7	52.3	51.1	49.6
15-17 years	37.5	38.7	37.8	37.8	37.6	36.0	33.8	32.1	30.4	28.7
18-19 years	88.6	94.4	94.5	92.1	91.5	89.1	86.5	83.6	82.0	80.3
White	50.8	52.8	51.8	51.1	51.1	50.1	48.4	46.3	45.4	44.6
15-17 years	29.5	30.7	30.1	30.3	30.7	30.0	28.6	27.1	25.9	24.8
18-19 years	78.0	83.5	83.8	82.1	82.1	81.2	78.8	75.9	74.6	73.5
Black	112.8	115.5	112.4	108.6	104.5	96.1	91.7	88.2	85.4	81.0
15-17 years	82.3	84.1	81.3	79.8	76.3	69.7	64.9	60.8	56.8	52.0
18-19 years	152.9	158.6	157.9	151.9	148.3	137.1	133.0	130.1	126.9	122.8

[1] Includes races other than White and Black.

Source: U.S. National Center for Health Statistics, *Monthly Vital Statistics Report*, Vol. 49, No. 1, Supplement.

No. 72. Live Births by State: 1999

[Number of births, except rate. Registered births. Excludes births to nonresidents of the United States. By race of mother. See Appendix III]

State	All races [1]	White		Black		Hispanic [2]	Birth rate [3]	Fertility rate [4]
		Total	Non-Hispanic	Total	Non-Hispanic			
United States..	**3,959,417**	**3,132,501**	**2,346,450**	**605,970**	**588,981**	**764,339**	**14.5**	**65.9**
Alabama........	62,122	41,747	40,190	19,753	19,719	1,588	14.2	63.3
Alaska.........	9,950	6,565	6,066	441	427	594	16.1	74.3
Arizona.........	81,145	70,946	38,853	2,729	2,600	32,011	17.0	81.1
Arkansas	36,729	28,421	26,448	7,680	7,666	1,968	14.4	67.7
California	518,508	421,541	172,336	35,403	34,250	249,364	15.6	69.5
Colorado........	62,167	56,711	40,705	2,899	2,793	16,282	15.3	69.8
Connecticut......	43,310	36,277	28,226	5,383	4,993	6,323	13.2	61.9
Delaware	10,676	7,696	6,863	2,671	2,643	857	14.2	61.7
Dist. of Columbia ...	7,522	2,200	1,411	5,167	5,116	790	14.5	60.0
Florida	197,023	146,696	106,383	45,078	44,083	41,484	13.0	65.1
Georgia	126,717	81,297	70,016	42,133	41,532	10,557	16.3	68.8
Hawaii	17,038	3,999	3,340	460	425	2,210	14.4	68.7
Idaho..........	19,872	19,212	16,810	78	74	2,356	15.9	73.2
Illinois	182,068	140,267	103,430	34,239	34,023	36,959	15.0	68.0
Indiana.........	86,031	75,534	70,896	9,300	9,262	4,365	14.5	65.2
Iowa	37,558	35,363	33,261	1,164	1,116	1,844	13.1	62.3
Kansas.........	38,782	34,611	30,030	2,855	2,823	4,272	14.6	67.5
Kentucky	54,403	48,791	47,837	4,977	4,948	951	13.7	61.5
Louisiana	67,136	38,587	36,936	27,267	27,036	1,538	15.4	67.7
Maine..........	13,616	13,242	12,449	106	86	135	10.9	49.4
Maryland	71,967	44,385	40,400	24,260	24,048	4,088	13.9	60.4
Massachusetts.....	80,939	67,328	60,744	8,168	6,548	8,797	13.1	58.5
Michigan........	133,607	105,354	91,860	24,044	23,692	6,230	13.5	60.7
Minnesota.......	65,970	57,518	50,952	4,016	3,921	3,316	13.8	62.6
Mississippi	42,684	22,665	22,171	19,406	19,398	451	15.4	67.9
Missouri	75,432	62,592	60,350	11,273	11,231	2,260	13.8	63.0
Montana........	10,785	9,376	8,954	35	32	318	12.2	59.8
Nebraska	23,907	21,685	18,851	1,268	1,257	2,293	14.3	66.6
Nevada	29,362	25,036	15,575	2,194	2,117	9,268	16.2	78.3
New Hampshire....	14,041	13,628	12,753	139	121	357	11.7	50.8
New Jersey.......	114,105	84,444	64,762	21,133	19,151	21,313	14.0	64.5
New Mexico	27,191	22,864	9,168	497	465	13,827	15.6	72.2
New York	255,612	183,874	124,484	53,381	47,512	53,004	14.0	63.6
North Carolina	113,795	81,236	71,496	28,428	28,286	9,871	14.9	67.6
North Dakota......	7,639	6,743	6,463	87	84	121	12.1	57.3
Ohio	152,584	127,733	124,221	22,087	21,572	3,422	13.6	61.4
Oklahoma........	49,010	38,684	34,159	4,629	4,466	3,919	14.6	68.9
Oregon.........	45,204	41,417	34,247	904	878	6,904	13.6	64.8
Pennsylvania.....	145,347	121,104	113,655	20,363	20,000	7,161	12.1	57.4
Rhode Island......	12,366	10,787	7,362	984	856	1,893	12.5	57.2
South Carolina....	54,948	34,985	33,315	19,069	19,030	1,720	14.1	62.1
South Dakota	10,524	8,671	8,505	89	88	179	14.4	67.7
Tennessee	77,803	60,004	57,589	16,498	16,471	2,432	14.2	63.5
Texas..........	349,245	298,081	139,861	40,097	39,515	157,736	17.4	77.6
Utah	46,290	44,040	38,551	265	254	5,425	21.7	93.1
Vermont	6,567	6,473	6,297	40	35	40	11.1	49.2
Virginia.........	95,469	68,509	62,054	22,173	22,034	6,520	13.9	59.6
Washington.......	79,586	68,273	55,433	3,331	3,043	10,359	13.8	62.1
West Virginia.....	20,728	19,799	19,679	752	746	96	11.5	54.7
Wisconsin.......	68,208	58,770	54,828	6,505	6,446	4,041	13.0	59.3
Wyoming........	6,129	5,740	5,225	72	69	530	12.8	60.8

[1] Includes other races not shown separately.   [2] Persons of Hispanic origin may be of any race. Births by Hispanic origin of mother.   [3] Per 1,000 estimated population.   [4] Per 1,000 women aged 15-44 years estimated.

Source: U.S. National Center for Health Statistics, *Vital Statistics of the United States*, annual; and *National Vital Statistics Reports (NVSR)* (formerly *Monthly Vital Statistics Report*, Vol. 48, No. 3).

No. 73. Total Fertility Rate and Intrinsic Rate of Natural Increase: 1960 to 1999

[Based on race of child and registered births only, thru 1979. Beginning 1980, based on race of mother. Beginning 1970, excludes births to nonresidents of United States. The *total fertility rate* is the number of births that 1,000 women would have in their lifetime if, at each year of age, they experienced the birth rates occurring in the specified year. A total fertility rate of 2,110 represents "replacement level" fertility for the total population under current mortality conditions (assuming no net immigration). The *intrinsic rate of natural increase* is the rate that would eventually prevail if a population were to experience, at each year of age, the birth rates and death rates occurring in the specified year and if those rates remained unchanged over a long period of time. Minus sign (-) indicates decrease. See also Appendix III]

Annual average and year	Total fertility rate			Intrinsic rate of natural increase			Annual average and year	Total fertility rate			Intrinsic rate of natural increase		
	Total	White	Black and other	Total	White	Black and other		Total	White	Black and other	Total	White	Black and other
1960-64	3,449	3,326	4,326	18.6	17.1	27.7	1982	1,828	1,767	2,107	-5.2	-7.0	3.0
1965-69	2,622	2,512	3,362	8.2	6.4	18.6	1983	1,799	1,741	2,066	-5.8	-7.5	2.2
1970-74	2,094	1,997	2,680	-0.7	-2.5	9.1	1984	1,807	1,749	2,071	-5.6	-7.3	2.1
1975-79	1,774	1,685	2,270	-6.6	-8.5	3.0	1985	1,844	1,787	2,109	-4.8	-6.5	2.7
1980-84	1,819	1,731	2,262	-5.4	-7.3	3.0	1986	1,838	1,776	2,136	-4.9	-6.7	2.8
1985-88	1,870	1,769	2,339	-4.2	-6.3	4.3	1987	1,872	1,805	2,198	-4.1	-6.1	4.0
							1988	1,934	1,857	2,298	-2.9	-5.1	5.7
1970	2,480	2,385	3,067	6.0	4.5	14.4	1989	2,014	1,931	2,433	-1.4	-3.6	7.4
1971	2,267	2,161	2,920	2.6	0.8	12.6	1990	2,081	2,003	2,480	-0.1	-2.3	8.3
1972	2,010	1,907	2,628	-2.0	-3.9	8.6	1991	2,073	1,996	2,480	-0.2	-2.4	8.2
1973	1,879	1,783	2,443	-4.5	-6.5	5.7	1992	2,065	1,994	2,442	-0.4	-2.5	7.5
1974	1,835	1,749	2,339	-5.4	-7.2	4.0	1993	2,046	1,982	2,385	-0.7	-1.9	3.7
1975	1,774	1,686	2,276	-6.7	-8.6	3.0	1994	2,036	1,985	2,300	(NA)	(NA)	(NA)
1976	1,738	1,652	2,223	-7.4	-9.3	2.1	1995	2,019	1,989	2,175	(NA)	(NA)	(NA)
1977	1,790	1,703	2,279	-6.2	-8.1	3.2	1996	2,040	2,019	2,149	(NA)	(NA)	(NA)
1978	1,760	1,668	2,265	-6.8	-8.8	2.9	1997	2,040	2,017	2,158	(NA)	(NA)	(NA)
1979	1,808	1,716	2,310	-5.7	-7.7	3.8	1998	2,058	2,041	2,171	(NA)	(NA)	(NA)
1980	1,840	1,773	2,177	-5.1	-7.0	4.0	1999	2,075	2,065	2,147	(NA)	(NA)	(NA)
1981	1,812	1,748	2,118	-5.6	-7.4	3.0							

NA Not available. [1] Data for 1984 and earlier includes races other than Black.

Source: U.S. National Center for Health Statistics, *Vital Statistics of the United States*, annual; and unpublished data.

No. 74. Projected Fertility Rates by Race, Origin, and Age Group: 2000 and 2010

[For definition of total fertility rate, see headnote, Table 73. Birth rates represent live births per 1,000 women in age group indicated. Projections are based on middle fertility assumptions. For explanations of methodology, see text, Section 1, Population]

Age group	All races [1]		White		Black		American Indian, Eskimo, Aleut		Asian and Pacific Islander		Hispanic [2]	
	2000	2010	2000	2010	2000	2010	2000	2010	2000	2010	2000	2010
Total fertility rate	2,055	2,123	2,019	2,098	2,124	2,140	2,503	2,451	2,275	2,252	2,911	2,818
Birth rates:												
10 to 14 years old	1.2	1.3	0.8	0.9	3.4	3.5	2.0	2.0	0.7	0.7	2.4	2.3
15 to 19 years old	56.5	60.2	50.0	54.3	93.5	95.6	94.0	93.6	30.0	29.6	99.4	95.7
20 to 24 years old	112.5	115.8	108.4	112.6	136.2	137.1	163.6	159.6	84.5	83.7	181.1	175.2
25 to 29 years old	112.7	115.7	114.8	118.5	94.2	95.5	120.6	118.6	136.6	134.5	151.6	146.7
30 to 34 years old	85.1	87.8	86.8	90.0	62.3	63.4	78.2	77.3	129.8	128.2	94.3	91.6
35 to 39 years old	35.5	36.7	35.4	36.6	28.9	28.9	34.1	33.7	60.3	59.0	43.5	41.9
40 to 44 years old	6.9	7.3	6.8	7.1	6.1	6.0	7.4	7.4	13.9	13.8	10.5	9.9
45 to 49 years old	0.3	0.3	0.3	0.3	0.3	0.3	0.3	0.3	0.9	0.9	0.6	0.6

[1] Includes other races not shown separately. [2] Persons of Hispanic origin may be of any race.

Source: U.S. Census Bureau, Population Division Working Paper No. 38.

No. 75. Birth Rates by Live-Birth Order and Race: 1980 to 1999

[**Births per 1,000 women 15 to 44 years old in specified racial group.** Live-birth order refers to number of children born alive. Figures for births of order not stated are distributed. See also headnote, Table 70]

Live-birth order	All races [1]					White					Black				
	1980	1990	1995	1998	1999	1980	1990	1995	1998	1999	1980	1990	1995	1998	1999
Total	68.4	70.9	65.6	65.6	65.9	65.6	68.3	64.4	64.6	65.1	84.9	86.8	72.3	71.0	70.1
First birth	29.5	29.0	27.3	26.4	26.6	28.8	28.4	26.9	26.1	26.4	33.7	32.4	28.7	27.0	26.5
Second birth	21.8	22.8	21.1	21.4	21.5	21.3	22.4	21.1	21.5	21.6	24.7	25.6	20.7	21.1	20.9
Third birth	10.3	11.7	10.5	10.8	10.9	9.6	11.1	10.3	10.7	10.8	14.0	15.6	12.0	12.3	12.4
Fourth birth [2]	3.9	4.5	4.0	4.2	4.2	3.4	4.0	3.8	3.9	4.0	6.5	7.4	5.7	5.7	5.7
Fifth birth	1.5	1.7	1.5	1.5	1.5	1.3	1.4	1.3	1.3	1.4	2.9	3.2	2.6	2.6	2.5
Sixth and seventh	1.0	1.0	0.9	0.9	0.9	0.8	0.8	0.7	0.8	0.8	2.1	2.0	1.8	1.7	1.7
Eighth and over	0.4	0.3	0.3	0.3	0.3	0.3	0.2	0.2	0.2	0.2	0.9	0.5	0.6	0.6	0.6

[1] Includes other races not shown separately. [2] 1996 data represents "fourth child and over."

Source: U.S. National Center for Health Statistics, *Vital Statistics of the United States*, annual; and *National Vital Statistics Reports (NVSR)* (formerly *Monthly Vital Statistics Report*).

No. 76. Births to Teens, Unmarried Mothers, and Prenatal Care: 1990 to 1999

[In percent. Represents registered births. See headnote, Table 69]

Characteristics	1990	1994	1995	1996	1997	1998	1999
Percent of births to teenage mothers	**12.8**	**13.1**	**13.1**	**12.9**	**12.7**	**12.5**	**12.3**
White	10.9	11.3	11.5	11.3	11.2	11.1	10.9
Black	23.1	23.2	23.1	22.8	22.2	21.5	20.7
American Indian, Eskimo, Aleut	19.5	21.0	21.4	20.9	20.8	20.9	20.2
Asian and Pacific Islander [1]	5.7	5.7	5.6	5.3	5.2	5.4	5.1
Filipino	6.1	6.0	6.2	6.1	5.9	6.2	5.9
Chinese	1.2	1.0	0.9	0.9	0.9	0.9	0.9
Japanese	2.9	2.8	2.5	2.5	2.2	2.4	2.1
Hawaiian	18.4	19.6	19.1	18.4	18.6	18.8	18.2
Other	(NA)	6.4	6.3	5.8	5.7	5.8	5.5
Hispanic origin [2]	16.8	17.8	17.9	17.4	17.0	16.9	16.7
Mexican	17.7	18.6	18.8	18.1	17.7	17.5	17.4
Puerto Rican	21.7	23.2	23.5	23.1	22.3	21.9	21.1
Cuban	7.7	7.3	7.7	7.6	7.4	6.9	7.7
Central and South American	9.0	10.4	10.6	10.5	10.5	10.3	10.0
Other and unknown Hispanic	(NA)	20.8	20.1	19.8	19.8	20.2	19.5
Percent births to unmarried mothers	**26.6**	**32.6**	**32.2**	**32.4**	**32.4**	**32.8**	**33.0**
White	16.9	25.4	25.3	25.7	25.8	26.3	26.8
Black	66.7	70.4	69.9	69.8	69.2	69.1	68.9
American Indian, Eskimo, Aleut	53.6	57.0	57.2	58.0	58.7	59.3	58.9
Asian and Pacific Islander [1]	(NA)	16.2	16.3	16.7	15.6	15.6	15.4
Filipino	15.9	18.5	19.5	19.4	19.5	19.7	21.1
Chinese	5.0	7.2	7.9	9.2	6.5	6.4	6.9
Japanese	9.6	11.2	10.8	11.4	10.1	9.7	9.9
Hawaiian	45.0	48.6	49.0	49.9	49.1	51.1	50.4
Hispanic origin [2]	36.7	43.1	40.8	40.7	40.9	41.6	42.2
Mexican	33.3	40.8	38.1	37.9	38.9	39.6	40.1
Puerto Rican	55.9	60.2	60.0	60.7	59.4	59.5	59.6
Cuban	18.2	22.9	23.8	24.7	24.4	24.8	26.4
Central and South American	41.2	45.9	44.1	44.7	41.8	42.0	43.7
Percent of mothers beginning prenatal care 1st trimester	**74.2**	**80.2**	**81.3**	**81.9**	**82.5**	**82.8**	**83.2**
White	77.7	82.8	83.6	84.0	84.7	84.8	85.1
Black	60.7	68.3	70.4	71.4	72.3	73.3	74.1
American Indian, Eskimo, Aleut	57.9	65.2	66.7	67.7	68.1	68.8	69.5
Asian and Pacific Islander [1]	(NA)	79.7	79.9	81.2	82.1	83.1	83.7
Filipino	77.1	81.3	80.9	82.5	83.3	84.2	84.2
Chinese	81.3	86.2	85.7	86.8	87.4	88.5	88.5
Japanese	87.0	89.2	89.7	89.3	89.3	90.2	90.7
Hawaiian	65.8	77.0	75.9	78.5	78.0	78.8	79.6
Hispanic origin [2]	60.2	68.9	70.8	72.2	73.7	74.3	74.4
Mexican	57.8	67.3	69.1	70.7	72.1	72.8	73.1
Puerto Rican	63.5	71.7	74.0	75.0	76.5	76.9	77.7
Cuban	84.8	90.1	89.2	89.2	90.4	91.8	91.4
Central and South American	61.5	71.2	73.2	75.0	76.9	78.0	77.6
Percent of mothers beginning prenatal care 3d trimester or no care	**6.0**	**4.4**	**4.2**	**4.0**	**3.9**	**3.9**	**3.8**
White	4.9	3.6	3.5	3.3	3.2	3.3	3.2
Black	10.9	8.2	7.6	7.3	7.3	7.0	6.6
American Indian, Eskimo, Aleut	12.9	9.8	9.5	8.6	8.6	8.5	8.2
Asian and Pacific Islander [1]	(NA)	4.1	4.3	3.9	3.8	3.6	3.5
Filipino	4.5	3.6	4.1	3.3	3.3	3.1	2.8
Chinese	3.4	2.7	3.0	2.5	2.4	2.2	2.0
Japanese	2.9	1.9	2.3	2.2	2.7	2.1	2.1
Hawaiian	8.7	4.7	5.1	5.0	5.4	4.7	4.0
Hispanic origin [2]	12.0	7.6	7.4	6.7	6.2	6.3	6.3
Mexican	13.2	8.3	8.1	7.2	6.7	6.8	6.7
Puerto Rican	10.6	6.5	5.5	5.7	5.4	5.1	5.0
Cuban	2.8	1.6	2.1	1.6	1.5	1.2	1.4
Central and South American	10.9	6.5	6.1	5.5	5.0	4.9	5.2
Percent of births with low birth weight [3]	**7.0**	**7.3**	**7.3**	**7.4**	**7.5**	**7.6**	**7.6**
White	5.7	6.1	6.2	6.3	6.5	6.5	6.6
Black	13.3	13.2	13.1	13.0	13.0	13.0	13.1
American Indian, Eskimo, Aleut	6.1	6.4	6.6	6.5	6.8	6.8	7.1
Asian and Pacific Islander [1]	(NA)	6.8	6.9	7.1	7.2	7.4	7.4
Filipino	7.3	7.8	7.8	7.9	8.3	8.2	8.3
Chinese	4.7	4.8	5.3	5.0	5.1	5.3	5.2
Japanese	6.2	6.9	7.3	7.3	6.8	7.5	7.9
Hawaiian	7.2	7.2	6.8	6.8	7.2	7.2	7.7
Hispanic origin [2]	6.1	6.2	6.3	7.4	6.4	6.4	6.4
Mexican	5.5	5.8	5.8	5.9	6.0	6.0	5.9
Puerto Rican	9.0	9.1	9.4	9.2	9.4	9.7	9.3
Cuban	5.7	6.3	6.5	6.5	6.8	6.5	6.8
Central and South American	5.8	6.0	6.2	6.0	6.3	6.5	6.4

NA Not available. [1] Includes other races not shown separately. [2] Hispanic persons may be of any race. Includes other types, not shown separately. [3] Births less than 2,500 grams (5 lb.-8 oz.).

Source: U.S. National Center for Health Statistics, *Vital Statistics of the United States*, annual; and *National Vital Statistics Reports (NVSR)* (formerly *Monthly Vital Statistics Report*).

No. 77. Births to Unmarried Women by Race of Child and Age of Mother: 1990 to 1999

[Excludes births to nonresidents of United States. Marital status is inferred from a comparison of the child's and parents' surnames on the birth certificate for those states that do not report on marital status. No estimates included for misstatements on birth records or failures to register births. See also Appendix III]

Race of child and age of mother	1990	1995	1997	1998	1999	Race of child and age of mother	1990	1995	1997	1998	1999
NUMBER (1,000)						30 to 34 years	10.1	10.6	9.9	9.6	9.5
Total [1]	1,165	1,254	1,257	1,294	1,308	35 to 39 years	(NA)	(NA)	4.8	4.7	4.8
White	647	785	793	821	840	40 years and over	(NA)	(NA)	1.1	1.1	1.1
Black	473	421	415	421	417						
Under 15 years.	11	11	10	9	9	**AS PERCENT OF ALL BIRTHS IN RACIAL GROUPS**					
15 to 19 years	350	376	376	381	374						
20 to 24 years	404	432	439	460	476	**Total**	28.0	32.2	32.4	32.8	33.0
25 to 29 years	230	229	235	243	247	White	20.1	25.3	25.8	26.3	26.8
30 to 34 years	118	133	125	125	125	Black	65.2	69.9	69.2	69.1	68.9
35 to 39 years	(NA)	(NA)	60	61	63						
40 years and over	(NA)	(NA)	14	14	14	**BIRTH RATE** [2]					
						Total [1][3]	43.8	45.1	44.0	44.3	44.4
PERCENT DISTRIBUTION [1]						White [3]	31.8	37.5	37.0	37.5	38.1
Total	100.0	100.0	100.0	100.0	100.0	Black [3]	93.9	75.9	73.4	73.3	71.5
White	55.6	62.6	63.1	63.5	64.1						
Black	40.6	33.6	33.0	32.6	31.9	15 to 19 years	42.5	44.4	42.2	41.5	40.4
						20 to 24 years	65.1	70.3	71.0	72.3	72.9
Under 15 years.	0.9	0.9	0.8	0.7	0.7	25 to 29 years	56.0	56.1	56.2	58.4	60.2
15 to 19 years	30.0	30.0	29.9	29.4	28.6	30 to 34 years	37.6	39.6	39.0	39.1	39.3
20 to 24 years	34.7	34.4	34.9	35.6	36.4	35 to 39 years	(NA)	(NA)	19.0	19.0	19.3
25 to 29 years	19.7	18.3	18.7	18.8	18.9	40 to 44 years	(NA)	(NA)	4.6	4.6	4.6

NA Not available. [1] Includes other races not shown separately. [2] Rate per 1,000 unmarried women (never-married, widowed, and divorced) estimated as of July 1. [3] Covers women aged 15 to 44 years.

Source: U.S. National Center for Health Statistics, *Vital Statistics of the United States*, annual; and *National Vital Statistics Reports (NVSR)* (formerly *Monthly Vital Statistics Report*).

No. 78. Live Births by Plurality of Birth and Ratios and Race of Mother: 1994 to 1999

Plurality and race of mother	1994	1995	1996	1997	1998	1999
NUMBER						
Live births, total [1]	3,952,767	3,899,589	3,891,494	3,880,894	3,941,553	3,959,417
White	3,121,004	3,098,885	3,093,057	3,072,640	3,118,727	3,132,501
Black	636,391	603,139	594,781	599,913	609,902	605,970
Live births in single deliveries [1]	3,851,109	3,797,880	3,784,805	3,770,020	3,823,258	3,837,789
White	3,041,559	3,018,184	3,007,997	2,984,532	3,024,693	3,035,757
Black	617,689	585,787	577,057	581,394	590,372	586,027
Live births in twin deliveries [1]	97,064	96,736	100,750	104,137	110,670	114,307
White	75,318	76,196	79,677	82,090	87,163	90,191
Black	18,344	17,000	17,285	17,989	19,001	19,374
Live births in higher-order multiple [1]	4,594	4,973	5,939	6,737	7,625	7,321
White	4,127	4,505	5,383	6,018	6,871	6,553
Black	358	352	439	530	529	569
RATIO PER 1,000 LIVE BIRTHS						
All multiple births [1]	25.7	26.1	27.4	28.6	30.0	30.7
White	25.5	26.0	27.5	28.7	30.2	30.9
Black	29.4	28.8	29.8	30.9	32.0	32.9
Twin births [1]	24.6	24.8	25.9	26.8	28.1	28.9
White.	24.1	24.6	25.8	26.7	27.9	28.8
Black	28.8	28.2	29.1	30.0	31.2	32.0
RATIO PER 100,000 LIVE BIRTHS						
Higher-order multiple births [1]	116.2	127.5	152.6	173.6	193.5	184.9
White	132.2	145.4	174.0	195.9	220.3	209.2
Black	56.3	58.4	73.8	88.3	86.7	93.9

[1] Includes races other than White and Black.

Source: U.S. National Center for Health Statistics, Advance report of Final Natality Statistics, and *National Vital Statistics Reports (NVSR)* (formerly *Monthly Vital Statistics Report*).

No. 79. Low Birth Weight and Births to Teenage Mothers and to Unmarried Women—States: 1990 to 1999

[Represents registered births. Excludes births to nonresidents of the United States. Based on 100 percent of births in all states and the District of Columbia. See Appendix III]

State	Percent of births with low birth weight [1]			Births to teenage mothers percent of total			Births to unmarried women percent of total		
	1990	1995	1999	1990	1995	1999	1990	1995	1999
U.S...........	7.0	7.3	7.6	12.8	13.1	14.5	28.0	32.2	33.0
AL..............	8.4	9.0	9.3	18.2	18.5	14.2	30.1	34.5	33.3
AK..............	4.8	5.3	5.8	9.7	11.2	16.1	26.2	29.9	33.2
AZ..............	6.4	6.8	6.9	14.2	15.1	17.0	32.7	38.2	38.8
AR..............	8.2	8.2	8.6	19.7	19.6	14.4	29.4	32.9	35.2
CA..............	5.8	6.1	6.1	11.6	12.4	15.6	[2]31.6	32.1	32.9
CO..............	8.0	8.4	8.3	11.3	12.1	15.3	21.2	24.9	25.4
CT..............	6.6	7.1	7.6	8.2	8.6	13.2	[2]26.6	30.6	29.0
DE..............	7.6	8.4	8.6	11.9	13.2	14.2	29.0	34.9	38.8
DC..............	15.1	13.4	13.1	17.8	16.3	14.5	64.9	65.8	61.7
FL..............	7.4	7.7	8.2	13.9	13.7	13.0	31.7	35.8	37.5
GA..............	8.7	8.8	8.7	16.7	16.3	16.3	32.8	35.2	36.6
HI..............	7.1	7.0	7.6	10.5	10.1	14.4	24.8	29.2	32.8
ID..............	5.7	5.9	6.2	12.3	14.0	15.9	16.7	19.9	21.6
IL..............	7.6	7.9	8.0	13.1	12.9	15.0	31.7	33.8	34.1
IN..............	6.6	7.5	7.9	14.5	14.7	14.5	26.2	31.9	34.5
IA..............	5.4	6.0	6.2	10.2	11.0	13.1	21.0	25.2	27.5
KS..............	6.2	6.4	7.1	12.3	13.1	14.6	21.5	25.9	28.6
KY..............	7.1	7.6	8.2	17.5	17.2	13.7	23.6	28.5	30.4
LA..............	9.2	9.7	10.0	17.6	19.1	15.4	36.8	42.4	44.8
ME..............	5.1	6.1	6.0	10.8	10.3	10.9	22.6	27.8	31.3
MD..............	7.8	8.5	9.0	10.5	10.3	13.9	[2]29.6	33.3	34.9
MA..............	5.9	6.3	7.1	8.0	7.5	13.1	24.7	25.6	26.5
MI..............	7.6	7.7	8.0	13.5	12.5	13.5	[2]26.2	34.3	33.1
MN..............	5.1	5.9	6.1	8.0	8.4	13.8	20.9	23.9	25.9
MS..............	9.6	9.8	10.3	21.3	22.2	15.4	40.5	45.3	45.9
MO..............	7.1	7.6	7.7	14.4	14.4	13.8	28.6	32.1	34.1
MT..............	6.2	5.8	6.8	11.5	12.6	12.2	[2]23.7	26.5	30.0
NE..............	5.3	6.3	6.7	9.8	10.0	14.3	20.7	24.3	25.9
NV..............	7.2	7.4	7.6	12.6	13.7	16.2	[2]25.4	42.0	35.7
NH..............	4.9	5.5	6.2	7.2	7.6	11.7	16.9	22.2	24.2
NJ..............	7.0	7.6	8.2	8.4	8.2	14.0	24.3	27.6	28.5
NM..............	7.4	7.5	7.7	16.3	18.4	15.6	35.4	42.6	45.1
NY..............	7.6	7.6	7.8	9.1	9.3	14.0	[2]33.0	37.9	36.6
NC..............	8.0	8.7	8.9	16.2	15.2	14.9	29.4	31.4	33.2
ND..............	5.5	5.3	6.2	8.6	9.6	12.1	18.4	23.5	27.5
OH..............	7.1	7.6	7.9	13.8	13.7	13.6	[2]28.9	33.0	34.1
OK..............	6.6	7.0	7.4	16.2	17.1	14.6	25.2	30.5	33.2
OR..............	5.0	5.5	5.4	12.0	13.0	13.6	25.7	28.9	30.4
PA..............	7.1	7.4	7.9	10.9	10.8	12.1	28.6	32.4	32.9
RI..............	6.2	6.8	7.3	10.5	10.1	12.5	26.3	31.1	34.3
SC..............	8.7	9.3	9.8	17.1	17.3	14.1	32.7	37.4	39.0
SD..............	5.1	5.6	5.9	10.8	11.4	14.4	22.9	28.0	31.8
TN..............	8.2	8.7	9.2	17.6	16.9	14.2	30.2	33.1	34.7
TX..............	6.9	7.1	7.4	15.6	16.6	17.4	[2]17.5	30.0	31.3
UT..............	5.7	6.3	6.8	10.3	10.8	21.7	13.5	15.7	16.7
VT..............	5.3	5.4	5.7	8.5	8.2	11.1	20.1	24.9	28.9
VA..............	7.2	7.7	7.8	11.7	11.4	13.9	26.0	29.3	29.7
WA..............	5.3	5.5	5.8	10.8	11.5	13.8	23.7	26.7	28.1
WV..............	7.1	7.9	8.0	17.8	17.2	11.5	25.4	30.5	31.7
WI..............	5.9	6.0	6.7	10.2	10.5	13.0	24.2	27.4	29.2
WY..............	7.4	7.4	8.4	13.6	15.2	12.8	19.8	26.4	29.0
Puerto Rico	(NA)	(NA)	11.4	(NA)	(NA)	15.3	(NA)	(NA)	(NA)
Virgin Islands	(NA)	(NA)	10.1	(NA)	(NA)	14.0	(NA)	(NA)	(NA)
Guam	(NA)	(NA)	7.8	(NA)	(NA)	26.5	(NA)	(NA)	(NA)
American Samoa.	(NA)	(NA)	3.6	(NA)	(NA)	27.2	(NA)	(NA)	(NA)
Northern Marianas. ...	(NA)	(NA)	8.2	(NA)	(NA)	20.0	(NA)	(NA)	(NA)

NA Not available.   [1] Less than 2,500 grams (5 pounds-8 ounces).   [2] Marital status of mother is inferred.

Source: U.S. National Center for Health Statistics, *Vital Statistics of the United States*, annual; and *National Vital Statistics Reports (NVSR)* (formerly *Monthly Vital Statistics Report*).

U.S. Census Bureau, Statistical Abstract of the United States: 2001

No. 80. Live Births by Place of Delivery, Median and Low Birth Weight, and Prenatal Care: 1990 to 1999

[Represents registered births. Excludes births to nonresidents of the United States. For total number of births, see Table 70. See Appendix III]

Item	1990	1992	1993	1994	1995	1996	1997	1999
Births attended (1,000):								
In hospital [1]	4,110	4,022	3,959	3,912	3,861	3,891	3,881	3,923
By physician, not in hospital	14	10	8	7	6	6	5	5
By midwife and other, not in hospital [2]	21	21	20	21	21	20	20	21
Median birth weight [3]	7 lb.-7 oz.	7 lb.-7 oz.	7 lb.-7 oz.	(NA)	(NA)	7 lb.-7 oz.	7 lb.-7 oz.	(NA)
Percent of births with low birth weight . . .	7.0	7.1	7.2	7.3	7.3	7.4	7.5	7.6
White.	5.7	5.8	6.0	6.1	6.2	6.3	6.5	6.6
Black.	13.3	13.3	13.3	13.2	13.1	13.0	13.0	13.1
Percent of births by period in which prenatal care began:								
1st trimester	74.2	77.7	78.9	80.2	81.3	81.9	82.5	83.2
3d trimester or no prenatal care	6.0	5.2	4.8	4.4	4.2	4.0	3.9	3.8

NA Not available. [1] Includes all births in hospitals or institutions and in clinics. [2] Includes births with attendant not specified. [3] Median birth weight based on race of mother; prior to 1990, based on race of child.

Source: U.S. National Center for Health Statistics, *Vital Statistics of the United States,* annual, and *National Vital Statistics Reports* (formerly Monthly Vital Statistics Report), and unpublished data.

No. 81. Cesarean Section Deliveries by Age of Mother: 1990 to 1999

[**In thousands (4,111 represents 4,111,000), except rate.** 1990 excludes data for Oklahoma, which did not report method of delivery on the birth certificate]

Age of mother	1990	1995	1999	Age of mother	1990	1995	1999
Births by method of delivery.	4,111	3,900	3,959	Repeat	53	46	51
Vaginal.	3,111	3,064	3,064	Not stated.	16	4	4
After previous cesarean	84	112	98	Hispanic births by method of			
Cesarean deliveries	914	807	862	delivery (1,000)	595	680	764
Primary.	575	510	542	Vaginal.	458	540	599
Repeat	339	297	320	After previous cesarean	10	17	17
Not stated.	85	29	33	Cesarean deliveries	123	137	161
White births by method of delivery .	3,252	3,099	3,133	Primary.	76	83	94
Vaginal.	2,454	2,435	2,426	Repeat	47	54	67
After previous cesarean	67	91	77	Not stated.	14	3	4
Cesarean deliveries	733	640	679	Cesarean delivery rate [1]	22.7	20.8	22.0
Primary.	459	401	424	White.	23.0	20.8	21.9
Repeat	274	239	255	Black	22.1	21.8	23.2
Not stated.	66	24	27	Primary [2]	16.0	14.7	15.5
				White	16.1	14.6	15.3
Black births by method of delivery. .	679	603	606	Black	15.7	15.7	16.5
Vaginal.	517	469	462	Rate of vaginal cesarean birth			
After previous cesarean	13	16	15	after previous cesarean [3]	19.9	27.5	23.4
Cesarean deliveries	146	130	139	White	19.7	27.6	23.2
Primary.	93	84	88	Black	20.3	26.1	23.2

[1] Percent of all live births by cesarean delivery. [2] Number of primary cesareans per 100 live births to women who have not had a previous cesarean. [3] Number of vaginal births after previous cesarean delivery per 100 live births to women with a previous cesarean delivery.

Source: U.S. National Center for Health Statistics, *Vital Statistics of the United States,* annual.

No. 82. Women Who Have Had a Child in the Last Year by Age and Labor Force Status: 1980 to 1998

[**3,247 represents 3,247,000.** See headnote, Table 83]

Year	Total, 18 to 44 years old			18 to 29 years old			30 to 44 years old		
	Number (1,000)	In the labor force		Number (1,000)	In the labor force		Number (1,000)	In the labor force	
		Number (1,000)	Percent		Number (1,000)	Percent		Number (1,000)	Percent
1980	3,247	1,233	38	2,476	947	38	770	287	37
1981	3,381	1,411	42	2,499	1,004	40	881	407	46
1982	3,433	1,508	44	2,445	1,040	43	988	469	48
1983	3,625	1,563	43	2,682	1,138	42	942	425	45
1984	3,311	1,547	47	2,375	1,058	45	936	489	52
1985	3,497	1,691	48	2,512	1,204	48	984	488	50
1986	3,625	1,805	50	2,452	1,185	48	1,174	620	53
1987	3,701	1,881	51	2,521	1,258	50	1,180	623	53
1988 [1]	3,667	1,866	51	2,384	1,177	49	1,283	688	54
1990 [1]	3,913	2,068	53	2,568	1,275	50	1,346	793	59
1992 [1]	3,688	1,985	54	2,346	1,182	50	1,342	802	60
1994 [1]	3,890	2,066	53	2,389	1,209	51	1,50ı	857	57
1995 [1]	3,696	2,034	55	2,252	1,150	51	1,444	884	61
1998 [1]	3,671	2,155	59	(NA)	(NA)	(NA)	(NA)	(NA)	(NA)

NA Not available. [1] Lower age limit is 15 years old.

Source: U.S. Census Bureau, *Current Population Reports,* P20-482; and unpublished data.

No. 83. Women Who Have Had a Child in the Last Year by Age: 1980 to 1998

[**3,247 represents 3,247,000.** Excludes births to nonresidents of the United States. Data are by place of residence. Metropolitan Statistical Areas (MSAs), Consolidated Metropolitan Statistical Areas (CMSAs), and New England County Metropolitan Areas (NECMAs) are defined by the U.S. Office of Management and Budget as of June 30, 1990. See Appendix II for definitions and components]

Age of mother	Women who had a child in last year (1,000)			Total births per 1,000 women			First births per 1,000 women		
	1980	1990	1998	1980	1990	1998	1980	1990	1998
Total	**3,247**	**3,913**	**3,671**	**71.1**	**67.0**	**60.7**	**28.5**	**26.4**	**24.6**
15 to 29 years old [1] . . .	2,476	2,568	2,274	103.7	90.8	81.7	48.6	43.2	40.2
15 to 19 years old . .	(NA)	338	460	(NA)	39.8	48.0	(NA)	30.1	29.3
20 to 24 years old . .	1396	1038	864	96.6	113.4	98.2	(NA)	51.8	50.4
25 to 29 years old . .	1,081	1,192	950	114.8	112.1	100.5	(NA)	46.2	41.8
30 to 44 years old	770	1,346	1,397	35.4	44.7	42.7	6.3	10.6	11.3
30 to 34 years old . .	519	892	843	60.0	80.4	82.4	(NA)	21.9	23.8
35 to 39 years old . .	192	377	437	26.9	37.3	38.5	(NA)	6.5	8.7
40 to 44 years old . .	59	77	117	9.9	8.6	10.5	(NA)	1.2	2.6

NA Not available.   [1] For 1980-88, 18 to 29 years old.

Source: U.S. Census Bureau, *Current Population Reports*, P20-375, P20-454, P20-470, and P20-499.

No. 84. Characteristics of Women Who Have Had a Child in the Last Year: 1995 and 1998

[**As of June.** Covers civilian noninstitutional population. Since the number of women who had a birth during the 12-month period was tabulated and not the actual numbers of births, some small underestimation of fertility for this period may exist due to the omission of: (1) multiple births, (2) two or more live births spaced within the 12-month period (the woman is counted only once), (3) women who had births in the period and who did not survive to the survey date, and (4) women who were in institutions and therefore not in the survey universe. These losses may be somewhat offset by the inclusion in the CPS of births to immigrants who did not have their children born in the United States and births to nonresident women. These births would not have been recorded in the vital registration system. Based on Current Population Survey (CPS); see text, Section 1 and Appendix III]

Characteristic	1995			1998		
	Women who have had a child in the last year			Women who have had a child in the last year		
	Number of women (1,000)	Total births per 1,000 women	First births per 1,000 women	Number of women (1,000)	Total births per 1,000 women	First births per 1,000 women
Total [1]	**60,225**	**61.4**	**23.2**	**60,519**	**60.7**	**24.6**
White	48,603	59.2	22.6	48,487	60.8	24.2
Black	8,617	70.6	26.4	8,809	62.9	27.8
Hispanic [2]	6,632	79.6	25.0	7,359	84.0	36.1
Currently married	31,616	85.5	30.3	30,903	81.8	29.7
Married, spouse present	29,202	87.2	31.4	28,344	85.5	31.4
Married, spouse absent [3]	2,414	64.5	17.4	2,559	40.7	11.8
Widowed or divorced	5,762	28.4	4.1	5,430	26.4	6.4
Never married	22,846	36.3	18.0	24,185	41.3	22.1
Educational attainment:						
Less than high school	12,629	57.3	19.6	13,048	60.8	23.5
High school, 4 years	18,404	67.4	25.5	17,536	59.0	21.9
College: 1 or more years	29,192	59.3	23.2	29,935	61.6	26.7
No degree	12,724	56.1	21.2	12,626	54.6	21.7
Associate degree.	4,663	56.9	19.2	4,413	65.3	28.6
Bachelor's degree	8,884	65.3	27.0	9,762	64.2	29.1
Graduate or professional degree .	2,921	59.2	26.8	3,134	76.2	36.6
Labor force status:						
Employed	39,989	46.5	20.9	40,957	47.6	19.8
Unemployed	3,287	53.5	22.8	2,808	73.6	33.5
Not in labor force	16,949	98.1	28.5	16,754	90.5	34.8
Occupation of employed women:						
Managerial-professional	11,059	46.2	22.3	12,044	55.3	23.2
Technical, sales, admin. support . . .	16,997	48.6	21.5	16,801	45.9	21.7
Service workers	7,612	44.0	16.6	7,796	42.0	14.5
Farming, forestry, and fishing	501	41.0	27.9	467	30.1	4.0
Precision prod, craft, repair.	813	56.6	37.5	784	36.9	15.6
Operators, fabricators, laborers	3,007	39.5	17.8	3,064	46.0	13.4
Family income:						
Under $10,000	6,957	91.0	32.8	5,631	73.3	29.5
$10,000 to $19,999	8,159	64.3	25.8	6,917	74.3	30.6
$20,000 to $24,999	4,542	60.6	20.3	3,902	77.3	36.4
$25,000 to $29,999	4,364	57.0	18.9	3,848	61.4	20.8
$30,000 to $34,999	4,076	60.6	24.3	3,928	58.6	21.6
$35,000 to $49,999	9,949	59.1	20.8	9,478	55.1	21.9
$50,000 to $74,999	9,720	52.5	23.3	11,003	60.3	24.1
$75,000 and over	7,088	53.1	19.2	9,627	50.2	21.7

[1] Includes women of other races and women with family income not reported, not shown separately.   [2] Persons of Hispanic origin may be of any race.   [3] Includes separated women.

Source: U.S. Census Bureau, *Current Population Reports*, P20-375, P20-499, and unpublished data..

Vital Statistics 67

No. 85. Number of Pregnancies, Live Births, and Induced Abortions by Age and Race of Woman: 1980 to 1996

[Due to rounding, figures may not add to totals]

Age and race of woman	1980	1985	1990	1991	1992	1993	1994	1995	1996
ALL PREGNANCIES									
Total [1]	**5,912**	**6,144**	**6,778**	**6,674**	**6,596**	**6,494**	**6,373**	**6,245**	**6,240**
Under 15 years	29	30	29	29	30	30	30	28	26
15 to 19 years	1,146	981	1,013	975	939	928	923	904	893
20 to 24 years	1,956	1,891	1,847	1,843	1,813	1,762	1,682	1,602	1,570
25 to 29 years	1,626	1,764	1,908	1,827	1,771	1,701	1,637	1,598	1,617
30 to 34 years	844	1,045	1,319	1,313	1,326	1,332	1,333	1,322	1,312
35 to 39 years	258	373	562	581	603	622	642	659	683
40 years and over	54	60	100	106	113	119	127	132	140
Race:									
White	4,585	4,733	5,117	5,006	4,924	4,834	4,755	4,692	(NA)
All other	1,328	1,411	1,660	1,668	1,671	1,660	1,618	1,553	(NA)
LIVE BIRTHS									
Total	**3,612**	**3,761**	**4,158**	**4,111**	**4,065**	**4,000**	**3,953**	**3,900**	**3,891**
Race:									
White	2,936	3,038	3,290	3,241	3,202	3,150	3,121	3,099	3,093
All other	676	723	868	870	863	850	832	801	798
INDUCED ABORTIONS									
Total	**1,554**	**1,589**	**1,609**	**1,557**	**1,529**	**1,500**	**1,431**	**1,364**	**1,366**
Under 15 years	15	17	13	12	13	12	12	11	10
15 to 19 years	445	399	351	314	295	289	276	264	264
20 to 24 years	549	548	532	533	526	514	478	442	434
25 to 29 years	304	336	360	348	341	332	316	308	318
30 to 34 years	153	181	216	213	213	211	205	196	195
35 to 39 years	67	87	108	107	110	111	111	110	112
40 years and over	21	21	29	29	31	31	32	32	33
Race:									
White	1,094	1076	1,039	982	944	911	861	820	(NA)
All other	460	513	570	574	585	589	570	544	(NA)

NA Not available. [1] Includes fetal losses not shown.

Source: U.S. National Center for Health Statistics, *Vital and Health Statistics, Trends in Pregnancies and Pregnancy Rates by Outcome: 1976-96*, Series 21, No. 56.

No. 86. Numbers and Rates of Pregnancies, Live Births, Induced Abortions, and Fetal Losses for Teenagers by Age, Race, and Hispanic Origin: 1996

Pregnancy outcome and race and Hispanic origin	Number (1,000)				Rate per 1,000 women			
	10-14 years old	15-19 years old			10-14 years old	15-19 years old		
		Total	15-17 years old	18-19 years old		Total	15-17 years old	18-19 years old
ALL RACES [1]								
All pregnancies	26	893	372	521	2.8	98.7	67.8	146.4
Live births	11	492	186	306	1.2	54.4	33.8	86.0
Induced abortions	10	264	104	160	1.1	29.2	19.0	44.9
Fetal losses [2]	4	137	82	55	0.5	15.2	15.0	15.5
NON-HISPANIC								
White:								
All pregnancies	7	416	163	253	1.1	68.1	43.9	105.6
Live births	3	229	76	153	0.4	37.6	20.6	63.7
Induced abortions	3	117	46	71	0.5	19.1	12.5	29.4
Fetal losses [2]	1	70	40	30	0.2	11.4	10.8	12.4
Black:								
All pregnancies	12	242	106	136	8.7	177.8	128.1	254.4
Live births	5	128	55	73	3.8	94.2	66.6	136.6
Induced abortions	5	90	36	54	3.9	65.9	43.7	100.1
Fetal losses [2]	1	24	15	9	1.0	17.7	17.7	17.7
HISPANIC [3]								
All pregnancies	5	183	74	110	4.3	157.1	105.0	235.4
Live births	3	119	48	71	2.6	101.8	69.0	151.1
Induced abortions	2	45	17	28	1.3	38.6	24.7	59.5
Fetal losses [2]	1	20	8	12	0.4	16.7	11.3	24.8

[1] Includes races other than White and Black. [2] Spontaneous fetal losses from recognized pregnancies of all gestational periods as reported by women in the 1995 National Survey of Family Growth charted by the National Center for Health Statistics. The rate of pregnancy loss depends on the degree to which losses at very early gestations are detected. [3] Includes all persons of Hispanic origin of any race.

Source: U.S. National Center for Health Statistics, *Trends in Pregnancies and Pregnancy Rates by Outcome: Estimates for the United States, 1976-96*, Series 21, No. 56.

No. 87. Contraceptive Use by Women, 15 to 44 Years of Age: 1995

[60,201 represents 60,201,000. Based on samples of the female population of the United States; see source for details. See Appendix III]

Contraceptive status and method	All women [1]	Age			Race			Marital status		
		15-24 years	25-34 years	35-44 years	Non-Hispanic White	Non-Hispanic Black	His-panic	Never mar-ried	Cur-rently mar-ried	For-merly married
All women (1,000)	**60,201**	**18,002**	**20,758**	**21,440**	**42,522**	**8,210**	**6,702**	**22,679**	**29,673**	**7,849**
PERCENT DISTRIBUTION										
Sterile [2]	29.7	2.6	25.0	57.0	30.2	31.5	28.4	6.9	43.2	45.1
Surgically sterile	27.9	1.8	23.6	54.0	28.5	29.7	26.3	5.7	41.1	42.5
Nonsurgically sterile [3]	1.7	0.7	1.3	2.8	1.6	1.8	2.0	1.1	2.0	2.2
Pregnant, postpartum	4.6	5.9	6.9	1.3	4.3	4.5	6.3	3.1	6.4	1.9
Seeking pregnancy.	4.0	2.1	6.2	3.5	3.7	4.6	4.0	1.5	6.4	2.1
Other nonusers	22.3	44.4	13.3	12.6	21.1	23.1	26.3	46.8	4.7	18.4
Never had intercourse	10.9	30.8	3.4	1.4	10.4	8.9	12.1	28.9	-	-
No intercourse in last month [4] .	6.2	7.0	5.3	6.5	5.7	7.2	8.6	11.5	0.5	12.7
Had intercourse in last month [4] .	5.2	6.6	4.6	4.7	5.0	7.0	5.6	6.4	4.2	5.7
Nonsurgical contraceptors	39.7	45.0	49.1	26.1	41.2	36.1	35.1	41.8	39.7 .	32.4
Pill	17.3	23.1	23.7	6.3	18.8	14.8	13.6	20.4	15.6	14.6
IUD	0.5	0.1	0.6	0.8	0.5	0.5	0.9	0.3	0.7	0.4
Diaphragm.	1.2	0.2	1.2	2.0	1.5	0.5	0.4	0.5	1.8	0.9
Condom	13.1	13.9	15.0	10.7	13.0	12.5	12.1	13.9	13.3	10.1
Periodic abstinence	1.5	0.5	1.8	2.0	1.6	0.7	1.3	0.6	2.3	0.7
Natural family planning	0.2	-	0.3	0.3	0.3	-	0.1	-	0.4	-
Withdrawal.	2.0	1.6	2.3	1.9	2.1	0.9	2.0	1.5	2.3	1.8
Other methods [5]	3.9	5.6	4.2	2.1	3.4	6.2	4.7	4.6	3.3	3.9

- Represents or rounds to zero. [1] Includes other races, not shown separately. [2] Total sterile includes male sterile for unknown reasons. [3] Persons sterile from illness, accident, or congenital conditions. [4] Data refer to no intercourse in the 3 months prior to interview. [5] Includes implants, injectables, morning-after-pill, suppository, Today™ sponge, and less frequently used methods.
Source: U.S. National Center for Health Statistics, special tabulations from the 1995 National Survey of Family Growth.

No. 88. Women 15-44 Years of Age Who Have Ever Had a Live Birth and Use of Maternity Leave for the Most Recent Birth: 1995

Characteristics of the mother	Number (1,000)	Percent distribution				Did not take leave [1]		
		Total	Not em-ployed	Em-ployed	Took mater-nity leave	Not needed	Not offered	Other reasons
All women	**34,958**	**100.0**	**48.0**	**52.0**	**37.3**	**2.3**	**0.9**	**11.6**
AGE AT TIME OF BIRTH								
15-19 years old.	3,436	100.0	71.9	28.1	14.8	0.7	0.1	12.5
20-24 years old.	10,094	100.0	52.8	47.2	29.8	1.3	1.3	14.9
25-29 years old.	11,629	100.0	44.8	55.2	41.1	2.7	0.8	10.5
30-44 years old.	9,799	100.0	38.3	61.7	48.3	3.5	0.8	9.1
YEAR OF CHILD'S BIRTH								
1991-95.	13,999	100.0	43.2	56.8	43.5	2.2	0.9	10.3
1981-90.	15,344	100.0	47.4	52.6	37.2	2.7	0.8	11.8
1980 and before	5,616	100.0	61.5	38.5	22.0	1.6	0.9	14.0
MARITAL STATUS AT TIME OF BIRTH								
Never married.	6,379	100.0	58.4	41.6	26.8	0.8	1.0	13.0
Married	26,439	100.0	44.9	55.1	40.3	2.8	0.8	11.1 ·
Formerly married.	2,140	100.0	54.3	45.7	31.1	0.8	1.3	12.5
BIRTH ORDER OF CHILD								
First	10,901	100.0	35.8	64.2	46.9	1.8	1.1	14.4
Second	13,965	100.0	47.7	52.3	38.1	2.6	1.0	10.7
Third or higher	10,092	100.0	61.5	38.5	25.8	2.5	0.4	9.7
EDUCATION AT INTERVIEW [2]								
No high school diploma or GED [3]	4,961	100.0	69.6	30.4	16.5	0.7	0.4	12.8
High school diploma or GED	14,295	100.0	48.8	51.2	36.2	1.6	1.0	12.4
Some college, no bachelor's degree	7,967	100.0	40.1	59.9	44.4	2.6	1.1	11.8
Bachelor's degree or higher	5,929	100.0	32.8	67.2	52.8	5.6	0.9	7.9
RACE AND HISPANIC ORIGIN								
Hispanic	4,372	100.0	57.8	42.2	28.9	1.1	0.8	11.4
Non-Hispanic White.	24,009	100.0	44.7	55.3	39.6	3.0	0.9	12.0
Non-Hispanic Black	5,149	100.0	53.5	46.5	34.5	0.4	1.1	10.6
Non-Hispanic other	1,428	100.0	53.7	46.3	34.8	1.5	0.6	9.4

[1] The group labeled "not needed" includes women who did not need to take maternity leave: (1) Due to the timing of their birth relative to their job schedule. (2) Due to the nature of their jobs. (3) Because they decided to quit their jobs after delivery. The group labeled "not offered" includes: (1) Women whose employers did not offer (or denied) maternity leave at all. (2) Women whose job benefits did not include maternity leave. The final group labeled "other reasons" includes women who decided to quit their jobs before delivery, who could not afford to take maternity leave for personal or financial reasons, or who continued to work right after delivery. [2] Limited to women 22-44 years of age at time of interview. [3] GED is general equivalency diploma.
Source: U.S. National Center for Health Statistics, *Fertility, Family Planning, and Women's Health: New data from the 1995 National Survey of Family Growth, Vital and Health Statistics*, Series 23, No. 19, 1997.

Vital Statistics 69

No. 89. Live Births—Mothers Who Smoked During Pregnancy: 1998

[Excludes California, Indiana, New York State (but includes New York City), and South Dakota, which did not require reporting of tobacco use during pregnancy]

Smoking measure and race of mother	Total	Age of mother					
		15-19 years	20-24 years	25-29 years	30-34 years	35-39 years	40-54 years
All races [1]	3,186,186	403,166	793,176	877,765	707,569	332,045	64,409
White.	2,492,290	274,055	592,477	709,323	587,178	273,519	51,979
Black	548,653	115,957	171,505	124,996	82,730	40,880	8,582
PERCENT DISTRIBUTION							
All races smoker	100.0	100.0	100.0	100.0	100.0	100.0	100.0
10 cigarettes or less	68.6	77.4	70.2	65.8	64.1	61.9	59.1
11-20 cigarettes	27.5	20.4	26.5	30.0	30.9	32.2	33.4
21 cigarettes or more.	3.8	2.2	3.3	4.4	5.0	5.8	7.2
White smoker	100.0	100.0	100.0	100.0	100.0	100.0	100.0
10 cigarettes or less	66.1	75.5	67.8	63.4	61.3	58.4	55.5
11-20 cigarettes	29.7	22.2	28.7	32.1	33.2	35.1	36.0
21 cigarettes or more.	4.1	2.2	3.4	4.4	6	7	8
Black smoker.	100.0	100.0	100.0	100.0	100.0	100.0	100.0
10 cigarettes or less	83.0	89.8	85.7	81.6	79.1	77.8	73.6
11-20 cigarettes	15	9.4	13	16.2	18.5	19.3	23.2
21 cigarettes or more.	2.0	1	1.5	2.1	2.2	2.8	-

- Represents zero. [1] Includes races other than White and Black.

Source: U.S. National Center for Health Statistics, National Vital Statistics Reports (NVSR) (formerly *Monthly Vital Statistical Report*).

No. 90. Percent Low Birthweight by Smoking Status, Age, and Race of Mother: 1998

[Low birthweight is defined as weight of less than 2,500 grams (5 lb. 8 oz.). Excludes California, Indiana, New York State (but includes New York City), and South Dakota, which did not require reporting of tobacco use during pregnancy]

Smoking status and race of mother	All ages	Under 15 years	Age of mother						
			15-19 years			20-24 years	25-29 years	30-34 years	35-39 years
			Total	15-17 years	18-19 years				
All races [1]	7.8	13.4	9.9	10.8	9.4	7.8	6.9	7.2	8.6
Smoker.	12.0	14.1	11.6	12.2	11.4	10.5	11.0	13.6	16.9
Nonsmoker	7.2	13.3	9.5	10.5	8.9	7.3	6.3	6.5	7.6
White	6.7	11.2	8.3	9.0	7.9	6.6	5.9	6.3	7.5
Smoker.	10.7	13.0	10.9	11.4	10.7	9.8	9.7	11.6	14.3
Nonsmoker	6.0	10.8	7.5	8.4	7.0	5.8	5.4	5.7	6.7
Black.	13.1	15.7	13.8	14.5	13.4	12.1	12.2	13.8	16.0
Smoker.	20.9	(B)	17.2	18.3	16.7	16.2	20.5	25.4	29.1
Nonsmoker	12.3	15.6	13.5	14.2	13.0	11.7	11.3	12.3	13.7

B Base data too small to meet statistical standards of reliability. [1] Includes races other than White and Black.

Source: U.S. National Center for Health Statistics, *National Vital Statistics Reports (NVSR)* (formerly *Monthly Vital Statistical Report*).

No. 91. Live Births to Mothers With Selected Complications of Labor and/or Delivery and Rates by Age of Mother: 1999

[Rates are number of live births with specified complication per 1,000 live births in specified group]

Complication	Complication reported	Age of mother						
		All ages	Under 20 years	20-24 years	25-29 years	30-34 years	35-39 years	40-54 years
All races [1]								
Febrile.	59,904	15.3	18.5	15.6	15.9	14.5	12.3	11.1
Meconium, moderate/heavy	213,698	54.7	59.7	55.2	53.5	52.5	55.1	55.5
Premature rupture of membrane	100,130	25.6	26.7	24.3	25.1	25.8	27.3	30.9
Abruption placenta	21,999	5.6	5.4	5.2	5.3	5.8	7.0	8.6
Placenta previa.	12,492	3.2	1.1	1.7	2.8	4.3	6.5	8.9
Other excessive bleeding	21,930	5.6	5.2	5.2	5.5	5.8	6.4	8.2
Seizures during labor.	1,331	0.3	0.7	0.4	0.3	0.2	0.3	0.3
Precipitous labor	77,848	19.9	14.3	18.9	19.8	22.1	23.6	23.3
Prolonged labor	30,683	7.9	8.4	8.0	7.8	7.8	7.3	7.9
Dysfunctional labor	105,795	27.1	26.5	25.5	27.4	27.7	28.2	31.2
Breech/Malpresentation	152,084	38.9	29.2	31.5	39.1	44.7	50.4	58.1
Cephalopelvic disproportion.	71,604	18.3	17.4	16.7	19.2	19.2	18.6	20.6
Cord Prolapse	7,773	2.0	1.6	1.8	1.9	2.1	2.5	2.8
Anesthetic complication [2]	2,299	0.6	0.4	0.5	0.7	0.7	0.8	0.9
Fetal distress [2]	140,756	39.6	43.7	38.5	38.0	38.6	41.7	49.7

[1] Includes races other than White and Black. [2] Texas does not report this complication.

Source: U.S. National Center for Health Statistics, *Vital Statistics of the United States,* annual; and unpublished data.

No. 92. Abortions—Number, Rate, and Ratio by Race: 1975 to 1997

Year	All races				White				Black and other			
	Women 15-44 years old (1,000)	Abortions			Women 15-44 years old (1,000)	Abortions			Women 15-44 years old (1,000)	Abortions		
		Num-ber (1,000)	Rate per 1,000 women	Ratio per 1,000 live births [1]		Num-ber (1,000)	Rate per 1,000 women	Ratio per 1,000 live births [1]		Num-ber (1,000)	Rate per 1,000 women	Ratio per 1,000 live births [1]
1975 ..	47,606	1,034	21.7	331	40,857	701	17.2	276	6,749	333	49.3	565
1979 ..	52,016	1,498	28.8	420	44,266	1,062	24.0	373	7,750	435	56.2	625
1980 ..	53,048	1,554	29.3	428	44,942	1,094	24.3	376	8,106	460	56.5	642
1981 ..	53,901	1,577	29.3	430	45,494	1,108	24.3	377	8,407	470	55.9	645
1982 [2] .	54,679	1,574	28.8	428	46,049	1,095	23.8	373	8,630	479	55.5	646
1983 [2] .	55,340	1,575	28.5	436	46,506	1,084	23.3	376	8,834	491	55.5	670
1984 ..	56,061	1,577	28.1	423	47,023	1,087	23.1	366	9,038	491	54.3	646
1985 [2] .	56,754	1,589	28.0	422	47,512	1,076	22.6	360	9,242	513	55.5	659
1986 [2] .	57,483	1,574	27.4	416	48,010	1,045	21.8	350	9,473	529	55.9	661
1987 ..	57,964	1,559	27.1	405	48,288	1,017	21.1	338	9,676	542	56.0	648
1988 ..	58,192	1,591	27.3	401	48,325	1,026	21.2	333	9,867	565	57.3	638
1989 [2] .	58,365	1,567	26.8	380	48,104	1,006	20.9	309	10,261	561	54.7	650
1990 [2] .	58,700	1,609	27.4	389	48,224	1,039	21.5	318	10,476	570	54.4	655
1991 ..	59,080	1,557	26.3	379	48,406	982	20.3	303	10,674	574	53.8	661
1992 [2] .	59,020	1,529	25.9	380	48,161	943	19.6	298	10859	585	53.9	681
1993 [2] .	59,143	1,500	25.4	378	48,137	911	18.9	291	11,007	589	53.5	700
1994 [2] .	59,284	1,431	24.1	364	48,121	861	17.9	277	11,163	570	51.1	699
1995 ..	59,442	1,364	22.9	351	48,140	820	17.0	265	11,302	544	48.1	686
1996 ..	59,606	1,366	22.9	351	48,120	800	16.6	259	11,486	566	49.2	701
1997 ..	59,688	1,328	22.2	340	48,081	773	16.1	250	11,607	555	47.8	680

[1] Live births are those which occurred from July 1 of year shown through June 30 of the following year (to match time of conception with abortions). Births are classified by race of child 1972-1988, and by race of mother after 1988.   [2] Total numbers of abortions in 1983 and 1986 have been estimated by interpolation; 1989, 1990, 1993, and 1994 have been estimated using trends in CDC data.

No. 93. Abortions by Selected Characteristics: 1990 to 1997

[Number of abortions from surveys conducted by source; characteristics from the U.S. Centers for Disease Control's (CDC) annual abortion surveillance summaries, with adjustments for changes in states reporting data to the CDC each year. Total number of abortions in 1990 have been estimated using trends in CDC data]

Characteristic	Number (1,000)			Percent distribution			Abortion ratio [1]		
	1990	1995	1997	1990	1995	1997	1990	1995	1997
Total abortions	1,609	1,364	1,328	100	100	100	280	260	254
Age of woman:									
Less than 15 years old	13	11	10	1	1	1	515	480	496
15 to 19 years old	351	264	254	22	19	19	403	348	345
20 to 24 years old	532	442	420	33	32	32	328	317	306
25 to 29 years old	360	308	313	22	23	24	224	225	225
30 to 34 years old	216	196	189	13	14	14	196	179	175
35 to 39 years old	108	110	109	7	8	8	249	220	207
40 years old and over.	29	32	34	2	2	3	354	310	290
Race of woman:									
White.	1,039	820	773	65	60	58	241	210	200
Black and other	570	544	555	35	40	42	396	409	405
Marital status of woman: [2]									
Married	341	269	253	21	20	19	104	93	87
Unmarried	1,268	1,095	1,074	79	80	81	516	466	459
Number of prior live births:									
None.	780	614	562	49	45	42	316	277	262
One.	396	359	367	25	26	28	230	223	224
Two.	280	248	251	17	18	19	292	285	282
Three	102	95	97	6	7	7	279	284	282
Four or more.	50	48	50	3	4	4	223	228	236
Number of prior induced abortions:									
None.	891	721	680	55	53	51	(NA)	(NA)	(NA)
One.	443	383	376	28	28	28	(NA)	(NA)	(NA)
Two or more	275	260	271	17	19	20	(NA)	(NA)	(NA)
Weeks of gestation: [3]									
Less than 9 weeks	825	728	732	51	53	55	(NA)	(NA)	(NA)
9 to 10 weeks	416	317	292	26	23	22	(NA)	(NA)	(NA)
11 to 12 weeks	195	153	146	12	11	11	(NA)	(NA)	(NA)
13 weeks or more	173	166	157	11	12	12	(NA)	(NA)	(NA)

NA Not available.   [1] Number of abortions per 1,000 abortions and live births. Live births are those which occurred from July 1 of year shown through June 30 of the following year (to match time of conception with abortions).   [2] Separated women included with unmarried.   [3] Data not exactly comparable with prior years because of a change in the method of calculation.

Source of Tables 92 and 93: 1975-1988, S.K. Henshaw and J. Van Vort, eds., *Abortion Factbook, 1992 Edition: Readings, Trends, and State and Local Data to 1988,* The Alan Guttmacher Institute, New York, NY, 1992 (copyright); S.K. Henshaw and J. Van Vort, *Abortion Services in the United States, 1991 and 1992; Family Perspectives, 26:100, 1994;* and unpublished data.

No. 94. Abortions—Number and Rate by State: 1992 and 1996

[Number of abortions from surveys of hospitals, clinics, and physicians identified as providers of abortion services conducted by The Alan Guttmacher Institute. Abortion rates are computed per 1,000 women 15 to 44 years of age on July 1 of specified year]

State	Number (1,000) 1992	Number (1,000) 1996	Rate [1] 1992	Rate [1] 1996	State	Number (1,000) 1992	Number (1,000) 1996	Rate [1] 1992	Rate [1] 1996
U.S.	1,529	1,366	25.9	22.9	MO	14	11	11.6	9.1
AL	17	15	18.2	15.6	MT	3	3	18.2	15.6
AK	2	2	16.5	14.6	NE	6	4	15.7	12.3
AZ	21	19	24.1	19.8	NV	18	15	44.2	44.6
AR	7	6	13.5	11.4	NH	4	3	14.6	12.7
CA	304	238	42.1	33.0					
					NJ	55	63	31.0	35.8
CO	20	18	23.6	20.9	NM	6	5	17.7	14.4
CT	20	16	26.2	22.5	NY	195	168	46.2	41.1
DE	6	4	35.2	24.1	NC	36	34	22.4	20.2
DC	21	21	138.4	154.5	ND	1	1	10.7	9.4
FL	85	94	30.0	32.0					
					OH	50	43	19.5	17.0
GA	40	37	24.0	21.1	OK	9	8	12.5	11.8
HI	12	7	46.0	27.3	OR	16	15	23.9	21.6
ID	2	2	7.2	6.1	PA	50	40	18.6	15.2
IL	68	69	25.4	26.1	RI	7	5	30.0	24.4
IN	16	15	12.0	11.2					
					SC	12	10	14.2	11.6
IA	7	6	11.4	9.4	SD	1	1	6.8	6.5
KS	13	11	22.4	18.9	TN	19	18	16.2	14.8
KY	10	8	11.4	9.6	TX	97	91	23.1	20.7
LA	14	15	13.4	14.7	UT	4	4	9.3	7.8
ME	4	3	14.7	9.7					
					VT	3	2	21.2	17.1
MD	31	31	26.4	26.3	VA	35	30	22.7	18.9
MA	41	41	28.4	29.3	WA	33	26	27.7	20.9
MI	56	49	25.2	22.3	WV	3	3	7.7	6.6
MN	16	15	15.6	13.9	WI	15	14	13.6	12.3
MS	8	4	12.4	7.2	WY	-	-	4.3	2.7

- Represents or rounds to zero. [1] Rate per 1,000 women, 15 to 44 years old.

Source: S.K. Henshaw and J. Van Vort, *Abortion Services in the United States, 1991 and 1992, Family Planning Perspectives,* 26:100, 1994; and unpublished data.

No. 95. Average Lifetime in Years by Race by State: 1989-91

State	Total	White	Black	State	Total	White	Black
U.S.	75.37	76.13	69.16	MT	76.23	76.72	(S)
AL	73.64	75.01	69.23	NE	76.92	77.21	(S)
AZ	76.10	76.42	70.84	NV	74.18	74.44	(S)
AR	74.33	75.20	68.93	NH	76.72	76.68	(S)
CA	75.86	75.92	69.65				
				NJ	75.42	76.46	68.47
CO	76.96	77.06	72.41	NM	75.74	76.08	(S)
CT	76.91	77.44	70.84	NY	74.68	75.61	69.33
DE	74.76	75.76	69.26	NC	74.48	75.89	69.38
DC	67.99	76.09	64.44	ND	77.62	77.99	(S)
FL	75.84	76.82	68.77				
				OH	75.32	75.93	70.15
GA	73.61	75.24	68.79	OK	75.10	75.21	70.85
HI	78.21	77.92	(S)	OR	76.44	76.51	(S)
ID	76.88	76.89	(S)	PA	75.38	76.15	68.27
IL	74.90	76.16	67.46	RI	76.54	76.80	(S)
IN	75.39	75.82	69.80				
				SC	73.51	75.33	68.82
IA	77.29	77.38	(S)	SD	76.91	77.91	(S)
KS	76.76	77.06	71.22	TN	74.32	75.27	68.97
KY	74.37	74.65	70.16	TX	75.14	75.75	69.79
LA	73.05	74.87	68.62	UT	77.70	77.77	(S)
ME	76.35	76.35	(S)				
				VT	76.54	76.50	(S)
MD	74.79	76.30	69.69	VA	75.22	76.34	70.05
MA	76.72	76.90	72.45	WA	76.82	76.92	71.34
MI	75.04	76.18	68.49	WV	74.26	74.37	69.75
MN	77.76	77.97	(S)	WI	76.87	77.18	70.96
MS	73.03	74.78	69.41	WY	76.21	76.34	(S)
MO	75.25	76.02	68.81				

S Does not meet standards of reliability and precision.

Source: U.S. National Center for Health Statistics, *for 1989-91,* Volume II.

No. 96. Expectation of Life at Birth, 1970 to 1999, and Projections, 2000 to 2010

[**In years.** Excludes deaths of nonresidents of the United States]

Year	Total			White			Black and other			Black		
	Total	Male	Female	Total	Male	Female	Total	Male	Female	Total	Male	Female
1970.	70.8	67.1	74.7	71.7	68.0	75.6	65.3	61.3	69.4	64.1	60.0	68.3
1975.	72.6	68.8	76.6	73.4	69.5	77.3	68.0	63.7	72.4	66.8	62.4	71.3
1980.	73.7	70.0	77.4	74.4	70.7	78.1	69.5	65.3	73.6	68.1	63.8	72.5
1982.	74.5	70.8	78.1	75.1	71.5	78.7	70.9	66.8	74.9	69.4	65.1	73.6
1983.	74.6	71.0	78.1	75.2	71.6	78.7	70.9	67.0	74.7	69.4	65.2	73.5
1984.	74.7	71.1	78.2	75.3	71.8	78.7	71.1	67.2	74.9	69.5	65.3	73.6
1985.	74.7	71.1	78.2	75.3	71.8	78.7	71.0	67.0	74.8	69.3	65.0	73.4
1986.	74.7	71.2	78.2	75.4	71.9	78.8	70.9	66.8	74.9	69.1	64.8	73.4
1987.	74.9	71.4	78.3	75.6	72.1	78.9	71.0	66.9	75.0	69.1	64.7	73.4
1988.	74.9	71.4	78.3	75.6	72.2	78.9	70.8	66.7	74.8	68.9	64.4	73.2
1989.	75.1	71.7	78.5	75.9	72.5	79.2	70.9	66.7	74.9	68.8	64.3	73.3
1990.	75.4	71.8	78.8	76.1	72.7	79.4	71.2	67.0	75.2	69.1	64.5	73.6
1991.	75.5	72.0	78.9	76.3	72.9	79.6	71.5	67.3	75.5	69.3	64.6	73.8
1992.	75.8	72.3	79.1	76.5	73.2	79.8	71.8	67.7	75.7	69.6	65.0	73.9
1993.	75.5	72.2	78.8	76.3	73.1	79.5	71.5	67.3	75.5	69.2	64.6	73.7
1994.	75.7	72.3	79.0	76.4	73.2	79.6	71.7	67.5	75.8	69.6	64.9	74.1
1995.	75.8	72.5	78.9	76.5	73.4	79.6	71.9	67.9	75.7	69.6	65.2	73.9
1996.	76.1	73.0	79.0	76.8	73.8	79.6	72.6	68.9	76.1	70.3	66.1	74.2
1997 `.	76.5	73.6	79.4	77.1	74.3	79.9	(NA)	(NA)	(NA)	71.1	67.2	74.7
1998 [1].	76.7	73.8	79.5	77.3	74.5	80.0	(NA)	(NA)	(NA)	71.3	67.6	74.8
1999 [2].	77.0	74.1	79.7	77.5	74.7	80.2	(NA)	(NA)	(NA)	72.2	68.7	75.4
Projections:												
2000	77.1	74.2	79.9	77.7	74.8	80.4	(NA)	(NA)	(NA)	72.4	68.9	75.6
2005	77.8	74.9	80.7	78.3	75.4	81.1	(NA)	(NA)	(NA)	73.5	69.9	76.8
2010	78.5	75.6	81.4	79.0	76.1	81.8	(NA)	(NA)	(NA)	74.5	70.9	77.8

NA Not available.   [1] The 1998 life table values are based upon an 85 percent sample of deaths.   [2] Based on middle mortality assumptions; for details, see source. Source: U.S. Census Bureau, Population Division Working Paper No. 38.

Source: Except as noted, U.S. National Center for Health Statistics, *Vital Statistics of the United States*, annual, and *National Vital Statistics Reports (NVSR)* (formerly *Monthly Vital Statistics Reports*).

No. 97. Selected Life Table Values: 1979 to 1998

Age and sex	Total [1]			White			Black		
	1979-1981	1990	1998	1979-1981	1990	1998	1979-1981	1990	1998
AVERAGE EXPECTATION OF LIFE IN YEARS									
At birth: Male.	70.1	71.8	73.8	70.8	72.7	74.5	64.1	64.5	67.6
Female	77.6	78.8	79.5	78.2	79.4	80.0	72.9	73.6	74.8
Age 20: Male.	51.9	53.3	55.0	52.5	54.0	55.5	46.4	46.7	49.5
Female	59.0	59.8	60.3	59.4	60.3	60.8	54.9	55.3	56.2
Age 40: Male.	33.6	35.1	36.4	34.0	35.6	36.8	29.5	30.1	31.9
Female	39.8	40.6	41.1	40.2	41.0	41.4	36.3	36.8	37.5
Age 50: Male.	25.0	26.4	27.6	25.3	26.7	27.9	22.0	22.5	23.9
Female	30.7	31.3	31.8	31.0	31.6	32.0	27.8	28.2	28.8
Age 65: Male.	14.2	15.1	16.0	14.3	15.2	16.1	13.3	13.2	14.3
Female	18.4	18.9	19.2	18.6	19.1	19.3	17.1	17.2	17.4
EXPECTED DEATHS PER 1,000 ALIVE AT SPECIFIED AGE [2]									
At birth: Male.	13.9	10.3	(NA)	12.3	8.6	(NA)	23.0	19.7	(NA)
Female	11.2	8.2	(NA)	9.7	6.6	(NA)	19.3	16.3	(NA)
Age 20: Male.	1.8	1.6	(NA)	1.8	1.4	(NA)	2.2	2.7	(NA)
Female	0.6	0.5	(NA)	0.6	0.5	(NA)	0.7	0.7	(NA)
Age 40: Male.	3.0	3.1	(NA)	2.6	2.7	(NA)	6.9	7.1	(NA)
Female	1.6	1.4	(NA)	1.4	1.2	(NA)	3.2	3.1	(NA)
Age 50: Male.	7.8	6.2	(NA)	7.1	5.6	(NA)	14.9	12.8	(NA)
Female	4.2	3.5	(NA)	3.8	3.2	(NA)	7.7	6.6	(NA)
Age 65: Male.	28.2	12.9	(NA)	27.4	23.0	(NA)	38.5	36.8	(NA)
Female	14.3	13.5	(NA)	13.6	12.8	(NA)	21.6	21.4	(NA)
NUMBER SURVIVING TO SPECIFIED AGE PER 1,000 BORN ALIVE									
Age 20: Male.	973	979	(NA)	975	981	(NA)	961	963	(NA)
Female	982	986	(NA)	984	988	(NA)	972	976	(NA)
Age 40: Male.	933	938	(NA)	940	946	(NA)	885	880	(NA)
Female	965	971	(NA)	969	975	(NA)	941	944	(NA)
Age 50: Male.	890	899	(NA)	901	912	(NA)	801	801	(NA)
Female	941	950	(NA)	947	957	(NA)	896	904	(NA)
Age 65: Male.	706	741	(NA)	724	760	(NA)	551	571	(NA)
Female	835	851	(NA)	848	864	(NA)	733	751	(NA)

NA Not available.   [1] Includes other races not shown separately.   [2] See footnote 1, Table 98.

Source: U.S. National Center for Health Statistics, *U.S. Life Tables and Actuarial Tables, 1959-61, 1969-71, and 1979-81; Vital Statistics of the United States*, annual; and unpublished data.

Vital Statistics 73

No. 98. Expectation of Life and Expected Deaths by Race, Sex, and Age: 1998

Age (years)	Expectation of life in years					Expected deaths per 1,000 alive at specified age [1]				
		White		Black			White		Black	
	Total	Male	Female	Male	Female	Total	Male	Female	Male	Female
At birth	76.7	74.5	80.0	67.6	74.8	7.21	6.48	5.42	15.79	12.85
1	76.3	74.0	79.4	67.7	74.8	0.55	0.49	0.44	1.16	0.90
2	75.3	73.0	78.5	66.8	73.8	0.36	0.36	0.28	0.67	0.52
3	74.3	72.1	77.5	65.8	72.9	0.26	0.25	0.21	0.52	0.44
4	73.4	71.1	76.5	64.9	71.9	0.21	0.21	0.17	0.42	0.29
5	72.4	70.1	75.5	63.9	70.9	0.20	0.20	0.15	0.39	0.31
6	71.4	69.1	74.5	62.9	69.9	0.19	0.19	0.14	0.37	0.27
7	70.4	68.1	73.5	61.9	69.0	0.18	0.18	0.13	0.34	0.24
8	69.4	67.1	72.5	60.9	68.0	0.17	0.17	0.13	0.30	0.22
9	68.4	66.2	71.6	60.0	67.0	0.15	0.15	0.12	0.25	0.20
10	67.4	65.2	70.6	59.0	66.0	0.13	0.13	0.11	0.21	0.19
11	66.4	64.2	69.6	58.0	65.0	0.14	0.13	0.12	0.20	0.18
12	65.5	63.2	68.6	57.0	64.0	0.18	0.19	0.14	0.29	0.19
13	64.5	62.2	67.6	56.0	63.0	0.27	0.31	0.19	0.48	0.23
14	63.5	61.2	66.6	55.0	62.1	0.39	0.47	0.26	0.74	0.27
15	62.5	60.2	65.6	54.1	61.1	0.52	0.65	0.33	1.02	0.32
16	61.5	59.3	64.6	53.1	60.1	0.64	0.81	0.40	1.28	0.38
17	60.6	58.3	63.7	52.2	59.1	0.73	0.94	0.44	1.52	0.43
18	59.6	57.4	62.7	51.3	58.1	0.80	1.04	0.45	1.74	0.49
19	58.7	56.4	61.7	50.4	57.2	0.85	1.11	0.44	1.93	0.54
20	57.7	55.5	60.8	49.5	56.2	0.89	1.18	0.42	2.16	0.61
21	56.8	54.6	59.8	48.6	55.2	0.94	1.26	0.41	2.40	0.69
22	55.8	53.6	58.8	47.7	54.3	0.97	1.30	0.40	2.57	0.76
23	54.9	52.7	57.8	46.8	53.3	0.98	1.30	0.41	2.65	0.82
24	53.9	51.8	56.8	45.9	52.4	0.97	1.27	0.42	2.65	0.86
25	53.0	50.8	55.9	45.1	51.4	0.96	1.23	0.44	2.62	0.91
26	52.0	49.9	54.9	44.2	50.5	0.95	1.20	0.46	2.61	0.97
27	51.1	49.0	53.9	43.3	49.5	0.96	1.19	0.48	2.61	1.04
28	50.1	48.0	52.9	42.4	48.6	0.98	1.21	0.51	2.64	1.11
29	49.2	47.1	52.0	41.5	47.6	1.03	1.25	0.54	2.71	1.20
30	48.2	46.1	51.0	40.6	46.7	1.08	1.31	0.57	2.78	1.30
31	47.3	45.2	50.0	39.7	45.7	1.13	1.37	0.61	2.86	1.40
32	46.3	44.3	49.1	38.8	44.8	1.19	1.44	0.66	2.96	1.51
33	45.4	43.3	48.1	38.0	43.9	1.27	1.52	0.72	3.10	1.65
34	44.4	42.4	47.1	37.1	42.9	1.35	1.60	0.79	3.26	1.80
35	43.5	41.5	46.2	36.2	42.0	1.44	1.69	0.86	3.43	1.96
36	42.6	40.5	45.2	35.3	41.1	1.53	1.79	0.93	3.62	2.12
37	41.6	39.6	44.2	34.4	40.2	1.63	1.90	1.00	3.85	2.29
38	40.7	38.7	43.3	33.6	39.3	1.74	2.03	1.07	4.15	2.48
39	39.8	37.7	42.3	32.7	38.4	1.88	2.19	1.15	4.50	2.70
40	38.8	36.8	41.4	31.9	37.5	2.03	2.36	1.24	4.88	2.93
41	37.9	35.9	40.4	31.0	36.6	2.18	2.54	1.34	5.29	3.16
42	37.0	35.0	39.5	30.2	35.7	2.35	2.73	1.44	5.76	3.42
43	36.1	34.1	38.5	29.4	34.8	2.53	2.94	1.55	6.32	3.69
44	35.2	33.2	37.6	28.5	33.9	2.73	3.17	1.67	6.96	3.97
45	34.3	32.3	36.7	27.7	33.1	2.95	3.42	1.80	7.71	4.30
46	33.4	31.4	35.7	26.9	32.2	3.20	3.71	1.95	8.52	4.65
47	32.5	30.5	34.8	26.2	31.4	3.47	4.01	2.13	9.31	4.99
48	31.6	29.6	33.9	25.4	30.5	3.75	4.33	2.35	10.01	5.32
49	30.7	28.8	32.9	24.7	29.7	4.04	4.66	2.60	10.65	5.65
50	29.8	27.9	32.0	23.9	28.8	4.36	5.03	2.88	11.34	6.01
51	29.0	27.0	31.1	23.2	28.0	4.73	5.44	3.19	12.16	6.43
52	28.1	26.2	30.2	22.5	27.2	5.13	5.90	3.51	13.06	6.93
53	27.2	25.3	29.3	21.8	26.4	5.58	6.43	3.85	14.02	7.51
54	26.4	24.5	28.4	21.1	25.6	6.10	7.04	4.23	15.04	8.15
55	25.5	23.7	27.6	20.4	24.8	6.69	7.76	4.66	16.08	8.84
56	24.7	22.9	26.7	19.7	24.0	7.36	8.58	5.16	17.19	9.59
57	23.9	22.0	25.8	19.0	23.2	8.09	9.47	5.71	18.49	10.39
58	23.1	21.3	25.0	18.4	22.5	8.88	10.42	6.30	20.06	11.26
59	22.3	20.5	24.1	17.8	21.7	9.73	11.44	6.93	21.85	12.20
60	21.5	19.7	23.3	17.1	21.0	10.68	12.56	7.65	23.87	13.24
61	20.7	18.9	22.5	16.5	20.2	11.74	13.84	8.48	25.92	14.35
62	20.0	18.2	21.6	16.0	19.5	12.88	15.26	9.36	27.72	15.44
63	19.2	17.5	20.8	15.4	18.8	14.07	16.82	10.28	29.04	16.45
64	18.5	16.8	20.1	14.9	18.1	15.29	18.48	11.23	29.98	17.41
65	17.8	16.1	19.3	14.3	17.4	16.51	20.16	12.19	30.64	18.28
70	14.3	12.8	15.6	11.5	14.1	25.51	31.60	19.41	43.07	28.47
75	11.3	10.0	12.2	9.2	11.3	37.99	47.05	30.07	61.44	41.10
80	8.6	7.5	9.1	7.1	8.7	59.23	73.21	49.50	86.29	60.15

[1] Based on the proportion of the cohort who are alive at the beginning of an indicated age interval who will die before reaching the end of that interval. For example, out of every 1,000 people alive and exactly 50 years old at the beginning of the period, between 4 and 5 (4.44) will die before reaching their 51st birthdays.

Source: U.S. National Center for Health Statistics, *Vital Statistics of the United States*, annual; and *National Vital Statistics Report*, Vol. 47, No. 28, and unpublished data.

No. 99. Deaths and Death Rates by Sex and Race: 1980 to 1998

[1,990 represents 1,990,000. Rates are per 1,000 population for specified groups. Excludes deaths of nonresidents of the United States and fetal deaths. For explanation of age-adjustment, see text, this section. The standard population for this table is the total population of the United States enumerated in 1940. See Appendix III]

Sex and race	1980	1985	1989	1990	1991	1992	1993	1994	1995	1996	1997	1998
Deaths [1] (1,000) . . .	**1,990**	**2,086**	**2,150**	**2,148**	**2,170**	**2,176**	**2,269**	**2,279**	**2,312**	**2,315**	**2,314**	**2,338**
Male [1] (1,000)	1,075	1,098	1,114	1,113	1,122	1,122	1,162	1,163	1,173	1,164	1,154	1,157
Female [1] (1,000)	915	989	1,036	1,035	1,048	1,053	1,107	1,116	1,139	1,151	1,160	1,180
White (1,000)	1,739	1,819	1,854	1,853	1,869	1,874	1,951	1,960	1,987	1,993	1,996	2,016
Male (1,000)	934	950	951	951	956	957	988	989	997	992	987	990
Female (1,000)	805	869	903	902	912	917	963	971	990	1,001	1,010	1,026
Black (1,000)	233	244	268	266	270	269	282	282	286	282	277	278
Male (1,000)	130	134	146	145	147	147	154	153	154	149	144	143
Female (1,000)	103	111	121	120	122	123	129	129	132	133	132	135
Death rates [1]	**8.8**	**8.8**	**8.7**	**8.6**	**8.6**	**8.5**	**8.8**	**8.8**	**8.8**	**8.7**	**8.6**	**8.6**
Male [1]	9.8	9.5	9.3	9.2	9.1	9.0	9.2	9.2	9.1	9.0	8.8	8.8
Female [1]	7.9	8.1	8.2	8.1	8.1	8.1	8.4	8.4	8.5	8.5	8.5	8.5
White	8.9	9.0	8.9	8.9	8.9	8.8	9.1	9.1	9.1	9.1	9.0	9.0
Male	9.8	9.6	9.4	9.3	9.3	9.2	9.4	9.3	9.3	9.2	9.1	9.0
Female	8.1	8.4	8.5	8.5	8.5	8.4	8.8	8.8	8.9	9.0	9.0	9.0
Black	8.8	8.5	8.9	8.8	8.6	8.5	8.8	8.6	8.6	8.4	8.1	8.1
Male	10.3	9.9	10.3	10.1	10.0	9.8	10.1	9.9	9.8	9.4	8.9	8.8
Female	7.3	7.3	7.6	7.5	7.4	7.4	7.6	7.5	7.6	7.5	7.4	7.5
Age-adjusted [1]	**5.9**	**5.5**	**5.3**	**5.2**	**5.1**	**5.0**	**5.1**	**5.1**	**5.0**	**4.9**	**4.8**	**4.7**
Male [1]	7.8	7.2	6.9	6.8	6.7	6.6	6.6	6.5	6.5	6.2	6.0	5.9
Female [1]	4.3	4.1	4.0	3.9	3.9	3.8	3.9	3.9	3.9	3.8	3.8	3.7
White	5.6	5.2	5.0	4.9	4.9	4.8	4.9	4.8	4.8	4.7	4.6	4.5
Male	7.5	6.9	6.5	6.4	6.3	6.2	6.3	6.2	6.1	5.9	5.7	5.6
Female	4.1	3.9	3.8	3.7	3.7	3.6	3.7	3.6	3.6	3.6	3.6	3.6
Black	8.4	7.9	8.1	7.9	7.8	7.7	7.9	7.7	7.7	7.4	7.1	6.9
Male	11.1	10.5	10.8	10.6	10.5	10.3	10.5	10.3	10.2	9.7	9.1	8.8
Female	6.3	5.9	5.9	5.8	5.8	5.7	5.8	5.7	5.7	5.6	5.5	5.4

[1] Includes other races, not shown separately.
Source: U.S. National Center for Health Statistics, *Vital Statistics of the United States*, annual; and *National Vital Statistics Reports (NVSR)* (formerly *Monthly Vital Statistics Report*).

No. 100. Death Rates by Age, Sex, and Race: 1970 to 1998

[Number of deaths per 100,000 population in specified group. See headnote, Table 99]

Sex, year, and race	All ages [1]	Under 1 yr. old	1-4 yr. old	5-14 yr. old	15-24 yr. old	25-34 yr. old	35-44 yr. old	45-54 yr. old	55-64 yr. old	65-74 yr. old	75-84 yr. old	85 yr. old and over
MALE [2]												
1970	1,090	2,410	93	51	189	215	403	959	2,283	4,874	10,010	17,822
1980	977	1,429	73	37	172	196	299	767	1,815	4,105	8,817	18,801
1990	918	1,083	52	29	147	204	310	610	1,553	3,492	7,889	18,057
1995	914	844	45	27	141	205	333	599	1,417	3,285	7,377	17,979
1997	881	813	40	24	124	160	266	551	1,337	3,191	7,116	17,462
1998	876	818	38	23	119	152	259	543	1,297	3,144	7,019	16,763
White:												
1980	983	1,230	66	35	167	171	257	699	1,729	4,036	8,830	19,097
1990	931	896	46	26	131	176	268	549	1,467	3,398	7,845	18,268
1995	932	718	39	25	122	178	288	535	1,331	3,199	7,321	18,153
1997	906	678	35	22	109	140	235	496	1,252	3,123	7,086	17,767
1998	905	682	32	21	106	133	231	486	1,216	3,082	7,012	17,122
Black:												
1980	1,034	2,587	111	47	209	407	690	1,480	2,873	5,131	9,232	16,099
1990	1,008	2,112	86	41	252	431	700	1,261	2,618	4,946	9,130	16,955
1995	981	1,591	78	40	249	417	721	1,273	2,438	4,611	8,779	16,729
1997	894	1,672	67	35	216	309	524	1,114	2,320	4,298	8,297	16,084
1998	868	1,693	69	35	194	277	475	1,074	2,238	4,136	8,259	15,442
FEMALE [2]												
1970	808	1,864	75	32	68	102	231	517	1,099	2,580	6,678	15,518
1980	785	1,142	55	24	58	76	159	413	934	2,145	5,440	14,747
1990	812	856	41	19	49	74	138	343	879	1,991	4,883	14,274
1995	847	690	36	18	48	78	150	328	841	1,986	4,883	14,492
1997	849	661	32	17	46	70	141	316	815	1,959	4,821	14,492
1998	854	681	31	16	44	68	142	310	788	1,968	4,832	14,428
White:												
1970	813	1,615	66	30	62	84	193	463	1,015	2,471	6,699	15,980
1980	806	963	49	23	56	65	138	373	876	2,067	5,402	14,980
1990	847	690	36	18	46	62	117	309	823	1,924	4,839	14,401
1995	891	572	31	17	44	64	126	294	788	1,925	4,831	14,639
1997	898	546	28	16	44	60	121	285	766	1,901	4,786	14,681
1998	907	571	27	15	41	58	121	277	740	1,918	4,816	14,705
Black:												
1970	829	3,369	129	44	112	231	533	1,044	1,986	3,861	6,692	10,707
1980	733	2,124	84	31	71	150	324	768	1,561	3,057	6,212	12,367
1990	748	1,736	68	28	69	160	299	639	1,453	2,866	5,688	13,310
1995	759	1,342	63	27	70	167	328	619	1,350	2,824	5,840	13,472
1997	743	1,384	51	27	62	135	287	590	1,307	2,740	5,669	13,702
1998	738	1,363	54	23	57	128	280	574	1,262	2,702	5,748	13,450

[1] Includes unknown age.   [2] Includes other races not shown separately.
Source: U.S. National Center for Health Statistics, *Vital Statistics of the United States*, annual; *National Vital Statistics Reports (NVSR)* (formerly *Monthly Vital Statistics Report*); and unpublished data.

Vital Statistics   75

No. 101. Deaths and Death Rates by State: 1990 to 1998

[By state of residence. Excludes deaths of nonresidents of the United States, except as noted. Caution should be used in comparing death rates by state; rates are affected by the population composition of the area. See also Appendix III]

State	Number of deaths (1,000)							Rate per 1,000 population [1]						
	1990	1993	1994	1995	1996	1997	1998	1990	1993	1994	1995	1996	1997	1998
United States..	2,148	2,269	2,279	2,312	2,315	2,314	2,337	8.6	8.8	8.8	8.8	8.7	8.6	8.6
Alabama.........	39	41	42	42	43	43	44	9.7	9.9	9.9	10.0	10.0	10.0	10.1
Alaska..........	2	2	2	3	3	3	3	4.0	3.8	4.0	4.2	4.3	4.2	4.2
Arizona.........	29	33	34	35	37	37	38	7.9	8.2	8.4	8.4	8.3	8.1	8.2
Arkansas	25	27	26	27	27	28	28	10.5	10.9	10.7	10.8	10.6	11.0	10.8
California	214	222	224	224	223	225	227	7.2	7.0	7.1	7.1	7.0	7.0	6.9
Colorado........	22	24	24	25	26	26	27	6.6	6.7	6.6	6.7	6.7	6.6	6.7
Connecticut......	28	29	29	29	30	29	30	8.4	8.9	8.9	9.0	9.0	9.0	9.1
Delaware	6	6	6	6	7	7	7	8.7	8.7	9.0	8.8	9.0	8.9	8.8
Dist. of Columbia ...	7	7	7	7	7	6	6	12.0	11.6	12.6	12.4	12.2	11.6	11.6
Florida	134	147	149	153	153	155	158	10.4	10.7	10.7	10.8	10.7	10.5	10.1
Georgia	52	56	57	58	59	59	60	8.0	8.1	8.0	8.1	8.0	7.9	7.9
Hawaii..........	7	7	7	8	8	8	8	6.1	6.2	6.2	6.4	6.7	6.7	6.8
Idaho..........	7	8	8	9	9	9	9	7.4	7.6	7.5	7.3	7.3	7.4	7.5
Illinois	103	107	107	108	106	103	104	9.0	9.2	9.1	9.2	9.0	8.7	8.7
Indiana.........	50	52	52	53	53	53	53	8.9	9.1	9.1	9.2	9.1	9.1	9.1
Iowa...........	27	28	28	28	28	28	28	9.7	9.9	9.8	9.9	9.8	9.7	9.9
Kansas.........	22	24	23	24	24	24	24	9.0	9.2	9.1	9.3	9.3	9.2	9.2
Kentucky........	35	37	37	37	37	38	38	9.5	9.7	9.7	9.6	9.6	9.7	9.6
Louisiana	38	40	39	40	40	40	40	8.9	9.3	9.0	9.1	9.1	9.2	9.2
Maine..........	11	12	12	12	11	12	12	9.0	9.3	9.4	9.5	9.4	9.7	9.8
Maryland	38	40	41	42	42	42	42	8.0	8.7	8.2	8.3	8.3	8.2	8.2
Massachusetts.....	53	56	55	55	55	55	55	8.8	9.4	9.1	9.1	9.1	8.9	9.0
Michigan........	79	83	83	84	84	83	85	8.5	8.7	8.7	8.8	8.7	8.5	8.7
Minnesota.......	35	36	37	38	37	37	37	7.9	8.0	8.0	8.1	8.0	7.9	7.9
Mississippi	25	26	27	27	27	28	28	9.8	10.1	10.0	10.0	9.8	10.1	10.1
Missouri	50	54	54	54	54	54	55	9.8	10.8	10.2	10.2	10.1	10.1	10.1
Montana........	7	7	7	8	8	8	8	8.6	8.9	8.6	8.8	8.8	8.8	9.1
Nebraska.......	15	15	15	15	15	15	15	9.4	9.6	9.3	9.3	9.4	9.2	9.1
Nevada	9	11	12	13	13	13	14	7.8	7.8	8.2	8.2	8.2	8.0	8.3
New Hampshire....	8	9	9	9	9	9	9	7.7	7.9	7.8	8.0	8.1	8.1	8.0
New Jersey.......	70	73	72	74	73	72	72	9.1	9.2	9.1	9.3	9.2	9.0	8.8
New Mexico......	11	12	12	13	12	13	13	7.0	7.3	7.3	7.4	7.3	7.3	7.4
New York	169	171	169	168	164	159	157	9.4	9.4	9.3	9.3	9.0	8.7	8.6
North Carolina.....	57	62	63	65	66	66	68	8.6	9.0	8.9	9.0	9.1	8.9	9.0
North Dakota......	6	6	6	6	6	6	6	8.9	9.3	9.2	9.3	9.3	9.2	9.3
Ohio	99	103	103	106	105	105	106	9.1	9.1	9.3	9.5	9.4	9.4	9.4
Oklahoma........	30	32	32	33	33	34	34	9.7	10.1	9.9	10.0	10.0	10.2	10.1
Oregon.........	25	28	27	28	29	29	29	8.8	9.0	8.9	9.0	9.0	8.9	9.0
Pennsylvania......	122	126	128	128	129	128	127	10.3	10.5	10.6	10.6	10.7	10.6	10.6
Rhode Island......	10	10	9	10	10	10	10	9.5	9.7	9.4	9.8	9.6	9.9	9.8
South Carolina.....	30	32	32	34	34	34	35	8.5	8.6	8.8	9.1	9.2	9.0	9.1
South Dakota.....	6	7	7	7	7	7	7	9.1	9.6	9.4	9.5	9.3	9.3	9.3
Tennessee	46	49	51	51	51	53	53	9.5	9.7	9.8	9.8	9.7	9.8	9.8
Texas..........	125	135	136	138	140	143	143	7.4	7.5	7.4	7.4	7.3	7.3	7.2
Utah	9	10	10	11	11	12	12	5.3	5.5	5.5	5.6	5.6	5.6	5.6
Vermont	5	5	5	5	5	5	5	8.2	8.5	8.2	8.5	8.3	8.6	8.4
Virginia.........	48	52	52	53	54	54	54	7.8	8.0	8.0	8.0	8.0	8.0	8.0
Washington.......	37	40	40	41	42	41	43	7.6	8.0	7.5	7.5	7.6	7.4	7.5
West Virginia......	19	20	20	20	20	21	21	10.8	11.0	11.1	11.1	11.2	11.5	11.5
Wisconsin.......	43	45	44	45	45	45	46	8.7	8.7	8.7	8.8	8.7	8.7	8.8
Wyoming	3	3	3	4	4	4	3,853	7.1	7.5	7.3	7.7	7.5	7.8	8.0
Puerto Rico.......	(NA)	(NA)	(NA)	(NA)	(NA)	29	(NA)	(NA)	(NA)	(NA)	(NA)	(NA)	7.6	(NA)
Virgin Islands......	(NA)	(NA)	(NA)	(NA)	(NA)	1	(NA)	(NA)	(NA)	(NA)	(NA)	(NA)	5.4	(NA)
Guam	(NA)	(NA)	(NA)	(NA)	(NA)	1	(NA)	(NA)	(NA)	(NA)	(NA)	(NA)	4.2	(NA)

NA Not available. [1] Rates based on enumerated resident population as of April 1 for 1990; estimated resident population as of July 1 for all other years.

Source: U.S. National Center for Health Statistics, *Vital Statistics of the United States*, annual; *National Vital Statistics Reports (NVSR)* (formerly *Monthly Vital Statistics Report*).

No. 102. Infant, Maternal, and Neonatal Mortality Rates and Fetal Mortality Ratios by Race: 1980 to 1998

[Deaths per 1,000 live births, except as noted. Excludes deaths of nonresidents of United States. Rate for live births tabulated according to race of mother, for infant and neonatal mortality rates. Beginning 1989, race for live births tabulated according to race of mother, for maternal mortality rates and mortality rates. See also Appendix III]

Item	1980	1990	1993	1994	1995	1996	1997	1998
Infant deaths [1]	12.6	9.2	8.4	8.0	7.6	7.3	7.2	7.2
White	10.9	7.6	6.8	6.6	6.3	6.0	6.0	6.0
Black and other	20.2	15.5	14.1	13.5	(NA)	(NA)	(NA)	(NA)
Black	22.2	18.0	16.5	15.8	15.1	14.2	13.7	14.3
Maternal deaths [2]	9.2	8.2	7.5	8.3	7.1	7.6	8.4	(NA)
White	6.7	5.4	4.8	6.2	4.2	5.1	5.8	(NA)
Black and other	19.8	19.1	17.6	16.2	18.5	16.9	18.3	(NA)
Black	21.5	22.4	20.5	18.5	22.1	20.3	20.8	(NA)
Neonatal deaths [3]	8.5	5.8	5.3	5.1	4.9	4.7	4.7	4.8
White	7.4	4.8	4.3	4.2	4.1	3.9	3.9	4.0
Black and other	13.2	9.9	9.0	8.6	(NA)	(NA)	(NA)	(NA)
Black	14.6	11.6	10.7	10.2	9.8	9.2	9.0	9.5

NA Not available.   [1] Represents deaths of infants under 1 year old, exclusive of fetal deaths.   [2] Per 100,000 live births from deliveries and complications of pregnancy, childbirth, and the puerperium. Deaths are classified according to the ninth revision of the *International Classification of Diseases;* earlier years classified according to the revision in use at the time; see text, this section.   [3] Represents deaths of infants under 28 days old, exclusive of fetal deaths.

No. 103. Infant Deaths and Infant Mortality Rates by Cause of Death: 1980 to 1998

[Excludes deaths of nonresidents of the United States. Deaths classified according to ninth revision of *International Classification of Diseases*. See also Appendix III]

Cause of death	1980	1990	1992	1993	1994	1995	1996	1997	1998
Total:									
Number	45,526	38,351	34,628	33,466	31,710	29,583	28,487	27,692	28,371
Percent distribution	100	100	100	100	100	100	100	97	100
Infant mortality rate [1]	12.6	9.2	8.4	8.0	7.6	7.3	7.1	7.2	7.2
Congenital anomalies:									
Number	9,220	8,239	7,449	7,129	6,854	6,554	6,381	6,063	6,212
Percent distribution	20	21	22	21	22	22	(NA)	21	22
Infant mortality rate [1]	2.6	2.0	1.8	1.7	1.7	1.6	1.6	1.6	1.6
Disorders relating to short gestation and unspecified low birth weight:									
Number	3,648	4,013	4,035	4,310	4,254	3,933	3,902	3,727	4,101
Percent distribution	8	10	12	13	13	13	(NA)	13	14
Infant mortality rate [1]	1.0	1.0	1.1	1.1	1.0	1.0	1.0	1.0	1.0
Sudden infant death syndrome:									
Number	5,510	5,417	4,891	4,669	4,073	3,397	3,050	2,705	2,822
Percent distribution	12	14	14	14	13	11	(NA)	9	10
Infant mortality rate [1]	1.5	1.3	1.2	1.0	0.9	0.8	0.7	0.6	0.7
Respiratory distress syndrome:									
Number	4,989	2,850	2,063	1,815	1,567	1,454	1,362	1,262	1,295
Percent distribution	11	7	6	5	5	5	(NA)	4	5
Infant mortality rate [1]	1.4	0.7	0.5	0.4	0.4	0.4	0.3	0.3	0.3
Newborn affected by maternal complications of pregnancy:									
Number	1,572	1,655	1,461	1,343	1,296	1,309	1,249	1,242	1,343
Percent distribution	4	4	4	4	4	4	(NA)	4	5
Infant mortality rate [1]	0.4	0.4	0.3	0.3	0.3	0.3	0.3	0.3	0.3
Newborn affected by complications of placenta, cord, and membranes:									
Number	985	975	993	994	948	962	949	927	961
Percent distribution	2	3	3	3	3	3	(NA)	3	3
Infant mortality rate [1]	0.3	0.2	0.2	0.2	(NA)	0.2	0.2	0.2	0.2
Accidents and adverse effects:									
Number	1,166	930	819	898	889	787	804	753	754
Percent distribution	3	2	2	3	3	3	(NA)	3	3
Infant mortality rate [1]	0.3	0.2	0.2	0.2	(NA)	0.2	0.2	0.2	0.2
Infections specific to the perinatal period:									
Number	971	875	901	772	828	788	756	756	815
Percent distribution	2	2	3	2	3	3	(NA)	3	3
Infant mortality rate [1]	0.3	0.2	0.2	0.2	(NA)	0.2	0.2	0.2	0.2
Pneumonia and influenza:									
Number	1,012	634	600	530	559	492	496	397	441
Percent distribution	2	2	2	2	2	2	(NA)	1	2
Infant mortality rate [1]	0.3	0.2	0.1	0.1	(NA)	0.1	0.1	0.1	0.1
Intrauterine hypoxia and birth asphyxia:									
Number	1,497	762	613	549	537	475	428	456	461
Percent distribution	3	2	2	2	2	2	(NA)	2	2
Infant mortality rate [1]	0.4	0.2	0.1	0.1	(NA)	0.1	0.1	0.1	0.1
All other causes:									
Number	14,956	12,001	10,803	10,457	9,905	9,432	9,110	9,404	9,166
Percent distribution	33	31	31	31	30	32	(NA)	33	32
Infant mortality rate [1]	4.1	2.9	2.6	2.5	(NA)	2.3	2.4	2.5	2.3

NA Not available.   [1] Deaths of infants under 1 year old per 1,000 live births.

Source of Tables 102-103: U.S. National Center for Health Statistics, *Vital Statistics of the United States*, annual; *National Vital Statistics Reports (NVSR)* (formerly *Monthly Vital Statistics Report);* and unpublished data.

Vital Statistics **77**

No. 104. Infant Mortality Rates by Race—States: 1980 to 1998

[**Deaths per 1,000 live births, by place of residence.** Represents deaths of infants under 1 year old, exclusive of fetal deaths. Excludes deaths of nonresidents of the United States. See Appendix III]

State	Total [1]				White				Black			
	1980	1990	1995	1998	1980	1990	1995	1998	1980	1990	1995	1998
U.S................	12.6	9.2	7.6	7.2	11.0	7.3	6.3	6.0	21.4	18.0	15.1	14.3
Alabama	15.1	10.8	9.8	10.2	11.6	8.1	7.1	7.7	21.6	16.0	15.2	15.5
Alaska	12.3	10.5	7.7	5.9	9.4	7.6	6.1	4.7	19.5	(B)	(B)	(S)
Arizona	12.4	8.8	7.5	7.5	11.8	7.8	7.2	6.9	18.4	20.6	17.0	20.0
Arkansas	12.7	9.2	8.8	8.9	10.3	8.4	7.2	7.6	20.0	13.9	14.3	14.0
California	11.1	7.9	6.3	5.8	10.6	7.0	5.8	5.3	18.0	16.8	14.4	13.7
Colorado	10.1	8.8	6.5	6.7	9.8	7.8	6.0	6.4	19.1	19.4	16.8	16.0
Connecticut	11.2	7.9	7.2	7.0	10.2	6.3	6.5	5.6	19.1	17.6	12.6	17.4
Delaware	13.9	10.1	7.5	9.6	9.8	9.7	6.0	6.9	27.9	20.1	13.1	18.7
District of Columbia	25.0	20.7	16.2	12.5	17.8	-	(B)	(S)	26.7	24.6	19.6	15.5
Florida	14.6	9.6	7.5	7.2	11.8	6.7	6.0	5.9	22.8	16.8	13.0	12.3
Georgia	14.5	12.4	9.4	8.5	10.8	7.4	6.5	6.0	21.0	18.3	15.1	13.4
Hawaii	10.3	6.7	5.8	6.9	11.6	6.1	(B)	5.3	(S)	(S)	(B)	(S)
Idaho	10.7	8.7	6.1	7.2	10.7	8.6	5.8	7.1	(NA)	(B)	(B)	(S)
Illinois	14.8	10.7	9.4	8.4	11.7	7.9	7.2	6.4	26.3	22.4	18.7	17.2
Indiana	11.9	9.6	8.4	7.6	10.5	7.9	7.3	6.5	23.4	17.4	17.5	17.3
Iowa	11.8	8.1	8.2	6.6	11.5	7.9	7.8	6.2	27.2	21.9	21.2	18.3
Kansas	10.4	8.4	7.0	7.0	9.5	8.0	6.2	7.0	20.6	17.7	17.6	10.0
Kentucky	12.9	8.5	7.6	7.5	12.0	8.2	7.4	6.8	22.0	14.3	10.7	15.4
Louisiana	14.3	11.1	9.8	9.1	10.5	8.1	6.2	5.7	20.6	16.7	15.3	14.0
Maine	9.2	6.2	6.5	6.3	9.4	6.7	6.3	6.4	(B)	(B)	(B)	(S)
Maryland	14.0	9.5	8.9	8.6	11.6	6.8	6.0	5.2	20.4	17.1	15.3	15.3
Massachusetts	10.5	7.0	5.2	5.1	10.1	6.1	4.7	4.9	16.8	11.9	9.0	8.3
Michigan	12.8	10.7	8.3	8.2	10.6	7.4	6.2	6.3	24.2	21.6	17.3	16.8
Minnesota	10.0	7.3	6.7	5.9	9.6	6.7	6.0	5.1	20.0	23.7	17.6	13.4
Mississippi	17.0	12.1	10.5	10.1	11.1	7.4	7.0	6.3	23.7	16.2	14.7	14.8
Missouri	12.4	9.4	7.4	7.7	11.1	7.9	6.4	6.1	20.7	18.2	13.8	16.8
Montana	12.4	9.0	7.0	7.4	11.8	6.0	7.0	7.2	(NA)	(B)	(B)	(S)
Nebraska	11.5	8.3	7.4	7.3	10.7	6.9	7.3	6.7	25.2	18.9	(B)	19.4
Nevada	10.7	8.4	5.7	7.0	10.0	8.2	5.5	6.0	20.6	14.2	(B)	17.3
New Hampshire	9.9	7.1	5.5	4.4	9.9	6.0	5.5	4.3	22.5	(B)	(B)	(S)
New Jersey	12.5	9.0	6.6	6.4	10.3	6.4	5.3	5.0	21.9	18.4	13.3	12.8
New Mexico	11.5	9.0	6.2	7.2	11.3	7.6	6.1	6.9	23.1	(B)	(B)	(S)
New York	12.5	9.6	7.7	6.3	10.8	7.4	6.2	5.3	20.0	18.1	13.9	10.9
North Carolina	14.5	10.6	9.2	9.3	12.1	8.0	6.7	6.5	20.0	16.5	15.9	17.6
North Dakota	12.1	8.0	7.2	8.6	11.7	7.2	6.7	8.2	27.5	(B)	(B)	(S)
Ohio	12.8	9.8	8.7	8.0	11.2	7.8	7.3	7.0	23.0	19.5	17.5	14.2
Oklahoma	12.7	9.2	8.3	8.5	12.1	9.1	8.0	8.1	21.8	14.3	15.1	13.5
Oregon	12.2	8.3	6.1	5.4	12.2	7.0	5.9	5.3	15.9	(B)	(B)	(S)
Pennsylvania	13.2	9.6	7.8	7.1	11.9	7.4	6.2	5.8	23.1	20.5	17.6	15.4
Rhode Island	11.0	8.1	7.2	7.0	10.9	7.0	7.0	6.2	(B)	(B)	(B)	(S)
South Carolina	15.6	11.7	9.6	9.6	10.8	8.1	6.7	6.0	22.9	17.3	14.6	16.2
South Dakota	10.9	10.1	9.5	9.1	9.0	8.0	7.9	7.5	(NA)	(B)	(B)	(S)
Tennessee	13.5	10.3	9.3	8.2	11.9	7.3	6.8	6.3	19.3	17.9	17.9	15.0
Texas	12.2	8.1	6.5	6.4	11.2	6.7	5.9	5.8	18.8	14.7	11.7	11.6
Utah	10.4	7.5	5.4	5.6	10.5	6.0	5.3	5.7	27.3	(B)	(B)	(S)
Vermont	10.7	6.4	6.0	7.0	10.7	5.9	6.2	6.8	(B)	(B)	(B)	(S)
Virginia	13.6	10.2	7.8	7.7	11.9	7.4	5.7	5.7	19.8	19.5	15.3	14.9
Washington	11.8	7.8	5.9	5.7	11.5	7.3	5.6	5.2	16.4	20.6	16.2	13.5
West Virginia	11.8	9.9	7.9	8.0	11.4	8.1	7.6	8.0	21.5	(B)	(B)	(S)
Wisconsin	10.3	8.2	7.3	7.2	9.7	7.7	6.3	6.0	18.5	19.0	18.6	18.7
Wyoming	9.8	8.6	7.7	7.2	9.3	7.5	6.8	5.8	25.9	(S)	(B)	(S)

- Represents zero.   B Base figure too small to meet statistical standards for reliability.   NA Not available.   S Figure does not meet publication standards.   [1] Includes other races, not shown separately.

Source: U.S. National Center for Health Statistics, *Vital Statistics of the United States,* annual; and unpublished data.

U.S. Census Bureau, Statistical Abstract of the United States: 2001

No. 105. Deaths and Death Rates by Selected Causes: 1990 to 1998

[**2,148.5 represents 2,148,500.** Excludes deaths of nonresidents of the United States, except as noted. Deaths classified according to ninth revision of *International Classification of Diseases;* for earlier years, classified according to revision in use at that time. See also Appendix III]

Cause of death	Deaths (1,000)				Crude death rate per 100,000 population [1]			
	1990	1995	1997	1998	1990	1995	1997	1998
All causes	2,148.5	2,312.1	2,314.2	2,337.3	863.8	880.0	864.7	864.7
Major cardiovascular diseases	916.0	951.4	944.1	940.6	368.3	362.1	352.8	348.0
Diseases of heart.............	720.1	737.6	727.0	724.9	289.5	280.7	271.6	268.2
Percent of total	33.5	31.9	31.4	31.0	33.5	31.9	31.4	31.0
Rheumatic fever and rheumatic heart disease	6.0	5.1	5.0	4.8	2.4	2.0	1.9	1.8
Hypertensive heart disease [2]	23.4	25.0	26.6	27.7	9.5	9.5	9.9	10.3
Ischemic heart disease	489.2	481.3	466.1	459.8	196.7	183.2	174.2	170.1
Other diseases of endocardium . . .	13.0	16.2	17.7	18.5	5.2	6.2	6.6	6.9
All other forms of heart disease . . .	188.4	207.4	209.2	211.6	75.8	78.9	78.2	78.3
Hypertension [2].................	9.2	12.5	13.5	14.3	3.7	4.8	5.1	5.3
Cerebrovascular diseases	144.1	158.0	159.8	158.4	57.9	60.1	59.7	58.6
Atherosclerosis	18.0	16.7	16.1	15.3	7.3	6.4	6.0	5.7
Other	24.6	26.6	27.8	27.7	9.9	10.1	10.4	10.2
Malignancies [3]	505.3	538.5	539.6	541.5	203.2	204.9	201.6	200.3
Percent of total.............	23.5	23.3	23.3	23.2	23.5	23.3	23.3	23.2
Of respiratory and intrathoracic organs	146.4	156.4	158.5	159.7	58.9	59.5	59.2	59.1
Of digestive organs and peritoneum	120.8	126.6	127.1	128.7	48.6	48.2	47.5	47.6
Of genital organs	57.5	60.5	59.0	58.4	23.1	23.0	22.0	21.6
Of breast	43.7	44.2	42.3	42.1	17.6	16.8	15.8	15.6
Of urinary organs	20.7	22.6	23.4	23.8	8.3	8.6	8.7	8.8
Leukemia	18.6	20.1	20.3	20.3	7.5	7.7	7.6	7.5
Accidents and adverse effects	92.0	93.3	95.6	97.8	37.0	35.5	35.7	36.2
Motor vehicle	46.8	43.4	43.5	43.5	18.8	16.5	16.2	16.1
All other	45.2	50.0	52.2	54.3	18.2	19.0	19.5	20.1
Chronic obstructive pulmonary diseases and allied conditions	86.7	102.9	109.0	112.6	34.9	39.2	40.7	41.7
Bronchitis, chronic and unspecified . .	3.6	3.3	3.1	3.0	1.4	1.3	1.1	1.1
Emphysema	15.7	16.9	17.5	17.6	6.3	6.4	6.5	6.5
Asthma...................	4.8	5.6	5.4	5.4	1.9	2.1	2.0	2.0
Other	62.6	77.0	83.0	86.6	25.2	29.3	31.0	32.0
Pneumonia and influenza	79.5	82.9	86.4	91.9	32.0	31.6	32.3	34.0
Pneumonia	77.4	82.3	85.7	90.1	31.1	31.3	32.0	33.4
Influenza.................	2.1	0.6	0.7	1.7	0.8	0.2	0.3	0.6
Diabetes mellitus.............	47.7	59.3	62.6	64.8	19.2	22.6	23.4	24.0
Suicide	30.9	31.3	30.5	30.6	12.4	11.9	11.4	11.3
Chronic liver disease and cirrhosis	25.8	25.2	25.2	25.2	10.4	9.6	9.4	9.3
Other infectious and parasitic diseases .	32.2	50.3	23.3	20.3	13.0	19.1	8.7	7.5
Homicide and legal intervention	24.9	22.9	19.8	18.3	10.0	8.7	7.4	6.8
Nephritis, nephrotic syndrome, and nephrosis	20.8	23.7	25.3	26.2	8.3	9.0	9.5	9.7
Septicemia.................	19.2	21.0	22.4	23.7	7.7	8.0	8.4	8.8
Certain conditions originating in the perinatal period	17.7	13.5	13.1	13.4	7.1	5.1	4.9	5.0
Congenital anomalies.............	13.1	11.9	11.9	11.9	5.3	4.5	4.5	4.4
Benign neoplasms [4]	6.8	7.8	7.7	7.9	2.7	3.0	2.9	2.9
Ulcer of stomach and duodenum	6.2	5.5	5.1	4.7	2.5	2.1	1.9	1.7
Hernia of abdominal cavity and intestinal obstruction [5]...........	5.8	6.2	6.5	6.6	2.3	2.4	2.4	2.5
Anemias..................	4.1	4.6	4.5	4.5	1.6	1.7	1.7	1.7
Cholelithiasis and other disorders of gall bladder................	3.0	2.8	2.8	2.8	1.2	1.0	1.0	1.0
Nutritional deficiencies	3.0	3.6	3.9	4.1	1.2	1.4	1.5	1.5
Tuberculosis	1.8	1.3	1.2	1.1	0.7	0.5	0.4	0.4
Infections of kidney	1.3	0.9	0.8	0.8	0.5	0.3	0.3	0.3
Viral hepatitis	1.6	3.4	4.1	4.8	0.6	1.3	1.5	1.8
Meningitis.................	1.0	0.8	0.8	0.8	0.4	0.3	0.3	0.3
Acute bronchitis and bronchiolitis	0.6	0.5	0.5	0.5	0.3	0.2	0.2	0.2
Hyperplasia of prostate	0.5	0.4	0.4	0.4	0.2	0.2	0.2	0.2
Symptoms, signs, and ill-defined conditions..................	24.1	27.3	25.8	26.0	9.7	10.4	9.6	9.6
All other causes................	172.9	214.1	235.4	247.6	69.5	81.5	88.0	91.6

[1] 1990 based on resident population enumerated as of April 1. Other years based on resident population estimated as of July 1. [2] With or without renal disease. [3] Includes other types of malignancies not shown separately. [4] Includes neoplasms of unspecified nature; beginning 1980 also includes carcinoma in situ. [5] Without mention of hernia.

Source: U.S. National Center for Health Statistics, *Vital Statistics of the United States,* annual; and *National Vital Statistics Report (NVSR)* (formerly *Monthly Vital Statistics Report*); and unpublished data.

U.S. Census Bureau, Statistical Abstract of the United States: 2001

No. 106. Age-Adjusted Death Rates by Selected Causes: 1990 to 1998

[Rates per 100,000 population. For explanation of age-adjustment, see text, this section. The standard population for this table is the total population of the United States enumerated in 1940. See also headnote, Table 105]

Cause of death	1990	1993	1994	1995	1996	1997	1998
All causes	**520.2**	**513.3**	**507.4**	**503.9**	**491.6**	**479.1**	**471.7**
Major cardiovascular diseases	189.8	181.8	176.8	174.9	170.7	166.1	161.2
Diseases of heart	152.0	145.3	140.4	138.3	134.5	130.5	126.6
Rheumatic fever and rheumatic heart disease	1.5	1.3	1.2	1.1	1.1	1.0	1.0
Hypertensive heart disease [1]	4.8	4.9	5.0	5.1	5.2	5.2	5.3
Ischemic heart disease	102.6	94.9	91.4	89.5	86.7	82.9	79.5
Acute myocardial infraction	53.7	47.5	45.6	43.8	42.0	39.7	38.0
Other diseases of endocardium	2.5	2.6	2.6	2.6	2.7	2.7	2.7
Old myocardial infarction and other	47.8	46.5	45.0	44.9	44.0	42.5	40.9
Hypertension [1]	1.9	2.2	2.2	2.3	2.3	2.3	2.4
Cerebrovascular diseases	27.7	26.5	26.5	26.7	26.4	25.9	25.1
Atherosclerosis	2.7	2.4	2.3	2.3	2.2	2.1	1.9
Intracerebral/intracranial hemorrhage	5.2	5.1	5.0	5.1	5.2	5.6	5.5
Cerebral thrombosis	3.3	2.5	2.4	2.2	2.0	1.8	1.6
Cerebral embolism	0.1	0.1	0.1	0.1	0.1	0.1	0.1
Malignancies [2]	135.0	132.6	131.5	129.9	127.9	125.6	123.6
Of respiratory and intrathoracic organs	41.4	40.8	40.1	39.7	39.3	38.7	38.2
Of digestive organs and peritoneum	30.2	29.5	29.3	29.1	28.5	28.2	28.1
Of genital organs	13.6	13.2	13.2	12.8	12.5	12.0	11.7
Of breast	12.7	11.8	11.6	11.5	11.0	10.5	10.2
Of urinary organs	5.1	5.0	5.1	5.1	5.1	5.0	5.0
Leukemia	5.0	4.9	4.9	4.8	4.8	4.7	4.6
Of lip, oral cavity, and pharynx	2.4	2.3	2.1	2.1	2.1	2.0	2.0
Accidents and adverse effects	32.5	30.3	30.3	30.5	30.4	30.1	30.1
Motor vehicle	18.5	16.0	16.1	16.3	16.2	15.9	15.6
All other	14.0	14.4	14.2	14.2	14.2	14.2	14.4
Chronic obstructive pulmonary diseases and allied conditions [3]	19.7	21.4	21.0	20.8	21.0	21.1	21.3
Bronchitis, chronic and unspecified	0.8	0.8	0.7	0.6	0.6	0.6	0.5
Emphysema	3.7	3.9	3.7	3.6	3.6	3.6	3.6
Asthma	1.4	1.4	1.5	1.5	1.5	1.4	1.4
Other	13.7	15.2	15.1	15.0	15.2	15.5	15.7
Pneumonia and influenza	14.0	13.5	13.0	12.9	12.8	12.9	13.2
Pneumonia	13.7	13.3	12.8	12.8	12.7	12.8	13.0
Influenza	0.3	0.2	0.2	0.1	0.1	0.1	0.2
Diabetes mellitus	11.7	12.4	12.9	13.3	13.6	13.5	13.6
Suicide	11.5	11.3	11.2	11.2	10.8	10.6	10.4
Chronic liver disease and cirrhosis	8.6	7.9	7.9	7.6	7.5	7.4	7.2
Homicide and legal intervention	10.2	10.7	10.3	9.4	8.5	8.0	7.3
Nephritis, nephrotic syndrome, and renal failure	3.9	4.1	3.9	4.0	3.9	4.1	4.4
Acute glomerulonephritis/nephrotic syndrome	0.1	(NA)	0.1	-	-	-	-
Septicemia	4.1	4.1	4.0	4.1	4.1	4.2	4.4
Other infectious and parasitic diseases	12.0	15.9	17.5	17.6	13.0	7.6	6.5
Benign neoplasms [4]	1.7	1.7	1.7	1.7	1.7	1.6	1.6
Ulcer of stomach and duodenum	1.3	1.2	1.2	1.0	0.9	0.9	0.8
Hernia of abdominal cavity and intestinal obstruction [5]	1.1	1.0	1.1	1.0	1.0	1.0	1.0
Anemias	0.9	0.9	0.9	0.9	0.8	0.8	0.8
Cholelithiasis and other disorders of gallbladder	0.6	0.5	0.5	0.5	0.5	0.5	0.5
Nutritional deficiencies	0.5	0.5	0.5	0.5	0.5	0.5	0.5
Tuberculosis	0.5	0.4	0.4	0.3	0.3	0.3	0.2
Tuberculosis of respiratory system	0.4	0.3	0.3	0.2	0.2	0.2	0.2
Other tuberculosis	0.1	0.1	0.1	0.1	0.1	0.1	0.1
Infections of kidney	0.2	0.2	0.2	0.2	0.2	0.1	0.1
Viral hepatitis	0.5	0.8	0.9	1.0	1.1	1.2	1.4
Meningitis	0.3	0.3	0.3	0.2	0.3	0.3	0.2
Acute bronchitis and bronchiolitis	0.1	0.1	0.1	0.1	0.1	0.1	0.1
Hyperplasia of prostate	0.1	0.1	0.1	0.1	0.1	0.1	0.1
Symptoms, signs, and ill-defined conditions	7.3	7.4	6.8	7.2	6.6	6.4	6.2
Meningococcal infection	0.1	0.1	0.1	0.1	0.1	0.1	0.1
Angina pectoris	0.2	0.2	0.2	0.1	0.1	0.1	0.1
Appendicitis	0.1	0.1	0.1	0.1	0.1	0.1	0.1
Complications of pregnancy, childbirth	0.1	0.1	0.1	0.1	0.1	0.1	0.1
Congenital anomalies	5.0	4.6	4.5	4.4	4.3	4.2	4.2
Perinatal period conditions	6.9	5.9	4.8	5.4	5.3	5.3	5.5
Birth trauma, intrauterine hypoxia, etc.	1.5	1.0	0.9	0.9	0.8	0.8	0.8

- Represents or rounds to zero.   NA Not available.   [1] With or without renal disease.   [2] Includes other types of malignancies not shown separately.   [3] Prior to 1980, data are shown for bronchitis, emphysema, and asthma.   [4] Includes neoplasms of unspecified nature; also includes carcinoma in situ.   [5] Without mention of hernia.

Source: U.S. National Center for Health Statistics, *Vital Statistics of the United States*, annual; and *National Vital Statistics Report (NVSR)* (formerly *Monthly Vital Statistics Report*); and unpublished data.

No. 107. Deaths by Selected Causes and Selected Characteristics: 1998

[Excludes deaths of nonresidents of the United States. Deaths classified according to ninth revision of *International Classification of Diseases*. See also Appendix III]

Age, sex, and race	Total [1]	Heart disease	Cancer	Accidents and adverse effects	Cerebro-vascular diseases	Chronic obstructive pulmonary diseases [2]	Pneumonia	Suicide	Chronic liver disease, cirrhosis	Diabetes mellitus	Homicide and legal intervention
ALL RACES [3]											
Both sexes, total [4]	2,337,256	724,859	541,532	97,835	158,448	112,584	90,147	30,575	25,192	64,751	18,272
Under 1 years old	28,371	609	78	754	296	39	435	-	16	2	322
1 to 4 years old	5,251	214	365	1,935	57	49	143	-	1	6	399
5 to 14 years old	7,791	326	1,013	3,254	82	152	107	324	4	20	460
15 to 24 years old	30,627	1,057	1,699	13,349	178	239	205	4,135	22	137	5,506
25 to 34 years old	42,516	3,207	4,385	12,045	670	328	530	5,365	506	636	4,565
35 to 44 years old	88,866	13,593	17,022	15,127	2,650	884	1,383	6,837	3,370	1,885	3,567
45 to 54 years old	146,479	35,056	45,747	10,946	5,709	2,828	2,146	5,131	5,744	4,386	1,744
55 to 64 years old	233,724	65,068	87,024	7,340	9,653	10,162	3,795	2,963	5,279	8,705	766
65 to 74 years old	458,982	135,295	154,753	8,892	23,912	31,102	10,853	2,597	5,655	16,490	468
75 to 84 years old	681,663	226,769	158,517	12,711	54,428	43,718	28,344	2,355	3,703	20,529	318
85 years old and over	612,575	243,609	70,916	11,372	60,804	23,076	42,201	851	887	11,955	101
WHITE											
Both sexes, total [4]	2,015,984	635,549	470,139	82,178	136,855	104,061	79,992	27,648	21,771	51,706	9,241
Under 1 years old	18,561	405	68	511	198	20	251	-	11	2	188
1 to 4 years old	3,628	136	289	1,388	34	23	96	-	-	5	199
5 to 14 years old	5,613	224	802	2,336	58	78	77	274	3	17	267
15 to 24 years old	22,296	693	1,371	11,170	128	129	131	3,434	17	86	2,262
25 to 34 years old	30,080	2,138	3,417	9,745	445	168	340	4,559	401	427	2,110
35 to 44 years old	65,347	9,702	13,234	12,281	1,698	578	913	6,278	2,737	1,341	1,961
45 to 54 years old	112,156	26,733	36,605	8,727	3,721	2,231	1,551	4,753	4,671	3,104	1,044
55 to 64 years old	189,312	52,095	72,770	6,071	7,007	9,028	2,978	2,793	4,479	6,334	504
65 to 74 years old	394,664	115,449	135,114	7,700	19,473	28,791	9,217	2,456	5,123	12,885	333
75 to 84 years old	612,181	203,633	142,444	11,571	48,202	41,232	25,427	2,262	3,488	17,212	242
85 years old and over	561,836	224,310	64,016	10,580	55,887	21,776	39,010	824	838	10,293	83
BLACK											
Both sexes, total [4]	278,440	78,294	61,193	12,801	18,237	7,205	8,293	1,977	2,697	11,378	8,420
Under 1 years old	8,726	166	8	223	90	16	147	-	5	-	123
1 to 4 years old	1,397	64	60	470	20	24	43	-	1	1	187
5 to 14 years old	1,815	89	165	761	22	64	27	31	1	3	163
15 to 24 years old	7,159	325	248	1,654	41	105	60	488	3	49	3,095
25 to 34 years old	10,804	986	767	1,810	197	143	161	546	59	193	2,296
35 to 44 years old	21,005	3,561	3,196	2,400	865	286	431	388	487	507	1,486
45 to 54 years old	30,265	7,513	7,787	1,872	1,762	547	537	262	873	1,105	631
55 to 64 years old	38,813	11,573	12,302	1,047	2,263	994	725	110	640	2,062	229
65 to 74 years old	55,607	17,480	16,848	978	3,696	1,968	1,348	89	432	3,137	116
75 to 84 years old	59,415	19,997	13,793	928	5,134	2,045	2,338	50	162	2,855	68
85 years old and over	43,341	16,517	6,015	646	4,142	1,013	2,472	11	32	1,466	18

- Represents zero. [1] Includes other causes, not shown separately. [2] Includes allied conditions. [3] Includes other races, not shown separately. [4] Includes those deaths with age not stated.

Source: U.S. National Center for Health Statistics, *Vital Statistics of the United States,* annual.

Vital Statistics   81

[Excludes deaths of nonresidents of the United States. Deaths classified according to ninth revision of *International Classification of Diseases.* See also Appendix III]

Age and leading cause of death	Number of deaths			Death rate per 100,000 population		
	Total	Male	Female	Total	Male	Female
All ages [1]	**2,337,256**	**1,157,260**	**1,179,996**	**864.7**	**876.4**	**853.5**
1 to 4 yrs. old, total	**5,251**	**2,920**	**2,331**	**34.6**	**37.6**	**31.4**
Leading causes of death:						
Accidents	1,935	1,155	780	12.7	14.9	10.5
Congenital anomalies	564	287	277	3.7	3.7	3.7
Malignant neoplasms (cancer).	365	189	176	2.4	2.4	2.4
Homicide and legal intervention	399	223	176	2.6	2.9	2.4
Heart disease	214	114	100	1.4	1.5	1.3
HIV infection [2]	(NA)	(NA)	(NA)	(NA)	(NA)	(NA)
Pneumonia and influenza	146	73	73	1.0	0.9	1.0
Certain conditions originating in the perinatal period	75	37	38	0.5	0.5	0.5
Septicemia	89	54	35	0.6	0.7	0.5
Cerebrovascular diseases	57	(NA)	32	0.4	(NA)	0.4
5 to 14 yrs. old, total.	**7,791**	**4,686**	**3,105**	**19.9**	**23.4**	**16.2**
Leading causes of death:						
Accidents	3,254	2,086	1,158	8.3	10.4	6.1
Malignant neoplasms (cancer).	1,013	582	431	2.6	2.9	2.3
Homicide and legal intervention	460	257	203	1.2	1.3	1.1
Congenital anomalies	371	197	174	0.9	1.0	0.9
Suicide	324	241	83	0.8	1.2	0.4
Heart disease	326	191	135	0.8	1.0	0.7
HIV infections [2]	(NA)	(NA)	(NA)	(NA)	(NA)	(NA)
Chronic obstructive pulmonary diseases .	152	88	64	0.4	0.4	0.3
Pneumonia and influenza	121	57	64	0.3	0.3	0.3
Benign neoplasms & carcinoma in situ . .	84	46	38	0.2	0.2	0.2
15 to 24 yrs. old, total.	**30,627**	**22,717**	**7,910**	**82.3**	**119.3**	**43.5**
Leading causes of death:						
Accidents	13,349	9,887	3,462	35.9	51.9	19.1
Homicide and legal intervention	5,506	4,720	786	14.8	24.8	4.3
Suicide	4,135	3,532	603	11.1	18.5	3.3
Malignant neoplasms (cancer).	1,699	1,029	670	4.6	5.4	3.7
Heart disease	1,057	672	385	2.8	3.5	2.1
HIV infection [2]	194	93	101	0.5	0.5	0.6
Congenital anomalies	450	256	194	1.2	1.3	1.1
Chronic obstructive pulmonary disease . .	239	149	90	0.6	0.8	0.5
Pneumonia and influenza	215	109	106	0.6	0.6	0.6
Cerebrovascular diseases	178	109	(NA)	0.5	0.6	(NA)
25 to 44 yrs. old, total.	**131,382**	**86,354**	**45,028**	**157.7**	**208.8**	**107.4**
Leading causes of death:						
HIV infection [2]	8,658	6,509	2,149	10.4	15.7	5.1
Accidents	27,172	20,232	6,940	32.6	48.9	16.5
Malignant neoplasms (cancer).	21,407	9,684	11,723	25.7	23.4	28.0
Heart disease	16,800	11,796	5,004	20.2	28.5	11.9
Suicide	12,202	9,700	2,502	14.6	23.5	6.0
Homicide and legal intervention	8,132	6,210	1,922	9.8	15.0	4.6
Chronic liver disease and cirrhosis	3,876	2,670	1,206	4.7	6.5	2.9
Cerebrovascular diseases	3,320	1,703	1,617	4.0	4.1	3.9
Diabetes mellitus	2,521	1,507	1,014	3.0	3.6	2.4
Pneumonia and influenza	1,931	1,118	813	2.3	2.7	1.9
45 to 64 yrs. old, total.	**380,203**	**231,861**	**148,342**	**664.0**	**836.9**	**501.9**
Leading causes of death:						
Malignant neoplasms (cancer).	132,771	70,736	62,035	231.9	255.3	209.9
Heart disease	100,124	70,138	29,986	174.9	253.2	101.5
Accidents	18,286	12,971	5,315	31.9	46.8	18.0
Cerebrovascular diseases	15,362	8,466	6,896	26.8	30.6	23.3
Chronic obstructive pulmonary diseases .	12,990	6,737	6,253	22.7	24.3	21.2
Diabetes mellitus	13,091	7,139	5,952	22.9	25.8	20.1
Chronic liver disease and cirrhosis	11,023	8,031	2,992	19.3	29.0	10.1
HIV infection [2]	4,099	3,352	(NA)	7.2	12.1	(NA)
Suicide	8,094	6,201	1,893	14.1	22.4	6.4
Pneumonia and influenza	6,023	3,589	2,434	10.5	13.0	8.2
65 yrs. old and over, total	**1,753,220**	**792,612**	**960,608**	**5,096.4**	**5,582**	**4,755**
Leading causes of death:						
Heart disease	605,673	270,637	335,036	1,760.6	1,906	1,658
Malignant neoplasms (cancer).	384,186	199,794	184,392	1,116.8	1,407	913
Cerebrovascular diseases	139,144	50,616	88,528	404.5	356.5	438.2
Chronic obstructive pulmonary diseases .	97,896	49,376	48,520	284.6	347.8	240.2
Pneumonia and influenza	82,989	35,790	47,199	241.2	252.1	233.6
Diabetes millitus	48,974	20,862	28,112	142.4	146.9	139.1
Accidents	32,975	16,176	16,799	95.9	113.9	83.2
Alzheimer's disease.	22,416	6,913	15,503	65.2	48.7	76.7
Nephritis, nephrotic syndrome, and nephrosis	22,640	10,533	12,107	65.8	74.2	59.9
Septicemia	19,012	7,687	11,325	55.3	54.1	56.1

NA Not available.   [1] Includes those deaths with age not stated.   [2] Human immunodeficiency virus.

Source: U.S. National Center for Health Statistics, *Vital Statistics of the United States,* annual; and unpublished data.

No. 109. Death Rates by Leading Cause—States: 1997

[Deaths per 100,000 resident population enumerated as of April 1. By place of residence. Excludes nonresidents of the United States. Causes of death classified according to ninth revisions of International Classification of Diseases]

State	Total [1]	Heart disease	Cancer	Cerebro-vascular dis-eases [2]	Acci-dents and adverse effects	Motor vehicle acci-dents	Chronic obstruc-tive pulmo-nary dis-eases [2]	Diabetes mellitus	HIV [3]	Suicide	Homicide
U.S...	864.7	268.2	200.3	58.6	36.2	16.1	41.7	24.0	5.0	11.3	6.8
AL	1,001.5	309.7	222.4	67.3	50.6	25.3	45.6	30.1	4.0	13.1	10.5
AK	422.6	91.9	106.0	24.9	40.9	11.7	18.2	10.4	(S)	21.0	8.0
AZ	813.7	225.8	181.6	52.9	47.7	20.2	51.4	21.6	3.0	17.2	9.5
AR	1,103.7	333.3	234.8	92.8	50.7	26.8	49.0	25.5	2.6	13.6	9.2
CA	696.0	213.5	157.4	50.5	28.4	11.6	37.8	17.9	4.4	10.5	7.4
CO....	658.3	167.3	146.4	43.8	38.5	16.7	46.2	14.3	2.1	15.4	4.7
CT	899.6	294.4	217.0	59.5	32.6	10.4	38.0	20.3	5.1	7.8	4.4
DE	889.9	257.8	222.2	49.4	38.9	15.6	44.0	31.2	7.4	9.1	4.0
DC	1,158.7	317.7	259.4	60.2	39.6	10.7	30.2	36.9	47.8	8.2	41.9
FL	1,054.3	342.8	255.9	67.6	39.4	19.7	54.9	27.0	10.4	14.6	7.3
GA....	792.8	235.1	171.8	54.4	41.3	21.7	35.9	18.2	9.1	10.8	8.8
HI.....	665.1	206.0	165.0	55.2	25.1	10.4	22.3	16.9	1.8	9.7	2.3
ID.....	741.7	197.1	170.0	57.3	46.5	21.9	43.9	19.4	(S)	16.4	2.8
IL.....	865.1	272.4	204.5	59.5	32.3	12.6	37.7	22.7	4.1	8.6	9.2
IN.....	906.0	279.4	214.5	66.0	37.3	17.7	46.8	24.2	1.7	11.8	7.0
IA......	970.9	319.6	224.6	77.1	38.2	16.1	50.3	23.0	(S)	11.5	2.3
KS	915.3	274.1	194.4	69.6	43.8	20.9	45.6	24.4	1.0	12.4	6.0
KY	972.3	302.9	225.5	63.2	43.6	20.9	49.9	27.8	2.0	13.4	6.4
LA	919.3	271.6	214.2	57.8	44.4	22.5	35.8	41.8	8.3	11.0	13.6
ME....	965.6	286.3	234.6	63.3	36.0	14.5	61.8	26.8	(S)	15.8	2.3
MD.....	820.4	232.5	198.6	51.3	27.2	12.6	33.3	28.1	9.8	9.7	11.3
MA.....	893.9	260.4	224.7	54.0	21.7	7.9	41.4	22.8	3.5	8.2	2.0
MI	852.3	285.3	197.6	58.8	31.9	15.0	38.8	24.8	2.8	9.9	7.9
MN.....	787.8	198.3	186.2	60.5	36.6	14.3	36.9	23.2	1.2	9.7	2.5
MS.....	1,007.3	346.6	216.5	66.0	62.4	35.0	41.5	23.1	5.1	12.0	13.0
MO.....	1,005.6	330.4	226.9	71.7	45.1	21.1	50.1	25.6	2.7	12.8	7.9
MT.....	884.0	227.8	207.3	65.8	52.4	24.9	57.4	22.4	(S)	17.9	3.1
NE.....	922.3	284.7	197.1	69.6	40.7	20.8	47.2	20.3	1.4	12.3	3.4
NV.....	797.9	235.8	201.7	46.5	38.1	20.0	54.2	13.3	4.2	22.7	9.8
NH.....	806.5	239.1	205.4	52.1	28.9	11.8	48.3	22.4	(S)	13.0	(S)
NJ	895.8	288.2	222.2	50.4	27.3	9.6	34.4	28.6	9.0	7.2	4.1
NM.....	731.5	185.4	157.8	41.4	57.3	22.2	44.0	24.3	2.4	17.1	9.7
NY.....	874.7	327.5	203.1	42.8	25.7	9.3	35.4	19.8	12.1	7.5	5.4
NC.....	889.2	258.3	203.5	72.1	43.4	22.2	42.5	26.1	5.8	11.4	8.9
ND.....	919.5	272.3	209.8	72.2	46.4	18.5	42.6	29.8	(S)	11.3	(S)
OH.....	941.7	297.6	222.5	59.9	31.6	12.9	48.2	30.8	2.0	9.9	4.0
OK...	1,023.3	337.6	212.4	68.4	48.1	23.2	52.3	27.7	2.5	14.1	6.9
OR.....	887.0	221.1	212.4	79.9	42.8	16.8	49.1	26.1	1.7	16.6	4.4
PA	1,064.3	345.1	248.5	68.5	38.1	13.8	46.6	29.2	4.0	11.4	5.3
RI.....	994.5	310.6	250.9	59.8	24.5	8.7	45.9	26.4	2.6	8.7	2.4
SC	896.0	261.4	200.9	75.6	47.0	25.9	40.9	25.8	7.0	11.7	9.2
SD	930.3	285.6	211.9	72.9	48.8	22.4	42.9	27.9	(S)	15.6	(S)
TN	981.1	304.1	220.8	72.9	48.4	22.5	48.6	24.8	4.3	13.7	9.1
TX	734.5	216.5	163.5	49.7	37.6	19.1	33.4	24.8	4.7	10.8	7.4
UT	562.3	137.2	112.9	37.9	34.0	18.8	23.0	22.3	(S)	16.0	3.0
VT	857.9	242.7	205.3	55.8	36.6	13.9	42.3	22.5	(S)	14.6	(S)
VA	799.7	235.9	189.8	56.2	34.4	13.9	36.5	19.6	4.5	12.2	6.6
WA.....	739.0	202.4	180.6	60.3	34.3	13.2	42.2	21.1	2.0	12.4	4.1
WV.....	1,150.0	380.0	260.8	67.1	46.4	20.7	63.3	39.9	1.1	12.8	4.9
WI	868.4	262.0	208.7	69.8	36.8	14.5	39.5	24.4	1.1	11.4	3.7
WY.....	780.6	218.5	175.7	60.1	48.0	28.1	49.9	23.9	(S)	18.1	(S)

S Figure does not meet publication standards. [1] Includes other causes not shown separately. [2] Includes allied conditions. [3] Human immunodeficiency virus.

Source: U.S. National Center for Health Statistics, *National Vital Statistics Report (NVSR)*.

U.S. Census Bureau, Statistical Abstract of the United States: 2001

No. 110. Estimated Persons Living With Acquired Immunodeficiency Syndrome (AIDS) by Selected Characteristics: 1994 to 1999

[These numbers do not represent actual cases of persons living with AIDS. Rather, these numbers are point estimates of persons living with AIDS derived by subtracting the estimated cumulative number of deaths in persons with AIDS from the estimated cumulative number of persons with AIDS. Estimated AIDS cases and estimated deaths are adjusted for reporting delays and for redistribution of cases initially reported with no identified risk, but not for incomplete reporting. See source, "Technical notes"]

Characteristic	1994	1995	1996	1997	1998	1999
Total	197,060	216,010	239,382	267,311	292,286	317,368
RACE/ETHNICITY						
White, not Hispanic.	86,417	91,302	98,119	106,734	114,079	121,485
Black, not Hispanic.	71,818	81,152	92,167	105,142	117,110	128,941
Hispanic	36,448	40,891	46,016	51,927	57,201	62,573
Asian/Pacific Islander	1,457	1,613	1,854	2,082	2,304	2,579
American Indian/Alaska Native	668	723	804	888	966	1,068
MALE ADULT/ADOLESCENT EXPOSURE CATEGORY						
Male total.	161,081	174,361	191,410	212,348	231,022	249,951
Men who have sex with men	94,694	100,938	110,272	121,981	132,441	143,108
Injecting drug use.	40,046	44,345	48,763	53,812	58,118	62,418
Men who have sex with men and inject drugs . . .	14,884	15,687	16,453	17,698	18,682	19,553
Hemophilia/coagulation disorder	1,699	1,729	1,740	1,788	1,825	1,853
Heterosexual contact.	7,903	9,760	12,174	14,907	17,627	20,495
Receipt of blood transfusion, blood components, or tissue	914	963	1,035	1,140	1,253	1,375
Risk not reported or identified	940	937	974	1,023	1,080	1,151
FEMALE ADULT/ADOLESCENT EXPOSURE CATEGORY						
Female total.	32,702	38,234	44,484	51,386	57,578	63,682
Injecting drug use.	16,244	18,352	20,357	22,661	24,457	26,122
Hemophilia/coagulation disorder	108	137	164	201	229	248
Heterosexual contact.	15,131	18,478	22,566	26,974	31,187	35,445
Receipt of blood transfusion, blood components, or tissue	843	888	980	1,088	1,203	1,318
Risk not reported or identified	376	379	416	463	504	548
Pediatric [1] exposure category	3,277	3,415	3,487	3,577	3,682	3,732

[1] Less than 13 years old.

Source: Centers for Disease Control and Prevention, HIV/AIDS Surveillance Report, annual.

No. 111. Death Rates From Heart Disease by Sex and Age: 1980 to 1998

[Deaths per 100,000 population in specified age groups. Beginning 1970, excludes deaths of nonresidents of the United States. Beginning 1980, deaths classified according to the ninth revision of the International Classification of Diseases. For earlier years, classified according to the revision in use at the time; see text, this section. See Appendix III]

Age at death and selected type of heart disease	Male					Female				
	1980	1990	1995	1997	1998	1980	1990	1995	1997	1998
Total U.S. rate [1]	369	298	283	272	267	305	282	279	271	268
25 to 34 years	11	10	11	11	10	5	5	6	6	6
35 to 44 years old.	69	48	47	44	42	21	15	17	17	16
45 to 54 years old.	283	183	169	158	149	85	61	56	54	52
55 to 64 years old.	747	537	465	435	405	272	216	194	182	173
65 to 74 years old.	1,728	1,250	1,102	1,031	996	829	617	558	529	524
75 to 84 years old.	3,834	2,968	2,615	2,444	2,382	2,497	1,894	1,715	1,617	1,587
85 years old and over	8,753	7,418	7,040	6,659	6,354	7,351	6,478	6,268	6,014	5,898
Persons 45 to 54 years old:										
Ischemic heart.	217.3	123.8	107.5	98.0	90.9	52.2	33.6	29.4	27.8	25.3
Rheumatic heart	3.1	1.1	0.7	0.8	0.9	4.3	1.9	1.3	1.3	1.1
Hypertensive heart [2].	8.3	7.6	8.8	9.4	8.9	5.5	4.3	3.9	4.2	4.0
Persons 55 to 64 years old:										
Ischemic heart.	581.1	375.4	312.6	286.0	264.7	189.0	135.4	116.8	108.2	101.3
Rheumatic heart	6.2	3.4	2.2	2.0	1.8	9.2	4.7	3.4	2.9	3.1
Hypertensive heart [2].	21.8	18.1	18.2	18.2	19.1	13.3	10.9	9.3	9.6	9.6
Persons 65 to 74 years old:										
Ischemic heart.	1,355.5	898.5	770.5	712.1	684.1	605.3	415.2	362.8	336.5	329.3
Rheumatic heart	11.8	7.1	4.5	4.3	4.0	18.6	10.5	8.3	7.5	7.5
Hypertensive heart [2].	44.3	33.2	30.9	31.6	31.4	36.2	25.9	22.1	21.7	22.4
Persons 75 to 84 years old:										
Ischemic heart.	2,953.7	2,129.6	1,824.0	1,688.0	1,636.6	1,842.7	1,287.6	1,116.3	1,032.3	1,007.8
Rheumatic heart	16.7	12.3	10.7	10.3	9.1	25.4	22.5	17.9	15.9	15.2
Hypertensive heart [2].	90.7	67.9	59.7	58.5	59.3	101.1	69.7	62.4	61.4	61.6
Persons 85 years old and over:										
Ischemic heart.	6,501.6	5,120.7	4,674.4	4,370.7	4,145.7	5,280.6	4,257.8	3,948.8	3,711.0	3,594.8
Rheumatic heart	19.5	18.7	21.5	21.0	17.2	25.8	33.3	28.8	29.2	28.6
Hypertensive heart [2].	180.3	154.3	154.9	161.4	159.2	250.8	212.1	223.2	235.7	235.7

[1] Includes persons under 25 years old, not shown separately.   [2] With or without renal disease.

Source: U.S. National Center for Health Statistics, Vital Statistics of the United States, annual; and unpublished data.

No. 112. Death Rates From Cancer by Sex and Age: 1990 to 1998

[Deaths per 100,000 population in the specified age groups. See headnote, Table 111]

Age at death and selected type of cancer	Male 1990	1995	1996	1997	1998	Female 1990	1995	1996	1997	1998
Total [1]	221.3	219.5	217.2	214.6	213.6	186.0	191.0	190.2	189.2	187.7
25 to 34 years	12.6	11.7	11.5	11.5	10.9	12.6	12.2	12.6	11.7	11.7
35 to 44 years	38.5	36.5	35.6	34.5	34.4	48.1	44.0	42.9	43.1	42.1
45 to 54 years	162.5	143.7	140.7	138.0	136.5	155.5	140.7	135.2	132.3	128.2
55 to 64 years	532.9	480.5	469.1	453.4	441.1	375.2	357.5	349.6	343.2	331.6
65 to 74 years	1,122.2	1,089.9	1,080.9	1,058.4	1,045.5	677.4	690.7	685.2	676.8	675.2
75 to 84 years	1,914.4	1,842.3	1,802.7	1,770.2	1,745.6	1,010.3	1,061.5	1,060.0	1,050.6	1,048.6
85 years old and over	2,739.9	2,837.3	2,733.1	2,712.5	2,562.6	1,372.1	1,429.1	1,426.8	1,439.2	1,412.5
Persons, 35 to 44 years old:										
Respiratory, intrathoracic	9.1	7.6	7.8	7.5	7.5	5.4	5.1	5.3	5.6	5.5
Digestive organs, peritoneum	8.9	8.9	8.7	8.5	8.4	5.5	5.5	5.5	5.7	5.6
Breast	(B)	(B)	(B)	(B)	(B)	17.8	15.0	14.2	14.0	13.4
Genital organs	0.6	0.7	0.6	0.6	0.7	7.3	6.7	6.5	6.3	6.4
Lymphatic and hematopoietic tissues, excl. leukemia	4.5	4.9	4.6	4.3	3.9	2.1	2.3	2.2	2.3	1.9
Urinary organs	1.5	1.5	1.4	1.3	1.5	0.6	0.7	0.6	0.7	0.7
Lip, oral cavity, and pharynx	1.3	1.1	1.1	1.1	1.0	0.3	0.4	0.4	0.4	0.4
Leukemia	2.5	2.4	2.1	2.1	2.5	2.2	1.7	1.7	1.7	1.7
Persons, 45 to 54 years old:										
Respiratory, intrathoracic	63.0	49.9	48.5	45.2	43.6	35.3	30.1	29.0	27.5	26.7
Digestive organs, peritoneum	40.4	37.3	36.6	38.4	39.4	23.3	21.0	20.2	20.1	20.8
Breast	0.3	0.3	0.2	0.2	0.2	45.4	41.4	38.8	37.8	35.8
Genital organs	2.9	2.6	2.9	2.7	2.6	19.4	17.6	16.4	17.1	16.6
Lymphatic and hematopoietic tissues, excl. leukemia	10.9	11.0	10.3	10.9	10.2	6.0	6.2	6.2	5.8	5.6
Urinary organs	7.2	7.1	6.9	7.0	7.2	2.9	2.8	2.8	3.0	2.6
Lip, oral cavity, and pharynx	5.9	5.3	4.9	5.0	4.8	1.6	1.3	1.2	1.4	1.3
Leukemia	5.6	4.8	5.1	4.9	4.6	4.1	3.5	3.5	3.5	3.3
Persons, 55 to 64 years old:										
Respiratory, intrathoracic	232.6	196.1	190.7	182.7	176.4	107.6	104.8	102.2	100.7	99.7
Digestive organs, peritoneum	124.0	120.9	117.1	115.4	112.5	69.3	66.0	63.6	62.7	61.3
Breast	0.6	0.7	0.6	0.7	0.5	78.6	69.8	67.4	64.4	62.2
Genital organs	27.9	23.6	22.2	20.5	20.1	40.1	37.2	37.1	36.1	35.1
Lymphatic and hematopoietic tissues, excl. leukemia	27.2	27.7	27.8	27.6	26.5	16.7	18.6	18.6	18.9	17.2
Urinary organs	23.5	21.9	22.1	21.6	21.7	8.8	9.1	8.7	8.7	8.5
Lip, oral cavity, and pharynx	16.2	12.7	12.8	11.7	12.1	4.7	4.3	4.1	3.7	3.7
Leukemia	14.7	14.5	14.0	13.8	12.8	8.8	8.7	8.5	8.7	7.9
Persons, 65 to 74 years old:										
Respiratory, intrathoracic	447.3	432.4	424.6	418.8	416.4	181.7	205.0	209.0	212.0	215.3
Digestive organs, peritoneum	267.4	256.9	255.0	252.4	250.9	153.0	149.9	147.1	141.8	143.5
Breast	1.1	1.1	1.2	1.2	0.9	111.7	103.3	99.1	94.1	93.3
Genital organs	123.5	110.0	107.8	98.7	92.6	71.0	66.7	65.9	65.6	64.6
Lymphatic and hematopoietic tissues, excl. leukemia	56.8	61.3	61.6	63.5	61.9	39.5	44.0	43.0	43.5	42.8
Urinary organs	50.7	50.9	52.7	51.6	52.2	19.8	19.8	20.0	20.0	19.7
Lip, oral cavity, and pharynx	21.5	19.3	19.1	19.2	18.0	8.3	7.5	6.6	7.0	6.5
Leukemia	36.0	37.2	37.1	37.4	36.8	18.8	18.9	20.0	19.2	18.9
Persons, 75 to 84 years old:										
Respiratory, intrathoracic	594.4	573.4	566.9	562.9	553.2	194.5	245.1	251.1	258.9	262.8
Digestive organs, peritoneum	468.0	418.7	418.7	415.7	412.1	293.3	283.4	280.5	274.2	271.5
Breast	1.6	2.4	2.3	2.1	2.5	146.3	142.0	139.8	132.1	131.4
Genital organs	358.5	333.9	321.7	301.3	291.6	95.3	96.3	95.0	93.5	93.7
Lymphatic and hematopoietic tissues, excl. leukemia	104.5	109.3	113.4	114.1	112.6	71.2	80.3	80.2	80.7	82.4
Urinary organs	107.5	105.4	101.0	102.5	101.3	38.5	39.3	39.9	39.8	39.2
Lip, oral cavity, and pharynx	26.1	23.2	21.1	20.5	21.8	11.6	10.3	10.5	10.4	10.2
Leukemia	71.9	75.1	71.4	71.6	71.9	38.8	39.9	40.8	37.9	39.4
Persons, 85 years old and over:										
Respiratory, intrathoracic	538.0	543.2	543.2	568.8	532.5	142.8	187.5	190.6	203.2	202.5
Digestive organs, peritoneum	699.5	644.0	644.0	628.2	598.8	497.6	478.8	478.3	477.9	469.9
Breast	2.4	4.2	4.2	3.3	4.0	196.8	203.7	204.9	198.5	194.7
Genital organs	750.0	821.5	775.2	767.4	705.0	115.6	120.5	117.5	117.3	114.6
Lymphatic and hematopoietic tissues, excl. leukemia	140.5	154.2	153.7	148.8	153.1	90.0	100.4	98.0	103.9	98.3
Urinary organs	186.3	192.2	192.8	186.0	186.4	68.5	68.4	67.4	70.8	67.8
Lip, oral cavity, and pharynx	37.4	34.1	29.6	29.1	29.9	17.5	17.7	16.3	16.7	18.2
Leukemia	116.0	123.0	120.7	115.7	102.2	65.0	65.5	64.6	65.3	65.8

B Base figure too small to meet statistical standards for reliability. [1] Includes persons under 25 years of age and malignant neoplasms of other and unspecified sites, not shown separately.

Source: U.S. National Center for Health Statistics, *Vital Statistics of the United States,* annual; and unpublished data.

Vital Statistics 85

No. 113. Death Rates From Accidents and Violence by Race and Sex: 1990 to 1998

[Rates are per 100,000 population. Excludes deaths of nonresidents of the United States. Deaths classified according to the ninth revision of the *International Classification of Diseases*. See text, this section. See Appendix III]

Cause of death	White						Black					
	Male			Female			Male			Female		
	1990	1995	1998	1990	1995	1998	1990	1995	1998	1990	1995	1998
Motor vehicle accidents	26.1	22.6	21.9	11.4	10.8	10.7	28.1	24.6	22.2	9.4	9.0	9.4
All other accidents	23.6	24.7	26.0	12.4	13.5	15.5	32.7	31.6	29.3	13.4	13.5	12.8
Suicide.	22.0	21.4	20.3	5.3	(NA)	4.8	12.0	(NA)	10.2	2.3	(NA)	1.8
Homicide	9.0	(NA)	6.1	2.8	(NA)	2.2	69.2	56.3	42.1	13.5	(NA)	8.6

NA Not available.

No. 114. Deaths and Death Rates From Accidents by Type: 1980 to 1998

[See headnote, Table 113, and Appendix III]

Type of accident	Deaths (number)					Rate per 100,000 population				
	1980	1990	1996	1997	1998	1980	1990	1996	1997	1998
Total	**105,718**	**91,983**	**(NA)**	**(NA)**	**(NA)**	**46.7**	**37.0**	**(NA)**	**35.7**	**36.2**
Motor vehicle accidents	53,172	46,814	43,649	43,458	43,501	23.5	18.8	16.5	16.2	16.1
Traffic	51,930	45,827	42,522	42,340	42,191	22.9	18.4	16.0	15.8	15.6
Nontraffic	1,242	987	1,127	1,118	1,310	0.5	0.4	0.4	0.4	0.5
Water-transport accidents	1,429	923	675	758	692	0.6	0.4	0.3	0.3	0.3
Air and space transport accidents . .	1,494	941	1,061	734	692	0.7	0.4	0.4	0.3	0.3
Railway accidents	632	663	565	527	515	0.3	0.3	0.2	0.2	0.2
Accidental falls	13,294	12,313	14,986	15,447	16,274	5.9	5.0	5.6	5.8	6.0
Accidental drowning.	6,043	3,979	3,488	3,561	3,964	2.7	1.6	1.3	1.3	1.5
Accidents caused by—										
Fires and flames	5,822	4,175	3,741	3,490	3,255	2.6	1.7	1.4	1.0	1.0
Firearms, unspecified and other . .	1,667	1,175	947	820	726	0.7	0.5	0.4	0.3	0.3
Handguns.	288	241	187	161	140	0.1	0.1	0.1	0.1	0.1
Electric current	1,095	670	482	488	548	0.5	0.3	0.2	0.2	0.2
Accidental poisoning by—										
Drugs and medicines	2,492	4,506	8,431	9,099	9,838	1.1	1.8	3.2	3.4	3.6
Other solid and liquid substances .	597	549	441	488	417	0.3	0.2	0.2	0.2	0.2
Gases and vapors	1,242	748	638	576	546	0.5	0.3	0.2	0.2	0.2
Complications due to medical procedures.	2,282	2,669	2,919	3,043	3,228	1.0	1.1	1.1	1.1	1.2
Inhalation and ingestion of objects . .	3,249	3,303	3,206	3,275	3,515	1.4	1.3	1.2	1.2	1.3

NA Not available.

Source of Tables 113-114: U.S. National Center for Health Statistics, *Vital Statistics of the United States*, annual; and unpublished data.

No. 115. Homicide Rates by Race, Sex, and Age: 1997 and 1998

[Rate per 100,000 population]

Age	White				Black			
	Male		Female		Male		Female	
	1997	1998	1997	1998	1997	1998	1997	1998
Total [1]	**6.7**	**6.1**	**2.3**	**2.2**	**47.1**	**42.1**	**9.3**	**8.6**
Under 1 year.	7.8	6.7	4.6	5.9	18.1	21.8	21.6	22.1
1-4 yrs..	1.9	1.7	1.6	1.6	7.1	9.5	5.5	7.0
5-9 yrs..	0.7	0.5	0.6	0.7	2.1	2.1	1.9	1.6
10-14 yrs..	1.4	1.3	0.6	1.0	5.6	4.4	2.3	2.6
15-19 yrs..	11.1	10.2	2.9	2.4	85.3	71.0	10.6	9.8
20-24 yrs..	15.4	14.4	3.5	3.2	146.0	126.7	16.4	15.8
25-29 yrs..	12.5	11.2	3.3	3.3	99.6	92.5	15.8	15.3
30-34 yrs..	10.3	9.2	3.5	3.3	66.9	57.9	15.0	12.9
35-39 yrs..	8.3	7.9	3.2	3.2	51.8	46.5	14.2	13.6
40-44 yrs..	7.3	7.2	2.5	3.0	41.9	40.0	12.1	10.3
45-49 yrs..	6.4	5.7	2.4	2.2	37.1	31.4	8.3	7.9
50-54 yrs..	5.2	4.7	1.7	1.6	24.4	27.5	4.8	3.9
55-59 yrs..	5.0	4.1	1.8	1.5	19.5	20.7	4.3	3.3
60-64 yrs..	4.0	3.5	1.3	1.2	20.7	17.1	5.7	(B)
65-69 yrs..	3.4	3.0	1.4	1.4	14.0	12.7	4.3	(B)
70-74 yrs..	3.1	2.7	1.9	1.5	14.8	11.7	(B)	(B)
75-79 yrs..	3.1	2.8	1.9	1.5	15.4	13.9	(B)	(B)
80-84 yrs..	3.1	3.0	2.1	2.3	(B)	(B)	(B)	(B)
85 yrs. and over.	5.2	2.8	2.7	2.0	(B)	(B)	(B)	(B)

B Base figure too small to meet statistical standards for reliability of a derived figure.   [1] Includes persons under 15 years old, not shown separately.

Source: U.S. National Center for Health Statistics, *Vital Statistics of the United States*, annual.

86   Vital Statistics

No. 116. Deaths—Life Years Lost and Mortality Costs by Age, Sex, and Cause: 1998

[*Life years lost:* Number of years person would have lived in absence of death. *Mortality cost:* value of lifetime earnings lost by persons who die prematurely, discounted at 6 percent]

Characteristic	Num-ber of deaths (1,000)	Life years lost [1] Total (1,000)	Per death	Mortality cost [2] Total (mil.)	Per death	Characteristic	Num-ber of deaths (1,000)	Life years lost [1] Total (1,000)	Per death	Mortality cost [2] Total (mil.)	Per death
Total, 1998 . .	**2,337**	**37,959**	**16.2**	**391,290**	**167,444**	Heart disease. . .	354	4,818	13.6	79,487	224,628
Under 5 yrs. old .	34	2,564	76.3	28,013	833,170	Cancer	282	4,325	15.3	51,467	182,470
5 to 14 yrs. old. .	8	537	68.9	7,924	1,017,102	Cerebrovascular					
15 to 24 yrs. old .	31	1,792	58.5	37,917	1,238,041	diseases	61	750	12.3	7,355	120,296
25 to 44 yrs. old .	131	5,650	43.0	133,550	1,016,498	Accidents and					
45 to 64 yrs. old .	326	9,884	30.3	145,852	446,900	adverse effects .	63	2,193	34.8	48,812	775,530
65 yrs. old and						Other	397	7,883	19.9	97,809	246,408
over	1,807	17,532	9.7	38,034	21,047						
Heart disease. . .	725	9,151	12.6	112,162	154,748	**Female . . . . .**	**1,180**	**17,989**	**15.2**	**106,360**	**90,143**
Cancer	542	8,944	16.5	81,201	149,950	Under 5 yrs. old .	15	1,185	79.4	10,597	710,441
Cerebrovascular						5 to 14 yrs. old. .	3	225	72.6	2,652	854,119
diseases	158	1,868	11.8	11,373	71,778	15 to 24 yrs. old .	8	496	62.7	7,840	991,157
Accidents and						25 to 44 yrs. old .	45	2,065	45.9	34,590	768,195
adverse effects .	98	3,248	33.2	61,550	629,827	45 to 64 yrs. old .	95	4,188	44.3	39,544	418,442
Other	814	14,748	18.1	125,005	153,501	65 yrs. old and					
Male	**1,157**	**19,969**	**17.3**	**284,930**	**246,279**	over	1,014	9,830	9.7	11,137	10,979
Under 5 yrs. old .	19	1,379	73.7	17,416	931,033	Heart disease. . .	371	4,333	11.7	32,675	88,086
5 to 14 yrs. old. .	5	312	66.6	5,272	1,125,097	Cancer	259	4,619	17.8	29,734	114,599
15 to 24 yrs. old .	23	1,296	57.1	30,077	1,324,005	Cerebrovascular					
25 to 44 yrs. old .	86	3,585	41.5	98,959	1,145,973	diseases	97	1,118	11.5	4,017	41,290
45 to 64 yrs. old .	232	5,695	24.6	106,308	458,499	Accidents and					
65 yrs. old and						adverse effects .	35	1,054	30.3	12,738	366,192
over	793	7,702	9.7	26,897	33,934	Other	417	6,864	16.4	27,196	65,152

[1] Based on life expectancy at year of death. [2] Cost estimates based on the person's age, sex, life expectancy at the time of death, labor force participation rates, annual earnings, value of homemaking services, and a 4 percent discount rate by which to convert to present worth the potential aggregate earnings lost over the years.

Source: Institute for Health and Aging, University of California, San Francisco, CA, unpublished data.

No. 117. Marriages and Divorces: 1970 to 1998

Year	Marriages [1] Number (1,000)	Total	Men, 15 yrs. old and over [2]	Women, 15 yrs. old and over [2]	Unmarried women 15 yrs. old and over	15 to 44 yrs. old	Divorces and annulments Number (1,000)	Total [2]	Married women, 15 yrs. old and over
1970	2,159	10.6	31.1	28.4	76.5	140.2	708	3.5	14.9
1975	2,153	10.0	27.9	25.6	66.9	118.5	1,036	4.8	20.3
1980	2,390	10.6	28.5	26.1	61.4	102.6	1,189	5.2	22.6
1984	2,477	10.5	28.0	25.8	59.5	99.0	1,169	5.0	21.5
1985	2,413	10.1	27.0	24.9	57.0	94.9	1,190	5.0	21.7
1986	2,407	10.0	26.6	24.5	56.2	93.9	1,178	4.9	21.2
1987	2,403	9.9	26.3	24.3	55.7	92.4	1,166	4.8	20.8
1988	2,396	9.8	26.0	24.0	54.6	91.0	1,167	4.8	20.7
1989	2,403	9.7	25.8	23.9	54.2	91.2	1,157	4.7	20.4
1990	2,443	9.8	26.0	24.1	54.5	91.3	1,182	4.7	20.9
1991	2,371	9.4	(NA)	(NA)	54.2	86.8	1,189	4.7	20.9
1992	2,362	9.3	(NA)	(NA)	53.3	88.2	1,215	4.8	21.2
1993	2,334	9.0	(NA)	(NA)	52.3	86.8	1,187	4.6	20.5
1994	2,362	9.1	(NA)	(NA)	51.5	84.0	1,191	4.6	20.5
1995	2,336	8.9	(NA)	(NA)	50.8	83.0	1,169	4.4	19.8
1996	2,344	8.8	(NA)	(NA)	49.7	81.5	1,150	4.3	19.5
1997	2,384	8.9	(NA)	(NA)	(NA)	(NA)	1,163	4.3	(NA)
1998	2,244	8.3	(NA)	(NA)	(NA)	(NA)	1,135	4.2	(NA)

NA Not available. [1] Beginning 1980, includes nonlicensed marriages registered in California. [2] Rates for 1981-88 are revised and may differ from rates published previously.

Source: U.S. National Center for Health Statistics, *Vital Statistics of the United States,* annual; and *National Vital Statistics Reports* (formerly Monthly Vital Statistics Report), and unpublished data.

Vital Statistics 87

No. 118. Marriages and Divorces—Number and Rate by State: 1990 to 1998

[2,443.0 represents 2,443,000. By place of occurance]

State	Marriages [1] Number (1,000) 1990	1995	1998	Rate per 1,000 population [2] 1990	1995	1998	Divorces [3] Number (1,000) 1990	1995	1998	Rate per 1,000 population [2] 1990	1995	1998
U.S.	2,443.0	2,336.0	2,258.0	9.8	8.9	8.3	1,182.0	1,169.0	850.8	4.7	4.4	4.3
Alabama	43.3	42.0	49.9	10.6	9.9	11.4	25.3	26.0	26.3	6.1	6.1	5.9
Alaska.	5.7	5.5	5.9	10.2	9.0	9.6	2.9	3.0	3.2	5.5	5.0	4.8
Arizona	37.0	38.9	37.9	10.0	9.2	7.9	25.1	27.6	25.8	6.9	6.6	5.8
Arkansas	35.7	36.6	38.4	15.3	14.7	15.1	16.8	16.0	15.4	6.9	6.5	6.3
California [4]	236.7	199.6	194.1	7.9	6.3	5.9	128.0	(NA)	(NA)	4.3	(NA)	(NA)
Colorado	31.5	34.3	31.4	9.8	9.2	7.7	18.4	(NA)	(NA)	5.5	(NA)	(NA)
Connecticut	27.8	22.6	19.9	7.9	6.7	6.1	10.3	10.6	9.6	3.2	2.9	3.2
Delaware	5.6	5.4	5.0	8.4	7.5	6.7	3.0	3.7	3.4	4.4	5.1	4.9
Dist. of Columbia. .	4.7	3.5	2.4	8.2	6.4	4.6	2.7	1.9	1.1	4.5	3.4	3.6
Florida.	142.3	144.3	139.5	10.9	10.2	9.2	81.7	79.5	80.1	6.3	5.6	5.3
Georgia	64.4	61.5	59.8	10.3	8.5	7.7	35.7	37.2	35.8	5.5	5.2	4.8
Hawaii.	18.1	18.8	20.8	16.4	15.8	17.5	5.2	5.5	4.8	4.6	4.6	4.6
Idaho	15.0	15.5	15.5	13.9	13.3	12.4	6.6	6.8	7.0	6.5	5.8	5.4
Illinois	97.1	83.2	84.5	8.8	7.0	7.0	44.3	38.8	40.5	3.8	3.3	3.2
Indiana	54.3	50.4	34.6	9.6	8.7	5.8	(NA)	(NA)	(NA)	(NA)	(NA)	(NA)
Iowa	24.8	22.0	23.5	9.0	7.8	8.2	11.1	10.5	9.5	3.9	3.7	3.7
Kansas	23.4	22.1	20.9	9.2	8.6	7.9	12.6	10.7	10.7	5.0	4.2	4.0
Kentucky	51.3	47.6	44.3	13.5	12.3	11.2	21.8	22.9	22.4	5.8	5.9	5.8
Louisiana.	41.2	40.8	42.2	9.6	9.4	9.6	(NA)	(NA)	(NA)	(NA)	(NA)	(NA)
Maine	11.8	10.8	10.5	9.7	8.7	8.4	5.3	5.5	5.1	4.3	4.4	4.4
Maryland	46.1	42.8	37.5	9.7	8.5	7.3	16.1	15.0	16.4	3.4	3.0	2.9
Massachusetts . . .	47.8	43.6	39.2	7.9	7.2	6.4	16.8	13.5	16.5	2.8	2.2	2.2
Michigan	76.1	71.0	66.1	8.2	7.4	6.7	40.2	39.9	38.9	4.3	4.2	4.0
Minnesota	33.7	32.8	32.2	7.7	7.1	6.7	15.4	15.8	15.3	3.5	3.4	3.3
Mississippi	24.3	21.5	20.6	9.4	8.0	7.4	14.4	13.1	13.0	5.5	4.8	4.7
Missouri.	49.3	44.9	43.8	9.6	8.4	8.0	26.4	26.8	25.8	5.1	5.0	4.9
Montana	7.0	6.6	6.4	8.6	7.6	7.2	4.1	4.2	3.4	5.1	4.8	4.7
Nebraska.	12.5	12.1	12.3	8.0	7.4	7.4	6.5	6.3	6.4	4.0	3.8	3.8
Nevada	123.4	134.8	143.9	99.0	88.1	79.5	13.3	12.4	14.8	11.4	8.1	6.8
New Hampshire . .	10.6	9.6	7.3	9.5	8.4	6.1	5.3	4.9	7.0	4.7	4.2	4.1
New Jersey	58.0	52.4	48.4	7.6	6.7	5.9	23.6	24.3	25.3	3.0	3.1	3.0
New Mexico.	13.2	15.1	13.4	8.8	9.0	7.7	7.7	11.3	8.0	4.9	6.7	6.5
New York.	169.3	147.4	115.9	8.6	8.1	6.4	57.9	56.0	45.8	3.2	3.1	3.1
North Carolina . . .	52.1	61.6	63.8	7.8	8.6	8.3	34.0	37.0	36.8	5.1	5.1	4.8
North Dakota	4.8	4.6	4.2	7.5	7.2	6.6	2.3	2.2	2.1	3.6	3.4	3.5
Ohio	95.8	90.1	85.6	9.0	8.1	7.6	51.0	48.7	46.0	4.7	4.4	4.3
Oklahoma	33.2	28.5	25.9	10.6	8.7	7.7	24.9	21.8	20.0	7.7	6.7	6.5
Oregon	25.2	25.7	26.0	8.9	8.2	7.9	15.9	15.0	15.2	5.5	4.8	4.5
Pennsylvania	86.8	75.8	74.2	7.1	6.3	6.2	40.1	39.4	38.5	3.3	3.3	3.3
Rhode Island	8.1	7.4	7.5	8.1	7.5	7.6	3.8	3.7	3.2	3.7	3.7	3.7
South Carolina . . .	55.8	44.6	41.5	15.9	12.1	10.7	16.1	14.8	14.6	4.5	4.0	3.8
South Dakota	7.7	7.3	6.7	11.1	10.0	9.2	2.6	2.9	2.6	3.7	4.0	3.9
Tennessee	66.6	82.3	81.2	13.9	15.7	14.8	32.3	33.1	34.5	6.5	6.3	6.0
Texas	182.8	188.5	188.9	10.5	10.1	9.4	94.0	99.9	(NA)	5.5	5.3	5.0
Utah	19.0	21.6	21.5	11.2	11.1	10.1	8.8	8.9	8.8	5.1	4.6	4.2
Vermont	6.1	6.1	5.9	10.9	10.3	9.9	2.6	2.8	2.6	4.5	4.8	4.7
Virginia	71.3	67.9	64.3	11.4	10.3	9.4	27.3	28.9	30.0	4.4	4.4	4.2
Washington	48.6	42.0	41.2	9.5	7.7	7.2	28.8	29.7	28.8	5.9	5.5	5.2
West Virginia	13.2	11.2	11.7	7.2	6.1	6.5	9.7	9.4	9.3	5.3	5.1	5.2
Wisconsin	41.2	36.3	35.1	7.9	7.1	6.7	17.8	17.5	17.7	3.6	3.4	3.3
Wyoming	4.8	5.2	4.7	10.7	10.7	9.7	3.1	3.2	2.8	6.6	6.7	6.7

NA Not available. [1] Data are counts of marriages performed, except as noted. [2] Based on total population residing in area; population enumerated as of April 1 for 1980; estimated as of July 1 for all other years. [3] Includes annulments. [4] Marriage data include nonlicensed marriages registered.

Source: U.S. National Center for Health Statistics, *Vital Statistics of the United States*, annual; *National Vital Statistics Reports (NVSR)* (formerly *Monthly Vital Statistical Report*).

Health and Nutrition

This section presents statistics on health expenditures and insurance coverage, including medicare and medicaid, medical personnel, hospitals, nursing homes and other care facilities, injuries, diseases, disability status, nutritional intake of the population, and food consumption. Summary statistics showing recent trends on health care and discussions of selected health issues are published annually by the U.S. National Center for Health Statistics (NCHS) in *Health, United States.* Data on national health expenditures, medical costs, and insurance coverage are compiled by the U.S. Centers for Medicare & Medicaid Services (CMS) (formerly Health Care Financing Administration), and appear in the quarterly *Health Care Financing Review* and in the annual *Medicare and Medicaid Statistical Supplement* to the *Health Care Financing Review.* Statistics on health insurance are also collected by NCHS and are published in Series 10 of *Vital and Health Statistics.* U.S. Census Bureau also publishes data on insurance coverage. Statistics on health facilities are collected by NCHS and are published in Series 14 of *Vital and Health Statistics.* Statistics on hospitals are published annually by the Health Forum, L.L.C., an American Hospital Association Company, in *Hospital Statistics.* Primary sources for data on nutrition are the quarterly *National Food Review* and the annual *Food Consumption, Prices, and Expenditures,* both issued by the U.S. Department of Agriculture. NCHS also conducts periodic surveys of nutrient levels in the population, including estimates of food and nutrient intake, overweight and obesity, hypercholesterolemia, hypertension, and clinical signs of malnutrition.

National health expenditures—CMS compiles estimates of national health expenditures (NHE) to measure spending for health care in the United States. The NHE accounts are structured to show spending by type of expenditure (i.e., hospital care, physician and clinical care, dental care, and other professional care;

home health care; retail sales of prescription drugs; other medical nondurables; vision products and other medical durables; nursing home care and other personal health expenditures; plus nonpersonal health expenditures for such items as public health, research, construction of medical facilities, administration, and the net cost of private health insurance) and by source of funding (e.g., private health insurance, out-of-pocket payments, and a range of public programs including medicare, medicaid, and those operated by the Department of Veterans Affairs (VA)).

Data used to estimate health expenditures come from existing sources which are tabulated for other purposes. The type of expenditure estimates rely upon statistics produced by such groups as the American Hospital Association, the Census Bureau, and the Department of Health and Human Services (HHS). Source of funding estimates are constructed using administrative and statistical records from the medicare and medicaid programs, the Department of Defense and VA medical programs, the Social Security Administration, Census Bureau's *Governmental Finances,* state and local governments, other HHS agencies, and other nongovernment sources. Detailed descriptions of sources and methods are available on the HCFA home page at <www.hcfa.gov/stats/nhe-oact/lessons>. The most recent analysis of health care expenditure estimates, are published in the Health Care Financing Review's annual article on national health expenditures. Portions of this report are also on <www.hcfa.gov/stats/nhe-oact/>.

Medicare and medicaid—Since July 1966, the federal medicare program has provided two coordinated plans for nearly all people age 65 and over: (1) A hospital insurance plan which covers hospital and related services and (2) a voluntary supplementary medical insurance plan, financed partially by monthly premiums

Health and Nutrition   89

paid by participants, which partly covers physicians' and related medical services. Such insurance also applies, since July 1973, to disabled beneficiaries of any age after 24 months of entitlement to cash benefits under the social security or railroad retirement programs and to persons with end stage renal disease.

Medicaid is a health insurance program for certain low-income people. These include: certain low-income families with children; aged, blind, or disabled people on Supplemental Security Income; certain low-income pregnant women and children; and people who have very high medical bills. Medicaid is funded and administered through a state-federal partnership. Although there are broad federal requirements for medicaid, states have a wide degree of flexibility to design their program. States have authority to establish eligibility standards, determine what benefits and services to cover, and set payment rates. All states, however, must cover these basic services: inpatient and outpatient hospital services, laboratory and X-ray services, skilled nursing and home health services, doctor's services, family planning, and periodic health checkups, diagnosis and treatment for children.

Health resources—Hospital statistics based on data from the American Hospital Association's yearly survey are published annually in *Hospital Statistics* and cover all hospitals accepted for registration by the Association. To be accepted for registration, a hospital must meet certain requirements relating to number of beds, construction, equipment, medical and nursing staff, patient care, clinical records, surgical and obstetrical facilities, diagnostic and treatment facilities, laboratory services, etc. Data obtained from NCHS cover all U.S. hospitals which meet certain criteria for inclusion. The criteria are published in *Vital and Health Statistics* reports, Series 13. NCHS defines a hospital as a nonfederal short-term general or special facility with six or more inpatient beds with an average stay of less than 60 days.

Statistics on the demographic characteristics of persons employed in the health occupations are compiled by the U.S.

Bureau of Labor Statistics and reported in *Employment and Earnings* (monthly) (see Table 593, Section 12, Labor Force, Employment, and Earnings). Data based on surveys of health personnel and utilization of health facilities providing long-term care, ambulatory care, and hospital care are presented in NCHS Series 13 and Series 14, *Data on Health Resources Utilization and Data on Health Resources: Manpower and Facilities.* Statistics on patient visits to health care providers, as reported in health interviews, appear in NCHS Series 10, *National Health Interview Survey Data.*

The CMS's *Health Care Financing Review* and its annual *Medicare and Medicaid Statistical Supplement* present data for hospitals and nursing homes as well as extended care facilities and home health agencies. These data are based on records of the medicare program and differ from those of other sources because they are limited to facilities meeting federal eligibility standards for participation in medicare.

Disability and illness—General health statistics, including morbidity, disability, injuries, preventive care, and findings from physiological testing are collected by NCHS in its National Health Interview Survey and its National Health and Nutrition Examination Surveys and appear in *Vital and Health Statistics,* Series 10 and 11, respectively. The Department of Labor compiles statistics on occupational injuries (see Section 12, Labor Force, Employment, and Wealth). Annual incidence data on notifiable diseases are compiled by the Public Health Service (PHS) at its Centers for Disease Control and Prevention in Atlanta, Georgia, and are published as a supplement to its *Morbidity and Mortality Weekly Report.* The list of diseases is revised annually and includes those which, by mutual agreement of the states and PHS, are communicable diseases of national importance.

Nutrition—Statistics on annual per capita consumption of food and its nutrient value are estimated by the U.S. Department of Agriculture and published quarterly in *National Food Review.* Historical data can be found in *Food Consumption, Prices, and Expenditures,*

90   Health and Nutrition

issued annually. Statistics on food insufficiency and food and nutrient intake are collected by NCHS to estimate the diet of the nation's population. NCHS also collects physical examination data to assess the population's nutritional status, including growth, overweight/obesity, nutritional deficiencies, and prevalence of nutrition-related conditions, such as hypertension, hypercholesterolemia, and diabetes.

Statistical reliability—For discussion of statistical collection, estimation, and sampling procedures and measures of reliability applicable to data from NCHS and CMS, see Appendix III.

No. 119. National Health Expenditures—Summary, 1960 to 1999, and Projections, 2000 to 2010

[In billions of dollars (27 represents $27,000,000,000). Includes Puerto Rico and outlying areas]

Year	Total expenditures [1]	Private expenditures			Public expenditures			Health services and supplies				
		Total [2]	Out-of-pocket	Insurance	Total	Federal	State and local	Total [3]	Hospital care	Physician and clinical services	Prescription drugs	Nursing home care
1960	27	20	13	6	7	3	4	25	9	5	3	1
1961	29	21	13	7	7	3	4	27	10	6	3	1
1962	31	23	14	7	8	4	4	29	11	6	3	1
1963	34	25	15	8	9	4	5	31	12	7	3	1
1964	38	28	17	9	9	4	5	34	13	8	3	1
1965	41	31	18	10	10	5	6	37	14	8	4	1
1966	45	32	19	10	14	7	6	41	16	9	4	2
1967	51	32	19	10	19	12	7	47	18	10	4	2
1968	57	36	21	12	22	14	8	53	21	11	5	3
1969	65	40	23	13	24	16	9	59	24	12	5	4
1970	73	45	25	16	28	18	10	67	28	14	5	4
1971	81	50	26	18	31	20	11	75	31	16	6	5
1972	91	56	29	21	35	23	12	84	34	17	6	6
1973	101	61	32	23	39	25	14	93	39	19	7	6
1974	114	67	35	26	46	30	16	106	45	22	7	7
1975	130	75	37	30	55	36	19	121	52	25	8	9
1976	149	87	41	37	62	42	20	139	60	28	9	10
1977	169	99	45	45	70	47	23	160	68	33	9	11
1978	189	110	48	52	80	54	26	179	76	35	10	13
1979	214	124	53	60	90	61	29	203	87	41	11	15
1980	246	141	58	68	105	71	34	233	102	47	12	18
1981	285	164	66	81	121	83	38	271	119	55	13	20
1982	321	187	72	94	134	92	42	305	135	61	15	23
1983	354	206	79	104	147	102	46	336	146	68	17	25
1984	389	228	86	117	161	113	48	371	156	77	20	28
1985	427	252	96	130	175	122	52	409	167	90	22	31
1986	457	267	103	134	190	131	59	439	178	100	24	34
1987	497	289	109	147	209	143	66	477	192	112	27	36
1988	557	331	119	174	226	154	72	535	209	127	31	41
1989	622	370	126	205	252	172	79	598	229	142	35	46
1990	696	413	138	233	282	193	90	669	254	158	40	53
1991	761	441	143	253	320	222	99	734	279	175	45	58
1992	827	468	147	272	358	251	107	797	302	190	48	62
1993	888	497	149	296	390	274	116	856	320	201	51	66
1994	937	509	146	309	427	299	129	904	332	210	55	68
1995	987	529	149	322	458	324	134	954	344	220	61	75
1996	1,038	554	155	337	484	347	138	1,004	356	229	67	80
1997	1,094	588	166	356	506	362	144	1,056	368	241	75	85
1998	1,146	623	176	377	523	369	154	1,108	377	254	85	88
1999	1,211	662	187	401	549	385	164	1,171	391	269	100	90
2000, proj	1,311	722	202	438	589	413	176	1,268	416	289	117	96
2001, proj	1,424	793	221	485	631	442	189	1,378	443	312	136	103
2002, proj	1,542	865	239	531	677	473	203	1,493	472	337	155	111
2003, proj	1,666	940	258	580	726	507	219	1,614	505	363	176	119
2004, proj	1,790	1,014	277	628	775	540	236	1,734	535	389	197	127
2005, proj	1,919	1,088	296	675	831	578	253	1,860	567	414	220	136
2006, proj	2,051	1,160	315	721	891	618	273	1,988	597	439	245	145
2007, proj	2,186	1,231	336	765	955	662	293	2,119	627	463	272	154
2008, proj	2,327	1,303	358	807	1,024	710	315	2,257	657	489	302	163
2009, proj	2,478	1,380	382	853	1,098	760	337	2,403	688	517	333	173
2010, proj	2,637	1,458	404	903	1,179	816	363	2,558	721	546	366	183

[1] Includes medical research and medical facilities construction, not shown separately. [2] Includes other private expenditures, not shown separately. [3] Includes other objects of expenditure, not shown separately.

Source: U. S. Centers for Medicare & Medicaid Services, *Health Care Financing Review,* summer 2001.

Health and Nutrition 91

No. 120. National Health Expenditures by Type: 1990 to 1999

[In billions of dollars (695.6 represents $695,600,000,000), except percent. Includes Puerto Rico and outlying areas]

Type of expenditure	1990	1993	1994	1995	1996	1997	1998	1999
Total	**695.6**	**887.6**	**936.7**	**987.0**	**1,038.0**	**1,093.9**	**1,146.1**	**1,210.7**
Annual percent change [1]	11.8	7.3	5.5	5.4	5.2	5.4	4.8	5.6
Percent of gross domestic product	12.0	13.4	13.3	13.3	13.3	13.2	13.0	13.0
Private expenditures	**413.2**	**497.3**	**509.4**	**528.8**	**553.6**	**588.0**	**623.2**	**662.1**
Health services and supplies	401.6	483.6	495.9	516.3	540.4	573.1	607.7	646.6
Out-of-pocket payments	137.8	148.9	146.2	149.2	155.0	165.5	176.1	186.5
Insurance premiums [2]	232.6	295.7	308.9	322.3	337.4	355.6	376.8	401.2
Other	31.2	39.1	40.8	44.8	47.9	52.0	54.8	58.9
Medical research	1.0	1.4	1.4	1.4	1.6	1.6	2.0	2.1
Medical facilities construction	10.7	12.3	12.1	11.1	11.6	13.3	13.6	13.4
Public expenditures	**282.4**	**390.3**	**427.3**	**458.2**	**484.4**	**505.8**	**522.9**	**548.5**
Percent federal of public	68.2	70.3	69.9	70.7	71.5	71.5	70.6	70.1
Health services and supplies	267.6	372.2	408.3	438.1	463.4	483.3	500.2	524.2
Medicare [3]	110.2	148.3	166.2	184.8	200.3	211.2	211.4	213.6
Public assistance medical payments [4] . .	78.7	126.6	139.2	149.5	157.6	164.9	176.9	193.4
Temporary disability insurance [5]	0.1	0.1	0.1	0.1	0.1	0.1	0.1	0.1
Workers' compensation (medical) [5]	17.5	21.6	22.2	21.9	21.9	20.3	20.2	20.7
Defense Dept. hospital, medical.	10.4	12.1	11.8	12.1	12.0	12.1	12.2	12.5
Maternal, child health programs.	1.9	2.2	2.3	2.3	2.4	2.5	2.6	2.8
Public health activities	20.2	27.2	30.0	31.4	32.9	36.0	38.6	41.1
Veterans' hospital, medical care.	11.3	14.1	15.1	15.4	16.3	16.3	16.9	17.6
Medical vocational rehabilitation.	0.4	0.5	0.5	0.6	0.6	0.6	0.6	0.6
State and local hospitals [6]	13.1	14.2	15.3	14.0	13.5	13.3	13.7	14.1
Other [7]	3.8	5.3	5.6	6.0	5.9	6.1	7.0	7.8
Medical research	11.7	14.2	14.8	15.7	16.2	17.1	18.6	20.1
Medical facilities construction	3.1	3.9	4.2	4.4	4.8	5.4	4.1	4.2

[1] Change from immediate prior year. For explanation of average annual percent change, see Guide to Tabular Presentation. [2] Covers insurance benefits and amount retained by insurance companies for expenses, additions to reserves, and profits (net cost of insurance). [3] Represents expenditures for benefits and administrative cost from federal hospital and medical insurance trust funds under old-age, survivors, disability, and health insurance programs; see text, this section. [4] Payments made directly to suppliers of medical care (primarily medicaid). [5] Includes medical benefits paid under public law by private insurance carriers, state governments, and self-insurers. [6] Expenditures not offset by other revenues. [7] Covers expenditures for Substance Abuse and Mental Health Services Administration, Indian Health Service; school health and other programs.

Source: U.S. Centers for Medicare & Medicaid Services, *Health Care Financing Review*, summer 2001.

No. 121. National Health Expenditures by Object, 1990 to 1999, and Projections, 2000

[In billions of dollars (695.6 represents $695,600,000,000). Includes Puerto Rico and outlying areas]

Object of expenditure	1990	1993	1994	1995	1996	1997	1998	1999	2000, proj.
Total	**695.6**	**887.6**	**936.7**	**987.0**	**1,038.0**	**1,093.9**	**1,146.1**	**1,210.7**	**1,311.1**
Spent by—									
Consumers	370.4	444.5	455.1	471.5	492.5	521.1	552.9	587.7	640.9
Out-of-pocket	137.8	148.9	146.2	149.2	155.0	165.5	176.1	186.5	202.5
Private insurance.	232.6	295.7	308.9	322.3	337.4	355.6	376.8	401.2	438.4
Government.	282.4	390.3	427.3	458.2	484.4	505.8	522.9	548.5	589.4
Other [1]	42.8	52.7	54.3	57.3	61.1	66.9	70.3	74.4	80.8
Spent for—									
Health services and supplies.	669.2	855.8	904.2	954.4	1,003.8	1,056.5	1,107.9	1,170.8	1,268.2
Personal health care expenses	609.4	775.8	816.5	865.7	911.9	958.8	1,002.3	1,057.7	1,143.9
Hospital care.	253.9	320.0	332.4	343.6	355.9	367.7	377.1	390.9	415.8
Physician and clinical services	157.5	201.2	210.4	220.5	229.3	240.9	254.2	269.4	289.2
Dental services	31.5	38.9	41.4	44.5	46.8	50.2	53.1	56.1	60.3
Other professional services [2]	18.2	24.5	25.7	28.5	30.9	33.4	35.9	37.9	41.2
Home health care.	12.6	21.9	26.1	30.5	33.6	34.5	33.5	33.1	36.6
Prescription drugs	40.3	51.3	54.6	60.8	67.2	75.1	85.2	99.6	116.9
Other medical products [3]	33.1	36.2	37.6	39.8	42.4	44.1	45.0	47.6	50.6
Nursing home care.	52.7	65.7	68.3	74.6	79.9	85.1	88.0	90.0	96.2
Other personal health care.	9.7	16.2	20.0	23.0	25.9	27.9	30.2	33.2	37.1
Government administration and net cost of private health insurance [4]	39.6	52.8	57.7	57.2	59.0	61.6	67.0	72.0	80.0
Government public health activities.	20.2	27.2	30.0	31.4	32.9	36.0	38.6	41.1	44.2
Medical research [5]	12.7	15.6	16.3	17.1	17.8	18.7	20.5	22.2	24.3
Medical facilities construction	13.7	16.2	16.2	15.5	16.4	18.7	17.7	17.6	18.7

[1] Includes nonpatient revenues, privately funded construction, and industrial inplant. [2] Includes services of registered and practical nurses in private duty, podiatrists, optometrists, physical therapists, clinical psychologists, chiropractors, naturopaths, and Christian Science practitioners. [3] Includes expenditures for other nondurable medical products plus durable medical equipment such as eyeglasses, hearing aids, orthopedic appliances, artificial limbs, crutches, wheelchairs. [4] Includes administrative expenses of federally financed health programs. [5] Research and development expenditures of drug companies and other manufacturers and providers of medical equipment and supplies are excluded from research expenditures, but are included in the expenditure class in which the product falls.

Source: U.S. Centers for Medicare & Medicaid Services, *Health Care Financing Review*, summer 2001.

No. 122. Health Services and Supplies—Per Capita Consumer Expenditures by Object: 1990 to 1999

[In dollars, except percent. Based on Social Security Administration estimates of total U.S. population as of July 1, including Armed Forces and federal employees abroad and civilian population of outlying areas. Excludes research and construction]

Object of expenditure	1990	1993	1994	1995	1996	1997	1998	1999
Total, national	**2,633**	**3,258**	**3,410**	**3,564**	**3,715**	**3,874**	**4,025**	**4,215**
Annual percent change [1]	10.7	6.2	4.6	4.5	4.2	4.3	3.9	4.7
Hospital care	999	1,218	1,253	1,283	1,317	1,348	1,370	1,407
Physician and clinical services	620	766	793	823	849	884	924	970
Dental services	124	148	156	166	173	184	193	202
Other professional services [2]	71	93	97	107	114	122	130	136
Home health care	49	83	98	114	124	127	122	119
Prescription drugs	159	195	206	227	249	276	310	358
Other nondurable medical products	88	89	91	95	100	102	104	111
Durable medical equipment [2]	42	49	50	53	57	59	59	61
Nursing home care	207	250	258	278	296	312	320	324
Other personal health care	38	62	75	86	96	102	110	120
Government administration and net cost of private health insurance	156	201	218	214	218	226	243	259
Government public health activities	80	104	113	117	122	132	140	148
Total, private consumer [3]	**1,457**	**1,693**	**1,716**	**1,761**	**1,823**	**1,911**	**2,009**	**2,116**
Hospital care	427	472	460	454	451	458	477	492
Physician and clinical services	386	480	489	499	511	532	552	574
Dental services	120	141	149	158	165	175	184	192
Other professional services [2]	47	60	62	69	75	82	89	95
Home health care	20	28	31	36	42	48	53	55
Prescription drugs	132	159	166	182	198	219	243	280
Other nondurable medical products	86	86	88	91	96	98	100	106
Durable medical equipment [2]	33	37	37	38	41	42	42	44
Nursing home care	90	88	86	95	99	104	111	113
Net cost of private health insurance	116	143	149	139	145	153	158	165

[1] Change from immediate prior year. [2] See footnotes for corresponding objects in Table 121. [3] Represents out-of-pocket payments and private health insurance.

No. 123. Government Expenditures for Health Services and Supplies: 1999

[In millions of dollars (524,240 represents $524,240,000,000). Includes Puerto Rico and outlying areas. Excludes medical research and construction]

Type of service	Total [1]	Federal	State and local	Medicare [2] (OASDHI)	Public assistance [3]	Other health services			
						Veterans	Defense Dept. [4]	Workers' compensation [5]	
Total [1]	**524,240**	**366,859**	**157,381**	**213,550**	**193,351**	**17,599**	**12,543**	**20,720**	
Hospital care	232,581	185,236	47,345	121,365	69,128	13,278	9,220	7,448	
Physician and clinical services	87,184	72,789	14,395	54,665	18,711	969	2,101	6,347	
Prescription drugs	21,656	12,450	9,206	1,953	18,683	25	475	423	
Nursing home care	54,143	35,580	18,564	9,636	42,718	1,789	-	-	
Gov't administration	25,106	15,304	9,801	7,620	12,866	74	159	4,080	
Public health activities . . .	41,130	4,359	36,772	-	-	-	-	-	

- Represents zero. [1] Includes other items not shown separately. [2] Covers hospital and medical insurance payments and administrative costs under old-age, survivors, disability, and health insurance program. [3] Covers medicaid and other medical public assistance. Excludes funds paid into medicare trust fund by states to cover premiums for public assistance recipients and medically indigent persons. [4] Includes care for retirees and military dependents. [5] Medical benefits.

No. 124. Personal Health Care—Third Party Payments and Private Consumer Expenditures, 1990 to 1999, and Projections, 2000

[In billions of dollars (609.4 represents $609,400,000,000), except percent. See headnote, Table 125]

Item	1990	1993	1994	1995	1996	1997	1998	1999	2000, proj
Personal health care expenditures	609.4	775.8	816.5	865.7	911.9	958.8	1,002.3	1,057.7	1,143.9
Third party payments, total	**471.7**	**626.9**	**670.3**	**716.6**	**756.9**	**793.3**	**826.1**	**871.2**	**941.5**
Percent of personal health care	77.4	80.8	82.1	82.8	83.0	82.7	82.4	82.4	82.3
Private insurance payments	203.2	258.0	269.3	285.0	298.2	313.8	333.2	355.3	387.4
Government expenditures	237.8	330.4	360.8	387.4	411.5	428.2	439.1	458.0	490.7
Other [1]	30.6	38.5	40.2	44.1	47.2	51.3	53.8	57.9	63.3
Private consumer expenditures [2]	**341.0**	**406.9**	**415.6**	**434.2**	**453.2**	**479.3**	**509.4**	**541.8**	**589.9**
Percent met by private insurance . . .	59.6	63.4	64.8	65.6	65.8	65.5	65.4	65.6	65.7
Hospital care	108.5	123.9	121.9	121.5	122.0	125.0	131.3	136.7	147.5
Percent met by private insurance . . .	89.6	89.8	90.9	91.4	91.4	91.2	91.0	90.8	91.3
Physician and clinical services	98.1	126.0	129.8	133.5	138.1	145.0	151.8	159.3	169.8
Percent met by private insurance . . .	69.0	76.4	78.4	80.5	80.5	80.2	80.3	80.7	80.6
Prescription drugs	33.7	41.7	43.9	48.7	53.5	59.6	66.9	77.9	91.5
Percent met by private insurance . . .	29.3	33.3	37.9	44.0	47.9	50.9	53.3	55.1	56.1

[1] Includes nonpatient revenues and industrial inplant health services. [2] Includes expenditures not shown separately. Represents out-of-pocket payments and private health insurance benefits. Excludes net cost of insurance.

Source of Tables 122-124: U.S. Centers for Medicare & Medicaid Services, *Health Care Financing Review*, summer 2001.

Health and Nutrition 93

No. 125. Personal Health Care Expenditures by Object and Source of Payment: 1999

[In millions of dollars (1,057,722 represents $1,057,722,000,000), except as indicated. Includes Puerto Rico and outlying areas. Covers all expenditures for health services and supplies, except net cost of insurance and administration, government public health activities, and expenditures of philanthropic agencies for fund raising activities]

Object of expenditure		Private payments					Govern-ment	Third party pay-ments[2]
	Total	Total	Consumer					
			Total	Out of pocket payments	Private health insurance	Other[1]		
Total	1,057,722	599,718	541,790	186,531	355,259	57,928	458,004	871,191
Hospital care.	390,933	158,352	136,671	12,566	124,105	21,682	232,581	378,367
Physician and clinical services	269,360	182,176	159,325	30,682	128,643	22,851	87,184	238,678
Dental services	56,050	53,478	53,343	25,649	27,694	135	2,572	30,401
Other professional services[3]	37,886	29,403	26,294	11,379	14,915	3,109	8,483	26,506
Home health care	33,054	16,943	15,221	8,962	6,259	1,722	16,111	24,092
Prescription drugs	99,562	77,906	77,906	34,946	42,961	-	21,656	64,616
Other nondurable medical products.	30,708	29,496	29,496	29,496	-	-	1,212	1,212
Durable medical equipment	16,874	12,097	12,097	8,940	3,157	-	4,777	7,934
Nursing home care.	90,046	35,903	31,436	23,911	7,526	4,466	54,143	66,136
Other personal health care	33,249	3,963	-	-	-	3,963	29,285	33,249

- Represents zero.   [1] Includes nonpatient revenues and industrial plant.   [2] Covers private health insurance, other private payments, and government.   [3] See footnotes for corresponding items on Table 121.

Source: U.S. Centers for Medicare & Medicaid Services, *Health Care Financing Review*, summer 2000.

No. 126. Hospital Care and Physician and Clinical Service Expenditures by Source of Payment: 1990 to 1999

[In billions of dollars (253.9 represents $253,900,000,000)]

Source of payment	Hospital care					Physician and clinical services				
	1990	1995	1997	1998	1999	1990	1995	1997	1998	1999
Total	253.9	343.6	367.7	377.1	390.9	157.5	220.5	240.9	254.2	269.4
Out-of-pocket payments	11.2	10.5	11.0	11.8	12.6	30.4	26.3	28.7	29.9	30.7
Third-party payments	242.7	333.1	356.6	365.3	378.4	127.1	194.2	212.2	224.3	238.7
Private health insurance	97.2	111.0	113.9	119.5	124.1	67.7	107.3	116.2	121.9	128.6
Other private funds	10.4	14.6	17.9	19.9	21.7	11.3	17.6	20.1	21.1	22.9
Government	135.1	207.5	224.8	225.9	232.6	48.1	69.4	75.9	81.3	87.2
Federal	102.6	167.4	183.5	181.5	185.2	38.7	56.1	62.6	67.7	72.8
State and local	32.5	40.1	41.4	44.5	47.3	9.4	13.2	13.3	13.7	14.4
Medicare[1]	67.8	108.5	124.1	121.8	121.4	30.2	41.7	47.4	51.3	54.7
Medicaid[2]	27.6	54.3	58.0	60.8	66.5	7.0	14.8	16.2	16.7	17.7

[1] Medicare expenditures come from federal funds.   [2] Medicaid expenditures come from federal and state and local funds.

Source: U.S. Centers for Medicare & Medicaid Services, *Health Care Financing Review*, summer 2001.

No. 127. Retail Prescription Drug Sales: 1995 to 2000

[2,125 represents 2,125,000,000]

Sales outlet	Number of prescriptions (millions)					Retail sales (bil. dol.)				
	1995	1997	1998	1999	2000	1995	1997	1998	1999	2000
Total	2,125	2,316	2,481	2,707	2,843	68.6	89.1	103.0	121.7	140.7
Traditional chain	914	1,038	1,129	1,246	1,336	27.4	36.4	43.1	51.6	59.7
Independent.	666	646	651	680	682	20.0	22.5	24.8	28.1	30.4
Mass merchant.	238	254	272	289	293	7.2	8.9	10.4	12.0	13.1
Supermarkets.	221	269	306	357	389	7.0	9.8	11.4	13.4	16.9
Mail order	86	109	123	134	144	7.0	11.4	13.4	16.6	20.6

Source: National Association of Chain Drug Stores, Alexandria, VA, *The Chain Pharmacy Industry Profile, 2000* (copyright).

No. 128. Personal Health Care Expenditures by State, 1990 to 1998, and by Selected Object, 1998

[In millions of dollars (612,245 represents $612,245,000,000). This series of state health expenditures (SHE) uses the same definitions and, to the extent possible, the same data sources as does the national health expenditures series. For health services, this structure clusters spending according to the establishment providing those services. For retail purchases of medical products, it groups spending according to product classification. Thus, SHE is establishment-based, grouping services together according to place of service or of product sale rather than according to type of service. Establishment-based expenditures are those in which spending is located in the state of the provider rather than in the beneficiary's state of residence. Because people are able to cross state borders to receive health care services, health care spending by provider location is not necessarily an accurate reflection of spending on behalf of persons residing in that state]

State	1990	1995	1996	1997	Total [1]	Hospital care	Physician and other professional services	Prescription drugs	Nursing home care
U.S.	612,245	876,212	920,970	965,701	1,016,383	380,050	296,102	90,648	87,826
AL.........	9,163	13,654	14,537	15,519	16,056	6,618	4,609	1,552	1,064
AK.........	1,347	1,921	2,042	2,133	2,299	986	568	133	42
AZ.........	8,562	12,352	13,146	13,834	14,782	4,977	5,135	1,397	839
AR.........	4,925	7,149	7,539	8,033	8,463	3,324	2,225	903	776
CA.........	74,369	99,215	102,378	105,790	110,057	34,948	44,239	7,537	5,626
CO.........	7,740	11,395	12,004	12,776	13,669	4,850	4,314	970	904
CT.........	10,013	13,662	13,952	14,600	15,221	4,686	4,292	1,354	2,264
DE.........	1,728	2,619	2,698	2,915	3,106	1,166	792	300	290
DC.........	3,564	4,184	4,223	4,205	4,258	2,585	781	180	245
FL.........	35,789	51,328	54,404	56,754	59,724	19,742	18,985	6,204	4,880
GA.........	15,303	23,096	24,489	25,940	27,219	10,396	8,510	2,460	1,545
HI.........	2,745	4,168	4,427	4,452	4,658	1,775	1,594	311	204
ID.........	1,697	2,758	2,994	3,194	3,397	1,236	935	334	264
IL.........	27,618	39,000	40,738	42,267	44,305	17,996	11,975	3,964	3,924
IN.........	12,692	18,388	18,727	20,207	21,259	8,515	5,613	2,058	2,337
IA.........	6,067	8,513	9,073	9,496	10,198	4,084	2,457	945	1,186
KS.........	5,540	7,989	8,417	8,890	9,394	3,580	2,538	854	920
KY.........	7,820	11,790	12,651	13,592	14,414	5,731	3,785	1,564	1,283
LA.........	9,975	14,673	15,272	15,946	16,500	7,139	4,249	1,507	1,248
ME.........	2,695	3,908	4,242	4,554	4,925	1,846	1,219	456	476
MD.........	11,755	16,838	17,824	18,596	19,646	7,313	5,978	1,678	1,695
MA.........	19,027	25,997	27,033	28,471	30,039	11,305	8,322	2,172	3,568
MI.........	22,133	31,089	32,888	34,435	35,647	14,641	9,186	3,885	2,459
MN.........	11,462	16,826	17,776	18,858	20,313	6,540	7,183	1,491	1,964
MS.........	4,729	7,447	7,997	8,431	8,882	3,848	2,212	962	687
MO.........	12,690	18,024	18,900	19,783	20,911	8,828	5,310	1,814	2,002
MT.........	1,628	2,445	2,496	2,680	2,838	1,224	695	234	222
NE.........	3,531	5,091	5,500	5,721	6,095	2,597	1,367	626	697
NV.........	2,806	4,471	4,795	5,170	5,606	1,865	1,918	478	164
NH.........	2,558	3,779	4,033	4,333	4,658	1,559	1,405	391	425
NJ.........	20,169	29,504	30,865	31,580	32,695	11,191	9,506	3,545	3,233
NM.........	2,917	4,430	4,839	5,075	5,344	2,317	1,415	402	257
NY.........	53,926	75,183	78,503	81,100	85,785	32,636	20,103	7,122	10,586
NC.........	13,748	21,966	23,773	25,584	27,327	10,987	7,106	2,566	2,347
ND.........	1,639	2,373	2,461	2,542	2,680	1,282	612	192	287
OH.........	26,896	37,246	39,470	40,552	42,581	16,763	11,024	3,898	4,978
OK.........	6,357	9,454	10,095	10,419	10,988	4,218	2,978	1,056	954
OR.........	6,247	9,182	9,637	10,259	10,840	3,545	3,285	918	838
PA.........	32,635	45,050	46,398	48,853	51,322	20,213	13,434	5,035	5,883
RI.........	2,728	3,783	3,900	4,149	4,515	1,702	1,095	400	468
SC.........	6,806	10,616	11,199	12,363	13,204	5,597	3,254	1,315	907
SD.........	1,513	2,301	2,479	2,635	2,842	1,257	747	201	286
TN.........	12,213	18,820	20,026	21,154	22,021	8,276	6,719	2,129	2,001
TX.........	37,682	56,504	60,410	64,245	67,750	25,322	20,071	6,023	4,346
UT.........	3,233	4,807	5,229	5,622	5,944	2,290	1,648	564	300
VT.........	1,172	1,762	1,821	1,933	2,066	712	563	183	177
VA.........	13,252	18,712	19,899	21,103	22,261	8,689	6,265	2,130	1,546
WA.........	11,276	16,810	17,461	18,214	19,292	6,362	5,908	1,603	1,492
WV.........	3,930	6,024	6,314	6,692	7,037	2,955	1,793	776	515
WI.........	11,441	16,739	17,738	18,738	19,945	7,252	5,844	1,745	2,110
WY.........	793	1,179	1,260	1,313	1,407	582	343	133	113

[1] Includes other expenditures not shown separately.

Source: U.S. Centers for Medicare & Medicaid Services, <http://www.hcfa.gov/stats/nhe-oact/stateestimates/Tables98/AllPayer.csv>; (accessed 23 January 2001).

No. 129. Consumer Price Indexes of Medical Care Prices: 1980 to 2000

[1982-1984=100. Indexes are annual averages of monthly data based on components of consumer price index for all urban consumers; for explanation, see text, Section 14, Prices]

Year	Medical care services						Medical care commodities		Annual percent change [3]		
	Medical care, total	Total [1]	Professional services			Hospital and related services	Total [2]	Prescription drugs and medical supplies	Medical care, total	Medical care services	Medical care commodities
			Total [1]	Physicians	Dental						
1980....	74.9	74.8	77.9	76.5	78.9	69.2	75.4	72.5	11.0	11.3	9.3
1985....	113.5	113.2	113.5	113.3	114.2	116.1	115.2	120.1	6.3	6.1	7.2
1990....	162.8	162.7	156.1	160.8	155.8	178.0	163.4	181.7	9.0	9.3	8.4
1993....	201.4	202.9	184.7	191.3	188.1	231.9	195.0	223.0	5.9	6.5	3.7
1994....	211.0	213.4	192.5	199.8	197.1	245.6	200.7	230.6	4.8	5.2	2.9
1995....	220.5	224.2	201.0	208.8	206.8	257.8	204.5	235.0	4.5	5.1	1.9
1996....	228.2	232.4	208.3	216.4	216.5	269.5	210.4	242.9	3.5	3.7	2.9
1997....	234.6	239.1	215.4	222.9	226.6	278.4	215.3	249.3	2.8	2.9	2.3
1998....	242.1	246.8	222.2	229.5	236.2	287.5	221.8	258.6	3.2	3.2	3.0
1999....	250.6	255.1	229.2	236.0	247.2	299.5	230.7	273.4	3.5	3.4	4.0
2000....	260.8	266.0	237.7	244.7	258.5	317.3	238.1	285.4	4.1	4.3	3.2

[1] Includes other services not shown separately. [2] Includes other commodities not shown separately. [3] Percent change from the immediate prior year.

Source: U.S. Bureau of Labor Statistics, CPI Detailed Report, January 2001

No. 130. Average Annual Expenditures Per Consumer Unit for Health Care: 1985 to 1999

[In dollars, except percent. See text, Section 13, Income, Expenditures, and Wealth and headnote, Table 659. For composition of regions, see map, inside front cover]

Item	Health care, total					Percent distribution		
	Amount	Percent of total expenditures	Health insurance	Medical services	Drugs and medical supplies [1]	Health insurance	Medical services	Drugs and medical supplies [1]
1985	1,108	4.7	375	496	238	33.8	44.8	21.5
1990	1,480	5.2	581	562	337	39.3	38.0	22.8
1995	1,732	5.4	860	512	360	49.7	29.6	20.8
1996	1,770	5.2	827	543	400	46.7	30.7	22.6
1997	1,841	5.3	881	531	428	47.9	28.8	23.2
1998	1,903	5.4	913	542	448	48.0	28.5	23.5
1999	1,959	5.3	923	558	479	47.1	28.5	24.5
Age of reference person:								
Under 25 years old	551	2.5	233	184	133	42.3	33.4	24.1
25 to 34 years old..........	1,170	3.2	597	351	222	51.0	30.0	19.0
35 to 44 years old..........	1,631	3.8	746	531	355	45.7	32.6	21.8
45 to 54 years old..........	2,183	4.7	942	754	486	43.2	34.5	22.3
55 to 64 years old..........	2,450	6.2	1,063	751	636	43.4	30.7	26.0
65 to 74 years old..........	2,991	10.0	1,572	574	845	52.6	19.2	28.3
75 years old and over	3,052	13.3	1,534	632	887	50.3	20.7	29.1
Race of reference person:								
White and other	2,078	5.4	972	602	504	46.8	29.0	24.3
Black	1,093	4.0	564	239	291	51.6	21.9	26.6
Origin of reference person:								
Hispanic	1,119	3.4	534	313	273	47.7	28.0	24.4
Non-Hispanic	2,036	5.4	958	580	498	47.1	28.5	24.5
Region of residence:								
Northeast	1,804	4.7	840	568	395	46.6	31.5	21.9
Midwest	2,087	5.7	1,009	559	519	48.3	26.8	24.9
South	1,956	5.9	926	524	505	47.3	26.8	25.8
West..................	1,982	4.6	896	600	466	45.7	30.6	23.8
Size of consumer unit:								
One person	1,336	6.0	614	346	376	46.0	25.9	28.1
Two or more persons.......	2,214	5.1	1,049	644	521	47.4	29.1	23.5
Two persons.............	2,475	6.4	1,177	648	650	47.6	26.2	26.3
Three persons	1,946	4.5	903	607	437	46.4	31.2	22.5
Four persons	2,070	4.2	996	677	397	48.1	32.7	19.2
Five persons or more	2,024	4.3	958	647	419	47.3	32.0	20.7
Income before taxes:								
Complete income reporters [2] ...	2,042	5.2	945	579	517	46.3	28.4	25.3
Quintiles of income:								
Lowest 20 percent	1,248	7.4	600	266	382	48.1	21.3	30.6
Second 20 percent.....	1,912	7.7	899	447	565	47.0	23.4	29.6
Third 20 percent	1,960	5.9	959	522	478	48.9	26.6	24.4
Fourth 20 percent......	2,222	4.8	1,049	650	523	47.2	29.3	23.5
Highest 20 percent	2,862	3.8	1,217	1,009	636	42.7	35.3	22.2
Incomplete reporters of income .	1,716	5.6	854	492	370	49.8	28.7	21.6

[1] Includes prescription and nonprescription drugs. [2] A complete reporter is a consumer unit providing values for at least one of the major sources of income.

Source: Bureau of Labor Statistics, Consumer Expenditure Survey, annual.

[In millions (28.5 represents 28,500,000). As of July 1. Includes Puerto Rico and outlying areas and enrollees in foreign countries and unknown place of residence]

Item	1980	1985	1990	1995	1996	1997	1998	1999
Total	28.5	31.1	34.2	37.5	38.1	38.4	38.8	39.1
Aged	25.5	28.2	30.9	33.1	33.4	33.6	33.8	33.9
Disabled	3.0	2.9	3.3	4.4	4.6	4.8	5.0	5.2
Hospital insurance	28.1	30.6	33.7	37.1	37.7	38.1	38.4	38.7
Aged	25.1	27.7	30.5	32.7	33.0	33.2	33.4	33.5
Disabled	3.0	2.9	3.3	4.4	4.6	4.8	5.0	5.2
Supplementary medical insurance	27.4	30.0	32.6	35.7	36.1	36.5	36.8	37.0
Aged	24.7	27.3	29.7	31.7	32.0	32.2	32.3	32.4
Disabled	2.7	2.7	2.9	3.9	4.2	4.3	4.5	4.6

Source: U.S. Centers for Medicare & Medicaid Services, Office of the Actuary, "Medicare Enrollment Trends 1966-1999"; published 16 November 2000; <http://www.hcfa.gov/stats/enrltrnd.htm>.

No. 132. Medicare Disbursements by Type of Beneficiary: 1980 to 2000

[In millions of dollars (35,025 represents $35,025,000,000). For years ending Sept. 30. Distribution of benefits by type is estimated and subject to change]

Type of beneficiary	1980	1990	1995	1996	1997	1998	1999	2000
Total disbursements	35,025	109,709	180,096	194,263	210,342	213,412	211,959	219,275
Hospital insurance disbursements [1]	24,288	66,687	114,883	125,317	137,789	137,140	131,441	130,284
Benefits	23,776	65,721	113,394	123,908	136,007	134,321	129,107	125,992
Aged	20,951	58,503	100,107	109,379	120,239	118,467	113,321	110,142
Disabled	2,825	7,218	13,288	14,529	15,768	15,854	15,786	15,850
Disabled	2,654	6,467	12,320	13,474	14,659	14,791	14,731	14,768
ESRD [2]	171	751	968	1,055	1,109	1,063	1,056	1,082
Peer review activity	14	191	189	180	168	188	177	236
Administrative expenses [3]	497	774	1,300	1,229	1,614	1,653	1,978	2,350
Supplementary medical insurance disbursements [1]	10,737	43,022	65,213	68,946	72,553	76,272	80,518	88,991
Benefits	10,144	41,498	63,490	67,165	71,117	75,782	79,151	88,876
Aged	8,497	36,837	54,830	57,807	60,989	65,118	67,996	76,507
Disabled	1,647	4,661	8,660	9,358	10,128	10,664	11,154	12,369
Disabled	1,256	3,758	7,363	7,943	8,604	9,156	9,668	10,750
ESRD [2]	391	903	1,297	1,415	1,524	1,508	1,486	1,619
Peer review activity	-	-	2	11	16	33	36	43
Administrative expenses	593	1,524	1,722	1,771	1,420	1,435	1,510	1,779

- Represents zero. [1] Beginning 1998 home health agency transfers are excluded from total supplementary medical insurance disbursements and included in total hospital insurance disbursements. [2] Represents persons entitled because of End Stage Renal Disease only. Benefits for those who have ESRD but would be entitled due to their aged or disabled status are included in aged and disabled benefits. [3] Includes costs of experiments and demonstration projects. Includes costs of the health care fraud and abuse control program.

Source: U.S. Centers for Medicare & Medicaid Services, unpublished data.

No. 133. Medicare Trust Funds: 1980 to 2000

[In billions of dollars (23.9 represents $23,900,000,000)]

Type of trust fund	1980	1985	1990	1995	1996	1997	1998	1999	2000
HOSPITAL INSURANCE (HI)									
Net contribution income [1]	23.9	47.7	72.2	103.3	115.9	119.5	130.7	140.3	154.5
Interest received [2]	1.1	[3]3.4	8.5	10.8	10.2	9.6	9.3	10.1	11.7
Benefit payments	25.1	47.5	66.2	116.4	128.6	137.8	[4]134.0	[4]128.8	[4]128.5
Assets, end of year	13.7	[5]20.5	98.9	130.3	124.9	115.6	120.4	141.4	177.5
SUPPLEMENTARY MEDICAL INSURANCE (SMI)									
Net premium income	3.0	5.6	11.3	19.7	18.8	19.3	[6]20.9	[6]19.0	20.6
Transfers from general revenue	7.5	18.3	33.0	39.0	65.0	60.2	[6]64.1	[6]59.1	65.9
Interest received [2]	0.4	1.2	1.6	1.6	1.8	2.5	2.7	2.8	3.5
Benefit payments	10.6	22.9	42.5	65.0	68.6	72.8	[4]76.1	[4]80.7	[4]88.9
Assets, end of year	4.5	10.9	15.5	13.1	28.3	36.1	46.2	44.8	44.0

[1] Includes income from taxation of benefits beginning in 1995. Includes premiums from aged ineligibles enrolled in HI. [2] Includes recoveries of amounts reimbursed from the trust fund. [3] Reflects interest on interfund borrowing. [4] Monies tranferred to the SMI trust fund for home health agency costs, as provided for by P.L. 105-33, are included in HI benefit payments but excluded from SMI benefit payments. [5] Excludes $10.6 billion lent to the OASI Trust Fund (see Table 526). [6] Premiums withheld from check and associated general revenue contributions that were to occur on Jan. 3, 1999, actually occurred on December 31, 1998. These amounts are therefore excluded from 1999 data.

Source: U.S. Centers for Medicare & Medicaid Services, Annual Report of the Board of Trustees of the Federal Hospital Insurance Trust Fund and Annual Report of the Board of Trustees of the Federal Supplementary Medical Insurance Trust Fund.

Health and Nutrition 97

No. 134. Medicare—Persons Served and Reimbursements: 1990 to 1998

[24,809 represents 24,809,000. Persons served are enrollees who use covered services, incurred expenses greater than the applicable deductible amounts and for whom medicare paid benefits. Reimbursements are amounts paid to providers for covered services. Excluded are retroactive adjustments resulting from end of fiscal year cost settlements and certain lump-sum interim payments. Also excluded are beneficiary (or third party payor) liabilities for applicable deductibles, coinsurance amounts, and charges for noncovered services. Includes data for enrollees living in outlying territories and foreign countries]

Type of coverage and service	Unit	Persons 65 years old and over			Disabled persons [1]		
		1990	1995	1998	1990	1995	1998
Persons served, total [2]	1,000....	**24,809**	**27,379**	**25,931**	**2,390**	**3,333**	**3,641**
Hospital insurance [2]	1,000....	6,367	7,147	6,840	680	933	961
Inpatient hospital	1,000....	5,906	6,148	6,074	644	844	899
Skilled-nursing services	1,000....	615	1,186	1,443	23	54	75
Home health services	1,000....	1,818	3,185	2,641	122	272	225
Supplementary medical insurance [2]	1,000....	24,687	27,234	25,605	2,365	3,299	3,596
Physicians' and other medical services	1,000....	24,193	26,621	25,083	2,249	3,184	3,452
Outpatient services	1,000....	14,055	17,597	18,150	1,496	2,281	2,619
Home health services	1,000....	38	42	1,339	-	-	131
Persons served per 1,000 enrollees, total [2]	Rate	**802**	**826**	**767**	**734**	**759**	**725**
Hospital insurance [2]	Rate	209	218	205	209	212	191
Inpatient hospital	Rate	194	188	182	198	192	179
Skilled-nursing services	Rate	20	36	43	7	12	15
Home health services	Rate	60	97	79	38	62	45
Supplementary medical insurance [2]	Rate	832	858	793	804	837	804
Physicians' and other medical services	Rate	815	839	776	764	808	772
Outpatient services	Rate	474	554	562	508	579	586
Home health services	Rate	1	1	42	-	-	29
Reimbursements, total	Mil. dol ..	**88,778**	**138,948**	**146,355**	**11,239**	**21,024**	**23,855**
Per person served	Dollars ...	3,578	5,075	5,644	4,703	6,308	6,552
Hospital insurance	Mil. dol. ..	54,244	89,631	90,511	6,694	12,752	13,624
Inpatient hospital	Mil. dol. ..	48,952	68,213	71,899	6,346	11,079	12,342
Skilled-nursing services	Mil. dol. ..	1,886	7,504	11,074	85	374	603
Home health services	Mil. dol. ..	3,406	13,914	7,534	264	1,300	678
Supplementary medical insurance	Mil. dol. ..	34,533	49,317	55,844	4,545	8,272	10,231
Physicians' and other medical services	Mil. dol. ..	27,379	37,069	38,685	2,831	4,888	5,749
Outpatient services	Mil. dol. ..	7,077	12,045	12,972	1,714	3,384	3,994
Home health services	Mil. dol. ..	78	203	4,187	-	-	489

- Represents or rounds to zero.   [1] Age under 65; includes persons enrolled because of end-stage renal disease (ESRD) only.
[2] Persons are counted once for each type of covered service used, but are not double counted in totals.

Source: U.S. Centers for Medicare & Medicaid Serivces, *Medicare Program Statistics*, annual; and unpublished data.

No. 135. Medicare Benefits by Type of Provider: 1980 to 2000

[In millions of dollars (23,776 represents $23,776,000,000). For years ending Sept. 30. Distribution of benefits by type is estimated and subject to change]

Type of provider	1980	1990	1995	1996	1997	1998	1999	2000
Hospital insurance benefits, total	23,776	65,721	113,394	123,908	136,007	134,321	129,107	125,992
Inpatient hospital	22,860	57,012	81,095	84,513	88,541	86,942	85,696	86,566
Skilled nursing facility	392	2,761	8,683	10,416	12,388	13,377	11,488	10,593
Home health agency	524	3,295	15,715	17,157	17,938	14,115	8,994	4,552
Hospice	(NA)	318	1,854	1,969	2,082	2,080	2,494	2,818
Managed care	(NA)	2,335	6,047	9,853	15,059	17,807	20,435	21,463
Supplementary medical insurance benefits, total	10,144	41,498	63,490	67,165	71,117	75,782	79,151	88,876
Physician fee schedule	(NA)	(NA)	31,110	31,569	31,958	32,338	33,379	35,947
Durable medical equipment	(NA)	(NA)	3,576	3,785	4,112	4,104	4,278	4,573
Carrier lab [1]	(NA)	(NA)	2,819	2,654	2,414	2,166	2,085	2,201
Other carrier [2]	(NA)	(NA)	4,513	4,883	5,452	5,854	6,400	7,164
Hospital [3]	(NA)	(NA)	8,448	8,683	9,251	8,977	8,473	8,439
Home health	(NA)	(NA)	223	236	246	189	405	4,570
Intermediary lab [4]	(NA)	(NA)	1,437	1,338	1,419	1,478	1,517	1,622
Other intermediary [5]	(NA)	(NA)	5,110	5,664	6,372	6,543	5,642	6,013
Managed care	(NA)	(NA)	6,253	8,353	9,893	14,132	16,970	18,348

NA Not available.   [1] Lab services paid under the lab fee schedule performed in a physician's office lab or an independent lab.   [2] Includes free-standing ambulatory surgical centers facility costs, ambulance, and supplies.   [3] Includes the hospital facility costs for medicare Part B services which are predominantly in the outpatient department. The physician reimbursement associated with these services is included on the "Physician Fee Schedule" line.   [4] Lab fee services paid under the lab fee schedule performed in a hospital outpatient department.   [5] Includes ESRD free-standing dialysis facility payments and payments to rural health clinics, outpatient rehabilitation facilities, psychiatric hospitals, and federally qualified health centers.

Source: U.S. Centers for Medicare & Medicaid Services, unpublished data.

No. 136. Medicare—Summary by State and Other Area: 1995 and 2000

[For fiscal year ending in year shown. (37,535 represents 37,535,000)]

State and area	Enrollment [1] (1,000) 1995	2000	Payments [2] (mil. dol.) 1995	2000	State and area	Enrollment [1] (1,000) 1995	2000	Payments [2] (mil. dol.) 1995	2000
All areas ..	37,535	39,140	176,884	214,868	MO	833	854	3,821	4,274
U.S.....	36,758	38,286	175,976	213,555	MT.........	130	135	489	575
					NE.........	249	252	840	1,225
AL.........	642	677	3,042	3,885	NV.........	194	229	894	1,069
AK.........	34	40	133	189	NH.........	156	167	597	628
AZ.........	602	658	2,717	2,938	NJ.........	1,168	1,195	5,603	6,767
AR.........	423	436	1,638	2,083	NM.........	211	229	710	854
CA.........	3,633	3,837	20,406	23,621	NY.........	2,630	2,694	13,904	18,653
CO.........	421	458	1,835	2,338	NC.........	1,027	1,111	4,276	5,942
CT.........	502	512	2,584	3,291	ND.:......	103	103	412	501
DE.........	101	110	445	430	OH.........	1,666	1,692	7,282	9,310
DC.........	78	76	1,164	784	OK.........	488	504	2,178	2,137
FL.........	2,628	2,771	14,828	19,221	OR.........	469	484	1,685	1,853
GA.........	833	898	4,090	4,111	PA	2,071	2,088	10,796	13,257
HI.........	149	162	580	622	RI	168	170	772	1,075
ID	150	161	463	639	SC.........	509	555	1,926	2,947
IL.........	1,617	1,629	7,276	7,309	SD	117	119	563	584
IN	823	845	3,491	4,720	TN	771	815	4,083	4,907
IA	474	476	1,527	1,453	TX	2,080	2,223	11,504	14,538
KS	383	389	1,545	1,915	UT	187	201	708	918
KY	586	615	2,401	3,153	VT	83	88	284	315
LA	581	597	3,448	4,383	VA	818	876	2,979	4,038
ME	201	213	707	793	WA	688	725	2,603	2,843
MD.........	602	635	2,868	3,998	WV	330	336	1,208	1,656
MA.........	933	954	5,496	5,466	WI	762	777	2,673	3,496
MI	1,347	1,389	6,237	6,269	WY	60	64	180	247
MN	631	648	2,378	3,109	PR	477	525	875	1,224
MS	397	414	1,723	2,248	Other areas .	300	330	33	89

[1] Hospital and/or medical insurance enrollment for 1995 as of July and for 2000 as of September.   [2] Distribution of benefit payments by state is based on a methodology which considered actual payments to health maintenance organizations and estimated payments for other providers of medicare services.

Source: U.S. Centers for Medicare & Medicaid Services; "Medicare Beneficiaries Enrolled as of July 1 of each year. Years 1995-1998"; published 29 July 1999; <http://www.hcfa.gov/stats/histenr1.htm> and "Medicare Estimated Benefit Payments by State for Fiscal Year 2000"; <http://www.hcfa.gov/stats/BENEPAY/bnpay00i.htm>.

No. 137. Medicaid—Selected Characteristics of Persons Covered: 1999

[In thousands, except percent (27,688 represents 27,688,000). Represents number of persons as of March of following year who were enrolled at any time in year shown. Person did not have to receive medical care paid for by medicaid in order to be counted. See headnote, Table 522]

Poverty status	Total [1]	White	Black	Hispanic [2]	Under 18 years old	18-44 years old	45-64 years old	65 years and over
Persons covered, total......	27,688	18,540	7,443	5,895	14,278	7,327	3,167	2,917
Below poverty level...........	12,884	7,868	4,322	2,997	7,129	3,398	1,406	950
Above poverty level	14,804	10,672	3,121	2,898	7,149	3,929	1,761	1,967
Percent of population covered..	10.1	8.3	21.0	18.1	19.9	8.7	5.3	8.9
Below poverty level..........	39.9	35.9	51.7	40.3	58.9	27.6	30.1	30.0
Above poverty level	6.1	5.3	11.6	11.5	12.0	4.1	3.2	6.7

[1] Includes other races not shown separately.   [2] Persons of Hispanic origin may be of any race.

Source: U.S. Census Bureau, Current Population Reports, P60-210, earlier reports; and unpublished data.

No. 138. Medicaid—Selected Utilization Measures: 1980 to 1998

[In thousands (2,255 represents 2,255,000). For year ending September 30. Includes Virgin Islands. See text, this section]

Measure	1980	1985	1990	1994	1995	1996	1997	1998
General hospitals:								
Recipients discharged	2,255	2,390	3,261	3,890	3,743	3,300	3,135	2,793
Total days of care	24,089	29,562	27,471	28,941	25,711	23,072	21,532	19,091
Nursing facilities: [1]								
Total recipients	1,395	1,375	1,461	1,639	1,667	1,594	1,497	1,555
Total days of care	273,497	277,996	360,044	400,785	400,123	409,663	388,985	384,549
Intermediate care facilities: [2]								
Total recipients	121	147	146	159	151	140	146	124
Total days of care	250,124	47,324	49,730	54,105	56,878	56,625	62,423	50,636

[1] Includes skilled nursing facilities and intermediate care facilities for all other than the mentally retarded.   [2] Mentally retarded.

Source: U.S. Centers for Medicare & Medicaid Services, Office of Information Systems, Statistical Report on Medical Care: Eligibles, Recipients, Payments, and Services.

Health and Nutrition 99

No. 139. Medicaid—Recipients and Payments: 1990 to 1998

[For year ending September 30 (25,255 represents 25,255,000). Includes Puerto Rico and outlying areas. Medical vendor payments are those made directly to suppliers of medical care]

Basis of eligibility and type of service	Recipients (1,000)					Payments (mil. dol.)				
	1990	1995	1996	1997	1998	1990	1995	1996	1997	1998
Total [1]	25,255	36,282	36,118	34,872	40,649	64,859	120,141	121,685	124,430	142,318
Age 65 and over	3,202	4,119	4,285	3,955	3,964	21,508	36,527	36,947	37,721	40,602
Blindness	83	92	95	(NA)	(NA)	434	848	869	(NA)	(NA)
Disabled [2]	3,635	5,767	6,126	6,129	6,638	23,969	48,570	51,196	54,130	60,375
AFDC [3] program	17,230	24,767	23,866	22,594	26,872	17,690	31,487	29,819	29,851	37,639
Other and unknown	1,105	1,537	1,746	2,195	3,176	1,257	2,708	2,853	2,727	3,702
Inpatient services in—										
General hospital	4,593	5,561	5,362	4,746	4,273	16,674	26,331	25,176	23,143	21,499
Mental hospital	92	84	93	87	135	1,714	2,511	2,040	2,009	2,801
Intermediate care facilities, mentally retarded	147	151	140	136	126	7,354	10,383	9,555	9,798	9,482
Nursing facility services [4]	1,461	1,667	1,594	1,603	1,646	17,693	29,052	29,630	30,504	31,892
Physicians	17,078	23,789	22,861	21,170	18,555	4,018	7,360	7,238	7,041	6,070
Dental	4,552	6,383	6,208	5,935	4,965	593	1,019	1,028	1,036	901
Other practitioner	3,873	5,528	5,343	5,142	4,342	372	986	1,094	979	587
Outpatient hospital	12,370	16,712	15,905	13,632	12,158	3,324	6,627	6,504	6,169	5,759
Clinic	2,804	5,322	5,070	4,713	5,285	1,688	4,280	4,222	4,252	3,921
Laboratory [5]	8,959	13,064	12,607	11,074	9,381	721	1,180	1,208	1,033	939
Home health [6]	719	1,639	1,727	1,861	1,225	3,404	9,406	10,868	12,237	2,702
Prescribed drugs	17,294	23,723	22,585	20,954	19,338	4,420	9,791	10,697	11,972	13,522
Family planning	1,752	2,501	2,366	2,091	2,011	265	514	474	418	449
Prepaid health care	(NA)	(NA)	(NA)	(NA)	20,203	(NA)	(NA)	(NA)	(NA)	19,296

NA Not available. [1] Recipient data do not add due to small number of recipients that are reported in more than one category. Includes recipients of, and payments for, other care not shown separately. [2] Permanently and totally. Beginning 1997, includes blind. [3] Aid to families with dependent children includes children, adults, and foster care. [4] Nursing facility services includes skilled nursing facility services and intermediate care facility services for all other than the mentally retarded. [5] Includes radiological services. [6] Data for 1998 not comparable with earlier years.

Source: U.S. Centers for Medicare & Medicaid Services, Office of Information Systems, *Statistical Report on Medical Care: Eligibles, Recipients, Payments, and Services.*

No. 140. Medicaid—Summary by State and Other Area: 1995 and 1998

[For year ending September 30 (36,282 represents 36,282,000). Data for 1998 includes managed care recipients and capitation payments]

State and area	Recipients [1] (1,000)		Payments [2] (mil. dol)		State and area	Recipients [1] (1,000)		Payments [2] (mil. dol)	
	1995	1998	1995	1998		1995	1998	1995	1998
All areas	36,282	40,649	120,141	142,318	MO	695	734	2,039	2,570
U.S.	35,210	39,666	119,885	142,058	MT	99	101	326	381
					NE	168	211	608	753
AL	539	527	1,455	1,902	NV	105	128	350	482
AK	68	75	252	330	NH	97	94	473	606
AZ	494	508	218	1,644	NJ	790	813	3,813	4,219
AR	353	425	1,376	1,376	NM	287	329	714	882
CA	5,017	7,082	10,521	14,237	NY	3,035	3,073	22,066	24,296
CO	294	345	1,063	1,439	NC	1,084	1,168	3,175	4,014
CT	380	381	2,125	2,421	ND	61	62	297	341
DE	79	101	324	420	OH	1,533	1,291	5,585	6,121
DC	138	166	532	731	OK	394	342	1,055	1,178
FL	1,735	1,905	4,802	5,686	OR	462	511	1,327	1,378
GA	1,147	1,222	3,076	3,012	PA	1,230	1,523	4,633	6,080
HI	52	185	258	507	RI	135	153	673	919
ID	115	123	360	425	SC	496	595	1,438	2,019
IL	1,552	1,364	5,600	6,173	SD	74	90	305	356
IN	559	607	1,878	2,564	TN	1,466	1,844	2,772	3,167
IA	304	315	1,036	1,289	TX	2,582	2,325	6,565	7,140
KS	256	242	831	916	UT	160	216	464	619
KY	641	644	1,945	2,425	VT	100	124	320	351
LA	785	721	2,708	2,384	VA	681	653	1,833	2,118
ME	153	170	760	747	WA	639	1,413	1,461	2,044
MD	414	561	2,019	2,489	WV	389	343	1,169	1,243
MA	728	908	3,972	4,609	WI	460	519	1,894	2,206
MI	1,168	1,363	3,409	4,345	WY	51	46	171	192
MN	473	538	2,550	2,924	PR	1,055	964	244	250
MS	520	486	1,266	1,442	VI	17	20	12	10

[1] Persons who had payments made on their behalf at any time during the fiscal year. [2] Payments are for fiscal year and reflect federal and state contribution payments. Data exclude disproportionate hospital share payments.

Source: Centers for Medicare & Medicaid Services, Office of Information Systems, *Statistical Report on Medical Care: Eligibles, Recipients, Payments, and Services.*

100   Health and Nutrition

No. 141. Medicaid Managed Care Enrollment by State and Other Area: 1991 to 1998

[For year ending June 30. (28,280 represents 28,280,000)]

State and area	Total medi-caid (1,000)	Managed care enrollment Number (1,000)	Managed care enrollment Percent of total	State and area	Total medi-caid (1,000)	Managed care enrollment Number (1,000)	Managed care enrollment Percent of total	State and area	Total medi-caid (1,000)	Managed care enrollment Number (1,000)	Managed care enrollment Percent of total
1991	28,280	2,696	9.5	IL.	1,309	176	13.4	NC.	815	559	68.5
1995	33,373	9,800	29.4	IN	404	233	57.6	ND.	42	22	51.8
				IA	207	191	92.1	OH.	1,032	293	28.3
1998,				KS	171	84	49.3	OK.	310	154	49.6
total . .	30,897	16,574	53.6	KY	518	325	62.7	OR.	338	300	88.6
				LA	753	41	5.4	PA	1,325	905	68.2
U.S.	30,010	15,760	52.5	ME.	153	16	10.6	RI	118	74	63.2
AL	511	362	70.9	MD.	457	306	67.0	SC.	443	16	3.5
AK	66	-	-	MA.	851	533	62.6	SD.	62	44	70.5
AZ	432	368	85.1	MI	1,106	753	68.0	TN	1,269	1,269	100.0
AR	333	186	55.9	MN.	429	225	52.5	TX	1,719	438	25.4
CA	4,901	2,246	45.8	MS.	384	154	39.9	UT	124	113	91.2
CO	218	216	99.0	MO	607	252	41.5	VT	108	52	48.3
CT	307	221	71.8	MT	67	66	98.4	VA	499	299	60.0
DE	81	62	76.7	NE	152	111	72.7	WA	789	718	91.0
DC	113	51	45.2	NV	91	35	38.7	WV	309	131	42.5
FL	1,418	916	64.5	NH.	73	7	10.0	WI	397	195	49.0
GA	883	674	76.3	NJ	643	377	58.6	WY	35	-	-
HI	164	132	80.4	NM.	243	194	79.7	PR	870	814	93.5
ID	89	31	34.8	NY	2,140	634	29.6	VI	17	-	-

- Represents zero.

Source: U.S. Centers for Medicare & Medicaid Services, "National Summary of Medicaid Managed Care Programs and Enrollment, June 30, 1998;" published 8 April 1999; <http://32.97.224.53:8°/medicaid/trends98.htm>; and "Medicaid Managed Care Penetration Rates by State - 6/30/98"; published 8 April 1999; <http://32.97.224.53:80/medicaid/mcsten98.htm>.

No. 142. Health Maintenance Organizations (HMOs): 1980 to 2000

[As of January 1, except 1980 as of June 30 (9.1 represents 9,100,000). An HMO is a prepaid health plan delivering comprehensive care to members through designated providers, having a fixed periodic payment for health care services, and requiring members to be in a plan for a specified period of time (usually 1 year). A group HMO delivers health services through a physician group that is controlled by the HMO unit or contracts with one or more independent group practices to provide health services. An individual practice association (IPA) HMO contracts directly with physicians in independent practice, and/or contracts with one or more associations of physicians in independent practice, and/or contracts with one or more multispecialty group practices. Data are based on a census of HMOs]

Model type	Number of plans					Model type	Enrollment [1] (mil.)				
	1980	1990	1995	1999	2000		1980	1990	1995	1999	2000
Total	235	572	550	643	568	Total	9.1	33.0	46.2	81.3	80.9
IPA	97	360	323	309	278	IPA	1.7	13.7	17.4	32.8	33.4
Group	138	212	107	126	102	Group	7.4	19.3	12.9	15.9	15.2
Mixed	(NA)	(NA)	120	208	188	Mixed	(NA)	(NA)	15.9	32.6	32.3

NA Not available. [1] 1980-95 excludes enrollees participating in open-ended plans; 1999 and 2000 include open-ended enrollment.

No. 143. Persons Enrolled in Health Maintenance Organizations (HMOs) by State: 1990 and 2000

[80,899 represents 80,899,000. Data are based on a census of health maintenance organizations. Data for 1990 are for pure HMO enrollment at midyear. Data for 2000 are for pure and open-ended enrollment as of January 1]

State	Number 2000 (1,000)	Percent of population 1990	Percent of population 2000	State	Number 2000 (1,000)	Percent of population 1990	Percent of population 2000	State	Number 2000 (1,000)	Percent of population 1990	Percent of population 2000
US [1] . . .	80,899	13.5	29.7	KS	476	7.9	17.9	ND.	16	1.7	2.5
				KY	1,247	5.7	31.5	OH.	2,831	13.3	25.1
AL	315	5.3	7.2	LA	744	5.4	17.0	OK.	492	5.5	14.7
AK	-	-	-	ME.	279	2.6	22.3	OR.	1,362	24.7	41.1
AZ	1,476	16.2	30.9	MD.	2,270	14.2	43.9	PA	4,065	12.5	33.9
AR	265	2.2	10.4	MA.	3,272	26.5	53.0	RI	377	20.6	38.1
CA	17,741	30.7	53.5	MI	2,670	15.2	27.1	SC.	386	1.9	9.9
CO	1,603	20.0	39.5	MN.	1,427	16.4	29.9	SD.	49	3.3	6.7
CT	1,465	19.9	44.6	MS.	30	-	1.1	TN	1,807	3.7	33.0
DE	165	17.5	22.0	MO	1,927	8.2	35.2	TX	3,705	6.9	18.5
DC	183	(NA)	35.2	MT	61	1.0	7.0	UT	752	13.9	35.3
FL	4,748	10.6	31.4	NE	187	5.1	11.2	VT	27	6.4	4.6
GA	1,353	4.8	17.4	NV	425	8.5	23.5	VA	1,269	6.1	18.5
HI	355	21.6	30.0	NH.	405	9.6	33.7	WA	876	14.6	15.2
ID	99	1.8	7.9	NJ	2,520	12.3	30.9	WV	187	3.9	10.3
IL	2,551	12.6	21.0	NM.	656	12.7	37.7	WI	1,588	21.7	30.2
IN	736	6.1	12.4	NY	6,511	15.1	35.8	WY	7	-	1.4
IA	212	10.1	7.4	NC.	1,365	4.8	17.8				

- Represents zero. NA Not available. [1] Data for 2000 include Guam and Puerto Rico.

Source of Tables 142 and 143: InterStudy Publications, St. Paul, MN, The InterStudy Competitive Edge, annual (copyright).

Health and Nutrition 101

No. 144. Health Insurance Coverage Status by Selected Characteristics: 1990 to 1999

[Persons as of following year for coverage in the year shown (248.9 represents 248,900,000). Government health insurance includes medicare, medicaid, and military plans. Based on Current Population Survey; see text, Section 1, Population, and Appendix III]

Characteristic	Number (mil.)							Percent			
	Total persons	Covered by private or government health insurance					Not covered by health insurance	Covered by private or government health insurance			Not covered by health insurance
		Private		Government							
		Total[1]	Total	Group health[2]	Medicare	Medicaid		Total[1]	Private	Medicaid	
1990	248.9	214.2	182.1	150.2	32.3	24.3	34.7	86.1	73.2	9.7	13.9
1995[3]	264.3	223.7	185.9	161.5	34.7	31.9	40.6	84.6	70.3	12.1	15.4
1997[3]	269.1	225.6	188.5	165.1	35.6	29.0	43.4	83.9	70.1	10.8	16.1
1998[3]	271.7	227.5	190.9	168.6	35.9	27.9	44.3	83.7	70.2	10.3	16.3
1999, total[3][4]	274.1	231.5	194.6	172.0	36.1	27.9	42.6	84.5	71.0	10.2	15.5
Age:											
Under 18 years	72.3	62.3	49.8	46.6	0.4	14.5	10.0	86.1	68.9	20.0	13.9
Under 6 years	23.6	20.3	15.4	14.7	0.1	5.7	3.3	86.1	65.2	24.0	13.9
6 to 11 years	24.8	21.5	17.2	16.2	0.1	5.0	3.3	86.7	69.3	20.2	13.3
12 to 17 years	24.0	20.5	17.3	15.7	0.1	3.8	3.4	85.7	72.1	15.9	14.4
18 to 24 years	26.5	18.8	16.4	13.5	0.2	2.6	7.7	71.0	62.0	10.0	29.0
25 to 34 years	37.8	29.0	26.6	25.2	0.3	2.3	8.8	76.8	70.3	6.2	23.2
35 to 44 years	44.8	37.4	34.6	32.4	0.9	2.3	7.4	83.5	77.3	5.2	16.5
45 to 54 years	36.6	31.7	29.4	27.5	1.1	1.7	4.9	86.6	80.4	4.6	13.4
55 to 64 years	23.4	20.0	17.7	15.7	2.0	1.5	3.4	85.5	75.5	6.3	14.5
65 years and over	32.6	32.2	20.1	11.2	31.2	2.9	0.4	98.7	61.5	8.9	1.3
Sex: Male	133.9	111.9	95.7	85.9	15.6	12.1	22.1	83.5	71.4	9.1	16.5
Female	140.2	119.7	98.9	86.1	20.4	15.8	20.5	85.4	70.6	11.3	14.6
Race: White	224.8	192.9	166.2	145.9	31.4	18.7	31.9	85.8	73.9	8.3	14.2
Black	35.5	28.0	19.8	18.4	3.6	7.5	7.5	78.8	55.8	21.1	21.2
Asian and Pacific Islander	10.9	8.7	7.3	6.6	0.8	1.1	2.3	79.2	66.7	10.0	20.8
Hispanic origin[5]	32.8	21.9	15.4	14.2	2.0	5.9	11.0	66.6	47.0	18.1	33.4
Household income:											
Less than $25,000	64.6	49.1	26.5	17.8	17.6	17.6	15.6	75.9	41.0	27.2	24.1
$25,000-$49,999	77.1	63.1	54.2	47.7	10.7	6.7	14.0	81.9	70.2	8.6	18.2
$50,000-$74,999	56.9	50.2	47.3	44.0	3.8	2.0	6.7	88.2	83.1	3.6	11.8
$75,000 or more	75.5	69.2	66.7	62.7	3.9	1.6	6.3	91.7	88.4	2.1	8.3
Persons below poverty	32.3	21.8	8.3	5.5	4.3	12.9	10.4	67.7	25.8	39.9	32.4

[1] Includes other government insurance, not shown separately. Persons with coverage counted only once in total, even though they may have been covered by more that one type of policy. [2] Related to employment of self or other family members. [3] Beginning 1995, data based on 1990 census adjusted population controls. [4] Includes other races not shown separately. [5] Persons of Hispanic origin may be of any race.

No. 145. Persons With and Without Health Insurance Coverage by State: 1999

[231,533 represents 231,533,000. Based on the Current Population Survey and subject to sampling error; see text, Section 1. Population, and Appendix III]

State	Total persons covered (1,000)	Total persons not covered		Children not covered		State	Total persons covered (1,000)	Total persons not covered		Children not covered	
		Number (1,000)	Percent of total	Number (1,000)	Percent of total			Number (1,000)	Percent of total	Number (1,000)	Percent of total
U.S.	231,533	42,554	15.5	10,023	13.9	MO	5,003	473	8.6	78	5.4
						MT	732	168	18.6	45	18.9
AL	3,801	632	14.3	122	10.6	NE	1,480	179	10.8	40	8.9
AK	509	120	19.1	33	16.2	NV	1,532	400	20.7	131	22.1
AZ	3,838	1,035	21.2	308	22.0	NH	1,127	128	10.2	21	5.9
AR	2,183	378	14.7	81	11.8	NJ	7,015	1,090	13.4	196	9.8
CA	27,057	6,901	20.3	1,726	18.3	NM	1,335	463	25.8	150	27.7
CO	3,516	710	16.8	187	16.0	NY	15,464	3,044	16.4	551	11.5
CT	3,005	327	9.8	84	9.2	NC	6,355	1,154	15.4	234	12.4
DE	679	87	11.4	14	6.7	ND	543	72	11.8	16	10.4
DC	437	80	15.4	19	17.2	OH	10,046	1,247	11.0	267	8.9
FL	12,159	2,893	19.2	583	16.5	OK	2,698	571	17.5	137	17.0
GA	6,550	1,260	16.1	262	12.6	OR	2,912	498	14.6	117	13.2
HI	1,080	135	11.1	34	10.6	PA	10,674	1,111	9.4	219	7.6
ID	1,014	239	19.1	72	20.5	RI	915	68	6.9	18	6.9
IL	10,448	1,718	14.1	404	12.1	SC	3,145	673	17.6	175	19.4
IN	5,261	638	10.8	135	8.9	SD	621	83	11.8	17	9.1
IA	2,599	234	8.3	46	6.2	TN	4,900	637	11.5	131	9.4
KS	2,300	317	12.1	84	12.5	TX	15,380	4,665	23.3	1,343	24.1
KY	3,332	566	14.5	126	13.7	UT	1,846	305	14.2	82	11.4
LA	3,328	968	22.5	280	24.6						
ME	1,120	151	11.9	21	6.7	VT	531	74	12.3	12	8.0
MD	4,457	597	11.8	114	9.5	VA	5,875	967	14.1	243	14.1
MA	5,546	648	10.5	140	9.1	WA	4,799	898	15.8	188	13.3
MI	8,996	1,132	11.2	284	9.7	WV	1,456	300	17.1	50	13.8
MN	4,417	386	8.0	100	7.4	WI	4,806	595	11.0	167	10.7
MS	2,304	458	16.6	117	15.5	WY	405	78	16.1	19	14.5

Source of Tables 144 and 145: U.S. Census Bureau, Current Population Reports, P60-211; and unpublished data.

No. 146. Percent of Private Establishments Offering Health Insurance and Employees Enrolled: 1998

[Health insurance plan. An insurance plan that provides hospital and/or physician coverage to an employee or retiree for a single premium. Based on the Medical Expenditure Panel Survey—Insurance Component; for details on sample survey, see source]

Firm size and industry group	Percent of all establishments offering one or more major health plans	Percent of establishments offering health insurance that offer—				Private employees		
		Any managed care plan [1]	Exclusive provider plan [2]	Preferred provider plan [3]	Insurance to retirees over age 65	Percent working in establishments offering health insurance	Percent of eligible employees enrolled in health insurance	Percent enrolled in employer's plan
Total	55.2	86.4	38.6	60.9	15.4	87.0	85.3	66.2
Less than 10 employees	35.9	80.0	33.1	49.3	4.3	51.2	82.8	64.7
10 to 24 employees	66.7	86.1	35.7	55.3	7.2	70.6	79.0	60.0
25 to 99 employees	83.8	89.6	35.6	62.4	11.5	86.6	78.7	58.2
100 to 999 employees.	94.1	91.7	37.4	69.4	18.7	96.7	82.8	62.3
1,000 or more employees	99.2	93.4	52.6	80.2	41.2	99.1	89.4	71.4
Agriculture, forestry, and fishing . .	28.1	71.3	27.2	46.7	9.5	61.4	78.0	57.8
Mining	83.1	70.7	24.0	56.2	25.0	94.7	95.2	89.6
Construction	43.1	83.1	32.4	53.8	6.3	72.4	80.4	60.7
Manufacturing	71.9	90.1	40.7	60.2	14.6	96.1	91.3	84.0
Transportation, communication. and utilities	64.4	89.0	46.3	67.8	32.2	93.3	91.5	77.3
Wholesale trade	69.6	86.6	35.7	62.0	14.8	93.1	90.8	77.7
Retail trade	54.9	87.5	39.7	62.8	17.4	81.9	79.3	49.9
Finance, insurance, and real estate	64.4	91.8	49.1	73.7	38.2	93.5	85.1	73.2
Services	53.5	84.8	36.3	57.4	7.9	85.1	81.9	59.8

[1] Either a preferred provider or exclusive provider plan. for all nonemergency care in order for costs to be covered. incentive to use a particular subset of providers. [2] A plan that requires the enrollee to use a limited subset of providers [3] A plan that allows the enrollee to use any provider but has a costs

Source: U.S. Agency for Healthcare Research and Quality, "Private-Sector Data by Firm Size, Industry Group, Ownership, Age of Firm and Other Characteristics: United States: 1998"; <http://www.meps.ahrq.gov/mepsdata/ic/1998/index198.htm>.

No. 147. Medical Care Benefit Coverage and Average Monthly Employee Contributions: 1980 to 1997

[Covers full-time employees in private nonfarm establishments. Based on a sample survey of establishments; for details, see source and headnotes, Tables 628 and 629]

Item	Medium and large establishments					Small establishments			
	1980	1991	1993	1995	1997	1990	1992	1994	1996
Percent of full-time employees participating . .	97	83	82	77	76	69	71	66	64
PERCENT DISTRIBUTION OF PARTICIPATING FULL-TIME EMPLOYEES									
Fee arrangement, total.	100	100	100	100	100	100	100	100	100
Traditional fee-for-service [1]	(NA)	67	50	37	27	74	68	55	36
Preferred provider organization [2]	(NA)	16	26	34	40	13	18	24	35
Health maintenance organization [3]	(NA)	17	23	27	33	14	14	19	27
Other	(NA)	(Z)	1	1	1	-	(Z)	1	2
Individual coverage:									
Employee contributions not required	(NA)	49	37	33	31	58	53	46	48
Employee contributions required	26	51	61	67	69	42	47	52	52
Family coverage:									
Employee contributions not required	(NA)	31	21	22	20	33	27	19	24
Employee contributions required	46	69	76	78	80	67	73	75	75
AVERAGE MONTHLY EMPLOYEE CONTRIBUTION (dol.)									
Individual coverage:									
Total.	(NA)	27	32	34	39	25	37	41	43
Non-HMO [4]	(NA)	26	31	33	42	25	36	39	43
HMO	(NA)	29	32	36	34	25	39	49	41
Family coverage:									
Total.	(NA)	97	107	118	130	109	151	160	182
Non-HMO [4]	(NA)	92	102	112	132	104	147	151	181
HMO	(NA)	118	122	133	126	135	168	190	182

- Represents zero.   NA Not available.   Z Less than 0.5 percent.   [1] These plans pay for specific medical procedures as expenses are incurred.   [2] Groups of hospitals and physicians that contract to provide comprehensive medical services at prearranged prices. To encourage use of organization members, the health plan limits reimbursement rates when participants use nonmember services.   [3] Includes federally qualified and other HMOs that deliver comprehensive health care on a prepayment rather than fee-for-service basis.   [4] Includes traditional fee-for-service plans, preferred provider plans, and exclusive provider organization plans.

Source: U.S. Bureau of Labor Statistics, News, USDL 98-240, June 15, 1998; News, USDL 99-02, January 7, 1999; and earlier releases.

Health and Nutrition   103

No. 148. Health Care Employer Firms—Establishments, Receipts, Payroll, and Employees by Kind of Business (NAICS Basis): 1997

Kind of business	NAICS code [1]	Estab- lish- ments (number)	Receipts		Annual payroll		Paid em- ployees for pay period including March 12 (1,000)
			Total (mil. dol.)	Per paid employee (dol.)	Total (mil. dol.)	Per paid employee (dol.)	
TAXABLE FIRMS							
Ambulatory health care services	621	440,200	310,012	82,796	137,979	36,851	3,744.3
Offices of physicians	6211	195,449	171,629	109,238	84,977	54,086	1,571.1
Offices of dentists	6212	114,178	48,482	75,556	18,227	28,405	641.7
Offices of other healtḥ practitioneṛs [2]	6213	88,886	28,282	69,560	10,457	25,718	406.6
Offices of chiropractors	62131	30,487	6,570	71,648	1,886	20,569	91.7
Offices of optometrists	62132	17,875	6,362	79,978	1,773	22,295	79.5
Offices of PT/OT/speech therapy & audiology [3]	62134	14,277	8,684	61,357	4,377	30,924	141.5
Outpatient care centers	6214	11,828	17,306	99,572	5,502	31,655	173.8
Medical & diagnostic laboratories	6215	9,076	16,317	107,819	5,402	35,693	151.3
Home health care services	6216	16,315	21,474	31,510	10,941	16,054	681.5
Other ambulatory health care services	6219	4,468	6,521	55,162	2,475	20,933	118.2
Hospitals [2]	622	1,345	40,146	78,475	13,886	27,143	511.6
General medical & surgical hospitals	6221	792	34,213	81,215	11,570	27,466	421.3
Nursing & residential care facilities [2]	623	32,833	55,844	37,610	24,626	16,585	1,484.8
Nursing care facilities	6231	12,517	44,485	38,332	20,193	17,400	1,160.5
Community care facilities for the elderly	6233	11,637	7,088	36,151	2,533	12,920	196.1
TAX-EXEMPT FIRMS							
Ambulatory health care services [2]	621	15,181	45,428	67,871	17,884	26,719	669.3
Outpatient care centers	6214	9,940	31,561	91,086	11,158	32,202	346.5
Home health care services	6216	3,375	10,104	37,775	5,426	20,286	267.5
Hospitals	622	5,340	339,032	76,679	141,910	32,096	4,421.5
General medical & surgical hospitals	6221	4,695	319,920	77,928	131,054	31,923	4,105.3
Psychiatric & substance abuse hospitals	6222	412	10,689	53,173	6,983	34,737	201.0
Other specialty hospitals	6223	233	8,423	73,176	3,874	33,655	115.1
Nursing & residential care facilities [2]	623	24,526	37,235	37,768	17,527	17,778	985.9
Nursing care facilities	6231	3,088	15,249	38,445	7,396	18,647	396.6
Residential mental retardation/ health facilities [2]	6232	12,940	7,973	32,401	4,126	16,768	246.1
Residential mental retardation facilities	62321	9,287	5,270	29,958	2,791	15,866	175.9
Community care facilities for the elderly	6233	3,951	9,304	41,167	3,742	16,556	226.0

[1] North American Industry Classification System, see text, Section 15, Business Enterprise. [2] Includes other kinds of business not shown separately. [3] Offices of physical, occupational and speech therapists, and audiologists.

Source: U.S. Census Bureau, *1997 Economic Census, Health Care and Social Assistance*, Series EC97562A-US, issued October 1999.

No. 149. Annual Receipts/Revenue for Health Care Industries: 1998 and 1999

[In millions of dollars (399,556 represents $399,556,000,000). Based on the North American Industry Classification System (NAICS), see text, Section 15, Business Enterprise. All firms in NAICS 6211, 6212, 6213, and 6215 are defined as taxable. Estimates for the nonemployer portion are derived from administrative records data provided by other federal agencies. These data are available only at the total revenue level. Estimates for tax-exempt firms are derived only from a sample of employer firms]

Kind of business	NAICS code	Total, all firms [1]		Employer firms			
					1999		
		1998	1999	1998, total	Total	Taxable firms	Tax- exempt firms
Ambulatory health care services	621	399,556	417,501	374,348	390,511	342,972	47,539
Offices of physicians	6211	192,663	201,795	181,579	190,049	190,049	(X)
Offices of dentists	6212	53,158	56,395	51,476	54,592	54,592	(X)
Offices of other health practitioners [2]	6213	37,790	39,216	30,018	30,902	30,902	(X)
Offices of chiropractors	62131	7,908	8,312	6,946	7,291	7,291	(X)
Offices of optometrists	62132	7,455	7,932	6,885	7,318	7,318	(X)
Offices of PT/OT/speech therapy & audiology [3]	62134	10,173	9,715	9,003	8,574	8,574	(X)
Outpatient care centers	6214	52,447	55,990	51,851	55,329	22,234	33,095
Medical & diagnostic laboratories	6215	19,236	20,355	18,501	19,546	19,546	(X)
Home health care services	6216	31,942	30,583	30,579	29,148	19,492	9,656
Other ambulatory health care services	6219	12,321	13,167	10,345	10,945	6,157	4,787
Hospitals	622	397,373	413,035	397,373	413,035	42,593	370,442
General medical & surgical hospitals	6221	(NA)	(NA)	370,862	385,480	35,310	350,170
Psychiatric & substance abuse hospitals	6222	(NA)	(NA)	14,686	15,379	4,383	10,996
Other specialty hospitals	6223	(NA)	(NA)	11,825	12,176	2,900	9,276
Nursing and residential care facilities	623	100,132	102,301	98,984	101,049	59,569	41,480
Nursing care facilities	6231	(NA)	(NA)	63,085	63,128	46,270	16,858
Residential mental retardation/health facilities [2]	6232	(NA)	(NA)	12,479	13,113	3,906	9,207
Residential mental retardation facilities	62321	(NA)	(NA)	8,287	8,608	2,628	5,981
Community care facilities for the elderly	6233	(NA)	(NA)	18,041	19,346	8,742	10,603

NA Not available.   X Not applicable.   [1] Includes taxable nonemployer firms, not shown separately.   [2] Includes other kinds of business not shown separately.   [3] Offices of physical, occupational and speech therapists, and audiologists.

Source: U.S. Census Bureau, *Service Annual Survey, 1999*.

No. 150. Receipts for Selected Health Service Industries by Source of Revenue: 1998 and 1999

[In millions of dollars (181,579 represents $181,579,000,000). Based on the North American Industry Classification System (NAICS), see text, Section 15, Business Enterprise. Based on a sample of employer firms only and does not include nonemployer revenue]

Source of revenue	Offices of physicians (NAICS 6211)		Offices of dentists (NAICS 6212)		Hospitals (NAICS 622)		Nursing and residential care facilities (NAICS 623)	
	1998	1999	1998	1999	1998	1999	1998	1999
Total	181,579	190,049	51,476	54,592	397,373	413,035	98,984	101,049
Medicare	42,839	44,934	(S)	(S)	132,174	134,311	12,891	11,670
Medicaid	12,216	12,856	1,168	1,209	47,250	50,050	39,879	41,645
Other government [1]	1,759	1,842	(S)	(S)	21,349	21,648	5,600	5,988
Worker's compensation	6,787	6,880	(S)	(S)	4,635	4,614	(S)	(S)
Private insurance	85,828	90,466	26,599	28,395	135,269	143,402	5,976	6.193
Patient (out-of-pocket)	20,507	21,258	22,474	23,638	20,943	22,383	[2]24,336	[2]25,290
Other patient care sources, n.e.c [3]	6,815	6,928	436	472	13,251	13,237	2,972	3,095
Nonpatient care revenue	4,828	4,886	(S)	(S)	22,501	23,389	7,305	7,140

S Figure does not meet publication standards. [1] Veterans, National Institute of Health, Indian Affairs, etc. [2] Represents payment from patients and their families plus patients' assigned social security benefits. [3] N.e.c. represents not elsewhere classified.

Source: U.S. Census Bureau, *Service Annual Survey: 1999.*

No. 151. Employment in the Health Service Industries: 1980 to 2000

[In thousands (5,278 represents 5,278,000). See headnote Table 609]

Industry	1987 SIC code [1]	1980	1990	1995	1998	1999	2000
Health services [2]	80	5,278	7,814	9,230	9,853	9,977	10,095
Offices and clinics of MDs	801	802	1,338	1,609	1,806	1,875	1,924
Offices and clinics of dentists	802	(NA)	513	592	646	667	686
Offices and clinics of other practitioners	804	96	277	397	448	441	439
Nursing and personal care facilities	805	997	1,415	1,691	1,772	1,786	1,796
Skilled nursing care facilities	8051	(NA)	989	1,253	1,355	1,364	1,366
Intermediate care facilities	8052	(NA)	200	211	201	203	206
Other, n.e.c [3]	8059	(NA)	227	227	215	219	224
Hospitals	806	2,750	3,549	3,772	3,930	3,974	3,990
General medical and surgical hospitals	8062	(NA)	3,268	3,474	3,631	3,674	3,689
Psychiatric hospitals	8063	(NA)	104	91	79	75	74
Specialty hospitals, exc. psychiatric	8069	(NA)	176	208	221	224	228
Medical and dental laboratories	807	(NA)	166	190	199	203	209
Home health care services	808	(NA)	291	629	666	636	643

NA Not available. [1] Based on the 1987 Standard Industrial Classification code; see text, Section 15, Business Enterprise. [2] Includes other industries not shown separately. [3] N.e.c. means not elsewhere classified.

Source: U.S. Bureau of Labor Statistics, *Employment and Earnings,* monthly, March and June issues.

No. 152. Registered Nurses by Employment Status: 1992 to 2000

[As of March (2,240 represents 2,240,000). Based on a sample and subject to sampling variability; see source for details]

Year	Total (1,000)	Percent—		
		Employed full time	Employed part time	Not employed
1992	2,240	57.0	25.7	17.3
1996	2,559	59.0	23.7	17.3
2000	2,697	58.5	23.2	18.3

Source: U.S. Dept. of Health and Human Services, Health Resources and Services Administration, *The Registered Nurse Population, National Sample Survey of Registered Nurses-March 2000, Preliminary Findings,* February 2001.

No. 153. Physicians by Selected Activity: 1980 to 1999

[In thousands (467.7 represents 467,700). As of Dec. 31, except 1990 as of Jan. 1, and as noted. Includes Puerto Rico and outlying areas]

Activity	1980	1990	1995	1996	1997	1998	1999
Doctors of medicine, total.	467.7	615.4	720.3	737.8	756.7	777.9	797.6
Professionally active	435.5	560.0	646.0	663.9	684.6	707.0	720.9
Place of medical education:							
U.S. medical graduates	343.6	437.2	492.2	505.7	519.7	533.4	542.2
Foreign medical graduates [1]	91.8	122.8	153.8	158.3	164.9	173.7	178.7
Sex: Male	386.7	463.9	505.9	515.6	527.0	538.9	544.1
Female.	48.7	96.1	140.1	148.3	157.7	168.1	176.7
Active nonfederal	417.7	539.5	624.9	643.5	665.2	688.0	702.8
Patient care	361.9	487.8	564.1	580.7	603.7	606.4	610.7
Office-based practice	271.3	359.9	427.3	445.8	458.2	468.8	473.2
General and family practice	47.8	57.6	59.9	61.8	62.0	64.6	66.2
Cardiovascular diseases	6.7	10.7	13.7	14.3	15.0	15.1	15.6
Dermatology	4.4	6.0	7.0	7.2	7.4	7.6	7.8
Gastroenterology	2.7	5.2	7.3	7.6	7.9	7.9	8.2
Internal medicine	40.5	57.8	72.6	77.9	81.4	83.3	84.6
Pediatrics	17.4	26.5	33.9	35.5	36.8	38.4	40.5
Pulmonary diseases	2.0	3.7	5.0	4.9	5.0	4.9	5.7
General surgery	22.4	24.5	24.1	25.4	27.9	27.5	26.8
Obstetrics and gynecology	19.5	25.5	29.1	29.9	30.1	31.2	31.1
Ophthalmology	10.6	13.1	14.6	14.9	15.1	15.6	15.2
Orthopedic surgery	10.7	14.2	17.1	17.6	18.5	18.5	17.0
Otolaryngology	5.3	6.4	7.1	7.2	7.4	7.5	7.3
Plastic surgery	2.4	3.8	4.6	5.0	5.3	5.3	5.1
Urological surgery	6.2	7.4	8.0	8.2	8.4	8.4	8.2
Anesthesiology	11.3	17.8	23.8	24.9	25.6	26.2	26.6
Diagnostic radiology	4.2	9.8	12.8	13.3	14.1	14.2	14.3
Emergency medicine	(NA)	8.4	11.7	12.3	12.5	13.3	13.9
Neurology	3.2	5.6	7.6	7.9	8.2	8.5	8.1
Pathology, anatomical/clinical	6.0	7.3	9.0	9.7	10.2	10.0	10.1
Psychiatry	15.9	20.0	23.3	24.4	24.5	25.0	24.4
Other specialty	31.9	28.8	35.0	35.8	35.0	35.9	36.4
Hospital-based practice	90.6	127.9	136.8	134.9	145.3	137.6	137.2
Residents and interns [2]	59.6	89.9	93.7	90.6	95.8	92.3	92.5
Full-time hospital staff	31.0	38.0	43.1	44.3	49.5	45.3	44.8
Other professional activity [3]	35.2	39.0	40.3	42.8	41.5	41.6	41.2
Not classified	20.6	12.7	20.6	20.0	20.0	40.0	50.9
Federal	17.8	20.5	21.1	20.4	19.4	19.0	18.1
Patient care	14.6	16.1	18.1	18.2	16.9	15.3	14.7
Other professional activity [3]	3.2	4.4	3.0	2.2	2.4	3.7	3.4
Inactive/unknown address	32.1	55.4	74.3	73.8	72.1	70.8	76.8
Doctors of osteopathy [4]	18.8	30.9	35.7	37.3	38.9	40.8	43.5

NA Not available. [1] Foreign medical graduates received their medical education in schools outside the United States and Canada. [2] Includes clinical fellows. [3] Includes medical teaching, administration, research, and other. [4] As of July. Total DOs. Data from American Osteopathic Association, Chicago, IL.
Source: Except as noted, American Medical Association, Chicago, IL, *Physician Characteristics and Distribution in the U.S.*, annual (copyright).

No. 154. Active Nonfederal Physicians and Nurses by State: 1999

[As of December. Excludes doctors of osteopathy, federally-employed persons, and physicians with addresses unknown. Includes all physicians not classified according to activity status]

State	Physicians Total	Physicians Rate [1]	Nurses Total	Nurses Rate [1]	State	Physicians Total	Physicians Rate [1]	Nurses Total	Nurses Rate [1]
United States. .	693,345	254	2,271,340	833	Missouri	12,695	232	53,890	985
Alabama	8,733	200	33,680	771	Montana	1,683	191	7,850	889
Alaska	1,054	170	7,350	1,186	Nebraska	3,679	221	14,950	897
Arizona	9,714	203	36,660	767	Nevada	3,209	177	11,420	631
Arkansas	4,906	192	19,890	780	New Hampshire	2,813	234	10,860	904
California	82,176	248	176,360	532	New Jersey	24,525	301	65,730	807
Colorado	9,914	244	31,230	770	New Mexico	3,717	214	12,600	724
Connecticut	11,859	361	32,660	995	New York	71,840	395	170,930	939
Delaware	1,791	238	8,440	1,120	North Carolina	18,166	237	71,550	935
District of Columbia .	3,935	758	8,290	1,597	North Dakota	1,420	224	7,460	1,177
Florida	36,760	243	131,800	872	Ohio	26,731	237	103,980	924
Georgia	16,470	211	56,680	728	Oklahoma	5,614	167	20,500	610
Hawaii	3,184	269	9,540	805	Oregon	7,519	227	29,580	892
Idaho	1,944	155	7,520	601	Pennsylvania	35,148	293	136,360	1,137
Illinois	31,928	263	110,270	909	Rhode Island	3,362	339	11,680	1,179
Indiana	11,753	198	49,360	831	South Carolina	8,294	213	32,410	834
Iowa	5,009	175	31,220	1,088	South Dakota	1,379	188	7,400	1,009
Kansas	5,424	204	23,660	891	Tennessee	13,626	248	49,210	897
Kentucky	8,382	212	33,190	838	Texas	41,084	205	132,110	659
Louisiana	10,975	251	35,370	809	Utah	4,312	202	13,870	651
Maine	2,913	232	13,600	1,085	Vermont	1,860	313	5,160	869
Maryland	19,592	379	44,210	855	Virginia	16,717	243	57,560	837
Massachusetts	26,062	422	72,840	1,180	Washington	13,616	237	44,740	777
Michigan	22,246	226	83,370	845	West Virginia	3,962	219	16,130	893
Minnesota	12,125	254	51,970	1,088	Wisconsin	12,167	232	47,520	905
Mississippi	4,533	164	21,700	784	Wyoming	825	172	5,030	1,049

[1] Per 100,000 resident population. Based on U.S. Census Bureau estimates as of July 1, 1999.
Source: Physicians: American Medical Association, Chicago, IL, *Physician Characteristics and Distribution in the U.S.*, annual (copyright); Nurses: U.S. Dept. of Health and Human Services, Health Resources and Services Administration, unpublished data.

106 Health and Nutrition

No. 155. Health Professions—Practitioners and Schools: 1990 to 1999

[Data on the number of total schools and enrollment are reported as of the beginning of the academic year; all other school data are reported as of the end of the academic year. Data are based on reporting by health professions schools]

Year	Medi-cine	Oste-opathy	Registered nursing Total	Bacca-laureate	Associ-ate degree	Diploma	Licensed practical nursing	Den-tistry [1]	Optom-etry	Phar-macy
ACTIVE PERSONNEL (1,000)										
1990	540	28	1,790	[2]682	[3]1,107	([3])	(NA)	148	26	162
1995	637	36	2,116	[2]881	[3]1,235	([3])	(NA)	153	29	182
1997 [4]	685	39	2,203	[2]935	[3]1,267	([3])	(NA)	157	30	185
1998	707	41	2,239	[2]958	[3]1,281	([3])	(NA)	158	(NA)	(NA)
NUMBER OF SCHOOLS [5]										
1990	126	15	1,470	489	829	152	1,154	58	17	74
1995	125	16	1,516	521	876	119	(NA)	54	17	75
1997	125	19	(NA)	(NA)	(NA)	(NA)	(NA)	55	17	81
1998	125	19	(NA)	(NA)	(NA)	(NA)	(NA)	55	17	81
1999	125	19	(NA)	(NA)	(NA)	(NA)	(NA)	(NA)	17	(NA)
TOTAL ENROLLMENT										
1990	65,016	6,615	201,458	74,865	106,175	20,418	46,720	16,412	4,723	23,013
1995	67,072	8,146	268,350	112,659	135,895	19,796	59,428	16,353	5,201	27,667
1997	67,276	8,961	238,244	103,213	122,242	12,789	(NA)	16,570	5,210	28,027
1998	66,900	9,434	(NA)	(NA)	(NA)	(NA)	(NA)	16,926	(NA)	28,345
1999	66,517	9,882	(NA)	(NA)	(NA)	(NA)	(NA)	(NA)	5,313	28,646
GRADUATES										
1990	15,398	1,529	66,088	18,571	42,318	5,199	35,417	4,233	1,115	6,956
1995	15,888	1,843	97,052	31,254	58,749	7,049	44,234	3,908	1,219	7,837
1997	15,923	2,009	(NA)	(NA)	(NA)	(NA)	(NA)	3,930	(NA)	7,772
1998	16,314	2,096	(NA)	(NA)	(NA)	(NA)	(NA)	4,041	1,237	7,400
1999	16,143	2,193	(NA)	(NA)	(NA)	(NA)	(NA)	(NA)	(NA)	(NA)

NA Not available. [1] Personnel data exclude dentists in military service, U.S. Public Health Service, and U.S. Dept. of Veterans Affairs. [2] Includes nurses with advanced degrees. [3] Diploma nurses included with associate degree nurses. [4] Data for medicine, nursing, dentistry, and osteopathy for 1997; other occupations are for 1996. [5] Some nursing schools offer more than one type of program. Numbers shown for nursing are number of nursing programs.

Source: U.S. National Center for Health Statistics, *Health United States*, annual.

No. 156. Percent Distribution of Number of Visits to Health Care Professionals by Selected Characteristics: 1997 and 1998

[Covers ambulatory visits to doctor's offices and emergency departments, and home health care visits during a 12-month period. Based on the redesigned National Health Interview Survey, a sample survey of the civilian noninstitutionalized population. Data presented in this table are not comparable with data on physician contacts presented in previous editions of the source or the *Statistical Abstract*]

Characteristic	None 1997	None 1998	1-3 visits 1997	1-3 visits 1998	4-9 visits 1997	4-9 visits 1998	10 or more visits 1997	10 or more visits 1998
All persons [1]	16.5	15.9	46.2	46.8	23.6	23.8	13.7	13.5
Age:								
Under 6 years	5.0	4.9	44.9	46.7	37.0	36.6	13.0	11.8
6-17 years	15.3	15.0	58.7	58.4	19.3	20.3	6.8	6.3
18-44 years	21.7	21.6	46.7	47.7	19.0	18.6	12.6	12.2
45-64 years	16.9	15.9	42.9	43.6	24.7	24.3	15.5	16.2
65 years and over	8.9	7.3	34.7	34.1	32.5	35.3	23.8	23.4
Sex: [1]								
Male	21.3	20.7	47.1	47.3	20.6	21.2	11.0	10.8
Female	11.8	11.3	45.4	46.4	26.5	26.3	16.3	16.0
Race and Hispanic origin: [1]								
White, non-Hispanic	14.7	14.2	46.6	47.1	24.4	24.6	14.3	14.0
Black, non-Hispanic	16.9	16.5	46.1	46.5	23.1	23.2	13.8	13.8
Hispanic	24.9	24.0	42.3	44.8	20.3	19.7	12.5	11.5

[1] Estimates are age adjusted to the year 2000 standard using six age groups: Under 18 years, 18-44 years, 45-54 years, 55-64 years, 65-74 years, and 75 years and over.

Source: U.S. National Center for Health Statistics, *Health, United States, 2000*.

Health and Nutrition 107

No. 157. Medical Practice Characteristics by Selected Specialty: 1985 to 1998

[Dollar figures in thousands (112.2 represents $112,200). Based on a sample telephone survey of nonfederal office and hospital based patient care physicians, excluding residents. For details see source. For definition of mean, see Guide to Tabular Presentation]

Specialty	1985	1990	1994	1995	1996	1997	1998
MEAN HOURS IN PATIENT CARE PER WEEK							
All physicians [1]	51.3	53.3	52.1	51.3	53.4	53.2	51.7
General/Family practice	53.6	55.0	51.9	52.9	53.5	53.1	51.3
Internal medicine	52.4	55.7	56.6	53.9	57.2	56.0	54.3
Surgery	51.2	53.1	53.4	53.2	54.2	55.0	51.7
Pediatrics	50.6	52.4	51.6	50.4	51.0	51.6	48.6
Obstetrics/Gynecology	56.9	60.4	58.1	54.6	60.5	59.9	59.9
MEAN NET INCOME							
All physicians [1]	112.2	164.3	182.4	195.5	199.0	199.6	194.4
General/Family practice	77.9	102.7	121.2	131.2	139.1	140.9	142.5
Internal medicine	102.0	152.5	174.9	185.7	185.7	193.9	182.1
Surgery	155.0	236.4	255.2	269.4	275.2	261.4	268.2
Pediatrics	76.2	106.5	126.2	140.5	140.6	143.5	139.6
Obstetrics/Gynecology	124.3	207.3	200.4	244.3	231.0	228.7	214.4
MEAN PROFESSIONAL EXPENSES							
All physicians [1]	102.7	150.0	183.1	201.6	217.6	228.6	261.9
General/Family practice	96.5	134.5	190.5	179.4	210.7	205.5	263.0
Internal medicine	90.0	139.2	186.4	200.4	192.2	238.2	259.7
Surgery	135.7	201.0	249.9	265.1	307.2	312.5	325.8
Pediatrics	87.3	138.0	157.8	208.5	212.4	224.8	187.3
Obstetrics/Gynecology	131.9	212.6	196.8	266.9	267.1	306.6	375.9
MEAN LIABILITY PREMIUM							
All physicians [1]	10.5	14.5	15.1	15.0	14.1	14.2	16.8
General/Family practice	6.8	7.8	10.2	9.0	8.4	12.0	10.9
Internal medicine	5.8	9.2	8.6	9.4	8.9	9.4	16.5
Surgery	16.6	22.8	22.3	23.3	21.7	19.7	22.8
Pediatrics	4.7	7.8	7.6	7.9	8.3	12.3	9.0
Obstetrics/Gynecology	23.5	34.3	37.4	38.6	35.2	33.0	35.8

[1] Includes other specialties not shown separately.
Source: American Medical Association, Chicago IL, *Physician Socioeconomic Statistics, 1999-2000* (copyright) and *Physician Socioeconomic Statistics, 2000-2002* (copyright).

No. 158. Ambulatory Care Visits to Physicians' Offices and Hospital Outpatient and Emergency Departments: 1999

[944.1 represents 944,100,000. Based on the annual National Ambulatory Medical Care Survey and National Hospital Ambulatory Medical Care Survey and subject to sampling error; see source for details]

Characteristic	Number of visits (mil.)				Visits per 100 persons			
	Total	Physician offices	Out-patient dept.	Emer-gency dept.	Total	Physician offices	Out-patient dept.	Emer-gency dept.
Total	944.1	756.7	84.6	102.8	347	279	31	38
Age:								
Under 15 years old	157.3	116.9	18.6	21.9	261	194	31	36
15 to 24 years old	85.6	59.7	10.4	15.5	226	157	27	41
25 to 44 years old	240.1	186.0	22.3	31.8	291	226	27	39
45 to 64 years old	240.7	201.9	20.9	17.9	410	344	36	31
65 to 74 years old	106.0	92.6	7.0	6.5	596	521	39	36
75 years old and over	114.2	99.5	5.5	9.2	779	679	37	63
Sex:								
Male	393.3	311.2	33.6	48.5	297	235	25	37
Female	550.8	445.6	51.1	54.2	396	320	37	39
Race:								
White	796.8	654.7	63.5	78.6	357	293	29	35
Black/African-American	113.0	74.0	17.8	21.2	322	211	51	60
Asian/Native Hawaiian/Other Pacific Islander	30.3	25.5	2.7	2.1	277	233	25	19
American Indian/Alaska Native	2.6	1.3	[1]0.4	[1]0.9	106	54	[1]15	[1]37
More than one race reported	1.5	1.3	[1]0.2	([1])	(NA)	(NA)	(NA)	(NA)
Region:								
Northeast	212.5	171.4	21.6	19.4	404	326	41	37
Midwest	203.7	154.1	22.9	26.8	305	231	34	40
South	317.0	252.5	25.5	38.9	329	262	27	40
West	210.9	178.7	14.6	17.6	378	320	26	32
Primary source of payment:								
Private insurance	490.5	417.6	32.9	39.9	(X)	(X)	(X)	(X)
Medicare	184.6	156.7	12.5	15.4	(X)	(X)	(X)	(X)
Medicaid	94.6	56.8	19.9	17.9	(X)	(X)	(X)	(X)
Worker's compensation	19.6	15.6	0.9	3.1	(X)	(X)	(X)	(X)
Self pay	64.9	40.7	7.6	16.6	(X)	(X)	(X)	(X)
No charge	9.4	7.2	[1]1.7	[1]0.5	(X)	(X)	(X)	(X)
Other	43.8	35.6	4.8	3.3	(X)	(X)	(X)	(X)
Unknown	36.7	26.5	4.3	5.9	(X)	(X)	(X)	(X)

NA Not available.   X Not applicable.   [1] Figures do not meet standard of reliability or precision.
Source: U.S. National Center for Health Statistics, *Advance Data*, Nos. 320, 321, and 322; June 25, 2001; June 26, 2001; and July 10, 2001.

No. 159. Visits to Office-Based Physicians and Hospital Outpatient Departments by Diagnosis: 1995 and 1999

[307.0 represents 307,000,000. See headnote, Table 158]

Leading diagnoses [1]	Number (mil.) 1995	Number (mil.) 1999	Rate per 1,000 persons [2] 1995	Rate per 1,000 persons [2] 1999	Leading diagnoses [1]	Number (mil.) 1995	Number (mil.) 1999	Rate per 1,000 persons [2] 1995	Rate per 1,000 persons [2] 1999
MALE					**FEMALE**				
All ages	307.0	344.7	2,406	2,602	All ages	457.3	496.6	3,404	3,566
Under 15 years old [3]	75.2	71.3	2,471	2,315	Under 15 years old [3]	71.4	64.2	2,457	2,183
Routine infant or child health check	10.4	12.4	341	402	Routine infant or child health check	10.2	11.4	351	386
Otitis media	9.8	7.3	322	236	Acute upper respiratory infections [4]	9.1	7.2	313	245
Acute upper respiratory infections [4]	7.7	7.2	252	233	Otitis media	8.5	5.3	293	181
Attention deficit disorder	1.3	2.4	41	78	Acute pharyngitis	2.8	1.8	95	60
Acute pharyngitis	2.4	2.0	80	64	Asthma	1.4	1.7	50	58
15 to 44 years old [3]	90.8	99.0	1,540	1,662	15 to 44 years old [3]	173.9	179.4	2,888	2,947
Acute upper respiratory infections [4]	3.7	3.5	63	59	Normal pregnancy	22.2	19.1	369	313
Essential hypertension	1.8	3.1	31	52	Acute upper respiratory infections [4]	6.4	6.6	107	108
Allergic rhinitis.	1.6	2.9	28	49	Allergic rhinitis.	2.0	5.0	34	83
General medical examination	4.5	2.8	76	47	General medical examination .	7.4	4.6	123	76
Chronic sinusitis	1.6	2.0	26	34	Gynecological examination . .	2.6	4.6	44	76
45 to 64 years old [3]	69.8	90.8	2,795	3,202	45 to 64 years old [3]	104.6	132.0	3,911	4,359
Essential hypertension	4.3	6.5	172	230	Essential hypertension	5.2	7.8	193	258
Diabetes mellitus	2.7	5.4	109	189	Diabetes mellitus	3.5	4.4	131	146
Ischemic heart disease	2.3	2.1	93	74	Acute upper respiratory infections [4]	2.4	3.5	91	117
Malignant neoplasms	2.2	2.1	88	73	Malignant neoplasms	3.2	3.4	120	112
Disorders of lipoid metabolism	0.9	2.0	34	72	Allergic rhinitis.	1.5	3.3	55	107
65 years old and over [3]	71.2	83.7	5,405	6,080	65 years old and over [3]	107.5	121.0	5,861	6,470
Essential hypertension	3.8	6.4	286	462	Essential hypertension	7.7	9.7	421	518
Malignant neoplasms	4.8	5.7	365	415	Cataract	4.6	5.7	254	307
Diabetes mellitus	2.7	4.1	209	298	Diabetes mellitus	3.8	5.3	206	281
Ischemic heart disease	3.3	4.1	252	296	Malignant neoplasms	4.3	4.1	234	219
Cataract	2.3	3.3	177	240	Heart disease, excluding ischemic.	4.2	3.7	227	197

[1] Based on the International Classification of Diseases, 9th Revision, Clinical Modification, (ICD-9-CM). [2] Based on U.S. Census Bureau estimated civilian population as of July 1. [3] Includes other first-listed diagnoses, not shown separately. [4] Excluding pharyngitis.

Source: U.S. National Center for Health Statistics, Advance Data, Nos. 321 and 322, June 26. 2001 and July 10, 2001.

No. 160. Visits to Hospital Emergency Departments by Diagnosis: 1999

[48,546 represents 48,546,000. See headnote, Table 158]

Leading diagnoses [1]	Number (1,000)	Rate per 1,000 persons [2]	Leading diagnoses [1]	Number (1,000)	Rate per 1,000 persons [2]
MALE			**FEMALE**		
All ages.	48,546	366	All ages.	54,219	389
Under 15 years old [3]	11,710	380	Under 15 years old [3].	10,173	349
Acute upper respiratory infections [4] . . .	1,157	38	Otitis media	1,108	38
Otitis media	1,036	34	Acute upper respiratory infections [4] . . .	890	30
Open wound of head	772	25	Contusions with intact skin surfaces . . .	545	19
Contusions with intact skin surfaces . . .	554	18	Open wound of head	395	13
Asthma	445	14	Pyrexia of unknown origin	366	13
15 to 44 years old [3]	22,234	373	15 to 44 years old [3]	25,103	412
Contusions with intact skin surfaces . . .	1,211	20	Abdominal pain	1,253	21
Open wound of hand and fingers	1,012	17	Complications of pregnancy, child-birth, and the puerperium	1,242	20
Open wound, excluding head, hand, and fingers.	916	15	Contusions with intact skin surfaces . . .	1,015	17
Open wound of head	682	11	Acute upper respiratory infections [4] . . .	784	13
Acute upper respiratory infections [4] . . .	502	8	Urinary tract infection, site not specified.	639	10
45 to 64 years old [3]	8,290	292	45 to 64 years old [3]	9,506	317
Chest pain	581	20	Chest pain	595	20
Contusions with intact skin surfaces . . .	284	10	Abdominal pain	400	13
Abdominal pain	283	10	Contusions with intact skin surfaces . . .	390	13
Open wound of hand and fingers	247	9	Chronic and unspecified bronchitis	284	9
Open wound, excluding head, hand, and fingers	178	6	Urinary tract infection, site not specified	204	7
65 years old and over [3]	6,312	459	65 years old and over [3]	9,347	500
Heart disease, excluding ischemic	449	33	Heart disease, excluding ischemic	537	29
Chest pain	391	28	Chest pain	534	29
Ischemic heart disease.	239	17	Contusions with intact skin surfaces . . .	300	16
Pneumonia.	219	16	Abdominal pain	241	13
Chronic and unspecified bronchitis	174	13	Urinary tract infection, site not specified.	241	13

[1] Based on the International Classification of Diseases, 9th Revision, Clinical Modification, (ICD-9-CM). [2] Based on U.S. Census Bureau estimated civilian population as of July 1. [3] Includes other first-listed diagnoses, not shown separately. [4] Excluding pharyngitis.

Source: U.S. National Center for Health Statistics, Advance Data, No. 320, June 25, 2001.

U.S. Census Bureau, Statistical Abstract of the United States: 2001

No. 161. Hospitals—Summary Characteristics: 1980 to 1999

[For beds, 1,365 represents 1,365,000. Covers hospitals accepted for registration by the American Hospital Association; see text, this section. Short-term hospitals have an average patient stay of less than 30 days; long-term, an average stay of longer duration. Special hospitals include obstetrics and gynecology; eye, ear, nose, and throat; rehabilitation; orthopedic; and chronic and other special hospitals except psychiatric, tuberculosis, alcoholism, and chemical dependency hospitals]

Item	1980	1985	1990	1994	1995	1996	1997	1998	1999
NUMBER									
All hospitals	6,965	6,872	6,649	6,374	6,291	6,201	6,097	6,021	5,890
With 100 beds or more	3,755	3,805	3,620	3,492	3,376	3,347	3,267	3,216	3,140
Nonfederal [1]	6,606	6,529	6,312	6,067	5,992	5,911	5,812	5,746	5,626
Community hospitals [2]	5,830	5,732	5,384	5,229	5,194	5,134	5,057	5,015	4,956
Nongovernmental nonprofit	3,322	3,349	3,191	3,139	3,092	3,045	3,000	3,026	3,012
For profit	730	805	749	719	752	759	797	771	747
State and local government	1,778	1,578	1,444	1,371	1,350	1,330	1,260	1,218	1,197
Long-term general and special	157	128	131	110	112	112	125	125	129
Psychiatric	534	610	757	696	657	636	601	579	516
Tuberculosis	11	7	4	5	3	3	4	3	4
Federal	359	343	337	307	299	290	285	275	264
BEDS (1,000)									
All hospitals [3]	1,365	1,318	1,213	1,128	1,081	1,062	1,035	1,013	994
Rate per 1,000 population [4]	6.0	5.5	4.9	4.3	4.1	4.0	3.9	3.7	3.6
Beds per hospital	196	190	182	177	172	171	170	168	169
Nonfederal [1]	1,248	1,197	1,113	1,044	1,004	989	973	956	939
Community hospitals [2]	988	1,001	927	902	873	862	853	840	830
Rate per 1,000 population [4]	4.3	4.2	3.7	3.5	3.3	3.3	3.2	3.1	3.0
Nongovernmental nonprofit	692	707	657	637	610	598	591	588	587
For profit	87	104	102	101	106	109	115	113	107
State and local government	209	189	169	164	157	155	148	139	136
Long-term general and special	39	31	25	19	19	19	17	18	20
Psychiatric	215	169	158	121	110	106	100	95	87
Tuberculosis	2	1	(Z)	1	(Z)	(Z)	(Z)	(Z)	(Z)
Federal	117	112	98	84	78	73	62	57	55
AVERAGE DAILY CENSUS (1,000)									
All hospitals	1,060	910	844	745	710	685	673	662	657
Community hospitals [2]	747	649	619	568	548	531	528	525	526
Nongovernmental nonprofit	542	476	455	413	393	379	376	377	381
For profit	57	54	54	50	55	56	60	60	58
State and local government	149	119	111	104	100	96	92	87	86
EXPENSES (bil. dol.) [5]									
All hospitals	91.9	153.3	234.9	310.8	320.3	330.5	342.3	355.5	372.9
Nonfederal [1]	84.0	141.0	219.6	290.8	300.0	308.3	319.6	332.9	349.2
Community hospitals [2]	76.9	130.5	203.7	275.8	285.6	293.8	305.8	318.8	335.2
Nongovernmental nonprofit	55.8	96.1	150.7	204.2	209.6	216.0	225.3	238.0	251.5
For profit	5.8	11.5	18.8	23.4	26.7	28.4	31.2	31.7	31.2
State and local government	15.2	22.9	34.2	48.1	49.3	49.4	49.3	49.1	52.5
Long-term general and special	1.2	1.9	2.7	2.3	2.2	2.3	2.5	2.6	2.8
Psychiatric	5.8	8.3	12.9	12.3	11.7	12.0	11.0	11.2	11.0
Tuberculosis	0.1	0.1	0.1	0.7	0.4	(Z)	0.1	(Z)	(Z)
Federal	7.9	12.3	15.2	20.0	20.2	22.3	22.7	22.6	23.7
PERSONNEL (1,000) [6]									
All hospitals	3,492	3,625	4,063	4,270	4,273	4,276	4,333	4,407	4,369
Nonfederal [1]	3,213	3,326	3,760	3,969	3,971	3,981	4,036	4,071	4,074
Community hospitals [2]	2,873	2,997	3,420	3,692	3,714	3,725	3,790	3,831	3,838
Nongovernmental nonprofit	2,086	2,216	2,533	2,719	2,702	2,711	2,765	2,834	2,862
For profit	189	221	273	301	343	359	385	383	362
State and local government	598	561	614	672	670	654	640	614	614
Long-term general and special	56	58	55	38	38	40	37	37	42
Psychiatric	275	263	280	233	215	212	204	198	191
Tuberculosis	3	2	1	1	1	1	1	1	1
Federal	279	299	303	301	301	295	296	336	295
Outpatient visits (mil.)	263.0	282.1	368.2	453.6	483.2	505.5	520.6	545.5	573.5
Emergency	82.0	80.1	92.8	96.0	99.9	97.6	97.4	99.0	103.8

Z Less than 500 beds or $50 million. [1] Includes hospital units of institutions. [2] Short term (average length of stay less than 30 days) general and special (e.g., obstetrics and gynecology; eye, ear, nose and throat; rehabilitation etc. except psychiatric, tuberculosis, alcoholism and chemical dependency). Excludes hospital units of institutions. [3] Beginning 1990, number of beds at end of reporting period; prior years, average number in 12 month period. [4] Based on Census Bureau estimated resident population as of July 1. Estimates reflect revisions based on the 1990 Census of Population. [5] Excludes new construction. [6] Includes full-time equivalents of part-time personnel.

Source: Health Forum, An American Hospital Association Company, Chicago, IL, *Hospital Statistics 2001 Edition*, and prior years (copyright).

No. 162. Average Cost to Community Hospitals Per Patient: 1980 to 1999

[In dollars, except percent. Covers nonfederal short-term general or special hospitals (excluding psychiatric or tuberculosis hospitals and hospital units of institutions). Total cost per patient based on total hospital expenses (payroll, employee benefits, professional fees, supplies, etc.). Data have been adjusted for outpatient visits]

Type of expense and hospital	1980	1985	1990	1993	1994	1995	1996	1997	1998	1999
Average cost per day, total	245	460	687	881	931	968	1,006	1,033	1,067	1,103
Annual percent change [1]	12.9	11.9	7.8	7.4	5.7	4.0	2.6	3.3	3.3	
Nongovernmental nonprofit	246	463	692	898	950	994	1,042	1,074	1,111	1,140
For profit	257	501	752	914	924	947	946	962	968	999
State and local government	239	433	635	800	859	878	903	914	949	1,007
Average cost per stay, total	1,851	3,245	4,947	6,132	6,230	6,216	6,225	6,262	6,386	6,512
Nongovernmental nonprofit	1,902	3,307	5,001	6,178	6,257	6,279	6,344	6,393	6,526	6,608
For profit	1,676	3,033	4,727	5,643	5,529	5,425	5,207	5,219	5,262	5,350
State and local government	1,750	3,106	4,838	6,206	6,513	6,445	6,419	6,475	6,612	6,923

[1] Change from immediate prior year.

Source: Health Forum, An American Hospital Association Company, Chicago, IL, *Hospital Statistics 2001 Edition* (copyright).

No. 163. Community Hospitals—States: 1990 to 1999

[Beds: 928.1 represents 928,100. For definition of community hospitals see footnote 2, Table 161]

State	Number of hospitals			Beds (1,000)			Patients admitted (1,000)		Average daily census [1] (1,000)		Outpatient visits (mil.)	
	1990	1995	1999	1990	1995	1999	1995	1999	1995	1999	1995	1999
United States	5,384	5,194	4,956	928.1	872.7	829.6	30,945	32,359	547.6	525.5	414.3	495.3
Alabama	120	115	109	18.6	18.3	16.3	642	670	10.7	9.9	6.4	7.8
Alaska	16	17	17	1.2	1.3	1.3	40	41	0.7	0.7	0.8	1.0
Arizona	61	61	61	9.9	9.9	10.6	427	511	5.6	6.5	4.0	4.9
Arkansas	86	85	83	10.9	10.1	10.1	342	375	6.0	6.0	3.6	4.0
California	445	424	395	80.5	75.0	73.7	3,029	3,244	45.0	46.8	39.5	44.8
Colorado	69	69	67	10.4	9.3	9.3	340	383	5.4	5.3	5.5	6.4
Connecticut	35	34	35	9.6	7.5	7.9	338	338	5.5	5.7	5.7	6.8
Delaware	8	8	6	2.0	1.9	2.0	81	87	1.5	1.3	1.4	1.3
District of Columbia	11	12	12	4.5	3.8	3.5	154	138	2.7	2.7	1.2	1.4
Florida	224	212	203	50.7	49.7	49.4	1,772	2,020	29.4	30.5	16.9	19.7
Georgia	163	160	154	25.7	26.1	24.8	859	824	15.8	15.4	9.6	10.8
Hawaii	18	21	22	2.9	3.0	2.3	97	99	2.4	2.1	2.1	2.4
Idaho	43	41	42	3.2	3.4	3.5	104	120	1.8	1.9	1.7	2.2
Illinois	210	207	198	45.8	42.0	37.7	1,452	1,509	25.0	22.6	20.6	23.9
Indiana	113	115	111	21.8	19.4	19.2	699	683	11.3	11.0	11.8	13.1
Iowa	124	116	115	14.3	12.6	11.8	361	359	7.1	6.8	6.2	8.6
Kansas	138	132	131	11.8	10.8	11.6	291	326	5.8	6.1	4.0	5.0
Kentucky	107	104	105	15.9	15.1	15.0	534	570	9.0	9.0	6.1	8.0
Louisiana	140	130	122	19.1	19.1	16.8	622	627	10.6	9.5	8.0	9.5
Maine	39	39	37	4.5	4.0	3.7	142	146	2.6	2.4	2.5	2.8
Maryland	52	50	49	13.6	12.6	11.6	574	577	8.8	8.3	4.9	5.9
Massachusetts	101	96	79	21.7	18.9	16.3	751	739	13.0	11.5	13.5	15.7
Michigan	176	167	145	33.9	29.6	26.1	1,120	1,084	19.3	17.2	19.2	22.4
Minnesota	152	142	134	19.4	17.4	16.5	496	535	11.3	11.1	5.7	6.5
Mississippi	103	97	96	12.9	12.6	13.2	388	416	7.6	8.0	3.2	3.5
Missouri	135	126	118	24.3	21.9	20.3	714	743	12.6	11.6	9.9	14.6
Montana	55	55	53	4.6	4.2	4.7	96	98	2.7	3.2	1.3	2.5
Nebraska	90	91	85	8.5	7.9	8.3	183	199	4.5	5.0	2.5	3.0
Nevada	21	20	22	3.4	3.6	3.7	149	198	2.2	2.7	1.4	2.1
New Hampshire	27	29	28	3.5	3.4	3.0	110	109	2.1	1.6	1.8	2.4
New Jersey	95	92	81	28.9	29.9	24.6	1,068	1,069	21.4	16.9	12.8	16.1
New Mexico	37	36	36	4.2	3.7	3.4	156	164	2.1	2.0	2.5	3.1
New York	235	230	218	74.7	73.9	68.9	2,398	2,406	59.1	53.0	38.9	45.7
North Carolina	120	119	114	22.0	22.7	23.4	833	931	15.5	15.7	8.8	11.5
North Dakota	50	43	41	4.4	4.2	3.9	89	87	2.7	2.3	1.3	1.6
Ohio	190	180	167	43.1	37.8	34.2	1,375	1,359	22.2	20.2	22.0	24.9
Oklahoma	111	110	109	12.4	11.5	11.1	368	411	6.1	6.2	3.8	4.6
Oregon	70	64	59	8.1	7.2	6.6	296	318	3.8	3.9	5.8	6.7
Pennsylvania	238	225	210	52.6	48.5	43.0	1,810	1,755	33.8	29.2	26.9	29.3
Rhode Island	12	11	11	3.2	2.7	2.4	119	117	1.8	1.7	1.7	1.9
South Carolina	69	66	64	11.3	11.3	11.6	410	479	7.2	7.7	4.7	6.4
South Dakota	53	50	48	4.2	4.6	4.3	94	97	3.0	2.9	1.0	1.6
Tennessee	134	126	121	23.6	20.9	20.6	740	752	12.5	11.8	7.4	9.5
Texas	428	416	408	59.2	57.2	56.8	2,029	2,303	31.1	32.9	22.7	28.3
Utah	42	42	42	4.4	4.2	4.2	171	189	2.2	2.4	3.2	4.4
Vermont	15	14	14	1.7	1.8	1.7	55	51	1.3	1.1	1.0	1.4
Virginia	97	96	89	20.0	18.6	17.3	699	724	11.5	11.3	7.2	8.7
Washington	91	88	86	12.0	10.8	11.1	467	491	6.0	6.5	8.4	10.0
West Virginia	59	59	58	8.4	8.1	8.1	271	289	4.9	4.9	4.0	5.1
Wisconsin	129	127	123	18.6	17.0	15.9	550	553	10.2	9.3	8.2	10.5
Wyoming	27	25	23	2.2	2.0	1.8	43	45	1.1	1.0	0.7	0.9

[1] Inpatients receiving treatment each day; excludes newborn.

Source: Health Forum, An American Hospital Association Company, Chicago, IL, *Hospital Statistics 2001 Edition*, and prior years (copyright).

Health and Nutrition   111

No. 164. Hospital Use Rates by Type of Hospital: 1980 to 1999

Type of hospital	1980	1985	1990	1995	1996	1997	1998	1999
Community hospitals: [1]								
Admissions per 1,000 population [2]	159	141	125	118	117	118	118	119
Admissions per bed.	37	33	34	35	36	37	38	39
Average length of stay [3] (days)	7.6	7.1	7.2	6.5	6.2	6.1	6.0	5.9
Outpatient visits per admission	5.6	6.5	9.7	13.4	14.1	14.3	14.9	15.3
Outpatient visits per 1,000 population [2]	890	919	1,208	1,577	1,658	1,681	1,755	1,817
Surgical operations (million [4])	18.8	20.1	21.9	23.2	23.6	24.2	25.3	26.3
Number per admission	0.5	0.6	0.7	0.7	0.8	0.8	0.8	0.8
Nonfederal psychiatric:								
Admissions per 1,000 population [2]	2.5	2.5	2.9	2.7	2.7	2.7	2.7	2.5
Days in hospital per 1,000 population [2]	295	224	190	124	117	109	103	96

[1] For definition of community hospitals, see footnote 2, Table 161. [2] Based on U.S. Census Bureau estimated resident population as of July 1. Estimates reflect revisions based on the 1990 Census of Population. [3] Number of inpatient days divided by number of admissions. [4] 18.8 represents 18,800,000.

Source: Health Forum, An American Hospital Association Company, Chicago, IL, *Hospital Statistics 2001 Edition*, and prior years (copyright).

No. 165. Hospital Utilization Rates: 1980 to 1999

[37,832 represents 37,832,000. Represents estimates of inpatients discharged from noninstitutional, short-stay hospitals, exclusive of federal hospitals. Excludes newborn infants. Based on sample data collected from the National Hospital Discharge Survey, a sample survey of hospital records of patients discharged in year shown; subject to sampling variability. Comparisons beginning 1990 with data for earlier years should be made with caution as estimates of change may reflect improvements in the survey design rather than true changes in hospital use]

Sex	1980	1985	1990	1994	1995	1996	1997	1998	1999
Patients discharged (1,000)	37,832	35,056	30,788	30,843	30,722	30,545	30,914	31,827	32,132
Patients discharged per 1,000 persons,									
total [1]	168	148	122	117	116	114	114	117	117
Male	139	124	100	96	94	92	93	93	95
Female	194	171	143	138	136	135	135	139	138
Days of care per 1,000 persons, total [1]	1,217	954	784	674	620	597	582	589	581
Male	1,068	849	694	599	551	533	508	517	510
Female	1,356	1,053	869	745	686	657	653	658	649
Average stay (days)	7.3	6.5	6.4	5.7	5.4	5.2	5.1	5.1	5.0
Male	7.7	6.9	6.9	6.2	5.8	5.8	5.5	5.5	5.4
Female	7.0	6.2	6.1	5.4	5.0	4.9	4.8	4.7	4.7

[1] Based on U.S. Census Bureau estimated civilian population as of July 1. Estimates for 1980 and 1985 do not reflect revisions based on the 1990 Census of Population. Beginning with 1990 data, rates are based on the U.S. Census Bureau estimates of the civilian population that have been adjusted for net underenumeration in the 1990 Census.

Source: U.S. National Center for Health Statistics, *Vital and Health Statistics*, Series 13; and unpublished data.

No. 166. Hospital Discharges and Days of Care: 1995 and 1999

[30,722 represents 30,722,000. See headnote, Table 165. For composition of regions, see map, inside front cover]

Age and region	Discharges				Days of care per 1,000 persons [1]		Average stay (days)	
	Number (1,000)		Per 1,000 persons [1]					
	1995	1999	1995	1999	1995	1999	1995	1999
Total	30,722	32,132	116	117	620	581	5.4	5.0
Age:								
Under 1 year old	790	827	198	209	1,083	1,107	5.5	5.3
1 to 4 years old	744	729	46	47	153	159	3.3	3.4
5 to 14 years old	872	902	22	22	99	102	4.5	4.6
15 to 24 years old	2,943	2,852	80	74	271	246	3.4	3.3
25 to 34 years old	4,201	3,829	102	99	354	331	3.5	3.3
35 to 44 years old	3,449	3,411	81	76	381	334	4.7	4.4
45 to 64 years old	6,168	6,899	119	117	657	586	5.5	5.0
65 to 74 years old	4,832	4,883	260	271	1,685	1,578	6.5	5.8
75 years old and over	6,724	7,799	459	482	3,248	3,013	7.1	6.3
Race:								
White	19,951	20,757	91	92	491	460	5.4	5.0
Black	3,887	3,788	113	105	658	572	5.8	5.4
Asian/Pacific Islander	486	470	51	43	278	213	5.4	5.0
American Indian/Eskimo/ Aleut	107	211	46	85	240	479	5.2	5.6
Region:								
Northeast	7,051	6,952	136	133	858	763	6.3	5.7
Midwest	6,994	7,368	113	116	586	535	5.2	4.6
South	11,373	12,007	122	123	643	611	5.3	5.0
West	5,303	5,805	91	93	410	430	4.5	4.6

[1] Based on U.S. Census Bureau estimated civilian population that has been adjusted for the net underenumeration in the 1990 Census of Population.

Source: U.S. National Center for Health Statistics, *Vital and Health Statistics*, Series 13; and unpublished data.

No. 167. Hospital Discharges and Days of Care by Sex: 1999

[12,748 represents 12,748,000. Represents estimates of inpatients discharged from noninstitutional, short-stay hospitals, exclusive of federal hospitals. See headnote, Table 165]

Age and first-listed diagnosis	Discharges Number (1,000)	Per 1,000 persons [1]	Days of care per 1,000 persons [1]	Average stay (days)	Age and first-listed diagnosis	Discharges Number (1,000)	Per 1,000 persons [1]	Days of care per 1,000 persons [1]	Average stay (days)
MALE					FEMALE				
All ages [2]	**12,748**	**103.4**	**565**	**5.5**	**All ages** [2]	**19,384**	**132.2**	**614**	**4.6**
Under 18 years [3]	1,592	43.0	198	4.6	Under 18 years [3]	1,458	41.3	173	4.2
Pneumonia	233	6.3	22	3.5	Pneumonia	174	4.9	18	3.6
Injuries and poisoning	182	4.9	[4]22	[4]4.5	Injuries and poisoning	122	3.5	[4]14	[4]4.1
Asthma	121	3.3	8	2.4	Asthma	82	2.3	6	2.4
18 to 44 years [3]	2,521	46.0	223	4.8	18 to 44 years [3]	6,980	126.4	410	3.2
Injuries and poisoning	449	8.2	38	4.6	Delivery	3,650	66.1	163	2.5
Serious mental illness [5]	275	5.0	43	8.6	Serious mental illness [5]	283	5.1	38	7.5
Alcohol and drug [6]	197	3.6	17	4.8	Injuries and poisoning	261	4.7	20	4.2
Diseases of heart	164	3.0	11	3.6					
45 to 64 years [3]	3,390	118.5	603	5.1	45 to 64 years [3]	3,508	115.4	570	4.9
Diseases of heart	815	28.5	111	3.9	Diseases of heart	484	15.9	68	4.3
Injuries and poisoning	271	9.5	51	5.4	Injuries and poisoning	255	8.4	46	5.5
Malignant neoplasms	183	6.4	44	6.8	Malignant neoplasms	211	6.9	47	6.8
Serious mental illness [5]	115	4.0	40	10.0	Serious mental illness [5]	140	4.6	41	8.8
65 to 74 years [3]	2,310	283.5	1,640	5.8	65 to 74 years [3]	2,573	260.0	1,527	5.9
Diseases of heart	616	75.6	354	4.7	Diseases of heart	537	54.3	268	4.9
Malignant neoplasms	185	22.7	152	6.7	Injuries and poisoning	176	17.8	109	6.1
Injuries and poisoning	145	17.8	107	6.0	Malignant neoplasms	154	15.5	106	6.8
Pneumonia	122	14.9	89	6.0	Cerebrovascular diseases	128	13.0	68	5.2
Cerebrovascular diseases	116	14.3	70	4.9	Pneumonia	120	12.1	73	6.0
75 years old and older [3]	2,935	481.8	3,046	6.3	75 years old and older [3]	4,865	481.4	2,993	6.2
Diseases of heart	694	113.9	584	5.1	Diseases of heart	1,041	103.0	542	5.3
Pneumonia	250	41.0	281	6.9	Injuries and poisoning	502	49.7	308	6.2
Injuries and poisoning	201	32.9	234	7.1	Pneumonia	326	32.2	223	6.9
Cerebrovascular diseases	187	30.7	169	5.5	Cerebrovascular diseases	272	26.9	151	5.6
Malignant neoplasms	172	28.2	216	7.7	Malignant neoplasms	209	20.6	168	8.1

[1] Based on Census Bureau estimated civilian population as of July 1. Population figures are adjusted for net underenumeration using the 1990 National Population Adjustment Matrix from the U.S. Census Bureau. [2] Average length of stay and rates per 1,000 population are age-adjusted to the year 2000, standard using six age groups; Under 18 years, 18-44 years, 45-54 years, 55-64 years, 65-74 years, and 75 years and over. [3] Includes other first-listed diagnoses not shown separately. [4] Estimates are considered unreliable. [5] Excludes discharges from other types of facilities such as the Dept. of Veterans Affairs or long-term hospitals. [6] Includes abuse, dependence, and withdrawal. Excludes discharges from other types of facilities such as the Dept. of Veterans Affairs or day treatment programs.

Source: U.S. National Center for Health Statistics, *Health, United States, 2001*.

No. 168. Organ Transplants and Grafts: 1990 to 2000

[As of end of year. Based on reports of procurement programs and transplant centers in the United States, except as noted]

Procedure	Number of procedures						Number of centers		Number of people waiting, 2000	1-year patient survival rates, 1999 (percent)
	1990	1995	1996	1997	1998	1999	1990	2000		
Transplant: [1]										
Heart	2,095	2,344	2,319	2,266	2,309	2,162	148	142	4,164	82.8
Heart-lung	52	69	38	63	47	48	79	83	209	53.3
Lung	203	870	812	925	860	873	70	77	3,732	72.4
Liver	2,631	3,819	3,918	4,005	4,356	4,596	85	121	17,132	78.2
Kidney	9,358	10,954	11,228	11,536	12,229	12,400	232	246	50,426	90.0
Kidney-pancreas	459	915	857	845	968	933	(NA)	(NA)	2,553	92.2
Pancreas	60	103	157	193	230	358	84	133	1,032	80.3
Intestine	1	21	14	22	28	36	(NA)	38	151	50.9
Multi-organ	71	124	172	195	180	120	(NA)	(NA)	(NA)	(NA)
Cornea grafts [2]	40,631	44,652	46,300	45,493	(NA)	45,765	[3]107	(NA)	(NA)	(NA)
Bone grafts	350,000	450,000	475,000	(NA)	500,000	650,000	30	(NA)	(X)	(NA)
Skin grafts [4]	5,500	5,500	9,000	(NA)	9,000	10,000	25	(NA)	(X)	(NA)

NA Not available.   X Not applicable.   [1] Kidney-pancreas and heart-lung transplants are each counted as one organ. All other multi-organ transplants, excluding kidney-pancreas and heart-lung, are included in the multi-organ row. The data and analyses reported in the 2000 Annual Report of the U.S. Scientific Registry of Transplant Recipients and the Organ Procurement and Transplantation Network have been supplied by UNOS under contract with HHS. The authors alone are responsible for the reporting and interpretation of these data.   [2] 1990, number of procedures and eye banks include Canada.   [3] Eye banks.   [4] Procedure data are shown in terms of square feet.

Source: Transplants, *2000 Annual Report of the U.S. Scientific Registry for Transplant Recipients and the Organ Procurement and Transplantation Network: Transplant Data: 1990-1999*. U.S. Department of Health and Human Services, Health Resources and Services Administration, Office of Special Programs, Division of Transplantation, Rockville, MD; United Network for Organ Sharing, Richmond, VA; American Association of Tissue Banks, McLean, VA; and Eye Bank Association of America, Washington, DC; and unpublished data.

Health and Nutrition 113

No. 169. Procedures for Inpatients Discharged From Short-Stay Hospitals: 1990 to 1999

[23,051 represents 23,051,000. Excludes newborn infants and discharges from federal hospitals. See headnote, Table 165]

Sex and type of procedure	Number of procedures (1,000)				Rate per 1,000 population [1]			
	1990	1995	1998	1999	1990	1995	1998	1999
Surgical procedures, total [2]	23,051	22,530	23,780	23,833	92.4	86.2	87.1	86.5
Cardiac catheterization	995	1,068	1,202	1,271	4.0	4.1	4.4	4.6
Removal of coronary artery obstruction [3]	285	434	926	1,069	1.2	1.7	3.4	3.9
Reduction of fracture [4]	609	577	610	628	2.4	2.2	2.2	2.3
Coronary artery bypass graft	392	573	553	571	1.6	2.2	2.0	2.1
Male, total [2]	8,538	8,388	8,757	8,949	70.6	65.9	65.7	66.5
Cardiac catheterization	620	660	716	758	5.1	5.2	5.4	5.6
Removal of coronary artery obstruction [3]	200	285	594	708	1.7	2.2	4.4	5.3
Coronary artery bypass graft	286	423	396	389	2.4	3.3	3.0	2.9
Female, total [2]	14,513	14,142	15,022	14,884	113.0	105.3	107.5	105.6
Repair of current obstetric laceration	795	964	1,093	1,116	6.2	7.2	7.8	7.9
Cesarean section	945	785	900	841	7.4	5.8	6.4	6.0
Hysterectomy	591	583	645	616	4.6	4.3	4.6	4.4
Diagnostic and other nonsurgical procedures [5]	17,455	17,278	17,720	17,482	70.0	66.1	64.9	63.5
Angiocardiography and arteriography [6]	1,735	1,834	1,961	2,034	7.0	7.0	7.2	7.4
Diagnostic ultrasound	1,608	1,181	1,123	1,022	6.4	4.5	4.1	3.7
Respiratory therapy	1,164	1,127	1,109	1,117	4.7	4.3	4.1	4.1
CAT scan [7]	1,506	967	986	871	6.0	3.7	3.6	3.2
Male, total [5]	7,378	7,261	7,431	7,421	61.0	57.1	55.7	55.1
Angiocardiography and arteriography [6]	1,051	1,076	1,115	1,145	8.7	8.5	8.4	8.5
Respiratory therapy	586	572	564	560	4.9	4.5	4.2	4.2
CAT scan [7]	736	473	462	408	6.1	3.7	3.5	3.0
Female, total [5]	10,077	10,016	10,290	10,061	78.5	74.6	73.6	71.4
Manual assisted delivery	750	866	975	802	5.9	6.5	7.0	5.7
Fetal EKG and fetal monitoring	1,377	935	835	756	10.8	7.0	6.0	5.4
Diagnostic ultrasound	941	682	635	571	7.3	5.1	4.5	4.1

[1] Based on Census Bureau estimated civilian population as of July 1. Beginning 1998 population figures are adjusted for net underenumeration using the 1990 National Population Adjustment Matrix from the Census Bureau. [2] Includes other types of surgical procedures not shown separately. [3] Beginning 1998 includes separately coded "insertion of stent." [4] Excluding skull, nose, and jaw. [5] Includes other nonsurgical procedures not shown separately. [6] Using contrast material. [7] Computerized axial tomography.

Source: U.S. National Center for Health Statistics, *Vital and Health Statistics*, series 13; and unpublished data.

No. 170. Hospital Utilization Measures for HIV Patients: 1985 to 1999

[HIV represents human immunodeficiency virus. See headnote, Table 165]

Measure of utilization	Unit	1985	1990	1995	1997	1998	1999
Number of patients discharged [1]	1,000	23	146	249	178	189	180
Rate of patient discharges [2]	Rate	1.0	5.8	9.4	6.6	6.9	6.5
Number of days of care	1,000	387	2,188	2,326	1,448	1,503	1,310
Rate of days of care [2]	Rate	16.3	86.9	87.6	53.5	55.0	47.5
Average length of stay [3]	Days	17.1	14.9	9.3	8.1	8.0	7.3

[1] Comparisons beginning 1990 with data for earlier years should be made with caution as estimates of change may reflect improvements in the 1988 sample design rather than true changes in hospital use. [2] Per 10,000 population. Based on Census Bureau estimated civilian population as of July 1. Population estimates for the 1980's do not reflect revised estimates based on the 1990 Census of Population. Beginning 1900 rates are based on civilian population estimates that have been adjusted for net underenumeration in the 1990 Census. [3] For similar data on all patients, see Table 165.

Source: National Center for Health Statistics, *Vital and Health Statistics*, Series 13; and unpublished data.

No. 171. Skilled Nursing Facilities: 1980 to 1999

[448 represents 448,000. Covers facilities and beds certified for participation under medicare as of midyear. Includes facilities which have transfer agreements with one or more participating hospitals, and are engaged primarily in providing skilled nursing care and related services for the rehabilitation of injured, disabled, or sick persons]

Item	Unit	1980	1990	1995	1996	1997	1998	1999
Skilled nursing facilities	Number	5,155	9,008	13,281	14,177	14,860	15,037	14,913
Beds	1,000	448	512	657	672	685	723	837
Per 1,000 medicare enrollees [1]	Rate	16.0	15.2	17.7	17.8	18.0	18.8	21.6

[1] Based on total number of beneficiaries enrolled in the medicare hospital insurance program as of July 1 of year stated.

Source: U.S. Health Care Financing Administration, *Medicare Participating Providers and Suppliers of Health Services, 1980*; and unpublished data.

No. 172. Home Health and Hospice Care Agencies by Selected Characteristics: 1998

[In percent, except as Indicated (13.3 represents 13,300). Based on the National Home and Hospice Care Survey. Home health care is provided to individuals and families in their place of residence. Hospice care is available in both the home and inpatient settings. See source for details. For composition of regions see map, inside front cover]

Agency characteristic	Agencies, total	Current patients [1]			Discharges [2]		
		Total	Home health care	Hospice care	Total	Home health care	Hospice care
Total (1,000)	13.3	1,961.6	1,881.8	79.8	8,117.7	7,621.8	496.0
PERCENT DISTRIBUTION							
Ownership:							
Proprietary	53.9	46.1	47.1	23.0	38.4	39.1	26.7
Voluntary nonprofit	36.2	45.4	44.2	73.0	54.3	53.2	69.9
Government and other	9.9	8.5	8.7	[3]4.1	7.4	7.6	[3]3.4
Certification:							
Medicare	84.3	84.0	83.5	96.6	92.9	92.8	93.9
Medicaid	85.1	85.1	84.8	92.3	89.3	89.3	90.0
Region:							
Northeast	16.7	34.4	35.4	10.7	33.9	34.8	18.7
Midwest	25.8	21.5	21.4	23.9	25.6	25.7	22.9
South	42.0	33.9	33.4	44.6	26.4	25.9	33.3
West	15.5	10.2	9.7	20.8	14.2	13.つ	25.1

[1] Patients on the rolls of the agency as of midnight the day prior to the survey.   [2] Patients removed from the rolls of the agency during the 12 months prior to the day of the survey. A patient could be included more than once if the individual had more than one episode of care during the year.   [3] Figure does not meet standard of reliability or precision.

Source: U.S. National Center for Health Statistics, unpublished data.

No. 173. Home Health and Hospice Care Patients by Selected Characteristics: 1998

[In percent, except as Indicated (1,961.6 represents 1,961,600). See headnote, Table 172]

Item	Current patients [1]			Discharges [2]		
	Total	Home health care	Hospice care	Total	Home health care	Hospice care
Total (1,000)	1,961.6	1,881.8	79.8	8,117.7	7,621.8	496.0
PERCENT DISTRIBUTION						
Age: [3]						
Under 45 years old	15.1	15.5	4.6	14.7	15.3	5.9
45-54 years old	7.1	7.1	6.4	7.1	7.1	6.7
55-64 years old	8.8	8.7	10.6	8.3	8.1	11.2
65 years old and over	69.1	68.7	78.4	70.0	69.6	76.1
65-69 years old	8.2	8.3	7.2	9.7	9.7	9.2
70-74 years old	11.6	11.5	15.5	13.0	12.8	16.7
75-79 years old	14.5	14.4	16.8	17.0	17.1	16.8
80-84 years old	15.5	15.5	16.2	13.9	13.8	15.2
85 years old and over	19.2	19.1	22.7	16.3	16.2	18.2
Sex:						
Male	34.0	33.6	42.7	38.4	37.7	47.9
Female	66.0	66.4	57.3	61.6	62.3	52.1
Race:						
White	70.0	69.5	82.7	67.8	67.0	79.8
Black and other	13.5	13.6	9.9	12.9	13.0	9.3
Black	12.9	13.0	8.9	11.7	11.8	8.0
Unknown	16.6	17.0	7.4	19.3	20.0	[4]10.9
Marital status: [3]						
Married	30.3	29.7	44.6	39.7	38.9	48.9
Widowed	32.7	32.5	35.8	28.3	28.1	32.0
Divorced or separated	4.9	4.8	8.5	4.5	4.4	5.1
Never married	17.0	17.4	7.5	15.1	15.7	7.2
Unknown	15.1	15.6	[4]3.6	12.5	12.9	[4]6.8
Primary admission diagnosis:						
Neoplasms	6.1	3.9	57.5	10.9	7.3	65.7
Endocrine, nutritional and metabolic and immunity disorders	7.9	8.2	(4)	5.1	5.4	(4)
Diseases of the nervous system and sense organs	7.7	7.6	9.5	4.3	4.3	4.9
Diseases of the circulatory system	23.0	23.5	12.6	24.3	25.2	11.4
Diseases of the respiratory system	8.0	7.5	10.6	8.3	8.4	6.2
Diseases of the musculoskeletal system and connective tissue	7.9	8.2	(4)	8.3	8.8	(4)
Injuries and poisoning	8.5	8.9	(4)	9.3	9.9	(4)

[1] Patients on the rolls of the agency as of midnight the day prior to the survey.   [2] Patients removed from the rolls of the agency during the 12 months prior to the day of the survey. A patient could be included more than once if the individual had more than one episode of care during the year.   [3] For current patients, current age or marital status; for discharged patients, age or marital status at time of discharge.   [4] Figure does not meet standard of reliability or precision.

Source: U.S. National Center for Health Statistics, unpublished data.

U.S. Census Bureau, Statistical Abstract of the United States: 2001

No. 174. Elderly Home Health Patients: 1998

[1,293 represents 1,293,000. Covers the civilian population 65 years old and over who are home health care patients. Age of patient is based on age at the time of interview. Home health care is provided to individuals and families in their place of residence. Based on the 1998 National Home and Hospice Care Survey]

Item	Current patients [1] Number (1,000)	Current patients [1] Percent	Discharges [2] Number (1,000)	Discharges [2] Percent	Item	Current patients [1] Number (1,000)	Current patients [1] Percent	Discharges [2] Number (1,000)	Discharges [2] Percent
Total 65 yrs. old & over	**1,293**	**100.0**	**5,301**	**100.0**	Own income	69	5.4	84	1.6
Received help with—					Medicare	953	73.8	4,659	87.9
Bathing or showering	645	49.9	2,152	40.6	Medicaid	141	10.9	186	3.5
Dressing	554	42.8	1,784	33.7					
Eating	115	8.9	330	6.2	Services rendered: [5]				
Transferring in/out of a bed or chair	352	27.2	1,225	23.1	Nursing services	1,015	78.6	4,800	90.5
Using the toilet room	269	20.8	921	17.4	Social services	151	11.7	714	13.5
					Counseling	70	5.4	191	3.6
Doing light housework	471	36.4	1,173	22.1	Medications	66	5.1	252	4.8
Managing money	26	2.0	(3)	(3)	Physical therapy	277	21.5	1,664	31.4
Shopping for groceries or clothes	176	13.6	192	3.6					
Using the telephone	48	3.7	75	1.4	Homemaker-household services	312	24.2	587	11.1
Preparing meals	261	20.2	515	9.7	Nutrition services	49	3.8	118	2.2
Taking medications	228	17.6	655	12.4	Physician services	28	2.2	87	1.6
Primary source of payment [4]:					Occupational therapy	68	5.3	399	7.5
Private insurance	52	4.0	310	5.9	Speech therapy/audiology	(3)	(3)	[3] 73	[3] 1.4

[1] Patients on the rolls of the agency as of midnight the day prior to the survey. [2] Patients removed from the rolls of the agency during the 12 months prior to the day of the survey. A patient could be included more than once if the individual had more than one episode of care during the year. [3] Figure does not meet standard of reliability or precision. [4] For current patients, the expected source; for discharges the actual source for the entire episode. [5] For current patients, services currently being provided; for discharges services provided during the 30 days prior to discharge.

Source: U.S. National Center for Health Statistics, unpublished data.

No. 175. Nursing Homes—Selected Characteristics: 1985 to 1999

[Beds: 1,624 represents 1,624,000. Covers nursing and related care homes in the conterminous United States that had three or more beds, were staffed for use by residents, and routinely provided nursing and personal care services. Excludes places providing only room and board and places serving specific health problems. Based on the 1999 National Nursing Home Survey, a two-stage survey sample of nursing homes and their residents. Subject to sampling variability. For composition of regions, see map, inside front cover]

Characteristic	Beds Nursing homes	Beds Number (1,000)	Beds Per nursing home	Current residents Number (1,000)	Occupancy rate [1]	Full-time equivalent employment Administrative, medical, and therapeutic Number (1,000)	Administrative, medical, and therapeutic Rate per 100 beds	Nursing Number (1,000)	Nursing Rate per 100 beds
1985	19,100	1,624	85	1,491	91.8	89.4	5.5	704	43.4
1995	16,700	1,771	106	1,549	87.4	90.5	5.1	916	51.7
1997	17,000	1,821	107	1,609	88.4	100.0	5.5	950	52.2
1999, total	**18,000**	**1,965**	**109**	**1,627**	**82.8**	**96.6**	**4.9**	**961**	**48.9**
Ownership:									
Proprietary	12,000	1,291	108	1,048	81.2	60.2	4.6	597	46.2
Voluntary nonprofit	4,800	523	109	446	85.3	29.1	5.6	280	53.5
Government and other	1,200	151	126	133	88.1	7.4	4.7	84	55.6
Certification:									
Medicare and medicaid certified	14,700	1,698	116	1,414	83.3	83.2	4.9	842	49.6
Medicare only	[2] 600	49	82	37	75.5	2.8	5.7	26	53.1
Medicaid only	2,100	177	89	143	80.8	9.0	5.1	75	42.4
Not certified	[2] 500	40	80	33	82.5	1.6	4.0	18	45.0
Bed size:									
Less than 50 beds	2,000	72	36	59	81.9	7.1	9.9	43	59.7
50-99 beds	7,000	503	72	414	82.3	28.8	5.7	252	50.1
100-199 beds	7,500	998	133	826	82.8	45.0	4.5	476	47.7
200 beds or more	1,400	392	280	328	83.7	15.7	4.0	190	48.5
Region:									
Northeast	3,200	443	138	382	86.2	21.7	4.9	244	55.1
Midwest	6,000	619	103	498	80.4	28.3	4.6	272	43.9
South	6,000	652	109	531	81.6	30.5	4.7	311	47.7
West	2,800	251	90	215	85.7	16.1	6.4	133	53.0
Affiliation: [3]									
Chain	10,800	1,179	109	977	82.9	58.7	5.0	556	47.2
Independent	7,200	781	108	646	82.7	37.7	4.8	404	51.7

[1] Number of residents divided by number of available beds multiplied by 100. [2] Figure does not meet standards of reliability or precision. [3] Excludes a small number of homes, beds, and residents with unknown affiliation.

Source: U.S. National Center for Health Statistics, unpublished data.

No. 176. Nursing Home Residents 65 Years Old and Over by Selected Characteristics: 1997

[1,465 represents 1,465,000. Covers nursing and related care homes in the conterminous United States that had three or more beds, were staffed for use by residents, and routinely provided nursing and personal care services. Excludes places providing only room and board and places serving specific health problems. Based on the National Nursing Home Survey, a two-stage survey sample of nursing homes and their residents. Subject to sampling variability]

Characteristic [1]	Number (1,000)	Percent distri- bution	Item	Percent of elderly residents	Functional status	Percent of elderly residents receiving assistance
Total [2]	**1,465**	**100.0**	Type of aids used:		ADLs: [9]	
			Wheelchair	62.3	Bathing, showering	96.2
Male	372	25.4	Walker	25.2	Dressing	87.2
Female	1,093	74.6			Eating	45.0
					Transferring in or	
65 to 74 years	198	13.5	Vision impaired	27.1	out of beds or chair	25.4
75 to 84 years	528	36.1	Hearing impaired	23.7	Using toilet room	56.2
85 years and over	738	50.4				
			Type of nursing care:		IADLs: [10]	
White	1,295	88.4	Skilled care [3]	47.8	Care of personal	
Black	137	9.4	Intermediate care [4]	47.8	possessions	77.1
			Residential care [5]	3.6	Managing money	72.2
Hispanic	32	2.2			Securing personal	
Non-Hispanic	1,340	91.5	Primary source		items	76.2
			of payment: [6]		Using telephone	62.2
Living quarters:			Private sources [7]	28.2		
Private residence	472	32.2	Medicare	29.7		
Retirement home	34	2.3	Medicaid	38.2		
Board and care and/or			Other [8]	3.8		
residential facility	67	4.6				
Nursing home	179	12.2				
Hospital	651	44.5				
Mental health facility	19	1.3				

[1] At time of admission. [2] Includes other and/or unknown, not shown separately. [3] Skilled care indicates the greatest degree of medical care. Every patient is under the supervision of a physician and the facility has a transfer agreement with a nearby hospital. Twenty-four hour nursing care is provided with a physician on call to furnish medical care in case of emergency. [4] Intermediate care is provided to individuals who do not require the degree of care or treatment normally given by a hospital or skilled nursing facility, but who do require health-related institutionalized care above the level of room and board. [5] Residential care usually means providing residents with room, board, laundry services, some forms of personal care, and recreational activities and social services. [6] In month before interview. [7] Includes private insurance, own income, family support, social security benefits, and retirement funds. [8] Includes supplemental security income, welfare, religious organizations, foundations, agencies, Veterans Administration contract, pensions, or other compensation, payment source not yet determined, and other and unknown sources. [9] Activities of daily living. [10] Instrumental activities of daily living.

Source: U.S. National Center for Health Statistics, *Advance Data*, No. 312, April 25, 2000.

No. 177. Mental Health Facilities—Summary by Type of Facility: 1998

[Beds: 261.9 represents 261,900. Facilities, beds and inpatients as of year-end; Excludes private psychiatric office practice and psychiatric service modes of all types in hospitals or outpatient clinics of federal agencies other than U.S. Dept. of Veterans Affairs. Excludes data from Puerto Rico, Virgin Islands, Guam, and other territories]

Type of facility	Number of facilities	Inpatient beds		Inpatients		Inpatient care episodes [2]
		Total (1,000)	Rate [1]	Total (1,000)	Rate [1]	
Total	**3,729**	**261.9**	**97.3**	**215.9**	**80.3**	**2,099**
Mental hospitals:						
State and county	229	63.5	23.6	57.0	21.2	186
Private [3]	809	67.1	24.9	51.9	19.3	527
General hospitals [4]	1,593	54.3	20.2	37.0	13.8	1,137
Veterans Administration [5]	123	13.3	4.9	10.9	4.0	128
Other [6]	975	63.7	23.7	59.1	22.0	121

[1] Rate per 100,000 population. Based on Census Bureau estimated civilian population as of July 1. [2] "Inpatient care episodes" is defined as the number of residents in inpatient facilities at the beginning of the year plus the total additions to inpatient facilities during the year. [3] Includes residential treatment centers for emotionally disturbed children. [4] Nonfederal hospitals with separate psychiatric services. [5] Includes U.S. Department of Veterans Affairs (VA) neuropsychiatric hospitals, VA general hospitals with separate psychiatric settings and VA freestanding psychiatric outpatient clinics. [6] Includes free-standing psychiatric outpatient facilities that provide only psychiatric outpatient services and other multiservice mental health facilities with two or more settings, which are not elsewhere classified, as well as freestanding partial care facilities which only provide psychiatric partial care services. Number of facilities data also include freestanding psychiatric partial care facilities.

Source: U.S. Substance Abuse and Mental Health Services Administration, Center for Mental Health Services, unpublished data.

U.S. Census Bureau, Statistical Abstract of the United States: 2001

No. 178. Injury and Poisoning Episodes and Conditions by Age and Sex: 1998

[34,020 represents 34,020,000. Covers all medically attended injuries and poisonings occurring during the 3-month period prior to the survey interview. There may be more than one condition per episode. Based on the redesigned National Health Interview Survey, a sample survey of the civilian noninstitutionalized population; see Appendix III]

External cause and nature of injury	Total	Both sexes Total, age-adjusted [1]	Under 12 years old	12 to 21 years old	22 to 44 years old	45 to 64 years old	65 years old and over	Male, total	Female, total
EPISODES									
Number (1,000)	34,020	(X)	5,335	6,424	12,389	6,205	3,667	19,142	14,878
Annual rate per 1,000 population, total [2]	126.5	126.3	110.8	167.5	132.4	109.5	113.8	145.7	108.1
Fall	39.1	39.3	41.8	38.7	31.4	32.8	68.9	36.3	41.8
Struck by or against a person or an object	18.2	18.0	20.1	41.4	17.0	8.0	8.7	24.3	12.3
Transportation [3]	16.6	16.5	10.8	29.9	18.8	13.9	7.6	18.1	15.1
Overexertion	17.4	17.4	3.5	17.8	23.3	24.6	7.9	21.0	13.9
Cutting, piercing instruments	10.5	10.5	8.0	8.4	14.7	10.2	5.3	16.0	[4]5.3
Poisoning	6.1	6.1	11.0	6.4	4.8	4.6	5.2	6.2	6.1
CONDITIONS [5]									
Annual rate per 1,000 population, total [2]	148.2	148.2	117.9	189.5	156.3	134.2	145.6	166.3	131.0
Sprains/strains	38.3	38.4	10.1	54.6	48.5	44.6	20.3	40.9	35.9
Open wounds	27.1	26.9	41.8	27.3	26.9	19.3	19.6	37.1	17.6
Fractures	22.8	22.9	17.9	32.3	20.5	19.6	31.3	25.2	20.5
Contusions	17.2	17.3	8.8	21.6	15.8	14.9	32.5	15.7	18.5

X Not applicable.   [1] Data were age-adjusted by the direct method to the 2000 projected population.   [2] Includes other items not shown separately.   [3] Includes the categories "Motor vehicle traffic"; "Pedal cycle, other"; "Pedestrian, other", and "Transport, other."   [4] Figure does not meet standard of reliability or precision   [5] Poisoning episodes are assumed to have a single condition resulting from the episode.
Source: U.S. National Center for Health Statistics, unpublished data.

No. 179. Injuries Associated With Consumer Products: 1998

[For products associated with more than 40,000 injuries in 1998. Estimates calculated from a representative sample of hospitals with emergency treatment departments in the United States. Data are estimates of the number of emergency room treated cases nationwide associated with various products. Product involvement does not necessarily mean the product caused the accident. Products were selected from the U.S. Consumer Product Safety Commission's National Electronic Injury Surveillance System]

Product	Number	Product	Number
Home workshop equipment:		Other doors (excl. garage)	342,302
Saws (hand or power)	98,707	Ceilings and walls	251,722
Hammers	42,426	Household cabinets, racks, and shelves	242,078
		Nails, screws, tacks, or bolts	183,068
Household packaging and containers:		Windows	143,138
Household containers and packaging	202,252	Porches, balconies, open-side floors	138,123
Bottles and jars	87,201	Fences or fence posts	124,202
		Glass doors	40,721
Housewares:			
Knives	454,246	Personal use items:	
Tableware and flatware	122,306	Footwear	99,436
		Jewelry	61,977
Home furnishing: [1]			
Beds	437,980	Yard and garden equipment:	
Tables	316,733	Lawn mowers	76,337
Chairs	286,020		
Bathtubs and showers	181,837	Sports and recreation equipment:	
Ladders	157,219	Bicycles	577,621
Sofas, couches, davenports, etc.	124,258	Trampolines	95,239
Carpets, rugs	117,588	Swings or swing sets	81,984
Toilets	48,964	Playground climbing equipment	78,219
		Swimming pools	81,079
Home structures, construction: [2]		All-terrain vehicles	73,900
Stairs or steps	989,977	Skateboards	54,532
Floors or flooring materials	986,093	Slides or sliding boards	49,540

[1] Includes accessories.   [2] Includes materials.

No. 180. Costs of Unintentional Injuries: 1999

[469.0 represents $469,000,000,000. Covers costs of deaths or disabling injuries together with vehicle accidents and fires]

Cost	Amount (bil. dol.) Total [1]	Motor vehicle	Work	Home	Other	Percent distribution Total [1]	Motor vehicle	Work	Home	Other
Total	469.0	181.5	122.6	101.7	78.4	100.0	100.0	100.0	100.0	100.0
Wage and productivity losses [2]	245.6	66.1	63.9	66.7	52.5	52.4	36.4	52.1	65.6	67.0
Medical expense	77.4	20.1	19.9	21.8	16.7	16.5	11.1	16.2	21.4	21.3
Administrative expenses [3]	77.6	53.3	23.5	4.6	4.3	16.5	29.4	19.2	4.5	5.5
Motor vehicle damage	40.2	40.2	2.0	(NA)	(NA)	8.6	22.1	1.6	(NA)	(NA)
Employer cost [4]	20.0	1.8	11.0	4.2	3.4	4.3	1.0	9.0	4.1	4.3
Fire loss	8.2	(NA)	2.3	4.4	1.5	1.7	(NA)	1.9	4.3	1.9

NA Not available.   [1] Excludes duplication between work and motor vehicle ($15.2 billion in 1999).   [2] Actual loss of wages and household production, and the present value of future earnings lost.   [3] Home and other costs may include costs of administering medical treatment claims for some motor-vehicle injuries filed through health insurance plans.   [4] Estimate of the uninsured costs incurred by employers, representing the money value of time lost by noninjured workers.
Source of Tables 179 and 180: National Safety Council, Itasca, IL, Injury Facts, 2000 Edition (copyright).

118   Health and Nutrition

No. 181. Specified Reportable Diseases—Cases Reported: 1980 to 1999

[190.9 represents 190,900. Figures should be interpreted with caution. Although reporting of some of these diseases is incomplete, the figures are of value in indicating trends of disease incidence. Includes cases imported from outside the United States]

Disease	1980	1985	1990	1994	1995	1996	1997	1998	1999
AIDS [1]	(²)	8,249	41,595	78,279	71,547	66,885	58,492	46,521	45,104
Botulism [3]	89	122	92	1^3	97	119	132	87	114
Brucellosis (undulant fever)	183	153	85	119	98	112	98	79	82
Chickenpox [4] (1,000)	190.9	178.2	173.1	151.2	120.6	83.5	93.6	82.5	46.0
Cholera	9	4	6	39	23	4	6	17	6
Cryptosporidiosis	(²)	(²)	(²)	(²)	(²)	(²)	2,566	3,793	2,361
Diphtheria	3	3	4	2	-	2	4	1	1
Escherichia coli 0157:H7	(²)	(²)	(²)	1,420	2,139	2,741	2,555	3,161	4,513
Haemophilus influenza	(²)	(²)	(²)	1,174	1,180	1,170	1,162	1,194	1,309
Hansen disease (Leprosy)	223	361	198	136	144	112	122	108	108
Hepatitis: B (serum) (1,000)	19.0	26.6	21.1	12.5	10.8	10.6	10.4	10.3	7.7
A (infectious) (1,000)	29.1	23.2	31.4	29.8	31.6	31.0	30.0	23.2	17.0
C/Non-A, non-B (1,000) [5]	(²)	4.2	2.6	4.4	4.6	3.7	3.8	3.5	3.1
Legionellosis	(²)	830	1,370	1,615	1,241	1,198	1,163	1,355	1,108
Lyme disease	(²)	(²)	(²)	13,043	11,700	16,455	12,801	16,801	16,273
Malaria	2,062	1,049	1,292	1,229	1,419	1,800	2,001	1,611	1,666
Measles (1,000)	13.5	2.8	27.8	1.0	0.3	0.5	0.1	0.1	0.1
Meningococcal infections	2,840	2,479	2,451	2,886	3,243	3,437	3,308	2,725	2,501
Mumps (1,000)	8.6	3.0	5.3	1.5	0.9	0.8	0.7	0.7	0.4
Pertussis [6] (1,000)	1.7	3.6	4.6	4.6	5.1	7.8	6.6	7.4	7.3
Plague	18	17	2	17	9	5	4	9	9
Poliomyelitis, acute [7]	9	7	6	8	6	5	3	1	-
Psittacosis	124	119	113	38	64	42	33	47	16
Rabies, animal	6,421	5,565	4,826	8,147	7,811	6,982	8,105	7,259	6,730
Rabies, human	-	1	1	6	5	3	2	1	-
Rubella [8]	3,904	630	1,125	227	128	238	181	364	276
Salmonellosis [9] (1,000)	33.7	65.3	48.6	43.3	46.0	45.5	41.9	43.7	40.6
Shigellosis [10] (1,000)	19.0	17.1	27.1	29.8	32.1	26.0	23.1	23.6	17.5
Tetanus	95	83	64	51	41	36	50	41	40
Toxic-shock syndrome	(²)	384	322	192	191	145	157	138	113
Trichinosis	131	61	129	32	29	11	13	19	12
Tuberculosis [11] (1,000)	27.7	22.2	25.7	24.4	22.9	21.3	19.9	18.4	17.5
Typhoid fever	510	402	552	441	369	396	365	375	346
Typhus fever:									
Tick-borne (Rocky Mt. spotted fever)	1,163	714	651	465	590	831	409	365	579
Sexually transmitted diseases:									
Gonorrhea (1,000)	1,004	911	690	418	393	326	325	356	360
Syphilis (1,000)	69	68	134	82	69	53	47	38	36
Chlamydia (1,000)	(²)	(²)	(²)	(²)	478	499	527	604	657
Chancroid (1,000)	0.8	2.1	4.2	0.8	0.6	0.4	0.2	0.2	0.1

- Represents zero. [1] Acquired immunodeficiency syndrome was not a notifiable disease until 1984. Figures are shown for years in which cases were reported to the CDC. Beginning 1994, based on revised classification system and expanded surveillance case definition. [2] Disease was not notifiable. [3] Includes foodborne, infant, wound, and unspecified cases. [4] Chickenpox was taken off the nationally notifiable list in 1991 but many states continue to report. [5] Includes some persons positive for antibody to hepatitis C virus who do not have hepatitis. [6] Whooping cough. [7] Revised. Data subject to annual revisions. [8] German measles. [9] Excludes typhoid fever. [10] Bacillary dysentery. [11] Newly reported active cases.

Source: U.S. Centers for Disease Control and Prevention, Atlanta, GA, *Summary of Notifiable Diseases, United States, 1999, Morbidity and Mortality Weekly Report*, Vol. 48, No. 53, April 6, 2001.

No. 182. Children Immunized Against Specified Diseases: 1995 to 1999

[In percent. Covers civilian noninstitutionalized population ages 19 months to 35 months. Based on estimates from the National Immunization Survey. The health care providers of the children are contacted to verify and/or complete vaccination information. Results are based on race/ethnic status of the child]

Vaccination	1995, total	1998, total	1999					
			Total	White non-Hispanic	Hispanic	Black non-Hispanic	American Indian/ Alaskan Native [1]	Asian/ Pacific Islander [1]
Diphtheria-tetanus-pertussis (DTP)/ diphtheria-tetanus:								
3+ doses	95	96	96	97	95	94	95	97
4+ doses	79	84	83	86	80	79	80	87
Polio: 3+ doses	88	91	90	90	89	87	88	90
Hib [2]: 3+ doses	92	93	94	95	92	92	91	90
Measles, mumps, rubella vaccine	88	92	92	92	90	90	92	93
Hepatitis B: 3+ doses	68	87	88	89	87	87	(NA)	88
Varicella [3]	(NA)	43	58	56	61	58	(NA)	64
4+ DTP/3+ polio/1+ MCV [4]	76	81	80	82	77	75	78	82
4+ DTP/3+ polio/1+ MCV/3+ hiB [4]	74	79	78	81	75	74	75	77

NA Not available. [1] Non-Hispanic. [2] Haemophilus B. [3] Data collection for varicella (chicken pox) began in July 1996. [4] MCV=Measles containing vaccine.

Source: U.S. Centers for Disease Control and Prevention, Atlanta, GA, *Morbidity and Mortality Weekly Report*, Vol. 49, No. 26, July 7, 2000; and "Immunization Coverage in the U.S."; <http://www.cdc.gov/nip/coverage/default.htm>.

U.S. Census Bureau, Statistical Abstract of the United States: 2001

No. 183. AIDS Cases Reported by Patient Characteristic: 1981 to 2000

[Provisional. For cases reported in the year shown. Includes Puerto Rico, Virgin Islands, Guam, and U.S. Pacific Islands. Acquired immunodeficiency syndrome (AIDS) is a specific group of diseases or conditions which are indicative of severe immunosuppression related to infection with the human immunodeficiency virus (HIV). For data on AIDS deaths, see Table 110. Data are subject to retrospective changes and may differ from those data in Table 181]

Characteristic	1981-2000, total	2000	Characteristic	1981-2000, total	2000
Total [1]	774,467	42,156	Transmission category:		
			Males, 13 years and over	635,451	31,501
Age:			Men who have sex with men.	355,409	13,562
Under 5 years old	6,872	(NA)	Injecting drug use	140,536	5,922
5 to 12 years old.	2,036	(NA)	Men who have sex with men and		
13 to 19 years old	4,061	(NA)	injecting drug use	48,989	1,548
20 to 29 years old	128,726	(NA)	Hemophilia/coagulation disorder	4,907	93
30 to 39 years old	345,822	(NA)	Heterosexual contact [2].	20,235	2,030
40 to 49 years old	202,901	(NA)	Heterosexual contact with injecting		
50 to 59 years old	61,310	(NA)	drug user.	9,225	519
60 years old and over	22,734	(NA)	Transfusion [3]	4,971	144.
Sex:			Undetermined [4]	51,179	7,683
Male	640,022	31,588	Females, 13 years and over	130,104	10,459
Female	134,441	10,568	Injecting drug use	52,991	2,609
Race/ethnic group:			Hemophilia/coagulation disorder	283	3
Non-Hispanic White	331,160	13,392	Heterosexual contact [2].	31,910	3,004
Non-Hispanic Black	292,522	19,890	Heterosexual contact with injecting		
Hispanic	141,694	8,173	drug user.	20,610	977
Asian/Pacific Islander	5,728	380	Transfusion [3]	3,806	138
American Indian/Alaska Native. . . .	2,337	204	Undetermined [4]	20,504	3,728

NA Not available. [1] Includes persons with characteristics unknown. [2] Includes persons who have had heterosexual contact with a person with human immunodeficiency virus (HIV) infection or at risk of HIV infection. [3] Receipt of blood transfusion, blood components, or tissue. [4] Includes persons for whom risk information is incomplete (because of death, refusal to be interviewed, or loss to followup), persons still under investigation, men reported only to have had heterosexual contact with prostitutes, and interviewed persons for whom no specific risk is identified.

Source: U.S. Centers for Disease Control and Prevention, Atlanta, GA, *HIV/AIDS Surveillance Report*, Volume 12, No. 2.

No. 184. AIDS, Syphilis, Tuberculosis, and Measles Cases Reported by State: 1999

[Diseases selected are those included in the Healthy People 2000 Indicators series]

State	AIDS	Syphilis	Tuber-culosis	Measles	State	AIDS	Syphilis	Tuber-culosis	Measles
U.S. . . .	[1]45,104	35,628	17,531	100	MO	531	395	208	-
AL	476	1,018	314	-	MT.	13	3	14	.r
AK	15	13	61	-	NE.	67	24	18	-
AZ	880	833	262	1	NV.	242	92	93	1
AR	194	364	181	5	NH.	46	17	19	1
CA	5,445	2,859	3,606	17	NJ	2,043	800	571	-
CO	319	91	88	-	NM.	93	80	64	-
CT	586	126	121	2	NY.	7,703	4,094	1,837	5
DE	186	72	34	-	NC.	794	1,713	488	-
DC	838	458	70	-	ND.	7	-	7	-
FL	5,468	2,957	1,277	2	OH.	547	364	317	-
GA	1,678	1,973	665	-	OK.	148	538	208	-
HI	100	11	184	3	OR.	225	37	123	12
ID	25	13	16	-	PA	1,967	932	454	-
IL.	1,557	1,967	825	2	RI	107	55	53	-
IN	363	802	150	2	SC	959	925	315	-
IA	87	37	58	-	SD	16	3	21	-
KS	171	95	69	-	TN	759	1,734	382	-
KY	277	302	209	2	TX	3,181	3,699	1,649	7
LA	854	1,423	357	-	UT	155	49	40	-
ME.	80	1	23	-	VT	20	3	3	-
MD.	1,525	1,385	294	-	VA	943	722	334	18
MA.	1,454	385	270	8	WA	360	204	258	5
MI	649	778	351	6	WV	69	15	41	-
MN.	190	71	201	1	WI	152	190	110	-
MS.	421	906	215	-	WY	15	-	3	-

- Represents zero. [1] Includes 104 cases among persons with unknown state of residence.

Source: U.S. Centers for Disease Control and Prevention, Atlanta, GA, *Summary of Notifiable Diseases, United States, 1999, Morbidity and Mortality Weekly Report*, Vol. 48, No. 53, April 6, 2001.

120   Health and Nutrition

No. 185. Disability Status of Children Under 15 Years Old: 1997

[For period August through November 1997 (11,656 represents 11,656,000). Covers civilian noninstitutional population and members of the Armed Forces living off post or with their families on post. The criteria for presence of disability varied by age. In general, a disability is considered a reduced ability to perform tasks one would normally do at a given stage in life. Based on the Survey of Income and Program Participation; for details, see source]

Age and disability status	Number (1,000)	Percent distribution	Age and disability status	Number (1,000)	Percent distribution
Children under 3 years old	11,656	100.0	Children 6 to 14 years old	36,605	100.0
With a disability	196	1.7	With a disability	3,944	10.8
With a developmental delay	191	1.6	With a severe disability [1]	1,619	4.4
Difficulty moving arms or legs	35	0.3	Difficulty doing regular schoolwork. . .	2,313	6.3
Children 3 to 5 years old.	11,935	100.0	With a learning disability	1,805	4.9
With a disability	454	3.8	With a developmental disability [2] . . .	320	0.9
With a developmental delay	355	3.0	Difficulty with one or more ADLs [3] . . .	223	0.6
Difficulty running or playing	207	1.7	Needs personal assistance	208	0.6

[1] Children who (1) used an ambulatory aid; (2) had serious difficulty seeing, hearing, or speaking; (3) needed help with one or more ADLs (see Table 187); or had a developmental disability or a developmental condition. [2] A child was considered to have a developmental disability if a "yes" response was received to a question about the presence of mental retardation or to a question about the presence of some other developmental disability such as autism or cerebral palsy. [3] See headnote, Table 187.

No. 186. Disability Status of Persons 15 Years Old and Over: 1997

[In thousands, except as noted (212,642 represents 212,642,000). See headnote, Table 185]

Disability status	Total	15 to 21 years	22 to 44 years	45 to 54 years	55 to 64 years	65 to 79 years	80 years and over
Total	212,642	27,128	93,905	35,891	23,155	24,911	7,652
Persons with any disability	46,534	2,821	11,234	7,624	7,874	11,416	5,564
Percent of total	21.9	10.4	12.0	21.2	34.0	45.8	72.7
With a severe disability . . . . [1]	30,855	1,379	7,101	4,886	5,701	7,504	4,284
Difficulty with one or more ADLs [1] . . .	7,750	111	1,121	1,053	1,289	2,363	1,813
Needs personal assistance	3,869	100	592	444	557	1,054	1,123
Difficulty with one or more IADLs [1]	12,185	341	2,117	1,493	1,720	3,580	2,934
Needs personal assistance with one or more ADLs or IADLs [1]	9,353	324	1,629	1,056	1,174	2,620	2,551

[1] See headnote, Table 187.

No. 187. Receipt of Personal Assistance by Persons With Disabilities: 1997

[9,291 represents 9,291,000. See headnote, Table 185. ADLs are activities of daily living and include getting around inside the home, getting in or out of a bed or chair, taking a bath or shower, dressing, eating, and using the toilet. IADLs are instrumental activities of daily living and include going outside the home, keeping track of money and bills, preparing meals, doing light housework, and using the telephone]

Relationship of first helper to person receiving assistance	Persons 15 years old and over				Persons 65 years old and over			
	Receiving assistance with an ADL or an IADL		Receiving assistance with an ADL		Receiving assistance with an ADL or an IADL		Receiving assistance with an ADL	
	Number (1,000)	Percent distribution	Number (1,000)	Percent distribution	Number (1,000)	Percent distribution	Number (1,000)	Percent distribution
Persons receiving assistance	9,291	100.0	3,774	100.0	5,048	100.0	2,145	100.0
Household member	4,895	52.7	2,299	60.9	2,242	44.4	1,198	55.9
Not a household member	4,395	47.3	1,475	39.1	2,806	55.6	947	44.1
Spouse	2,851	30.7	1,453	38.5	1,436	28.5	800	37.3
Daughter	1,703	18.3	664	17.6	1,298	25.7	497	23.2
Son	784	8.4	279	7.4	581	11.5	181	8.4
Parent.	1,087	11.7	336	8.9	2	(Z)	2	0.1
Other relative	1,049	11.3	301	8.0	637	12.6	206	9.6
Nonrelative.	1,014	10.9	346	9.2	510	10.1	163	7.6
Paid help	803	8.6	395	10.5	583	11.6	295	13.8

Z Less than 0.05 percent.

Source of Tables 185-187: U.S. Census Bureau, unpublished data.

U.S. Census Bureau, Statistical Abstract of the United States: 2001

No. 188. Substance Abuse Treatment Facilities and Clients: 1995 to 1999

[As of October 1. Based on the Uniform Facility Data Set (UFDS) survey, a census of all known facilities that provide substance abuse treatment in the United States and associated jurisdictions. Selected missing data for responding facilities were imputed]

Item	Number	Type of care and type of problem	Number of clients, 1998	Client characteristic	Number of clients, 1998
FACILITIES		Total	1,038,378	Total	1,038,378
1995	10,746	Outpatient rehab	915,798	Under 18 yrs	100,322
1996	10,641	24-hour rehab	108,627	18 to 24 yrs	182,986
1997	10,860	24-hour detoxification . . .	13,953	25 to 34 yrs	282,467
1998	13,455			35 to 44 yrs	293,561
1999	15,239			45 to 64 yrs	162,795
				65 yrs and over	16,247
CLIENTS					
1995	1,009,127	Drug only	279,224	Male	715,479
1996	940,141	Alcohol only	245,589	Female	322,899
1997	929,086	Both alcohol & drug	513,565		
1998	1,038,378			White, non-Hispanic	605,793
		Total with a drug problem [1]	792,789	Black, non-Hispanic	247,840
				Hispanic	140,499
		Total with an alcohol problem [2]	759,154	Asian, Pacific Islander . .	9,300
				American Indian [3]	26,724
				Other	8,222

[1] The sum of clients with a drug problem and clients with both diagnoses. [2] The sum of clients with an alcohol problem and clients with both diagnoses. [3] Includes Alaskan Native.

Source: U.S. Substance Abuse and Mental Health Services Administration, *Uniform Facility Data Set (UFDS): Annual surveys for 1995, 1996, 1997, 1998 and 1999.*

No. 189. Drug Use by Type of Drug and Age Group: 1985 to 1999

[In percent. Current users are those who used drugs at least once within month prior to this study. Based on a representative sample of the U.S. population age 12 and older, including persons living in households and in some group quarters such as dormitories and homeless shelters. The national trends in substance use presented in the 1999 report (and below) are based on data from a sample of 13,000 respondents using paper questionnaires similar to those used in prior years. Due to changes in the 1999 survey results shown in Table 190 are not comparable to data shown here. For further details, see source. Subject to sampling variability; see source]

Age and type of drug	Ever used [1]				Current user					
	1985	1990	1995	1998	1985	1990	1995	1997	1998	1999
12 YEARS OLD AND OVER										
Any illicit drug	34.4	34.2	34.2	35.8	12.1	6.7	6.1	6.4	6.2	7.0
Marijuana and hashish	29.4	30.5	31.0	33.0	9.7	5.4	4.7	5.1	5.0	5.4
Cocaine	11.2	11.2	10.3	10.6	3.0	0.9	0.7	0.7	0.8	0.8
Crack	(NA)	1.5	1.8	2.0	(NA)	0.3	0.2	0.3	0.2	0.2
Inhalants	7.9	5.7	5.7	5.8	0.6	0.4	0.4	0.4	0.3	0.3
Hallucinogens	6.9	7.9	9.5	9.9	1.2	0.4	0.7	0.8	0.7	0.7
PCP	2.0	2.0	3.2	3.5	(NA)	(NA)	-	0.1	-	-
LSD	4.6	5.8	7.5	7.9	(NA)	(NA)	0.3	0.2	0.3	0.2
Heroin	0.9	0.8	1.2	1.1	0.1	-	0.1	0.2	0.1	0.1
Stimulants [2]	7.3	5.5	4.9	4.4	1.8	0.6	0.4	0.3	0.3	0.3
Sedatives [2]	4.8	2.8	2.7	2.1	0.5	0.2	0.2	0.1	0.1	0.1
Tranquilizers [2]	7.6	4.0	3.9	3.5	2.2	0.6	0.4	0.4	0.3	0.4
Analgesics [2]	7.6	6.3	6.1	5.3	1.4	0.9	0.6	0.7	0.8	1.0
Alcohol	84.9	82.2	82.3	81.3	60.2	52.6	52.2	51.4	51.7	52.0
"Binge" alcohol use [3]	(NA)	(NA)	(NA)	(NA)	20.2	14.4	15.8	15.3	15.6	15.1
Cigarettes	78.0	75.4	71.8	69.7	38.7	32.6	28.8	29.6	27.7	29.7
Smokeless tobacco	(NA)	17.5	17.0	17.2	(NA)	3.9	3.3	3.2	2.0	2.2
12 to 17 YEARS OLD										
Marijuana and hashish	20.1	12.7	16.2	17.0	10.2	4.4	8.2	9.4	8.3	7.0
Cocaine	4.7	2.6	2.0	2.2	1.5	0.6	0.8	1.0	0.8	0.7
Alcohol	56.1	48.8	40.6	37.3	41.2	32.5	21.1	20.5	19.1	19.0
"Binge" alcohol use [3]	(NA)	(NA)	(NA)	(NA)	21.9	(NA)	7.9	8.3	7.7	7.8
Cigarettes	50.7	45.1	38.1	35.8	29.4	22.4	20.2	19.9	18.2	15.9
18 TO 25 YEARS OLD										
Marijuana and hashish	57.6	50.4	41.4	44.6	21.7	12.7	12.0	12.8	13.8	16.4
Cocaine	24.3	19.3	9.8	10.0	8.1	2.3	1.3	1.2	2.0	1.9
Alcohol	(NA)	87.6	84.4	83.2	70.1	62.8	61.3	58.4	60.0	60.2
"Binge" alcohol use [3]	(NA)	(NA)	(NA)	(NA)	34.4	(NA)	29.9	28.0	31.7	31.1
Cigarettes	75.3	70.7	67.7	68.8	47.4	40.9	35.3	40.6	41.6	41.0
26 TO 34 YEARS OLD										
Marijuana and hashish	54.1	56.5	51.8	47.9	19.0	9.5	6.7	6.0	5.5	6.4
Cocaine	23.6	25.4	21.6	17.1	6.3	1.9	1.2	0.9	1.2	1.0
Alcohol	(NA)	(NA)	90.1	88.2	70.6	64.4	63.0	60.2	60.9	61.9
Cigarettes	84.7	84.1	75.8	71.8	45.7	42.4	34.7	33.7	32.5	34.4
35 YEARS OLD AND OVER										
Marijuana and hashish	13.9	19.6	25.3	29.4	2.6	2.4	1.8	2.6	2.5	2.5
Cocaine	4.1	5.9	8.6	10.4	0.5	0.2	0.4	0.5	0.5	0.6
Alcohol	(NA)	83.5	87.1	86.6	57.5	49.5	52.6	52.8	51.7	53.4
Cigarettes	82.2	79.0	77.5	75.2	35.5	28.9	27.2	27.9	25.1	28.5

- Represents or rounds to zero. NA Not available. [1] Comparable data for 1999 are not available. [2] Nonmedical use; does not include over-the-counter drugs. [3] Binge use is defined as drinking five or more drinks on the same occasion on at least one day in the past 30 days.

Source: U.S. Substance Abuse and Mental Health Services Administration, *National Household Survey on Drug Abuse,* annual.

122   Health and Nutrition

No. 190. Estimated Use of Selected Drugs by State: 1999

[15,193 represents 15,193,000. Current users are those persons 12 years old and over who used drugs at least once within month prior to this study. Based on national sample of respondents (see also headnote, Table 189). The state estimates were produced by combining the prevalence rate based on the state sample data and the prevalence rate based on a national regression model applied to local-area county and census block group/tract-level estimates from the state. The parameters of the regression model are estimated from the entire national sample. For comparison purposes, the data shown here display estimates for all 50 states and the District of Columbia utilizing the modeled estimates for all 51 areas]

State	Estimated current users (1,000)					Current users as percent of population				
	Any illicit drug [1]	Mari- juana	Any illicit drug other than majijuana [1]	Ciga- rettes	Binge alcohol [2]	Any illicit drug [1]	Mari- juana	Any illicit drug other than majijuana [1]	Ciga- rettes	Binge alcohol [2]
U.S.	15,193	11,476	6,645	57,296	44,486	6.9	5.2	3.0	25.9	20.1
AL.	184	129	95	1,013	621	5.1	3.6	2.6	28.0	17.2
AK.	52	35	18	127	105	10.7	7.2	3.7	26.4	21.8
AZ.	267	203	130	919	725	7.1	5.4	3.4	24.4	19.2
AR.	106	80	55	614	399	5.0	3.7	2.6	28.8	18.7
CA.	2,110	1,598	887	5,247	4,692	8.3	6.3	3.5	20.6	18.4
CO.	310	273	113	821	738	9.3	8.1	3.4	24.6	22.1
CT.	208	139	96	625	558	7.7	5.2	3.6	23.2	20.7
DE.	53	43	21	180	142	8.5	6.9	3.4	28.9	22.8
DC.	32	31	14	106	74	7.6	7.4	3.4	24.9	17.5
FL.	843	696	360	3,146	2,181	6.8	5.6	2.9	25.2	17.5
GA.	363	267	172	1,649	1,132	5.8	4.3	2.7	26.4	18.1
HI.	69	59	22	217	201	7.1	6.0	2.2	22.4	20.8
ID.	68	48	29	259	197	6.4	4.5	2.8	24.5	18.7
IL.	670	514	283	2,647	2,122	6.9	5.3	2.9	27.2	21.8
IN.	369	259	144	1,425	988	7.5	5.3	2.9	29.0	20.1
IA.	131	83	57	648	582	5.5	3.5	2.4	27.2	24.4
KS.	127	88	59	532	471	5.9	4.1	2.7	24.9	22.1
KY.	198	128	103	1,080	612	6.0	3.9	3.1	33.1	18.7
LA.	202	132	101	976	768	5.7	3.7	2.8	27.5	21.7
ME.	74	65	35	269	209	7.1	6.2	3.4	25.8	20.0
MD.	226	215	103	939	649	5.3	5.1	2.4	22.1	15.3
MA.	514	399	199	1,289	1,244	10.1	7.8	3.9	25.3	24.4
MI.	628	454	260	2,299	1,709	8.0	5.7	3.3	29.1	21.7
MN.	263	233	106	1,137	946	6.7	5.9	2.7	29.0	24.2
MS.	131	85	56	648	413	5.8	3.8	2.5	28.8	18.3
MO.	297	229	117	1,374	1,026	6.6	5.1	2.6	30.6	22.8
MT.	59	48	22	193	170	7.7	6.2	2.9	25.3	22.3
NE.	76	58	36	336	344	5.6	4.2	2.6	24.7	25.3
NV.	143	86	59	430	331	9.6	5.8	4.0	28.9	22.2
NH.	69	62	26	256	208	7.0	6.3	2.6	25.7	20.9
NJ.	511	338	208	1,582	1,328	7.7	5.1	3.1	23.7	19.9
NM.	130	106	57	394	315	8.9	7.2	3.9	27.0	21.6
NY.	1,030	738	463	3,768	3,062	7.0	5.0	3.1	25.5	20.7
NC.	392	315	169	1,876	1,038	6.3	5.0	2.7	30.0	16.6
ND.	29	23	13	151	153	5.4	4.3	2.4	28.3	28.7
OH.	606	436	256	2,832	2,074	6.5	4.7	2.8	30.6	22.4
OK.	140	98	83	821	500	5.1	3.6	3.0	30.2	18.4
OR.	214	187	97	716	525	7.7	6.7	3.5	25.7	18.9
PA.	707	493	299	2,682	2,160	7.0	4.9	3.0	26.6	21.4
RI.	71	63	26	223	175	8.7	7.7	3.1	27.2	21.4
SC.	166	126	78	802	539	5.4	4.1	2.5	25.9	17.4
SD.	37	27	15	153	155	6.0	4.4	2.4	25.0	25.3
TN.	254	186	117	1,319	788	5.5	4.0	2.5	28.7	17.1
TX.	850	594	447	3,868	3,373	5.4	3.8	2.8	24.5	21.3
UT.	104	82	59	322	258	6.2	4.9	3.5	19.2	15.4
VT.	35	29	15	119	107	6.8	5.7	3.0	23.6	21.2
VA.	264	231	131	1,297	1,021	4.7	4.1	2.4	23.2	18.3
WA.	398	328	158	1,202	839	8.4	7.0	3.4	25.5	17.8
WV.	80	60	45	479	271	5.1	3.8	2.9	30.9	17.4
WI.	306	255	119	1,177	1,141	7.0	5.9	2.7	27.1	26.3
WY.	30	24	13	103	101	7.3	5.8	3.2	24.7	24.2

[1] Any illicit drug indicates use at least once of marijuana/hashish, cocaine (including crack), inhalants, hallucinogens (including PCP and LSD), heroin, or any prescription-type psychotherapeutic used nonmedically. Any illicit drug other than marijuana indicates use at least once of any of these listed drugs, regardless of marijuana/hashish use; marijuana/hashish users who also have used any of the other listed drugs are included. [2] Binge use is defined as drinking five or more drinks on the same occasion on at least one day in the past 30 days. By "occasion" is meant at the same time or within a couple hours of each other.

Source: U.S. Substance Abuse and Mental Health Services Administration, National Household Survey on Drug Abuse. 1999.

Health and Nutrition 123

No. 191. Current Cigarette Smoking: 1985 to 1998

[In percent. Prior to 1995, a current smoker is a person who has smoked at least 100 cigarettes and who now smokes. Beginning 1995, definition includes persons who smoke only "some days." Excludes unknown smoking status. Based on the National Health Interview Survey; for details, see Appendix III]

Sex, age, and race	1985	1990	1995	1998	Sex, age, and race	1985	1990	1995	1998
Total smokers, age-adjusted [1]	**29.9**	**25.3**	**24.6**	**24.0**	Black, total	39.9	32.5	28.5	29.0
					18 to 24 years	27.2	21.3	[2]14.6	19.7
Male	32.2	28.0	26.5	25.9	25 to 34 years	45.6	33.8	25.1	25.2
Female	27.9	22.9	22.7	22.1	35 to 44 years	45.0	42.0	36.3	36.2
					45 to 64 years	46.1	36.7	33.9	37.3
White male	31.3	27.6	26.2	26.0	65 years and over	27.7	21.5	28.5	16.3
Black male	40.2	32.8	29.4	29.0	Female, total	27.9	22.8	22.6	21.9
					18 to 24 years	30.4	22.5	21.8	24.5
White female	27.9	23.5	23.4	23.0	25 to 34 years	32.0	28.2	26.4	24.6
Black female	30.9	20.8	23.5	21.1	35 to 44 years	31.5	24.8	27.1	26.4
					45 to 64 years	29.9	24.8	24.0	22.5
Total smokers	**30.1**	**25.5**	**24.7**	**24.1**	65 years and over	13.5	11.5	11.5	11.2
Male, total	32.6	28.4	27.0	26.4	White, total	27.7	23.4	23.1	22.6
18 to 24 years	28.0	26.6	27.8	31.3	18 to 24 years	31.8	25.4	24.9	28.0
25 to 34 years	38.2	31.6	29.5	28.6	25 to 34 years	32.0	28.5	27.3	26.9
35 to 44 years	37.6	34.5	31.5	30.2	35 to 44 years	31.0	25.0	27.0	26.7
45 to 64 years	33.4	29.3	27.1	27.7	45 to 64 years	29.7	25.4	24.3	22.5
65 years and over	19.6	14.6	14.9	10.4	65 years and over	13.3	11.5	11.7	11.2
White, total	31.7	28.0	26.6	26.3	Black, total	31.0	21.2	23.5	21.0
18 to 24 years	28.4	27.4	28.4	34.1	18 to 24 years	23.7	10.0	[2]8.8	8.3
25 to 34 years	37.3	31.6	29.9	29.2	25 to 34 years	36.2	29.1	26.7	21.5
35 to 44 years	36.6	33.5	31.2	29.6	35 to 44 years	40.2	25.5	31.9	30.0
45 to 64 years	32.1	28.7	26.3	27.0	45 to 64 years	33.4	22.6	27.5	25.3
65 years and over	18.9	13.7	14.1	10.0	65 years and over	14.5	11.1	13.3	11.5

[1] Estimates are age adjusted to the year 2000 standard using five age groups: 18-24 years, 25-34 years, 35-44 years, 45-64 years, 65 years and over. [2] Data have a relative standard error of 20-30 percent.

Source: U.S. National Center for Health Statistics, *Health, United States, 2000.*

No. 192. Current Cigarette Smoking by Sex and State: 1999

[In percent. Current cigarette smoking is defined as persons who reported having smoked 100 or more cigarettes during their lifetime and who currently smoke every day or some days. Based on the Behavioral Risk Factor Surveillance System, a telephone survey of health behaviors of the civilian, noninstitutionalized U.S. population, 18 years old and over; for details, see source]

State	Total	Male	Female	State	Total	Male	Female	State	Total	Male	Female
U.S. [1] . .	**22.7**	**24.2**	**20.9**	KS	21.1	24.3	18.1	ND	22.2	23.4	21.0
				KY	29.7	33.9	25.9	OH	27.6	29.3	26.0
AL	23.5	26.1	21.2	LA	23.6	26.9	20.7	OK	25.2	26.7	23.9
AK	27.2	25.3	29.4	ME	23.3	27.7	19.2	OR	21.5	22.9	20.1
AZ	20.0	23.6	16.7	MD	20.3	22.2	18.6	PA	23.2	24.3	22.2
AR	27.2	29.7	25.0	MA	19.4	19.5	19.2	RI	22.4	23.3	21.6
CA	18.7	22.0	15.5	MI	25.1	26.6	23.7	SC	23.6	28.4	19.3
CO	22.5	22.8	22.1	MN	19.5	21.7	17.3	SD	22.5	23.1	21.9
CT	22.8	25.4	20.4	MS	23.0	27.4	19.0	TN	24.9	25.7	24.1
DE	25.4	27.6	23.5	MO	27.1	30.6	23.9	TX	22.4	27.4	17.7
DC	20.6	21.5	19.8	MT	20.2	18.5	21.9	UT	13.9	16.6	11.4
FL	20.7	22.3	19.2	NE	23.3	27.5	19.5	VT	21.8	22.9	20.7
GA	23.7	28.3	19.5	NV	31.5	32.8	30.3	VA	21.2	21.3	21.2
HI	18.6	20.1	17.0	NH	22.4	21.7	23.1	WA	22.4	24.0	20.8
ID	21.5	22.5	20.6	NJ	20.7	22.0	19.4	WV	27.1	30.2	24.4
IL	24.2	26.9	21.8	NM	22.5	24.1	20.9	WI	23.7	23.0	24.3
IN	27.0	31.0	23.3	NY	21.9	22.8	21.1	WY	23.9	25.8	22.0
IA	23.5	26.6	20.7	NC	25.2	27.7	23.0				

[1] Represents median value among the states and DC.

Source: U.S. Centers for Disease Control and Prevention, Atlanta, GA, *Morbidity and Mortality Weekly Report*, Vol. 49, No. 43, November 3, 2000.

No. 193. Use of Mammography for Women 40 Years Old and Over by Patient Characteristics: 1990 to 1998

[Percent of women having a mammogram within the past 2 years. Covers civilian noninstitutional population. Based on National Health Interview Survey; see Appendix III]

Characteristic	1990	1994	1998	Characteristic	1990	1994	1998
Total [1]	**51.4**	**60.9**	**66.9**	Years of school completed:			
40 to 49 years old	55.1	61.3	63.4	Less than 12 years	36.4	48.2	54.5
50 years old and over.	49.7	60.6	68.9	12 years	52.7	61.0	66.7
50 to 64 years old	56.0	66.5	73.7	13 years or more	62.8	69.7	72.8
65 years old and over	43.4	55.0	63.8				
White, non-Hispanic	52.7	61.3	68.0	Poverty status: [3]			
Black, non-Hispanic	46.0	64.4	66.0	Below poverty	23.7	44.4	50.5
Hispanic origin [2]	45.2	51.9	60.2	At or above poverty	54.8	64.8	69.3

[1] Includes all other races not shown separately and unknown education level and poverty status. [2] Persons of Hispanic origin may be of any race. [3] For explanation of poverty level, see text, Section 13, Income, Expenditures, and Wealth.

Source: U.S. National Center for Health Statistics, *Health United States, 2000.*

124   Health and Nutrition

No. 194. Cancer—Estimated New Cases, 2001, and Survival Rates, 1980-82 to 1989-96

[1,268 represents 1,268,000. The 5-year relative survival rate, which is derived by adjusting the observed survival rate for expected mortality, represents the likelihood that a person will not die from causes directly related to their cancer within 5 years. Survival data shown are based on those patients diagnosed while residents of an area listed below during the time periods shown. Data are based on information collected as part of the National Cancer Institute's Surveillance, Epidemiology and End Results (SEER) program, a collection of population-based registries in Connecticut, New Mexico, Utah, Iowa, Hawaii, Atlanta, Detroit, Seattle-Puget Sound, and San Francisco-Oakland]

Site	Estimated new cases,[1] 2001 (1,000)			5-year relative survival rates (percent)							
				White				Black			
	Total	Male	Female	1980-82	1983-85	1986-88	1989-96	1980-82	1983-85	1986-88	1989-96
All sites [2]	1,268	643	625	52.1	53.9	56.7	61.5	39.7	39.8	42 6	48.9
Lung	170	91	79	13.5	13.9	13.5	14.4	12.2	11.4	11.9	11.3
Breast [3]	194	2	192	77.1	79.3	83.9	86.3	65.8	63.5	69.4	71.4
Colon and rectum	135	67	68	54.8	57.6	60.8	62.1	46.4	47.9	52.3	52.2
Colon	98	46	52	55.7	58.4	61.5	62.6	49.1	49.3	52.6	52.2
Rectum	37	21	16	52.9	55.9	59.2	60.7	38.0	43.5	51.1	52.3
Prostate	198	198	(X)	74.5	76.3	82.7	94.1	64.7	63.9	69.3	86.7
Bladder	54	39	15	79.0	78.3	80.6	81.9	58.9	59.3	62.0	63.7
Corpus uteri	38	(X)	38	82.8	84.6	84.4	85.6	54.5	53.9	56.7	56.9
Non-Hodgkin's lymphoma [4]	56	31	25	51.9	54.4	52.9	52.6	50.0	44.9	49.9	41.9
Oral cavity and pharynx	30	20	10	55.5	55.3	55.3	56.2	30.8	35.0	34.8	34.6
Leukemia [4]	32	18	14	39.6	41.7	43.9	45.4	33.2	33.4	37.2	34.0
Melanoma of skin	51	29	22	83.1	84.8	87.8	88.5	60.9	74.4	67.5	70.0
Pancreas	29	14	15	2.8	2.9	3.2	4.2	4.7	5.4	6.0	3.9
Kidney	31	19	12	51.2	55.8	57.5	61.5	56.1	54.6	53.2	58.0
Stomach	22	13	8	16.4	16.2	19.1	19.5	19.4	18.8	19.0	21.6
Ovary	23	(X)	23	38.8	40.2	42.0	50.1	38.3	41.7	38.5	47.5
Cervix uteri [5]	13	(X)	13	68.0	70.3	71.7	71.6	61.2	60.2	55.3	58.6

X Not applicable. [1] Estimates provided by American Cancer Society are based on rates from the National Cancer Institute's SEER program. [2] Includes other sites not shown separately. [3] Survival rates for female only. [4] All types combined. [5] Invasive cancer only.

Source: U.S. National Institutes of Health, National Cancer Institute, *Cancer Statistics Review, 1973-1997.*

No. 195. Cancer—Estimated New Cases and Deaths by State: 2001

[In thousands (1,268.0 represents 1,268,000). Excludes basal and squamous cellskin cancers and in situ carcinomas except urinary bladder]

State	New cases [1]			Deaths			State	New cases [1]			Deaths		
	Total [2]	Lung	Female breast	Total [2]	Lung	Female breast		Total [2]	Lung	Female breast	Total [2]	Lung	Female breast
U.S.	1,268.0	169.5	192.2	553.4	157.4	40.2	MO	28.4	4.3	3.8	12.4	4.0	0.8
							MT	4.3	0.6	0.6	1.9	0.5	0.1
AL	22.6	3.1	2.9	9.9	2.9	0.6	NE	7.5	0.9	1.2	3.3	0.9	0.2
AK	1.6	0.2	0.2	0.7	0.2	0.1	NV	9.2	1.3	1.2	4.0	1.2	0.2
AZ	21.3	2.8	3.2	9.3	2.6	0.7	NH	5.8	0.8	0.8	2.5	0.7	0.2
AR	14.1	2.2	1.9	6.1	2.0	0.4							
CA	117.4	14.2	18.8	51.2	13.2	3.9	NJ	41.2	5.0	6.7	18.0	4.6	1.4
							NM	6.9	0.8	1.1	3.0	0.7	0.2
CO	14.3	1.6	2.1	6.2	1.5	0.4	NY	83.2	10.0	14.2	36.3	9.3	3.0
CT	16.0	2.0	2.5	7.0	1.9	0.5	NC	37.3	5.4	5.5	16.3	5.0	1.1
DE	4.0	0.6	0.6	1.8	0.5	0.1	ND	3.1	0.4	0.5	1.3	0.3	0.1
DC	2.8	0.3	0.6	1.2	0.3	0.1							
FL	91.6	12.9	12.5	40.0	12.0	2.6	OH	58.2	8.1	8.9	25.4	7.5	1.9
							OK	16.6	2.6	2.5	7.3	2.4	0.5
GA	31.1	4.4	5.0	13.6	4.1	1.0	OR	16.7	2.3	2.4	7.3	2.1	0.5
HI	4.7	0.6	0.6	2.0	0.6	0.1	PA	68.4	8.9	10.3	29.8	8.2	2.2
ID	5.0	0.6	0.8	2.2	0.6	0.2	RI	5.6	0.8	0.8	2.4	0.7	0.2
IL	56.8	7.4	9.1	24.8	6.9	1.9							
IN	29.3	4.2	4.4	12.8	3.9	0.9	SC	18.8	2.6	2.8	8.2	2.4	0.6
							SD	3.6	0.4	0.5	1.6	0.4	0.1
IA	14.8	1.9	2.3	6.5	1.8	0.5	TN	28.8	4.3	4.2	12.6	4.0	0.9
KS	12.1	1.6	1.7	5.3	1.5	0.4	TX	78.9	11.0	12.3	34.4	10.2	2.6
KY	21.1	3.4	2.9	9.2	3.2	0.6	UT	5.6	0.4	1.0	2.5	0.4	0.2
LA	21.7	2.9	3.3	9.5	2.7	0.7							
ME	6.9	1.0	1.0	3.0	0.9	0.2	VT	2.9	0.4	0.4	1.2	0.4	0.1
							VA	30.5	4.2	4.6	13.3	3.9	1.0
MD	23.5	3.2	4.0	10.3	3.0	0.8	WA	24.8	3.3	3.6	10.8	3.1	0.8
MA	31.3	4.0	4.6	13.7	3.7	1.0	WV	10.9	1.7	1.5	4.8	1.5	0.3
MI	45.3	6.2	6.8	19.8	5.7	1.4	WI	25.0	3.0	3.6	10.9	2.8	0.7
MN	20.6	2.4	3.2	9.0	2.3	0.7	WY	2.2	0.3	0.3	1.0	0.2	0.1
MS	13.9	2.0	2.0	6.1	1.9	0.4							

[1] Estimates are offered as a rough guide and should be interpreted with caution. They are calculated according to the distribution of estimated 2001 cancer deaths by state. [2] Includes other types of cancer, not shown separately.

Source: American Cancer Society, Inc., Atlanta, Georgia, *Cancer Facts and Figures—2001* (copyright).

No. 196. Cumulative Percent Distribution of Population by Height and Sex: 1988-94

[Height was measured without shoes. Based on sample and subject to sampling variability; see source]

Height	Males						Females					
	20-29 years	30-39 years	40-49 years	50-59 years	60-69 years	70-79 years	20-29 years	30-39 years	40-49 years	50-59 years	60-69 years	70-79 years
Percent under—												
4'8"	-	-	-	-	-	-	0.6	0.1	-	-	0.2	1.7
4'9"	-	-	-	-	-	-	0.7	0.2	0.3	0.1	0.7	3.3
4'10"	-	-	-	-	0.1	-	1.2	0.7	0.7	1.9	1.7	4.9
4'11"	-	-	-	-	0.1	0.1	3.1	2.6	1.7	3.1	4.4	9.8
5'	0.1	-	0.2	-	0.4	0.1	6.0	5.5	5.3	6.6	9.9	15.4
5'1"	0.1	-	0.4	0.1	0.5	0.6	11.5	10.4	9.9	11.9	19.0	28.9
5'2"	0.5	0.8	0.7	0.2	0.7	1.9	21.8	18.5	18.8	24.4	34.3	45.6
5'3"	1.3	1.4	0.9	1.0	2.2	2.7	34.3	30.7	31.9	38.6	48.3	61.2
5'4"	3.4	2.2	1.7	2.5	5.8	7.8	48.9	42.9	49.2	52.6	65.5	74.5
5'5"	6.9	5.1	5.6	6.0	9.4	16.5	62.7	59.1	64.3	69.9	76.5	85.9
5'6"	11.7	10.1	12.1	11.7	15.8	27.3	74.0	71.8	77.0	81.6	87.8	93.9
5'7"	20.8	18.9	19.6	20.5	27.4	39.5	84.7	84.1	87.0	89.3	92.5	97.3
5'8"	32.0	28.3	28.0	32.6	38.6	53.4	92.4	91.6	94.5	95.6	96.7	99.2
5'9"	46.3	44.3	42.1	43.9	55.1	68.7	96.2	95.6	97.3	99.0	99.3	99.9
5'10"	58.7	58.0	58.1	60.6	68.8	79.5	98.6	98.1	98.9	99.6	99.8	100.0
5'11"	70.1	70.4	71.1	75.2	81.4	89.2	99.5	99.5	99.4	100.0	100.0	100.0
6'	81.2	79.7	81.5	85.4	90.0	94.1	100.0	100.0	100.0	100.0	100.0	100.0
6'1"	87.4	86.2	89.0	92.4	95.2	97.2	100.0	100.0	100.0	100.0	100.0	100.0
6'2"	94.7	92.4	94.4	96.4	98.2	99.3	100.0	100.0	100.0	100.0	100.0	100.0
6'3"	97.9	98.1	97.2	98.2	99.5	99.9	100.0	100.0	100.0	100.0	100.0	100.0

- Represents or rounds to zero.

Source: U.S. National Center for Health Statistics, unpublished data.

No. 197. Percent of U.S. Adults Who Were Overweight and Percent Who Were Obese: 1998

[Percent who are overweight includes those who are obese and represent those who have a body mass index (BMI) equal to or above 25. Percent who are obese represent those who have a BMI equal to or above 30. BMI is a measure that adjusts body weight for height. It is calculated as weight in kilograms divided by height in meters squared. These estimates are based on definitions provided in the *Dietary Guidelines for Americans*, published by the U.S. Dept. of Agriculture and the U.S. Dept. of Health and Human Services. Based on the National Health Interview Survey; for details, see Appendix III]

Characteristic	Both sexes		Males		Females	
	Overweight	Obese	Overweight	Obese	Overweight	Obese
All ages (age-adjusted) [1]	55.3	20.0	63.6	20.0	47.2	20.0
All ages (unadjusted) [1]	55.2	20.0	63.6	20.0	47.2	20.0
18-24 years old.	37.5	12.6	43.6	11.5	31.4	13.7
25-44 years old.	54.2	20.0	64.9	20.7	43.6	19.4
45-64 years old.	64.2	24.7	72.3	24.6	56.4	24.8
65 years old and over	55.6	17.3	60.5	16.3	51.8	18.0
Hispanic	62.9	25.1	68.3	24.4	57.1	25.6
White, Non-Hispanic	53.4	18.4	63.3	18.9	43.7	17.9
Black, Non-Hispanic.	67.1	29.6	68.0	25.8	66.1	32.6
Asian/Pacific Islander, non-Hispanic .	32.0	5.8	36.4	7.2	28.0	4.6
Educational attainment:						
Fewer than 9 grades	62.0	24.1	63.3	21.5	60.5	26.7
Grades 9 - 11	61.0	25.1	63.1	22.4	58.9	28.0
General equivalency degree	61.7	27.4	67.5	26.5	54.6	28.8
High school graduate	57.2	21.1	64.9	21.1	50.5	21.0
Some college - no degree	56.0	20.6	66.1	21.8	46.6	19.4
Associate of Arts - Technical	55.9	20.0	65.2	21.4	46.9	19.0
Associate of Arts - Academic	53.1	18.7	65.4	17.0	44.0	20.0
Bachelor of Arts or Science	48.7	14.6	61.2	15.9	35.9	13.2
Graduate degree	43.3	12.5	54.5	13.5	29.8	11.1

[1] Age-specific rates are unadjusted; all other estimates were adjusted to the 2000 projected population.

Source: U.S. National Center for Health Statistics, unpublished data.

No. 198. Percentage of Adults Engaging in Leisure-Time Physical Activity: 1998

[In percent. Covers persons 18 years old and over. Based on responses to questions about physical activity in prior month from the Behavioral Risk Factor Age-adjusted Surveillance System. Estimates are age-adjusted to the year 2000 standard population. Based on a survey sample of approximately 147,000 persons in 50 states and the District of Columbia in 1998]

Characteristic	Persons who meet recommended activity [1]	Persons with insufficient activity [2]	Persons who are physically inactive [3]	Characteristic	Persons who meet recommended activity [1]	Persons with insufficient activity [2]	Persons who are physically inactive [3]
Total...........	25.3	45.8	28.9	30 to 44 years old ...	24.7	47.4	27.9
				45 to 64 years old ...	23.9	44.7	31.4
Male...........	26.4	46.8	26.9	65 to 74 years old ...	23.6	40.5	35.9
Female.........	24.4	44.8	30.8	75 years old and over...........	25.3	26.8	47.9
White, non-Hispanic ...	26.4	47.3	26.3				
Black, non-Hispanic....	20.9	43.9	35.2	School years completed:			
Hispanic	20.8	38.6	40.6	Less than 12 years ...	15.7	34.4	49.9
Other	25.6	44.6	29.8	12 years	21.3	44.5	34.2
				Some college (13-15 years)	26.9	48.1	24.9
Males:				College (16 or more years)	33.5	49.9	16.6
18 to 29 years old ...	27.7	54.2	18.1				
30 to 44 years old ...	22.8	52.7	24.5				
45 to 64 years old ...	25.4	44.1	30.5	Household income:			
65 to 74 years old ...	32.1	36.8	31.1	Less than $10,000...	19.7	36.5	43.8
75 years old and over...........	32.1	26.9	41.0	$10,000 to $19,999 ...	19.3	40.5	40.2
				$20,000 to $34,999 ..	22.8	45.0	32.2
Females:				$35,000 to $49,999 ...	26.9	48.5	24.6
18 to 29 years old ...	24.5	50.0	25.5	$50,000 and over ...;	33.5	49.0	17.6

[1] Recommended activity is physical activity at least five times/week x 30 minutes/time or vigorous physical activity for 20 minutes at a time at least three times/week. [2] Persons whose reported physical activity does not meet recommended level. [3] Persons with no reported physical activity.

Source: U.S. National Center for Chronic Disease Prevention and Health Promotion, unpublished data.

No. 199. Households and Persons Having Problems With Access to Food: 1995 to 1999

[100,445 represents 100,445,000. Food secure means that a household had access at all times to enough food for an active healthy life, with no need for recourse to emergency food sources or other extraordinary coping behaviors to meet their basic food needs. A food insecure household did not have this same access to enough food to fully meet basic needs at all times. Food insecure households with hunger were those with one or more household members who were hungry at least sometime during the period due to inadequate resources for food. The omission of homeless persons may be a cause of underreporting. The federal food security measure was developed through a collaborative process between private nongovernment experts, academic researchers, and a federal interagency working group, with leadership from the U.S. Dept. of Agriculture and the U.S. Dept. of Health and Human Services. The severity of food insecurity and hunger in households is measured through a series of questions about experiences and behaviors known to characterize households that are having difficulty meeting basic food needs. These experiences and behaviors generally occur in an ordered sequence as the severity of food insecurity increases. As resources become more constrained, adults in typical households first worry about having enough food, then they stretch household resources and juggle other necessities, then decrease the quality and variety of household members' diets, then decrease the frequency and quantity of adults' food intake, and finally decrease the frequency and quantity of children's food intake. All questions refer to the previous 12 months and include a qualifying phrase reminding respondents to report only those occurrences that resulted from inadequate financial resources. Restrictions to food intake due to dieting or busy schedules are excluded. Data are from the Food Security Supplement to the Current Population Survey (CPS); for details about the CPS, see text, Section 1, Population, and Appendix III]

Household food security level	Number (1,000)				Percent distribution			
	1995	1998 [1]	1998 [2]	1999	1995	1998 [1]	1998 [2]	1999
Households, total	100,445	103,480	103,309	104,684	100.0	100.0	100.0	100.0
Food secure	90,097	92,972	91,121	94,154	89.7	89.8	88.2	89.9
Food insecure	10,348	10,509	12,188	10,529	10.3	10.2	11.8	10.1
Without hunger...........	6,402	6,820	8,353	7,420	6.4	6.6	8.1	7.1
With hunger.............	3,946	3,689	3,835	3,109	3.9	3.6	3.7	3.0
Adult members...........	191,063	197,423	197,084	198,900	100.0	100.0	100.0	100.0
Food secure	172,862	178,631	174,964	179,960	90.5	90.5	88.8	90.5
Food insecure	18,200	18,792	22,120	18,941	9.5	9.5	11.2	9.5
Without hunger...........	11,611	12,657	15,632	13,869	6.1	6.4	7.9	7.0
With hunger.............	6,589	6,135	6,488	5,072	3.4	3.1	3.3	2.5
Child members...........	70,279	71,463	71,282	71,418	100.0	100.0	100.0	100.0
Food secure	58,048	59,090	57,255	59,344	82.6	82.7	80.3	83.1
Food insecure	12,231	12,373	14,027	12,074	17.4	17.3	19.7	16.9
Without hunger...........	8,131	9,114	10,658	9,368	11.6	12.8	15.0	13.1
With hunger [3]...........	4,100	3,259	3,369	2,707	5.8	4.6	4.7	3.8

[1] Adjusted data. These data are comparable to those of earlier years. [2] Data as collected. These data are comparable to those for 1999. [3] Most of these children did not, themselves, face hunger, but adults or older children in the household did.

Source: U.S. Dept. of Agriculture, Food and Nutrition Service, Household Food Security in the United States, 1999, Food Assistance and Nutrition Research Report #8; fall 2000.

Health and Nutrition 127

No. 200. Healthy Eating Indexes by Selected Food Groups and Dietary Guidelines: 1996

[Healthy Eating Index is comprised of the sum of 10 dietary component indices for a maximum possible score of 100. A score of 80 or above was judged to reflect a "good" diet. Each of the dietary components has a scoring range of zero to 10. Individuals with an intake at the recommended level received a maximum score of 10 points. A score of zero was assigned when no foods in a particular group were eaten. Intermediate scores were calculated proportionately. The indexes for grains, vegetables, fruits, milk, and meat groups measure the degree to which a person's diet conforms to the U.S. Department of Agriculture's (USDA) "Food Guide Pyramid" serving recommendations. The index was applied to USDA one-day food and nutrient intake data from the Continuing Survey of Food Intakes by Individuals. The data are based on a representative sample of individuals two years old and over excluding women who were pregnant or lactating at the time of the survey]

Food group and dietary guideline	Average score on one day	Percent receiving score of 10	Perfect score of 10 [1]	Score of zero
Healthy Eating Index. . . .	63.8	[2]12.2	(X)	(X)
Grains [3]	6.7	22.2	6-11 servings	No servings
Vegetables [4]	6.3	31.8	3-5 servings	No servings
Fruits [4]	3.8	17.1	2-4 servings	No servings
Milk [5]	5.4	25.5	2-3 servings	No servings
Meat [6]	6.4	26.4	2-3 servings	No servings
Total fat [7]	6.9	37.5	30% or less energy from fat	45% or more energy from fat
Saturated fat [7]	6.4	40.1	Less than 10% energy from saturated fat	15% or more energy from saturated fat
Cholesterol	7.9	71.9	300 mg. or less	450 mg. or more
Sodium	6.3	34.7	2,400 mg. or less	4,800 mg or more
Variety [8]	7.6	53.0	8 different food items over 1 day	Fewer than 4 items over 1 day

X Not applicable.   [1] Depends on recommended energy intake. All amounts listed are based on a per day basis.   [2] Percent receiving a score of 80 or higher.   [3] One serving: a slice of bread, one-half cup of cooked pasta, or one-half cup of cooked cereal grains.   [4] One serving: one-half cup of cooked vegetables, 1 cup of raw leafy vegetables, or one-half cup of raw nonleafy chopped vegetables. Fruits are similar.   [5] One serving: one cup of milk or equivalent.   [6] Includes eggs, nuts, and some legumes. One serving: 2.5 ounces of lean meat or equivalent.   [7] Consumption of specified fat as a percentage of total food energy intake.   [8] Amount of variety in a person's diet over a 1-day period.

Source: U.S. Department of Agriculture, Center for Nutrition Policy and Promotion, unpublished data.

No. 201. Nutrition—Nutrients in Foods Available for Civilian Consumption Per Capita Per Day: 1970 to 1999

[Computed by the Center for Nutrition Policy and Promotion (CNPP). Based on Economic Research Service (ERS) estimates of per capita quantities of food available for consumption from "Food Consumption, Prices, and, Expenditures," on imputed consumption data for foods no longer reported by ERS, and on CNPP estimates of quantities of produce from home gardens. Food supply estimates do not reflect loss of food or nutrients from further marketing or home processing. Enrichment and fortification levels of iron, zinc, thiamin, riboflavin, niacin, vitamin A, vitamin B_6, vitamin B_{12}, and ascorbic acid are included]

Nutrient	Unit	1970-79	1980-89	1990-99	1995	1999
Food energy	Calories	3,200	3,400	3,700	3,700	3,800
Carbohydrate	Grams	387	411	478	481	500
Dietary fiber	Grams	19	20	23	23	24
Protein	Grams	95	98	108	108	111
Total fat [1]	Grams	149	156	159	158	164
Saturated	Grams	51	52	51	51	52
Monounsaturated	Grams	60	63	67	67	70
Polyunsaturated	Grams	28	31	33	33	34
Cholesterol	Milligrams	440	420	410	410	430
Vitamin A	Micrograms RE [2]	1,540	1,560	1,710	1,720	1,780
Carotenes	Micrograms RE [2]	550	590	730	730	800
Vitamin E	Milligrams α-TE [3]	13.9	15.5	17.3	17.1	17.8
Vitamin C	Milligrams	110	117	127	127	132
Thiamin.	Milligrams	2.2	2.5	2.9	2.9	3.0
Riboflavin	Milligrams	2.5	2.7	2.9	2.9	2.9
Niacin	Milligrams	24.0	28.0	32.0	32.0	33.0
Vitamin B_6	Milligrams	2.0	2.2	2.4	2.5	2.5
Folate.	Micrograms.	310	343	432	384	641
Vitamin B_{12}	Micrograms.	8.9	8.1	8.0	8.1	8.1
Calcium	Milligrams	910	910	970	970	990
Phosphorus	Milligrams	1,470	1,520	1,660	1,650	1,690
Magnesium	Milligrams	330	340	380	380	390
Iron	Milligrams	16.1	19.4	23.1	23.1	23.6
Zinc	Milligrams	12.9	13.9	15.2	15.3	15.5
Copper	Milligrams	1.6	1.8	1.9	1.9	2.0
Potassium	Milligrams	3,490	3,530	3,790	3,760	3,890
Selenium.	Milligrams	130	139	162	158	178
Sodium [4]	Milligrams	1,360	1,350	1,370	1,370	1,360

[1] Includes other types of fat not shown separately.   [2] Retinol equivalents.   [3] Alpha-Tocopherol equivalents.   [4] Does not include amount from processed foods; underestimates actual availability.

Source: U.S. Dept. of Agriculture, Center for Nutrition Policy and Promotion. Data published by Economic Research Service in Food Consumption, Prices, and Expenditures, annual.

No. 202. Per Capita Consumption of Major Food Commodities: 1980 to 1999

[In pounds, retail weight, except as indicated. Consumption represents the residual after exports, nonfood use and ending stocks are subtracted from the sum of beginning stocks, domestic production, and imports. Based on Census Bureau estimated population]

Commodity	Unit	1980	1985	1990	1995	1997	1998	1999
Red meat, total (boneless, trimmed weight) [1][2]	Pounds	126.4	124.9	112.3	115.1	111.0	115.6	117.7
Beef	Pounds	72.1	74.6	63.9	64.4	63.8	64.9	65.8
Veal	Pounds	1.3	1.5	0.9	0.8	0.9	0.7	0.6
Lamb and mutton	Pounds	1.0	1.1	1.0	0.9	0.8	0.9	0.9
Pork	Pounds	52.1	47.7	46.4	49.0	45.5	49.2	50.5
Poultry (boneless, trimmed weight) [2]	Pounds	40.8	45.5	56.3	62.9	64.2	65.0	68.3
Chicken	Pounds	32.7	36.4	42.4	48.8	50.3	50.8	54.2
Turkey	Pounds	8.1	9.1	13.8	14.1	13.9	14.2	14.1
Fish and shellfish (boneless, trimmed weight)	Pounds	12.4	15.0	15.0	14.9	14.5	14.8	15.2
Eggs	Number	271	255	234	235	239	247	255
Shell	Number	236	217	186	175	173	176	181
Processed	Number	35	39	48	60	66	71	74
Dairy products, total [3]	Pounds	543.2	593.7	568.3	583.8	577.6	581.7	597.9
Fluid milk products [4]	Gallons	27.9	27.1	26.2	24.9	24.6	24.3	24.2
Beverage milks	Gallons	27.6	26.7	25.7	24.3	24.0	23.7	23.6
Plain whole milk	Gallons	16.5	13.9	10.2	8.4	8.2	8.0	8.0
Plain reduced-fat milk (2%)	Gallons	6.3	7.9	9.1	8.2	7.7	7.5	7.5
Plain light and skim milks	Gallons	3.1	3.2	5.0	6.2	6.6	6.6	6.4
Flavored whole milk	Gallons	0.6	0.4	0.3	0.3	0.3	0.3	0.4
Flavored milks other than whole	Gallons	0.6	0.7	0.8	0.8	0.9	1.0	1.0
Buttermilk	Gallons	0.5	0.5	0.4	0.3	0.3	0.3	0.3
Yogurt (excl. frozen)	1/2 pints	4.6	7.3	7.4	9.4	9.5	9.3	9.1
Fluid cream products [5]	1/2 pints	10.5	13.5	14.3	15.8	17.0	17.3	18.3
Cream [6]	1/2 pints	6.3	8.2	8.7	9.5	10.7	10.9	11.7
Sour cream and dips	1/2 pints	3.4	4.3	4.7	5.5	5.6	5.7	5.8
Condensed and evaporated milks	Pounds	7.0	7.5	7.9	6.9	6.6	6.2	6.6
Whole milk	Pounds	3.8	3.6	3.2	2.3	2.6	2.0	2.1
Skim milk	Pounds	3.3	3.8	4.8	4.5	4.0	4.1	4.5
Cheese [7]	Pounds	17.5	22.5	24.6	27.3	28.0	28.3	29.8
American [8]	Pounds	9.6	12.2	11.1	11.8	12.0	12.2	13.0
Cheddar	Pounds	6.9	9.8	9.0	9.1	9.6	9.6	10.1
Italian [8]	Pounds	4.4	6.5	9.0	10.4	11.0	11.3	11.8
Mozzarella	Pounds	3.0	4.6	6.9	8.1	8.4	8.8	9.2
Other [8]	Pounds	3.4	3.9	4.5	5.0	5.0	4.8	5.0
Swiss	Pounds	1.3	1.3	1.4	1.1	1.0	1.1	1.1
Cream and Neufchatel	Pounds	1.0	1.2	1.7	2.1	2.3	2.3	2.4
Cottage cheese, total	Pounds	4.5	4.1	3.4	2.7	2.7	2.7	2.7
Lowfat	Pounds	0.8	1.0	1.2	1.2	1.3	1.3	1.3
Frozen dairy products	Pounds	26.4	27.9	28.4	29.4	28.8	29.6	29.3
Ice cream	Pounds	17.5	18.1	15.8	15.7	16.4	16.6	16.8
Lowfat ice cream	Pounds	7.1	6.9	7.7	7.5	7.9	8.3	7.9
Sherbet	Pounds	1.2	1.3	1.2	1.3	1.3	1.3	1.3
Frozen yogurt	Pounds	(NA)	(NA)	2.8	3.5	2.1	2.2	2.1
Fats and oils:								
Total, fat content only	Pounds	56.9	64.1	63.0	66.3	64.9	65.6	68.5
Butter (product weight)	Pounds	4.5	4.9	4.4	4.5	4.2	4.5	4.8
Margarine (product weight)	Pounds	11.3	10.8	10.9	9.2	8.6	8.3	8.1
Lard (direct use)	Pounds	2.3	1.6	1.6	1.6	1.9	2.0	2.0
Edible beef tallow (direct use)	Pounds	1.1	2.0	0.6	2.7	2.2	3.2	3.7
Shortening	Pounds	18.2	22.9	22.2	22.5	20.9	21.0	21.6
Salad and cooking oils	Pounds	21.2	23.5	25.2	26.8	28.5	27.8	29.4
Other edible fats and oils	Pounds	1.5	1.6	1.2	1.6	1.1	1.3	1.6
Flour and cereal products [9]	Pounds	144.7	156.5	181.0	192.8	200.9	198.4	201.9
Wheat flour	Pounds	116.9	124.6	136.0	141.8	149.5	146.0	148.4
Rice, milled	Pounds	9.4	9.1	15.8	18.9	18.4	18.9	19.4
Corn products	Pounds	12.9	17.2	21.4	25.3	27.0	27.4	28.4
Oat products	Pounds	3.9	4.0	6.5	5.5	4.7	4.5	4.5
Breakfast cereals [10]	Pounds	12.0	12.8	15.4	17.1	16.3	15.6	15.5
Ready-to-eat	Pounds	9.7	10.5	12.6	14.6	13.8	13.3	13.1
Ready-to-cook	Pounds	2.3	2.3	2.9	2.5	2.5	2.3	2.4
Caloric sweeteners, total [11]	Pounds	123.0	128.8	136.9	149.8	154.0	155.1	158.4
Sugar, refined cane and beet	Pounds	83.6	62.7	64.4	65.5	66.5	66.9	67.9
Corn sweeteners [12]	Pounds	38.2	64.8	71.1	83.0	86.1	86.8	89.1
High-fructose corn syrup	Pounds	19.0	45.2	49.6	58.4	62.4	63.8	66.2
Other:								
Cocoa beans	Pounds	3.4	4.6	5.4	4.6	5.1	5.5	5.7
Coffee (green beans)	Pounds	10.3	10.5	10.3	8.0	9.3	9.5	10.0
Peanuts (shelled)	Pounds	4.8	6.3	6.0	5.7	5.9	5.9	6.4
Tree nuts (shelled)	Pounds	1.8	2.5	2.4	1.9	2.1	2.2	2.7

NA Not available. [1] Excludes edible offals. [2] Excludes shipments to Puerto Rico and the other U.S. possessions. [3] Milk-equivalent, milkfat basis. Includes butter. [4] Fluid milk figures are aggregates of commercial sales and milk produced and consumed on farms. [5] Includes eggnog, not shown separately. [6] Heavy cream, light cream, and half and half. [7] Excludes full-skim American, cottage, pot, and baker's cheese. [8] Includes other cheeses not shown separately. [9] Includes rye flour and barley products not shown separately. Excludes quantities used in alcoholic beverages. [10] Partially overlaps flour and cereal products category. [11] Dry weight. Includes edible syrups (maple, molasses, etc.) and honey not shown separately. [12] Includes glucose and dextrose not shown separately.

Source: U.S. Department of Agriculture, Economic Research Service, *Food Consumption, Prices, and Expenditures, 1970-1999*; and *Agricultural Outlook*, monthly.

Health and Nutrition 129

[In pounds, farm weight. Domestic food use of fresh fruits and vegetables reflects the fresh-market share of commodity production plus imports and minus exports]

Commodity	1980	1985	1990	1994	1995	1996	1997	1998	1999
Fruits and vegetables, total [1]	606.7	627.7	656.0	705.6	694.3	710.8	717.9	707.2	719.0
Fruits, total	270.4	270.0	272.6	290.9	284.8	290.2	296.9	284.4	297.9
Fresh fruits	104.7	110.5	116.3	126.3	124.1	128.1	131.9	131.7	132.5
Noncitrus	78.7	89.0	95.0	101.3	100.0	103.2	104.9	104.2	111.8
Apples	19.2	17.3	19.6	19.6	18.9	19.0	18.4	19.4	18.8
Bananas	20.8	23.5	24.4	28.1	27.4	28.0	27.6	28.6	31.4
Cantaloupes	5.8	8.5	9.2	8.5	9.1	10.4	10.7	10.9	11.4
Grapes	3.9	6.8	7.9	7.3	7.5	6.9	8.0	7.3	8.2
Peaches and nectarines	7.1	5.5	5.5	5.5	5.4	4.4	5.6	4.7	5.3
Pears	2.6	2.8	3.2	3.5	3.4	3.1	3.5	3.4	3.4
Pineapples	1.5	1.5	2.0	2.0	1.9	1.9	2.4	2.8	3.1
Plums and prunes	1.5	1.4	1.5	1.6	0.9	1.5	1.5	1.2	1.3
Strawberries	2.0	3.0	3.2	4.1	4.2	4.4	4.2	4.0	4.5
Watermelons	10.7	13.5	13.3	15.2	15.4	16.8	15.8	14.6	15.8
Other [2]	3.6	5.2	5.2	5.9	5.9	6.8	7.2	7.3	8.1
Fresh citrus	26.1	21.5	21.4	25.0	24.1	24.9	27.0	27.1	20.7
Oranges	14.3	11.6	12.4	13.1	12.0	12.8	14.2	14.9	8.6
Grapefruit	7.3	5.5	4.4	6.1	6.1	5.9	6.3	6.0	5.9
Other [3]	4.5	4.4	4.6	5.8	6.0	6.2	6.5	6.2	6.2
Processed fruits	165.7	159.5	156.2	164.7	160.8	162.1	165.0	153.1	165.3
Frozen fruits [4]	3.1	3.3	3.8	3.8	4.2	4.0	3.7	4.2	3.7
Dried fruits [5]	11.2	12.8	12.1	12.8	12.8	11.3	10.8	12.4	10.5
Canned fruits [6]	24.6	20.9	21.0	22.0	17.5	18.8	20.4	17.4	19.6
Fruit juices [7]	126.1	122.2	119.0	126.6	125.9	127.8	129.3	118.8	131.0
Vegetables, total	336.2	357.7	383.5	414.6	409.4	420.6	421.0	418.0	421.2
Fresh vegetables	149.1	156.0	167.1	184.6	179.1	184.1	188.9	185.5	192.1
Asparagus (all uses)	0.3	0.5	0.6	0.6	0.6	0.6	0.7	0.7	0.9
Broccoli	1.4	2.6	3.4	4.5	4.4	4.6	5.1	5.2	6.0
Cabbage	8.1	8.8	8.8	9.4	8.4	8.6	9.4	8.8	8.1
Carrots	6.2	6.5	8.3	12.8	11.3	12.6	14.4	13.5	13.6
Cauliflower	1.1	1.8	2.2	2.0	1.7	1.7	1.8	1.5	2.1
Celery (all uses)	7.4	6.9	7.2	7.4	6.9	6.4	6.1	6.0	6.2
Corn	6.5	6.4	6.7	8.2	7.9	8.5	8.4	9.5	9.9
Cucumbers	3.9	4.4	4.7	5.4	5.7	6.0	6.5	6.6	6.9
Head lettuce	25.6	23.7	27.8	25.3	22.5	21.9	24.3	22.0	25.3
Mushrooms	1.2	1.8	2.0	2.0	2.1	2.1	2.4	2.5	2.5
Onions	11.4	13.6	15.1	17.1	18.0	18.7	19.1	18.3	18.6
Snap beans	1.3	1.3	1.1	1.6	1.7	1.5	1.4	1.7	1.9
Bell peppers (all uses)	2.9	3.8	4.5	6.5	6.3	7.2	6.6	6.5	6.7
Potatoes	51.1	46.3	46.8	50.2	49.9	50.7	49.4	47.9	49.2
Sweetpotatoes (all uses)	4.4	5.4	4.6	4.7	4.5	4.6	4.5	4.1	4.0
Tomatoes	12.8	14.9	15.5	16.4	17.1	17.7	17.1	17.9	17.8
Other fresh vegetables [8]	3.5	7.3	7.8	10.5	10.1	10.7	11.8	12.8	12.4
Processed vegetables	187.1	201.8	216.4	230.2	230.4	236.5	232.2	232.5	229.1
Selected vegetables for freezing	51.5	64.5	66.8	78.4	79.9	84.6	83.0	81.8	82.5
Selected vegetables for canning	102.8	99.2	111.5	112.3	110.8	109.5	107.8	109.3	105.7
Vegetables for dehydrating [9]	10.5	12.8	14.6	14.3	14.7	17.8	17.1	18.3	16.0
Potatoes for chips	16.5	17.6	16.4	16.7	16.6	16.7	16.2	15.1	16.3
Pulses [10]	5.8	7.6	7.1	8.4	8.4	8.0	8.1	7.9	8.6

[1] Excludes wine grapes. [2] Apricots, avocados, cherries, cranberries, kiwifruit, mangoes, papayas, and honeydew melons.
[3] Lemons, limes, tangerines, and tangelos. [4] Apples, apricots, blackberries, blueberries, boysenberries, cherries, loganberries, peaches, plums, prunes, raspberries, and strawberries. [5] Apples, apricots, dates, figs, peaches, pears, prunes, and raisins.
[6] Apples, apricots, cherries, olives, peaches, pears, pineapples, plums, and prunes. [7] Apple, cranberry, grape, grapefruit, lemon, lime, orange, pineapple, and prunes. [8] Artichokes, Brussels sprouts, eggplant, escarole, endive, garlic, romaine, leaf lettuce, radishes, and spinach. [9] Onions and potatoes. [10] Dry peas, lentils, and dry edible beans.

No. 204. Per Capita Consumption of Selected Beverages by Type: 1980 to 1999

[In gallons. See headnote, Table 202]

Commodity	1980	1985	1990	1994	1995	1996	1997	1998	1999
Nonalcoholic	(NA)	(NA)	128.3	130.6	129.9	132.4	134.8	138.7	145.1
Milk (plain and flavored)	27.6	26.7	25.7	24.8	24.3	24.3	24.0	23.7	23.6
Whole	17.0	14.3	10.5	9.2	8.8	8.7	8.5	8.3	8.4
Reduced-fat, light, and skim	10.5	12.3	15.2	15.6	15.6	15.7	15.5	15.4	15.2
Tea	7.3	7.1	6.9	8.2	8.0	7.8	7.4	8.4	8.4
Coffee	26.7	27.4	26.9	21.1	20.5	22.5	23.7	24.3	25.7
Bottled water	2.4	4.5	8.0	10.7	11.6	12.5	13.1	16.0	18.1
Carbonated soft drinks	35.1	35.7	46.2	48.9	48.0	47.4	47.7	48.8	50.8
Diet	5.1	7.1	10.7	11.5	11.0	10.8	10.8	11.3	11.7
Regular	29.9	28.7	35.6	37.5	37.0	36.6	36.8	37.6	39.1
Fruit juices	9.5	7.8	7.9	8.6	8.7	8.9	9.5	8.6	9.6
Fruit drinks, cocktails, and ades	(NA)	(NA)	6.3	7.4	7.8	8.0	8.3	7.9	7.9
Canned iced tea	(NA)	(NA)	0.1	0.6	0.7	0.7	0.8	0.7	0.7
Vegetable juices	(NA)	(NA)	0.3	0.3	0.3	0.3	0.3	0.3	0.3
Alcoholic (adult population)	42.8	40.7	39.5	36.6	35.9	36.1	36.1	36.1	36.3
Beer	36.6	34.6	34.4	32.2	31.6	31.6	31.5	31.7	31.9
Wine [1]	3.2	3.5	2.9	2.5	2.6	2.7	2.8	2.6	2.7
Distilled spirits	3.0	2.6	2.2	1.8	1.8	1.8	1.8	1.8	1.8

NA Not available. [1] Beginning 1985, includes wine coolers.

Source of Tables 203 and 204: U.S. Dept. of Agriculture, Economic Research Service, Food Consumption, Prices, and Expenditures, annual; and Agricultural Outlook, monthly.

130 Health and Nutrition

Education

This section presents data primarily concerning formal education as a whole, at various levels, and for public and private schools. Data shown relate to the school-age population and school enrollment, educational attainment, education personnel, and financial aspects of education. In addition, data are shown for charter schools, computer usage in schools, distance education, and adult education. The chief sources are the decennial census of population and the Current Population Survey (CPS), both conducted by the U.S. Census Bureau (see text, Section 1, Population); annual, biennial, and other periodic surveys conducted by the National Center for Education Statistics (NCES), a part of the U.S. Department of Education; and surveys conducted by the National Education Association.

The censuses of population have included data on school enrollment since 1840 and on educational attainment since 1940. The CPS has reported on school enrollment annually since 1945 and on educational attainment periodically since 1947.

The NCES is continuing the pattern of statistical studies and surveys conducted by the U.S. Office of Education since 1870. The annual *Digest of Education Statistics* provides summary data on pupils, staff, finances, including government expenditures, and organization at the elementary, secondary, and higher education levels. It is also a primary source for detailed information on federal funds for education, projections of enrollment, graduates, and teachers. *The Condition of Education,* issued annually, presents a summary of information on education of particular interest to policymakers. NCES also conducts special studies periodically.

The census of governments, conducted by the Census Bureau every 5 years (for the years ending in "2" and "7"), provides data on school district finances and state and local government expenditures for education. Reports published by the

Bureau of Labor Statistics contain data relating civilian labor force experience to educational attainment (see also Tables 571, 595, and 604 in Section 12, Labor Force, Employment, and Earnings).

Types and sources of data—The statistics in this section are of two general types. One type, exemplified by data from the Census Bureau, is based on direct interviews with individuals to obtain information about their own and their family members' education. Data of this type relate to school enrollment and level of education attained, classified by age, sex, and other characteristics of the population. The school enrollment statistics reflect attendance or enrollment in any regular school within a given period; educational attainment statistics reflect the highest grade completed by an individual, or beginning 1992, the highest diploma or degree received.

For enrollment data starting in October 1994, the CPS used 1990 census population controls plus adjustment for undercount. Also the survey changed from paper to computer assisted technology. For years 1981 through 1993, 1980 census population controls were used; 1971 through 1980, 1970 census population controls had been used. These changes had little impact on summary measures (e.g., medians) and proportional measures (e.g., enrollment rates); however, use of the controls may have significant impact on absolute numbers.

The second type, generally exemplified by data from the NCES and the National Education Association, is based on reports from administrators of educational institutions and of state and local agencies having jurisdiction over education. Data of this type relate to enrollment, attendance, staff, and finances for the nation, individual states, and local areas.

Unlike the NCES, the Census Bureau does not regularly include specialized vocational, trade, business, or correspondence

Education 131

schools in its surveys. The NCES includes nursery schools and kindergartens that are part of regular grade schools in their enrollment figures. The Census Bureau includes all nursery schools and kindergartens. At the higher education level, the statistics of both agencies are concerned with institutions granting degrees or offering work acceptable for degree-credit, such as junior colleges.

School attendance—All states require that children attend school. While state laws vary as to the ages and circumstances of compulsory attendance, generally they require that formal schooling begin by age 6 and continue to age 16.

Schools—The NCES defines a school as "a division of the school system consisting of students composing one or more grade groups or other identifiable groups, organized as one unit with one or more teachers to give instruction of a defined type, and housed in a school plant of one or more buildings. More than one school may be housed in one school plant, as is the case when the elementary and secondary programs are housed in the same school plant."

Regular schools are those which advance a person toward a diploma or degree. They include public and private nursery schools, kindergartens, graded schools, colleges, universities, and professional schools.

Public schools are schools controlled and supported by local, state, or federal governmental agencies; private schools are those controlled and supported mainly by religious organizations or by private persons or organizations.

The Census Bureau defines *elementary* schools as including grades 1 through 8; *high* schools as including grades 9 through 12; and *colleges* as including junior or community colleges, regular 4-year colleges, and universities and graduate or professional schools. Statistics reported by the NCES and the National Education Association by type of organization, such as elementary level and secondary level, may not be strictly comparable with those from the Census Bureau because the grades included at the two levels vary, depending on the level assigned to the middle or junior high school by the local school systems.

School year—Except as otherwise indicated in the tables, data refer to the school year which, for elementary and secondary schools, generally begins in September of the preceding year and ends in June of the year stated. For the most part, statistics concerning school finances are for a 12-month period, usually July 1 to June 30. Enrollment data generally refer to a specific point in time, such as fall, as indicated in the tables.

Statistical reliability—For a discussion of statistical collection, estimation, and sampling procedures and measures of statistical reliability applicable to the Census Bureau and the NCES data, see Appendix III.

No. 205. School Enrollment: 1965 to 2010

[In thousands (54,394 represents 54,394,000). As of fall]

Year	All levels			K through grade 8		Grades 9 through 12		College[1]	
	Total	Public	Private	Public	Private	Public	Private	Public	Private
1965	54,394	46,143	8,251	30,563	4,900	11,610	1,400	3,970	1,951
1970	59,838	52,322	7,516	32,558	4,052	13,336	1,311	6,428	2,153
1975	61,004	53,654	7,350	30,515	3,700	14,304	1,300	8,835	2,350
1980	58,305	50,335	7,971	27,647	3,992	13,231	1,339	9,457	2,640
1981	57,916	49,691	8,225	27,280	4,100	12,764	1,400	9,647	2,725
1982	57,591	49,262	8,330	27,161	4,200	12,405	1,400	9,696	2,730
1983	57,432	48,935	8,497	26,981	4,315	12,271	1,400	9,683	2,782
1984	57,150	48,686	8,465	26,905	4,300	12,304	1,400	9,477	2,765
1985	57,226	48,901	8,325	27,034	4,195	12,388	1,362	9,479	2,768
1986	57,709	49,467	8,242	27,420	4,116	12,333	1,336	9,714	2,790
1987	58,254	49,982	8,272	27,933	4,232	12,076	1,247	9,973	2,793
1988	58,485	50,349	8,136	28,501	4,036	11,687	1,206	10,161	2,894
1989	59,436	51,120	8,316	29,152	4,162	11,390	1,193	10,578	2,961
1990	60,267	52,061	8,206	29,878	4,095	11,338	1,137	10,845	2,974
1991	61,605	53,356	8,248	30,506	4,074	11,541	1,125	11,310	3,049
1992	62,686	54,208	8,478	31,088	4,212	11,735	1,163	11,385	3,103
1993	63,241	54,654	8,587	31,504	4,280	11,961	1,191	11,189	3,116
1994	63,986	55,245	8,741	31,898	4,360	12,213	1,236	11,134	3,145
1995	64,764	55,933	8,831	32,341	4,465	12,500	1,197	11,092	3,169
1996[1]	65,762	56,732	9,030	32,764	4,486	12,847	1,297	11,120	3,247
1997[1]	66,490	57,323	9,167	33,073	4,552	13,054	1,308	11,196	3,306
1998[1]	67,008	57,711	9,297	33,346	4,597	13,193	1,327	11,176	3,373
1999, proj.	67,656	58,436	9,220	33,488	4,599	13,369	1,339	11,579	3,282
2000, proj.	68,124	58,821	9,303	33,521	4,611	13,505	1,352	11,795	3,340
2001, proj.	68,516	59,148	9,368	33,557	4,616	13,619	1,363	11,972	3,389
2002, proj.	68,787	59,376	9,411	33,543	4,614	13,753	1,377	12,080	3,420
2003, proj.	69,050	59,594	9,457	33,442	4,600	13,931	1,395	12,221	3,462
2004, proj.	69,303	59,806	9,499	33,237	4,572	14,199	1,422	12,370	3,505
2005, proj.	69,538	59,997	9,540	33,051	4,546	14,423	1,444	12,523	3,550
2006, proj.	69,771	60,178	9,592	32,915	4,527	14,537	1,455	12,726	3,610
2007, proj.	69,979	60,327	9,654	32,835	4,517	14,530	1,455	12,962	3,682
2008, proj.	70,149	60,434	9,715	32,825	4,515	14,393	1,441	13,216	3,759
2009, proj.	70,317	60,543	9,774	32,877	4,522	14,232	1,425	13,434	3,827
2010, proj.	70,506	60,675	9,830	32,999	4,539	14,069	1,409	13,607	3,882

[1]Data for 1996, 1997, and 1998 are based on new classification system. See footnote 1, Table 264.

Source: U.S. National Center for Education Statistics, *Digest of Education Statistics*, annual, and *Projections of Education Statistics*, annual.

No. 206. School Expenditures by Type of Control and Level of Instruction in Constant (1999-2000) Dollars: 1960 to 2000

[In millions of dollars (137,473 represents $137,473,000,000). For school years ending in year shown. Total expenditures for public elementary and secondary schools include current expenditures, interest on school debt and capital outlay. Data deflated by the Consumer Price Index, wage earners, and clerical workers through 1975; thereafter, all urban consumers, on a school year basis (supplied by the National Center for Education Statistics). See also Appendix III]

Year	Elementary and secondary schools				Colleges and universities		
	Total	Total	Public	Private[1]	Total	Public	Private
1960	137,473	96,294	89,957	6,338	41,179	22,491	18,688
1970	306,805	193,530	182,326	11,204	113,275	72,755	40,520
1975	355,189	225,036	211,961	13,075	130,153	88,145	42,008
1980	361,177	224,961	209,261	15,701	136,216	90,354	45,862
1985	396,404	239,132	219,284	19,848	157,273	101,967	55,306
1986	419,251	251,720	231,184	20,536	167,531	109,010	58,521
1987	444,372	266,647	244,883	21,764	177,725	113,465	64,260
1988	457,966	274,742	252,383	22,359	183,224	116,706	66,517
1989	484,557	292,478	269,569	22,909	192,079	121,679	70,401
1990	508,677	307,945	283,679	24,266	200,732	128,510	72,222
1991	521,655	314,686	290,035	24,651	206,969	132,020	74,949
1992	530,369	320,013	295,270	24,743	210,356	133,107	77,249
1993	541,722	325,857	300,437	25,419	215,866	136,798	79,067
1994	552,551	332,879	307,176	25,703	219,672	138,443	81,229
1995	567,193	340,367	314,029	26,338	226,826	143,614	83,212
1996	580,300	348,716	321,761	26,955	231,584	145,462	86,122
1997	598,885	361,100	333,614	27,486	237,785	148,722	89,063
1998, prel.	624,053	378,292	349,927	28,365	245,760	153,548	92,212
1999, prel.	641,191	387,780	359,281	28,500	253,410	156,799	96,611
2000, prel.	646,800	389,000	360,600	28,400	257,800	159,700	98,100

[1] Estimated.

Source: U.S. National Center for Education Statistics, *Digest Education Statistics*, annual.

Education 133

No. 207. School Enrollment, Faculty, Graduates, and Finances With Projections: 1995 to 2004

[As of fall, except as indicated (50,502 represents 50,502,000)]

Item	Unit	1995	1999, proj.	2000, proj.	2001, proj.	2002, proj.	2003, proj.	2004, proj.
ELEMENTARY AND SECONDARY SCHOOLS								
School enrollment, total	1,000...	50,502	52,781	52,989	53,155	53,287	53,367	53,429
Kindergarten through grade 8	1,000...	36,806	38,085	38,132	38,172	38,157	38,042	37,809
Grades 9 through 12	1,000...	13,697	14,696	14,857	14,982	15,130	15,325	15,620
Public	1,000...	44,840	46,857	47,026	47,176	47,296	47,373	47,436
Kindergarten through grade 8	1,000...	32,341	33,488	33,521	33,557	33,543	33,442	33,237
Grades 9 through 12	1,000...	12,500	13,369	13,505	13,619	13,753	13,931	14,199
Private	1,000...	5,662	5,924	5,963	5,979	5,991	5,995	5,993
Kindergarten through grade 8	1,000...	4,465	4,597	4,611	4,616	4,614	4,600	4,572
Grades 9 through 12	1,000...	1,197	1,327	1,352	1,363	1,377	1,395	1,422
Enrollment rate:								
5 and 6 year olds	Percent	96.0	96.0	(NA)	(NA)	(NA)	(NA)	(NA)
7 to 13 year olds	Percent	98.9	98.7	(NA)	(NA)	(NA)	(NA)	(NA)
14 to 17 year olds	Percent	96.3	95.8	(NA)	(NA)	(NA)	(NA)	(NA)
Classroom teachers, total [1]	1,000...	2,978	3,304	3,252	3,269	3,281	3,296	3,312
Public	1,000...	2,598	2,907	2,850	2,865	2,877	2,891	2,905
Private	1,000...	380	397	402	403	404	405	407
High school graduates, total [2]	1,000...	2,540	2,839	2,837	2,886	2,929	2,935	2,944
Public	1,000...	2,273	2,545	2,542	2,585	2,624	2,630	2,637
Public schools: [2]								
Average daily attendance (ADA)	1,000...	41,502	43,383	43,582	43,720	43,832	43,903	43,962
Current dollars:								
Teachers' average salary	Dol.	37,704	42,414	44,047	45,400	46,663	48,046	(NA)
Current school expenditure	Bil. dol.	255.1	330.3	352.2	369.8	385.0	401.7	(NA)
Per pupil in ADA	Dol.	6,147	7,613	8,081	8,458	8,783	9,150	(NA)
Constant (1998-99) dollars:								
Teachers' average salary	Dol.	40,152	41,394	42,069	42,367	42,443	42,565	(NA)
Current school expenditure	Bil. dol.	271.7	322.3	336.4	345.1	350.2	355.9	(NA)
Per pupil in ADA	Dol.	6,546	7,430	7,718	7,893	7,989	8,106	(NA)
HIGHER EDUCATION								
Enrollment, total	1,000...	14,262	14,861	15,135	15,361	15,500	15,683	15,874
Male	1,000...	6,343	6,392	6,481	6,565	6,614	6,681	6,749
Full time	1,000...	3,807	3,861	3,917	3,972	3,998	4,040	4,080
Part time	1,000...	2,535	2,531	2,563	2,592	2,616	2,642	2,670
Female	1,000...	7,919	8,469	8,655	8,796	8,886	9,001	9,125
Full time	1,000...	4,321	4,640	4,748	4,839	4,890	4,968	5,050
Part time	1,000...	3,598	3,829	3,906	3,958	3,997	4,033	4,075
Public	1,000...	11,092	11,579	11,795	11,972	12,080	12,221	12,370
Four-year institutions	1,000...	5,815	6,041	6,157	6,253	6,313	6,392	6,471
Two-year institutions	1,000...	5,278	5,537	5,638	5,718	5,767	5,829	5,899
Private	1,000...	3,169	3,282	3,340	3,389	3,420	3,462	3,505
Four-year institutions	1,000...	2,955	3,076	3,131	3,177	3,206	3,245	3,285
Two-year institutions	1,000...	215	206	209	213	214	217	220
Undergraduate	1,000...	12,232	12,818	13,079	13,294	13,419	13,584	13,753
Graduate	1,000...	1,732	1,760	1,775	1,786	1,799	1,813	1,832
First-time professional	1,000...	298	283	281	281	283	285	289
Full-time equivalent	1,000...	10,335	10,787	10,992	11,166	11,266	11,408	11,555
Public	1,000...	7,752	8,104	8,261	8,393	8,467	8,573	8,684
Private	1,000...	2,583	2,684	2,731	2,773	2,799	2,835	2,871
Faculty, total	1,000...	932	1,004	1,013	(NA)	(NA)	(NA)	(NA)
Public	1,000...	657	715	721	(NA)	(NA)	(NA)	(NA)
Private	1,000...	275	289	291	(NA)	(NA)	(NA)	(NA)
Degrees conferred, total [2]	1,000...	2,248	2,266	2,281	2,297	2,316	2,344	2,363
Associate's	1,000...	555	559	569	571	577	581	583
Bachelor's	1,000...	1,165	1,185	1,194	1,210	1,220	1,240	1,253
Master's	1,000...	406	398	396	396	399	402	406
Doctorate's	1,000...	45	45	45	45	45	45	45
First-professional	1,000...	77	78	77	75	75	75	76

NA Not available.   [1] Full-time equivalents.   [2] For school year ending June the following year.

Source: U.S. National Center for Education Statistics, *Digest of Education Statistics*, annual, and *Projections of Educational Statistics*, annual.

134   Education

No. 208. Federal Funds for Education and Related Programs: 1998 to 2000

[In millions of dollars (76,909.2 represents $76,909,200,000), except percent. For fiscal years ending in September. Figures represent on-budget funds]

Level, agency, and program	1998	1999	2000 [1]
Total, all programs	**76,909.2**	**83,137.9**	**90,658.9**
Percent of federal budget outlays	4.7	4.9	5.1
Elementary/secondary education programs	**37,486.2**	**39,937.9**	**43,968.0**
Department of Education [1]	16,001.8	17,026.7	20,757.8
Grants for the disadvantaged	7,817.8	7,554.2	8,379.3
School improvement programs	1,367.8	1,328.0	2,662.7
Indian education	52.7	56.8	80.9
Special education	3,658.4	4,444.1	5,432.3
Vocational and adult education	1,451.3	1,364.0	1,546.9
Education reform—Goals 2000 [2]	746.5	887.1	1,124.9
Department of Agriculture [2]	9,090.0	9,367.9	9,856.1
Child nutrition programs	8,564.9	8,877.9	9,354.1
Special milk program [3]			
Agricultural Marketing Service—commodities [4]	400.0	400.0	400.0
Department of Defense [2]	1,312.2	1,379.0	1,369.8
Overseas dependents schools	821.8	882.3	864.7
Section VI schools [5]	319.3	329.1	329.3
Department of Health and Human Services	5,137.2	5,429.9	6,039.6
Head Start	4,347.4	4,658.0	5,267.0
Social security student benefits [2]	715.7	709.9	725.6
Department of the Interior [2]	578.8	593.3	670.6
Mineral Leasing Act and other funds	44.5	37.7	52.1
Indian Education	533.3	554.6	617.5
Department of Justice	196.2	204.8	231.6
Inmate programs	195.2	201.8	227.6
Department of Labor	4,644.0	5,402.0	4,524.0
Job Corps	1,188.0	1,253.0	1,003.0
Department of Veterans Affairs	411.3	417.9	423.1
Vocational rehab for disabled veterans	406.0	411.6	416.7
Other agencies and programs	114.7	116.5	115.3
Higher education programs [2]	**15,799.6**	**17,639.5**	**19,887.0**
Department of Education	12,122.3	13,715.6	15,833.9
Student financial assistance	7,878.8	9,124.7	9,363.3
Federal Family Education Loans	2,272.0	2,805.5	4,030.7
Department of Agriculture	36.6	29.7	30.7
Department of Commerce	3.6	3.6	3.7
Department of Defense	934.4	983.2	1,001.7
Tuition assistance for military personnel	286.0	280.5	269.8
Service academies [6]	111.0	115.1	114.7
Senior ROTC	301.0	321.8	337.1
Professional development education	236.4	265.7	280.1
Department of Health and Human Services [2]	788.2	880.2	965.8
Health professions training programs	289.5	301.7	341.9
National Health Service Corps scholarships	30.1	28.5	30.6
National Institutes of Health training grants [7]	428.0	509.2	550.2
Department of the Interior	153.6	132.2	149.3
Shared revenues, Mineral Leasing Act and other receipts—estimated education share	71.0	47.8	60.9
Indian programs	82.6	84.4	88.4
Department of State	283.0	290.0	260.0
Department of Transportation	59.9	60.3	64.2
Department of Veterans Affairs [2]	1,005.7	1,123.2	1,143.1
Post-Vietnam veterans	9.0	3.7	3.1
All-volunteer-force educational assistance	882.2	988.7	991.6
Other agencies and programs [2]	412.2	421.5	434.6
National Endowment for the Humanities	29.7	28.5	29.9
National Science Foundation	359.0	369.0	378.0
United States Information Agency [8]			
Other education programs [2]	**5,148.5**	**5,318.0**	**5,766.8**
Department of Education [2]	2,893.7	3,123.3	3,420.0
Administration	403.5	439.9	516.0
Rehabilitative services and handicapped research	2,482.2	2,675.2	2,891.0
Department of Agriculture	410.7	428.3	412.6
Department of Health and Human Services	162.0	181.0	214.0
Department of Justice	32.9	33.8	28.8
Department of State	49.2	56.9	63.3
Department of the Treasury [2]	96.0	65.0	81.0
Other agencies and programs [2]	1,504.0	1,429.7	1,547.0
Agency for International Development	340.3	313.0	340.0
Library of Congress	331.0	350.0	365.0
National Endowment for the Arts	2.2	6.3	4.0
National Endowment for the Humanities	62.6	63.2	63.3
Research programs at universities and related institutions [2]	**18,475.0**	**20,242.5**	**21,017.1**
Department of Agriculture	415.4	536.3	474.8
Department of Defense	1,769.5	1,787.6	1,614.4
Department of Energy	3,499.6	3,713.8	3,945.1
Department of Health and Human Services	7,775.5	9,022.3	9,244.0
National Aeronautics and Space Administration	1,922.1	1,944.1	2,163.8
National Science Foundation	2,147.9	2,359.0	2,518.0

[1] Estimated. [2] Includes other programs and agencies, not shown separately. [3] The Special Milk Program is included in the Child Nutrition Program. [4] Purchased under Section 32 of the Act of August 1935 for use in child nutrition programs. [5] Program provides for the education of dependents of federal employees residing on federal property where free public education is unavailable in the nearby community. [6] Instructional costs only including academics, audiovisual, academic computer center, faculty training, military training, physical education, and libraries. [7] Includes alcohol, drug abuse, and mental health training programs. [8] Program transferred to the Department of State in fiscal year 1998.

Source: U.S. National Center for Education Statistics, Digest of Education Statistics, 2000.

Education   135

No. 209. School Enrollment by Age: 1970 to 1999

[As of October (60,357 represents 60,357,000). Covers civilian noninstitutional population enrolled in nursery school and above. Based on Current Population Survey, see text, Section 1, Population]

Age	1970	1980	1985	1990	1994	1995	1996	1997	1998	1999
ENROLLMENT (1,000)										
Total 3 to 34 years old. .	60,357	57,348	58,013	60,588	66,427	66,939	67,317	69,041	69,277	69,601
3 and 4 years old	1,461	2,280	2,801	3,292	3,917	4,042	3,959	4,194	4,164	4,273
5 and 6 years old	7,000	5,853	6,697	7,207	7,752	7,901	7,893	7,964	7,902	7,774
7 to 13 years old	28,943	23,751	22,849	25,016	26,768	27,003	26,936	27,616	27,846	28,209
14 and 15 years old.	7,869	7,282	7,362	6,555	7,519	7,651	7,598	7,744	7,653	7,741
16 and 17 years old.	6,927	7,129	6,654	6,098	6,895	6,997	7,220	7,538	7,456	7,611
18 and 19 years old.	3,322	3,788	3,716	4,044	4,180	4,274	4,539	4,618	4,914	4,840
20 and 21 years old.	1,949	2,515	2,708	2,852	3,133	3,025	3,017	3,231	3,197	3,256
22 to 24 years old	1,410	1,931	2,068	2,231	2,724	2,545	2,605	2,754	2,607	2,664
25 to 29 years old	1,011	1,714	1,942	2,013	2,070	2,216	2,265	2,223	2,216	2,018
30 to 34 years old	466	1,105	1,218	1,281	1,468	1,284	1,286	1,159	1,322	1,215
35 years old and over . . .	(NA)	1,290	1,766	2,439	2,845	2,830	2,979	2,989	2,831	2,794
ENROLLMENT RATE										
Total 3 to 34 years old. .	56.4	49.7	48.3	50.2	53.3	53.7	54.1	55.6	55.8	56.0
3 and 4 years old	20.5	36.7	38.9	44.4	47.3	48.7	48.3	52.6	52.1	54.2
5 and 6 years old	89.5	95.7	96.1	96.5	96.7	96.0	94.0	96.6	95.6	96.0
7 to 13 years old.	99.2	99.3	99.2	99.6	99.3	98.9	97.7	99.1	98.9	98.7
14 and 15 years old.	98.1	98.2	98.1	99.0	98.8	98.9	98.0	98.9	98.4	98.2
16 and 17 years old.	90.0	89.0	91.7	92.5	94.4	93.6	92.8	94.3	93.9	93.6
18 and 19 years old.	47.7	46.4	51.6	57.3	60.2	59.4	61.5	61.5	62.2	60.6
20 and 21 years old.	31.9	31.0	35.3	39.7	44.9	44.9	44.4	45.9	44.8	45.3
22 to 24 years old	14.9	16.3	16.9	21.0	24.1	23.2	24.8	26.4	24.9	24.5
25 to 29 years old	7.5	9.3	9.2	9.7	10.8	11.6	11.9	11.8	11.9	11.1
30 to 34 years old	4.2	6.4	6.1	5.8	6.7	6.0	6.1	5.7	6.6	6.2
35 years old and over . . .	(NA)	1.4	1.6	2.1	2.3	2.2	2.3	2.3	2.1	1.8

NA Not available.

Source: U.S. Census Bureau, Current Population Reports, P20-533; and earlier reports.

No. 210. School Enrollment by Race, Hispanic Origin, and Age: 1980 to 1999

[47,673 represents 47,673,000. See headnote, Table 209]

Age	White			Black			Hispanic origin [1]		
	1980	1990	1999	1980	1990	1999	1980	1990	1999
ENROLLMENT (1,000)									
Total 3 to 34 years old	47,673	48,899	54,457	8,251	8,854	10,917	4,263	6,073	9,672
3 and 4 years old	1,844	2,700	3,330	371	452	688	172	249	526
5 and 6 years old	4,781	5,750	6,038	904	1,129	1,257	491	835	1,362
7 to 13 years old	19,585	20,076	22,021	3,598	3,832	4,614	2,009	2,794	4,308
14 and 15 years old	6,038	5,265	6,095	1,088	1,023	1,232	568	739	1,070
16 and 17 years old	5,937	4,858	5,942	1,047	962	1,204	454	592	975
18 and 19 years old	3,199	3,271	3,859	494	596	688	226	329	543
20 and 21 years old	2,206	2,402	2,610	242	305	426	111	213	222
22 to 24 years old	1,669	1,781	2,112	196	274	335	93	121	263
25 to 29 years old	1,473	1,706	1,530	187	162	266	84	130	247
30 to 34 years old	942	1,090	920	124	119	207	54	72	156
35 years old and over	1,104	2,096	2,255	186	238	365	(NA)	145	265
ENROLLMENT RATE									
Total 3 to 34 years old	48.9	49.5	55.2	53.9	51.9	58.1	49.8	47.4	51.1
3 and 4 years old	36.3	44.9	53.7	38.2	41.6	56.2	28.5	29.8	36.9
5 and 6 years old	95.8	96.5	95.6	95.4	96.3	97.4	94.5	94.8	93.9
7 to 13 years old	99.2	99.6	98.7	99.4	99.8	98.5	99.2	99.4	98.6
14 and 15 years old	98.3	99.1	98.2	97.9	99.2	98.2	94.3	99.0	97.6
16 and 17 years old	88.6	92.5	93.5	90.6	91.7	93.4	81.8	85.4	88.1
18 and 19 years old	46.3	57.1	60.4	45.7	55.2	57.4	37.8	44.1	44.5
20 and 21 years old	31.9	41.0	45.6	23.4	28.4	39.4	19.5	27.2	22.6
22 to 24 years old	16.4	20.2	24.1	13.6	20.0	21.6	11.7	9.9	15.0
25 to 29 years old	9.2	9.9	10.5	8.8	6.1	10.4	6.9	6.3	9.1
30 to 34 years old	6.3	5.9	5.8	6.8	4.4	7.8	5.1	3.6	5.6
35 years old and over	1.3	2.1	1.9	1.8	2.1	2.5	(NA)	2.1	2.3

NA Not available. [1] Persons of Hispanic origin may be of any race.

Source: U.S. Census Bureau, Current Population Reports, P20-533; and earlier reports.

No. 211. Enrollment in Public and Private Schools: 1960 to 1999

[In millions (39.0 represents 39,000,000), except percent. As of October. For civilian noninstitutional population. For 1960, 5 to 34 years old; for 1970 to 1985, 3 to 34 years old; beginning 1986, for 3 years old and over]

Year	Public						Private					
	Total	Nursery	Kindergarten	Elementary	High School	College	Total	Nursery	Kindergarten	Elementary	High School	College
1960	39.0	(NA)	(¹)	27.5	9.2	2.3	7.2	(NA)	(¹)	4.9	1.0	1.3
1970	52.2	0.3	2.6	30.0	13.5	5.7	8.1	0.8	0.5	3.9	1.2	1.7
1975	52.8	0.6	2.9	27.2	14.5	7.7	8.2	1.2	0.5	3.3	1.2	2.0
1980	(NA)	0.6	2.7	24.4	(NA)	(NA)	(NA)	1.4	0.5	3.1	(NA)	(NA)
1982	49.2	0.7	2.7	24.4	13.0	8.4	8.2	1.4	0.6	3.0	1.1	2.6
1983	48.7	0.8	2.7	24.2	12.8	8.2	9.0	1.5	0.7	3.0	1.2	2.6
1984	49.0	0.8	3.0	24.1	12.7	8.5	8.3	1.6	0.5	2.7	1.1	2.4
1985	49.0	0.9	3.2	23.8	12.8	8.4	9.0	1.6	0.6	3.1	1.2	2.5
1986 ²	51.2	0.8	3.4	24.2	13.0	9.8	9.4	1.7	0.6	3.0	1.2	2.9
1987 ²	51.7	0.8	3.4	24.8	12.7	10.0	8.9	1.7	0.6	2.8	1.1	2.8
1988 ²	52.2	0.9	3.4	25.5	12.2	10.3	8.9	1.8	0.5	2.8	1.0	2.8
1989 ²	52.5	0.9	3.3	25.9	12.1	10.3	8.9	1.9	0.6	2.7	0.8	2.9
1990 ²	53.8	1.2	3.3	26.6	11.9	10.7	9.2	2.2	0.6	2.7	0.9	2.9
1991 ²	54.5	1.1	3.5	26.6	12.2	11.1	9.4	1.8	0.6	3.0	1.0	3.0
1992 ²	55.0	1.1	3.5	27.1	12.3	11.1	9.4	1.8	0.6	3.1	1.0	3.0
1993 ²	56.0	1.2	3.5	27.7	12.6	10.9	9.4	1.8	0.7	2.9	1.0	3.0
1994 ²	58.6	1.9	3.3	28.1	13.5	11.7	10.7	2.3	0.6	3.4	1.1	3.3
1995 ²	58.7	2.0	3.2	28.4	13.7	11.4	11.1	2.4	0.7	3.4	1.2	3.3
1996 ²	59.5	1.9	3.4	28.1	14.1	12.0	10.8	2.3	0.7	3.4	1.2	3.2
1997 ²	61.6	2.3	3.3	29.3	14.6	12.1	10.5	2.2	0.7	3.1	1.2	3.3
1998 ²	60.8	2.3	3.1	29.1	14.3	12.0	11.3	2.3	0.7	3.4	1.2	3.6
1999 ²	60.8	2.3	3.2	29.2	14.4	11.7	11.4	2.3	0.7	3.6	1.3	3.5
Percent White:												
1960	85.7	(NA)	(¹)	84.3	88.2	92.2	95.7	(NA)	(¹)	95.3	96.7	96.3
1970	84.5	59.5	84.4	83.1	85.6	90.7	93.4	91.1	88.2	94.1	96.1	92.8
1980	(NA)	68.2	80.7	80.9	(NA)	(NA)	(NA)	89.0	87.0	90.7	(NA)	(NA)
1990	79.8	71.7	78.3	78.9	79.2	84.1	87.4	89.6	83.2	88.2	89.4	85.0
1995	78.0	71.3	76.9	77.5	76.9	81.9	85.0	88.7	84.1	86.1	86.0	81.1
1999	77.2	69.2	76.5	77.1	77.7	78.8	84.3	87.4	81.2	85.2	87.0	80.9

NA Not available. ¹ Included in elementary school. ² See Table 268 for college enrollment 35 years old and over. Also data beginning 1986 based on a revised edit and tabulation package.

Source: U.S. Census Bureau, *Current Population Reports*, P20-533; and earlier reports.

No. 212. School Enrollment by Sex and Level: 1960 to 1999

[In millions (46.3 represents 46,300,000). As of Oct. For the civilian noninstitutional population. For 1960, persons 5 to 34 years old; 1970-1979, 3 to 34 years old; beginning 1980, 3 years old and over. Elementary includes kindergarten and grades 1-8; high school, grades 9-12; and college, 2-year and 4-year colleges, universities, and graduate and professional schools. Data for college represent degree-credit enrollment]

Year	All levels ¹			Elementary			High school			College		
	Total	Male	Female	Total	Male	Female	Total	Male	Female	Total	Male	Female
1960	46.3	24.2	22.0	32.4	16.7	15.7	10.2	5.2	5.1	3.6	2.3	1.2
1970	60.4	31.4	28.9	37.1	19.0	18.1	14.7	7.4	7.3	7.4	4.4	3.0
1975	61.0	31.6	29.4	33.8	17.3	16.5	15.7	8.0	7.7	9.7	5.3	4.4
1980	58.6	29.6	29.1	30.6	15.8	14.9	14.6	7.3	7.3	11.4	5.4	6.0
1981	59.9	30.3	29.6	31.0	15.9	15.0	14.7	7.5	7.3	12.1	5.8	6.3
1982	59.4	30.0	29.4	30.7	15.8	14.9	14.2	7.2	7.0	12.3	5.9	6.4
1983	59.3	30.1	29.2	30.6	15.7	14.8	14.1	7.1	7.0	12.4	6.0	6.3
1984	58.9	29.9	29.0	30.3	15.6	14.7	13.9	7.1	6.8	12.3	6.0	6.3
1985	59.8	30.0	29.7	30.7	15.7	15.0	14.1	7.2	6.9	12.5	5.9	6.6
1986 ²	60.5	30.6	30.0	31.1	16.1	15.0	14.2	7.2	7.0	12.7	6.0	6.7
1987	60.6	30.7	29.9	31.6	16.3	15.3	13.8	7.0	6.8	12.7	6.0	6.7
1988	61.1	30.7	30.5	32.2	16.6	15.6	13.2	6.7	6.4	13.1	5.9	7.2
1989	61.5	30.8	30.7	32.5	16.7	15.8	12.9	6.6	6.3	13.2	6.0	7.2
1990	63.0	31.5	31.5	33.2	17.1	16.0	12.8	6.5	6.4	13.6	6.2	7.4
1991	63.9	32.1	31.8	33.8	17.3	16.4	13.1	6.8	6.4	14.1	6.4	7.6
1992	64.6	32.2	32.3	34.3	17.7	16.6	13.3	6.8	6.5	14.0	6.2	7.8
1993	65.4	32.9	32.5	34.8	17.9	16.9	13.6	7.0	6.6	13.9	6.3	7.6
1994	69.3	34.6	34.6	35.4	18.2	17.2	14.6	7.4	7.2	15.0	6.8	8.2
1995	69.8	35.0	34.8	35.7	18.3	17.4	15.0	7.7	7.3	14.7	6.7	8.0
1996	70.3	35.1	35.2	35.5	18.3	17.3	15.3	7.9	7.4	15.2	6.8	8.4
1997	72.0	35.9	36.2	36.3	18.7	17.6	15.8	8.0	7.7	15.4	6.8	8.6
1998	72.1	36.0	36.1	36.4	18.7	17.7	15.6	7.9	7.6	15.5	6.9	8.6
1999	72.4	36.3	36.1	36.7	18.8	17.9	15.9	8.2	7.7	15.2	7.0	8.2

¹ Beginning 1970, includes nursery schools, not shown separately. ² Revised. Data beginning 1986, based on a revised edit and tabulation package.

Source: U.S. Census Bureau, *Current Population Reports*, P20-533; and earlier reports.

Education 137

No. 213. School Enrollment by Control and Level: 1980 to 1998

[In thousands (58,305 represents 58,305,000). As of fall. Data are for regular day schools and exclude independent nursery schools and kindergartens, residential schools for exceptional children, subcollegiate departments of colleges, federal schools for Indians, and federally operated schools on federal installations. College data include degree-credit and nondegree-credit enrollment. For projections, see Table 205]

Control of school and level	1980	1990	1991	1992	1993	1994	1995	1996	1997	1998
Total.............	58,305	60,267	61,605	62,686	63,241	63,986	64,764	65,762	66,490	67,008
Public.............	50,335	52,061	53,356	54,208	54,654	55,245	55,933	56,731	57,323	57,711
Private.............	7,971	8,206	8,248	8,478	8,587	8,741	8,831	9,030	9,166	9,297
Kindergarten through 8 ..	31,639	33,973	34,580	35,300	35,784	36,258	36,806	37,250	37,625	37,941
Public.............	27,647	29,878	30,506	31,088	31,504	31,898	32,341	32,764	33,073	33,344
Private.............	3,992	4,095	4,074	4,212	4,280	4,360	4,465	4,486	4,552	4,597
Grades 9 through 12....	14,570	12,475	12,666	12,898	13,152	13,449	13,697	14,144	14,362	14,518
Public.............	13,231	11,338	11,541	11,735	11,961	12,213	12,500	12,847	13,054	13,191
Private.............	1,339	1,137	1,125	1,163	1,191	1,236	1,197	1,297	1,308	1,327
College[1].............	12,097	13,819	14,359	14,487	14,305	14,279	14,262	14,368	14,503	14,550
Public.............	9,457	10,845	11,310	11,385	11,189	11,134	11,092	11,120	11,196	11,176
Private.............	2,640	2,974	3,049	3,103	3,116	3,145	3,169	3,247	3,306	3,373

[1] Beginning 1996, reflects new classification of institutions. See footnote 1, Table 264.

Source: U.S. National Center for Education Statistics, *Digest of Education Statistics*, annual.

No. 214. Students Who Are Foreign Born or Who Have Foreign-Born Parents: 1999

[In thousands (48,789 represents 48,789,000), except percent. As of October. Covers civilian noninstitutional population enrolled in elementary school and above. Based on Current Population Survey, see text, Section 1, Population, and Appendix III]

Characteristic	All students	Students with at least one foreign-born parent						
		Total		Foreign-born student		Native student	
		Number	Percent	Number	Percent	Number	Percent
ELEMENTARY AND HIGH SCHOOL							
Total[1].....................	48,789	9,731	19.9	2,494	5.1	7,237	14.8
White.............................	38,115	6,867	18.0	1,666	4.4	5,201	13.6
White, non-Hispanic.............	31,123	2,290	7.4	467	1.5	1,823	5.9
Black.............................	7,924	839	10.6	240	3.0	599	7.6
Asian and Pacific Islander	2,181	1,914	87.8	553	25.3	1,361	62.5
Hispanic[2].........................	7,378	4,820	65.3	1,288	17.5	3,532	47.9
COLLEGE, 1 TO 4 YEARS							
Total[1].....................	12,046	2,496	20.7	1,280	10.6	1,216	10.1
White.............................	9,481	1,525	16.1	648	6.8	877	9.3
White, non-Hispanic.............	8,410	832	9.9	297	3.5	535	6.4
Black.............................	1,726	268	15.5	167	9.7	101	5.9
Asian and Pacific Islander	743	676	91.0	450	60.6	226	30.4
Hispanic[2].........................	1,136	725	63.8	378	33.3	347	30.5
GRADUATE SCHOOL							
Total[1].....................	3,157	794	25.1	498	15.8	296	9.4
White.............................	2,571	455	17.7	225	8.8	230	8.9
White, non-Hispanic.............	2,408	348	14.5	158	6.6	190	7.9
Black.............................	271	54	20.0	42	15.8	12	4.2
Asian and Pacific Islander	298	283	94.8	228	76.4	55	18.5
Hispanic[2].........................	170	110	64.7	68	39.7	42	25.0

[1] Includes other races, not shown separately. [2] Persons of Hispanic origin may be of any race.

Source: U.S. Census Bureau, *Current Population Reports*, P20-533.

No. 215. Educational Attainment by Race and Hispanic Origin: 1960 to 2000

[In percent. For persons 25 years old and over. 1960, 1970, and 1980 as of April 1 and based on sample data from the censuses of population. Other years as of March and based on the Current Population Survey; see text, Section 1, Population, and Appendix III. See Table 216 for data by sex]

Year	Total [1]	White	Black	Asian and Pacific Islander	Hispanic [2] Total [3]	Hispanic [2] Mexican	Hispanic [2] Puerto Rican	Hispanic [2] Cuban
HIGH SCHOOL GRADUATE OR MORE [4]								
1960	41.1	43.2	20.1	(NA)	(NA)	(NA)	(NA)	(NA)
1970	52.3	54.5	31.4	(NA)	32.1	24.2	23.4	43.9
1980	66.5	68.8	51.2	(NA)	44.0	37.6	40.1	55.3
1985	73.9	75.5	59.8	(NA)	47.9	41.9	46.3	51.1
1990	77.6	79.1	66.2	80.4	50.8	44.1	55.5	63.5
1995	81.7	83.0	73.8	(NA)	53.4	46.5	61.3	64.7
1996	81.7	82.8	74.3	83.2	53.1	46.9	60.4	63.8
1997	82.1	83.0	74.9	84.9	54.7	48.6	61.1	65.2
1998	82.8	83.7	76.0	(NA)	55.5	48.3	63.8	67.8
1999	83.4	84.3	77.0	84.7	56.1	49.7	63.9	70.3
2000	84.1	84.9	78.5	85.7	57.0	51.0	64.3	73.0
COLLEGE GRADUATE OR MORE [4]								
1960	7.7	8.1	3.1	(NA)	(NA)	(NA)	(NA)	(NA)
1970	10.7	11.3	4.4	(NA)	4.5	2.5	2.2	11.1
1980	16.2	17.1	8.4	(NA)	7.6	4.9	5.6	16.2
1985	19.4	20.0	11.1	(NA)	8.5	5.5	7.0	13.7
1990	21.3	22.0	11.3	39.9	9.2	5.4	9.7	20.2
1995	23.0	24.0	13.2	(NA)	9.3	6.5	10.0	19.4
1996	23.6	24.3	13.6	41.7	9.3	6.5	11.0	18.8
1997	23.9	24.6	13.3	42.2	10.3	7.5	10.7	19.7
1998	24.4	25.0	14.7	(NA)	11.0	7.5	11.9	22.2
1999	25.2	25.9	15.4	42.4	10.9	7.1	11.1	24.8
2000	25.6	26.1	16.5	43.9	10.6	6.9	13.0	23.0

NA Not available.   [1] Includes other races, not shown separately.   [2] Persons of Hispanic origin may be of any race.
[3] Includes persons of other Hispanic origin, not shown separately.   [4] Through 1990, completed 4 years of high school or more and 4 years of college or more.

Source: U.S. Census Bureau, *U.S. Census of Population, U.S. Summary*, PC80-1-C1 and *Current Population Report* P20-536, earlier reports, and unpublished data. Internet site <http://www.census.gov/population/www/socdemo/educ-attn.html>.

No. 216. Educational Attainment by Race, Hispanic Origin, and Sex: 1960 to 2000

[In percent. See Table 215 for headnote and totals for both sexes]

Year	All races [1] Male	All races [1] Female	White Male	White Female	Black Male	Black Female	Asian and Pacific Islander Male	Asian and Pacific Islander Female	Hispanic [2] Male	Hispanic [2] Female
HIGH SCHOOL GRADUATE OR MORE [3]										
1960	39.5	42.5	41.6	44.7	18.2	21.8	(NA)	(NA)	(NA)	(NA)
1970	51.9	52.8	54.0	55.0	30.1	32.5	(NA)	(NA)	37.9	34.2
1980	67.3	65.8	69.6	68.1	50.8	51.5	(NA)	(NA)	67.3	65.8
1985	74.4	73.5	76.0	75.1	58.4	60.8	(NA)	(NA)	48.5	47.4
1990	77.7	77.5	79.1	79.0	65.8	66.5	84.0	77.2	50.3	51.3
1995	81.7	81.6	83.0	83.0	73.4	74.1	(NA)	(NA)	52.9	53.8
1996	81.9	81.6	82.7	82.8	74.3	74.2	86.0	80.7	53.0	53.3
1997	82.0	82.2	82.9	83.2	73.5	76.0	(NA)	(NA)	54.9	54.6
1998	82.8	82.9	83.6	83.8	75.2	76.7	(NA)	(NA)	55.7	55.3
1999	83.4	83.4	84.2	84.3	76.7	77.2	86.9	82.8	56.0	56.3
2000	84.2	84.0	84.8	85.0	78.7	78.3	88.2	83.4	56.6	57.5
COLLEGE GRADUATE OR MORE [3]										
1960	9.7	5.8	10.3	6.0	2.8	3.3	(NA)	(NA)	(NA)	(NA)
1970	13.5	8.1	14.4	8.4	4.2	4.6	(NA)	(NA)	7.8	4.3
1980	20.1	12.8	21.3	13.3	8.4	8.3	(NA)	(NA)	9.4	6.0
1985	23.1	16.0	24.0	16.3	11.2	11.0	(NA)	(NA)	9.7	7.3
1990	24.4	18.4	25.3	19.0	11.9	10.8	44.9	35.4	9.8	8.7
1995	26.0	20.2	27.2	21.0	13.6	12.9	(NA)	(NA)	10.1	8.4
1996	26.0	21.4	26.9	21.8	12.4	14.6	46.4	37.3	10.3	8.3
1997	26.2	21.7	27.0	22.3	12.5	13.9	(NA)	(NA)	10.6	10.1
1998	26.5	22.4	27.3	22.8	13.9	15.4	(NA)	(NA)	11.1	10.9
1999	27.5	23.1	28.5	23.5	14.2	16.4	46.2	39.0	10.7	11.0
2000	27.8	23.6	28.5	23.9	16.3	16.7	47.6	40.7	10.7	10.6

NA Not available.   [1] Includes other races, not shown separately.   [2] Persons of Hispanic origin may be of any race.
[3] Through 1990, completed 4 years of high school or more and 4 years of college or more.

Source: U.S. Census Bureau, *U.S. Census of Population, 1960, 1970, and 1980, Vol. 1*; and *Current Population Reports* P20-536; earlier reports, and unpublished data. Internet site <http://www.census.gov/population/www/socdemo/educ-attn.html>.

No. 217. Educational Attainment by Selected Characteristic: 2000

[For persons 25 years old and over (175,230 represents 175,230,000). As of March. Based on the Current Population Survey; see text, Section 1, Population, and Appendix III. For composition of regions, see map inside front cover]

Characteristic	Population (1,000)	Percent of population—highest level					
		Not a high school graduate	High school graduate	Some college, but no degree	Associate's degree [1]	Bachelor's degree	Advanced degree
Total persons	175,230	15.8	33.1	17.6	7.8	17.0	8.6
Age:							
25 to 34 years old...........	37,786	11.8	30.6	19.5	8.8	22.7	6.6
35 to 44 years old...........	44,805	11.4	33.7	18.4	9.5	18.4	8.6
45 to 54 years old...........	36,630	11.1	31.0	18.7	9.0	18.7	11.5
55 to 64 years old...........	23,387	18.3	35.7	16.3	6.2	13.1	10.4
65 to 74 years old...........	17,796	26.4	37.4	14.2	4.5	10.4	7.1
75 years old or over	14,825	35.4	34.1	13.2	3.9	8.7	4.7
Sex:							
Male....................	83,611	15.8	31.9	17.4	7.1	17.8	10.0
Female..................	91,620	16.0	34.3	17.7	8.4	16.3	7.3
Race:							
White	147,067	15.1	33.4	17.4	8.0	17.3	8.8
Black	20,036	21.5	35.2	20.0	6.8	11.4	5.1
Other	8,127	16.6	23.8	14.0	7.3	25.2	13.2
Hispanic origin:							
Hispanic	17,150	43.0	27.9	13.5	5.0	7.3	3.3
Non-Hispanic.............	158,080	13.0	33.7	18.0	8.1	18.1	9.1
Region:							
Northeast	34,145	15.0	35.3	13.5	7.7	18.0	10.5
Midwest	40,079	13.1	35.5	18.2	8.3	16.8	8.0
South	62,292	18.3	34.0	17.1	7.0	15.7	7.8
West....................	38,713	15.7	27.4	21.1	8.6	18.6	8.6
Marital status:							
Never married...........	26,045	14.9	29.9	17.8	7.5	21.5	8.4
Married spouse present...	109,296	13.4	33.0	17.4	8.2	18.3	9.8
Married spouse absent [2]	2,560	28.0	32.8	14.6	5.5	11.6	7.3
Separated	4,141	24.6	38.0	17.8	6.3	10.1	3.2
Widowed................	13,641	35.8	36.1	13.1	4.9	6.8	3.2
Divorced................	19,549	13.8	35.4	21.6	8.8	13.3	7.0
Civilian labor force status:							
Employed	114,600	9.7	31.8	18.8	9.0	20.4	10.4
Unemployed.............	3,908	23.5	36.0	18.7	7.0	10.2	4.7
Not in the labor force........	56,095	28.3	35.9	14.8	5.4	10.7	5.0

[1] Includes vocational degrees.   [2] Excludes those separated.

Source: U.S. Census Bureau, *Current Population Reports*, P20-536; and unpublished data.

No. 218. Earnings by Highest Degree Earned: 1999

[For persons 18 years old and over with earnings. Persons as of March, the following year. Based on Current Population Survey; see text, Section 1, Population, and Appendix III. For definition of mean, see Guide to Tabular Presentation]

Characteristic	Total persons	Level of highest degree							
		Not a high school graduate	High school graduate only	Some college, no degree	Associate's	Bachelor's	Master's	Professional	Doctorate
MEAN EARNINGS (dol.)									
All persons [1]	32,356	16,121	24,572	26,958	32,152	45,678	55,641	100,987	86,833
Age:									
25 to 34 years old....	29,901	16,916	24,040	26,914	28,088	39,768	46,768	58,043	60,852
35 to 44 years old....	36,900	18,984	27,444	34,219	35,370	50,153	56,816	100,240	94,936
45 to 54 years old....	41,465	19,707	28,883	36,935	37,508	54,922	62,158	116,327	87,659
55 to 64 years old....	38,577	22,212	27,558	34,240	35,703	50,141	57,580	132,326	97,214
65 years old and over .	24,263	12,121	18,704	19,052	17,609	30,624	35,639	104,055	78,333
Sex:									
Male.............	40,257	18,855	30,414	33,614	40,047	57,706	68,367	120,352	97,357
Female...........	23,551	12,145	18,092	20,241	25,079	42,378	59,792		61,136
White.............	33,326	16,623	25,270	27,674	32,686	46,894	55,622	103,450	87,746
Male.............	41,598	19,320	31,279	34,825	41,010	59,606	68,831	123,086	97,076
Female...........	23,756	12,405	18,381	20,188	24,928	32,507	41,845	57,314	64,080
Black.............	24,979	13,569	20,991	24,101	28,772	37,422	48,777	75,509	(B)
Male.............	28,821	16,391	25,849	27,538	31,885	42,530	54,642	(B)	(B)
Female...........	21,694	10,734	16,506	21,355	26,787	33,184	44,761	(B)	(B)
Hispanic [2]	22,096	16,106	20,704	23,115	29,329	36,212	50,576	64,029	(B)
Male.............	24,970	18,020	23,736	27,288	36,740	42,733	60,013	(B)	(B)
Female...........	18,187	12,684	16,653	18,782	22,695	29,249	41,118	(B)	(B)

B Base figure too small to meet statistical standards for reliability of a derived figure.   [1] Includes other races, not shown separately.   [2] Persons of Hispanic origin may be of any race.

Source: U.S. Census Bureau, *Current Population Reports*, P20-536.

No. 219. Educational Attainment by State: 1990 and 2000

[In percent. As of March 2000 and April 1990. For persons 25 years old and over, except as indicated. Based on the 1990 Census of Population and the Current Population Survey; see text, Section 1, Population, and Appendix III]

State	1990						2000	
	Not a high school graduate	High school graduate or more	Bachelor's degree or more			Drop-outs [1]	High school graduate or more	College graduate or more
			Total	Bachelor's degree	Advanced degree			
United States	**24.8**	**75.2**	**20.3**	**13.1**	**7.2**	**11.2**	**84.1**	**25.6**
Alabama	33.1	66.9	15.7	10.1	5.5	12.6	77.5	20.4
Alaska	13.4	86.6	23.0	15.0	8.0	10.9	90.4	28.1
Arizona	21.3	78.7	20.3	13.3	7.0	14.4	85.1	24.6
Arkansas	33.7	66.3	13.3	8.9	4.5	11.4	81.7	18.4
California	23.8	76.2	23.4	15.3	8.1	14.2	81.2	27.5
Colorado	15.6	84.4	27.0	18.0	9.0	9.8	89.7	34.6
Connecticut	20.8	79.2	27.2	16.2	11.0	9.0	88.2	31.6
Delaware	22.5	77.5	21.4	13.7	7.7	10.4	86.1	24.0
District of Columbia	26.9	73.1	33.3	16.1	17.2	13.9	83.2	38.3
Florida	25.6	74.4	18.3	12.0	6.3	14.3	84.0	22.8
Georgia	29.1	70.9	19.3	12.9	6.4	14.1	82.6	23.1
Hawaii	19.9	80.1	22.9	15.8	7.1	7.5	87.4	26.3
Idaho	20.3	79.7	17.7	12.4	5.3	10.4	86.2	20.0
Illinois	23.8	76.2	21.0	13.6	7.5	10.6	85.5	27.1
Indiana	24.4	75.6	15.6	9.2	6.4	11.4	84.6	17.1
Iowa	19.9	80.1	16.9	11.7	5.2	6.6	89.7	25.5
Kansas	18.7	81.3	21.1	14.1	7.0	8.7	88.1	27.3
Kentucky	35.4	64.6	13.6	8.1	5.5	13.3	78.7	20.5
Louisiana	31.7	68.3	16.1	10.5	5.6	12.5	80.8	22.5
Maine	21.2	78.8	18.8	12.7	6.1	8.3	89.3	24.1
Maryland	21.6	78.4	26.5	15.6	10.9	10.9	85.7	32.3
Massachusetts	20.0	80.0	27.2	16.6	10.6	8.5	85.1	32.7
Michigan	23.2	76.8	17.4	10.9	6.4	10.0	86.2	23.0
Minnesota	17.6	82.4	21.8	15.6	6.3	6.4	90.8	31.2
Mississippi	35.7	64.3	14.7	9.7	5.1	11.8	80.3	18.7
Missouri	26.1	73.9	17.8	11.7	6.1	11.4	86.6	26.2
Montana	19.0	81.0	19.8	14.1	5.7	8.1	89.6	23.8
Nebraska	18.2	81.8	18.9	13.1	5.9	7.0	90.4	24.6
Nevada	21.2	78.8	15.3	10.1	5.2	15.2	82.8	19.3
New Hampshire	17.8	82.2	24.4	16.4	7.9	9.4	88.1	30.1
New Jersey	23.3	76.7	24.9	16.0	8.8	9.6	87.3	30.1
New Mexico	24.9	75.1	20.4	12.1	8.3	11.7	82.2	23.6
New York	25.2	74.8	23.1	13.2	9.9	9.9	82.5	28.7
North Carolina	30.0	70.0	17.4	12.0	5.4	12.5	79.2	23.2
North Dakota	23.3	76.7	18.1	13.5	4.5	4.6	85.5	22.6
Ohio	24.3	75.7	17.0	11.1	5.9	8.9	87.0	24.6
Oklahoma	25.4	74.6	17.8	11.8	6.0	10.4	86.1	22.5
Oregon	18.5	81.5	20.6	13.6	7.0	11.8	88.1	27.2
Pennsylvania	25.3	74.7	17.9	11.3	6.6	9.1	85.7	24.3
Rhode Island	28.0	72.0	21.3	13.5	7.8	11.1	81.3	26.4
South Carolina	31.7	68.3	16.6	11.2	5.4	11.7	83.0	19.0
South Dakota	22.9	77.1	17.2	12.3	4.9	7.7	91.8	25.7
Tennessee	32.9	67.1	16.0	10.5	5.4	13.4	79.9	22.0
Texas	27.9	72.1	20.3	13.9	6.5	12.9	79.2	23.9
Utah	14.9	85.1	22.3	15.4	6.8	8.7	90.7	26.4
Vermont	19.2	80.8	24.3	15.4	8.9	8.0	90.0	28.8
Virginia	24.8	75.2	24.5	15.4	9.1	10.0	86.6	31.9
Washington	16.2	83.8	22.9	15.9	7.0	10.6	91.8	28.6
West Virginia	34.0	66.0	12.3	7.5	4.8	10.9	77.1	15.3
Wisconsin	21.4	78.6	17.7	12.1	5.6	7.1	86.7	23.8
Wyoming	17.0	83.0	18.8	13.1	5.7	6.9	90.0	20.6

[1] For persons 16 to 19 years old. A dropout is a person who is not in regular school and who has not completed the 12th grade or received a general equivalency degree.

Source: U.S. Census Bureau, *1990 Census of Population*, CPH-L-96, and *Current Population Reports*, P20-536.

Education 141

No. 220. Nonfatal Crimes Against Students: 1997 and 1998

[For students aged 12 through 18 (2,721.2 represents 2,721,200). For crimes occurring at school or going to or from school. Based on the National Crime Victimization Survey; see Appendix III]

Student characteristic	1997				1998			
			Violent				Violent	
	Total	Theft	Total	Serious [1]	Total	Theft	Total	Serious [1]
Total (1,000).	2,721.2	1,666.0	1,055.2	201.8	2,715.6	1,562.3	1,153.2	252.7
RATE PER 1,000 STUDENTS								
Total [2].	102	63	40	8	101	58	43	9
Sex:								
Male.	114	64	50	10	111	59	52	10
Female.	91	61	29	5	91	58	33	8
Age:								
12 to 14 years old.	123	69	54	10	125	65	60	14
15 to 18 years old.	86	58	29	6	83	53	30	6
Race/ethnicity:								
White, non-Hispanic	111	67	43	7	105	60	45	9
Black, non-Hispanic.	95	59	36	[3]8	111	64	48	12
Hispanic	76	44	32	10	82	48	34	[3]1
Other, non-Hispanic.	91	72	[3]19	[3]5	89	57	32	[3]4
Urbanicity: [4]								
Urban.	105	63	42	12	117	68	49	13
Suburban	111	66	46	8	97	56	40	7
Rural	79	55	24	[3]2	93	50	43	11
Household income:								
Less than $7,500	64	31	32	[3]3	110	56	53	[3]17
$7,500 to $14,999.	93	53	40	[3]6	97	38	59	[3]12
$15,000 to $24,999	107	65	42	9	126	64	62	10
$25,000 to $34,999	114	71	43	7	102	50	52	15
$35,000 to $49,999	105	56	49	11	86	57	29	[3]6
$50,000 to $74,999	110	75	35	8	110	68	42	10
$75,000 and over	125	84	41	[3]7	112	75	37	[3]6

[1] Includes rape, sexual assault, robbery and aggravated assault. [2] Includes those whose race/ethnicity or incomes are unknown. [3] Estimate based on fewer than 10 cases. [4] Urban: The largest city (or groupings of cities) of an MSA; suburban: those portions of metro areas outside central cities; rural: Places outside MSAs.

Source: U.S. National Center for Education Statistics and U.S. Bureau of Justice Statistics. *Indicators of School Crime and Safety 2000,* October 2000, NCES 2001-017; and earlier issues.

No. 221. Public Schools Reporting Criminal Incidents to the Police: 1996-97

[In percent. For crimes that took place in school buildings, on school buses or grounds, and places holding school-sponsored events. Based on the National Center for Education Statistics' Fast Response Survey System; see source for details]

School characteristic	Any incidents					Serious violent incidents [2]				
	Total	City [1]	Urban fringe [1]	Town [1]	Rural [1]	Total	City [1]	Urban fringe [1]	Town [1]	Rural [1]
Total	56.7	59.3	58.4	63.2	46.9	10.1	16.8	11.2	5.4	7.8
Instructional level:										
Elementary school	45.1	46.9	47.0	52.6	34.2	4.2	6.1	3.3	2.0	5.1
Middle school	74.1	86.7	78.8	70.0	62.0	18.7	35.8	21.7	7.0	15.0
High school	76.9	88.8	84.0	84.2	64.1	20.6	48.0	33.0	12.7	9.4
School enrollment:										
Less than 300	37.8	(B)	(B)	44.9	38.0	3.9	(B)	(B)	8.8	2.5
300 to 999	59.6	54.2	59.2	67.3	56.8	9.3	12.5	9.0	3.2	13.9
1,000 or more	89.1	93.1	86.7	86.5	(B)	32.9	44.2	29.8	15.9	(B)
Minority enrollment:										
Less than 5 percent	46.7	(B)	47.2	53.9	40.8	5.8	(B)	5.9	3.3	7.3
5 to 19 percent	57.7	52.0	62.9	64.0	45.0	10.9	14.5	11.3	10.6	6.8
20 to 49 percent	58.1	54.7	58.5	66.7	53.3	11.1	19.1	10.1	5.0	8.0
50 percent or more	68.3	64.8	62.3	81.5	74.9	14.7	17.6	17.8	4.4	11.6
Free/reduced price lunch eligibility:										
Less than 20 percent	54.4	50.6	57.3	64.2	41.2	8.6	12.2	9.9	7.1	5.6
21 to 34 percent	53.2	56.0	65.5	57.2	39.5	11.7	18.4	13.3	7.1	11.6
35 to 49 percent	59.4	76.1	53.3	63.1	52.5	11.6	34.2	8.6	3.0	8.6
50 to 74 percent	58.8	60.8	54.7	66.6	52.0	8.9	22.9	10.3	2.0	2.3
75 percent or more	59.2	58.5	(B)	(B)	(B)	10.2	8.4	(B)	(B)	(B)

B Base figure too small to meet statistical standards for reliability of a derived figure. [1] City: central city of an MSA; urban fringe: a place within an MSA but not its central city; town: a place outside an MSA, with a population greater than or equal to 2,500 and defined as urban by the U.S. Census Bureau; rural: a place with a population under 2,500 and defined as urban by the U.S. Census Bureau. [2] Includes murder, rape or other sexual battery, suicide, physical attack or fight with a weapon, or robbery.

Source: U.S. National Center for Education Statistics and U.S. Bureau of Justice Statistics. *Indicators of School Crime and Safety 1999,* September 1999, NCES 1999-057.

No. 222. Children Whose Parents Are Involved in School Activities: 1999

[In percent, except as indicated (23,355 represents 23,355,000). Based on the National Household Education Survey; see source for details]

Parental involvement	Students in grades K to 5					Students in grades 6 to 8				
	Total	Two-parent families	One-parent families			Total	Two-parent families	One-parent families		
			Total	Mother	Father			Total	Mother	Father
Total students, 1999 (1,000)	23,355	15,841	7,514	6,634	880	11,252	7,747	3,506	3,010	496
Any adult attending a meeting	84.9	88.6	77.1	77.3	75.7	81.1	85.3	72.0	71.2	77.0
Only mother attended	39.4	25.7	68.2	77.3	(X)	38.7	28.5	61.2	71.2	(X)
Only father attended	5.7	4.1	8.9	(X)	75.7	6.9	5.1	10.9	(X)	77.0
Both attended	39.8	58.7	(X)	(X)	(X)	35.6	51.7	(X)	(X)	(X)
Any adult attending a conference	87.7	89.4	84.1	85.1	76.7	71.1	72.3	68.5	68.1	70.8
Only mother attended	52.0	41.0	75.1	85.1	(X)	41.0	33.1	58.8	68.1	(X)
Only father attended	6.4	5.1	9.0	(X)	76.7	7.1	5.8	10.0	(X)	70.8
Both attended	29.4	43.3	(X)	(X)	(X)	23.0	33.4	(X)	(X)	(X)
Any adult attending a class event	70.8	74.0	64.1	63.1	71.2	67.8	72.6	57.3	55.9	66.1
Only mother attended	31.5	20.0	55.7	63.1	(X)	24.6	14.1	48.0	55.9	(X)
Only father attended	5.1	3.6	8.3	(X)	71.2	5.3	3.5	9.3	(X)	66.1
Both attended	34.2	50.4	(X)	(X)	(X)	37.9	55.0	(X)	(X)	(X)
Any adult acted as a volunteer	48.9	55.5	34.8	36.3	23.1	31.7	36.1	21.9	22.1	20.6
Only mother attended	37.0	39.3	32.1	36.3	(X)	21.8	23.0	19.0	22.1	(X)
Only father attended	3.2	3.4	2.7	(X)	23.1	3.1	3.1	2.9	(X)	20.6
Both attended	8.6	12.7	(X)	(X)	(X)	6.8	9.9	(X)	(X)	(X)
Number of activities at least one parent participated in:										
None	3.5	2.2	6.5	6.2	8.3	7.3	4.4	13.7	14.1	11.2
One	7.4	5.7	11.0	11.1	10.3	11.7	11.0	13.4	13.9	10.8
Two	19.7	17.6	24.3	24.2	25.0	25.8	24.8	27.9	28.0	27.3
Three	32.0	31.7	32.5	31.7	39.0	32.2	33.5	29.2	28.5	33.5
Four	37.4	42.9	25.7	26.8	17.4	23.0	26.2	15.7	15.5	17.2
Number of activities both parents participated in:										
None	24.0	24.0	(X)	(X)	(X)	27.0	27.0	(X)	(X)	(X)
One	21.7	21.7	(X)	(X)	(X)	24.8	24.8	(X)	(X)	(X)
Two	26.0	26.0	(X)	(X)	(X)	24.2	24.2	(X)	(X)	(X)
Three	21.5	21.5	(X)	(X)	(X)	19.5	19.5	(X)	(X)	(X)
Four	6.7	6.7	(X)	(X)	(X)	4.5	4.5	(X)	(X)	(X)

X Not applicable.
Source: U S. National Center for Education Statistics, *National Household Education Survey*, 1999.

No. 223. Children's Involvement in Home Literacy Activities: 1993 and 1999

[In percent, except number of children (8,579 represents 8,579,000). For children 3 to 5 years old not yet enrolled in kindergarten who participated in activities with a family member. Based on the National Education Household Survey; see source. See also Table 226]

Characteristic	Children (1,000)		Read to [1]		Told a story [1]		Taught letters, words, or numbers [1]		Visited a library [2]	
	1993	1999	1993	1999	1993	1999	1993	1999	1993	1999
Total	8,579	8,549	78	81	43	50	58	64	38	36
Age:										
3 years old	3,889	3,827	79	81	46	52	57	65	34	33
4 years old	3,713	3,722	78	81	41	49	58	63	41	39
5 years old	976	1,001	76	79	36	44	58	64	38	41
Race/ethnicity:										
White, non-Hispanic	5,902	5,296	85	89	44	53	58	65	42	39
Black, non-Hispanic	1,271	1,258	66	71	39	45	63	68	29	35
Hispanic	1,026	1,421	58	61	38	40	54	55	26	25
Other	381	574	73	81	50	53	59	69	43	43
Mother's home language: [3]										
English	7,805	7,599	81	84	44	52	58	66	39	39
Not English	603	683	42	48	36	31	52	45	26	19
Mother's highest education: [3]										
Less than high school	1,036	952	60	61	37	36	56	60	22	18
High school	3,268	2,556	76	76	41	48	56	63	31	30
Vocational ed. or some college	2,624	2,586	83	85	45	52	60	67	44	40
College degree	912	1,455	90	91	48	55	56	65	55	50
Graduate/professional training or degree	569	734	90	93	50	54	60	62	59	48
Family type:										
Two parents	6,226	5,997	81	85	44	52	57	64	41	40
None or one parent	2,353	2,553	71	72	41	44	59	65	30	29
Poverty status:										
Above threshold	6,323	6,575	82	85	44	52	57	66	41	40
Below threshold	2,256	1,975	68	69	39	42	59	58	28	24

[1] Three or more times in the past week.   [2] At least once in the past month.   [3] Excludes children with no mother in the household and no female guardian
Source: U.S. National Center for Education Statistics, *Statistical Brief*, NCES 2000-026, November 1999.

Education 143

No. 224. Children Who Speak a Language Other Than English at Home: 1979 to 1999

[In percent, except total. For children 5 to 17 years old (3.8 represents 3,800,000). For children reported to speak English less than "very well." Based on the Current Population Survey; see text Section 1, Population, and Appendix III]

Characteristic	1979	1989	1992	95 [1]	1999 [1]
Children who speak another language at home (mil.) . .	3.8	5.3	6.4	6.7	8.8
Percent of children 5 to 17 years old	8.5	12.6	14.2	14.1	16.7
Race and Hispanic origin:					
White, non-Hispanic	3.2	3.5	3.7	3.6	3.9
Black, non-Hispanic	1.3	2.4	4.2	3.0	4.5
Hispanic [2]	75.1	71.2	76.6	73.9	70.9
Other, non-Hispanic [3]	44.1	53.4	58.3	45.5	51.0
Region: [4]					
Northeast	10.5	13.5	16.2	15.1	17.7
Midwest	3.7	4.9	5.6	5.9	7.5
South	6.8	10.7	11.1	11.7	14.3
West	17.0	24.2	27.2	26.4	28.8
Children who speak another language at home and have difficulty speaking English (mil.)	1.3	1.9	2.2	2.4	2.6
Percent of children 5 to 17 years old	2.8	4.4	4.9	5.1	5.0
Race and Hispanic origin:					
White, non-Hispanic	0.5	0.8	0.6	0.7	1.0
Black, non-Hispanic	0.3	0.5	1.3	0.9	1.0
Hispanic [2]	28.7	27.4	29.9	31.0	23.4
Other, non-Hispanic [3]	19.8	20.4	21.0	14.1	11.7
Region: [4]					
Northeast	2.9	4.8	5.3	5.0	4.4
Midwest	1.1	1.3	1.6	2.3	2.0
South	2.2	3.8	3.5	3.4	3.6
West	6.5	8.8	10.4	11.4	10.5

[1] Reflects revised interviewing techniques and/or change in population controls to the 1990 census-based estimates. [2] Persons of Hispanic origin may be of any race. [3] Includes mostly Asian/Pacific Islanders, but also American Indian/Alaska Native children. [4] For composition of regions, see map, inside front cover.

Source: Federal Interagency Forum on Child and Family Statistics, *America's Children: Key National Indicators of Well-Being*, 2001.

No. 225. Preprimary School Enrollment—Summary: 1970 to 1999

[As of October. Civilian noninstitutional population (10,949 represents 10,949,000). Includes public and nonpublic nursery school and kindergarten programs. Excludes 5 year olds enrolled in elementary school. Based on Current Population Survey; see text, Section 1, Population, and Appendix III]

Item	1970	1975	1980	1985	1990	1995	1997	1998	1999
NUMBER OF CHILDREN (1,000)									
Population, 3 to 5 years old	10,949	10,183	9,284	10,733	11,207	12,518	12,121	12,078	11,920
Total enrolled [1]	4,104	4,954	4,878	5,865	6,659	7,739	7,861	7,788	7,844
Nursery	1,094	1,745	1,981	2,477	3,378	4,331	4,438	4,512	4,506
Public	332	570	628	846	1,202	1,950	2,207	2,212	2,209
Private	762	1,174	1,353	1,631	2,177	2,381	2,231	2,300	2,298
Kindergarten	3,010	3,211	2,897	3,388	3,281	3,408	3,422	3,276	3,338
Public	2,498	2,682	2,438	2,847	2,767	2,799	2,847	2,674	2,777
Private	511	528	459	541	513	608	..575	602	560
White	3,443	4,105	3,994	4,757	5,389	6,144	6,086	5,985	6,093
Black	586	731	725	919	964	1,236	1,356	1,346	1,264
Hispanic [2]	(NA)	(NA)	370	496	642	1,040	1,142	1,170	1,189
3 years old	454	683	857	1,035	1,205	1,489	1,529	1,498	1,505
4 years old	1,007	1,418	1,423	1,765	2,086	2,553	2,665	2,666	2,768
5 years old	2,643	2,852	2,598	3,065	3,367	3,697	3,667	3,624	3,571
ENROLLMENT RATE									
Total enrolled [1]	37.5	48.6	52.5	54.6	59.4	61.8	64.8	64.5	65.8
White	37.8	48.6	52.7	54.7	59.7	63.0	64.1	63.6	65.3
Black	34.9	48.1	51.8	55.8	57.8	58.9	68.6	68.6	67.9
Hispanic [2]	(NA)	(NA)	43.3	43.3	49.0	51.1	52.5	54.0	53.2
3 years old	12.9	21.5	27.3	28.8	32.6	35.9	38.7	37.6	39.0
4 years old	27.8	40.5	46.3	49.1	56.0	61.6	66.1	66.6	68.8
5 years old	69.3	81.3	84.7	86.5	88.8	87.5	88.6	88.7	88.5

NA Not available. [1] Includes races not shown separately. [2] Persons of Hispanic origin may be of any race. The method of identifying Hispanic children was changed in 1980 from allocation based on status of mother to status reported for each child. The number of Hispanic children using the new method is larger.

Source: U.S. Census Bureau, *Current Population Reports*, P20-533.

144   Education

No. 226. Children's School Readiness Skills: 1993 and 1999

[In percent. For children 3 to 5 years old not yet enrolled in kindergarten. Based on the National Education Household Survey; see source for details. See also Table 223]

Characteristic	Recognizes all letters 1993	Recognizes all letters 1999	Counts to 20 or higher 1993	Counts to 20 or higher 1999	Writes name 1993	Writes name 1999	Reads or pretends to read storybooks 1993	Reads or pretends to read storybooks 1999	Has three to four skills 1993	Has three to four skills 1999
Total	21	24	52	57	50	51	72	74	35	39
Age:										
3 years old	11	15	37	41	22	24	66	70	15	20
4 years old	28	28	62	67	70	70	75	76	49	50
5 years old	36	44	78	81	84	87	81	77	65	69
Sex:										
Male	19	21	49	54	47	47	68	70	32	35
Female	23	27	56	60	53	56	76	77	39	43
Race/ethnicity:										
White, non-Hispanic	23	25	56	60	52	54	76	79	39	42
Black, non-Hispanic	18	25	53	60	45	49	63	66	31	35
Hispanic	10	14	32	41	42	43	59	57	22	25
Other	22	30	49	59	52	57	70	79	36	48
Mother's home language:										
English	22	25	55	60	51	53	73	76	37	41
Not English	9	8	24	25	38	34	52	45	17	14
Mother's highest education:										
Less than high school	8	7	30	36	40	32	55	53	19	15
High school	17	17	48	48	48	49	70	69	30	31
Vocational education or some college	23	25	59	60	51	52	79	79	39	42
College degree	31	35	68	73	58	61	84	84	52	54
Graduate/professional training or degree	39	40	68	73	59	64	83	83	55	57
Mother's employment status:										
Employed	23	24	57	59	52	53	75	75	39	40
Unemployed	17	15	41	53	46	39	67	64	29	32
Not in the labor force	18	24	49	54	47	50	68	73	32	38
Family type:										
Two parents	22	26	54	58	51	53	74	75	37	41
None or one parent	18	19	49	54	47	48	65	69	31	33
Poverty status:										
Above threshold	24	28	57	62	53	56	74	77	40	45
Below threshold	12	10	41	39	41	37	64	63	23	19

Source: U.S. National Center for Education Statistics, *Home Literacy Activities and Signs of Children's Emerging Literacy, 1993 and 1999*, NCES 2000-026, November 1999.

No. 227. Charter Schools—Creation Status by Year of Opening: 1999

[Charter schools are public schools that come into existence through a contract with either a state agency or local school board. In 1998-99 they enrolled about 252,000 students in 27 states with open charter schools, or 0.8% of students in public schools in those states. Based on a survey; see source for details]

Item	Total	Creation status (percent) All schools	New	Pre-existing Public	Pre-existing Private
All charter schools	975	100.0	72.2	17.7	10.1
Opened in—					
1998-99	318	100.0	76.4	15.0	8.6
1997-98	252	100.0	82.5	9.9	7.5
1996-97	171	100.0	66.7	17.5	15.8
1995-96	145	100.0	64.1	20.7	15.2
1994-95 or earlier	94	100.0	53.2	43.6	3.2

Source: U.S. Department of Education, Office of Education Research and Improvement, *The State of Charter Schools 2000, Fourth-Year Report*, January 2000.

U.S. Census Bureau, Statistical Abstract of the United States: 2001

No. 228. Public Elementary and Secondary Schools—Summary: 1980 to 2000

[For school year ending in year shown, except as indicated (48,041 represents 48,041,000). Data are estimates]

Item	Unit	1980	1985	1990	1995	1998	1999	2000
School districts, total	Number.	16,044	15,812	15,552	14,947	14,858	14,904	15,001
ENROLLMENT								
Population 5-17 years old [1]	1,000. . .	48,041	44,787	44,949	48,205	50,504	50,914	51,257
Percent of resident population	Percent .	21.4	19.0	18.2	18.5	18.9	18.8	18.8
Fall enrollment [2]	1,000. . .	41,778	39,354	40,527	43,898	45,885	46,274	46,540
Percent of population 5-17 years old [3]	Percent .	87.0	87.9	90.2	91.1	90.9	90.9	90.8
Elementary [3]	1,000. . .	24,397	23,830	26,253	28,148	29,228	29,092	29,195
Secondary [4]	1,000. . .	17,381	15,524	14,274	15,750	16,657	17,182	17,345
Average daily attendance (ADA)	1,000. . .	38,411	36,530	37,573	40,792	42,678	42,894	43,162
High school graduates	1,000. . .	2,762	2,424	2,327	2,282	2,435	2,478	2,511
INSTRUCTIONAL STAFF								
Total [5]	1,000. . .	2,521	2,473	2,685	2,924	3,116	3,188	3,272
Classroom teachers.	1,000. . .	2,211	2,175	2,362	2,568	2,745	2,813	2,886
Average salaries:								
Instructional staff.	Dollar . .	16,715	24,666	32,638	38,339	41,272	42,488	43,768
Classroom teachers.	Dollar . .	15,970	23,600	31,367	36,685	39,454	40,580	41,724
REVENUES								
Revenue receipts	Mil. dol. .	97,635	141,013	208,656	273,255	322,501	340,194	352,480
Federal	Mil. dol. .	9,020	9,533	13,184	18,764	22,262	23,774	24,305
State	Mil. dol. .	47,929	69,107	100,787	129,958	158,419	169,064	178,773
Local	Mil. dol. .	40,686	62,373	94,685	124,533	141,820	147,356	149,402
Percent of total:								
Federal	Percent .	9.2	6.8	6.3	6.9	6.9	7.0	6.9
State	Percent .	49.1	49.0	48.3	47.6	49.1	49.7	50.7
Local	Percent .	41.7	44.2	45.4	45.6	44.0	43.3	42.4
EXPENDITURES								
Total	Mil. dol. .	96,105	139,382	209,698	276,584	327,541	348,345	360,303
Current expenditures (day schools) .	Mil. dol. .	85,661	127,230	186,583	242,995	283,283	298,687	308,443
Other current expenditures [6]	Mil. dol. .	1,859	2,109	3,341	5,564	6,662	6,749	6,981
Capital outlay.	Mil. dol. .	6,504	7,529	16,012	21,646	29,328	34,496	35,692
Interest on school debt	Mil. dol. .	2,081	2,514	3,762	6,379	8,268	8,413	9,186
Percent of total:								
Current expenditures (day schools) .	Percent .	89.1	91.3	89.0	87.9	86.5	85.7	85.6
Other current expenditures [6]	Percent .	1.9	1.5	1.6	2.0	2.0	1.9	1.9
Capital outlay.	Percent .	6.8	5.4	7.6	7.8	9.0	9.9	9.9
Interest on school debt	Percent .	2.2	1.8	1.8	2.3	2.5	2.4	2.5
In current dollars:								
Revenue receipts per pupil enrolled.	Dollar . .	2,337	3,583	5,149	6,225	7,028	7,352	7,574
Current expenditures per pupil enrolled.	Dollar . .	2,050	3,233	4,604	5,535	6,174	6,455	6,627
In constant (2000) dollars: [7]								
Revenue receipts per pupil enrolled .	Dollar . .	5,099	5,734	6,863	7,007	7,359	7,566	7,574
Current expenditures per pupil enrolled.	Dollar . .	4,473	5,173	6,137	6,231	6,464	6,643	6,627

[1] Estimated resident population as of July 1 of the previous year, except 1980 and 1990 population enumerated as of April 1. Estimates reflect revisions based on the 1990 Census of Population. [2] Fall enrollment of the previous year. [3] Kindergarten through grade 6. [4] Grades 7 through 12. [5] Full-time equivalent. [6] Current expenses for summer schools, adult education, post-high school vocational education, personnel retraining, etc., when operated by local school districts and not part of regular public elementary and secondary day-school program. [7] Compiled by U.S. Census Bureau. Deflated by the Consumer Price Index, all urban consumers (for school year) supplied by U.S. National Center for Education Statistics.

Source: Except as noted, National Education Association, Washington, DC, Estimates of School Statistics Database (copyright).

[Enrollment in thousands (46,398 represents 46,398,000). Data reported by schools, rather than school districts]

Enrollment size of school	Number of schools					Enrollment [1]				
	Total	Elementary [2]	Secondary [3]	Combined [4]	Other [5]	Total	Elementary [2]	Secondary [3]	Combined [4]	Other [5]
Total	91,062	63,574	22,103	3,770	1,615	46,398	30,300	15,031	994	73
PERCENT										
Total	100.0	100.0	100.0	100.0	100.0	100.0	100.0	100.0	100.0	100.0
Under 100 students	10.1	6.2	15.4	42.0	60.8	0.9	0.6	1.0	5.9	19.4
100 to 199 students	9.5	8.7	10.6	16.5	18.4	2.7	2.8	2.2	8.2	19.0
200 to 299 students	11.2	12.2	8.3	9.5	10.3	5.4	6.5	2.9	8.1	18.8
300 to 399 students	13.1	15.4	7.4	7.0	5.3	8.8	11.3	3.7	8.4	13.8
400 to 499 students	13.2	15.8	7.1	5.2	2.4	11.3	14.8	4.5	8.0	7.7
500 to 599 students	11.5	13.7	6.3	5.3	1.3	12.1	15.7	4.9	10.0	5.1
600 to 699 students	8.5	9.7	5.8	4.3	-	10.5	13.1	5.3	9.5	-
700 to 799 students	6.2	6.8	5.2	2.5	0.2	8.8	10.6	5.6	6.3	1.1
800 to 999 students	7.1	6.9	8.7	3.0	0.6	12.0	12.7	11.0	9.4	3.5
1,000 to 1,499 students . . .	6.1	4.1	12.8	3.1	0.4	13.9	9.9	22.1	12.3	3.6
1,500 to 1,999 students . . .	2.1	0.5	7.0	1.1	-	6.8	1.7	17.0	6.2	-
2,000 to 2,999 students . . .	1.2	0.1	4.7	0.4	0.2	5.4	0.3	15.6	3.2	2.8
3,000 or more students . . .	0.2	(Z)	0.9	0.3	0.2	1.5	0.1	4.3	4.5	5.3
Average enrollment	(X)	(X)	(X)	(X)	(X)	524	478	707	290	135

- Represents zero.   X Not applicable.   Z Less than 0.05 percent.   [1] Data for those schools reporting enrollment.
[2] Includes schools beginning with grade 6 or below and with no grade higher than 8.   [3] Includes schools with no grade lower than 7.   [4] Includes schools with both elementary and secondary grades.   [5] Includes special education, alternative, and other schools not classified by grade span.

Source: U.S. National Center for Education Statistics, *Digest of Education Statistics*, annual.

No. 230. Public Elementary and Secondary School Building Conditions: 1999

[In percent. Based on survey and subject to sampling error; see source]

Characteristic	Schools with at least one building feature inadequate [1][2]	Schools with inadequate building features [2]				
		Roofs	Exterior walls, finishes, windows, and doors	Plumbing	Heating, ventilation, and air conditioning	Electric power
All public schools	50	22	24	25	29	22
School instructional level:						
Elementary school	49	22	23	24	28	21
High school	56	26	27	28	34	25
Combined	54	18	31	25	34	20
School enrollment size:						
Less than 300	55	24	31	28	29	23
300 to 599	50	22	21	27	32	21
600 or more	49	22	23	20	26	22
Region: [3]						
Northeast	39	16	18	19	22	14
Midwest	51	20	28	25	27	19
South	51	25	22	24	28	22
West.	57	27	26	32	40	32
Percent minority enrollment:						
5 percent or less	48	21	26	22	28	18
6 to 20 percent	49	25	23	26	29	18
21 to 50 percent	46	17	17	23	25	19
More than 50 percent	59	28	29	29	34	32
Percent of students in school eligible for free or reduced- price lunch:						
Less than 20 percent	45	18	21	23	28	18
20 to 39 percent	45	21	21	23	26	20
40 to 69 percent	53	22	25	23	29	21
70 percent or more	63	32	30	32	35	30

[1] Includes other conditions, not shown separately.   [2] Based on ratings of fair, poor, and replace by school district respondent.   [3] For composition of regions, see map, inside front cover.

Source: U.S. National Center for Education Statistics, Fast Response Survey System, *Condition of America's Public School Facilities, 1999*, NCES 2000-032, June 2000.

Education 147

No. 231. Public Elementary and Secondary School Enrollment by State: 1980 to 1999

[In thousands (27,647 represents 27,647,000), except rate. As of fall. Includes unclassified students]

State	Enrollment								Enrollment rate [2]			
	K through grade 8 [1]				Grades 9 through 12							
	1980	1990	1998	1999, prel.	1980	1990	1998	1999, prel.	1980	1990	1998	1999, prel.
United States . . .	27,647	29,878	33,346	33,488	13,231	11,338	13,193	13,369	86.2	91.2	91.4	91.4
Alabama.	528	527	542	539	231	195	206	202	87.6	93.2	95.6	95.5
Alaska	60	85	97	96	26	29	38	39	94.0	97.4	94.0	91.4
Arizona.	357	479	623	624	157	161	226	229	88.9	93.3	92.7	89.9
Arkansas	310	314	319	318	138	123	133	133	90.3	95.8	93.4	93.5
California	2,730	3,615	4,270	4,337	1,347	1,336	1,656	1,702	87.1	92.6	93.2	94.0
Colorado.	374	420	501	507	172	154	198	202	92.2	94.6	91.5	91.1
Connecticut.	364	347	399	404	168	122	145	150	83.3	90.2	92.1	90.8
Delaware	62	73	80	80	37	27	33	33	79.5	87.2	66.9	85.3
District of Columbia .	71	61	57	60	29	19	15	17	91.8	100.6	103.4	113.5
Florida	1,042	1,370	1,704	1,725	468	492	634	656	84.4	92.6	90.7	91.0
Georgia	742	849	1,029	1,044	327	303	372	379	86.8	93.7	96.3	96.3
Hawaii	110	123	135	133	55	49	53	53	83.4	87.4	88.6	88.9
Idaho	144	160	169	169	59	61	76	77	95.4	96.9	94.2	95.2
Illinois	1,335	1,310	1,452	1,462	649	512	560	565	82.6	86.9	87.8	88.0
Indiana.	708	676	697	699	347	279	292	289	88.0	90.4	89.3	88.6
Iowa	351	345	337	336	183	139	162	161	88.4	92.1	92.3	92.6
Kansas	283	320	327	326	133	117	145	146	88.7	92.5	91.7	91.8
Kentucky	464	459	464	459	206	177	191	190	83.7	90.5	91.8	91.8
Louisiana	544	586	558	548	234	199	210	209	80.2	88.1	87.0	86.4
Maine.	153	155	151	149	70	60	60	60	91.6	96.5	93.8	93.7
Maryland	493	527	607	607	258	188	235	239	83.9	89.1	89.0	87.9
Massachusetts. . . .	676	604	705	706	346	230	258	265	88.6	88.8	90.6	90.3
Michigan.	1,227	1,145	1,245	1,245	570	440	475	481	86.9	90.3	90.9	90.5
Minnesota.	482	546	587	580	272	211	270	274	87.2	91.3	90.7	89.9
Mississippi	330	372	365	365	147	131	137	135	79.6	91.3	90.7	91.0
Missouri	567	588	651	649	277	228	263	265	83.8	86.5	87.9	88.2
Montana.	106	111	110	107	50	42	50	50	92.9	94.1	92.6	92.3
Nebraska	189	198	200	197	91	76	91	91	86.6	88.7	88.2	87.6
Nevada	101	150	229	240	49	51	82	86	93.4	98.6	94.1	93.4
New Hampshire	112	126	147	147	55	46	58	60	85.3	89.1	90.3	89.7
New Jersey.	820	784	936	954	426	306	333	335	81.5	85.9	87.8	88.3
New Mexico	186	208	232	229	85	94	96	96	89.5	94.4	89.5	89.1
New York	1,838	1,828	2,028	2,034	1,033	770	849	854	80.8	86.6	89.2	89.5
North Carolina.	786	783	921	935	343	304	334	341	90.1	94.8	90.6	90.7
North Dakota.	77	85	77	75	40	33	38	38	85.9	92.6	93.6	93.3
Ohio	1,312	1,258	1,301	1,296	645	514	541	540	84.8	88.0	87.6	87.3
Oklahoma.	399	425	448	447	179	154	181	180	92.9	95.1	96.2	96.5
Oregon.	319	340	380	378	145	132	163	167	88.5	90.6	89.6	89.7
Pennsylvania.	1,231	1,172	1,267	1,262	678	496	549	555	80.4	83.5	84.9	84.9
Rhode Island.	98	102	112	114	51	37	42	43	80.1	87.5	88.2	87.3
South Carolina.	426	452	478	484	193	170	187	183	88.1	93.9	94.5	94.9
South Dakota.	86	95	91	90	42	34	42	41	87.4	89.9	88.2	88.4
Tennessee	602	598	665	664	252	226	241	252	87.8	93.5	93.3	94.1
Texas.	2,049	2,511	2,868	2,896	851	872	1,077	1,096	92.4	98.4	97.9	97.8
Utah	250	325	329	329	93	122	153	151	98.2	97.8	96.6	96.6
Vermont	66	71	73	72	29	25	32	32	87.9	94.3	96.9	97.4
Virginia.	703	728	815	817	307	270	309	317	90.7	94.2	93.6	93.4
Washington.	515	613	696	695	242	227	302	309	91.7	94.1	91.9	91.5
West Virginia.	270	224	206	203	113	98	92	88	92.6	95.7	96.9	96.4
Wisconsin	528	566	601	596	303	232	279	281	82.1	86.1	86.5	86.4
Wyoming	70	71	64	62	28	27	31	30	97.3	97.7	96.5	95.5

[1] Data include a small number of prekindergarten students. [2] Percent of persons 5-17 years old. Based on enumerated resident population as of April 1, 1980, and 1990, and estimated resident population as of July 1 for other years. Data not adjusted for revisions based on the 1990 Census of Population.

Source: U.S. National Center for Education Statistics, *Digest of Education Statistics*, annual.

U.S. Census Bureau, Statistical Abstract of the United States: 2001

No. 232. Public Elementary and Secondary School Enrollment by Grade: 1980 to 1999

[In thousands (40,877 represents 40,877,000). As of fall of year. Kindergarten includes nursery schools]

Grade	1980	1985	1990	1992	1993	1994	1995	1996	1997	1998	1999, prel.
Pupils enrolled	40,877	39,422	41,217	42,823	43,4u5	44,111	44,840	45,611	46,127 · 46,539		46,857
Kindergarten and grades 1 to 8 .	27,647	27,034	29,878	31,088	31,504	31,898	32,341	32,764	33,073	33,346	33,488
Kindergarten	2,689	3,192	3,610	3,817	3,922	4,047	4,173	4,202	4,198	4,172	4,148
First	2,894	3,239	3,499	3,542	3,529	3,593	3,671	3,770	3,755	3,727	3,684
Second	2,800	2,941	3,327	3,431	3,429	3,440	3,507	3,600	3,689	3,681	3,655
Third	2,893	2,895	3,297	3,361	3,437	3,439	3,445	3,524	3,597	3,696	3,690
Fourth	3,107	2,771	3,248	3,342	3,361	3,426	3,431	3,454	3,507	3,592	3,686
Fifth	3,130	2,776	3,197	3,325	3,350	3,372	3,438	3,453	3,458	3,520	3,604
Sixth	3,038	2,789	3,110	3,303	3,356	3,381	3,395	3,494	3,492	3,497	3,564
Seventh	3,085	2,938	3,067	3,299	3,355	3,404	3,422	3,464	3,520	3,530	3,541
Eighth	3,086	2,982	2,979	3,129	3,249	3,302	3,356	3,403	3,415	3,480	3,497
Unclassified [1]	924	511	543	539	515	494	502	401	442	451	418 ·
Grades 9 to 12	13,231	12,388	˙1,338	11,735	11,961	12,213	12,500	12,847	13,054	13,193	13,369
Ninth	3,377	3,439	3,169	3,352	3,487	3,604	3,704	3,801	3,819	3,856	3,935
Tenth	3,368	3,230	2,896	3,027	3,050	3,131	3,237	3,323	3,376	3,382	3,415
Eleventh	3,195	2,866	2,612	2,656	2,751	2,748	2,826	2,930	2,972	3,021	3,034
Twelfth	2,925	2,550	2,381	2,431	2,424	2,488	2,487	2,586	2,673	2,722	2,782
Unclassified [1]	366	303	282	269	248	242	245	206	214	212	203

[1] Includes ungraded and special education.

Source: U.S. National Center for Education Statistics, *Digest of Education Statistics*, annual.

No. 233. School Enrollment Below Postsecondary—Summary by Sex, Race, and Hispanic Origin: 1999

[In thousands (57,191 represents 57,191,000), except percent and rate. As of October. Covers civilian noninstitutional population enrolled in nursery school through high school. Based on Current Population Survey, see text, Section 1, Population, and Appendix III]

Characteristic		Sex		Race and Hispanic origin				
				White			Asian and Pacific Islander	
	Total [1]	Male	Female	Total	Non-Hispanic	Black		Hispanic [2]
All students	57,191	29,300	27,892	44,578	36,474	9,285	2,580	8,829
Nursery	4,578	2,311	2,267	3,590	3,044	729	205	585
Full day	2,293	1,169	1,124	1,621	1,713	525	109	271
Part day	2,285	1,142	1,144	1,968	1,332	204	96	314
Kindergarten	3,824	1,958	1,867	2,956	2,307	632	195	666
Elementary	32,873	16,867	16,006	25,616	20,779	5,388	1,461	5,088
High school	15,916	8,164	7,752	12,416	10,344	2,536	719	2,290
Students in public schools . . .	49,339	25,258	24,079	37,919	30,259	8,556	2,253	8,081
Nursery	2,269	1,128	1,141	1,571	1,146	569	96	458
Full day	1,072	567	504	745	624	380	56	217
Part day	1,198	561	637	826	522	189	40	241
Kindergarten	3,167	1,609	1,557	2,422	1,839	558	148	594
Elementary	29,264	14,979	14,284	22,552	17,960	5,002	1,343	4,829
High school	14,638	7,542	7,097	11,374	9,314	2,427	666	2,200
Population 15 to 17 years old: Percent below modal grade [3] .	30.8	36.2	25.1	30.0	28.9	34.8	25.6	36.5
Students, 10th to 12th grade: Annual dropout rate	4.7	4.3	5.1	4.4	3.8	6.0	4.8	7.1
Population 18 to 24 years old . .	26,042	12,906	13,136	20,865	17,080	3,827	1,130	3,954
Dropouts	3,413	1,818	1,594	2,680	1,404	613	58	1,340
High school graduates	21,127	10,201	10,926	16,755	14,812	2,907	1,019	2,325
Enrolled in college	9,259	4,396	4,863	7,151	6,735	ˎ1,142	626	740

[1] Includes other races, not shown separately. [2] Persons of Hispanic origin may be of any race. [3] The modal grade is the grade most common for a given age.

Source: U.S. Census Bureau, *Current Population Reports*, P20-533.

U.S. Census Bureau, Statistical Abstract of the United States: 2001

No. 234. Employed Students by Selected Characteristic: 1997-98

[In percent. For students 14 to 16 years old at the beginning of the 1997-98 school year who held a job with an employer during the school year or following summer. Excludes freelance work, such as babysitting or mowing lawns. Based on the National Longitudinal Survey of Youth 1997; see source for details]

Characteristic	Students with an employer job	Students who worked during the school year [1]			
		Total	School year and summer	School year only	Summer only [2]
Total, age 14 [3]	33.4	18.3	15.1	3.2	15.1
Male	39.2	21.8	17.3	4.5	17.4
Female.	27.3	14.7	12.8	1.9	12.6
White, non-Hispanic	38.3	22.4	18.8	3.6	15.9
Black, non-Hispanic	22.5	9.3	6.9	2.4	13.2
Hispanic origin.	24.3	12.9	10.0	2.9	11.4
Enrolled in grade 8	28.8	12.3	10.1	2.2	16.5
Enrolled in grade 9	35.7	20.4	16.8	3.6	15.3
Total, age 15 [3]	60.1	39.0	34.7	4.2	21.1
Male	62.4	41.5	37.6	3.9	20.9
Female.	57.5	36.1	31.5	4.6	21.4
White, non-Hispanic	65.0	42.3	37.9	4.4	22.7
Black, non-Hispanic	47.6	30.5	27.5	2.9	17.2
Hispanic origin.	54.1	36.2	31.1	5.1	17.9
Enrolled in grade 9	54.9	33.9	29.1	4.8	21.0
Enrolled in grade 10	63.3	41.1	36.9	4.2	22.2
Total, age 16 [3]	73.9	58.4	51.8	6.5	15.5
Male	74.6	56.8	49.9	6.9	17.8
Female.	73.1	59.9	53.7	6.2	13.2
White, non-Hispanic	79.8	64.5	57.9	6.7	15.3
Black, non-Hispanic	59.4	45.4	38.9	6.5	14.0
Hispanic origin.	62.8	43.4	36.5	7.0	19.3
Enrolled in grade 10	68.1	50.2	42.7	7.5	18.0
Enrolled in grade 11	78.2	63.3	56.5	6.8	14.9

[1] September 1997 through May 1998, excluding last week of December and first week of January. [2] June, July, and August 1998. [3] Includes other races, not shown separately.

Source: U.S. Bureau of Labor Statistics, *Employment Experience of Youths: Results from a Longitudinal Survey*, USDL 00-353, December 7, 2000.

No. 235. Elementary and Secondary Schools—Teachers and Pupil-Teacher Ratios: 1980 to 1998

[In thousands (2,485 represents 2,485,000), except ratios. As of fall. Data are for full-time equivalents. Schools are classified by type of organization, rather than by grade group; elementary includes kindergarten and secondary includes junior high]

Item	Total			Public			Private		
	Total	Elementary	Secondary	Total	Elementary	Secondary	Total	Elementary	Secondary
Number of teachers:									
1980	2,485	1,401	1,084	2,184	1,189	995	301	212	89
1985	2,549	1,483	1,066	2,206	1,237	969	343	246	97
1990	2,753	1,683	1,070	2,398	1,429	969	355	254	101
1991	2,787	1,722	1,065	2,432	1,468	964	355	254	101
1992	2,822	1,752	1,070	2,459	1,492	967	363	260	103
1993	2,870	1,775	1,095	2,504	1,513	991	366	262	104
1994	2,926	1,791	1,135	2,552	1,525	1,027	374	266	108
1995	2,978	1,794	1,184	2,598	1,525	1,073	380	269	111
1996	3,054	1,856	1,198	2,667	1,582	1,085	387	274	113
1997	3,134	1,928	1,206	2,746	1,653	1,093	388	275	113
1998	3,217	1,978	1,239	2,826	1,701	1,125	391	277	114
Pupil-teacher ratio:									
1980	18.6	20.1	16.6	18.7	20.4	16.8	17.7	18.8	15.0
1985	17.6	19.1	15.6	17.9	19.5	15.8	16.2	17.1	14.0
1990	16.9	18.5	14.3	17.2	18.9	14.6	14.7	16.1	11.3
1991	17.0	18.4	14.6	17.3	18.8	15.0	14.7	16.0	11.1
1992	17.1	18.4	14.8	17.4	18.8	15.2	14.6	16.2	11.3
1993	17.1	18.5	14.7	17.4	18.9	15.1	14.8	16.3	11.5
1994	17.1	18.6	14.4	17.3	19.0	14.8	14.9	16.4	11.4
1995	17.0	18.9	14.0	17.3	19.3	14.4	14.9	16.6	10.8
1996	16.8	18.4	14.2	17.1	18.9	14.4	14.9	16.4	11.5
1997	16.6	18.1	14.2	16.8	18.3	14.5	15.1	16.6	11.6
1998	16.3	17.8	14.0	16.5	18.0	14.2	15.2	16.6	11.6

Source: U.S. National Center for Education Statistics, *Digest of Education Statistics*, annual.

150 Education

No. 236. Public Elementary and Secondary School Teachers—Selected Characteristics: 1993-94

[For school year (280 represents 280,000). Based on survey and subject to sampling error; for details, see source. Excludes prekindergarten teachers. See Table 260 for similar data on private school teachers]

Characteristic	Unit	Age Under 30 years old	30 to 39 years old	40 to 49 years old	Over 50 years old	Sex Male	Fe-male	Race/ethnicity White [1]	Black [1]	His-panic
Total teachers [2]	1,000 . .	280	573	1,070	637	694	1,867	2,217	188	109
Highest degree held:										
Bachelor's	Percent .	83.9	59.4	46.3	40.9	46.2	54.1	51.8	48.4	62.8
Master's	Percent .	14.5	36.6	47.0	50.4	45.7	40.6	42.5	44.6	29.8
Education specialist.	Percent .	1.0	3.0	5.4	6.1	5.1	4.4	4.4	5.4	4.6
Doctorate	Percent .	0.1	0.3	0.7	1.4	1.3	0.5	0.7	0.9	1.4
Full-time teaching experience:										
Less than 3 years	Percent .	47.8	10.5	4.3	1.3	8.9	10.0	9.4	8.5	16.7
3 to 9 years	Percent .	52.2	48.7	16.9	7.3	21.6	26.9	25.5	20.8	32.1
10 to 20 years	Percent .	(X)	40.8	47.5	24.2	29.9	37.0	35.1	35.5	34.1
20 years or more	Percent .	(X)	(X)	31.3	67.1	39.6	26.1	30.0	35.2	17.1
Full-time teachers.	1,000 . .	259	518	974	590	643	1,698	2,012	182	103
Earned income	Dol. . . .	27,151	31,596	38,106	42,243	41,031	34,781	36,576	36,200	35,197
Salary	Dol. . . .	24,737	29,270	35,751	39,931	36,182	33,384	34,221	33,889	32,996

X Not applicable.   [1] Non-Hispanic.   [2] Includes teachers with no degrees and associates degrees, not shown separately.

Source: U.S. National Center for Education Statistics, *Digest of Education Statistics,* 1997; and unpublished data.

No. 237. Public Elementary and Secondary Schools—Number and Average Salary of Classroom Teachers, 1980 to 2000, and by State, 2000

[Estimates for school year ending in June of year shown (2,211 represents 2,211,000). Schools classified by type of organization rather than by grade-group; elementary includes kindergarten]

Year and state	Teachers [1] (1,000) Total	Ele-men-tary	Sec-ond-ary	Avg. salary ($1,000) All teach-ers	Ele-men-tary	Sec-ond-ary	Year and state	Teachers [1] (1,000) Total	Ele-men-tary	Sec-ond-ary	Avg. salary ($1,000) All teach-ers	Ele-men-tary	Sec-ond-ary
1980	2,211	1,206	1,005	16.0	15.6	16.5	ME	15.5	10.7	4.7	35.6	35.3	36.1
1985	2,175	1,212	963	23.6	23.2	24.2	MD	50.5	28.3	22.1	44.0	43.3	45.0
1990	2,362	1,390	972	31.4	30.8	32.0	MA	68.0	29.2	38.8	46.3	46.3	46.3
1991	2,409	1,436	974	33.1	32.5	33.9	MI	96.1	49.9	46.2	48.7	48.7	48.7
1992	2,429	1,466	963	34.1	33.5	34.8	MN	56.0	29.5	26.5	39.8	40.6	39.2
1993	2,466	1,496	970	35.0	34.4	35.9	MS	30.8	17.0	13.8	31.9	31.4	32.5
1994	2,512	1,517	995	35.7	35.2	36.6	MO	63.7	32.8	30.9	35.7	35.0	36.3
1995	2,568	1,535	1,033	36.7	36.2	37.5	MT	10.4	7.1	3.3	32.1	31.7	32.9
1996	2,607	1,562	1,045	37.7	37.3	38.4	NE	20.4	11.9	8.5	33.3	33.3	33.3
1997	2,673	1,608	1,065	38.5	38.2	39.1	NV	17.5	10.6	6.9	39.4	39.1	39.8
1998	2,745	1,652	1,093	39.5	39.1	40.0	NH	14.0	9.6	4.4	37.7	37.7	37.7
1999	2,813	1,673	1,140	40.6	40.3	41.2	NJ	94.4	59.4	35.0	52.2	51.2	54.2
2000, U.S.	2,886	1,720	1,165	41.7	41.5	42.4	NM	20.3	14.3	6.0	32.6	32.3	33.2
AL	47.0	28.5	18.5	36.7	36.7	36.7	NY	203.4	101.7	101.7	50.2	49.8	51.8
AK	7.9	5.3	2.6	47.3	47.3	47.3	NC	79.8	50.2	29.6	39.4	39.2	39.7
AZ	44.5	34.3	10.2	35.7	35.7	35.7	ND	8.0	5.1	2.9	29.9	29.5	30.1
AR	28.7	14.1	14.6	33.4	32.5	34.3	OH	114.0	76.8	37.2	41.4	41.1	42.1
CA	284.6	210.5	74.2	47.7	47.6	50.0	OK	41.5	21.6	19.9	31.3	31.1	31.5
CO	40.8	20.4	20.4	38.2	38.7	39.0	OR	28.4	19.7	8.7	40.9	40.9	41.0
CT	40.4	28.9	11.5	51.8	51.2	53.3	PA	114.5	60.0	54.5	48.3	48.1	48.6
DE	7.6	3.7	3.9	44.4	44.3	44.6	RI	12.1	7.1	5.0	47.0	47.0	47.1
DC	4.8	3.3	1.5	47.1	47.6	46.4	SC	43.5	30.5	13.1	36.1	35.8	36.7
FL	132.6	67.7	64.9	36.7	36.7	36.7	SD	9.3	6.4	2.8	29.1	29.1	29.0
GA	90.7	53.4	37.3	41.0	40.4	41.8	TN	55.5	40.3	15.2	36.3	36.0	37.3
HI	11.1	6.0	5.1	40.6	40.6	40.6	TX	267.9	136.6	131.3	37.6	37.4	38.1
ID	13.6	7.0	6.7	35.2	35.2	35.1	UT	22.2	11.5	10.6	34.9	34.9	35.4
IL	127.0	90.0	37.1	46.5	44.5	51.3	VT	8.5	4.4	4.1	37.7	38.3	36.8
IN	58.7	31.5	27.2	41.9	41.9	41.8	VA	87.6	52.8	34.7	38.1	36.9	40.1
IA	33.9	15.9	18.0	35.7	34.7	36.5	WA	50.3	28.1	22.2	41.0	41.1	40.9
KS	33.2	16.9	16.3	38.5	38.5	38.5	WV	20.9	14.5	6.5	35.0	34.7	35.6
KY	40.1	28.3	11.8	36.4	35.8	37.7	WI	57.4	39.3	18.1	41.2	40.9	41.7
LA	49.4	34.3	15.1	33.1	33.1	33.1	WY	6.8	3.3	3.5	34.1	34.1	34.1

[1] Full-time equivalent.

Source: National Education Association, Washington, DC, Estimates of School Statistics Database (copyright).

Education 151

No. 238. Average Salary and Wages Paid in Public School Systems: 1980 to 2000

[In dollars. For school year ending in year shown. Data reported by a stratified sample of school systems enrolling 300 or more pupils. Data represent unweighted means of average salaries paid school personnel reported by each school system]

Position	1980	1985	1990	1995	1996	1997	1998	1999	2000
ANNUAL SALARY									
Central office administrators:									
Superintendent (contract salary) . . .	39,344	56,954	75,425	90,198	94,229	98,106	101,519	106,122	112,158
Deputy/assoc. superintendent	37,440	52,877	69,623	81,266	84,077	88,564	90,226	92,936	97,251
Assistant superintendent	33,452	48,003	62,698	75,236	77,007	80,176	82,339	86,005	88,913
Administrators for—									
Finance and business	27,147	40,344	52,354	61,323	63,840	65,797	67,724	71,387	73,499
Instructional services	29,790	43,452	56,359	66,767	68,463	70,788	73,058	75,680	79,023
Public relations/information	24,021	35,287	44,926	53,263	53,860	55,928	57,224	59,214	60,655
Staff personnel services	29,623	44,182	56,344	65,819	67,760	70,088	71,073	73,850	76,608
Subject area supervisors	23,974	34,422	45,929	54,534	56,145	58,776	60,359	61,083	63,103
School building administrators:									
Principals:									
Elementary.	25,165	36,452	48,431	58,589	60,922	62,903	64,653	67,348	69,407
Junior high/middle	27,625	39,650	52,163	62,311	64,452	66,859	68,740	71,499	73,877
Senior high.	29,207	42,094	55,722	66,596	69,277	72,410	74,380	76,768	79,839
Assistant principals:									
Elementary.	20,708	30,496	40,916	48,491	50,537	52,284	53,206	54,306	56,419
Junior high/middle	23,507	33,793	44,570	52,942	54,355	56,451	57,768	59,238	60,842
Senior high.	24,816	35,491	46,486	55,556	57,555	59,739	60,999	62,691	64,811
Classroom teachers.	15,913	23,587	31,278	37,264	38,706	39,580	40,133	41,351	42,213
Auxiliary professional personnel:									
Counselors	18,847	27,593	35,979	42,486	44,073	45,365	46,162	47,287	48,195
Librarians	16,764	24,981	33,469	40,418	41,761	43,315	44,310	45,680	46,732
School nurses	13,788	19,944	26,090	31,066	32,786	33,720	34,619	35,520	35,540
Secretarial/clerical personnel:									
Central office:									
Secretaries.	10,331	15,343	20,238	23,935	24,809	25,709	26,316	27,540	28,405
Accounting/payroll clerks.	10,479	15,421	20,088	24,042	25,009	25,881	26,249	27,630	28,498
Typists/data entry clerks	8,359	12,481	16,125	18,674	19,447	20,726	21,633	22,474	22,853
School building level:									
Secretaries.	8,348	12,504	16,184	19,170	20,076	20,709	21,215	21,831	22,630
Library clerks	6,778	9,911	12,152	14,381	14,791	15,349	15,742	16,033	16,509
HOURLY WAGE RATE									
Other support personnel:									
Teacher aides:									
Instructional	4.06	5.89	7.43	8.77	9.04	9.25	9.46	9.80	10.00
Noninstructional	3.89	5.60	7.08	8.29	8.52	8.88	8.82	9.31	9.77
Custodians	4.88	6.90	8.54	10.05	10.35	10.65	10.79	11.22	11.35
Cafeteria workers	3.78	5.42	6.77	7.89	8.15	8.30	8.56	8.82	9.02
Bus drivers	5.21	7.27	9.21	10.69	11.04	11.50	11.55	12.04	12.48

Source: Educational Research Service, Arlington, VA, *National Survey of Salaries and Wages in Public Schools*, annual, Vols. 2 and 3. (All rights reserved. Copyright.)

No. 239. Public School Employment: 1982 and 1998

[In thousands (3,082 represents 3,082,000). Covers full-time employment. Excludes Hawaii. 1982 also excludes District of Columbia and New Jersey. 1982 based on sample survey of school districts with 250 or more students. 1998 based on sample survey of school districts with 100 or more employees; see source for sampling variability]

Occupation	1982					1998				
	Total	Male	Female	White [1]	Black [1]	Total	Male	Female	White [1]	Black [1]
All occupations	3,082	1,063	2,019	2,498	432	3,890	1,040	2,850	3,028	515
Officials, administrators	41	31	10	36	3	50	27	23	42	5
Principals and assistant										
principals.	90	72	19	76	11	105	53	52	81	16
Classroom teachers [2]	1,680	534	1,146	1,435	186	2,157	544	1,613	1,805	208
Elementary schools	798	129	669	667	98	1,079	151	928	895	103
Secondary schools	706	363	343	619	67	795	331	464	677	73
Other professional staff	235	91	144	193	35	277	61	216	228	32
Teachers aides [3]	215	14	200	146	45	389	43	346	257	78
Clerical, secretarial staff.	210	4	206	177	19	266	11	255	203	29
Service workers [4]	611	316	295	434	132	646	301	345	411	147

[1] Excludes individuals of Hispanic origin. [2] Includes other classroom teachers, not shown separately. [3] Includes technicians. [4] Includes craftworkers and laborers.

Source: U.S. Equal Employment Opportunity Commission, *Elementary-Secondary Staff Information (EEO-5)*, biennial.

No. 240. Public Elementary and Secondary School Price Indexes: 1975 to 1998

[1983=100. **For years ending June 30.** Reflects prices paid by public elementary-secondary schools. For explanation of average annual percent change, see Guide to Tabular Presentation]

Year	Personnel compensation					Contracted services, supplies and equipment						
	Index, total	Total	Profes-sional salaries	Nonpro-fessional salaries	Fringe benefits	Total	Serv-ices	Sup-plies and materi-als	Equip-ment replace-ment	Library materi-als and text-books	Utilities	Fixed costs
1975 ..	52.7	53.4	56.0	55.6	40.9	50.4	55.7	58.0	53.7	53.8	34.5	45.2
1980 ..	76.6	75.9	76.7	77.8	71.0	79.2	77.4	85.9	79.6	82.1	71.1	77.9
1984 ..	105.1	106.0	105.7	104.5	108.3	101.7	105.6	99.6	103.4	107.8	94.3	105.4
1985 ..	112.1	113.7	113.4	111.3	117.1	106.0	112.4	103.2	107.2	111.0	96.1	110.8
1986 ..	118.5	121.1	121.4	117.6	123.3	108.3	117.4	103.0	109.3	120.8	93.7	116.2
1987 ..	123.3	127.4	128.4	121.9	128.8	107.5	123.7	101.5	112.9	126.5	75.3	122.7
1988 ..	129.8	134.5	135.5	127.5	137.0	111.7	126.1	105.9	113.4	140.0	78.1	128.4
1989 ..	136.3	141.6	142.2	133.3	147.0	116.1	131.8	112.0	116.0	149.4	75.1	134.6
1990 ..	144.5	150.0	150.1	139.4	159.3	123.5	137.7	119.2	121.2	171.7	82.1	140.3
1991 ..	152.3	158.3	158.1	146.5	169.8	129.6	142.5	122.7	125.7	189.4	92.6	144.9
1992 ..	158.5	165.5	165.9	152.4	175.8	131.9	148.0	122.5	128.5	199.0	90.8	148.9
1993 ..	162.2	169.6	169.3	155.1	184.5	133.9	151.5	121.9	131.8	205.6	90.4	153.8
1994 ..	167.1	175.2	175.1	159.3	190.2	136.5	154.0	122.7	135.4	218.4	90.6	158.8
1995 ..	170.9	179.2	178.9	163.7	194.9	139.3	157.2	124.4	138.7	230.7	89.7	163.9
1996 ..	177.3	185.6	185.7	169.2	200.3	145.9	161.8	138.7	143.2	227.9	91.0	169.1
1997 ..	181.7	190.2	190.2	174.5	204.2	149.4	165.2	137.7	145.2	238.0	100.1	172.9
1998 ..	184.5	193.3	193.3	177.9	207.6	150.8	168.0	137.7	144.2	245.3	98.1	177.0

Source: Research Associates of Washington, Arlington, VA, *Inflation Measures for Schools, Colleges, and Libraries*, annual (copyright).

No. 241. Finances of Public Elementary and Secondary School Systems by Enrollment-Size Group: 1997-98

[In millions of dollars (327,202 represents $327,202,000,000), except as Indicated. Data are estimates, subject to sampling variability. For details, see source. See also Appendix III]

Item	All school systems	School systems with enrollment of—						
		50,000 or more	25,000 to 49,999	15,000 to 24,999	7,500 to 14,999	5,000 to 7,499	3,000 to 4,999	Under 3,000
Fall enrollment (1,000)	46,127	9,113	5,302	4,431	6,896	4,219	5,427	10,738
General revenue	327,202	64,456	35,698	28,854	48,238	30,513	39,100	80,343
From federal sources	21,790	5,338	2,474	1,782	2,946	1,634	2,108	5,508
Through state	19,753	4,972	2,277	1,653	2,612	1,513	1,889	4,838
Compensatory programs	6,995	2,036	811	592	915	519	653	1,469
Handicapped programs	2,790	476	292	238	400	235	273	875
Child nutrition programs	5,961	1,623	761	556	809	475	585	1,154
Direct	2,037	366	197	130	334	121	219	670
From state sources [1]	160,178	30,978	18,535	15,940	24,184	14,063	17,586	38,893
General formula assistance	112,205	19,549	12,550	11,556	17,246	10,091	12,942	28,271
Handicapped programs	9,426	2,056	1,185	861	1,380	760	909	2,274
From local sources	145,234	28,140	14,689	11,132	21,108	14,816	19,406	35,942
Taxes	97,932	14,754	10,051	7,291	14,780	10,856	14,004	26,196
Contributions from parent gov't	24,369	9,839	2,114	1,862	3,012	1,866	2,570	3,107
From other local governments.	3,047	382	285	196	285	233	441	1,225
Current charges	8,653	1,336	905	770	1,313	824	1,088	2,416
School lunch	4,770	671	508	456	770	492	652	1,220
Other	11,233	1,828	1,335	1,014	1,718	1,037	1,303	2,998
General expenditure	331,445	65,157	35,965	29,110	48,607	30,997	39,777	81,833
Current spending	287,075	56,989	30,774	25,000	42,101	26,801	34,171	71,239
By function:								
Instruction	174,709	34,955	18,494	15,306	25,871	16,567	21,117	42,398
Support services	96,100	18,390	10,405	8,199	13,859	8,848	11,283	25,115
Other current spending.	16,267	3,643	1,875	1,495	2,372	1,385	1,771	3,726
By object:								
Total salaries and wages	186,092	36,769	20,416	16,609	27,644	17,662	22,354	44,638
Total employee benefits	48,626	10,284	5,146	4,218	7,373	4,544	5,712	11,348
Other	52,357	9,936	5,213	4,172	7,085	4,594	6,104	15,253
Capital outlay	35,874	6,659	4,322	3,403	5,248	3,333	4,453	8,456
Interest on debt	7,402	1,480	821	664	1,079	695	1,016	1,648
Payments to other governments	1,094	28	48	43	178	168	137	491
Debt outstanding	144,057	28,024	15,279	12,964	21,378	13,974	20,258	32,180
Long-term.	141,591	27,944	15,131	12,815	21,045	13,744	19,823	31,088
Short-term	2,466	80	147	149	333	230	435	1,092
Long-term debt issued	32,648	5,502	3,027	2,747	5,307	3,748	5,317	7,000
Long-term debt retired	15,573	3,192	1,402	1,064	2,515	1,663	2,354	3,383

[1] Includes other sources, not shown separately.

Source: U.S. Census Bureau, Internet site <http://www.census.gov/govs/www/school.html>.

No. 242. Public Elementary and Secondary Estimated Finances, 1980 to 2000, and by State, 2000

[In millions of dollars (101,724 represents $101,724,000,000), except as noted. For school years ending in June of year shown]

Year and state	Receipts Total	Revenue receipts Total	Source Federal	State	Local	Non-revenue receipts [1]	Expenditures Total [2]	Per capita [3] (dol.)	Current expenditures Elementary and secondary day schools	Average per pupil in ADA [4] Amount (dol.)	Rank
1980	101,724	97,635	9,020	47,929	40,686	4,089	96,105	427	85,661	2,230	(X)
1985	146,976	141,013	9,533	69,107	62,373	5,963	139,382	591	127,230	3,483	(X)
1990	218,126	208,656	13,184	100,787	94,685	9,469	209,698	850	186,583	4,966	(X)
1993	263,460	247,912	17,381	115,924	114,606	15,548	248,898	976	219,297	5,538	(X)
1994	275,121	259,587	18,434	119,443	121,710	15,534	262,485	1,018	230,773	5,749	(X)
1995	288,501	273,255	18,764	129,958	124,533	15,246	276,584	1,062	242,995	5,957	(X)
1996	305,749	286,521	19,324	137,488	129,709	19,228	292,489	1,113	254,505	6,139	(X)
1997	323,116	303,014	20,202	147,855	134,957	20,102	310,705	1,171	269,643	6,394	(X)
1998	343,347	322,501	22,262	158,419	141,820	20,846	327,541	1,223	283,283	6,638	(X)
1999	366,575	340,194	23,774	169,064	147,356	26,381	348,345	1,289	298,687	6,963	(X)
2000, total	**378,575**	**352,480**	**24,305**	**178,773**	**149,402**	**26,095**	**360,303**	**1,321**	**308,443**	**7,146**	**(X)**
Alabama	5,140	4,085	427	2,636	1,023	1,054	4,441	1,016	3,611	5,118	47
Alaska	1,342	1,198	150	761	286	144	1,319	2,129	1,217	10,711	2
Arizona	4,922	4,440	324	2,186	1,930	482	4,894	1,024	3,869	4,866	49
Arkansas	2,663	2,591	213	1,630	748	72	2,868	1,124	2,479	5,625	46
California	44,621	43,311	3,352	27,248	12,712	1,310	42,517	1,283	35,482	5,232	38
Colorado	4,801	4,276	235	1,908	2,133	525	4,560	1,124	3,740	5,695	45
Connecticut	6,118	6,111	289	2,609	3,213	7	6,118	1,864	5,434	10,286	4
Delaware	1,030	1,010	75	666	269	20	993	1,318	911	8,653	11
Dist. Columbia	719	719	120	-	600	-	683	1,317	639	9,933	5
Florida	19,320	17,731	1,435	9,015	7,280	1,589	17,471	1,156	13,970	6,536	31
Georgia	10,070	9,082	601	4,677	3,804	987	10,176	1,307	8,471	6,387	34
Hawaii	1,508	1,349	133	1,184	32	159	1,421	1,198	1,158	6,777	26
Idaho	1,577	1,504	106	917	482	73	1,483	1,184	1,327	5,756	43
Illinois	15,760	13,969	903	3,816	9,250	1,791	14,823	1,222	12,468	6,720	27
Indiana	8,442	8,099	366	4,103	3,631	342	7,942	1,336	6,594	7,254	19
Iowa	3,724	3,520	151	1,857	1,511	204	3,417	1,191	2,988	6,386	35
Kansas	3,595	3,357	207	2,163	987	238	3,327	1,254	2,997	7,149	21
Kentucky	4,637	4,628	372	2,924	1,331	9	4,571	1,154	4,064	7,053	22
Louisiana	5,382	4,772	557	2,425	1,790	611	4,834	1,106	4,282	6,039	40
Maine	1,714	1,664	103	770	791	50	1,714	1,368	1,594	8,173	12
Maryland	7,343	7,048	379	2,809	3,859	296	7,041	1,361	6,075	7,704	16
Massachusetts	9,222	9,221	464	3,966	4,791	1	8,946	1,449	8,464	9,366	7
Michigan	16,818	15,074	1,009	10,885	3,180	1,744	14,025	1,422	12,673	8,099	13
Minnesota	8,033	7,157	335	4,292	2,529	876	7,991	1,673	6,405	8,015	14
Mississippi	2,929	2,580	362	1,411	807	350	2,697	974	2,299	4,905	48
Missouri	7,326	6,573	448	2,480	3,646	753	6,191	1,132	5,229	6,234	37
Montana	1,096	1,066	118	478	470	30	1,086	1,230	966	6,801	25
Nebraska	1,912	1,896	100	820	976	15	1,905	1,143	1,722	6,576	29
Nevada	2,696	2,167	108	661	1,398	530	2,514	1,389	1,813	6,283	36
New Hampshire	1,571	1,486	55	127	1,304	85	1,469	1,223	1,282	6,840	24
New Jersey	12,820	12,725	405	4,849	7,471	95	12,861	1,579	12,217	10,504	3
New Mexico	2,190	2,090	263	1,562	265	100	2,134	1,227	1,901	6,513	32
New York	32,094	30,630	2,030	14,007	14,593	1,464	31,829	1,749	27,929	10,807	1
North Carolina	8,373	7,892	596	5,411	1,884	481	8,227	1,075	7,147	6,185	39
North Dakota	727	695	80	280	335	33	574	905	520	4,621	50
Ohio	16,600	15,000	870	6,500	7,630	1,600	14,420	1,281	11,800	7,152	20
Oklahoma	4,106	3,887	336	2,390	1,161	218	3,717	1,107	3,533	6,026	41
Oregon	5,687	4,098	258	2,336	1,505	1,588	5,568	1,679	4,690	9,910	6
Pennsylvania	15,557	15,546	861	6,374	8,312	11	13,882	1,157	13,159	7,823	15
Rhode Island	1,232	1,232	54	469	709	-	1,296	1,308	1,241	8,773	9
South Carolina	5,178	4,648	368	2,386	1,894	530	4,869	1,253	3,997	6,400	33
South Dakota	881	820	85	300	436	61	814	1,111	693	5,737	44
Tennessee	5,429	5,160	467	2,480	2,214	269	5,159	941	4,868	5,780	42
Texas	30,976	27,938	2,358	12,290	13,289	3,039	29,574	1,475	24,319	6,588	28
Utah	2,418	2,416	167	1,507	743	1	2,386	1,120	1,921	4,282	51
Vermont	912	890	40	682	169	22	806	1,358	730	7,352	18
Virginia	7,158	6,658	363	2,519	3,777	500	7,932	1,154	6,973	6,543	30
Washington	7,865	7,502	576	4,936	1,990	363	9,039	1,570	6,553	6,992	23
West Virginia	2,516	2,412	217	1,515	680	105	2,743	1,518	2,470	9,238	8
Wisconsin	9,016	7,780	356	4,154	3,270	1,236	8,294	1,580	6,923	8,718	10
Wyoming	807	775	59	404	312	32	740	1,543	635	7,391	17

- Represents or rounds to zero. X Not applicable. [1] Amount received by local education agencies from the sales of bonds and real property and equipment, loans, and proceeds from insurance adjustments. [2] Includes interest on school debt and other current expenditures not shown separately. [3] Based on U.S. Census Bureau estimated resident population, as of July 1, the previous year, except 1980 and 1990 population enumerated as of April 1. [4] Average daily attendance.

Source: National Education Association, Washington, DC, Estimates of School Statistics Database (copyright).

[In percent. As of fall. Excludes special education, vocational education, and alternative schools. Based on sample and subject to sampling error; see source for details]

School characteristic	Percent of schools with Internet access				Percent of instructional classrooms with Internet access				Students per instructional computer with Internet access, 2000	Schools with Internet available to students outside of regular school hours, 2000
	1995	1998	1999	2000	1995	1998	1999	2000		
Total [1]	50	89	95	98	8	51	64	77	7	54
Instructional level:										
Elementary	46	88	94	97	8	51	62	76	8	46
Secondary	65	94	98	100	8	52	67	79	5	80
Size of enrollment:										
Less than 300	39	87	96	96	9	54	71	83	4	49
300 to 999	52	89	94	98	8	53	64	78	7	53
1,000 or more	69	95	96	99	4	45	58	70	7	79
Percent minority enrollment:										
Less than 6 percent	52	91	95	98	9	57	74	85	6	46
6 to 20 percent	58	93	97	100	10	59	78	83	6	59
21 to 49 percent........	55	91	96	98	9	52	64	79	7	54
50 percent or more......	39	82	92	96	3	37	43	64	8	61
Percent of students eligible for free or reduced-price lunch:										
Less than 35 percent	60	92	95	99	9	57	73	82	6	58
35 to 49 percent.........	48	93	98	99	6	60	69	81	6	47
50 to 74 percent.........	41	88	96	97	6	41	61	77	7	52
75 percent or more......	31	79	89	94	3	38	38	60	9	56

[1] Includes combined schools.

Source: U.S. National Center for Education Statistics, *Internet Access in U.S. Public Schools and Classrooms: 1994-2000,* NCES 2001-071, May 2001.

No. 244. Advanced Telecommunications in Private Schools: 1995 and 1999

[For fall 1995 and school year 1998-99. Based on the Fast Response Survey System; for details, see source]

Characteristic	Number of students per computer		Internet access (percent)						Percent of schools without access that plan to have access in the future, 1999	Percent of teachers using computers for teaching, 1999
			Schools with access		Instructional rooms with access		Students enrolled in schools with access			
	1995	1999	1995	1999	1995	1999	1995	1999		
All private schools .	9	6	25	67	5	25	41	81	46	45
Affiliation:										
Catholic............	10	7	35	83	4	27	43	86	74	48
Other religious	9	7	16	54	2	18	30	72	41	41
Nonsectarian	6	4	32	66	13	41	59	84	38	49
Instructional level:										
Elementary	9	7	23	64	3	21	32	77	46	45
Secondary.........	7	5	57	90	6	32	70	97	31	47
Combined.........	8	5	19	64	8	28	41	80	46	44
Size of enrollment:										
Less than 150	7	5	13	48	2	16	16	60	38	41
150 to 299.........	9	7	27	77	3	17	28	77	60	43
300 or more........	9	6	50	85	8	34	56	87	77	47
Minority enrollment:										
Less than 6 percent ..	9	7	24	59	3	28	38	83	13	41
6 to 20 percent......	7	6	29	75	9	27	51	86	71	46
21 to 49 percent.....	8	6	29	76	3	32	44	85	59	45
50 percent or more ...	11	8	18	52	2	10	24	59	59	47

[1] Percent of teachers using computers or advanced telecommunications (e.g. networked computers and interactive television) for teaching.

Source: U.S. National Center for Education Statistics, *Advanced Telecommunications in U.S. Private Schools, fall 1995 and 1998-99,* NCES 97-394 and 2001-037.

Education 155

No. 245. Computers for Student Instruction in Elementary and Secondary Schools: 2000-2001

[53,006 represents 53,006,000. Market Data Retrieval collects student use computer information in elementary and secondary schools nationwide through a comprehensive annual technology survey that utilizes both mail, telephone, and Internet data methods]

Level	Total schools	Total enroll-ment (1,000)	Number of com-puters[1] (1,000)	Stu-dents per com-puter	Schools with a local area network (LAN) (percent)	Schools, by location of computer[2] (percent) Class-rooms	Com-puter lab	Library/ media center	Schools with high speed Internet access[2][3] (percent)
U.S. total	**111,134**	**53,066**	**12,169**	**4.4**	**84.8**	**82.3**	**75.2**	**77.7**	**67.4**
Public schools, total......	89,508	47,841	11,297	4.2	87.3	86.5	76.3	81.7	72.2
Elementary..........	52,475	23,801	5,094	4.7	85.6	84.8	70.3	81.4	67.4
Middle/Junior high	13,714	8,864	2,129	4.2	90.7	88.1	87.8	90.4	78.8
Senior high..........	16,192	12,770	3,404	3.8	91.2	90.1	86.1	83.3	82.0
K-12/other	7,127	2,405	671	3.6	84.1	87.6	76.6	62.8	70.5
Catholic schools, total	8,135	2,654	428	6.2	76.5	56.0	76.7	59.5	43.5
Elementary..........	6,746	1,963	303	6.5	73.0	53.3	73.8	53.9	37.7
Secondary	1,223	631	116	5.5	94.0	67.7	91.0	86.7	70.9
K-12/other	166	60	9	6.8	83.6	67.9	75.5	62.3	49.0
Other private schools, total .	13,491	2,570	444	5.8	63.8	55.3	59.0	43.7	34.7
Elementary..........	6,694	1,085	174	6.3	60.7	58.9	53.2	36.5	31.7
Secondary	1,056	231	63	3.7	82.9	63.7	82.7	65.0	53.4
K-12/other	5,741	1,253	207	6.1	64.1	47.9	61.4	48.5	34.0

[1] Includes estimates for schools not reporting number of computers.   [2] Statistics based on responses of those indicating location of Internet access computers.   [3] High speed includes Internet connection types: T1, T3, cable modem, digital satellite.

Source: Market Data Retrieval, Shelton, CT, unpublished data (copyright).

No. 246. Public School Teachers Using Computers or the Internet for Classroom Instruction During Class Time: 1999

[In percent. Based on the Fast Survey Response System conducted in the spring of 1999 and subject to sampling error; see source]

Characteristic	Teachers using computers or Internet for class-room in-struction[1]	Teacher assigns to a moderate or large extent Com-puter applica-tions[2]	Practice drills	Research using the Internet	Solve problems and analyze data	Research using CD-ROM	Produce multi-media reports/ projects	Graph-ical presen-tation of materials	Demon-stration/ simu-lations
Teachers with access to computers or the Internet at school ...	66	41	31	30	27	27	24	19	17
School instructional level:									
Elementary school ...	68	41	39	25	31	27	22	17	15
Secondary school	60	42	12	41	20	27	27	23	21
Percent of students in school eligible for free or reduced-price school lunch:									
Less than 11 percent..	71	55	26	39	25	32	29	26	22
11 to 30 percent.....	65	45	29	35	29	27	23	18	16
31 to 49 percent.....	65	39	33	29	26	30	23	16	17
50 to 70 percent.....	62	33	33	25	27	24	25	19	13
71 percent or more ...	64	31	35	18	27	19	22	19	16
Hours of professional development:									
0 hours............	41	21	19	20	14	16	16	10	8
1-8 hours	56	36	26	28	24	24	20	16	13
9-32 hours.........	72	47	35	32	30	31	26	21	19
More than 32 hours...	82	55	43	42	41	34	37	31	29

[1] Includes corresponding with others (e.g. authors, experts) via e-mail or Internet, not shown separately.   [2] For example, word processing or spreadsheets.

Source: U.S. National Center for Education Statistics, Fast Response Survey System, Teacher Use of Computers and the Internet in Public Schools, NCES 2000-090, April 2000.

No. 247. Student Use of Computers at School: 1984 to 1997

[In percent. As of October. Based on the Current Population Survey and subject to sampling error; see Appendix III and source]

Characteristic	1984, total	1989, total	1993, total	1997 Total	Prekinder-garten and kinder-garden	Grades 1-8	Grades 9-12	1st to 4th year of college	5th or later year of college
Total	27.3	42.7	59.0	68.8	36.5	79.3	70.5	64.7	55.5
Sex:									
Male	29.0	43.5	59.4	70.1	37.1	79.5	71.3	67.8	59.9
Female	25.5	41.9	58.7	67.6	35.7	79.0	69.6	62.2	52.1
Race/ethnicity:									
White, non-Hispanic	30.0	45.7	61.6	71.1	38.7	84.0	71.9	64.3	53.8
Black, non-Hispanic	16.8	32.6	51.5	66.3	33.5	71.6	72.9	69.2	55.8
Hispanic	18.6	34.9	52.3	61.5	31.0	68.3	63.1	63.3	54.7
Other	28.6	42.7	59.0	65.3	32.7	74.9	63.6	63.1	68.9
Household income:									
Less than $5,000.	18.7	36.7	51.2	62.1	25.4	69.6	67.9	61.1	74.1
$5,000 to $9,999	21.0	36.1	53.3	63.5	35.1	70.1	61.6	69.8	74.8
$10,000 to $14,999	22.4	38.4	56.4	66.2	33.3	74.1	68.2	64.1	70.5
$15,000 to $19,999	25.9	41.5	58.1	65.9	33.0	74.9	66.7	62.1	69.4
$20,000 to $24,999	26.7	42.4	56.4	66.9	34.2	74.9	69.2	64.0	65.8
$25,000 to $29,999	30.5	46.1	60.0	68.5	38.9	77.7	72.0	63.1	53.7
$30,000 to $34,999	30.5	44.2	59.1	67.6	34.6	79.9	70.4	55.2	47.7
$35,000 to $39,999	32.3	45.2	60.7	69.0	34.6	79.9	70.1	61.5	55.2
$40,000 to $49,999	32.8	44.7	59.3	70.5	34.7	81.6	74.1	63.3	52.0
$50,000 to $74,999	35.5	47.0	62.6	71.7	39.3	84.0	72.8	67.2	48.5
$75,000 or more	36.0	51.2	64.6	72.1	43.2	85.7	71.6	68.1	50.1
Control of school:									
Public	27.4	43.3	60.2	70.2	40.1	79.0	70.5	63.4	56.7
Private.	26.5	38.9	52.1	60.7	29.6	82.1	69.6	70.4	53.0

Source: U.S. National Center for Education Statistics, *Digest of Education Statistics*, 1998.

No. 248. Children and Youth With Disabilities Served by Selected Programs: 1991 to 2000

[For school year ending in year shown (4,361.8 represents 4,361,800). Excludes outlying areas. Through 1994, includes children with disabilities served under Chapter 1 of ESEA (Elementary and Secondary Education Act), SOP (State Operated Programs); beginning 1995, Individuals with Disabilities ACT (IDEA), Parts B and C]

Item	1991	1994	1995	1996	1997	1998	1999	2000
NUMBER (1,000)								
Total	4,361.8	4,779.4	4,907.5	5,079.0	5,230.8	5,397.0	5,539.9	5,683.7
Specific learning disabilities.	2,144.0	2,427.7	2,510.2	2,601.9	2,674.4	2,754.5	2,815.7	2,872.0
Speech impairments	987.8	1,018.0	1,020.3	1,026.9	1,048.7	1,063.6	1,074.2	1,090.0
Mental retardation	551.5	553.8	570.5	585.6	593.6	603.3	610.7	614.4
Emotional disturbance	390.8	415.0	428.0	439.2	446.3	454.4	462.8	470.1
Multiple disabilities.	97.6	109.7	89.6	94.5	99.4	107.3	107.8	113.0
Hearing impairments	59.2	64.7	65.2	68.0	68.8	69.7	70.9	71.7
Orthopedically impairments	49.3	56.9	60.5	63.2	66.3	67.4	69.4	71.4
Other health impairments	56.3	83.1	107.1	134.2	161.4	191.1	221.8	254.1
Visually impaired.	23.7	24.8	24.7	25.5	25.8	26.0	26.1	26.6
Autism.	(NA)	19.1	22.7	29.1	34.4	42.5	54.1	65.4
Deaf-blind	1.5	1.4	1.3	1.4	1.2	1.4	1.6	1.8
Traumatic brain injury [1]	(NA)	5.4	7.3	9.6	10.5	11.9	13.0	13.9
Developmental delay [1]	(NA)	(NA)	(NA)	(NA)	(NA)	3.8	11.9	19.3
PERCENT DISTRIBUTION								
Specific learning disabilities.	49.2	50.8	51.2	51.2	51.1	51.0	50.8	50.5
Speech impairments	22.6	21.3	20.8	20.2	20.0	19.7	19.4	19.2
Mental retardation	12.6	11.6	11.6	11.5	11.3	11.2	11.0	10.8
Emotional disturbance	9.0	8.7	8.7	8.6	8.5	8.4	8.4	8.3
Multiple disabilities.	2.2	2.3	1.8	1.9	1.9	2.0	1.9	2.0
Hearing impairments	1.4	1.4	1.3	1.3	1.3	1.3	1.3	1.3
Orthopedically impairments	1.1	1.2	1.2	1.2	1.3	1.2	1.3	1.3
Other health impairments	1.3	1.7	2.2	2.6	3.1	3.5	4.0	4.5
Visually impaired.	0.5	0.5	0.5	0.5	0.5	0.5	0.5	0.5
Autism.	(NA)	0.4	0.5	0.6	0.7	0.8	1.0	1.2
Deaf-blind	(Z)	(Z)	(Z)	(Z)	(Z)	(Z)	(Z)	(Z)
Traumatic brain injury [1]	(NA)	0.1	0.1	0.2	0.2	0.2	0.2	0.2
Developmental delay [1]	(NA)	(NA)	(NA)	(NA)	(NA)	0.1	0.2	0.3

NA Not available. Z less than 0.05 percent. [1] For children 3 to 9 years old.

Source: U.S. Department of Education, Office of Special Education Programs, Data Analysis System (DANS).

Education 157

No. 249. Private Schools: 1997-98

[5,076.1 represents 5,076,100. Based on the Private School Survey, conducted every 2 years; see source for details. For composition of regions, see map, inside front cover]

Characteristic	Schools				Students (1,000)				Teachers (1,000)			
	Num-ber	Ele-mentary	Sec-ondary	Com-bined	Num-ber	Ele-mentary	Sec-ondary	Com-bined	Num-ber	Ele-mentary	Sec-ondary	Com-bined
Total	27,402	16,623	2,487	8,292	5,076.1	2,824.8	798.3	1,452.9	376.5	180.5	60.9	135.2
School type:												
Catholic.	8,182	6,800	1,121	262	2,514.7	1,833.1	606.4	75.2	144.6	97.7	40.2	6.7
Parochial	4,778	4,526	204	47	1,346.0	1,245.7	86.2	14.0	72.4	65.4	6.0	1.0
Diocesan	2,556	2,011	480	65	829.3	533.8	278.2	17.3	47.4	28.5	17.5	1.4
Private.	848	262	437	150	339.5	53.5	242.1	43.9	24.8	3.8	16.7	4.3
Other religious . . .	13,195	6,830	697	5,668	1,764.4	731.3	112.2	921.0	143.1	55.2	10.2	77.7
Conservative												
Christian.	4,978	1,700	143	3,135	737.0	219.4	22.3	495.3	56.8	15.9	1.7	39.3
Affiliated.	3,287	2,166	292	830	551.5	281.8	58.7	211.0	46.4	22.4	5.5	18.4
Unaffiliated	4,929	2,964	262	1,703	475.9	230.1	31.2	214.6	39.9	16.9	3.0	20.0
Nonsectarian	6,025	2,993	670	2,362	797.0	260.5	79.7	456.8	88.8	27.6	10.5	50.8
Regular	2,705	1,523	266	915	553.4	168.9	56.4	328.1	57.4	16.5	7.3	33.6
Special emphasis	2,070	1,290	236	545	158.6	80.6	14.4	63.7	17.0	9.1	1.6	6.3
Special education . .	1,250	181	168	901	85.0	11.0	9.0	65.0	14.5	2.1	1.6	10.8
Program emphasis:												
Regular elem/sec .	22,363	14,495	1,973	5,895	4,684.0	2,679.9	753.5	1,250.6	330.2	164.5	55.8	109.9
Montessori.	1,144	950	(B)	186	69.9	55.7	(B)	13.5	7.5	6.3	0.1	1.2
Special program emphasis	589	273	66	250	100.1	35.4	15.5	49.3	9.8	3.5	1.4	4.8
Special education .	1,387	204	178	1,005	93.5	12.4	9.7	71.3	16.0	2.3	1.7	12.0
Vocational/tech . . .	(B)	(B)	(B)	(B)	(B)	(B)	(B)	(B)	(B)	(B)	(B)	(B)
Early childhood. . .	160	148	(B)	(B)	7.9	7.4	-	(B)	0.6	0.5	(B)	(B)
Alternative	1,745	553	253	938	118.8	34.1	17.9	66.9	12.3	3.3	1.8	7.2
Size:												
Less than 150 . . .	15,573	9,041	1,046	5,486	918.9	555.2	58.2	305.5	96.2	50.6	7.7	37.9
150 to 299.	6,656	4,860	446	1,349	1,439.3	1,050.7	98.8	289.9	99.3	64.5	9.3	25.5
300 to 499.	3,125	1,994	408	722	1,197.2	760.0	159.6	277.7	78.6	42.8	12.8	23.1
500 to 749.	1,339	615	297	427	800.4	357.8	181.6	261.0	53.1	17.5	12.9	22.7
750 or more.	711	113	290	308	720.2	101.1	300.2	318.9	49.2	5.0	18.2	26.1
Region:												
Northeast	6,325	3,872	795	1,658	1,287.0	751.1	261.1	274.9	100.3	47.7	21.4	31.2
Midwest	7,423	5,299	604	1,520	1,345.6	896.9	240.7	208.0	88.6	53.2	16.7	18.7
South	8,111	4,014	564	3,533	1,510.3	631.8	153.4	725.1	121.9	46.0	12.1	63.7
West.	5,542	3,437	524	1,580	933.2	545.0	143.2	245.0	65.7	33.5	10.7	21.5

- Represents zero.   B Does not meet standard of reliability or precision.

Source: U.S. National Center for Education Statistics, Office of Educational Research and Improvement, *Private School Universe Survey, 1997-98*, NCES 1999-319.

No. 250. Private Elementary and Secondary School Teachers—Selected Characteristics: 1993-94

[For school year (65 represents 65,000). Based on survey and subject to sampling error; for details, see source. See Table 236 for similar data on public school teachers]

Characteristic	Unit	Age				Sex		Race/ethnicity		
		Under 30 years old	30 to 39 years old	40 to 49 years old	Over 50 years old	Male	Fe-male	White [1]	Black [1]	His-panic
Total teachers [2] . . .	1,000 . . .	65	94	131	88	93	285	348	12	12
Highest degree held:										
Bachelor's	Percent .	78.8	63.1	54.0	47.2	47.3	62.8	59.4	55.8	57.4
Master's	Percent .	10.8	25.7	35.1	40.5	40.6	26.3	30.2	26.4	19.9
Education specialist .	Percent .	1.0	2.6	3.4	3.8	2.6	3.0	2.6	4.8	4.4
Doctorate	Percent .	0.2	1.4	2.0	2.6	4.3	0.8	1.6	1.0	2.3
Full-time teaching experience:										
Less than 3 years . .	Percent .	54.9	21.7	12.6	7.2	21.7	20.6	20.4	26.9	25.5
3 to 9 years	Percent .	44.9	51.2	29.8	13.4	28.2	35.8	33.6	34.9	41.8
10 to 20 years	Percent .	0.1	27.1	45.5	30.2	28.7	29.9	30.0	27.9	21.6
20 years or more . . .	Percent .	(Z)	(Z)	12.1	49.2	21.4	13.7	16.0	10.3	11.1
Full-time teachers	1,000 . . .	53	82	103	62	70	231	277	9	9
Earned income	Dol.	18,384	21,344	22,190	24,113	27,196	20,007	21,578	23,094	22,912
Salary	Dol.	16,062	19,108	20,631	22,500	23,003	18,815	19,717	20,333	20,740

Z Less than 0.05 percent.   [1] Non-Hispanic.   [2] Includes teachers with no degrees and associates degrees, not shown separately.

Source: U.S. National Center for Education Statistics, *Digest of Education Statistics*, 1997.

158 Education

No. 251. Scholastic Assessment Test (SAT) Scores and Characteristics of College-Bound Seniors: 1967 to 2000

[For school year ending in year shown. Data are for the SAT I: Reasoning Tests. SAT I: Reasoning Test replaced the SAT in March 1994. Scores between the two tests have been equated to the same 200-800 scale and are thus comparable. Scores for 1995 and prior years have been recentered and revised]

Type of test and characteristic	Unit	1967	1970	1975	1980	1985	1990	1995	1998	1999	2000
AVERAGE TEST SCORES [1]											
Verbal, total [2]	Point	543	537	512	502	509	500	504	505	505	505
Male	Point	540	536	515	506	514	505	505	509	509	507
Female	Point	545	538	509	498	503	496	502	502	502	504
Math, total [2]	Point	516	512	498	492	500	501	506	512	511	514
Male	Point	535	531	518	515	522	521	525	531	531	533
Female	Point	495	493	479	473	480	483	490	496	495	498
PARTICIPANTS											
Total [3]	1,000	(NA)	(NA)	996	922	977	1,026	1,068	1,173	1,220	1,260
Male	Percent	(NA)	(NA)	49.9	48.2	48.3	47.8	46.4	46.2	46.1	46.2
White	Percent	(NA)	(NA)	86.0	82.1	81.0	73.0	69.2	67.0	66.9	66.4
Black	Percent	(NA)	(NA)	7.9	9.1	7.5	10.0	10.7	11.0	11.1	11.2
Obtaining scores [1] of—											
600 or above:											
Verbal	Percent	(NA)	(NA)	(NA)	(NA)	(NA)	20.3	21.9	21.0	21.2	21.1
Math	Percent	(NA)	(NA)	(NA)	(NA)	(NA)	20.4	23.4	23.7	23.7	24.2
Below 400:											
Verbal	Percent	(NA)	(NA)	(NA)	(NA)	(NA)	17.3	16.4	16.1	16.1	15.9
Math	Percent	(NA)	(NA)	(NA)	(NA)	(NA)	15.8	16.0	15.3	15.7	14.7
Selected intended area of study:											
Business and commerce	Percent	(NA)	(NA)	11.5	18.6	21.0	20.9	13.3	13.6	13.8	13.6
Engineering	Percent	(NA)	(NA)	6.7	11.1	11.7	10.2	8.8	8.6	8.5	8.5
Social science	Percent	(NA)	(NA)	7.7	7.8	7.5	12.6	11.6	10.5	10.5	10.6
Education	Percent	(NA)	(NA)	9.1	6.1	4.7	7.5	8.1	8.9	8.9	8.8

NA Not available. [1] Minimum score 200; maximum score, 800. [2] 1967 and 1970 are estimates based on total number of persons taking SAT. [3] 996 represents 996,000.

Source: College Entrance Examination Board, New York, NY, *National College-Bound Senior*, annual (copyright).

No. 252. ACT Program Scores and Characteristics of College-Bound Students: 1970 to 2000

[For academic year ending in year shown. Except as indicated, test scores and characteristics of college-bound students. Through 1980, data based on 10 percent sample; thereafter, based on all ACT tested graduating seniors]

Type of test and characteristic	Unit	1970	1975	1980	1985	1990 [1]	1995 [1]	1997 [1]	1998 [1]	1999 [1]	2000 [1]
TEST SCORES [2]											
Composite	Point	19.9	18.6	18.5	18.6	20.6	20.8	21.0	21.0	21.0	21.0
Male	Point	20.3	19.5	19.3	19.4	21.0	21.0	21.1	21.2	21.1	21.2
Female	Point	19.4	17.8	17.9	17.9	20.3	20.7	20.8	20.9	20.9	20.9
English	Point	18.5	17.7	17.9	18.1	20.5	20.2	20.3	20.4	20.5	20.5
Male	Point	17.6	17.1	17.3	17.6	20.1	19.8	19.9	19.9	20.0	20.0
Female	Point	19.4	18.3	18.3	18.6	20.9	20.6	20.7	20.8	20.9	20.9
Math	Point	20.0	17.6	17.4	17.2	19.9	20.2	20.6	20.8	20.7	20.7
Male	Point	21.1	19.3	18.9	18.6	20.7	20.9	21.3	21.5	21.4	21.4
Female	Point	18.8	16.2	16.2	16.0	19.3	19.7	20.1	20.2	20.2	20.2
Reading [3]	Point	19.7	17.4	17.2	17.4	(NA)	21.3	21.3	21.4	21.4	21.4
Male	Point	20.3	18.7	18.2	18.3	(NA)	21.1	21.2	21.1	21.1	21.2
Female	Point	19.0	16.4	16.4	16.6	(NA)	21.4	21.5	21.6	21.6	21.5
Science reasoning [4]	Point	20.8	21.1	21.1	21.2	(NA)	21.0	21.1	21.1	21.0	21.0
Male	Point	21.6	22.4	22.4	22.6	(NA)	21.6	21.7	21.8	21.5	21.6
Female	Point	20.0	20.0	20.0	20.0	(NA)	20.5	20.6	20.6	20.6	20.6
PARTICIPANTS [5]											
Total [6]	1,000	788	714	822	739	817	945	959	995	1,019	1,065
Male	Percent	52	46	45	46	46	44	44	43	43	43
White	Percent	(NA)	77	83	82	79	75	76	76	76	76
Black	Percent	4	7	8	8	9	10	10	11	11	11
Obtaining composite scores of— [7]											
27 or above	Percent	14	14	13	14	12	13	14	14	14	14
18 or below	Percent	21	33	33	32	35	34	33	33	33	32
Planned educational major:											
Business [8]	Percent	18	21	20	21	20	14	11	12	11	11
Engineering	Percent	8	6	8	9	9	9	8	7	7	6
Social science [9]	Percent	10	9	6	7	10	9	8	9	9	8
Education	Percent	16	12	9	6	8	9	9	10	10	9

NA Not available. [1] Beginning 1990, not comparable with previous years because a new version of the ACT was introduced. Estimated average composite scores for prior years: 1989, 20.6; 1988, 1987, and 1986, 20.8. [2] Minimum score, 1; maximum score, 36. [3] Prior to 1990, social studies; data not comparable with previous years. [4] Prior to 1990, natural sciences; data not comparable with previous years. [5] Beginning 1985, data are for seniors who graduated in year shown and had taken the ACT in their junior or senior years. Data by race are for those responding to the race question. [6] 788 represents 788,000. [7] Prior to 1990, 26 or above and 15 or below. [8] Includes political and persuasive (e.g. sales) fields through 1975; 1980 and 1985 business and commerce; thereafter, business and management and business and office. [9] Includes religion through 1975.

Source: ACT, Inc., Iowa City, IA, *High School Profile Report*, annual.

Education   159

No. 253. Proficiency Test Scores for Selected Subjects by Characteristic: 1977 to 1999

[Based on The National Assessment of Educational Progress Tests which are administered to a representative sample of students in public and private schools. Test scores can range from 0 to 500, except as indicated. For details, see source]

Test and year	Total	Sex Male	Sex Female	Race White[1]	Race Black[1]	Hispanic origin	Less than high school	High school	More than high school Total	Some college	College graduate
READING											
9 year olds:											
1979-80	215	210	220	221	189	190	194	213	226	(NA)	(NA)
1987-88	212	208	216	218	189	194	193	211	220	(NA)	(NA)
1998-99	212	209	215	221	186	193	199	206	220	(NA)	(NA)
13 year olds:											
1979-80	259	254	263	264	233	237	239	254	271	(NA)	(NA)
1987-88	258	252	263	261	243	240	247	253	265	(NA)	(NA)
1998-99	259	254	265	267	238	244	238	251	270	(NA)	(NA)
17 year olds:											
1979-80	286	282	289	293	243	261	262	278	299	(NA)	(NA)
1987-88	290	286	294	295	274	271	267	282	300	(NA)	(NA)
1998-99	288	282	295	295	264	271	265	274	298	(NA)	(NA)
WRITING[2]											
4th graders:											
1983-84	204	201	208	211	182	189	179	192	217	208	218
1987-88	206	199	213	215	173	190	194	199	212	211	212
1995-96	207	200	214	216	182	191	190	203	(NA)	205	214
8th graders:											
1983-84	267	258	276	272	247	247	258	261	276	271	278
1987-88	264	254	274	269	246	250	254	258	271	275	271
1995-96	264	251	276	271	242	246	245	258	(NA)	270	274
11th graders:											
1983-84	290	281	299	297	270	259	274	284	299	298	300
1987-88	291	282	299	296	275	274	276	285	298	296	299
1995-96	283	275	292	289	267	269	260	275	(NA)	287	291
MATHEMATICS											
9 year olds:											
1977-78	219	217	220	224	192	203	200	219	231	230	231
1985-86	222	222	222	227	202	205	201	218	231	229	231
1998-99	232	233	231	239	211	213	214	224	(NA)	237	240
13 year olds:											
1977-78	264	264	265	272	230	238	245	263	280	273	284
1985-86	269	270	268	274	249	254	252	263	278	274	280
1998-99	276	277	275	283	251	259	256	264	(NA)	279	286
17 year olds:											
1977-78	300	304	297	306	268	276	280	294	313	305	317
1985-86	302	305	299	308	279	283	279	293	310	305	314
1998-99	208	210	207	215	283	293	289	299	(NA)	308	317
SCIENCE											
9 year olds:											
1976-77	220	222	218	230	175	192	199	223	233	237	232
1985-86	224	227	221	232	196	199	204	220	235	236	235
1998-99	229	231	228	240	199	206	213	218	(NA)	234	237
13 year olds:											
1976-77	247	251	244	256	208	213	224	245	264	260	266
1985-86	251	256	247	259	222	226	229	245	262	258	264
1998-99	256	259	253	266	227	227	229	243	(NA)	261	268
17 year olds:											
1976-77	290	297	282	298	240	262	265	284	304	296	309
1985-86	289	295	282	298	253	259	258	277	300	295	304
1998-99	295	300	291	306	254	276	264	281	(NA)	297	307
HISTORY, 1993-94											
4th graders	205	203	206	215	177	180	177	197	(NA)	214	216
8th graders:	259	259	259	267	239	243	241	251	(NA)	264	270
12th graders	286	288	285	292	265	267	263	276	(NA)	287	296
GEOGRAPHY, 1993-94											
4th graders	206	208	203	218	168	183	186	197	(NA)	216	216
8th graders	260	262	258	270	229	239	238	250	(NA)	265	272
12th graders	285	288	281	291	258	268	263	274	(NA)	286	294
CIVICS, 1997-98[3]											
4th graders	150	149	151	159	132	126	124	153	(NA)	150	153
8th graders	150	148	152	159	133	127	123	144	(NA)	143	160
12th graders	150	148	152	158	131	130	124	140	(NA)	145	160

NA Not available.   [1] Non-Hispanic.   [2] Writing scores revised from previous years; previous writing scores were recorded on a 0 to 400 rather than 0 to 500 scale.   [3] Civics uses a scale of 0 to 300.

Source: U.S. National Center for Education Statistics, Digest of Education Statistics, annual, and NAEP 1998 Civics Report Card for the Nation.

160   Education

No. 254. Advanced Placement Program—Summary: 1999 and 2000

[Includes exams taken by candidates abroad. In 2000 this represents 29,993 examinations taken by 20,664 students in 695 schools abroad. Minus sign (-) indicates decrease]

Item	Program total				2000				
	Schools repre-sented, 2000	Exams taken		Percent change, 1999-00	Grade level of test taker			Sex of test taker	
		1999	2000		10th grade	11th grade	12th grade	Male	Female
Exams taken, total [1]	(X)	1,149,515	1,272,317	11	68,317	437,502	729,659	589,005	683,312
By subject area:									
Art History	828	9,038	9,721	8	887	2,493	6,084	3,372	6,349
Art, Drawing	1,253	4,204	4,675	11	68	918	3,542	1,957	2,718
Art, General	1,975	8,769	9,172	5	126	1,434	7,329	3,340	5,832
Biology	6,410	82,592	86,826	5	6,622	31,729	45,936	36,578	50,248
Calculus AB	9,657	127,744	137,276	7	1,229	18,185	114,794	72,620	64,656
Calculus BC	3,066	30,724	34,142	11	617	5,983	26,846	21,076	13,066
Chemistry.	4,865	48,899	52,786	8	2,306	26,776	22,571	29,598	23,188
Computer Science—A . .	2,033	12,218	13,646	12	1,600	5,167	6,528	11,384	2,262
Computer Science—AB .	1,271	6,619	6,876	4	667	2,554	3,447	6,136	740
Economics-Micro	1,380	14,867	17,464	17	316	2,407	14,248	10,189	7,275
Economics-Macro	1,624	20,014	23,761	19	259	2,914	19,946	13,619	10,142
English Language/ Composition	5,274	97,370	114,049	17	1,186	81,674	28,770	42,889	71,160
English Literature/ Composition	10,021	176,221	190,643	8	168	11,721	174,558	69,009	121,634
Environmental Science . .	939	9,209	13,698	49	325	4,123	8,803	5,996	7,702
European History	3,347	54,759	59,708	9	28,080	9,307	20,862	28,841	30,867
French Language	2,909	15,031	15,493	3	755	3,998	10,173	4,812	10,681
French Literature	389	1,547	1,655	7	51	336	1,215	484	1,171
German Language	1,146	3,584	3,784	6	214	907	2,486	1,799	1,985
Government and Politics—U.S.	3,862	57,015	66,370	16	1,948	6,799	56,228	32,456	33,914
Government and Politics—Comparative . .	801	7,463	8,246	10	721	1,037	6,306	4,477	3.769
International English Language	65	4,633	5,844	26	18	60	74	2,354	3,490
Latin—Vergil	573	3,399	3,439	1	280	1,552	1,533	1,781	1,658
Latin—Literature	415	2,212	2,343	6	129	1,020	1,141	1,144	1,199
Music Theory	1,311	4,820	5,304	10	377	1,566	3,209	2,697	2,607
Physics—B	2,928	27,685	30,967	12	472	10,257	19,552	20,108	10,859
Physics—Mechanics . . .	1,929	14,419	15,634	8	75	1,717	13,514	11,632	4,002
Physics—Electricity and Magnetism	1,173	7,102	7,465	5	46	691	6,570	5,862	1,603
Psychology.	1,928	28,291	34,035	20	716	9,152	23,355	11,731	22,304
Spanish Language	4,936	58,340	64,380	10	5,669	22,103	33,932	22,878	41,502
Spanish Literature	984	7,998	8,829	10	448	2,718	5,329	2,813	6,016
Statistics	2,242	25,240	34,118	35	1,073	6,502	25,734	17,425	16,693
U.S. History	8,184	177,489	189,968	7	10,869	159,702	15,044	87,948	102,020
Candidates taking exams [1] .	(X)	704,298	768,586	9	61,778	291,921	387,904	341,993	426,593

X Not applicable.   [1] Includes candidates and exams taken in other grades not shown separately.

Source: The College Board, New York, NY, Advanced Placement Program, *National Summary Report*, 2000 (copyright).

No. 255. Foreign Language Enrollment in Public High Schools: 1970 to 1994

[In thousands (13,301.9 represents 13,301,900), except percent. As of fall, for grades 9 through 12]

Language	1970	1974	1976	1978	1982	1985	1990	1994
Total enrollment.	13,301.9	13,648.9	13,952.1	13,941.4	12,879.3	12,466.5	11,099.6	11,847.5
Enrolled in all foreign languages	3,779.3	3,294.5	3,174.0	3,200.1	2,909.8	4,028.9	4,256.9	5,001.9
Percent of all students.	28.4	24.1	22.7	23.0	22.6	32.3	38.4	42.2
Enrolled in modern foreign languages [1].	3,514.1	3,127.3	3,023.5	3,048.3	2,740.2	3,852.0	4,093.0	4,813.0
Spanish	1,810.8	1,678.1	1,717.0	1,631.4	1,562.8	2,334.4	2,611.4	3,219.8
French.	1,230.7	977.9	888.4	856.0	858.0	1,133.7	1,089.4	1,105.9
German	410.5	393.0	352.7	330.6	266.9	312.2	295.4	326.0
Italian	27.3	40.2	45.6	45.5	44.1	47.3	40.4	43.8
Japanese	(NA)	(NA)	(NA)	(NA)	6.2	8.6	25.1	42.3
Russian	20.2	15.1	11.3	8.8	5.7	6.4	16.5	16.4
Percent of all students [1]	26.4	22.9	21.7	21.9	21.3	30.9	36.9	40.6
Spanish	13.6	12.3	12.3	11.7	12.1	18.7	23.5	27.2
French	9.3	7.2	6.4	6.1	6.7	9.1	9.8	9.3
German	3.1	2.9	2.5	2.4	2.1	2.5	2.7	2.8
Italian	0.2	0.3	0.3	0.3	0.3	0.4	0.4	0.4
Japanese	(NA)	(NA)	(NA)	(NA)	0.1	0.1	0.2	0.4
Russian	0.2	0.1	0.1	0.1	(Z)	0.1	0.2	0.1

NA Not available.   Z Less than 0.05 percent.   [1] Includes other foreign languages, not shown separately.

Source: The American Council on the Teaching of Foreign Languages, Yonkers, NY, *Foreign Language Enrollments in Public Secondary Schools, Fall 1994.*

U.S. Census Bureau, Statistical Abstract of the United States: 2001

No. 256. Public High School Graduates by State: 1980 to 2000

[In thousands (2,747.7 represents 2,747,000). For school year ending in year shown]

State	1980	1990	1995	2000 est.	State	1980	1990	1995	2000 est.
United States...	2,747.7	2,320.3	2,273.1	2,545.3	Missouri	62.3	49.0	49.0	53.5
					Montana	12.1	9.4	10.1	10.9
Alabama	45.2	40.5	35.0	37.9	Nebraska	22.4	17.7	18.0	22.1
Alaska	5.2	5.4	5.9	7.0	Nevada	8.5	9.5	10.4	13.9
Arizona	28.6	32.1	30.0	42.4	New Hampshire	11.7	10.8	10.1	10.4
Arkansas	29.1	26.5	25.1	26.6					
California	249.2	236.3	259.1	303.2	New Jersey	94.6	69.8	67.7	68.9
					New Mexico	18.4	14.9	15.4	17.3
Colorado	36.8	33.0	32.6	38.1	New York	204.1	143.3	134.4	141.8
Connecticut	37.7	27.9	26.3	29.9	North Carolina	70.9	64.8	57.0	61.5
Delaware	7.6	5.6	5.6	6.4					
District of Columbia	5.0	3.6	2.7	2.5	North Dakota	9.9	7.7	8.0	8.6
Florida	87.3	88.9	89.2	99.9	Ohio	144.2	114.5	102.1	115.0
Georgia	61.6	56.6	56.3	66.6	Oklahoma	39.3	35.6	33.1	36.8
Hawaii	11.5	10.3	9.4	10.2	Oregon	29.9	25.5	26.6	28.7
Idaho	13.2	12.0	14.7	15.7	Pennsylvania	146.5	110.5	106.0	114.2
Illinois	135.6	108.1	104.6	111.2					
Indiana	73.1	60.0	56.3	58.4	Rhode Island	10.9	7.8	7.7	7.5
					South Carolina	38.7	32.5	30.2	34.5
Iowa	43.4	31.8	31.7	34.1	South Dakota	10.7	7.7	8.5	9.4
Kansas	30.9	25.4	25.8	29.0	Tennessee	49.8	46.1	43.8	41.7
Kentucky	41.2	38.0	36.6	37.0	Texas	171.4	172.5	171.8	213.0
Louisiana	46.3	36.1	36.5	35.2	Utah	20.0	21.2	26.3	32.3
Maine	15.4	13.8	11.8	12.9					
					Vermont	6.7	6.1	5.9	6.8
Maryland	54.3	41.6	41.8	48.1	Virginia	66.6	60.6	58.2	66.9
Massachusetts	73.8	55.9	48.0	50.5	Washington	50.4	45.9	49.9	57.2
Michigan	124.3	93.8	85.5	100.6	West Virginia	23.4	21.9	20.3	19.6
Minnesota	64.9	49.1	50.5	57.6	Wisconsin	69.3	52.0	52.7	59.4
Mississippi	27.6	25.2	23.0	26.4	Wyoming	6.1	5.8	5.9	6.3

Source: U.S. National Center for Education Statistics. *Digest of Education Statistics*, annual.

No. 257. High School Dropouts by Race and Hispanic Origin: 1975 to 1999

[In percent. As of October]

Item	1975	1980	1985	1990 [1]	1992	1993	1994	1995	1996	1997	1998	1999
EVENT DROPOUTS [2]												
Total [3]	5.8	6.0	5.2	4.0	4.3	4.2	5.0	5.4	4.7	4.3	4.4	4.7
White	5.4	5.6	4.8	3.8	4.1	4.1	4.7	5.1	4.5	4.2	4.4	4.4
Male	5.0	6.4	4.9	4.1	3.8	4.1	4.6	5.4	4.8	4.9	4.4	4.1
Female	5.8	4.9	4.7	3.5	4.4	4.1	4.9	4.8	4.1	3.5	4.4	4.7
Black	8.7	8.3	7.7	5.1	4.9	5.4	6.2	6.1	6.3	4.8	5.0	6.0
Male	8.3	8.0	8.3	4.1	3.3	5.7	6.5	7.9	4.6	4.6		5.2
Female	9.0	8.5	7.2	6.0	6.7	5.0	5.7	4.4	7.8	5.7	5.5	6.8
Hispanic [4]	10.9	11.5	9.7	8.0	7.9	5.4	9.2	11.6	8.4	8.6	8.4	7.1
Male	10.1	16.9	9.3	8.7	5.8	5.7	8.4	10.9	9.2	10.4	8.6	6.9
Female	11.6	6.9	9.8	7.2	8.6	5.0	10.1	12.5	7.6	6.7	8.2	7.3
STATUS DROPOUTS [5]												
Total [3]	15.6	15.6	13.9	13.6	12.7	12.7	13.3	13.9	12.8	13.0	13.9	13.1
White	13.9	14.4	13.5	13.5	12.2	12.2	12.7	13.6	12.5	12.4	13.7	12.8
Male	13.5	15.7	14.7	14.2	13.3	13.0	13.6	14.3	12.9	13.8	15.7	13.9
Female	14.2	13.2	12.3	12.8	11.1	11.5	11.7	13.0	12.1	10.9	11.7	11.8
Black	27.3	23.5	17.6	15.1	16.3	16.4	15.5	14.4	16.0	16.7	17.1	16.0
Male	27.8	26.0	18.8	13.6	15.5	15.6	17.5	14.2	17.4	17.5	20.5	16.3
Female	26.9	21.5	16.6	16.2	17.1	17.2	13.7	14.6	14.7	16.1	14.3	15.7
Hispanic [4]	34.9	40.3	31.5	37.3	33.9	32.7	34.7	34.7	34.5	30.6	34.4	33.9
Male	32.6	42.6	35.8	39.8	38.4	34.7	36.1	34.2	36.2	33.2	39.7	36.4
Female	36.8	38.1	27.0	34.5	29.6	31.0	33.1	35.4	32.7	27.6	28.6	31.1

[1] Beginning 1990 reflects new editing procedures for cases with missing data on school enrollment. [2] Percent of students who drop out in a single year without completing high school. For grades 10 to 12. [3] Includes other races, not shown separately. [4] Persons of Hispanic origin may be of any race. [5] Percent of the population who have not completed high school and are not enrolled, regardless of when they dropped out. For persons 18 to 24 years old.

Source: U.S. Census Bureau, *Current Population Reports*, P20-533.

No. 258. High School Dropouts by Age, Race, and Hispanic Origin: 1970 to 1999

[As of October (4,670 represents 4,670,000). For persons 14 to 24 years old. See Table 260 for definition of dropouts]

Age and race	Number of dropouts (1,000)					Percent of population				
	1970	1980	1990	1995	1999	1970	1980	1990	1995	1999
Total dropouts [1][2] ..	4,670	5,212	3,854	3,963	3,966	12.2	12.0	10.1	9.9	9.4
16 to 17 years	617	709	418	406	416	8.0	8.8	6.3	5.4	5.1
18 to 21 years	2,138	2,578	1,921	1,980	2,048	16.4	15.8	13.4	14.2	13.5
22 to 24 years	1,770	1,798	1,458	1,491	1,364	18.7	15.2	13.8	13.6	12.6
White [2]	3,577	4,169	3,127	3,098	3,123	10.8	11.3	10.1	9.7	9.3
16 to 17 years	485	619	334	314	334	7.3	9.2	6.4	5.4	5.3
18 to 21 years	1,618	2,032	1,516	1,530	1,587	14.3	14.7	13.1	13.8	13.1
22 to 24 years	1,356	1,416	1,235	1,181	1,093	16.3	14.0	14.0	13.4	12.5
Black [2]	1,047	934	611	605	691	22.2	16.0	10.9	10.0	10.8
16 to 17 years	125	80	73	70	63	12.8	6.9	6.9	5.8	4.9
18 to 21 years	500	486	345	328	383	30.5	23.0	16.0	15.8	16.8
22 to 24 years	397	346	185	194	229	37.8	24.0	13.5	12.5	14.8
Hispanic [2][3]	(NA)	919	1,122	1,355	1,472	(NA)	29.5	26.8	24.7	23.9
16 to 17 years	(NA)	92	89	94	105	(NA)	16.6	12.9	10.7	9.5
18 to 21 years	(NA)	470	502	652	708	(NA)	40.3	32.9	29.9	32.1
22 to 24 years	(NA)	323	523	598	632	(NA)	40.6	42.8	37.4	36.1

NA Not available. [1] Includes other groups not shown separately. [2] Includes persons 14 to 15 years, not shown separately. [3] Persons of Hispanic origin may be of any race.

Source: U.S. Census Bureau, *Current Population Reports*, P20-533; and earlier reports.

No. 259. Enrollment Status by Race, Hispanic Origin, and Sex: 1975 and 1999

[As of October (15,693 represents 15,693,000). For persons 18 to 21 years old. For the civilian noninstitutional population. Based on the Current Population Survey; see text, Section 1, Population, and Appendix III]

Characteristic	Total persons 18 to 21 years old (1,000)		Percent distribution							
			Enrolled in high school		High school graduates				Not high school graduates	
					Total		In college			
	1975	1999	1975	1999	1975	1999	1975	1999	1975	1999
Total [1]	15,693	15,187	5.7	9.6	78.0	76.9	33.5	43.7	16.3	13.5
White	13,448	12,104	4.7	9.0	80.6	77.8	34.6	44.4	14.7	13.1
Black	1,997	2,280	12.5	13.0	60.4	70.3	24.9	36.0	27.0	16.8
Hispanic [2]	899	2,204	12.0	12.3	57.2	55.5	24.4	22.4	30.8	32.1
Male [1]	7,584	7,616	7.4	11.3	76.6	74.4	35.4	41.7	15.9	14.3
White	6,545	6,128	6.2	10.9	79.7	75.3	36.9	41.8	14.1	13.8
Black	911	1,089	15.9	15.1	55.0	67.3	23.9	36.9	29.0	17.7
Hispanic [2]	416	1,130	17.3	15.0	54.6	51.9	25.2	20.1	27.9	33.2
Female [1]	8,109	7,571	4.2	7.8	79.2	79.5	31.8	45.8	16.6	12.6
White	6,903	5,977	3.2	7.2	81.4	80.4	32.4	47.0	15.3	12.4
Black	1,085	1,191	9.7	11.0	65.0	73.0	25.8	35.0	25.4	16.0
Hispanic [2]	484	1,073	7.6	9.6	59.3	59.4	23.6	24.8	33.1	31.0

[1] Includes other races not shown separately. [2] Persons of Hispanic origin may be of any race.

Source: U.S. Census Bureau, *Current Population Reports*, P20-533; and earlier reports.

No. 260. Employment Status of High School Graduates and School Dropouts: 1980 to 2000

[In thousands (11,622 represents 11,622,000), except percent. As of October. For civilian noninstitutional population 16 to 24 years old. Based on Current Population Survey; see text, Section 1, Population, and Appendix III]

Employment status, sex, and race	Graduates [1]				Dropouts [3]			
	1980	1990	1995 [2]	2000 [2]	1980	1990	1995 [2]	2000 [2]
Civilian population	11,622	8,370	6,627	7,351	5,254	3,800	3,876	3,776
In labor force	9,795	7,107	5,530	6,195	3,549	2,506	2,443	2,612
Percent of population	84.3	84.9	83.4	84.3	67.5	66.0	63.0	69.2
Employed	8,567	6,279	4,863	5,632	2,651	1,993	1,894	2,150
Percent of labor force	87.5	88.3	87.9	90.9	74.7	79.5	77.5	82.3
Unemployed	1,228	828	667	563	898	513	549	463
Unemployment rate, total [4]	12.5	11.7	12.1	9.1	25.3	20.5	22.5	17.7
Male	13.5	11.1	11.7	9.3	23.5	18.8	19.2	16.3
Female	11.5	12.3	12.5	8.8	28.7	23.5	28.8	20.3
White	10.8	9.0	10.5	7.2	21.6	17.0	19.1	15.0
Black	26.1	26.0	20.3	18.1	43.9	43.3	48.0	33.2
Not in labor force	1,827	1,262	1,097	1,156	1,705	1,294	1,433	1,163
Percent of population	15.7	15.1	16.6	15.7	32.5	34.1	37.0	30.8

[1] For persons not enrolled in college who have completed 4 years of high school only. [2] See footnote 2, Table 567. [3] For persons not in regular school and who have not completed the 12th grade nor received a general equivalency degree. [4] Includes other races not shown separately.

Source: U.S. Bureau of Labor Statistics, Bulletin 2307; *News*, USDL 01-94, April 13, 2001; and unpublished data.

Education 163

No. 261. General Educational Development (GED) Credentials Issued: 1974 to 1999

[GEDs issued in thousands (295 represents 295,000). Includes outlying areas]

Year	GEDs issued	Percent distribution by age of test taker				
		19 years old or under	20 to 24 years old	25 to 29 years old	30 to 34 years old	35 years old and over
1974	295	35	27	13	9	17
1975	342	33	26	14	9	18
1980	488	37	27	13	8	15
1985	427	33	26	15	10	16
1990	419	35	25	14	10	17
1993	476	33	27	14	11	16
1994	499	34	26	13	10	16
1995	513	37	25	13	10	15
1996	514	40	25	13	9	15
1997	471	41	25	12	8	14
1998	496	43	25	11	8	14
1999	516	43	25	11	8	14

Source: U.S. National Center for Education Statistics, *Digest of Education Statistics*, 2000.

No. 262. College Enrollment of Recent High School Graduates: 1960 to 1999

[High school graduates in thousands (1,679 represents 1,679,000). For persons 16 to 24 who graduated from high school in the preceding 12 months. Includes persons receiving GEDs. Based on surveys and subject to sampling error]

Year	Number of high school graduates					Percent enrolled in college [2]				
	Total [1]	Male	Female	White	Black	Total [1]	Male	Female	White	Black
1960	1,679	756	923	1,565	(NA)	45.1	54.0	37.9	45.8	(NA)
1965	2,659	1,254	1,405	2,417	(NA)	50.9	57.3	45.3	51.7	(NA)
1970	2,757	1,343	1,414	2,461	(NA)	51.8	55.2	48.5	52.0	(NA)
1975	3,186	1,513	1,673	2,825	(NA)	50.7	52.6	49.0	51.2	(NA)
1980	3,089	1,500	1,589	2,682	361	49.3	46.7	51.8	49.9	41.8
1982	3,100	1,508	1,592	2,644	384	50.6	49.0	52.1	52.0	36.5
1983	2,964	1,390	1,574	2,496	392	52.7	51.9	53.4	55.0	38.5
1984	3,012	1,429	1,583	2,514	438	55.2	56.0	54.5	57.9	40.2
1985	2,666	1,286	1,380	2,241	333	57.7	58.6	56.9	59.4	42.3
1986	2,786	1,331	1,455	2,307	386	53.8	55.9	51.9	56.0	36.5
1987	2,647	1,278	1,369	2,207	337	56.8	58.4	55.3	56.6	51.9
1988	2,673	1,334	1,339	2,187	382	58.9	57.0	60.8	60.7	45.0
1989	2,454	1,208	1,245	2,051	337	59.6	57.6	61.6	60.4	52.8
1990	2,355	1,169	1,185	1,921	341	59.9	57.8	62.0	61.5	46.3
1991	2,276	1,139	1,137	1,867	320	62.4	57.6	67.1	64.6	45.6
1992	2,398	1,216	1,182	1,900	353	61.7	59.6	63.8	63.4	47.9
1993	2,338	1,118	1,219	1,910	302	62.6	59.7	65.4	62.8	55.6
1994	2,517	1,244	1,273	2,065	318	61.9	60.6	63.2	63.6	50.9
1995	2,599	1,238	1,361	2,088	356	61.9	62.6	61.4	62.6	51.4
1996	2,660	1,297	1,363	2,092	416	65.0	60.1	69.7	65.8	55.3
1997	2,769	1,354	1,415	2,228	394	67.0	63.5	70.3	67.5	59.6
1998	2,810	1,452	1,358	2,227	393	65.6	62.4	69.1	65.8	62.1
1999	2,897	1,474	1,423	2,287	453	62.9	61.4	64.4	62.8	59.2

NA Not available. [1] Includes other races, not shown separately. [2] As of October.
Source: U.S. National Center for Education Statistics, *Digest of Education Statistics*, annual.

No. 263. College Enrollment by Sex and Attendance Status: 1983 to 1998

[As of fall. In thousands (12,465 represents 12,465,000)]

Sex and age	1983		1988		1993		1997		1998 [1]	
	Total	Part time	Total	Part time	Total	Part time	Total	Part time	Total	Part time
Total	12,465	5,204	13,055	5,619	14,305	6,177	14,345	6,023	14,549	5,968
Male	6,024	2,264	6,002	2,340	6,427	2,537	6,330	2,491	6,387	2,445
14 to 17 years old	102	16	55	5	83	10	55	9	88	18
18 to 19 years old	1,256	158	1,290	132	1,224	138	1,392	258	1,481	238
20 to 21 years old	1,241	205	1,243	216	1,294	209	1,359	298	1,335	280
22 to 24 years old	1,158	382	1,106	378	1,260	392	1,190	427	1,130	374
25 to 29 years old	1,115	624	875	485	950	564	964	494	952	503
30 to 34 years old	570	384	617	456	661	484	439	281	436	271
35 years old and over	583	494	816	668	955	739	931	724	966	762
Female	6,441	2,940	7,053	3,278	7,877	3,640	8,015	3,532	8,163	3,522
14 to 17 years old	142	16	115	17	93	6	113	39	103	21
18 to 19 years old	1,496	179	1,536	195	1,416	172	1,622	264	1,799	243
20 to 21 years old	1,125	204	1,278	218	1,414	279	1,484	297	1,476	281
22 to 24 years old	884	378	932	403	1,263	493	1,263	436	1,192	408
25 to 29 years old	947	658	932	633	1,058	689	1,017	601	1,022	622
30 to 34 years old	721	553	698	499	811	575	659	446	655	428
35 years old and over	1,126	953	1,563	1,313	1,824	1,427	1,859	1,450	1,916	1,519

[1] In this table, data beginning in 1998 reflect the new classification of institutions. See footnote 1, Table 264.
Source: U.S. National Center for Education Statistics, *Digest of Education Statistics*, annual.

No. 264. Higher Education—Summary: 1970 to 1998

[Institutions, staff, and enrollment as of fall (474 represents 474,000). Finances for fiscal year ending in the following year. Covers universities, colleges, professional schools, junior and teachers colleges, both publicly and privately controlled, regular session. Includes estimates for institutions not reporting. See also Appendix III]

Item	Unit	1970	1980	1985	1990	1994	1995	1996	1997	1998
ALL INSTITUTIONS										
Number of institutions [1]	Number.	2,556	3,231	3,340	3,559	3,688	3,706	4,009	4,064	4,070
4-year	Number .	1,665	1,957	2,029	2,141	2,215	2,244	2,267	2,309	2,343
2-year	Number .	891	1,274	1,311	1,418	1,473	1,462	1,742	1,755	1,727
Instructional staff—										
(Lecturer or above) [2]	1,000...	474	686	715	817	915	932	932	990	995
Percent full-time	Percent .	78	66	64	61	(NA)	59	59	57	(NA)
Total enrollment [3]	1,000...	8,581	12,097	12,247	13,819	14,279	14,262	14,368	14,502	14,549
Male	1,000...	5,044	5,874	5,818	6,284	6,372	6,343	6,353	6,396	6,387
Female	1,000...	3,537	6,223	6,429	7,535	7,907	7,919	8,015	8,106	8,163
4-year institutions	1,000...	6,262	7,571	7,716	8,579	8,749	8,769	8,804	8,897	9,033
2-year institutions	1,000...	2,319	4,526	4,531	5,240	5,530	5,493	5,563	5,606	5,516
Full-time	1,000...	5,816	7,098	7,075	7,821	8,138	8,129	8,303	8,438	8,582
Part-time	1,000...	2,765	4,999	5,172	5,998	6,141	6,133	6,065	6,064	5,968
Public	1,000...	6,428	9,457	9,479	10,845	11,134	11,092	11,120	11,196	11,176
Private	1,000...	2,153	2,640	2,768	2,974	3,145	3,169	3,247	3,306	3,373
Undergraduate [4]	1,000...	7,376	10,475	10,597	11,959	12,263	12,232	12,327	12,451	12,477
Men	1,000...	4,254	5,000	4,962	5,380	5,422	5,401	5,421	5,469	5,463
Women	1,000...	3,122	5,475	5,635	6,579	6,840	6,831	6,906	6,982	7,014
First-time freshmen	1,000...	2,063	2,588	2,292	2,257	2,133	2,169	2,274	2,219	2,218
First professional	1,000...	173	278	274	273	295	298	298	298	303
Men	1,000...	159	199	180	167	174	174	173	170	169
Women	1,000...	15	78	94	107	121	124	126	129	134
Graduate [4]	1,000...	1,031	1,343	1,376	1,586	1,721	1,732	1,742	1,753	1,770
Men	1,000...	630	675	677	737	776	768	759	758	755
Women	1,000...	400	670	700	849	946	965	983	996	1,015
Current funds revenues [5]	Mil. dol.	23,879	65,585	100,438	149,766	189,121	197,973	(NA)	(NA)	(NA)
Tuition and fees	Mil. dol.	5,021	13,773	23,117	33,117	37,434	51,507	55,260	(NA)	(NA)
Federal government	Mil. dol.	4,190	9,748	12,705	18,236	23,243	23,939	(NA)	(NA)	(NA)
State government	Mil. dol.	6,503	20,106	29,912	39,481	44,343	45,693	(NA)	(NA)	(NA)
Auxiliary enterprises	Mil. dol.	3,125	7,287	10,674	14,903	18,336	18,868	(NA)	(NA)	(NA)
Current funds expenditures [5]	Mil. dol .	23,375	64,053	97,536	146,088	182,969	190,476	(NA)	(NA)	(NA)
Educational and general [6]	Mil. dol.	17,616	50,074	76,128	114,140	144,158	151,446	(NA)	(NA)	(NA)
Auxiliary enterprises	Mil. dol.	2,988	7,288	10,528	14,272	17,205	17,599	(NA)	(NA)	(NA)
Endowment (market value)	Mil. dol.	13,714	23,465	50,281	72,049	109,707	128,837	(NA)	(NA)	(NA)
2-YEAR INSTITUTIONS										
Number of institutions [1][7]	Number.	891	1,274	1,311	1,418	1,473	1,462	1,742	1,755	1,727
Public	Number .	654	945	932	972	1,036	1,047	1,088	1,092	1,075
Private	Number .	237	329	379	446	437	415	654	663	652
Instructional staff—										
(Lecturer or above) [2]	1,000...	92	192	211	(NA)	(NA)	285	285	307	(NA)
Enrollment [3][4]	1,000...	2,319	4,526	4,531	5,240	5,530	5,493	5,563	5,606	5,516
Public	1,000...	2,195	4,329	4,270	4,996	5,308	5,278	5,314	5,361	5,272
Private	1,000...	124	198	261	244	221	215	249	245	244
Male	1,000...	1,375	2,047	2,002	2,233	2,323	2,329	2,359	2,390	2,345
Female	1,000...	945	2,479	2,529	3,007	3,207	3,164	3,204	3,216	3,172
Current funds revenue [5]	Mil. dol .	2,504	8,505	12,293	18,021	22,977	24,614	(NA)	(NA)	(NA)
Tuition and fees	Mil. dol.	413	1,618	2,618	4,029	5,643	6,323	(NA)	(NA)	(NA)
State government	Mil. dol.	926	3,961	5,659	8,001	9,252	9,848	(NA)	(NA)	(NA)
Local government	Mil. dol.	701	1,623	2,027	3,044	4,139	4,324	(NA)	(NA)	(NA)
Current funds expenditures	Mil. dol .	2,327	8,212	11,976	17,494	22,078	23,522	(NA)	(NA)	(NA)
Education and general [6]	Mil. dol.	2,073	7,608	11,118	16,270	20,616	22,053	(NA)	(NA)	(NA)
Instruction	Mil. dol.	1,205	3,764	5,398	7,903	9,829	10,312	(NA)	(NA)	(NA)

NA Not available. [1] Beginning 1980, number of institutions includes count of branch campuses. Due to revised survey procedures, data beginning 1990 are not comparable with previous years. Beginning 1996 data reflect a new classification of institutions; this classification includes some additional, primarily 2-year, colleges than before and excludes a few institutions that did not award degrees. Includes institutions that were eligible to participate in Title IV federal financial aid programs. [2] Due to revised survey methods, data beginning 1990 not comparable with previous years. [3] Beginning 1980, branch campuses counted according to actual status, e.g., 2-year branch in 2-year category; previously a 2-year branch included in university category. [4] Includes unclassified students. (Students taking courses for credit, but are not candidates for degrees.) [5] Includes items not shown separately. [6] Data for 1970 are not strictly comparable with later years. [7] Beginning 1980, includes schools accredited by the National Association of Trade and Technical Schools. See footnote 1 for information pertaining to data beginning 1996.

Source: U.S. National Center for Education Statistics, *Digest of Education Statistics*, annual; *Projections of Education Statistics*, annual; and unpublished data.

Education 165.

No. 265. College Enrollment by Selected Characteristics: 1990 to 1997

[In thousands (13,818.6 represents 13,818,600). As of fall. Totals may differ from other tables because of adjustments to underreported and nonreported racial/ethnic data. Nonresident alien students are not distributed among racial/ethnic groups]

Characteristic	1990	1991	1992	1993	1994	1995	1996 [1]	1997 [1]
Total	13,818.6	14,359.0	14,487.4	14,304.8	14,278.8	14,261.8	14,367.5	14,502.3
Male	6,283.9	6,501.8	6,524.0	6,427.5	6,371.9	6,342.5	6,352.8	6,396.0
Female	7,534.7	7,857.1	7,963.4	7,877.4	7,906.9	7,919.2	8,014.7	8,106.3
Public	10,844.7	11,309.6	11,384.6	11,189.1	11,133.7	11,092.4	11,120.5	11,196.1
Private	2,973.9	3,049.4	3,102.8	3,115.7	3,145.1	3,169.4	3,247.0	3,306.2
2-year	5,240.1	5,651.9	5,722.4	5,565.9	5,529.7	5,492.5	5,563.3	5,605.6
4-year	8,578.6	8,707.1	8,765.0	8,738.9	8,749.1	8,769.3	8,804.2	8,896.8
Undergraduate	11,959.2	12,439.3	12,537.7	12,324.0	12,262.6	12,232.0	12,326.9	12,450.6
Graduate	1,586.2	1,639.1	1,668.7	1,688.4	1,721.5	1,732.0	1,742.3	1,753.5
First professional . . .	273.4	280.5	280.9	292.4	294.7	297.6	298.3	298.3
White [2]	10,722.5	10,989.8	10,875.4	10,600.0	10,427.0	10,311.2	10,263.9	10,266.1
Male	4,861.0	4,962.2	4,884.6	4,755.0	4,650.7	4,594.1	4,552.2	4,548.8
Female	5,861.5	6,027.6	5,990.8	5,845.1	5,776.3	5,717.2	5,711.7	5,717.4
Public	8,385.4	8,622.2	8,492.8	8,226.6	8,056.3	7,945.4	7,871.9	7,857.8
Private	2,337.0	2,367.5	2,382.6	2,373.4	2,370.6	2,365.9	2,392.0	2,408.3
2-year	3,954.3	4,198.8	4,131.2	3,960.6	3,861.7	3,794.0	3,780.8	3,770.0
4-year	6,768.1	6,791.0	6,744.3	6,639.5	6,565.3	6,517.2	6,483.1	6,496.1
Undergraduate	9,272.6	9,507.7	9,387.6	9,100.4	8,916.0	8,805.6	8,769.5	8,783.9
Graduate	1,228.4	1,258.0	1,267.2	1,273.8	1,286.8	1,282.3	1,272.6	1,261.8
First professional . . .	221.5	224.0	220.6	225.9	224.2	223.3	221.7	220.4
Black [2]	1,247.0	1,335.4	1,392.9	1,412.8	1,448.6	1,473.7	1,505.6	1,551.0
Male	484.7	. 517.0	536.9	543.7	549.7	555.9	564.1	579.8
Female	762.3	818.4	856.0	869.1	898.9	917.8	941.4	971.3
Public	976.4	1,053.4	1,100.5	1,114.3	1,144.6	1,160.6	1,177.4	1,205.3
Private	270.6	281.9	292.3	298.5	304.1	313.0	328.1	345.8
2-year	524.3	577.6	601.6	599.0	615.0	621.5	636.0	654.6
4-year	722.8	757.7	791.2	813.7	833.6	852.2	869.6	896.4
Undergraduate	1,147.2	1,229.3	1,280.6	1,290.4	1,317.3	1,333.6	1,358.6	1,398.1
Graduate	83.9	88.9	94.1	102.2	110.6	118.6	125.5	131.6
First professional . . .	15.9	17.2	18.2	20.2	20.7	21.4	21.5	21.4
Hispanic	782.4	866.6	955.0	988.8	1,045.6	1,093.8	1,166.1	1,218.5
Male	353.9	390.5	427.7	441.2	464.0	480.2	506.6	525.8
Female	428.5	476.0	527.3	547.6	581.6	613.7	659.5	692.7
Public	671.4	742.1	822.3	851.3	898.7	937.1	990.7	1,031.6
Private	111.0	124.5	132.7	137.5	146.8	156.8	175.4	186.9
2-year	424.2	483.7	545.0	556.8	582.9	608.4	657.3	688.5
4-year	358.2	382.9	409.9	432.0	462.7	485.5	508.8	530.0
Undergraduate	724.6	804.2	887.8	918.1	968.3	1,012.0	1,079.4	1,125.9
Graduate	47.2	50.9	55.3	57.9	63.9	68.0	72.8	78.7
First professional . . .	10.7	11.4	12.0	12.8	13.4	13.8	13.9	13.9
American Indian [2]	102.8	113.7	119.3	121.7	127.4	131.3	137.6	142.5
Male	43.1	47.6	50.2	51.2	53.0	54.8	57.2	59.0
Female	59.7	66.1	69.1	70.5	74.4	76.5	80.4	83.4
Public	90.4	100.2	103.3	106.4	110.7	113.8	118.8	123.6
Private	12.4	13.6	15.9	15.3	16.6	17.5	18.8	18.8
2-year	54.9	62.6	64.4	63.2	66.2	65.6	70.2	71.0
4-year	47.9	51.2	54.9	58.5	61.2	65.7	67.3	71.5
Undergraduate	95.5	105.8	110.9	112.7	117.4	120.7	126.5	130.8
Graduate	6.2	6.6	7.0	7.3	8.1	8.5	8.9	9.4
First professional . . .	1.1	1.3	1.5	1.7	1.8	2.1	2.2	2.3
Asian [2]	572.4	637.2	697.0	724.4	774.3	797.4	828.2	859.2
Male	294.9	325.1	351.5	363.1	385.0	393.3	405.5	417.7
Female	277.5	312.0	345.6	361.3	389.3	404.1	422.6	441.5
Public	461.0	516.3	565.9	586.3	622.1	638.0	657.9	680.4
Private	111.5	120.9	131.1	138.2	152.2	159.4	170.3	178.8
2-year	215.2	255.7	289.5	295.0	312.5	314.9	327.0	340.7
4-year	357.2	381.5	407.5	429.4	461.8	482.4	501.1	518.5
Undergraduate	500.5	558.7	613.0	634.2	674.1	692.2	717.6	743.7
Graduate	53.2	57.6	61.5	65.2	72.6	75.6	79.1	82.6
First professional . . .	18.7	20.8	22.5	25.0	27.6	29.6	31.4	32.9
Nonresident alien . .	391.5	416.4	447.7	457.1	455.9	454.4	466.3	465.0
Male	246.3	259.4	273.1	273.4	269.5	264.3	267.2	264.9
Female	145.2	157.0	174.6	183.7	186.4	190.1	199.0	200.1
Public	260.0	275.3	299.5	304.3	301.2	297.5	303.8	297.3
Private	131.4	141.0	148.1	152.7	154.7	156.9	162.5	167.7
2-year	67.1	73.5	90.6	91.2	91.4	88.1	92.0	80.7
4-year	324.3	342.8	357.0	365.9	364.5	366.2	374.3	384.3
Undergraduate	218.7	233.6	257.9	268.2	269.4	267.6	275.3	268.2
Graduate	167.3	177.0	183.6	182.0	179.5	179.5	183.3	189.4
First professional . . .	5.4	5.8	6.2	6.9	7.0	7.3	7.6	7.5

[1] Beginning 1996 data reflect a new classification of institutions; this classification includes some additional, primarily 2-year, colleges than before and excludes a few institutions that did not award degrees. [2] Non-Hispanic.

Source: U.S. National Center for Education Statistics, *Digest of Education Statistics,* annual.

No. 266. Degree-Granting Institutions, Number, and Enrollment by State: 1997

[14,502 represents 14,502,000. Number of institutions beginning in academic year. Opening fall enrollment of resident and extension students attending full time or part time. Excludes students taking courses for credit by mail, radio, or TV, and students in branches of U.S. institutions operated in foreign countries. See Appendix III]

State	Number of institutions[1]	Enrollment (1,000)							Minority enrollment			Nonresident alien
		Total	Male	Female	Public	Private	Full time	White[2]	Total[3]	Black[2]	Hispanic	
United States . . .	4,064	14,502	6,396	8,106	11,196	3,306	8,438	10,266	3,771	1,551	1,218	465
Alabama	79	219	95	123	194	25	152	155	59	54	2	5
Alaska	8	28	11	17	27	1	12	22	6	1	1	(Z)
Arizona	67	293	131	162	261	32	142	209	76	10	45	8
Arkansas	47	112	47	65	101	11	73	89	21	17	1	2
California	396	1,958	865	1,093	1,664	294	937	956	930	153	406	72
Colorado	70	252	114	138	213	39	138	200	46	9	25	6
Connecticut	42	153	67	86	95	58	83	120	27	12	8	6
Delaware	10	45	19	26	36	8	26	35	9	7	1	1
District of Columbia	17	72	32	40	5	68	50	35	28	21	3	9
Florida	140	658	285	373	535	124	325	421	216	93	99	22
Georgia	104	306	131	175	235	71	209	203	94	79	5	9
Hawaii	20	62	27	34	46	16	36	15	41	2	1	6
Idaho	15	62	27	34	50	11	42	57	4	(Z)	2	1
Illinois	172	726	317	410	537	190	379	501	206	95	68	19
Indiana	96	296	134	162	225	71	199	253	33	19	7	10
Iowa	64	181	81	100	128	53	125	161	13	5	3	7
Kansas	59	178	81	97	160	18	97	148	24	9	8	5
Kentucky	63	179	74	105	146	33	120	158	17	13	1	3
Louisiana	85	219	92	128	189	30	157	143	71	59	5	6
Maine	35	56	22	34	38	18	32	53	3	1	-	1
Maryland	58	261	109	152	217	44	131	167	84	61	7	10
Massachusetts	129	413	180	233	175	238	265	315	72	25	19	25
Michigan	110	550	239	311	459	91	285	436	95	62	12	18
Minnesota	115	270	120	150	203	67	170	239	24	8	4	7
Mississippi	46	131	55	76	119	12	97	86	43	40	1	2
Missouri	112	303	132	170	191	112	175	253	42	27	6	8
Montana	28	44	20	24	39	5	34	38	5	(Z)	1	1
Nebraska	37	112	50	61	89	22	69	99	9	4	2	3
Nevada	14	76	34	42	73	3	27	56	18	5	7	2
New Hampshire	26	64	27	37	35	29	39	59	4	1	1	1
New Jersey	59	326	142	184	261	64	179	218	96	39	33	12
New Mexico	44	109	46	63	101	8	56	58	49	3	37	2
New York	319	1,024	435	590	568	457	670	666	314	138	104	44
North Carolina	121	374	160	214	302	72	236	273	94	77	5	7
North Dakota	21	39	19	20	35	4	32	35	3	(Z)	(Z)	1
Ohio	177	537	236	301	405	132	341	447	73	52	8	17
Oklahoma	46	177	80	97	155	23	108	132	37	13	5	8
Oregon	54	170	78	92	144	26	94	142	22	3	6	6
Pennsylvania	253	588	263	325	335	253	407	487	84	49	12	18
Rhode Island	12	72	32	40	37	35	47	60	9	3	3	3
South Carolina	61	176	73	103	149	28	114	127	47	42	2	3
South Dakota	25	39	18	22	33	6	29	35	4	(Z)	(Z)	1
Tennessee	83	250	108	141	194	56	168	199	46	38	3	5
Texas	194	969	442	527	846	124	534	582	359	98	210	28
Utah	21	158	78	80	119	39	98	142	11	1	5	5
Vermont	25	36	16	21	21	16	26	34	2	(Z)	1	1
Virginia	92	365	159	206	302	63	208	265	91	62	9	8
Washington	72	315	140	176	275	41	187	247	58	13	13	10
West Virginia	34	88	39	49	76	12	62	80	6	4	1	2
Wisconsin	66	298	133	166	244	54	183	262	29	13	7	7
Wyoming	9	30	13	17	29	1	17	27	2	(Z)	1	-
U.S. military[4]	12	83	70	13	83	-	20	66	17	11	3	1

- Represents zero.   Z Fewer than 500.   [1] Branch campuses counted as separate institutions.   [2] Non-Hispanic.
[3] Includes other races not shown separately.   [4] Service schools.
Source: U.S. National Center for Education Statistics, *Digest of Education Statistics*, annual.

No. 267. Postsecondary Institutions Offering Distance Education: 1997-98

[Distance education refers to courses delivered to off-campus locations via audio, video or computer technologies. Based on the Postsecondary Education Quick Information System; see source for details]

Institutional characteristic	Institutions		Enrollments in distance education courses			
				In college level credit-granting courses		
	Total	Offering distance education	Total	Total	Undergraduate	Graduate[1]
Total[2]	5,010	1,680	1,661,100	1,363,670	1,082,380	281,300
Public, 2-year	1,230	760	714,160	690,700	690,550	(B)
Public, 4-year	610	480	711,350	452,600	289,520	163,080
Private, 4-year	2,050	390	222,350	208,590	90,520	118,070
Less than 3,000 students	3,800	730	382,060	270,400	177,150	93,250
3,000 to 9,999	820	610	477,470	461,880	413,770	48,100
10,000 or more	400	350	801,570	631,400	491,460	139,950

B Base too small to meet statistical standards for reliability of a derived figure.   [1] Includes first-professional level courses.
[2] Includes private 2-year institutions, not reported separately. Too few offered distance education to make a reliable estimate.
Source: U.S. National Center for Education Statistics, *Distance Education at Postsecondary Education Institutions*, December 1999, NCES 2000-013.

Education 167

No. 268. College Enrollment by Sex, Age, Race, and Hispanic Origin: 1980 to 1999

[In thousands (11,387 represents 11,387,000). As of October for the civilian noninstitutional population. 14 years old and over. Based on the Current Population Survey; see text, Section 1, Population, and Appendix III]

Characteristic	1980	1985	1990 [1]	1992	1993	1994	1995	1996	1997	1998	1999
Total [2]	11,387	12,524	13,621	14,035	13,898	15,022	14,715	15,226	15,436	15,546	15,203
Male [3]	5,430	5,906	6,192	6,192	6,324	6,764	6.703	6,820	6,843	6.905	6.956
18 to 24 years	3,604	3,749	3,922	3,912	3,994	4,152	4,089	4,187	4,374	4,403	4,397
25 to 34 years	1,325	1,464	1,412	1,392	1,406	1,589	1,561	1,523	1,509	1,500	1,458
35 years old and over	405	561	772	789	873	958	985	1,013	899	953	1,024
Female [3]	5,957	6,618	7,429	7,844	7,574	8,258	8.013	8.406	8,593	8.641	8,247
18 to 24 years	3,625	3,788	4,042	4,429	4,199	4,576	4,452	4,582	4,829	4,919	4,863
25 to 34 years	1,378	1,599	1,749	1,732	1,688	1,830	1,788	1,920	1,760	1,915	1,637
35 years old and over	802	1,100	1,546	1,575	1 616	1,766	1,684	1,765	1,892	1.732	1,675
White [3]	9,925	10,781	11,488	11,710	11,434	12,222	12,021	12,189	12,442	12,401	12,053
18 to 24 years	6,334	6,500	6,635	6,916	6,763	7,118	7,011	7,123	7,495	7,541	7,446
25 to 34 years	2,328	2,604	2,698	2,582	2,505	2,735	2,686	2,644	2,522	2,568	2,345
35 years old and over	1,051	1,448	2,023	2,053	2,068	2,267	2,208	2,254	2,297	2,199	2,174
Male	4,804	5,103	5,235	5,210	5,222	5,524	5,535	5,453	5,552	5,602	5,562
Female	5,121	5,679	6,253	6,499	6,212	6,698	6,486	6,735	6,890	6,799	6,491
Black [3]	1,163	1,263	1,393	1,424	1,545	1,800	1,772	1,901	1,903	2,016	1,998
18 to 24 years	688	734	894	886	861	1.001	988	983	1,085	1,115	1,146
25 to 34 years	289	295	258	302	386	440	426	519	423	539	453
35 years old and over	156	213	207	208	284	323	334	354	372	340	354
Male	476	552	587	527	636	745	710	764	723	770	833
Female	686	712	807	897	909	1,054	1,062	1,136	1,180	1,247	1,164
Hispanic origin [3][4]	443	580	748	918	995	1,187	1,207	1,223	1,260	1,363	1,307
18 to 24 years	315	375	435	586	602	662	745	706	806	820	740
25 to 34 years	118	189	168	214	249	312	250	310	254	336	334
35 years old and over	(NA)	(NA)	130	102	129	205	193	184	151	198	226
Male	222	279	364	388	442	529	568	529	555	550	568
Female	221	299	384	530	553	659	639	692	704	814	739

NA Not available. [1] Beginning 1990, based on a revised edit and tabulation package. [2] Includes other races not shown separately. [3] Includes persons 14 to 17 years old, not shown separately. [4] Persons of Hispanic origin may be of any race.

Source: U.S. Census Bureau, *Current Population Reports*, P20-533; and earlier reports.

No. 269. Foreign (Nonimmigrant) Student Enrollment in College: 1976 to 2000

[For fall of the previous year (179 represents 179,000)]

Region of origin	Enrollment (1,000)									Percent enrolled in—					
										Engineering		Science[1]		Business	
	1976	1980	1985	1990	1995	1997	1998	1999	2000	1980	1998	1980	1998	1980	1998
All regions	179	286	342	387	453	458	481	491	515	25	16	8	8	16	21
Africa	25	36	40	25	21	22	23	26	30	20	14	9	8	19	21
Nigeria	11	16	18	4	2	2	2	3	4	19	14	9	8	22	18
Asia [2]	97	165	200	245	292	291	308	308	315	32	18	8	8	16	21
China: Taiwan	11	18	23	31	36	30	31	31	29	17	15	15	6	17	24
Hong Kong	12	10	11	11	13	11	10	9	8	22	15	9	5	26	30
India	10	9	15	26	34	31	34	37	42	31	35	16	8	21	16
Indonesia	1	2	7	9	12	12	13	12	11	27	21	7	2	21	41
Iran	20	51	17	7	3	2	2	2	2	45	30	7	16	11	7
Japan	7	12	13	30	45	46	47	46	47	7	4	5	4	19	19
Malaysia	2	4	22	14	14	15	15	12	9	13	34	14	3	22	32
Saudi Arabia	3	10	8	4	4	4	5	5	5	30	31	4	4	14	13
South Korea	3	5	16	22	34	37	43	39	41	17	11	11	6	15	14
Thailand	7	7	7	7	11	13	15	12	11	17	16	6	4	26	38
Europe	14	23	33	46	65	68	72	74	78	15	9	9	9	14	22
Latin America [3]	30	42	49	48	47	50	51	55	62	20	13	8	6	14	25
Mexico	5	6	6	7	9	9	10	10	11	16	16	7	5	11	25
Venezuela	5	10	10	3	4	5	5	5	5	30	14	8	5	11	24
North America	10	16	16	19	23	24	23	23	24	8	6	6	8	13	13
Canada	10	15	15	18	23	23	23	23	24	8	6	6	8	12	13
Oceania	3	4	4	4	4	4	4	4	5	5	5	7	6	16	22

[1] Physical and life sciences. [2] Includes countries not shown separately. [3] Includes Central America, Caribbean, and South America.

Source: Institute of International Education, New York, NY, *Open Doors*, annual (copyright).

168 Education

No. 270. College Enrollment—Summary by Sex, Race, and Hispanic Origin: 1999

[In thousands (15,203 represents 15,203,000), except percent. As of October. Covers civilian noninstitutional population 15 years old and over enrolled in colleges and graduate schools. Based on Current Population Survey, see text, Section 1, Population, and Appendix III]

Characteristic	Total [1]	Sex		Race and Hispanic origin				
		Male	Female	White		Black	Asian and Pacific Islander	Hispanic [2]
				Total	Non-Hispanic			
Total enrollment	15,203	6,956	8,247	12,053	10,818	1,998	1,042	1,307
15 to 17 years old	151	78	73	87	80	45	16	7
18 to 19 years old	3,520	1,648	1,872	2,849	2,574	430	223	297
20 to 21 years old	3,120	1,525	1,595	2,520	2,324	391	192	196
22 to 24 years old	2,620	1,224	1,396	2,077	1,837	327	211	247
25 to 29 years old	1,940	911	1,029	1,475	1,283	254	187	207
30 to 34 years old	1,156	547	608	870	755	198	71	127
35 years old and over	2,698	1,023	1,674	2,174	1,965	355	142	226
Type of school:								
2-year	3,794	1,637	2,157	3,002	2,490	534	213	534
15 to 19 years old	1,187	537	649	944	794	170	70	155
20 to 24 years old	1,175	536	639	937	783	140	87	157
25 years old and over	1,432	563	868	1,119	913	228	56	223
4-year	8,252	3,916	4,336	6,480	5,920	1,192	530	603
15 to 19 years old	2,439	1,166	1,273	1,956	1,835	305	163	139
20 to 24 years old	3,867	1,902	1,965	3,094	2,837	508	255	263
25 years old and over	1,946	849	1,097	1,427	1,248	380	112	200
Graduate school	3,157	1,403	1,755	2,571	2,408	272	298	170
15 to 24 years old	742	333	409	598	566	70	67	33
25 to 34 years old	1,211	584	627	976	921	88	135	56
35 years old and over	1,204	486	719	992	921	111	96	80
Public	11,659	5,185	6,474	9,186	8,158	1,586	779	1,093
2-year	3,482	1,486	1,996	2,765	2,297	482	191	490
4-year	6,207	2,876	3,331	4,838	4,388	903	417	486
Graduate	1,970	823	1,147	1,583	1,473	201	172	117
Percent of students:								
Employed full-time	33.1	33.9	32.4	33.9	33.6	34.8	20.7	37.1
Employed part-time	30.3	28.9	31.5	32.0	32.8	21.7	28.1	24.6

[1] Includes other races, not shown separately. [2] Persons of Hispanic origin may be of any race.

Source: U.S. Census Bureau, *Current Population Reports*, P20-533.

No. 271. Higher Education Registrations in Foreign Languages: 1970 to 1998

[As of fall (1,111.5 represents 1,111,500)]

Item	1970	1974	1977	1980	1983	1986	1990	1995	1998
Registrations [1] (1,000)	1,111.5	946.6	933.5	924.8	966.0	1,003.2	1,184.1	1,138.8	1,193.8
Index (1960=100)	171.8	146.3	144.3	142.9	149.3	155.0	183.0	176.0	184.5
By selected language (1,000):									
Spanish	389.2	362.2	376.7	379.4	386.2	411.3	533.9	606.3	656.6
French	359.3	253.1	246.1	248.4	270.1	275.3	272.5	205.4	199.1
German	202.6	152.1	135.4	126.9	128.2	121.0	133.3	96.3	89.0
Italian	34.2	33.0	33.3	34.8	38.7	40.9	49.7	43.8	49.3
Japanese	6.6	9.6	10.7	11.5	16.1	23.5	45.7	44.7	43.1
Chinese	6.2	10.7	9.8	11.4	13.2	16.9	19.5	26.5	28.5
Latin	27.6	25.2	24.4	25.0	24.2	25.0	28.2	25.9	26.1
Russian	36.2	32.5	27.8	24.0	30.4	34.0	44.6	24.7	23.8
Ancient Greek	16.7	24.4	25.8	22.1	19.4	17.6	16.4	16.3	16.4
Hebrew	16.6	22.4	19.4	19.4	18.2	15.6	13.0	13.1	15.8
American Sign Language	(X)	(X)	(X)	(X)	(X)	(X)	1.6	4.3	11.4
Portuguese	5.1	5.1	5.0	4.9	4.4	5.1	6.2	6.5	6.9
Arabic	1.3	2.0	3.1	3.5	3.4	3.4	3.5	4.4	5.5

X Not applicable. [1] Includes other foreign languages, not shown separately.

Source: Association of Departments of Foreign Languages, New York, NY, *ADFL Bulletin*, Vol. 31, No. 2, and earlier issues (copyright).

Education 169

No. 272. College Freshmen—Summary Characteristics: 1970 to 2000

[In percent, except as indicated (12.8 represents $12,800). As of fall for first-time full-time freshmen in 4-year colleges and universities. Based on sample survey and subject to sampling error; see source]

Characteristic	1970	1980	1985	1990	1995	1997	1998	1999	2000
Sex:									
Male	52.1	48.8	48.9	46.9	45.6	45.5	45.5	45.3	45.2
Female	47.9	51.2	51.1	53.1	54.4	54.5	54.5	54.7	54.8
Applied to three or more colleges	(NA)	31.5	35.4	42.9	44.4	44.1	46.2	47.7	50.5
Average grade in high school:									
A- to A+	19.6	26.6	28.7	29.4	36.1	41.2	39.8	42.7	42.9
B- to B+	62.5	58.2	57.1	57.0	54.2	51.2	52.3	50.7	50.5
C to C+	17.7	14.9	14.0	13.4	9.6	7.6	7.7	6.5	6.5
D	0.3	0.2	0.2	0.2	0.1	0.1	0.1	0.1	0.1
Political orientation:									
Liberal	35.7	21.0	22.4	24.6	22.9	23.1	23.3	23.6	24.8
Middle of the road	43.4	57.0	53.1	51.7	51.3	52.0	53.1	53.4	51.9
Conservative	17.3	19.0	21.3	20.6	21.8	21.0	19.9	19.3	18.9
Probable field of study:									
Arts and humanities	(NA)	10.5	10.1	10.5	11.2	10.9	11.8	11.3	12.1
Biological sciences	(NA)	4.5	4.5	4.9	8.3	8.0	7.0	7.2	6.6
Business	(NA)	21.2	24.6	21.1	15.4	15.6	16.4	16.4	16.7
Education	(NA)	8.4	6.9	10.3	10.1	10.2	11.1	10.6	11.0
Engineering	(NA)	11.2	11.0	9.7	8.1	9.6	8.2	9.0	8.7
Physical science	(NA)	3.2	3.2	2.8	3.1	2.7	2.4	2.3	2.6
Social science	(NA)	8.2	9.4	11.0	9.9	9.3	9.5	9.7	10.0
Professional	(NA)	15.5	13.1	13.0	16.5	15.1	14.5	13.1	11.6
Technical [1]	(NA)	3.1	2.4	1.1	1.2	1.6	1.8	1.9	2.1
Data processing/computer programming	(NA)	1.7	1.7	0.7	0.8	1.1	1.2	1.4	1.5
Other [1]	(NA)	14.0	15.1	15.8	16.0	16.6	17.3	18.0	17.9
Communications	(NA)	2.4	2.8	2.9	1.8	2.1	2.2	2.4	2.7
Computer science	(NA)	2.6	2.4	1.7	2.2	3.0	3.4	3.7	3.7
Recipient of financial aid:									
Pell grant	(NA)	30.9	18.2	20.0	18.8	19.0	19.3	18.4	16.9
Supplemental educational opportunity grant	(NA)	8.9	5.6	6.7	6.4	5.9	6.5	6.8	5.8
State scholarship or grant	(NA)	16.7	15.1	16.7	17.2	17.9	19.1	20.9	21.9
College grant	(NA)	16.3	23.9	26.3	32.7	34.2	34.7	35.9	32.5
Federal guaranteed student loan	(NA)	22.3	23.0	21.8	31.0	27.7	28.4	28.7	26.2
Perkins loan [2]	(NA)	10.4	7.1	8.2	10.5	10.5	11.0	10.6	9.5
College loan	(NA)	4.6	3.9	6.1	10.6	11.8	12.3	13.1	11.4
College work-study grant	(NA)	17.0	12.4	12.4	15.7	15.0	15.3	15.8	13.2
Median family income ($1,000)	12.8	24.5	37.3	46.6	54.8	58.3	58.9	61.6	64.4

NA Not available. [1] Includes other fields, not shown separately. [2] National Direct Student Loan prior to 1990.

Source: The Higher Education Research Institute, University of California, Los Angeles, CA, *The American Freshman: National Norms*, annual.

No. 273. Students Enrolled in Postsecondary Institution by Disability Status and Selected Student Characteristics: 1995-96

[In percent, except total (16,678 represents 16,678,000). Based on the National Postsecondary Student Aid Study; see source for details]

Student characteristic	Undergraduate			Graduate and first-professional		
	All students	Disabled students[1]	Nondisabled students	All students	Disabled students[1]	Nondisabled students
Total (in thousands)	**16,678**	**892**	**15,786**	**2,784**	**89**	**2,695**
Age	100.0	100.0	100.0	100.0	100.0	100.0
15 to 23	54.9	46.0	55.5	9.2	7.6	9.3
24 to 29	17.9	13.6	18.1	42.7	32.3	43.0
30 or older	27.2	40.4	26.4	48.1	60.0	47.7
Sex	100.0	100.0	100.0	100.0	100.0	100.0
Male	44.1	50.0	43.8	45.7	31.3	46.2
Female	55.9	50.0	56.2	54.3	68.7	53.8
Race/ethnicity of student	100.0	100.0	100.0	100.0	100.0	100.0
White, non-Hispanic	71.4	80.9	70.8	80.6	73.9	80.9
Black, non-Hispanic	11.6	7.1	11.9	6.4	10.7	6.2
Hispanic	10.3	7.7	10.5	4.9	9.8	4.7
Asian/Pacific Islander	5.3	1.8	5.5	8.1	5.6	8.2
American Indian/Alaskan Native	0.9	2.1	0.8	(B)	(B)	(B)
Other	0.5	0.4	0.5	(B)	(B)	(B)
Attendance status	100.0	100.0	100.0	100.0	100.0	100.0
Full-time	40.5	38.7	40.6	32.5	34.2	32.5
Part-time	59.5	61.3	59.4	67.5	65.8	67.5

B Base too small to meet statistical standards of reliability of a derived figure. [1] Disabled students are those who reported that they had one or more of the following conditions: a specific learning disability, a visual handicap, hard of hearing, deafness, a speech disability, an orthopedic handicap, or a health impairment.

Source: U.S. National Center for Education Statistics, *Digest of Education Statistics, 2000*.

[1983=100. For years ending June 30. Reflects prices paid by colleges and universities]

Year	Index, total	Personnel compensation				Contracted services, supplies, and equipment					
		Total	Professional salaries	Nonprofessional salaries	Fringe benefits	Total	Services	Supplies and materials	Equipment	Library acquisitions	Utilities
1970 ..	39.5	42.1	47.7	38.8	24.7	31.9	42.8	37.6	41.9	25.7	16.3
1973 ..	46.7	49.8	54.3	47.6	34.7	37.6	49.9	41.1	46.5	37.7	20.2
1974 ..	49.9	52.8	57.2	50.6	38.6	41.4	52.2	46.5	49.4	41.6	24.8
1975 ..	54.3	56.3	60.3	54.6	42.9	48.5	56.8	58.0	58.3	46.7	31.8
1976 ..	57.8	60.0	63.5	59.0	47.8	51.3	59.1	60.7	61.7	52.1	34.4
1977 ..	61.5	63.5	66.4	63.1	52.8	55.7	62.6	63.8	64.8	56.8	40.5
1978 ..	65.7	67.6	69.9	68.1	58.4	60.2	66.6	66.6	69.3	63.2	45.9
1979 ..	70.5	72.4	74.1	73.4	64.5	65.1	71.2	71.7	74.7	70.0	50.3
1980 ..	77.5	78.4	79.4	80.2	72.6	75.0	77.0	84.6	81.6	77.8	64.1
1981 ..	85.8	85.8	86.3	87.7	81.8	85.9	85.2	95.6	89.6	85.9	79.7
1982 ..	93.9	93.5	93.7	94.6	91.5	94.9	94.2	100.4	96.4	93.5	92.4
1983 ..	100.0	100.0	100.0	100.0	100.0	100.0	100.0	100.0	100.0	100.0	100.0
1984 ..	104.8	105.4	104.7	105.1	108.3	103.0	104.9	99.7	102.3	105.3	102.5
1985 ..	110.8	112.0	111.4	109.2	117.7	107.1	110.8	103.0	104.8	111.3	105.3
1986 ..	116.3	118.8	118.2	112.8	127.7	109.0	115.1	102.6	107.2	121.2	103.1
1987 ..	120.9	125.4	125.0	116.3	137.4	107.4	119.7	99.0	108.9	132.9	91.0
1988 ..	126.2	131.7	130.9	120.6	147.2	109.8	123.0	101.1	120.5	140.5	87.7
1989 ..	132.8	139.6	138.8	125.3	158.8	112.8	128.8	108.3	115.1	153.5	85.3
1990 ..	140.8	148.3	147.6	130.3	171.4	118.7	134.0	114.3	119.6	167.0	90.1
1991 ..	148.2	156.5	155.6	135.4	184.3	123.3	139.8	116.4	123.3	179.8	92.4
1992 ..	153.5	162.4	160.8	140.2	194.3	126.9	145.7	115.2	126.3	193.9	93.3
1993 ..	158.0	167.6	165.0	144.2	204.3	129.4	149.5	113.2	128.6	204.3	94.7
1994 ..	163.3	173.3	170.3	148.2	213.6	133.9	154.8	114.3	130.8	216.2	98.7
1995 ..	168.3	179.1	176.1	152.5	221.4	136.1	158.0	115.7	133.5	228.8	96.8
1996 ..	173.3	184.1	181.7	157.3	224.5	141.3	163.8	130.1	137.0	245.0	93.3
1997 ..	178.6	189.0	187.2	162.1	226.7	148.0	167.3	128.6	139.3	260.9	106.1
1998 ..	184.9	195.9	193.6	168.0	236.7	152.5	172.8	126.2	141.3	275.9	111.1

Source: Research Associates of Washington, Arlington, VA, *Inflation Measures for Schools, Colleges, and Libraries*, annual (copyright).

No. 275. Finances of Public Colleges, 1990 to 1997, and by State, 1998

[For academic years ending in year shown (7,959.7 represents 7,959,700). Data provided by the state higher education finance officers, except as noted]

State	FTE [1] enrollment (1,000)	Appropriations for current operations [2] (mil. dol.)	Net tuition revenues (mil. dol.) [3]	State	FTE [1] enrollment (1,000)	Appropriations for current operations [2] (mil. dol.)	Net tuition revenues (mil. dol.) [3]
Total, 1990	7,959.7	33,853.9	11,264.7	Michigan	311.1	1,837.3	1,422.0
Total, 1993	8,397.1	35,172.0	15,746.3	Minnesota	156.9	941.6	400.6
Total, 1994	8,334.0	36,497.0	16,623.4	Mississippi	107.4	468.6	228.4
Total, 1995	8,262.7	38,655.2	17,406.8	Missouri	131.2	801.7	493.5
Total, 1996	8,267.1	40,077.5	18,465.2	Montana	33.4	117.4	92.4
Total, 1997	8,304.3	42,143.0	19,443.0	Nebraska	66.4	329.7	128.3
Total, 1998	**8,386.9**	**44,484.6**	**20,210.6**	Nevada	42.0	266.6	61.6
Alabama	168.7	643.1	439.1	New Hampshire	27.0	87.6	175.0
Alaska	17.1	156.0	38.1	New Jersey [4]	181.5	1,149.3	610.2
Arizona	168.1	865.4	339.1	New Mexico	67.6	390.1	100.1
Arkansas...........	76.8	376.2	181.5	New York	424.3	2,264.5	1,124.8
California...........	1,344.6	7,202.8	1,345.6	North Carolina	241.2	1,652.2	375.1
Colorado...........	138.5	540.7	462.7	North Dakota	29.8	136.8	63.6
Connecticut	55.7	467.0	223.2	Ohio	335.1	1,578.9	1,165.3
Delaware...........	27.4	151.2	186.8	Oklahoma	111.5	612.5	228.8
District of Columbia....	2.9	37.8	9.9	Oregon	102.2	479.0	274.0
Florida	403.5	1,992.1	575.2	Pennsylvania	274.9	1,479.6	1,387.6
Georgia	222.2	1,471.5	449.1	Rhode Island	24.8	141.0	110.9
Hawaii	30.0	201.7	59.1	South Carolina	127.9	550.2	392.0
Idaho	41.0	230.7	59.9	South Dakota	20.8	93.0	70.0
Illinois	364.4	2,078.4	546.9	Tennessee..........	158.3	723.6	355.1
Indiana	178.4	897.9	586.8	Texas	635.3	3,236.4	1,366.1
Iowa	108.9	615.5	310.5	Utah...............	84.6	420.7	153.3
Kansas............	100.4	531.7	234.5	Vermont	15.0	47.4	123.2
Kentucky...........	114.4	512.5	267.6	Virginia	220.2	990.4	688.1
Louisiana	137.6	545.3	340.3	Washington	194.6	978.5	341.5
Maine	26.8	169.8	104.6	West Virginia	62.0	206.0	164.1
Maryland...........	152.9	763.4	511.4	Wisconsin	184.1	1,085.9	473.6
Massachusetts.......	114.2 ·	825.9	323.6	Wyoming...........	21.1	141.5	45.9

[1] Full-time equivalent (FTE). Credit and noncredit program enrollment including summer session. Excludes medical enrollments. [2] State and local appropriations. Includes aid to students attending in-state public institutions. Excludes sums for research, agriculture stations and cooperative extension, and hospitals and medical schools. [3] Excludes appropriated aid to students attending in-state public institutions. [4] Estimated by source.

Source: Research Associates of Washington, Arlington, VA, *State Profiles: Financing Public Higher Education*, annual (copyright).

Education **171**

No. 276. Federal Student Financial Assistance: 1995 to 2001

[35,450 represents ($35,450,000,000. For award years July 1 of year shown to the following June 30. Funds utilized exclude operating costs, etc., and represent funds given to students]

Award year impact data	1995	1996	1997	1998	1999	2000	2001, est.
FUNDS UTILIZED (mil. dol.)							
Total	35,450	38,849	40,074	43,072	43,469	46,933	(NA)
Federal Pell Grants	5,445	5,764	6,331	7,233	7,191	7,883	9,095
Federal Supplemental Educational Opportunity Grant	764	762	811	855	784	799	875
Federal Work-Study	764	776	906	913	1,044	1,123	1,216
Federal Perkins Loan	1,029	1,022	1,062	1,070	1,058	1,058	1,058
Federal Direct Student Loan (FDSL)	8,296	9,796	9,873	10,933	10,972	10,960	(NA)
Federal Family Education Loans (FFEL)	19,152	20,729	21,091	22,068	22,420	25,110	(NA)
NUMBER OF AWARDS (1,000)							
Total	13,667	14,516	14,652	15,187	15,257	15,822	(NA)
Federal Pell Grants	3,612	3,666	3,733	3,855	3,759	3,832	3,937
Federal Supplemental Educational Opportunity Grant	1,083	1,191	1,116	1,163	1,118	1,139	1,203
Federal Work-Study	702	691	746	744	930	1,000	1,000
Federal Perkins Loan	688	674	679	669	698	698	676
Federal Direct Student Loan (FDSL)	2,339	2,762	2,775	3,017	3,026	2,915	(NA)
Federal Family Education Loans (FFEL)	5,243	5,531	5,603	5,739	5,726	6,238	(NA)
AVERAGE AWARD (dol.)							
Total	2,594	2,676	2,735	2,836	2,849	2,966	(NA)
Federal Pell Grants	1,507	1,572	1,696	1,876	1,913	2,057	2,310
Federal Supplemental Educational Opportunity Grant	706	640	727	735	701	701	727
Federal Work-Study	1,087	1,123	1,215	1,228	1,123	1,123	1,215
Federal Perkins Loan	1,497	1,516	1,564	1,600	1,516	1,516	1,565
Federal Direct Student Loan (FDSL)	3,548	3,547	3,558	3,624	3,626	3,760	(NA)
Federal Family Education Loans (FFEL)	3,653	3,748	3,764	3,845	3,916	4,025	(NA)
COHORT DEFAULT RATE [1]							
Federal Perkins Loan	12.6	13.0	12.5	11.5	11.5	(X)	(X)
FFEL/FDSL Combined Rates	10.4	9.6	8.8	6.9	(X)	(X)	(X)

NA Not available.   X Not applicable.   [1] As of June 30. Represents the percent of borrowers entering repayment status in year shown who defaulted in the following year.

Source: U.S. Dept. of Education, Office of Postsecondary Education, unpublished data.

No. 277. Student Borrowing Status for Higher Education: 1997

[In percent, except amount borrowed. Represents borrowing status in 1997 of 1992-93 bachelor's degree recipients. Based on the 1993 Baccalaureate and Beyond Longitudinal Study; see source for details]

Item	Did not borrow	Borrowed as— Undergraduate only	Borrowed as— Graduate only	Borrowed as— Both	Average amount borrowed (dol.)
Total	43.7	42.1	6.5	7.7	15,612
Bachelor's degree-granting institution:					
Public, 4-year	46.4	40.2	6.7	6.7	13,623
Private, not-for-profit, 4-year	39.1	44.8	6.3	9.9	19,528
Other	34.8	55.1	3.4	6.7	13,266
Undergraduate borrowing:					
Did not borrow	87.1	(X)	12.9	(X)	27,123
Borrowed	(X)	84.6	(X)	15.4	14,116
Highest enrollment after bachelor's:					
None	49.0	51.0	(X)	(X)	10,475
Master's degree	33.8	23.9	17.6	24.7	16,940
First-professional degree	12.2	4.7	44.8	38.3	57,430
Doctoral degree	26.6	14.9	31.1	27.4	32,284
Other that graduate degree	49.6	50.4	(X)	(X)	9,339
Highest degree earned after bachelor's: [1]					
None	45.8	45.9	3.8	4.6	13,247
Master's	30.8	15.7	24.0	29.5	20,767
First-professional	9.5	4.1	45.2	41.1	63,372
All others, except doctoral degree	46.8	43.3	4.7	5.3	12,268

X Not applicable.   [1] Excludes doctoral degree recipients. Too few recipients for a reliable estimate.

Source: U.S. National Center for Education Statistics, *Debt Burden Four Years After College*, NCES 2000-188, August 2000.

No. 278. Institutions of Higher Education—Charges: 1985 to 2000

[In dollars. Estimated. For the entire academic year ending in year shown. Figures are average charges per full-time equivalent student. Room and board are based on full-time students]

Academic. control and year	Tuition and required fees [1]				Board rates [2]				Dormitory charges			
	All institutions	2-yr. colleges	4-yr. colleges	Other 4-yr. schools	All institutions	2-yr. colleges	4-yr. colleges	Other 4-yr. schools	All institutions	2-yr. colleges	4-yr. colleges	Other 4-yr. schools
Public: .												
1985	971	584	1,386	1,117	1,241	1,302	1,276	1,201	1,196	921	1,237	1,200
1990	1,356	756	2,035	1,608	1,635	1,581	1,728	1,561	1,513	962	1,561	1,554
1994	1,942	1,125	2,820	2,360	1,880	1,681	1,993	1,828	1,873	1,190	1,897	1,958
1995	2,057	1,192	2,977	2,499	1,949	1,712	2,108	1,866	1,959	1,232	1,992	2,044
1996	2,179	1,239	3,151	2,660	2,020	1,681	2,192	1,937	2,057	1,297	2,104	2,133
1997	2,271	1,276	3,323	2,778	2,111	1,789	2,282	2,025	2,148	1,339	2,187	2,232
1998	2,360	1,314	3,486	2,877	2,228	1,795	2,438	2,130	2,225	1,401	2,285	2,312
1999	2,427	1,323	3,645	2,974	2,346	1,828	2,576	2,245	2,328	1,450	2,408	2,407
2000, prel. .	2,507	1,336	3,774	3,090	2,361	1,844	2,624	2,234	2,434	1,542	2,514	2,512
Private:												
1985	5,315	3,485	6,843	5,135	1,462	1,294	1,647	1,405	1,426	1,424	1,753	1,309
1990	8,174	5,196	10,348	7,778	1,948	1,811	2,339	1,823	1,923	1,663	2,411	1,774
1994	10,572	6,370	13,874	10,100	2,434	1,970	2,946	2,278	2,490	2,067	3,277	2,261
1995	11,111	6,914	14,537	10,653	2,509	2,023	3,035	2,362	2,587	2,233	3,469	2,347
1996	11,864	7,094	15,605	11,297	2,606	2,098	3,218	2,429	2,738	2,371	3,680	2,473
1997	12,498	7,236	16,552	11,871	2,663	2,181	3,142	2,520	2,878	2,537	3,826	2,602
1998	12,801	7,464	17,229	12,338	2,762	2,785	3,132	2,648	2,954	2,672	3,756	2,731
1999	13,368	7,852	18,226	12,809	2,865	2,884	3,188	2,765	3,074	2,581	3,914	2,849
2000, prel. .	14,175	8,107	19,312	13,467	2,882	2,922	3,157	2,791	3,219	2,739	4,063	2,973

[1] For in-state students. [2] Beginning 1990, rates reflect 20 meals per week, rather than meals served 7 days a week.

Source: U.S. National Center for Education Statistics. *Digest of Education Statistics*, annual.

No. 279. Voluntary Financial Support of Higher Education: 1990 to 2000

[For school years ending in years shown (9,800 represents $9,800,000,000); enrollment as of fall of preceding year. Voluntary support, as defined in Gift Reporting Standards, excludes income from endowment and other invested funds as well as all support received from federal, state, and local governments and their agencies and contract research]

Item	Unit	1990	1994	1995	1996	1997	1998	1999	2000
Estimated support, total	Mil. dol.	9,800	12,350	12,750	14,250	16,000	18,400	20,400	23,200
Individuals	Mil. dol	4,770	6,210	6,540	7,440	8,500	10,000	10,740	12,220
Alumni.	Mil. dol	2,540	3,410	3,600	4,040	4,650	5,500	5,930	6,800
Business corporations	Mil. dol	2,170	2,510	2,560	2,800	3,050	3,250	3,610	4,150
Foundations	Mil. dol	1,920	2,540	2,460	2,815	3,200	3,800	4,530	5,080
Fundraising consortia and other organizations	Mil. dol	700	850	940	940	1,000	1,050	1,190	1,380
Religious organizations	Mil. dol	240	240	250	255	250	300	330	370
Current operations	Mil. dol	5,440	6,710	7,230	7,850	8,500	9,000	9,900	11,270
Capital purposes.	Mil. dol	4,360	5,640	5,520	6,400	7,500	9,400	10,500	11,930
Enrollment, higher education. . .	1,000 .		13,309	14,078	14,044	14,021	14,031	14,108	14,258	14,564
Support per student.	Dollars .		736	877	908	1,016	1,140	1,304	1,431	1,593
In 1999-2000 dollars	Dollars .		981	1,016	1,022	1,113	1,214	1,364	1,472	1,593
Expenditures, higher education .	Bil. dol .		150.56	189.73	201.52	210.86	220.44	230.94	243.68	257.31
Expenditures per student	Dollars .		11,312	13,477	14,350	15,038	15,711	15,370	16,894	17,668
In 1999-2000 dollars	Dollars .		15,071	15,615	16,148	16,472	16,730	17,125	17,580	17,668
Institutions reporting support . .	Number.	1,056	992	1,086	1,104	1,061	1,061	938	945
Total support reported	Mil. dol.	8,214	10,326	10,992	12,251	13,801	15,771	17,229	19,419
Private 4-year institutions	Mil. dol	5,072	6,103	6,500	7,163	8,023	9,118	9,848	11,047
Public 4-year institutions.	Mil. dol	3,056	4,138	4,382	4,943	5,654	6,556	7,252	8,254
2-year colleges.	Mil. dol .	85	84	110	145	124	98	129	117

Source: Council for Aid to Education, New York, NY. *Voluntary Support of Education*, annual.

No. 280. Average Salaries for College Faculty Members: 1998 to 2000

[In thousands of dollars (53.6 represents $53,600). For academic year ending in year shown. Figures are for 9 months teaching for full-time faculty members in 4-year institutions. Fringe benefits averaged in 1998, $13,200 in public institutions and $15,800 in private institutions, in 1999, $13,200 in public institutions and $16,600 in private institutions, and in 2000, $14,200 in public institutions and $17,200 in private institutions]

Type of control and academic rank	1998	1999	2000	Type of control and academic rank	1998	1999	2000
Public: All ranks.	53.6	55.9	57.7	Private: [1] All ranks.	61.5	63.5	66.3
Professor	68.0	71.3	74.4	Professor	81.8	83.9	88.4
Associate professor	51.2	53.4	55.3	Associate professor	54.5	56.3	59.0
Assistant professor	42.4	44.1	45.8	Assistant professor	44.9	46.8	48.8
Instructor	32.4	33.3	34.4	Instructor	34.5	36.1	37.5

[1] Excludes church-related colleges and universities.

Source: American Association of University Professors, Washington, DC, *AAUP Annual Report on the Economic Status of the Profession*.

No. 281. Employees in Higher Education Institutions by Sex and Occupation: 1976 to 1997

[In thousands (1,863.8 represents 1,863,800). As of fall. Based on survey and subject to sampling error; see source]

Year and status	Total	Professional staff									Non-profes-sional staff, total
		Total	Executive, administrative, and managerial		Faculty [1]		Research/instruction assistants		Other		
			Male	Female	Male	Female	Male	Female	Male	Female	
1976, total	1,863.8	1,073.1	74.6	26.6	460.6	172.7	106.5	53.6	87.5	91.0	790.7
Full time	1,339.9	709.4	72.0	25.0	326.8	107.2	18.6	9.4	76.2	74.1	630.5
Part time	523.9	363.7	2.6	1.7	133.7	65.4	87.9	44.2	11.3	16.9	160.2
1991, total	2,545.2	1,595.5	85.4	59.3	525.6	300.7	119.1	78.6	165.4	261.3	949.8
Full time	1,812.9	1,031.8	82.9	56.2	366.2	169.4	(NA)	(NA)	142.2	214.8	781.1
Part time	732.3	563.7	2.5	3.1	159.4	131.2	119.1	78.6	23.2	46.4	168.7
1997, total [2]	2,752.5	1,835.9	81.9	69.4	587.4	402.4	125.9	96.9	187.6	284.4	916.6
Full time	1,828.5	1,104.8	78.9	65.6	363.9	204.8	(NA)	(NA)	159.3	232.3	723.7
Part time	924.0	731.1	3.0	3.8	223.5	197.6	125.9	96.9	28.3	52.1	192.9

NA Not available.   [1] Instruction and research.   [2] In this table, data beginning in 1997 reflect the new classification of institutions. See footnote 1, Table 264.

Source: U.S. National Center for Education Statistics, *Fall Staff in Postsecondary Institutions, 1995* and *1997*, March 1998 and January 2000.

No. 282. Faculty in Institutions of Higher Education: 1970 to 1997

[In thousands (474 represents 474,000), except percent. As of fall. Based on survey and subject to sampling error; see source]

Year	Employment status			Control		Level		Percent		
	Total	Full time	Part time	Public	Private	4-Year	2-Year	Part time	Public	2-Year
1970	474	369	104	314	160	382	92	22	66	19
1975	628	440	188	443	185	467	161	30	71	26
1980	686	450	236	495	191	494	192	34	72	28
1985	715	459	256	503	212	504	211	36	70	30
1987 [1]	793	523	270	553	240	548	246	34	70	31
1989	824	524	300	577	247	584	241	36	70	29
1991	826	536	291	581	245	591	235	35	70	28
1993	915	546	370	650	265	626	289	40	71	32
1995	932	551	381	657	275	647	285	41	70	31
1997 [2]	990	569	421	695	295	683	307	43	70	31

[1] Data beginning 1987 not comparable to prior years.   [2] In this table, data beginning in 1997 reflect the new classification of institutions. See footnote 1, Table 264.

Source: U.S. National Center for Education Statistics, *Fall Staff in Postsecondary Institutions, 1995* and *1997*, March 1998 and January 2000.

No. 283. Salary Offers to Candidates for Degrees: 1998 to 2000

[In dollars. Data are average beginning salaries based on offers made by business, industrial, government, nonprofit, and educational employers to graduating students. Data from representative colleges throughout the United States]

Field of study	Bachelor's			Master's [1]			Doctor's		
	1998	1999	2000	1998	1999	2000	1998	1999	2000
Accounting.	32,825	34,644	36,710	36,492	38,152	39,839	(NA)	(NA)	(NA)
Business administration/ management [2]	31,454	33,310	36,357	51,231	50,095	50,276	(NA)	(NA)	[3]65,865
Marketing.	29,231	31,901	33,373	[3]53,563	[3]54,530	[3]45,593	(NA)	(NA)	(NA)
Engineering:									
Civil.	35,335	36,076	37,932	41,584	42,265	44,587	[3]54,167	[3]58,571	[3]54,588
Chemical	45,104	46,929	48,890	[3]48,593	[3]52,068	[3]54,473	62,343	67,333	68,161
Computer	43,865	45,666	50,182	51,610	58,673	[3]57,087	[3]64,417	[3]57,471	[3]77,700
Electrical	43,282	45,180	48,613	53,534	57,162	60,828	66,716	70,848	74,423
Mechanical	41,260	43,275	45,952	48,695	51,879	53,581	[3]58,922	64,283	[3]69,830
Nuclear [4]	[3]41,517	[3]42,986	[3]47,070	[3]45,090	[3]54,000	[3]64,986	(NA)	(NA)	(NA)
Petroleum.	49,926	50,440	50,367	[3]50,760	[3]55,375	[3]50,369	(NA)	(NA)	(NA)
Engineering technology . .	39,390	38,182	40,110	(NA)	(NA)	(NA)	(NA)	(NA)	(NA)
Chemistry	33,892	34,111	35,942	[3]37,145	[3]38,779	[3]46,389	54,219	56,885	62,901
Mathematics.	36,203	37,253	41,761	[3]41,186	[3]41,964	[3]46,453	[3]52,368	[3]58,917	[3]60,237
Physics	[3]36,139	40,025	42,455	[3]42,964	[3]50,552	[3]32,722	45,601	[3]60,288	[3]46,500
Humanities.	28,447	27,861	33,117	(NA)	(NA)	(NA)	(NA)	(NA)	(NA)
Social sciences [5]	27,149	28,608	30,933	(NA)	(NA)	(NA)	(NA)	(NA)	(NA)
Computer science	41,949	44,649	49,055	52,648	51,438	61,377	[3]62,500	[3]58,688	[3]71,846

NA Not available.   [1] Candidates with 1 year or less of full-time nonmilitary employment.   [2] For master's degree, offers are after nontechnical undergraduate degree.   [3] Fewer than 50 offers reported.   [4] Includes engineering physics.   [5] Excludes economics.

Source: National Association of Colleges and Employers, Bethlehem, PA, Salary Survey. *A Study of Beginning Offers*, annual (copyright).

174   Education

No. 284. Earned Degrees Conferred by Level and Sex: 1960 to 1998

[In thousands (477 represents 477,000), **except percent.** Includes Alaska and Hawaii]

Year ending	All degrees		Associate's		Bachelor's		Master's		First professional		Doctor's	
	Total	Percent male	Male	Female	Male	Female	Male	Female	Male	Female	Male	Female
1960	477	65.8	(NA)	(NA)	254	138	51	24	(NA)	(NA)	9	1
1965	660	61.5	(NA)	(NA)	282	212	81	40	27	1	15	2
1970	1,271	59.2	117	89	451	341	126	83	33	2	26	4
1975	1,666	56.0	191	169	505	418	162	131	49	7	27	7
1980	1,731	51.1	184	217	474	456	151	147	53	17	23	10
1981	1,752	50.3	189	228	470	465	147	149	53	19	23	10
1982	1,788	49.8	197	238	473	480	146	150	52	20	22	10
1983	1,815	49.6	204	246	479	490	145	145	51	22	22	11
1984	1,819	49.6	203	250	482	492	144	141	51	23	22	11
1985	1,828	49.3	203	252	483	497	143	143	50	25	22	11
1986	1,830	49.0	196	250	486	502	144	145	49	25	22	12
1987	1,823	48.4	191	245	481	510	141	148	47	25	22	12
1988	1,835	48.0	190	245	477	518	145	154	45	25	23	12
1989	1,873	47.3	186	250	483	535	149	161	45	26	23	13
1990	1,940	46.6	191	264	492	560	154	171	44	27	24	14
1991	2,025	45.8	199	283	504	590	156	181	44	28	25	15
1992	2,108	45.6	207	297	521	616	162	191	45	29	26	15
1993	2,167	45.5	212	303	533	632	169	200	45	30	26	16
1994	2,206	45.1	215	315	532	637	176	211	45	31	27	17
1995	2,218	44.9	218	321	526	634	179	219	45	31	27	18
1996	2,248	44.2	220	336	522	642	179	227	45	32	27	18
1997	2,288	43.6	224	347	521	652	181	238	46	33	27	19
1998	2,298	43.2	218	341	520	664	184	246	45	34	27	19

NA Not available.   [1] First-professional degrees are included with bachelor's degrees.   [2] Data beginning in 1996 reflect the new classification of institutions. See footnote 1, Table 264.

Source: U.S. National Center for Education Statistics. *Digest of Education Statistics,* annual.

No. 285. Degrees Earned by Level and Race/Ethnicity: 1981 to 1998

[For school year ending in year shown. Data exclude some institutions not reporting field of study and are slight undercounts of degrees awarded]

Level of degree and race/ethnicity	Total						Percent distribution	
	1981	1985	1990	1995	1997 [1]	1998 [1]	1981	1998 [1]
Associate's degrees, total	410,174	429,815	450,263	538,545	563,620	555,538	100.0	100.0
White, non-Hispanic	339,167	355,343	369,580	419,323	424,364	411,336	82.7	74.0
Black, non-Hispanic	35,330	35,791	35,327	47,142	55,260	55,008	8.6	9.9
Hispanic	17,800	19,407	22,195	36,013	42,645	45,627	4.3	8.2
Asian or Pacific Islander	8,650	9,914	13,482	20,717	24,829	25,047	2.1	4.5
American Indian Alaskan Native	2,584	2,953	3,530	5,492	5,927	6,220	0.6	1.1
Nonresident alien	6,643	6,407	6,149	9,858	10,595	12,300	1.6	2.2
Bachelor's degrees, total	934,800	968,311	1,048,631	1,158,788	1,168,023	1,183,033	100.0	100.0
White, non-Hispanic	807,319	826,106	884,376	913,377	898,224	900,317	86.4	76.1
Black, non-Hispanic	60,673	57,473	61,063	87,203	94,053	98,132	6.5	8.3
Hispanic	21,832	25,874	32,844	54,201	61,941	65,937	2.3	5.6
Asian or Pacific Islander	18,794	25,395	39,248	60,478	67,969	71,592	2.0	6.1
American Indian Alaskan Native	3,593	4,246	4,392	6,606	7,409	7,894	0.4	0.7
Nonresident alien	22,589	29,217	26,708	36,923	38,427	39,161	2.4	3.3
Master's degrees, total	294,183	280,421	322,465	397,052	414,882	429,296	100.0	100.0
White, non-Hispanic	241,216	223,628	251,690	292,784	302,541	307,587	82.0	71.6
Black, non-Hispanic	17,133	13,939	15,446	24,171	28,224	30,097	5.8	7.0
Hispanic	6,461	6,864	7,950	12,907	15,187	16,215	2.2	3.8
Asian or Pacific Islander	6,282	7,782	10,577	16,842	18,477	21,088	2.1	4.9
American Indian Alaskan Native	1,034	1,256	1,101	1,621	1,924	2,049	0.4	0.5
Nonresident alien	22,057	26,952	35,701	48,727	48,529	52,260	7.5	12.2
Doctor's degrees, total	32,839	32,307	38,113	44,427	45,394	45,925	100.0	100.0
White, non-Hispanic	25,908	23,934	25,880	27,826	28,344	28,747	78.9	62.6
Black, non-Hispanic	1,265	1,154	1,153	1,667	1,847	2,066	3.9	4.5
Hispanic	456	677	788	984	1,098	1,270	1.4	2.8
Asian or Pacific Islander	877	1,106	1,235	2,690	2,607	2,334	2.7	5.1
American Indian Alaskan Native	130	119	99	130	173	187	0.4	0.4
Nonresident alien	4,203	5,317	8,958	11,130	11,325	11,321	12.8	24.7
First-professional degrees, total	71,340	71,057	70,744	75,800	77,815	78,353	100.0	100.0
White, non-Hispanic	64,551	63,219	60,240	59,402	59,852	59,273	90.5	75.6
Black, non-Hispanic	2,931	3,029	3,410	4,747	5,251	5,483	4.1	7.0
Hispanic	1,541	1,884	2,427	3,231	3,553	3,547	2.2	4.5
Asian or Pacific Islander	1,456	1,816	3,362	6,397	7,037	7,712	2.0	9.8
American Indian Alaskan Native	192	248	257	412	511	561	0.3	0.7
Nonresident alien	669	861	1,048	1,611	1,611	1,777	0.9	2.3

[1] In this table, data beginning in 1997 reflect the new classification of institutions. See footnote 1, Table 264.

Source: U.S. National Center for Education Statistics. *Digest of Education Statistics,* annual.

U.S. Census Bureau, Statistical Abstract of the United States: 2001

No. 286. Degrees and Awards Earned Below Bachelor's by Field: 1998

[Covers associate degrees and other awards based on postsecondary curriculums of less than 4 years in institutions of higher education]

Field of study	Less than 1-year awards		1- to less than 4-year awards		Associate degrees	
	Total	Women	Total	Women	Total	Women
Total	112,340	60,910	137,015	79,954	558,555	340,942
Agriculture and natural resources	1,854	410	2,085	661	6,673	2,214
Architecture and related programs	2	2	29	19	265	175
Area, ethnic, and cultural studies	162	116	137	115	104	79
Biological/life sciences	62	20	36	16	2,113	1,331
Business management and administrative services [1]	18,930	13,733	25,756	21,168	96,915	70,910
Communications and communications technologies	449	193	583	242	3,970	1,818
Computer and information sciences	4,873	2,474	4,425	2,100	13,870	6,243
Construction trades	1,989	166	4,041	174	2,172	117
Consumer and personal services	3,357	2,539	6,636	4,976	7,744	3,102
Education	1,045	770	951	807	9,278	7,104
Engineering and engineering technologies	3,557	542	8,006	1,035	34,897	4,541
English language and literature/letters	187	130	22	13	1,609	1,066
Foreign languages and literatures	293	187	46	36	543	326
Health professions and related sciences	34,430	26,098	42,399	36,422	92,031	77,771
Home economics and vocational home economics	5,221	3,892	4,898	4,447	8,292	7,595
Law and legal studies	661	557	1,523	1,271	7,797	6,854
Liberal/general studies and humanities	232	132	522	329	186,248	115,636
Library science	103	95	47	44	96	82
Mathematics	2	1	2	1	844	353
Mechanics and repairers	5,733	801	15,815	807	10,616	715
Multi/interdisciplinary studies	821	527	66	44	9,401	4,860
Parks, recreation, leisure, and fitness	108	71	147	65	895	383
Physical sciences	108	55	150	59	2,286	1,187
Precision production trades	3,509	642	9,862	1,539	11,085	2,534
Protective services	13,184	2,929	3,326	881	19,002	6,182
Psychology	74	69	40	34	1,765	1,161
Public administration and services	373	271	429	327	4,156	3,464
R.O.T.C. and military technologies	-	-	-	-	22	1
Social sciences and history	33	21	99	46	4,196	2,632
Theological studies, religion and philosophy	133	65	525	240	664	298
Transportation and material moving	8,869	2,349	677	100	1,009	157
Visual and performing arts	1,122	565	2,806	1,402	14,980	8,207
Undistributed and unclassified	864	488	929	534	3,017	1,844

- Represents zero.   [1] Includes marketing

Source: U.S. National Center for Education Statistics, Digest of Education Statistics, 2000.

No. 287. Bachelor's Degrees Earned by Field: 1971 to 1998

Field of study	1971	1980	1990	1995	1998 [1]	Percent female	
						1971	1998 [1]
Total	839,730	929,417	1,051,344	1,160,134	1,184,406	43.4	56.1
Agriculture and natural resources	12,672	22,802	12,900	19,841	23,284	4.2	40.7
Architecture and environmental design	5,570	9,132	9,364	8,756	7,652	11.9	35.1
Area, ethnic and cultural studies	2,582	2,840	4,613	5,706	6,153	52.4	66.8
Biological sciences/life sciences	35,743	46,370	37,204	55,984	65,868	29.1	55.1
Business and management	114,729	184,867	248,698	234,323	233,119	9.1	48.5
Communications [2]	10,802	28,616	51,308	48,803	50,114	35.3	60.1
Computer and information sciences	2,388	11,154	27,257	24,404	26,852	13.6	26.7
Education	176,307	118,038	105,112	106,079	105,968	74.5	75.2
Engineering [2]	50,046	68,893	81,322	78,154	73,910	0.8	16.9
English language and literature/letters	64,342	32,541	47,519	51,901	49,708	65.6	66.9
Foreign languages and literatures	20,536	12,089	12,386	13,775	14,451	74.0	70.0
Health sciences	25,226	63,920	58,302	79,855	84,379	77.1	82.1
Home economics	11,167	18,411	14,491	15,345	17,296	97.3	88.6
Law and legal studies	545	683	1,592	2,032	2,017	5.0	71.8
Liberal/general studies	7,481	23,196	27,985	33,356	33,202	33.6	64.3
Library and archival sciences	1,013	398	77	50	73	92.0	76.7
Mathematics	24,937	11,872	15,176	13,723	12,328	37.9	46.5
Multi/interdisciplinary studies	6,286	11,277	16,267	26,033	26,163	22.8	66.1
Parks and recreation	1,621	5,753	4,582	12,889	16,781	34.7	50.2
Philosophy, religion, and theology	11,890	13,276	12,068	12,854	14,110	25.5	33.1
Physical sciences [3]	21,412	23,410	16,066	19,177	19,416	13.8	38.4
Protective services	2,045	15,015	15,354	24,157	25,076	9.2	40.4
Psychology	38,187	42,093	53,952	72,083	73,972	44.4	74.4
Public administration and services	5,466	16,644	13,908	18,586	20,408	68.4	81.0
R.O.T.C. and military technologies	357	38	196	27	3	0.3	-
Social sciences [3]	155,324	103,662	118,083	128,154	125,040	36.8	49.2
Visual and performing arts	30,394	40,892	39,934	48,690	52,077	59.7	58.7
Unclassified [4]	662	1,535	5,628	5,397	4,986	0.9	25.8

- Represents zero.   [1] In this table, data beginning in 1998 reflect the new classification of institutions. See footnote 1, Table 264.   [2] Includes technologies.   [3] Includes history.   [4] Includes precision production trades and transportation and materials moving.

Source: U.S. National Center for Education Statistics, Digest of Education Statistics, annual.

No. 288. Master's and Doctorate's Degrees Earned by Field: 1971 to 1998

Level and field of study	1971	1980	1990	1995	1998 [1]	Percent female 1971	Percent female 1998 [1]
MASTER'S DEGREES							
Total	230,509	298,081	324,301	397,629	430,164	40.1	57.1
Agriculture and natural resources	2,457	3,976	3,382	4,252	4,475	5.9	43.0
Architecture and related programs	1,705	3,139	3,499	3,923	4,347	13.8	41.6
Area, ethnic and cultural studies	1,032	852	1,212	1,639	1,617	38.3	56.2
Biological sciences/life sciences	5,728	6,510	4,869	5,393	6,261	33.6	52.4
Business management and administrative services	25,977	54,484	76,676	93,809	102,171	3.9	38.6
Communications and technologies	1,856	3,082	4,362	5,609	6,175	34.6	61.3
Computer and information sciences	1,588	3,647	9,677	10,326	11,246	10.3	29.0
Education	87,666	101,819	84,881	101,242	114,691	56.2	76.4
Engineering and engineering technologies . .	16,443	16,243	24,772	29,670	27,088	1.1	19.9
English language and literature/letters	10,686	6,189	6,567	7,845	7,795	60.6	66.1
Foreign languages	5,217	2,854	2,760	3,136	2,927	64.2	68.2
Health sciences	5,749	15,704	20,321	31,243	39,260	55.3	77.7
Home economics	1,452	2,690	2,100	2,864	2,914	93.9	83.0
Law and legal studies	955	1,817	1,888	2,511	3,228	4.8	35.9
Liberal arts and sciences, general studies and humanities	885	2,646	1,999	2,565	2,801	44.6	63.5
Library science	7,001	5,374	4,341	5,057	4,871	81.3	79.2
Mathematics	5,695	3,382	4,146	4,181	3,643	27.1	41.0
Multi/interdisciplinary studies	821	2,306	2,834	2,457	2,677	25.0	59.8
Parks and recreation	218	647	529	1,755	2,024	29.8	48.0
Philosophy, religion, and theology	4,036	5,126	6,265	6,620	5,999	27.1	40.4
Physical sciences and science technologies	6,367	5,219	5,449	5,753	5,361	13.3	35.9
Protective services	194	1,805	1,151	1,706	2,000	10.3	41.4
Psychology	5,717	9,938	10,730	13,921	13,747	40.6	73.1
Public administration and services	7,785	17,560	17,399	23,501	25,144	50.0	72.1
R.O.T.C. and military technologies	2	46	-	124	-	-	-
Social sciences [2]	16,539	12,176	11,634	14,845	14,938	28.5	46.7
Visual and performing arts	6,675	8,708	8,481	10,277	11,145	47.4	58.8
Unclassified [3]	63	142	2,377	1,405	1,619	-	34.1
DOCTORATE'S DEGREES							
Total	32,107	32,615	38,371	44,446	46,010	14.3	42.0
Agriculture and natural resources	1,086	991	1,295	1,264	1,302	2.9	28.5
Architecture and related programs	36	79	103	141	131	8.3	38.9
Area, ethnic and cultural studies	144	151	131	186	181	16.7	47.5
Biological sciences/life sciences	3,645	3,636	3,844	4,645	4,961	16.3	42.5
Business management and administrative services	757	753	1,093	1,394	1,290	2.8	31.4
Communications and technologies	145	193	273	321	359	13.1	52.4
Computer and information sciences	128	240	627	884	858	2.3	16.3
Education	6,041	7,314	6,502	6,905	6,729	21.0	63.2
Engineering and engineering technology . . .	3,638	2,507	4,981	6,128	5,994	0.6	12.2
English language and literature/letters	1,650	1,294	1,078	1,561	1,639	28.8	59.1
Foreign languages	988	755	724	905	959	34.6	57.7
Health sciences	466	786	1,536	2,069	2,484	16.5	62.5
Home economics	123	192	301	388	424	61.0	74.5
Law and legal studies	20	40	111	88	66	-	43.9
Liberal arts and sciences, general studies and humanities	32	192	63	90	87	31.3	50.6
Library science	39	73	42	55	48	28.2	64.6
Mathematics	1,249	763	966	1,226	1,259	7.6	25.7
Multi/interdisciplinary studies	59	209	272	238	508	6.8	44.3
Parks and recreation	2	21	35	149	129	50.0	41.9
Philosophy, religion, and theology	866	1,693	1,756	2,098	2,045	5.8	20.0
Physical sciences and science technologies	4,390	3,089	4,164	4,483	4,571	5.6	25.2
Protective services	1	18	38	26	39	-	35.9
Psychology	2,144	3,395	3,811	3,822	4,073	24.0	67.5
Public administration and services	174	342	508	556	499	24.1	55.3
Social sciences [2]	3,660	3,230	3,010	3,725	4,127	13.9	40.8
Visual and performing arts	621	655	849	1,080	1,163	22.2	51.3
Unclassified [3]	3	4	258	19	85	-	41.2

- Represents zero. [1] In this table, data beginning in 1998 reflect the new classification of institutions. See footnote 1, Table 264. [2] Includes history. [3] Includes precision production trades and transportation and materials moving.

Source: U.S. National Center for Education Statistics, *Digest of Education Statistics*, annual.

Education 177

No. 289. First Professional Degrees Earned in Selected Professions: 1970 to 1998

[First professional degrees include degrees which require at least 6 years of college work for completion (including at least 2 years of preprofessional training). See Appendix III]

Type of degree and sex of recipient	1970	1975	1980	1985	1990	1994	1995	1996	1997	1998
Medicine (M.D.):										
Institutions conferring degrees	86	104	112	120	124	121	119	119	118	117
Degrees conferred, total	8,314	12,447	14,902	16,041	15,075	15,368	15,537	15,341	15,571	15,424
Percent to women	8.4	13.1	23.4	30.4	34.2	37.9	38.8	40.9	41.4	41.6
Dentistry (D.D.S. or D.M.D.):										
Institutions conferring degrees	48	52	58	59	57	53	53	53	52	53
Degrees conferred, total	3,718	4,773	5,258	5,339	4,100	3,787	3,897	3,697	3,784	4,032
Percent to women	0.9	3.1	13.3	20.7	30.9	38.5	36.4	35.8	36.9	38.2
Law (LL.B. or J.D.):										
Institutions conferring degrees	145	154	179	181	182	185	183	183	184	185
Degrees conferred, total	14,916	29,296	35,647	37,491	36,485	40,044	39,349	39,828	40,079	39,331
Percent to women	5.4	15.1	30.2	38.5	42.2	43.0	42.6	43.5	43.7	44.4
Theological (B.D., M.Div., M.H.L.):										
Institutions conferring degrees	(NA)	(NA)	(NA)	(NA)	(NA)	186	192	184	178	190
Degrees conferred, total	5,298	5,095	7,115	7,221	5,851	5,967	5,978	5,879	5,859	5,873
Percent to women	2.3	6.8	13.8	18.5	24.8	24.8	25.7	25.2	26.2	26.1

NA Not available.

Source: U.S. National Center for Education Statistics, *Digest of Education Statistics*, annual.

No. 290. Participation in Adult Education: 1994-95 and 1998-99

[In thousands (189,543 represents 189,543,000), except percent. For the civilian noninstitutional population 17 years old and over not enrolled full time in elementary or secondary school at the time of the survey. Adult education is considered any enrollment in any educational activity at any time in the prior 12 months, except full-time enrollment in a higher education credential program. Based on survey and subject to sampling error; see source for details]

Characteristic	Adult population (1,000)	Participants in adult education					
		Number taking adult ed. courses (1,000)	Percent of total	Reason for taking course (percent) [1]			
				Personal/ social	Advance on the job	Train for a new job	Complete degree or diploma
Total, 1995	189,543	76,261	40	44	54	11	10
Total, 1999	194,434	88,809	46	43	54	12	11
Age:							
17 to 24 years old	25,276	13,029	52	34	32	20	23
25 to 34 years old	34,880	19,431	56	38	56	16	11
35 to 44 years old	45,258	23,047	51	41	62	13	9
45 to 54 years old	37,153	18,972	51	44	65	6	7
55 to 64 years old	24,309	9,003	37	49	56	7	9
65 years old and over	27,559	5,328	19	76	22	-	4
Sex:							
Male	92,946	40,204	43	34	59	11	13
Female	101,488	48,605	48	50	50	12	9
Race/ethnicity:							
White, non-Hispanic	143,679	65,547	46	45	56	11	10
Black, non-Hispanic	22,129	10,803	49	42	52	15	13
Hispanic	19,491	7,981	41	35	45	14	11
Other non-Hispanic races	9,135	4,478	49	35	49	14	19
Marital status:							
Never married	41,530	20,773	50	34	45	17	18
Currently married	118,568	55,966	47	46	58	10	9
Other	34,337	12,070	35	45	55	11	8
Children under 18 in household:							
Yes	83,365	43,060	52	41	55	12	12
No	111,070	45,749	41	44	53	11	10
Educational attainment:							
Up to 8th grade	11,078	1,527	14	41	39	3	21
9th to 12th grade	21,375	5,578	26	35	28	15	21
High school diploma or GED	53,488	19,693	37	39	52	12	7
Vocational school after high school	6,319	2,629	42	44	57	11	5
Some college	35,147	18,220	52	48	46	14	15
Associate's degree	11,377	6,735	59	38	60	15	14
Bachelor's or higher	55,651	34,426	62	45	63	9	8
Labor force status:							
Employed	132,227	70,849	54	37	63	12	11
Unemployed	7,963	3,433	43	39	23	32	22
Not in the labor force	54,244	14,527	27	72	17	7	10

- Represents or rounds to zero. [1] Reason for taking at least one course. Includes duplication. Excludes other reasons, not shown separately.

Source: U.S. National Center for Education Statistics, *1995* and *1999 National Household Education Surveys*.

178 Education

Law Enforcement, Courts, and Prisons

This section presents data on crimes committed, victims of crimes, arrests, and data related to criminal violations and the criminal justice system. The major sources of these data are the Bureau of Justice Statistics (BJS), the Federal Bureau of Investigation (FBI), and the Administrative Office of the U.S. Courts. BJS issues several reports, including *Sourcebook of Criminal Justice Statistics, Criminal Victimization in the United States, Prisoners in State and Federal Institutions, Children in Custody, Census of State Correctional Facilities and Survey of Prison Inmates, Census of Jails and Survey of Jail Inmates, Parole in the United States, Capital Punishment,* and the annual *Expenditure and Employment Data for the Criminal Justice System.* The Federal Bureau of Investigation's major annual report is *Crime in the United States,* which presents data on reported crimes as gathered from state and local law enforcement agencies.

Legal jurisdiction and law enforcement—Law enforcement is, for the most part, a function of state and local officers and agencies. The U.S. Constitution reserves general police powers to the states. By act of Congress, federal offenses include only offenses against the U.S. government and against or by its employees while engaged in their official duties and offenses which involve the crossing of state lines or an interference with interstate commerce. Excluding the military, there are 52 separate criminal law jurisdictions in the United States: 1 in each of the 50 states, 1 in the District of Columbia, and the federal jurisdiction. Each of these has its own criminal law and procedure and its own law enforcement agencies. While the systems of law enforcement are quite similar among the states, there are often substantial differences in the penalties for like offenses.

Law enforcement can be divided into three parts: Investigation of crimes and arrests of persons suspected of committing them; prosecution of those charged with crime; and the punishment or treatment of persons convicted of crime.

Crime—There are two major approaches taken in determining the extent of crime. One perspective is provided by the FBI through its Uniform Crime Reporting Program (UCR). The FBI receives monthly and annual reports from law enforcement agencies throughout the country, currently representing 95 percent of the national population. Each month, city police, sheriffs, and state police file reports on the number of index offenses that become known to them.

The FBI Crime Index offenses are as follows: *Murder and nonnegligent manslaughter* is based on police investigations, as opposed to the determination of a medical examiner or judicial body, includes willful felonious homicides and excludes attempts and assaults to kill, suicides, accidental deaths, justifiable homicides, and deaths caused by negligence; *forcible rape* includes forcible rapes and attempts; *robbery* includes stealing or taking anything of value by force or violence or threat of force or violence and includes attempted robbery; *aggravated assault* includes assault with intent to kill; *burglary* includes any unlawful entry to commit a felony or a theft and includes attempted burglary and burglary followed by larceny; *larceny* includes theft of property or articles of value without use of force and violence or fraud and excludes embezzlement, "con games," forgery, etc.; *motor vehicle theft* includes all cases where vehicles are driven away and abandoned but excludes vehicles taken for temporary use and returned by the taker. Arson was added as the eighth Index offense in April 1979 following a Congressional mandate. *Arson* includes any willful or malicious burning or attempt to burn, with or without intent to defraud, a dwelling house, public building, motor vehicle or aircraft, personal property of another, etc.

The monthly Uniform Crime Reports also contain data on crimes cleared by arrest and on characteristics of persons arrested

Law Enforcement, Courts, and Prisons 179

for all criminal offenses. In summarizing and publishing crime data, the FBI depends primarily on the adherence to the established standards of reporting for statistical accuracy, presenting the data as information useful to persons concerned with the problem of crime and criminal law enforcement.

National Crime Victimization Survey (NCVS)—A second perspective on crime is provided by this survey of the Bureau of Justice Statistics. Details about the crimes come directly from the victims. No attempt is made to validate the information against police records or any other source.

The NCVS measures rape, robbery, assault, household and personal larceny, burglary, and motor vehicle theft. The NCVS includes offenses reported to the police, as well as those not reported.

Police reporting rates (percent of victimizations) varied by type of crime. In 1994, for instance, 32 percent of the rapes/sexual assaults were reported; 55 percent of the robberies; 40 percent of assaults; 33 percent of personal thefts; 51 percent of the household burglaries; and 78 percent of motor vehicle thefts.

Murder and kidnaping are not covered. Commercial burglary and robbery were dropped from the program during 1977. The so-called victimless crimes, such as drunkenness, drug abuse, and prostitution, also are excluded, as are crimes for which it is difficult to identify knowledgeable respondents or to locate data records.

Crimes of which the victim may not be aware also cannot be measured effectively. Buying stolen property may fall into this category, as may some instances of embezzlement. Attempted crimes of many types probably are under recorded for this reason. Events in which the victim has shown a willingness to participate in illegal activity also are excluded.

In any encounter involving a personal crime, more than one criminal act can be committed against an individual. For example, a rape may be associated with a robbery or a household offense, such as a burglary, can escalate into something more serious in the event of a personal confrontation. In classifying the survey-measured crimes, each criminal incident has been counted only once—by the most serious act that took place during the incident and ranked in accordance with the seriousness classification system used by the Federal Bureau of Investigation. The order of seriousness for crimes against persons is as follows: Rape, robbery, assault, and larceny. Personal crimes take precedence over household offenses.

A *victimization*, basic measure of the occurrence of crime, is a specific criminal act as it affects a single victim. The number of victimizations is determined by the number of victims of such acts. Victimization counts serve as key elements in computing rates of victimization. For crimes against persons, the rates are based on the total number of individuals age 12 and over or on a portion of that population sharing a particular characteristic or set of traits. As general indicators of the danger of having been victimized during the reference period, the rates are not sufficiently refined to represent true measures of risk for specific individuals or households.

An *incident* is a specific criminal act involving one or more victims; therefore the number of incidents of personal crimes is lower than that of victimizations.

Courts—Statistics on criminal offenses and the outcome of prosecutions are incomplete for the country as a whole, although data are available for many states individually. The only national compilations of such statistics were made by the Census Bureau for 1932 to 1945 covering a maximum of 32 states and by the Bureau of Justice Statistics for 1986, 1988, 1990, and 1992 based on a nationally representative sample survey.

The bulk of civil and criminal litigation in the country is commenced and determined in the various state courts. Only when the U.S. Constitution and acts of Congress specifically confer jurisdiction upon the federal courts may civil or criminal litigation be heard and decided by them. Generally, the federal courts have

U.S. Census Bureau, Statistical Abstract of the United States: 2001

jurisdiction over the following types of cases: Suits or proceedings by or against the United States; civil actions between private parties arising under the Constitution, laws, or treaties of the United States; civil actions between private litigants who are citizens of different states; civil cases involving admiralty, maritime, or prize jurisdiction; and all matters in bankruptcy. The Administrative Office of the United States Courts has compiled statistics on the caseload of the federal courts annually since 1940.

There are several types of courts with varying degrees of legal jurisdiction. These jurisdictions include original, appellate, general, and limited or special. A court of original jurisdiction is one having the authority initially to try a case and pass judgment on the law and the facts; a court of appellate jurisdiction is one with the legal authority to review cases and hear appeals; a court of general jurisdiction is a trial court of unlimited original jurisdiction in civil and/or criminal cases, also called a "major trial court"; a court of limited or special jurisdiction is a trial court with legal authority over only a particular class of cases, such as probate, juvenile, or traffic cases.

The 94 federal courts of original jurisdiction are known as the U.S. district courts. One or more of these courts is established in every state and one each in the District of Columbia, Puerto Rico, the Virgin Islands, the Northern Mariana Islands, and Guam. Appeals from the district courts are taken to intermediate appellate courts of which there are 13, known as U.S. courts of appeals and the United States Court of Appeals for the Federal Circuit. The Supreme Court of the United States is the final and highest appellate court in the federal system of courts.

Juvenile offenders—For statistical purposes, the FBI and most states classify as juvenile offenders persons under the age of 18 years who have committed a crime or crimes.

Delinquency cases are all cases of youths referred to a juvenile court for violation of a law or ordinance or for seriously "antisocial" conduct. Several types of facilities are available for those adjudicated delinquent, ranging from the short-term physically unrestricted environment to the long-term very restrictive atmosphere.

Prisoners—Data on prisoners in federal and state prisons and reformatories were collected annually by the Census Bureau until 1950, by the Federal Bureau of Prisons until 1971, transferred then to the Law Enforcement Assistance Administration, and, in 1979, to the Bureau of Justice Statistics. Adults convicted of criminal activity may be given a prison or jail sentence. A *prison* is a confinement facility having custodial authority over adults sentenced to confinement of more than 1 year. A *jail* is a facility, usually operated by a local law enforcement agency, holding persons detained pending adjudication and/or persons committed after adjudication to 1 year or less. Nearly every state publishes annual data either for its whole prison system or for each separate state institution.

Statistical reliability—For discussion of statistical collection, estimation and sampling procedures, and measures of statistical reliability pertaining to the National Crime Victimization Survey and Uniform Crime Reporting Program, see Appendix III.

U.S. Census Bureau, Statistical Abstract of the United States: 2001

No. 291. Crimes and Crime Rates by Type of Offense: 1980 to 1999

[13,408 represents 13,408,000. Data refer to offenses known to the police. Rates are based on Census Bureau estimated resident population as of July 1; 1980 and 1990, enumerated as of April 1. See source for details. Minus sign (-) indicates decrease. For definitions of crimes, see text, this section]

Item and year	Total	Violent crime Total	Murder [1]	Forcible rape	Robbery	Aggravated assault	Property crime Total	Burglary	Larceny/ theft	Motor vehicle theft
Number of offenses (1,000):										
1980	13,408	1,345	23.0	83.0	566	673	12,064	3,795	7,137	1,132
1985	12,431	1,329	19.0	88.7	498	723	11,103	3,073	6,926	1,103
1986	13,212	1,489	20.6	91.5	543	834	11,723	3,241	7,257	1,224
1987	13,509	1,484	20.1	91.1	518	855	12,025	3,236	7,500	1,289
1988	13,923	1,566	20.7	92.5	543	910	12,357	3,218	7,706	1,433
1989	14,251	1,646	21.5	94.5	578	952	12,605	3,168	7,872	1,565
1990	14,476	1,820	23.4	102.6	639	1,055	12,656	3,074	7,946	1,636
1991	14,873	1,912	24.7	106.6	688	1,093	12,961	3,157	8,142	1,662
1992	14,438	1,932	23.8	109.1	672	1,127	12,506	2,980	7,915	1,611
1993	14,145	1,926	24.5	106.0	660	1,136	12,219	2,835	7,821	1,563
1994	13,990	1,858	23.3	102.2	619	1,113	12,132	2,713	7,880	1,539
1995	13,863	1,799	21.6	97.5	581	1,099	12,064	2,594	7,998	1,472
1996	13,494	1,689	19.7	96.3	536	1,037	11,805	2,506	7,905	1,394
1997	13,195	1,636	18.2	96.2	499	1,023	11,559	2,461	7,744	1,354
1998	12,486	1,534	17.0	93.1	447	977	10,952	2,333	7,376	1,243
1999	11,635	1,431	15.5	89.1	410	916	10,205	2,100	6,957	1,147
Rate per 100,000 population:										
1980	5,950.0	596.6	10.2	36.8	251.1	298.5	5,353.3	1,684.1	3,167.0	502.2
1985	5,207.1	556.6	7.9	37.1	208.5	302.9	4,650.5	1,287.3	2,901.2	462.0
1986	5,480.4	617.7	8.6	37.9	225.1	346.1	4,862.6	1,344.6	3,010.3	507.8
1987	5,550.0	609.7	8.3	37.4	212.7	351.3	4,940.3	1,329.6	3,081.3	529.4
1988	5,664.2	637.2	8.4	37.6	220.9	370.2	5,027.1	1,309.2	3,134.9	582.9
1989	5,741.0	663.1	8.7	38.1	233.0	383.4	5,077.9	1,276.3	3,171.3	630.4
1990	5,820.3	731.8	9.4	41.2	257.0	424.1	5,088.5	1,235.9	3,194.8	657.8
1991	5,897.8	758.1	9.8	42.3	272.7	433.3	5,139.7	1,252.0	3,228.8	659.0
1992	5,660.2	757.5	9.3	42.8	263.6	441.8	4,902.7	1,168.2	3,103.0	631.5
1993	5,484.4	746.8	9.5	41.1	255.9	440.3	4,737.6	1,099.2	3,032.4	606.1
1994	5,373.5	713.6	9.0	39.3	237.7	427.6	4,660.0	1,042.0	3,026.7	591.3
1995	5,275.9	684.6	8.2	37.1	220.9	418.3	4,591.3	987.1	3,043.8	560.4
1996	5,086.6	636.5	7.4	36.3	201.9	390.9	4,450.1	944.8	2,979.7	525.5
1997	4,930.0	611.3	6.8	35.9	186.3	382.3	4,318.7	919.4	2,893.4	506.0
1998	4,619.3	567.5	6.3	34.5	165.4	361.3	4,051.8	863.0	2,729.0	459.8
1999	4,266.8	524.7	5.7	32.7	150.2	336.1	3,742.1	770.0	2,551.4	420.7

[1] Includes nonnegligent manslaughter.

Source: U.S. Federal Bureau of Investigation, *Crime in the United States*, annual. See also <http://www.fbi.gov/ucr/Cius99/99crime/99cius.pdf>.

No. 292. Crimes and Crime Rates by Type and Area: 1999

[In thousands (11,635 represents 11,635,000), except rate. Rate per 100,000 population; see headnote, Table 291. Estimated totals based on reports from city and rural law enforcement agencies representing 96 percent of the national population. For definitions of crimes, see text, this section]

Type of crime	United States Total	United States Rate	Metropolitan areas [1] Total	Metropolitan areas [1] Rate	Other cities Total	Other cities Rate	Rural areas Total	Rural areas Rate
Total	11,635	4,267	9,989	4,600	1,012	4,561	633	1,901
Violent crime	1,431	525	1,268	584	89	403	73	221
Murder and nonnegligent manslaughter	16	6	13	6	1	4	1	4
Forcible rape	89	33	74	34	7	34	8	23
Robbery	410	150	391	180	13	59	6	17
Aggravated assault	916	336	789	363	68	307	59	177
Property crime	10,204	3,742	8,722	4,016	923	4,158	560	1,680
Burglary	2,100	770	1,742	802	174	783	184	552
Larceny-theft	6,957	2,551	5,923	2,727	699	3,151	335	1,005
Motor vehicle theft	1,147	421	1,056	487	50	224	41	124

[1] For definition, see Appendix II.

Source: U.S. Federal Bureau of Investigation, *Crime in the United States*, annual. See also <http://www.fbi.gov/ucr/Cius99/99crime/99cius.pdf>.

No. 293. Crime Rates by State, 1997 to 1999, and by Type, 1999

[Offenses known to the police per 100,000 population. Based on Census Bureau estimated resident population as of July 1. For definitions of crimes, see text, this section]

State	1997, total	1998, total	1999 Total	Violent crime Total	Murder[1]	Forcible rape	Robbery	Aggravated assault	Property crime Total	Burglary	Larceny/ theft	Motor vehicle theft
United States	4,930	4,619	4,267	525	5.7	32.7	150	336	3,742	770	2,551	421
Alabama	4,890	4,597	4,412	490	7.9	34.6	121	327	3,922	884	2,737	301
Alaska.	5,273	4,777	4,363	632	8.6	83.5	91	448	3,732	612	2,691	429
Arizona	7,195	6,575	5,897	551	8.0	28.9	153	362	5,345	1,034	3,511	801
Arkansas	4,719	4,283	4,043	425	5.6	27.8	79	313	3,618	850	2,506	261
California	4,865	4,343	3,805	627	6.0	28.2	181	412	3,178	675	1,994	508
Colorado	4,650	4,488	4,063	341	4.6	41.4	75	219	3,723	665	2,693	365
Connecticut	3,984	3,787	3,389	346	3.3	19.9	124	199	3,044	588	2,112	344
Delaware [2]	5,783	5,363	4,835	734	3.2	70.2	198	463	4,101	696	3,002	404
District of Columbia [3] . .	9,839	8,836	8,067	1,628	46.4	47.8	644	889	6,439	976	4,181	1,282
Florida	7,272	6,886	6,206	854	5.7	46.3	212	591	5,352	1,200	3,535	617
Georgia	5,792	5,463	5,149	534	7.5	29.8	166	330	4,615	917	3,182	515
Hawaii.	6,023	5,333	4,838	235	3.7	29.9	88	113	4,602	795	3,414	393
Idaho	3,925	3,715	3,149	245	2.0	33.3	18	192	2,904	610	2,143	152
Illinois [4]	5,141	4,859	4,507	733	7.7	34.2	219	471	3,774	712	2,632	430
Indiana	4,466	4,169	3,766	375	6.6	27.0	109	232	3,391	715	2,335	341
Iowa	3,816	3,501	3,224	280	1.5	27.2	37	215	2,944	593	2,172	179
Kansas [4]	5,152	4,872	4,439	383	6.0	40.1	77	260	4,056	824	3,004	228
Kentucky [4]	3,127	3,116	2,878	301	5.4	26.3	80	189	2,578	611	1,749	218
Louisiana	6,449	6,098	5,747	733	10.7	33.1	174	515	5,014	1,093	3,425	496
Maine	3,132	3,041	2,875	112	2.2	19.1	19	72	2,763	601	2,027	135
Maryland	5,653	5,366	4,919	743	9.0	30.0	264	441	4,176	836	2,848	492
Massachusetts	3,675	3,436	3,263	551	2.0	26.9	96	426	2,712	534	1,763	415
Michigan	4,917	4,683	4,325	575	7.0	49.2	143	376	3,750	778	2,398	576
Minnesota	4,414	4,047	3,597	274	2.8	42.7	82	147	3,323	580	2,465	278
Mississippi	4,630	4,384	4,270	349	7.7	41.7	112	188	3,921	1,051	2,381	489
Missouri.	4,815	4,826	4,579	500	6.6	26.3	131	337	4,079	777	2,881	420
Montana [4]	4,409	4,359	4,070	207	2.6	28.3	26	150	3,863	429	3,220	215
Nebraska.	4,284	4,405	4,108	430	3.6	24.8	76	326	3,678	610	2,742	327
Nevada	6,065	5,281	4,654	570	9.1	52.1	233	276	4,084	974	2,386	724
New Hampshire	2,640	2,420	2,282	97	1.5	28.7	21	45	2,185	308	1,765	113
New Jersey	4,057	3,654	3,400	412	3.5	17.3	175	216	2,988	577	1,977	434
New Mexico	6,907	6,719	5,962	835	9.8	54.3	148	622	5,128	1,235	3,426	467
New York.	3,911	3,589	3,279	589	5.0	19.6	241	324	2,691	512	1,858	320
North Carolina	5,492	5,322	5,175	542	7.2	28.2	158	349	4,633	1,287	3,012	334
North Dakota	2,711	2,681	2,393	67	1.6	22.4	9	34	2,326	369	1,794	163
Ohio	4,510	4,328	3,996	316	3.5	36.7	128	148	3,680	773	2,559	348
Oklahoma	5,495	5,004	4,684	508	6.9	40.9	83	378	4,176	1,027	2,788	361
Oregon	6,270	5,647	5,002	375	2.7	36.8	86	249	4,627	807	3,409	411
Pennsylvania	3,432	3,273	3,114	421	4.9	27.3	156	233	2,693	467	1,899	327
Rhode Island	3,654	3,518	3,582	287	3.6	39.5	80	164	3,295	640	2,249	407
South Carolina	6,134	5,777	5,324	847	6.6	40.8	148	651	4,477	1,020	3,086	372
South Dakota	3,245	2,624	2,645	167	2.5	45.8	14	105	2,477	444	1,916	118
Tennessee	5,512	5,034	4,694	695	7.1	44.0	157	487	3,999	937	2,602	461
Texas	5,481	5,112	5,032	560	6.1	38.0	147	370	4,472	950	3,063	459
Utah	5,996	5,506	4,977	276	2.1	37.8	54	181	4,701	685	3,669	347
Vermont [4]	2,828	3,139	2,817	114	2.9	22.9	11	77	2,704	596	1,955	154
Virginia	3,876	3,660	3,374	315	5.7	25.0	101	183	3,059	472	2,326	261
Washington	5,926	5,867	5,256	377	3.0	47.1	101	226	4,878	950	3,342	587
West Virginia	2,469	2,547	2,721	351	4.4	18.6	37	291	2,370	570	1,592	208
Wisconsin [4]	3,678	3,543	3,296	246	3.4	20.1	85	138	3,051	488	2,299	263
Wyoming	4,181	3,808	3,455	232	2.3	28.5	15	186	3,223	489	2,609	124

[1] Includes nonnegligent manslaughter. [2] Forcible rape figures furnished by the state-level uniform crime reporting (UCR) Program administered by the Delaware State Bureau of Investigation were not in accordance with the national UCR guidelines; therefore, it was necessary that the forcible rape count be estimated. [3] Includes offenses reported by the police at the National Zoo. [4] Complete data were not available; therefore, it was necessary for the crime counts to be estimated for Illinois, Kansas, Kentucky, Montana, and New Hampshire for all years shown and for Vermont for 1997 and Wisconsin for 1998.

Source: U.S. Federal Bureau of Investigation, *Crime in the United States*, annual. See also <http://www.fbi.gov/ucr/Cius99/99crime/99cius.pdf>.

Law Enforcement, Courts, and Prisons 183

No. 294. Crime Rates by Type—Selected Large Cities: 1999

[Offenses known to the police per 100,000 population. Based on U.S. Census Bureau estimated resident population as of July 1. For definitions of crimes, see text, this section]

City ranked by population size, 1999 [1]	Crime index, total	Violent crime					Property crime			
		Total	Murder	Forcible rape	Robbery	Aggra-vated assault	Total	Burglary	Larceny/ theft	Motor vehicle. theft
New York, NY	4,031.0	1,062.6	8.9	22.9	485.8	545.0	2,968.4	544.7	1,889.4	534.3
Los Angeles, CA	4,588.7	1,283.2	11.6	35.3	394.8	841.5	3,305.5	589.6	2,039.8	676.1
Chicago, IL	(NA)	(NA)	22.7	(NA)	716.4	993.5	6,332.8	1,067.8	3,986.3	1,278.8
Houston, TX	7,271.2	1,187.3	13.3	41.3	460.7	672.0	6,083.9	1,365.4	3,645.6	1,073.0
Philadelphia, PA	7,291.3	1,604.5	20.3	65.1	773.6	745.5	5,686.8	978.3	3,474.6	1,233.9
San Diego, CA	4,003.6	598.4	4.6	28.7	146.3	418.8	3,405.3	530.3	2,108.7	766.3
Phoenix, AZ	7,720.2	832.0	17.5	32.6	311.5	470.4	6,888.3	1,299.2	4,124.1	1,465.0
San Antonio, TX	6,793.4	561.0	8.5	53.0	148.1	351.4	6,232.4	968.3	4,769.0	495.1
Dallas, TX	9,615.7	1,414.3	17.5	60.7	582.5	753.5	8,201.4	1,798.5	4,767.0	1,635.9
Detroit, MI	10,416.5	2,253.9	42.6	81.0	802.4	1,328.0	8,162.6	1,874.7	3,542.3	2,745.6
Las Vegas, NV	5,184.9	664.9	11.8	57.7	338.3	257.0	4,520.0	1,098.2	2,362.5	1,059.4
San Jose, CA	2,943.9	580.9	2.9	39.6	82.9	455.6	2,363.0	306.6	1,729.9	326.5
Honolulu, HI	4,925.0	253.6	4.3	27.1	104.7	117.6	4,671.3	702.4	3,507.6	461.2
Indianapolis, IN	5,322.1	1,016.2	14.9	55.9	342.3	603.2	4,305.8	1,313.6	2,276.4	715.9
San Francisco, CA	5,725.1	866.3	8.5	25.5	459.2	373.1	4,858.9	730.3	3,338.7	789.9
Jacksonville, FL	7,151.7	1,034.2	11.8	65.3	242.4	714.6	6,117.5	1,373.9	4,049.3	694.3
Columbus, OH	9,101.9	854.6	10.5	94.7	449.4	300.0	8,247.2	2,092.4	5,141.8	1,013.1
Baltimore, MD	(NA)	(NA)	(NA)	(NA)	(NA)	(NA)	(NA)	(NA)	(NA)	(NA)
El Paso, TX	5,791.9	686.0	2.2	29.7	114.6	539.5	5,105.9	400.1	4,336.0	369.8
Memphis, TN	8,368.1	1,410.5	19.3	112.8	609.2	669.2	6,957.6	2,132.5	3,567.4	1,257.7
Charlotte-Mecklenburg, NC	8,829.6	1,345.3	13.9	43.3	416.1	872.0	7,484.3	1,705.0	4,378.4	800.9
Milwaukee, WI	7,929.3	1,043.4	21.3	46.8	539.5	435.7	6,885.9	1,112.4	4,497.2	1,276.3
Austin, TX	6,904.1	497.9	3.7	34.4	178.8	280.9	6,406.3	1,204.2	4,733.5	468.6
Boston, MA	6,288.5	1,302.1	5.6	60.4	442.3	793.8	4,986.4	612.0	3,161.8	1,212.6
Seattle, WA	9,164.7	767.3	8.3	34.6	302.4	422.0	8,397.4	1,191.4	5,614.7	1,591.3
Nashville, TN	8,883.7	1,607.3	13.0	88.0	374.8	1,131.5	7,276.4	1,331.3	4,991.1	954.0
Washington, DC	8,061.7	1,627.7	46.4	47.8	644.3	889.2	6,433.9	976.3	4,175.9	1,281.7
Denver, CO	5,256.0	570.8	12.4	48.9	203.7	305.9	4,685.2	1,061.4	2,644.1	979.7
Portland, OR	8,133.7	1,236.6	6.9	66.8	278.6	884.3	6,897.1	1,199.8	4,775.8	921.4
Fort Worth, TX	7,487.5	851.1	13.4	57.3	290.0	490.3	6,636.4	1,504.6	4,350.3	781.5
Cleveland, OH	6,743.3	1,215.3	15.7	101.6	610.2	487.8	5,528.0	1,455.3	2,584.4	1,488.2
Oklahoma City, OK	9,323.5	859.3	11.8	84.0	224.6	538.9	8,464.2	1,696.6	6,001.4	766.2
Tucson, AZ	8,992.4	913.9	7.6	52.0	271.8	582.4	8,078.5	1,289.5	5,762.3	1,026.8
New Orleans, LA	7,676.9	1,273.2	33.9	60.1	586.7	592.5	6,403.7	1,207.7	3,667.9	1,528.0
Kansas City, MO	11,630.8	1,749.1	26.4	74.3	558.3	1,090.1	9,881.7	1,939.4	6,422.0	1,520.3
Virginia Beach, VA	3,676.1	238.5	2.7	24.4	115.8	95.5	3,437.6	464.7	2,808.8	164.1
Long Beach, CA	4,152.2	744.9	10.5	27.2	358.2	349.0	3,407.2	767.8	1,870.7	768.7
Albuquerque, NM	9,766.1	1,250.7	11.4	52.4	396.7	790.2	8,515.4	1,620.5	5,777.9	1,116.9
Atlanta, GA	13,488.5	2,729.5	34.8	78.0	990.1	1,626.6	10,759.0	2,083.9	6,893.4	1,781.7
Sacramento, CA	6,610.8	752.0	13.2	34.9	353.6	350.4	5,858.7	1,171.7	3,599.5	1,087.6
Fresno, CA	7,137.5	992.2	6.4	39.6	313.9	632.2	6,145.3	1,093.9	3,902.1	1,149.4
Tulsa, OK	7,396.1	1,162.1	10.7	61.4	231.8	858.2	6,234.0	1,713.7	3,676.8	843.5
Miami, FL	10,723.8	2,105.0	16.9	30.3	823.7	1,234.2	8,618.8	1,962.5	5,123.8	1,532.5
Omaha, NE	7,048.2	1,238.8	9.1	46.7	257.8	925.2	5,809.4	944.2	3,902.1	963.0
Oakland, CA	8,370.2	1,550.0	16.2	82.2	589.9	861.7	6,820.2	1,372.2	4,158.3	1,289.8
Mesa, AZ	6,168.2	578.5	2.4	36.4	100.4	439.3	5,589.7	1,062.6	3,753.5	773.6
Minneapolis, MN	8,635.2	1,388.7	13.2	126.7	588.8	659.9	7,246.5	1,562.6	4,597.8	1,086.1
Colorado Springs, CO	5,189.8	525.0	6.8	64.4	141.3	312.4	4,664.8	811.0	3,525.7	328.0
Pittsburgh, PA	6,123.5	877.6	14.1	39.8	455.5	368.2	5,245.9	897.5	3,427.2	921.1
St. Louis, MO	13,998.2	2,233.0	38.1	42.2	819.2	1,333.5	11,765.2	2,304.9	7,510.7	1,949.6
Cincinnati, OH	6,431.6	737.4	8.3	73.7	357.9	297.5	5,694.2	1,297.2	3,898.3	498.8
Wichita, KS	6,312.9	579.9	8.1	50.9	210.7	310.3	5,733.0	1,200.8	4,029.1	503.2
Toledo, OH	7,409.6	688.4	4.8	49.4	290.3	343.9	6,721.2	1,506.0	4,329.0	886.2
Arlington, TX	6,242.0	627.5	3.5	35.1	175.6	413.3	5,614.5	1,022.8	4,038.5	553.2
Santa Ana, CA	3,597.2	588.8	4.8	31.2	278.6	274.1	3,008.3	394.9	1,876.7	736.7
Buffalo, NY	6,868.5	1,077.2	10.6	58.5	489.3	518.8	5,791.4	1,470.8	3,327.5	993.1
Anaheim, CA	3,373.9	547.3	5.3	28.4	156.3	357.3	2,826.6	547.6	1,820.5	458.5
Tampa, FL	10,929.2	2,254.0	10.6	79.5	792.3	1,371.6	8,675.1	2,056.4	4,659.3	1,959.4
Corpus Christi, TX	7,136.5	870.4	5.3	67.9	135.9	661.3	6,266.1	1,233.2	4,503.9	528.9
Newark, NJ	7,881.2	1,813.7	25.7	38.4	906.3	843.3	6,067.5	1,150.4	2,954.4	1,962.7
Riverside, CA	4,385.7	776.0	11.3	26.9	236.1	499.7	3,609.7	845.9	2,155.4	608.3
Raleigh, NC	7,099.4	772.2	6.1	35.0	281.0	450.2	6,327.2	1,315.2	4,504.4	507.6
St. Paul, MN	7,064.3	849.2	5.4	76.9	297.7	469.2	6,215.1	1,367.2	4,117.1	730.7
Anchorage, AK	5,023.2	652.9	7.4	62.1	154.4	429.1	4,370.3	598.6	3,286.4	485.3
Louisville, KY	5,964.7	862.9	14.4	24.1	450.9	373.4	5,101.7	1,331.0	2,991.9	778.8
Aurora, CO	5,646.7	568.1	4.3	71.1	177.8	314.9	5,078.6	895.1	3,393.0	790.4
Birmingham, AL	8,148.1	1,118.5	30.7	83.4	369.4	635.0	7,029.5	1,516.7	4,735.0	777.8
Stockton, CA	6,790.6	1,152.4	13.1	53.4	371.0	714.9	5,638.2	1,016.2	3,743.7	878.3
Lexington, KY	6,101.7	786.5	9.9	58.8	217.9	499.9	5,315.3	1,020.8	3,914.6	379.9

NA Not available. [1] Resident population estimated by the FBI. [2] The rates for forcible rape, violent crime, and crime index are not shown because the forcible rape figures were not in accordance with national Uniform Crime Reporting guidelines.

Source: U.S. Federal Bureau of Investigation, *Crime in the United States*, annual. See also <http://www.fbi.gov/ucr/Cius99/99crime/99cius.pdf>.

No. 295. Murder Victims—Circumstances and Weapons Used or Cause of Death: 1990 to 1999

[Based solely on police investigation. For definition of murder, see text, this section]

Characteristic	1990	1995	1998	1999	Characteristic	1990	1995	1998	1999
Murders, total...	20,273	20,232	14,209	13,011	Other motives	19.4	21.6	16.4	21.0
Percent distribution...	100.0	100.0	100.0	100.0	Unknown	24.8	28.9	30.9	29.6
CIRCUMSTANCES					TYPE OF WEAPON OR CAUSE OF DEATH				
Felonies, total	20.8	17.7	17.7	17.0	Guns	64.3	68.2	64.8	65.2
Robbery	9.2	9.3	8.7	8.1	Handguns	49.8	55.8	52.0	51.2
Narcotics	6.7	5.1	4.8	4.5	Cutting or stabbing	17.4	12.6	13.3	13.2
Sex offenses	1.1	0.2	0.7	0.6	Blunt objects [1]	5.4	4.5	5.3	5.8
Other felonies	3.7	3.2	3.4	3.9	Personal weapons [2]	5.5	5.9	6.8	6.8
Suspected felonies	0.7	0.6	0.7	0.5	Strangulations, asphyxiations	2.0	1.8	2.2	2.3
Argument, total	34.4	31.2	34.3	31.9	Fire	1.4	0.8	0.9	1.0
Property or money	2.5	1.7	1.7	1.6	All other [3]	4.0	6.1	6.7	5.8
Romantic triangle	2.0	1.4	1.3	1.1					
Other arguments	29.8	28.2	31.3	29.2					

[1] Refers to club, hammer, etc. [2] Hands, fists, feet, etc. [3] Includes poison, drowning, explosives, narcotics, and unknown.
Source: U.S. Federal Bureau of Investigation, *Crime in the United States*, annual. See also <http://www.fbi.gov/ucr/Cius99/99crime/99cius.pdf> (released 15 October 2000).

No. 296. Murder Victims by Age, Sex, and Race: 1999

Age	Total	Sex			Race			
		Male	Female	Unknown	White	Black	Other	Unknown
Total	13,011	9,811	3,185	15	6,519	5,984	384	124
Percent distribution	100.0	75.4	24.5	0.1	50.1	46.0	3.0	1.0
Under 18 yrs. old	1,506	990	516	-	772	649	69	16
18 yrs. old and over	11,289	8,681	2,603	5	5,635	5,260	313	81
Infant (under 1 yr. old)	218	110	108	-	121	85	7	5
1 to 4 yrs. old	296	151	145	-	162	115	14	5
5 to 8 yrs. old	100	46	54	-	54	37	9	-
9 to 12 yrs. old	79	40	39	-	55	19	4	1
13 to 16 yrs. old	460	347	113	-	228	208	20	4
17 to 19 yrs. old	1,309	1,118	191	-	548	717	39	5
20 to 24 yrs. old	2,314	1,940	374	-	959	1,294	48	13
25 to 29 yrs. old	1,832	1,507	324	1	752	1,014	49	17
30 to 34 yrs. old	1,410	1,065	343	2	678	688	34	10
35 to 39 yrs. old	1,328	942	386	-	715	567	36	10
40 to 44 yrs. old	1,099	782	317	-	597	462	32	8
45 to 49 yrs. old	727	540	186	1	417	275	29	6
50 to 54 yrs. old	471	339	131	1	299	142	24	6
55 to 59 yrs. old	304	224	80	-	205	86	12	1
60 to 64 yrs. old	223	161	62	-	155	60	6	2
65 to 69 yrs. old	187	126	61	-	137	42	8	-
70 to 74 yrs. old	148	78	70	-	113	29	5	1
75 yrs. old and over	290	155	135	-	212	69	6	3
Age unknown	216	140	66	10	112	75	2	27

- Represents zero.
Source: U.S. Federal Bureau of Investigation, *Crime in the United States*, annual. See also <http://www.fbi.gov/ucr/Cius99/99crime/99cius.pdf> (released 15 October 2000).

No. 297. Homicide Victims by Race and Sex: 1980 to 1998

[Rates per 100,000 resident population in specified group. Excludes deaths to nonresidents of United States. Deaths classified according to the ninth revision of the *International Classification of Diseases*; see text, Section 2, Vital Statistics]

Year	Homicide victims					Homicide rate [2]				
	Total [1]	White		Black		Total [1]	White		Black	
		Male	Female	Male	Female		Male	Female	Male	Female
1980	24,278	10,381	3,177	8,385	1,898	10.7	10.9	3.2	66.6	13.5
1985	19,893	8,122	3,041	6,616	1,666	8.3	8.2	2.9	48.4	11.0
1986	21,731	8,567	3,123	7,634	1,861	9.0	8.6	3.0	55.0	12.1
1987	21,103	7,979	3,149	7,518	1,969	8.7	7.9	3.0	53.3	12.6
1988	22,032	7,994	3,072	8,314	2,089	9.0	7.9	2.9	58.0	13.2
1989	22,909	8,337	2,971	8,888	2,074	9.2	8.2	2.8	61.1	12.9
1990	24,932	9,147	3,006	9,981	2,163	10.0	9.0	2.8	69.2	13.5
1991	26,513	9,581	3,201	10,628	2,330	10.5	9.3	3.0	72.0	14.2
1992	25,488	9,456	3,012	10,131	2,187	10.0	9.1	2.8	67.5	13.1
1993	26,009	9,054	3,232	10,640	2,297	10.1	8.6	3.0	69.7	13.6
1994	24,926	9,055	2,921	10,083	2,124	9.6	8.5	2.6	65.1	12.4
1995	22,895	8,336	3,028	8,847	1,936	8.7	7.8	2.7	56.3	11.1
1996	20,971	7,570	2,747	8,183	1,800	7.9	7.0	2.5	51.5	10.2
1997	19,846	7,343	2,570	7,601	1,652	7.4	6.7	2.3	47.1	9.3
1998	18,272	6,707	2,534	6,873	1,547	6.8	6.1	2.2	42.1	8.6

[1] Includes races not shown separately. [2] Rate based on enumerated population figures as of April 1 for 1980 and 1990; July 1 estimates for other years.
Source: U.S. National Center for Health Statistics, *Vital Statistics of the United States*, annual; and *National Vital Statistics Reports (NVSR)* (formerly *Monthly Vital Statistics Report*); and unpublished data.

Law Enforcement, Courts, and Prisons   185

No. 298. Forcible Rape—Number and Rate: 1980 to 1999

[For definition of rape, see text, this section]

Item	1980	1990	1992	1993	1994	1995	1996	1997	1998	1999
NUMBER										
Total	82,990	102,560	109,060	106,010	102,220	97,460	96,250	96,153	93,144	89,107
By force	63,599	86,541	93,825	92,360	89,297	85,249	84,053	84,931	82,823	79.503
Attempt	19,391	16,019	15,235	13,650	12,923	12,211	12,197	11,222	10,321	9.604
RATE										
Per 100,000 population	36.8	41.2	42.8	41.1	39.3	37.1	36.3	35.9	34.5	32.7
Per 100,000 females	71.6	80.5	83.5	80.3	76.7	72.5	71.0	70.4	67.4	63.9
Per 100,000 females 12 years old and over	86.3	96.6	100.5	96.4	92.0	87.1	85.3	84.4	80.7	76.5
AVERAGE ANNUAL PERCENT CHANGE IN RATE [1]										
Per 100,000 population	6.1	8.1	1.2	-4.0	-4.4	-5.6	-2.2	-1.0	-4.1	-5.2
Per 100,000 females 12 years old and over	6.0	8.2	-0.4	-4.1	-4.6	-5.3	-2.1	-1.0	-4.5	-5.3

[1] Represents annual average from prior year shown except for 1980, from 1979 and for 1990, from 1989.

Source: U.S. Federal Bureau of Investigation, *Population-at-Risk Rates and Selected Crime Indicators*, annual.

No. 299. Robbery and Property Crimes by Type and Selected Characteristic: 1990 to 1999

[For definition of crime, see text, this section]

Characteristic of offenses	Number of offenses (1,000)				Rate per 100,000 inhabitants				Average value lost (dol.)	
	1990	1995	1998	1999	1990	1995	1998	1999	1998	1999
Robbery, total [1]	**639**	**581**	**447**	**410**	**257.0**	**220.9**	**165.4**	**150.2**	**980**	**1,131**
Type of crime:										
Street or highway	359	315	220	198	144.2	120.0	81.3	72.6	751	856
Commercial house	73	71	61	56	29.5	27.2	22.7	20.2	1,348	1,549
Gas station	18	13	10	9	7.1	5.1	3.6	3.2	532	627
Convenience store	39	30	26	25	15.6	11.4	9.6	9.1	582	620
Residence	62	63	54	50	25.1	24.0	20.2	18.3	1,076	1,231
Bank	9	9	9	8	3.8	3.5	3.2	2.9	4,489	4.552
Weapon used:										
Firearm	234	238	171	163	94.1	90.6	63.2	59.9	(NA)	(NA)
Knife or cutting instrument	76	53	39	35	30.7	20.1	14.5	12.7	(NA)	(NA)
Other dangerous weapon	61	53	58	41	24.5	20.2	21.5	14.9	(NA)	(NA)
Strongarm	268	236	179	171	107.7	90.0	66.3	62.3	(NA)	(NA)
Burglary, total	**3,074**	**2,595**	**2,333**	**2,100**	**1,235.9**	**987.6**	**863.0**	**770.0**	**1,331**	**1,458**
Forcible entry	2,150	1,737	1,521	1,350	864.5	661.2	562.8	495.0	(NA)	(NA)
Unlawful entry	678	657	652	605	272.8	250.1	241.4	221.8	(NA)	(NA)
Attempted forcible entry	245	201	159	145	98.7	76.4	58.9	53.2	(NA)	(NA)
Residence	2,033	1,736	1,563	1,394	817.4	660.6	578.5	511.3	1,283	1,441
Nonresidence	1,041	859	769	706	418.5	327.0	284.5	258.7	1,428	1,490
Occurred during the night	1,135	905	790	699	456.4	344.4	287.2	256.2	(NA)	(NA)
Occurred during the day	1,151	1,000	894	798	462.8	380.5	317.4	292.7	(NA)	(NA)
Larceny-theft, total	**7,946**	**8,001**	**7,376**	**6,957**	**3,194.8**	**3,044.9**	**2,729.0**	**2,551.4**	**632**	**678**
Pocket picking	81	51	44	43	32.4	19.4	16.4	15.8	410	451
Purse snatching	82	51	42	40	32.8	19.5	15.7	14.8	373	392
Shoplifting	1,291	1,205	1,094	1,003	519.1	458.4	404.9	367.8	143	165
From motor vehicles	1,744	1,940	1,937	1,789	701.3	738.5	716.5	656.1	600	693
Motor vehicle accessories	1,185	964	738	724	476.3	367.0	273.1	265.5	419	451
Bicycles	443	501	375	326	178.2	190.5	138.9	119.5	260	338
From buildings	1,118	1,004	990	947	449.4	382.1	366.4	347.2	1,026	1,015
From coin-operated machines	63	50	44	46	25.4	18.9	16.3	17.0	327	376
Other	1,940	2,235	2,110	2,039	780.0	850.5	780.7	747.8	881	912
Motor vehicles, total [2]	**1,636**	**1,473**	**1,243**	**1,147**	**657.8**	**560.5**	**459.8**	**420.7**	**5,911**	**6,104**
Automobiles	1,304	1,154	939	856	524.3	439.2	347.2	314.1	(NA)	(NA)
Trucks and buses	238	240	231	215	95.5	91.2	88.5	78.8	(NA)	(NA)

NA Not available.   [1] Includes other crimes not shown separately.   [2] Includes other types of motor vehicles not shown separately.

Source: U.S. Federal Bureau of Investigation, *Population-at-Risk Rates and Selected Crime Indicators*, annual.

U.S. Census Bureau, Statistical Abstract of the United States: 2001

No. 300. Hate Crimes—Number of Incidents, Offenses, Victims, and Known Offenders by Bias Motivation: 1999

[The FBI collected statistics on hate crimes from 12,096 law enforcement agencies representing over 233 million inhabitants in 1999. Hate crime offenses cover incidents motivated by race, religion, sexual orientation, ethnicity/national origin, and disability]

Bias motivation	Incidents reported	Offenses	Victims [1]	Known offenders [2]
Total bias motivations	7,943	9,384	9,892	7,347
Race, total	4,340	5,293	5,542	4,412
Anti-White	791	981	1,007	1,023
Anti-Black	2,983	3,574	3,715	2,887
Anti-American Indian/Alaskan native	48	50	51	42
Anti-Asian/Pacific Islander	304	369	385	294
Anti-multiracial group	214	319	384	166
Ethnicity/national origin, total	840	1,026	1,057	921
Anti-Hispanic	475	588	601	576
Anti-other ethnicity/national origin	365	438	456	345
Religion, total	1,416	1,539	1,694	609
Anti-Jewish	1,111	1,199	1,290	434
Anti-Catholic	36	41	41	18
Anti-Protestant	50	52	53	20
Anti-Islamic	32	34	34	14
Anti-other religious group	152	173	225	99
Anti-multireligious group	31	35	46	21
Anti-atheism/agnosticism/etc	4	5	5	3
Sexual orientation, total	1,321	1,492	1,563	1,375
Anti-male homosexual	920	1,030	1,076	1,043
Anti-female homosexual	185	215	228	149
Anti-homosexual	179	206	218	154
Anti-heterosexual	14	16	16	15
Anti-bisexual	23	25	25	14
Disability, total	20	22	24	22
Anti-physical	10	11	13	9
Anti-mental	10	11	11	13
Multiple bias	6	12	12	8

[1] The term "victim" may refer to a person, business, institution, or a society as a whole. [2] The term "known offender" does not imply that the identity of the suspect is known but only that an attribute of the suspect is identified which distinguishes him/her from an unknown offender.

Source: U.S. Federal Bureau of Investigation, *Hate Crime Statistics*, annual; and <http://www.fbi.gov/ucr/99hate.pdf> (released 15 October 2000) and subsequent updates because of late data submissions.

No. 301. Hate Crimes Reported by State: 1999

[See headnote, Table 300]

State	Number of participating agencies	Population covered (1,000)	Agencies submitting incidents	Incidents reported	State	Number of participating agencies	Population covered (1,000)	Agencies submitting incidents	Incidents reported
United States...	12,096	232,905	1,838	7,944	Missouri	209	4,280	27	84
Alabama	(¹)	(¹)	(¹)	(¹)	Montana	87	750	8	27
Alaska	1	258	1	5	Nebraska	233	1,527	9	35
Arizona	87	4,530	17	252	Nevada	37	1,809	6	75
Arkansas	191	2,539	2	8	New Hampshire	90	591	16	20
California	718	33,133	244	1,949	New Jersey	564	8,143	250	617
Colorado	235	4,057	41	154	New Mexico	59	1,177	2	16
Connecticut	98	3,188	55	138	New York	505	18,188	17	590
Delaware	52	753	10	37	North Carolina	464	7,526	15	31
District of Columbia	1	519	1	4	North Dakota	82	493	1	2
Florida	482	15,044	93	267	Ohio	350	8,029	67	232
Georgia	56	867	6	36	Oklahoma	299	3,352	23	42
Hawaii	(¹)	(¹)	(¹)	(¹)	Oregon	238	3,314	27	123
Idaho	120	1,251	22	34	Pennsylvania	1,133	11,711	34	185
Illinois	55	4,705	55	247	Rhode Island	48	991	9	41
Indiana	143	3,079	19	111	South Carolina	339	3,883	34	73
Iowa	222	2,798	20	31	South Dakota	117	725	6	14
Kansas	1	332	1	41	Tennessee	352	4,362	61	133
Kentucky	250	2,743	36	71	Texas	938	20,018	75	266
Louisiana	172	3,728	3	6	Utah	122	2,130	20	59
Maine	165	1,248	6	22	Vermont	43	499	10	16
Maryland	146	5,171	33	230	Virginia	373	5,892	50	215
Massachusetts	305	5,395	108	450	Washington	231	5,612	45	230
Michigan	607	9,370	154	413	West Virginia	246	1,465	19	34
Minnesota	311	4,765	56	225	Wisconsin	363	5,248	20	49
Mississippi	88	1,239	2	2	Wyoming	68	479	2	2

[1] Did not report.

Source: U.S. Federal Bureau of Investigation, *Hate Crime Statistics*, annual; and <http://www.fbi.gov/ucr/99hate.pdf> (released 15 October 2000) and subsequent updates because of late data submissions.

U.S. Census Bureau. Statistical Abstract of the United States: 2001

No. 302. Criminal Victimizations and Victimization Rates: 1996 to 1999

[Based on National Crime Victimization Survey; see text, this section, and Appendix III]

Type of crime	Number of victimizations (1,000)				Victimization rates [1]			
	1996	1997	1998	1999	1996	1997	1998	1999
All crimes, total	36,796	34,788	31,307	28,780	(X)	(X)	(X)	(X)
Personal crimes [2]	9,443	8,971	8,412	7,565	43.5	40.8	37.9	33.7
Crimes of violence	9,125	8,614	8,116	7,357	42.0	39.2	36.6	32.8
Completed violence	2,700	2,679	2,564	2,278	12.4	12.2	11.6	10.1
Attempted/threatened violence	6,425	5,935	5,553	5,079	29.6	27.0	25.0	22.6
Rape/sexual assault	307	311	333	383	1.4	1.4	1.5	1.7
Rape/attempted rape	197	194	200	201	0.9	0.9	0.9	0.9
Rape	98	115	110	141	0.4	0.5	0.5	0.6
Attempted rape	99	79	89	60	0.5	0.4	0.4	0.3
Sexual assault	110	117	133	182	0.5	0.5	0.6	0.8
Robbery	1,134	944	886	810	5.2	4.3	4.0	3.6
Completed/property taken	757	607	610	530	3.5	2.8	2.7	2.4
With injury	250	243	170	189	1.1	1.1	0.8	0.8
Without injury	508	363	439	341	2.3	1.7	2.0	1.5
Attempted to take property	377	337	277	280	1.7	1.5	1.2	1.2
With injury	79	73	70	78	0.4	0.3	0.3	0.3
Without injury	298	265	207	202	1.4	1.2	0.9	0.9
Assault	7,683	7,359	6,897	6,164	35.4	33.5	31.1	27.4
Aggravated	1,910	1,883	1,674	1,503	8.8	8.6	7.5	6.7
With injury	513	595	547	449	2.4	2.7	2.5	2.0
Threatened with weapon	1,397	1,288	1,126	1,054	6.4	5.9	5.1	4.7
Simple	5,773	5,476	5,224	4,660	26.6	24.9	23.5	20.8
With minor injury	1,240	1,258	1,175	998	5.7	5.7	5.3	4.4
Without injury	4,533	4,218	4,048	3,662	20.9	19.2	18.2	16.3
Personal theft [3]	318	357	296	208	1.5	1.6	1.3	0.9
Property crimes	27,353	25,817	22,895	21,215	266.3	248.3	217.4	198.0
Household burglary	4,845	4,635	4,054	3,652	47.2	44.6	38.5	34.1
Completed	4,056	3,893	3,380	3,064	39.5	37.4	32.1	28.6
Attempted forcible entry	789	742	674	587	7.7	7.1	6.4	5.5
Motor vehicle theft	1,387	1,433	1,138	1,068	13.5	13.8	10.8	10.0
Completed	938	1,007	822	808	9.1	9.7	7.8	7.5
Attempted	449	426	316	260	4.4	4.1	3.0	2.4
Theft	21,120	19,749	17,703	16,495	205.7	189.9	168.1	153.9
Completed [4]	20,303	18,960	17,074	15,964	197.7	182.3	162.1	149.0
Attempted	818	789	629	532	8.0	7.6	6.0	5.0

X Not applicable.   [1] Per 1,000 persons age 12 or older or per 1,000 households.   [2] The victimization survey cannot measure murder because of the inability to question the victim.   [3] Includes pocket picking, purse snatching, and attempted purse snatching.   [4] Includes thefts in which the amount taken was not ascertained.

Source: U.S. Bureau of Justice Statistics, *Criminal Victimization,* annual; and *Criminal Victimization 1999, Changes 1998-99 with Trends 1993-99,* Series NCJ-182734. See also <http://www.ojp.usdoj.gov/bjs/pub/pdf/cv99.pdf>.

No. 303. Victimization Rates by Type of Violent Crime and Characteristic of the Victim: 1999

[Rate per 1,000 persons age 12 years or older. Based on National Crime Victimization Survey; see text, this section, and Appendix III]

Characteristic	All crime	Crimes of violence			Assault			Personal theft
		All crimes of violence	Rape/ sexual assault	Robbery	Total	Aggra- vated	Simple	
Total	33.7	32.8	1.7	3.6	27.1	6.7	20.8	0.9
Male	37.9	37.0	0.4	5.0	31.6	8.7	22.9	0.9
Female	29.7	28.8	3.0	2.3	23.6	4.8	18.8	0.9
12 to 15 yrs. old	77.5	74.4	4.0	6.7	63.7	13.1	50.6	3.1
16 to 19 yrs. old	78.9	77.4	6.9	8.2	62.3	16.8	45.5	[1]1.5
20 to 24 yrs. old	69.5	68.5	4.3	7.7	56.4	16.7	39.7	[1]1.0
25 to 34 yrs. old	37.4	36.3	1.7	4.1	30.5	8.3	22.2	1.2
35 to 49 yrs. old	25.6	25.2	0.8	2.8	21.6	4.7	16.9	[1]0.4
50 to 64 yrs. old	15.0	14.4	[1]0.2	1.9	12.3	1.8	10.5	[1]0.6
65 yrs. old and over	4.4	3.8	[1]0.1	[1]0.7	3.0	1.1	1.9	[1]0.6
White	32.7	31.9	1.6	3.1	27.2	6.2	21.1	0.8
Black	42.9	41.6	2.6	7.7	31.3	10.6	20.8	1.3
Other	26.0	24.5	[1]1.7	[1]2.5	20.3	5.7	14.6	[1]1.5
Hispanic	35.3	33.8	1.9	5.6	26.3	8.9	17.4	1.5
Non-Hispanic	33.3	32.4	1.7	3.4	27.3	6.4	20.9	0.9
Household income:								
Less than $7,500	59.5	57.5	4.3	8.1	45.1	14.5	30.6	[1]1.9
$7,500-$14,999	45.6	44.5	1.6	6.9	35.9	10.0	26.0	[1]1.1
$15,000-$24,999	36.1	35.3	3.2	4.8	27.2	7.2	20.1	[1]0.8
$25,000-$34,999	39.1	37.9	1.2	3.1	33.7	6.9	26.7	1.2
$35,000-$49,999	30.8	30.3	1.6	3.5	25.3	5.5	19.7	[1]0.5
$50,000-$74,999	33.7	33.3	1.5	2.2	29.7	7.1	22.6	[1]0.4
$75,000 or more	24.1	22.9	0.8	1.8	20.3	4.0	16.3	1.2

[1] Based on 10 or fewer sample cases.

Source: U.S. Bureau of Justice Statistics, *Criminal Victimization,* annual; and *Criminal Victimization 1999, Changes 1998-99 with Trends 1993-99,* Series NCJ-182734. See also <http://www.ojp.usdoj.gov/bjs/pub/pdf/cv99.pdf>.

No. 304. Victim-Offender Relationship in Crimes of Violence by Characteristics of the Criminal Incident: 1999

[In percent. Covers only crimes of violence. Based on National Crime Victimization Survey; see text, this section, and Appendix III]

Characteristics of incident	Total	Rape/ sexual assault	Robbery	Assault Total	Aggra- vated[1]	Simple
Total	100	100	100	100	100	100
Victim/offender relationship: [2]						
Relatives	12	11	6	10	8	10
Well-known	37	37	19	29	26	30
Casual acquaintance	11	21	7	17	15	17
Stranger	41	31	69	44	51	43
Time of day: [3]						
6 a.m. to 6 p.m.	54	28	46	57	46	60
6 p.m. to midnight	33	41	38	32	40	30
Midnight to 6 a.m.	11	24	15	9	12	8
Location of crime:						
At or near victim's home or lodging	26	28	29	26	29	25
Friend's/relative's/neighbor's home	8	34	4	7	7	7
Commercial places	14	9	4	15	10	17
Parking lots/garages	7	4	15	7	8	6
School	15	5	7	17	9	19
Streets other than near victim's home	17	12	32	16	26	13
Other [4]	12	8	11	13	11	13
Victim's activity:						
At work or traveling to or from work	21	10	14	23	15	25
School	13	8	10	14	8	16
Activities at home	23	33	19	23	24	22
Shopping/errands	4	2	10	4	5	3
Leisure activities away from home	22	33	19	21	29	19
Traveling	9	5	18	8	13	7
Other	8	8	9	8	7	8
Distance from victim's home:						
Inside home or lodging	14	28	17	13	13	13
Near victim's home	15	5	14	16	19	15
1 mile or less	19	19	28	18	21	17
5 miles or less	23	17	20	24	21	25
50 miles or less	24	25	17	25	21	26
More than 50 miles	3	3	4	3	4	3
Weapons:						
No weapons present	74	94	48	76	4	100
Weapons present	26	6	52	24	96	-
Firearm	7	1	25	6	23	-
Other type of weapon [5]	18	4	27	18	73	-

- Represents zero. [1] An aggravated assault is any assault in which an offender possesses or uses a weapon or inflicts serious injury. [2] Excludes "don't know" relationships. [3] Excludes "not known and not available" time of day. [4] Includes areas on public transportation or inside station, in apartment yard, park, field, playground, or other areas. [5] Includes knives, other sharp objects, blunt objects, and other types of weapons.

Source: U.S. Bureau of Justice Statistics, *Criminal Victimization*, annual; and *Criminal Victimization 1999, Changes 1998-99 with Trends 1993-99*, Series NCJ-182734. See also <http://www.ojp.usdoj.gov/bjs/pub/pdf/cv99.pdf>.

No. 305. Property Victimization Rates by Selected Household Characteristic: 1999

[Victimizations per 1,000 households. Based on National Crime Victimization Survey; see text, this section, and Appendix III]

Characteristic	Total	Burglary	Motor vehicle theft	Theft
Total	198.0	34.1	10.0	153.9
Race:				
White	190.0	31.5	9.0	149.5
Black	249.9	52.6	16.0	181.2
Other	206.3	31.2	11.6	163.6
Ethnicity:				
Hispanic	232.5	37.2	17.3	178.0
Non-Hispanic	194.6	33.7	9.3	151.5
Household income:				
Less than $7,500	220.8	67.0	6.2	147.6
$7,500-$14,999	200.1	44.2	10.1	145.9
$15,000-$24,999	214.9	38.9	11.2	164.9
$25,000-$34,999	199.1	37.1	10.4	151.7
$35,000-$49,999	207.6	30.9	11.7	165.0
$50,000-$74,999	213.6	24.1	10.3	179.1
$75,000 or more	220.4	23.1	9.7	187.7
Residence:				
Urban	256.3	46.2	15.9	194.2
Suburban	181.4	27.1	8.5	145.8
Rural	159.8	32.6	5.7	121.5
Form of tenure:				
Home owned	170.4	26.5	8.4	135.5
Home rented	251.9	48.9	13.0	190.0

Source: U.S. Bureau of Justice Statistics, *Criminal Victimization*, annual; and *Criminal Victimization 1999, Changes 1998-99 with Trends 1993-99*, Series NCJ-182734. See also <http://www.ojp.usdoj.gov/bjs/pub/pdf/cv99.pdf>.

No. 306. Violence by Intimate Partners by Sex, 1993 to 1998, and by Type of Crime, 1998

[Violent acts covered include murder, rape, sexual assault, robbery, and aggravated and simple assault. Intimate partners involve current spouses, former spouses, current boy/girlfriends, and former boy/girlfriends. Based on the National Criminal Victimization Survey; see text, this section, and Appendix III. Homicide data were obtained from the Federal Bureau of Investigation]

Year and type of crime	All persons		Females		Males	
	Number	Rate per 100,000 [1]	Number	Rate per 100,000 [1]	Number	Rate per 100,000 [1]
1993	1,235,660	584.2	1,072,090	982.0	163,570	159.8
1994	1,179,360	551.8	1,003,180	908.9	176,180	170.4
1995	1,069,190	495.7	953,700	855.8	115,490	110.8
1996	1,030,020	472.6	879,290	781.7	150,730	142.9
1997	956,330	433.8	848,480	747.3	107,850	100.9
1998, total	**1,033,660**	**465.9**	**876,340**	**766.8**	**157,330**	**146.2**
Murder	1,830	0.8	1,320	1.2	510	0.5
Rape or sexual assault	63,490	28.6	63,490	55.6	(B)	(B)
Robbery	103,940	46.8	101,830	89.1	(B)	(B)
Aggravated assault	187,970	84.7	140,050	122.5	47,910	44.5
Simple assault	676,440	304.9	569,650	498.4	106,790	99.2

B Base figure too small to meet statistical standards for reliability of derived figure. In this case, 10 or fewer sample cases. [1] Rates are the number of victimizations per 100,000 persons.
Source: U.S. Bureau of Justice Statistics, *Intimate Partner Victimization*, Series NCJ 178247, May 2000.

No. 307. Nonfatal Violent Victimizations With Injury by Victim Characteristics: Period 1992-98

[Violent acts covered include rape, sexual assault, robbery, and aggravated and simple assault whether completed or not. Based on the National Criminal Victimization Survey; see text, this section, and Appendix III]

Victim characteristics	Number of violent victimizations (1,000)			Rate per 1,000 persons			Percent of victims of violent crime	
	All victimizations	With injury [1]	With severe injury [2]	All victimizations	With injury [1]	With severe injury [2]	With injury [1]	With severe injury [2]
All victims of violence [3]	**71,408**	**18,037**	**2,409**	**47.2**	**11.9**	**1.6**	**25.3**	**3.4**
Sex:								
Male	40,792	9,024	1,580	55.8	12.3	2.2	22.1	3.9
Female	30,615	9,013	830	39.3	11.6	1.1	29.4	2.7
Race/ethnicity:								
White [4]	51,578	12,448	1,493	45.6	11.0	1.3	24.1	2.9
Black [4]	9,953	2,909	552	56.5	16.5	3.1	29.2	5.5
American Indian [4]	837	294	49	113.0	39.6	6.6	35.1	5.9
Asian, Pacific Islander [4]	1,232	307	38	26.5	6.6	0.8	25.0	3.1
Hispanic	6,953	1,877	253	51.1	13.8	1.9	27.0	3.6
Age:								
12 to 14 years	8,959	2,442	161	110.2	30.1	2.0	27.3	1.8
15 to 17 years	8,367	2,297	267	106.7	29.3	3.4	27.5	3.2
18 to 21 years	10,337	3,092	468	102.3	30.6	4.6	29.9	4.5
22 to 24 years	6,448	1,790	233	84.4	23.4	3.0	27.8	3.6
25 to 34 years	16,354	4,039	603	56.9	14.0	2.1	24.7	3.7
35 to 49 years	15,919	3,401	501	37.8	8.1	1.2	21.4	3.1
50 to 64 years	3,948	745	143	16.1	3.0	0.6	18.9	3.6
65 years or older	1,075	231	33	4.9	1.1	0.1	21.5	3.0
Education:								
Grade school or less	2,011	512	30	46.7	11.9	0.7	25.5	1.5
Junior high school	10,778	3,066	285	69.0	19.6	1.8	28.4	2.6
High school	30,615	8,643	1,374	46.2	13.0	2.1	28.2	4.5
College	27,248	5,575	697	43.3	8.9	1.1	20.5	2.6
Marital status:								
Never married	40,450	10,919	1,466	87.4	23.6	3.2	27.0	3.6
Married	18,175	3,188	390	23.0	4.0	0.5	17.5	2.1
Separated/divorced	11,738	3,672	522	74.1	23.2	3.3	31.3	4.4
Widowed	848	197	29	8.9	2.1	0.3	23.2	3.4
Annual household income:								
Less than $10,000	11,665	3,922	654	73.0	24.6	4.1	33.6	5.6
$10,000 to $19,999	12,807	3,542	469	54.8	15.2	2.0	27.7	3.7
$20,000 to $29,999	10,285	2,565	377	48.5	12.1	1.8	24.9	3.7
$30,000 to $39,999	9,323	2,022	217	46.5	10.1	1.1	21.7	2.3
$40,000 to $49,999	6,424	1,468	184	43.9	10.0	1.3	22.9	2.9
$50,000 or more	14,510	2,862	297	39.6	7.8	0.8	19.7	2.1
Location of residence:								
Urban	26,718	6,985	1,064	60.5	15.8	2.4	26.1	4.0
Suburban	33,365	7,975	933	44.8	10.7	1.3	23.9	2.8
Rural	11,324	3,077	413	34.9	9.5	1.3	27.2	3.6

[1] Includes rapes/sexual assaults with unspecified types of injuries. [2] Includes gunshot or knife wounds, broken bones, loss of teeth, internal injuries, loss of consciousness, and undetermined injuries requiring 2 or more days of hospitalization. [3] Injury data were reported for 99.9 percent of violent victimizations for 1992 through 1998. Data were reported on gender for 100 percent; on race and ethnicity for 98.9 percent; on age for 100 percent; on education for 99.0 percent; on marital status for 99.7 percent; on household income for 91.0 percent; and on location of residence for 100 percent. [4] Excludes Hispanics.
Source: U.S. Bureau of Justice Statistics, *Injuries from Violent Crime, 1992-98*, Series NCJ 168633, June 2001.

No. 308. Persons Arrested by Charge and Selected Characteristics: 1999

[10,618.7 represents 10,618,700. Represents arrests (not charges) reported by approximately 9,600 agencies with a total 1999 population of approximately 195 million as estimated by FBI]

Offense charged	Total arrests (1,000)					Percent—		
	Total	White	Black	American Indian or Alaskan Native	Asian or Pacific Islander	Total (1,000)	Under 15 yrs. old	Under 18 yrs. old
Total	10,618.7	7,125.4	3,244.4	132.9	116.0	10,661.7	5.2	16.6
Serious crimes [1]	1,701.1	1,062.9	592.1	19.6	26.4	1,704.3	10.4	27.5
Murder and nonnegligent manslaughter	11.7	5.1	6.2	0.1	0.2	11.7	1.2	9.7
Forcible rape	21.4	12.9	8.1	0.2	0.3	21.5	6.3	16.5
Robbery	95.1	39.2	54.2	0.5	1.2	95.2	7.6	27.5
Aggravated assault	359.7	220.2	130.9	3.8	4.9	360.3	5.0	14.1
Burglary	214.4	144.3	65.4	2.1	2.7	214.7	12.5	32.8
Larceny/theft	880.8	575.4	278.6	11.6	15.3	882.7	12.5	31.0
Motor vehicle theft	106.1	57.1	45.9	1.1	1.9	106.2	8.9	34.9
Arson	11.9	8.8	2.9	0.1	0.1	12.0	35.1	52.8
All other nonserious crimes	8,917.6	6,062.5	2,652.3	113.3	89.6	8,957.4	4.2	14.4
Other assaults	950.8	608.7	318.6	12.8	10.6	952.7	7.6	16.6
Forgery and counterfeiting	81.2	52.3	27.2	0.5	1.2	81.3	0.8	6.1
Fraud	297.3	184.2	109.2	1.2	2.7	298.0	1.6	5.6
Embezzlement	13.1	8.2	4.6	0.1	0.2	13.1	0.5	9.5
Stolen property—buying, receiving, possessing	88.0	48.8	37.4	0.7	1.0	88.1	6.1	22.8
Vandalism	203.5	150.8	47.3	3.0	2.4	203.9	18.1	41.0
Weapons; carrying, possessing etc.	130.9	76.6	51.9	0.9	1.5	131.1	7.7	23.9
Prostitution and commercialized vice	76.0	44.4	29.5	0.5	1.6	76.1	0.2	1.4
Sex offenses (except forcible rape and prostitution)	68.0	50.6	15.8	0.8	0.9	68.1	9.0	17.7
Drug abuse violations	1,218.8	744.7	459.6	6.5	7.9	1,220.5	1.9	12.3
Gambling	13.2	5.7	7.0	-	0.4	13.2	1.0	9.5
Offenses against family and children	94.9	63.0	29.2	1.0	1.7	99.2	2.1	6.2
Driving under the influence	982.4	855.8	101.6	14.7	10.4	1,000.1	-	1.5
Liquor laws	567.9	443.5	106.9	13.6	4.0	570.3	2.0	19.8
Drunkenness	480.5	395.5	71.2	11.7	2.1	481.6	0.4	3.1
Disorderly conduct	489.4	313.8	165.6	6.8	3.2	490.3	9.4	25.4
Vagrancy	26.6	13.6	12.2	0.6	0.1	26.6	1.6	10.0
Suspicion	4.9	3.4	1.5	-	-	4.9	6.7	23.2
Curfew and loitering law violations	118.6	86.1	29.6	1.4	1.5	118.8	27.4	100.0
Runaways	103.3	79.9	18.4	1.2	3.8	103.4	39.1	100.0
All other offenses (except traffic)	2,908.4	1,832.9	1,008.0	35.2	32.4	2,916.1	2.9	10.5

- Represents zero or rounds to zero.   [1] Includes arson.

Source: U.S. Federal Bureau of Investigation, Crime in the United States, annual. See also <http://www.fbi.gov/ucr/Cius99/99crime/99cius.pdf>.

No. 309. Juvenile Arrests for Selected Offenses: 1980 to 1999

[169,439 represents 169,439,000. Juveniles are persons under 18 years of age]

Offense	1980	1990	1992	1993	1994	1995	1996	1997	1998	1999
Number of contributing agencies	8,178	10,765	11,058	10,277	10,693	10,037	10,026	9,472	9,589	9,502
Population covered (1,000)	169,439	204,543	217,754	213,705	208,035	206,762	195,805	194,925	194,612	195,324
NUMBER										
Violent crime, total	77,220	97,103	118,358	122,434	125,141	123,131	104,455	100,273	90,201	81,715
Murder	1,475	2,661	3,025	3,473	3,114	2,812	2,184	1,887	1,587	1,131
Forcible rape	3,668	4,971	5,451	5,490	4,873	4,556	4,228	4,127	3,988	3,544
Robbery	38,529	34,944	42,639	44,598	47,046	47,240	39,788	36,419	29,989	26,125
Aggravated assault	33,548	54,527	67,243	68,873	70,108	68,523	58,255	57,840	54,637	50,915
Weapon law violations	21,203	33,123	49,903	54,414	52,278	46,506	40,145	39,358	34,122	31,307
Drug abuse, total	86,685	66,300	73,232	90,618	124,931	149,236	148,783	155,444	148,066	138,774
Sale and manufacturing	13,004	24,575	25,331	27,635	32,746	34,077	32,558	30,761	29,312	26,134
Heroin/cocaine	1,318	17,511	17,881	18,716	20,327	19,187	17,465	15,855	15,094	12,686
Marijuana	8,876	4,372	4,853	6,144	8,812	10,682	11,489	11,208	10,808	10,770
Synthetic narcotics	465	346	663	455	465	701	614	671	813	722
Dangerous nonnarcotic drugs	2,345	2,346	1,934	2,320	3,142	3,507	2,990	3,027	2,597	1,956
Possession	73,681	41,725	47,901	62,983	92,185	115,159	116,225	124,683	118,754	112,640
Heroin/cocaine	2,614	15,194	16,855	17,726	21,004	21,253	17,560	18,328	16,278	13,445
Marijuana	64,465	20,940	25,004	37,915	61,003	82,015	87,712	94,046	91,467	89,523
Synthetic narcotics	1,524	1,155	897	1,008	1,227	2,047	1,713	1,987	1,916	1,581
Dangerous nonnarcotic drugs	5,078	4,436	5,145	6,334	8,951	9,844	9,240	10,322	9,093	8,091

Source: U.S. Federal Bureau of Investigation, Crime in the United States, annual. See also <http://www.fbi.gov/ucr/Cius99/99crime/99cius.pdf>.

U.S. Census Bureau, Statistical Abstract of the United States: 2001

No. 310. Drug Use by Arrestees in Major U.S. Cities by Type of Drug and Sex: 1999

[Percent testing positive. Based on data from the Arrestee Drug Abuse Monitoring Program]

City	Male				Female			
	Any drug [1]	Marijuana	Cocaine	Heroin	Any drug [1]	Marijuana	Cocaine	Heroin
Albuquerque, NM	63.9	36.9	42.5	13.6	73.9	24.4	56.1	30.6
Atlanta, GA	76.7	44.4	51.3	4.3	77.2	33.5	62.0	4.5
Chicago, IL . . .	74.4	44.6	41.7	20.1	76.9	26.5	64.3	32.4
Cleveland, OH	71.0	43.3	40.3	4.3	67.5	27.8	50.0	7.5
Dallas, TX.	60.5	39.2	34.3	4.5	56.1	26.6	40.1	6.7
Denver, CO.	66.8	43.7	40.6	3.4	69.1	34.1	50.7	2.9
Detroit, MI.	65.3	47.9	27.0	8.6	68.9	26.2	45.9	16.4
Houston, TX	59.5	38.2	35.7	6.2	43.3	22.8	23.3	6.9
Indianapolis, IN	64.1	48.0	33.7	2.5	69.2	37.5	45.1	4.8
Las Vegas, NV	59.6	28.0	30.3	4.6	71.5	23.1	49.5	8.7
Los Angeles, CA	62.4	32.3	35.6	5.5	61.6	21.0	36.7	8.2
Miami, FL	66.0	36.2	49.2	3.4	(NA)	(NA)	(NA)	(NA)
New Orleans, LA	69.2	39.6	43.8	13.5	58.6	24.9	41.4	7.0
New York, NY	74.7	40.8	44.2	15.2	81.3	26.2	65.1	21.1
Oklahoma City, OK	64.2	47.9	25.5	1.6	64.8	39.3	34.5	3.3
Philadelphia, PA.	69.8	41.2	39.3	14.8	76.0	25.6	59.8	14.2
Phoenix, AZ	64.4	36.2	31.6	7.6	66.6	25.6	43.2	11.6
Portland, OR	63.8	34.5	22.7	12.9	68.2	23.4	33.2	18.9
Sacramento, CA.	68.3	44.0	15.8	4.4	74.6	33.1	30.1	5.1
San Antonio, TX.	49.5	35.6	22.5	9.6	30.9	15.6	18.7	10.2
San Diego, CA.	63.8	36.3	16.5	9.0	66.5	29.0	22.6	10.9
San Jose, CA	55.4	34.3	13.7	4.0	60.5	26.3	19.7	13.2
Seattle, WA.	65.9	39.0	33.4	13.9	69.8	28.4	48.2	20.3
Tucson, AZ	68.0	45.1	39.9	8.6	58.0	23.7	41.1	9.0
Washington, DC	68.9	34.9	37.7	16.0	(NA)	(NA)	(NA)	(NA)

NA Not available. [1] Includes other drugs not shown separately.

Source: U.S. National Institute of Justice, *1999 Annual Report on Drug Use Among Adult and Juvenile Arrestees*, June 2000.

No. 311. Drug Arrest Rates for Drug Abuse Violations, 1990 to 1999, and by Region, 1999

[Rate per 100,000 inhabitants. Based on Census Bureau estimated resident population as of July 1, except 1990, enumerated as of April 1. For composition of regions, see map, inside front cover]

Offense	1990	1995	1998	1999				
				Total	North-east	Midwest	South	West
Drug arrest rate, total	435.3	564.7	610.5	583.7	736.9	364.0	553.8	635.9
Sale and/or manufacture	139.0	140.7	138.6	126.4	218.2	71.3	105.3	115.9
Heroin or cocaine [1]	93.7	83.7	77.0	70.1	158.3	23.9	57.5	47.7
Marijuana.	26.4	32.7	34.0	33.8	46.9	29.9	29.3	31.7
Synthetic or manufactured drugs	2.7	3.9	5.6	6.3	3.5	2.6	11.2	5.2
Other dangerous nonnarcotic drugs . .	16.2	20.3	22.1	16.1	9.5	15.1	7.2	31.2
Possession	296.3	423.9	471.9	457.3	518.7	292.6	448.5	520.1
Heroin or cocaine [1]	144.4	157.4	156.1	142.4	202.3	55.3	122.3	172.6
Marijuana.	104.9	192.7	234.5	237.0	291.0	186.4	280.9	180.0
Synthetic or manufactured drugs	6.6	8.5	10.5	10.4	6.0	5.5	14.1	12.3
Other dangerous nonnarcotic drugs . .	40.4	65.4	70.8	67.6	19.4	45.3	31.3	155.1

[1] Includes other derivatives such as morphine, heroin, and codeine.

Source: U.S. Federal Bureau of Investigation, *Crime in the United States*, annual. See also <http://www.fbi.gov/ucr/Cius99/99crime/ 99cius.pdf>.

No. 312. Federal Drug Seizures by Type of Drug: 1990 to 2000

[In pounds. For fiscal years ending in year shown. Reflects the combined drug seizure effort of the Drug Enforcement Administration, the Federal Bureau of Investigation, the U.S. Customs Services, and beginning October 1993 the U.S. Border Patrol within the jurisdiction of the United States as well as maritime seizures by the U.S. Coast Guard. Based on reports to the Federal-Wide Drug Seizure System, which eliminates duplicate reporting of a seizure involving more than one federal agency]

Drug	1990	1993	1994	1995	1996	1997	1998	1999	2000
Total	1,238,425	1,845,998	2,397,037	2,913,227	3,181,573	3,338,276	3,836,416	4,948,698	5,476,199
Heroin.	1,704	3,516	2,883	2,971	3,373	3,121	3,519	2,732	3,044
Cocaine.	235,891	244,315	309,928	233,447	254,437	252,329	266,089	296,934	235,299
Cannabis.	500,415	799,083	1,042,113	1,338,405	1,461,881	1,541,413	1,783,404	2,324,516	2,618,928
Marijuana	483,353	773,004	1,040,999	1,306,528	1,429,786	1,488,362	1,782,808	2,322,838	2,594,940
Hashish	17,062	26,080	1,114	31,876	32,096	53,051	596	1,678	23,988

Source: U.S. Drug Enforcement Administration, unpublished data from Federal-Wide Drug Seizure System.

No. 313. Immigration and Naturalization Service Enforcement Activities: 1990 to 1998

[1,169.9 represents 1,169,900. For fiscal years ending in year shown. See text, Section 8, State and Local Government Finances and Employment]

Item	Unit	1990	1992	1993	1994	1995	1996	1997	1998
Deportable aliens located	1,000	1,169.9	1,258.5	1,327.3	1,094.7	1,394.6	1,650.0	1,536.5	1,679.4
Border Patrol	1,000	1,103.4	1,199.6	1,263.5	1,031.7	1,324.2	1,549.9	1,413.0	1,555.8
Southwestern border	1,000	(NA)	1,145.6	1,212.9	979.1	1,271.4	1,507.0	1,368.7	1,516.7
Mexican	1,000	1,054.8	1,168.9	1,230.1	999.9	1,293.5	1,523.1	1,387.7	1,522.9
Canadian	1,000	5.7	6.2	5.2	3.4	3.5	2.7	2.9	2.3
Other	1,000	42.8	24.4	28.1	28.4	27.2	24.0	22.4	30.5
Number of seizures by Border Patrol	Number	17,275	11,391	10,995	9,134	9,327	11,129	11,792	14,401
Value of seizures by Border Patrol	Mil. dol.	843.6	1,247.9	1,382.9	1,598.1	2,011.8	1,255.4	1,094.6	1,405.0
Narcotics	Mil. dol.	797.8	1,216.8	1,337.8	1,555.7	1,965.3	1,208.8	1,046.3	1,340.0
Aliens expelled:									
Formal removals [1]	1,000	30.0	43.7	42.5	45.6	50.9	69.6	114.3	172.5
Voluntary departures [2]	1,000	1,022.5	1,105.8	1,243.3	1,029.1	1,313.7	1,573.4	1,440.6	1,569.8

NA Not available.   [1] Include deportations, exclusions, and removals.   [2] Includes aliens under docket control required to depart and voluntary departures not under docket control.

Source: U.S. Immigration and Naturalization Service, *Statistical Yearbook*, annual; and unpublished data.

No. 314. Authorized Intercepts of Communication—Summary: 1980 to 1999

[Data for jurisdictions with statutes authorizing or approving interception of wire or oral communication]

Item	1980	1985	1990	1991	1992	1993	1994	1995	1996	1997	1998	1999
Jurisdictions: [1]												
With wiretap statutes	28	32	40	41	41	41	41	41	46	45	45	45
Reporting interceptions	22	22	25	23	23	23	18	19	24	24	26	28
Intercept applications authorized	564	784	872	856	919	976	1,154	1,058	1,149	1,186	1,329	1,350
Intercept installations	524	722	812	802	846	938	1,100	1,024	1,035	1,094	1,245	1,277
Federal	79	235	321	349	332	444	549	527	574	563	562	595
State	445	487	491	453	514	494	551	497	461	531	683	682
Intercepted communications, average [2]	1,058	1,320	1,487	1,584	1,861	1,801	2,139	2,028	1,969	2,081	1,858	1,921
Incriminating	315	275	321	290	347	364	373	459	422	418	350	390
Persons arrested [3]	1,871	2,469	2,057	2,364	2,685	2,428	2,852	2,577	2,464	3,086	3,450	4,372
Convictions [3]	259	660	420	605	607	413	772	494	502	542	911	654
Major offense specified:												
Gambling	199	206	116	98	66	96	86	95	114	98	93	60
Drugs	282	434	520	536	634	679	876	732	821	870	955	978
Homicide and assault	13	25	21	21	35	28	19	30	41	31	55	62
Other	70	119	215	201	184	173	173	201	173	187	228	250

[1] Jurisdictions include federal government, states, and District of Columbia.   [2] Average per authorized installation.
[3] Based on information received from intercepts installed in year shown; additional arrests/convictions will occur in subsequent years but are not shown here.

Source: Administrative Office of the U.S. Courts, *Report on Applications for Orders Authorizing or Approving the Interception of Wire, Oral or Electronic Communications* (Wiretap Report), annual.

No. 315. Background Checks for Firearm Transfers: 1994 to 1999

[In thousands (22,254 represents 22,254,000), except rates. For "Interim period" of 1994 to November 29, 1998, covered handgun purchases from licensed firearm dealers; beginning November 29, 1998 (effective date for the Brady Handgun Violence Prevention Act, P.L. 103-159,1993) covers the transfer of both handguns and long guns from a federal firearms licensee, as well as purchases from pawnshops and retail gun shops]

Inquiries and rejections	1994-1999, period[1]	Interim period					Permanent Brady	
		1994	1995	1996	1997	1998 [2]	Dec, 1998 [3]	1999
Applications and rejections:								
Applications received	22,254	2,483	2,706	2,593	2,574	2,384	893	8,621
Applications rejected	536	62	41	70	69	70	20	204
Rejection rate	2.4	2.5	1.5	2.7	2.7	2.9	2.2	2.4

[1] Represents from the Inception of the Brady Act on March 1, 1994 to 1999.   [2] For period January 1 to November 29, 1998.
[3] For period November 30 to December 31, 1999. Counts are from the National Instant Criminal Background Check System and may include multiple transactions for the same application.

Source: U.S. Bureau of Justice Statistics, *Background Checks for Firearm Transfers, 1999*, Series NCJ 180882, June 2000.

Law Enforcement, Courts, and Prisons   193

No. 316. General Purpose Law Enforcement Agencies—Number and Employment: 1999

[Includes both full-time and part-time employees. State police data are based on the 49 primary law enforcement agencies; excludes agencies that perform primarily court-related duties]

Type of agency	Number of agencies [1]	Number of employees					
		Full-time			Part-time		
		Total	Sworn	Civilian	Total	Sworn	Civilian
Total	16,661	932,780	677,933	254,847	84,171	37,062	47,109
Local police.	13,524	556,631	436,182	120,449	63,575	27,824	35,751
Sheriff	3,088	290,707	185,859	104,848	19,670	9,238	10,432
State police.	49	85,442	55,892	29,550	926	-	926

- Represents zero. [1] The number of agencies reported here is the result of a weighted sample and not an exact enumeration.
Source: U.S. Bureau of Justice Statistics, *Law Enforcement Management and Administrative Statistics, 1999*, Series NCJ 184481, November 2000.

No. 317. U.S. Population Who Had Contact With Police by Age and Reason for Contact: 1999

[43,705 represents 43,705,000. Persons having multiple contacts or more than one reason for any single contact appear in table more than once; therefore, number of contacts may not add to total. Covers persons 16 years old and over. Based on the Police-Public Contact Survey of 94,717 persons; data subject to sampling variability]

Reason for contact	Number having contact (1,000)	Number of persons who had contact with police per 1,000 residents							
		All persons	16 to 17 years	18 to 19 years	20 to 24 years	25 to 29 years	30 to 39 years	40 to 49 years	50 years and over
Contact with police for any reason .	43,705	209	229	343	313	263	235	222	131
Respondent contacted police:									
Report a crime	8,373	40	24	51	56	52	50	48	23
Witness to a crime.	1,393	7	7	9	9	9	9	8	3
Ask for assistance	5,227	25	14	19	28	33	34	29	17
Report a neighborhood problem . . .	4,001	19	5	9	15	22	27	25	14
Witness to an accident	1,674	8	5	13	10	11	10	9	5
Other reasons.	4,031	19	10	18	18	20	21	27	15
Police contacted respondent:									
Motor vehicle stop	22,732	109	130	225	203	155	121	102	54
Involved in an accident	3,355	16	29	29	21	18	14	15	13
Witness to an accident	766	4	[1]3	7	5	4	4	4	2
Victim of crime	921	4	4	9	9	4	5	4	2
Witness to a crime.	1,368	7	10	8	11	7	7	8	4
Suspect in a crime.	1,314	6	22	23	16	6	5	5	2
Serve warrant.	345	2	[1]2	[1]2	6	2	2	1	[1]0
Crime prevention	615	3	4	[1]2	2	3	4	3	2
Other reasons.	5,289	25	39	39	29	27	29	30	16

[1] Based on a sample of 10 or fewer cases.
Source: U.S. Bureau of Justice Statistics, *Contacts Between Police and the Public Findings from the 1999 National Survey*, Series NCJ 184957, February 2001.

No. 318. Drivers Stopped by Police by Sex, Race, and Ethnicity by Age and Cause: 1999

[19,277 represents 19,277,000. Covers drivers 16 years old and over. Based on the Police-Public Contact Survey of 94,717 persons; data subject to sampling variability]

Characteristic of driver	Drivers stopped at least once		Reason police gave for traffic stop—percent distribution					
	Number	Percent of all drivers	Speeding	Vehicle defect	Roadside check for drinking drivers	Record check	Driver suspected of something	Other traffic offense
All drivers, total	19,277	10.3	51.2	11.4	2.3	9.2	2.3	22.7
Male	11,722	12.5	49.3	12.5	2.5	8.3	3.0	23.6
Female.	7,555	8.2	54.1	9.6	1.9	10.6	1.4	21.3
White.	14,846	10.4	53.7	10.4	2.5	9.1	2.3	21.0
Black	2,232	12.3	43.4	13.4	[1]1.4	11.0	2.4	28.1
Hispanic	1,615	8.8	42.1	15.4	[1]1.3	9.7	3.0	27.9
Other	584	8.7	45.6	15.9	[1]1.2	[1]4.0	2.3	[1]30.7
16 to 19 years old	2,032	18.2	52.3	12.1	0.7	4.4	6.1	23.6
20 to 29 years old	5,560	16.8	53.5	13.5	2.0	7.2	2.3	20.8
30 to 39 years old	4,526	11.3	51.4	11.5	2.1	10.2	1.8	22.2
40 to 49 years old	3,764	9.4	51.0	10.4	2.6	9.8	1.6	23.4
50 to 59 years old	2,094	7.7	48.8	8.8	3.8	13.4	1.8	22.6
60 years old and over . . .	1,302	3.8	43.1	7.6	3.3	13.2	[1]1.4	29.9

[1] Based on a sample of 10 or fewer cases.
Source: U.S. Bureau of Justice Statistics, *Contacts Between Police and the Public Findings from the 1999 National Survey*, Series NCJ 184957, February 2001.

No. 319. Justifiable Homicide by Police and Police Officers Murdered by Felons: 1980 to 1998

[The killing of a felon is considered justified when it is done to prevent the imminent death or serious bodily injury to the officer or another person. Excludes negligent homicides, justifiable homicides by private citizens, and murders in which the victim is some-one other than an officer slain in the line of duty]

Year	Felons killed by police in justifiable homicides							Police officers killed by felons				
			Percent of killed felons							Percent of murdered officers		
	Number	Rate [1]	Male	Female	White	Black	Other race	Number	Rate [2]	White	Black	Other race
1980	457	2.49	97.8	2.2	51	48	1	104	26.44	86.5	13.5	-
1981	381	2.06	99.2	0.8	54	45	1	91	22.86	84.6	14.3	1.1
1982	376	2.00	98.1	1.9	52	46	2	92	22.81	83.7	15.2	1.1
1983	406	2.14	99.0	1.0	54	44	2	80	17.80	83.0	12.5	3.8
1984	332	1.73	97.9	2.1	58	41	1	72	15.41	84.7	13.9	1.4
1985	321	1.65	97.8	2.2	61	35	4	78	16.57	89.0	10.3	1.3
1986	298	1.52	98.7	1.3	58	40	2	66	13.87	89.4	10.6	-
1987	296	1.50	98.0	2.0	64	34	2	74	15.40	90.4	9.6	-
1988	339	1.70	98.2	1.8	59	39	2	78	16.06	91.0	9.0	-
1989	362	1.80	95.9	4.1	60	38	2	66	13.30	89.4	10.6	-
1990	379	1.88	96.6	3.4	62	36	2	66	12.61	80.0	18.5	1.5
1991	359	1.76	95.8	4.2	54	43	3	71	13.26	87.3	12.7	-
1992	414	2.01	97.8	2.2	60	38	2	64	11.76	82.3	16.1	1.6
1993	453	2.17	96.9	3.1	55	42	3	70	12.64	85.7	14.3	-
1994	459	2.18	95.9	4.1	57	40	3	79	14.07	84.2	15.0	1.3
1995	382	1.80	98.7	1.3	59	38	3	74	12.61	83.8	12.2	4.1
1996	355	1.65	97.7	2.3	61	37	2	61	10.25	80.0	14.5	5.5
1997	361	1.66	96.7	3.3	63	35	2	70	11.32	80.0	16.9	3.1
1998	367	1.67	97.5	2.5	62	35	3	61	9.51	86.9	11.5	1.6

- Represents zero. [1] Rate per 1,000,000 persons. [2] Rate per 100,000 sworn police officers.

Source: U.S. Bureau of Justice Statistics, *Policing and Homicide, 1976-98: Justifiable Homicide by Police, Police Officers Murdered by Felons*, Series NCJ 180987, March 2001.

No. 320. Law Enforcement Officers Killed and Assaulted: 1990 to 1999

[Covers officers killed feloniously and accidentally in line of duty; includes federal officers. For composition of regions, see map, inside front cover]

Item	1990	1992	1993	1994	1995	1996	1997	1998	1999
OFFICERS KILLED									
Total killed	133	130	129	141	133	112	132	142	107
Northeast	13	16	12	17	16	17	14	6	11
Midwest	20	15	27	30	19	21	25	19	17
South	69	68	57	54	63	46	55	70	56
West	23	23	22	31	32	18	31	36	22
Puerto Rico	8	8	11	9	2	10	7	9	1
Outlying areas, foreign countries	-	-	-	-	1	-	-	2	-
Feloniously killed	66	64	70	79	74	61	70	61	42
Firearms	57	55	67	78	62	57	67	58	41
Handgun	48	44	51	66	43	50	49	40	25
Rifle	8	9	13	8	14	6	12	17	11
Shotgun	1	2	3	4	5	1	6	1	5
Knife	3	1	-	-	2	1	2	1	-
Bomb	-	1	-	-	8	-	-	1	-
Personal weapons	2	1	-	-	-	1	1	-	1
Other	4	6	3	1	2	2	-	1	1
Accidentally killed	67	66	59	62	59	51	62	81	65
ASSAULTS									
Population (1,000) [1]	197,426	215,494	197,551	215,501	191,759	165,264	184,825	193,098	196,315
Number of—									
Agencies represented	9,343	10,653	8,814	10,246	8,503	7,803	8,120	8,153	8,174
Police officers	410,131	456,177	424,054	469,426	428,379	371,964	411,015	452,361	470,145
Total assaulted	72,091	81,150	62,933	64,967	57,762	46,608	52,149	60,673	55,026
Firearm	3,651	4,445	3,880	3,174	2,354	1,878	2,110	2,126	1,783
Knife or cutting instrument . . .	1,647	2,093	1,486	1,510	1,356	871	971	1,098	990
Other dangerous weapon . . .	7,423	8,599	7,155	7,197	6,414	5,069	5,800	7,415	7,392
Hands, fists, feet, etc.	59,370	66,013	50,412	53,086	47,638	38,790	43,268	50,034	44,861

- Represents zero. [1] Represents the number of persons covered by agencies shown.

Source: U.S. Federal Bureau of Investigation, *Law Enforcement Officers Killed and Assaulted*, annual.

Law Enforcement, Courts, and Prisons 195

No. 321. U.S. Supreme Court—Cases Filed and Disposition: 1980 to 1999

[Statutory term of court begins first Monday in October]

Action	1980	1990	1993	1994	1995	1996	1997	1998	1999
Total cases on docket	5,144	6,316	7,786	8,100	7,565	7,602	7,692	8,083·	8,445
Appellate cases on docket	2,749	2,351	2,442	2,515	2,456	2,430	2,432	2,387	2,413
From prior term	527	365	342	377	361	375	347	326	321
Docketed during present term	2,222	1,986	2,100	2,138	2,095	2,055	2,085	2,061	2,092
Cases acted upon	2,324	2,042	2,099	2,185	2,130	2,124	2,142	2,092	2,096
Granted review	167	114	78	83	92	74	75	72	78
Denied, dismissed, or withdrawn	1,999	1,802	1,947	2,016	1,945	1,955	1,990	1,940	1,958
Summarily decided	90	81	34	52	62	66	36	44	34
Cases not acted upon	425	309	343	330	326	306	290	295	317
Pauper cases on docket	2,371	3,951	5,332	5,574	5,098	5,165	5,253	5,689	6,024
Cases acted upon	2,027	3,436	4,621	4,983	4,514	4,613	4,616	4,951	5,273
Granted review	17	27	21	10	13	13	14	9	14
Denied, dismissed, or withdrawn	1,968	3,369	4,566	4,955	4,439	4,582	4,581	4,926	5,239
Summarily decided	32	28	30	14	55	15	14	11	16
Cases not acted upon	344	515	711	591	584	552	637	738	751
Original cases on docket	24	14	12	11	11	7	7	7	8
Cases disposed of during term	7	3	1	2	5	2	1	2	-
Total cases available for argument	264	201	145	136	145	140	138	124	124
Cases disposed of	162	131	105	97	93	92	97	94	87
Cases argued	154	125	99	94	90	90	96	90	83
Cases dismissed or remanded without argument	8	6	6	3	3	2	1	4	4
Cases remaining	102	70	40	39	52	48	41	30	37
Cases decided by signed opinion	144	121	93	91	87	87	93	84	81
Cases decided by per curiam opinion	8	4	6	3	3	3	1	4	2
Number of signed opinions	123	112	84	82	75	80	91	75	74

- Represents zero.   [1] Includes cases granted review and carried over to next term, not shown separately.

Source: Office of the Clerk, Supreme Court of the United States, unpublished data.

No. 322. U.S. District Courts—Civil Cases Commenced and Pending: 1996 to 1999

[For years ending June 30]

Type of case	Cases commenced				Cases pending			
	1996	1997	1998	1999	1996	1997	1998	1999
Cases total [1]	272,661	265,151	261,262	251,511	243,703	259,536	269,119	246,920
Contract actions [1]	33,413	38,858	44,205	46,721	26,999	31,613	32,403	35,415
Recovery of overpayments [2]	3,583	8,070	15,188	18,822	2,301	3,881	6,129	9,733
Real property actions	6,276	5,761	5,655	5,787	4,486	3,951	3,971	3,931
Tort actions	67,029	52,710	52,218	39,785	65,823	72,250	84,073	63,683
Personal injury [1]	63,222	48,266	48,356	35,962	62,087	68,154	80,114	59,899
Personal injury product liability [1]	38,170	23,294	28,325	17,196	34,096	36,621	50,838	31,927
Asbestos	6,760	8,184	9,718	7,413	2,037	2,438	1,576	1,686
Other personal injury	25,052	24,972	20,031	18,766	27,991	3,533	29,276	27,972
Personal property damage	3,807	4,444	3,862	3,823	3,736	4,096	3,959	3,784
Actions under statutes [1]	165,922	167,807	159,172	159,205	144,094	151,655	148,630	158,163
Civil rights [1]	40,476	43,166	42,750	41,453	42,545	46,096	46,718	45,348
Employment	22,150	23,707	23,804	22,948	24,212	26,669	27,097	26,043
Bankruptcy suits	4,737	4,217	3,905	3,875	3,938	3,648	2,921	2,597
Commerce (ICC rates, etc.)	1,622	483	528	650	760	504	510	486
Environmental matters	1,158	973	1,007	882	1,869	1,630	1,602	1,406
Prisoner petitions	69,352	64,262	55,120	56,037	50,353	50,392	44,905	42,302
Forfeiture and penalty	2,255	2,301	2,431	2,207	1,989	1,905	1,959	1,787
Labor laws	15,068	15,320	15,039	14,325	11,742	12,199	11,807	11,265
Protected property rights [3]	6,800	7,511	7,660	8,082	6,273	6,765	7,037	7,344
Securities commodities and exchanges	1,741	1,737	2,166	2,684	2,872	2,591	2,998	3,538
Social security laws	8,517	13,047	13,955	14,511	9,153	12,978	14,844	14,407
Tax suits	2,078	2,294	1,733	1,280	1,646	1,668	1,507	1,254
Freedom of information	465	400	436	350	496	435	416	386

[1] Includes other types not shown separately.   [2] Includes enforcement of judgments in student loan cases, and overpayments of veterans benefits.   [3] Includes copyright, patent, and trademark rights.

Source: Administrative Office of the U.S. Courts, *Statistical Tables for the Federal Judiciary*, annual.

U.S. Census Bureau, Statistical Abstract of the United States: 2001

No. 323. U.S. District Courts—Offenders Convicted and Sentenced to Prison and Length of Sentence: 1999

Most serious offense of conviction	Offenders convicted	Convicted offenders sentenced to prison	Mean length of sentence (mo.)	Most serious offense of conviction	Offenders convicted	Convicted offenders sentenced to prison	Mean length of sentence (mo.)
Total [1]	66,055	47,659	57.8	Possession	1,527	1,577	83.4
Violent offenses	2,781	2,489	87.7	Trafficking and manufacturing	22,748	20,117	74.8
Property offenses	12,712	7,204	24.0	Public-order offenses	17,097	14,683	48.7
Fraudulent offenses [2]	10,493	6,067	22.3	Regulatory offenses	1,093	627	26.1
Embezzlement	1,012	469	14.2	Other offenses	16,004	14,056	49.7
Fraud [3]	7,892	4,789	23.5	Weapons	3,623	3,191	98.7
Forgery	137	53	20.5	Immigration	9,306	8,427	30.7
Other offenses [2]	2,219	1,137	33.1	Tax law violations [4]	608	344	21.0
Larceny	1,412	641	27.1	Misdemeanors	9,115	1,556	10.7
Drug offenses [2]	24,275	21,694	75.4				

[1] Total may include offenders for whom offense category could not be determined.   [2] Includes offenses not shown separately.   [3] Excludes tax fraud.   [4] Includes tax fraud.

Source: U.S. Bureau of Justice Statistics, Compendium of Federal Justice Statistics, 1999. Series NCJ 186179. April 2001.

No. 324. U.S. District Courts—Civil Rights-Related Complaints and Disposition: 1990 to 1999

[Covers civil rights complaints related to employment, housing, welfare, or voting rights, but excludes prisoner petitions]

Year	Complaints				Disposition				
		Jurisdiction				Percent of cases disposed			
		Cases involving U.S. government		Private cases	Cases disposed	Dismissed		Judgement	
	Total	Plaintiff	Defendant			Total	Settled	Total	Trial
1990	18,793	747	1,736	16,310	17,811	65.6	30.7	34.4	7.8
1991	19,892	816	1,532	16,992	17,975	67.2	31.5	32.9	7.6
1992	24,233	639	1,773	21,821	25,094	65.9	31.5	34.1	7.3
1993	27,655	747	1,970	24,938	23,416	67.5	31.5	32.4	6.6
1994	32,622	718	2,268	29,636	26,596	69.4	34.8	30.6	6.7
1995	36,600	668	2,358	33,574	30,175	69.4	33.4	30.6	6.0
1996	42,007	486	2,433	39,088	34,986	69.7	33.7	30.3	5.7
1997	43,278	561	2,356	40,361	38,131	70.5	34.2	29.5	5.2
1998	42,354	672	2,366	38,835	40,185	70.9	35.2	29.2	4.9
1999	41,304	714	2,399	38,191	42,134	(NA)	(NA)	(NA)	(NA)

NA Not available.

Source: U.S. Bureau of Justice Statistics, Civil Rights Complaints in U.S. District Courts, 1990-98, Series NCJ 173427, January 2000; and Administrative Office of the U.S. Courts, Judicial Business of the U.S. Courts, 1999.

No. 325. Federal Prosecutions of Public Corruption: 1980 to 1999

[As of Dec. 31. Prosecution of persons who have corrupted public office in violation of Federal Criminal Statutes]

Prosecution status	1980	1985	1990	1991	1992	1993	1994	1995	1996	1997	1998	1999
Total: [1]												
Indicted	727	1,157	1,176	1,452	1,189	1,371	1,165	1,051	984	1,057	1,174	1,134
Convicted	602	997	1,084	1,194	1,081	1,362	969	878	902	853	1,014	1,065
Awaiting trial	213	256	300	346	380	403	332	323	244	327	340	329
Federal officials:												
Indicted	123	563	615	803	624	627	571	527	456	459	442	480
Convicted	131	470	583	665	532	595	488	438	459	392	414	460
Awaiting trial	16	90	103	149	139	133	124	120	64	83	85	101
State officials:												
Indicted	72	79	96	115	81	113	99	61	109	51	91	115
Convicted	51	66	79	77	92	133	97	61	83	49	58	80
Awaiting trial	28	20	28	42	24	39	17	23	40	20	37	44
Local officials:												
Indicted	247	248	257	242	232	309	248	236	219	255	277	237
Convicted	168	221	225	180	211	272	202	191	190	169	264	219
Awaiting trial	82	49	98	88	91	132	96	89	60	118	90	95

[1] Includes individuals who are neither public officials nor employees but who were involved with public officials or employees in violating the law, not shown separately.

Source: U.S. Department of Justice, Federal Prosecutions of Corrupt Public Officials, 1970-1980 and Report to Congress on the Activities and Operations of the Public Integrity Section, annual.

U.S. Census Bureau, Statistical Abstract of the United States: 2001

No. 326. Delinquency Cases Disposed by Juvenile Courts by Reason for Referral: 1988 to 1998

[In thousands (1,190 represents 1,190,000), except rate. A delinquency offense is an act committed by a juvenile for which an adult could be prosecuted in a criminal court. Disposition of a case involves taking a definite action such as waiving the case to criminal court, dismissing the case, placing the youth on probation, placing the youth in a facility for delinquents, or such actions as fines, restitution, and community service]

Reason for referral	1988	1989	1990	1991	1992	1993	1994	1995	1996	1997	1998
All delinquency offenses .	1,190	1,220	1,317	1,412	1,482	1,522	1,666	1,767	1,829	1,814	1,753
Case rate [1]	47.0	48.3	51.4	54.1	55.4	55.7	60	62.6	64.1	62.9	60.3
Violent offenses.	70	78	94	105	113	117	131	137	132	111	103
Criminal homicide.	2	2	2	2	2	3	3	3	2	2	2
Forcible rape	4	5	5	6	6	7	7	7	7	6	6
Robbery	22	23	28	31	33	34	38	40	38	33	30
Aggravated assault	43	48	59	66	72	73	83	87	84	69	65
Property offenses.	518	535	564	613	618	592	608	631	640	610	549
Burglary	132	134	145	154	159	150	146	142	145	139	126
Larceny	325	327	341	381	381	372	391	424	434	412	371
Motor vehicle theft	55	67	71	72	71	63	62	53	52	50	44
Arson	7	7	7	7	8	8	10	11	9	9	8
Delinquency offenses	601	608	660	693	751	813	927	998	1,057	1,093	1,102
Simple assault	109	115	132	143	163	177	198	218	232	255	263
Vandalism	84	85	99	112	118	119	130	126	127	119	119
Drug law violations	81	78	71	65	72	92	131	165	184	190	192
Obstruction of justice.	75	75	80	76	80	97	112	121	139	150	148
Other [2]	253	255	278	298	318	328	356	367	375	379	380

[1] Number of cases disposed per 1,000 youth (ages 10 to 17) at risk.   [2] Includes such offenses as stolen property offenses, trespassing, weapons offenses, other sex offenses, liquor law violations, disorderly conduct, and miscellaneous offenses.

Source: National Center for Juvenile Justice, Pittsburgh, PA, *Juvenile Court Statistics*, annual.

No. 327. Delinquency Cases and Case Rates by Sex and Race: 1992 to 1998

[A delinquency offense is an act committed by a juvenile for which an adult could be prosecuted in a criminal court. Disposition of a case involves taking a definite action such as waiving the case to criminal court, dismissing the case, placing the youth on probation, placing the youth in a facility for delinquents, or such actions as fines, restitution, and community service. Offenses may not add to total sex and race categories due to rounding]

Sex, race, and offense	Number of cases			Case rate [1]		
	1992	1997	1998	1992	1997	1998
Male, total	1,195,100	1,386,700	1,330,700	87.1	93.7	89.2
Person	243,500	294,400	292,200	17.8	19.9	19.6
Property	692,900	656,300	606,000	50.5	44.3	40.6
Drugs	63,600	160,800	162,000	4.6	10.9	10.9
Public order	195,100	275,200	270,500	14.2	18.6	18.1
Female, total	286,800	427,700	422,700	22.0	30.5	29.9
Person	65,000	105,000	111,200	5.0	7.5	7.9
Property	167,200	206,500	192,500	12.9	14.7	13.6
Drugs	8,700	28,900	30,500	0.7	2.1	2.2
Public order	45,900	87,300	88,500	3.5	6.2	6.3
White, total	974,800	1,213,200	1,182,000	45.5	52.9	51.2
Person	177,200	242,700	249,900	8.3	10.6	10.8
Property	604,400	604,000	559,100	28.2	26.3	24.2
Drugs	37,300	127,800	131,500	1.7	5.6	5.7
Public order	155,900	238,700	241,400	7.3	10.4	10.5
Black, total	452,900	538,800	508,100	112.8	124.0	115.2
Person	121,400	145,300	141,600	30.2	33.4	32.1
Property	221,000	223,800	205,500	55.1	51.5	46.6
Drugs	33,400	57,500	56,000	8.3	13.2	12.7
Public order	77,100	112,200	105,100	19.2	25.8	23.8
Other races, total	54,200	62,300	63,300	41.6	40.2	39.9
Person	9,900	11,500	11,900	7.6	7.4	7.5
Property	34,800	35,000	33,900	26.7	22.6	21.4
Drugs	1,700	4,300	4,900	1.3	2.8	3.1
Public order	7,900	11,500	12,500	6.0	7.4	7.9

[1] Cases per 1,000 youth at risk.

Source: National Center for Juvenile Justice, Pittsburgh, PA, *Juvenile Court Statistics*, annual.

U.S. Census Bureau, Statistical Abstract of the United States: 2001

No. 328. Child Abuse and Neglect Cases Substantiated and Indicated— Victim Characteristics: 1990 to 1998

[Based on reports alleging child abuse and neglect that were referred for investigation by the respective child protective services agency in each state. The reporting period may be either calendar or fiscal year. The majority of states provided duplicated counts. Also, varying number of states reported the various characteristics presented below. A substantiated case represents a type of investigation disposition that determines that there is sufficient evidence under state law to conclude that maltreatment occurred or that the child is at risk of maltreatment. An indicated case represents a type of disposition that concludes that there was a reason to suspect maltreatment had occurred]

Item	1990 Number	1990 Percent	1996 Number	1996 Percent	1997 Number	1997 Percent	1998 Number	1998 Percent
TYPES OF SUBSTANTIATED MALTREATMENT								
Victims, total [1] [2]	**690,658**	(X)	**955,516**	(X)	**790,157**	(X)	**861,602**	(X)
Neglect	338,770	49.1	493,158	51.6	431,563	54.6	461,274	53.5
Physical abuse	186,801	27.0	224,967	23.5	192,872	24.4	195,891	22.7
Sexual abuse	119,506	17.3	117,058	12.3	96,070	12.2	99,278	11.5
Emotional maltreatment	45,621	6.6	55,199	5.8	48,407	6.1	51,618	6.0
Medical neglect	(NA)	(NA)	25,412	2.7	18,524	2.3	20,338	2.4
SEX OF VICTIM								
Victims, total [2]	**742,519**	100.0	**855,713**	100.0	**799,395**	100.0	**760,438**	100.0
Male	323,339	43.5	336,315	39.3	315,045	39.9	359,568	47.3
Female	369,919	49.8	371,700	43.4	348,001	44.0	388,187	51.0
AGE OF VICTIM								
Victims, total [2]	**731,282**	100.0	**863,466**	100.0	**789,303**	100.0	**767,749**	100.0
1 year and younger	97,101	13.3	90,752	10.5	83,819	10.6	105,097	13.7
2 to 5 years old	172,791	23.6	185,375	21.5	166,523	21.1	187,522	24.4
6 to 9 years old	157,681	21.6	178,802	20.7	165,845	21.0	193,316	25.2
10 to 13 years old	135,130	18.5	141,009	16.3	130,346	16.5	151,126	19.7
14 to 17 years old	103,383	14.1	110,751	12.8	97,050	12.3	111,894	14.6
18 and over	4,880	0.7	5,995	0.7	2,954	0.4	4,210	0.5

NA Not available.   X Not applicable.   [1] More than one type of maltreatment may be substantiated per child. Therefore, totals for this category will add up to more than 100 percent. Victim totals and maltreatment types are based on subset of states which reported both the number of child victims and maltreatment incidences by type for that year.   [2] Includes other and unknown not shown separately.

No. 329. Child Abuse and Neglect Cases Reported and Investigated by State: 1998

[Based on reports alleging child abuse and neglect that were referred for investigation by the respective child protective services agency in each state. The reporting period may be either calendar or fiscal year. The majority of states provide duplicated counts]

State	Population under 18 years old	Number of reports [1]	Number of children subject of an investigation [1]	Number of child victims [2]	State	Population under 18 years old	Number of reports [1]	Number of children subject of an investigation [1]	Number of child victims [2]
U.S. [3]	**69,872,059**	**1,851,267**	**2,972,862**	**903,395**	MO	1,406,616	48,119	75,178	12,556
AL	1,084,135	24,413	35,912	16,668	MT	224,403	9,676	19,004	3,292
AK	192,261	11,202	11,326	7,138	NE	445,642	8,272	14,641	4,219
AZ	1,263,404	34,930	60,610	8,983	NV	467,107	13,705	23,229	8,014
AR	653,721	20,511	29,572	8,578	NH	298,610	6,391	8,974	1,159
CA	8,911,372	122,622	413,372	157,683	NJ	1,990,439	75,988	75,988	9,851
CO	1,040,580	28,573	39,141	7,010	NM	504,210	12,781	13,403	4,241
CT	790,715	31,221	40,905	16,923	NY	4,502,611	142,174	240,655	83,537
DE	179,071	6,473	9,693	2,894	NC	1,919,774	125,862	125,862	37,357
DC	102,959	4,077	9,862	4,916	ND	162,611	4,221	7,098	(NA)
FL	3,539,932	125,359	186,967	82,119	OH	2,844,005	84,657	135,628	58,070
GA	2,022,351	47,007	74,180	24,567	OK	879,367	34,790	60,340	16,584
HI	298,327	2,129	3,568	2,185	OR	825,170	17,300	27,680	10,147
ID	351,158	10,100	26,682	7,936	PA	2,859,828	22,589	22,589	5,392
IL	3,187,332	64,357	110,658	35,657	RI	237,917	8,117	9,863	3,448
IN	1,517,366	102,155	102,155	18,962	SC	959,296	20,000	38,238	8,432
IA	722,139	19,412	28,072	7,311	SD	200,937	5,313	5,313	2,647
KS	697,452	18,480	26,751	5,312	TN	1,331,402	32,286	32,286	9,930
KY	988,293	63,439	63,439	22,875	TX	5,629,200	121,183	172,718	39,925
LA	1,191,412	27,117	45,318	13,773	UT	701,300	16,931	27,222	7,990
ME	291,585	4,121	9,030	3,579	VT	141,347	1,883	1,973	887
MD	1,287,190	31,091	55,964	14,234	VA	1,644,678	32,902	49,026	9,766
MA	1,457,703	37,091	52,899	27,559	WA	1,472,490	32,880	47,281	12,926
MI	2,551,615	62,659	156,425	22,744	WV	404,254	16,350	64,483	7,793
MN	1,259,447	16,197	24,844	10,572	WI	1,351,044	22,232	22,232	8,168
MS	756,875	18,002	32,404	6,079	WY	129,406	1,927	2,209	807

NA Not available.   [1] The number of children subject of an investigation is calculated from the total number of children by disposition and is a national estimate for the 50 states and the District of Columbia based on submissions from reporting states.   [2] Victims are defined as children subject of a substantiated or indicated maltreatment. In 1998, Ohio included "In Need of Services," and North Dakota did not use these dispositions.   [3] Includes estimates for states that did not report.

Source of Tables 328 and 329: U.S. Department of Health and Human Services, National Center on Child Abuse and Neglect, National Child Abuse and Neglect Data System, *Child Maltreatment 1998: Reports From the States to the National Child Abuse and Neglect System,* April 2000.

Law Enforcement, Courts, and Prisons   199

No. 330. Jail Inmates by Sex, Race, and Hispanic Origin: 1990 to 2000

[Data are for midyear. Excludes federal and state prisons or other correctional institutions; institutions exclusively for juveniles; state-operated jails in Alaska, Connecticut, Delaware, Hawaii, Rhode Island, and Vermont; and other facilities which retain persons for less than 48 hours. **As of June 30.** Data based on the Annual Survey of Jails, which is a sample survey and subject to sampling variability]

Characteristic	1990	1994	1995	1996	1997	1998	1999	2000
Total inmates.	405,320	486,474	507,044	518,492	567,079	592,462	605,943	621,149
Male	365,821	431,300	448,000	454,700	498,678	520,581	528,998	543,120
Female	37,198	48,500	51,300	55,700	59,296	63,791	67,487	70,414
White non-Hispanic. . . .	169,600	190,100	203,300	215,700	230,300	244,900	249,900	260,500
Black non-Hispanic.	172,300	213,400	220,600	213,100	237,900	244,000	251,800	256,300
Hispanic.	58,100	74,900	74,400	80,900	88,900	91,800	93,800	94,100
Other [1]	5,400	8,100	8,800	8,800	10,000	11,800	10,400	10,200

[1] Includes American Indians, Alaska Natives, Asians, and Pacific Islanders.

Source: U.S. Bureau of Justice Statistics, through 1994, *Jail Inmates*, annual; beginning 1995, *Prison and Jail Inmates at Midyear*, annual.

No. 331. State and Federal Correctional Facilities—Inmates and Staff: 1990 and 1995

[Covers all state and federal correctional institutions or places of confinement such as prisons, prison farms, boot camps, and community based halfway houses and work release centers. Excludes jails and other regional detention centers, private facilities, facilities for the military, Immigration and Naturalization Service, Bureau of Indian Affairs, U.S. Marshall Service, and correctional hospital wards not operated by correctional authorities]

Characteristic	1990	1995	Characteristic	1990	1995
FACILITIES			INMATES		
Total	1,287	1,500	Total	715,649	1,023,572
Type of facility:			Male.	675,624	961,210
Confinement.	1,037	1,196	Female	40,025	62,362
Community.	250	304	Type of facility:		
Federal	80	125	Confinement.	698,570	992,333
State.	1,207	1,375	Community.	17,079	31,239
Size of facility:			Federal	56,821	81,930
Fewer than 500.	816	854	State.	658,828	941,642
500-999.	260	286	Custody level:		
1,000-2,499.	185	306	Maximum/close/high.	150,205	202,174
2,500 or more.	26	54	Medium	292,372	415,688
Age of facility:			Minimum/low	219,907	366,227
Less than 10 years	314	497	Not classified	53,165	39,483
10-19 years old.	163	273			
20-49 years old.	373	366	STAFF		
50-99 years old.	379	310	Total	264,201	347,320
100 years old or more	58	45	Federal.	18,451	25,379
Not reported	-	9	State	245,750	321,941

- Represents zero.

Source: U.S. Bureau of Justice Statistics, *Census of State and Federal Correctional Facilities, 1995.*

No. 332. Federal and State Prisoners by Sex: 1980 to 1999

[Based on U.S. Census Bureau estimated resident population, as of **December 31.** Includes all persons under jurisdiction of federal and state authorities rather than those in the custody of such authorities. Represents inmates sentenced to maximum term of more than a year]

Year	Total	Rate [1]	State	Male	Female	Year	Total	Rate [1]	State	Male	Female
1980	315,974	139	295,363	303,643	12,331	1990	739,980	297	689,577	699,416	40,564
1981	353,673	154	331,504	339,375	14,298	1991	789,610	313	732,914	745,808	43,802
1982	395,516	171	371,864	379,075	16,441	1992	846,277	332	780,571	799,776	46,501
1983	419,346	179	393,015	401,870	17,476	1993	932,074	359	857,675	878,037	54,037
1984	443,398	188	415,796	424,193	19,205	1994	1,016,691	389	936,896	956,566	60,125
1985	480,568	202	447,873	459,223	21,345	1995	1,085,022	411	1,001,359	1,021,059	63,963
1986	522,084	217	485,553	497,540	24,544	1996	1,137,722	427	1,048,907	1,068,123	69,599
1987	560,812	231	521,289	533,990	26,822	1997	1,195,498	445	1,100,511	1,121,663	73,835
1988	603,732	247	560,994	573,587	30,145	1998	1,245,402	461	1,141,720	1,167,802	77,600
1989	680,907	276	633,739	643,643	37,264	1999	1,305,393	476	1,191,118	1,222,799	82,594

[1] Rate per 100,000 estimated population.

Source: U.S. Bureau of Justice Statistics, *Prisoners in State and Federal Institutions on December 31*, annual.

No. 333. State Prisons Expenditures by State: 1996

[In millions of dollars (22,033.2 represents $22,033,200,000), except as indicated. For fiscal year ending in year indicated]

State	Total expenditures	Operating expenditures	Capital expenditures	Operating expenditures per inmate (dol.) Per year	Per day	State	Total expenditures	Operating expenditures	Capital expenditures	Operating expenditures per inmate (dol.) Per year	Per day
U.S...	22,033.2	20,737.9	1,295.3	20,142	55.18	MO	262.8	249.4	13.4	12,832	35.16
AL	169.0	165.8	3.2	7,987	21.88	MT	42.4	41.9	0.6	20,782	56.94
AK	116.7	112.4	4.3	32,415	88.81	NE	69.9	67.9	2.0	22,271	61.02
AZ	418.1	409.2	8.9	19,091	52.30	NV	122.0	119.0	2.9	15,370	42.11
AR	133.7	124.5	9.2	13,341	36.55	NH	43.0	42.4	0.5	20,839	57.09
CA	3,031.0	2,918.8	112.2	21,385	58.59	NJ	839.3	827.1	12.2	30,773	84.31
CO	249.8	234.5	15.3	21,020	57.59	NM	125.6	123.9	1.7	29,491	80.80
CT	497.8	475.4	22.5	31,912	87.43	NY	2,220.6	1,948.8	271.8	28,426	77.88
DE	88.0	87.3	0.7	17,987	49.28	NC	756.8	733.8	23.1	25,303	69.32
DC	213.7	212.1	1.6	21,296	58.34	ND	10.7	10.6	0.2	17,154	47.00
FL. ...	1,224.9	1,100.7	124.3	17,327	47.47	OH	1,014.9	873.6	141.3	19,613	53.74
GA	560.4	547.5	12.9	15,933	43.65	OK	198.3	193.6	4.7	10,601	29.04
HI. ...	87.4	83.9	3.5	23,318	63.88	OR	254.3	253.4	0.9	31,837	87.22
ID. ...	57.0	55.0	1.9	16,277	44.60	PA	978.8	902.2	76.5	28,063	76.88
IL. ...	740.4	732.8	7.6	19,351	53.02	RI. ...	109.6	108.7	0.9	35,739	97.92
IN. ...	338.2	325.7	12.5	20,188	55.31	SC	315.5	277.9	37.7	13,977	38.29
IA. ...	146.1	143.8	2.3	24,286	66.54	SD	34.2	33.6	0.6	17,787	48.73
KS	170.8	158.5	12.4	22,242	60.94	TN	350.6	349.2	1.4	22,904	62.75
KY	208.7	198.8	9.9	16,320	44.71	TX	1,713.9	1,565.2	148.7	12,215	33.47
LA	316.2	313.5	2.8	12,304	33.71	UT	113.4	111.8	1.6	32,361	88.66
ME	51.7	48.2	3.5	33,711	92.36	VT	33.5	33.4	0.1	31,094	85.19
MD	520.3	480.9	39.4	22,247	60.95	VA	476.7	452.4	24.4	16,306	44.67
MA	309.7	304.5	5.2	26,002	71.24	WA	357.9	311.1	46.7	26,662	73.05
MI. ...	1,167.6	1,161.1	6.5	28,067	76.89	WV	46.9	43.7	3.2	17,245	47.25
MN	186.0	184.4	1.6	37,825	103.63	WI. ...	360.4	313.4	47.1	27,771	76.08
MS	148.9	143.9	4.9	11,156	30.56	WY	29.0	27.0	2.0	19,456	53.30

Source: U.S. Bureau of Justice Statistics, *State Prison Expenditures, 1996*, Series NCJ 172211, August 1999.

No. 334. Prisoners Under Jurisdiction of State and Federal Correctional Authorities—Summary by State: 1980 to 1999

[For years ending December 31]

State	1980	1990	1998	1999, advance Total	Percent change, 1998-1999	State	1980	1990	1998	1999, advance Total	Percent change, 1998-1999
U.S. [1] ..	329,821	773,919	1,300,573	1,366,721	3.4	MO	5,726	14,943	24,974	26,155	4.7
AL	6,543	15,665	22,676	24,658	8.7	MT	739	1,425	2,734	2,954	8.0
AK [2] ..	822	2,622	4,097	3,949	-3.6	NE	1,446	2,403	3,676	3,688	0.3
AZ [3] ..	4,372	14,261	25,515	25,986	1.8	NV	1,839	5,322	9,651	9,494	-1.6
AR	2,911	7,322	10,638	11,415	7.3	NH	326	1,342	2,169	2,257	4.1
CA	24,569	97,309	161,904	163,067	0.7	NJ	5,884	21,128	31,121	31,493	1.2
CO	2,629	7,671	14,312	15,670	9.5	NM	1,279	3,187	5,078	5,124	0.9
CT [2] ..	4,308	10,500	17,605	18,639	5.9	NY	21,815	54,895	70,001	[5]73,233	2.6
DE [2] ..	1,474	3,471	5,558	[4]6,983	(X)	NC	15,513	18,411	31,961	31,086	-2.7
DC [2] ..	3,145	9,947	9,829	8,652	-12.0	ND	253	483	915	943	3.1
FL [3] ..	20,735	44,387	67,224	69,596	3.5	OH	13,489	31,822	48,450	46,842	-3.3
GA [3] ..	12,178	22,411	39,262	42,091	7.2	OK [6] ..	4,796	12,285	20,892	22,393	7.2
HI [2] ..	985	2,533	4,924	4,903	-0.4	OR	3,177	6,492	8,981	9,810	9.2
ID [3] ..	817	1,961	4,083	[5]4,842	12.9	PA	8,171	22,290	36,377	36,525	0.4
IL [3] ..	11,899	27,516	43,051	44,660	3.7	RI [2] ..	813	2,392	3,445	3,003	-12.8
IN	6,683	12,736	19,197	19,309	0.6	SC	7,862	17,319	21,764	22,008	1.1
IA [3] ..	2,481	3,967	7,394	7,232	-2.2	SD	635	1,341	2,422	2,506	3.5
KS	2,494	5,775	8,183	8,567	4.7	TN	7,022	10,388	17,738	[5]22,502	4.5
KY	3,588	9,023	14,987	15,317	2.2	TX	29,892	50,042	144,510	[5]163,190	1.9
LA	8,889	18,599	32,228	34,066	5.7	UT	932	2,496	4,453	[5]5,426	4.2
ME	814	1,523	1,691	1,716	1.5	VT [2] ..	480	1,049	1,473	1,536	4.3
MD	7,731	17,848	22,572	23,095	2.3	VA	8,920	17,593	30,276	32,453	7.2
MA [3][6]	3,185	8,345	11,799	11,356	-3.8	WA	4,399	7,995	14,161	14,590	3.0
MI [3][6]	15,124	34,267	45,879	46,617	1.6	WV	1,257	1,565	3,478	3,532	1.6
MN	2,001	3,176	5,572	5,969	7.1	WI	3,980	7,465	18,403	20,417	10.9
MS	3,902	8,375	16,678	18,247	9.4	WY	534	1,110	1,571	1,713	9.0

X Not applicable. [1] State-level data excludes federal inmates. [2] Includes both jail and prison inmates (state has combined jail and prison system). [3] Numbers are for custody rather than jurisdiction counts. [4] Reporting criteria were expanded in 1999 to include home confinement clients in supervised custody facilities. Comparable counts for 1998 were not available. [5] Reporting criteria changed in 1999; percent calculated based on counts adjusted for comparable reporting. [6] 1980 and 1990, data are for custody counts; thereafter, jurisdiction counts are reported.

Source: U.S. Bureau of Justice Statistics, *Prisoners in 1999*, Series NCJ 183476; and earlier reports.

[As of December 31, except jail counts as June 30]

Year	Total [1]	Percent of adult population	Probation	Jail	Prison	Parole	Male	Female
1980	1,840,400	(NA)	1,118,097	[2]182,288	319,598	220,438	(NA)	(NA)
1981	2,006,600	(NA)	1,225,934	[2]195,085	360,029	225,539	(NA)	(NA)
1982	2,192,600	(NA)	1,357,264	207,853	402,914	224,604	(NA)	(NA)
1983	2,475,100	(NA)	1,582,947	221,815	423,898	246,440	(NA)	(NA)
1984	2,689,200	(NA)	1,740,948	233,018	448,264	266,992	(NA)	(NA)
1985	3,011,400	1.7	1,968,712	254,986	487,593	300,203	2,606,000	405,500
1986	3,239,400	1.8	2,114,621	272,735	526,436	325,638	2,829,100	410,300
1987	3,459,600	1.9	2,247,158	294,092	562,814	355,505	3,021,000	438,600
1988	3,714,100	2.0	2,356,483	341,893	607,766	407,977	3,223,000	491,100
1989	4,055,600	2.2	2,522,125	393,303	683,367	456,803	3,501,600	554,000
1990	4,348,000	2.3	2,670,234	403,019	743,382	531,407	3,746,300	601,700
1991	4,535,600	2.4	2,728,472	424,129	792,535	590,442	3,913,000	622,600
1992	4,762,600	2.5	2,811,611	441,781	850,566	658,601	4,050,300	712,300
1993	4,944,000	2.6	2,903,061	455,500	909,381	676,100	4,215,800	728,200
1994	5,141,300	2.7	2,981,022	479,800	990,147	690,371	4,377,400	763,900
1995	5,335,100	2.8	3,077,861	499,300	1,078,542	679,421	4,513,000	822,100
1996	5,482,700	2.8	3,164,996	510,400	1,127,528	679,733	4,629,900	852,800
1997	5,725,800	2.9	3,296,513	557,974	1,176,564	694,787	4,825,300	900,500
1998	6,126,300	3.1	3,670,591	584,372	1,224,469	696,385	(NA)	(NA)
1999, advance	6,317,900	3.1	3,773,624	596,485	1,283,902	712,713	(NA)	(NA)

NA Not available.   [1] Totals may not add due to individuals having multiple correctional statuses.   [2] Estimated.

Source: U.S. Bureau of Justice Statistics, Correctional Populations in the United States, annual.

No. 336. Prisoners Under Sentence of Death by Characteristic: 1980 to 1999

[As of December 31. Excludes prisoners under sentence of death who remained within local correctional systems pending exhaustion of appellate process or who had not been committed to prison]

Characteristic	1980	1989	1990	1991	1992	1993	1994	1995	1996	1997	1998	1999
Total [1]	688	2,243	2,346	2,466	2,575	2,727	2,905	3,064	3,242	3,328	3,465	3,527
White	418	1,308	1,368	1,450	1,508	1,575	1,653	1,732	1,833	1,864	1,917	1,948
Black and other	270	935	978	1,016	1,067	1,152	1,252	1,332	1,409	1,464	1,548	1,579
Under 20 years	11	6	8	14	12	13	19	20	17	16	16	16
20 to 24 years	173	191	168	179	188	211	231	264	288	275	273	251
25 to 34 years	334	1,080	1,110	1,087	1,078	1,066	1,088	1,068	1,088	1,077	1,108	1,108
35 to 54 years	186	917	1,006	1,129	1,212	1,330	1,449	1,583	1,711	1,809	1,897	1,958
55 years and over	10	56	64	73	85	96	103	119	138	151	171	194
Years of school completed:												
7 years or less	68	183	178	173	181	185	186	191	196	205	208	201
8 years	74	178	186	181	180	183	198	195	201	206	218	221
9 to 11 years	204	739	775	810	836	885	930	979	1,040	1,069	1,122	1,142
12 years	162	695	729	783	831	887	939	995	1,037	1,084	1,128	1,157
More than 12 years	43	192	209	222	232	244	255	272	282	288	301	307
Unknown	163	263	279	313	315	332	382	422	486	476	488	499
Marital status:												
Never married	268	956	998	1,071	1,132	1,222	1,320	1,412	1,507	1,555	1,645	1,689
Married	229	610	632	663	663	671	707	718	739	740	752	731
Divorced [2]	217	684	726	746	780	823	863	924	996	1,033	1,068	1,107
Time elapsed since sentencing:												
Less than 12 months	185	231	231	252	265	262	280	287	306	262	293	259
12 to 47 months	389	809	753	718	720	716	755	784	816	844	816	800
48 to 71 months	102	408	438	441	444	422	379	423	447	456	482	499
72 months and over	38	802	934	1,071	1,146	1,316	1,476	1,560	1,673	1,766	1,874	1,969
Legal status at arrest:												
Not under sentence	384	1,301	1,345	1,415	1,476	1,562	1,662	1,764	1,881	1,957	2,036	2,088
Parole or probation [3]	115	585	578	615	702	754	800	866	894	880	879	886
Prison or escaped	45	94	128	102	101	102	103	110	112	116	127	125
Unknown	170	270	305	321	296	298	325	314	355	375	423	428

[1] Revisions to the total number of prisoners were not carried to the characteristics except for race.   [2] Includes persons married but separated, widows, widowers, and unknown.   [3] Includes prisoners on mandatory conditional release, work release, leave, AWOL, or bail. Covers 28 prisoners in 1990, and 29 in 1991 and 1992, 33 in 1993 and 1995, 31 in 1994 and 1996, 30 in 1997, 26 in 1998, and 21 in 1999.

Source: U.S. Bureau of Justice Statistics, Capital Punishment, annual.

No. 337. Movement of Prisoners Under Sentence of Death: 1980 to 1999

[Prisoners reported under sentence of death by civil authorities. The term "under sentence of death" begins when the court pronounces the first sentence of death for a capital offense]

Status	1980	1989	1990	1991	1992	1993	1994	1995	1996	1997	1998	1999
Under sentence of death, Jan. 1	595	2,117	2,243	2,346	2,465	2,580	2,727	2,905	3,064	3,242	3,328	3,465
Received death sentence [1][2]	203	251	244	266	265	282	306	310	299	256	285	272
White	125	133	147	163	147	146	162	168	174	146	145	157
Black	77	114	94	101	114	130	136	138	119	106	132	104
Dispositions other than executions	101	102	108	116	124	108	112	105	99	89	93	112
Executions	-	16	23	14	31	38	31	56	45	74	68	98
Under sentence of death, Dec. 31 [1][2]	688	2,243	2,346	2,466	2,575	2,727	2,890	3,054	3,242	3,335	3,452	3,527
White	425	1,308	1,368	1,450	1,508	1,575	1,645	1,730	1,833	1,876	1,906	1,948
Black	268	898	940	1,016	1,029	1,111	1,197	1,275	1,358	1,406	1,486	1,514

- Represents zero. [1] Includes races other than White or Black. [2] Revisions to total number of prisoners under death sentence not carried to this category.

Source: U.S. Bureau of Justice Statistics, *Capital Punishment*, annual.

No. 338. Prisoners Executed Under Civil Authority by Sex and Race: 1930 to 2000

[Excludes executions by military authorities. The Army (including the Air Force) carried out 160 (148 between 1942 and 1950; 3 each in 1954, 1955, and 1957; and 1 each in 1958, 1959, and 1961). Of the total, 106 were executed for murder (including 21 involving rape), 53 for rape, and 1 for desertion. The Navy carried out no executions during the period]

Year or period	Total [1]	Male	Female	White	Black	Executed for murder Total [1]	White	Black
All years, 1930-2000	4,542	4,484	37	2,173	2,315	3,692	1,884	1,770
1930 to 1939	1,667	1,656	11	827	816	1,514	803	687
1940 to 1949	1,284	1,272	12	490	781	1,064	458	595
1950 to 1959	717	709	8	336	376	601	316	280
1960 to 1967	191	190	1	98	93	155	87	68
1968 to 1976	-	-	-	-	-	-	-	-
1977 to 2000	683	657	5	422	249	683	422	254
1985	18	-	-	11	7	18	11	7
1986	18	18	-	11	7	18	11	7
1987	25	25	-	13	12	25	13	12
1988	11	11	-	6	5	11	6	5
1989	16	16	-	8	8	16	8	8
1990	23	23	-	16	7	23	16	7
1991	14	14	-	7	7	14	7	7
1992	31	31	-	19	11	31	19	11
1993	38	38	-	23	14	38	23	14
1994	31	31	-	20	11	31	20	11
1995	56	56	-	33	22	56	33	22
1996	45	45	-	31	14	45	31	14
1997	74	74	-	45	27	74	45	27
1998	68	66	2	48	18	68	48	18
1999	98	98	-	61	33	98	61	33
2000	85	83	2	48	36	85	48	36

- Represents zero. [1] Includes races other than White or Black. [2] Includes 25 armed robbery, 20 kidnapping, 11 burglary, 8 espionage (6 in 1942 and 2 in 1953), and 6 aggravated assault.

Source: Through 1978, U.S. Law Enforcement Assistance Administration; thereafter, U.S. Bureau of Justice Statistics, *Correctional Populations in the United States*, annual; and *Capital Punishment*, annual.

No. 339. Prisoners Under Sentence of Death and Executed Under Civil Authority by State: 1977 to 2000

[Alaska, District of Columbia, Hawaii, Iowa, Maine, Massachusetts, Michigan, Minnesota, New York, North Dakota, Rhode Island, Vermont, West Virginia, and Wisconsin are jurisdictions without a death penalty]

State	1977 to 2000	1997	1998	1999	2000
U.S.	683	74	68	98	85
AL	23	3	1	2	5
AZ	22	2	4	7	3
AR	23	4	1	4	2
CA	8	-	1	2	1
DE	11	-	-	2	1
FL	50	1	4	1	6
GA	23	-	1	-	-
ID	1	-	-	-	-
IL	12	2	1	1	-
IN	7	1	1	1	-
KY	2	1	-	1	-
LA	26	1	-	1	1
MD	3	1	1	-	-
MS	4	-	-	-	-
MO	46	6	3	9	5
NE	3	1	-	-	-
NV	8	-	1	1	-
NC	16	-	3	4	1
OK	30	1	4	6	11
OR	2	1	-	-	-
PA	3	-	-	1	-
SC	25	2	7	4	1
TN	1	-	-	-	1
TX	239	37	20	35	40
UT	6	-	1	-	-
VA	81	9	13	14	8
WA	3	-	1	-	-
WY	1	-	-	-	-

- Represents zero.

Source: Through 1978, U.S. Law Enforcement Assistance Administration; thereafter, U.S. Bureau of Justice Statistics, *Capital Punishment*, annual.

Law Enforcement, Courts, and Prisons 203

No. 340. Fire Losses—Total and Percent Change: 1980 to 1999

[Includes allowance for uninsured and unreported losses but excludes losses to government property and forests. Represents incurred losses]

Year	Total (mil. dol.)	Per capita [1]	Year	Total (mil. dol.)	Per capita [1]	Year	Total (mil. dol.)	Per capita [1]
1980	5,579	24.56	1987	8,504	34.96	1994	12,778	49.09
1981	5,625	24.53	1988	9,626	39.11	1995	11,887	45.24
1982	5,894	25.61	1989	9,514	38.33	1996	12,544	47.30
1983	6,320	27.20	1990	9,495	38.07	1997	12,940	48.33
1984	7,602	32.35	1991	11,302	44.83	1998	11,510	45.59
1985	7,753	32.70	1992	13,588	53.29	1999	11,482	42.11
1986	8,488	35.21	1993	11,331	43.96			

[1] Based on U.S. Census Bureau resident population as of July 1.

Source: Insurance Information Institute, New York, NY, *Insurance Facts*, annual (copyright).

No. 341. Fires—Number and Loss by Type and Property Use: 1996 to 1999

[Number of 1,975 represents 1,975,000 and property loss of 9,406 represents $9,406,000,000. Based on annual sample survey of fire departments. No adjustments were made for unreported fires and losses. Property loss includes direct property loss only]

Type and property use	Number (1,000)				Property loss (mil. dol.)			
	1996	1997	1998	1999	1996	1997	1998	1999
Fires, total.	1,975	1,795	1,755	1,823	9,406	8,525	8,629	10,024
Structure	578	552	517	523	7,933	7,087	6,717	8,490
Outside of structure [1]	63	57	62	64	91	99	497	123
Brush and rubbish	766	662	653	724	-	-	-	-
Vehicle.	414	397	381	369	1,333	1,269	1,337	1,324
Other.	154	127	142	143	49	70	78	87
Structure by property use:								
Public assembly	16	15	16	16	330	327	354	412
Educational	9	8	8	8	65	58	84	71
Institutional	8	8	9	8	24	25	23	23
Stores and offices	27	27	25	29	665	612	462	659
Residential.	428	407	381	383	4,962	4,585	4,391	5,092
1-2 family units [2]	324	303	283	283	4,121	3,735	3,642	4,123
Apartments.	93	93	86	88	748	718	631	842
Other residential [3]	11	11	12	12	93	132	118	127
Storage [4]	41	36	36	36	949	577	687	[5]1,375
Industry, utility, defense [4] . .	18	17	16	18	[6]733	723	496	671
Special structures	31	34	26	25	205	180	220	187

- Represents zero. [1] Includes outside storage, crops, timber, etc. 1998 property loss data include $390 million loss in timber from Florida wildfires. [2] Includes mobile homes. [3] Includes hotels and motels, college dormitories, boarding houses, etc. [4] Data underreported as some incidents were handled by private fire brigades or fixed suppression systems which do not report. [5] Includes estimated losses of $515 million due to two power plant fires. [6] Includes $280 million in property in a storage property fire in New Orleans, Louisiana, in 1996.

Source: National Fire Protection Association, Quincy, MA, "1999 U.S. Fire Loss," *NFPA Journal*, September 2000, and prior issues (copyright 2000).

No. 342. Fires and Property Loss for Incendiary and Suspicious Fires and Civilian Fire Deaths and Injuries by Selected Property Type: 1996 to 1999

[Based on sample survey of fire departments]

Characteristic	1996	1997	1998	1999	Characteristic	1996	1997	1998	1999
NUMBER (1,000)					CIVILIAN FIRE DEATHS				
					Deaths, total [2].	4,990	4,050	4,035	3,570
Structure fires, total .	578	552	517	523					
Structure fires of incendiary or suspicious origin	85	78	76	72	Residential property.	4,080	3,390	3,250	2,920
					One- and two-family dwellings	3,470	2,700	2,775	2,375
Fires of incendiary origin .	52	52	47	44	Apartments.	565	660	445	520
Fires of suspicious origin.	33	26	29	28	Vehicles	710	480	575	470
PROPERTY LOSS [1] (mil. dol.)					CIVILIAN FIRE INJURIES				
					Injuries, total [2]	25,550	23,750	23,100	21,875
Structure fires, total .	7,933	7,087	6,717	8,490	Residential property.	19,300	17,775	17,175	16,425
Structure fires of incendiary or suspicious origin	1,405	1,309	1,249	1,281	One- and two-family dwellings	13,700	12,300	11,800	11,550
					Apartments.	5,175	5,000	5,000	4,500
Fires of incendiary origin .	897	802	816	828	Vehicles	2,225	2,125	2,225	1,850
Fires of suspicious origin.	508	507	433	453					

[1] Direct property loss only. [2] Includes other not shown separately.

Source: National Fire Protection Association, Quincy, MA, "1999 U.S. Fire Loss," *NFPA Journal*, September 2000, and prior issues (copyright 2000).

Geography and Environment

This section presents a variety of information on the physical environment of the United States, starting with basic area measurement data and ending with climatic data for selected weather stations around the country. The subjects covered between those points are mostly concerned with environmental trends but include related subjects such as land use, water consumption, air pollutant emissions, toxic releases, oil spills, hazardous waste sites, municipal waste and recycling, threatened and endangered wildlife, and the environmental industry.

The information in this section is selected from a wide range of federal agencies that compile the data for various administrative or regulatory purposes, such as the Environmental Protection Agency, U.S. Geological Survey, National Oceanic and Atmospheric Administration (NOAA), Natural Resources Conservation Service, and General Services Administration.

Area—For the 1990 census, area measurements were calculated by computer based on the information contained in a single, consistent geographic database, the TIGER® file (described below), rather than relying on historical, local, and manually calculated information. This especially affects water area figures reported in 1990; these had only included those bodies of water of at least 40 acres and those streams with a width of at least one-eighth of a statute mile from 1940 to 1980. Water area figures for 1990 increased because the data reflected all water recorded in the Census Bureau's geographic database including coastal, Great Lakes, and territorial waters.

Geography—The U.S. Geological Survey conducts investigations, surveys, and research in the fields of geography, geology, topography, geographic information systems, mineralogy, hydrology, and geothermal energy resources as well as natural hazards. The U.S. Geological Survey provides United States cartographic data

through the Earth Sciences Information Center, water resources data through the National Water Data Exchange (NAWDEX), and a variety of research and Open-File reports which are announced monthly in *New Publications of the U.S. Geological Survey.*

In a joint project with the U.S. Census Bureau, during the 1980s, the U.S. Geological Survey provided the basic information on geographic features for input into a national geographic and cartographic database prepared by the Census Bureau, called the TIGER® (Topologically Integrated Geographic Encoding and Referencing) database. Since then, using a variety of sources, the Census Bureau has updated these features and their related attributes (names, descriptions, etc.) and inserted current information on the boundaries, names, and codes of legal and statistical geographic entities; very few of these updates added aerial water features, however. Maps prepared by the Census Bureau using the TIGER database show the names and boundaries of entities and are available on a current basis. An inventory is available for the 1990 census, both on computer tape and CD-ROM as the *1990 TIGER/GICS (Geographic Identification Code Scheme)* and for the 1997 economic censuses in the *Geographic Reference Manual* (EC97-R-1). The Census Bureau maintains a current inventory of governmental units and their legal boundaries primary through its Boundary and Annexation Survey. The information is available to the public in several files, all available on line: TIGER/Line®, TIGER/CTSI, TIGER/GICS, and several series of maps for Census 2000: P.L. County Block Maps, Census Tract Outline Maps, and Voting District/State Legislative District Outline Maps.

An inventory of the nation's land resources by type of use/cover was conducted by the National Resource Recovery Conservation Service (formerly the Soil Conservation Service) every 5 years

U.S. Census Bureau, Statistical Abstract of the United States: 2001

beginning in 1982. The most recent survey results, which were published in the 1997 National Resources Inventory, cover all nonfederal land in Puerto Rico, the Virgin Islands, and the United States except Alaska. Tables 345 and 346 provide results from the survey.

Environment—The principal federal agency responsible for pollution abatement and control activities is the Environmental Protection Agency (EPA). It is responsible for establishing and monitoring national air quality standards, water quality activities, solid and hazardous waste disposal, and control of toxic substances. Many of these series now appear on the EPA Web site at the Center for Environmental Information and Statistics and can be accessed at <http://www.epa.gov/ceis/>.

National Ambient Air Quality Standards (NAAQS) for suspended particulate matter, sulfur dioxide, photochemical oxidants, carbon monoxide, and nitrogen dioxide were originally set by the EPA in April 1971. Every 5 years, each of the NAAQS is reviewed and revised if new health or welfare data indicates that a change is necessary. The standard for photochemical oxidants, now called ozone, was revised in February 1979. Also, a new NAAQS for lead was promulgated in October 1978 and for suspended particulate matter in 1987. Table 355 gives some of the health-related standards for the six air pollutants having NAAQS. Data gathered from state networks are periodically submitted to EPA's National Aerometric Information Retrieval System (AIRS) for summarization in annual reports on the nationwide status and trends in air quality; for details, see *National Air Quality and Emissions Trends Report, 1998.*

The Toxics Release Inventory (TRI), published by the U.S. EPA, is a valuable source of information regarding toxic chemicals that are being used, manufactured, treated, transported, or released into the environment. Two rules, Section 313 of the Emergency Planning and Community Right-To-Know Act (EPCRA) and Section 6607 of the Pollution Prevention

Act (PPA), mandate that a publicly accessible toxic chemical database be developed and maintained by U.S. EPA. This database, known as the TRI, contains information concerning waste management activities and the release of toxic chemicals by facilities that manufacture, process, or otherwise use said materials.

Data on the release of these chemicals are collected from manufacturing facilities and facilities added in 1998 that have the equivalent of 10 or more full-time employees and meet the established thresholds for manufacturing, processing, or "otherwise use" of listed chemicals. Facilities must report their releases and other waste management quantities. Federal facilities have been required to report since 1994, regardless of industry classification. In May 1997, EPA added seven new industry sectors that reported to the TRI for the first time in July 1999 for the 1998 reporting year.

Climate—NOAA, through the National Weather Service and the National Environmental Satellite, Data, and Information Service, is responsible for data on climate. NOAA maintains about 11,600 weather stations, of which over 3,000 produce autographic precipitation records, about 600 take hourly readings of a series of weather elements, and the remainder record data once a day. These data are reported monthly in the *Climatological Data* and *Storm Data,* published monthly, and annually in the *Local Climatological Data* (published by location for major cities).

The normal climatological temperatures, precipitation, and degree days listed in this publication are derived for comparative purposes and are averages for the 30-year period, 1961-90. For stations that did not have continuous records for the entire 30 years from the same instrument site, the normals have been adjusted to provide representative values for the current location. The information in all other tables is based on data from the beginning of the record at that location through 1999, except as noted.

Figure 6.1
Waste Recovery of Selected Materials in Municipal Solid Wastes: 1999

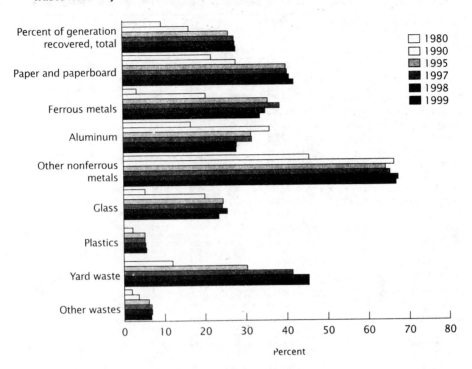

Source: Chart prepared by U.S. Census Bureau. For data, see Table 360.

Figure 6.2
Toxic Chemical Releases by Industry: 1998

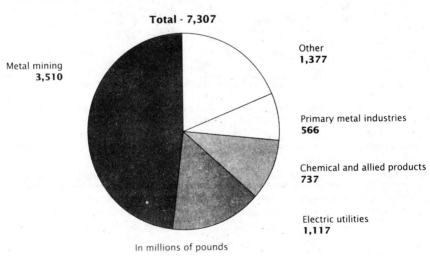

In millions of pounds

Source: Chart prepared by U.S. Census Bureau. For data, see Table 363.

Geography and Environment   207

No. 343. Land and Water Area of States and Other Entities: 1990

[One square mile=2.59 square kilometers. Excludes territorial water, which was included in the 1993 edition of the *Statistical Abstract*]

State and other area	Total area Sq. mi.	Total area Sq. km.	Land area Sq. mi.	Land area Sq. km.	Water area Total Sq. mi.	Water area Total Sq. km.	Water area Inland sq. mi.	Water area Coastal sq. mi.	Water area Great Lakes sq. mi.
United States . . .	3,717,796	9,629,091	3,536,278	9,158,960	181,518	470,131	78,937	42,528	60,052
Alabama	52,237	135,293	50,750	131,443	1,486	3,850	968	-.519	-
Alaska.	615,230	1,593,444	570,374	1,477,268	44,856	116,177	17,501	27,355	-
Arizona	114,006	295,276	113,642	294,333	364	943	364	-	-
Arkansas	53,182	137,742	52,075	134,875	1,107	2,867	1,107	-	-
California.	158,869	411,470	155,973	403,971	2,895	7,499	2,674	222	-
Colorado	104,100	269,618	103,729	268,658	371	960	371	-	-
Connecticut	5,544	14,358	4,845	12,550	698	1,808	161	538	-
Delaware	2,396	6,206	1,955	5,062	442	1,144	71	371	-
District of Columbia . . .	68	177	61	159	7	18	7	-	-
Florida.	59,928	155,214	53,937	139,697	5,991	15,517	4,683	1,308	-
Georgia	58,977	152,750	57,919	150,010	1,058	2,740	1,011	47	-
Hawaii.	6,459	16,729	6,423	16,636	36	93	36	-	-
Idaho	83,574	216,456	82,751	214,325	823	2,131	823	-	-
Illinois	57,918	150,007	55,593	143,987	2,325	6,021	750	-	1,575
Indiana	36,420	94,328	35,870	92,904	550	1,424	315	-	235
Iowa	56,276	145,754	55,875	144,716	401	1,038	401	-	-
Kansas	82,282	213,110	81,823	211,922	459	1,189	459	-	-
Kentucky	40,411	104,665	39,732	102,907	679	1,759	679	-	-
Louisiana.	49,651	128,595	43,566	112,836	6,085	15,759	4,153	1,931	-
Maine	33,741	87,388	30,865	79,939	2,876	7,449	2,263	613	-
Maryland	12,297	31,849	9,775	25,316	2,522	6,533	680	1,842	-
Massachusetts	9,241	23,934	7,838	20,300	1,403	3,634	424	979	-
Michigan	96,705	250,465	56,809	147,136	39,895	103,329	1,704	-	38,192
Minnesota	86,943	225,182	79,617	206,207	7,326	18,975	4,780	-	2,546
Mississippi	48,286	125,060	46,914	121,506	1,372	3,553	781	591	-
Missouri.	69,709	180,546	68,898	178,446	811	2,100	811	-	-
Montana	147,046	380,849	145,556	376,991	1,490	3,859	1,490	-	-
Nebraska.	77,358	200,358	76,878	199,113	481	1,245	481	-	-
Nevada	110,567	286,367	109,806	284,396	761	1,971	761	-	-
New Hampshire	9,283	24,044	8,969	23,231	314	813	314	-	-
New Jersey	8,215	21,277	7,419	19,215	796	2,062	371	425	-
New Mexico	121,598	314,939	121,364	314,334	234	605	234	-	-
New York.	.53,989	139,833	47,224	122,310	6,766	17,523	1,888	976	3,901
North Carolina	52,672	136,421	48,718	126,180	3,954	10,241	3,954	-	-
North Dakota	70,704	183,123	68,994	178,695	1,710	4,428	1,710	-	-
Ohio	44,828	116,103	40,953	106,067	3,875	10,036	376	-	3,499
Oklahoma	69,903	181,048	68,679	177,877	1,224	3,171	1,224	-	-
Oregon	97,132	251,571	96,002	248,646	1,129	2,925	1,050	80	-
Pennsylvania	46,058	119,291	44,820	116,083	1,239	3,208	490	-	749
Rhode Island	1,231	3,189	1,045	2,707	186	482	168	18	-
South Carolina	31,189	80,779	30,111	77,988	1,078	2,791	1,006	72	-
South Dakota	77,121	199,744	75,896	196,571	1,225	3,174	1,225	-	-
Tennessee	42,146	109,158	41,219	106,758	926	2,400	926	-	-
Texas	267,277	692,248	261,914	678,358	5,363	13,890	4,959	404	-
Utah . . . .·. . . .	84,904	219,902	82,168	212,815	2,736	7,086	2,736	-	-
Vermont	9,615	24,903	9,249	23,956	366	947	366	-	-
Virginia	42,326	109,625	39,598	102,558	2,729	7,067	1,000	1,728	-
Washington	70,637	182,949	66,581	172,445	4,055	10,503	1,545	2,511	-
West Virginia	24,231	62,759	24,087	62,384	145	375	145	-	-
Wisconsin	65,499	169,643	54,314	140,672	11,186	28,971	1,831	-	9,355
Wyoming	97,818	253,349	97,105	251,501	714	1,848	714	-	-
Other areas:									
Puerto Rico.	3,508	9,085	3,427	8,875	81	210	65	16	-
American Samoa . . .	90	233	77	200	13	33	7	6	-
Guam	217	561	210	543	7	18	7	-	-
No. Mariana Islands .	189	490	179	464	10	26	2	8	-
Palau. . . . . . *. . . .	241	624	177	458	64	165	40	24	-
U.S. Virgin Islands . .	171	443	134	346	37	96	17	20	-

- Represents or rounds to zero.

Source: U.S. Census Bureau, *1990 Census of Population and Housing*, Series CPH-2; and unpublished data from the TIGER/Geographic Information Control System (TIGER/GICS) computer file. Corrections have been made subsequent to the 1990 census reports.

No. 344. Total and Federally Owned Land by State: 1999

[As of end of fiscal year; see text, Section 8, State and Local Government Finances and Employment. Total land area figures are not comparable with those in Table 343]

State	Total (1,000 acres)	Not owned by federal government (1,000 acres)	Owned by federal government [1] Acres (1,000)	Owned by federal government [1] Percent	State	Total (1,000 acres)	Not owned by federal government (1,000 acres)	Owned by federal government [1] Acres (1,000)	Owned by federal government [1] Percent
United States...	2,271,343	1,641,078	630,266	27.7	Missouri	44,248	42,154	2,095	4.7
Alabama	32,678	31,444	1,234	3.8	Montana	93,271	67,488	25,783	27.6
Alaska	365,482	137,486	227,996	62.4	Nebraska	49,032	48,385	647	1.3
Arizona	72,688	40,299	32,389	44.6	Nevada	70,264	12,038	58,226	82.9
Arkansas	33,599	30,361	3,238	9.6	New Hampshire	5,769	5,010	759	13.2
California	100,207	56,493	43,713	43.6	New Jersey	4,813	4,695	119	2.5
Colorado	66,486	42,246	24,239	36.5	New Mexico	77,766	51,140	26,626	34.2
Connecticut	3,135	3,121	14	0.5	New York	30,681	30,575	106	0.3
Delaware	1,266	1,258	8	0.6	North Carolina	31,403	29,047	2,356	7.5
District of Columbia	39	30	9	22.7	North Dakota	44,452	42,681	1,771	4.0
Florida	34,721	31,655	3,066	8.8	Ohio	26,222	25,830	392	1.5
Georgia	37,295	35,431	1,864	5.0	Oklahoma	44,088	42,764	1,323	3.0
Hawaii	4,106	3,487	618	15.1	Oregon	61,599	29,284	32,315	52.5
Idaho	52,933	19,854	33,079	62.5	Pennsylvania	28,804	28,135	670	2.3
Illinois	35,795	35,221	574	1.6	Rhode Island	677	673	4	0.6
Indiana	23,158	22,657	501	2.2	South Carolina	19,374	18,267	1,107	5.7
Iowa	35,860	35,665	195	0.5	South Dakota	48,882	46,220	2,662	5.4
Kansas	52,511	51,837	673	1.3	Tennessee	26,728	25,070	1,658	6.2
Kentucky	25,512	24,278	1,234	4.8	Texas	168,218	165,649	2,568	1.5
Louisiana	28,868	27,709	1,159	4.0	Utah	52,697	18,692	34,005	64.5
Maine	19,848	19,679	168	0.8	Vermont	5,937	5,565	372	6.3
Maryland	6,319	6,152	167	2.6	Virginia	25,496	23,212	2,284	9.0
Massachusetts	5,035	4,963	72	1.4	Washington	42,694	30,541	12,152	28.5
Michigan	36,492	32,413	4,079	11.2	West Virginia	15,411	14,232	1,178	7.6
Minnesota	51,206	47,000	4,206	8.2	Wisconsin	35,011	33,139	1,872	5.3
Mississippi	30,223	28,575	1,647	5.5	Wyoming	62,343	31,272	31,071	49.8

[1] Excludes trust properties.

Source: U.S. General Services Administration, *Summary Report on Real Property Owned by the United States Throughout the World,* annual.

No. 345. Nonfederal Developed Land Use by State and Other Area: 1997

[In thousands of acres (1,944,130 represents 1,944,130,000), except percent. Excludes Alaska and District of Columbia]

State and other area	Total surface area	Developed land Total	Developed land Percent of total	Developed land Change, 1992-97	State and other area	Total surface area	Developed land Total	Developed land Percent of total	Developed land Change, 1992-97
Total	1,944,130	98,252	5.0	11,217	Montana	94,110	1,032	1.1	76
					Nebraska	49,510	1,206	2.5	55
United States	1,941,823	97,745	5.0	11,105	Nevada	70,763	381	0.6	27
Alabama	33,424	2,252	6.8	315	New Hampshire	5,941	589	10.0	63
Arizona	72,964	1,491	2.1	114	New Jersey	5,216	1,778	34.1	214
Arkansas	34,037	1,409	4.2	169	New Mexico	77,823	1,153	1.5	217
California	101,510	5,456	5.4	553	New York	31,361	3,184	10.2	318
Colorado	66,625	1,652	2.5	113	North Carolina	33,709	3,856	11.5	507
Connecticut	3,195	874	27.4	39	North Dakota	45,251	992	2.2	33
Delaware	1,534	226	14.8	23	Ohio	26,445	3,611	13.7	365
Florida	37,534	5,185	13.9	825	Oklahoma	44,738	1,926	4.4	177
Georgia	37,741	3,957	10.5	852	Oregon	62,161	1,222	2.0	104
Hawaii	4,158	180	4.4	7	Pennsylvania	28,995	3,983	13.8	545
Idaho	53,488	755	1.5	92	Rhode Island	813	201	24.7	7
Illinois	36,059	3,181	8.9	247	South Carolina	19,939	2,097	10.6	362
Indiana	23,156	2,260	9.8	195	South Dakota	49,358	960	2.0	58
Iowa	36,017	1,702	4.8	69	Tennessee	26,974	2,371	8.8	402
Kansas	52,661	1,940	3.7	97	Texas	171,052	8,567	5.1	894
Kentucky	25,863	1,738	6.8	237	Utah	54,339	662	1.3	81
Louisiana	31,377	1,624	5.2	134	Vermont	6,154	318	5.2	12
Maine	20,966	712	3.4	111	Virginia	27,087	2,626	9.7	344
Maryland	7,870	1,236	15.8	178	Washington	44,035	2,065	4.7	241
Massachusetts	5,339	1,479	27.8	212	West Virginia	15,508	874	5.7	177
Michigan	37,349	3,546	9.5	364	Wisconsin	35,920	2,418	6.8	188
Minnesota	54,010	2,186	4.1	232	Wyoming	62,603	644	1.1	34
Mississippi	30,527	1,474	4.9	206					
Missouri	44,614	2,517	5.7	224	Caribbean	2,307	507	22.0	112

Source: U.S. Department of Agriculture, National Resource and Conservation Service, and Iowa State University, Statistical Laboratory, *1997 National Resources Inventory,* reissued December 2000.

Geography and Environment 209

No. 346. Land Cover/Use by State: 1997

[In thousands of acres (1,944,130 represents 1,944,130,000), except percent. Excludes Alaska and District of Columbia]

State and other area	Total surface area	Rural land, total	Percent of total	Crop- land	CRP land [1]	Pasture land	Range- land	Forest land	Other rural land
					Rural land				
Total........	1,944,130	1,393,760	71.7	376,998	32,696	119,992	405,977	406,955	51,142
United States ...	1,941,823	1,392,098	71.7	376,630	32,696	119,549	405,832	406,315	51,077
Alabama.........	33,424	28,950	86.6	2,954	522	3,528	74	21,261	612
Arizona.........	72,964	40,858	56.0	1,212	-	73	32,323	4,216	3,035
Arkansas	34,037	28,638	84.1	7,625	230	5,351	38	15,011	384
California	101,510	47,555	46.8	9,635	173	1,049	18,269	13,936	4,494
Colorado........	66,625	40,850	61.3	8,770	1,890	1,211	24,574	3,442	964
Connecticut......	3,195	2,178	68.2	204	-	112	-	1,759	103
Delaware	1,534	988	64.4	485	1	24	-	352	128
Florida	37,534	25,498	67.9	2,752	120	4,231	3,229	12,536	2,630
Georgia	37,741	30,648	81.2	4,757	595	2,865	-	21,560	872
Hawaii	4,158	3,565	85.7	246	-	36	1,009	1,635	639
Idaho..........	53,488	18,618	34.8	5,517	785	1,315	6,501	3,948	553
Illinois..........	36,059	31,675	87.8	24,011	726	2,502	-	3,784	652
Indiana.........	23,158	20,069	86.7	13,407	378	1,830	-	3,781	674
Iowa	36,017	33,673	93.5	25,310	1,739	3,572	-	2,182	870
Kansas.........	52,661	49,685	94.3	26,524	2,849	2,322	15,728	1,546	716
Kentucky	25,863	22,327	86.3	5,178	332	5,686	-	10,667	465
Louisiana	31,377	24,664	78.6	5,659	140	2,385	277	13,226	2,976
Maine...........	20,966	18,794	89.6	413	30	123	-	17,691	537
Maryland	7,870	4,808	61.1	1,616	19	478	-	2,373	321
Massachusetts.....	5,339	3,394	63.6	277	-	119	-	2,744	254
Michigan........	37,349	29,426	78.8	8,540	321	2,032	-	16,354	2,178
Minnesota.......	54,010	45,356	84.0	21,414	1,544	3,434	-	16,248	2,716
Mississippi	30,527	26,429	86.6	5,352	799	3,679	-	16,209	389
Missouri	44,614	39,358	88.2	13,751	1,606	10,849	88	12,431	634
Montana........	94,110	64,958	69.0	15,171	2,721	3,443	36,751	5,431	1,443
Nebraska	49,510	47,187	95.3	19,469	1,245	1,801	23,089	826	757
Nevada	70,763	10,079	14.2	701	2	279	8,372	305	420
New Hampshire	5,941	4,353	73.3	134	-	94	-	3,932	193
New Jersey.......	5,216	2,766	53.0	589	1	111	-	1,698	367
New Mexico	77,823	50,071	64.3	1,875	467	231	39,990	5,467	2,041
New York	31,361	26,702	85.1	5,417	54	2,722	-	17,702	808
North Carolina	33,709	24,592	73.0	5,639	131	2,039	-	15,959	824
North Dakota.....	45,251	41,442	91.6	25,004	2,802	1,129	10,689	454	1,363
Ohio	26,445	22,070	83.5	11,627	324	2,006	-	7,081	1,032
Oklahoma........	44,738	40,610	90.8	9,737	1,138	7,963	14,033	7,281	459
Oregon.........	62,161	28,858	46.4	3,762	483	1,961	9,286	12,643	724
Pennsylvania......	28,995	23,816	82.1	5,471	90	1,845	-	15,478	932
Rhode Island.....	813	458	56.3	22	-	25	-	387	24
South Carolina.....	19,939	16,018	80.3	2,574	263	1,197	-	11,188	797
South Dakota	49,358	44,411	90.0	16,738	1,686	2,108	21,876	518	1,484
Tennessee	26,974	22,597	83.8	4,644	374	4,990	-	12,042	547
Texas...........	171,052	155,530	90.9	26,938	3,906	15,914	95,745	10,816	2,211
Utah	54,339	17,599	32.4	1,679	216	695	10,733	1,883	2,392
Vermont.........	6,154	5,183	84.2	607	-	338	-	4,150	88
Virginia.........	27,087	19,886	73.4	2,918	71	2,995	-	13,316	587
Washington.......	44,035	28,508	64.7	6,656	1,017	1,193	5,857	12,835	951
West Virginia......	15,508	13,252	85.5	864	-	1,527	-	10,582	279
Wisconsin........	35,920	30,374	84.6	10,613	661	2,994	-	14,448	1,658
Wyoming	62,603	32,773	52.4	2,174	247	1,146	27,302	1,004	900
Caribbean........	2,307	1,662	72.0	368	-	443	-	640	65

- Represents or rounds to zero.   [1] Conservation Reserve Program (CRP). A federal program established under the Food Security Act of 1985 to assist private landowners to convert highly erodible cropland to vegetative cover for 10 years.

Source: U.S. Department of Agriculture, National Resource and Conservation Service, and Iowa State University, Statistical Laboratory, Summary Report, 1997 National Resources Inventory, revised December 2000. See also <http://www.nhq.nrcs.usda.gov/NRI/1997/summaryreport.pdf>.

No. 347. Extreme and Mean Elevations by State and Other Area

[One foot=.305 meter]

State and other area	Highest point Name	Elevation Feet	Meters	Lowest point Name	Elevation Feet	Meters	Approximate mean elevation Feet	Meters
U.S.	**Mt. McKinley (AK)**	**20,320**	**6,198**	**Death Valley (CA).**	**-282**	**-86**	**2,500**	**763**
AL	Cheaha Mountain	2,405	733	Gulf of Mexico	(¹)	(¹)	500	153
AK	Mount McKinley	20,320	6,198	Pacific Ocean	(¹)	(¹)	1,900	580
AZ	Humphreys Peak	12,633	3,853	Colorado River	70	21	4,100	1,251
AR	Magazine Mountain	2,753	840	Ouachita River	55	17	650	198
CA	Mount Whitney	14,494	4,419	Death Valley	-282	-86	2,900	885
CO	Mt. Elbert	14,433	4,402	Arkansas River	3,350	1,022	6,800	2,074
CT	Mt. Frissell on South slope.	2,380	726	Long Island Sound	(¹)	(¹)	500	153
DE	Ebright Road, ² New Castle County	448	137	Atlantic Ocean	(¹)	(¹)	60	18
DC	Tenleytown at Reno Reservoir	410	125	Potomac River	1	(Z)	150	46
FL	Sec. 30, T6N, R20W, Walton County	345	105	Atlantic Ocean	(¹)	(¹)	100	31
GA	Brasstown Bald	4,784	1,459	Atlantic Ocean	(¹)	(¹)	600	183
HI	Puu Wekiu	13,796	4,208	Pacific Ocean	(¹)	(¹)	3,030	924
ID	Borah Peak	12,662	3,862	Snake River	710	217	5,000	1,525
IL	Charles Mound	1,235	377	Mississippi River	279	85	600	183
IN	Franklin Twp., Wayne Co .	1,257	383	Ohio River	320	98	700	214
IA	Sec. 29, T100N, R41W, Osceola County ³	1,670	509	Mississippi River	480	146	1,100	336
KS	Mount Sunflower	4,039	1,232	Verdigris River	679	207	2,000	610
KY	Black Mountain	4,139	2,162	Mississippi River	257	78	750	229
LA	Driskill Mountain	535	163	New Orleans	-8	-2	100	31
ME	Mount Katahdin	5,267	1,606	Atlantic Ocean	(¹)	(¹)	600	183
MD	Backbone Mountain	3,360	1,025	Atlantic Ocean	(¹)	(¹)	350	107
MA	Mount Greylock	3,487	1,064	Atlantic Ocean	(¹)	(¹)	500	153
MI	Mount Arvon	1,979	604	Lake Erie	571	174	900	275
MN	Eagle Mountain, Cook Co .	2,301	702	Lake Superior	600	183	1,200	366
MS	Woodall Mountain	806	246	Gulf of Mexico	(¹)	(¹)	300	92
MO	Taum Sauk Mountain	1,772	540	St. Francis River	230	70	800	244
MT	Granite Peak	12,799	3,904	Kootenai River	1,800	549	3,400	1,037
NE	Johnson Twp., Kimball Co .	5,424	1,654	Missouri River	840	256	2,600	793
NV	Boundary Peak	13,140	4,007	Colorado River	479	146	5,500	1,678
NH	Mount Washington	6,288	1,918	Atlantic Ocean	(¹)	(¹)	1,000	305
NJ	High Point	1,803	550	Atlantic Ocean	(¹)	(¹)	250	76
NM	Wheeler Peak	13,161	4,014	Red Bluff Reservoir	2,842	867	5,700	1,739
NY	Mount Marcy	5,344	1,630	Atlantic Ocean	(¹)	(¹)	1,000	305
NC	Mount Mitchell	6,684	2,039	Atlantic Ocean	(¹)	(¹)	700	214
ND	White Butte, Slope Co . . .	3,506	1,069	Red River	750	229	1,900	580
OH	Campbell Hill	1,549	472	Ohio River	455	139	850	259
OK	Black Mesa	4,973	1,517	Little River	289	88	1,300	397
OR	Mount Hood	11,239	3,428	Pacific Ocean	(¹)	(¹)	3,300	1,007
PA	Mount Davis	3,213	980	Delaware River	(¹)	(¹)	1,100	336
RI	Jerimoth Hill	812	248	Atlantic Ocean	(¹)	(¹)	200	61
SC	Sassafras Mountain	3,560	1,086	Atlantic Ocean	(¹)	(¹)	350	107
SD	Harney Peak	7,242	2,209	Big Stone Lake	966	295	2,200	671
TN	Clingmans Dome	6,643	2,026	Mississippi River	178	54	900	275
TX	Guadalupe Peak	8,749	2,668	Gulf of Mexico	(¹)	(¹)	1,700	519
UT	Kings Peak	13,528	4,126	Beaverdam Wash	2,000	610	6,100	1,861
VT	Mount Mansfield	4,393	1,340	Lake Champlain	95	29	1,000	305
VA	Mount Rogers	5,729	1,747	Atlantic Ocean	(¹)	(¹)	950	290
WA	Mount Rainier	14,410	4,395	Pacific Ocean	(¹)	(¹)	1,700	519
WV	Spruce Knob	4,861	1,483	Potomac River	240	73	1,500	458
WI	Timms Hill	1,951	595	Lake Michigan	579	177	1,050	320
WY	Gannett Peak	13,804	4,210	Belle Fourche River	3,099	945	6,700	2,044
Other areas: Puerto Rico	Cerro de Punta	4,390	1,339	Atlantic Ocean	(¹)	(¹)	1,800	549
American Samoa . . .	Lata Mountain	3,160	964	Pacific Ocean	(¹)	(¹)	1,300	397
Guam	Mount Lamlam	1,332	406	Pacific Ocean	(¹)	(¹)	330	101
Virgin Is. . . .	Crown Mountain	1,556	475	Atlantic Ocean	(¹)	(¹)	750	229

Z Less than 0.5 meter.   ¹ Sea level.   ² At DE-PA state line.   ³ "Sec." denotes section; "T," township; "R," range; "N," north; and "W," west.

Source: U.S. Geological Survey, for highest and lowest points, *Elevations and Distances in the United States, 1990;* for mean elevations, 1983 edition.

Geography and Environment   211

No. 348. U.S. Wetland Resources and Deepwater Habitats by Type: 1986 and 1997

[In thousands of acres (144,673.3 represents 144,677,300). Wetlands and deepwater habitats are defined separately because the term wetland does not include permanent water bodies. Deepwater habitats are permanently flooded land lying below the deepwater boundary of wetlands. Deepwater habitats include environments where surface water is permanent and often deep, so that water, rather than air, is the principal medium within which the dominant organisms live, whether or not they are attached to the substrate. As in wetlands, the dominant plants are hydrophytes; however, the substrates are in general terms. Wetlands are lands where saturation with water is the dominant factor determining the nature of soil development and the types of plant and animal communities living in the soil and on its surface. The single feature that most wetlands share is soil or substrate that is at least periodically saturated with or covered by water. Wetlands are lands transitional between terrestrial and aquatic systems where the water table is usually at or near the surface or the land is covered by shallow water]

Wetland or deepwater category	1986	1997	Change, 1986 to 1997
All wetlands and deepwater habitats, total	**144,673.3**	**144,136.8**	**-536.5**
All deepwater habitats, total	38,537.6	38,645.1	107.5
Lacustrine [1]	14,608.9	14,725.3	116.4
Riverine [2]	6,291.1	6,255.9	-35.2
Estuarine subtidal [3]	17,637.6	17,663.9	26.3
All wetlands, total	106,135.7	105,491.7	-644
Intertidal wetlands [4]	5,336.6	5,326.2	-10.4
Marine intertidal	133.1	130.9	-2.2
Estuarine intertidal nonvegetated	580.4	580.1	-0.3
Estuarine intertidal vegetated	4,623.1	4,615.2	-7.9
Freshwater wetlands	100,799.1	100,165.5	-633.6
Freshwater nonvegetated	5,251.0	5,914.3	663.3
Freshwater vegetated	95,548.1	94,251.2	-1,296.9
Freshwater emergent [5]	26,383.3	25,157.1	-1,226.2
Freshwater forested [6]	51,929.6	50,728.5	-1,201.1
Freshwater shrub [7]	17,235.2	18,365.6	1,130.4

[1] The lacustrine system includes deepwater habitats with all of the following characteristics: (1) situated in a topographic depression or a dammed river channel; (2) lacking trees, shrubs, persistent emergents, emergent mosses, or lichens with greater than 30 percent coverage; (3) total area exceeds 20 acres.　[2] The riverine system includes deepwater habitats contained within a channel, with the exception of habitats with water containing ocean derived salts in excess of 0.5 parts per thousand.　[3] The estuarine system consists of deepwater tidal habitats and adjacent tidal wetland that are usually semi-enclosed by land but have open, partly obstructed, or sporadic access to the open ocean, and in which ocean water is at least occasionally diluted by freshwater runoff from the land. Subtidal is where the substrate is continuously submerged by marine or estuarine waters.　[4] Intertidal is where the substrate is exposed and flooded by tides. Intertidal includes the splash zone of coastal waters.　[5] Emergent wetlands are characterized by erect, rooted, herbaceous hydrophytes, excluding mosses and lichens. This vegetation is present for most of the growing season in most years. These wetlands are usually dominated by perennial plants.　[6] Forested wetlands are characterized by woody vegetation that is 20 feet tall or taller.　[7] Shrub wetlands include areas dominated by woody vegetation less than 20 feet tall. The species include true shrubs, young trees, and trees or shrubs that are small or stunted because of environmental conditions.
Source: U.S. Fish and Wildlife Service, *Status and Trends of Wetlands in the Conterminous United States, 1986 to 1997,* January 2001.

No. 349. Water Areas for Selected Major Bodies of Water: 1990

[Includes only that portion of body of water under the jurisdiction of the United States, excluding Hawaii. One square mile=2.59 square kilometers]

Body of water and state	Area Sq. mi.	Area Sq. km.	Body of water and state	Area Sq. mi.	Area Sq. km.
Atlantic Coast water bodies:			San Francisco Bay (CA)	264	684
Chesapeake Bay (MD-VA)	2,747	7,115	Willapa Bay (WA)	125	325
Pamlico Sound (NC)	1,622	4,200	Hood Canal (WA)	117	303
Long Island Sound (CT-NY)	914	2,368	Interior water bodies:		
Delaware Bay (DE-NJ)	614	1,591	Lake Michigan (IL-IN-MI-WI)	22,342	57,866
Cape Cod Bay (MA)	598	1,548	Lake Superior (MI-MN-WI) [1]	20,557	53,243
Albemarle Sound (NC)	492	1,274	Lake Huron (MI) [1]	8,800	22,792
Biscayne Bay (FL)	218	565	Lake Erie (MI-NY-OH-PA) [1]	5,033	13,036
Buzzards Bay (MA)	215	558	Lake Ontario (NY) [1]	3,446	8,926
Tangier Sound (MD-VA)	172	445	Great Salt Lake (UT)	1,836	4,756
Currituck Sound (NC)	116	301	Green Bay (MI-WI)	1,396	3,617
Pocomoke Sound (MD-VA)	111	286	Lake Okeechobee (FL)	663	1,717
Chincoteague Bay (MD-VA)	105	272	Lake Sakakawea (ND)	563	1,459
			Lake Oahe (ND-SD)	538	1,394
Gulf Coast water bodies:			Lake of the Woods (MN) [1]	462	1,196
Mississippi Sound (AL-LA-MS)	813	2,105	Lake Champlain (NY-VT) [1]	414	1,072
Laguna Madre (TX)	733	1,897	Alaska water bodies:		
Lake Pontchartrain (LA)	631	1,635	Chatham Strait	1,559	4,039
Florida Bay (FL)	616	1,596	Prince William Sound	1,382	3,579
Breton Sound (LA)	511	1,323	Clarence Strait	1,199	3,107
Mobile Bay (AL)	310	802	Iliamna Lake	1,022	2,646
Lake Borgne (LA-MS)	271	702	Frederick Sound	792	2,051
Matagorda Bay (TX)	253	656	Sumner Strait	791	2,048
Atchafalaya Bay (LA)	245	635	Stephens Passage	702	1,819
Galveston Bay (TX)	236	611	Kvichak Bay	640	1,659
Tampa Bay (FL)	212	549	Montague Strait	463	1,198
Pacific Coast water bodies:			Becharof Lake	447	1,158
Puget Sound (WA)	808	2,092	Icy Strait	436	1,130

[1] Area measurements for Lake Champlain, Lake Erie, Lake Huron, Lake Ontario, Lake St. Clair, Lake Superior, and Lake of the Woods include only those portions under the jurisdiction of the United States.
Source: U. S. Census Bureau, unpublished data from the Census TIGER® database.

No. 350. Flows of Largest U.S. Rivers—Length, Discharge, and Drainage Area

River	Location of mouth	Source stream (name and location)	Length (miles)[1]	Average discharge at mouth (1,000 cubic ft. per second)	Drainage area (1,000 sq. mi.)
Missouri	Missouri	Red Rock Creek, MT	2,540	76.2	[2]529
Mississippi	Louisiana	Mississippi River, MN	[3]2,340	[4]593	[2,5]1,150
Yukon	Alaska	McNeil River, Canada	1,980	225	[2]328
St. Lawrence	Canada	North River, MN	1,900	348	[2]396
Rio Grande	Mexico-Texas	Rio Grande, CO	1,900	-	336
Arkansas	Arkansas	East Fork Arkansas River, CO	1,460	41	161
Colorado	Mexico	Colorado River, CO	1,450	-	246
Atchafalaya[6]	Louisiana	Tierra Blanca Creek, NM	1,420	58	95.1
Ohio	Illinois-Kentucky	Allegheny River, PA	1,310	281	203
Red	Louisiana	Tierra Blanca Creek, NM	1,290	56	93.2
Brazos	Texas	Blackwater Draw, NM	1,280	-	45.6
Columbia	Oregon-Washington	Columbia River, Canada	1,240	265	[2]258
Snake	Washington	Snake River, WY	1,040	56.9	108
Platte	Nebraska	Grizzly Creek, CO	990	-	84.9
Pecos	Texas	Pecos River, NM	926	-	44.3
Canadian	Oklahoma	Canadian River, CO	906	-	46.9
Tennessee	Kentucky	Courthouse Creek, NC	886	68	40.9
Colorado (of Texas)	Texas	Colorado River, TX	862	-	42.3
North Canadian	Oklahoma	Corrumpa Creek, NM	800	-	17.6
Mobile	Alabama	Tickanetley Creek, GA	774	67.2	44.6
Kansas	Kansas	Arikaree River, CO	743	-	59.5
Kuskokwim	Alaska	South Fork Kuskokwim River, AK	724	67	48
Yellowstone	North Dakota	North Folk Yellowstone River, WY	692	-	70
Tanana	Alaska	Nabesna River, AK	659	41	44.5
Gila	Arizona	Middle Fork Gila River, NM	649	-	58.2

- Represents zero.   [1] From source to mouth.   [2] Drainage area includes both the United States and Canada.   [3] The length from the source of the Missouri River to the Mississippi River and thence to the Gulf of Mexico is about 3,710 miles.   [4] Includes about 167,000 cubic ft. per second diverted from the Mississippi into the Atchafalaya River but excludes the flow of the Red River.   [5] Excludes the drainage areas of the Red and Atchafalaya Rivers.   [6] In east-central Louisiana, the Red River flows into the Atchafalaya River, a distributary of the Mississippi River. Data on average discharge, length, and drainage area include the Red River, but exclude all water diverted into the Atchafalaya from the Mississippi River.

Source: U.S. Geological Survey, *Largest Rivers in the United States*, Open File Report 87-242, May 1990.

No. 351. U.S. Water Withdrawals and Consumptive Use Per Day by End Use: 1940 to 1995

[Includes Puerto Rico. Withdrawal signifies water physically withdrawn from a source. Includes fresh and saline water; excludes water used for hydroelectric power]

Year	Total (bil. gal.)	Per capita[1] (gal.)	Irrigation (bil. gal.)	Public supply[2] Total (bil. gal.)	Public supply[2] Per capita[3] (gal.)	Rural[4] (bil. gal.)	Industrial and misc.[5] (bil. gal.)	Steam electric utilities (bil. gal.)
WITHDRAWALS								
1940	140	1,027	71	10	75	3.1	29	23
1950	180	1,185	89	14	145	3.6	37	40
1955	240	1,454	110	17	148	3.6	39	72
1960	270	1,500	110	21	151	3.6	38	100
1965	310	1,602	120	24	155	4.0	46	130
1970	370	1,815	130	27	166	4.5	47	170
1975	420	1,972	140	29	168	4.9	45	200
1980	440	1,953	150	34	183	5.6	45	210
1985	399	1,650	137	38	189	7.8	31	187
1990	408	1,620	137	41	195	7.9	30	195
1995	402	1,500	134	43	192	8.9	26	190
CONSUMPTIVE USE								
1960	61	339	52	3.5	25	2.8	3.0	0.2
1965	77	403	66	5.2	34	3.2	3.4	0.4
1970	87	427	73	5.9	36	3.4	4.1	0.8
1975	96	451	80	6.7	38	3.4	4.2	1.9
1980	100	440	83	7.1	38	3.9	5.0	3.2
1985	92	380	74	[6]	[6]	9.2	6.1	6.2
1990	94	370	76	[6]	[6]	8.9	6.7	4.0
1995	100	374	81	[6]	[6]	9.9	4.8	3.7

[1] Based on U.S. Census Bureau resident population as of July 1.   [2] Includes commercial water withdrawals.   [3] Based on population served.   [4] Rural farm and nonfarm household and garden use, and water for farm stock and dairies.   [5] For 1940 to 1960, includes manufacturing and mineral industries, rural commercial industries, air-conditioning, resorts, hotels, motels, military and other state and federal agencies, and miscellaneous; thereafter, includes manufacturing, mining and mineral processing, ordnance, construction, and miscellaneous.   [6] Public supply consumptive use included in end-use categories.

Source: 1940-1960, U.S. Bureau of Domestic Business Development, based principally on committee prints, *Water Resources Activities in the United States*, for the Senate Committee on National Water Resources, U.S. Senate, thereafter, U.S. Geological Survey, *Estimated Use of Water in the United States in 1995*, circular 1200, and previous quinquennial issues.

[In millions of gallons per day (401,500 represents 401,500,000,000), except as noted. Figures may not add due to rounding. Withdrawal signifies water physically withdrawn from a source. Includes fresh and saline water]

State or other area	Water withdrawn								Consumptive use,[1] fresh water
		Per capita (gal. per day) fresh	Source		Selected major uses				
	Total		Ground water	Surface water	Irrigation	Public supply[2]	Industrial	Thermo-electric	
U.S.[2]	401,500	1,280	77,500	324,000	134,000	43,600	26,200	190,000	100,000
Alabama	7,100	1,670	445	6,650	139	875	753	5,200	532
Alaska	329	350	132	196	0.6	90	197	30	25
Arizona	6,830	1,620	2,840	3,990	5,670	846	197	62	3,830
Arkansas	8,800	3,540	5,460	3,340	5,940	419	187	1,780	4,140
California	45,900	1,130	14,700	31,300	28,900	5,740	802	9,630	25,500
Colorado	13,800	3,690	2,270	11,600	12,700	732	191	115	5,230
Connecticut	4,450	389	166	4,290	28	448	11	3,940	97
Delaware	1,500	1,050	110	1,390	48	101	64	1,270	71
District of Columbia	10	18	0.5	9.7	-	-	0.5	9.7	15
Florida	18,200	509	4,340	13,800	3,470	2,360	649	11,600	2,780
Georgia	5,820	799	1,190	4,630	722	1,250	676	3,070	1,170
Hawaii	1,930	853	531	1,400	652	218	20	970	542
Idaho	15,100	13,000	2,830	12,300	13,000	254	76	-	4,360
Illinois	19,900	1,680	953	19,000	180	1,950	527	17,100	857
Indiana	9,140	1,570	709	8,430	116	784	2,410	5,690	505
Iowa	3,030	1,070	528	2,510	39	418	301	2,130	290
Kansas	5,240	2,040	3,510	1,720	3,380	384	77	1,260	3,620
Kentucky	4,420	1,150	226	4,190	12	521	375	3,450	318
Louisiana	9,850	2,270	1,350	8,500	769	677	2,580	5,480	1,930
Maine	326	178	80	246	27	135	16	136	48
Maryland	7,730	289	246	7,480	57	907	331	6,360	150
Massachusetts	5,510	189	351	5,160	82	759	88	4,570	180
Michigan	12,100	1,260	862	11,200	227	1,490	1,910	8,370	667
Minnesota	3,390	736	714	2,680	157	573	438	2,090	417
Mississippi	3,200	1,140	2,590	614	1,740	377	294	375	1,570
Missouri	7,030	1,320	891	6,140	567	757	63	5,550	692
Montana	8,860	10,200	217	8,640	8,550	161	80	22	1,960
Nebraska	10,500	6,440	6,200	4,350	7,550	328	175	2,350	7,020
Nevada	2,300	1,480	896	1,400	1,640	479	95	27	1,340
New Hampshire	1,320	388	81	1,240	6.3	130	50	1,110	35
New Jersey	6,110	269	580	5,530	125	1,120	486	4,360	210
New Mexico	3,510	2,080	1,700	1,800	2,990	337	69	55	1,980
New York	16,800	567	1,010	15,800	30	3,140	321	13,100	469
North Carolina	9,290	1,070	535	8,750	239	939	385	7,420	713
North Dakota	1,120	1,750	122	1,000	117	85	17	819	181
Ohio	10,500	944	905	9,620	27	1,560	650	8,190	791
Oklahoma	2,040	543	1,220	822	864	597	285	124	716
Oregon	7,910	2,520	1,050	6,860	6,170	572	379	9.0	3,210
Pennsylvania	9,680	802	860	8,820	16	1,730	1,930	5,930	565
Rhode Island	411	138	27	383	2.3	121	7.3	275	19
South Carolina	6,200	1,690	322	5,880	53	614	703	4,810	321
South Dakota	460	631	187	273	269	97	32	5.3	249
Tennessee	10,100	1,920	435	9,640	24	831	868	8,300	233
Texas	29,600	1,300	8,780	20,800	9,450	3,420	2,920	13,500	10,500
Utah	4,460	2,200	790	3,670	3,530	506	253	48	2,200
Vermont	565	967	50	515	3.9	66	12	452	24
Virginia	8,260	826	358	7,900	30	911	622	6,620	218
Washington	8,860	1,620	1,760	7,100	6,470	1,300	652	376	3,080
West Virginia	4,620	2,530	146	4,470	-	217	1,330	3,010	352
Wisconsin	7,250	1,420	759	6,490	169	692	453	5,820	443
Wyoming	7,060	14,700	335	6,720	6,590	100	118	220	2,800
Puerto Rico	2,840	154	135	2,680	107	443	15	2,260	187
Virgin Islands	202	113	0.7	201	-	7.8	20	173	1.9

- Represents zero. [1] Water that has been evaporated, transpired, or incorporated into products, plant or animal tissue; and therefore, is not available for immediate reuse. [2] Includes Puerto Rico and Virgin Islands.

Source: U.S. Geological Survey, *Estimated Use of Water in the United States in 1995*, circular 1200. Next update will include data for 2000.

No. 353. U.S. Water Quality Conditions by Type of Waterbody: 1998

[Section 305(b) of the Clean Water Act requires states and other jurisdictions to assess the health of their waters and the extent to which their waters support water quality standards. Section 305(b) requires that states submit reports describing water quality conditions to the Environmental Protection Agency every 2 years. Water quality standards have three elements (designated uses, criteria developed to protect each use, and an antidegradation policy. For information on survey methodology and assessment criteria, see report]

Item	Rivers and streams (miles)	Lakes, reservoirs, and ponds (acres)	Estuaries (sq. miles)	Great Lakes shoreline (miles)	Ocean shoreline (miles)
Total size.................	3,662,255	41,593,748	90,465	5,521	66,645
Amount accessed [1]...........	842,426	17,390,370	28,687	4,950	3,130
Percent of total size	23	42	32	90	5
Amount accessed as—					
Good [2]	463,441	7,927,486	13,439	85	2,496
Good but threatened [3].........	85,544	1,565,175	2,766	103	257
Polluted [4]	291,264	7,897,110	12,482	4,762	377
Percent of accessed as—					
Good [2]	55	46	47	2	80
Good but threatened [3].........	10	9	10	2	8
Polluted [4]	35	45	44	96	12
Amount impaired by leading sources of pollution: [5]					
Agriculture.................	170,750	2,417,801	1,827	133	48
Atmospheric deposition	(NA)	616,701	2,922	1,017	(NA)
Forestry	20,020	(NA)	(NA)	(NA)	(NA)
Habitat modification............	18,451	417,662	(NA)	(NA)	(NA)
Hydromodification.............	57,763	1,179,344	531	(NA)	(NA)
Industrial discharges/point sources..	13,795	502,760	1,926	140	52
Irrigated crop production	31,156	410,204	(NA)	(NA)	(NA)
Land disposal of wastes.........	19,928	381,073	1,508	(NA)	117
Municipal point sources	29,087	866,116	3,528	120	96
Natural sources	33,004	654,812	5,223	(NA)	(NA)
Nonirrigated crop production......	46,484	553,064	(NA)	(NA)	(NA)
Resource extraction	25,231	(NA)	585	(NA)	(NA)
Urban runoff and storm sewers	32,310	931,567	3,482	134	236

NA Not available. [1] Includes waterbodies accessed as not attainable for one or more uses. Most states do not assess all their waterbodies during the 2-year reporting cycle, but use a "rotating basin approach" whereby all waters are monitored over a set period of time. [2] Based on assessment of available data, water quality supports all designated uses. Water quality meets narrative and/or numberic criteria adopted to protect and support a designated use. [3] Although all assessed uses are currently met, data show a declining trend in water quality. Projections based on this trend indicate water quality will be impaired in the future, unless action is taken to prevent further degradation. [4] Impaired or not attainable. The reporting state or jurisdiction has performed a "use-attainability analysis" and demonstrated that support of one or more designated beneficial uses is not attainable due to specific biological, chemical, physical, or economic/social conditions. [5] Excludes unknown and natural sources.
Source: U.S. Environmental Protection Agency, *National Water Quality Inventory: 1998 Report to Congress*, June 2000.

No. 354. Oil Spills in U.S. Water—Number and Volume: 1996 to 1999

[3,117,831 represents 3,117,831,000. Based on reported discharges into U.S. navigable waters, including territorial waters (extending 3 to 12 miles from the coastline), tributaries, the contiguous zone, onto shoreline, or into other waters that threaten the marine environment. Data found in Marine Safety Management System]

Spill characteristic	Number of spills				Spill volume (1,000 gal.)			
	1996	1997	1998	1999	1996	1997	1998	1999
Total..........	9,335	8,624	8,315	8,539	3,117,831	942,574	885,303	1,172,449
Size of spill (gallons):								
1-100	8,904	8,299	7,962	8,212	43,434	39,082	38,093	39,119
101-1,000	322	243	259	240	114,831	81,895	86,606	86,530
1,001-3,000	57	40	54	42	102,008	78,117	96,743	74,582
3,001-5,000	20	14	15	18	86,389	58,016	64,609	73,798
5,001-10,000	12	15	15	10	92,163	109,288	108,148	66,274
10,001-50,000	15	11	8	12	351,106	282,176	216,335	301,510
50,001-100,000	-	1	-	4	-	84,000	-	245,406
100,000-1,000,000	5	1	2	1	2,327,900	210,000	274,769	285,230
1,000,000 and over...	-	-	-	-	-	-	-	-
Waterbody:								
Atlantic ocean	119	87	109	148	27,980	40,857	6,674	29,440
Pacific ocean	491	505	644	758	29,209	32,841	192,775	150,694
Gulf of Mexico	2,403	2,341	2,190	1,756	45,145	105,462	181,372	45,786
Great Lakes........	228	156	119	129	3,507	4,311	3,006	906
Lakes.............	19	29	25	31	52	210,270	63	624
Rivers and canals....	1,984	1,821	1,944	1,924	475,550	182,676	280,651	504,264
Bays and sounds	793	811	891	1,299	1,092,207	46,450	24,234	136,650
Harbors...........	992	858	790	907	288,252	45,932	97,223	105,213
Other	2,306	2,016	1,603	1,587	1,155,929	273,775	99,305	198,872
Source:								
Tankship	122	124	104	92	219,311	22,429	56,673	8,414
Tankbarge	313	252	220	227	1,163,258	165,649	248,089	158,997
All other vessels.....	5,151	4,971	4,848	5,361	298,451	192,801	316,473	409,084
Facilities	509	838	937	1,019	406,384	204,935	166,269	367,537
Pipelines	17	32	45	25	978,392	224,122	47,863	36,140
All other nonvessels ..	552	486	571	571	23,527	72,208	32,584	147,704
Unknown...........	2,671	1,921	1,590	1,244	28,508	60,430	17,352	44,593

- Represents or rounds to zero.
Source: U.S. Coast Guard, <http://www.uscg.mil/hq/g-m/nmc/response/stats/Summary.htm> (accessed 05 December 2001).

Geography and Environment **215**

No. 355. National Ambient Air Pollutant Concentrations: 1990 to 1999

[Data represent annual composite averages of pollutant based on daily 24-hour averages of monitoring stations, except carbon monoxide is based on the second-highest, nonoverlapping, 8-hour average; ozone, average of the second-highest daily maximum 1-hour value; and lead, quarterly average of ambient lead levels. Based on data from the Aerometric Information Retrieval System. µg/m³=micrograms of pollutant per cubic meter of air; ppm=parts per million]

Pollutant	Unit	Monitoring stations, number	Air quality standard [1]	1990	1994	1995	1996	1997	1998	1999
Carbon monoxide	ppm	388	[2]9	5.8	5.1	4.6	4.3	3.9	3.8	3.7
Ozone	ppm	703	[3]12	0.112	0.107	0.112	0.105	0.105	0.110	0.107
Ozone	ppm	705	[4]0.08	0.085	0.084	0.087	0.083	0.082	0.086	0.085
Sulfur dioxide	ppm	480	.03	0.0081	0.0069	0.0056	0.0056	0.0054	0.0053	0.0052
Particulates (PM-10)	µg/m³	954	[5]50	29.2	26.0	24.8	23.9	23.8	23.6	23.9
Nitrogen dioxide	ppm	230	.053	0.020	0.020	0.019	0.018	0.018	0.018	0.018
Lead	µg/m³	175	[6]1.5	0.1	0.05	0.05	0.04	0.04	0.04	0.04

[1] Refers to the primary National Ambient Air Quality Standard that protects the public health. [2] Based on 8-hour standard of 9 ppm. [3] Based on 1-hour standard of 0.12 ppm. [4] Based on 8-hour standard of 0.08 ppm. [5] The particulates (PM-10) standard replaced the previous standard for total suspended particulates in 1987. [6] Based on 3-month standard of 1.5 µg/m³.
Source: U.S. Environmental Protection Agency, National Air Quality and Emissions Trends Report, annual.

No. 356. National Air Pollutant Emissions: 1970 to 1998

[In thousands of tons, except as indicated. PM-10=Particulate matter of less than 10 microns. Methodologies to estimate data for 1970 to 1980 period and 1985 to present emissions differ. Beginning with 1985, the estimates are based on a modified National Acid Precipitation Assessment Program inventory]

Year	PM-10	PM-10, fugitive dust [1]	Sulfur dioxide	Nitrogen dioxides	Volatile organic compounds	Carbon monoxide	Lead (tons)
1970	13,042	(NA)	31,161	20,928	30,982	129,444	220,869
1975	7,671	(NA)	28,011	22,632	26,079	116,757	159,659
1980	7,119	(NA)	25,905	24,384	26,336	117,434	74,153
1985	4,831	40,614	23,658	23,198	24,428	117,013	22,890
1986	4,642	46,298	22,886	22,808	23,617	111,688	14,763
1987	4,758	37,711	22,661	23,068	23,470	110,798	7,681
1988	5,598	55,474	23,135	24,124	24,306	118,729	7,053
1989	4,811	48,253	23,293	23,893	22,513	106,439	5,468
1990	5,057	24,905	23,660	24,049	20,936	98,523	4,975
1991	4,725	24,836	23,041	24,249	21,102	100,872	4,169
1992	4,610	24,862	22,806	24,596	20,659	97,630	3,810
1993	4,528	23,478	22,466	24,961	20,868	98,160	3,916
1994	4,751	26,162	21,870	25,372	21,535	102,643	4,047
1995	4,579	22,491	19,181	24,921	20,817	93,353	3,929
1996	4,732	28,309	19,121	24,676	18,736	95,479	3,899
1997	4,743	29,482	19,622	24,824	18,876	94,410	3,952
1998	4,450	30,292	19,647	24,454	17,917	89,454	3,973

NA Not available. [1] Sources such as agricultural tilling, construction, mining and quarrying, paved roads, unpaved roads, and wind erosion.

No. 357. Air Pollutant Emissions by Pollutant and Source: 1998

[In thousands of tons, except as indicated. See headnote, Table 356]

Source	Particulates [1]	Sulfur dioxide	Nitrogen oxides	Volatile organic compounds	Carbon monoxide	Lead (tons)
Total emissions	34,741	19,647	24,454	17,917	89,454	3,973
Fuel combustion, stationary sources	1,091	16,721	10,189	893	5,374	503
Electric utilities	302	13,217	6,103	54	417	68
Industrial	245	2,895	2,969	161	1,114	19
Other fuel combustion	544	609	1,117	678	3,843	416
Residential	432	127	742	654	3,699	6
Industrial processes	607	1,458	786	1,417	3,624	2,327
Chemical and allied product manufacturing	65	299	152	396	1,129	175
Metals processing	171	444	88	75	1,495	2,098
Petroleum and related industries	32	345	138	496	368	(NA)
Other	339	370	408	450	632	54
Solvent utilization	6	1	2	5,278	2	(NA)
Storage and transport	94	3	7	1,324	80	(NA)
Waste disposal and recycling	310	42	97	433	1,154	620
Highway vehicles	257	326	7,765	5,325	50,386	19
Light-duty gas vehicles and motorcycles	56	130	2,849	2,832	27,039	12
Light-duty trucks	40	99	1,917	2,015	18,726	7
Heavy-duty gas vehicles	8	11	323	257	3,067	-
Diesels	152	85.3	2,676	222	1,554	(NA)
Off highway [2]	461	1,084	5,280	2,461	19,914	503
Miscellaneous [3]	31,916	12	328	786	8,920	(NA)

- Represents or rounds to zero. NA Not available. [1] Represents both PM-10 and PM-10 fugitive dust; see Table 356. [2] Includes emissions from farm tractors and other farm machinery, construction equipment, industrial machinery, recreational marine vessels, and small general utility engines such as lawn mowers. [3] Includes emissions such as from forest fires and other kinds of burning, various agricultural activities, fugitive dust from paved and unpaved roads, and other construction and mining activities, and natural sources.
Source of Tables 356 and 357: U.S. Environmental Protection Agency, National Air Pollutant Emission Trends, 1900-1998, EPA-454/R-00-002.

No. 358. Emissions of Greenhouse Gases by Type and Source: 1990 to 1999

[Emission estimates were mandated by Congress through Section 1605(a) of the Energy Policy Act of 1992 (Title XVI). Gases that contain carbon can be measured either in terms of the full molecular weight of the gas or just in terms of their carbon content]

Type and source	Unit	1990	1994	1995	1996	1997	1998	1999
Carbon dioxide:								
Carbon content, total [1]	Mil. metric tons	1,350.5	1,422 5	1,434.7	1,484.1	1,505.2	1,507.4	1,526.8
Energy sources	Mil. metric tons	1,325.0	1,393.7	1,404.7	1,453.6	1,474.1	1,476.3	1,495.0
Methane:								
Gas, total [1]	Mil. metric tons	31.74	31.17	31.18	30.16	30.11	29.29	28.77
Energy sources	Mil. metric tons	11.94	11.16	11.38	10.88	11.03	10.70	10.56
Landfills	Mil. metric tons	11.40	10.83	10.63	10.32	9.97	9.45	9.11
Agricultural sources	Mil. metric tons	8.29	9.05	9.03	8.83	8.98	9.00	8.96
Nitrous oxide, total [1]	1,000 metric tons	1,168	1,310	1,257	1,246	1,226	1,223	1,224
Agriculture	1,000 metric tons	844	927	859	846	865	874	870
Energy sources	1,000 metric tons	211	255	269	266	269	272	279
Industrial sources	1,000 metric tons	96	110	111	116	74	58	57
Chloroflurocarbons (CFCs) gases [2]	1,000 metric tons	202	109	102	67	51	49	41
CFC-11	1,000 metric tons	54	37	36	27	25	25	24
CFC-12	1,000 metric tons	113	58	52	36	23	21	14
CFC-113	1,000 metric tons	26	9	9	(Z)	(Z)	(Z)	(Z)
Other CFCs	1,000 metric tons	9	5	5	4	3	3	3
Halons	1,000 metric tons	2.8	2.7	2.9	3.0	3.0	3.0	3.0
Hydrofluorocarbons:	1,000 metric tons							
HFC-23	1,000 metric tons	3.0	3.0	2.0	3.0	3.0	3.4	2.6
HFC-125	1,000 metric tons	(Z)	0.3	0.5	0.7	0.9	1.1	1.3
HFC-134a	1,000 metric tons	1.0	6.3	14.3	19.0	23.5	26.9	30.3
HFC-143a	1,000 metric tons	(Z)	0.1	0.1	0.2	0.3	0.5	0.7
Perfluorocarbons:	1,000 metric tons							
CF-4	1,000 metric tons	3	2	2	3	3	3	2
C-2 F-6	1,000 metric tons	3	2	2	2	2	2	2
C-4 F-10	1,000 metric tons	1	-	1	1	1	1	1
Sulfur hexafluoride	1,000 metric tons	(Z)	(Z)	(Z)	(Z)	(Z)	(Z)	(Z)
	1,000 metric tons	1	1	2	2	2	2	1

- Represents or rounds to zero.   Z Less than 500 metric tons.   [1] Includes minor sources not shown separately.   [2] Covers principally CFC-11, CFC-12, and CFC-113.

Source: U.S. Energy Information Administration, *Emissions of Greenhouse Gases in the United States,* annual.

No. 359. Municipal Solid Waste Generation, Recovery, and Disposal: 1980 to 1999

[In millions of tons (151.5 represents 151,500,000), except as indicated. Covers post-consumer residential and commercial solid wastes which comprise the major portion of typical municipal collections. Excludes mining, agricultural and industrial processing, demolition and construction wastes, sewage sludge, and junked autos and obsolete equipment wastes. Based on material-flows estimating procedure and wet weight as generated]

Item and material	1980	1990	1993	1994	1995	1996	1997	1998	1999
Waste generated	151.5	205.2	211.8	214.2	211.4	209.2	216.4	223.0	229.9
Per person per day (lb.)	3.7	4.5	4.5	4.5	4.4	4.3	4.4	4.5	4.6
Materials recovered	14.5	33.6	43.8	50.8	54.9	57.3	59.4	61.6	63.9
Per person per day (lb.)	0.35	0.7	0.9	1.1	1.1	1.2	1.2	1.3	1.3
Combustion for energy recovery	2.7	29.7	30.9	31.2	34.5	36.1	36.7	34.4	34.0
Per person per day (lb.)	0.06	0.7	0.7	0.7	0.7	0.7	0.8	0.7	0.7
Combustion without energy recovery	11.0	2.2	1.6	1.3	1.0	(¹)	(¹)	(¹)	(¹)
Per person per day (lb.)	0.27	0.05	0.03	0.03	0.02	(¹)	(¹)	(¹)	(¹)
Landfill, other disposal	123.3	139.7	135.5	130.9	120.9	115.8	120.4	127.1	131.9
Per person per day (lb.)	3.0	3.1	2.9	2.8	2.5	2.4	2.5	2.6	2.7
Percent distribution of generation:									
Paper and paperboard	36.1	35.4	36.6	37.7	38.6	38.1	38.5	37.7	38.1
Glass	9.9	6.4	6.4	6.2	6.1	5.9	5.5	5.6	5.5
Metals	9.6	8.1	7.5	7.6	7.5	7.7	7.7	7.6	7.8
Plastics	5.2	8.3	9.0	9.0	8.9	9.4	9.9	10.0	10.5
Rubber and leather	2.8	2.8	2.7	2.9	2.9	3.0	3.0	3.1	2.7
Textiles	1.7	2.8	3.2	3.4	3.5	3.7	3.8	3.9	3.9
Wood	4.4	6.0	5.8	5.3	4.9	5.2	5.3	5.3	5.3
Food wastes	8.7	10.1	10.0	10.0	10.3	10.4	10.1	11.2	10.9
Yard wastes	18.2	17.1	15.7	14.7	14.0	13.3	12.8	12.4	12.1
Other wastes	3.4	3.0	3.0	3.2	3.3	3.3	3.4	3.2	3.2

[1] Combustion without energy recovery is no longer available separately.

Source: Franklin Associates, Ltd., Prairie Village, KS, *Characterization of Municipal Solid Waste in the United States: 1999.* Prepared for the U.S. Environmental Protection Agency.

U.S. Census Bureau, Statistical Abstract of the United States: 2001

No. 360. Generation and Recovery of Selected Materials in Municipal Solid Waste: 1980 to 1999

[In millions of tons, except as indicated (151.5 represents 151,500,000). Covers post-consumer residential and commercial solid wastes which comprise the major portion of typical municipal collections. Excludes mining, agricultural and industrial processing, demolition and construction wastes, sewage sludge, and junked autos and obsolete equipment wastes. Based on material-flows estimating procedure and wet weight as generated]

Item and material	1980	1990	1993	1994	1995	1996	1997	1998	1999
Waste generated, total	151.5	205.2	211.8	214.2	211.4	209.2	216.4	223.0	229.9
Paper and paperboard.	54.7	72.7	77.4	80.8	81.7	79.7	83.3	84.2	87.5
Ferrous metals	11.6	12.6	11.9	11.8	11.6	11.8	12.3	12.4	13.3
Aluminum	1.8	2.8	2.9	3.0	3.0	3.0	3.0	3.1	3.1
Other nonferrous metals.	1.1	1.1	1.1	1.4	1.3	1.3	1.3	1.4	1.4
Glass	15.0	13.1	13.6	13.4	12.8	12.3	12.0	12.5	12.6
Plastics.	7.9	17.1	19.0	19.3	18.9	19.8	21.5	22.4	24.2
Yard waste	27.5	35.0	33.3	31.5	29.7	27.9	27.7	27.7	27.7
Other wastes	31.9	50.7	52.5	53.1	52.4	53.5	55.3	59.3	60.1
Materials recovered, total	14.5	33.6	43.8	50.8	54.9	57.3	59.4	61.6	63.9
Paper and paperboard.	11.9	20.2	25.5	29.5	32.7	33.2	33.6	34.4	36.7
Ferrous metals	0.4	2.6	3.9	4.0	4.1	4.4	4.7	4.3	4.5
Aluminum	0.3	1.0	1.0	1.2	0.9	0.9	1.0	0.9	0.9
Other nonferrous metals.	0.5	0.7	0.7	1.0	0.8	0.8	0.8	0.9	0.9
Glass	0.8	2.6	3.0	3.1	3.1	3.2	2.9	3.2	2.9
Plastics.	-	0.4	0.7	0.9	1.0	1.1	1.1	1.2	1.4
Yard waste	-	4.2	6.9	8.0	9.0	10.4	11.5	12.6	12.6
Other wastes	0.6	1.8	2.1	3.1	3.2	3.3	3.8	4.1	4.0
Percent of generation recovered, total	9.6	16.4	20.7	23.7	26.0	27.4	27.4	27.6	27.8
Paper and paperboard.	21.8	27.8	32.9	36.5	40.0	41.6	40 3	40.8	41.9
Ferrous metals	3.4	20.4	32.8	33.9	35.5	37.2	38.4	34.9	33.6
Aluminum	16.7	35.9	35.7	37.8	31.4	31.5	31.6	27.9	27.8
Other nonferrous metals.	45.5	66.4	63.1	73.3	64.3	66.7	65.4	67.4	66.9
Glass	5.3	20.0	22.1	23.3	24.5	25.8	24.3	25.5	23.4
Plastics.	-	2.2	3.5	4.9	5.2	5.4	5.2	5.4	5.6
Yard waste	-	12.0	20.8	25.4	30.3	37.2	41.4	45.3	45.3
Other wastes	1.9	3.6	4.0	5.9	6.1	6.2	6.8	6.9	6.7

- Represents zero.

Source: Franklin Associates, Ltd., Prairie Village, KS, *Characterization of Municipal Solid Waste in the United States: 1999.* Prepared for the U.S. Environmental Protection Agency.

No. 361. Curbside Recycling Programs—Number and Population Served by Region: 1995 to 1999

[For composition of regions, see map, inside front cover. 1998 data are not available]

Region	Number of programs			Population served [1]					
				Total (1,000)			Percent		
	1995	1997	1999	1995	1997	1999	1995	1997	1999
Total	7,375	8,969	9,349	121,335	136,229	139,826	46	51	52
Northeast	2,210	3,406	3,414	37,256	43,200	43,162	72	83	83
South.	1,281	1,344	1,581	31,521	36,952	37,914	34	39	39
Midwest	2,985	3,357	3,477	25,487	26,970	30,106	41	43	48
West	899	862	877	27,071	29,107	28,644	49	50	48

[1] Calculated using population of states reporting data.

Source: Franklin Associates, Ltd., Prairie Village, KS, *Characterization of Municipal Solid Waste in the United States: 1999.* Prepared for the U.S. Environmental Protection Agency. Also in *Biocycle Magazine.*

No. 362. Toxic Chemical Releases and Transfers by Media: 1988 to 1999

[In millions of pounds (3,213.1 represents 3,213,100,000), except as indicated. Based on reports filed as required by Section 313 of the Emergency Planning and Community Right-to-Know Act (EPCRA, or Title III of the Superfund Amendments and Reauthorization Act of 1986), Public Law 99-499. Owners and operators of facilities that are classified within Standard Classification Code groups 20 through 39, have 10 or more full-time employees, and that manufacture, process, or otherwise uses any listed toxic chemical in quantities greater than the established threshold in the course of a calendar year are covered and required to report]

Media	Core chemicals [1]					
	1988	1995	1996	1997	1998	1999
Total facilities reporting	19,829	20,110	19,778	19,443	19,193	18,573
Total releases	**3,213.1**	**1,937.6**	**1,892.1**	**1,904.3**	**1,813.2**	**1,749.7**
On-site releases	2,790.4	1,644.3	1,563.0	1,459.0	1,391.1	1,294.0
Air emissions	2,180.6	1,204.2	1,106.7	989.3	926.7	858.5
Surface water	41.9	17.0	16.2	18.0	17.3	14.3
Underground injection	161.9	154.7	138.7	131.4	114.7	109.3
Releases to land	405.9	-	138.1	131.2	114.6	109.2
Off-site releases	422.7	293.3	329.1	445.3	422.1	455.7
Total transfers off-site for further waste management	(NA)	3,041.3	2,927.9	2,980.3	2,759.9	2,840.6
Tranfers to recycling	(NA)	2,202.4	2,145.4	2,144.1	1,963.7	2,030.9
Transfers to energy recovery	(NA)	489.8	448.2	470.0	439.5	469.5
Transfers to treatment	331.8	200.2	183.1	213.7	209.3	200.0
Transfers to POTWs [2]	231.6	146.7	150.2	152.4	146.8	140.1
Other off-site transfers	43.0	2.2	1.0	-	0.6	0.2
Total production-related waste managed	(NA)	17,688.6	17,399.7	17,772.6	18,102.1	18,769.0
Recycled on-site	(NA)	5,877.3	5,907.9	6,212.2	6,574.3	6,485.0
Recycled off-site	(NA)	2,285.6	2,185.3	2,156.2	2,028.8	2,099.6
Energy recovery on-site	(NA)	2,591.8	2,562.4	2,543.6	2,594.5	2,572.2
Energy recovery off-site	(NA)	477.6	486.7	484.0	444.6	467.0
Treated on-site	(NA)	4,183.5	4,080.7	4,181.1	4,306.4	5,103.7
Treated off-site	(NA)	394.1	360.7	371.8	384.9	369.6
Quantity released on- and off-site	(NA)	1,878.6	1,816.1	1,823.7	1,768.7	1,671.7

- Represents or rounds to zero.   NA Not available.   [1] Chemicals covered for all reporting years. Excludes chemicals removed from the list, those added in 1990, 1991, 1994, and 1995 and aluminum oxide, ammonia, hydrochloric acid, and sulfuric acid.   [2] POTW (Publicly Owned Treatment Work) is a wastewater treatment facility that is owned by a state or municipality.

No. 363. Toxic Chemical Releases by Industry: 1999

[In millions of pounds (7,754.8 represents 7,754,800,000), except as indicated. "Original Industries" include owners and operators of facilities that are classified within Standard Classification Code groups 20 through 39, have 10 or more full-time employees, and that manufacture, process, or otherwise uses any listed toxic chemical in quantities greater than the established threshold in the course of a calendar year are covered and required to report. Beginning in 1998, additional industries (listed below as "New Industries") were required to report]

Industry	1987 SIC [1] code	Total facilities (number)	Total on- and off-site releases [2]	Air emissions	Surface water discharges	Surface impoundments	Other on-site land disposal	Total on-site releases	Off-site releases/transfers off-site to disposal
Total	(X)	**22,639**	**7,754.8**	**2,029.4**	**258.9**	**1,231.2**	**3,040.3**	**7,292.6**	**462.2**
ORIGINAL INDUSTRIES									
Total [3]	(X)	**20,698**	**2,309.3**	**1,175.1**	**253.6**	**73.8**	**142.5**	**1,951.9**	**357.4**
Food and kindred products	20	1,615	123.2	59.8	50.2	0.3	0.1	116.3	7.0
Tobacco products	21	23	3.7	2.8	0.2	-	-	2.9	0.8
Textile mill products	22	241	9.8	8.5	0.2	0.1	0.1	9.1	0.7
Apparel and other textile products	23	15	0.5	0.4	-	-	-	0.4	0.1
Lumber and wood products	24	830	35.2	34.1	0.1	-	-	34.4	0.8
Furniture and fixtures	25	352	15.3	15.2	-	-	-	15.2	0.1
Paper and allied products	26	438	225.6	186.0	19.1	3.2	0.3	220.4	5.2
Printing and publishing	27	213	20.7	20.5	-	-	-	20.6	0.1
Chemical and allied products	28	3,759	663.4	288.2	77.1	29.1	4.2	609.3	54.2
Petroleum and coal products	29	410	69.9	48.0	15.7	0.3	0.1	67.0	2.9
Rubber and misc. plastic products	30	1,831	103.5	91.6	-	-	-	92.2	11.3
Leather and leather products	31	72	4.4	2.2	0.1	-	-	2.3	2.1
Stone, clay, glass products	32	668	42.1	32.9	0.1	0.1	0.1	36.7	5.4
Primary metal industries	33	1,912	591.1	106.6	62.5	35.9	130.4	399.9	191.2
Fabricated metals products	34	2,846	80.4	57.3	2.4	-	0.3	60.5	19.9
Industrial machinery and equipment	35	1,100	15.4	10.8	0.1	-	0.2	11.4	4.0
Electronic, electric equipment	36	1,167	39.4	16.9	4.4	-	-	22.3	17.1
Transportation equipment	37	1,295	104.0	91.7	0.2	-	0.3	92.6	11.4
Instruments and related products	38	240	10.6	8.5	1.3	-	-	9.8	0.7
Miscellaneous	39	307	10.2	8.8	-	-	-	8.9	1.3
NEW INDUSTRIES									
Total	(X)	**1,941**	**5,445.5**	**854.3**	**5.3**	**1,157.4**	**2,897.8**	**5,340.8**	**104.8**
Metal mining	10	108	3,977.0	4.5	0.4	1,027.3	2,892.9	3,974.8	2.2
Coal mining	12	50	11.8	1.8	0.2	2.5	0.3	11.8	-
Electric utilities	49	625	1,162.5	841.9	4.5	125.4	4.6	1,104.6	58.0
Chemical wholesalers	5169	428	2.0	1.3	-	-	-	1.3	0.6
Petroleum bulk terminals	5171	532	4.3	4.0	-	-	-	4.1	0.2
RCRA/solvent recovery	4953/7369	198	288.0	0.8	0.1	2.2	-	244.2	43.8

- Represents or rounds to zero.   X Not applicable.   [1] Standard Industrial Classification, see text, Section 12, Labor Force. Employment, and Earnings.   [2] Includes media of release (injection, landfills, etc), not shown separately.   [3] Includes industries with no specific industry identified, not shown separately.

Source of Tables 362 and 363: U.S. Environmental Protection Agency, *1999 Toxics Release Inventory*. See also <http://www.epa.gov/tri/tri99/pdr/199pdr.pdf> (released April 2001).

No. 364. Toxic Releases by State: 1988 to 1999

[In millions of pounds (3,213.1 represents 3,213,100,000). Excludes delisted chemicals, chemicals added in 1990, 1991, 1994, and 1995 and aluminum oxide, ammonia, hydrochloric acid, and sulfuric acid. See headnote, Table 362]

State and outlying area	Core chemicals					State and outlying area	Core chemicals				
	1988	1996	1997	1998	1999		1988	1996	1997	1998	1999
Total	3,213.1	1,892.1	1,904.3	1,813.2	1,732.5	MT.........	35.6	47.2	42.6	50.4	48.8
U.S. total...	3,197.6	1,882.9	1,895.9	1,805.7	1,726.2	NE.........	17.1	8.8	13.9	10.2	8.9
						NV.........	2.4	3.3	4.0	3.7	4.0
AL.........	111.0	90.0	80.1	67.0	63.1	NH.........	14.0	2.3	2.4	2.3	2.4
AK.........	3.7	1.7	0.8	0.3	0.2	NJ.........	48.4	12.3	13.5	11.8	13.1
AZ.........	66.3	45.9	30.6	53.5	50.2	NM.........	30.4	42.8	40.1	23.8	20.0
AR.........	41.0	31.5	50.2	40.3	40.4	NY.........	100.9	28.2	29.1	22.7	22.9
CA.........	110.3	35.5	27.9	27.3	28.1	NC.........	124.3	63.4	55.3	49.0	45.9
CO.........	15.7	3.0	2.8	3.3	3.1	ND.........	1.2	0.8	0.8	1.1	1.0
CT.........	38.5	7.3	8.4	6.1	4.4	OH.........	205.8	128.6	132.0	128.4	118.3
DE.........	8.7	4.9	5.9	5.9	5.3	OK.........	30.5	15.3	15.4	14.1	13.5
DC.........	-	-	-	-	-	OR.........	21.8	23.5	23.8	26.1	25.5
FL.........	33.1	34.2	31.7	30.9	31.7	PA.........	136.2	87.0	96.0	90.3	87.3
GA.........	85.8	43.0	53.2	46.9	44.7	RI.........	7.8	2.3	2.1	1.6	1.2
HI.........	0.8	0.4	0.3	0.3	0.3	SC.........	66.0	48.6	52.1	49.8	57.1
ID.........	7.3	13.8	12.9	12.8	14.8	SD.........	2.4	1.4	1.3	1.4	1.1
IL.........	140.7	82.2	91.8	83.7	81.0	TN.........	126.8	100.0	89.9	78.1	76.6
IN.........	184.5	101.1	111.8	107.1	114.6	TX.........	322.1	186.2	179.3	172.6	168.2
IA.........	43.0	19.4	20.2	25.1	25.7	UT.........	123.8	77.7	98.5	99.6	82.7
KS.........	30.4	17.5	18.9	17.4	19.8	VT.........	1.7	0.4	0.3	0.2	0.3
KY.........	65.7	33.3	35.1	30.7	35.9	VA.........	112.4	39.9	41.4	39.9	39.1
LA.........	129.6	105.8	93.8	92.2	77.4	WA.........	30.6	22.1	24.6	24.3	17.0
ME.........	15.5	5.6	6.3	6.6	4.8	WV.........	39.7	17.6	15.3	16.3	12.0
MD.........	20.2	9.3	9.8	8.8	9.1	WI.........	62.3	33.1	33.9	33.9	31.9
MA.........	32.2	7.0	6.3	6.5	5.0	WY.........	2.0	1.2	1.3	1.3	1.6
MI.........	141.1	81.9	75.1	73.6	63.8						
MN.........	55.9	17.2	15.6	15.0	14.5	Guam......	-	-	-	-	-
MS.........	59.7	47.1	46.4	40.8	39.8	Puerto Rico ...	12.9	7.9	7.2	6.6	5.7
MO.........	91.1	50.2	53.1	48.7	47.9	Virgin Islands .	2.6	1.2	1.2	0.9	0.5

- Represents zero.

Source: U.S. Environmental Protection Agency, *1999 Toxics Release Inventory.* See also <http://www.epa.gov/tri/tri99/pdr/199pdr.pdf> (released April 2001).

No. 365. Hazardous Waste Sites on the National Priority List by State: 2000

[As of December 31. Includes both proposed and final sites listed on the National Priorities List for the Superfund program as authorized by the Comprehensive Environmental Response, Compensation, and Liability Act of 1980 and the Superfund Amendments and Reauthorization Act of 1986]

State and outlying area	Total sites	Rank	Percent distribution	Federal	Non-federal	State and outlying area	Total sites	Rank	Percent distribution	Federal	Non-federal
Total	1,292	(X)	(X)	166	1,126	Montana.........	14	30	1.1	-	14
						Nebraska........	10	39	0.8	1	9
United States ...	1,279	(X)	100.0	165	1,114	Nevada..........	1	49	0.1	-	1
Alabama.........	15	27	1.2	3	12	New Hampshire....	19	20	1.5	1	18
Alaska..........	7	44	0.5	6	1	New Jersey.......	113	1	8.8	8	105
Arizona.........	10	39	0.8	3	7	New Mexico......	12	32	0.9	1	11
Arkansas........	12	32	0.9	-	12	New York........	88	4	6.9	4	84
California.......	99	2	7.7	24	75	North Carolina....	25	15	2.0	2	23
Colorado........	17	22	1.3	3	14	North Dakota.....	-	50	-	-	-
Connecticut......	16	24	1.3	1	15	Ohio............	35	11	2.7	5	30
Delaware........	17	22	1.3	1	16	Oklahoma.......	12	32	0.9	1	11
District of Columbia .	1	(X)	0.1	1	-	Oregon..........	12	32	0.9	2	10
Florida.........	53	6	4.1	6	47	Pennsylvania.....	97	3	7.6	6	91
Georgia.........	15	27	1.2	2	13	Rhode Island.....	12	32	0.9	2	10
Hawaii	3	45	0.7	2	1	South Carolina....	25	15	2.0	2	23
Idaho	9	41	0.7	2	7	South Dakota.....	2	47	0.2	1	1
Illinois.........	44	8	3.4	5	39	Tennessee.......	14	30	1.1	4	10
Indiana.........	29	14	2.3	-	29	Texas..........	38	10	3.0	4	34
Iowa...........	16	24	1.3	1	15	Utah...........	20	19	1.6	4	16
Kansas.........	12	32	0.9	2	10	Vermont.........	8	43	0.6	-	8
Kentucky........	15	27	1.2	1	14	Virginia.........	31	13	2.4	11	20
Louisiana........	16	24	1.3	1	15	Washington......	48	7	3.8	14	34
Maine..........	12	32	0.9	3	9	West Virginia.....	9	41	0.7	2	7
Maryland........	18	21	1.4	8	10	Wisconsin........	41	9	3.2	-	41
Massachusetts....	33	12	2.6	8	25	Wyoming	2	48	0.2	1	1
Michigan........	69	5	5.4	1	68						
Minnesota.......	25	15	2.0	2	23	Guam..........	2	(X)	(X)	1	1
Mississippi......	3	45	0.2	-	3	Puerto Rico......	9	(X)	(X)	-	9
Missouri........	25	15	2.0	3	22	Virgin Islands.....	2	(X)	(X)	-	2

- Represents zero.   X Not applicable.

Source: U.S. Environmental Protection Agency, *Supplementary Materials: National Priorities List, Proposed Rule,* December 2000.

No. 366. Environmental Industry—Revenues and Employment by Industry Segment: 1990 to 2000

[148.2 represents $148,200,000,000. Covers approximately 59,000 private and public companies engaged in environmental activities]

Industry segment	Revenue (bil. dol.)					Employment (1,000)				
	1990	1995	1998	1999	2000	1990	1995	1998	1999	2000
Industry total	148.2	179.2	189.8	196.5	201.7	1,174.3	1,327.0	1,357.6	1,389.7	1,425.2
Analytical services [1]	1.5	1.2	1.1	1.2	1.2	20.2	14.1	13.6	13.9	13.8
Wastewater treatment works [2]	18.3	23.1	25.6	26.7	27.3	95.0	101.5	107.5	111.3	113.5
Solid waste management [3]	26.1	32.5	36.1	37.2	38.2	209.5	243.4	250.7	254.8	261.7
Hazardous waste management [4]	6.3	6.2	5.7	5.3	5.2	56.9	52.5	46.1	43.8	42.6
Remediation/industrial services	11.1	11.1	11.0	11.2	11.7	107.2	98.1	113.5	115.5	120.3
Consulting & engineering	12.5	15.5	15.8	16.4	16.0	144.2	180.2	171.5	177.2	173.2
Water equipment & chemicals	13.5	16.5	19.1	20.0	21.2	97.9	110.2	128.3	133.4	141.5
Instrument manufacturing	2.0	3.0	3.3	3.2	3.3	18.8	26.2	27.7	26.2	27.2
Air pollution control equipment [5]	13.1	14.8	16.5	17.1	17.7	82.7	107.2	113.2	117.3	121.0
Waste management equipment [6]	8.7	9.9	9.5	9.7	9.9	88.8	93.8	75.7	74.6	76.2
Process & prevention technology	0.4	0.8	1.0	1.0	1.1	8.9	19.5	26.7	28.9	31.5
Water utilities [7]	19.8	25.3	28.8	29.4	30.3	104.7	118.2	126.4	128.9	132.9
Resource recovery [8]	13.1	16.9	13.3	14.4	14.9	118.4	136.0	125.0	128.8	132.6
Environmental energy sources [9]	1.8	2.4	3.0	3.6	3.8	21.1	26.1	31.7	35.1	37.2

[1] Covers environmental laboratory testing and services. [2] Mostly revenues collected by municipal entities. [3] Covers such activities as collection, transportation, transfer stations, disposal, landfill ownership and management for solid waste. [4] Transportation and disposal of hazardous, medical and nuclear waste. [5] Includes stationery and mobile sources. [6] Includes vehicles, containers, liners, processing, and remediation equipment. [7] Revenues generated from the sale of water. [8] Revenues generated from the sale of recovered metals, paper, plastic, etc. [9] Includes solar, wind, geothermal, and conservation devices.

Source: Environmental Business International, Inc., San Diego, CA, Environmental Business Journal, monthly (copyright).

No. 367. Threatened and Endangered Wildlife and Plant Species—Number: 2001

[As of April. Endangered species: One in danger of becoming extinct throughout all or a significant part of its natural range. Threatened species: One likely to become endangered in the foreseeable future]

Item	Mammals	Birds	Reptiles	Amphibians	Fishes	Snails	Clams	Crustaceans	Insects	Arachnids	Plants
Total listings	340	273	115	27	125	32	71	21	46	12	739
Endangered species, total	314	253	78	18	81	21	63	18	37	12	593
United States	63	78	14	10	70	20	61	18	33	12	592
Foreign	251	175	64	8	11	1	2	-	4	-	1
Threatened species, total	26	20	37	9	44	11	8	3	9	-	146
United States	9	14	22	8	44	11	8	3	9	-	144
Foreign	17	6	15	1	-	-	-	-	-	-	2

- Represents zero.

Source: U.S. Fish and Wildlife Service, Endangered Species Bulletin, bimonthly; and <http://ecos.fws.gov/tess/html/boxscore.html> (accessed 22 May 2001).

No. 368. Tornadoes, Floods, Tropical Storms, and Lightning: 1990 to 2000

Weather type	1990	1991	1992	1993	1994	1995	1996	1997	1998	1999	2000
Tornadoes, number [1]	1,133	1,132	1,298	1,176	1,082	1,235	1,170	1,148	(NA)	(NA)	(NA)
Lives lost, total	53	39	39	33	69	30	25	67	130	(NA)	(NA)
Most in a single tornado	29	17	12	7	22	6	5	27	34	(NA)	(NA)
Floods and flash floods:											
Lives lost	142	61	62	103	91	80	131	117	136	(NA)	(NA)
North Atlantic tropical storms and hurricanes [2]	14	8	7	8	7	19	13	7	14	12	15
Number of hurricanes reaching U.S. mainland	-	1	1	1	-	2	2	1	3	3	-
Total direct deaths from tropical storms and hurricanes	123	17	28	273	1,175	121	138	4	(NA)	(NA)	(NA)
Direct deaths on U.S. mainland	10	17	26	9	38	29	33	4	23	70	5
Property loss in U.S. (mil. dol.)	57	1,500	26,500	57	973	3,729	3,600	100	7.299	5.862	27
Lightning:											
Deaths	74	73	41	43	74	85	52	42	(NA)	(NA)	(NA)
Injuries	252	432	292	295	577	510	309	306	(NA)	(NA)	(NA)

- Represents zero. NA Not available. [1] A violent, rotating column of air descending from a cumulonimbus cloud in the form of a tubular- or funnel-shaped cloud, usually characterized by movements along a narrow path and wind speeds from 100 to over 300 miles per hour. Also known as a "twister" or "waterspout." [2] Source: National Hurricane Center, Coral Gables, FL, unpublished data. Tropical storms have maximum winds of 39 to 73 miles per hour; hurricanes have maximum winds of 74 miles per hour or higher.

Source: Except as noted, U.S. National Oceanic and Atmospheric Administration, Storm Data, monthly.

Geography and Environment 221

No. 369. Major U.S. Weather Disasters: 1980 to 2000

[4.0 represents $4,000,000,000. Covers only weather related disasters costing $1 billion or more]

Event	Description	Time period	Esti- mated cost (bil. dol.)	Deaths
Southern drought/heat wave	Severe drought and heat over south-central and south- eastern states cause significant agricultural losses	Spring-summer 2000	over 4.0	140
Western fire season	Severe fire season in western states due to drought and frequent winds	Spring-summer 2000	over 2.0	5
Hurricane Floyd	Category 2 hurricane in NC, causing severe flooding in NC and some flooding in SC, VA, MD, PA, NY, DE, RI, CT, MA, and VT	Sept. 1999	6.0	75
Drought/heat wave	Drought/heatwave over eastern U.S.	Summer 1999	1.0	256
Oklahoma-Kansas tornadoes	Category F4-F5 tornados hit OK, KS, TX, and TN	May 1999	1.0	55
Arkansas-Tennessee tornados	Two outbreaks of tornadoes in 6-day period	January 1999	1.3	31
Texas flooding	Severe flooding in southeast Texas from 2 heavy rain events with 10-20 in. totals	Oct.-Nov. 1998	1.0	31
Hurricane Georges	Category 2 hurricane in Puerto Rico, Florida Keys, and Gulf coasts of LA, MS, AL, and FL	Sept. 1998	3-4	16
Hurricane Bonnie	Category 3 hurricane in eastern NC and VA	August 1998	1.0	2
Southern drought/heat wave	Severe drought and heat wave from TX/OK eastward to the Carolinas	Summer 1998	6.0	200
Minnesota severe storms/hail	Very damaging severe thunderstorms with large hail over wide areas of Minnesota	May 1998	1.5	1
Southeast severe weather	Tornadoes and flooding related to strong El Nino in the southeast	Winter/spring 1998	1.0	Over 130
Northeast ice storm	Intense ice storm hits ME, NH, VT, and NY	January 1998	1.4	16
Northern plains flooding	Severe flooding in Dakotas and Minnesota due to heavy spring snowmelt	April-May 1997	2.0	11
MS and OH valleys flooding and tornadoes	Tornadoes and severe flooding hit the states of AR, MO, MS, TN, IL, IN, KY, OH, and WV	March 1997	1.0	67
West Coast flooding	Flooding from rains and snowmelt in CA, WA, OR, ID, NV, & MT	Dec. 1996-Jan. 1999	2-3	36
Hurricane Fran	Category 3 hurricane in NC and VA	Sept. 1996	5.0	37
Southern Plains severe drought	Drought in agricultural areas of TX & OK	Fall 1995- summer 1996	Over 4	(NA)
Pacific Northwest severe flooding	Flooding from heavy rain & snowmelt in OR, WA, ID, and MT.	Feb. 1996	1.0	9
Blizzard of '96 followed by flooding	Heavy snowstorm followed by severe flooding in Appalachians, Mid-Atlantic, and Northeast	Jan. 1996	3.0	187
Hurricane Opal	Category 3 hurricane in FL, AL, parts of GA, TN, & Carolinas.	Oct. 1995	Over 3	27
Hurricane Marilyn	Category 2 hurricane in Virgin Islands	Sept. 1995	2.1	13
TX/OK/LA/MS severe weather and flooding	Flooding, hail, & tornadoes across TX, OK, parts of LA, MS, Dallas & New Orleans hardest hit	May 1995	5-6	32
California flooding	Flooding from frequent winter storms across much of CA	Jan.-Mar. 1995	3.0	27
Western Fire Season	Severe fire season in western states due to dry weather.	Summer-fall 1994	1.0	(NA)
Texas flooding	Flooding from torrential rain & thunderstorms across south- east TX	Oct. 1994	1.0	19
Tropical Storm Alberto	Flooding due to 10 to 25 inch rain across GA, AL, part of FL.	July 1994	1.0	32
Southeast ice storm	Intense ice storm in pts of TX, OK, AR, LA, MS, AL, TN, GA, SC, NC, & VA	Feb. 1994	3.0	9
California wildfires	Out-of-control wildfires over southern CA	Fall 1993	1.0	4
Midwest flooding	Extreme flooding across central U.S.	Summer 1993	15-20	48
Drought/heat wave	Extreme drought/heatwave across southeastern U.S.	Summer 1993	1.0	(NA)
Storm/blizzard	"Storm of the Century" hits entire eastern seaboard	Mar. 1993	3-6	270
Nor'easter of 1992	Slow-moving storm batters northeast U.S. coast, New England hardest hit	Dec. 1992	1-2	19
Hurricane Iniki	Category 4 hurricane hit Hawaiian island of Kauai	Sept. 1992	1.8	7
Hurricane Andrew	Category 4 hurricane hit FL & LA	Aug. 1992	27.0	58
Oakland Firestorm	Oakland, CA firestorm due to low humidity & high winds.	Oct. 1991	1.5	25
Hurricane Bob	Category 2 hurricane—mainly coastal NC, Long Island, & New England.	Aug. 1991	1.5	18
TX/OK/LA/AR Flooding	Torrential rains cause flooding along Trinity, Red, and Arkansas rivers	May 1990	1.0	13
Hurricane Hugo	Category 4 hurricane hit Puerto Rico & Virgin Islands, devastated NC & SC	Sept. 1989	Over 9	86
Drought/Heat Wave	Drought/heatwave over central & eastern U.S.	Summer 1988	40.0	5,000- 10,000
Hurricane Juan	Category 1 hurricane, flooding most severe problem, hit LA and southeast U.S.	Oct.-Nov. 1985	1.5	63
Hurricane Elena	Category 3 hurricane across FL to LA	Aug.-Sept. 1985	1.3	4
Florida Freeze	Severe freeze central/northern FL, damage to citrus indus- try.	Jan. 1985	1.2	-
Florida Freeze	Severe freeze central/northern FL, damage to citrus indus- try.	Dec. 1983	2.0	-
Hurricane Alicia	Category 3 hurricane across TX	Aug. 1983	3.0	21
Drought/heat wave	Drought/heatwave over central & eastern U.S.	June-Sept. 1980	20.0	10,000

- Represents zero.   NA Not available or not reported.

Source: U.S. National Oceanic and Atmospheric Administration, National Climatic Data Center. *"Billion Dollar U.S. Weather Disasters, 1980-2000"* (release date: May 14, 2001) <http://www.ncdc.noaa.gov/ol/reports/billionz.html>.

222   Geography and Environment

No. 370. Highest and Lowest Temperatures by State Through 1999

State	Highest temperatures			Lowest temperatures		
	Station	Temperature (F)	Date	Station	Temperature (F)	Date
U.S.	**Greenland Ranch, CA**	**134**	**Jul. 10, 1913**	**Prospect Creek, AK**	**-80**	**Jan. 23, 1971**
AL	Centerville	112	Sep. 5, 1925	New Market	-27	Jan. 30, 1966
AK	Fort Yukon	100	[1]Jun. 27, 1915	Prospect Creek Camp	-80	Jan. 23, 1971
AZ	Lake Havasu City	128	Jun. 29, 1994	Hawley Lake	-40	Jan. 7, 1971
AR	Ozark	120	Aug. 10, 1936	Pond	-29	Feb. 13, 1905
CA	Greenland Ranch	134	Jul. 10, 1913	Boca	-45	Jan. 20, 1937
CO	Bennett	118	Jul. 11, 1888	Maybell	-61	Feb. 1, 1985
CT	Danbury	106	Jul. 15, 1995	Falls Village	-32	Feb. 16, 1943
DE	Millsboro	110	Jul. 21, 1930	Millsboro	-17	Jan. 17, 1893
FL	Monticello	109	Jun. 29, 1931	Tallahassee	-2	Feb. 13, 1899
GA	Greenville	112	Aug. 20, 1983	CCC Camp F-16	-17	[1]Jan. 27, 1940
HI	Pahala	100	Apr. 27, 1931	Mauna Kea Obs. 111.2	12	May 17, 1979
ID	Orofino	118	Jul. 28, 1934	Island Park Dam	-60	Jan. 18, 1943
IL	East St. Louis	117	Jul. 14, 1954	Congerville	-36	Jan. 5, 1999
IN	Collegeville	116	Jul. 14, 1936	New Whiteland	-36	Jan. 19, 1994
IA	Keokuk	118	Jul. 20, 1934	Elkader	-47	[2]Feb. 3, 1996
KS	Alton (near)	121	[2]Jul. 24, 1936	Lebanon	-40	Feb. 13, 1905
KY	Greensburg	114	Jul. 28, 1930	Shelbyville	-37	Jan. 19, 1994
LA	Plain Dealing	114	Aug. 10, 1936	Minden	-16	Feb. 13, 1899
ME	North Bridgton	105	[2]Jul. 10, 1911	Van Buren	-48	Jan. 19, 1925
MD	Cumberland & Frederick	109	[2]Jul. 10, 1936	Oakland	-40	Jan. 13, 1912
MA	New Bedford & Chester	107	Aug. 2, 1975	Chester	-35	Jan. 12, 1981
MI	Mio	112	Jul. 13, 1936	Vanderbilt	-51	Feb. 9, 1934
MN	Moorhead	114	[2]Jul. 6, 1936	Tower	-60	Feb. 2, 1996
MS	Holly Springs	115	Jul. 29, 1930	Corinth	-19	Jan. 30, 1966
MO	Warsaw & Union	118	[2]Jul. 14, 1954	Warsaw	-40	Feb. 13, 1905
MT	Medicine Lake	117	Jul. 5, 1937	Rogers Pass	-70	Jan. 20, 1954
NE	Minden	118	[2]Jul. 24, 1936	Camp Clarke	-47	Feb. 12, 1899
NV	Laughlin	125	Jun. 29, 1994	San Jacinto	-50	Jan. 8, 1937
NH	Nashua	106	Jul. 4, 1911	Mt. Washington	-47	Jan. 29, 1934
NJ	Runyon	110	Jul. 10, 1936	River Vale	-34	Jan. 5, 1904
NM	Waste Isolat Pilot Plt	122	Jun. 27, 1994	Gavilan	-50	Feb. 1, 1951
NY	Troy	108	Jul. 22, 1926	Old Forge	-52	[2]Feb. 18, 1979
NC	Fayetteville	110	Aug. 21, 1983	Mt. Mitchell	-34	Jan. 21, 1985
ND	Steele	121	Jul. 6, 1936	Parshall	-60	Feb. 15, 1936
OH	Gallipolis (near)	113	[2]Jul. 21, 1934	Milligan	-39	Feb. 10, 1899
OK	Tipton	120	[2]Jun. 27, 1994	Watts	-27	Jan. 18, 1930
OR	Pendleton	119	Aug. 10, 1898	Seneca	-54	[2]Feb. 10, 1933
PA	Phoenixville	111	[2]Jul. 10, 1936	Smethport	-42	[1]Jan. 5, 1904
RI	Providence	104	Aug. 2, 1975	Kingston	-23	Jan. 11, 1942
SC	Camden	111	[2]Jun. 28, 1954	Caesars Head	-19	Jan. 21, 1985
SD	Gannvalley	120	Jul. 5, 1936	McIntosh	-58	Feb. 17, 1936
TN	Perryville	113	[2]Aug. 9, 1930	Mountain City	-32	Dec. 30, 1917
TX	Seymour	120	Aug. 12, 1936	Seminole	-23	[2]Feb. 8, 1933
UT	Saint George	117	Jul. 5, 1985	Peter's Sink	-69	Feb. 1, 1985
VT	Vernon	105	Jul. 4, 1911	Bloomfield	-50	Dec. 30, 1933
VA	Balcony Falls	110	Jul. 15, 1954	Mtn. Lake Bio. Stn.	-30	Jan. 22, 1985
WA	Ice Harbor Dam	118	[2]Aug. 5, 1961	Mazama & Winthrop	-48	Dec. 30, 1968
WV	Martinsburg	112	[2]Jul. 10, 1936	Lewisburg	-37	Dec. 30, 1917
WI	Wisconsin Dells	114	Jul. 13, 1936	Couderay	-55	Feb. 4, 1996
WY	Basin	114	Jul. 12, 1900	Riverside R.S.	-66	Feb. 9, 1933

[1] Estimated.   [2] Also on earlier dates at the same or other places.

Source: U.S. National Oceanic and Atmospheric Administration, <http://www.ncdc.noaa.gov/ol/climate/severeweather/temperatures.html> (released 03 March 2000).

Geography and Environment   223

No. 371. Normal Daily Mean, Maximum, and Minimum Temperatures— Selected Cities

[In Fahrenheit degrees. Airport data except as noted. Based on standard 30-year period, 1961 through 1990]

State	Station	Daily mean temperature			Daily maximum temperature			Daily minimum temperature		
		Jan.	July	Annual average	Jan.	July	Annual average	Jan.	July	Annual average
AL	Mobile	49.9	82.3	67.5	59.7	91.3	77.4	40.0	73.2	57.4
AK	Juneau	24.2	56.0	40.6	29.4	63.9	46.9	19.0	48.1	34.1
AZ	Phoenix	53.6	93.5	72.6	65.9	105.9	85.9	41.2	81.0	59.3
AR	Little Rock	39.1	81.9	61.8	49.0	92.4	72.5	29.1	71.5	51.0
CA	Los Angeles	56.8	69.1	63.0	65.7	75.3	70.4	47.8	62.8	55.5
	Sacramento	45.2	75.7	60.8	52.7	93.2	73.5	37.7	58.1	48.1
	San Diego	57.4	71.0	64.2	65.9	76.2	70.8	48.9	65.7	57.6
	San Francisco	48.7	62.7	57.1	55.6	71.6	65.2	41.8	53.9	49.0
CO	Denver	29.7	73.5	50.3	43.2	88.2	64.2	16.1	58.6	36.2
CT	Hartford	24.6	73.7	49.9	33.2	85.0	60.2	15.8	62.2	39.5
DE	Wilmington	30.6	76.4	54.2	38.7	85.6	63.6	22.4	67.1	44.8
DC	Washington	34.6	80.0	58.0	42.3	88.5	66.9	26.8	71.4	49.2
FL	Jacksonville	52.4	81.6	68.0	64.2	91.4	78.9	40.5	71.9	57.1
	Miami	67.2	82.6	75.9	75.2	89.0	82.8	59.2	76.2	69.0
GA	Atlanta	41.0	78.8	61.3	50.4	88.0	71.2	31.5	69.5	51.3
HI	Honolulu	72.9	80.5	77.2	80.1	87.5	84.4	65.6	73.5	70.0
ID	Boise	29.0	74.0	50.9	36.4	90.2	62.8	21.6	57.7	39.1
IL	Chicago	21.0	73.2	49.0	29.0	83.7	58.6	12.9	62.6	39.5
	Peoria	21.6	75.5	50.7	29.9	85.7	60.4	13.2	65.4	41.0
IN	Indianapolis	25.5	75.4	52.3	33.7	85.5	62.1	17.2	65.2	42.4
IA	Des Moines	19.4	76.6	49.9	28.1	86.7	59.8	10.7	66.5	40.0
KS	Wichita	29.5	81.4	56.2	39.8	92.8	67.4	19.2	69.9	45.0
KY	Louisville	31.7	77.2	56.1	40.3	87.0	66.0	23.2	67.3	46.0
LA	New Orleans	51.3	81.9	68.1	60.8	90.6	77.6	41.8	73.1	58.5
ME	Portland	20.8	68.6	45.4	30.3	78.8	54.9	11.4	58.3	35.8
MD	Baltimore	31.8	77.0	55.1	40.2	87.2	65.0	23.4	66.8	45.2
MA	Boston	28.6	73.5	51.3	35.7	81.8	59.0	21.6	65.1	43.6
MI	Detroit	22.9	72.3	48.6	30.3	83.3	58.1	15.6	61.3	39.0
	Sault Ste. Marie	12.9	63.8	39.7	21.1	76.3	49.6	4.6	51.3	29.8
MN	Duluth	7.0	66.1	38.5	16.2	77.1	47.9	-2.2	55.1	29.0
	Minneapolis-St. Paul	11.8	73.6	44.9	20.7	84.0	54.3	2.8	63.1	35.3
MS	Jackson	44.1	81.5	64.2	55.6	92.4	76.4	32.7	70.5	52.0
MO	Kansas City	25.7	78.5	53.6	34.7	88.7	63.6	16.7	68.2	43.7
	St. Louis	29.3	79.8	56.1	37.7	89.3	65.4	20.8	70.4	46.7
MT	Great Falls	21.2	68.2	44.8	30.6	83.3	56.4	11.6	53.2	33.1
NE	Omaha	21.1	76.9	50.6	31.3	87.9	61.5	10.9	65.9	39.5
NV	Reno	32.9	71.6	50.8	45.1	91.9	66.8	20.7	51.3	34.7
NH	Concord	18.6	69.5	45.1	29.8	82.4	57.0	7.4	56.5	33.1
NJ	Atlantic City	30.9	74.7	53.0	40.4	84.5	63.2	21.4	64.8	42.8
NM	Albuquerque	34.2	78.5	56.2	46.8	92.5	70.1	21.7	64.4	42.2
NY	Albany	20.6	71.8	47.4	30.2	84.0	58.1	11.0	59.6	36.6
	Buffalo	23.6	71.1	47.7	30.2	80.2	55.8	17.0	61.9	39.5
	New York [1]	31.5	76.8	54.7	37.6	85.2	62.3	25.3	68.4	47.1
NC	Charlotte	39.3	79.3	60.1	49.0	88.9	70.4	29.6	69.6	49.7
	Raleigh	38.9	78.1	59.3	48.9	88.0	70.1	28.8	68.1	48.4
ND	Bismarck	9.2	70.4	41.6	20.2	84.4	53.8	-1.7	56.4	29.4
OH	Cincinnati	28.1	75.1	53.2	36.6	85.5	63.2	19.5	64.8	43.2
	Cleveland	24.8	71.9	49.6	31.9	82.4	58.7	17.6	61.4	40.5
	Columbus	26.4	73.2	51.4	34.1	83.7	61.2	18.5	62.7	41.6
OK	Oklahoma City	35.9	82.0	60.0	46.7	93.4	71.1	25.2	70.6	48.8
OR	Portland	39.6	68.2	53.6	45.4	79.9	62.6	33.7	56.5	44.5
PA	Philadelphia	30.4	76.7	54.3	37.9	86.1	63.4	22.8	67.2	45.1
	Pittsburgh	26.1	72.1	50.3	33.7	82.6	59.9	18.5	61.6	40.7
RI	Providence	27.9	72.7	50.4	36.6	82.1	59.8	19.1	63.2	41.0
SC	Columbia	43.8	80.8	63.1	55.3	91.6	75.1	32.1	70.0	50.9
SD	Sioux Falls	13.8	74.3	45.5	24.3	86.3	56.8	3.3	62.3	34.2
TN	Memphis	39.7	82.6	62.3	48.5	92.3	72.1	30.9	72.9	52.4
	Nashville	36.2	79.3	59.1	45.9	89.5	69.8	26.5	68.9	48.4
TX	Dallas-Fort Worth	43.4	85.3	65.4	54.1	96.5	76.3	32.7	74.1	54.6
	El Paso	42.8	82.3	63.2	56.1	96.1	77.5	29.4	68.4	49.0
	Houston	50.4	82.6	67.9	61.0	92.7	78.6	39.7	72.4	57.3
UT	Salt Lake City	27.9	77.9	52.0	36.4	92.2	63.6	19.3	63.7	40.3
VT	Burlington	16.3	70.5	44.6	25.1	81.2	54.0	7.5	59.7	35.2
VA	Norfolk	39.1	78.2	59.2	47.3	86.4	67.8	30.9	70.0	50.6
	Richmond	35.7	78.0	57.7	45.7	88.4	68.8	25.7	67.5	46.6
WA	Seattle-Tacoma	40.1	65.2	52.0	45.0	75.2	59.4	35.2	55.2	44.6
	Spokane	27.1	68.8	47.3	33.2	83.1	57.5	20.8	54.4	36.9
WV	Charleston	32.1	75.1	55.0	41.2	85.7	65.8	23.0	64.4	44.2
WI	Milwaukee	18.9	70.9	46.1	26.1	79.9	54.3	11.6	62.0	37.9
WY	Cheyenne	26.5	68.4	45.6	37.7	82.2	58.0	15.2	54.6	33.2
PR	San Juan	77.0	82.6	80.2	83.2	88.5	86.4	70.8	76.8	74.0

[1] City office data.

Source: U.S. National Oceanic and Atmospheric Administration, Climatography of the United States, No. 81.

U.S. Census Bureau, Statistical Abstract of the United States: 2001

No. 372. Highest Temperature of Record—Selected Cities

[In Fahrenheit degrees. Airport data, except as noted. For period of record through 1999]

State	Station	Length of record (yr.)	Jan.	Feb.	Mar.	Apr.	May	June	July	Aug.	Sept.	Oct.	Nov.	Dec.	Annual
AL	Mobile.........	58	84	82	90	94	100	102	104	102	99	93	87	81	104
AK	Juneau	55	57	57	61	72	82	86	90	83	73	61	56	54	90
AZ	Phoenix........	62	88	92	100	105	113	122	121	116	118	107	93	88	122
AR	Little Rock	58	83	85	91	95	98	105	112	108	106	97	86	80	112
CA	Los Angeles	64	88	92	95	102	97	104	97	98	110	106	101	94	110
	Sacramento	49	70	76	88	95	105	115	114	110	108	101	87	72	115
	San Diego	59	88	90	93	98	96	101	95	98	111	107	97	88	111
	San Francisco	72	72	78	85	92	97	106	105	100	103	99	85	75	106
CO	Denver	61	73	76	84	90	96	104	104	101	97	89	79	75	104
CT	Hartford........	45	65	73	89	96	99	100	102	101	99	91	81	76	102
DE	Wilmington......	52	75	78	86	94	96	100	102	101	100	91	85	75	102
DC	Washington	58	79	82	89	95	99	101	104	105	101	94	86	79	105
FL	Jacksonville	58	85	88	91	95	100	103	105	102	100	96	88	84	105
	Miami.........	57	88	89	92	96	96	98	98	98	97	95	89	87	98
GA	Atlanta	51	79	80	89	93	95	101	105	102	98	95	84	79	105
HI	Honolulu	30	88	88	88	91	93	92	94	93	95	94	93	89	95
ID	Boise	60	63	71	81	92	98	109	111	110	102	94	78	65	111
IL	Chicago........	41	65	71	88	91	93	104	104	101	99	91	78	71	104
	Peoria	60	70	72	86	92	93	105	103	103	100	90	81	71	105
IN	Indianapolis	60	71	75	85	89	93	102	104	102	100	90	81	74	104
IA	Des Moines	60	65	73	91	93	98	103	105	108	101	95	81	69	108
KS	Wichita	47	75	87	89	96	100	110	113	110	107	95	85	83	113
KY	Louisville	52	77	77	86	91	95	102	106	101	104	92	84	76	106
LA	New Orleans	53	83	85	89	92	96	100	101	102	101	94	87	84	102
ME	Portland	59	64	64	88	85	94	98	99	103	95	88	74	71	103
MD	Baltimore.......	49	75	79	89	94	98	101	104	105	100	92	83	77	105
MA	Boston	48	66	70	89	94	95	100	102	102	100	90	79	76	102
MI	Detroit.........	41	62	70	81	89	93	104	102	100	98	91	77	69	104
	Sault Ste. Marie ...	59	45	49	75	85	89	93	97	98	95	80	67	60	98
MN	Duluth	58	52	55	78	88	90	94	97	97	95	86	71	55	97
	Minneapolis-St. Paul.	61	58	60	83	95	96	102	105	102	98	90	77	68	105
MS	Jackson........	36	82	85	89	94	99	105	106	104	104	95	88	84	106
MO	Kansas City	27	69	77	86	93	95	105	107	109	102	92	82	70	109
	St. Louis	42	76	85	89	93	94	102	107	107	104	94	85	76	107
MT	Great Falls......	62	67	70	78	89	93	101	105	106	98	91	76	69	106
NE	Omaha	63	69	78	89	97	99	105	114	110	104	96	83	72	114
NV	Reno	58	70	75	83	89	96	103	104	105	101	91	77	70	105
NH	Concord	58	68	67	89	95	97	98	102	101	98	90	80	73	102
NJ	Atlantic City	56	78	75	87	94	99	106	104	102	99	90	84	77	106
NM	Albuquerque......	60	69	76	85	89	98	107	105	101	100	91	77	72	107
NY	Albany	53	65	68	89	92	94	99	100	99	100	89	82	71	100
	Buffalo	56	72	70	81	94	90	96	97	99	98	87	80	74	99
	New York [1]......	131	72	75	86	96	99	101	106	104	102	94	84	75	106
NC	Charlotte	60	78	81	90	93	100	103	103	103	104	98	85	78	104
	Raleigh	55	79	84	92	95	97	104	105	105	104	98	88	80	105
ND	Bismarck	60	62	69	81	93	98	107	109	109	105	95	79	65	109
OH	Cincinnati.......	38	69	74	84	89	93	102	103	102	98	88	81	75	103
	Cleveland	58	73	71	83	88	92	104	103	102	101	90	82	77	104
	Columbus	60	74	74	85	89	94	102	100	101	100	90	80	76	102
OK	Oklahoma City	46	80	92	93	100	104	105	110	110	107	96	87	86	110
OR	Portland	59	63	71	80	90	100	100	107	107	105	92	73	65	107
PA	Philadelphia	58	74	74	87	94	97	100	104	101	100	96	81	73	104
	Pittsburgh	47	69	73	82	89	91	98	103	100	97	87	82	74	103
RI	Providence......	46	69	72	85	98	95	97	102	104	100	86	78	77	104
SC	Columbia.......	52	84	84	91	94	101	107	107	107	101	101	90	83	107
SD	Sioux Falls.......	54	66	70	87	94	100	110	108	108	104	94	81	63	110
TN	Memphis	58	78	81	85	94	99	104	108	105	103	95	85	81	108
	Nashville	60	78	84	86	91	97	106	107	104	105	94	84	79	107
TX	Dallas-Fort Worth ..	46	88	95	96	95	103	113	110	108	108	102	89	88	113
	El Paso	60	80	83	89	98	104	114	112	108	104	96	87	80	114
	Houston	30	84	91	91	95	99	103	104	107	102	96	89	85	107
UT	Salt Lake City	71	62	69	78	86	95	104	107	106	100	89	75	69	107
VT	Burlington	56	66	62	84	91	93	100	100	101	94	85	75	67	101
VA	Norfolk	51	78	82	88	97	100	101	103	104	99	95	86	80	104
	Richmond	70	80	83	93	96	100	104	105	102	103	99	86	81	105
WA	Seattle-Tacoma....	55	64	70	75	85	93	96	100	99	98	89	74	64	100
	Spokane	52	59	63	71	90	96	101	103	108	98	86	67	56	108
WV	Charleston	52	79	78	89	94	93	98	104	101	102	92	85	80	104
WI	Milwaukee	59	62	68	82	91	93	101	103	103	98	89	77	64	103
WY	Cheyenne	64	66	71	74	83	90	100	100	96	95	83	75	69	100
PR	San Juan........	45	92	96	96	97	96	97	95	97	97	98	96	94	98

[1] City office data.

Source: U.S. National Oceanic and Atmospheric Administration, *Comparative Climatic Data*, annual.

U.S. Census Bureau, Statistical Abstract of the United States: 2001

No. 373. Lowest Temperature of Record—Selected Cities

[In **Fahrenheit degrees**. Airport data, except as noted. For period of record through 1998]

State	Station	Length of record (yr.)	Jan.	Feb.	Mar.	Apr.	May	June	July	Aug.	Sept.	Oct.	Nov.	Dec.	Annual
AL	Mobile	58	3	11	21	32	43	49	60	59	42	30	22	8	3
AK	Juneau	55	-22	-22	-15	6	25	31	36	27	23	11	-5	-21	-22
AZ	Phoenix	62	17	22	25	32	40	50	61	60	47	34	25	22	17
AR	Little Rock	58	-4	-5	11	28	40	46	54	52	37	29	17	-1	-5
CA	Los Angeles	64	23	32	34	39	43	48	49	51	47	41	34	32	23
	Sacramento	49	23	23	26	31	36	41	48	49	43	36	26	18	18
	San Diego	59	29	36	39	41	48	51	55	57	51	43	38	34	29
	San Francisco	72	24	25	30	31	36	41	43	42	38	34	25	20	20
CO	Denver	61	-25	-30	-11	-2	22	30	43	41	17	3	-8	-25	-30
CT	Hartford	45	-26	-21	-6	9	28	37	44	36	30	17	1	-14	-26
DE	Wilmington	52	-14	-6	2	18	30	41	48	43	36	24	14	-7	-14
DC	Washington	58	-5	4	11	24	34	47	54	49	39	29	16	1	-5
FL	Jacksonville	58	7	19	23	34	45	47	61	63	48	36	21	11	7
	Miami	57	30	32	32	46	53	60	69	68	68	51	39	30	30
GA	Atlanta	51	-8	5	10	26	37	46	53	55	36	28	3	-	-8
HI	Honolulu	30	53	53	55	57	60	65	66	67	66	61	57	54	53
ID	Boise	60	-17	-15	6	19	22	31	35	34	23	11	-3	-25	-25
IL	Chicago	41	-27	-19	-8	7	24	36	40	41	28	17	1	-25	-27
	Peoria	60	-25	-19	-10	14	25	39	47	41	26	19	-2	-23	-25
IN	Indianapolis	60	-27	-21	-7	16	28	37	44	41	28	17	-2	-23	-27
IA	Des Moines	60	-24	-26	-22	9	30	38	47	40	26	14	-4	-22	-26
KS	Wichita	47	-12	-21	-2	15	31	43	51	48	31	18	1	-16	-21
KY	Louisville	52	-22	-19	-1	22	31	42	50	46	33	23	-1	-15	-22
LA	New Orleans	53	14	16	25	32	41	50	60	60	42	35	24	11	11
ME	Portland	59	-26	-39	-21	8	23	33	40	33	23	15	3	-21	-39
MD	Baltimore	49	-7	-3	6	20	32	40	50	45	35	25	13	-	-7
MA	Boston	48	-12	-4	6	16	34	45	50	47	38	28	15	-7	-12
MI	Detroit	41	-21	-15	-4	10	25	36	41	38	29	17	9	-10	-21
	Sault Ste. Marie	59	-36	-35	-24	-2	18	26	36	29	25	16	-10	-31	-36
MN	Duluth	58	-39	-39	-29	-5	17	27	35	32	22	8	-23	-34	-39
	Minneapolis-St. Paul	61	-34	-32	-32	2	18	34	43	39	26	13	-17	-29	-34
MS	Jackson	36	2	10	15	27	38	47	51	55	35	26	17	4	2
MO	Kansas City	27	-17	-19	-10	12	30	42	51	43	31	17	1	-23	-23
	St. Louis	42	-18	-10	-5	22	31	43	51	47	36	23	1	-16	-18
MT	Great Falls	62	-37	-35	-29	-6	15	31	36	30	20	-11	-25	-43	-43
NE	Omaha	63	-23	-21	-16	5	27	38	44	43	25	13	-9	-23	-23
NV	Reno	58	-16	-16	-2	13	18	25	33	24	20	8	1	-16	-16
NH	Concord	58	-33	-37	-16	8	21	30	35	29	21	10	-5	-22	-37
NJ	Atlantic City	56	-10	-11	5	12	25	37	42	40	32	20	10	-7	-11
NM	Albuquerque	60	-17	-5	8	19	28	40	52	50	37	21	-7	-7	-17
NY	Albany	53	-28	-21	-21	10	26	36	40	34	24	16	5	-22	-28
	Buffalo	56	-16	-20	-7	12	26	35	43	38	32	20	9	-10	-20
	New York [1]	131	-6	-15	3	12	32	44	52	50	39	28	5	-13	-15
NC	Charlotte	60	-5	5	4	24	32	45	53	53	39	24	11	2	-5
	Raleigh	55	-9	-	11	23	31	38	48	46	37	19	11	4	-9
ND	Bismarck	60	-44	-43	-31	-12	15	30	35	33	11	-10	-30	-43	-44
OH	Cincinnati	38	-25	-11	-11	15	27	39	47	43	31	16	1	-20	-25
	Cleveland	58	-20	-15	-5	10	25	31	41	38	32	19	3	-15	-20
	Columbus	60	-22	-13	-6	14	25	35	43	39	31	20	5	-17	-22
OK	Oklahoma City	46	-4	-3	3	20	37	47	53	51	36	16	11	-8	-8
OR	Portland	59	-2	-3	19	29	29	39	43	44	34	26	13	6	-3
PA	Philadelphia	58	-7	-4	7	19	28	44	51	44	35	25	15	1	-7
	Pittsburgh	47	-22	-12	-1	14	26	34	42	39	31	16	-1	-12	-22
RI	Providence	46	-13	-7	1	14	29	41	48	40	33	20	6	-10	-13
SC	Columbia	52	-1	5	4	26	34	44	54	53	40	23	12	4	-1
SD	Sioux Falls	54	-36	-31	-23	5	17	33	38	34	22	9	-17	-28	-36
TN	Memphis	58	-4	-11	12	29	38	48	52	48	36	25	9	-13	-13
	Nashville	60	-17	-13	2	23	34	42	51	47	36	26	-1	-10	-17
TX	Dallas-Fort Worth	46	4	7	15	29	41	51	59	56	43	29	20	-1	-1
	El Paso	60	-8	8	14	23	31	46	57	56	41	25	1	5	-8
	Houston	30	12	20	22	31	44	52	62	60	48	29	19	7	7
UT	Salt Lake City	71	-22	-30	2	14	25	35	40	37	27	16	-14	-21	-30
VT	Burlington	56	-30	-30	-20	2	24	33	39	35	25	15	-2	-26	-30
VA	Norfolk	51	-3	8	18	28	36	45	54	49	45	27	20	7	-3
	Richmond	70	-12	-10	11	23	31	40	51	46	35	21	10	-1	-12
WA	Seattle-Tacoma	55	-	1	11	29	28	38	43	44	35	28	6	6	-
	Spokane	52	-22	-24	-7	17	24	33	37	35	24	10	-21	-25	-25
WV	Charleston	52	-16	-12	-	19	26	33	46	41	34	17	6	-12	-16
WI	Milwaukee	59	-26	-26	-10	12	21	33	40	44	28	18	-5	-20	-26
WY	Cheyenne	64	-29	-34	-21	-8	16	25	38	36	8	-1	-16	-28	-34
PR	San Juan	45	61	62	60	64	66	69	69	70	69	67	66	63	60

- Represents zero.   [1] City office data.

Source: U.S. National Oceanic and Atmospheric Administration, *Comparative Climatic Data*, annual.

U.S. Census Bureau, Statistical Abstract of the United States: 2001

No. 374. Normal Monthly and Annual Precipitation—Selected Cities

[In Inches. Airport data, except as noted. Based on standard 30-year period, 1961 through 1990]

State	Station	Jan.	Feb.	Mar.	Apr.	May	June	July	Aug.	Sept.	Oct.	Nov.	Dec.	Annual
AL	Mobile	4.76	5.46	6.41	4.48	5.74	5.04	6.85	6.96	5.91	2.94	4.10	5.31	63.96
AK	Juneau	4.54	3.75	3.28	2.77	3.42	3.15	4.16	5.32	6.73	7.84	4.91	4.44	54.31
AZ	Phoenix	0.67	0.68	0.88	0.22	0.12	0.13	0.83	0.96	0.86	0.65	0.66	1.00	7.66
AR	Little Rock	3.42	3.61	4.91	5.49	5.17	3.57	3.60	3.26	4.05	3.75	5.20	4.83	50.86
CA	Los Angeles	2.40	2.51	1.98	0.72	0.14	0.03	0.01	0.15	0.31	0.34	1.76	1.66	12.01
	Sacramento	3.73	2.87	2.57	1.16	0.27	0.12	0.05	0.07	0.37	1.08	2.72	2.51	17.52
	San Diego	1.80	1.53	1.77	0.79	0.19	0.07	0.02	0.10	0.24	0.37	1.45	1.57	9.90
	San Francisco	4.35	3.17	3.06	1.37	0.19	0.11	0.03	0.05	0.20	1.22	2.86	3.09	19.70
CO	Denver	0.50	0.57	1.28	1.71	2.40	1.79	1.91	1.51	1.24	0.98	0.87	0.64	15.40
CT	Hartford	3.41	3.23	3.63	3.85	4.12	3.75	3.19	3.65	3.79	3.57	4.04	3.91	44.14
DE	Wilmington	3.03	2.91	3.43	3.39	3.84	3.55	4.23	3.40	3.43	2.88	3.27	3.48	40.84
DC	Washington	2.72	2.71	3.17	2.71	3.66	3.38	3.80	3.91	3.31	3.02	3.12	3.12	38.63
FL	Jacksonville	3.31	3.93	3.68	2.77	3.55	5.69	5.60	7.93	7.05	2.90	2.19	2.72	51.32
	Miami	2.01	2.08	2.39	2.85	6.21	9.33	5.70	7.58	7.63	5.64	2.66	1.83	55.91
GA	Atlanta	4.75	4.81	5.77	4.26	4.29	3.56	5.01	3.66	3.42	3.05	3.86	4.33	50.77
HI	Honolulu	3.55	2.21	2.20	1.54	1.13	0.50	0.59	0.44	0.78	2.28	3.00	3.80	22.02
ID	Boise	1.45	1.07	1.29	1.24	1.08	0.81	0.35	0.43	0.80	0.75	1.48	1.36	12.11
IL	Chicago	1.53	1.36	2.69	3.64	3.32	3.78	3.66	4.22	3.82	2.41	2.92	2.47	35.82
	Peoria	1.51	1.42	2.91	3.77	3.70	3.99	4.20	3.10	3.87	2.65	2.69	2.44	36.25
IN	Indianapolis	2.32	2.46	3.79	3.70	4.00	3.49	4.47	3.64	2.87	2.63	3.23	3.34	39.94
IA	Des Moines	0.96	1.11	2.33	3.36	3.66	4.46	3.78	4.20	3.53	2.62	1.79	1.32	33.12
KS	Wichita	0.79	0.96	2.43	2.38	3.81	4.31	3.13	3.02	3.49	2.22	1.59	1.20	29.33
KY	Louisville	2.86	3.30	4.66	4.23	4.62	3.46	4.51	3.54	3.16	2.71	3.70	3.64	44.39
LA	New Orleans	5.05	6.01	4.90	4.50	4.56	5.84	6.12	6.17	5.51	3.05	4.42	5.75	61.88
ME	Portland	3.53	3.33	3.67	4.08	3.62	3.44	3.09	2.87	3.09	3.90	5.17	4.55	44.34
MD	Baltimore	3.05	3.12	3.38	3.09	3.72	3.67	3.69	3.92	3.41	2.98	3.32	3.41	40.76
MA	Boston	3.59	3.62	3.69	3.60	3.25	3.09	2.84	3.24	3.06	3.30	4.22	4.01	41.51
MI	Detroit	1.76	1.74	2.55	2.95	2.92	3.61	3.18	3.43	2.89	2.10	2.67	2.82	32.62
	Sault Ste. Marie	2.42	1.74	2.30	2.35	2.71	3.14	2.71	3.61	3.69	3.23	3.45	2.88	34.23
MN	Duluth	1.22	0.80	1.91	2.25	3.03	3.82	3.61	3.99	3.84	2.49	1.80	1.24	30.00
	Minneapolis-St. Paul.	0.95	0.88	1.94	2.42	3.39	4.05	3.53	3.62	2.72	2.19	1.55	1.08	28.32
MS	Jackson	5.24	4.70	5.82	5.57	5.05	3.18	4.51	3.77	3.55	3.26	4.81	5.91	55.37
MO	Kansas City	1.09	1.10	2.51	3.12	5.04	4.72	4.38	4.01	4.86	3.29	1.92	1.58	37.62
	St. Louis	1.81	2.12	3.58	3.50	3.97	3.72	3.85	2.85	3.12	2.68	3.28	3.03	37.51
MT	Great Falls	0.91	0.57	1.10	1.41	2.52	2.39	1.24	1.54	1.24	0.78	0.66	0.85	15.21
NE	Omaha	0.74	0.77	2.04	2.66	4.52	3.87	3.51	3.24	3.72	2.28	1.49	1.02	29.86
NV	Reno	1.07	0.99	0.71	0.38	0.69	0.46	0.28	0.32	0.39	0.38	0.87	0.99	7.53
NH	Concord	2.51	2.53	2.72	2.91	3.14	3.15	3.23	3.32	2.81	3.23	3.66	3.16	36.37
NJ	Atlantic City	3.46	3.06	3.62	3.56	3.33	2.64	3.83	4.14	2.93	2.82	3.58	3.32	40.29
NM	Albuquerque	0.44	0.46	0.54	0.52	0.50	0.59	1.37	1.64	1.00	0.89	0.43	0.50	8.88
NY	Albany	2.36	2.27	2.93	2.99	3.41	3.62	3.18	3.47	2.95	2.83	3.23	2.93	36.17
	Buffalo	2.70	2.31	2.68	2.87	3.14	3.55	3.08	4.17	3.49	3.09	3.83	3.67	38.58
	New York [1]	3.42	3.27	4.08	4.20	4.42	3.67	4.35	4.01	3.89	3.56	4.47	3.91	47.25
NC	Charlotte	3.71	3.84	4.43	2.68	3.82	3.39	3.92	3.73	3.50	3.36	3.23	3.48	43.09
	Raleigh	3.48	3.69	3.77	2.59	3.92	3.68	4.01	4.02	3.19	2.86	2.98	3.24	41.43
ND	Bismarck	0.45	0.43	0.77	1.67	2.18	2.72	2.14	1.72	1.49	0.90	0.49	0.51	15.47
OH	Cincinnati	2.59	2.69	4.24	3.75	4.28	3.84	4.24	3.35	2.88	2.86	3.46	3.15	41.33
	Cleveland	2.04	2.19	2.91	3.14	3.49	3.70	3.52	3.40	3.44	2.54	3.17	3.09	36.63
	Columbus	2.18	2.24	3.27	3.21	3.93	4.04	4.31	3.72	2.96	2.15	1.98	2.86	38.09
OK	Oklahoma City	1.13	1.56	2.71	2.77	5.22	4.31	2.61	2.60	3.84	3.23	1.98	1.40	33.36
OR	Portland	5.35	3.85	3.56	2.39	2.06	1.48	0.63	1.09	1.75	2.67	5.34	6.13	36.30
PA	Philadelphia	3.21	2.79	3.46	3.62	3.75	3.74	4.28	3.80	3.42	2.62	3.34	3.38	41.41
	Pittsburgh	2.54	2.39	3.41	3.15	3.59	3.71	3.75	3.21	2.97	2.36	2.85	2.92	36.85
RI	Providence	3.88	3.61	4.05	4.11	3.76	3.33	3.18	3.63	3.48	3.69	4.43	4.38	45.53
SC	Columbia	4.42	4.12	4.82	3.28	3.68	4.80	5.50	6.09	3.67	3.04	2.90	3.59	49.91
SD	Sioux Falls	0.51	0.64	1.64	2.52	3.03	3.40	2.68	2.85	3.02	1.78	1.09	0.70	23.86
TN	Memphis	3.73	4.35	5.41	5.46	4.93	3.57	3.79	3.43	3.53	3.01	5.10	5.74	52.10
	Nashville	3.58	3.81	4.85	4.37	4.88	3.57	3.97	3.46	3.46	2.62	4.12	4.61	47.30
TX	Dallas-Fort Worth	1.83	2.18	2.77	3.50	4.88	2.98	2.31	2.21	3.39	3.52	2.29	1.84	33.70
	El Paso	0.40	0.41	0.29	0.20	0.25	0.67	1.54	1.58	1.70	0.76	0.44	0.57	8.81
	Houston	3.29	2.96	2.92	3.21	5.24	4.96	3.60	3.49	4.89	4.27	3.79	3.45	46.07
UT	Salt Lake City	1.11	1.23	1.91	2.12	1.80	0.93	0.81	0.86	1.28	1.44	1.29	1.40	16.18
VT	Burlington	1.82	1.63	2.23	2.76	3.12	3.47	3.65	4.06	3.30	2.88	3.13	2.42	34.47
VA	Norfolk	3.78	3.47	3.70	3.06	3.81	3.82	5.06	4.40	3.34	3.53	3.17	3.26	43.16
	Richmond	3.24	3.16	3.61	2.96	3.84	3.62	5.03	4.40	1.88	3.23	5.83	5.91	37.19
WA	Seattle-Tacoma	5.38	3.99	3.54	2.33	1.70	1.50	0.76	1.14	1.88	3.23	2.15	2.42	16.49
	Spokane	1.98	1.49	1.49	1.18	1.41	1.26	0.67	0.72	0.73	0.99	2.15	2.42	16.49
WV	Charleston	2.91	3.04	3.63	3.31	3.94	3.59	4.99	4.01	3.24	2.89	3.59	3.39	42.53
WI	Milwaukee	1.60	1.45	2.67	3.50	2.84	3.24	3.47	3.53	3.38	2.41	2.51	2.33	32.93
WY	Cheyenne	0.40	0.39	1.03	1.37	2.39	2.08	2.09	1.69	1.27	0.74	0.53	0.42	14.40
PR	San Juan	2.81	2.15	2.35	3.76	5.93	4.00	4.37	5.32	5.28	5.71	5.94	4.72	52.34

[1] City office data.

Source: U.S. National Oceanic and Atmospheric Administration, *Climatography of the United States*, No. 81.

[Airport data, except as noted. For period of record through 1999]

State	Station	Length of record (yr.)	Jan.	Feb.	Mar.	Apr.	May	June	July	Aug.	Sept.	Oct.	Nov.	Dec.	Annual
AL	Mobile	58	11	10	10	8	9	11	16	14	10	6	8	10	122
AK	Juneau	55	18	17	18	17	17	15	17	18	21	24	20	21	223
AZ	Phoenix	60	4	4	4	2	1	1	4	5	3	3	3	4	36
AR	Little Rock	57	10	9	10	10	10	8	8	7	7	7	8	9	104
CA	Los Angeles	64	6	6	6	3	1	1	1	(Z)	1	2	3	5	35
	Sacramento	60	10	9	9	5	3	1	(Z)	(Z)	1	3	7	9	58
	San Diego	59	7	6	7	4	2	1	(Z)	-	1	2	4	6	42
	San Francisco	72	11	10	10	6	3	1	(Z)	(Z)	1	4	7	10	63
CO	Denver	61	6	6	9	9	11	9	9	9	6	5	6	5	89
CT	Hartford	45	11	10	12	11	12	11	10	10	10	9	11	12	127
DE	Wilmington	52	11	10	11	11	11	10	9	9	8	8	9	10	116
DC	Washington	58	10	9	11	10	11	9	10	9	8	7	8	9	113
FL	Jacksonville	58	8	8	8	6	8	13	14	15	13	9	7	8	116
	Miami	57	7	6	6	6	10	15	16	18	17	14	8	7	131
GA	Atlanta	65	12	10	11	9	9	10	12	9	8	7	8	10	115
HI	Honolulu	50	9	9	9	9	7	6	7	6	7	9	9	10	97
ID	Boise	60	12	10	10	8	8	6	2	3	4	6	10	11	90
IL	Chicago	41	11	9	12	13	11	10	10	9	9	9	11	11	125
	Peoria	60	9	8	11	12	12	10	9	8	9	8	9	10	114
IN	Indianapolis	60	12	10	13	12	12	10	9	9	8	8	10	12	126
IA	Des Moines	60	8	7	10	11	11	11	9	9	9	7	7	8	108
KS	Wichita	46	5	5	8	8	11	9	8	8	8	6	5	6	86
KY	Louisville	52	11	11	13	12	12	10	10	8	8	7	10	11	124
LA	New Orleans	51	10	9	9	7	8	11	14	13	10	6	7	10	114
ME	Portland	59	11	10	11	12	12	11	10	9	9	9	12	11	129
MD	Baltimore	49	11	9	11	11	11	9	9	9	8	8	9	10	114
MA	Boston	48	12	10	12	11	12	10	9	10	9	9	11	12	127
MI	Detroit	41	13	11	13	13	11	10	10	9	10	9	12	13	135
	Sault Ste. Marie	58	19	14	13	11	11	11	10	11	13	14	17	19	165
MN	Duluth	58	12	9	11	10	12	13	12	11	12	10	11	11	134
	Minneapolis-St. Paul	61	9	7	10	10	11	12	10	10	10	8	9	9	115
MS	Jackson	36	11	9	10	8	9	8	11	10	8	6	8	10	109
MO	Kansas City	27	7	7	10	11	12	10	8	9	8	7	8	7	105
	St. Louis	42	9	8	11	11	11	9	9	8	8	8	9	9	111
MT	Great Falls	62	9	8	9	9	12	12	8	8	7	6	7	8	101
NE	Omaha	63	6	7	9	10	12	11	9	9	8	6	6	6	100
NV	Reno	57	6	6	6	4	4	3	2	2	3	3	5	6	51
NH	Concord	58	11	9	11	11	12	11	10	10	9	9	11	11	126
NJ	Atlantic City	56	11	10	11	11	10	9	9	9	8	7	9	10	113
NM	Albuquerque	60	4	4	5	3	4	4	9	10	6	5	3	4	61
NY	Albany	53	13	11	12	12	13	11	10	10	10	9	12	12	135
	Buffalo	56	20	17	16	14	13	11	10	10	11	12	16	19	168
	New York [1]	130	11	10	11	11	11	10	11	10	8	8	9	10	121
NC	Charlotte	60	10	10	11	9	9	10	11	10	7	7	8	10	111
	Raleigh	55	10	10	10	9	10	10	11	10	8	7	8	9	113
ND	Bismarck	60	8	7	8	8	10	11	9	8	7	6	6	8	96
OH	Cincinnati	52	12	11	13	13	12	11	10	9	8	8	11	12	130
	Cleveland	58	16	14	15	15	13	11	10	10	10	11	14	16	155
	Columbus	60	13	12	14	13	13	11	11	9	8	9	11	13	137
OK	Oklahoma City	60	5	6	7	8	10	9	6	6	7	7	5	6	83
OR	Portland	59	18	16	17	15	12	9	4	5	7	12	18	19	153
PA	Philadelphia	59	11	9	11	11	11	10	9	9	8	8	9	10	117
	Pittsburgh	47	16	14	15	14	13	12	11	10	10	10	13	16	152
RI	Providence	46	11	10	12	11	11	11	9	9	9	9	11	12	124
SC	Columbia	52	10	10	10	8	9	10	12	11	8	6	7	9	110
SD	Sioux Falls	54	6	7	9	10	11	11	10	9	8	6	6	6	99
TN	Memphis	49	10	9	11	10	9	9	9	7	7	6	9	10	106
	Nashville	58	11	11	12	11	11	10	10	9	8	7	9	11	119
TX	Dallas-Fort Worth	46	7	7	7	8	9	7	5	5	7	6	6	6	79
	El Paso	60	4	3	2	2	2	3	8	8	6	4	3	4	49
	Houston	30	11	9	9	7	8	9	9	9	9	7	8	9	105
UT	Salt Lake City	71	10	9	10	10	8	5	5	6	5	6	8	9	91
VT	Burlington	56	15	11	13	12	14	12	12	13	12	12	14	15	154
VA	Norfolk	51	11	10	11	10	10	9	11	10	8	8	8	9	116
	Richmond	62	10	9	11	9	11	9	11	9	8	7	8	9	114
WA	Seattle-Tacoma	55	19	16	17	14	11	9	5	6	9	13	18	19	155
	Spokane	52	14	11	11	9	10	8	5	5	6	8	13	15	113
WV	Charleston	52	15	14	15	14	13	12	13	11	9	8	12	14	151
WI	Milwaukee	59	12	10	12	12	12	11	11	9	9	9	10	11	125
WY	Cheyenne	64	6	6	9	10	12	11	11	10	8	6	6	6	101
PR	San Juan	44	17	13	12	13	16	15	19	18	18	17	19	19	197

- Represents zero.   Z Less than 1/2 day.   [1] City office data.

Source: U.S. National Oceanic and Atmospheric Administration, *Comparative Climatic Data*, annual.

228 Geography and Environment

No. 376. Snow and Ice Pellets—Selected Cities

[In inches. Airport data, except as noted. For period of record through 1999. T denotes trace]

State	Station	Length of record (yr)	Jan.	Feb.	Mar.	Apr.	May	June	July	Aug.	Sept.	Oct.	Nov.	Dec.	Annual
AL	Mobile	57	0.1	0.1	0.1	T	T	-	T	-	-	-	T	0.1	0.4
AK	Juneau	55	26.2	19.3	15.1	3.3	T	T	-	-	T	1	12.4	22.3	99.6
AZ	Phoenix	62	T	T	-	T	T	T	-	-	-	-	T	-	T
AR	Little Rock	56	2.4	1.5	0.5	T	T	T	-	-	-	T	0.2	0.6	5.2
CA	Los Angeles	62	T	T	T	-	-	-	-	-	-	-	-	T	T
	Sacramento	50	T	T	T	-	T	-	-	-	-	-	-	T	T
	San Diego	59	T	-	T	T	-	-	-	-	-	-	T	T	T
	San Francisco	69	-	-	T	T	-	-	-	-	-	-	-	-	T
CO	Denver	61	8.1	7.5	12.5	8.9	1.6	-	T	T	1.6	3.7	9.1	7.3	60.3
CT	Hartford	42	13.0	12.0	10.0	1.5	-	T	-	-	-	0.1	2.1	10.3	49.0
DE	Wilmington	49	6.8	6.1	3.3	0.2	T	T	T	-	-	0.1	0.9	3.3	20.7
DC	Washington	56	5.4	5.3	2.3	T	T	T	T	T	-	-	0.8	2.8	16.6
FL	Jacksonville	58	T	-	-	T	-	T	T	-	-	-	-	-	T
	Miami	57	-	-	-	-	T	-	-	-	-	-	-	-	T
GA	Atlanta	62	0.9	0.5	0.4	T	-	-	-	-	-	T	-	0.2	2.0
HI	Honolulu	52	-	-	-	-	-	-	-	-	-	-	-	-	-
ID	Boise	60	6.4	3.7	1.7	0.6	0.1	T	T	T	T	0.1	2.3	5.8	20.7
IL	Chicago	40	11.2	8.0	6.9	1.6	0.1	-	T	-	T	0.4	1.9	.8	38.1
	Peoria	56	6.8	5.3	4.1	0.8	T	-	T	-	T	0.1	2.0	5.9	25.0
IN	Indianapolis	68	6.8	5.6	3.4	0.5	-	T	-	T	-	0.2	1.9	5.1	23.5
IA	Des Moines	57	8.3	7.2	6.0	1.8	-	T	T	-	T	0.3	3.1	6.7	33.4
KS	Wichita	46	4.2	4.1	2.8	0.2	T	T	T	T	T	-	1.3	3.2	15.8
KY	Louisville	52	5.4	4.6	3.3	0.1	T	T	T	T	-	0.1	1.0	2.2	16.7
LA	New Orleans	50	-	0.1	T	T	T	-	-	-	-	-	T	0.1	0.2
ME	Portland	59	19.6	16.7	13.0	2.9	0.2	-	-	-	T	0.2	3.3	14.6	70.5
MD	Baltimore	49	6.2	6.7	3.9	0.1	T	-	T	-	-	-	1	3.1	21.0
MA	Boston	62	12.9	11.7	8.1	0.9	-	-	-	T	-	-	1.3	7.5	42.4
MI	Detroit	41	10.7	9.2	7.0	1.7	T	-	T	-	T	0.2	2.8	9.6	41.2
	Sault Ste. Marie	56	29.0	18.4	14.7	5.8	0.5	T	T	T	0.1	2.4	15.6	31.0	117.5
MN	Duluth	56	17.9	11.5	13.7	6.7	0.7	T	T	T	0.1	1.5	12.9	15.4	80.4
	Minneapolis-St. Paul	61	10.6	8.1	10.7	2.8	0.1	T	T	T	T	0.5	7.8	9.4	50.0
MS	Jackson	36	0.5	0.2	0.2	-	-	-	-	-	-	-	-	0.1	1.0
MO	Kansas City	65	5.7	4.4	3.4	0.8	T	T	T	-	T	0.1	1.2	4.4	20.0
	St. Louis	63	5.5	4.4	3.9	0.5	-	T	T	-	-	T	1.4	3.7	19.4
MT	Great Falls	62	9.6	8.3	10.6	7.2	1.7	0.3	T	0.1	1.5	3.4	7.4	8.1	58.2
NE	Omaha	64	7.3	6.7	6.3	1.0	0.1	T	-	-	T	0.3	2.6	5.6	29.9
NV	Reno	54	5.8	5.2	4.3	1.2	0.8	-	-	-	-	0.3	2.4	4.3	24.3
NH	Concord	58	18.0	14.2	11.2	2.5	0.1	T	-	-	T	0.1	4.0	13.7	63.8
NJ	Atlantic City	51	5.0	5.3	2.5	0.3	T	T	T	-	-	T	0.4	2.2	15.7
NM	Albuquerque	60	2.5	2.1	1.8	0.6	T	T	T	T	T	0.1	1.2	2.6	10.9
NY	Albany	53	16.5	13.9	11.5	2.5	0.1	T	T	-	T	0.2	4.2	14.3	63.2
	Buffalo	56	24.4	17.8	12.0	3.2	0.2	T	T	T	T	0.3	11.0	22.6	91.5
	New York [1]	131	7.5	8.5	5.1	0.9	T	-	T	-	-	-	0.9	5.4	28.3
NC	Charlotte	60	2.0	1.6	1.2	T	T	T	-	-	-	T	0.1	0.5	5.4
	Raleigh	55	2.3	2.5	1.3	-	T	T	T	-	-	-	0.1	0.8	7.0
ND	Bismarck	60	7.8	7.0	8.5	4.1	0.9	T	T	T	T	0.2	1.8	7.0	44.3
OH	Cincinnati	52	7.2	5.7	4.6	0.5	-	T	T	-	-	0.3	2	3.7	24.0
	Cleveland	58	13.4	12.0	10.5	2.4	0.1	T	T	-	T	0.6	5.2	11.8	56.0
	Columbus	52	8.9	6.1	4.7	0.9	-	T	T	-	T	0.1	2.2	5.3	28.2
OK	Oklahoma City	60	3.1	2.4	1.5	T	T	T	T	-	T	-	0.5	1.8	9.3
OR	Portland	55	3.2	1.1	0.4	T	-	T	-	-	-	-	0.7	3.2	6.5
PA	Philadelphia	57	6.0	6.5	3.6	0.3	T	-	T	-	-	-	0.4	3.5	20.3
	Pittsburgh	47	11.8	9.1	8.8	1.7	0.1	T	T	T	T	0.4	3.5	8.1	43.5
RI	Providence	46	9.8	9.9	7.4	0.7	0.2	-	-	-	-	0.1	1.1	6.8	36.0
SC	Columbia	52	0.4	0.8	0.2	T	-	-	-	T	-	-	T	0.3	1.7
SD	Sioux Falls	54	6.9	8.2	9.4	2.8	T	T	T	-	T	0.8	5.8	7.1	41.0
TN	Memphis	49	2.2	1.4	0.8	T	T	T	-	-	-	T	0.1	0.6	5.1
	Nashville	57	3.7	3.0	1.5	-	T	-	T	-	T	-	0.4	1.4	10.0
TX	Dallas-Fort Worth	43	1.1	0.9	0.2	T	T	-	-	-	-	T	0.1	0.2	2.5
	El Paso	57	1.3	0.8	0.4	0.3	T	T	T	-	T	-	0.9	1.6	5.3
	Houston	65	0.2	0.2	T	T	T	T	T	-	-	-	T	T	0.4
UT	Salt Lake City	71	13.7	10.0	9.3	4.9	0.6	T	T	T	0.1	1.3	6.8	11.8	58.5
VT	Burlington	56	19.4	16.5	13.4	4.1	0.2	-	T	-	-	0.2	6.7	17.7	78.2
VA	Norfolk	49	2.8	3.0	1.0	-	T	T	-	T	-	-	-	0.9	7.7
	Richmond	60	4.8	4.0	2.4	0.1	T	-	-	-	-	T	0.4	2.0	13.7
WA	Seattle-Tacoma	52	4.9	1.6	1.3	0.1	T	-	T	-	-	T	1.1	2.4	11.4
	Spokane	52	15.5	7.6	3.9	0.6	0.1	T	-	-	T	0.4	6.2	14.5	48.8
WV	Charleston	49	11.1	8.7	5.4	0.9	-	T	T	T	-	0.2	2.4	5.3	34.0
WI	Milwaukee	59	14.1	9.5	8.4	1.8	0.1	T	T	T	T	0.2	3.1	10.1	47.3
WY	Cheyenne	64	6.6	6.2	11.8	9.3	3.2	0.2	T	T	0.9	3.7	7.1	6.2	55.2
PR	San Juan	44	-	-	-	-	-	-	-	-	-	T	-	-	T

- Represents zero or rounds to zero.   [1] City office data.

Source: U.S. National Oceanic and Atmospheric Administration, *Comparative Climatic Data*, annual.

U.S. Census Bureau, Statistical Abstract of the United States: 2001

No. 377. Sunshine, Average Wind Speed, Heating and Cooling Degree Days, and Average Relative Humidity—Selected Cities

[Airport data, except as noted. For period of record through 1998, except as noted. M=morning. A=afternoon]

State	Station	Avg % possible sunshine Length of record (yr.)	Annual	Wind Length of record (yr.)	Annual	Jan.	July	Heating degree days	Cooling degree days	Length of record (yr.)	Annual M	Annual A	Jan. M	Jan. A	July M	July A
AL	Mobile	47	60	50	8.8	10.1	6.9	1,702	2,627	36	87	59	82	63	90	62
AK	Juneau	47	23	53	8.3	8.0	7.5	8,897	-	32	79	69	76	73	78	66
AZ	Phoenix	57	81	53	6.2	5.3	7.1	1,350	4,162	38	50	23	65	32	43	20
AR	Little Rock	35	60	56	7.8	8.4	6.7	3,155	2,005	34	83	57	80	62	86	55
CA	Los Angeles	60	72	50	7.5	6.7	7.9	1,458	727	39	79	65	71	61	86	68
	Sacramento	49	73	48	7.9	7.2	8.9	2,749	1,237	12	82	46	90	70	76	29
	San Diego	55	72	58	7.0	6.0	7.5	1,256	984	38	77	63	72	58	82	67
	San Francisco	68	71	71	10.6	7.2	13.6	3,016	145	39	84	62	86	67	86	60
CO	Denver	61	67	47	8.6	8.6	8.3	6,020	679	35	67	40	63	49	68	34
CT	Hartford	41	52	44	8.4	9.0	7.3	6,151	677	39	77	52	72	56	79	51
DE	Wilmington	47	55	50	9.0	9.8	7.8	4,937	1,046	51	78	55	75	60	79	54
DC	Washington	48	55	50	9.4	10.0	8.3	4,047	1,549	38	75	53	70	56	76	53
FL	Jacksonville	47	61	49	7.9	8.1	7.0	1,434	2,551	62	89	56	87	58	89	59
	Miami	46	68	49	9.2	9.5	7.9	200	4,198	34	83	61	84	59	83	63
GA	Atlanta	61	59	60	9.1	10.4	7.7	2,991	1,667	38	82	56	79	60	88	59
HI	Honolulu	47	74	49	11.3	9.4	13.1	-	4,474	29	72	56	81	61	68	51
ID	Boise	56	58	59	8.7	8.0	8.4	5,861	754	59	69	43	80	70	54	22
IL	Chicago	37	52	40	10.4	11.7	8.4	6,536	752	40	80	61	78	69	82	57
	Peoria	52	53	55	9.9	11.0	7.8	6,148	982	39	83	63	80	70	87	61
IN	Indianapolis	64	51	50	9.6	10.9	7.5	5,615	1,014	39	84	62	81	71	87	60
IA	Des Moines	46	55	49	10.7	11.4	8.9	6,497	1,036	37	80	61	77	68	83	59
KS	Wichita	39	62	45	12.2	12.0	11.3	4,791	1,628	45	80	56	79	64	79	50
KY	Louisville	47	53	51	8.3	9.5	6.8	4,514	1,288	38	81	59	77	65	85	58
LA	New Orleans	47	60	50	8.2	9.3	6.1	1,513	2,655	50	88	64	85	67	91	66
ME	Portland	54	55	58	8.7	9.1	7.6	7,378	268	58	79	59	76	61	80	59
MD	Baltimore	45	58	48	8.9	9.6	7.7	4,707	1,137	45	77	54	72	57	80	53
MA	Boston	60	55	41	12.4	13.8	11.0	5,641	678	34	72	58	68	58	74	56
MI	Detroit	37	49	40	10.3	12.0	8.5	6,569	626	40	81	60	80	70	82	54
	Sault Ste. Marie	54	43	57	9.2	9.6	7.8	9,316	131	57	85	67	81	74	89	62
MN	Duluth	47	49	49	11.0	11.6	9.4	9,818	180	37	81	64	77	70	85	60
	Minneapolis-St. Paul	57	54	60	10.5	10.5	9.4	7,981	682	39	79	61	75	68	81	56
MS	Jackson	30	59	35	7.1	8.3	5.5	2,467	2,215	35	91	59	86	65	94	61
MO	Kansas City	23	59	26	10.6	11.2	9.2	5,393	1,288	26	81	61	77	65	85	60
	St. Louis	47	55	49	9.7	10.6	8.0	4,758	1,534	38	82	60	81	67	84	57
MT	Great Falls	57	51	57	12.6	14.9	10.0	7,741	388	37	68	46	67	61	68	31
NE	Omaha	49	59	62	10.5	10.9	8.8	6,300	1,072	34	81	60	79	66	85	60
NV	Reno	53	69	56	6.6	5.6	7.2	5,674	508	35	69	32	79	51	61	19
NH	Concord	54	55	56	6.7	7.3	5.7	7,554	328	33	81	54	76	59	84	51
NJ	Atlantic City	37	56	40	9.9	10.9	8.3	5,169	826	34	82	56	78	59	83	57
NM	Albuquerque	56	76	59	8.9	8.0	8.9	4,425	1,244	38	59	29	68	40	59	27
NY	Albany	57	49	60	8.9	9.8	7.5	6,894	507	33	80	58	76	63	81	55
	Buffalo	52	43	59	11.9	14.0	10.3	6,747	477	38	80	62	79	73	79	55
	New York [2]	42	64	61	9.3	10.7	7.6	4,805	1,096	64	72	56	68	60	75	55
NC	Charlotte	49	59	49	7.4	7.8	6.6	3,341	1,582	38	82	53	78	56	86	56
	Raleigh	47	59	49	7.6	8.4	6.7	3,457	1,417	34	85	54	79	55	89	58
ND	Bismarck	56	55	59	10.2	10.0	9.2	8,968	488	39	81	58	75	70	85	49
OH	Cincinnati	44	49	51	9.0	10.5	7.2	5,248	996	36	82	60	80	69	86	57
	Cleveland	54	45	57	10.5	12.2	8.6	6,201	621	38	80	62	78	70	82	57
	Columbus	46	48	49	8.3	9.8	6.5	5,708	797	39	80	59	77	68	84	56
OK	Oklahoma City	44	64	50	12.3	12.6	10.9	3,659	1,859	33	80	56	78	60	80	51
OR	Portland	47	39	50	7.9	10.0	7.6	4,522	371	58	85	59	85	75	82	45
PA	Philadelphia	55	56	58	9.5	10.3	8.2	4,954	1,101	39	76	55	73	59	79	54
	Pittsburgh	43	44	46	9.0	10.5	7.3	5,968	654	38	79	57	76	66	83	54
RI	Providence	42	55	45	10.4	11.1	9.4	5,884	606	35	75	55	71	57	77	56
SC	Columbia	48	60	50	6.8	7.2	6.3	2,649	1,966	32	87	51	83	55	89	54
SD	Sioux Falls	50	57	50	11.1	10.9	9.8	7,809	744	35	82	62	78	70	84	56
TN	Memphis	43	59	50	8.8	10.0	7.5	3,082	2,118	59	81	58	79	64	84	58
	Nashville	54	57	57	8.0	9.1	6.5	3,729	1,616	33	84	58	80	64	89	58
TX	Dallas-Fort Worth	42	64	45	10.7	11.0	9.8	2,407	2,603	35	82	57	80	61	81	50
	El Paso	53	80	56	8.8	8.3	8.3	2,708	2,094	38	56	27	65	35	61	29
	Houston	26	56	29	7.8	8.2	6.9	1,599	2,700	29	90	61	86	66	93	58
UT	Salt Lake City	69	62	69	8.8	7.5	9.5	5,765	1,047	39	67	43	79	69	52	22
VT	Burlington	52	44	55	9.0	9.8	8.0	7,771	388	33	77	59	73	64	79	53
VA	Norfolk	47	58	50	10.6	11.5	8.9	3,495	1,422	50	78	57	75	59	81	59
	Richmond	50	56	50	7.7	8.1	6.9	3,963	1,348	64	83	53	80	57	85	56
WA	Seattle-Tacoma [3]	51	38	50	8.9	9.6	8.2	4,908	190	39	83	62	81	74	81	49
	Spokane	48	48	51	8.9	8.8	8.6	6,842	398	39	78	52	85	79	65	28
WV	Charleston	47	48	51	5.9	7.1	4.8	4,646	1,031	51	83	56	78	63	90	59
WI	Milwaukee	55	52	58	11.5	12.6	9.7	7,324	479	38	80	65	76	69	82	62
WY	Cheyenne	60	64	41	12.9	15.3	10.4	7,326	285	39	65	45	57	50	70	38
PR	San Juan	40	76	43	8.4	8.4	9.7	-	5,558	43	79	65	82	64	79	67

- Represents zero. [1] Percent of days that are either clear or partly cloudy. Period of record through 1997. [2] Airport data for sunshine. [3] Does not represent airport data.

Source: U.S. National Oceanic and Atmospheric Administration, Comparative Climatic Data, annual.

Elections

This section relates primarily to presidential, congressional, and gubernatorial elections. Also presented are summary tables on congressional legislation; state legislatures; Black, Hispanic, and female officeholders; population of voting age; voter participation; and campaign finances.

Official statistics on federal elections, collected by the Clerk of the House, are published biennially in *Statistics of the Presidential and Congressional Election* and *Statistics of the Congressional Election.* Federal and state elections data appear also in *America Votes,* a biennial volume published by Congressional Quarterly, Inc., Washington, DC. Federal elections data also appear in the U.S. Congress, *Congressional Directory,* and in official state documents. Data on reported registration and voting for social and economic groups are obtained by the U.S. Census Bureau as part of the Current Population Survey (CPS) and are published in *Current Population Reports,* Series P20 (see text, Section 1).

Almost all federal, state, and local governmental units in the United States conduct elections for political offices and other purposes. The conduct of elections is regulated by state laws or, in some cities and counties, by local charter. An exception is that the U.S. Constitution prescribes the basis of representation in Congress and the manner of electing the President and grants to Congress the right to regulate the times, places, and manner of electing federal officers. Amendments to the Constitution have prescribed national criteria for voting eligibility. The 15th Amendment, adopted in 1870, gave all citizens the right to vote regardless of race, color, or previous condition of servitude. The 19th Amendment, adopted in 1919, further extended the right to vote to all citizens regardless of sex. The payment of poll taxes as a prerequisite to voting in federal elections was banned by the 24th Amendment in 1964. In 1971, as a result of the 26th Amendment, eligibility to vote in national elections was extended to all citizens, 18 years old and over.

Presidential election—The Constitution specifies how the President and Vice President are selected. Each state elects, by popular vote, a group of electors equal in number to its total of members of Congress. The 23d Amendment, adopted in 1961, grants the District of Columbia three presidential electors, a number equal to that of the least populous state. Subsequent to the election, the electors meet in their respective states to vote for President and Vice President. Usually, each elector votes for the candidate receiving the most popular votes in his or her state. A majority vote of all electors is necessary to elect the President and Vice President. If no candidate receives a majority, the House of Representatives, with each state having one vote, is empowered to elect the President and Vice President, again, with a majority of votes required.

The 22d Amendment to the Constitution, adopted in 1951, limits presidential tenure to two elective terms of 4 years each or to one elective term for any person who, upon succession to the Presidency, has held the office or acted as President for more than 2 years.

Congressional election—The Constitution provides that Representatives be apportioned among the states according to their population, that a census of population be taken every 10 years as a basis for apportionment, and that each state have at least one Representative. At the time of each apportionment, Congress decides what the total number of Representatives will be. Since 1912, the total has been 435, except during 1960 to 1962 when it increased to 437, adding one Representative each for Alaska and Hawaii. The total reverted to 435 after

U.S. Census Bureau, Statistical Abstract of the United States: 2001

reapportionment following the 1960 census. Members are elected for 2-year terms, all terms covering the same period. The District of Columbia, American Samoa, Guam, and the Virgin Islands each elect one nonvoting Delegate, and Puerto Rico elects a nonvoting Resident Commissioner.

The Senate is composed of 100 members, 2 from each state, who are elected to serve for a term of 6 years. One-third of the Senate is elected every 2 years. Senators were originally chosen by the state legislatures. The 17th Amendment to the Constitution, adopted in 1913, prescribed that Senators be elected by popular vote.

Voter eligibility and participation— The Census Bureau publishes estimates of the population of voting age and the percent casting votes in each state for Presidential and congressional election years. These voting-age estimates include a number of persons who meet the age requirement but are not eligible to vote, (e.g. aliens and some institutionalized˙ persons). In addition, since 1964, voter participation and voter characteristics data have been collected during November of election years as part of the CPS. These survey data include noncitizens in the voting age population estimates but exclude members of the Armed Forces and the institutional population.

Statistical reliability—For a discussion of statistical collection and estimation, sampling procedures, and measures of statistical reliability applicable to Census Bureau data, see Appendix III.

Figure 7.1
Vote Cast for President by Major Political Party
Millions of dollars

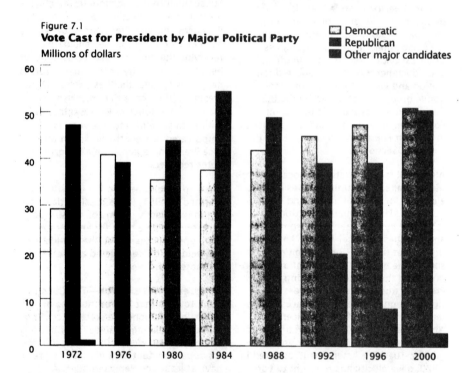

¹ 1972—American, John Schmitz; 1980—Independent, John Anderson; 1992—Independent; Ross Perot, 1996 Reform, Ross Perot. 2000—Green, Ralph Nader.

Source: Chart prepared by U.S. Census Bureau. For data, see Tables 378 and 379.

No. 378. Vote Cast for President by Major Political Party: 1940 to 2000

[Prior to 1960, excludes Alaska and Hawaii; prior to 1964, excludes DC. Vote cast for major party candidates include the votes of minor parties cast for those candidates]

Year	Candidates for President		Vote cast for President						
			Total popular vote[1] (1,000)	Democratic			Republican		
				Popular vote		Electoral vote	Popular vote		Electoral vote
	Democratic	Republican		Number (1,000)	Percent		Number (1,000)	Percent	
1940....	F. D. Roosevelt..	Willkie........	49,900	27,313	54.7	449	22,348	44.8	82
1944....	F. D. Roosevelt..	Dewey........	47,977	25,613	53.4	432	22,018	45.9	99
1948....	Truman.......	Dewey........	48,794	24,179	49.6	303	21,991	45.1	189
1952....	Stevenson.....	Eisenhower....	61,551	27,315	44.4	89	33,936	55.1	442
1956....	Stevenson.....	Eisenhower....	62,027	26,023	42.0	73	35,590	57.4	457
1960....	Kennedy......	Nixon........	68,838	34,227	49.7	303	34,108	49.5	219
1964..:.	Johnson......	Goldwater.....	70,645	43,130	61.1	486	27,178	38.5	52
1968....	Humphrey.....	Nixon........	73,212	31,275	42.7	191	31,785	43.4	301
1972....	McGovern.....	Nixon........	77,719	29,170	37.5	17	47,170	60.7	520
1976....	Carter........	Ford.........	81,556	40,831	50.1	297	39,148	48.0	240
1980....	Carter........	Reagan.......	86,515	35,484	41.0	49	43,904	50.7	489
1984....	Mondale.......	Reagan.......	92.653	37,577	40.6	13	54,455	58.8	525
1988....	Dukakis......	Bush........	91,595	41,809	45.6	111	48,886	53.4	426
1992....	Clinton.......	Bush........	104,425	44,909	43.0	370	39,104	37.4	168
1996....	Clinton.......	Dole.........	96,278	47,402	49.2	379	39,199	40.7	159
2000 ...	Gore.........	Bush........	105,397	50,992	48.4	266	50,455	47.9	271

[1] Include votes for minor party candidates, independents, unpledged electors, and scattered write-in votes.

Source: Congressional Quarterly, Inc., Washington, DC, *America at the Polls 2*, 1965, and *America Votes*, biennial, (copyright).

No. 379. Vote Cast for Leading Minority Party Candidates for President: 1940 to 2000

[See headnote, Table 378]

Year	Candidate	Party	Popular vote (1,000)	Candidate	Party	Popular vote (1,000)
1940 ..	Norman Thomas ...	Socialist..........	116	Roger Babson.....	Prohibition.........	59
1944 ..	Norman Thomas ...	Socialist..........	79	Claude Watson....	Prohibition.........	75
1948 ..	Strom Thurmond ...	States' Rights.......	1,176	Henry Wallace.....	Progressive........	1,157
1952 ..	Vincent Hallinan....	Progressive........	140	Stuart Hamblen....	Prohibition.........	73
1956 ..	T. Coleman Andrews.	States' Rights.......	111	Eric Hass.........	Socialist Labor......	44
1960 ..	Eric Hass........	Socialist Labor......	48	Rutherford Decker..	Prohibition.........	46
1964 ..	Eric Hass........	Socialist Labor......	45	Clifton DeBerry....	Socialist Workers...	33
1968 ..	George Wallace....	American Independent.	9,906	Henning Blomen...	Socialist Labor.....	53
1972 ..	John Schmitz......	American..........	1,099	Benjamin Spock....	People's..........	79
1976 ..	Eugene McCarthy ..	Independent	757	Roger McBride.....	Libertarian........	173
1980 ..	John Anderson	Independent	5,720	Ed Clark.........	Libertarian.........	921
1984 ..	David Bergland	Libertarian........	228	Lyndon H. LaRouche	Independent	79
1988 ..	Ron Paul........	Libertarian........	432	Lenora B. Fulani...	New Alliance.......	217
1992 ..	H. Ross Perot.....	Independent	19,742	Andre Marrou.....	Libertarian.........	292
1996 ..	H. Ross Perot.....	Reform Party	8,085	Ralph Nader......	Green............	685
2000 ..	Ralph Nader......	Green............	2,883	Pat Buchanan.....	Reform...........	449

Source: Congressional Quarterly, Inc. Washington, DC, *America at the Polls 1920-1996*, 1997; and *America Votes*, biennial (copyright).

No. 380. Democratic and Republican Percentages of Two-Party Presidential Vote by Selected Characteristics of Voters: 1992 and 1996

[In percent. Covers citizens of voting age living in private housing units in the contiguous United States. Percentages for Democratic Presidential vote are computed by subtracting the percentage Republican vote from 100 percent; third-party or independent votes are not included as valid data. Data are from the National Election Studies and are based on a sample and subject to sampling variability; for details, see source]

Characteristic	1992		1996		Characteristic	1992		1996	
	Demo- cratic	Repub- lican	Demo- cratic	Repub- lican		Demo- cratic	Repub- lican	Demo- cratic	Repub- lican
Total [1]	58	42	58	42	Race:				
					White...........	53	47	54	46
Year of birth:					Black...........	94	6	99	1
1959 or later......	58	42	58	42					
1943 to 1958	58	42	58	42	Education:				
1927 to 1942	56	44	56	44	Grade school ...	68	32	82	18
1911 to 1926......	62	38	64	36	High school.......	62	38	60	40
1895 to 1910	58	42	57	43	College	52	48	49	51
Sex:									
Male	55	45	51	50	Union household.....	68	32	75	25
Female	61	39	65	35	Nonunion household ..	57	43	54	46

[1] Includes other characteristics, not shown separately.

Source: Center for Political Studies, University of Michigan, Ann Arbor, MI, unpublished data (copyright).

Elections 233

No. 381. Electoral Vote Cast for President by Major Political Party—States: 1960 to 2000

[D=Democratic, R=Republican. For composition of regions, see map, inside front cover]

State	1960[1]	1964	1968[2]	1972[3]	1976[4]	1980	1984	1988[5]	1992	1996	2000
Democratic	303	486	191	17	297	49	13	111	370	379	266
Republican	219	52	301	520	240	489	525	426	168	159	271
Northeast:											
Democratic	121	126	102	14	86	4	-	53	106	106	102
Republican	12	-	24	108	36	118	113	60	-	-	4
Midwest:											
Democratic	71	149	31	-	58	10	10	29	100	100	68
Republican	82	-	118	145	87	135	127	108	29	29	61
South:											
Democratic	101	121	45	3	149	31	3	8	68	80	15
Republican	50	47	77	165	20	138	174	168	116	104	168
West:											
Democratic	10	90	13	-	4	4	-	21	96	93	81
Republican	75	5	82	102	97	98	111	90	23	26	38
AL	[1]D-5	R-10	([2])	R-9	D-9	R-9	R-9	R-9	R-9	R-9	R-9
AK	R-3	D-3	R-3	R-3	R-3	R-3	R-3	R-3	R-3	R-3	R-3
AZ	R-4	R-5	R-5	R-6	R-6	R-6	R-7	R-7	R-8	D-8	R-8
AR	D-8	D-6	([2])	R-6	D-6	R-6	R-6	R-6	D-6	D-6	R-6
CA	R-32	D-40	R-40	R-45	R-45	R-45	R-47	R-47	D-54	D-54	D-54
CO	R-6	D-6	R-6	R-7	R-7	R-7	R-8	R-8	D-8	R-8	R-8
CT	D-8	D-8	D-8	R-8	R-8	R-8	R-8	R-8	D-8	D-8	D-8
DE	D-3	D-3	R-3	R-3	D-3	R-3	R-3	R-3	D-3	D-3	D-3
DC	(X)	D-3	D-3	D-3	D-3	D-3	D-3	D-3	D-3	D-3	D-2
FL	R-10	D-14	R-14	R-17	D-17	R-17	R-21	R-21	R-25	D-25	R-25
GA	D-12	R-12	([2])	R-12	D-12	D-12	R-12	R-12	D-13	R-13	R-13
HI	D-3	D-4	D-4	R-4	D-4	D-4	R-4	D-4	D-4	D-4	D-4
ID	R-4	D-4	R-4	R-4	R-4	R-4	R-4	R-4	R-4	R-4	R-4
IL	D-27	D-26	R-26	R-26	R-26	R-26	R-24	R-24	D-22	D-22	D-22
IN	R-13	D-13	R-13	R-13	R-13	R-13	R-12	R-12	R-12	R-12	R-12
IA	R-10	D-9	R-9	R-8	R-8	R-8	R-8	D-8	D-7	D-7	D-7
KS	R-8	D-7	R-7	R-7	R-7	R-7	R-7	R-7	R-6	R-6	R-6
KY	R-10	D-9	R-9	R-9	D-9	R-9	R-9	R-9	D-8	D-8	R-8
LA	D-10	R-10	([2])	R-10	D-10	R-10	R-10	R-10	D-9	D-9	R-9
ME	R-5	D-4	D-4	R-4	R-4	R-4	R-4	R-4	D-4	D-4	D-4
MD	D-9	D-10	D-10	R-10	D-10	R-10	R-10	R-10	D-10	D-10	D-10
MA	D-16	D-14	D-14	D-14	D-14	R-14	R-13	D-13	D-12	D-12	D-12
MI	D-20	D-21	D-21	R-21	R-21	R-21	R-20	R-20	D-18	D-18	D-18
MN	D-11	D-10	D-10	R-10	D-10	D-10	D-10	D-10	D-10	D-10	D-10
MS	([1])	R-7	([2])	R-7	D-7	R-7	R-7	R-7	R-7	R-7	R-7
MO	D-13	D-12	R-12	R-12	D-12	R-12	R-11	R-11	D-11	D-11	R-11
MT	R-4	D-4	R-4	R-4	R-4	R-4	R-4	R-4	D-3	R-3	R-3
NE	R-6	D-5	R-5	R-5	R-5	R-5	R-5	R-5	R-5	R-5	R-5
NV	D-3	D-3	R-3	R-3	R-3	R-3	R-4	R-4	D-4	D-4	R-4
NH	R-4	D-4	R-4	R-4	R-4	R-4	R-4	R-4	R-4	D-4	R-4
NJ	D-16	D-17	R-17	R-17	R-17	R-17	R-16	R-16	D-15	D-15	D-15
NM	D-4	D-4	R-4	R-4	R-4	R-4	R-5	R-5	D-5	D-5	D-5
NY	D-45	D-43	D-43	R-41	D-41	R-41	R-36	R-36	D-33	D-33	D-33
NC	D-14	D-13	[2]R-12	R-13	D-13	R-13	R-13	R-13	R-14	R-14	R-14
ND	R-4	D-4	R-4	R-3	R-3	R-3	R-3	R-3	R-3	R-3	R-3
OH	R-25	D-26	R-26	R-25	D-25	R-25	R-23	R-23	D-21	D-21	R-21
OK	[1]R-7	D-8	R-8	R-8	R-8	R-8	R-8	R-8	R-8	R-8	R-8
OR	R-6	D-6	R-6	R-6	R-6	R-6	R-7	D-7	D-7	D-7	D-7
PA	D-32	D-29	D-29	R-27	D-27	R-27	R-25	R-25	D-23	D-23	D-23
RI	D-4	D-4	D-4	R-4	D-4	D-4	R-4	D-4	D-4	D-4	D-4
SC	D-8	R-8	R-8	R-8	D-8	R-8	R-8	R-8	R-8	R-8	R-8
SD	R-4	D-4	R-4	R-4	R-4	R-4	R-3	R-3	R-3	R-3	R-3
TN	R-11	D-11	R-11	R-10	D-10	R-10	R-11	R-11	D-11	D-11	R-11
TX	D-24	D-25	D-25	R-26	D-26	R-26	R-29	R-29	R-32	R-32	R-32
UT	R-4	D-4	R-4	R-4	R-4	R-4	R-5	R-5	R-5	R-5	R-5
VT	R-3	D-3	R-3	R-3	R-3	R-3	R-3	R-3	D-3	D-3	D-3
VA	R-12	D-12	R-12	[3]R-11	R-12	R-12	R-12	R-12	R-13	R-13	R-13
WA	R-9	D-9	D-9	R-9	[4]R-8	R-9	R-10	D-10	D-11	D-11	D-11
WV	D-8	D-7	D-7	R-6	D-6	D-6	R-6	[5]D-5	D-5	D-5	R-5
WI	R-12	D-12	R-12	R-11	D-11	R-11	R-11	D-11	D-11	D-11	D-11
WY	R-3	D-3	R-3	R-3	R-3	R-3	R-3	R-3	R-3	R-3	R-3

- Represents zero. [1] Excludes 15 electoral votes cast for Harry F. Byrd as follows: AL 6, MS 8, and OK 1. [2] Excludes 46 electoral votes cast for American Independent George C. Wallace as follows: AL 10, AR 6, GA 12, LA 10, MS 7, and NC 1. [3] Excludes one electoral vote cast for Libertarian John Hospers in Virginia. [4] Excludes one electoral vote cast for Ronald Reagan in Washington. [5] Excludes one electoral vote cast for Lloyd Bentsen for President in West Virginia.

Source: 1956-72, U.S. Congress, Clerk of the House, *Statistics of the Presidential and Congressional Election*, quadrennial; 1976-96, Congressional Quarterly, Inc., Washington D.C. *America Votes*, biennial (copyright).

234 Elections

Figure 7.2
Presidential Electoral Vote by State: 2000

Democrat

Republican

ME 4

VT 3

NH 4

MA 12

RI 4

CT 8

NY 33

NJ 15

DE 3

MD 10

DC 2

PA 23

VA 13

NC 14

SC 8

FL 25

WV 5

GA 13

OH 21

KY 8

MI 18

TN 11

AL 9

IN 12

MS 7

IL 22

MO 11

AR 6

LA 9

WI 3

MN 10

IA 7

OK 8

TX 32

KS 6

ND 3

SD 3

NE 5

CO 8

NM 5

MT 3

WY 3

UT 5

AZ 8

ID 4

NV 4

WA 11

OR 7

CA 54

AK 3

HI 4

Source: Chart prepared by U.S. Census Bureau, for data see Table 381.

Elections 235

No. 382. Popular Vote Cast for President by Political Party—States: 1996 and 2000

[In thousands 96,278 represents 96,278,000, except percent]

State	1996				2000				
								Percent of total vote	
	Total [1]	Demo-cratic Party	Repub-lican Party	Perot (Reform Party)	Total [1]	Demo-cratic Party	Repub-lican Party	Demo-cratic Party	Repub-lican Party
United States. .	96,278	47,402	39,199	8,085	105,397	50,992	50,455	48.4	47.9
Alabama.	1,534	662	769	92	1,666	693	941	41.6	56.5
Alaska	242	80	123	26	286	79	167	27.7	58.6
Arizona.	1,404	653	622	112	1,532	685	782	44.7	51.0
Arkansas	884	475	325	70	922	423	473	45.9	51.3
California	10,019	5,120	3,828	698	10,966	5,861	4,567	53.4	41.7
Colorado.	1,511	671	692	100	1,741	738	884	42.4	50.8
Connecticut.	1,393	736	483	140	1,460	816	561	55.9	38.4
Delaware	271	140	99	29	328	180	137	55.0	41.9
District of Columbia .	186	158	17	4	202	172	18	85.2	9.0
Florida	5,304	2,547	2,245	484	5,963	2,912	2,913	48.8	48.8
Georgia	2,299	1,054	1,081	146	2,597	1,116	1,420	43.0	54.7
Hawaii	360	205	114	27	368	205	138	55.8	37.5
Idaho.	492	165	257	63	502	139	337	27.6	67.2
Illinois	4,311	2,342	1,587	346	4,742	2,589	2,019	54.6	42.6
Indiana.	2,136	887	1,007	224	2,199	902	1,246	41.0	56.6
Iowa	1,234	620	493	105	1,316	639	634	48.5	48.2
Kansas.	1,074	388	583	93	1,072	399	622	37.2	58.0
Kentucky	1,389	637	623	120	1,544	639	872	41.4	56.5
Louisiana	1,784	928	713	123	1,766	792	928	44.9	52.6
Maine.	606	313	186	86	652	320	287	49.1	44.0
Maryland	1,781	966	682	116	2,020	1,141	814	56.5	40.3
Massachusetts.	2,557	1,572	718	227	2,703	1,616	879	59.8	32.5
Michigan.	3,849	1,990	1,481	337	4,233	2,170	1,953	51.3	46.1
Minnesota.	2,193	1,120	766	258	2,439	1,168	1,110	47.9	45.5
Mississippi	894	394	440	52	994	405	573	40.7	57.6
Missouri	2,158	1,026	890	217	2,360	1,111	1,190	47.1	50.4
Montana.	407	168	180	55	411	137	240	33.4	58.4
Nebraska	677	237	363	71	697	232	434	33.3	62.2
Nevada	464	204	199	44	609	280	302	46.0	49.5
New Hampshire. . . .	499	246	196	48	569	266	274	46.8	48.1
New Jersey.	3,076	1,652	1,103	262	3,187	1,789	1,284	56.1	40.3
New Mexico	556	273	233	32	599	287	286	47.9	47.8
New York	6,316	3,756	1,933	503	6,822	4,108	2,403	60.2	35.2
North Carolina.	2,516	1,108	1,226	168	2,911	1,258	1,631	43.2	56.0
North Dakota.	266	107	125	33	288	95	175	33.1	60.7
Ohio	4,534	2,148	1,860	483	4,702	2,184	2,350	46.4	50.0
Oklahoma.	1,207	488	582	131	1,234	474	744	38.4	60.3
Oregon.	1,378	650	538	121	1,534	720	714	47.0	46.5
Pennsylvania.	4,506	2,216	1,801	431	4,913	2,486	2,281	50.6	46.4
Rhode Island.	390	233	105	44	409	250	131	61.0	31.9
South Carolina.	1,152	506	573	64	1,383	566	786	40.9	56.8
South Dakota	324	139	151	31	316	119	191	37.6	60.3
Tennessee	1,894	909	864	106	2,076	982	1,062	47.3	51.1
Texas.	5,612	2,460	2,736	379	6,408	2,434	3,800	38.0	59.3
Utah	666	222	362	66	771	203	515	26.3	66.8
Vermont	258	138	80	31	294	149	120	50.6	40.7
Virginia.	2,417	1,091	1,138	160	2,739	1,217	1,437	44.4	52.5
Washington.	2,254	1,123	841	201	2,487	1,248	1,109	50.2	44.6
West Virginia.	636	328	234	72	648	295	336	45.6	51.9
Wisconsin.	2,196	1,072	845	227	2,599	1,243	1,237	47.8	47.6
Wyoming	212	78	105	26	218	60	148	27.7	67.8

[1] Includes other parties.

Source: Congressional Quarterly, Inc., Washington, DC, *America Votes*, biennial (copyright).

U.S. Census Bureau, Statistical Abstract of the United States: 2001

No. 383. Vote Cast for United States Senators, 1998 and 2000, and Incumbent Senators, 2000—States

[D=Democrat; R=Republican]

State	1998 Total (1,000)[1]	1998 Percent for leading party	2000 Total (1,000)[1]	2000 Percent for leading party	Incumbent senators and year term expires — Name, party, and year	Incumbent senators and year term expires — Name, party, and year
Alabama	1,293	R-63.2	(X)	(X)	Jeff Sessions (R) 2003	Richard C. Shelby (R) 2005
Alaska	222	R-74.5	(X)	(X)	Frank H. Murkowski (R) 2005	Ted Stevens (R) 2003
Arizona	1,013	R-68.7	1,397	R-79.3	John McCain (R) 2005	Jon Kyl (R) 2007
Arkansas	701	D-55.1	(X)	(X)	Blanche Lincoln (D) 2005	Tim Hutchinson (R) 2003
California	8,315	D-53.1	10,624	D-55.8	Barbara Boxer (D) 2005	Dianne Feinstein (D) 2007
Colorado	1,327	R-62.5	(X)	(X)	Ben N. Campbell (R) 2005	Wayne Allard (R) 2003
Connecticut	964	D-65.1	1,311	D-63.2	Christopher J. Dodd (D) 2005	Joseph I. Lieberman (D) 2007
Delaware	(X)	(X)	327	D-55.5	Joseph R. Biden Jr. (D) 2003	Thomas R. Carper (D) 2007
Florida	3,900	D-62.5	5,857	D-51.0	Bob Graham (D) 2005	Bill Nelson (D) 2007
Georgia	1,754	R-52.4	2,429	D-58.2	Paul Coverdell (R) 2005	Zell Miller (D) 2007
Hawaii	398	D-79.2	346	D-72.7	Daniel K. Akaka (D) 2007	Daniel K. Inouye (D) 2005
Idaho	378	R-69.5	(X)	(X)	Larry E. Craig (R) 2003	Michael D. Crapo (R) 2005
Illinois	3,395	R-50.3	(X)	(X)	Peter Fitzgerald (R) 2005	Richard J. Durbin (D) 2003
Indiana	1,589	D-63.7	2,145	R-66.6	Evan Bayh (D) 2005	Richard G. Lugar (R) 2005
Iowa	948	R-68.4	(X)	(X)	Tom Harkin (D) 2003	Charles E. Grassley (R) 2005
Kansas	727	R-65.3	(X)	(X)	* Sam Brownback (R) 2005	* Pat Roberts (R) 2003
Kentucky	1,145	R-49.7	(X)	(X)	Jim Bunning (R) 2005	Mitch McConnell (R) 2003
Louisiana[2]	969	D-64.0	(X)	(X)	John B. Breaux (D) 2005	Mary Landrieu (D) 2003
Maine	(X)	(X)	635	R-68.9	Susan Collins (R) 2003	Olympia J. Snowe (R) 2007
Maryland	1,507	D-70.5	1,947	D-63.2	Barbara A. Mikulski (D) 2005	Paul S. Sarbanes (D) 2007
Massachusetts	(X)	(X)	2,599	D-72.7	Edward M. Kennedy (D) 2007	John F. Kerry (D) 2003
Michigan	(X)	(X)	4,168	D-49.5	Carl Levin (D) 2003	Debbie Stabenow (D) 2007
Minnesota	(X)	(X)	2,420	D-48.8	Paul David Wellstone (D) 2003	Mark Dayton (D) 2007
Mississippi	(X)	(X)	994	R-65.9	Thad Cochran (R) 2003	Trent Lott (R) 2007
Missouri	1,577	R-52.7	2,362	D-50.5	Christopher S. Bond (R) 2005	Mel Carnahan (D) 2007
Montana	(X)	(X)	412	R-50.6	Max Baucus (D) 2003	Conrad Burns (R) 2007
Nebraska	(X)	(X)	692	D-51.0	Chuck Hagel (R) 2003	Ben Nelson (D) 2007
Nevada	436	D-47.9	600	R-55.1	Harry Reid (D) 2005	John Ensign (R) 2007
New Hampshire	315	R-67.8	(X)	(X)	Judd Gregg (R) 2005	Robert C. Smith (R) 2003
New Jersey	(X)	(X)	3,016	D-50.1	Robert G. Torricelli (D) 2003	Jon Corzine (D) 2007
New Mexico	(X)	(X)	590	D-61.7	Jeff Bingaman (D) 2007	Pete V. Domenici (R) 2003
New York	4,671	D-54.6	6,780	D-55.3	Hillary Rodham Clinton (D) 2007	Charles E. Schumer (D) 2005
North Carolina	2,012	D-51.2	(X)	(X)	John Edwards (D) 2005	Jesse Helms (R) 2003
North Dakota	213	D-63.2	288	D-61.4	Byron L. Dorgan (D) 2005	Kent Conrad (D) 2007
Ohio	3,404	R-56.5	4,449	R-59.9	George V. Voinovich (R) 2005	Mike DeWine (R) 2007
Oklahoma	860	R-66.4	(X)	(X)	James Inhofe (R) 2003	Don Nickles (R) 2005
Oregon	1,118	D-61.1	(X)	(X)	Gordon Smith (R) 2003	Ron Wyden (D) 2005
Pennsylvania	2,958	R-61.3	4,736	R-52.4	Rick Santorum (R) 2007	Arlen Specter (R) 2005
Rhode Island	(X)	(X)	392	R-56.8	Jack Reed (D) 2003	Lincoln Chafee (R) 2007
South Carolina	1,068	D-52.7	(X)	(X)	Ernest F. Hollings (D) 2005	Strom Thurmond (R) 2003
South Dakota	262	D-62.1	(X)	(X)	Thomas A. Daschle (D) 2005	Tim Johnson (D) 2003
Tennessee	(X)	(X)	1,929	R-65.1	Fred Thompson (R) 2003	Bill Frist (R) 2007
Texas	(X)	(X)	6,277	R-65.0	Kay Bailey Hutchison (R) 2007	Phil Gramm (R) 2003
Utah	495	R-64.0	770	R-65.6	Robert F. Bennett (R) 2005	Orrin G. Hatch (R) 2007
Vermont	214	D-72.2	289	R-65.6	Patrick J. Leahy (D) 2005	James M. Jeffords (R) 2007
Virginia	(X)	(X)	2,718	R-52.3	George F. Allen (R) 2007	John W. Warner (R) 2003
Washington	1,889	D-58.4	2,461	D-48.7	Patty Murray (D) 2005	Maria Cantwell (D) 2007
West Virginia	(X)	(X)	603	D-77.8	Robert C. Byrd (D) 2007	John D. Rockefeller IV (D) 2003
Wisconsin	1,761	D-50.5	2,540	D-61.5	Herb Kohl (D) 2007	Russell Feingold (D) 2005
Wyoming	(X)	(X)	214	R-73.8	Mike Enzi (R) 2003	Craig Thomas (R) 2007

X Not applicable.   [1] Includes vote cast for minor parties.   [2] Louisiana holds an open-primary election with candidates from all parties running on the same ballot. Any candidate who receives a majority is elected.

Source: Congressional Quarterly, Inc., Washington, D.C. *America Votes*, biennial (copyright).

Elections   237

No. 384. Apportionment of Membership in House of Representatives by State: 1790 to 2000

[Total membership includes Representatives assigned to newly admitted states after the apportionment acts. Population figures used for apportionment purposes are those determined for states by each decennial census. No reapportionment based on 1920 population census. For method of calculating apportionment and a short history of apportionment, see House Report 91-1314, 91st Congress, 2d session, The Decennial Population Census and Congressional Apportionment]

State	1790	1800	1810	1820	1830	1840	1850	1860	1870	1880	1890	1900	1910	1930	1940	1950	1960	1970	1980	1990	2000
U.S.	106	142	186	213	242	232	237	243	293	332	357	391	435	435	435	437	435	435	435	435	435
AL	(X)	(X)	[1]1	3	5	7	7	6	8	8	9	9	10	9	9	9	8	7	7	7	7
AK	(X)	(X)	(X)	(X)	(X)	(X)	(X)	(X)	(X)	(X)	(X)	(X)	(X)	(X)	(X)	[1]1	1	1	1	1	1
AZ	(X)	(X)	(X)	(X)	(X)	(X)	(X)	(X)	(X)	(X)	(X)	(X)	[2]1	1	2	2	3	4	5	6	8
AR	(X)	(X)	(X)	(X)	[1]1	1	2	3	4	5	6	7	7	7	7	6	4	4	4	4	4
CA	(X)	(X)	(X)	(X)	(X)	[1]2	2	3	4	6	7	8	11	20	23	30	38	43	45	52	53
CO	(X)	(X)	(X)	(X)	(X)	(X)	(X)	(X)	[1]1	1	2	3	4	4	4	4	4	5	6	6	7
CT	7	7	7	6	6	4	4	4	4	4	4	5	5	6	6	6	6	6	6	6	5
DE	1	1	2	1	1	1	1	1	1	1	1	1	1	1	1	1	1	1	1	1	1
FL	(X)	(X)	(X)	(X)	(X)	[1]1	1	1	2	2	2	3	4	5	6	8	12	15	19	23	25
GA	2	4	6	7	9	8	8	7	9	10	11	11	12	10	10	10	10	10	10	11	13
HI	(X)	(X)	(X)	(X)	(X)	(X)	(X)	(X)	(X)	(X)	(X)	(X)	(X)	(X)	(X)	[1]1	2	2	2	2	2
ID	(X)	(X)	(X)	(X)	(X)	(X)	(X)	(X)	(X)	[1]1	1	1	2	2	2	2	2	2	2	2	2
IL	(X)	(X)	[1]1	1	3	7	9	14	19	20	22	25	27	27	26	25	24	24	22	20	19
IN	(X)	(X)	[1]1	3	7	10	11	11	13	13	13	13	13	12	11	11	11	11	10	10	9
IA	(X)	(X)	(X)	(X)	(X)	[1]2	2	6	9	11	11	11	11	9	8	8	7	6	6	5	5
KS	(X)	(X)	(X)	(X)	(X)	(X)	(X)	1	3	7	8	8	8	7	6	6	5	5	5	4	4
KY	2	6	10	12	13	10	10	9	10	11	11	11	11	9	9	8	7	7	7	6	6
LA	(X)	(X)	[1]1	3	3	4	4	5	6	6	6	7	8	8	8	8	8	8	8	7	7
ME	(X)	(X)	(X)	7	8	7	6	5	5	4	4	4	4	3	3	3	2	2	2	2	2
MD	8	9	9	9	8	6	6	5	6	6	6	6	6	6	6	6	7	8	8	8	8
MA	14	17	20	13	12	10	11	10	11	12	13	14	16	15	14	14	12	12	11	10	10
MI	(X)	(X)	(X)	(X)	[1]1	3	4	6	9	11	12	12	13	17	17	18	19	19	18	16	15
MN	(X)	(X)	(X)	(X)	(X)	(X)	[1]2	2	3	5	7	9	10	9	9	9	8	8	8	8	8
MS	(X)	(X)	[1]1	1	2	4	5	5	6	7	7	8	8	7	7	6	5	5	5	5	4
MO	(X)	(X)	(X)	1	2	5	7	9	13	14	15	16	16	13	13	11	10	10	9	9	9
MT	(X)	(X)	(X)	(X)	(X)	(X)	(X)	(X)	(X)	[1]1	1	1	2	2	2	2	2	2	2	1	1
NE	(X)	(X)	(X)	(X)	(X)	(X)	(X)	[1]1	1	3	6	6	6	5	4	4	3	3	3	3	3
NV	(X)	(X)	(X)	(X)	(X)	(X)	(X)	[1]1	1	1	1	1	1	1	1	1	1	1	2	2	3
NH	4	5	6	6	5	4	3	3	3	2	2	2	2	2	2	2	2	2	2	2	2
NJ	5	6	6	6	6	5	5	5	7	7	8	10	12	14	14	14	15	15	14	13	13
NM	(X)	(X)	(X)	(X)	(X)	(X)	(X)	(X)	(X)	(X)	(X)	(X)	[2]1	1	2	2	2	2	3	3	3
NY	10	17	27	34	40	34	33	31	33	34	34	37	43	45	45	43	41	39	34	31	29
NC	10	12	13	13	13	9	8	7	8	9	9	10	10	11	12	12	11	11	11	12	13
ND	(X)	(X)	(X)	(X)	(X)	(X)	(X)	(X)	(X)	[1]1	1	2	3	2	2	2	2	1	1	1	1
OH	(X)	[1]1	6	14	19	21	21	19	20	21	21	21	22	24	23	23	24	23	21	19	18
OK	(X)	(X)	(X)	(X)	(X)	(X)	(X)	(X)	(X)	(X)	(X)	[1]5	8	9	8	6	6	6	6	6	5
OR	(X)	(X)	(X)	(X)	(X)	(X)	[1]1	1	1	1	2	2	3	3	4	4	4	4	5	5	5
PA	8	13	18	23	26	28	24	25	24	27	28	30	32	36	34	33	30	27	25	23	21
RI	2	2	2	2	2	2	2	2	2	2	2	2	3	2	2	2	2	2	2	2	2
SC	6	8	9	9	9	7	6	4	5	7	7	7	7	6	6	6	6	6	6	6	6
SD	(X)	(X)	(X)	(X)	(X)	(X)	(X)	(X)	(X)	[1]2	2	2	3	2	2	2	2	2	1	1	1
TN	[1]1	3	6	9	13	11	10	8	10	10	10	10	10	9	10	9	9	8	9	9	9
TX	(X)	(X)	(X)	(X)	(X)	[1]2	2	4	6	11	13	16	18	21	21	22	23	24	27	30	32
UT	(X)	(X)	(X)	(X)	(X)	(X)	(X)	(X)	(X)	(X)	[1]1	1	2	2	2	2	2	2	3	3	3
VT	2	4	6	5	5	4	3	3	3	2	2	2	1	1	1	1	1	1	1	1	1
VA	19	22	23	22	21	15	13	11	9	10	10	10	10	9	9	10	10	10	10	11	11
WA	(X)	(X)	(X)	(X)	(X)	(X)	(X)	(X)	[1]1	2	3	5	6	6	7	7	7	8	9	9	9
WV	(X)	(X)	(X)	(X)	(X)	(X)	(X)	[1]3	4	4	5	6	6	6	6	6	5	4	4	3	3
WI	(X)	(X)	(X)	(X)	(X)	[1]2	3	6	8	9	10	11	11	10	10	10	10	10	9	9	8

X Not applicable.   [1] Assigned after apportionment.   [2] Included in apportionment in anticipation of statehood.

Source: U.S. Census Bureau, unpublished data. See also <http://www.census.gov/population/www/censusdata/apportionment.html>.

No. 385. Vote Cast for United States Representatives by Major Political Party—States: 1990 to 2000

[In thousands, except percent (61,513 represents 61,513,000). In each state, totals represent the sum of votes cast in each Congressional District or votes cast for Representative at Large in states where only one member is elected. In all years there are numerous districts within the state where either the Republican or Democratic party had no candidate. In some states the Republican and Democratic vote includes votes cast for the party candidate by endorsing parties]

State	1990 Total[1]	1990 Democratic	1990 Republican	1990 Percent for leading party	1996 Total[1]	1996 Democratic	1996 Republican	1996 Percent for leading party	2000 Total[1]	2000 Democratic	2000 Republican	2000 Percent for leading party
U.S. [2]	61,513	32,565	27,648	D-52.9	65,897	31,482	32,255	R-48.9	97,226	46,521	46,954	R-48.3
AL	1,017	690	315	D-67.9	1,215	545	666	R-54.8	1,439	486	849	R-59.0
AK	192	92	99	R-51.7	223	77	140	R-62.6	274	45	191	R-69.6
AZ [3]	966	345	621	R-64.3	1,004	407	574	R-57.1	1,466	558	855	R-58.3
AR	665	369	296	D-55.5	525	169	320	R-60.9	633	355	277	D-56.2
CA	7,287	3,568	3,347	D-49.0	7,990	4,040	3,510	D-50.6	10,438	5,407	4,446	D-51.8
CO	1,001	504	487	D-50.3	1,274	533	716	R-56.2	1,624	496	969	R-59.7
CT	1,037	489	546	R-52.6	954	496	442	D-51.9	1,313	699	595	D-53.2
DE	177	116	58	D-65.5	181	57	120	R-66.4	313	96	212	R-67.6
DC [3,4]	160	98	42	D-61.7	(NA)	(NA)	(NA)	(NA)	(NA)	(NA)	(NA)	(NA)
FL [3,4]	2,378	1,213	1,163	D-51.0	1,213	581	558	D-47.9	5,011	1,976	2,852	R-56.9
GA	1,394	855	539	D-61.3	1,632	592	1,040	R-63.7	2,417	918	1,498	R-62.0
HI	341	216	118	D-63.3	397	261	119	D-65.7	340	221	111	D-65.0
ID	315	183	131	D-58.2	379	169	205	R-54.0	493	142	333	R-67.5
IL	3,077	1,646	1,349	D-53.5	3,215	1,566	1,625	R-50.5	4,393	2,454	1,907	D-55.8
IN	1,514	831	683	D-54.9	1,576	673	862	R-54.7	2,157	953	1,141	R-52.9
IA	792	401	385	D-50.6	901	338	552	R-61.3	1,276	532	717	R-56.2
KS	781	394	387	D-50.4	727	272	450	R-61.9	1,038	328	658	R-63.4
KY	764	353	397	R-52.0	1,099	456	637	R-58.0	1,435	562	825	R-57.5
LA	106	106	-	D-100.0	310	213	97	D-68.7	1,202	360	747	R-62.1
ME	517	284	233	D-55.0	415	281	125	D-67.7	638	423	203	D-66.2
MD	1,091	566	517	D-51.9	1,482	792	690	D-53.5	1,927	1,061	856	D-55.1
MA	2,051	1,420	567	D-69.2	1,742	1,306	413	D-75.0	2,347	1,968	343	D-83.8
MI	2,434	1,321	1,089	D-54.3	2,985	1,469	1,438	D-49.2	4,070	2,178	1,787	D-53.5
MN	1,781	1,042	736	D-58.5	2,040	1,090	863	D-53.5	2,364	1,234	993	D-52.2
MS	369	299	69	D-81.2	551	263	232	D-47.7	986	496	468	D-50.3
MO	1,353	728	625	D-53.8	1,572	788	748	D-50.1	2,326	1,136	1,136	D-48.8
MT	317	157	160	R-50.5	332	147	176	R-53.0	411	190	211	R-51.5
NE	587	277	309	R-52.7	526	105	393	R-74.7	683	178	487	R-71.2
NV	313	144	151	R-48.2	410	79	275	R-67.1	585	225	331	R-56.5
NH	291	141	149	R-51.2	318	124	190	R-59.8	556	239	303	R-54.5
NJ	1,827	837	911	R-49.9	1,815	902	858	R-49.7	2,988	1,532	1,384	R-51.3
NM	359	146	214	R-59.5	498	228	246	R-49.5	588	300	274	R-51.0
NY	3,662	1,830	1,662	D-50.0	4,267	2,278	1,858	D-53.4	5,824	3,190	2,466	D-54.8
NC	2,011	1,076	935	D-53.5	1,904	827	1,014	R-53.3	2,780	1,194	1,515	R-54.5
ND	234	153	81	D-65.2	213	120	88	D-56.2	286	151	127	D-52.9
OH	3,418	1,807	1,590	D-52.9	3,375	1,594	1,752	R-51.9	4,518	2,067	2,203	R-48.8
OK	857	519	338	D-60.6	859	314	538	R-62.7	1,088	337	702	R-64.5
OR	1,053	667	342	D-63.4	1,090	631	402	D-57.9	1,440	790	607	D-54.9
PA	2,851	1,293	1,552	R-54.5	2,896	1,381	1,472	R-50.8	4,554	2,279	2,229	D-50.0
RI	347	182	165	D-52.5	293	204	77	D-69.5	384	247	89	D-64.4
SC	670	383	275	D-57.2	974	370	580	R-59.6	1,321	525	730	R-55.2
SD	257	174	83	D-67.6	259	64	194	R-75.1	315	78	231	R-73.4
TN	717	369	289	D-51.5	914	412	470	R-51.4	1,854	819	992	R-53.5
TX	3,278	1,763	1,496	D-53.8	3,462	1,531	1,787	R-51.6	5,986	2,799	2,932	R-49.0
UT	442	234	191	D-52.9	471	127	304	R-64.6	759	305	427	R-56.2
VT	210	6	83	I-56.0	215	(X)	71	R-32.9	283	15	52	I-76.4
VA	1,153	663	411	D-57.5	1,149	514	542	R-47.2	2,422	1,060	1,132	R-46.7
WA	1,313	696	596	D-53.0	1,858	980	819	D-52.8	2,382	1,246	998	D-52.3
WV	375	251	123	D-67.1	351	283	29	D-80.6	580	421	109	D-72.6
WI	1,256	597	652	R-51.9	1,673	762	880	R-52.6	2,506	1,188	1,311	R-52.3
WY	158	71	87	R-55.1	174	67	101	R-57.8	212	61	142	R-66.8

- Represents zero.   NA Not available.   X Not applicable.   [1] Includes vote cast for minor parties. Total for 1996 includes results from 431 districts, including 14 where members were elected without major party opposition (7 won by the Republicans and 7 by the Democrats). In four districts (three in Louisiana and 1 in Florida) candidates ran unopposed and no vote was recorded. [2] Includes vote cast for nonvoting Delegate at Large in District of Columbia, except for 1994 and 1996. [3] State law does not require tabulation of votes for unopposed candidates. [4] In 1990 Districts 8, 10, 12, 13, and 16 were unopposed; in 1994 Districts 4, 10, 13, 14, 18, and 23 were unopposed; in 1996 District 4 was unopposed.

Source: Congressional Quarterly, Inc., Washington, DC, *America Votes*, biennial (copyright).

No. 386. Vote Cast for United States Representatives by Major Political Party—Congressional Districts: 2000

[In some states the Democratic and Republican vote includes votes cast for the party candidate by endorsing parties]

State and district	Democratic candidate Name	Percent of total	Republican candidate Name	Percent of total	State and district	Democratic candidate Name	Percent of total	Republican candidate Name	Percent of total
AL	(X)	(X)	(X)	(X)	44th..	Oden	37.9	Bono	59.2
1st..	(¹)	(¹)	Callahan	91.3	45th..	Crisell	32.4	Rohrabacher	62.1
2d..	Woods	29.2	Everett	68.2	46th..	Sanchez	60.2	Tuchman	35.0
3d..	(¹)	(¹)	Riley	86.9	47th..	Graham	30.1	Cox	65.6
4th..	Folsom	37.4	Aderholt	60.6	48th..	Kouvelis	28.3	Issa	61.4
5th..	Cramer, Jr..	88.8	(¹)	(¹)	49th..	Davis	49.6	Bilbray	46.2
6th..	(¹)	(¹)	Bachus	87.9	50th..	Filner	68.3	Divine	27.6
7th..	Hilliard.	74.6	Martin	23.2	51st..	Barraza	30.4	Cunningham	64.3
AK	Greene	16.5	Young	69.6	52d..	Barkacs	31.3	Hunter	64.7
AZ	(X)	(X)	(X)	(X)	CO	(X)	(X)	(X)	(X)
1st..	Mendoza	42.4	Flake	53.6	1st..	DeGette	68.7	Thomas	27.3
2d..	Pastor	68.5	Barenholtz	26.9	2d..	Udall	55.0	Cox	38.6
3d..	Scharer	31.4	Stump	65.7	3d..	Imrie	29.1	McInnis	65.8
4th..	Jankowski	32.7	Shadegg	64.0	4th..	(¹)	(¹)	Schaffer	79.5
5th..	Cunningham.	35.3	Kolbe	60.1	5th..	(¹)	(¹)	Hefley	82.7
6th..	Nelson	35.6	Hayworth	61.4	6th..	Toltz	42.1	Tancredo	53.9
AR	(X)	(X)	(X)	(X)	CT	(X)	(X)	(X)	(X)
1st..	Berry	60.1	Myshka	39.7	1st..	Larson	71.9	Backlund	28.1
2d..	Snyder	57.5	Thomas	42.5	2d..	Gejdenson	49.4	Simmons	48.8
3d..	(¹)	(¹)	Hutchinson..	(²)	3d..	DeLauro	71.9	Gold	27.5
4th..	Ross	51.0	Dickey	49.0	4th..	Sanchez	40.9	Shays	57.6
CA	(X)	(X)	(X)	(X)	5th..	Maloney	53.6	Nielsen	44.3
1st..	Thompson	65.0	Chase	28.0	6th..	Valenti	32.9	Johnson	62.6
2d..	Morgan	28.2	Herger	65.7	DE	Miller	30.8	Castle	67.6
3d..	Kent	40.4	Ose	56.2	FL	(X)	(X)	(X)	(X)
4th..	Norberg	31.5	Doolittle	63.4	1st..	(¹)	(¹)	Scarborough	99.5
5th..	Matsui	68.7	Payne	26.1	2d..	Boyd	72.1	Dodd	27.9
6th..	Woolsey	64.3	McAuliffe	28.3	3d..	Brown	57.6	Carroll	42.4
7th..	Miller	76.5	Hoffman	21.1	4th..	Sullivan	31.2	Crenshaw	67.0
8th..	Pelosi	84.4	Sparks	11.7	5th..	Thurman	64.3	Enwall	35.7
9th..	Lee	85.0	Washington	9.8	6th..	(¹)	(¹)	Stearns	100.0
10th..	Tauscher	52.6	Hutchinson.	44.2	7th..	Vaughen	36.8	Mica	63.2
11th..	Santos	38.1	Pombo	57.8	8th..	Chapin	49.2	Keller	50.8
12th..	Lantos	74.5	Garza	20.8	9th..	(¹)	(¹)	Bilirakis	81.9
13th..	Stark	70.4	Goetz	24.3	10th..	(¹)	(¹)	Young	75.7
14th..	Eshoo	70.2	Quraishi	25.8	11th..	Davis	84.6	(¹)	(¹)
15th..	Honda	54.3	Cunneen	42.2	12th..	Stedem	43.0	Putnam	57.0
16th..	Lofgren	72.1	Thayn	23.3	13th..	Dunn	36.1	Miller	63.8
17th..	Farr	68.6	Engler	24.7	14th..	(¹)	(¹)	Goss	85.2
18th..	Condit	67.1	Wilson	31.3	15th..	Kurth	39.2	Weldon	58.8
19th..	Rosenberg	31.7	Radanovich	64.9	16th..	Brown	37.2	Foley	60.2
20th..	Dooley	52.3	Rodriguez	45.5	17th..	Meek	100.0	(¹)	(¹)
21st..	Martinez	24.8	Thomas	71.6	18th..	(¹)	(¹)	Ros Lehtinen	100.0
22d..	Capps	53.1	Stoker	44.3	19th..	Wexler	71.6	Thompson	28.4
23d..	Case	40.7	Gallegly	54.1	20th..	Deutsch	99.9	(¹)	(¹)
24th..	Sherman	66.0	Doyle	29.8	21st..	(¹)	(¹)	Diaz-Balart	100.0
25th..	Gold	33.2	McKeon	62.2	22d..	Bloom	49.9	Shaw	50.1
26th..	Berman	84.1	(¹)	(¹)	23d..	Hastings	76.3	Lambert	23.7
27th..	Schiff	52.7	Rogan	43.8	GA	(X)	(X)	(X)	(X)
28th..	Nelson	39.9	Dreier	56.8	1st..	Griggs	30.9	Kingston	69.1
29th..	Waxman	75.7	Scileppi	19.2	2d..	Bishop, Jr..	53.5	Glenn	46.5
30th..	Becerra	83.3	Goss	11.8	3d..	Notti	36.5	Collins	63.5
31st..	Solis	79.4	(¹)	(¹)	4th..	McKinney	60.7	Warren	39.3
32d..	Dixon	83.5	Williamson	12.1	5th..	Lewis	77.2	Schwab	22.8
33d..	Roybal-Allard	84.5	Miller	11.5	6th..	DeHart	25.2	Isakson	74.8
34th..	Napolitano	71.3	Canales	22.5	7th..	Kahn	44.7	Barr	55.3
35th..	Waters	86.5	McGill	10.8	8th..	Marshall	41.1	Chambliss	58.9
36th..	Harman	48.4	Kuykendall	46.6	9th..	Harrington	24.8	Deal	75.2
37th..	Millender-McDonald	82.3	Van	11.3	10th..	Freeman	36.8	Norwood	63.2
38th..	Schipske	47.5	Horn	48.4	11th..	(¹)	-	Linder	100.0
39th..	Kanel	31.3	Royce	62.9	HI	(X)	(X)	(X)	(X)
40th..	(¹)	(¹)	Lewis	79.9	1st..	Abercrombie..	69.0	Meyers	28.6
41st..	Favila	37.4	Miller	58.9	2d..	Mink	61.6	Francis	36.0
42d..	Baca	59.8	Pirozzi	35.1	ID	(X)	(X)	(X)	(X)
43d..	(¹)	(¹)	Calvert	73.7	1st..	Pall	31.4	Otter	64.8
					2d..	Williams	25.9	Simpson	70.7

See footnotes at end of table.

U.S. Census Bureau, Statistical Abstract of the United States: 2001

No. 386. Vote Cast for United States Representatives by Major Political Party—Congressional Districts: 2000—Con.

[See headnote, p. 240]

State and district	Democratic candidate Name	Percent of total	Republican candidate Name	Percent of total
IL....	(X)	(X)	(X)	(X)
1st	Rush	87.8	Wardingley	12.2
2d	Jackson Jr.	89.8	Gordon III	10.2
3d	Lipinski	75.6	Groth	24.4
4th	Gutierrez	88.6	(1)	(1)
5th	Blagojevich	87.3	(1)	(1)
6th	Christensen	41.1	Hyde	58.9
7th	Davis	85.9	Dallas	14.1
8th	Pressl	39.0	Crane	61.0
9th	Schakowsky	76.4	Driscoll	23.6
10th	Gash	48.8	Kirk	51.2
11th	Stevenson	43.6	Weller	56.4
12th	Costello	100.0	(1)	(1)
13th	Mason	33.8	Biggert	66.2
14th	Deljonson	26.0	Hastert	74.0
15th	Kelleher	46.8	Johnson	53.2
16th	Hendrickson	33.3	Manzullo	66.7
17th	Evans	54.9	Baker	45.1
18th	Harant	32.9	LaHood	67.1
19th	Phelps	64.6	Eatherly	35.4
20th	Cooper	36.9	Shimkus	63.1
IN....	(X)	(X)	(X)	(X)
1st	Visclosky	71.6	Reynolds	27.0
2d	Rock	38.8	Pence	50.9
3d	Roemer	51.6	Chocola	47.4
4th	Foster	35.4	Souder	62.3
5th	Goodnight	37.5	Buyer	60.9
6th	Griesey	26.4	Burton	70.3
7th	Graf	31.8	Kerns	64.8
8th	Perry	45.3	Hostettler	52.7
9th	Hill	54.2	Bailey	43.8
10th	Carson	58.5	Scott	39.7
IA....	(X)	(X)	(X)	(X)
1st	Simpson	36.1	Leach	61.8
2d	Smith	43.7	Nussle	55.4
3d	Boswell	62.8	Marcus	33.7
4th	Huston	36.7	Ganske	61.4
5th	Palecek	29.2	Latham	68.8
KS....	(X)	(X)	(X)	(X)
1st	(1)	(1)	Moran	89.3
2d	Wiles	29.3	Ryun	67.4
3d	Moore	50.0	Kline	46.9
4th	Nolla	42.0	Tiahrt	54.4
KY....	(X)	(X)	(X)	(X)
1st	Roy	42.0	Whitfield	58.0
2d	Pedigo	31.4	Lewis	67.7
3d	Jordan	44.2	Northup	52.9
4th	Lucas	54.3	Bell	43.5
5th	Bailey	26.4	Rogers	73.6
6th	Baesler	34.8	Fletcher	52.8
LA[3]	(X)	(X)	(X)	(X)
1st	Armato	12.6	Vitter	80.5
2d	Jefferson	(3)	(1)	(1)
3d	(1)	(1)	Tauzin	78.0
4th	Green	25.1	McCrery	70.5
5th	Beall	23.9	Cooksey	69.1
6th	Rogillio	29.7	Baker	68.0
7th	John	83.3	(1)	(1)
ME....	(X)	(X)	(X)	(X)
1st	Allen	59.8	Amero	36.5
2d	Baldacci	73.4	Campbell	26.6
MD....	(X)	(X)	(X)	(X)
1st	Bozman	35.5	Gilchrest	64.4
2d	Bosley	31.3	Ehrlich	68.6
3d	Cardin	75.7	Harby	24.0
4th	Wynn	87.2	Kimble	12.6
5th	Hoyer	65.1	Hutchins	34.9
6th	DeArmon	39.3	Bartlett	60.6
7th	Cummings	87.1	Kondner	12.8
8th	Lierman	45.5	Morella	52.0
MA....	(X)	(X)	(X)	(X)
1st	Olver	65.3	Abair	28.4
2d	Neal	77.5	(1)	(1)
3d	McGovern	76.5	(1)	(1)
4th	Frank	70.8	Travis	20.0
5th	Meehan	74.4	(1)	(1)
6th	Tierney	67.6	McCarthy	27.5
7th	Markey	75.6	(1)	(1)
8th	Capuano	71.0	(1)	(1)
9th	Moakley	71.2	Jeghelian	18.0
10th	Delahunt	70.5	Bleicken	24.4
MI....	(X)	(X)	(X)	(X)
1st	Stupak	58.4	Yob	40.4
2d	Shrauger	33.2	Hoekstra	64.4
3d	Steele	33.1	Ehlers	65.0
4th	Hollenbeck	29.1	Camp	68.0
5th	Barcia	74.3	Actis	23.9
6th	Bupp	29.2	Upton	67.9
7th	Crittendon	35.7	Smith	61.1
8th	Byrum	48.7	Rogers	48.8
9th	Kildee	61.1	Garrett	35.9
10th	Bonior	64.4	Turner	33.2
11th	Frumin	40.5	Knollenberg	55.8
12th	Levin	64.3	Baron	32.1
13th	Rivers	64.7	Berry	32.1
14th	Conyers Jr.	89.1	Ashe	9.3
15th	Kilpatrick	88.6	Boyd-Fields	9.0
16th	Dingell	71.0	Morse	26.5
MN....	(X)	(X)	(X)	(X)
1st	Rieder	41.6	Gutknecht	56.4
2d	Minge	48.0	Kennedy	48.1
3d	Shuff	29.8	Ramstad	67.6
4th	McCollum	48.0	Runbeck	30.9
5th	Sabo	69.2	Taylor	22.8
6th	Luther	49.6	Kline	48.0
7th	Peterson	68.7	Menze	29.3
8th	Oberstar	67.8	Lemen	25.8
MS....	(X)	(X)	(X)	(X)
1st	Grist	28.6	Wicker	69.8
2d	Thompson	65.1	Caraway	31.2
3d	Thrash	25.7	Pickering	73.2
4th	Shows	58.1	Lampton	39.8
5th	Taylor	78.8	McDonnell	18.2
MO....	(X)	(X)	(X)	(X)
1st	Clay	75.2	Billingsly	21.5
2d	House	42.4	Akin	55.3
3d	Gephardt	57.8	Federer	39.7
4th	Skelton	66.9	Noland	31.3
5th	McCarthy	68.8	Gordon	28.6
6th	Danner	46.8	Graves, Jr.	50.9
7th	Christrup	23.9	Blunt	73.9
8th	Camp	28.9	Emerson	69.3
9th	Carroll	38.3	Hulshof	59.3
MT....	Keenan	46.3	Rehberg	51.5
NE....	(X)	(X)	(X)	(X)
1st	Jacobsen	31.0	Bereuter	66.2
2d	Kiel	31.1	Terry	65.8
3d	Reynolds	15.7	Osborne	82.0
NV....	(X)	(X)	(X)	(X)
1st	Berkley	51.7	Porter	44.2
2d	Cahill	29.8	Gibbons	64.2
NH....	(X)	(X)	(X)	(X)
1st	Clark	45.1	Sununu	52.9
2d	Brannen	40.7	Bass	56.2
NJ....	(X)	(X)	(X)	(X)
1st	Andrews	76.2	Cathcart	21.2
2d	Janosik	31.9	LoBiondo	66.4
3d	Levin	41.2	Saxton	57.3
4th	Gusciora	35.1	Smith	63.2
5th	Mercurio	30.4	Roukema	65.4
6th	Pallone Jr.	67.5	Kennedy	29.8
7th	Connelly	45.6	Ferguson	51.6
8th	Pascrell Jr.	67.0	Fusco	30.3
9th	Rothman	67.9	Tedeschi	30.0
10th	Payne	87.5	Weber	12.1
11th	Scollo	29.6	Frelinghuysen	68.0
12th	Holt	48.7	Zimmer	48.5
13th	Menendez	78.7	de Leon	18.6

See footnotes at end of table.

U.S. Census Bureau, Statistical Abstract of the United States: 2001

No. 386. Vote Cast for United States Representatives by Major Political Party—Congressional Districts: 1998—Con.

[See headnote. p. 240]

State and district	Democratic candidate Name	Percent of total	Republican candidate Name	Percent of total
NM	(X)	(X)	(X)	(X)
1st.	Kelly	43.3	Wilson	50.3
2d.	Montoya	41.9	Skeen	58.1
3d.	Udall	67.2	Lutz	32.8
NY	(X)	(X)	(X)	(X)
1st.	Seltzer	36.1	Grucci, Jr.	41.2
2d.	Israel	40.0	Johnson	29.1
3d.	Lamagna	32.8	King	43.8
4th.	McCarthy	50.7	Becker	29.8
5th.	Ackerman	52.0	Elkowitz	22.9
6th.	Meeks	66.7	(1)	(1)
7th.	Crowley	51.0	Birtley	16.0
8th.	Nadler	61.5	Henry	11.9
9th.	Weiner	52.3	Dear	22.2
10th.	Towns	66.5	Brown	3.8
11th.	Owens	64.0	Cleary	4.3
12th.	Velazquez	60.9	Markgraf	7.5
13th.	Johnstone	27.8	Fossella	47.7
14th.	Maloney	59.4	Rhodes	18.8
15th.	Rangel	70.8	Suero	3.9
16th.	Serrano	71.9	Justice	2.8
17th.	Engel	68.0	McManus	6.9
18th.	Lowey	55.6	Vonglis	23.2
19th.	Graham	30.7	Kelly	50.1
20th.	Feiner	32.6	Gilman	50.7
21st.	McNulty	59.0	Pillsworth	22.6
22d.	McCallion	25.6	Sweeney	54.3
23d.	Englebrecht	17.0	Boehlert	49.5
24th.	Tallon	18.8	McHugh	58.0
25th.	Gavin	25.4	Walsh	52.1
26th.	Hinchey	50.7	Moppert	31.7
27th.	Pecoraro	24.8	Reynolds	51.2
28th.	Slaughter	59.4	Johns	26.3
29th.	LaFalce	46.8	Sommer	27.9
30th.	Fee	25.0	Quinn	45.6
31st.	Peters	18.9	Houghton	60.1
NC	(X)	(X)	(X)	(X)
1st.	Clayton	65.6	Kratzer	32.9
2d.	Etheridge	58.3	Haynes	40.9
3d.	McNairy	37.3	Jones	61.4
4th.	Price	61.6	Ward	36.6
5th.	(1)	(1)	Burr	92.8
6th.	(1)	(1)	Coble	91.0
7th.	McIntyre	69.7	Adams	28.9
8th.	Taylor	44.0	Hayes	55.0
9th.	McGuire	30.0	Myrick	68.6
10th.	Parker	29.5	Ballenger	68.2
11th.	Neill	42.1	Taylor	55.1
12th.	Watt	64.8	Mitchell	33.3
ND	(1)	(1)	Dorso	44.5
OH	(X)	(X)	(X)	(X)
1st.	Cranley	44.6	Chabot	53.0
2d.	Sanders	23.1	Portman	73.6
3d.	Hall	83.0	(1)	(1)
4th.	Dickman	29.0	Oxley	67.4
5th.	Edmon	25.5	Gillmor	69.8
6th.	Strickland	57.7	Azinger	40.3
7th.	Minor	25.1	Hobson	67.6
8th.	Parks	26.2	Boehner	71.0
9th.	Kaptur	74.8	Bryan	21.9
10th.	Kucinich	75.0	Smith	22.0
11th.	Tubbs Jones	84.8	Sykora	11.2
12th.	O'Shaughnessy	43.8	Tiberi	52.9
13th.	Brown	64.6	Jeric	32.0
14th.	Sawyer	64.8	Wood	31.0
15th.	Buckel	27.9	Pryce	67.5
16th.	Smith	26.8	Regula	69.2
17th.	Traficant	50.0	Alberty	22.7
18th.	Guthrie	33.5	Ney	64.4
19th.	Blanchard	31.9	LaTourette	64.8
OK	(X)	(X)	(X)	(X)
1st.	Lowe	29.2	Largent	69.3
2d.	Carson	54.9	Ewing	41.8
3d.	(1)	(1)	Watkins	86.6
4th.	Weatherford	31.2	Watts, Jr.	64.9
5th.	McWatters	27.2	Istook, Jr.	68.4
6th.	Beutler	39.2	Lucas	59.3
OR	(X)	(X)	(X)	(X)
1st.	Wu	58.3	Starr	38.0
2d.	Ponsford	26.1	Walden	73.6
3d.	Blumenauer	66.8	Pollock	23.6
4th.	DeFazio	68.0	Lindsey	30.6
5th.	Hooley	56.8	Boquist	43.1
PA	(X)	(X)	(X)	(X)
1st.	Brady	88.3	Kush	11.7
2d.	Fattah	98.0	(1)	(1)
3d.	Borski	68.7	Dougherty	31.3
4th.	Van Horne	41.0	Hart	59.0
5th.	(1)	(1)	Peterson	85.6
6th.	Holden	66.3	Kopel	33.7
7th.	Lennon	35.2	Weldon	64.8
8th.	Strouse	38.7	Greenwood	59.2
9th.	(1)	(1)	Shuster	100.0
10th.	Casey	47.4	Sherwood	52.6
11th.	Kanjorski	66.4	Urban	33.6
12th.	Murtha	70.8	Choby	27.5
13th.	Hoeffel	52.8	Greenleaf	45.7
14th.	Coyne	100.0	(1)	(1)
15th.	O'Brien	46.7	Toomey	53.3
16th.	Yorczyk	33.1	Pitts	66.9
17th.	Herrmann	28.5	Gekas	71.5
18th.	Doyle	69.4	Stephens	30.6
19th.	Sanders	26.5	Platts	72.6
20th.	Mascara	64.4	Davis	35.6
21st.	Flitter	39.2	English	60.8
RI	(X)	(X)	(X)	(X)
1st.	Kennedy	66.6	Cabral	33.2
2d.	Langevin	62.2	Tingle	14.0
SC	(X)	(X)	(X)	(X)
1st.	Brack	35.7	Brown	60.3
2d.	Frederick	40.8	Spence	57.0
3d.	Brightharp	29.3	Graham	67.8
4th.	(1)		DeMint	79.6
5th.	Spratt	58.8	Gullick	39.5
6th.	Clyburn	71.8	Ellison	26.0
SD	Hohn	24.9	Thune	73.4
TN	(X)	(X)	(X)	(X)
1st.	(1)	(1)	Jenkins	100.0
2d.	(1)	(1)	Duncan, Jr.	89.3
3d.	Callaway	34.6	Wamp	63.9
4th.	Dunaway	33.1	Hilleary	65.8
5th.	Clement	72.5	Scott	24.5
6th.	Gordon	62.1	Charles	35.7
7th.	Sims	29.1	Bryant	69.6
8th.	Tanner	72.3	Yancy	27.7
9th.	Ford, Jr.	100.0	(1)	(1)

See footnotes at end of table.

U.S. Census Bureau, Statistical Abstract of the United States: 2001

[See headnote, p. 240]

State and district	Democratic candidate Name	Percent of total	Republican candidate Name	Percent of total	State and district	Democratic candidate Name	Percent of total	Republican candidate Name	Percent of total
TX	(X)	(X)	(X)	(X)	1st...	Davies	37.0	Davis	57.5
1st...	Sandlin	55.8	Willingham	43.4	2d...	Wagner	48.0	Schrock	52.0
2d...	Turner	91.1	(¹)	(¹)	3d...	Scott	97.7	(¹)	(¹)
3d...	Zachary	25.7	Johnson	71.6	4th...	Sisisky	98.9	(¹)	(¹)
4th...	Hall	60.3	Newton	37.9	5th...	Boyd, Jr.	30.7	(¹)	(¹)
5th...	Coggins	44.4	Sessions	54.0	6th...	(¹)	(¹)	Goodlatte	99.3
6th...	(¹)	(¹)	Barton	88.1	7th...	Stewart	33.0	Cantor	66.9
7th...	Sell	24.4	Culberson	73.9	8th...	Moran	63.3	Miller	34.1
8th...	(¹)	(¹)	Brady	91.6	9th...	Boucher	69.8	Osborne	30.1
9th...	Lampson	59.2	Williams	39.7	10th...	(¹)	(¹)	Wolf	84.2
10th...	Doggett	84.6	(¹)	(¹)	11th...	Corrigan	34.3	Davis	61.9
11th...	Edwards	54.8	Farley	44.3	WA	(X)	(X)	(X)	(X)
12th...	Greene	36.0	Granger	62.7	1st...	Inslee	54.6	McDonald	42.6
13th...	Clinesmith	31.1	Thornberry	67.6	2d...	Larsen	50.0	Koster	45.9
14th...	Sneary	40.3	Paul	59.7	3d...	Baird	56.4	Matson	40.6
15th...	Hinojosa	88.5	(¹)	(¹)	4th...	Davis	37.3	Hastings	60.9
16th...	Reyes	68.3	Power	30.2	5th...	Keefe	38.9	Nethercutt, Jr.	57.3
17th...	Stenholm	59.0	Clements	35.5	6th...	Dicks	64.7	Lawrence	31.1
18th...	Jackson-Lee	76.5	Levy	22.2	7th...	McDermott	72.8	(¹)	(¹)
19th...	(¹)	(¹)	Combest	91.6	8th...	Behrens-Benedict	35.6	Dunn	62.2
20th...	Gonzalez	87.7	(¹)	(¹)	9th...	Smith	61.7	Vance	35.0
21st...	Green	22.2	Smith	75.9	WV	(X)	(X)	(X)	(X)
22d...	Matranga	36.2	DeLay	60.4	1st...	Mollohan	87.8	(¹)	(¹)
23d...	Garza	38.8	Bonilla	59.3	2d...	Humphreys	45.9	Capito	48.5
24th...	Frost	61.8	Wright	36.7	3d...	Rahall II.	91.3	(¹)	(¹)
25th...	Bentsen	60.1	Sudan	38.5	WI.	(X)	(X)	(X)	(X)
26th...	Love	25.6	Armey	72.5	1st...	Thomas	33.3	Ryan	66.6
27th...	Ortiz	63.4	Ahumada	33.9	2d...	Baldwin	51.4	(¹)	(¹)
28th...	Rodriguez	89.0	(¹)	(¹)	3d...	Kind	63.7	Tully	35.9
29th...	Green	73.3	Vu	25.6	4th...	Kleczka	60.8	Riener	37.8
30th...	Johnson	91.8	(¹)	(¹)	5th...	Barrett	77.7	Smith	22.0
UT	(X)	(X)	(X)	(X)	6th...	Flaherty	34.9	Petri	65.0
1st...	Collinwood	27.2	Hansen	69.0	7th...	Obey	63.3	Cronin	36.7
2d...	Matheson	55.9	Smith	41.3	8th...	Reich	25.3	Green	74.6
3d...	Dunn	37.3	Cannon	58.5				Sensenbrenner, Jr.	74.0
VT¹⁰	Diamond-stone	5.3	Kerin	18.3	9th...	Clawson	25.9		
VA	(X)	(X)	(X)	(X)	WY	Green	28.6	Cubin	66.8

- Represents zero.   X Not applicable.   ¹ No candidate.   ² According to state law, it is not required to tabulate votes for unopposed candidates.   ³ Louisiana holds an open-primary election with candidates from all parties running on the same ballot. Any candidate who receives a majority is elected; if no candidate receives 50 percent, there is a run-off election in November between the top two finishers.

Source: Congressional Quarterly Inc., *Congressional Quarterly Weekly Report* (copyright).

No. 387. Composition of Congress by Political Party: 1973 to 2001

[D=Democratic, R=Republican. Data for beginning of first session of each Congress (as of January 3), except as noted. Excludes vacancies at beginning of session]

Year	Party and President	Congress	House Majority party	House Minority party	House Other	Senate Majority party	Senate Minority party	Senate Other
1973 [1,2]	R (Nixon)	93d	D-239	R-192	1	D-56	R-42	2
1975 [3]	R (Ford)	94th	D-291	R-144	2	D-60	R-37	2
1977 [4]	D (Carter)	95th	D-292	R-143	-	D-61	R-38	1
1979 [4]	D (Carter)	96th	D-276	R-157	-	D-58	R-41	1
1981 [4]	R (Reagan)	97th	D-243	R-192	1	R-53	D-46	1
1983	R (Reagan)	98th	D-269	R-165	-	R-54	D-46	-
1985	R (Reagan)	99th	D-252	R-182	-	R-53	D-47	-
1987	R (Reagan)	100th	D-258	R-177	-	D-55	R-45	-
1989	R (Bush)	101st	D-259	R-174	-	D-55	R-45	-
1991 [5]	R (Bush)	102d	D-267	R-167	1	D-56	R-44	-
1993 [5]	D (Clinton)	103d	D-258	R-176	1	D-57	R-43	-
1995 [5]	D (Clinton)	104th	R-230	D-204	1	R-52	D-48	-
1996 [5]	D (Clinton)	104th	R-236	D-197	1	R-53	D-46	-
1997 [5,6]	D (Clinton)	105th	R-226	D-207	2	R-55	D-45	-
1999	D (Clinton)	106th	R-222	D-212	1	R-54	D-45	1
2001	R (Bush)	107th	R-221	D-210	2	D-50	R-49	1

- Represents zero.   ¹ Senate had one Independent and one Conservative-Republican.   ² House had one Independent-Democrat.   ³ Senate had one Independent, one Conservative-Republican, and one undecided (New Hampshire).   ⁴ Senate had one Independent.   ⁵ House had one Independent-Socialist.   ⁶ As of beginning of second session.

Source: U.S. Congress, Joint Committee on Printing, *Congressional Directory*, annual; beginning 1977, biennial.

Elections   243

No. 388. Composition of Congress by Political Party Affiliation—States: 1993 to 2001

[Figures are for the beginning of the first session (as of January 3), except as noted. Dem.=Democratic; Rep.=Republican]

State	Representatives								Senators							
	103rd Cong.,[2] 1993		105th Cong.,[2 3 4] 1997		106th Cong.,[2 3 4] 1999		107th Cong.,[2 3 6 7] 2001		103rd Cong., 1993		104th Cong.,[3 5] 1995		106st Cong.,[1] 1999		107th Cong.,[2 3 6 7] 2001	
	Dem.	Rep.	Dem.	Rep.	Dem.	Rep.	Dem.	Rep.	Dem.	Rep.	Dem.	Rep.	Dem.	Rep.	Dem.	Rep.
U.S. . . .	258	176	206	228	212	222	210	221	57	43	45	55	45	55	50	49
AL.	4	3	2	5	2	5	2	5	2	-	-	2	-	2	-	2
AK.	-	1	-	1	-	1	-	1	-	2	-	2	-	2	-	2
AZ.	3	3	1	5	1	5	1	5	1	1	-	2	-	2	-	2
AR.	2	2	2	2	2	2	3	-	2	-	1	1	·, 1	1	1	1
CA.	30	22	29	23	28	24	32	20	2	-	2	-	2	-	2	-
CO.	2	4	2	4	2	4	2	4	1	1	-	2	-	2	-	2
CT.	3	3	4	2	4	2	3	3	2	-	2	-	2	-	2	-
DE.	-	1	-	1	-	1	-	1	1	1	1	1	1	1	2	-
FL.	10	13	8	15	8	15	8	15	1	1	1	1	1	1	2	-
GA.	7	4	3	8	3	8	3	8	1	1	1	1	1	1	2	-
HI.	2	-	2	-	2	-	2	-	2	-	2	-	2	-	2	-
ID.	1	1	-	2	-	2	-	2	-	2	-	2	-	2	-	2
IL.	12	8	10	10	10	10	10	10	2	-	2	-	1	1	1	1
IN.	7	3	4	6	4	6	4	6	-	2	-	2	1	1	1	1
IA.	1	4	1	4	1	4	1	4	1	1	1	1	1	1	1	1
KS.	2	2	-	4	1	3	1	3	-	2	-	2	-	2	-	2
KY.	4	2	1	5	1	5	1	5	1	1	1	1	-	2	-	2
LA.	4	3	2	5	2	5	2	5	2	-	2	-	2	-	2	-
ME	1	1	2	-	2	-	2	-	1	1	-	2	-	2	-	2
MD	4	4	4	4	4	4	4	4	2	-	2	-	2	-	2	-
MA	8	2	10	-	10	-	9	-	2	-	2	-	2	-	2	-
MI	10	6	10	6	10	6	9	7	2	-	1	1	1	1	2	-
MN	6	2	6	2	6	2	5	3	1	1	1	1	1	1	2	-
MS	5	-	2	3	3	2	3	2	-	2	-	2	-	2	-	2
MO	6	3	5	4	5	4	4	5	-	2	-	2	-	2	1	1
MT	1	-	-	1	-	1	-	1	1	1	1	1	1	1	1	1
NE	1	2	-	3	-	3	-	3	2	-	1	1	1	1	1	1
NV	1	1	-	2	1	1	1	1	2	-	2	-	2	-	1	1
NH	1	1	-	2	-	2	-	2	-	2	-	2	-	2	-	2
NJ	7	6	6	7	7	6	7	6	2	-	2	-	2	-	2	-
NM	1	2	-	3	1	2	1	2	1	1	1	1	1	1	1	1 -
NY.	18	13	18	13	19	12	19	12	1	1	1	1	2	-	2	-
NC	8	4	6	6	5	7	5	7	-	2	-	2	1	1	1	1
ND	1	-	1	-	1	-	1	-	2	-	2	-	2	-	2	-
OH	10	9	8	11	8	11	8	11	2	-	1	1	-	2	-	2
OK	4	2	-	6	-	6	1	5	1	1	-	2	-	2	-	2
OR	4	1	4	1	4	1	4	1	-	2	1	1	1	1	1	1
PA	11	10	11	10	11	10	10	11	1	1	-	2	-	2	-	2
RI	1	1	2	-	2	-	2	-	1	1	1	1	1	1	1	1
SC.	3	3	2	4	2	4	2	4	1	1	1	1	1	1	1	1
SD.	1	-	-	1	-	1	-	1	1	1	2	-	2	-	2	-
TN.	6	3	4	5	4	5	4	5	2	-	-	2	-	2	-	2
TX.	21	9	17	13	17	13	17	13	1	1	-	2	-	2	-	2
UT.	2	1	-	3	-	3	1	2	-	2	-	2	-	2	-	2
VT.	-	-	-	-	-	-	-	-	1	1	1	1	1	1	1	-
VA.	7	4	6	5	6	5	3	7	1	1	1	1	1	1	-	2
WA	8	1	3	6	5	4	6	3	1	1	1	1	1	1	2	-
WV	3	-	3	-	3	-	2	1	2	-	2	-	2	-	2	-
WI	4	5	5	4	5	4	5	4	2	-	2	-	2	-	2	-
WY	-	1	-	1	-	1	-	1	-	2	-	2	-	2	-	2

- Represents zero.   [1] Alabama and Indiana had one vacancy each.   [2] Vermont had one Independent-Socialist Representative.   [3] As of beginning of second session.   [4] California had one vacancy.   [5] Oregon had one vacancy.   [6] Massachusetts and Arkansas had one vacancy each.   [7] Vermont and Virginia had one Independent Representative each.

Source: U.S. Congress, Joint Committee on Printing, Congressional Directory, biennial; and unpublished data.

U.S. Census Bureau, Statistical Abstract of the United States: 2001

No. 389. Members of Congress—Incumbents Reelected: 1964 to 2000

	Representatives						Senators					
	Incumbent candidates						Incumbent candidates					
			Re-elected		Defeated in—				Re-elected		Defeated in—	
Year	Retire-ments [1]	Total	Num-ber	Per-cent of candi-dates	Pri-mary	General election	Retire-ments [1]	Total	Num-ber	Per-cent of candi-dates	Pri-mary	General election
PRESIDENTIAL-YEAR ELECTIONS												
1964	33	397	344	86.6	8	45	2	33	28	84.8	1	4
1968	23	409	396	96.8	4	9	6	28	20	71.4	4	4
1972	40	390	365	93.6	12	13	6	27	20	74.1	2	5
1976	47	384	368	95.8	3	13	8	25	16	64.0	-	9
1980	34	398	361	90.7	6	31	5	29	16	55.2	4	9
1984	22	411	392	95.4	3	16	4	29	26	89.7	-	3
1988	23	409	402	98]	1	6	6	27	23	85.2	-	4
1992	65	368	325	88.3	[2]19	[3]24	7	28	23	82.1	1	4
1996	50	384	361	94.0	2	21	13	21	19	90.5	1	1
2000	32	403	394	97.8	3	6	5	29	23	79.3	-	6
MIDTERM ELECTIONS												
1966	22	411	362	88.1	8	41	3	32	28	87.5	3	1
1970	29	401	379	94.5	10	12	4	31	24	77.4	1	6
1974	43	391	343	87.7	8	40	7	27	23	85.2	2	2
1978	49	382	358	93.7	5	19	10	25	15	60.0	3	7
1982	40	393	354	90.1	[2]10	29	3	30	28	93.3	-	2
1986	40	394	385	97.7	3	6	6	28	21	75.0	-	7
1990	27	406	390	96.1	1	15	3	32	31	96.9	-	1
1994	48	387	349	90.2	4	34	9	26	24	92.3	-	2
1998	23	404	395	97.8	1	6	5	29	26	89.7	-	3

- Represents zero.   [1] Does not include persons who died or resigned before the election.   [2] Number of incumbents defeated in primaries by other incumbents due to redistricting: six in 1982 and four in 1992.   [3] Five incumbents defeated in general election by other incumbents due to redistricting.

Source: Ornstein, Norman J., Thomas E. Mann, and Michael J. Malbin, *Vital Statistics on Congress, 1993-1994*, Beginning 1995, Congressional Quarterly, Inc., Washington, DC, *America Votes*, biennial (copyright).

No. 390. Members of Congress—Selected Characteristics: 1981 to 1999

[As of beginning of first session of each Congress, (January 3). Figures for Representatives exclude vacancies]

Members of congress and year	Male	Fe-male	Black [1]	API [2]	His-panic [3]	Age [4] (in years)					Seniority [5]				
						Under 40	40 to 49	50 to 59	60 to 69	70 and over	Less than 2 yrs.	2 to 9 yrs.	10 to 19 yrs.	20 to 29 yrs.	30 yrs. or more
REPRESENTATIVES															
97th Cong., 1981	416	19	[6]18	3	6	94	142	132	54	13	77	231	96	23	8
98th Cong., 1983	413	21	[6]21	3	8	86	145	132	57	14	83	224	88	28	11
99th Cong., 1985	412	22	[6]21	3	10	71	154	131	59	19	49	237	104	34	10
100th Cong., 1987. . . .	412	23	[6]23	4	11	63	153	137	56	26	51	221	114	37	12
101st Cong., 1989. . . .	408	25	[6]24	5	10	41	163	133	74	22	39	207	139	35	13
102d Cong., 1991	407	28	[6]26	3	11	39	152	134	86	24	55	178	147	44	11
103d Cong., 1993 [8] . . .	388	47	[6]38	4	17	47	151	128	89	15	118	141	132	32	12
104th Cong., 1995. . . .	388	47	[7]40	4	17	53	155	135	79	13	92	188	110	36	9
106th Cong., 1999. . . .	379	56	[7]39	(NA)	(NA)	23	116	173	87	35	41	236	104	46	7
SENATORS															
97th Cong., 1981	98	2	-	3	-	9	35	36	14	6	19	51	17	11	2
98th Cong., 1983	98	2	-	2	-	7	28	39	20	6	5	61	21	10	3
99th Cong., 1985	98	2	-	2	-	4	27	38	25	6	8	56	27	7	2
100th Cong., 1987. . . .	98	2	-	2	-	5	30	36	22	7	14	41	36	7	2
101st Cong., 1989. . . .	98	2	-	2	-	-	30	40	22	8	23	22	43	10	2
102d Cong., 1991	98	2	-	2	-	-	23	46	24	7	5	34	47	10	4
103d Cong., 1993 [8] . . .	93	7	1	2	-	1	16	48	22	12	15	30	39	11	5
104th Cong., 1995. . . .	92	8	1	2	-	1	14	41	27	17	12	38	30	15	5
106th Cong., 1999. . . .	91	9	-	(NA)	(NA)	-	14	38	35	13	8	39	33	14	6

- Represents zero.   NA Not available.   [1] Source: Joint Center for Political and Economic Studies, Washington, DC. *Black Elected Officials: Statistical Summary*, annual (copyright).   [2] Asian and Pacific Islanders. Source: Library of Congress. Congressional Research Service, "Asian Pacific Americans in the United States Congress", Report 94-767 GOV.   [3] Source: National Association of Latino Elected and Appointed Officials, Washington, DC, *National Roster of Hispanic Elected Officials*, annual.   [4] Some members do not provide date of birth.   [5] Represents consecutive years of service.   [6] Includes District of Columbia delegate but not Virgin Islands Delegate.   [7] Includes members elected to fill vacant seats through June 14, 1993.   [8] Includes District of Columbia and Virgin Islands delegate.

Source: Except as noted, compiled by U.S. Census Bureau from data published in *Congressional Directory*, biennial.

No. 391. U.S. Congress—Measures Introduced and Enacted and Time in Session: 1983 to 1999

[Excludes simple and concurrent resolutions]

Item	98th Cong., 1983-84	99th Cong., 1985-86	100th Cong., 1989-90	101st Cong., 1991-92	102d Cong., 1991-92	103d Cong., 1993-94	104th Cong., 1995-96	105th Cong., 1996-97	106th Cong., 1998-99
Measures introduced	11,156	9,885	9,588	6,664	6,775	8,544	6,808	7,732	9,158
Bills	10,134	8,697	8,515	5,977	6,212	7,883	6,545	7,532	8,968
Joint resolutions	1,022	1,188	1,073	687	563	661	263	200	190
Measures enacted	677	483	761	666	609	473	337	404	604
Public	623	466	713	650	589	465	333	394	580
Private	54	17	48	16	20	8	4	10	24
HOUSE OF REPRESENTATIVES									
Number of days	266	281	298	281	280	265	290	251	272
Number of hours	1,705	1,794	1,659	1,688	1,796	1,887	2,445	2,001	2,179
Number of hours per day	6.4	6.4	5.6	6.0	6.4	7.1	8.4	8.0	8.0
SENATE									
Number of days	281	313	307	274	287	291	343	296	303
Number of hours	1,951	2,531	2,341	2,254	2,292	2,514	2,876	2,188	2,200
Number of hours per day	6.9	8.1	7.6	8.2	8.0	8.6	8.4	7.4	7.3

Source: U.S. Congress, *Congressional Record* and *Daily Calendar*, selected issues.

No. 392. Congressional Bills Vetoed: 1961 to 1999

Period	President	Total vetoes	Regular vetoes	Pocket vetoes	Vetoes sustained	Bills passed over veto
1961-63	Kennedy	21	12	9	21	-
1963-69	Johnson	30	16	14	30	-
1969-74	Nixon	43	26	17	36	7
1974-77	Ford	66	48	18	54	12
1977-81	Carter	31	13	18	29	2
1981-89	Reagan	78	39	39	69	9
1989-93	Bush	44	29	15	43	1
1993-99	Clinton	30	30	-	28	2

- Represents zero.

Source: U.S. Congress, Senate Library, *Presidential Vetoes ... 1789-1968*; U.S. Congress, *Calendars of the U.S. House of Representatives and History of Legislation*, annual.

No. 393. Number of Governors by Political Party Affiliation: 1970 to 2001

[Reflects figures after inaugurations for each year]

Year	Democratic	Republican	Independent/ other	Year	Democratic	Republican	Independent/ other	Year	Democratic	Republican	Independent/ other
1970	18	32	-	1990	29	21	-	1996	18	31	1
1975	36	13	1	1991 [1]	29	19	2	1997	17	32	1
1980	31	19	-	1992	28	20	2	1998	17	32	1
1985	34	16	-	1993	30	18	2	1999	17	31	2
1988	27	23	-	1994	29	19	2	2000	17	31	2
1989	28	22	-	1995	19	30	1	2001	19	31	-

- Represents zero. [1] Reflects result of runoff election in Arizona in February 1991.

Source: National Governors' Association, Washington, DC, 1970-87 and 1991-99, *Directory of Governors of the American States, Commonwealths & Territories*, annual; and 1988-90, *Directory of Governors*, annual. (copyright).

No. 394. Vote Cast for and Governor Elected by State: 1990 to 2000

[In thousands, except percent (1,216 represents 1,216,000). D=Democratic, R=Republican, I=Independent]

State	1990 Total vote [1]	1990 Percent leading party	1996 Total vote [1]	1996 Percent leading party	1998 Total vote [1]	1998 Percent leading party	2000 Total vote [1]	2000 Percent leading party	Candidate elected at most recent election
AL	1,216	R-52.1	(X)	(X)	1,318	D-57.7	(X)	(X)	Donald Siegelman
AK	195	I-38.9	(X)	(X)	220	D-51.3	(X)	(X)	Tony Knowles
AZ	[2]941	[2]R-52.4	(X)	(X)	1,018	R-60.9	(X)	(X)	Jane Dee Hull
AR	696	D-57.5	(X)	(X)	706	R-59.8	(X)	(X)	Mike Huckabee
CA	7,699	R-49.2	(X)	(X)	8,385	D-58.0	(X)	(X)	Gray Davis
CO	1,011	D-61.9	(X)	(X)	1,321	R-49.1	(X)	(X)	Bill Owens
CT	1,141	I-40.4	(X)	(X)	1,000	R-62.9	(X)	(X)	John G. Rowland
DE	(X)	(X)	271	D-69.5	(X)	(X)	324	D-59.2	Ruth Ann Minner
FL	3,531	D-56.5	(X)	(X)	3,964	R-55.3	(X)	(X)	Jeb Bush
GA	1,450	D-52.9	(X)	(X)	1,793	D-52.5	(X)	(X)	Roy Barnes
HI	340	D-59.8	(X)	(X)	408	D-50.1	(X)	(X)	Benjamin J. Cayetano
ID	321	D-68.2	(X)	(X)	381	R-67.7	(X)	(X)	Dirk Kempthorne
IL	3,257	R-50.7	(X)	(X)	3,359	R-51.0	(X)	(X)	George Ryan
IN	(X)	(X)	2,110	D-51.5	(X)	(X)	2,179	D-56.6	Frank L. O'Bannon
IA	976	R-60.6	(X)	(X)	956	D-52.3	(X)	(X)	Tom Vilsack
KS [2]	783	D-48.6	(X)	(X)	743	R-73.4	(X)	(X)	Bill Graves
KY [2]	(X)	(X)	984	D-50.9	(X)	(X)	580	D-60.7	Paul E. Patton
LA	(X)	(X)	1,550	R-63.5	(X)	(X)	1,295	R-62.2	Mike Foster
ME	522	R-46.7	(X)	(X)	421	R-18.9	(X)	(X)	Angus King
MD	1,111	D-59.8	(X)	(X)	1,536	D-55.1	(X)	(X)	Parris N. Glendening
MA	2,343	R-50.2	(X)	(X)	1,903	R-50.8	(X)	(X)	Argeo Paul Cellucci
MI	2,565	R-49.8	(X)	(X)	3,027	R-62.2	(X)	(X)	John Engler
MN	1,807	R-49.6	(X)	(X)	2,091	R-34.3	(X)	(X)	Jesse Ventura
MS [2]	(X)	(X)	819	R-55.6	(X)	(X)	764	D-49.6	Ronnie Musgrove
MO	(X)	(X)	2,143	D-57.2	(X)	(X)	2,347	D-49.1	Bob Holden
MT	(X)	(X)	405	R-79.2	(X)	(X)	410	R-51.0	Judy Martz
NE	587	D-49.9	(X)	(X)	545	R-53.9	(X)	(X)	Mike Johanns
NV	321	D-64.8	(X)	(X)	434	R-51.6	(X)	(X)	Kenny Guinn
NH	295	R-60.3	497	D-57.2	319	D-66.1	565	D-48.7	Jeanne Shaheen
NJ [3]	2,254	D-61.2	(X)	(X)	2,418	R-46.9	(X)	(X)	Christine Todd Whitman
NM	411	D-54.6	(X)	(X)	499	R-54.5	(X)	(X)	Gary E. Johnson
NY	4,057	D-53.2	(X)	(X)	4,735	R-54.3	(X)	(X)	George E. Pataki
NC	(X)	(X)	2,566	D-56.0	(X)	(X)	2,942	D-52.0	Mike Easley
ND	(X)	(X)	264	R-66.2	(X)	(X)	289	R-55.0	John Hoeven
OH	3,478	R-55.7	(X)	(X)	3,354	R-50.0	(X)	(X)	Bob Taft
OK	911	D-57.4	(X)	(X)	874	R-57.9	(X)	(X)	Frank Keating
OR	1,113	D-45.7	(X)	(X)	1,113	D-64.4	(X)	(X)	John Kitzhaber
PA	3,025	D-67.7	(X)	(X)	3,025	R-57.4	(X)	(X)	Tom Ridge
RI	357	D-74.1	(X)	(X)	306	R-51.0	(X)	(X)	Lincoln C. Almond
SC	761	R-69.5	(X)	(X)	1,071	D-53.2	(X)	(X)	Jim Hodges
SD	257	R-58.9	(X)	(X)	260	R-64.0	(X)	(X)	William J. Janklow
TN	790	D-60.8	(X)	(X)	976	R-68.6	(X)	(X)	Don Sundquist
TX	3,893	D-49.5	(X)	(X)	3,738	R-68.2	(X)	(X)	George W. Bush
UT	(X)	(X)	672	R-75.0	(X)	(X)	762	R-55.8	Michael O. Leavitt
VT	211	R-51.8	255	D-70.5	218	D-55.7	293	D-50.5	Howard Dean
VA [3]	1,789	D-50.1	(X)	(X)	1,736	R-55.8	(X)	(X)	James S. Gilmore
WA	(X)	(X)	2,237	D-58.0	(X)	(X)	2,470	D-58.4	Gary Locke
WV	(X)	(X)	629	R-51.6	(X)	(X)	648	D-50.1	Bob Wise
WI	1,380	R-58.2	(X)	(X)	1,756	R-59.7	(X)	(X)	Tommy G. Thompson
WY	160	D-65.4	(X)	(X)	175	R-55.6	(X)	(X)	Jim Geringer

X Not applicable.   [1] Includes minor party and scattered votes.   [2] Voting years 1987, 1991, and 1995.   [3] Voting years 1989, 1993, and 1997.

Source: Congressional Quarterly Inc., Washington, D.C., *America Votes*, biennial; and unpublished data (copyright).

Elections   247

No. 395. Composition of State Legislatures by Political Party Affiliation: 1994 to 2000

[Data reflect election results in year shown for most states; and except as noted, results in previous year for other states. Figures reflect immediate results of elections, including holdover members in state houses which do not have all of their members running for re-election. Dem.=Democrat, Rep.=Republican. In general, Lower House refers to body consisting of state Representatives; Upper House, of state Senators]

State	Lower House								Upper House							
	1994 [1,2]		1996 [1,2]		1998 [1]		2000 [3]		1994 [1,4]		1996 [6]		1998 [4]		2000 [7]	
	Dem.	Rep.	Dem.	Rep.	Dem.	Rep.	Dem.	Rep.	Dem.	Rep.	Dem.	Rep.	Dem.	Rep.	Dem.	Rep.
U.S.	2,817	2,603	2,886	2,539	2,903	2,580	2,818	2,600	1,021	905	998	931	1,041	963	995	931
AL [8]	74	31	72	33	71	34	67	36	23	12	22	12	22	13	23	12
AK [9]	17	22	16	24	15	25	13	27	8	12	7	13	6	14	6	14
AZ [10]	22	38	22	38	22	38	24	36	11	19	12	18	12	18	15	15
AR [9]	88	12	86	13	86	14	70	30	28	7	28	6	28	7	27	8
CA [9]	39	40	43	37	42	37	50	29	21	17	25	15	23	16	26	13
CO [9]	24	41	24	41	24	41	28	37	16	19	15	20	15	20	18	17
CT [10]	90	61	97	54	96	55	100	51	17	19	19	17	19	17	21	15
DE [9]	14	27	14	27	13	28	15	26	12	9	13	8	13	8	13	8
FL [9]	63	57	59	61	57	63	43	77	19	21	17	23	17	23	15	25
GA [10]	114	65	106	74	102	78	104	74	35	20	34	22	34	22	34	24
HI [9]	44	7	39	12	39	12	32	19	23	2	23	2	23	2	24	3
ID [10]	13	57	11	59	11	59	9	61	8	27	5	30	5	30	3	32
IL [11]	54	64	60	58	60	58	62	56	26	33	28	31	28	31	27	32
IN [9]	44	56	50	50	50	50	53	47	20	30	19	31	19	31	18	32
IA [9]	36	64	46	54	46	54	44	56	27	23	21	29	22	28	20	30
KS [9]	45	80	48	77	48	77	46	79	13	27	13	27	13	2.	10	30
KY [9]	64	36	64	36	64	36	66	34	21	17	20	18	20	18	18	20
LA [8]	86	17	76	28	78	27	71	32	33	6	25	14	25	14	26	13
ME [10]	77	74	81	69	81	69	81	69	16	18	19	15	19	15	17	17
MD [8]	100	41	100	41	99	41	106	35	32	15	32	15	32	15	33	14
MA [10]	125	34	134	25	130	29	136	24	30	10	34	6	31	8	34	6
MI [9]	53	56	58	52	58	51	53	56	16	22	16	22	16	22	14	22
MN [9]	71	63	70	64	70	64	65	69	43	21	42	24	42	24	39	26
MS [8]	89	31	86	33	84	36	86	33	36	14	34	18	34	18	34	18
MO [9]	87	76	88	75	85	76	87	76	19	15	19	15	19	15	15	16
MT [9]	33	67	35	65	35	65	42	58	19	31	16	34	16	33	19	31
NE [12]	(12)	(12)	(12)	(12)	(12)	(12)	(12)	(12)	(12)	(12)	(12)	(12)	(12)	(12)	(12)	(12)
NV [9]	21	21	25	17	25	17	27	15	8	13	9	12	9	12	9	12
NH [10]	112	286	143	255	147	248	143	255	6	18	9	15	9	15	11	13
NJ [9]	28	52	30	50	32	48	32	48	16	24	16	24	16	24	16	24
NM [9]	46	24	42	28	42	28	42	28	27	15	25	17	25	17	24	18
NY [10]	94	56	96	54	95	52	99	51	25	36	26	35	26	35	25	36
NC [10]	52	68	59	61	59	61	62	58	26	24	30	20	30	20	35	15
ND [13]	23	75	26	72	26	71	29	69	20	29	19	30	18	29	17	32
OH [9]	43	56	39	60	39	60	40	59	13	20	12	21	12	20	12	20
OK [9]	65	36	65	36	65	36	53	48	35	13	33	15	33	15	30	18
OR [9]	26	34	29	31	29	31	27	33	11	19	10	20	10	20	14	16
PA [10]	101	102	99	104	99	104	99	104	21	29	20	30	20	30	20	28
RI [10]	84	16	84	16	84	16	85	15	40	10	41	9	42	8	44	6
SC [9]	58	62	53	70	52	71	54	69	29	17	26	20	25	21	22	24
SD [10]	24	46	23	47	22	48	20	50	16	19	13	22	13	22	11	24
TN [9]	59	40	61	38	61	38	61	38	18	15	18	15	18	15	18	15
TX [9]	89	61	82	68	82	68	77	72	17	14	14	16	14	17	15	16
UT [9]	20	55	20	55	21	54	25	50	10	19	9	20	9	20	9	20
VT [10]	86	61	89	57	89	57	62	83	12	18	17	13	17	13	16	14
VA [9]	52	47	53	46	51	48	47	52	22	18	20	20	19	21	18	22
WA [9]	38	60	45	53	41	57	49	49	25	24	23	26	23	26	25	24
WV [9]	69	30	74	25	74	26	75	25	26	8	25	9	25	9	28	6
WI [9]	48	51	47	52	46	51	43	56	16	17	17	16	17	16	18	15
WY [9]	13	47	17	43	17	43	14	46	10	20	9	21	9	21	10	20

[1] Status as of December 7, 1994. [2] Excludes one Independent each for AK, CA, LA, and VA; two Independents each for MS and VT; four Independents for SC; members of political parties other than Democratic, Republican, or Independent (one in MA and VT, and two in NH) one undecided in GA; and one vacancy each in LA, MI, and WV; one vacancy each for GA, NH, TX, and WI; two vacancies each for CT and MA; and three vacancies for NV. [3] Excludes one Independent each for NH and VA; two for GA; three each for ME and MS; five for VT; one vacancy each for CA, MI, NH, SC and two vacancies in AL. [4] Excludes one Independent for CA and one vacancy each for AL and NJ. [5] Excludes two Independents for CA; and one vacancy each for CA and PA. [6] Excludes one Independent in ME, two Independents in CA, one vacancy in GA, two vacancies in MS, and three vacancies in MN. [7] Excludes one Independent each for ME and MN; one vacancy each in CA and OH; two vacancies for MI and PA; three vacancies for MO. [8] Members of both houses serve 4-year terms. [9] Upper House members serve 4-year terms and Lower House members serve 2-year terms. [10] Members of both houses serve 2-year terms. [11] Illinois—4 and 2 year term depending on district. [12] Nebraska—4 year term. [13] North Dakota—By the 2001 session all Senators and Representatives will be serving 4-year terms.

Source: The Council of State Governments, Lexington, KY, State Elective Officials and the Legislatures, biennial (copyright); thereafter, National Conference of State Legislatures, Denver, CO, unpublished data.

No. 396. Political Party Control of State Legislatures by Party: 1975 to 2000

[As of beginning of year. Until 1972 there were two nonpartisan legislatures in Minnesota and Nebraska. Since then only Nebraska has had a nonpartisan legislature]

Year	Legislatures under—			Year	Legislatures under—			Year	Legislatures under—		
	Demo-cratic control	Split control or tie	Re-publican control		Demo-cratic control	Split control or tie	Re-publican control		Demo-cratic control	Split control or tie	Re-publican control
1975...	37	7	5	1987...	28	12	9	1995...	18	12	19
1977...	36	8	5	1989 [2]	28	13	8	1996...	16	15	18
1979...	30	7	12	1990...	29	11	9	1997...	20	11	18
1981...	28	6	15	1992...	29	14	6	1999...	20	12	17
1983 [1]	34	4	11	1993...	25	16	8	2000...	16	15	18
1985...	27	11	11	1994...	24	17	8				

[1] Two 1984 midterm recall elections resulted in a change in control of the Michigan State Senate. At the time of the 1984 election, therefore, Democrats controlled 33 legislatures.   [2] A party change during the year by a Democratic representative broke the tie in the Indiana House of Representatives, giving the Republicans control of both chambers.
Source: National Conference of State Legislatures, Denver, CO, *State Legislatures*, periodic.

No. 397. Women Holding State Public Offices by Office and State: 2000

[As of January. For data on women in U.S. Congress, see Table 390]

State	State-wide elective executive office [1]	State legisla-ture	State	State-wide elective executive office [1]	State legisla-ture	State	State-wide elective executive office [1]	State legisla-ture
United States .	92	1,672	Kentucky	-	16	North Dakota . . .	4	26
Alabama	3	11	Louisiana	1	23	Ohio	2	27
Alaska	1	11	Maine	-	52	Oklahoma	4	15
Arizona	5	32	Maryland	1	55	Oregon	-	27
Arkansas	2	21	Massachusetts . .	2	52	Pennsylvania . . .	1	32
California	2	31	Michigan	2	36	Rhode Island . . .	-	37
Colorado	1	34	Minnesota	4	57	South Carolina . .	1	18
Connecticut	4	56	Mississippi	-	22	South Dakota . . .	4	15
Delaware	3	15	Missouri	2	44	Tennessee	1	23
Florida	1	39	Montana	2	37	Texas	2	33
Georgia	2	46	Nebraska	2	12	Utah	2	22
Hawaii	1	17	Nevada	3	22	Vermont	1	57
Idaho.	1	27	New Hampshire. .	1	135	Virginia	-	23
Illinois	2	44	New Jersey	1	19	Washington	4	60
Indiana	3	27	New Mexico	3	31	West Virginia . . .	-	24
Iowa	2	31	New York	1	45	Wisconsin.	-	31
Kansas	2	54	North Carolina. . .	1	31	Wyoming	2	17

- Represents zero.   [1] Excludes women elected to the judiciary, women appointed to state cabinet-level positions, women elected to executive posts by the legislature, and elected members of university Board of Trustees or board of education.
Source: Center for the American Woman and Politics, Eagleton Institute of Politics, Rutgers University, New Brunswick, NJ, information releases, copyright.

No. 398. Public Confidence Levels in Selected Public and Private Institutions: 1999

[Based on a sample survey of 2,719 persons 18 years old and over conducted during the spring and subject to sampling variability; see source]

Institution	Level of confidence				
	A great deal	Quite a lot	Some	Very little	Can't say/ no answer
Religious organizations	31.9	29.5	26.7	9.7	2.1
Private higher education (colleges or univ.)	22.9	35.6	26.6	8.1	6.9
Private elementary or secondary education	17.0	33.8	32.5	10.3	6.4
Youth development and recreation organizations	33.0	38.9	20.1	4.9	3.0
Federated charitable appeals	16.1	28.8	33.2	16.4	5.6
Health organizations	15.0	27.5	35.4	12.8	9.3
Environmental organizations	13.3	25.7	36.0	15.8	9.2
Human service organizations	29.0	38.7	23.6	5.5	3.2
Private and community foundations	8.7	26.5	36.2	12.5	16.2
Public /society benefit organizations [1]	10.9	22.5	41.4	18.4	6.8
International/foreign organizations [2]	7.7	19.9	38.5	20.9	13.0
Small businesses	16.4	38.1	33.4	8.7	3.5
Military	22.2	35.0	29.4	10.8	2.6
Public higher educ. (colleges or univ.)	19.1	42.4	28.7	7.4	2.4
Public elementary or secondary education	15.9	35.0	32.6	14.9	1.5
Organized labor	9.9	18.1	39.1	27.5	5.4
Media (e.g. newspapers, TV, radio)	7.6	20.7	37.4	32.5	1.8
Work-related organizations.	6.6	23.5	47.1	14.7	8.2
Major corporations	7.4	21.5	43.5	23.0	4.6
State government.	7.9	23.1	45.0	21.6	2.4
Political organizations, parties.	4.3	14.5	37.3	40.5	3.4
Local government.	8.7	24.1	42.8	22.0	2.4
Federal government	7.9	19.5	43.4	26.9	2.3
Congress	6.4	15.8	40.2	34.9	2.7

[1] Civil rights, social justice, or community improvement organizations.   [2] Culture exchange or relief organizations.
Source: Saxon-Harold, Susan K.E., Murray Weitzman, and the Gallup Organization, Inc., *Giving & Volunteering in the United States: 1999 Edition.* (Copyright and published by INDEPENDENT SECTOR, Washington, DC, 2000.)

Elections 249

No. 399. Black Elected Officials by Office, 1970 to 1999, and State, 1999

[As of January 1999, no Black elected officials had been identified in Hawaii, Idaho, Maine, Montana, North Dakota, South Dakota, or Wyoming]

State	Total	U.S. and state legisla- tures[1]	City and county offices[2]	Law enforce- ment[3]	Educa- tion[4]	State	Total	U.S. and state legisla- tures[1]	City and county offices[2]	Law enforce- ment[3]	Educa- tion[4]
1970 (Feb.)	1,469	179	715	213	362	MA	31	6	20	2	3
1980 (July)	4,890	326	2,832	526	1,206	MI	338	22	144	54	118
1990 (Jan.)	7,335	436	4,485	769	1,645	MN	16	1	4	6	5
1995 (Jan.)	8,385	604	4,954	987	1,840	MS	850	46	575	97	132
1996 (Jan.)	8,545	606	5,023	994	1,922	MO	201	17	149	12	23
1997 (Jan.)	8,617	613	5,056	996	1,952	NE	4	1	1	-	2
1998 (Jan.)	8,830	614	5,210	998	2,008	NV	13	5	4	2	2
1999 (Jan.)	8,896	618	5,354	997	1,927	NH	3	3	-	-	-
						NJ	239	16	133	1	89
AL	725	36	540	53	96	NM	4	1	-	2	1
AK	3	-	2	-	1	NY	305	32	73	75	125
AZ	13	2	1	4	6	NC	506	27	359	28	92
AR	504	15	297	65	127	OH	284	18	199	25	42
CA	237	10	66	77	84	OK	105	6	80	3	16
CO	21	5	5	10	1	OR	7	4	1	2	-
CT	68	15	43	3	7	PA	164	19	57	60	28
DE	24	4	16	1	3	RI	10	9	1	-	-
DC	199	[5]2	192	-	5	SC	542	34	333	8	167
FL	216	23	146	33	14	TN	172	17	105	25	25
GA	584	48	394	40	102	TX	479	18	319	42	100
IL	627	27	314	56	230	UT	1	-	-	1	-
IN	84	14	50	12	8	VT	1	1	-	-	-
IA	14	1	8	1	4	VA	251	16	137	16	82
KS	19	7	5	4	3	WA	21	2	9	9	1
KY	62	4	47	5	6	WV	19	4	12	3	-
LA	714	32	398	123	161	WI	31	8	14	4	5
MD	185	40	101	33	11						

- Represents zero. [1] Includes elected state administrators. [2] County commissioners and councilmen, mayors, vice mayors, aldermen, regional officials, and other. [3] Judges, magistrates, constables, marshals, sheriffs, justices of the peace, and other. [4] Members of state education agencies, college boards, school boards, and other. [5] Includes one shadow representative.

Source: Joint Center for Political and Economic Studies, Washington, DC, *Black Elected Officials: A Statistical Summary*, annual (copyright) and <http://www.jointcenter.org/databank/graphs/98eo.pdf> and <http://www.jointcenter.org/databank/graphs/99beo.pdf> (accessed 17 April 2001).

No. 400. Hispanic Public Elected Officials by Office, 1985 to 2000, and State, 2000

[As of September. For states not shown, no Hispanic public officials had been identified]

State	Total	State execu- tives and legisla- tors[1]	County and munici- pal officials	Judicial and law enforce- ment	Educa- tion and school boards	State	Total	State execu- tives and legisla- tors[1]	County and munici- pal officials	Judicial and law enforce- ment	Educa- tion and school boards
1985 (Sept.)	3,147	129	1,316	517	1,185	LA	3	-	1	2	-
1987 (Sept.)	3,317	138	1,412	568	1,199	MA	13	3	7	-	3
1988 (Sept.)	3,360	135	1,425	574	1,226	MI	8	2	5	-	1
1989 (Sept.)	3,783	143	1,724	575	1,341	MN	3	1	1	1	-
1990 (Sept.)	4,004	144	1,819	583	1,458	MO	1	-	1	-	-
1991 (Sept.)	4,202	151	1,867	596	1,588	MT	1	-	-	1	-
1992 (Sept.)	4,994	150	1,908	628	2,308	NE	3	1	2	-	-
1993 (Sept.)	5,170	182	2,023	633	2,332	NV	4	1	2	1	-
1994 (Sept.)	5,459	199	2,197	651	2,412	NH	1	1	-	-	-
2000	5,205	223	1,846	454	2,682	NJ	77	6	46	-	25
CA	767	33	317	37	380	NM	618	48	316	74	180
CO	154	11	92	9	42	NY	76	14	16	8	38
CT	26	5	17	-	4	NC	1	1	-	-	-
DE	3	1	2	-	-	OH	7	-	5	2	-
DC	1	-	1	-	-	OR	6	-	5	-	1
FL	90	17	57	11	5	PA	5	1	2	1	1
GA	3	-	3	-	-	RI	3	2	1	-	-
HI	2	1	1	-	-	TX	1,828	42	768	280	738
ID	2	-	2	-	-	UT	3	1	2	-	-
IL	1,190	7	34	-	[2]1,149	VA	1	-	-	-	1
IN	10	1	7	1	1	WA	12	3	6	-	3
IA	1	-	1	-	-	WI	12	1	6	3	2
KS	6	2	4	-	-	WY	4	1	3	-	-

- Represents zero. [1] Includes U.S. Representatives, not shown separately. [2] Includes local school council members in the Chicago area.

Source: National Association of Latino Elected and Appointed Officials, Washington, DC, *National Roster of Hispanic Elected Officials*, annual.

No. 401. Voting-Age Population, Percent Reporting Registered, and Voted: 1980 to 2000

[As of November. Covers civilian noninstitutional population 18 years old and over. Includes aliens. Figures are based on Current Population Survey (see text, Section 1, Population, and Appendix III) and differ from those in Table 403 based on population estimates and official vote counts]

Characteristic	VAP (mil.) 1980	1988	1990	1994	1996	1998	2000	Reg. Pres. 1980	1992	1996	2000	Reg. Cong. 1986	1990	1994	1998	Voted Pres. 1980	1992	1996	2000	Voted Cong. 1986	1990	1994	1998
Total [1]	157.1	178.1	182.1	190.3	193.7	198.2	202.6	66.9	68.2	65.9	63.9	64.3	62.2	62.0	62.1	59.2	61.3	54.2	54.7	46.0	45.0	44.6	41.9
18 to 20 years old	12.3	10.7	10.8	10.3	10.8	11.4	11.9	44.7	48.3	45.6	40.5	35.4	35.4	37.2	32.1	35.7	38.5	31.2	28.4	18.6	18.4	16.5	13.5
21 to 24 years old	15.9	14.8	14.0	14.9	13.9	14.1	14.9	52.7	55.3	51.2	49.3	46.6	43.3	45.5	43.1	45.7	46.0	33.4	24.2	22.0	22.3	19.2	28.0
25 to 34 years old	35.7	42.7	42.7	41.1	40.1	38.6	37.3	62.0	60.6	56.9	54.7	55.8	52.0	51.5	52.4	54.6	53.2	43.1	43.7	35.1	33.8	32.2	40.7
35 to 44 years old	25.6	35.2	37.9	41.9	43.3	44.4	44.5	70.6	69.2	66.5	63.8	67.9	65.5	63.3	62.4	64.4	63.6	54.9	55.0	49.3	48.4	46.0	53.6
45 to 64 years old	43.6	45.9	46.9	50.9	53.7	57.4	61.4	75.8	75.3	73.5	71.2	74.8	71.4	71.0	73.1	69.3	70.0	(NA)	64.1	58.7	55.8	56.0	59.5
65 years old and over	24.1	28.8	29.9	31.1	31.9	32.7	32.8	74.6	78.0	77.0	76.1	76.9	78.5	75.6	75.4	65.1	70.1	(NA)	67.6	60.9	60.3	60.7	59.5
Male	74.1	84.5	86.6	91.0	92.6	95.2	97.1	66.6	66.9	64.4	62.2	63.4	61.2	60.8	60.6	59.1	60.2	52.8	53.1	45.8	44.6	44.4	41.4
Female	83.0	93.6	95.5	99.3	101.0	103.0	105.5	67.1	69.3	67.3	65.6	65.0	63.1	63.2	63.5	59.4	62.3	55.5	56.2	46.1	45.4	44.9	42.4
White	137.7	152.9	155.6	160.3	162.8	165.8	168.7	68.4	70.1	67.7	65.6	65.3	63.8	64.2	63.9	60.9	63.6	56.0	56.4	47.0	46.7	46.9	43.3
Black	16.4	19.7	20.4	21.8	22.5	23.3	24.1	60.0	63.9	63.5	63.6	64.0	58.8	58.3	60.2	50.5	54.0	50.6	53.5	43.2	39.2	37.0	39.6
Hispanic [2]	8.2	12.9	13.8	17.5	18.4	20.3	21.6	36.3	35.0	35.7	34.9	35.9	32.3	30.0	33.7	29.9	28.9	26.7	27.5	24.2	21.0	19.1	20.0
Region: [3]																							
Northeast	35.5	37.9	38.1	38.4	38.3	38.5	38.9	64.8	67.0	64.7	63.7	62.0	61.0	60.9	60.8	58.5	61.2	54.5	55.2	44.4	45.2	45.2	41.2
Midwest	41.5	43.3	43.9	44.5	45.2	45.9	46.4	73.8	74.6	71.6	70.2	70.7	68.2	68.7	68.2	65.8	67.2	59.3	60.9	49.5	48.6	48.8	47.3
South	50.6	60.7	62.4	66.4	68.1	70.1	71.8	64.8	67.2	65.9	64.5	63.0	61.3	60.7	62.7	55.6	59.0	52.2	53.5	43.0	42.4	40.5	38.6
West	29.5	36.2	37.7	41.0	42.1	43.7	45.5	63.3	63.6	60.8	56.9	60.8	57.7	58.1	56.0	57.2	58.5	51.8	49.9	48.4	45.0	46.4	42.3
School years completed:																							
8 years or less	22.7	19.1	17.7	14.7	14.1	13.3	12.9	53.0	43.9	40.7	36.1	50.5	44.0	40.1	40.2	42.6	35.1	28.1	26.8	32.7	27.7	23.2	24.6
High school:																							
1 to 3 years	22.5	21.1	21.0	20.7	21.0	21.0	20.1	54.6	50.4	47.9	45.9	52.4	47.9	44.7	43.4	45.6	[4]41.2	33.8	33.6	33.8	30.9	[4]27.0	25.0
4 years [5]	61.2	70.0	71.5	64.9	65.2	65.6	66.3	66.4	64.9	62.2	60.1	62.9	60.0	58.9	58.6	58.9	[5]57.5	49.1	49.4	44.1	42.2	[4]40.5	37.1
College:																							
1 to 3 years [6]	26.7	34.3	36.3	[5]50.4	50.9	52.9	55.3	74.4	75.4	72.9	70.0	70.0	68.7	68.4	68.3	67.2	[6]68.7	60.5	60.3	49.9	50.0	[6]49.1	46.2
4 years or more [7]	24.0	33.6	35.6	[6]39.4	42.5	45.4	48.0	84.3	84.8	80.4	77.3	77.8	77.3	76.3	75.1	79.9	[7]81.0	73.0	72.0	62.5	62.5	[7]63.1	57.2
Employed	95.0	113.8	115.5	122.6	125.6	135.7	133.4	68.7	69.9	67.0	64.7	64.4	62.6	62.9	62.6	61.8	63.8	55.2	55.5	45.7	45.1	45.2	41.2
Unemployed	6.9	5.8	6.7	6.5	6.4	5.2	5.2	50.3	53.7	52.5	46.1	50.6	44.6	46.4	48.5	41.2	46.2	37.2	35.1	31.2	27.9	28.3	28.4
Not in labor force	55.2	58.5	59.9	61.2	61.6	62.5	64.2	65.8	66.8	65.1	63.8	65.4	63.4	61.9	62.1	57.0	58.7	54.1	54.5	48.2	46.7	45.3	44.5

NA Not available. [1] Includes other races not shown separately. [2] Hispanic persons may be of any race. [3] For composition of regions, see map, inside cover. [4] Represents those who completed 9th to 12th grade, but have no high school diploma. [5] High school graduate. [6] Some college or associate degree. [7] Bachelor's or advanced degree.

Source: U.S. Census Bureau, Current Population Reports, P20-453 and P20-466; and unpublished data.

U.S. Census Bureau, Statistical Abstract of the United States: 2001

No. 402. Persons Reported Registered and Voted by State: 2000

[See headnote, Table 401]

State	Voting-age population (1,000)	Percent of voting-age population		State	Voting-age population (1,000)	Percent of voting-age population	
		Registered	Voted			Registered	Voted
U.S.....	202,609	63.9	54.7	MO	4,066	74.3	65.4
AL	3,278	73.6	59.6	MT	658	70.0	62.2
AK	412	72.5	65.5	NE	1,205	71.8	58.9
AZ	3,524	53.3	46.7	NV	1,377	52.3	46.5
AR	1,893	59.4	49.4	NH	902	69.6	63.3
CA	24,749	52.8	46.4	NJ	6,109	63.2	55.2
CO	3,049	64.1	53.6	NM	1,261	59.5	51.3
CT	2,415	62.5	55.2	NY	13,725	58.6	51.0
DE	567	67.9	62.2	NC	5,629	66.1	53.2
DC	407	72.4	65.6	ND	449	91.1	69.8
FL	11,633	60.5	51.6	OH	8,301	67.0	58.1
GA	5,775	61.1	49.0	OK	2,457	68.3	58.3
HI	855	47.0	39.7	OR	2,515	68.2	60.8
ID	927	61.4	53.9	PA	8,950	65.3	55.7
IL	8,859	66.7	56.8	RI	729	69.7	60.1
IN	4,380	68.5	58.5	SC	2,929	68.0	58.9
IA	2,110	72.2	64.1	SD	530	70.9	58.7
KS	1,908	67.7	60.2	TN	4,173	62.1	52.3
KY	2,996	69.7	54.9	TX	14,533	61.4	48.2
LA	3,143	75.4	64.6	UT	1,472	64.7	56.3
ME	979	80.3	69.2	VT	458	72.0	63.3
MD	3,812	65.6	57.1	VA	5,177	64.1	57.2
MA	4,614	70.3	60.1	WA	4,314	66.1	58.6
MI	7,231	69.1	60.1	WV	1,405	63.1	52.1
MN	3,506	76.7	67.8	WI	3,884	76.5	67.8
MS	2,029	72.2	59.8				

Source: U.S. Census Bureau, Current Population Reports, P20-466, and unpublished data.

No. 403. Participation in Elections for President and U.S. Representatives: 1932 to 1998

[As of November. Estimated resident population 21 years old and over, 1932-70, except as noted, and 18 years old and over thereafter; includes Armed Forces. Prior to 1960, excludes Alaska and Hawaii. District of Columbia is included in votes cast for President beginning 1964 and in votes cast for Representative from 1972 to 1998]

Year	Resident population (incl. aliens) of voting age (1,000)	Votes cast				Year	Resident population (incl. aliens) of voting age (1,000)	Votes cast			
		For President [2] (1,000)	Percent of voting-age population	For U.S. Representatives (1,000)	Percent of voting-age population			For President [2] (1,000)	Percent of voting-age population	For U.S. Representatives (1,000)	Percent of voting-age population
1932	75,768	39,758	52.5	37,657	49.7	1966	116,638	(X)	(X)	52,908	45.4
1934	77,997	(X)	(X)	32,256	41.4	1968	120,285	73,212	60.9	66,288	55.1
1936	80,174	45,654	56.9	42,886	53.5	1970	124,498	(X)	(X)	54,173	43.5
1938	82,354	(X)	(X)	36,236	44.0	1972	140,777	77,719	55.2	71,430	50.7
1940	84,728	49,900	58.9	46,951	55.4	1974	146,338	(X)	(X)	52,495	35.9
1942	86,465	(X)	(X)	28,074	32.5	1976	152,308	81,556	53.5	74,422	48.9
1944	85,654	47,977	56.0	45,103	52.7	1978	158,369	(X)	(X)	55,332	34.9
1946	92,659	(X)	(X)	34,398	37.1	1980	163,945	86,515	52.8	77,995	47.6
1948	95,573	48,794	51.1	45,933	48.1	1982	169,643	(X)	(X)	64,514	38.0
1950	98,134	(X)	(X)	40,342	41.1	1984	173,995	92,653	53.3	83,231	47.8
1952	99,929	61,551	61.6	57,571	57.6	1986	177,922	(X)	(X)	59,619	33.5
1954	102,075	(X)	(X)	42,580	41.7	1988	181,956	91,595	50.3	81,786	44.9
1956	104,515	62,027	59.3	58,426	55.9	1990	185,812	(X)	(X)	61,513	33.1
1958	106,447	(X)	(X)	45,818	43.0	1992	189,524	104,425	55.1	96,239	50.8
1960	109,672	68,838	62.8	64,133	58.5	1994	193,650	(X)	(X)	70,781	36.6
1962	112,952	(X)	(X)	51,267	45.4	1996	196,928	96,278	49.0	89,863	45.8
1964	114,090	70,645	61.9	65,895	57.8	1998	198,228	(X)	(X)	65,897	32.9

X Not applicable. [1] Population 18 and over in Georgia, 1944-70, and in Kentucky, 1956-70; 19 and over in Alaska and 20 and over in Hawaii, 1960-70. [2] Source: 1932-58, U.S. Congress, Clerk of the House, Statistics of the Presidential and Congressional Election, biennial.

Source: Except as noted, U.S. Census Bureau, Current Population Reports, P25-1085; Congressional Quarterly Inc., Washington, DC, America Votes, biennial (copyright).

No. 404. Resident Population of Voting Age and Percent Casting Votes— States: 1994 to 2000

[As of November. **Estimated population, 18 years old and over.** Includes Armed Forces stationed in each state, aliens, and institutional population]

State	Voting-age population							Percent casting votes for—				
				2000, (1,000)				Presidential electors		U.S. Representatives		
	1994 (1,000)	1996 (1,000)	1998 (1,000)	Total	Female	Black	His-panic[1]	1996	2000	1996	1998	2000
U.S.	193,650	196,928	198,228	202,609	105,523	24,132	21,598	49.0	52.0	45.6	33.2	48.0
AL.	3,138	3,221	3,252	3,278	1,771	859	27	47.7	50.8	46.6	37.4	43.9
AK.	429	423	413	412	210	13	12	56.9	69.2	53.6	54.1	66.5
AZ.	2,923	3,321	3,362	3,524	1,789	114	910	45.4	43.5	63.9	29.9	41.6
AR.	1,817	1,854	1,855	1,893	996	331	51	47.5	48.7	57.1	28.3	33.4
CA.	23,225	23,095	23,696	24,749	12,817	1,678	6,514	43.3	44.3	57.8	33.7	42.2
CO	2,713	2,841	2,954	3,049	1,535	116	478	53.1	57.1	52.1	43.1	53.2
CT.	2,486	2,471	2,438	2,415	1,268	317	139	56.4	60.4	48.0	39.1	54.4
DE.	534	551	555	567	299	111	20	49.6	57.7	52.4	32.5	55.2
DC	452	428	392	407	216	258	26	42.7	49.4	44.1	(NA)	(NA)
FL.	10,856	11,055	11,275	11,633	6,100	1,467	2,162	48.0	51.3	40.9	10.8	43.1
GA	5,159	5,432	5,581	5,775	3,078	1,956	169	42.6	45.0	47.0	29.2	41.8
HI	900	875	855	855	442	16	29	40.8	42.9	46.9	46.5	39.8
ID	803	847	881	927	480	4	58	58.2	54.0	52.6	43.0	53.1
IL	8,712	8,703	8,659	8,859	4,652	1,342	771	49.2	53.5	50.8	37.1	49.6
IN	4,298	4,346	4,377	4,380	2,223	286	79	48.9	50.2	52.5	36.0	49.2
IA	2,112	2,135	2,102	2,110	1,061	81	89	57.7	62.3	47.7	42.8	60.4
KS.	1,889	1,896	1,868	1,908	981	103	50	56.6	56.2	47.1	38.9	54.4
KY.	2,857	2,926	2,956	2,996	1,597	230	71	47.5	51.5	52.3	37.2	47.9
LA.	3,100	3,117	3,114	3,143	1,709	892	61	56.9	56.2	56.2	10.0	38.2
ME	931	943	938	979	514	6	4	64.5	66.5	56.9	44.2	65.2
MD	3,750	3,786	3,861	3,812	1,974	1,165	131	46.7	53.0	62.8	38.4	50.5
MA	4,564	4,677	4,594	4,614	2,403	311	251	55.3	58.6	56.1	37.9	50.9
MI	6,983	7,177	7,227	7,231	3,713	891	156	54.5	58.5	53.2	41.3	56.3
MN	3,362	3,417	3,443	3,506	1,785	95	50	64.3	69.5	55.6	59.2	67.4
MS	1,905	1,966	1,975	2,029	1,086	611	25	45.6	49.0	60.9	27.9	48.6
MO	3,902	3,981	3,967	4,066	2,165	449	38	54.2	58.0	54.8	39.6	57.2
MT	623	647	654	658	329	1	13	62.9	62.3	55.3	50.7	62.3
NE.	1,192	1,211	1,193	1,205	626	46	56	56.1	57.8	40.7	44.1	56.7
NV.	1,088	1,204	1,298	1,377	683	112	220	39.3	44.2	41.8	31.6	42.5
NH	843	869	874	902	461	13	14	58.0	63.1	48.8	36.4	61.6
NJ	5,974	6,023	6,059	6,109	3,190	787	583	51.2	52.2	43.0	30.0	48.9
NM	1,167	1,216	1,253	1,261	670	36	484	46.0	47.4	(NA)	39.7	46.6
NY.	13,646	13,610	13,440	13,725	7,112	2,181	1,706	46.5	49.7	43.2	31.8	42.4
NC	5,364	5,512	5,536	5,629	3,003	1,315	255	45.8	51.7	36.9	34.4	49.4
ND	467	475	460	449	228	2	3	56.3	64.1	45.7	46.3	63.5
OH	8,313	8,334	8,263	8,301	4,385	934	106	54.3	56.6	38.1	40.8	54.4
OK	2,394	2,423	2,426	2,457	1,302	115	76	49.9	50.2	40.1	35.4	44.2
OR	2,311	2,404	2,474	2,515	1,296	34	193	57.5	61.0	42.5	44.1	57.3
PA	9,212	9,150	8,942	8,950	4,663	764	248	49.0	54.9	44.5	32.4	50.9
RI	764	754	726	729	390	38	30	52.0	56.1	42.3	40.4	52.7
SC.	2,740	2,792	2,817	2,929	1,575	662	62	41.5	47.2	44.3	34.6	45.1
SD.	522	533	529	530	266	5	4	61.1	59.6	45.6	48.9	59.2
TN.	3,913	4,009	4,080	4,173	2,137	658	67	47.1	49.7	46.1	22.4	44.4
TX.	13,166	13,748	14,080	14,533	7,454	1,397	4,414	41.2	44.1	36.8	24.6	41.2
UT.	1,246	1,347	1,408	1,472	748	4	104	50.3	52.3	46.4	33.4	51.5
VT.	429	442	444	458	238	1	3	58.6	64.2	15.1	48.5	61.8
VA.	4,967	5,058	4,969	5,177	2,745	1,010	234	47.5	52.9	48.8	23.1	46.8
WA	4,000	4,112	4,179	4,314	2,261	123	167	54.7	57.6	38.3	44.5	55.2
WV	1,389	1,401	1,401	1,405	750	45	7	45.0	46.1	45.1	25.1	41.2
WI	3,777	3,819	3,790	3,884	1,972	147	159	57.4	66.9	48.6	44.2	64.5
WY	343	348	346	350	175	1	19	60.1	62.3	62.4	50.4	60.6

NA Not available. [1] Persons of Hispanic origin may be of any race.

Source: Compiled by U.S. Census Bureau. Population data from U.S. Census Bureau, *Current Population Reports*, P25-1117 and Statistical Brief (SB/96-2); votes cast from Elections Research Center, Chevy Chase, MD, *America Votes*, biennial, (copyright); and Congressional Quarterly Inc., Washington, DC (copyright).

Elections 253

No. 405. Political Party Financial Activity by Major Political Party: 1981 to 2000

[In millions of dollars (39.3 represents $39,300,000). Covers financial activity during 2-year calendar period indicated. Some political party financial activities, such as building funds and state and local election spending, are not reported to the source. Also excludes contributions earmarked to federal candidates through the party organizations, since some of those funds never passed through the committees' accounts]

Year and type of committee	Democratic				Republican			
	Receipts, net [1]	Dis-burse-ments, net [1]	Contribu-tions to candi-dates	Monies spent on behalf of party's nomi-nees [2]	Receipts, net [1]	Dis-burse-ments, net [1]	Contribu-tions to candi-dates	Monies spent on behalf of party's nomi-nees [2]
1981-82	39.3	40.1	1.7	3.3	215.0	214.0	5.6	14.3
1983-84	98.5	97.4	2.6	9.0	297.9	300.8	4.9	20.1
1985-86	64.8	65.9	1.7	9.0	255.2	258.9	3.4	14.3
1987-88	125.7	119.6	1.8	17.9	257.5	251.4	3.4	22.7
1989-90	85.8	90.9	1.5	8.7	206.3	213.5	2.9	10.7
1991-92	187.5	180.5	1.9	28.1	267.3	256.1	3.0	33.9
1993-94, total	151.1	149.9	2.2	21.2	254.4	243.7	3.0	20.6
1995-96, total	221.6	214.3	2.2	22.6	416.5	408.5	3.7	31.0
1997-98, total	160.0	155.3	1.2	18.6	285.0	275.9	2.6	15.7
1999-00, total [3]	**275.2**	**265.8**	**1.4**	**21.0**	**465.8**	**427.0**	**2.3**	**29.6**
National committee	124.0	122.0	-	13.5	212.8	187.4	0.4	23.7
Senatorial committee	40.5	41.5	0.3	0.1	51.5	50.7	0.4	-
Congressional committee	48.4	49.3	0.6	2.6	97.3	95.4	0.7	3.7
State and local	149.3	140.0	0.5	4.7	176.6	165.9	0.8	2.2

- Represents zero.   [1] Excludes monies transferred between affiliated committees.   [2] Monies spent in the general election. Minus sign (-) indicates refunds for expenditures.   [3] Excludes "Other national" activity.

Source: U.S. Federal Election Commission, *FEC Reports on Financial Activity, Final Report, Party and Non-Party Political Committees*, biennial.

No. 406. National Party Nonfederal Activity: 1996 to 2000

[During the 2000 election cycle, both major parties raised record amounts of nonfederal or "soft money." Soft money is used to pay a portion of the overhead expenses of party organizations, as well as other shared expenses that benefit both federal and nonfederal elections. In addition, it is used for issue advocacy, as well as generic party advertising. It may also be transferred from national committees to state and local party committees as well as being used to support construction and maintenance of party headquarters.]

Year and type of committee	Democratic		Republican	
	Receipts	Disbursements	Receipts	Disbursements
1996				
Total	123,877,924	121,826,562	138,199,706	149,658,099
National	101,905,186	100,483,977	113,127,010	114,401,973
Senatorial	14,176,392	14,061,273	29,395,329	29,362,653
Congressional	12,340,824	11,822,790	18,530,773	28,746,879
1998				
Total	92,811,927	92,987,711	131,615,116	127,730,744
National	56,966,353	57,411,879	74,805,286	74,325,722
Senatorial	25,880,538	25,858,673	37,866,845	37,283,103
Congressional	16,865,410	16,617,533	26,914,059	24,092,993
2000				
Total	245,202,519	244,848,838	249,861,645	252,785,565
National	136,563,419	135,332,105	166,207,843	163,521,510
Senatorial	63,717,982	63,300,415	44,652,709	44,633,117
Congressional	56,702,023	57,997,220	47,295,736	52,925,581

Source: U.S. Federal Election Commission, FEC Index of Independent Expenditures, 1987-88, May 1989; press release of May 19, 1989; and unpublished data.

No. 407. Political Action Committees—Number by Committee Type: 1980 to 2000

[As of December 31]

Committee type	1980	1985	1990	1995	1996	1997	1998	1999	2000
Total.................	2,551	3,992	4,172	4,016	4,079	3,844	3,798	3,835	3,706
Corporate	1,206	1,710	1,795	1,674	1,642	1,597	1,567	1,548	1,523
Labor	297	388	346	334	332	332	321	318	316
Trade/membership/health	576	695	774	815	838	825	821	844	812
Nonconnected	374	1,003	1,062	1,020	1,103	931	935	972	902
Cooperative	42	54	59	44	41	42	39	38	39
Corporation without stock	56	142	136	129	123	117	115	115	114

Source: U.S. Federal Election Commission, press release of January 2001.

No. 408. Political Action Committees—Financial Activity Summary by Committee Type: 1995 to 2000

[In millions of dollars (437.5 represents $437,500,000). Covers financial activity during 2-year calendar period indicated. Data have not been adjusted for transfers between affiliated committees]

Committee type	Receipts			Disbursements [1]			Contributions to candidates		
	1995-96	1997-98	1999-00	1995-96	1997-98	1999-00	1995-96	1997-98	1999-00
Total..............	437.5	502.6	604.9	430.0	470.8	579.4	217.9	219.9	259.8
Corporate	133.8	144.1	164.5	130.6	137.6	158.3	78.2	78.0	91.5
Labor	104.1	111.3	136.0	99.8	98.2	128.7	48.0	44.6	51.6
Trade/membership/health ..	106.0	119.6	142.9	105.4	114.4	137.2	60.2	62.3	71.8
Nonconnected	81.2	114.3	144.3	81.3	107.8	139.6	24.0	28.2	37.3
Cooperative	3.9	4.5	3.7	4.2	4.3	3.3	3.0	2.4	2.4
Corporation without stock ..	8.5	8.8	13.6	8.7	8.5	12.2	4.5	4.4	5.3

[1] Comprises contributions to candidates, independent expenditures, and other disbursements.

Source: U.S. Federal Election Commission, *FEC Reports on Financial Activity, Final Report, Party and Non-Party Political Committees,* biennial.

No. 409. Presidential Campaign Finances—Federal Funds for General Election: 1980 to 1996

[In millions of dollars (62.7 represents $62,700,000). Based on FEC certifications, audit reports, and Dept. of Treasury reports]

1980		1988		1992		1996	
Candidate	Amount	Candidate	Amount	Candidate	Amount	Candidate	Amount
Total ..,....	62.7	Total........	92.2	Total........	110.4	Total........	152.6
Anderson [1]	4.2	Bush........	46.1	Bush........	55.2	Clinton	61.8
Carter	29.4	Dukakis......	46.1	Clinton	55.2	Dole	61.8
Reagan	29.2	Perot	-	Perot	29.0		

- Represents zero. [1] John Anderson, as the candidate of a new party, was permitted to raise funds privately. Total receipts for the Anderson campaign, including federal funds, were $17.6 million, and total expenditures were $15.6 million.

Source: U.S. Federal Election Commission, periodic press releases.

No. 410. Presidential Campaign Finances—Primary Campaign Receipts and Disbursements: 1987 to 1996

[In millions of dollars (213.8 represents $213,800,000). Covers campaign finance activity during 2-year calendar period indicated. Covers candidates who received federal matching funds or who had significant financial activity]

Item	Total			Democratic			Republican		
	1987-88 [1]	1991-92 [2]	1995-96	1987-88	1991-92	1995-96	1987-88	1991-92	1995-96
Receipts, total [3] ...	213.8	125.2	243.9	91.9	70.0	46.2	116.0	49.7	187.0
Individual contributions.	141.1	82.4	126.4	59.4	44.7	31.3	76.8	34.4	93.1
Federal matching funds............	65.7	41.5	56.0	30.1	24.4	14.0	34.7	15.0	41.6
Disbursements....	210.7	118.7	(NA)	90.2	64.4	(NA)	114.6	48.8	(NA)

NA Not available. [1] Includes a minor party candidate who sought several party nominations and a Democratic candidate who did not receive federal matching funds, but who had significant financial activity. [2] Includes other parties, not shown separately. [3] Includes other types of receipts, not shown separately.

Source: U.S. Federal Election Commission, *FEC Reports on Financial Activity, Final Report, Presidential Pre-Nomination Campaigns,* quadrennial.

U.S. Census Bureau, Statistical Abstract of the United States: 2001

No. 411. Congressional Campaign Finances—Receipts and Disbursements: 1995 to 2000

[Covers all campaign finance activity during 2-year calendar period indicated for primary, general, run-off, and special elections, for 1995-96 relates to 1,680 House of Representatives candidates and 198 Senate candidates. Data have been adjusted to eliminate transfers between all committees within a campaign. For further information on legal limits of contributions, see Federal Election Campaign Act of 1971, as amended]

Item	House of representatives						Senate					
	Amount (mil. dol.)			Percent distribution			Amount (mil. dol.)			Percent distribution		
	1995-96	1997-98	1999-00	1995-96	1997-98	1999-00	1995-96	1997-98	1999-00	1995-96	1997-98	1999-00
Total receipts [1]	500.0	489.2	604.4	100	100	100	285.1	287.1	434.2	100	100	100
Individual contributions	272.9	253.2	312.8	55	52	52	166.9	166.5	250.0	59	58	58
Other committees	155.0	158.5	192.8	31	32	32	45.6	48.1	51.9	16	17	12
Candidate loans	42.0	46.8	60.0	8	10	10	40.3	52.2	88.6	14	18	20
Candidate contributions	7.0	5.3	6.1	1	1	1	16.4	1.3	18.4	.6	(Z)	4
Democrats	233.1	233.4	286.7	46	47	47	126.5	134.1	230.4	44	47	53
Republicans	266.9	255.8	317.7	53	52	53	157.7	153.0	203.8	55	53	47
Others	5.4	4.5	6.0	1	1	1	0.9	0.4	2.8	(Z)	(Z)	1
Incumbents	279.8	293.6	359.6	56	60	60	81.8	135.5	130.6	29	47	30
Challengers [2]	119.1	92.8	125.4	24	19	21	79.2	113.9	97.5	28	40	22
Open seats [2]	101.1	102.7	119.3	14	21	20	124.1	37.7	206.0	44	13	47
Total disbursements	472.5	448.3	566.6	95	100	94	287.5	287.9	431.9	100	100	100
Democrats	221.1	211.1	266.9	44	47	47	127.4	134.6	226.3	44	47	52
Republicans	251.4	237.2	299.7	50	53	53	159.1	152.9	205.7	55	53	48
Others	5.3	4.2	5.7	1	1	1	0.9	0.4	2.7	(Z)	(Z)	1
Incumbents	258.1	257.2	324.9	51	57	57	85.4	137.3	130.2	30	48	30
Challengers [2]	119.6	94.7	123.6	24	21	22	78.9	112.5	97.2	27	39	23
Open seats [2]	100.2	100.6	118.0	20	22	21	123.1	38.1	204.5	43	13	47

Z Less than $50,000 or 0.5 percent.   [1] Includes other types of receipts, not shown separately.   [2] Elections in which an incumbent did not seek re-election.

Source: U.S. Federal Election Commission, *FEC Reports on Financial Activity, Final Report, U.S. Senate and House Campaigns*, biennial.

No. 412. Contributions to Congressional Campaigns by Political Action Committees (PAC) by Type of Committee: 1983 to 2000

[In millions of dollars. Covers amounts given to candidates in primary, general, run-off, and special elections during the 2-year calendar period indicated. For number of political action committees, see Table 407]

Type of committee	Total [1]	Democrats	Republicans	Incumbents	Challengers	Open seats [2]
HOUSE OF REPRESENTATIVES						
1983-84	75.7	46.3	29.3	57.2	11.3	7.2
1985-86	87.4	54.7	32.6	65.9	9.1	12.4
1987-88	102.2	67.4	34.7	82.2	10.0	10.0
1989-90	108.5	72.2	36.2	87.5	7.3	13.6
1991-92	127.4	85.4	41.7	94.4	12.2	20.8
1993-94	132.4	88.2	43.9	101.4	12.7	18.3
1995-96	159.8	79.4	79.7	117.2	21.4	20.1
1997-98	158.7	77.6	80.9	123.9	14.8	19.7
1999-00, total [3]	195.9	99.2	96.2	152.2	20.2	23.0
Corporate	63.1	22.2	40.7	55.3	2.4	5.3
Trade association [4]	55.7	22.5	33.0	46.3	3.5	5.7
Labor	44.0	40.3	3.6	30.5	8.1	5.3
Nonconnected [5]	27.4	11.5	15.8	15.3	5.8	6.2
SENATE						
1983-84	29.7	14.0	15.6	17.9	6.3	5.4
1985-86	45.3	20.2	25.1	23.7	10.2	11.4
1987-88	45.7	24.2	21.5	28.7	8.0	9.0
1989-90	41.2	20.2	21.0	29.5	8.2	3.5
1991-92	51.2	29.0	22.2	31.9	9.4	10.0
1997-98, total [3]	48.1	20.7	27.3	34.3	6.6	7.2
1999-00, total [3]	61.3	23.9	37.4	42.7	7.2	11.3
Corporate	26.8	7.5	19.3	20.7	1.5	4.6
Trade association [4]	15.7	5.1	10.6	11.7	1.2	2.8
Labor	7.5	7.0	0.5	3.2	2.8	1.5
Nonconnected [5]	9.5	3.6	5.9	5.8	1.5	2.2

[1] Includes other parties, not shown separately.   [2] Elections in which an incumbent did not seek re-election.   [3] Includes other types of political action committees not shown separately.   [4] Includes membership organizations and health organizations.   [5] Represents "ideological" groups as well as other issue groups not necessarily ideological in nature.

Source: U.S. Federal Election Commission, *FEC Reports on Financial Activity, Party and Non-Party Political Committees, Final Report*, biennial.

State and Local Government Finances and Employment

This section presents data on revenues, expenditures, debt, and employment of state and local governments. Nationwide statistics relating to state and local governments, their numbers, finances, and employment are compiled primarily by the U.S. Census Bureau through a program of censuses and surveys. Every fifth year (for years ending in "2" and "7") the Census Bureau conducts a census of governments involving collection of data for all governmental units in the United States. In addition, the Census Bureau conducts annual surveys which cover all the state governments and a sample of local governments.

Annually, the Census Bureau releases information on the Internet which presents financial data for the federal government, nationwide totals for state and local governments, and state-local data by states. Also released annually is a series on state, city, county, and school finances and on state and local public employment. There is also a series of quarterly data releases covering tax revenue and finances of major public employee retirement systems.

Basic information for Census Bureau statistics on governments is obtained by mail canvass from state and local officials; however, financial data for each of the state governments and for many of the large local governments are compiled from their official records and reports by Census Bureau personnel. In over two-thirds of the states, all or part of local government financial data are obtained through central collection arrangements with state governments. Financial data on the federal government are primarily based on the *Budget* published by the Office of Management and Budget (see text, Section 9, Federal Government Finances and Employment).

Governmental units—The governmental structure of the United States includes, in addition to the federal government and the states, thousands of local governments—counties, municipalities, townships, school districts, and numerous kinds of "special districts." In 1997, 87,453 local governments were identified by the census of governments (see Tables 413-415). As defined by the census, governmental units include all agencies or bodies having an organized existence, governmental character, and substantial autonomy. While most of these governments can impose taxes, many of the special districts—such as independent public housing authorities and numerous local irrigation, power, and other types of districts—are financed from rentals, charges for services, benefit assessments, grants from other governments, and other nontax sources. The count of governments excludes semi-autonomous agencies through which states, cities, and counties sometimes provide for certain functions—for example, "dependent" school systems, state institutions of higher education, and certain other "authorities" and special agencies which are under the administrative or fiscal control of an established governmental unit.

Finances—The financial statistics relate to government fiscal years ending June 30 or at some date within the 12 previous months. The following governments are exceptions and are included as though they were part of the June 30 group; ending September 30, the state governments of Alabama and Michigan, the District of Columbia, and Alabama school districts; and ending August 31, the state government of Texas and Texas school districts. New York State ends its fiscal year on March 31. The federal government ended the fiscal year June 30 until 1976 when its fiscal year, by an act of Congress, was revised to extend from Oct. 1 to Sept. 30. A 3-month quarter (July 1 to Sept. 30, 1976) bridged the transition.

Nationwide government finance statistics have been classified and presented in

State and Local Government Finances and Employment 257

terms of uniform concepts and categories, rather than according to the highly diverse terminology, organization, and fund structure utilized by individual governments.

Statistics on governmental finances distinguish among general government, utilities, liquor stores, and insurance trusts. *General government* comprises all activities except utilities, liquor stores, and insurance trusts. Utilities include government water supply, electric light and power, gas supply, and transit systems. Liquor stores are operated by 17 states and by local governments in 6 states. Insurance trusts relate to employee retirement, unemployment compensation, and other social insurance systems administered by the federal, state, and local governments.

Data for cities or counties relate only to municipal or county and their dependent agencies and do not include amounts for other local governments in the same geographic location. Therefore, expenditure figures for "education" do not include spending by the separate school districts which administer public schools within most municipal or county areas. Variations in the assignment of governmental responsibility for public assistance, health, hospitals, public housing, and other functions to a lesser degree also have an important effect upon reported amounts of city or county expenditure, revenue, and debt.

Employment and payrolls—These data are based mainly on mail canvassing of state and local governments. Payroll includes all salaries, wages, and individual fee payments for the month specified, and employment relates to all persons on governmental payrolls during a pay period of the month covered— including paid officials, temporary help, and (unless otherwise specified) part-time as well as full-time personnel. Beginning 1986, statistics for full-time equivalent employment have been computed with a formula using hours worked by part-time employees. A payroll based formula was used prior to 1985. Full-time equivalent employment statistics were not computed for 1985. Figures shown for individual governments cover major dependent agencies such as institutions of higher education, as well as the basic central departments and agencies of the government.

Statistical reliability—For a discussion of statistical collection and estimation, sampling procedures, and measures of statistical reliability applicable to Census Bureau data, see Appendix III.

No. 413. Number of Governmental Units by Type: 1942 to 1997

Type of government	1942	1952 [1]	1962	1967	1972	1977	1982	1987	1992	1997
Total	155,116	116,807	91,237	81,299	78,269	79,913	81,831	83,237	85,006	87,504
U.S. government	1	1	1	1	1	1	1	1	1	1
State government	48	50	50	50	50	50	50	50	50	50
Local governments	155,067	116,756	91,186	81,248	78,218	79,862	81,780	83,186	84,955	87,453
County	3,050	3,052	3,043	3,049	3,044	3,042	3,041	3,042	3,043	3,043
Municipal	16,220	16,807	18,000	18,048	18,517	18,862	19,076	19,200	19,279	19,372
Township and town	18,919	17,202	17,142	17,105	16,991	16,822	16,734	16,691	16,656	16,629
School district	108,579	67,355	34,678	21,782	15,781	15,174	14,851	14,721	14,422	13,726
Special district	8,299	12,340	18,323	21,264	23,885	25,962	28,078	29,532	31,555	34,683

[1] Adjusted to include units in Alaska and Hawaii which adopted statehood in 1959.

Source: U.S. Census Bureau, *Census of Governments, Government Organization,* Series (GC(1)-1).

U.S. Census Bureau. Statistical Abstract of the United States: 2001

No. 414. Number of Local Governments by Type—States: 1997

State	All governmental units [1]	County	Municipal	Township [1]	School district	Special district [2] Total [3]	Special district [2] Natural resources	Special district [2] Fire protection	Special district [2] Housing [4]
United States	87,453	3,043	19,372	16,629	13,726	34,683	6,983	5,601	3,469
Alabama	1,131	67	446	-	127	491	71	5	154
Alaska	175	12	149	-	-	14	-	-	13
Arizona	637	15	87	-	231	304	79	152	-
Arkansas	1,516	75	491	-	311	639	232	74	126
California	4,607	57	471	-	1,069	3,010	472	369	79
Colorado	1,869	62	269	-	180	1,358	168	249	96
Connecticut	583	-	30	149	17	387	1	65	94
Delaware	336	3	57	-	19	257	236	-	3
Dist. of Columbia	2	-	1	-	-	1	-	-	-
Florida	1,081	66	394	-	95	526	132	56	105
Georgia	1,344	156	535	-	180	473	36	2	206
Hawaii	19	3	1	-	-	15	14	-	-
Idaho	1,147	44	200	-	114	789	182	144	10
Illinois	6,835	102	1,288	1,433	944	3,068	935	827	113
Indiana	3,198	91	569	1,008	294	1,236	134	2	63
Iowa	1,876	99	950	-	394	433	249	68	26
Kansas	3,950	105	627	1,370	324	1,524	260	-	204
Kentucky	1,366	119	434	-	176	637	131	144	17
Louisiana	467	60	302	-	66	39	3	-	-
Maine	832	16	22	467	98	229	16	-	30
Maryland	420	23	156	-	-	241	156	-	20
Massachusetts	861	12	44	307	85	413	18	16	252
Michigan	2,775	83	534	1,242	584	332	82	2	-
Minnesota	3,501	87	854	1,794	360	406	114	-	176
Mississippi	936	82	295	-	164	395	251	-	62
Missouri	3,416	114	944	324	537	1,497	181	273	143
Montana	1,144	54	128	-	362	600	125	159	12
Nebraska	2,894	93	535	455	681	1,130	84	419	126
Nevada	205	16	19	-	17	153	35	16	5
New Hampshire	575	10	13	221	166	165	10	14	21
New Jersey	1,421	21	324	243	552	281	16	200	2
New Mexico	881	33	99	-	96	653	609	-	6
New York	3,413	57	615	929	686	1,126	2	912	-
North Carolina	952	100	527	-	-	325	155	-	94
North Dakota	2,758	53	363	1,341	237	764	80	289	38
Ohio	3,597	88	941	1,310	666	592	97	60	73
Oklahoma	1,799	77	592	-	578	552	98	20	105
Oregon	1,493	36	240	-	258	959	195	263	22
Pennsylvania	5,070	66	1,023	1,546	516	1,919	7	-	91
Rhode Island	119	-	8	31	4	76	3	34	26
South Carolina	716	46	269	-	91	310	48	97	45
South Dakota	1,810	66	309	956	177	302	107	60	34
Tennessee	940	93	343	-	14	490	112	-	100
Texas	4,700	254	1,177	-	1,087	2,182	428	103	395
Utah	683	29	230	-	40	384	77	24	17
Vermont	691	14	49	237	279	112	14	20	10
Virginia	483	95	231	-	1	156	47	-	-
Washington	1,812	39	275	-	296	1,202	163	402	45
West Virginia	704	55	232	-	55	362	15	-	39
Wisconsin	3,059	72	583	1,266	442	696	184	-	171
Wyoming	654	23	97	-	56	478	119	61	-

- Represents zero. [1] Includes "town" governments in the six New England States and in Minnesota, New York, and Wisconsin. [2] Single function districts. [3] Includes other special districts not shown separately. [4] Includes community development.

No. 415. County, Municipal, and Township Governments by Population Size: 1997

[Number of governments as of January 1997. Population enumerated as of July 1, 1994. Consolidated city-county governments are classified as municipal rather than county governments. Township governments include "towns" in the six New England States, Minnesota, New York, and Wisconsin]

Population-size group	County governments Number, 1997	County governments Population, 1994 Number (1,000)	County governments Population, 1994 Percent	Municipal governments Number, 1997	Municipal governments Population, 1994 Number (1,000)	Municipal governments Population, 1994 Percent	Township governments Number, 1997	Township governments Population, 1994 Number (1,000)	Township governments Population, 1994 Percent
Total	3,043	236,107	100	19,372	161,605	100	16,629	54,662	100
250,000 or more	183	128,741	55	66	46,417	29	4	1,758	3
100,000 to 299,999	264	40,234	17	142	20,687	13	31	4,259	8
50,000 to 99,999	378	26,583	11	346	23,595	15	84	5,626	10
25,000 to 49,999	604	21,543	9	590	20,623	13	257	8,750	16
10,000 to 24,999	908	15,047	6	1,378	21,606	13	744	11,509	21
5,000 to 9,999	413	3,105	1	1,618	11,504	7	1,064	7,403	14
2,500 to 4,999	178	668	-	2,096	7,426	5	1,836	6,422	12
1,000 to 2,499	86	165	-	3,723	5,965	4	3,606	5,766	11
Less than 1,000	29	21	-	9,413	3,782	2	9,003	3,169	6

- Represents or rounds to zero.

Source of Tables 414 and 415: U.S. Census Bureau, Census of Governments, Government Organization, Series (GC(1)-1).

State and Local Government Finances and Employment   259

No. 416. Government Current Receipts and Expenditures in the National Income and Product Accounts: 1980 to 2000

[In billions of dollars (767.1 represents $767,100,000,000). For explanation of national income, see text, Section 13, Income, Expenditures, and Wealth]

Item	1980	1990	1995	1996	1997	1998	1999	2000
Current receipts	**767.1**	**1,607.7**	**2,117.1**	**2,269.1**	**2,440.0**	**2,613.8**	**2,786.1**	**3,023.9**
Personal tax and nontax receipts	304.2	609.6	778.3	869.7	968.8	1,070.4	1,159.2	1,288.2
Corporate profits tax accruals	84.8	140.6	211.0	223.6	237.2	238.8	253.0	271.5
Indirect business tax and nontax accruals	212.0	447.3	594.6	620.0	646.2	681.3	713.1	762.7
Contributions for social insurance	166.2	410.1	533.2	555.8	587.8	623.3	660.7	701.5
Current expenditures	**812.0**	**1,778.0**	**2,293.7**	**2,384.5**	**2,462.4**	**2,529.3**	**2,624.8**	**2,772.5**
Consumption expenditures	469.4	965.7	1,133.9	1,171.8	1,223.3	1,261.4	1,328.0	1,422.7
Transfer payments (net)	275.0	583.1	869.9	916.0	945.0	965.9	1,000.1	1,050.0
To persons	270.2	573.1	860.1	902.4	934.4	955.0	988.4	1,036.0
To the rest of the world (net)	4.8	10.0	9.8	13.6	10.6	11.0	11.6	14.0
Net interest paid[1]	53.2	204.3	268.0	274.4	275.3	278.8	263.8	262.6
Interest paid	89.1	297.8	357.5	366.6	371.2	372.2	359.5	362.8
To persons and business[1]	76.4	257.1	300.1	299.0	283.2	281.1	264.3	255.2
To the rest of the world	12.7	40.8	57.4	67.6	88.1	91.1	95.1	107.7
Less: Interest received by government[1]	35.9	93.6	89.5	92.2	96.0	93.4	95.7	100.3
Less: Dividends received by government	0.1	0.2	0.3	0.3	0.3	0.4	0.4	0.4
Subsidies less current surplus of government enterprises	14.5	25.3	22.2	22.6	19.1	23.5	33.3	37.6
Subsidies	9.7	26.8	33.2	33.7	33.0	35.4	44.0	44.1
Less: Current surplus of government enterprises	-4.8	1.5	11.1	11.1	13.9	11.8	10.7	6.5
Less: Wage accruals less disbursements	-	0.1	-	-	-	-	-	-
Current surplus or deficit (-), national income and product accounts	**-44.9**	**-170.3**	**-176.7**	**-115.4**	**-22.3**	**84.5**	**161.3**	**251.4**
Social insurance funds	-12.5	46.9	23.9	19.4	31.6	58.6	96.1	117.7

- Represents zero. [1] Prior to 1960, interest paid to persons and business (and interest received by government are not shown separately but are included in interest paid.

No. 417. All Government Consumption Expenditures and Gross Investment by Type in the National Income and Product Accounts: 1980 to 2000

[In billions of dollars (569.7 represents $569,700,000,000). For explanation of national income, see text, Section 13, Income, Expenditures, and Wealth]

Item	1980	1990	1995	1996	1997	1998	1999	2000
All government consumption expenditures & gross investment	**569.7**	**1,181.4**	**1,372.0**	**1,421.9**	**1,487.9**	**1,538.5**	**1,632.5**	**1,741.0**
Federal	**245.3**	**508.4**	**521.5**	**531.6**	**538.2**	**539.2**	**564.0**	**590.2**
National defense	**169.6**	**374.9**	**350.6**	**357.0**	**352.6**	**349.1**	**364.5**	**375.4**
Consumption expenditures	145.3	308.9	297.5	302.4	304.2	299.7	311.8	321.9
Durable goods	12.8	30.9	21.0	21.0	21.1	21.1	22.1	22.5
Nondurable goods	10.1	11.0	6.3	7.7	7.5	6.9	8.1	10.4
Services	122.4	267.0	270.2	273.7	275.6	271.7	281.6	289.0
Gross investment	24.3	65.9	53.1	54.6	48.4	49.4	52.7	53.5
Structures	3.2	6.1	6.3	6.7	5.7	5.4	5.3	5.3
Equipment and software	21.1	59.8	46.9	47.9	42.7	44.0	47.4	48.2
Nondefense	**75.6**	**133.6**	**170.9**	**174.6**	**185.6**	**190.1**	**199.5**	**214.8**
Consumption expenditures	63.5	111.0	141.8	142.9	152.7	153.4	157.8	171.8
Durable goods	-0.4	-0.1	0.9	1.1	1.2	-0.4	1.0	1.3
Nondurable goods	5.6	4.6	6.5	6.1	7.9	8.1	5.8	6.9
Services	58.4	106.4	134.3	135.7	143.6	145.6	151.0	163.6
Gross investment	12.0	22.6	29.2	31.7	32.9	36.7	41.7	43.0
Structures	7.1	8.0	10.8	11.1	9.7	11.2	11.5	10.8
Equipment and software	4.9	14.6	18.4	20.5	23.2	25.5	30.1	32.2
State and local	**324.4**	**673.0**	**850.5**	**890.4**	**949.7**	**999.3**	**1,068.5**	**1,150.8**
Consumption expenditures	260.5	545.8	694.7	726.5	766.4	808.3	858.4	929.0
Durable goods	4.7	10.6	12.7	13.1	13.8	14.8	15.7	16.9
Nondurable goods	28.3	53.6	72.9	79.9	81.7	83.4	91.8	110.9
Services	227.5	481.5	609.0	633.6	670.9	710.1	750.8	801.2
Gross investment	64.0	127.2	155.8	163.8	183.3	191.0	210.1	221.8
Structures	55.1	98.5	117.3	122.5	139.3	142.4	157.3	165.0
Equipment and software	8.9	28.7	38.6	41.3	44.0	48.6	52.9	56.8
Addenda:								
Compensation of general government employees	295.7	609.4	735.8	759.4	790.0	819.7	855.8	904.1
Federal	102.5	193.9	206.9	211.0	213.2	215.3	221.8	233.4
State and local	193.2	415.5	528.9	548.4	576.8	604.4	634.0	670.7

See footnotes at end of Table 418.

Source of Tables 416 and 417: U.S. Bureau of Economic Analysis. <http://www.bea.doc.gov/bea/dn/nipaweb/index.htm> (accessed 21 August 2001).

[In billions of chained (1996) dollars (1,292.5 represents $1,292,500,000,000). For explanation of national income, see text, Section 13, Income, Expenditures, and Wealth]

Item	1987	1990	1992	1993	1994	1995	1996	1997	1998	1999	2000
All government consumption expenditures and gross investment by type [1]	1,292.5	1,387.3	1,410.0	1,398.8	1,400.1	1,406.4	1,421.9	1,455.4	1,483.3	1,531.8	1,572.6
Federal	597.8	606.8	595.1	572.0	551.3	536.5	531.6	529.6	525.4	536.7	545.9
National defense	450.2	443.2	417.1	394.7	375.9	361.9	357.0	347.7	341.6	348.6	349.0
Consumption expenditures	373.2	369.7	350.6	336.1	320.5	308.7	302.4	298.5	290.6	294.7	294.5
Durable goods [2]	37.8	33.4	29.8	27.5	23.4	21.1	21.0	21.2	21.3	22.4	22.6
Nondurable goods	13.0	10.7	10.1	9.3	8.5	6.9	7.7	7.7	8.0	8.9	9.3
Services	320.9	325.0	310.3	299.1	288.5	280.7	273.7	269.6	261.4	263.6	262.9
Compensation of general government employees, except own-account investment [3]	176.2	172.9	162.2	155.0	147.0	139.0	133.1	128.3	124.3	120.9	120.3
Consumption of general government fixed capital [4]	53.8	61.2	63.8	64.1	63.9	63.4	63.0	62.7	62.4	62.5	62.6
Other services	92.3	91.6	84.8	80.4	77.9	78.5	77.7	78.7	74.8	80.3	80.2
Gross investment	76.3	73.2	66.4	58.6	55.4	53.2	54.6	49.1	51.0	54.1	54.7
Structures	11.2	7.7	6.3	5.7	6.2	6.5	6.7	5.5	5.1	4.8	4.6
Equipment and software	65.7	65.4	60.0	52.8	49.2	46.8	47.9	43.6	45.9	49.4	50.3
Nondefense	146.5	163.0	177.9	177.3	175.5	174.6	174.6	181.8	183.8	188.1	196.7
Consumption expenditures	125.4	140.1	150.0	147.8	148.0	145.7	142.9	148.6	146.5	146.2	154.2
Durable goods [2]	-0.9	-0.7	-0.1	0.5	1.0	0.8	1.1	1.3	-0.2	1.2	1.5
Nondurable goods	2.9	4.6	6.1	6.4	6.2	6.4	6.1	7.9	8.3	5.6	7.7
Commodity Credit Corporation inventory change	-4.7	-2.5	-1.3	-1.0	-1.2	-0.4	-0.4	-0.1	0.3	-0.2	2.0
Other nondurables	7.6	7.1	7.4	7.4	7.4	6.8	6.5	8.0	8.1	5.8	5.7
Services	121.5	135.6	143.6	140.5	140.4	138.5	135.7	139.4	138.5	139.3	146.0
Compensation of general government employees, except own-account investment [3]	77.0	83.2	84.5	84.1	81.8	78.5	76.4	75.9	76.7	77.2	79.5
Consumption of general government fixed capital [4]	11.2	13.3	14.6	15.2	15.9	16.7	18.0	19.6	21.4	23.9	26.4
Other services	34.6	39.9	44.7	41.5	42.9	43.3	41.3	44.0	40.4	38.5	40.5
Gross investment	21.5	23.5	28.0	29.5	27.6	29.0	31.7	33.3	37.5	42.5	42.9
Structures	11.6	9.3	11.6	12.4	11.2	11.1	11.1	9.4	10.6	10.6	9.5
Equipment and software	10.6	14.2	16.5	17.2	16.5	17.9	20.5	23.9	27.0	32.1	33.9
State and local	695.6	781.1	815.3	827.0	848.9	869.9	890.4	925.8	957.7	994.7	1,026.3
Consumption expenditures	577.3	638.9	667.8	680.4	697.5	711.3	726.5	745.7	771.9	794.5	821.4
Durable goods [2]	9.7	10.9	12.1	12.3	12.4	12.7	13.1	13.9	15.0	15.9	17.0
Nondurable goods	51.6	57.8	65.0	68.6	72.8	75.6	79.9	82.3	88.4	93.9	99.9
Services	516.2	570.3	590.6	599.4	612.3	623.1	633.6	649.5	668.8	685.3	705.4
Compensation of general government employees, except own-account investment [3]	465.0	507.1	516.5	521.6	527.9	536.5	542.3	550.9	559.9	566.1	577.0
Consumption of general government fixed capital [4]	45.8	52.7	57.6	60.0	62.5	65.3	68.2	71.7	75.7	80.2	84.8
Other services	10.7	13.6	17.1	18.2	21.8	21.3	23.0	26.8	33.0	39.0	43.7
Gross investment	118.8	142.2	147.4	146.6	151.4	158.6	163.8	180.2	185.8	200.4	205.0
Structures	99.9	114.5	118.7	116.1	117.0	120.9	122.5	134.7	134.0	142.8	143.5
Equipment and software	20.3	28.4	29.4	31.0	34.6	37.8	41.3	45.4	52.3	58.4	63.1
Residual	-7.5	-4.4	-1.3	-1.1	-0.5	-0.6	-	-	-1.1	-2.8	-5.3
Addenda:											
Compensation of general government employees [3]	723.1	769.2	769.3	767.1	763.5	761.3	759.4	763.4	769.4	773.4	786.3
Federal	255.9	258.4	248.6	240.8	230.4	219.0	211.0	205.7	202.6	199.8	201.7
State and local	469.5	512.4	521.9	527.1	533.6	542.4	548.4	557.7	566.8	573.6	584.7

- Represents zero. [1] Gross government investment consists of general government and government enterprise expenditures for fixed assets; inventory investment is included in government consumption expenditures. [2] Consumption expenditures for durable goods excludes expenditures classified as investment, except for goods transferred to foreign countries by the federal government. [3] Compensation of government employees engaged in new own-account investment and related expenditures for goods and services are classified as investment in structures and in software. The compensation of all general government employees is shown in the addenda. [4] Consumption of fixed capital, or depreciation, is included in government consumption expenditures as a partial measure of the value of the services of general government fixed assets; use of depreciation assumes a zero net return.

Source: U.S. Bureau of Economic Analysis, <http://www.bea.doc.gov/bea/dn/nipaweb/index.htm> (accessed 21 August 2001).

State and Local Government Finances and Employment 261

No. 419. Federal Grants-in-Aid Summary: 1970 to 2001

[24,065 represents $24,065,000,000, except as indicated. For fiscal year ending in year shown; see text, this section. Minus sign (-) indicates decrease]

Year	Current dollars							Constant (1996) dollars	
			Grants to individuals		Grants as percent of—				
	Total grants (mil. dol.)	Annual percent change [1]	Total (mil. dol.)	Percent of total grants	State/local govt. expenditures from own sources [2]	Federal outlays	Gross domestic product	Total grants (bil. dol.)	Annual percent change [1]
1970	24,065	19.3	8,717	36.2	29.1	12.3	2.4	92.9	10.3
1975	49,791	14.8	16,752	33.6	34.8	15.0	3.2	136.5	3.5
1980	91,385	9.6	32,619	35.7	39.9	15.5	3.3	168.5	-1.3
1985	105,852	8.5	49,321	46.6	29.6	11.2	2.6	147.0	4.9
1990	135,325	11.0	75,685	55.9	25.2	10.8	2.4	157.9	6.6
1992	178,065	15.2	110,016	61.8	28.7	12.9	2.9	195.4	12.6
1993	193,612	8.7	121,519	62.8	29.6	13.7	3.0	207.3	6.1
1994	210,596	8.8	131,123	62.3	30.9	14.4	3.0	220.7	6.5
1995	224,991	6.8	141,183	62.8	31.5	14.8	3.1	229.8	4.1
1996	227,811	1.3	142,802	62.7	30.8	14.6	3.0	227.8	-0.9
1997	234,160	2.8	144,189	61.6	30.2	14.6	2.9	229.2	0.6
1998	246,128	5.1	155,854	63.3	30.3	14.9	2.8	237.5	3.6
1999	267,081	8.5	167,677	62.8	31.4	15.7	2.9	253.3	6.7
2000	284,659	6.6	177,139	62.2	31.3	15.9	2.9	262.5	3.6
2001, est . .	316,265	11.1	199,441	63.1	(NA)	17.0	3.1	283.2	7.9

NA Not available. [1] Average annual percent change from prior year shown. For explanation, see Guide to Tabular Presentation. 1970, change from 1969. [2] Outlays as defined in the national income and product accounts.

Source: U. S. Office of Management and Budget, based on *Historical Tables* and *Analytical Prospectives, Budget of the United States Government*, annual.

No. 420. Federal Aid to State and Local Governments: 1970 to 2001

[In millions of dollars (24,065 represents $24,065,000,000). For fiscal year ending in year shown; see text, this section. Includes trust funds]

Program	1970	1980	1990	1995	1998	1999	2000	2001 est.
Grant-in-aid shared revenue [1]	[2]24,065	91,385	135,325	224,991	246,128	267,061	284,659	316,265
National defense	37	93	241	68	12	1	2	2
Energy	25	499	461	492	424	462	433	479
Natural resources and environment	411	5,363	3,745	4,148	3,758	4,103	4,595	5,092
Environmental Protection Agency	194	4,603	2,874	2,912	2,746	2,960	3,490	3,595
Agriculture	604	569	1,285	780	668	659	724	842
Commerce and Housing Credit	4	3	-	5	9	5	3	6
Transportation [1]	4,599	13,022	19,174	25,787	26,144	28,904	32,222	35,264
Airports [3]	83	590	1,220	1,826	1,511	1,565	1,624	2,221
Highways [3]	4,395	9,208	14,171	19,475	19,791	22,590	24,711	26,426
Urban mass transit [3]	104	3,129	3,730	4,353	4,221	4,188	5,262	5,417
Community and regional development [1]	1,780	6,486	4,965	7,230	7,653	9,332	8,665	8,739
Appalachian regional development	184	335	124	182	180	136	125	108
Community development block grants	(X)	3,902	2,818	4,333	4,621	4,804	4,955	4,940
Education, employment, training, social services [1]	6,417	21,862	23,359	34,125	36,502	38,217	42,125	46,844
Compensatory education for the disadvantaged	1,470	3,370	4,437	6,785	7,800	7,534	8,511	8,432
School improvement programs	86	523	1,080	1,288	1,260	1,255	2,394	2,936
Bilingual and immigrant education	-	166	152	189	204	284	319	370
Federally affected areas impact aid	622	622	799	803	724	1,076	875	1,121
Vocational and adult education	285	854	1,287	1,449	1,425	1,338	1,448	1,669
Payments to states for Family Support Activities	81	383	265	953	4,451	4,707	5,453	6,055
Social services-block grants to states	574	2,763	2,749	2,797	2,437	1,993	1,827	1,906
Children and family services programs	390	1,548	2,618	4,463	5,054	5,421	5,843	6,325
Training and employment assistance	954	6,191	3,042	3,620	3,399	3,436	2,957	3,641
Office of libraries.	105	158	127	129	121	129	152	155
Health [1]	3,849	15,758	43,890	93,587	105,833	113,969	124,843	141,793
Alcohol, drug abuse, and mental health [4] . . .	146	679	1,241	2,444	2,236	2,214	1,931	2,027
Grants to states for medicaid [4]	2,727	13,957	41,103	89,070	101,234	108,042	117,921	128,853
Income security [1]	5,795	18,495	35,189	55,122	58,870	64,178	63,200	69,627
Family support payments to states [4]	4,142	6,888	12,246	17,133	2,171	2,756	2,906	3,439
Food stamps-administration	559	412	2,130	2,740	3,673	3,362	3,508	3,558
Child nutrition and special milk programs [4] . .	380	3,388	4,871	7,897	8,436	8,740	9,060	9,755
Housing assistance [4]	436	3,435	9,516	18,416	19,668	22,830	19,974	21,501
Veterans benefits and services [4]	18	90	134	253	288	517	434	445
Administration of justice.	42	529	574	1,222	3,658	4,793	5,120	4,465
General government [5]	479	8,616	2,309	2,172	2,309	2,141	2,287	2,653

- Represents or rounds to zero. X Not applicable. [1] Includes items not shown separately. [2] Includes $5 million for international affairs subsequently provided to a private institution. [3] Trust funds. [4] Includes grants for payments to individuals. [5] Includes general purpose fiscal assistance.

Source: U.S. Office of Management and Budget, *Historical Tables, Budget of the United States Government*, annual.

No. 421. Federal Aid to State and Local Governments—Selected Programs by State: 2000

[In millions of dollars (291,943 represents $291,943,000,000), except per capita. For fiscal year ending September 30]

State and outlying area	Department of Agriculture						Department of Education				
	Food and nutrition service							Office of Special Education and Rehabilitative Services			
	Federal aid, total [1]	Total	Child nutrition programs [2]	Food stamp program [3]	Special supplemental food program (WIC)	Other	Total	Education for the disadvantaged	Special education	Rehabilitation services & disability research	Other
United States [4]	291,943	19,792	8,993	3,494	3,948	3,357	26,654	8,362	5,089	2,625	10,578
Alabama	4,570	336	171	30	63	71	499	139	85	50	225
Alaska	2,260	93	25	7	18	43	227	27	17	15	168
Arizona	4,501	350	178	33	85	54	577	127	66	44	340
Arkansas	2,657	238	106	23	44	64	264	90	49	37	88
California	33,158	2,323	1,203	229	673	218	3,112	1,082	493	262	1,274
Colorado	3,273	188	89	21	39	39	322	75	69	35	143
Connecticut	3,771	148	71	24	33	21	275	79	67	20	108
Delaware	818	56	25	6	8	17	83	22	14	9	37
District of Columbia	2,963	50	26	8	10	6	159	31	19	24	85
Florida	11,676	828	484	78	178	89	1,154	408	273	12	461
Georgia	7,192	560	328	55	105	71	597	187	122	76	212
Hawaii	1,221	92	38	13	25	16	162	21	21	11	108
Idaho	1,229	101	36	9	18	38	128	29	22	16	62
Illinois	11,271	681	341	94	151	94	1,059	328	244	121	365
Indiana	5,142	297	139	37	66	55	483	125	113	59	185
Iowa	2,639	178	75	17	30	56	251	57	54	28	113
Kansas	2,315	165	91	10	26	38	262	70	56	25	111
Kentucky	4,720	315	155	31	59	69	422	143	74	47	157
Louisiana	5,248	444	241	38	75	90	524	194	77	41	213
Maine	1,850	95	33	7	12	44	134	38	29	16	51
Maryland	5,538	256	130	38	50	39	407	108	104	38	157
Massachusetts	7,500	283	153	35	59	35	545	154	143	52	196
Michigan	9,486	695	228	235	115	117	917	345	172	89	310
Minnesota	4,599	296	149	36	47	63	385	98	94	43	151
Mississippi	3,420	371	164	36	56	116	345	132	50	41	123
Missouri	5,671	340	165	46	63	66	468	117	101	65	185
Montana	1,439	84	30	9	14	32	168	30	17	14	107
Nebraska	1,682	130	61	13	18	38	156	25	58	14	59
Nevada	1,244	80	39	7	19	15	108	25	29	13	43
New Hampshire	1,116	54	18	7	9	21	93	20	24	11	38
New Jersey	8,212	343	172	61	68	42	635	184	164	56	230
New Mexico	2,774	182	97	12	33	41	381	69	90	26	195
New York	30,038	1,277	667	212	272	126	1,744	698	287	165	593
North Carolina	7,911	526	274	52	96	104	650	157	140	78	275
North Dakota	1,155	65	24	6	9	25	117	22	12	12	72
Ohio	10,560	524	248	79	120	76	911	315	165	119	312
Oklahoma	3,587	308	142	39	58	68	407	98	61	40	208
Oregon	3,597	414	98	43	51	222	295	85	69	38	103
Pennsylvania	12,765	567	262	98	124	84	1,150	447	256	114	334
Rhode Island	1,526	55	25	6	12	13	100	28	22	11	38
South Carolina	4,017	291	151	24	60	56	369	105	80	44	139
South Dakota	1,131	84	29	9	13	32	137	22	15	12	88
Tennessee	6,160	379	187	38	86	67	482	133	111	66	172
Texas	17,350	1,529	892	156	331	150	2,032	752	347	192	740
Utah	1,910	164	75	34	31	25	205	38	49	24	94
Vermont	900	52	15	10	9	18	81	20	14	11	36
Virginia	4,615	330	128	65	71	67	550	119	131	66	234
Washington	5,707	389	146	43	85	115	510	132	99	55	224
West Virginia	2,542	159	68	12	28	51	229	76	36	27	90
Wisconsin	4,504	277	118	35	55	69	469	137	93	58	182
Wyoming	1,014	40	15	3	7	15	88	19	14	9	46
Outlying areas	4,879	1,617	169	1,224	161	64	826	379	76	71	299
Puerto Rico	4,225	1,550	146	1,211	146	47	719	349	42	66	262

See footnotes at end of table.

U.S. Census Bureau, Statistical Abstract of the United States: 2001

[In millions of dollars (2,209 represents $2,209,000,000). For fiscal year ending September 30]

State and outlying area	FEMA, [5] total	Department of Housing and Urban Development							Department of Labor		
			Public housing programs						State unem- ployment insur- ance and employ- ment service	Employ- ment & Training Admin- istration workforce Invest- ment Act
		Total	Commu- nity develop- ment block grants	Low rent block	Section 8 pro- grams	Housing certi- ficate pro- gram	Capital pro- grams	Other	Total [6]		
United States [4]	2,209	32,356	4,972	2,914	379	15,972	3,690	4,428	5,149	2,965	1,852
Alabama	58	427	62	80	-	160	76	49	82	42	35
Alaska	6	206	13	7	-	26	4	157	39	28	8
Arizona	17	337	56	14	3	131	16	118	74	39	31
Arkansas	8	213	36	19	-	107	24	28	52	27	22
California	525	3,443	560	101	23	2,101	185	474	814	428	337
Colorado	11	435	52	12	7	208	35	121	62	40	16
Connecticut	4	530	51	46	21	323	40	49	70	51	13
Delaware	4	88	7	9	1	49	4	18	18	11	6
District of Columbia	3	429	56	43	24	150	90	67	39	17	19
Florida	211	1,117	197	83	11	612	59	156	182	98	74
Georgia	71	858	128	85	11	332	205	98	139	67	65
Hawaii	5	177	34	9	-	87	12	35	37	17	17
Idaho	5	80	17	-	-	46	1	15	31	22	7
Illinois	26	1,705	259	200	16	859	246	124	226	136	79
Indiana	5	495	84	31	4	252	32	90	72	48	17
Iowa	24	200	51	1	-	106	7	35	38	27	6
Kansas	10	165	39	9	-	75	14	28	37	22	11
Kentucky	17	395	66	36	2	203	50	38	68	31	32
Louisiana	19	467	86	50	3	194	67	68	75	35	36
Maine	10	195	45	7	-	105	6	32	25	17	6
Maryland	11	682	93	48	11	384	66	79	94	61	26
Massachusetts	13	1,313	148	86	12	841	91	135	104	75	23
Michigan	15	857	178	49	5	412	75	138	191	116	57
Minnesota	46	515	96	26	1	247	70	76	71	48	15
Mississippi	19	266	46	20	-	131	29	41	53	25	25
Missouri	12	499	100	26	22	239	52	60	80	51	24
Montana	18	121	15	3	1	38	5	58	28	16	10
Nebraska	8	132	27	7	-	66	12	20	24	17	4
Nevada	5	146	20	13	-	78	9	26	39	28	7
New Hampshire	4	118	21	5	-	75	8	9	18	12	5
New Jersey	44	1,362	127	143	43	758	193	98	153	104	42
New Mexico	6	176	25	5	-	73	8	65	46	23	21
New York	73	4,049	452	712	9	1,897	634	344	372	199	155
North Carolina	288	715	96	79	14	302	63	162	103	69	24
North Dakota	69	129	50	1	-	35	2	40	30	23	6
Ohio	15	1,324	214	130	13	647	181	139	175	94	70
Oklahoma	16	394	55	19	1	145	19	155	45	26	16
Oregon	19	324	45	12	-	191	17	58	89	53	30
Pennsylvania	32	1,689	287	227	39	642	344	150	213	146	56
Rhode Island	2	249	22	14	-	146	16	51	23	16	5
South Carolina	31	308	53	24	7	167	23	34	67	35	25
South Dakota	6	130	35	2	-	40	3	51	18	10	7
Tennessee	33	496	60	78	10	220	77	51	97	54	36
Texas	51	1,653	332	91	31	786	216	198	299	154	134
Utah	6	137	25	3	-	62	3	44	43	32	6
Vermont	5	76	12	2	-	47	3	12	14	9	3
Virginia	30	573	73	50	5	346	39	60	92	55	30
Washington	38	504	83	29	7	242	38	106	135	85	38
West Virginia	10	190	40	13	1	100	14	23	44	19	22
Wisconsin	14	434	89	12	17	212	30	74	88	64	17
Wyoming	2	48	6	1	-	18	2	22	18	10	6
Outlying areas	118	758	150	120	6	258	176	48	103	30	70
Puerto Rico	94	687	148	99	6	232	162	41	93	26	64

See footnotes at end of table.

U.S. Census Bureau, Statistical Abstract of the United States: 2001

No. 421. Federal Aid to State and Local Governments—Selected Programs by State: 2000—Con.

[In millions of dollars (159,344 represents $159,344,000,000). For fiscal year ending September 30]

State and outlying area	Department of Health and Human Services						Department of Transportation				
		Admininstation for children									
	Total	Tempo-rary assis-tance to needy families	Children & family services (Head Start)	Foster care and adop-tion assis-tance	Health care financ-ing admin-istration	Other	Total	High-way trust fund	Federal transit admin-istration	Other	Federal aid, other
United States [4]	159,344	13,140	5,378	4,594	119,308	16,925	32,379	24,149	5,087	3,143	14,060
Alabama	2,362	83	84	17	1,965	214	580	473	14	93	226
Alaska	901	41	24	11	348	477	420	336	7	77	369
Arizona	2,250	218	97	52	1,619	265	578	436	49	93	317
Arkansas	1,487	68	53	27	1,208	131	316	277	12	27	79
California	18,643	3,341	607	961	12,127	1,607	3,240	1,967	871	401	1,058
Colorado	1,533	113	64	37	1,105	214	427	297	83	48	294
Connecticut	2,186	202	47	111	1,638	188	466	399	60	7	92
Delaware	384	30	11	11	281	51	133	120	8	5	52
District of Columbia	1,018	79	60	36	639	204	326	131	171	24	938
Florida	6,371	552	182	159	4,713	765	1,415	1,104	212	99	397
Georgia	3,810	244	148	62	2,706	650	911	710	132	69	246
Hawaii	545	69	20	22	355	79	131	82	39	10	74
Idaho	592	42	23	8	453	66	199	172	7	20	93
Illinois	5,972	439	255	348	4,165	766	1,251	858	278	115	353
Indiana	2,863	216	77	56	2,287	227	669	571	58	40	257
Iowa	1,475	130	45	44	1,109	148	349	305	16	28	124
Kansas	1,235	92	56	29	929	129	331	304	12	15	111
Kentucky	2,721	183	88	43	2,208	199	598	519	27	53	183
Louisiana	3,030	130	109	59	2,524	208	489	404	39	46	200
Maine	1,110	61	25	41	872	112	182	146	28	8	98
Maryland	3,343	180	124	109	1,698	1,233	530	378	106	46	216
Massachusetts	4,329	350	99	88	3,381	411	618	484	97	37	296
Michigan	5,383	728	188	175	3,888	404	990	847	78	65	440
Minnesota	2,476	218	73	74	1,811	299	542	423	56	64	268
Mississippi	1,932	48	127	12	1,583	161	294	272	6	16	140
Missouri	3,249	227	108	60	2,533	320	843	669	89	84	182
Montana	534	33	28	10	359	104	310	260	28	22	174
Nebraska	919	54	30	23	698	114	220	195	10	15	95
Nevada	500	39	18	16	329	97	210	149	19	42	157
New Hampshire	587	27	13	12	459	76	141	123	4	14	101
New Jersey	4,358	188	117	67	3,571	416	1,089	588	459	41	229
New Mexico	1,287	138	52	21	944	133	293	263	10	20	403
New York	19,444	1,306	365	666	15,962	1,145	2,086	1,133	761	192	994
North Carolina	4,526	315	126	77	3,581	428	837	756	28	53	265
North Dakota	434	20	21	11	320	63	211	187	5	19	100
Ohio	6,305	566	204	234	4,704	597	967	743	136	88	339
Oklahoma	1,838	95	76	38	1,293	336	369	320	18	31	210
Oregon	1,849	157	63	36	1,419	173	361	287	46	28	244
Pennsylvania	7,481	398	187	294	5,905	697	1,283	848	267	167	349
Rhode Island	866	84	19	16	683	63	170	133	16	20	61
South Carolina	2,383	96	65	23	1,989	210	401	363	17	21	167
South Dakota	415	15	25	6	296	74	202	180	4	18	139
Tennessee	3,735	172	90	24	3,191	258	586	483	45	58	354
Texas	8,984	482	352	106	7,068	975	2,264	1,783	308	172	538
Utah	856	55	32	21	635	113	333	230	79	24	166
Vermont	465	44	14	17	350	40	135	115	9	11	72
Virginia	2,193	140	142	61	1,498	353	634	507	49	78	212
Washington	3,117	283	96	39	2,348	350	702	477	163	61	313
West Virginia	1,355	68	41	21	1,100	125	363	286	12	66	192
Wisconsin	2,750	210	84	101	2,078	277	279	172	59	48	193
Wyoming	211	10	15	2	151	33	204	181	2	21	403
Outlying areas	751	61	309	-	235	146	358	273	56	28	348
Puerto Rico	684	56	293	-	219	116	292	223	56	13	107

- Represents or rounds to zero. [1] Includes programs not shown separately. [2] Includes "special milk program." [3] For Puerto Rico, amount shown is for nutritional assistance grant program, all other amounts are grant payments for food stamp administration. [4] Totals include outlying areas and include undistributed amounts not shown separately. [5] FEMA = Federal Emergency Management Agency. [6] Includes other not shown separately.

Source: U.S. Census Bureau, *Federal Aid to States For Fiscal Year 2000*, Series FAS/00. <http://www.census.gov/govs/www/cffr.html>.

State and Local Government Finances and Employment 265

No. 422. State and Local Government Receipts and Current Expenditures in the National Income and Product Accounts: 1980 to 2000

[In billions of dollars (316.6 represents $316,600,000,000). For explanation of national income, see text, Section 13, Income, Expenditures, and Wealth]

Item	1980	1990	1992	1993	1994	1995	1996	1997	1998	1999	2000
Receipts.............	316.6	663.4	772.2	823.2	873.8	917.9	960.4	1,011.3	1,072.3	1,142.7	1,230.1
Personal tax and nontax											
receipts.............	53.9	136.0	156.4	164.7	174.8	186.5	199.6	216.9	234.9	249.7	274.1
Income taxes.........	42.6	107.7	119.6	126.0	133.4	142.5	152.9	167.6	182.8	194.8	216.3
Non axes............	5.0	15.6	22.5	23.4	25.0	27.1	29.2	31.1	33.1	35.1	37.3
Other...............	6.3	12.8	14.3	15.3	16.4	17.0	17.5	18.2	19.1	19.8	20.5
Corporate profits tax accruals...	14.5	22.5	24.4	26.9	30.0	31.7	33.0	34.2	35.1	36.6	40.2
Indirect business tax and nontax											
accruals [1].........	172.3	383.4	429.2	454.8	480.1	501.6	524.9	552.5	583.1	617.5	661.2
Sales taxes.........	82.9	183.2	202.2	216.0	230.9	243.6	255.6	269.3	284.9	307.1	331.7
Property taxes......	68.8	161.1	182.8	191.1	197.6	203.5	211.4	220.3	229.2	238.5	248.5
Contributions for social											
insurance...........	3.6	10.0	13.1	14.1	14.5	13.6	12.5	10.8	10.0	9.6	9.9
Federal grants-in-aid......	72.3	111.4	149.1	162.6	174.5	184.5	190.4	196.8	209.1	229.3	244.6
Current expenditures....	307.8	660.8	777.2	821.7	865.2	902.5	939.0	980.3	1,030.6	1,092.7	1,170.5
Consumption expenditures	260.5	545.8	601.6	629.5	662.6	694.7	726.5	766.4	808.4	855.0	918.0
Transfer payments to persons..	51.2	127.8	180.1	195.4	206.9	217.8	224.3	227.5	234.1	252.0	267.8
Net interest paid.........	-5.4	-6.3	2.8	5.6	4.4	0.5	0.9	-0.9	-0.6	-3.0	-4.5
Interest received by											
government..........	24.7	66.7	62.2	59.1	61.3	67.3	69.5	73.5	74.5	78.1	81.1
Less: Dividends received.....	0.1	0.2	0.2	0.2	0.2	0.3	0.3	0.3	0.4	0.4	0.4
Subsidies.............	0.4	0.4	0.4	0.4	0.3	0.3	0.3	0.4	0.4	0.5	0.5
Less: Current surplus of											
government enterprises......	-1.2	6.7	7.6	8.9	8.8	10.5	12.8	12.8	11.3	11.4	11.0
Current surplus or deficit.	8.8	2.6	-4.9	1.5	8.6	15.3	21.4	31.0	41.7	50.0	59.6
Social insurance funds.......	1.3	2.0	3.1	4.2	4.6	4.0	2.7	1.1	0.4	-0.4	-0.4
Other................	7.5	0.7	-8.1	-2.7	4.0	11.4	18.7	29.9	41.3	50.4	60.1

[1] Includes other items not shown separately.

Source: U.S. Bureau of Economic Analysis, *National Income and Product Accounts of the United States, 1929-97*, (forthcoming), and *Survey of Current Business*, May 2001.

No. 423. State and Local Government Consumption Expenditures and Transfers in the National Income and Product Accounts: 1980 to 2000

[In billions of dollars (324.4 represents $324,400,000,000). For explanation of national income, see text, Section 13, Income, Expenditures, and Wealth]

Expenditure	1980	1985	1990	1994	1995	1996	1997	1998	1999	2000
Consumption expenditures and gross investment [1]...	324.4	464.9	673.0	806.8	850.5	890.4	949.7	1,000.3	1,065.8	1,148.6
Consumption expenditures......	260.5	380.5	545.8	662.6	694.7	726.5	766.4	808.4	855.0	918.0
Durable goods [2].........	4.7	7.4	10.6	12.2	12.7	13.1	13.8	15.0	15.9	17.1
Nondurable goods..........	28.3	38.1	53.6	66.7	72.9	79.9	81.7	83.6	91.3	109.5
Services................	227.5	335.0	481.5	583.7	609.0	633.6	670.9	709.8	747.7	791.4
Gross investment..........	64.0	84.4	127.2	144.2	155.8	163.8	183.3	191.9	210.9	230.6
Structures..............	55.1	67.6	98.5	108.7	117.3	122.5	139.3	144.0	157.5	169.6
Equipment..............	8.9	16.8	28.7	35.5	38.6	41.3	44.0	48.0	53.4	61.0
Transfers..............	51.2	77.3	127.8	206.9	217.8	224.3	227.5	234.1	252.0	(NA)
Benefits from social insurance										
funds.................	2.8	4.9	9.2	11.0	10.7	10.9	10.7	10.3	10.5	(NA)
Temporary disability insurance..	0.8	1.4	2.2	2.2	2.1	2.0	2.0	2.1	2.1	(NA)
Public assistance............	44.0	67.2	111.1	185.8	195.8	201.9	205.0	210.9	227.7	(NA)
Medical care.............	24.9	42.4	78.2	144.9	155.0	163.6	168.3	174.1	189.0	(NA)
Medicaid.............	23.9	39.7	73.1	139.4	149.6	158.2	163.1	169.2	183.9	(NA)
Family assistance [3].......	12.5	15.2	19.2	23.2	22.6	20.3	17.7	17.0	17.8	(NA)
Supplemental security income..	2.0	2.3	3.8	3.8	3.8	3.6	3.7	3.9	4.3	(NA)
General assistance.........	1.4	2.2	2.9	3.4	3.5	3.3	3.3	3.3	3.3	(NA)
Energy assistance.........	1.3	2.1	1.6	2.0	1.5	1.3	1.4	1.3	1.4	(NA)
Other [4]...............	1.7	3.0	5.4	8.6	9.4	9.7	10.6	11.4	11.9	(NA)
Education..............	2.4	3.5	5.3	7.6	8.7	9.1	9.1	9.9	10.7	(NA)
Employment and training.......	1.7	0.9	0.9	1.1	1.1	0.9	1.0	1.1	1.1	(NA)
Other [5]...............	0.3	0.7	1.2	1.4	1.5	1.6	1.6	1.8	2.0	(NA)

NA Not available. [1] Gross government investment consists of general government and government enterprise expenditures for fixed assets; inventory investment is included in government consumption expenditures. [2] Consumption expenditures for durable goods excludes expenditures classified as investment, except for goods transferred to foreign countries by the federal government. [3] Consists of aid to families with dependent children. Beginning with 1996, assistance programs operating under the Personal Responsibility and Work Opportunity Act of 1996. [4] Consists of emergency assistance and medical insurance premium payments paid on behalf of indigents. [5] Consists largely of foster care, veterans benefits, Alaska dividends, and crime victim payments.

Source: U.S. Bureau of Economic Analysis, *National Income and Product Accounts of the United States 1929-97*, (forthcoming), and *Survey of Current Business*, May 2001.

No. 424. State and Local Governments—Summary of Finances: 1980 to 1998

[In millions of dollars (451,537 represents $451,537,000,000), except as indicated. For fiscal year ending in year shown; see text, this section. Local government amounts are estimates subject to sampling variation; see Appendix III and source]

Item	Total (mil. dol.)				Per capita [1] (dol.)			
	1980	1990	1997	1998	1980	1990	1997	1998
Revenue [2]	451,537	1,032,115	1,616,495	1,720,889	1,993	4,150	6,037	6,368
From federal government	83,029	136,802	244,847	255,048	367	550	914	944
Public welfare	24,921	59,961	124,284	128,470	110	241	464	475
Highways	8,980	14,368	19,871	20,241	40	58	74	75
Education	14,435	23,233	35,986	38,922	64	93	134	144
Health and hospitals	2,513	5,904	12,745	13,856	11	24	48	51
Housing and community development	3,905	9,655	17,009	18,239	17	39	64	67
Other and unallocable	28,275	23,683	34,951	35,319	125	95	131	131
From state and local sources	368,509	895,313	1,371,649	1,465,841	1,627	3,600	5,123	5,424
General, net intergovernmental	299,293	712,700	1,044,391	1,110,714	1,321	2,865	3,901	4,110
Taxes	223,463	501,619	728,304	773,963	986	2,017	2,720	2,864
Property	68,499	155,613	218,877	230,150	302	626	817	852
Sales and gross receipts	79,927	177,885	261,418	274,883	353	715	976	1,017
Individual income	42,080	105,640	159,042	175,630	186	425	594	650
Corporation income	13,321	23,566	33,820	34,412	59	95	126	127
Other	19,636	38,915	55,146	58,888	87	156	206	218
Charges and miscellaneous	75,830	211,081	316,087	336,751	335	849	1,181	1,246
Utility and liquor stores	25,560	58,642	78,186	81,127	113	236	292	300
Water supply system	6,766	17,674	26,895	27,473	30	71	100	102
Electric power system	11,387	29,268	36,008	37,812	50	118	134	140
Transit system	2,397	5,216	7,300	7,546	11	21	27	28
Gas supply system	1,809	3,043	4,088	4,188	8	12	15	15
Liquor stores	3,201	3,441	3,895	4,107	14	14	15	15
Insurance trust revenue [3]	43,656	123,970	249,072	274,001	193	498	930	1,014
Employee retirement	25,441	94,268	199,655	237,472	112	379	746	879
Unemployment compensation	13,529	18,441	34,780	23,153	60	74	130	86
Direct expenditure	432,328	972,662	1,456,698	1,525,762	1,908	3,911	5,441	5,646
By function:								
Direct general expenditure [3]	367,340	834,786	1,246,121	1,314,496	1,622	3,356	4,654	4,864
Education	133,211	288,148	418,416	450,365	588	1,159	1,563	1,666
Elementary and secondary	92,930	202,009	293,961	318,065	410	812	1,098	1,177
Higher education	33,919	73,418	106,061	112,874	150	295	396	418
Highways	33,311	61,057	82,062	87,214	147	245	306	323
Public welfare	45,552	110,518	199,970	204,640	201	444	747	757
Health	8,387	24,223	42,226	44,391	37	97	158	164
Hospitals	23,787	50,412	68,218	69,633	105	203	255	258
Police protection	13,494	30,577	47,389	50,475	60	123	177	187
Fire protection	5,718	13,186	19,323	20,269	25	53	72	75
Correction	6,448	24,635	39,882	42,479	28	100	149	157
Natural resources	5,509	12,330	16,607	17,492	24	50	62	65
Sanitation and sewerage	13,214	28,453	41,349	41,765	58	114	154	155
Housing and community development	6,062	15,479	23,530	24,697	27	62	88	91
Parks and recreation	6,520	14,326	20,720	22,365	29	58	77	83
Financial administration	6,719	16,217	24,400	25,914	30	65	91	96
Interest on general debt [4]	14,747	49,739	62,169	64,554	65	200	232	239
Utility and liquor stores [4]	36,191	77,801	99,453	102,865	160	313	371	381
Water supply system	9,228	22,101	31,176	32,069	41	89	116	119
Electric power system	15,016	30,997	34,470	35,264	66	125	129	130
Gas supply system	1,715	2,989	3,895	4,645	8	12	15	17
Transit system	7,641	18,788	26,675	27,542	34	76	100	102
Liquor stores	2,591	2,926	3,236	3,346	11	12	12	12
Insurance trust expenditure [3]	28,797	63,321	111,124	108,400	127	255	415	401
Employee retirement	14,008	38,355	72,840	80,222	56	154	272	297
Unemployment compensation	12,070	16,499	27,158	17,779	53	66	101	66
By character and object:								
Current operation	307,811	700,131	1,068,783	1,129,257	1,359	2,815	3,992	4,179
Capital outlay	62,894	123,069	171,414	181,871	278	495	640	673
Construction	51,492	89,114	130,475	135,546	227	358	487	502
Equipment, land, and existing structures	11,402	33,955	40,938	46,326	50	137	153	171
Assistance and subsidies	15,222	27,227	33,455	31,636	67	109	125	117
Interest on debt (general and utility)	17,604	58,914	71,922	74,597	78	237	289	276
Insurance benefits and repayments	28,797	63,321	111,124	108,400	127	255	415	401
Expenditure for salaries and wages	163,896	341,158	468,947	495,139	723	1,372	1,751	1,832
Debt outstanding, year end	335,603	860,584	1,224,510	1,283,560	1,481	3,460	4,573	4,750
Long-term	322,456	841,278	1,207,873	1,266,308	1,423	3,382	4,511	4,686
Short-term	13,147	19,306	16,636	17,252	58	78	62	64
Long-term debt:								
Issued	42,364	108,468	151,260	204,351	187	436	565	756
Retired	17,404	64,831	109,288	144,636	77	261	408	535

[1] 1980 and 1990 based on enumerated resident population as of April 1. Other years based on estimated resident population as of July 1; see Table 2. [2] Aggregates exclude duplicative transactions between state and local governments; see source. [3] Includes amounts not shown separately. [4] Interest on utility debt included in "utility expenditure." For total interest on debt, see "Interest on debt (general and utility)."

Source: U.S. Census Bureau, 1980-90, *Government Finances*, GF, No. 5, annual; thereafter, <http://www.census.gov/govs/www/estimate.html> (accessed 02 July 2001).

State and Local Government Finances and Employment 267

[In millions of dollars (1,720,889 represents $1,720,889,000,000) except as indicated. For fiscal year ending in year shown; see text, this section. Local government amounts are estimates subject to sampling variation; see Appendix III and source]

Item	Total [1]	State and local — State	State and local — Local	Per capita [2] (dol.) — State and local	Per capita [2] (dol.) — State	Per capita [2] (dol.) — Local
Revenue [2]	1,720,889	1,103,239	909,661	6,368	4,090	3,366
Intergovernmental revenue	255,048	240,789	306,270	944	893	1,133
Total revenue from own sources	1,465,841	862,450	603,391	5,424	3,197	2,233
General revenue from own sources	1,110,714	622,734	487,980	4,110	2,309	1,806
Taxes [3]	773,963	473,051	300,912	2,864	1,754	1,113
Property	230,150	10,659	219,492	852	40	812
Individual income	175,630	160,115	15,515	650	594	57
Corporation income	34,412	31,089	3,323	127	115	12
Sales and gross receipts	274,883	226,643	48,240	1,017	840	179
General	188,753	155,272	33,481	698	576	124
Selective [3]	86,131	71,371	14,759	319	265	55
Motor fuel	29,247	28,345	902	108	105	3
Alcoholic beverages	4,047	3,765	282	15	14	1
Tobacco products	7,956	7,748	209	29	29	1
Public utilities	16,796	8,796	8,001	62	33	30
Motor vehicle and operators' licenses	16,143	14,919	1,223	60	55	5
Death and gift	6,971	6,939	32	26	26	-
Charges and miscellaneous [3]	336,751	149,682	187,068	1,246	555	692
Current charges [3]	201,554	76,219	125,335	746	283	464
Education [3]	56,689	43,258	13,431	210	160	50
School lunch sales	4,781	16	4,766	18	-	18
Higher education	47,504	42,719	4,785	176	158	18
Natural resources	2,796	1,768	1,028	10	7	4
Hospitals	50,652	16,600	34,052	187	62	126
Sewerage	22,717	41	22,677	84	-	84
Solid waste management	9,617	406	9,211	36	2	34
Parks and recreation	5,690	1,073	4,616	21	4	17
Housing and community development	4,064	414	3,650	15	2	14
Airports	9,522	768	8,754	35	3	32
Sea and inland port facilities	2,239	643	1,597	8	2	6
Highways	6,331	3,946	2,386	23	15	9
Interest earnings	65,417	32,715	32,702	242	121	121
Special assessments	3,778	41	3,737	14	-	14
Sale of property	2,178	495	1,683	8	2	6
Utility and liquor store revenue	81,127	7,687	73,439	300	29	272
Insurance trust revenue	274,001	232,029	41,972	1,014	860	155
Expenditure	1,529,308	929,952	884,759	5,659	3,448	3,274
Intergovernmental expenditure	3,546	278,853	10,095	13	1,034	37
Direct expenditure	1,525,762	651,098	874,664	5,646	2,414	3,237
General expenditure [3]	1,314,496	548,800	765,696	4,864	2,035	2,833
Education [3]	450,365	118,563	331,802	1,666	440	1,228
Elementary and secondary education	318,065	2,886	315,179	1,177	11	1,166
Higher education	112,874	96,251	16,623	418	357	62
Public welfare	204,640	172,119	32,521	757	638	120
Hospitals	69,633	28,486	41,148	258	106	152
Health	44,391	23,130	21,261	164	86	79
Highways	87,214	51,971	35,243	323	193	130
Police protection	50,475	7,165	43,310	187	27	160
Fire protection	20,269	-	20,269	75	-	75
Corrections	42,479	28,679	13,800	157	106	51
Natural resources	17,492	12,883	4,609	65	48	17
Sewerage	25,647	1,132	24,515	95	4	91
Solid waste management	16,118	1,988	14,130	60	7	52
Housing and community development	24,697	2,414	22,284	91	9	82
Governmental administration	70,727	29,692	41,035	262	110	152
Parks and recreation	22,365	3,893	18,472	83	14	68
Interest on general debt	64,554	26,776	37,778	239	99	140
Utility	99,519	8,365	91,154	368	31	337
Liquor store expenditure	3,346	2,820	526	12	10	2
Insurance trust expenditure	108,400	91,113	17,287	401	338	64
By character and object:						
Current operation	1,129,257	446,440	682,817	4,179	1,655	2,527
Capital outlay	181,871	64,441	117,430	673	239	435
Construction	135,546	50,542	85,004	502	187	315
Equip., land, and existing structures	46,326	13,899	32,426	171	52	120
Assistance and subsidies	31,636	21,515	10,121	117	80	37
Interest on debt (general and utility)	74,597	27,590	47,008	276	102	174
Insurance benefits and repayments	108,400	91,113	17,287	401	338	64
Expenditure for salaries and wages [4]	495,139	139,970	355,170	1,832	519	1,314

- Represents or rounds to zero. [1] Based on estimated resident population as of July 1. See Table 2. [2] Aggregates exclude duplicative transactions between levels of government; see source. [3] Includes amounts not shown separately. [4] Included in items shown above.

Source: U.S. Census Bureau, <http://www.census.gov/pub/ govs/www/index.html> (accessed 07 July 2001), and unpublished data.

No. 426. State and Local Governments—Capital Outlays: 1985 to 1998

[In millions of dollars (79,898 represents $79,898,000,000), except percent. For fiscal year ending in year shown; see text. this section. Local government amounts are subject to sampling variation; see Appendix III and source]

Level and function	1985	1990	1993	1994	1995	1996	1997	1998
State & local governments, total	79,898	123,102	135,899	137,501	151,440	158,911	171,414	181,871
Annual percent change [1]	13.1	4.9	5.3	0.5	1.2	10.1	4.9	6.1
Direct expenditure	656,188	972,695	1,210,097	1,260,642	1,347,763	1,393,714	1,456,698	1,525,762
Percent of direct expenditure	12.2	12.7	11.2	10.9	11.2	11.4	11.8	11.9
By function: Education [2]	13,477	25,997	31,359	29,012	35,708	40,302	44,077	49,332
Higher education	4,629	18,057	22,102	19,693	24,808	28,868	32,210	36,198
Elementary and secondary	8,358	7,441	8,949	8,959	10,461	11,006	11,279	12,590
Highways	23,900	33,867	36,980	39,503	42,561	43,453	44,962	48,067
Health and hospitals	2,709	3,848	5,291	5,157	4,883	5,166	5,065	5,692
Natural resources	1,736	2,545	2,137	2,349	2,891	3,042	3,041	3,206
Housing [3]	3,217	3,997	4,891	4,066	4,527	4,704	5,490	5,544
Air transportation	1,875	3,434	5,413	5,170	3,802	3,814	4,877	5,004
Water transportation [4]	717	924	996	1,483	1,101	1,246	1,376	1,252
Sewerage	5,926	8,356	10,261	7,989	8,894	9,326	9,589	9,061
Parks and recreation	2,196	3,877	3,849	3,919	4,085	4,869	5,577	6,154
Utilities	13,435	16,601	15,942	18,180	19,028	18,755	20,107	20,357
Water	4,160	6,873	6,500	6,893	7,466	7,381	8,721	8,644
Electric	5,247	3,976	3,760	4,030	3,715	3,522	3,459	3,026
Transit	3,830	310	428	290	340	318	399	986
Gas	198	5,443	5,254	6,966	7,507	7,533	7,528	7,701
Other	10,711	19,657	18,780	20,673	23,961	24,233	27,254	28,202
State governments, total	30,657	45,524	50,152	52,895	57,829	58,927	59,599	64,441
Annual percent change [1]	16.3	5.6	4.9	0.1	5.5	9.3	1.9	8.1
Direct expenditure	269,171	397,291	529,167	550,276	596,325	607,594	629,049	651,098
Percent of direct expenditure	11.4	11.5	9.5	9.6	9.7	9.7	9.5	9.9
By function: Education [2]	4,711	7,253	8,868	8,594	10,042	10,445	10,915	11,970
Highways	17,827	24,850	28,207	29,995	31,687	32,198	32,726	35,008
Health and hospitals	1,038	1,531	2,025	2,375	2,402	2,375	2,253	2,274
Natural resources	1,076	1,593	1,455	1,702	1,956	2,044	2,058	2,199
Housing [3]	38	119	174	193	187	263	225	202
Air transportation	280	339	519	389	356	356	446	339
Water transportation [4]	274	202	250	297	223	305	269	305
Sewerage	187	333	684	774	853	913	474	639
Parks and recreation	351	601	694	692	650	706	938	1,293
Utilities	1,825	2,605	1,827	2,124	2,226	2,627	2,361	2,758
Other	3,051	6,098	5,449	5,760	7,246	6,716	6,934	7,454
Local governments, total	49,241	77,578	85,747	84,606	93,611	99,984	111,814	117,430
Annual percent change [1]	16.2	4.5	5.5	-1.3	10.6	6.8	11.8	5.0
Direct expenditure	386,753	575,404	680,930	710,366	751,438	786,120	827,648	874,664
Percent of direct expenditure	12.7	13.5	12.6	11.9	12.5	12.7	13.5	13.4
By function: Education [2]	8,766	18,744	22,491	20,418	25,667	29,858	33,162	37,362
Highways	6,073	9,017	8,773	9,508	10,874	11,255	12,235	13,059
Health and hospitals	1,671	2,316	3,266	2,782	2,481	2,790	2,811	3,418
Natural resources	660	952	682	647	935	998	983	1,007
Housing [3]	3,179	3,878	4,717	3,872	4,340	4,441	5,265	5,342
Air transportation	1,595	3,095	4,894	4,781	3,446	3,458	4,431	4,665
Water transportation [4]	443	722	746	1,185	877	941	1,107	947
Sewerage	5,738	8,023	9,578	7,215	8,040	8,413	9,116	8,422
Parks and recreation	1,845	3,276	3,155	3,228	3,435	4,163	4,639	4,861
Utilities	11,610	13,996	14,115	16,056	16,801	16,149	17,746	17,599
Other	7,660	13,559	13,331	14,913	16,715	17,518	20,320	20,748

[1] Change from prior year shown. [2] Includes other education. [3] Includes community development. [4] Includes terminals.
Source: U.S. Census Bureau, 1985-90 *Historical Statistics on Governmental Finances and Employment*; and *Government Finances*, Series GF, No. 5, annual; thereafter, <http://www.census.gov/govs/www/index.html> (accessed 20 July 2001).

No. 427. State and Local Governments—Expenditure for Public Works: 1990 to 1998

[In millions of dollars (138,851 represents $138,851,000,000). Public works include expenditures on highways, airports, water transport terminals, and sewerage, solid waste management, water supply, and mass transit systems. Represents direct expenditures excluding intergovernmental grants]

Item	Total	Highways	Airport transportation	Water transport and terminals	Sewerage	Solid waste management	Water supply	Mass transit
1990, total	138,851	61,057	6,484	1,968	18,309	10,144	22,101	18,788
State	43,787	36,464	635	504	636	891	136	4,521
Local	95,064	24,593	5,848	1,464	17,673	9,253	21,966	14,267
Capital expenditures (percent)	44	55	53	47	46	18	31	29
1995, total	180,148	77,109	8,397	2,309	23,583	14,990	28,041	25,719
State	56,392	46,893	783	604	1,462	1,658	178	4,814
Local	123,756	30,216	7,614	1,706	22,121	13,331	27,863	20,904
Capital expenditures (percent)	41	55	45	48	38	13	27	29
1997, total	194,207	82,062	10,136	2,809	25,667	15,682	31,176	26,675
State	58,593	48,773	883	739	1,098	1,677	164	5,260
Local	135,614	33,289	9,253	2,070	24,570	14,005	31,012	21,415
Capital expenditures (percent)	40	55	48	49	37	10	28	28
1998, total	201,833	87,214	10,459	2,785	25,647	16,118	32,069	27,542
State	62,556	51,971	810	830	1,132	1,988	172	5,653
Local	139,277	35,243	9,649	1,955	24,515	14,130	31,897	21,889
Capital expenditures (percent)	40	55	48	45	35	11	27	28

Source: U.S. Census Bureau, 1990, *Government Finances*, Series GF, No. 5, annual; thereafter, <http://www.census.gov govs/www/index.html> (accessed 20 July 2001).

State and Local Government Finances and Employment 269

No. 428. State and Local Governments—Revenue by State: 1998

[In millions of dollars ($1,720,889 represents $1,720,889,000,000). For fiscal year ending in year shown; see text, this section]

State	Total revenue [1]	General revenue Total	Intergovernmental from federal government	General revenue own sources	Taxes Total	Property	Sales and gross receipts	Individual income	Motor vehicle	Other taxes
United States...	1,720,889	1,365,762	255,048	1,110,714	773,963	230,150	274,883	210,042	14,884	44,004
Alabama	22,400	18,233	4,331	13,902	8,337	1,084	4,220	2,131	199	703
Alaska	11,022	9,662	1,250	8,412	2,013	706	265	276	47	720
Arizona	26,119	18,716	3,534	15,182	11,072	3,166	5,063	2,391	136	316
Arkansas	12,759	10,465	2,469	7,996	5,438	904	2,570	1,643	104	218
California	232,302	174,427	32,552	141,875	98,716	24,722	33,848	33,372	1,643	5,130
Colorado	23,967	19,703	3,154	16,550	10,971	3,161	4,023	3,153	182	453
Connecticut	23,730	20,808	3,326	17,482	14,487	5,018	4,721	3,941	223	585
Delaware	5,520	4,648	747	3,902	2,394	335	257	1,010	31	760
District of Columbia	5,904	5,257	1,619	3,638	2,889	695	934	1,083	19	158
Florida	88,919	68,158	9,722	58,436	37,955	13,131	19,702	1,271	865	2,986
Georgia	40,284	34,292	6,251	28,041	19,506	5,000	7,671	6,057	170	607
Hawaii	8,259	6,790	1,324	5,466	3,929	599	2,003	1,145	105	77
Idaho	6,598	5,353	951	4,401	2,869	763	964	897	102	143
Illinois	69,393	57,567	9,915	47,651	35,635	13,318	11,377	8,949	865	1,127
Indiana	28,721	26,036	4,117	21,919	14,747	5,055	4,473	4,805	134	279
Iowa	15,418	13,685	2,366	11,319	7,459	2,416	2,385	2,066	307	284
Kansas	13,916	12,435	1,942	10,493	7,375	2,150	2,742	2,050	130	303
Kentucky	21,621	17,450	3,900	13,549	9,355	1,568	3,429	3,393	195	770
Louisiana	25,396	20,525	4,248	16,277	10,062	1,537	5,450	1,810	105	1,160
Maine	7,993	6,768	1,508	5,260	4,012	1,634	1,145	1,013	85	134
Maryland	31,918	25,206	3,939	21,267	16,052	4,248	4,065	6,686	170	884
Massachusetts	41,013	35,575	6,917	28,658	21,706	6,981	4,462	9,387	244	632
Michigan	58,305	50,267	9,135	41,132	28,211	8,503	8,851	9,164	726	967
Minnesota	36,337	27,883	4,398	23,485	16,489	4,737	5,050	5,503	552	647
Mississippi	14,643	11,931	3,009	8,923	5,661	1,309	2,857	1,091	127	277
Missouri	29,107	23,264	4,717	18,546	13,320	3,033	5,368	4,005	254	659
Montana	4,960	4,246	1,135	3,111	2,016	886	278	522	61	269
Nebraska	10,971	8,016	1,417	6,599	4,576	1,589	1,531	1,116	87	252
Nevada	11,178	8,080	1,051	7,028	4,764	1,105	2,992	-	102	565
New Hampshire	6,172	5,067	917	4,150	2,863	1,831	498	298	59	177
New Jersey	56,498	47,184	6,621	40,563	30,010	14,156	7,676	6,798	404	975
New Mexico	11,483	9,258	2,033	7,226	4,580	573	2,380	979	123	526
New York	171,133	134,624	29,095	105,529	78,485	24,445	20,653	29,743	738	2,906
North Carolina	47,529	35,449	6,848	28,601	19,298	4,090	6,821	7,124	412	850
North Dakota	4,205	3,520	980	2,539	1,626	490	660	260	40	177
Ohio	70,553	52,698	9,783	42,915	30,827	8,740	9,465	10,623	674	1,324
Oklahoma	17,388	13,744	2,623	11,121	7,497	1,151	3,020	2,108	589	628
Oregon	22,841	17,704	4,045	13,659	8,135	2,532	835	3,718	320	730
Pennsylvania	72,674	57,667	11,161	46,506	33,631	9,232	10,035	9,907	695	3,762
Rhode Island	6,074	5,261	1,144	4,117	3,079	1,243	901	805	52	78
South Carolina	22,014	17,239	3,585	13,654	8,388	2,331	3,072	2,301	118	566
South Dakota	4,185	3,246	857	2,389	1,592	573	814	38	48	118
Tennessee	30,314	22,361	5,541	16,820	11,292	2,538	6,826	768	287	873
Texas	100,422	83,522	16,087	67,435	46,315	17,333	23,551	-	1,082	4,349
Utah	12,902	9,649	1,873	7,777	5,163	1,183	2,167	1,559	70	184
Vermont	3,473	3,144	751	2,393	1,720	762	427	412	36	84
Virginia	39,139	30,561	4,216	26,345	18,169	5,543	5,320	5,851	396	1,059
Washington	42,381	29,961	4,829	25,132	17,283	5,498	10,195	-	366	1,224
West Virginia	9,878	8,114	2,162	5,952	3,953	777	1,591	1,088	83	415
Wisconsin	37,049	26,848	4,107	22,741	16,643	5,249	4,786	5,728	271	610
Wyoming	3,909	3,496	847	2,649	1,395	526	493	-	53	323

See footnotes at end of table.

No. 428. State and Local Governments—Revenue by State: 1998—Con.

[In millions of dollars (336,751 represents $336,751,000,000). For fiscal year ending in year shown; see text, this section]

State	General revenue								Utility and liquor stores	Insurance trust revenue
	Current charges and miscellaneous revenue									
	Current charges					Miscellaneous revenue				
	Total	Total	Education	Hospitals	Sewerage	Total	Interest earnings	Special assessment		
United States	336,751	201,554	56,689	50,652	22,717	135,196	65,417	3,778	81,127	274,001
Alabama	5,565	4,092	1,098	2,124	193	1,473	769	12	1,773	2,395
Alaska	6,399	768	122	55	52	5,631	2,210	3	250	1,110
Arizona	4,110	2,209	844	190	305	1,901	911	54	2,314	5,089
Arkansas	2,558	1,704	489	727	141	853	444	9	494	1,799
California	43,159	26,760	5,277	5,587	3,114	16,399	7,828	1,112	12,524	45,352
Colorado	5,579	3,579	1,330	535	357	1,999	1,079	65	1,290	2,973
Connecticut	2,995	1,508	466	292	168	1,487	693	29	458	2,463
Delaware	1,508	737	300	41	104	770	322	-	138	734
District of Columbia . .	749	372	15	108	100	377	143	-	406	241
Florida	20,481	11,818	2,076	2,694	1,281	8,663	3,626	864	4,605	16,156
Georgia	8,535	5,542	1,125	2,454	510	2,994	1,302	19	2,529	3,463
Hawaii	1,537	1,058	206	145	136	479	289	14	182	1,287
Idaho	1,532	1,024	235	358	79	509	301	7	182	1,064
Illinois	12,016	6,472	2,153	813	691	5,544	3,092	77	2,437	9,389
Indiana	7,172	4,711	2,052	1,465	434	2,461	1,127	24	1,230	1,455
Iowa	3,860	2,632	1,006	1,039	217	1,228	517	15	599	1,134
Kansas	3,118	1,963	640	598	159	1,155	632	78	702	779
Kentucky	4,194	2,231	879	436	227	1,963	1,301	12	1,122	3,050
Louisiana	6,215	4,069	891	2,191	184	2,146	1,037	3	751	4,120
Maine	1,248	652	214	55	112	596	249	2	173	1,052
Maryland	5,215	3,031	1,345	58	489	2,184	910	113	613	6,099
Massachusetts	6,952	3,258	1,035	195	579	3,694	1,528	36	1,909	3,529
Michigan	12,921	7,971	3,115	1,543	1,151	4,950	2,128	91	1,792	6,246
Minnesota	6,996	3,823	1,176	771	385	3,172	1,500	268	1,254	7,200
Mississippi	3,262	2,304	557	1,276	120	958	453	4	647	2,065
Missouri	5,227	3,203	1,195	864	374	2,024	1,211	16	1,119	4,724
Montana	1,095	591	259	49	10	504	306	37	103	611
Nebraska	2,023	1,275	493	335	96	748	395	31	1,977	978
Nevada	2,264	1,512	274	440	189	752	448	35	420	2,679
New Hampshire	1,287	664	320	3	64	623	425	3	317	789
New Jersey	10,553	5,715	1,528	492	961	4,838	1,849	11	1,123	8,192
New Mexico	2,645	1,174	388	399	91	1,472	775	11	293	1,932
New York	27,045	15,881	2,220	4,608	1,222	11,163	4,846	119	5,977	30,532
North Carolina	9,303	6,791	1,692	2,890	744	2,512	1,689	13	2,652	9,428
North Dakota	913	579	241	16	23	334	157	33	77	607
Ohio	12,089	7,400	3,003	1,268	1,310	4,689	2,204	83	2,171	15,684
Oklahoma	3,624	2,508	871	828	178	1,116	624	5	892	2,752
Oregon	5,523	3,066	841	632	407	2,457	962	102	921	4,216
Pennsylvania	12,874	7,406	2,678	959	1,214	5,469	2,823	67	2,662	12,345
Rhode Island	1,038	442	207	2	58	595	307	1	107	706
South Carolina	5,266	4,000	925	2,069	192	1,265	776	18	1,709	3,065
South Dakota	797	400	134	36	42	397	225	5	149	790
Tennessee	5,528	4,235	1,004	1,812	406	1,293	739	4	4,893	3,060
Texas	21,120	12,506	3,891	3,327	1,680	8,614	4,570	48	5,816	11,084
Utah	2,614	1,611	636	336	127	1,003	543	4	1,221	2,032
Vermont	673	407	259	1	34	266	149	2	166	163
Virginia	8,176	5,111	1,711	1,254	582	3,066	1,566	5	1,340	7,237
Washington	7,849	5,380	1,450	1,208	771	2,469	1,185	75	3,545	8,875
West Virginia	1,999	1,156	374	254	104	843	452	2	184	1,580
Wisconsin	6,098	3,706	1,337	520	491	2,393	1,248	101	788	9,412
Wyoming	1,253	549	113	305	29	705	553	37	130	283

- Represents or rounds to zero.   ¹ Includes items not shown separately.

Source: U.S. Census Bureau. <http://www.census.gov/govs/www/estimate98.html> (accessed 20 July 2001).

U.S. Census Bureau, Statistical Abstract of the United States: 2001

No. 429. State and Local Governments—Expenditures and Debt by State: 1998

[In millions of dollars (1,529,308 represents $1,529,308,000,000), except as indicated. For fiscal year ending in year shown; see text, this section]

State	Total expenditure [1]	Total Amount	Per capita [2] (dol.)	Total direct general expenditures	Education and social services — Education	Education and social services — Public welfare	Education and social services — Health and hospitals	Highways	Police protection	Fire protection	Corrections
United States..	1,529,308	1,318,042	5,659	1,314,496	450,365	204,640	114,024	87,214	50,475	20,269	42,479
Alabama	21,652	18,583	4,976	18,583	6,629	3,063	2,996	1,231	609	227	356
Alaska.	7,754	6,867	12,608	6,763	1,532	664	255	641	163	56	157
Arizona	22,180	18,642	4,752	18,642	6,515	2,558	885	1,303	932	357	865
Arkansas	11,102	10,102	4,374	10,101	3,748	1,807	1,029	952	314	110	248
California	204,411	170,055	6,254	167,985	52,190	24,902	15,740	6,620	8,270	3,253	5,810
Colorado	21,437	18,478	5,401	18,469	6,830	2,403	1,051	1,553	749	301	742
Connecticut	20,792	18,300	6,353	18,300	5,451	3,007	1,492	1,014	625	353	480
Delaware	4,440	4,054	5,968	4,053	1,505	502	236	343	140	18	142
Dist. of Columbia. .	6,140	4,454	11,786	4,454	755	1,188	442	145	283	112	303
Florida.	74,609	66,491	5,005	66,491	19,659	8,454	5,788	4,746	3,344	1,340	2,923
Georgia	38,645	33,262	5,060	33,262	12,306	4,772	3,921	2,116	1,078	439	1,240
Hawaii.	7,466	6,607	6,274	6,595	1,636	919	506	333	208	89	121
Idaho	5,730	5,185	4,655	5,185	1,925	629	506	493	179	66	156
Illinois	65,041	55,827	5,389	55,825	19,324	8,162	3,946	3,671	2,678	1,041	1,445
Indiana	26,856	24,581	4,546	24,559	10,234	3,459	2,305	1,698	710	358	628
Iowa	15,132	13,868	5,289	13,837	5,459	1,992	1,508	1,449	366	121	251
Kansas	12,695	11,333	4,810	11,333	4,371	1,149	1,051	1,286	418	148	310
Kentucky	18,765	16,609	4,770	16,609	5,576	3,331	1,059	1,345	416	186	412
Louisiana.	22,326	19,864	5,117	19,864	6,336	2,936	2,952	1,405	769	253	541
Maine	6,668	6,138	5,343	6,130	2,029	1,417	374	475	149	72	101
Maryland	26,452	23,448	5,156	23,448	8,536	3,347	1,064	1,368	949	415	902
Massachusetts . . .	39,758	34,083	6,471	33,916	9,816	5,977	2,214	2,809	1,187	695	882
Michigan	54,521	48,552	5,552	48,482	19,846	6,940	4,141	2,826	1,634	571	1,577
Minnesota	30,468	27,019	6,447	27,019	9,044	5,140	1,784	2,245	791	245	524
Mississippi	13,219	11,886	4,805	11,886	4,098	1,772	1,781	1,168	341	130	254
Missouri.	24,512	21,918	4,508	21,918	8,015	3,380	1,912	1,753	812	353	596
Montana	4,444	4,005	5,050	4,005	1,466	481	296	424	102	34	99
Nebraska.	9,507	7,419	5,724	7,409	2,969	1,132	553	715	189	116	170
Nevada	9,776	8,590	5,606	8,584	2,560	784	688	805	421	170	368
New Hampshire . .	5,633	5,092	4,749	5,092	1,806	977	162	432	165	89	88
New Jersey	50,916	44,573	6,289	44,513	16,183	5,681	2,301	2,636	1,918	604	1,381
New Mexico	9,787	8,777	5,644	8,777	3,108	1,320	773	1,066	303	111	272
New York.	153,512	128,864	8,454	128,227	35,964	27,052	10,806	6,219	5,139	2,022	4,088
North Carolina . . .	38,974	33,826	5,165	33,826	11,925	5,202	4,923	2,294	1,125	383	1,141
North Dakota	3,562	3,266	5,582	3,266	1,136	495	93	412	62	50	41
Ohio	60,171	50,576	5,354	50,572	18,253	8,647	4,162	3,316	1,926	959	1,641
Oklahoma	14,723	12,767	4,409	12,726	5,126	1,714	1,268	1,002	396	230	445
Oregon	20,826	17,021	6,345	17,021	5,878	2,337	1,437	1,199	587	309	676
Pennsylvania	65,955	57,160	5,495	57,061	20,888	10,708	3,361	3,601	1,973	419	1,898
Rhode Island	5,654	4,933	5,723	4,911	1,650	1,000	212	244	173	131	127
South Carolina . . .	19,873	17,070	5,175	17,070	6,104	2,957	2,747	816	538	168	548
South Dakota	3,409	3,133	4,663	3,133	1,049	424	140	500	81	27	74
Tennessee	28,632	22,441	5,270	22,441	7,297	3,980	2,846	1,667	808	339	595
Texas	93,270	81,312	4,732	81,312	32,852	10,350	7,738	5,279	2,920	1,134	3,579
Utah	11,649	9,863	5,545	9,863	3,841	1,051	664	1,153	331	102	286
Vermont	3,307	3,020	5,595	3,010	1,171	556	72	301	70	29	39
Virginia	33,120	30,075	4,878	30,074	11,071	3,823	2,260	2,556	1,049	468	1,040
Washington	37,888	30,853	6,661	30,824	10,433	4,336	3,248	2,157	899	577	892
West Virginia	9,141	7,999	5,045	7,999	2,864	1,649	473	850	144	49	146
Wisconsin	29,462	26,279	5,642	26,151	10,398	3,847	1,459	2,222	960	421	822
Wyoming	3,347	2,920	6,973	2,918	1,008	268	401	358	82	23	59

See footnotes at end of table.

U.S. Census Bureau, Statistical Abstract of the United States: 2001

No. 429. State and Local Governments—Expenditures and Debt by State: 1998—Con.

[In millions of dollars (25,647 represents $25,647,000,000), except as indicated. For fiscal year ending in year shown; see text, this section]

State	General expenditure							Utility and liquor store expenditures	Employee retirement expenditure	Debt outstanding
	Environment and housing									
	Sewerage	Solid waste management	Parks and recreation	Housing and community development	Governmental administration	Interest on general debt	Other general expenditure			
United States	25,647	16,118	22,365	24,697	70,727	64,554	120,923	102,865	80,222	1,283,560
Alabama	244	186	290	305	775	620	1,052	1,896	985	13,224
Alaska	78	52	60	158	508	434	2,004	326	451	7,448
Arizona	447	231	533	265	1,255	862	1,636	2,232	999	21,972
Arkansas	129	116	120	102	464	306	655	457	360	6,095
California	3,903	2,124	2,756	4,576	10,916	7,518	19,408	17,212	12,162	161,486
Colorado	315	83	593	312	1,011	1,161	1,366	1,599	1,193	20,936
Connecticut	229	337 ·	168	403	1,064	1,246	2,430	648	1,341	22,510
Delaware	99	58	51	87	332	279	260	145	175	4,983
District of Columbia . . .	132	32	73	126	300	233	329	1,188	432	4,834
Florida	1,271	1,416	1,535	1,095	3,965	3,825	7,131	5,238	2,137	71,809
Georgia	656	406	485	546	1,757	1,103	2,437	3,724	1,411	25,409
Hawaii	110	108	181	233	433	485	1,233	261	452	7,845
Idaho	109	77	68	42	288	164	483	175	208	2,879
Illinois	1,089	408	1,797	1,504	3,020	3,307	4,431	3,974	4,154	58,855
Indiana	500	191	301	334	1,229	857	1,758	1,238	839	16,127
Iowa	264	125	202	130	623	340	1,006	620	492	6,508
Kansas	142	85	150	83	656	493	991	688	542	9,276
Kentucky	292	164	222	165	709	1,205	1,528	885	903	20,947
Louisiana	302	226	419	220	1,004	951	1,548	842	1,470	16,667
Maine	107	86	45	92	317	253	612	144	300	5,258
Maryland	535	433	648	571	1,389	1,233	2,058	931	1,421	23,324
Massachusetts	1,018	326	255	1,137	1,629	2,129	3,843	2,793	2,165	46,320
Michigan	1,323	454	580	220	2,331	2,052	3,987	2,032	3,070	38,963
Minnesota	474	276	627	872	1,491	1,355	2,150	1,453	1,581	26,862
Mississippi	107	93	126	115	598	440	864	641	591	7,566
Missouri	434	107	355	341	1,111	873	1,875	1,251	1,070	15,989
Montana	44	51	42	57	263	206	440	97	222	3,449
Nebraska	94	71	124	91	339	203	644	1,828	218	6,463
Nevada	154	12	330	119	671	543	959	568	357	11,291
New Hampshire	70	86	48	83	287	448	352	322	162	6,606
New Jersey	913	1,007	1,007	734	2,583	2,266	5,300	2,018	2,830	46,560
New Mexico	99	99	186	78	491	335	536	414	523	6,600
New York	1,891	1,880	1,558	2,744	6,086	8,287	14,489	11,024	10,583	155,710
North Carolina	479	546	498	437	1,366	1,061	2,445	3,200	1,579	25,570
North Dakota	22	30	87	60	135	115	527	89	85	1,948
Ohio	1,322	516	776	1,008	2,989	1,794	3,263	2,515	4,899	33,949
Oklahoma	208	132	262	124	632	450	739	912	832	9,428
Oregon	441	128	291	381	1,178	661	1,519	1,364	1,692	13,391
Pennsylvania	1,122	507	540	1,126	2,753	3,490	4,675	3,665	3,568	61,863
Rhode Island	99	49	68	116	268	317	458	147	326	6,483
South Carolina	149	202	255	189	733	578	1,086	1,730	824	15,145
South Dakota	43	24	81	36	177	152	324	144 ·	115	3,032
Tennessee	383	312	541	437	966	789	1,480	5,035	859	16,451
Texas	1,493	762	1,030	1,212	3,665	3,933	5,364	6,856	4,264	83,658
Utah	155	104	217	117	689	370	783	1,320	309	12,848
Vermont	37	36	25	57	193	148	276	173	72	2,734
Virginia	626	503	512	561	1,763	1,510	2,333	1,510	1,363	29,024
Washington	729	407	662	521	1,471	1,306	3,185	3,957	1,376	35,005
West Virginia	116	43	89	73	453	506	547	225	369	6,917
Wisconsin	613	384	439	295	1,210	1,229	1,852	949	1,768	23,174
Wyoming	34	25	54	10	190	135	271	207	127	2,166

[1] Includes items not shown separately.   [2] Based on estimated resident population as of July 1.

Source: U.S. Census Bureau, <http://www.census.gov/govs/www/estimate98.html> (accessed 23 July 2001).

State and Local Government Finances and Employment   273

[In millions of dollars (1,720,889 represents $1,720,889,000,000), except as indicated. For fiscal year ending in year shown; see text, this section]

State	Revenue [1]						Expenditures [1]		Debt outstanding	
	All revenue	Per capita [2] (dol.)	General revenue	Per capita [2] (dol.)	From state/ local sources	Per capita [2] (dol.)	Direct general expendi- tures	Per capita [2] (dol.)	Total	Per capita [2] (dol.)
United States ...	1,720,889	6,368	1,365,762	5,054	1,465,841	5,424	1,314,496	4,864	1,283,560	4,750
Alabama	22,400	5,148	18,233	4,190	18,069	4,153	18,583	4,271	13,224	3,039
Alaska	11,022	17,922	9,662	15,711	9,772	15,889	6,763	10,996	7,448	12,111
Arizona	26,119	5,597	18,716	4,010	22,585	4,839	18,642	3,994	21,972	4,708
Arkansas	12,759	5,027	10,465	4,123	10,290	4,054	10,101	3,980	6,095	2,401
California	232,302	7,108	174,427	5,337	199,750	6,112	167,985	5,140	161,486	4,941
Colorado	23,967	6,038	19,703	4,964	20,813	5,244	18,469	4,653	20,936	5,275
Connecticut	23,730	7,250	20,808	6,358	20,404	6,234	18,300	5,591	22,510	6,877
Delaware	5,520	7,419	4,648	6,248	4,773	6,415	4,053	5,448	4,983	6,698
District of Columbia	5,904	11,332	5,257	10,090	4,285	8,225	4,454	8,548	4,834	9,279
Florida	88,919	5,964	68,158	4,572	79,197	5,312	66,491	4,460	71,809	4,817
Georgia	40,284	5,275	34,292	4,490	34,033	4,456	33,262	4,355	25,409	3,327
Hawaii	8,259	6,941	6,790	5,706	6,935	5,828	6,595	5,542	7,845	6,592
Idaho	6,598	5,360	5,353	4,348	5,647	4,587	5,185	4,212	2,879	2,339
Illinois	69,393	5,749	57,567	4,769	59,478	4,928	55,825	4,625	58,855	4,876
Indiana	28,721	4,861	26,036	4,407	24,604	4,164	24,559	4,157	16,127	2,730
Iowa	15,418	5,389	13,685	4,783	13,052	4,562	13,837	4,837	6,508	2,275
Kansas	13,916	5,273	12,435	4,712	11,974	4,537	11,333	4,294	9,276	3,515
Kentucky	21,621	5,496	17,450	4,436	17,721	4,505	16,609	4,222	20,947	5,325
Louisiana	25,396	5,821	20,525	4,704	21,148	4,847	19,864	4,553	16,667	3,820
Maine	7,993	6,405	6,768	5,423	6,485	5,197	6,130	4,912	5,258	4,213
Maryland	31,918	6,222	25,206	4,914	27,979	5,454	23,448	4,571	23,324	4,547
Massachusetts	41,013	6,675	35,575	5,790	34,096	5,550	33,916	5,520	46,320	7,539
Michigan	58,305	5,937	50,267	5,119	49,170	5,007	48,482	4,937	38,963	3,968
Minnesota	36,337	7,689	27,883	5,900	31,939	6,758	27,019	5,717	26,862	5,684
Mississippi	14,643	5,323	11,931	4,337	11,635	4,229	11,886	4,321	7,566	2,750
Missouri	29,107	5,353	23,264	4,278	24,390	4,485	21,918	4,031	15,989	2,940
Montana	4,960	5,637	4,246	4,825	3,825	4,347	4,005	4,551	3,449	3,920
Nebraska	10,971	6,605	8,016	4,826	9,554	5,752	7,409	4,461	6,463	3,891
Nevada	11,178	6,409	8,080	4,633	10,126	5,806	8,584	4,922	11,291	6,474
New Hampshire	6,172	5,204	5,067	4,272	5,255	4,431	5,092	4,293	6,606	5,570
New Jersey	56,498	6,979	47,184	5,828	49,877	6,161	44,513	5,498	46,560	5,751
New Mexico	11,483	6,622	9,258	5,339	9,450	5,450	8,777	5,062	6,608	3,806
New York	171,133	9,424	134,624	7,414	142,038	7,822	128,227	7,061	155,710	8,575
North Carolina	47,529	6,299	35,449	4,698	40,681	5,391	33,826	4,483	25,570	3,389
North Dakota	4,205	6,591	3,520	5,517	3,224	5,054	3,266	5,120	1,948	3,054
Ohio	70,553	6,278	52,698	4,689	60,771	5,408	50,572	4,500	33,949	3,021
Oklahoma	17,388	5,207	13,744	4,116	14,764	4,422	12,726	3,811	9,428	2,824
Oregon	22,841	6,959	17,704	5,394	18,796	5,727	17,021	5,186	13,391	4,080
Pennsylvania	72,674	6,055	57,667	4,805	61,513	5,125	57,061	4,754	61,863	5,154
Rhode Island	6,074	6,148	5,261	5,325	4,930	4,990	4,911	4,971	6,483	6,562
South Carolina	22,014	5,733	17,239	4,489	18,429	4,799	17,070	4,445	15,145	3,944
South Dakota	4,185	5,726	3,246	4,440	3,329	4,553	3,133	4,286	3,032	4,147
Tennessee	30,314	5,580	22,361	4,116	24,773	4,560	22,441	4,131	16,451	3,028
Texas	100,422	5,094	83,522	4,237	84,335	4,278	81,312	4,125	83,658	4,244
Utah	12,902	6,141	9,649	4,593	11,029	5,249	9,863	4,694	12,848	6,115
Vermont	3,473	5,876	3,144	5,320	2,722	4,605	3,010	5,092	2,734	4,627
Virginia	39,139	5,765	30,561	4,502	34,923	5,144	30,074	4,430	29,024	4,275
Washington	42,381	7,451	29,961	5,267	37,552	6,602	30,824	5,419	35,005	6,154
West Virginia	9,878	5,452	8,114	4,478	7,716	4,258	7,999	4,415	6,917	3,818
Wisconsin	37,049	7,095	26,848	5,141	32,942	6,308	26,151	5,008	23,174	4,438
Wyoming	3,909	8,143	3,496	7,282	3,062	6,379	2,918	6,080	2,166	4,512

[1] Includes items not shown separately.   [2] Based on estimated resident population as of July 1.

Source: U.S. Census Bureau, <http://www.census.gov/govs/www/estimate98.html> (accessed 20 July 2001); and unpublished data.

No. 431. State and Local Governments—Indebtedness: 1980 to 1998

[In billions of dollars (335.6 represents $335,600,000,000), except per capita. For fiscal year ending in year shown; see text, this section. Local government amounts are estimates subject to sampling variation; see Appendix III and source]

Item	Total	Per capita [1] (dol.)	Local schools [2]	Utilities	All other	Short-term	Net long term	Debt issued	Debt retired
			Long-term						
			Debt outstanding				Long term		
1980: Total	335.6	1,481	32.3	55.2	235.0	13.1	262.9	42.4	17.4
State	122.0	540	3.8	4.6	111.5	2.1	79.8	16.4	5.7
Local	213.6	943	28.5	50.6	123.5	11.0	183.1	25.9	11.7
1990: Total	860.6	3,459	60.4	134.8	646.1	19.3	477.0	108.5	64.8
State	318.3	1,282	4.4	12.3	298.8	2.8	125.5	43.5	22.9
Local	542.3	2,180	56.0	122.4	347.4	16.5	351.5	65.0	42.0
1994: Total	1,074.7	4,129	143.5	164.9	438.0	26.7	672.8	207.8	166.6
State	411.0	1,582	10.4	16.7	162.0	4.9	200.8	78.5	61.3
Local	663.7	2,550	86.2	148.2	276.0	21.8	472.0	129.3	105.3
1995: Total	1,115.3	4,244	118.2	163.9	756.0	27.0	835.3	129.3	95.1
State	427.2	1,629	11.3	17.0	345.0	6.1	205.3	52.6	37.5
Local	688.1	2,619	107.0	146.9	411.0	20.9	629.9	76.8	57.6
1996: Total	1,169.7	4,411	130.7	170.3	844.7	24.0	751.6	141.1	106.5
State	452.4	1,709	11.2	16.3	419.1	5.8	220.3	60.2	42.4
Local	717.3	2,705	119.5	154.0	425.6	18.2	531.3	80.9	64.1
1997: Total	1,224.5	4,573	139.0	179.1	889.8	16.6	797.7	151.3	109.3
State	456.7	1,705	11.7	16.0	426.8	2.1	222.6	54.4	41.1
Local	767.9	2,867	127.3	163.1	463.0	14.5	575.1	96.6	68.2
1998: Total	1,283.6	4,750	159.2	182.8	924.3	17.3	842.6	204.4	144.6
State	483.1	1,788	13.6	16.7	450.6	2.2	237.2	83.4	58.1
Local	800.4	2,962	145.5	166.1	473.8	15.1	605.4	120.9	86.5

[1] 1980 and 1990 based on enumerated resident population as of April 1; other years based on estimated resident population as of July 1; see Table 2. [2] Includes debt for education activities other than higher education.

Source: U.S. Census Bureau, *1980-90, State and Local Government Finance Estimates*, annual; thereafter, <http://www.census.gov/govs/www/estimate.html> (accessed 24 July 2001).

No. 432. Long Term Municipal New Issues for State and Local Governments: 1980 to 2000

[In billions of dollars (45.6 represents $45,600,000,000)]

Item	1980	1985	1990	1994	1995	1996	1997	1998	1999	2000
Long-term municipal new issues [1]	45.6	202.4	125.9	162.2	156.2	181.5	214.3	279.7	219.2	194.3
General obligation	13.7	39.6	40.2	55.6	60.2	64.2	72.2	92.6	69.8	65.2
Revenue	31.9	162.8	85.7	106.7	96.0	117.3	142.1	187.1	149.4	129.1
Competitive	19.3	27.8	30.2	49.5	41.0	47.0	47.8	65.2	52.8	48.7
Negotiated	26.4	174.6	95.9	112.8	115.4	134.5	166.5	214.5	166.4	145.6
States with largest issuance: [2]										
California	3.6	25.3	15.7	25.4	20.2	24.9	27.7	33.9	26.5	22.9
New York	2.9	12.7	16.9	18.8	18.8	20.8	27.4	36.3	19.8	19.1
Texas	3.8	21.2	6.5	10.3	10.4	11.6	15.3	18.1	17.7	14.7
Florida	2.2	13.2	5.9	7.7	9.1	10.0	10.5	14.7	10.8	10.1
Illinois	2.3	9.2	6.3	7.9	6.6	8.8	9.6	10.1	12.4	8.9
All Others	30.8	120.8	74.6	92.1	91.1	105.4	123.8	166.6	132.0	118.6
Type of issuer: [3]										
City, town, or village	8.5	36.5	22.7	26.6	27.9	30.2	34.8	44.3	33.0	29.3
College or university	0.2	2.9	1.5	2.4	2.5	4.5	3.3	4.6	4.1	3.8
County/parish	4.6	15.8	10.0	17.2	13.3	16.8	15.5	21.2	17.1	12.7
Direct issuer	-	0.4	0.2	0.6	0.4	1.4	0.8	2.1	2.0	2.6
District	3.9	15.6	15.2	21.7	22.4	27.8	33.7	43.6	34.1	27.8
Local authority	9.2	51.1	20.7	26.3	27.9	33.5	41.5	53.9	43.2	33.1
State authority	14.1	68.1	40.6	47.6	47.2	53.0	66.0	85.2	68.1	64.2
State	5.1	12.1	15.0	19.8	14.6	14.3	18.7	24.7	17.6	20.8
Refunding	1.6	70.5	25.3	49.8	47.5	45.4	81.2	120.8	66.3	19.1
New Capital	45.6	202.4	125.9	162.3	156.2	181.5	214.3	279.7	219.2	194.3
General use of proceeds:										
Airports	0.4	3.0	5.2	4.3	4.7	5.2	6.4	10.2	5.5	7.4
Combined utilities	0.3	2.4	1.0	1.2	0.7	1.2	1.5	1.8	1.0	0.3
Economic development	0.2	2.5	2.1	4.2	2.5	1.8	2.9	3.5	3.6	2.9
Education	4.0	20.4	20.5	26.9	28.5	34.4	42.7	56.5	47.6	39.9
Health care	3.1	30.0	12.6	13.8	11.5	16.6	22.1	33.4	22.0	14.4
Industrial development	1.0	2.9	1.9	2.1	3.2	2.8	3.5	3.6	3.5	3.4
Multifamily housing	2.5	20.2	3.1	4.9	6.1	6.6	5.4	6.4	6.1	6.2
Nursing homes/life care retirement	0.3	1.2	1.6	2.4	1.9	1.5	3.6	4.8	4.9	1.8
Other miscellaneous	11.1	37.3	36.2	48.8	44.2	55.2	57.0	71.5	58.4	52.8
Pollution control	2.3	10.0	2.5	7.0	5.0	5.0	5.6	9.7	8.9	4.8
Electric & public power	4.4	23.2	5.2	6.3	4.8	5.7	6.5	15.6	4.9	5.7
Single family housing	10.6	16.4	12.5	10.5	10.0	10.5	13.6	12.9	12.6	12.0
Solid waste/resource recovery	0.4	3.8	3.0	3.8	3.3	1.6	3.6	2.4	1.2	0.5
Student loans	0.2	4.0	0.4	3.3	4.4	4.2	3.9	4.9	5.3	7.6
Transportation	1.3	11.0	7.6	9.4	11.3	9.1	16.6	20.5	16.0	15.9
Water, sewer, and gas facilities	3.1	13.4	9.3	12.5	13.2	14.5	18.2	20.9	16.4	11.3
Waterfront/seaports	0.5	1.5	0.5	0.8	0.8	1.3	1.2	0.9	1.2	1.1

- Represents or rounds to zero. [1] Excludes issues with a final maturity of less than 13 months, private placements, and not-for-profit cooperative utilities. [2] Ranked by 1997 Long Term Municipal New Issue Volume. [3] Includes outlying areas.

Source: Thomson Financial Securities Data Company, Newark, NJ, Municipal New Issues Database (copyright).

State and Local Government Finances and Employment **275**

No. 433. Bond Ratings for State Governments by State: 2000

[As of fourth quarter. Key to investment grade ratings are in declining order of quality. The ratings from AA to CCC may be modified by the addition of a plus or minus sign to show relative standing within the major rating categories. *S&P:* AAA, AA, A, BBB, BB, B, CCC, CC, C; *Moody's:* Aaa, Aa, A, Baa, Ba, B, Caa, Ca, C; Numerical modifiers 1, 2, and 3 are added to letter-rating. *Fitch:* AAA, AA, A, BBB, BB, B, CCC, CC, C]

State	Standard & Poor's	Moody's	Fitch	State	Standard & Poor's	Moody's	Fitch
Alabama	AA	Aa3	AA	Montana	AA-	Aa3	(1)
Alaska	(1)	Aa2	AA	Nebraska	(1)	(1)	(1)
Arizona	(1)	(1)	(1)	Nevada	AA	Aa2	AA
Arkansas	AA	Aa2	AAA	New Hampshire	AA+	Aa2	AA+
California	AA	Aa2	AA	New Jersey	AA+	Aa1	AA+
Colorado	(1)	(1)	(1)	New Mexico	AA+	Aa1	(1)
Connecticut	AA	Aa2	AA	New York	AA	A2	AA
Delaware	AAA	Aaa	(1)	North Carolina	AAA	Aaa	AAA
Florida	AA+	Aa2	AA	North Dakota	AA-	(1)	(1)
Georgia	AAA	Aaa	AAA	Ohio	AA+	Aa1	AA+
Hawaii	A+	Aa3	AA-	Oklahoma	AA	Aa3	AA
Idaho	(1)	(1)	(1)	Oregon	AA	Aa2	AA
Illinois	AA	Aa2	AA+	Pennsylvania	AA	Aa2	AA
Indiana	AA+	(1)	(1)	Rhode Island	AA-	Aa3	AA
Iowa	(1)	(1)	(1)	South Carolina	AAA	Aaa	AAA
Kansas	AA+	(1)	(1)	South Dakota	(1)	(1)	(1)
Kentucky	AA	(1)	(1)	Tennessee	AA+	Aa1	AAA
Louisiana	A	A2	A	Texas	AA	Aa1	AA+
Maine	AA+	Aa2	AA+	Utah	AAA	Aaa	AAA
Maryland	AAA	Aaa	AAA	Vermont	AA+	Aa1	AA+
Massachusetts	AA-	Aa2	AA-	Virginia	AAA	Aaa	AAA
Michigan	AAA	Aaa	AA+	Washington	AA+	A¹1	AA+
Minnesota	AAA	Aaa	AAA	West Virginia	AA-	Aa3	AA-
Mississippi	AA	Aa3	AA	Wisconsin	AA	Aa2	AA+
Missouri	AAA	Aaa	AAA	Wyoming	AA	(1)	(1)

[1] Not reviewed.

Sources: Standard & Poor's, New York, NY; Moody's Investors Service, New York, NY (copyright); and Fitch IBCA, New York, NY (copyright).

No. 434. Bond Ratings for City Governments by Largest Cities: 2000

[As of fourth quarter. For key to ratings, see headnote in table above]

Cities ranked by 1998 population	Standard & Poor's	Moody's	Fitch IBCA	Cities ranked by 1998 population	Standard & Poor's	Moody's	Fitch IBCA
New York, NY	A	A2	A+	Fresno, CA	(1)	A2	(1)
Los Angeles, CA	AA	Aa2	AA	Honolulu, HI	AA-	Aa3	AA
Chicago, IL	A+	A1	AA-	Tulsa, OK	AA	Aa2	(1)
Houston, TX	AA-	Aa3	AA	Omaha, NE	AAA	Aaa	(1)
Philadelphia, PA	BBB	Baa1	AAA	Miami, FL	BB	Baa3	(1)
San Diego, CA	AA	Aa1	AA+	Oakland, CA	A+	A1	A+
Phoenix, AZ	AA+	Aa1	(1)	Mesa, AZ	AA-	A1	AAA
San Antonio, TX	AA+	Aa2	(1)	Minneapolis, MN	AAA	Aaa	(1)
Dallas, TX	AAA	Aaa	(1)	Colorado Springs, CO	AA	Aa3	(1)
Detroit, MI	A-	Baa1	AAA	Pittsburgh, PA	(1)	A3	(1)
San Jose, CA	(1)	[2]Aa1	(1)	St. Louis, MO	A-	A3	A-
San Francisco, CA	AA	Aa3	AA	Cincinnati, OH	AA+	Aa1	(1)
Indianapolis, IN	AAA	Aaa	AAA	Wichita, KS	AA	Aa2	(1)
Jacksonville, FL	AA	Aa2	AA	Toledo, OH	A	A3	(1)
Columbus, OH	AAA	Aaa	AA	Arlington, TX	AA	Aa2	(1)
Baltimore, MD	A+	A1	A+	Santa Ana, CA	(1)	(1)	(1)
El Paso, TX	AA	Aa3	AAA	Buffalo, NY	BBB	Baa2	(1)
Memphis, TN	AA	Aa2	AA	Anaheim, CA	AA	Aa2	(1)
Milwaukee, WI	AA	Aa2	AA+	Tampa, FL	(1)	[2]Aa3	(1)
Boston, MA	AA-	Aa3	AA-	Corpus Christi, TX	A+	A3	AA-
Austin, TX	AA+	Aa2	(1)	Newark, NJ	(1)	Baa1	(1)
Seattle, WA	AA+	Aaa	(1)	Riverside, CA	(1)	(1)	(1)
Washington, DC	BBB+	Baa1	BBB	Raleigh, NC	AAA	Aaa	AAA
Nashville-Davidson, TN	AA	Aa2	(1)	St. Paul, MN	AA+	Aa2	AA+
Charlotte, NC	AAA	Aaa	(1)	Louisville, KY	AA-	Aa3	(1)
Portland, OR	(1)	Aaa	(1)	Anchorage, AK	(1)	Aa3	(1)
Denver, CO	AA+	Aa2	AA+	Birmingham, AL	AA	Aa3	AA
Cleveland, OH	A+	A1	A	Aurora, CO	AA	Aa2	AAA
Fort Worth, TX	AA+	Aa2	(1)	Lexington-Fayette, KY	AA+	Aa2	(1)
Oklahoma City, OK	AA	Aa2	(1)	Stockton, CA	(1)	(1)	(1)
New Orleans, LA	BBB+	Baa2	(1)	St Petersburg, FL	A+	(1)	(1)
Tucson, AZ	AA	Aa2	(1)	Jersey City, NJ	BBB	Baa3	(1)
Kansas City, MO	AA	Aa3	(1)	Rochester, NY	AA	A2	(1)
Virginia Beach, VA	AA	Aa1	AA+	Akron, OH	AA-	A1	AA-
Long Beach, CA	AA-	[2]Aa3	(1)	Norfolk, VA	AA	A1	AA
Albuquerque, NM	AA-	Aa3	(1)	Baton Rouge, LA	(1)	(1)	(1)
Sacramento, CA	AA	Aa2	(1)	Mobile, AL	(1)	A2	(1)
Atlanta, GA	AA	Aa3	(1)	Richmond, VA	AA	A1	AA

[1] Not reviewed. [2] Issuer rating.

Sources: Standard & Poor's, New York, NY; Moody's Investors Service, New York, NY (copyright); and Fitch IBCA, New York, NY (copyright).

U.S. Census Bureau, Statistical Abstract of the United States: 2001

No. 435. State Resources, Expenditures, and Balances: 2000 and 2001

[In millions of dollars (964,378 represents $964,378,000,000). For fiscal year ending in year shown; see text: this section. General funds exclude special funds earmarked for particular purposes, such as highway trust funds and federal funds; they support most on-going broad-based state services and are available for appropriation to support any governmental activity. Minus sign (-) indicates deficit]

State	Expenditures by fund source					State general fund					
	Total. 2000	2001 [1]				Resources [3] [4]		Expenditures [4]		Balance [5]	
		Total [2]	General fund	Federal funds	Other state funds	2000	2001 [1]	2000	2001 [1]	2000	2001 [1]
Total	964,378	1,034,418	494,629	272,442	242,752	538,485	498,427	504,707	477,462	30,481	17,487
United States . .	945,271	1,013,220	487,018	268,062	233,545	531,289	498,427	497,593	477,462	30,399	17,487
Alabama	14,730	17,280	5,248	5,545	6,487	5,317	5,268	5,215	5,248	101	20
Alaska.	5,245	5,750	2,300	1,928	1,355	2,262	2,290	2,262	2,290	6.	6.
Arizona	14,924	15,858	6,385	3,788	5,398	6,216	6,572	6,012	6,467	203	104
Arkansas	10,093	10,855	3,261	2,480	5,015	3,177	3,261	3,177	3,261	-	-
California	122,167	140,623	78,816	41,199	15,560	75,861	86,266	66,494	79,708	6·9,367	6·6,557
Colorado	12,267	13,372	5,285	3,132	4,516	6,791	7,218	5,992	6,682	6·798	6·537
Connecticut	18,096	18,204	11,281	3,230	2,361	11,214	11,914	10,913	11,413	300	501
Delaware	5,015	5,268	2,482	780	1,850	2,584	2,569	2,246	2,467	338	102
Florida.	48,808	51,217	20,049	10,749	18,604	19,044	20,465	18,554	20,465	490	-
Georgia	25,865	25,738	14,472	9,710	892	15,581	17,279	13,782	14,770	6·2,509	6·1,128
Hawaii.	6,784	7,523	3,391	1,066	2,553	3,473	3,716	3,201	3,385	272	330
Idaho	3,636	4,221	1,844	1,364	1,008	1,863	2,024	1,681	1,844	182	180
Illinois	35,084	38,304	18,087	7,954	10,797	24,600	25,747	23,084	24,547	1,517	1,200
Indiana	16,881	16,537	7,526	4,312	4,664	10,691	10,570	8,967	9,742	1,098	392
Iowa	11,652	11,487	4,882	2,865	3,707	4,939	4,877	4,763	4,869	176	8
Kansas	8,416	9,130	4,429	2,530	1,814	4,746	4,864	4,368	4,434	378	430
Kentucky	12,653	13,783	7,040	4,953	1,790	6,782	7,124	6,549	7,124	175	-
Louisiana	15,636	16,618	6,134	4,782	5,593	5,966	6,216	5,909	6,227	6·81	6.
Maine	4,846	5,985	2,696	1,786	1,405	2,610	2,662	2,317	2,648	301	19
Maryland	18,316	20,007	10,110	4,278	5,147	9,958	10,590	9,022	10,215	936	375
Massachusetts . . .	26,532	26,764	17,709	5,921	1,886	21,326	20,700	20,828	20,596	297	104
Michigan	34,947	37,274	9,741	9,777	17,433	10,015	9,831	9,803	9,831	212	-
Minnesota	18,447	21,373	13,216	4,337	3,485	13,602	14,239	11,476	13,131	6·2,125	6·1,108
Mississippi	9,655	10,711	3,596	3,514	3,094	3,460	3,634	3,435	3,633	26	1
Missouri.	16,015	17,087	7,812	4,871	4,062	7,537	7,921	7,350	7,812	187	109
Montana	2,783	3,146	1,249	1,252	645	1,277	1,371	1,105	1,264	170	104
Nebraska.	5,801	5,692	2,459	1,574	1,659	2,660	2,787	2,344	2,462	316	204
Nevada	4,594	5,413	1,629	1,182	2,502	1,744	1,918	1,608	1,875	168	106
New Hampshire . .	3,395	3,494	1,078	1,004	1,351	1,032	1,081	1,028	1,081	4	-
New Jersey	29,672	31,769	20,768	6,888	3,043	21,147	22,338	19,459	21,057	6.	6.
New Mexico	8,269	9,110	3,810	2,837	2,463	3,421	3,855	3,390	3,718	-	-
New York.	73,573	79,466	37,063	24,724	16,136	38,337	40,800	37,170	39,702	6·1,167	6·1,098
North Carolina . . .	25,837	24,851	14,050	6,134	4,017	14,100	13,720	13,854	13,720	-	-
North Dakota	2,256	2,267	826	835	584	833	864	773	826	60	38
Ohio	38,816	44,134	21,477	5,832	15,610	20,272	21,128	19,244	20,739	196	190
Oklahoma	10,595	11,880	5,065	3,407	3,190	4,825	5,077	4,545	4,819	280	259
Oregon	10,655	12,481	4,841	2,972	4,234	5,277	5,381	5,183	4,920	94	461
Pennsylvania	38,465	42,106	19,892	12,504	8,675	20,014	20,260	19,295	19,979	611	313
Rhode Island	4,271	4,794	2,215	1,521	914	2,344	2,585	2,231	2,472	92	113
South Carolina . . .	16,892	18,148	5,759	6,672	5,012	5,730	5,794	5,156	5,644	6·574	6·150
South Dakota	2,109	2,304	794	910	596	800	823	771	805	-	6
Tennessee	15,809	17,902	7,568	6,719	3,430	6,682	7,244	6,593	7,231	52	-
Texas	49,465	52,462	29,232	15,113	8,117	58,598	(NA)	56,266	(NA)	2,332	(NA)
Utah	6,561	7,155	3,792	1,625	1,723	3,477	3,792	3,364	3,792	113	-
Vermont	2,231	2,381	866	887	582	905	899	855	897	-	-
Virginia	22,364	22,997	10,850	3,726	8,179	11,935	12,652	11,282	12,339	653	314
Washington	21,481	20,785	10,627	5,656	3,737	10,705	11,273	10,220	10,788	485	486
West Virginia	6,482	6,710	2,240	2,537	1,642	2,802	2,870	2,639	2,864	148	-
Wisconsin	26,185	20,804	11,076	4,700	5,028	12,100	11,324	11,294	11,030	6·836	6·293
Wyoming	-	-	-	-	-	660	777	518	630	6·142	6·147
Puerto Rico	19,107	21,198	7,611	4,380	9,207	7,196	(NA)	7,114	(NA)	82	(NA)

- Represents zero.   NA Not available.   [1] Estimated.   [2] Includes bonds not shown separately.   [3] Includes funds budgeted, adjustments, and balances from previous year.   [4] May or may not include budget stabilization fund transfers, depending on state accounting practices.   [5] Resources less expenditures. Total excludes Puerto Rico.   [6] Ending balance includes the balance in a budget stabilization fund.

Source: Expenditures by fund from National Association of State Budget Officers, Washington, DC, 2000 State Expenditure Report, and State General Fund from National Governors' Association and NASBO, Fiscal Survey of the States, semi-annual (copyright).

State and Local Government Finances and Employment   277

No. 436. State Governments—Summary of Finances: 1980 to 1998

[In millions of dollars (293,356 represents $293,356,000,000), except where indicated. For fiscal year ending in year shown; see text; this section]

Item	Total (mil. dol.) 1980	1990	1997	1998	Per capita [1] (dollars) 1980	1990	1997	1998
Borrowing and revenue	293,356	672,994	1,093,486	1,179,301	1,299	2,712	4,094	4,371
Borrowing	16,394	40,532	54,064	83,439	73	163	202	309
Revenue	276,962	632,462	1,039,422	1,095,862	1,226	2,549	3,890	4,063
General revenue	233,592	517,720	814,382	864,863	1,034	2,087	3,048	3,206
Taxes	137,075	300,779	443,335	474,392	607	1,212	1,659	1,759
Sales and gross receipts	67,855	147,404	215,737	227,343	300	594	807	843
General	43,168	99,929	147,069	155,971	191	403	550	578
Motor fuels	9,722	19,379	27,132	28,345	43	78	102	105
Alcoholic beverages	2,478	3,191	3,698	3,765	11	13	14	14
Tobacco products	3,738	5,541	7,451	7,748	17	22	28	29
Other	8,750	19,365	30,387	31,513	39	78	114	117
Licenses	8,690	18,849	28,217	29,668	38	76	106	110
Motor vehicles	4,936	9,850	12,965	13,667	22	40	49	51
Corporations in general	1,388	3,096	5,882	6,135	6	12	22	23
Other	2,366	5,903	9,370	9,866	10	24	35	37
Individual income	37,089	96,076	144,668	160,746	164	387	541	596
Corporation net income	13,321	21,751	30,662	31,094	59	88	115	115
Property	2,892	5,775	10,297	10,650	13	23	39	39
Other	7,227	10,922	13,754	14,891	32	44	51	55
Charges and miscellaneous	32,190	90,612	140,454	149,682	142	365	526	555
Intergovernmental revenue	64,326	126,329	230,592	240,789	285	509	863	893
From federal government	61,892	118,353	215,421	224,444	274	477	806	832
Public welfare	24,680	59,397	123,087	127,356	109	239	461	472
Education	12,765	21,271	33,663	36,138	57	86	126	134
Highways	8,860	13,931	19,346	19,659	39	56	72	73
Health and hospitals	2,309	5,475	11,676	12,579	10	22	44	47
Other	13,278	17,279	27,649	28,712	69	96	103	106
From local governments	2,434	7,976	15,171	16,345	11	32	57	61
Utility revenue	1,304	3,305	4,046	4,205	6	13	15	16
Liquor store revenue	2,765	2,907	3,292	3,483	12	12	12	13
Insurance trust revenue [2]	39,301	108,530	217,703	223,311	174	437	815	828
Employee retirement	21,146	78,898	168,184	186,885	94	318	629	693
Unemployment compensation	13,468	18,370	34,882	23,051	60	74	131	85
Expenditure and debt redemption	263,494	592,213	935,208	988,507	1,166	2,386	3,500	3,665
Expenditure	257,812	572,318	893,827	930,037	1,141	2,306	3,345	3,448
General expenditure	228,223	508,284	788,176	827,654	1,010	2,048	2,950	3,068
Education	87,939	184,935	275,821	294,814	389	745	1,032	1,093
Public welfare	44,219	104,971	203,204	207,926	196	423	760	771
Health	6,485	20,029	33,880	35,067	29	81	127	130
Hospitals	11,370	22,637	29,313	28,928	50	91	110	107
Highways	25,044	44,249	60,204	63,620	111	178	225	236
Police protection	2,263	5,166	7,501	8,038	10	21	28	30
Correction	4,449	17,266	29,043	30,601	20	70	109	113
Natural resources	4,346	9,909	12,909	13,541	19	40	48	50
Housing and community development	601	2,856	3,839	3,982	3	12	14	15
Other and unallocable	41,507	96,266	132,462	141,137	184	388	496	523
Utility expenditure	2,401	7,131	7,783	8,365	11	29	29	31
Liquor store expenditure	2,206	2,452	2,697	2,820	10	10	10	10
Insurance trust expenditure	24,981	54,452	95,172	91,198	111	219	356	338
Employee retirement	10,256	29,562	56,570	63,087	45	119	212	234
Unemployment compensation	12,006	16,423	27,475	17,712	53	66	103	66
By character and object:								
Intergovernmental expenses	84,504	175,028	264,207	278,853	374	705	989	1,034
Direct expenditure	173,307	397,291	629,620	651,183	767	1,601	2,356	2,414
Current operation	108,131	258,046	425,898	446,440	479	1,040	1,594	1,655
Capital outlay	23,325	45,524	59,658	64,441	103	183	223	239
Construction	19,736	34,803	46,991	50,542	87	140	176	187
Other capital outlay	(X)	(X)	12,667	13,899	(X)	(X)	47	52
Land and existing structure	1,345	3,471	(NA)	(NA)	6	14	-	-
Equipment	2,243	7,250	(NA)	(NA)	10	29	-	-
Assistance and subsidies	9,818	16,902	21,867	21,515	43	68	82	80
Interest on debt	7,052	22,367	27,025	27,590	31	90	101	102
Insurance benefits [3]	24,981	54,452	95,171	91,198	111	219	356	338
Debt redemption	5,682	19,895	41,381	58,470	25	80	155	217
Debt outstanding, year-end	121,958	318,254	455,698	483,117	540	1,282	1,705	1,791
Long-term	119,821	315,490	453,556	480,948	530	1,271	1,697	1,783
Full-faith and credit	49,364	74,972	119,514	124,653	219	302	447	462
Nonguaranteed	70,457	240,518	334,042	356,294	312	969	1,250	1,321
Short-term	2,137	2,764	2,142	2,169	9	11	8	8
Net long-term [4]	79,810	125,524	222,393	237,107	353	506	832	879
Full-faith and credit only	39,357	63,481	109,513	114,890	174	256	410	426

- Represents zero. NA Not available. X Not applicable. [1] 1980 and 1990 based on enumerated resident population as of April 1; other years based on estimated resident population as of July 1. [2] Includes other items not shown separately. [3] Includes repayments. [4] Less cash and investment assets specifically held for redemption of long-term debt.

Source: U.S. Census Bureau, *State Government Finances*, Series GF, No. 3, annual; <http://www.census.gov/ftp/pub/govs/www/state.html> (accessed 08 August 2001).

No. 437. State Governments—Revenue by State: 1999

[In millions of dollars (1,152,870 represents $1,152,870,000,000), except as noted. For fiscal year ending in year shown; see text, this section. Includes local shares of state imposed taxes. N.e.c. = Not elsewhere classified]

State	Total revenue [1]	General revenue Total	Per capita [2] Total (dol.)	Per capita [2] Rank	Intergovernmental revenue Total	Intergovernmental revenue From federal government	Charges and miscellaneous Total	Charges and miscellaneous Current charges	Charges and miscellaneous Miscellaneous general revenue	Insurance trust revenue
United States . .	1,152,870	906,076	3,329	(X)	253,692	238,941	152,441	79,308	73,133	236,838
Alabama	15,501	13,093	2,996	35	4,282	4,240	2,779	1,985	794	2,263
Alaska.	7,313	5,941	9,582	1	1,223	1,220	3,813	314	3,499	1,346
Arizona	15,122	13,077	2,737	46	3,662	3,393	1,872	777	1,095	2,023
Arkansas	10,361	8,449	3,312	24	2,471	2,457	1,369	869	501	1,912
California	154,017	119,408	3,603	18	33,721	31,150	13,299	8,097	5,203	34,394
Colorado	14,158	11,747	2,896	40	2,959	2,941	2,220	1,279	941	2,411
Connecticut	16,437	14,920	4,546	6	3,147	3,141	2,150	1,003	1,146	1,495
Delaware	4,540	4,060	5,385	2	764	738	1,265	538	728	472
Florida.	49,209	39,222	2,596	49	9,091	8,723	6,333	2,179	4,155	9,981
Georgia	27,639	21,445	2,754	45	5,871	5,822	3,113	1,665	1,447	6,193
Hawaii.	6,646	5,615	4,738	3	1,265	1,253	1,183	801	382	1,032
Idaho	4,870	3,847	3,073	32	961	957	715	347	368	970
Illinois	43,294	35,686	2,942	39	9,365	8,548	5,110	2,130	2,980	7,608
Indiana	19,149	17,729	2,983	36	4,481	4,327	3,512	2,120	1,393	1,420
Iowa	11,629	9,208	3,209	29	2,467	2,378	1,872	1,180	691	2,321
Kansas	8,687	7,597	2,863	43	1,885	1,854	1,123	648	474	1,090
Kentucky	16,853	13,584	3,429	22	3,860	3,847	2,368	1,355	1,013	3,269
Louisiana.	17,786	14,603	3,340	23	4,589	4,530	3,523	2,252	1,271	3,177
Maine	5,888	4,857	3,876	13	1,440	1,430	876	343	533	958
Maryland	19,613	16,240	3,140	31	3,798	3,669	2,941	1,520	1,420	3,281
Massachusetts . . .	28,120	25,664	4,156	8	5,454	5,103	5,477	1,684	3,793	2,374
Michigan	46,724	36,791	3,730	14	8,770	8,361	6,165	3,714	2,451	9,412
Minnesota	25,089	19,131	4,006	12	4,045	3,990	2,605	1,222	1,383	5,958
Mississippi	10,701	8,972	3,240	27	3,099	2,983	1,299	848	451	1,573
Missouri.	19,505	15,770	2,884	41	4,733	4,690	2,473	1,245	1,228	3,735
Montana	3,725	3,121	3,534	20	1,152	1,134	623	311	312	569
Nebraska.	5,576	5,089	3,055	33	1,420	1,400	1,006	514	493	487
Nevada	7,573	5,013	2,771	44	984	933	599	332	267	2,531
New Hampshire . .	4,024	3,108	2,588	50	1,112	948	925	431	494	649
New Jersey	39,150	29,708	3,648	16	7,120	6,748	5,662	3,020	2,642	8,957
New Mexico.	8,757	7,161	4,115	9	2,071	2,019	1,635	636	999	1,596
New York.	102,242	80,042	4,399	7	31,479	25,519	9,862	4,391	5,471	19,909
North Carolina . . .	34,064	25,312	3,308	25	7,613	7,118	3,282	2,002	1,261	8,752
North Dakota	2,936	2,552	4,025	11	873	851	572	408	164	384
Ohio	51,273	33,207	2,950	38	9,309	9,072	5,719	3,363	2,356	17,615
Oklahoma	11,935	9,684	2,884	41	2,796	2,717	1,471	984	487	1,966
Oregon	15,666	11,889	3,585	19	3,526	3,469	3,021	1,371	1,651	3,566
Pennsylvania	49,482	38,859	3,240	27	10,261	10,184	7,010	4,150	2,859	9,822
Rhode Island	5,478	3,994	4,030	10	1,303	1,229	796	306	491	1,473
South Carolina . . .	14,566	12,378	3,185	30	3,882	3,580	2,334	1,622	713	1,413
South Dakota	2,886	2,179	2,972	37	807	795	501	202	299	707
Tennessee	16,904	14,635	2,669	47	5,568	5,495	1,870	1,394	476	2,268
Texas	71,649	52,545	2,621	48	16,310	15,665	10,560	4,616	5,944	19,104
Utah	8,742	7,043	3,307	26	1,827	1,809	1,562	1,049	513	1,591
Vermont	3,055	2,730	4,596	5	833	802	509	297	212	295
Virginia	26,138	20,867	3,036	34	4,047	3,929	5,257	3,108	2,149	4,998
Washington	28,737	20,242	3,517	21	4,695	4,620	3,209	2,005	1,204	8,208
West Virginia	8,034	6,584	3,644	17	2,123	2,082	1,159	599	560	1,403
Wisconsin	28,334	19,262	3,669	15	4,271	4,197	3,364	1,977	1,387	9,072
Wyoming	3,092	2,215	4,614	4	908	880	495	106	389	837

See footnotes at end of table.

U.S. Census Bureau, Statistical Abstract of the United States: 2001

No. 437. State Governments—Revenue by State: 1999—Con.

[See headnote, page 279]

State	All taxes Total	Per capita [2] Total (dol.)	Rank	Total property taxes	Sales and gross receipts taxes Total	General sales taxes Total	Selective sales taxes [3] Total	Alcoholic beverages and tobacco sales	Insurance premiums	Motor fuels sales	Public utilities
United States...	499,943	1,837	(X)	11,654	239,367	164,378	74,989	12,070	9,595	29,169	8,869
Alabama	6,032	1,380	46	164	3,129	1,649	1,480	188	188	498	459
Alaska	905	1,460	2	49	132	-	132	60	28	38	4
Arizona	7,543	1,579	39	268	4,295	3,310	985	211	152	585	34
Arkansas	4,609	1,807	34	454	2,228	1,602	626	122	68	380	-
California	72,388	2,184	12	3,843	28,320	22,684	5,635	1,173	1,264	3,034	43
Colorado	6,568	1,619	44	-	2,521	1,704	817	94	121	516	8
Connecticut	9,624	2,932	1	-	4,821	3,218	1,603	175	178	545	168
Delaware	2,031	2,693	5	-	274	-	274	36	51	103	24
Florida	23,799	1,575	41	961	17,920	13,881	4,039	1,029	336	1,577	640
Georgia	12,462	1,600	38	44	5,371	4,349	1,023	226	230	566	-
Hawaii	3,167	2,672	3	-	1,915	1,447	468	81	54	74	121
Idaho	2,171	1,734	23	-	1,008	702	306	34	52	212	3
Illinois	21,211	1,749	28	210	9,995	5,949	4,046	559	218	1,329	1,213
Indiana	9,736	1,638	27	4	4,676	3,308	1,368	120	157	664	6
Iowa	4,868	1,697	20	-	2,368	1,646	722	110	114	341	-
Kansas	4,589	1,729	21	47	2,239	1,687	552	124	78	326	1
Kentucky	7,357	1,857	15	371	3,394	2,086	1,308	83	213	445	-
Louisiana	6,491	1,485	45	26	3,689	2,001	1,687	136	240	537	14-
Maine	2,541	2,028	22	43	1,160	829	331	111	42	173	-
Maryland	9,501	1,837	18	250	4,031	2,300	1,732	153	178	680	154
Massachusetts	14,732	2,386	6	-	4,735	3,270	1,466	346	336	637	-
Michigan	21,857	2,216	7	1,581	9,296	7,230	2,066	740	199	1,075	-
Minnesota	12,482	2,613	4	9	5,295	3,404	1,890	243	179	581	-
Mississippi	4,574	1,652	36	1	3,028	2,230	798	97	112	395	1
Missouri	8,564	1,566	40	17	3,918	2,716	1,202	138	217	663	-
Montana	1,346	1,524	35	228	304	-	304	30	39	160	17
Nebraska	2,662	1,598	29	5	1,252	855	396	64	34	264	3
Nevada	3,430	1,896	13	83	2,925	1,830	1,095	79	117	237	8
New Hampshire	1,071	892	50	1	517	-	517	85	57	120	57
New Jersey	16,926	2,079	14	1	7,983	5,054	2,928	494	293	483	1,091
New Mexico	3,454	1,985	10	38	1,957	1,452	504	60	81	247	7
New York	38,701	2,127	11	-	12,820	7,970	4,850	845	717	505	1,629
North Carolina	14,436	1,887	16	-	5,869	3,342	2,527	228	291	1,146	340
North Dakota	1,106	1,745	19	2	637	333	305	29	21	105	27
Ohio	18,179	1,615	37	17	8,685	5,873	2,812	375	357	1,371	693
Oklahoma	5,417	1,613	31	-	2,081	1,376	705	137	144	384	16
Oregon	5,341	1,611	30	-	665	-	665	205	54	397	8
Pennsylvania	21,589	1,800	24	176	10,054	6,659	3,395	501	432	747	670
Rhode Island	1,895	1,912	17	1	924	561	363	71	32	119	66
South Carolina	6,161	1,585	43	8	3,086	2,347	739	155	80	351	36
South Dakota	871	1,188	49	-	681	462	219	31	35	108	2
Tennessee	7,197	1,312	47	-	5,531	4,218	1,313	158	257	770	5
Texas	25,676	1,281	48	-	21,003	13,104	7,899	1,107	751	2,592	450
Utah	3,654	1,715	32	-	1,851	1,376	475	73	78	313	-
Vermont	1,388	2,337	33	386	447	206	242	28	20	57	9
Virginia	11,563	1,682	42	27	4,186	2,395	1,792	132	245	795	110
Washington	12,338	2,143	8	2,155	9,060	7,254	1,807	438	239	718	261
West Virginia	3,302	1,827	25	3	1,768	897	870	41	98	237	196
Wisconsin	11,628	2,215	9	82	4,890	3,265	1,625	309	106	909	295
Wyoming	812	1,691	26	99	429	347	82	7	10	63	2

See footnotes at end of table.

U.S. Census Bureau, Statistical Abstract of the United States: 2001

No. 437. State Governments—Revenue by State: 1999—Con.

[See headnote, page 279]

State	License taxes					Income			Other taxes	
	Total	Corporation license	Hunting and fishing license	Motor vehicle and operators license	Occupancy and business license, n.e.c.	Total	Individual income	Corporation net income	Total[3]	Death and gift
United States...	30,440	6,359	1,076	15,372	6,233	203,530	172,764	30,766	14,952	7,493
Alabama	454	123	17	201	102	2,140	1,907	233	144	63
Alaska.	85	1	18	34	30	212	-	212	428	2
Arizona	246	7	15	157	56	2,644	2,098	545	89	89
Arkansas	219	11	20	114	55	1,646	1,434	212	62	33
California	3,122	33	75	1,804	1,101	36,192	30,732	5,459	912	878
Colorado	292	5	60	177	43	3,656	3,355	301	100	65
Connecticut	361	13	4	255	78	4,084	3,610	475	357	250
Delaware	676	460	1	30	169	1,003	771	233	77	27
Florida.	1,503	126	13	990	297	1,267	-	1,267	2,147	650
Georgia	423	35	22	258	68	6,490	5,697	793	134	111
Hawaii.	93	3	-	64	16	1,121	1,069	52	36	29
Idaho	204	1	24	109	38	943	847	96	16	11
Illinois	1,254	121	24	840	257	9,351	7,247	2,104	401	347
Indiana	218	5	14	140	44	4,689	3,699	990	149	149
Iowa	469	33	20	325	69	1,950	1,715	235	81	73
Kansas	234	25	14	155	30	1,950	1,696	254	120	70
Kentucky	487	173	18	190	91	2,844	2,532	312	260	81
Louisiana	508	301	19	112	69	1,822	1,536	286	447	96
Maine	124	3	12	68	35	1,167	1,020	147	46	30
Maryland	381	11	11	199	157	4,583	4,178	405	256	126
Massachusetts . . .	428	22	6	293	54	9,286	8,037	1,250	282	174
Michigan	1,153	12	45	815	208	9,366	6,953	2,414	461	175
Minnesota	879	4	42	619	196	6,085	5,306	779	213	58
Mississippi	282	72	12	131	55	1,213	983	230	50	31
Missouri.	603	102	26	273	163	3,904	3,627	277	121	119
Montana	117	1	29	56	22	573	483	90	124	18
Nebraska.	174	6	13	88	50	1,207	1,072	135	25	17
Nevada	345	19	7	123	104	-	-	-	78	41
New Hampshire . .	132	4	7	70	42	319	63	256	102	49
New Jersey	757	149	11	395	135	7,658	6,324	1,334	528	423
New Mexico	194	2	14	140	32	974	810	164	292	22
New York.	917	73	26	661	90	23,464	20,576	2,888	1,499	1,071
North Carolina . . .	875	227	16	482	128	7,507	6,586	921	186	183
North Dakota . . .	84	-	11	43	29	276	182	94	108	7
Ohio	1,380	394	27	626	301	7,943	7,192	752	154	141
Oklahoma	750	39	13	584	101	2,258	2,070	187	328	89
Oregon	526	6	29	353	121	4,034	3,710	324	116	48
Pennsylvania	2,313	1,116	44	788	294	7,948	6,410	1,538	1,097	761
Rhode Island	90	12	2	53	21	829	763	66	52	47
South Carolina . . .	425	37	14	115	116	2,556	2,298	257	88	57
South Dakota	109	2	16	34	50	51	-	51	30	26
Tennessee	692	323	19	252	85	732	160	571	243	89
Texas	3,711	2,128	62	981	460	-	-	-	962	256
Utah	138	2	18	84	32	1,641	1,461	180	23	8
Vermont	65	1	5	37	18	433	383	50	57	23
Virginia	482	28	20	314	108	6,502	6,088	414	366	154
Washington	565	13	28	301	170	-	-	-	556	70
West Virginia	161	8	17	86	27	1,183	920	263	187	27
Wisconsin	659	60	73	303	210	5,833	5,162	671	163	117
Wyoming	82	6	22	50	4	-	-	-	202	10

- Represents or rounds to zero.   X Not applicable.   [1] Duplicate intergovernmental transactions are excluded.   [2] Based on estimated resident population as of July 1.   [3] Includes amounts not shown separately.

Source: U.S. Census Bureau, <http://www.census.gov/govs/www/index.html> (accessed 24 July 2001).

State and Local Government Finances and Employment 281

U.S. Census Bureau, Statistical Abstract of the United States: 2001

No. 438. State Governments—Expenditures and Debt by State: 1999

[In millions of dollars (998,365 represents $998,365,000,000) except as indicated. For fiscal year ending in year shown; see text, this section]

State	Total expendi-ture [1]	Total Amount	Per capita [2] (dol.)	Inter-govern-mental	Direct expenditures Total [3]	Educa-tion	Public welfare	Health and hospi-tals	High-ways	Police protec-tion
United States.....	998,365	889,475	3,268	304,933	584,542	126,185	182,238	54,391	56,242	7,810
Alabama	14,702	13,289	3,041	3,631	9,658	2,613	3,195	1,602	733	89
Alaska...........	6,141	5,572	8,987	1,029	4,543	664	683	126	553	52
Arizona...........	14,278	13,127	2,747	5,944	7,183	1,832	1,409	569	1,145	140
Arkansas.........	8,943	8,372	3,282	2,650	5,723	1,438	1,895	690	564	66
California.........	133,673	120,178	3,626	58,350	61,828	13,290	17,049	6,150	3,446	932
Colorado	13,148	11,699	2,884	3,520	8,179	2,364	2,146	405	888	70
Connecticut	15,213	13,340	4,064	2,811	10,529	1,388	2,830	1,437	690	128
Delaware.........	3,941	3,671	4,869	721	2,950	680	502	248	294	61
Florida...........	42,459	39,735	2,630	13,438	26,297	3,755	8,498	2,868	3,331	340
Georgia..........	23,203	21,579	2,771	6,677	14,902	4,004	4,834	913	1,567	166
Hawaii............	6,266	5,651	4,769	153	5,498	1,778	934	522	282	5
Idaho	4,230	3,777	3,017	1,213	2,563	570	691	128	313	35
Illinois...........	38,314	34,358	2,833	10,803	23,555	4,228	8,261	2,702	1,948	313
Indiana	18,614	17,437	2,934	6,248	11,190	3,731	3,456	591	1,203	179
Iowa	10,321	9,543	3,326	2,873	6,670	1,793	1,977	690	811	75
Kansas	8,371	7,678	2,893	2,806	4,872	1,381	1,247	420	814	46
Kentucky	14,778	13,327	3,365	3,249	10,078	2,214	3,556	663	1,291	126
Louisiana.........	15,706	14,051	3,214	3,645	10,406	2,242	2,930	1,665	967	177
Maine	4,865	4,386	3,501	858	3,528	547	1,394	322	338	43
Maryland.........	17,593	15,540	3,005	4,064	11,476	2,361	3,600	968	919	211
Massachusetts	28,030	25,820	4,181	6,752	19,068	2,468	5,775	1,887	2,070	377
Michigan	38,798	35,123	3,561	16,030	19,092	5,642	5,910	1,665	1,283	264
Minnesota	20,388	18,410	3,855	7,005	11,405	2,919	4,365	519	871	106
Mississippi	9,927	9,073	3,276	3,019	6,054	1,275	2,014	660	741	57
Missouri..........	16,525	15,346	2,806	4,442	10,904	2,064	3,686	1,128	1,113	133
Montana	3,512	3,136	3,551	708	2,427	570	486	224	386	25
Nebraska.........	5,184	4,962	2,978	1,487	3,474	949	1,106	236	485	46
Nevada	6,103	5,280	2,919	2,089	3,191	744	760	179	427	48
New Hampshire	3,594	3,101	2,582	478	2,623	477	858	137	320	34
New Jersey	32,058	25,831	3,172	7,799	18,032	3,832	4,497	1,555	1,396	298
New Mexico........	8,089	7,434	4,273	2,366	5,068	1,103	1,339	607	922	70
New York..........	92,584	78,720	4,326	30,383	48,337	5,913	19,707	4,209	3,125	421
North Carolina	26,830	24,611	3,217	8,542	16,068	3,908	4,715	1,393	2,150	317
North Dakota	2,675	2,459	3,879	557	1,902	491	587	35	250	13
Ohio.............	41,113	33,285	2,957	12,015	21,269	5,212	7,124	1,838	1,943	203
Oklahoma	10,655	9,249	2,754	2,982	6,267	1,779	1,719	466	769	31
Oregon	13,965	11,635	3,509	3,672	7,963	1,578	2,711	697	657	117
Pennsylvania	44,237	38,517	3,211	10,948	27,570	5,725	9,583	1,865	2,739	752
Rhode Island	4,378	3,730	3,764	595	3,135	552	1,036	238	232	32
South Carolina	14,483	12,641	3,253	3,355	9,286	2,166	3,116	1,305	848	174
South Dakota	2,272	2,106	2,873	472	1,634	296	434	106	280	18
Tennessee.........	15,890	14,900	2,717	4,175	10,725	2,484	4,204	1,145	1,098	114
Texas	54,761	49,591	2,474	15,024	34,567	7,889	11,018	3,540	3,927	319
Utah	7,810	7,214	3,387	1,812	5,403	1,679	1,289	547	586	69
Vermont	2,603	2,456	4,135	699	1,757	411	549	56	207	24
Virginia	22,739	21,155	3,078	6,500	14,655	3,585	3,182	1,755	2,194	189
Washington	24,230	20,616	3,582	6,117	14,499	3,852	4,564	1,657	1,083	143
West Virginia	7,336	6,343	3,510	1,577	4,765	941	1,666	211	786	42
Wisconsin	20,466	18,315	3,489	7,888	10,427	2,563	2,910	750	937	99
Wyoming..........	2,373	2,107	4,389	762	1,345	243	243	103	322	18

See footnotes at end of table.

U.S. Census Bureau, Statistical Abstract of the United States: 2001

No. 438. State Governments—Expenditures and Debt by State: 1999—Con.

[See headnote, page 282]

State	General expenditure								Debt outstanding		
	Direct expenditures							Insurance trust expenditures	Cash and security holdings	Total	Per capita [2] (dol.)
	Corrections	Natural resources	Parks and recreation	Governmental administration	Interest on general debt	Utility expenditures	Liquor stores expenditures				
United States..	30,770	13,601	3,843	32,558	27,785	8,779	2,967	97,144	2,265,945	510,486	1,876
Alabama	277	202	15	336	198	-	142	1,271	24,769	4,467	1,022
Alaska	153	254	10	314	218	28	-	540	43,254	3,911	6,312
Arizona	676	149	40	412	150	26	-	1,125	35,724	2,725	570
Arkansas	221	157	54	266	116	-	-	571	14,828	2,488	975
California	3,734	2,060	252	4,804	2,541	106	-	13,389	295,496	53,975	1,628
Colorado	589	171	51	353	251	7	-	1,443	27,392	4,059	1,001
Connecticut	523	90	27	782	1,028	198	-	1,676	27,616	17,505	5,334
Delaware	202	77	51	295	235	43	-	227	10,046	3,713	4,927
Florida	2,105	1,212	126	1,749	1,031	46	-	2,678	89,348	17,825	1,180
Georgia	884	411	125	588	391	-	-	1,624	48,517	6,269	805
Hawaii	134	73	36	286	487	-	-	615	13,453	5,421	4,573
Idaho	167	125	16	213	118	-	42	411	10,602	2,031	1,623
Illinois	1,110	318	118	1,118	1,712	-	-	3,956	76,813	26,582	2,192
Indiana	473	187	57	424	307	-	-	1,177	29,171	7,056	1,187
Iowa	206	213	18	383	85	-	69	709	22,509	2,472	862
Kansas	232	166	7	299	20	-	-	693	10,328	1,482	559
Kentucky	330	272	103	567	440	12	-	1,439	30,845	7,422	1,874
Louisiana	381	334	258	452	406	3	-	1,652	32,707	7,152	1,636
Maine	78	120	10	190	178	-	51	428	11,240	3,875	3,093
Maryland	732	324	171	742	476	362	-	1,692	43,586	11,201	2,166
Massachusetts	592	199	115	1,047	1,902	117	-	2,094	52,800	35,798	5,797
Michigan	1,465	358	106	686	892	-	423	3,252	69,711	16,189	1,641
Minnesota	277	398	102	696	425	-	-	1,978	49,462	5,485	1,149
Mississippi	221	200	50	221	165	-	126	729	18,275	3,224	1,165
Missouri	486	243	41	637	500	-	-	1,179	39,728	8,903	1,628
Montana	94	159	13	177	148	-	31	346	7,568	2,355	2,668
Nebraska	124	126	26	142	106	-	-	222	8,625	1,820	1,092
Nevada	215	64	15	256	233	45	-	779	16,283	2,997	1,657
New Hampshire	78	34	6	159	340	-	252	241	9,092	5,427	4,518
New Jersey	1,000	210	294	1,140	1,176	1,657	-	4,570	74,526	27,932	3,430
New Mexico	208	119	44	299	170	-	-	655	27,867	3,158	1,815
New York	2,200	340	401	3,393	3,480	5,092	-	8,771	181,471	76,562	4,208
North Carolina	896	458	168	694	437	-	-	2,219	67,346	8,227	1,075
North Dakota	37	81	8	82	69	-	-	215	6,323	1,329	2,098
Ohio	1,312	313	144	1,023	855	-	282	7,546	129,083	14,963	1,329
Oklahoma	423	158	59	378	204	267	-	1,139	21,980	5,564	1,657
Oregon	445	268	41	687	271	4	128	2,198	28,102	5,738	1,730
Pennsylvania	1,359	480	132	1,126	1,694	-	737	4,982	97,789	17,658	1,472
Rhode Island	141	34	38	225	271	57	-	591	11,074	5,464	5,515
South Carolina	437	191	46	286	216	666	-	1,176	23,539	5,082	1,308
South Dakota	58	77	21	92	116	-	-	166	7,060	2,105	2,871
Tennessee	347	185	112	409	206	4	-	986	27,391	3,321	606
Texas	2,577	648	54	1,350	871	-	-	5,170	170,804	14,736	735
Utah	217	136	24	420	179	-	81	515	15,733	3,781	1,775
Vermont	39	55	7	126	120	3	28	115	4,280	2,116	3,565
Virginia	808	165	63	819	860	8	246	1,330	53,996	11,877	1,728
Washington	663	473	64	480	572	-	254	3,336	62,684	11,080	1,925
West Virginia	125	135	48	313	203	5	40	947	8,874	3,689	2,042
Wisconsin	643	281	49	522	657	-	-	2,151	67,834	11,225	2,138
Wyoming	75	98	10	99	61	-	35	231	8,402	1,046	2,181

- Represents or rounds to zero.   [1] Duplicate intergovernmental transactions are excluded.   [2] Based on estimated resident population as of July 1.   [3] Includes amounts not shown separately.

Source: U.S. Census Bureau, <http://www.census.gov/govs/www/index.html>.

State and Local Government Finances and Employment   283

No. 439. Local Governments—Revenue by State: 1998

[In millions of dollars (909,661 represents $909,661,000,000), except as noted. For fiscal year ending in year shown; see text, this section]

State	Total revenue[1]	General revenue Total	Per capita[2] (dol.)	Intergovernmental revenue Total	From federal government	From state governments	Taxes Total[3]	Property	General, sales and gross receipts	Income	Motor licenses
United States .	909,661	794,250	2,939	306,270	30,604	275,666	300,912	219,492	48,240	18,838	1,222
Alabama	11,174	9,418	2,164	3,923	356	3,567	2,603	944	1,226	94	22
Alaska	2,869	2,575	4,187	1,056	174	882	827	657	148	-	9
Arizona	14,667	12,033	2,578	5,334	523	4,812	4,123	2,914	1,055	-	3
Arkansas	5,283	4,751	1,872	2,111	111	2,000	1,382	894	468	-	-
California	141,787	117,809	3,605	56,128	4,138	51,990	31,003	20,851	7,337	-	-
Colorado	13,480	11,778	2,967	3,401	387	3,014	5,073	3,152	1,705	-	29
Connecticut	9,606	8,752	2,674	2,706	316	2,390	5,094	5,018	-	-	1
Delaware	1,638	1,477	1,985	734	50	684	412	335	2	43	-
Dist. of Columbia .	5,904	5,257	10,090	1,619	1,619	-	2,889	695	934	1,083	19
Florida	49,817	44,028	2,953	14,062	1,800	12,263	15,442	12,146	2,775	-	33
Georgia	23,385	20,394	2,670	6,841	624	6,217	7,916	4,962	2,679	-	-
Hawaii	1,667	1,485	1,248	317	155	162	753	599	91	-	43
Idaho.	3,073	2,941	2,389	1,268	93	1,175	811	763	12	-	4
Illinois	39,820	34,667	2,872	11,843	1,707	10,136	15,864	13,112	2,266	-	114
Indiana	16,081	14,791	2,504	5,410	333	5,078	5,631	5,052	65	443	1
Iowa	8,254	7,730	2,702	3,016	249	2,767	2,656	2,416	171	31	12
Kansas	7,920	7,099	2,690	2,528	110	2,418	2,713	2,104	552	-	3
Kentucky	8,393	7,242	1,841	3,059	309	2,750	2,240	1,204	171	641	23
Louisiana	11,242	10,328	2,367	3,673	275	3,398	3,980	1,514	2,251	-	4
Maine	3,113	3,010	2,412	906	102	803	1,642	1,591	5	-	25
Maryland	15,161	13,420	2,616	4,208	535	3,672	6,862	4,006	222	2,168	-
Massachusetts . .	19,284	16,277	2,649	6,962	989	5,973	7,218	6,981	91	-	-
Michigan	33,452	29,813	3,036	15,510	948	14,561	7,694	6,934	48	493	1
Minnesota	18,045	16,243	3,437	6,676	510	6,166	4,985	4,727	117	-	5
Mississippi	6,575	6,074	2,208	2,601	193	2,409	1,421	1,307	59	-	-
Missouri	13,982	12,275	2,257	4,367	494	3,873	5,097	3,017	1,568	276	13
Montana	1,991	1,922	2,184	743	103	640	689	658	3	-	12
Nebraska	6,491	4,342	2,614	1,290	155	1,135	1,942	1,584	214	-	14
Nevada	5,961	5,568	3,192	2,243	195	2,047	1,651	1,033	365	-	-
New Hampshire. .	2,678	2,615	2,205	409	53	356	1,854	1,830	-	-	-
New Jersey	27,928	27,264	3,368	8,667	594	8,073	14,405	14,153	26	30	-
New Mexico	4,550	4,257	2,455	2,312	237	2,075	1,006	536	429	-	-
New York	104,743	88,625	4,880	30,025	2,973	27,051	42,330	24,445	8,230	8,327	124
North Carolina. .	22,487	19,785	2,622	8,316	567	7,749	5,429	4,090	1,086	-	23
North Dakota . . .	1,619	1,530	2,398	631	118	513	548	487	50	-	-
Ohio	33,325	31,303	2,785	11,734	1,092	10,642	13,184	8,723	1,154	2,890	94
Oklahoma	7,591	6,946	2,080	2,720	187	2,533	2,196	1,151	1,010	-	2
Oregon	10,957	10,235	3,118	4,484	723	3,761	3,136	2,532	164	-	11
Pennsylvania . . .	35,653	32,316	2,693	13,035	1,625	11,411	13,002	9,083	348	2,319	-
Rhode Island . . .	2,330	2,173	2,199	691	79	612	1,258	1,241	1	-	-
South Carolina . .	9,766	8,779	2,286	3,098	273	2,825	2,705	2,319	178	-	14
South Dakota . . .	1,723	1,559	2,133	504	105	399	759	573	153	-	17
Tennessee	17,415	12,052	2,218	4,053	345	3,708	4,296	2,538	1,506	-	78
Texas	57,169	50,011	2,537	16,036	2,088	13,948	21,686	17,333	3,667	-	243
Utah	5,911	4,794	2,282	1,952	200	1,752	1,665	1,183	394	-	-
Vermont	1,442	1,290	2,182	364	24	340	762	752	3	-	-
Virginia	18,455	16,528	2,435	5,670	593	5,077	7,626	5,522	1,409	-	111
Washington	20,775	17,255	3,034	6,955	651	6,304	5,476	3,451	1,512	-	109
West Virginia . . .	3,653	3,492	1,927	1,649	93	1,556	941	774	33	-	1
Wisconsin.	17,423	16,092	3,082	7,725	398	7,327	5,493	5,173	199	-	1
Wyoming	1,953	1,856	3,867	705	35	670	540	427	90	-	9

See footnotes at end of table.

284   State and Local Government Finances and Employment

[See headnote, page 284]

State	General revenue								Utility revenue	Liquor store revenue	Insurance trust revenue
	Current charges and miscellaneous general revenue										
	Current charges					Miscellaneous general revenue					
	Total	Total	Education	Hospital	Sewerage	Total	Interest	Special assessment			
United States....	187,068	125,335	13,431	34,052	22,677	61,733	32,702	3,737	72,815	625	41,972
Alabama	2,892	2,197	238	1,273	193	695	356	12	1,631	-	126
Alaska	691	462	29	55	52	229	177	3	228	-	66
Arizona	2,575	1,464	204	190	305	1,112	609	54	2,294	-	341
Arkansas	1,258	888	122	384	141	371	201	9	494	-	37
California	30,678	19,092	1,207	3,604	3,113	11,586	5,325	1,112	12,364	-	11,614
Colorado	3,304	2,287	208	500	357	1,017	612	65	1,290	-	412
Connecticut	953	565	57	14	168	388	187	29	435	-	419
Delaware	331	221	12	-	104	110	70	-	129	-	31
District of Columbia	749	372	15	108	100	377	143	-	406	-	241
Florida	14,523	9,738	1,109	2,573	1,281	4,785	2,613	863	4,599	-	1,190
Georgia	5,636	3,983	197	2,240	510	1,654	885	19	2,529	-	462
Hawaii	415	264	-	-	136	151	79	11	182	-	-
Idaho	861	696	43	345	79	165	73	7	131	-	1
Illinois	6,960	4,390	736	559	691	2,570	1,558	77	2,437	-	2,716
Indiana	3,750	2,636	258	1,458	434	1,114	442	24	1,230	-	60
Iowa	2,057	1,518	383	607	217	539	270	15	505	-	20
Kansas	1,858	1,193	207	399	159	664	391	73	702	-	120
Kentucky	1,943	998	91	165	227	945	751	12	1,122	-	30
Louisiana	2,675	1,946	68	1,219	184	729	506	3	744	-	170
Maine	462	337	21	52	112	126	60	2	102	-	-
Maryland	2,350	1,547	406	-	483	803	420	113	394	124	1,224
Massachusetts	2,097	1,559	153	165	579	538	242	36	1,833	-	1,173
Michigan	6,609	4,222	612	645	1,151	2,387	1,011	91	1,278	-	2,360
Minnesota	4,582	2,657	254	699	385	1,925	932	268	1,075	179	548
Mississippi	2,051	1,521	177	1,032	120	530	285	4	498	-	2
Missouri	2,811	2,001	373	600	374	809	491	16	1,119	-	588
Montana	490	295	48	44	40	194	100	37	69	-	-
Nebraska	1,109	781	140	260	96	328	184	31	1,977	-	172
Nevada	1,674	1,180	67	433	189	494	288	24	393	-	-
New Hampshire	351	253	33	-	64	98	40	3	62	-	1
New Jersey	4,192	2,657	469	212	934	1,536	552	11	652	-	12
New Mexico	939	537	68	134	91	402	212	11	293	-	-
New York	16,270	11,432	682	2,953	1,219	4,838	2,071	116	3,698	-	12,420
North Carolina	6,040	4,811	367	2,478	744	1,229	794	13	2,346	307	51
North Dakota	351	172	37	-	23	178	73	33	77	-	12
Ohio	6,385	4,219	783	659	1,308	2,166	1,185	83	1,743	-	280
Oklahoma	2,030	1,463	191	672	178	567	344	5	618	-	27
Oregon	2,614	1,746	295	275	407	868	409	102	721	-	1
Pennsylvania	6,279	3,770	498	26	1,213	2,510	1,622	67	1,886	-	1,451
Rhode Island	224	155	17	-	56	69	40	1	98	-	59
South Carolina	2,976	2,385	177	1,437	192	591	358	18	982	-	5
South Dakota	296	201	21	32	42	96	59	5	134	15	14
Tennessee	3,703	2,925	317	1,442	406	777	472	4	4,893	-	471
Texas	12,289	8,177	1,145	2,328	1,680	4,111	2,740	48	5,816	-	1,343
Utah	1,177	676	61	39	127	501	279	4	1,118	-	-
Vermont	164	101	16	-	34	63	23	2	138	-	15
Virginia	3,232	2,165	213	244	582	1,068	659	5	1,082	-	845
Washington	4,823	3,479	220	900	771	1,345	678	75	3,250	-	269
West Virginia	902	572	34	213	104	329	241	2	137	-	24
Wisconsin	2,874	1,981	314	83	491	893	490	84	788	-	543
Wyoming	611	448	40	300	29	163	98	37	91	-	6

- Represents or rounds to zero.   [1] Duplicate intergovernmental transactions are excluded.   [2] Based on estimated resident population as of July.   [3] Includes items not shown separately.

Source: U.S. Census Bureau, <http://www.census.gov/govs/www/estimate.html>; and unpublished data.

State and Local Government Finances and Employment   285

[In millions of dollars, (884,759 represents $884,759,000,000), except as indicated. For fiscal year ending in year shown; see text, this section]

State	Total expenditure [1]	Total amount	Per capita [2] (dol.)	General expenditure							
				Selected functions (direct expenditures)							
				Total [3]	Education	Public welfare	Health	Hospitals	Highways	Police protection	Fire protection
United States . .	884,759	775,791	3,274	765,696	331,802	32,521	21,261	41,148	35,243	43,310	20,269
Alabama	11,350	9,534	2,609	9,527	4,209	36	260	1,245	534	524	227
Alaska.	2,830	2,516	4,601	2,516	944	9	64	58	115	114	56
Arizona	14,177	11,898	3,038	11,596	4,781	450	115	258	560	808	357
Arkansas	5,107	4,639	2,012	4,639	2,441	10	35	352	307	252	110
California.	134,498	113,790	4,115	112,357	40,048	9,863	4,555	5,815	3,517	7,238	3,253
Colorado	13,350	11,564	3,364	11,524	4,580	528	142	516	826	686	301
Connecticut	8,909	8,252	2,722	8,247	4,191	124	94	18	349	511	353
Delaware	1,568	1,444	2,107	1,441	889	1	10	-	67	89	18
Dist. of Columbia. .	6,140	4,454	11,786	4,454	755	1,188	149	293	145	283	112
Florida.	48,116	42,550	3,228	42,366	16,208	294	460	2,997	1,730	3,009	1,340
Georgia.	23,258	19,330	3,045	19,292	8,699	81	627	2,371	842	931	439
Hawaii.	1,741	1,481	1,463	1,481	-	12	21	-	84	203	89
Idaho	3,054	2,917	2,481	2,912	1,375	35	40	336	205	145	66
Illinois	39,256	33,722	3,252	33,682	15,312	407	495	1,011	1,721	2,372	1,041
Indiana	15,563	14,233	2,634	14,164	6,649	428	127	1,599	614	533	358
Iowa	8,249	7,684	2,883	7,601	3,747	96	226	644	732	301	121
Kansas	7,548	6,827	2,860	6,801	3,210	61	149	401	489	373	148
Kentucky	8,232	7,334	2,093	7,333	3,507	41	270	184	283	300	186
Louisiana.	10,862	9,895	2,490	9,891	4,287	54	71	1,293	477	603	253
Maine	2,907	2,810	2,329	2,809	1,529	34	18	56	170	110	72
Maryland	13,715	12,808	2,673	12,677	6,340	93	257	-	542	760	415
Massachusetts . . .	19,186	15,552	3,123	14,979	7,468	70	78	223	621	935	695
Michigan	32,614	29,987	3,321	29,846	14,681	523	1,655	749	1,739	1,403	571
Minnesota	18,155	16,462	3,841	16,379	6,318	1,089	365	836	1,424	690	245
Mississippi.	6,761	6,238	2,458	6,236	2,847	25	50	1,054	460	287	130
Missouri.	13,379	11,907	2,460	11,903	6,033	112	188	679	749	696	353
Montana	1,898	1,832	2,157	1,828	997	28	39	42	92	78	34
Nebraska.	6,044	4,144	3,639	4,136	2,072	39	31	306	303	152	116
Nevada	6,292	5,807	3,608	5,803	1,919	86	97	424	472	377	·170
New Hampshire . .	2,679	2,576	2,259	2,507	1,336	140	20	-	138	133	89
New Jersey	26,664	26,049	3,293	25,715	12,567	1,242	273	278	1,016	1,671	604
New Mexico	4,454	4,040	2,569	4,021	2,049	43	29	157	201	249	111
New York.	98,228	87,049	5,409	81,629	29,792	8,698	2,072	4,335	3,493	4,752	2,022
North Carolina . .	22,577	19,363	2,992	19,083	8,263	863	1,133	2,508	337	879	383
North Dakota	1,589	1,494	2,491	1,481	666	34	16	-	147	51	50
Ohio	32,325	29,996	2,876	29,843	13,127	1,627	1,612	771	1,499	1,734	959
Oklahoma	7,517	6,838	2,251	6,836	3,456	11	88	649	367	368	230
Oregon	11,070	9,764	3,373	9,761	4,404	35	472	346	558	480	309
Pennsylvania	35,225	31,630	2,935	31,616	15,601	1,608	1,483	129	1,002	1,281	419
Rhode Island . . .	2,218	2,047	2,245	2,046	1,150	6	4	-	54	148	131
South Carolina . . .	9,465	8,392	2,465	8,367	4,061	10	178	1,310.	161	378	168
South Dakota	1,661	1,511	2,273	1,506	757	14	12	28	181	64	27
Tennessee	17,819	12,529	3,280	12,490	5,008	133	178	1,591	593	711	339
Texas	56,653	49,354	2,874	48,933	25,257	229	1,189	3,270	1,824	2,635	1,134
Utah	5,902	4,659	2,809	4,653	2,262	24	141	27	241	270	102
Vermont	1,357	1,212	2,297	1,211	773	1	5	-	115	39	29
Virginia	18,271	16,719	2,691	16,698	7,597	797	407	214	522	875	468
Washington	21,065	17,239	3,703	17,201	6,931	31	549	1,118	1,088	760	577
West Virginia . . .	3,529	3,325	1,947	3,319	1,981	1	64	207	43	100	49
Wisconsin	17,844	16,683	3,417	16,652	7,945	1,153	636	150	1,410	900	421
Wyoming	1,886	1,710	3,928	1,709	786	6	17	299	85	71	23

See footnotes at end of table.

U.S. Census Bureau, Statistical Abstract of the United States: 2001

[See headnote, page 286]

| State | General expenditure | | | | | | | | | | |
| | Selected functions (direct expenditures) | | | | | | | | | | |
	Correction	Parks and recreation	Housing and community development	Sewerage	Solid waste	Governmental administration	Interest on general debt	Other general expenditure	Utility expenditures	Insurance trust expenditure	Debt outstanding
United States	13,800	18,472	22,284	24,515	14,130	41,035	37,778	68,129	91,154	17,287	800,443
Alabama	104	270	302	244	183	457	417	515	1,751	65	9,058
Alaska	1	47	110	78	52	165	209	494	302	12	3,649
Arizona	206	502	263	446	198	868	711	1,075	2,204	75	19,165
Arkansas	52	74	98	119	106	215	183	285	457	11	3,710
California	2,449	2,539	4,428	3,822	1,457	7,269	5,098	11,007	17,127	3,580	111,236
Colorado	160	551	271	315	71	679	924	975	1,593	193	17,299
Connecticut	-	149	352	229	188	387	263	1,037	447	210	4,783
Delaware	-	19	44	99	16	64	66	60	102	22	1,213
District of Columbia	303	73	126	132	32	300	233	329	1,188	499	4,834
Florida	993	1,427	984	1,266	1,410	2,299	2,786	5,162	5,169	397	54,840
Georgia	413	327	467	656	404	1,236	717	1,083	3,724	204	19,369
Hawaii	-	131	110	109	108	164	139	311	261	-	2,135
Idaho	33	50	38	86	77	164	53	211	135	1	996
Illinois	424	1,684	1,460	1,058	375	1,970	1,693	2,659	3,974	1,560	33,540
Indiana	194	252	273	499	169	794	567	1,110	1,238	91	9,423
Iowa	70	186	127	264	121	286	224	458	555	11	4,479
Kansas	86	144	82	142	85	397	414	620	688	33	7,865
Kentucky	124	118	148	277	131	250	778	735	877	21	14,134
Louisiana	186	164	216	302	188	581	526	690	839	127	9,573
Maine	29	36	63	106	79	144	85	280	97	-	1,784
Maryland	162	434	467	480	415	691	619	1,002	456	344	12,788
Massachusetts	275	148	903	459	282	576	353	1,891	2,683	951	13,487
Michigan	306	540	181	1,323	415	1,679	1,179	2,902	1,637	989	22,815
Minnesota	252	528	826	474	248	843	1,046	1,196	1,288	239	21,530
Mississippi	44	70	106	107	93	366	284	314	522	2	4,892
Missouri	141	317	279	433	102	601	395	827	1,251	221	7,897
Montana	12	35	28	44	50	97	72	180	67	-	1,191
Nebraska	51	98	89	94	71	211	96	405	1,828	71	4,555
Nevada	167	313	108	154	7	467	369	672	485	-	8,410
New Hampshire	28	40	37	68	75	133	63	208	102	1	1,238
New Jersey	386	395	585	885	855	1,440	1,038	2,501	604	11	19,346
New Mexico	77	145	70	92	96	214	183	306	414	-	4,028
New York	1,931	1,199	2,556	1,872	1,770	2,640	4,593	9,904	6,070	5,109	82,455
North Carolina	189	376	383	479	524	743	675	1,347	2,961	14	18,693
North Dakota	10	79	49	22	30	66	63	198	89	6	1,091
Ohio	391	683	884	1,128	491	1,981	944	2,013	2,253	75	19,766
Oklahoma	54	215	116	208	128	285	286	376	658	22	5,477
Oregon	287	258	309	441	108	517	336	901	1,242	64	7,662
Pennsylvania	715	419	1,105	1,121	454	1,666	2,287	2,328	2,948	647	45,469
Rhode Island	-	34	103	58	26	73	48	211	109	62	1,131
South Carolina	125	209	160	149	198	457	356	444	1,071	3	9,954
South Dakota	17	61	27	43	24	89	34	128	130	6	964
Tennessee	235	420	430	383	295	613	584	976	5,032	259	13,260
Texas	1,067	977	1,185	1,493	652	2,417	3,025	2,579	6,856	442	69,250
Utah	99	192	102	155	93	336	210	402	1,243	-	9,413
Vermont	-	16	21	37	26	51	26	73	143	3	625
Virginia	330	457	482	576	474	1,050	851	1,598	1,267	284	18,196
Washington	327	602	413	729	357	1,009	762	1,949	3,715	111	24,716
West Virginia	26	40	60	116	39	172	251	170	182	22	3,484
Wisconsin	256	392	272	605	258	757	592	905	949	212	12,453
Wyoming	18	38	4	34	25	106	72	125	173	2	1,122

- Represents or rounds to zero.   [1] Duplicate intergovernmental transactions are excluded.   [2] Based on estimated resident population as of July 1.   [3] Includes items not shown separately.

Source: U.S. Census Bureau, <http://www.census.gov/govs/www/esti96.html> (accessed 26 April 1999); and unpublished data.

U.S. Census Bureau, Statistical Abstract of the United States: 2001

No. 441. Estimated State and Local Taxes Paid by a Family of Four in Selected Cities: 1999

[Data based on average family of four (two wage earners and two school age children) owning their own home and living in a city where taxes apply. Comprises state and local sales, income, auto, and real estate taxes. For definition of median, see Guide to Tabular Presentation]

City	Total taxes paid, by gross family income level (dollars)					Total taxes paid as percent of income				
	$25,000	$50,000	$75,000	$100,000	$150,000	$25,000	$50,000	$75,000	$100,000	$150,000
Albuquerque, NM . . .	1,554	3,565	6,117	8,687	14,014	6.2	7.1	8.2	8.7	9.3
Atlanta, GA	1,733	4,283	7,276	9,920	15,427	6.9	8.6	9.7	9.9	10.3
Baltimore, MD	1,567	5,144	8,142	10,977	16,199	6.3	10.3	10.9	11.0	10.8
Boston, MA	2,021	5,056	8,087	10,805	16,874	8.1	10.1	10.8	10.8	11.2
Charlotte, NC	1,885	4,288	7,029	9,763	15,177	7.5	8.6	9.4	9.8	10.1
Chicago, IL	2,110	4,279	6,748	8,894	13,165	8.4	8.6	9.0	8.9	8.8
Columbus, OH	2,069	4,438	7,274	10,076	15,960	8.3	8.9	9.7	10.1	10.6
Denver, CO	1,412	3,253	5,210	6,954	10,352	5.6	6.5	6.9	7.0	6.9
Detroit, MI	2,218	4,849	7,621	10,187	15,412	8.9	9.7	10.2	10.2	10.3
Honolulu, HI	2,172	4,512	7,368	10,010	15,449	8.7	9.0	9.8	10.0	10.3
Houston, TX	1,567	2,812	4,374	5,628	7,965	6.3	5.6	5.8	5.6	5.3
Indianapolis, IN . . .	1,847	3,610	5,593	7,403	11,020	7.4	7.2	7.5	7.4	7.3
Jacksonville, FL . . .	1,217	2,477	4,020	5,239	7,667	4.9	5.0	5.4	5.2	5.1
Kansas City, MO . . .	1,938	4,077	6,451	8,656	13,622	7.8	8.2	8.6	8.7	9.1
Las Vegas, NV	1,487	2,405	3,592	4,516	6,441	5.9	4.8	4.8	4.5	4.3
Los Angeles, CA . . .	1,973	3,968	7,269	10,626	17,650	7.9	7.9	9.7	10.6	11.8
Memphis, TN	1,582	2,588	4,022	5,196	7,736	6.3	5.2	5.4	5.2	5.2
Milwaukee, WI	2,253	5,265	8,264	10,990	16,405	9.0	10.5	11.0	11.0	10.9
Minneapolis, MN . . .	1,657	4,734	8,151	11,195	17,595	6.6	9.5	10.9	11.2	11.7
New Orleans, LA . . .	1,364	3,417	5,843	7,900	12,011	5.5	6.8	7.8	7.9	8.0
New York City, NY . .	1,987	5,522	9,557	13,422	21,364	7.9	11.0	12.7	13.4	14.2
Oklahoma City, OK . .	1,986	4,042	6,505	8,751	13,594	7.9	8.1	8.7	8.8	9.1
Omaha, NE	1,880	4,070	6,836	9,424	15,199	7.5	8.1	9.1	9.4	10.1
Philadelphia, PA. . . .	3,339	6,218	9,235	12,021	17,534	13.4	12.4	12.3	12.0	11.7
Phoenix, AZ	1,881	3,703	5,916	8,068	13,221	7.5	7.4	7.9	8.1	8.8
Portland, ME	2,804	6,227	10,316	13,960	21,654	11.2	12.5	13.8	14.0	14.4
Seattle, WA	2,207	3,729	5,657	7,124	10,350	8.8	7.5	7.5	7.1	6.9
Virginia Beach, VA . .	2,413	4,578	7,217	9,493	14,404	9.7	9.2	9.6	9.5	9.6
Washington, DC . . .	2,157	4,680	7,944	11,007	17,058	8.6	9.4	10.6	11.0	11.4
Wichita, KS	1,852	3,814	6,511	8,924	13,957	7.4	7.6	8.7	8.9	9.3
Average [1]	2,024	4,296	6,968	9,371	14,397	8.1	8.6	9.3	9.4	9.6
Median [1]	1,938	4,160	6,836	9,424	14,565	7.8	8.3	9.1	9.4	9.7

[1] Based on selected cities and District of Columbia. For complete list of cities, see Table 442.

Source: Government of the District of Columbia, Department of Finance and Revenue, *Tax Rates and Tax Burdens in the District of Columbia: A Nationwide Comparison,* annual.

No. 442. Residential Property Tax Rates in Selected Cities: 1999

[Effective tax rate is amount each jurisdiction considers based upon assessment level used. Assessment level is ratio of assessed value to assumed market value. Nominal rate is announced rates it levied at taxable value of house]

City	Effective tax rate per $100		Assessment level (percent)	Nominal rate per $100	City	Effective tax rate per $100		Assessment level (percent)	Nominal rate per $100
	Rank	Rate				Rank	Rate		
Bridgeport, CT	1	4.55	70.0	6.50	Memphis, TN	28	1.43	15.0	9.50
Newark, NJ.	2	3.60	14.7	24.53	Houston, TX	29	1.42	4.0	35.45
Manchester, NH.	3	3.34	100.0	3.34	Wilmington, DE	30	1.34	100.0	1.34
Milwaukee, WI.	4	3.12	101.0	3.09	Boston, MA	31	1.33	100.0	1.33
Philadelphia, PA	5	2.84	100.0	2.84	Minneapolis, MN	32	1.30	11.5	11.30
Portland, ME	6	2.65	93.3	2.84	Billings, MT.	33	1.29	88.3	1.46
Des Moines, IA	7	2.64	32.0	8.26	Little Rock, AR	34	1.18	89.9	1.31
Baltimore, MD	8	2.53	100.0	2.53	Wichita, KS.	35	1.15	18.3	6.30
Sioux Falls, SD	9	2.52	56.5	4.46	Albuquerque, NM. . . .	36	1.13	94.1	1.20
Detroit, MI	10	2.37	85.0	2.79	Seattle, WA	37	1.12	11.0	10.21
Jacksonville, FL.	11	2.33	40.0	5.82	Oklahoma City, OK . . .	37	1.12	91.7	1.22
Providence, RI	12	2.13	100.0	2.13	Louisville, KY	39	1.11	33.0	3.37
Omaha, NE	13	2.03	92.3	2.20	Virginia Beach, VA . . .	40	1.11	19.0	5.83
Fargo, ND	14	2.02	4.1	49.32	Las Vegas, NV	41	1.09	35.0	3.11
Atlanta, GA.	15	1.96	34.5	5.68	Charlotte, NC	42	1.02	44.4	2.30
Burlington, VT.	16	1.93	40.0	4.83	Jackson, MS.	43	0.96	100.0	0.96
Boise City, ID	17	1.83	96.0	1.91	Washington, DC	44	0.95	10.0	9.45
Anchorage, AK	18	1.77	98.1	1.81	Charleston, WV	45	0.91	60.0	1.51
New Orleans, LA. . . .	19	1.72	95.0	1.82	New York City, NY . . .	46	0.83	7.6	10.88
Columbus, OH	19	1.72	81.3	2.12	Los Angeles, CA	47	0.80	75.0	1.06
Phoenix, AZ	21	1.70	10.0	17.00	Birmingham, AL.	48	0.77	10.0	7.72
Indianapolis, IN	22	1.70	10.0	16.97	Denver, CO	49	0.73	9.5	7.73
Portland, OR.	23	1.68	10.0	16.76	Cheyenne, WY	50	0.67	9.7	6.89
Kansas City, MO	24	1.67	29.7	5.63	Honolulu, HI	51	0.37	100.0	0.37
Columbia, SC	25	1.58	25.0	6.31					
Chicago, IL.	26	1.55	76.4	2.03	Unweighted average .	(X)	1.69	55.5	6.80
Salt Lake City, UT . . .	27	1.48	99.0	1.49	Median	(X)	1.55	(X)	(X)

X Not applicable.

Source: Government of the District of Columbia, Department of Finance and Revenue, *Tax Rates and Tax Burdens in the District of Columbia: A Nationwide Comparison,* annual.

No. 443. Gross Revenue From Parimutuel and Amusement Taxes and Lotteries by State: 1999

[In millions of dollars (37,532 represents $37,532,000,000). For fiscal years; see text, this section]

State	Gross revenue (mil. dol.)	Amusement taxes [1]	Parimutuel taxes	Lottery revenue Total [2] (mil. dol.)	Apportionment of funds (percent) Prizes	Administration	Proceeds available from ticket sales
United States ...	37,532	3,292	382	33,858	19,581	2,010	12,266
Alabama	4	-	4	(X)	(X)	(X)	(X)
Alaska	2	2	(X)	(X)	(X)	(X)	(X)
Arizona	254	1	3	251	144	27	80
Arkansas	6	-	6	(X)	(X)	(X)	(X)
California	2,392	(X)	64	2,328	1,307	165	856
Colorado	420	73	6	341	225	33	83
Connecticut	1,175	291	11	873	517	81	275
Delaware	332	(X)	-	332	75	6	251
Florida	2,036	(X)	51	1,985	1,057	129	800
Georgia	1,816	(X)	(X)	1,816	1,060	112	645
Hawaii	(X)	(X)	(X)	(X)	(X)	(X)	(X)
Idaho	90	(X)	(X)	90	52	17	21
Illinois	1,788	375	37	1,376	813	64	499
Indiana	622	(X)	4	618	384	30	204
Iowa	320	154	3	163	102	23	38
Kansas	185	1	4	180	107	21	52
Kentucky	574	-	27	547	349	34	164
Louisiana	739	462	5	272	149	18	105
Maine	142	(X)	5	137	81	15	41
Maryland	1,091	10	1	1,080	582	106	392
Massachusetts	3,032	7	8	3,018	2,205	64	749
Michigan	1,609	(X)	13	1,596	924	51	621
Minnesota	427	63	1	363	235	69	59
Mississippi	187	187	(X)	(X)	(X)	(X)	(X)
Missouri	647	165	(X)	483	282	40	160
Montana	29	(X)	-	28	15	6	7
Nebraska	79	6	1	72	39	16	17
Nevada	634	634	(X)	(X)	(X)	(X)	(X)
New Hampshire	192	2	4	186	116	6	63
New Jersey	1,894	326	-	1,568	869	49	650
New Mexico	93	3	1	89	47	22	20
New York	3,416	1	37	3,378	1,872	98	1,409
North Carolina	(X)	(X)	(X)	(X)	(X)	(X)	(X)
North Dakota	11	11	(X)	(X)	(X)	(X)	(X)
Ohio	2,167	(X)	17	2,150	1,260	75	816
Oklahoma	13	8	4	(X)	(X)	(X)	(X)
Oregon	1,529	-	1	1,528	756	214	558
Pennsylvania	1,579	1	30	1,548	869	59	620
Rhode Island	646	(X)	6	640	504	6	131
South Carolina	35	35	(X)	(X)	(X)	(X)	(X)
South Dakota	122	-	2	120	15	7	98
Tennessee	(X)	(X)	(X)	(X)	(X)	(X)	(X)
Texas	2,608	23	13	2,572	1,329	101	1,142
Utah	(X)	(X)	(X)	(X)	(X)	(X)	(X)
Vermont	70	(X)	-	70	42	8	20
Virginia	925	-	(X)	925	552	117	257
Washington	475	-	2	473	296	63	114
West Virginia	264	(X)	8	256	113	25	117
Wisconsin	406	1	3	402	237	31	135
Wyoming	-	(X)	-	(X)	(X)	(X)	(X)

- Represents or rounds to zero.   X Not applicable.   [1] Represents nonlicense taxes.   [2] Excludes commissions.

Source: U.S. Census Bureau, unpublished data; <http://www.census.gov/govs/state/99lottery.html>.

No. 444. Lottery Sales—Type of Game: 1980 to 2000

[In millions of dollars (2,393 represents $2,393,000,000). For fiscal years]

Game	1980	1985	1990	1995	1997	1998	1999	2000
Total ticket sales	2,393	9,035	20,017	31,931	35,486	35,588	35,966	37,201
Passive [1]	206	88	(NA)	(NA)	(NA)	(NA)	(NA)	(NA)
Instant [2]	527	1,296	5,204	11,511	14,217	13,882	13,933	15,459
Three-digit [3]	1,554	3,376	4,572	5,737	5,639	5,643	5,237	5,341
Four-digit [3]	55	693	1,302	1,941	2,111	2,232	2,655	2,711
Lotto [4]	52	3,583	8,563	10,594	9,996	9,854	9,794	9,160
Other [5]	(NA)	(NA)	409	2,148	3,523	3,978	4,347	4,530
State proceeds (net income) [6]	978	3,735	7,703	11,100	11,959	12,102	11,255	11,404

NA Not available.   [1] Also known as draw game or ticket. Player must match his ticket to winning numbers drawn by lottery. Players cannot choose their numbers.   [2] Player scratches a latex section on ticket which reveals instantly whether ticket is a winner.   [3] Players choose and bet on three or four digits, depending on game, with various payoffs for different straight order or mixed combination bets.   [4] Players typically select six digits out of a large field of numbers. Varying prizes are offered for matching three through six numbers drawn by lottery.   [5] Includes break-open tickets, spiel, keno, video lottery, etc.   [6] Sales minus prizes and expenses equal net government income.

Source: TLF Publications, Inc., Boyds, MD, 2000 World Lottery Almanac annual; LaFleur's Fiscal 2000 Lottery Special Report; (copyright).

State and Local Government Finances and Employment   289

[In millions of dollars (60,056 represents $60,056,000,000). For fiscal years ending in year shown; see text, this section. Cities ranked by size of population estimated as of July 1, 1998, except Honolulu ranked by county population. Data reflect inclusion of fiscal activity of dependent school systems where applicable]

Cities ranked by 1998 population	Total revenue	General revenue — Total	Intergovernmental — Total	Intergov. — From federal government	Intergov. — From state/local government	Intergov. — From local government	Own sources — Total	Taxes — Total	Taxes — Property	Sales and gross receipts — Total	Sales — General sales	Sales — Public utilities	Current charges — Total	Current charges — Parks and recreation	Current charges — Sewerage[1]	Miscellaneous — Total	Miscellaneous — Interest earnings	Utility revenue[2]	Employee retirement revenue
New York City, NY [3]	60,056	44,918	17,230	2,321	14,793	116	27,688	20,542	7,327	4,051	3,069	303	5,026	41	876	2,120	733	2,718	12,420
Los Angeles, CA	9,731	4,783	873	360	418	94	3,909	2,078	712	916	297	527	1,321	72	414	510	319	2,700	2,249
Chicago, IL	5,472	4,336	1,252	349	902	-	3,084	1,812	650	977	163	422	782	-	125	490	301	281	856
Houston, TX	2,658	1,815	156	118	36	3	1,659	957	467	457	292	126	516	20	274	187	112	289	573
Philadelphia, PA [3]	5,348	3,976	1,615	406	1,079	130	2,361	1,766	333	154	97	-	452	12	192	143	102	655	716
San Diego, CA	1,969	1,477	401	205	111	86	1,076	502	143	300	165	41	259	38	137	143	143	204	287
Phoenix, AZ	1,806	1,447	466	134	297	35	981	463	129	304	203	60	370	22	64	147	86	162	196
San Antonio, TX	1,909	800	125	32	80	13	675	333	162	158	108	16	215	23	94	127	95	1,060	49
Dallas, TX	1,814	1,484	137	109	26	2	1,347	604	310	280	173	79	540	32	145	203	144	160	170
Detroit, MI	3,485	2,019	878	263	576	39	1,141	677	266	45	-	45	285	19	206	179	76	204	1,262
Honolulu, HI [3]	1,156	1,025	181	108	72	1	844	517	404	66	-	21	220	16	113	107	56	130	-
San Jose, CA	1,342	1,024	124	25	64	35	900	515	137	228	121	90	270	17	93	115	56	14	303
Indianapolis, IN [3]	1,301	1,263	283	53	223	7	980	591	479	32	-	-	281	18	34	108	56	7	30
San Francisco, CA [3]	5,299	3,823	1,427	151	1,271	5	2,396	1,281	504	448	231	65	824	40	141	291	174	277	1,199
Jacksonville, FL [3]	1,966	907	101	34	66	1	807	430	238	178	98	69	173	4	49	204	169	816	243
Baltimore, MD [3]	2,646	1,992	1,064	45	951	69	928	703	467	42	-	24	119	8	61	105	63	64	591
Columbus, OH	956	826	132	52	72	8	694	405	28	10	-	-	215	6	132	74	38	130	-
El Paso, TX	558	367	43	29	11	-	324	180	98	77	-	14	99	4	32	44	29	54	137
Memphis, TN	2,473	1,226	795	23	436	335	431	233	184	37	59	14	133	55	38	65	33	1,007	241
Milwaukee, WI	1,082	709	379	73	305	1	330	168	158	-	-	-	100	1	35	61	37	53	320
Boston, MA [3]	2,275	2,015	906	80	825	2	1,109	835	774	35	-	-	172	-	103	102	32	93	166
Washington, DC [3]	5,300	4,998	1,393	1,341	-	51	3,605	2,889	695	934	557	198	372	29	100	344	113	61	139
Austin, TX	1,471	595	84	52	31	1	511	267	136	118	88	15	202	15	91	42	20	683	193
Seattle, WA	1,577	966	130	46	79	5	836	497	167	202	107	82	265	40	119	74	32	440	171
Nashville-Davidson, TN [3]	2,229	1,437	310	14	296	-	1,127	749	426	249	217	8	230	10	79	148	123	738	55
Cleveland, OH	1,019	738	180	92	88	-	558	361	64	19	-	-	121	5	17	76	35	280	-
Denver, CO [3]	1,753	1,487	200	25	176	-	1,286	536	139	339	299	15	619	38	60	131	84	128	138
Portland, OR	738	674	97	31	34	32	577	336	212	44	-	33	150	11	101	91	48	63	-
Fort Worth, TX	670	423	40	-	40	-	383	242	138	72	67	-	89	4	46	52	30	106	-
New Orleans, LA	889	769	161	64	97	-	608	339	155	165	107	35	176	7	39	93	45	53	141
Oklahoma City, OK	608	551	64	39	25	10	487	303	30	267	244	20	133	11	40	50	33	51	66
Tucson, AZ	629	474	192	53	129	61	282	192	31	151	129	16	58	11	-	32	18	87	6
Charlotte, NC	731	661	149	29	59	9	512	237	184	27	-	3	181	23	76	95	74	30	67
Kansas City, MO [3]	998	715	86	59	18	-	629	426	69	196	87	68	128	11	41	76	55	66	40
Virginia Beach, VA [3]	990	945	352	16	334	1	593	469	316	116	35	38	74	15	36	50	37	45	218

- Represents or rounds to zero. [1] Includes solid waste management. [2] Includes water, electric, and transit. [3] Represents, in effect, city-county consolidated government.

Source: U.S. Census Bureau, Government Finances, 1997-98. See also <http://www.census.gov/govs/estimate/98allpub.pdf> (issued September 2001).

No. 446. City Governments—Expenditures and Debt for Largest Cities: 1998

[In millions of dollars (51,850 represents $51,850,000,000). For fiscal year ending in year shown; see headnote; see text, this section. Regarding intercity comparisons, see text, this section]

Cities ranked by 1998 population	Total expenditure	Total direct expenditure	General expenditure: Total	Education	Housing and community development	Public welfare	Health and hospitals	Police protection	Fire protection	Correction	Highways	Parks and recreation	Sewerage	Solid waste management	Governmental administration [1]	Interest on general debt	Utility expenditure [2]	Employee retirement expenditure	Debt outstanding total
New York City, NY [3]	51,850	48,110	42,041	10,110	2,255	7,764	4,146	2,743	1,053	1,210	1,261	500	1,005	785	823	2,337	4,700	5,108	50,305
Los Angeles, CA	8,010	7,954	4,879	13	235	-	31	886	342	1	131	219	399	151	286	372	2,235	896	9,225
Chicago, IL	5,053	5,018	4,084	1	177	136	128	972	272	-	372	53	109	183	133	501	319	651	8,783
Houston, TX	2,616	2,602	2,066	-	59	-	83	398	205	22	213	114	355	51	84	184	424	125	5,600
Philadelphia, PA [3]	4,879	4,756	3,786	18	160	319	693	412	143	231	90	101	180	93	296	129	706	387	3,961
San Diego, CA	1,801	1,794	1,466	-	110	-	1	224	93	-	51	101	350	71	64	197	247	88	3,131
Phoenix, AZ	1,730	1,722	1,415	14	79	-	-	231	118	-	93	120	184	53	91	62	276	39	4,652
San Antonio, TX.	1,822	1,818	858	28	16	34	36	152	90	-	70	95	127	37	30	80	935	28	3,679
Dallas, TX.	1,590	1,559	1,273	-	31	1	22	201	91	5	81	113	188	35	61	80	192	124	2,642
Detroit, MI. [3]	2,890	2,811	1,926	7	110	-	104	304	101	-	206	115	83	117	200	121	391	573	2,642
Honolulu, HI. [3]	1,207	1,207	996	-	80	-	11	140	53	-	43	73	95	82	94	73	211	-	1,684
San Jose, CA	1,049	1,037	886	-	115	-	-	144	70	-	56	84	94	60	58	145	86	76	1,611
Indianapolis, IN [3]	1,376	1,366	1,037	1	92	46	293	109	45	-	88	52	77	29	112	264	45	39	2,357
San Francisco, CA [3]	4,924	4,761	4,013	103	99	403	787	285	163	45	123	193	95	19	242	208	593	319	5,863
Jacksonville, FL [3]	1,846	1,767	1,102	-	16	12	42	121	72	85	34	67	99	87	61	61	670	74	4,570
Baltimore, MD [3]	2,082	2,079	1,844	712	68	2	80	209	105	41	112	55	99	38	114	28	72	165	1,329
Columbus, OH	918	903	780	-	25	-	35	162	105	-	58	51	38	12	52	28	138	-	1,451
El Paso, TX.	500	497	375	-	11	-	22	81	36	8	23	27	38	38	28	27	92	33	655
Memphis, TN.	2,375	2,357	1,288	653	25	-	8	144	80	-	45	86	64	38	22	47	993	114	872
Milwaukee, WI.	867	836	700	-	72	-	17	156	73	-	74	5	110	37	42	233	34	134	504
Boston, MA	2,194	1,967	1,924	652	89	105	79	204	113	78	74	28	132	32	51	75	34	236	1,152
Washington, DC [3]	5,243	5,074	4,623	755	126	1,188	442	283	112	303	145	73	41	24	284	34	121	432	4,545
Austin, TX.	1,169	1,169	569	-	14	7	59	79	53	-	20	38	110	77	45	127	549	51	4,281
Seattle, WA.	1,598	1,470	1,054	-	65	-	16	129	77	15	140	150	72	45	83	35	460	73	1,806
Nashville-Davidson, TN [3]	2,345	2,345	1,470	455	-	22	121	104	67	40	37	166	18	27	76	327	792	83	2,917
Cleveland, OH [3]	1,065	1,061	762	-	70	-	40	151	69	-	58	53	50	28	91	20	303	-	1,873
Denver, CO [3]	1,540	1,482	1,399	-	28	179	21	120	62	6	70	83	160	2	103	63	90	52	1,238
Portland, OR.	814	811	673	-	40	-	-	93	53	-	72	71	31	18	47	32	77	64	906
Fort Worth, TX.	538	536	401	-	11	-	10	92	43	-	55	35	63	20	41	20	89	45	1,198
New Orleans, LA	876	876	740	-	78	2	28	106	42	46	21	20	37	26	70	63	87	49	759
Oklahoma City, OK.	588	588	526	-	28	-	-	89	79	-	47	98	-	53	26	32	54	8	751
Tucson, AZ	600	600	425	-	35	5	1	70	34	-	43	24	-	25	53	76	159	15	1,292
Charlotte, NC	697	686	527	-	21	1	-	98	44	28	43	74	30	28	16	56	160	10	1,093
Kansas City, MO [3]	843	819	717	-	53	-	63	124	55	5	43	74	47	20	49	56	69	57	837
Virginia Beach, VA [3]	998	998	920	462	7	20	27	53	24	16	22	38	28	22	28	43	78	-	-

- Represents or rounds to zero.   [1] Excludes public buildings.   [2] Includes water, electric, and transit.   [3] Represents, in effect, city-county consolidated government.

Source: U.S. Census Bureau, unpublished data.

No. 447. County Governments—Revenue for Largest Counties: 1997

[In millions of dollars (14,216 represents $14,216,000,000). For fiscal year ending in year shown; see text, this section]

Counties ranked by 1997 population	Total revenue [1]	General revenue — Total [1]	Intergovernmental — Total	From federal government — Total [1]	From federal — Housing and community development	From state government — Total	From state — Public welfare	From state — Health and hospitals	From local govt.	General revenue from own sources — Total	Taxes — Total [1]	Taxes — Property	Sales and gross receipts — Total	Sales and gross receipts — General sales	Current charges — Total	Current charges — Parks and recreation	Current charges — Sewerage [1]	Current charges — Hospitals [1]	Miscellaneous general revenue — Total	Miscellaneous — Interest earnings
Los Angeles, CA	14,218	11,538	8,140	241	207	7,680	4,287	1,187	219	3,398	1,825	1,661	96	43	839	84	39	396	734	237
Cook, IL	2,447	2,058	385	18	18	365	163	52	2	1,673	1,216	781	422	272	357	30	–	194	99	65
Harris, TX	1,592	1,592	325	42	–	227	126	214	55	1,268	757	702	20	–	254	3	56	73	257	228
San Diego, CA	2,341	2,285	1,684	76	57	1,521	830	185	87	602	339	280	25	21	162	2	85	–	101	29
Orange, CA	2,637	2,255	1,241	28	20	1,142	418	11	70	1,014	293	223	48	46	281	12	3	–	440	204
Maricopa, AZ	1,573	1,573	923	57	15	842	354	331	24	650	318	305	–	–	229	7	–	143	102	71
Wayne, MI	1,487	1,411	762	97	5	583	94	–	82	648	246	240	–	–	286	2	63	–	117	33
Metropolitan Dade, FL [2]	4,233	4,015	725	278	87	441	1	60	6	3,290	1,168	784	324	77	1,664	19	418	608	457	266
Dallas, TX	984	967	226	2	–	202	86	123	22	742	365	329	3	–	313	–	–	247	63	49
King, WA	1,622	1,557	366	37	12	222	–	73	107	1,191	773	382	293	240	320	16	240	–	98	65
Santa Clara, CA	1,716	1,716	1,136	32	6	1,065	605	123	39	580	338	305	4	3	152	2	11	89	90	49
San Bernardino, CA	1,914	1,732	1,275	76	15	1,146	712	5	54	457	198	171	18	14	155	8	–	38	104	60
Broward, FL	1,256	1,220	175	40	9	130	–	110	5	1,045	519	427	66	–	366	14	44	–	160	121
Riverside, CA	1,602	1,602	1,099	30	11	984	530	–	86	502	233	196	21	17	117	3	130	30	152	70
Middlesex, MA	125	64	38	–	–	33	–	148	3	28	12	–	–	–	11	–	33	5	5	84
Cuyahoga, OH	1,234	1,234	529	9	7	515	255	39	5	705	389	216	140	131	218	3	–	195	98	44
Suffolk, NY	1,763	1,679	474	18	–	431	211	163	25	1,205	1,010	399	595	593	123	7	3	–	72	34
Alameda, CA	1,846	1,498	964	18	4	894	563	28	43	544	313	191	104	98	128	7	16	38	103	110
Bexar, TX	681	680	171	4	2	154	114	54	13	509	237	217	6	–	155	3	–	137	117	64
Tarrant, TX	577	577	169	11	–	145	57	57	13	408	252	229	–	–	84	20	–	56	72	48
Nassau, NY	2,443	2,443	654	50	25	604	292	103	–	1,789	1,352	669	680	670	324	6	9	183	113	23
Allegheny, PA	1,082	1,011	551	27	21	523	125	219	160	460	239	227	10	–	175	10	–	18	46	31
Oakland, MI	773	708	433	8	7	265	25	125	29	275	178	165	1	–	53	–	10	2	44	23
Sacramento, CA	1,956	1,737	910	27	22	853	485	108	14	827	333	179	–	–	319	16	155	–	175	100
Hennepin, MN	1,194	1,194	452	31	7	407	247	98	57	742	366	363	117	96	294	6	51	207	82	50
Clark, NV	1,910	1,697	372	54	4	280	–	53	25	1,325	578	212	–	–	576	3	58	270	171	137
Franklin, OH	650	648	305	3	–	276	92	3	4	343	259	175	236	82	33	–	2	–	51	41
St. Louis, MO	504	478	52	14	–	33	6	97	–	426	351	72	71	63	28	3	–	–	47	35
Palm Beach, FL	1,051	1,019	130	33	14	96	–	3	–	890	435	313	272	233	285	25	145	187	170	84
Erie, NY	1,278	1,239	316	–	–	298	208	3	12	923	543	216	106	–	300	1	4	40	80	40
Milwaukee, WI	1,069	871	481	105	12	369	136	26	7	390	207	159	318	313	150	15	–	–	33	8
Fairfax, VA	2,817	2,342	429	64	33	358	31	103	7	1,913	1,520	1,207	46	46	292	–	181	–	101	84
Hillsborough, FL	1,352	1,270	253	52	16	201	62	16	–	1,017	407	305	188	111	438	15	43	217	172	94
Westchester, NY	1,659	1,653	404	25	–	360	223	60	19	1,248	703	454	246	239	500	20	11	347	46	33

- Represents or rounds to zero.   [1] Includes solid waste management.   [2] Represents, in effect, city-county consolidated government.

Source: U.S. Census Bureau, 1997 Finances of County Government Series, (GC97(4)-3, quinquennial, and unpublished data.

No. 448. County Governments—Expenditures, and Debt for Largest Counties: 1997

[In millions of dollars (12,630 represents $12,630,000,000). For fiscal year ending in year shown; see text, this section. See headnote, Table 447]

Counties ranked by 1997 population	Total expenditure	Total direct expenditure	General expenditure Total	Education	Housing and community development	Public welfare	Health	Hospitals	Police protection	Correction	Governmental administration	General public buildings	Highways	Parks and recreation	Natural resources	Sewerage and solid waste management	Interest on general debt	Utility expenditure	Employee retirement expenditure[1]	Debt outstanding
Los Angeles, CA	12,630	11,930	11,704	443	244	4,095	846	1,443	1,085	642	1,100	91	164	217	151	197	425	39	887	6,098
Cook, IL	2,065	2,049	1,922	1	15	19	32	649	58	279	416	50	89	88	39	39	97		143	1,796
Harris, TX	1,629	1,629	1,629		19	22	101	434	125	178	199	28	137	30	7	198	259	9	98	5,559
San Diego, CA	2,508	2,450	2,401	105	60	801	275		105	175	371	4	63	12	53	119	62			1,110
Orange, CA	2,182	2,116	2,072	102	20	523	183	182	130	131	345	22	66	63	50	57	251		110	3,764
Maricopa, AZ	1,583	1,358	1,358	20	19	521	38	84	62	92	192		70	164	120	227	66			1,040
Wayne, MI	1,491	1,362	1,411		6	106	294		25	145	160	8	96	25			57		80	985
Metropolitan Dade, FL	4,442	4,438	4,007		205	65		710	326	190	240		105	98	19	569	336	435	5	6,460
Dallas, TX	942	938	937		5	13	98	422	23	170	108	19	12	64	34	255	43	340		719
King, WA	1,694	1,662	1,353		14	5	217	66	69	71	247	15	100	38	2	16	141			2,053
Santa Clara, CA	1,896	1,787	1,896	111	6	493	169	286	44	186	270	39	53	13	31	96	53	6	80	827
San Bernardino, CA	1,962	1,867	1,876	111	16	656	110	294	119	90	155	5	32	46	10	137	54	111		1,260
Broward, FL	1,203	1,159	1,092		15	27	78		124	96	113	21	39	6	77	104	134	2		2,484
Riverside, CA	1,570	1,451	1,568	125	33	466	105	106	110	110	174	15	60				75		47	1,284
Middlesex, MA	107	107	60					7		40	5									4
Cuyahoga, OH	1,179	1,171	1,179	219	9	228	206	334	16	65	128	33	34	12	4	12	85	131		1,750
Suffolk, NY	1,841	1,617	1,710	28	4	350	132		339	70	92		32	51	84	51	68			1,563
Alameda, CA	1,783	1,681	1,672		9	471	187	202	37	119	184	3	37	154	7	84	69		110	746
Bexar, TX	650	604	649		2	49	35	289	18	58	58	1	15	4		7	98		1	1,188
Tarrant, TX	550	549	550		10	11	66	205	13	60	70	10	76	54	3		56			935
Nassau, NY	2,812	2,517	2,795	288	25	440	111	285	452	150	108	180	22	61		129	140	17	43	2,843
Allegheny, PA	1,056	961	1,013	27	24	126	177	96	23	59	100	10	96	9	42	129	86		18	1,430
Oakland, MI	691	681	657		7	3	160	7	29	98	85	10	110	21	5	172	30	16	75	2,383
Sacramento, CA	1,780	1,749	1,695	64	102	518	129		74	68	173	23	57	121	30	61	117	10		531
Hennepin, MN	1,136	1,133	1,136		6	187	184	282	48	78	100		203	17		70	23	352		3,830
Clark, NV	2,122	2,111	1,770		10	49	211	281	172	50	123	1	37	24		4	145		1	552
Franklin, OH	662	638	661		5	150			16	26	79	37	35	37		2	36			399
St Louis, MO	506	338	498		14		29		41	65	92	44	38	106	36	163	23		8	1,606
Palm Beach, FL	1,102	1,072	1,025		12	22	27	182	124	46	154	12	81	55		31	106	77		481
Erie, NY	1,255	986	1,220	68	4	489	43	97	29	67	42	14	24	39			30	35		565
Milwaukee, WI	948	948	742		6		35		18	30	71	20	51		9	202	138	129		2,554
Fairfax, VA	2,720	2,679	2,470	1,161		211	114		114	30	62	13	68		40	82	110	77	126	2,313
Hillsborough, FL	1,329	1,319	1,236		50	145	36	303	97	55	57		27	33		118	80	93		709
Westchester, NY	1,728	1,520	1,695	68	19	59	75	352	17	86	97	28	29		14	35	43	33	80	812
Contra Costa, CA	1,183	1,174	1,102	47	52	430	118	202	43	57	109	1	55	16	11	65	52	37		860
Pinellas, FL	625	595	588		8	11	55		64	43	106									

- Represents or rounds to zero.   [1] Includes water, electric, and transit.

Source: U.S. Census Bureau. 1997 Finances of County Government. Series (GC97(4)-3. quinquennial. and unpublished data

No. 449. Governmental Employment and Payrolls: 1980 to 1999

[Employees in thousands (16,213 represents 16,213,000), payroll in millions of dollars (19,935 represents $19,935,000,000). For 1980 to 1995 as of October; later years as of March. 1996 data are not available. Covers both full-time and part-time employees. Local government data are estimates subject to sampling variation; see Appendix III and source]

Type of government	1980	1985	1990	1992	1993	1994	1995	1997	1998	1999
EMPLOYEES (1,000)										
Total	16,213	16,690	18,369	18,745	18,823	19,420	19,521	19,540	19,854	20,306
Federal (civilian) [1]	2,898	3,021	3,105	3,047	2,999	2,952	2,895	2,807	2,765	2,799
State and local	13,315	13,669	15,263	15,698	15,824	16,468	16,626	16,733	17,089	17,506
Percent of total	82	82	83	84	84	85	85	86	86	86
State	3,753	3,984	4,503	4,595	4,673	4,694	4,719	4,733	4,758	4,818
Local	9,562	9,685	10,760	11,103	11,151	11,775	11,906	12,000	12,271	12,689
Counties	1,853	1,891	2,167	2,253	2,253	(NA)	(NA)	2,425	(NA)	(NA)
Municipalities	2,561	2,467	2,642	2,665	2,644	(NA)	(NA)	2,755	(NA)	(NA)
School districts	4,270	4,416	4,950	5,134	(NA)	(NA)	(NA)	455	(NA)	(NA)
Townships	394	392	418	424	(NA)	(NA)	(NA)	5,675	(NA)	(NA)
Special districts	484	519	585	627	(NA)	(NA)	(NA)	691	(NA)	(NA)
OCTOBER PAYROLLS (mil. dol.)										
Total	19,935	28,945	39,228	43,120	(NA)	(NA)	(NA)	49,156	51,568	54,363
Federal (civilian) [1]	5,205	7,580	8,999	9,937	(NA)	(NA)	(NA)	9,744	10,115	10,478
State and local	14,730	21,365	30,229	33,183	34,540	36,545	37,714	39,412	41,453	43,886
Percent of total	74	74	77	77	(NA)	(NA)	(NA)	80	80	81
State	4,285	6,329	9,083	9,828	10,288	10,666	10,927	11,413	11,845	12,565
Local	10,445	15,036	21,146	23,355	24,252	25,878	26,787	27,999	29,608	31,321
Counties	1,936	2,819	4,192	4,698	4,839	(NA)	(NA)	5,750	(NA)	(NA)
Municipalities	2,951	4,191	5,564	6,207	6,328	(NA)	(NA)	7,146	(NA)	(NA)
School districts	4,683	6,746	9,551	10,394	(NA)	(NA)	(NA)	869	(NA)	(NA)
Townships	330	446	642	685	(NA)	(NA)	(NA)	12,579	(NA)	(NA)
Special districts	546	834	1,197	1,370	(NA)	(NA)	(NA)	1,654	(NA)	(NA)

NA Not available. [1] Includes employees outside the United States.

Source: U.S. Census Bureau, *Historical Statistics on Governmental Finances and Employment*, and *Public Employment*, series GE, No. 1, annual; <http://www.census.gov/govs/www/apes.html> (accessed 20 July 2001).

No. 450. All Governments—Employment and Payroll by Function: 1999

[Employees in thousands (20,306 represents 20,306,000), payroll in millions of dollars (54,365 represents $54,365,000,000). As of March 1999. Covers full-time and part-time employees. Local government data are estimates subject to sampling variation; see Appendix III and source]

Function	Employees (1,000)					October payrolls (mil. dol.)				
	Total	Federal (civilian) [1]	State and local			Total	Federal (civilian) [1]	State and local		
			Total	State	Local			Total	State	Local
Total	20,306	2,799	17,506	4,818	12,689	54,363	10,478	43,886	12,565	31,321
National defense [2]	713	713	(X)	(X)	(X)	2,459	2,459	(X)	(X)	(X)
Postal Service	876	876	(X)	(X)	(X)	2,936	2,936	(X)	(X)	(X)
Space research and technology	19	19	(X)	(X)	(X)	106	106	(X)	(X)	(X)
Elem. and secondary educ.	6,788	(X)	6,788	55	6,733	16,468	(X)	16,468	144	16,323
Higher education	2,589	(X)	2,589	2,065	524	5,459	(X)	5,459	4,512	948
Other education	121	11	110	110	(X)	350	49	301	301	(X)
Health	569	135	434	175	259	1,723	598	1,124	508	616
Hospitals	1,175	156	1,019	435	584	3,217	555	2,662	1,163	1,499
Public welfare	521	9	512	229	283	1,325	43	1,283	611	671
Social insurance administration	162	67	96	96	(X)	568	283	285	285	(X)
Police protection	1,018	104	914	100	814	3,520	514	3,006	351	2,655
Fire protection	376	(X)	376	(X)	376	1,103	(X)	1,103	(X)	1,103
Correction	715	31	684	457	228	2,101	118	1,982	1,326	657
Streets & highways	569	3	566	251	315	1,579	17	1,562	750	812
Air transportation	91	50	41	3	38	442	309	133	11	122
Water transport/terminals	27	14	13	5	8	86	43	43	16	27
Solid waste management	117	(X)	117	2	115	298	(X)	298	7	291
Sewerage	130	(X)	130	1	128	381	(X)	381	6	375
Parks & recreation	367	25	342	38	304	642	86	556	79	477
Natural resources	391	184	207	164	43	1,298	767	531	434	97
Housing & community dev.	141	17	125	-	125	414	79	335	-	335
Water supply	169	-	169	1	169	467	-	467	3	463
Electric power	79	-	79	6	74	310	-	310	29	280
Gas supply	11	-	11	-	11	30	-	30	-	30
Transit	210	(X)	210	29	181	752	(X)	752	118	634
Libraries	171	4	167	1	166	282	20	262	1	261
State liquor stores	8	(X)	8	8	(X)	16	(X)	16	16	(X)
Financial administration	549	137	412	169	244	1,594	516	1,078	494	584
Other government administration	463	22	441	60	381	870	86	784	173	611
Judicial and legal	455	56	399	148	250	1,540	280	1,260	535	725
Other & unallocable	716	166	549	212	337	2,026	611	1,415	692	723

- Represents or rounds to zero. X Not applicable. [1] Includes employees outside the United States. [2] Includes international relations.

Source: U.S. Census Bureau, <http://www.census.gov/pub/govs/www/apes.html> (accessed 05 August 2001).

No. 451. State and Local Government—Employer Costs Per Hour Worked: 2000

[In dollars. As of March. Based on a sample. see source for details. For additional data. see Table 626]

Occupation and industry	Total compensation	Wages and salaries	Benefits Total	Paid leave	Supplemental pay	Insurance	Retirement and savings	Legally required benefits	Other [1]
Total workers	**$29.05**	**$20.57**	**$8.48**	**$2.26**	**$0.25**	**$2.38**	**$1.84**	**$1.70**	**$0.05**
Occupational group:									
White-collar occupations	32.17	23.36	8.81	2.33	0.14	2.51	1.96	1.82	0.05
Prof. specialty & technical	38.15	28.48	9.67	2.3	0.15	2.68	2.37	2.1	0.07
Professional specialty	39.41	29.55	9.86	2.31	0.13	2.75	2.46	2.13	0.07
Teachers	42.18	32.02	10.16	2.18	0.07	2.9	2.74	2.2	0.09
Technical	24.76	17.08	7.68	2.25	0.4	1.92	1.38	1.7	0.04
Executive, admin., & managerial	36.2	25.44	10.76	3.64	0.18	2.6	2.23	2.07	0.03
Admin. support including clerical	18.52	12.38	6.14	1.7	0.1	2.14	1.04	1.14	0.03
Blue-collar occupations	22.78	15.05	7.72	2.18	0.36	2.28	1.31	1.57	0.03
Service occupations	22.05	14.29	7.76	2.06	0.53	2.01	1.73	1.38	0.06
Industry group:									
Services	30.61	22.37	8.25	2.04	0.16	2.44	1.84	1.73	0.05
Health services	23.74	16.03	7.7	2.4	0.6	1.91	1.08	1.68	0.04
Hospitals	24.31	16.42	7.88	2.47	0.59	1.96	1.11	1.71	0.04
Educational services	31.86	23.54	8.32	1.97	0.09	2.5	1.96	1.74	0.06
Elementary and secondary education	31.23	23.13	8.1	1.77	0.07	2.62	1.91	1.66	0.07
Higher education	34.18	25.17	9	2.52	0.17	2.18	2.14	1.98	(Z)
Public administration	26.26	17.47	8.79	2.65	0.38	2.25	1.88	1.59	0.05

Z Cost per hour worked is less than one cent. [1] Includes severance pay and supplemental unemployment benefits.
Source: U.S. Bureau of Labor Statistics, *Compensation and Working Conditions, Fall 2000.*

No. 452. State and Local Governments—Full-Time Employment and Salary by Sex, and Race/Ethnic Group: 1973 to 1997

[As of June 30. (3,809 represents 3,809,000). Excludes school systems and educational institutions. Based on reports from state governments (44 in 1973; 48 in 1975, 1976, and 1979; 47 in 1977 and 1983; 45 in 1978; 42 in 1980; 49 in 1981 and 1984 through 1987; and 50 in 1989 through 1991) and a sample of county, municipal, township, and special district jurisdictions employing 15 or more nonelected, nonappointed full-time employees. Data for 1993 only for state and local governments with 100 or more employees. Data for 1974, 1982, 1988, 1992, and 1994 not available. For definition of median, see Guide to Tabular Presentation]

Year and occupation	Employment (1,000) Total	Male	Female	White [1]	Minority Total [2]	Black [1]	Hispanic [3]	Median annual salary ($1,000) Male	Female	White [1]	Minority Total [2]	Black [1]	Hispanic [3]
1973	3,809	2,486	1,322	3,115	693	523	125	9.6	7.0	8.8	7.5	7.4	7.4
1975	3,899	2,436	1,464	3,102	797	602	147	11.3	8.2	10.2	8.8	8.6	8.9
1976	4,369	2,724	1,645	3,490	880	664	165	11.8	8.6	10.7	9.2	9.1	9.4
1977	4,415	2,737	1,678	3,480	935	705	175	12.4	9.1	11.3	9.7	9.5	9.9
1978	4,447	2,711	1,736	3,481	966	723	181	13.3	9.7	12.0	10.4	10.1	10.7
1979	4,576	2,761	1,816	3,568	1,008	751	192	14.1	10.4	12.8	10.9	10.6	11.4
1980	3,987	2,350	1,637	3,146	842	619	163	15.2	11.4	13.8	11.8	11.5	12.3
1981	4,665	2,740	1,925	3,591	1,074	780	205	17.7	13.1	16.1	13.5	13.3	14.7
1983	4,492	2,674	1,818	3,423	1,069	768	219	20.1	15.3	18.5	15.9	15.6	17.3
1984	4,580	2,700	1,880	3,458	1,121	799	233	21.4	16.2	19.6	17.4	16.5	18.4
1985	4,742	2,789	1,952	3,563	1,179	835	248	22.3	17.3	20.6	18.4	17.5	19.2
1986	4,779	2,797	1,982	3,549	1,230	865	259	23.4	18.1	21.5	19.6	18.7	20.2
1987	4,849	2,818	2,031	3,600	1,249	872	268	24.2	18.9	22.4	20.9	19.3	21.1
1989	5,257	3,030	2,227	3,863	1,394	961	308	26.1	20.6	24.1	22.1	20.7	22.7
1990	5,374	3,071	2,302	3,918	1,456	994	327	27.3	21.8	25.2	23.3	22.0	23.8
1991	5,459	3,110	2,349	3,965	1,494	1,011	340	28.4	22.7	26.4	23.8	22.7	24.5
1993	5,024	2,820	2,204	3,588	1,436	948	341	30.6	24.3	28.5	25.9	24.2	26.8
1997, total	**5,205**	**2,898**	**2,307**	**3,676**	**1,529**	**973**	**392**	**34.6**	**27.9**	**32.2**	**30.2**	**27.4**	**29.5**
Officials/administrators	296	197	99	247	49	31	12	54.8	47.2	52.5	50.7	49.7	50.7
Professionals	1,291	605	686	974	317	183	71	42.3	36.6	39.1	37.3	35.5	37.0
Technicians	456	265	191	338	118	68	33	34.4	27.8	31.7	29.7	28.4	28.7
Protective service	969	813	156	704	265	171	77	35.0	29.2	34.6	32.2	30.5	36.5
Paraprofessionals	369	100	269	221	148	111	27	25.1	22.6	24.1	22.8	21.1	23.0
Admin. support	882	117	765	590	292	179	83	25.3	23.5	23.7	23.6	23.4	23.5
Skilled craft	406	385	21	302	104	62	31	31.9	26.4	31.5	31.2	31.0	32.2
Service/maintenance	536	416	120	299	237	168	56	25.7	19.9	24.9	23.9	22.8	24.4
1999, total	**5,332**	**2,939**	**2,393**	**3,723**	**1,609**	**1,012**	**417**	**37.0**	**29.9**	**34.8**	**31.1**	**29.6**	**31.2**
Officials/administrators	307	201	106	253	54	34	13	58.7	51.0	56.4	53.9	52.4	53.7
Professionals	1,353	622	731	1,005	348	201	78	45.6	38.8	42.0	40.1	37.8	38.5
Technicians	454	263	191	332	122	70	34	37.0	29.9	34.4	31.6	30.3	31.8
Protective service	1,020	843	177	729	290	185	86	37.7	31.4	37.2	35.4	32.9	39.5
Paraprofessionals	374	99	275	222	152	113	29	27.3	24.3	26.0	23.8	22.9	25.7
Admin. support	890	120	770	593	297	181	86	27.2	25.1	25.3	25.5	25.2	25.1
Skilled craft	399	378	21	295	103	61	32	33.7	28.3	33.0	33.1	31.7	32.8
Service/maintenance	535	413	122	293	242	167	60	27.6	21.2	26.6	25.1	24.4	26.0

[1] Non-Hispanic. [2] Includes other minority groups not shown separately. [3] Persons of Hispanic origin may be of any race.
Source: U.S. Equal Employment Opportunity Commission. *State and Local Government Information Report,* biennially.

State and Local Government Finances and Employment 295

No. 453. State and Local Government Full-Time Equivalent Employment by Selected Function and State: 1999

[In thousands (1,541.4 represents 1,541,400). For March. Local government amounts are estimates subject to sampling variation; see Appendix III and source]

State	Education Total		Education Elem. & secondary		Education Higher education		Public welfare		Health		Hospitals	
	Total	Local	State	Local	State	Local	State	Local	State	Local	State	Local
United States	**1,541.4**	**6,023.3**	**44.9**	**5,720.5**	**1,398.8**	**302.8**	**225.4**	**261.7**	**169.2**	**224.3**	**414.9**	**536.5**
Alabama	36.5	92.7	-	92.7	33.1	-	3.8	1.5	5.3	4.3	11.3	25.0
Alaska	7.8	15.5	3.1	15.5	4.2	-	2.0	0.2	0.6	0.6	0.2	0.3
Arizona	26.7	98.4	-	87.8	23.8	10.6	5.9	1.9	2.1	2.8	0.7	4.6
Arkansas	21.1	59.2	-	59.2	18.2	-	3.7	0.1	4.9	0.3	4.6	4.9
California	127.4	648.4	-	577.2	122.8	71.2	3.5	54.9	10.6	36.9	29.7	60.5
Colorado	35.7	83.8	-	82.3	34.4	1.5	1.9	5.1	1.1	2.6	3.8	9.6
Connecticut	20.0	69.7	3.6	69.7	13.5	-	4.7	1.9	2.0	1.4	10.5	-
Delaware	7.2	14.7	-	14.7	6.9	-	1.6	-	1.7	0.2	2.2	-
District of Columbia	-	10.2	(X)	9.4	(X)	0.8	(X)	1.0	(X)	1.3	(X)	4.1
Florida	48.5	290.1	-	267.7	46.5	22.3	12.5	5.8	18.0	5.5	6.0	28.8
Georgia	46.0	186.1	-	186.0	39.2	0.1	9.1	0.6	3.7	14.3	11.9	33.4
Hawaii	31.4	-	24.2	-	7.0	-	0.8	0.1	2.9	0.2	3.2	-
Idaho	10.3	30.3	-	29.3	9.7	1.0	1.7	0.1	1.3	0.8	1.0	4.7
Illinois	55.9	257.4	-	237.3	52.9	20.1	12.5	6.8	3.1	7.1	14.9	14.3
Indiana	47.3	126.4	-	126.4	46.1	-	5.0	1.4	1.7	3.0	5.0	23.4
Iowa	24.7	72.2	-	66.1	23.5	6.1	2.8	1.3	0.3	2.1	7.4	10.2
Kansas	19.3	78.1	-	72.0	18.7	6.1	2.7	0.6	0.9	3.3	2.9	6.1
Kentucky	27.4	94.3	-	94.3	23.4	-	6.4	0.7	1.7	4.6	4.6	4.3
Louisiana	31.9	103.9	-	103.5	28.3	0.3	6.0	0.4	6.0	1.2	22.2	16.8
Maine	7.1	33.0	-	33.0	5.9	-	2.0	0.4	1.2	0.7	0.4	0.8
Maryland	27.8	109.6	-	100.9	25.8	8.7	7.3	2.7	5.9	4.2	5.8	-
Massachusetts	23.4	137.1	-	136.1	22.4	1.1	7.4	2.3	7.7	3.0	8.8	3.0
Michigan	66.0	212.6	0.6	200.5	65.0	12.0	12.9	2.0	1.7	8.1	12.8	11.0
Minnesota	37.2	117.0	-	117.0	33.3	-	2.6	11.1	2.2	3.9	4.8	10.8
Mississippi	19.2	76.8	-	70.9	17.6	5.9	3.1	0.8	3.1	0.2	10.6	22.2
Missouri	31.5	124.1	-	118.7	29.4	5.4	8.0	2.8	3.3	4.4	13.0	9.3
Montana	7.7	19.9	-	19.8	7.3	0.1	1.5	0.5	0.9	0.6	0.6	0.6
Nebraska	10.5	41.6	-	38.8	10.0	2.9	2.8	1.2	0.8	0.6	4.6	3.9
Nevada	7.4	29.5	-	29.5	7.2	-	1.0	0.4	1.2	0.7	1.0	5.0
New Hampshire	7.0	28.3	-	28.3	6.7	-	1.4	2.2	0.9	0.1	0.8	0.4
New Jersey	43.9	187.8	12.8	177.8	27.4	10.0	5.7	11.4	2.7	3.7	15.0	3.7
New Mexico	18.4	46.0	-	42.0	17.5	4.0	1.4	0.4	2.2	0.3	5.7	0.7
New York	49.4	445.6	-	413.6	44.7	32.1	6.7	49.5	9.5	17.7	48.4	53.1
North Carolina	47.1	181.4	-	166.3	44.2	15.2	1.4	13.6	2.6	14.8	15.9	23.3
North Dakota	6.9	13.6	-	13.6	6.6	-	0.4	1.0	1.2	0.3	1.1	-
Ohio	67.0	236.7	-	230.4	64.8	6.3	2.1	24.8	3.6	16.0	12.2	13.9
Oklahoma	26.8	78.6	-	78.4	24.8	0.3	6.6	0.2	4.0	1.3	3.5	10.1
Oregon	16.2	69.3	-	61.5	15.2	7.8	5.4	0.9	1.9	4.0	6.7	2.8
Pennsylvania	51.9	220.2	-	213.9	49.1	6.2	11.9	21.1	1.4	4.9	14.1	0.2
Rhode Island	6.6	22.8	0.4	22.8	5.5	-	1.6	0.2	1.4	0.1	1.3	-
South Carolina	28.6	87.4	-	87.4	25.9	-	5.0	0.3	7.8	2.0	8.9	21.6
South Dakota	5.0	18.1	-	17.8	4.6	0.4	0.9	0.3	0.5	0.2	1.0	0.6
Tennessee	36.1	112.6	-	112.6	34.1	-	5.3	2.7	3.1	3.5	10.0	20.2
Texas	93.6	555.8	-	524.4	88.9	31.4	21.5	3.1	14.6	18.2	33.3	45.0
Utah	25.9	44.3	-	44.3	24.9	-	3.2	0.5	1.5	1.7	5.1	0.9
Vermont	4.7	16.1	-	16.1	4.3	-	1.1	-	0.5	-	0.2	-
Virginia	46.7	159.8	-	158.6	43.9	1.3	2.0	6.6	5.2	5.9	13.4	3.5
Washington	50.3	87.4	-	87.4	46.8	-	5.0	1.0	5.4	3.3	7.6	9.5
West Virginia	13.2	41.2	-	41.2	11.7	-	0.1	-	0.7	1.2	1.7	3.6
Wisconsin	29.6	120.9	-	111.2	28.3	9.8	1.1	13.2	1.9	6.1	3.9	1.6
Wyoming	3.2	16.5	-	14.7	3.1	1.8	0.8	-	0.5	0.2	1.0	4.5

See footnote at end of table.

296   State and Local Government Finances and Employment

No. 453. State and Local Government Full-Time Equivalent Employment by Selected Function and State: 1999—Con.

[In thousands. For March. Local government amounts are estimates subject to sampling variation; see Appendix III and source]

State	Highways		Police protection		Fire protection		Corrections		Parks and recreation		Government administration	
	State	Local	State	Local	State	Local	State	Local	State	Local	State	Local
United States . . .	**246.2**	**296.1**	**98.2**	**750.8**	**(X)**	**289.6**	**451.7**	**221.0**	**32.1**	**205.4**	**361.8**	**640.1**
Alabama	3.5	7.0	1.4	11.1	(X)	5.5	4.4	2.6	0.6	3.3	7.1	8.4
Alaska	2.7	0.8	0.4	1.1	(X)	0.6	1.3	0.1	0.1	0.3	2.7	2.2
Arizona	3.0	4.5	1.8	14.4	(X)	5.1	8.9	3.8	0.4	4.0	5.4	16.2
Arkansas	3.5	3.6	1.1	6.6	(X)	2.4	3.7	1.5	0.7	0.9	2.8	6.1
California	19.5	21.3	12.4	82.4	(X)	29.8	47.1	28.8	3.0	31.7	28.8	91.4
Colorado	3.0	5.1	1.3	10.9	(X)	4.4	5.4	3.3	0.2	6.1	5.8	10.0
Connecticut	3.6	4.0	1.7	8.5	(X)	4.5	8.8	-	0.2	2.3	7.8	4.6
Delaware	1.4	0.4	0.9	1.5	(X)	0.3	2.3	-	0.2	0.3	2.5	1.1
District of Columbia .	(X)	0.5	(X)	4.2	(X)	1.6	(X)	2.9	(X)	0.6	(X)	2.0
Florida	10.3	12.9	4.0	49.4	(X)	19.9	31.9	13.9	1.1	16.0	25.0	37.4
Georgia	6.2	7.6	2.2	20.9	(X)	8.9	18.6	7.2	1.6	4.1	5.0	19.1
Hawaii	0.9	1.0	-	3.5	(X)	1.7	2.3	-	0.2	1.7	3.9	2.2
Idaho	1.7	1.7	0.5	2.8	(X)	1.0	1.6	1.0	0.2	0.7	2.2	3.2
Illinois	8.3	12.5	3.9	41.3	(X)	15.9	15.8	9.2	0.7	15.2	11.1	31.1
Indiana	4.3	7.1	2.0	14.2	(X)	7.0	6.0	4.6	0.1	3.5	4.3	15.0
Iowa	2.9	5.6	1.0	5.9	(X)	1.7	3.1	1.0	0.1	1.8	4.6	5.8
Kansas	3.4	5.1	1.0	7.9	(X)	2.7	3.5	2.2	0.5	2.0	4.5	6.9
Kentucky	5.4	3.5	2.1	7.6	(X)	5.1	3.5	2.6	1.6	1.4	8.8	6.8
Louisiana	5.7	5.0	1.1	14.2	(X)	4.4	6.8	5.4	1.2	2.9	5.7	10.7
Maine	2.6	1.8	0.4	2.9	(X)	1.3	1.2	0.6	0.1	0.6	2.1	3.0
Maryland	4.7	5.3	2.4	15.2	(X)	6.1	11.4	2.8	0.6	6.4	8.8	8.9
Massachusetts	4.4	6.4	4.7	18.0	(X)	12.6	6.9	5.4	1.0	2.0	13.3	9.5
Michigan	3.0	9.5	3.2	21.6	(X)	7.9	17.8	5.1	0.5	4.7	6.4	23.3
Minnesota	5.1	7.5	0.9	9.7	(X)	2.1	3.6	4.0	0.6	4.4	6.0	12.9
Mississippi	3.3	5.4	1.2	7.4	(X)	3.1	4.1	1.5	0.4	0.9	2.1	7.7
Missouri	6.6	7.2	2.4	14.9	(X)	6.9	11.5	2.2	0.6	4.1	7.1	10.8
Montana	1.9	1.2	0.4	1.8	(X)	0.6	1.0	0.5	0.1	0.4	1.6	2.3
Nebraska	2.3	2.9	0.7	3.8	(X)	1.2	1.9	1.0	0.3	1.0	1.6	4.1
Nevada	1.6	1.6	0.7	5.4	(X)	2.1	3.1	1.6	0.2	2.4	2.7	5.7
New Hampshire	1.9	1.8	0.4	2.8	(X)	1.6	1.2	0.5	0.2	0.4	1.7	1.7
New Jersey	7.3	10.5	3.8	29.3	(X)	7.2	9.4	6.5	1.7	5.0	19.5	18.8
New Mexico	2.4	1.8	0.6	4.7	(X)	1.8	4.2	1.3	0.7	2.0	4.7	4.7
New York	13.6	26.8	5.7	79.1	(X)	23.4	35.3	26.1	2.7	10.2	36.4	41.7
North Carolina	11.9	4.2	3.4	19.4	(X)	6.3	19.1	3.8	0.9	5.2	10.2	11.1
North Dakota	0.9	1.0	0.2	1.2	(X)	0.3	0.5	0.2	0.1	0.8	1.3	1.4
Ohio	7.5	13.8	2.6	29.2	(X)	15.0	17.9	7.8	0.7	8.4	11.9	33.6
Oklahoma	3.0	6.1	1.8	9.1	(X)	4.2	6.0	1.0	1.0	2.2	5.6	6.2
Oregon	3.5	4.4	1.4	7.0	(X)	3.5	4.3	3.5	0.4	2.7	8.4	7.2
Pennsylvania	13.4	12.0	5.5	25.3	(X)	6.2	14.8	10.9	1.3	3.9	13.6	32.0
Rhode Island	0.8	0.9	0.3	2.8	(X)	2.5	1.8	-	0.1	0.5	2.7	1.6
South Carolina	4.9	2.7	3.2	9.9	(X)	3.8	8.9	1.9	0.6	2.7	3.5	7.7
South Dakota	1.0	1.5	0.3	1.4	(X)	0.4	0.9	0.5	0.1	0.5	1.2	1.6
Tennessee	4.7	6.5	1.9	15.3	(X)	6.6	6.3	4.8	1.1	4.2	5.3	11.0
Texas	14.7	19.7	3.6	54.5	(X)	19.3	46.8	21.6	1.0	12.9	16.8	41.0
Utah	1.8	1.7	0.8	4.7	(X)	1.7	2.9	1.0	0.3	2.5	3.4	4.3
Vermont	1.0	1.2	0.5	0.8	(X)	0.3	0.9	-	0.1	0.2	1.5	0.9
Virginia	10.3	4.4	2.5	15.2	(X)	7.2	15.6	6.3	0.9	6.6	8.0	14.0
Washington	6.4	6.9	2.2	11.6	(X)	6.5	7.5	4.3	0.6	4.2	5.7	15.3
West Virginia	6.2	0.9	1.0	2.6	(X)	1.0	1.2	0.4	0.6	0.8	3.6	3.7
Wisconsin	2.0	8.9	0.9	14.5	(X)	4.5	7.9	3.6	0.2	3.2	6.1	11.2
Wyoming	1.8	0.6	0.2	1.4	(X)	0.4	0.7	0.3	0.1	0.6	1.0	1.0

- Represents or rounds to zero. X Not applicable.

Source: U.S. Census Bureau, <http://www.census.gov/pub/govs/www/apes.html> (accessed 05 August 2001).

State and Local Government Finances and Employment   297

No. 454. State and Local Government Employment and Average Earnings by State: 1990 and 1999

[In thousands (3,840 represents 3,840,000) except as noted. For March]

State	Full-time equivalent employment (1,000) State 1990	1999	Local [1] 1990	1999	Full-time equivalent employment per 10,000 population [2] State 1990	1999	Local [1] 1990	1999	Average March earnings [3] (dol.) State 1990	1999	Local [1] 1990	1999
United States . . .	3,840	4,034	9,239	10,715	154	149	371	396	2,472	3,236	2,364	3,236
Alabama.	79	81	148	180	196	186	367	414	2,196	2,754	1,749	2,754
Alaska	22	23	21	26	401	369	385	418	3,543	3,836	3,491	3,836
Arizona.	50	63	136	173	137	135	370	372	2,334	2,978	2,540	2,978
Arkansas	43	51	78	95	182	203	330	376	1,922	2,649	1,545	2,649
California	325	350	1,091	1,262	109	107	367	386	3,209	4,227	3,073	4,227
Colorado.	54	62	130	162	165	156	395	407	2,765	3,649	2,292	3,649
Connecticut.	58	63	98	107	178	194	299	326	3,018	3,650	2,854	3,650
Delaware	21	23	17	20	314	303	250	273	2,245	3,035	2,458	3,035
District of Columbia .	(X)	(X)	57	43	(X)	(X)	939	826	(X)	(X)	3,024	(X)
Florida	160	180	497	559	123	120	384	375	2,095	3,023	2,247	3,023
Georgia	112	116	270	333	173	151	418	436	2,037	2,827	1,872	2,827
Hawaii	49	53	13	14	445	443	120	118	2,317	2,810	2,536	2,810
Idaho.	19	24	37	50	186	195	372	403	2,100	2,889	1,772	2,889
Illinois	145	140	416	474	127	116	364	393	2,520	3,375	2,463	3,375
Indiana.	89	82	196	231	161	138	354	391	2,496	2,835	2,036	2,835
Iowa	57	53	107	117	207	185	387	408	2,936	3,548	2,024	3,548
Kansas.	50	43	104	125	200	164	421	475	2,077	2,967	1,979	2,967
Kentucky	75	70	114	144	204	178	310	367	2,141	2,935	1,823	2,935
Louisiana	85	96	155	184	200	219	368	422	2,047	2,590	1,713	2,590
Maine.	22	20	42	50	179	161	345	400	2,352	2,856	1,978	2,856
Maryland	89	89	159	182	186	173	333	355	2,609	3,206	2,776	3,206
Massachusetts.	93	87	196	228	155	142	325	371	2,541	3,549	2,554	3,549
Michigan.	144	137	316	344	155	140	340	350	2,858	3,786	2,646	3,786
Minnesota.	70	71	163	199	160	150	374	422	2,936	3,777	2,552	3,777
Mississippi	47	54	105	137	183	197	407	496	1,824	2,641	1,543	2,641
Missouri	74	93	171	207	145	170	334	381	1,965	2,575	2,052	2,575
Montana	17	19	35	33	211	213	434	373	2,072	2,671	1,959	2,671
Nebraska	29	30	68	76	186	178	430	455	2,075	2,400	2,089	2,400
Nevada	19	23	42	62	160	133	348	352	2,502	3,296	2,574	3,296
New Hampshire. . . .	16	19	33	43	145	157	301	361	2,352	3,003	2,215	3,003
New Jersey.	112	130	304	317	145	160	393	390	2,859	3,997	2,698	3,997
New Mexico	40	44	57	71	262	254	379	407	2,100	2,676	1,783	2,676
New York	285	250	866	904	158	137	482	498	2,997	3,803	2,795	3,803
North Carolina.	107	125	244	311	161	165	368	413	2,372	2,922	2,065	2,922
North Dakota.	15	16	20	22	234	246	314	341	2,057	2,661	2,138	2,661
Ohio	139	137	385	451	128	122	355	402	2,510	3,263	2,236	3,263
Oklahoma.	65	64	116	132	208	192	369	393	1,975	2,715	1,761	2,715
Oregon.	52	55	100	122	184	168	353	371	2,302	3,133	2,322	3,133
Pennsylvania.	127	147	361	378	107	122	304	315	2,437	3,338	2,403	3,338
Rhode Island.	21	20	27	35	205	200	266	350	2,586	3,631	2,656	3,631
South Carolina.	79	79	116	153	227	206	333	399	1,956	2,560	1,848	2,560
South Dakota	13	13	24	27	192	177	349	362	1,979	2,688	1,733	2,688
Tennessee	79	81	175	215	163	150	358	395	2,055	2,748	1,883	2,748
Texas.	223	269	706	879	131	136	415	445	2,192	2,822	1,952	2,822
Utah	37	49	51	72	216	232	294	341	2,000	2,784	2,092	2,784
Vermont	13	13	18	22	233	215	312	364	2,302	3,215	2,090	3,215
Virginia	117	114	221	259	188	168	356	381	2,267	3,119	2,248	3,119
Washington.	91	109	164	188	187	191	336	330	2,459	3,407	2,515	3,407
West Virginia.	34	33	59	61	188	181	326	335	1,919	2,564	1,862	2,564
Wisconsin.	67	63	183	211	136	121	375	404	2,503	3,537	2,372	3,537
Wyoming	11	11	24	28	239	230	539	586	2,045	2,541	2,110	2,541

X Not applicable.   [1] Estimates subject to sampling variation; see Appendix III and source.   [2] Based on estimated resident population as of July 1.   [3] For full-time employees.

Source: U.S. Census Bureau, *1990 Public Employment,* Series GE, No. 1, annual; thereafter, <http://www.census.gov/pub/govs/www/apes.html> (accessed 15 August 2001).

No. 455. City Government Employment and Payroll—Largest Cities: 1990 and 2000

[In thousands (456.2 represents 456,200). 1998 for March; 1990 for October. See footnote 3. Table 445, for areas representing city-county consolidated governments]

Cities ranked by 1998 population	Total employment (1,000)		Full-time equivalent employment [1]				Payroll (mil. dol.)		Average earnings for full-time employees (dol.)	
			Total (1,000)		Per 10,000 population [1]					
	1990	2000	1990	2000	1990	2000	1990	2000	1990	2000
New York, NY [2] [3]	456.2	458.1	394.6	429.3	539	579	1,091.7	1,708.8	2,783	4,150
Los Angeles, CA	51.3	49.4	50.8	48.4	146	134	176.5	230.1	3,488	4,793
Chicago, IL	41.6	41.3	41.6	40.7	149	145	124.9	171.3	3,002	4,239
Houston, TX	19.6	25.2	19.6	24.9	120	139	40.4	75.2	2,061	3,037
Philadelphia, PA.	32.4	31.1	31.9	30.0	201	209	89.1	109.2	2,843	3,637
San Diego, CA.	10.4	12.3	9.8	11.4	88	94	28.8	46.9	3,019	4,201
Phoenix, AZ	11.9	13.0	11.4	12.7	116	106	31.7	50.3	2,876	4,024
San Antonio, TX.	13.4	16.9	12.8	15.7	134	141	28.4	48.0	2,227	3,160
Dallas, TX.	14.9	15.6	14.5	15.2	144	141	28.2	50.4	1,945	3,332
Detroit, MI.	22.1	40.7	21.2	36.1	206	372	49.8	132.1	2,390	3,693
Honolulu, HI	9.9	9.8	9.2	9.1	110	104	23.7	30.9	2,600	3,435
San Jose, CA	5.9	7.6	4.9	6.9	62	80	16.0	36.3	3,453	5,569
San Francisco, CA.	25.8	27.7	25.7	27.7	356	371	93.8	141.6	3,648	5,112
Indianapolis, IN	12.8	12.4	12.5	12.0	171	161	23.1	36.7	1,910	3,115
Jacksonville, FL	10.8	10.1	9.8	9.7	154	140	23.8	35.6	2,582	3,815
Columbus, OH	7.7	9.1	7.5	8.8	118	131	17.8	30.1	2,416	3,478
Baltimore, MD [2]	29.7	30.8	29.1	29.2	395	452	73.2	95.3	2,540	3,361
El Paso, TX. [2]	4.9	5.9	4.8	5.8	94	95	9.5	15.6	1,973	2,701
Memphis, TN [2]	21.7	28.2	21.1	26.9	341	446	47.6	80.3	2,287	3,024
Milwaukee, WI.	9.0	7.9	8.6	7.7	137	133	20.6	28.5	2,431	3,706
Boston, MA [2]	20.9	23.3	20.9	22.0	363	396	49.8	80.2	2,391	3,734
Austin, TX.	10.0	10.6	9.6	10.1	203	183	20.9	31.2	2,186	3,128
Seattle, WA.	11.2	11.4	10.2	10.3	198	192	32.3	48.3	3,274	4,726
Washington, DC [2] [3]	49.6	37.7	47.9	36.5	789	697	138.7	139.4	2,930	3,863
Nashville-Davidson, TN [2]	17.9	20.6	16.9	19.6	347	385	41.8	62.3	2,510	3,235
Charlotte, NC	5.0	5.2	4.8	5.1	115	100	11.5	17.1	2,399	3,408
Portland, OR.	4.8	6.2	4.5	5.4	97	108	14.6	23.4	3,305	4,416
Denver, CO.	13.0	14.5	11.9	13.7	254	274	31.1	47.3	2,649	3,534
Cleveland, OH.	8.9	10.1	8.2	9.4	163	189	20.6	27.8	2,521	2,989
Fort Worth, TX.	5.5	6.1	5.2	5.7	117	117	11.1	18.9	2,171	3,394
Oklahoma City, OK.	4.8	5.1	4.5	4.8	101	102	10.5	16.0	2,430	3,457
New Orleans, LA	9.8	10.5	9.6	10.1	194	216	15.5	24.4	1,623	2,446
Tucson, AZ	5.0	7.1	4.7	5.8	114	127	11.5	16.0	2,528	2,787
Kansas City, MO	6.4	6.8	6.3	6.6	145	150	14.9	21.3	2,390	3,246
Virginia Beach, VA [2]	14.4	19.7	13.1	17.4	334	402	28.4	43.4	2,232	2,679
Long Beach, CA	5.7	6.1	5.4	5.7	126	132	17.7	25.7	3,413	4,855
Albuquerque, NM	6.9	7.1	6.2	6.6	161	157	12.2	18.3	2,040	2,868
Las Vegas, NV	1.9	2.6	2.0	2.5	77	61	4.9	11.2	2,563	4,681
Sacramento, CA.	4.2	4.4	3.9	4.0	105	100	11.3	17.0	3,021	4,400
Atlanta, GA.	8.3	8.8	8.1	8.6	205	213	18.4	25.6	2,286	2,974
Fresno, CA.	2.9	3.2	2.7	3.1	77	79	7.9	12.7	2,944	4,073
East Baton Rouge Parish, LA.	6.0	7.1	5.0	6.0	132	152	11.0	14.7	2,255	2,653
Tulsa, OK.	4.4	4.5	4.2	4.5	115	117	10.5	13.7	2,555	3,126
Omaha, NE.	2.9	3.4	2.7	2.9	79	78	7.9	10.6	3,051	3,874
Miami, FL.	4.3	3.8	4.0	3.6	113	99	14.6	15.1	3,771	4,276
Oakland, CA.	4.6	4.2	4.1	4.2	111	116	15.3	24.8	3,948	5,861
Mesa, AZ	2.3	3.5	2.3	3.3	81	93	6.8	13.4	2,898	4,072
Minneapolis, MN	6.4	6.3	5.7	5.8	154	164	15.2	21.3	2,815	3,866
Colorado Springs, CO.	5.9	7.4	5.3	6.9	188	200	13.3	25.3	2,618	3,747
Pittsburgh, PA	5.9	4.4	5.6	4.3	152	126	12.3	15.3	2,240	3,593
St. Louis, MO	7.8	8.0	7.4	7.6	186	225	17.0	24.1	2,363	3,176
Cincinnati, OH.	7.0	6.5	6.3	6.4	173	189	16.1	21.3	2,634	3,504
Wichita, KS.	2.7	3.6	2.6	3.1	87	93	5.4	9.3	2,083	3,072
Toledo, OH.	3.0	2.8	3.0	2.8	91	89	8.6	10.0	2,847	3,628
Arlington, TX.	1.8	3.0	1.8	2.4	68	79	4.5	7.1	2,538	3,090
Santa Ana, CA.	2.0	2.5	1.7	2.2	58	71	6.8	10.1	4,144	5,606
Buffalo, NY [2]	13.1	11.4	12.4	10.5	379	348	31.3	43.4	2,596	4,457
Anaheim, CA.	3.7	3.2	2.6	2.5	99	86	8.6	11.5	3,728	5,267
Tampa, FL	4.3	4.3	4.2	4.2	151	145	10.5	14.1	2,505	3,370
Corpus Christi, TX	3.2	3.5	3.0	3.3	116	117	5.9	8.6	2,009	2,675
Newark, NJ	5.1	5.5	4.9	5.2	177	195	8.3	22.3	1,698	4,371
Riverside, CA	2.0	2.1	2.0	1.9	88	72	7.0	8.0	3,459	4,625
Raleigh, NC	3.0	3.2	3.0	2.9	141	113	5.0	8.9	2,297	3,114
St. Paul, MN	3.6	4.2	3.4	3.2	124	125	10.5	13.3	3,265	4,189
Louisville, KY.	4.5	4.6	4.3	4.3	159	169	9.1	11.8	2,180	2,844
Anchorage, AK	8.8	10.1	7.9	9.0	351	352	28.4	34.6	3,706	3,973
Birmingham, AL.	3.9	4.2	3.8	4.1	142	163	8.4	11.5	2,243	2,799
Aurora, CO.	1.9	2.5	1.9	2.5	84	98	4.8	9.0	2,586	3,682
Lexington-Fayette, KY.	3.0	4.0	3.0	3.6	133	150	6.0	10.2	1,929	2,910
Stockton, CA.	2.0	2.3	1.0	1.9	47	80	5.0	7.1	3,554	4,054
St. Petersburg, FL	3.0	3.2	3.0	3.0	125	125	7.0	9.9	2,412	3,366
Jersey City, NJ	4.0	4.1	3.0	3.7	131	159	10.0	15.3	3,172	4,323
Plano, TX.	(NA)	2.0	(NA)	1.8	(NA)	81	(NA)	6.4	(NA)	3,702
Rochester, NY	9.0	11.1	8.0	10.7	347	491	27.0	37.5	3,315	3,546
Akron, OH.	6.0	2.9	5.0	2.7	224	126	11.0	9.2	2,255	3,460
Norfolk, VA [2]	10.5	14.5	9.8	12.0	376	557	21.9	32.8	2,268	2,758
Lincoln, NE.	4.0	2.7	3.0	2.5	156	118	7.0	8.2	2,367	3,382

NA Not available.   [1] 1990 based on enumerated population as of April 1, 1990.   [2] Includes city-operated elementary and secondary schools.   [3] Includes city-operated university or college.

Source: U.S. Census Bureau, City Employment, GE-90-2, and unpublished data. <http://www.census.gov/govs/www/apesloc.html> (accessed 15 August 2001).

State and Local Government Finances and Employment   299

No. 456. County Government Employment and Payroll—Largest Counties: 2000

[For March. See text, this section]

Counties ranked by 1998 population	Total employ-ment (1,000)	Per 10,000 popu-lation [1]	Pay-roll (mil. dol.)	Avg. earn-ings (dol.)	Counties ranked by 1998 population	Total employ-ment (1,000)	Per 10,000 popu-lation [1]	Pay-roll (mil. dol.)	Avg. earn-ings (dol.)
Los Angeles, CA	98.8	102	396.7	4,274	Kent, MI	2.7	46	7.6	3,141
Cook, IL	28.9	56	99.3	3,445	Tulsa, OK	1.5	26	3.3	2,378
Harris, TX	19.8	61	59.5	3,063	Delaware, PA	3.2	59	7.3	2,248
Maricopa, AZ	15.3	54	43.7	2,934	Summit, OH	3.9	71	9.8	2,560
San Diego, CA	19.5	65	66.3	3,651	Bernalillo, NM	1.6	29	4.0	2,717
Orange, CA	24.3	83	81.4	3,623	Hidalgo, TX	1.9	36	4.0	2,174
Miami-Dade, FL	36.0	163	130.3	3,817	Gwinnett, GA	3.8	68	11.4	3,243
Wayne, MI	6.7	32	25.8	3,914	Bristol, MA	0.8	15	2.4	3,204
Dallas, TX	12.5	58	36.4	3,055	Camden, NJ	5.5	100	18.6	3,707
King, WA	15.8	86	52.1	3,812	Jefferson, CO	2.8	50	8.8	3,464
Santa Clara, CA	14.9	87	65.3	4,655	Union, NJ	4.5	71	11.9	3,373
San Bernardino, CA	20.6	115	67.6	3,664	El Paso, CO	2.2	42	6.1	3,006
Broward, FL	11.0	72	37.0	3,437	Ocean, NJ	3.7	64	10.8	3,600
Riverside, CA	16.6	104	54.2	3,534	Passaic, NJ	4.1	73	14.1	4,169
Alameda, CA	12.1	79	51.1	4,619	Ramsey, MN	3.9	74	13.6	3,898
Cuyahoga, OH	16.1	116	49.2	3,065	New Castle, DE	1.7	32	5.4	3,690
Suffolk, NY	12.9	82	51.9	4,686	Lake, IN	2.4	42	4.4	2,241
Tarrant, TX	6.9	50	19.0	2,811	Anne Arundel, MD	14.7	275	49.9	3,983
Bexar, TX	9.5	67	23.6	2,619	Arapahoe, CO	1.9	38	5.7	3,245
Nassau, NY	18.9	130	71.3	4,295	Plymouth, MA	0.6	13	2.0	3,487
Allegheny, PA	7.0	54	17.6	2,605	Brevard, FL	3.9	79	9.3	2,644
Oakland, MI	4.5	36	15.6	3,697	Morris, NJ	3.5	67	10.6	3,622
Clark, NV	16.6	131	60.3	4,169	Will, IL	1.9	40	5.8	3,221
Sacramento, CA	13.3	110	50.3	4,094	Onondaga, NY	5.9	118	15.7	2,946
Hennepin, MN	13.0	103	41.5	3,815	Lancaster, PA	2.4	50	5.5	2,675
Palm Beach, FL	8.6	82	27.0	3,200	Polk, FL	4.2	88	10.4	2,649
Franklin, OH	6.6	64	19.2	2,962	Jefferson, LA	10.6	214	25.8	2,692
St Louis, MO	4.2	41	12.9	3,215	Lucas, OH	4.2	91	11.9	2,957
Erie, NY	10.9	105	33.4	3,578	Sedgwick, KS	2.4	53	7.1	3,015
Fairfax, VA	35.3	348	117.5	3,746	Douglas, NE	1.9	41	5.2	2,918
Hillsborough, FL	16.2	132	34.4	2,993	Genesee, MI	2.2	40	6.4	3,674
Contra Costa, CA	10.7	104	44.7	4,779	Sonoma, CA	6.2	125	23.5	4,581
Milwaukee, WI	8.5	88	26.5	3,314	Johnson, KS	3.4	71	9.0	3,101
Westchester, NY	6.9	70	26.6	4,240	Collin, TX	1.1	26	2.8	2,557
Du Page, IL	3.9	41	11.8	3,360	Stanislaus, CA	5.7	121	18.4	3,733
Pinellas, FL	6.2	69	18.5	3,039	Dane, WI	2.3	49	7.2	3,610
Shelby, TN	13.1	143	35.1	2,842	Volusia, FL	3.3	63	7.3	2,776
Bergen, NJ	5.8	48	13.0	3,178	Chester, PA	2.4	54	6.3	2,859
Salt Lake, UT	5.8	53	13.4	3,252	Burlington, NJ	3.8	77	9.3	3,027
Hamilton, OH	5.9	68	15.3	2,679	Spokane, WA	1.8	44	11.1	6,181
Montgomery, MD	37.4	342	123.1	4,619	Washington, OR	1.6	38	5.5	3,688
Orange, FL	9.9	115	28.0	3,092	Mobile, AL	2.1	51	4.4	2,137
Pima, AZ	8.0	91	20.0	2,859	Lee, FL	3.0	75	9.3	3,230
Macomb, MI	3.0	35	8.9	3,333	Kane, IL	1.3	32	3.5	2,755
Prince Georges, MD	29.4	338	90.8	3,564	Santa Barbara, CA	5.8	130	20.5	4,010
Fresno, CA	8.6	108	26.0	3,293	Guilford, NC	13.0	295	32.3	2,862
Essex, NJ	5.6	66	19.3	4,048	Denton, TX	1.2	31	3.2	2,735
Fulton, GA	7.9	104	25.0	3,356	Solano, CA	3.1	72	10.2	3,736
Ventura, CA	8.6	113	31.5	3,829	York, PA	2.1	55	5.0	2,407
Baltimore, MD	23.3	287	63.8	3,227	Stark, OH	2.9	74	6.6	2,372
Montgomery, PA	3.5	47	9.2	2,783	Westmoreland, PA	2.4	63	5.4	2,394
Middlesex, NJ	4.5	55	14.4	3,881	Knox, TN	9.4	226	19.8	2,462
Monroe, NY	7.0	83	20.4	3,430	Monterey, CA	5.5	136	17.5	3,534
Travis, TX	3.5	49	10.6	3,057	Hillsborough, NH	0.7	17	1.8	2,974
El Paso, TX	4.0	56	10.4	2,685	Polk, IA	2.1	57	6.4	3,313
San Mateo, CA	6.2	83	24.6	4,415	Berks, PA	2.6	67	5.5	2,391
Pierce, WA	3.4	47	13.0	4,216	Tulare, CA	5.2	139	15.7	3,262
Jefferson, KY	3.5	51	8.9	2,610	Greenville, SC	2.1	56	4.9	2,506
Jefferson, AL	4.8	72	14.7	3,122	Waukesha, WI	1.5	40	4.5	3,242
Jackson, MO	2.1	30	5.0	2,519	Seminole, FL	2.5	67	6.7	2,926
Norfolk, MA	0.6	8	1.6	2,977	Pulaski, AR	1.2	34	2.8	2,406
Oklahoma, OK	2.6	37	4.4	1,860	Dakota, MN	1.8	47	5.7	3,706
Kern, CA	9.2	136	30.3	3,504	Fort Bend, TX	1.0	30	2.5	2,579
Multnomah, OR	6.0	83	15.0	3,050	Utah, UT	0.8	22	2.0	2,884
Mecklenburg, NC	23.8	334	58.2	2,834	Clackamas, OR	2.2	59	7.1	3,755
Lake, IL	3.2	48	9.6	3,277	Mercer, NJ	3.7	87	10.5	3,691
Monmouth, NJ	5.7	85	18.3	3,673	Butler, OH	2.2	64	5.5	2,607
Dekalb, GA	6.5	104	19.5	3,170	Orange, NY	3.2	87	9.4	3,267
Bucks, PA	2.5	40	7.3	3,181	Clark, WA	1.4	43	4.8	3,476
Snohomish, WA	2.4	41	9.3	3,906	Cameron, TX	1.4	41	2.8	2,156
Wake, NC	17.8	277	44.7	2,876	Pasco, FL	2.6	77	6.1	2,457
Cobb, GA	3.9	66	11.9	3,353	Adams, CO	1.6	48	5.0	3,273
Montgomery, OH	4.9	82	14.4	3,065	Charleston, SC	2.5	73	5.8	2,622
Hudson, NJ	3.8	62	9.7	2,923	Nueces, TX	1.6	50	3.6	2,283
San Joaquin, CA	7.4	123	22.6	3,509	Allen, IN	1.6	45	4.0	2,868

[1] 1999 based on estimated resident population as of March, 1998.

Source: U.S. Census Bureau, unpublished data. <http://www.census.gov/govs/www/apesloc.html> (accessed 15 August 2001).

Section 9
Federal Government Finances and Employment

This section presents statistics relating to the financial structure and the civilian employment of the federal government. The fiscal data cover taxes, other receipts, outlays, and debt. The principal sources of fiscal data are the *Budget of the United States Government* and related documents, published annually by the Office of Management and Budget (OMB), and the Department of the Treasury's *United States Government Annual Report* and its *Appendix.* Detailed data on tax returns and collections are published annually by the Internal Revenue Service. The personnel data relate to staffing and payrolls. They are published by the Office of Personnel Management and the Bureau of Labor Statistics. The primary source for data on public lands is *Public Land Statistics*, published annually by the Bureau of Land Management, Department of the Interior. Data on federally owned land and real property are collected by the General Services Administration and presented in its annual *Inventory Report on Real Property Owned by the United States Throughout the World.*

Budget concept—Under the unified budget concept, all federal monies are included in one comprehensive budget. These monies comprise both federal funds and trust funds. Federal funds are derived mainly from taxes and borrowing and are not restricted by law to any specific government purpose. Trust funds, such as the Unemployment Trust Fund, collect certain taxes and other receipts for use in carrying out specific purposes or programs in accordance with the terms of the trust agreement or statute. Fund balances include both cash balances with Treasury and investments in U.S. securities. Part of the balance is obligated, part unobligated. Prior to 1985, the budget totals, under provisions of law, excluded some federal activities—including the Federal Financing Bank, the Postal Service, the Synthetic Fuels Corporation, and the lending activities of the Rural Electrification Administration. The Balanced Budget

and Emergency Deficit Control Act of 1985 (P.L.99-177) repealed the off-budget status of these entities and placed social security (federal old-age and survivors insurance and the federal disability insurance trust funds) off-budget. Though social security is now off-budget and, by law, excluded from coverage of the congressional budget resolutions, it continues to be a federal program.

Receipts arising from the government's sovereign powers are reported as governmental receipts; all other receipts, i.e., from business-type or market-oriented activities, are offset against outlays. Outlays are reported on a checks-issued (net) basis (i.e., outlays are recorded at the time the checks to pay bills are issued).

Debt concept—For most of U.S. history, the total debt consisted of debt borrowed by the Treasury (i.e., public debt). The present debt series, includes both public debt and agency debt. The *gross federal debt* includes money borrowed by the Treasury and by various federal agencies; it is the broadest generally used measure of the federal debt. *Total public debt* is covered by a statutory debt limitation and includes only borrowing by the Treasury.

Treasury receipts and outlays—All receipts of the government, with a few exceptions, are deposited to the credit of the U.S. Treasury regardless of ultimate disposition. Under the Constitution, no money may be withdrawn from the Treasury unless appropriated by the Congress.

The day-to-day cash operations of the federal government clearing through the accounts of the U.S. Treasury are reported in the *Daily Treasury Statement.* Extensive detail on the public debt is published in the *Monthly Statement of the Public Debt of the United States.*

Budget receipts such as taxes, customs duties, and miscellaneous receipts, which are collected by government agencies,

U.S. Census Bureau, Statistical Abstract of the United States: 2001

and outlays represented by checks issued and cash payments made by disbursing officers as well as government agencies are reported in the *Daily Treasury Statement of Receipts and Outlays of the United States Government* and in the Treasury's *United States Government Annual Report* and its *Appendix*. These deposits in and payments from accounts maintained by government agencies are on the same basis as the unified budget.

The quarterly *Treasury Bulletin* contains data on fiscal operations and related Treasury activities, including financial statements of government corporations and other business-type activities.

Income tax returns and tax collections—Tax data are compiled by the Internal Revenue Service of the Treasury Department. The *Annual Report of the Commissioner and Chief Counsel of the Internal Revenue Service* gives a detailed account of tax collections by kind of tax and by regions, districts, and states. The agency's annual *Statistics of Income* reports present detailed data from individual income tax returns and corporation income tax returns. The quarterly *Statistics of Income Bulletin* has, in general, replaced the supplemental *Statistics of Income* publications which presented data on such diverse subjects as tax-exempt organizations, unincorporated businesses, fiduciary income tax and estate tax returns, sales of capital assets by individuals, international income and taxes reported by corporations and individuals, and estate tax wealth.

Employment and payrolls—The Office of Personnel Management collects employment and payroll data from all departments and agencies of the federal government, except the Central Intelligence Agency, the National Security Agency, and the Defense Intelligence Agency. Employment figures represent the number of persons who occupied civilian positions at the end of the report month shown and who are paid for personal services rendered for the federal government, regardless of the nature of appointment or method of payment. Federal payrolls include all payments for personal services rendered during the report month and payments for accumulated annual leave of employees who separate from the service. Since most federal employees are paid on a biweekly basis, the calendar month earnings are partially estimated on the basis of the number of work days in each month where payroll periods overlap.

Federal employment and payroll figures are published by the Office of Personnel Management in its *Federal Civilian Workforce Statistics—Employment and Trends*. It also publishes biennial employment data for minority groups, data on occupations of white- and blue-collar workers, and data on employment by geographic area; reports on salary and wage distribution of federal employees are published annually. General schedule is primarily white-collar; wage system primarily blue-collar. Data on federal employment are also issued by the Bureau of Labor Statistics in its *Monthly Labor Review* and in Employment and Earnings and by the U.S. Census Bureau in its annual *Public Employment*.

Public lands—The data on applications, entries, selections, patents, and certifications refer to transactions which involve the disposal, under the public land laws (including the homestead laws), of federal public lands to nonfederal owners. In general, original entries and selections are applications to secure title to public lands which have been accepted as properly filed (i.e., allowed). Some types of applications, however, are not reported until issuance of the final certificate, which passes equitable title to the land to the applicant.

No. 457. Federal Budget—Summary: 1945 to 2001

[In billions of dollars (45.2 represents $45,159,000,000), except percent. For fiscal years ending in year shown; see text, Section 8, State and Local Government Finances and Employment. The Balanced Budget and Emergency Deficit Control Act of 1985 put all the previously off-budget federal entities into the budget and moved social security off-budget. Minus sign (-) indicates deficit or decrease]

Year	Receipts	Outlays	Surplus or deficit (-)	Outlays as percent of GDP [1]	Gross federal debt [2] Total	Federal gov't account	Held by the public Total	Federal Reserve System	As percent of GDP [1]
1945	45.2	92.7	-47.6	41.9	260.1	24.9	235.2	21.8	117.5
1950	39.4	42.6	-3.1	15.6	256.9	37.8	219.0	18.3	93.9
1955	65.5	68.4	-3.0	17.3	274.4	47.8	226.6	23.6	69.4
1960	92.5	92.2	0.3	17.7	290.5	53.7	236.8	26.5	56.0
1965	116.8	118.2	-1.4	17.2	322.3	61.5	260.8	39.1	46.9
1970	192.8	195.6	-2.8	19.3	380.9	97.7	283.2	57.7	37.6
1975	279.1	332.3	-53.2	21.3	541.9	147.2	394.7	85.0	34.7
1976	298.1	371.8	-73.7	21.4	629.0	151.6	477.4	94.7	36.2
TQ [3]	81.2	96.0	-14.7	20.9	643.6	148.1	495.5	96.7	35.4
1977	355.6	409.2	-53.7	20.7	706.4	157.3	549.1	105.0	35.8
1978	399.6	458.7	-59.2	20.7	776.6	169.5	607.1	115.5	35.0
1979	463.3	504.0	-40.7	20.1	829.5	189.2	640.3	115.6	33.1
1980	517.1	590.9	-73.8	21.6	909.1	197.1	711.9	120.8	33.3
1981	599.3	678.2	-79.0	22.2	994.8	205.4	789.4	124.5	32.5
1982	617.8	745.8	-128.0	23.1	1,137.3	212.7	924.6	134.5	35.2
1983	600.6	808.4	-207.8	23.5	1,371.7	234.4	1,137.3	155.5	39.9
1984	666.5	851.9	-185.4	22.1	1,564.7	257.6	1,307.0	155.1	40.8
1985	734.1	946.4	-212.3	22.9	1,817.5	310.2	1,507.4	169.8	43.9
1986	769.2	990.5	-221.2	22.5	2,120.6	379.9	1,740.8	190.9	48.2
1987	854.4	1,004.1	-149.8	21.6	2,346.1	456.2	1,889.9	212.0	50.5
1988	909.3	1,064.5	-155.2	21.2	2,601.3	549.5	2,051.8	229.2	51.9
1989	991.2	1,143.7	-152.5	21.2	2,868.0	677.1	2,190.0	220.1	53.1
1990	1,032.0	1,253.2	-221.2	21.8	3,206.6	794.7	2,411.8	234.4	55.9
1991	1,055.0	1,324.4	-269.4	22.3	3,598.5	909.2	2,689.3	258.6	60.7
1992	1,091.3	1,381.7	-290.4	22.2	4,002.1	1,002.1	3,000.1	296.4	64.4
1993	1,154.4	1,409.5	-255.1	21.5	4,351.4	1,102.6	3,248.8	325.7	66.3
1994	1,258.6	1,461.9	-203.3	21.0	4,643.7	1,210.2	3,433.4	355.2	66.9
1995	1,351.8	1,515.8	-164.0	20.7	4,921.0	1,316.2	3,604.8	374.1	67.2
1996	1,453.1	1,560.6	-107.5	20.3	5,181.9	1,447.4	3,734.5	390.9	67.3
1997	1,579.3	1,601.3	-22.0	19.6	5,369.7	1,596.9	3,772.8	424.5	65.6
1998	1,721.8	1,652.6	69.2	19.1	5,478.7	1,757.1	3,721.6	458.2	63.2
1999	1,827.5	1,702.9	124.6	18.7	5,606.1	1,973.2	3,632.9	496.6	61.4
2000	2,025.2	1,788.8	236.4	18.2	5,629.0	2,218.9	3,410.1	511.4	57.3
2001, est	2,136.9	1,856.2	280.7	18.0	5,625.0	2,450.8	3,174.2	(NA)	54.5

NA Not available. [1] Gross domestic product as of fiscal year; for calendar year GDP, see Section 13, Income, Expenditures, and Wealth. [2] See text, this section, for discussion of debt concept. [3] Prior to fiscal year 1977 the federal fiscal years began on July 1 and ended on June 30. In calendar year 1976 the July-September period was a separate accounting period (known as the transition quarter or TQ) to bridge the period required to shift to the new fiscal year.
Source: U.S. Office of Management and Budget, *Historical Tables*, annual.

No. 458. Federal Budget Outlays—Defense, Human and Physical Resources, and Net Interest Payments: 1980 to 2001

[In billions of dollars (590.9 represents $590,947,000,000). For fiscal year ending in year shown. Minus sign (-) indicates offsets]

Outlays	1980	1985	1990	1995	1997	1998	1999	2000	2001, est.
Federal outlays, total	590.9	946.4	1,253.2	1,515.8	1,601.3	1,652.6	1,702.9	1,788.8	1,856.2
National defense	134.0	252.7	299.3	272.1	270.5	268.5	274.9	294.5	299.1
Human resources	313.4	471.8	619.3	923.8	1,002.3	1,033.4	1,058.7	1,115.3	1,201.4
Education, training, employment, and social services	31.8	29.3	38.8	54.3	53.0	55.0	56.2	59.2	65.3
Health	23.2	33.5	57.7	115.4	123.8	131.4	141.1	154.5	175.3
Medicare	32.1	65.8	98.1	159.9	190.0	192.8	190.4	197.1	219.3
Income security	86.6	128.2	147.1	220.5	230.9	233.2	237.7	247.9	262.6
Social security	118.5	188.6	248.6	335.8	365.3	379.2	390.0	409.4	433.6
Veterans benefits and services	21.2	26.3	29.1	37.9	39.3	41.8	43.2	47.1	45.4
Physical resources	66.0	56.8	126.0	59.1	59.9	74.7	81.9	84.7	87.6
Energy	10.2	5.6	3.3	4.9	1.5	1.3	0.9	-1.1	-0.7
Natural resources and environment	13.9	13.4	17.1	21.9	21.2	22.3	24.0	25.0	27.4
Commerce and housing credit	9.4	4.3	67.6	-17.8	-14.6	1.0	2.6	3.2	-0.8
Transportation	21.3	25.8	25.8	39.4	40.8	40.3	42.5	46.9	51.1
Community and regional development	11.3	7.7	8.5	10.7	11.1	9.8	11.9	10.6	10.6
Net interest	52.5	129.5	184.4	232.2	244.0	241.2	229.7	223.2	206.4
International affairs	12.7	16.2	13.8	16.4	15.2	13.1	15.2	17.2	17.5
Agriculture	8.8	25.6	12.0	9.8	9.0	12.2	23.0	36.6	25.9
Administration of justice	4.6	6.3	10.0	16.2	20.2	22.8	25.9	27.8	29.4
General government	13.0	11.6	10.6	14.0	12.9	15.7	15.8	13.5	16.8
Undistributed offsetting receipts	-19.9	-32.7	-36.6	-44.5	-50.0	-47.2	-40.4	-42.6	-47.7

Source: U. S. Office of Management and Budget, *Historical Tables*, annual.

Federal Government Finances and Employment **303**

U.S. Census Bureau, Statistical Abstract of the United States: 2001

Figure 9.1
Federal Budget Summary: 1980 to 2001

Receipts, outlays, and surplus or deficit

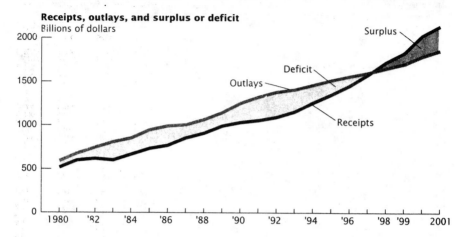

Outlays and federal debt as a percent of gross domestic product

Gross federal debt

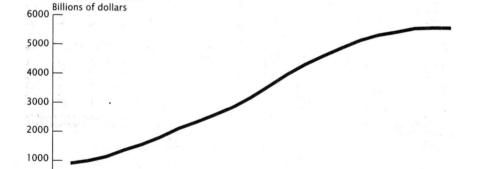

Source: Charts prepared by U.S. Bensus Bureau. For data, see Table 457.

304 Federal Government Finances and Employment

No. 459. Federal Receipts by Source: 1990 to 2001

[In billions of dollars (1,032.0 represents $1,031,969,000,000). For fiscal years ending in year shown; see text, Section 8, State and Local Government Finances and Employment. Receipts reflect collections. Covers both federal funds and trust funds; see text, this section. Excludes government-sponsored but privately-owned corporations, Federal Reserve System, District of Columbia government, and money held in suspense as deposit funds]

Source	1990	1995	1997	1998	1999	2000	2001, est.
Total receipts [1]	1,032.0	1,351.8	1,579.3	1,721.8	1,827.5	2,025.2	2,136.9
Individual income taxes	466.9	590.2	737.5	828.6	879.5	1,004.5	1,072.9
Corporation income taxes	93.5	157.0	182.3	188.7	184.7	207.3	213.1
Social insurance and retirement receipts	380.0	484.5	539.4	571.8	611.8	652.9	689.7
Excise taxes	35.3	57.5	56.9	57.7	70.4	68.9	71.1
Social insurance and retirement receipts [1]	380.0	484.5	539.4	571.8	611.8	652.9	689.7
Employment and general retirement	353.9	451.0	506.8	540.0	580.9	620.5	655.5
Old-age & survivors ins. (off-budget)	255.0	284.1	336.7	358.8	383.6	411.7	430.9
Disability insurance (off-budget)	26.6	67.0	55.3	57.0	60.9	68.9	73.0
Hospital insurance	68.6	96.0	110.7	119.9	132.3	135.5	147.2
Railroad retirement/pension fund	2.3	2.4	2.4	2.6	2.6	2.7	2.7
Railroad social security equivalent account	1.4	1.5	1.6	1.8	1.5	1.7	1.7
Unemployment insurance	21.6	28.9	28.2	27.5	26.5	27.6	29.6
Total excise taxes [1]	35.3	57.5	56.9	57.7	70.4	68.9	71.1
Federal funds	15.6	26.9	27.8	21.7	19.3	22.7	24.0
Alcohol	5.7	7.2	7.3	7.2	7.4	8.1	7.7
Tobacco	4.1	5.9	5.9	5.7	5.4	7.2	7.5
Telephone	3.0	3.8	4.5	4.9	5.2	5.7	5.9
Ozone depleting chemicals/products	0.4	0.6	0.1	0.1	0.1	0.1	0.1
Transportation fuels	(X)	8.5	7.1	0.6	0.8	0.8	0.8
Trust funds	19.8	30.5	29.1	36.0	51.1	46.2	47.2
Highway	13.9	22.6	23.9	26.6	39.3	35.0	35.4
Airport and airway	3.7	5.5	4.0	8.1	10.4	9.7	10.4
Black lung disability	0.7	0.6	0.6	0.6	0.6	0.5	0.6
Inland waterway	0.1	0.1	0.1	0.1	0.1	0.1	0.1
Hazardous substance superfund	0.8	0.9	0.1	(Z)	(Z)	(Z)	(Z)
Oil spill liability	0.1	0.2	(Z)	(Z)	(Z)	0.2	(Z)
Aquatic resources	0.2	0.3	0.3	0.3	0.4	0.3	0.4
Vaccine injury compensation	0.2	0.1	0.1	0.1	0.1	0.1	0.1

X Not applicable.   Z $50 million or less.   [1] Totals reflect interfund and intragovernmental transactions and/or other functions, not shown separately.

Source: U.S. Office of Management and Budget, *Historical Tables*, annual.

No. 460. Federal Trust Fund Receipts, Outlays, and Balances: 1998 to 2000

[In billions of dollars (932 represents $932,000,000,000). For fiscal years ending in year shown. Receipts deposited. Outlays on a checks-issued basis less refunds collected. Balances: That which have not been spent. See text, this section, for discussion of the budget concept and trust funds]

Description	Income			Outlays			Balances [1]		
	1998	1999	2000	1998	1999	2000	1998	1999	2000
Total [2]	932	1,002	1,053	771	789	829	1,669	1,876	2,100
Airport and airway trust fund	9	11	11	6	8	9	9	12	14
Federal employees health benefits fund	17	18	20	17	19	20	6	6	6
Fed./civ. employees retirement funds	73	76	77	44	45	46	461	492	523
Federal old-age, survivors and disability insurance trust funds	481	517	564	382	393	412	730	855	1,007
Foreign military sales trust fund	14	12	11	14	12	11	-	6	6
Highway trust fund	29	39	35	25	29	33	18	29	31
Health insurance trust funds:									
Medicare:									
Fed. hospital ins. trust fund	138	153	160	137	132	130	117	138	168
Federal supplemental medical insurance	83	86	91	77	81	91	41	46	46
Military retirement fund	38	38	39	31	32	33	146	152	158
Railroad retirement trust funds	10	9	10	8	8	8	17	14	16
Unemployment trust funds	32	32	33	24	25	24	71	78	87
Veterans life insurance trust funds	2	2	2	2	2	2	14	14	14
Other trust funds [3]	10	9	11	9	13	9	33	35	35

- Represents or rounds to zero.   [1] Balances available on a cash basis (rather than an authorization basis) at the end of the year. Balances are primarily invested in federal debt securities.   [2] Includes funds not shown separately.   [3] Effective August 9, 1989, the permanent insurance fund of the FDIC was classified under law as a federal fund.

Source: U.S. Office of Management and Budget, *Analytical Perspectives*, annual.

No. 461. Federal Budget Outlays in Constant (1996) Dollars: 1980 to 2001

[Dollar amounts in billions of dollars (1,093 represents $1,093,000,000,000). For fiscal year ending in year shown; see text, Section 8, State and Local Government Finances and Employment. Given the inherent imprecision in deflating outlays, the data shown in constant dollars present a reasonable perspective—not precision. The deflators and the categories that are deflated are as comparable over time as feasible. Minus sign (-) indicates offset]

Outlays	1980	1990	1995	1996	1997	1998	1999	2000	2001, est.
Constant (1996) dollar outlays, total	1,093	1,484	1,552	1,561	1,569	1,599	1,620	1,660	1,678
National defense [1]	245	355	282	266	265	260	260	270	269
Nondefense, total:									
Payments for individuals	514	687	893	909	930	945	951	980	1,019
Direct payments [2]	454	596	744	762	785	791	788	811	835
Grants to state and local gov'ts.	60	91	149	148	146	154	163	169	184
All other grants	108	67	81	80	84	83	90	94	99
Net Interest [2]	94	214	237	241	239	233	219	209	189
All other [2]	173	209	106	102	100	122	136	145	143
Undistributed offsetting receipts [2]	-42	-48	-47	-38	-49	-45	-37	-38	-41
Total nondefense	847	1,129	1,270	1,295	1,304	1,339	1,360	1,389	1,409
Total outlays as percent of GDP	21.6	21.8	20.7	20.3	19.6	19.1	18.7	18.2	18.0
National defense [1]	4.9	5.2	3.7	3.5	3.3	3.1	3.0	3.0	2.9
Nondefense, total:									
Payments for individuals	10.2	10.2	11.9	11.8	11.6	11.3	10.9	10.7	10.9
Direct payments [2]	9.0	8.8	10.0	9.9	9.8	9.4	9.1	8.9	8.9
Grants to state and local governments	1.2	1.3	2.0	1.9	1.8	1.8	1.9	1.8	2.0
All other grants	2.1	1.0	1.1	1.0	1.0	1.0	1.1	1.1	1.1
Net Interest [2]	1.9	3.2	3.2	3.1	3.0	2.8	2.5	2.3	2.0
All other [2]	3.2	2.9	1.4	1.3	1.2	1.5	1.6	1.6	1.5
Total nondefense	16.7	16.6	17.0	16.8	16.3	16.0	15.6	15.2	15.1
Percent of outlays, total	100.0	100.0	100.0	100.0	100.0	100.0	100.0	100.0	100.0
National defense [1]	22.7	23.9	17.9	17.0	16.9	16.2	16.1	16.5	16.1
Payments for individuals	47.1	46.6	57.7	58.3	59.3	59.1	58.6	58.8	60.7
Direct payments [2]	41.6	40.5	48.1	48.8	50.0	49.4	48.6	48.7	49.7
Grants to state and local governments	5.5	6.2	9.6	9.5	9.3	9.7	10.0	10.1	11.0
All other grants	9.9	4.6	5.2	5.1	5.3	5.2	5.6	5.8	6.1
Net Interest [2]	8.9	14.7	15.3	15.4	15.2	14.6	13.5	12.5	11.1
All other [2]	14.8	13.1	6.8	6.5	6.3	7.7	8.5	8.9	8.6
Undistributed offsetting receipts [2]	-3.4	-2.9	-2.9	-2.4	-3.1	-2.9	-2.4	-2.4	-2.6

[1] Includes a small amount of grants to state and local governments and direct payments for individuals. [2] Includes some off-budget amounts; most of the off-budget amounts are direct payments for individuals (social security benefits).
Source: U.S. Office of Management and Budget, *Historical Tables*, annual.

No. 462. Federal Outlays by Agency: 1990 to 2001

[In billions of dollars (1,253.2 represents $1,253,198,000,000). See headnote, Table 457]

Department or other unit	1990	1995	1998	1999	2000	2001, est.
Total outlays	1,253.2	1,515.8	1,652.6	1,703.0	1,788.8	1,856.2
Legislative Branch	2.2	2.6	2.6	2.6	2.9	3.1
The Judiciary Branch	1.6	2.9	3.5	3.8	4.1	4.3
Agriculture	46.0	56.7	53.9	62.8	75.7	69.6
Commerce	3.7	3.4	4.0	5.0	7.8	5.5
Defense-Military	289.8	259.6	256.1	261.4	281.2	283.9
Education	23.0	31.2	31.5	32.3	33.9	36.7
Energy	12.1	17.6	14.4	16.0	15.0	16.7
Health and Human Services	175.5	303.1	350.6	359.7	382.6	430.5
Housing and Urban Development	20.2	29.0	30.2	32.7	30.8	37.3
Interior	5.8	7.5	7.3	7.8	8.0	8.7
Justice	6.5	10.8	16.2	18.3	19.6	20.7
Labor	25.2	32.1	30.0	32.5	31.4	38.2
State	4.8	6.3	5.4	6.5	6.9	9.3
Transportation	28.7	38.8	39.5	41.8	46.0	50.6
Treasury	255.2	348.6	390.1	386.7	391.2	388.5
Veterans Affairs	29.0	37.8	41.8	43.2	47.1	45.2
Corps of Engineers	3.3	3.7	3.8	4.2	4.3	4.6
Other Defense-Civil Programs	21.7	28.0	31.2	32.0	32.9	34.4
Environmental Protection Agency	5.1	6.4	6.3	6.8	7.2	7.5
Executive Office of the President	0.2	0.2	0.2	0.4	0.3	0.3
Federal Emergency Management Administration	2.2	3.1	2.1	4.0	3.1	3.1
General Services Administration	-0.1	0.8	1.1	(Z)	(Z)	0.6
International Assistance Programs	10.1	11.1	9.0	10.1	12.1	11.4
National Aeronautics and Space Administration	12.4	13.4	14.2	13.7	13.4	13.8
National Science Foundation	1.8	2.8	3.2	3.3	3.5	4.0
Office of Personnel Management	31.9	41.3	46.3	47.5	48.7	51.0
Social Security Administration (on-budget)	18.1	31.8	38.1	40.6	45.6	41.1
Social Security Administration (off-budget)	245.0	330.4	370.1	379.2	396.2	421.9
Undistributed offsetting receipts	-98.9	-137.6	-161.0	-159.1	-172.8	-190.2

Z $50 million or less.
Source: U.S. Office of Management and Budget, *Historical Tables*, annual.

U.S. Census Bureau, Statistical Abstract of the United States: 2001

No. 463. Federal Outlays by Detailed Function: 1990 to 2001

[In billions of dollars (1,253.2 represents $1,253,198,000,000)]

Superfunction and function	1990	1995	1998	1999	2000	2001, est.
Outlays, total	**1,253.2**	**1,515.8**	**1,652.6**	**1,702.9**	**1,788.8**	**1,856.2**
National defense.	299.3	272.1	268.5	274.9	294.5	299.1
Department of Defense-Military.	289.8	259.4	256.1	261.4	281.2	283.9
Military personnel	75.6	70.8	69.0	69.5	76.0	72.1
Operation and maintenance	88.3	91.1	93.5	96.4	105.9	110.4
Procurement	81.0	55.0	48.2	48.8	51.7	52.7
Research, development, test, and evaluation. . . .	37.5	34.6	37.4	37.4	37.6	38.0
Military construction	5.1	6.8	6.0	5.5	5.1	5.2
Family housing.	3.5	3.6	3.9	3.7	3.4	3.7
Atomic energy defense activities.	9.0	11.8	11.3	12.4	12.2	13.7
International affairs	13.8	16.4	13.1	15.2	17.2	17.5
International devel. & humanitarian assist.	5.5	7.6	5.4	5.7	6.5	7.0
International security assistance	8.7	5.3	5.1	5.5	6.4	6.3
Conduct of foreign affairs	3.1	4.2	3.3	4.2	4.7	6.7
Foreign information and exchange activities	1.1	1.4	1.2	1.2	0.8	0.9
International financial programs	-4.5	-2.0	-1.9	-1.3	-1.2	-3.5
General science, space and technology	14.4	16.7	18.2	18.1	18.6	19.7
General science and basic research	2.8	4.1	5.4	5.7	6.2	6.9
Space flight, research, and supporting activities. . . .	11.6	12.6	12.9	12.4	12.4	12.9
Energy	3.3	4.9	1.3	0.9	-1.1	-0.7
Energy supply	2.0	3.6	0.2	-0.1	-2.1	-1.7
Energy conservation.	0.4	0.7	0.6	0.6	0.7	0.7
Emergency energy preparedness	0.4	0.2	0.2	0.2	0.2	0.2
Energy information, policy, and regulation.	0.6	0.5	0.2	0.2	0.2	0.2
Natural resources and environment [1]	17.1	21.9	22.3	24.0	25.0	27.4
Water resources	4.4	4.6	4.7	4.7	5.1	5.4
Conservation and land management	3.6	5.3	5.5	5.7	5.9	6.8
Recreational resources	1.9	2.7	2.8	3.4	3.4	3.8
Pollution control and abatement	5.2	6.5	6.4	6.9	7.4	7.7
Agriculture	12.0	9.8	12.2	23.0	36.6	25.9
Farm income stabilization	9.8	7.0	9.3	20.0	33.5	22.1
Agricultural research and services.	2.2	2.8	2.9	3.0	3.2	3.8
Commerce and housing credit [1]	67.6	-17.8	1.0	2.6	3.2	-0.8
Mortgage credit	3.8	-1.0	-2.9	0.4	-3.3	1.3
Postal Service	2.1	-1.8	0.3	1.1	2.1	2.7
Deposit insurance	57.9	-17.8	-4.4	-5.3	-3.1	-1.0
Transportation [1]	29.5	39.4	40.3	42.5	46.9	51.1
Ground transportation	19.0	25.3	26.0	28.1	31.7	34.5
Air transportation	7.2	10.0	10.6	10.7	10.6	12.0
Water transportation	3.2	3.7	3.5	3.5	4.4	4.4
Community and regional development.	8.5	10.7	9.8	11.9	10.6	10.6
Community development	3.5	4.7	5.1	5.1	5.5	5.5
Area and regional development	2.9	2.7	2.5	2.3	2.5	2.8
Disaster relief and insurance	2.1	3.3	2.1	4.4	2.6	2.3
Educ./training/employment/& soc. services [1]	38.8	54.3	55.0	56.2	59.2	65.3
Elementary, secondary, and vocational education. . .	9.9	14.7	16.6	17.6	20.6	23.5
Higher education	11.1	14.2	12.1	11.6	10.1	9.6
Research and general education aids	1.6	2.1	2.3	2.3	2.5	3.0
Training and employment	5.6	7.4	6.6	6.8	6.8	8.1
Social services	9.7	14.9	16.3	16.9	18.0	19.6
Health.	57.7	115.4	131.4	141.1	154.5	175.3
Health care services.	47.6	101.9	116.3	124.5	136.2	154.2
Health research and training	8.6	11.6	13.1	14.4	16.0	18.5
Consumer and occupational health and safety	1.5	1.9	2.0	2.2	2.3	2.5
Medicare	98.1	159.9	192.8	190.4	197.1	219.3
Income security [1]	147.1	220.5	233.2	237.7	247.9	262.6
Gen. retirement & disability ins. (exc. soc. sec.). . . .	5.1	5.1	4.6	1.9	5.0	5.6
Federal employee retirement and disability	52.0	65.9	73.5	75.1	77.2	81.2
Unemployment compensation	18.9	23.6	22.1	23.6	23.0	27.8
Housing assistance	15.9	27.5	28.7	27.7	28.8	31.0
Food and nutrition assistance.	24.0	37.6	33.6	33.1	32.5	35.0
Social security	248.6	335.8	379.2	390.0	409.4	433.6
Veterans benefits and services [1]	29.1	37.9	41.8	43.2	47.1	45.4
Income security for veterans	15.2	19.0	21.3	22.2	24.9	22.4
Veterans education, training and rehabilitation.	0.3	1.1	1.1	1.3	1.3	1.7
Hospital and medical care for veterans	12.1	16.4	17.5	18.2	19.5	20.8
Veterans housing.	0.5	0.3	0.8	0.6	0.3	-1.0
Administration of justice	10.0	16.2	22.8	25.9	27.8	29.4
General government	10.6	14.0	15.7	15.8	13.5	16.8
Net interest [1]	184.4	232.2	241.2	229.7	223.2	206.4
Interest on Treasury debt securities (gross).	264.7	332.4	363.8	353.5	362.0	357.9
Interest received by on-budget trust funds	-46.3	-59.9	-67.2	-66.6	-69.1	-73.7
Interest received by off-budget trust funds	-16.0	-33.3	-46.6	-52.1	-59.8	-68.9
Undistributed offsetting receipts	-36.6	-44.5	-47.2	-40.4	-42.6	-47.7

[1] Includes functions not shown separately.

Source: U.S. Office of Management and Budget, *Historical Tables*, annual.

No. 464. Tax Expenditures Estimates Selected by Function: 2000 to 2003

[In millions of dollars (6,200 represents $6,200,000,000). For years ending Sept. 30. Tax expenditures are defined as *revenue losses* attributable to provisions of the federal tax laws which allow a special exclusion, exemption, or deduction from gross income or which provide a special credit, a preferential rate of tax, or a deferral of liability. Covers only tax expenditures of $3.0 billion or more in 2003]

Function and provision	2000	2002	2003
International affairs:			
Current law tax expenditures:			
Extraterritorial income exclusion	(X)	4,810	5,150
Deferral of income from controlled foreign corporations [1]	6,200	7,000	7,450
Total, current law income tax expenditures	16,630	18,340	18,910
General science, space, and technology:			
Current law tax expenditures:			
Credit for increasing research activities	1,630	6,760	5,390
Total, current law income tax expenditures	3,310	8,440	7,160
Commerce and housing:			
Current law tax expenditures:			
Financial institutions and insurance:			
Exclusion of interest on life insurance savings	13,950	16,520	17,990
Housing:			
Deductibility of mortgage interest on owner-occupied homes	60,270	65,750	68,050
Deduct. of state & local property tax on owner-occupied homes . . .	22,140	25,570	27,220
Capital gains exclusion on home sales	18,540	19,670	20,260
Exception from passive loss rules for $25,000 of rental loss	4,720	4,220	4,000
Credit for low-income housing investments	3,210	3,460	3,600
Accelerated depreciation on rental housing [1]	4,740	5,520	5,830
Commerce:			
Capital gains (except agri., timber, iron ore, and coal) [1]	40,520	42,950	44,220
Step-up basis of capital gains at death	27,090	29,370	30,540
Accelerated depreciation of machinery and equipment [1]	30,660	35,400	37,680
Graduated corporation income tax rate [1]	6,480	7,140	7,460
Total, current law income tax expenditures	242,455	266,700	277,810
Education, training, employment, and social services:			
Current law tax expenditures:			
Education:			
HOPE tax credit	4,210	4,610	4,280
Deductibility of charitable contributions (education)	2,730	2,930	3,090
Training, employment, and social services:			
Deduct. of charitable contrib., other than educ. and health	20,150	22,030	23,160
Total, current law income tax expenditures	36,030	38,770	40,410
Health:			
Current law income tax expenditures:			
Exc. of employer contrib. for med. ins. premiums & med. care	76,530	92,230	99,800
Workers' compensation insurance premiums	4,620	5,090	5,350
Deductibility of medical expenses	4,250	4,870	5,170
Deductibility of charitable contributions (health)	2,910	3,100	3,270
Total, current law income tax expenditures	91,080	108,620	117,750
Income security:			
Current law tax expenditures:			
Exclusion of workers' compensation benefits	5,120	5,810	6,070
Child credit	19,330	18,980	18,410
Earned income tax credit	4,644	4,963	5,225
Total, current law income tax expenditures	147,604	159,053	165,675
Social Security:			
Current law tax expenditures:			
Exclusion of social security benefits:			
Social Security benefits for retired workers	18,250	19,930	20,520
Social Security benefits for disabled	2,640	3,160	3,490
Social Security benefits for dependents and survivors	3,910	4,210	4,440
Total, current law income tax expenditures	24,800	27,300	28,450
Veterans benefits and services:			
Current law tax expenditures:			
Exclusion of veterans death benefits and disability compensation	3,090	3,460	3,640
Total, current law income tax expenditures	3,280	3,670	3,860
General purpose fiscal assistance:			
Current law tax expenditures:			
Exclusion of interest on public purpose state and local bonds	22,600	23,510	23,980
Deductibility of nonbusiness state and local taxes	42,650	48,730	51,780
Total, current law income tax expenditures	67,720	74,800	78,340

X Not applicable.   [1] Normal tax method.

Source: U.S. Office of Management and Budget, *Budget of the United States Government*, annual.

No. 465. United States Government—Balance Sheet: 1990 to 2000

[In millions of dollars (70,415 represents $70,415,000,000). For fiscal year ending in year shown]

Item	1990	1995	1999	2000
Assets, total	**70,415**	**89,349**	**170,378**	**180,798**
Cash and monetary assets, total	6C.839	84,080	103,507	98,401
U.S. Treasury operating cash:				
Federal Reserve account	7,638	8,620	6,641	8,459
Tax and loan note accounts	32,517	29,329	49,817	44,199
Special drawing rights (SDR):				
Total holdings	10,666	11,035	10,284	10,316
SDR's certificates issued to Federal Reserve Banks	-8,518	-10,168	-7,200	-3,200
Monetary assets with IMF [1]	8,883	14,682	19,982	13,690
Other cash and monetary assets:				
U.S. Treasury monetary assets	1,572	356	30	
Cash and other assets held outside the Treasury Account	8,079	29,697	18,341	18,960
U.S. Treasury time deposits	(NA)	528	5,612	5,977
Loan financing accounts:				
Guaranteed loans	(NA)	-12,714	-18,518	-22,956
Direct loans	(NA)	19,732	83,894	105,459
Miscellaneous asset accounts	9,576	-1,748	1,496	-107
Total assets and excess of liabilities over assets	**2,479,165**	**3,674,266**	**3,690,740**	**3,467,468**
Excess of liabilities over assets at beginning of fiscal year	2,188,926	3,421,723	3,645,730	3,520,361
Add: Total deficit for fiscal year	220,388	163,916	-124,360	-236,897
Subtotal	2,409,314	3,585,639	3,521,370	3,283,464
Deduct: Other transactions not applied to surplus or deficit	*564*	*722*	*1,009*	*-3,207*
Excess of liabilities over assets at close of fiscal year	2,408,750	3,584,917	3,520,361	3,286,671
Liabilities, total	**2,479,165**	**3,674,266**	**3,690,740**	**3,467,468**
Federal securities, total	3,266,073	4,920,944	5,606,080	5,629,009
Treasury debt securities, total	3,293,124	4,893,989	5,577,575	5,601,336
Treasury debt securities outstanding	3,233,313	4,973,985	5,656,271	5,674,178
Premium and discount on public debt securities	-59,811	-79,996	-78,696	-72,842
Agency securities outstanding	32,758	26,955	28,505	27,672
Deduct: Net Federal securities held as investments by government accounts	*795,907*	*1,317,645*	*1,973,160*	*2,218,896*
Equals: Borrowing from the public, total	2,470,166	3,603,299	3,632,920	3,410,113
Accrued interest payable	43,799	50,611	42,603	44,211
Special drawing rights allocated by IMF [1]	6,823	7,380	6,799	6,359
Deposit fund liabilities	8,306	8,186	3,998	2,826
Miscellaneous liability accounts (checks outstanding, etc.)	9,882	4,790	4,420	3,959

Represents zero.   NA Not available.   [1] IMF = International Monetary Funds.

Source: U.S. Dept of Treasury, *United States Government Annual Report.*

No. 466. Federal Participation in the Credit Market: 1970 to 2000

[In millions of dollars (11.3 represents $11,300,000), except percents]

Item	1970	1980	1990	1995	1996	1997	1998	1999	2000, est.
Total, federal and federally assisted borrowing	**11.3**	**103.2**	**261.6**	**197.5**	**219.6**	**96.1**	**7.3**	**-27.9**	**-76.0**
Federal borrowing from the public	3.5	71.6	220.9	171.3	129.7	38.3	-51.2	-88.7	-170.9
Guaranteed borrowing	7.8	31.6	40.7	26.2	89.9	57.8	58.5	60.8	94.9
Total, federal and federally assisted lending	**10.8**	**55.8**	**43.5**	**27.8**	**93.9**	**70.6**	**65.3**	**74.2**	**104.8**
Direct loans	3.0	24.2	2.8	1.6	4.0	12.8	6.8	13.4	9.9
Guaranteed loans	7.8	31.6	40.7	26.2	89.9	57.8	58.5	60.8	94.9
Total net borrowing in credit market	88.2	336.9	704.1	720.4	727.1	713.5	975.3	1,091.4	(NA)
Federal borrowing participation rate (percent)	12.8	30.6	37.2	27.4	30.2	13.5	0.7	-2.6	(NA)
Total net lending in credit market	88.2	336.9	704.1	720.4	727.1	713.5	975.3	1091.4	(NA)
Federal lending participation rate (percent)	12.2	16.6	6.2	3.9	12.9	9.9	6.7	6.8	(NA)

NA Not available.

Source: U.S. Office of Management and Budget, *Analytical Perspectives,* annual.

No. 467. Summary of Federal Debt: 1990 to 1999

[In millions of dollars ($3,266,073 represents $3,266,073,000,000). As of end of fiscal year]

Item	1990	1995	1997	1998	1999
Debt outstanding, total	3,266,073	5,000,945	5,446,333	5,555,565	5,685,181
Public debt securities	3,233,313	4,973,983	5,413,146	5,526,193	5,656,271
Agency securities	32,758	26,962	33,187	29,372	28,910
Securities held by–					
Government accounts, total	795,907	1,320,800	1,605,557	1,769,497	1,989,705
Public debt securities	795,762	1,320,784	1,598,459	1,765,580	1,989,072
Agency securities	145	16	7,098	3,917	634
The public, total	2,470,166	3,680,145	3,840,776	3,786,068	3,695,476
Public debt securities	2,437,551	3,653,199	3,814,687	3,760,613	3,667,199
Agency securities	32,613	26,946	26,089	25,455	28,276
Interest-bearing public debt, total	3,210,943	4,950,644	5,407,528	5,518,681	5,647,241
Marketable, total	2,092,759	3,260,447	3,439,616	3,331,030	3,232,998
Treasury bills	482,454	742,462	701,909	637,648	653,165
Treasury notes	1,218,081	1,980,343	2,122,172	2,009,115	1,828,775
Treasury bonds	377,224	522,643	576,151	610,444	643,695
Treasury inflation-indexed notes	(Z)	(Z)	24,384	58,823	92,365
Federal Financing Bank	15,000	15,000	15,000	15,000	15,000
Nonmarketable, total	1,118,184	1,690,197	1,967,912	2,187,651	2,414,242
U.S. savings bonds	122,152	181,181	182,665	180,816	180,019
Foreign series: Government	36,041	40,950	34,909	35,079	30,970
Government account series, total	779,412	1,324,270	1,606,478	1,777,329	2,005,166
Airport and airway trust fund	14,312	11,145	6,360	8,550	12,414
Bank insurance fund	8,438	20,117	26,329	27,445	28,359
Employees life insurance fund	9,561	15,839	18,038	19,377	20,755
Exchange stabilization fund	1,863	2,399	15,460	15,981	12,382
Federal disability insurance trust fund	11,254	35,150	63,513	76,947	92,622
Federal employees retirement funds	223,229	357,539	407,202	440,145	474,692
Federal hospital insurance trust fund	98,249	129,864	116,621	118,250	153,767
Federal Housing Administration	6,678	6,277	13,643	14,518	15,152
Fed. old-age & survivors insurance trust fund	203,717	447,947	567,445	653,282	762,226
Fed. S&L Corp., resolution fund	929	528	1,806	2,087	2,304
Fed. supplementary medical insur. trust fund	14,286	13,513	34,464	39,502	26,528
Government life insurance fund	184	106	(Z)	(Z)	(Z)
Highway trust fund	9,530	8,954	22,341	17,928	28,083
National service life insurance fund	10,917	11,954	12,023	12,008	11,954
Postal Service fund	3,063	1,249	860	1,000	-
Railroad retirement account	8,356	12,129	17,486	19,764	22,347
Treasury deposit funds	304	130	74	71	71
Unemployment trust fund	50,186	47,098	61,880	70,598	77,357
Other	106,376	202,332	222,933	239,878	264,153
State and local government series	161,248	113,368	111,863	164,431	168,091
Domestic series	18,886	29,995	29,995	29,995	29,995
Other	447	432	1	1	1
MATURITY DISTRIBUTION					
Amount outstanding, privately held	1,841,903	2,870,781	2,998,846	2,856,637	2,726,011
Maturity class:					
Within 1 year	626,297	1,002,875	1,017,913	940,572	915,146
1-5 years	630,144	1,157,492	1,206,993	1,105,175	946,041
5-10 years	267,573	290,111	321,622	319,331	331,115
10-20 years	82,713	87,297	154,205	157,347	149,703
20 years and over	235,176	333,006	298,113	334,212	298,750

- Represents zero.   Z Less than $500,000.

Source: U.S. Department of the Treasury, *Treasury Bulletin*, quarterly.

No. 468. U.S. Savings Bonds: 1980 to 1999

[In billions of dollars ($73 represents $73,000,000,000), except percent. As of end of fiscal year; see text, Section 8, State and Local Government Finances and Employment]

Item	1980	1990	1991	1992	1993	1994	1995	1996	1997	1998	1999
Amounts outstanding, total [1]	73	123	134	149	167	177	182	184	183	181	180
Funds from sales	5	8	9	14	17	9	7	6	5	5	6
Accrued discounts	4	8	10	9	9	9	9	10	9	9	9
Redemptions [2]	17	8	8	7	8	9	12	2	2	14	14
Percent of total outstanding	23.0	6.1	5.6	5.0	4.7	5.3	6.5	1.4	1.1	7.9	7.9

[1] Interest-bearing debt only for amounts end of year.   [2] Matured and unmatured bonds.

Source: U.S. Dept. of the Treasury, *Treasury Bulletin*, quarterly.

U.S. Census Bureau, Statistical Abstract of the United States: 2001

No. 469. Federal Funds—Summary Distribution by State: 1999

[In millions of dollars ($1,637,170 represents $1,637,170,000,000). For year ending Sept. 30. Data for grants, salaries and wages and direct payments to individuals are on an expenditures basis; procurement is on obligation basis]

State	Federal funds		Defense	Non-defense	Direct payments to individuals	Procure-ment	Grants to state and local govern-ments	Salaries and wages
	Total [1]	Per capita [2] (dol.)						
United States [3] . . .	1,637,170	5,740	238,224	1,398,947	920,780	223,324	308,530	184,537
Alabama	29,217	6,570	5,534	23,683	16,820	4,691	4,833	2,873
Alaska.	5,953	9,496	1,712	4,242	1,322	1,108	2,174	1,349
Arizona	29,244	5,700	6,585	22,659	16,390	5,286	4,704	2,865
Arkansas	14,828	5,546	1,132	13,696	10,284	587	2,778	1,178
California	175,751	5,189	29,256	146,495	94,881	26,955	36,080	17,835
Colorado	22,918	5,328	4,585	18,334	11,191	4,349	3,591	3,787
Connecticut	19,517	5,731	2,674	16,843	11,390	2,699	4,033	1,396
Delaware	3,959	5,053	425	3,534	2,550	149	838	422
District of Columbia . . .	28,254	49,391	2,521	25,733	3,881	7,491	4,675	12,208
Florida	92,776	5,805	13,460	79,317	63,899	8,594	12,149	8,135
Georgia	42,460	5,187	8,499	33,961	23,137	5,102	7,520	6,700
Hawaii.	9,015	7,441	3,473	5,542	3,960	1,278	1,348	2,429
Idaho	7,009	5,417	625	6,384	3,664	1,347	1,270	728
Illinois	60,008	4,832	3,973	56,035	38,572	3,999	11,228	6,210
Indiana	28,723	4,724	2,506	26,218	19,220	2,192	5,108	2,204
Iowa	14,751	5,041	896	13,855	9,934	1,115	2,714	988
Kansas	14,260	5,304	2,048	12,212	8,797	1,297	2,323	1,844
Kentucky	24,444	6,048	2,683	21,761	14,286	2,747	4,687	2,724
Louisiana	25,955	5,808	3,399	22,556	15,296	3,096	5,300	2,264
Maine	7,849	6,157	1,303	6,546	4,419	881	1,770	779
Maryland	45,089	8,513	8,596	36,493	18,453	10,551	6,911	9,174
Massachusetts	40,824	6,430	5,607	35,217	22,661	6,006	9,070	3,087
Michigan	46,823	4,711	2,345	44,478	31,216	2,374	10,107	3,126
Minnesota	22,992	4,674	1,927	21,065	14,251	2,090	4,753	1,897
Mississippi	18,358	6,454	2,943	15,416	11,145	1,978	3,517	1,718
Missouri.	35,687	6,378	6,020	29,668	20,260	6,053	5,939	3,437
Montana	5,917	6,558	390	5,527	3,466	288	1,474	689
Nebraska.	9,611	5,617	908	8,703	6,370	486	1,720	1,035
Nevada	8,626	4,317	1,081	7,545	5,475	836	1,340	976
New Hampshire	5,802	4,695	689	5,113	3,570	523	1,238	471
New Jersey	43,469	5,166	4,405	39,064	27,748	4,106	7,876	3,739
New Mexico	14,470	7,954	1,714	12,755	5,612	4,134	3,032	1,692
New York.	110,333	5,814	5,585	104,748	63,982	6,909	31,564	7,879
North Carolina	41,367	5,139	5,858	35,508	24,767	2,555	8,518	5,527
North Dakota	5,245	8,166	506	4,738	3,289	238	1,101	616
Ohio	57,355	5,052	5,099	52,256	37,196	4,867	10,665	4,627
Oklahoma	20,613	5,974	3,714	16,899	12,139	1,940	3,583	2,951
Oregon	16,553	4,838	824	15,729	10,491	790	3,684	1,589
Pennsylvania	73,715	6,002	6,057	67,658	47,877	6,284	13,940	5,615
Rhode Island	6,876	6,559	918	5,958	3,996	584	1,574	722
South Carolina	22,294	5,557	3,499	18,796	12,877	2,774	4,163	2,481
South Dakota	5,138	6,807	344	4,794	3,187	279	1,088	584
Tennessee	33,560	5,899	2,250	31,310	19,138	5,217	6,372	2,833
Texas	106,493	5,107	20,564	85,928	57,039	18,981	18,346	12,126
Utah	10,037	4,494	1,934	8,103	4,773	1,597	2,065	1,603
Vermont	3,362	5,523	346	3,017	1,793	320	929	320
Virginia	62,709	8,859	24,543	38,166	23,747	21,321	5,163	12,477
Washington	33,897	5,751	6,130	27,767	17,948	4,664	6,345	4,940
West Virginia	11,739	6,491	352	11,387	7,424	622	2,729	963
Wisconsin	24,300	4,531	1,231	23,069	15,986	1,460	5,254	1,600
Wyoming	3,220	6,521	326	2,894	1,457	323	1,022	417

[1] Includes other programs not shown separately. [2] Based on Census Bureau resident population as of July 1. [3] Includes outlying areas, not shown separately.

Source: U.S. Census Bureau, Consolidated Federal Funds Report, annual.

Federal Government Finances and Employment 311

No. 470. Per Capita Federal Balance of Payments by State: 1990 to 1999

[For year ending Sept. 30. Represents federal spending within the borders of the 50 states, including defense and excluding interest payments on the federal debt. Each state runs a balance of payments surplus or deficit with the federal government. Put another way, each state indirectly subsidizes or is being subsidized by the other states]

State	1990	1995	1997	1998	1999					
					Amount	Rank	Spend-ing	Defense	Non-defense	Social security
Alabama	1,948	1,629	1,717	1,863	$2,091	9	6,610	4,519	1,320	1,964
Alaska	1,025	1,063	1,969	2,155	2,777	6	7,649	4,872	2,194	3,786
Arizona	1,163	853	387	493	904	20	5,617	4,713	1,361	1,689
Arkansas	1,163	1,057	1,348	1,534	1,633	13	5,871	4,238	595	1,772
California	-481	-255	-463	-600	-685	39	4,909	5,593	943	1,439
Colorado	960	-233	-530	-444	-620	38	5,303	5,923	1,408	1,884
Connecticut	-1,898	-2,466	-2,438	-2,432	-2,840	50	5,224	8,064	1,046	1,156
Delaware	-1,861	-1,415	-1,025	-1,050	-1,025	43	4,851	5,876	615	1,458
District of Columbia	28,482	33,259	36,318	37,804	42,514	(X)	49,965	7,451	6,295	39,471
Florida	57	258	354	128	47	31	6,121	6,074	1,058	1,392
Georgia	-218	85	-77	-111	-29	32	5,493	5,523	1,322	1,626
Hawaii	1,056	908	1,718	1,981	1,982	10	5,937	3,955	2,391	1,441
Idaho	1,342	552	569	817	829	21	5,178	4,349	1,166	1,616
Illinois	-1,588	-1,687	-1,717	-1,535	-1,669	47	4,592	6,260	354	1,442
Indiana	-478	-789	-495	-374	-399	35	4,686	5,085	493	1,318
Iowa	366	53	255	548	750	22	5,820	5,071	325	2,409
Kansas	318	46	-40	187	373	25	5,832	5,459	898	2,083
Kentucky	1,192	1,363	1,613	2,073	1,595	14	6,111	4,516	970	1,702
Louisiana	1,147	1,439	1,636	1,312	1,576	15	6,008	4,432	788	1,815
Maine	821	1,262	1,599	1,668	1,324	16	5,539	4,215	1,110	1,399
Maryland	1,306	1,731	1,802	2,148	1,770	12	8,334	6,564	1,895	3,768
Massachusetts	89	-304	-622	-793	-895	42	5,361	6,256	836	1,528
Michigan	-1,070	-1,411	-1,387	-1,231	-1,042	44	4,682	5,724	265	1,197
Minnesota	-680	-1,454	-1,433	-1,568	-1,294	45	4,775	6,069	432	1,713
Mississippi	2,364	2,409	2,333	2,351	2,684	7	6,589	3,905	1,285	1,877
Missouri	1,633	1,457	1,212	1,269	1,187	18	6,544	5,358	1,293	1,966
Montana	1,764	1,774	2,189	2,454	3,109	2	7,389	4,279	596	3,939
Nebraska	587	-166	-157	125	320	27	5,624	5,304	657	2,177
Nevada	-991	-1,420	-1,625	-1,802	-1,583	46	4,355	5,938	944	1,172
New Hampshire	-1,644	-1,430	-1,498	-1,565	-1,787	48	4,067	5,854	576	1,189
New Jersey	-2,404	-2,079	-2,006	-2,054	-2,342	49	4,362	6,705	504	1,097
New Mexico	3,906	3,651	3,603	3,778	3,944	1	7,992	4,048	2,655	2,678
New York	-1,068	-943	-702	-854	-890	41	4,944	5,834	305	1,370
North Carolina	-179	-41	53	66	146	30	5,287	5,141	898	1,415
North Dakota	2,167	1,870	2,644	2,568	3,043	4	7,690	4,647	1,005	3,745
Ohio	-186	-438	-412	-369	-344	34	4,827	5,171	514	1,275
Oklahoma	1,028	1,233	1,642	1,755	1,866	11	6,198	4,332	1,255	1,864
Oregon	-25	-436	-412	-441	-483	36	4,752	5,235	354	1,564
Pennsylvania	-222	166	167	218	256	28	5,531	5,275	563	1,450
Rhode Island	141	495	649	754	528	23	5,504	4,976	824	1,409
South Carolina	1,592	1,119	1,023	1,159	1,265	17	5,810	4,546	1,438	1,346
South Dakota	1,682	1,053	1,659	1,838	2,327	8	7,276	4,949	638	3,720
Tennessee	700	742	776	1,000	961	19	6,071	5,110	686	2,029
Texas	-100	-54	-142	-252	-189	33	5,377	5,566	1,037	1,801
Utah	1,503	734	46	9	230	29	4,324	4,094	725	1,854
Vermont	-623	18	39	167	343	26	5,061	4,719	587	1,690
Virginia	2,454	2,970	2,779	2,969	3,069	3	8,825	5,756	3,685	2,851
Washington	264	-31	-143	-355	-533	37	5,339	5,872	1,377	1,490
West Virginia	1,627	2,415	2,387	2,710	2,808	5	6,724	3,916	419	2,036
Wisconsin	-715	-1,149	-953	-886	-887	40	4,521	5,409	284	1,333
Wyoming	836	294	617	243	386	24	6,338	5,951	769	3,062

X Not applicable.

Source: Jay H. Walder and Herman B. Leonard, Taubman Center for State and Local Government and John F. Kennedy School of Government, Harvard University, The Federal Budget and the States, annual.

No. 471. Tax Returns Filed—Examination Coverage: 1988 to 1999

[In thousands (103,251 represents 103,251,000, except as indicated. Return classification as Schedule C or C-EZ (nonfarm sole proprietorships) or Schedule F (farm proprietorships) for audit examination purposes was based on the largest source of income on the return and certain other characteristics. Therefore, some returns with business activity are reflected in the nonbusiness individual income tax return statistics in the table below (and vise versa), so that the statistics for the number of returns with Schedule C is not comparable to the number of nonfarm sole proprietorship returns in Table 713. Series completely revised starting with fiscal year 1988]

Year and item	Returns filed [1]	Returns examined					Average tax and penalty per return (dollars)		
		Total	Percent coverage	By—			Revenue agents [3]	Tax auditors	Service centers
				Revenue agents	Tax auditors	Service centers [2]			
INDIVIDUAL RETURNS									
1988	103,251	1,621	1.57	353	532	736	997,696	2,188	1,950
1989	107,029	1,385	1.29	243	543	599	246,371	1,827	1,649
1990	109,868	1,145	1.04	202	517	426	309,566	1,962	2,432
1991	112,3.5	1,313	1.17	200	500	613	664,440	2,398	2,738
1992	113,829	1,206	1.06	210	537	459	1,365,896	2,280	2,539
1993	114,719	1,059	0.92	251	506	303	103,250	2,625	2,974
1994	113,754	1,226	1.08	364	456	406	246,785	3,113	1,963
1995	114,683	1,919	1.67	339	459	1,122	204,616	3,497	1,404
1996	116,060	1,942	1.67	252	509	1,180	818,753	3,051	1,714
1997	118,363	1,519	1.28	210	506	804	802,549	3,460	2,963
1998	120,342	1,193	0.99	168	383	625	177,830	3,372	2,760
1999 [4]									
Individual, total	122,547	1,100	0.9	124	236	716	322,230	3,265	2,085
1040A, TPI under $25,000 [5]	44,323	601	1.36	13	53	524	56,542	2,821	2,171
Non 1040, TPI under $25,000 [5]	13,110	76	0.58	8	23	43	16,289	2,361	1,691
TPI $25,000 under $50,000 [5]	28,832	103	0.36	12	47	40	24,148	2,013	1,422
TPI $50,000 under $100,000 [5]	20,873	78	0.37	12	40	23	44,723	2,596	1,136
TPI $100,000 and over [5]	7,025	80	1.14	32	21	26	480,050	5,344	4,046
Sch C—TGR under $25,000 [6]	2,547	68	2.69	6	19	41	8,555	2,758	1,433
Sch C—TGR $25,000 under $100,000 [6]	3,267	42	1.3	10	22	9	65,763	5,170	1,547
Sch C—TGR $100,000 and over [6]	1,876	45	2.4	29	10	6	136,064	9,088	2,699
Sch F—TGR under $100,000 [6]	417	3	0.68	1	1	1	8,802	2,782	819
Sch F—TGR $100,000 and over [6]	277	3	1.23	2	1	2	31,217	3,841	1,206
Corporation (except S Corporation)	2,523	39	1.55	50	(NA)	2	4,704,095	(NA)	5,732
Fiduciary	3,398	6	0.19	2	(NA)	4	1,887,997	(NA)	634
Estate	110	9	8.46	10	(NA)	0.4	116,993	(NA)	6,837
Gift	261	2	0.91	2	(NA)	0.001	190,791	(NA)	(NA)
Employment	29,132	24	0.08	21	2	0.3	121,026	5,959	1031
Excise	822	13	1.53	11	1	(NA)	48,884	9183	(NA)
Windfall profit	(NA)	(NA)	-	(NA)	(NA)	(NA)	(NA)	48	(NA)
Misc. taxable		0.3	-	0.02	(NA)	0.0006	372,816	(NA)	2,609
Partnerships	1,861	8	0.43	6	(NA)	2	(NA)	(NA)	(NA)
S Corporations (nontaxable)	2,600	21	0.81	20	(NA)	0.7	(NA)	(NA)	(NA)
Miscellaneous nontaxable [7]	(NA)	5	(NA)	0.03	(NA)	(NA)	(NA)	(NA)	(NA)

- Represents zero.   NA Not available.   [1] Returns filed in previous calendar year.   [2] Includes taxpayer contacts by correspondence.   [3] Mostly reflects coordinated examination of large corporations and related returns.   [4] Includes activities to protect release of funds in Treasury in response to taxpayer efforts to recoup tax previously assessed and paid with penalty.   [5] Total positive income, i.e., excludes losses.   [6] TGR = Total gross receipts.   [7] Includes Domestic International Sales Corporations, Interest Charge Domestic International Sales Corporations, Real Estate Investment Mortgage Conduits, and other.

Source: U.S. Internal Revenue Service, *IRS Data Book, 1999*, Publication 55B.

No. 472. Internal Revenue Gross Collections by Source: 1980 to 1999

[For fiscal year ending in year shown; see text, Section 8, State and Local Government Finances and Employment]

Source of revenue	Collections (bil. dol.)					Percent of total				
	1980	1990	1995	1998	1999	1980	1990	1995	1998	1999
All taxes	519	1,078	1,389	1,769	1,904	100.0	100.0	100.0	100.0	100.0
Individual income taxes	288	540	676	928	1,002	54.9	50.1	48.7	52.5	52.6
Withheld by employers	224	388	534	647	694	43.1	36.0	38.4	36.6	36.4
Employment taxes [1]	128	367	465	558	599	24.7	34.0	33.5	31.5	31.4
Old-age and disability insurance	123	358	455	547	587	23.6	33.2	32.8	30.9	30.9
Unemployment insurance	3	6	6	6	7	0.6	0.6	0.4	0.4	0.3
Corporation income taxes	72	110	174	213	216	13.9	10.2	12.5	12.0	11.4
Estate and gift taxes	7	12	15	25	28	1.3	1.1	1.1	1.4	1.5
Excise taxes	25	49	59	45	55	4.7	4.5	4.2	3.3	2.6

[1] Includes railroad retirement, not shown separately.

Source: U.S. Internal Revenue Service, *Annual Report*, and Bureau of Alcohol, Tobacco, and Firearms, *Alcohol and Tobacco Tax Collections*.

No. 473. Federal Individual Income Tax Returns With Adjusted Gross Income (AGI)—Summary: 1990 and 1998

[Includes Puerto Rico and Virgin Islands. Includes returns of resident aliens, based on a sample of unaudited returns as filed. Data are not comparable for all years because of tax changes and other changes, as indicated. See *Statistics of Income, Individual Income Tax Returns* publications for a detailed explanation. See Appendix III]

Item	Number of returns (1,000)		Amount (mil. dol.)		Average amount (dollars)	
	1990	1998	1990	1998	1990	1998
Total returns	113,717	124,771	3,405,427	5,415,973	29,947	43,407
Adjusted gross income (AGI)	113,717	124,771	3,405,427	5,415,973	29,947	43,407
Salaries and wages	96,730	106,535	2,599,401	3,879,762	26,873	36,418
Taxable interest received	70,370	67,232	227,084	178,334	3,227	2,653
Tax-exempt interest	3,917	4,778	40,228	50,223	10,270	10,511
Dividends in AGI	22,904	30,423	80,169	118,480	3,500	3,894
Business or profession net income	11,222	13,083	161,657	226,145	14,405	17,285
Business or profession net loss	3,416	4,022	20,227	23,745	5,921	5,904
Net capital gain in AGI	9,217	20,957	123,783	455,223	13,430	21,722
Net capital loss in AGI	5,071	4,734	9,552	9,139	1,884	1,931
Sales of property other than capital assets, net gain	866	829	6,300	6,208	7,275	7,489
Sales of property other than capital assets, net loss	825	891	4,829	7,784	5,853	8,736
Pensions and annuities in AGI	17,014	20,473	159,294	280,650	9,363	13,708
Unemployment compensation in AGI	8,014	7,083	15,453	16,815	1,928	2,374
Social security benefits in AGI	5,083	8,941	19,687	68,703	3,873	7,684
Rent net income	3,934	4,339	25,886	40,610	6,580	9,359
Rent net loss	5,163	4,845	33,450	28,874	6,479	5,960
Royalty net income	1,171	1,131	4,534	5,938	3,872	5,250
Royalty net loss	49	53	126	198	2,571	3,736
Partnerships and S Corporations net income [1]	3,210	4,032	112,030	240,836	34,900	59,731
Partnerships and S Corporations net loss [1]	2,767	2,152	45,007	53,482	16,266	24,852
Estate or trust net income	445	485	4,633	10,495	10,411	21,639
Estate or trust net loss	74	45	468	1,031	6,324	22,911
Farm net income	996	673	11,395	8,809	11,441	13,089
Farm net loss	1,325	1,419	11,829	16,743	8,928	11,799
Statutory adjustments, total	16,648	21,998	33,974	51,531	2,041	2,343
Individual Retirement Arrangements	5,224	3,868	9,858	8,188	1,887	2,117
Student loan interest deduction	(NA)	3,764	(NA)	1,731	(NA)	460
Medical savings accounts	(NA)	42	(NA)	62	(NA)	1,476
Self-employed retirement plans	824	1,177	6,778	11,040	8,226	9,380
Deduction for self-employment tax	11,006	13,756	9,921	15,960	901	1,160
Self-employment health insurance	2,754	3,381	1,627	4,693	591	1,388
Exemptions, total [2]	227,549	245,593	465,985	650,347	2,048	2,648
Deductions, total	112,796	123,763	789,942	1,135,918	7,003	9,178
Standard deductions	80,621	85,576	331,457	459,457	4,111	5,369
Returns with additional standard deductions for age 65 or older or for blindness	10,954	11,082	10,616	14,057	969	1,268
Itemized deductions, total [3]	32,175	38,186	458,485	676,460	14,250	17,715
Medical and dental expenses	5,091	5,560	21,457	31,984	4,215	5,753
Taxes paid	31,594	37,576	140,011	241,783	4,432	6,435
Interest paid	29,395	32,024	208,354	271,624	7,088	8,482
Home mortgage interest paid	26,679	31,627	189,233	254,397	7,093	8,044
Charitable contributions	29,230	33,836	57,243	109,240	1,958	3,229
Taxable income	93,148	100,801	2,263,661	3,780,838	24,302	37,508
Income tax before credits	93,089	100,798	453,128	813,569	4,868	8,071
Tax credits, total [2]	12,484	34,272	6,831	30,056	547	877
Child care credit	6,144	6,128	2,549	2,661	415	434
Elderly and disabled credit	340	180	62	36	182	200
Child tax credit	(NA)	24,811	(NA)	15,143	(NA)	610
Education credit	(NA)	4,653	(NA)	3,377	(NA)	726
Foreign tax credit	772	2,995	1,682	4,677	2,179	1,562
General business credit	263	272	616	732	2,342	2,691
Income tax after credits	89,844	93,027	446,296	783,513	4,967	8,422
Income tax, total [4]	89,862	93,048	447,127	788,542	4,976	8,475
Minimum tax	(NA)	(NA)	(NA)	(NA)	(NA)	(NA)
Alternative minimum tax	132	853	830	5,015	6,288	5,879
Earned income credit	12,555	19,705	7,512	31,592	598	1,603
Used to offset income tax before credits	5,702	5,919	1,617	2,232	284	377
Used to offset other taxes	1,355	3,165	659	2,358	486	745
Excess earned income credit (refundable)	8,698	16,279	5,266	27,002	605	1,659
Tax payments, total	104,816	117,835	495,922	893,418	4,731	7,582
Excess social security tax withheld	931	1,304	905	1,524	972	1,169
Estimated tax payments	12,806	13,072	91,607	177,751	7,153	13,598
Payments with requests for extension of filing time	1,305	1,541	16,704	45,640	12,800	29,617
Taxes due at time of filing	26,987	28,430	56,561	102,151	2,096	3,593
Tax overpayments, total	83,508	93,435	88,479	167,987	1,060	1,798
Overpayment refunds	80,514	90,233	78,103	144,446	970	1,601

NA Not available.   [1] S Corporations are certain small corporations with up to 35 shareholders.   [2] Includes items not shown separately. Beginning 1996, total exemptions amount is after limitation.   [3] Beginning 1996, total itemized deductions are after limitation.   [4] Includes minimum tax or alternative minimum tax.

Source: U.S. Internal Revenue Service, *Statistics of Income Bulletin,* and *Statistics of Income, Individual Income Tax Returns,* annual.

No. 474. Individual Income Tax Returns—Number, Income Tax, and Average Tax by Size of Adjusted Gross Income: 1995 and 1998

[In billions of dollars (4,189.4 represents $4,189,400,000,000), except as indicated]

Size of adjusted gross income	Number of returns (1,000) 1995	Number of returns (1,000) 1998, prel.	Adjusted gross income (AGI) 1995	Adjusted gross income (AGI) 1998, prel.	Taxable income 1995	Taxable income 1998, prel.	Income tax total [1] 1995	Income tax total [1] 1998, prel.	Tax as percent of AGI [2] 1995	Tax as percent of AGI [2] 1998, prel.	Average tax ($1,000) [2] 1995	Average tax ($1,000) [2] 1998, prel.
Total	118,218	124,771	4,189.4	5,416.0	2,813.8	3,780.8	588.4	788.5	14.1	14.6	6.8	8.5
Less than $1,000 [3]	3,204	2,845	-53.9	-52.1	0.1	-	0.1	0.1	-0.2	-0.2	0.2	0.4
$1,000-$2,999	6,526	5,753	13.0	11.5	0.9	0.9	0.2	0.1	1.2	1.1	0.1	0.1
$3,000-$4,999	5,860	5,615	23.2	22.4	1.3	1.3	0.2	0.2	1.0	0.9	0.1	0.1
$5,000-$6,999	5,680	5,250	34.0	31.5	2.9	3.1	0.4	0.5	1.3	1.5	0.2	0.3
$7,000-$8,999	5,593	5,110	44.9	40.8	6.7	5.6	1.0	0.8	2.2	1.8	0.3	0.3
$9,000-$10,999 . . .	5,372	5,313	53.7	53.0	10.7	10.2	1.6	1.5	3.0	2.7	0.5	0.5
$11,000-$12,999 . . .	5,555	5,085	66.6	61.0	17.2	14.7	2.6	2.0	3.9	3.3	0.8	0.7
$13,000-$14,999 . .	5,344	5,215	74.8	73.0	23.9	20.9	3.2	2.7	4.3	3.7	0.9	0.9
$15,000-$16,999 . .	4,837	4,815	77.3	77.0	29.2	26.9	3.8	3.4	4.9	4.5	1.1	1.1
$17,000-$18,999 . .	4,402	4,638	79.3	83.4	34.0	33.5	4.3	4.1	5.5	5.0	1.3	1.3
$19,000-$21,999 . .	6,507	6,514	133.4	133.4	64.9	60.5	8.6	7.3	6.5	5.5	1.5	1.5
$22,000-$24,999 . .	5,610	5,858	131.8	137.5	71.1	70.5	10.1	9.0	7.6	6.5	1.9	1.9
$25,000-$29,999 . .	7,848	8,192	215.2	224.6	125.1	127.5	18.5	17.0	8.6	7.6	2.4	2.3
$30,000-$39,999 . .	12,380	13,135	430.5	456.2	270.6	282.9	42.4	40.3	9.9	8.8	3.5	3.2
$40,000-$49,999 . .	9,099	9,974	406.6	447.1	269.4	294.9	43.6	44.8	10.7	10.0	4.8	4.5
$50,000-$74,999 . .	13,679	15,887	828.3	969.8	579.8	675.3	100.3	108.9	12.1	11.2	8.2	6.9
$75,000-$99,999 . .	5,374	7,221	458.5	618.5	335.0	452.3	67.7	85.2	14.8	13.8	16.0	11.8
$100,000-$199,999 .	4,075	6,266	532.0	822.6	411.6	636.0	97.2	143.7	18.3	17.5	31.3	22.9
$200,000-$499,999 .	1,007	1,606	292.1	463.6	249.4	395.5	74.6	111.5	25.6	24.1	95.0	69.5
$500,000-$999,999 .	178	307	120.3	207.6	106.6	185.1	36.3	58.5	30.2	28.2	258.2	190.6
$1,000,000 or more .	87	172	227.6	533.5	203.5	483.3	71.5	146.8	31.4	27.5	1,077.0	854.0

- Represents or rounds to zero.   [1] Consists of income after credits, and alternative minimum tax.   [2] Computed using taxable returns only.   [3] In addition to low income taxpayers, this size class (and others) includes taxpayers with "tax preferences," not reflected in adjusted gross income or taxable income which are subject to the "alternative minimum tax" (included in total income tax).

Source: U.S. Internal Revenue Service. *Statistics of Income Bulletin*, quarterly and *Statistics of Income, Individual Income Tax Returns*, annual.

No. 475. Individual Income Tax Returns—Itemized Deductions and Statutory Adjustments by Size of Adjusted Gross Income: 1998

[Preliminary]

Item	Unit	Total	Under $10,000	$10,000 to $19,999	$20,000 to $29,999	$30,000 to $39,999	$40,000 to $49,999	$50,000 to $99,999	$100,000 and over
Returns with itemized deductions:									
Number [1]	1,000	38,186	605	2,015	3,231	4,072	4,570	16,074	7,619
Amount	Mil. dol	676,460	6,721	21,665	34,115	45,383	54,394	243,287	270,894
Medical and dental expenses:									
Returns	1,000	5,560	366	1,054	1,047	880	659	1,353	199
Amount	Mil. dol	31,984	2,447	6,713	5,015	3,897	3,091	7,817	3,004
Taxes paid:									
Returns, total	1,000	37,576	535	1,864	3,127	3,992	4,504	15,961	7,594
State, local income taxes	1,000	31,908	278	1,265	2,507	3,348	3,898	13,931	6,680
Real estate taxes	1,000	33,633	434	1,500	2,592	3,419	3,962	14,632	7,094
Amount, total	Mil. dol	241,783	1,059	3,554	6,941	10,955	14,767	79,124	125,383
State, local income taxes	Mil. dol	152,638	189	837	2,401	4,758	7,469	44,617	92,367
Real estate taxes	Mil. dol	79,978	797	2,497	4,056	5,523	6,400	30,734	29,970
Interest paid:									
Returns	1,000	32,024	374	1,293	2,473	3,343	3,925	14,124	6,492
Amount	Mil. dol	271,624	2,433	7,427	14,540	20,104	24,748	107,709	94,665
Home mortgages interest:									
Returns	1,000	31,627	360	1,279	2,452	3,314	3,903	14,038	6,281
Amount	Mil. dol	254,397	2,357	7,267	14,356	19,736	24,360	105,669	80,652
Contributions:									
Returns	1,000	33,836	377	1,507	2,590	3,412	3,972	14,721	7,257
Amount	Mil. dol	109,240	371	2,156	4,161	5,504	6,530	31,977	58,542
Employee business expense:									
Returns	1,000	11,605	57	389	842	1,296	1,619	5,419	1,982
Amount	Mil. dol	41,570	174	1,248	2,818	4,492	4,976	17,295	10,567
Returns with statutory adjus'mts: [2]									
Returns	1,000	21,998	2,957	3,225	3,137	2,645	2,211	5,112	2,711
Amount of adjustments	Mil. dol	51,531	2,035	3,544	4,460	4,192	3,668	12,731	20,900
Payments to IRAs: [3]									
Returns	1,000	3,868	164	396	643	642	444	1,050	529
Amount	Mil. dol	8,188	254	709	1,228	1,248	934	2,321	1,496
Payments to Keogh plans:									
Returns	1,000	1,177	12	28	49	67	72	367	584
Amount	Mil. dol	11,040	29	59	130	221	287	2,044	8,270
Alimony paid:									
Returns	1,000	591	22	50	59	55	54	188	163
Amount	Mil. dol	6,878	244	318	420	335	370	1,712	3,480

[1] After limitations.   [2] Includes disability income exclusion, employee business expenses, moving expenses, forfeited interest penalty, alimony paid, deduction for expense of living abroad, and other data not shown separately.   [3] Individual Retirement Account.

Source: U.S. Internal Revenue Service. *Statistics of Income Individual Income Tax Returns*, annual.

Federal Government Finances and Employment   315

No. 476. Federal Individual Income Tax Returns—Adjusted Gross Income (AGI) by Source of Income and Income Class for Taxable Returns: 1998

[In millions of dollars (93,048 represents $93,048,000,000), except as indicated. Minus sign (-) indicates net loss was greater than net income. See headnote. Table 473]

Item	Total [1]	Under $10,000	$10,000 to $19,999	$20,000 to $29,999	$30,000 to $39,999	$40,000 to $49,999	$50,000 to $99,999	$100,000 and over
Number of returns (1,000)	93,048	8,261	15,365	15,365	12,779	9,876	23,055	8,347
Source of income:								
Adjusted gross income (AGI)	5,160,224	47,311	232,203	382,997	444,055	442,747	1,585,000	2,025,912
Salaries and wages	3,624,306	40,729	168,576	305,555	363,056	365,944	1,266,733	1,113,714
Percent of AGI for taxable returns	70.2	86.1	72.6	79.8	81.8	82.7	79.9	55.0
Interest received	166,135	3,668	13,848	13,373	12,069	10,299	39,416	73,463
Dividends in AGI	113,810	1,636	4,383	4,724	5,189	5,355	24,067	68,454
Business; profession, net profit less loss	180,423	1,343	6,963	10,657	12,634	12,570	48,019	88,237
Pensions and annuities in AGI. .	265,382	2,716	28,285	34,193	29,931	26,660	90,946	52,652
Sales of property, [2] net gain less loss	440,078	4,523	3,819	4,890	6,195	6,672	41,324	372,656
Rents and royalties, net income less loss	23,518	156	752	508	882	-387	1,774	19,833
Other sources, [3] net	393,306	-7,163	7,551	12,547	18,012	19,169	85,395	257,793
Percent of all returns: [4]								
Number of returns	74.6	6.6	12.3	12.3	10.2	7.9	18.5	6.7
Adjusted gross income	95.3	0.9	4.3	7.1	8.2	8.2	29.3	37.4
Salaries and wages	93.4	1.0	4.3	7.9	9.4	9.4	32.6	28.7
Interest received	93.2	2.1	7.8	7.5	6.8	5.8	22.1	41.2
Dividends in AGI	96.1	1.4	3.7	4.0	4.4	4.5	20.3	57.8
Business; profession, net profit less loss	89.1	0.7	3.4	5.3	6.2	6.2	23.7	43.7
Pensions and annuities in AGI . . .	94.6	1.0	10.1	12.2	10.7	9.5	32.4	18.8
Sales of property [2] net gain less loss	99.0	1.0	0.9	1.1	1.4	1.5	9.3	83.8

[1] Includes a small number of taxable returns with no adjusted gross income.   [2] Includes sales of capital assets and other property; net gain less loss.   [3] Excludes rental passive losses disallowed in the computation of adjusted gross income; net income less loss.   [4] Without regard to taxability.

Source: U.S. Internal Revenue Service, Statistics of Income, Individual Income Tax Returns, annual.

No. 477. Federal Individual Income Tax Returns by State: 1998

State	Number of returns [1] (1,000)	Adjusted gross income (AGI) [2]	Income tax Total [3] (mil. dol.)	Income tax Per capita [4] (dol.)	State	Number of returns [1] (1,000)	Adjusted gross income (AGI) [2]	Income tax Total [3] (mil. dol.)	Income tax Per capita [4] (dol.)
U.S.	125,394	5,381,508	792,296	2,931	MO	2,492	96,350	13,150	2,418
					MT	410	12,696	1,498	1,702
AL	1,880	66,477	8,565	1,968	NE	796	30,330	4,012	2,413
AK	329	12,585	1,828	2,977	NV	874	40,373	6,319	3,617
AZ	2,037	84,085	11,692	2,504	NH	599	27,685	4,143	3,496
AR	1,096	35,790	4,400	1,734	NJ	3,924	212,727	35,182	4,335
CA	14,197	662,213	99,025	3,031	NM	768	25,134	3,068	1,766
CO	1,974	89,915	13,328	3,356	NY	8,268	406,381	66,088	3,636
CT	1,626	99,010	17,962	5,486	NC	3,516	136,960	18,059	2,393
DE	364	16,252	2,328	3,129	ND	300	9,664	1,185	1,857
DC	272	13,461	2,236	4,275	OH	5,473	211,365	28,694	2,560
FL	7,076	298,976	46,836	3,140	OK	1,436	48,922	6,151	1,838
GA	3,471	144,775	20,416	2,672	OR	1,522	60,751	7,898	2,406
HI	554	20,874	2,580	2,163	PA	5,654	233,941	33,771	2,814
ID	534	18,762	2,242	1,824	RI	472	19,581	2,692	2,725
IL	5,636	265,945	42,129	3,498	SC	1,748	62,047	7,839	2,044
IN	2,765	109,636	15,035	2,549	SD	344	11,489	1,541	2,088
IA	1,335	49,309	6,223	2,174	TN	2,492	93,660	13,129	2,417
KS	1,200	48,374	6,530	2,484	TX	8,694	356,997	55,056	2,786
KY	1,694	60,045	7,620	1,936	UT	896	34,954	4,157	1,980
LA	1,847	64,332	8,630	1,975	VT	288	10,797	1,397	2,364
ME	584	20,600	2,601	2,091	VA	3,198	145,882	21,133	3,112
MD	2,460	118,590	16,964	3,304	WA	2,670	126,665	20,128	3,538
MA	3,011	156,030	25,152	4,092	WV	740	23,574	2,813	1,553
MI	4,498	196,297	28,748	2,928	WI	2,514	103,179	13,955	2,671
MN	2,298	103,137	14,557	3,081	WY	229	9,382	1,433	2,979
MS	1,154	35,837	4,266	1,550	Other [5]	1,185	38,713	5,909	(NA)

NA Not available.   [1] Includes returns constructed by Internal Revenue Service for certain self-employment tax returns.   [2] Less deficit.   [3] Includes additional tax for tax preferences, self-employment tax, tax from investment credit recapture and other income-related taxes.   Total is before earned income credit.   [4] Based on resident population as of July 1.   [5] Includes returns filed from Army Post Office and Fleet Post Office addresses by members of the armed forces stationed overseas; returns by other U.S. citizens abroad; and returns filed by residents of Puerto Rico with income from sources outside of Puerto Rico or with income earned as U.S. Government employees.

Source: U.S. Internal Revenue Service, Statistics of Income Bulletin, quarterly.

U.S. Census Bureau, Statistical Abstract of the United States: 2001

No. 478. Federal Individual Income Tax—Tax Liability and Effective and Marginal Tax Rates for Selected Income Groups: 1990 to 1999

[Refers to income after exclusions. Effective rate represents tax liability divided by stated income. The marginal tax rate is the percentage of the first additional dollar of income which would be paid in income tax. Computations assume the low income allowance, standard deduction, zero bracket amount, or itemized deductions equal to 10 percent of adjusted gross income, whichever is greatest. Excludes self-employment tax]

Adjusted gross income	1990	1994	1995	1996	1997	1998	1999
TAX LIABILITY							
Single person, no dependents:							
$5,000	-	-306	-314	-323	-332	-341	-347
$10,000	705	563	540	518	480	455	427
$20,000	2,205	2,063	2,040	2,018	1,980	1,958	1,943
$25,000	2,988	2,813	2,790	2,768	2,730	2,708	2,693
$35,000	5,718	5,093	4,973	4,846	4,692	4,559	4,479
$50,000	9,498	8,957	8,865	8,766	8,654	8,549	8,483
$75,000	16,718	15,555	15,418	15,270	15,107	14,951	14,852
Married couple, two dependents: [1]							
$5,000	-700	-1,500	-1,800	-2,000	-2,000	-2,000	-2,000
$10,000	-953	-2,528	-3,110	-3,556	-3,556	-3,756	-3,816
$20,000	926	-359	-832	-1,324	-1,414	-1,811	-1,958
$25,000	1,703	1,275	929	479	389	-8	-155
$35,000	3,203	2,828	2,768	2,715	2,625	2,565	2,520
$50,000	5,960	5,078	5,018	4,965	4,875	4,815	4,770
$75,000	12,386	11,216	11,030	10,831	10,576	10,371	10,224
EFFECTIVE RATE							
Single person, no dependents:							
$5,000 [2]	-	-6.1	-6.3	-6.5	-6.6	-6.8	-6.9
$10,000	7.1	5.6	5.4	5.2	4.8	4.6	4.3
$20,000	11.0	10.3	10.2	10.1	9.9	9.8	9.7
$25,000	12.0	11.3	11.2	11.1	10.9	10.8	10.8
$35,000	16.3	14.6	14.2	13.8	13.4	13.0	12.8
$50,000	19.0	17.9	17.7	17.5	17.3	17.1	17.0
$75,000	22.3	20.7	20.6	20.4	20.1	19.9	19.8
Married couple, two dependents: [2]							
$5,000 [3]	-14.0	-30.0	-36.0	-40	-40	-40.0	-40.0
$10,000 [4]	-9.5	-25.3	-31.1	-35.6	-35.6	-37.6	38.2
$20,000 [4]	4.6	-1.8	-4.2	-6.6	-7.1	-9.1	-9.8
$25,000	6.8	5.1	3.7	1.9	1.6	-	-0.6
$35,000	9.2	8.1	7.9	7.8	7.5	7.3	7.2
$50,000	11.9	10.2	10.0	9.9	9.8	9.6	9.5
$75,000	16.5	15.0	14.7	14.4	14.1	13.8	13.6
MARGINAL TAX RATE							
Single person, no dependents:							
$5,000	-	7.7	-	-	-	-	-
$10,000	15	15	15	15	15	22.7	22.7
$20,000	15	15	15	15	15	15	15
$25,000	28	15	15	15	15	15	15
$35,000	28	28	28	28	28	28	28
$50,000	28	28	28	28	28	28	28
$75,000	33	31	31	31	31	31	31
Married couple, two dependents: [1]							
$5,000 [3]	-14	-30	-36	-40	-40	-40	-40
$10,000 [4]	-	-	-	-	-	-	-
$20,000 [4]	25	32.7	35.2	36.1	36.1	36.1	36.1
$25,000	15	32.7	35.2	36.1	36.1	36.1	36.1
$35,000	15	15	15	15	15	15	15
$50,000	28	15	15	15	15	15	15
$75,000	28	28	28	28	28	28	28

- Represents zero. [1] Only one spouse is assumed to work. [2] Beginning 1994, refundable earned income credit. [3] Refundable earned income credit. [4] Refundable earned income credit.

Source: U.S. Dept. of the Treasury, Office of Tax Analysis, unpublished data.

Federal Government Finances and Employment **317**

No. 479. Federal Individual Income Tax—Current Income Equivalent to 1995 Constant Income for Selected Income Groups: 1990 to 1999

[Constant 1995 dollar incomes calculated by using the NIPA Chain-Type Price Index for Person Consumption Expenditures (1996 = 100) 1990, 85.63; 1994, 95.70; 1995, 97.90; 1996, 100.0; 1997, 101.98; 1998, 102.93; and 1999, 104.57]

Adjusted gross income	1990	1994	1995	1996	1997	1998	1999
REAL INCOME EQUIVALENT							
Single person, no dependents:							
$5,000	4,280	4,790	4,900	5,000	5,100	5,150	5,230
$10,000	8,560	9,570	9,790	10,000	10,200	10,290	10,460
$20,000	17,130	19,140	19,580	20,000	20,400	20,590	20,910
$25,000	21,410	23,930	24,480	25,000	25,500	25,730	26,140
$35,000	29,970	33,500	34,270	35,000	35,690	36,030	36,600
$50,000	42,820	47,850	48,950	50,000	50,990	51,470	52,290
$75,000	64,220	71,780	73,430	75,000	76,490	77,200	78,430
Married couple, two dependents: [1]							
$5,000	4,280	4,790	4,900	5,000	5,100	5,150	5,230
$10,000	8,560	9,570	9,790	10,000	10,200	10,290	10,460
$20,000	17,130	19,140	19,580	20,000	20,400	20,590	20,910
$25,000	21,410	23,930	24,480	25,000	25,500	25,730	26,140
$35,000	29,970	33,500	34,270	35,000	35,690	36,030	36,600
$50,000	42,820	47,850	48,950	50,000	50,990	51,470	52,290
$75,000	64,220	71,780	73,430	75,000	76,490	77,200	78,430
EFFECTIVE RATE (percent)							
Single person, no dependents:							
$5,000 [2]	-	-6.4	-6.4	-6.5	-6.5	-6.6	-6.6
$10,000	5.7	5.2	5.2	5.2	5.0	4.9	4.9
$20,000	10.4	10.1	10.1	10.1	10.0	9.9	9.9
$25,000	11.3	11.1	11.1	11.1	11.0	10.9	11.0
$35,000	14.6	13.9	13.9	13.8	13.7	13.5	13.5
$50,000	18.0	17.6	17.6	17.5	17.5	17.3	17.3
$75,000	21.0	20.4	20.4	20.4	20.3	20.2	20.2
Married couple, two dependents: [1]							
$5,000 [3]	-14.0	-30.0	-36.0	-40.0	-40.0	-40.0	-40.0
$10,000 [4]	-11.1	-26.4	-31.8	-35.6	-34.9	-36.5	-36.5
$20,000 [4]	1.2	-3.3	-5.0	-6.6	-6.2	-7.8	-7.8
$25,000	5.4	3.9	3.0	1.9	2.2	1.0	1.0
$35,000	8.2	7.8	7.8	7.8	7.6	7.5	7.5
$50,000	10.2	9.9	9.9	9.9	9.9	9.8	9.8
$75,000	15.1	14.5	14.5	14.4	14.3	14.2	14.1
MARGINAL TAX RATE (percent)							
Single person, no dependents:							
$5,000	-	-	-	-	-	-	-
$10,000	15.0	15.0	15.0	15.0	15.0	15.0	15.0
$20,000	15.0	15.0	15.0	15.0	15.0	15.0	15.0
$25,000	15.0	15.0	15.0	15.0	15.0	15.0	15.0
$35,000	28.0	28.0	28.0	28.0	28.0	28.0	28.0
$50,000	28.0	28.0	28.0	28.0	28.0	28.0	28.0
$75,000	33.0	31.0	31.0	31.0	31.0	31.0	31.0
Married couple, two dependents: [1]							
$5,000 [3]	-14.0	-30.0	-36.0	-40.0	-40.0	-40.0	-40.0
$10,000 [4]	-	-	-	-	-	-	-
$20,000	25.0	32.7	35.2	36.1	36.1	36.1	36.1
$25,000	15.0	32.7	35.2	36.1	36.1	36.1	36.1
$35,000	15.0	15.0	15.0	15.0	15.0	15.0	15.0
$50,000	15.0	15.0	15.0	15.0	15.0	15.0	15.0
$75,000	28.0	28.0	28.0	28.0	28.0	28.0	28.0

- Represents zero. [1] Only one spouse is assumed to work. [2] Beginning 1994, refundable earned income credit. [3] Refundable earned income credit. [4] Refundable earned income credit.

Source: U.S. Dept. of the Treasury, Office of Tax Analysis, unpublished data.

No. 480. Paid Full-Time Federal Civilian Employment, All Areas: 1990 to 2000

[As of March 31. Excludes employees of Congress and federal courts, maritime seamen of Dept. of Commerce, and small number for whom rates were not reported. See text, this section, for explanation of general schedule and wage system]

Compensation authority	Employees (1,000)				Average pay			
	1990	1995	1999	2000	1990	1995	1999	2000
Total	2,697	2,620	2,483	(NA)	31,174	(NA)	47,569	(NA)
General Schedule	1,506	1,417	1,234	1,216	31,239	40,568	46,744	49,428
Wage System	369	269	214	205	26,565	32,084	35,767	37,082
Postal pay system [1]	661	753	798	(NA)	29,264	33,665	36,413	(NA)
Other	161	181	237	250	41,149	53,839	62,519	66,248

NA Not available. [1] Source: Employees—U.S. Postal Service, Annual Report of the Postmaster General. Average pay—U.S. Postal Service, Comprehensive Statement of Postal Operations, annual.

Source: Except as noted, U.S. Office of Personnel Management, Pay Structure of the Federal Civil Service, annual.

No. 481. Federal Civilian Employment by Branch and Agency: 1990 to 2000

[For fiscal year ending in year shown; excludes Central Intelligence Agency, National Security Agency; and, as of November 1984, the Defense Intelligence Agency; and, as of October 1996, the National Imagery and Mapping Agency]

Agency	1990	1999	2000	Percent change, 1999-00
Total, all agencies	3,128,267	2,749,239	2,708,101	-1.5
Legislative Branch, total	37,495	30,353	31,157	2.6
Judicial Branch	23,605	32,196	32,186	-
Executive Branch, total	3,067,167	2,686,690	2,644,758	-1.6
Executive Departments	2,065,542	1,614,097	1,592,200	-1.4
State	25,288	25,892	27,983	8.1
Treasury	158,655	143,088	143,508	0.3
Defense	1,034,152	690,706	676,268	-2.1
Justice	83,932	124,885	125,970	0.9
Interior	77,679	72,541	73,818	1.8
Agriculture	122,594	104,661	104,466	-0.2
Commerce	69,920	60,765	47,652	-21.6
Labor	17,727	15,913	16,040	0.8
Health & Human Services	123,959	61,403	62,605	2.0
Housing & Urban Development	13,596	10,273	10,319	0.4
Transportation	67,364	64,135	63,598	-0.8
Energy	17,731	15,820	15,692	-0.8
Education	4,771	4,770	4,734	-0.8
Veterans Affairs [1]	248,174	219,245	219,547	0.1
Independent agencies:				
Armed Forces Retirement Home	966	801	765	-4.5
Board of Gov Fed Reserve System	1,525	1,688	1,644	-2.6
Commodity Futures Trading Comm	542	574	574	-
Consumer Product Safety Comm	520	483	479	-0.8
Environmental Protection Agency	17,123	18,590	18,036	-3.0
Equal Employment Opportunity Comm	2,880	2,945	2,780	-5.6
Federal Communications Commission	1,778	1,978	1,965	-0.7
Federal Deposit Insurance Corporation	17,641	7,492	6,958	-7.1
Fed Emergency Managmt Agency	3,137	5,521	4,813	-12.8
Federal Trade Commission	988	982	1,019	3.8
General Services Administration	20,277	14,199	14,334	1.0
Int Boun & Wat Comm (U.S. & Mexico)	260	286	268	-6.3
National Archives & Recds Admin	3,120	2,612	2,702	3.4
National Aeronautics & Space Admin	24,872	18,647	18,819	0.9
Natl Labor Relations Board	2,263	1,897	2,054	8.3
Natl Science Foundation	1,318	1,271	1,247	-1.9
Nuclear Regulatory Commission	3,353	2,862	2,858	-0.1
Office of Personnel Management	6,636	3,689	3,780	2.5
Panama Canal Commission	8,240	9,060	6	-99.9
Peace Corps	1,178	1,097	1,065	-2.9
Railroad Retirement Board	1,772	1,252	1,176	-6.1
Securities & Exchange Comm	2,302	2,866	2,955	3.1
Small Business Administration	5,128	4,575	4,150	-9.3
Smithsonian Institution, summary	5,092	5,271	5,065	-3.9
Social Security Admin	[2] (X)	64,008	64,474	0.7
Tennessee Valley Authority	28,392	13,321	13,145	-1.3
U.S. Information Agency	8,555	6,318	2,436	-61.4
U.S. Postal Service	816,886	866,342	860,726	-0.6

- Represents zero.   X Not applicable.   [1] Formerly Veterans Administration.   [2] Included with HHS.

Source: U.S. Office of Personnel Management, *Federal Civilian Workforce Statistics— Employment and Trends*, bimonthly.

No. 482. Federal Employment Trends—Individual Characteristics: 1990 to 1999

[In percents, except as indicated]

Characteristics	1990	1992	1993	1994	1995	1996	1997	1998	1999
Average age (years) [1]	42.3	43.0	43.8	44.1	44.3	44.8	45.2	45.6	46.3
Average length of service (years) [1]	13.4	14.1	14.9	15.2	15.5	15.9	16.3	16.6	17.1
Retirement eligible:									
Civil Service Retirement System [2]	8.0	10.0	10.0	10.0	10.0	11.0	12.0	13.0	16.6
Federal Employees Retirement System	3.0	3.0	4.0	5.0	5.0	6.0	7.0	8.0	(NA)
College-conferred [3]	35.0	36.0	37.0	38.0	39.0	39.0	40.0	40.0	40.5
Race and national origin:									
Total minorities	27.4	27.9	28.2	28.5	28.9	29.1	29.4	29.7	30.4
Black	16.7	16.7	16.7	16.7	16.8	16.7	16.7	16.7	17.1
Hispanic	5.4	5.5	5.6	5.7	5.9	6.1	6.2	6.4	6.6
Disabled	7.0	7.0	7.0	7.0	7.0	7.0	7.0	7.0	7.1
Veterans preference	30.0	28.0	27.0	27.0	26.0	26.0	25.0	25.0	24.2
Vietnam Era veterans	17.0	16.0	16.0	17.0	17.0	17.0	15.0	14.0	13.7
Retired military	4.9	4.4	4.3	4.3	4.2	4.3	4.2	3.9	3.9

NA Not available.   [1] Represents full-time permanent employees.   [2] Represents full-time permanent employees under the Civil Service Retirement System (excluding hires since January 1984), and the Federal Employees Retirement System (since January 1984).   [3] Bachelor's degree or higher.

Source: U.S. Office of Personnel Management, Office of Workforce Information, *The Fact Book, Federal Civilian Workforce Statistics*, annual. See also <http://www.opm.gov/feddata/00factbook.pdf> (released October 2000).

Federal Government Finances and Employment   **319**

No. 483. Federal Civilian Employment and Annual Payroll by Branch: 1970 to 2000

[Employment in thousands (2,997 represents 2,997,000); payroll in millions of dollars (27,322 represents $27,322,000,000). Average annual employment. For fiscal year ending in year shown; see text, Section 8, State and Local Government Finances and Employment. Includes employees in U.S. territories and foreign countries. Data represent employees in active-duty status, including intermittent employees. Annual employment figures are averages of monthly figures. Excludes Central Intelligence Agency, National Security Agency, and, as of November 1984, the Defense Intelligence Agency, and as of October 1996, the National Imagery and Mapping Agency]

Year	Employment						Payroll				
	Total	Percent of U.S. employed [1]	Executive		Legisla- tive	Judicial	Total	Executive		Legisla- tive	Judicial
			Total	Defense				Total	Defense		
1970	[2]2,997	3.8	2,961	1,263	29	7	27,322	26,894	11,264	338	89
1971	2,899	3.7	2,861	1,162	31	7	29,475	29,007	11,579	369	98
1972	2,882	3.5	2,842	1,128	32	8	31,626	31,102	12,181	411	112
1973	2,822	3.3	2,780	1,076	33	9	33,240	32,671	12,414	447	121
1974	2,825	3.3	2,781	1,041	35	9	35,661	35,035	12,789	494	132
1975	2,877	3.4	2,830	1,044	37	10	39,126	38,423	13,418	549	154
1976	2,879	3.2	2,831	1,025	38	11	42,259	41,450	14,699	631	179
1977	2,855	3.1	2,803	997	39	12	45,895	44,975	15,696	700	219
1978	2,875	3.0	2,822	987	40	13	49,921	48,899	16,995	771	251
1979	2,897	2.9	2,844	974	40	13	53,590	52,513	18,065	817	260
1980	[2]2,987	3.0	2,933	971	40	14	58,012	56,841	18,795	883	288
1981	2,909	2.9	2,855	986	40	15	63,793	62,510	21,227	922	360
1982	2,871	2.9	2,816	1,019	39	16	65,503	64,125	22,226	980	398
1983	2,878	2.9	2,823	1,033	39	16	69,878	68,420	23,406	1,013	445
1984	2,935	2.8	2,879	1,052	40	17	74,616	73,084	25,253	1,081	451
1985	3,001	2.8	2,944	1,080	39	18	80,599	78,992	28,330	1,098	509
1986	3,047	2.8	2,991	1,089	38	19	82,598	80,941	29,272	1,112	545
1987	3,075	2.7	3,018	1,084	38	19	85,543	83,797	29,786	1,153	593
1988	3,113	2.7	3,054	1,073	38	21	88,841	86,960	29,609	1,226	656
1989	3,133	2.7	3,074	1,067	38	22	92,847	90,870	30,301	1,266	711
1990	[2]3,233	2.7	3,173	1,060	38	23	99,138	97,022	31,990	1,329	787
1991	3,101	2.7	3,038	1,015	38	25	104,273	101,965	32,956	1,434	874
1992	3,106	2.6	3,040	1,004	39	27	108,054	105,402	31,486	1,569	1,083
1993	3,043	2.5	2,976	952	39	28	114,323	111,523	32,755	1,609	1,191
1994	2,993	2.4	2,928	900	37	28	116,138	113,264	32,144	1,613	1,260
1995	2,943	2.4	2,880	852	34	28	118,304	115,328	31,753	1,598	1,379
1996	2,881	2.3	2,819	811	32	29	119,321	116,385	31,569	1,519	1,417
1997	2,816	2.2	2,755	768	31	30	119,603	116,693	31,431	1,515	1,396
1998	2,783	2.1	2,721	730	31	31	121,964	118,800	30,315	1,517	1,647
1999	2,789	2.1	2,726	703	30	32	124,990	121,732	30,141	1,560	1,699
2000	[2]2,879	2.1	2,816	681	31	32	130,832	127,472	29,607	1,619	1,741

[1] Civilian only. See Table 567.   [2] Includes 33,000 temporary census workers.
Source: U.S. Office of Personnel Management, *Federal Civilian Workforce Statistics—Employment and Trends*, bimonthly; and unpublished data.

No. 484. Federal Executive Branch (Non-Postal) Employment by Race and National Origin: 1990 to 2000

[As of Sept. 30. Covers total employment for only Executive branch agencies participating in OPMs Central Personnel Data File (CPDF)]

Pay system	1990	1995	1998	1999	2000
All personnel	2,150,359	1,960,577	1,804,591	1,766,298	1,755,689
White, non-Hispanic	1,562,846	1,394,690	1,269,790	1,236,698	1,224,836
General schedule and related	1,218,188	1,101,108	1,010,793	979,803	961,261
Grades 1-4 ($13,870 - $24,833)	132,028	79,195	61,909	58,381	55,067
Grades 5-8 ($21,370 - $38,108)	337,453	288,755	255,344	246,759	239,128
Grades 9-12 ($32,380 - $61,040)	510,261	465,908	425,617	413,989	404,649
Grades 13-15 ($55,837 - $100,897)	238,446	267,250	267,923	260,674	262,417
Total executives/senior pay levels [1]	9,337	13,307	13,634	13,856	14,332
Wage pay system	244,220	186,184	157,639	151,585	146,075
Other pay systems	91,101	94,091	87,724	91,454	103,168
Black	356,867	327,302	300,661	298,694	298,701
General schedule and related	272,657	258,586	242,587	241,422	241,135
Grades 1-4 ($13,870-$24,833)	65,077	41,381	30,668	28,530	26,895
Grades 5-8 ($21,370 - $38,108)	114,993	112,962	103,985	101,742	99,937
Grades 9-12 ($32,380 - $61,040)	74,985	79,795	79,999	81,410	82,809
Grades 13-15 ($55,837 - $100,897)	17,602	24,448	27,935	29,740	31,494
Total executives/senior pay levels [1]	479	942	1,044	1,103	1,180
Wage pay system	72,755	55,637	45,492	44,076	42,590
Other pay systems	10,976	12,137	11,538	12,093	13,796
Hispanic	115,170	115,964	115,545	114,743	115,247
General schedule and related	83,218	86,762	89,155	89,367	89,911
Grades 1-4 ($13,870 - $24,833)	15,738	11,081	9,213	8,874	8,526
Grades 5-8 ($21,370 - $38,108)	28,727	31,152	31,877	31,544	31,703
Grades 9-12 ($32,380 - $61,040)	31,615	34,056	35,864	36,474	36,813
Grades 13-15 ($55,837 - $100,897)	7,138	10,473	12,201	12,475	12,869
Total executives/senior pay levels [1]	154	382	454	487	547
Wage pay system	26,947	22,128	19,341	17,781	16,926
Other pay systems	4,851	6,692	6,595	7,108	7,863
American Indian, Alaska Natives, Asians, and Pacific	115,476	122,621	118,595	116,163	116,905

[1] General schedule pay rates and Senior Pay Levels effective as of January 1999.
Source: Office of Personnel Management, Central Personnel Data File.

No. 485. Paid Civilian Employment in the Federal Government: 1998

[As of December 31 (2,758 represents 2,758,000). Excludes Central Intelligence Agency, Defense Intelligence Agency, seasonal and on-call employees, and National Security Agency]

State	Total (1,000)	Percent Defense	Percent change, 1996-98	State	Total (1,000)	Percent Defense	Percent change, 1996-98
United States......	2,758	23.7	0.8	Missouri............	57	15.8	-1.7
Alabama............	52	42.3	-	Montana............	11	9.1	-
Alaska.............	14	28.6	-	Nebraska...........	15	20.0	-
Arizona............	43	18.6	7.5	Nevada.............	13	15.4	8.3
Arkansas...........	21	19.0	5.0	New Hampshire......	8	12.5	-
California..........	265	26.4	-1.5	New Jersey.........	65	23.1	-4.4
Colorado...........	54	20.4	3.8	New Mexico.........	26	26.9	-
Connecticut........	23	13.0	4.5	New York...........	139	8.6	-
Delaware...........	5	20.0	-	North Carolina......	57	29.8	3.6
District of Columbia..	181	7.2	-2.2	North Dakota.......	8	25.0	-
Florida	116	23.3	3.6	Ohio...............	87	27.6	1.2
Georgia	88	35.2	1.1	Oklahoma..........	43	46.5	2.4
Hawaii	24	70.8	-	Oregon.............	30	10.0	7.1
Idaho	11	9.1	-	Pennsylvania.......	113	24.8	0.9
Illinois.............	98	14.3	1.0	Rhode Island.......	11	36.4	-
Indiana............	38	23.7	-5.0	South Carolina.....	27	37.0	3.8
Iowa..............	20	5.0	-	South Dakota.......	10	10.0	-
Kansas............	25	20.0	-	Tennessee..........	52	13.5	-
Kentucky...........	31	22.6	-8.8	Texas..............	175	25.7	1.7
Louisiana..........	35	22.9	2.9	Utah...............	28	42.9	-3.4
Maine.............	13	38.5	-	Vermont	6	8.3	-
Maryland...........	131	25.2	4.0	Virginia............	147	55.8	-2.6
Massachusetts......	56	12.5	3.7	Washington.........	63	34.9	1.6
Michigan...........	59	13.6	7.3	West Virginia	18	11.1	-
Minnesota..........	35	5.7	6.1	Wisconsin..........	31	9.7	6.9
Mississippi.........	25	40.0	4.2	Wyoming...........	6	16.7	-

- Represents zero or rounds to zero.

Source: U.S. Office of Personnel Management, *Biennial Report of Employment by Geographic Area.*

No. 486. Federal General Schedule Employee Pay Increases: 1965 to 2000

[Percent change from prior year shown, except 1965, change from 1964. Represents legislated pay increases. For some years data based on range for details see source]

Date	Pay increase	Date	Pay increase	Date	Pay increase
1965.............	3.6	1976.............	5.2	1989...........	4.1
1966.............	2.9	1977.............	7.0	1990...........	3.6
1967.............	4.5	1978.............	5.5	1991...........	4.1
1968.............	4.9	1979.............	7.0	1992...........	4.2
1969.............	9.1	1980.............	9.1	1993...........	3.7
1970.............	6.0	1981.............	4.8	1994...........	-
1971.............	6.0	1982.............	4.0	1995...........	2.0
1972.............	5.5	1984.............	4.0	1996...........	2.0
1972.............	5.1	1985.............	3.5	1997...........	2.3
1973.............	4.8	1986.............	-	1998...........	2.3
1974.............	5.5	1987.............	3.0	1999...........	3.1
1975.............	5.0	1988.............	2.0	2000...........	3.8

- Represents zero.

Source: U.S. Office of Personnel Management, *Pay Structure of the Federal Civil Service,* annual.

No. 487. Turnover Data for the Executive Branch—All Areas: 1985 to 1999

[Turnover data exclude Legislative and Judicial branches, U.S. Postal Service, Postal Rate Commission]

Year	Accessions Total	Accessions New hires	Separations Total	Separations Quits	Total employment Average	Change from prior year	Percent change
1985	541,787	451,516	484,742	185,453	2,210,487	32,214	1.5
1986	466,191	379,267	478,595	182,124	2,207,807	-2,680	-0.1
1987	515,958	431,687	440,797	176,813	2,207,828	21	(Z)
1988	463,413	375,561	448,025	175,374	2,226,642	18,814	0.9
1989	515,759	435,911	483,850	172,376	2,233,981	7,339	0.3
1990	819,554	716,066	799,237	165,099	2,348,458	114,477	5.1
1991	495,123	351,112	515,673	134,175	2,224,389	-124,069	-5.3
1992	430,021	290,883	446,126	129,167	2,238,635	14,246	0.6
1993	382,399	253,374	423,830	127,140	2,189,416	-49,219	-2.2
1994	317,509	219,026	398,134	111,096	2,114,387	-75,029	-3.4
1995	345,166	222,025	457,246	91,909	2,037,890	-76,542	-3.6
1996	266,473	199,463	356,566	80,922	1,960,892	-76,953	-3.8
1997	283,517	208,725	333,431	81,574	1,895,295	-65,597	-3.3
1998	320,830	242,637	321,292	84,124	1,855,112	-40,183	-2.1
1999	423,500	346,988	372,778	129,196	1,846,170	-8,942	-0.5

Z Less than 0.05 percent.

Source: U.S. Office of Personnel Management, *Monthly Report of Federal Civilian Employment.*

U.S. Census Bureau, *Statistical Abstract of the United States: 2001*

No. 488. Accessions to and Separations From Employment in the Federal Government: 1995 and 2000

[As of September 30. Turnover data exclude Legislative and Judicial branches, U.S. Postal Service, Postal Rate Commission.]

Agency	Accessions				Separations			
	Number		Rate		Number		Rate	
	1995	2000	1995	2000	1995	2000	1995	2000
Total, all agencies	556,695	1,380,937	19.2	48.8	638,733	1,233,364	22.1	43.6
Legislative Branch, total [1]	1,074	1,233	6.6	9.2	1,985	1,689	12.2	12.6
General Accounting Office	39	219	0.9	6.8	392	452	8.9	13.9
Government Printing Office	77	199	1.8	6.3	318	284	7.6	8.9
Library of Congress	540	322	11.6	7.4	642	509	13.8	11.6
Judicial Branch	-	-	-	-	-	-	-	-
Executive Branch, total	555,621	1,379,704	19.3	49.0	636,748	1,231,675	22.1	43.7
Executive Office of the President	384	450	24.3	27.3	373	395	23.6	23.9
Executive Departments	257,125	1,148,804	14.0	65.6	422,606	998,722	23.0	57
State	3,338	3,649	13.3	13.1	3,919	2,649	15.6	9.5
Treasury	24,532	49,878	15.0	33.1	52,634	49,254	32.2	32.6
Defense	104,088	94,329	12.2	13.8	155,722	105,734	18.3	75.5
Justice	14,958	9,985	14.9	8.0	7,496	7,397	7.5	5.9
Interior	12,936	19,008	17.1	27.0	16,147	14,110	21.4	20
Agriculture [2]	25,365	27,440	23.3	27.7	41,384	27,535	37.9	27.7
Commerce [2]	5,900	892,415	15.8	434.2	6,460	742,789	17.3	361.4
Labor	1,438	1,709	8.7	10.7	2,003	1,599	12.2	10
Health & Human Services [3]	8,774	11,129	9.3	17.9	78,780	8,698	83.7	14
Housing & Urban Development	489	1,004	4.0	9.8	1,952	993	15.8	9.7
Transportation	2,673	3,089	4.2	4.9	4,740	4,212	7.4	6.6
Energy	2,087	1,260	10.5	8.0	2,671	1,355	13.4	8.6
Education	683	531	13.8	11.2	354	321	7.2	6.8
Veterans Affairs [4]	49,864	33,771	19.0	15.5	48,344	32,650	18.5	14.9
Independent agencies [1]	298,112	230,450	28.6	21.7	213,769	232,558	20.5	21.9
Board of Governors, Fed RSRV System	231	184	13.7	11.2	199	254	11.8	15.4
Environmental Protection Agency	2,232	1,011	12.3	5.6	2,078	1,469	11.5	8.1
Equal Employment Opportunity Comm	129	86	4.5	2.9	156	161	5.4	5.5
Federal Deposit Insurance Corporation	360	425	2.2	5.9	4,404	1,044	26.8	14.5
Fed Emergency Management Agency	3,165	1,124	60.2	22.0	3,059	2,180	58.2	42.7
General Services Administration	292	815	1.7	5.8	2,552	691	14.8	4.9
National Aeronautics & Space Admin	2,004	1,745	8.9	9.4	3,673	1,627	16.2	8.7
National Archives & Records Admin	583	510	20.0	19.2	307	366	10.5	13.8
Nuclear Regulatory Commission	98	239	3.0	8.4	263	251	8.0	8.8
Office of Personnel Management	506	703	10.3	18.7	1,407	640	28.6	17
Panama Canal Comm	1,744	332	19.6	14.6	1,246	8,530	14.0	374.8
Railroad Retirement Board	46	39	2.9	3.2	185	115	11.6	9.6
Securities and Exchange Commission	584	607	21.1	21.0	356	461	12.8	16
Small Business Administration	1,065	879	18.1	20.3	2,799	1,251	47.6	28.9
Smithsonian Institution	707	620	13.1	12.1	980	860	18.2	16.8
Tennessee Valley Authority	674	875	4.1	6.6	2,873	1,013	17.3	7.6
U.S. Information Agency	356	138	4.7	5.6	836	174	11.0	7.1
U.S. International Dev. Coop. Agency	333	181	.8.6	7.6	665	268	17.2	11.2
U.S. Postal Service	210,447	210,915	25.0	24.3	179,494	204,015	21.3	23.5

- Represents or rounds to zero.   [1] Includes other branches, or other agencies, not shown separately.   [2] 2000 includes census enumerators for the 2000 Census.   [3] Sizable changes due to the Social Security Administration which was separated from the Department of Health and Human Services to become an independent agency effective April 1995.   [4] Formerly Veterans Administration.

Source: U.S. Office of Personnel Management, *Federal Civilian Workforce Statistics—Employment and Trends*, bimonthly.

No. 489. Federal Land and Buildings Owned and Leased and Predominant Land Usage: 1990 to 1999

[For fiscal years ending in years shown; see text, Section 8, State and Local Government Finances and Employment. Covers federal real property throughout the world, except as noted. Cost of land figures represent total cost of property owned in year shown. For further details see source. For data on federal land by state, see Table 344]

Item	Unit	1990	1995	1996	1997	1998	1999
Federally owned:							
Land, worldwide	1,000 acres	650,014	549,670	563,278	563,231	655,042	630,648
United States	1,000 acres	649,802	549,474	563,129	563,081	654,885	630,266
Buildings	1,000	(NA)	(NA)	(NA)	(NA)	(NA)	(NA)
United States	1,000	446	424	430	430	420	419
Buildings floor area (sq. ft.)	Mil. sq/ft	(NA)	(NA)	(NA)	(NA)	(NA)	(NA)
United States	Mil. sq/ft	2,859	2,793	2,930	2,935	2,911	2,875
Costs	Mil. dol.	187,865	199,387	217,857	222,391	244,273	238,327
Land	Mil. dol.	(NA)	18,972	22,952	22,914	26,450	17,257
Buildings	Mil. dol.	(NA)	113,018	123,897	128,530	130,858	132,981
Structures and facilities	Mil. dol.	(NA)	67,398	71,008	70,946	86,965	88,090
Federally leased:							
Land, worldwide	1,000 acres	994	1,385	1,373	1,374	1,306	1,400
United States	1,000 acres	938	1,351	1,339	1,340	1,272	1,342
Buildings	1,000	(NA)	(NA)	(NA)	(NA)	(NA)	(NA)
United States	Number	47,291	77,896	77,232	76,761	76,357	(NA)
Buildings floor area (sq. ft.)	Mil. sq/ft	(NA)	(NA)	(NA)	(NA)	(NA)	(NA)
United States	Mil. sq/ft	234	275	277	276	276	301
Annual rental	Mil. dol.	2,590	3,633	3,739	3,613	3,628	(NA)
United States	Mil. dol.	2,125	3,174	3,214	3,212	3,226	(NA)

NA Not available.

Source: U.S. General Services Administration, *Inventory Report on Real Property Owned by the United States Throughout the World*, annual.

Section 10
National Defense and Veterans Affairs

This section presents data on national defense and its human and financial costs; active and reserve military personnel; ships, equipment, and aircraft; and federally sponsored programs and benefits for veterans. The principal sources of these data are the annual *Selected Manpower Statistics* and the *Atlas/Data Abstract for the United States and Selected Areas* issued by the Office of the Secretary of Defense; *Annual Report of Secretary of Veterans Affairs, Department of Veterans Affairs,* and *The Budget of the United States Government,* Office of Management and Budget. For more data on expenditures, personnel, and ships, see Section 30.

Department of Defense (DOD)—The Department of Defense is responsible for providing the military forces of the United States. It includes the Office of the Secretary of Defense, the Joint Chiefs of Staff, the Army, the Navy, the Air Force, and the defense agencies. The President serves as Commander in Chief of the Armed Forces; from him, the authority flows to the Secretary of Defense and through the Joint Chiefs of Staff to the commanders of unified and specified commands (e.g., U.S. Strategic Command).

Reserve components—Reserve personnel of the Armed Forces consist of the Army National Guard, Army Reserve, Naval Reserve, Marine Corps Reserve, Air National Guard, Air Force Reserve, and Coast Guard Reserve. They provide trained personnel available for active duty in the Armed Forces in time of war or national emergency and at such other times as authorized by law.

The National Guard has dual federal-state responsibilities and uses jointly provided equipment, facilities, and budget support. The President is empowered to mobilize the National Guard and to use such of the Armed Forces as he considers necessary to enforce federal authority in any state.

The ready reserve includes selected reservists who are intended to assist active forces in a war and the individual ready reserve who, in a major war, would be used to fill out active and reserve units and later would be a source of combat replacements; a portion of the ready reserve serves in an active status. The standby reserve cannot be called to active duty unless the Congress gives explicit approval. The retired reserve represents a low potential for mobilization.

Department of Veterans Affairs (VA)—The Department of Veterans Affairs administers laws authorizing benefits for eligible former and present members of the Armed Forces and for the beneficiaries of deceased members. Veterans benefits available under various acts of Congress include compensation for service-connected disability or death; pensions for nonservice-connected disability or death; vocational rehabilitation, education, and training; home loan insurance; life insurance; health care; special housing and automobiles or other conveyances for certain disabled veterans; burial and plot allowances; and educational assistance to families of deceased or totally disabled veterans, servicemen missing in action, or prisoners of war. Since these benefits are legislated by Congress, the dates they were enacted and the dates they apply to veterans may be different from the actual dates the conflicts occurred.

VA estimates of veterans cover all persons with active duty service during periods of war or armed conflict and until 1982 include those living outside the United States.

U.S. Census Bureau, Statistical Abstract of the United States: 2001

No. 490. National Defense Outlays and Veterans Benefits: 1960 to 2001

[For fiscal year ending in year shown; see text, Section 8, State and Local Government Finances and Employment. Includes outlays of Department of Defense, Department of Veterans Affairs, and other agencies for activities primarily related to national defense and veterans programs. For explanation of average annual percent change, see Guide to Tabular Presentation. Minus sign (-) indicates decline]

Year	National defense and veterans outlays				Annual percent change [1]			Defense outlays, percent of—	
		Defense outlays							
	Total outlays (bil. dol.)	Current dollars (bil. dol.)	Constant (1996) dollars (bil. dol.)	Veterans outlays (bil. dol.)	Total outlays	Defense outlays	Veterans outlays	Federal outlays	Gross domestic product [2]
1960	53.5	48.1	280.3	5.4	2.5	2.4	3.1	52.2	9.3
1965	56.3	50.6	267.7	5.7	-6.8	-7.6	0.7	42.8	7.4
1970	90.4	81.7	336.6	8.7	0.3	-1.0	13.6	41.8	8.1
1975	103.1	86.5	239.5	16.6	11.2	9.0	24.0	26.0	5.5
1980	155.1	134.0	244.7	21.1	13.9	15.2	6.3	22.7	4.9
1985	279.0	252.7	329.9	26.3	10.3	11.1	2.7	26.7	6.1
1990	328.4	299.3	354.3	29.1	-1.6	-1.4	-3.2	23.9	5.2
1991	304.6	273.3	309.3	31.3	-7.2	-8.7	7.6	20.6	4.6
1992	332.4	298.4	327.0	34.1	12.0	12.4	8.0	21.6	4.8
1993	326.8	291.1	314.1	35.7	-1.9	-2.4	4.6	20.7	4.4
1994	319.2	281.6	297.9	37.6	-2.3	-3.2	5.4	19.3	4.1
1995	310.0	272.1	281.8	37.9	-2.9	-3.4	0.8	17.9	3.7
1996	302.7	265.8	265.8	37.0	-2.3	-2.3	-2.4	17.0	3.5
1997	309.8	270.5	265.3	39.3	2.3	1.8	6.3	16.9	3.3
1998	310.2	268.5	260.4	41.8	0.1	-0.8	6.3	16.2	3.1
1999	320.2	274.9	263.1	43.2	3.2	2.4	3.4	16.1	3.0
2000	337.4	294.5	273.8	46.8	5.4	5.7	8.3	16.2	3.0
2001, est	337.7	299.1	269.2	46.4	0.1	0.2	-0.7	15.9	2.9

[1] Change from prior year shown; for 1960, change from 1955. [2] Represents fiscal year GDP; for definition, see text, Section 13. Income, Expenditures, and Wealth.

No. 491. Federal Budget Outlays for Defense Functions: 1980 to 2001

[In billions of dollars (134.0 represents $134,000,000,000), except percent. For fiscal year ending in year shown; see text, Section 8, State and Local Government Finances and Employment. Minus sign (-) indicates decline]

Defense function	1980	1990	1993	1994	1995	1996	1997	1998	1999	2000	2001; est.
Outlays total	134.0	299.3	291.1	281.6	272.1	265.8	270.5	268.5	274.9	294.5	299.1
Percent change [1]	15.2	-1.4	-2.4	-3.2	-3.4	-2.3	1.8	-0.8	2.4	7.1	1.6
Defense Dept., military	130.9	289.8	278.6	268.6	259.4	253.2	258.3	256.1	261.4	281.2	283.9
Military personnel	40.9	75.6	75.9	73.1	70.8	66.7	69.7	69.0	69.5	76.0	72.1
Operation, maintenance	44.8	88.3	94.1	87.9	91.1	88.8	92.5	93.5	96.4	105.9	110.4
Procurement	29.0	81.0	69.9	61.8	55.0	48.9	47.7	48.2	48.8	51.7	52.7
Research and development	13.1	37.5	37.0	34.8	34.6	36.5	37.0	37.4	37.4	37.6	38.0
Military construction	2.5	5.1	4.8	5.0	6.8	6.7	6.2	6.0	5.5	5.1	5.2
Family housing	1.7	3.5	3.3	3.3	3.6	3.8	4.0	3.9	3.7	3.4	3.7
Other [2]	-1.1	-1.2	-6.4	2.7	-2.4	1.8	1.2	-1.9	0.1	1.6	1.8

[1] Change from immediate prior year. [2] Revolving and management funds, trust funds, special foreign currency program, allowances, and offsetting receipts.

No. 492. National Defense—Budget Authority and Outlays: 1980 to 2001

[In billions of dollars (143.9 represents $143,900,000,000), except percent. For fiscal year ending in year shown, except as noted; see text, Section 8, State and Local Government Finances and Employment]

Item	1980	1990	1994	1995	1996	1997	1998	1999	2000	2001, est.
Defense (Budget authority) [1]	143.9	303.3	263.3	266.4	266.2	270.4	271.3	292.3	304.1	310.6
Department of Defense-Military	140.7	293.0	251.4	255.7	254.6	258.0	258.6	278.6	290.5	295.1
Atomic energy defense activities [1]	3.0	9.7	10.9	10.1	10.7	11.4	11.7	12.6	12.4	14.1
Defense-related activities	0.2	0.6	1.1	0.6	0.9	1.0	1.0	1.1	1.2	1.5
Defense (Outlays) [1]	134.0	299.3	281.6	272.1	265.8	270.5	268.5	274.9	294.5	299.1
Department of Defense-Military	130.9	289.8	268.6	259.4	253.2	258.3	256.1	261.4	281.2	283.9
Atomic energy defense activities [1]	2.9	9.0	11.9	11.8	11.6	11.3	11.3	12.4	12.2	13.7
Defense-related activities	0.2	0.6	1.1	0.8	0.9	0.9	1.1	1.1	1.1	1.5

[1] Includes defense budget authority, balances, and outlays by other departments.

Source of Tables 490-492: U.S. Office of Management and Budget, *Historical Tables*, annual.

Figure 10.1
National Defense Outlays as a Percent of Federal Outlays and Gross Domestic Product: 1980 to 2001

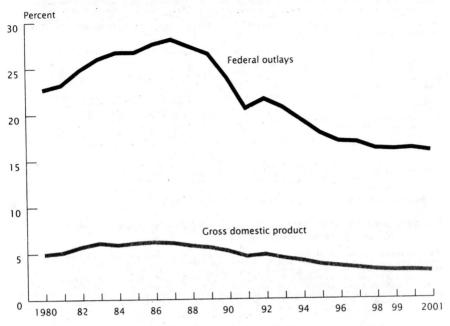

Source: Charts prepared by U.S. Census Bureau. For data, see Table 490.

Figure 10.2
U.S. Military Personnel on Active Duty Abroad: 2000

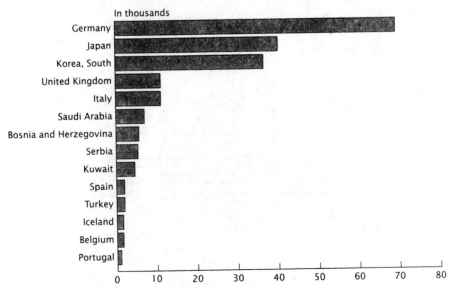

Source: Charts prepared by U.S. Census Bureau. For data, see Table 503.

National Defense and Veterans Affairs   325

No. 493. Military Prime Contract Awards to All Businesses by Program: 1980 to 1999

[In billions of dollars (83.7 represents $83,700,000,000). Net values for fiscal year ending in year shown; see text, Section 8. State and Local Government Finances and Employment. Includes all new prime contracts; debit or credit changes in contracts are also included. Actions cover official awards, amendments, or other changes in prime contracts to obtain military supplies, services, or construction. Excludes term contracts and contracts which do not obligate a firm total dollar amount or fixed quantity, but includes job orders, task orders, and delivery orders against such contracts]

DOD procurement program	1980	1990	1993	1994	1995	1996	1997	1998	1999
Total	83.7	144.7	138.3	132.2	131.4	132.2	128.4	128.8	135.2
Intragovernmental [1]	10.2	10.0	12.9	11.1	12.3	13.0	11.5	9.9	11.6
For work outside the U.S.	5.4	7.1	5.8	5.6	5.6	6.4	6.4	5.6	7.4
Educ. and nonprofit institutions	1.5	3.5	3.4	3.3	3.3	3.3	3.6	3.5	3.9
With business firms for work in the U.S. [2]	66.7	123.8	116.0	112.0	110.0	109.5	106.9	109.7	112.2
Major hard goods	41.0	79.1	64.5	59.2	56.0	55.1	52.5	56.0	57.5
Aircraft	12.5	24.0	23.0	23.5	18.8	20.3	18.4	20.8	23.3
Electronics and communication equip.	9.6	18.5	14.2	12.4	12.3	11.5	12.1	10.7	10.7
Missiles and space systems	7.9	17.1	12.1	11.6	10.6	10.2	9.5	9.9	9.5
Ships	6.0	10.3	9.0	6.8	9.1	7.1	6.8	8.6	7.8
Tanks, ammo. and weapons	5.1	9.2	6.2	4.9	5.3	5.9	5.7	6.0	6.2
Services	5.9	14.6	17.5	17.7	18.6	19.2	20.2	21.2	23.7

[1] Covers only purchases from other federal agencies and reimbursable purchases on behalf of foreign governments.
[2] Includes Department of Defense. Includes other business not shown separately. Contracts awarded for work in U.S. possessions, and other areas subject to complete sovereignty of United States; contracts in a classified location; and any intragovernmental contracts entered into overseas.

Source: U.S. Dept. of Defense, *Prime Contract Awards*, semiannual.

No. 494. Department of Defense Contract Awards, Payroll, and Civilian and Military Personnel—States: 2000

[For years ending Sept. 30. Contracts refer to awards made in year specified; expenditures relating to awards may extend over several years. Civilian employees include United States citizen and foreign national direct hire civilians subject to Office of Management and Budget (OMB) ceiling controls and civilian personnel involved in civil functions in the United States. Excludes indirect hire civilians and those direct hire civilian not subject to OMB ceiling controls. Military personnel include active duty personnel based ashore. Excludes personnel temporarily shore-based in a transient status, or afloat. Payroll outlays include the gross earnings of civilian and active duty military personnel for services rendered to the government and for cash allowances for benefits. Excludes employer's share of employee benefits, accrued military retirement benefits and most permanent change of station costs]

State	Contract awards [1] (mil. dol.)	Payroll (mil. dol.)	Personnel 1,000 Civilian	Personnel 1,000 Military	State	Contract awards [1] (mil. dol.)	Payroll (mil. dol.)	Personnel 1,000 Civilian	Personnel 1,000 Military
AL	3,298	2,376	20.2	11.1	MT	87	290	1.1	3.5
AK	831	902	4.8	15.7	NE	238	660	3.2	7.6
AZ	4,547	1,995	8.2	21.3	NV	276	818	2.0	7.7
AR	343	772	3.6	4.7	NH	398	262	1.0	0.7
CA	18,100	11,362	60.8	146.3	NJ	2,944	1,518	14.2	8.5
CO	2,214	2,395	11.0	29.1	NM	654	1,106	7.0	11.0
CT	2,177	541	2.6	6.5	NY	3,839	1,776	11.1	19.6
DE	95	329	1.4	3.7	NC	1,199	4,653	15.4	90.9
DC	1,899	1,218	12.6	13.0	ND	134	405	3.3	7.2
FL	6,470	6,887	26.4	60.9	OH	3,077	2,189	23.4	6.8
GA	3,665	4,934	30.4	66.0	OK	1,401	2,391	21.4	24.6
HI	1,160	2,537	17.9	40.4	OR	284	556	3.0	0.6
ID	213	399	1.4	4.2	PA	3,967	2,217	25.7	3.1
IL	1,609	2,361	12.7	32.1	RI	418	502	4.3	3.4
IN	1,611	929	9.3	1.1	SC	1,055	2,449	8.9	39.6
IA	621	272	1.5	0.4	SD	87	266	1.7	3.1
KS	891	1,136	5.5	15.5	TN	1,077	1,165	6.7	2.4
KY	910	1,856	6.1	35.8	TX	12,145	8,659	39.3	109.9
LA	1,938	1,403	8.6	15.5	UT	950	1,044	13.5	4.8
ME	772	571	5.8	2.7	VT	243	96	0.6	-
MD	4,977	3,726	32.0	30.4	VA	13,637	11,407	79.6	133.3
MA	4,737	826	6.9	2.3	WA	2,192	4,035	23.1	48.9
MI	1,446	867	7.7	1.0	WV	74	271	1.8	0.6
MN	1,458	440	2.5	0.7	WI	768	456	3.0	0.6
MS	1,557	1,392	9.5	16.6	WY	100	226	1.0	3.3
MO	4,508	1,604	9.4	16.2					

- Represents zero.   [1] Military awards for supplies, services, and construction. Net value of contracts of over $25,000 for work in each state and DC. Figures reflect impact of prime contracting on state distribution of defense work. Often the state in which a prime contractor is located in is not the state where the subcontracted work is done. See also headnote, Table 502. Undistributed civilians and military personnel, their payrolls, and prime contract awards for performance in classified locations are excluded.

Source: U.S. Dept. of Defense. *Atlas/Data Abstract for the United States and Selected Areas*, annual.

326 National Defense and Veterans Affairs

No. 495. Worldwide Military Expenditures in Current and Constant (1997) Dollars: 1990 to 1997

[In billions of dollars (1,090 represents $1,090,000,000,000). For military expenditures and Armed Forces by country, see Section 30, Comparative International Statistics. GNP = Gross national product]

Country group	1990	1991	1992	1993	1994	1995	1996	1997
CURRENT DOLLARS								
Expenditures, total [1]	1,090	1,010	856	819	813	798	810	842
United States	306	280	305	298	288	279	271	276
Percent of total	28.1	27.7	35.6	36.4	35.4	35.0	33.5	32.8
Developed countries [2]	883	817	649	637	628	600	597	610
Developing countries [2]	206	196	207	182	185	198	212	232
NATO countries [3]	488	465	486	477	467	454	451	457
CONSTANT (1997) DOLLARS								
Expenditures, total [1]	1,280	1,150	949	885	860	826	823	842
United States	359	317	338	321	305	289	276	276
Percent of total	28.0	27.6	35.6	36.3	35.5	35.0	33.5	32.8
Developed countries [2]	1,030	925	719	688	664	621	607	610
Developing countries [2]	242	222	230	197	196	205	216	232
NATO countries [3]	572	527	538	515	494	470	458	457
Percent of GNP	4.5	4.0	3.4	3.1	2.9	2.7	2.6	2.6
United States	5.2	4.7	4.8	4.5	4.1	3.8	3.5	3.3
Developed countries [2]	4.5	4.0	3.3	3.2	3.0	2.7	2.6	2.5
Developing countries [2]	4.6	4.0	3.6	2.9	2.7	2.7	2.7	2.7
NATO countries [3]	4.1	3.7	3.7	3.5	3.2	3.0	2.8	2.7

[1] Includes countries not shown separately.   [2] Twenty-eight developed countries; see Table 496 for selected countries; for complete list, see source.   [3] North Atlantic Treaty Organization.

No. 496. Arms Trade in Constant (1997) Dollars—Selected Countries: 1990 to 1997

[In millions of dollars (70 represents $70,000,000, except percent. Because some countries exclude arms imports or exports from their trade statistic and their "total" imports and exports are therefore understated, and because arms transfers may be estimated independently of trade data, the ratio of arms to total imports or exports may be overstated and may even exceed 100 percent]

Country	1990	1995	1996	1997	Country	1990	1995	1996	1997
EXPORTERS [1]					IMPORTERS [1]				
Australia	70	52	295	30	Algeria	375	249	132	480
Belarus	(NA)	176	203	490	Australia	1,405	1,346	1,322	925
Belgium	223	124	325	110	Brazil	199	269	346	430
Bulgaria	94	145	112	120	China, Mainland	468	854	1,627	500
Canada	732	647	559	550	China, Taiwan	1,171	1,553	1,728	9,200
China: Mainland	2,694	673	635	1,100	Egypt	1,522	2,174	1,728	1,600
Czech Republic	(NA)	104	102	90	Germany	2,694	880	915	750
France	6,090	2,692	3,558	5,900	Greece	849	497	661	850
Germany	1,874	1,760	1,322	750	Iran	2,225	342	356	850
India	12	5	5	90	Israel	1,640	802	940	1,100
Israel	820	906	763	370	Italy	492	404	488	430
Italy	234	228	163	700	Japan	1,874	1,864	2,440	2,600
Korea, North	246	62	112	701	Korea, South	1,113	1,967	1,322	1,100
Netherlands	234	352	366	500	Kuwait	316	1,346	1,728	2,000
Poland	269	41	71	60	Malaysia	82	854	203	725
Russia	(NA)	3,935	3,152	2,300	Netherlands	995	425	686	460
Singapore	35	31	41	90	Pakistan	1,405	570	275	600
South Africa	59	166	356	370	Qatar	117	52	5	625
Spain	410	414	224	525	Saudi Arabia	8,900	10,350	9,862	11,600
Sweden	849	1,010	1,220	900	Spain	703	425	661	430
Switzerland	70	145	203	50	Thailand	457	777	635	950
Ukraine	(NA)	249	203	500	Turkey	1,522	1,760	1,627	1,600
United Arab Emirates	6	10	81	40	United Arab Emirates	1,874	1,346	1,118	1,400
United Kingdom	5,387	5,488	6,303	6,600	United Kingdom	1,522	984	1,525	2,100
United States	25,650	23,710	23,380	31,800	United States	2,108	1,035	1,220	1,600

NA Not available.   [1] Includes countries not shown separately.

Source of Tables 495 and 496: U.S. Arms Control and Disarmament Agency, World Military Expenditures and Arms Transfers, annual.

U.S. Census Bureau, Statistical Abstract of the United States: 2001

No. 497. U.S. Military Sales and Assistance to Foreign Governments: 1990 to 1998

[In millions of dollars (16,614 represents $16,614,000,000). For fiscal year ending in year shown; see text, Section 8, State and Local Government Finances and Employment. Department of Defense (DOD) sales deliveries cover deliveries against sales orders authorized under Arms Export Control Act, as well as earlier and applicable legislation. For details regarding individual programs, see source]

Item	1990	1991	1992	1993	1994	1995	1996	1997	1998
Military sales agreements	16,614	17,324	13,901	31,109	13,292	8,950	10,295	8,782	8,231
Military constr. sales agrmts	636	799	148	660	58	25	83	30	341
Military sales deliveries [1]	7,718	8,777	10,054	11,314	9,467	11,940	11,574	19,233	13,523
Military sales financing	4,758	4,693	4,274	4,124	3,917	3,712	3,836	3,530	3,420
Military assistance programs [2] . . .	137	177	116	651	328	123	340	70	93
Military assist. program delivery [3] .	27	150	82	60	5	10	25	114	59
IMET program/deliveries [3]	43	46	42	43	22	26	39	43	36

[1] Includes military construction sales deliveries.　[2] Also includes Military Assistance Service Funded (MASF) program data, Section 506(a) drawdown authority, and MAP Merger Funds.　[3] Includes Military Assistance Service Funded (MASF) program data and Section 506(a) drawdown authority.

No. 498. U.S. Military Sales Deliveries by Country: 1990 to 1998

[In millions of dollars (8,065 represents $8,065,000,000). For fiscal years ending in year shown. See text, Section 8, State and Local Government Finances and Employment. Represents Department of Defense military sales]

Country	1990	1991	1992	1993	1994	1995	1996	1997	1998
Total [1]	8,065	9,191	10,389	11,666	9,736	12,158	11,716	19,331	13,905
Australia	384	205	156	259	354	308	229	197	344
China: Taiwan	455	549	711	818	845	1,353	853	5,696	1,490
Egypt	368	482	1,027	1,239	890	1,536	1,112	1,181	584
Germany	366	476	510	356	152	236	378	211	191
Greece	114	124	163	226	236	221	210	717	414
Israel	146	238	720	782	412	328	386	504	1,618
Italy	61	61	52	72	181	54	77	51	43
Japan	272	518	571	380	785	753	786	512	420
Kuwait	52	75	815	840	217	476	628	1,391	325
Netherlands	397	387	236	114	140	157	397	174	347
Saudi Arabia	874	2,742	2,387	3,453	1,992	3,568	2,854	4,660	3,959
South Korea	328	230	309	306	381	442	342	483	956
Turkey	761	627	703	756	937	374	483	1,167	541

[1] Includes countries not shown.

Source of Tables 497 and 498: U.S. Defense Security Cooperation Agency (DSCA) Fact Book, *Foreign Military Sales, Foreign Military Construction Sales*, and *Military Assistance Facts*, annual.

No. 499. Military and Civilian Personnel and Expenditures: 1990 to 1999

Item	1990	1995	1996	1997	1998	1999
Personnel, total [1] (1,000)	3,693	3,391	3,252	3,081	2,943	2,863
Active duty military	1,185	1,085	1,056	1,045	1,004	1,003
Expenditures, total (mil. dol.) [2]	209,904	209,695	211,740	205,764	208,843	218,861
Prime contract awards [3] (mil. dol.)	121,254	109,005	109,408	106,561	109,386	114,875
Major area of work (mil. dol.):						•
Aircraft, fixed wing	6,329	7,543	8,950	5,432	12,904	7,733
Guided missiles	928	495	625	2,831	417	654

[1] Includes those based ashore and excludes those temporarily shore-based, in a transient status, or afloat.　[2] Includes expenditures not shown separately.　[3] Represents contract awards over $25,000.

Source: U.S. Dept. of Defense, *Atlas/Data Abstract for the United States and Selected Areas*, annual.

No. 500. Department of Defense Manpower: 1950 to 2000

[In thousands (1,459 represents 1,459,000. As of end of fiscal year; see text, Section 8, State and Local Government Finances and Employment. Includes National Guard, Reserve, and retired regular personnel on extended or continuous active duty. Excludes Coast Guard. Other officer candidates are included under enlisted personnel]

Year	Total [1][2]	Army Total [2]	Army White	Army Black	Army Officers	Army Enlisted	Navy [3] Total [2]	Navy White	Navy Black	Navy Officers	Navy Enlisted	Marine Corps Total [2]	Marine Corps White	Marine Corps Black	Marine Corps Officers	Marine Corps Enlisted	Air Force Total [2]	Air Force White	Air Force Black	Air Force Officers	Air Force Enlisted
1950	1,459	593	(NA)	(NA)	73	519	381	(NA)	(NA)	45	333	74	(NA)	(NA)	7	67	411	(NA)	(NA)	57	354
1955	2,935	1,109	(NA)	(NA)	122	986	661	(NA)	(NA)	75	583	205	(NA)	(NA)	18	187	960	(NA)	(NA)	137	823
1960	2,475	873	(NA)	(NA)	101	770	617	(NA)	(NA)	70	545	171	(NA)	(NA)	16	154	815	(NA)	(NA)	130	683
1965	2,654	969	(NA)	(NA)	112	855	670	(NA)	(NA)	78	588	190	(NA)	(NA)	17	173	825	(NA)	(NA)	132	690
1970	3,065	1,323	(NA)	(NA)	167	1,153	691	(NA)	(NA)	81	606	260	(NA)	(NA)	25	235	791	(NA)	(NA)	130	657
1971	2,713	1,124	(NA)	(NA)	149	972	622	(NA)	(NA)	75	542	212	(NA)	(NA)	22	191	755	(NA)	(NA)	126	625
1972	2,322	811	(NA)	(NA)	121	687	587	(NA)	(NA)	73	511	198	(NA)	(NA)	20	178	726	(NA)	(NA)	122	600
1973	2,252	801	(NA)	(NA)	116	682	564	(NA)	(NA)	71	490	196	(NA)	(NA)	19	177	691	(NA)	(NA)	115	572
1974	2,162	783	(NA)	(NA)	106	674	546	(NA)	(NA)	67	475	189	(NA)	(NA)	19	170	644	(NA)	(NA)	110	529
1975	2,128	784	(NA)	(NA)	103	678	535	(NA)	(NA)	66	466	196	(NA)	(NA)	19	177	613	(NA)	(NA)	105	503
1976	2,082	779	(NA)	(NA)	98	678	525	(NA)	(NA)	64	458	192	(NA)	(NA)	19	174	585	(NA)	(NA)	100	481
1977	2,075	782	(NA)	(NA)	98	680	530	(NA)	(NA)	63	462	192	(NA)	(NA)	19	173	571	(NA)	(NA)	96	470
1978	2,062	772	(NA)	(NA)	98	670	530	(NA)	(NA)	63	463	191	(NA)	(NA)	18	172	570	(NA)	(NA)	95	470
1979	2,027	759	(NA)	(NA)	97	657	523	(NA)	(NA)	62	457	185	(NA)	(NA)	18	167	559	(NA)	(NA)	96	459
1980	2,051	777	503	229	99	674	527	436	55	63	460	188	142	39	18	170	558	460	80	98	456
1981	2,083	781	502	232	102	675	540	443	58	65	470	191	145	38	18	172	570	468	83	99	467
1982	2,109	780	504	230	103	673	553	450	62	67	481	192	149	38	19	173	583	476	87	102	476
1983	2,123	780	512	220	106	669	558	462	66	68	485	194	152	37	20	174	592	483	88	105	483
1984	2,138	780	520	215	108	668	565	455	67	69	491	196	153	36	20	176	597	486	89	106	486
1985	2,151	781	523	211	110	667	571	459	70	71	495	198	152	37	20	178	602	488	90	108	489
1986	2,169	781	524	210	110	667	581	464	75	72	504	199	151	38	20	179	608	491	92	109	495
1987	2,174	781	519	212	108	668	587	467	81	72	510	200	150	38	20	179	607	489	92	107	495
1988	2,138	772	507	213	107	660	593	466	85	72	516	197	147	38	20	177	576	462	88	105	467
1989	2,130	770	497	218	107	658	593	461	91	72	516	197	146	38	20	177	571	458	87	104	463
1990	2,044	732	466	213	104	624	579	446	93	72	503	197	145	38	20	177	535	428	82	100	431
1991	1,986	711	452	204	104	603	570	439	92	71	495	194	144	36	20	174	510	409	77	97	409
1992	1,807	610	388	173	95	511	542	415	88	69	468	185	138	30	19	165	470	377	70	90	376
1993	1,705	572	365	158	88	480	510	390	84	66	439	178	134	28	18	160	444	357	65	84	356
1994	1,610	541	344	147	85	453	469	355	78	62	403	174	131	28	18	156	426	341	62	81	341
1995	1,518	509	322	137	83	422	435	326	75	59	372	175	130	28	18	157	400	318	58	78	318
1996	1,472	491	(NA)	(NA)	81	407	417	(NA)	(NA)	57	355	174	(NA)	(NA)	18	157	389	(NA)	(NA)	76	309
1997	1,439	492	(NA)	(NA)	79	408	396	(NA)	(NA)	56	335	174	(NA)	(NA)	18	156	377	(NA)	(NA)	74	299
1998	1,407	484	(NA)	(NA)	78	401	382	(NA)	(NA)	55	323	173	(NA)	(NA)	18	155	367	(NA)	(NA)	72	292
1999	1,386	479	(NA)	(NA)	77	398	373	(NA)	(NA)	54	315	173	(NA)	(NA)	18	155	361	(NA)	(NA)	70	286
2000	1,384	482	(NA)	(NA)	77	401	373	(NA)	(NA)	54	315	173	(NA)	(NA)	18	155	356	(NA)	(NA)	69	282

NA Not available. [1] Beginning 1980, excludes Navy Reserve personnel on active duty for Training and Administration of Reserves (TARS). From 1969, the full-time Guard and Reserve. [2] Includes Cadets and other not shown separately. [3] Prior to 1980, includes Navy Reserve personnel on active duty for Training and Administration of Reserves (TARS).

Source: U.S. Dept. of Defense, Selected Manpower Statistics, annual.

U.S. Census Bureau, Statistical Abstract of the United States: 2001

No. 501. United States Military and Civilian Personnel in Installations: 1999

[As of September 30. MC represents Marine Corps]

State	Military personnel				Civilian personnel			
	Total	Army	Navy/MC	Air Force	Total [1]	Army	Navy/MC	Air Force
U.S.	1,014,166	386,369	324,613	303,184	633,600	208,006	179,340	151,406
AL.	11,272	6,116	573	4,583	20,955	16,603	40	2,713
AK.	15,684	6,196	85	9,403	4,247	2,333	7	1,622
AZ.	21,240	5,358	4,559	11,323	8,117	3,338	414	3,337
AR.	4,888	369	110	4,409	3,570	2,585	6	865
CA.	109,697	7,697	80,572	21,428	64,086	6,899	34,986	12,376
CO	29,247	15,002	955	13,290	11,118	2,661	46	5,055
CT.	4,412	38	4,265	109	2,593	450	1,136	256
DE.	3,898	13	13	3,872	1,370	184	-	1,102
DC	13,240	4,600	4,974	3,666	12,651	4,357	7,015	993
FL.	50,731	2,982	23,223	24,526	26,322	2,594	12,731	7,739
GA	62,714	49,340	4,096	9,278	30,678	11,295	4,409	11,987
HI	32,354	14,692	13,179	4,483	16,318	4,293	8,864	2,026
ID	4,326	40	76	4,210	1,411	604	54	691
IL	35,674	716	29,283	5,675	12,988	6,537	1,793	2,923
IN	991	416	411	164	9,266	1,436	3,164	1,160
IA	443	234	115	94	1,514	938	4	519
KS.	16,354	13,264	179	2,911	5,457	3,914	3	1,069
KY.	36,149	35,713	228	208	8,734	7,030	185	223
LA.	15,246	8,367	1,515	5,364	7,815	4,168	1,503	1,667
ME	2,136	242	1,781	113	5,520	320	4,509	290
MD	29,859	7,548	14,085	8,226	32,101	12,037	15,633	2,313
MA	2,535	318	489	1,728	6,970	2,225	305	3,132
MI	1,085	488	389	208	7,664	4,614	26	1,208
MN	862	321	320	221	2,418	1,333	26	782·
MS	12,069	500	3,255	8,314	9,434	3,586	2,740	2,785
MO	17,184	11,489	1,901	3,794	9,516	5,675	240	1,200
MT	3,663	26	15	3,622	1,113	442	1	604
NE.	7,988	90	558	7,340	3,323	1,406	14	1,534
NV.	7,721	91	1,003	6,627	2,068	305	334	1,199
NH	376	18	201	157	1,028	506	45	305
NJ.	7,116	958	847	5,311	14,549	9,627	2,312	1,593
NM	11,642	420	252	10,970	6,915	2,931	62	3,568
NY.	20,532	17,219	2,636	677	11,365	6,886	178	2,439
NC	86,594	38,831	38,431	9,332	16,311	5,959	7,084	1,210
ND	7,499	27	6	7,466	1,638	409	1	1,112
OH	7,668	578	525	6,565	23,544	1,311	82	12,335
OK	25,234	14,889	841	9,504	20,187	4,116	88	14,567
OR	933	200	368	365	2,908	2,072	19	786
PA.	3,261	1,252	1,604	405	25,772	7,883	8,696	1,603
RI	3,415	97	3,160	158	4,352	264	3,743	239
SC.	38,289	11,963	17,329	8,997	9,495	2,542	3,746	1,708
SD.	3,171	38	8	3,125	1,264	485	1	711
TN.	2,679	378	1,800	501	4,939	2,468	1,029	948
TX.	108,835	60,945	6,909	40,981	39,993	16,050	1,788	17,716
UT.	4,844	331	148	4,365	12,419	2,079	22	8,849
VT.	125	24	16	85	525	253	2	229
VA.	80,132	25,696	40,420	14,016	78,973	19,519	36,004	4,238
WA	32,398	17,367	7,751	7,280	22,322	5,015	14,162	1,877
WV	614	208	299	107	1,713	1,216	76	398
WI	578	294	142	142	3,119	2,069	11	914
WY	3,496	7	3	3,486	932	184	1	691

- Represents zero.   [1] Includes other DOD organizations not shown separately.

Source: U.S. Dept. of Defense, *Selected Manpower Statistics*, annual.

No. 502. Military Personnel on Active Duty by Location: 1980 to 1999

[In thousands (2,051 represents 2,051,000). As of end of fiscal year; see text, Section 8, State and Local Government Finances and Employment]

Item	1980	1985	1990	1993	1994	1995	1996	1997	1998	1999
Total.	2,051	2,151	2,044	1,705	1,611	1,518	1,472	1,439	1,407	1,386
Shore-based [1]	1,840	1,920	1,794	1,505	1,431	1,351	1,317	1,294	1,267	1,241
Afloat [2]	211	231	252	200	180	167	155	145	140	145
United States [3]	1,562	1,636	1,437	1,397	1,324	1,280	1,231	1,211	1,147	1,133
Foreign countries	488	516	609	308	287	238	240	227	260	253

[1] Includes Navy personnel temporarily on shore.　[2] Includes Marine Corps.　[3] Includes outlying areas.

Source: U.S. Dept. of Defense, *Selected Manpower Statistics*, annual.

No. 503. U.S. Military Personnel on Active Duty in Selected Foreign Countries: 2000

[As of end of fiscal year]

Country	2000	Country	2000	Country	2000
In foreign countries [1] .	**257,817**	El Salvador	27	Norway.	81
Ashore	212,858	France	67	Oman.	251
Afloat	44,959	Germany.	69,203	Pakistan	22
Argentina	26	Greece	678	Panama	20
Australia	175	Greenland	125	Peru.	425
Austria	18	Haiti.	21	Philippines.	79
Bahamas, The	24	Honduras	351	Portugal	1,005
Bahrain.	949	Hungary	375	Qatar	52
Belgium	1,554	Iceland	1,636	Rep. of Korea	36,565
Bolivia	20	India.	20	Russia	101
Bosnia and Herzegovina . . .	5,708	Indonesia	51	Saudi Arabia	7,053
Brazil	38	Israel	36	Singapore	411
Canada.	156	Italy	11,190	South Africa	34
Chile	26	Jamaica	11	Spain	2,007
China	74	Japan.	40,159	Switzerland	19
Colombia.	224	Jordan	29	Thailand	526
Croatia	138	Kenya.	21	Tunisia	12
Cuba (Guantanamo)	688	Korea, Republic of	36,565	Turkey	2,006
Cyprus	41	Kuwait	4,602	Ukraine	16
Denmark	26	Macedonia	347	United Arab Emirates.	402
Diego Garcia	625	Mexico	29	United Kingdom	11,207
Ecuador	20	Netherlands.	659	Venezuela	28
Egypt	499	New Zealand	6	Zambabwe	8

[1] Includes areas not shown separately.

Source: U.S. Department of Defense, *Selected Manpower Statistics*, annual.

No. 504. Coast Guard Personnel on Active Duty: 1970 to 1998

[As of end of fiscal year; see text, Section 8, State and Local Government Finances and Employment]

Year	Total	Officers	Cadets	Enlisted	Year	Total	Officers	Cadets	Enlisted
1970.	37,689	5,512	653	31,524	1993.	39,234	7,628	907	30,699
1975.	36,788	5,630	1,177	29,981	1994.	37,802	7,656	881	29,265
1980.	39,381	6,463	877	32,041	1995.	36,731	7,462	841	28,401
1985.	38,595	6,775	733	31,087	1996.	35,229	7,270	830	27,129
1990.	36,939	6,876	927	29,136	1997.	34,890	7,100	845	26,945
1991.	38,377	7,192	900	30,285	1998.	35,293	7,119	811	27,363
1992.	39,388	7,507	919	30,962					

Source: U.S. Dept. of Transportation, *Annual Report of the Secretary of Transportation*.

No. 505. U.S. Active Duty Military Deaths by Manner of Death: 1980 to 1999

Manner of death	1980-99	1980	1990	1991	1992	1993	1994	1995	1996	1997	1998	1999
Deaths, total	**32,912**	**2,391**	**1,526**	**1,787**	**1,332**	**1,245**	**1,109**	**1,055**	**1,008**	**864**	**815**	**761**
Accident	19,488	1,577	864	931	712	672	548	572	518	463	420	411
Illness	5,974	401	275	323	253	215	217	167	180	177	156	126
Homicide	1,803	161	71	108	112	89	86	59	65	43	28	34
Self-inflicted	4,539	236	250	233	222	246	231	242	210	159	155	110
Pending/undetermined.	545	15	42	44	32	13	8	9	14	22	53	80
Hostile deaths	563	1	24	148	1	10	19	6	21	-	3	-
Deaths per 100,000	(X)	116.6	74.7	90.0	73.7	73.0	68.9	69.5	68.5	60.1	57.9	54.9
Nonhostile deaths per 100,000	(X)	116.5	73.5	82.5	73.7	72.4	67.7	69.1	67.1	60.1	57.7	54.9
Accidents per 100,000.	(X)	76.9	42.3	46.9	39.4	39.4	34.0	37.7	35.2	32.2	29.9	29.7
Illnesses per 100,000.	(X)	19.6	13.5	16.3	14.0	12.6	13.5	11.0	12.2	12.3	11.1	9.1
Homicides per 100,000	(X)	7.9	3.5	5.4	6.2	5.2	5.3	3.9	4.4	3.0	2.0	2.5
Self-inflicted per 100,000	(X)	11.5	12.2	11.7	12.3	14.4	14.3	15.9	14.3	11.1	11.0	7.9

- Represents zero.　X Not applicable.

Source: U.S. Dept. of Defense, *DOD Worldwide U.S. Active Duty Military Personnel*.

National Defense and Veterans Affairs　331

No. 506. Armed Forces Personnel—Summary of Major Conflicts

[For Revolutionary War, number of personnel serving not known, but estimates range from 184,000 to 250,000; for War of 1812, 286,730 served; for Mexican War, 78,718 served. Dates of the major conflicts may differ from those specified in various laws providing benefits for veterans]

Item	Unit	Civil War [1]	Spanish-American War	World War I	World War II	Korean conflict	Vietnam conflict
Personnel serving [2]	1,000....	2,213	307	4,735	[3]16,113	[4]5,720	[5]8,744
Average duration of service	Months...	20	8	12	33	.19	23
Service abroad: Personnel serving	Percent	(NA)	[6]29	53	73	[7]56	(NA)
Average duration [8]	Months...	(NA)	1.5	6	16	13	(NA)
Casualties: [9] Battle deaths [2]	1,000....	140	(Z)	53	292	34	[10]47
Other deaths	1,000....	224	2	63	114	3	11
Wounds not mortal [2]	1,000....	282	2	204	671	103	[10]153
Draftees: Classified	1,000....	777	(X)	24,234	36,677	9,123	[5]75,717
Examined	1,000....	522	(X)	3,764	17,955	3,685	[5]8,611
Rejected	1,000....	160	(X)	803	6,420	1,189	[5]3,880
Inducted	1,000....	46	(X)	2,820	10,022	1,560	[5]1,759

NA Not available. X Not applicable. Z Fewer than 500. [1] Union forces only. Estimates of the number serving in Confederate forces range from 600,000 to 1.5 million. [2] Source: U.S. Department of Defense, *Selected Manpower Statistics*, annual. [3] Covers Dec. 1, 1941, to Dec. 31, 1946. [4] Covers June 25, 1950, to July 27, 1953. [5] Covers Aug. 4, 1964, to Jan. 27, 1973. [6] Army and Marines only. [7] Excludes Navy. Covers July 1950 through Jan. 1955. Far East area only. [8] During hostilities only. [9] For periods covered, see footnotes 3, 4, and 5. [10] Covers Jan. 1, 1961, to Jan. 27, 1973. Includes known military service personnel who have died from combat related wounds.

Source: Except as noted, the President's Commission on Veterans' Pensions, Veterans' *Benefits in the United States*, Vol. I, 1956; and U.S. Dept. of Defense, unpublished data.

No. 507. Enlisted Military Personnel Accessions: 1990 to 1997

[In thousands (461.1 represents 461,100). For years ending Sept. 30]

Branch of service	1990	1995	1996	1997	Branch of service	1990	1995	1996	1997
Total	**461.1**	**357.3**	**367.6**	**380.1**	Navy	135.3	93.4	91.3	93.3
First enlistments	216.4	160.0	174.6	184.6	First enlistments	62.1	36.4	39.2	43.7
Reenlistments	237.0	180.8	181.0	187.4	Reenlistments	58.6	41.4	40.6	41.6
Reserves to active duty	15.6	16.6	12.0	8.1	Marine Corps	47.7	46.7	48.7	50.0
					First enlistments	32.9	34.4	34.5	35.1
Army	181.7	135.9	146.0	162.3	Reenlistments	14.4	11.9	0.4	14.7
First enlistments	84.8	57.7	69.7	75.3	Air Force	104.4	81.3	81.6	74.5
Reenlistments	96.5	77.7	76.2	87.0	First enlistments	36.6	31.4	31.2	30.5
					Reenlistments	67.5	49.7	50.3	44.0

Source: U.S. Dept. of Defense, *Selected Manpower Statistics*, annual.

No. 508. Military Personnel on Active Duty: 1990 to 2000

[In thousands (2,043.7 represents 2,043,700). As of Sept. 30]

Rank/grade	1990	1995	1996	1997	1998	1999	2000
Total [1]	**2,043.7**	**1,518.2**	**1,471.7**	**1,438.6**	**1,406.8**	**1,385.7**	**1,384.3**
Recruit—E-1	97.6	63.4	69.3	74.1	73.6	81.2	80.0
Private—E-2	140.3	99.7	99.0	100.8	99.0	93.9	99.0
Pvt. 1st class—E-3	280.1	197.1	200.4	196.0	194.7	190.5	196.3
Corporal—E-4	427.8	317.2	283.8	264.8	262.9	262.9	251.0
Sergeant—E-5	361.5	261.4	254.8	250.6	239.9	229.5	229.5
Staff Sgt.—E-6	239.1	180.5	172.6	169.6	163.7	162.9	164.9
Sgt. 1st class—E-7	134.1	109.3	107.7	104.7	100.4	97.1	97.7
Master Sgt.—E-8	38.0	28.8	28.8	27.6	26.6	25.8	26.0
Sgt. Major—E-9	15.3	11.1	10.7	10.8	10.5	10.4	10.2
Warrant Officer—W-1	3.2	2.0	2.1	2.0	2.1	2.2	2.1
Chief Warrant—W-4	3.0	2.2	2.0	1.9	2.0	2.1	2.0
2d Lt.—0-1	31.9	25.6	25.2	24.8	23.8	24.9	26.4
1st Lt.—0-2	37.9	26.1	25.8	25.5	26.2	25.4	24.7
Captain—0-3	106.6	84.3	81.0	78.3	73.8	69.8	68.1
Major—0-4	53.2	43.9	43.9	43.1	43.3	43.5	43.2
Lt. Colonel—0-5	32.3	28.7	28.2	28.0	28.6	28.0	27.5
Colonel—0-6	14.0	11.7	11.6	11.4	11.3	11.3	11.3
Brig. General—0-7	0.5	0.4	0.4	0.4	0.4	0.4	0.4
Major General—0-8	0.4	0.3	0.3	0.3	0.3	0.3	0.3
Lt. General—0-9	0.1	0.1	0.1	0.1	0.1	0.1	0.1
General—0-10	(Z)	(Z)	(Z)	(Z)	(Z)	(Z)	(Z)

Z Fewer than 50. [1] Includes cadets and midshipmen and warrant officers, W-2 and W-3.

Source: U.S. Dept. of Defense, *Selected Manpower Statistics*, annual, and Office of the Comptroller, unpublished data.

No. 509. Military Reserve Personnel: 1990 to 2000

[As of end of fiscal year. The Ready Reserve includes the Selected Reserve which is scheduled to augment active forces during times of war or national emergency, and the Individual Ready Reserve which, during times of war or national emergency, would be used to fill out Active, Guard and Reserve units, and which would also be a source for casualty replacements; Ready Reservists serve in an active status (except for the Inactive National Guard - a very small pool within the Army National Guard). The Standby Reserve cannot be called to active duty except in situations where those members are the only available assets with specific required specialties. The Retired Reserve is categorized into three groups, based on age and length of retirement, prioritized for mobilization purposes]

Reserve status and branch of service	1990	1995	1996	1997	1998	1999	2000
Total reserves [1]	1,688,674	1,674,164	1,564,387	1,474,167	1,382,348	1,316,984	1,276,843
Ready reserve	1,658,707	1,648,388	1,536,641	1,450,974	1,353,428	1,288,844	1,251,452
Standby reserve	29,967	25,776	27,746	23,193	28,920	28,140	25,391
Retired reserve	462,371	505,905	529,669	549,845	562,088	564,358	573,305

[1] Less retired reserves.

Source: U.S. Dept. of Defense, *Official Guard and Reserve Manpower Strengths and Statistics*, quarterly.

No. 510. Ready Reserve Personnel Profile—Race: 1990 to 2000

Item	Race					Percent distribution			
	Total	White	Black	Asian	American Indian	White	Black	Asian	American Indian
1990	1,641,475	1,289,367	271,470	14,616	7,695	78.7	16.4	0.9	0.5
1991	1,758,144	1,377,583	290,241	17,966	9,111	78.5	16.4	1.0	0.5
1992	1,857,801	1,443,155	308,807	19,944	9,180	77.8	16.5	1.1	0.5
1993	1,840,650	1,425,255	309,699	21,089	9,068	77.5	16.7	1.1	0.5
1994	1,779,436	1,366,387	297,519	22,190	8,870	76.9	16.6	1.2	0.5
1995	1,633,497	1,254,592	273,847	21,792	8,591	76.9	16.7	1.3	0.5
1996	1,522,451	1,166,628	249,114	21,240	8,226	76.7	16.3	1.4	0.6
1997	1,437,722	1,102,234	229,950	21,412	8,115	76.8	15.9	1.5	0.6
1998	1,340,557	1,022,851	209,814	21,411	7,531	76.4	15.5	1.6	0.6
1999	1,288,844	969,248	201,969	22,293	7,349	76.0	15.8	1.8	0.6
2000	1,251,452	980,037	202,574	22,610	7,589	75.3	15.9	2.1	0.7

Source: U.S. Dept. of Defense, *Official Guard and Reserve Manpower Strengths and Statistics*, annual.

No. 511. National Guard—Summary: 1980 to 1999

[As of end of fiscal year; see text, Section 8, State and Local Government Finances and Employment. Includes Puerto Rico]

Item	Unit	1980	1985	1990	1994	1995	1996	1997	1998	1999
Army National Guard:										
Units	Number	3,379	4,353	4,055	6,000	5,872	5,643	5,500	5,415	5,360
Personnel [1]	1,000	368	438	444	397	375	373	370	362	357
Number of females	1,000	(NA)	(NA)	(NA)	(NA)	(NA)	(NA)	(NA)	(NA)	38
Funds obligated [2]	Bil. dol.	1.8	4.4	5.2	6.0	6.0	5.9	5.7	6.0	6.5
Value of equipment	Bil. dol.	7.6	18.8	29.0	31.0	33.0	33.0	33.0	33.0	34.0
Air National Guard:										
Units	Number	1,054	1,184	1,339	1,665	1,604	1,588	(NA)	1,541	1,541
Personnel [1]	1,000	96	109	118	114	110	110	108	108	107
Number of females	1,000	(NA)	(NA)	(NA)	(NA)	(NA)	(NA)	(NA)	(NA)	15
Funds obligated [2]	Bil. dol.	1.7	2.8	3.2	3.1	4.2	4.6	4.5	4.4	4.8
Value of equipment (est.) [3]	Bil. dol.	5.2	21.4	26.4	40.2	38.3	40.1	42.0	41.0	43.0

NA Not available. [1] Officers and enlisted personnel. [2] Federal funds; includes personnel, operations, maintenance, and military construction. [3] Beginning 1985, increase due to repricing of aircraft to current year dollars to reflect true replacement value. Beginning 1994 includes value of aircraft and support equipment.

Source: National Guard Bureau, *Annual Review of the Chief, National Guard Bureau*; and unpublished data.

U.S. Census Bureau, Statistical Abstract of the United States: 2001

No. 512. Summary of U.S. Military Force Structure: 1993 to 1999 and Projections to 2001

Item	1993	1994	1995	1996	1997	1998	1999	2000	2001
DEPARTMENT OF DEFENSE (DOD) STRATEGIC FORCES [1]									
Land-based ICBMs: [2]									
Minuteman II (1 warhead each) plus Minuteman III (3 warheads each)	737	625	535	530	530	500	500	500	500
Peacekeeper (10 warheads each)	50	50	50	50	50	50	50	50	34
Heavy bombers (PAI): [3]									
B-52	84	64	74	56	56	56	56	56	56
B-1 [4]	84	84	60	60	60	70	74	80	82
B-2	-	3	6	9	10	12	13	16	16
Submarine-launched ballistic missiles: [2]									
Poseidon (C-3) and Trident (C-4) missiles on pre-Ohio-class submarines	96	48	-	-	-	.	.	.	.
Trident (C-4 and D-5) missiles on Ohio-class submarines	312	336	360	384	408	432	432	432	432
DOD AIRLIFT AND SEALIFT FORCES									
Intertheater Airlift (PMAI): [5]									
C-5	109	107	104	104	104	104	104	104	104
C-141	214	214	199	187	163	143	136	104	88
KC-10 [6]	57	54	54	54	54	54	54	54	54
C-17	2	9	17	22	24	30	37	46	58
Intratheater Airlift (PMAI): [5]									
C-130 [7]	380	424	428	432	430	425	425	425	425
Sealift ships (Active): [8]									
Tankers	20	18	18	12	13	10	10	10	10
Cargo	40	51	51	49	48	43	49	52	57
Sealift ships, reserve:									
RRF [9]	97	93	77	82	87	88	87	87	69
SPECIAL OPERATIONS FORCES									
Army:									
Special forces groups, (Active)	5	5	5	5	5	5	5	5	5
Special forces groups, (National Guard)	2	2	2	2	2	2	2	2	2
Special forces groups, (Reserve)	2	-	-	-	-	-	-	-	-
Psychological operations groups (Active)	1	1	1	1	1	1	1	1	1
Special operations aviation regiments	1	1	1	1	1	1	1	1	1
Ranger regiments	1	1	1	1	1	1	1	1	1
Civil affairs battalions (Active)	1	1	1	1	1	1	1	1	1
Civil affairs brigades (Reserve)	9	9	9	9	9	8	8	8	8
Civil affairs commands (Reserve)	3	3	3	3	3	4	4	4	4
Air Force:									
Special operations wings/groups:									
Active	3	3	3	3	3	3	3	3	3
National Guard	1	1	1	1	1	1	1	1	1
Special operations wing (Reserve)	1	1	1	1	1	1	1	1	1
Special tactics groups	1	1	1	1	1	1	1	1	1
Naval:									
Special boat squadrons	2	2	2	2	2	2	2	2	2

- Represents or rounds to zero. [1] Force levels shown are for the ends of the fiscal years in question. The actual force levels for FY 2000 and FY 2001 will depend on future decisions. [2] Number of operational missiles. Not in maintenance or overhaul status. [3] PAI=Primary aircraft inventory. PAI excludes backup and attrition reserve aircrafts as well as aircraft in depot maintenance. Total inventory counts will be higher than the PAI figures given here. [4] B-1 are accountable under START I but will not be accountable under START II. [5] PMAI = Primary mission aircraft inventory for active and reserve components. The numbers shown reflect only combat support and industrial funded PMAI aircraft and not developments/test or training aircraft. [6] Includes 37 KC-10s allocated to an airlift code. [7] Does not include Department of the Navy aircraft. [8] Includes fast sea lift (FSS), afloat prepositioning, and common-user (charter) ships, plus (through FY 1998) aviation support ships. For FY 1999 on, includes LMSR and ready reserve force (RRF) ships tendered to the Military sealift command (MSC). FSS and LMSR vessels are maintained in a reserve, 4-day ready status. [9] The RRF includes vessels assigned to 4-, 5-, 10-, or 20-day reactivation readiness groups. The ship counts shown exclude RRF vessels tendered to the MSC. Inventory figures for FY 1999, FY 2000, and FY 2001 include aviation support ships.

Source: U.S. Dept. of Defense, *Annual Report to the President and the Congress.*

No. 513. Veterans by Sex, Period of Service, and by States: 1999

[In thousands (24,679 represents 24,679,000). As of end of fiscal year; see text, Section 8, State and Local Government Finances and Employment. Estimated starting with veteran's place of residence as of April 1, 1980, based on 1980 Census of Population data, extended to later years on the basis of estimates of veteran interstate migration, separations from the Armed Forces, and mortality; not directly comparable with earlier estimates previously published by the VA. Excludes 602,000 whose active-duty military service of less than 2 years occurred since Sept. 30, 1980, and who failed to satisfy the minimum service requirement. Also excludes a small number of National Guard personnel or reservists who incurred service-connected disabilities while on an initial tour of active duty for training only]

| State | Total veterans [1] | | | World War I | World War II | Korean conflict | Vietnam era [1] | Persian Gulf War |
	Both sexes	Male	Female					
United States.	24,679	23,445	1,234	3	5,922	4,034	8,079	2,188
Alabama.	408	387	21	-	95	72	133	49
Alaska	63	58	5	-	6	7	29	4
Arizona.	443	416	27	-	113	78	146	32
Arkansas	246	234	12	-	62	41	79	28
California	2,666	2,514	152	-	608	444	925	185
Colorado.	363	340	23	-	72	59	140	31
Connecticut.	313	299	15	-	82	51	96	21
Delaware	75	71	4	-	18	12	24	7
District of Columbia	46	42	3	-	12	9	14	5
Florida.	1,652	1,559	93	-	501	301	491	126
Georgia	661	624	36	-	121	98	244	67
Hawaii	112	104	8	-	22	18	42	10
Idaho	107	101	5	-	25	16	35	11
Illinois	999	960	39	-	249	160	310	89
Indiana.	564	541	23	-	128	88	178	55
Iowa	273	263	10	-	68	47	84	28
Kansas.	246	236	10	-	60	41	84	20
Kentucky	350	336	14	-	82	56	116	37
Louisiana	349	332	17	-	86	57	113	41
Maine.	148	140	8	-	32	23	50	15
Maryland	505	473	32	-	106	77	170	42
Massachusetts.	549	522	26	-	151	92	162	36
Michigan.	898	858	40	-	205	132	284	91
Minnesota.	437	420	17	-	95	69	147	35
Mississippi	221	210	11	-	55	39	66	30
Missouri	556	533	24	-	132	94	180	52
Montana	89	84	5	-	21	15	30	10
Nebraska	158	150	8	-	37	29	50	16
Nevada	184	174	10	-	40	35	65	10
New Hampshire	130	122	8	-	27	20	45	11
New Jersey	682	655	27	-	190	118	196	47
New Mexico	165	154	11	-	37	26	59	16
New York	1,422	1,360	62	-	370	228	404	133
North Carolina	684	647	37	-	151	110	230	66
North Dakota.	55	52	3	-	12	10	18	6
Ohio	1,124	1,076	48	-	275	173	347	112
Oklahoma	324	310	14	-	81	58	114	27
Oregon	356	337	19	-	85	54	124	30
Pennsylvania	1,283	1,229	54	-	356	207	373	113
Rhode Island	102	97	5	-	29	17	31	8
South Carolina	367	347	20	-	78	58	128	41
South Dakota	70	67	4	-	16	13	21	9
Tennessee	495	474	21	-	110	79	169	50
Texas.	1,556	1,475	81	-	341	251	567	145
Utah	129	124	5	-	33	22	43	11
Vermont	60	56	4	-	12	9	20	6
Virginia.	676	629	48	-	135	110	254	60
Washington.	607	570	37	-	125	95	229	49
West Virginia	188	181	6	-	50	33	58	20
Wisconsin	481	460	21	-	112	75	149	44
Wyoming	43	41	2	-	10	7	16	4

- Represents or rounds to zero. [1] Excludes reservists.

Source: U.S. Dept. of Veterans Affairs, Management Sciences Service (008B2), *Annual Report of the Secretary of Veterans Affairs.*

No. 514. Veterans Living by Age and by Service: 1999

[In thousands, except as indicated. As of July 1. Includes Puerto Rico. Estimated. Excludes 573,000 whose active military service of less than 2 years occurred since Sept. 30, 1980. See headnote, Table 513]

| Age | Total veterans | Wartime veterans | | | | | |
		Total [1]	Gulf War	Vietnam era	Korean conflict	World War II	World War I
All ages	26,178	18,945	2,200	8,113	4,064	5,940	3
Under 35 years old.	1,941	1,362	1,362	-	-	-	-
35-39 years old	1,387	286	274	12	-	-	-
40-44 years old	1,749	691	222	518	-	-	-
45-49 years old	2,391	1,996	202	1,949	-	-	-
50-54 years old	3,546	3,330	99	3,310	-	-	-
55-59 years old	2,472	1,494	30	1,485	-	-	-
60-64 years old	2,363	899	9	385	583	-	-
60 years old and over . . .	12,693	9,786	11	840	4,064	5,940	-

- Represents or rounds to zero. [1] Veterans who served in more than one wartime period are counted only once.

Source: U.S. Dept. of Veterans Affairs, Office of Policy and Planning, *Veteran Population*, annual.

National Defense and Veterans Affairs 335

No. 515. Disabled Veterans Receiving Compensation: 1980 to 2000

[In thousands (2,274 represents 2,274,000), except as indicated. As of end of fiscal year; see text, Section 8, State and Local Government Finances and Employment. Represents veterans receiving compensation for service-connected disabilities. Totally disabled refers to veterans with any disability, mental or physical, deemed to be total and permanent which prevents the individual from maintaining a livelihood and are rated for disability at 100 percent]

Military service	1980	1990	1993	1994	1995	1996	1997	1998	1999	2000
Disabled, all periods [1]	2,274	2,184	2,198	2,218	2,236	2,253	2,263	2,277	2,294	2,308
Peace-time	262	444	471	492	514	529	539	550	561	567
World War I [1]	30	3	1	1	1	(Z)	(Z)	(Z)	(Z)	(Z)
World War II	1,193	876	769	731	692	655	616	578	541	505
Korea	236	209	198	195	191	187	182	179	175	171
Vietnam	553	652	682	694	705	714	724	729	736	741
Persian Gulf	(X)	(X)	76	106	134	168	202	241	282	325
Compensation (mil. dol.)	6,104	9,284	10,545	11,056	11,644	11,072	13,004	13,791	14,542	15,489

X Not applicable.   Z Less than 500.   [1] Includes Spanish-American War and Mexican Border service, not shown separately.

Source: U.S. Dept. of Veterans Affairs, *Annual Report of the Secretary of Veterans Affairs;* and unpublished data.

No. 516. Veterans Benefits—Expenditures by Program: 1980 to 1998

[In millions of dollars (23,187 represents $23,187,000,000). For fiscal years ending in year shown; see text, Section 8, State and Local Government Finances and Employment. Beginning with fiscal year 1990, data are for outlays]

Program	1980	1990	1992	1993	1994	1995	1996	1997	1998
Total	23,187	28,998	33,900	35,460	37,401	37,775	36,915	39,277	41,776
Medical programs	6,042	11,582	13,815	14,603	15,430	16,255	16,337	16,900	17,575
Construction	300	661	639	622	695	641	698	597	515
General operating expenses	605	811	920	904	906	954	961	1,063	877
Compensation and pension	11,044	14,674	16,282	16,882	17,188	17,765	17,056	19,284	20,289
Vocational rehabilitation and education	2,350	452	695	863	1,119	1,127	1,212	1,287	1,310
All other [1]	2,846	818	1,549	1,586	2,062	1,034	652	145	1,209

[1] Includes insurance and indemnities, and miscellaneous funds and expenditures. (Excludes expenditures from personal funds of patients.)

Source: U.S. Dept. of Veterans Affairs, *Trend Data,* annual.

No. 517. Veterans Compensation and Pension Benefits—Number on Rolls by Period of Service and Status: 1980 to 2000

[As of Sept. 30. Living refers to veterans receiving compensation for disability incurred or aggravated while on active duty and war veterans receiving pension and benefits for nonservice connected disabilities. Deceased refers to deceased veterans whose dependents were receiving pensions and compensation benefits]

Period of service and veteran status	1980	1990	1995	1996	1997	1998	1999	2000
Total	4,646	3,584	3,330	3,308	3,281	3,263	3,252	3,236
Living veterans	3,195	2,746	2,669	2,671	2,667	2,668	2,673	2,672
Service connected	2,273	2,184	2,236	2,253	2,263	2,277	2,294	2,308
Nonservice connected	922	562	433	418	404	391	379	364
Deceased veterans	1,451	838	662	637	614	595	579	564
Service connected	358	320	307	306	305	303	304	307
Nonservice connected	1,093	518	355	332	309	291	274	257
Prior to World War I	14	4	2	2	2	1	1	1
Living	(Z)	(Z)	(Z)	(Z)	(Z)	(Z)	(Z)	(Z)
World War I	692	198	89	74	61	51	42	34
Living	198	18	3	2	1	1	(Z)	(Z)
World War II	2,520	1,723	1,307	1,237	1,165	1,097	1,031	968
Living	1,849	1,294	961	902	842	785	730	676
Korean conflict [1]	446	390	368	360	351	342	333	323
Living	317	305	290	285	278	271	264	255
Peacetime	312	495	559	574	582	592	602	607
Living	262	444	514	529	539	550	561	567
Vietnam era [2]	662	774	868	889	913	932	953*	969
Living	569	685	766	784	804	819	835	848
Persian Gulf War [3]	(X)	(X)	138	173	207	247	290	334
Living	(X)	(X)	134	169	203	242	283	326

X Not applicable.   Z Fewer than 500.   [1] Service during period June 27, 1950, to Jan. 31, 1955.   [2] Service from Aug. 5, 1964, to May 7, 1975.   [3] Service from August 2, 1990, to the present.

Source: U.S. Dept. of Veterans Affairs, *Annual Report of the Secretary of Veterans Affairs;* and unpublished data.

Section 11
Social Insurance and Human Services

This section presents data related to governmental expenditures for social welfare; governmental programs for old-age, survivors, disability, and health insurance (OASDHI); governmental employee retirement; private pension plans; government unemployment and temporary disability insurance; federal supplemental security income payments and aid to the needy; child and other welfare services; and federal food programs. Also included here are selected data on workers compensation and vocational rehabilitation, child support, child care, charity contributions, and philanthropic trusts and foundations.

The principal sources for these data are the Social Security Administrations quarterly *Social Security Bulletin* and the *Annual Statistical Supplement to the Social Security Bulletin* which present current data on many of the programs.

Social insurance under the Social Security Act—Programs established by the Social Security Act provide protection against wage loss resulting from retirement, prolonged disability, death, or unemployment, and protection against the cost of medical care during old age and disability. The federal OASDI program provides monthly benefits to retired or disabled insured workers and their dependents and to survivors of insured workers. To be eligible, a worker must have had a specified period of employment in which OASDI taxes were paid. The age of eligibility for full retirement benefits has been 65 years old for many years. However, for persons born in 1938 or later that age will gradually increase until it reaches age 67 for those born after 1959. Reduced benefits may be obtained as early as age 62. The worker's spouse is under the same limitations. Survivor benefits are payable to dependents of deceased insured workers. Disability benefits are payable to an insured worker under age 65 with a prolonged disability and to the disabled worker's dependents on the same basis as dependents of

retired workers. Disability benefits are provided at age 50 to the disabled widow or widower of a deceased worker who was fully insured at the time of death. Disabled children, aged 18 or older, of retired, disabled, or deceased workers are also eligible for benefits. A lump sum benefit is generally payable on the death of an insured worker to a spouse or minor children. For information on the medicare program, see Section 3, Health and Nutrition.

Retirement, survivors, disability, and hospital insurance benefits are funded by a payroll tax on annual earnings (up to a maximum of earnings set by law) of workers, employers, and the self-employed. The maximum taxable earnings are adjusted annually to reflect increasing wage levels (see Table 525). Effective January 1994, there is no dollar limit on wages and self-employment income subject to the hospital insurance tax. Tax receipts and benefit payments are administered through federal trust funds. Special benefits for uninsured persons; hospital benefits for persons aged 65 and over with specified amounts of social security coverage less than that required for cash benefit eligibility; and that part of the cost of supplementary medical insurance not financed by contributions from participants are financed from federal general revenues.

Unemployment insurance is presently administered by the U.S. Employment and Training Administration and each state's employment security agency. By agreement with the U.S. Secretary of Labor, state agencies also administer unemployment compensation for eligible ex-military personnel and federal employees. Under state unemployment insurance laws, benefits related to the individual's past earnings are paid to unemployed eligible workers. State laws vary concerning the length of time benefits are paid and their amount. In most states, benefits are payable for 26 weeks and, during periods

Social Insurance and Human Services 337

U.S. Census Bureau, Statistical Abstract of the United States: 2001

of high unemployment, extended benefits are payable under a federal-state program to those who have exhausted their regular state benefits. Some states also supplement the basic benefit with allowances for dependents.

Unemployment insurance is funded by a federal unemployment tax levied on the taxable payrolls of most employers. Taxable payroll under the federal act and 12 state laws is the first $7,000 in wages paid each worker during a year. Forty-one states have taxable payrolls above $7,000. Employers are allowed a percentage credit of taxable payroll for contributions paid to states under state unemployment insurance laws. The remaining percent of the federal tax finances administrative costs, the federal share of extended benefits, and advances to states. About 97 percent of wage and salary workers are covered by unemployment insurance.

Retirement programs for government employees—The Civil Service Retirement System (CSRS) and the Federal Employees' Retirement System (FERS) are the two major programs providing age and service, disability, and survivor annuities for federal civilian employees. In general, employees hired after December 31, 1983, are covered under FERS and the social security program (OASDHI), and employees on staff prior to that date are members of CSRS and are covered under medicare. CSRS employees were offered the option of transferring to FERS during 1987 and 1998. There are separate retirement systems for the uniformed services (supplementing OASDHI) and for certain special groups of federal employees. State and local government employees are covered for the most part by state and local retirement systems similar to the federal CSRS. In many jurisdictions these benefits supplement OASDHI coverage.

Workers' compensation—All states provide protection against work-connected injuries and deaths, although some states exclude certain workers (e.g., domestic help). Federal laws cover federal employees, private employees in the District of Columbia, and longshoremen and harbor workers. In addition, the Social Security Administration and the Department of

Labor administer "black lung" benefits programs for coal miners disabled by pneumoconiosis and for specified dependents and survivors. Specified occupational diseases are compensable to some extent. In most states, benefits are related to the worker's salary. The benefits may or may not be augmented by dependents' allowances or automatically adjusted to prevailing wage levels.

Income support—Income support programs are designed to provide benefits for persons with limited income and resources. The Supplemental Security Income (SSI) program and Temporary Assistance for Needy Families (TANF) program are the major programs providing monthly payments. In addition, a number of programs provide money payments or in-kind benefits for special needs or purposes. Several programs offer food and nutritional services. Also, various federal-state programs provide energy assistance, public housing, and subsidized housing to individuals and families with low incomes. General assistance may also be available at the state or local level.

The SSI program, administered by the Social Security Administration, provides income support to persons aged 65 or older and blind or disabled adults and children. Eligibility requirements and federal payment standards are nationally uniform. Most states supplement the basic SSI payment for all or selected categories of persons.

The Personal Responsibility and Work Opportunity Reconciliation Act of 1996 contained provisions that replaced the Aid to Families With Dependent Children (AFDC), Job Opportunities and Basic Skills (JOBS), and Emergency Assistance programs with the Temporary Assistance for Needy Families block grant program. This law contains strong work requirements, comprehensive child support enforcement, support for families moving from welfare to work, and other features. The TANF became effective as soon as each state submitted a complete plan implementing TANF, but no later than July 1, 1997. The AFDC program provided cash assistance based on need, income, resources, and family size.

U.S. Census Bureau, Statistical Abstract of the United States: 2001

Federal food stamp program—Under the food stamp program, single persons and those living in households meeting nationwide standards for income and assets may receive coupons redeemable for food at most retail food stores. The monthly amount of coupons a unit receives is determined by household size and income. Households without income receive the determined monthly cost of a nutritionally adequate diet for their household size. This amount is updated to account for food price increases. Households with income receive the difference between the amount of a nutritionally adequate diet and 30 percent of their income, after certain allowable deductions.

To qualify for the program, a household must have less than $2,000 in disposable assets ($3,000 if one member is aged 60 or older), gross income below 130 percent of the official poverty guidelines for the household size, and net income below 100 percent of the poverty guidelines. Households with a person aged 60 or older or a disabled person receiving SSI, social security, state general assistance, or veterans' disability benefits may have gross income exceeding 130 percent of the poverty guidelines. All households in which all members receive TANF or SSI are categorically eligible for food stamps without meeting these income or resource criteria. Households are certified for varying lengths of time, depending on their income sources and individual circumstances.

Health and welfare services—Programs providing health and welfare services are aided through federal grants to states for child welfare services, vocational rehabilitation, activities for the aged, maternal and child health services, maternity and infant care projects, comprehensive health services, and a variety of public health activities. For information about the medicaid program, see Section 3, Health and Nutrition.

Noncash benefits—The U.S. Census Bureau annually collects data on the characteristics of recipients of noncash (in-kind) benefits to supplement the collection of annual money income data in the Current Population Survey (see text, Section 1, Population, and Section 14, Prices). Noncash benefits are those benefits received in a form other than money which serve to enhance or improve the economic well-being of the recipient. As for money income, the data for noncash benefits are for the calendar year prior to the date of the interview. The major categories of noncash benefits covered are public transfers (e.g., food stamps, school lunch, public housing, and medicaid) and employer or union-provided benefits to employees.

Statistical reliability—For discussion of statistical collection, estimation, and sampling procedures and measures of statistical reliability applicable to HHS and Census Bureau data, see Appendix III.

U.S. Census Bureau, Statistical Abstract of the United States: 2001

No. 518. Government Transfer Payments to Individuals—Summary: 1970 to 1999

[In billions of dollars (69.3 represents $69,300,000,000)]

Year	Total	Retirement & disability insurance benefits	Medical payments	Income maintenance benefits	Unemployment insurance benefits	Veterans benefits	Federal education & training assistance payments [1]	Other [2]
1970	69.3	34.3	13.0	9.9	4.2	7.5	0.4	0.1
1975	159.3	72.0	30.7	21.5	18.2	14.0	1.0	1.9
1980	262.7	128.8	62.0	34.3	18.7	14.7	4.1	0.2
1985	394.7	197.2	114.6	44.4	15.9	16.6	5.5	0.6
1990	561.4	263.9	189.1	63.5	18.2	17.7	7.3	1.8
1991	635.7	285.7	223.5	72.5	26.9	18.1	7.3	1.8
1992	714.8	304.7	257.3	84.6	39.7	18.6	8.0	2.0
1993	760.6	320.8	284.7	90.3	34.9	19.4	9.1	1.4
1994	792.8	334.8	308.3	95.6	24.1	19.7	8.6	1.8
1995	841.0	350.0	337.5	100.4	21.9	20.5	9.0	1.6
1996	883.0	364.6	361.3	102.5	22.5	21.4	8.6	2.1
1997	914.9	379.4	379.6	100.3	20.3	22.2	11.5	1.7
1998	933.4	391.9	384.9	100.5	19.9	23.2	11.2	1.9
1999	964.2	402.8	399.1	104.1	20.8	24.1	11.3	2.0

[1] See footnote 9, Table 519.   [2] See footnote 10, Table 519.

No. 519. Government Transfer Payments to Individuals by Type: 1990 to 1999

[In millions of dollars (561,399 represents $561,399,000,000)]

Item	1990	1994	1995	1996	1997	1998	1999
Total	**561,399**	**792,815**	**841,041**	**883,042**	**914,942**	**933,394**	**964,173**
Retirement & disability insurance benefit payments	263,854	334,773	350,027	364,623	379,415	391,873	402,844
Old age, survivors, & disability insurance..	244,135	312,145	327,667	341,987	356,602	369,291	379,905
Railroad retirement and disability	7,221	7,963	8,028	8,085	8,193	8,225	8,203
Worker's compensation payments (federal & state)	8,618	10,734	10,530	10,795	10,606	10,313	10,374
Other government disability insurance & retirement [1]	3,880	3,931	3,802	3,756	4,014	4,044	4,362
Medical payments.................	189,099	308,292	337,532	361,342	379,557	384,877	399,060
Medicare...................	107,929	160,891	180,283	195,581	209,198	208,755	208,081
Public assistance medical care [2]	78,176	144,886	155,017	163,629	168,288	174,079	188,972
Military medical insurance [3]	2,994	2,515	2,232	2,132	2,071	2,043	2,007
Income maintenance benefit payments....	63,481	95,642	100,444	102,494	100,288	100,475	104,137
Supplemental Security Income (SSI).....	16,670	26,269	27,726	28,903	29,154	30,322	31,024
Family assistance [4]	19,187	23,163	22,637	20,325	17,717	17,012	17,760
Food stamps	14,741	22,842	22,447	21,955	18,732	16,463	15,492
Other income maintenance [5]	12,883	23,368	27,634	31,311	34,685	36,678	39,861
Unemployment insurance benefit payments..	18,208	24,055	21,864	22,480	20,299	19,934	20,765
State unemployment insurance compensation.................	17,644	23,072	20,975	21,614	19,469	19,183	20,016
Unemployment compensation for federal civilian employees	215	378	339	326	281	252	223
Unemployment compensation for railroad employees...................	89	63	62	65	72	61	65
Unemployment compensation for veterans.	144	398	320	279	259	241	231
Other unemployment compensation [6]	116	144	168	196	218	197	230
Veterans benefit payments............	17,687	19,705	20,545	21,430	22,233	23,170	24,076
Veterans pension and disability	15,550	16,936	17,565	18,286	19,061	20,068	20,887
Veterans readjustment [7]	257	853	1,086	1,138	1,234	1,203	1,358
Veterans life insurance benefits	1,868	1,904	1,883	1,997	1,929	1,891	1,823
Other assistance to veterans [8]	12	12	11	9	9	8	8
Federal education & training assistance payments [9]	7,300	8,562	9,007	8,568	11,481	11,189	11,264
Other payments to individuals [10]	1,770	1,786	1,622	2,105	1,669	1,876	2,027

[1] Consists largely of temporary disability payments and black lung payments.   [2] Consists of medicaid and other medical vendor payments.   [3] Consists of payments made under the TriCare Management Program (formerly called CHAMPUS) for the medical care of dependents of active duty military personnel and of retired military personnel and their dependents at nonmilitary medical facilities.   [4] Through 1995, consists of Emergency Assistance and Aid to Families With Dependent Children. Beginning with 1998, consists of benefits— generally known as Temporary Assistance for Needy Families— provided under the Personal Responsibility and Work Opportunity Reconciliation Act of 1996. For 1996-97, consists of payments under all three of these programs.   [5] Consists largely of general assistance, refugee assistance, foster home care and adoption assistance, earned income tax credits, and energy assistance.   [6] Consists of trade readjustment allowance payments, Redwood Park benefit payments, public service employment benefit payments, and transitional benefit payments.   [7] Consists largely of veterans' readjustment benefit payments, educational assistance to spouses and children of disabled or deceased veterans, payments to paraplegics, and payments for autos and conveyances for disabled veterans.   [8] Consists largely of state and local government payments to veterans.   [9] Excludes veterans. Consists largely of federal fellowship payments (National Science Foundation fellowships and traineeships, subsistence payments to state maritime academy cadets, and other federal fellowships), interest subsidy on higher education loans, basic educational opportunity grants, and Job Corps payments.   [10] Consists largely of Bureau of Indian Affairs payments, education exchange payments, Alaska Permanent Fund dividend payments, compensation of survivors of public safety officers, compensation of victims of crime, disaster relief payments, compensation for Japanese internment, and other special payments to individuals.

Source of Tables 518 and 519: U.S. Bureau of Economic Analysis, "Regional Accounts Data, Annual State Personal Income"; <http://www.bea.doc.gov/bea/regional/spi/>; (accessed 23 May 2001).

No. 520. Government Transfer Payments to Individuals by State: 1990 to 1999

[In millions of dollars (561,399 represents $561,399,000,000)]

State	1990, total	1995, total	1999							
			Total	Retirement & disability insurance benefits	Medical payments	Income maintenance benefits	Unemployment insurance benefits	Veterans benefits	Federal education & training assistance payments[1]	Other[2]
U.S.	561,399	841,041	964,173	402,844	399,060	104,137	20,765	24,076	11,264	2,027
AL.	8,738	13,395	15,723	6,796	6,116	1,812	215	557	219	8
AK.	1,294	1,860	2,573	440	592	249	123	80	15	1,075
AZ.	7,864	12,653	15,173	7,100	5,651	1,383	189	529	226	96
AR.	5,459	8,063	9,391	4,222	3,454	1,008	189	411	102	6
CA.	65,912	96,576	107,700	39,571	42,783	18,996	2,734	2,052	1,455	109
CO	5,796	9,273	10,509	4,600	4,226	945	156	411	154	18
CT.	8,121	12,470	13,854	5,664	6,353	1,191	361	194	85	6
DE.	1,364	2,148	2,532	1,234	944	207	55	63	27	2
DC	1,676	2,318	2,529	588	1,338	420	63	62	51	8
FL.	33,029	52,572	60,987	28,104	25,017	4,722	704	1,824	580	35
GA	11,843	19,042	21,888	9,195	8,554	2,747	302	791	288	12
HI	2,139	3,480	3,753	1,544	1,293	616	135	123	40	2
ID	1,849	2,836	3,459	1,748	1,145	275	113	121	51	6
IL	25,216	36,032	39,567	17,397	15,610	4,286	1,176	601	466	30
IN	11,363	16,191	18,844	9,236	7,254	1,469	266	369	239	12
IA	6,065	8,215	9,345	4,860	3,251	694	191	210	132	8
KS.	5,264	7,298	8,226	4,106	2,965	657	155	227	107	9
KY.	8,343	12,503	14,807	6,435	5,783	1,748	262	414	159	6
LA	9,284	15,257	16,643	5,811	7,800	2,170	175	448	231	7
ME	2,814	4,203	4,932	2,030	2,057	497	92	204	48	3
MD	9,168	13,513	15,962	6,690	6,897	1,484	299	410	170	11
MA.	16,490	23,068	26,204	9,416	12,974	2,133	832	574	263	12
MI.	22,351	29,984	35,272	15,438	14,516	3,521	877	557	348	16
MN	9,469	13,241	14,978	6,645	6,082	1,342	359	368	165	17
MS	5,609	8,648	10,075	3,979	4,102	1,381	118	334	147	14
MO	11,277	17,029	19,960	8,774	8,403	1,766	298	493	213	13
MT	1,893	2,636	2,854	1,488	885	245	67	116	40	12
NE.	3,141	4,425	5,382	2,589	2,083	407	49	184	68	3
NV.	2,479	4,217	5,310	2,666	1,835	384	193	183	43	7
NH	2,013	3,461	3,749	1,789	1,528	228	31	134	37	2
NJ.	18,376	27,593	30,259	13,455	12,565	2,358	1,114	479	273	15
NM.	2,786	4,586	5,570	2,267	2,026	766	92	253	89	78
NY.	54,178	82,755	93,031	29,327	47,585	12,104	1,624	1,135	1,222	35
NC	12,658	21,054	25,828	11,169	10,427	2,654	455	846	256	20
ND	1,510	1,940	2,220	1,085	823	155	34	59	40	24
OH	26,578	36,753	40,367	19,207	15,657	3,592	665	819	403	25
OK	6,615	9,937	11,370	5,162	4,194	1,125	141	573	158	16
OR	6,374	9,529	11,443	5,504	3,976	994	450	371	132	16
PA	32,238	45,821	52,674	22,460	22,598	4,711	1,474	966	446	19
RI	2,776	4,027	4,626	1,771	2,096	438	155	107	57	3
SC	6,724	10,621	13,075	5,779	5,076	1,409	204	441	151	13
SD	1,445	2,061	2,356	1,104	878	187	15	95	30	47
TN.	10,814	17,338	20,577	8,307	9,131	1,997	359	586	183	14
TX.	29,214	49,155	57,931	22,213	25,264	6,430	1,255	1,938	774	56
UT.	2,594	3,892	4,665	2,224	1,692	393	103	123	117	14
VT.	1,163	1,743	2,060	893	809	230	46	56	24	1
VA.	10,174	15,539	18,386	8,937	6,521	1,717	180	771	249	11
WA	10,973	16,608	19,244	8,759	6,838	1,708	983	707	214	34
WV	5,125	7,426	8,265	4,127	2,869	790	138	258	79	4
WI	10,941	14,829	16,622	8,163	6,107	1,289	468	399	178	18
WY	819	1,225	1,422	777	435	106	31	49	20	3

[1] Excludes veterans. Consists largely of federal fellowship payments (National Science Foundation, fellowships and traineeships, subsistence payments to state maritime academy cadets, and other federal fellowships), interest subsidy on higher education loans, basic educational opportunity grants, and Job Corps payments.   [2] Consists largely of Bureau of Indian Affairs payments, education exchange payments, Alaska Permanent Fund dividend payments, compensation of survivors of public safety officers, compensation of victims of crime, disaster relief payments, compensation for Japanese internment, and other special payments to individuals.

Source: U.S. Bureau of Economic Analysis, "Regional Accounts Data, Annual State Personal Income"; <http://www.bea.doc.gov/bea/regional/spi/>; (accessed 23 May 2001).

Social Insurance and Human Services 341

No. 521. Number of Persons With Income by Specified Sources of Income: 1999

[In thousands (195,636 represents 195,636,000). Persons 16 years old and over as of March 2000. Based on Current Population Survey; see text, Sections 1, Population and 13, Income, Expenditures, and Wealth, and Appendix III]

Source of income	Total persons with income	Under 65 years old	65 years old and over	White	Black	Hispanic origin [1]
Total	195,636	163,658	31,978	164,355	22,499	18,793
Earnings	148,847	143,326	5,522	124,535	17,335	15,474
Wages and salary	140,107	135,520	4,586	116,736	16,792	14,852
Nonfarm self-employment	11,632	10,743	888	10,263	818	792
Farm self-employment	1,837	1,568	269	1,755	43	58
Unemployment compensation	5,260	5,148	112	4,453	607	681
Workers compensation	1,833	1,764	70	1,545	210	208
Social security, railroad retirement . . .	37,794	8,610	29,184	33,192	3,695	2,094
Supplemental Security Income (SSI) . .	4,895	3,603	1,292	3,249	1,336	666
Public assistance	2,756	2,684	73	1,627	961	594
TANF/Welfare (AFDC) only [2]	1,776	1,748	28	970	685	406
Other assistance only	832	790	42	582	212	156
Both	148	146	2	75	64	33
Veterans payments	2,512	1,376	1,136	2,146	300	87
Survivors benefits	2,687	931	1,756	2,405	205	81
Company or union	1,272	280	992	1,164	72	37
Disability benefits	1,616	1,438	178	1,281	275	127
Company or union	482	436	46	392	83	33
Pensions	15,135	4,634	10,501	13,620	1,226	441
Company or union	9,441	2,463	6,978	8,604	667	291
Federal government	1,298	376	921	1,090	168	34
Military retirement	933	562	371	841	72	23
State or local government	2,836	988	1,849	2,496	291	62
Interest	104,493	84,953	19,540	93,566	6,646	5,145
Dividends	40,564	33,550	7,014	37,104	1,825	1,054
Rents, royalties, estates or trusts	12,437	9,426	3,011	11,210	621	628
Education	7,525	7,500	25	6,068	1,028	587
Pell grant only	1,356	1,350	7	969	308	152
Other government only	1,124	1,114	10	861	182	97
Scholarships only	2,098	2,098	-	1,814	163	134
Child support	5,146	5,123	23	4,135	859	444
Alimony	462	413	49	439	14	30
Financial assistance	1,987	1,888	99	1,563	269	144
Other income	1,216	961	255	1,046	93	63
Combinations of income types:						
Government transfer payments	54,384	24,016	30,368	45,752	6,844	4,077
Public assistance or SSI	7,314	5,982	1,333	4,692	2,154	1,209
Property income [3]	109,908	89,438	20,470	98,270	7,008	5,518

- Represents or rounds to zero. [1] Persons of Hispanic origin may be of any race. [2] TANF-Temporary assistance for needy families program; AFDC=Aid to Families with Dependent Children program. [3] Includes estates and trusts reported as survivor benefits.

Source: U.S. Census Bureau, "Table PINC-09. Source of Income in 1999—Number With Income and Mean Income of Specified Type in 1999 of People 16 Years Old and Over, by Race, Hispanic Origin, and Sex"; published 5 October 2000; <http://ferret.bls.census.gov/macro/032000/perinc/new09000.htm>.

No. 522. Households Receiving Means-Tested Noncash Benefits: 1980 to 1999

[In thousands (82,368 represents 82,368,000), except percent. Households as of March of following year. Covers civilian noninstitutional population, including persons in the Armed Forces living off post or with their families on post. A means-tested benefit program requires that the household's income and/or assets fall below specified guidelines in order to qualify for benefits. There are general trends toward underestimation of noncash beneficiaries. Households are classified according to poverty status of family or nonfamily householder; for explanation of poverty level, see text, Section 13, Income, Expenditures, and Wealth. Data for 1980 and 1990 based on 1980 census population controls; beginning 1995, based on 1990 census population controls. Based on Current Population Survey; see text, Section 1, Population, and Appendix III]

Type of benefit received	1980	1990	1995	1998	1999			
						Below poverty level		Above poverty level
					Total	Number	Percent of total	
Total households	82,368	94,312	99,627	103,874	104,705	11,936	100	92,769
Receiving at least one noncash benefit . .	14,266	16,098	21,148	19,807	18,996	6,989	59	12,007
Not receiving cash public assistance . .	7,860	8,819	13,335	13,461	12,999	3,952	33	9,047
Receiving cash public assistance [1] . . .	6,407	7,279	7,813	6,346	5,997	3,037	25	2,960
Total households receiving—								
Food stamps	6,769	7,163	8,388	6,357	5,738	3,682	31	2,056
School lunch	5,532	6,252	8,607	8,120	7,258	2,959	25	4,299
Public housing	2,777	4,339	4,846	4,808	4,447	2,488	21	1,959
Medicaid	8,287	10,321	14,111	13,363	13,477	5,309	44	8,168

[1] Households receiving money from Aid to Families With Dependent Children program (beginning 1998, Temporary Assistance for Needy Families program), Supplemental Security Income program or other public assistance programs.

Source: U.S. Census Bureau, "Table NC1. Means-Tested Noncash Benefits Received by Households, by Selected Household Characteristics, Race and Hispanic Origin, and Poverty Status: 1999"; published 8 January 2001; <http://ferret.bls.census.gov/macro/032000/noncash/1000.htm>; and Current Population Reports, P-60 reports.

No. 523. Government Expenditures for Income-Tested Benefits by Type of Benefit: 1980 to 1998

[In millions of dollars (104,676 represents $104,676,000,000). For years ending September 30. Programs covered provide cash, goods, or services to persons who make no payment and render no service in return. In case of many programs, including family cash welfare, food and housing programs, job and training programs and some educational programs, some recipients must work or study. Most of the programs base eligibility on individual, household, or family income, but some use group or area income tests; and a few offer help on the basis of presumed need. Constant dollar figures are based on the Consumer Price Index for all Urban Consumers.]

Level of government and year	Total spending — Current dollars	Total spending — Constant (1998) dollars	Medical benefits	Cash aid	Food benefits	Housing benefits	Education benefits	Jobs/training	Services	Energy aid
TOTAL										
1980	104,676	207,231	64,537	56,865	26,818	19,017	10,247	17,235	9,103	3,407
1985	143,294	217,245	74,955	57,059	30,914	21,396	15,115	6,028	8,302	3,475
1990	212,578	265,405	108,397	67,738	31,345	21,909	17,966	5,296	10,597	2,158
1991	251,896	301,724	131,652	73,813	35,117	22,712	18,458	5,783	11,892	2,298
1992	296,403	344,585	157,919	81,173	39,820	28,160	16,527	6,387	12,538	2,061
1993	312,331	352,697	161,546	84,468	41,034	28,553	17,028	6,023	12,233	1,812
1994	348,770	383,854	177,654	95,002	41,687	28,351	17,103	6,070	15,792	2,195
1995	366,669	392,253	186,816	97,989	41,323	29,176	17,215	5,817	12,119	1,800
1996	370,769	385,319	184,923	96,083	40,617	29,052	17,020	4,868	11,454	1,301
1997	379,971	385,910	189,008	94,537	37,932	29,347	17,809	4,036	11,813	1,428
1998	391,733	391,729	196,389	94,562	35,511	29,511	18,126	3,856	12,453	1,321
FEDERAL										
1980	80,043	158,464	38,405	37,571	25,913	19,017	9,681	17,075	7,394	3,407
1985	105,064	159,285	42,268	37,123	29,354	21,396	14,427	5,905	5,384	3,428
1990	151,514	189,166	62,708	45,502	29,803	21,909	17,181	4,963	5,099	2,003
1991	177,953	213,154	74,805	50,634	33,545	22,712	17,903	5,257	6,236	2,163
1992	208,273	242,129	91,470	56,635	38,142	25,486	15,813	5,834	6,790	1,959
1993	223,595	252,492	96,044	60,245	39,266	27,051	16,163	5,388	6,674	1,732
1994	246,374	271,158	103,112	69,774	39,739	26,574	16,109	5,350	8,389	2,110
1995	258,457	276,491	108,489	72,662	39,365	26,689	16,193	4,949	6,431	1,713
1996	263,550	273,893	108,003	72,758	38,622	26,497	16,028	4,199	6,560	1,225
1997	269,754	273,971	109,471	72,971	35,927	26,853	16,767	3,855	6,764	1,363
1998	277,332	277,330	113,779	73,872	33,451	26,897	16,989	3,785	7,300	1,257
STATE AND LOCAL										
1980	24,633	48,767	26,132	19,294	905	. . .	566	160	1,709	-
1985	38,230	57,960	32,687	19,936	1,560	. . .	688	123	2,918	47
1990	61,064	76,239	45,689	22,236	1,542	. . .	785	333	5,498	155
1991	73,943	88,570	56,847	23,179	1,572	2,674	655	526	5,656	135
1992	88,130	102,456	66,449	24,538	1,678	1,502	714	553	5,748	102
1993	88,736	100,204	65,502	24,223	1,768	1,777	865	635	5,629	80
1994	102,396	112,696	74,542	25,228	1,948	2,487	994	720	7,403	85
1995	108,212	115,762	78,327	25,327	1,958	2,555	1,022	868	5,688	87
1996	107,219	111,426	76,920	23,325	1,995	2,494	992	669	4,894	76
1997	110,216	111,938	79,537	21,566	2,005	2,494	1,042	181	5,049	65
1998	114,401	114,399	82,610	20,690	2,060	2,614	1,137	71	5,153	64

- Represents or rounds to zero.

Source: Library of Congress, Congressional Research Service, "Cash and Noncash Benefits for Persons With Limited Income: Eligibility Rules, Recipient and Expenditure Data, FY1996-FY1998"; CRS Report RL 30401: December 15, 1999.

U.S. Census Bureau, Statistical Abstract of the United States: 2001

No. 524. Cash and Noncash Benefits for Persons With Limited Income: 1997 and 1998

[For years ending September 30, except as noted (379,971 represents $379,971,000,000). Programs covered provide cash, goods, or services to persons who make no payment and render no service in return. In case of many programs, including family cash welfare, food and housing programs, job and training programs and some educational programs, some recipients must work or study. Most of the programs base eligibility on individual, household, or family income, but some use group or area income tests; and a few offer help on the basis of presumed need]

Program	Average monthly recipients (1,000)		Expenditures (mil. dol.)					
			Total		Federal		State and local	
	1997	1998	1997	1998	1997	1998	1997	1998
Total.	(X)	(X)	379,971	391,733	269,754	277,332	110,216	114,401
Medical care [1]	(X)	(X)	186,100	196,391	107,787	113,779	78,313	82,612
Medicaid [2][3]	40,160	41,360	167,359	177,364	94,738	100,177	72,621	77,187
Veterans [4][5]	(NA)	153	9,220	9,603	9,220	9,603	-	-
General assistance [5]	(NA)	(NA)	5,268	4,956	-	-	5,268	4,956
Indian health services [2][3]	1,430	1,458	2,057	2,099	2,057	2,099	-	-
Maternal and child health services	23,900	(NA)	1,105	1,102	681	678	424	424
Consolidated health centers [2]	8,300	8,450	802	825	802	825	-	-
Cash aid [1]	(X)	(X)	93,082	94,562	71,848	73,872	21,234	20,690
Supplemental Security Income [3][6]	6,984	7,199	32,395	33,601	28,667	29,656	3,728	3,945
TANF/AFDC [3][7]	10,936	8,770	23,179	21,513	12,494	11,286	10,685	10,227
Earned income tax credit (refunded portion) [8] . .	58,143	58,197	23,200	25,300	23,200	25,300	-	-
Foster care	289	306	6,794	7,033	3,692	3,730	3,102	3,303
General assistance [8]	700	(NA)	3,200	2,625	-	-	3,200	2,625
Pensions for needy veterans [9][10]	747	712	3,066	3,071	3,066	3,071	-	-
Food benefits [1]	(X)	(X)	37,348	35,511	35,374	33,451	1,974	2,060
Food stamps [3][11]	24,200	21,000	24,772	22,384	22,868	20,397	1,904	1,987
School lunch program [12][13]	15,100	15,300	5,044	5,196	5,044	5,196	(NA)	(NA)
Women, infants and children [3][14]	7,400	7,400	3,846	3,896	3,846	3,896	-	-
School breakfast [12]	6,000	6,100	1,180	1,266	1,180	1,266	-	-
Child and adult care food program [15]	(NA)	1,800	1,199	1,404	1,199	1,404	-	-
Nutrition program for elderly [16]	(NA)	(NA)	685	700	615	627	70	73
Housing benefits [1]	(X)	(X)	28,896	29,511	26,440	26,897	2,456	2,614
Low-income housing asst. (Sec. 8) [17]	2,943	3,001	16,393	16,114	16,393	16,114	-	-
Low-rent public housing [17][18]	1,372	1,295	4,384	3,899	4,384	3,899	(NA)	(NA)
Rural housing loans [19][20]	41	55	2,706	3,830	2,706	3,830	-	-
Interest reduction payments [17]	494	477	604	618	604	618	-	-
Home investment partnerships [3][20][21] . . .	73	75	3,817	4,062	1,373	1,461	2,444	2,601
Education aid [1]	(X)	(X)	17,535	18,128	16,509	16,991	1,026	1,137
Pell grants [22][23]	3,665	3,732	5,660	6,274	5,660	6,274	-	-
Head Start	794	822	4,976	5,434	3,981	4,347	995	1,087
Stafford loans [22]	4,882	4,956	4,610	3,770	4,610	3,770	-	-
Federal Work-Study Program [22][23]	691	945	617	830	617	830	-	-
Services [1]	(X)	(X)	11,631	12,453	6,660	7,300	4,971	5,153
Social services (Title 20) [24]	(NA)	(NA)	6,400	5,885	2,500	2,299	3,900	3,586
Child care and development block grant [25] . . .	(NA)	(NA)	3,378	4,690	2,307	3,123	1,071	1,567
Jobs and training [1]	(X)	(X)	3,973	3,857	3,796	3,785	178	71
Training for disadvantaged adults and youth [26]	483	499	1,022	1,085	1,022	1,085	-	-
Job Corps	65	70	1,154	1,246	1,154	1,246	-	-
Summer youth employment program [27]	493	530	871	871	871	871	-	-
Energy assistance [1]	(X)	(X)	1,406	1,321	1,342	1,257	64	64
Low-income energy assistance [3][28]	(NA)	(NA)	1,221	1,132	1,221	1,132	(NA)	(NA)

- Represents zero.   NA Not available.   X Not applicable.   [1] Includes other programs not shown separately.   [2] Recipient data represent unduplicated annual number.   [3] Expenditures include administrative expenses.   [4] Medical care for veterans with a nonservice-connected disability.   [5] Estimated expenditures.   [6] Includes state-administered SSI supplements.   [7] Aid to families with dependent children program and its successor, Temporary Assistance for Needy Families (TANF). Excludes data for foster care program and child support operations (cost and collections).   [8] Estimated recipients.   [9] Estimated recipients as of September.   [10] Includes dependents and survivors.   [11] Includes Puerto Rico's nutritional assistance program.   [12] Free and reduced-price segments.   [13] Includes estimate of commodity assistance.   [14] Special supplemental food program for women, infants and children.   [15] Recipient data are numbers of children receiving free or reduced-price meals and snacks in child care centers and estimates of children in family day care homes with incomes below 185 percent of poverty.   [16] No income test required but preference given to those with greatest need.   [17] Recipient data represent units eligible for payment at end of year.   [18] Includes operating subsidies and HUD-administered Indian housing.   [19] Recipient data represent total families or dwelling units during year.   [20] Expenditure data represent amounts obligated.   [21] Recipient data are housing units provided or rehabilitated.   [22] Recipient data are total numbers for the school year ending in year shown.   [23] Expenditure data are appropriations available for school year ending the fiscal year named.   [24] Nonfederal expenditure data are rough estimates.   [25] Recipient data are estimated number of children served. P.L. 104-193 ended AFDC and its related child care programs and established a new mandatory child care block grant.   [26] Recipient data are total number of participants.   [27] Total participants (June-August).   [28] Households served during the year with heating and winter crisis aid. federal funds include amounts transferred to other programs serving the needy.

Source: Library of Congress. Congressional Research Service, "Cash and Noncash Benefits for Persons With Limited Income: Eligibility Rules, Recipient, and Expenditure Data, FY1996-FY1998"; CRS Report RL30401; December 15, 1999.

No. 525. Social Security—Covered Employment, Earnings, and Contribution Rates: 1980 to 2000

[140.4 represents 140,400,000. Includes Puerto Rico, Virgin Islands, American Samoa, and Guam. Represents all reported employment. Data are estimated. OASDHI=Old-age, survivors, disability, and health insurance; SMI=Supplementary medical insurance]

Item	Unit	1980	1985	1990	1994	1995	1996	1997	1998	1999	2000
Workers with insured status [1]	Million . . .	140.4	150.9	164.0	170.7	172.9	174.8	177.5	179.5	182.2	184.6
Male	Million . . .	76.6	80.7	86.5	89.1	90.0	90.9	92.0	92.8	• 94.0	95.0
Female	Million . . .	63.8	70.1	77.5	81.6	82.9	84.0	85.5	86.7	88.3	89.6
Under 25 years old . . .	Million . . .	25.7	22.0	21.3	19.0	18.8	18.5	18.8	19.2	19.9	20.4
25 to 34 years old. . . .	Million . . .	36.5	40.1	41.6	39.8	39.4	38.8	38.2	37.4	36.8	36.3
35 to 44 years old. . . .	Million . . .	23.0	29.9	36.4	39.7	40.5	41.3	41.8	42.2	42.4	42.4
45 to 54 years old. . . .	Million . . .	18.6	19.2	22.8	28.2	29.5	30.7	31.9	33.1	34.4	35.8
55 to 59 years old. . . .	Million . . .	9.3	9.0	8.7	9.5	9.7	10.1	10.7	11.3	11.8	12.2
60 to 64 years old. . . .	Million . . .	8.2	8.8	8.8	8.4	8.4	8.5	8.8	8.9	9.2	9.4
65 to 69 years old. . . .	Million . . .	7.0	7.5	8.2	8.1	8.1	8.1	8.0	7.9	7.9	8.0
70 years old and over .	Million . . .	12.1	14.3	16.3	18.1	18.5	18.8	19.3	19.6	19.8	20.1
Workers reported with—											
Taxable earnings [2] . .	Million . . .	113	120	134	138	141	144	147	149	151	153
Maximum earnings [2] . .	Million . . .	10	8	8	8	8	9	9	9	9	10
Earnings in covered employment [2]	Bil. dol . . .	1,329	1,942	2,704	3,169	3,359	3,568	3,848	4,141	4,432	4,733
Reported taxable [2] . .	Bil. dol . . .	1,178	1,725	2,359	2,785	2,920	3,076	3,287	3,517	3,736	3,987
Percent of total	Percent . . .	88.6	88.8	87.2	87.9	86.9	86.2	85.4	84.9	84.3	84.2
Average per worker:											
Total earnings [2] . .	Dollars. . .	11,761	16,125	20,227	22,929	23,814	24,863	26,236	27,697	29,314	30,924
Taxable earnings [2] .	Dollars. . .	10,430	14,326	17,642	20,152	20,700	21,431	22,415	23,525	24,714	26,052
Annual maximum taxable earnings [3]	Dollars. . .	25,900	39,600	51,300	60,600	61,200	62,700	65,400	68,400	72,600	76,200
Contribution rates for OASDHI: [4]											
Each employer and employee. . . , ...	Percent . .	6.13	7.05	7.65	7.65	7.65	7.65	7.65	7.65	7.65	7.65
Self-employed [5]	Percent . .	8.10	14.10	15.30	15.30	15.30	15.30	15.30	15.30	15.30	15.30
SMI, monthly premium [6] .	Dollars. . .	9.60	15.50	28.60	41.10	46.10	42.50	43.80	43.80	45.50	45.50

[1] Estimated number fully insured for retirement and/or survivor benefits as of end of year. [2] Includes self-employment. [3] Beginning 1994 upper limit on earnings subject to HI taxes was repealed. [4] As of January 1, 2001, each employee and employer pays 7.65 percent and the self-employed pay 15.3 percent. [5] Self-employed pays 11.8 percent in 1985. The additional amount is supplied from general revenues. Beginning 1990, self-employed pays 15.3 percent, and half of the tax is deductible for income tax purposes and for computing self-employment income subject to social security tax. [6] 1980, as of July 1; beginning 1985, as of January 1. As of January 1, 2001, the monthly premium is $50.00.

Source: U.S. Social Security Administration, *Annual Statistical Supplement* to the *Social Security Bulletin*; and unpublished data.

No. 526. Social Security Trust Funds: 1980 to 2000

[In billions of dollars (103.5 represents $103,500,000,000)]

Type of trust fund	1980	1985	1990	1995	1996	1997	1998	1999	2000
Old-age and survivors insurance (OASI):									
Net contribution income [1]	103.5	180.2	272.4	310.1	328.0	357.4	380.4	407.3	433.0
Interest received [2]	1.8	1.9	16.4	32.8	35.7	39.8	44.5	49.8	57.5
Benefit payments [3]	105.1	167.2	223.0	291.6	302.9	316.3	326.8	334.4	352.7
Assets, end of year	22.8	[4]35.8	214.2	458.5	514.0	589.1	681.6	798.8	931.0
Disability insurance (DI):									
Net contribution income [1]	13.3	17.4	28.7	54.7	57.7	56.5	59.5	63.9	71.8
Interest received [2]	0.5	0.9	0.9	2.2	3.0	4.0	4.8	5.7	6.9
Benefit payments [3]	15.5	18.8	24.8	40.9	44.2	45.7	48.2	51.4	55.0
Assets, end of year	3.6	[5]6.3	11.1	37.6	52.9	66.4	80.8	97.3	118.5

[1] Includes deposits by states and deductions for refund of estimated employee-tax overpayment. Beginning in 1985, includes government contributions on deemed wage credits for military service in 1957 and later. Includes tax credits on net earnings from self-employment in 1985-89. Includes taxation of benefits beginning in 1985. [2] In 1985-90, includes interest on advance tax transfers. Beginning 1985, includes interest on reimbursement for unnegotiated checks. Data for 1985 reflect interest on interfund borrowing. [3] Includes payments for vocational rehabilitation services furnished to disabled persons receiving benefits because of their disabilities. Beginning in 1985, amounts reflect deductions for unnegotiated benefit checks. [4] Includes $13.2 billion borrowed from the DI and HI Trust Funds (see Table 133). [5] Excludes $2.5 billion lent to the OASI Trust Fund.

Source: U.S. Social Security Administration, *Annual Report of Board of Trustees, OASI, DI, HI, and SMI Trust Funds.* Also published in *Social Security Bulletin,* quarterly.

No. 527. Social Security (OASDI)—Benefits by Type of Beneficiary: 1980 to 2000

[35,585 represents 35,585,000. A person eligible to receive more than one type of benefit is generally classified or counted only once as a retired-worker beneficiary. OASDI=Old-age, survivors, and disability insurance. See also headnote, Table 525 and Appendix III]

Type of beneficiary	1980	1985	1990	1994	1995	1996	1997	1998	1999	2000
Number of benefits [1] (1,000)	35,585	37,058	39,832	42,883	43,387	43,737	43,971	44,246	44,596	45,415
Retired workers [2] (1,000)	19,562	22,432	24,838	26,408	26,898	26,673	27,275	27,511	27,775	28,499
Disabled workers [3] (1,000)	2,859	2,657	3,011	3,963	4,185	4,386	4,508	4,698	4,879	5,042
Wives and husbands [2 4] (1,000)	3,477	3,375	3,367	3,337	3,290	3,194	3,129	3,054	2,987	2,963
Children (1,000)	4,607	3,319	3,187	3,654	3,734	3,803	3,772	3,769	3,795	3,803
Under age 18	3,423	2,699	2,497	2,887	2,956	3,010	2,970	2,963	2,970	2,976
Disabled children [5]	450	526	600	673	686	697	705	713	721	729
Students [6]	733	94	89	94	92	96	97	93	104	98
Of retired workers	639	457	422	440	442	443	441	439	442	459
Of deceased workers	2,610	1,917	1,776	1,864	1,884	1,898	1,893	1,884	1,885	1,878
Of disabled workers	1,358	945	989	1,350	1,409	1,463	1,438	1,446	1,468	1,466
Widowed mothers [7] (1,000)	562	372	304	283	275	242	230	221	212	203
Widows and widowers [2 8] (1,000)	4,411	4,863	5,111	5,232	5,226	5,210	5,053	4,990	4,944	4,901
Parents [2] (1,000)	15	10	6	4	4	4	4	3	3	3
Special benefits [9] (1,000)	93	32	7	2	1	1	(Z)	(Z)	(Z)	(Z)
AVERAGE MONTHLY BENEFIT, CURRENT DOLLARS										
Retired workers [2]	341	479	603	697	720	745	765	780	804	844
Retired worker and wife [2]	567	814	1,027	1,184	1,221	1,262	1,295	1,318	1,357	1,420
Disabled workers [3]	371	484	587	661	682	704	722	733	754	786
Wives and husbands [2 4]	164	236	298	343	354	369	379	386	398	416
Children of retired workers	140	198	259	309	322	337	349	358	373	395
Children of deceased workers	240	331	406	456	469	487	500	510	526	550
Children of disabled workers	110	142	164	178	183	194	201	208	216	228
Widowed mothers [7]	246	332	409	464	478	515	532	545	566	595
Widows and widowers, nondisabled [2] .	311	433	556	655	680	699	731	749	775	810
Parents [2]	276	378	482	570	591	614	638	651	674	704
Special benefits [9]	105	138	167	187	192	197	201	204	209	217
AVERAGE MONTHLY BENEFIT, CONSTANT (2000) DOLLARS [10]										
Retired workers [2]	688	763	784	810	816	817	825	828	831	844
Retired worker and wife [2]	1,143	1,296	1,336	1,376	1,384	1,385	1,397	1,399	1,403	1,420
Disabled workers [3]	748	771	763	768	773	772	779	778	780	786
Wives and husbands [2 4]	331	376	388	399	401	404	409	410	411	416
Children of deceased workers	484	527	528	530	532	534	539	541	544	550
Widowed mothers [7]	496	529	532	539	542	565	574	579	585	595
Widows and widowers, nondisabled [2] .	627	689	723	761	771	766	789	795	801	810
Number of benefits awarded (1,000)	4,215	3,796	3,717	3,940	3,882	3,793	3,866	3,800	3,917	4,290
Retired workers [2]	1,620	1,690	1,665	1,625	1,609	1,581	1,719	1,631	1,690	1,961
Disabled workers [3]	389	377	468	632	646	624	587	608	620	622
Wives and husbands [2 4]	469	440	379	345	322	302	319	311	322	385
Children	1,174	714	695	824	809	798	757	763	773	777
Widowed mothers [7]	108	72	58	55	52	49	44	42	42	40
Widows and widowers [2 8]	452	502	452	459	445	438	440	444	470	505
Parents [2]	1	(Z)	(Z)	(Z)	(Z)	(Z)	(Z)	(Z)	(Z)	(Z)
Special benefits [9]	1	1	(Z)	(Z)	(Z)	(Z)	(Z)	(Z)	(Z)	(Z)
BENEFIT PAYMENTS DURING YEAR (bil. dol.)										
Total [11]	120.5	186.2	247.8	316.8	332.6	347.1	362.0	375.0	385.8	407.6
Monthly benefits [12]	120.1	186.0	247.6	316.6	332.4	346.9	361.8	374.8	385.6	407.4
Retired workers [2]	70.4	116.8	156.8	196.4	205.3	213.4	223.6	232.3	238.5	253.5
Disabled workers [3]	12.8	16.5	22.1	33.7	36.6	39.6	41.1	43.5	46.5	49.8
Wives and husbands [2 4]	7.0	11.1	14.5	17.4	17.9	18.2	18.6	18.9	18.8	19.4
Children	10.5	10.7	12.0	15.4	16.1	17.1	17.6	18.1	18.6	19.3
Under age 18	7.4	8.5	9.0	11.4	11.9	12.6	13.0	13.3	13.6	14.1
Disabled children [5]	1.0	1.8	2.5	3.4	3.6	3.8	4.0	4.2	4.4	4.6
Students [6]	2.1	0.4	0.5	0.6	0.6	0.6	0.6	0.7	0.7	0.7
Of retired workers	1.1	1.1	1.3	1.6	1.7	1.8	1.9	1.9	2.0	2.1
Of deceased workers	7.4	7.8	8.6	10.3	10.7	11.2	11.7	11.9	12.1	12.5
Of disabled workers	2.0	1.8	2.2	3.4	3.7	4.0	4.1	4.2	4.4	4.7
Widowed mothers [7]	1.6	1.5	1.4	1.6	1.6	1.5	1.5	1.4	1.4	1.4
Widows and widowers [2 8]	17.6	29.3	40.7	52.1	54.8	57.0	59.3	60.5	61.8	63.9
Parents [2]	0.1	0.1	(Z)	(Z)	(Z)	(Z)	(Z)	(Z)	(Z)	(Z)
Special benefits [9]	0.1	0.1	(Z)	(Z)	(Z)	(Z)	(Z)	(Z)	(Z)	(Z)
Lump sum	0.4	0.2	0.2	0.2	0.2	0.2	0.2	0.2	0.2	0.2

Z Fewer than 500 or less than $50 million.   [1] Number of benefit payments in current-payment status, i.e., actually being made at a specified time with no deductions or with deductions amounting to less than a month's benefit.   [2] 62 years and over.   [3] Disabled workers under age 65.   [4] Includes wife beneficiaries with entitled children in their care and entitled divorced wives.   [5] 18 years old and over. Disability began before age 18.   [6] Full-time students aged 18-21 through 1984 and aged 18 and 19 beginning 1985.   [7] Includes surviving divorced mothers with entitled children in their care and widowed fathers with entitled children in their care.   [8] Includes widows aged 60-61, surviving divorced wives aged 60 and over, disabled widows and widowers aged 50 and over; and widowers aged 60-61.   [9] Benefits for persons aged 72 and over not insured under regular or transitional provisions of Social Security Act.   [10] Constant dollar figures are based on the consumer price index (CPI-U) for December as published by the U.S. Bureau of Labor Statistics.   [11] Represents total disbursements of benefit checks by the U.S. Dept. of the Treasury during the years specified.   [12] Distribution by type estimated.

Source: U.S. Social Security Administration, Annual Statistical Supplement to the Social Security Bulletin; and unpublished data.

No. 528. Social Security—Beneficiaries, Annual Payments, and Average Monthly Benefit, 1990 to 2000 and by State and Other Areas, 2000

[39,832 represents 39,832,000. Number of beneficiaries in current-payment status and average monthly benefit as of December. Data based on 10-percent sample of administrative records. See also headnote, Table 527, and Appendix III]

Year, state, and other area	Number of beneficiaries (1,000)				Annual payments [2] (mil. dol.)				Average monthly benefit (dol.)		
	Total	Retired workers and dependents [1]	Survivors	Disabled workers and dependents	Total	Retired workers and dependents [1]	Survivors	Disabled workers and dependents	Retired workers [3]	Disabled workers	Widows and widowers [4]
1990	39,832	28,369	7,197	4,266	247,796	172,042	50,951	24,803	603	587	557
1995	43,380	30,139	7,379	5,862	332,581	224,381	67,302	40,898	720	682	680
1997	43,976	30,649	7,171	6,156	361,970	243,590	72,721	45,659	765	722	731
1998	44,247	30,819	7,091	6,338	374,772	252,659	73,940	48,173	780	734	749
1999	44,599	31,035	7,038	6,526	385,525	258,885	75,309	51,331	804	755	775
2000, total [5]	45,417	31,761	6,981	6,675	407,431	274,645	77,848	54,938	845	787	810
United States	44,324	31,090	6,763	6,471	401,044	271,185	76,233	53,625	(NA)	(NA)	(NA)
Alabama	827	516	146	165	6,942	4,186	1,483	1,272	797	756	733
Alaska	55	35	10	10	465	291	94	80	825	777	765
Arizona	791	575	106	111	7,163	5,026	1,187	950	857	817	838
Arkansas	517	332	86	100	4,250	2,633	845	772	777	738	714
California	4,208	3,046	598	564	38,138	26,460	6,864	4,814	854	799	843
Colorado	535	376	78	81	4,698	3,148	882	667	822	779	818
Connecticut	579	436	72	70	5,711	4,219	896	597	926	814	899
Delaware	135	96	19	19	1,268	872	229	167	880	814	868
District of Columbia	74	52	13	10	579	384	112	83	714	732	675
Florida	3,193	2,381	414	398	28,700	20,622	4,751	3,328	840	792	835
Georgia	1,106	712	186	209	9,503	5,947	1,872	1,683	812	767	745
Hawaii	184	143	23	18	1,628	1,230	246	152	834	804	783
Idaho	194	140	28	26	1,697	1,176	310	211	822	772	825
Illinois	1,842	1,320	291	232	17,530	12,060	3,477	1,993	885	816	872
Indiana	994	695	154	144	9,380	6,336	1,846	1,198	883	796	863
Iowa	540	396	82	62	4,891	3,417	968	505	843	764	830
Kansas	440	317	67	56	4,057	2,821	789	448	865	765	858
Kentucky	739	438	130	172	6,203	3,505	1,324	1,373	792	782	727
Louisiana	711	429	154	128	5,906	3,350	1,562	995	783	790	741
Maine	251	170	34	47	2,075	1,360	371	344	776	717	765
Maryland	723	519	115	89	6,622	4,541	1,292	789	850	821	819
Massachusetts	1,064	759	140	165	9,696	6,691	1,656	1,350	849	778	842
Michigan	1,645	1,138	262	245	15,892	10,585	3,151	2,157	909	847	870
Minnesota	739	545	108	86	6,633	4,673	1,252	708	835	770	817
Mississippi	516	303	92	121	4,101	2,364	855	883	762	733	687
Missouri	1,005	687	154	164	8,881	5,876	1,699	1,306	832	770	805
Montana	158	111	24	23	1,376	926	267	182	819	776	802
Nebraska	284	209	42	33	2,533	1,778	493	262	828	744	833
Nevada	287	212	35	40	2,609	1,849	402	358	851	835	847
New Hampshire	200	145	26	30	1,849	1,298	306	245	860	788	858
New Jersey	1,352	1,000	188	165	13,521	9,712	2,319	1,489	933	845	897
New Mexico	281	191	46	43	2,303	1,508	456	338	788	762	758
New York	3,006	2,147	416	443	28,691	19,916	4,912	3,862	897	833	861
North Carolina	1,350	906	193	251	11,651	7,652	1,977	2,021	814	761	743
North Dakota	114	81	21	12	972	645	232	95	788	748	775
Ohio	1,918	1,334	327	257	17,724	11,698	3,877	2,149	862	789	843
Oklahoma	594	408	100	86	5,141	3,358	1,081	703	805	773	784
Oregon	568	420	77	72	5,200	3,684	908	609	855	779	850
Pennsylvania	2,357	1,708	371	279	22,121	15,315	4,464	2,342	868	803	851
Rhode Island	192	139	23	30	1,739	1,237	259	243	845	764	846
South Carolina	689	448	107	134	5,908	3,760	1,060	1,088	812	772	736
South Dakota	136	97	23	16	1,124	766	240	118	774	711	763
Tennessee	996	642	165	188	8,537	5,332	1,699	1,505	811	757	755
Texas	2,638	1,811	481	346	22,883	14,963	5,139	2,781	821	780	787
Utah	242	178	34	30	2,152	1,530	386	236	848	771	860
Vermont	105	73	14	18	918	624	159	135	831	756	813
Virginia	1,035	704	161	169	9,060	5,929	1,741	1,390	821	784	770
Washington	845	618	114	114	7,898	5,564	1,366	968	879	792	865
West Virginia	390	233	76	81	3,488	1,947	837	705	833	833	774
Wisconsin	900	665	127	107	8,347	5,936	1,522	889	864	781	852
Wyoming	77	56	10	11	690	485	118	87	841	798	826
Puerto Rico	665	362	120	183	3,940	1,941	826	1,173	555	667	498
Guam	11	7	2	1	63	39	17	7	591	683	567
American Samoa	5	2	1	2	28	9	9	10	502	596	419
Virgin Islands	13	10	2	2	97	67	17	12	710	726	637
Northern Mariana Islands	2	1	1	(Z)	8	4	3	1	478	410	368
Abroad	393	287	91	16	2,226	1,381	735	110	510	683	551

NA Not available.   Z Fewer than 500.   [1] Includes special benefits for persons aged 72 and over not insured under regular or transitional provisions of Social Security Act.   [2] Unnegotiated checks not deducted. Through 1997 includes lump-sum payments to survivors of deceased workers.   [3] Excludes persons with special benefits.   [4] Nondisabled only.   [5] Includes those with state or area unknown.

Source: U.S. Social Security Administration, Social Security Bulletin, quarterly.

Social Insurance and Human Services   347

No. 529. Public Employee Retirement Systems—Participants and Finances: 1980 to 1999

[For fiscal year of retirement system, except data for the Thrift Savings Plan are for calendar year (4,629 represents 4,629,000)]

Retirement plan	Unit	1980	1985	1990	1994	1995	1996	1997	1998	1999, proj.
TOTAL PARTICIPANTS [1]										
Federal retirement systems:										
Defined benefit:										
Civil Service Retirement System	1,000	4,629	4,919	4,167	3,808	3,731	3,663	3,518	3,423	(NA)
Federal Employees Retirement System [2]	1,000	(X)	(X)	1,180	1,764	1,512	1,615	1,679	1,757	(NA)
Military Service Retirement System [3]	1,000	3,380	3,672	3,763	3,451	3,387	3,372	3,367	3,368	(NA)
Thrift Savings Plan [4]	1,000	(X)	(X)	1,625	2,119	2,195	2,254	2,303	2,300	(NA)
State and local retirement systems [5] [6]	1,000	(NA)	15,234	16,858	13,290	14,734	15,153	15,194	16,215	(NA)
ACTIVE PARTICIPANTS										
Federal retirement systems:										
Defined benefit:										
Civil Service Retirement System	1,000	2,700	2,800	1,826	1,443	1,525	1,343	1,189	1,099	(NA)
Federal Employees Retirement System [2]	1,000	(X)	(X)	1,136	1,375	1,318	1,447	1,497	1,547	(NA)
Military Service Retirement System [3]	1,000	2,050	2,192	2,130	1,666	1,572	1,525	1,491	1,459	(NA)
Thrift Savings Plan [4]	1,000	(X)	(X)	1,419	1,876	1,930	1,987	2,011	1,800	(NA)
State and local retirement systems [5] [6]	1,000	(NA)	10,364	11,345	11,849	12,524	13,051	12,817	13,059	(NA)
ASSETS										
Total	Bil. dol.	258	529	1,047	1,519	1,655	1,854	2,110	2,403	(NA)
Federal retirement systems	Bil. dol.	73	154	326	494	537	581	631	686	(NA)
Defined benefit	Bil. dol.	73	154	318	468	502	534	570	608	616
Civil Service Retirement System	Bil. dol.	73	142	220	294	311	329	344	361	374
Federal Employees Retirement System [2]	Bil. dol.	(X)	(X)	18	50	60	70	83	97	91
Military Service Retirement System [3]	Bil. dol.	(7)	12	80	124	131	135	143	150	151
Thrift Savings Plan [4]	Bil. dol.	(X)	(X)	8	26	35	47	61	77	(NA)
State and local retirement systems [5]	Bil. dol.	185	374	721	1,025	1,118	1,273	1,479	1,717	(NA)
CONTRIBUTIONS										
Total	Bil. dol.	83	106	103	121	127	129	139	137	(NA)
Federal retirement systems	Bil. dol.	19	54	61	67	67	66	73	73	(NA)
Defined benefit	Bil. dol.	19	54	59	62	61	60	66	65	65
Civil Service Retirement System	Bil. dol.	19	27	28	31	31	32	33	33	33
Federal Employees Retirement System [2]	Bil. dol.	(X)	(X)	4	6	6	6	7	6	6
Military Service Retirement System [3]	Bil. dol.	(7)	27	27	25	24	22	26	26	26
Thrift Savings Plan [4]	Bil. dol.	(X)	(X)	2	5	6	6	7	8	(NA)
State and local retirement systems [5]	Bil. dol.	64	52	42	54	60	63	66	64	(NA)
BENEFITS										
Total	Bil. dol.	39	62	89	124	125	135	142	152	(NA)
Federal retirement systems	Bil. dol.	27	40	53	65	66	70	73	76	(NA)
Defined benefit	Bil. dol.	27	40	53	64	65	69	72	74	(NA)
Civil Service Retirement System	Bil. dol.	15	23	31	36	37	39	41	42	43
Federal Employees Retirement System [2]	Bil. dol.	(X)	(X)	(Z)	(Z)	1	1	1	1	1
Military Service Retirement System [3]	Bil. dol.	12	17	22	28	28	29	30	31	(NA)
Thrift Savings Plan [4]	Bil. dol.	(X)	(X)	(Z)	1	1	1	1	2	(NA)
State and local retirement systems [5]	Bil. dol.	12	22	36	59	59	65	69	76	(NA)

NA Not available.   X Not applicable.   Z Less than $500 million.   [1] Includes active, separated vested, retired employees, and survivors.   [2] The Federal Employees Retirement System was established June 6, 1986.   [3] Includes nondisability and disability retirees, surviving families, and all active personnel with the exception of active reserves.   [4] The Thrift Savings Plan (a defined contribution plan) was established April 1, 1987.   [5] Excludes state and local plans that are fully supported by employee contributions.   [6] Not adjusted for double counting of individuals participating in more than one plan.   [7] The Military Retirement System was unfunded until October 1, 1984.

Source: Employee Benefit Research Institute, Washington, DC, EBRI Databook on Employee Benefits, Fourth Edition, and unpublished data (copyright).

No. 530. Federal Civil Service Retirement: 1980 to 2000

[As of Sept. 30 or for year ending Sept. 30 (2,720 represents 2,720,000). Covers both Civil Service Retirement System and Federal Employees Retirement System]

Item	Unit	1980	1985	1990	1995	1996	1997	1998	1999	2000
Employees covered [1]	1,000	2,720	2,750	2,945	2,668	2,629	2,681	2,658	2,668	2,764
Annuitants, total	1,000	1,675	1,955	2,143	2,311	2,333	2,352	2,369	2,368	2,376
Age and service	1,000	905	1,122	1,288	1,441	1,459	1,474	1,488	1,491	1,501
Disability	1,000	343	332	297	263	260	257	253	246	242
Survivors	1,000	427	501	558	607	614	621	628	631	633
Receipts, total [2]	Mil. dol.	24,389	40,790	52,689	65,684	67,339	70,227	72,156	74,522	75,967
Employee contributions	Mil. dol.	3,686	4,679	4,501	4,498	4,398	4,358	4,274	4,381	4,637
Federal government contributions	Mil. dol.	15,562	22,301	27,368	33,130	33,991	35,386	36,188	36,561	37,722
Disbursements, total [3]	Mil. dol.	14,977	23,203	31,416	38,435	39,711	41,722	43,058	43,932	45,194
Age and service annuitants [4]	Mil. dol.	12,639	19,414	26,495	32,070	32,970	34,697	35,806	36,492	37,546
Survivors	Mil. dol.	1,912	3,158	4,366	5,864	6,221	6,518	6,763	6,978	7,210
Average monthly benefit:										
Age and service	Dollars	992	1,189	1,369	1,643	1,698	1,749	1,796	1,830	1,885
Disability	Dollars	723	881	1,008	1,164	1,184	1,204	1,216	1,221	1,240
Survivors	Dollars	392	528	653	819	849	881	905	923	952
Cash and security holdings	Bil. dol.	73.7	142.3	238.0	366.2	394.1	422.2	451.3	481.3	508.1

[1] Excludes employees in leave without pay status.   [2] Includes interest on investments.   [3] Includes refunds, death claims, and administration.   [4] Includes disability annuitants.

Source: U.S. Office of Personnel Management, Civil Service Retirement and Disability Trust Fund Annual Report.

348   Social Insurance and Human Services

No. 531. State and Local Government Retirement Systems—Beneficiaries and Finances: 1990 to 1999

[In billions of dollars, except as indicated (4,026 represents 4,026,000). For fiscal years closed during the 12 months ending June 30]

Year and level of government	Num- ber of benefi- ciaries (1,000)	Receipts					Benefits and withdrawals			Cash and security holdings
		Total	Employee contri- butions	Government contributions		Earn- ings on invest- ments	Total	Ben- efits	With- drawals	
				State	Local					
1990: All systems	4,026	111.3	13.9	14.0	18.6	64.9	38.4	36.0	2.4	721
State-administered	3,232	89.2	11.6	14.0	11.5	52.0	29.6	27.6	2.0	575
Locally administered	794	22.2	2.2	(Z)	7.0	12.9	8.8	8.4	0.4	145
1995: All systems	4,979	148.8	18.6	16.6	24.4	89.2	61.4	58.8	2.7	1,118
State-administered	4,025	123.3	15.7	16.2	15.4	76.0	48.0	45.8	2.2	914
Locally administered	954	25.5	2.9	0.4	9.0	13.3	13.5	13.0	0.5	204
1998: All systems	5,381	263.4	21.8	18.9	23.5	199.2	80.5	76.5	4.0	1,717
State-administered	4,423	213.7	18.3	18.6	16.2	160.7	63.0	59.7	3.3	1,423
Locally administered	958	49.6	3.5	0.3	7.3	38.5	17.5	16.8	0.7	293
1999: All systems	5,506	264.3	23.6	17.2	23.4	200.0	85.7	81.8	3.9	1,907
State-administered	4,522	220.7	19.8	16.9	15.4	168.5	67.4	64.3	3.1	1,582
Locally administered	984	43.6	3.8	0.3	8.0	31.5	18.3	17.5	0.8	325

Z Less than $50 million.

Source: U.S. Census Bureau. Through 1995. *Finances of Employee-Retirement Systems of State and Local Governments.* Series GF, No. 2, annual; beginning 1998. "Federal, State, and Local Governments, State and Local Government Public Employee Retirement Systems"; <http://www.census.gov/govs/www/retire.html>.

No. 532. Private Pension Plans—Summary by Type of Plan: 1990 to 1997

[712.3 represents 712,300. "Pension plan" is defined by the Employee Retirement Income Security Act (ERISA) as "any plan, fund, or program which was heretofore or is hereafter established or maintained by an employer or an employee organization, or by both, to the extent that such plan (a) provides retirement income to employees, or (b) results in a deferral of income by employees for periods extending to the termination of covered employment or beyond, regardless of the method of calculating the contributions made to the plan, the method of calculating the benefits under the plan, or the method of distributing benefits from the plan." A defined benefit plan provides a definite benefit formula for calculating benefit amounts - such as a flat amount per year of service or a percentage of salary times years of service. A defined contribution plan is a pension plan in which the contributions are made to an individual account for each employee. The retirement benefit is dependent upon the account balance at retirement. The balance depends upon amounts contributed, investment experience, and, in the case of profit sharing plans, amounts which may be allocated to the account due to forfeitures by terminating employees. Employee Stock Ownership Plans (ESOP) and 401(k) plans (see Table 535) are included among defined contribution plans. Data are based on Form 5500 series reports filed with the Internal Revenue Service]

Item	Unit	Total				Defined contribution plan				Defined benefit plan			
		1990	1995	1996	1997	1990	1995	1996	1997	1990	1995	1996	1997
Number of plans [1] [2] [3]	1,000	712.3	693.4	696.2	720.0	599.2	623.9	632.6	660.5	113.1	69.5	63.7	59.5
Total participants [2] [3]	Million	76.9	87.5	91.7	95.0	38.1	47.7	50.6	54.6	38.8	39.7	41.1	40.4
Active participants [2] [4]	Million	61.8	66.2	67.9	70.7	35.5	42.7	44.6	48.0	26.3	23.5	23.3	22.7
Contributions [5]	Bil. dol.	98.8	158.8	169.5	177.9	75.8	117.4	133.7	148.1	23.0	41.4	35.8	29.9
Benefits [6]	Bil. dol.	129.4	183.0	213.4	232.5	63.0	97.9	116.5	135.3	66.4	85.1	96.9	97.2

[1] Excludes all plans covering only one participant.   [2] Includes double counting of workers in more than one plan.   [3] Total participants include active participants, vested separated workers, and retirees   [4] Any workers currently in employment covered by a plan and who are earning or retaining credited service under a plan. Includes any nonvested former employees who have not yet incurred breaks in service.   [5] Includes both employer and employee contributions.   [6] Benefits paid directly from trust and premium payments made from plan to insurance carriers. Excludes benefits paid directly by insurance carriers.

Source: U.S. Dept. of Labor, Pension and Welfare Benefits Administration. *Private Pension Plan Bulletin*, No. 10 winter 2001 and unpublished data.

No. 533. Percent of Full-Time Employees Participating in Retirement Plans: 1991 to 1997

[In percent. Covers full-time employees in medium and large private nonfarm establishments. Based on a sample survey of establishments; for details, see source and headnote, Table 628]

Type of retirement plan	1991	1993	1995	1997
Total [1]	78	78	80	79
Defined benefit	59	56	52	50
Defined contribution	48	49	55	57
401(k) plans [2]	44	43	54	55

[1] Some employees participate in both defined benefit and defined contribution plans, but are counted just once in total   [2] A 401(k) plan is a qualified retirement plan that allows participants to have a portion of their compensation (otherwise payable in cash) contributed pretax to a retirement account on their behalf.

Source: U.S. Bureau of Labor Statistics. *News.* USDL 99-02, January 7, 1999

No. 534. Pension Plan Coverage of Workers by Selected Characteristics: 1999

[65,484 represents 65,484,000. Covers workers as of March 2000 who had earnings in 1999. Based on Current Population Survey; see text, Section 1, Population, and Appendix III]

Sex and age	Number with coverage (1,000)				Percent of total workers			
	Total [1]	White	Black	Hispanic [2]	Total [1]	White	Black	Hispanic [2]
Total	65,484	55,511	7,206	4,348	44.0	44.5	41.6	28.1
Male..............	36,111	31,210	3,397	2,492	46.0	46.7	42.4	27.9
Under 65 years old	35,259	30,441	3,343	2,462	46.8	47.6	42.8	28.0
15 to 24 years old	1,771	1,551	135	211	13.6	14.1	9.4	11.0
25 to 44 years old	19,322	16,404	2,014	1,488	50.8	51.5	47.3	29.7
45 to 64 years old	14,166	12,485	1,194	763	58.6	59.4	56.5	40.9
65 years old and over	851	769	54	29	26.6	26.4	27.8	21.5
Female..............	29,373	24,301	3,809	1,857	41.7	42.0	40.8	28.3
Under 65 years old	28,863	23,843	3,766	1,835	42.4	42.8	41.3	28.4
15 to 24 years old	1,431	1,167	204	138	11.8	11.7	12.2	10.4
25 to 44 years old	15,420	12,482	2,171	1,140	45.6	46.0	44.0	31.3
45 to 64 years old	12,011	10,194	1,392	557	54.3	54.6	55.0	37.2
65 years old and over	510	458	42	21	21.8	22.0	20.4	22.0

[1] Includes other races, not shown separately. [2] Hispanic persons may be of any race.

Source: U.S. Census Bureau, "Current Population Survey, Annual Demographic Survey, March Supplement"; published 8 January 2001; <http://ferret.bls.census.gov/macro/032000/noncash/8000.htm>.

No. 535. 401(k) Plans—Summary: 1985 to 1996

[10,339 represents 10,339,000. A 401(k) plan is a qualified retirement plan that allows participants to have a portion of their compensation (otherwise payable in cash) contributed pretax to a retirement account on their behalf]

Item	1985	1990	1991	1992	1993	1994	1995	1996
Number of plans [1]	29,869	97,614	111,314	139,704	154,527	174,945	200,813	230,808
Active participants [2] (1,000)	10,339	19,548	19,126	22,404	23,138	26,206	28,061	30,843
Assets (bil. dol.).............	144	385	440	553	616	675	864	1,062
Contributions (bil. dol.)	24	49	52	64	69	76	87	104
Benefits (bil. dol.)............	16	32	33	43	44	51	62	78
Percentage of all private defined contribution plans:								
Assets	34	54	53	58	58	62	65	(NA)
Contributions	46	65	64	69	68	72	74	(NA)
Benefits	35	51	51	58	57	62	64	(NA)

NA Not available. [1] Excludes single-participant plans. [2] May include some employees who are eligible to participate in the plan but have not elected to join. 401(k) participants may participate in one or more additional plans.

Source: Employee Benefit Research Institute, Washington, DC, EBRI Databook on Employee Benefits, Fourth Edition (copyright).

No. 536. State Unemployment Insurance by State and Other Area: 1999

[6,951 represents 6,951,000. See headnote, Table 537. For state data on insured unemployment, see Table 606]

State or other area	Benefi-ciaries, first payments (1,000)	Benefits paid (mil. dol.)	Avg. weekly unemploy-ment benefits (dol.)	State or other area	Benefi-ciaries, first payments (1,000)	Benefits paid (mil. dol.)	Avg. weekly unemploy-ment benefits (dol.)	State or other area	Benefi-ciaries, first payments (1,000)	Benefits paid (mil. dol.)	Avg. weekly unemploy-ment benefits (dol.)
Total .	6,951	20,270	212	KY	104	240	201	OH	228	688	224
AL	128	192	156	LA	74	187	162	OK	45	121	209
AK	46	123	182	ME	33	81	192	OR	143	429	223
AZ	71	150	157	MD	97	271	205	PA	402	1,350	251
AR	77	162	197	MA	182	822	279	RI	44	141	246
CA	1,048	2,634	158	MI	323	880	238	SC	96	194	185
CO	55	159	241	MN	100	357	279	SD	8	16	170
CT	109	372	225	MS	55	110	153	TN	151	323	184
DE	23	56	204	MO	132	293	175	TX	359	1,189	225
DC	17	60	235	MT	25	56	181	UT	38	98	205
FL	223	670	212	NE	26	55	177	VT	18	45	203
GA	163	281	199	NV	65	192	216	VA	92	179	187
HI	31	130	278	NH	15	35	208	WA	190	906	276
ID	44	102	200	NJ	256	1,077	277	WV	52	129	198
IL	307	1,169	241	NM	30	86	178	WI	209	475	223
IN	112	271	210	NY	417	1,639	232	WY	11	27	201
IA	81	180	227	NC	216	428	219	PR	117	237	103
KS	53	158	237	ND	12	40	201	VI	2	4	173

Source: U.S. Employment and Training Administration, Unemployment Insurance Financial Data Handbook.

350 Social Insurance and Human Services

No. 537. State Unemployment Insurance—Summary: 1980 to 1999

[3,356 represents 3,356,000. Includes unemployment compensation for state and local government employees where covered by state law]

Item	Unit	1980	1985	1990	1993	1994	1995	1996	1997	1998	1999
Insured unemployment, avg. weekly..	1,000...	3,356	2,617	2,522	2,751	2,670	2,572	2,596	2,323	2,222	2,188
Percent of covered employment [1]..	Percent .	3.9	2.9	2.4	2.6	2.5	2.3	2.3	2.0	1.9	1.8
Percent of civilian unemployed....	Percent .	43.9	31.5	35.8	30.8	33.4	34.7	35.9	34.5	35.8	37.2
Unemployment benefits, avg. weekly .	Dollars .	100	128	162	180	182	187	189	193	200	212
Percent of weekly wage	Percent .	36.6	35.3	36.0	36.0	35.7	35.5	34.5	33.5	32.9	31.6
Weeks compensated............	Million .	149.0	119.3	116.0	125.6	123.4	118.3	119.0	106.6	101.4	100.6
Beneficiaries, first payments	1,000...	9,992	8,372	8,629	7,884	7,959	8,035	7,990	7,325	7,332	6,951
Average duration of benefits [2].....	Weeks .	14.9	14.2	13.4	15.9	15.5	14.7	14.9	14.6	13.8	14.5
Claimants exhausting benefits......	1,000...	3,072	2,572	2,323	3,204	2,977	2,662	2,739	2,485	2,266	2,300
Percent of first payment [3].......	Percent .	33.2	31.2	29.4	39.2	36.3	34.3	33.4	32.8	31.8	31.4
Contributions collected [4]	Bil. dol..	11.4	19.3	15.2	19.8	21.8	22.0	21.6	21.2	19.8	19.2
Benefits paid...............	Bil. dol..	14.2	14.7	18.0	21.8	21.5	21.2	21.8	19.7	19.4	20.3
Funds available for benefits [5]	Bil. dol..	6.6	10.1	37.9	28.0	31.3	35.4	38.6	43.8	48.0	50.3
Average employer contribution rate [6] .	Percent .	2.37	3.13	1.95	2.51	2.55	2.44	2.28	2.13	1.92	1.76

[1] Insured unemployment as percent of average covered employment in preceding year.   [2] Weeks compensated divided by first payment.   [3] Based on first payments for 12-month period ending June 30.   [4] Contributions from employers; also employees in states which tax workers.   [5] End of year. Sum of balances in state clearing accounts, benefit-payment accounts, and state accounts in federal unemployment trust funds.   [6] As percent of taxable wages.
Source: U.S. Employment and Training Administration, *Unemployment Insurance Financial Data Handbook.*

No. 538. Persons With Work Disability by Selected Characteristics: 2000

[In thousands, except percent (16,744 represents 16,744,000). As of March. Covers civilian noninstitutional population and members of Armed Forces living off post or with their families on post. Persons are classified as having a work disability if they (1) have a health problem or disability which prevents them from working or which limits the kind or amount of work they can do; (2) have a service-connected disability or ever retired or left a job for health reasons; (3) did not work in survey reference week or previous year because of long-term illness or disability; or (4) are' under age 65, and are covered by medicare or receive Supplemental Security Income. Based on Current Population Survey; see text, Section 1, Population, and Appendix III]

Age and participation status in assistance programs	Total [1]	Male	Female	White	Black	Hispanic [2]
Persons with work disability	**16,744**	**8,192**	**8,552**	**12,856**	**3,230**	**1,588**
16 to 24 years old..................	1,347	643	703	924	356	133
25 to 34 years old..................	2,062	902	1,160	1,465	520	243
35 to 44 years old..................	3,768	1,983	1,785	2,932	721	367
45 to 54 years old..................	4,516	2,383	2,133	3,464	820	378
55 to 64 years old..................	5,051	2,280	2,771	4,070	813	468
Percent work disabled of total population ...	9.5	9.5	9.5	8.9	14.5	7.8
16 to 24 years old..................	3.9	3.7	4.1	3.4	6.9	2.6
25 to 34 years old..................	5.5	4.9	6.1	4.9	10.2	4.3
35 to 44 years old..................	8.5	9.1	7.9	8.0	12.7	7.4
45 to 54 years old..................	12.4	13.4	11.4	11.3	20.1	12.5
55 to 64 years old..................	21.6	20.1	22.6	20.2	35.1	26.8
Percent of work disabled—						
Receiving social security income............	31.8	34.3	29.4	32.6	30.8	27.9
Receiving food stamps	17.3	13.7	20.8	13.9	29.2	24.0
Covered by medicaid................	32.1	28.0	36.0	28.6	46.0	43.8
Residing in public housing	6.2	4.8	7.6	4.1	14.2	8.4
Residing in subsidized housing	3.7	2.6	4.8	3.0	6.0	5.2

[1] Includes other races not shown separately.   [2] Hispanic persons may be of any race.
Source: U.S. Census Bureau, unpublished data.

No. 539. Vocational Rehabilitation—Summary: 1980 to 1999

[For year ending September 30 (1,076 represents $1,076,000,000). Includes Puerto Rico, Guam, Virgin Islands, American Samoa, Northern Mariana Islands, and the Republic of Palau. State agencies, using matching state and federal funds, provide vocational rehabilitation services to eligible individuals with disabilities to enable them to prepare for and engage in gainful employment. Services may include counseling, guidance and work related placement services, physical and mental restoration, training and rehabilitation technology]

Item	Unit	1980	1985	1990	1994	1995	1996	1997	1998	1999
Federal and state expenditures [1]........	Mil. dol..	1,076	1,452	1,910	2,517	2,714	2,844	3,046	3,081	3,138
Federal expenditures...............	Mil. dol..	817	1,100	1,525	1,891	2,054	2,104	2,164	2,232	2,287
Applicants processed for program eligibility.	1,000...	717	594	625	675	625	578	617	624	608
Percent accepted into program	Percent .	58	60	57	72	76	76	79	75	80
Total persons rehabilitated [2]...........	1,000...	277	228	216	203	210	213	212	224	232
Rehabilitation rate [3]...............	Percent .	64	64	62	49	46	61	61	62	63
Severely disabled persons rehabilitated [2] [4]	1,000...	143	135	146	149	159	166	168	185	197
Rehabilitation rate [3]...............	Percent .	61	62	62	49	46	60	60	61	62
Percent of total persons rehabilitated ...	Percent .	51	59	68	74	76	78	79	83	85
Persons served, total [5].............	1,000...	1,095	932	938	1,194	1,250	1,226	1,267	1,211	1,202
Persons served, severely disabled [4] [5]...	1,000...	606	581	640	882	940	951	1,005	988	1,015
Percent of total persons served......	Percent .	55	62	68	74	75	78	79	82	84

[1] Includes expenditures only under the basic support provisions of the Rehabilitation Act.   [2] Persons successfully placed into gainful employment.   [3] Persons rehabilitated as a percent of all active case closures (whether rehabilitated or not); beginning 1996, as a percent of persons who required services.   [4] An individual with a severe disability is an individual whose severe physical or mental impairment seriously limits one or more functional capacities in terms of an employment outcome, and whose vocational rehabilitation can be expected to require multiple vocational rehabilitation services over an extended period of time.   [5] Includes active cases accepted for rehabilitation services during year plus active cases on hand at beginning of year.
Source: U.S. Dept. of Education, Rehabilitation Services Administration, *Caseload Statistics of State Vocational Rehabilitation Agencies in Fiscal Years*, and *State Vocational Rehabilitation Agency Program Data in Fiscal Years*, both annual.

No. 540. Workers' Compensation Payments: 1980 to 1999

[In billions of dollars, except as indicated (79 represents 79,000,000). See headnote. Table 541]

Item	1980	1985	1990	1993	1994	1995	1996	1997	1998	1999
Workers covered [1] (mil.)	79	84	106	106	109	113	115	118	121	124
Premium amounts paid [2]	**22.3**	**29.2**	**53.1**	**60.8**	**60.5**	**57.1**	**55.3**	**52.5**	**52.8**	**53.3**
Private carriers [2]	15.7	19.5	35.1	35.6	34.0	31.6	30.5	29.5	30.1	30.2
State funds	3.0	3.5	8.0	10.9	11.2	10.5	10.2	9.5	9.8	10.1
Federal programs [3]	1.1	1.7	2.2	2.5	2.5	2.6	2.6	2.6	2.7	2.7
Self-insurers	2.4	4.5	7.9	11.8	12.8	12.5	12.0	11.0	10.2	10.4
Annual benefits paid [2]	**13.6**	**22.2**	**38.2**	**45.3**	**44.6**	**43.4**	**41.8**	**41.1**	**42.3**	**43.4**
By private carriers [2]	7.0	12.3	22.2	24.1	22.3	21.1	20.4	21.0	22.8	23.9
From state funds [4]	4.3	5.7	8.8	10.6	10.8	11.0	10.6	10.3	10.3	10.2
Employers' self-insurance [5]	2.3	4.1	7.2	10.6	11.5	11.2	10.8	9.8	9.2	9.3
Type of benefit:										
Medical/hospitalization	3.9	7.5	15.2	17.5	17.2	16.7	16.6	15.7	16.4	18.1
Compensation payments	9.7	14.7	23.1	27.8	27.5	26.7	25.3	25.4	25.9	25.4
Percent of covered payroll: [1]										
Workers' compensation costs [6][7]	1.96	1.82	2.18	2.17	2.05	1.83	1.67	1.47	1.37	1.29
Benefits [7]	1.07	1.30	1.57	1.62	1.51	1.39	1.26	1.15	1.09	1.05

[1] Data for years 1980 and 1985 not comparable with later years. [2] Premium and benefit amounts include estimated payments under insurance policy deductible provisions. Deductible benefits are allocated to private carriers and state funds. [3] Includes federal employer compensation program and that portion of federal black lung benefits program financed from employer contributions. [4] Net cash and medical benefits paid by competitive and exclusive state funds and by federal workers' compensation programs, including black lung benefit program. [5] Cash and medical benefits paid by self-insurers, plus value of medical benefits paid by employers carrying workers' compensation policies that exclude standard medical coverage. [6] Premiums written by private carriers and state funds, and benefits paid by self-insurers increased by 5-10 percent from 1980 to 1990 and by 11 percent for 1993-99 for administrative costs. Also includes benefits paid and administrative costs of federal system for government employees. [7] Excludes programs financed from general revenue—black lung benefits and supplemental pensions in some states.

Source: 1980-1993, U.S. Social Security Administration, *Annual Statistical Supplement* to the *Social Security Bulletin.* Beginning 1994, National Academy of Social Insurance, Washington, DC. *Workers' Compensation: Benefits, Coverage, and Costs,* annual.

No. 541. Workers' Compensation Payments by State: 1990 to 1999

[In millions of dollars (38,238 represents $38,238,000,000). Calendar-year data, except fiscal-year data for federal civilian and other programs and for some states with state funds. Payments represent compensation and medical benefits and include insurance losses paid by private insurance carriers (compiled from state workers' compensation agencies and A.M. Best Co); disbursements of state funds (compiled from the A.M. Best Co. and state workers' compensation agencies); and self-insurance payments, based on information from the National Association of Insurance Commissioners and the source's estimates. Includes benefit payments under Longshore and Harbor Workers' Compensation Act for states in which such payments are made]

State	1990	1995	1997	1998	1999	State	1990	1995	1997	1998	1999
Total [1]	38,238	43,373	41,147	42,312	43,371	Nevada	339	365	341	335	363
						New Hampshire	169	169	155	164	171
Alabama	444	516	530	615	596	New Jersey	844	[2]972	923	955	987
Alaska	113	115	130	129	138	New Mexico	228	145	120	117	117
Arizona	371	386	428	418	428	New York	1,752	[2]2,780	2,618	2,557	2,782
Arkansas	229	187	157	164	166	North Carolina	480	495	618	766	710
California	6,065	[2]7,177	7,074	7,374	7,856	North Dakota	60	71	77	81	77
Colorado	595	584	674	657	702	Ohio	1,960	2,162	2,030	2,069	2,019
Connecticut	694	[2]733	732	711	722	Oklahoma	369	580	547	520	465
Delaware	75	[2]103	121	119	105						
						Oregon	573	463	417	433	399
District of Columbia	86	113	82	76	82	Pennsylvania	2,019	[2]2,663	2,471	2,418	2,441
Florida	1,976	2,518	2,318	2,208	2,080	Rhode Island	219	[2]138	138	145	153
Georgia	735	699	713	808	816	South Carolina	277	[2]353	459	484	512
Hawaii	216	326	255	233	211	South Dakota	56	70	74	73	80
Idaho	105	148	213	237	230	Tennessee	463	396	433	518	514
Illinois	1,607	1,438	1,577	1,687	1,720	Texas	2,896	[2]2,006	1,377	1,489	1,678
Indiana	350	361	438	482	522	Utah	187	140	192	220	219
Iowa	231	233	273	292	284	Vermont	61	65	87	95	104
Kansas	266	[2]290	313	318	326	Virginia	507	557	534	591	581
Kentucky	383	498	380	410	431	Washington	883	1,129	1,234	1,309	1,418
Louisiana	575	516	420	428	429	West Virginia	389	529	617	629	665
Maine	380	286	271	246	250	Wisconsin	561	651	594	622	652
Maryland	505	522	1,082	1,127	1,169	Wyoming	49	74	68	74	71
Massachusetts	1,235	[2]775	653	641	634						
Michigan	1,205	[2]1,585	1,332	1,367	1,393	Federal programs:					
Minnesota	582	[2]733	738	732	745	Civilian employ-					
Mississippi	198	[2]218	231	235	254	ees	1,448	1,880	1,901	1,955	2,009
Missouri	496	733	527	589	593	Black lung					
Montana	150	140	168	171	145	benefits [3]	1,435	1,222	1,103	1,035	981
Nebraska	137	141	185	182	173	Other [4]	11	(NA)	(NA)	(NA)	(NA)

NA Not available. [1] Total for 1995 includes an amount for benefits under deductible provisions not distributed by state. [2] Includes benefits under deductible provisions. [3] Includes payments by Social Security Administration and by Department of Labor. [4] Primarily payments made to dependents of reservists who died while on active duty in the Armed Forces.

Source: 1990, U.S. Social Security Administration, *Social Security Bulletin,* summer 1995, and selected prior issues. Beginning 1995, National Academy of Social Insurance, Washington, DC. *Workers' Compensation: Benefits, Coverage, and Costs,* annual.

No. 542. Supplemental Security Income—Recipients and Payments: 1980 to 1999

[As of December, except total payments, calendar year (4,142 represents 4,142,000). See also Appendix III]

Program	Unit	1980	1985	1990	1994	1995	1996	1997	1998	1999
Recipients, total [1]	1,000 . . .	4,142	4,138	4,817	6,296	6,514	6,614	6,495	6,566	6,557
Aged	1,000 . . .	1,808	1,504	1,454	1,466	1,446	1,413	1,363	1,332	1,308
Blind	1,000 . . .	78	82	84	85	84	82	81	80	79
Disabled	1,000 . . .	2,256	2,551	3,279	4,745	4,984	5,119	5,052	5,154	5,169
Payments, total [2]	Mil. dol .	7,941	11,060	16,599	25,877	27,628	28,792	29,052	30,216	30,959
Aged	Mil. dol .	2,734	3,035	3,736	4,367	4,467	4,507	4,532	4,425	4,725
Blind	Mil. dol .	190	264	334	372	376	372	375	366	391
Disabled	Mil. dol .	5,014	7,755	12,521	21,131	22,779	23,906	24,006	25,305	25,722
Average monthly payment, total [1]	Dollars . .	168	226	299	351	358	363	351	359	368
Aged	Dollars .	128	164	213	243	251	261	268	277	289
Blind	Dollars .	213	274	342	364	370	379	382	390	401
Disabled	Dollars . .	198	261	337	384	389	391	373	380	388

[1] Persons with a federal SSI payment and/or federally administered state supplementation.   [2] Includes payments not distributed by reason for eligibility.

No. 543. Supplemental Security Income (SSI)—Recipients and Payments by State and Other Area: 1995 to 1999

[Recipients as of December; payments for calendar year (6,514 represents 6,514,000). Data cover federal SSI payments and/or federally-administered state supplementation. For explanation of methodology, see Appendix III]

State and other area	Recipients (1,000)			Payments for year (mil. dol.)			State and other area	Recipients (1,000)			Payments for year (mil. dol.)		
	1995	1998	1999	1995	1998	1999		1995	1998	1999	1995	1998	1999
Total . . .	6,514	6,566	6,557	27,037	29,408	30,106	MO	114	112	111	431	459	463
U.S.	6,513	6,563	6,556	27,035	29,405	30,104	MT	14	14	14	53	55	56
AL	165	163	160	600	651	659	NE	21	21	21	76	83	84
AK	7	8	8	27	32	35	NV	21	23	24	79	95	101
AZ	73	78	79	288	329	340	NH	11	11	11	39	46	47
AR	94	90	88	326	340	339	NJ	144	145	146	594	646	665
CA	1,032	1,042	1,066	5,391	5,769	6,168	NM	45	46	46	166	183	187
CO	57	56	55	217	231	230	NY	589	608	609	2,724	3,055	3,118
CT	45	47	48	181	203	211	NC	191	194	192	639	717	720
DE	11	12	12	40	48	50	ND	9	9	8	29	30	30
DC	20	20	20	83	89	91	OH	248	249	243	1,044	1,132	1,125
FL	338	362	367	1,300	1,515	1,564	OK	74	73	73	266	293	297
GA	199	199	197	692	767	773	OR	47	49	51	183	206	219
HI	19	20	20	82	94	98	PA	265	276	278	1,159	1,306	1,339
ID	17	17	18	63	71	73	RI	24	26	27	100	117	124
IL	267	255	251	1,160	1,180	1,177	SC	111	110	108	384	420	423
IN	89	90	88	348	378	380	SD	14	13	13	47	50	49
IA	42	41	40	148	157	157	TN	180	170	166	648	670	666
KS	38	37	36	141	148	151	TX	404	409	408	1,391	1,542	1,557
KY	165	172	172	635	708	720	UT	20	20	20	80	87	87
LA	182	174	168	717	740	727	VT	13	13	13	50	51	51
ME	31	29	29	96	107	111	VA	130	133	132	471	525	530
MD	82	86	87	332	383	389	WA	92	97	98	398	453	469
MA	164	167	167	700	772	788	WV	68	71	71	276	313	316
MI	210	213	210	896	975	983	WI	112	90	87	487	371	363
MN	62	64	64	235	262	266	WY	6	6	6	21	23	23
MS	141	135	131	504	528	517	N. Mariana .	1	1	1	2	3	3

Source of Tables 542 and 543: U.S. Social Security Administration, *Social Security Bulletin*, quarterly, and *Annual Statistical Supplement* to the *Social Security Bulletin*.

No. 544. Temporary Assistance for Needy Families (TANF)—Families and Recipients: 1980 to 2000

[In thousands (3,712 represents 3,712,000). Average monthly families and recipients for calendar year, except 2000 for Jan.-June period. Prior to TANF, the cash assistance program to families was called Aid to Families with Dependent Children (1980-1996). Under the new welfare law (Personal Responsibility and Work Opportunity Reconciliation Act of 1996), the program became TANF. See text, this section. Includes Puerto Rico, Guam, and Virgin Islands

Year	Families	Recipients	Year	Families	Recipients	Year	Families	Recipients
1980	3,712	10,774	1988	3,749	10,915	1995	4,791	13,418
1982	3,542	10,258	1989	3,799	10,993	1996	4,434	12,321
1983	3,686	10,761	1990	4,057	11,695	1997	3,740	10,376
1984	3,714	10,831	1991	4,467	12,930	1998	3,050	8,347
1985	3,701	10,855	1992	4,829	13,773	1999	2,512	6,722
1986	3,763	11,038	1993	5,012	14,205	2000	2,266	5,890
1987	3,776	11,027	1994	5,033	14,161			

Source: U.S. Administration for Children and Families, unpublished data.

U.S. Census Bureau, Statistical Abstract of the United States: 2001

No. 545. Temporary Assistance for Needy Families (TANF)—Recipients by State and Other Area: 1995 to 2000

[In thousands (4,791 represents 4,791,000). Average monthly families and recipients for calendar year, except as noted. See headnote, Table 544]

State or other area	Families 1995	Families 1999	Families 2000 [1]	Recipients 1995	Recipients 1999	Recipients 2000 [1]	State or other area	Families 1995	Families 1999	Families 2000 [1]	Recipients 1995	Recipients 1999	Recipients 2000 [1]
Total .	4,791	2,512	2,266	13,418	6,722	5,890	MT.	11	5	5	33	14	14
U.S.	4,734	2,483	2,230	13,242	6,633	5,785	NE.	15	8	10	41	25	28
AL	45	20	19	114	49	56	NV.	16	7	7	41	18	15
AK	12	8	8	36	25	25	NH.	10	6	6	27	15	14
AZ	68	34	33	185	89	83	NJ.	110	59	52	310	155	131
AR	24	12	12	62	29	29	NM.	34	25	24	103	79	71
CA.	916	592	499	2,675	1,662	1,300	NY.	452	310	258	1,241	793	723
CO.	38	13	11	106	35	29	NC.	123	55	46	305	124	99
CT	61	32	28	169	78	66	ND.	5	3	3	14	8	8
DE.	11	6	6	24	17	18	OH.	222	104	100	592	263	252
DC.	26	19	20	72	50	46	OK.	44	14	11	120	40	25
FL	224	77	67	606	184	151	OR.	38	17	17	101	44	43
GA.	138	45	53	378	113	140	PA .	201	101	90	582	280	238
HI	22	16	15	66	45	44	RI .	22	18	16	60	49	45
ID	9	1	1	24	3	2	SC.	48	17	16	127	41	37
IL.	233	112	90	684	335	183	SD.	6	3	3	17	8	7
IN	62	37	35	177	108	97	TN.	102	57	56	271	153	146
IA	35	21	20	97	58	53	TX.	269	115	126	730	311	338
KS	28	13	12	77	34	36	UT.	16	7	8	44	22	24
KY	74	41	39	184	95	89	VT.	10	6	6	27	18	16
LA	77	36	27	251	101	85	VA .	70	36	31	179	86	71
ME.	21	13	11	59	30	28	WA .	101	61	57	283	166	154
MD.	80	25	29	220	63	72	WV .	38	11	11	102	31	32
MA.	97	51	44	263	122	100	WI .	71	18	17	202	44	38
MI	195	89	75	578	244	207	WY .	5	1	1	14	2	1
MN.	61	41	39	178	121	115	PR .	54	27	32	164	79	92
MS.	51	12	15	140	28	33	GU .	2	2	3	8	7	10
MO	88	49	47	249	129	125	VI.	1	1	1	5	3	3

[1] January-June period only.

Source: U.S. Administration for Children and Families, unpublished data.

No. 546. Temporary Assistance for Needy Families (TANF)—Expenditures by Type: 1999

[In millions of dollars (22,585 represents $22,585,000,000). Represents federal and state funds expended in fiscal year 1999]

State	Total [1]	Percent federal funds	Type of expenditure — Cash and work based assistance [2]	Work activities	Child care	State	Total [1]	Percent federal funds	Type of expenditure — Cash and work based assistance [2]	Work activities	Child care
U.S.	22,585	50	13,449	1,754	1,995	MO	317	60	165	41	43
AL	91	57	35	15	14	MT.	41	61	25	5	1
AK	88	43	64	10	5	NE.	116	74	68	17	6
AZ	240	59	122	14	12	NV.	65	58	28	1	2
AR	72	63	24	22	5	NH.	60	47	36	4	5
CA.	6,252	54	4,290	312	412	NJ.	450	33	302	32	48
CO.	160	44	55	9	11	NM.	130	69	108	-	3
CT	385	52	199	16	104	NY.	3,652	42	2,347	180	182
DE.	59	55	24	10	12	NC.	394	57	176	4	44
DC.	128	40	80	17	16	ND.	33	72	22	2	1
FL	484	23	306	105	34	OH.	656	37	380	5	69
GA.	410	57	207	31	35	OK.	151	57	58	31	27
HI	168	52	149	6	-	OR.	286	68	177	54	20
ID	27	46	4	2	1	PA	1,038	53	530	72	47
IL.	840	49	574	33	117	RI	164	58	115	8	14
IN	188	36	85	13	15	SC.	107	66	39	23	4
IA	175	65	92	24	6	SD.	22	58	11	3	1
KS	176	61	46	8	7	TN.	209	58	110	34	5
KY	208	61	120	21	16	TX.	591	57	233	47	35
LA	128	54	67	14	5	UT.	80	68	41	26	4
ME.	109	63	74	10	7	VT.	65	58	52	(Z)	4
MD.	328	46	189	50	26	VA	258	50	140	61	22
MA.	632	43	331	35	87	WA	504	42	317	39	34
MI	1,034	54	435	152	309	WV	58	25	33	3	3
MN.	377	47	234	45	50	WI	322	48	91	80	60
MS.	44	48	27	7	2	WY	14	24	10	2	2

- Represents zero.   Z Less than $500,000.   [1] Includes other types of expenditures not shown separately.   [2] "Work-based" assistance is money earned by TANF recipients in return for community service jobs or work experience.

Source: U.S. Administration for Children and Families, Temporary Assistance for Needy Families (TANF) Program, Third Annual Report to Congress, August 2000.

354   Social Insurance and Human Services

No. 547. Child Support—Award and Recipiency Status of Custodial Parent: 1997

[In thousands except as noted (13,987 represents 13,987,000). Custodial parents 15 years and older with own children under 21 years of age present from absent parents as of spring 1998. Covers civilian noninstitutional population. Based on Current Population Survey; see text, Section 1, Population, and Appendix III. For definition of mean, see Guide to Tabular Presentation]

Award and recipiency status	All custodial parents				Custodial parents below the poverty level			
	Total				Total			
	Number	Percent distribu- tion	Mothers	Fathers	Number	Percent distribu- tion	Mothers	Fathers
Total	13,987	(X)	11,905	2,082	4,038	(X)	3,816	222
With child support agreement or award . . .	7,876	(X)	7,080	796	2,101	(X)	2,021	81
Supposed to receive payments in 1997. .	7,006	100.0	6,331	674	1,794	100.0	1,723	72
Actually received payments in 1997 . .	4,720	67.4	4,335	385	978	54.5	947	31
Received full amount	2,863	40.9	2,650	213	436	24.3	415	21
Received partial payments	1,857	26.5	1,685	172	542	30.2	532	10
Did not receive payments in 1997. . . .	2,286	32.6	1,996	289	816	45.5	776	41
Child support not awarded	6,111	(X)	4,825	1,286	1,937	(X)	1,795	141
MEAN INCOME AND CHILD SUPPORT								
Received child support payments in 1997:								
Mean total money income (dol.)	24,741	(X)	23,249	41,529	7,222	(X)	7,306	(B)
Mean child support received (dol.)	3,622	(X)	3,655	3,251	2,317	(X)	2,290	(B)
Received the full amount due:								
Mean total money income (dol.) . . .	27,533	(X)	25,899	47,815	6,977	(X)	7,226	(B)
Mean child support received (dol.) . .	4,719	(X)	4,780	3,955	3,646	(X)	3,663	(B)
Received partial payments:								
Mean total money income (dol.) . . .	20,435	(X)	19,083	33,712	7,418	(X)	7,369	(B)
Mean child support received (dol.) . .	1,931	(X)	1,886	2,375	1,247	(X)	1,217	(B)
Received no payments in 1997:								
Mean total money income (dol.)	18,370	(X)	16,659	30,179	6,336	(X)	6,108	(B)
Without child support agreement or award:								
Mean total money income (dol.)	19,925	(X)	15,643	35,986	5,673	(X)	5,657	(B)

B Base too small to meet statistical standards for reliability.   X Not applicable.

Source: U.S. Census Bureau, Current Population Reports, P60-212.

No. 548. Child Support Enforcement Program—Caseload and Collections: 1980 to 1999

[For years ending Sept. 30 (5,432 represents 5,432,000). Includes Puerto Rico, Guam, and the Virgin Islands. The child support enforcement program locates absent parents, establishes paternity of children born out-of-wedlock, and establishes and enforces support orders. By law, these services are available to all families that need them. The program is operated at the state and local government level but 68 percent of administrative costs are paid by the federal government. Child support collected for families not receiving Temporary Assistance for Needy Families (TANF) goes to the family to help it remain self-sufficient. Most of the child support collected on behalf of TANF families goes to federal and state governments to offset TANF payments. Based on data reported by state agencies. Minus sign (-) indicates net outlay]

Item	Unit	1980	1985	1990	1995	1996	1997	1998	1999
Total cases	1,000 . . .	5,432	8,401	12,796	19,162	19,319	19,057	19,419	17,330
Paternities established, total	1,000 . . .	144	232	393	659	734	814	848	845
Support orders established, total [1]	1,000 . . .	374	669	1,022	1,051	1,093	1,260	1,148	1,221
FINANCES									
Collections, total [2]	Mil. dol .	1,478	2,694	6,010	10,827	12,020	13,364	14,348	15,843
TANF/FC collections [2]	Mil. dol .	603	1,090	1,750	2,689	2,855	2,843	2,650	2,482
State share	Mil. dol .	274	415	620	939	1,014	1,159	1,089	1,048
Incentive payments to states	Mil. dol .	72	145	264	400	409	410	396	377
Federal share	Mil. dol .	246	341	533	822	888	1,046	961	922
Non-TANF collections	Mil. dol .	874	1,604	4,260	8,138	9,165	10,521	11,698	13,362
Administrative expenditures, total .	Mil. dol .	466	814	1,606	3,012	3,049	3,428	3,585	4,039
State share	Mil. dol .	117	243	545	918	1,014	1,100	1,200	1,359
Federal share	Mil. dol .	349	571	1,061	2,095	2,035	2,328	2,385	2,680
Program savings, total	Mil. dol .	127	86	-190	-852	-738	-813	-1,139	-1,692
State share	Mil. dol .	230	317	338	421	409	469	286	66
Federal share	Mil. dol .	-103	-231	-528	-1,273	-1,147	-1,282	-1,424	-1,758

[1] Through 1990 includes modifications to orders.   [2] Collections for current assistance cases where the children are: (1) recipients of TANF under Title IV-A of the Social Security Act or (2) entitled to Foster Care (FC) maintenance under Title IV-E of the Social Security Act plus collections distributed as assistance reimbursements. Includes medical support and payments to families of current assistance not shown separately.

Source: U.S. Department of Health and Human Services, Office of Child Support Enforcement, Annual Report to Congress.

Social Insurance and Human Services   355

No. 549. Federal Food Programs: 1980 to 2000

[21.1 represents 21,100,000. For years ending Sept. 30; see text, Section 8, State and Local Government Finances and Employment. Program data include Puerto Rico, Virgin Islands, Guam, American Samoa, Northern Marianas, and the former Trust Territory when a federal food program was operated in these areas. Participation data are average monthly figures except as noted. Participants are not reported for the commodity distribution programs. Cost data are direct federal benefits to recipients; they exclude federal administrative payments and applicable state and local contributions. Federal costs for commodities and cash-in-lieu of commodities are shown separately from direct cash benefits for those programs receiving both]

Program	Unit	1980	1985	1990	1995	1997	1998	1999	2000
Food stamp:									
Participants	Million . .	21.1	19.9	20.1	26.6	22.9	19.8	18.2	17.2
Federal cost.	Mil. dol. .	8,721	10,744	14,187	22,765	19,550	16,889	15,755	14,985
Monthly average coupon value per recipient .	Dollars . .	34.47	44.99	58.92	71.26	71.27	71.12	72.20	72.75
Nutrition assistance program for Puerto Rico: [1]									
Federal cost.	Mil. dol. .	(X)	825	937	1,131	1,174	1,204	1,236	1,268
National school lunch program (NSLP):									
Free lunches served	Million . .	1,671	1,657	1,662	2,090	2,194	2,198	2,207	2,204
Reduced-price lunches served	Million . .	308	255	273	309	347	362	392	409
Children participating [2]	Million . .	26.6	23.6	24.1	25.7	26.3	26.6	26.9	27.2
Federal cost.	Mil. dol. .	2,279	2,578	3,214	4,466	4,934	5,102	5,314	5,489
School breakfast (SB):									
Children participating [2].	Million . .	3.6	3.4	4.1	6.3	6.9	7.1	7.4	7.5
Federal cost.	Mil. dol. .	288	379	596	1,049	1,214	1,272	1,345	1,393
Special supplemental food program (WIC): [3]									
Participants	Million . .	1.9	3.1	4.5	6.9	7.4	7.4	7.3	7.2
Federal cost.	Mil. dol. .	584	1,193	1,637	2,517	2,815	2,808	2,853	2,847
Child and adult care (CC): [4]									
Participants [5]	Million . .	0.7	1.0	1.5	2.4	2.5	2.6	2.7	2.7
Federal cost. [6]	Mil. dol. .	207	390	720	1,296	1,393	1,372	1,438	1,495
Summer feeding (SF): [6]									
Children participating [7].	Million . .	1.9	1.5	1.7	2.1	2.2	2.2	2.2	2.1
Federal cost.	Mil. dol. .	104	103	145	212	217	234	238	233
Federal cost of commodities donated to— [8]									
Child nutrition (NSLP, CC, SF, and SB)	Mil. dol. .	930	840	646	733	661	774	754	697

X Not applicable.   [1] Puerto Rico was included in the food stamp program until June 30, 1982.   [2] Average monthly participation (excluding summer months of June through August). Includes children in public and private elementary and secondary schools and in residential child care institutes.   [3] WIC serves pregnant and postpartum women, infants, and children up to age five.   [4] Program provides year-round subsidies to feed preschool children in child care centers and family day care homes. Certain care centers serving disabled or elderly adults also receive meal subsidies.   [5] Average quarterly daily attendance at participating institutions.   [6] Program provides free meals to children in poor areas during summer months.   [7] Peak month (July) average daily attendance at participating institutions.   [8] Includes the federal cost of commodity entitlements, cash-in-lieu of commodities, and bonus foods.

No. 550. Federal Food Stamp Program by State: 1995 to 2000

[26,619 represents 26,619,000. Participation data are average monthly number. For years ending Sept. 30. Food stamp costs are for benefits only and exclude administrative expenditures]

State	Persons (1,000)			Benefits (mil. dol.)			State	Persons (1,000)			Benefits (mil. dol.)		
	1995	1999	2000	1995	1999	2000		1995	1999	2000	1995	1999	2000
Total [1] . .	26,619	18,183	17,163	22,765	15,755	14,985	MO	576	408	420	488	348	358
U.S. . .	26,579	18,146	17,125	22,714	15,702	14,928	MT	71	61	59	57	52	51
							NE.	105	92	82	77	66	61
AL.	525	405	396	441	346	344	NV.	99	62	61	91	56	57
AK.	45	41	38	50	49	46	NH	58	37	36	44	31	28
AZ.	480	257	259	414	233	240							
AR.	272	253	247	212	210	206							
CA.	3,175	2,027	1,832	2,473	1,796	1,639	NJ.	551	385	345	506	346	304
CO	252	173	156	217	145	127	NM	239	178	169	196	144	140
CT.	226	178	165	169	150	138	NY.	2,183	1,541	1,439	2,065	1,464	1,361
DE.	57	39	32	47	32	31	NC	614	505	488	495	435	403
DC	94	84	81	93	82	77	ND	41	33	32	32	26	25
FL.	1,395	933	882	1,307	813	772	OH	1,155	640	610	1,017	535	520
							OK	375	271	253	315	221	209
GA	816	617	559	700	514	489	OR	289	224	234	254	190	198
HI	125	125	118	177	180	166	PA.	1,173	835	777	1,006	704	656
ID	80	57	58	59	45	46	RI	93	76	74	82	61	59
IL	1,151	820	779	1,056	767	777							
IN	470	298	300	382	255	269							
IA	184	129	123	141	103	100	SC.	364	309	295	297	251	249
KS.	184	115	117	144	80	83	SD.	50	44	43	40	37	37
KY.	520	396	403	413	337	337	TN.	662	511	496	554	425	415
LA	711	516	500	629	463	448	TX.	2,558	1,401	1,333	2,246	1,255	1,215
ME	132	109	102	112	89	81	UT.	119	88	82	90	73	68
							VT.	59	44	41	46	34	32
MD	399	264	219	365	237	199	VA.	546	362	336	450	282	262
MA	410	261	232	315	205	182	WA	476	307	295	417	260	241
MI	971	683	611	806	515	457	WV	309	247	227	253	208	185
MN	308	208	196	240	172	164	WI	320	182	193	220	124	129
MS	480	288	276	383	232	226	WY	34	23	22	28	19	19

[1] Includes Guam and the Virgin Islands. Several outlying areas receive nutrition assistance grants in lieu of food stamp assistance (e.g., Puerto Rico, American Samoa and the Northern Marianas).

Source of Tables 549 and 550: U.S. Dept. of Agriculture, Food and Nutrition Service. In "Annual Historical Review of FNS Programs" and unpublished data.

356   Social Insurance and Human Services

No. 551. Selected Characteristics of Food Stamp Households and Participants: 1990 to 1999

[For years ending September 30. Data for 1990-1992 exclude Guam and the Virgin Islands. Based on a sample of households from the Food Stamp Quality Control System]

Year	Households				Participants		
		Percent of total				Percent of total	
	Total (1,000)	With children	With elderly [1]	With disabled [2]	Total (1,000)	Children	Elderly [1]
1990	7,803	60.3	18.1	8.9	20,411	49.6	7.7
1991	8,855	60.4	16.4	9.0	22,963	52.0	7.0
1992	10,049	62.2	15.4	9.5	25,743	51.9	6.6
1993	10.791	62.1	15.5	10.7	27,595	51.5	6.8
1994	11,091	61.1	15.8	12.5	28,009	51.4	7.0
1995	10,883	59.7	16.0	18.9	26,955	51.5	7.1
1996	10,552	59.5	16.2	20.2	25,926	51.0	7.3
1997	9,452	58.3	17.6	22.3	23,117	51.4	7.9
1998	8,246	58.3	18.2	24.4	19,969	52.8	8.2
1999	7,670	55.7	20.1	26.5	18,149	51.5	9.4

[1] Persons 60 years old and over. [2] Beginning 1995, disabled households are defined as households with at least one member under age 65 who received SSI, or at least one member age 18 to 61 who received social security, veterans benefits, or other government benefits as a result of a disability. For years prior to 1995, disabled households are defined as households with SSI but no members over age 59. The substantial increase in the percentage of households with a disabled member between 1994 and 1995 is due in part to the change in the definition of disabled households. Using the previous definition, 13.3 percent of households included a disabled person in fiscal year 1995.

No. 552. Food Stamp Households and Participants—Summary: 1999

[For year ending September 30. Based on a sample of 47,553 households from the Food Stamp Quality Control System]

Household type and income source	Households		Age, sex, race, and Hispanic origin	Participants	
	Number (1,000)	Percent		Number (1,000)	Percent
Total	7,670	100.0	Total [1]	18,149	100.0
With children	4,275	55.7	Children	9,354	51.5
Single-parent households	2,928	38.2	Under 5 years old	3,025	16.7
Married-couple households	964	12.6	5 to 17 years old	6,329	34.9
Other.	702	9.1	Adults	8,789	48.5
With elderly	1,543	20.1	18 to 35 years old	3,785	20.9
Living alone	1,212	15.8	36 to 59 years old	3,305	18.2
Not living alone	330	4.3	60 years old and over	1,699	9.4
Disabled	2,031	26.5			
Living alone	1,162	15.1	Male	7,226	39.8
Not living alone	869	11.3	Female.	10,878	59.9
Earned income	2,058	26.8	White, non-Hispanic	7,363	40.6
Wages and salaries	1,914	25.0	Black, non-Hispanic	6,543	36.1
Unearned income	6,069	79.1	Hispanic	3,279	18.1
TANF [2]	2,096	27.3	Asian	564	3.1
Supplemental Security Income . . .	2,315	30.2	Native American.	281	1.5
Social security.	1,897	24.7	Other	119	0.7
No income	649	8.5			

[1] Includes persons of unknown age not shown separately. [2] Temporary Assistance for Needy Families (TANF) program.

Source of Tables 551 and 552: U.S. Dept. of Agriculture, Food and Nutrition Service, *Characteristics of Food Stamp Households: Fiscal Year 1999*, December 2000.

No. 553. Head Start—Summary: 1980 to 2000

[376 represents 376,000. For years ending September 30; see text, Section 8, State and Local Government Finances and Employment]

Year	Enrollment (1,000)	Appropriation (mil. dol.)	Age and race	Enrollment, 2000 (percent)	Item	Number
1980	376	735	Under 3 years old	6	Average cost per child:	
1985	452	1,075	3 years old.	33	1995	$4,534
1990	541	1,552	4 years old.	56	1999	$5,403
1991	583	1,952	5 years old and over . . .	5	2000	$5,951
1992	621	2,202				
1993	714	2,776			Paid staff (1,000):	
1994	740	3,326	White	30	1995	147
1995	751	3,534	Black	35	1999	172
1996	752	3,569	Hispanic	29	2000	180
1997	794	3,981	American Indian	3	Volunteers (1,000):	
1998	822	4,347	Asian	2	1995	1,235
1999	826	4,658	Hawaiian/		1999	1,327
2000	858	5,267	Pacific Islander	1	2000	1,252

Source: U.S. Administration for Children and Families, "Head Start Statistical Fact Sheet;" <http://www2.acf.dhhs.gov/programs/hsb/research/index.htm>.

U.S. Census Bureau, Statistical Abstract of the United States: 2001

No. 554. Social Assistance—Taxable Establishments, Receipts, Payroll, and Employees by Kind of Business: 1997

[18,051 represents $18,051,000,000]

Kind of business	NAICS code [1]	All firms		Employer firms			
		Establishments (number)	Receipts (mil. dol.)	Establishments (number)	Receipts (mil. dol.)	Annual payroll (mil. dol.)	Paid employees [2] (1,000)
Social assistance	624	583,203	18,051	56,691	12,599	5,766	491.1
Individual & family services	6241	43,070	3,228	9,843	2,636	1,113	68.8
Child & youth services	62411	(NA)	(NA)	1,648	539	210	11.5
Services for elderly & disabled persons . .	62412	(NA)	(NA)	2,976	807	394	32.2
Other individual & family services	62419	(NA)	(NA)	5,219	1,290	508	25.1
Community/emergency & other relief services	6242	1,682	136	344	112	29	1.6
Community food services	62421	(NA)	(NA)	95	18	4	0.4
Community housing services	62422	(NA)	(NA)	167	74	21	1.0
Emergency & other relief services	62423	(NA)	(NA)	82	20	4	0.2
Vocational rehabilitation services	6243	5,762	1,514	2,549	1,432	676	32.0
Child day care services	6244	532,689	13,172	43,955	8,419	3,948	388.7

NA Not available.   [1] North American Industry Classification System, 1997; see text, Section 15, Business Enterprise.   [2] For pay period including March 12.

No. 555. Social Assistance—Tax-Exempt Establishments, Receipts, Payroll, and Employees by Kind of Business: 1997

[44,756 represents $44,756,000,000. Covers establishments with payroll only]

Kind of business	NAICS code [1]	Establishments (number)	Receipts (mil. dol.)	Annual payroll (mil. dol)	Paid employees [2] (1,000)
Social assistance	624	69,737	44,756	18,628	1,253.1
Individual & family services	6241	36,364	26,453	10,781	642.6
Child & youth services	62411	11,086	7,719	3,171	172.0
Services for elderly & disabled persons	62412	9,960	8,217	3,260	226.7
Other individual & family services	62419	15,318	10,516	4,350	243.9
Community/emergency & other relief services . .	6242	9,606	6,085	1,739	100.8
Community food services	62421	2,988	1,598	324	23.0
Community housing services	62422	4,737	2,954	1,079	60.2
Emergency & other relief services	62423	1,881	1,534	336	17.7
Vocational rehabilitation services	6243	5,668	6,462	3,093	269.7
Child day care services	6244	18,099	5,757	3,015	240.0

[1] North American Industry Classification System, 1997; see text, Section 15, Business Enterprise.   [2] For pay period including March 12.

Source of Tables 554 and 555: U.S. Census Bureau, *1997 Economic Census, Health Care and Social Assistance*, Series EC97S62A-US, issued October 1999 and *Nonemployer Statistics*.

No. 556. Social Assistance Services—Revenue for Employer Firms: 1998 and 1999

[In millions of dollars (60,816 represents $60,816,000,000). Based on the North American Industry Classification System (NAICS), see text, Section 15, Business Enterprise]

Kind of business	NAICS code	Total		Taxable firms		Tax-exempt firms	
		1998	1999	1998	1999	1998	1999
Social assistance	624	60,816	66,191	13,170	14,878	47,646	51,313
Individual and family services	6241	30,554	33,174	2,601	2,979	27,953	30,195
Child and youth services	62411	8,294	8,937	581	696	7,713	8,241
Services for elderly and disabled persons . . .	62412	9,566	10,259	794	862	8,772	9,397
Other individual and family services	62419	12,694	13,979	1,226	1,422	11,468	12,557
Community/ emergency and other relief services	6242	6,416	6,981	198	215	6,217	6,765
Community food services	62421	1,766	1,949	(S)	(S)	1,678	1,855
Community housing services	62422	3,221	3,469	95	104	3,127	3,365
Emergency and other relief services	62423	1,428	1,563	(S)	(S)	1,413	1,545
Vocational rehabilitation services	6243	8,719	9,373	1,563	1,741	7,155	7,632
Child day care services	6244	15,127	16,663	8,807	9,943	6,320	6,720

S Figure does not meet publication standards.

Source: U.S. Census Bureau, *Service Annual Survey, 1999.*

No. 557. Child Care Arrangements of Preschool Children by Type of Arrangement: 1991 to 1999

[In percent, except as indicated (8,428 represents 8,428,000). Estimates are based on children 3 to 5 years old who have not entered kindergarten. Based on interviews from a sample survey of the civilian, noninstitutional population in households with telephones; see source for details]

Characteristic	Children		Type of nonparental arrangement [1]			With parental care only
	Number (1,000)	Percent distribution	In relative care	In nonrelative care	In center-based program [2]	
1991, total	8,428	100.0	16.9	14.8	52.8	31.0
1995, total	9,232	100.0	19.4	16.9	55.1	25.9
1999, total	**8,549**	**100.0**	**23.3**	**15.9**	**59.3**	**23.3**
Age:						
3 years old	3,827	44.8	25.1	16.5	45.6	30.7
4 years old	3,722	43.5	22.3	15.3	68.9	18.3
5 years old	1,001	11.7	20.3	16.2	76.1	13.5
Race-ethnicity:						
White, non-Hispanic	5,296	61.9	18.8	19.3	59.4	23.6
Black, non-Hispanic	1,258	14.7	36.0	8.0	72.5	13.1
Hispanic	1,421	16.6	25.9	12.7	44.4	33.6
Other	574	6.7	31.0	9.9	66.0	17.5
Household income:						
Less than $10,001	1,126	13.2	28.9	12.8	56.6	26.6
$10,001 to $20,000	1,395	16.3	29.5	12.9	51.1	28.1
$20,001 to $30,000	1,327	15.5	27.7	12.2	50.8	29.6
$30,001 to $40,000	1,050	12.3	23.3	14.9	54.5	25.3
$40,001 to $50,000	792	9.3	20.9	14.2	59.7	23.1
$50,001 to $75,000	1,351	15.8	17.3	20.5	65.5	19.0
$75,001 or more	1,509	17.7	16.2	21.9	74.0	13.4

[1] Columns do not add to 100.0 because some children participated in more than one type of nonparental arrangement.
[2] Center-based programs include day care centers, head start programs, preschools, prekindergarten, and nursery schools.

Source: U.S. National Center for Education Statistics, *Digest of Education Statistics, 2000.*

No. 558. Licensed Child Care Centers and Family Child Care Providers by State: 2000

[Centers as of February; family child care providers as of August]

State	Licensed child care centers	Licensed family child care providers	State	Licensed child care centers	Licensed family child care providers
United States	**105,564**	**304,700**	Missouri	1,515	2,720
			Montana	251	1,525
Alabama	1,432	2,840	Nebraska	746	3,397
Alaska	225	2,258	Nevada	406	645
Arizona	2,299	4,206	New Hampshire	936	449
Arkansas	1,935	1,802			
California	13,385	41,590	New Jersey	3,700	5,100
			New Mexico	636	299
Colorado	2,594	5,372	New York	3,632	21,752
Connecticut	1,648	4,341	North Carolina	3,895	5,330
Delaware	296	1,835	North Dakota	116	2,325
District of Columbia	360	234			
Florida	6,232	8,210	Ohio	3,370	11,923
			Oklahoma	1,964	4,278
Georgia	2,454	6,999	Oregon	868	9,300
Hawaii	500	501	Pennsylvania	3,625	4,850
Idaho	504	1,203	Rhode Island	402	914
Illinois	3,022	9,992			
Indiana	681	3,456	South Carolina	1,779	1,848
			South Dakota	196	1,047
Iowa	1,526	5,062	Tennessee	3,152	2,830
Kansas	1,378	7,623	Texas	7,966	14,517
Kentucky	2,040	4,804	Utah	302	1,844
Louisiana	2,110	12,855			
Maine	904	2,400	Vermont	528	1,420
			Virginia	2,456	4,976
Maryland	2,345	11,239	Washington	1,974	7,211
Massachusetts	2,341	10,710	West Virginia	400	4,216
Michigan	4,837	15,746	Wisconsin	2,289	7,615
Minnesota	1,575	15,559	Wyoming	208	646
Mississippi	1,629	886			

Source: Children's Foundation, Washington, DC, *Child Care Center Licensing Study and Family Child Care Licensing Study,* annual (copyright).

No. 559. Charity Contributions—Average Dollar Amount: 1991 to 1998

[Estimates cover households' contribution activity (both cash and in-kind) for the year and are based on respondents' replies as to contribution and volunteer activity of household. For 1998, based on a sample survey of 2,553 persons 18 years old and over conducted during the spring of the following year and subject to sampling variability; see source]

Year and age	All contributing households		Contributors and volunteers		Household income	All contributing households		Contributors and volunteers	
	Average amount (dol.)	Percent of household income	Average amount (dol.)	Percent of household income		Average amount (dol.)	Percent of household income	Average amount (dol.)	Percent of household income
1991	899	2.2	1,155	2.6	1998—				
1995	1,017	2.2	1,279	2.6	Under $10,000	329	5.2	419	6.3
					$10,000-$19,999	495	3.3	633	4.2
1998, total	1,075	2.1	1,339	2.5	$20,000-$29,999	552	2.2	650	2.6
18-24 years	478	1.2	598	1.4	$30,000-$39,999	734	2.1	886	2.5
25-34 years	768	1.5	875	1.8	$40,000-$49,999	951	2.1	1,073	2.4
35-44 years	1,071	1.9	1,273	2.2	$50,000-$59,999	1,041	1.9	1,189	2.2
45-54 years	1,375	2.2	1,720	2.6	$60,000-$74,999	1,696	2.6	1,948	3.0
55-64 years	1,345	2.5	1,716	3.2	$75,000-$99,999	1,394	1.6	1,748	2.0
65-74 years	897	2.5	1,212	3.0	$100,000 and over	2,550	2.2	3,029	2.6
75 years and over	1,242	4.6	1,781	5.7					
					Itemizers [1]	1,509	2.4	1,791	2.8
White	1,174	2.2	1,466	2.7	Claimed charitable				
Black	658	1.8	789	2.1	deduction	1,798	2.7	2,084	3.1
					Didn't claim charitable deduction	426	0.9	487	1.1
Hispanic [2]	504	1.1	500	1.2	Nonitemizers	619	1.7	774	2.0

[1] Persons who itemized their deductions on their 1998 federal tax returns.   [2] Hispanic persons may be of any race.

No. 560. Charity Contributions—Percent of Households Contributing by Dollar Amount, 1991 to 1998, and Type of Charity, 1998

[In percent, except as noted. See headnote, Table 559]

Annual amount of household contributions	All households			Givers			Type of charity	1998	
	1991	1995	1998	1991	1995	1998		Percentage of households	Average contribution [1] (dol.)
None	27.8	31.5	29.9	(X)	(X)	(X)	Arts, culture, humanities	11.5	221
Givers	72.2	68.5	70.1	100.0	100.0	100.0	Education	12.6	382
$1 to $100	14.9	15.2	15.6	24.9	24.3	22.2	Environment	12.4	194
$101 to $200	8.1	7.2	8.8	13.5	11.6	12.5	Health	20.8	234
$201 to $300	7.3	5.7	6.9	12.2	9.2	9.9	Human services	27.3	250
$301 to $400	3.3	4.7	5.6	5.6	7.5	8.0	International	4.5	279
$401 to $500	3.2	5.2	4.3	5.4	8.3	6.1	Private, community		
$501 to $600	2.6	3.0	3.3	4.4	4.7	4.7	foundations	4.8	271
$601 to $700	2.5	2.6	2.6	4.2	4.1	3.7	Public, societal benefit	11.1	134
$701 to $999	3.4	3.7	4.3	5.7	6.0	6.1	Recreation - adults	5.0	144
$1,000 or more	14.5	15.2	18.8	24.2	24.3	26.8	Religion	45.2	1,002
Not reported	12.4	5.9	(X)	(X)	(X)	(X)	Youth development	21.4	174

X Not applicable.   [1] Average contribution per contributing household.

Source of Tables 559 and 560: Hodgkinson, Virginia, Murray Weitzman, and the Gallup Organization, Inc., *Giving and Volunteering in the United States: 1992 and 1996 Editions.* (Copyright and published by INDEPENDENT SECTOR, Washington, DC, fall 1992 and 1996.) and Saxon-Harrold, Susan K.E., Murray Weitzman, and the Gallup Organization, Inc., *Giving and Volunteering in the United States: 1999 Edition.* (Copyright and published by INDEPENDENT SECTOR, Washington, DC, 2000.)

No. 561. Private Philanthropy Funds by Source and Allocation: 1980 to 2000

[In billions of dollars (48.6 represents $48,600,000,000). Estimates for sources of funds based on U.S. Internal Revenue Service reports of individual charitable deductions, household surveys of giving by Independent Sector, and, for 1980 and 1985, an econometric model. For corporate giving, data are corporate charitable deductions from the US Internal Revenue Service and the contributions made by corporate foundations as reported by the Foundation Center. Data about foundation donations are based upon surveys of foundations and data provided by the Foundation Center. Estimates of the allocation of funds were derived from surveys of nonprofits conducted by various sources]

Source and allocation	1980	1985	1990	1992	1993	1994	1995	1996	1997	1998	1999	2000
Total funds	48.6	71.7	101.4	110.4	116.5	119.2	124.0	138.6	153.8	172.1	190.8	203.5
Individuals	40.7	57.4	81.0	87.7	92.0	92.5	95.4	107.6	118.6	133.0	145.0	152.1
Foundations [1]	2.8	4.9	7.2	8.6	9.5	9.7	10.6	12.0	13.9	17.0	20.5	24.5
Corporations	2.3	4.6	5.5	5.9	6.5	7.0	7.3	7.5	8.6	8.5	9.7	10.9
Charitable bequests	2.9	4.8	7.6	8.2	8.5	10.0	10.7	11.5	12.6	13.6	15.6	16.0
Allocation:												
Religion	22.2	38.2	49.8	51.0	52.9	56.4	58.1	61.9	64.7	68.2	71.2	74.3
Health	5.3	7.7	9.9	10.2	10.8	11.5	12.6	13.9	14.0	16.9	18.0	18.8
Education	5.0	8.2	12.4	14.3	15.4	16.6	17.6	19.2	22.2	25.3	27.5	28.2
Human service	4.9	8.5	11.8	11.6	12.5	11.7	11.7	12.2	12.7	16.1	17.4	18.0
Arts, culture and humanities	3.2	5.1	7.9	9.3	9.6	9.7	10.0	10.9	10.6	10.5	11.1	11.5
Public/societal benefit	1.5	2.2	4.9	5.0	5.4	6.1	7.1	7.6	8.4	10.9	11.0	11.6
Environment/wildlife	(2)	(2)	2.5	2.9	3.0	3.3	3.8	3.8	4.1	5.3	5.8	6.2
International	(2)	(2)	1.3	1.5	1.6	1.9	1.8	1.7	2.0	2.1	2.6	2.7
Unallocated [3]	4.6	-2.9	-3.0	-0.5	-0.9	-4.4	-7.0	-5.2	1.4	-2.4	-2.5	32.2
Gifts to foundations	2.0	4.7	3.8	5.0	6.3	6.3	8.5	12.6	14.0	19.2	28.8	(2)

[1] Data from Foundation Center.   [2] Included in "Unallocated."   [3] Money received by charities but not allocated to sources.
Source: AAFRC Trust for Philanthropy, Indianapolis, IN, *Giving USA,* annual (copyright).

No. 562. Foundations—Number and Finances: 1975 to 1999

[30.1 represents $30,100,000,000. Covers nongovernmental nonprofit organizations with funds and programs managed by their own trustees or directors, whose goals were to maintain or aid social, educational, religious, or other activities deemed to serve the common good. Excludes organizations that make general appeals to the public for funds, act as trade associations for industrial or other special groups, or do not currently award grants. Constant dollar figures based on Consumer Price Index, all urban consumers, supplied by US Bureau of Labor Statistics. Minus sign (-) indicates decrease]

| | | Assets | | | | Grants [2] | | | | Grants received | | | |
| | | Current dollars | | Constant (1975) dollars | | Current dollars | | Constant (1975) dollars | | Current dollars | | Constant (1975) dollars | |
Year	Number of foundations	Amount (bil. dol)	Percent change[1]	Amount (bil. dol)	Percent change[1]	Amount (bil. dol)	Percent change[1]	Amount (bil. dol)	Percent change[1]	Amount (bil. dol)	Percent change[1]	Amount (bil. dol)	Percent change[1]
1975	21,877	30.1	(X)	30.1	(X)	1.9	(X)	1.9	(X)	(NA)	(X)	(NA)	(X)
1980	22,088	48.2	15.8	31.5	2.0	3.4	20.4	2.2	6.0	2.0	-10.4	1.6	-21.1
1985	25,639	102.1	37.8	51.0	33.1	6.0	19.6	3.0	15.5	4.7	40.8	2.9	35.9
1990	32,401	142.5	3.6	58.7	-1.7	8.7	9.7	3.6	4.1	5.0	-10.0	2.5	-14.6
1991	33,356	162.9	14.3	64.4	9.7	9.2	6.1	3.6	1.8	5.5	9.9	2.6	5.6
1992	35,765	176.8	8.5	67.8	5.4	10.2	10.9	3.9	7.6	6.2	13.1	2.9	9.7
1993	37,571	189.2	7.0	70.5	3.9	11.1	8.8	4.1	5.7	7.8	25.6	3.5	21.9
1994	38,807	195.8	3.5	71.1	0.9	11.3	1.6	4.1	-0.9	8.1	4.2	3.6	1.5
1995	40,140	226.7	15.8	80.0	12.6	12.3	8.6	4.3	5.6	10.3	27.0	4.4	23.5
1996	41,588	267.6	18.0	91.8	14.6	13.8	12.9	4.8	9.6	16.0	56.1	6.7	51.7
1997	44,146	329.9	23.3	110.4	20.3	16.0	15.5	5.4	12.8	15.8	-1.2	6.4	-4.5
1998	46,832	385.1	16.7	127.1	15.1	19.5	21.7	6.4	19.7	22.6	42.6	9.0	40.4
1999	50,201	448.6	16.5	(NA)	(NA)	23.3	19.8	(NA)	(NA)	32.1	42.1	(NA)	(NA)

NA Not available. X Not applicable. [1] Percent change from immediate preceding year. [2] Includes grants, scholarships. and employee matching gifts.

Source: The Foundation Center, New York, NY, FC Stats; <http://fdncenter.org/fcstats/index.html>, (copyright).

No. 563. Foundations—Number and Finances by Asset Size: 1999

[448,612 represents $448,612,000,000. Figures are for latest year reported by foundations. See headnote, Table 562]

| Asset size | Number | Assets (mil. dol.) | Gifts received (mil. dol.) | Expenditures (mil. dol.) | Grants (mil. dol.) | Percent distribution | | | | |
						Number	Assets	Gifts received	Expenditures	Grants
Total	50,201	448,612	32,077	28,911	23,321	100.0	100.0	100.0	100.0	100.0
Under $50,000	7,553	128	389	509	466	15.1	(Z)	1.3	1.8	2.1
$50,000-$99,999	3,413	250	106	147	127	6.8	0.1	0.3	0.5	0.5
$100,000-$249,999	6,842	1,139	252	334	287	13.6	0.3	0.8	1.2	1.2
$250,000-$499,999	6,224	2,253	357	428	368	12.4	0.5	1.1	1.5	1.6
$500,000-$999,999	6,759	4,857	528	663	549	13.5	1.1	1.6	2.3	2.4
$1,000,000-$4,999,999	12,142	27,510	2,562	2,702	2,260	24.2	6.1	8.0	9.3	9.7
$5,000,000-$9,999,999	3,019	21,137	1,896	1,899	1,562	6.0	4.7	5.9	6.6	6.7
$10,000,000-$49,999,999	3,204	67,517	4,912	5,093	4,052	6.4	15.1	15.3	17.6	17.4
$50,000,000-$99,999,999	494	34,462	2,373	2,339	1,873	1.0	7.7	7.4	8.1	8.0
$100,000,000-$249,999,999	345	51,947	3,115	3,228	2,584	0.7	11.6	9.7	11.2	11.1
$250,000,000 or more	206	237,409	15,584	11,569	9,194	0.4	52.9	48.6	40.0	39.4

Z Less than 0.05 percent.

Source: The Foundation Center, New York, NY. Foundation Yearbook, annual (copyright).

No. 564. Foundations—Grants Reported by Subject Field and Recipient Organization: 1999

[11,574 represents $11,574,000,000. Covers grants of $10,000 or more in size. Based on reports of 1,016 foundations. Grant sample dollar value represented half of all grant dollars awarded by private, corporate, and community foundations. For definition of foundations, see headnote, Table 562]

| Subject field | Number of grants | | Dollar value | | Recipient organization | Number of grants | | Dollar value | |
	Number	Percent distribution	Amount (mil. dol.)	Percent distribution		Number	Percent distribution	Amount (mil. dol.)	Percent distribution
Total	108,169	100.0	11,574	100.0	Arts/humanities organizations	4,035	3.7	407	3.5
Arts and culture	15,878	14.7	1,554	13.4	Community improvement				
Education	22,063	20.4	2,822	24.4	organizations	5,484	5.1	590	5.1
Environment & animals	6,416	5.9	732	6.3	Educational institutions	28,452	26.3	4,070	35.2
Health	12,776	11.8	1,982	17.1	Colleges & universities	13,108	12.1	2,111	18.2
Human services	26,905	24.9	1,869	16.2	Educational support				
International affairs,					agencies	6,763	6.3	971	8.4
development & peace	2,917	2.7	346	3.0	Schools	6,152	5.7	514	4.4
Public/societal benefit	13,379	12.4	1,321	11.4	Environmental agencies	4,139	3.8	442	3.8
Science and technology	2,426	2.2	412	3.6	Hospitals/medical care				
Social sciences	1,811	1.7	262	2.3	facilities	4,162	3.8	623	5.4
Religion	3,447	3.2	263	2.3	Human service agencies	20,787	19.2	1,318	11.4
Other	151	0.1	11	0.1	Museums/historical societies	4,578	4.2	591	5.1

Source: The Foundation Center, New York, NY. Foundation Giving Trends, annual (copyright).

U.S. Census Bureau, Statistical Abstract of the United States: 2001

No. 565. Percent of Adult Population Doing Volunteer Work: 1998

[Volunteers are persons who worked in some way to help others for no monetary pay during the previous year. Based on a sample survey of 2,553 persons 18 years old and over conducted during the spring of the following year and subject to sampling variability; see source]

Age, sex, race, and Hispanic origin	Percent of population volunteering	Average hours volunteered per week	Educational attainment and household income	Percent of population volunteering	Average hours volunteered per week	Type of activity	Percent of population involved in activity
Total..........	55.5	3.5	Elementary school......	29.4	(B)	Arts, culture, humanities..	8.6
			Some high school.......	43.0	3.9	Education............	17.3
18-24 years old....	45.8	3.0	High school graduate....	43.2	2.8	Environment..........	9.2
25-34 years old....	54.9	3.5	Technical, trade, or			Health..............	11.4
35-44 years old....	67.3	3.7	business school........	53.5	3.5	Human services.......	15.9
45-54 years old....	62.7	3.8	Some college.........	67.2	4.8		
55-64 years old....	50.3	3.3	College graduate.......	67.7	3.1	Informal............	24.4
65-74 years old....	46.6	3.6				International, foreign....	2.5
75 years old and over.	43.0	3.1	Under $10,000.........	42.1	3.4	Political organizations...	4.6
			$10,000-$19,999.......	42.2	2.9	Private, community	
Male............	49.4	3.6	$20,000-$29,999.......	43.7	4.0	foundations........	3.4
Female..........	61.7	3.4	$30,000-$39,999.......	54.4	3.4		
			$40,000-$49,999.......	67.5	3.6	Public and societal benefit.	7.9
White...........	58.6	3.5	$50,000-$59,999.......	62.8	4.3	Recreation - adults......	8.6
Black...........	46.6	4.7	$60,000-$74,999.......	71.2	2.9	Religion............	22.8
			$75,000-$99,999.......	64.2	3.5	Work-related organizations.	*0.3
Hispanic [1]......	46.4	2.1	$100,000 or more......	70.5	3.5	Youth development.....	17.6

B Base figure too small to meet statistical standards for reliability.   [1] Hispanic persons may be of any race.

Source: Saxon-Harrold, Susan K.E., Murray Weitzman, and the Gallup Organization, Inc., *Giving and Volunteering in the United States: 1999 Edition.* (Copyright and published by INDEPENDENT SECTOR, Washington, DC, 2000.)

No. 566. Community Service Participation of Students in Grades 6 Through 12: 1996 and 1999

[12,627 represents 12,627,000. Based on the National Household Education Survey, a sample survey of approximately 55,000 households with telephones in the civilian, noninstitutional population; for details, see source]

Characteristic	Students participating in community service (1,000) 1996	1999	Percent students participating in community service 1996	1999	Characteristic	Students participating in community service (1,000) 1996	1999	Percent students participating in community service 1996	1999
Total [1]............	12,627	14,063	49	52	Parent's highest level of education:				
Student's grade:					Less than high school....	834	1,013	34	37
Grades 6 through 8......	5,462	5,610	47	48	High school graduate or				
Grades 9 and 10.......	3,370	3,955	45	50	equivalent...........	3,273	3,125	42	45
Grades 11 and 12......	3,795	4,486	56	61	Voc/tech education after				
Sex:					high school or some				
Male...............	5,971	6,446	45	47	college............	3,617	3,930	48	50
Female..............	6,656	7,617	53	57	College graduate.......	2,250	2,710	58	62
Race/ethnicity:					Graduate or professional				
White, non-Hispanic.....	9,113	9,759	53	56	school............	2,653	3,285	64	65
Black, non-Hispanic.....	1,761	1,993	43	47	School type:				
Hispanic............	1,246	1,587	38	39	Public.............	11,056	12,331	47	50
Other race-ethnicity....	506	724	50	53	Private:				
					Church-related.......	1,270	1,286	69	72
					Not church-related....	301	446	57	68

[1] Includes students with no grade reported.

Source: U.S. National Center for Education Statistics, *Statistics in Brief*, November 1999 (NCES 2000-028).

U.S. Census Bureau, Statistical Abstract of the United States: 2001

Section 12

Labor Force, Employment, and Earnings

This section presents statistics on the labor force; its distribution by occupation and industry affiliation; and the supply of, demand for, and conditions of labor. The chief source of these data is the Current Population Survey (CPS) conducted by the U.S. Census Bureau for the Bureau of Labor Statistics (BLS). Comprehensive historical and current data are available from the BLS Internet site <http://www.bls.gov/cps/home.htm>. These data are published on a current basis by the BLS monthly publication *Employment and Earnings*. Detailed data on the labor force are also available from the Census Bureaus decennial census of population.

Types of data—Most statistics in this section are obtained by two methods: household interviews or questionnaires and reports of establishment payroll records. Each method provides data which the other cannot suitably supply. Population characteristics, for example, are readily obtainable only from the household survey, while detailed industrial classifications can be readily derived only from establishment records.

Household data are obtained from a monthly sample survey of the population. The CPS is used to gather data for the calendar week including the 12th of the month and provides current comprehensive data on the labor force (see text, Section 1, Population). The CPS provides information on the work status of the population without duplication since each person is classified as employed, unemployed, or not in the labor force. Employed persons holding more than one job are counted only once, according to the job at which they worked the most hours during the survey week.

Monthly, quarterly, and annual data from the CPS are published by the Bureau of Labor Statistics in *Employment and Earnings*. Data presented include national totals of the number of persons in the civilian labor force by sex, race, Hispanic origin, and age; the number employed; hours of work; industry and occupational groups; and the number unemployed, reasons for, and duration of unemployment. Annual data shown in this section are averages of monthly figures for each calendar year, unless otherwise specified.

The CPS also produces annual estimates of employment and unemployment for each state, 50 large metropolitan statistical areas, and selected cities. These estimates are published by BLS in its annual *Geographic Profile of Employment and Unemployment*. More detailed geographic data (e.g., for counties and cities) are provided by the decennial population censuses.

Data based on establishment records are compiled by BLS and cooperating state agencies as part of an ongoing Current Employment Statistics program. Survey data, gathered monthly from a sample of employers through mail questionnaires or electronic interviewing, are supplemented by data from other government agencies and adjusted at intervals to data from government social insurance program reports. The estimates exclude self-employed persons, private household workers, unpaid family workers, agricultural workers, and the Armed Forces. In March 2000, reporting establishments employed 6 million manufacturing workers (31 percent of the total manufacturing employment at the time), 18 million workers in private nonmanufacturing industries (20 percent of the total in private nonmanufacturing), and 15 million federal, state, and local government employees (72 percent of total government).

The establishment survey counts workers each time they appear on a payroll during the reference period (as with the CPS, the week including the 12th of the month). Thus, unlike the CPS, a person with two jobs is counted twice. The establishment survey is designed to provide detailed industry information for the nation,

U.S. Census Bureau, Statistical Abstract of the United States: 2001

states, and metropolitan areas on non-farm wage and salary employment, average weekly hours, and average hourly and weekly earnings. Establishment survey data also are published in *Employment and Earnings*. Historical national data are available on the site <http://www.bls.gov/ces/home.htm>.

In June 2000, BLS began to phase in a comprehensive sample redesign of the establishment survey, changing from a quota sample to a probability-based sample. Probability-based sample estimates for the wholesale trade industry were published at that time. In June 2001, estimates for the mining, construction, and manufacturing industries were published under the new sample design for the first time. Redesigned samples for the remaining industry divisions will be phased in during the next 2 years. More information on the sample redesign appears in "BLS Establishment Estimates Revised to Incorporate March 1999 Benchmarks" and "BLS Establishment Estimates Revised to Incorporate March 2000 Benchmarks" in the June 2000 and June 2001 issues, respectively, of *Employment and Earnings*, as well as the Establishment Data portion of the Explanatory Notes and Estimates of Error section of *Employment and Earnings*.

Labor force—According to the CPS definitions, the civilian labor force comprises all civilians in the noninstitutional population 16 years and over classified as "employed" or "unemployed" according to the following criteria: Employed civilians comprise (a) all civilians, who, during the reference week, did any work for pay or profit (minimum of an hour's work) or worked 15 hours or more as unpaid workers in a family enterprise and (b) all civilians who were not working but who had jobs or businesses from which they were temporarily absent for noneconomic reasons (illness, weather conditions, vacation, labor-management dispute, etc.) whether they were paid for the time off or were seeking other jobs. Unemployed persons comprise all civilians who had no employment during the reference week, who made specific efforts to find a job within the previous 4 weeks (such as applying directly to an employer or to a public employment service or checking

with friends) and who were available for work during that week, except for temporary illness. Persons on layoff from a job and expecting recall also are classified as unemployed. All other civilian persons, 16 years old and over, are "not in the labor force."

Beginning in 1982, changes in the estimation procedures and the introduction of 1980 census data caused substantial increases in the population and estimates of persons in all labor force categories. Rates on labor force characteristics, however, were essentially unchanged. In order to avoid major breaks in series, some 30,000 labor force series were adjusted back to 1970. The effect of the 1982 revisions on various data series and an explanation of the adjustment procedure used are described in "Revisions in the Current Population Survey in January 1982," in the February 1982 issue of *Employment and Earnings*. The revisions did not, however, smooth out the breaks in series occurring between 1972 and 1979, and data users should make allowances for them in making certain data comparisons.

Beginning in January 1994, several changes were introduced into the CPS that effect all data comparisons with prior years. These changes include the results of a major redesign of the survey questionnaire and collection methodology, revisions to some of the labor force concepts and definitions, and the introduction of 1990 census population controls, adjusted for the estimated undercount. An explanation of the changes and their effects on the labor force data appears in "Revisions in the Current Population Survey Effective January 1994" in the February 1994 issue of *Employment and Earnings*.

Beginning 1996, 1990 census population controls, adjusted for the estimated undercount, were extended back to January 1990. A discussion of the changes and their effects on the labor force data appears in "Revisions In Household Survey Data Effective February 1996" in the March 1996 issue of *Employment and Earnings*.

Beginning in January 1997, the CPS reflects updated 1990 census-based population controls. The greatest impact of the new population controls was on estimates for persons of Hispanic origin. An explanation of the changes and their effects on labor force estimates appear in "Revisions in the Current Population Survey Effective January 1997" in the February 1997 issue of *Employment and Earnings*.

Beginning in January 1998, the CPS reflects the introduction of new composite estimation procedures and revised 1990 census-based population controls. An explanation of the changes and their effects on labor force estimates appear in "Revisions in the Current Population Survey Effective January 1998" in the February 1998 issue of *Employment and Earnings*.

Beginning in January 1999 and January 2000, the CPS reflects the introduction of revised 1990 census-based population controls that incorporate newly updated information on immigration. An explanation of the changes and their effects on labor force estimates appear in "Revisions in the Current Population Survey Effective January 1999" and "Revisions in the Current Population Survey Effective January 2000" in the February 1999 and February 2000 issues, respectively, of *Employment and Earnings*.

Hours and earnings—Average hourly earnings, based on establishment data, are gross earnings (i.e., earnings before payroll deductions) and include overtime premiums; they exclude irregular bonuses and value of payments in kind. Hours are those for which pay was received. Wages and salaries from the CPS consist of total monies received for work performed by an employee during the income year. It includes wages, salaries, commissions, tips, piece-rate payments, and cash bonuses earned before deductions were made for taxes, bonds, union dues, etc. Persons who worked 35 hours or more are classified as working full time.

Industry and occupational groups— Industry data derived from the CPS for 1983-91 utilize the 1980 census industrial classification developed from the 1972 SIC. CPS data from 1971 to 1982

were based on the 1970 census classification system which was developed from the 1967 SIC. Most of the industry categories were not affected by the change in classification.

Establishments responding to the establishment survey are classified according to the *Standard Industrial Classification (SIC) Manual*. See text, Section 15, Business Enterprise, for information about the SIC manual.

The occupational classification system used in the 1980 census and in the CPS for 1983-91, evolved from the 1980 Standard Occupational Classification (SOC) system, first introduced in 1977. Occupational categories used in the 1980 census classification system are so radically different from the 1970 census system used in the CPS through 1982, that their implementation represented a break in historical data series. In cases where data have not yet been converted to the 1980 classifications and still reflect the 1970 classifications (e.g., Table 704), comparisons between the two systems should not be made. To help users bridge the data gap, a limited set of estimates was developed for the 1972-82 period based on the new classifications. The estimates were developed by means of applying conversion factors created by double coding a 20-percent sample of CPS occupational records for 6 months during 1981-82. For further details, contact BLS.

Beginning in January 1992, the occupational and industrial classification system used in the 1990 census were introduced into the CPS. (These systems were largely based on the 1980 Standard Occupational Classification and the 1987 Standard Industrial Classification.) There were a few breaks in comparability between the 1980 and 1990 census-based systems, particularly within the "technical, sales, and administrative support" categories. The most notable changes in industry classification were the shift of several industries from "business services" to "professional services" and the splitting of some industries into smaller, more detailed categories. A number of industry titles were changed as well, with no change in content.

Labor Force, Employment, and Earnings   365

Productivity—BLS publishes data on productivity as measured by output per hour (labor productivity), output per combined unit of labor and capital input (multifactor productivity), and, for manufacturing industries, output per combined unit of capital, labor, energy, materials, and purchased service inputs. Labor productivity and related indexes are published for the business sector as a whole and its major subsectors: nonfarm business, manufacturing, nonfinancial corporations, and over 450 specific industries. Multifactor productivity and related measures are published for the private business sector and its major subsectors. Productivity indexes which take into account capital, labor, energy, materials, and service inputs are published for the 18 major industry groups which comprise the manufacturing sector, the utility services industry group, for 108 three-digit SIC manufacturing industries, and railroad transportation. The major sector data are published in the BLS quarterly news release, *Productivity and Costs* and in the annual *Multifactor Productivity Measures* release. Industry productivity measures are published annually in the news releases *Productivity and Costs, Manufacturing Industries, and Productivity and Costs, Services - Producing and Mining Industries*. Detailed information on methods, limitations, and data sources appears in the BLS *Handbook of Methods*, BLS Bulletin 2490 (1997), Chapters 10 and 11.

Unions—As defined here, unions include traditional labor unions and employee associations similar to labor unions. Data on union membership status provided by BLS are for employed wage and salary workers and relate to their principal job. Earnings by union membership status are usual weekly earnings of full-time wage and salary workers. The information is collected through the Current Population Survey. Collective bargaining settlements data are available for bargaining situations involving 1,000 or more workers in private industry and state and local government.

Work stoppages—Work stoppages include all strikes and lockouts known to BLS which last for at least 1 full day or shift and involve 1,000 or more workers. All stoppages, whether or not authorized by a union, legal or illegal, are counted. Excluded are work slowdowns and instances where employees report to work late or leave early to attend mass meetings or mass rallies.

Seasonal adjustment—Many economic statistics reflect a regularly recurring seasonal movement which can be estimated on the basis of past experience. By eliminating that part of the change which can be ascribed to usual seasonal variation (e.g., climate or school openings and closings), it is possible to observe the cyclical and other nonseasonal movements in the series. However, in evaluating deviations from the seasonal pattern—that is, changes in a seasonally adjusted series—it is important to note that seasonal adjustment is merely an approximation based on past experience. Seasonally adjusted estimates have a broader margin of possible error than the original data on which they are based, since they are subject not only to sampling and other errors, but also are affected by the uncertainties of the adjustment process itself.

Statistical reliability—For discussion of statistical collection, estimation, sampling procedures, and measures of statistical reliability applicable to Census Bureau and BLS data, see Appendix III.

No. 567. Employment Status of the Civilian Population: 1960 to 2000

[In thousands (117,245 represents 117,245,000), except as indicated. Annual averages of monthly figures. For the civilian noninstitutional population 16 years old and over. Based on Current Population Survey; see text, Section 1, Population, and Appendix III]

Year	Civilian noninsti- tutional population	Civilian labor force			Employ- ment/ population ratio [1]	Unemployed		Not in labor force	
		Total	Percent of population	Employed		Number	Percent of labor force	Number	Percent of population
1960	117,245	69,628	59.4	65,778	56.1	3,852	5.5	47,617	40.6
1970	137,085	82,771	60.4	78,678	57.4	4,093	4.9	54,315	39.6
1980	167,745	106,940	63.8	99,303	59.2	7,637	7.1	60,806	36.2
1981	170,130	108,670	63.9	100,397	59.0	8,273	7.6	61,460	36.1
1982	172,271	110,204	64.0	99,526	57.8	10,678	9.7	62,067	36.0
1983	174,215	111,550	64.0	100,834	57.9	10,717	9.6	62,665	36.0
1984	176,383	113,544	64.4	105,005	59.5	8,539	7.5	62,839	35.6
1985	178,206	115,461	64.8	107,150	60.1	8,312	7.2	62,744	35.2
1986	180,587	117,834	65.3	109,597	60.7	8,237	7.0	62,752	34.7
1987	182,753	119,865	65.6	112,440	61.5	7,425	6.2	62,888	34.4
1988	184,613	121,669	65.9	114,968	62.3	6,701	5.5	62,944	34.1
1989	186,393	123,869	66.5	117,342	63.0	6,528	5.3	62,523	33.5
1990 [2] . . .	189,164	125,840	66.5	118,793	62.8	7,047	5.6	63,324	33.5
1991	190,925	126,346	66.2	117,718	61.7	8,628	6.8	64,578	33.8
1992	192,805	128,105	66.4	118,492	61.5	9,613	7.5	64,700	33.6
1993	194,838	129,200	66.3	120,259	61.7	8,940	6.9	65,638	33.7
1994 [2] . . .	196,814	131,056	66.6	123,060	62.5	7,996	6.1	65,758	33.4
1995	198,584	132,304	66.6	124,900	62.9	7,404	5.6	66,280	33.4
1996	200,591	133,943	66.8	126,708	63.2	7,236	5.4	66,647	33.2
1997 [2] . . .	203,133	136,297	67.1	129,558	63.8	6,739	4.9	66,837	32.9
1998 [2] . . .	205,220	137,673	67.1	131,463	64.1	6,210	4.5	67,547	32.9
1999 [2] . . .	207,753	139,368	67.1	133,488	64.3	5,880	4.2	68,385	32.9
2000 [2] . . .	209,699	140,863	67.2	135,208	64.5	5,655	4.0	68,836	32.8

[1] Civilian employed as a percent of the civilian noninstitutional population.   [2] Data not strictly comparable with data for earlier years, See text, this section, and February 1994, March 1996, February 1997, 1998, 1999, and 2000 issues of *Employment and Earnings.*

Source: U.S. Bureau of Labor Statistics, Bulletin 2307; and *Employment and Earnings*, monthly.

No. 568. Civilian Labor Force and Participation Rates With Projections: 1980 to 2008

[106.9 represents 106,900,000. For civilian noninstitutional population 16 years old and over. Annual averages of monthly figures. Rates are based on annual average civilian noninstitutional population of each specified group and represent proportion of each specified group in the civilian labor force. Based on Current Population Survey; see text, Section 1, Population, and Appendix III]

Race, sex, and age	Civilian labor force (millions)						Participation rate (percent)					
	1980	1990 [1]	1995	1999 [1]	2000 [1]	2008, proj.	1980	1990 [1]	1995	1999 [1]	2000 [1]	2008, proj.
Total [2]	106.9	125.8	132.3	139.4	140.9	154.6	63.8	66.5	66.6	67.1	67.2	67.6
White	93.6	107.4	112.0	116.5	117.6	126.7	64.1	66.9	67.1	67.3	67.4	67.9
Male	54.5	59.6	61.1	63.4	63.9	67.7	78.2	77.1	75.7	75.6	75.4	74.5
Female	39.1	47.8	50.8	53.1	53.7	59.0	51.2	57.4	59.0	59.6	59.8	61.5
Black	10.9	13.7	14.8	16.4	16.6	19.1	61.0	64.0	63.7	65.8	65.8	66.3
Male	5.6	6.8	7.2	7.7	7.8	8.9	70.3	71.0	69.0	68.7	69.0	68.3
Female	5.3	6.9	7.6	8.7	8.8	10.2	53.1	58.3	59.5	63.5	63.2	64.6
Hispanic [3]	6.1	10.7	12.3	14.7	15.4	19.6	64.0	67.4	65.8	67.7	68.6	67.7
Male	3.8	6.5	7.4	8.5	8.9	11.0	81.4	81.4	79.1	79.8	80.6	77.9
Female	2.3	4.2	4.9	6.1	6.4	8.6	47.4	53.1	52.6	55.9	56.9	57.9
Male	61.5	69.0	71.4	74.5	75.2	81.1	77.4	76.4	75.0	74.7	74.7	73.7
16 to 19 years	5.0	4.1	4.0	4.3	4.3	4.8	60.5	55.7	54.8	52.9	53.0	52.9
20 to 24 years	8.6	7.9	7.3	7.3	7.6	8.3	85.9	84.4	83.1	81.9	82.6	81.4
25 to 34 years	17.0	19.9	18.7	17.3	17.1	17.1	95.2	94.1	93.0	93.3	93.4	93.2
35 to 44 years	11.8	17.5	19.2	20.4	20.3	18.3	95.5	94.3	92.3	92.8	92.6	92.3
45 to 54 years	9.9	11.1	13.4	15.4	16.0	19.0	91.2	90.7	88.8	88.8	88.6	88.8
55 to 64 years	7.2	6.6	6.5	7.5	7.6	10.8	72.1	67.8	66.0	67.9	67.3	69.4
65 years and over . .	1.9	2.0	2.2	2.3	2.4	2.8	19.0	16.3	16.8	16.9	17.5	17.8
Female	45.5	56.8	60.9	64.9	65.6	73.4	51.5	57.5	58.9	60.0	60.2	61.9
16 to 19 years	4.4	3.7	3.7	4.0	4.1	4.6	52.9	51.6	52.2	51.0	51.3	52.4
20 to 24 years	7.3	6.8	6.3	6.6	6.8	7.5	68.9	71.3	70.3	73.2	73.3	74.6
25 to 34 years	12.3	16.1	15.5	14.8	14.6	15.3	65.5	73.5	74.9	76.4	76.3	79.0
35 to 44 years	8.6	14.7	16.6	17.5	17.5	16.6	65.5	76.4	77.2	77.2	77.3	80.0
45 to 54 years	7.0	9.1	11.8	14.0	14.5	17.8	59.9	71.2	74.4	76.7	76.8	80.0
55 to 64 years	4.7	4.9	5.4	6.2	6.4	9.8	41.3	45.2	49.2	51.5	51.8	57.7
65 years and over . .	1.2	1.5	1.6	1.7	1.8	1.9	8.1	8.6	8.8	8.9	9.4	9.1

[1] See footnote 2, Table 567.   [2] Includes other races, not shown separately.   [3] Persons of Hispanic origin may be of any race.

Source: U.S. Bureau of Labor Statistics, *Employment and Earnings*, monthly, January issues; *Monthly Labor Review*, November 1999; and unpublished data.

No. 569. Employment Status of the Civilian Population: 1970 to 2000

[In thousands (137,085 represents 137,085,000), except as indicated. Annual averages of monthly figures. For the civilian noninstitutional population 16 years old and over. Based on Current Population Survey; see text, Section 1, Population, and Appendix III]

Year, sex, race, and Hispanic origin	Civilian noninstitu- tional popula- tion	Civilian labor force			Employ- ment/ popu- lation ratio [1]	Unemployed		Not in labor force	
		Total	Percent of popula- tion	Employed		Number	Percent of labor force	Number	Percent of population
Total: [2]									
1970	137,085	82,771	60.4	78,678	57.4	4,093	4.9	54,315	39.6
1980	167,745	106,940	63.8	99,303	59.2	7,637	7.1	60,806	36.2
1985	178,206	115,461	64.8	107,150	60.1	8,312	7.2	62,744	35.2
1990 [3]	189,164	125,840	66.5	118,793	62.8	7,047	5.6	63,324	33.5
1995	198,584	132,304	66.6	124,900	62.9	7,404	5.6	66,280	33.4
1998 [3]	205,220	137,673	67.1	131,463	64.1	6,210	4.5	67,547	32.9
1999 [3]	207,753	139,368	67.1	133,488	64.3	5,880	4.2	68,385	32.9
2000 [3]	209,699	140,863	67.2	135,208	64.5	5,655	4.0	68,836	32.8
Male:									
1970	64,304	51,228	79.7	48,990	76.2	2,238	4.4	13,076	20.3
1980	79,398	61,453	77.4	57,186	72.0	4,267	6.9	17,945	22.6
1985	84,469	64,411	76.3	59,891	70.9	4,521	7.0	20,058	23.7
1990 [3]	90,377	69,011	76.4	65,104	72.0	3,906	5.7	21,367	23.6
1995	95,178	71,360	75.0	67,377	70.8	3,983	5.6	23,818	25.0
1998 [3]	98,758	73,959	74.9	70,693	71.6	3,266	4.4	24,799	25.1
1999 [3]	99,722	74,512	74.7	71,446	71.6	3,066	4.1	25,210	25.3
2000 [3]	100,731	75,247	74.7	72,293	71.8	2,954	3.9	25,484	25.3
Female:									
1970	72,782	31,543	43.3	29,688	40.8	1,855	5.9	41,239	56.7
1980	88,348	45,487	51.5	42,117	47.7	3,370	7.4	42,861	48.5
1985	93,736	51,050	54.5	47,259	50.4	3,791	7.4	42,686	45.5
1990 [3]	98,787	56,829	57.5	53,689	54.3	3,140	5.5	41,957	42.5
1995	103,406	60,944	58.9	57,523	55.6	3,421	5.6	42,462	41.1
1998 [3]	106,462	63,714	59.8	60,771	57.1	2,944	4.6	42,748	40.1
1999 [3]	108,031	64,855	60.0	62,042	57.4	2,814	4.3	43,175	40.0
2000 [3]	108,968	65,616	60.2	62,915	57.7	2,701	4.1	43,352	39.8
White:									
1970	122,174	73,556	60.2	70,217	57.5	3,339	4.5	48,618	39.8
1980	146,122	93,600	64.1	87,715	60.0	5,884	6.3	52,523	35.9
1985	153,679	99,926	65.0	93,736	61.0	6,191	6.2	53,753	35.0
1990 [3]	160,625	107,447	66.9	102,261	63.7	5,186	4.8	53,178	33.1
1995	166,914	111,950	67.1	106,490	63.8	5,459	4.9	54,965	32.9
1998 [3]	171,478	115,415	67.3	110,931	64.7	4,484	3.9	56,064	32.7
1999 [3]	173,085	116,509	67.3	112,235	64.8	4,273	3.7	56,577	32.7
2000 [3]	174,428	117,574	67.4	113,475	65.1	4,099	3.5	56,854	32.6
Black:									
1973	14,917	8,976	60.2	8,128	54.5	846	9.4	5,941	39.8
1980	17,824	10,865	61.0	9,313	52.2	1,553	14.3	6,959	39.0
1985	19,664	12,364	62.9	10,501	53.4	1,864	15.1	7,299	37.1
1990 [3]	21,477	13,740	64.0	12,175	56.7	1,565	11.4	7,737	36.0
1995	23,246	14,817	63.7	13,279	57.1	1,538	10.4	8,429	36.3
1998 [3]	24,373	15,982	65.6	14,556	59.7	1,426	8.9	8,391	34.4
1999 [3]	24,855	16,365	65.8	15,056	60.6	1,309	8.0	8,490	34.2
2000 [3]	25,218	16,603	65.8	15,334	60.8	1,269	7.6	8,615	34.2
Hispanic: [4]									
1980	9,598	6,146	64.0	5,527	57.6	620	10.1	3,451	36.0
1985	11,915	7,698	64.6	6,888	57.8	811	10.5	4,217	35.4
1990 [3]	15,904	10,720	67.4	9,845	61.9	876	8.2	5,184	32.6
1995	18,629	12,267	65.8	11,127	59.7	1,140	9.3	6,362	34.2
1998 [3]	21,070	14,317	67.9	13,291	63.1	1,026	7.2	6,753	32.1
1999 [3]	21,650	14,665	67.7	13,720	63.4	945	6.4	6,985	32.3
2000 [3]	22,393	15,368	68.6	14,492	64.7	876	5.7	7,025	31.4
Mexican:									
1986 [3]	7,377	4,941	67.0	4,387	59.5	555	11.2	2,436	33.0
1990 [3]	9,752	6,707	68.8	6,146	63.0	561	8.4	3,045	31.2
1995 [3]	11,609	7,765	66.9	7,016	60.4	750	9.7	3,844	33.1
1998 [3]	13,216	9,096	68.8	8,431	63.8	664	7.3	4,121	31.2
1999 [3]	13,582	9,267	68.2	8,656	63.7	611	6.6	4,315	31.8
2000 [3]	14,386	9,955	69.2	9,364	65.1	591	5.9	4,430	30.8
Puerto Rican:									
1986 [3]	1,494	804	53.8	691	46.3	113	14.0	690	46.2
1990 [3]	1,718	960	55.9	870	50.6	91	9.5	758	44.1
1995 [3]	1,896	1,098	57.9	974	51.4	123	11.2	798	42.1
1998 [3]	2,080	1,249	60.0	1,145	55.0	104	8.3	832	40.0
1999 [3]	2,058	1,269	61.6	1,165	56.6	104	8.2	789	38.3
2000 [3]	2,025	1,278	63.1	1,196	59.1	82	6.4	747	36.9
Cuban:									
1986 [3]	842	570	67.7	533	63.3	36	6.4	272	32.3
1990 [3]	918	603	65.7	559	60.9	44	7.2	315	34.3
1995 [3]	1,019	613	60.2	568	55.7	45	7.4	406	39.8
1998 [3]	1,062	651	61.3	612	57.6	39	6.0	411	38.7
1999 [3]	1,141	714	62.6	681	59.7	33	4.6	427	37.4
2000 [3]	1,104	680	61.6	650	58.9	30	4.4	424	38.4

[1] Civilian employed as a percent of the civilian noninstitutional population.   [2] Includes other races, not shown separately.
[3] See footnote 2, Table 567.   [4] Persons of Hispanic origin may be of any race. Includes persons of other Hispanic origin, not shown separately.

Source: U.S. Bureau of Labor Statistics, Bulletin 2307; and Employment and Earnings, monthly, January issues.

No. 570. Civilian Labor Force—Percent Distribution by Sex and Age: 1970 to 2000

[82,771 represents 82,771,000. For civilian noninstitutional population 16 years old and over. Annual averages of monthly figures. Based on Current Population Survey; see text, Section 1, Population, and Appendix III]

Year and sex	Civilian labor force (1,000)	Percent distribution						
		16 to 19 years	20 to 24 years	25 to 34 years	35 to 44 years	45 to 54 years	55 to 64 years	65 yrs. and over
Total: 1970	82,771	8.8	12.8	20.6	19.9	20.5	13.6	3.9
1980 ¹	106,940	8.8	14.9	27.3	19.1	15.8	11.2	2.9
1990 ¹	125,840	6.2	11.7	28.6	25.5	16.1	9.2	2.7
1995 ¹	132,304	5.9	10.3	25.8	27.0	19.1	9.0	2.9
1999 ¹	139,368	6.0	10.0	23.1	27.2	21.1	9.8	2.9
2000 ¹	140,863	5.9	10.2	22.5	26.9	21.6	9.9	3.0
Male: 1970	51,228	7.8	11.2	22.1	20.4	20.3	13.9	4.2
1980 ¹	61,453	8.1	14.0	27.6	19.3	16.1	11.8	3.1
1990 ¹	69,011	5.9	11.4	2P.8	25.3	16.1	9.6	2.9
1995 ¹	71,360	5.7	10.3	26.2	26.9	18.8	9.1	3.1
1999 ¹	74,512	5.8	9.8	23.2	27.4	20.7	10.0	3.1
2000 ¹	75,247	5.7	10.0	22.7	27.0	21.2	10.1	3.2
Female: 1970	31,543	10.3	15.5	18.1	18.9	20.7	13.2	3.3
1980 ¹	45,487	9.6	16.1	26.9	19.0	15.4	10.4	2.6
1990 ¹	56,829	6.5	12.0	28.3	25.8	16.1	8.7	2.6
1995 ¹	60,944	6.1	10.4	25.5	27.2	19.4	8.8	2.7
1999 ¹	64,855	6.2	10.2	22.9	27.0	21.6	9.6	2.6
2000 ¹	65,616	6.2	10.3	22.2	26.7	22.1	9.8	2.7

¹ See footnote 2, Table 567.
Source: U.S. Bureau of Labor Statistics, Bulletin 2307, and Employment Earnings, monthly, January issues.

No. 571. Civilian Labor Force and Participation Rates by Educational Attainment, Sex, Race, and Hispanic Origin: 1992 to 2000

[102,387 represents 102,387,000. As of March. For the civilian noninstitutional population 25 to 64 years of age. See Table 604 for unemployment data. Based on Current Population Survey; see text, Section 1, Population, and Appendix III]

Year, sex, and race	Civilian labor force					Participation rate ¹				
		Percent distribution								
	Total (1,000)	Less than high school diploma	High school graduate, no degree	Less than a bachelor's degree	College graduate	Total	Less than high school diploma	High school graduates, no degree	Less than a bachelor's degree	College graduate
Total: ²										
1992	102,387	12.2	36.2	25.2	26.4	79.0	60.3	78.3	83.5	88.4
1995 ³	106,519	10.8	33.1	27.8	28.3	79.3	59.8	77.3	83.2	88.7
1997 ³	110,514	10.9	33.0	27.4	28.6	80.1	61.7	82.5	83.7	88.5
1998 ³	111,857	10.7	32.8	27.4	29.1	80.2	63.0	78.4	83.5	88.0
1999 ³	112,542	10.3	32.3	27.4	30.0	80.0	62.7	78.1	83.0	87.6
2000 ³	114,052	9.8	31.8	27.9	30.4	80.3	62.7	78.4	83.2	87.8
Male:										
1992 . . .	55,917	13.9	34.7	23.8	27.5	88.6	75.1	89.0	91.8	93.7
1995 ³ . .	57,454	12.2	32.3	25.7	29.7	87.4	72.0	86.9	90.1	93.8
1997 ³ . .	59,268	12.8	32.2	25.8	29.2	87.7	75.2	86.4	90.6	93.5
1998 ³ . .	59,905	12.3	32.3	25.8	29.6	87.8	75.3	86.7	90.0	93.4
1999 ³ . .	60,030	11.7	32.0	25.8	30.5	87.5	74.4	86.6	89.4	93.0
2000 ³ . .	60,510	11.1	31.8	26.1	30.9	87.5	74.9	86.2	88.9	93.3
Female:										
1992 . . .	46,469	10.2	37.9	26.9	25.0	70.0	45.6	69.1	76.2	82.2
1995 ³ . .	49,065	9.1	34.1	30.2	26.6	71.5	47.2	68.9	77.3	82.8
1997 ³ . .	51,246	8.7	34.0	29.3	28.0	72.8	47.1	71.4	77.6	83.2
1998 ³ . .	51,953	8.8	33.3	29.3	28.6	73.0	49.8	70.9	77.8	82.3
1999 ³ . .	52,512	8.7	32.7	29.2	29.5	72.8	50.5	70.4	77.4	81.9
2000 ³ . .	53,541	8.4	31.8	30.0	29.8	73.5	50.4	71.2	78.3	82.0
White:										
1992 . . .	87,656	11.3	36.1	25.5	27.1	79.8	61.5	78.7	83.8	88.7
1995 ³ . .	90,192	10.0	32.8	27.8	29.3	80.1	61.6	77.9	83.4	88.8
1997 ³ . .	93,179	10.4	32.8	27.3	29.5	81.0	63.8	79.2	83.9	89.0
1998 ³ . .	93,527	10.2	32.7	27.4	29.8	80.6	63.8	78.6	83.5	88.3
1999 ³ . .	94,216	9.8	32.2	27.2	30.8	80.6	64.2	78.5	83.3	87.9
2000 ³ . .	95,073	9.5	31.8	27.7	31.0	80.8	64.2	78.7	83.1	87.9
Black:										
1992 . . .	10,936	19.2	40.3	24.9	15.6	74.4	55.4	76.9	83.4	89.1
1995 ³ . .	11,695	14.1	38.6	29.6	17.7	74.2	51.0	74.5	82.8	90.9
1997 ³ . .	12,253	14.3	37.8	31.3	16.6	74.9	52.9	75.0	83.8	89.0
1998 ³ . .	12,893	14.3	37.3	30.1	18.2	77.7	59.3	77.0	85.0	88.8
1999 ³ . .	12,945	13.0	37.2	30.4	19.5	76.5	55.1	76.5	82.9	88.6
2000 ³ . .	13,383	11.8	36.1	31.5	20.7	77.9	55.5	77.0	84.2	90.3
Hispanic: ⁴										
1992 . . .	7,702	39.1	30.2	19.3	11.4	73.8	64.6	77.5	84.2	87.1
1995 ³ . .	9,298	38.9	28.2	21.3	11.6	73.2	64.7	75.9	81.9	87.9
1997 ³ . .	10,556	37.4	28.1	22.1	12.4	75.9	66.4	79.4	85.3	87.7
1998 ³ . .	10,922	37.3	29.1	20.3	13.3	75.8	67.9	78.8	82.3	86.9
1999 ³ . .	11,129	36.5	29.2	21.4	12.9	75.7	67.0	79.0	84.0	85.0
2000 ³ . .	11,800	37.1	29.4	21.0	12.5	76.9	69.9	78.5	83.5	87.0

¹ See headnote, Table 568.   ² Includes other races, not shown separately.   ³ See footnote 2, Table 567.   ⁴ Persons of Hispanic origin may be of any race.
Source: U.S. Bureau of Labor Statistics, unpublished data.

U.S. Census Bureau, Statistical Abstract of the United States: 2001

No. 572. Characteristics of the Civilian Labor Force by State: 2000

[In thousands (140,863 represents 140,863,000), except ratio and rate. Preliminary. For civilian noninstitutional population, 16 years old and over. Annual averages of monthly figures. Because of separate processing and weighting procedures, the totals for the United States may differ from results obtained by aggregating totals for states]

State	Total Number	Total Female	Employed Total	Employed Female	Employed/population ratio [1]	Unemployed Total Number	Unemployed Total Female	Unemployed Rate [2] Total	Unemployed Rate [2] Male	Unemployed Rate [2] Female	Participation rate [3] Male	Participation rate [3] Female
United States...	140,863	65,616	135,208	62,915	64.5	5,655	2,701	4.0	3.9	4.1	74.7	60.2
Alabama	2,154	1,030	2,055	981	60.4	99	49	4.6	4.5	4.8	70.7	56.9
Alaska	322	150	301	141	68.6	21	9	6.6	7.2	6.0	79.3	67.8
Arizona	2,347	1,076	2,256	1,029	62.2	91	47	3.9	3.5	4.4	73.6	56.6
Arkansas	1,238	575	1,183	549	59.8	55	26	4.4	4.4	4.5	69.6	56.1
California	17,091	7,776	16,246	7,376	63.7	845	401	4.9	4.8	5.2	75.6	59.1
Colorado	2,276	1,041	2,213	1,013	70.5	63	29	2.7	2.8	2.7	79.6	65.5
Connecticut	1,746	833	1,707	811	67.3	39	21	2.3	2.0	2.6	75.4	62.9
Delaware	409	197	393	189	66.8	16	8	4.0	4.0	4.0	76.0	63.8
District of Columbia	279	144	263	136	63.6	16	8	5.8	5.8	5.7	70.8	64.7
Florida	7,490	3,461	7,221	3,324	60.4	269	137	3.6	3.3	4.0	70.1	55.7
Georgia	4,173	1,993	4,019	1,910	67.4	154	83	3.7	3.3	4.2	77.4	63.3
Hawaii	595	290	570	279	64.1	26	11	4.3	4.9	3.7	71.7	62.6
Idaho	658	299	626	285	65.8	32	15	4.9	4.8	4.9	76.7	61.9
Illinois	6,419	3,017	6,140	2,891	66.7	279	126	4.4	4.5	4.2	77.1	63.1
Indiana	3,084	1,383	2,984	1,336	65.9	100	47	3.2	3.1	3.4	76.8	59.8
Iowa	1,563	726	1,522	705	69.4	41	21	2.6	2.4	2.9	76.9	65.7
Kansas	1,411	680	1,359	655	67.9	52	24	3.7	3.8	3.6	75.7	65.7
Kentucky	1,982	936	1,900	897	61.7	82	40	4.1	4.0	4.2	71.3	57.9
Louisiana	2,030	966	1,917	910	58.3	112	55	5.5	5.4	5.7	70.5	54.2
Maine	689	328	665	317	66.6	24	11	3.5	3.5	3.5	74.4	63.9
Maryland	2,805	1,326	2,697	1,278	67.2	108	48	3.9	4.1	3.6	75.7	64.3
Massachusetts	3,237	1,534	3,151	1,492	65.6	86	42	2.6	2.6	2.7	73.8	61.4
Michigan	5,201	2,385	5,016	2,299	66.5	185	87	3.6	3.5	3.6	76.7	61.5
Minnesota	2,739	1,303	2,649	1,268	72.6	90	35	3.3	3.8	2.7	80.1	70.3
Mississippi	1,326	649	1,251	610	60.0	75	39	5.7	5.4	6.0	71.5	57.0
Missouri	2,930	1,390	2,828	1,336	67.9	101	54	3.5	3.1	3.9	76.8	64.3
Montana	479	223	456	212	65.9	24	10	4.9	5.2	4.6	74.4	64.3
Nebraska	924	443	897	428	71.5	28	14	3.0	2.8	3.2	78.6	69.0
Nevada	986	446	946	428	67.2	40	17	4.1	4.2	3.9	77.2	63.0
New Hampshire	686	324	666	314	71.0	19	9	2.8	2.8	2.8	79.8	66.7
New Jersey	4,188	1,933	4,030	1,854	64.1	157	78	3.8	3.5	4.0	75.5	58.4
New Mexico	833	398	792	380	60.1	40	18	4.9	5.2	4.5	69.8	57.2
New York	8,941	4,214	8,533	4,025	60.3	408	189	4.6	4.6	4.5	71.0	56.1
North Carolina	3,958	1,869	3,814	1,793	65.7	144	76	3.6	3.3	4.1	75.3	61.6
North Dakota	339	164	329	161	68.6	10	4	3.0	3.6	2.4	75.3	67.0
Ohio	5,783	2,754	5,546	2,637	64.3	237	116	4.1	4.0	4.2	73.9	60.9
Oklahoma	1,648	766	1,598	744	62.5	50	21	3.0	3.2	2.8	72.2	57.3
Oregon	1,803	830	1,715	794	65.8	87	35	4.9	5.4	4.3	76.4	62.2
Pennsylvania	5,972	2,778	5,722	2,668	61.6	250	110	4.2	4.4	4.0	72.2	57.1
Rhode Island	505	246	484	236	64.3	21	10	4.1	4.0	4.2	74.5	60.6
South Carolina	1,985	973	1,909	933	63.0	77	40	3.9	3.6	4.1	72.5	59.5
South Dakota	401	191	392	187	71.0	9	4	2.3	2.5	2.0	77.8	67.7
Tennessee	2,798	1,294	2,688	1,236	62.7	110	58	3.9	3.5	4.5	71.8	59.1
Texas	10,325	4,613	9,887	4,401	65.3	437	213	4.2	3.9	4.6	77.5	59.4
Utah	1,104	479	1,068	461	70.0	36	17	3.2	3.0	3.6	82.0	62.7
Vermont	332	161	322	157	68.3	10	4	2.9	3.0	2.8	76.1	65.3
Virginia	3,610	1,700	3,530	1,665	66.6	80	35	2.2	2.3	2.1	75.6	61.3
Washington	3,045	1,442	2,888	1,368	65.1	158	75	5.2	5.2	5.2	75.2	62.6
West Virginia	825	393	779	373	53.9	46	19	5.5	6.1	4.9	63.5	51.3
Wisconsin	2,935	1,372	2,831	1,323	70.2	104	48	3.5	3.6	3.5	77.3	68.3
Wyoming	267	122	257	118	69.2	10	5	3.9	4.0	3.7	79.0	65.1

[1] Civilian employment as a percent of civilian noninstitutional population. [2] Percent unemployed of the civilian labor force.
[3] Percent of civilian noninstitutional population of each specified group in the civilian labor force.

Source: U.S. Bureau of Labor Statistics, "Local Area Unemployment Statistics, Geographic Profile" Internet site <http://www.bls.gov/lau>.

No. 573. Civilian Labor Force by Selected Metropolitan Area: 2000

[140,863 represents 140,863,000. For the civilian noninstitutional population 16 years old and over. Annual averages of monthly figures. Data are derived from the Local Area Unemployment Statistics Program. For composition of metropolitan areas, see Appendix II]

Metropolitan areas ranked by labor force size, 2000	Civilian labor force (1,000)	Unemployment rate [1]	Metropolitan areas ranked by labor force size, 2000	Civilian labor force (1,000)	Unemployment rate [1]
U.S. total	140,863	4.0	Indianapolis, IN MSA	854	2.5
Los Angeles-Long Beach, CA PMSA . . .	4,761	5.4	Columbus, OH MSA.............	851	2.5
Chicago, IL PMSA	4,273	4.2	Sacramento, CA PMSA...........	813	4.0
New York, NY PMSA	4,201	5.3	Charlotte-Gastonia-Rock Hill,		
Washington, DC-MD-VA-WV PMSA. . . .	2,695	2.4	NC-SC MSA	807	3.3
Philadelphia, PA-NJ PMSA	2,503	4.0	Milwaukee-Waukesha, WI PMSA	803	3.8
Detroit, MI PMSA................	2,343	3.2	Fort Lauderdale, FL PMSA	779	3.7
Atlanta, GA MSA................	2,262	3.0	San Antonio, TX MSA............	776	3.4
Houston, TX PMSA	2,163	4.1	Las Vegas, NV-AZ MSA	768	4.2
Dallas, TX PMSA................	1,967	3.1	Norfolk-Virginia Beach-Newport News,		
Boston, MA-NH PMSA	1,800	2.2	VA-NC MSA	743	2.6
Minneapolis-St. Paul, MN-WI MSA	1,718	2.6	Austin-San Marcos, TX MSA	738	2.0
Phoenix-Mesa, AZ MSA	1,563	2.7	Salt Lake City-Ogden, UT MSA	707	3.1
Riverside-San Bernardino, CA PMSA . .	1,523	5.1	Nashville, TN MSA..............	663	2.8
Orange County, CA PMSA..........	1,513	2.5	Bergen-Passaic, NJ PMSA	663	3.7
San Diego, CA MSA..............	1,405	3.0	Middlesex-Somerset-Hunterdon,		
Nassau-Suffolk, NY PMSA	1,401	3.0	NJ PMSA	655	2.7
Seattle-Bellevue-Everett, WA PMSA . . .	1,397	3.7	Raleigh-Durham-Chapel Hill, NC MSA . .	649	1.8
St. Louis, MO-IL MSA.............	1,364	3.7	Greensboro-Winston-Salem-High Point,		
Baltimore, MD PMSA	1,316	4.4	NC MSA...................	649	2.9
Oakland, CA PMSA	1,245	2.9	Grand Rapids-Muskegon-Holland,		
Tampa-St. Petersburg-Clearwater,			MI MSA	628	3.1
FL MSA	1,233	2.6	New Orleans, LA MSA	608	5.0
Pittsburgh, PA MSA	1,154	4.1	Hartford, CT MSA	596	2.4
Denver, CO PMSA...............	1,150	2.3	Providence-Fall River-Warwick,		
Cleveland-Lorain-Elyria, OH PMSA	1,126	4.4	RI-MA MSA.................	574	4.0
Portland-Vancouver, OR-WA PMSA. . . .	1,069	3.9	Louisville, KY-IN MSA............	570	3.4
Miami, FL PMSA	1,054	5.3	Rochester, NY MSA.............	565	4.0
Newark, NJ PMSA...............	1,021	3.7	Memphis, TN-AR-MS MSA	560	3.9
Kansas City, MO-KS MSA	1,005	3.3	Jacksonville, FL MSA	559	3.1
San Jose, CA PMSA	1,004	2.0	Buffalo-Niagara Falls, NY MSA.	557	5.0
San Francisco, CA PMSA	986	2.1	Oklahoma City, OK MSA...........	552	2.4
Fort Worth-Arlington, TX PMSA	917	3.2	Monmouth-Ocean, NJ PMSA	523	3.5
Orlando, FL MSA................	897	2.6	Richmond-Petersburg, VA MSA	520	1.9
Cincinnati, OH-KY-IN PMSA	856	3.5	West Palm Beach-Boca Raton, FL MSA.	518	4.4

[1] Percent unemployed of the civilian labor force.

Source: U.S. Bureau of Labor Statistics, Local Area Unemployment Statistics program.

No. 574. School Enrollment and Labor Force Status: 1980 and 2000

[In thousands (37,103 represents 37,103,000), except percent. As of October. For the civilian noninstitutional population 16 to 24 years old. Based on Current Population Survey; see text, Section 1, Population, and Appendix III]

Characteristic	Population		Civilian labor force		Employed		Unemployed		
	1980	2000 [1]	1980	2000 [1]	1980	2000 [1]	1980, total	2000 [1] Total	2000 [1] Rate [2]
Total, 16 to 24 years [3]	37,103	34,568	24,918	22,627	21,454	20,675	3,464	1,952	8.6
Enrolled in school [3]	15,713	18,313	7,454	9,183	6,433	8,457	1,021	726	7.9
16 to 19 years	11,126	12,267	4,836	5,273	4,029	4,735	807	538	10.2
20 to 24 years	4,587	6,046	2,618	3,910	2,404	3,722	214	187	4.8
Sex:									
Male	7,997	8,988	3,825	4,341	3,259	3,977	566	364	8.4
Female	7,716	9,325	3,629	4,842	3,174	4,480	455	361	7.5
College level	7,664	9,593	3,996	5,811	3,632	5,513	364	298	5.1
Full-time.	6,396	8,011	2,854	4,411	2,554	4,169	300	242	5.5
Race:									
White	13,242	14,557	6,687	7,751	5,889	7,197	798	554	7.1
Below college	6,566	6,883	3,095	2,890	2,579	2,566	516	324	11.2
College level	6,678	7,675	3,592	4,861	3,310	4,631	282	230	4.7
Black.	2,028	2,631	595	1,008	406	871	189	137	13.6
Below college	1,282	1,395	294	380	174	287	120	93	24.6
College level	747	1,236	300	628	230	585	70	44	7.0
Not enrolled [3]	21,390	16,255	17,464	13,444	15,021	12,218	2,443	1,226	9.1
White	18,103	12,996	15,121	10,992	13,318	10,175	1,803	817	7.4
Black	2,864	2,592	2,055	1,897	1,451	1,543	604	354	18.7

[1] See footnote 2, Table 567. [2] Percent of civilian labor force in each category. [3] Includes other races, not shown separately.

Source: U.S. Bureau of Labor Statistics, Bulletin 2307; News, USDL 01-94, April 13, 2001; and unpublished data.

No. 575. Labor Force Participation Rates by Marital Status, Sex, and Age: 1970 to 2000

[Annual averages of monthly figures. See Table 572 for definition of participation rate. Based on Current Population Survey; see text, Section 1, Population, and Appendix III]

Marital status and year	Male participation rate							Female participation rate						
	Total	16-19 years	20-24 years	25-34 years	35-44 years	45-64 years	65 and over	Total	16-19 years	20-24 years	25-34 years	35-44 years	45-64 years	65 and over
Single:														
1970	65.5	54.6	73.8	87.9	86.2	75.7	25.2	56.8	44.7	73.0	81.4	78.6	73.0	19.7
1980	72.6	59.9	81.3	89.2	82.2	66.9	16.8	64.4	53.6	75.2	83.3	76.9	65.6	13.9
1985	73.8	56.3	81.5	89.4	84.6	65.5	15.6	66.6	52.3	76.3	82.4	80.8	67.9	9.8
1990 [1]	74.8	55.1	81.6	89.9	84.5	67.3	15.7	66.7	51.7	74.5	80.9	80.8	66.2	12.1
1994 [1]	73.9	53.6	80.5	88.4	83.1	67.8	17.8	66.7	51.4	73.6	78.9	78.7	68.8	12.7
1995	73.7	54.4	80.3	88.7	81.4	67.0	17.9	66.8	52.2	72.9	80.2	79.5	67.3	11.6
1996	73.3	52.8	79.8	89.1	82.1	67.4	18.2	67.1	51.5	73.3	80.9	79.4	68.5	12.2
1997 [1]	73.1	51.9	80.1	89.0	82.1	68.5	14.8	67.9	51.0	75.1	82.3	80.1	70.8	11.5
1998 [1]	73.3	52.9	79.7	89.1	82.5	70.2	15.2	68.5	52.4	75.3	83.0	80.9	69.9	9.7
1999 [1]	73.4	52.5	79.7	89.5	83.5	70.6	17.3	68.7	51.1	76.1	84.2	80.8	69.6	9.9
2000 [1]	73.5	52.7	80.5	89.4	82.8	69.7	17.1	69.0	51.3	76.3	84.1	80.9	70.0	10.8
Married: [2]														
1970	86.1	92.3	94.7	98.0	98.1	91.2	29.9	40.5	37.8	47.9	38.8	46.8	44.0	7.3
1980	80.9	91.3	96.9	97.5	97.2	84.3	20.5	49.8	49.3	61.4	58.8	61.8	46.9	7.3
1985	78.7	91.0	95.6	97.4	96.8	81.7	16.8	53.8	49.6	65.7	65.8	68.1	49.4	6.6
1990 [1]	78.6	92.1	95.6	96.9	96.7	82.6	17.5	58.4	49.5	66.1	69.6	74.0	56.5	8.5
1994 [1]	77.4	88.7	94.2	95.9	95.6	81.9	18.1	60.7	48.9	65.8	71.6	75.8	61.9	9.4
1995	77.5	89.2	94.9	96.3	95.4	82.4	18.0	61.0	51.6	64.7	72.0	75.7	62.7	9.1
1996	77.6	84.4	94.5	96.4	95.4	83.2	18.3	61.2	48.6	66.0	71.7	75.8	63.7	9.0
1997 [1]	77.7	84.6	94.9	96.1	95.7	83.6	18.3	61.6	50.1	66.1	71.9	76.0	64.6	8.9
1998 [1]	77.6	83.8	95.0	96.4	95.8	83.7	17.5	61.2	49.8	66.1	71.6	74.5	64.9	8.9
1999 [1]	77.5	83.2	93.7	96.5	95.9	83.4	18.3	61.2	49.8	64.5	70.9	74.6	65.3	9.6
2000 [1]	77.3	79.6	94.0	96.7	95.8	83.1	19.0	61.3	53.4	64.2	70.5	74.8	65.4	10.1
Other: [3]														
1970	60.7	(B)	90.4	93.7	91.1	78.5	19.3	40.3	48.6	60.3	64.6	68.8	61.9	10.0
1980	67.5	(B)	92.6	94.1	91.9	73.3	13.7	43.6	50.0	68.4	76.5	77.1	60.2	8.2
1985	68.7	(B)	95.1	93.7	91.8	72.8	11.4	45.1	51.9	66.2	76.9	81.6	61.0	7.5
1990 [1]	68.9	(B)	93.1	93.0	90.7	74.9	12.0	47.2	53.9	65.4	77.0	82.1	65.0	8.4
1994 [1]	66.8	(B)	91.0	90.3	88.6	72.6	11.9	47.5	46.2	66.6	74.3	80.4	67.6	8.7
1995	66.2	(B)	92.7	90.9	88.2	72.4	12.1	47.4	55.8	67.2	77.1	80.7	67.2	8.4
1996	66.4	(B)	90.6	92.0	88.8	73.1	11.5	48.1	42.6	70.7	78.5	82.1	67.7	8.0
1997 [1]	67.4	60.8	89.9	92.1	89.6	74.7	13.2	48.6	49.7	70.4	80.2	81.9	68.6	8.1
1998 [1]	66.9	66.2	89.1	93.0	89.1	73.7	13.1	48.8	50.4	73.7	81.0	82.8	68.6	8.4
1999 [1]	65.9	(B)	90.2	92.3	88.7	73.4	12.3	49.1	45.3	73.6	82.4	83.4	69.1	8.4
2000 [1]	66.6	60.4	87.7	93.2	89.8	74.0	12.7	49.4	45.8	74.0	83.2	82.9	69.7	8.7

B Percentage not shown where base is less than 35,000.   [1] See footnote 2, Table 567.   [2] Spouse present.   [3] Widowed, divorced, and married (spouse absent).

Source: U.S. Bureau of Labor Statistics, Bulletins 2217 and 2340; and unpublished data.

No. 576. Marital Status of Women in the Civilian Labor Force: 1970 to 2000

[Annual averages of monthly figures (31,543 represents 31,543,000). For civilian noninstitutional population 16 years old and over. Based on the Current Population Survey; see text, Section 1, Population, and Appendix III]

Year	Female labor force (1,000)				Female participation rate [3]			
	Total	Single	Married [1]	Other [2]	Total	Single	Married [1]	Other [2]
1970	31,543	7,265	18,475	5,804	43.3	56.8	40.5	40.3
1975	37,475	9,125	21,484	6,866	46.3	59.8	44.3	40.1
1980	45,487	11,865	24,980	8,643	51.5	64.4	49.9	43.6
1982	47,755	12,460	25,971	9,324	52.6	65.1	51.1	44.8
1983	48,503	12,659	26,468	9,376	52.9	65.0	51.8	44.4
1984	49,709	12,867	27,199	9,644	53.6	65.6	52.8	44.7
1985	51,050	13,163	27,894	9,993	54.5	66.6	53.8	45.1
1986	52,413	13,512	28,623	10,277	55.3	67.2	54.9	45.6
1987	53,658	13,885	29,381	10,393	56.0	67.4	55.9	45.7
1988	54,742	14,194	29,921	10,627	56.6	67.7	56.7	46.2
1989 [4]	56,030	14,377	30,548	11,104	57.4	68.0	57.8	47.0
1990 [4]	56,829	14,612	30,901	11,315	57.5	66.7	58.4	47.2
1991	57,178	14,681	31,112	11,385	57.4	66.2	58.5	46.8
1992	58,141	14,872	31,700	11,570	57.8	66.2	59.3	47.1
1993 [4]	58,795	15,031	31,980	11,784	57.9	66.2	59.4	47.2
1994 [4]	60,239	15,333	32,888	12,018	58.8	66.7	60.7	47.5
1995	60,944	15,467	33,359	12,118	58.9	66.8	61.0	47.4
1996	61,857	15,842	33,618	12,397	59.3	67.1	61.2	48.1
1997 [4]	63,036	16,492	33,802	12,742	59.8	67.9	61.6	48.6
1998 [4]	63,714	17,087	33,857	12,771	59.8	68.5	61.2	48.8
1999 [4]	64,855	17,575	34,372	12,909	60.0	68.7	61.2	49.1
2000 [4]	65,616	17,847	34,631	13,138	60.2	69.0	61.3	49.4

[1] Husband present.   [2] Widowed, divorced, or separated.   [3] See Table 572 for definition of participation rate.   [4] See footnote 2, Table 567.

Source: U.S. Bureau of Labor Statistics, Bulletin 2307; and unpublished data.

No. 577. Employment Status of Women by Marital Status and Presence and Age of Children: 1970 to 2000

[7.0 represents 7,000,000. As of March. For the civilian noninstitutional persons 16 years and over. Based on the Current Population Survey; see text, Section 1, Population, and Appendix III]

Item	Total			With any children								
				Total			Children 6 to 17 only			Children under 6		
	Single	Mar-ried [1]	Other [2]	Single	Mar-ried [1]	Other [2]	Single	Mar-ried [1]	Other [2]	Single	Mar-ried [1]	Other [2]
IN LABOR FORCE (mil.)												
1970	7.0	18.4	5.9	(NA)	10.2	1.9	(NA)	6.3	1.3	(NA)	3.9	0.6
1980	11.2	24.9	8.8	0.6	13.7	3.6	0.2	8.4	2.6	0.3	5.2	1.0
1985	12.9	27.7	10.3	1.1	14.9	4.0	0.4	8.5	2.9	0.7	6.4	1.1
1990	14.0	31.0	11.2	1.5	16.5	4.2	0.6	9.3	3.0	0.9	7.2	1.2
1995	15.0	33.6	12.0	2.1	18.0	4.6	0.8	10.2	3.3	1.3	7.8	1.3
1997 [3] ...	16.2	33.9	12.8	2.8	18.2	4.7	1.0	10.6	3.4	1.8	7.6	1.3
1998 [3] ...	16.9	34.1	12.9	3.0	18.1	4.5	1.2	10.5	3.3	1.8	7.7	1.2
1999 [3] ...	17.5	34.3	13.0	3.1	17.9	4.6	1.2	10.6	3.3	1.8	7.2	1.3
2000 [3] ...	17.8	35.0	13.2	3.1	18.2	4.5	1.2	10.8	3.4	1.8	7.3	1.1
PARTICIPATION RATE [4]												
1970	53.0	40.8	39.1	(NA)	39.7	60.7	(NA)	49.2	66.9	(NA)	30.3	52.2
1980	61.5	50.1	44.0	52.0	54.1	69.4	67.6	61.7	74.6	44.1	45.1	60.3
1985	65.2	54.2	45.6	51.6	60.8	71.9	64.1	67.8	77.8	46.5	53.4	59.7
1990	66.4	58.2	46.8	55.2	66.3	74.2	69.7	73.6	79.7	48.7	58.9	63.6
1995	65.5	61.1	47.3	57.5	70.2	75.3	67.0	76.2	79.5	53.0	63.5	66.3
1997 [3] ...	66.8	62.1	48.7	68.1	71.1	79.1	74.0	77.6	81.1	65.1	63.6	74.2
1998 [3] ...	68.1	61.8	49.4	72.5	70.6	79.7	81.2	76.8	82.7	67.3	63.7	72.5
1999 [3] ...	68.1	61.6	49.4	73.4	70.1	80.4	82.6	77.1	81.8	68.1	61.8	77.1
2000 [3] ...	68.6	62.0	50.2	73.9	70.6	82.7	79.7	77.2	85.0	70.5	62.8	76.6
EMPLOYMENT (mil.)												
1970	6.5	17.5	5.6	(NA)	9.6	1.8	(NA)	6.0	1.2	(NA)	3.6	0.6
1980	10.1	23.6	8.2	0.4	12.8	3.3	0.2	8.1	2.4	0.2	4.8	0.9
1985	11.6	26.1	9.4	0.9	13.9	3.5	0.3	8.1	2.6	0.5	5.9	0.9
1990	12.9	29.9	10.5	1.2	15.8	3.8	0.5	8.9	2.7	0.7	6.9	1.1
1995	13.7	32.3	11.3	1.8	17.2	4.2	0.7	9.8	3.1	1.1	7.3	1.2
1997 [3] ...	14.7	32.8	12.1	2.3	17.5	4.3	0.9	10.3	3.1	1.4	7.3	1.1
1998 [3] ...	15.6	33.0	12.2	2.5	17.4	4.2	1.1	10.1	3.1	1.4	7.3	1.1
1999 [3] ...	16.2	33.4	12.3	2.7	17.3	4.3	1.1	10.4	3.1	1.6	7.0	1.1
2000 [3] ...	16.4	34.0	12.7	2.7	17.6	4.3	1.1	10.6	3.2	1.6	7.1	1.1
UNEMPLOY-MENT RATE [5]												
1970	7.1	4.8	4.8	(NA)	6.0	7.2	(NA)	4.8	5.9	(NA)	7.9	9.8
1980	10.3	5.3	6.4	23.2	5.9	9.2	15.6	4.4	7.9	29.2	8.3	12.8
1985	10.2	5.7	8.5	23.8	6.6	12.1	15.4	5.5	10.6	28.5	8.0	16.1
1990	8.2	3.5	5.7	18.4	4.2	8.5	14.5	3.8	7.7	20.8	4.8	10.2
1995	8.7	3.9	5.8	16.6	4.3	8.1	11.8	3.6	7.1	19.5	5.3	10.8
1997 [3] ...	8.8	3.2	5.8	16.9	3.5	9.0	13.5	2.9	7.9	18.8	4.4	11.7
1998 [3] ...	7.5	3.2	5.0	15.1	3.8	6.7	11.8	3.2	5.3	17.5	4.5	10.6
1999 [3] ...	7.4	2.8	5.0	11.7	2.9	6.2	8.9	2.4	4.5	13.6	3.7	10.7
2000 [3] ...	7.3	2.7	4.3	11.0	2.9	5.1	8.7	2.6	4.8	12.6	3.5	5.9

NA Not available. [1] Husband present. [2] Widowed, divorced, or separated. [3] See footnote 2, Table 567. [4] Percent of women in each specific category in the labor force. [5] Unemployed as a percent of civilian labor force in specified group.
Source: U.S. Bureau of Labor Statistics, Bulletin 2307; and unpublished data.

No. 578. Labor Force Participation Rates for Wives, Husband Present by Age of Own Youngest Child: 1975 to 2000

[As of March. For civilian noninstitutional population 16 years old and over. For definition of participation rate, see Table 577. Based on Current Population Survey; see text, Section 1, Population, and Appendix III]

Presence and age of child	Total			White			Black		
	1975	1985	2000 [1]	1975	1985	2000 [1]	1975	1985	2000 [1]
Wives, total	44.4	54.2	62.0	43.6	53.3	61.3	54.1	63.8	70.9
No children under 18	43.8	48.2	54.7	43.6	47.5	54.4	47.6	55.2	60.9
With children under 18	44.9	60.8	70.6	43.6	59.9	69.8	58.4	71.7	80.9
Under 6, total...........	36.7	53.4	62.8	34.7	52.1	61.5	54.9	69.6	78.0
Under 3.............	32.7	50.5	59.0	30.7	49.4	57.5	50.1	66.2	74.2
1 year or under	30.8	49.4	58.3	29.2	48.6	57.6	50.0	63.7	72.3
2 years...........	37.1	54.0	61.9	35.1	52.7	59.8	56.4	69.9	80.1
3 to 5 years	42.2	58.4	68.4	40.1	56.6	67.4	61.2	73.8	82.5
3 years...........	41.2	55.1	66.0	39.0	52.7	65.2	62.7	72.3	80.4
4 years...........	41.2	59.7	69.7	38.7	58.4	68.7	64.9	70.6	82.0
5 years...........	44.4	62.1	70.6	43.8	59.9	69.4	56.3	79.1	88.0
6 to 13 years	51.8	68.2	75.3	50.7	67.7	75.0	65.7	73.3	84.3
14 to 17 years	53.5	67.0	80.6	53.4	66.6	81.0	52.3	74.4	79.6

[1] See footnote 2, Table 567.
Source: U.S. Bureau of Labor Statistics, Bulletin 2340; and unpublished data.

Labor Force, Employment, and Earnings 373

No. 579. Families With Own Children—Employment Status of Parents: 1995 and 2000

[Annual average of monthly figures (33,544 represents 33,544,000). For families with own children. Based on the Current Population Survey, see text, Section 1, Population, and Appendix III]

Characteristic	Number (1,000) 1995	Number (1,000) 2000	Percent distribution 1995	Percent distribution 2000	Characteristic	Number (1,000) 1995	Number (1,000) 2000	Percent distribution 1995	Percent distribution 2000
WITH OWN CHILDREN UNDER 18					Father employed, not mother	2,921	3,001	22.5	22.0
					Neither parent employed	517	380	4.0	2.8
Total families	33,544	34,340	100.0	100.0					
Parent(s) employed	29,659	31,601	88.4	92.0	Families maintained by women [1]	4,360	4,668	100.0	100.0
No parent employed	3,886	2,739	11.6	8.0	Mother employed	3,142	3,715	72.1	79.6
					Mother not employed	1,219	954	27.9	20.4
Married-couple families	24,604	24,915	100.0	100.0					
Parent(s) employed	23,643	24,282	96.1	97.5	Families maintained by men [1]	908	1,086	100.0	100.0
Mother employed	16,629	17,012	67.6	68.3	Father employed	766	929	84.3	85.6
Both parents employed	15,491	15,996	63.0	64.2	Father not employed	143	157	15.7	14.4
Mother employed, not father	1,137	1,016	4.6	4.1	**WITH OWN CHILDREN UNDER 6**				
Father employed, not mother	7,014	7,270	28.5	29.2					
Neither parent employed	962	633	3.9	2.5	**Total families**	15,275	14,958	100.0	100.0
					Parent(s) employed	13,267	13,708	86.9	91.6
Families maintained by women [1]	7,433	7,613	100.0	100.0	No parent employed	2,007	1,249	13.1	8.4
Mother employed	4,755	5,751	64.0	75.5					
Mother not employed	2,678	1,862	36.0	24.5	Married-couple families	11,604	11,287	100.0	100.0
					Parent(s) employed	11,159	11,034	96.2	97.8
Families maintained by men [1]	1,507	1,812	100.0	100.0	Mother employed	7,066	6,765	60.9	59.9
Father employed	1,261	1,568	83.7	86.5	Both parents employed	6,646	6,421	57.3	56.9
Father not employed	245	244	16.3	13.5	Mother employed, not father	421	344	3.6	3.0
WITH OWN CHILDREN 6 to 17					Father employed, not mother	4,092	4,269	35.3	37.8
					Neither parent employed	445	254	3.8	2.2
Total families	18,270	19,382	100.0	100.0					
Parent(s) employed	16,391	17,892	89.7	92.3	Families maintained by women [1]	3,073	2,945	100.0	100.0
No parent employed	1,878	1,490	10.3	7.7	Mother employed	1,613	2,036	52.5	69.1
					Mother not employed	1,460	909	47.5	30.9
Married-couple families	13,001	13,628	100.0	100.0					
Parent(s) employed	12,484	13,248	96.0	97.2	Families maintained by men [1]	598	726	100.0	100.0
Mother employed	9,562	10,247	73.6	75.2	Father employed	496	639	82.8	88.0
Both parents employed	8,846	9,575	68.0	70.3	Father not employed	102	87	17.1	12.0
Mother employed, not father	717	672	5.5	4.9					

[1] No spouse present.
Source: U.S. Bureau of Labor Statistics, *News*, USDL 97-195, June 16, 1997; and USDL 01-103, April 19, 2001.

No. 580. Employed Civilians and Weekly Hours: 1980 to 2000

[In thousands (99,303 represents 99,303,000, except as indicated. For civilian noninstitutional population 16 years old and over. Annual averages of monthly figures. Based on Current Population Survey; see text, Section 1, Population, and Appendix III]

Item	1980	1990 [1]	1995	1996	1997 [1]	1998 [1]	1999 [1]	2000 [1]
Total employed	99,303	118,793	124,900	126,708	129,558	131,463	133,488	135,208
Age:								
16 to 19 years old	7,710	6,581	6,419	6,500	6,661	7,051	7,172	7,276
20 to 24 years old	14,087	13,401	12,443	12,138	12,380	12,557	12,891	13,321
25 to 34 years old	27,204	33,935	32,356	32,077	31,809	31,394	30,865	30,501
35 to 44 years old	19,523	30,817	34,202	35,051	35,908	36,278	36,728	36,697
45 to 54 years old	16,234	19,525	24,378	25,514	26,744	27,587	28,635	29,717
55 to 64 years old	11,586	11,189	11,445	11,739	12,296	12,872	13,315	13,627
65 years old and over	2,960	3,346	3,666	3,690	3,761	3,725	3,882	4,070
Class of worker:								
Nonagriculture	95,938	115,570	121,460	123,264	126,159	128,085	130,207	131,903
Wage and salary worker	88,525	106,598	112,448	114,171	116,983	119,019	121,323	123,128
Self-employed	7,000	8,719	8,902	8,971	9,056	8,962	8,790	8,674
Unpaid family workers	413	253	110	122	120	103	95	101
Agriculture	3,364	3,223	3,440	3,443	3,399	3,378	3,281	3,305
Wage and salary worker	1,425	1,740	1,814	1,869	1,890	2,000	1,944	2,034
Self-employed	1,642	1,378	1,580	1,518	1,457	1,341	1,297	1,233
Unpaid family workers	297	105	45	56	51	38	40	38
Weekly hours:								
Nonagriculture:								
Wage and salary workers	38.1	39.2	39.2	39.2	39.4	39.2	39.5	39.6
Self-employed	41.2	40.8	39.4	39.6	39.7	39.6	40.1	40.0
Unpaid family workers	34.7	34.0	33.5	34.1	32.6	34.0	33.4	32.3
Agriculture:								
Wage and salary workers	41.6	41.2	41.1	41.5	41.6	40.6	41.1	41.0
Self-employed	49.3	46.8	43.5	43.1	42.7	43.3	43.3	43.0
Unpaid family workers	38.6	38.5	42.0	38.0	44.3	36.2	36.6	37.5

[1] See footnote 2, Table 567.
Source: U.S. Bureau of Labor Statistics, *Employment and Earnings*, monthly, January issues; and unpublished data.

No. 581. Employed Workers Actively Seeking a New Job: 1999

[In thousands (117,930 represents 117,930,000), except rate. As of February. For employed wage and salary workers 16 old and over (except as indicated) responding to the question on actively seeking work in the prior 3 months. Based on the Current Population Survey; see text, Section 1, Population, and Appendix III]

Characteristic	Total employed	Persons responding to search question			Characteristic	Total employed	Persons responding to search question		
		Total	Actively seeking work	Percent			Total	Actively seeking work	Percent
Total	117,930	114,898	5,131	4.5	Professional specialty .	18,617	18,265	839	4.6
Age:					Technical and related support	4,079	4,029	194	4.8
16 to 19 years old. . . .	6,600	6,360	377	5.9	Sales	13,324	12,912	686	5.3
20 to 24 years old. . . .	12,108	11,692	855	7.3	Administrative support,				
25 to 34 years old. . . .	28,836	28,126	1,631	5.8	including clerical	18,241	17,787	774	4.3
35 to 44 years old. . . .	32,390	31,649	1,387	4.4	Private household. . . .	614	482	28	5.8
45 to 54 years old. . . .	24,518	23,966	672	2.8	Protective service . . .	2,490	2,405	81	3.4
55 to 64 years old. . . .	10,754	10,475	177	1.7	Service, except private				
65 years old and over .	2,724	2,629	32	1.2	households and protective	13,368	12,923	633	4.9
Sex: Male	61,095	59,541	2,712	4.6	Precision production,				
Female	56,835	55,357	2,419	4.4	craft, and repair	12,576	12,287	476	3.9
Educational attainment: [1]					Machine operators,				
Less than high school diploma	9,644	9,275	246	2.7	assemblers, and inspectors	7,189	7,003	255	3.6
High school diploma, no college	31,207	30,425	897	2.9	Transportation and material moving occu-				
Some college or associate degree	28,075	27,486	1,262	4.6	pations	4,859	4,734	188	4.0
Bachelor's degree or more	30,297	29,660	1,493	5.0	Handlers, equipment cleaners, helpers and laborers	4,754	4,585	227	5.0
Occupation:					Farming, forestry and				
Executive, administrative, and managerial .	16,237	15,957	671	4.2	fishing	1,582	1,529	78	5.1

[1] Persons 25 years old and over.

Source: U.S. Bureau of Labor Statistics, Current Population Survey, February 1999, unpublished data.

No. 582. Persons At Work by Hours Worked: 2000

[129,592 represents 129,592,000. For civilian noninstitutional population 16 years old and over. Annual averages of monthly figures. Based on Current Population Survey; see text, Section 1, Population, and Appendix III]

Hours of work	Persons at work (1,000)			Percent distribution		
	Total	Agriculture industries	Non-agriculture industries	Total	Agriculture industries	Non-agriculture industries
Total	129,592	3,159	126,433	100.0	100.0	100.0
1 to 34 hours	29,620	887	28,732	22.9	28.1	22.7
1 to 4 hours	1,215	63	1,152	0.9	2.0	0.9
5 to 14 hours	4,685	216	4,469	3.6	6.8	3.5
15 to 29 hours.	14,863	408	14,455	11.5	12.9	11.4
30 to 34 hours.	8,856	201	8,655	6.8	6.4	6.8
35 hours and over.	99,973	2,272	97,701	77.1	71.9	77.3
35 to 39 hours.	8,583	174	8,409	6.6	5.5	6.7
40 hours	50,981	837	50,144	39.3	26.5	39.7
41 hours and over	40,409	1,261	39,149	31.2	39.9	31.0
41 to 48 hours	14,602	256	14,346	11.3	8.1	11.3
49 to 58 hours	15,084	389	14,695	11.6	12.3	11.6
60 hours and over	10,723	616	10,107	8.3	19.5	8.0
Average weekly hours:						
Total at work	39.7	41.7	39.7	(X)	(X)	(X)
Persons usually working full time .	43.4	47.8	43.3	(X)	(X)	(X)

X Not applicable.

Source: U.S. Bureau of Labor Statistics, Employment and Earnings, monthly, January. 2000 issue.

No. 583. Persons With a Job but Not at Work: 1980 to 2000

[In thousands (5,881 represents 5,881,000), except percent. For civilian noninstitutional population 16 years old and over. Annual averages of monthly figures. Based on Current Population Survey; see text, Section 1, Population, and Appendix III]

Reason for not working	1980	1985	1990 [1]	1993	1994 [1]	1995	1996	1997 [1]	1998 [1]	1999 [1]	2000 [1]
All industries, number	**5,881**	**5,789**	**6,160**	**6,041**	**5,619**	**5,582**	**5,768**	**5,555**	**5,586**	**5,407**	**5,616**
Percent of employed	5.9	5.4	5.2	5.0	4.6	4.5	4.6	4.3	4.2	4.1	4.2
Reason for not working:											
Vacation	3,320	3,338	3,529	3,328	2,877	2,982	3,085	2,942	3,033	2,899	3,071
Illness	1,426	1,308	1,341	1,295	1,184	1,084	1,090	1,114	1,095	1,096	1,145
Bad weather	155	141	90	153	165	122	256	146	130	104	88
Industrial dispute	105	42	24	24	15	21	11	20	10	7	14
All other	876	960	1,177	1,241	1,378	1,373	1,325	1,334	1,318	1,300	1,298

[1] See footnote 2, Table 567.

Source: U.S. Bureau of Labor Statistics, Employment and Earnings, monthly, January issues; and unpublished data.

Labor Force, Employment, and Earnings 375

No. 584. Self-Employed Workers by Industry and Occupation: 1980 to 2000

[In thousands (8,642 represents 8,642,000). For civilian noninstitutional population 16 years old and over. Annual averages of monthly figures. Data from 1990 forward are not fully comparable with data for prior years because of the introduction of the occupational and industrial classification used in the 1990 census. Based on the Current Population Survey; see text, Section 1, Population, and Appendix III]

Item	1980	1990 [1]	1995	1996	1997 [1]	1998 [1]	1999 [1]	2000 [1]
Total self-employed	8,642	10,097	10,482	10,490	10,513	10,303	10,087	9,907
Industry: Agriculture	1,642	1,378	1,580	1,518	1,457	1,341	1,297	1,233
Nonagriculture	7,000	8,719	8,902	8,971	9,056	8,962	8,790	8,674
Mining	28	24	16	15	14	21	16	16
Construction	1,173	1,457	1,460	1,496	1,492	1,519	1,545	1,581
Manufacturing	358	427	433	406	422	428	380	343
Transportation and public utilities	282	301	396	432	438	430	429	399
Trade	1,899	1,851	1,772	1,760	1,761	1,640	1,621	1,498
Finance, insurance, and real estate	458	630	660	674	629	609	661	693
Services	2,804	4,030	4,166	4,189	4,300	4,317	4,138	4,145
Occupation:								
Managerial and professional specialty	(NA)	3,050	3,147	3,288	3,432	3,400	3,298	3,119
Technical, sales, and administrative support	(NA)	2,240	2,341	2,304	2,219	2,117	2,111	2,083
Service occupations	(NA)	1,207	1,190	1,198	1,179	1,198	1,136	1,202
Precision production, craft, and repair	(NA)	1,675	1,618	1,595	1,651	1,697	1,665	1,722
Operators, fabricators, and laborers	(NA)	567	631	634	629	584	607	555
Farming, forestry, and fishing	(NA)	1,358	1,556	1,471	1,403	1,307	1,270	1,226

NA Not available.   [1] See footnote 2, Table 567.

Source: U.S. Bureau of Labor Statistics, Bulletin 2307; Employment and Earnings, monthly, January issues, and unpublished data.

No. 585. Self-Employed Persons With Home-Based Businesses: 1997

[4,125 represents 4,125,000. As of May. For persons at work 16 years and over in nonagricultural industries who worked in home-based businesses as part of their primary job. Based on the Current Population Survey; see text Section 1, Population, and Appendix III]

Characteristic	Total [1] (1,000)	Percent distribution by hours worked at home			Mean hours	
		Less than 8 hours	8 hours or more		Worked at home	Total at work on primary job
			Total	35 hours or more		
Total	4,125	30.4	69.6	29.3	23.0	37.3
SEX						
Male	2,157	36.2	63.8	25.5	20.4	42.1
Female	1,968	24.2	75.8	33.5	25.9	31.9
RACE AND HISPANIC ORIGIN						
White	3,868	30.5	69.5	29.0	22.9	36.9
Black	135	29.2	70.8	47.0	29.1	42.7
Hispanic origin [2]	156	27.8	72.2	31.3	23.8	35.9
OCCUPATION						
Managerial and professional	1,714	28.3	71.7	28.2	23.1	37.0
Exec., admin., and managerial	1,014	28.3	71.7	29.0	23.8	39.6
Professional	700	28.3	71.7	27.1	22.1	33.2
Technical, sales and administrative [3]	1,016	33.4	66.6	22.5	19.5	32.0
Sales	722	34.4	65.6	24.1	20.2	35.8
Administrative support	259	33.1	66.9	15.5	16.7	20.1
Service	616	12.0	88.0	58.3	36.9	42.1
Precision production, craft, and repair	564	50.1	49.9	15.1	14.8	41.9
Operators, fabricators, and laborers	215	36.1	63.9	22.4	20.0	38.0
INDUSTRY						
Construction	726	49.5	50.5	14.3	14.3	44.3
Manufacturing	193	13.6	86.4	38.5	29.1	36.5
Transportation and public utilities	132	52.8	47.2	18.0	14.9	35.7
Wholesale trade	185	28.9	71.1	30.2	22.3	39.4
Retail trade	532	38.9	61.1	19.2	19.1	30.5
Finance, insurance, and real estate	291	22.5	77.5	23.6	20.9	34.5
Services	2,054	23.0	77.0	37.8	27.4	36.8

[1] Includes persons who worked at home but did not report the number of hours worked. These persons are excluded from the distribution.   [2] Persons of Hispanic origin may be of any race.   [3] Includes other occupations, not shown separately.

Source: U.S. Bureau of Labor Statistics, News, USDL 98-93, March 11, 1998.

No. 586. Multiple Jobholders: 2000

[Annual average of monthly figures (7,556 represents 7,556,000). For the civilian noninstitutional population 16 years old and over. Multiple jobholders are employed persons who, either 1) had jobs as wage or salary workers with two employers or more; 2) were self-employed and also held a wage and salary job; or 3) were unpaid family workers on their primary jobs but also held wage and salary job. Based on the Current Population Survey; see text, Section 1, Population, and Appendix III]

Characteristic	Total		Male		Female	
	Number (1,000)	Percent of employed	Number (1,000)	Percent of employed	Number (1,000)	Percent of employed
Total [1]	7,556	5.6	3,968	5.5	3,588	5.7
Age:						
16 to 19 years old.................	346	4.8	145	3.9	201	5.6
20 to 24 years old.................	752	5.6	337	4.8	415	6.6
25 to 54 years old.................	5,614	5.8	3,011	5.8	2,604	5.8
55 to 64 years old.................	695	5.1	379	5.1	317	5.1
65 years old and over	148	3.6	95	4.1	52	3.1
Race and Hispanic origin:						
White	6,462	5.7	3,433	5.6	3,029	5.8
Black	818	5.3	396	5.5	422	5.2
Hispanic origin [2]	490	3.4	298	3.5	192	3.2
Marital status:						
Married, spouse present.............	4,156	5.4	2,499	5.8	1,656	4.9
Widowed, divorced, or separated.........	1,299	6.1	469	5.3	830	6.6
Single, never married...............	2,101	5.7	1,000	5.0	1,102	6.6
Full- or part-time status:						
Primary job full time, secondary job part time ..	4,173	(X)	2,409	(X)	1,764	(X)
Both jobs part time	1,595	(X)	518	(X)	1,077	(X)
Both jobs full time	317	(X)	210	(X)	106	(X)
Hours vary on primary or secondary job	1,429	(X)	811	(X)	618	(X)

X Not applicable.   [1] Includes a small number of persons who work part time on their primary job and full time on their secondary job(s), not shown separately. Includes other races, not shown separately.   [2] Persons of Hispanic origin may be of any race.

Source: U.S. Bureau of Labor Statistics, *Employment and Earnings,* monthly, January 2001 issue.

No. 587. Average Number of Jobs Held From Ages 18 to 34: 1978 to 1998

[In percent. For persons 33 to 41 in 1998. A job is an uninterrupted period of work with a particular employer. Educational attainment as of 1998. Based on the National Longitudinal Survey of Youth 1979; see source for details]

Sex and educational attainment	Total [1]	Number of jobs held by age—		
		Age 18 to 24 years old	Age 25 to 29 years old	Age 30 to 34 years old
Total [2]	9.2	5.6	3.0	2.4
Less than a high school diploma.................	9.3	5.2	3.0	2.4
High school graduates, no college.................	8.7	5.2	2.8	2.4
Less than a bachelor's degree	9.6	5.8	3.2	2.5
Bachelor's degree or more.................	9.7	6.3	3.0	2.4
Male	9.6	5.8	3.2	2.6
Less than a high school diploma..............	10.7	6.1	3.5	2.8
High school graduates, no college..............	9.1	5.5	3.1	2.5
Less than a bachelor's degree	10.0	6.0	3.4	2.6
Bachelor's degree or more...................	9.3	6.0	2.9	2.4
Female	8.8	5.4	2.8	2.3
Less than a high school diploma..............	7.4	4.0	2.2	2.0
High school graduates, no college..............	8.2	4.8	2.5	2.3
Less than a bachelor's degree	9.2	5.6	3.0	2.4
Bachelor's degree or more.................	10.1	6.6	3.1	2.3
White, non-Hispanic.......................	9.4	5.8	3.0	2.4
Less than a high school diploma..............	9.8	5.6	3.1	2.6
High school graduates, no college..............	8.7	5.3	2.8	2.4
Less than a bachelor's degree	9.9	6.0	3.2	2.5
Bachelor's degree or more.................	9.8	6.4	3.0	2.3
Black, non-Hispanic.......................	8.5	4.7	2.9	2.5
Less than a high school diploma..............	8.0	3.9	2.7	2.2
High school graduates, no college..............	8.4	4.5	2.9	2.5
Less than a bachelor's degree	8.5	5.0	2.9	2.4
Bachelor's degree or more.................	9.4	6.0	3.1	2.7
Hispanic origin	8.7	5.0	2.9	2.4
Less than a high school diploma..............	8.8	4.9	2.8	2.2
High school graduates, no college..............	8.6	5.0	2.8	2.4
Less than a bachelor's degree	8.6	5.1	3.0	2.3
Bachelor's degree or more.................	8.9	5.3	2.7	2.6

[1] Jobs held in more than one age category were counted in each category, but only once in the total.   [2] Includes other races, not shown separately.

Source: U.S. Bureau of Labor Statistics, *Number of Jobs Held, Labor Market Activity, and Earnings Growth Over Two Decades: Results from a Longitudinal Survey,* USDL 00-119, April 25, 2000.

Labor Force, Employment, and Earnings   377

No. 588. Distribution of Workers by Tenure With Current Employer by Selected Characteristic: 2000

[120,303 represents 120,303,000. As of February. For employed wage and salary workers 16 years old and over. Based on the Current Population Survey and subject to sampling error; see source and Appendix III]

Characteristic	Number employed (1,000)	Percent distribution by tenure with current employer								Median years [1]
		12 months or less	13 to 23 months	2 years	3 to 4 years	5 to 9 years	10 to 14 years	15 to 19 years	20 years or more	
Total [2]	120,303	26.8	8.0	5.3	16.1	17.1	11.0	6.1	9.5	3.5
AGE AND SEX										
16 to 19 years old	6,713	75.1	11.9	6.9	5.8	0.3	-	-	-	0.7
20 years old and over	113,590	24.0	7.7	5.3	16.7	18.1	11.7	6.4	10.1	4.0
20 to 24 years old	12,535	54.7	13.0	9.3	17.5	5.5	(Z)	-	-	1.1
25 to 34 years old	28,560	31.1	10.3	7.1	21.9	21.2	7.4	0.9	(Z)	2.6
35 to 44 years old	32,625	19.4	6.9	4.5	16.9	21.2	15.5	9.5	6.1	4.8
45 to 54 years old	25,650	13.7	5.4	3.3	13.0	17.7	14.9	10.0	21.8	8.2
55 to 64 years old	11,326	11.2	3.9	3.3	11.7	16.8	15.8	9.8	27.5	10.0
65 years old and over	2,893	12.9	4.9	2.7	12.6	16.9	15.4	9.2	25.5	9.5
Male	62,306	25.6	7.7	5.3	15.8	17.3	10.9	6.5	11.0	3.8
16 to 19 years old	3,401	73.8	12.2	7.7	6.0	0.4	-	-	-	0.7
20 years old and over	58,905	22.9	7.4	5.2	16.4	18.2	11.5	6.8	11.6	4.2
20 to 24 years old	6,499	52.0	12.7	9.2	19.8	6.1	0.1	-	-	1.2
25 to 34 years old	15,222	29.4	10.0	7.3	21.8	22.1	8.4	0.9	(Z)	2.7
35 to 44 years old	17,023	17.9	6.4	4.2	15.7	20.9	16.4	11.1	7.3	5.4
45 to 54 years old	12,858	13.1	5.0	3.2	11.7	16.8	13.0	10.8	26.3	9.5
55 to 64 years old	5,841	11.2	3.9	3.2	11.4	16.9	14.5	8.2	30.6	10.2
65 years old and over	1,461	14.4	3.4	2.5	12.2	18.5	12.7	8.1	28.0	9.1
Female	57,997	28.1	8.3	5.4	16.4	17.0	11.1	5.7	8.0	3.3
16 to 19 years old	3,312	76.5	11.7	6.0	5.6	0.1	-	-	-	0.7
20 years old and over	54,685	25.2	8.1	5.3	17.1	18.0	11.8	6.0	8.5	3.7
20 to 24 years old	6,037	57.6	13.3	9.4	15.0	4.8	-	-	-	1.0
25 to 34 years old	13,338	33.0	10.7	6.8	22.0	20.2	6.3	1.0	-	2.5
35 to 44 years old	15,601	21.0	7.4	4.9	18.2	21.5	14.4	7.8	4.8	4.3
45 to 54 years old	12,791	14.4	5.9	3.5	14.3	18.7	16.8	9.2	17.3	7.3
55 to 64 years old	5,485	11.3	3.8	3.4	11.9	16.6	17.2	11.6	24.3	9.9
65 years old and over	1,432	11.5	6.4	2.8	12.9	15.3	18.0	10.3	22.8	9.7
RACE AND HISPANIC ORIGIN										
White	100,624	26.2	8.0	5.2	16.0	17.1	11.2	6.3	9.8	3.6
Male	52,890	24.9	7.6	5.3	15.7	17.2	11.0	6.6	11.5	3.9
Female	47,735	27.6	8.5	5.2	16.4	17.0	11.4	6.0	7.9	3.4
Black	14,199	29.3	7.0	6.1	15.6	17.6	10.0	5.3	9.2	3.4
Male	6,546	29.0	7.2	6.0	15.1	17.8	10.1	6.2	8.6	3.3
Female	7,653	29.5	6.8	6.1	16.1	17.4	9.8	4.5	9.8	3.3
Hispanic origin [3]	13,767	30.7	8.3	7.7	18.1	16.6	8.8	4.3	5.5	2.8
Male	7,971	28.7	8.0	7.6	17.7	17.6	9.6	4.8	6.0	3.0
Female	5,796	33.4	8.6	7.9	18.7	15.3	7.7	3.7	4.7	2.5

- Represents zero.   Z Less than 0.05 percent.   [1] For definition of median, see Guide to Tabular Presentation.   [2] Includes other races, not shown separately.   [3] Persons of Hispanic origin may be of any race.
Source: U. S. Bureau of Labor Statistics, News, USDL 00-245, August 29, 2000; and unpublished data.

No. 589. Part-Time Workers by Reason: 2000

[In thousands (29,620 represents 29,620,000), except hours. For persons working 1 to 34 hours per week. For civilian noninstitutional population 16 years old and over. Annual average of monthly figures. Based on the Current Population Survey and subject to sampling error; see text, Section 1, Population, and Appendix III]

Reason	All industries			Nonagricultural industries		
	Total	Usually work—		Total	Usually work—	
		Full time	Part time		Full time	Part time
Total working fewer than 35 hours	29,620	9,020	20,599	28,732	8,757	19,975
Economic reasons	3,190	1,313	1,877	3,045	1,236	1,810
Slack work or business conditions	1,927	1,041	886	1,835	989	846
Could find only part-time work	944	-	944	924	-	924
Seasonal work	142	96	47	115	75	40
Job started or ended during the week	177	177	-	171	171	-
Noneconomic reasons	26,429	7,707	18,722	25,687	7,521	18,165
Child-care problems	872	94	779	860	93	767
Other family or personal obligations	5,617	735	4,882	5,461	718	4,743
Health or medical limitations	727	-	727	696	-	696
In school or training	6,321	91	6,231	6,181	89	6,093
Retired or Social Security limit on earnings	1,940	-	1,940	1,819	-	1,819
Vacation or personal day	3,223	3,223	-	3,169	3,169	-
Holiday, legal, or religious	427	427	-	422	422	-
Weather related curtailment	299	299	-	257	257	-
Other	7,003	2,839	4,164	6,821	2,775	4,046
Average hours per week:						
Economic reasons	23.3	23.9	22.8	23.3	24.0	22.9
Noneconomic reasons	21.3	25.2	19.7	21.4	25.3	19.8

- Represents or rounds to zero.
Source: U.S. Bureau of Labor Statistics, Employment and Earnings, monthly, January 2001 issue.

378   Labor Force, Employment, and Earnings

No. 590. Displaced Workers by Selected Characteristics: 2000

[In percent, except total (3,275 represents 3,275,000). As of February. For persons 20 years old and over with tenure of 3 years or more who lost or left a job between January 1997 and December 1999 because of plant closings or moves, slack work, or the abolishment of their positions. Data revised since originally published. Based on Current Population Survey and subject to sampling error; see source and Appendix III]

		Employment status			Reason for job loss		
Characteristic	Total (1,000)	Employed	Un-employed	Not in the labor force	Plant or company closed down or moved	Slack work	Position or shift abolished
Total [1]	3,275	73.5	10.4	16.1	49.4	21.6	29.0
20 to 24 years old	100	87.7	3.7	8.7	49.8	29.5	20.7
25 to 54 years old	2,503	79.5	10.3	10.2	48.3	22.1	29.6
55 to 64 years old	517	56.0	13.6	30.4	56.6	15.3	28.1
65 years old and over	155	26.3	5.2	68.6	43.1	29.0	27.9
Males	1,765	78.9	9.6	11.5	47.1	24.0	28.9
20 to 24 years old	75	86.6	4.9	8.4	43.4	36.1	20.5
25 to 54 years old	1,331	85.1	9.1	5.8	46.2	24.0	29.8
55 to 64 years old	279	62.9	13.3	23.8	56.3	17.4	26.3
65 years old and over	80	23.6	10.0	66.4	33.5	34.6	31.9
Females	1,511	67.3	11.3	21.4	52.1	18.7	29.1
20 to 24 years old	25	(2)	(2)	(2)	(2)	(2)	(2)
25 to 54 years old	1,172	73.2	11.7	15.1	50.7	19.9	29.4
55 to 64 years old	238	47.9	14.0	38.1	57.0	12.8	30.2
65 years old and over	75	29.1	-	70.9	53.4	23.0	23.6
White	2,778	74.4	9.9	15.7	48.9	20.9	30.3
Black	363	72.2	12.8	15.0	53.2	26.5	20.3
Hispanic origin [3]	346	69.7	13.0	17.3	50.4	32.1	17.5

- Represents zero.   [1] Includes other races, not shown separately.   [2] Data not shown where base is less than 75,000.
[3] Persons of Hispanic origin may be of any race.
Source: U.S. Bureau of Labor Statistics, *News*, USDL 00-223, August 9, 2000.

No. 591. Labor Force Status of Persons With a Work Disability by Age: 2000

[In percent, except as indicated (21,379 represents 21,379,000). As of March. For civilians 16 to 74 who have a condition which prevents then from working or limits the amount of work they can do. Data from the Current Population Survey and subject to sampling error; see text, Section 1, Population, and Appendix III]

Labor force status	Total	Age						
		16 to 24 years old	25 to 34 years old	35 to 44 years old	45 to 54 years old	55 to 64 years old	65 to 69 years old	70 to 74 years old
Number (1,000)	21,379	1,393	2,114	3,840	4,588	5,154	2,146	2,143
In labor force	26.2	40.4	42.2	36.0	32.2	17.3	12.9	5.2
Employed	23.7	33.4	37.8	32.0	30.2	16.1	12.3	4.7
Full-time	15.3	18.0	26.7	22.3	21.9	9.8	2.5	1.4
Not in labor force	73.8	59.6	57.8	64.0	67.8	82.7	87.1	94.8
Unemployment rate	9.3	17.3	10.4	11.1	6.1	7.0	4.7	8.7

Source: U.S. Census Bureau Internet site <http://www.census.gov/hhes/www/disable/disabcps.html> (accessed 20 August 2001).

No. 592. Persons Not in the Labor Force: 2000

[In thousands (68,836 represents 68,836,000). Annual average of monthly figures. For the civilian noninstitutional population 16 years old and over. Based on the Current Population Survey; see text, Section 1, Population, and Appendix III]

Status and reason		Age			Sex	
	Total	16 to 24 years old	25 to 54 years old	55 years old and over	Male	Female
Total not in the labor force	68,836	11,738	18,953	38,146	25,484	43,352
Do not want a job now [1]	64,459	10,107	17,007	37,345	23,627	40,832
Want a job now	4,377	1,631	1,945	801	1,856	2,521
In the previous year—						
Did not search for a job	2,675	903	1,143	629	1,068	1,607
Did search for a job [2]	1,703	728	802	172	788	914
Not available for work now	550	280	237	33	217	334
Available for work now, not looking for work	1,152	448	565	139	572	581
Reason for not currently looking for work:						
Discouraged over job prospects [3]	260	79	143	39	160	100
Family responsibilities	118	26	83	10	23	96
In school or training	185	158	26	1	97	88
Ill health or disability	95	15	58	22	49	46
Other [4]	493	171	255	68	243	250

[1] Includes some persons who are not asked if they want a job.   [2] Persons who had a job in the prior 12 months must have searched since the end of that job.   [3] Includes such things as believes no work available, could not find work, lacks necessary schooling or training, employer thinks too young or old, and other types of discrimination.   [4] Includes such things as child care and transportation problems.
Source: U.S. Bureau of Labor Statistics, *Employment and Earnings*, monthly, January 2001 issue.

Labor Force, Employment, and Earnings   379

[100,834 represents 100,834,000. For civilian noninstitutional population 16 years old and over. Annual average of monthly figures. Based on Current Population Survey; see text, Section 1, Population, and Appendix III. Persons of Hispanic origin may be of any race. See headnote, Table 584]

Occupation	1983				2000 [1]			
	Total employed (1,000)	Percent of total			Total employed (1,000)	Percent of total		
		Female	Black	Hispanic		Female	Black	Hispanic
Total...............................	100,834	43.7	9.3	5.3	135,208	46.5	11.3	10.7
Managerial and professional specialty	23,592	40.9	5.6	2.6	40,887	49.8	8.2	5.0
Executive, administrative, and managerial [2].........	10,772	32.4	4.7	2.8	19,774	45.3	7.6	5.4
Officials and administrators, public	417	38.5	8.3	3.8	651	52.7	13.1	7.0
Financial managers	357	38.6	3.5	3.1	784	50.1	6.1	4.3
Personnel and labor relations managers	106	43.9	4.9	2.6	226	61.8	7.9	4.0
Purchasing managers.....................	82	23.6	5.1	1.4	123	41.3	7.0	3.2
Managers, marketing, advertising and public relations ..	396	21.8	2.7	1.7	755	37.6	4.2	4.2
Administrators, education and related fields	415	41.4	11.3	2.4	848	67.0	13.5	5.7
Managers, medicine and health	91	57.0	5.0	2.0	752	77.9	9.7	5.4
Managers, properties and real estate	305	42.8	5.5	5.2	552	50.9	8.2	7.2
Management-related occupations	2,966	40.3	5.8	3.5	4,932	56.5	9.5	5.4
Accountants and auditors	1,105	38.7	5.5	3.3	1,592	56.7	8.9	5.1
Professional specialty [2]	12,820	48.1	6.4	2.5	21,113	53.9	8.7	4.6
Architects................................	103	12.7	1.6	1.5	215	23.5	1.6	5.5
Engineers [2]	1,572	5.8	2.7	2.2	2,093	9.9	5.7	3.7
Aerospace engineers	80	6.9	1.5	2.1	78	9.7	5.4	3.6
Chemical engineers	67	6.1	3.0	1.4	85	10.4	5.1	1.0
Civil engineers......................	211	4.0	1.9	3.2	288	9.7	6.1	2.7
Electrical and electronic..............	450	6.1	3.4	3.1	725	9.8	6.3	3.6
Industrial engineers	210	11.0	3.3	2.4	244	15.3	6.4	4.0
Mechanical	259	2.8	3.2	1.1	342	6.3	4.7	3.7
Mathematical and computer scientists [2].........	463	29.6	5.4	2.6	2,074	31.4	8.1	3.7
Computer systems analysts, scientists	276	27.8	6.2	2.7	1,797	29.2	8.0	3.6
Operations and systems researchers and analysts ...	142	31.3	4.9	2.2	227	45.5	10.9	4.4
Natural scientists [2]........................	357	20.5	2.6	2.1	566	33.5	5.4	3.2
Chemists, except biochemists...............	98	23.3	4.3	1.2	153	30.3	11.0	2.2
Biological and life scientists	55	40.8	2.4	1.8	114	45.4	4.0	6.0
Medical scientists	(3)	(3)	(3)	(3)	84	49.5	4.6	4.6
Health diagnosing occupations [2].............	735	13.3	2.7	3.3	1,038	27.1	5.2	3.4
Physicians	519	15.8	3.2	4.5	719	27.9	6.3	3.7
Dentists	126	6.7	2.4	1.0	168	18.7	3.4	2.2
Health assessment and treating occupations	1,900	85.8	7.1	2.2	2,966	85.7	9.0	3.4
Registered nurses	1,372	95.8	6.7	1.8	2,111	92.8	9.5	2.8
Pharmacists	158	26.7	3.8	2.6	208	46.5	3.3	3.8
Dietitians	71	90.8	21.0	3.7	97	89.9	18.4	4.8
Therapists [2]	247	76.3	7.6	2.7	478	74.7	8.1	5.0
Respiratory therapists	69	69.4	6.5	3.7	78	62.4	10.8	5.3
Physical therapists	55	77.0	9.7	1.5	144	61.1	6.5	6.8
Speech therapists	51	90.5	1.5	-	102	93.5	4.5	2.0
Physicians' assistants	51	36.3	7.7	4.4	72	57.6	5.6	7.8
Teachers, college and university........	606	36.3	4.4	1.8	961	43.7	6.4	4.6
Teachers, except college and university [2]...........	3,365	70.9	9.1	2.7	5,353	75.4	10.4	5.2
Prekindergarten and kindergarten	299	98.2	11.8	3.4	626	98.5	13.3	8.0
Elementary school	1,350	83.3	11.1	3.1	2,177	83.3	11.3	5.6
Secondary school....................	1,209	51.8	7.2	2.3	1,319	57.9	8.9	4.2
Special education...................	81	82.2	10.2	2.3	362	82.6	9.2	3.2
Counselors, educational and vocational	184	53.1	13.9	3.2	258	70.2	17.1	5.3
Librarians, archivists, and curators	213	84.4	7.8	1.6	263	84.4	6.0	5.8
Librarians	193	87.3	7.9	1.8	232	85.2	6.7	6.6
Social scientists and urban planners [2].........	261	46.8	7.1	2.1	450	58.9	7.8	4.1
Economists..........................	98	37.9	6.3	2.7	139	53.3	6.3	4.4
Psychologists	135	57.1	8.6	1.1	265	64.6	8.1	4.0
Social, recreation, and religious workers [2].........	831	43.1	12.1	3.8	1,492	56.4	17.4	6.4
Social workers........................	407	64.3	18.2	6.3	828	72.4	22.7	8.5
Recreation workers....................	65	71.9	15.7	2.0	126	71.0	9.5	4.9
Clergy	293	5.6	4.9	1.4	369	13.8	14.1	4.5
Lawyers and judges......................	651	15.8	2.7	1.0	926	29.7	5.7	4.1
Lawyers.............................	612	15.3	2.6	0.9	881	29.6	5.4	3.9
Writers, artists, entertainers, and athletes [2]	1,544	42.7	4.8	2.9	2,439	50.0	6.9	5.6
Authors	62	46.7	2.1	0.9	138	54.1	7.7	2.2
Technical writers	(3)	(3)	(3)	(3)	70	64.2	2.1	1.7
Designers	393	52.7	3.1	2.7	738	57.2	4.0	6.3
Musicians and composers	155	28.0	7.9	4.4	161	34.1	13.5	6.0
Actors and directors	60	30.8	6.6	3.4	139	41.5	12.8	6.1
Painters, sculptors, craft-artists, and artist printmakers	186	47.4	2.1	2.3	238	46.5	6.8	4.2
Photographers........................	113	20.7	4.0	3.4	148	32.6	5.7	5.9
Editors and reporters	204	48.4	2.9	2.1	288	55.8	5.0	3.0
Public relations specialists	157	50.1	6.2	1.9	205	61.1	10.8	5.5
Announcers..........................	(3)	(3)	(3)	(3)	54	10.7	10.5	6.0
Athletes	58	17.6	9.4	1.7	90	19.8	10.9	5.5

See footnotes at end of table.

U.S. Census Bureau, Statistical Abstract of the United States: 2001

[100,834 represents 100,834,000. For civilian noninstitutional population 16 years old and over. Annual average of monthly figures. Based on Current Population Survey; see text, Section 1, Population, and Appendix III. Persons of Hispanic origin may be of any race. See headnote, Table 584]

Occupation	1983				2000 [1]			
	Total employed (1,000)	Percent of total			Total employed (1,000)	Percent of total		
		Female	Black	Hispanic		Female	Black	Hispanic
Technical, sales, and administrative support	31,265	64.6	7.6	4.3	39,442	63.8	11.4	8.9
Technicians and related support	3,053	48.2	8.2	3.1	4,385	51.7	11.2	6.9
Health technologists and technicians [2]	1,111	84.3	12.7	3.1	1,724	80.5	15.0	8.2
Clinical laboratory technologists and technicians	255	76.2	10.5	2.9	342	75.0	18.0	7.5
Dental hygienists	66	98.6	1.6	-	112	98.5	2.4	1.7
Radiologic technicians	101	71.7	8.6	4.5	161	69.2	10.8	7.7
Licensed practical nurses	443	97.0	17.7	3.1	374	93.6	20.0	5.0
Engineering and related technologists and technicians [2]	822	18.4	6.1	3.5	1,002	20.4	10.0	6.1
Electrical and electronic technicians	260	12.5	8.2	4.6	468	16.9	11.0	7.1
Drafting occupations	273	17.5	5.5	2.3	219	23.4	6.2	4.7
Surveying and mapping technicians	(3)	(3)	(3)	(3)	79	7.4	6.5	7.8
Science technicians [2]	202	29.1	6.6	2.8	270	41.4	8.7	8.4
Biological technicians	52	37.7	2.9	2.0	108	59.5	7.1	8.2
Chemical technicians	82	26.9	9.5	3.5	71	21.2	7.2	7.6
Technicians, except health, engineering, and science [2]	917	35.3	5.0	2.7	1,389	40.5	7.9	5.7
Airplane pilots and navigators	69	2.1	-	1.6	129	3.7	1.9	4.3
Computer programmers	443	32.5	4.4	2.1	699	26.5	8.1	3.5
Legal assistants	128	74.0	4.3	3.6	387	84.4	8.4	9.8
Sales occupations	11,818	47.5	4.7	3.7	16,340	49.6	8.8	8.5
Supervisors and proprietors	2,958	28.4	3.6	3.4	4,937	40.3	6.6	7.3
Sales representatives, finance and business services [2]	1,853	37.2	2.7	2.2	2,934	44.5	7.6	4.9
Insurance sales	551	25.1	3.8	2.5	577	42.5	6.5	4.4
Real estate sales	570	48.9	1.3	1.5	787	54.3	5.3	5.0
Securities and financial services sales	212	23.6	3.1	1.1	600	31.3	8.2	3.4
Advertising and related sales	124	47.9	4.5	3.3	165	61.9	9.2	5.7
Sales representatives, commodities, except retail	1,442	15.1	2.1	2.2	1,581	27.5	2.8	6.4
Sales workers, retail and personal services	5,511	69.7	6.7	4.8	6,782	63.5	12.3	11.4
Cashiers	2,009	84.4	10.1	5.4	2,939	77.5	16.5	13.5
Sales-related occupations	54	58.7	2.8	1.3	107	69.1	9.3	2.2
Administrative support, including clerical	16,395	79.9	9.6	5.0	18,717	79.0	13.7	9.7
Supervisors	676	53.4	9.3	5.0	710	60.3	17.0	9.4
Computer equipment operators	605	63.9	12.5	6.0	323	48.6	16.6	7.4
Computer operators	597	63.7	12.1	6.0	321	48.7	16.6	7.4
Secretaries, stenographers, and typists [2]	4,861	98.2	7.3	4.5	3,328	98.0	9.9	8.6
Secretaries	3,891	99.0	5.8	4.0	2,623	98.9	8.5	8.7
Typists	906	95.6	13.8	6.4	551	94.6	17.8	9.3
Information clerks	1,174	88.9	8.5	5.5	2,071	88.0	11.3	10.4
Receptionists	602	96.8	7.5	6.6	1,017	96.7	9.7	11.6
Records processing occupations, except financial [2]	866	82.4	13.9	4.8	1,119	81.5	16.9	10.6
Order clerks	188	78.1	10.6	4.4	305	77.1	24.4	12.4
Personnel clerks, except payroll and time keeping	64	91.1	14.9	4.6	84	82.5	18.7	4.8
Library clerks	147	81.9	15.4	2.5	152	87.0	10.8	6.5
File clerks	287	83.5	16.7	6.1	338	80.2	15.3	12.0
Records clerks	157	82.8	11.6	5.6	227	85.9	13.4	10.7
Financial records processing [2]	2,457	89.4	4.6	3.7	2,269	91.8	9.2	7.3
Bookkeepers, accounting, and auditing clerks	1,970	91.0	4.3	3.3	1,719	92.2	7.8	6.1
Payroll and time keeping clerks	192	82.2	5.9	5.0	174	91.3	8.7	8.4
Billing clerks	146	88.4	6.2	3.9	198	92.2	16.3	12.4
Cost and rate clerks	96	75.6	5.9	5.3	42	77.9	9.4	10.9
Billing, posting, and calculating machine operators	(3)	(3)	(3)	(3)	134	91.7	16.8	12.3
Duplicating, mail and other office machine operators	68	62.6	16.0	6.1	55	54.2	16.8	9.6
Communications equipment operators	256	89.1	17.0	4.4	167	84.3	21.8	10.7
Telephone operators	244	90.4	17.0	4.3	156	83.9	22.9	10.4
Mail and message distributing occupations	799	31.6	18.1	4.5	978	41.2	21.9	7.7
Postal clerks, except mail carriers	248	36.7	26.2	5.2	304	54.4	32.4	6.2
Mail carrier, postal service	259	17.1	12.5	2.7	340	30.6	14.7	5.9
Mail clerks, except postal service	170	50.0	15.8	5.9	178	54.0	22.6	11.2
Messengers	122	26.2	16.7	5.2	157	23.9	16.7	10.4
Material recording, scheduling, and distributing [2] [4]	1,562	37.5	10.9	6.6	2,052	46.7	15.3	12.8
Dispatchers	157	41.7	11.4	4.3	269	51.7	15.1	9.0
Production coordinators	182	44.0	6.1	2.2	227	58.5	12.0	6.6
Traffic, shipping, and receiving clerks	421	22.6	9.1	11.1	661	33.8	16.1	17.5
Stock and inventory clerks	532	38.7	13.3	5.5	460	44.9	15.1	13.1
Expediters	112	57.5	8.4	4.3	310	66.5	13.4	10.5
Adjusters and investigators	675	69.9	11.1	5.1	1,818	75.5	17.5	10.1
Insurance adjusters, examiners, and investigators	199	65.0	11.5	3.3	451	73.9	14.6	7.0
Investigators and adjusters, except insurance	301	70.1	11.3	4.8	1,097	76.0	17.0	11.5
Eligibility clerks, social welfare	69	88.7	12.9	9.4	94	89.2	16.1	9.5
Bill and account collectors	106	66.4	8.5	6.5	176	69.4	28.2	9.5
Miscellaneous administrative support [2]	2,397	85.2	12.5	5.9	3,826	83.9	14.3	10.4
General office clerks	648	80.6	12.7	5.2	864	83.6	12.9	10.5
Bank tellers	480	91.0	7.5	4.3	431	90.0	13.7	8.2
Data entry keyers	311	93.6	18.6	5.6	749	83.5	18.8	11.2
Statistical clerks	96	75.7	7.5	3.4	104	88.5	15.8	8.4
Teachers' aides	348	93.7	17.8	12.6	710	91.0	12.8	14.4

See footnotes at end of table.

U.S. Census Bureau, Statistical Abstract of the United States: 2001

[100,834 represents 100,834,000. For civilian noninstitutional population 16 years old and over. Annual average of monthly figures. Based on Current Population Survey; see text, Section 1, Population, and Appendix III. Persons of Hispanic origin may be of any race. See headnote, Table 584]

Occupation	1983				2000 [1]			
	Total employed (1,000)	Percent of total			Total employed (1,000)	Percent of total		
		Female	Black	Hispanic		Female	Black	Hispanic
Service occupations	13,857	60.1	16.6	6.8	18,278	60.4	18.1	15.7
Private household [2]	980	96.1	27.8	8.5	792	95.5	14.9	31.7
Child care workers	408	96.9	7.9	3.6	275	97.5	11.6	19.9
Cleaners and servants	512	95.8	42.4	11.8	500	94.8	16.9	37.7
Protective service	1,672	12.8	13.6	4.6	2,399	19.0	19.6	8.7
Supervisors, protective service	127	4.7	7.7	3.1	201	15.1	13.9	7.8
Supervisors, police and detectives	58	4.2	9.3	1.2	116	14.3	10.5	3.0
Firefighting and fire prevention	189	1.0	6.7	4.1	248	3.8	8.7	5.4
Firefighting occupations	170	1.0	7.3	3.8	233	3.0	9.0	5.0
Police and detectives	545	9.4	13.1	4.0	1,060	16.5	18.3	8.4
Police and detectives, public service	412	5.7	9.5	4.4	560	12.1	13.0	10.1
Sheriffs, bailiffs, and other law enforcement officers	87	13.2	11.5	4.0	156	19.2	20.2	5.8
Correctional institution officers	146	17.8	24.0	2.8	344	22.5	25.9	6.9
Guards	711	20.6	17.0	5.6	889	27.0	25.7	10.0
Guards and police, except public service	602	13.0	18.9	6.2	745	20.1	27.5	10.6
Service except private household and protective [2]	11,205	64.0	16.0	6.9	15,087	65.1	18.0	16.0
Food preparation and service occupations [2]	4,860	63.3	10.5	6.8	6,327	57.7	11.9	17.2
Bartenders	338	48.4	2.7	4.4	365	51.8	2.0	13.2
Waiters and waitresses	1,357	87.8	4.1	3.6	1,440	76.7	4.4	11.0
Cooks	1,452	50.0	15.8	6.5	2,076	43.3	17.6	21.6
Food counter, fountain, and related occupations	326	76.0	9.1	6.7	357	67.9	12.6	11.8
Kitchen workers, food preparation	138	77.0	13.7	8.1	317	71.1	13.0	12.3
Waiters' and waitresses' assistants	364	38.8	12.6	14.2	670	51.4	10.5	18.8
Health service occupations	1,739	89.2	23.5	4.8	2,557	89.5	31.4	10.1
Dental assistants	154	98.1	6.1	5.7	218	96.4	5.1	10.6
Health aides, except nursing	316	86.8	16.5	4.8	356	82.6	26.4	8.7
Nursing aides, orderlies, and attendants	1,269	88.7	27.3	4.7	1,983	89.9	35.2	10.4
Cleaning and building service occupations [2]	2,736	38.8	24.4	9.2	3,127	45.0	22.2	23.4
Maids and housemen	531	81.2	32.3	10.1	650	81.3	27.7	28.3
Janitors and cleaners	2,031	28.6	22.6	8.9	2,233	36.3	20.9	22.5
Personal service occupations [2]	1,870	79.2	11.1	6.0	3,077	80.5	14.8	10.8
Barbers	92	12.9	8.4	12.1	108	25.3	27.8	12.7
Hairdressers and cosmetologists	622	88.7	7.0	5.7	820	91.2	10.9	10.7
Attendants, amusement and recreation facilities	131	40.2	7.1	4.3	246	39.4	9.9	6.0
Public transportation attendants	63	74.3	11.3	5.9	127	80.9	12.3	7.9
Welfare service aides	77	92.5	24.2	10.5	99	82.2	30.3	12.7
Family child care providers	(NA)	(NA)	(NA)	(NA)	457	97.7	14.8	13.3
Early childhood teachers' assistants	(NA)	(NA)	(NA)	(NA)	480	95.2	17.4	10.6
Precision production, craft, and repair	12,328	8.1	6.8	6.2	14,882	9.1	8.0	13.9
Mechanics and repairers	4,158	3.0	6.8	5.3	4,875	5.1	8.2	10.7
Mechanics and repairers, except supervisors [2]	3,906	2.8	7.0	5.5	4,652	5.0	8.3	10.8
Vehicle and mobile equipment mechanics/repairers [2]	1,683	0.8	6.9	6.0	1,787	1.6	7.1	13.1
Automobile mechanics	800	0.5	7.8	6.0	860	1.2	7.3	15.6
Aircraft engine mechanics	95	2.5	4.0	7.6	126	6.1	8.3	9.0
Electrical and electronic equipment repairers [2]	674	7.4	7.3	4.5	999	11.5	10.7	7.8
Data processing equipment repairers	98	9.3	6.1	4.5	342	15.4	9.8	4.8
Telephone installers and repairers	247	9.9	7.8	3.7	295	13.1	11.6	9.5
Construction trades	4,289	1.8	6.6	6.0	6,120	2.6	7.0	16.4
Construction trades, except supervisors	3,784	1.9	7.1	6.1	5,153	2.7	7.2	18.1
Carpenters	1,160	1.4	5.0	5.0	1,467	1.7	6.0	16.3
Extractive occupations	196	2.3	3.3	6.0	128	1.9	3.6	7.8
Precision production occupations	3,685	21.5	7.3	7.4	3,759	25.0	9.5	14.4
Operators, fabricators, and laborers	16,091	26.6	14.0	8.3	18,319	23.6	15.4	17.5
Machine operators, assemblers, and inspectors [2]	7,744	42.1	14.0	9.4	7,319	36.9	14.7	19.3
Textile, apparel, and furnishings machine operators [2]	1,414	82.1	18.7	12.5	854	69.2	18.3	33.0
Textile sewing machine operators	806	94.0	15.5	14.5	425	78.4	16.3	40.6
Pressing machine operators	141	66.4	27.1	14.2	81	66.6	13.9	49.9
Fabricators, assemblers, and hand working occupations	1,715	33.7	11.3	8.7	2,070	33.5	13.9	17.1
Production inspectors, testers, samplers, and weighers	794	53.8	13.0	7.7	703	48.5	16.3	17.3
Transportation and material moving occupations	4,201	7.8	13.0	5.9	5,557	10.0	16.5	11.9
Motor vehicle operators	2,978	9.2	13.5	6.0	4,222	11.5	16.7	11.8
Trucks drivers	2,195	3.1	12.3	5.7	3,088	4.7	14.4	12.5
Transportation occupations, except motor vehicles	212	2.4	6.7	3.0	183	3.5	13.7	3.6
Material moving equipment operators	1,011	4.8	12.9	6.3	1,152	5.4	16.0	13.7
Industrial truck and tractor operators	369	5.6	19.6	8.2	569	7.0	22.1	18.4
Handlers, equipment cleaners, helpers, and laborers [2]	4,147	16.8	15.1	8.6	5,443	19.8	15.3	20.7
Freight, stock, and material handlers	1,488	15.4	15.3	7.1	2,015	22.4	17.7	14.6
Laborers, except construction	1,024	19.4	16.0	8.6	1,307	20.8	15.5	18.4
Farming, forestry, and fishing	3,700	16.0	7.5	8.2	3,399	20.6	4.9	23.7
Farm operators and managers	1,450	12.1	1.3	0.7	1,125	25.4	0.9	3.0
Other agricultural and related occupations	2,072	19.9	11.7	14.0	2,115	18.9	7.1	36.1
Farm workers	1,149	24.8	11.6	15.9	768	18.7	4.7	47.4
Forestry and logging occupations	126	1.4	12.8	2.1	109	8.4	4.4	7.8
Fishers, hunters, and trappers	53	4.5	1.8	2.5	51	11.9	3.6	2.0

- Represents or rounds to zero.   NA Not available.   [1] See footnote 2, Table 567.   [2] Includes other occupations, not shown separately.   [3] Level of total employment below 50,000.   [4] Includes clerks.

Source: U.S. Bureau of Labor Statistics, Employment and Earnings, monthly, January issues; and unpublished data.

No. 594. Employment Projections by Occupation: 1998 and 2008

[In thousands (299 represents 299,000), **except percent and rank**. Estimates based on the Current Employment Statistics estimates; the Occupational Employment Statistics estimates; and the Current Population Survey. See source for methodological assumptions]

Occupation	Employment (1,000) 1998	Employment (1,000) 2008	Change Number (1,000)	Change Percent	Quartile rank by 1997 median hourly earnings [1]	Education and training category
FASTEST GROWING						
Computer engineers	299	622	323	108	1	Bachelor's degree
Computer support specialists	429	869	439	102	1	Associate degree
Systems analysts	617	1,194	577	94	1	Bachelor's degree
Database administrators	87	155	67	77	1	Bachelor's degree
Desktop publishing specialists	26	44	19	73	2	Long-term on-the-job training
Paralegals and legal assistants	136	220	84	62	2	Associate degree
Personal care and home health aides	746	1,179	433	58	4	Short-term on-the-job training
Medical assistants	252	398	146	58	3	Moderate-term on-the-job training
Social and human service assistants	268	410	141	53	3	Moderate-term on-the-job training
Physician assistants	66	98	32	48	1	Bachelor's degree
Data processing equipment repairers	79	117	37	47	2	Postsecondary vocational training
Residential counselors	190	278	88	46	3	Bachelor's degree
Electronic semiconductor processors	63	92	29	45	2	Moderate-term on-the-job training
Medical records and health information technicians	92	133	41	44	3	Associate degree
Physical therapy assistants and aides	82	118	36	44	3	Associate degree
Engineering, natural science, and computer and information systems managers	326	468	142	43	1	Work experience plus bachelors or higher degree
Respiratory therapists	86	123	37	43	2	Associate degree
Dental assistants	229	325	97	42	3	Moderate-term on-the-job training
Surgical technologists	54	77	23	42	2	Postsecondary vocational training
Securities, commodities, and financial services sales agents	303	427	124	41	1	Bachelor's degree
Dental hygienists	143	201	58	41	1	Associate degree
Occupational therapy assistants and aides	19	26	7	40	2	Associate degree
Cardiovascular technologists and technicians	21	29	8	39	2	Associate degree
Correctional officers	383	532	148	39	2	Long-term on-the-job training
Speech-language pathologists and audiologists	105	145	40	38	1	Masters degree
Social workers	604	822	218	36	2	Bachelor's degree
Bill and account collectors	311	420	110	35	3	Short-term on-the-job training
Ambulance drivers and attendants, except EMTs	19	26	7	35	3	Short-term on-the-job training
Biological scientists	81	109	28	35	1	Doctoral degree
Occupational therapists	73	98	25	34	1	Bachelor's degree
LARGEST JOB GROWTH						
Systems analysts	617	1,194	577	94	1	Bachelor's degree
Retail salespersons	4,056	4,620	563	14	4	Short-term on-the-job training
Cashiers	3,198	3,754	556	17	4	Short-term on-the-job training
General managers and top executives	3,362	3,913	551	16	1	Work experience plus bachelors or higher degree
Truck drivers light and heavy	2,970	3,463	493	17	2	Short-term on-the-job training
Office clerks, general	3,021	3,484	463	15	3	Short-term on-the-job training
Registered nurses	2,079	2,530	451	22	1	Associate degree
Computer support specialists	429	869	439	102	1	Associate degree
Personal care and home health aides	746	1,179	433	58	4	Short-term on-the-job training
Teacher assistants	1,192	1,567	375	31	4	Short-term on-the-job training
Janitors and cleaners, including maids and housekeeping cleaners	3,184	3,549	365	11	4	Short-term on-the-job training
Nursing aides, orderlies, and attendants	1,367	1,692	325	24	4	Short-term on-the-job training
Computer engineers	299	622	323	108	1	Bachelor's degree
Teachers, secondary school	1,426	1,749	322	23	1	Bachelor's degree
Office and administrative support supervisors and managers	1,611	1,924	313	19	2	Work experience in a related occupation
Receptionists and information clerks	1,293	1,599	305	24	3	Short-term on-the-job training
Waiters and waitresses	2,019	2,322	303	15	4	Short-term on-the-job training
Guards	1,027	1,321	294	29	4	Short-term on-the-job training
Marketing and sales worker supervisors	2,584	2,847	263	10	2	Work experience in a related occupation
Food counter, fountain, and related workers	2,025	2,272	247	12	4	Short-term on-the-job training
Child care workers	905	1,141	236	26	4	Short-term on-the-job training
Laborers, landscaping and groundskeeping	1,130	1,364	234	21	3	Short-term on-the-job training
Social workers	604	822	218	36	2	Bachelor's degree
Hand packers and packagers	984	1,197	213	22	4	Short-term on-the-job training
Teachers, elementary school	1,754	1,959	205	12	1	Bachelor's degree
Blue-collar worker supervisors	2,198	2,394	196	9	1	Work experience in a related occupation
College and university faculty	865	1,061	195	23	1	Doctoral degree

[1] Quartile ranks based on the Occupational Employment Statistics hourly earnings. Ranks: 1 = $16.25 and over; 2 = $10.89 to $16.14; 3 = $7.78 to $10.88; 4 = below $7.77.

Source: U.S. Bureau of Labor Statistics, *Monthly Labor Review*, November 1999.

Labor Force, Employment, and Earnings **383**

No. 595. Occupations of the Employed by Selected Characteristics: 2000

[In thousands (59,215 represents 59,215,000). Annual averages of monthly figures. For civilian noninstitutional population 25 to 64 years old. Based on Current Population Survey; see text, Section 1, Population, and Appendix III]

Sex, race, and educational attainment	Total employed	Managerial/professional	Tech./sales/administrative	Service[1]	Precision production[2]	Operators/fabricators[3]	Farming, forestry, fishing
Male, total[4]	59,215	18,709	11,180	4,908	11,731	10,753	1,934
Less than a high school diploma	6,444	303	447	834	1,904	2,342	615
High school graduates, no college	18,416	2,100	2,974	1,849	5,386	5,390	718
Less than a bachelor's degree	15,606	3,744	3,844	1,603	3,629	2,404	383
College graduates	18,748	12,562	3,916	622	813	616	218
White	50,400	16,390	9,572	3,660	10,410	8,607	1,761
Less than a high school diploma	5,450	261	387	596	1,692	1,972	543
High school graduates, no college	15,536	1,869	2,539	1,316	4,831	4,331	649
Less than a bachelor's degree	13,192	3,314	3,258	1,238	3,185	1,838	360
College graduates	16,222	10,946	3,388	510	702	466	209
Black	5,929	1,213	1,031	934	915	1,712	125
Less than a high school diploma	701	25	44	160	151	269	52
High school graduates, no college	2,239	163	314	421	406	881	54
Less than a bachelor's degree	1,792	306	422	286	296	468	14
College graduates	1,197	719	251	67	60	94	5
Female, total[4]	51,328	18,495	19,518	7,978	1,184	3,611	542
Less than a high school diploma	4,100	255	832	1,707	202	985	120
High school graduates, no college	16,134	2,330	7,581	3,634	553	1,833	202
Less than a bachelor's degree	15,443	4,569	7,724	2,067	303	635	145
College graduates	15,651	11,341	3,381	570	127	157	76
White	42,084	15,682	16,327	5,902	943	2,714	517
Less than a high school diploma	3,169	214	685	1,237	160	760	112
High school graduates, no college	13,264	2,026	6,548	2,665	455	1,380	191
Less than a bachelor's degree	12,584	3,880	6,320	1,553	231	459	141
College graduates	13,067	9,562	2,773	447	96	115	73
Black	6,732	1,864	2,386	1,666	150	652	13
Less than a high school diploma	688	32	102	388	21	140	4
High school graduates, no college	2,282	235	821	796	69	354	8
Less than a bachelor's degree	2,273	532	1,137	418	46	139	1
College graduates	1,488	1,064	326	64	13	20	1

[1] Includes private household workers. [2] Includes craft and repair. [3] Includes laborers. [4] Includes other races, not shown separately.

Source: U.S. Bureau of Labor Statistics, unpublished data.

No. 596. Employment by Industry: 1980 to 2000

[In thousands (99,303 represents 99,303,000), except percent. See headnote, Table 570. Data for 1990, and also beginning 1995, not strictly comparable with other years due to changes in industrial classification]

Industry	1980	1990[1]	1995[1]	1999[1]	2000[1] Total	2000[1] Percent Female	2000[1] Percent Black	2000[1] Percent Hispanic[2]
Total employed	99,303	118,793	124,900	133,488	135,208	46.5	11.3	10.7
Agriculture	3,364	3,223	3,440	3,281	3,305	26.4	4.2	22.5
Mining	979	724	627	565	521	13.7	5.2	8.3
Construction	6,215	7,764	7,668	8,987	9,433	9.7	6.7	14.9
Manufacturing	21,942	21,346	20,493	20,070	19,940	32.5	10.3	12.3
Transportation, communication, and other public utilities	6,525	8,168	8,709	9,554	9,740	28.7	15.7	9.4
Wholesale and retail trade	20,191	24,622	26,071	27,572	27,832	47.2	9.6	12.2
Wholesale trade	3,920	4,669	4,986	5,189	5,421	30.4	7.6	11.9
Retail trade	16,270	19,953	21,086	22,383	22,411	51.2	10.1	12.3
Finance, insurance, real estate	5,993	8,051	7,983	8,815	8,727	58.5	10.5	6.9
Services[3]	28,752	39,267	43,953	48,687	49,695	62.1	12.8	9.1
Business and repair services[3]	3,848	7,485	7,526	9,046	9,661	37.4	12.0	11.0
Advertising	191	277	267	284	280	55.2	6.6	6.6
Services to dwellings and buildings	370	827	829	820	862	51.6	16.3	27.0
Personnel supply services	235	710	853	1,066	1,063	59.9	22.8	11.2
Computer and data processing	221	805	1,136	2,079	2,496	31.8	7.4	3.6
Detective/protective services	213	378	506	593	574	25.6	24.3	10.6
Automobile services	952	1,457	1,459	1,583	1,626	14.9	11.0	16.2
Personal services[3]	3,839	4,733	4,375	4,488	4,515	70.0	13.8	18.6
Private households	1,257	1,036	971	940	894	92.1	15.7	29.8
Hotels and lodging places	1,149	1,818	1,495	1,541	1,443	57.9	16.7	21.0
Entertainment and recreation	1,047	1,526	2,238	2,649	2,582	42.3	9.9	9.6
Professional and related services[3]	19,853	25,351	29,661	32,370	32,784	70.0	13.2	7.1
Hospitals	4,036	4,700	4,961	5,117	5,028	76.3	17.5	6.4
Health services, except hospitals	3,345	4,673	5,967	6,529	6,569	79.7	15.4	7.8
Elementary, secondary schools	5,550	5,994	6,653	7,451	7,629	76.0	12.0	8.2
Colleges and universities	2,108	2,637	2,768	2,919	2,903	54.3	10.8	6.3
Social services	1,590	2,239	2,979	3,426	3,519	81.9	19.3	9.2
Legal services	776	1,215	1,335	1,365	1,362	58.5	6.7	6.5
Public administration[4]	5,342	5,627	5,957	5,958	6,015	44.9	16.6	7.3

[1] See footnote 2, Table 567. [2] Persons of Hispanic origin may be of any race. [3] Includes industries not shown separately. [4] Includes workers involved in uniquely governmental activities, e.g., judicial and legislative.

Source: U.S. Bureau of Labor Statistics, Employment and Earnings, monthly, January issues; and unpublished data.

384   Labor Force, Employment, and Earnings

No. 597. Employment Projections by Industry: 1998 to 2008

[**140,515 represents 140,515,000.** Estimates based on the Current Employment Statistics estimates; the Occupational Employment Statistics estimates; and the Current Population Survey. See source for methodological assumptions. Minus sign (-) indicates decline]

Industry	1987 SIC code [1]	Employment (1,000)		Change (1,000), 1998-2008	Average annual rate of change, 1998-2008
		1998	2008		
Total	(X)	140,515	160,795	20,281	1.4
MOST RAPID GROWTH					
Computer and data processing services	737	1,599	3,472	1,872	8.1
Health services, n.e.c. [2]	807-809	1,209	2,018	809	5.3
Residential care	836	747	1,171	424	4.6
Management and public relations	874	1,034	1,500	466	3.8
Personnel supply services	736	3,230	4,623	1,393	3.7
Miscellaneous equipment rental and leasing	735	258	369	111	3.6
Museums, botanical and zoological gardens	84	93	131	39	3.6
Research and testing services	873	614	861	247	3.4
Miscellaneous transportation services	473,474,478	236	329	94	3.4
Security and commodity brokers	62	645	900	255	3.4
Miscellaneous business services	732,733,738	2,278	3,172	893	3.4
Offices of health practitioners	801-804	2,949	4,098	1,150	3.3
Automobile parking, repair, and services ... [2]	752-754	944	1,300	356	3.2
Amusement and recreation services, n.e.c. [2]	791,9	1,217	1,653	436	3.1
Water and sanitation	494-497	196	263	67	3.0
Local and interurban passenger transit	41	468	622	154	2.9
Individual and miscellaneous social services	832,839	923	1,223	300	2.9
Child day care services	835	605	800	196	2.8
Job training and related services	833	369	484	114	2.7
Landscape and horticultural services	078	460	603	142	2.7
Veterinary services	074	196	255	59	2.7
Producers, orchestras, and entertainers	792	176	225	49	2.5
Cable and pay television services	484	181	230	49	2.4
Commercial sports	794	127	160	34	2.4
Engineering and architectural services	871	905	1,140	235	2.3
Nondepository; holding and investment offices	61,67	906	1,141	235	2.3
Miscellaneous transportation equipment	375,379	76	96	20	2.3
Nursing and personal care facilities	805	1,762	2,213	451	2.3
Automotive rentals, without drivers	751	200	250	50	2.3
Services to buildings	734	950	1,187	237	2.3
MOST RAPID DECLINE					
Crude petroleum, natural gas, and gas liquids	131,132	143	77	-66	-6.0
Apparel	231-238	547	350	-197	-4.4
Coal mining	12	92	59	-32	-4.2
Footwear except rubber and plastic	313,4	38	25	-13	-4.1
Federal electric utilities	(X)	30	20	-10	-4.1
Metal cans and shipping containers	341	37	25	-12	-3.8
Watches, clocks and parts	387	7	5	-2	-3.7
Tobacco products	21	41	30	-11	-3.1
Metal mining	10	50	37	-13	-3.0
Luggage, handbags, and leather products, n.e.c. [2]	311,315-317,319	45	34	-11	-2.7
Blast furnaces and basic steel products	331	232	177	-55	-2.7
Petroleum refining	291	96	75	-21	-2.5
Weaving, finishing, yarn and thread mills	221-224, 226,228	320	251	-69	-2.4
Private households	88	962	759	-203	-2.3
Forestry, fishing, hunting, and trapping	08,09	48	38	-10	-2.3
Hydraulic cement	324	17	14	-4	-2.3
Electrical industrial apparatus	362	153	122	-31	-2.3
Railroad transportation	40	231	185	-46	-2.2
Knitting mills	225	159	128	-32	-2.2
Primary nonferrous smelting and refining	333	39	32	-8	-2.1
Service industries for the printing trade	279	50	41	-9	-2.0
Engines and turbines	351	84	69	-15	-1.9
Household appliances	363	117	96	-20	-1.9
Household audio and video equipment	365	82	67	-14	-1.9
Combined utilities	493	159	131	-27	-1.9
Jewelry, silverware, and plated ware	391	50	42	-8	-1.8
Ordnance and ammunition	348	41	34	-7	-1.8
Tires and inner tubes	301	79	66	-13	-1.8
Electric distribution equipment	361	82	70	-13	-1.7
Photographic equipment and supplies	386	81	69	-12	-1.6

X Not applicable.   [1] Based on the 1987 Standard Industrial Classification; see text, Section 15, Business Enterprise.
[2] N.e.c. means not elsewhere classified.

Source: U.S. Bureau of Labor Statistics. *Monthly Labor Review*, November 1999.

No. 598. Unemployed Workers—Summary: 1980 to 2000

[In thousands (7,637 represents 7,637,000), except as indicated. For civilian noninstitutional population 16 years old and over. Annual averages of monthly figures. For data on unemployment insurance, see Table 537]

Age, sex, race, Hispanic origin	1980	1985	1990 [1]	1995	1997 [1]	1998 [1]	1999 [1]	2000 [1]
UNEMPLOYED								
Total [2]	7,637	8,312	7,047	7,404	6,739	6,210	5,880	5,655
16 to 19 years old	1,669	1,468	1,212	1,346	1,271	1,205	1,162	1,093
20 to 24 years old	1,835	1,738	1,299	1,244	1,152	1,081	1,042	1,025
25 to 44 years old	2,964	3,681	3,323	3,390	2,989	2,677	2,432	2,309
45 to 64 years old	1,075	1,331	1,109	1,269	1,199	1,125	1,120	1,096
65 years and over	94	93	105	153	127	122	124	131
Male	4,267	4,521	3,906	3,983	3,577	3,266	3,066	2,954
16 to 19 years old	913	806	667	744	694	686	633	604
20 to 24 years old	1,076	944	715	673	636	583	562	549
25 to 44 years old	1,619	1,950	1,803	1,776	1,504	1,308	1,195	1,143
45 to 64 years old	600	766	662	697	674	621	606	576
65 years and over	58	55	59	94	69	69	70	82
Female	3,370	3,791	3,140	3,421	3,162	2,944	2,814	2,701
16 to 19 years old	755	661	544	602	577	519	529	489
20 to 24 years old	760	794	584	571	516	498	480	476
25 to 44 years old	1,345	1,732	1,519	1,615	1,486	1,370	1,238	1,167
45 to 64 years old	473	566	447	574	525	503	513	521
65 years and over	36	39	46	60	58	53	54	49
White [3]	5,884	6,191	5,186	5,459	4,836	4,484	4,273	4,099
16 to 19 years old	1,291	1,074	903	952	912	876	844	805
20 to 24 years old	1,364	1,235	899	866	765	731	720	684
Black [3]	1,553	1,864	1,565	1,538	1,560	1,426	1,309	1,269
16 to 19 years old	343	357	268	325	302	281	268	239
20 to 24 years old	426	455	349	311	327	301	273	290
Hispanic [3][4]	620	811	876	1,140	1,069	1,026	945	876
16 to 19 years old	145	141	161	205	197	214	196	181
20 to 24 years old	138	171	167	209	206	194	171	162
Full-time workers	6,269	6,793	5,677	5,909	5,395	4,916	4,669	4,502
Part-time workers	1,369	1,519	1,369	1,495	1,344	1,293	1,211	1,153
UNEMPLOYMENT RATE (percent) [5]								
Total [2]	7.1	7.2	5.6	5.6	4.9	4.5	4.2	4.0
16 to 19 years old	17.8	18.6	15.5	17.3	16.0	14.6	13.9	13.1
20 to 24 years old	11.5	11.1	8.8	9.1	8.5	7.9	7.5	7.1
25 to 44 years old	6.0	6.2	4.9	4.8	4.2	3.8	3.5	3.3
45 to 64 years old	3.7	4.5	3.5	3.4	3.0	2.7	2.6	2.5
65 years and over	3.1	3.2	3.0	4.0	3.3	3.2	3.1	3.1
Male	6.9	7.0	5.7	5.6	4.9	4.4	4.1	3.9
16 to 19 years old	18.3	19.5	16.3	18.4	16.9	16.2	14.7	14.0
20 to 24 years old	12.5	11.4	9.1	9.2	8.9	8.1	7.7	7.3
25 to 44 years old	5.6	5.9	4.8	4.7	3.9	3.4	3.2	3.1
45 to 64 years old	3.5	4.5	3.7	3.5	3.1	2.8	2.6	2.4
65 years and over	3.1	3.1	3.0	4.3	3.0	3.1	3.0	3.4
Female	7.4	7.4	5.5	5.6	5.0	4.6	4.3	4.1
16 to 19 years old	17.2	17.6	14.7	16.1	15.0	12.9	13.2	12.1
20 to 24 years old	10.4	10.7	8.5	9.0	8.1	7.8	7.2	7.0
25 to 44 years old	6.4	6.6	4.9	5.0	4.6	4.2	3.8	3.6
45 to 64 years old	4.0	4.6	3.2	3.3	2.8	2.6	2.5	2.5
65 years and over	3.1	3.3	3.1	3.7	3.6	3.3	3.2	2.8
White [3]	6.3	6.2	4.8	4.9	4.2	3.9	3.7	3.5
16 to 19 years old	15.5	15.7	13.5	14.5	13.6	12.6	12.0	11.4
20 to 24 years old	9.9	9.2	7.3	7.7	6.9	6.5	6.3	5.8
Black [3]	14.3	15.1	11.4	10.4	10.0	8.9	8.0	7.6
16 to 19 years old	38.5	40.2	30.9	35.7	32.4	27.6	27.9	24.7
20 to 24 years old	23.6	24.5	19.9	17.7	18.3	16.8	14.6	15.0
Hispanic [3][4]	10.1	10.5	8.2	9.3	7.7	7.2	6.4	5.7
16 to 19 years old	22.5	24.3	19.5	24.1	21.6	21.3	18.6	16.7
20 to 24 years old	12.1	12.6	9.1	11.5	10.3	9.4	8.3	7.5
Experienced workers [6]	6.9	6.8	5.3	5.4	4.7	4.3	4.0	3.9
Women maintaining families	9.2	10.4	8.3	8.0	8.1	7.2	6.4	5.9
Married men, wife present [2]	4.2	4.3	3.4	3.3	2.7	2.4	2.2	2.0
White	3.9	4.0	3.1	3.0	2.5	2.2	2.1	2.1
Black	7.4	8.0	6.2	5.0	4.3	3.9	3.8	3.7
Percent without work for—								
Fewer than 5 weeks	43.2	42.1	46.3	36.5	37.7	42.2	43.7	45.0
5 to 10 weeks	23.4	22.2	23.5	22.0	21.9	22.1	21.8	23.0
11 to 14 weeks	9.0	8.0	8.5	9.6	9.9	9.3	9.3	8.9
15 to 26 weeks	13.8	12.3	11.7	14.6	14.8	12.3	12.8	11.8
27 weeks and over	10.7	15.4	10.0	17.3	15.8	14.1	12.3	11.4
Unemployment duration, average (weeks)	11.9	15.6	12.0	16.6	15.8	14.5	13.4	12.6

[1] See footnote 2, Table 567. [2] Includes other races, not shown separately. [3] Includes other ages, not shown separately. [4] Persons of Hispanic origin may be of any race. [5] Unemployed as percent of civilian labor force in specified group. [6] Wage and salary workers.

Source: U.S. Bureau of Labor Statistics, *Employment and Earnings*, monthly, January issues; and unpublished data.

No. 599. Use of Traditional Methods of Job Searching: 1994 to 1999

[In percent. For December. For the civilian noninstitutionalized population 16 and over who are unemployed active jobseekers. Based on the Current Population Survey; see text, Section 1, Population, and Appendix III]

Job search method	1994	1995	1996	1997	1998	1999
Contacted: Employer directly	67.4	65.1	64.7	67.3	64.5	65.1
Public employment agency	20.4	20.1	18.9	19.1	20.4	15.9
Private employment agency	7.2	7.1	7.5	6.6	6.6	7.0
Friends or relatives	15.7	18.0	16.6	14.6	13.5	13.4
School employment center	2.3	1.9	2.3	2.7	2.3	1.6
Sent out resumes/filled out applications	40.2	46.9	48.3	46.6	48.3	47.6
Checked union/professional registers	2.7	2.4	2.5	1.7	1.5	1.9
Placed or answered ads	16.7	17.7	17.3	16.3	14.5	12.5
Used other active search methods.	3.5	2.9	3.9	4.6	4.4	5.7

Source: U.S. Bureau of Labor Statistics, *Monthly Labor Review*, October 2000.

No. 600. Internet Job Search Rates by Labor Force Status and Selected Characteristic: 1998

[In percent. For December. For the civilian noninstitutionalized population 16 and over. Represents persons who responded they used the Internet regularly to search for jobs. Based on the Current Population Survey; see text, Section 1, Population, and Appendix III]

Characteristic	Employed			Unemployed		Not in the labor force		
	Total	Working	Absent [1]	On layoff	Job-seeker	Retired	Disabled	Other
INTERNET USE FOR JOB SEARCH								
White	5.6	7.1	6.8	4.9	16.5	0.3	1.7	3.9
Black	4.8	6.3	6.8	5.4	9.2	0.1	0.7	2.8
Hispanic [2]	3.2	4.0	3.7	(Z)	7.2	(Z)	0.3	2.0
Men	6.5	7.6	8.7	3.9	15.2	0.4	1.8	5.7
Women	4.7	6.5	5.6	6.6	14.7	0.2	1.1	3.1
Internet job search from:								
Home	4.0	5.2	5.4	2.9	11.0	0.3	1.1	2.6
Outside the home	1.8	2.3	2.1	1.9	4.6	(Z)	0.4	1.4
Any source	5.5	7.1	7.0	4.8	15.0	0.3	1.4	3.8
INTERNET JOB SEARCH RATES AMONG THOSE WITH ACCESS								
Computer in the home:								
White.	9.9	11.0	11.4	9.6	31.2	1.3	6.8	6.4
Black.	12.5	13.6	18.1	(B)	33.3	0.8	1.2	6.5
Hispanic [2].	8.4	9.6	10.1	(B)	20.5	(Z)	1.9	4.8
Men	11.8	12.4	15.2	9.6	30.9	1.7	7.7	9.8
Women	8.5	9.9	9.4	9.4	31.5	0.9	4.4	5.2
Internet access from home: [3]								
White.	14.1	15.5	16.1	17.0	47.9	2.4	11.2	8.6
Black.	20.7	21.4	(B)	(B)	64.0	2.0	(B)	11.0
Hispanic [2].	15.5	16.7	(B)	(B)	(B)	-	(B)	10.7
Men	16.8	17.5	20.6	17.4	48.5	3.0	12.2	13.3
Women	12.2	14.1	12.8	(B)	50.9	1.6	8.5	7.2
Internet use from any location:								
White.	15.4	16.0	16.6	21.2	49.6	3.5	17.1	10.6
Black.	23.0	22.8	30.3	(B)	51.1	(B)	(B)	16.3
Hispanic [2].	18.0	18.7	13.8	(B)	51.5	(B)	(B)	11.9
Men	17.9	18.0	22.3	17.6	49.1	4.1	21.0	13.9
Women	14.4	15.1	14.1	(B)	50.8	2.9	13.6	9.8

- Represents zero. B Data not shown where base is less than 75,000. Z Less than 0.5 percent [1] Absent from work due. for example, to vacation, or illness. [2] Persons of Hispanic origin may be of any race. [3] Someone in the household uses the Internet from home.

Source: U.S. Bureau of Labor Statistics, *Monthly Labor Review*, October 2000.

U.S. Census Bureau, Statistical Abstract of the United States: 2001

No. 601. Unemployed Persons by Sex and Reason: 1980 to 2000

[In thousands (4,267 represents 4,267,000). For civilian noninstitutional population 16 years old and over. Annual averages of monthly figures. Based on Current Population Survey; see text, Section 1, Population, and Appendix III]

Sex and reason	1980	1985	1990 [1]	1992	1993	1994 [1]	1995	1996	1997 [1]	1998 [1]	1999 [1]	2000 [1]
Male, total	4,267	4,521	3,906	5,523	5,055	4,367	3,983	3,880	3,577	3,266	3,066	2,954
Job losers [2]	2,649	2,749	2,257	3,593	3,150	2,416	2,190	2,158	1,902	1,703	1,563	1,499
Job leavers	438	409	528	495	507	408	407	372	414	368	389	384
Reentrants	776	876	806	978	939	1,265	1,113	1,076	1,004	931	895	855
New entrants	405	487	315	457	459	278	273	273	257	264	219	216
Female, total	3,370	3,791	3,140	4,090	3,885	3,629	3,421	3,356	3,162	2,944	2,814	2,701
Job losers [2]	1,297	1,390	1,130	1,796	1,699	1,399	1,286	1,212	1,135	1,119	1,059	993
Job leavers	453	468	513	507	469	383	417	402	381	366	394	391
Reentrants	1,152	1,380	1,124	1,307	1,259	1,521	1,412	1,435	1,334	1,201	1,111	1,102
New entrants	468	552	373	480	459	326	306	307	312	257	250	215

[1] See footnote 2, Table 567.   [2] Beginning 1994, persons who completed temporary jobs are identified separately and are included as job losers.

Source: U.S. Bureau of Labor Statistics, *Employment and Earnings*, monthly, January issues; and Bulletin 2307; and unpublished data.

No. 602. Unemployment Rates by Industry, 1980 to 2000, and by Sex, 1980 and 2000

[In percent. For civilian noninstitutional population 16 years old and over. Annual averages of monthly figures. Rate represents unemployment as a percent of labor force in each specified group. Data for 1985-90 not strictly comparable with other years due to changes in industrial classification]

Industry	1980	1985	1990 [1]	1995 [1]	1999 [1]	2000 [1]	Male 1980	Male 2000 [1]	Female 1980	Female 2000 [1]
All unemployed [2]	7.1	7.2	5.6	5.6	4.2	4.0	6.9	3.9	7.4	4.1
Industry: [3]										
Agriculture	11.0	13.2	9.8	11.1	8.9	7.5	9.7	7.0	15.1	8.9
Mining	6.4	9.5	4.8	5.2	5.7	3.9	6.7	4.3	4.5	1.5
Construction	14.1	13.1	11.1	11.5	7.0	6.4	14.6	6.5	8.9	5.2
Manufacturing	8.5	7.7	5.8	4.9	3.6	3.6	7.4	3.1	10.8	4.7
Transportation and public utilities	4.9	5.1	3.9	4.5	3.0	3.1	5.1	2.9	4.4	3.4
Wholesale and retail trade	7.4	7.6	6.4	6.5	5.2	5.0	6.6	4.4	8.3	5.7
Finance, insurance, and real estate	3.4	3.5	3.0	3.3	2.3	2.3	3.2	2.0	3.5	2.5
Services	5.9	6.2	5.0	5.4	4.1	3.8	6.3	3.9	5.8	3.7
Government	4.1	3.9	2.7	2.9	2.1	2.0	3.9	1.9	4.3	2.1

[1] See footnote 2, Table 567.   [2] Includes the self-employed, unpaid family workers, and persons with no previous work experience, not shown separately.   [3] Covers unemployed wage and salary workers.

Source: U.S. Bureau of Labor Statistics, *Employment and Earnings*, monthly, January issues.

No. 603. Unemployment by Occupation, 1990 to 2000, and by Sex, 2000

[7,047 represents 7,047,000. For civilian noninstitutional population 16 years old and over. Annual averages of monthly data. Rate represents unemployment as a percent of the labor force for each specified group. Based on Current Population Survey; see text, Section 1, Population, and Appendix III. See also headnote, Table 584]

Occupation	Number (1,000) 1990 [1]	1995 [1]	2000 [1]	Unemployment rate 1990 [1]	1995 [1]	2000 [1] Total	2000 [1] Male	2000 [1] Female
Total [2]	7,047	7,404	5,655	5.6	5.6	4.0	3.9	4.1
Managerial and professional specialty	666	880	725	2.1	2.4	1.7	1.6	1.9
Executive, administrative, and managerial	350	420	356	2.3	2.4	1.8	1.7	1.9
Professional specialty	316	460	369	2.0	2.5	1.7	1.6	1.9
Technical sales, and administrative support	1,641	1,744	1,464	4.3	4.5	3.6	3.1	3.8
Technicians and related support	116	113	97	2.9	2.8	2.2	2.3	2.0
Sales occupations	720	795	684	4.8	5.0	4.0	2.9	5.1
Administrative support, including clerical	804	836	684	4.1	4.3	3.5	4.0	3.4
Service occupations	1,139	1,378	1,023	6.6	7.5	5.3	5.3	5.3
Private household	47	99	58	5.6	10.7	6.9	9.1	6.8
Protective service	74	86	65	3.6	3.7	2.6	2.3	3.9
Service except private household and protective	1,018	1,193	900	7.1	7.9	5.6	6.3	5.3
Precision production, craft, and repair	861	860	554	5.9	6.0	3.6	3.5	4.3
Mechanics and repairers	175	182	129	3.8	4.0	2.6	2.5	4.3
Construction trades	483	501	312	8.5	9.0	4.9	4.8	6.8
Other precision production, craft, and repair	202	177	113	4.7	4.2	2.8	2.5	3.8
Operators, fabricators, and laborers	1,714	1,618	1,228	8.7	8.2	6.3	5.9	7.5
Machine operators, assemblers, inspectors	727	629	455	8.1	7.4	5.9	4.9	7.4
Transportation and material moving occupations	329	329	253	6.3	6.0	4.4	4.2	5.8
Handlers, equipment cleaners, helpers, laborers	657	660	520	11.6	11.7	8.7	8.7	8.6
Construction laborers	177	179	133	18.1	18.7	11.6	11.6	11.9
Farming, forestry, and fishing	237	311	215	6.4	7.9	6.0	5.5	7.7

[1] See footnote 2, Table 567.   [2] Includes persons with no previous work experience and those whose last job was in the Armed Forces.

Source: U.S. Bureau of Labor Statistics, *Employment and Earnings*, monthly, January issues.

No. 604. Unemployed and Unemployment Rates by Educational Attainment, Sex, Race, and Hispanic Origin: 1992 to 2000

[6,846 represents 6,846,000. As of March. For the civilian noninstitutional population 25 to 64 years old. See Table 571 for civilian labor force and participation rate data. Based on Current Population Survey; see text, Section 1, Population, and Appendix III]

Year, sex, and race	Unemployed (1,000)					Unemployment rate [1]				
	Total	Less than high school diploma	High school graduates, no degree	Less than a bachelor's degree	College graduate	Total	Less than high school diploma	High school graduate, no degree	Less than a bachelor's degree	College graduate
Total: [2]										
1992 ...	6,846	1,693	2,851	1,521	782	6.7	13.5	7.7	5.9	2.9
1995 ...	5,065	1,150	1,833	1,329	753	4.8	10.0	5.2	4.5	2.5
1999 [3] ...	3,942	895	1,445	961	640	3.5	7.7	4.0	3.1	1.9
2000 [3] ...	3,750	883	1,364	966	537	3.3	7.9	3.8	3.0	1.5
Male:										
1992	4,207	1,151	1,709	854	493	7.5	14.8	8.8	6.4	3.2
1995	2,925	765	1,064	656	440	5.1	10.9	5.7	4.4	2.6
1999 [3]	2,121	491	782	495	353	3.5	7.0	4.1	3.2	1.9
2000 [3]	2,027	475	749	494	308	3.3	7.1	3.9	3.1	1.6
Female:										
1992	2,639	542	1,142	666	289	5.7	11.4	6.5	5.3	2.5
1995	2,140	385	770	673	313	4.4	8.6	4.6	4.5	2.4
1999 [3]	1,821	404	663	466	287	3.5	8.8	3.9	3.0	1.9
2000 [3]	1,723	407	615	472	229	3.2	9.1	3.6	2.9	1.4
White:										
1992	5,247	1,285	2,146	1,176	641	6.0	12.9	6.8	5.3	2.7
1995	3,858	831	1,362	1,054	612	4.3	9.2	4.6	4.2	2.3
1999 [3]	2,886	651	1,034	716	484	3.1	7.0	3.4	2.8	1.7
2000 [3]	2,812	676	1,006	723	407	3.0	7.5	3.3	2.7	1.4
Black:										
1992	1,353	361	619	291	81	12.4	17.2	14.1	10.7	4.8
1995	905	225	377	218	86	7.7	13.7	8.4	6.3	4.1
1999 [3]	810	201	321	204	84	6.3	12.0	6.7	5.2	3.3
2000 [3]	717	164	305	179	68	5.4	10.4	6.3	4.3	2.5
Hispanic: [4]										
1992	757	408	224	88	36	9.8	13.6	9.6	5.9	4.2
1995	746	393	211	102	40	8.0	10.9	8.1	5.2	3.7
1999 [3]	620	315	179	89	36	5.6	7.8	5.5	3.7	2.5
2000 [3]	647	363	159	78	47	5.5	8.3	4.6	3.1	3.2

[1] Percent unemployed of the civilian labor force.   [2] Includes other races, not shown separately.   [3] See footnote 2, Table 567.   [4] Persons of Hispanic origin may be of any race.

Source: U.S. Bureau of Labor Statistics, unpublished data.

No. 605. Unemployed Persons by Reason of Unemployment: 2000

[5,655 represents 5,655,000. Annual averages of monthly data. Based on Current Population Survey; see text, Section 1, Population, and Appendix III]

Age, sex, and reason	Total unemployed (1,000)	Percent distribution by duration				
		Less than 5 weeks	5 to 14 weeks	15 weeks and over		
				Total	15 to 26 weeks	27 weeks or longer
Total 16 years old and over	5,655	45.0	31.9	23.1	11.8	11.4
16 to 19 years old	1,093	53.8	32.9	13.3	8.0	5.3
Total 20 years old and over	4,562	42.9	31.6	25.5	12.6	12.8
Males	2,350	42.0	31.7	26.3	12.5	13.8
Job losers and persons who completed temporary jobs	1,398	43.7	32.3	24.0	12.9	11.1
On temporary layoff	484	56.4	31.8	11.7	8.0	3.7
Not on temporary layoff	914	37.0	32.5	30.5	15.5	15.0
Permanent job losers	609	33.9	33.4	32.7	16.6	16.1
Persons who completed temporary jobs	306	43.1	30.7	26.1	13.2	12.9
Job leavers	324	48.3	31.0	20.7	9.5	11.2
Reentrants	574	35.4	30.8	33.8	13.1	20.7
New entrants	54	29.7	29.2	41.2	15.8	25.3
Females	2,212	43.8	31.6	24.6	12.8	11.8
Job losers and persons who completed temporary jobs	934	43.9	32.2	23.9	13.9	10.0
On temporary layoff	302	56.0	31.7	12.3	8.7	3.6
Not on temporary layoff	632	38.1	32.5	29.4	16.4	13.1
Permanent job losers	441	34.9	33.3	31.8	17.8	14.1
Persons who completed temporary jobs	191	45.6	30.5	23.9	13.1	10.8
Job leavers	340	49.6	30.5	19.9	9.8	10.1
Reentrants	860	41.9	31.2	26.9	13.1	13.8
New entrants	78	37.8	33.6	28.6	8.6	20.0

Source: U.S. Bureau of Labor Statistics, *Employment and Earnings*, monthly, January 2000 issue.

Labor Force, Employment, and Earnings 389

No. 606. Total Unemployed and Insured Unemployed by State: 1980 to 2000

[7,637 represents 7,637,000. For civilian noninstitutional population 16 years old and over. Annual averages of monthly figures. Total unemployment estimates based on the Current Population Survey; see text, Section 1, Population, and Appendix III. U.S. totals derived by independent population controls; therefore state data may not add to U.S. totals]

State	Total unemployed								Insured unemployed [3]			
	Number (1,000)				Percent [1]				Number (1,000)		Percent [4]	
	1980	1990 [2]	1995 [2]	2000 [2]	1980	1990 [2]	1995 [2]	2000 [2]	1998	1999	1998	1999
United States ...	7,637	7,047	7,404	5,655	7.1	5.6	5.6	4.0	[5]2,221.7	[5]2,187.9	[5]1.9	[5]1.8
Alabama........	147	130	129	99	8.8	6.9	6.3	4.6	30.3	28.4	1.7	1.6
Alaska.........	18	19	22	21	9.7	7.0	7.3	6.6	12.1	12.9	5.0	5.1
Arizona.........	83	99	112	91	6.7	5.5	5.1	3.9	19.0	21.2	1.0	1.0
Arkansas	76	78	59	55	7.6	7.0	4.9	4.4	26.2	24.9	2.5	2.3
California	790	874	1,211	845	6.8	5.8	7.8	4.9	365.5	367.0	2.7	2.7
Colorado........	88	89	88	63	5.9	5.0	4.2	2.7	16.7	15.9	0.9	0.8
Connecticut......	94	95	94	39	5.9	5.2	5.5	2.3	30.8	31.2	2.0	1.9
Delaware	22	19	17	16	7.7	5.2	4.3	4.0	6.1	5.5	1.6	1.4
District of Columbia .	24	22	25	16	7.3	6.6	8.9	5.8	6.8	6.5	1.7	1.6
Florida	251	390	376	269	5.9	6.0	5.5	3.6	74.3	73.1	1.2	1.1
Georgia	163	182	177	154	6.4	5.5	4.9	3.7	33.0	32.6	1.0	0.9
Hawaii	21	16	34	26	4.9	2.9	5.9	4.3	12.6	10.7	2.5	2.1
Idaho..........	34	29	32	32	7.9	5.9	5.4	4.9	13.0	12.5	2.6	2.4
Illinois	459	369	312	279	8.3	6.2	5.2	4.4	103.6	104.0	1.9	1.8
Indiana.........	252	149	146	100	9.6	5.3	4.7	3.2	30.9	28.6	1.1	1.0
Iowa	82	62	54	41	5.8	4.3	3.5	2.6	16.4	17.9	1.2	1.3
Kansas.........	53	57	59	52	4.5	4.5	4.4	3.7	13.1	14.7	1.1	1.2
Kentucky	133	104	100	82	8.0	5.9	5.4	4.1	26.1	24.9	1.6	1.5
Louisiana	121	117	135	112	6.7	6.3	6.9	5.5	22.7	25.9	1.3	1.4
Maine..........	39	33	37	24	7.8	5.2	5.7	3.5	11.3	9.8	2.1	1.8
Maryland	140	122	139	108	6.5	4.7	5.1	3.9	34.5	30.2	1.6	1.4
Massachusetts.....	162	195	170	86	5.6	6.0	5.4	2.6	63.4	66.2	2.1	2.2
Michigan........	534	350	253	185	12.4	7.6	5.3	3.6	90.7	79.7	2.1	1.8
Minnesota.......	125	117	96	90	5.9	4.9	3.7	3.3	31.2	29.9	1.3	1.2
Mississippi	79	90	77	75	7.5	7.6	6.1	5.7	18.7	18.4	1.8	1.7
Missouri........	167	151	135	101	7.2	5.8	4.8	3.5	41.3	40.1	1.7	1.6
Montana........	23	24	26	24	6.1	6.0	5.9	4.9	8.2	7.8	2.4	2.2
Nebraska	31	18	24	28	4.1	2.2	2.6	3.0	6.8	7.0	0.8	0.8
Nevada	27	33	43	40	6.2	4.9	5.4	4.1	17.9	18.3	2.1	2.0
New Hampshire....	22	36	25	19	4.7	5.7	4.0	2.8	3.8	3.7	0.7	0.7
New Jersey......	260	206	261	157	7.2	5.1	6.4	3.8	90.7	91.0	2.6	2.5
New Mexico	42	46	50	40	7.5	6.5	6.3	4.9	11.4	11.0	1.7	1.7
New York	597	467	541	408	7.5	5.3	6.3	4.6	173.1	157.5	2.2	2.0
North Carolina....	187	144	158	144	6.6	4.2	4.3	3.6	50.4	51.3	1.4	1.4
North Dakota......	15	13	11	10	5.0	4.0	3.3	3.0	3.6	4.1	1.2	1.4
Ohio	426	310	266	237	8.4	5.7	4.8	4.1	72.1	68.1	1.4	1.3
Oklahoma.......	66	86	73	50	4.8	5.7	4.7	3.0	12.7	14.2	1.0	1.0
Oregon.........	107	83	80	87	8.3	5.6	4.8	4.9	43.0	42.4	2.9	2.8
Pennsylvania.....	425	315	343	250	7.8	5.4	5.9	4.2	140.6	136.5	2.7	2.6
Rhode Island.....	34	35	34	21	7.2	6.8	7.0	4.1	13.3	13.2	3.1	3.0
South Carolina.....	96	83	94	77	6.9	4.8	5.1	3.9	24.7	25.7	1.5	1.5
South Dakota	16	13	11	9	4.9	3.9	2.9	2.3	2.3	2.1	0.7	0.6
Tennessee	152	126	140	110	7.3	5.3	5.2	3.9	42.0	39.9	1.7	1.6
Texas..........	352	544	579	437	5.2	6.3	6.0	4.2	110.5	124.6	1.3	1.4
Utah	40	35	35	36	6.3	4.3	3.6	3.2	9.4	10.1	1.0	1.1
Vermont	16	15	14	10	6.4	5.0	4.2	2.9	5.8	5.3	2.2	1.9
Virginia.........	128	141	157	80	5.0	4.3	4.5	2.2	24.1	22.2	0.8	0.7
Washington......	156	125	179	158	7.9	4.9	6.4	5.2	77.1	77.6	3.2	3.1
West Virginia.....	74	64	62	46	9.4	8.4	7.9	5.5	15.9	16.1	2.5	2.4
Wisconsin........	167	114	106	104	7.2	4.4	3.7	3.5	51.2	50.3	2.0	1.9
Wyoming	9	13	12	10	4.0	5.5	4.8	3.9	3.2	3.1	1.5	1.5

[1] Total unemployment as percent of civilian labor force.   [2] See footnote 2, Table 567.   [3] Source: U.S. Employment and Training Administration, *Unemployment Insurance, Financial Handbook*, annual updates.   [4] Insured unemployment as percent of average covered employment in the previous year.   [5] Includes 58,000 in Puerto Rico and the Virgin Islands in 1998 and 59,100 in 1999.

Source: Except as noted, U.S. Bureau of Labor Statistics, *Geographic Profile of Employment and Unemployment*, annual.

No. 607. Nonfarm Establishments—Employees, Hours, and Earnings by Industry: 1980 to 2000

[90,406 represents 90,406,000. Based on data from establishment reports. Includes all full- and part-time employees who worked during, or received pay for, any part of the pay period reported. Excludes proprietors, the self-employed, farm workers, unpaid family workers, private household workers, and Armed Forces. Establishment data shown here conform to industry definitions in the 1987 Standard Industrial Classification and are adjusted to March 1999 employment benchmarks, and reflect historical corrections to previously published data. Based on the Current Employment Statistics Program; see Appendix III]

Item and year	Total	Goods-producing				Service-producing						
		Total	Mining	Construction	Manufacturing	Total	Transportation and public utilities	Wholesale trade	Retail trade	Finance, insurance, and real estate	Services	Government
EMPLOYEES (1,000)												
1980	90,406	25,658	1,027	4,346	20,285	64,748	5,146	5,292	15,018	5,160	17,890	16,241
1985	97,387	24,842	927	4,668	19,248	72,544	5,233	5,727	17,315	5,948	21,927	16,394
1990	109,403	24,905	709	5,120	19,076	84,497	5,777	6,173	19,601	6,709	27,934	18,304
1993	110,713	23,352	610	4,668	18,075	87,361	5,811	5,981	19,773	6,757	30,197	18,841
1994	114,163	23,908	601	4,986	18,321	90,256	5,984	6,162	20,507	6,896	31,579	19,128
1995	117,191	24,265	581	5,160	18,524	92,925	6,132	6,378	21,187	6,806	33,117	19,305
1996	119,608	24,493	580	5,418	18,495	95,115	6,253	6,482	21,597	6,911	34,454	19,419
1997	122,690	24,962	596	5,691	18,675	97,727	6,408	6,648	21,966	7,109	36,040	19,557
1998	125,865	25,414	590	6,020	18,805	100,451	6,611	6,800	22,295	7,389	37,533	19,823
1999	128,786	25,482	535	6,404	18,543	103,304	6,826	6,924	22,788	7,569	39,027	20,170
2000	131,418	25,662	538	6,687	18,437	105,756	6,993	7,054	23,136	7,618	40,384	20,572
PERCENT DISTRIBUTION												
1980	100.0	28.4	1.1	4.8	22.4	71.6	5.7	5.9	16.6	5.7	19.8	18.0
1985	100.0	25.5	1.0	4.8	19.8	74.5	5.4	5.9	17.8	6.1	22.5	16.8
1990	100.0	22.8	0.6	4.7	17.4	77.2	5.3	5.6	17.9	6.1	25.5	16.7
1993	100.0	21.1	0.6	4.2	16.3	78.9	5.2	5.4	17.9	6.1	27.3	17.0
1994	100.0	20.9	0.5	4.4	16.0	79.1	5.2	5.4	18.0	6.0	27.7	16.8
1995	100.0	20.7	0.5	4.4	15.8	79.3	5.2	5.4	18.1	5.8	28.3	16.5
1996	100.0	20.5	0.5	4.5	15.5	79.5	5.2	5.4	18.1	5.8	28.8	16.2
1997	100.0	20.3	0.5	4.6	15.2	79.7	5.2	5.4	17.9	5.8	29.4	15.9
1998	100.0	20.2	0.5	4.8	14.9	79.8	5.3	5.4	17.7	5.9	29.8	15.7
1999	100.0	19.8	0.4	5.0	14.4	80.2	5.3	5.4	17.7	5.9	30.3	15.7
2000	100.0	19.5	0.4	5.1	14.0	80.5	5.3	5.4	17.6	5.8	30.7	15.7
WEEKLY HOURS [1]												
1980	35.3	(NA)	43.3	37.0	39.7	(NA)	39.6	38.4	30.2	36.2	32.6	(NA)
1985	34.9	(NA)	43.4	37.7	40.5	(NA)	39.5	38.4	29.4	36.4	32.5	(NA)
1990	34.5	(NA)	44.1	38.2	40.8	(NA)	38.4	38.1	28.8	35.8	32.5	(NA)
1993	34.5	(NA)	44.3	38.5	41.4	(NA)	39.3	38.2	28.8	35.8	32.5	(NA)
1994	34.7	(NA)	44.8	38.9	42.0	(NA)	39.7	38.4	28.9	35.8	32.5	(NA)
1995	34.5	(NA)	44.7	38.9	41.6	(NA)	39.4	38.3	28.8	35.9	32.4	(NA)
1996	34.4	(NA)	45.3	39.0	41.6	(NA)	39.6	38.3	28.8	35.9	32.4	(NA)
1997	34.6	(NA)	45.4	39.0	42.0	(NA)	39.7	38.4	28.9	36.1	32.6	(NA)
1998	34.6	(NA)	43.9	38.9	41.7	(NA)	39.5	38.3	29.0	36.4	32.6	(NA)
1999	34.5	(NA)	43.8	39.1	41.7	(NA)	38.7	38.3	29.0	36.2	32.6	(NA)
2000	34.5	(NA)	44.9	39.3	41.5	(NA)	38.5	38.5	28.9	36.3	32.7	(NA)
HOURLY EARNINGS [1]												
1980	6.66	(NA)	9.17	9.94	7.27	(NA)	8.87	6.95	4.88	5.79	5.85	(NA)
1985	8.57	(NA)	11.98	12.32	9.54	(NA)	11.40	9.15	5.94	7.94	7.90	(NA)
1990	10.01	(NA)	13.68	13.77	10.83	(NA)	12.92	10.79	6.75	9.97	9.83	(NA)
1993	10.83	(NA)	14.60	14.38	11.74	(NA)	13.55	11.74	7.29	11.35	10.78	(NA)
1994	11.12	(NA)	14.88	14.73	12.07	(NA)	13.78	12.06	7.49	11.83	11.04	(NA)
1995	11.43	(NA)	15.30	15.09	12.37	(NA)	14.13	12.43	7.69	12.32	11.39	(NA)
1996	11.44	(NA)	15.62	15.47	12.77	(NA)	14.45	12.87	7.99	12.80	11.79	(NA)
1997	11.45	(NA)	16.15	16.04	13.17	(NA)	14.92	13.45	8.33	13.34	12.28	(NA)
1998	11.46	(NA)	16.91	16.61	13.49	(NA)	15.31	14.07	8.74	14.07	12.84	(NA)
1999	11.47	(NA)	17.09	17.18	13.91	(NA)	15.69	14.58	9.08	14.62	13.36	(NA)
2000	11.48	(NA)	17.14	17.86	14.38	(NA)	16.22	15.18	9.45	15.07	13.88	(NA)
WEEKLY EARNINGS [1]												
1980	235	(NA)	397	368	289	(NA)	351	267	147	210	191	(NA)
1985	299	(NA)	520	464	386	(NA)	450	351	175	289	257	(NA)
1990	345	(NA)	603	526	442	(NA)	496	411	194	357	319	(NA)
1993	374	(NA)	647	554	486	(NA)	533	448	210	406	350	(NA)
1994	386	(NA)	667	573	507	(NA)	547	463	216	424	359	(NA)
1995	394	(NA)	684	587	515	(NA)	557	476	221	442	369	(NA)
1996	407	(NA)	708	603	531	(NA)	572	493	230	460	382	(NA)
1997	425	(NA)	733	626	553	(NA)	592	516	241	482	400	(NA)
1998	442	(NA)	742	646	563	(NA)	605	539	253	512	419	(NA)
1999	457	(NA)	749	672	580	(NA)	607	558	263	529	436	(NA)
2000	474	(NA)	770	702	597	(NA)	624	584	273	547	454	(NA)

NA Not available. [1] Average hours and earnings. Private production and related workers in mining, manufacturing, and construction; nonsupervisory employees in other industries.

Source: U.S. Bureau of Labor Statistics, *Employment and Earnings*, monthly, June issues and Internet site <http://www.bls.gov/ces/home.htm>

Labor Force, Employment, Earnings   391

No. 608. Employees in Nonfarm Establishments—States: 1990 to 2000

[In thousands (109,403 represents 109,403,000). For coverage, see headnote, Table 607. National totals differ from the sum of the state figures because of differing benchmarks among states and differing industrial and geographic stratification. Based on 1987 *Standard Industrial Classification Manual*, see text, Section 15, Business Enterprise]

State	1990	1995	2000 Total [1]	Construction	Manufacturing	Transportation and public utilities	Wholesale and retail trade	Finance, insurance, and real estate	Services	Government
United States ...	109,403	117,191	131,418	6,687	18,437	6,993	30,190	7,618	40,384	20,572
Alabama.	1,636	1,804	1,934	105	361	96	447	92	472	353
Alaska	238	262	284	14	14	27	58	13	73	75
Arizona.	1,483	1,796	2,248	162	215	109	526	144	717	367
Arkansas	924	1,069	1,162	54	251	70	267	46	279	191
California	12,500	12,422	14,519	734	1,944	746	3,301	823	4,627	2,321
Colorado.	1,521	1,834	2,215	161	205	144	525	142	685	339
Connecticut.	1,624	1,562	1,693	65	262	79	366	141	537	242
Delaware	348	366	421	25	59	17	92	50	121	57
District of Columbia .	686	643	647	11	11	19	49	32	300	224
Florida	5,387	5,996	7,076	389	487	358	1,757	444	2,642	994
Georgia	2,992	3,402	3,993	207	587	268	982	207	1,132	603
Hawaii	528	533	552	[2]24	17	42	137	33	183	115
Idaho	385	477	560	36	77	28	142	24	143	109
Illinois	5,288	5,593	6,029	266	944	354	1,365	401	1,855	834
Indiana.	2,522	2,787	3,010	153	688	149	710	141	751	412
Iowa	1,226	1,358	1,478	64	261	73	358	86	392	242
Kansas.	1,089	1,198	1,346	65	210	86	320	64	348	245
Kentucky	1,471	1,643	1,825	87	322	109	430	77	472	309
Louisiana	1,590	1,772	1,931	132	184	113	455	87	538	375
Maine.	535	538	604	30	85	24	150	32	182	100
Maryland	2,171	2,183	2,449	156	180	115	556	138	858	445
Massachusetts.	2,985	2,977	3,319	130	436	144	748	228	1,209	424
Michigan.	3,970	4,274	4,679	211	980	181	1,094	205	1,317	684
Minnesota.	2,127	2,379	2,669	119	440	135	632	161	779	396
Mississippi	937	1,075	1,157	55	234	57	257	43	273	234
Missouri	2,345	2,521	2,758	141	403	180	648	167	788	426
Montana.	297	351	389	20	25	22	103	18	116	81
Nebraska	730	816	910	44	120	58	218	61	252	154
Nevada	621	786	1,029	88	44	56	215	47	446	121
New Hampshire. . . .	508	540	621	25	106	22	164	33	188	83
New Jersey	3,635	3,601	3,996	157	462	272	935	265	1,316	589
New Mexico	580	682	744	45	43	37	173	32	216	183
New York	8,212	7,892	8,632	329	874	430	1,749	748	3,034	1,464
North Carolina	3,118	3,460	3,947	234	782	181	900	187	1,034	626
North Dakota.	266	302	327	16	25	19	82	17	92	73
Ohio	4,882	5,221	5,642	254	1,085	250	1,357	308	1,591	784
Oklahoma.	1,196	1,316	1,485	61	182	85	342	73	425	288
Oregon.	1,247	1,418	1,603	86	243	80	394	94	439	266
Pennsylvania	5,170	5,253	5,698	251	926	301	1,275	326	1,872	727
Rhode Island.	451	440	476	19	73	17	109	31	163	64
South Carolina.	1,545	1,646	1,877	117	347	95	447	82	464	323
South Dakota	289	344	379	18	50	17	92	26	105	70
Tennessee	2,193	2,499	2,738	127	508	178	645	131	745	399
Texas.	7,095	8,023	9,444	561	1,086	591	2,247	525	2,720	1,566
Utah	724	908	1,077	73	131	61	252	57	310	185
Vermont	258	270	298	15	49	12	68	12	92	50
Virginia.	2,896	3,070	3,507	211	389	186	767	189	1,132	623
Washington.	2,143	2,347	2,717	162	350	147	653	137	781	484
West Virginia.	630	688	736	34	81	37	164	30	226	143
Wisconsin.	2,292	2,559	2,834	126	617	133	636	149	766	405
Wyoming	199	219	239	18	11	14	55	8	55	61

[1] Includes mining, not shown separately. [2] Hawaii includes mining with construction.

Source: U.S. Bureau of Labor Statistics, *Employment and Earnings*, monthly, May issues. Compiled from data supplied by cooperating state agencies.

No. 609. Nonfarm Industries—Employees and Earnings: 1980 to 2000

[Annual averages of monthly figures (90,406 represents 90,406,000). Covers all full- and part-time employees who worked during, or received pay for, any part of the pay period including the 12th of the month. For mining and manufacturing, data refer to production and related workers; for construction, to employees engaged in actual construction work; and for other industries, to nonsupervisory employees and working supervisors. See also headnote, Table 607]

Industry	1987 SIC [1] code	All employees (1,000)			Production workers					
					Total (1,000)			Average hourly earnings (dollars)		
		1980	1990	2000	1980	1990	2000	1980	1990	2000
Total	(X)	90,406	109,403	131,418	(NA)	(NA)	(NA)	(NA)	(NA)	(NA)
Private sector [2].	(X)	74,166	91,098	110,846	60,331	73,774	90,850	6.66	10.01	13.74
Mining	(B)	1,027	709	538	762	509	401	9.17	13.68	17.14
Metal mining	10	98	58	44	74	46	34	10.26	14.05	19.04
Coal mining	12	246	147	80	204	119	66	10.86	16.71	19.40
Oil and gas extraction.	13	560	395	304	389	261	218	8.59	12.94	16.76
Nonmetallic minerals, except fuels . .	14	123	110	110	96	83	83	7.52	11.58	15.62
Construction.	(C)	4,346	5,120	6,687	3,421	3,974	5,175	9.94	13.77	17.86
General building contractors . .	15	1,173	1,298	1,505	900	938	1,050	9.22	13.01	17.20
Heavy construction, except building . .	16	895	770	886	720	643	740	9.20	13.34	17.33
Special trade contractors.	17	2,278	3,051	4,296	1,802	2,393	3,385	10.63	14.20	18.20
Manufacturing.	(D)	20,285	19,076	18,437	14,214	12,947	12,642	7.27	10.83	14.38
Durable goods	(X)	12,159	11,109	11,085	8,416	7,363	7,569	7.75	11.35	14.93
Lumber and wood products [3]	24	704	733	821	587	603	671	6.57	9.08	11.80
Logging	241	88	85	76	71	70	62	8.64	11.22	13.48
Sawmills and planing mills	242	215	198	181	190	172	157	6.70	9.22	11.79
Millwork, plywood, and structural members.	243	206	262	328	170	210	262	6.44	9.04	11.93
Wood containers	244	43	45	56	37	38	48	4.95	6.64	9.50
Mobile homes . . . [3]	2451	46	41	70	36	33	57	6.08	8.67	12.07
Furniture and fixtures [3]	25	466	506	555	376	400	441	5.49	8.52	11.75
Household furniture	251	301	289	295	253	241	251	5.12	7.87	11.07
Office furniture	252	51	68	77	40	51	55	5.91	9.64	13.04
Partitions and fixtures . . . . . [3]	254	63	78	89	47	57	66	6.68	9.77	12.36
Stone, clay, and glass products [3]	32	629	556	566	486	432	440	7.50	11.12	14.32
Flat glass	321	18	17	15	14	13	13	9.65	15.15	19.26
Glass and glassware, pressed and blown	322	124	83	64	105	72	51	7.97	12.40	16.01
Products of purchased glass	323	45	60	64	32	46	49	6.50	9.75	12.95
Cement, hydraulic.	324	31	18	18	25	14	13	10.55	13.90	19.49
Structural clay products	325	46	36	33	34	28	26	6.14	9.55	12.62
Pottery and related products.	326	47	39	37	39	31	29	6.25	9.62	12.17
Concrete, gypsum, and plaster	327	204	206	245	157	157	191	7.45	10.76	14.04
Primary metal industries [3]	33	1,142	756	695	878	574	545	9.77	12.92	16.50
Blast furnaces and basic steel products	331	512	276	225	396	212	176	11.39	14.82	19.46
Iron and steel foundries	332	209	132	123	167	105	101	8.20	11.55	15.53
Primary nonferrous metals	333	71	46	37	53	34	29	10.63	14.36	18.45
Nonferrous rolling and drawing	335	211	172	169	151	124	129	8.81	12.29	15.05
Nonferrous foundries (castings).	336	90	84	97	72	66	79	7.30	10.21	13.42
Fabricated metal products [3]	34	1,609	1,419	1,532	1,194	1,045	1,153	7.45	10.83	13.86
Metal cans and shipping containers . .	341	75	50	36	63	43	30	9.84	14.27	17.01
Cutlery, handtools, and hardware . . .	342	164	131	118	125	96	91	7.02	10.78	12.66
Plumbing and heating, exc. electric . .	343	71	60	61	52	43	43	6.59	9.75	12.50
Fabricated structural metal products. .	344	506	427	501	351	303	367	7.27	10.16	13.34
Screw machine products	345	109	96	106	84	73	83	6.96	10.70	14.29
Metal forgings and stampings . . . [3]	346	260	225	251	205	178	198	8.56	12.70	16.39
Industrial machinery and equipment [3] . .	35	2,517	2,095	2,128	1,614	1,260	1,347	8.00	11.77	15.63
Engines and turbines	351	135	89	86	87	58	58	9.73	14.55	17.96
Farm and garden machinery.	352	169	106	103	116	78	72	8.78	10.99	14.82
Construction and related machinery. .	353	389	229	240	255	141	153	8.60	11.92	14.58
Metalworking machinery	354	398	330	333	290	236	237	8.13	12.27	16.42
Special industry machinery.	355	194	159	169	125	94	89	7.53	11.90	16.35
General industrial machinery.	356	300	247	251	196	158	158	7.95	11.32	14.67
Computer and office equipment. . . .	357	420	438	363	181	137	156	6.75	11.51	18.45
Refrigeration and service machinery.	358	175	177	214	120	125	152	7.23	10.93	13.58
Electronic and other elec. equip. [3]	36	1,771	1,673	1,704	(⁴)	1,055	1,054	(⁴)	10.30	13.80
Electric distribution equipment.	361	117	97	85	82	67	58	6.96	10.15	13.38
Electrical industrial apparatus	362	232	169	148	163	119	99	(⁴)	10.00	13.20
Household appliances	363	162	124	117	128	99	96	6.95	10.26	13.67
Electric lighting and wiring equip	364	211	189	184	157	136	132	6.43	10.12	13.41
Household audio and video equip . .	365	109	85	81	79	59	52	6.42	9.68	12.57
Communications equipment	366	(⁴)	264	271	(⁴)	133	119	(⁴)	11.03	14.09
Electronic components and accessories . . . . [3]	367	539	582	667	325	329	389	6.05	10.00	14.11
Transportation equipment [3]	37	1,881	1,989	1,841	1,220	1,224	1,226	9.35	14.08	19.04
Motor vehicles and equipment	371	789	812	1,011	575	617	770	9.85	14.56	19.58
Aircraft and parts	372	633	712	459	344	345	222	9.28	14.79	20.75
Ship and boat building and repairing .	373	221	188	168	176	141	126	8.22	10.94	14.39
Railroad equipment.	374	71	33	33	53	25	24	9.93	13.41	17.70
Guided missiles, space vehicles, and parts	376	111	185	88	35	57	22	9.22	14.39	20.34
Instruments and related products	38	1,022	1,006	847	(⁴)	499	421	(⁴)	11.29	14.62
Search and navigation equipment . . .	381	(⁴)	284	160	(⁴)	94	40	(⁴)	14.62	17.39
Measuring and controlling devices . . .	382	(⁴)	323	293	(⁴)	180	146	(⁴)	10.68	14.80
Medical instruments and supplies . . .	384	(⁴)	246	285	(⁴)	144	16⁵	(⁴)	9.85	13.26
Ophthalmic goods	385	44	43	32	31	30	22	5.30	8.18	11.26

See footnotes at end of table.

Labor Force, Employment, and Earnings 393

U.S. Census Bureau, Statistical Abstract of the United States: 2001

[Annual averages of monthly figures (90,406 represents 90,406,000). Covers all full- and part-time employees who worked during, or received pay for, any part of the pay period including the 12th of the month. For mining and manufacturing, data refer to production and related workers; for construction, to employees engaged in actual construction work; and for other industries, to nonsupervisory employees and working supervisors. See also headnote, Table 607]

| Industry | 1987 SIC [1] code | All employees (1,000) | | | Production workers | | | | | |
| | | | | | Total (1,000) | | | Average hourly earnings (dollars) | | |
		1980	1990	2000	1980	1990	2000	1980	1990	2000
Photographic equipment and supplies	386	135	100	71	67	43	41	8.83	14.08	18.81
Watches, clocks, watchcases, and parts	387	22	11	6	17	8	5	5.24	7.70	11.84
Misc. manufacturing industries [3]	39	418	375	396	313	272	271	5.46	8.61	11.65
Jewelry, silverware, and plated ware	391	56	52	49	40	37	33	5.76	9.23	12.30
Toys and sporting goods	394	117	104	108	88	76	72	5.01	7.94	11.15
Pens, pencils, office and art supplies	395	37	34	29	27	24	20	5.58	8.89	11.87
Costume jewelry and notions	396	(4)	33	18	(4)	25	14	(4)	7.40	10.80
Nondurable goods [3]	(X)	8,127	7,968	7,353	5,798	5,584	5,073	6.56	10.12	13.53
Food and kindred products [3]	20	1,708	1,661	1,672	1,175	1,194	1,249	6.85	9.62	12.41
Meat products	201	358	422	505	298	359	429	6.99	7.94	10.24
Dairy products	202	175	155	145	96	95	102	6.86	10.56	14.43
Preserved fruits and vegetables	203	246	247	223	202	206	186	5.94	8.95	12.11
Grain mill products	204	144	128	123	99	89	87	7.67	11.52	15.26
Bakery products	205	230	213	202	139	133	141	7.14	10.85	13.10
Sugar and confectionery products	206	108	99	89	81	78	71	6.56	10.26	14.42
Fats and oils	207	44	31	29	32	22	20	7.03	10.10	13.68
Beverages	208	234	184	185	105	78	91	8.12	13.51	16.39
Tobacco products	21	69	49	36	54	36	25	7.74	16.23	19.07
Cigarettes [3]	211	46	35	24	35	26	15	9.23	19.57	25.34
Textile mill products [3]	22	848	691	541	737	593	458	5.07	8.02	10.95
Broadwoven fabric mills, cotton	221	150	91	63	135	82	56	5.25	8.31	11.22
Broadwoven fabric mills, synthetics	222	116	77	56	104	68	48	5.30	8.63	11.73
Broadwoven fabric mills, wool	223	19	17	9	16	14	7	5.21	8.61	11.67
Narrow fabric mills	224	23	24	20	20	20	16	4.63	7.39	10.12
Knitting mills	225	224	205	132	194	179	112	4.77	7.37	10.16
Textile finishing, except wool	226	74	62	58	62	50	49	5.39	8.45	11.08
Carpets and rugs	227	54	61	65	44	50	54	5.20	8.25	10.96
Yarn and thread mills	228	125	103	82	113	92	74	4.76	7.68	10.50
Apparel and other textile products [3]	23	1,264	1,036	650	1,079	869	517	4.56	6.57	9.09
Men's and boys' suits and coats	231	77	50	21	67	42	17	5.34	7.34	9.32
Men's and boys' furnishings	232	362	274	141	310	235	115	4.23	6.06	8.54
Women's and misses outerwear	233	417	328	195	360	274	152	4.61	6.26	8.40
Women's and children's undergarments	234	90	62	22	76	51	18	4.15	6.18	8.71
Girls' and children's outerwear	236	64	56	18	55	47	15	4.20	5.95	8.61
Paper and allied products [3]	26	685	697	661	519	522	501	7.84	12.31	16.21
Papermills	262	178	180	141	133	136	110	9.05	15.10	21.03
Paperboard mills	263	65	52	47	51	40	36	9.28	15.26	21.07
Paperboard containers and boxes	265	205	209	219	157	162	170	6.94	10.39	13.73
Misc. converted paper products	267	220	241	244	163	174	177	6.89	10.79	14.13
Printing and publishing [3]	27	1,252	1,569	1,556	699	871	830	7.53	11.24	14.30
Newspapers	271	420	474	445	164	166	148	7.72	11.17	14.05
Periodicals	272	90	129	146	16	47	51	7.16	11.95	15.98
Books	273	101	121	129	52	66	60	6.76	10.10	13.99
Commercial printing	275	410	552	565	304	401	401	7.85	11.52	14.47
Blankbooks and bookbinding	278	62	72	62	51	56	46	5.78	8.83	11.27
Chemicals and allied products [3]	28	1,107	1,086	1,027	626	600	582	8.30	13.54	17.94
Industrial inorganic chemicals	281	161	138	98	88	70	55	9.07	14.66	19.58
Plastics materials and synthetics	282	205	180	148	137	116	100	8.21	13.97	18.60
Drugs	283	196	237	305	97	105	140	7.69	12.90	17.99
Soap, cleaners, and toilet goods	284	141	159	158	86	98	100	7.67	11.71	15.21
Paints and allied products	285	65	61	53	33	31	28	7.39	11.99	15.13
Industrial organic chemicals	286	174	155	121	88	86	73	9.67	15.97	21.01
Agricultural chemicals	287	72	56	53	45	34	32	8.12	13.73	18.10
Petroleum and coal products [3]	29	198	157	131	125	103	76	10.10	16.24	21.47
Petroleum refining	291	155	118	86	93	75	46	10.94	17.58	24.75
Asphalt paving and roofing materials	295	31	27	31	24	21	23	7.69	12.87	16.46
Rubber and misc. plastics products [3]	30	764	888	1,005	588	687	781	6.58	9.76	12.77
Tires and inner tubes	301	115	84	81	81	62	61	9.74	15.42	19.97
Rubber and plastics footwear	302	22	11	4	20	9	3	4.43	6.66	10.31
Leather and leather products [3]	31	233	133	74	197	109	55	4.58	6.91	10.12
Leather tanning and finishing	311	19	15	13	16	12	11	6.10	9.04	12.95
Footwear, except rubber	314	144	74	29	123	63	23	4.42	6.61	9.80
Luggage	316	16	11	11	12	8	8	4.90	6.91	8.76
Handbags and personal leather goods	317	30	15	7	25	12	3	4.33	6.08	8.83
Transp. and public utilities [3]	(E)	5,146	5,777	6,993	4,293	4,781	5,825	8.87	12.92	16.22
Railroad transportation	40	532	279	220	(4)	(4)	(4)	(4)	(4)	(4)
Class I railroads, plus Amtrak [5]	4011	482	241	194	(4)	(4)	(4)	[6]9.92	16.08	17.95
Local and interurban passenger transit	41	265	338	498	244	308	458	6.34	9.23	12.12
Trucking and warehousing	42	(4)	1,395	1,839	(NA)	1,215	1,614	(4)	11.68	14.29
Water transportation	44	211	177	201	(4)	(4)	(4)	(4)	(4)	(4)
Transportation by air	45	(4)	968	1,282	(4)	(4)	(4)	(4)	(4)	(4)
Pipelines, except natural gas	46	21	19	13	15	14	9	10.50	17.04	22.77
Transportation services	47	(4)	336	472	159	270	390	6.94	10.38	14.52

See footnotes at end of table.

[Annual averages of monthly figures (90,406 represents 90,406,000). Covers all full- and part-time employees who worked during, or received pay for, any part of the pay period including the 12th of the month. For mining and manufacturing, data refer to production and related workers; for construction, to employees engaged in actual construction work; and for other industries, to nonsupervisory employees and working supervisors. See also headnote, Table 607]

Industry	1987 SIC [1] code	All employees (1,000)			Production workers					
					Total (1,000)			Average hourly earnings (dollars)		
		1980	1990	2000	1980	1990	2000	1980	1990	2000
Communication [3]	48	1,357	1,309	1,612	1,014	978	1,191	8.50	13.51	17.79
Telephone communication	481	1,072	913	1,106	779	658	795	8.72	14.13	18.00
Radio and television broadcasting	483	192	234	251	154	193	203	7.44	12.71	18.77
Cable and other pay television services	484	[4]	126	220	[4]	105	176	[4]	10.50	15.45
Electric, gas, and sanitary services [3]	49	829	957	857	678	759	689	8.90	15.23	21.47
Electric services	491	391	454	356	316	351	285	9.12	15.80	22.50
Gas production and distribution	492	168	165	127	138	129	100	8.27	14.25	19.67
Combination utility services	493	197	193	152	162	156	123	9.64	17.58	25.57
Sanitary services	495	50	115	185	44	99	151	7.16	11.55	18.17
Wholesale trade	(F)	5,292	6,173	7,054	4,328	4,959	5,628	6.95	10.79	15.18
Retail trade [3]	(G)	15,018	19,601	23,136	13,484	17,358	20,358	4.88	6.75	9.45
General merchandise stores	53	2,245	2,540	2,753	2,090	2,380	2,574	4.77	6.83	9.47
Food stores	54	2,384	3,215	3,515	2,202	2,953	3,172	6.24	7.31	9.38
Automotive dealers and service stations	55	1,689	2,063	2,414	1,430	1,718	2,016	5.66	8.92	13.05
Apparel and accessory stores	56	957	1,183	1,199	820	991	995	4.30	6.25	9.31
Furniture and home furnishings stores	57	606	820	1,118	502	670	926	5.53	8.53	12.72
Eating and drinking places	58	4,626	6,509	8,065	4,256	5,905	7,257	3.69	4.97	6.93
Finance, insurance, real estate	(H)	5,160	6,709	7,618	3,907	4,860	5,572	5.79	9.97	15.07
Depository institutions	60	[4]	2,251	2,043	[4]	1,632	1,474	[4]	8.43	11.72
Nondepository institutions	61	[4]	373	689	[4]	270	451	[4]	10.40	15.71
Security and commodity brokers	62	227	424	745	[4]	[4]	[4]	[4]	[4]	[4]
Insurance carriers	63	1,224	1,462	1,592	854	982	1,236	6.29	11.18	17.59
Insurance, agents, brokers, service	64	464	663	770	[4]	[4]	[4]	[4]	[4]	[4]
Real estate	65	989	1,315	1,537	[4]	[4]	[4]	[4]	[4]	[4]
Holding and other investment offices	67	115	221	242	[4]	[4]	[4]	[4]	[4]	[4]
Services [3]	(I)	17,890	27,934	40,384	15,921	24,387	35,249	5.85	9.83	13.88
Hotels and other lodging places	70	1,076	1,631	1,910	[4]	[4]	[4]	[4]	[4]	[4]
Hotels and motels	701	1,038	1,578	1,851	954	1,398	1,625	4.45	6.98	9.65
Personal services [3]	72	818	1,104	1,276	[4]	[4]	[4]	[4]	[4]	[4]
Laundry, cleaning, garment services	721	356	426	457	318	379	400	4.47	6.82	9.10
Beauty shops	723	284	372	427	264	333	378	4.26	7.10	10.22
Business services [3]	73	2,564	5,139	9,746	[4]	4,522	8,640	[4]	9.48	13.89
Advertising	731	153	235	293	116	169	213	8.07	13.51	19.72
Personnel supply services	736	543	1,535	3,834	[4]	[4]	[4]	[4]	[4]	[4]
Employment agencies	7361	[4]	246	416	[4]	[4]	[4]	[4]	[4]	[4]
Help supply services	7363	[4]	1,288	3,419	[4]	1,245	3,293	[4]	8.09	11.07
Computer and data processing services	737	304	772	1,941	254	603	1,562	7.16	15.11	23.36
Prepackaged software	7372	[4]	113	318	[4]	[4]	[4]	[4]	[4]	[4]
Data processing and preparation	7374	[4]	197	284	[4]	[4]	[4]	[4]	[4]	[4]
Auto repair, services, and parking	75	571	914	1,198	488	756	986	6.10	8.77	11.90
Automotive repair shops	753	350	524	660	297	429	531	6.52	9.67	13.36
Motion pictures	78	[4]	408	631	[4]	344	536	[4]	10.95	15.26
Motion picture theaters	783	124	112	132	[4]	[4]	[4]	[4]	[4]	[4]
Amusement and recreation services	79	[4]	1,076	1,771	[4]	944	1,553	[4]	8.11	10.11
Health services [3]	80	5,278	7,814	10,139	4,712	6,948	8,984	5.68	10.41	14.75
Offices and clinics of medical doctors	801	802	1,338	1,933	[4]	1,105	1,596	[4]	10.58	15.46
Nursing and personal care facilities	805	997	1,415	1,791	898	1,279	1,608	4.17	7.24	10.72
Hospitals	806	2,750	3,549	4,019	2,522	3,248	3,684	6.06	11.79	16.49
Home health care services	808	[4]	291	642	[4]	269	590	[4]	8.72	12.44
Legal services	81	498	908	1,011	427	748	806	7.35	14.16	20.12
Educational services	82	1,138	1,661	2,355	[4]	[4]	[4]	[4]	[4]	[4]
Social services	83	1,134	1,734	2,963	990	1,494	2,556	4.26	7.11	9.91
Membership organizations	86	1,539	1,946	2,441	[4]	[4]	[4]	[4]	[4]	[4]
Engineering and management services	87	[4]	2,478	3,413	[4]	1,886	2,586	[4]	13.56	19.05
Government	(J)	16,241	18,304	20,572	(NA)	(NA)	(NA)	(NA)	(NA)	(NA)
Federal government	(X)	2,866	3,085	2,777	(NA)	(NA)	(NA)	(NA)	(NA)	(NA)
State government	(X)	3,610	4,305	4,746	(NA)	(NA)	(NA)	(NA)	(NA)	(NA)
Local government	(X)	9,765	10,914	13,049	(NA)	(NA)	(NA)	(NA)	(NA)	(NA)

NA Not available.   X Not applicable.   [1] 1987 Standard Industrial Classification, see text, Section 15, Business Enterprise.
[2] Excludes government.   [3] Includes industries not shown separately.   [4] Included in totals; not available separately.   [5] For changes in "Class I" classification, see text, Section 23, Transportation.   [6] Includes all employees except executives, officials, and staff assistants who received pay during the month.

Source: U.S. Bureau of Labor Statistics, *Employment and Earnings*, monthly, June issues and Internet site <http://www.bls.gov/ces/home.htm>.

Labor Force, Employment, and Earnings   395

No. 610. Employers With Selected Work-Based Learning Activities by Establishment Size and Type: 1997

[In percent. Based on survey of private establishments with 20 or more employees. Excludes nonprofits, government, and corporate headquarters. Subject to sampling error; see source]

Establishment and size type	All activities	At least one activity	Internship	Job shadowing	Cooperative education	Mentoring	Registered apprenticeship
Total	0.8	41.9	20.6	14.8	14.4	9.5	7.8
Establishment size:							
20 to 49 employees.	1.3	35.2	17.0	14.6	12.2	9.2	8.1
50 to 99 employees.	-	47.1	18.9	13.0	15.4	7.7	7.4
100 to 249 employees	0.2	54.2	29.3	14.9	19.1	10.6	7.4
250 employees or more	0.4	68.5	48.6	24.6	24.0	19.4	7.4
Establishment type:							
Construction, manufacturing and transportation	-	39.7	16.6	9.0	11.1	5.2	12.3
Wholesale/retail trade	1.7	38.3	17.1	13.9	18.0	11.4	7.7
Services	0.1	50.5	31.0	22.6	11.6	11.1	3.1

- Represents zero.

Source: U.S. National Center for Education Statistics, *Vocational Education in the United States: Toward 2000*, NCES 2000-029.

No. 611. Adults Taking Work-Related Adult Education Classes: 1995 and 1999

[In thousands (178,618 represents 178,618,000), except percent. For the civilian noninstitutional population 16 years old and over not enrolled in elementary or secondary school. Excludes retired persons over 70 who did not work for pay in the prior year. Excludes classes such as basic skills, personal development, etc. See also Table 290]

Occupation	1995			1999		
	Total population	Participants		Total population	Participants	
		Number	Percent		Number	Percent
Total	178,618	39,655	22	183,498	44,815	24
Health assessment, treatment	2,337	1,667	71	3,034	2,207	73
Health diagnosing	859	576	67	884	578	65
Teacher, below college	5,414	2,837	52	6,778	3,512	52
Other professional [1]	7,903	3,739	47	9,864	4,991	51
Executive, administrative, managerial . . .	13,098	5,509	42	28,665	10,704	37
College teacher.	1,254	511	41	2,582	1,080	42
Technical and related support	5,240	2,268	43	7,314	3,021	41
Miscellaneous.	2,311	819	35	2,161	337	16
Administrative support, including clerical.	22,968	6,646	29	22,276	5,789	26
Sales workers.	18,179	4,214	23	14,626	3,325	23
Service	20,080	4,192	21	18,192	3,393	19
Precision production, craft and repair . . .	12,667	2,811	22	11,179	1,634	15
Transportation and materials moving. . . .	5,311	825	16	5,476	959	18
Machine operators, assemblers and inspectors	9,484	1,392	15	10,121	1,873	19
Agriculture, forestry and fishing	2,336	270	12	2,532	394	16
Handlers, equipment cleaning, helpers and laborers	2,456	273	11	3,874	206	5
No job in the past year.	46,720	1,107	2	33,939	814	2

[1] For example, includes engineers, scientists, and social scientists.

Source: U.S. National Center for Education Statistics, *Adult Participation in Work-Related Courses, 1994-95*, October 1998, NCES 98-309; and National Household Education Survey, spring 1999.

No. 612. Annual Indexes of Output Per Hour for Selected Three-Digit SIC Industries: 1988 to 1999

[See text, this section. Minus sign (-) indicates decrease]

Industry	1987 SIC code [1]	Indexes (1987=100) 1988	1990	1995	1997	1998	1999	Average annual percent change [2]
Mining:								
Bituminous coal and lignite mining	122	111.7	118.7	155.9	176.6	188.0	192.2	5.6
Crude petroleum and natural gas	131	101.0	97.0	119.4	125.2	127.4	132.3	2.4
Manufacturing:								
Meat products.	201	100.1	97.1	102.3	102.5	102.3	102.2	0.2
Dairy products	202	108.4	107.3	116.4	119.3	119.3	114.1	1.1
Preserved fruits and vegetables	203	97.0	95.6	109.1	110.7	117.8	120.0	1.5
Grain mill products.	204	101.3	105.4	115.4	118.2	126.2	130.4	2.2
Bakery products	205	96.8	92.7	97.3	99.1	100.8	107.5	0.6
Sugar and confectionery products	206	99.5	103.2	108.3	116.7	123.0	130.0	2.2
Beverages	208	105.6	117.0	133.5	135.5	136.4	132.4	2.4
Miscellaneous food and kindred products.	209	107.0	99.2	102.9	104.1	112.7	116.3	1.3
Broadwoven fabric mills, cotton	221	99.6	103.1	134.0	131.2	136.2	138.7	2.8
Knitting mills.	225	96.6	107.5	138.3	138.0	135.9	144.8	3.1
Yarn and thread mills	228	102.1	110.2	137.4	150.4	153.0	169.5	4.5
Men's and boys' furnishings	232	100.1	102.1	123.4	162.1	174.7	187.0	5.4
Women's and misses' outerwear	233	101.4	104.1	135.5	149.9	151.9	174.5	4.7
Miscellaneous fabricated textile products	239	96.6	99.9	109.2	119.2	117.2	129.2	2.2
Sawmills and planing mills	242	100.7	99.8	110.2	116.9	118.7	125.4	1.9
Millwork, plywood, and structural members. . . .	243	98.8	98.0	92.7	89.1	91.3	90.7	-0.8
Wood buildings and mobile homes	245	97.8	103.1	97.0	100.3	99.2	96.8	-0.3
Miscellaneous wood products	249	95.9	107.7	115.4	123.4	131.2	141.3	2.9
Household furniture	251	99.4	104.5	116.9	121.3	125.8	128.7	2.1
Partitions and fixtures.	254	95.7	95.6	101.2	121.1	125.6	127.0	2.0
Paper mills.	262	103.9	102.3	118.6	112.0	114.9	122.7	1.7
Paperboard containers and boxes	265	99.7	101.3	105.1	109.7	113.5	113.5	1.1
Miscellaneous converted paper products	267	101.1	101.4	113.3	119.5	122.9	127.3	2.0
Newspapers	271	96.9	90.6	79.0	79.0	83.6	86.3	-1.2
Periodicals	272	97.9	93.9	87.8	100.1	115.0	115.1	1.2
Books	273	99.1	96.6	101.6	102.6	101.0	105.4	0.4
Miscellaneous publishing	274	96.7	92.2	94.8	114.5	119.5	128.3	2.1
Blankbooks and bookbinding	278	95.6	99.4	108.7	114.2	116.4	123.3	1.8
Industrial inorganic chemicals	281	105. .	106.8	109.3	116.8	145.8	170.7	4.6
Plastics materials and synthetics	282	98.8	100.9	128.3	135.4	142.2	145.7	3.2
Drugs:	283	101.0	103.8	10€ 7	112.4	104.3	104.8	0.4
Soaps, cleaners, and toilet goods	284	102.0	103.8	118.6	126.4	122.7	116.8	1.3
Industrial organic chemicals.	286	109.9	101.4	98.6	111.2	105.7	111.3	0.9
Miscellaneous chemical products	289	95.4	97.3	107.8	120.3	120.6	128.1	2.1
Petroleum refining	291	105.3	109.2	132.3	149.2	155.7	169.5	4.5
Tires and inner tubes	301	102.9	103.0	131.1	149.1	144.2	145.5	3.2
Fabricated rubber products, n.e.c. [3]	306	104.2	109.0	121.5	125.3	132.3	140.8	2.9
Miscellaneous plastics products, n.e.c. [3] . . .	308	100.5	105.7	121.0	129.9	133.8	141.2	2.9
Glass and glassware, pressed or blown.	322	100.6	104.8	115.7	128.3	135.2	143.6	3.1
Concrete, gypsum, and plaster products	327	100.8	102.3	104.5	107.6	112.8	114.4	1.1
Miscellaneous nonmetallic mineral products . . .	329	103.0	95.4	107.8	114.6	114.7	114.6	1.1
Blast furnace and basic steel products	331	112.6	109.7	142.6	155.0	151.0	148.9	3.4
Iron and steel foundries	332	104.0	106.1	112.7	120.8	121.1	126.2	2.0
Nonferrous rolling and drawing.	335	95.5	92.7	99.2	111.3	115.2	122.7	1.7
Nonferrous foundries (castings)	336	102.6	104.0	117.8	127.0	131.5	130.8	2.3
Cutlery, handtools, and hardware	342	97.8	97.3	111.3	114.6	115.7	123.9	1.8
Fabricated structural metal products	344	100.4	98.8	105.8	111.9	112.7	112.7	1.0
Metal forgings and stampings	346	101.5	95.6	99.0	109.3	120.2	125.9	2.2
Metal services, n.e.c. [3]	347	108.3	104.7	127.7	124.4	127.3	127.9	2.1
Miscellaneous fabricated metal products	349	101.4	97.5	106.6	107.7	111.5	110.3	0.8
Engines and turbines	351	106.8	106.5	122.7	136.9	145.9	151.2	3.5
Farm and garden machinery	352	106.3	116.5	134.7	141.2	148.5	125.5	1.9
Construction and related machinery	353	106.5	107.0	122.1	132.5	137.5	137.2	2.7
Metalworking machinery	354	101.0	101.1	114.8	119.2	119.8	123.5	1.8
Special industry machinery	355	104.6	107.5	132.3	131.7	125.1	139.3	2.8
General industrial machinery	356	105.9	101.5	109.0	110.0	111.2	111.4	0.9
Computer and office equipment	357	121.4	138.1	469.4	960.2	1350.6	1840.2	27.5
Refrigeration and service machinery	358	102.1	103.6	112.7	115.0	121.4	123.2	1.8
Industrial machinery, n.e.c. [3]	359	106.5	107.3	138.8	129.3	127.5	134.3	2.5
Electric distribution equipment	361	105.4	106.3	143.0	142.8	147.5	146.6	3.2
Electrical industrial apparatus	362	104.6	107.7	150.8	164.2	162.3	162.9	4.1
Household appliances	363	103.0	105.8	127.3	142.9	150.3	150.2	3.4
Electric lighting and wiring equipment	364	101.9	99.9	113.7	121.8	129.2	132.4	2.4
Communications equipment	366	110.2	123.8	200.6	275.3	276.0	327.1	10.4
Electronic components and accessories	367	109.0	133.4	401.5	613.4	768.0	1070.0	21.8
Miscellaneous electrical equipment & supplies .	369	102.8	90.6	114.1	128.3	135.3	140.7	2.9
Motor vehicles and equipment	371	103.2	102.4	106.7	116.3	125.2	136.5	2.6
Aircraft and parts.	372	100.6	98.9	107.9	114.7	140.1	139.6	2.8
Ship and boat building and repairing.	373	99.4	103.7	98.0	105.3	102.0	112.6	1.0
Guided missiles, space vehicles, parts	376	104.1	116.5	121.0	136.5	142.4	158.2	3.9

See footnotes at end of table.

U.S. Census Bureau, Statistical Abstract of the United States: 2001

[See text, this section. Minus sign (-) indicates decrease]

Industry	1987 SIC code [1]	Indexes (1987=100)						Average annual percent change [2]
		1988	1990	1995	1997	1998	1999	
Search and navigation equipment	381	104.8	112.7	149.5	149.5	149.1	139.7	2.8
Measuring and controlling devices	382	103.7	106.4	146.4	142.4	143.5	152.9	3.6
Medical instruments and supplies	384	105.2	116.9	131.5	147.4	158.6	160.2	4.0
Photographic equipment & supplies	386	105.6	107.8	129.5	121.5	124.8	147.2	3.3
Toys and sporting goods	394	104.8	108.1	113.6	125.7	131.6	124.0	1.8
Miscellaneous manufactures	399	102.1	106.5	108.1	109.4	108.5	111.2	0.9
Transportation:								
Railroad transportation	4011	108.4	118.5	156.2	169.8	173.3	182.3	5.1
Trucking, except local [4]	4213	105.2	111.1	125.4	132.4	129.9	131.6	2.3
United states postal service [5]	431	99.9	104.0	106.5	108.3	109.7	110.3	0.8
Air transportation [4]	4512, 13, 22 (pt.)	99.5	92.9	108.6	111.6	110.7	108.3	0.7
Utilities:								
Telephone communications	481	106.2	113.3	148.1	160.9	170.3	189.1	5.5
Radio and television broadcasting	483	103.1	104.9	109.6	101.1	100.7	101.8	0.1
Cable and other pay TV services	484	102.1	92.6	84.5	84.7	83.5	81.5	-1.7
Electric utilities	491, 3 (pt.)	104.9	110.1	135.0	150.5	160.1	162.7	4.1
Gas utilities	492, 3 (pt.)	108.3	105.8	137.1	158.6	144.4	145.0	3.1
Trade:								
Lumber and other building materials dealers	521	101.3	104.3	117.8	121.8	134.2	142.3	3.0
Paint, glass, and wallpaper stores	523	103.0	106.8	130.9	134.8	163.5	163.2	4.2
Hardware stores	525	110.3	115.3	115.5	119.0	137.8	149.3	3.4
Retail nurseries, lawn and garden supply stores	526	107.1	84.7	117.4	127.5	133.7	151.2	3.5
Department stores	531	100.1	96.8	115.9	128.8	135.5	147.4	3.3
Variety stores	533	102.6	154.4	211.3	257.7	268.7	319.5	10.2
Miscellaneous general merchandise stores	539	101.3	118.6	167.3	170.3	185.7	195.2	5.7
Grocery stores	541	99.6	96.6	93.9	91.7	92.2	95.4	-0.4
Retail bakeries	546	90.4	91.2	83.0	67.6	68.1	83.8	-1.5
New and used car dealers	551	103.6	106.7	108.1	108.8	108.7	111.9	0.9
Auto and home supply stores	553	103.5	103.6	109.1	108.1	113.0	116.0	1.2
Gasoline service stations	554	103.2	103.0	127.2	126.1	133.9	140.6	2.9
Men's and boy's wear stores	561	106.6	115.6	121.4	136.3	145.2	154.6	3.7
Women's clothing stores	562	99.5	106.6	139.9	157.3	176.1	190.5	5.5
Family clothing stores	565	103.1	107.8	141.8	150.2	153.1	156.5	3.8
Shoe stores	566	103.3	107.2	139.2	148.4	145.0	151.1	3.5
Furniture and homefurnishings stores	571	99.5	104.6	117.4	124.2	127.2	134.1	2.5
Household appliance stores	572	99.1	104.3	138.4	153.5	181.4	183.9	5.2
Radio, television, computer, and music stores	573	119.0	121.1	199.3	218.4	260.3	314.6	10.0
Eating and drinking places	581	103.0	104.5	102.0	101.6	102.0	104.3	0.4
Drug and proprietary stores	591	102.9	106.3	111.1	119.7	125.6	129.8	2.2
Liquor stores	592	98.4	105.9	104.7	109.9	116.5	113.5	1.1
Used merchandise stores	593	106.1	103.0	120.6	140.3	163.6	181.9	5.1
Miscellaneous shopping goods stores	594	101.7	107.2	123.1	129.1	138.8	145.2	3.2
Nonstore retailers	596	106.2	111.1	152.4	186.5	208.0	222.2	6.9
Fuel dealers	598	95.6	84.5	111.4	109.0	105.8	115.1	1.2
Retail stores, n.e.c. [3]	599	106.1	114.5	127.0	147.8	157.3	161.0	4.0
Finance and services:								
Commercial banks	602	102.8	107.7	126.4	133.0	132.6	135.2	2.5
Hotels and motels	701	97.7	96.2	110.5	108.2	111.6	113.5	1.1
Laundry, cleaning, and garment services	721	97.3	102.3	106.6	109.0	116.2	121.8	1.7
Photographic studios, portrait	722	103.3	98.2	116.2	114.1	121.6	105.0	0.4
Beauty shops	723	95.4	97.5	104.8	108.5	110.5	113.3	1.0
Funeral services and crematories	726	102.7	91.2	100.2	101.9	104.2	99.7	(Z)
Automotive repair shops	753	106.1	107.9	121.6	117.2	124.9	127.6	2.1
Motion picture theaters	783	107.8	118.1	105.0	103.4	106.1	110.5	0.8

Z Less than 0.05 percent. [1] 1987 Standard Industrial Classification; see text, Section 15, Business Enterprise. [2] Average annual percent change, 1987 to 1999, based on compound rate formula. [3] N.e.c. means not elsewhere classified. [4] Refers to output per employee. [5] Refers to output per full-time equivalent employee years on fiscal basis.

Source: U.S. Bureau of Labor Statistics, Internet site <http://www.bls.gov/lpc/home.htm>.

No. 613. Productivity and Related Measures: 1980 to 2000

[See text, this section. Minus sign (-) indicates decrease]

Item	1980	1985	1990	1995	1996	1997	1998	1999	2000
INDEXES (1992=100)									
Output per hour, business sector	80.4	88.7	95.2	'02.6	105.4	107.8	110.8	113.8	118.6
Nonfarm business	82.0	89.3	95.3	102.8	105.4	107.5	110.4	113.2	118.1
Manufacturing	70.1	82.3	92.9	109.0	112.8	117.6	124.0	129.6	138.5
Output, [1] business sector	69.8	83.1	97.6	111.5	116.4	122.5	128.6	134.8	142.4
Nonfarm business	70.2	83.0	97.8	111.8	116.7	122.7	129.0	135.1	142.8
Manufacturing	75.3	86.0	97.3	113.4	117.0	124.1	130.4	135.2	142.9
Hours, [2] business sector	86.8	93.6	102.6	108.7	110.4	113.6	116.1	118.4	120.0
Nonfarm business	85.6	93.0	102.7	108.8	110.7	114.1	116.8	119.3	120.9
Manufacturing	107.5	104.6	104.8	104.0	103.7	105.5	105.2	104.3	103.2
Compensation per hour, [3] business sector	54.2	72.9	90.7	106.7	110.1	113.5	119.6	125.1	131.4
Nonfarm business	54.6	73.2	90.5	106.6	109.8	113.1	119.0	124.2	130.5
Manufacturing	55.6	75.1	90.8	107.9	109.3	111.4	117.3	122.0	128.4
Real hourly compensation, [3] business sector	89.4	92.7	96.5	99.3	99.8	100.7	104.6	107.1	108.9
Nonfarm business	90.0	93.1	96.3	99.2	99.5	100.3	104.0	106.4	108.1
Manufacturing	91.6	95.5	96.6	100.4	99.0	98.8	102.6	104.5	106.4
Unit labor costs, [4] business sector	67.4	82.1	95.3	104.1	104.5	105.3	108.0	109.9	110.7
Nonfarm business	66.5	82.0	95.0	103.7	104.2	105.2	107.7	109.7	110.5
Manufacturing	79.3	91.3	97.8	99.0	96.9	94.7	94.6	94.1	92.7
ANNUAL PERCENT CHANGE [5]									
Output per hour, business sector	-0.3	2.0	1.3	0.7	2.8	2.3	2.8	2.8	4.2
Nonfarm business	-0.3	1.3	1.1	0.9	2.5	2.0	2.7	2.6	4.3
Manufacturing	0.4	3.6	2.9	3.8	3.5	4.3	5.4	4.5	6.9
Output, [1] business sector	-1.1	4.2	1.5	3.1	4.4	5.2	5.0	4.8	5.6
Nonfarm business	-1.1	3.9	1.4	3.4	4.3	5.1	5.1	4.8	5.7
Manufacturing	-4.2	2.8	0.7	4.3	3.1	6.1	5.1	3.7	5.7
Hours, [2] business sector	-0.9	2.2	0.2	2.4	1.6	2.9	2.2	2.0	1.3
Nonfarm business	-0.8	2.5	0.3	2.4	1.7	3.1	2.4	2.2	1.3
Manufacturing	-4.6	-0.7	-2.1	0.4	-0.3	1.7	-0.3	-0.8	-1.1
Compensation per hour, [3] business sector	10.8	4.9	5.7	2.1	3.2	3.1	5.3	4.6	5.0
Nonfarm business	10.8	4.7	5.5	2.1	3.0	3.0	5.2	4.4	5.1
Manufacturing	12.0	5.5	4.8	2.1	1.3	1.9	5.3	4.0	5.2
Real hourly compensation, [3] business sector	-0.3	1.5	0.6	-0.4	0.4	0.9	3.9	2.4	1.6
Nonfarm business	-0.3	1.2	0.4	-0.4	0.3	0.8	3.8	2.3	1.6
Manufacturing	0.8	2.0	-0.2	-0.4	-1.4	-0.2	3.8	1.9	1.8
Unit labor costs, [4] business sector	11.1	2.9	4.3	1.4	0.4	0.8	2.5	1.8	0.8
Nonfarm business	11.1	3.3	4.3	1.2	0.5	0.9	2.5	1.8	0.7
Manufacturing	11.6	1.8	1.9	-1.7	-2.1	-2.3	-0.1	-0.5	-1.6

[1] Refers to gross sectoral product, annual weighted. [2] Hours at work of all persons engaged in the business and nonfarm business sectors (employees, proprietors, and unpaid family workers); employees' and proprietors' hours in manufacturing. [3] Wages and salaries of employees plus employers' contributions for social insurance and private benefit plans. Also includes an estimate of same for self-employed. Real compensation deflated by the consumer price index for all urban consumers; see text, Section 14, Prices. [4] Hourly compensation divided by output per hour. [5] All changes are from the immediate prior year.
Source: U.S. Bureau of Labor Statistics, News USDL 01-132, Productivity and Costs; and Internet site <http://www.bls.gov lpc/home.htm>.

No. 614. Workers Using Computers on the Job: 1993 and 1997

[In percent, except as indicated (51,106 represents 51,106,000). For workers 18 years old and over. Based on the Current Population Survey and subject to sampling error; see Appendix III and source]

Characteristic	Number using computers (1,000)	Percent of total	Type of application							
			Analysis/ spread-sheets	Book-keeping/ inven-tory	Com-munica-tions [2]	Data-bases	Desktop publish-ing	Sales and telemar-keting	Word proces-sing
Total, 1993	51,106	45.8	36.1	45.0	38.7	34.5	22.3	16.2	44.4
Total, 1997	63,885	49.8	40.9	66.4	47.0	34.1	26.1	22.1	57.0
Age:									
18 to 24 years old	6,007	37.1	28.2	70.3	35.3	23.4	18.4	23.5	43.1
25 to 29 years old	7,984	52.5	41.7	69.8	46.6	35.0	25.8	23.4	58.3
30 to 39 years old	18,864	53.3	44.0	67.0	49.1	35.4	28.3	24.0	58.5
40 to 49 years old	18,182	54.9	43.6	65.8	48.6	36.9	27.1	20.6	58.9
50 to 59 years old	10,092	50.7	39.1	62.8	49.0	33.5	26.1	19.6	58.8
60 years old and over	2,755	32.6	33.5	62.1	42.2	28.8	21.6	21.3	54.1
Sex: Male	30,336	44.1	46.5	64.3	51.4	36.8	29.4	24.6	53.9
Female	33,549	56.5	35.8	68.3	43.1	31.6	23.1	19.9	59.8
Occupation:									
Executive, admin., managerial	14,528	77.5	60.1	76.3	61.4	47.2	32.6	30.9	74.5
Professional specialty	13,900	71.7	44.4	45.1	55.8	37.8	40.3	9.8	68.7
Teachers, below college	2,961	60.3	33.1	31.9	39.7	27.5	42.3	4.6	73.6
Teachers, college and univ.	759	79.9	51.5	27.1	74.6	40.2	41.3	5.4	83.5
Technical/related support	3,226	75.1	42.9	51.8	49.4	36.9	26.1	7.7	49.6
Sales workers	8,277	54.8	38.4	83.0	43.0	31.3	21.0	57.2	46.1
Admin. support, inc. clerical	14,235	77.6	31.4	75.0	39.4	28.3	17.0	15.9	56.2
Service workers	2,752	16.4	15.7	52.3	27.6	17.4	9.6	11.0	34.4
Precision prod., craft/repair	3,501	25.0	29.6	62.8	31.6	22.5	18.2	11.1	29.0
Operators, laborers [3]	3,154	17.3	19.1	63.1	21.3	14.6	12.6	9.2	17.4
Farming, forestry and fishing	311	9.3	40.2	79.3	22.8	33.0	11.2	19.1	33.7

[1] Includes other applications, not shown separately. A person may be counted in more than one application. [2] Includes bulletin boards and electronic mail. [3] Includes fabricators.
Source: U.S. National Center for Education Statistics, Digest of Education Statistics, 1994 and 1998.

Labor Force, Employment, and Earnings 399

No. 615. Annual Total Compensation and Wages and Salary Accruals Per Full-Time Equivalent Employee by Industry: 1990 to 1999

[In dollars. Wage and salary accruals include executives' compensation, bonuses, tips, and payments-in-kind; total compensation includes in addition to wages and salaries, employer contributions for social insurance, employer contributions to private and welfare funds, director's fees, jury and witness fees, etc. Based on the 1987 Standard Industrial Classification Code (SIC); See text, Section 15, Business Enterprise]

Industry	Annual total compensation				Annual wages and salary			
	1990	1995	1998	1999	1990	1995	1998	1999
Domestic industries	31,940	37,742	41,639	43,283	26,259	30,911	35,034	36,555
Private industries	30,822	36,322	40,260	41,927	25,853	30,310	34,631	36,187
Agriculture, forestry, and fishing	18,475	21,022	23,553	24,281	15,996	18,166	20,701	21,288
Mining.	45,872	56,523	61,811	65,144	38,024	46,583	52,465	55,369
Construction	33,833	37,285	39,996	41,545	27,871	30,431	34,625	36,127
Manufacturing	36,958	44,713	48,382	50,641	30,054	35,779	40,830	42,862
Transportation	36,459	40,732	43,536	44,673	28,900	32,349	35,991	37,189
Communications.	46,281	59,952	66,315	72,873	38,751	48,979	56,086	62,148
Electric, gas, and sanitary services.	48,097	59,478	65,158	68,387	39,557	48,751	54,975	58,034
Wholesale trade	37,031	44,508	50,178	52,718	31,499	37,808	43,606	45,856
Retail trade	18,626	21,189	23,861	24,706	15,990	18,246	20,602	21,414
Finance, insurance, and real estate	37,501	49,272	60,044	63,225	31,982	41,661	52,403	55,357
Services	28,807	34,043	37,716	39,266	24,697	29,084	32,759	34,197
Government	37,218	44,951	49,139	50,782	28,176	33,962	37,227	38,594

Source: U.S. Bureau of Economic Analysis, *National Income and Product Accounts of the United States, 1929-94;* and *Survey of Current Business,* May 2001.

No. 616. Average Hourly and Weekly Earnings by Private Industry Group: 1980 to 2000

[Average earnings include overtime. Data are for production and related workers in mining, manufacturing, and construction, and nonsupervisory employees in other industries. Excludes agriculture. See headnote, Table 607]

Private industry group	Current dollars					Constant (1982) dollars [1]				
	1980	1985	1990	1995	2000	1980	1985	1990	1995	2000
TOTAL AVERAGE HOURLY EARNINGS										
Total	6.66	8.57	10.01	11.43	13.74	7.78	7.77	7.52	7.39	7.88
Mining	9.17	11.98	13.68	15.30	17.14	10.71	10.86	10.28	9.90	9.83
Construction	9.94	12.32	13.77	15.09	17.86	11.61	11.17	10.35	9.76	10.25
Manufacturing	7.27	9.54	10.83	12.37	14.38	8.49	8.65	8.14	8.00	8.25
Transportation, public utilities	8.87	11.40	12.92	14.13	16.22	10.36	10.34	9.71	9.14	9.31
Wholesale trade	6.95	9.15	10.79	12.43	15.18	8.12	8.30	8.11	8.04	8.71
Retail trade	4.88	5.94	6.75	7.69	9.45	5.70	5.39	5.07	4.97	5.42
Finance, insurance, real estate	5.79	7.94	9.97	12.32	15.07	6.76	7.20	7.49	7.97	8.65
Services	5.85	7.90	9.83	11.39	13.88	6.83	7.16	7.39	7.37	7.96
TOTAL AVERAGE WEEKLY EARNINGS										
Total	235	299	345	394	474	275	271	259	255	272
Mining	397	520	603	684	770	464	471	453	442	442
Construction	368	464	526	587	702	430	421	395	380	403
Manufacturing	289	386	442	515	597	337	350	332	333	342
Transportation, public utilities	351	450	496	557	624	410	408	373	360	358
Wholesale trade	267	351	411	476	584	312	319	309	308	335
Retail trade	147	175	194	221	273	172	158	146	143	157
Finance, insurance, real estate	210	289	357	442	547	245	262	268	286	314
Services	191	257	319	369	454	223	233	240	239	260

[1] Earnings in current dollars divided by the Consumer Price Index (CPI-W) on a 1982 base; see text, Section 14, Prices.

Source: U.S. Bureau of Labor Statistics, *Employment and Earnings,* monthly, March and June issues; and Internet site <http://www.bls.gov/ces/home.htm>.

No. 617. Annual Percent Changes in Earnings and Compensation: 1980 to 2000

[Annual percent change from immediate prior year. Minus sign (-) indicates decrease]

Item	1980	1985	1990	1995	1996	1997	1998	1999	2000
Current dollars:									
Hourly earnings, total [1]	8.1	3.0	3.6	2.8	3.4	3.9	4.1	3.6	3.9
Hourly earnings, manufacturing [2]	8.5	3.8	3.3	2.5	3.2	3.1	2.4	3.0	3.5
Compensation per employee-hour [3] . . .	10.7	4.6	5.5	2.1	3.1	3.0	5.2	4.4	5.1
Constant (1982) dollars:									
Hourly earnings, total [1]	-4.8	-0.4	-1.6	-0.1	0.5	1.6	2.6	1.4	0.4
Hourly earnings, manufacturing [2]	-4.5	0.3	-1.7	-0.4	0.4	0.9	1.1	0.7	-
Compensation per employee-hour [3] . . .	-0.4	1.2	0.4	-0.4	0.3	0.8	3.7	2.2	1.6

- Represents or rounds to zero. [1] Production or nonsupervisory workers on private nonfarm payrolls. [2] Production and related workers. [3] Nonfarm business sector.

Source: U.S. Bureau of Labor Statistics, News USDL 01-132, *Productivity and Costs;* and Internet site <http://www.bls.gov/lpc/home.htm>.

No. 618. Mean Hourly Earnings and Weekly Hours for Metro and Nonmetro Areas by Selected Characteristics: 1998

[Covers civilian workers in private industry establishments and state and local governments in the 50 states and DC. Excludes private households, federal government, and agriculture. Based on establishment survey; see source for details]

Item	Mean hourly earnings (dol.) [1]			Mean weekly hours		
	Total	Metro areas [2]	Nonmetro areas	Total	Metro areas [2]	Nonmetro areas
Total	15.72	16.40	12.31	36.5	36.4	37.1
Private industry	14.95	15.67	11.16	36.5	36.3	37.2
State and local government	18.59	19.23	15.90	36.6	36.6	36.6
WORKER CHARACTERISTIC						
White-collar occupations	19.39	19.93	15.65	36.7	36.7	36.9
Professional specialty and technical	24.10	24.58	20.76	36.4	36.4	36.3
Professional	25.90	26.35	22.75	36.3	36.3	36.2
Technical	17.83	18.43	13.37	36.8	36.8	36.6
Executive, administrative, and managerial	27.78	28.35	22.56	40.0	40.1	39.7
Executive, administrators, and managers	31.73	32.69	24.25	40.3	40.4	39.8
Management related	21.88	22.14	18.45	39.6	39.6	39.5
Sales	13.28	14.12	9.10	33.0	32.6	35.3
Administrative support	12.00	12.23	10.41	37.0	37.0	37.5
Blue-collar occupations	12.90	13.31	11.36	38.5	38.4	38.9
Precision production, craft, and repair	16.58	17.14	14.09	39.8	39.8	40.0
Machine operators, assemblers, and inspectors	11.59	11.96	10.49	39.6	39.5	39.7
Transportation and material moving	13.72	13.85	13.01	37.9	38.1	37.2
Handlers, equipment cleaners, helpers and laborers	9.69	9.84	9.17	35.9	35.5	37.2
Service occupations	9.52	9.90	8.20	33.0	32.6	34.6
Protective service	14.36	14.88	11.84	38.0	37.7	39.4
Food service	6.76	6.91	6.31	30.1	29.2	33.0
Health service	8.77	9.02	7.85	33.7	34.0	32.5
Cleaning and building service	9.03	9.23	8.06	35.1	34.8	36.9
Personal service	9.27	9.63	8.58	29.6	27.8	34.1
Full time	16.40	17.17	12.64	39.6	39.6	39.7
Part time	9.25	9.37	8.50	21.1	21.1	20.9
Union [3]	17.76	18.14	15.18	36.9	36.7	38.0
Nonunion	15.10	15.84	11.70	36.4	36.3	36.9
Time [4]	15.66	16.33	12.34	36.4	36.3	37.0
Incentive [4]	17.14	17.91	11.21	38.6	38.4	40.0
ESTABLISHMENT CHARACTERISTIC						
Goods producing [5]	16.00	17.00	12.37	39.8	39.8	40.0
Service producing [5]	14.40	15.05	10.12	35.0	34.9	35.2
50 to 99 workers	13.04	13.48	11.14	35.2	35.1	35.2
100 to 499 workers	14.21	14.66	12.19	36.3	36.3	36.6
500 to 999 workers	16.45	16.94	14.55	37.3	37.1	38.2
1,000 to 2,499 workers	16.51	18.25	11.30	36.8	36.3	38.5
2,500 workers or more	20.07	20.09	18.96	37.3	37.2	39.7
GEOGRAPHIC REGION [6]						
New England	17.38	17.75	14.75	35.1	35.2	34.2
Middle Atlantic	18.10	18.39	13.58	35.8	35.7	36.2
East North Central	16.08	16.55	13.55	36.2	36.2	36.5
West North Central	14.85	15.83	12.10	36.5	36.5	36.4
South Atlantic	14.40	14.89	12.00	37.1	37.0	37.7
East South Central	11.87	13.88	9.97	37.7	36.9	38.6
West South Central	14.62	14.86	13.08	37.2	37.2	37.1
Mountain	14.58	14.73	13.99	36.4	36.5	36.0
Pacific	17.86	18.04	14.96	36.2	36.2	35.6

[1] Earnings are straight time hourly wages or salary, including incentive pay, cost-of-living adjustments, and hazard pay. Excludes premium pay for overtime, vacations and holidays, nonproduction bonuses and tips. [2] Metropolitan areas defined as of 1994. [3] Workers whose wages are determined through collective bargaining. [4] Time worker wages are based solely on an hourly rate or salary. Incentive workers wages are based at least in part on productivity payments such as piece rates or commissions. [5] For private industry only. [6] Composition of regions: NEW ENGLAND: Maine, New Hampshire, Vermont, Massachusetts, Rhode Island, Connecticut. MIDDLE ATLANTIC: New York, New Jersey, and Pennsylvania. EAST NORTH CENTRAL: Ohio, Indiana, Illinois, Michigan, Wisconsin. WEST NORTH CENTRAL: Minnesota, Iowa, Missouri, North Dakota, South Dakota, Nebraska, and Kansas. SOUTH ATLANTIC: Delaware, Maryland, District of Columbia, Virginia, West Virginia. North Carolina, South Carolina, Georgia, Florida. EAST SOUTH CENTRAL: Kentucky, Tennessee, Alabama, Mississippi. WEST SOUTH CENTRAL: Arkansas, Louisiana, Oklahoma, and Texas. MOUNTAIN: Montana, Idaho, Wyoming, Colorado, New Mexico, Arizona, Utah, Nevada. PACIFIC: Washington, Oregon, California, Alaska, and Hawaii.

Source: U.S. Bureau of Labor Statistics, *National Compensation Survey: Occupational Wages in the United States, 1998*, Bulletin 2529, September 2000.

No. 619. Average Annual Pay by State: 1998 and 1999

[In dollars, except percent change. For workers covered by state unemployment insurance laws and for federal civilian workers covered by unemployment compensation for federal employees, approximately 99 percent of wage and salary civilian employment in 1999. Excludes most agricultural workers on small farms, all Armed Forces, elected officials in most states, railroad employees, most domestic workers, most student workers at school, employees of certain nonprofit organizations, and most self-employed individuals. Pay includes bonuses, cash value of meals and lodging, and tips and other gratuities]

State	Average annual pay 1998	Average annual pay 1999 [1]	Percent change, 1998-99	State	Average annual pay 1998	Average annual pay 1999 [1]	Percent change, 1998-99
United States......	31,945	33,313	4.3	Missouri	28,907	29,958	3.6
Alabama	27,042	28,069	3.8	Montana	22,648	23,253	2.7
Alaska	33,847	34,034	0.6	Nebraska	25,539	26,633	4.3
Arizona...........	29,322	30,523	4.1	Nevada...........	30,203	31,213	3.3
Arkansas..........	24,425	25,371	3.9	New Hampshire	30,944	32,139	3.9
California..........	35,348	37,564	6.3	New Jersey	39,516	(NA)	(NA)
Colorado..........	32,248	34,192	6.0	New Mexico.......	25,711	26 270	2.2
Connecticut	40,895	42,653	4.3	New York	40,684	42,133	3.6
Delaware..........	33,969	35,102	3.3	North Carolina	28,176	29,453	4.5
District of Columbia....	48,462	50,742	4.7	North Dakota	22,990	23,753	3.3
Florida	28,184	28,911	2.6	Ohio.............	30,392	31,396	3.3
Georgia	30,856	32,339	4.8	Oklahoma	25,122	25,748	2.5
Hawaii	29,036	29,771	2.5	Oregon	29,544	30,867	4.5
Idaho	24,868	26,042	4.7	Pennsylvania	31,584	32,694	3.5
Illinois............	34,715	36,279	4.5	Rhode Island	30,156	31,177	3.4
Indiana...........	29,108	30,027	3.2	South Carolina	26,161	27,124	3.7
Iowa.............	26,026	26,939	3.5	South Dakota......	22,751	23,765	4.5
Kansas...........	26,845	28,029	4.4	Tennessee........	28,462	29,518	3.7
Kentucky..........	26,697	27,748	3.9	Texas	31,515	32,895	4.4
Louisiana.........	26,910	27,221	1.2	Utah.............	26,873	27,884	3.8
Maine............	25,875	26,887	3.9	Vermont	26,611	27,595	3.7
Maryland..........	33,301	34,472	3.5	Virginia	31,373	33,015	5.2
Massachusetts	37,774	40,331	6.8	Washington	33,076	35,736	8.0
Michigan	34,521	35,734	3.4	West Virginia	25,276	26,008	2.9
Minnesota	32,075	33,487	4.4	Wisconsin	28,531	29,597	3.7
Mississippi........	23,822	24,392	2.4	Wyoming	24,725	25,639	3.7

NA Not available. [1] Preliminary. 1999 U.S. total includes an estimate for New Jersey.

Source: U.S. Bureau of Labor Statistics, News USDL 00-339, November 17, 2000, Average Annual Pay by State and Industry.

No. 620. Average Annual Pay by Selected Metropolitan Area: 1998 and 1999

[In dollars. Metropolitan areas ranked by average pay 1998. Includes data for Metropolitan Statistical Areas and Primary Metropolitan Statistical Areas defined as of June 1999. In the New England areas, the New England County Metropolitan Area (NECMA) definitions were used. See source for details. See also headnote, Table 619]

Metropolitan area	1998	1999, prel.[1]	Metropolitan area	1998	1999, prel.[1]
Metropolitan areas	33,407	34,868	Dutchess County, NY	33,568	35,256
San Jose, CA................	51,397	61,110	Saginaw-Bay City-Midland, MI......	33,330	33990
New York, NY................	50,381	52,351	Monmouth-Ocean, NJ	33,233	(NA)
San Francisco, CA	45,644	50,169	Rochester, MN	33,125	35,025
New Haven-Bridgeport-Stamford-			Sacramento, CA	32,979	34,266
Waterbury-Danbury, CT	44,812	47,142	Brazoria, TX	32,945	33,266
Middlesex-Somerset-Hunterdon, NJ ..	44,567	(NA)	Charlotte-Gastonia-Rock Hill, NC-SC ..	32,897	34,325
Newark, NJ	42,906	(NA)	Portland-Vancouver, OR-WA	32,840	34,380
Trenton, NJ	41,612	(NA)	Raleigh-Durham-Chapel Hill, NC	32,821	34,866
Washington, DC-MD-VA-WV.......	40,585	42,601	Baltimore, MD	32,731	33,837
Bergen-Passaic, NJ............	40,110	(NA)	Springfield, IL................	32,610	33,990
Jersey City, NJ...............	40,079	(NA)	Indianapolis, IN	32,487	33,665
Seattle-Bellevue-Everett, WA	39,849	43,921	Cleveland-Lorain-Elyria, OH	32,354	33,437
Detroit, MI..................	39,497	40,836	St. Louis, MO-IL..............	32,256	33,345
Oakland, CA	38,559	40,975	San Diego, CA	32,210	34,690
Hartford, CT.................	38,490	39,954	Cincinnati, OH-KY-IN...........	32,206	33,626
Boston-Worcester-Lawrence-Lowell-			Milwaukee-Waukesha, WI	32,130	33,375
Brockton, MA-NH	38,335	40,903	Rochester, NY	32,084	32,588
Boulder-Longmont, CO	37,817	40,002	Yolo, CA	32,025	32,341
Chicago, IL..................	37,745	39,536	Ventura, CA..................	31,973	33,927
Kokomo, IN	37,532	39,653	West Palm Beach-Boca Raton, FL...	31,877	32,609
Dallas, TX...................	37,309	39,281	Fort Worth-Arlington, TX	31,662	32,961
Wilmington-Newark, DE-MD	36,758	37,990	Bloomington-Normal, IL	31,437	32,888
Houston, TX	36,729	38,114	Richmond-Petersburg, VA	31,404	33,012
Los Angeles-Long Beach, CA	36,571	37,748	Cedar Rapids, IA	31,375	32,441
Philadelphia, PA-NJ...........	36,231	(NA)	Pittsburgh, PA	31,369	33,057
Nassau-Suffolk, NY...........	35,783	36,944	Racine, WI	31,348	32,532
Orange County, CA...........	35,717	37,487	Memphis, TN-AR-MS............	31,285	32,591
Minneapolis-St. Paul, MN-WI	35,624	37,248	Kansas City, MO-KS	31,276	33,026
Denver, CO	35,606	38,133	Decatur, IL..................	31,239	32,061
Anchorage, AK...............	35,459	35,707	Phoenix-Mesa, AZ	31,197	32,430
Atlanta, GA	35,405	37,341	Dayton-Springfield, OH	31,196	32,362
Austin-San Marcos, TX	35,347	38,930	Columbus, OH................	31,166	32,428
New London-Norwich, CT........	34,618	35,409	Albany-Schenectady-Troy, NY	31,078	31,901
Flint, MI	34,580	35,658	Grand Rapids-Muskegon-Holland, MI ..	31,060	31,913
Ann Arbor, MI................	34,331	35,733	Lansing-East Lansing, MI........	30,945	32,434
Huntsville, AL................	33,789	34,225	Miami, FL	30,867	32,059

NA Not available. [1] Preliminary. 1999 U.S. total includes an estimate for New Jersey.

Source: U.S. Bureau of Labor Statistics, News USDL 00-349, November 28, 2000, Average Annual Pay Levels in Metropolitan Areas.

No. 621. Full-Time Wage and Salary Workers—Number and Earnings: 1985 to 2000

[In current dollars of usual weekly earnings. Data represent annual averages (77,002 represents 77,002,000). See text, this section, and headnote Table 584, for a discussion of occupational data. Based on Current Population Survey; see text, Section 1, Population, and Appendix III. For definition of median, see Guide to Tabular Presentation]

Characteristic	Number of workers (1,000)				Median weekly earnings (dol.)			
	1985	1990 [1]	1995 [1]	2000 [1]	1985	1990 [1]	1995 [1]	2000 [1]
All workers [2]	77,002	85,804	89,282	99,917	343	412	479	576
Male	45,589	49,564	51,222	56,273	406	481	538	646
16 to 24 years old	6,956	6,824	6,118	6,786	240	282	303	376
25 years old and over	38,632	42,740	45,104	49,487	442	512	588	700
Female	31,414	36,239	38,060	43,644	277	346	406	491
16 to 24 years old	5,621	5,227	4,366	5,147	210	254	275	342
25 years old and over	25,793	31,012	33,695	38,497	296	369	428	515
White	66,481	72,811	74,874	82,475	355	424	494	591
Male	40,030	42,797	43,747	47,578	417	494	566	669
Female	26,452	30,014	31,127	34,897	281	353	415	500
Black	8,393	9,820	10,596	12,556	277	329	383	468
Male	4,367	4,983	5,279	5,989	304	361	411	503
Female	4,026	4,837	5,317	6,568	252	308	355	429
Hispanic origin [3]	(NA)	7,812	8,719	11,738	(NA)	304	329	396
Male	(NA)	5,000	5,597	7,261	(NA)	318	350	414
Female	(NA)	2,812	3,122	4,477	(NA)	278	305	364
Occupation, male:								
Managerial and professional	11,078	12,255	13,684	15,875	583	729	829	994
Exec., admin., managerial	5,835	6,389	7,172	8,142	593	740	833	1,014
Professional specialty	5,243	5,866	6,512	7,733	571	719	827	977
Technical, sales, and administrative support	8,803	9,677	9,894	10,828	420	493	556	655
Tech. and related support	1,563	1,762	1,688	1,882	472	567	641	761
Sales	4,227	4,692	5,000	5,583	431	502	579	684
Admin. support, incl. clerical	3,013	3,224	3,206	3,363	391	436	489	563
Service	3,947	4,602	4,779	5,284	272	317	357	414
Private household	13	12	15	20	(B)	(B)	(B)	(B)
Protective	1,327	1,531	1,691	1,771	391	477	552	659
Other service	2,607	3,059	3,073	3,493	230	271	300	357
Precision production [4]	10,026	10,259	10,046	11,075	408	486	534	628
Mechanics and repairers	3,752	3,687	3,658	4,024	400	475	538	649
Construction trades	3,308	3,650	3,541	4,341	394	478	507	599
Other	2,966	2,922	2,847	2,709	433	508	574	651
Operators, fabricators and laborers	10,585	11,464	11,529	11,837	325	375	413	487
Machine operators, assemblers, and inspectors	4,403	4,594	4,576	4,240	341	387	421	495
Transportation and material moving	3,459	3,752	3,870	4,221	369	416	482	558
Handlers, equipment cleaners, helpers, and laborers	2,724	3,118	3,083	3,376	261	306	328	394
Farming, forestry, and fishing	1,150	1,306	1,290	1,374	216	261	294	347
Occupation, female:								
Managerial and professional	8,302	10,575	12,609	15,580	399	510	605	709
Exec., admin., managerial	3,492	4,758	5,803	7,226	383	484	570	686
Professional specialty	4,810	5,816	6,806	8,354	408	534	632	725
Technical, sales, and administrative support	14,622	16,290	16,004	17,424	269	331	383	452
Tech. and related support	1,200	1,476	1,506	1,769	331	417	480	541
Sales	2,929	3,554	3,862	4,550	226	290	330	407
Admin. support, incl. clerical	10,494	11,260	10,636	11,105	270	332	384	449
Service	3,963	4,577	4,838	5,736	185	230	264	316
Private household	330	305	324	348	130	171	193	261
Protective	156	217	266	341	278	405	438	500
Other service	3,477	4,055	4,249	5,047	188	230	264	314
Precision production [4]	906	900	957	1,088	268	316	371	445
Mechanics and repairers	144	139	150	203	392	458	550	627
Construction trades	53	50	66	88	265	393	400	475
Other	709	711	741	796	253	299	346	414
Operators, fabricators, and laborers	3,482	3,722	3,462	3,574	216	261	297	351
Machine operators, assemblers, and inspectors	2,778	2,878	2,559	2,396	216	259	296	355
Transportation and material moving	189	227	261	366	252	314	354	407
Handlers, equipment cleaners, helpers and laborers	514	616	642	812	209	249	284	320
Farming, forestry, and fishing	138	175	190	242	185	216	249	294

B Data not shown where base is less than 50,000.   NA Not available.   [1] See footnote 2, Table 567.   [2] Includes other races, not shown separately.   [3] Persons of Hispanic origin may be of any race.   [4] Includes craft and repair.

Source: U.S. Bureau of Labor Statistics, Bulletin 2307, and *Employment and Earnings*, monthly, January issues; and unpublished data.

Labor Force, Employment, and Earnings   403

No. 622. Workers With Earnings by Occupation of Longest Held Job and Sex: 1999

[70,387 represents 70,387,000. As of March 2000, covers persons 15 years old and over. Based on Current Population Survey; see text, Section 1, Population, and Appendix III. For definition of median, see Guide to Tabular Presentation]

Major occupation of longest job held	All workers				Full-time, year-round			
	Women		Men		Women		Men	
	Number (1,000)	Median earnings	Number (1,000)	Median earnings	Number (1,000)	Median earnings	Number (1,000)	Median earnings
Total [1]	**70,387**	**18,389**	**78,460**	**30,104**	**40,404**	**26,324**	**57,511**	**36,476**
Executive, administrators, and managerial	9,404	31,912	11,243	51,274	7,302	36,141	9,831	55,261
Professional specialty	11,858	31,339	9,938	50,366	7,061	37,533	7,869	54,616
Technical and related support	2,604	25,274	2,236	38,025	1,775	30,001	1,732	41,700
Sales	9,675	11,428	8,793	31,355	4,436	23,778	6,437	38,267
Admin. support, incl. clerical	16,356	19,337	4,270	24,592	10,063	24,581	2,887	31,767
Precision production, craft and repair	1,527	20,397	13,866	30,734	1,067	24,946	10,854	34,429
Machine operators, assemblers, and inspectors	3,062	15,066	5,082	25,617	1,959	18,928	4,031	29,156
Transportation and material moving	639	13,863	5,400	26,080	279	20,720	3,901	30,754
Handlers, equipment cleaners, helpers, and laborers	1,283	11,852	5,110	14,446	597	18,432	2,613	21,206
Service workers	13,034	9,846	8,671	15,171	5,527	16,306	4,988	24,289
Private household	1,090	5,035	57	(B)	325	11,820	14	(B)
Service, except private household	11,944	10,278	8,614	15,243	5,203	16,538	4,973	24,342
Farming, forestry, and fishing	855	6,280	3,180	12,126	269	13,230	1,756	18,949

B Base less than 75,000.   [1] Includes people whose longest job was in the Armed Forces.

Source: U.S. Census Bureau, *Current Population Reports* P60-209.

No. 623. Employment Cost Index (ECI), Compensation by Industry and Occupation: 1982 to 2000

[As of December. The ECI is a measure of the rate of change in employee compensation (wages, salaries, and employer costs for employee benefits). Data are not seasonally adjusted; 1982 and 1985 based on fixed employment counts from 1970 Census of Population; 1990 based on fixed employment counts from the 1980 Census of Population; Beginning 1995 based primarily on 1990 Occupational Employment Survey]

Item	Indexes (June 1989=100)						Percent change for 12 months ending Dec.—				
	1982	1985	1990	1995	1999	2000	1985	1990	1995	1999	2000
Civilian workers [1]	**74.8**	**86.8**	**107.6**	**127.2**	**144.6**	**150.6**	**4.3**	**4.9**	**2.7**	**3.4**	**4.1**
Workers, by occupational group:											
White-collar occupations	72.9	85.8	108.3	128.0	146.3	152.5	4.9	5.2	2.9	3.5	4.2
Blue-collar occupations	78.2	88.4	106.5	125.8	140.6	146.5	3.3	4.4	2.5	3.3	4.2
Service occupations	74.3	87.2	108.0	127.4	144.8	150.0	3.9	5.1	2.5	3.4	3.6
Workers, by industry division:											
Manufacturing	76.9	87.8	107.2	128.3	143.6	149.3	3.3	5.1	2.6	3.4	4.0
Nonmanufacturing	73.9	86.4	107.8	126.8	144.7	150.7	4.7	4.9	2.8	3.4	4.1
Service industries	70.5	84.1	110.2	129.4	146.5	152.4	4.7	6.3	2.4	3.4	4.0
Public administration [2]	71.9	85.4	108.7	128.3	144.4	148.3	4.9	5.3	3.3	3.2	2.7
State and local government	**70.8**	**84.6**	**110.4**	**129.3**	**144.6**	**148.9**	**5.6**	**5.8**	**2.9**	**3.4**	**3.0**
Workers, by occupational group:											
White-collar occupations	70.4	84.2	110.9	129.1	144.0	148.3	5.8	6.0	2.9	3.4	3.0
Blue-collar workers	73.9	86.7	108.7	128.0	142.5	147.2	5.3	4.8	2.6	3.4	3.3
Workers, by industry division:											
Service industries	70.0	84.0	111.3	129.6	144.5	148.9	5.9	6.3	2.8	3.4	3.0
Schools	69.0	83.6	111.6	129.8	144.7	149.0	6.2	6.0	2.8	3.4	3.0
Elementary and secondary	68.6	83.6	112.1	130.1	144.1	148.1	6.4	6.3	2.8	3.4	2.8
Colleges and universities	(NA)	(NA)	110.2	128.7	146.5	151.7	(NA)	5.3	2.5	3.5	3.5
Services, excluding schools [3]	73.1	85.2	110.2	129.4	143.8	148.8	4.7	6.8	3.0	3.6	3.5
Public administration [2]	71.9	85.4	108.7	128.3	144.4	148.3	4.9	5.3	3.3	3.2	2.7
Private industry workers [4]	**75.8**	**87.3**	**107.0**	**126.7**	**144.6**	**150.9**	**3.9**	**4.6**	**2.6**	**3.4**	**4.4**
Workers, by occupational group:											
White-collar occupations	73.7	86.4	107.4	127.6	146.9	153.6	4.9	4.9	2.8	3.5	4.6
Blue-collar occupations	78.4	88.5	106.4	125.6	140.5	146.4	3.1	4.4	2.4	3.3	4.2
Service occupations	76.3	88.4	107.3	125.2	142.6	148.1	3.0	4.7	1.9	3.3	3.9
Workers, by industry division:											
Manufacturing	76.9	87.8	107.2	128.3	143.6	149.3	3.3	5.1	2.6	3.4	4.0
Nonmanufacturing	75.1	87.0	106.9	125.9	144.5	151.1	4.3	4.5	2.7	3.4	4.6
Service industries	(NA)	84.1	109.3	129.4	147.6	154.1	(NA)	6.2	2.2	3.4	4.4
Business services	(NA)	(NA)	107.4	126.3	151.9	158.4	(NA)	6.0	2.7	4.1	4.3
Health services	(NA)	83.7	110.8	132.2	144.2	150.6	(NA)	6.8	2.7	3.7	4.4
Hospitals	(NA)	(NA)	110.7	131.3	144.6	151.1	(NA)	7.0	2.1	3.4	4.5
Workers by bargaining status:											
Union	79.6	90.1	106.2	127.7	141.2	146.9	2.6	4.3	2.8	2.7	4.0
Nonunion	74.3	86.3	107.3	126.5	145.2	151.6	4.6	4.8	2.7	3.6	4.4

NA Not available.   [1] Includes private industry and state and local government workers and excludes farm, household, and federal government workers.   [2] Consists of legislative, judicial, administrative, and regulatory activities.   [3] Includes library, social, and health services. Formerly called hospitals and other services.   [4] Excludes farm and household workers.

Source: U.S. Bureau of Labor Statistics, *News, Employment Cost Index*, quarterly; and Internet site <http://www.bls.gov/ncs/ect/home.htm>

No. 624. Federal Minimum Wage Rates: 1950 to 2000

Year	Value of the minimum wage		Year	Value of the minimum wage	
	Current dollars	Constant (2000) dollars [1]		Current dollars	Constant (2000) dollars [1]
1950	0.75	5.36	1976	2.30	6.96
1952	0.75	4.87	1977	2.30	6.54
1953	0.75	4.84	1978	2.65	7.00
1954	0.75	4.80	1979	2.90	6.88
1955	0.75	4.82	1980	3.10	6.48
1956	1.00	6.33	1981	3.35	6.35
1957	1.00	6.13	1982	3.35	5.98
1958	1.00	5.96	1983	3.35	5.79
1959	1.00	5.92	1984	3.35	5.55
1960	1.00	5.82	1985	3.35	5.36
1961	1.15	6.62	1986	3.35	5.26
1962	1.15	6.56	1987	3.35	5.08
1963	1.25	7.03	1988	3.35	4.88
1964	1.25	6.94	1989	3.35	4.65
1965	1.25	6.83	1990	3.80	5.01
1966	1.25	6.64	1991	4.25	5.37
1967	1.40	7.22	1992	4.25	5.22
1968	1.60	7.92	1993	4.25	5.06
1969	1.60	7.51	1994	4.25	4.94
1970	1.60	7.10	1995	4.25	4.80
1971	1.60	6.80	1996	4.75	5.21
1972	1.60	6.59	1997	5.15	5.53
1973	1.60	6.21	1998	5.15	5.44
1974	2.00	6.99	1999	5.15	5.32
1975	2.10	6.72	2000	5.15	5.15

[1] Adjusted for inflation using the CPI-U; see text, Section 14, Prices.

Source: U.S. Employment Standards Administration, Internet site: <http://www.dol.gov/dol/esa/public/minwage/main.htm> (accessed 29 August 01).

No. 625. Workers Paid Hourly Rates by Selected Characteristics: 2000

[Data are annual averages (72,744 represents 72,744,000). For employed wage and salary workers. Based on Current Population Survey; see text, Section 1, Population, and Appendix III]

Characteristic	Number of workers [1] (1,000)			Percent of all workers paid hourly rates			Median hourly earnings of workers paid hourly rates [2]
	Total paid hourly rates	At or below $5.15			At or below $5.15		
		Total	At $5.15	Below $5.15	Total	At $5.15	Below $5.15	
Total, 16 years and over [3]	72,744	2,710	866	1,844	3.7	1.2	2.5	$9.91
16 to 24 years	16,938	1,447	510	938	8.5	3.0	5.5	7.21
16 to 19 years	6,698	848	340	508	12.7	5.1	7.6	6.37
25 years and over	55.806	1,263	357	906	2.3	0.6	1.6	10.93
Male, 16 years and over	36,228	954	322	632	2.6	0.9	1.7	10.85
16 to 24 years	8,743	548	202	346	6.3	2.3	4.0	7.59
16 to 19 years	3,362	351	142	209	10.4	4.2	6.2	6.57
25 years and over	27,485	406	120	286	1.5	0.4	1.0	12.41
Women, 16 years and over	36,516	1,757	544	1,212	4.8	1.5	3.3	9.03
16 to 24 years	8,194	899	308	592	11.0	3.8	7.2	6.97
16 to 19 years	3,336	497	198	299	14.9	5.9	9.0	6.22
25 years and over	28,321	857	237	621	3.0	0.8	2.2	9.89
White	59,374	2,242	687	1,555	3.8	1.2	2.6	9.98
Black	10,105	361	148	213	3.6	1.5	2.1	9.27
Hispanic origin [4]	9,847	318	129	189	3.2	1.3	1.9	8.50
Full-time workers [5]	55,701	1,025	289	736	1.8	0.5	1.3	10.76
Part-time workers [5]	16,909	1,673	577	1,096	9.9	3.4	6.5	7.14
Private sector industries	63,951	2,543	789	1,754	4.0	1.2	2.7	9.76
Goods-producing [6]	19,303	207	98	109	1.1	0.5	0.6	11.17
Service-producing [7]	44,647	2,337	691	1,646	5.2	1.5	3.7	8.95
Public sector	8,793	167	78	89	1.9	0.9	1.0	11.90

[1] Excludes the incorporated self-employed. [2] For definition of median, see Guide to Tabular Presentation. [3] Includes races not shown separately. Also includes a small number of multiple jobholders whose full- part- time status can not be determined for their principal job. [4] Persons of Hispanic origin may be of any race. [5] Working fewer than 35 hours per week. [6] Includes agriculture, mining, construction, and manufacturing. [7] Includes transportation and public utilities; wholesale trade; finance, insurance, and real estate; private households; and other service industries.

Source: U.S. Bureau of Labor Statistics, Employment and Earnings, January 2001.

No. 626. Employer Costs for Employee Compensation Per Hour Worked: 2001

[In dollars. As of March, for private industry workers. Based on a sample of establishments; see source for details]

Compensation component	Total	Goods producing [1]	Service producing [2]	Manufacturing	Non-manufacturing	Union members	Non-union members	Full-time workers	Part-time workers
Total compensation	**20.81**	**24.40**	**19.74**	**24.30**	**20.12**	**27.80**	**19.98**	**23.55**	**11.65**
Wages and salaries	15.18	16.86	14.68	16.66	14.89	18.36	14.81	16.91	9.41
Total benefits	5.63	7.55	5.06	7.64	5.23	9.45	5.18	6.64	2.25
Paid leave	1.37	1.60	1.30	1.85	1.28	1.92	1.31	1.67	0.37
Vacation	0.68	0.81	0.64	0.92	0.63	0.98	0.64	(NA)	(NA)
Holiday	0.47	0.59	0.44	0.68	0.43	0.64	0.45	(NA)	(NA)
Sick	0.17	0.13	0.18	0.15	0.17	0.22	0.16	(NA)	(NA)
Other	0.06	0.08	0.05	0.10	0.05	0.08	0.05	(NA)	(NA)
Supplemental pay	0.61	1.07	0.48	1.09	0.52	1.12	0.55	0.74	0.18
Premium pay	0.24	0.54	0.15	0.58	0.17	0.66	0.19	(NA)	(NA)
Shift pay	0.05	0.08	0.05	0.11	0.04	0.15	0.04	(NA)	(NA)
Nonproduction bonuses	0.32	0.44	0.29	0.41	0.31	0.30	0.32	(NA)	(NA)
Insurance	1.28	1.85	1.11	1.93	1.15	2.48	1.14	1.55	0.36
Health insurance	1.16	1.68	1.01	1.75	1.05	2.26	1.04	(NA)	(NA)
Retirement and savings	0.62	0.83	0.55	0.75	0.59	1.52	0.51	0.75	0.15
Defined benefit	0.21	0.38	0.16	0.29	0.20	1.08	0.11	(NA)	(NA)
Defined contributions	0.40	0.46	0.39	0.46	0.39	0.45	0.40	(NA)	(NA)
Legally required	1.73	2.14	1.60	1.95	1.68	2.34	1.65	1.89	1.18
Social Security	1.26	1.43	1.21	1.42	1.23	1.56	1.23	(NA)	(NA)
Federal unemployment	0.03	0.03	0.03	0.03	0.03	0.03	0.03	(NA)	(NA)
State unemployment	0.09	0.12	0.09	0.10	0.09	0.13	0.09	(NA)	(NA)
Workers compensation	0.33	0.56	0.27	0.40	0.32	0.62	0.30	(NA)	(NA)
Other benefits [3]	0.02	0.05	-	0.07	-	0.07	0.02	0.03	-

- Represents or rounds to zero. NA Not available. [1] Mining, construction, and manufacturing. [2] Transportation, communications, and public utilities, wholesale and retail trade, finance, insurance, and real estate, and services. [3] Includes severance pay, and supplemental unemployment benefits.

Source: U.S. Bureau of Labor Statistics, *News, Employer Costs for Employee Compensation*, USDL, 01-194, June 29, 2001.

No. 627. Employees With Employer- or Union-Provided Pension Plans or Group Health Plans: 1999

[Total in thousands (148,983 represents 148,983,000). As of March 2000, for wage and salary workers 15 years old and over. Based on Current Population Survey; see text, Section 1, Population, and Appendix III. Data based on 1990 population controls]

Occupation	Total (1,000)	Percent— Included in pension plan	Percent— With group health plan	Characteristic	Total (1,000)	Percent— Included in pension plan	Percent— With group health plan
Total	**148,983**	**44.0**	**53.4**	**AGE**			
Executive, admin., managerial	20,658	58.3	68.2	Total	148,983	44.0	53.4
Professional specialty	21,796	62.1	66.6	15 to 24 years	25,237	12.7	21.9
				25 to 44 years old	71,897	48.3	58.5
Technical/related support	4,842	56.5	67.0	45 to 64 years	46,305	56.5	64.2
Sales workers	18,483	31.8	42.9	65 years and over	5,544	24.6	40.1
Admin. support, inc. clerical	20,671	49.1	56.1	**WORK EXPERIENCE**			
				Worked	148,983	44.0	53.4
Precision prod., craft/repair	15,401	44.3	57.2	Full time	119,158	51.5	62.4
				50 weeks or more	97,952	56.6	67.7
Mach. operators, assemblers [1]	8,148	46.7	60.8	27 to 49 weeks	12,294	35.7	47.5
Transportation/material moving	6,041	42.5	57.8	26 weeks or fewer	8,913	16.8	24.2
Handlers, equipment cleaners [2]	6,399	26.7	37.8	Part time	29,825	13.9	17.6
				50 weeks or more	13,766	19.3	22.5
Service workers	21,717	24.2	33.7	27 to 49 weeks	6,379	14.8	18.1
Private households	1,147	2.4	8.9	26 weeks or fewer	9,679	5.6	10.1
Other	20,571	25.4	35.1	**EMPLOYER SIZE**			
				Under 25 persons	43,242	17.0	29.3
Farming, forestry and fishing	4,064	10.7	21.5	25 to 99 persons	19,018	37.7	52.7
				100 to 499 persons	20,194	50.9	62.8
Armed Forces	761	71.6	39.6	500 to 999 persons	7,875	57.7	67.4
				Over 1,000 persons	58,654	61.6	66.2

[1] Includes inspectors. [2] Includes helpers and laborers.

Source: U.S. Census Bureau Internet site <http://ferret.bls.census.gov/macro/032000/noncash/toc.htm>.

[In percent. Covers full-time employees in private industry. Medium and large establishments exclude establishments with fewer than 100 workers. Covers only benefits for which the employer pays part or all of the premium or expenses involved, except unpaid family leave. Based on a sample survey of establishments; for details, see source. For data on employee benefits in small establishments, see Table 629]

Employee benefit program	All employees	Professional, technical and related	Clerical and sales	Blue collar and service	Employee benefit program	All employees	Professional, technical and related	Clerical and sales	Blue collar and service
Paid time off:					Tax-deferred savings:				
Holidays	89	89	91	88	With employer contribution	46	56	51	38
Vacations	95	96	97	94	With no employer contribution	9	11	8	8
Personal leave	20	23	33	13					
Funeral leave	81	84	85	76	Income continuation plans:				
Jury duty leave	87	92	89	83	Severance pay	36	48	43	26
Military leave	47	60	50	38	Supplemental unemployment benefits	5	2	2	7
Sick leave	56	73	7ᴜ	38					
Family leave	2	3	3	1	Family benefits:				
					Child care	10	14	10	7
Unpaid family leave	93	95	96	91	Adoption assistance	10	16	12	6
					Long-term care insurance	7	10	11	4
Disability benefits:					Flexible workplace	2	5	3	(Z)
Short-term disability	55	54	52	58					
Long-term disability	43	62	52	28	Health promotion programs:				
					Wellness programs	36	44	36	32
Insurance:					Employee assistance programs	61	75	63	52
Medical care	76	79	78	74	Fitness center	21	31	19	16
Dental care	59	64	59	56					
Vision care	26	28	25	24	Miscellaneous benefits:				
Life insurance	87	94	91	81	Job-related travel accident insurance	42	56	46	32
					Nonproduction bonuses	42	43	43	40
Retirement	79	89	81	72	Subsidized commuting	6	10	7	3
Defined benefit	50	52	49	50	Educational assistance:				
Defined contribution	57	70	63	46	Job-related	67	81	68	58
Savings and thrift	39	49	45	30	Nonjob related	20	25	18	18
Deferred profit sharing	13	15	15	12					
Employee stock ownership	4	6	6	3					
Money purchase pension	8	12	6	6					

Z Less than 0.5 percent.
Source: U.S. Bureau of Labor Statistics, News, USDL 99-02, January 7, 1999.

No. 629. Employee Benefits in Small Establishments: 1996

[In percent. Covers full-time employees in private industry. Small establishments are establishments with fewer than 100 workers. Covers only benefits for which the employer pays part or all of the premium or expenses involved, except certain tax deferred earnings arrangements. Based on a sample survey of establishments; for details, see sources. For data on employee benefits in medium and large establishments, see Table 628]

Employee benefit program	All employees	Professional, technical and related	Clerical and sales	Blue collar and service	Employee benefit program	All employees	Professional, technical and related	Clerical and sales	Blue collar and service
Paid time off:					Income contribution plans:				
Holidays	80	86	91	71	Severance pay	15	23	19	9
Vacations	86	90	95	79	Supplemental unemployment benefits	(Z)	(NA)	(Z)	(Z)
Personal leave	14	21	18	8					
Funeral leave	51	60	60	42	Family benefits:				
Jury duty leave	59	74	68	47	Employer assistance for child care	2	4	2	(Z)
Military leave	18	25	22	12	Employer provided funds	1	2	2	(Z)
Sick leave	50	66	64	35	On-site child care	1	2	(Z)	(Z)
Family leave	2	3	3	1	Off-site child care	1	2	(Z)	(Z)
Insurance:									
Short-term disability	29	32	33	25	Health promotion programs:				
Long-term disability	22	39	30	10	Wellness programs	8	11	9	5
Medical care	64	76	69	56	Employee assistance programs	14	18	19	10
Fee-for-service [1]	36	31	34	41	Fitness center	4	6	5	3
HMO [1]	27	27	28	25					
PPO [1]	35	41	36	32	Miscellaneous benefits:				
Dental care	31	40	35	24	Job-related travel accident insurance	12	17	16	7
Life insurance	62	72	68	54	Nonproduction bonuses	44	44	46	43
Retirement	46	56	53	37	Subsidized commuting	1	3	2	1
Defined benefit	15	12	16	15	Educational assistance:				
Defined contribution	38	51	46	28	Job-related	38	56	45	27
Tax deferred earnings arrangements:					Nonjob related	5	6	6	4
With employer contribution	24	30	31	17					
With no employer contribution	4	8	4	3					

NA Not available.   Z Less than 0.5 percent.   [1] Percent of participants receiving medical care insurance.
Source: U.S. Bureau of Labor Statistics, News, USDL 98-240, June 15, 1998.

Labor Force, Employment, and Earnings   407

No. 630. Workers Killed or Disabled on the Job: 1970 to 1999

[Data for 1999 are preliminary estimates (13.8 represents 13,800). Excludes homicides and suicides. Estimates based on data from the U.S. National Center for Health Statistics, State vital statistics departments, state industrial commissions and beginning 1992, Bureau of Labor Statistics, Census of Occupational Fatalities. Numbers of workers based on data from the U.S. Bureau of Labor Statistics]

Year	Deaths							Deaths, **1999**		
	Total		Manufacturing		Non-manufacturing		Dis-abling injur-ies [2] (mil.)	Year and industry group	Num-ber (1,000)	Rate [1]	Dis-abling injur-ies, **1999** [2] (1,000)
	Num-ber (1,000)	Rate [1]	Num-ber (1,000)	Rate [1]	Num-ber (1,000)	Rate [1]					
1970 ...	13.8	18	1.7	9	12.1	21	2.2	**Total**	[3]5,100	3.8	**3,800**
1975 ...	13.0	15	1.6	9	11.4	17	2.2	Agriculture [4]	770	22.5	150
1980 ...	13.2	13	1.7	8	11.5	15	2.2	Mining and quarrying [5] ..	130	23.1	20
1985 ...	11.5	11	1.2	6	10.3	12	2.0	Construction.........	1,190	14.0	400
1990 ...	10.1	9	1.0	5	9.1	9	3.9	Manufacturing........	600	3.0	670
1994 ...	5.3	4	0.7	4	4.3	4	3.5	Transportation and			
1995 ...	5.0	4	0.6	4	4.3	4	3.6	utilities............	850	10.7	370
1996 ...	5.0	4	0.7	3	4.3	4	3.9	Trade [6]	450	1.6	710
1997 ...	5.1	4	0.7	3	4.4	4	3.8	Services [7]	640	1.4	900
1998 ...	5.1	4	0.6	3	4.5	4	3.8	Government.........	470	2.3	580
1999 ...	5.1	4	0.6	3	4.5	4	3.8				

[1] Per 100,000 workers.   [2] Disabling injury defined as one which results in death, some degree of physical impairment, or renders the person unable to perform regular activities for a full day beyond the day of the injury. Due to change in methodology, data beginning 1990 not comparable with prior years.   [3] Includes deaths where industry is not known.   [4] Includes forestry and fishing.   [5] Includes oil and gas extraction.   [6] Includes wholesale and retail trade.   [7] Includes finance, insurance, and real estate.

Source: National Safety Council, Itasca, IL, *Accident Facts*, annual through 1998 edition; thereafter, *Injury Facts*, annual, (copyright).

No. 631. Worker Deaths, Injuries, and Production Time Lost: 1995 to 1999

[45.7 represents 45,700. Data may not agree with Table 630 because data here are not revised]

Item	Deaths (1,000)			Disabling injuries [1] (mil.)			Production time lost (mil. days)					
							In the current year			In future years [2]		
	1995	1998	1999	1995	1998	1999	1995	1998	1999	1995	1998	1999
All accidents	45.7	42.7	45.7	9.9	9.5	10.4	225	220	240	455	420	440
On the job	5.3	5.1	5.1	3.6	3.8	3.8	75	80	80	65	60	60
Off the job.............	40.4	37.6	40.6	6.3	5.7	6.6	150	140	160	390	360	380
Motor vehicle	22.9	21.0	21.0	1.2	1.1	1.1	(NA)	(NA)	(NA)	(NA)	(NA)	(NA)
Public nonmotor vehicle ...	7.5	7.0	9.1	2.3	2.3	3.0	(NA)	(NA)	(NA)	(NA)	(NA)	(NA)
Home	10.0	9.6	10.5	2.8	2.3	2.5	(NA)	(NA)	(NA)	(NA)	(NA)	(NA)

NA Not available.   [1] See footnote 2, Table 630, for a definition of disabling injuries.   [2] Based on an average of 5,850 days lost in future years per fatality and 565 days lost in future years per permanent injury.

Source: National Safety Council, Itasca, IL, *Accident Facts*, annual through 1998 edition; thereafter, *Injury Facts*, annual, (copyright).

No. 632. Industries With the Highest Total Case Incidence Rates for Nonfatal Injuries and Illnesses: 1998 and 1999

[Rates per 100 full-time employees. Industries shown are those with the highest rates for 1999. For nonfarm employment data, see Table 609. Rates refer to any occupational injury or illness resulting in (1) lost workday cases or (2) nonfatal cases without lost workdays. Incidence rates were calculated as: Number of injuries and illnesses divided by total hours worked by all employees during year multiplied by 200,000 as base for 100 full-time equivalent workers (working 40 hours per week, 50 weeks a year)]

Industry	1987 SIC [1] code	1998	1999	Industry	1987 SIC [1] code	1998	1999
Private industry	(X)	6.7	6.3	Canned and cured fish and seafoods .	2091	11.9	16.6
				Truck trailers	3715	23.4	16.6
Meat packing plants	2011	29.3	26.7	Secondary nonferrous metals	334	18.0	16.3
Motor vehicles and car bodies.....	3711	23.9	22.7	Aluminum die-castings...........	3363	17.6	16.2
Metal sanitary ware.........	3431	20.0	22.6	Metal heat treating	3398	12.1	16.2
Gray and ductile iron foundries	3321	25.1	21.9	Brick and structural clay tile	3251	13.4	16.1
Ship building and repairing	3731	22.4	20.2	Primary nonferrous metals, n.e.c. [2] ...	3339	10.1	16.0
Automotive stampings	3465	21.1	20.1	Prefabricated metal buildings	3448	15.8	15.8
Steel foundries, n.e.c. [2]	3325	20.8	19.3	Structural wood members, n.e.c.....	2439	14.4	15.7
Prefabricated wood buildings	2452	14.8	19.0	Leather tanning and finishing	311	12.7	15.7
Aluminum foundries..........	3365	18.2	18.3	Wood pallets and skids	2448	14.7	15.5
Truck and bus bodies..........	3713	19.6	18.0	Plastics plumbing fixtures........	3088	8.6	15.4
Iron and steel forgings..........	3462	16.7	17.8	Fabricated structural metal	3441	17.6	15.2
Mobile homes	2451	21.3	17.3	Public building and related furniture ..	253	15.6	14.9
Travel trailers and campers	3792	15.7	17.1	Millwork	2431	15.2	14.8

X Not applicable.   [1] 1987 Standard Industrial Classification; see text, Section 15, Business Enterprise.   [2] N.e.c. means not elsewhere classified.

Source: U.S. Bureau of Labor Statistics, *Occupational Injuries and Illnesses in the United States by Industry*, annual.

No. 633. Nonfatal Occupational Injury and Illness Incidence Rates: 1998 and 1999

[Rates per 100 full-time employees. For nonfarm employment data, see Table 632. Rates refer to any occupational injury or illness resulting in (1) lost workday cases or (2) nonfatal cases without lost workdays. Incidence rates were calculated as: Number of injuries and illnesses divided by total hours worked by all employees during year multiplied by 200,000 as base for 100 full-time equivalent workers (working 40 hours per week, 50 weeks a year)]

Industry	1987 SIC [1] code	1998	1999	Industry	1987 SIC [1] code	1998	1999
Private sector [2]	(X)	6.7	6.3	Trucking and warehousing	42	8.4	8.7
Agriculture, forestry, fishing [2]	A	7.9	7.3	Water transportation	44	7.5	8.0
Mining [3]	B	4.9	4.4	Transportation by air	45	14.5	13.3
Metal mining [3]	10	5.2	5.0	Pipelines, except natural gas	46	2.2	5.1
Coal mining [3]	12	8.2	7.4	Transportation services	47	3.4	3.8
Oil and gas extraction	13	4.1	3.5	Communications	48	3.0	3.1
Nonmetallic minerals, exc. fuels	14	4.6	4.3	Electric, gas, sanitary services	49	6.3	6.1
Construction	C	8.8	8.6	**Wholesale and retail trade**	F, G	6.5	6.1
General building contractors	15	8.4	8.0	Wholesale trade	F	6.5	6.3
Heavy construction, except building	16	8.2	7.8	Retail trade	G	6.5	6.1
Special trade contractors	17	9.1	8.9	**Finance, insurance, real estate**	H	1.9	1.8
Manufacturing	D	9.7	9.2	Depository institutions	60	1.5	1.5
Durable goods	(X)	10.7	10.1	Nondepository institutions	61	1.2	1.0
Lumber and wood products	24	13.2	13.0	Security and commodity brokers	62	0.6	0.6
Furniture and fixtures	25	11.4	11.5	Insurance carriers	63	1.9	1.9
Stone, clay, and glass products	32	11.8	10.7	Insurance agents, brokers, and service	64	1.1	0.9
Primary metal industries	33	14.0	12.9	Real estate	65	4.0	3.9
Fabricated metal products	34	13.9	12.6	Holding and other investment offices	67	1.7	1.4
Industrial machinery and equip	35	9.5	8.5	**Services [4]**	I	5.2	4.9
Electronic/other electric equip	36	5.9	5.7	Hotels and other lodging places	70	7.3	7.8
Transportation equipment	37	14.6	13.7	Personal services	72	3.1	3.0
Instruments/related products	38	4.0	4.0	Business services	73	3.6	3.0
Miscellaneous manufacturing industries	39	8.1	8.4	Auto repair, services, and parking	75	5.2	6.1
Nondurable goods	(X)	8.2	7.8	Miscellaneous repair services	76	6.4	5.2
Food and kindred products	20	13.6	12.7	Motion pictures	78	3.5	2.9
Tobacco products	21	6.4	5.5	Amusement and recreation services	79	8.2	6.7
Textile mill products	22	6.7	6.4	Health services	80	7.7	7.5
Apparel and other textile products	23	6.2	5.8	Legal services	81	0.8	1.0
Paper and allied products	26	7.1	7.0	Educational services	82	3.1	2.9
Printing and publishing	27	5.4	5.0	Social services	83	6.4	5.6
Chemicals and allied products	28	4.2	4.4	Museums, botanical, zoological gardens	84	8.1	7.0
Petroleum and coal products	29	3.9	4.1	Membership organizations	86	2.9	3.1
Rubber and misc. plastics products	30	11.2	10.1	Engineering and management services	87	2.1	1.7
Leather and leather products	31	9.8	10.3				
Transportation/public utilities [3]	E	7.3	7.3				
Railroad transportation [3]	40	3.4	3.6				
Local passenger transit	41	8.8	9.1				

X Not applicable. [1] 1987 Standard Industrial Classification; see text, Section 15, Business Enterprise. [2] Excludes farms with fewer than 11 employees. [3] Data conforming to OSHA definitions for employers in the railroad industry and for mining operators in coal, metal, and nonmetal mining. Independent mining contractors are excluded from the coal, metal, and nonmetal mining industries. [4] Includes categories not shown separately.

Source: U.S. Bureau of Labor Statistics, *Occupational Injuries and Illnesses in the United States by Industry,* annual.

No. 634. Fatal Work Injuries by Cause: 1999

[For the 50 states and DC. Based on the 1999 Census of Fatal Occupational Injuries. Due to methodological differences, data differ from those in Table 630. For details, see source]

Cause	Number of fatalities	Percent distribution	Cause	Number of fatalities	Percent distribution
Total	**6,023**	**100**	Contacts with objects and equipment [1]	1,029	17
			Struck by object [1]	585	10
Transportation accidents [1]	2,613	43	Struck by falling objects	358	6
Highway accidents [1]	1,491	25	Struck by flying object	55	1
Collision between vehicles, mobile equipment	711	12	Caught in or compressed by—		
Noncollision accidents	388	6	Equipment or objects	302	5
Nonhighway accident (farm, industrial premises)	353	6	Collapsing materials	128	2
Aircraft accidents	227	4	Falls	717	12
Workers struck by a vehicle	377	6	Exposure to harmful substances or environments [1]	529	9
Water vehicle accidents	102	2	Contact with electric current	278	5
Railway accidents	56	1	Exposure to caustic, noxious or allergenic substances	106	2
Assaults and violent acts [1]	893	15	Oxygen deficiency	93	2
Homicides [1]	645	11	Drowning, submersion	75	1
Shooting	506	8	Fires and explosions	216	4
Stabbing	60	1	Other events and exposures	26	(Z)
Self-inflicted injury	208	3			

Z Less than 0.5 percent. [1] Includes other causes, not shown separately.

Source: U.S. Bureau of Labor Statistics, *USDL News,* Bulletin 00-236, August 17, 2000.

Labor Force, Employment, and Earnings 409

No. 635. Fatal Occupational Injuries by Industry and Event: 1999

[For the 50 states and the District of Columbia. Based on the 1999 Census of Fatal Occupational Injuries. Due to methodological differences, data differ from those in Table 630. For details, see source]

Industry	1987 SIC[1] code	Fatal-ities[2]	Event or exposure—percent distribution					Rate[5]
			Trans-portation incidents	Assaults/violent acts	Contact with objects[3]	Falls	Expo-sure[4]	
Total...................	(X)	6,023	43.4	14.8	17.1	11.9	8.8	4.5
Private industry	(X)	5,461	42.3	14.2	18.2	12.5	8.9	4.8
Agriculture, forestry, fishing	A	807	50.6	8.2	24.7	5.2	9.8	24.1
Mining[6]	B	121	28.9	-	47.1	6.6	7.4	21.5
Coal mining.................	12	35	14.3	-	62.9	-	-	41.7
Oil and gas extraction	13	50	34.0	-	32.0	-	10.0	15.2
Construction	C	1,190	26.9	1.9	20.6	31.8	14.8	14.0
General building contractors	15	183	24.0	2.7	18.0	43.2	8.2	-
Heavy construction, except building.................	16	280	48.2	-	28.2	6.8	13.6	-
Special trade contractors	17	709	18.9	2.3	18.6	39.1	16.9	-
Manufacturing[6]	D	719	27.7	7.0	35.5	12.0	8.9	3.6
Food and kindred products.....	20	83	36.1	7.2	25.3	15.7	14.5	5.1
Lumber and wood products	24	190	28.9	3.2	57.4	4.7	3.2	23.1
Transportation and public utilities[6] ...	E	1,006	71.4	8.8	9.6	2.8	5.4	12.7
Local passenger transit	41	102	37.3	55.9	4.9	-	-	17.2
Trucking and warehousing	42	605	81.8	4.0	8.8	2.1	2.5	22.6
Transportation by air	45	74	86.5	-	6.8	-	-	8.6
Electric, gas, sanitary services	49	86	50.0	-	15.1	-	19.8	8.4
Wholesale trade	F	237	56.5	12.7	16.5	8.0	4.6	4.6
Retail trade[6].................	G	507	25.4	57.8	4.3	5.7	3.7	2.3
Food stores.................	54	115	13.0	81.7	-	-	-	3.3
Automotive dealer and service stations	55	82	46.3	29.3	11.0	-	-	3.7
Eating and drinking places	58	145	13.8	73.1	-	5.5	5.5	2.2
Finance, insurance, real estate......	H	105	37.1	41.0	-	7.6	10.5	1.2
Services[6]...................	I	732	42.1	24.2	10.2	11.1	8.5	1.9
Business services............	73	161	43.5	23.6	8.7	14.3	8.1	-
Auto repair, services, and parking	75	132	31.1	32.6	21.2	4.5	3.8	8.4
Government...............	J	562	53.6	20.5	5.9	6.0	7.7	2.8

- No data reported or data do not meet publication standards.   X Not applicable.   [1] 1987 Standard Industrial Classification code, see text Section 15, Business Enterprise.   [2] Includes 37 fatalities for which there was insufficient information to determine industry classification. Includes fatalities caused by other events and exposures, not shown separately.   [3] Includes equipment.   [4] Exposure to harmful substances or environments.   [5] Rate per 100,000 employed civilians 16 years old and over.   [6] Includes other industries, not shown separately.

Source: U.S. Bureau of Labor Statistics, *USDL News,* 00-236, August 17, 2000; and unpublished data.

No. 636. Work Stoppages: 1960 to 2000

[**896 represents 896,000.** Excludes work stoppages involving fewer than 1,000 workers and lasting less than 1 day. Information is based on reports of labor disputes appearing in daily newspapers, trade journals, and other public sources. The parties to the disputes are contacted by telephone, when necessary, to clarify details of the stoppages]

Year	Number of work stop-pages[1]	Workers involved[2] (1,000)	Days idle		Year	Number of work stop-pages[1]	Workers involved[2] (1,000)	Days idle	
			Number[3] (1,000)	Percent estimated working time[4]				Number[3] (1,000)	Percent estimated working time[4]
1960......	222	896	13,260	0.09	1984......	62	376	8,499	0.04
1965......	268	999	15,140	0.10	1985......	54	324	7,079	0.03
1969......	412	1,576	29,397	0.16	1986......	69	533	11,861	0.05
1970......	381	2,468	52,761	0.29	1987......	46	174	[5]4,481	0.02
1971......	298	2,516	35,538	0.19	1988......	40	118	[5]4,381	0.02
1972......	250	975	16,764	0.09	1989......	51	452	16,996	0.07
1973......	317	1,400	16,260	0.08	1990......	44	185	5,926	0.02
1974......	424	1,796	31,809	0.16	1991......	40	392	4,584	0.02
1975......	235	965	17,563	0.09	1992......	35	364	3,989	0.01
1976......	231	1,519	23,962	0.12	1993......	35	182	3,981	0.01
1977......	298	1,212	21,258	0.10	1994......	45	322	5,020	0.02
1978......	219	1,006	23,774	0.11	1995......	31	192	5,771	0.02
1979......	235	1,021	20,409	0.09	1996......	37	273	4,889	0.02
1980......	187	795	20,844	0.09	1997......	29	339	4,497	0.01
1981......	145	729	16,908	0.07	1998......	34	387	5,116	0.02
1982......	96	656	9,061	0.04	1999......	17	73	1,996	0.01
1983......	81	909	17,461	0.08	2000......	39	394	20,419	0.06

[1] Beginning in year indicated.   [2] Workers counted more than once if involved in more than one stoppage during the year.   [3] Resulting from all stoppages in effect in a year, including those that began in an earlier year.   [4] Agricultural and government employees are included in the total working time; private household and forestry and fishery employees are excluded.   [5] Revised since originally published.

Source: U.S. Bureau of Labor Statistics, *Work Stopages Summary,* USDL 01-41, February 9, 2001.

No. 637. Labor Union Membership by Sector: 1983 to 2000

[17,717.4 represents 17,717,400. See headnote, Table 639]

Sector	1983	1985	1990	1995	1996	1997	1998	1999	2000
TOTAL (1,000)									
Wage and salary workers:									
Union members	17,717.4	16,996.1	16,739.8	16,359.6	16,269.4	16,109.9	16,211.4	16,476.7	16,258.2
Covered by unions	20,532.1	19,358.1	19,057.8	18,346.3	18,158.1	17,923.0	17,918.3	18,182.3	17,944.1
Public sector workers:									
Union members	5,737.2	5,743.1	6,485.0	6,927.4	6,854.4	6,746.7	6,905.3	7,058.1	7,110.5
Covered by unions	7,112.2	6,920.6	7,691.4	7,986.6	7,829.7	7,668.0	7,814.7	7,966.3	7,975.6
Private sector workers:									
Union members	11,980.2	11,253.0	10,254.8	9,432.1	9,415.0	9,363.3	9,306.1	9,418.6	9,147.7
Covered by unions	13,419.9	12,437.5	11,366.4	10,359.8	10,328.4	10,255.0	10,103.6	10,216.0	9,968.5
PERCENT									
Wage and salary workers:									
Union members	20.1	18.0	16.1	14.9	14.5	14.1	13.9	13.9	13.5
Covered by unions	23.3	20.5	18.3	16.7	16.2	15.6	15.4	15.3	14.9
Public sector workers:									
Union members	36.7	35.7	36.5	37.7	37.6	37.2	37.5	37.3	37.5
Covered by unions	45.5	43.1	43.3	43.5	43.0	42.3	42.5	42.1	42.0
Private sector workers:									
Union members	16.5	14.3	11.9	10.3	10.0	9.7	9.5	9.4	9.0
Covered by unions	18.5	15.9	13.2	11.3	11.0	10.6	10.3	10.2	9.8

Source: The Bureau of National Affairs, Inc., Washington, DC, *Union Membership and Earnings Data Book: Compilations from the Current Population Survey (2001 edition)*, (copyright by BNA PLUS); authored by Barry Hirsch of Trinity University, San Antonio, TX and David Macpherson of Florida State University. Internet site <http://www.bna.com/bnaplus/databook.html>.

No. 638. Union Members by Selected Characteristics: 2000

[Annual averages of monthly data (120,786 represents 120,786,000). Covers employed wage and salary workers 16 years old and over. Excludes self-employed workers whose businesses are incorporated although they technically qualify as wage and salary workers. Based on Current Population Survey, see text, Section 1, Population, and Appendix III]

Characteristic	Employed wage and salary workers			Median usual weekly earnings [3] (dol.)			
	Total (1,000)	Percent Union members [1]	Percent Represented by unions [2]	Total	Union members [1]	Represented by unions [2]	Not represented by unions
Total [4]	120,786	13.5	14.9	576	696	691	542
16 to 24 years old	20,166	5.0	5.7	361	437	436	355
25 to 34 years old	28,406	11.9	13.1	550	627	624	529
35 to 44 years old	32,470	14.9	16.3	631	716	712	614
45 to 54 years old	25,651	18.8	20.7	671	755	752	639
55 to 64 years old	11,204	17.8	19.6	617	727	723	592
65 years and over	2,889	8.4	9.7	442	577	565	422
Men	62,853	15.2	16.5	646	739	737	620
Women	57,933	11.5	13.1	491	616	613	472
White	100,455	13.0	14.4	591	716	711	565
Men	53,105	14.9	16.1	669	757	755	641
Women	47,350	10.9	12.5	500	631	627	482
Black	14,544	17.1	18.9	468	596	590	436
Men	6,701	19.1	20.7	503	619	614	479
Women	7,843	15.4	17.3	429	564	555	408
Hispanic [5]	13,609	11.4	12.8	396	584	580	377
Men	7,884	12.3	13.5	414	631	620	394
Women	5,725	10.2	11.8	364	489	492	346
Full-time workers	99,917	14.8	16.3	576	696	691	542
Part-time workers	20,619	6.8	7.7	(X)	(X)	(X)	(X)
Managerial and professional specialty	35,378	12.8	14.9	836	840	834	836
Technical sales, and admin. support	36,124	8.6	9.7	506	598	590	497
Service occupations	16,953	13.2	14.4	355	554	542	327
Precision, production, craft, and repair	12,716	21.9	22.9	613	784	778	570
Operators, fabricators, and laborers	17,642	19.8	20.9	446	605	602	411
Farming, forestry, and fishing	1,974	4.5	5.5	334	516	506	325
Agricultural wage and salary workers	1,821	2.1	2.5	347	(B)	(B)	344
Private nonagri. wage and salary workers	99,989	9.1	9.9	555	664	657	537
Mining	499	10.9	11.4	768	746	748	774
Construction	6,666	18.3	19.0	584	814	810	529
Manufacturing	19,167	14.8	15.6	595	630	628	587
Transportation and public utilities	7,508	24.0	25.6	679	768	762	639
Wholesale and retail trade, total	25,133	4.7	5.2	444	518	514	439
Finance, insurance, and real estate	7,488	1.6	2.1	620	596	593	621
Services	33,528	5.6	6.6	543	567	574	540
Government	18,976	37.5	42.0	665	730	726	609

B Data not shown where base is less than 50,000.   X Not applicable.   [1] Members of a labor union or an employee association similar to a labor union.   [2] Members of a labor union or an employee association similar to a union as well as workers who report no union affiliation but whose jobs are covered by a union or an employee association contract.   [3] For full-time employed wage and salary workers.   [4] Includes races not shown separately. Also includes a small number of multiple jobholders whose full- and part-time status can not be determined for their principal job.   [5] Persons of Hispanic origin may be of any race.

Source: U.S. Bureau of Labor Statistics, *Employment and Earnings*, monthly, January 2001 issue.

Labor Force, Employment, and Earnings   411

No. 639. Labor Union Membership by State: 1983 and 2000

[Annual averages of monthly figures (17,717.4 represents 17,717,400). For wage and salary workers in agriculture and non-agriculture. Data represent union members by place of residence. Based on the Current Population Survey and subject to sampling error. For methodological details, see source]

State	Union members (1,000)		Workers covered by unions (1,000)		Percent of workers—					
					Union members		Covered by unions		Private manufacturing sector union members	
	1983	2000	1983	2000	1983	2000	1983	2000	1983	2000
United States..	17,717.4	16,258.2	20,532.1	17,944.1	20.1	13.5	23.3	14.9	27.8	14.8
Alabama [1]	228.2	180.8	268.2	197.6	16.9	9.6	19.8	10.5	25.9	14.4
Alaska	41.7	56.8	49.2	64.3	24.9	21.9	29.3	24.8	23.3	11.8
Arizona [1]	125.0	129.7	156.4	147.8	11.4	6.4	14.3	7.3	7.8	5.2
Arkansas [1]	82.2	61.5	103.2	70.9	11.0	5.8	13.8	6.7	18.7	4.7
California	2,118.9	2,295.1	2,505.2	2,546.0	21.9	16.0	25.9	17.7	21.0	7.4
Colorado.	177.9	173.2	209.6	193.0	13.6	9.0	16.0	10.0	13.1	13.5
Connecticut.	314.0	245.8	345.1	262.5	22.7	16.3	25.0	17.4	28.1	15.4
Delaware	49.2	46.9	54.1	51.7	20.1	13.3	22.1	14.6	27.3	19.8
District of Columbia	52.4	35.9	69.4	40.2	19.5	14.7	25.9	16.5	17.6	14.8
Florida [1]	393.7	433.6	532.9	553.6	10.2	6.8	13.8	8.7	11.3	4.3
Georgia [1]	267.0	228.1	345.1	267.0	11.9	6.3	15.3	7.4	16.9	9.5
Hawaii	112.6	123.5	124.9	129.1	29.2	24.8	32.4	26.0	35.6	11.6
Idaho [1]	41.3	40.7	53.7	48.0	12.5	7.6	16.2	9.0	19.0	9.2
Illinois	1,063.8	1,046.3	1,205.1	1,100.6	24.2	18.6	27.4	19.5	32.4	20.3
Indiana.	503.3	418.4	544.5	460.6	24.9	15.6	27.0	17.1	48.7	22.1
Iowa [1]	185.9	181.8	231.3	215.1	17.2	13.6	21.5	16.1	40.3	24.0
Kansas [1]	125.2	108.5	170.4	134.5	13.7	9.0	18.7	11.2	25.5	19.2
Kentucky	223.7	208.0	259.8	234.5	17.9	12.0	20.8	13.6	37.4	23.4
Louisiana [1]	204.2	121.9	267.8	154.8	13.8	7.1	18.1	9.0	24.9	15.5
Maine.	88.0	78.1	100.4	92.2	21.0	14.0	24.0	16.6	24.8	22.6
Maryland	346.5	353.3	423.1	405.5	18.5	14.6	22.6	16.7	29.2	18.8
Massachusetts.	603.2	406.3	661.4	444.9	23.7	14.3	26.0	15.7	26.7	8.7
Michigan.	1,005.4	938.3	1,084.6	985.3	30.4	20.8	32.8	21.8	46.2	28.8
Minnesota.	393.9	419.0	439.4	434.3	23.2	18.2	25.9	18.8	22.3	13.9
Mississippi [1]	79.4	67.7	99.7	104.3	9.9	6.0	12.5	9.3	18.9	12.6
Missouri	374.4	337.9	416.7	365.3	20.8	13.2	23.2	14.2	36.6	21.8
Montana.	49.5	51.2	55.5	57.8	18.3	13.9	20.5	15.7	33.0	13.8
Nebraska [1]	80.6	64.9	94.8	89.4	13.6	8.4	16.0	11.5	19.1	13.1
Nevada [1]	90.0	150.9	106.7	165.3	22.4	17.1	26.6	18.8	10.8	7.0
New Hampshire	48.5	59.8	60.8	66.7	11.5	10.4	14.4	11.6	10.6	7.1
New Jersey	822.1	762.0	918.2	800.7	26.9	20.8	30.0	21.8	31.4	18.5
New Mexico	52.6	56.2	70.6	69.7	11.8	8.1	15.8	10.1	11.9	3.0
New York	2,155.6	1,958.0	2,385.9	2,036.4	32.5	25.5	36.0	26.5	31.0	19.9
North Carolina [1]	178.7	124.1	238.1	148.4	7.6	3.6	10.2	4.4	6.9	2.7
North Dakota [1]	28.4	17.6	35.1	21.1	13.2	6.5	16.3	7.8	27.4	12.4
Ohio	1,011.0	879.0	1,125.0	955.1	25.1	17.3	27.9	18.8	40.9	24.3
Oklahoma	131.5	93.8	168.2	108.0	11.5	6.8	14.7	7.8	25.2	11.6
Oregon.	222.9	234.4	261.9	251.0	22.3	16.1	26.2	17.2	28.7	11.3
Pennsylvania.	1,195.7	869.6	1,350.0	925.7	27.5	16.9	31.1	18.0	42.3	18.5
Rhode Island.	85.8	79.6	93.7	82.5	21.5	18.2	23.5	18.8	16.9	10.9
South Carolina [1]	69.6	70.3	100.6	88.8	5.9	4.0	8.6	5.1	5.5	4.6
South Dakota [1]	26.8	18.2	34.8	22.2	11.5	5.5	14.9	6.7	19.0	5.2
Tennessee [1]	252.4	211.5	300.9	238.8	15.1	8.9	18.0	10.0	21.4	11.9
Texas [1]	583.7	505.4	712.8	645.1	9.7	5.8	11.9	7.4	16.1	8.5
Utah [1]	81.6	69.3	100.9	84.9	15.2	7.3	18.9	9.0	14.9	5.8
Vermont	25.9	28.2	31.5	33.9	12.6	10.3	15.3	12.4	13.5	8.4
Virginia [1]	268.3	179.1	346.1	227.0	11.7	5.6	15.1	7.1	21.2	10.5
Washington.	419.9	470.8	499.7	516.1	27.1	18.2	32.3	19.9	35.5	23.0
West Virginia.	142.7	102.9	160.6	111.4	25.3	14.3	28.5	15.5	41.3	34.8
Wisconsin.	465.5	446.0	526.7	473.1	23.8	17.6	26.9	18.7	36.0	19.7
Wyoming [1]	27.1	17.9	31.8	21.6	13.9	8.3	16.2	10.0	14.6	8.7

[1] Right to work state.

Source: The Bureau of National Affairs, Inc., Washington, DC, *Union Membership and Earnings Data Book: Compilations from the Current Population Survey (2001 edition)*, (copyright by BNA PLUS); authored by Barry Hirsch of Trinity University, San Antonio. TX, and David Macpherson of Florida State University. Internet site <http://www.bna.com/bnaplus/databook.html>.

412 Labor Force, Employment, and Earnings

Section 13

Income, Expenditures, and Wealth

This section presents data on gross domestic product (GDP), gross national product (GNP), national and personal income, saving and investment, money income, poverty, and national and personal wealth. The data on income and expenditures measure two aspects of the U.S. economy. One aspect relates to the national income and product accounts (NIPAs), a summation reflecting the entire complex of the nation's economic income and output and the interaction of its major components; the other relates to the distribution of money income to families and individuals or consumer income.

The primary source for data on GDP, GNP, national and personal income, gross saving and investment, and fixed reproducible tangible wealth is the *Survey of Current Business,* published monthly by the Bureau of Economic Analysis (BEA). A comprehensive revision to the NIPAs was released beginning in October 1999. Discussions of the revision appeared in the August, September, October, December 1999, and the April 2000 issues of the *Survey of Current Business.* Summary historical estimates appeared in the August 2000 issue of the *Survey of Current Business.* Detailed historical data will appear in forthcoming *National Income and Product Accounts of the United States, 1929-97* report to be issued in 2001.

Sources of income distribution data are the decennial censuses of population and the Current Population Survey (CPS), both products of the U.S. Census Bureau (see text, Section 1). Annual data on income of families, individuals, and households are presented in *Current Population Reports, Consumer Income,* P60 Series.

Data on individuals' saving and assets are published by the Board of Governors of the Federal Reserve System in the quarterly *Flow of Funds Accounts.* The Board also periodically conducts the *Survey of Consumer Finances,* which presents financial information on family assets and net

worth. Detailed information on personal wealth is published periodically by the Internal Revenue Service (IRS) in *SOI Bulletin.*

National income and product—Gross domestic product is the total output of goods and services produced by labor and property located in the United States, valued at market prices. GDP can be viewed in terms of the expenditure categories that comprise its major components—purchases of goods and services by consumers and government, gross private domestic investment, and net exports of goods and services. The goods and services included are largely those bought for final use (excluding illegal transactions) in the market economy. A number of inclusions, however, represent imputed values, the most important of which is rental value of owner-occupied housing. GDP, in this broad context, measures the output attributable to the factors of production located in the United States. Gross state product (GSP) is the gross market value of the goods and services attributable to labor and property located in a state. It is the state counterpart of the nation's gross domestic product.

In January 1996, BEA replaced its fixed-weighted index as the featured measure of real GDP with an index based on chain-type annual weights. Changes in this measure of real output and prices are calculated as the average of changes based on weights for the current and preceding years. (Components of real output are weighted by price, and components of prices are weighted by output.) These annual changes are "chained" (multiplied) together to form a time series that allows for the effects of changes in relative prices and changes in the composition of output over time. Quarterly and monthly changes are also based on annual weights. The new output indexes are

Income, Expenditures, and Wealth   413

expressed as 1996=100, and for recent years, in 1996 dollars; the new price indexes are based to 1996=100.

Chained (1996) dollar estimates of most components of GDP are not published for periods prior to 1987, because during periods far from the base period, the levels of the components may provide misleading information about their contributions to an aggregate. Values are published in index form (1996=100) for 1929 to the present to allow users to calculate the percent changes for all components, changes which are accurate for all periods. In addition, the Bureau of Economic Analysis publishes estimates of the contribution of major components to the percent change in GDP for all periods.

Gross national product measures the output attributable to all labor and property supplied by United States residents. GNP differs from "national income" mainly in that GNP includes allowances for depreciation and for indirect business taxes (sales and property taxes); see Table 646.

In December 1991, the Bureau of Economic Analysis began featuring gross domestic product rather than gross national product as the primary measure of U.S. production. GDP is now the standard measure of growth because it is the appropriate measure for much of the short-term monitoring and analysis of the economy. In addition, the use of GDP facilitates comparisons of economic activity in the United States with that in other countries.

National income is the aggregate of labor and property earnings which arises in the current production of goods and services. It is the sum of employee compensation, proprietors' income, rental income of persons, corporate profits, and net interest. It measures the total factor costs of the goods and services produced by the economy. Income is measured before deduction of taxes.

Capital consumption adjustment for corporations and for nonfarm sole proprietorships and partnerships is the difference between capital consumption based on income tax returns and capital consumption measured using empirical evidence on prices of used equipment and structures in resale markets, which have shown that depreciation for most types of assets approximates a geometric pattern. The tax return data are valued at historical costs and reflect changes over time in service lives and depreciation patterns as permitted by tax regulations. *Inventory valuation adjustment* represents the difference between the book value of inventories used up in production and the cost of replacing them.

Personal income is the current income received by persons from all sources minus their personal contributions for social insurance. Classified as "persons" are individuals (including owners of unincorporated firms), nonprofit institutions that primarily serve individuals, private trust funds, and private noninsured welfare funds. Personal income includes transfers (payments not resulting from current production) from government and business such as social security benefits, public assistance, etc., but excludes transfers among persons. Also included are certain nonmonetary types of income—chiefly estimated net rental value to owner-occupants of their homes and the value of services furnished without payment by financial intermediaries. Capital gains (net losses) are excluded.

Disposable personal income is personal income less personal tax and nontax payments. It is the income available to persons for spending or saving. Personal tax and nontax payments are tax payments (net of refunds) by persons (except personal contributions for social insurance) that are not chargeable to business expense and certain personal payments to general government that are treated like taxes. Personal taxes include income, estate and gift, and personal property taxes and motor vehicle licenses. Nontax payments include passport fees, fines and forfeitures, and donations.

Consumer Expenditure Survey—The Consumer Expenditure Survey program was begun in late 1979. The principal objective of the survey is to collect current consumer expenditure data which provide a continuous flow of data on the buying habits of American consumers. The data are necessary for future revisions of the Consumer Price Index.

414   Income, Expenditures, and Wealth

The survey conducted by the Census Bureau for the Bureau of Labor Statistics consists of two components: (1) An interview panel survey in which the expenditures of consumer units are obtained in five interviews conducted every 3 months, and (2) a diary or recordkeeping survey completed by participating households for two consecutive 1-week periods.

Each component of the survey queries an independent sample of consumer units representative of the U.S. total population.

Over 52 weeks of the year, 5,000 consumer units are sampled for the diary survey. Each consumer unit keeps a diary for two 1-week periods yielding approximately 10,000 diaries a year. The interview sample is selected on a rotating panel basis, targeted at 5,000 consumer units per quarter. Data are collected in 88 urban and 16 rural areas of the country that are representative of the U.S. total population. The survey includes students in student housing. Data from the two surveys are combined; integration is necessary to permit analysis of total family expenditures because neither the diary nor quarterly interview survey was designed to collect a complete account of consumer spending.

Distribution of money income to families and individuals—Money income statistics are based on data collected in various field surveys of income conducted since 1936. Since 1947, the Census Bureau has collected the data on an annual basis and published them in *Current Population Reports*, P60 Series. In each of the surveys, field representatives interview samples of the population with respect to income received during the previous year. Money income as defined by the Census Bureau differs from the BEA concept of "personal income."

Data on consumer income collected in the CPS by the Census Bureau cover money income received (exclusive of certain money receipts such as capital gains) before payments for personal income taxes, social security, union dues, medicare deductions, etc. Therefore, money income does not reflect the fact that some families receive part of their income in the form of noncash benefits (see Section 12) such as food stamps, health benefits, and subsidized housing; that some farm families receive noncash benefits in the form of rent-free housing and goods produced and consumed on the farm; or that noncash benefits are also received by some nonfarm residents which often take the form of the use of business transportation and facilities, full or partial payments by business for retirement programs, medical and educational expenses, etc. These elements should be considered when comparing income levels. For data on noncash benefits, see Section 12. None of the aggregate income concepts (GDP, national income, or personal income) is exactly comparable with money income, although personal income is the closest.

In October 1983, the Census Bureau began to collect data under the new Survey of Income and Program Participation (SIPP). The information supplied by this survey is expected to provide better measures of the status and changes in income distribution and poverty of households and persons in the United States. The data collected in SIPP will be used to study federal and state aid programs (such as food stamps, welfare, medicaid, and subsidized housing), to estimate program costs and coverage, and to assess the effects of proposed changes in program eligibility rules or benefit levels. The core questions are repeated at each interview and cover labor force activity, the types and amounts of income received, and participation status in various programs. The core also contains questions covering attendance in post-secondary schools and private health insurance coverage. Various supplements or topical modules covering areas such as educational attainment, assets and liabilities, and pension plan coverage are periodically included.

Poverty—Families and unrelated individuals are classified as being above or below the poverty level using the poverty index originated at the Social Security Administration in 1964 and revised by Federal Interagency Committees in 1969 and 1980.

The poverty index is based solely on money income and does not reflect the fact that many low-income persons receive noncash benefits such as food stamps, medicaid, and public housing. The index is based on the Department of Agriculture's 1961 Economy Food Plan and reflects the different consumption requirements of families based on their size and composition. The poverty thresholds are updated every year to reflect changes in the Consumer Price Index. The following technical changes to the thresholds were made in 1981: (1) distinctions based on sex of householder have been eliminated, (2) separate thresholds for farm families have been dropped, and (3) the matrix has been expanded to families of nine or more persons from the old cutoff of seven or more persons. These changes have been incorporated in the calculation of poverty data beginning with 1981. In the recent past, the Census Bureau has published a number of technical papers that presented experimental poverty estimates based on income definitions that counted the value of selected government noncash benefits. The Census Bureau has also published annual reports on after-tax income (see Tables 664 and 665). The annual income and poverty reports (P60 Series) have brought together the benefit and tax data that previously appeared in the separate reports. These reports have shown the distribution of income among households and the prevalence of poverty under the official definition of money income and under definitions that add or subtract income components. In addition, in July 1999, the Census Bureau released a report (P60-205) that showed the effect of using experimental poverty following the recommendations of a National Academy of Sciences panel on redefining our nation's poverty measure.

Statistical reliability—For a discussion of statistical collection and estimation, sampling procedures, and measures of statistical reliability pertaining to Census Bureau data, see Appendix III.

U.S. Census Bureau, Statistical Abstract of the United States: 2001

No. 640. Gross Domestic Product in Current and Real (1996) Dollars: 1960 to 2000

[In billions of dollars (527.4 represents $527,400,000,000). For explanation of gross domestic product and chained dollars, see text, this section]

Item	1960	1970	1980	1985	1987	1988	1989	1990	1991	1992	1993	1994	1995	1996	1997	1998	1999	2000
CURRENT DOLLARS																		
Gross domestic product	527.4	1,039.7	2,795.6	4,213.0	4,742.5	5,108.3	5,489.1	5,803.2	5,986.2	6,318.9	6,642.3	7,054.3	7,400.5	7,813.2	8,318.4	8,790.2	9,299.2	9,963.1
Personal consumption expenditures	332.3	648.9	1,762.9	2,712.6	3,105.3	3,356.6	3,596.7	3,831.5	3,971.2	4,209.7	4,454.7	4,716.4	4,969.0	5,237.5	5,529.3	5,850.9	6,268.7	6,757.3
Durable goods	43.3	85.0	214.2	363.3	419.7	450.2	467.8	467.6	443.0	470.8	513.4	560.8	589.7	616.5	642.5	693.9	761.3	820.3
Nondurable goods	152.9	272.0	696.1	928.8	1,015.3	1,082.9	1,165.4	1,246.1	1,278.8	1,322.9	1,375.2	1,438.0	1,497.3	1,574.1	1,641.6	1,707.6	1,845.5	2,010.0
Services	136.1	292.0	852.7	1,420.6	1,670.3	1,823.5	1,963.5	2,117.8	2,249.4	2,415.9	2,566.1	2,717.6	2,882.0	3,047.0	3,245.2	3,449.3	3,661.9	3,927.0
Gross private domestic investment	78.9	152.4	477.9	736.3	781.5	821.1	872.9	861.7	800.2	866.6	955.1	1,097.1	1,143.8	1,242.7	1,390.5	1,549.9	1,650.1	1,832.7
Fixed investment	75.7	150.4	484.2	714.5	754.3	802.7	845.2	847.2	800.4	851.6	934.0	1,034.6	1,110.7	1,212.7	1,327.7	1,472.9	1,606.8	1,778.2
Change in business inventories	3.2	2.0	-6.3	21.8	27.1	18.5	27.7	14.5	-0.2	15.0	21.1	62.6	33.0	30.0	62.9	77.0	43.3	54.5
Net exports of goods and services	2.4	1.2	-14.9	-114.2	-142.3	-106.3	-80.7	-71.4	-20.7	-27.9	-60.5	-87.1	-84.3	-89.0	-89.3	-151.5	-254.0	-370.7
Exports	25.3	57.0	278.9	303.0	365.6	446.9	509.0	557.2	601.6	636.8	658.0	725.1	818.6	874.2	966.4	966.0	990.2	1,097.3
Imports	22.8	55.8	293.8	417.2	507.9	553.2	589.7	628.6	622.3	664.6	718.5	812.1	902.8	963.1	1,055.8	1,117.5	1,244.2	1,468.0
Government consumption expenditures and gross investment	113.8	237.1	569.7	878.3	997.9	1,036.9	1,100.2	1,181.4	1,235.5	1,270.5	1,293.0	1,327.9	1,372.0	1,421.9	1,487.9	1,540.9	1,634.4	1,743.7
Federal	65.9	116.4	245.3	413.4	460.4	462.6	482.6	508.4	527.4	534.5	527.3	521.1	521.5	531.6	538.2	540.6	568.6	595.2
National defense	55.2	90.9	169.6	312.4	351.2	355.9	363.2	374.9	384.5	378.5	364.9	355.1	350.6	357.0	352.6	349.2	365.0	377.0
State and local	47.9	120.7	324.4	464.9	537.5	574.3	617.7	673.0	708.1	736.0	765.7	806.8	850.5	890.4	949.7	1,000.3	1,065.8	1,148.6
CHAINED (1996) DOLLARS																		
Gross domestic product	2,376.7	3,578.0	4,900.9	5,717.1	6,113.3	6,368.4	6,591.8	6,707.9	6,676.4	6,880.0	7,062.6	7,347.7	7,543.8	7,813.2	8,159.5	8,515.7	8,875.8	9,318.5
Personal consumption expenditures	1,510.8	2,317.5	3,193.0	3,820.9	4,113.4	4,279.5	4,393.7	4,474.5	4,466.6	4,594.5	4,748.9	4,928.1	5,075.6	5,237.5	5,423.9	5,678.7	5,978.8	6,294.3
Durable goods	(NA)	(NA)	(NA)	(NA)	455.2	481.5	491.7	487.1	454.9	479.0	518.3	557.7	583.5	616.5	657.3	727.3	817.8	896.0
Nondurable goods	(NA)	(NA)	(NA)	(NA)	1,274.5	1,315.1	1,351.0	1,369.6	1,364.0	1,389.7	1,430.3	1,485.1	1,529.0	1,574.1	1,619.9	1,684.8	1,779.4	1,869.0
Services	(NA)	(NA)	(NA)	(NA)	2,379.3	2,477.2	2,546.0	2,616.2	2,651.8	2,729.7	2,802.5	2,886.2	2,963.4	3,047.0	3,147.0	3,269.4	3,390.8	3,543.9
Gross private domestic investment	272.8	436.2	655.3	863.4	879.3	902.8	906.5	907.3	829.5	899.8	977.9	1,107.0	1,140.6	1,242.7	1,393.3	1,566.8	1,669.7	1,839.8
Fixed investment	(NA)	(NA)	(NA)	(NA)	856.0	887.1	911.2	894.6	832.5	886.5	958.4	1,045.9	1,109.2	1,212.7	1,328.6	1,485.3	1,621.4	1,771.7
Change in business inventories	(NA)	(NA)	(NA)	(NA)	29.6	18.4	29.6	16.5	-1.0	17.1	20.0	66.8	30.4	30.0	63.8	80.2	45.3	60.9
Net exports of goods and services	(NA)	(NA)	(NA)	(NA)	-156.2	-112.1	-79.4	-56.5	-15.8	-19.8	-59.1	-86.5	-78.4	-89.0	-113.3	-221.0	-322.4	-412.4
Exports	87.5	159.3	334.8	341.6	408.0	473.5	529.4	575.7	613.2	651.0	672.7	732.8	808.2	874.2	981.5	1,003.6	1,033.0	1,126.3
Imports	108.0	223.1	324.8	490.7	564.2	585.6	608.8	632.2	629.0	670.8	731.8	819.4	886.6	963.1	1,094.8	1,224.6	1,355.3	1,538.7
Government consumption expenditures and gross investment	661.3	931.1	1,020.9	1,190.5	1,292.5	1,307.5	1,343.5	1,387.3	1,403.4	1,410.0	1,398.8	1,400.1	1,406.4	1,421.9	1,455.4	1,486.4	1,536.1	1,579.2
Federal	(NA)	(NA)	(NA)	(NA)	597.8	586.9	594.7	606.8	604.9	595.1	572.0	551.3	536.5	531.6	529.6	526.9	540.1	548.2
National defense	(NA)	(NA)	(NA)	(NA)	450.2	446.8	443.3	443.2	438.4	417.1	394.7	375.9	361.9	357.0	347.7	341.7	348.5	349.1
State and local	(NA)	(NA)	(NA)	(NA)	695.6	721.4	749.5	781.1	798.9	815.3	827.0	848.9	869.9	890.4	925.8	959.2	995.6	1,030.5

NA Not available.

Source: U.S. Bureau of Economic Analysis, National Income and Product Accounts, 1929-97, (forthcoming); and Survey of Current Business, May 2001.

Income, Expenditures, and Wealth   417

No. 641. Gross Domestic Product in Current and Real (1996) Dollars by Industry: 1990 to 1999

[In billions of dollars (5,803.2 represents $5,803,200,000,000). Data are based on the 1987 SIC. Data include nonfactor charges (capital consumption allowances, indirect business taxes, etc.) as well as factor charges against gross product; corporate profits and capital consumption allowances have been shifted from a company to an establishment basis]

Industry	Current dollars				Chained (1996) dollars			
	1990	1995	1998	1999	1990	1995	1998	1999
Gross domestic product [1]	5,803.2	7,400.5	8,790.2	9,299.2	6,707.9	7,543.8	8,515.7	8,875.8
Private industries.	4,996.7	6,411.1	7,684.4	8,140.8	5,736.8	6,508.7	7,499.9	7,860.7
Agriculture, forestry, and fishing	108.3	109.8	127.2	125.4	118.5	123.1	144.0	150.9
Farms	79.6	73.2	80.8	74.2	84.2	85.5	100.2	106.3
Agricultural services	28.7	36.7	46.5	51.2	34.6	37.6	43.2	44.4
Mining	111.9	95.7	105.6	111.8	105.8	113.0	126.2	121.9
Metal mining	5.2	6.5	5.1	5.5	4.4	5.5	7.3	8.6
Coal mining	11.8	10.7	11.3	11.3	7.5	10.1	12.5	13.1
Oil and gas extraction	87.1	69.3	77.4	82.8	87.5	88.6	94.9	89.1
Nonmetallic minerals, except fuels	7.8	9.1	11.8	12.3	8.1	9.1	11.5	11.4
Construction	248.7	290.3	378.1	416.4	290.7	299.6	345.8	361.1
Manufacturing	1,040.6	1,289.1	1,436.0	1,500.8	1,102.3	1,284.7	1,446.4	1,529.4
Durable goods	586.6	729.8	833.4	877.8	585.1	714.9	892.4	970.5
Lumber and wood products	32.2	42.3	41.4	44.1	45.1	41.6	39.5	40.8
Furniture and fixtures	15.6	19.5	24.1	25.9	18.1	20.7	22.7	23.6
Stone, clay, and glass products	25.3	32.4	38.2	41.0	29.4	32.8	35.9	36.9
Primary metal industries	43.2	53.0	54.1	54.9	43.7	49.6	54.7	60.7
Fabricated metal products	69.4	87.2	102.2	105.5	76.1	90.8	96.7	95.9
Industrial machinery	118.2	132.8	150.8	158.2	93.5	124.7	187.0	216.6
Electronic & other electric equipment .	105.7	146.9	172.8	186.6	68.6	128.7	225.1	276.8
Motor vehicles and equipment	47.3	98.2	107.2	114.5	68.7	103.2	107.0	110.4
Other transportation equipment	60.5	47.7	59.2	59.6	75.7	49.4	57.5	56.3
Instruments and related products	49.3	47.2	57.7	60.0	68.9	52.6	49.2	48.8
Misc. manufacturing industries	19.8	22.7	25.7	27.6	22.8	23.3	24.6	26.0
Nondurable goods	454.0	559.2	602.6	623.1	520.2	570.3	557.9	566.9
Food and kindred products	96.4	121.1	124.8	131.4	109.5	133.3	115.0	117.1
Tobacco manufactures	11.9	15.1	16.8	19.9	14.5	15.7	11.5	7.0
Textile mill products	22.0	24.8	25.4	25.3	22.8	26.0	23.6	22.9
Apparel and other textile products . . .	25.4	27.3	25.8	25.5	27.3	28.0	25.0	23.6
Paper and allied products	45.0	58.9	55.1	57.0	52.5	52.2	55.3	56.0
Printing and publishing	73.1	80.8	94.0	99.0	102.9	89.2	84.0	84.3
Chemicals and allied products	109.9	150.8	168.4	176.3	131.1	148.0	159.8	168.6
Petroleum and coal products	31.7	29.0	32.9	28.6	22.9	26.9	26.6	34.9
Rubber and misc. plastic products . . .	33.9	46.1	55.1	55.8	34.0	47.0	53.8	54.4
Leather and leather products	4.7	5.3	4.2	4.2	5.2	5.3	4.0	4.0
Transportation and public utilities	490.9	642.6	728.0	779.6	525.0	634.5	686.4	752.3
Transportation	177.4	233.4	287.8	303.4	180.6	225.1	257.1	272.4
Railroad transportation	19.8	23.6	25.4	23.4	18.1	22.7	23.9	22.8
Local & interurban passenger transit. .	9.1	12.4	16.2	17.1	12.8	13.2	15.6	17.2
Trucking and warehousing	69.4	89.0	109.3	116.6	68.1	86.6	90.7	95.7
Water transportation	10.0	11.6	14.1	14.4	10.2	11.3	13.5	12.5
Transportation by air	45.3	67.7	88.2	95.0	46.9	62.9	79.0	87.5
Pipelines, except natural gas.	5.5	5.5	6.1	6.6	5.7	5.0	6.5	7.2
Transportation services	18.2	23.5	28.5	30.2	19.5	23.4	28.2	30.1
Communications.	148.1	202.3	234.1	260.2	155.2	202.4	232.0	264.6
Telephone and telegraph	119.4	151.6	173.9	195.1	117.1	147.6	180.9	215.1
Radio and television broadcasting . . .	28.7	50.7	60.2	65.1	37.5	55.2	51.4	51.9
Electric, gas, and sanitary services	165.4	206.9	206.0	216.0	190.0	207.2	197.4	216.3
Wholesale trade	376.1	500.6	610.9	643.3	395.1	483.0	665.3	709.3
Retail trade.	507.8	648.8	796.8	856.4	559.5	641.4	805.5	847.3
Finance, insurance, and real estate	1,010.3	1,347.2	1,689.5	1,792.1	1,250.6	1,393.0	1,605.9	1,692.1
Depository institutions	171.3	227.4	292.7	305.3	244.0	242.4	249.5	255.0
Nondepository institutions	23.3	34.1	48.4	45.3	26.3	33.4	53.1	52.5
Security and commodity brokers	42.3	77.7	135.3	152.1	42.0	76.5	153.7	207.8
Insurance carriers	64.8	120.2	154.4	165.0	112.2	129.9	139.9	142.6
Insurance agents, brokers & services . . .	37.7	47.2	52.6	56.9	61.4	49.9	48.5	50.5
Real estate	665.7	832.6	969.2	1,034.0	763.4	852.8	933.5	973.5
Services	1,071.5	1,462.4	1,837.1	1,986.9	1,361.9	1,510.4	1,704.4	1,772.6
Hotels and other lodging places	46.3	61.7	76.0	83.5	55.2	62.7	65.5	67.3
Personal services	38.0	46.7	55.4	58.2	46.4	48.1	52.2	53.1
Business services	203.9	302.0	447.1	510.8	241.3	313.9	417.4	463.5
Auto repair, services, and garages. . . .	50.3	65.1	80.9	86.8	61.9	65.9	74.8	78.3
Motion pictures	17.7	22.4	28.8	29.8	21.2	23.6	27.8	27.2
Amusement and recreation services. . . .	36.5	53.5	72.2	78.7	45.0	55.6	67.4	70.7
Health services	314.4	433.1	492.6	514.2	423.2	444.3	462.0	463.5
Legal services	82.7	101.1	116.4	125.1	108.8	105.1	107.0	111.9
Educational services	39.6	55.7	66.7	71.1	50.3	58.5	61.2	61.2
Social services & membership organizations	30.1	47.4	57.1	61.3	38.0	49.3	52.0	53.0
Other services	149.2	194.4	251.5	272.8	191.3	199.9	233.9	241.9
Government	806.6	989.5	1,105.8	1,158.4	1,008.2	1,017.1	1,049.8	1,070.4
Federal	300.2	342.3	360.7	375.4	384.7	354.3	348.4	352.6
State and local	506.4	647.2	745.2	783.0	624.1	662.9	701.3	717.7

[1] Includes private households and statistical discrepancy, not shown separately.

Source: U.S. Bureau of Economic Analysis, *National Income and Product Accounts, 1929-97*, (forthcoming); and *Survey of Current Business*, December 2000.

418   Income, Expenditures, and Wealth

No. 642. Gross Domestic Product in Current and Real (1996) Dollars by Type of Product and Sector: 1990 to 2000

[In billions of dollars (5,803 represents $5,803,000,000,000). For explanation of chained dollars, see text, this section]

Item	1990	1992	1993	1994	1995	1996	1997	1998	1999	2000
CURRENT DOLLARS										
Gross domestic product ...	**5,803**	**6,319**	**6,642**	**7,054**	**7,401**	**7,813**	**8,318**	**8,790**	**9,299**	**9,963**
PRODUCT										
Goods.............	2,266	2,391	2,503	2,680	2,798	2,951	3,145	3,316	3,510	3,793
Durable goods..........	1,002	1,027	1,108	1,197	1,273	1,351	1,469	1,578	1,678	1,844
Nondurable goods.........	1,264	1,365	1,395	1,483	1,525	1,600	1,676	1,738	1,832	1,950
Services	3,011	3,416	3,594	3,783	3,985	4,191	4,442	4,673	4,935	5,254
Structures	526	512	546	592	617	671	731	801	854	916
SECTOR										
Business	4,842	5,242	5,518	5,887	6,190	6,556	7,011	7,426	7,872	8,460
Nonfarm...............	4,762	5,162	5,444	5,803	6,117	6,464	6,922	7,345	7,798	8,387
Farm..............	80	81	74	84	73	92	88	81	74	73
Households and institutions......	238	280	297	313	330	349	363	385	402	422
General government	723	797	827	855	880	909	945	979	1,025	1,081
Federal	260	283	287	287	287	292	295	299	310	327
State and local	464	515	540	567	593	617	649	681	716	753
CHAINED (1996) DOLLARS										
Gross domestic product ...	**6,708**	**6,880**	**7,063**	**7,348**	**7,544**	**7,813**	**8,160**	**8,516**	**8,876**	**9,319**
PRODUCT										
Goods.............	2,404	2,455	2,548	2,708	2,814	2,951	3,146	3,340	3,544	3,811
Durable goods............	1,007	1,015	1,094	1,179	1,265	1,351	1,491	1,638	1,781	1,970
Nondurable goods	1,400	1,445	1,457	1,531	1,549	1,600	1,655	1,704	1,769	1,853
Services	3,692	3,847	3,917	4,010	4,098	4,191	4,308	4,427	4,563	4,723
Structures	615	585	603	631	633	671	707	752	777	801
SECTOR										
Business	5,524	5,669	5,838	6,112	6,296	6,556	6,882	7,216	7,557	7,975
Nonfarm.................	5,441	5,575	5,753	6,014	6,210	6,464	6,779	7,115	7,450	7,866
Farm...............	84	96	86	100	86	92	104	100	106	106
Households and institutions......	292	309	320	331	342	349	361	372	378	386
General government	895	905	906	906	907	909	917	929	942	962
Federal	331	326	320	310	299	292	288	286	287	292
State and local	565	579	587	596	608	617	629	642	655	669

Source: U.S. Bureau of Economic Analysis, *National Income and Product Accounts of the United States, 1929-97,* (forthcoming); and *Survey of Current Business,* May 2001.

No. 643. GDP Components in Current Dollars—Annual Percent Change: 1990 to 2000

[Change from previous year; for 1990, change from 1989. For explanation of chained dollars, see text, this section. Minus sign (-) indicates decrease]

Item	1990	1992	1993	1994	1995	1996	1997	1998	1999	2000
Gross domestic product (GDP) .	**5.7**	**5.6**	**5.1**	**6.2**	**4.9**	**5.6**	**6.5**	**5.7**	**5.8**	**7.1**
Personal consumption expenditures...	6.5	6.0	5.6	5.9	5.4	5.4	5.6	5.8	7.1	7.8
Durable goods...............	-	6.3	9.1	9.2	5.2	4.5	4.2	8.0	9.7	7.8
Nondurable goods............	6.9	3.5	3.9	4.6	4.1	5.1	4.3	4.0	8.1	8.9
Services	7.9	7.4	6.2	5.9	6.0	5.7	6.5	6.3	6.2	7.2
Gross private domestic investment	-1.3	8.3	10.2	14.9	4.2	8.7	11.9	11.5	6.5	11.1
Fixed investment	0.2	6.4	9.7	10.8	7.4	9.2	9.5	10.9	9.1	10.7
Nonresidential............	2.8	2.8	9.0	9.7	10.2	9.0	11.1	10.8	8.6	13.2
Structures............	4.7	-6.1	4.2	4.5	9.1	9.9	13.7	10.7	0.8	13.5
Producers' durable equipment .	1.9	6.7	10.8	11.6	10.6	8.7	10.3	10.8	11.3	13.1
Residential	-6.5	17.7	11.7	13.6	-0.1	9.7	4.8	11.3	10.5	3.0
Exports of goods and services	9.5	5.8	3.3	10.2	12.9	6.8	10.6	-	2.5	10.8
Exports of goods	7.2	5.2	2.5	10.8	14.6	5.9	11.4	-1.0	2.5	12.8
Exports of services	15.5	7.4	5.4	8.7	8.9	9.0	8.5	2.3	2.5	6.1
Imports of goods and services	6.6	6.8	8.1	13.0	11.2	6.7	9.6	5.8	11.3	18.0
Imports of goods..............	4.9	8.8	8.8	14.2	12.0	6.7	9.5	5.1	12.7	19.1
Imports of services	14.6	-1.5	5.0	7.7	7.2	6.6	10.3	9.5	4.6	12.2
Govt. consumption expenditures and gross investment	7.4	2.8	1.8	2.7	3.3	3.6	4.6	3.6	6.1	6.7
Federal	5.4	1.4	-1.4	-1.2	0.1	1.9	1.2	0.4	5.2	4.7
National defense	3.2	-1.6	-3.6	-2.7	-1.3	1.8	-1.2	-1.0	4.5	3.3
Nondefense	12.0	9.2	4.1	2.2	3.0	2.1	6.3	3.1	6.3	7.2
State and local..............	9.0	3.9	4.0	5.4	5.4	4.7	6.7	5.3	6.5	7.8

- Represents or rounds to zero.

Source: U.S. Bureau of Economic Analysis, *National Income and Product Accounts of the United States, 1929-97,* (forthcoming); and *Survey of Current Business,* May 2001.

Income, Expenditures, and Wealth 419

No. 644. Gross State Product in Current and Real (1996) Dollars: 1990 to 1998

[In billions of dollars (5,706.7 represents $5,706,700,000,000). For definition of gross state product or chained dollars, see text, this section]

State	Current dollars					Chained (1996) dollars [1]				
	1990	1995	1996	1997	1998	1990	1995	1996	1997	1998
United States........	5,706.7	7,309.5	7,715.9	8,240.3	8,745.2	6,630.7	7,434.0	7,715.9	8,120.9	8,537.7
Alabama	71.5	95.3	99.0	104.7	109.8	83.2	96.4	99.0	103.3	107.0
Alaska.............	24.8	24.2	24.8	25.5	24.2	27.7	25.6	24.8	25.1	24.4
Arizona	68.8	104.6	113.1	123.1	133.8	78.9	105.5	113.1	121.7	131.8
Arkansas	38.4	53.6	56.5	59.1	61.6	44.2	54.5	56.5	58.7	60.7
California...........	798.2	924.6	971.8	1,043.7	1,118.9	926.6	940.1	971.8	1,028.9	1,093.9
Colorado	74.6	109.2	117.5	129.7	141.8	87.0	111.5	117.5	127.5	138.1
Connecticut	98.9	119.0	124.7	134.8	142.1	117.3	121.1	124.7	132.5	138.1
Delaware	20.3	27.4	28.7	31.2	33.7	25.0	28.0	28.7	30.0	32.0
District of Columbia	40.4	48.4	48.5	50.6	54.1	50.9	49.7	48.5	49.5	51.7
Florida.............	258.0	344.4	365.8	391.1	418.9	303.4	350.1	365.8	384.2	405.4
Georgia	141.3	202.8	218.4	233.8	253.8	164.7	205.6	218.4	230.2	245.8
Hawaii	32.3	37.3	37.5	38.8	39.7	38.1	38.0	37.5	38.0	38.0
Idaho	17.7	27.0	27.9	29.1	30.9	20.0	27.3	27.9	29.1	31.0
Illinois	276.5	359.8	376.5	402.3	425.7	318.5	364.5	376.5	397.0	416.1
Indiana	111.0	148.6	155.3	163.8	174.4	127.2	150.3	155.3	162.2	170.9
Iowa	56.2	72.2	77.5	81.6	84.6	63.8	73.6	77.5	81.6	84.5
Kansas	51.6	64.0	68.0	73.1	77.0	59.9	65.5	68.0	72.3	75.5
Kentucky	67.9	91.4	95.5	101.4	107.2	77.5	92.8	95.5	100.3	104.3
Louisiana	95.0	114.1	120.1	127.2	129.3	108.4	119.0	120.1	124.6	128.8
Maine	23.5	28.1	29.1	30.6	32.3	27.8	28.4	29.1	30.2	31.3
Maryland	115.0	139.7	145.4	155.0	164.8	137.0	142.4	145.4	152.1	159.0
Massachusetts	159.9	197.1	209.6	223.5	239.4	187.1	200.2	209.6	219.8	232.9
Michigan	190.7	253.9	264.8	280.2	294.5	224.9	258.1	264.8	277.0	288.0
Minnesota	100.4	131.8	141.5	152.3	161.4	116.5	133.8	141.5	150.6	157.9
Mississippi	39.2	54.4	56.3	59.3	62.2	44.9	55.2	56.3	58.5	60.7
Missouri............	104.8	139.7	146.8	155.2	162.8	122.8	142.1	146.8	153.1	158.4
Montana	13.4	17.7	18.2	19.1	19.4	15.5	18.0	18.2	18.8	19.5
Nebraska...........	33.6	44.3	48.0	49.8	51.7	38.7	45.5	48.0	49.5	51.0
Nevada	31.6	49.1	54.0	58.5	63.0	37.1	49.7	54.0	57.0	59.9
New Hampshire	23.9	32.4	35.0	38.1	41.3	27.3	32.6	35.0	37.9	41.0
New Jersey	216.9	271.3	285.5	303.6	319.2	253.5	274.9	285.5	297.9	308.0
New Mexico	27.2	42.0	43.8	46.5	47.7	29.4	42.5	43.8	46.3	48.6
New York	502.1	597.8	634.2	669.4	706.9	593.3	·609.3	634.2	657.2	687.7
North Carolina	141.2	194.5	204.0	220.9	235.8	162.8	197.4	204.0	217.8	227.6
North Dakota	11.7	14.7	16.1	16.2	17.2	13.4	15.2	16.1	16.2	17.2
Ohio	230.1	295.2	305.6	325.2	341.1	266.0	298.7	305.6	321.4	333.6
Oklahoma	57.7	69.4	73.9	78.3	81.7	66.0	71.1	73.9	77.2	80.3
Oregon	57.9	81.3	91.9	98.8	104.8	66.6	81.6	91.9	98.7	105.8
Pennsylvania	249.7	318.1	328.7	347.2	364.0	291.3	322.1	328.7	341.3	353.1
Rhode Island	21.6	25.6	26.4	29.2	30.4	25.5	26.0	26.4	28.6	29.4
South Carolina	66.1	86.5	89.2	94.5	100.4	76.0	87.3	89.2	93.6	97.9
South Dakota	13.1	18.4	19.5	20.0	21.2	15.2	18.9	19.5	20.0	21.2
Tennessee	95.0	136.6	141.8	150.7	159.6	110.5	138.4	141.8	148.6	155.0
Texas	388.1	515.4	555.6	606.9	645.6	439.6	529.3	555.6	597.6	640.3
Utah	31.3	46.4	51.6	56.1	59.6	36.3	47.1	51.6	55.1	58.1
Vermont	11.8	14.0	14.7	15.5	16.3	13.4	14.1	14.7	15.3	15.9
Virginia	148.1	189.0	200.0	213.4	230.8	174.4	192.5	200.0	209.4	221.7
Washington	115.6	151.5	162.0	176.2	192.9	136.8	154.2	162.0	173.5	187.0
West Virginia	28.3	36.3	37.2	38.5	39.9	31.7	36.5	37.2	38.0	38.8
Wisconsin	100.4	133.7	141.0	149.3	157.8	115.2	135.1	141.0	148.3	155.3
Wyoming	13.4	·15.7	17.1	17.8	17.5	14.4	16.6	17.1	17.5	17.8

[1] For chained (1996) dollar estimates, states will not add to U.S. total.

Source: U.S. Bureau of Economic Analysis, *Survey of Current Business*, June 2000.

No. 645. Gross State Product in Chained (1996) Dollars by Industry: 1998

[In billions of dollars (8,537.7 represents $8,537,700,000,000). For definition of gross state product or chained dollars, see text, this section. Industries based on 1987 Standard Industrial Classification]

State	Total [1]	Farms, forestry, fisher-ies [2]	Con-struction	Manu-facturing	Trans-portation, public utilities	Whole-sale trade	Retail trade	Finance, insur-ance, real estate	Serv-ices	Govern-ment [3]
United States [4] ..	8,537.7	142.9	342.9	1,448.7	726.0	664.0	795.7	1,606.7	1,708.1	984.9
Alabama.	107.0	2.4	4.4	22.3	9.4	7.9	11.4	14.3	17.3	16.3
Alaska	24.4	0.4	1.0	1.0	4.3	0.8	1.8	2.7	3.0	4.8
Arizona.	131.8	2.2	7.5	21.9	9.8	9.7	14.2	23.9	26.1	15.4
Arkansas	60.7	2.8	2.3	14.4	6.4	4.3	6.9	6.7	9.0	7.1
California	1,093.9	23.2	38.0	160.5	78.3	84.3	104.5	240.3	242.3	118.2
Colorado.	138.1	2.3	7.5	15.3	16.7	9.8	13.7	23.4	29.5	16.7
Connecticut.	138.1	0.9	4.6	23.7	8.8	10.6	10.8	38.3	29.0	11.5
Delaware	32.0	0.3	0.9	5.2	1.6	1.4	2.3	12.9	4.6	2.9
District of Columbia . .	51.7	-	0.5	1.2	2.5	0.7	1.4	8.8	17.2	19.4
Florida	405.4	7.4	18.8	30.6	35.6	34.3	47.9	86.5	94.5	49.1
Georgia	245.8	4.0	9.5	41.9	28.1	25.4	23.1	38.4	44.9	29.6
Hawaii	38.0	0.5	1.5	1.0	4.0	1.7	4.3	8.9	8.0	8.3
Idaho	31.0	2.0	1.7	6.7	2.6	2.2	3.2	3.7	4.8	4.0
Illinois	416.1	5.6	16.6	74.2	38.6	36.2	34.5	83.0	86.9	39.4
Indiana	170.9	3.0	8.0	54.7	12.9	11.7	15.9	21.6	26.3	16.2
Iowa	84.5	5.6	3.4	21.0	6.6	6.7	7.3	11.8	12.6	9.2
Kansas.	75.5	3.3	3.0	13.2	8.3	6.8	7.9	9.6	12.6	9.7
Kentucky	104.3	2.8	4.1	28.2	8.4	7.2	10.2	11.3	15.7	13.7
Louisiana	128.8	1.4	6.0	18.4	11.7	8.3	11.2	15.5	20.1	14.4
Maine	31.3	0.6	1.4	5.2	2.3	2.1	3.9	5.6	5.9	4.2
Maryland	159.0	1.4	8.1	13.3	12.6	11.2	14.9	33.4	36.5	27.6
Massachusetts.	232.9	1.3	7.8	34.3	14.3	19.2	19.2	54.9	60.6	21.3
Michigan.	288.0	2.7	11.7	78.6	18.9	23.9	28.8	40.9	52.7	28.6
Minnesota.	157.9	3.9	7.0	29.3	11.8	14.7	15.1	28.4	31.0	15.9
Mississippi	60.7	1.9	2.5	13.5	5.9	4.0	6.7	6.6	9.8	9.1
Missouri	158.4	2.7	7.2	31.5	16.5	13.3	15.7	23.4	30.5	17.2
Montana	19.5	1.0	0.9	1.5	2.3	1.4	2.1	2.6	3.7	3.0
Nebraska	51.0	3.9	2.3	7.0	5.5	4.5	4.5	7.3	9.0	6.9
Nevada	59.9	0.5	5.2	2.8	4.9	3.3	6.5	10.7	17.8	6.3
New Hampshire	41.0	0.3	1.5	10.8	2.5	2.9	3.9	8.7	7.3	3.2
New Jersey.	308.0	1.6	10.6	40.4	29.9	32.6	23.6	71.2	68.4	30.0
New Mexico	48.6	1.1	2.0	9.3	3.5	2.3	4.6	6.1	8.1	7.9
New York	687.7	3.0	19.6	74.3	55.2	47.2	48.5	220.2	150.4	69.2
North Carolina	227.6	5.4	9.9	55.8	17.2	16.7	21.8	36.1	35.7	28.7
North Dakota.	17.2	1.9	0.8	1.5	1.6	1.7	1.7	2.2	2.9	2.4
Ohio	333.6	4.0	12.7	87.2	25.2	26.6	33.0	50.7	58.3	34.9
Oklahoma	80.3	2.0	2.6	14.2	8.0	5.5	8.5	9.5	13.9	12.4
Oregon.	105.8	3.1	5.0	30.0	7.0	8.9	8.9	14.7	17.0	11.4
Pennsylvania	353.1	3.3	13.4	72.8	31.3	24.3	32.5	63.4	75.5	35.0
Rhode Island	29.4	0.2	1.0	4.5	2.3	1.7	2.6	7.2	6.2	3.5
South Carolina	97.9	1.2	4.7	23.8	7.4	6.7	11.0	13.4	15.3	14.2
South Dakota	21.2	2.2	0.8	3.0	1.6	1.6	2.0	4.0	3.2	2.5
Tennessee	155.0	1.8	6.2	32.3	12.3	13.3	18.2	22.1	31.1	17.4
Texas.	640.3	8.8	28.3	96.8	70.7	56.7	60.1	88.3	116.9	68.3
Utah	58.1	0.7	3.2	8.9	5.0	4.0	6.2	9.6	10.9	8.1
Vermont	15.9	0.4	0.7	3.0	1.3	1.0	1.6	2.7	3.3	1.9
Virginia.	221.7	2.0	9.4	29.8	20.7	13.8	19.5	39.1	47.4	38.9
Washington.	187.0	5.0	8.7	25.0	16.0	15.2	18.4	32.5	41.1	24.8
West Virginia.	38.8	0.3	1.7	6.4	4.6	2.3	3.9	4.3	6.4	5.6
Wisconsin	155.3	3.9	6.5	43.2	10.7	11.1	14.3	23.8	25.4	16.4
Wyoming	17.8	0.4	0.7	1.0	2.3	0.7	1.3	1.9	1.7	2.2

- Represents zero.   [1] Includes mining not shown separately.   [2] Includes agricultural services.   [3] Includes federal civilian and military and state and local government.   [4] States will not add to U.S. total as chained-dollar estimates are usually not additive.

Source: U.S. Bureau of Economic Analysis, *Survey of Current Business*, June 2000.

Income, Expenditures, and Wealth   421

No. 646. Relation of GDP, GNP, Net National Product, National Income, Personal Income, Disposable Personal Income, and Personal Saving: 1990 to 2000

[In billions of dollars (5,803.2 represents $5,803,200,000,000). For definitions, see text, this section]

Item	1990	1994	1995	1996	1997	1998	1999	2000
Gross domestic product.	5,803.2	7,054.3	7,400.5	7,813.2	8,318.4	8,790.2	9,299.2	9,963.1
Plus: Receipts of factor income from the rest of the world [1]	188.3	184.3	232.3	245.6	281.3	285.4	305.9	370.6
Less: Payments of factor income to the rest of the world [2].	159.3	167.5	211.9	227.5	274.2	288.9	316.9	374.9
Equals: Gross national product.	5,832.2	7,071.1	7,420.9	7,831.2	8,325.4	8,786.7	9,288.2	9,958.7
Less: Consumption of fixed capital	711.3	874.9	911.7	956.2	1,013.3	1,077.3	1,161.0	1,257.1
Equals: Net national product [3]	5,120.9	6,196.2	6,509.1	6,875.0	7,312.1	7,709.3	8,127.1	8,701.6
Less: Indirect business tax and nontax liability.	447.3	575.3	594.6	620.0	646.2	679.6	718.1	769.6
Plus: Subsidies [4].	25.3	25.2	22.2	22.6	19.1	21.5	28.4	27.9
Equals: National income [3]	4,642.1	5,556.8	5,876.7	6,210.4	6,618.4	7,038.1	7,469.7	8,002.0
Less: Corporate profits [5].	408.6	573.2	668.8	754.0	833.8	815.0	856.0	946.2
Net interest.	452.4	380.5	389.8	386.3	423.9	482.7	507.1	567.2
Contributions for social insurance	410.1	508.4	533.2	555.8	587.8	622.1	662.1	705.6
Wage accruals less disbursements . . .	0.1	17.6	16.4	3.6	-2.9	2.1	5.2	-
Plus: Personal interest income.	772.4	742.4	792.5	810.6	864.0	940.8	963.7	1,034.3
Personal dividend income	165.4	234.7	254.0	297.4	334.9	351.1	370.3	396.6
Government transfer payments to persons	573.1	810.1	860.1	902.4	934.4	954.3	986.5	1,037.1
Business transfer payments to persons	21.3	23.7	25.8	26.4	27.9	28.7	29.7	30.7
Equals: Personal income	4,903.2	5,888.0	6,200.9	6,547.4	6,937.0	7,391.0	7,789.6	8,281.7
Less: Personal tax and nontax payments.	609.6	722.6	778.3	869.7	968.8	1,070.9	1,152.0	1,291.9
Equals: Disposable personal income. .	4,293.6	5,165.4	5,422.6	5,677.7	5,968.2	6,320.0	6,637.7	6,989.8
Less: Personal outlays	3,959.3	4,849.9	5,120.2	5,405.6	5,715.3	6,054.7	6,490.1	6,998.3
Equals: Personal saving.	334.3	315.5	302.4	272.1	252.9	265.4	147.6	-8.5

- Represents zero.   [1] Consists largely of receipts by U.S. residents of interest and dividends and reinvested earnings of foreign affiliates of U.S. corporations.   [2] Consists largely of payments to foreign residents of interest and dividends and reinvested earnings of U.S. affiliates of foreign corporations.   [3] Includes items not shown separately.   [4] Less current surplus of government enterprises.   [5] With inventory valuation and capital consumption adjustments.

Source: U.S. Bureau of Economic Analysis, *National Income and Product Accounts of the United States, 1929-97,* (forthcoming); and *Survey of Current Business,* May 2001.

No. 647. Selected Per Capita Income and Product Items in Current and Real (1996) Dollars: 1960 to 2000

[In dollars. Based on U.S. Census Bureau estimated population including Armed Forces abroad; based on quarterly averages. For explanation of chained dollars, see text, this section]

Year	Current dollars					Chained (1996) dollars			
	Gross domestic product	Gross national product	Personal income	Disposable personal income	Personal consumption expenditures	Gross domestic product	Gross national product	Disposable personal income	Personal consumption expenditures
1960	2,918	2,935	2,283	2,026	1,838	13,148	13,232	9,210	8,358
1965	3,705	3,733	2,868	2,567	2,286	15,583	15,702	10,965	9,764
1970	5,069	5,101	4,101	3,591	3,164	17,446	17,556	12,823	11,300
1975	7,571	7,632	6,166	5,470	4,771	18,911	19,065	14,393	12,551
1976	8,363	8,442	6,765	5,960	5,272	19,771	19,953	14,873	13,155
1977	9,221	9,315	7,432	6,519	5,803	20,481	20,685	15,256	13,583
1978	10,313	10,412	8,302	7,253	6,425	21,383	21,584	15,845	14,035
1979	11,401	11,547	9,247	8,033	7,091	21,821	22,096	16,120	14,230
1980	12,276	12,431	10,205	8,869	7,741	21,521	21,791	16,063	14,021
1981	13,614	13,765	11,301	9,773	8,453	21,830	22,066	16,265	14,069
1982	14,035	14,192	11,922	10,364	8,954	21,184	21,418	16,328	14,105
1983	15,085	15,242	12,576	11,036	9,757	21,902	22,116	16,673	14,741
1984	16,636	16,786	13,853	12,215	10,569	23,288	23,494	17,799	15,401
1985	17,664	17,771	14,738	12,941	11,373	23,970	24,112	18,229	16,020
1986	18,501	18,565	15,425	13,555	12,029	24,565	24,649	18,641	16,541
1987	19,529	19,585	16,317	14,246	12,787	25,174	25,246	18,870	16,938
1988	20,845	20,920	17,433	15,312	13,697	25,987	26,080	19,522	17,463
1989	22,188	22,271	18,593	16,235	14,539	26,646	26,742	19,833	17,760
1990	23,215	23,331	19,614	17,176	15,327	26,834	26,962	20,058	17,899
1991	23,691	23,789	20,126	17,710	15,717	26,423	26,529	19,919	17,677
1992	24,741	24,833	21,105	18,616	16,482	26,938	27,039	20,318	17,989
1993	25,735	25,829	21,735	19,121	17,259	27,363	27,461	20,384	18,399
1994	27,068	27,132	22,593	19,820	18,097	28,194	28,257	20,709	18,910
1995	28,131	28,208	23,571	20,613	18,888	28,676	28,753	21,055	19,294
1996	29,428	29,496	24,660	21,385	19,727	29,428	29,496	21,385	19,727
1997	31,029	31,055	25,876	22,262	20,625	30,436	30,468	21,838	20,232
1998	32,489	32,476	27,317	23,359	21,625	31,474	31,472	22,672	20,989
1999	34,063	34,023	28,534	24,314	22,962	32,512	32,485	23,191	21,901
2000	36,174	36,158	30,069	25,379	24,534	33,833	33,826	23,640	22,853

Source: U.S. Bureau of Economic Analysis, *National Income and Product Accounts of the United States, 1929-97,* (forthcoming); and *Survey of Current Business,* May 2001.

No. 648. Personal Consumption Expenditures in Current and Real (1996) Dollars by Type: 1990 to 1999

[In billions of dollars (3,831.5 represents $3,831,500,000,000). For definition of "chained" dollars, see text, this section]

Expenditure	Current dollars				Chained (1996) dollars			
	1990	1995	1998	1999	1990	1995	1998	1999
Total expenditures [1]	**3,831.5**	**4,969.0**	**5,850.9**	**6,268.7**	**4,474.5**	**5,075.6**	**5,678.7**	**5,978.8**
Food and tobacco [1].	677.9	802.5	900.2	963.8	774.4	825.1	858.8	887.8
Food purchased for off-premise consumption	401.6	459.8	504.2	531.8	452.4	473.7	488.6	506.9
Purchased meals and beverages [2] . . .	227.8	287.5	332.2	356.3	261.8	294.6	315.3	329.9
Tobacco products	41.0	46.7	54.4	66.0	52.0	48.1	46.2	43.4
Clothing, accessories, and jewelry [1]	261.7	317.3	368.3	397.2	258.2	312.9	376.3	411.5
Shoes	31.5	37.1	41.7	43.3	32.0	36.8	42.2	45.0
Clothing.	172.4	210.4	244.4	263.4	165.1	207.2	249.8	273.3
Jewelry and watches	30.3	38.1	44.2	48.8	30.1	36.7	47.8	54.0
Personal care.	53.7	67.4	80.5	86	60.1	68.3	78.2	81.9
Housing [1]	585.6	740.8	858.2	906.2	696.2	763.7	807.7	828.3
Owner-occupied nonfarm dwellings-space rent	410.7	529.3	622.7	661.1	488.3	546.1	586.7	605.7
Tenant-occupied nonfarm dwellings-space rent.	148.7	177.0	193.8	200.6	174.6	181.6	182.9	183.7
Household operation [1]	433.6	555	643.8	682.5	476.8	564.2	641.1	681.9
Furniture [3]	38.4	47.5	56.4	60.3	42.2	48.1	56.6	60.6
Semidurable house furnishings [4] . . .	22.5	29.7	35.2	38.3	21.8	29.0	36.8	40.5
Cleaning and polishing preparations . .	38.9	47.3	53.5	57.1	42.4	48.5	52.1	54.6
Household utilities	141.1	175.0	185.8	189.8	162.8	180.8	186.1	189.4
Electricity	74.2	91.0	96.1	96.2	83.2	92.5	99.6	100.3
Gas.	26.8	31.5	32.4	32.7	29.5	32.8	30.8	30.9
Water and other sanitary services . .	27.1	38.4	44.5	46.5	37.1	39.8	42.1	43.0
Fuel oil and coal	12.9	14.1	12.8	14.4	13.1	15.7	14.0	15.5
Telephone and telegraph.	60.5	87.8	113	121.7	62.6	88.1	114.4	126.3
Medical care [1]	619.7	888.6	1040.9	1102.6	807.6	907.8	997.0	1,030.0
Drug preparations and sundries [5] . . .	65.4	92.1	121.8	136.8	80.3	94.1	117.4	127.2
Physicians	140.4	192.4	221.2	232.3	183.3	193.8	213.7	219.5
Dentists	32.4	46.5	55	57.8	44.8	48.7	50.5	50.6
Hospitals and nursing homes [6]	265	370.9	428.7	451.8	340.5	381.5	410.4	422.3
Health insurance	37.7	58	61.3	64.6	66	58.9	61	62.7
Medical care [7]	31.7	46.4	51.7	55.2	47.9	47.1	48.2	50.2
Personal business [1]	284.7	406.8	533.7	586.2	363.2	424.4	485.9	520.4
Expense of handling life insurance [8] . .	55.0	81.8	92.2	98	71.2	87	82.9	83.7
Legal services	40.9	48	58.7	62.3	51.9	49.7	53.9	54.7
Funeral and burial expenses	9.5	13.3	16.3	16.2	12.9	14.0	14.9	14.4
Transportation [1]	455.4	560.3	648.6	705.5	532.2	574.7	656.0	698.3
User-operated transportation [1]	419.0	517.8	599.4	654.6	493.5	532.3	608.5	649.1
New autos	89.7	82.2	87.8	97.3	104.0	83.5	88.4	98.8
Net purchases of used autos	29.3	50.0	55.3	58.7	42.0	51.2	57.7	60.3
Tires, tubes, accessories, etc.	29.9	36.9	41.7	44.8	29.7	36.8	42.3	45.7
Repair, greasing, washing, parking, storage, rental, and leasing	84.9	122.2	153.1	162.1	100.8	124.5	148.3	153.9
Gasoline and oil	107.3	113.3	115.2	128.3	113.1	120.2	131.2	134.2
Purchased local transportation	8.4	10.4	12.1	12.3	10.8	11.4	12.0	12.3
Mass transit systems	5.8	7.1	8.0	8.2	7.4	7.8	8.0	8.3
Taxicab	2.6	3.2	4.1	4.0	3.4	3.6	4.0	4.0
Purchased intercity transportation [1]. . .	28.1	32.1	37.2	38.7	28.1	31.0	35.6	37.0
Railway (commutation)	0.7	0.6	0.7	0.7	0.9	0.7	0.7	0.7
Bus	1.3	1.6	2.1	2.2	1.3	1.6	2.0	2.0
Airline	22.7	25.5	29.5	30.7	22.0	24.3	28.2	29.5
Recreation [1][9]	284.9	401.6	489.8	534.9	292.6	398.7	507.3	567.5
Magazines, newspapers, and sheet music	21.6	26.2	32.5	37.0	27.2	27.2	31.5	35.0
Nondurable toys and sport supplies . .	32.8	47.2	57.3	63.1	33.7	47.4	60.7	71.1
Video and audio products, including musical instruments and computer goods	52.9	77.0	90.7	99.1	33.0	67.3	122.1	154.3
Computers, peripherals, and software	8.9	21.0	28.6	31.9	2.1	14.6	60.8	92.3
Education and research	83.7	114.5	139.4	148.9	107.6	119.2	130.0	133.9
Higher education.	43.8	62.9	73.2	76.7	60.1	65.6	67.9	69.1
Religious and welfare activities	97.1	134.9	162.6	170.2	115.3	138.7	154.0	156.1
Foreign travel and other, net.	-6.3	-20.7	-15.2	-15.4	-5.3	-21.4	-11.2	-10.8
Foreign travel by U.S. residents	42.7	54.1	68.9	72.9	51.7	55.3	69.3	71.5
Less: Expenditures in the United States by nonresidents	51.6	75.4	85.6	89.9	60.1	77.4	82.4	84.2

[1] Includes other expenditures not shown separately. [2] Consists of purchases (including tips) of meals and beverages from retail, service, and amusement establishments; hotels; dining and buffet cars; schools; school fraternities; institutions; clubs; and industrial lunch rooms. Includes meals and beverages consumed both on and off-premise. [3] Includes mattresses and bedsprings. [4] Consists largely of textile house furnishings including piece goods allocated to house furnishing use. Also includes lamp shades, brooms, and brushes. [5] Excludes drug preparations and related products dispensed by physicians, hospitals, and other medical services. [6] Consists of (1) current expenditures (including consumption of fixed capital) allocated to house nursing homes and (2) payments by patients to proprietary and government hospitals and nursing homes. [7] Consists of (1) premiums, less benefits and dividends, for health hospitalization and accidental death and dismemberment insurance provided by commercial insurance carriers and (2) administrative expenses (including consumption of fixed capital) of Blue Cross and Blue Shield plans and of other independent prepaid and self-insured health plans. [8] Consists of (1) operating expenses of life insurance carriers and private noninsured pension plans and (2) premiums less benefits and dividends of fraternal benefit societies. Excludes expenses allocated by commercial carriers to accident and health insurance. [9] For additional details, see Table 1233.

Source: U.S. Bureau of Economic Analysis, *National Income and Product Accounts of the United States, 1929-97*, (forthcoming); and *Survey of Current Business*, May 2001.

No. 649. Personal Income and Its Disposition: 1990 to 2000

[In billions of dollars (4,903.2 represents $4,903,200,000,000), except as indicated. For definition of personal income and chained dollars, see text, this section]

Item	1990	1994	1995	1996	1997	1998	1999	2000
Personal income	4,903.2	5,888.0	6,200.9	6,547.4	6,937.0	7,391.0	7,789.6	8,281.7
Wage and salary disbursements	2,754.6	3,236.7	3,424.7	3,626.5	3,888.9	4,190.7	4,470.0	4,769.4
Goods-producing industries [1]	754.4	824.0	863.6	908.2	975.1	1,038.6	1,089.2	1,153.2
Manufacturing.	561.4	620.3	647.5	673.7	718.4	756.6	782.4	815.9
Distributive industries [2]	633.6	738.4	782.1	822.4	879.6	949.1	1,020.3	1,107.3
Service industries [3]	849.9	1,070.4	1,156.3	1,254.9	1,369.9	1,510.3	1,636.0	1,748.0
Government	516.7	603.9	622.7	641.0	664.3	692.7	724.4	760.9
Other labor income.	390.0	507.5	497.0	490.0	475.4	485.5	501.0	524.0
Proprietors' income [4]	381	476.6	497.7	544.7	581.2	620.7	663.5	710.4
Rental income of persons [5]	49.1	110.3	117.9	129.7	128.3	135.4	143.4	140.0
Personal dividend income	165.4	234.7	254.0	297.4	334.9	351.1	370.3	396.6
Personal interest income	772.4	742.4	792.5	810.6	864	940.8	963.7	1,034.3
Transfer payments to persons	594.4	833.9	885.9	928.8	962.2	983.0	1,016.2	1,067.8
Less: Personal contributions for social insurance	203.7	254.1	268.8	280.4	297.9	316.2	338.5	360.7
Less: Personal tax and nontax payments.	609.6	722.6	778.3	869.7	968.8	1,070.9	1,152.0	1,291.9
Equals: Disposable personal income. .	4,293.6	5165.4	5422.6	5677.7	5968.2	6,320.0	6637.7	6,989.8
Less: Personal outlays	3,959.3	4,849.9	5,120.2	5,405.6	5,715.3	6,054.7	6,490.1	6,998.3
Personal consumption expenditures . .	3,831.5	4,716.4	4,969.0	5,237.5	5,529.3	5,850.9	6,268.7	6,757.3
Interest paid by persons	115.8	117.9	134.7	149.9	164.8	179.8	194.8	212.2
Personal transfer payments to the rest of the world (net).	12.0	15.6	16.5	18.2	21.2	24.0	26.6	28.8
Equals: Personal saving.	334.3	315.5	302.4	272.1	252.9	265.4	147.6	-8.5
Addenda: Disposable personal income: Total, billions of chained (1996) dollars.	5,014.2	5,397.2	5,539.1	5,677.7	5,854.5	6,134.1	6,331.0	6,511.0
Per capita (dollars): Current dollars	17,176.0	19,820.0	20,613.0	21,385.0	22,262.0	23,359.0	24,314.0	25,379.0
Chained (1996) dollars	20,058.0	20,709.0	21,055.0	21,385.0	21,838.0	22,672.0	23,191.0	23,640.0
Personal saving as percentage of disposable personal income	7.8	6.1	5.6	4.8	4.2	4.2	2.2	-0.1

[1] Comprises agriculture, forestry, fishing, mining, construction, and manufacturing. [2] Comprises transportation, communication, public utilities, and trade. [3] Comprises finance, insurance, real estate, services, and rest of world. [4] With capital consumption and inventory valuation adjustments. [5] With capital consumption adjustment.

Source: U.S. Bureau of Economic Analysis, *National Income and Product Accounts of the United States, 1929-97*, (forthcoming); and *Survey of Current Business*, May 2001.

No. 650. Gross Saving and Investment: 1990 to 2000

[In billions of dollars (977.7 represents $977,700,000,000)]

Item	1990	1994	1995	1996	1997	1998	1999	2000
Gross saving	977.7	1,155.9	1,257.5	1,349.3	1,502.3	1,654.4	1,717.6	1,825.1
Gross private saving	1,016.2	1,199.3	1,266.0	1,290.4	1,343.7	1,375.7	1,343.5	1,297.1
Personal saving.	334.3	315.5	302.4	272.1	252.9	265.4	147.6	-8.5
Undistributed corporate profits [1]	102.4	151.6	203.6	232.7	261.3	218.9	229.4	265
Undistributed profits	95.3	151.8	203.3	205	220	162.1	196.4	244.4
Inventory valuation adjustment	-12.9	-12.4	-18.3	3.1	8.4	17.0	-9.1	-12.9
Capital consumption adjustment . . .	19.9	12.2	18.6	24.6	32.9	39.9	42.1	33.5
Corporate consumption of fixed capital	391.1	482.7	512.1	543.5	581.5	624.3	676.9	739.4
Noncorporate consumption of fixed capital	188.4	231.9	231.5	238.5	250.9	265.1	284.5	301.1
Wage accruals less disbursements . . .	-	17.6	16.4	3.6	-2.9	2.1	5.2	-
Gross government saving	-38.6	-43.4	-8.5	58.9	158.6	278.7	374.0	528.0
Federal	-104.3	-130.9	-108	-51.5	33.4	137.4	217.3	351.6
State and local	65.7	87.5	99.4	110.4	125.1	141.2	156.8	176.4
Gross investment	1,008.2	1,214.4	1,284	1,382.1	1,532.1	1,629.6	1,645.6	1,741.3
Gross private domestic investment	861.7	1,097.1	1,143.8	1,242.7	1,390.5	1,549.9	1,650.1	1,832.7
Gross government investment	215.8	225.6	238.2	250.1	264.6	278.8	308.7	336.6
Net foreign investment	-69.2	-108.3	-98.0	-110.7	-123.1	-199.1	-313.2	-427.9
Statistical discrepancy.	30.6	58.5	26.5	32.8	29.7	-24.8	-71.9	-83.7
Addendum: Gross saving as a percentage of gross national product	16.8	16.3	16.9	17.2	18	18.8	18.5	18.3

- Represents or rounds to zero. [1] With inventory valuation and capital consumption adjustments.

Source: U.S. Bureau of Economic Analysis, *National Income and Product Accounts of the United States, 1929-97*, (forthcoming); and *Survey of Current Business*, May 2001.

No. 651. Personal Income in Current and Constant (1996) Dollars by State: 1980 to 2000

[In billions of dollars (2,313.9 represents $2,313,900,000,000), except percent. 2000 preliminary. Represents a measure of income received from all sources during the calendar year by residents of each state. Data exclude federal employees overseas and U.S. residents employed by private U.S. firms on temporary foreign assignment. Totals may differ from those in Tables 646, 647, and 649. For definition of average annual percent change, see Guide to Tabular Presentation]

State	Current dollars				Constant (1996) dollars [1]				Average annual percent change		Percent distribution	
	1980	1990	1999	2000	1980	1990	1999	2000	1990-99	1999-2000	1990	2000
United States ..	2,313.9	4,885.5	7,784.1	8,351.5	4,191.1	5,705.4	7,424.1	7,779.0	3.0	4.8	100.0	100.0
Alabama	30.8	64.1	100.4	104.4	55.8	74.9	95.7	97.2	2.8	1.5	1.3	1.2
Alaska	6.0	12.6	17.7	18.8	10.9	14.7	16.9	17.6	1.6	3.8	0.3	0.2
Arizona	26.3	63.3	120.3	131.2	47.6	73.9	114.7	122.2	5.0	6.5	1.3	1.6
Arkansas	17.4	34.2	56.7	59.5	31.4	39.9	54.1	55.4	3.4	2.4	0.7	0.7
California	286.3	655.6	989.6	1,093.2	518.5	765.6	943.8	1,018.3	2.4	7.9	13.4	13.1
Colorado	31.4	65.1	127.9	141.7	57.0	76.0	122.0	132.0	5.4	8.2	1.3	1.7
Connecticut ...	38.7	87.9	129.8	138.4	70.1	102.7	123.8	128.9	2.1	4.1	1.8	1.7
Delaware	6.4	14.5	23.1	24.5	11.6	16.9	22.1	22.8	3.0	3.4	0.3	0.3
District of Columbia	7.9	16.1	20.3	21.4	14.3	18.8	19.4	19.9	0.3	2.8	0.3	0.3
Florida	98.9	258.5	419.8	449.8	179.1	301.9	400.4	419.0	3.2	4.6	5.3	5.4
Georgia	46.5	115.4	212.8	228.7	84.2	134.8	203.0	213.0	4.7	5.0	2.4	2.7
Hawaii	11.1	24.9	32.6	34.2	20.2	29.1	31.1	31.8	0.8	2.3	0.5	0.4
Idaho	8.3	16.1	28.6	31.3	15.0	18.7	27.3	29.1	4.3	6.7	0.3	0.4
Illinois	126.7	237.6	377.6	400.6	229.4	277.5	360.2	373.2	2.9	3.6	4.9	4.8
Indiana	51.9	97.9	155.4	164.2	94.0	114.3	148.3	153.0	2.9	3.2	2.0	2.0
Iowa	28.2	48.3	73.5	78.2	51.0	56.4	70.1	72.8	2.4	4.0	1.0	0.9
Kansas	23.8	45.1	70.9	74.8	43.1	52.7	67.6	69.7	2.8	3.0	0.9	0.9
Kentucky	30.2	57.2	92.0	98.2	54.6	66.8	87.7	91.5	3.1	4.2	1.2	1.2
Louisiana	37.3	64.2	99.9	104.3	67.6	75.0	95.2	97.1	2.7	2.0	1.3	1.2
Maine	9.5	21.5	30.8	32.7	17.2	25.1	29.4	30.4	1.7	3.6	0.4	0.4
Maryland	47.5	110.4	168.2	179.4	86.0	129.0	160.4	167.1	2.5	4.2	2.3	2.1
Massachusetts ...	61.3	139.8	219.4	241.2	111.1	163.2	209.2	224.7	2.8	7.4	2.9	2.9
Michigan	96.0	177.1	277.2	294.3	173.8	206.8	264.4	274.1	2.8	3.7	3.6	3.5
Minnesota	42.2	87.8	146.8	157.9	76.4	102.5	140.0	147.1	3.5	5.1	1.8	1.9
Mississippi	17.9	33.9	57.3	59.7	32.4	39.6	54.6	55.6	3.6	1.8	0.7	0.7
Missouri	46.2	91.0	144.4	153.6	83.7	106.3	137.7	143.0	2.9	3.9	1.9	1.8
Montana	7.2	12.4	19.4	20.4	13.1	14.5	18.5	19.0	2.8	2.4	0.3	0.2
Nebraska	14.6	28.6	45.1	47.6	26.4	33.4	43.0	44.4	2.8	3.2	0.6	0.6
Nevada	9.5	25.2	56.1	61.0	17.3	29.4	53.5	56.8	6.9	6.2	0.5	0.7
New Hampshire...	9.2	23.0	37.6	41.2	16.6	26.9	35.9	38.4	3.3	6.9	0.5	0.5
New Jersey	86.9	192.1	290.0	311.2	157.4	224.4	276.6	289.9	2.4	4.8	3.9	3.7
New Mexico	11.0	22.7	38.0	40.4	19.9	26.6	36.2	37.6	3.5	3.8	0.5	0.5
New York	194.9	419.7	616.9	655.6	353.0	490.2	588.3	610.6	2.0	3.8	8.6	7.8
North Carolina...	48.6	115.6	202.1	218.9	88.1	135.0	192.8	203.9	4.0	5.8	2.4	2.6
North Dakota ...	5.3	10.1	14.7	16.1	9.6	11.8	14.1	15.0	2.0	6.6	0.2	0.2
Ohio	109.1	204.1	305.9	322.4	197.6	238.4	291.7	300.3	2.3	3.0	4.2	3.9
Oklahoma	29.1	51.0	77.1	81.2	52.8	59.6	73.5	75.6	2.4	2.8	1.0	1.0
Oregon	26.9	52.2	89.4	97.0	48.8	60.9	85.3	90.3	3.8	6.0	1.1	1.2
Pennsylvania ...	120.5	235.8	343.3	362.8	218.2	275.4	327.4	337.9	1.9	3.2	4.8	4.3
Rhode Island ...	9.2	20.3	29.1	31.1	16.7	23.7	27.7	29.0	1.8	4.6	0.4	0.4
South Carolina ...	24.4	56.2	91.5	97.6	44.2	65.6	87.2	90.9	3.2	4.2	1.1	1.2
South Dakota	5.6	11.3	18.4	19.7	10.2	13.2	17.5	18.4	3.2	4.9	0.2	0.2
Tennessee	38.3	82.3	140.1	149.3	69.3	96.1	133.6	139.0	3.7	4.1	1.7	1.8
Texas	142.8	297.6	537.9	581.2	258.6	347.5	513.0	541.3	4.4	5.5	6.1	7.0
Utah	12.5	25.9	49.6	53.4	22.6	30.3	47.3	49.7	5.1	5.2	0.5	0.6
Vermont........	4.5	10.2	15.3	16.4	8.1	11.9	14.6	15.3	2.3	4.2	0.2	0.2
Virginia	54.6	127.6	204.8	220.6	98.9	149.0	195.3	205.5	3.0	5.2	2.6	2.6
Washington	45.3	98.1	174.9	185.8	82.1	114.6	166.8	173.1	4.3	3.8	2.0	2.2
West Virginia	15.9	26.1	37.8	39.6	28.9	30.5	36.1	36.9	1.9	2.4	0.5	0.5
Wisconsin.......	47.9	89.0	143.7	151.4	86.7	104.0	137.1	141.0	3.1	2.9	1.8	1.8
Wyoming	5.6	8.2	12.6	13.4	10.1	9.5	12.1	12.5	2.7	3.9	0.2	0.2

[1] Implicit price deflator for personal consumption expenditures is used as a deflator.

Source: U.S. Bureau of Economic Analysis, Survey of Current Business, May 2001, and unpublished data.

U.S. Census Bureau, Statistical Abstract of the United States: 2001

No. 652. Personal Income Per Capita in Current and Constant (1996) Dollars by State: 1980 to 2000

[2000 preliminary. See headnote, Table 651]

State	Current dollars			Constant (1996) dollars [1]			Income rank		
	1980	1990	2000	1980	1990	2000	1980	1990	2000
United States ...	10,183	19,584	29,676	18,444	22,870	27,642	(X)	(X)	(X)
Alabama........	7,892	15,832	23,471	14,295	18,489	21,862	46	42	44
Alaska..........	14,807	22,719	30,064	26,819	26,532	28,003	1	6	15
Arizona.........	9,590	17,211	25,578	17,370	20,099	23,825	29	35	37
Arkansas	7,586	14,509	22,257	13,740	16,944	20,731	49	49	47
California	12,029	21,889	32,275	21,788	25,562	30,062	3	8	8
Colorado........	10,809	19,703	32,949	19,578	23,009	30,690	13	19	7
Connecticut......	12,439	26,736	40,640	22,530	31,223	37,854	2	1	1
Delaware	10,803	21,636	31,255	19,567	25,267	29,112	14	9	12
District of Columbia .	12,347	26,627	37,383	22,364	31,095	34,820	(X)	(X)	(X)
Florida	10,049	19,855	28,145	18,201	23,187	26,216	21	17	23
Georgia	8,474	17,738	27,940	15,349	20,715	26,025	37	29	24
Hawaii	11,512	22,391	28,221	20,851	26,149	26,286	10	7	22
Idaho..........	8,735	15,866	24,180	15,821	18,529	22,522	36	41	41
Illinois	11,077	20,756	32,259	20,063	24,239	30,048	8	10	9
Indiana.........	9,449	17,625	27,011	17,115	20,583	25,159	31	30	31
Iowa	9,671	17,380	26,723	17,517	20,297	24,891	27	33	33
Kansas.........	10,038	18,182	27,816	18,181	21,233	25,909	22	23	27
Kentucky	8,231	15,484	24,294	14,909	18,082	22,629	40	44	40
Louisiana	8,833	15,223	23,334	15,999	17,778	21,734	34	45	45
Maine...........	8,408	17,479	25,623	15,229	20,412	23,866	38	31	36
Maryland	11,230	23,023	33,872	20,341	26,887	31,550	9	5	5
Massachusetts.....	10,673	23,223	37,992	19,332	27,120	35,387	12	4	2
Michigan........	10,369	19,022	29,612	18,781	22,214	27,582	15	20	17
Minnesota.......	10,320	20,011	32,101	18,692	23,369	29,900	16	16	10
Mississippi	7,076	13,164	20,993	12,817	15,373	19,554	50	50	50
Missouri	9,390	17,751	27,445	17,008	20,730	25,564	30	28	28
Montana........	9,143	15,524	22,569	16,560	18,129	21,022	33	43	46
Nebraska	9,272	18,088	27,829	16,794	21,123	25,921	32	25	26
Nevada	11,780	20,674	30,529	21,337	24,143	28,436	5	12	14
New Hampshire....	9,915	20,713	33,332	17,959	24,189	31,047	23	11	6
New Jersey......	11,778	24,766	36,983	21,333	28,922	34,448	4	2	3
New Mexico	8,402	14,960	22,203	15,218	17,471	20,681	39	47	48
New York	11,095	23,315	34,547	20,096	27,228	32,179	7	3	4
North Carolina.....	8,247	17,367	27,194	14,938	20,281	25,330	42	34	30
North Dakota......	8,095	15,880	25,068	14,662	18,545	23,349	47	40	38
Ohio	10,103	18,792	28,400	18,299	21,946	26,453	25	21	19
Oklahoma.......	9,580	16,214	23,517	17,352	18,935	21,905	28	38	43
Oregon.........	10,196	18,253	28,350	18,468	21,316	26,406	18	22	20
Pennsylvania......	10,151	19,823	29,539	18,386	23,150	27,514	17	18	18
Rhode Island......	9,742	20,194	29,685	17,645	23,583	27,650	26	14	16
South Carolina.....	7,794	16,050	24,321	14,117	18,743	22,654	48	39	39
South Dakota	8,142	16,238	26,115	14,747	18,963	24,325	45	37	35
Tennessee	8,319	16,821	26,239	15,068	19,644	24,440	41	36	34
Texas...........	9,957	17,458	27,871	18,035	20,388	25,960	20	32	25
Utah...........	8,464	14,996	23,907	15,331	17,513	22,268	44	46	42
Vermont	8,702	18,055	26,901	15,762	21,085	25,057	35	26	32
Virginia..........	10,176	20,538	31,162	18,431	23,985	29,026	19	13	13
Washington.......	10,913	20,026	31,528	19,766	23,387	29,367	11	15	11
West Virginia......	8,172	14,579	21,915	14,802	17,026	20,413	43	48	49
Wisconsin........	10,161	18,160	28,232	18,404	21,208	26,297	24	24	21
Wyoming	11,753	17,996	27,230	21,288	21,016	25,363	6	27	29

X Not applicable.   [1] Implicit price deflator for personal consumption expenditures is used as a deflator.

Source: U.S. Bureau of Economic Analysis, *Survey of Current Business*, May 2001, and unpublished data.

No. 653. Disposable Personal Income Per Capita in Current and Constant (1996) Dollars by State: 1980 to 2000

[In dollars, except percent. 2000 preliminary]

State	Current dollars			Constant (1996) dollars [1]			Percent of U.S. average		
	1980	1990	2000	1980	1990	2000	1980	1990	2000
United States	8,848	17,146	25,090	16,026	20,023	23,370	100.0	100.0	100.0
Alabama.	6,996	14,097	20,487	12,672	16,463	19,083	79.1	82.2	81.7
Alaska	12,738	19,937	26,171	23,072	23,283	24,377	144.0	116.3	104.3
Arizona.	8,493	15,247	21,947	15,383	17,806	20,442	96.0	88.9	87.5
Arkansas	6,741	12,988	19,479	12,210	15,168	18,144	76.2	75.8	77.6
California	10,497	19,027	26,808	19,013	22,220	24,970	118.6	111.0	106.8
Colorado.	9,347	17,251	27,573	16,930	20,146	25,683	105.6	100.6	109.9
Connecticut.	10,655	23,279	32,556	19,299	27,186	30,324	120.4	135.8	129.8
Delaware	8,984	18,612	26,305	16,272	21,735	24,502	101.5	108.6	104.8
District of Columbia	10,480	22,921	30,243	18,982	26,767	28,170	118.4	133.7	120.5
Florida	8,857	17,731	24,090	16,042	20,707	22,439	100.1	103.4	96.0
Georgia	7,442	15,537	23,712	13,479	18,144	22,086	84.1	90.6	94.5
Hawaii	10,054	19,428	24,570	18,210	22,688	22,886	113.6	113.3	97.9
Idaho	7,779	14,071	20,889	14,090	16,432	19,457	87.9	82.1	83.3
Illinois	9,519	18,042	27,167	17,241	21,070	25,305	107.6	105.2	108.3
Indiana	8,246	15,398	22,941	14,936	17,982	21,368	93.2	89.8	91.4
Iowa	8,366	15,295	23,154	15,153	17,862	21,567	94.6	89.2	92.3
Kansas.	8,674	16,009	23,808	15,711	18,696	22,176	98.0	93.4	94.9
Kentucky	7,267	13,623	20,845	13,162	15,909	19,416	82.1	79.5	83.1
Louisiana	7,709	13,681	20,508	13,963	15,977	19,102	87.1	79.8	81.7
Maine.	7,502	15,414	21,929	13,588	18,001	20,426	84.8	89.9	87.4
Maryland	9,530	19,712	28,147	17,261	23,020	26,217	107.7	115.0	112.2
Massachusetts.	9,121	19,915	30,998	16,521	23,257	28,873	103.1	116.2	123.5
Michigan.	9,009	16,589	25,027	16,318	19,373	23,311	101.8	96.8	99.7
Minnesota.	8,867	17,328	26,857	16,060	20,236	25,016	100.2	101.1	107.0
Mississippi	6,347	11,927	18,686	11,496	13,929	17,405	71.7	69.6	74.5
Missouri	8,195	15,611	23,526	14,843	18,231	21,913	92.6	91.1	93.8
Montana	8,009	13,785	19,690	14,506	16,098	18,340	90.5	80.4	78.5
Nebraska	8,099	16,071	23,857	14,669	18,768	22,221	91.5	93.7	95.1
Nevada	10,348	18,112	26,105	18,743	21,151	24,315	117.0	105.6	104.0
New Hampshire.	8,757	18,450	28,719	15,861	21,546	26,750	99.0	107.6	114.5
New Jersey.	10,137	21,503	30,560	18,361	25,112	28,465	114.6	125.4	121.8
New Mexico	7,520	13,396	19,472	13,621	15,644	18,137	85.0	78.1	77.6
New York	9,480	19,899	28,296	17,171	23,238	26,356	107.1	116.1	112.8
North Carolina.	7,208	15,257	23,219	13,056	17,817	21,627	81.5	89.0	92.5
North Dakota.	7,085	14,320	22,229	12,833	16,723	20,705	80.1	83.5	88.6
Ohio	8,797	16,442	24,023	15,934	19,201	22,376	99.4	95.9	95.7
Oklahoma.	8,329	14,264	20,449	15,086	16,658	19,047	94.1	83.2	81.5
Oregon.	8,788	16,003	23,822	15,917	18,689	22,189	99.3	93.3	94.9
Pennsylvania.	8,817	17,433	25,117	15,970	20,359	23,395	99.7	101.7	100.1
Rhode Island	8,520	17,795	25,448	15,432	20,781	23,703	96.3	103.8	101.4
South Carolina.	6,880	14,199	21,048	12,462	16,582	19,605	77.8	82.8	83.9
South Dakota	7,362	14,846	23,301	13,335	17,337	21,704	83.2	86.6	92.9
Tennessee	7,449	15,193	23,154	13,492	17,743	21,567	84.2	88.6	92.3
Texas.	8,616	15,600	24,248	15,606	18,218	22,586	97.4	91.0	96.6
Utah	7,515	13,219	20,719	13,612	15,437	19,299	84.9	77.1	82.6
Vermont	7,663	15,838	23,007	13,880	18,496	21,430	86.6	92.4	91.7
Virginia	8,784	17,899	26,078	15,910	20,903	24,290	99.3	104.4	103.9
Washington.	9,544	17,761	26,855	17,287	20,742	25,014	107.9	103.6	107.0
West Virginia.	7,162	12,997	19,258	12,972	15,178	17,938	80.9	75.8	76.8
Wisconsin.	8,811	15,817	23,795	15,959	18,471	22,164	99.6	92.2	94.8
Wyoming	10,166	16,077	23,179	18,413	18,775	21,590	114.9	93.8	92.4

[1] Constant dollars based on the implicit price deflator for personal consumption expenditures.

Source: U.S. Bureau of Economic Analysis, *Survey of Current Business*, May 2001, unpublished data.

Income, Expenditures, and Wealth 427

No. 654. Personal Income by Selected Large Metropolitan Area: 1997 to 1999

[As defined June 30, 1994. CMSA=Consolidated Metropolitan Statistical Area; MSA=Metropolitan Statistical Area; PMSA=Primary Metropolitan Statistical Area. See Appendix II]

Metropolitan area ranked by 1999 income	Personal income				Per capita personal income			
	1997 (mil. dol.)	1998 (mil. dol.)	1999 (mil. dol.)	Annual percent change, 1998-99	1997 (dol.)	1998 (dol.)	1999 (dol.)	Percent of national average, 1999
United States	6,928,545	7,383,476	7,784,137	5.4	25,874	27,321	28,546	100.0
New York-No. New Jersey-Long Island, NY-NJ-CT-PA CMSA	690,088	733,999	774,748	5.6	34,663	36,705	38,539	135.0
Los Angeles-Riverside-Orange County, CA CMSA	397,751	425,958	449,834	5.6	25,558	26,966	28,050	98.3
New York, NY PMSA	298,362	318,126	338,168	6.3	34,492	36,653	38,814	136.0
Chicago-Gary-Kenosha, IL-IN-WI CMSA	268,636	287,137	300,846	4.8	30,661	32,544	33,857	118.6
San Francisco-Oakland-San Jose, CA CMSA. .	235,703	254,671	280,844	10.3	35,081	37,378	40,858	143.1
Chicago, IL PMSA	248,178	265,552	278,241	4.8	31,452	33,406	34,743	121.7
Los Angeles-Long Beach, CA PMSA	235,075	251,637	263,815	4.8	25,758	27,281	28,276	99.1
Washington-Baltimore, DC-MD-VA-WV CMSA	231,206	246,577	263,429	6.8	32,095	33,918	35,797	125.4
Boston-Worcester-Lawrence-Lowell-Brockton, MA-NH NECMA	185,695	199,622	214,141	7.3	31,869	34,044	36,285	127.1
Philadelphia-Wilmington-Atlantic City, PA-NJ-DE-MD CMSA.	175,748	185,987	194,352	4.5	29,404	31,067	32,397	113.5
Washington, DC-MD-VA-WV PMSA	158,227	169,627	182,032	7.3	34,384	36,390	38,403	134.5
Detroit-Ann Arbor-Flint, MI CMSA	152,659	161,651	170,312	5.4	28,052	29,645	31,140	109.1
Philadelphia, PA-NJ PMSA	146,477	154,869	161,501	4.3	29,635	31,316	32,627	114.3
Dallas-Fort Worth, TX CMSA	135,784	149,021	159,469	7.0	29,067	31,082	32,482	113.8
Houston-Galveston-Brazoria, TX CMSA	123,660	135,062	141,745	4.9	28,708	30,691	31,543	110.5
Detroit, MI PMSA	126,336	133,887	140,825	5.2	28,278	29,956	31,472	110.3
Houston, TX PMSA	112,925	123,578	129,901	5.1	29,393	31,470	32,386	113.5
Atlanta, GA MSA	105,565	116,171	125,302	7.9	29,064	31,028	32,486	113.8
Seattle-Tacoma-Bremerton, WA CMSA	101,627	111,582	121,483	8.9	30,177	32,600	35,052	122.8
Dallas, TX PMSA	96,196	105,999	113,794	7.4	30,859	33,096	34,690	121.5
Nassau-Suffolk, NY PMSA	95,132	99,841	104,197	4.4	35,771	37,372	38,751	135.7
Minneapolis-St. Paul, MN-WI MSA.	88,287	95,516	101,242	6.0	31,587	33,746	35,250	123.5
Miami-Fort Lauderdale, FL CMSA	89,755	94,768	99,018	4.5	24,870	25,902	26,682	93.5
Orange County, CA PMSA	81,395	87,626	93,333	6.5	30,536	32,171	33,805	118.4
Seattle-Bellevue-Everett, WA PMSA	76,080	84,641	93,116	10.0	33,484	36,616	39,880	139.7
Cleveland-Akron, OH CMSA	79,514	83,910	87,042	3.7	27,267	28,809	29,905	104.8
Denver-Boulder-Greeley, CO CMSA.	72,098	78,651	85,396	8.6	31,103	33,287	35,318	123.7
Oakland, CA PMSA.	72,106	77,261	83,769	8.4	31,741	33,374	35,666	124.9
San Francisco, CA PMSA.	70,441	77,548	83,769	8.0	42,150	46,071	49,695	174.1
Phoenix-Mesa, AZ MSA	71,071	77,606	83,228	7.2	25,013	26,480	27,617	96.7
San Diego, CA MSA	70,957	76,840	83,183	8.3	26,067	27,779	29,489	103.3
Baltimore, MD PMSA	70,139	74,017	78,309	5.8	28,343	29,834	31,434	110.1
St. Louis, MO-IL MSA	71,103	75,109	78,051	3.9	27,798	29,321	30,382	106.4
San Jose, CA PMSA	61,593	66,341	76,850	15.8	37,981	40,406	46,649	163.4
Newark, NJ PMSA	67,668	72,186	75,676	4.8	34,830	37,055	38,715	135.6
New Haven-Bridgprt-Stamford-Danbury-Waterbury, CT PMSA.	65,653	70,443	73,991	5.0	40,378	43,207	45,267	158.6
Denver, CO PMSA	60,223	65,665	71,359	8.7	31,678	33,906	36,058	126.3
Riverside-San Bernardino, CA PMSA	61,591	66,105	70,604	6.8	20,201	21,210	22,060	77.3
Pittsburgh, PA MSA.	63,415	65,697	68,977	5.0	26,878	28,014	29,587	103.6
Cleveland-Lorain-Elyria, OH PMSA	61,890	65,269	67,683	3.7	27,763	29,339	30,472	106.7
Portland-Salem, OR-WA CMSA	57,575	61,203	64,589	5.5	27,216	28,462	29,615	103.7
Tampa-St. Petersburg-Clearwater, FL MSA . . .	57,336	60,882	64,120	5.3	25,769	27,006	28,145	98.6
Cincinnati-Hamilton, OH-KY-IN CMSA	51,476	55,058	57,819	5.0	26,612	28,259	29,485	103.3
Portland-Vancouver, OR-WA PMSA	50,433	53,638	56,616	5.6	28,164	29,471	30,672	107.4
Bergen-Passaic, NJ PMSA	49,184	51,584	54,521	5.7	36,883	38,568	40,623	142.3
Miami, FL PMSA	49,081	51,561	53,811	4.4	23,020	23,972	24,733	86.6
Kansas City, MO-KS MSA	46,607	49,923	53,072	6.3	27,128	28,737	30,225	105.9
Milwaukee-Racine, WI CMSA	46,826	49,469	51,847	4.8	28,473	30,070	31,457	110.2
Sacramento-Yolo, CA CMSA.	43,278	46,428	49,736	7.1	25,771	27,190	28,568	100.1
Cincinnati, OH-KY-IN PMSA	43,593	46,662	48,996	5.0	27,133	28,849	30,105	105.5
Indianapolis, IN MSA	40,994	44,507	46,904	5.4	27,240	29,304	30,523	106.9
Milwaukee-Waukesha, WI PMSA	41,976	44,379	46,512	4.8	28,760	30,405	31,805	111.4
Fort Worth-Arlington, TX PMSA.	39,589	43,022	45,675	6.2	25,473	27,028	28,035	98.2
Sacramento, CA PMSA	39,412	42,394	45,530	7.4	25,796	27,276	28,718	100.6

Source: U.S. Bureau of Economic Analysis, Survey of Current Business, June 2001.

Flow of Funds Accounts—Composition of Individuals' Savings: 1990 to 1999

[In billions of dollars (567.7 represents 567,700,000,000). Combined statement for households, farm business, and nonfarm noncorporate business. Minus sign (-) indicates decrease]

Composition of savings	1990	1992	1993	1994	1995	1996	1997	1998	1999
Increase in financial assets	567.7	448.4	439.7	502.4	485.9	497.0	441.2	586.6	556.6
Foreign deposits	1.4	1.2	-1.1	3.1	4.6	12.4	6.3	-0.3	4.3
Checkable deposits and currency	-19.4	103.7	56.4	-24.2	-53.9	-50.7	-32.8	59.2	-14.2
Time and savings deposits	48.5	-76.9	-106.5	-4.0	173.2	175.7	190.2	202.3	115.6
Money market fund shares	26.9	-40.9	-0.3	13.5	98.8	56.6	89.7	145.4	103.9
Securities	179.0	179.3	140.8	151.4	-129.4	-107.2	-277.9	-275.0	-81.4
Open market paper	6.2	-3.3	15.6	1.2	1.3	7.4	3.6	4.2	5.3
U.S. government securities	114.2	78.9	-16.3	290.2	-48.0	27.7	-161.8	-153.8	100.7
Municipal securities	27.7	-27.0	-32.1	-50.2	-43.5	-22.2	53.6	15.3	48.3
Corporate and foreign bonds	43.1	2.3	31.3	30.5	95.0	46.2	75.4	60.4	32.3
Corporate equities [1]	-39.6	-5.6	-62.8	-187.6	-228.8	-347.2	-507.1	-462.7	-401.7
Mutual fund shares	27.5	133.9	205.1	67.4	94.7	180.8	258.4	261.6	133.6
Life insurance reserves	26.5	29.1	37.1	35.5	45.8	44.5	59.3	53.3	58.6
Pension fund reserves	249.4	244.3	267.9	254.4	235.4	247.6	304.4	303.9	287.4
Investment in bank personal trusts	32.9	-7.1	0.9	17.8	4.0	-8.6	-56.3	-48.0	-31.1
Miscellaneous assets	22.4	15.7	44.5	54.9	107.3	126.7	158.2	145.8	113.6
Gross investment in tangible assets	806.3	793.8	864.4	958.8	979.9	1,061.1	1,092.5	1,206.1	1,364.1
Minus: Consumption of fixed capital	593.5	639.0	649.2	690.6	709.3	729.6	755.7	784.7	840.7
Equals: Net investment in tangible assets	212.9	154.8	215.2	268.2	270.5	331.5	336.9	421.4	523.4
Net increase in liabilities	241.5	168.6	246.2	324.8	407.3	484.7	533.9	641.7	757.3
Mortgage debt on nonfarm homes	212.3	168.9	159.4	182.6	179.5	241.2	251.0	382.3	431.7
Other mortgage debt [2]	1.4	-39.4	-29.4	-29.6	-8.5	53.6	83.7	79.3	89.8
Consumer credit	11.9	6.1	58.4	124.9	138.9	88.8	52.5	67.6	94.4
Policy loans	4.1	5.7	5.6	7.8	10.5	4.5	3.2	0.1	-5.3
Security credit	-3.7	-1.6	22.6	-1.1	3.5	15.8	36.8	21.6	69.7
Other liabilities [2]	15.5	28.9	29.6	40.2	83.5	80.8	106.7	90.7	77.0
Personal saving with consumer durables [3]	539.1	434.7	408.7	445.7	349.1	343.8	244.2	366.3	322.7
Personal saving, without consumer durable [3]	466.3	379.6	323.0	332.7	223.8	202.7	88.3	170.7	101.7
Personal saving (NIPA, excludes consumer durables) [4]	334.3	413.7	350.8	315.6	302.4	272.1	271.1	229.7	156.3

[1] Only directly held and those in closed-end funds. Other equities are included in mutual funds, life insurance and pension reserves, and bank personal trusts. [2] Includes corporate farms. [3] Flow of Funds measure. [4] National Income and Product Accounts measure.

Source: Board of Governors of the Federal Reserve System, *Flow of Funds Accounts*, quarterly.

Annual Expenditure Per Child by Husband-Wife Families by Family Income and Expenditure Type: 2000

[In dollars. Expenditures based on data from the 1990-92 Consumer Expenditure Survey updated to 2000 dollars using the Consumer Price Index. Excludes expenses for college. For more on the methodology, see report cited below]

Age of child	Expenditure type							
	Total	Housing	Food	Transportation	Clothing	Health care	Child care and education	Miscellaneous [1]
INCOME: LESS THAN $38,000								
Less than 2 yrs. old	6,280	2,400	880	770	380	440	800	610
3 to 5 yrs. old	6,420	2,370	980	750	370	420	900	630
6 to 8 yrs. old	6,520	2,290	1,260	870	410	490	530	670
9 to 11 yrs. old	6,530	2,070	1,510	950	450	530	320	700
12 to 14 yrs. old	7,380	2,310	1,590	1,070	760	540	230	880
15 to 17 yrs. old	7,280	1,860	1,720	1,440	670	570	380	640
INCOME: $38,000-$64,000								
Less than 2 yrs. old	8,740	3,250	1,060	1,150	440	580	1,310	950
3 to 5 yrs. old	8,980	3,220	1,220	1,130	430	560	1,450	970
6 to 8 yrs. old	8,990	3,140	1,550	1,250	480	630	930	1,010
9 to 11 yrs. old	8,950	2,920	1,830	1,330	530	690	610	1,040
12 to 14 yrs. old	9,690	3,150	1,840	1,450	890	690	450	1,220
15 to 17 yrs. old	9,860	2,710	2,050	1,830	790	730	770	980
INCOME: MORE THAN $64,000								
Less than 2 yrs. old	13,000	5,160	1,400	1,610	580	670	1,980	1,600
3 to 5 yrs. old	13,280	5,130	1,580	1,590	570	640	2,160	1,610
6 to 8 yrs. old	13,160	5,050	1,910	1,710	620	730	1,490	1,650
9 to 11 yrs. old	13,020	4,830	2,220	1,790	680	790	1,030	1,680
12 to 14 yrs. old	13,870	5,070	2,330	1,910	1,120	790	790	1,860
15 to 17 yrs. old	14,260	4,620	2,450	2,310	1,020	840	1,390	1,630

[1] Expenses include personal care items, entertainment, and reading materials.

Source: Dept. of Agriculture, Center for Nutrition Policy and Promotion, *Expenditures on Children by Families, 2000 Annual Report*. See also <http://www.usda.gov/cnpp/Crc/Crc2000.pdf>.

Income, Expenditures, and Wealth   429

No. 657. Average Annual Expenditures of All Consumer Units by Type of Expenditure: 1990 to 1999

[In dollars. Based on Consumer Expenditure Survey. Data are averages for the noninstitutional population. Expenditures reported here are out-of-pocket]

Type	1990	1993	1994	1995	1996	1997	1998	1999
Number of consumer units (1,000)	96,968	100,049	102,210	103,024	104,212	105,576	107,182	108,465
Total expenditures	28,381	30,692	31,751	32,277	33,797	34,819	35,535	37,027
Food	4,296	4,399	4,411	4,505	4,698	4,801	4,810	5,031
Food at home	2,485	2,735	2,712	2,803	2,876	2,880	2,780	2,915
Meats, poultry, fish, and eggs . . .	668	734	732	752	737	743	723	749
Dairy products	295	295	289	297	312	314	301	322
Fruits and vegetables	408	444	437	457	490	476	472	500
Other food at home	746	827	825	856	889	895	858	896
Food away from home	1,811	1,664	1,698	1,702	1,823	1,921	2,030	2,116
Alcoholic beverages	293	268	279	277	309	309	309	318
Housing	8,703	9,636	10,106	10,465	10,747	11,272	11,713	12,057
Shelter	4,836	5,415	5,686	5,932	6,064	6,344	6,680	7,016
Fuels, utilities, public services	1,890	2,112	2,189	2,193	2,347	2,412	2,405	2,377
Apparel and services	1,618	1,676	1,644	1,704	1,752	1,729	1,674	1,743
Transportation	5,120	5,453	6,044	6,016	6,382	6,457	6,616	7,011
Vehicle purchase	2,129	2,319	2,725	2,639	2,815	2,736	2,964	3,305
Gasoline and motor oil	1,047	977	986	1,006	1,082	1,098	1,017	1,055
Other transportation	1,944	1,843	1,953	2,016	2,058	2,230	2,206	2,254
Health care	1,480	1,776	1,755	1,732	1,770	1,841	1,903	1,959
Entertainment	1,422	1,626	1,567	1,612	1,834	1,813	1,746	1,891
Reading	153	166	165	163	159	164	161	159
Tobacco products, smoking supplies . .	274	268	259	269	255	264	273	300
Personal insurance and pensions	2,593	2,908	2,957	2,967	3,060	3,223	3,381	3,436
Life and other personal insurance	345	399	398	374	353	379	398	394
Pensions and Social Security	2,248	2,509	2,559	2,593	2,707	2,844	2,982	3,042

Source: U.S. Bureau of Labor Statistics, *Consumer Expenditures in 1999*; and earlier reports.

No. 658. Average Annual Expenditures of All Consumer Units by Metropolitan Area: 1998-99

[In dollars. Metropolitan areas defined June 30, 1983, CMSA=Consolidated Metropolitan Statistical Area; MSA=Metropolitan Statistical Area; PMSA=Primary Metropolitan Statistical Area. See text, Section 1, Population, and Appendix II. See headnote, Table 657]

Metropolitan area	Total expendi-tures [1]	Food	Housing			Transportation			Health care
			Total [1]	Shelter	Utility, fuels [2]	Total [1]	Vehicle purchases	Gasoline and motor oil	
Anchorage, AK MSA	50,945	6,267	17,366	10,522	2,614	9,284	3,812	1,300	2,324
Atlanta, GA MSA	38,726	4,449	13,739	8,136	3,053	8,058	3,814	1,074	1,835
Baltimore, MD MSA	39,787	5,165	13,489	8,169	2,356	6,347	2,801	1,012	1,581
Boston-Lawrence-Salem, MA-NH CMSA	39,286	4,904	14,611	9,478	2,419	6,312	2,645	923	1,686
Chicago-Gary-Lake County, IL-IN-WI CMSA	38,156	5,092	13,732	8,408	2,647	6,233	2,779	928	1,951
Cincinnati-Hamilton, OH-KY-IN CMSA .	37,392	4,994	12,072	6,933	2,341	6,857	3,108	1,029	2,280
Cleveland-Akron-Lorain, OH CMSA . . .	37,692	4,940	11,944	6,942	2,523	7,133	3,471	916	1,661
Dallas-Fort Worth, TX CMSA	44,225	6,490	13,228	7,358	2,909	7,835	3,687	1,272	2,148
Denver-Boulder-Greeley, CO CMSA . .	44,414	5,172	15,415	9,726	2,200	8,233	3,116	1,107	1,915
Detroit-Ann Arbor, MI CMSA	38,120	5,580	13,018	7,599	2,607	7,162	2,854	1,054	1,701
Honolulu, HI MSA	42,472	6,300	14,672	10,076	2,032	5,354	999	1,060	2,188
Houston-Galveston-Brazoria, TX CMSA	43,043	5,624	13,109	7,167	2,882	9,569	5,039	1,243	1,919
Kansas City, MO-Kansas City, KS CMSA	36,955	5,115	11,421	6,538	2,597	7,789	3,948	1,155	2,043
Los Angeles-Long Beach, CA PMSA . .	43,225	5,204	15,934	10,087	2,267	7,551	2,976	1,157	1,757
Miami-Fort Lauderdale, FL CMSA	38,144	4,791	13,963	8,443	2,723	7,425	2,840	1,085	1,481
Milwaukee, WI PMSA	36,863	4,344	13,147	8,249	2,277	7,271	3,643	1,022	2,050
Minneapolis-St. Paul, MN-WI MSA . . .	48,444	5,778	14,973	8,811	2,284	8,847	4,175	1,172	2,262
New York-Northern New Jersey-Long Island, NY-NJ-CT CMSA	44,016	6,265	16,180	10,552	2,592	6,972	2,655	877	1,863
Philadelphia-Wilmington-Trenton, PA-NJ-DE-MD CMSA	40,149	4,753	14,783	9,239	2,841	7,896	3,865	869	1,781
Phoenix-Mesa, AZ MSA	40,193	4,981	12,893	7,725	2,458	8,212	4,035	1,016	2,007
Pittsburgh-Beaver Valley, PA CMSA . .	34,517	4,981	9,992	4,945	2,426	5,795	2,443	862	1,932
Portland-Vancouver, OR-WA CMSA . . .	43,331	5,855	13,847	8,708	2,160	8,117	4,123	1,103	1,837
San Diego, CA MSA	44,235	5,292	16,270	10,461	1,977	8,550	3,988	1,177	1,850
San Francisco-Oakland-San Jose, CA CMSA	51,016	6,963	18,059	11,886	2,193	8,186	3,164	1,232	1,792
Seattle-Tacoma, WA CMSA	44,078	6,080	14,899	9,387	2,263	7,650	2,867	1,216	1,931
St. Louis-East St. Louis-Alton, MO-IL CMSA	36,111	5,270	11,304	6,435	2,681	7,014	3,582	970	1,985
Tampa-St. Petersburg-Clearwater, FL MSA	32,932	4,750	11,044	6,258	2,457	5,986	2,602	900	2,294
Washington, DC-MD-VA MSA	46,797	5,358	16,381	10,472	2,640	8,171	3,914	1,040	2,202

[1] Includes expenditures not shown separately. [2] Includes public services.

Source: U.S. Bureau of Labor Statistics, *Consumer Expenditures*, annual; and Internet site <http://stats.bls.gov/csxmsa.htm#y9899> (released 21 December 2000).

No. 659. Average Annual Expenditures of All Consumer Units by Race, Hispanic Origin, and Age of Householder: 1999

[In dollars. Based on Consumer Expenditure Survey. Data are averages for the noninstitutional population. Expenditures reported here are out-of-pocket]

Item	All consumer units	Black	His-panic	Under 25 yrs.	25 to 34 yrs.	35 to 44 yrs.	45 to 54 yrs.	55 to 64 yrs.	65 yrs. and over
Expenditures, total	**37,027**	**27,374**	**33,105**	**21,725**	**36,181**	**42,836**	**46,538**	**39,427**	**26,553**
Food	5,031	4,146	5,493	3,354	5,140	6,109	5,945	5,056	3,511
Food at home	2,915	2,665	3,556	1,828	2,890	3,537	3,340	2,920	2,266
Cereals and bakery products	448	405	495	271	432	561	509	433	357
Cereals and cereal products	160	168	204	102	170	211	175	140	116
Bakery products	288	236	291	169	262	350	335	294	242
Meats, poultry, fish, and eggs	749	878	1,097	469	751	897	878	761	563
Beef	220	225	331	155	221	266	257	230	154
Pork	157	200	230	93	154	185	185	165	121
Other meats	97	94	128	61	95	119	111	94	77
Poultry	136	172	206	82	148	162	160	136	96
Fish and seafood	106	151	142	59	103	125	130	102	87
Eggs	32	36	60	19	31	40	34	35	27
Dairy products	322	233	377	195	322	410	354	305	255
Fresh milk and cream	122	87	165	78	124	158	130	107	99
Other dairy products	200	146	211	117	198	252	224	198	156
Fruits and vegetables	500	439	663	283	475	572	563	525	450
Fresh fruits	152	128	216	77	136	173	173	161	149
Fresh vegetables	149	116	224	79	146	161	168	171	131
Processed fruits	113	108	134	77	105	133	129	108	100
Processed vegetables	86	86	89	49	87	104	93	86	71
Other food at home	896	710	924	610	910	1,097	1,037	895	641
Nonalcoholic beverages	242	201	279	167	236	301	301	241	158
Food away from home	2,116	1,482	1,937	1,526	2,250	2,572	2,605	2,136	1,245
Alcoholic beverages	318	158	269	369	365	384	320	330	172
Housing	12,057	9,705	11,001	6,585	12,520	14,215	14,513	12,093	8,946
Shelter	7,016	5,500	6,778	4,140	7,613	8,605	8,534	6,660	4,578
Owned dwellings	4,525	2,674	3,186	596	3,936	6,110	6,203	4,813	2,973
Mortgage interest and charges	2,547	1,660	1,919	311	2,694	3,990	3,642	2,328	745
Property taxes	1,123	620	634	168	751	1,297	1,444	1,380	1,149
Rented dwellings	2,027	2,683	3,420	3,296	3,447	2,121	1,532	1,206	1,182
Other lodging	464	142	171	248	230	374	799	641	423
Utilities, fuels, and public services	2,377	2,403	2,124	1,166	2,249	2,587	2,819	2,608	2,145
Natural gas	270	296	228	92	238	283	304	327	284
Electricity	899	894	743	426	811	969	1,074	997	848
Fuel oil and other fuels	74	41	30	14	47	72	94	80	102
Telephone	849	934	872	562	924	950	1,008	869	614
Water and other public services	285	239	251	72	229	313	339	335	298
Household operations	666	457	470	181	772	830	606	476	746
Personal services	323	283	269	121	573	500	148	60	311
Other household expenses	343	173	201	60	199	330	459	416	435
Housekeeping supplies	498	362	445	221	441	604	574	570	423
Household furnishings and equipment	1,499	984	1,184	877	1,445	1,590	1,980	1,779	1,054
Household textiles	114	93	110	41	101	114	169	111	106
Furniture	365	304	352	283	435	403	446	382	205
Floor coverings	44	22	27	11	37	37	52	94	31
Major appliances	183	147	158	91	176	192	215	196	175
Miscellaneous household equipment	692	364	453	405	615	754	968	853	438
Apparel and services	1,743	1,877	2,071	1,192	2,047	2,053	2,048	1,722	1,070
Men and boys	421	369	525	238	519	517	517	406	219
Women and girls	655	726	651	422	709	764	817	671	416
Children under 2 years old	67	72	114	99	139	80	40	41	17
Footwear	303	464	490	234	374	373	327	308	165
Other apparel products and services	297	245	291	199	306	319	347	296	253
Transportation	7,011	5,106	6,801	5,037	7,150	8,041	9,010	7,330	4,385
Vehicle purchases (net outlay)	3,305	2,374	3,362	2,859	3,500	3,807	4,117	3,406	1,911
Cars and trucks, new	1,628	903	1,352	857	1,377	1,722	2,079	2,109	1,304
Cars and trucks, used	1,641	1,471	1,959	1,974	2,034	2,058	1,988	1,283	606
Gasoline and motor oil	1,055	757	1,116	708	1,066	1,259	1,349	1,093	644
Other vehicle expenses	2,254	1,683	1,979	1,253	2,249	2,565	3,085	2,339	1,443
Vehicle finance charges	320	267	276	209	402	394	431	320	104
Maintenance and repair	664	475	586	402	554	743	890	724	519
Vehicle insurance	756	591	672	408	705	806	1,052	803	566
Public transportation	397	292	344	217	335	411	459	492	387
Health care [1]	1,959	1,093	1,119	551	1,170	1,631	2,183	2,450	3,019
Entertainment [2]	1,891	935	1,245	1,149	1,776	2,254	2,368	2,176	1,239
Personal care products and services	408	401	404	254	381	471	475	449	333
Reading	159	81	71	70	116	157	210	195	163
Education	635	410	366	1,277	453	637	1,125	552	139
Tobacco products and smoking supplies	300	208	172	220	295	370	395	329	148
Miscellaneous	889	601	697	370	745	984	1,104	1,041	807
Cash contributions	1,190	544	679	186	589	1,074	1,426	1,762	1,640
Personal insurance and pensions	3,436	2,107	2,718	1,110	3,433	4,455	5,415	3,941	980
Life and other personal insurance	394	308	191	61	238	418	616	533	333
Pensions and social security	3,042	1,799	2,528	1,049	3,195	4,037	4,799	3,408	647
Personal taxes [1]	**3,588**	**1,562**	**2,334**	**845**	**3,065**	**3,963**	**5,363**	**6,628**	**1,256**

[1] For additional health care expenditures, see Table 130.   [2] For additional recreation expenditures, see Section 26, Arts, Entertainment, and Recreation.

Source: U.S. Bureau of Labor Statistics, *Consumer Expenditures in 1999*.

Income, Expenditures, and Wealth   431

No. 660. Average Annual Expenditures of All Consumer Units by Region and Size of Unit: 1999

[For composition of regions, see map, inside front cover. See headnote, Table 657]

Item	Region				Size of consumer unit				
	North-east	Mid west	South	West	One person	Two per-sons	Three per-sons	Four per-sons	Five or more
Expenditures, total	38,446	36,337	33,328	42,364	22,404	$38,895	42,885	49,119	47,581
Food	5,480	4,865	4,615	5,462	2,685	5,085	5,770	7,021	7,716
Food at home	3,084	2,740	2,729	3,245	1,449	2,843	3,412	4,098	4,966
Cereals and bakery products	487	428	416	485	222	423	535	658	754
Cereals and cereal products	170	149	153	174	73	141	191	248	300
Bakery products	317	280	263	311	149	282	343	410	454
Meats, poultry, fish, and eggs	830	655	739	793	340	743	875	1,020	1,377
Beef	238	209	212	229	91	218	261	298	428
Pork	147	151	170	151	67	158	182	204	306
Other meats	115	96	89	95	48	95	109	143	166
Poultry	162	105	136	147	63	129	162	192	254
Fish and seafood	133	71	100	130	55	110	126	140	163
Eggs	36	24	31	41	16	32	34	43	61
Dairy products	361	307	290	355	155	307	377	469	567
Fresh milk and cream	135	120	112	129	58	104	145	188	238
Other dairy products	226	187	178	226	98	202	232	281	329
Fruits and vegetables	564	438	451	584	264	509	563	678	805
Fresh fruits	177	131	129	192	85	154	169	202	248
Fresh vegetables	168	123	132	184	76	158	171	196	226
Processed fruits	136	100	101	125	60	113	126	158	184
Processed vegetables	84	84	89	84	42	85	97	121	147
Other food at home	843	912	832	1,029	468	861	1,063	1,273	1,462
Nonalcoholic beverages	224	243	233	270	128	234	287	344	382
Food away from home	2,396	2,126	1,887	2,216	1,236	2,243	2,357	2,923	2,750
Alcoholic beverages	367	324	256	365	286	378	314	291	259
Housing	13,365	11,526	10,338	14,201	8,207	12,171	13,618	15,954	14,992
Shelter	8,255	6,492	5,541	8,829	5,143	6,952	7,803	9,069	8,568
Owned dwellings	5,312	4,452	3,542	5,470	2,309	4,608	5,341	6,936	6,074
Mortgage interest and charges	2,628	2,385	2,027	3,474	1,004	2,264	3,247	4,558	4,015
Property taxes	1,843	1,213	765	962	731	1,238	1,184	1,505	1,282
Rented dwellings	2,423	1,599	1,645	2,743	2,517	1,745	2,003	1,599	2,108
Other lodging	520	441	354	616	317	599	459	534	385
Utilities, fuels, and public services	2,455	2,401	2,445	2,177	1,551	2,432	2,732	3,017	3,160
Natural gas	363	378	157	253	184	268	305	326	397
Electricity	844	829	1,087	726	566	934	1,025	1,162	1,196
Fuel oil and other fuels	189	65	42	35	45	91	79	94	75
Telephone	846	858	862	822	592	847	994	1,050	1,094
Water and other public services	213	272	296	342	165	292	330	385	398
Household operations	658	587	555	933	469	489	810	1,189	837
Personal services	288	327	264	441	193	108	478	760	518
Other household expenses	370	260	291	492	276	381	331	429	319
Housekeeping supplies	502	541	458	512	238	542	551	726	711
Household furnishings and equipment	1,496	1,506	1,339	1,749	807	1,756	1,723	1,953	1,717
Household textiles	118	122	94	134	69	127	135	131	147
Furniture	364	336	352	418	198	389	428	533	443
Floor coverings	44	47	40	46	21	61	50	49	39
Major appliances	200	181	171	189	109	215	190	239	210
Small appliances, misc. housewares	104	108	85	118	69	137	94	104	92
Miscellaneous household equipment	666	711	597	844	340	826	826	898	786
Apparel and services	1,817	1,591	1,598	2,070	933	1,645	1,982	2,698	2,690
Men and boys	434	452	351	487	175	399	461	708	743
Women and girls	684	574	628	760	337	674	734	1,007	897
Children under 2 years old	69	60	69	69	10	33	131	117	168
Footwear	301	272	298	347	135	262	352	491	582
Other apparel products and services	329	233	253	407	276	277	303	376	300
Transportation	6,466	6,939	6,863	7,802	3,536	7,427	8,726	9,486	9,665
Vehicle purchases (net outlay)	2,706	3,382	3,466	3,495	1,507	3,525	4,172	4,584	4,702
Cars and trucks, new	1,516	1,451	1,777	1,681	753	2,004	2,006	1,916	2,001
Cars and trucks, used	1,179	1,905	1,647	1,755	728	1,493	2,113	2,605	2,672
Gasoline and motor oil	907	1,038	1,069	1,180	565	1,065	1,280	1,440	1,556
Other vehicle expenses	2,315	2,169	2,043	2,625	1,215	2,333	2,869	3,046	2,952
Vehicle finance charges	232	337	362	314	120	301	468	483	505
Maintenance and repair	661	572	613	847	382	693	807	883	862
Vehicle insurance	825	722	709	807	429	784	952	1,009	963
Public transportation	538	349	286	503	250	505	405	415	455
Health care [1]	1,804	2,087	1,956	1,962	1,336	2,475	1,946	2,070	2,024
Entertainment [2]	1,828	2,067	1,567	2,268	1,040	2,038	2,291	2,638	2,236
Personal care products and services	404	401	385	457	254	434	474	519	516
Reading	195	166	117	189	122	185	171	182	136
Education	939	568	452	728	421	507	795	1,013	874
Tobacco products and smoking supplies	318	346	302	232	189	301	372	387	385
Miscellaneous	858	875	793	1,081	688	907	1,091	999	942
Cash contributions	1,113	1,163	1,141	1,365	1,018	1,542	1,071	921	1,158
Personal insurance and pensions	3,494	3,418	2,946	4,181	1,689	3,798	4,264	4,941	3,988
Life and other personal insurance	403	378	411	379	133	454	475	643	497
Pensions and social security	3,092	3,041	2,535	3,801	1,556	3,345	3,790	4,298	3,491
Personal taxes	3,819	4,388	2,483	4,193	2,218	3,622	3,892	6,612	2,866

[1] For additional health care expenditures, see Table 130.   [2] For additional recreation expenditures, see Section 26, Arts, Entertainment, and Recreation.

Source: U.S. Bureau of Labor Statistics, Consumer Expenditures in 1999.

No. 661. Money Income of Households—Percent Distribution by Income Level, Race, and Hispanic Origin, in Constant (1999) Dollars: 1970 to 1999

[Constant dollars based on CPI-U deflator. Households as of March of following year. Based on Current Population Survey; see text, Sections 1 and 13, and Appendix III. For definition of median, see Guide to Tabular Presentation]

Year	Number of house-holds (1,000)	Percent distribution							Median income (dollars)
		Under $10,000	$10,000-$14,999	$15,000-$24,999	$25,000-$34,999	$35,000-$49,999	$50,000-$74,999	$75,000 and over	
ALL HOUSEHOLDS [1]									
1970	64,778	12.9	7.4	14.5	15.2	21.2	18.7	10.1	35,232
1980	82,368	11.6	8.2	15.3	13.9	18.4	19.4	13.1	35,851
1985	88,458	11.8	7.8	15.1	13.6	17.6	18.4	15.8	36,568
1990	94,312	11.0	7.4	14.3	13.7	17.5	18.5	17.6	38,168
1995	99,627	10.8	8.0	15.0	13.6	16.6	18.0	17.9	37,251
1996	101,018	11.0	8.1	14.6	13.4	16.1	18.3	18.5	37,686
1997	102,528	10.6	7.8	14.6	12.9	16.3	18.3	19.7	38,411
1998	103,874	10.1	7.6	13.8	13.1	15.8	18.7	20.9	39,744
1999	104,705	9.2	7.3	14.1	12.7	15.8	18.4	22.6	40,816
WHITE									
1970	57,575	11.7	6.9	13.9	15.1	21.9	19.7	10.9	36,696
1980	71,872	10.1	7.6	14.9	14.0	18.9	20.5	14.1	37,822
1985	76,576	10.1	7.4	14.6	13.7	18.0	19.3	16.9	38,565
1990	80,968	9.2	7.0	14.1	13.8	17.9	19.3	18.7	39,809
1995	84,511	9.3	7.6	14.7	13.6	16.9	18.7	19.1	39,099
1996	85,059	9.3	7.7	14.4	13.4	16.4	19.1	19.7	39,459
1997	86,106	9.1	7.5	14.3	12.8	16.4	19.0	21.0	40,453
1998	87,212	8.5	7.2	13.5	13.1	16.0	19.5	22.1	41,816
1999	87,671	7.8	7.0	13.9	12.6	16.0	19.1	23.7	42,504
BLACK									
1970	6,180	23.4	12.2	20.2	15.8	15.0	9.9	3.6	22,336
1980	8,847	24.0	13.0	18.9	13.8	14.3	11.0	5.0	21,790
1985	9,797	24.5	11.1	18.7	13.3	14.3	11.5	6.6	22,945
1990	10,671	24.8	10.8	16.2	13.5	14.8	12.3	7.6	23,805
1995	11,577	22.0	11.0	17.6	14.2	14.5	12.6	8.0	24,480
1996	12,109	21.8	11.4	17.0	13.9	14.5	13.2	8.2	24,934
1997	12,474	20.7	10.4	17.9	13.9	15.0	13.6	8.5	26,002
1998	12,579	21.1	10.3	17.3	13.6	14.3	13.4	10.0	25,911
1999	12,849	18.5	10.1	16.4	13.7	14.7	14.0	12.6	27,910
HISPANIC [2]									
1970	(NA)	(NA)	(NA)	(NA)	(NA)	(NA)	(NA)	(NA)	(NA)
1980	3,906	15.2	10.4	20.2	16.1	16.5	14.9	6.8	27,634
1985	5,213	16.4	11.4	18.9	15.3	16.7	13.2	8.1	27,041
1990	6,220	15.4	10.8	18.4	15.7	17.3	13.6	8.8	28,463
1995	7,939	17.9	11.5	20.4	15.2	14.5	12.6	7.8	24,990
1996	8,225	16.1	11.4	19.9	15.4	15.4	12.7	8.9	26,445
1997	8,590	16.1	10.5	19.5	15.0	16.5	12.5	10.0	27,640
1998	9,060	14.7	10.7	17.8	16.2	15.6	14.3	10.7	28,956
1999	9,319	11.9	9.7	18.9	15.8	16.7	15.2	11.9	30,735

NA Not available. [1] Includes other races not shown separately. [2] Persons of Hispanic origin may be of any race.

No. 662. Money Income of Households—Median Income by Race and Hispanic Origin, in Current and Constant (1999) Dollars: 1980 to 1999

[In dollars. See headnote, Table 661]

Year	Median income in current dollars					Median income in constant (1999) dollars				
	All house-holds [1]	White	Black	Asian, Pacific Islander	His-panic [2]	All house-holds [1]	White	Black	Asian, Pacific Islander	His-panic [2]
1980	17,710	18,684	10,764	(NA)	13,651	35,851	37,822	21,790	(NA)	27,634
1985	23,618	24,908	14,819	(NA)	17,465	36,568	38,565	22,945	(NA)	27,041
1986 [3]	24,897	26,175	15,080	(NA)	18,352	37,845	39,788	22,922	(NA)	27,897
1987 [3]	26,061	27,458	15,672	(NA)	19,336	38,220	40,268	22,984	(NA)	28,357
1988	27,225	28,781	16,407	32,267	20,359	38,340	40,532	23,105	45,441	28,672
1989	28,906	30,406	18,083	36,102	21,921	38,836	40,852	24,295	48,505	29,452
1990	29,943	31,231	18,676	38,450	22,330	38,168	39,809	23,805	49,012	28,463
1991	30,126	31,569	18,807	36,449	22,691	36,850	38,615	23,005	44,584	27,756
1992 [4]	30,636	32,209	18,755	37,801	22,597	36,379	38,246	22,270	44,887	26,833
1993	31,241	32,960	19,533	38,347	22,886	36,019	38,001	22,521	44,211	26,386
1994	32,264	34,028	21,027	40,482	23,421	36,270	38,253	23,638	45,507	26,329
1995	34,076	35,766	22,393	40,614	22,860	37,251	39,099	24,480	44,397	24,990
1996	35,492	37,161	23,482	43,276	24,906	37,686	39,459	24,934	45,952	26,445
1997	37,005	38,972	25,050	45,249	26,628	38,411	40,453	26,002	46,969	27,640
1998	38,885	40,912	25,351	46,637	28,330	39,744	41,816	25,911	47,667	28,956
1999	40,816	42,504	27,910	51,205	30,735	40,816	42,504	27,910	51,205	30,735

NA Not available. [1] Includes other races not shown separately. [2] Persons of Hispanic origin may be of any race. [3] Beginning 1987, data based on revised processing procedures and not directly comparable with prior years. [4] Based on 1990 census population controls.

Source of Tables 661 and 662: U.S. Census Bureau, *Current Population Reports*, P60-209; and Internet site <http://www.census.gov/hhes/income/histinc/h05.html> (released 20 September 2001).

Income, Expenditures, and Wealth 433

No. 663. Money Income of Households—Distribution by Income Level and Selected Characteristics: 1999

Characteristic	Number of house- holds (1,000)	Number (1,000)							Median income (dollars)
		Under $10,000	$10,000- $14,999	$15,000- $24,999	$25,000- $34,999	$35,000- $49,999	$50,000- $74,999	$75,000 and over	
Total [1]	104,705	9,656	7,660	14,720	13,271	16,539	19,272	23,586	40,816
Age of householder:									
15 to 24 years.	5,860	1,043	605	1,255	1,049	930	640	337	25,171
25 to 34 years	18,627	1,229	1,011	2,448	2,752	3,489	4,157	3,540	42,174
35 to 44 years	23,955	1,315	973	2,538	2,831	4,066	5,503	6,729	50,873
45 to 54 years	20,927	1,255	844	1,754	1,989	3,210	4,494	7,382	56,917
55 to 64 years	13,592	1,422	917	1,499	1,525	2,113	2,491	3,625	44,597
65 years and over	21,745	3,393	3,311	5,225	3,125	2,731	1,987	1,974	22,812
White	87,671	6,856	6,100	12,154	11,071	13,999	16,731	20,760	42,504
Black	12,849	2,368	1,299	2,109	1,755	1,886	1,804	1,629	27,910
Hispanic [2]	9,319	1,106	900	1,761	1,471	1,553	1,413	1,114	30,735
Region:									
Northeast	20,087	1,931	1,536	2,740	2,358	2,865	3,536	5,121	41,984
Midwest	24,508	2,077	1,670	3,385	2,924	3,996	4,996	5,461	42,679
South	37,303	3,841	2,968	5,503	5,044	5,986	6,460	7,502	37,442
West	22,808	1,807	1,486	3,093	2,946	3,692	4,280	5,504	42,720
Size of household:									
One person	26,724	5,650	4,101	5,529	3,966	3,449	2,402	1,627	21,083
Two persons	34,666	1,995	2,003	4,997	4,755	5,915	6,934	8,067	43,342
Three persons	17,152	1,001	686	1,937	1,854	2,856	3,880	4,937	51,190
Four persons	15,309	575	458	1,207	1,440	2,490	3,635	5,505	59,768
Five persons	6,981	272	251	638	783	1,177	1,580	2,279	54,440
Six persons	2,445	102	107	261	282	423	508	761	51,887
Seven or more persons	1,428	60	55	151	190	229	334	410	52,146
Type of household:									
Family households	72,025	3,737	3,264	8,479	8,513	12,062	15,462	20,509	49,940
Married-couple	55,311	1,317	1,669	5,439	5,961	9,194	13,032	18,698	56,827
Male householder, wife absent	4,028	216	229	537	598	831	807	810	41,838
Female householder, husband absent	12,687	2,203	1,365	2,503	1,955	2,037	1,622	1,001	26,164
Nonfamily households . . .	32,680	5,919	4,397	6,241	4,758	4,477	3,810	3,077	24,566
Male householder	14,641	1,950	1,378	2,551	2,325	2,372	2,164	1,900	30,753
Female householder . .	18,039	3,969	3,019	3,690	2,432	2,105	1,646	1,178	19,917
Educational attainment of householder: [3]									
Total	98,845	8,613	7,055	13,465	12,222	15,609	18,632	23,249	42,038
Less than 9th grade	6,800	1,786	1,181	1,517	919	662	502	233	17,261
9th to 12th grade (no diploma).	8,974	1,845	1,258	1,957	1,340	1,232	944	400	21,737
High school graduate	30,846	2,838	2,580	5,206	4,461	5,444	5,870	4,448	35,744
Some college, no degree . .	17,986	1,051	999	2,477	2,370	3,312	3,810	3,966	44,149
Associate degree	7,755	352	410	836	1,009	1,330	1,821	1,996	49,279
Bachelor's degree or more	26,484	743	626	1,472	2,124	3,628	5,685	12,205	69,804
Bachelor's degree	17,144	526	469	1,063	1,594	2,577	3,799	7,115	64,406
Master's degree	6,336	137	104	325	388	788	1,446	3,148	74,476
Professional degree	1,651	34	45	57	79	160	193	1,082	100,000
Doctorate degree	1,353	44	9	27	63	103	246	860	97,325
Work experience of householder:									
Total	104,705	9,656	7,660	14,720	13,271	16,539	19,272	23,586	40,816
Worked	75,166	3,102	3,214	8,449	9,468	13,121	16,646	21,165	50,246
Worked at full-time jobs .	65,248	1,790	2,285	6,800	8,094	11,715	15,096	19,467	52,261
50 weeks or more	55,487	658	1,438	5,173	6,708	10,216	13,556	17,739	55,619
27 to 49 weeks	6,316	414	493	1,021	899	1,020	1,131	1,338	38,868
26 weeks or less	3,445	718	354	606	487	480	409	391	26,001
Worked at part-time jobs	9,918	1,312	930	1,649	1,374	1,406	1,551	1,698	32,586
50 weeks or more	5,153	455	467	876	681	796	881	997	36,594
27 to 49 weeks	2,198	266	206	373	339	276	380	359	32,015
26 weeks or less	2,567	590	257	400	354	334	290	342	26,079
Did not work	29,539	6,554	4,446	6,271	3,803	3,418	2,626	2,421	20,627

[1] Includes other races not shown separately. [2] Persons of Hispanic origin may be of any race. [3] Persons 25 years old and over.

Source: U.S. Census Bureau, *Current Population Reports*, P60-209, *Money Income in the United States: 1999*. See also <http://www.census.gov/prod/2000pubs/p60-209.pdf>.

No. 664. Household Income Before and After Taxes in Current and Constant (1999) Dollars: 1980 to 1999

[In dollars, except as indicated. Households as of March of the following year. Income in current and 1999 CPI-U-X1 adjusted dollars]

Year	Number of house-holds (1,000)	Current dollars				Constant (1999) dollars			
		Mean		Median		Mean		Median	
		Before taxes	After taxes	Before taxes	After taxes	Before taxes	After taxes	Before taxes	After taxes
1980	82,368	21,063	16,272	17,710	14,551	42,638	32,939	35,850	29,456
1985 [1]	88,458	29,066	22,646	23,618	19,401	45,004	35,063	36,568	30,039
1990	94,312	37,403	29,188	29,943	24,546	47,677	37,205	38,168	31,288
1991 [2]	95,669	37,922	29,640	30,126	24,955	46,386	36,256	36,850	30,525
1992 [2]	96,426	38,840	30,425	30,636	25,474	46,121	36,128	36,379	30,249
1993 [3]	97,107	41,428	32,092	31,241	26,112	47,764	37,000	36,019	30,106
1994 [4]	98,990	43,133	33,315	32,264	26,973	48,488	37,451	36,270	30,322
1995 [5]	99,627	44,938	34,592	34,076	28,249	49,125	37,815	37,251	30,881
1996	101,018	47,123	36,008	35,492	29,312	50,036	38,234	37,686	31,124
1997	102,528	49,692	37,656	37,005	30,648	51,581	39,087	38,411	31,813
1998	103,874	51,855	38,963	38,885	32,064	53,000	39,824	39,744	32,772
1999	104,705	54,842	40,761	40,816	33,676	54,842	40,761	40,816	33,676

[1] Recording of amounts for earnings from longest job increased to $299,999. Full implementation of 1980 census-based sample design. [2] Implementation of 1990 census population controls. [3] Data collection method changed from paper and pencil to computer assisted interviewing. In addition, the March 1994 income supplement was revised to allow for the coding of different income amounts on selected questionnaire items. Limits either increased or decreased in the following categories: earnings increased to $999,999; social security increased to $49,999; supplemental security income and public assistance increased to $24,999; veterans' benefits increased to $99,999; child support and alimony decreased to $49,999. [4] Introduction of 1990 census sample design. [5] Full implementation of the 1990 census-based sample design and metropolitan definitions, 7,000 household sample reduction, and revised race edits.

Source: U.S. Census Bureau, Internet site <http://www.census.gov/hhes/income/histinc/rdi02.html> (accessed 7 May 2001).

No. 665. Mean-Taxes Paid and Taxes Paid as a Percentage of Total Mean Before-Tax Income by Type of Tax in Current and Constant (1999) Dollars: 1980 to 1999

[Households as of March of the following year. Mean taxes paid in current and 1999 CPI-U-X1 adjusted dollars]

Type of tax and year	Number (1,000)	Mean taxes paid		As a per-cent of mean before-tax income	Type of tax and year	Number (1,000)	Mean taxes paid		As a per-cent of mean before-tax income
		Current dollars (dollars)	Constant 1999 dollars (dollars)				Current dollars (dollars)	Constant 1999 dollars (dollars)	
One or more taxes paid:					1994 [4]	63,626	2,194	2,466	4.1
1980	76,171	5,180	10,486	23.1	1995 [5]	64,827	2,296	2,510	4.2
1985	81,943	6,947	10,756	22.5	1996	65,856	2,467	2,620	4.3
1990	87,597	8,896	11,340	22.4	1997	67,164	2,674	2,776	4.5
1991	88,636	9,007	11,017	22.3	1998	68,924	2,898	2,962	4.7
1992	89,232	9,178	10,898	22.2	1999	70,643	3,138	3,138	4.8
1993	89,561	10,217	11,780	23.1	FICA payroll taxes:				
1994	91,540	10,768	12,105	23.4	1980	62,061	1,114	2,255	5.3
1995	92,754	11,292	12,344	23.7	1985 [1]	66,090	1,894	2,933	5.6
1996	94,236	12,118	12,867	24.3	1990	70,942	2,692	3,431	6.2
1997	95,850	13,077	13,574	24.9	1991 [2]	71,466	2,807	3,434	6.3
1998	97,254	13,990	14,299	25.5	1992 [2]	72,516	2,889	3,431	6.3
1999	98,755	15,151	15,151	26.3	1993 [3]	72,264	2,961	3,414	6.1
Federal income taxes:					1994 [4]	74,050	3,107	3,493	6.1
1980	61,316	4,011	8,119	15.3	1995 [5]	75,096	3,193	3,491	6.1
1985 [1]	68,019	4,675	7,238	13.2	1996	76,724	3,330	3,536	6.0
1990	70,255	5,806	7,401	12.4	1997	77,999	3,508	3,641	6.1
1991 [2]	69,842	5,901	7,218	12.3	1998	79,150	3,686	3,767	6.1
1992 [2]	68,957	6,029	7,159	12.1	1999	80,626	3,868	3,868	6.1
1993 [3]	68,786	7,098	8,184	13.3	Property taxes on own home:				
1994 [4]	69,501	7,591	8,533	13.5	1980	52,328	575	1,164	2.3
1995 [5]	70,926	7,935	8,674	13.7	1985 [1]	53,298	811	1,256	2.3
1996	72,009	8,637	9,171	14.3	1990	58,472	1,125	1,434	2.5
1997	73,941	9,445	9,804	14.9	1991 [2]	59,403	1,119	1,369	2.5
1998	74,354	10,121	10,345	15.2	1992 [2]	59,838	1,213	1,440	2.6
1999	76,041	11,096	11,096	15.9	1993 [3]	60,554	1,230	1,418	2.5
State income taxes:					1994 [4]	62,121	1,257	1,413	2.4
1980	52,591	859	1,739	3.3	1995 [5]	63,377	1,361	1,488	2.5
1985 [1]	57,033	1,330	2,059	3.8	1996	64,559	1,433	1,522	2.6
1990	61,875	1,710	2,180	3.8	1997	65,998	1,390	1,443	2.3
1991 [2]	62,314	1,761	2,154	3.8	1998	66,859	1,586	1,621	2.6
1992 [2]	62,247	1,837	2,181	3.9	1999	68,207	1,584	1,584	2.4
1993 [3]	62,459	2,045	2,358	4.4					

[1] See footnote 1, Table 664.   [2] See footnote 2, Table 664.   [3] See footnote 3, Table 664.   [4] See footnote 4, Table 664.
[5] See footnote 5, Table 664.

Source: U.S. Census Bureau, Internet site <http://www.census.gov/hhes/income/histinc/rdi02.html> (accessed 7 May 2001).

Income, Expenditures, and Wealth   435

Money Income of Households—Median Income and Income Level by Household Type: 1999

[See headnote, Table 661]

Item	Family households					Nonfamily households		
	All house-holds	Total	Married couple	Male house-holder, wife absent	Female house-holder, husband absent	Total [1]	Single-person household	
							Male house-holder	Female house-holder
MEDIAN INCOME (dollars)								
All households...............	**40,816**	**49,940**	**56,827**	**41,838**	**26,164**	**24,566**	**26,852**	**17,347**
White	42,504	51,912	57,242	42,401	29,629	25,161	27,375	17,720
Black	27,910	33,805	50,758	37,825	19,133	19,860	22,022	14,036
Hispanic [2]	30,735	33,077	37,583	34,320	20,765	20,462	19,637	10,787
NUMBER (1,000)								
All households...............	**104,705**	**72,025**	**55,311**	**4,028**	**12,687**	**32,680**	**14,641**	**18,039**
Under $5,000...................	3,010	1,547	585	88	874	1,463	648	815
$5,000 to $9,999................	6,646	2,190	732	129	1,329	4,456	1,302	3,154
$10,000 to $14,999	7,660	3,263	1,670	229	1,365	4,397	1,378	3,019
$15,000 to $19,999	7,482	4,189	2,563	264	1,361	3,294	1,232	2,062
$20,000 to $24,999	7,238	4,291	2,875	273	1,143	2,948	1,320	1,629
$25,000 to $34,999	13,272	8,513	5,960	598	1,955	4,757	2,326	2,433
$35,000 to $49,999	16,540	12,062	9,193	831	2,037	4,477	2,373	2,105
$50,000 to $74,999	19,272	15,463	13,033	807	1,622	3,810	2,164	1,646
$75,000 to $99,999	10,755	9,321	8,298	402	621	1,435	862	571
$100,000 and over	12,831	11,187	10,399	407	381	1,644	1,038	607

[1] Includes other nonfamily households not shown separately.   [2] Persons of Hispanic origin may be of any race.

Source: U.S. Census Bureau, *Current Population Reports*, P60-209, *Money Income in the United States: 1999*. See also <http://www.census.gov/prod/2000pubs/p60-209.pdf>.

No. 667. Money Income of Households—Median Income by State in Constant (1999) Dollars: 1990 to 1999

[**Constant dollars based on the CPI-U-X1 deflator.** Data based on the Current Population Survey; see text, Sections 1 and 13, and Appendix III. The CPS is designed to collect reliable data on income primarily at the national level and secondarily at the regional level. When the income data are tabulated by state, the estimates are considered less reliable and, therefore, particular caution should be used when trying to interpret the results]

State	1990	1995 [1]	1997	1998	1999	State	1990	1995 [1]	1997	1998	1999
U.S. ...	**38,168**	**37,251**	**38,411**	**39,744**	**40,816**						
						MO	34,839	38,070	37,942	41,089	41,466
AL	29,773	28,413	33,153	37,067	36,213	MT......	29,796	30,343	30,322	32,274	31,244
AK......	50,092	52,422	49,818	51,812	51,509	NE......	35,031	35,997	36,011	37,217	38,787
AZ......	37,251	33,739	33,984	37,909	37,119	NV......	40,819	39,446	40,331	40,634	41,680
AR......	29,045	28,219	27,156	28,276	29,762	NH......	52,013	42,821	42,556	45,951	46,167
CA......	42,434	40,457	41,203	41,838	43,744						
						NJ	49,373	48,017	49,846	50,926	49,930
CO......	39,175	44,499	44,876	47,628	48,346	NM.....	31,917	28,413	31,229	32,240	32,475
CT......	49,547	43,993	45,657	47,535	50,798	NY......	40,268	36,105	37,159	38,220	40,058
DE......	39,265	38,182	44,669	42,374	46,839	NC......	33,561	34,959	37,202	36,630	37,340
DC......	34,916	33,613	33,071	34,171	38,686	ND......	32,203	31,799	32,864	30,973	32,877
FL......	34,015	32,517	33,688	35,680	35,876						
						OH......	38,257	38,197	37,507	39,785	39,617
GA......	35,131	37,276	38,056	39,519	39,433	OK......	31,082	28,763	32,543	34,472	32,919
HI	49,612	46,844	42,490	41,729	44,373	OR......	37,324	39,763	38,663	39,930	40,713
ID	32,256	35,721	34,674	37,490	35,906	PA......	36,972	37,741	38,943	39,877	37,995
IL.......	41,480	41,618	42,852	44,132	46,392	RI	40,749	38,654	36,119	41,585	42,936
IN	34,324	36,496	40,367	40,608	40,929						
						SC......	36,628	31,780	35,564	34,002	36,563
IA	34,783	38,829	35,067	37,837	41,238	SD......	31,320	32,334	30,823	33,510	35,982
KS......	38,134	33,168	37,857	37,522	37,476	TN......	28,797	31,719	31,800	34,844	36,536
KY......	31,586	32,588	37,053	37,053	33,901	TX......	35,982	35,024	36,408	36,573	38,978
LA......	28,559	30,553	34,524	32,436	32,695	UT......	38,421	39,879	44,401	45,277	46,094
ME......	35,008	37,013	34,018	36,427	38,932						
						VT......	39,640	36,976	36,385	40,242	41,630
MD.....	49,530	44,865	48,459	51,121	52,310	VA......	44,707	39,597	44,590	44,312	45,750
MA.....	46,203	42,168	43,620	43,280	44,192	WA	40,932	38,882	46,256	48,468	45,639
MI	38,160	39,820	40,214	42,745	46,238	WV	28,217	27,198	28,533	27,294	29,433
MN.....	40,108	41,467	44,182	48,984	47,240	WI	39,147	44,771	41,100	42,240	45,825
MS.....	25,720	29,011	29,582	29,763	32,540	WY	37,552	34,467	34,693	36,029	37,395

[1] Full implementation of the 1990 census-based sample design and metropolitan definitions, 7,000 household sample reduction, and revised race edits.

Source: U.S. Census Bureau, *Current Population Reports*, P60-209; and <http://www.census.gov/hhes/income/histinc/ho8.html> (released 20 September 2000).

No. 668. Money Income of Families—Percent Distribution by Income Level, Race, and Hispanic Origin, in Constant (1999) Dollars: 1980 to 1999

[Constant dollars based on CPI-U deflator. Families as of March of following year. Beginning with 1980, based on householder concept and restricted to primary families. Based on Current Population Survey; see text, Sections 1 and 13, and Appendix III. For definition of median, see Guide to Tabular Presentation]

Year	Number of families (1,000)	Under $10,000	$10,000-$14,999	$15,000-$24,999	$25,000-$34,999	$35,000-$49,999	$50,000-$74,999	$75,000 and over	Median income (dollars)
ALL FAMILIES [1]									
1980	60,309	6.1	6.1	13.6	14.0	20.3	23.5	16.4	42,557
1985	63,558	7.1	5.7	13.5	13.5	18.9	21.8	19.5	42,943
1990	66,322	6.7	5.4	12.3	13.2	18.6	21.8	22.1	45,064
1995	69,597	6.5	5.8	13.0	13.4	17.6	21.2	22.4	44,395
1997	70,884	6.6	5.3	12.7	12.4	17.3	21.4	24.4	46,262
1998	71,551	6.3	5.1	12.1	12.5	16.4	21.7	25.9	47,769
1999	72,031	5.7	4.8	12.0	11.9	16.5	21.2	27.9	48,950
WHITE									
1980	52,710	4.8	5.2	12.9	13.9	20.9	24.7	17.6	44,340
1985	54,991	5.6	5.0	12.8	13.4	19.4	22.8	20.9	45,136
1990	56,803	5.0	4.6	11.9	13.2	19.0	22.8	23.5	47,055
1995	58,872	5.0	5.2	12.5	13.3	17.9	22.2	24.0	46,619
1997	59.515	5.2	4.7	12.1	12.3	17.4	22.2	26.2	48,531
1998	60,077	4.9	4.6	11.3	12.5	16.7	22.5	27.⌣	50,106
1999	60,256	4.4	4.2	11.6	11.8	16.7	22.1	29.3	51,224
BLACK									
1980	6,317	16.3	13.3	19.5	14.5	16.2	13.7	6.4	25,656
1985	6,921	19.3	10.8	18.8	14.0	15.5	13.7	8.0	25,991
1990	7,471	19.3	11.3	15.6	13.5	16.2	14.5	9.6	27,307
1995	8,055	17.7	10.2	17.2	14.4	15.8	14.4	10.3	28,389
1997	8,408	16.4	9.5	17.7	13.6	15.8	16.3	10.7	29,690
1998	8,452	15.6	9.0	18.1	13.4	14.9	16.1	12.8	30,053
1999	8,664	14.6	9.1	16.0	13.6	15.3	15.8	15.6	31,778
ASIAN AND PACIFIC ISLANDER									
1990	1,536	6.2	3.9	10.8	10.3	14.7	21.5	32.6	53,851
1995	2,125	7.0	6.0	9.6	11.3	15.7	22.1	28.3	50,675
1997	2,381	5.4	5.2	8.7	9.6	17.5	21.4	32.1	53,820
1998	2,459	7.3	3.6	9.4	10.3	15.3	20.2	34.0	53,993
1999	2,506	6.6	4.8	9.0	9.1	14.8	18.5	37.1	56,316
HISPANIC ORIGIN [2]									
1980	3,235	11.3	10.3	20.2	16.9	17.8	16.2	7.2	29,790
1985	4,206	13.1	11.1	19.2	15.6	17.6	14.5	9.0	29,460
1990	4,981	12.7	10.8	18.8	15.5	17.7	14.6	9.9	29,867
1995	6,287	14.2	11.3	21.4	16.0	15.1	13.4	8.6	26,859
1997	6,961	13.0	10.6	19.9	15.3	17.0	13.1	11.0	29,211
1998	7,273	11.8	10.1	18.8	17.0	16.0	15.2	11.2	30,262
1999	7,561	10.0	8.9	19.7	15.9	16.7	15.9	12.8	31,663

[1] Includes other races not shown separately.   [2] Persons of Hispanic origin may be of any race.

No. 669. Money Income of Families—Median Income by Race and Hispanic Origin in Current and Constant (1999) Dollars: 1980 to 1999

[See headnote, Table 668]

Year	Median income in current dollars					Median income in constant (1999) dollars				
	All families [1]	White	Black	Asian, Pacific Islander	His-panic [2]	All families [1]	White	Black	Asian, Pacific Islander	His-panic [2]
1980	21,023	21,904	12,674	(NA)	14,716	42,557	44,340	25,656	(NA)	29,790
1985 [3]	27,735	29,152	16,786	(NA)	19,027	42,943	45,137	25,990	(NA)	29,460
1986	29,458	30,809	17,604	(NA)	19,995	44,778	46,832	26,759	(NA)	30,394
1987 [4]	30,970	32,385	18,406	(NA)	20,300	45,419	47,494	26,993	(NA)	29,771
1988	32,191	33,915	19,329	36,560	21,769	45,334	47,762	27,221	51,487	30,657
1989	34,213	35,975	20,209	40,351	23,446	45,967	48,334	27,152	54,214	31,501
1990	35,353	36,915	21,423	42,246	23,431	45,064	47,055	27,307	53,850	29,867
1991	35,939	37,783	21,548	40,974	23,895	43,961	46,216	26,358	50,119	29,228
1992 [5]	36,573	38,670	21,103	42,255	23,555	43,429	45,919	25,059	50,176	27,971
1993 [6]	36,959	39,300	21,542	44,456	23,654	42,612	45,311	24,837	51,255	27,272
1994 [7]	38,782	40,884	24,698	46,122	24,318	43,597	45,960	27,764	51,848	27,337
1995 [8]	40,611	42,646	25,970	46,356	24,5.0	44,395	46,620	28,390	50,675	26,859
1996	42,300	44,756	26,522	49,105	26,179	44,915	47,523	28,162	52,141	27,797
1997	44,568	46,754	28,602	51,850	28,142	46,262	48,531	29,689	53,821	29,212
1998	46,737	49,023	29,404	52,826	29,608	47,769	50,106	30,053	53,993	30,262
1999	48,950	51,224	31,778	56,316	31,663	48,950	51,224	31,778	56,316	31,663

NA Not available.   [1] Includes other races not shown separately.   [2] Persons of Hispanic origin may be of any race.
[3] Recording of amounts for earnings from longest job increased to $299,999.   [4] Implementation of a new March CPS processing system.   [5] Implementation of 1990 census population controls.   [6] See text, Section 13, for information on data collection change.   [7] Introduction of 1990 census sample design.   [8] Full implementation of the 1990 census-based sample design and metropolitan definitions, 7,000 household sample reduction, and revised race edits.

Source of Tables 668 and 669: U.S. Census Bureau, Current Population Reports, P60-209; and Internet site <http://www.census.gov/hhes/income/histinc/h05.html> (released 20 September 2001).

Income, Expenditures, and Wealth   437

No. 670. Share of Aggregate Income Received by Each Fifth and Top 5 Percent of Families: 1980 to 1999

[Families as of March of the following year. Income in constant 1999 CPI-U adjusted dollars]

Year	Number of families (1,000)	Income at selected positions (dollars) Upper limit of each fifth Lowest	Second	Third	Fourth	Top 5 percent	Percent distribution of aggregate income Lowest 5th	Second 5th	Third 5th	Fourth 5th	Highest 5th	Top 5 percent
1980	60,309	21,053	35,446	50,203	70,446	111,337	5.3	11.6	17.6	24.4	41.1	14.6
1985	63,558	20,570	35,435	51,330	74,674	122,264	4.8	11.0	16.9	24.3	43.1	16.1
1986	64,491	21,281	36,634	53,385	76,870	126,774	4.7	10.9	16.9	24.1	43.4	16.5
1987 [1]	65,204	21,409	36,931	53,970	78,211	127,515	4.6	10.7	16.8	24.0	43.8	17.2
1988	65,837	21,268	36,872	54,219	78,732	129,564	4.6	10.7	16.7	24.0	44.0	17.2
1989	66,090	21,501	37,619	54,817	80,008	132,962	4.6	10.6	16.5	23.7	44.6	17.9
1990	66,322	21,473	37,022	53,587	78,380	130,473	4.6	10.8	16.6	23.8	44.3	17.4
1991	67,173	20,794	35,609	52,598	77,051	125,774	4.5	10.7	16.6	24.1	44.2	17.1
1992 [2]	68,216	19,846	35,237	52,248	76,056	125,884	4.3	10.5	16.5	24.0	44.7	17.6
1993 [3]	68,506	19,565	34,588	51,917	77,010	130,492	4.1	9.9	15.7	23.3	47.0	20.3
1994 [4]	69,313	20,167	35,186	52,835	78,689	134,947	4.2	10.0	15.7	23.3	46.9	20.1
1995	69,597	20,847	36,058	53,549	78,993	135,178	4.4	10.1	15.8	23.2	46.5	20.0
1996	70,241	20,897	36,436	54,244	79,972	135,913	4.2	10.0	15.8	23.1	46.8	20.3
1997	70,884	21,368	37,368	55,654	83,040	142,290	4.2	9.9	15.7	23.0	47.2	20.7
1998	71,551	22,077	38,524	57,257	85,541	148,406	4.2	9.9	15.7	23.0	47.3	20.7
1999	72,031	22,826	39,600	59,400	88,082	155,040	4.3	9.9	15.6	23.0	47.2	20.3

[1] Implementation of a new March CPS processing system. [2] Based on 1990 census population controls. [3] See text, Section 13, for explanation of changes in data collection method. [4] Introduction of new 1990 census sample design.

Source: U.S. Census Bureau, Current Population Reports, P60-209; and Internet site <http://www.census.gov/hhes/income/histinc/f02.html> (released 30 October 2000).

No. 671. Money Income of Families—Distribution by Family Characteristics and Income Level: 1999

[See headnote, Table 668. For composition of regions, see inside front cover]

Characteristic	Number of families (1,000)	Income level (1,000) Under $10,000	$10,000 to $14,999	$15,000 to $24,999	$25,000 to $34,999	$35,000 to $49,999	$50,000 to $74,999	$75,000 and over	Median income (dollars)
All families	**72,031**	**4,144**	**3,485**	**8,678**	**8,550**	**11,861**	**15,236**	**20,076**	**48,950**
Age of householder:									
15 to 24 years old	3,353	713	343	670	603	500	339	185	24,031
25 to 34 years old	13,009	1,035	751	1,683	1,666	2,290	3,036	2,548	43,309
35 to 44 years old	18,708	869	620	1,805	1,960	3,079	4,506	5,868	54,933
45 to 54 years old	15,804	530	501	993	1,188	2,268	3,699	6,625	65,303
55 to 64 years old	9,569	505	431	891	944	1,589	2,042	3,167	54,249
65 years old and over	11,588	491	838	2,636	2,189	2,135	1,615	1,682	33,148
White	60,256	2,637	2,514	6,970	7,090	10,046	13,303	17,695	51,224
Black	8,664	1,264	793	1,383	1,176	1,326	1,369	1,354	31,778
Hispanic origin [1]	7,561	757	674	1,489	1,202	1,263	1,206	971	31,663
Northeast	13,439	790	626	1,507	1,461	2,003	2,713	4,338	52,390
Midwest	16,850	834	664	1,775	1,813	2,936	4,052	4,777	51,767
South	26,192	1,693	1,463	3,424	3,401	4,412	5,251	6,548	44,979
West	15,550	828	732	1,972	1,875	2,510	3,221	4,413	48,918
Type of family:									
Married-couple families	55,315	1,328	1,693	5,471	5,963	9,214	13,034	18,613	56,676
Male householder, wife absent	4,028	316	286	581	653	762	776	655	37,396
Female householder, husband absent	12,687	2,501	1,507	2,625	1,935	1,885	1,426	808	23,732
Unrelated subfamilies	571	187	83	158	69	48	18	7	15,716
Education attainment of householder: [2]									
Total	**68,678**	**3,431**	**3,142**	**8,008**	**7,947**	**11,361**	**14,897**	**19,891**	**50,571**
Less than 9th grade	4,385	557	646	1,132	801	593	447	209	23,668
9th to 12th grade (no diploma)	5,989	798	613	1,335	1,066	1,015	823	339	27,050
High school graduate (includes equivalency)	21,702	1,183	1,060	2,997	3,106	4,356	5,076	3,925	42,995
Some college, no degree	12,747	469	423	1,395	1,458	2,469	3,083	3,450	50,967
Associate degree	5,560	166	178	473	601	946	1,492	1,706	56,602
Bachelor's degree or more	18,295	259	222	676	916	1,983	3,976	10,263	81,140
Bachelor's degree	11,743	167	168	500	696	1,429	2,742	6,041	76,059
Master's degree	4,395	54	45	142	144	418	962	2,630	85,632
Professional degree	1,174	18	6	22	42	86	119	882	100,000
Doctorate degree	982	19	3	13	34	51	154	708	100,000

[1] Persons of Hispanic origin may be of any race. [2] Persons 25 years old and over.

Source: U.S. Census Bureau, Current Population Reports, P60-209. See also <http://www.census.gov/prod/2000pubs/p60-209.pdf>.

438 Income, Expenditures, and Wealth

No. 672. Money Income of Families—Work Experience by Income Level: 1999

[See headnote, Table 668]

Characteristic	Number of families (1,000)	Income level (1,000)							Median income (dollars)
		Under $10,000	$10,000 to $14,999	$15,000 to $24,999	$25,000 to $34,999	$35,000 to $49,999	$50,000 to $74,999	$75,000 and over	
All families.	**72,031**	**4,144**	**3,485**	**8,678**	**8,550**	**11,861**	**15,236**	**20,076**	**48,950**
Number of earners:									
No earners.	9,321	1,849	1,143	2,381	1,523	1,177	708	541	21,789
One earner.	21,333	1,916	1,841	4,165	3,437	3,645	3,103	3,226	32,383
Two earners or more	41,377	379	501	2,132	3,591	7,039	11,425	16,309	64,289
Two earners	32,235	340	461	1,949	3,157	5,925	9,031	11,372	60,802
Three earners	6,766	35	33	154	376	936	1,858	3,375	74,899
Four earners or more	2,376	5	8	29	58	177	537	1,562	91,186
Work experience of householder:									
Total.	**72,031**	**4,144**	**3,485**	**8,678**	**8,550**	**11,861**	**15,236**	**20,076**	**48,950**
Worked.	54,379	1,932	1,835	4,998	5,727	9,019	12,949	17,918	56,288
Worked at full-time jobs	47,401	1,170	1,411	4,080	4,802	7,916	11,625	16,396	58,502
50 weeks or more	40,573	408	883	3,067	3,919	6,881	10,443	14,973	61,396
27 to 49 weeks	4,360	240	301	624	553	673	866	1,102	44,492
26 weeks or less	2,468	524	226	388	330	361	317	322	27,722
Worked at part-time jobs.	6,978	761	424	919	925	1,103	1,324	1,522	41,029
50 weeks or more	3,603	229	211	500	408	624	750	883	45,883
27 to 49 weeks	1,555	159	101	195	243	215	318	323	39,905
26 weeks or less	1,820	373	113	223	275	264	256	317	32,821

No. 673. Median Income of Families by Type of Family in Current and Constant (1999) Dollars: 1980 to 1999

[See headnote, Table 668]

Year	Current dollars					Constant (1999) dollars				
		Married-couple families			Female householder, no husband present		Married-couple families			Female householder, no husband present
	Total	Total	Wife in paid labor force	Wife not in paid labor force		Total	Total	Wife in paid labor force	Wife not in paid labor force	
1980	21,023	23,141	26,879	18,972	17,519	10,408	42,557	46,844	54,411	38,405	35,464	21,069
1985	27,735	31,100	36,431	24,556	22,622	13,660	42,943	48,153	56,407	38,021	35,026	21,150
1990	35,353	39,895	46,777	30,265	29,046	16,932	45,064	50,853	59,625	38,578	37,024	21,583
1991	35,939	40,995	48,169	30,075	28,351	16,692	43,961	50,145	58,920	36,788	34,679	20,418
1992 [1] . . .	36,573	41,890	49,775	30,174	27,576	17,025	43,429	49,742	59,106	35,830	32,745	20,216
1993 [2] . . .	36,959	43,005	51,204	30,218	26,467	17,443	42,612	49,582	59,035	34,840	30,515	20,111
1994 [2] . . .	38,782	44,959	53,309	31,176	27,751	18,236	43,597	50,541	59,928	35,047	31,196	20,500
1995 [3] . . .	40,611	47,062	55,823	32,375	30,358	19,691	44,395	51,447	61,024	35,392	33,187	21,526
1996	42,300	49,707	58,381	33,748	31,600	19,911	44,915	52,780	61,990	35,834	33,554	21,142
1997	44,568	51,591	60,669	36,027	32,960	21,023	46,262	53,552	62,975	37,396	34,213	21,822
1998	46,737	54,180	63,751	37,161	35,681	22,163	47,769	55,377	65,159	37,982	36,469	22,652
1999	48,950	56,676	66,529	38,626	37,396	23,732	48,950	56,676	66,529	38,626	37,396	23,732

[1] Based on 1990 census population controls. [2] See text, Section 13, for information on data collection change. [3] Introduction of 1990 census sample design.

No. 674. Married-Couple Families—Number and Median Income by Work Experience of Husbands and Wives and Presence of Children: 1998

[As of March 1999. Based on Current Population Survey; see text, Sections 1 and 13, and Appendix III]

Work experience of husband or wife	Number (1,000)					Median income (dollars)				
	All married-couple families	No related children	One or more related children under 18 years old			All married-couple families	No related children	One or more related children under 18 years old		
			Total	One child	Two children or more			Total	One child	Two children or more
All married-couple families . . .	**54,778**	**28,552**	**26,226**	**10,077**	**16,150**	**54,180**	**51,323**	**57,022**	**59,033**	**55,674**
Husband worked	43,705	18,822	24,883	9,429	15,454	60,867	64,090	58,730	60,784	57,118
Wife worked	32,873	14,289	18,584	7,459	11,125	65,411	68,878	62,817	65,261	61,561
Wife year-round, full-time worker.	19,132	9,139	9,993	4,421	5,572	70,918	73,284	68,438	71,474	66,482
Wife did not work	10,832	4,532	6,300	1,970	4,329	45,541	49,128	42,079	42,063	42,084
Husband year-round, full-time worker .	36,285	14,576	21,709	8,155	13,554	63,750	68,930	60,883	62,429	59,910
Wife worked	27,799	11,555	16,244	6,491	9,753	68,075	72,342	65,140	67,325	63,693
Wife year-round, full-time worker.	16,703	7,774	8,929	3,932	4,997	72,930	76,459	70,515	73,502	68,203
Wife did not work	8,486	3,021	5,465	1,663	3,801	48,514	52,355	45,372	43,373	45,996
Husband did not work	11,073	9,730	1,343	647	696	28,488	28,819	26,196	27,388	25,168
Wife worked	3,019	2,230	789	393	396	38,818	41,883	31,098	35,727	28,875
Wife year-round, full-time worker.	1,666	1,194	472	230	242	43,080	45,437	36,102	40,107	32,030
Wife did not work	8,055	7,500	554	254	300	25,657	26,029	19,116	19,903	17,312

Source of Tables 672-674: U.S. Census Bureau, *Current Population Reports,* P60-206; and <http://www.census.gov/hhes/income/histinc/index.htm> (accessed 17 May 2000).

No. 675. Money Income of Persons—Selected Characteristics by Income Level: 1999

[**Persons as of March of following year.** Covers persons 15 years old and over. For definition of median, see Guide to Tabular Presentation. For composition of regions, see map, inside front cover]

Characteristic	All persons (1,000)	Persons with income									
		Number (1,000)									
		Total (1,000)	Under $5,000 [1]	$5,000 to $9,999	$10,000 to $14,999	$15,000 to $24,999	$25,000 to $34,999	$35,000 to $49,999	$50,000 to $74,999	$75,000 and over	Median income (dollars)
MALE											
Total	103,114	96,023	8,341	8,695	9,380	17,386	14,566	15,235	12,557	9,863	27,275
15 to 24 years old	19,503	14,428	5,123	2,843	2,089	2,561	1,152	453	149	57	8,302
25 to 34 years old	18,563	17,974	685	995	1,419	4,011	3,724	3,798	2,230	1,112	29,864
35 to 44 years old	22,135	21,654	831	1,004	1,370	3,324	3,754	4,468	4,055	2,849	36,217
45 to 54 years old	17,890	17,477	597	992	989	2,151	2,447	3,456	3,608	3,236	40,939
55 to 64 years old	11,137	10,804	580	926	872	1,602	1,575	1,817	1,693	1,739	33,648
65 yr. old and over	13,886	13,686	526	1,935	2,641	3,736	1,914	1,242	822	870	19,079
Northeast	19,343	18,025	1,642	1,558	1,716	2,990	2,574	2,853	2,467	2,226	28,789
Midwest	23,907	22,714	1,950	1,983	1,866	3,911	3,632	4,002	3,162	2,208	29,268
South	36,543	33,762	2,953	3,197	3,634	6,468	5,339	5,215	3,908	3,050	25,926
West	23,320	21,521	1,796	1,956	2,165	4,017	3,022	3,166	3,021	2,380	27,185
White	86,443	81,574	6,710	6,789	7,746	14,515	12,458	13,292	11,130	8,933	28,564
Black	11,687	10,067	1,170	1,452	1,138	2,165	1,492	1,348	865	437	20,579
Hispanic [2]	11,327	10,045	931	1,259	1,701	2,729	1,427	1,093	617	287	18,234
Education attainment of householder: [3]											
Total	83,611	81,595	3,218	5,852	7,291	14,825	13,414	14,782	12,408	9,806	31,613
Less than 9th grade	5,918	5,610	394	1,503	1,207	1,536	531	287	108	45	13,438
9th to 12th grade [4]	7,298	6,900	499	1,026	1,287	1,890	1,123	704	259	112	17,707
High school graduate [5]	26,651	25,960	1,144	1,818	2,572	5,963	5,302	5,076	2,978	1,109	27,240
Some college, no degree	14,540	14,266	495	792	998	2,567	2,711	3,218	2,251	1,234	32,724
Associate degree	5,952	5,878	165	224	378	890	1,063	1,405	1,199	554	36,632
Bachelor's degree or more	23,251	22,981	521	489	848	1,979	2,684	4,092	5,614	6,753	52,240
Bachelor's degree	14,909	14,729	353	351	660	1,422	1,954	2,939	3,626	3,424	47,325
Master's degree	5,166	5,102	108	86	116	381	513	789	1,409	1,702	58,933
Professional degree	1,752	1,736	36	28	48	95	120	183	254	972	81,934
Doctorate degree	1,425	1,414	25	24	25	81	98	182	324	655	70,452
FEMALE											
Total	110,660	99,613	17,797	17,559	13,667	19,849	12,939	9,663	5,466	2,674	15,311
15 to 24 years old	19,040	13,957	5,765	2,989	1,986	2,185	694	250	56	33	6,689
25 to 34 years old	19,223	17,411	2,585	1,997	2,179	4,109	3,161	2,075	845	459	19,396
35 to 44 years old	22,670	21,098	3,305	2,307	2,265	4,410	3,507	2,875	1,671	759	20,683
45 to 54 years old	18,741	17,579	2,179	2,013	1,766	3,507	3,025	2,650	1,666	772	22,588
55 to 64 years old	12,250	11,277	2,050	1,929	1,421	2,186	1,377	1,124	785	406	15,917
65 yr. old and over	18,735	18,291	1,912	6,324	4,050	3,452	1,175	689	443	246	10,943
Northeast	21,661	19,773	3,389	3,565	2,542	3,870	2,411	1,971	1,284	741	15,780
Midwest	25,293	23,470	4,278	3,896	3,251	4,905	3,166	2,179	1,257	539	15,508
South	39,170	34,861	6,185	6,470	4,990	7,055	4,558	3,214	1,597	792	14,734
West	24,537	21,509	3,944	3,629	2,884	4,018	2,804	2,300	1,328	602	15,547
White	91,138	82,781	14,950	14,283	11,401	16,524	10,603	8,086	4,593	2,342	15,362
Black	14,167	12,432	1,970	2,535	1,781	2,523	1,768	1,124	543	189	14,771
Hispanic [2]	11,466	8,749	1,973	1,928	1,436	1,750	817	516	231	97	11,314
Education attainment of householder: [3]											
Total	91,620	85,657	12,031	14,571	11,681	17,664	12,245	9,413	5,410	2,641	17,082
Less than 9th grade	6,261	5,272	1,111	2,178	1,087	678	123	67	23	6	8,238
9th to 12th grade [4]	8,377	7,342	1,425	2,400	1,580	1,340	403	143	33	20	9,625
High school graduate [5]	31,435	29,199	4,401	5,673	4,784	7,433	3,988	1,986	674	261	14,695
Some college, no degree	16,213	15,473	2,008	2,028	1,961	3,666	2,721	1,800	895	393	19,665
Associate degree	7,740	7,384	911	823	831	1,592	1,449	1,144	456	178	21,959
Bachelor's degree or more	21,595	20,984	2,176	1,469	1,437	2,955	3,561	4,273	3,329	1,784	31,642
Bachelor's degree	14,931	14,450	1,677	1,131	1,108	2,267	2,722	2,776	1,863	906	28,594
Master's degree	5,230	5,138	402	275	264	546	710	1,213	1,210	518	39,744
Professional degree	834	808	60	27	45	81	84	165	131	214	45,510
Doctorate degree	599	587	37	36	20	61	45	118	125	145	46,499

[1] Includes persons with income deficit. [2] Persons of Hispanic origin may be of any race. [3] Persons 25 years and over. [4] No diploma attained. [5] Includes high school equivalency.

Source: U.S. Census Bureau, *Current Population Reports*, Series P60-209. See also <http://www.census.gov/prod/2000pubs/p60-209.pdf>.

440 Income, Expenditures, and Wealth

No. 676. Median Income of Persons With Income in Constant (1999) Dollars by Sex, Race, and Hispanic Origin: 1980 to 1999

[Persons as of March of following year. Constant dollars based on CPI-U deflator. Persons 15 years old and over]

Item	Male					Female				
	1980	1990	1995	1998	1999	1980	1990	1995	1998	1999
NUMBER WITH INCOME (1,000)										
All races	78,661	88,220	92,066	94,948	96,023	80,826	92,245	96,007	98,694	99,613
White	69,420	76,480	79,022	80,896	81,574	70,573	78,566	80,608	82,063	82,781
Black	7,387	8,820	9,339	9,776	10,067	8,596	10,687	11,607	12,272	12,432
Asian and Pacific Islander.	(NA)	2,235	3,095	3,500	3,572	(NA)	2,333	3,025	3,591	3,568
Hispanic [1]	3,996	6,767	8,577	9,617	10,045	3,617	5,903	7,478	8,405	8,749
Non-Hispanic White.	65,564	69,987	70,754	71,707	72,027	67,084	72,939	73,506	74,106	74,496
MEDIAN INCOME IN CONSTANT (1998) DOLLARS)										
All races	25,364	25,867	24,664	27,077	27,275	9,959	12,836	13,261	14,749	15,311
White	26,980	26,985	26,121	28,257	28,564	10,014	13,151	13,464	14,940	15,362
Black	16,212	16,402	17,497	19,748	20,579	9,271	10,615	11,982	13,427	14,771
Asian and Pacific Islander.	(NA)	24,721	24,228	25,679	27,731	(NA)	14,131	14,061	15,564	16,840
Hispanic [1]	19,553	17,170	16,223	17,638	18,234	8,917	9,600	9,760	11,102	11,314
Non-Hispanic White.	27,694	27,989	27,855	30,522	30,594	10,081	13,487	14,001	15,553	15,922

NA Not available.   [1] Persons of Hispanic origin may be of any race.

No. 677. Average Earnings of Year-Round Full-Time Workers by Educational Attainment: 1999

[In dollars. For persons 18 years old and over as of March 2000]

Sex and age		High school				College		
	All workers	Less than 9th grade	9th to 12th grade (no diploma)	High school graduate (includes equivalency)	Some college, no degree	Associate degree	Bachelor's degree or more
Male, total.	40,257	18,743	18,908	30,414	33,614	40,047	66,810
18 to 24 years old	13,215	12,925	9,175	15,001	11,743	17,991	21,161
25 to 34 years old	35,282	18,128	19,895	29,162	32,803	34,392	50,164
35 to 44 years old	46,000	21,466	23,886	34,151	43,174	45,108	70,594
45 to 54 years old	53,411	21,159	26,479	36,484	46,916	47,041	80,024
55 to 64 years old	49,646	20,292	29,125	35,224	42,896	43,349	79,097
65 years old and over. . . .	31,910	12,830	15,366	26,484	21,324	20,393	54,497
Female, total.	23,551	12,392	12,057	18,092	20,241	25,079	36,755
18 to 24 years old	10,590	10,051	6,851	10,729	9,345	13,279	19,007
25 to 34 years old	23,872	12,765	13,023	17,373	20,828	22,925	34,195
35 to 44 years old	26,632	13,223	13,145	19,573	25,099	26,802	40,012
45 to 54 years old	28,683	12,871	14,799	21,682	26,396	28,638	41,096
55 to 64 years old	25,876	13,975	20,006	20,502	25,517	28,088	37,801
65 years old and over. . . .	13,739	6,778	10,751	10,766	16,359	15,168	21,506

No. 678. Per Capita Money Income in Current and Constant (1999) Dollars by Race and Hispanic Origin: 1970 to 1999

[In dollars. Constant dollars based on CPI-U deflator. As of March of following year]

Year	Current dollars					Constant (1999) dollars				
	All races [1]	White	Black	Asian, Pacific Islander	His-panic [2]	All races [1]	White	Black	Asian, Pacific Islander	His-panic [2]
1970	3,177	3,354	1,869	(NA)	(NA)	12,816	13,530	7,539	(NA)	(NA)
1980	7,787	8,233	4,804	(NA)	4,865	15,763	16,666	9,725	(NA)	9,848
1985 [3]	11,013	11,671	6,840	(NA)	6,613	17,052	18,071	10,591	(NA)	10,239
1990	14,387	15,265	9,017	(NA)	8,424	18,339	19,458	11,494	(NA)	10,738
1991	14,617	15,510	9,170	(NA)	8,662	17,880	18,972	11,217	(NA)	10,595
1992 [4]	14,847	15,785	9,239	(NA)	8,591	17,630	18,744	10,971	(NA)	10,201
1993	15,777	16,800	9,863	15,691	8,830	18,190	19,369	11,371	18,091	10,180
1994 [5]	16,555	17,611	10,650	16,902	9,435	18,610	19,798	11,972	19,001	10,606
1995 [6]	17,227	18,304	10,982	16,567	9,300	18,832	20,009	12,005	18,111	10,167
1996	18,136	19,181	11,899	17,921	10,048	19,257	20,367	12,635	19,029	10,669
1997	19,241	20,425	12,351	18,226	10,773	19,972	21,201	12,820	18,919	11,182
1998	20,120	21,394	12,957	18,709	11,434	20,564	21,867	13,243	19,122	11,687
1999	21,181	22,375	14,397	21,134	11,621	21,181	22,375	14,397	21,134	11,621

NA Not available.   [1] Includes other races not shown separately.   [2] Persons of Hispanic origin may be of any race.
[3] Beginning 1985, data based on revised Hispanic population controls.   [4] Based on 1990 population controls.   [5] Introduction to new 1990 census sample design.   [6] Full implementation of the 1990 census-based sample design.

Source of Tables 676-678: U.S. Census Bureau, Current Population Reports, P60-209; and Internet site, <http://www.census.gov/hhes/income/histinc/index.html> (released 7 February 2001).

Income, Expenditures, and Wealth   441

No. 679. Persons Below Poverty Level and Below 125 Percent of Poverty Level: 1970 to 1999

[Persons as of March of the following year. Based on Current Population Survey; See text, Sections 1 and 13, and Appendix III]

Year	Number below poverty level (1,000)					Percent below poverty level					Below 125 percent of poverty level	
	All races [1]	White	Black	Asian and Pacific Islander	His-panic [2]	All races [1]	White	Black	Asian and Pacific Islander	His-panic [2]	Num-ber (1,000)	Percent of total population
1970	25,420	17,484	7,548	(NA)	(NA)	12.6	9.9	33.5	(NA)	(NA)	35,624	17.6
1975	25,877	17,770	7,545	(NA)	2,991	12.3	9.7	31.3	(NA)	26.9	37,182	17.6
1976	24,975	16,713	7,595	(NA)	2,783	11.8	9.1	31.1	(NA)	24.7	35,509	16.7
1977	24,720	16,416	7,726	(NA)	2,700	11.6	8.9	31.3	(NA)	22.4	35,659	16.7
1978	24,497	16,259	7,625	(NA)	2,607	11.4	8.7	30.6	(NA)	21.6	34,155	15.8
1979 [3]	26,072	17,214	8,050	(NA)	2,921	11.7	9.0	31.0	(NA)	21.8	36,616	16.4
1980	29,272	19,699	8,579	(NA)	3,491	13.0	10.2	32.5	(NA)	25.7	40,658	18.1
1981	31,822	21,553	9,173	(NA)	3,713	14.0	11.1	34.2	(NA)	26.5	43,748	19.3
1982	34,398	23,517	9,697	(NA)	4,301	15.0	12.0	35.6	(NA)	29.9	46,520	20.3
1983 [4]	35,303	23,984	9,882	(NA)	4,633	15.2	12.1	35.7	(NA)	28.0	47,150	20.3
1984	33,700	22,955	9,490	(NA)	4,806	14.4	11.5	33.8	(NA)	28.4	45,288	19.4
1985	33,064	22,860	8,926	(NA)	5,236	14.0	11.4	31.3	(NA)	29.0	44,166	18.7
1986	32,370	22,183	8,983	(NA)	5,117	13.6	11.0	31.1	(NA)	27.3	43,486	18.2
1987 [5]	32,221	21,195	9,520	1,021	5,422	13.4	10.4	32.4	16.1	28.0	43,032	17.9
1988	31,745	20,715	9,356	1,117	5,357	13.0	10.1	31.3	17.3	26.7	42,551	17.5
1989	31,528	20,785	9,302	939	5,430	12.8	10.0	30.7	14.1	26.2	42,653	17.3
1990	33,585	22,326	9,837	858	6,006	13.5	10.7	31.9	12.2	28.1	44,837	18.0
1991	35,708	23,747	10,242	996	6,339	14.2	11.3	32.7	13.8	28.7	47,527	18.9
1992 [6]	38,014	25,259	10,827	985	7,592	14.8	11.9	33.4	12.7	29.6	50,592	19.7
1993	39,265	26,226	10,877	1,134	8,126	15.1	12.2	33.1	15.3	30.6	51,801	20.0
1994	38,059	25,379	10,196	974	8,416	14.5	11.7	30.6	14.6	30.7	50,401	19.3
1995	36,425	24,423	9,872	1,411	8,574	13.8	11.2	29.3	14.6	30.3	48,761	18.5
1996	36,529	24,650	9,694	1,454	8,697	13.7	11.2	28.4	14.5	29.4	49,310	18.5
1997	35,574	24,396	9,116	1,468	8,308	13.3	11.0	26.5	14.0	27.1	47,853	17.8
1998	34,476	23,454	9,091	1,360	8,070	12.7	10.5	26.1	12.5	25.6	46,036	17.0
1999	32,258	21,922	8,360	1,163	7,439	11.8	9.8	23.6	10.7	22.8	44,286	16.2

NA Not available. [1] Includes other races not shown separately. [2] Persons of Hispanic origin may be of any race. [3] Population controls based on 1980 census; see text, Sections 1 and 13. [4] Beginning 1983, data based on revised Hispanic population controls and not directly comparable with prior years. [5] Beginning 1987, data based on revised processing procedures and not directly comparable with prior years. [6] Beginning 1992, based on 1990 population controls.

Source: U.S. Census Bureau, *Current Population Reports*, P60-210. See also <http://www.census.gov/prod/2000pubs/p60-210.pdf>.

No. 680. Children Below Poverty Level by Race and Hispanic Origin: 1970 to 1999

[Persons as of March of the following year. Covers only related children in families under 18 years old. Based on Current Population Survey; see text, Sections 1 and 13, and Appendix III]

Year	Number below poverty level (1,000)					Percent below poverty level				
	All races [1]	White	Black	Asian and Pacific Islander	His-panic [2]	All races [1]	White	Black	Asian and Pacific Islander	His-panic [2]
1970	10,235	6,138	3,922	(NA)	(NA)	14.9	10.5	41.5	(NA)	(NA)
1975	10,882	6,748	3,884	(NA)	1,619	16.8	12.5	41.4	(NA)	33.1
1976	10,081	6,034	3,758	(NA)	1,424	15.8	11.3	40.4	(NA)	30.1
1977	10,028	5,943	3,850	(NA)	1,402	16.0	11.4	41.6	(NA)	28.0
1978	9,722	5,674	3,781	(NA)	1,354	15.7	11.0	41.2	(NA)	27.2
1979	9,993	5,909	3,745	(NA)	1,505	16.0	11.4	40.8	(NA)	27.7
1980	11,114	6,817	3,906	(NA)	1,718	17.9	13.4	42.1	(NA)	33.0
1981	12,068	7,429	4,170	(NA)	1,874	19.5	14.7	44.9	(NA)	35.4
1982	13,139	8,282	4,388	(NA)	2,117	21.3	16.5	47.3	(NA)	38.9
1983 [3]	13,427	8,534	4,273	(NA)	2,251	21.8	17.0	46.2	(NA)	37.7
1984	12,929	8,086	4,320	(NA)	2,317	21.0	16.1	46.2	(NA)	38.7
1985	12,483	7,838	4,057	(NA)	2,512	20.1	15.6	43.1	(NA)	39.6
1986	12,257	7,714	4,037	(NA)	2,413	19.8	15.3	42.7	(NA)	37.1
1987 [4]	12,275	7,398	4,234	432	2,606	19.7	14.7	44.4	22.7	38.9
1988	11,935	7,095	4,148	458	2,576	19.0	14.0	42.8	23.5	37.3
1989	12,001	7,164	4,257	368	2,496	19.0	14.1	43.2	18.9	35.5
1990	12,715	7,696	4,412	356	2,750	19.9	15.1	44.2	17.0	37.7
1991	13,658	8,316	4,637	348	2,977	21.1	16.1	45.6	17.1	39.8
1992 [5]	14,521	8,752	5,015	352	3,440	21.6	16.5	46.3	16.0	39.0
1993	14,961	9,123	5,030	358	3,666	22.0	17.0	45.9	17.6	39.9
1994	14,610	8,826	4,787	308	3,956	21.2	16.3	43.3	17.9	41.1
1995	13,999	8,474	4,644	532	3,938	20.2	15.5	41.5	18.6	39.3
1996	13,764	8,488	4,411	553	4,090	19.8	15.5	39.5	19.1	39.9
1997	13,422	8,441	4,116	608	3,865	19.2	15.4	36.8	19.9	36.4
1998	12,845	7,935	4,073	542	3,670	18.3	14.4	36.4	17.5	33.6
1999	11,510	7,123	3,644	348	3,382	16.3	12.9	32.7	11.5	29.9

NA Not available. [1] Includes other races not shown separately. [2] Persons of Hispanic origin may be of any race. [3] Beginning 1983, data based on revised Hispanic population controls and not directly comparable with prior years. [4] Beginning 1987, data based on revised processing procedures and not directly comparable with prior years. [5] Beginning 1992, based on 1990 population controls.

Source: U.S. Census Bureau, *Current Population Reports*, P60-210. See also <http://www.census.gov/prod/2000pubs/p60-210.pdf>.

No. 681. Weighted Average Poverty Thresholds by Size of Unit: 1980 to 1999

[In dollars. For information on the official poverty thresholds; see text, this section]

Size of family unit	1980[1]	1990	1993	1994	1995	1996	1997	1998	1999
One person (unrelated individual) . . .	4,190	6,652	7,363	7,547	7,763	7,995	8,183	8,316	8,501
Under 65 years	4,290	6,800	7,518	7,710	7,929	8,163	8,350	8,480	8,667
65 years and over	3,949	6,268	6,930	7,108	7,309	7,525	7,698	7,818	7,990
Two persons	5,363	8,509	9,414	9,661	9,933	10,233	10,473	10,634	10,869
Householder under 65 years	5,537	8,794	9,728	9,976	10,259	10,564	10,805	10,972	11,214
Householder 65 years and over . . .	4,983	7,905	8,740	8,967	9,219	9,491	9,712	9,862	10,075
Three persons	6,565	10,419	11,522	11,821	12,158	12,516	12,802	13,003	13,290
Four persons	8,414	13,359	14,763	15,141	15,569	16,036	16,400	16,660	17,029
Five persons	9,966	15,792	17,449	17,900	18,408	18,952	19,380	19,680	20,127
Six persons	11,269	17,839	19,718	20,235	20,804	21,389	21,886	22,228	22,727
Seven persons	12,761	20,241	22,383	22,923	23,552	24,268	24,802	25,257	25,912
Eight persons	14,199	22,582	24,838	25,427	26,237	27,091	27,593	28,166	28,967
Nine or more persons	16,896	26,848	29,529	30,300	31,280	31,971	32,566	33,339	34,417

[1] Poverty levels for nonfarm families.

Source: U.S. Census Bureau, *Current Population Reports*, P60-210; and Internet site <http://www.census.gov/hhes/poverty/histpov/hstpov1.html> (released 26 September 2000).

No. 682. Persons Below Poverty Level by Selected Characteristics: 1999

[Persons as of March 1999. Based on Current Population Survey; see text, Sections 1 and 13, and Appendix III. For composition of regions, see map, inside front cover]

Age and region	Number below poverty level (1,000)					Percent below poverty level				
	All races [1]	White	Black	Asian and Pacific Islander	His-panic [2]	All races [1]	White	Black	Asian and Pacific Islander	His-panic [2]
Total	32,258	21,922	8,360	1,163	7,439	11.8	9.8	23.6	10.7	22.8
Under 18 years old	12,109	7,568	3,759	361	3,506	16.9	13.5	33.1	11.8	30.3
18 to 24 years old	4,603	3,125	1,165	239	941	17.3	14.8	29.3	20.0	23.8
25 to 34 years old	3,968	2,792	893	176	1,121	10.5	9.2	17.3	9.3	19.8
35 to 44 years old	3,733	2,614	945	108	811	8.3	7.1	16.6	5.9	16.3
45 to 54 years old	2,466	1,749	538	122	422	6.7	5.7	13.1	8.5	14.0
55 to 59 years old	1,179	890	231	36	141	9.2	8.0	17.9	9.4	14.2
60 to 64 years old	1,033	776	204	37	140	9.8	8.5	19.8	11.4	18.5
65 years old and over . . .	3,167	2,409	626	85	358	9.7	8.3	22.7	10.6	20.4
65 to 74 years old	1,577	1,127	360	56	221	8.9	7.3	22.2	10.9	19.5
75 years old and over .	1,591	1,283	260	29	137	10.7	9.6	23.5	10.1	22.0
Northeast	5,678	3,770	1,594	248	1,203	10.9	8.7	24.3	12.8	26.2
Midwest	6,210	4,109	1,495	108	422	9.8	7.5	26.4	8.8	16.3
South	12,538	7,666	4,462	220	2,428	13.1	10.4	23.2	11.6	22.3
West	7,833	6,377	509	586	3,386	12.6	12.2	18.3	10.0	23.2

[1] Includes other races not shown separately.   [2] Persons of Hispanic origin may be of any race.

Source: U.S. Census Bureau, *Current Population Reports*, P60-210; and unpublished data.

No. 683. Persons 65 Years Old and Over Below Poverty Level: 1980 to 1999

[Persons as of March of following year. Based on the Current Population Survey, see text, Sections 1 and 13, and Appendix III]

Characteristic	Number below poverty level (1,000)					Percent below poverty level				
	1980	1990	1995	1998	1999	1980	1990	1995	1998	1999
Total	3,871	3,658	3,318	3,386	3,167	15.7	12.2	10.5	10.5	9.7
White	3,042	2,707	2,572	2,555	2,409	13.6	10.1	9.0	8.9	8.3
Black	783	860	629	718	626	38.1	33.8	25.4	26.4	22.7
Asian and Pacific Islander.	(NA)	62	89	97	85	(NA)	12.1	14.3	12.4	10.6
Hispanic [1]	179	245	342	356	358	30.8	22.5	23.5	21.0	20.4
In families	(NA)	1,172	1,058	1,234	1,071	(NA)	5.8	5.0	5.7	4.9
Unrelated individuals	(NA)	2,479	2,260	2,150	2,095	(NA)	24.7	21.4	20.4	19.7

NA Not available.   [1] Persons of Hispanic origin may be of any race.

Source: U.S. Census Bureau, *Current Population Reports*, P60-210; and earlier reports.

No. 684. Persons Below Poverty Level by State: 1980 to 1999

[Based on the Current Population Survey; see text, Sections 1 and 13, and Appendix III. The CPS is designed to collect reliable data on income primarily at the national level and secondarily at the regional level. When the income data are tabulated by state, the estimates are considered less reliable and, therefore, particular caution should be used when trying to interpret the results; for additional detail, see source]

State	Number below poverty level (1,000)					Percent below poverty level				
	1980	1990 [1]	1995	1998	1999	1980	1990 [1]	1995	1998	1999
United States	29,272	33,585	36,425	34,476	32,258	13.0	13.5	13.8	12.7	11.8
Alabama..........	810	779	882	609	671	21.2	19.2	20.1	14.5	15.1
Alaska............	36	57	45	60	47	9.6	11.4	7.1	9.4	7.6
Arizona...........	354	484	700	812	579	12.8	13.7	16.1	16.6	12.0
Arkansas	484	472	376	377	375	21.5	19.6	14.9	14.7	14.7
California	2,619	4,128	5,342	5,118	4,677	11.0	13.9	16.7	15.4	13.8
Colorado..........	247	461	335	363	351	8.6	13.7	8.8	9.2	8.3
Connecticut........	255	196	318	310	235	8.3	6.0	9.7	9.5	7.1
Delaware	68	48	74	80	79	11.8	6.9	10.3	10.3	10.4
District of Columbia	131	120	122	114	77	20.9	21.1	22.2	22.3	14.9
Florida	1,692	1,896	2,321	1,923	1,867	16.7	14.4	16.2	13.1	12.4
Georgia	727	1,001	878	1,034	1,005	13.9	15.8	12.1	13.5	12.9
Hawaii	81	121	122	131	132	8.5	11.0	10.3	10.9	10.9
Idaho............	138	157	167	165	175	14.7	14.9	14.5	13.0	13.9
Illinois	1,386	1,606	1,459	1,234	1,206	12.3	13.7	12.4	10.1	9.9
Indiana...........	645	714	545	547	395	11.8	13.0	9.6	9.4	6.7
Iowa	311	289	352	257	211	10.8	10.4	12.2	9.1	7.5
Kansas...........	215	259	273	250	318	9.4	10.3	10.8	9.6	12.2
Kentucky	701	628	572	521	470	19.3	17.3	14.7	13.5	12.1
Louisiana	868	952	849	821	823	20.3	23.6	19.7	19.1	19.2
Maine............	158	162	138	131	135	14.6	13.1	11.2	10.4	10.6
Maryland	389	468	520	359	356	9.5	9.9	10.1	7.2	7.3
Massachusetts.......	542	626	665	528	722	9.5	10.7	11.0	8.7	11.7
Michigan..........	1,194	1,315	1,174	1,097	977	12.9	14.3	12.2	11.0	9.7
Minnesota..........	342	524	427	498	346	8.7	12.0	9.2	10.3	7.2
Mississippi	591	684	630	486	444	24.3	25.7	23.5	17.6	16.1
Missouri...........	625	700	484	531	633	13.0	13.4	9.4	9.8	11.6
Montana...........	102	134	133	153	140	13.2	16.3	15.3	16.6	15.6
Nebraska..........	199	167	159	211	180	13.0	10.3	9.6	12.3	10.9
Nevada	70	119	173	195	216	8.3	9.8	11.1	10.6	11.3
New Hampshire.......	63	68	60	119	96	7.0	6.3	5.3	9.8	7.7
New Jersey.........	659	711	617	693	631	9.0	9.2	7.8	8.6	7.8
New Mexico	268	319	457	371	371	20.6	20.9	25.3	20.4	20.7
New York	2,391	2,571	3,020	3,068	2,603	13.8	14.3	16.5	16.7	14.1
North Carolina......	877	829	877	1,039	1,017	15.0	13.0	12.6	14.0	13.5
North Dakota........	99	87	76	97	80	15.5	13.7	12.0	15.1	13.0
Ohio	1,046	1,256	1,285	1,253	1,347	9.8	11.5	11.5	11.2	12.0
Oklahoma..........	406	481	548	458	414	13.9	15.6	17.1	14.1	12.7
Oregon...........	309	267	360	503	427	11.5	9.2	11.2	15.0	12.6
Pennsylvania........	1,142	1,328	1,464	1,338	1,101	9.8	11.0	12.2	11.3	9.4
Rhode Island........	97	71	102	112	97	10.7	7.5	10.6	11.6	9.9
South Carolina.......	534	548	744	527	445	16.8	16.2	19.9	13.7	11.7
South Dakota	127	93	103	77	54	18.8	13.3	14.5	10.8	7.7
Tennessee	884	833	846	749	659	19.6	16.9	15.5	13.4	11.9
Texas............	2,247	2,684	3,270	2,994	3,007	15.7	15.9	17.4	15.1	15.0
Utah	148	143	168	190	122	10.0	8.2	8.4	9.0	5.7
Vermont...........	62	61	61	58	58	12.0	10.9	10.3	9.9	9.7
Virginia...........	647	705	648	589	542	12.4	11.1	10.2	8.8	7.9
Washington.........	538	434	677	512	539	12.7	8.9	12.5	8.9	9.5
West Virginia........	297	328	300	312	276	15.2	18.1	16.7	17.8	15.7
Wisconsin..........	403	448	449	449	461	8.5	9.3	8.5	8.8	8.6
Wyoming	49	51	59	51	56	10.4	11.0	12.2	10.6	11.6

[1] Beginning 1990, data based on revised processing procedures and not directly comparable with prior years.

Source: U.S. Census Bureau, Current Population Reports, P60-210, and <http://www.census.gov/hhes/poverty/histpov/hstpov21.html> (accessed 11 November 2000).

444 Income, Expenditures, and Wealth

No. 685. Families Below Poverty Level and Below 125 Percent of Poverty by Race and Hispanic Origin: 1970 to 1999

[Families as of March of the following year. Based on Current Population Survey, see text, Sections 1 and 13, and Appendix III]

Year	Number below poverty level (1,000)				Percent below poverty level				Below 125 percent of poverty level	
	All races [1]	White	Black	His-panic [2]	All races [1]	White	Black	His-panic [2]	Number (1,000)	Percent
1970	5,260	3,708	1,481	(NA)	10.1	8.0	29.5	(NA)	7,516	14.4
1975	5,450	3,838	1,513	627	9.7	7.7	27.1	25.1	7,974	14.2
1976	5,311	3,560	1,617	598	9.4	7.1	27.9	23.1	7,647	13.5
1977	5,311	3,540	1,637	591	9.3	7.0	28.2	21.4	7,713	13.5
1978	5,280	3,523	1,622	559	9.1	6.9	27.5	20.4	7,417	12.8
1979 [3]	5,461	3,581	1,722	614	9.2	6.9	27.8	20.3	7,784	13.1
1980	6,217	4,195	1,826	751	10.3	8.0	28.9	23.2	8,764	14.5
1981	6,851	4,670	1,972	792	11.2	8.8	30.8	24.0	9,568	15.7
1982	7,512	5,118	2,158	916	12.2	9.6	33.0	27.2	10,279	16.7
1983 [4]	7,647	5,220	2,161	981	12.3	9.7	32.3	25.9	10,358	16.7
1984	7,277	4,925	2,094	991	11.6	9.1	30.9	25.2	9,901	15.8
1985	7,223	4,983	1,983	1,074	11.4	9.1	28.7	25.5	9,753	15.3
1986	7,023	4,811	1,987	1,085	10.9	8.6	28.0	24.7	9,476	14.7
1987 [5]	7,005	4,567	2,117	1,168	10.7	8.1	29.4	25.5	9,338	14.3
1988	6,874	4,471	2,089	1,141	10.4	7.9	28.2	23.7	9,284	14.1
1989	6,784	4,409	2,077	1,133	10.3	7.8	27.8	23.4	9,267	14.0
1990	7,098	4,622	2,193	1,244	10.7	8.1	29.3	25.0	9,564	14.4
1991	7,712	5,022	2,343	1,372	11.5	8.8	30.4	26.5	10,244	15.3
1992 [6]	8,144	5,255	2,484	1,529	11.9	9.1	31.1	26.7	10,959	16.1
1993	8,393	5,452	2,499	1,625	12.3	9.4	31.3	27.3	11,203	16.4
1994	8,053	5,312	2,212	1,724	11.6	9.1	27.3	27.8	10,771	15.5
1995	7,532	4,994	2,127	1,695	10.8	8.5	26.4	27.0	10,223	14.7
1996	7,708	5,059	2,206	1,748	11.0	8.6	26.1	26.4	10,476	14.9
1997	7,324	4,990	1,985	1,721	10.3	8.4	23.6	24.7	10,032	14.2
1998	7,186	4,829	1,981	1,648	10.0	8.0	23.4	22.7	9,714	13.6
1999	6,676	4,377	1,898	1,525	9.3	7.3	21.9	20.2	9,320	12.9

NA Not available.   [1] Includes other races not shown separately.   [2] Persons of Hispanic origin may be of any race.   [3] Population controls based on 1980 census; see text, this section.   [4] Beginning 1983, data based on revised Hispanic population controls and not directly comparable with prior years.   [5] Beginning 1987, data based on revised processing procedures and not directly comparable with prior years.   [6] Beginning 1992, based on 1990 population controls.

Source: U.S. Census Bureau, *Current Population Reports,* P60-210.

No. 686. Families Below Poverty Level by Selected Characteristics: 1999

Characteristic	Number below poverty level (1,000)				Percent below poverty level			
	All races [1]	White	Black	Hispanic [2]	All races [1]	White	Black	Hispanic [2]
Total	6,676	4,377	1,898	1,525	9.3	7.3	21.9	20.2
Age of householder:								
15 to 24 years old	942	536	361	215	29.3	22.6	53.3	33.7
25 to 34 years old	1,857	1,189	563	510	14.3	11.5	28.7	24.7
35 to 44 years old	1,635	1,118	437	411	8.7	7.2	18.8	18.8
45 to 54 years old	896	598	232	197	5.7	4.5	13.2	15.3
55 to 64 years old	704	497	156	109	7.4	6.0	16.6	15.1
65 years old and over	604	418	137	77	5.2	4.1	14.1	12.3
Education of householder: [3]								
No high school diploma . . .	2,247	1,531	586	832	21.7	18.6	33.8	28.2
High school diploma, no college	1,980	1,357	542	289	9.1	7.4	20.5	15.9
Some college, less than Bachelor's degree	1,078	658	347	133	5.9	4.3	14.9	9.8
Bachelor's degree or more .	391	273	48	50	2.1	1.7	3.8	6.6
Work experience of house-holder:								
Total [4]	6,066	3,955	1,758	1,447	10.0	7.9	22.9	20.9
Worked during year	3,622	2,351	1,071	872	7.0	5.4	16.9	15.3
Year-round, full-time	1,247	851	329	371	3.1	2.6	7.2	9.0
Not year-round, full-time .	2,375	1,500	743	500	19.5	15.2	41.4	32.1
Did not work	2,444	1,604	687	575	28.6	23.7	51.3	46.7

[1] Includes other races not shown separately.   [2] Hispanic persons may be of any race.   [3] Householder 25 years old and over.   [4] Persons 16-64 years old.

Source: U.S. Census Bureau, *Current Population Reports,* P60-210; and unpublished data.

U.S. Census Bureau, Statistical Abstract of the United States: 2001

No. 687. Nonfinancial Assets Held by Families by Type of Asset: 1998

[**Median value in thousands of dollars.** Constant dollar figures are based on consumer price index for all urban consumers published by U.S. Bureau of Labor Statistics. Families include one-person units and, as used in this table, are comparable to the Census Bureau household concept. For definition of family, see text, Section 1, Population. Based on Survey of Consumer Finance; see Appendix III. For data on financial assets, see Table 1167. For definition of median, see Guide to Tabular Presentation]

Age of family head and family income	Total	Vehicles	Primary resi- dence	Other residen- tial property	Equity in nonresi- dential property	Business equity	Other	Any non- financial asset
PERCENT OF FAMILIES OWNING ASSET								
All families, total	**96.8**	**82.8**	**66.2**	**12.8**	**8.6**	**11.5**	**8.5**	**89.9**
Age of family head:								
Under 35 years old.	94.8	78.3	38.9	3.5	2.7	7.2	7.3	83.3
35 to 44 years old	97.6	85.8	67.1	12.2	7.5	14.7	8.8	92.0
45 to 54 years old	96.7	87.5	74.4	16.2	12.2	16.2	9.2	92.9
55 to 64 years old	98.2	88.7	80.3	20.4	10.4	14.3	8.5	93.8
65 to 74 years old	98.5	83.4	81.5	18.4	15.3	10.1	10.3	92.0
75 years old and over.	96.4	69.8	77.0	13.6	8.1	2.7	7.0	87.2
Family income:								
Less than $10,000	83.8	51.3	34.5	(B)	(B)	3.8	2.6	62.7
$10,000 to $24,999	96.4	78.0	51.7	5.8	5.0	5.0	5.6	85.9
$25,000 to $49,999	99.2	89.6	68.2	11.4	7.6	10.3	9.4	95.6
$50,000 to $99,999	100.0	93.6	85.0	19.0	12.0	15.0	10.2	98.0
$100,000 and more	100.0	88.7	93.3	37.3	22.6	34.7	17.1	98.9
Current work status of householder:								
Working for someone else	98.2	87.6	63.5	10.6	6.7	5.5	8.8	92.4
Self-employed	99.2	89.5	81.3	25.3	17.7	63.4	13.3	98.1
Retired.	94.7	73.3	72.4	14.3	10.1	3.6	6.4	85.2
Other not working	85.7	58.5	35.8	4.5	(B)	3.7	(B)	66.3
Tenure:								
Owner occupied	100.0	90.6	100.0	16.8	11.3	14.5	9.5	100.0
Renter occupied or other.	90.7	67.6	(X)	5.1	3.3	5.4	6.4	70.1
MEDIAN VALUE [1] ($1,000)								
All families, total	**123.5**	**10.8**	**100.0**	**65.0**	**38.0**	**60.0**	**10.0**	**97.8**
Age of family head:								
Under 35 years old.	28.9	8.9	84.0	42.5	25.0	34.0	5.0	22.7
35 to 44 years old	128.0	11.4	101.0	45.0	20.0	62.5	8.0	103.5
45 to 54 years old	178.9	12.8	120.0	74.0	45.0	100.0	14.0	126.8
55 to 64 years old	198.2	13.5	110.0	70.0	54.0	62.5	28.0	126.9
65 to 74 years old	165.2	10.8	95.0	75.0	45.0	61.1	10.0	109.9
75 years old and over.	135.0	7.0	85.0	103.0	54.0	40.0	10.0	96.1
Family income:								
Less than $10,000	11.7	4.0	51.0	(B)	(B)	37.5	5.0	16.3
$10,000 to $24,999	46.2	5.7	71.9	70.0	25.0	31.1	5.0	43.7
$25,000 to $49,999	112.0	10.2	85.0	50.0	28.0	37.5	6.0	83.5
$50,000 to $99,999	233.2	16.6	130.0	60.0	30.0	56.0	12.0	156.3
$100,000 and more	665.6	26.8	240.0	132.0	114.1	230.0	36.0	380.0
Current work status of householder:								
Working for someone else	112.4	11.2	98.0	50.0	24.0	30.0	7.0	89.6
Self-employed	329.3	15.5	150.0	85.0	80.0	100.0	50.0	256.6
Retired.	134.5	8.6	89.0	100.0	50.0	50.0	10.0	97.8
Other not working	18.0	7.2	90.0	64.6	(B)	39.0	(B)	28.5
Tenure:								
Owner occupied	193.3	13.2	100.0	65.0	45.0	75.0	13.0	130.6
Renter occupied or other.	11.6	6.2	(X)	64.6	15.0	31.0	5.0	7.2

B Base too small to meet statistical standards for reliability of derived figure.   X Not applicable.   [1] Median value of financial asset for families holding such assets.

Source: Board of Governors of the Federal Reserve System, *Federal Reserve Bulletin*, January 2000, and unpublished revisions.

No. 688. Family Net Worth—Mean and Median Net Worth in Constant (1998) Dollars by Selected Family Characteristics: 1992 to 1998

[Net worth in thousands of constant (1998) dollars (212.7 represents $212,700). Constant dollar figures are based on consumer price index for all urban consumers published by U.S. Bureau of Labor Statistics. Families include one-person units and as used in this table are comparable to the Census Bureau household concept. Based on Survey of Consumer Finance; see Appendix III. For definition of median, see Guide to Tabular Presentation]

Family characteristic	1992			1995			1998		
	Percent of families	Net worth		Percent of families	Net worth		Percent of families	Net worth	
		Mean	Median		Mean	Median		Mean	Median
All families	**100.0**	**212.7**	**56.5**	**100.0**	**224.8**	**60.9**	**100.0**	**282.5**	**71.6**
Age of family head:									
Under 35 years old.	25.8	53.1	10.4	24.8	47.4	12.7	23.3	65.9	9.0
35 to 44 years old	22.8	152.7	50.9	23.0	152.8	54.9	23.3	196.2	63.4
45 to 54 years old	16.2	304.4	89.3	17.9	313.0	100.8	19.2	362.7	105.5
55 to 64 years old	13.2	384.9	130.2	12.5	404.7	122.4	12.8	530.2	127.5
65 to 74 years old	12.6	326.1	112.3	12.0	369.3	117.9	11.2	465.5	146.5
75 years old and over.	9.4	244.4	99.2	9.8	273.8	98.8	10.2	310.2	125.6
Family income in constant (1998) dollars:[1]									
Less than $10,000	14.8	32.1	2.9	15.1	46.6	4.8	12.6	40.0	3.6
$10,000 to $24,999	27.0	69.8	27.1	25.4	80.3	31.0	24.8	85.6	24.8
$25,000 to $49,999	29.8	131.4	55.6	31.0	124.0	56.7	28.8	135.4	60.3
$50,000 to $99,999	20.7	245.6	129.9	21.0	258.1	126.6	25.2	275.5	152.0
$100,000 and more	7.6	1,300.8	481.9	7.4	1,411.9	511.4	8.6	1,727.8	510.8
Education of householder:									
No high school diploma.	20.4	80.2	21.3	18.5	89.6	24.0	16.5	79.1	20.9
High school diploma.	30.0	127.7	43.9	31.7	141.3	54.7	31.9	157.8	53.8
Some college	17.8	195.8	65.9	19.0	201.2	49.7	18.5	237.8	73.9
College degree	31.9	387.0	112.1	30.7	407.2	110.9	33.2	528.2	146.4
Current work status of householder:									
Working for someone else. . . .	54.8	139.6	44.7	58.3	145.2	51.9	59.2	168.9	52.4
Self-employed	10.9	682.3	164.7	10.3	742.0	165.5	11.3	919.8	248.1
Retired.	26.0	214.0	80.7	25.0	239.4	86.2	24.4	307.2	113.0
Other not working	8.3	72.2	4.5	6.5	62.9	3.9	5.1	76.5	3.6
Region:									
Northeast	20.2	240.0	73.2	19.8	266.9	88.0	19.3	302.4	94.2
Midwest	24.4	198.0	65.0	23.9	210.0	69.2	23.6	248.8	80.3
South	34.6	160.4	39.4	35.1	197.6	46.6	35.7	267.5	61.3
West	20.9	290.2	81.4	21.2	247.1	58.1	21.3	327.1	61.3
Tenure:									
Owner occupied	63.9	307.4	112.8	64.7	321.3	110.5	66.2	403.5	132.1
Renter occupied or other. . . .	36.1	45.1	3.7	35.3	47.9	5.2	33.8	45.1	4.2

[1] Income for year preceding the survey.

Source: Board of Governors of the Federal Reserve System, *Federal Reserve Bulletin,* January 2000, and unpublished data.

Figure 13.1

Percent of Persons Below Poverty Level: 1980 to 1999

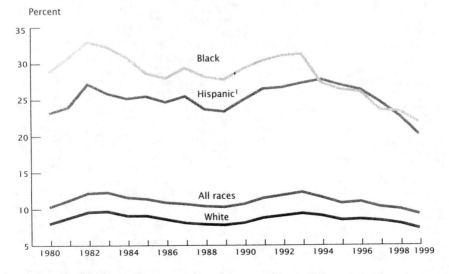

[1] Persons of Hispanic origin maybe of any race.
Source: Chart prepared by U.S. Census Bureau. For data, see Table 685.

Income, Expenditures, and Wealth   447

No. 689. Household and Nonprofit Organization Sector Balance Sheet: 1980 to 2000

[In billions of dollars (10,989 represents $10,989,000,000,000). As of December 31. For details of financial assets and liabilities, see Table 1175]

Item	1980	1990	1993	1994	1995	1996	1997	1998	1999	2000
Assets	10,989	24,315	28,353	29,372	32,487	35,363	39,508	43,382	49,218	48,978
Tangible assets [1]	4,381	9,326	9,908	10,229	10,697	11,187	11,914	12,776	13,819	15,243
Real estate	3,421	7,415	7,818	8,039	8,425	8,842	9,500	10,263	11,134	12,309
Consumer durable goods	934	1,853	2,014	2,111	2,189	2,259	2,324	2,419	2,587	2,827
Financial assets [1]	6,607	14,989	18,445	19,143	21,790	24,176	27,594	30,606	35,398	33,736
Deposits	1,517	3,253	3,157	3,116	3,309	3,457	3,642	4,030	4,210	4,583
Checkable deposits and currency.................	251	409	593	563	504	444	398	444	389	310
Time and savings deposits	1,203	2,466	2,210	2,186	2,337	2,482	2,636	2,821	2,937	3,238
Money market fund shares	62	365	338	348	445	495	571	726	841	995
Credit market instruments [1]	425	1,518	1,673	1,954	1,946	2,119	2,076	2,032	2,303	2,171
U.S. government securities......	165	555	652	963	910	1,023	901	741	925	789
Treasury	160	469	603	800	734	738	603	473	510	306
Savings bonds...........	73	126	172	180	185	187	187	187	186	185
Corporate equities	875	1,795	3,216	3,047	4,071	4,687	5,910	6,672	8,750	6,579
Mutual fund shares............	46	457	965	997	1,159	1,495	1,941	2,375	3,106	3,026
Pension fund reserves..........	970	3,460	4,664	4,979	5,833	6,582	7,725	8,760	9,748	9,848
Equity in noncorporate business	2,198	3,275	3,229	3,445	3,684	3,889	4,164	4,415	4,705	4,916
Liabilities	1,455	3,747	4,397	4,720	5,096	5,444	5,828	6,335	6,958	7,560
Credit market instruments	1,404	3,625	4,217	4,535	4,898	5,222	5,560	6,039	6,578	7,169
Home mortgages	935	2,532	3,001	3,178	3,368	3,579	3,828	4,204	4,620	5,022
Consumer credit.............	355	805	859	984	1,123	1,212	1,264	1,332	1,426	1,569
Net worth	9,533	20,568	23,956	24,652	27,391	29,919	33,680	37,047	42,260	41,418
Memo:										
Replacement cost value of structures:										
Residential	2,548	4,599	5,330	5,748	6,012	6,352	6,706	7,168	7,677	8,199
Households	2,363	4,337	5,053	5,459	5,718	6,050	6,394	6,843	7,337	7,855
Farm households	112	150	161	170	174	179	184	192	201	203
Nonprofit organizations	73	112	116	120	121	124	127	134	138	142
Nonresidential (nonprofits)	267	475	537	572	596	624	663	707	744	799
Disposable personal income	2,116	4,363	5,047	5,304	5,505	5,780	6,092	6,441	6,775	7,085
Owners' equity in household real estate.	2,010	4,075	4,102	4,103	4,262	4,429	4,732	5,003	5,402	6,015

[1] Includes types of assets and/or liabilities not shown separately.
Source: Board of Governors of the Federal Reserve System, *Balance Sheets for the U.S. Economy.*

No. 690. Net Stock of Fixed Reproducible Tangible Wealth in Current and Real (1996) Dollars: 1980 to 1999

[In billions of dollars (10,297 represents $10,297,000,000,000). As of December 31]

Item	1980	1990	1993	1994	1995	1996	1997	1998	1999
CURRENT DOLLARS									
Net stock	10,297	18,187	20,397	21,618	22,617	23,701	24,925	26,246	27,866
Private......................	7,213	12,760	14,318	15,204	15,909	16,723	17,653	18,670	19,882
Nonresidential equipment........	1,420	2,542	2,829	2,992	3,183	3,352	3,520	3,729	4,011
Information processing and related equipment	225	663	760	803	850	906	975	1,050	1,183
Industrial equipment..........	525	893	964	1,011	1,075	1,119	1,157	1,199	1,241
Transportation equipment	306	472	557	604	651	690	717	768	840
Other equipment	319	513	547	575	607	637	672	713	747
Nonresidential structures	2,256	4,081	4,499	4,739	4,941	5,175	5,487	5,749	6,036
Nonresidential buildings, excluding farm.............	1,169	2,514	2,817	2,992	3,125	3,286	3,499	3,742	3,991
Utilities	695	1,005	1,109	1,148	1,190	1,229	1,265	1,285	1,311
Residential.................	3,537	6,087	6,935	7,414	7,723	8,131	8,581	9,124	9,766
Housing units	2,898	4,963	5,653	6,059	6,302	6,625	6,995	7,451	7,984
Government	2,151	3,612	4,086	4,322	4,533	4,725	4,943	5,145	5,423
Equipment.................	300	559	645	672	686	692	694	698	727
Structures.................	1,952	3,053	3,441	3,651	3,847	4,033	4,249	4,446	4,696
Federal....................	653	1,087	1,229	1,279	1,314	1,343	1,367	1,383	1,429
Defense..................	483	743	842	874	885	891	893	891	910
State and local..............	1,498	2,525	2,857	3,043	3,219	3,382	3,576	3,762	3,994
Consumer durable goods...........	934	1,815	1,993	2,092	2,176	2,254	2,329	2,431	2,561
Motor vehicles	257	574	599	629	647	663	673	706	753
Furniture and household equipment .	459	823	924	968	1,011	1,053	1,096	1,141	1,193
Other	203	417	470	495	519	537	560	583	615
CHAINED (1996) DOLLARS									
Net stock	14,269	20,650	21,796	22,291	22,829	23,450	24,126	24,915	25,812
Private......................	9,950	14,562	15,345	15,694	16,075	16,521	17,010	17,574	18,197
Nonresidential equipment........	1,855	2,723	2,915	3,036	3,183	3,354	3,555	3,796	4,097
Nonresidential structures	3,177	4,704	4,887	4,939	5,008	5,094	5,198	5,317	5,427
Residential..................	4,921	7,142	7,547	7,720	7,884	8,074	8,261	8,474	8,705
Government	3,127	4,192	4,445	4,512	4,585	4,668	4,749	4,836	4,936
Federal....................	969	1,291	1,327	1,326	1,326	1,334	1,329	1,328	1,332
State and local..............	2,156	2,901	3,117	3,185	3,259	3,334	3,420	3,508	3,603
Consumer durable goods..........	1,198	1,899	2,010	2,087	2,170	2,262	2,369	2,511	2,695

Source: U.S. Bureau of Economic Analysis, *Fixed Assets and Consumer Durable Goods in the United States, 1925-97* (forthcoming); and *Survey of Current Business,* September 2000.

Section 14
Prices

This section presents indexes of producer and consumer prices, actual prices for selected commodities, and energy prices. The primary sources of these data are monthly publications of the Department of Labor, Bureau of Labor Statistics (BLS), which include *Monthly Labor Review, Consumer Price Index, Detailed Report, Producer Price Indexes,* and *U.S. Import and Export Price Indexes.* The Department of Commerce, Bureau of Economic Analysis is the source for gross domestic product measures.

Producer price index (PPI)—This index, dating from 1890, is the oldest continuous statistical series published by BLS. It is designed to measure average changes in prices received by producers of all commodities, at all stages of processing, produced in the United States.

The index has undergone several revisions (see *Monthly Labor Review,* February 1962, April 1978, and August 1988). It is now based on approximately 10,000 individual products and groups of products along with about 100,000 quotations per month. Indexes for the net output of manufacturing and mining industries have been added in recent years. Prices used in constructing the index are collected from sellers and generally apply to the first significant large-volume commercial transaction for each commodity—i.e., the manufacturer's or other producer's selling price or the selling price on an organized exchange or at a central market.

The weights used in the index represent the total net selling value of commodities produced or processed in this country. Values are f.o.b. (free on board) production point and are exclusive of excise taxes. Effective with the release of data for January 1988, many important producer price indexes were changed to a new reference base year, 1982=100, from 1967=100. The reference year of the PPI shipment weights has been taken primarily from the 1987 Census of Manufactures. For further detail regarding the PPI, see the BLS *Handbook of Methods,* Bulletin 2490 (April 1997), Chapter 16. The PPI Web page is <http://stats.bls.gov/ppihome.htm>.

Consumer price indexes (CPI)—The CPI is a measure of the average change in prices over time in a "market basket" of goods and services purchased either by urban wage earners and clerical workers or by all urban consumers. In 1919, BLS began to publish complete indexes at semiannual intervals, using a weighting structure based on data collected in the expenditure survey of wage-earner and clerical-worker families in 1917-19 (BLS Bulletin 357, 1924). The first major revision of the CPI occurred in 1940, with subsequent revisions in 1953, 1964, 1978, 1987, and 1998.

Beginning with the release of data for January 1988 in February 1988, most consumer price indexes shifted to a new reference base year. All indexes previously expressed on a base of 1967=100, or any other base through December 1981, have been rebased to 1982-84=100. The expenditure weights are based upon data tabulated from the Consumer Expenditure Surveys for 1993, 1994, and 1995.

BLS publishes CPIs for two population groups: (1) a CPI for all urban consumers (CPI-U) which covers approximately 80 percent of the total population; and (2) a CPI for urban wage earners and clerical workers (CPI-W) which covers 32 percent of the total population. The CPI-U includes, in addition to wage earners and clerical workers, groups which historically have been excluded from CPI coverage, such as professional, managerial, and technical workers; the self-employed; short-term workers; the unemployed; and retirees and others not in the labor force.

The current CPI is based on prices of food, clothing, shelter, fuels, transportation fares, charges for doctors' and dentists' services, drugs, etc. purchased for day-to-day living. Prices are collected in 87 areas across the country from over 50,000 housing units and 23,000 establishments. Area selection was based on the 1990 census. All taxes directly associated with the purchase and use of items are included in the index. Prices of food, fuels, and a few other items are obtained every month in all 87 locations. Prices of most other commodities and services are collected monthly in the three largest geographic areas and every other month in other areas.

In calculating the index, each item is assigned a weight to account for its relative importance in consumers' budgets. Price changes for the various items in each location are then averaged. Local data are then combined to obtain a U.S. city average. Separate indexes are also published for regions, area size-classes, cross-classifications of regions and size-classes, and for 26 local areas, usually consisting of the Metropolitan Statistical Area (MSA); see Appendix II. Area definitions are those established by the Office of Management and Budget in 1983. Definitions do not include revisions made since 1992. Area indexes do not measure differences in the level of prices among cities; they only measure the average change in prices for each area since the base period. For further detail regarding the CPI, see the BLS *Handbook of Methods,* Bulletin 2490, Chapter 17; the *Consumer Price Index,* and the CPI home page: <http://stats.bls.gov/cpihome.htm>. In January 1983, the method of measuring home-ownership costs in the CPI-U was changed to a rental equivalence approach. This treatment calculates homeowner costs of shelter based on the implicit rent owners would pay to rent the homes they own. The rental equivalence approach was introduced into the CPI-W in 1985. The CPI-U was used to prepare the consumer price tables in this section.

Other price indexes—Chain-weighted price indexes, produced by the Bureau of Economic Analysis (BEA), are weighted averages of the detailed price indexes used in the deflation of the goods and services that make up the gross domestic product (GDP) and its major components. Growth rates are constructed for years and quarters using quantity weights for the current and preceding year or quarter; these growth rates are used to move the index for the preceding period forward a year or quarter at a time. The gross domestic purchases chained price index measures the average price of goods and services purchased in the United States. It differs from the GDP chained price index, which measures of the average price of goods produced in the United States, by excluding net exports. All chain-weighted price indexes are expressed in terms of the reference year value 1996=100.

Measures of inflation—Inflation is defined as a time of generally rising prices for goods and factors of production. The Bureau of Labor Statistics samples prices of items in a representative market basket and publishes the result as the CPI. The media invariably announce the inflation rate as the percent change in the CPI from month to month. A much more meaningful indicator of inflation is the percent change from the same month of the prior year. The producer price index measures prices at the producer level only. The PPI shows the same general pattern of inflation as does the CPI but is more volatile. The PPI can be roughly viewed as a leading indicator. It often tends to foreshadow trends that later occur in the CPI.

Other measures of inflation include the gross domestic purchases chain-weighted price index, the index of industrial materials prices; the Dow Jones Commodity Spot Price Index; Futures Price Index; the Employment Cost Index, the Hourly Compensation Index, or the Unit Labor Cost Index as a measure of the change in cost of the labor factor-of production; and changes in long-term interest rates that are often used to measure changes in the cost of the capital factor of production.

International price indexes—The BLS International Price Program produces export and import price indexes for nonmilitary goods traded between the United States and the rest of the world.

The export price index provides a measure of price change for all products sold by U.S. residents to foreign buyers. The import price index provides a measure of price change for goods purchased from other countries by U.S. residents. The reference period for the indexes is 1995=100, unless otherwise indicated. The product universe for both the import and export indexes includes raw materials, agricultural products, semifinished manufactures, and finished manufactures, including both capital and consumer goods. Price data for these items are collected primarily by mail questionnaire. In nearly all cases, the data are collected directly from the exporter or importer, although in a few cases, prices are obtained from other sources.

To the extent possible, the data gathered refer to prices at the U.S. border for exports and at either the foreign border or the U.S. border for imports. For nearly all products, the prices refer to transactions completed during the first week of the month. Survey respondents are asked to indicate all discounts, allowances, and rebates applicable to the reported prices, so that the price used in the calculation of the indexes is the actual price for which the product was bought or sold.

In addition to general indexes for U.S. exports and imports, indexes are also published for detailed product categories of exports and imports. These categories are defined according to the five-digit level of detail for the Bureau of Economic Analysis End-Use Classification, the three-digit level of detail for the Standard International Trade Classification (SITC), and the four-digit level of detail for the Harmonized System. Aggregate import indexes by country or region of origin are also available.

No. 691. Purchasing Power of the Dollar: 1950 to 2000

[Indexes: PPI, 1982=$1.00; CPI, 1982-84=$1.00. Producer prices prior to 1961 and consumer prices prior to 1964 exclude Alaska and Hawaii. Producer prices based on finished goods index. Obtained by dividing the average price index for the 1982=100, PPI; 1982-84=100, CPI base periods (100.0) by the price index for a given period and expressing the result in dollars and cents. Annual figures are based on average of monthly data]

Year	Annual average as measured by—		Year	Annual average as measured by—		Year	Annual average as measured by—	
	Producer prices	Consumer prices		Producer prices	Consumer prices		Producer prices	Consumer prices
1950	$3,546	$4,151	1967	2.809	2.993	1984	0.964	0.961
1951	3.247	3.846	1968	2.732	2.873	1985	0.955	0.928
1952	3.268	3.765	1969	2.632	2.726	1986	0.969	0.913
1953	3.300	3.735				1987	0.949	0.880
1954	3.289	3.717	1970	2.545	2.574	1988	0.926	0.846
1955	3.279	3.732	1971	2.469	2.466	1989	0.880	0.807
1956	3.195	3.678	1972	2.392	2.391	1990	0.839	0.766
1957	3.077	3.549	1973	2.193	2.251	1991	0.822	0.734
1958	3.012	3.457	1974	1.901	2.029	1992	0.812	0.713
1959	3.021	3.427	1975	1.718	1.859			
						1993	0.802	0.692
1960	2.994	3.373	1976	1.645	1.757	1994	0.797	0.675
1961	2.994	3.340	1977	1.546	1.649	1995	0.782	0.656
1962	2.985	3.304	1978	1.433	1.532	1996	0.762	0.638
1963	2.994	3.265	1979	1.289	1.380	1997	0.759	0.623
1964	2.985	3.220	1980	1.136	1.215	1998	0.766	0.614
1965	2.933	3.166	1981	1.041	1.098	1999	0.752	0.600
1966	2.841	3.080	1982	1.000	1.035	2000	0.725	0.581
			1983	0.984	1.003			

Source: U.S. Bureau of Labor Statistics. Monthly data in U.S. Bureau of Economic Analysis, *Survey of Current Business.*

U.S. Census Bureau, Statistical Abstract of the United States. 2001

Figure 14.1
**Annual Percent Change in Consumer
Price Indexes: 1990 to 2000**

Source: Chart prepared by U.S. Census Bureau. For data, see Table 692.

Figure 14.2
**Annual Percent Change in Producer Price Indexes
by Stage of Processing: 1990 to 2000**

Source: Chart prepared by U.S. Census Bureau. For data, see Table 697.

452   Prices

No. 692. Consumer Price Indexes (CPI-U) by Major Groups: 1980 to 2000

[**1982-84=100.** Represents annual averages of monthly figures. Reflects buying patterns of all urban consumers. Minus sign (-) indicates decrease. See text, this section]

Year	All items	Com- modi- ties	Energy	Food	Shelter	Apparel and upkeep	Trans- porta- tion	Medi- cal care	Fuel oil	Elec- tricity	Utility (piped) gas	Tele- phone services
1980	82.4	86.8	81.0	87.7	75.8	65.7	90.9	83.1	74.9	77.7	81.9	86.0
1987	113.6	113.5	121.3	75.8	110.0	95.1	110.6	105.4	130.1	116.5	115.1	107.7
1988	118.3	118.2	127.1	75.8	111.5	94.5	115.4	108.7	138.6	116.0	119.4	111.5
1989	124.0	125.1	132.8	80.3	114.7	97.1	118.6	114.1	149.3	117.2	125.0	116.7
1990	130.7	132.4	140.0	98.6	117.4	97.3	124.1	120.5	162.8	117.7	130.4	122.8
1991	136.2	136.3	146.3	92.4	121.8	98.5	128.7	123.8	177.0	119.7	134.9	126.6
1992	140.3	137.9	151.2	88.0	124.2	100.3	131.9	126.5	190.1	120.4	138.3	129.1
1993	144.5	140.9	155.7	87.2	126.7	106.5	133.7	130.4	201.4	121.2	141.5	131.5
1994	148.2	144.3	160.5	85.6	126.7	108.5	133.4	134.3	211.0	123.1	144.6	133.8
1995	152.4	148.4	165.7	84.8	129.6	102.9	132.0	139.1	220.5	124.0	147.1	136.4
1996	156.9	153.3	171.0	97.0	131.8	107.2	131.7	143.0	228.2	125.9	150.1	139.9
1997	160.5	157.3	176.3	96.9	132.5	114.6	132.9	144.3	234.6	127.7	152.7	141.8
1998	163.0	160.7	182.1	84.8	127.4	112.4	133.0	141.6	242.1	127.0	156.7	141.9
1999	166.6	164.1	187.3	86.6	126.5	113.0	131.3	144.4	250.6	100.1	161.1	144.4
2000	172.2	167.8	193.4	130.3	128.5	132.0	129.6	153.3	260.8	98.5	165.6	(NA)
PERCENT CHANGE [1]												
1980	13.5	8.6	17.6	39.0	15.5	19.2	7.1	17.9	11.0	2.5	8.9	12.3
1987	3.6	4.1	4.7	2.3	-0.4	-4.6	4.4	3.0	6.6	-0.6	2.9	3.2
1988	4.1	4.1	4.8	-	1.4	-0.6	4.3	3.1	6.5	-0.4	3.7	3.5
1989	4.8	5.8	4.5	5.9	2.9	2.8	2.8	5.0	7.7	1.0	4.7	4.7
1990	5.4	5.8	5.4	22.8	2.4	0.2	4.6	5.6	9.0	0.4	4.3	5.2
1991	4.2	2.9	4.5	-6.3	3.7	1.2	3.7	2.7	8.7	1.7	3.5	3.1
1992	3.0	1.2	3.3	-4.8	2.0	1.8	2.5	2.2	7.4	0.6	2.5	2.0
1993	3.0	2.2	3.0	-0.9	2.0	6.2	1.4	3.1	5.9	0.7	2.3	1.9
1994	2.6	2.4	3.1	-1.8	-	1.9	-0.2	3.0	4.8	1.6	2.2	1.7
1995	2.8	2.8	3.2	-0.9	2.3	-5.2	-1.0	3.6	4.5	0.7	1.7	1.9
1996	3.0	3.3	3.2	14.4	1.7	4.2	-0.2	2.8	3.5	1.5	2.0	2.6
1997	2.3	2.6	3.1	-C.1	0.5	6.9	0.9	0.9	2.8	1.4	1.7	1.4
1998	1.6	2.2	3.3	-12.5	-3.8	-1.9	0.1	-1.9	3.2	-21.1	2.6	0.1
1999	2.2	2.1	2.9	2.1	-0.7	0.5	-1.3	2.0	3.5	-0.6	2.8	1.8
2000	3.4	2.3	3.3	50.5	1.6	16.8	-1.3	6.2	4.1	-1.6	2.8	-100.0

- Represents zero.   NA Not available.   [1] Change from prior year.

Source: Bureau of Labor Statistics, *Monthly Labor Review and Handbook of Labor Statistics*, periodic.

No. 693. Consumer Price Indexes (CPI-U)—Selected Areas: 2000

[**1982-84=100, except as indicated.** Represents annual averages of monthly figures. Local area CPI indexes are byproducts of the national CPI program. Each local index has a smaller sample size than the national index and is therefore, subject to substantially more sampling and other measurement error. As a result, local area indexes show greater volatility than the national index, although their long-term trends are similar. Area definitions are those established by the Office of Management and Budget in 1983. For further detail see the U.S. Bureau of Labor Statistics Handbook of Methods, Bulletin 2285, Chapter 19, the Consumer Price Index, and Report 736, the CPI: 1987 Revision. See also text, this section]

Area	All items	Food and bever- ages	Food	Hous- ing	Apparel and upkeep	Trans- porta- tion	Medical care	Fuel and other utilities
U.S. city average	172.2	168.4	167.8	169.6	129.6	153.3	260.8	137.9
Anchorage, AK MSA	150.9	151.7	152.3	134.2	124.5	150.5	272.1	143.8
Atlanta, GA MSA	170.6	171.8	176.5	171.0	132.3	137.6	264.2	155.6
Boston, MA MSA	183.6	174.8	175.3	179.6	139.6	152.2	348.6	131.9
Chicago-Gary, IL-IN CMSA	173.8	171.4	170.4	175.3	112.5	148.4	259.5	134.4
Cincinnati-Hamilton, OH-KY-IN CMSA	164.8	156.4	154.7	158.2	127.2	148.8	253.9	132.2
Cleveland-Akron-Lorain, OH CMSA	168.0	172.9	174.7	166.1	123.1	152.0	233.9	139.8
Dallas-Fort Worth, TX CMSA	164.7	169.2	166.4	152.6	137.5	152.3	243.2	135.8
Denver-Boulder-Greely, CO CMSA	173.2	160.5	162.0	170.2	90.6	179.3	303.7	138.1
Detroit-Ann Arbor-Flint, MI CMSA	169.8	163.9	163.3	161.7	127.9	162.5	257.4	129.8
Honolulu, HI MSA	176.3	164.8	164.8	177.9	103.5	169.6	239.8	147.4
Houston-Galveston-Brazoria, TX CMSA	154.2	157.7	156.9	137.2	146.5	142.4	242.9	111.3
Kansas City, MO-KS CMSA	166.6	165.0	166.1	161.5	118.5	147.5	245.1	142.6
Los Angeles-Anaheim-Riverside, CA CMSA	171.6	173.6	171.4	170.8	117.0	154.2	252.2	155.6
Miami-Fort Lauderdale, FL CMSA	167.8	174.8	175.2	158.6	151.1	158.6	241.2	116.8
Milwaukee, WI PMSA	168.6	168.9	169.8	166.4	119.7	149.4	257.7	124.9
Minneapolis-St. Paul, MN-WI MSA	170.1	177.9	175.0	156.2	138.2	157.6	249.7	135.2
New York-Northern New Jersey-Long Island, NY-NJ-CT CMSA	182.5	172.8	171.9	186.1	123.7	160.0	275.1	126.1
Philadelphia-Wilmington-Trenton, PA-NJ-DE- MD CMSA	176.5	161.4	160.5	176.9	102.6	160.6	278.7	133.4
Pittsburgh, PA MSA	168.0	159.3	157.8	165.5	157.7	139.6	248.7	149.2
Portland, OR MSA	178.0	158.4	158.5	178.1	135.3	165.2	247.3	146.1
San Diego, CA MSA	182.8	169.2	167.2	190.5	131.3	162.4	256.5	139.5
San Francisco-Oakland-San Jose, CA CMSA	180.2	175.1	175.7	197.0	115.4	143.1	242.9	185.0
Seattle-Tacoma, WA CMSA	179.2	173.7	174.2	184.8	126.6	159.6	246.6	131.5
St. Louis-East St. Louis, MO-IL CMSA	163.1	166.8	165.1	155.0	120.9	150.6	256.8	136.1
Tampa-St. Petersburg-Clearwater, FL MSA [1]	145.7	142.3	141.4	139.4	158.9	134.0	199.0	124.2
Washington-Baltimore, DC-MD-VA-WV CMSA [2]	107.6	105.5	105.6	128.9	98.2	107.3	109.7	112.8

[1] 1987=100.   [2] 1997=100; except "Apparel and upkeep" and "Transportation," 1996=100.

Source: U.S. Bureau of Labor Statistics, *Monthly Labor Review* and *CPI Detailed Report*, January issues.

No. 694. Consumer Price Indexes for All Urban Consumers (CPI-U) for Selected Items and Groups: 1980 to 2000

[1982-84 = 100. Annual averages of monthly figures. See headnote, Table 692]

Item	1980	1990	1994	1995	1996	1997	1998	1999	2000
All items	**82.4**	**130.7**	**148.2**	**152.4**	**156.9**	**160.5**	**163.0**	**166.6**	**172.2**
Food and beverages	86.7	132.1	144.9	148.9	153.7	157.7	161.1	164.6	168.4
Food	86.8	132.4	144.3	148.4	153.3	157.3	160.7	164.1	167.8
Food at home	88.4	132.3	144.1	148.8	154.3	158.1	161.1	164.2	167.9
Cereals and bakery products	83.9	140.0	163.0	167.5	174.0	177.6	181.1	185.0	188.3
Cereals and cereal products	84.2	141.1	164.8	167.1	168.9	169.5	171.5	175.0	175.9
Cereals	76.3	158.6	190.6	192.5	190.0	187.5	189.9	195.2	198.0
Rice, pasta, and cornmeal	90.9	122.0	139.7	140.2	144.2	148.8	150.5	151.9	150.7
Bakery products	83.8	139.2	161.9	167.4	176.1	181.1	185.4	189.4	194.1
White bread	85.9	136.4	159.0	165.5	177.5	183.8	187.3	192.5	199.1
Cookies, cakes, and cupcakes	81.5	142.7	165.1	169.1	174.1	179.2	181.2	185.0	187.9
Meats, poultry, fish and eggs	92.0	130.0	137.2	138.8	144.8	148.5	147.3	147.9	154.5
Meats	92.7	128.5	135.4	135.5	140.2	144.4	141.6	142.3	150.7
Beef and veal	98.4	128.8	136.0	134.9	134.5	136.8	136.5	139.2	148.1
Ground beef excl. canned	104.6	118.1	119.7	116.1	114.3	116.4	116.1	118.4	125.2
Pork	81.9	129.8	133.9	134.8	148.2	155.9	148.5	145.9	156.5
Bacon	73.5	113.4	118.1	120.0	148.9	164.0	152.0	151.5	177.5
Chops	82.9	140.2	144.2	144.2	153.0	155.2	146.8	143.5	152.2
Ham	85.5	132.4	139.3	139.6	149.2	156.3	150.0	147.0	152.7
Poultry	93.7	132.5	141.5	143.5	152.4	156.6	157.1	157.9	159.8
Fresh whole chicken	94.4	134.9	140.1	142.2	152.6	158.5	159.6	161.8	162.9
Fresh, frozen chicken parts	91.7	135.9	145.6	146.0	155.0	157.4	157.2	156.8	157.7
Fish and seafood	87.5	146.7	163.7	171.6	173.1	177.1	181.7	185.3	190.4
Canned fish and seafood	93.7	119.5	123.8	125.5	125.9	128.4	132.6	131.5	127.4
Eggs	88.6	124.1	114.3	120.5	142.1	140.0	135.4	128.1	131.9
Dairy products	90.9	126.5	131.7	132.8	142.1	145.5	150.8	159.6	160.7
Fruits and vegetables	82.1	149.0	165.0	177.7	183.9	187.5	198.2	203.1	204.6
Fresh fruits and vegetables	81.8	(NA)	186.7	206.0	211.8	215.4	231.2	237.2	238.8
Fresh fruits	84.8	170.9	201.2	219.0	234.4	236.3	246.5	266.3	258.3
Apples	92.1	147.5	174.0	183.5	202.3	199.6	202.3	200.1	212.6
Bananas	91.5	138.2	143.6	153.8	159.0	159.6	160.9	159.4	162.5
Oranges, tangerines	72.6	160.6	189.9	224.5	239.3	226.1	251.5	337.0	257.0
Fresh vegetables	79.0	151.1	172.3	193.1	189.2	194.6	215.8	209.3	219.4
Potatoes	81.0	162.6	174.3	174.7	180.6	174.2	185.2	193.1	196.3
Lettuce	77.8	150.3	170.3	221.2	185.7	200.1	229.1	208.3	228.1
Tomatoes	81.9	160.8	173.5	188.3	198.2	213.6	239.2	224.1	234.7
Processed fruits and vegetables.	82.6	(NA)	134.5	137.5	144.4	147.9	(NA)	(NA)	(NA)
Coffee	111.6	117.5	140.4	163.1	149.2	168.0	163.4	154.8	154.0
Food away from home	83.4	(NA)	145.7	149.0	152.7	157.0	161.1	165.1	169.0
Alcoholic beverages.	86.4	129.3	151.5	153.9	158.5	162.8	165.7	169.7	174.7
Alcoholic beverages at home	87.3	123.0	142.5	143.1	146.8	149.5	150.6	153.7	158.1
Beer and ale	84.8	123.6	143.4	143.9	147.4	148.2	148.5	151.9	156.8
Distilled spirits	89.8	125.7	144.3	145.7	147.5	150.8	152.7	156.2	162.3
Wine	89.5	114.4	133.3	133.6	139.3	145.5	147.3	149.4	151.6
Alcoholic beverages away from home	82.9	144.4	171.6	176.5	182.7	189.4	195.0	201.0	207.1
Housing	81.1	128.5	144.8	148.5	152.8	156.8	160.4	163.9	169.6
Shelter	81.0	140.0	160.5	165.7	171.0	176.3	182.1	187.3	193.4
Renters' cost	(NA)	146.7	169.4	174.3	180.2	186.4	(NA)	(NA)	(NA)
Rent, residential	80.9	138.4	154.0	157.8	162.0	166.7	(NA)	(NA)	(NA)
Tenants' insurance	78.9	130.6	145.8	150.9	154.7	159.2	(NA)	(NA)	(NA)
Homeowners' costs	(NA)	144.6	165.5	171.0	176.5	181.5	(NA)	(NA)	(NA)
Owners' equivalent rent	(NA)	144.8	165.8	171.3	176.8	181.9	187.8	192.9	198.7
Household insurance.	(NA)	135.3	152.3	157.4	161.0	165.3	(NA)	(NA)	(NA)
Maintenance and repair	82.4	122.2	130.8	135.3	139.0	143.7	(NA)	(NA)	(NA)
Fuels and other utilities.	75.4	111.6	122.8	123.7	127.5	130.8	128.5	128.8	137.9
Fuels	74.8	104.5	111.7	111.5	115.2	117.9	113.7	113.5	122.8
Fuel oil and other	86.1	99.3	88.8	88.1	99.2	99.8	90.0	91.4	129.7
Fuel oil	87.7	98.6	85.6	84.8	97.0	96.9	84.8	86.6	130.3
Gas (piped) and electricity	71.4	109.3	119.2	119.2	122.1	125.1	121.2	120.9	128.0
Electricity	75.8	117.4	126.7	128.6	129.6	131.8	132.5	127.4	128.5
Utility (piped) gas	65.7	97.3	108.5	102.9	107.2	114.6	112.4	113.0	132.0
Telephone services	77.7	117.7	123.1	124.0	125.9	127.7	(NA)	100.1	98.5
Local charges	72.8	149.3	156.9	160.4	160.8	163.1	165.7	168.7	175.6
Interstate toll charges	83.3	68.2	75.2	74.9	77.9	77.3	75.5	73.4	68.0
Intrastate toll charges	85.2	95.1	90.2	86.0	89.4	93.9	95.7	94.7	90.7
Water and sewerage maintenance	74.0	150.2	190.6	196.5	204.5	210.0	217.3	222.0	227.5
Cable television.	(NA)	158.4	197.4	200.7	212.6	228.7	245.2	254.6	266.8
Refuse collection.	(NA)	171.2	231.4	241.2	246.0	250.5	256.7	263.8	269.8

See footnotes at end of table.

U.S. Census Bureau, Statistical Abstract of the United States: 2001

[1982-84 = 100. Annual averages of monthly figures. See headnote, Table 692]

Item	1980	1990	1994	1995	1996	1997	1998	1999	2000
Household furnishings and operations	86.3	113.3	121.0	123.0	124.7	125.4	126.6	126.7	128.2
Furniture and bedding	88.0	115.7	128.2	130.9	134.1	134.5	135.0	134.9	134.4
Bedroom furniture	83.5	118.5	135.1	136.4	139.3	141.5	141.3	141.0.	138.4
Video and audio equipment.	100.7	80.8	76.0	73.9	71.3	99.4	101.1	100.7	101.0
Television	104.6	74.6	69.9	68.1	64.5	61.7	59.2	54.9	49.9
Video products other than TV.	(NA)	91.5	73.8	70.3	66.3	63.4	(NA)	92.1	88.6
Audio products	97.7	93.2	93.8	92.1	90.7	88.9	85.2	81.7	80.2
Housekeeping supplies	83.2	125.2	132.3	137.1	141.1	143.1	145.7	148.1	153.4
Postage	76.2	125.1	145.3	160.3	160.3	160.3	160.3	165.1	165.1
Apparel and upkeep	90.9	124.1	133.4	132.0	131.7	132.9	133.0	131.3	129.6
Apparel commodities	92.9	122.0	130.4	128.7	128.2	129.1	(NA)	(NA)	(NA)
Apparel commodities less footwear	93.0	122.8	131.2	129.3	128.5	129.4	129.3	127.8	126.2
Men's and boy's apparel	89.4	120.4	126.4	126.2	127.7	130.1	131.8	131.1	129.7
Women's and girl's apparel.	96.0	122.6	130.9	126.9	124.7	126.1	126.0	123.3	121.5
Infants' and toddlers'	85.5	125.8	128.1	127.2	129.7	129.0	126.1	129.0	130.6
Footwear	91.8	117.4	126.0	125.4	126.6	127.6	128.0	125.7	123.8
Transportation	83.1	120.5	134.3	139.1	143.0	144.3	141.6	144.4	153.3
Private transportation	84.2	118.8	131.4	136.3	140.0	141.0	137.9	140.5	149.1
New vehicles.	88.5	121.4	137.6	141.0	143.7	144.3	143.4	142.9	142.8
New cars	88.4	121.0	136.0	139.0	141.4	141.7	140.7	139.6	139.6
New trucks	(NA)	121.6	141.7	145.9	149.5	151.4	151.1	152.0	151.7
Used cars.	62.3	117.6	141.7	156.5	157.0	151.1	150.6.	152.0	155.8
Motor fuel	97.4	101.2	98.5	100.0	106.3	106.2	92.2	100.7	129.3
Automobile maintenance and repair.	81.5	130.1	150.2	154.0	158.4	162.7	167.1	171.9	177.3
Automobile insurance	82.0	177.9	224.8	234.3	243.9	251.6	254.3	253.8	256.7
Vehicle rental, registration, other.	78.3	148.1	174.2	177.9	181.1	185.4	102.5	103.8	107.3
Public transportation	69.0	142.6	172.0	175.9	181.9	186.7	190.3	197.7	209.6
Airline fares.	68.0	148.4	185.5	189.7	192.5	199.2	205.3	218.8	239.4
Other intercity transportation	73.1	143.3	152.8	153.3	156.0	155.1	160.4	160.6	156.3
Intracity transportation.	69.7	133.5	152.7	157.5	173.2	175.8	174.2	172.4	174.9
Medical care	74.9	162.8	211.0	220.5	228.2	234.6	242.1	250.6	260.8
Medical care commodities.	75.4	163.4	200.7	204.5	210.4	215.3	221.8	230.7	238.1
Prescription drugs	72.5	181.7	230.6	235.0	242.9	249.3	258.6	273.4	285.4
Nonprescription drugs, medical sup.	(NA)	120.6	138.1	140.5	143.1	145.4	147.7	148.5	149.5
Medical care services.	74.8	162.7	213.4	224.2	232.4	239.1	246.8	255.1	266.0
Professional medical services.	77.9	156.1	192.5	201.0	208.3	215.4	222.2	229.2	237.7
Physicians' services	76.5	160.8	199.8	208.8	216.4	222.9	229.5	236.0	244.7
Dental services	78.9	155.8	197.1	206.8	216.5	226.6	236.2	247.2	258.5
Eye care	(NA)	117.3	133.0	137.0	139.3	141.5	144.1	145.5	149.7
Hospital and related services	69.2	178.0	245.6	257.8	269.5	278.4	287.5	299.5	317.3
Recreation.	(NA)	(NA)	(NA)	(NA)	(NA)	(NA)	(NA)	102.0	103.3
Photography	(NA)	(NA)	(NA)	(NA)	(NA)	(NA)	(NA)	99.4	99.2
Sporting goods, equipment	88.5	114.9	122.2	123.5	123.4	122.6	121.9	120.3	119.0
Sport vehicles, including bicycles	87.9	115.3	122.3	125.3	125.7	124.5	125.3	128.7	130.9
Other recreational goods	(NA)	(NA)	(NA)	(NA)	(NA)	(NA)	97.1	92.3	87.8
Toys, hobbies, and playground equipment . .	(NA)	(NA)	(NA)	(NA)	(NA)	(NA)	97.2	91.7	87.4
Pets, pet products and services.	(NA)	(NA)	(NA)	(NA)	(NA)	(NA)	101.5	103.4	106.1
Pet supplies and expenses	83.3	124.6	130.9	132.3	139.0	142.7	143.5	144.5	144.3
Recreation services.	(NA)	(NA)	(NA)	(NA)	(NA)	(NA)	102.4	106.9	111.7
Recreational reading materials.	(NA)	(NA)	(NA)	(NA)	(NA)	179.0	184.1	186.1	188.3
Club membership.	(NA)	117.0	130.7	132.8	133.3	132.1	(NA)	105.8	108.9
Admissions	83.8	151.2	175.2	182.3	192.1	198.9	205.5	216.5	230.5
Tobacco and smoking products	72.0	181.5	220.0	225.7	232.8	243.7	274.8	355.8	394.9
Personal care.	81.9	130.4	144.6	147.1	150.1	152.7	156.7	161.1	165.6
Personal care services	83.7	132.8	147.9	151.5	156.6	162.4	166.0	171.4	178.1
Education and communication.	70.9	170.2	223.2	235.5	247.5	259.7	(NA)	101.2	102.5
Education	(NA)	(NA)	(NA)	(NA)	(NA)	97.3	102.1	107.0	112.5
School books and supplies	71.4	171.3	205.5	214.4	226.9	238.4	250.8	261.7	279.9
Tuition and other school fees.	71.2	175.7	239.8	253.8	267.1	280.4	294.2	308.4	324.0
College tuition	70.8	175.0	249.8	264.8	279.8	294.1	306.5	318.7	331.9
Elementary and high school tuition	72.3	182.8	242.6	259.2	272.8	288.1	307.9	327.3	349.9
Day care and nursery school	(NA)	(NA)	119.6	124.5	129.4	134.3	140.9	148.1	156.3
All commodities	86.0	122.8	133.8	136.4	139.9	141.8	141.9	144.4	149.2
All commodities less food.	85.7	117.4	127.9	129.8	132.6	133.4	132.0	134.0	139.2
Energy	86.0	102.1	104.6	105.2	110.1	111.5	102.9	106.6	124.6

NA Not available.

Source: U.S. Bureau of Labor Statistics, *Monthly Labor Review* and *CPI Detailed Report*, January issues.

No. 695. Cost of Living Index—Selected Metropolitan Areas: Fourth Quarter 2000

[Measures relative price levels for consumer goods and services in participating areas for a mid-management standard of living. The nationwide average equals 100, and each index is read as a percent of the national average. The index does not measure inflation, but compares prices at a single point in time. Excludes taxes. Metropolitan areas as defined by the Office of Management and Budget. For definitions and components of MSAs, see source for details]

Metropolitan areas (MA)	Composite index (100%)	Grocery items (16%)	Housing (28%)	Utilities (8%)	Transportation (10%)	Health care (5%)	Misc. goods and services (33%)
Anniston, AL MSA	93.1	94.8	91.2	99.6	88.3	81.3	95.6
Birmingham, AL MSA	94.7	90.5	86.4	108.0	97.3	94.8	99.8
Decatur, AL MSA	93.1	94.6	89.5	90.0	100.4	90.5	94.3
Dothan, AL MSA	91.6	97.3	80.4	83.8	90.7	88.2	101.0
Florence, AL MSA	89.8	90.3	82.0	92.1	89.4	87.7	96.0
Huntsville, AL MSA	96.1	98.0	87.4	85.1	103.7	100.3	102.2
Mobile, AL MSA	96.4	96.5	92.3	105.7	103.0	82.7	97.7
Montgomery, AL MSA	97.5	95.5	93.8	108.4	107.2	94.5	96.4
Tuscaloosa, AL MSA	99.4	95.4	95.3	95.5	98.3	103.0	105.5
Anchorage, AK MSA	122.9	124.9	132.0	82.8	109.1	160.4	122.3
Nonmetropolitan areas:							
Fairbanks, AK	120.1	118.4	109.2	154.1	113.7	166.8	116.8
Kodiak, AK	129.1	139.4	128.4	152.6	114.3	153.3	119.9
Flagstaff, AZ-UT MSA	108.3	104.3	122.0	93.1	116.4	116.8	98.6
Las Vegas, NV-AZ MSA:							
Lake Havasu City, AZ	99.2	102.9	99.9	109.1	111.0	99.0	90.9
Phoenix-Mesa, AZ MSA:							
Phoenix, AZ	102.5	104.9	100.9	101.2	109.1	118.8	98.6
Tucson, AZ MSA	99.6	108.7	99.8	111.9	102.2	116.0	88.8
Yuma, AZ	95.4	98.8	86.1	147.1	107.2	98.5	85.2
Fayetteville-Springdale-Rogers, AR MSA	89.7	86.3	87.7	89.2	93.9	85.6	92.4
Fort Smith, AR-OK MSA	86.9	86.6	77.4	88.2	90.7	86.8	93.8
Jonesboro, AR MSA	87.0	91.3	79.6	93.5	85.7	86.3	90.1
Little Rock-North Little Rock, AR MSA	88.0	89.9	81.4	98.0	83.7	88.2	91.6
Fresno, CA MSA	106.0	107.3	95.6	125.0	113.8	115.5	105.7
Los Angeles-Long Beach, CA PMSA	144.7	113.6	230.5	105.4	113.3	121.1	109.6
Riverside-San Bernardino, CA PMSA:							
Riverside City, CA	106.6	108.7	100.8	111.1	111.8	119.7	105.9
Sacramento, CA PMSA	118.8	117.0	130.5	118.1	120.1	160.7	103.1
San Diego, CA MSA	127.3	125.8	157.7	125.4	124.2	131.4	102.9
San Francisco, CA PMSA	199.2	123.4	392.8	133.0	130.6	165.2	113.8
Visalia-Tulare-Porterville, CA MSA	104.9	104.6	96.6	104.1	117.9	113.8	107.0
Colorado Springs, CO MSA	99.9	100.3	105.5	83.8	108.7	121.2	92.9
Denver, CO PMSA	107.1	109.5	119.9	79.5	106.6	130.0	98.5
Fort Collins-Loveland, CO MSA:							
Fort Collins, CO	103.7	109.0	115.2	77.3	104.2	114.5	96.1
Grand Junction, CO MSA	100.1	104.7	97.7	89.5	104.2	104.1	100.7
Pueblo, CO MSA	91.9	110.3	78.5	96.0	89.0	104.5	92.3
New Haven-Meriden, CT PMSA	123.8	106.1	144.8	160.2	110.6	115.0	111.2
Dover, DE MSA	104.2	107.5	96.4	123.5	97.2	97.1	107.6
Wilmington-Newark, DE-MD PMSA	110.7	109.7	111.4	131.4	102.0	120.1	106.9
Washington DC-MD-VA-WV PMSA	112.9	110.0	124.2	91.7	112.7	121.4	108.6
Daytona Beach, FL MSA	96.8	104.1	93.1	99.4	104.3	97.4	93.3
Fort Walton Beach FL, MSA	100.3	96.3	104.7	89.6	100.8	103.0	100.4
Jacksonville, FL MSA	93.3	101.8	88.2	91.2	97.0	91.0	93.3
Orlando, FL MSA	99.7	105.7	94.7	106.3	95.8	111.1	98.9
Panama City, FL MSA	97.5	101.5	97.2	95.4	109.0	106.6	91.5
Pensacola, FL MSA	97.8	98.7	93.3	87.9	103.3	107.4	100.4
Sarasota-Bradenton, FL MSA:							
Sarasota, FL	105.1	100.5	111.0	110.1	103.4	105.3	101.5
Tallahassee, FL MSA	109.0	105.7	109.9	112.0	106.6	104.5	110.4
Tampa-St. Petersburg-Clearwater, FL MSA	96.4	102.9	91.8	107.7	92.2	92.1	96.4
Tampa, FL	102.5	106.01	99.5	105.1	102.7	106.6	102.0
West Palm Beach-Boca Raton, FL	104.2	106.3	97.1	102.4	107.7	107.5	108.1
Albany, GA MSA	94.3	97.6	84.8	101.8	95.3	88.1	99.7
Atlanta, GA MSA:							
Atlanta, GA	103.2	101.9	109.4	93.2	101.9	106.9	100.8
Augusta-Aiken, GA-SC MSA	94.2	104.5	82.5	92.5	95.5	98.4	98.5
Boise City, ID MSA	98.9	95.7	100.6	84.6	102.6	112.6	99.2
Pocatello, ID	94.9	104.7	80.9	89.2	104.4	100.5	99.7
Bloomington-Normal, IL MSA	105.3	100.0	99.9	118.6	104.1	103.8	109.7
Champaign-Urbana, IL MSA	105.5	100.4	103.4	119.6	101.2	98.4	108.7
Chicago, IL PMSA:							
Joliet/Will County, IL	104.6	105.6	107.0	102.0	111.1	109.2	100.1
Decatur, IL MSA	93.5	91.6	88.3	101.1	97.3	80.4	97.9
Peoria-Pekin, IL MSA	100.2	98.0	95.8	93.0	99.9	92.5	108.0
Rockford, IL MSA	101.4	102.1	103.9	93.5	9.9	111.7	99.8
Springfield, IL MSA	94.3	96.9	96.6	99.2	86.0	100.9	91.3
Bloomington, IN MSA	100.0	106.0	91.9	94.5	93.9	102.6	106.8
Elkhart-Goshen, IN MSA	96.1	96.1	92.1	108.5	94.2	97.1	96.8
Evansville-Henderson, IN-KY MSA	93.7	92.7	93.0	89.4	96.4	93.7	95.1
Indianapolis, IN MSA:							
Lafayette, IN MSA	94.1	92.4	90.0	101.6	93.0	96.4	96.6

See footnotes at end of table.

U.S. Census Bureau, Statistical Abstract of the United States: 2001

[See headnote, page 456]

Metropolitan areas (MA)	Composite index (100%)	Grocery items (16%)	Housing (28%)	Utilities (8%)	Transportation (10%)	Health care (5%)	Misc. goods and services (33%)
Muncie, IN MSA	97.4	94.8	101.3	97.3	99.3	94.4	95.3
South Bend, IN MSA	93.3	87.6	92.2	109.4	88.1	99.5	93.8
Cedar Rapids, IA MSA	97.5	89.6	89.1	126.0	100.0	91.8	101.8
Waterloo-Cedar Falls, IA MSA	97.3	98.0	88.9	110.4	107.5	97.4	97.7
Lawrence, KS MSA	100.1	93.0	107.4	101.0	100.4	87.7	98.8
Wichita, KS MSA	100.4	97.7	95.6	112.7	99.7	106.3	102.0
Cincinnati, OH-KY-IN PMSA:							
Covington, KY	93.4	97.2	84.2	100.1	94.4	97.7	96.8
Clarksville-Hopkinsville, TN-KY MSA:	95.8	91.2	89.8	101.1	96.8	89.5	102.6
Evansville-Henderson, IN-KY MSA	94.6	101.7	99.9	79.7	91.6	86.7	92.4
Lexington, KY MSA	97.1	103.0	94.9	83.0	95.3	97.3	99.9
Louisville, KY-IN MSA	97.6	94.8	90.9	104.2	114.3	89.9	99.3
Baton Rouge, LA MSA	105.8	106.8	102.6	131.1	103.8	97.3	103.9
Lafayette, LA MSA	99.6	93.3	108.0	92.9	101.2	89.5	98.2
Lake Charles, LA MSA	100.6	89.9	104.4	132.2	103.6	92.6	95.1
Monroe, LA MSA	96.9	88.9	94.7	122.5	97.9	89.8	97.3
New Orleans, LA MSA	99.3	105.9	86.9	135.9	108.5	103.3	94.5
Shreveport-Bossier City, LA MSA	91.3	89.0	85.9	90.4	91.2	89.8	97.5
Cumberland, MD-WV MSA	97.9	89.1	99.9	97.9	87.8	90.1	104.7
Boston, MA-NH PMSA:							
Boston PMSA (MA Part)	133.1	117.0	170.8	126.4	119.8	131.1	114.9
Grand Rapids-Muskegon-Holland, MI MSA	111.0	107.4	127.9	88.5	111.0	97.7	105.9
Lansing-East Lansing, MI MSA	98.1	101.1	99.3	78.6	91.8	97.9	102.4
Minneapolis-St Paul, MN-WI MSA:							
Minneapolis, MN	112.9	100.6	122.1	111.8	110.9	131.6	109.0
St Paul, MN	112.4	101.7	120.6	116.1	113.0	129.4	107.0
Rochester, MN MSA	99.7	96.4	94.9	88.7	103.5	117.0	104.3
St Cloud, MN MSA	96.7	96.4	85.0	104.7	101.7	100.2	102.8
Hattiesburg, MS MSA	95.0	92.5	91.3	120.7	91.1	90.4	95.0
Jackson, MS MSA	92.4	81.2	90.7	108.2	97.6	78.4	96.1
Columbia, MO MSA	97.2	95.2	97.3	85.7	98.5	97.7	100.3
Joplin, MO MSA	89.1	88.5	92.0	83.7	79.6	102.4	89.0
St Joseph, MO MSA	92.9	89.0	87.9	90.8	92.6	97.7	98.9
St Louis, MO-IL MSA	96.7	93.8	88.6	97.0	104.2	104.8	101.5
Springfield, MO MSA	92.5	93.5	88.4	82.1	92.9	97.6	97.1
Billings, MT MSA	99.2	99.8	94.5	100.2	100.1	106.5	101.3
Great Falls, MT MSA	102.6	107.4	115.6	82.5	97.0	90.7	97.7
Missoula, MT MSA	103.6	112.1	95.5	102.2	101.3	103.5	107.3
Lincoln, NE MSA	98.6	98.4	99.3	88.8	98.4	99.6	100.4
Omaha, NE-IA MSA	95.3	93.5	90.4	107.2	100.2	95.9	95.9
Las Vegas, NV-AZ MSA:							
Las Vegas, NV MSA	108.9	113.9	112.2	87.4	117.6	118.3	104.8
Reno, NV MSA	110.9	117.6	113.7	92.6	122.2	128.5	103.5
Manchester, NH PMSA	101.9	100.7	91.9	144.7	96.2	104.8	102.0
Albuquerque, NM MSA:							
Albuquerque, NM	101.8	111.3	100.6	92.7	102.9	103.7	99.9
Las Cruces, NM MSA	96.3	101.6	90.4	96.6	91.0	97.9	99.9
Santa Fe, NM MSA:							
Santa Fe, NM	116.5	103.9	146.0	91.7	112.7	129.5	102.7
Binghamton, NY MSA	97.9	98.3	87.8	133.0	96.5	92.9	98.8
Buffalo-Niagara Falls, NY MSA	103.7	115.9	85.7	183.3	97.8	94.1	97.0
Glens Falls, NY MSA	106.1	109.2	85.9	167.1	103.0	98.5	108.9
Nassau-Suffolk, NY PMSA	140.0	125.2	175.2	149.3	110.3	144.2	123.3
New York, NY PMSA	235.2	143.5	475.2	166.1	117.4	179.4	136.9
Asheville, NC MSA	100.5	101.3	98.8	94.6	107.1	90.5	102.5
Charlotte-Gastonia-Rock Hill, NC-SC MSA	97.9	101.9	91.2	94.9	103.8	97.7	100.7
Fayetteville, NC MSA	100.1	108.1	85.7	103.0	98.2	100.2	108.4
Greensboro-Winston-Salem-High Point, NC MSA	92.6	96.2	88.0	94.5	93.8	91.4	94.1
Greensboro, NC	95.2	95.0	94.9	94.4	101.0	98.5	93.6
Greenville, NC MSA	100.0	94.7	106.1	125.4	92.6	96.8	93.9
Jacksonville, NC MSA	92.9	94.9	80.2	115.2	85.6	93.4	99.5
Raleigh-Durham-Chapel Hill, NC MSA:							
Raleigh, NC	104.6	101.8	108.2	99.6	97.0	111.1	105.5
Rocky Mount, NC MSA	98.2	101.1	85.8	130.1	97.8	100.8	99.2
Wilmington, NC MSA	105.2	107.2	115.2	101.8	88.5	96.2	103.0
Bismarck, ND MSA	96.6	100.1	90.0	95.7	102.6	92.7	99.6
Fargo-Moorhead, ND-MN MSA	98.6	98.2	93.7	100.8	99.9	104.8	101.1
Nonmetropolitan areas:							
Minot, ND	93.1	95.4	88.9	96.5	90.3	83.1	97.1
Akron, OH PMSA	98.1	104.0	86.6	127.2	97.5	103.2	97.5
Cincinnati, OH-KY-IN PMSA:							
Cincinnati, OH	98.8	99.4	90.2	109.8	99.2	94.0	103.8
Cleveland-Lorain-Elyria, OH PMSA	107.2	105.5	106.6	130.6	104.3	118.8	102.0
Dayton-Springfield, OH MSA	95.4	95.4	85.4	113.6	93.8	100.6	99.3
Lima, OH MSA	96.0	103.7	88.7	100.6	87.8	86.1	101.2
Mansfield, OH MSA	95.2	100.6	86.4	127.2	94.5	88.6	93.5
Toledo, OH MSA	101.3	110.1	90.3	126.2	96.5	99.9	102.0
Youngstown-Warren, OH MSA	92.3	96.4	85.8	126.2	84.8	83.7	91.2

See footnotes at end of table.

U.S. Census Bureau, Statistical Abstract of the United States: 2001

No. 695. Cost of Living Index—Selected Metropolitan Areas: Fourth Quarter 2000—Con.

[See headnote, page 456]

Metropolitan areas (MA)	Com-posite index (100%)	Grocery items (16%)	Housing (28%)	Utilities (8%)	Trans-por-tation (10%)	Health care (5%)	Misc. goods and services (33%)
Enid, OK MSA..........................	94.2	96.6	80.5	100.2	95.0	92.3	103.2
Lawton, OK MSA......................	95.1	96.5	85.2	93.8	102.6	90.8	101.6
Oklahoma City, OK MSA.............	93.5	88.2	85.7	99.7	96.3	97.3	99.8
Tulsa, OK MSA........................	92.4	97.9	79.7	108.7	90.5	105.7	95.2
Corvallis, OR MSA....................	109.6	97.0	122.6	103.0	111.9	128.3	102.7
Portland-Vancover, OR-WA PMSA....	105.3	102.8	101.5	93.0	117.5	124.9	106.1
Salem, OR PMSA......................	103.6	99.0	103.9	91.2	103.2	122.7	105.9
Lancaster, PA MSA....................	97.2	93.0	91.5	104.1	106.7	94.1	100.1
Philadelphia, PA-NJ PMSA...........	120.9	105.0	145.6	120.2	116.5	101.8	112.2
Pittsburgh, PA MSA	103.0	99.1	98.4	131.4	98.1	95.6	104.6
Williamsport, PA MSA	94.1	96.9	84.2	106.6	94.4	88.8	98.9
York, PA MSA:							
Hanover, PA........................	99.8	89.9	105.9	121.6	98.5	83.8	96.9
York County, PA	103.0	96.9	105.1	119.0	110.1	92.7	99.8
Charleston-North Charleston, SC MSA.	102.8	102.8	107.0	97.0	95.7	102.2	102.9
Columbia, SC MSA....................	93.8	101.0	90.0	105.5	85.5	94.6	93.2
Myrtle Beach, SC MSA................	96.8	101.7	93.6	81.2	95.9	95.0	101.4
Sumter, SC MSA......................	95.1	103.8	81.0	99.7	95.2	92.3	102.0
Sioux Falls, SD MSA..................	97.4	95.9	91.3	115.0	102.9	95.8	97.5
Chattanooga, TN-GA MSA............	99.5	102.7	100.3	88.7	94.1	88.6	103.1
Clarksville-Hopkinsville, TN-KY MSA:.	90.9	89.9	84.7	88.7	102.1	93.0	93.5
Jackson, TN MSA	95.4	101.6	84.2	87.2	102.3	86.7	103.2
Johnson City-Kingsport-Bristol, TN-VA MSA:							
Johnson City, TN	90.5	87.9	93.6	100.9	84.1	83.5	89.7
Kingsport, TN......................	88.0	95.7	87.3	76.2	88.0	90.4	87.4
Knoxville, TN MSA	93.0	98.3	87.1	94.1	91.0	91.3	96.1
Memphis, TN-AR-MS MSA.............	90.1	98.6	82.8	90.1	98.2	88.2	90.0
Nashville, TN MSA:							
Nashville-Franklin, TN	92.6	97.1	87.2	82.4	97.0	84.2	97.5
Abilene, TX MSA......................	93.8	85.2	86.8	101.1	98.9	97.5	100.1
Amarillo, TX MSA......................	92.0	90.9	85.4	83.8	98.1	94.7	97.8
Beaumont-Port Arthur, TX MSA......	94.9	95.0	89.6	87.5	100.7	103.7	98.2
Brownsville-Harlingen-San Benito, TX MSA......	92.3	91.4	73.9	106.4	100.7	103.3	100.7
Dallas, TX PMSA......................	99.5	96.2	96.6	99.0	104.4	102.2	101.7
El Paso, TX MSA......................	93.9	102.8	80.2	109.3	103.3	90.1	95.2
Fort Worth-Arlington, TX PMSA:							
Houston, TX PMSA:							
Houston, TX PMSA	94.7	92.5	83.3	108.1	105.6	111.5	96.4
Killeen-Temple, TX MSA	92.0	86.8	86.1	103.8	97.7	104.8	93.1
Longview-Marshall, TX MSA..........	89.9	88.2	88.3	81.7	88.1	92.7	94.2
Lubbock, TX MSA	90.9	87.0	81.4	86.5	104.1	101.6	96.3
McAllen-Edinburg-Mission, TX MSA...	90.8	80.1	83.9	115.0	87.8	94.5	96.4
Odessa-Midland, TX MSA:							
Odessa, TX	89.4	85.8	79.2	90.6	95.6	99.9	95.9
San Angelo, TX MSA	92.4	85.6	82.8	84.9	96.7	96.2	103.8
San Antonio, TX MSA	91.8	85.0	86.8	91.6	97.0	93.8	100.5
Sherman-Denison, TX MSA	95.5	93.4	86.4	99.0	97.9	101.5	101.8
Tyler, TX MSA	90.9	90.9	80.1	105.9	89.8	95.3	96.0
Victoria, TX MSA	88.1	82.0	85.2	102.6	93.5	91.7	87.8
Waco, TX MSA	93.7	87.6	84.9	105.4	101.0	97.5	98.5
Provo-Orem, UT MSA.................	98.7	107.0	96.7	83.0	108.5	92.7	98.1
Salt Lake City-Ogden, UT MSA......	99.3	111.7	94.6	74.1	99.9	98.7	103.4
Burlington, VT MSA...................	110.2	110.0	111.9	129.7	102.3	113.2	106.2
Lynchburg, VA	93.6	94.2	94.7	82.2	86.3	98.2	96.7
Norfolk-Virginia Beach-Newport News VA-NC MSA .	97.8	100.4	90.5	122.9	102.8	103.4	94.3
Hampton Roads-Southeast VA	97.0	95.0	91.9	112.1	109.8	91.7	95.7
Richmond-Petersburg, VA MSA.......	102.5	95.1	110.9	112.6	102.2	93.7	97.8
Roanoke, VA MSA	90.7	93.0	89.7	76.3	88.0	93.8	94.3
Bellingham, WA MSA	108.7	105.6	117.4	89.5	106.7	121.5	106.0
Olympia, WA PMSA...................	103.7	105.3	104.4	83.4	107.0	130.4	102.1
Richland-Kennewick-Pasco, WA MSA	100.8	102.4	101.2	77.2	109.3	124.9	99.1
Spokane, WA MSA....................	101.1	103.6	98.9	75.8	104.3	119.2	104.6
Tacoma, WA MSA	101.5	112.8	93.1	79.8	108.4	126.1	102.7
Yakima, WA MSA	103.1	105.6	106.1	79.0	99.0	131.1	102.2
Huntington-Ashland, WV-KY-OH MSA	97.2	103.2	91.9	82.5	99.8	92.8	102.3
Appleton-Oshkosh-Neenah, WI MSA .	101.5	95.4	104.7	107.8	95.0	97.6	102.7
Eau Claire, WI MSA	95.8	98.8	88.1	100.3	100.5	110.3	96.3
Green Bay, WI MSA	97.0	89.1	97.7	103.9	98.5	105.5	96.8
Sheboygan, WI MSA	94.6	96.7	88.1	104.1	103.5	91.4	94.6
Wausau, WI MSA.....................	95.3	95.0	91.5	103.1	96.3	105.5	95.0
Cheyenne, WY MSA...................	99.1	113.1	90.4	95.0	98.6	104.1	100.0

Source: ACCRA, 4232 King St., Alexandria, VA 22302-1507, *ACCRA Cost of Living Index*, Fourth Quarter 2000 (copyright)

No. 696. Annual Percent Changes From Prior Year in Consumer Prices— United States and OECD Countries: 1990 to 1999

[Covers member countries of Organization for Economic Cooperation (OECD). For consumer price indexes for OECD countries, see Section 30, Comparative International Statistics]

Country	1990	1993	1994	1995	1996	1997	1998	1999
United States	5.4	3.0	2.6	2.8	2.9	2.3	1.6	2.3
OECD	5.8	4.2	4.4	5.5	5.1	4.4	3.8	3.3
Australia.	7.3	1.8	1.9	4.6	2.6	0.3	0.9	1.2
Canada	4.8	1.9	0.2	2.2	1.6	1.6	1.0	1.7
Japan	3.1	1.2	0.7	-0.1	0.1	1.7	0.6	-0.1
New Zealand.	6.1	1.3	1.8	3.8	2.3	1.2	1.3	-0.1
Austria	3.3	3.6	3.0	2.2	1.5	1.3	0.9	0.2
Belgium	3.4	2.8	2.4	1.5	2.1	1.6	1.0	1.2
Denmark.	2.7	1.3	2.0	2.1	2.1	2.2	1.8	2.4
Finland.	6.1	2.2	1.1	0.8	0.6	1.2	1.4	1.1
France	3.4	2.1	1.7	1.8	2.0	1.2	0.8	0.4
Greece	20.4	14.4	10.7	8.9	8.2	5.5	4.8	2.8
Ireland	3.3	1.4	2.3	2.5	1.7	1.4	2.4	1.4
Italy [1]	6.1	4.2	3.9	5.4	4.0	2.0	2.0	1.5
Luxembourg	3.7	3.6	2.2	1.9	1.3	1.4	1.0	1.3
Netherlands	2.5	2.6	2.8	1.9	2.0	2.2	2.0	2.2
Norway.	4.1	2.3	1.4	2.5	1.3	2.6	2.3	2.5
Portugal [2]	13.4	6.7	5.4	4.2	3.1	2.3	2.8	2.8
Spain	6.7	4.6	4.7	4.7	3.6	2.0	1.8	2.4
Sweden	10.5	4.7	2.4	2.9	0.8	0.9	0.4	0.1
Switzerland.	5.4	3.3	0.9	1.8	0.8	0.5	-	0.6
Turkey [2]	60.3	66.1	105.2	89.1	80.4	85.7	84.6	63.9
United Kingdom	9.5	1.6	2.5	3.4	2.4	3.1	3.4	1.6
Germany.	2.7	4.5	2.7	1.8	1.4	1.9	0.9	0.7

- Represents or rounds to zero.   [1] Households of wage and salary earners.   [2] Excludes rent.
Source: Organization for Economic Cooperation and Development, Paris, France, *Main Economic Indicators*, monthly (copyright).

No. 697. Producer Price Indexes by Stage of Processing: 1980 to 2000

[1982=100. Minus sign (-) indicates decline. See text, this section]

Year	Crude materials			Crude nonfood materials except fuel	Intermediate materials, supplies, and components	Finished goods		Consumer foods		Finished consumer goods excl. food
	Total	Foodstuffs and feedstuffs	Fuel			Consumer goods	Capital equipment	Crude	Processed	
1980	95.3	104.6	69.4	91.8	90.3	88.6	85.8	93.9	92.3	87.1
1981	103.0	103.9	84.8	109.8	98.6	96.6	94.6	104.4	97.2	96.1
1982	100.0	100.0	100.0	100.0	100.0	100.0	100.0	100.0	100.0	100.0
1983	101.3	101.8	105.1	98.8	100.6	101.3	102.8	102.4	100.9	101.2
1984	103.5	104.7	105.1	101.0	103.1	103.3	105.2	111.4	104.9	102.2
1985	95.8	94.8	102.7	94.3	102.7	103.8	107.5	102.9	104.8	103.3
1986	87.7	93.2	92.2	76.0	99.1	101.4	109.7	105.6	107.4	98.5
1987	93.7	96.2	84.1	88.5	101.5	103.6	111.7	107.1	109.6	100.7
1988	96.0	106.1	82.1	85.9	107.1	106.2	114.3	109.8	112.7	103.1
1989	103.1	111.2	85.3	95.8	112.0	112.1	118.8	119.6	118.6	108.9
1990	108.9	113.1	84.8	107.3	114.5	118.2	122.9	123.0	124.4	115.3
1991	101.2	105.5	82.9	97.5	114.4	120.5	126.7	119.3	124.4	118.7
1992	100.4	105.1	84.0	94.2	114.7	121.7	129.1	107.6	124.4	120.8
1993	102.4	108.4	87.1	94.1	116.2	123.0	131.4	114.4	126.5	121.7
1994	101.8	106.5	82.4	97.0	118.5	123.3	134.1	111.3	127.9	121.6
1995	102.7	105.8	72.1	105.8	124.9	125.6	136.7	118.8	129.8	124.0
1996	113.8	121.5	92.6	105.7	125.7	129.5	138.3	129.2	133.8	127.6
1997	111.1	112.2	101.3	103.5	125.6	130.2	138.2	126.6	135.1	128.2
1998 . . . . . ▸	96.8	103.9	86.7	84.5	123.0	128.9	137.6	127.2	134.8	126.4
1999	98.2	98.7	91.2	91.1	123.2	132.0	137.6	125.5	135.9	130.5
2000 prel	119.8	100.2	133.4	118.2	129.1	138.1	138.8	123.3	138.2	138.4
PERCENT CHANGE[1]										
1980	10.9	4.6	21.1	22.0	15.2	14.3	10.7	1.7	6.3	18.5
1981	8.1	-0.7	22.2	21.6	9.2	9.0	10.3	11.2	5.3	10.3
1982	-2.9	-3.8	17.9	19.6	1.4	3.5	5.7	-4.2	2.9	4.1
1983	1.3	1.8	5.1	-8.9	0.6	1.3	2.8	2.4	0.9	1.2
1984	2.2	2.8	-	-1.2	2.5	2.0	2.3	8.8	4.0	1.0
1985	-7.4	-9.5	-2.3	2.2	-0.4	0.5	2.2	-7.6	-0.1	1.1
1986	-8.5	-1.7	-10.2	-6.6	-3.5	-2.3	2.0	2.6	2.5	-4.6
1987	6.8	3.2	-8.8	-19.4	2.4	2.2	1.8	1.4	2.0	2.2
1988	2.5	10.3	-2.4	16.4	5.5	2.5	2.3	2.5	2.8	2.4
1989	7.4	4.8	3.9	-2.9	4.6	5.6	3.9	8.9	5.2	5.6
1990	5.6	1.7	-0.6	12.0	2.2	5.4	3.5	2.8	4.9	5.9
1991	-7.1	-6.7	-2.2	-9.1	-0.1	1.9	3.1	-3.0	-	2.9
1992	-0.8	-0.4	1.3	-3.4	0.3	1.0	1.9	-9.8	-	1.8
1993	2.0	3.1	3.7	-0.1	1.3	1.1	1.8	6.3	1.7	0.7
1994	-0.6	-1.8	-5.4	3.1	2.0	0.2	2.1	-2.7	1.1	-0.1
1995	0.9	-0.7	-12.5	9.1	5.4	1.9	1.9	6.7	1.5	2.0
1996	10.8	14.8	28.4	-0.1	0.6	3.1	1.2	8.8	3.1	2.9
1997	-2.4	-7.7	9.4	-2.1	-0.1	0.5	-0.1	-2.0	1.0	0.5
1998	-12.9	-7.4	-14.4	-18.4	-2.1	-1.0	-0.4	0.5	-0.2	-1.4
1999	1.4	-5.0	5.2	7.8	0.2	2.4	-	-1.3	0.8	3.2
2000	22.0	1.5	46.3	29.7	4.8	4.6	0.9	-1.8	1.7	6.1

- Represents or rounds to zero.   [1] Change from prior year.
Source: U.S. Bureau of Labor Statistics, *Producer Price Indexes*, monthly and annual.

Prices   459

No. 698. Producer Price Indexes by Stage of Processing: 1990 to 2000

[1982=100, except as indicated]

Stage of processing	1990	1994	1995	1996	1997	1998	1999	2000
Finished goods	**119.2**	**125.5**	**127.9**	**131.3**	**131.8**	**1ᴗᴗ.7**	**133.0**	**138.0**
Finished consumer goods	**118.2**	**123.3**	**125.6**	**129.5**	**130.2**	**128.9**	**132.0**	**138.1**
Finished consumer foods	**124.4**	**126.8**	**129.0**	**133.6**	**134.5**	**134.3**	**135.1**	**137.1**
Fresh fruits and melons	118.1	82.7	85.8	100.8	99.4	90.5	103.6	90.8
Fresh and dry vegetables	118.1	129.0	144.4	135.0	123.1	139.5	118.0	126.7
Eggs for fresh use (Dec. 1991=100)	(NA)	80.9	86.3	105.1	97.1	90.1	77.9	84.9
Bakery products	141.0	160.0	164.3	169.8	173.9	175.8	178.0	182.4
Milled rice	102.5	118.3	113.1	129.4	127.3	124.9	121.3	100.7
Pasta products (June 1985=100)	114.1	127.1	125.0	127.4	125.1	122.6	122.1	121.6
Beef and veal	116.0	103.6	100.9	100.2	102.8	99.4	106.3	113.6
Pork	119.8	101.4	101.5	120.9	123.1	96.6	96.0	113.3
Processed young chickens	111.0	113.3	113.5	121.5	118.6	125.2	113.4	110.4
Processed turkeys	107.6	108.5	104.9	105.5	101.0	95.2	94.8	98.9
Finfish and shellfish	147.2	161.4	170.8	165.9	178.1	183.2	190.9	198.0
Dairy products	117.2	119.4	119.7	130.4	128.1	138.2	139.2	133.8
Processed fruits and vegetables	124.7	121.1	122.4	127.6	126.4	125.7	128.1	128.5
Confectionery end products	140.0	156.9	160.7	166.9	168.3	168.7	170.4	170.8
Soft drinks	122.3	127.0	133.1	134.0	133.2	134.8	137.9	144.1
Roasted coffee	113.0	128.2	146.5	129.2	152.9	143.9	134.7	133.5
Shortening and cooking oils	123.2	138.6	142.5	138.5	137.8	143.4	140.4	132.3
Finished consumer goods excluding foods . . .	**115.3**	**121.6**	**124.0**	**127.6**	**128.2**	**126.4**	**130.5**	**138.4**
Alcoholic beverages	117.2	124.8	128.5	132.8	135.1	135.2	136.7	140.5
Women's apparel	116.1	119.7	119.6	119.9	120.5	122.3	123.9	124.1
Men's and boy's apparel	120.2	128.5	130.3	132.1	132.7	133.2	133.1	133.2
Girls', children's, and infants' apparel	115.3	119.9	121.6	122.4	122.9	121.8	118.2	117.7
Textile house furnishings	109.5	117.3	119.5	122.3	122.6	123.1	122.7	122.0
Footwear	125.6	135.5	139.2	141.6	143.7	144.7	144.5	145.0
Residential electric power (Dec. 1990=100)	(NA)	109.8	111.8	112.8	112.8	110.7	109.5	110.8
Residential gas (Dec. 1990=100)	(NA)	108.8	104.4	110.4	116.5	114.0	114.3	135.6
Gasoline	78.7	61.7	63.7	72.8	71.9	53.4	64.7	94.8
Fuel oil No. 2	73.3	56.0	56.6	69.5	64.8	48.1	56.1	93.5
Pharmaceutical preps, ethical (prescription)	200.8	250.0	257.0	265.4	273.5	322.9	335.0	344.9
Pharmaceutical preps, proprietary (over-counter) . . .	156.8	183.2	186.5	185.1	184.8	184.5	186.0	187.6
Soaps and synthetic detergents	117.7	121.4	122.9	125.2	126.4	126.1	126.3	128.2
Cosmetics and other toilet preparations	121.6	128.7	129.0	130.2	130.6	132.9	135.4	137.2
Tires, tubes, and tread	96.8	98.6	100.2	97.0	95.2	94.0	92.9	93.0
Sanitary papers and health products	135.3	133.2	144.4	149.9	147.1	145.1	144.3	146.3
Newspaper circulation	144.1	174.9	185.6	198.8	201.9	202.9	207.1	209.3
Periodical circulation	150.3	171.1	176.6	180.6	188.1	193.8	196.9	199.2
Book publishing	153.4	175.8	185.0	193.9	200.1	205.9	213.0	217.5
Household furniture	125.1	138.0	141.8	144.5	146.2	148.4	150.5	152.7
Floor coverings	119.0	121.5	123.7	126.6	128.0	128.3	127.2	129.4
Household appliances	110.8	112.8	112.4	112.7	110.1	108.9	108.5	107.4
Home electronic equipment	82.7	80.3	78.9	79.0	77.1	75.9	73.7	71.8
Household glassware	132.5	147.4	153.2	157.3	161.3	162.7	163.9	166.0
Household flatware	122.1	133.9	138.3	138.4	138.5	139.2	139.7	142.6
Lawn and garden equipment, except tractors	123.0	128.4	130.4	132.3	132.2	131.7	132.0	131.8
Passenger cars	118.3	133.9	134.1	135.4	133.6	131.9	131.3	132.7
Toys, games, and children's vehicles	118.1	122.4	124.3	125.3	125.2	124.4	123.1	121.8
Sporting and athletic goods	112.6	120.1	122.0	123.3	124.7	126.2	126.2	126.0
Tobacco products	221.4	224.7	231.3	237.4	248.9	283.6	374.0	397.2
Mobile homes	117.5	137.0	145.6	149.8	152.2	154.3	158.4	161.3
Jewelry, platinum, and karat gold	122.8	127.3	127.8	129.4	129.2	128.1	127.1	127.2
Costume jewelry and novelties	125.3	134.1	135.1	136.9	139.9	139.6	140.1	141.5
Capital Equipment	**122.9**	**134.1**	**136.7**	**138.3**	**138.2**	**137.6**	**137.6**	**138.8**
Agricultural machinery and equipment	121.7	137.0	142.9	146.8	149.0	150.4	152.1	153.3
Construction machinery and equipment	121.6	133.7	136.7	139.8	142.2	145.2	147.2	148.6
Metal cutting machine tools	129.8	143.1	148.0	152.6	156.0	159.9	160.7	161.9
Metal forming machine tools	128.7	141.9	145.7	149.6	153.9	157.6	159.7	162.0
Tools, dies, jigs, fixtures, and industrial molds	117.2	131.4	133.8	136.2	138.1	138.8	139.8	141.1
Pumps, compressors, and equipment	119.2	135.2	139.4	143.5	146.5	149.0	151.7	154.1
Industrial material handling equipment	115.0	122.4	125.3	127.4	129.7	131.3	132.9	134.6

See footnote at end of table.

U.S. Census Bureau, Statistical Abstract of the United States: 2001

No. 698. Producer Price Indexes by Stage of Processing: 1990 to 2000—Con.

[1982=100, except as indicated]

Stage of processing	1990	1994	1995	1996	1997	1998	1999	2000
Capital Equipment—Continued								
Electronic computers (Dec. 1990=100)	(NA)	58.0	51.8	42.4	33.2	24.7	87.2	73.0
Textile machinery	128.8	144.9	146.7	148.4	152.1	152.7	154.2	156.2
Paper industries machinery (June 1982=100)	134.8	147.5	151.0	153.8	157.4	160.3	162.6	164.7
Printing trades machinery	124.9	130.9	133.6	136.8	138.8	141.5	141.0	142.2
Transformers and power regulators	120.9	125.3	128.9	129.7	129.5	131.0	132.6	135.7
Communication/related equip. (Dec. 1985=100)	106.1	110.8	112.1	113.0	114.0	114.0	112.7	110.7
X-ray and electromedical equipment	109.8	112.4	111.8	109.9	107.4	106.7	104.3	101.8
Oil field and gas field machinery	102.4	110.8	114.1	117.8	122.8	125.8	126.5	128.3
Mining machinery and equipment	121.0	131.1	135.6	139.0	140.3	142.2	144.2	146.1
Office and store machines and equipment	109.5	111.3	111.5	112.0	112.4	112.3	112.3	112.9
Commercial furniture	133.4	144.7	148.2	151.7	154.3	155.2	156.6	158.3
Light motor trucks	130.0	157.1	159.0	160.3	158.9	155.1	157.5	157.5
Heavy motor trucks	120.3	138.7	144.1	144.1	140.4	142.1	146.5	148.1
Truck trailers	110.8	122.2	131.7	130.7	130.3	135.0	136.3	139.4
Civilian aircraft (Dec. 1985=100)	115.3	135.4	141.8	147.3	150.0	150.1	151.7	159.5
Ships (Dec. 1985=100)	110.1	131.1	132.8	138.7	143.7	145.7	145.8	146.4
Railroad equipment	118.6	129.2	134.8	137.2	134.7	134.9	135.2	135.7
Intermediate materials, supplies, and components	**114.5**	**118.5**	**124.9**	**125.7**	**125.6**	**123.0**	**123.2**	**129.1**
Intermediate foods and feeds	**113.3**	**114.8**	**114.8**	**128.1**	**125.4**	**116.1**	**111.1**	**111.7**
Flour	103.6	110.4	123.0	136.8	118.7	109.2	104.3	103.9
Refined sugar	122.7	118.2	119.3	123.7	123.6	119.8	121.0	110.1
Confectionery materials	101.2	112.4	109.1	107.9	105.4	93.8	94.0	94.0
Crude vegetable oils	115.8	135.0	130.0	118.1	116.6	131.1	90.2	74.3
Prepared animal feeds	107.4	111.3	109.1	135.3	132.9	107.9	98.3	102.9
Intermediate materials less foods and feeds.	**120.9**	**127.1**	**135.2**	**134.0**	**134.2**	**133.5**	**123.9**	**130.1**
Synthetic fibers	106.7	104.1	109.4	111.3	111.1	109.8	103.8	107.3
Processed yarns and threads	112.6	108.4	112.8	114.7	114.0	112.7	108.6	107.9
Gray fabrics	117.2	116.8	121.2	121.4	121.9	121.6	114.4	113.2
Leather	177.5	179.6	191.4	177.9	182.7	178.5	176.3	181.6
Liquefied petroleum gas	77.4	58.2	65.1	84.7	84.5	60.1	73.7	127.2
Commercial electric power	115.3	128.8	131.7	131.6	131.7	130.5	129.1	131.5
Industrial electric power	119.6	129.2	130.8	131.6	130.8	130.0	128.9	131.5
Commercial natural gas (Dec. 1990=100)	(NA)	103.7	96.5	103.2	109.8	106.6	108.1	133.7
Industrial natural gas (Dec. 1990=100)	(NA)	99.5	90.9	98.9	109.3	104.2	103.3	139.2
Natural gas to electric utilities (Dec. 1990=100)	(NA)	90.2	87.7	90.4	96.9	80.5	81.6	120.6
Jet fuels	76.0	53.9	55.0	66.7	62.9	46.0	52.5	88.5
No. 2 Diesel fuel	74.1	56.0	57.0	70.0	64.5	47.3	57.3	93.3
Residual fuel	57.7	48.2	52.6	59.8	59.5	43.8	51.5	84.8
Industrial chemicals	113.2	114.3	128.4	126.7	126.4	121.6	118.9	129.1
Prepared paint	124.8	135.3	142.1	147.2	152.1	155.0	157.4	161.0
Paint materials	136.3	132.1	139.4	141.3	141.5	143.8	144.1	148.4
Medicinal and botanical chemicals	102.2	125.4	128.3	128.6	133.4	135.0	142.2	146.3
Fats and oils, inedible	88.1	110.6	126.9	133.3	132.3	116.9	88.4	70.0
Mixed fertilizers	103.3	105.7	111.1	114.7	113.6	115.3	113.7	112.4
Nitrogenates	92.3	112.3	129.4	130.5	132.3	108.2	94.6	118.3
Phosphates	96.5	95.5	109.1	116.3	110.4	112.5	112.0	96.8
Other agricultural chemicals	119.9	140.8	144.3	146.1	147.8	149.7	144.5	146.0
Plastic resins and materials	124.1	122.4	143.5	133.1	137.3	125.6	125.8	141.8
Synthetic rubber	111.9	108.9	126.3	122.2	119.3	117.2	113.9	119.2
Plastic construction products	117.2	122.9	133.8	130.9	128.2	126.2	128.0	135.8
Unsupported plastic film, sheet, and shapes	119.0	122.8	135.6	132.7	131.7	128.1	127.5	131.4
Plastic parts and components for manufacturing . . .	112.9	113.5	115.9	117.5	117.2	117.1	117.4	117.4
Softwood lumber	123.8	198.1	178.5	189.5	206.5	182.4	196.0	178.6
Hardwood lumber	131.0	168.3	167.0	163.9	174.1	178.7	177.3	185.8
Millwork	130.4	162.4	163.8	166.6	170.9	171.1	174.7	176.4
Plywood	114.2	158.6	165.3	156.4	159.3	157.6	176.4	157.8
Woodpile	151.3	115.9	183.2	133.1	128.6	122.0	119.7	145.4
Paper	128.8	126.0	159.0	149.4	143.9	146.0	141.8	149.9
Paperboard	135.7	140.5	183.1	155.1	144.4	151.7	153.2	176.6
Paper boxes and containers	129.9	136.1	163.8	153.9	144.7	154.7	158.0	172.7
Building paper and board	112.2	144.1	144.9	137.2	129.6	132.8	141.6	138.8

See footnotes at end of table.

U.S. Census Bureau, Statistical Abstract of the United States: 2001

No. 698. Producer Price Indexes by Stage of Processing: 1990 to 2000—Con.

[1982=100, except as indicated]

Stage of processing	1990	1994	1995	1996	1997	1998	1999	2000
Intermediate materials less foods and feeds—Continued								
Commercial printing (June 1982=100)	128.0	136.5	144.5	148.3	148.7	152.1	152.2	155.2
Foundry and forge shop products	117.2	123.9	129.3	132.6	134.1	135.0	135.1	136.6
Steel mill products	112.1	113.4	120.1	115.6	116.4	113.9	105.3	108.5
Primary nonferrous metals	133.4	115.7	146.8	126.2	126.2	106.7	101.5	113.8
Aluminum mill shapes	127.9	127.7	160.4	144.8	147.5	142.1	138.1	149.1
Copper and brass mill shapes	174.6	167.3	195.2	179.0	177.3	153.4	151.2	162.7
Nonferrous wire and cable	142.6	139.3	151.5	147.5	148.1	140.9	135.6	143.9
Metal containers	114.0	108.1	117.2	110.0	108.1	108.7	106.4	106.8
Hardware	125.9	137.5	141.1	143.8	145.6	147.0	148.7	151.2
Plumbing fixtures and brass fittings	144.3	159.6	166.0	171.1	174.5	175.1	176.7	180.5
Heating equipment	131.6	142.5	147.5	151.2	152.4	153.2	154.0	155.5
Fabricated structural metal products	121.8	127.3	135.1	137.8	140.3	142.5	143.3	144.9
Fabricated ferrous wire products (June 1982=100)	114.6	122.6	125.7	126.8	128.0	130.1	130.6	130.0
Other miscellaneous metal products	120.7	122.7	124.9	125.7	126.2	126.2	125.5	125.9
Mechanical power transmission equipment	125.3	140.5	146.9	151.5	154.8	157.7	161.1	163.9
Air conditioning and refrigeration equipment	122.1	127.0	130.2	132.7	132.6	134.6	135.5	135.3
Metal valves, excluding fluid power (Dec. 1982=100) . . .	125.3	140.3	145.3	149.8	153.3	156.6	160.2	162.2
Ball and roller bearings	130.6	145.7	152.0	157.8	162.9	165.2	166.8	168.7
Wiring devices	132.2	141.5	147.2	151.2	154.0	154.2	152.5	153.0
Motors, generators, motor generator sets	132.9	140.2	143.9	145.6	144.7	145.8	145.9	146.2
Switchgear and switchboard equipment	124.4	136.8	140.3	142.6	145.6	148.3	151.0	152.9
Electronic components and accessories	118.4	116.6	113.6	108.9	104.0	100.1	98.2	97.2
Internal combustion engines	120.2	132.9	135.6	138.8	140.1	140.7	143.0	143.8
Machine shop products	124.3	129.7	131.3	133.6	135.2	136.3	136.8	137.9
Flat glass	107.5	110.5	113.2	110.0	108.4	107.2	106.4	109.8
Cement	103.7	119.5	128.1	134.0	139.4	145.7	150.6	150.2
Concrete products	113.5	124.6	129.4	133.2	136.0	140.1	143.7	147.8
Asphalt felts and coatings	97.1	95.3	100.0	100.0	99.9	99.6	99.2	104.0
Gypsum products	105.2	136.1	154.5	154.0	170.8	177.2	208.0	201.4
Glass containers	120.4	127.5	130.5	129.1	125.7	125.9	125.9	127.4
Motor vehicle parts	111.2	114.3	116.0	116.2	115.4	114.6	114.0	113.5
Aircraft engines and engine parts (Dec. 1985=100)	113.5	130.7	132.8	134.7	135.7	136.9	138.5	140.8
Aircraft parts and auxiliary equipment, n.e.c. [1] (June 1985=100)	117.7	134.0	135.7	139.3	141.3	142.6	143.7	145.2
Photographic supplies	127.6	124.7	126.8	129.8	130.0	128.9	128.3	125.2
Medical/surgical/personal aid devices	127.3	140.4	141.3	143.1	143.1	143.3	144.6	146.0
Crude materials for further processing	108.9	101.8	102.7	113.8	111.1	96.7	98.2	119.8
Crude foodstuffs and feedstuffs	113.1	106.5	105.8	121.5	112.2	103.8	98.7	100.2
Wheat	87.6	104.8	118.6	136.6	108.2	87.8	79.5	80.3
Corn	100.9	100.1	109.0	158.5	110.1	91.7	78.2	76.4
Slaughter cattle	122.5	105.8	99.5	95.8	97.9	92.5	97.6	104.1
Slaughter hogs	94.1	65.9	70.2	88.6	87.0	52.2	53.8	72.7
Slaughter broilers/fryers	119.5	127.7	129.1	148.0	137.2	151.8	134.5	127.6
Slaughter turkeys	116.9	119.6	120.3	121.5	112.9	110.4	120.0	120.7
Fluid milk	100.8	95.7	93.6	107.9	97.5	112.6	106.3	92.0
Soybeans	100.8	106.0	102.2	127.9	131.0	103.4	80.1	83.4
Cane sugar, raw	119.2	115.2	119.7	118.6	116.8	117.2	113.7	102.2
Crude nonfood materials	101.5	94.8	96.8	104.5	106.4	88.3	94.3	129.0
Raw cotton	118.2	121.3	156.2	130.0	116.5	111.0	87.4	95.2
Leaf tobacco	95.8	100.2	102.5	105.1	(NA)	104.6	101.6	(NA)
Cattle hides	217.8	200.9	209.9	186.5	196.1	153.3	141.9	169.5
Coal	97.5	96.7	95.0	94.5	96.3	93.1	90.7	87.9
Natural gas	80.4	78.8	66.6	91.2	101.7	83.7	91.2	150.7
Crude petroleum	71.0	47.1	51.1	62.2	57.5	35.7	50.3	85.6
Logs and timber	142.8	219.1	220.4	206.8	214.4	208.2	202.0	196.3
Wastepaper	138.9	209.5	371.1	141.6	163.3	146.0	183.6	282.2
Iron ore	83.3	82.7	91.8	96.7	96.3	95.5	94.9	94.6
Iron and steel scrap	166.0	192.9	202.7	191.1	188.9	164.9	139.2	142.4
Nonferrous metal ores (Dec. 1983=100)	98.3	81.4	101.6	90.2	82.2	66.9	63.1	67.6
Copper base scrap	181.3	155.5	193.5	166.3	157.7	116.3	108.2	123.9
Aluminum base scrap	172.6	172.9	209.4	173.4	195.1	162.8	161.7	177.1
Construction sand, gravel, and crushed stone	125.4	137.9	142.3	145.6	148.2	152.7	157.2	163.2

NA Not available.   [1] N.e.c. Not elsewhere classified.

Source: U.S. Bureau of Labor Statistics, *Producer Price Indexes*, monthly and annual

462   Prices

No. 699. Producer Price Indexes for the Net Output of Selected Industries: 1996 to 2000

[Indexes are based on selling prices reported by establishments of all sizes by probability sampling. Manufacturing industries selected by shipment value. N.e.c.= not elsewhere classified. See text, Section 22, Domestic Trade]

Industry	SIC code [1]	Index base [2]	1996	1997	1998	1999	2000
MINING							
Iron ores.	1011	12/84	95.7	95.3	94.5	94.0	93.7
Copper ores	1021	06/88	117.0	110.4	76.8	71.3	87.5
Lead and zinc ores.	1031	12/85	109.4	138.6	107.0	111.8	118.8
Gold ores	1041	06/85	117.0	100.9	90.0	85.6	84.2
Metal mining services	1081	12/85	112.5	116.8	122.2	120.2	108.5
Metal ores, n.e.c.	1099	12/85	110.5	100.8	89.9	82.9	85.6
Bituminous coal and lignite.	1211	12/81	95.0	95.9	93.0	90.6	87.9
Anthracite mining	1231	12/79	158.6	159.0	160.1	158.7	157.5
Coal Mining Services	1241	06/85	109.2	108.1	108.1	107.7	108.2
Crude petroleum and natural gas liquids.	1331	06/96	(X)	115.6	86.1	102.6	171.6
Drilling oil and gas wells	1381	12/85	115.1	143.7	154.6	133.1	136.9
Oil and gas exploration services	1382	12/85	103.7	105.6	114.5	92.7	80.4
Oil and gas field services, n.e.c.	1389	12/85	108.2	112.7	113.6	112.9	123.0
Dimension stone	1411	06/85	132.2	138.2	142.2	145.9	153.4
Crushed and broken limestone.	1422	12/83	132.4	134.5	137.4	140.6	145.6
Crushed and broken granite, n.e.c.	1423	12/83	156.5	159.7	166.4	172.5	182.5
Crushed and broken stone, n.e.c.	1429	12/83	143.0	145.4	147.9	149.9	153.1
Construction sand and gravel.	1442	06/82	151.1	155.3	163.0	169.0	175.6
Industrial sand.	1446	06/82	136.6	138.9	142.2	145.2	148.0
Kaolin and ball clay	1455	06/84	116.5	117.1	115.8	113.3	113.4
Clay and related minerals, n.e.c.	1459	06/84	130.2	131.7	133.4	133.5	135.7
Potash, soda, and borate minerals	1474	12/84	121.2	117.4	118.9	113.6	111.6
Chemicals and fertilizer mineral mining, n.e.c.	1479	12/89	91.8	92.7	93.4	95.0	90.1
Nonmetallic minerals (except fuels) services	1481	06/85	103.4	104.7	104.7	106.5	107.3
Miscellaneous nonmetallic minerals	1499	06/85	130.3	133.5	136.7	138.0	138.7
MANUFACTURING							
Meat packing plants	2011	12/80	110.9	113.5	101.4	104.2	113.4
Sausage and other prepared meats.	2013	12/82	115.5	118.8	113.3	118.8	121.3
Poultry slaughtering and processing	2015	12/81	127.1	124.7	127.1	119.8	118.4
Natural and processed cheese	2022	06/81	119.6	115.7	126.1	124.3	117.9
Dry, condensed, and evaporated milk products	2023	12/83	139.5	138.7	146.4	142.4	140.9
Ice cream and frozen desserts	2024	06/83	130.5	135.1	142.6	150.0	150.4
Fluid milk	2026	12/82	134.3	133.6	140.4	145.9	141.8
Canned specialties.	2032	12/82	157.7	163.0	165.6	168.6	171.6
Canned fruits, vegetables, preserves, jams, and jellies	2033	06/81	138.4	137.7	136.9	138.2	139.2
Pickled fruits/veg./veg. sauces/seasonings/salad dressings . . .	2035	06/81	160.9	161.2	162.2	163.2	163.6
Frozen fruits and vegetables	2037	06/81	141.5	139.2	138.6	141.8	141
Frozen specialties	2038	12/82	135.7	136.8	137.0	137.4	136.1
Flour and other grain mill products	2041	06/83	133.3	114.3	103.3	97.1	97.1
Cereal breakfast foods	2043	12/83	174.5	168.2	161.4	159.5	159.6
Wet corn milling.	2046	06/85	133.6	123.6	107.1	101.3	102.6
Dog and cat food	2047	12/85	130.7	132.1	132.3	132.2	131.3
Prepared animal feeds, n.e.c.	2048	12/80	119.8	112.2	95.2	86.7	88.9
Bread and other bakery products, except cookies and crackers	2051	06/80	195.7	199.7	201.4	204.5	211.4
Cookies and crackers	2052	06/83	161.4	167.0	170.3	171.0	171.9
Candy and other confectionery products, and chewing gum . .	2064	06/83	143.8	146.2	146.8	149.4	151
Soybean oil mill products.	2075	12/79	98.6	103.2	86.7	68.0	69.3
Malt beverages	2082	06/82	127.7	128.0	128.1	131.4	136
Bottled and canned soft drinks	2086	06/81	141.2	140.5	142.4	145.7	152.0
Flavoring extracts and syrups, n.e.c.	2087	12/85	127.7	130.7	131.4	133.6	137.3
Fresh or frozen packaged fish	2092	12/82	140.0	145.2	151.7	160.9	171.5
Coffee	2095	06/81	138.7	161.8	153.3	145.8	144.3
Potato and corn chips, and similar snacks	2096	06/91	106.5	109.4	111.1	112.7	115.9
Macaroni, spaghetti, and noodles	2098	06/85	127.4	125.5	122.7	122.3	121.9
Food preparations, n.e.c.	2099	12/85	124.1	127.5	128.5	128.9	129.2
Cigarettes.	2111	12/82	210.5	223.3	260.4	356.7	379.2
Cigars	2121	12/82	201.8	228.5	242.7	259.6	268.9
Cotton broadwoven fabric	2211	12/80	119.1	118.5	117.4	114.1	110.6
Manmade fiber and silk broadwoven fabric	2221	06/81	113.0	115.0	114.8	108.6	108.7
Narrow fabric mills	2241	06/84	121.2	122.7	123.8	124.3	125.4
Knit outerwear.	2253	12/84	117.9	118.6	118.9	116.4	117.3
Carpet and rugs.	2273	06/90	104.4	105.9	106.4	105.6	107.7
Spun yarn.	2281	12/82	106.1	104.7	102.5	96.9	95.5
Men's and boys' separate trousers and slacks. . . .	2325	12/81	133.1	133.4	136.5	137.0	134.8
Women's, misses', and juniors' dresses	2335	12/80	125.4	126.0	127.0	126.3	125.8
Women's, misses', and juniors' outerwear, n.e.c.	2339	06/83	108.4	110.9	111.2	112.6	113.0
House furnishings, n.e.c.	2392	06/83	120.4	120.5	119.5	118.8	117.7
Automotive trimmings, apparel findings, and related products	2396	12/83	117.2	120.1	124.0	122.6	124.5
Logging camps and logging contractors	2411	12/81	185.8	191.2	188.2	182.8	177.4
Sawmills and planing mills	2421	12/80	152.0	163.1	151.7	157.4	148.0
Millwork	2431	06/83	153.6	156.4	157.2	160.0	161.3
Wood kitchen cabinets	2434	06/84	147.3	150.4	153.1	155.7	159.8
Softwood plywood	2436	12/80	139.5	142.4	142.5	164.7	140.7
Mobile homes	2451	06/81	155.3	157.8	159.9	164.2	167.1
Wood household furniture, except upholstered.	2511	12/79	189.7	192.3	195.8	200.5	204.1
Upholstered wood household furniture	2512	06/82	136.3	138.1	140.1	142.0	144.5
Nonwood office furniture	2522	12/79	192.4	193.5	191.6	191.8	193.5
Public building and related furniture.	2531	12/84	133.7	135.9	135.9	136.8	138.5

See footnotes at end of table

U.S. Census Bureau, Statistical Abstract of the United States: 2001

[See headnote, page 463]

Industry	SIC code [1]	Index base [2]	1996	1997	1998	1999	2000
Paper mills	2621	06/81	152.2	143.2	144.4	139.7	148.9
Paperboard mills	2631	12/82	169.8	158.2	165.1	167.0	192.2
Corrugated and solid fiber boxes.	2653	03/80	168.7	154.9	168.8	175.5	196.8
Folding paperboard boxes	2657	12/83	143.4	142.2	143.6	142.3	145.4
Paper coated and laminated, n.e.c.	2672	06/93	110.5	110.1	109.6	109.8	111.5
Plastics, foil and coated paper bags	2673	12/83	158.6	160.9	156.5	159.0	168.6
Sanitary paper products	2676	06/83	150.3	147.8	146.0	145.1	147.7
Newspaper publishing.	2711	12/79	306.9	317.7	328.5	339.3	350.6
Periodical publishing.	2721	12/79	253.2	263.2	276.8	284.9	292.8
Book publishing	2731	12/80	224.7	232.1	238.0	247.6	254.4
Miscellaneous publishing	2741	06/84	174.5	181.1	187.8	194.5	201.3
Commercial printing, lithographic.	2752	06/82	149.0	149.8	153.3	153.2	156.0
Commercial printing, n.e.c..	2759	06/82	158.2	159.4	160.9	162.6	166.1
Manifold business forms	2761	12/83	168.4	165.8	167.1	170.5	184.9
Industrial inorganic chemicals, n.e.c.	2819	12/82	136.0	135.5	132.3	129.2	132.7
Plastic materials and resins	2821	12/80	149.6	153.9	139.5	142.8	164.6
Noncellulosic manmade fibers	2824	06/81	109.3	107.7	106.6	98.9	101.6
Medicinal chemicals and botanical products (in bulk)	2833	06/82	129.8	134.2	136.3	143.2	147.8
Pharmaceutical preparations	2834	06/81	253.9	259.1	289.9	298.5	306.9
In vivo and In vitro diagnostics	2835	03/80	166.6	167.4	177.8	184.5	190.0
Biological products, except diagnostics.	2836	06/91	111.2	112.3	115.8	126.1	127.5
Soap and other detergents.	2841	06/83	123.8	124.6	124.8	125.9	127.4
Specialty cleaning, polishing and sanitation preparations. . . .	2842	06/83	129.6	130.8	132.6	135.1	138.1
Toilet preparations	2844	03/80	168.5	168.9	171.7	174.8	175.5
Paints and allied products	2851	06/83	147.4	152.1	154.9	157.3	160.7
Cyclic (coal tar) crudes and intermediates, organic dyes and pigments	2865	12/82	118.3	115.2	109.3	110.1	125.0
Industrial organic chemicals, n.e.c.	2869	12/82	171.2	171.5	168.0	169.1	185.8
Agricultural chemicals, n.e.c.	2879	06/82	136.5	137.6	139.4	135.4	136.4
Adhesives and sealants.	2891	12/83	146.1	148.8	151.4	151.7	153.5
Chemicals and chemical preparations, n.e.c..	2899	06/85	130.3	133.2	134.3	134.8	135.7
Petroleum refining	2911	06/85	85.3	83.1	62.3	73.6	111.7
Tires and inner tubes	3011	06/81	105.2	103.4	102.2	100.4	100.4
Fabricated rubber products, n.e.c.	3069	06/83	130.6	132.1	132.4	132.2	132.8
Unsupported plastic film and sheet	3081	06/93	108.9	108.3	103.8	103.2	107.3
Plastic bottles	3085	06/93	107.0	107.1	105.5	106.1	110.4
Plastic foam products	3086	06/93	110.7	109.7	108.6	108.6	110.2
Custom compounding of purchased plastic resins	3087	06/93	108.1	106.7	107.4	104.2	110.9
Plastic products n.e.c..	3089	06/93	106.4	106.3	106.3	106.7	107.6
Products of purchased glass	3231	06/83	126.3	127.1	127.5	128.4	131.7
Concrete products	3272	12/79	148.1	151.6	156.7	161.0	166.4
Ready-mixed concrete.	3273	06/81	135.2	138.0	142.3	145.6	150.2
Blast furnaces and steel mills.	3312	06/82	114.0	114.2	111.4	102.0	104.2
Cold finishing of steel shapes - mfpm.	3316	06/82	116.4	116.7	114.7	110.3	113.5
Steel pipe and tubes - mfpm	3317	06/82	126.7	131.8	132.7	127.1	132.2
Gray iron foundries	3321	12/80	141.5	143.0	143.3	144.5	147.1
Primary copper	3331	06/80	144.8	137.3	106.2	102.2	112.6
Secondary nonferrous metals.	3341	06/80	94.0	94.5	85.9	84.8	88.4
Rolling, drawing and extruding of copper	3351	12/80	151.1	149.9	131.9	130.0	137.7
Aluminum sheet, plate, foil and welded tube products	3353	06/81	148.4	152.9	145.5	139.5	150.3
Nonferrous wire drawing and insulating	3357	12/82	153.7	154.5	148.1	143.7	153.3
Metal cans	3411	06/81	112.0	110.4	110.2	107.8	108.1
Hardware, n.e.c..	3429	06/85	123.7	125.0	126.0	127.4	129.8
Fabricated structural metal.	3441	06/82	130.7	132.8	136.8	139.1	142.0
Metal doors, sash and trim.	3442	06/83	151.1	152.5	152.9	153.6	156.1
Fabricated plate work (boiler shops)	3443	03/80	159.1	161.9	164.7	167.2	168.9
Sheet metal work	3444	12/82	137.7	138.6	139.9	140.1	141.8
Bolts, nuts, screws, rivets, and washers	3452	06/82	124.2	125.6	127.0	126.4	126.5
Automotive stampings.	3465	12/82	112.5	112.8	112.1	110.4	110.6
Metal stampings, n.e.c.	3469	06/84	127.3	128.5	128.9	128.6	128.7
Metal coating and allied services.	3479	12/84	118.0	118.4	119.1	118.8	119.1
Industrial valves.	3491	06/91	114.8	117.3	119.7	122.4	124.0
Fabricated metal products, n.e.c.	3499	06/85	128.5	129.9	131.8	131.8	133.0
Turbines and turbine generator sets.	3511	06/82	145.7	146.9	146.9	148.7	149.6
Internal combustion engines, n.e.c.	3519	12/82	134.3	135.7	136.2	138.1	139.0
Farm machinery and equipment	3523	12/82	136.7	138.8	140.4	142.2	143.9
Lawn and garden equipment	3524	12/82	125.9	126.0	124.9	124.5	124.4
Construction machinery	3531	12/80	161.6	164.4	167.8	170.8	172.7
Special tools, dies, jigs, fixtures and industrial molds	3544	06/81	142.5	144.1	144.9	145.8	147.0
Special industry machinery, n.e.c.	3559	12/81	160.5	163.3	166.0	168.2	169.4
Pumps and pumping equipment	3561	12/83	146.1	150.4	153.3	156.2	158.6
General industrial machinery, n.e.c.	3569	12/84	147.0	149.5	151.3	153.8	156.8
Electronic computers.	3571	12/90	45.2	36.5	29.1	91.1	80.8
Computer storage devices	3572	12/92	57.6	51.1	45.3	95.0	85.0
Computer peripheral equipment, n.e.c.	3577	12/93	93.1	90.5	84.5	80.1	78.8
Refrigeration and heating equipment	3585	12/82	128.2	129.2	131.3	131.5	130.6
Service industry machinery, n.e.c.	3589	06/82	154.6	159.3	161.7	164.0	165.9
Machinery, except electrical, not elsewhere classified	3599	06/84	123.4	125.4	126.9	127.6	129.7
Switchgear and switchboard apparatus	3613	06/85	133.6	135.0	138.2	141.0	143.4
Electric motors and generators	3621	06/83	139.1	138.6	139.8	139.9	140.4
Relays and industrial controls.	3625	06/85	133.6	137.8	140.4	142.8	144.4

See footnotes at end of table.

No. 699. Producer Price Indexes for the Net Output of Selected Industries: 1996 to 2000—Con.

[See headnote, page 463]

Industry	SIC code [1]	Index base [2]	1996	1997	1998	1999	2000
Household audio & video equipment	3651	03/80	82.4	80.5	79.7	77.8	76.1
Telephone & telegraph apparatus	3661	12/85	119.7	119.4	117.9	115.8	113.1
Radio and television broadcast and communication equipment . .	3663	12/91	104.2	105.7	105.5	104.1	101.5
Printed circuit boards	3672	06/91	95.9	95.0	93.9	92.2	91.6
Semiconductors and related devices	3674	06/81	84.8	76.7	70.6	97.4	91.1
Electronic components, n.e.c	3679	06/82	114.9	114.2	114.2	113.8	114.5
Electrical equipment for internal combustion engines	3694	12/82	128.2	128.8	127.9	127.4	127.6
Electrical equipment and supplies, not elsewhere classified	3699	12/85	118.0	118.5	117.5	118.6	118.5
Motor vehicles and passenger car bodies	3711	06/82	140.4	138.7	136.8	137.6	138.7
Truck and bus bodies	3713	12/82	149.9	153.5	155.3	157.0	160.2
Motor vehicle parts and accessories	3714	12/82	114.0	113.1	112.6	112.0	111.6
Aircraft	3721	12/85	140.5	142.3	142.6	144.1	150.5
Aircraft engines and engine parts	3724	12/85	133.4	134.8	135.7	136.8	139.5
Aircraft parts and auxiliary equipment, n.e.c	3728	06/85	136.3	139.0	140.9	142.2	143.3
Ship building and repairing	3731	12/85	130.1	133.3	134.8	135.4	137.2
Railroad equipment	3743	06/84	129.6	127.4	127.5	128.1	128.6
Search, detection, navigation, and guidance systems and aeronautical and nautical nav syst	3812	12/91	105.5	107.0	109.0	109.0	108.8
Industrial process control instruments	3823	06/83	142.2	147.7	149.9	151.0	152.3
Electrical measuring and integrating instruments	3825	12/83	134.2	135.0	135.1	135.5	137.4
Laboratory analytical instruments	3826	12/85	115.9	117.5	118.4	116.9	118.8
Surgical and medical instruments and apparatus	3841	06/82	130.9	129.0	127.9	127.4	127.2
Surgical, orthopedic and prosthetic appliances and supplies	3842	06/83	156.1	158.1	160.5	163.0	166.3
Electromedical equipment	3845	06/85	107.9	104.7	103.8	101.4	98.7
Photographic equipment and supplies	3861	12/83	114.9	113.5	110.0	106.7	106.1
Sporting and athletic goods, n.e.c	3949	12/85	125.3	127.5	129.1	128.8	127.8
Signs and advertising displays	3993	12/85	132.1	134.3	136.2	139.1	140.7
Manufacturing industries, n.e.c	3999	12/85	125.0	124.6	125.1	126.1	127.2

SERVICES

Industry	SIC code [1]	Index base [2]	1996	1997	1998	1999	2000
Railroads, line haul operations	4011	12/84	111.5	112.1	113.4	113.0	114.5
Local trucking without storage	4212	06/93	102.9	104.6	104.8	106.3	109.9
Trucking, except local	4213	06/92	107.6	110.7	114.1	118.0	123.4
Local trucking with storage	4214	06/93	11.9	112.2	113.0	113.2	114.1
Courier services, except by air	4215	12/92	113.0	116.4	122.2	126.0	130.4
Farm product warehousing and storage	4221	12/92	102.4	102.9	104.1	107.1	110.7
Refrigerated warehousing and storage	4222	12/91	104.6	105.1	105.5	106.4	108.1
General warehousing and storage	4225	06/93	104.3	105.5	107.2	111.5	113.4
United States Postal Service	4311	06/89	132.3	132.3	132.3	135.3	135.2
Deep sea foreign transportation of freight	4412	06/88	114.1	113.1	116.4	134.0	156.9
Domestic deep sea transportation of freight	4424	06/88	122.0	124.5	120.9	124.3	129.8
Freight transportation on the Great Lakes-St Lawrence Seaway . .	4432	12/91	104.6	106.4	107.4	107.4	107.4
Water transportation of freight, n.e.c	4449	12/90	109.9	105.9	107.4	111.2	117.9
Marine cargo handling	4491	12/91	101.6	103.7	105.0	106.7	109.1
Tugging and towing services	4492	12/92	110.9	113.3	115.7	119.7	124.2
Air transportation, scheduled	4512	12/89	148.1	153.9	152.6	161.2	186.4
Air courier services	4513	12/89	113.9	115.1	113.2	117.3	128.0
Air transportation, nonscheduled	4522	06/92	105.0	104.5	106.0	109.2	114.7
Airports, flying fields, and airport services	4581	06/92	106.6	109.7	112.5	116.2	122.0
Crude petroleum pipelines	4612	06/86	104.7	96.0	96.8	95.5	101.0
Refined petroleum pipelines	4613	06/86	104.3	105.3	104.8	104.9	105.3
Travel agencies	4724	12/89	109.9	114.5	112.5	112.0	121.8
Freight transportation arrangement	4731	12/94	101.5	101.4	99.8	99.2	100.3
Telephone communications, except radiotelephone	4813	06/95	99.9	99.6	98.5	96.0	93.9
Radio broadcasting	4832	06/88	140.6	148.5	151.2	162.3	170.1
Cable and other pay television services	4841	06/93	103.3	108.3	112.4	116.2	120.9
Electric power and natural gas utilities	4981	12/90	111.1	112.0	110.4	109.5	114.4
Scrap and waste materials	5093	12/86	147.6	152.7	131.7	127.9	152.3
Life insurance carriers	6311	12/98	(X)	(X)	(X)	100.4	99.3
Property and casualty insurance	6331	06/98	(X)	(X)	(X)	100.8	102
Operators and lessors of nonresidential buildings	6512	12/95	99.6	101.0	103.1	105.9	108.9
Real estate agents and managers	6531	12/95	99.6	100.8	102.5	104.4	107.5
Hotels and motels	7011	06/93	110.1	115.6	119.8	124.9	128.7
Advertising agencies	7311	06/95	101.7	103.8	105.3	107.4	109.9
Building cleaning and maintenance services, n.e.c.	7349	12/94	102.4	104.5	105.6	108.0	111.1
Employment agencies	7361	06/94	103.0	104.5	106.4	109.9	111.8
Help supply services	7363	06/94	105.1	106.9	109.1	111.1	113.5
Prepackaged software	7372	12/97	(X)	(X)	100.6	100.1	101.4
Truck rental and leasing, without drivers	7513	06/91	106.5	104.5	104.7	104.2	108.9
Passenger car rental, without drivers	7514	12/91	119.3	130.5	132.5	129.4	135.3
Offices and clinics of doctors of medicine	8011	12/93	107.6	109.0	11.2	113.8	115.7
Skilled and intermediate care facilities	8053	12/94	110.0	114.7	119.4	124.1	130.8
General medical and surgical hospitals	8062	12/92	112.5	113.6	114.5	116.6	119.6
Psychiatric hospitals	8063	12/92	113.7	112.0	108.2	109.2	109.1
Specialty hospitals, except psychiatric	8069	12/92	113.6	114.7	117.1	120.0	123.9
Medical laboratories	8071	06/94	105.3	106.1	106.4	105.9	107.8
Home health care services	8082	12/96	(X)	103.3	106.1	107.1	111.0
Legal services	8111	12/96	(X)	102.5	106.2	108.7	112.1
Engineering design, analysis, and consulting services	8711	12/96	(X)	102.3	105.0	107.9	110.8
Architectural design, analysis, and consulting services	8712	12/96	(X)	102.0	105.5	111.8	115.7
Accounting, auditing, and bookkeeping services	8721	06/95	102.9	105.7	108.2	111.9	115.3

X Not applicable.   [1] Standard Industrial Classification code.   [2] Index based year equals 100.

Source: U.S. Bureau of Labor Statistics, *Producer Price Indexes*, monthly.

No. 700. Chain-Type Price Indexes For Personal Consumption Expenditures PCE): 1980 to 2000

[1996=100. For explanation of "chain-type," see text, Section 13, Income, Expenditures, and Wealth]

Item	1980	1985	1990	1995	1998	1999	2000
Personal consumption expenditures .	55.2	71.0	85.6	97.9	103.0	104.9	107.4
Durable goods.	76.5	88.6	96.0	101.1	95.4	93.1	91.5
Motor vehicles and parts	61.0	74.2	83.8	98.4	99.0	99.3	99.8
Furniture and household equipment	106.3	116.3	113.6	104.5	90.4	85.2	81.4
Nondurable goods	65.3	77.3	91.0	97.9	101.4	103.7	107.6
Food.	60.8	72.9	88.2	97.3	104.1	106.1	108.7
Clothing and shoes	86.5	93.3	103.5	101.4	98.0	96.4	95.2
Gasoline, fuel oil, and other energy goods.	90.6	93.3	95.2	93.7	88.2	95.4	123.2
Gasoline and oil	91.4	92.8	94.8	94.2	87.9	95.7	122.4
Fuel oil and coal	87.4	97.6	98.6	89.6	91.5	92.9	129.7
Services.	45.9	64.4	81.0	97.3	105.5	108.0	110.8
Housing.	47.1	66.7	84.1	97.0	106.3	109.4	112.6
Household operation	56.3	81.8	87.6	98.1	100.8	100.6	102.4
Transportation	51.9	65.5	81.8	98.4	104.9	106.4	109.4
Medical care	37.2	55.9	76.0	97.9	104.5	107.0	110.1
Recreation.	53.7	67.9	83.3	96.8	105.8	108.8	112.8
Addenda:							
Energy goods and services.	75.5	90.3	92.5	95.6	93.2	96.9	114.2
PCE less food and energy	52.4	69.2	84.7	98.2	103.5	105.1	106.8

Source: U.S. Bureau of Economic Analysis, *The National Income and Product Accounts of the United States,* 1929-94, Vol. 2; and *Survey of Current Business,* August 1997 and May 1999.

No. 701. Chain-Type Price Indexes for Gross Domestic Product: 1980 to 2000

[1996=100. For explanation of "chain-type," see text Section 13, Income, Expenditures, and Wealth]

Item	1980	1985	1990	1995	1998	1999	2000
Gross domestic product.	57.1	73.7	86.5	98.1	103.2	104.8	107.0
Personal consumption expenditures.	55.2	71.0	85.6	97.9	103.0	104.9	107.4
Durable goods	76.5	88.6	96.0	101.1	95.4	93.1	91.5
Nondurable goods.	65.3	77.3	91.0	97.9	101.4	103.7	107.6
Services.	45.9	64.4	81.0	97.3	105.5	108.0	110.8
Gross private domestic investment	73.0	85.3	95.1	100.3	98.9	98.8	99.9
Fixed investment.	71.8	84.5	94.7	100.1	99.2	99.1	100.4
Nonresidential	77.4	89.6	98.2	100.9	97.1	95.8	96.3
Structures.	60.0	74.1	85.8	97.4	107.7	110.2	114.6
Producers' durable equipment	86.6	96.3	102.9	102.1	93.8	91.5	91.0
Residential.	58.7	72.2	85.5	97.9	105.6	109.6	113.6
Exports of goods and services	83.3	88.7	96.8	101.3	96.3	95.9	97.4
Exports of goods	94.7	95.6	101.4	102.7	94.3	93.0	94.0
Exports of services.	58.4	73.4	86 5	98.0	101.3	103.3	106.5
Imports of goods and services	90.5	85.0	99.4	101.8	91.3	91.8	95.5
Imports of goods	95.9	88.8	102.0	102.5	90.2	90.3	94.5
Imports of services.	69.0	69.5	88.3	98.3	97.1	99.9	100.5
Government consumption expenditures [1] . .	55.8	73.8	85.2	97.6	103.7	106.4	110.4
Federal.	57.5	75.7	83.8	97.2	102.6	105.3	108.6
National defense	57.9	77.2	84.6	96.9	102.2	104.8	108.0
Nondefense	56.0	71.5	82.0	97.9	103.4	106.3	109.7
State and local.	67.1	72.4	87.7	97.7	107.7	111.8	115.7

[1] And gross investment.

Source: U.S. Bureau of Economic Analysis, *The National Income and Product Accounts of the United States, 1929-97,* (forthcoming); and *Survey of Current Business,* May 2001.

No. 702. Commodity Research Bureau Futures Price Index: 1980 to 2000

[1967=100. Index computed daily. Represents unweighted geometric average of commodity futures prices (through 6 months forward) of 17 major commodity futures markets. Represents end-of-year index]

Item	1980	1985	1990	1992	1993	1994	1995	1996	1997	1998	1999	2000
All commodities	308.5	229.2	222.6	205.9	212.4	229.7	237.1	247.9	229.1	191.2	205.1	227.8
Softs [1]	426.0	398.2	276.0	232.4	246.9	352.3	354.4	322.2	408.7	344.8	280.9	254.4
Industrials	324.6	211.7	245.5	224.7	235.0	263.6	272.5	266.3	210.9	185.3	192.9	211.0
Grains and oilseeds [2]	312.1	198.5	171.2	196.9	193.8	191.2	218.6	284.7	210.7	172.8	156.6	174.9
Energy	(NA)	96.5	246.0	192.6	151.8	173.8	180.0	224.0	180.4	135.0	221.0	355.8
Oilseeds [3]	314.6	245.4	223.6	218.8	239.8	259.9	277.5	307.9	([3])	([3])	([3])	([3])
Livestock and meats	217.4	206.9	226.2	179.8	201.4	192.3	192.4	241.7	238.1	186.7	239.6	253.6
Metals (precious)	531.4	256.6	257.8	228.5	242.2	273.9	276.0	271.3	249.3	234.3	253.4	265.7

NA Not available. [1] Prior to 1997, reported as Imported. [2] Prior to 1997, reported as Grains. [3] Incorporated into Grains and Oilseeds beginning 1997.

Source: Bridge Commodity Research Bureau (CRB), Chicago, IL, *CRB Commodity Index Report,* weekly (copyright).

No. 703. Indexes of Spot Primary Market Prices: 1980 to 2000

[1967=100. Computed weekly for 1980; daily thereafter. Represents unweighted geometric average of price quotations of 23 commodities; much more sensitive to changes in market conditions than is a monthly producer price index]

Items and number of commodities	1980	1985	1990	1993	1994	1995	1996	1997	1998	1999	2000
All commodities (23)	**265.1**	**251.4**	**279.2**	**237.7**	**261.5**	**290.6**	**297.7**	**271.8**	**235.2**	**227.3**	**224.0**
Foodstuffs (10)	260.9	248.1	231.5	208.3	215.5	229.1	251.3	227.3	197.5	178.1	184.7
Raw industrials (13)	268.0	253.6	317.0	260.4	299.2	348.2	334.9	307.5	265.3	268.9	255.8
Livestock and products (5)	250.5	284.5	306.9	291.3	296.9	314.6	338.4	306.1	232.3	265.7	265.5
Metals (5)	257.9	220.2	313.9	236.2	262.1	306.7	296.7	269.8	218.5	261.6	214.3
Textiles and fibers (4)	234.7	220.8	259.4	205.3	252.6	286.0	274.6	261.5	237.5	223.8	245.7
Fats and oils (4)	229.5	273.1	193.3	190.1	209.6	228.3	245.7	257.1	236.0	174.8	163.6

Source: Bridge Commodity Research Bureau, Chicago, IL, *CRB Commodity Index Report*, weekly (copyright).

No. 704. Average Prices of Selected Fuels and Electricity: 1980 to 2000

[In dollars per unit, except electricity, in cents per kWh. Represents price to end-users, except as noted]

Type	Unit [1]	1980	1990	1993	1994	1995	1996	1997	1998	1999	2000
Crude oil, composite [2] . . .	Barrel	28.07	22.22	16.41	15.59	17.23	20.71	19.04	12.52	17.51	28.23
Motor gasoline: [3]											
Unleaded regular	Gallon.	1.25	1.16	1.11	1.11	1.15	1.23	1.23	1.06	1.17	1.51
Unleaded premium . . .	Gallon.	(NA)	1.35	1.30	1.31	1.34	1.41	1.42	1.25	1.36	1.69
No. 2 heating oil.	Gallon.	0.97	1.06	0.91	0.88	0.87	0.99	0.98	0.85	0.88	1.31
No. 2 diesel fuel.	Gallon.	0.82	0.73	0.60	0.55	0.56	0.68	0.64	0.49	0.58	0.94
Residual fuel oil	Gallon.	0.61	0.44	0.34	0.35	0.39	0.46	0.42	0.31	0.37	0.60
Natural gas, residential . .	1,000 cu/ft . .	3.68	5.80	6.16	6.41	6.06	6.34	6.94	6.82	6.69	7.71
Electricity, residential. . . .	kWh	5.36	7.83	8.32	8.38	8.40	8.36	8.43	8.26	8.16	8.21

NA Not available. [1] See headnote. [2] Refiner acquisition cost. [3] Average, all service.

Source: U.S. Energy Information Administration, *Monthly Energy Review*.

No. 705. Weekly Food Cost by Type of Family: 1990 and 2000

[In dollars. Assumes that food for all meals and snacks is purchased at the store and prepared at home. See source for details on estimation procedures]

Family type	December 1990				December 2000			
	Thrifty plan	Low-cost plan	Moderate-cost plan	Liberal-plan	Thrifty-plan	Low-cost plan	Moderate-cost plan	Liberal-plan
FAMILIES								
Family of two:								
20-50 years.	48.10	60.60	74.70	92.70	60.60	78.20	96.40	120.00
51 years and over	45.60	58.30	71.80	85.80	57.60	75.20	93.10	111.50
Family of four:								
Couple, 20-50 years and children—								
1-2 and 3-5 years	70.10	87.30	106.60	131.00	88.40	112.60	137.60	169.40
6-8 and 9-11 years	80.10	102.60	128.30	154.40	101.90	132.60	165.30	199.20
INDIVIDUALS [1]								
Child:								
1-2 years	12.70	15.40	18.00	21.80	16.10	19.80	23.20	28.20
3-5 years	13.70	16.80	20.70	24.90	17.30	21.70	26.80	32.10
6-8 years	16.60	22.20	27.90	32.50	21.50	28.80	35.90	41.70
9-11 years	19.80	25.30	32.50	37.60	25.30	32.70	41.80	48.40
Male:								
12-14 years.	20.60	28.60	35.70	42.00	26.20	36.90	45.70	53.80
15-19 years.	21.40	29.60	36.80	42.60	27.00	38.00	47.40	54.70
20-50 years.	22.90	29.30	36.60	44.30	28.90	37.90	47.20	57.20
51 years and over	20.90	27.90	34.30	41.10	26.40	36.10	44.50	53.40
Female:								
12-19 years.	20.80	24.80	30.10	36.30	26.30	31.80	38.60	46.70
20-50 years.	20.80	25.80	31.30	40.00	26.20	33.20	40.40	51.90
51 years and over	20.60	25.10	31.00	36.90	26.00	32.30	40.10	48.00

[1] The costs given are for individuals in four-person families. For individuals in other size families, the following adjustments are suggested: one-person, add 20 percent; two-person, add 10 percent; three-person, add 5 percent; five- or six-person, subtract 5 percent; seven- (or more) person, subtract 10 percent.

Source: U.S. Dept. of Agriculture, *Agricultural Research Service,* monthly.

Prices 467

No. 706. Food—Retail Prices of Selected Items: 1990 to 2000

[In dollars per pound, except as indicated. As of December]

Food	1990	1993	1994	1995	1996	1997	1998	1999	2000
Cereals and bakery products:									
Flour, white, all purpose	0.24	0.22	0.23	0.24	0.30	0.28	0.28	0.27	0.28
Rice, white, lg. grain, raw	0.49	0.50	0.53	0.55	0.55	0.58	0.54	0.50	(NA)
Spaghetti and macaroni	0.85	0.84	0.87	0.88	0.84	0.88	0.88	0.88	0.88
Bread, whole wheat	(NA)	1.12	1.12	1.15	1.30	1.30	1.32	1.36	1.36
Meats, poultry, fish and eggs:									
Ground beef, 100% beef	1.63	1.57	1.38	1.40	1.42	1.39	1.39	1.53	1.63
Ground beef, lean and extra lean	(NA)	2.25	2.14	2.04	2.05	2.06	2.08	2.15	2.33
Sirloin steak, bone-in	3.65	3.69	(NA)	(NA)	(NA)	(NA)	(NA)	(NA)	(NA)
T-bone steak	5.45	5.77	5.86	5.92	5.87	6.07	6.40	6.71	6.82
Pork:									
Bacon, sliced	2.28	2.02	1.89	2.17	2.64	2.61	2.58	2.75	3.03
Chops, center cut, bone-in	3.32	3.24	3.03	3.29	3.44	3.39	3.03	3.21	3.46
Sausage	2.42	1.99	1.85	1.92	2.15	2.08	2.43	2.50	2.75
Poultry:									
Chicken, fresh, whole	0.86	0.91	0.90	0.94	1.00	1.00	1.06	1.05	1.08
Chicken breast, bone-in	2.00	2.17	1.91	1.95	2.09	1.99	2.11	2.08	2.14
Turkey, frozen, whole	0.96	0.95	0.98	0.99	1.02	0.98	0.95	0.98	0.99
Tuna, light, chunk, canned	2.11	2.04	2.02	2.00	2.03	2.03	2.22	2.03	1.92
Eggs, Grade A, large, (dozen)	1.00	0.87	0.87	1.16	1.31	1.17	1.09	0.92	0.96
Dairy products:									
Milk, fresh, whole, fortified (1/2 gal.)	1.39	1.43	1.44	1.48	1.65	1.61	(NA)	(NA)	(NA)
Butter, salted, grade AA, stick	1.92	1.61	1.54	1.73	2.17	2.46	3.18	2.27	2.80
Ice cream, prepack., bulk, reg. (1/2 gal.)	2.54	2.59	2.62	2.68	2.94	3.02	3.30	3.40	3.66
Fresh fruits and vegetables:									
Apples, red Delicious	0.77	0.78	0.72	0.83	0.89	0.90	0.85	0.92	0.82
Bananas	0.43	0.41	0.46	0.45	0.48	0.46	0.51	0.49	0.49
Oranges, navel	0.56	0.56	0.55	0.64	0.59	0.58	0.61	0.64	0.62
Grapefruit	0.56	0.50	0.47	0.49	0.55	0.53	0.55	0.58	0.58
Grapes, thompson seedless	(NA)	1.96	2.13	1.86	(NA)	2.19	(NA)	2.40	2.36
Lemons	0.97	1.05	1.04	1.12	1.14	1.06	1.37	1.41	1.11
Pears, Anjou	0.79	0.89	(NA)	(NA)	1.06	0.85	0.98	1.03	(NA)
Potatoes, white	0.32	0.36	0.34	0.38	0.33	0.37	0.38	0.40	0.35
Tomatoes, field grown	0.86	1.31	1.43	1.51	1.21	1.62	1.80	1.41	1.57
Cabbage	0.39	0.37	0.45	0.41	0.40	0.46	0.42	0.42	(NA)
Carrots, short trimmed and topped	0.44	0.41	0.48	0.53	0.54	0.50	0.54	0.52	(NA)
Celery	0.49	0.49	0.52	0.54	0.44	0.57	0.53	0.56	(NA)
Cucumbers	0.56	0.93	0.69	0.53	0.60	0.58	(NA)	0.84	(NA)
Onions, dry yellow	(NA)	0.48	0.43	0.41	0.46	0.46	(NA)	(NA)	(NA)
Peppers, sweet	(NA)	1.26	1.52	1.32	0.81	1.54	1.46	1.53	(NA)

NA Not available.

Source: U.S. Bureau of Labor Statistics, *Monthly Labor Review* and *CPI Detailed Report*, January issues.

No. 707. Import Price Indexes—Selected Commodities: 1990 to 2000

[1995 = 100. Indexes are weighted by the 1990 Tariff Schedule of the United States Annotated, a scheme for describing and reporting product composition and value of U.S. imports. Import prices are based on U.S. dollar prices paid by importer. F.o.b. = free on board; c.i.f. = cost, insurance, and freight; n.e.s. = not elsewhere specified]

Commodity	1990	1994	1995 [1]	1996	1997	1998	1999	2000
All commodities	90.3	95.8	100.8	100.1	98.2	92.6	92.4	99.6
Food and live animals	84.9	93.9	100.1	94.7	103.7	98.0	93.3	91.3
Meat	116.3	105.9	99.1	90.4	101.9	98.3	94.5	99.1
Fish	77.9	97.6	101.6	97.5	103.6	109.4	104.3	109.1
Crustaceans; fresh, chilled, frozen, salted or dried	73.3	97.7	103.4	95.0	103.5	106.4	99.0	113.5
Beverages and tobacco	86.1	98.2	99.7	103.6	107.5	109.6	110.4	113.0
Crude materials	82.4	86.3	99.8	94.3	97.4	87.7	90.3	90.7
Mineral fuels and related products	92.9	96.9	105.1	110.6	104.6	77.6	92.7	172.0
Crude petroleum and petroleum products	91.7	96.4	105.4	111.0	104.0	73.4	91.3	171.0
Natural gas	112.7	95.4	101.2	108.2	113.3	111.9	106.5	195.4
Chemicals and related products	88.3	92.0	100.7	98.8	96.4	93.6	90.6	94.1
Intermediate manufactured products	88.8	90.2	99.8	99.2	96.8	94.0	92.0	97.6
Machinery and transport equipment	90.2	97.6	100.6	98.6	95.7	91.8	90.3	89.6
Computer equipment and office machines	119.2	104.0	100.4	91.7	81.2	70.4	63.1	60.0
Computer equipment	143.0	109.1	99.7	93.0	80.8	66.5	54.7	50.5
Telecommunications [2]	102.0	99.2	100.5	97.3	93.4	89.4	87.6	84.6
Electrical machinery and equipment	92.0	98.9	101.6	95.5	90.2	84.5	82.7	83.3
Road vehicles	84.3	96.6	100.0	100.4	100.8	101.1	102.3	102.8
Miscellaneous manufactured articles	92.1	98.2	100.4	100.7	100.2	98.6	97.8	96.9
Plumbing, heating & lighting fixtures	95.3	96.4	100.4	99.5	96.2	96.0	93.0	92.7
Furniture and parts	93.7	98.2	100.7	100.8	102.9	100.2	98.7	97.3
Articles of apparel and clothing	97.6	99.2	100.1	101.5	101.5	102.6	102.7	101.8	100.7
Footwear	97.2	98.4	100.0	101.3	101.1	100.7	100.7	100.3

[1] June 1995 may not equal 100 because indexes were reweighted to an "average" trade value in 1995. [2] Includes sound recording and reproducing equipment.

Source: U.S. Bureau of Labor Statistics, *U.S. Import and Export Price Indexes*, monthly.

No. 708. Export Price Indexes—Selected Commodities: 1990 to 2000

[**1990=100.** Indexes are weighted by 1980 export values according to the Schedule B classification system of the U.S. Census Bureau. Prices used in these indexes were collected from a sample of U.S. manufacturers of exports and are factory transaction prices, except as noted. F.a.s. = free alongside ship. N.e.s. = not elsewhere specified. F.o.b. = free on board]

Commodity	1990	1994	1995 [1]	1996	1997	1998	1999	2000
All commodities.	**91.5**	**94.8**	**100.5**	**1 .1.4**	**99.3**	**96.1**	**94.5**	**96.3**
Food and live animals	89.0	88.7	97.4	122.0	98.5	90.9	89.2	87.4
Meat	84.9	92.5	99.9	101.6	95.3	97.8	91.5	109.3
Fish	83.6	83.3	103.2	89.4	85.3	80.7	118.5	96.9
Cereals and cereal preparations	90.6	84.9	95.4	145.6	92.3	82.6	75.9	71.6
Wheat	80.4	65.4	91.1	129.3	87.1	75.4	69.7	68.4
Maize	97.6	94.9	98.0	165.3	90.4	80.9	73.3	68.4
Fruits and vegetables	83.6	89.8	96.2	105.7	101.6	98.4	98.5	87.8
Feeding stuff for animals	93.2	101.4	98.3	122.5	127.2	95.0	86.7	94.1
Miscellaneous food products	100.4	98.3	101.3	103.2	103.5	105.0	107.0	106.8
Beverages and tobacco	86.4	98.7	99.9	100.6	100.8	99.9	101.2	101.7
Tobacco and tobacco manufactures	86.6	98.6	100.0	100.6	100.9	99.7	101.2	101.8
Crude materials	80.4	86.4	104.1	90.3	93.4	82.0	74.9	84.4
Raw hides and skins	105.1	94.3	103.4	95.7	100.8	84.8	79.0	86.7
Oil seeds and oleaginous fruits	97.0	112.7	96.6	127.0	134.6	102.6	79.2	86.3
Cork and wood	66.4	97.3	102.1	94.7	93.2	82.0	82.0	86.7
Pulp and waste paper	64.7	61.1	111.6	56.8	65.9	64.0	66.0	97.6
Textile fibers	81.8	83.7	106.9	91.1	83.4	79.3	68.6	69.6
Cotton textile fibers	83.4	81.4	107.9	90.2	80.6	78.7	65.6	62.4
Crude fertilizers and minerals	101.9	97.3	99.4	96.8	97.8	97.0	93.5	93.3
Metalliferous ores and metal scrap	83.4	76.2	104.2	89.3	91.7	76.6	70.7	78.2
Ferrous waste and scrap	85.2	81.6	99.6	93.3	93.5	74.2	63.2	70.4
Nonferrous base metal waste and scrap	85.3	79.6	100.2	86.8	89.2	70.1	66.3	74.8
Mineral fuels and related materials	100.1	96.0	102.0	109.1	110.9	103.2	102.0	144.9
Coal, coke and briquettes	103.2	96.8	100.3	103.1	102.0	100.1	98.3	93.8
Crude petroleum and petroleum products	99.9	95.7	103.6	113.7	119.4	106.8	107.6	168.2
Animal and vegetable oils, fats and waxes	86.6	92.5	96.5	95.4	94.7	107.9	76.6	67.1
Chemicals and related products	85.6	86.9	102.6	97.1	96.5	92.6	91.2	95.5
Organic chemicals	81.7	79.8	106.8	87.8	84.9	77.1	75.2	88.8
Hydrocarbons, n.e.s. and derivatives, f.a.s.	82.9	82.0	115.7	90.8	95.0	75.0	78.4	106.5
Alcohols, phenols, phenol-alcohols, & deriv., f.a.s.	77.4	71.8	105.9	88.0	81.5	80.2	73.6	80.4
Chemical materials and products, n.e.s.	85.9	94.6	100.0	102.0	103.9	100.6	99.6	99.1
Intermediate manufactured products	86.9	90.9	100.8	97.9	98.2	97.9	96.8	100.3
Rubber manufactures	84.9	93.7	99.8	102.8	103.2	101.9	105.5	104.4
Paper and paperboard products	81.1	78.4	103.3	87.3	83.5	83.8	83.4	89.8
Textiles	89.7	96.1	101.1	103.8	103.3	103.2	99.2	98.6
Nonmetallic mineral manufactures	91.1	98.1	100.1	101.2	104.3	106.7	106.3	106.5
Nonferrous metals	88.4	81.6	99.7	93.4	93.4	88.1	85.0	100.1
Manufactures of metals, n.e.s.	88.0	94.7	100.1	101.5	104.4	107.0	108.7	109.4
Machinery and transport equipment [2]	95.3	99.4	100.0	100.9	100.6	98.7	97.6	97.3
Power generating machinery [3]	86.5	97.7	99.4	104.3	106.0	107.1	109.6	112.0
Rotating electric plant and parts thereof, n.e.s.	89.2	96.2	100.4	102.4	103.1	103.1	102.7	102.7
Machinery specialized for particular industries	88.0	97.3	99.9	102.7	104.2	105.2	106.1	106.5
Agricultural machinery and parts [4]	90.3	98.7	100.3	102.0	102.8	103.1	103.8	104.8
Civil engineering and contractors, plant and equip.	87.6	97.1	100.2	101.5	103.1	105.8	107.5	107.3
Metalworking machinery	89.0	98.8	100.0	102.3	104.3	108.4	108.8	107.6
General industrial machines, parts, n.e.s.	89.2	98.4	99.4	102.5	105.2	106.1	107.3	108.2
Computer equipment and office machines	132.0	106.5	100.8	93.7	84.7	76.5	71.6	68.2
Computer equipment	148.1	111.0	101.5	90.1	79.1	73.8	67.0	63.0
Telecommunications [5]	94.1	100.9	100.3	101.1	99.6	98.7	96.9	96.9
Electrical machinery and equipment	96.8	99.9	100.7	99.1	96.5	92.1	88.6	85.7
Electronic valves, diodes, transistors & integr. cir.	101.6	101.0	101.7	97.9	91.8	84.4	79.1	74.9
Road vehicles	92.1	98.4	99.8	101.0	101.8	101.9	102.5	103.9
Miscellaneous manufactured articles	91.7	99.1	99.9	100.8	101.7	100.8	101.0	101.0

[1] June 1995 may not equal 100 because indexes were reweighted to an "average" trade value in 1995.   [2] Excludes military and commercial aircraft.   [3] Includes equipment.   [4] Excludes tractors.   [5] Includes sound recording and reproducing equipment.

Source: U.S. Bureau of Labor Statistics, *U.S. Import and Export Price Indexes,* monthly.

No. 709. Refiner/Reseller Sales Price of Gasoline by State: 1997 to 1999

[In cents per gallon. As of March. Represents all refinery and gas plant operators' sales through company-operated retail outlets. Gasoline prices exclude excise taxes]

State	Gasoline excise taxes 1999	Average, all grades			Midgrade			Premium		
		1997	1998	1999	1997	1998	1999	1997	1998	1999
United States	(NA)	70.3	65.7	63.2	75.1	70.6	68.1	79.4	78.7	76.0
Alabama	18	67.6	68.5	61.7	70.3	72.5	65.6	75.7	80.8	73.8
Alaska	8	90.8	103.6	93.8	101.7	103.5	101.6	101.9	111.3	109.7
Arizona	18	78.5	75.0	73.9	85.3	80.8	79.2	90.1	91.0	90.5
Arkansas	21	66.2	62.9	56.6	68.9	69.3	62.9	73.6	77.1	71.2
California	18	79.4	66.3	79.9	84.4	70.7	83.6	90.4	79.8	92.7
Colorado	22	72.4	69.4	66.0	76.0	75.4	72.2	79.7	83.1	82.7
Connecticut	25	73.4	68.7	64.2	78.0	74.3	70.3	82.0	83.9	79.3
Delaware	23	71.6	65.9	57.8	74.7	73.0	63.7	80.5	80.8	72.4
District of Columbia . .	20	82.1	(D)	(D)	80.7	(D)	(D)	86.7	(D)	(D)
Florida	13	70.0	65.7	61.2	72.9	70.8	66.2	79.3	78.3	73.3
Georgia	8	66.2	60.1	56.3	69.1	64.7	60.8	74.0	73.4	69.4
Hawaii	16	102.5	113.9	103.9	106.2	116.2	106.8	111.7	125.4	115.1
Idaho	25	79.6	70.1	66.5	82.7	76.7	73.1	88.2	84.2	81.4
Illinois	19	71.0	66.6	65.8	78.6	70.4	68.6	81.6	79.3	80.9
Indiana	15	67.8	64.8	62.1	71.6	69.4	67.9	76.6	75.8	75.1
Iowa	20	68.8	64.6	59.1	72.6	69.0	63.0	75.3	72.9	67.1
Kansas	20	66.5	62.6	57.3	72.0	67.2	62.8	73.2	73.2	68.5
Kentucky	16	69.2	66.0	64.2	73.2	70.8	69.4	77.2	79.7	78.0
Louisiana	20	65.8	66.9	59.0	70.4	72.4	64.3	72.1	80.6	72.1
Maine	22	71.1	71.1	63.4	75.8	78.3	70.5	79.2	87.4	80.0
Maryland	24	73.7	68.5	59.7	76.2	73.2	64.7	81.1	79.7	71.1
Massachusetts	21	74.6	69.3	60.6	80.5	75.8	66.3	83.2	83.3	74.4
Michigan	19	68.3	63.8	59.9	72.6	69.9	66.6	76.9	76.1	72.7
Minnesota	20	71.6	73.6	68.0	74.4	77.0	70.4	78.2	84.9	78.2
Mississippi	18	65.5	68.6	61.7	69.9	73.2	64.9	73.6	82.4	74.5
Missouri	17	68.9	60.4	57.0	75.0	66.2	62.9	77.0	74.8	72.0
Montana	28	77.4	75.9	58.3	79.9	80.3	(NA)	86.6	84.3	69.2
Nebraska	24	68.7	65.6	59.2	73.0	69.2	63.0	76.0	76.6	69.8
Nevada	24	78.1	69.5	79.6	81.7	79.6	86.1	87.3	83.1	94.8
New Hampshire	20	76.7	67.9	62.5	81.3	75.0	68.3	86.7	93.8	77.2
New Jersey	11	70.7	68.4	63.4	79.2	72.4	67.8	80.6	81.4	76.1
New Mexico	19	73.0	72.6	64.6	76.0	79.4	70.9	80.9	85.7	78.5
New York	22	74.4	66.7	59.9	79.4	72.3	65.6	83.8	79.3	72.9
North Carolina	22	67.3	63.1	57.9	70.1	67.5	62.0	75.2	76.9	71.7
North Dakota	21	70.4	72.4	66.9	75.9	78.0	72.1	79.1	77.9	70.2
Ohio	22	68.4	67.1	66.7	72.2	72.2	72.5	77.6	79.8	79.8
Oklahoma	17	64.4	61.6	57.1	70.7	65.3	60.9	71.5	71.3	67.5
Oregon	24	75.7	66.2	75.0	82.4	73.6	83.0	86.8	82.4	92.2
Pennsylvania	26	69.1	60.8	54.4	72.3	65.5	58.7	77.4	74.1	67.0
Rhode Island	29	72.6	64.3	57.5	77.3	69.8	63.3	81.6	78.1	71.9
South Carolina	16	66.6	61.6	56.5	69.2	66.7	61.5	74.7	75.2	70.4
South Dakota	22	70.9	70.6	64.3	73.4	71.8	66.7	79.1	81.0	77.8
Tennessee	20	67.5	64.5	58.0	70.5	69.0	62.3	75.3	77.5	71.2
Texas	20	63.8	63.2	57.4	69.9	69.1	62.5	72.2	77.0	70.6
Utah	25	79.3	65.5	67.8	81.9	69.0	71.2	85.7	77.9	80.4
Vermont	20	77.6	67.5	63.6	81.9	73.7	67.8	86.5	82.0	75.7
Virginia	18	69.4	66.5	60.6	72.0	71.3	65.0	77.2	79.0	73.6
Washington	23	76.5	65.2	70.9	81.8	73.1	78.3	87.6	83.3	88.7
West Virginia	21	71.3	66.6	59.6	74.3	71.9	63.6	79.8	79.9	73.1
Wisconsin	26	68.6	65.1	62.6	73.2	70.7	68.3	76.5	75.0	74.2
Wyoming	14	75.4	74.1	67.8	81.9	79.9	71.6	83.8	82.7	79.1

D Withheld to avoid disclosure of individual company data. NA Not available.

Source: U.S. Energy Information, *Petroleum Marketing Monthly.*

Section 15
Business Enterprise

This section relates to the place and behavior of the business firm and to business initiative in the American economy. It includes data on the number, type, and size of businesses; financial data of domestic and multinational U.S. corporations; business investments, expenditures, and profits; and sales and inventories.

The principal sources of these data are the *Survey of Current Business*, published by the Bureau of Economic Analysis (BEA), the *Federal Reserve Bulletin*, issued by the Board of Governors of the Federal Reserve System, the annual *Statistics of Income (SOI)* reports of the Internal Revenue Service (IRS), and the Census Bureau's Economic Census, *County Business Patterns*, and *Quarterly Financial Report for Manufacturing, Mining, and Trade Corporations (QFR)*.

Business firms—A firm is generally defined as a business organization under a single management and may include one or more establishments. The terms firm, business, company, and enterprise are used interchangeably throughout this section. A firm doing business in more than one industry is classified by industry according to the major activity of the firm as a whole.

The IRS concept of a business firm relates primarily to the legal entity used for tax reporting purposes. A sole proprietorship is an unincorporated business owned by one person and may include large enterprises with many employees and hired managers and part-time operators. A partnership is an unincorporated business owned by two or more persons, each of whom has a financial interest in the business. A corporation is a business that is legally incorporated under state laws. While many corporations file consolidated tax returns, most corporate tax returns represent individual corporations, some

of which are affiliated through common ownership or control with other corporations filing separate returns.

Economic census—The economic census is the major source of facts about the structure and functioning of the nation's economy. It provides essential information for government, business, industry, and the general public. It furnishes an important part of the framework for such composite measures as the gross domestic product estimates, input/output measures, production and price indexes, and other statistical series that measure short-term changes in economic conditions. The Census Bureau takes the economic census every 5 years, covering years ending in "2" and "7." The economic census forms an integrated program at 5-year intervals since 1967, and before that for 1963, 1958, and 1954. Prior to that time, the individual censuses were taken separately at varying intervals.

The economic census is collected on an establishment basis. A company operating at more than one location is required to file a separate report for each store, factory, shop, or other location. Each establishment is assigned a separate industry classification based on its primary activity and not that of its parent company. Establishments responding to the establishment survey are classified into industries on the basis of their principal product or activity (determined by annual sales volume) in accordance with the *North American Industry Classification System—United States, 1997 manual* (see below).

More detailed information about the scope, coverage, classification system, data items, and publications for each of the economic censuses and related surveys is published in the *Guide to the Economic Censuses and Related Statistics*. More information on the methodology, procedures, and history of the censuses is

Business Enterprise   471

available in the *History of the 1997 Economic Census* found on the Census Bureau Web site at <http://www.census.gov/prod/ec97/pol00-hec.pdf>.

Data from the 1997 Economic Census were released through the Census Bureau's American FactFinder service, on CD-ROM, and in Adobe Acrobat PDF reports available on the Census Bureau Web site. For more information on these various media of release, see the following page on the Census Bureau Web site <http://www.census.gov/epcd/www/econ97.html>.

North American Industry Classification System (NAICS)—The 1997 Economic Census is the first census to present data based on the new NAICS. Previous census data were based on the Standard Industrial Classification (SIC) system. This new system of industrial classification was developed by experts on classification in government and private industry under the guidance of the Office of Information and Regulatory Affairs, Office of Management and Budget.

There are 20 NAICS sectors, which are subdivided into 96 subsectors (three-digit codes), 313 industry groups (four-digit codes), and, as implemented in the United States, 1,170 industries (five- and six-digit codes). While many of the individual NAICS industries correspond directly to industries as defined under the SIC system, most of the higher level groupings do not.

Most of the 1997 Economic Census data are issued on a NAICS basis as seen in the industry and geographic series from the census. Other related census reports remain on an SIC basis due to use of administrative records and other methodological and data processing issues. Current survey data from the Census Bureau as well as other statistical agencies are converting over time to NAICS after benchmarking to the 1997 Economic Census where appropriate or implementation of data collection on a NAICS basis.

U.S. Census Bureau, Statistical Abstract of the United States: 2001

No. 710. Number of Returns, Receipts, and Net Income by Type of Business: 1980 to 1998

[**8,932 represents 8,932,000.** Covers active enterprises only. Figures are estimates based on sample of unaudited tax returns; see Appendix III. Minus sign (-) indicates net loss]

Item	Number of returns (1,000)			Business receipts [2] (bil. dol.)			Net income (less loss) [3] (bil. dol.)		
	Nonfarm propri- etor- ships [1]	Partner- ships	Corpora- tions	Nonfarm propri- etor- ships [1]	Partner- ships	Corpora- tions	Nonfarm propri- etor- ships [1]	Partner- ships	Corpora- tions
1980	8,932	1,380	2,711	411	286	6,172	55	8	239
1985	11,929	1,714	3,277	540	349	8,050	79	-9	240
1989	14,298	1,635	3,628	693	524	10,440	133	14	389
1990	14,783	1,554	3,717	731	541	10,914	141	17	371
1991	15,181	1,515	3,803	713	539	10,963	142	21	345
1992	15,495	1,485	3,869	737	571	11,272	154	43	402
1993	15,848	1,468	3,965	757	627	11,814	156	67	498
1994	16,154	1,494	4,342	791	732	12,858	167	82	577
1995	16,424	1,581	4,474	807	854	13,969	169	107	714
1996	16,955	1,654	4,631	843	1,042	14,890	177	145	806
1997	17,176	1,759	4,710	870	1,297	15,890	187	168	915
1998	17,409	1,855	4,849	918	1,534	16,543	202	187	838

[1] In 1980, represents individually owned businesses, including farms; thereafter, represents only nonfarm proprietors, i.e., business owners. [2] Excludes investment income except for partnerships and corporations in finance, insurance, and real estate before 1998. After 1997 finance and insurance, real estate, and management of companies included investment income for partnerships and corporations. Starting 1985, investment income no longer included for S corporations. [3] Net income (less loss) is defined differently by form of organization, basically as follows: (a) Proprietorships: Total taxable receipts less total business deductions, including cost of sales and operations, depletion, and certain capital expensing, excluding charitable contributions and owners' salaries; (b) Partnerships: Total taxable receipts (including investment income except capital gains) less deductions, including cost of sales and operations and certain payments to partners, excluding charitable contributions, oil and gas depletion, and certain capital expensing; (c) Corporations: Total taxable receipts (including investment income, capital gains, and income from foreign subsidiaries deemed received for tax purposes, except for S corporations beginning 1985) less business deductions, including cost of sales and operations, depletion, certain capital expensing, and officers' compensation excluding S corporation charitable contributions and investment expenses starting 1985; net income is before income tax.

Source: U.S. Internal Revenue Service, *Statistics of Income,* various publications.

No. 711. Number of Returns and Business Receipts by Size of Receipts: 1990 to 1998

[**3,717 represents 3,717,000.** Covers active enterprises only. Figures are estimates based on sample of unaudited tax returns; see Appendix III]

Size-class of receipts	Returns (1,000)					Business receipts [1] (bil. dol.)				
	1990	1995	1996	1997	1998	1990	1995	1996	1997	1998
Corporations.	3,717	4,474	4,631	4,710	4,849	10,914	13,969	14,890	15,890	16,543
Under $25,000 [2]	879	1,030	1,060	1,106	1,181	5	4	5	4	4
$25,000 to $49,999	252	288	286	306	287	9	11	11	11	11
$50,000 to $99,999	359	447	480	453	456	26	33	35	33	34
$100,000 to $499,999.	1,162	1,393	1,444	1,450	1,481	291	350	364	363	368
$500,000 to $999,999.	416	513	521	533	552	294	361	368	376	389
$1,000,000 or more	649	803	841	862	892	10,289	13,210	14,107	15,102	15,738
Partnerships	1,554	1,581	1,654	1,759	1,855	541	854	1,042	1,297	1,534
Under $25,000 [2]	963	931	956	987	1,038	4	4	4	4	4
$25,000 to $49,999	126	133	141	151	157	5	5	5	5	6
$50,000 to $99,999	133	142	146	165	157	10	10	10	12	11
$100,000 to $499,999.	222	245	268	294	320	51	56	61	68	73
$500,000 to $999,999.	52	59	64	68	77	36	42	45	48	54
$1,000,000 or more	57	69	80	94	107	435	738	917	1,160	1,385
Nonfarm proprietorships	14,783	16,424	16,955	17,176	17,409	731	807	843	870	918
Under $25,000 [2]	10,196	11,317	11,577	11,703	11,767	69	76	78	79	79
$25,000 to $49,999	1,660	1,983	2,091	2,111	2,112	58	71	74	75	75
$50,000 to $99,999	1,282	1,393	1,473	1,491	1,590	91	99	105	107	113
$100,000 to $499,999.	1,444	1,514	1,579	1,637	1,686	296	310	319	332	345
$500,000 to $999,999.	143	147	165	160	175	97	100	110	107	118
$1,000,000 or more	57	70	71	75	78	119	151	158	170	188

[1] Excludes investment income except for partnerships and corporations in finance, insurance, and real estate before 1998. After 1997 finance and insurance, real estate, and management of companies included investment income for partnerships and corporations. [2] Includes firms with no receipts.

Source: U.S. Internal Revenue Service, *Statistics of Income Bulletin;* and unpublished data.

No. 712. Number of Returns, Receipts, and Net Income by Type of Business and Industry: 1998

[17,409 represents 17,409,000. Covers active enterprises only. Figures are estimates based on sample of unaudited tax returns; see Appendix III. Based on the North American Industry Classification System. Minus sign (-) indicates net loss]

Industry	Number of returns (1,000)			Business receipts [1] (bil. dol.)			Net income (less loss) (bil. dol.)		
	Non-farm propri-etor-ships	Partner-ships	Corpo-rations	Non-farm propri-etor-ships	Partner-ships	Corpo-rations	Non-farm propri-etor-ships	Partner-ships	Corpora-tions
Total [2]	17,409	1,855	4,849	918	1,534	16,543	202	187	838
Agriculture, forestry, fishing, and hunting [3]	289	116	135	16	16	100	1	1	1
Mining	119	29	31	5	26	117	(Z)	4	1
Utilities	7	2	8	(Z)	49	451	(Z)	1	32
Construction	2,243	126	552	144	106	859	26	8	28
Special trade contractors	1,790	43	(NA)	98	15	(NA)	21	2	(NA)
Manufacturing	361	35	310	27	247	4,591	4	10	246
Wholesale and retail trade [4]	2,726	130	957	221	304	4,517	16	6	87
Wholesale trade	377	26	338	40	133	2,093	5	4	38
Retail trade [5]	2,350	104	616	181	171	2,420	11	2	49
Motor vehicle and parts dealers .	131	12	(NA)	29	41	(NA)	1	(Z)	(NA)
Food and beverage stores.	128	14	(NA)	32	29	(NA)	2	(Z)	(NA)
Gasoline stations	38	6	(NA)	26	11	(NA)	(Z)	1	(NA)
Transportation and warehousing	790	19	160	43	31	470	7	2	16
Information	212	22	101	6	98	668	2	-6	33
Broadcasting and telecommunica-tions	34	6	(NA)	1	67	(NA)	(Z)	-7	(NA)
Finance and insurance.	599	209	218	61	184	2,358	13	63	285
Real estate and rental and leasing. . .	872	812	522	43	111	176	18	40	9
Professional, scientific, and technical services [5]	2,431	118	624	108	148	541	46	39	18
Legal services.	318	32	(NA)	27	66	(NA)	13	26	(NA)
Accounting, tax preparation, bookkeeping, and payroll services.	394	15	(NA)	10	29	(NA)	5	6	(NA)
Management, scientific, and technical consulting services	564	23	(NA)	22	17	(NA)	12	4	(NA)
Management of companies and enterprises.	(NA)	12	31	(NA)	14	551	(NA)	5	57
Administrative and support and waste management and remediation services.	1,251	28	200	34	23	264	9	1	7
Educational services	293	5	37	4	1	23	1	(Z)	1
Health care and social assistance . . .	1,506	38	307	81	60	357	36	8	4
Ambulatory health care services. . .	760	28	(NA)	70	35	(NA)	32	7	(NA)
Arts, entertainment and recreation . . .	987	30	93	20	22	60	5	(Z)	2
Accommodation and food services. . .	303	58	245	33	79	296	2	3	8
Accommodation	56	20	(NA)	5	49	(NA)	(Z)	3	(NA)
Food services and drinking places .	246	38	(NA)	29	30	(NA)	2	1	(NA)
Other services [5]	2,070	64	300	66	14	143	15	1	5
Personal and laundry services	1,208	39	(NA)	29	7	(NA)	8	(Z)	(NA)
Religious, grantmaking, civic, professional, and similar organizations	213	(Z)	(NA)	3	(Z)	(NA)	1	(NA)	(NA)
Unclassified	348	2	(NA)	6	(Z)	(NA)	2	(Z)	(NA)

NA Not available.   Z Less than 500 or $500 million.   [1] Includes investment income for partnerships and corporations in finance and insurance, real estate, and management of companies industries. Excludes investment income for S corporations. [2] For corporations, includes businesses not allocable to individual industries.   [3] For corporations represents agricultural services only.   [4] For corporations includes trade business not identified as wholesale or retail.   [5] Includes other industries not shown separately.

Source: U.S. Internal Revenue Service, *Statistics of Income,* various publications.

No. 713. Nonfarm Sole Proprietorships—Selected Income and Deduction Items: 1980 to 1998

[In millions of dollars (21,996 represents $21,996,000,000), except as indicated. All figures are estimates based on sample. Tax law changes have affected the comparability of the data over time; see *Statistics of Income* reports for a description]

Item	1980	1990	1992	1993	1994	1995	1996	1997	1998
Number of returns (1,000)	8,932	14,783	15,495	15,848	16,154	16,424	16,955	17,176	17,409
Businesses with net income (1,000)	(NA)	11,222	11,720	11,872	12,187	12,213	12,524	12,703	13,080
Inventory, end of year	21,996	30,422	29,898	31,795	33,602	33,356	33,785	33,223	32,882
Business receipts	411,206	730,606	737,082	757,215	790,630	807,364	843,234	870,392	918,268
Income from sales and operations	407,169	719,008	725,666	746,306	778,494	796,597	831,546	858,453	905,138
Business deductions [1]	356,258	589,250	583,147	600,765	623,833	638,127	666,461	683,872	716,157
Cost of goods sold/operations [1]	209,890	291,010	274,220	289,578	301,004	306,959	316,421	319,557	341,133
Purchases	168,302	210,225	204,317	210,260	216,365	219,305	220,029	224,259	231,405
Labor costs	10,922	22,680	18,838	20,685	23,497	24,383	26,002	24,941	27,448
Materials and supplies	12,909	30,195	28,825	32,701	34,304	34,427	40,473	37,552	42,162
Commissions	3,333	8,816	10,457	8,707	9,029	9,592	10,792	10,986	10,722
Salaries and wages (net)	26,561	46,998	52,316	52,046	53,649	54,471	56,322	57,746	58,865
Car and truck expenses	13,378	21,766	23,920	26,714	30,845	32,785	36,700	38,728	39,716
Rent paid	9,636	23,392	25,148	25,008	26,769	27,503	28,516	29,326	30,460
Repairs	5,032	8,941	9,706	9,847	10,385	10,172	10,715	10,897	11,350
Taxes paid	7,672	10,342	12,618	13,062	13,600	13,471	13,736	13,774	13,731
Utilities	4,790	13,539	14,547	16,069	16,918	17,206	18,162	18,575	18,431
Insurance	6,003	13,358	13,260	13,173	13,289	12,978	13,195	13,299	12,938
Interest paid	7,190	13,312	10,406	9,431	9,170	10,057	10,567	10,884	11,159
Depreciation	13,953	23,735	23,274	24,964	26,158	26,738	27,883	28,625	29,136
Pension and profit sharing plans	141	586	528	636	605	649	707	728	757
Net income (less loss) [2]	54,947	141,430	153,960	156,459	166,799	169,262	176,756	186,644	202,275
Net income [2]	68,010	161,657	173,473	176,983	187,845	191,729	200,124	210,465	226,190

NA Not available. [1] Includes other amounts not shown separately. [2] After adjustment for the passive loss carryover from prior years. Therefore, "business receipts" minus "total deductions" do not equal "net income."

Source: U.S. Internal Revenue Service, *Statistics of Income Bulletin.*

No. 714. Partnerships—Selected Income and Balance Sheet Items: 1980 to 1998

[In billions of dollars (598 represents $598,000,000,000), except as indicated. Covers active partnerships only. All figures are estimates based on samples. See Appendix III]

Item	1980	1990	1992	1993	1994	1995	1996	1997	1998
Number of returns (1,000)	1,380	1,554	1,485	1,468	1,494	1,581	1,654	1,759	1,855
Number with net income (1,000)	774	854	856	870	890	955	1,010	1,092	1,171
Number of partners (1,000)	8,420	17,095	15,735	15,627	14,990	15,606	15,662	16,184	15,663
Assets [1][2]	598	1,735	1,907	2,118	2,295	2,719	3,368	4,171	5,127
Depreciable assets (net)	239	681	701	698	712	767	848	980	1,153
Inventories, end of year	33	57	62	71	76	88	137	147	176
Land	70	215	213	207	208	221	232	257	291
Liabilities [1][2]	489	1,415	1,508	1,620	1,662	1,886	2,235	2,658	3,151
Accounts payable	34	67	79	80	81	91	121	159	191
Short-term debt [3]	48	88	115	131	126	124	126	127	230
Long-term debt [4]	178	498	486	489	508	544	607	706	884
Nonrecourse loans	119	470	476	478	463	466	474	492	523
Partners' capital accounts [2]	109	320	399	499	633	832	1,133	1,513	1,976
Receipts [1]	292	566	597	656	762	890	1,089	1,354	1,603
Business receipts [5]	271	483	515	561	732	854	1,042	1,297	1,534
Interest received	11	21	16	16	19	31	33	41	51
Deductions [1]	284	550	554	589	680	784	943	1,186	1,416
Cost of goods sold/operations	114	243	249	273	335	395	486	625	737
Salaries and wages	22	56	62	65	70	80	94	115	143
Taxes paid	10	9	10	11	12	13	15	18	24
Interest paid	28	30	25	27	36	43	49	60	73
Depreciation	22	60	60	60	22	23	29	38	43
Net income (less loss)	8	17	43	67	82	107	145	168	187
Net income	45	116	122	137	151	179	228	262	298

[1] Includes items not shown separately. [2] Assets, liabilities, and partners' capital accounts are understated because not all partnerships file complete balance sheets. [3] Mortgages, notes, and bonds payable in less than 1 year. [4] Mortgages, notes, and bonds payable in 1 year or more. [5] Excludes investment income except for partnerships in finance, insurance, and real estate from 1994 to 1997. After 1997 finance and insurance, real estate, and management of companies included investment income for partnerships.

Source: U.S. Internal Revenue Service, *Statistics of Income,* various issues.

U.S. Census Bureau, Statistical Abstract of the United States: 2001

No. 715. Partnerships—Selected Items by Industry: 1998

[In millions of dollars (5,126,548 represents $5,126,548,000,000), except as indicated. Covers active partnerships only. Includes partnerships not allocable by industry. Figures are estimates based on samples. Based on the North American Industry Classification System. See Appendix III]

Year	Number of partnerships (1,000)			Number of partners (1,000)	Total assets [1]	Business receipts [2]	Total deductions	Net income less loss	Net income	Net loss
	Total	With net income	With net loss							
Total	1,855	1,171	684	15,663	5,126,548	1,533,753	1,416,323	186,705	297,875	111,171
Agriculture, forestry, fishing and hunting	116	66	50	535	57,397	15,572	19,608	500	4,149	3,649
Mining	29	19	10	1,063	83,716	25,712	25,317	4,202	8,556	4,354
Utilities	2	1	1	50	61,941	48,838	49,933	1,399	4,035	2,636
Construction	126	74	52	422	122,348	106,321	102,685	7,809	11,973	4,165
Manufacturing	35	18	17	225	199,073	247,439	246,462	10,237	18,574	8,337
Wholesale trade	26	17	10	102	45,765	133,261	131,257	3,838	5,303	1,464
Retail trade	104	54	50	310	55,379	170,809	171,936	1,884	4,665	2,781
Transportation and warehousing	19	12	7	308	54,565	31,010	31,388	1,506	3,488	1,983
Information	22	9	13	359	198,050	98,388	111,465	-5,773	16,205	21,978
Finance and insurance	209	161	48	3,374	2,375,852	184,489	121,221	63,268	74,310	11,042
Real estate & rental & leasing	812	522	291	7,207	1,437,933	110,831	76,862	40,188	70,435	30,248
Professional, scientific, and technical services	118	80	38	478	59,435	147,765	116,501	38,733	42,440	3,707
Management of companies	12	7	5	255	159,894	14,251	8,959	5,292	9,015	3,723
Admin/support and waste management/remediation services	28	17	12	80	13,516	22,841	23,209	1,213	2,112	898
Educational services	5	3	2	12	2,744	1,073	1,125	-14	117	131
Health care and social assistance	38	25	13	205	42,453	59,774	56,724	7,913	10,457	2,544
Arts, entertainment, & rec.	30	14	16	218	40,344	22,157	29,294	26	3,412	3,386
Accommodation and food services	58	31	27	296	107,864	78,969	78,894	3,375	6,946	3,572
Other services	64	41	22	162	7,160	14,128	13,359	1,070	1,638	568
Nature of business not allocable	2	1	1	4	1,117	126	125	39	45	6

[1] Total assets are understated because not all partnerships file complete balance sheets. [2] Finance and insurance, real estate, and management of companies includes investment income for partnerships.

Source: U.S. Internal Revenue Service, Statistics of Income, various issues.

No. 716. Corporate Funds—Sources and Uses: 1980 to 2000

[In billions of dollars (183 represents $183,000,000,000). Covers nonfarm nonfinancial corporate business. See text, this section]

Item	1980	1985	1990	1993	1994	1995	1996	1997	1998	1999	2000
Profits before tax (book)	183	173	236	305	381	422	459	494	487	537	595
-Profit tax accruals	67	70	95	105	128	136	150	158	159	166	185
-Dividends	45	72	118	149	158	178	201	216	238	248	264
+Consumption of fixed capital	159	323	371	408	445	472	504	540	575	622	667
=U.S. internal funds, book	231	354	393	459	540	579	612	660	665	744	813
+Foreign earnings retained abroad	19	26	51	56	39	59	60	59	64	70	89
+Inventory valuation adjustment (IVA)	-42	(Z)	-13	-4	-12	-18	3	8	17	-9	-16
=Internal funds + IVA	208	380	432	511	567	620	676	728	746	804	887
Gross investment	174	226	391	640	626	699	690	650	723	763	854
Capital expenditures [1]	269	393	450	525	593	666	685	784	847	907	1,021
Fixed investment [2]	265	376	438	499	544	618	659	718	770	864	967
Net financial investment	-95	-167	-59	115	33	33	5	-133	-124	-144	-167
Net acquisition of financial assets [1]	127	212	124	333	275	424	403	150	347	691	514
Foreign deposits	(-Z)	3	(-Z)	-1	1	2	11	-5	1	3	3
Checkable deposits and currency	3	11	16	14	19	31	37	31	-18	64	65
Time and savings deposits	(Z)	12	-16	22	-7	-25	1	-7	-5	1	7
Money market fund shares	4	-2	10	-3	7	25	10	24	45	36	27
U.S. government securities	1	3	-20	-1	3	10	-5	-41	1	-1	3
Municipal securities	5	3	-8	9	2	-20	-6	-4	2	-4	9
Mortgages	9	6	-2	-8	4	2	-4	26	20	15	8
Consumer credit	1	4	3	7	9	-2	-7	1	-4	5	2
Trade receivables	50	45	29	51	72	78	88	94	15	107	101
Miscellaneous assets [1]	54	123	113	236	163	316	263	35	289	463	292
U.S. direct investment abroad [3]	20	14	35	58	79	90	77	84	128	137	110
Net increase in liabilities [1]	222	380	184	218	242	391	398	283	471	836	681
Net funds raised in markets	80	95	59	61	79	169	80	152	151	338	294
Net new equity issues	10	-85	-63	21	-45	-58	-70	-114	-267	-143	-153
Credit market instruments [1]	70	180	122	40	124	227	149	266	418	482	447
Commercial paper	4	15	10	10	21	18	-1	14	24	37	48
Corporate bonds [3]	28	83	47	75	23	91	116	151	219	230	175
Bank loans n.e.c.	29	32	3	-11	43	67	39	71	81	73	75
Mortgages	-11	4	7	-17	3	16	-27	-22	41	88	72
Trade payables	29	43	28	36	77	81	50	65	-15	134	100
Miscellaneous liabilities [1]	110	245	96	115	86	141	260	57	330	357	280
Foreign direct investment in U.S.	13	18	59	20	45	54	72	101	154	240	212

Z Less than $500 million. [1] Includes other items not shown separately. [2] Nonresidential fixed investment plus residential fixed investment. [3] Through 1992:Q4, corporate bonds include net issues by Netherlands Antillean financial subsidiaries, and U.S. direct investment abroad excludes net inflows from those bond issues.

Source: Board of Governors of the Federal Reserve System, "Federal Reserve Statistical Release, Z.1, Flow of Funds Accounts of the United States"; published: 9 March 2001; <http://www.federalreserve.gov/releases/Z1/20010309/data.htm>.

No. 717. Nonfinancial Corporate Business-Sector Balance Sheet: 1990 to 2000

[In billions of dollars (9,814 represents $9,814,000,000,000).] Represents year-end outstandings. Tangible assets stated at either market value or replacement cost]

Item	1990	1993	1994	1995	1996	1997	1998	1999	2000
Assets	9,814	10,179	10,818	11,647	12,444	13,397	14,473	15,618	16,919
Tangible assets	6,235	5,970	6,339	6,686	6,984	7,590	8,249	8,624	9,458
Real estate [1]	3,442	2,918	3,091	3,226	3,378	3,805	4,270	4,427	4,872
Equipment and software [2]	1,892	2,118	2,240	2,390	2,515	2,645	2,799	2,948	3,254
Inventories [2]	901	935	1,007	1,070	1,091	1,140	1,180	1,249	1,332
Financial assets [3]	3,579	4,210	4,479	4,961	5,460	5,807	6,223	6,993	7,461
Checkable deposits and currency	167	203	222	253	290	321	302	366	431
Trade receivables	967	1,035	1,107	1,185	1,273	1,367	1,381	1,488	1,589
Liabilities [3]	4,729	5,389	5,627	6,010	6,379	6,629	7,083	7,880	8,491
Credit market instruments	2,516	2,555	2,685	2,912	3,095	3,360	3,778	4,294	4,741
Corporate bonds [4]	1,008	1,230	1,253	1,344	1,460	1,611	1,830	2,059	2,234
Bank loans n.e.c.	545	478	521	588	627	698	779	852	926
Other loans and advances	473	388	421	454	472	521	568	616	692
Trade payables	626	719	797	878	927	992	977	1,112	1,211
Net worth (market value)	5,085	4,791	5,191	5,637	6,065	6,768	7,390	7,737	8,428

[1] At market value. [2] At replacement (current) cost. [3] Includes items not shown separately. [4] Through 1992, corporate bonds include net issues by Netherlands Antillean financial subsidiaries.

Source: Board of Governors of the Federal Reserve System, "Federal Reserve Statistical Release, Z.1, Flow of Funds Accounts of the United States"; published: 9 March 2001; <http://www.federalreserve.gov/releases/Z1/20010309/data.htm>.

No. 718. Corporations—Selected Financial Items: 1980 to 1998

[In billions of dollars (7,617 represents $7,617,000,000,000), except as noted.] Covers active corporations only. All corporations are required to file returns except those specifically exempt. See source for changes in law affecting comparability of historical data. Based on samples; see Appendix III]

Item	1980	1990	1992	1993	1994	1995	1996	1997	1998
Number of returns (1,000)	2,711	3,717	3,869	3,965	4,342	4,474	4,631	4,710	4,849
Number with net income (1,000)	1,597	1,911	2,064	2,145	2,392	2,455	2,588	2,647	2,761
S Corporation returns [1] (1,000)	545	1,575	1,785	1,902	2,073	2,153	2,304	2,452	2,588
Assets [2]	7,617	18,190	20,002	21,816	23,446	26,014	28,642	33,030	37,347
Cash	529	771	806	812	853	962	1,097	1,299	1,336
Notes and accounts receivable	1,985	4,198	4,169	4,532	4,768	5,307	5,783	6,632	7,062
Inventories	535	894	915	947	1,126	1,045	1,079	1,114	1,139
Investments in govt. obligations	266	921	1,248	1,290	1,309	1,363	1,339	1,343	1,366
Mortgage and real estate	894	1,538	1,567	1,627	1,661	1,713	1,825	2,029	2,414
Other investments	1,214	4,137	4,971	5,701	6,265	7,429	8,657	10,756	13,201
Depreciable assets	2,107	4,318	4,755	4,969	5,284	5,571	5,923	6,208	6,541
Depletable assets	72	129	131	137	148	154	169	177	193
Land	93	210	221	230	239	242	254	262	271
Liabilities [2]	7,617	18,190	20,002	21,816	23,446	26,014	28,642	33,030	37,347
Accounts payable	542	1,094	1,605	1,466	1,606	1,750	1,905	2,111	2,501
Short-term debt [3]	505	1,803	1,560	1,569	1,831	2,034	2,328	2,582	3,216
Long-term debt [4]	987	2,665	2,742	2,871	3,100	3,335	3,651	4,072	4,813
Capital stock	417	1,585	1,881	2,042	2,132	2,194	2,278	2,951	3,244
Paid-in or capital surplus	532	2,814	3,656	4,223	4,790	5,446	6,427	7,253	8,610
Retained earnings [5]	1,070	1,410	1,431	1,662	1,698	2,191	2,519	3,113	3,373
Net worth [2][6]	1,944	4,739	5,700	(NA)	7,031	8,132	9,495	11,353	13,108
Receipts [2][6]	6,361	11,410	11,742	12,270	13,360	14,539	15,526	16,610	17,324
Business receipts [6][7]	5,732	9,860	10,360	10,866	11,884	12,786	13,659	14,461	15,010
Interest [8]	367	977	829	808	882	1,039	1,082	1,140	1,277
Rents and royalties	54	133	140	130	132	145	156	176	200
Deductions [2][6]	6,125	11,033	11,330	11,765	12,775	13,821	14,728	15,704	16,489
Cost of sales and operations [7]	4,205	6,611	6,772	7,052	7,625	8,206	8,707	9,114	9,362
Compensation of officers	109	205	221	226	282	304	319	336	357
Rent paid on business property	72	185	196	201	223	232	248	265	308
Taxes paid	163	251	274	290	322	326	341	350	355
Interest paid	345	825	597	546	611	744	771	866	967
Depreciation	157	333	346	364	403	437	474	513	542
Advertising	52	126	134	140	157	163	177	188	198
Net income (less loss) [6][9]	239	371	402	498	577	714	806	915	838
Net income	297	553	570	659	740	881	987	1,118	1,091
Deficit	58	182	168	161	162	166	180	202	253
Income subject to tax	247	366	378	437	494	565	640	684	663
Income tax before credits [10]	104	119	126	149	168	194	220	235	231
Tax credits	42	32	30	35	37	42	53	55	50
Foreign tax credit	25	25	22	23	25	30	40	42	37
Income tax after credits [11]	62	96	102	(NA)	136	156	171	184	182

NA Not available. [1] Represents certain small corporations with up to 75 shareholders (35 for 1990-1996; 15 in 1980), mostly individuals, electing to be taxed at the shareholder level. [2] Includes items not shown separately. [3] Payable in less than 1 year. [4] Payable in 1 year or more. [5] Appropriated and unappropriated. [6] Beginning 1990, receipts, deductions and net income of S corporations are limited to those from trade or business. Those from investments are excluded. [7] Beginning 1990, includes gross sales and cost of sales of securities, commodities, and real estate by exchanges, brokers, or dealers selling on their own accounts. Previously, net gain included in total receipts only. Excludes investment income. [8] Includes tax-exempt interest in state and local government obligations. [9] Excludes regulated investment companies. [10] Consists of regular (and alternative tax) only. [11] Includes minimum tax, alternative minimum tax, adjustments for prior year credits, and other income-related taxes.

Source: U.S. Internal Revenue Service, *Statistics of Income, Corporation Income Tax Returns*, annual.

U.S. Census Bureau. Statistical Abstract of the United States: 2001

No. 719. Corporations by Receipt-Size Class and Industry: 1998

[**Number of returns in thousands (4,849 represents 4,849,000); receipts and net income in billions of dollars (16,543 represents $16,543,000,000,000).** Covers active enterprises only. Figures are estimates based on a sample of unaudited tax returns; see Appendix III. The industrial distribution is based on the North American Industry Classification System and on data collected from establishments; see text, this section]

Industry	Total	Under $1 mil. [1]	$1 mil.- $4.9 mil.	$5 mil.- $9.9 mil.	$10 mil.- $49.9 mil.	$50 mil. or more
Total: [2]						
Number..........	4,849	3,956	661	110	98	24
Business receipts [3]	16,543	805	1,403	763	1,978	11,594
Net income (less loss)	838	8	36	23	81	691
Agriculture, forestry, fishing, and hunting:						
Number..........	135	120	12	2	1	(Z)
Business receipts [3]	100	20	25	11	19	25
Mining:						
Number..........	31	27	3	1	1	(Z)
Business receipts [3]	117	4	7	4	12	90
Utilities:						
Number..........	8	7	1	(Z)	(Z)	(Z)
Business receipts [3]	451	1	1	1	4	443
Construction:						
Number..........	552	420	102	16	11	1
Business receipts [3]	859	103	220	111	213	213
Manufacturing:						
Number..........	310	192	75	18	19	6
Business receipts [3]	4,591	52	174	125	389	3,851
Wholesale and retail trade:						
Number..........	957	657	213	39	40	8
Business receipts[3]	4,517	180	462	270	842	2,763
Transportation and warehousing:						
Number..........	160	129	23	4	3	1
Business receipts [3]	470	24	50	26	55	315
Information:						
Number..........	101	85	12	2	2	1
Business receipts[3]	668	14	24	14	38	578
Finance and insurance:						
Number..........	218	183	21	5	6	3
Business receipts [3]	2,358	29	48	33	128	2,119
Real estate and rental and leasing:						
Number..........	522	500	19	2	1	(Z)
Business receipts [3]	176	41	38	12	22	63
Professional, scientific, and technical services:						
Number..........	624	557	54	8	5	1
Business receipts [3]	541	97	108	53	95	188
Management of companies & enterprises:						
Number..........	31	25	2	1	2	(Z)
Business receipts [3]	551	1	7	10	32	501
Administrative and support and waste management and remediation services:						
Number..........	200	172	23	4	2	(Z)
Business receipts [3]	264	36	48	25	31	123
Educational services:						
Number..........	37	33	3	1	(Z)	(Z)
Business receipts [3]	23	5	5	5	3	5
Health care and social services:						
Number..........	307	260	39	5	3	(Z)
Business receipts[3]	357	73	75	33	49	126
Arts, entertainment, and recreation:						
Number..........	93	85	7	1	(Z)	(Z)
Business receipts [3]	60	15	13	4	7	20
Accommodation and food services:						
Number..........	245	211	31	2	1	(Z)
Business receipts[3]	296	54	58	16	25	143
Other services:						
Number..........	300	277	21	1	1	(Z)
Business receipts [3]	143	55	39	7	15	27

Z Less than 500 returns.   [1] Includes businesses without receipts.   [2] Includes businesses not allocable to individual industries.   [3] Includes investment income for partnerships and corporations in finance and insurance, real estate, and management of companies industries. Excludes investment income for S corporations (certain small corporations with up to 75 shareholders, mostly individuals, electing to be taxed at the shareholder level).

Source: U.S. Internal Revenue Service, *Statistics of Income*, various publications; and unpublished data.

No. 720. Corporations by Asset-Size Class and Industry: 1998

[In millions of dollars (110,589 represents $110,589,000,000), except number of returns. Covers active corporations only. Excludes corporations not allocable by industry. The industrial distribution is based on the North American Industry Classification System and on data collected from companies; see text, this section. Detail may not add to total because of rounding]

Industry	Total	Under $10 mil. [1]	$10-$24.9 mil.	$25-$49.9 mil.	$50-$99.9 mil.	$100-$249.9 mil.	$250 mil. and over
Agriculture, forestry, fishing, and hunting:							
Returns	135,107	134,320	520	130	73	44	19
Total receipts	110,589	74,915	8,557	5,325	6,409	7,537	7,845
Mining:							
Returns	31,467	30,436	474	192	120	94	150
Total receipts	131,072	23,287	5,545	4,148	4,015	8,033	86,044
Utilities:							
Returns	8,067	7,659	115	34	39	39	180
Total receipts	475,839	8,449	2,039	1,213	3,609	3,528	457,001
Construction:							
Returns	551,935	547,613	3,012	752	285	169	103
Total receipts	875,357	591,952	85,999	46,901	33,017	37,168	80,321
Manufacturing:							
Returns	309,912	295,333	7,205	2,864	1,650	1,360	1,500
Total receipts	4,967,763	582,431	197,273	155,943	163,487	261,654	3,606,976
Wholesale and retail trade:							
Returns	956,803	943,529	8,561	2,289	1,061	735	628
Total receipts	4,626,957	1,722,977	414,769	215,139	181,709	244,031	1,848,332
Transportation and warehousing:							
Returns	159,646	158,139	851	277	140	130	108
Total receipts	488,074	141,900	23,271	14,108	14,421	23,241	271,132
Information:							
Returns	100,977	98,663	1,070	393	275	225	352
Total receipts	759,064	87,878	16,647	10,963	14,297	23,494	605,785
Finance and insurance:							
Returns	218,193	200,493	3,743	2,825	2,729	3,348	5,056
Total receipts	2,357,692	209,789	20,272	22,236	29,222	65,249	2,010,923
Real estate and rental and leasing:							
Returns	521,917	517,486	2,919	838	357	184	132
Total receipts	205,765	108,350	13,390	8,803	6,864	8,958	59,400
Professional, scientific, and technical services:							
Returns	623,784	621,263	1,412	497	310	191	111
Total receipts	563,743	341,158	38,206	24,912	22,589	35,881	100,997
Management of companies & enterprises:							
Returns	30,931	25,091	907	1,140	1,393	1,377	1,022
Total receipts	550,818	81,927	1,563	3,556	8,799	19,625	435,347
Administrative and support and waste management and remediation services:							
Returns	200,449	199,696	393	138	90	64	67
Total receipts	277,178	145,255	14,438	8,197	15,475	18,049	75,764
Educational services:							
Returns	36,959	36,838	68	24	14	8	6
Total receipts	25,845	18,936	1,979	1,250	991	1,074	1,616
Health care and social assistance:							
Returns	307,258	306,345	485	177	119	68	63
Total receipts	372,532	233,203	12,807	9,320	9,969	10,840	96,392
Art, entertainment, and recreation:							
Returns	92,966	92,386	337	102	64	46	31
Total receipts	67,273	37,389	3,731	2,328	4,414	5,054	14,357
Accommodation and food services:							
Returns	245,334	244,212	620	188	97	104	112
Total receipts	317,528	146,842	12,452	7,377	7,148	14,270	129,439
Other services:							
Returns	300,313	299,861	273	85	44	20	29
Total receipts	148,370	113,964	5,464	4,132	3,132	2,430	19,248

[1] Includes returns with zero assets.

Source: U.S. Internal Revenue Service, Statistics of Income, Corporation Income Tax Returns, annual.

No. 721. Economic Census Summary (NAICS Basis): 1997

Kind of business	NAICS code [1]	All firms		Employer firms			
		Establishments (number)	Sales, receipts or shipments (mil. dol.)	Establishments (number)	Sales, receipts or shipments (mil. dol.)	Annual payroll (mil. dol.)	Paid employees [2] (1,000)
TAXABLE							
Mining	21	117,240	178,953	25,000	173,989	20,798	509.0
Oil & gas extraction.	211	90,006	107,147	8,312	102,837	5,511	110.9
Mining (except oil & gas)	212	13,391	51,585	7,348	51,253	9,422	229.3
Support activities for mining	213	13,843	20,222	9,340	19,899	5,866	168.8
Utilities.	22	31,406	412,228	15,513	411,713	36,595	702.7
Utilities	221	31,406	412,228	15,513	411,713	36,595	702.7
Elec. pwr. generation, transmsn. & distribution	2211	(NA)	(NA)	7,935	269,095	30,440	564.5
Natural gas distribution	2212	(NA)	(NA)	2,747	136,995	5,110	102.9
Water, sewage, & other systems	2213	(NA)	(NA)	4,831	5,623	1,045	35.3
Construction	23	2,546,680	945,682	656,448	858,581	174,185	5,664.8
Building, developing, & general contracting . .	233	611,859	421,524	199,289	386,926	42,546	1,343.0
Heavy construction	234	80,319	132,720	42,557	130,795	30,292	880.4
Special trade contractors	235	1,854,502	391,439	414,602	340,861	101,347	3,441.5
Manufacturing	31-33	666,609	3,854,381	363,753	3,842,061	572,101	16,888.0
Wholesale trade.	42	859,328	(NA)	453,470	4,059,658	214,915	5,796.6
Wholesale trade, durable goods	421	526,545	(NA)	290,629	2,179,717	133,237	3,398.3
Wholesale trade, nondurable goods	422	332,783	(NA)	162,841	1,879,940	81,678	2,398.3
Retail trade.	44-45	2,949,786	2,530,304	1,118,447	2,460,886	237,196	13,991.1
Motor vehicle & parts dealers	441	240,460	660,682	122,633	645,368	50,239	1,719.0
Furniture & home furnishings stores	442	104,578	74,093	64,725	71,691	9,959	482.8
Electronics & appliance stores.	443	71,486	70,210	43,373	68,561	7,064	345.0
Bldg. material & garden equip. & supp. dealers	444	121,912	229,489	93,117	227,566	25,609	1,117.9
Food & beverage stores.	445	239,290	410,287	148,528	401,764	40,581	2,893.1
Health & personal care stores	446	142,491	119,056	82,941	117,701	15,191	903.7
Gasoline stations	447	137,566	199,856	126,889	198,166	11,482	922.1
Clothing & clothing accessories stores	448	251,398	140,565	156,601	136,398	16,597	1,280.2
Sporting goods, hobby, book, & music stores	451	164,753	65,572	69,149	62,011	7,113	560.8
General merchandise stores	452	56,788	331,453	36,171	330,444	30,871	2,507.5
Miscellaneous store retailers	453	530,500	91,670	129,838	78,109	10,165	753.0
Nonstore retailers	454	888,564	137,370	44,482	123,107	12,323	506.0
Transportation & warehousing [3] [4]	48-49	823,908	347,673	178,025	318,245	82,346	2,920.8
Air transportation [3]	481	19,518	20,925	3,598	20,249	2,748	89.1
Rail transportation (not covered in the Economic Census)	482	(NA)	(NA)	(NA)	(NA)	(NA)	(NA)
Water transportation	483	9,047	24,405	1,921	24,019	2,834	72.9
Truck transnortation.	484	426,345	162,104	103,798	141,225	38,471	1,293.8
Transit & ground passenger transportation. . .	485	164,672	17,756	16,013	13,792	5,549	339.6
Pipeline transportation	486	2,604	26,877	2,311	26,837	2,661	49.3
Scenic & sightseeing transportation	487	4,240	1,963	2,325	1,893	492	23.9
Transportation support activities.	488	55,616	40,930	30,675	39,758	12,592	411.6
Postal Service (not covered in the Economic Census)	491	(NA)	(NA)	(NA)	(NA)	(NA)	(NA)
Couriers & messengers	492	131,523	41,808	10,887	39,812	14,072	530.8
Warehousing & storage	493	10,343	10,905	6,497	10,658	2,926	109.8
Information	51	288,500	628,981	114,475	623,214	129,482	3,066.2
Publishing industries	511	79,614	180,434	33,896	179,035	43,358	1,006.2
Motion picture & sound recording industries.	512	71,016	57,858	22,204	55,926	9,392	276.0
Broadcasting & telecommunications	513	80,486	347,676	43,480	346,316	63,480	1,434.5
Information & data processing services	514	57,384	43,014	14,895	41,937	13,252	349.5
Finance & insurance	52	1,074,360	2,234,737	395,203	2,197,771	264,551	5,835.2
Monetary authorities - central bank.	521	42	24,582	42	24,582	903	21.7
Credit intermediation & related activities	522	330,563	817,504	166,882	808,811	98,723	2,744.9
Security, commodity contracts & like activity. .	523	242,901	291,425	54,491	274,987	71,281	706.1
Insurance carriers & related activities	524	499,365	1,084,618	172,299	1,072,784	92,230	2,327.3
Funds, trusts, & other financial vehicles (part).	525	1,489	16,608	1,489	16,608	1,413	35.3
Real estate & rental & leasing	53	1,684,976	342,621	288,273	240,918	41,591	1,702.4
Real estate	531	1,557,556	252,120	221,650	153,275	27,947	1,117.2
Rental & leasing services	532	124,792	79,184	64,472	76,379	12,569	559.4
Lessors of other nonfinancial intangible asset	533	2,628	11,317	2,151	11,264	1,074	25.8
Professional, scientific, & technical services . .	54	3,265,160	660,707	615,305	579,542	225,376	5,212.7
Professional, scientific, & technical services. .	541	3,265,160	660,707	615,305	579,542	225,376	5,212.7
Legal services.	5411	383,682	136,785	173,716	127,052	49,060	1,012.1
Accounting/tax prep/bookkeep/payroll services	5412	407,005	65,942	97,512	61,117	26,104	966.5
Architectural, engineering & related services	5413	(NA)	(NA)	92,710	116,986	46,943	1,038.3
Specialized design services.	5414	116,132	17,224	26,436	14,254	4,088	113.0
Computer systems design & related services	5415	278,512	115,696	72,278	108,968	42,151	764.7

See footnotes at end of table.

Kind of business	NAICS code [1]	All firms		Employer firms			
		Establish-ments (number)	Sales, receipts or ship-ments (mil. dol.)	Establish-ments (number)	Sales, receipts or ship-ments (mil. dol.)	Annual payroll (mil. dol.)	Paid employ-ees [2] (1,000)
Management, sci & tech consulting services	5416	644,497	80,803	80,426	63,429	26,582	511.3
Scientific R&D services	5417	24,480	23,553	7,830	23,078	9,322	177.0
Advertising & related services	5418	135,133	53,937	38,832	49,290	16,012	417.2
Other professional/scientific/technical service	5419	979,072	42,933	25,565	15,368	5,115	212.7
Management of companies & enterprises	55	(NA)	(NA)	47,319	92,473	154,178	2,617.5
Admin/support waste mgt/ remediation services	56	1,168,621	312,912	276,393	295,936	137,337	7,347.4
Administrative & support services	561	1,131,846	272,821	260,025	256,591	128,438	7,066.7
Waste management & remediation services	562	36,775	40,091	16,368	39,346	8,899	280.7
Educational services	61	268,937	17,731	33,783	14,933	4,903	248.7
Health care & social assistance	62	1,698,979	449,806	531,069	418,602	182,256	6,231.8
Ambulatory health care services	621	1,047,100	334,762	440,200	310,012	137,979	3,744.3
Hospitals	622	1,345	40,146	1,345	40,146	13,886	511.6
Nursing & residential care facilities	623	67,331	56,847	32,833	55,844	24,626	1,484.8
Social assistance	624	583,203	18,051	56,691	12,599	5,766	491.1
Arts, entertainment, & recreation	71	772,981	99,455	79,636	85,088	26,104	1,207.4
Perform arts, spectator sports, & related ind	711	561,923	42,995	25,942	32,744	12,834	235.9
Museums, historical sites, & like institutions	712	2,592	521	787	484	122	7.3
Amusement, gambling, & recreation industries	713	208,466	55,938	52,907	51,861	13,147	964.2
Accommodation & food services	72	736,073	359,434	545,068	350,399	97,007	9,451.2
Accommodation	721	105,686	101,394	58,162	98,457	26,674	1,696.7
Traveler accommodation	7211	78,235	97,353	47,079	94,966	25,851	1,645.7
RV parks & recreational camps	7212	14,523	3,026	7,598	2,735	665	35.3
Rooming & boarding houses	7213	12,928	1,015	3,485	757	157	15.7
Food services & drinking places	722	630,387	258,040	486,906	251,942	70,334	7,754.6
Full-service restaurants	7221	230,732	114,592	191,245	112,450	34,435	3,641.4
Limited-service eating places	7222	246,138	109,298	214,774	107,788	27,483	3,327.0
Special food services	7223	77,690	20,706	28,062	19,408	5,766	464.9
Drinking places (alcoholic beverages)	7224	75,827	13,445	52,825	12,296	2,649	321.3
Other services (except public administration)	81	2,357,005	206,332	420,950	163,033	48,453	2,493.6
Repair & maintenance	811	800,207	122,886	235,466	105,154	29,875	1,276.4
Auxiliaries, exc corp, subsidiary, & regional managing offices		(NA)	(NA)	12,930	11,276	33,114	792.4
TAX-EXEMPT							
Professional, scientific, & technical services	54	(NA)	(NA)	5,824	15,709	6,023	148.5
Professional, scientific, & technical services	541	(NA)	(NA)	5,824	15,709	6,023	148.5
Legal services	5411	(NA)	(NA)	2,532	1,497	797	23.3
Scientific R&D services	5417	(NA)	(NA)	3,292	14,212	5,226	125.1
Educational services	61	(NA)	(NA)	7,153	5,506	1,461	72.4
Health care & social assistance	62	(NA)	(NA)	114,784	466,452	195,949	7,329.8
Ambulatory health care services	621	(NA)	(NA)	15,181	45,428	17,884	669.3
Hospitals	622	(NA)	(NA)	5,340	339,032	141,910	4,421.5
Nursing & residential care facilities	623	(NA)	(NA)	24,526	37,235	17,527	985.9
Social assistance	624	(NA)	(NA)	69,737	44,756	18,628	1,253.1
Arts, entertainment, & recreation	71	(NA)	(NA)	19,463	19,627	6,683	380.3
Perform arts, spectator sports, & related industries	711	(NA)	(NA)	4,624	4,876	1,622	90.8
Museums, historical sites, & like institutions	712	(NA)	(NA)	4,793	6,280	1,715	84.5
Amusement, gambling, & recreation industries	713	(NA)	(NA)	10,046	8,470	3,347	205.0
Other services (except public administration)	81	(NA)	(NA)	98,765	102,864	17,068	762.6

NA Not available.   [1] North American Industry Classification System, 1997.   [2] For pay period including March 12.   [3] Data do not include large certificated passenger carriers that report to the Office of Airline Statistics, U.S. Department of Transportation.   [4] Railroad transportation and U.S. Postal Service are out of scope for the 1997 Economic Census.

Source: U.S. Census Bureau, *1997 Economic Census, Geographic Area Series* and *Nonemployer Statistics.*

Business Enterprise   481

No. 722. Comparative Statistics for the United States (1987 SIC Basis): 1992 and 1997

[162.1 represents $162,100,000,000. Includes only establishments with payroll SIC = Standard Industrial Classification]

Industry	1987 SIC code	Establishments (number)		Sales/receipts/ revenues/ shipments (bil. dol.)		Annual payroll (bil. dol.)		Paid employees (1,000)	
		1992	1997	1992	1997	1992	1997	1992	1997
MINING									
Total	(X)	29,497	25,251	162.1	174.5	18.6	20.9	534.7	512.0
Metal mining	10	(NA)	696	9.9	11.5	(NA)	2.1	(NA)	48.5
Coal mining.	12	(NA)	1,820	27.1	24.0	(NA)	4.2	(NA)	93.0
Oil & gas extraction	13	20,290	17,219	111.5	122.1	8.9	11.1	262.9	272.8
Nonmetallic minerals, except fuels.	14	5,502	5,516	13.6	16.8	2.9	3.5	97.5	97.8
CONSTRUCTION									
Total	(X)	572,851	639,482	539.1	834.8	117.7	171.0	4,668.3	5,567.0
General building contractors.	15	168,407	184,517	220.2	365.6	27.1	39.9	1,096.9	1,269.3
Heavy construction, ex. building	16	37,180	39,542	98.5	127.0	23.7	29.2	799.4	851.6
Special trade contractors	17	367,263	415,423	220.3	342.4	66.9	101.9	2,772.0	3,446.2
MANUFACTURING									
Total	(X)	370,912	377,776	3,004.7	3,958.1	494.1	595.7	16,948.9	17,557.0
Food & kindred products	20	20,798	20,878	407.0	480.8	36.8	42.9	1,502.7	1,561.4
Tobacco products	21	114	105	35.2	(D)	1.5	(D)	38.0	(1)
Textile mill products	22	5,886	6,155	70.8	82.4	12.4	13.7	616.4	561.9
Apparel & other textile products	23	23,093	23,411	71.7	81.2	15.3	15.4	985.3	829.3
Lumber & wood products	24	35,807	36,735	81.6	111.9	13.9	18.7	655.8	757.3
Furniture & fixtures	25	11,658	12,095	43.8	61.5	10.2	13.3	471.1	523.9
Paper & allied products	26	6,416	6,496	133.2	(D)	20.5	(D)	626.3	(2)
Printing & publishing	27	65,392	62,355	166.2	210.9	41.1	50.1	1,492.1	1,534.3
Chemicals & allied products	28	12,004	12,371	305.4	400.1	32.5	37.2	848.6	820.2
Petroleum & coal products	29	2,124	2,147	150.2	175.8	5.0	5.5	114.4	106.1
Rubber & miscellaneous plastics products .	30	15,842	16,892	113.6	160.7	23.2	30.3	906.7	1,037.0
Leather & leather products.	31	2,040	1,839	9.7	(D)	1.8	(D)	101.1	(3)
Stone, clay, & glass products	32	16,254	16,393	62.5	87.2	13.1	16.3	468.8	505.4
Primary metal industries	33	6,501	6,275	138.3	188.7	22.2	26.8	662.1	692.2
Fabricated metal products	34	36,429	37,985	166.5	231.7	39.0	50.9	1,362.3	1,549.5
Industrial machinery & equipment	35	53,956	56,383	258.7	407.4	57.2	74.6	1,738.9	1,978.2
Electronic & other electric equipment	36	16,932	17,104	216.8	348.6	44.2	58.3	1,438.8	1,582.3
Transportation equipment	37	11,287	12,387	399.3	515.9	62.7	68.3	1,646.9	1,561.7
Instruments & related products	38	11,354	11,727	134.9	(D)	33.1	(D)	907.1	(2)
Miscellaneous manufacturing industries . . .	39	17,035	18,043	39.5	51.0	8.4	10.6	365.5	394.0
TRANSPORTATION AND PUBLIC UTILITIES									
Total	(X)	(NA)	293,575	(NA)	1,143.9	(NA)	199.7	(NA)	5,689.1
Local and interurban passenger transit. . . .	41	17,805	19,621	12.6	(D)	5.2	(D)	354.9	(2)
Trucking and warehousing	42	110,908	133,373	143.8	197.4	39.9	55.7	1,580.1	1,960.1
Water transportation	44	8,147	9,214	29.2	35.2	5.2	6.3	171.3	178.6
Transportation by air	45	(NA)	11,455	(NA)	47.4	(NA)	10.4	(NA)	362.4
Pipelines, except natural gas	46	844	861	7.1	7.2	0.8	0.8	16.8	13.5
Transportation services	47	46,593	52,409	23.9	(D)	7.9	(D)	329.2	(2)
Communications	48	39,244	44,319	230.7	349.2	47.1	64.0	1,294.2	1,450.0
Electric, gas, & sanitary services.	49	20,049	22,323	311.0	447.9	39.2	41.9	915.0	835.9
WHOLESALE TRADE									
Total	(X)	495,457	521,127	3,238.5	4,235.4	173.3	234.5	5,791.3	6,509.3
Durable goods.	50	·313,464	337,277	1,593.9	2,299.5	105.2	147.7	3,349.1	3,887.4
Nondurable goods	51	181,993	183,850	1,644.6	1,935.9	68.1	86.8	2,442.2	2,622.0
RETAIL TRADE									
Total	(X)	1,526,215	1,561,195	1,894.9	2,545.9	222.9	290.5	18,407.5	21,165.9
Building materials & garden supplies	52	69,483	67,469	98.8	146.2	11.8	16.7	665.7	830.4
General merchandise stores.	53	34,606	34,899	245.3	(D)	24.5	(D)	2,078.5	(2)
Food stores.	54	180,568	171,057	369.2	416.0	37.2	42.8	2,969.3	3,109.3
Automotive dealers & service stations	55	201,707	202,237	529.9	788.2	39.4	55.5	1,942.6	2,283.8
Apparel & accessory stores	56	145,490	126,863	101.7	116.6	12.0	13.6	1,144.6	1,116.1
Home furniture, furnishings, & equipment . .	57	110,073	115,124	93.2	136.1	11.9	16.3	702.2	861.6
Eating & drinking places	58	433,608	475,907	195.3	(D)	52.6	(D)	6,547.9	(2)
Miscellaneous retail	59	350,680	367,639	261.4	365.9	33.5	45.4	2,356.6	2,795.5
FINANCE, INSURANCE, AND REAL ESTATE									
Total	(X)	585,580	661,388	1,831.5	2,474.9	211.6	308.2	6,509.6	7,314.3
Depository institutions	60	104,505	109,851	532.1	(D)	57.3	(D)	2,100.1	(2)
Nondepository institutions	61	39,439	52,074	135.4	(D)	15.5	(D)	445.6	(2)
Security & commodity brokers	62	31,177	45,029	108.9	(D)	33.8	(D)	406.4	(2)
Insurance carriers.	63	38,977	40,717	796.0	997.4	50.5	66.8	1,516.6	1,614.2
Insurance agents, brokers, & services	64	121,662	131,582	51.7	75.3	18.9	25.5	635.5	713.1
Real estate	65	229,493	252,292	141.7	180.1	26.2	33.5	1,231.5	1,340.1
Holding & other investment offices.	67	20,327	29,843	65.8	138.7	9.2	14.4	173.8	257.8

See footnotes at end of table.

U.S. Census Bureau, Statistical Abstract of the United States: 2001

No. 722. Comparative Statistics for the United States (1987 SIC Basis): 1992 and 1997—Con.

[See headnote, page 482]

Industry	1987 SIC code	Establishments (number)		Sales/receipts/ revenues/ shipments (bil. dol.)		Annual payroll (bil. dol.)		Paid employees (1,000)	
		1992	1997	1992	1997	1992	1997	1992	1997
SERVICES (taxable firms only)									
Total	(X)	1,825,435	2,077,666	1,202.6	1,843.8	452.7	688.9	19,290.4	25,278.4
Hotels & other lodging places	70	48,619	55,992	69.2	97.9	19.6	26.6	1,489.1	1,685.7
Personal services.	72	197,101	204,455	43.3	53.1	14.4	17.8	1,217.6	1,302.6
Business services.	73	306,551	397,264	274.9	528.5	109.3	211.5	5,542.4	8,652.0
Auto repair, services, and parking	75	171,970	191,907	70.0	99.6	15.5	22.6	863.9	1,094.2
Miscellaneous repair services	76	71,576	66,607	30.7	37.3	9.7	11.4	428.1	418.7
Motion pictures	78	41,857	46,017	44.0	67.9	9.8	13.8	478.1	571.1
Amusement & recreation services	79	72,514	81,225	48.8	81.8	15.5	24.7	900.5	1,232.6
Health services	80	441,705	466,421	299.1	398.5	129.1	173.5	4,452.5	5,520.0
Legal services	81	151,737	165,757	101.1	122.6	39.3	47.4	923.6	956.1
Educational services.	82	14,735	21,283	7.2	12.4	2.5	4.2	133.3	188.6
Social services.	83	59,123	69,713	13.3	18.9	5.5	8.0	505.4	662.2
Museums, botanical, zoological gardens. . .	84	475	659	0.2	0.4	0.1	0.1	3.3	5.9
Membership organizations	86	(NA)	868	(NA)	2.0	(NA)	0.7	(NA)	25.2
Engineering & management services	87	232,885	292,162	192.8	302.0	79.3	121.7	2,271.5	2,931.6
Services, n.e.c [4].	89	14,587	(NA)	8.0	(NA)	3.1	(NA)	81.1	(NA)
AUXILIARIES									
Total	(X)	47,250	48,193	(NA)	41.3	137.1	178.2	3,229.7	3,284.1

D Withheld to avoid disclosure.   NA Not available.   X Not applicable.   [1] 25,000-49,999 employees.   [2] 100,000 employees or more.   [3] 50,000-99,000 employees.   [4] Not elsewhere classified.

Source: U.S. Census Bureau, *1997 Economic Census, Comparative Statistics, Core Business Statistics Series*, EC97X-C52, issued June 2000.

No. 723. Establishments, Employees and Payroll by Employment-Size Class: 1990 to 1999

[6,176 represents 6,176,000. Excludes government employees, railroad employees, self-employed persons, etc. An *establishment* is a single physical location where business is conducted or where services or industrial operations are performed]

Employment-size class	Unit	1990	1992	1993	1994	1995	1996	1997	1998	1999
Establishments, total	1,000 .	6,176	6,318	6,403	6,509	6,613	6,739	6,895	6,942	7,008
Under 20 employees	1,000 .	5,354	5,507	5,577	5,662	5,733	5,843	5,968	5,991	6,036
20 to 99 employees.	1,000 .	684	678	688	704	730	741	767	786	802
100 to 499 employees	1,000 .	122	118	123	128	135	138	143	147	152
500 to 999 employees	1,000 .	10	9	9	10	10	11	11	11	12
1,000 or more employees	1,000 .	6	6	6	6	6	6	6	6	7
Employees, total	1,000 .	93,476	92,801	94,789	96,733	100,335	102,199	105,299	108,118	110,706
Under 20 employees	1,000 .	24,373	25,000	25,233	25,373	25,785	26,115	26,883	27,131	27,289
20 to 99 employees.	1,000 .	27,414	27,030	27,443	28,138	29,202	29,697	30,631	31,464	32,193
100 to 499 employees	1,000 .	22,926	22,227	23,195	24,048	25,364	26,086	26,993	27,842	28,707
500 to 999 employees	1,000 .	6,551	6,270	6,449	6,663	7,021	7,274	7,422	7,689	7,923
1,000 or more employees	1,000 .	12,212	12,275	12,470	12,513	12,962	13,026	13,370	13,991	14,594
Annual payroll, total.	Bil. dol.	2,104	2,272	2,363	2,488	2,666	2,849	3,048	3,309	3,555
Under 20 employees	Bil. dol.	485	536	554	579	608	647	688	734	773
20 to 99 employees.	Bil. dol.	547	586	611	650	696	747	796	866	925
100 to 499 employees	Bil. dol.	518	550	582	621	675	730	786	858	931
500 to 999 employees	Bil. dol.	174	186	191	202	219	240	254	277	298
1,000 or more employees	Bil. dol.	381	413	424	436	467	485	524	575	628

Source: U.S. Census Bureau, *County Business Patterns*, annual.

Business Enterprise   483

No. 724. Establishments, Employees, and Payroll by Employment-Size Class and Industry: 1998 and 1999

[Establishments and employees in thousands (6,942 represents 6,942,000); payroll in billions of dollars. Covers establishments with payroll. Employees are for the week including March 12. Most government employees are excluded. Based on the North American Industry Classification System (NAICS), see text, this section. For statement on methodology, see Appendix III]

Industry	NAICS code	1998, total	1999 Total	Under 20 employees	20 to 99 employees	100 to 499 employees	500 to 999 employees	1,000 or more employees
Establishments, total	(X)	6,942	7,008	6,036	802	152	12	7
Agriculture, forestry, fishing & hunting	11	27	27	25	1	(Z)	(Z)	(Z)
Mining	21	25	24	19	3	1	(Z)	(Z)
Utilities	22	16	17	12	4	1	(Z)	(Z)
Construction	23	692	699	636	56	6	(Z)	(Z)
Manufacturing	31-33	366	360	241	84	30	3	1
Wholesale trade	42	454	450	385	57	8	(Z)	(Z)
Retail trade	44-45	1,113	1,111	970	116	24	(Z)	(Z)
Transportation and warehousing	48-49	186	187	157	25	5	(Z)	(Z)
Information	51	121	127	100	21	5	1	(Z)
Finance and insurance	52	412	418	373	37	6	1	1
Real estate and rental and leasing	53	292	298	283	13	2	(Z)	(Z)
Professional, scientific, and technical services	54	687	705	651	45	8	1	(Z)
Management of companies and enterprises	55	44	47	31	11	4	1	(Z)
Admin/support waste mgt/remediation services	56	351	350	292	41	15	1	1
Educational services	61	65	66	51	13	3	(Z)	(Z)
Health care and social assistance	62	649	650	557	71	18	2	2
Arts, entertainment, and recreation	71	103	103	85	15	2	(Z)	(Z)
Accommodation and food services	72	544	540	389	142	8	(Z)	(Z)
Other services (except public administration)	81	719	718	672	43	4	(Z)	(Z)
Auxiliaries (exc corporate, subsidiary & regional mgt)	95	14	15	9	4	1	(Z)	(Z)
Unclassified establishments	99	62	98	98	(Z)	(Z)	(Z)	(Z)
Employees, total	(X)	108,118	110,706	27,289	32,193	28,707	7,923	14,594
Agriculture, forestry, fishing & hunting	11	187	192	94	(D)	(D)	(D)	(D)
Mining	21	498	457	89	(D)	(D)	(D)	47
Utilities	22	682	667	61	167	230	97	112
Construction	23	5,798	6,202	2,498	2,132	1,151	204	217
Manufacturing	31-33	16,946	16,660	1,405	3,728	6,149	2,206	3,172
Wholesale trade	42	5,885	5,972	1,885	2,218	1,386	247	235
Retail trade	44-45	14,241	14,477	5,155	4,732	4,245	252	93
Transportation and warehousing	48-49	3,462	3,627	659	1,027	873	194	874
Information	51	3,142	3,235	452	872	1,045	389	477
Finance and insurance	52	5,770	5,965	1,669	1,455	1,285	540	1,016
Real estate and rental and leasing	53	1,813	1,874	1,002	479	290	(D)	(D)
Professional, scientific, and technical services	54	6,052	6,432	2,248	1,740	1,454	362	628
Management of companies and enterprises	55	2,704	2,788	168	473	902	460	785
Admin/support waste mgt/remediation services	56	7,775	8,367	1,165	1,814	2,991	843	1,553
Educational services	61	2,324	2,432	242	526	493	238	932
Health care and social assistance	62	13,758	13,865	2,855	2,883	3,387	1,176	3,564
Arts, entertainment, and recreation	71	1,584	1,640	338	608	399	101	195
Accommodation and food services	72	9,466	9,638	2,336	5,419	1,316	210	357
Other services (except public administration)	81	5,038	5,151	2,809	1,560	613	76	93
Auxiliaries (exc corporate, subsidiary & regional mgt)	95	916	959	58	161	326	199	215
Unclassified establishments	99	78	106	100	6	(D)	-	-
Annual payroll, total	(X)	3,309	3,555	773	925	931	298	628
Agriculture, forestry, fishing & hunting	11	5	5	2	(D)	(D)	(D)	(D)
Mining	21	22	21	3	(D)	(D)	(D)	2
Utilities	22	38	39	3	9	14	6	7
Construction	23	199	219	76	80	47	8	8
Manufacturing	31-33	607	626	42	122	214	83	164
Wholesale trade	42	234	250	73	90	60	12	14
Retail trade	44-45	260	282	95	99	80	5	3
Transportation and warehousing	48-49	109	117	19	30	27	7	34
Information	51	147	170	21	38	56	22	33
Finance and insurance	52	290	313	70	75	72	29	67
Real estate and rental and leasing	53	50	54	26	15	10	(D)	(D)
Professional, scientific, and technical services	54	278	311	96	91	77	20	28
Management of companies and enterprises	55	176	192	13	31	58	29	61
Admin/support waste mgt/remediation services	56	164	183	33	44	59	16	31
Educational services	61	52	57	5	11	11	4	26
Health care and social assistance	62	395	409	99	76	78	35	122
Arts, entertainment, and recreation	71	36	39	10	11	12	2	4
Accommodation and food services	72	110	117	27	57	19	4	9
Other services (except public administration)	81	96	102	52	31	15	2	2
Auxiliaries (exc corporate, subsidiary & regional mgt)	95	41	45	3	7	14	9	12
Unclassified establishments	99	1	3	3	1	(D)	(D)	-

- Represents zero.   D Data withheld to avoid disclosure.   (X) Not applicable.   Z Less than 500 establishments.

Source: U.S. Census Bureau, *County Business Patterns*, annual.

No. 725. Major Industries—Employer Firms, Employment, and Annual Payroll by Enterprise Size: 1998

[**5,579 represents 5,579,000.** Firms are an aggregation of all commonly-owned establishments of a parent enterprise or company within an industry. Employment is measured in March and payroll is annual leading to some enterprises with zero employment. Numbers in parentheses represent North American Industry Classification System codes, see text, this section]

Industry and data type	Unit	All industries—employment size of enterprise								
		Total	0	1 to 4	5 to 9	10 to 19	20 to 99	100 to 499	Less than 500	More than 500
Total [1]:										
Firms	1,000 . . .	5,579	712	2,664	1,012	600	494	80	5,563	16
Employment.	1,000 . . .	108,118	-	5,584	6,643	8,048	19,378	15,411	55,064	53,053
Annual payroll	Bil. dol . .	3,309	32	137	160	207	531	446	1,513	1,797
Construction (23):										
Firms	1,000 . . .	686	106	336	120	68	50	5	685	1
Employment.	1,000 . . .	5,799	-	701	784	915	1,838	882	5,120	679
Annual payroll	Bil. dol . .	199	4	17	21	28	65	35	170	29
Manufacturing (31-33):										
Firms	1,000 . . .	319	24	97	58	51	66	17	314	5
Employment.	1,000 . . .	16,946	-	220	391	697	2,747	2,960	7,015	9,931
Annual payroll	Bil. dol . .	607	2	5	10	19	83	95	214	393
Wholesale trade (42):										
Firms	1,000 . . .	363	36	163	67	46	41	8	360	3
Employment.	1,000 . . .	5,885	-	345	439	609	1,495	962	3,850	2,035
Annual payroll	Bil. dol . .	234	2	11	14	21	54	37	139	95
Retail trade (44-45):										
Firms	1,000 . . .	739	76	346	157	87	60	8	736	2
Employment.	1,000 . . .	14,242	-	766	1,034	1,147	2,228	1,215	6,390	7,852
Annual payroll	Bil. dol . .	260	2	12	17	21	54	30	136	124
Transportation & warehousing (48-49):										
Firms	1,000 . . .	155	24	74	23	16	15	3	154	1
Employment.	1,000 . . .	3,463	-	144	153	210	560	440	1,507	1,956
Annual payroll	Bil. dol . .	109	1	3	4	5	15	13	40	69
Information (51):										
Firms	1,000 . . .	75	12	31	12	9	8	2	74	1
Employment.	1,000 . . .	3,142	-	63	81	120	321	319	903	2,239
Annual payroll	Bil. dol . .	147	1	3	3	4	12	15	37	110
Finance & insurance (52):										
Firms	1,000 . . .	222	25	129	32	16	15	4	220	2
Employment.	1,000 . . .	5,770	-	262	203	208	604	603	1,881	3,890
Annual payroll	Bil. dol . .	290	2	8	8	10	27	28	81	209
Real estate & rental & leasing (53):										
Firms	1,000 . . .	242	34	147	33	15	10	2	241	1
Employment.	1,000 . . .	1,813	-	279	210	200	365	255	1,308	505
Annual payroll	Bil. dol . .	50	1	6	5	5	10	7	35	15
Professional, scientific & technical services (54):										
Firms	1,000 . . .	642	96	362	94	49	33	5	639	2
Employment.	1,000 . . .	6,052	-	698	610	653	1,210	841	4,011	2,041
Annual payroll	Bil. dol . .	278	5	24	22	27	59	43	180	98
Admin/support waste mgt/ remediation services (56):										
Firms	1,000 . . .	303	52	139	48	28	26	8	300	3
Employment.	1,000 . . .	7,775	-	286	314	374	1,020	1,353	3,348	4,427
Annual payroll	Bil. dol . .	164	2	6	7	8	23	26	73	90
Health care and social assistance (62):										
Firms	1,000 . . .	528	43	236	123	63	46	13	524	3
Employment.	1,000 . . .	13,758	-	530	807	838	1,815	2,464	6,454	7,305
Annual payroll	Bil. dol . .	395	3	19	26	28	51	55	183	213
Arts, entertainment & recreation (71):										
Firms	1,000 . . .	96	20	38	14	10	12	2	96	1
Employment.	1,000 . . .	1,584	-	76	91	139	471	331	1,108	476
Annual payroll	Bil. dol . .	36	1	4	2	2	8	9	27	9
Accommodation & food services (72):										
Firms	1,000 . . .	418	59	131	80	68	71	8	417	2
Employment.	1,000 . . .	9,467	-	303	533	934	2,662	1,376	5,808	3,659
Annual payroll	Bil. dol . .	110	2	3	5	9	28	15	62	48
Other services (except public administration) (81):										
Firms	1,000 . . .	659	56	366	132	62	38	4	658	1
Employment.	1,000 . . .	5,039	-	777	855	819	1,344	556	4,350	688
Annual payroll	Bil. dol . .	96	1	12	14	15	25	12	80	16

- Represents zero.　[1] Includes other industries not shown separately.

Source: U.S. Small Business Administration, Office of Advocacy, based on data provided by the U.S. Census Bureau.

No. 726. Employer Firms, Establishments, Employment and Annual Payroll by Enterprise Size: 1990 to 1998

[In thousands except as noted (5,074 represents 5,074,000). Firms are an aggregation of all commonly-owned establishments of a parent enterprise or company. Employment is measured in March and payroll is annual leading to some enterprises with zero employment. This table illustrates the changing importance of enterprise sizes over time, not job growth as enterprises can grow or decline and change enterprise size cells over time]

Item		All industries—employment size of enterprise						
	Total	0-4	5-9	10-19	20-99	100-499	Less than 500	More than 500
Firms:								
1990	5,074	3,021	952	563	454	70	5,060	14
1991	5,051	3,036	941	551	440	68	5,037	14
1992	5,095	3,075	946	552	439	69	5,081	14
1993	5,194	3,140	962	560	446	72	5,179	15
1994	5,277	3,208	965	563	452	73	5,262	15
1995	5,369	3,250	981	577	470	76	5,354	15
1996	5,478	3,328	996	586	476	76	5,462	16
1997	5,542	3,358	1,007	594	487	80	5,526	16
1998	5,579	3,376	1,012	600	494	80	5,563	16
Establishments:								
1990	6,176	3,032	971	600	590	255	5,448	728
1991	6,201	3,049	961	593	593	261	5,457	743
1992	6,319	3,082	965	606	635	284	5,572	747
1993	6,401	3,148	981	609	632	285	5,655	746
1994	6,509	3,218	983	609	631	284	5,725	784
1995	6,613	3,260	998	618	639	284	5,799	814
1996	6,738	3,338	1,013	625	636	281	5,893	846
1997	6,895	3,364	1,023	639	683	309	6,018	877
1998	6,942	3,383	1,026	640	675	307	6,030	911
Employment:								
1990	93,469	5,117	6,252	7,543	17,710	13,545	50,167	43,302
1991	92,308	5,151	6,175	7,387	17,146	13,143	49,003	43,305
1992	92,826	5,179	6,203	7,391	17,121	13,307	49,201	43,625
1993	94,774	5,258	6,314	7,498	17,421	13,825	50,316	44,458
1994	96,722	5,319	6,333	7,544	17,694	14,118	51,008	45,714
1995	100,315	5,395	6,440	7,734	18,422	14,660	52,653	47,662
1996	102,187	5,486	6,541	7,855	18,643	14,650	53,175	49,013
1997	105,299	5,546	6,610	7,962	19,110	15,317	54,545	50,754
1998	108,118	5,584	6,643	8,048	19,378	15,411	55,064	53,053
Annual payroll ($bil.):								
1990	2,104	117	114	144	352	279	1,007	1,097
1991	2,145	118	117	147	352	279	1,013	1,132
1992	2,272	125	122	153	369	298	1,067	1,205
1993	2,363	129	127	159	385	316	1,116	1,247
1994	2,488	135	132	166	408	336	1,176	1,312
1995	2,666	142	137	175	437	361	1,252	1,414
1996	2,849	151	145	185	465	384	1,330	1,518
1997	3,048	158	151	194	495	418	1,416	1,632
1998	3,309	168	160	207	531	446	1,513	1,797

Source: U.S. Small Business Administration, Office of Advocacy, based on data provided by the U.S. Census Bureau, unpublished data.

No. 727. Firm Births and Deaths by Employment Size of Enterprise: 1989-98

[For employment (3,211 represents 3,211,000). Data represent activity from March of the beginning year to March of the ending year. Establishments with no employment in the first quarter of the beginning year were excluded. This table provides the number of births and deaths of initial establishments (based on plant number) as an approximation of firm births and deaths]

Item	Births (initial locations)				Deaths (initial locations)			
	Total	Less than 20	Less than 500	More than 500	Total	Less than 20	Less than 500	More than 500
Firms:								
1989-1990	584,892	558,478	584,660	232	531,400	502,685	530,991	409
1990-1991	541,141	515,870	540,889	252	546,518	516,964	546,149	369
1991-1992	544,596	519,014	544,278	318	521,606	492,746	521,176	430
1992-1993	564,504	539,601	564,093	411	492,651	466,550	492,266	385
1993-1994	570,587	546,437	570,337	250	503,563	476,667	503,125	438
1994-1995	594,369	568,896	594,119	250	497,246	472,441	496,874	372
1995-1996	597,792	572,442	597,503	289	512,402	485,509	512,024	378
1996-1997	590,644	564,197	590,335	309	530,003	500,014	529,481	522
1997-1998	589,982	564,804	589,706	276	540,601	511,567	540,112	489
Employment (1,000):								
1989-1990	3,211	1,886	3,091	120	3,199	1,683	2,988	210
1990-1991	3,105	1,713	2,907	198	3,208	1,723	3,044	164
1991-1992	3,201	1,703	2,864	337	3,126	1,603	2,894	232
1992-1993	3,438	1,751	3,054	384	2,906	1,516	2,698	209
1993-1994	3,106	1,760	2,890	216	3,077	1,549	2,801	276
1994-1995	3,322	1,836	3,049	273	2,823	1,517	2,634	189
1995-1996	3,256	1,845	3,056	200	3,100	1,560	2,808	291
1996-1997	3,228	1,814	3,030	198	3,275	1,621	2,961	314
1997-1998	3,205	1,812	3,002	203	3,233	1,662	2,992	242

Source: U.S. Small Business Administration, Office of Advocacy, from data provided by U.S. Census Bureau, unpublished data.

No. 728. Minority- and Women-Owned Businesses—Summary: 1997

[20,822 represents 20,822,000. Includes individual proprietorships, partnerships and subchapter S corporations]

Group	All firms		Firms with paid employees			
	Firms (1,000)	Sales and receipts (mil. dol.)	Firms (1,000)	Sales and receipts (mil. dol.)	Employees (1,000)	Annual payroll (mil. dol.)
All firms	**20,822**	**18,553,243**	**5,295**	**17,907,940**	**103,360**	**2,936,493**
Black	823	71,215	93	56,378	718	14,322
Hispanic	1,200	186,275	212	158,675	1,389	29,830
Cuban	125	26,492	30	23,873	176	4,163
Mexican, Mexican American, Chicano	472	73,707	91	62,271	695	13,015
Puerto Rican	70	7,461	11	5,814	62	1,497
Spaniard	57	16,923	13	15,264	76	2,046
Hispanic Latin American	287	40,998	43	34,798	239	5,863
Other Spanish/Hispanic/Latino	188	20,694	24	16,654	140	3,247
American Indian and Alaska Natives	197	34,344	33	29,226	299	6,624
Asian and Pacific Islander	913	306,933	290	278,294	2,203	46,180
Asian Indian	167	67,503	67	61,760	491	12,586
Chinese	253	106,197	91	98,233	692	12,945
Filipino	85	11,078	15	8,966	110	2,667
Japanese	86	43,741	23	41,295	262	7,107
Korean	136	45,936	50	40,746	334	5,789
Vietnamese	98	9,323	19	6,768	79	1,166
Other Asian	71	19,016	22	16,801	202	3,136
Hawaiian	16	2,250	2	1,957	21	498
Other Pacific Islander	4	1,888	1	1,768	13	286
Women	5,417	818,669	847	717,764	7,076	149,116

Source: U.S. Census Bureau, *Minority- and Women-Owned Businesses, United States, 1997 Economic Census*, published 24 May 2001; <http://www.census.gov/epcd/mwb97/us/us.html>.

No. 729. Women-Owned Firms by Major Industry Group: 1997

[818,669,084 represents $818,669,084,000. Based on the 1987 Standard Industrial Classification code; see text, this section. Includes individual proprietorships, partnerships and subchapter S corporations]

Major industry group	All firms		Firms with paid employees			
	Firms [1] (number)	Sales and receipts ($1,000)	Firms [1] (number)	Sales and receipts ($1,000)	Employees (number)	Annual payroll ($1,000)
All Industries	**5,417,034**	**818,669,084**	**846,780**	**717,763,965**	**7,076,081**	**149,115,699**
Agric. services, forestry, and fishing	74,444	5,852,901	16,652	4,599,852	77,370	1,442,618
Mining	20,030	7,186,113	2,180	6,491,900	25,982	873,455
Construction [2]	157,173	67,632,059	65,707	63,738,665	518,142	15,302,000
Manufacturing	121,108	113,722,304	41,141	111,658,770	901,434	24,674,596
Transportation and public utilities	128,999	32,944,160	35,623	30,063,926	321,759	7,803,912
Wholesale trade	125,645	188,488,639	50,459	184,574,784	468,276	14,086,123
Retail trade	919,990	152,041,311	211,583	137,296,015	1,574,747	19,520,353
Finance, insurance, and real estate	479,469	56,021,358	66,375	38,920,419	276,045	7,549,811
Services	2,981,266	186,161,274	355,768	140,255,817	2,908,080	57,808,228
Industries not classified	411,596	8,618,965	3,979	163,817	4,246	54,604

[1] Firms may be classified in more than one industry group. [2] Includes SIC 6552, Subdividers and developers, formerly included in Real Estate.

Source: U.S. Census Bureau, *Women-Owned Businesses, 1997 Economic Census*, Series EC97CS-2.

No. 730. Black-Owned Firms by Major Industry Group: 1997

[71,214,662 represents $71,214,662,000. Based on the 1987 Standard Industrial Classification code; see text, this section. Includes individual proprietorships, partnerships and subchapter S corporations]

Major industry group	All firms		Firms with paid employees			
	Firms [1] (number)	Sales and receipts ($1,000)	Firms [1] (number)	Sales and receipts ($1,000)	Employees (number)	Annual payroll ($1,000)
All Industries	823,499	71,214,662	93,235	56,377,860	718,341	14,322,312
Agricultural services, forestry, and fishing .	12,464	417,169	1,356	259,649	5,457	77,198
Mining	231	21,551	16	12,867	186	5,319
Construction [2]	56,508	7,712,059	12,973	6,587,348	70,928	1,510,252
Manufacturing	10,447	3,682,510	1,931	3,463,861	26,624	652,787
Transportation and public utilities	71,586	6,376,645	6,184	4,252,240	47,289	909,470
Wholesale trade	8,120	5,818,734	2,139	5,573,907	13,746	471,320
Retail trade	87,568	13,803,266	14,074	12,244,399	125,480	1,497,111
Finance, insurance, and real estate	37,934	3,088,582	4,820	2,189,556	18,379	498,318
Services	437,646	25,925,092	43,529	19,503,488	388,398	8,212,775
Industries not classified	101,128	4,369,056	6,347	2,290,545	21,853	487,761

[1] Firms may be classified in more than one industry group.   [2] Includes SIC 6552, Subdividers and developers, formerly included in Real Estate.

Source: U.S. Census Bureau, *Survey of Minority-Owned Business Enterprises, Black, 1997 Economic Census*, Series EC97CS-3.

No. 731. Asian- and Pacific Islander-Owned Firms by Major Industry Group: 1997

[306,932,982 represents $306,932,982,000. Based on the 1987 Standard Industrial Classification code; see text, this section. Includes individual proprietorships, partnerships and subchapter S corporations]

Major industry group	All firms		Firms with paid employees			
	Firms [1] (number)	Sales and receipts ($1,000)	Firms [1] (number)	Sales and receipts ($1,000)	Employees (number)	Annual payroll ($1,000)
All Industries	912,960	306,932,982	289,999	278,294,345	2,203,079	46,179,519
Agric. services, forestry, and fishing . . .	12,988	1,140,670	1,927	791,843	11,359	226,707
Mining	660	253,329	87	229,059	1,007	33,447
Construction [2]	27,711	7,485,505	6,398	6,522,807	42,533	1,386,303
Manufacturing	23,242	28,952,417	10,553	28,271,707	238,167	5,513,875
Transportation and public utilities	37,501	5,625,483	5,916	4,427,646	52,441	1,220,240
Wholesale trade	50,400	105,466,223	30,095	102,902,082	211,510	6,128,070
Retail trade	195,691	67,895,241	106,264	62,467,158	644,644	7,497,710
Finance, insurance, and real estate . . .	68,765	11,398,069	9,429	7,585,054	42,243	1,185,688
Services	406,010	67,762,462	107,910	57,153,191	896,731	21,719,605
Industries not classified	90,509	10,953,582	11,937	7,943,797	62,443	1,267,874

[1] Firms may be classified in more than one industry group.   [2] Includes SIC 6552, Subdividers and developers, formerly included in Real Estate.

Source: U.S. Census Bureau, *Survey of Minority-Owned Business Enterprises, Asians and Pacific Islanders, 1997 Economic Census*, Series EC97CS-5.

No. 732. American Indian- and Alaska Native-Owned Firms by Major Industry Group: 1997

[34,343,907 represents $34,343,907,000. Based on the 1987 Standard Industrial Classification code; see text, this section. Includes individual proprietorships, partnerships and subchapter S corporations]

Major industry group	All firms		Firms with paid employees			
	Firms [1] (number)	Sales and receipts ($1,000)	Firms [1] (number)	Sales and receipts ($1,000)	Employees (number)	Annual payroll ($1,000)
All Industries	197,300	34,343,907	33,277	29,226,260	298,661	6,624,235
Agric. services, forestry, and fishing . . .	8,942	360,484	797	174,841	2,760	50,041
Mining	947	543,908	199	465,764	2,124	64,737
Construction [2]	27,435	5,384,815	6,012	4,648,924	38,419	1,021,524
Manufacturing	6,717	2,503,417	1,612	2,334,452	21,206	563,454
Transportation and public utilities	6,291	1,620,515	1,118	1,347,949	10,584	276,381
Wholesale trade	4,365	3,155,143	1,145	3,036,534	9,801	260,713
Retail trade	14,768	4,618,484	4,645	4,245,552	31,451	441,783
Finance, insurance, and real estate . . .	4,616	1,190,741	1,004	1,025,527	4,585	133,050
Services	34,144	5,202,704	4,826	4,497,918	66,627	1,541,895
Industries not classified	89,243	9,763,696	12,086	7,448,800	111,103	2,270,656

[1] Firms may be classified in more than one industry group.   [2] Includes SIC 6552, Subdividers and developers, formerly included in Real Estate.

Source: U.S. Census Bureau, *Survey of Minority-Owned Business Enterprises, American Indians and Alaska Natives, 1997 Economic Census*, Series EC97CS-6.

No. 733. Hispanic-Owned Firms by Major Industry Group: 1997

[186,274,582 represents $186,274,582,000. Based on the 1987 Standard Industrial Classification code; see text, this section. Includes individual proprietorships, partnerships and subchapter S corporations]

Major industry group	All firms		Firms with paid employees			
	Firms [1] (number)	Sales and receipts ($1,000)	Firms [1] (number)	Sales and receipts ($1,000)	Employees (number)	Annual payroll ($1,000)
All industries	1,199,896	186,274,582	211,884	158,674,537	1,388,746	29,830,028
Agric. services, forestry, and fishing. . .	40,040	2,279,397	5,925	1,309,733	25,955	416,702
Mining	1,909	429,446	325	367,442	3,569	97,854
Construction [2]	152,573	21,923,384	31,478	19,146,212	168,873	4,218,419
Manufacturing	25,552	28,684,759	10,173	27,719,404	171,738	4,549,598
Transportation and public utilities	84,544	8,293,935	12,735	5,605,332	79,682	1,587,106
Wholesale trade.	31,480	40,386,625	14,125	38,746,137	94,281	2,388,988
Retail trade	155,061	32,280,310	48,713	28,599,447	324,474	3,892,182
Finance, insurance, and real estate . . .	56,629	6,644,826	9,944	4,728,312	34,783	949,006
Services	500,449	39,177,767	70,838	30,406,573	463,889	11,297,362
Industries not classified	151,931	6,174,133	7,909	2,045,945	21,502	432,812

[1] Firms may be classified in more than one industry group.   [2] Includes SIC 6552, subdividers and developers, formerly included in real estate.

Source: U.S. Census Bureau, *Survey of Minority-Owned Business Enterprises, Hispanic, 1997 Economic Census*, Series EC97CS-4.

No. 734. Women-Owned and Minority-Owned Firms by Receipt Size: 1997

[5,417 represents 5,417,000. Based on the 1987 Standard Industrial Classification code; see text, this section. Covers firms with paid employees and firms with no paid employees. Includes individual proprietorships, partnerships and subchapter S corporations]

Receipts size	Women-owned		Black-owned		Hispanic-owned		Asian- and Pacific Islander-owned		American Indian and Native Alaskan-owned	
	Number of firms (1,000)	Sales and receipts (mil. dol.)	Number of firms (1,000)	Sales and receipts (mil. dol.)	Number of firms (1,000)	Sales and receipts (mil. dol.)	Number of firms (1,000)	Sales and receipts (mil. dol.)	Number of firms (1,000)	Sales and receipts (mil. dol.)
Total	5,417	818,669	823	71,215	1,200	186,275	913	306,933	197	34,344
Less than $5,000	1,631	3,850	248	582	263	664	152	424	50	163
$5,000 to $9,999	976	6,554	156	1,057	212	1,461	108	824	30	245
$10,000 to $24,999	1,115	17,220	189	2,898	273	4,214	147	2,587	42	786
$25,000 to $49,999	571	19,828	93	3,193	145	4,879	112	4,261	24	938
$50,000 to $99,999	399	27,942	59	4,117	107	7,296	110	8,291	18	1,458
$100,000 to $249,999 . . .	356	55,587	42	6,663	97	14,840	121	20,232	16	2,799
$250,000 to $499,999 . . .	169	59,127	19	6,647	48	16,879	71	25,280	8	2,926
$500,000 to $999,999 . . .	100	69,398	9	5,868	28	19,629	47	32,935	4	3,004
$1,000,000 or more	99	559,165	9	40,190	27	116,412	45	212,099	5	22,025

Source: U.S. Census Bureau, *1997 Economic Census, Survey of Women-Owned Business Enterprises* and *Survey of Minority-Owned Business Enterprises Company Statistics Series*.

No. 735. Women-Owned and Minority-Owned Firms With Paid Employees by Employment Size: 1997

[717,764 represents $717,764,000,000. Based on the 1987 Standard Industrial Classification code; see text, this section. Includes individual proprietorships, partnerships and subchapter S corporations]

Employment size	Women-owned				Black-owned				Hispanic-owned			
	Number of firms	Sales and receipts (mil. dol.)	Employees (1,000)	Annual payroll (mil. dol.)	Number of firms	Sales and receipts (mil. dol.)	Employees (1,000)	Annual payroll (mil. dol.)	Number of firms	Sales and receipts (mil. dol.)	Employees (1,000)	Annual payroll (mil. dol.)
All industries . .	846,780	717,764	7,076	149,116	93,235	56,378	718	14,322	211,884	158,675	1,389	29,830
No employees [1] . .	115,281	14,538	-	2,649	15,217	2,932	-	500	29,118	4,615	-	637
1 to 4 employees . .	444,121	103,568	924	17,055	49,262	8,647	97	1,699	111,727	27,562	217	4,115
5 to 9 employees . .	150,300	84,335	975	17,712	14,734	7,325	96	1,628	37,727	28,571	229	4,549
10 to 19 employees.	79,327	91,168	1,047	20,594	7,171	6,608	94	1,778	19,860	24,172	235	4,589
20 to 49 employees.	39,987	104,393	1,168	25,029	4,477	10,220	133	2,669	9,260	27,460	265	5,464
50 to 99 employees.	10,325	71,473	694	16,110	1,484	8,391	101	2,247	3,070	18,014	178	3,988
100 to 499 employees	6,566	113,056	1,213	25,909	836	10,263	147	2,917	1,006	22,789	177	4,658
500 employees or more	873	135,233	1,056	24,057	53	1,993	50	886	115	5,492	88	1,829

- Represents zero.   [1] Firms reported annual payroll, but did not report any employees on their payroll during specified period in 1997.

Source: U.S. Census Bureau, *1997 Economic Census, Survey of Women-Owned Business Enterprises* and *Survey of Minority-Owned Business Enterprises Company Statistics Series*.

Business Enterprise 489

No. 736. Women-Owned and Minority-Owned Firms by State: 1997

[5,417.0 represents 5,417,000. Based on the 1987 Standard Industrial Classification code; see text, this section. Covers firms with paid employees and firms with no paid employees. Includes individual proprietorships, partnerships and subchapter S corporations]

State	Women-owned Number of firms [1] (1,000)	Women-owned Sales and receipts (mil. dol.)	Black-owned Number of firms [1] (1,000)	Black-owned Sales and receipts (mil. dol.)	Hispanic-owned Number of firms [1] (1,000)	Hispanic-owned Sales and receipts (mil. dol.)	Asian- and Pacific Islander-owned Number of firms [1] (1,000)	Asian- and Pacific Islander-owned Sales and receipts (mil. dol.)	American Indian and Native Alaskan-owned Number of firms [1] (1,000)	American Indian and Native Alaskan-owned Sales and receipts (mil. dol.)
U.S, total ...	5,417.0	818,669	823.5	71,215	1,199.9	186,275	913.0	306,933	197.3	34,344
AL.........	69.5	10,230	19.1	1,009	2.9	397	3.3	1,387	3.5	460
AK.........	16.6	1,942	0.9	56	1.4	192	1.8	311	6.8	1,709
AZ.........	88.8	11,305	3.6	314	28.9	4,227	7.1	2,002	5.5	753
AR.........	42.6	6,490	6.7	387	2.6	190	1.5	397	2.3	438
CA.........	700.5	121,191	79.1	6,395	336.4	51,682	316.0	121,566	26.6	5,836
CO.........	114.8	13,763	4.9	513	20.9	3,068	9.0	2,060	3.4	515
CT.........	72.4	9,276	7.3	528	6.6	1,163	5.9	2,516	1.3	407
DE.........	13.7	1,831	2.7	185	0.9	504	1.5	510	0.3	55
DC.........	14.0	1,813	10.9	1,335	2.2	664	2.4	1,039	0.1	(D)
FL.........	337.8	48,261	59.7	4,092	193.9	35,351	33.8	10,467	10.5	1,519
GA	145.6	25,267	55.8	4,111	11.7	1,888	18.2	6,416	4.5	495
HI	25.8	3,253	0.6	34	4.2	277	50.6	14,523	0.5	48
ID	25.8	2,405	0.2	18	2.8	240	1.0	192	1.2	301
IL	239.7	44,273	41.2	3,913	31.0	4,815	36.9	14,728	3.9	664
IN	107.1	13,578	11.1	1,192	4.3	818	4.9	1,928	2.9	396
IA	57.5	8,093	1.4	233	1.3	233	1.7	342	0.9	97
KS.........	54.6	6,928	3.4	594	3.5	403	2.6	728	2.3	453
KY.........	66.0	9,877	5.6	659	1.5	283	2.6	1,293	3.1	243
LA.........	70.6	11,463	25.8	1,917	6.6	1,283	6.5	1,373	3.2	561
ME	30.6	3,212	0.3	28	0.5	52	0.6	162	1.4	161
MD	115.8	14,657	47.6	3,965	11.2	1,567	22.2	5,794	2.4	331
MA	142.7	16,753	11.8	1,013	12.7	1,623	12.7	4,183	3.4	295
MI	184.6	26,499	25.0	4,623	10.0	1,967	11.7	5,491	5.8	720
MN	108.4	13,458	4.0	523	3.6	392	5.4	1,712	2.4	515
MS	38.3	5,995	17.6	853	1.0	124	2.5	818	1.1	210
MO	103.6	15,000	13.7	1,261	4.1	587	5.0	1,350	4.1	626
MT	22.4	2,048	0.1	(D)	1.0	115	0.4	73	1.9	165
NE.........	33.5	4,537	1.6	129	1.4	141	0.9	224	0.8	100
NV	33.3	5,972	2.8	226	6.6	1,221	5.0	1,868	1.2	245
NH	27.3	3,113	0.3	32	0.7	117	1.2	587	1.0	157
NJ.........	155.3	30,001	26.5	2,160	36.1	5,107	41.4	16,734	2.4	364
NM	38.7	4,450	1.1	143	28.3	3,668	2.5	578	6.8	580
NY.........	394.0	59,497	86.5	5,067	104.2	10,311	123.3	31,611	6.4	1,417
NC	139.9	24,166	39.9	2,299	7.3	1,080	8.1	2,461	7.1	912
ND	12.4	1,167	0.1	(D)	0.4	22	0.3	63	0.8	147
OH	205.0	30,597	27.0	3,947	6.4	1,513	11.4	4,603	5.1	1,074
OK	67.5	8,912	5.3	333	4.3	772	4.0	898	15.1	2,646
OR	80.5	10,335	2.2	436	6.0	1,074	7.5	2,089	2.9	373
PA	203.0	34,043	19.8	1,994	7.9	1,273	17.4	4,944	5.2	505
RI	19.9	2,684	1.3	124	2.2	207	1.1	250	0.6	80
SC.........	64.2	10,634	23.2	1,409	2.0	251	3.5	814	2.2	200
SD.........	14.1	1,202	0.2	17	0.3	59	0.3	55	1.0	222
TN.........	99.8	14,538	20.2	1,645	3.6	684	5.3	1,763	3.7	546
TX.........	381.5	65,065	60.4	6,857	240.4	39,482	60.2	18,849	15.7	3,320
UT.........	42.0	5,096	0.4	23	4.7	455	2.4	599	1.4	140
VT.........	17.0	1,313	0.2	37	0.9	184	0.3	49	0.8	179
VA.........	132.2	17,486	33.5	3,408	13.7	1,809	22.4	4,439	3.3	622
WA	123.0	15,099	5.6	504	10.0	1,711	23.3	8,008	4.7	1,203
WV	30.2	3,299	1.1	88	0.9	96	1.2	532	1.0	127
WI	89.3	15,654	4.8	550	3.0	817	3.8	1,488	2.3	1,136
WY	11.1	945	0.2	13	1.2	117	0.3	66	0.5	(D)

D Data withheld to avoid disclosure.   [1] Number of firms may be distributed in more than one state; therefore the U.S. total is smaller than the addition of the states.

Source: U.S. Census Bureau, *1997 Economic Census, Survey of Women-Owned Business Enterprises* and *Survey of Minority-Owned Business Enterprises Company Statistics Series*.

No. 737. Business Starts and Employment Associated With Start: 1990 to 1999

[647 represents 647,000]

Item	1990	1992	1993	1994	1995	1996	1997	1998	1999
New incorporations (1,000)........	647	667	707	742	767	786	799	761	(NA)
Failures [1], total................	60,747	97,069	86,133	71,558	71,128	71,931	84,342	71,857	(NA)
Rate per 10,000 concerns......	74	110	109	86	82	80	89	76	(NA)
Current liabilities [2] (mil. dol.)	56,130	94,318	47,756	28,978	37,284	29,569	24,802	(NA)	(NA)
Business starts, total	**158,930**	**164,086**	**166,154**	**188,387**	**168,158**	**170,475**	**166,740**	**155,141**	**151,016**
Agriculture, forestry & fishing	2,295	2,160	2,195	2,644	2,199	2,295	2,275	2,451	2,732
Mining	1,054	805	772	680	564	589	655	588	467
Construction	20,801	18,259	17,533	18,213	16,980	18,624	18,513	17,016	15,775
Manufacturing	15,315	14,043	13,789	12,927	12,172	12,908	13,144	11,876	11,292
Transportation & public utilities	6,281	6,578	6,846	7,683	7,161	7,993	8,741	8,559	8,932
Wholesale trade	18,170	18,419	17,958	16,409	14,956	16,019	15,780	13,983	12,233
Retail trade	43,109	40,318	38,707	38,949	36,381	38,407	36,377	33,151	29,263
Finance, insurance & real estate	9,550	9,581	10,314	11,746	10,362	11,222	12,198	12,317	11,783
Services	38,471	40,555	41,349	49,328	44,586	50,077	50,253	48,500	47,643
Unclassifiable establishments	3,884	13,368	16,691	29,808	22,797	12,341	8,804	6,700	10,896
Employment, total	**827,012**	**800,827**	**780,804**	**758,134**	**738,606**	**846,973**	**939,310**	**906,105**	**926,899**
Agriculture, forestry & fishing	8,518	7,422	5,198	7,099	6,146	7,794	10,001	10,105	11,090
Mining	8,431	6,519	6,164	4,312	3,184	4,697	4,248	6,790	4,575
Construction	80,096	59,361	53,432	54,210	53,118	64,478	82,336	78,920	80,558
Manufacturing	139,506	122,483	119,487	105,255	104,660	108,644	125,007	111,507	114,248
Transportation & public utilities	45,373	45,227	44,885	41,617	43,583	50,072	59,144	59,972	70,284
Wholesale trade	75,914	79,247	78,924	66,186	59,933	69,001	73,281	70,297	67,802
Retail trade	207,752	203,698	191,484	174,270	176,159	200,354	211,007	195,802	183,907
Finance. insurance & real estate	54,872	56,665	57,199	55,857	54,610	61,185	70,982	75,113	73,139
Services	205,481	219,120	222,054	243,296	233,482	278,292	299,137	294,331	316,065
Unclassifiable establishments	1,069	1,085	1,977	6,032	3,731	2,456	4,167	3,268	5,231

NA Not available. [1] Includes concerns discontinued following assignment, voluntary or involuntary petition in bankruptcy, attachment, execution, foreclosure, etc. [2] Liabilities exclude long-term publicly held obligations; offsetting assets are not taken into account.

Source: The Dun & Bradstreet Corporation, Murray Hill, NJ 07974-0027, *Business Starts Record*, annual; *Business Failure Record*, annual; and *Monthly New Incorporations Report* (copyright).

No. 738. Bankruptcy Cases Filed by State: 1995 to 2000

[In thousands (858.1 represents 858,100). For years ending June 30. Covers only bankruptcy cases filed under the Bankruptcy Reform Act of 1978. **Bankruptcy:** legal recognition that a company or individual is insolvent and must restructure or liquidate. Petitions "filed" means the commencement of a proceeding through the presentation of a petition to the clerk of the court]

State	1995	1998	1999	2000	State	1995	1998	1999	2000
Total [1]........	858.1	1,429.5	1,392.0	1,276.9	Missouri	15.1	27.4	27.9	26.3
					Montana	2.1	3.7	3.7	3.3
Alabama	24.3	33.8	31.2	31.4	Nebraska	3.4	6.1	5.8	5.6
Alaska	0.9	1.4	1.5	1.4	Nevada	7.3	14.4	15.5	14.3
Arizona.........	14.8	24.7	23.7	21.7	New Hampshire ...	3.1	5.1	4.5	3.9
Arkansas........	7.9	16.5	16.8	16.3					
California.......	140.4	211.3	200.2	160.6	New Jersey	25.5	44.5	44.1	38.7
					New Mexico......	3.7	7.9	7.7	7.1
Colorado........	13.1	18.9	17.3	15.6	New York	48.8	76.9	74.4	61.7
Connecticut	8.5	13.5	13.2	11.4	North Carolina ...	14.0	26.5	26.8	25.8
Delaware........	1.4	2.7	3.9	4.9	North Dakota	1.2	2.1	2.2	2.0
District of Columb 'a.	1.4	2.8	2.8	2.6					
Florida	43.4	76.4	79.2	74.0	Ohio............	32.4	55.5	55.3	53.6
					Oklahoma	13.2	22.5	21.3	19.3
Georgia	42.1	62.6	59.3	57.9	Oregon..........	13.2	17.9	18.2	18.1
Hawaii	1.8	5.1	5.9	5.0	Pennsylvania	22.0	45.2	45.7	43.8
Idaho	3.7	7.5	7.3	7.3	Rhode Island	3.0	5.4	5.3	4.8
Illinois.........	39.2	64.6	66.6	62.3					
Indiana	22.3	38.5	38.9	37.5	South Carolina....	6.9	11.3	11.6	11.7
					South Dakota....	1.3	2.3	2.3	2.1
Iowa...........	5.9	9.7	8.9	8.2	Tennessee.......	35.5	52.6	48.2	47.1
Kansas.........	8.5	13.2	12.3	11.4	Texas	43.8	72.0	68.6	62.9
Kentucky........	13.0	22.1	21.4	20.8	Utah	6.9	13.5	14.0	14.4
Louisiana	13.4	23.2	22.5	23.1					
Maine..........	1.9	4.4	4.5	4.1	Vermont	0.9	1.9	1.9	1.6
Maryland........	16.3	34.5	34.1	31.1	Virginia	25.5	43.4	41.2	37.1
Massachusetts	14.3	22.1	20.9	16.7	Washington	18.6	33.6	32.4	31.2
Michigan	22.7	41.2	38.8	36.4	West Virginia	3.8	8.8	8.4	8.2
Minnesota	14.1	19.5	17.4	15.4	Wisconsin	11.8	19.6	18.9	18.0
Mississippi.	10.6	19.1	18.1	17.9	Wyoming........	1.2	2.1	2.2	2.0

[1] Includes outlying areas not shown separately.

Source: Administrative Office of the U.S. Courts, unpublished data.

U.S. Census Bureau, Statistical Abstract of the United States: 2001

No. 739. Bankruptcy Petitions Filed and Pending by Type and Chapter: 1990 to 2000

[For years ending June 30. Covers only bankruptcy cases filed under the Bankruptcy Reform Act of 1978. *Bankruptcy:* legal recognition that a company or individual is insolvent and must restructure or liquidate. Petitions "filed" means the commencement of a proceeding through the presentation of a petition to the clerk of the court; "pending" is a proceeding in which the administration has not been completed]

Item	1990	1993	1994	1995	1996	1997	1998	1999	2000
Total filed	725,484	918,734	845,257	858,104	1,042,110	1,316,999	1,429,451	1,391,964	1,276,922
Business [1]	64,688	66,428	56,74?	51,288	52,938	53,993	50,202	39,934	36,910
Nonbusiness [2]	660,796	852,306	788,509	806,816	989,172	1,263,006	1,379,249	1,352,030	1,240,012
Voluntary	723,886	917,350	844,087	856,991	1,040,915	1,315,782	1,428,550	1,391,130	1,276,146
Involuntary	1,598	1,384	1,170	1,113	1,195	1,217	901	834	776
Chapter 7 [3]	505,337	638,916	578,903	581,390	712,129	917,274	1,015,453	993,414	885,447
Chapter 9 [4]	7	9	17	12	10	9	5	3	8
Chapter 11 [5]	19,591	20,579	17,098	13,221	12,859	11,159	9,613	8,684	9,947
Chapter 12 [6]	1,351	1,434	976	904	1,063	1,006	845	829	732
Chapter 13 [7]	199,186	257,777	248,246	262,551	316,024	387,521	403,501	389,004	380,770
Section 304 [8]	12	19	17	26	24	29	34	30	18
Total pending	961,919	1,183,009	1,134,036	1,090,446	1,169,112	1,331,290	1,389,917	1,394,794	1,400,416

[1] Business bankruptcies include those filed under chapters 7, 9, 11, or 12.   [2] Bankruptcies include those filed under chapters 7, 11, or 13.   [3] Chapter 7, liquidation of nonexempt assets of businesses or individuals.   [4] Chapter 9, adjustment of debts of a municipality.   [5] Chapter 11, individual or business reorganization.   [6] Chapter 12, adjustment of debts of a family farmer with regular income, effective November 26, 1986.   [7] Chapter 13, adjustment of debts of an individual with regular income.   [8] Chapter 11 U.S.C., Section 304, cases ancillary to foreign proceedings.

Source: Administrative Office of the U.S. Courts, *Statistical Tables for the Federal Judiciary.*

No. 740. Small Business Administration Loans to Small Businesses: 1980 to 2000

[For fiscal year ending in year shown; see text, Section 8, State and Local Government Finances and Employment. A small business must be independently owned and operated, must not be dominant in its particular industry, and must meet standards set by the Small Business Administration as to its annual receipts or number of employees]

Item	Unit	1980	1985	1990	1995	1996	1997	1998	1999	2000
Loans, all businesses	1,000...	31.7	19.3	18.8	60.1	52.7	49.4	47.2	48.9	48.3
Loans, minority-owned businesses..	1,000...	6.0	2.8	2.4	10.4	10.1	10.6	10.9	12.1	12.1
Percent of all business loans....	Percent .	19	15	13	19	19	22	23	25	25
Value of total loans [1]	Mil. dol. .	3,858	3,217	4,354	9,854	10,177	10,904	10,795	12,143	12,143
Minority business loans [2]	Mil. dol. .	470	324	473	1,885	2,130	2,603	2,697	3,361	3,652

[1] Includes both SBA and bank portions of loans.   [2] SBA direct loans and guaranteed portion of bank loans only.

Source: U.S. Small Business Administration, Management Information Summary, unpublished data.

No. 741. Venture Capital Commitments by Source: 1980 to 2000

[In billions of dollars (2.1 represents $2,100,000,000), except as indicated. Venture capital commitment: investment in venture capital partnerships]

Source	1980	1985	1990	1994	1995	1996	1997	1998	1999	2000
Capital commitments	2.1	3.1	3.1	7.6	9.9	11.8	17.1	29.4	60.0	92.9
Corporations	0.4	0.5	0.2	0.7	0.5	2.3	4.3	3.5	8.5	3.4
Endowments & foundations......	0.3	0.3	0.4	1.7	2.0	1.4	2.8	1.9	10.3	19.6
Individuals & families.........	0.4	0.5	0.4	0.9	1.7	0.8	2.1	3.3	5.8	11.0
Financial & insurance.........	0.3	0.5	0.3	0.7	2.0	0.4	1.1	3.1	9.3	21.7
Pension funds	0.7	1.4	1.8	3.6	3.8	6.9	6.8	17.7	26.1	37.3
PERCENT DISTRIBUTION										
Corporations	21	15	7	9	5	20	25	12	14	4
Endowments & foundations......	15	10	14	22	20	12	17	6	17	21
Individuals & families.........	17	17	12	12	17	7	12	11	10	12
Financial & insurance.........	14	14	10	10	20	3	6	10	16	23
Pension funds	32	43	56	47	38	58	39	60	44	40

Source: Venture Economics Investor Services, Boston, MA, *Venture Capital Journal,* monthly.

492   Business Enterprise

No. 742. Mergers and Acquisitions—Summary: 1985 to 1999

[Covers transactions valued at $5 million or more. Values based on transactions for which price data revealed. *All activity* includes mergers, acquisitions, acquisitions of partial interest that involve a 40% stake in the target or an investment of at least $100 million, divestitures, and leveraged transactions that result in a change in ownership. *Divestiture:* sale of a business, division, or subsidiary by corporate owner to another party. *Leveraged buyout:* acquisition of a business in which buyers use mostly borrowed money to finance purchase price and incorporate debt into capital structure of business after change in ownership]

Item	Unit	1985	1990	1993	1994	1995	1996	1997	1998	1999
All activity:										
Number.	Number . .	1,719	4,239	3,722	4,383	4,981	5,639	8,770	9,634	9,599
Value	Bil. dol. . .	149.6	205.6	420.4	524.9	895.8	1,059.3	1,610.3	2,480.2	3,401.6
Divestitures:										
Number.	Number . .	780	1,907	1,993	2,005	2,227	2,423	3,189	3,304	3,184
Value	Bil. dol. . .	51	90.8	213.4	236.9	365.3	319.0	616.2	554.8	677.7
Leveraged buyouts:										
Number.	Number . .	154	177	621	173	206	169	198	238	344
Value	Bil. dol. . .	16.3	17.6	1.64	10.6	23.6	17.4	24.1	27.2	58.1
Foreign acquisitions of U.S. companies:										
Number	Number . .	259	773	(NA)	(NA)	80	73	441	483	566
Value	Bil. dol. . .	27.9	56.4	(NA)	(NA)	3.5	2.9	64.8	232.5	282.6
U.S. acquisitions overseas:										
Number	Number . .	91	392	197	207	317	364	539	746	651
Value	Bil. dol. . .	3.7	20.5	19.5	21.1	62.6	59.3	87.8	127.8	166.1

NA Not available.

No. 743. Mergers and Acquisitions by Industry: 1998

[See headnote Table 742]

Industry	U.S. company acquiring U.S. company		Foreign company acquiring U.S. company		U.S. company acquiring foreign company	
	Number	Value (mil. dol.)	Number	Value (mil. dol.)	Number	Value (mil. dol.)
Total activity [1]	3,882	1,378,564.6	483	232,505.1	746	127,760.9
Advertising services.	31	3,194.3	4	54.4	10	2,163.6
Agriculture, forestry, and fishing	17	4,087.3	3	415.0	10	1,477.4
Air transportation and shipping.	8	1,788.9	2	222.0	6	5,666.9
Amusement and recreation services	46	5,411.5	3	140.6	7	245.4
Chemicals	37	14,275.9	13	2,327.2	15	2,824.1
Commercial banks, bank holding companies .	253	241,677.7	1	9,082.1	13	1,878.2
Communications equipment	47	5,006.3	15	6,005.5	20	1,615.4
Construction firms	76	3,494.9	6	1,314.3	8	344.0
Credit institutions.	37	25,294.2	1	85.0	9	1,572.9
Drugs	52	9,071.8	16	2,734.0	13	1,428.2
Electric, gas, water distribution.	57	29,988.7	6	16,767.4	30	19,649.0
Electronic and electrical equipment.	101	26,438.6	25	2,938.6	29	11,996.4
Food and kindred products	56	11,089.3	10	359.1	23	5,380.5
Health services	117	23,417.1	5	1,886.2	6	148.5
Hotels and casinos	122	18,939.7	8	489.4	21	1,840.8
Insurance	96	61,680.2	16	7,068.5	23	4,289.8
Investment & commodity firms, dealers, exchanges	120	37,363.9	18	3,407.2	34	4,797.7
Machinery	90	24,549.5	7	228.4	19	1,369.7
Measuring, medical, photo equip; clocks	104	28,158.3	24	3,676.3	25	3,336.0
Metal and metal products	84	12,155.2	10	2,008.5	24	1,408.0
Mining	28	6,415.8	7	2,108.6	16	1,034.7
Motion picture production and distribution . . .	27	3,474.4	1	420.0	4	146.4
Oil and gas; petroleum refining	147	118,128.6	19	56,178.8	28	7,594.3
Paper and allied products	19	16,637.0	9	911.6	10	3,460.9
Prepackaged software	160	19,782.5	36	3,059.4	38	2,793.9
Printing, publishing, and allied services	39	8,007.2	11	9,751.8	7	411.6
Radio & television broadcasting stations	137	108,477.3	5	341.7	11	4,872.3
Real estate, mortgage bankers and brokers . .	482	46,668.9	46	4,577.5	24	5,275.9
Repair services.	18	2,657.0	1	14.8	3	1,411.5
Retail trade-eating and drinking places	37	3,597.6	4	220.5	1	81.9
Retail trade-food stores	13	15,186.9	6	3,383.5	(NA)	(NA)
Retail trade—general merchandise and apparel	23	20,812.6	1	6.0	2	220.0
Rubber & misc plastic products	36	9,836.0	4	122.9	11	522.1
Sanitary services.	26	23,760.0	1	14.5	2	486.4
Real estate, mortgage bankers and brokers . .	52	23,744.6	2	927.0	(NA)	(NA)
Stone, clay, glass and concrete products	23	3,843.7	3	792.5	9	3,846.1
Telecommunications.	101	206,600.2	15	13,086.6	29	4,904.3
Textile and apparel products	32	3,648.9	8	479.1	2	584.8
Transportation and shipping (except air)	60	2,613.3	10	4,065.5	21	1,681.9
Transportation equipment	34	21,649.7	9	43,520.0	19	2,497.2
Wholesale trade—durable goods	93	6,612.4	7	296.8	16	1,250.9
Wholesale trade—nondurable goods.	48	6,555.8	12	6,782.9	7	1,668.7

NA Not available. [1] Includes other industries not shown separately.

Source of Tables 742 and 743: Thomson Financial Securities Data, Newark, NJ, Merger & Corporate Transactions Database (copyright).

U.S. Census Bureau, Statistical Abstract of the United States: 2001

No. 744. Patents and Trademarks: 1980 to 2000

[In thousands (113.0 represents 113,000). **Calendar year data.** Covers patents issued to citizens of the United States and residents of foreign countries. For data on foreign countries, see Table 1350]

Type	1980	1985	1990	1995	1996	1997	1998	1999	2000
Patent applications filed.	113.0	127.1	176.7	228.8	211.6	233.0	261.4	289.5	(NA)
Inventions	104.3	117.0	164.6	212.4	195.2	215.3	243.0	270.2	295.9
Designs	7.8	9.6	11.3	15.4	15.2	16.5	17.1	17.8	18.3
Botanical plants	0.2	0.2	0.4	0.5	0.7	0.6	0.7	0.9	0.8
Reissues	0.6	0.3	0.5	0.6	0.6	0.5	0.6	0.7	(NA)
Patents issued	66.2	77.3	99.2	113.8	121.7	124.1	163.1	169.1	176.0
Inventions	61.8	71.7	90.4	101.4	109.6	112.0	147.5	153.5	157.5
Individuals	13.8	12.9	17.3	17.4	18.2	17.6	22.5	22.8	22.4
Corporations: United States	27.7	31.2	36.1	44.0	48.7	50.2	66.1	69.4	70.9
Foreign [1]	19.1	26.4	36.0	39.1	41.5	42.9	57.9	60.3	63.3
U.S. Government	1.2	1.1	1.0	1.0	0.9	0.9	1.0	1.0	0.9
Designs	3.9	5.1	8.0	11.7	11.4	11.4	14.8	14.7	17.4
Botanical plants	0.1	0.2	0.3	0.4	0.4	0.4	0.6	0.4	0.5
Reissues	0.3	0.3	0.4	0.3	0.3	0.3	0.3	0.4	0.5
U.S. residents [2]	40.8	43.3	52.8	64.4	69.3	69.9	90.6	94.0	96.9
Foreign country residents [2]	25.4	33.9	46.2	49.4	52.4	54.2	72.5	75.1	79.1
Percent of total	38.4	43.9	46.7	43.4	43.0	43.7	44.4	44.4	44.9
Other published documents [3]	(Z)	(Z)	0.1	0.1	0.1	0.1	0.1	0.1	0.1
Trademarks:									
Applications filed.	46.8	65.1	127.3	188.9	212.5	234.6	246.6	328.6	(NA)
Issued	24.7	71.7	60.8	92.5	145.2	145.2	136.1	191.9	(NA)
Trademarks	18.9	65.8	53.6	85.6	93.7	138.2	129.9	184.9	(NA)
Trademark renewals.	5.9	5.9	7.2	6.9	8.8	7.0	6.2	7.0	(NA)

NA Not available.   Z Less than 50.   [1] Includes patents to foreign governments.   [2] Includes patents for inventions, designs, botanical plants, and reissues.   [3] Includes Defensive Publications, a practice which began in November 1968 and ended in July 1986; and Statutory Invention Registrations, the current practice, which began May 1985. These documents are patent applications, which are published to provide the defensive properties of a patent, but do not have the enforceable rights of a patent.

Source: U.S. Patent and Trademark Office. Fiscal-year figures are published in the *Commissioner of Patents and Trademarks Annual Report.*

No. 745. Patents by State: 1999

[Includes only U.S. patents granted to residents of the United States and territories]

State	Total	Inventions	Designs	Botanical plants	Reissues	State	Total	Inventions	Designs	Botanical plants	Reissues
U.S. [1]	94,035	83,906	9,654	201	274	Missouri	1,087	931	147	8	1
Alabama	473	405	62	2	4	Montana	142	126	15	-	1
Alaska	66	53	13	-	-	Nebraska	229	191	36	2	-
Arizona	1,623	1,499	118	1	5	Nevada	356	295	56	-	5
Arkansas	226	188	37	-	1	New Hampshire. .	692	651	40	-	1
California	18,850	16,773	1,950	81	46	New Jersey	4,366	3,987	367	3	9
Colorado	1,987	1,813	168	-	6	New Mexico	357	339	15	-	3
Connecticut	2,026	1,795	223	-	8	New York	6,900	6,109	766	12	13
Delaware	442	417	20	1	4	North Carolina. . .	1,956	1,734	213	1	8
Dist. of Columbia .	63	55	6	-	2	North Dakota . . .	76	67	8	1	-
Florida	3,040	2,600	401	30	9	Ohio	4,001	3,360	628	3	10
Georgia	1,544	1,320	215	1	8	Oklahoma	545	496	48	-	1
Hawaii	97	83	9	5	-	Oregon	1,386	1,097	275	11	3
Idaho.	1,263	1,224	32	-	7	Pennsylvania . . .	4,077	3,752	307	10	8
Illinois	4,304	3,736	549	5	14	Rhode Island . . .	341	261	80	-	-
Indiana	1,706	1,439	260	1	6	South Carolina . .	653	560	92	-	1
Iowa	817	745	69	-	3	South Dakota . . .	78	66	12	-	-
Kansas	494	433	60	-	1	Tennessee	1,014	855	155	1	3
Kentucky	509	453	54	1	1	Texas	6,418	6,050	344	5	19
Louisiana	519	483	33	-	3	Utah	748	678	62	6	2
Maine	145	121	24	-	-	Vermont	363	340	22	-	1
Maryland	1,630	1,510	116	-	4	Virginia	1,149	1,043	101	2	3
Massachusetts . .	3,819	3,521	284	2	12	Washington	2,037	1,826	204	2	5
Michigan	4,031	3,681	333	2	15	West Virginia . . .	166	149	15	-	2
Minnesota	2,901	2,650	242	1	8	Wisconsin.	1,996	1,674	315	-	7
Mississippi	225	188	35	1	1	Wyoming	58	52	6	-	-

- Represents zero.   [1] Includes U.S. territories not shown separately.

Source: U.S. Patent and Trademark Office, Technology Assessment and Forecast Database.

No. 746. Patents by Industry: 1980 to 1999

[Based on the 1972 Standard Industrial Classification (SIC). Includes all patents for inventions granted to residents of the United States, its territories, and foreign citizens. Individual industries may not add to total since a patent may be recorded in more than one industry category. Except for total, data for all years have been revised to reflect the U.S. Patent Classification System as of December 1998]

Industry	SIC code	1980	1985	1990	1995	1998	1999
Total	(X)	61,819	71,661	90,364	101,419	147,519	153,487
Durable goods:							
Stone, clay, and glass products	32	1,221	1,307	1,638	1,575	2,113	2,321
Primary metals	33, 3462-3	706	780	913	902	968	1,029
Fabricated metal products [1]	34	5,012	5,560	6,771	5,908	7,715	8,385
Machinery, except electrical	35	14,325	16,841	19,144	21,148	33,300	34,580
Electronic and other electric equipment	36, 3825	10,737	13,892	19,088	25,302	37,649	40,110
Transportation equipment	37, 348	3,107	3,743	4,727	4,466	5,781	6,088
Instruments and related products [2]	38	7,443	8,938	12,297	14,502	21,037	20,531
Nondurable goods:							
Food and kindred products	20	484	546	730	601	649	919
Textile mill products	22	420	494	501	609	797	844
Chemicals and allied products	28	9,880	10,274	12,487	13,566	20,473	20,792
Oil and gas extraction, petroleum products . . .	13, 29	595	802	664	643	574	723
Rubber and miscellaneous plastics products . .	30	2,611	3,045	3,818	3,958	4,937	5,098
Other industries	(X)	5,279	5,440	7,586	8,241	11,532	12,069

X Not applicable.   [1] Excludes SIC groups 3462, 3463, and 348.   [2] Excludes SIC group 3825.

Source: U.S. Patent and Trademark Office. *Patenting Trends in the United States, State Country Report,* annual.

No. 747. Academic Patenting—Number of U.S. Universities and Colleges With Patent Awards and Number of Academic Patent Awards: 1985 to 1998

Year	Number of universities and colleges with patent awards			Number of academic patents granted		
	Total	Public	Private	Total	Public	Private
1985	111	64	47	589	311	232
1986	119	74	45	670	356	262
1987	122	70	52	819	399	363
1988	120	68	52	814	407	368
1989	147	87	60	1,228	661	526
1990	145	88	57	1,183	676	479
1991	152	94	58	1,342	798	511
1992	150	92	58	1,542	909	599
1993	159	98	61	1,620	939	648
1994	166	100	66	1,780	1,068	677
1995	164	101	63	1,879	1,191	654
1996	176	105	71	2,154	1,341	774
1997	172	106	66	2,436	1,510	880
1998	173	102	71	3,151	1,828	1,278

Source: 1985-97, U.S. Patent and Trademark Office. *Technology Assessment and Report, U.S. Universities and Colleges. 1969-97;* 1998, National Science Foundation, special tabulation.

No. 748. Copyright Registration by Subject Matter: 1990 to 2000

[In thousands (643.5 represents 643,500). For years ending September 30. Comprises claims to copyrights registered for both U.S. and foreign works]

Subject matter	1990	1995	1999	2000	Subject matter	1990	1995	1999	2000
Total	643.5	609.2	594.5	515.1	Sound recordings	37.5	34.0	38.0	34.2
Monographs [1]	179.7	196.0	207.5	169.7	Renewals	51.8	30.6	23.8	16.8
Semiconductor chip products .	1.0	0.8	0.5	0.7	Musical works [2]	185.3	163.6	155.2	138.9
Serials	111.5	88.7	75.6	69.0	Works of the visual arts [3] . . .	76.7	95.5	93.6	85.8

[1] Includes computer software and machine readable works.   [2] Includes dramatic works, accompanying music, choreography, pantomimes, motion pictures, and filmstrips.   [3] Two-dimensional works of fine and graphic art, including prints and art reproductions; sculptural works; technical drawings and models; photographs; commercial prints and labels; works of applied arts, cartographic works, and multimedia works.

Source: The Library of Congress, Copyright Office. *Annual Report.*

U.S. Census Bureau, Statistical Abstract of the United States: 2001

No. 749. Net Stock of Fixed Private Capital by Industry: 1990 to 1999

[In billions of dollars (12,760 represents $12,760,000,000,000). Estimates as of Dec. 31. Net stock estimates are presented in terms of current cost. Based on the 1987 Standard Industrial Classification]

Industry	1990	1995	1996	1997	1998	1999
Fixed private capital	**12,760**	**15,908**	**16,723**	**17,653**	**18,670**	**19,882**
Agriculture, forestry, and fishing	481	551	569	594	621	647
Farms	447	498	511	532	553	573
Housing	161	187	192	202	212	225
Other	285	311	319	329	341	348
Agricultural services, forestry, and fishing	35	53	59	62	68	74
Mining	431	455	483	538	529	535
Metal mining	29	34	36	36	36	37
Coal mining	32	39	41	43	44	47
Oil and gas extraction	350	360	384	435	424	425
Nonmetallic minerals, except fuels	19	21	22	23	25	27
Construction	82	101	109	116	127	139
Manufacturing	1,217	1,457	1,521	1,584	1,655	1,743
Durable goods	636	747	782	819	861	910
Lumber and wood products	25	29	31	31	32	32
Furniture and fixtures	11	13	14	14	15	16
Stone, clay, and glass products	40	44	46	49	53	56
Primary metal industries	116	126	129	131	134	137
Fabricated metal products	70	81	84	87	90	94
Industrial machinery and equipment	110	126	130	138	144	153
Electronic and other electric equipment	92	120	133	143	153	167
Motor vehicles and equipment	64	85	90	95	102	109
Other transportation equipment	51	55	55	57	60	64
Instruments and related products	45	54	56	59	62	64
Miscellaneous manufacturing industries	12	14	15	15	15	16
Nondurable goods	581	711	738	765	794	833
Food and kindred products	119	146	151	158	164	171
Tobacco products	9	9	10	10	10	10
Textile mill products	34	38	39	39	40	41
Apparel and other textile products	11	13	14	14	14	15
Paper and allied products	84	98	101	104	106	108
Printing and publishing	52	59	61	64	67	73
Chemicals and allied products	157	200	210	219	230	245
Petroleum and coal products	75	93	95	95	96	97
Rubber and miscellaneous plastics products	38	52	55	59	64	69
Leather and leather products	3	3	3	3	3	3
Transportation and public utilities	1,855	2,232	2,313	2,401	2,489	2,608
Transportation	582	692	721	747	769	808
Railroad transportation	304	337	349	352	348	343
Local and interurban passenger transit	21	25	27	28	28	30
Trucking and warehousing	71	99	104	113	118	127
Water transportation	35	37	38	39	40	43
Transportation by air	85	115	122	131	147	169
Pipelines, except natural gas	38	44	45	47	47	49
Transportation services	26	34	36	37	41	47
Communications	436	549	587	621	664	713
Telephone and telegraph	377	458	484	507	536	572
Radio and television	59	91	103	114	128	141
Electric, gas, and sanitary services	837	991	1,005	1,033	1,056	1,087
Electric services	609	696	701	718	728	743
Gas services	165	205	212	220	230	240
Sanitary services	63	89	92	95	99	105
Wholesale trade	286	379	405	435	465	497
Retail trade	391	514	550	582	618	665
Finance, insurance, and real estate	7,466	9,481	9,986	10,555	11,246	12,032
Depository institutions	236	268	275	285	299	308
Nondepository institutions	114	166	192	210	234	254
Security and commodity brokers	40	63	69	76	85	95
Insurance carriers	89	139	146	155	166	177
Insurance agents, brokers, and service	8	13	14	16	17	19
Real estate	6,944	8,779	9,232	9,747	10,369	11,091
Owner-occupied housing	4,337	5,718	6,050	6,396	6,827	7,356
Tenant-occupied housing	1,640	1,880	1,953	2,048	2,153	2,255
Other	967	1,102	1,229	1,303	1,389	1,480
Holding and other investment offices	35	52	59	66	77	88
Services	552	739	786	848	920	1,015
Hotels and other lodging places	105	125	136	147	160	173
Personal services	27	27	27	28	29	31
Business services	99	131	139	155	178	214
Auto repair, services, and parking	62	111	119	122	128	135
Miscellaneous repair services	9	12	13	14	15	16
Motion pictures	16	28	31	35	38	42
Amusement and recreation services	34	47	50	54	57	60
Other services	200	257	272	292	316	343
Health services	98	135	143	153	166	179
Legal services	18	19	20	21	22	24
Educational services	11	14	15	16	17	19
Other [1]	73	90	94	102	110	122

[1] Consists of social services, membership organizations, and miscellaneous professional services.

Source: U.S. Bureau of Economic Analysis, *Survey of Current Business*, September 2000.

No. 750. Gross Private Domestic Investment in Current and Real (1996) Dollars: 1990 to 2000

[In billions of dollars (861.7 represents $861,700,000,000)]

Item	1990	1994	1995	1996	1997	1998	1999	2000
CURRENT DOLLARS								
Gross private domestic investment . . .	861.7	1,097.1	1,143.8	1,242.7	1,390.5	1,538.7	1,636.7	1,767.5
Less: Consumption of fixed capital	579.5	714.6	743.6	781.9	832.4	884.3	953.3	1,029.9
Equals: Net private domestic investment .	282.2	382.5	400.1	460.8	558.1	654.4	683.4	737.6
Fixed investment	847.2	1,034.6	1,110.7	1,212.7	1,327.7	1,465.6	1,578.2	1,718.1
Less: Consumption of fixed capital . . .	579.5	714.6	743.6	781.9	832.4	884.3	953.3	1,029.9
Equals: Net fixed investment	267.7	320.0	367.1	430.8	495.2	581.3	624.9	688.2
Nonresidential.	630.3	748.6	825.1	899.4	999.4	1,101.2	1,174.6	1,293.1
Residential.	216.8	286.0	285.6	313.3	328.2	364.4	403.5	425.1
Change in private inventories	14.5	62.6	33.0	30.0	62.9	73.1	58.6	49.4
CHAINED (1996) DOLLARS								
Gross private domestic investment . . .	907.3	1,107.0	1,140.6	1,242.7	1,393.3	1,558.0	1,660.1	1,772.9
Less: Consumption of fixed capital	612.6	724.3	742.6	781.9	831.8	894.7	967.9	1,036.2
Equals: Net private domestic investment .	294.7	382.8	398.0	460.8	561.5	663.3	692.2	736.7
Fixed investment	894.6	1,045.9	1,109.2	1,212.7	1,328.6	1,480.0	1,595.4	1,716.2
Nonresidential.	641.7	744.6	817.5	899.4	1,009.3	1,135.9	1,228.6	1,350.7
Residential.	253.5	302.7	291.7	313.3	319.7	345.1	368.3	371.4
Change in private inventories	16.5	66.8	30.4	30.0	63.8	76.7	62.1	50.6

Source: U.S. Bureau of Economic Analysis, *National Income and Product Accounts, Volume 1, 1929-94*, and *Survey of Current Business*, August 1997, and August 2001.

No. 751. Capital Expenditures: 1998 and 1999

[In millions of dollars (970,897 represents $970,897,000,000). Based on the North American Industry Classification System (NAICS), see text, this section]

Item	NAICS code	All companies		Companies with employees		Nonemployer businesses	
		1998	1999	1998	1999	1998	1999
STRUCTURES AND EQUIPMENT							
Total	(X)	970,897	1,038,150	896,452	965,828	74,445	72,321
Structures	(X)	329,111	320,849	300,283	294,558	28,828	26,291
New	(X)	284,491	297,443	260,008	277,041	24,483	20,402
Used	(X)	44,620	23,406	40,275	17,517	4,345	5,889
Equipment	(X)	641,786	717,301	596,169	671,270	45,617	46,030
New	(X)	606,210	679,825	570,397	646,616	35,813	33,209
Used	(X)	35,577	37,476	25,773	24,655	9,804	12,821
CAPITAL LEASE AND CAPITALIZED INTEREST EXPENSES							
Capital leases.	(X)	16,533	17,736	15,631	17,190	902	546
Capitalized interest	(X)	(NA)	(NA)	9,799	9,611	(NA)	(NA)
INDUSTRY							
Total expenditures	(X)	(NA)	(NA)	896,452	965,828	(NA)	(NA)
Forestry, fishing, and agricultural services . . .	113-115	(NA)	(NA)	854	1,716	(NA)	(NA)
Mining.	21	(NA)	(NA)	40,424	30,536	(NA)	(NA)
Utilities	22	(NA)	(NA)	36,010	44,622	(NA)	(NA)
Construction.	23	(NA)	(NA)	26,867	23,110	(NA)	(NA)
Manufacturing.	31-33	(NA)	(NA)	203,587	196,013	(NA)	(NA)
Durable goods.	321, 327, 33	(NA)	(NA)	117,901	116,168	(NA)	(NA)
Nondurable goods	31, 322-326	(NA)	(NA)	85,685	79,845	(NA)	(NA)
Wholesale trade	42	(NA)	(NA)	29,169	33,434	(NA)	(NA)
Retail trade	44-45	(NA)	(NA)	57,276	63,661	(NA)	(NA)
Transportation and warehousing	48-49	(NA)	(NA)	51,287	55,128	(NA)	(NA)
Information.	51	(NA)	(NA)	96,487	120,237	(NA)	(NA)
Finance and insurance	52	(NA)	(NA)	118,173	127,168	(NA)	(NA)
Real estate and rental and leasing	53	(NA)	(NA)	85,184	97,621	(NA)	(NA)
Professional, scientific, and technical services	54	(NA)	(NA)	22,277	29,334	(NA)	(NA)
Management of companies and enterprises . .	55	(NA)	(NA)	1,821	6,687	(NA)	(NA)
Admin/support waste mgt/remediation services	56	(NA)	(NA)	13,110	17,199	(NA)	(NA)
Educational services	61	(NA)	(NA)	12,983	13,533	(NA)	(NA)
Health care and social assistance	62	(NA)	(NA)	47,109	51,294	(NA)	(NA)
Arts, entertainment, and recreation	71	(NA)	(NA)	8,994	12,946	(NA)	(NA)
Accommodation and food services	72	(NA)	(NA)	20,822	23,223	(NA)	(NA)
Other services (except public administration) .	81	(NA)	(NA)	20,627	16,140	(NA)	(NA)
Structure and equipment expenditures serving multiple industry categories.	(X)	(NA)	(NA)	3,392	2,225	(NA)	(NA)

NA Not available.   X Not applicable.

Source: U.S. Census Bureau, *Annual Capital Expenditures, 1999*, Series ACE.

No. 752. Composite Indexes of Leading, Coincident, and Lagging Economic Indicators: 1990 to 2000

Item	Unit	1990	1995	1997	1998	1999	2000
Leading index, composite	1996=100. . .	95.4	98.2	102.9	105.4	108.8	110.0
Average weekly hours, manufacturing. . .	Hours	40.8	41.6	42.0	41.8	41.7	41.6
Average weekly initial claims for unemployment insurance	1,000.	386.3	358.6	320.1	315.6	296.2	301.8
Manufacturers' new orders, consumer goods and materials (1996 dol.).	Mil. dol.	128,882	152,881	166,079	169,335	180,434	182,903
Vendor performance, slower deliveries diffusion index	Percent	47.9	52.8	53.9	51.1	53.2	53.3
Manufacturers' new orders, nondefense capital goods (1996 dol.)	Mil. dol.	36,515	40,986	47,870	51,315	54,711	63,333
Building permits, new private housing units	1,000.	1,155	1,336	1,442	1,619	1,664	1,602
Stock prices, 500 common stocks	1941-43=10 .	334.6	541.6	872.7	1,084.3	1,326.1	1,426.8
Money supply, M2 (1996 dol.)	Bil. dol.	3,770	3,644	3,846	4,083	4,318	4,475
Interest rate spread, 10-year Treasury bonds less federal funds	Percent	0.45	0.74	0.89	-0.09	0.67	-0.21
Index of consumer expectations	1966:1=100 .	70.2	83.2	97.7	98.3	99.3	102.7
Coincident index, composite.	1996=100. . .	88.7	97.2	103.9	108.3	112.1	115.8
Employees on nonagricultural payrolls	1,000.	109,404	117,188	122,676	125,845	128,901	131,757
Personal income less transfer payments (1996 dol.).	Bil. dol.	5,032	5,446	5,858	6,221	6,465	6,719
Industrial production	1992=100. . .	98.9	114.3	127.6	133.7	139.2	147.0
Manufacturing and trade sales (1996 dol.).	Mil. dol.	593,865	699,548	767,882	811,825	866,163	906,024
Lagging index, composite	1996=100. . .	101.8	98.8	100.4	102.0	103.3	106.1
Average duration of unemployment	Weeks.	12.0	16.6	15.8	14.5	13.4	12.6
Inventories to sales ratio, manufacturing and trade (1996 dol.) . . .	Ratio	1.47	1.41	1.36	1.36	1.32	1.31
Change in labor cost per unit of output, manufacturing	Percent	2.8	-2.4	-3.7	-0.1	-1.2	-1.3
Average prime rate	Percent	10.01	8.83	8.44	8.35	7.99	9.23
Commercial and industrial loans outstanding (1996 dol.)	Mil. dol.	603,150	559,563	601,346	682,686	751,479	845,121
Consumer installment credit to personal income ratio.	Percent	16.1	16.6	17.5	17.2	17.4	17.7
Change in consumer price index for services	Percent	5.8	3.4	2.9	2.5	2.5	3.8

Source: The Conference Board, New York, NY 10022-6601, *Business Cycle Indicators*, monthly (copyright).

No. 753. Business Cycle Expansions and Contractions—Months of Duration: 1919 to 2000

[A trough is the low point of a business cycle; a peak is the high point. Contraction, or recession, is the period from peak to subsequent trough; expansion is the period from trough to subsequent peak. Business cycle reference dates are determined by the National Bureau of Economic Research, Inc.]

Business cycle reference date				Contraction (trough from previous peak)	Expansion (trough to peak)	Length of cycle	
Trough		Peak				Trough from previous trough	Peak from previous peak
Month	Year	Month	Year				
March.	1919	January	1920	[1]7	10	[2]51	[1]17
July	1921	May.	1923	18	22	28	40
July	1924	October	1926	14	27	36	41
November	1927	August.	1929	13	21	40	34
March.	1933	May.	1937	43	50	64	93
June.	1938	February	1945	13	80	63	93
October	1945	November	1948	8	37	88	45
October	1949	July.	1953	11	45	48	56
May	1954	August.	1957	10	39	55	49
April	1958	April	1960	8	24	47	32
February	1961	December	1969	10	106	34	116
November	1970	November	1973	11	36	117	47
March.	1975	January	1980	16	58	52	74
July	1980	July.	1981	6	12	64	18
November	1982	July.	1990	16	92	28	108
March.	1991	(X)	(X)	8	(X)	100	(X)
Average, all cycles:							
1854 to 1991 (31 cycles).				18	35	53	[3]53
1854 to 1919 (16 cycles).				22	27	48	[4]49
1919 to 1945 (six cycles).				18	35	53	53
1945 to 1991 (nine cycles).				11	50	61	61
Average, peacetime cycles:							
1854 to 1991 (26 cycles).				19	29	48	[5]48
1854 to 1919 (14 cycles).				22	24	46	[6]47
1919 to 1945 (5 cycles) .				20	26	46	45
1945 to 1991 (7 cycles) .				11	43	53	53

X Not applicable. [1] Previous peak: August 1918. [2] Previous trough: December 1914. [3] 30 cycles. [4] 15 cycles. [5] 25 cycles. [6] 13 cycles.

Source: National Bureau of Economic Research, Inc., Cambridge, MA, "US Business Cycle Expansions and Contractions"; <http://www.nber.org/cycles.html>; (accessed: 17 August 2001).

No. 754. Industrial Production Indexes by Industry: 1990 to 2000

[1992=100. Data based on 1987 Standard Industrial Classification (SIC)]

Industry	SIC code	1990	1991	1993	1994	1995	1996	1997	1998	1999	2000
Total Index	(X)	98.9	97.0	103.5	109.1	114.3	119.6	127.7	134.0	139.6	147.5
Manufacturing	(D)	98.5	96.2	103.7	109.9	115.7	121.4	130.8	138.2	144.8	153.6
Durable goods	(X)	99.0	95.5	105.7	114.6	124.2	134.7	148.8	162.3	175.6	193.4
Lumber and products	24	101.6	94.5	100.8	105.9	107.9	110.5	114.1	118.7	122.4	118.2
Furniture and fixtures	25	100.9	94.8	105.6	108.9	112.2	114.0	122.3	131.1	137.0	142.9
Stone, clay, and glass products	32	105.0	97.2	101.9	107.9	110.8	117.8	121.8	127.6	131.6	134.5
Primary metals	33	104.0	96.7	105.1	113.7	116.2	119.6	125.4	127.8	130.4	133.5
Iron and steel	331,2	106.4	96.0	105.9	114.3	116.5	118.9	123.8	124.6	126.7	131.0
Fabricated metal products	34	101.2	96.2	104.4	112.2	116.4	120.1	126.1	130.3	131.9	135.5
Industrial, commercial machinery [1]	35	100.1	95.4	110.2	124.5	144.0	160.2	177.1	195.2	219.0	252.6
Computer and office equipment	357	81.4	82.3	122.2	152.2	211.6	301.8	421.9	593.9	936.6	1,343.6
Electrical machinery	36	87.7	89.6	109.8	131.4	165.9	206.6	264.3	321.0	399.4	550.8
Transportation equipment	37	102.3	96.5	104.4	108.4	108.0	109.6	119.0	128.8	131.4	130.9
Motor vehicles and parts	371	95.3	88.5	114.9	132.9	136.3	136.3	147.0	152.4	165.8	170.5
Autos and light trucks	371pt	99.3	91.0	113.0	129.4	128.2	128.8	137.4	104.6	153.8	153.0
Aerospace and miscellaneous	372-6,9	109.8	105.0	93.9	84.8	80.8	83.8	92.0	106.3	98.9	93.8
Instruments	38	98.4	99.8	100.8	99.7	103.2	108.0	110.5	114.9	119.7	122.2
Nondurable goods	(X)	97.9	97.0	101.6	104.8	106.6	107.4	112.3	114.4	115.4	116.9
Foods	20	97.0	98.4	102.0	103.6	105.7	105.3	107.0	110.8	112.5	114.6
Tobacco products	21	105.4	98.9	84.2	104.4	111.8	113.5	111.6	108.2	97.1	95.3
Textile mill products	22	93.2	92.7	105.2	110.6	110.1	108.6	108.9	107.6	104.0	100.1
Paper and products	26	96.0	96.8	103.4	107.0	107.6	107.3	113.3	115.1	117.2	116.1
Printing and publishing	27	103.1	99.1	100.5	100.6	101.2	101.8	107.6	107.4	106.8	110.0
Chemicals and products	28	97.3	96.4	101.1	103.9	106.1	108.4	116.8	121.4	126.1	128.3
Petroleum and products	29	100.3	99.1	102.9	102.7	104.5	106.9	111.1	113.6	115.3	117.0
Rubber and plastics products	30	92.2	90.7	106.9	116.5	119.7	123.3	131.8	136.3	139.7	142.2
Leather and products	31	107.8	98.4	100.9	93.6	87.0	88.0	87.1	78.7	72.9	69.7
Mining	C	104.8	102.6	100.0	102.3	102.0	103.5	105.3	103.0	98.0	99.9
Metal mining	10	93.1	93.3	98.7	100.5	101.8	104.3	108.8	108.1	99.9	96.8
Coal mining	12	103.7	100.1	94.0	103.0	102.6	105.0	108.2	109.7	107.8	108.9
Oil and gas extraction	13	106.4	104.7	101.1	101.6	100.4	101.6	102.6	98.7	92.5	95.0
Stone and earth minerals	14	103.3	96.7	102.3	108.6	112.9	114.9	120.1	123.9	124.9	126.1
Utilities	(X)	98.3	100.4	104.0	105.4	109.1	112.7	112.8	114.1	117.1	121.0
Electric	491,3pt	99.2	101.2	103.9	105.6	109.6	112.8	113.4	117.3	120.2	124.0
Gas	492.3pt	94.4	97.3	104.3	104.6	107.2	112.3	110.5	102.9	106.1	111.2

X Not applicable.   [1] Includes computer equipment.

Source: Board of Governors of the Federal Reserve System, *Federal Reserve Bulletin*, monthly; and *Industrial Production and Capacity Utilization*, Statistical Release G.17, monthly.

No. 755. Index of Manufacturing Capacity: 1980 to 2000

[1992 output=100. Annual figures are averages of monthly data. Capacity represents estimated quantity of output relative to output in 1992 which the *current* stock of plant and equipment in manufacturing industries was capable of producing. Primary processing industries comprise textiles, lumber, paper and pulp, petroleum, rubber, stone, clay, glass, primary metals, fabricated metals, and a portion of chemicals. Advanced processing industries comprise chemical products, food, beverages, tobacco, apparel, furniture, printing and publishing, leather, machinery, transportation equipment, instruments, ordnance, and miscellaneous industry groups]

Year	Index of capacity	Relation of output to capacity (percent) All manufacturing	Primary processing	Advanced processing	Year	Index of capacity	Relation of output to capacity (percent) All manufacturing	Primary processing	Advanced processing
1980	95	79	77	81	1991	123	78	79	78
1981	98	78	76	80	1992	126	79	82	78
1982	100	72	68	74	1993	129	80	84	79
1983	102	74	74	75	1994	133	82	87	80
1984	105	80	81	79	1995	140	83	86	80
1985	109	79	79	78	1996	149	82	84	80
1986	112	79	79	78	1997	158	83	85	81
1987	114	81	84	80	1998	169	81	82	81
1988	116	84	86	82	1999	179	80	83	79
1989	118	84	85	83	2000	188	81	85	80
1990	121	81	83	81					

Source: Board of Governors of the Federal Reserve System, *Industrial Production and Capacity Utilization*, G.17 (419), monthly.

U.S. Census Bureau, Statistical Abstract of the United States: 2001

No. 756. Manufacturing and Trade—Sales and Inventories: 1992 to 2000

[In billions of dollars (541 represents $541,000,000,000), except ratios. Data reflect changeover to North American Industry Classification System (NAICS)]

Item	1992	1993	1994	1995	1996	1997	1998	1999	2000
Sales, average monthly [1]	**541**	**567**	**610**	**654**	**687**	**723**	**743**	**787**	**843**
Manufacturing	242	252	270	290	300	320	325	337	357
Retail trade	154	165	179	188	200	209	220	239	257
Merchant wholesalers	144	151	161	176	187	195	198	212	230
Inventories [2]	**841**	**868**	**931**	**990**	**1,009**	**1,050**	**1,084**	**1,139**	**1,205**
Manufacturing	379	380	401	425	431	444	452	462	484
Retail trade	268	286	312	330	340	351	364	392	418
Merchant wholesalers	194	202	219	235	238	255	268	284	303
Inventory-sales ratios [3]	**1.53**	**1.51**	**1.47**	**1.48**	**1.46**	**1.42**	**1.44**	**1.41**	**1.40**
Manufacturing	1.56	1.51	1.44	1.44	1.43	1.37	1.39	1.35	1.33
Retail trade	1.68	1.69	1.67	1.73	1.68	1.65	1.63	1.59	1.58
Merchant wholesalers	1.31	1.31	1.30	1.30	1.28	1.27	1.33	1.30	1.29

[1] Averages of monthly not seasonally adjusted figures. [2] Seasonally adjusted end-of-year data. [3] Averages of seasonally adjusted monthly ratios.

Source: U.S. Council of Economic Advisors, *Economic Indicators*, May 2001.

No. 757. Manufacturing Corporations—Number, Assets, and Profits by Asset Size: 1990 to 2000

[Corporations and assets as of end of 4th quarter; profits for entire year. (2,629,458 represents $2,629,458,000,000). For corporations above a certain asset value based on complete canvass. The asset value for complete canvass was raised in 1988 to $50 million and in 1995 to $250 million. Asset sizes less than these values are sampled, except as noted. For details regarding methodology, see source for first quarter, 1988]

Year	Unit	Total	Under $10 mil. [1]	$10-$25 mil.	$25-$50 mil.	$50-$100 mil.	$100-$250 mil.	$250 mil.-$1 bil.	$1 bil. and over
Corporations:									
1990	Number	(NA)	(NA)	(NA)	(NA)	834	774	597	367
1995	Number	(NA)	(NA)	(NA)	(NA)	574	639	727	447
1996	Number	(NA)	(NA)	(NA)	(NA)	532	620	745	484
1997	Number	(NA)	(NA)	(NA)	(NA)	470	615	748	529
1998	Number	(NA)	(NA)	(NA)	(NA)	416	531	753	549
1999	Number	(NA)	(NA)	(NA)	(NA)	438	486	730	601
2000	Number	(NA)	(NA)	(NA)	(NA)	450	499	722	635
Assets:									
1990	Mil. dol	2,629,458	142,4·9	74,477	55,914	72,554	123,967	287,512	1,872,536
1995	Mil. dol	3,345,229	155,618	87,011	68,538	87,262	159,133	370,263	2,417,403
1996	Mil. dol	3,574,407	163,928	87,096	69,722	93,205	156,702	398,651	2,605,102
1997	Mil. dol	3,746,797	167,921	87,398	76,034	85,186	157,130	397,559	2,775,570
1998	Mil. dol	3,967,309	170,068	87,937	69,627	86,816	148,060	419,153	2,985,647
1999	Mil. dol	4,382,814	170,058	85,200	67,352	97,810	138,143	398,881	3,425,370
2000	Mil. dol	4,842,118	172,731	86,182	72,544	92,355	149,221	391,820	3,877,265
Net profit: [2]									
1990	Mil. dol	110,128	8,527	5,160	2,769	2,661	3,525	7,110	80,377
1995	Mil. dol	198,151	13,224	5,668	3,767	5,771	7,000	16,549	146,172
1996	Mil. dol	224,869	15,802	6,872	4,266	5,664	7,935	16,059	168,271
1997	Mil. dol	244,505	17,948	8,383	4,153	4,675	7,074	18,433	183,836
1998	Mil. dol	234,386	18,350	6,421	3,790	4,681	5,610	14,364	181,170
1999	Mil. dol	257,805	17,398	7,618	3,504	4,798	4,795	12,756	206,934
2000	Mil. dol	276,714	16,758	6,794	3,427	2,891	3,687	15,983	227,173

NA Not available. [1] Excludes estimates for corporations with less than $250,000 in assets at time of sample selection. [2] After taxes.

Source: U.S. Census Bureau, *Quarterly Financial Report for Manufacturing, Mining and Trade Corporations*.

No. 758. Corporate Profits, Taxes, and Dividends: 1990 to 2000

[In billions of dollars (409 represents $409,000,000,000). Covers corporations organized for profit and other entities treated as corporations. Represents profits to U.S. residents, without deduction of depletion charges and exclusive of capital gains and losses; intercorporate dividends from profits of domestic corporations are eliminated; net receipts of dividends, reinvested earnings of incorporated foreign affiliates, and earnings of unincorporated foreign affiliates are added]

Item	1990	1995	1996	1997	1998	1999	2000
Corporate profits with IVA and CCA..	409	669	754	834	815	856	946
Corporate profits with IVA	389	650	729	801	775	814	913
Profits before tax	402	668	726	792	758	823	926
Profits tax liability	141	211	224	237	245	256	284
Profits after tax	261	458	503	555	514	567	641
Dividends	166	254	298	335	352	371	397
Undistributed profits	95	203	205	220	162	196	244
Inventory valuation adjustment (IVA)	-13	-18	3	8	17	-9	-13
Capital consumption adjustment (CCA)	20	19	25	33	40	42	34
Addenda:							
Corporate profits after tax with IVA/CCA [1] . .	268	458	530	597	570	600	662
Net cash flow with inventory IVA/CCA [1]	494	716	776	843	843	906	1,005
Undistributed profits with IVA/CCA [1]	102	204	233	261	219	229	265
Consumption of fixed capital	391	512	544	582	624	677	739
Less: Inventory valuation adjustment (IVA) . .	-13	-18	3	8	17	-9	-13
Equals: Net cash flow	506	734	773	834	826	915	1,017

[1] Inventory valuation adjustment/capital consumption adjustment.

Source: U.S. Bureau of Economic Analysis, *National Income and Product Accounts of the United States, 1929-97,* forthcoming, and *Survey of Current Business,* July 2001.

No. 759. Corporate Profits Before Taxes by Industry: 1990 to 1999

[In millions of dollars (401,534 represents $401,534,000,000). Profits are without inventory valuation and capital consumption adjustments. Based on the 1987 Standard Industrial Classification Code. See headnote, Table 758]

Industry	1990	1993	1994	1995	1996	1997	1998	1999
Corporate profits before tax . . .	401,534	510,375	573,406	668,454	726,345	792,396	758,172	822,976
Domestic industries.	328,812	433,634	496,168	576,442	625,492	681,706	654,672	711,560
Agriculture, forestry, and fishing	1,638	1,911	1,385	1,842	2,950	3,059	3,104	4,355
Mining.	2,502	1,509	3,348	4,517	8,124	10,972	3,184	2,376
Construction.	10,922	10,148	13,650	17,265	21,932	25,696	32,758	36,229
Manufacturing.	113,552	107,711	144,709	172,518	175,789	192,312	167,600	183,909
Transportation and public utilities	45,931	69,300	82,954	85,894	92,023	83,991	82,532	89,700
Transportation	954	6,368	10,316	11,613	16,157	18,639	22,148	24,470
Communications	20,049	33,202	36,837	33,604	35,012	25,570	22,966	26,641
Electric, gas, and sanitary services . . .	24,928	29,730	35,801	40,677	40,854	39,782	37,418	38,589
Wholesale trade	21,201	30,614	36,883	35,546	41,588	46,315	50,905	58,455
Retail trade	24,896	41,831	49,187	47,471	54,806	62,648	76,512	84,784
Finance, insurance, and real estate	88,334	129,104	117,726	160,062	171,827	195,658	180,922	190,752
Services	19,836	41,506	46,326	51,327	56,453	61,055	57,155	61,000
Rest of the world [1]	72,722	76,741	77,238	92,012	100,853	110,690	103,500	111,416

[1] Consists of receipts by all U.S. residents, including both corporations and persons, , dividends from their incorporated foreign affiliates, their share of reinvested earnings of their incorporated foreign affiliates, and earnings of unincorporated foreign affiliates, net of corresponding payments.

No. 760. Corporate Profits With Inventory Valuation and Capital Consumption Adjustments—Financial and Nonfinancial Industries: 1990 to 2000

[In billions of dollars (408.6 represents $408,600,000,000). See headnote, Table 758]

Item	1990	1994	1995	1996	1997	1998	1999	2000
Corporate profits with IVA/CCA [1] . .	408.6	573.2	668.8	754.0	833.8	815.0	856.0	946.2
Domestic industries.	335.9	496.0	576.8	653.2	723.1	711.5	744.6	805.0
Rest of the world	72.7	77.2	92.0	100.9	110.7	103.5	111.4	141.2
Corporate profits with IVA [1]	388.6	561.0	650.2	729.4	800.8	775.1	813.9	912.7
Domestic industries.	315.9	483.7	558.2	628.6	690.2	671.6	702.5	771.5
Financial	91.6	114.7	154.3	165.3	185.7	164.8	172.0	193.6
Nonfinancial	224.3	369.0	403.8	463.3	504.5	506.8	530.4	577.9
Manufacturing	109.2	139.6	166.1	181.2	195.2	177.4	181.6	185.0
Transportation and public utilities . . .	44.4	82.9	85.8	91.4	85.0	83.9	88.4	100.8
Wholesale trade.	19.1	33.1	29.4	42.6	49.2	56.4	56.7	65.1
Retail trade	21.0	46.6	44.1	52.9	63.9	76.6	81.5	89.5
Other.	30.6	66.8	78.5	95.2	111.2	112.6	122.3	137.5
Rest of the world	72.7	77.2	92.0	100.9	110.7	103.5	111.4	141.2

[1] Inventory valuation adjustment and capital consumption adjustment.

Source of Tables , 59-760: U.S. Bureau of Economic Analysis, *National Income and Product Accounts of the United States, 1929-97,* forthcoming, and *Survey of Current Business,* July 2001.

Business Enterprise 501

[Averages of quarterly figures at annual rates. Manufacturing data exclude estimates for corporations with less than $250,000 in assets at time of sample selection. Data are not necessarily comparable from year to year due to changes in accounting procedures, industry classifications, sampling procedures, etc.; for detail, see source. Based on sample; see source for discussion of methodology. Based on Standard Industrial Classification code; see text, this section. Minus sign (-) indicates loss]

Industry	Ratio of profits to stockholders' equity (percent)				Profits per dollar of sales (cents)				Ratio of stockholders' equity to debt			
	1990	1995	1999	2000	1990	1995	1999	2000	1990	1995	1999	2000
Manufacturing corporations	10.6	16.0	16.4	15.3	3.9	5.6	6.2	6.2	1.3	1.4	1.3	1.4
Durable goods	7.9	15.4	16.2	12.8	3.0	5.2	6.1	5.4	1.6	1.8	1.6	1.7
Lumber and wood products	(NA)	12.6	24.5	9.5	(NA)	3.5	5.5	2.4	(NA)	1.8	1.1	1.2
Furniture and fixtures	(NA)	7.9	17.6	12.4	(NA)	2.2	4.4	3.1	(NA)	1.7	1.2	1.1
Stone, clay, and glass products	5.2	12.2	20.1	9.1	1.7	4.4	7.1	3.9	0.8	1.1	1.0	1.2
Primary metal industries	9.2	19.0	6.1	5.6	2.5	5.4	2.2	1.8	1.1	1.3	1.1	1.0
Iron and steel	6.1	14.8	0.7	-2.7	0.9	3.9	0.2	-0.9	0.6	1.3	1.0	0.9
Nonferrous metals	10.2	22.1	10.7	12.1	3.9	6.7	4.2	4.5	1.7	1.3	1.3	1.2
Fabricated metal products	11.7	13.0	18.2	14.9	3.3	3.5	5.9	4.8	1.3	1.2	1.2	1.2
Machinery, exc. electrical	8.1	12.1	14.8	15.4	4.3	4.3	5.8	6.4	2.2	1.8	1.8	1.7
Electrical and electronic equipment	7.5	18.8	13.3	12.1	3.0	8.3	7.5	8.4	1.6	2.4	2.4	3.2
Transportation equipment	3.8	17.4	23.6	13.2	1.2	4.5	5.7	3.6	1.9	2.1	1.3	1.3
Motor vehicles and equipment	-1.0	21.0	24.5	12.3	-0.5	4.7	5.4	3.1	2.2	2.6	1.3	1.2
Aircraft, guided missiles and parts	11.5	10.6	21.9	14.1	3.4	3.6	6.5	4.7	1.6	1.7	1.3	1.3
Instruments and related products	12.8	13.7	16.5	15.1	6.5	7.6	9.3	8.9	1.6	2.3	1.4	1.7
Miscellaneous manufacturing	(NA)	11.1	12.8	11.0	(NA)	3.2	4.1	3.5	(NA)	1.7	1.0	1.0
Nondurable goods	13.1	16.6	16.8	18.8	4.8	6.0	6.4	7.0	1.2	1.2	1.1	1.1
Food and kindred products [1]	16.1	18.4	24.1	24.3	4.0	5.4	6.4	6.4	0.8	1.0	0.8	0.8
Textile mill products	2.7	4.9	4.0	-2.7	0.6	1.3	1.1	-0.6	0.7	0.9	0.8	0.6
Apparel (includes leather)	(NA)	12.5	12.9	15.9	(NA)	2.7	2.8	3.3	(NA)	1.1	1.0	0.9
Paper and allied products	10.6	20.9	11.2	10.8	4.2	6.9	4.1	4.0	1.1	0.9	0.9	0.9
Printing and publishing	8.2	14.8	19.9	15.9	3.6	6.1	7.3	6.2	1.2	1.3	1.0	1.0
Chemicals and allied products	16.8	21.0	18.8	18.7	7.9	9.1	9.0	8.8	1.4	1.2	1.1	1.1
Industrial	13.1	16.2	11.1	11.1	6.6	6.6	5.0	5.0	1.4	1.0	0.8	0.9
Drugs	27.1	26.7	28.2	26.5	15.7	14.4	15.0	14.0	2.2	1.4	1.5	1.7
Residual of chemicals	(NA)	20.3	12.4	14.6	(NA)	7.6	5.6	6.1	(NA)	1.3	1.0	0.8
Petroleum and coal products	12.7	10.6	11.0	22.8	5.6	4.9	6.0	10.3	1.7	1.7	2.0	2.4
Rubber and misc. plastics products	6.9	15.3	13.2	9.4	1.8	4.1	3.8	2.6	1.0	1.3	1.0	1.0
Mining corporations [2]	8.2	2.1	1.9	13.0	5.8	1.9	1.7	10.8	1.3	1.4	1.1	1.3
Retail trade corporations [2]	8.4	10.0	14.8	10.8	1.0	1.1	2.6	1.9	0.6	1.0	1.1	1.1
Wholesale trade corporations [2]	5.0	9.1	9.0	10.1	0.6	1.2	1.3	1.5	1.0	0.8	1.1	1.1

NA Not available. [1] Tobacco included in food and kindred products. [2] Includes estimates for corporations with assets of $50 million and over at time of sample selection.

No. 762. Manufacturing Corporations—Selected Finances: 1980 to 2000

[In billions of dollars (1,913 represents $1,913,000,000,000). Data are not necessarily comparable from year to year due to changes in accounting procedures, industry classifications, sampling procedures, etc.; for detail, see source]

Year	All manufacturing corps.					Durable goods industries					Nondurable goods industries				
	Sales	Profits [1] Before taxes	After taxes	Stockholders' equity [1]	Debt [2]	Sales	Profits [1] Before taxes	After taxes	Stockholders' equity [1]	Debt [2]	Sales	Profits [1] Before taxes	After taxes	Stockholders' equity [1]	Debt [2]
1980	1,913	146	93	668	292	889	57	36	318	143	1,024	88	57	350	149
1985	2,331	137	88	866	454	1,143	62	39	421	167	1,189	76	49	445	267
1986	2,221	129	83	875	501	1,126	52	33	436	168	1,095	77	51	438	298
1987	2,378	173	116	901	553	1,178	78	53	444	229	1,200	95	63	457	324
1988	2,596	215	154	958	622	1,285	92	67	469	265	1,312	124	87	489	357
1989	2,745	188	135	999	733	1,357	75	56	501	308	1,389	113	80	498	425
1990	2,811	158	110	1,044	782	1,357	57	41	515	328	1,454	101	69	529	453
1991	2,761	99	66	1,064	814	1,304	14	7	507	338	1,457	85	59	557	476
1992 [3]	2,890	31	22	1,035	819	1,390	-34	-24	474	335	1,500	65	46	561	485
1993	3,015	118	83	1,040	819	1,490	39	27	483	327	1,525	79	56	557	492
1994	3,256	244	175	1,110	815	1,658	121	87	533	316	1,598	123	88	577	500
1995	3,528	275	198	1,241	862	1,808	131	94	614	333	1,721	144	104	627	529
1996	3,758	307	225	1,348	920	1,942	147	106	674	366	1,816	160	119	674	554
1997	3,922	331	244	1,464	953	2,076	167	121	744	386	1,847	164	123	721	566
1998	3,949	315	234	1,487	1,065	2,169	175	128	794	458	1,781	140	107	694	607
1999	4,149	355	258	1,637	1,199	2,314	199	140	928	551	1,835	157	117	709	648
2000	4,506	385	277	1,881	1,306	2,455	192	133	1,095	612	2,050	193	144	786	694

[1] Beginning 1998, profits before and after income taxes reflect inclusion of minority stockholders' interest in net income before and after income taxes. [2] Annual data are average debt for the year (using four end-of-quarter figures). [3] Data for 1992 (most significantly 1992:I qtr.) reflect the early adoption of Financial Accounting Standards Board Statement 106 (Employer's Accounting for Post-Retirement Benefits Other Than Pensions) by a large number of companies during the fourth quarter of 1992. Data for 1993: I qtr. also reflect adoption of Statement 106. Corporations must show the cumulative effect of a change in accounting principle in the first quarter of the year in which the change is adopted.

Source of Tables 761 and 762: 1980, U.S. Federal Trade Commission; thereafter, U.S. Census Bureau, *Quarterly Financial Report for Manufacturing, Mining, and Trade Corporations.* In U.S. Council of Economic Advisers, *Economic Report of the President,* annual.

No. 763. U.S. Multinational Companies—Gross Product: 1995 and 1998

[In millions of dollars (1,831,046 represents $1,831,046,000,000). Gross product measures valued added by a firm. Consists of nonbank U.S. parent companies and their nonbank foreign affiliates. A U.S. parent comprises the domestic operations of a multinational and is a U.S. person that owns or controls 10 percent or more of the voting securities, or the equivalent, of a foreign business enterprise. A U.S. person can be an incorporated business enterprise. A majority-owned foreign affiliate is a foreign business enterprise in which a U.S. parent company owns or controls 50 percent or more of the voting securities]

Industry	U.S. multinationals		U.S. parents		Majority-owned foreign affiliates	
	1995	1998	1995	1998	1995	1998
All industries.	1,831,046	2,119,380	1,365,470	1,608,645	465,576	510,735
Petroleum [1] . . . . , .	205,044	178,398	110,014	95,015	95,030	83,383
Petroleum and coal products [1]	181,124	139,515	90,232	71,839	90,892	67,676
Integrated refining and extraction	174,012	128,700	84,397	62,324	89,615	66,376
Manufacturing	1,023,697	1,107,546	723,182	788,728	300,515	318,818
Food and kindred products [1]	119,282	119,270	78,223	77,328	41,059	41,942
Beverages	67,783	67,886	41,797	40,438	25,986	27,448
Chemical and allied products [1]	182,827	204,906	116,949	128,339	65,878	76,567
Industrial chemicals	66,480	58,653	42,625	37,925	23,855	20,728
Drugs . . . . ,	73,723	92,709	46,894	55,785	26,829	36,924
Industrial machinery and equipment [1]	139,767	147,612	88,818	89,822	50,949	57,790
Computer and office equipment . . . . , ...	74,748	76,197	39,934	37,910	34,814	38,287
Electronic and other electric equipment [1]	103,693	117,095	77,286	91,818	26,407	25,277
Electronic components and accessories. . . . , .	51,981	43,946	36,495	33,667	15,486	10,279
Electronic and other electric equipment, nec [2] . .	25,132	35,236	21,236	27,548	3,896	7,688
Transportation equipment	202,108	243,249	152,834	182,179	49,274	61,070
Other manufacturing [1]	216,632	220,388	169,135	175,549	47,497	44,839
Paper and allied products	55,446	49,854	43,995	39,791	11,451	10,063
Instruments and related products	47,134	56,389	33,413	41,858	13,721	14,531
Wholesale trade	39,127	72,431	30,853	54,519	8,274	17,912
Durable goods	23,322	37,487	18,325	28,324	4,997	9,163
Nondurable goods.	15,804	34,943	12,527	26,194	3,277	8,749
Finance (exc dep inst), insurance & real estate [1] . . .	72,489	107,439	52,813	82,725	19,676	24,714
Finance, except depository institutions	22,370	57,166	18,205	47,499	4,165	9,667
Insurance	41,677	43,830	32,815	33,358	8,862	10,472
Services [1]	118,328	175,885	97,623	139,111	20,705	36,774
Business services [1]	51,915	94,395	38,667	67,079	13,248	27,316
Computer and data processing services	24,094	53,987	18,481	38,398	5,613	15,589
Other industries [1]	372,360	477,681	350,984	448,547	21,376	29,134
Transportation	70,372	77,558	67,277	73,691	3,095	3,867
Communication.	121,576	169,004	117,802	163,713	3,774	5,291
Electric, gas, and sanitary services.	73,136	102,384	71,128	96,921	2,008	5,463
Retail trade	85,616	(NA)	77,367	100,173	8,249	(D)

D Figure withheld to avoid disclosure pertaining to a specific organization or individual.   NA Not available.   [1] Includes other industries not shown separately.   [2] Not elsewhere classified.

Source: U.S. Bureau of Economic Analysis, *Survey of Current Business*, September 1998 and July 2000.

No. 764. U.S. Multinational Companies—Selected Characteristics: 1998

[Preliminary. In billions of dollars (9,700 represents $9,700,000,000,000), except as indicated. Consists of nonbank U.S. parent companies and their nonbank foreign affiliates. U.S. parent is a U.S. person that owns or controls directly or indirectly, 10 percent or more of the voting securities of an incorporated foreign business enterprise, or an equivalent interest in an unincorporated foreign business enterprise. A U.S. person can be an incorporated business enterprise. A foreign affiliate is a foreign business enterprise owned or controlled by a U.S. parent company]

Industry [1]	U.S. parents				Foreign affiliates				U.S. exports shipped to foreign affiliates	U.S. imports shipped from foreign affiliates
	Total assets	Sales	Employment (1,000)	Employee compensation	Total assets	Sales	Employment (1,000)	Employee compensation		
All industries.	9,700	5,026	20,068	926	4,001	2,443	8,388	271	217.2	187.6
Petroleum	406	289	436	28	342	340	242	12	5.7	11.1
Manufacturing	2,929	2,300	8,696	478	982	1,087	4,653	141	197.2	158.6
Food and kindred products .	259	239	750	32	129	133	647	15	5.2	3.0
Chemicals and allied products	507	344	966	69	236	201	609	24	23.4	13.1
Primary and fabricated metals.	134	130	629	28	52	44	228	7	3.8	4.6
Industrial machinery and equipment	323	309	1,092	62	131	173	602	22	46.4	36.2
Electronic and electric equipment	269	260	1,092	61	90	110	782	15	35.1	19.2
Transportation equipment. .	924	591	1,771	116	148	242	752	28	63.9	69.6
Other	514	427	2,396	109	196	185	1,032	31	19.3	12.9
Wholesale trade.	228	423	738	34	244	439	601	28	8.6	14.0
Finance (except depository institutions), insurance, real estate	4,227	628	1,200	92	1,794	154	240	14	0.9	0.4
Services	387	266	3,044	95	194	150	1,087	41	1.5	0.6
Other industries	1,522	1,121	5,954	200	444	272	1,566	36	3.3	2.9

[1] Represents industry of U.S. parent or industry of foreign affiliate.

Source: U.S. Bureau of Economic Analysis, *Survey of Current Business*, July 2000.

Business Enterprise   503

No. 765. Gross Product, Employment, and Capital Expenditures of Nonbank U.S. MNCs, U.S. Parents, and Foreign Affiliates: 1990 to 1998

[Gross product and capital expenditures in millions of dollars (1,717,488 represents $1,717,488,000,000); employees in thousands. MNC=Multinational company. MOFA=Majority-owned foreign affiliate. Minus sign (-) indicates decrease]

item	1990	1994	1995	1996	1997	1998	Percent change at annual rates		
							1989-97	1996-97	1997-98
GROSS PRODUCT									
MNCs worldwide:									
Parents and all affiliates .	(NA)	(NA)	(NA)	(NA)	(NA)	(NA)	(NA)	(NA)	(NA)
Parents and MOFAs....	(NA)	1,717,488	1,831,046	1,978,948	2,094,318	2,119,380	5.5	5.8	1.2
Parents	(NA)	1,313,792	1,365,470	1,480,638	1,573,451	1,608,645	5.3	6.3	2.2
Affiliates, total.	(NA)	(NA)	(NA)	(NA)	(NA)	(NA)	(NA)	(NA)	(NA)
MOFAs	356,033	403,696	465,576	498,310	520,867	510,735	6.3	4.5	-1.9
Other.	(NA)	(NA)	(NA)	(NA)	(NA)	(NA)	(NA)	(NA)	(NA)
EMPLOYEES									
MNCs worldwide:									
Parents and all affiliates .	25,264	25,670	25,921	26,334	27,851	28,456	1.2	5.8	2.2
Parents and MOFAs....	23,786	24,273	24,500	24,867	26,358	26,968	1.2	6.0	2.3
Parents	18,430	18,565	18,576	18,790	19,878	20,068	0.7	5.8	1.0
Affiliates, total.	6,834	7,105	7,345	7,544	7,973	8,398	2.3	5.7	5.2
MOFAs	5,356	5,707	5,924	6,077	6,480	6,900	3.0	6.6	6.5
Other.	1,478	1,398	1,421	1,467	1,493	1,488	-0.1	1.8	-0.3
CAPITAL EXPENDITURES									
MNCs worldwide:									
Parents and all affiliates .	(NA)	328,240	(NA)	(NA)	(NA)	(NA)	(NA)	(NA)	(NA)
Parents and MOFAs....	274,614	303,364	323,616	340,510	398,037	419,620	5.4	16.9	5.4
Parents	213,079	231,917	248,017	260,048	309,247	323,181	5.5	18.9	4.5
Affiliates, total.	(NA)	96,323	(NA)	(NA)	(NA)	(NA)	(NA)	(NA)	(NA)
MOFAs	61,535	71,447	75,599	80,462	88,790	96,439	5.3	10.4	8.6
Other.	(NA)	24,876	(NA)	(NA)	(NA)	(NA)	(NA)	(NA)	(NA)

NA Not available.
Source: U.S. Bureau of Economic Analysis, *Survey of Current Business*, July 2000.

No. 766. Nonbank U.S. Multinational Companies—U.S. Parents and MOFAs by Industry: 1995 and 1998

[In billions of dollars (1,365.5 represents $1,365,500,000,000), except as noted. Data are by industry of U.S. parent, except MOFA data for capital expenditures and employees are by industry of affiliate. MOFA=Majority-owned foreign affiliate]

Item	Parents				MOFAs			
	Gross product	Profit-type return	Capital expenditures	Number of employees (1,000)	Gross product	Profit-type return	Capital expenditures	Number of employees (1,000)
1995: All industries	1,365.5	266.3	248.0	18,576	465.6	114.9	75.6	5,924
Petroleum.	110.0	12.6	24.6	472	95.0	19.2	15.7	172
Manufacturing	723.2	145.2	112.2	9,080	300.5	79.4	45.5	4,144
Food and kindred products . .	78.2	20.7	10.5	1,134	41.1	10.4	4.4	530
Chemicals and allied products. .	116.9	29.4	20.0	1,051	65.9	23.0	9.9	662
Primary and fabricated metals. .	39.9	6.2	6.0	564	19.5	4.0	2.4	204
Industrial machinery and equip .	88.8	18.5	10.7	1,128	50.9	13.3	5.2	631
Electronic and other electric equipment	77.3	21.2	19.7	1,058	26.4	8.9	6.2	596
Transportation equipment.	152.8	20.0	21.6	1,708	49.3	8.9	11.2	767
Other manufacturing	169.1	29.1	23.9	2,438	47.5	10.9	6.2	754
Wholesale trade.	30.9	4.3	6.2	500	8.3	2.7	1.1	203
Finance (except depository institutions), insurance and real estate.	52.8	24.6	11.5	1,059	19.7	8.0	3.4	200
Services	97.6	12.5	17.1	2,226	20.7	3.0	2.8	506
Other industries	351.0	67.1	76.4	5,239	21.4	2.5	7.0	699
1998: All industries	1,608.6	351.7	323.2	20,068	510.7	127.7	96.4	6,900
Petroleum.	95.0	8.1	30.0	436	83.4	12.4	22.0	177
Manufacturing	788.7	160.6	127.6	8,696	318.8	88.5	43.1	3,977
Food and kindred products	77.3	22.1	10.2	750	41.9	11.5	4.4	435
Chemicals and allied products. .	128.3	31.2	25.2	966	76.6	31.3	9.5	544
Primary and fabricated metals. .	43.7	7.2	6.2	629	11.3	2.7	1.7	190
Industrial machinery and equip .	89.8	14.1	15.0	1,092	57.8	15.8	5.3	564
Electronic and other electric equipment	91.8	15.4	17.4	1,092	25.3	6.9	6.1	721
Transportation equipment.	182.2	38.8	28.6	1,771	61.1	11.1	8.1	642
Other manufacturing	175.5	31.8	25.1	2,396	44.8	9.2	8.0	882
Wholesale trade.	54.5	8.7	10.8	738	17.9	4.8	5.6	570
Finance (except depository institutions), insurance and real estate.	82.7	43.5	15.2	1,200	24.7	9.3	5.9	222
Services	139.1	23.6	24.6	3,044	36.8	7.3	8.2	963
Other industries	448.5	107.3	114.9	5,954	29.1	5.4	11.6	991

Source: U.S. Bureau of Economic Analysis, *Survey of Current Business*, September 1998 and July 2000.

Section 16
Science and Technology

This section presents statistics on scientific, engineering, and technological resources, with emphasis on patterns of research and development (R&D) funding and on scientific, engineering, and technical personnel; education; and employment. Also included are statistics on space program outlays and accomplishments. Principal sources of these data are the National Science Foundation (NSF) and the National Aeronautics and Space Administration (NASA).

NSF gathers data chiefly through recurring surveys. Current NSF publications containing data on funds for research and development and on scientific and engineering personnel include detailed statistical tables; issue briefs; and annual, biennial, triennial, and special reports. Titles or the areas of coverage of these reports include the following: *Science and Engineering Indicators; National Patterns of R&D Resources; Women, Minorities, and Persons with Disabilities in Science and Engineering*—science and technology data presented in chart and tabular form in a pocket-sized publication—*Federal Funds for Research and Development; Federal R&D Funding by Budget Function; Federal Support to Universities, Colleges, and Selected Nonprofit Institutions; Research and Development in Industry;* R&D expenditures and graduate enrollment and support in academic science and engineering; and characteristics of doctoral scientists and engineers and of recent graduates in the United States. Statistical surveys in these areas pose problems of concept and definition and the data should therefore be regarded as broad estimates rather than precise, quantitative statements. See sources for methodological and technical details.

The National Science Board's biennial *Science and Engineering Indicators* contains data and analysis of international and domestic science and technology, including measures of inputs and outputs.

The *Budget of the United States Government,* published by the U.S. Office of Management and Budget, contains summary financial data on federal R&D programs.

Research and development outlays— NSF defines research as "systematic study directed toward fuller scientific knowledge of the subject studied" and development as "the systematic use of scientific knowledge directed toward the production of useful materials, devices, systems, or methods, including design and development of prototypes and processes." National coverage of R&D expenditures is developed primarily from periodic surveys in four principal economic sectors: (1) *Government,* made up primarily of federal executive agencies; (2) *industry,* consisting of manufacturing and nonmanufacturing firms and the federally funded research and development centers (FFRDCs) they administer; (3) *universities and colleges,* composed of universities, colleges, and their affiliated institutions, agricultural experiment stations, and associated schools of agriculture and of medicine, and FFRDCs administered by educational institutions; and (4) *other nonprofit institutions,* consisting of such organizations as private philanthropic foundations, nonprofit research institutes, voluntary health agencies, and FFRDCs administered by nonprofit organizations. The R&D funds reported consist of current operating costs, including planning and administration costs, except as otherwise noted. They exclude funds for routine testing, mapping and surveying, collection of general-purpose data, dissemination of scientific information, and training of scientific personnel.

Scientists, engineers, and technicians—Scientists and engineers are defined as persons engaged in scientific and engineering work at a level requiring a knowledge of sciences equivalent at least to that acquired through completion of a 4-year college course. Technicians are defined as persons engaged in technical

U.S. Census Bureau, Statistical Abstract of the United States: 2001

work at a level requiring knowledge acquired through a technical institute, junior college, or other type of training less extensive than 4-year college training. Craftsmen and skilled workers are excluded.

Figure 16.1
Research and Development Expenditures: 1980 to 2000
Billions

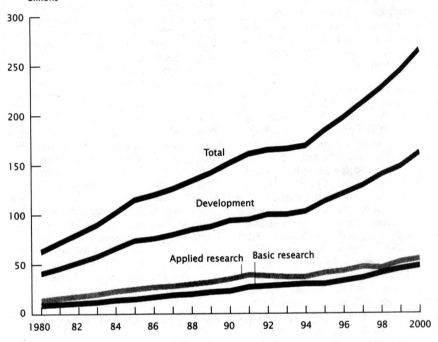

U.S. Census Bureau, Statistical Abstract of the United States: 2001

No. 767. R&D Expenditures: 1960 to 2000

[In millions of dollars (13,711 represents $13,711,000,000) except as indicated. For calendar years]

Year	Total	Sources of funds					Objective (percent of total)			Character of work		
		Federal govern-ment	In-dustry	Univer-sities/ colleges	Non-profit	Non-federal govern-ment[1]	Defense related[2]	Space re-lated[3]	Other	Basic research	Applied research	Devel-opment
1960....	13,711	8,915	4,516	67	123	90	53	3	44	1,286	3,065	9,360
1961....	14,564	9,484	4,757	75	148	101	50	6	44	1,512	3,123	9,930
1962....	15,636	10,138	5,124	84	179	112	49	7	45	1,824	3,698	10,116
1963....	17,519	11,645	5,456	96	197	125	42	14	43	2,115	3,865	11,540
1964....	19,103	12,764	5,888	114	200	138	37	19	43	2,396	4,201	12,506
1965....	20,252	13,194	6,549	136	225	150	33	21	45	2,664	4,374	13,215
1966....	22,072	14,165	7,331	165	252	160	32	20	47	2,930	4,653	14,490
1967....	23,346	14,563	8,146	200	271	168	35	14	49	3,168	4,848	15,332
1968....	24,666	14,964	9,008	221	290	185	35	14	52	3,376	5,137	16,154
1969....	25,996	15,228	10,011	233	316	208	35	11	54	3,491	5,454	17,051
1970....	26,271	14,984	10,449	259	343	237	33	10	56	3,594	5,752	16,925
1971....	26,952	15,210	10,824	290	366	262	33	10	59	3,720	5,833	17,399
1972....	28,740	16,039	11,715	312	393	282	33	8	59	3,850	6,147	18,743
1973....	30,952	16,587	13,299	343	422	302	32	7	62	4,099	6,655	20,197
1974....	33,359	17,287	14,885	393	474	320	29	7	64	4,511	7,344	21,504
1975....	35,671	18,533	15,824	432	534	348	28	8	65	4,875	8,091	22,706
1976....	39,435	20,292	17,702	480	592	369	27	8	66	5,373	8,976	25,085
1977....	43,421	22,155	19,642	569	662	394	27	7	67	6,075	9,670	27,677
1978....	48,774	24,468	22,457	679	727	443	26	6	69	6,998	10,710	31,067
1979....	55,457	27,303	26,097	785	791	482	25	6	70	7,864	12,117	35,475
1980....	63,273	30,035	30,929	920	871	519	24	5	71	8,825	13,745	40,703
1981....	72,267	33,714	35,948	1,058	967	581	24	5	70	9,844	16,393	46,030
1982....	80,848	37,233	40,692	1,207	1,095	621	26	5	68	10,863	18,286	51,698
1983....	90,075	41,576	45,264	1,357	1,220	658	28	4	67	12,110	20,394	57,571
1984....	102,344	46,571	52,187	1,514	1,351	721	29	3	67	13,503	22,517	66,323
1985....	114,778	52,748	57,962	1,743	1,491	834	30	3	66	14,885	25,403	74,489
1986....	120,337	54,711	60,991	2,019	1,647	969	32	3	65	17,287	27,251	75,799
1987....	126,299	58,548	62,576	2,262	1,849	1,065	32	3	65	18,551	27,914	79,833
1988....	133,930	60,180	67,977	2,527	2,081	1,165	30	3	66	19,813	29,545	84,572
1989....	141,914	60,489	74,966	2,852	2,333	1,274	28	4	68	21,908	32,279	87,727
1990....	152,051	61,669	83,208	3,187	2,589	1,399	25	4	70	23,069	34,974	94,008
1991....	160,914	60,822	92,300	3,457	2,852	1,483	23	4	73	27,201	38,632	95,081
1992....	165,358	60,923	96,229	3,568	3,113	1,525	22	4	74	27,628	37,938	99,793
1993....	165,714	60,515	96,549	3,708	3,387	1,556	22	4	74	28,754	37,285	99,676
1994....	169,214	60,790	99,203	3,936	3,664	1,621	20	4	76	29,578	36,613	103,023
1995....	183,611	62,961	110,870	4,108	3,924	1,750	19	5	77	29,560	40,999	113,053
1996....	197,330	63,392	123,412	4,430	4,238	1,858	18	4	78	32,812	43,169	121,348
1997....	212,379	64,783	136,231	4,846	4,593	1,926	17	4	79	36,270	47,211	128,898
1998....	226,872	66,827	147,867	5,183	5,007	1,987	16	4	81	41,294	45,702	139,875
1999....	244,143	67,711	163,397	5,562	5,390	2,083	15	3	83	44,625	51,632	147,886
2000,[4]..	264,622	69,627	181,040	5,969	5,789	2,197	14	3	83	47,903	55,041	161,679

[1] Nonfederal R&D expenditures to university and college performers. [2] R&D spending by the Department of Defense, including space activities, and a portion of the Department of Energy funds. [3] For the National Aeronautics and Space Administration only. [4] Preliminary.

Source: U.S. National Science Foundation, *National Patterns of R&D Resources*, annual.

No. 768. Federal Obligations for R&D in Current and Constant (1996) Dollars by Agency: 1980 to 2001

[In millions of dollars (29,830 represents $29,830,000,000). For fiscal years ending in year shown; see text, Section 8, State and Local Government Finances and Employment. Includes those agencies with obligations of $1 billion or more in 2000]

Agency	1980	1985	1990	1995	1997	1998	1999	2000, prel.	2001, prel.
CURRENT DOLLARS									
Obligations, total[1]............	29,830	48,360	63,559	68,187	69,827	72,101	75,341	79,470	81,526
Dept. of Defense	13,981	29,792	37,268	33,796	34,788	35,286	35,646	36,876	36,397
Dept. of Health and Human Services .	3,780	5,451	8,406	11,455	12,785	13,902	15,915	18,140	19,235
National Aeronautics and Space Administration.................	3,234	3,327	6,533	9,015	9,327	9,568	9,526	9,568	9,602
Dept. of Energy	4,754	4,966	5,631	6,145	5,604	5,874	6,010	6,306	6,793
National Science Foundation.......	882	1,346	1,690	2,149	2,249	2,289	2,506	2,656	3,180
Dept. of Agriculture	688	943	1,108	1,380	1,389	1,441	1,614	1,752	1,779
CONSTANT (1996) DOLLARS [2]									
Obligations, total............	53,278	65,804	73,863	69,550	68,660	69,730	71,856	74,361	74,719
Dept. of Defense	24,971	40,538	43,310	34,472	34,207	34,258	33,997	34,505	33,358
Dept. of Health and Human Services .	6,752	7,417	9,769	11,684	12,572	13,445	15,179	16,974	17,629
National Aeronautics and Space Administration.................	5,776	4,527	7,592	9,195	9,171	9,289	9,085	8,953	8,800
Dept. of Energy	8,490	6,757	6,544	6,268	5,510	5,703	5,732	5,901	6,226
National Science Foundation.......	1,575	1,831	1,964	2,192	2,211	2,223	2,390	2,485	2,914
Dept. of Agriculture	1,228	1,283	1,288	1,408	1,365	1,399	1,539	1,639	1,630

[1] Includes other agencies, not shown separately. [2] Based on gross domestic product implicit price deflator.
Source: U.S. National Science Foundation, *Federal Funds for Research and Development*, annual.

No. 769. Performance Sector of R&D Expenditures: 1995 to 2000

[In millions of dollars (183,611 represents $183,611,000,000). For calendar year. FFRDCs are federally funded research and development centers. For most academic institutions and the federal government before 1997 began on July 1 instead of October 1]

Year	Total	Federal government	Industry – Total	Industry Funded by – Federal government	Industry Funded by – Industry[1]	Industry FFRDCs	Universities and colleges – Total	Univ Funded by – Federal government	Univ Funded by – Non-federal government[2]	Univ Funded by – Industry	Univ Funded by – Universities & colleges	Univ Funded by – Non-profits	Universities & colleges FFRDCs[3]	Other nonprofit – Total	Other Funded by – Federal government	Other Funded by – Industry	Other Funded by – Nonprofits	Nonprofit FFRDCs
RESEARCH AND DEVELOPMENT TOTAL																		
1995	183,611	16,904	129,830	21,178	108,652	2,273	22,599	13,580	1,750	1,547	4,108	1,616	5,372	5,827	2,847	671	2,308	808
1996	197,330	16,585	142,371	21,356	121,015	2,297	23,686	14,067	1,858	1,667	4,430	1,665	5,410	6,209	2,906	730	2,574	772
1997	212,379	16,819	155,409	21,798	133,611	2,130	25,088	14,716	1,926	1,812	4,846	1,790	5,486	6,626	3,014	809	2,804	821
1998	226,872	17,362	167,102	22,086	145,016	2,078	26,664	15,589	1,987	1,971	5,183	1,934	5,589	7,234	3,281	880	3,073	843
1999	244,143	18,332	180,450	20,162	160,298	2,373	28,363	16,518	2,083	2,133	5,562	2,066	5,698	8,017	3,718	976	3,323	909
2000 prel.	264,622	19,143	197,280	19,635	177,645	2,575	30,154	17,475	2,197	2,310	5,969	2,203	5,801	8,750	4,079	1,085	3,586	918
BASIC RESEARCH																		
1995	29,560	2,689	5,569	190	5,379	530	15,137	9,628	1,069	945	2,509	987	2,661	2,899	1,170	390	1,338	75
1996	32,812	2,680	7,498	650	6,848	708	16,029	10,085	1,148	1,030	2,738	1,028	2,632	3,187	1,248	428	1,510	79
1997	36,270	2,746	9,795	1,029	8,766	625	17,015	10,608	1,190	1,119	2,993	1,105	2,660	3,322	1,317	449	1,557	108
1998	41,294	3,003	13,027	1,326	11,701	568	18,143	11,358	1,217	1,208	3,175	1,185	2,685	3,656	1,461	489	1,706	213
1999	44,625	3,312	14,024	1,211	12,813	649	19,439	12,154	1,281	1,312	3,421	1,271	2,759	4,092	1,705	542	1,845	351
2000 prel.	47,903	3,525	15,378	1,179	14,199	704	20,656	12,857	1,351	1,421	3,672	1,355	2,809	4,492	1,898	602	1,991	339
APPLIED RESEARCH																		
1995	40,999	4,952	26,919	3,164	23,755	535	5,653	2,774	558	494	1,311	516	1,119	1,692	934	170	589	129
1996	43,169	4,872	29,010	3,640	25,370	231	5,870	2,856	582	522	1,388	522	1,283	1,781	960	182	640	122
1997	47,211	4,997	32,430	2,648	29,782	213	6,152	2,900	604	568	1,519	561	1,364	1,926	1,011	205	711	128
1998	45,702	5,146	30,341	2,533	27,808	230	6,475	2,957	631	626	1,646	614	1,326	2,062	1,060	223	779	123
1999	51,632	5,503	35,367	3,440	31,927	274	6,814	3,075	658	673	1,756	652	1,276	2,284	1,194	247	842	114
2000 prel.	55,041	5,826	37,648	2,252	35,396	285	7,260	3,259	693	729	1,884	695	1,401	2,504	1,320	275	909	117
DEVELOPMENT																		
1995	113,053	9,262	97,342	17,824	79,518	1,208	1,809	1,177	123	108	288	113	1,592	1,236	744	111	381	603
1996	121,348	9,033	105,863	17,066	88,797	1,358	1,787	1,125	128	115	305	115	1,495	1,241	698	120	423	571
1997	128,898	9,077	113,184	18,121	95,063	1,292	1,921	1,207	132	125	333	123	1,462	1,378	687	155	536	585
1998	139,875	9,214	123,734	18,227	105,507	1,280	2,046	1,274	139	137	361	135	1,577	1,516	760	168	588	507
1999	147,886	9,517	131,060	15,512	115,548	1,450	2,110	1,290	144	148	385	143	1,663	1,641	819	187	636	445
2000 prel.	161,679	9,792	144,254	16,205	128,050	1,586	2,238	1,360	152	160	413	153	1,592	1,754	860	208	686	463

[1] For R&D funded by the federal government. FFRDCs are federally funded research and development centers. [2] Includes all nonfederal sources. [3] Includes all R&D expenditures of FFRDCs administered by academic institutions and funded by the federal government.

Source: National Science Foundation. Data derived from: *Research and Development in Industry*, annual; *Academic Research and Development Expenditures*, annual; and *Federal Funds for Research and Development*, annual.

No. 770. Performance Sector of R&D Expenditures by State: 1998

[In millions of dollars (226,872 represents $226,872,000,000). Industry R&D data refer to calendar years; other R&D data refer to fiscal years but may serve as approximation to calendar year data]

State	Industry					Universities and colleges						Other nonprofit institutions funded by federal government [5]
				Funded by—				Funded by—				
	Total R&D [1]	Federal government [2]	Total	Federal government [3]	Industry [4]	Total	Federal government	Non-federal government	Industry	U&Cs	Nonprofits	
U.S.	226,872	17,403	169,180	24,164	145,016	26,547	15,533	1,993	1,933	5,166	1,923	3,228
AL	1,926	753	707	180	527	442	282	7	30	82	40	24
AK	(D)	44	(D)	(D)	9	76	32	4	16	24	-	4
AZ	2,318	138	1,727	490	1,237	406	210	12	22	147	-	8
AR	283	46	118	(D)	(D)	117	41	33	8	27	15	2
CA	43,919	1,595	35,568	3,803	31,764	3,345	2,009	146	213	702	274	519
CO	4,565	202	3,565	1,237	2,329	489	332	26	27	68	36	55
CT	3,559	18	3,113	179	2,935	404	262	13	26	67	35	24
DE	2,556	4	2,476	13	2,463	73	36	5	4	19	9	3
DC	2,606	1,718	503	90	413	233	166	2	19	26	19	150
FL	4,773	750	3,300	889	2,411	713	356	81	52	184	40	11
GA	2,492	236	1,444	86	1,358	802	370	70	86	246	30	10
HI	242	55	17	(D)	(D)	148	87	37	11	13	-	22
ID	1,127	25	1,028	(D)	(D)	72	25	22	8	16	1	1
IL	8,830	72	6,892	136	6,755	1,046	587	57	60	262	81	62
IN	3,089	38	2,622	(D)	(D)	425	214	26	40	126	19	3
IA	1,054	33	634	(D)	(D)	358	167	53	31	89	18	4
KS	1,518	25	1,279	(D)	(D)	213	80	47	12	56	17	1
KY	645	7	427	(D)	(D)	210	80	15	19	86	9	2
LA	542	84	102	14	87	352	144	78	23	87	20	4
ME	159	11	82	(D)	(D)	35	14	2	7	11	1	31
MD	8,019	4,766	1,744	655	1,089	1,330	1,014	63	42	143	69	179
MA	13,382	301	10,604	2,419	8,185	1,343	987	32	107	99	118	707
MI	13,655	111	12,648	(D)	(D)	878	472	56	59	221	69	18
MN	3,818	38	3,321	334	2,986	365	206	48	25	56	29	94
MS	366	133	73	17	57	153	80	29	10	31	2	8
MO	1,868	49	1,313	(D)	(D)	484	278	24	30	109	43	22
MT	191	33	82	(D)	(D)	72	36	14	8	13	1	3
NE	315	29	93	(D)	(D)	186	63	47	17	55	5	7
NV	571	49	434	(D)	(D)	84	45	-5	5	24	4	4
NH	1,340	34	1,187	(D)	(D)	117	71	8	6	17	14	2
NJ	11,368	393	10,415	134	10,282	485	228	40	27	150	39	17
NM	3,032	396	1,205	(D)	(D)	229	152	13	13	46	5	15
NY	13,731	192	11,176	2,216	8,960	1,925	1,224	82	96	286	236	821
NC	4,560	236	3,362	12	3,350	899	516	129	121	96	36	64
ND	119	27	34	-	34	57	23	1	4	26	4	1
OH	6,970	698	5,338	605	4,732	808	444	74	88	152	49	125
OK	513	51	245	2	243	209	84	37	13	60	15	8
OR	1,910	88	1,492	26	1,467	310	203	33	10	38	25	21
PA	8,762	133	7,083	485	6,598	1,342	873	44	156	199	70	174
RI	1,677	•222	1,320	(D)	(D)	112	78	3	2	26	3	23
SC	989	45	695	(D)	(D)	246	113	27	11	83	11	3
SD	60	28	5	-	5	25	12	8	-	3	2	2
TN	2,503	38	2,040	(D)	(D)	346	208	37	20	54	28	28
TX	10,774	597	8,408	223	8,185	1,698	910	179	140	290	179	60
UT	1,495	135	1,109	181	928	249	165	18	14	43	10	1
VT	175	4	112	32	80	58	31	3	6	12	6	1
VA	4,934	1,480	2,707	1,614	1,093	491	289	49	46	77	30	44
WA	8,466	184	7,476	(D)	(D)	534	384	13	42	77	19	122
WV	421	97	225	(D)	(D)	63	25	3	5	27	4	1
WI	2,501	38	1,919	(D)	(D)	536	300	44	20	111	61	8
WY	65	12	2	-	2	49	18	5	3	21	1	3
Unknown	12,119	912	5,709	8,092	34,452	905	507	89	73	183	65	301

- Represents zero.   D Data withheld to avoid disclosing information about individual companies.   [1] Includes university and college Federally Funded Research and Development Centers (FFRDCs.) Nonprofit FFRDCs not shown separately.   [2] For R&D funded by the federal government.   [3] Includes performance at industry Federally Funded Research and Development Centers (FFRDCs). Nonprofit FFRDCs not shown separately.   [4] Includes all nonfederal sources.   [5] Data by state are for R&D funded by the federal government.

Source: U.S. National Science Foundation. Data derived from *Research and Development in Industry*, annual; *Academic Research and Development Expenditures*, annual; and *Federal Funds For Research and Development*, annual.

Science and Technology 509

No. 771. Federal Funding for R&D in Current and Constant (1996) Dollars by Selected Budget Functions: 1970 to 2001

[In millions of dollars (15,339 represents $15,339,000,000). For fiscal years ending in year shown; see text, Section 8, State and Local Government Finances and Employment. Excludes R&D plant. Represents budget authority. Functions shown are those for which $1 billion or more was authorized since 1995]

Function	1970	1980	1985	1990	1995	1996	1999	2000, prel.	2001, prel.
CURRENT DOLLARS									
Total [1]	15,339	29,739	49,887	63,781	68,791	73,569	77,637	80,733	82,730
Eight functions, percent of total	96.6	96.5	98.3	98.0	97.7	97.7	97.6	97.8	97.6
National defense	7,981	14,946	33,698	39,925	37,204	39,823	41,306	41,846	41,414
Health	1,084	3,694	5,418	8,308	11,407	13,576	15,553	17,762	18,858
Space research and technology [2]	3,606	2,738	2,725	5,765	7,916	8,196	8,245	8,447	8,732
Energy [2]	574	3,603	2,389	2,726	2,844	948	1,131	1,112	1,184
General science	452	1,233	1,862	2,410	2,794	4,360	4,690	4,885	5,529
Natural resources and environment	340	999	1,059	1,386	1,988	1,855	1,842	1,906	1,932
Transportation	535	887	1,030	1,045	1,833	1,833	1,725	1,570	1,665
Agriculture	238	585	836	950	1,194	1,249	1,288	1,405	1,450
CONSTANT (1996) DOLLARS [3]									
Total [1]	53,840	53,115	67,883	73,872	70,166	71,426	74,046	75,543	75,823
National defense	28,013	26,694	45,854	46,242	37,948	38,663	39,395	39,156	37,956
Health	3,805	6,598	7,372	9,622	11,635	13,181	14,834	16,620	17,283
Space research and technology [2]	12,657	4,890	3,708	6,677	8,074	7,959	7,864	7,904	8,003
Energy [2]	2,015	6,435	3,251	3,157	2,901	920	1,079	1,041	1,085
General science	1,587	2,202	2,534	2,791	2,850	4,233	4,473	4,571	5,087
Natural resources and environment	1,193	1,784	1,441	1,605	2,028	1,801	1,757	1,783	1,771
Transportation	1,878	1,584	1,402	1,210	1,870	1,780	1,645	1,469	1,526
Agriculture	835	1,045	1,138	1,100	1,218	1,213	1,228	1,315	1,329

[1] Includes other functions, not shown separately. [2] Beginning in FY 1998, a number of DOE programs were reclassified from energy (270). [3] Based on gross domestic product implicit price deflator.
Source: U.S. National Science Foundation, *Federal R&D Funding by Budget Function*, annual.

No. 772. National R&D Expenditures as a Percent of Gross Domestic Product by Country: 1981 to 1999

Year	Total R&D						Nondefense R&D [1]					
	United States	Japan	Unified Germany	France	United Kingdom	Italy	United States	Japan	Unified Germany	France	United Kingdom	Italy
1981	2.31	2.13	2.47	1.93	2.38	0.88	1.7	2.1	2.3	1.6	1.8	0.9
1985	2.72	2.58	2.75	2.22	2.24	1.12	1.9	2.6	2.6	1.8	1.8	1.1
1990	2.62	2.85	2.75	2.37	2.16	1.29	2.0	2.8	2.6	1.9	1.7	1.3
1994	2.40	2.63	2.26	2.34	2.07	1.05	1.9	2.6	2.2	2.0	1.8	1.0
1995	2.48	2.77	2.26	2.31	1.98	1.00	2.0	2.7	2.2	2.0	1.7	1.0
1996	2.53	2.80	2.26	2.30	1.91	1.01	2.1	2.8	2.2	2.0	1.6	1.0
1997	2.55	2.88	2.29	2.22	1.83	0.99	2.1	2.8	2.2	2.0	1.6	1.0
1998	2.58	3.01	2.31	2.18	1.83	1.02	2.2	3.0	2.2	2.0	1.6	1.0
1999	2.63	3.01	2.38	2.17	1.87	1.04	2.2	(NA)	2.3	(NA)	(NA)	(NA)

NA Not available. [1] Estimated.
Source: National Science Foundation, *National Patterns of R&D Resources*, annual; and Organization for Economic Cooperation and Development.

No. 773. R&D Expenditures in Science and Engineering at Universities and Colleges: 1981 to 1999

[In millions of dollars (6,847 represents $6,847,000,000)]

Characteristic	1981	1990	1999	Characteristic	1981	1990	1999
CURRENT DOLLARS				**CONSTANT (1996)[1]**			
Total	6,847	16,286	27,489	Total	11,090	18,863	26,217
Basic research	4,594	10,643	18,844	Basic research	7,441	12,327	17,972
Applied R&D	2,253	5,643	8,645	Applied R&D	3,649	6,536	8,245
Source of funds:				Source of funds:			
All governments	5,117	10,962	18,075	All governments	8,288	12,696	17,239
Institutions' own funds	1,004	3,006	5,366	Institutions' own funds	1,626	3,482	5,118
Industry	291	1,127	2,048	Industry	471	1,305	1,953
Other	435	1,191	2,000	Other	705	1,379	1,907
Fields:				Fields:			
Physical sciences	765	1,807	2,600	Physical sciences	1,239	2,093	2,480
Environmental sciences	550	1,069	1,690	Environmental sciences	891	1,238	1,612
Mathematical sciences	87	222	313	Mathematical sciences	141	257	299
Computer sciences	144	515	860	Computer sciences	233	596	820
Life sciences	3,695	8,726	15,591	Life sciences	5,985	10,107	14,870
Psychology	127	253	465	Psychology	206	293	443
Social sciences	366	703	1,262	Social sciences	593	814	1,204
Other sciences	145	336	452	Other sciences	235	389	431
Engineering	967	2,656	4,257	Engineering	1,566	3,076	4,060

[1] Based on gross domestic product implicit price deflator.
Source: U.S. National Science Foundation, *Survey of Research and Development Expenditures at Universities and Colleges*, annual.

No. 774. Federal Obligations to Universities and Colleges: 1970 to 1999

[In millions of dollars (3,237 represents $3,237,000,000) except percent. For fiscal years ending in year shown; see text, Section 8, State and Local Government Finances and Employment. Minus sign (-) indicates decrease]

Item	1970	1980	1990	1995	1997	1998	1999
CURRENT DOLLARS							
Federal obligations, total	3,237	8,299	15,226	(NA)	(NA)	(NA)	(NA)
Annual percent change [1]	-6.5	9.1	-1.8	(NA)	(NA)	(NA)	(NA)
Academic science/engineering obligations	2,188	4,791	10,471	14,461	15,096	16,094	18,058
Percent of total	67.6	57.7	68.8	(NA)	(NA)	(NA)	(NA)
Research and development	1,447	4,161	9,017	12,181	13,019	13,877	15,570
Research and development plant	45	38	142	341	276	157	173
Other science/engineering activities	696	593	1,312	1,939	1,801	2,060	2,315
Nonscience/engineering activities	1,049	3,508	4,755	(NA)	(NA)	(NA)	(NA)
CONSTANT (1996) DOLLARS [2]							
Federal obligations, total	11,361	14,822	17,694	(NA)	(NA)	(NA)	(NA)
Annual percent change [1]	-11.4	0.2	-5.4	(NA)	(NA)	(NA)	(NA)
Academic science/engineering obligations	7,678	8,557	12,168	14,750	14,807	15,565	17,223
Percent of total	67.6	57.7	68.8	(NA)	(NA)	(NA)	(NA)
Research and development	5,078	7,431	10,478	12,424	12,770	13,421	14,850
Research and development plant	157	67	165	348	271	151	165
Other science/engineering activities	2,444	1,058	1,525	1,978	1,767	1,993	2,208
Nonscience/engineering activities	3,682	6,265	5,526	(NA)	(NA)	(NA)	(NA)

NA Not available. [1] Percent change from immediate prior year. [2] Based on gross domestic product implicit price deflator.
Source: U.S. National Science Foundation, *Survey of Federal S&E Support to Universities, Colleges, and Nonprofit Institutions*, annual.

No. 775. Federal R&D Obligations to Selected Universities and Colleges: 1981 to 1999

[In millions of dollars (4,410.9 represents $4,410,900,000), except rank. For fiscal years ending in year shown; see text, Section 8, State and Local Government Finances and Employment. For the top 45 institutions receiving federal R&D funds in 1998. Awards to the administrative offices of university systems are excluded from totals for individual institutions because that allocation of funds is unknown, but those awards are included in "total all institutions"]

Major institution ranked by total 1998 federal R&D obligations	Obligations 1981	Obligations 1985	Obligations 1995	Obligations 1999	Rank 1981	Rank 1985	Rank 1995	Rank 1999
Total, all institutions [1]	4,410.9	6,246.2	12,180.9	15,569.9	(X)	(X)	(X)	(X)
45 institutions, percent of total	61.6	60.1	58.6	59.5	(X)	(X)	(X)	(X)
Johns Hopkins University	363.4	297.4	569.3	777.9	1	1	1	1
University of Washington	100.0	146.2	299.7	385.7	4	4	2	2
Stanford University	106.1	175.0	266.7	321.3	3	3	4	3
University of Pennsylvania	76.1	103.1	202.3	319.6	10	15	10	4
University of Michigan	74.0	108.0	243.6	315.9	11	11	5	5
University of California—San Diego	91.4	103.6	239.2	296.4	6	13	6	6
University of California—Los Angeles	94.9	128.2	216.4	275.2	5	5	7	7
Harvard University	87.8	109.4	191.5	265.6	7	9	13	8
Washington University	54.2	72.0	165.4	258.5	17	22	18	9
Massachusetts Institute of Technology	146.0	189.6	280.3	253.2	2	2	3	10
University of California—San Francisco	64.8	98.5	201.8	251.9	15	16	12	11
Columbia University—Main Division	83.7	127.3	185.7	251.6	9	6	14	12
University of Colorado	46.1	71.4	165.4	247.1	22	23	17	13
Yale University	73.5	109.2	179.5	246.0	12	10	15	14
University of Wisconsin—Madison	86.9	124.6	207.7	236.0	8	7	8	15
University of Minnesota	72.0	103.3	202.8	228.7	14	14	9	16
University of Pittsburgh	38.5	58.6	166.3	221.0	29	28	16	17
Duke University	44.3	69.2	155.0	210.7	23	26	20	18
Pennsylvania State University	47.1	76.7	152.5	207.8	21	19	21	19
Cornell University	72.7	120.0	202.2	203.8	13	8	11	20
University of North Carolina at Chapel Hill	38.4	63.1	156.3	199.3	30	27	19	21
University of California—Berkeley	64.1	106.7	142.4	189.9	16	12	23	22
University Southern California	49.2	89.7	152.2	189.9	20	17	22	23
University of Alabama—Birmingham	30.0	44.1	120.2	171.0	44	46	26	24
Case Western Reserve University	33.7	48.0	127.4	167.0	38	40	25	25
University of Chicago	54.0	71.2	106.7	155.6	18	24	31	26
University of Arizona	36.3	49.7	137.1	151.7	33	37	24	27
Baylor College of Medicine	35.1	45.8	84.1	149.4	35	45	43	28
University of Illinois—Urbana Champaign	53.6	83.1	115.7	145.5	19	18	28	29
California Institute of Technology	33.0	55.1	113.7	143.5	40	32	29	30
Northwestern University	32.4	48.3	101.9	138.6	47	39	32	31
University of Rochester	43.0	70.4	107.6	135.7	25	25	30	32
Boston University	27.0	46.2	86.1	131.2	51	43	41	33
University of Iowa	35.3	55.1	93.9	129.3	34	31	36	34
Emory University	17.4	27.0	75.8	128.5	72	70	49	35
University of California—Davis	31.8	43.2	98.9	128.4	42	47	33	36
The Scripps Research Institute	-	-	83.2	124.8	(NA)	(NA)	44	37
University of Texas at Austin	43.8	72.4	115.9	121.1	24	21	27	38
Vanderbilt University	27.4	39.9	94.4	118.2	49	48	35	39
Ohio State University	42.9	56.1	96.5	115.5	26	30	34	40
University of Utah	38.2	50.9	93.8	114.7	31	36	37	41
New York University	40.6	74.6	85.5	113.3	28	20	42	42
University of Florida	30.8	47.7	82.5	111.1	43	41	45	43
Indiana University	29.3	39.1	89.0	110.5	45	49	39	44
University of Virginia	24.3	37.4	79.0	109.8	52	52	48	45

- Represents zero. NA Not available. X Not applicable. [1] Includes other institutions, not shown separately.
Source: U.S. National Science Foundation, *Federal S&E Support to Universities and Colleges and Nonprofit Institutions*, annual.

Science and Technology 511

No. 776. Percentage of U.S. Scientific and Technical Articles Which Are Coauthored and Internationally Coauthored: 1989 to 1999

[Coauthorships are based on authors' corporate address. The database consists of the Institute of Scientific Information's Science and Social Science Citation Indexes (SCI, SSCI)]

Science field	Percentage coauthored				Percentage internationally coauthored			
	1989-91	1992-94	1995-97	1998-99	1989-91	1992-94	1995-97	1998-99
Science and engineering, total . . .	49.4	52.9	56.8	59.7	11.8	14.9	18.0	20.9
Physics	47.9	54.3	59.3	62.2	19.1	24.7	30.1	34.0
Chemistry	34.5	38.6	42.6	45.6	11.6	14.5	16.9	19.6
Earth & space science	53.3	58.2	63.1	67.2	20.2	24.2	28.7	33.1
Mathematics	42.8	46.8	49.6	52.3	21.0	24.3	26.8	30.2
Biology	34.5	38.6	42.5	49.0	11.6	14.5	16.9	19.4
Biomedical research	54.7	58.8	61.8	65.2	14.0	17.0	19.5	22.9
Clinical medicine	61.4	63.3	66.4	68.3	9.5	12.2	15.0	17.6
Engineering	39.3	43.3	47.0	51.2	11.5	13.8	16.5	20.2
Psychology	38.5	41.3	43.6	47.0	5.7	6.9	8.9	10.6
Social science	30.8	32.9	35.7	35.4	7.0	8.8	10.3	10.8
Health & professional fields	34.9	36.1	39.6	40.1	3.8	4.6	6.5	6.3

Source: CHI Research, Inc., Haddon Heights, NJ; and U.S. National Science Foundation, special tabulation.

No. 777. Citations on U.S. Patents to the U.S. Scientific and Technical Literature by Cited Field: 1990 to 2000

[Citations to articles with authors in different sectors are assigned fractionally to participating sectors. Citations are to articles published in a 12-year period, lagged by 3 years from the patent data. For example, 1997 citations are to articles published in 1993-95]

Science field	1990	1993	1994	1995	1996	1997	1998	1999	2000
Total	19,422	38,493	40,266	46,961	66,129	102,111	143,541	143,215	142,008
Physics	3,414	4,931	5,693	5,432	5,578	6,739	7,699	8,247	9,238
Chemistry	3,451	5,961	6,190	7,070	8,373	11,594	13,007	13,009	15,009
Earth & space science	138	122	152	164	238	259	369	440	434
Mathematics	7	23	22	26	34	48	52	42	48
Biology	544	868	1,172	1,336	2,017	2,244	3,683	4,515	4,063
Biomedical research	4,999	13,812	13,709	16,389	26,537	45,273	68,074	67,264	64,276
Clinical medicine	4,682	9,986	9,789	12,576	18,339	30,549	43,823	42,988	41,454
Engineering technology	2,187	2,790	3,538	3,969	5,014	5,418	6,838	6,720	7,496

Source: CHI Research, Inc., Haddon Heights, NJ; and U.S. National Science Foundation, special tabulation.

No. 778. Percentage of Citations to Foreign Articles in U.S. Scientific and Technical Public Publications: 1990 to 1999

[Citations are to 3 years' articles with 2-year lag. For example, 1997 citations are to articles published in 1993-1995]

Science field	1990	1992	1993	1994	1995	1996	1997	1998	1999
Total science & engineering . . .	29.6	30.4	31.0	31.7	32.1	32.9	33.5	34.0	35.1
Physics	34.4	34.6	35.5	36.9	38.0	39.4	40.9	41.3	43.3
Chemistry	36.4	37.3	37.6	38.6	38.1	39.3	40.7	41.8	41.9
Earth & space science	28.8	28.5	29.7	29.7	29.6	31.2	32.0	32.7	34.0
Mathematics	29.5	30.9	29.9	29.8	31.7	32.5	32.7	32.2	34.0
Biology	28.7	29.5	29.9	29.5	30.4	32.3	33.4	34.3	36.6
Biomedical research	29.8	30.4	30.9	31.5	31.6	32.0	32.3	32.4	33.1
Clinical medicine	30.0	31.4	32.0	32.8	33.4	34.2	34.5	35.4	36.6
Engineering technology	26.7	26.9	26.7	29.4	28.7	29.6	31.8	31.4	33.8
Psychology	17.8	17.5	17.7	17.7	18.2	19.2	20.2	20.6	21.3
Social science	14.7	14.4	14.7	15.1	15.6	16.9	17.2	17.2	17.1
Health & professional fields	9.5	9.3	9.8	9.9	9.9	10.1	10.7	10.7	11.9

Source: CHI Research, Inc., Haddon Heights, NJ; and U.S. National Science Foundation, special tabulation.

U.S. Census Bureau, Statistical Abstract of the United States: 2001

No. 779. Funds for Performance of Industrial R&D by Source of Funds and Selected Industries: 1997 to 1999

[In millions of dollars (157,539 represents $157,539,000,000). For calendar years. Covers basic research, applied research, and development]

Industry	NAICS [1] code	1997	1998	1999
CURRENT DOLLARS				
Total funds	(X)	157,539	169,180	182,823
Petroleum and coal products	324	(D)	1,395	615
Chemicals and allied products	325	16,492	18,969	20,246
Machinery	333	5,610	(D)	6,057
Navigational, measuring, electromedical, and control instruments	3345	8,030	11,232	14,337
Electrical equipment, appliances, and components	335	2,741	2,280	(D)
Motor vehicles, trailers, and parts	3361-3363	(D)	(D)	(D)
Aerospace products and parts	3364	17,865	16,359	14,425
All other [2]	(X)	(D)	(D)	(D)
Company funds	(X)	133,611	145,016	160,288
Petroleum and coal products	324	1,349	1,390	(D)
Chemicals	325	16,385	18,733	20,051
Machinery	333	5,470	5,831	5,658
Navigational, measuring, electromedical, and control instruments	3345	4,659	5,483	8,632
Electrical equipment, appliances, and components	335	2,580	2,139	3,820
Motor vehicles, trailers, and parts	3361-3363	14,340	13,781	17,987
Aerospace products and parts	3364	6,961	6,521	5,309
All other [2]	(X)	81,867	91,138	(D)
CONSTANT (1996) DOLLARS [3]				
Total funds	(X)	160,611	174,628	191,544
Petroleum and coal products	324	(D)	1,440	644
Chemicals	325	16,814	19,580	21,212
Machinery	333	5,719	(D)	6,346
Navigational, measuring, electromedical, and control instruments	3345	8,187	11,594	15,021
Electrical equipment, appliances, and components	335	2,794	2,353	(D)
Motor vehicles, trailers, and parts	3361-3363	(D)	(D)	(D)
Aerospace products and parts	3364	18,213	16,886	15,113
All other [2]	(X)	(D)	(D)	(D)
Company funds	(X)	136,216	149,686	167,934
Petroleum and coal products	324	1,375	1,435	(D)
Chemicals	325	16,705	19,336	21,007
Machinery	333	5,577	6,019	5,928
Navigational, measuring, electromedical, and control instruments	3345	4,750	5,660	9,044
Electrical equipment, appliances, and components	335	2,630	2,208	4,002
Motor vehicles, trailers, and parts	3361-3363	14,620	14,225	18,845
Aerospace products and parts	3364	7,097	6,731	5,562
All other [2]	(X)	83,463	94,073	(D)

D Figure withheld to avoid disclosure of information pertaining to a specific organization or individual. X Not applicable. [1] 1997 North American Industry Classification System; see text, Section 15, Business Enterprise. [2] All other manufacturing and nonmanufacturing. [3] Based on gross domestic product implicit price deflator.

Source: U.S. National Science Foundation, *Research and Development in Industry*, annual.

No. 780. R&D Funds in R&D-Performing Manufacturing Companies by Industry: 1997 to 1999

Industry	NAICS [1] code	Total R&D funds as a percent of net sales			Company R&D funds as a percent of net sales		
		1997	1998	1999	1997	1998	1999
Total [2]	(X)	3.9	3.7	3.7	3.3	3.2	3.2
Food	311	0.4	0.4	0.4	0.4	0.4	0.4
Paper, printing, and support activities	322, 326	(D)	(D)	(D)	1.4	1.0	1.4
Petroleum and coal products	324	(D)	0.8	0.4	0.5	0.8	(D)
Chemicals	325	5.5	6.3	5.2	5.5	6.2	5.1
Plastic and rubber products	326	1.3	2.0	1.9	1.3	2	1.9
Nonmetallic mineral products	327	1.9	1.3	(D)	1.9	(D)	1.5
Primary metals	331	0.8	(D)	0.4	0.6	0.5	0.4
Fabricated metal products	332	1.7	1.5	1.5	1.7	1.4	1.4
Machinery	333	3.2	(D)	3.5	3.1	3.1	3.3
Navigational, measuring, electromedical, and control instruments	3345	12.4	13.6	15.2	7.2	6.6	9.1
Electrical equipment, appliances, and components	335	3.1	2.9	(D)	2.9	2.7	2.3
Motor vehicles, trailers, and parts	3361-3367	(D)	(D)	(D)	3.7	2.2	2.9
Aerospace products and parts	3364	8.4	7.2	8.8	3.3	2.9	3.2

D Figure withheld to avoid disclosure of information pertaining to a specific organization or individual. X Not applicable. [1] 1997 North American Industry Classification System; see text, Section 15, Business Enterprise. [2] Includes all manufacturing industries.

Source: U.S. National Science Foundation, *Research and Development in Industry*, annual.

Figure 16.2
Funds for Performance of Industrial R&D: 1997 to 1999

☐ Total funds
■ Company funds

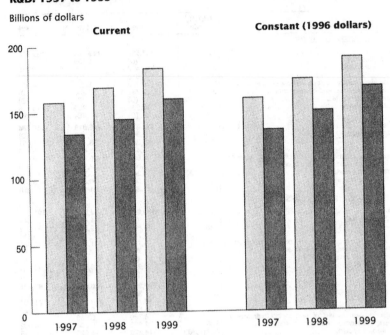

Billions of dollars

Current

Constant (1996 dollars)

Source: Chart prepared by U.S. Census Bureau. For data, see Table 779.

Figure 16.3
Federal Funding for Research—Percent Distribution by Field of Science: 2000

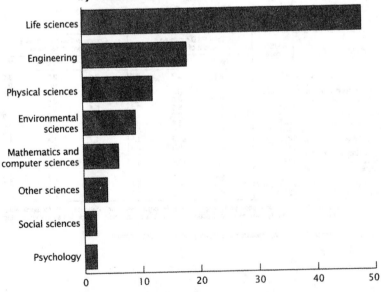

Source: Chart prepared by U.S. Census Bureau. For data, see Table 781.

514   Science and Technology

No. 781. Federal Obligations for Research in Current and Constant (1996) Dollars by Field of Science: 1980 to 2001

[In millions of dollars (11,597 represents $11,597,000,000). For fiscal years ending in year shown; see text, Section 8, State and Local Government Finances and Employment. Excludes R&D plant]

Field	1980	1985	1990	1995	1997	1998	1999	2000, prel.	2001, prel.
CURRENT DOLLARS									
Research, total	11,597	16,133	21,622	28,434	29,365	30,922	33,528	36,330	38,688
Basic	4,674	7,819	11,286	13,877	14,942	15,613	17,444	18,982	20,274
Applied......................	6,923	8,315	10,337	14,557	14,423	15,309	16,084	17,348	18,414
Life sciences	4,192	6,363	8,830	11,811	12,661	13,558	15,422	17,422	18,249
Psychology	199	327	449	623	545	591	633	720	752
Physical sciences	2,001	3,046	3,809	4,278	4,149	4,210	4,066	4,183	4,430
Environmental sciences	1,261	1,404	2,174	2,854	3,046	3,062	3,095	3,102	3,243
Mathematics and computer sciences ...	241	575	841	1,579	1,672	1,837	1,981	2,178	2,517
Engineering...................	2,830	3,618	4,227	5,708	5,690	5,895	6,263	6,548	7,089
Social sciences ....‚..........	524	460	630	679	696	806	855	902	996
Other sciences, n.e.c. [1]	350	342	664	902	905	964	1,212	1,273	1,412
CONSTANT (1996) DOLLARS [2]									
Research, total	20,713	21,953	25,128	29,003	28,804	29,906	31,977	33,995	35,458
Basic	8,348	10,639	13,116	14,154	14,656	15,100	16,637	17,762	18,581
Applied......................	12,365	11,314	12,013	14,848	14,148	14,806	15,340	16,233	16,877
Life sciences	7,488	8,658	10,261	12,047	12,419	13,112	14,709	16,302	16,725
Psychology	355	445	522	635	535	572	604	674	689
Physical sciences	3,573	4,145	4,426	4,364	4,070	4,071	3,878	3,914	4,060
Environmental sciences	2,252	1,910	2,526	2,911	2,987	2,961	2,952	2,903	2,972
Mathematics and computer sciences ...	430	782	977	1,611	1,640	1,776	1,889	2,038	2,307
Engineering...................	5,055	4,923	4,912	5,823	5,581	5,702	5,973	6,127	6,497
Social sciences ....‚..........	936	626	732	692	683	780	815	844	913
Other sciences, n.e.c. [1]	624	465	772	920	888	932	1,156	1,191	1,294

[1] N.e.c. = Not elsewhere classified.   [2] Based on gross domestic product implicit price deflator.

Source: U.S. National Science Foundation, *Federal Funds for Research and Development*, annual.

No. 782. R&D Scientists and Engineers—Employment and Cost by Industry: 1997 to 1999

[918.6 represents 918,600. Data are estimates; on average full-time-equivalent (FTE) basis]

Industry	NAICS [1] code	1997	1998	1999
EMPLOYED SCIENTISTS (1,000)				
Average FTE of scientists and engineers[2][3]..........	(X)	918.6	974.6	1,015.7
Chemicals	325	89.3	90.1	86.7
Machinery................................	333	100.4	104.1	74.1
Electrical equipment, appliances, and components	335	153.8	172.7	98.8
Motor vehicles, trailers, and parts.	3361-3363	64.0	63.5	69.2
Aerospace products and parts.	3364	85.8	71.7	60.9
CONSTANT (1996) DOLLARS [4] ($1,000)				
Cost per scientist or engineer [3][5]..................	(X)	168.6	168.7	171.8
Chemicals.................................	325	(D)	235	234.3
Machinery.................................	333	181.2	139.2	113.6
Electrical equipment, appliances, and components	335	157.2	146.2	(D)
Motor vehicles, trailers, and parts.	3361-3363	(D)	(D)	(D)
Aerospace products and parts.	3364	186.8	195.8	210.0

D Withheld to avoid disclosure.   X Not applicable.   [1] 1997 North American Industry Classification System; see text, Section 15, Business Enterprise.   [2] The mean number of FTE R&D scientists and engineers employed in January of the year shown and the following January.   [3] Includes industries not shown separately.   [4] Based on gross domestic product implicit price deflator.   [5] Represents the arithmetic mean of the numbers of R&D scientists and engineers reported in each industry for January in 2 consecutive years divided into total R&D expenditures in each industry.

Source: U.S. National Science Foundation, *Research and Development in Industry*, annual.

U.S. Census Bureau, Statistical Abstract of the United States: 2001

No. 783. Civilian Employment of Scientists, Engineers, and Technicians by Occupation and Industry: 1998

[In thousands (5,808.7 represents 5,808,700). Based on sample and subject to sampling error. For details, see source]

Occupation	Total [1]	Wage and salary workers								Self employed [5]
		Mining [2]	Construction	Manufacturing	Transportation [3]	Trade	Fire [4]	Services	Government	
Scientists, engineers, and technicians	5,808.7	57.7	84.0	1,444.9	263.8	305.7	284.9	2,316.2	692.8	358.4
Scientists	708.0	12.3	0.2	74.8	6.8	5.7	13.4	274.3	198.6	121.7
Physical scientists	199.8	9.1	0.2	54.2	3.7	3.0	0.4	75.4	45.7	8.0
Life scientists	173.5	3.3	(NA)	16.8	0.6	1.6	0.5	69.5	73.5	7.7
Mathematical scientists	14.0	-	-	2.0	0.1	0.1	0.8	6.9	4.1	(NA)
Social scientists	320.7	(NA)	(NA)	1.8	2.3	0.9	11.7	122.4	75.3	106.1
Computer systems analysts, engineers and scientists	1,530.5	5.3	3.5	214.6	66.9	100.6	187.1	714.1	124.2	114.1
Engineers [6]	1,461.8	17.1	35.4	667.0	77.3	47.4	11.2	390.4	166.1	49.9
Civil engineers	195.0	0.7	13.5	5.9	4.2	0.9	0.6	93.6	63.6	12.0
Electrical/electronics	357.0	0.4	6.8	163.4	35.4	14.9	1.3	87.1	32.1	15.6
Mechanical engineers	219.7	0.6	5.6	127.8	3.2	7.2	1.4	58.0	11.6	4.5
Engineering and science technicians	1,350.6	18.2	40.8	428.9	75.3	103.8	6.4	490.6	151.7	35.1
Electrical/electronics technicians	334.8	0.9	15.6	113.7	29.2	71.9	2.0	78.0	16.2	7.3
Engineering technicians	436.5	2.7	6.5	146.1	25.2	19.1	0.5	149.1	84.9	2.5
Drafters	283.2	2.8	17.0	84.2	12.9	7.4	1.0	130.4	9.8	17.6
Science technicians	227.4	10.1	0.4	84.7	6.3	5.4	2.6	86.3	28.6	3.1
Surveyors [7]	110.0	2.5	2.8	0.3	2.7	0.1	0.6	75.9	18.2	6.8
Computer programmers	647.8	2.2	1.2	59.4	34.9	48.2	66.1	370.9	34.0	30.8

- Represents zero. NA Not available. [1] Includes agriculture, forestry, and fishing not shown separately. [2] Includes oil and gas extraction. [3] Includes communications and public utilities. [4] Finance, insurance, and real estate. [5] Includes secondary jobs. [6] Includes kinds of engineers and technicians not shown separately. [7] Includes cartographers, photogrammetrists, and surveying and mapping technicians.

Source: U.S. Bureau of Labor Statistics, *National Industry-Occupation Employment Matrix* November 1999; and unpublished data. (Data collected biennially.)

No. 784. Graduate Science/Engineering Students in Doctorate-Granting Colleges: 1985 to 1999

[358.8 represents 358,800. As of fall. Includes outlying areas]

Field of science or engineering	Total (1,000)			Percent—							
				Female			Foreign		Part-time		
	1985	1990	1999	1985	1990	1999	1990	1999	1985	1990	1999
Total, all surveyed fields	358.8	403.3	432.7	124.2	152.4	194.9	101.9	110.1	117.4	126.9	123.2
Science/engineering	319.4	355.4	364.4	94.4	115.4	144.1	97.9	104.8	98.9	104.0	98.5
Engineering, total	90.7	100.6	95.5	10.4	13.7	18.6	36.7	40.3	36.1	36.4	29.4
Sciences, total	228.7	254.8	268.9	84.0	101.7	125.5	61.2	64.6	62.8	67.7	69.1
Physical sciences	29.5	32.6	29.5	6.1	7.7	8.5	12.1	10.9	3.5	3.7	3.3
Environmental	14.2	13.0	12.8	3.6	3.8	5.1	2.6	2.5	3.4	3.1	2.8
Mathematical sciences	15.5	17.7	14.3	4.5	5.4	5.1	6.3	5.6	4.3	4.4	3.1
Computer sciences	24.2	28.6	35.4	6.1	6.6	10.1	9.4	15.1	11.7	13.5	15.2
Agricultural sciences	10.9	10.7	11.2	2.8	3.1	4.5	3.1	2.5	2.0	1.9	2.5
Biological sciences	42.5	46.7	53.3	18.1	21.3	27.5	11.2	11.1	►7.0	7.1	7.9
Psychology	31.3	37.0	39.3	18.7	24.4	27.8	1.7	2.0	9.8	11.1	10.7
Social sciences	60.5	68.6	73.1	24.1	29.4	36.9	14.8	15.0	21.0	22.8	23.6
Health fields, total	39.3	48.0	68.3	29.8	36.9	50.7	4.1	5.3	18.4	22.8	24.7

Source: U.S. National Science Foundation, *Survey of Graduate Science Engineering Students and Postdoctorates,* annual.

U.S. Census Bureau, Statistical Abstract of the United States: 2001

No. 785. Science and Engineering Degree Recipients in 1995 and 1996

[In thousands (708.9 represents 708,900) except for percent. Based on survey a and subject to sampling error; see source for details]

Degree and field	Graduates 1995 and 1996 (1,000)	1996 [1] Percent distribution				Median salary [4] ($1,000)
		In school [2]	Employed		Not employed or not FT students	
			In S&E [3]	In other		
Bachelor's recipients	708.9	21	21	53	5	28.2
All science fields	593.8	23	12	60	5	26.0
Computer and information sciences	41.0	6	57	34	3	37.7
Mathematical sciences	26.8	19	15	63	3	29.8
Life and related sciences	139.0	31	11	53	5	22.8
Physical and related sciences	36.6	38	26	33	3	27.3
Psychology	138.0	24	6	65	5	22.3
Social and related sciences	212.4	18	6	70	6	26.4
All engineering fields	115.1	13	65	18	3	37.7
Aerospace and related engineering	3.0	22	48	27	2	34.0
Chemical engineering	11.6	17	65	14	4	39.3
Civil and architectural engineering	20.7	14	63	20	3	34.4
Electrical, electronics, computer, and communications engineering	32.9	10	70	16	4	40.5
Industrial engineering	5.8	8	66	24	2	37.6
Mechanical engineering	27.9	11	71	15	3	38.2
Other engineering	13.2	21	52	25	3	34.1
Master's recipients	149.5	21	49	27	3	41.5
All science fields	102.5	23	36	36	4	37.2
Computer and mathematical sciences	18.2	6	74	18	2	51.2
Mathematical sciences	7.9	27	37	32	3	39.7
Life and related sciences	15.3	32	37	27	4	32.4
Physical and related sciences	9.7	37	42	18	3	33.6
Psychology	26.4	22	29	43	5	29.7
Social and related sciences	25.1	26	15	54	5	35.0
All engineering fields	47.0	15	75	9	2	49.9
Aerospace and related engineering	1.5	31	54	15	1	48.8
Chemical engineering	2.0	33	61	4	2	47.6
Civil and architectural engineering	6.5	11	76	11	1	41.9
Electrical, electronics, computer, and communications engineering	16.2	15	77	7	1	55.0
Industrial engineering	3.2	13	70	16	1	49.9
Mechanical engineering	7.2	16	72	10	2	47.7
Other engineering	10.4	10	78	9	4	49.0

[1] As of April. [2] Full-time students. [3] In science and engineering. [4] For the principal job. Excludes full-time students, the self-employed, and persons whose principal job is less than 35 hours per week.
Source: National Science Foundation/SRS, *National Survey of Recent College Graduates: 1997.*

No. 786. Doctorates Conferred by Recipients' Characteristics: 1990 and 1998

[In percent, except as indicated]

Characteristic	1990, total	1998									
		All fields [1]	Engineering	Physical sciences [2]	Earth sciences	Mathematics	Computer sciences	Biological sciences [3]	Agricultural	Social sciences [4]	Psychology
Total conferred (number)	36,068	42,683	5,919	3,801	838	1,177	923	6,646	1,192	3,394	3,681
Male	63.7	58.0	87.0	77.0	73.0	75.0	83.0	56.0	72.0	59.0	33.0
Female	36.3	42.0	13.0	23.0	27.0	25.0	17.0	44.0	28.0	41.0	67.0
Median age [5]	33.9	33.7	31.6	29.8	33.7	30.7	33.2	31.1	34.6	33.8	32.5
CITIZENSHIP [6]											
Total conferred (number)	34,697	39,556	5,413	3,526	781	1,085	860	5,509	1,102	3,113	3,410
U.S. citizen	71.8	78.2	55.8	68.5	73.9	61.4	64.1	77.7	56.7	75.6	95.6
Foreign citizen	28.2	21.8	44.2	31.5	26.1	38.6	35.9	22.3	43.3	24.4	4.4
RACE/ETHNICITY [7]											
Total conferred (number)	26,604	30,914	3,021	4,211	577	666	551	4,279	625	2,352	3,259
White [8]	86.5	78.1	71.5	78.3	82.8	78.4	73.7	75.4	76.8	78.1	80.7
Black [8]	3.8	5.1	2.8	2.2	1.6	2.4	2.5	2.5	3.7	6.2	4.8
Asian/Pacific [8]	4.9	8.8	18.4	12.9	8.8	10.7	16.5	15.4	9.3	7.9	3.5
Indian/Alaskan [8]	0.4	0.6	0.4	0.5	0.5	0.5	0.5	0.3	1.4	0.5	1.0
Hispanic	3.1	4.2	3.6	2.6	2.8	4.1	2.5	3.9	6.1	4.5	6.4
Other/unknown	1.4	3.1	3.3	3.5	3.5	4.1	4.2	2.5	2.7	2.9	3.7

[1] Includes other fields, not shown separately. [2] Astronomy, physics, and chemistry. [3] Biochemistry, botany, microbiology, physiology, zoology, and related fields. [4] Anthropology, sociology, political science, economics, international relations, and related fields. [5] For definition of median, see Guide to Tabular Presentation. [6] For those with known citizenship. Includes those with temporary visas. [7] Excludes those with temporary visas. [8] Non-Hispanic.
Source: U.S. National Science Foundation, Division of Science Resources Studies, Survey of Earned Doctorates, *Selected Data on Science and Engineering Doctorate Awards,* annual.

U.S. Census Bureau, Statistical Abstract of the United States: 2001

No. 787. Space Vehicle Systems—Net Sales and Backlog Orders: 1965 to 1999

[In millions of dollars (2,449 represents $2,449,000,000). Backlog orders as of Dec. 31. Based on data from major companies engaged in manufacture of aerospace products. Includes parts but excludes engines and propulsion units]

Year	Net sales			Backlog orders			Year	Net sales			Backlog orders		
	Total	Military	Non-military	Total	Military	Non-military		Total	Military	Non-military	Total	Military	Non-military
1965 .	2,449	602	1,847	2,203	503	1,700	1994 .	10,594	5,707	4,887	12,888	6,732	6,156
1970 .	1,956	1,025	931	1,184	786	398	1995 .	11,314	4,782	6,532	15,650	5,872	9,778
1975 .	2,119	1,096	1,023	1,304	1,019	285	1996 .	11,698	5,613	6,085	23,004	9,125	13,879
1980 .	3,483	1,461	2,022	1,814	951	863	1997 .	13,410	4,916	8,494	23,357	8,790	14,567
1985 .	6,300	4,241	2,059	6,707	4,941	1,766	1998 .	9,490	4,227	5,264	20,371	7,970	12,402
1990 .	9,691	6,556	3,135	12,462	8,130	4,332	1999 .	9,022	5,107	3,915	21,026	10,036	10,989

Source: U.S. Census Bureau, *Current Industrial Reports*, MA-37D, *Aerospace Industry (Orders, Sales, and Backlog)* and, beginning 1994, Internet site <http://www.census.gov/cir/www>.

No. 788. Federal Outlays for General Science, Space, and Other Technology: 1970 to 2006

[In billions of dollars (4.5 represents $4,500,000,000). For fiscal years ending in year shown; see text, Section 8, State and Local Government Finances and Employment]

Year	Current dollars			Constant (1996) dollars		
	Total	General science/basic research	Space and other technologies	Total	General science/basic research	Space and other technologies
1970	4.5	0.9	3.6	18.5	3.9	14.6
1980	5.8	1.4	4.5	11.6	2.7	8.9
1985	8.6	2.0	6.6	12.8	3.0	9.8
1990	14.4	2.8	11.6	18.4	3.6	14.8
1995	16.7	4.1	12.6	17.3	4.3	13.0
1996	16.7	4.0	12.7	16.7	4.0	12.7
1997	17.2	4.1	13.1	16.9	4.0	12.9
1998	18.2	5.4	12.9	17.5	5.1	12.4
1999	18.1	5.7	12.4	17.0	5.3	11.7
2000	18.6	6.2	12.4	17.0	5.6	11.3
2001, est	19.7	6.9	12.9	17.6	6.1	11.5
2002, est	20.8	7.4	13.4	18.1	6.4	11.7
2003, est	21.4	7.7	13.7	18.2	6.5	11.8
2004, est	22.2	7.9	14.2	18.6	6.6	12.0
2005, est	22.6	8.0	14.6	18.6	6.6	12.1
2006, est	23.1	8.2	15.0	18.7	6.6	12.1

Source: U.S. Office of Management and Budget, *Budget of the United States, Historical Tables, Fiscal Year 2002*, annual.

No. 789. U.S. Commercial Space Industry Revenue by Type: 1996 to 2000

[In billions of dollars (19.6 represents $19,600,000,000). For calendar years]

Industry	1996	1997	1998	1999	2000, est.
Total	19.6	26.7	30.5	31.9	37.5
Satellite manufacturing [1]	7.3	10.3	11.8	10.0	10.0
Launch industry	3.2	3.6	3.5	3.5	5.8
Satellite services [1]	4.8	6.3	7.4	9.8	12.2
Ground equipment manufacturing [1]	4.3	6.5	7.8	8.6	9.5

[1] See footnotes for corresponding objects in Table 790.

No. 790. Worldwide Commercial Space Industry Revenue by Type: 1996 to 2000

[In billions of dollars (44.8 represents $44,800,000,000). For calendar years]

Industry	1996	1997	1998	1999	2000, est.
Total	44.8	57.5	63.9	69.1	82.6
Satellite manufacturing [1]	12.4	15.9	18.5	15.8	18.3
Launch industry	6.9	7.9	7.0	6.6	9.6
Satellite services [2]	15.8	21.2	24.5	30.7	37.0
Ground equipment manufacturing [3]	9.7	12.5	13.9	16.0	17.7

[1] Includes revenues from the construction and sale of satellites to both commercial and government. [2] Includes revenues derived from transponder leasing and subscription/retail services such as direct-to-home television and satellite mobile and data communications. [3] Includes revenues from the manufacture of gateways and satellite control stations, satellite news-gathering trucks, very small aperture terminals, direct-to-home television equipment and mobile satellite phones.

Source of Tables 789 and 790: Satellite Industry Association/Futron Corporation, Bethesda, MD, *1999 Satellite Survey* (copyright).

No. 791. National Aeronautics and Space Administration—Budget Authority: 1999 and Projections to 2004

[In millions of dollars (13,653.0 represents $13,653,000,000)]

Item	1999	2000	2001	2002	2003	2004
Budget authority, total.............	13,653.0	13,600.8	14,035.3	14,465.4	14,769.2	15,305.4
Human space flight......................	5,480.0	5,467.7	5,499.9	5,387.6	4,939.0	4,817.4
International space station	2,299.7	2,323.1	2,114.5	1,858.5	1,452.5	1,327.0
Space flight operations (space shuttle)	2,998.3	2,979.5	3,165.7	3,307.8	3,264.9	3,253.3
Payload utilization and operations	182.0	165.1	(NA)	(NA)	(NA)	(NA)
Payload and elv support................	(X)	(X)	90.2	90.3	91.5	97.0
Investments and support................	(X)	(X)	129.5	131.0	130.1	140.1
Science, aeronautics and technology	5,653.9	5,580.9	5,929.4	6,388.9	6,993.9	7,571.3
Space science	2,119.2	2,192.8	2,398.8	2,606.4	2,961.4	3,298.8
Life and microgravity sciences and applications	263.5	274.7	302.4	300.3	304.1	323.2
Earth science	1,413.8	1,443.4	1,405.8	1,332.5	1,293.3	1,303.4
Aerospace technology	1,338.9	1,124.9	1,193.0	1,548.9	1,948.8	2,244.7
Mission communication services	380.0	406.3	(NA)	(NA)	(NA)	(NA)
Space operations	(X)	(X)	529.4	500.8	386.3	301.2
Academic programs...................	138.5	138.8	100.0	100.0	100.0	100.0
Mission support	2,499.5	2,532.2	2,584.0	2,666.2	2,812.7	2,892.2
Safety, mission assurance, engineering and advanced concepts	35.6	43.0	47.5	51.5	51.5	51.5
Space communication services	185.8	89.7	(NA)	(NA)	(NA)	(NA)
Research and program management	2,109.6	2,217.6	2,290.6	2,383.7	2,482.2	2,569.7
Construction of facilities	168.5	181.9	245.9	231.0	279.0	271.0
Inspector General......................	19.6	20.0	22.0	22.7	23.6	24.5

NA Not available.   X Not applicable.

Source: U.S. National Aeronautics and Space Administration, <http://ifmp.nasa.gov/codeb/budget2002/2002websites.html>.

No. 792. NASA Space Shuttle Operations Expenditures: 1996 to 2001

[In millions of dollars (2,485.4 represents $2,485,400,000). Data are funding requirements for fiscal years shown]

Operation	1996	1997	1998	1999	2000	2001, est.
Total	2,485.4	2,464.9	2,369.4	2,998.3	2,979.5	3,165.7
Shuttle operations......................	2,485.4	2,464.9	2,369.4	2,426.7	2,490.7	2,672.8
Orbiter and integration	521.0	492.6	502.9	608.0	698.8	724.5
Propulsion........................	1,061.5	1,124.7	1,061.8	1,071.2	1,053.1	1,167.4
External tank......................	327.5	352.4	341.3	363.2	355.2	349.7
Space shuttle main engine...........	185.0	208.3	204.6	200.0	187.5	261.9
Reusable solid rocket motor............	395.7	412.8	380.4	339.0	356.7	418.3
Solid rocket booster	153.3	151.2	135.5	169.0	153.7	137.5
Mission and launch operations...........	902.9	847.6	804.7	747.5	738.8	780.9
Safety and performance upgrades	(X)	(X)	(X)	571.6	488.8	492.9
Orbiter improvements...................	(X)	(X)	(X)	234.8	183.7	327.2
Propulsion upgrades	(X)	(X)	(X)	175.7	213.2	60.2
Flight operations and launch site equipment...	(X)	(X)	(X)	147.6	80.9	90.0
Construction of facilities	(X)	(X)	(X)	13.5	11.0	15.5

X Not applicable.

Source: U.S. National Aeronautics and Space Administration, *NASA, 1996-97, Pocket Statistics,* annual; thereafter, <http://ifmp.nasa.gov/codeb/budget2002/2002websites.html>.

No. 793. World-Wide Successful Space Launches: 1957 to 2000

[Criterion of success is attainment of Earth orbit or Earth escape]

Country	Total, 1957-99	1957-64	1965-69	1970-74	1975-79	1980-84	1985-89	1990-94	1995-99	1999	2000
Total	4,042	289	586	555	607	605	550	466	384	73	82
Soviet Union/Russia [1] ...	2,598	82	302	405	461	483	447	283	135	26	35
United States	1,188	207	279	139	126	93	61	122	161	30	28
Japan	54	-	-	5	10	12	11	9	7	-	-
ESA [2].............	117	-	-	-	1	8	21	33	54	10	12
China.............	59	-	-	2	6	6	9	15	21	4	5
France	10	-	4	3	3	-	-	-	-	-	-
India	9	-	-	-	-	3	-	3	3	1	-
Israel	3	-	-	-	-	-	-	1	1	-	-
Ukraine [1]	2	(NA)	(NA)	(NA)	(NA)	(NA)	(NA)	(NA)	2	2	2
Australia...........	1	-	1	-	-	-	-	-	-	-	-
United Kingdom	1	-	-	1	-	-	-	-	-	-	-

- Represents zero.   NA Not available.   [1] Since Commonwealth of Independent States (CIS) barely exists, now show Russia as the successor to the Soviet space program and Ukraine separately.   [2] European Space Agency. Includes launches by Arianespace.

Source: Library of Congress, Congressional Research Service, Science Policy Research Division, *Space Activities of the United States, CIS, and Other Launching Countries/Organizations 1957-1994,* July 31, 1995; and forthcoming report.

Science and Technology 519

No. 794. Space Shuttle Launches—Summary: 1981 to July 2001

Flight number	Mission date	Orbiter name	Crew size (up/down)	Days/hours duration	Flight number	Mission date	Orbiter name	Crew size (up/down)	Days/hours duration
1	04/12/81	Columbia	2	2	61	12/2/93	Endeavour	7	11
2	11/12/81	Columbia	2	2	60	2/3/94	Discovery	6	8
3	03/22/82	Columbia	2	8	62	3/4/94	Columbia	5	14
4	06/27/82	Columbia	2	7	59	4/9/94	Endeavour	6	11
5	11/11/82	Columbia	4	5	65	7/8/94	Columbia	7	15
6	04/04/83	Challenger	4	5	64	9/9/94	Discovery	6	11
7	6/18/83	Challenger	5	6	68	9/30/94	Endeavour	6	11
8	8/30/83	Challenger	5	6	66	11/3/94	Atlantis	6	11
9	11/28/83	Columbia	6	10	63	2/3/95	Discovery	6	8
10	02/03/84	Challenger	5	8	67	3/2/95	Endeavour	7	17
11	04/06/84	Challenger	5	7	71	6/27/95	Atlantis	7/8	10
12	08/30/84	Discovery	6	7	70	7/13/95	Discovery	5	9
13	10/05/84	Challenger	7	8	69	9/7/95	Endeavour	5	11
14	11/08/84	Discovery	5	8	73	10/20/95	Columbia	7	16
15	01/24/85	Discovery	5	4	74	11/8/95	Atlantis	5	8
16	04/12/85	Discovery	7	7	72	1/11/96	Endeavour	6	9
17	04/29/85	Challenger	7	7	75	2/22/96	Columbia	7	16
18	06/17/85	Discovery	7	7	76	3/22/96	Atlantis	6/5	9
19	7/29/85	Challenger	7	8	77	5/19/96	Endeavour	6	10
20	8/27/85	Discovery	5	7	78	6/20/96	Columbia	7	17
21	10/3/85	Atlantis	5	4	79	9/16/96	Atlantis	6	10
22	10/30/85	Challenger	8	7	80	11/20/96	Columbia	5	18
23	11/26/85	Atlantis	7	7	81	01/12/97	Atlantis	6	10/05
24	1/12/86	Columbia	7	6	82	02/11/97	Discovery	7	10/00
25	1/28/86	Challenger	7	-	83	04/04/97	Columbia	7	03/23
26	9/29/88	Discovery	5	4	84	05/15/97	Atlantis	7/7	09/05
27	12/2/88	Atlantis	5	4	94	07/01/97	Columbia	7	15/07
29	3/13/89	Discovery	5	5	85	08/07/97	Discovery	5	11/20
30	5/4/89	Atlantis	5	4	86	09/25/97	Atlantis	7/7	10/19
28	8/8/89	Columbia	5	5	87	11/19/97	Columbia	6	15/17
34	10/18/89	Atlantis	5	5	89	01/22/98	Endeavor	7/7	08/20
33	11/22/89	Discovery	5	5	90	04/17/98	Columbia	7	15/22
32	1/9/90	Columbia	5	11	91	06/02/98	Discovery	6/7	09/19
36	2/28/90	Atlantis	5	4	95	11/20/98	Discovery	7	08/22
31	4/24/90	Discovery	5	5	88	12/04/98	Endeavor	6	11/19
41	10/6/90	Discovery	5	4	96	05/27/99	Discovery	7	09/19
38	11/15/90	Atlantis	5	5	93	07/23/99	Columbia	5	04/24
35	12/2/90	Columbia	7	9	103	12/19/99	Atlantis	7	07/23
37	4/5/91	Atlantis	5	6	99	02/11/00	Endeavor	6	11/04
39	4/28/91	Discovery	7	8	101	05/19/00	Atlantis	7	09/21
40	6/5/91	Columbia	7	9	106	09/08/00	Atlantis	7	11/19
43	8/2/91	Atlantis	5	9	92	10/11/00	Discovery	7	12/21
48	9/12/91	Discovery	5	5	98	12/02/00	Endeavor	5	10/20
44	11/24/91	Atlantis	6	7	97	02/07/01	Atlantis	5	12/21
42	1/22/92	Discovery	7	8	102	03/08/01	Discovery	7/7	12/20
45	3/24/92	Atlantis	7	9	100	04/19/01	Endeavor	7	11/20
49	5/7/92	Endeavour	7	9	104	07/12/01	Atlantis	5	12/19
50	6/25/92	Columbia	7	14					
46	7/31/92	Atlantis	7	8	FUTURE MISSIONS IN WORK				
47	9/12/92	Endeavour	7	8					
52	10/22/92	Columbia	6	10	105	10/05/2000	Discovery	7/7	7
53	12/2/92	Discovery	5	7	108	11/30/2000	Endeavor	7/7	10
54	1/13/93	Endeavour	5	6	109	1/18/2001	Columbia	7	11
56	4/8/93	Discovery	5	9	110	2/15/2001	Atlantis	7	9
55	4/26/93	Columbia	7	10	107	4/04/2002	Columbia	7	16
57	6/21/93	Endeavour	6	10	111	4/18/2002	Endeavor	4	10
51	9/12/93	Discovery	5	10					
58	10/18/93	Columbia	7	14					

- Represents zero.

Source: U.S. National Aeronautics and Space Administration, Internet site <http://www.ksc.nasa.gov/shuttle/missions/missions.html> (accessed 13 August 2001).

No. 795. Nobel Prize Laureates in Selected Sciences: 1901 to 1999

[Presented by location of award-winning research and by date of award]

Country	1901-1999 Total	Physics	Chemistry	Physiology/ Medicine	1901-1930	1931-1945	1946-1960	1961-1975	1976-1990	1991-1998	1999
Total	459	158	132	169	93	49	74	92	98	51	4
United States	199	70	47	82	6	14	38	41	63	36	3
United Kingdom	71	21	26	24	15	11	14	20	9	2	-
Germany [1]	61	17	29	15	27	11	4	8	7	3	-
France	25	11	7	7	13	2	-	5	2	3	-
Soviet Union	10	7	1	2	2	-	4	3	1	-	-
Japan	4	3	1	-	-	-	1	2	1	-	-
Other countries	89	29	21	39	30	11	13	13	15	7	1

- Represents zero. [1] Between 1946 and 1991, data are for the former West Germany only.

Source: U.S. National Science Foundation, unpublished data.

520 Science and Technology

This section presents statistics on farms and farm operators; land use; farm income, expenditures, and debt; farm output, productivity, and marketings; foreign trade in agricultural products; specific crops; and livestock, poultry, and their products.

The principal sources are the reports issued by the National Agricultural Statistics Service (NASS) and the Economic Research Service (ERS) of the U.S. Department of Agriculture. The information from the 1997 Census of Agriculture is available in printed form in the Volume 1, Geographic Area Series; in electronic format on CD-ROM; and on the Internet site <http://www.nass.usda.gov/census/>. The Department of Agriculture publishes annually *Agricultural Statistics*, a general reference book on agricultural production, supplies, consumption, facilities, costs, and returns. The ERS publishes data on farm assets, debt, and income on the Internet site <http://www.ers.usda.gov/briefing/farmincome/>. Sources of current data on agricultural exports and imports include *Foreign Agricultural Trade of the United States*, published by the ERS, and the reports of the U.S. Census Bureau, particularly *U.S. Imports of Merchandise on CD-ROM*, and *U.S. Exports of Merchandise on CD-ROM*.

The 45 field offices of the NASS collect data on crops, livestock and products, agricultural prices, farm employment, and other related subjects mainly through sample surveys. Information is obtained on some 75 crops and 50 livestock items as well as scores of items pertaining to agricultural production and marketing. State estimates and supporting information are sent to the Agricultural Statistics Board of NASS which reviews the estimates and issues reports containing state and national data. Among these reports are annual summaries such as *Crop Production*, *Crop Values*, *Agricultural Prices*, and *Livestock Production, Disposition and*

Income. For more information about concepts and methods underlying USDA's statistical series, see *Major Statistical Series of the U.S. Department of Agriculture* (Agricultural Handbook No. 671), a 12-volume set of publications.

Farms and farmland—The definitions of a farm have varied through time. Since 1850, when minimum criteria defining a farm for census purposes first were established, the farm definition has changed nine times. The current definition, first used for the 1974 census, is any place from which $1,000 or more of agricultural products were produced and sold, or normally would have been sold, during the census year.

Acreage designated as "land in farms" consists primarily of agricultural land used for crops, pasture, or grazing. It also includes woodland and wasteland not actually under cultivation or used for pasture or grazing, provided it was part of the farm operator's total operation. Land in farms includes acres set aside under annual commodity acreage programs as well as acres in the Conservation Reserve and Wetlands Reserve Programs for places meeting the farm definition. Land in farms is an operating unit concept and includes land owned and operated as well as land rented from others. All grazing land, except land used under government permits on a per-head basis, was included as "land in farms" provided it was part of a farm or ranch.

Since 1945, an evaluation of census coverage has been conducted for each census of agriculture to provide estimates of the completeness of census farm counts. According to coverage evaluation results, the past five censuses of agriculture included an average of 92 percent of U.S. farms and 98 percent of agriculture production. The 1997 coverage evaluation program was designed to measure four components of error in the census farm

Agriculture   521

counts. These components include under-count due to farms not on the mail list; overcount due to farms duplicated or enumerated more than once; undercount due to farms incorrectly classified as non-farms; and overcount due to nonfarms incorrectly classified as farms. The first component, mail list undercount, is by far the largest component of coverage error. The percentage of farms missed in the census varies considerably by state. In general, farms not on the mail list tended to be small in acreage, production, and sales of agricultural products. For more explanation about mail list compilation and census coverage, see Appendixes A and C, *1997 Census of Agriculture*, Volume 1, reports.

Farm income—The final agricultural sector output comprises cash receipts from farm marketings of crops and livestock, federal government payments made directly to farmers for farm-related activities, rental value of farm homes, value of farm products consumed in farm homes, and other farm-related income such as machine hire and custom work. Farm marketings represent quantities of agricultural products sold by farmers multiplied by prices received per unit of production at the local market. Information on prices received for farm products is generally obtained by the NASS Agricultural Statistics Board from surveys of firms (such as grain elevators, packers, and processors) purchasing agricultural commodities directly from producers. In some cases, the price information is obtained directly from the producers.

Crops—Estimates of crop acreage and production by the NASS are based on current sample survey data obtained from individual producers and objective yield

counts, reports of carlot shipments, market records, personal field observations by field statisticians, and reports from other sources. Prices received by farmers are marketing year averages. These averages are based on U.S. monthly prices weighted by monthly marketings during specific periods. U.S. monthly prices are state average prices weighted by marketings during the month. Marketing year average prices do not include allowances for outstanding loans, government purchases, deficiency payments or disaster payments.

All state prices are based on individual state marketing years, while U.S. marketing year averages are based on standard marketing years for each crop. For a listing of the crop marketing years and the participating states in the monthly program, see *Crop Values*. Value of production is computed by multiplying state prices by each state's production. The U.S. value of production is the sum of state values for all states. Value of production figures shown in Tables 827-830, 834, and 835 should not be confused with cash receipts from farm marketings which relate to sales during a calendar year, irrespective of the year of production.

Livestock—Annual inventory numbers of livestock and estimates of livestock, dairy, and poultry production prepared by the Department of Agriculture are based on information from farmers and ranchers obtained by probability survey sampling methods.

Statistical reliability—For a discussion of statistical collection and estimation, sampling procedures, and measures of statistical reliability pertaining to Department of Agriculture data, see Appendix III.

No. 796. Farms—Number and Acreage by Size of Farm: 1987 to 1997

[2,088 represents 2,088,000]

Size of farm	Number of farms (1,000)			Land in farms (mil. acres)			Cropland harvested (mil. acres)			Percent distribution, 1997		
	1987	1992	1997	1987	1992	1997	1987	1992	1997	Number of farms	All land in farms	Cropland harvested
Total	2,088	1,925	1,912	964.5	945.5	931.8	282.2	295.9	309.4	100.0	100.0	100.0
Under 10 acres	183	166	154	0.7	0.7	0.6	0.2	0.2	0.2	8.1	0.1	0.1
10 to 49 acres	412	388	411	11.1	10.3	11.0	3.9	3.5	3.6	21.5	1.2	1.2
50 to 99 acres	311	283	295	22.5	20.4	21.2	7.9	7.2	7.0	15.4	2.3	2.3
100 to 179 acres.	334	301	298	45.3	40.7	40.2	17.1	15.4	14.3	15.6	4.3	4.6
180 to 259 acres.	192	172	165	41.5	37.2	35.5	17.2	15.5	14.0	8.6	3.8	4.5
260 to 499 acres.	286	255	238	103.0	91.7	85.4	47.3	43.6	39.3	12.4	9.2	12.7
500 to 999 acres.	200	186	176	138.5	129.3	122.1	67.4	68.6	65.4	9.2	13.1	21.1
1,000 to 1,999 acres . .	102	102	101	138.8	139.0	138.8	61.1	69.3	73.8	5.3	14.9	23.9
2,000 acres and over. .	67	71	75	463.2	476.3	476.9	60.2	72.5	91.8	3.9	51.2	29.7

No. 797. Farms—Number and Acreage by Tenure of Operator: 1987 to 1997

[2,088 represents 2,088,000. Full owners own all the land they operate. Part owners own a part and rent from others the rest of the land they operate]

Item and year	Unit	Total	Full owner	Part owner	Tenant	Percent distribution			
						Total	Full owner	Part owner	Tenant
NUMBER OF FARMS									
1987	1,000. . . .	2,088	1,239	609	240	100.0	59.3	29.2	11.5
1992	1,000. . . .	1,925	1,112	597	217	100.0	57.7	31.0	11.3
1997	1,000. . . .	1,912	1,147	574	191	100.0	60.0	30.0	10.0
Under 50 acres	1,000. . . .	564	460	57	48	100.0	81.6	10.1	8.5
50 to 179 acres	1,000. . . .	593	409	131	53	100.0	69.0	22.1	8.9
180 to 499 acres	1,000. . . .	403	189	169	45	100.0	46.9	41.9	11.2
500 to 999 acres	1,000. . . .	176	50	103	23	100.0	28.4	58.5	13.0
1,000 acres or more	1,000. . . .	176	40	114	22	100.0	22.7	64.8	12.5
LAND IN FARMS									
1987	Mil. acres .	964	318	520	127	100.0	32.9	53.9	13.2
1992	Mil. acres .	946	296	527	123	100.0	31.3	55.7	13.0
1997	Mil. acres .	932	316	508	108	100.0	33.9	54.5	11.6

No. 798. Farm Operators—Tenure and Characteristics: 1992 and 1997

[In thousands, except as indicated (1,925 represents 1,925,000)]

Characteristic	All farms		Farms with sales of $10,000 and over		Characteristic	All farms		Farms with sales of $10,000 and over	
	1992	1997	1992	1997		1992	1997	1992	1997
Total operators	1,925	1,912	1,019	949	Tenant	217	191	148	126
White.	1,882	1,865	1,003	932	Principal occupation:				
Black.	19	18	5	4	Farming	1,053	962	754	675
American Indian, Eskimo,					Other	872	950	265	274
and Aleut	8	10	3	4	Place of residence: [2]				
Asian or Pacific Islander	8	9	5	5	On farm operated	1,379	1,362	736	681
Other.	8	10	3	3	Not on farm operated	409	413	215	201
Operators of Hispanic origin [1] .	21	28	8	11	Years on present farm: [2]				
Female	145	165	50	52	2 years or less	95	93	41	35
					3 to 4 years.	133	127	58	46
Under 25 years old	28	21	17	12	5 to 9 years	259	264	121	109
25 to 34 years old	179	128	112	72	10 years or more	1,113	1,114	648	616
35 to 44 years old	382	371	217	200	Days worked off farm: [2]				
45 to 54 years old	429	467	223	232	None	802	755	536	476
55 to 64 years old	430	427	229	212	Less than 100 days	165	165	104	98
65 years old and over.	478	497	220	222	100 to 199 days	162	168	76	76
Average age (years).	53.3	54.3	51.9	53.2	200 days or more	666	709	226	229
Full owner	1,112	1,147	422	404					
Part owner	597	574	448	419					

[1] Operators of Hispanic origin may be of any race.   [2] Excludes not reported.

Source of Tables 796-798: U.S. Dept. of Agriculture, National Agricultural Statistics Service, *Census of Agriculture: 1992,* Vol. 1; and *1997*, Vol. 1.

U.S. Census Bureau, Statistical Abstract of the United States: 2001

No. 799. Farms—Number, Acreage, and Value by Type of Organization: 1992 and 1997

[1,925 represents 1,925,000]

Item	Unit	Total [1]	Indi- vidual or family	Partner- ship	Corpor- ation	Total [1]	Indi- vidual or family	Partner- ship	Corpor- ation
						Percent distribution			
ALL FARMS									
Number of farms:									
1992	1,000 ...	1,925	1,653	187	73	100.0	85.9	9.7	3.8
1997	1,000 ...	1,912	1,643	169	84	100.0	85.9	8.8	4.4
Land in farms:									
1992	Mil. acres.	946	604	153	123	100.0	63.9	16.2	13.0
1997	Mil. acres.	932	585	149	131	100.0	62.8	16.0	14.1
Value of land and buildings: [2]									
1992	Bil. dol. ..	687	474	109	85	100.0	69.0	15.8	12.4
1997	Bil. dol. ..	860	593	133	114	100.0	69.0	15.5	13.3
Value of farm products sold:									
1992	Bil. dol. ..	163	88	29	44	100.0	54.1	18.0	27.2
1997	Bil. dol. ..	197	103	36	57	100.0	52.6	18.4	29.1
FARMS WITH SALES OF $10,000 AND OVER									
Number of farms:									
1992	1,000 ...	1,019	820	131	61	100.0	80.5	12.8	6.0
1997	1,000 ...	949	758	114	70	100.0	79.9	12.0	7.4
Land in farms:									
1992	Mil. acres.	822	512	143	119	100.0	62.2	17.4	14.4
1997	Mil. acres.	802	485	138	126	100.0	60.5	17.2	15.7

[1] Includes other types, not shown separately. [2] Based on a sample of farms.

No. 800. Corporate Farms—Characteristics by Type: 1997

[131.5 represents 131,500,000]

Item	Unit	All corpora- tions	Total	1-10 stock- holders	11 or more stock- holders	Total	1-10 stock- holders	11 or more stock- holders
			Family held corporations			Other corporations		
Farms	Number...	84,002	76,103	74,308	1,795	7,899	6,870	1,029
Percent distribution	Percent ...	100.0	90.6	88.5	2.1	9.4	8.2	1.2
Land in farms	Mil. acres..	131.5	119.6	109.6	10.0	11.9	8.8	3.1
Average per farm	Acres	1,565	1,571	1,474	5,571	1,507	1,284	2,994
Value of—								
Land and buildings [1]	Bil. dol. ...	113.7	99.3	91.6	7.7	14.4	9.3	5.1
Average per farm	$1,000	1,380	1,338	1,264	4,429	1,769	1,288	5,450
Farm products sold	Bil. dol. ...	56.9	45.9	40.8	5.1	11.0	7.3	3.8
Average per farm	$1,000 ...	677	603	548	2,862	1,395	1,057	3,649

[1] Based on a sample of farms.

No. 801. Farms—Number, Acreage, and Value of Sales by Size of Sales: 1997

[1,912 represents 1,912,000]

Value of products sold	Farms (1,000)	Total (mil.)	Average per farm	Total (mil. dol.)	Average per farm (dol.)	Farms	Acreage	Value of sales
		Acreage		Value of sales		Percent distribution		
Total	1,912	931.8	487	196,865	102,970	100.0	100.0	100.0
Less than $10,000	963	129.5	134	2,937	3,050	50.4	13.9	1.5
Less than $2,500	497	63.8	128	424	854	26.0	6.8	0.2
$2,500-$4,999	228	26.3	115	820	3,591	12.0	2.8	0.4
$5,000-$9,999	238	39.4	166	1,693	7,113	12.4	4.2	0.9
$10,000 or more	949	802.3	846	193,928	204,373	49.6	86.1	98.5
$10,000-$24,999	274	75.3	275	4,372	15,955	14.3	8.1	2.2
$25,000-$49,999	171	82.0	481	6,084	35,642	8.9	8.8	3.1
$50,000-$99,999	158	118.0	746	11,347	71,741	8.3	12.7	5.8
$100,000-$249,999	189	207.5	1,095	30,143	159,137	9.9	22.3	15.3
$250,000-$499,999	88	138.4	1,577	30,505	347,531	4.6	14.9	15.5
$500,000-$999,999	43	91.3	2,129	29,365	685,140	2.2	9.8	14.9
$1,000,000 or more	26	89.8	3,464	82,110	3,166,152	1.4	9.6	41.7

Source of Tables 799-801: U.S. Dept. of Agriculture, National Agricultural Statistics Service. *1997 Census of Agriculture,* Vol. 1.

[1,925 represents 1,925,000]

State	All farms								Farms with sales of $10,000 or more, 1997		
	Number of farms (1,000)		Land in farms (mil. acres)		Average size of farm (acres)		Total value [1] (mil. dol.)		Number of farms (1,000)	Land in farms (mil. acres)	Average size of farm (acres)
	1992	1997	1992	1997	1992	1997	1992	1997			
United States .	1,925	1,912	945.5	931.8	491	487	687,432	859,839	949	802.3	846
Alabama	38	41	8.5	8.7	223	210	8,350	12,340	13	5.2	406
Alaska	1	1	0.9	0.9	1,803	1,608	249	267	(Z)	0.7	3,088
Arizona	7	6	35.0	26.9	5,173	4,379	10,984	10,360	3	25.5	8,681
Arkansas	44	45	14.1	14.4	322	318	12,407	16,255	20	11.4	556
California	78	74	29.0	27.7	373	374	63,689	69,768	42	25.2	605
Colorado	27	28	34.0	32.6	1,252	1,154	14,568	19,993	15	28.9	1,943
Connecticut	3	4	0.4	0.4	105	97	2,138	2,104	1	0.2	159
Delaware	3	2	0.6	0.6	224	236	1,351	1,499	2	0.5	319
Florida	35	35	10.8	10.5	306	300	21,801	23,048	15	8.8	596
Georgia	41	40	10.0	10.7	246	265	11,437	15,842	16	7.5	468
Hawaii	5	5	1.6	1.4	298	263	3,854	3,460	2	1.3	572
Idaho	22	22	13.5	11.8	609	530	9,077	11,983	12	10.3	866
Illinois	78	73	27.3	27.2	351	372	41,844	56,475	50	25.6	515
Indiana	63	58	15.6	15.1	249	261	21,732	30,853	33	13.5	415
Iowa	97	91	31.3	31.2	325	343	38,063	51,438	67	29.2	435
Kansas	63	62	46.7	46.1	738	748	21,725	26,517	39	42.6	1,099
Kentucky	90	82	13.7	13.3	151	162	14,775	18,943	36	9.7	268
Louisiana	26	24	7.8	7.9	306	331	7,474	9,077	10	6.3	661
Maine	6	6	1.3	1.2	218	209	1,396	1,456	2	0.8	337
Maryland	13	12	2.2	2.2	171	178	6,570	6,825	6	1.8	295
Massachusetts . .	5	6	0.5	0.5	100	93	2,421	2,535	3	0.3	130
Michigan	47	46	10.1	9.9	217	215	11,517	16,490	23	8.1	359
Minnesota	75	73	25.7	26.0	342	354	23,319	29,927	47	23.0	486
Mississippi	32	31	10.2	10.1	318	323	7,952	10,555	10	6.9	658
Missouri	98	99	28.5	28.8	291	292	22,070	30,589	44	22.2	505
Montana	23	24	59.6	58.6	2,613	2,414	13,578	16,970	15	52.3	3,499
Nebraska	53	51	44.4	45.5	839	885	22,713	29,200	40	43.6	1,092
Nevada	3	3	9.3	6.4	3,205	2,266	2,347	2,474	1	6.2	4,209
New Hampshire. .	2	3	0.4	0.4	158	141	836	945	1	0.2	222
New Jersey	9	9	0.8	0.8	93	91	5,590	5,403	4	0.6	179
New Mexico	14	14	46.8	45.8	3,281	3,249	9,220	8,801	5	41.6	7,593
New York	32	32	7.5	7.3	231	228	9,130	9,117	17	5.7	334
North Carolina. . .	52	49	8.9	9.1	172	185	13,950	18,566	23	7.2	314
North Dakota . . .	31	31	39.4	39.4	1,267	1,290	13,163	15,635	23	36.4	1,590
Ohio	71	69	14.2	14.1	201	206	20,626	28,450	36	11.8	328
Oklahoma	67	74	32.1	33.2	480	448	15,754	20,188	30	26.7	899
Oregon	32	34	17.6	17.4	552	513	11,824	16,316	13	15.5	1,193
Pennsylvania . . .	45	45	7.2	7.2	160	158	14,752	16,891	25	5.4	221
Rhode Island . . .	1	1	0.1	0.1	76	75	313	325	(Z)	(Z)	107
South Carolina . .	20	20	4.5	4.6	221	228	5,093	6,558	6	2.9	470
South Dakota . . .	34	31	44.8	44.4	1,316	1,418	12,264	15,237	24	40.2	1,669
Tennessee	75	77	11.2	11.1	149	145	13,977	20,066	21	6.7	315
Texas	181	194	130.9	131.3	725	676	65,060	77,351	65	108.0	1,662
Utah	14	14	9.6	12.0	712	848	4,704	6,894	6	11.0	1,776
Vermont	5	6	1.3	1.3	235	217	1,730	1,876	3	1.0	321
Virginia	42	41	8.3	8.2	197	200	13,534	15,813	16	5.9	364
Washington	30	29	15.7	15.2	520	523	14,178	18,410	14	12.8	913
West Virginia . . .	17	18	3.3	3.5	192	194	2,810	3,790	4	1.5	401
Wisconsin.	68	66	15.5	14.9	228	227	14,285	18,504	40	12.4	309
Wyoming	9	9	32.9	34.1	3,772	3,692	5,242	7,460	6	30.9	5,349

Z Less than 500 farms or 50,000 acres.   [1] Value of land and buildings. Based on reports for a sample of farms.

Source: U.S. Dept. of Agriculture, National Agricultural Statistics Service, *1997 Census of Agriculture*, Vol. 1.

No. 803. Farms—Number and Acreage: 1980 to 2000

[**As of June 1 (2,440 represents 2,440,000).** Based on 1974 census definition; for definition of farms and farmland, see text of this section. Data for census years (indicated by italics) have been adjusted for underenumeration and are used as reference points along with data from acreage and livestock surveys in estimating data for other years. Minus sign (-) indicates decrease]

	Farms		Land in farms			Farms		Land in farms	
Year	Number (1,000)	Annual change [1] (1,000)	Total (mil. acres)	Average per farm (acres)	Year	Number (1,000)	Annual change [1] (1,000)	Total (mil. acres)	Average per farm (acres)
1980...	2,440	3	1,039	426	1995...	2,196	-1	963	438
1985...	2,293	-41	1,012	441	1996...	2,191	-6	959	438
1990...	2,146	-29	987	460	*1997...*	*2,191*	-	*956*	*436*
1992...	*2,108*	*-9*	*979*	*464*	1998...	2,191	1	954	435
1993...	2,202	94	969	440	1999...	2,192	1	947	432
1994...	2,198	-4	966	440	2000...	2,172	-20	943	434

- Represents or rounds to zero.   [1] Annual change from immediate preceding year.

No. 804. Farms—Number and Acreage by State: 1990 and 2000

[2,146 represents 2,146,000. See headnote, Table 803]

State	Farms (1,000)		Acreage (mil.)		Acreage per farm		State	Farms (1,000)		Acreage (mil.)		Acreage per farm	
	1990	2000	1990	2000	1990	2000		1990	2000	1990	2000	1990	2000
U.S........	2,146	2,172	987	943	460	434	Missouri......	108	109	30	30	281	275
							Montana......	25	28	61	57	2,449	2,054
Alabama.....	47	47	10	9	215	191	Nebraska.....	57	54	47	46	826	859
Alaska......	1	1	1	1	1,707	1,586	Nevada......	3	3	9	7	3,560	2,267
Arizona......	8	8	36	27	4,641	3,560	New Hampshire.	3	3	(Z)	(Z)	163	135
Arkansas.....	47	48	16	15	330	304	New Jersey....	8	10	1	1	107	86
California.....	85	88	31	28	362	318	New Mexico....	14	15	45	44	3,299	2,895
Colorado.....	27	29	33	32	1,249	1,090	New York......	39	38	8	8	218	203
Connecticut....	4	4	(Z)	(Z)	108	92	North Carolina...	62	57	10	9	156	161
Delaware......	3	3	1	1	207	223	North Dakota...	34	30	41	39	1,209	1,300
Florida......	41	44	11	10	266	234	Ohio.......	83	80	16	15	188	186
Georgia.....	48	50	13	11	260	222	Oklahoma.....	70	85	33	34	471	400
Hawaii.....	5	6	2	1	357	253	Oregon......	37	40	18	17	488	430
Idaho.......	22	25	14	12	628	486	Pennsylvania...	53	59	8	8	153	131
Illinois........	83	78	28	28	342	355	Rhode Island...	1	1	(Z)	(Z)	95	86
Indiana......	68	64	16	16	240	242	South Carolina...	25	24	5	5	208	196
Iowa.......	104	95	34	33	322	345	South Dakota...	35	33	44	44	1,266	1,354
Kansas.....	69	64	48	48	694	742	Tennessee.....	87	90	12	12	139	130
Kentucky.....	93	90	14	14	152	151	Texas........	196	226	132	130	673	575
Louisiana.....	32	30	9	8	278	275	Utah........	13	16	11	12	856	748
Maine.......	7	7	1	1	201	187	Vermont......	7	7	1	1	222	197
Maryland.....	15	12	2	2	148	169	Virginia......	46	49	9	9	193	178
Massachusetts..	6	6	1	1	100	93	Washington....	37	40	16	16	432	393
Michigan.....	54	52	11	10	200	200	West Virginia...	21	21	4	4	180	176
Minnesota.....	89	79	30	29	337	362	Wisconsin.....	80	77	18	16	220	210
Mississippi....	40	43	13	11	325	258	Wyoming......	9	9	35	35	3,899	3,761

Z Less than 500,000 acres.

Source of Tables 803 and 804: U.S. Dept. of Agriculture, National Agricultural Statistics Service, *Farm Numbers, 1975-80; Farms and Land in Farms, Final Estimates by States, 1979-1987; Farms and Land in Farms, Final Estimates, 1988-1992; Farms and Land in Farms, Final Estimates, 1993-1997*; and *Farms and Land In Farms,* February releases.

No. 805. Certified Organic Farmland Acreage and Livestock: 1992 to 1997

Item	Unit	1992	1995	1997	Crop	Certified organic acreage, 1997	
						Total (1,000)	Percent of total cropland
Certified growers.........	Number.	3,587	4,856	5,021	Total	1,347	0.16
					Pastureland and rangeland..	496	0.11
Certified organic acreage,					Cropland..............	850	0.23
total	1,000...	935	918	1,347			
Pastureland and rangeland.	1,000...	532	279	496			
Cropland.............	1,000...	403	639	850	Corn................	43	0.1
					Wheat...............	126	0.2
Certified animals:					Oats................	30	1.1
Beef cows	Number.	6,796	(NA)	4,429	Barley...............	30	0.5
Milk cows	Number.	2,265	(NA)	12,897	Spelt................	2	36.7
Hogs and pigs	Number.	1,365	(NA)	482	Buckwheat............	8	30.1
Sheep and lambs	Number.	1,221	(NA)	705	Soybeans.............	82	0.1
Layer hens	Number.	43,981	(NA)	537,826	Alfalfa...............	62	0.3
Broilers..............	Number.	17,382	(NA)	38,285	Grapes..............	19	1.9
Unclassified/other.......	Number.	(NA)	(NA)	226,105	Trees for maple syrup	14	11.5

NA Not available.

Source: U.S. Dept. of Agriculture, Economic Research Service, "U.S. certified organic farmland acreage and livestock, 1992-97"; published 4 April 2000; <http://www.ers.usda.gov/whatsnew/issues/organic/table4.htm>; and "Certified organic and total U.S. acreage, selected crops, 1995-1997"; published 4 April 2000; <http://www.ers.usda.gov/whatsnew/issues/organic/table5.htm>.

No. 806. Gross Farm Product—Summary: 1980 to 1999

[In billions of dollars (142.9 represents $142,900,000,000). For definition of gross product, see text, Section 13, Income, Expenditures, and Wealth. Minus sign (-) indicates decrease]

Item	1980	1985	1990	1992	1993	1994	1995	1996	1997	1998	1999
CURRENT DOLLARS											
Farm output, total..................	142.9	152.7	185.3	187.9	187.4	203.3	197.9	222.6	226.3	214.6	208.4
Cash receipts from farm marketings......	140.3	136.3	172.1	172.3	182.0	181.0	194.2	201.2	208.6	198.2	190.7
Farm housing.....................	5.1	5.0	5.1	5.3	5.6	5.9	6.0	6.2	6.4	6.7	7.0
Farm products consumed on farms	1.2	0.9	0.7	0.6	0.6	0.6	0.5	0.5	0.5	0.5	0.5
Other farm income	2.4	4.6	4.9	4.7	5.1	5.1	6.3	6.8	7.8	8.6	10.4
Change in farm inventories...........	-6.1	5.8	2.4	5.0	-5.9	10.8	-9.2	7.9	2.9	0.6	-0.2
Less: Intermediate goods and services purchased [1].....................	86.8	85.6	105.7	107.4	113.9	119.8	124.7	130.4	138.1	133.9	134.2
Equals: **Gross farm product**...........	56.1	67.1	79.6	80.5	73.6	83.6	73.2	92.2	88.3	80.8	74.2
Less: Consumption of fixed capital	18.6	21.0	22.1	23.4	23.5	23.7	24.6	25.4	26.3	27.4	29.2
Indirect business tax [2]	3.0	3.3	4.3	4.6	4.4	4.7	5.0	5.0	5.2	5.2	5.6
Plus: Subsidies to operators............	1.0	6.3	7.5	7.7	11.3	6.6	6.1	6.2	6.3	10.3	17.6
Equals: **Farm national income**	35.5	49.1	60.8	60.2	56.9	61.8	49.7	68.1	63.1	58.5	56.9
CHAINED (1996) DOLLARS [3]											
Farm output, total..................	(NA)	(NA)	200.8	213.6	208.3	227.1	217.9	222.6	237.5	238.4	243.9
Cash receipts from farm marketings......	(NA)	(NA)	186.3	195.9	202.6	202.9	214.7	201.2	218.7	220.5	224.3
Farm housing.....................	(NA)	(NA)	6.9	6.8	6.6	6.4	6.3	6.2	6.0	5.9	5.7
Farm products consumed on farms	(NA)	(NA)	0.6	0.6	0.6	0.6	0.5	0.5	0.5	0.5	0.5
Other farm income	(NA)	(NA)	5.7	5.6	6.0	5.8	7.0	6.8	8.2	9.6	12.4
Change in farm inventories...........	(NA)	(NA)	2.6	6.1	-7.9	13.0	-12.3	7.9	3.2	1.2	-
Less: Intermediate goods and services purchased [1].....................	(NA)	(NA)	117.0	118.8	122.8	127.7	132.3	130.4	134.4	138.0	138.4
Equals: **Gross farm product**	(NA)	(NA)	84.2	95.7	85.8	100.3	85.5	92.2	103.6	100.2	106.3

- Represents zero.   NA Not available.   [1] Includes rent paid to nonoperator landlords.   [2] Includes nontax liability.   [3] See text, Section 13, Income, Expenditures, and Wealth.

Source: U.S. Bureau of Economic Analysis, *National Income and Product Accounts of the United States 1929-97*, forthcoming and *Survey of Current Business*, August 2000.

No. 807. Value Added to Economy by Agricultural Sector: 1980 to 1999

[In billions of dollars (148.0 represents $148,000,000,000). Data are consistent with the net farm income accounts and include income and expenses related to the farm operator dwellings. The concept presented is consistent with that employed by the Organization for Economic Co-operation and Development]

Item	1980	1985	1990	1992	1993	1994	1995	1996	1997	1998	1999
Final agricultural sector output .	148.0	153.5	188.8	191.3	191.3	208.0	203.4	228.4	230.9	221.0	214.9
Final crop output (sales) [1]	64.4	74.1	83.3	88.9	82.4	100.3	95.7	115.6	112.3	102.1	93.1
Final animal output (sales) [1]........	70.3	68.7	90.2	87.1	92.0	89.7	87.7	92.0	96.5	94.2	95.1
Services and forestry	13.3	10.7	15.3	15.2	17.0	18.1	19.9	20.8	22.1	24.7	26.7
Machine hire and customwork.....	0.7	1.5	1.8	1.8	1.9	2.1	1.9	2.2	2.4	2.2	2.0
Forest products sold	1.0	1.4	1.9	2.2	2.5	2.6	2.8	2.6	2.8	3.0	2.9
Other farm income	0.6	3.2	4.5	4.1	4.6	4.3	5.8	6.2	6.9	8.7	10.8
Gross imputed rental value of farm dwellings	11.0	4.7	7.2	7.2	8.1	9.0	9.4	9.9	10.1	10.8	10.9
Less: Intermediate consumption outlays...................	77.0	73.5	92.9	93.4	100.7	104.9	109.7	113.2	121.0	118.5	120.8
Farm origin [2]	34.9	29.3	39.5	38.6	41.3	41.3	41.8	42.7	46.8	44.8	45.5
Feed purchased	21.0	16.9	20.4	20.1	21.4	22.6	23.8	25.2	26.3	25.0	24.5
Livestock and poultry purchased .	10.7	9.2	14.6	13.6	14.7	13.3	12.5	11.3	13.8	12.5	13.8
Manufactured inputs [2]	22.4	20.2	22.0	22.7	23.1	24.4	26.1	28.6	29.2	28.2	27.3
Fertilizers and lime............	9.5	7.5	8.2	8.3	8.4	9.2	10.0	10.9	10.9	10.6	9.9
Pesticides	3.5	4.3	5.4	6.5	6.7	7.2	7.7	8.5	9.0	9.0	8.6
Other intermediate expenses [2]	19.7	24.1	31.4	32.1	36.2	39.2	41.7	41.9	44.9	45.6	48.0
Repair and maintenance of capital items	7.1	6.4	8.6	8.5	9.2	9.1	9.5	10.3	10.4	10.4	10.5
Plus: Net government transactions [3] ..	-2.8	2.9	3.1	2.7	6.9	1.1	0.2	0.2	0.2	4.8	13.1
Direct Government payments	1.3	7.7	9.3	9.2	13.4	7.9	7.3	7.3	7.5	12.2	20.6
Property taxes	3.9	4.5	5.9	6.1	6.2	6.4	6.6	6.7	6.8	6.9	7.1
Equals: Gross value added	68.2	82.9	98.9	100.5	97.5	104.3	93.9	115.4	110.1	107.3	107.2
Less: Capital consumption	21.5	19.4	18.1	18.3	18.3	18.7	19.2	19.4	19.6	19.7	19.9
Equals: Net value added	46.7	63.5	80.8	82.2	79.2	85.6	74.7	96.0	90.6	87.5	87.3
Less: Employee compensation	8.3	8.5	12.5	12.3	13.2	13.5	14.3	15.2	16.0	16.9	17.5
Less: Net rent received by nonoperator landlords	6.1	7.7	10.2	11.2	10.9	11.8	10.9	12.9	12.8	12.7	12.9
Less: Real estate and nonreal estate interest......................	16.3	18.6	13.4	11.0	10.7	11.6	12.6	13.0	13.1	13.4	13.6
Equals: Net farm income.........	16.1	28.6	44.6	47.7	44.3	48.8	36.9	54.9	48.6	44.6	43.4

[1] Includes home consumption and value of inventory adjustment.   [2] Includes other outlays not shown separately.   [3] Direct Government payments minus motor vehicle registration and licensing fees and property taxes.

Source: U.S. Dept. of Agriculture, Economic Research Service, "United States and State Farm Income Data"; published 25 September 2000; <http://www.ers.usda.gov/Data/farmincome/finfidmu.htm>.

Agriculture   527

Figure 17.1
Changes in Farm Income Measures in the 1990s

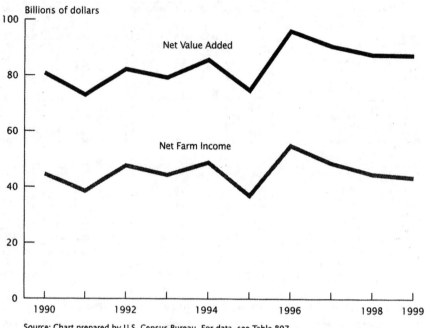

Source: Chart prepared by U.S. Census Bureau. For data, see Table 807.

Figure 17.2
Direct Government Payments to Agriculture: 1990 to 1999

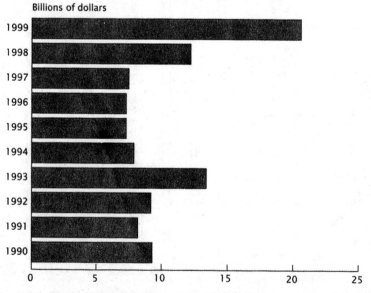

Source: Chart prepared by U.S. Census Bureau. For data, see Table 807.

528   Agriculture

No. 808. Farm Income—Cash Receipts From Farm Marketings: 1995 to 1999

[In millions of dollars (187,962 represents $187,962,000,000). Represents gross receipts from commercial market sales as well as net Commodity Credit Corporation loans. The source estimates and publishes individual cash receipt values only for major commodities and major producing states. The U.S. receipts for individual commodities, computed as the sum of the reported states, may understate the value of sales for some commodities. The degree of underestimation in some of the minor commodities can be substantial]

Commodity	1995	1997	1998	1999	Commodity	1995	1997	1998	1999
Total	187,962	207,596	196,575	188,610	Vegetables [1]	14,979	14,653	15,145	15,164
					Beans, dry.	567	530	595	574
Livestock and					Potatoes	2,481	2,226	2,368	2,698
products [1]	87,113	96,463	94,112	95,463	Carrots	545	536	483	682
Cattle and calves	34,044	36,000	33,415	36,522	Corn, sweet	647	671	693	695
Hogs	10,255	13,054	9,444	8,623	Lettuce	2,004	1,696	1,560	1,384
Dairy products	19,880	20,940	24,114	23,204	Onions	706	751	826	672
Broilers.	11,762	14,159	15,145	15,129	Tomatoes	1,584	1,646	1,764	1,834
Chicken eggs	3,893	4,540	4,439	4,323	Fresh	871	1,041	1,150	921
Turkeys	2,769	2,881	2,678	2,835	Processing	713	605	614	913
Horses/mules	662	1,799	1,914	938	Fruits/nuts [1]	11,097	13,134	12,238	12,975
Aquaculture [2]	797	707	781	(D)	Oranges	1,749	1,888	2,376	2,358
					Apples [3]	1,579	1,540	1,424	1,414
Crops [1]	100,849	111,134	102,463	93,146	Grapes [3]	1,860	2,876	2,560	2,732
Rice.	1,282	1,683	1,738	1,578	Wine	965	1,757	1,492	1,556
Wheat	9,054	8,710	7,128	5,690	Raisins	528	748	745	763
Corn	18,893	19,986	17,229	14,931	Strawberries.	812	904	1,003	1,119
Hay	3,288	4,585	3,799	3,351	Almonds	881	1,161	704	693
Sorghum grain.	1,377	1,552	950	846	Sugarbeets	1,071	1,160	1,181	1,218
Cotton	6,851	6,345	6,101	4,696	Cane for sugar. [3]	907	890	1,061	960
Tobacco	2,548	2,874	2,803	2,273	Forest products [4]	2,814	2,778	2,990	2,946
Peanuts	1,014	1,003	1,126	972	Greenhouse/nursery . .	10,336	11,879	12,041	12,239
Soybeans	13,868	18,116	15,671	11,922	Mushrooms	758	783	810	832

D Data withheld to avoid disclosure.   [1] Includes other commodities not shown separately.   [2] See also Table 861.
[3] Includes table grapes not shown separately.   [4] Timber, pulp, etc.

No. 809. Cash Receipts for Selected Commodities—Leading States: 1999

[36,522 represents $36,522,000,000. See headnote, Table 808]

State	Value of receipts (mil. dol.)	Percent of total receipts	Rank	State	Value of receipts (mil. dol.)	Percent of total receipts	Rank
Cattle and calves	36,522	100.0	(X)	Vegetables	15,164	100.0	(X)
Texas	6,124	16.8	1	California.	6,192	40.8	1
Nebraska	4,583	12.5	2	Florida	1,397	9.2	2
Kansas	4,521	12.4	3	Washington	836	5.5	3
Colorado	2,320	6.4	4	Idaho	754	5.0	4
Oklahoma	2,128	5.8	5	Arizona	608	4.0	5
Dairy products	23,204	100.0	(X)	Broilers	15,129	100.0	(X)
California.	4,090	17.6	1	Georgia	2,293	15.2	1
Wisconsin	3,160	13.6	2	Arkansas.	2,169	14.3	2
New York	1,737	7.5	3	Alabama	1,882	12.4	3
Pennsylvania	1,706	7.4	4	North Carolina	1,430	9.5	4
Minnesota	1,311	5.7	5	Mississippi.	1,323	8.7	5

X Not applicable.

No. 810. Balance Sheet of the Farming Sector: 1980 to 1999

[In billions of dollars, except as indicated (983 represents $983,000,000,000). As of December 31]

Item	1980	1985	1990	1992	1993	1994	1995	1996	1997	1998	1999
Assets	983	773	841	868	910	936	968	1,005	1,053	1,086	1,117
Real estate	783	586	619	641	678	704	740	770	808	842	870
Livestock and poultry [1] . . .	61	46	71	71	73	68	58	60	67	63	71
Machinery, motor vehicles [2]	80	83	86	85	86	88	89	90	90	90	89
Crops [3]	33	23	23	24	23	23	27	32	33	30	27
Purchased inputs	(NA)	1	3	4	4	5	3	4	5	5	4
Financial assets	27	33	38	43	46	48	49	49	50	55	56
Claims.	983	773	841	868	910	936	968	1,005	1,053	1,086	1,117
Debt	167	178	138	139	142	147	151	156	165	173	176
Real estate debt	90	100	75	75	76	78	79	82	85	90	94
Nonreal estate debt [4]	77	78	63	64	66	69	71	74	80	83	82
Equity	816	595	703	729	768	789	817	849	888	913	940
Farm debt/equity ratio (percent) . .	20.4	29.8	19.6	19.1	18.5	18.6	18.5	18.4	18.6	18.9	18.8
Farm debt/asset ratio (percent) . .	17.0	23.0	16.4	16.0	15.6	15.7	15.6	15.5	15.7	15.9	15.8

NA Not available.   [1] Excludes horses, mules, and broilers.   [2] Include only farm share value for trucks and autos.   [3] All non-CCC crops held on farms plus the value above loan rate for crops held under Commodity Credit Corporation.   [4] Excludes debt for nonfarm purposes.

Source of Tables 808-810: U.S. Dept. of Agriculture, Economic Research Service, "United States and State Farm Income Data"; published 25 September 2000; <http://www.ers.usda.gov/Data/farmincome/finfidmu.htm>; and "Farm Business Balance Sheet and Financial Ratios"; published 20 October 2000; <http://www.ers.usda.gov/Data/FarmBalanceSheet/fbsdmu.htm>.

Agriculture   529

No. 811. Farm Assets, Debt, and Income by State: 1998 and 1999

[Assets and debt, as of December 31 (1,085,525 represents $1,085,525,000,000). Farm income data are after inventory adjustment and include income and expenses related to the farm operator's dwelling]

State	Assets (mil. dol.)		Debt (mil. dol.)		Debt/asset ratio (percent)		Final agricultural sector output (mil. dol.)		Net farm income (mil. dol.)	
	1998	1999	1998	1999	1998	1999	1998	1999	1998	1999
United States..	1,085,525	1,116,604	172,862	176,431	15.9	15.8	221,007	214,927	44,623	43,398
Alabama	14,867	16,033	1,887	2,008	12.7	12.5	4,038	4,285	1,210	1,450
Alaska.	633	637	21	22	3.3	3.5	49	53	16	20
Arizona	29,198	31,127	1,398	1,450	4.8	4.7	2,473	2,520	667	708
Arkansas	21,235	21,867	4,196	4,315	19.8	19.7	5,903	5,995	1,568	1,831
California	82,096	84,603	16,522	17,173	20.1	20.3	26,110	26,670	5,779	4,986
Colorado	22,878	23,472	3,630	3,683	15.9	15.7	4,921	5,008	823	923
Connecticut	2,200	2,283	252	268	11.5	11.7	540	541	117	139
Delaware	1,695	1,728	367	375	21.7	21.7	877	839	126	121
Florida.	25,718	27,227	4,518	4,760	17.6	17.5	7,158	7,293	2,382	2,815
Georgia	20,192	21,750	3,503	3,551	17.4	16.3	6,143	6,150	.1,941	2,099
Hawaii.	3,766	3,644	265	258	7.0	7.1	546	567	65	63
Idaho	14,988	15,838	2,986	3,001	19.9	19.0	3,719	3,733	857	874
Illinois	69,141	68,153	9,346	9,499	13.5	13.9	8,766	7,457	1,462	1,007
Indiana	36,652	36,262	5,579	5,728	15.2	15.8	5,611	4,894	811	421
Iowa	69,460	69,544	12,663	13,035	18.2	18.7	12,153	10,812	2,242	1,450
Kansas	33,937	35,086	6,918	7,054	20.4	20.1	8,688	8,565	1,485	1,548
Kentucky	22,591	23,329	3,371	3,471	14.9	14.9	4,299	3,917	1,155	847
Louisiana	11,311	11,798	1,723	1,760	15.2	14.9	2,064	2,158	352	565
Maine	1,823	1,747	371	370	20.3	21.2	565	568	76	98
Maryland	6,994	7,300	1,078	1,088	15.4	14.9	1,764	1,751	307	337
Massachusetts . . .	3,034	3,219	357	375	11.8	11.7	478	461	57	65
Michigan	20,742	22,815	3,121	3,130	15.1	13.7	3,929	4,020	357	659
Minnesota	43,097	44,464	9,239	9,066	21.4	20.4	8,971	8,010	1,499	1,257
Mississippi	14,143	15,071	2,688	2,820	19.0	18.7	3,813	3,738	932	949
Missouri.	38,194	39,915	6,086	6,155	15.9	15.4	5,464	4,902	774	405
Montana	20,169	20,653	2,718	2,755	13.5	13.3	2,058	2,064	357	482
Nebraska.	39,763	41,093	8,941	9,143	22.5	22.3	9,827	9,429	1,833	1,651
Nevada	3,002	3,194	258	266	8.6	8.3	393	399	61	65
New Hampshire . .	938	955	94	104	10.1	10.9	181	181	16	25
New Jersey	5,705	5,748	477	495	8.4	8.6	887	852	132	127
New Mexico.	11,285	11,504	1,351	1,402	12.0	12.2	2,093	2,129	575	640
New York.	13,050	11,985	2,419	2,455	18.5	20.5	3,388	3,430	422	587
North Carolina . . .	22,196	23,551	3,678	3,675	16.6·	15.6	9,097	8,713	2,266	1,966
North Dakota	22,531	22,420	4,070	4,008	18.1	17.9	3,664	2,921	786	452
Ohio	34,797	34,203	4,131	4,249	11.9	12.4	5,798	5,130	1,280	803
Oklahoma	24,608	25,449	4,392	4,406	17.9	17.3	4,267	4,633	818	1,150
Oregon	17,847	18,201	2,540	2,579	14.2	14.2	3,627	3,652	494	323
Pennsylvania	21,282	21,951	2,710	2,759	12.7	12.6	4,670	4,479	665	627
Rhode Island	407	363	39	39	9.5	10.9	58	56	10	12
South Carolina . . .	8,486	8,350	974	988	11.5	11.8	1,660	1,659	324	422
South Dakota	21,728	23,125	4,143	4,182	19.1	18.1	4,264	3,974	.1,233	1,190
Tennessee	24,155	25,751	2,517	2,595	10.4	10.1	2,682	2,454	299	141
Texas	90,014	93,063	11,417	11,743	12.7	12.6	14,642	15,785	3,081	4,650
Utah	10,111	10,621	787	787	7.8	7.4	1,139	1,185	243	280
Vermont	2,507	2,563	˙385	382	15.4	14.9	594	600	120	141
Virginia	19,003	19,818	1,995	2,092	10.5	10.6	2,786	2,688	487	396
Washington	20,483	19,790	3,468	3,491	16.9	17.6	5,951	5,635	1,040	519
West Virginia	4,006	3,955	409	416	10.2	10.5	520	498	30	13
Wisconsin	28,075	29,923	5,817	5,931	20.7	19.8	6,744	6,385	876	879
Wyoming	8,775	9,446	1,051	1,076	12.0	11.4	933	1,041	74	173

Source: U.S. Dept. of Agriculture, Economic Research Service, "Uni⁺ᵊd States and State Farm Income Data"; published 25 September 2000; <http://www.ers.usda.gov/Data/farmincome/finfidmu.htm>; and "Farm Business Balance Sheet and Financial Ratios"; published 20 October 2000; <http://www.ers.usda.gov/Data/FarmBalanceSheet/fbsdmu.htm>.

530 Agriculture

No. 812. Farm Income—Farm Marketings, 1998 and 1999, and Principal Commodities, 1999 by State

[In millions of dollars (196,575 represents $196,575,000,000). Cattle include calves and greenhouse includes nursery]

State	1998			1999			State rank for total farm marketings and four principal commodities in order of marketing receipts
	Total	Crops	Live-stock and prod-ucts	Total	Crops	Live-stock and prod-ucts	
U.S...	**196,575**	**102,463**	**94,112**	**188,610**	**93,146**	**95,463**	**Cattle, dairy products, broilers, corn**
AL	3,296	709	2,587	3,438	662	2,777	23-Broilers, cattle, chicken eggs, greenhouse
AK	44	18	27	48	19	29	50-Greenhouse, dairy products, potatoes, hay
AZ	2,331	1,410	921	2,178	1,191	987	30-Cattle, dairy products, lettuce, cotton
AR	5,423	2,141	3,283	5,259	1,863	3,397	11-Broilers, rice, soybeans, cotton
CA	24,671	18,145	6,526	24,801	18,087	6,714	1-Dairy products, grapes, greenhouse, cattle
CO	4,371	1,529	2,842	4,354	1,338	3,016	16-Cattle, corn, dairy products, wheat
CT	482	298	184	482	302	180	44-Greenhouse, dairy products, chicken eggs, aquaculture
DE	776	167	609	718	153	566	40-Broilers, greenhouse, soybeans, dairy products
FL.	6,963	5,573	1,390	7,066	5,702	1,363	6-Oranges, greenhouse, sugar cane, dairy products
GA	5,418	2,017	3,400	5,241	1,907	3,334	12-Broilers, cotton, peanuts, chicken eggs
HI	514	423	90	533	447	86	42-Pineapples, sugar, greenhouse, macadamia nuts
ID	3,327	1,742	1,585	3,347	1,744	1,603	24-Dairy products, cattle, potatoes, wheat
IL	8,022	6,448	1,574	6,757	5,233	1,524	8-Corn, soybeans, hogs, cattle
IN	4,531	2,899	1,632	4,373	2,792	1,581	15-Corn, soybeans, hogs, dairy products
IA	11,053	6,300	4,753	9,716	5,004	4,712	3-Corn, hogs, soybeans, cattle
KS	7,946	3,408	4,539	7,616	2,607	5,009	5-Cattle, wheat, corn, sorghum grain
KY	3,773	1,603	2,171	3,456	1,298	2,158	22-Horses/mules, tobacco, cattle, broilers
LA	1,868	1,236	631	1,848	1,228	620	33-Sugar, cotton, rice, cattle
ME	510	215	295	515	229	286	43-Potatoes, dairy products, chicken eggs, aquaculture
MD	1,513	571	942	1,481	544	937	35-Broilers, greenhouse, dairy products, cattle
MA	422	314	108	396	295	101	45-Greenhouse, dairy products, cranberries, sweet corn
MI	3,506	2,186	1,320	3,470	2,139	1,331	21-Dairy products, greenhouse, soybeans, corn
MN	7,875	4,102	3,773	7,061	3,513	3,548	7-Dairy products, soybeans, corn, hogs
MS	3,436	1,271	2,164	3,174	1,031	2,143	25-Broilers, cotton, aquaculture, soybeans
MO	4,754	2,285	2,469	4,256	1,779	2,477	17-Cattle, soybeans, hogs, corn
MT	1,808	924	883	1,716	789	927	34-Wheat, cattle, barley, hay
NE	9,030	3,906	5,124	8,555	3,130	5,425	4-Cattle, corn, soybeans, hogs
NV	348	149	199	334	118	216	47-Cattle, dairy products, hay, greenhouse
NH	155	86	69	153	90	63	48-Greenhouse, dairy products, apples, cattle
NJ.	787	609	178	740	554	187	39-Greenhouse, horses/mules, dairy products, blueberries
NM	1,941	521	1,420	1,953	513	1,441	32-Cattle, dairy products, hay, pecans
NY	3,146	1,055	2,092	3,097	1,054	2,043	26-Dairy products, greenhouse, cattle, apples
NC	7,190	3,233	3,956	6,688	2,838	3,850	9-Broilers, hogs, greenhouse, tobacco
ND	2,913	2,359	555	2,759	2,112	647	28-Wheat, cattle, sunflower, soybeans
OH	4,918	3,064	1,854	4,429	2,643	1,786	14-Soybeans, corn, dairy products, greenhouse
OK	3,765	962	2,803	3,991	855	3,135	19-Cattle, broilers, wheat, hogs
OR	2,961	2,199	762	3,052	2,262	790	27-Greenhouse, cattle, dairy products, ryegrass
PA	4,161	1,252	2,909	4,070	1,193	2,877	18-Dairy products, cattle, greenhouse, chicken eggs
RI.	49	40	9	48	39	8	49-Greenhouse, dairy products, sweet corn, potatoes
SC	1,497	733	764	1,406	633	773	36-Broilers, greenhouse, turkeys, tobacco
SD	3,404	1,855	1,549	3,539	1,709	1,830	20-Cattle, soybeans, corn, wheat
TN	2,205	1,166	1,039	1,974	963	1,011	31-Cattle, broilers, dairy products, tobacco
TX	13,154	5,005	8,149	13,052	4,572	8,480	2-Cattle, cotton, greenhouse, broilers
UT	984	261	723	967	243	724	37-Cattle, dairy products, hay, greenhouse
VT	534	71	463	541	66	473	41-Dairy products, cattle, greenhouse, hay
VA	2,332	766	1,565	2,283	704	1,580	29-Broilers, cattle, dairy products, turkeys
WA	5,156	3,413	1,743	4,933	3,275	1,658	13-Dairy products, apples, cattle, potatoes
WV	396	61	335	387	53	334	46-Broilers, cattle, dairy products, turkeys
WI.	6,101	1,610	4,491	5,596	1,447	4,149	10-Dairy products, cattle, corn, potatoes
WY	848	168	680	852	172	680	38-Cattle, sugar beets, hay, sheep/lambs

Source: U.S. Dept. of Agriculture, Economic Research Service, "United States and State Farm Income Data"; published 25 September 2000; <http://www.ers.usda.gov/Data/farmincome/finfidmu.htm>.

No. 813. Indexes of Prices Received and Paid by Farmers: 1990 to 2000

[1990-92=100, except as noted]

Item	1990	1995	1999	2000	Item	1990	1995	1999	2000
Prices received,					Prices paid, total [2]	99	109	115	119
all products	**104**	**102**	**96**	**97**	Production	99	108	111	116
					Feed.	103	103	101	101
Crops...........	103	112	96	96	Livestock & poultry	102	82	95	109
Food grains	100	134	91	84	Seed	102	110	121	123
Feed grains and hay	105	112	86	88	Fertilizer	97	121	105	109
Cotton.............	107	127	85	77	Agricultural chemicals . ..	95	116	121	120
Tobacco	97	103	102	106	Fuels	100	89	93	133
Oil-bearing crops.......	105	104	83	86	Supplies & repairs......	96	112	121	124
Fruits and nuts	97	97	115	95	Autos and trucks.......	97	115	119	119
Commercial vegetables [1] .	102	121	108	114	Farm machinery	96	120	135	137
Potatoes & dry beans ...	133	107	101	105	Building materials	99	114	120	122
All other crops	(NA)	(NA)	108	108	Farm services........	96	115	116	118
					Rent...............	(NA)	117	113	113
Livestock and products	105	92	95	98	Interest.............	107	102	106	110
Meat animals	105	85	83	95	Taxes..............	95	109	120	123
Dairy products	105	98	110	92	Wage rates	96	114	135	138
Poultry and eggs.......	105	107	111	108	Parity ratio (1910-14=100) [3] . ..	51	45	40	39

NA Not available.   [1] Excludes potatoes and dry beans.   [2] Includes production items, interest, taxes, wage rates, and a family living component. The family living component is the Consumer Price Index for all urban consumers from the Bureau of Labor Statistics. See text, Section 14, Prices, and Table 692.   [3] Ratio of prices received by farmers to prices paid.
Source: U.S. Dept. of Agriculture, National Agricultural Statistics Service, *Agricultural Prices: Annual Summary.*

No. 814. Value of Selected Commodities Produced Under Contracts: 1999

[69,641 represents $69,641,000,000. Marketing contracts refer to verbal or written agreements between a buyer and a grower that set a price and determine an outlet for a specified quantity of a commodity before harvest or before the farmer markets the commodity. Production contracts involve paying the farmer a fee for providing management, labor, facilities, and equipment, while assigning ownership of the product to the contractor. Survey based estimates (see source) exclude Alaska and Hawaii and do not represent official U.S. Dept. of Agriculture estimates of farm sector activity]

Commodity	Value of production under contract (mil. dol.)	Percent of total production [1]	Commodity	Value of production under contract (mil. dol.)	Percent of total production [1]
Total	**69,641**	[2]**40**	Sugar beets	1,048	88
Marketing contracts [3]. . .	35,019	[2]20	Vegetables...... . ..	2,007	[4]20
Cattle	[4]1,695	[4]5	Production contracts [3] . .	34,622	[2]20
Corn............	1,926	13	Poultry and eggs [5]. . .	19,354	92
Cotton...........	1,746	37	Cattle	[4]6,730	[4]20
Fruits	6,624	64	Hogs............	5,179	53
Hogs............	[4]1,136	[4]12	Vegetables....... . .	1,534	[4]15
Soybeans	891	8			

[1] Represents percent of production under contract as percent of total commodity production, except as noted.   [2] Percent of total value of agricultural production.   [3] Includes other commodities not shown separately.   [4] Data have relative standard error between 25 and 49 percent.   [5] Data not available to estimate value of production for broilers.
Source: U.S. Dept. of Agriculture, Economic Research Service, data from Agricultural Resource Management Study, Phase 3.

No. 815. Civilian Consumer Expenditures for Farm Foods: 1980 to 1999

[In billions of dollars, except percent (264.4 represents $264,400,000,000). Excludes imported and nonfarm foods, such as coffee and seafood, as well as food consumed by the military, or exported]

Item	1980	1985	1990	1992	1993	1994	1995	1996	1997	1998	1999
Consumer expenditures, total ..	**264.4**	**345.4**	**449.8**	**474.5**	**489.2**	**512.2**	**529.5**	**546.7**	**566.5**	**585.0**	**618.4**
Farm value, total	81.7	86.4	106.2	105.1	109.6	109.6	113.8	122.2	121.9	119.6	120.5
Marketing bill, total [1]	182.7	259.0	343.6	369.4	379.6	402.6	415.7	424.5	444.6	465.4	497.9
Percent of total consumer expenditures	69.1	75.0	76.4	77.9	77.6	78.6	78.5	77.6	78.5	79.6	80.5
At-home expenditures [2]	180.1	220.8	276.2	289.6	294.9	308.7	316.9	328.0	339.2	346.8	365.0
Farm value.	65.9	66.6	80.2	76.9	76.4	75.3	76.1	81.6	79.0	77.0	77.6
Marketing bill [1]	114.2	154.2	196.0	212.7	218.5	233.4	240.8	246.4	260.2	269.8	287.4
Away-from-home expenditures	84.3	124.6	173.6	184.9	194.3	203.5	212.6	218.7	227.3	238.2	253.4
Farm value.	15.8	19.8	26.0	28.2	33.2	34.3	37.7	40.6	42.9	42.6	42.9
Marketing bill [1]	68.5	104.8	147.6	156.7	161.1	169.2	174.9	178.1	184.4	195.6	210.5
Marketing bill cost components:											
Labor cost	81.5	115.6	154.0	168.4	178.0	186.1	196.6	204.6	216.9	229.9	240.1
Packaging materials..........	21.0	26.9	36.5	40.1	40.9	43.3	48.2	47.7	48.7	50.4	50.9
Rail and truck transport	13.0	16.5	19.8	20.6	21.2	21.8	22.3	22.9	23.6	24.4	25.2
Corporate profits before taxes ...	9.9	10.4	13.2	15.7	18.1	20.9	19.5	20.7	22.3	23.3	26.2
Fuels and electricity	9.0	13.1	15.2	16.7	17.2	17.9	18.6	19.6	20.2	20.7	21.8
Advertising	7.3	12.5	17.1	18.0	18.6	19.3	19.8	20.9	22.1	22.6	23.8
Depreciation.............	7.8	15.4	16.3	16.2	17.2	18.1	19.9	20.1	21.0	21.5	22.6
Net interest	3.4	6.1	13.5	10.9	10.1	11.0	11.6	11.4	12.5	13.5	15.2
Net rent...............	6.8	9.3	13.9	17.2	17.9	18.9	19.8	21.0	21.8	22.6	23.9
Repairs...............	3.6	4.8	6.2	6.6	7.2	7.8	7.9	8.5	8.8	9.0	9.5
Taxes	8.3	11.7	15.7	17.5	18.2	18.7	19.1	19.4	19.8	20.4	21.5
Other	11.0	16.7	22.2	21.5	15.0	18.8	13.4	7.7	6.9	7.1	17.2

[1] The difference between expenditures for domestic farm-originated food products and the farm value or payment farmers received for the equivalent farm products.   [2] Food primarily purchased from retail food stores for use at home.
Source: U.S. Dept. of Agriculture, Economic Research Service, *Food Cost Review,* annual; *Food Review,* periodic; and *Agricultural Statistics,* annual.

No. 816. Indexes of Farm Production, Input Use, and Productivity: 1980 to 1996

[1992=100]

Item	1980	1985	1988	1989	1990	1991	1992	1993	1994	1995	1996
Farm output [1]	79	89	82 •	89	94	94	100	94	107	101	106
Livestock and products [2]	85	89	94	94	95	9᳌	100	101	107	110	109
Meat animals	98	94	97	97	96	99	100	100	103	104	100
Dairy products	85	94	96	95	98	98	100	99	114	115	115
Poultry and eggs	64	71	83	86	92	96	100	104	109	114	119
Crops [2]	75	89	75	86	92	92	100	89	106	96	103
Feed crops	76	100	62	85	88	86	100	76	102	83	98
Food grains	94	95	76	83	107	82	100	96	97	90	93
Oil crops	81	96	72	88	87	94	100	85	115	99	107
Cotton and cottonseed	68	82	96	75	96	109	100	100	122	110	117
Tobacco	102	87	78	80	94	96	100	94	85	93	80
Vegetables and melons	70	82	81	85	93	97	100	97	113	108	112
Fruits and nuts	90	86	102	98	97	96	100	107	111	102	102
Other crops	57	69	86	89	94	97	100	99	105	110	110
Farm input [3]	119	106	100	100	101	102	100	101	104	105	102
Farm labor	123	108	103	104	102	106	100	96	96	92	100
Farm real estate	113	107	99	101	100	100	100	98	100	99	101
Durable equipment	166	139	113	108	105	103	100	97	94	92	89
Energy	121	98	102	101	100	101	100	100	103	109	104
Agricultural chemicals [4]	119	97	91	94	95	100	100	105	106	90	97
Other purchased inputs [5]	117	99	99	103	103	104	100	110	117	121	116
Farm output per unit of input	66	84	83	90	93	92	100	94	103	97	104

[1] Annual production available for eventual human use. [2] Includes items not shown separately. [3] Based on physical quantities of resources used in production. [4] Includes fertilizer, lime, and pesticides. [5] Includes purchased services and miscellaneous inputs.

Source: U.S. Dept. of Agriculture, Economic Research Service, *Agricultural Outlook*, monthly. Also published in the U.S. Council of Economic Advisors, *Economic Report of the President*, annual.

No. 817. Agricultural Exports and Imports—Volume by Principal Commodities: 1990 to 2000

[In thousands of metric tons (2,707 represents 2,707,000)]

Exports	1990	1995	1999	2000	Imports	1990	1995	1999	2000
Animal products [1]	2,707	5,606	6,330	6,634	Fruits, nuts, vegetables	4,696	6,213	8,709	8,864
Wheat and products [2]	28,247	33,458	29,367	28,453	Bananas	3,094	3,664	4,295	4,031
Feed grains and products	61,526	67,403	58,932	55,716	Green coffee	1,174	953	1,234	1,297
Rice	2,534	3,275	2,938	3,147	Cocoa and products	716	620	924	999
Feeds and fodders	10,974	13,338	11,945	13,491	Red meat and poultry meat [5]	1,169	1,050	1,445	1,579
Protein meal	5,079	6,404	6,843	6,438					
Oilseeds and products [3]	15,820	23,596	24,147	27,938	Vegetable oils	1,204	1,509	1,645	1,845
Vegetable oils	1,226	2,532	2,455	2,040	Rubber, crude natural	840	1,044	1,144	1,232
Fruits, nuts, vegetables [4]	5,553	6,918	6,846	7,580	Sugar	1,858	1,599	1,612	1,464
Cotton and linters	1,733	2,118	754	1,552	Spices	129	155	211	212
Tobacco, unmanufactured	223	209	189	183	Tobacco, unmanufactured	173	190	222	216

[1] Includes meat and products, poultry meats, dairy products, and fats, oils and greases. Excludes live animals, hides, skins, and eggs. [2] Includes flour and bulgur. [3] Includes soybeans, sunflowerseeds, peanuts, cottonseed, safflowerseed, flaxseed, and nondefatted soybean flour. [4] Excludes fruit juices. [5] Excludes horsemeat.

Source: U.S. Dept. of Agriculture, Economic Research Service, *U.S. Agricultural Trade Update*, March 12, 2001; and *Foreign Agricultural Trade of the United States*, calendar year supplements.

No. 818. Agricultural Exports and Imports—Value: 1980 to 2000

[In billions of dollars, except percent (23.9 represents $23,900,000,000). Includes Puerto Rico. Excludes forest products and distilled liquors; includes crude rubber and similar gums (now mainly plantation products). Includes shipments under foreign aid programs]

Year	Trade balance	Exports, domestic products	Percent of all exports	Imports for consumption	Percent of all imports	Year	Trade balance	Exports, domestic products	Percent of all exports	Imports for consumption	Percent of all imports
1980	23.9	41.2	18	17.4	7	1995	26.1	56.3	10	30.3	4
1985	9.1	29.0	13	20.0	6	1996	26.9	60.4	10	33.5	4
1990	16.6	39.5	11	22.9	5	1997	21.1	57.2	9	36.2	4
1992	18.4	43.2	10	24.8	5	1998	14.9	51.8	8	36.9	4
1993	17.8	42.9	10	25.1	4	1999	10.8	48.5	8	37.7	4
1994	19.2	46.3	10	27.0	4	2000	12.6	51.6	7	39.0	3

Source: U.S. Dept. of Agriculture, Economic Research Service, *U.S. Agricultural Trade Update*, February 28, 2001; and *Foreign Agricultural Trade of the United States*, calendar year supplements. Also in *Agricultural Statistics*, annual.

Agriculture 533

No. 819. Agricultural Imports—Value by Selected Commodity, 1990 to 2000, and by Leading Countries of Origin, 2000

[In millions of dollars (22,920 represents $22,920,000,000)]

Commodity	1990	1995	1997	1998	1999	2000	Leading countries of origin, 2000
Total	**22,920**	**30,263**	**36,159**	**36,908**	**37,735**	**38,991**	**Canada, Mexico, Australia**
Competitive products.	17,346	21,799	26,807	27,925	29,746	31,228	Canada, Mexico, Australia
Cattle, live	978	1,413	1,124	1,144	1,000	1,152	Canada, Mexico, Australia
Beef and veal	1,872	1,447	1,609	1,842	2,136	2,400	Canada, Australia, New Zealand
Pork	938	686	754	682	753	997	Canada, Denmark, Poland
Dairy products	891	1,118	1,225	1,465	1,556	1,650	New Zealand, Canada, Italy
Fruits and preparations. .	2,218	2,249	2,847	2,852	3,540	3,469	Mexico, Chile, Costa Rica
Vegetables and preparations	2,317	3,189	3,706	4,374	4,583	4,735	Mexico, Canada, Spain
Wine.	917	1,153	1,711	1,876	2,186	2,209	France, Italy, Australia
Malt beverages	923	1,166	1,495	1,712	1,893	2,179	Mexico, Netherlands, Canada
Grains and feeds.	1,188	2,312	2,963	2,878	2,991	3,091	Canada, Italy, Thailand
Sugar and related products.	1,213	1,335	1,852	1,682	1,589	1,573	Canada, Mexico, United Kingdom
Oilseeds and products . .	952	1,748	2,127	2,075	1,850	1,855	Canada, Italy, Philippines
Noncompetitive products . .	5,574	8,464	9,353	8,984	7,989	7,763	Indonesia, Colombia, Canada
Coffee and products. . . .	1,915	3,263	3,886	3,431	2,899	2,701	Mexico, Colombia, Guatemala
Rubber, crude natural. . .	707	1,629	1,229	977	704	842	Indonesia, Thailand, Malaysia
Cocoa and products. . . .	1,072	1,106	1,471	1,666	1,522	1,404	Canada, Cote d'Ivoire, Indonesia
Bananas and plantains . .	939	1,140	1,220	1,202	1,209	1,130	Costa Rica, Ecuador, Colombia

Source: U.S. Dept. of Agriculture, Economic Research Service, *U.S. Agricultural Trade Update*, February 28, 2001; and *Foreign Agricultural Trade of the United States*, calendar year supplements.

No. 820. Imports' Share of Food Consumption by Commodity: 1990 to 1999

[In percent. Import share is the total quantity imported divided by the quantity available for domestic human food consumption. Calculated from supply and utilization balance sheets. A portion of the imports of some commodities is exported; therefore, the ratios presented here may overstate the importance of imports in domestic consumption for some commodity groups. Similarly, a portion of the imports of some commodities is diverted to such nonfood uses as feed, seed, alcohol and fuel production, and industrial uses. This too can overstate the importance of imports]

Commodity	1990	1995	1998	1999	Commodity	1990	1995	1998	1999
Red meat.	8.1	6.5	7.7	8.2	Grapes.	37.6	38.8	43.7	45.0
Beef	9.8	8.3	10.1	10.7	Fruit juice.	37.4	28.1	32.4	31.8
Pork	5.6	3.8	3.9	4.4	Orange.	27.9	19.2	24.1	22.9
Fish and shellfish	56.3	55.3	64.9	68.1	Apple.	63.9	53.7	60.2	60.8
Dairy products [1]	1.9	1.9	2.4	2.9	Fresh vegetables.	7.5	9.3	12.0	10.9
Cheese [2]	4.8	4.7	4.5	5.3	Cucumbers	33.7	38.3	40.2	39.7
Salad and cooking oils [3]	7.2	12.0	12.2	12.4	Peppers	19.7	19.1	24.8	24.7
Fresh fruits.	30.6	33.7	36.0	39.6	Tomatoes	20.5	30.5	38.6	33.7
Citrus.	3.4	7.1	8.4	13.4	Wheat [4].	4.6	7.7	11.3	10.2
Apples	4.7	7.7	6.5	7.3	Rice [5]	8.1	12.1	12.6	13.9
Bananas.	99.8	99.8	99.7	99.7	Cane and beet sugar [6]	24.5	12.4	17.6	13.9

[1] Milk equivalent of all dairy products calculated on a milkfat basis. [2] Natural equivalent of cheese and cheese products. Includes all types of cheese except full-skim American and cottage, pot, and baker's cheeses. [3] Olive and canola oil imports. [4] Flour and other wheat products included. Grain equivalent. [5] Rough equivalent. Includes milled rice converted to rough basis at annual extraction rate. [6] Import share is the quantity of imports for domestic consumption (net of re-exports) divided by domestic food consumption.

Source: U.S. Dept. of Agriculture, Economic Research Service, *Food Consumption, Prices, and Expenditures*, annual.

No. 821. Selected Farm Products—United States and World Production and Exports: 1995 to 2000

[In metric tons, except as indicated (59 represents 59,000,000). Metric ton=1.102 short tons or .984 long tons]

Commodity	Unit	Amount						United States as percent of world		
		United States			World					
		1995	1999	2000	1995	1999	2000	1995	1999	2000
PRODUCTION [1]										
Wheat	Million.	59	63	61	539	588	580	11.0	10.7	10.5
Corn for grain	Million.	188	240	253	515	606	583	36.5	39.6	43.4
Soybeans	Million.	59	72	75	125	159	170	47.4	45.3	44.1
Rice, milled.	Million.	5.6	6.5	6.0	371	408	399	1.5	1.6	1.5
Cotton [2]	Million bales [3].	19.7	13.9	17.0	85.9	84.9	87.2	23.0	16.4	19.5
EXPORTS [4]										
Wheat [5]	Million.	33.7	29.5	30.0	99.5	112.5	106.6	33.9	26.2	28.1
Corn	Million.	52.7	49.4	50.5	72.4	73.2	72.4	72.7	67.5	69.8
Soybeans	Million.	23.1	26.5	26.5	31.9	46.3	48.6	72.4	57.2	54.6
Rice, milled basis.	Million.	3.1	2.6	2.8	21.0	24.9	22.9	14.8	10.4	12.2
Cotton [2]	Million bales [3].	9.4	4.3	6.8	28.4	23.8	27.2	33.0	18.3	24.8

[1] Production years vary by commodity. In most cases, includes harvests from July 1 of the year shown through June 30 of the following year. [2] For production and trade years ending in year shown. [3] Bales of 480 lb. net weight. [4] Trade years may vary by commodity. Wheat, corn and soybean data are for trade year beginning in year shown. Rice data are for calendar year shown. [5] Includes wheat flour on a grain equivalent.

Source: U.S. Dept. of Agriculture, Foreign Agricultural Service, *Foreign Agricultural Commodity Circular Series*, periodic.

534 Agriculture

No. 822. Agricultural Exports—Value by Principal Commodities: 1990 to 2000

[In millions of dollars, except percent (39,540 represents $39,540,000,000). See headnote, Table 818]

Commodity	Value (mil. dol.)							Percent		
	1990	1995	1996	1997	1998	1999	2000	1990	1995	2000
Total agricultural exports [1]	39,540	56,347	60,417	57,217	51,815	48,485	51,580	100.0	100.0	100.0
Grains and feeds [1]	14,409	18,644	20,863	15,368	14,008	14,001	13,700	36.5	33.0	26.6
Feed grains and products	7,150	8,341	9,575	6,219	5,210	5,745	5,382	18.1	14.8	10.4
Corn	6,026	7,304	8,404	5,180	4,382	4,916	4,475	15.2	13.0	8.7
Wheat and products	4,035	5,734	6,466	4,302	3,905	3,806	3,583	10.2	10.2	6.9
Rice	801	996	1,029	932	1,208	944	835	2.0	1.8	1.6
Oilseeds and products [1]	5,728	8,953	10,823	12,093	9,495	8,172	8,566	14.4	15.8	16.6
Soybeans	3,548	5,400	7,324	7,379	4,835	4,517	5,244	9.0	9.6	10.2
Soybean oilcake and meal	979	986	1,430	1,865	1,604	1,070	1,163	2.5	1.8	2.3
Vegetable oils and waxes	832	1,852	1,406	1,802	2,272	1,628	1,259	2.1	3.2	2.4
Animals and animal products [1]	6,696	10,985	11,195	11,403	10,627	10,441	11,849	16.9	19.6	23.0
Hides and skins, incl. furskins	1,751	1,748	1,675	1,651	1,259	1,141	1,620	4.4	3.1	3.1
Cattle hides	1,369	1,465	1,327	1,337	993	927	1,283	3.5	2.6	2.5
Meats and meat products	2,558	4,522	4,590	4,597	4,371	4,834	5,365	6.5	8.0	10.4
Beef and veal	1,580	2,647	2,429	2,497	2,326	2,731	3,049	4.0	4.7	5.9
Fats, oils, and greases	424	827	593	541	647	507	384	1.1	1.5	0.7
Poultry and poultry products	906	2,345	2,828	2,779	2,530	2,119	2,261	2.3	4.2	4.4
Cotton, excluding linters	2,783	3,681	2,715	2,682	2,545	968	1,883	7.0	6.5	3.7
Tobacco, unmanufactured	1,441	1,400	1,390	1,553	1,459	1,294	1,222	3.6	2.5	2.4
Fruits and preparations	2,379	3,300	3,291	3,451	3,200	3,263	3,455	6.0	5.9	6.7
Fresh fruits	1,486	1,973	1,971	2,100	1,838	1,821	2,077	3.8	3.5	4.0
Vegetables and preparations	2,225	3,637	3,822	4,144	4,222	4,297	4,467	5.6	6.5	8.7
Nuts and preparations	976	1,410	1,626	1,446	1,360	1,184	1,330	2.5	2.5	2.6
Other	2,903	4,337	4,692	5,077	4,899	4,865	5,108	7.3	7.7	9.9

[1] Includes commodities not shown separately.

Source: U.S. Dept. of Agriculture, Economic Research Service, *U.S. Agricultural Trade Update*, March 12, 2001; and *Foreign Agricultural Trade of the United States*, calendar year supplements. Also in *Agricultural Statistics*, annual.

No. 823. Agricultural Exports—Value by Selected Countries of Destination: 1990 to 2000

[39,540 represents $39,540,000,000. See headnote, Table 818. Totals include transshipments through Canada, but transshipments are not distributed by country prior to 2000]

Country	Value (mil. dol.)							Percent		
	1990	1995	1996	1997	1998	1999	2000	1990	1995	2000
Total agricultural exports [1]	39,540	56,347	60,417	57,217	51,815	48,485	51,580	100.0	100.0	100.0
Asia [1]	17,718	28,212	28,547	25,699	20,984	20,299	22,362	44.8	50.1	43.4
Japan	8,146	11,164	11,695	10,525	9,104	8,936	9,324	20.6	19.8	18.1
Korea, South	2,650	3,758	3,871	2,863	2,268	2,460	2,604	6.7	6.7	5.0
Taiwan [2]	1,663	2,604	2,964	2,617	1,802	1,955	2,010	4.2	4.6	3.9
China [2]	818	2,634	2,089	1,614	1,358	862	1,724	2.1	4.7	3.3
Hong Kong	704	1,502	1,489	1,712	1,493	1,209	1,272	1.8	2.7	2.5
Indonesia	274	819	853	773	455	548	671	0.7	1.5	1.3
Philippines	381	767	893	874	722	789	902	1.0	1.4	1.7
Israel	304	485	617	537	365	423	482	0.8	0.9	0.9
Turkey	226	536	637	734	665	485	669	0.6	1.0	1.3
Western Europe [1][3]	7,396	9,065	9,700	9,728	8,267	7,142	6,705	18.7	16.1	13.0
European Union [4]	7,103	8,705	9,320	9,104	7,961	6,603	6,262	18.0	15.4	12.1
Belgium-Luxembourg	386	650	749	678	658	565	550	1.0	1.2	1.1
Netherlands	1,587	2,146	2,218	2,040	1,560	1,613	1,443	4.0	3.8	2.8
Germany	1,170	1,239	1,491	1,357	1,244	969	908	3.0	2.2	1.8
Spain [5]	939	1,270	1,124	1,156	1,047	712	610	2.4	2.3	1.2
United Kingdom	836	1,067	1,232	1,311	1,253	1,083	1,042	2.1	1.9	2.0
Italy	715	721	796	765	705	497	554	1.8	1.3	1.1
Latin America [1]	5,122	8,044	10,480	10,405	11,465	10,074	10,769	13.0	14.3	20.9
Mexico	2,561	3,541	5,445	5,178	6,160	5,634	6,545	6.5	6.3	12.7
Canada	4,225	5,804	6,138	6,784	7,009	7,066	7,650	10.7	10.3	14.8
Russia	(X)	1,046	1,328	1,204	835	730	598	(X)	1.9	1.2
Eastern Europe	537	293	438	284	271	171	170	1.4	0.5	0.3
Africa [1]	1,935	3,074	2,877	2,282	2,119	2,188	2,309	4.9	5.5	4.5
Egypt	692	1,448	1,319	964	914	1,061	1,046	1.8	2.6	2.0

X Not applicable. [1] Includes areas not shown separately. [2] See footnote, Table 1327. [3] Includes Canary Islands and Madeira Islands. [4] Includes France, Denmark, Greece, Ireland, and Portugal. Beginning 1995, also includes Austria, Finland, and Sweden. For consistency, data for all years are shown on same basis. [5] Includes Canary Islands and Spanish Africa, not elsewhere classified.

Source: U.S. Dept. of Agriculture, Economic Research Service, *Foreign Agricultural Trade of the United States*, calendar year supplements. Also in *Agricultural Statistics*, annual.

Agriculture 535

No. 824. Cropland Used for Crops and Acreages of Crops Harvested: 1980 to 2000

[In millions of acres, except as indicated (382 represents 382,000,000)]

Item	1980	1985	1990	1994	1995	1996	1997	1998	1999	2000
Cropland used for crops.....	382	372	341	339	332	346	349	345	344	343
Index (1977=100)........	101	98	90	90	88	92	92	91	91	91
Cropland harvested [1].........	342	334	310	310	302	314	321	315	316	312
Crop failure	10	7	6	7	8	10	7	10	8	10
Cultivated summer fallow	30	31	25	22	22	22	21	20	20	21
Cropland idled by all federal programs	(NA)	(NA)	62	49	55	34	33	30	30	31
Acres of crops harvested [2] ...	352	342	322	321	314	326	332	326	327	323

NA Not available. [1] Land supporting one or more harvested crops. [2] Area in principal crops harvested as reported by Crop Reporting Board plus acreages in fruits, vegetables for sale, tree nuts, and other minor crops.

Source: U.S. Dept. of Agriculture, Economic Research Service, *Economic Indicators of the Farm Sector: Production and Efficiency Statistics*, annual. Also in *Agricultural Statistics*, annual. Beginning 1994, *Agricultural Resources and Environmental Indicators*, periodic, and *AREI Updates: Cropland Use*, No. 12, annual.

No. 825. Percent of Corn, Soybean, and Cotton Acreage Planted With Genetically Modified Seed: 2000 and 2001

[In percent. Based on the June Agricultural Survey. Randomly selected farmers across the United States were asked if they planted corn, soybeans, or upland cotton seed that, through biotechnology, is resistant to herbicides, insects, or both. The states published individually below represent 82 percent of all corn planted acres, 90 percent of all soybean planted acres, and 83 percent of all upland cotton planted acres. Conventionally bred herbicide resistant varieties were excluded. Insect resistant varieties include only those containing bacillus thuringiensis (Bt). The acreage estimates are subject to sampling variability because all operations planting biotech varieties are not included in the sample]

State	Corn		State	Soybeans		State	Cotton	
	2000	2001		2000	2001		2000	2001
U.S., total	25	26	U.S., total	54	68	U.S., total	61	69
IL	17	16	AR	43	60	AR	70	78
IN	11	12	IL	44	64	CA	24	40
IA	30	32	IN	63	78	GA	82	85
KS..............	33	38	IA	59	73	LA	80	91
MI	12	17	KS	66	80	MS	78	86
MN	37	36	MI	50	59	NC	76	84
MO	28	32	MN	46	63	TX	46	49
NE..............	34	34	MS	48	63	Other states [1]	74	84
OH	9	11	MO............	62	69			
SD..............	48	47	NE	72	76			
WI..............	18	18	ND	22	49			
Other states [1]	17	20	OH	48	64			
			SD	68	80			
			WI	51	63			
			Other states [1]	54	64			

[1] Includes all other states in the specified commodity estimating program.

Source: U.S. Dept. of Agriculture, National Agricultural Statistics Service, *Acreage*, June 2001.

No. 826. Quantity of Pesticides Applied to Selected Crops: 1990 to 1997

[In million pounds of active ingredients, except as indicated]

Type of pesticide and commodity	1990	1991	1992	1993	1994	1995	1996	1997
Total	497.7	477.5	518.2	498.2	563.4	543.3	575.8	587.6
Herbicides	344.6	335.2	350.5	323.5	350.6	324.9	365.7	366.4
Insecticides	57.4	52.8	60.0	58.1	68.2	69.9	59.2	60.5
Fungicides	27.8	29.4	34.9	36.6	43.6	47.5	46.8	50.5
Other	67.9	60.1	72.7	80.0	101.1	101.0	104.0	110.2
Corn........................	240.7	233.2	245.2	220.5	233.0	201.3	227.7	229.3
Cotton......................	50.9	50.3	57.6	52.3	69.1	83.7	65.6	68.0
Wheat......................	17.8	13.8	19.7	19.1	23.8	21.5	32.9	25.7
Soybeans	74.4	70.4	67.8	64.4	69.5	68.7	78.1	84.5
Potatoes	43.8	35.6	41.6	50.5	64.2	53.1	49.5	58.5
Other vegetables.............	39.8	40.3	52.8	57.3	68.2	78.0	82.8	80.7
Citrus fruit	11.0	13.7	13.5	13.7	13.6	14.0	14.5	15.0
Apples	8.3	9.1	8.8	9.3	9.1	9.0	9.7	10.3
Other deciduous fruit	10.9	11.1	11.1	11.0	12.9	14.1	14.9	15.9
POUNDS OF ACTIVE INGREDIENT PER PLANTED ACRE								
Total	2.2	2.1	2.2	2.2	2.4	2.4	2.4	2.4
Herbicides	1.5	1.5	1.5	1.4	1.5	1.4	1.5	1.5
Insecticides	0.3	0.2	0.3	0.3	0.3	0.3	0.2	0.2
Fungicides	0.1	0.1	0.2	0.2	0.2	0.2	0.2	0.2
Other	0.3	0.3	0.3	0.4	0.4	0.4	0.4	0.5

Source: U.S. Dept. of Agriculture, Economic Research Service, *Production Practices for Major Crops in U.S. Agriculture, 1990-97*, Statistical Bulletin No. 969, August 2000.

536　Agriculture

No. 827. Principal Crops—Production, Supply, and Disappearance: 1990 to 2000

[74.2 represents 74,200,000. Marketing year beginning May 1 for hay, June 1 for wheat and barley, August 1 for cotton and rice, September 1 for soybeans, sorghum, and corn. Acreage, production, and yield of all crops periodically revised on basis of census data]

Crop and year	Acreage (mil.) Planted	Harvested	Yield per acre	Production	Farm price [1]	Farm value (mil. dol.)	Total supply [2]	Disappearance Total [3]	Exports	Ending stocks
Corn for grain:			Bu.	Mil. bu.	$/bu.			Mil. bu.		
1990	74.2	67.0	119	7,934	2.28	18,192	9,282	7,761	1,725	1,521
1995	71.5	65.2	114	7,400	3.24	24,118	8,974	8,548	2,228	426
1998	80.2	72.6	134	9,759	1.94	18,922	11,085	9,298	1,981	1,787
1999	77.4	70.5	134	9,431	1.82	17,104	11,232	9,515	1,937	1,718
2000	79.5	72.7	137	9,968	1.85	18,621	11,696	9,745	1,950	1,951
Soybeans:			Bu.	Mil. bu.	$/bu.			Mil. bu.		
1990	57.8	56.5	34.1	1,926	5.74	11,042	2,169	1,840	557	329
1995	62.5	61.5	35.3	2,174	6.72	14,617	2,516	2,333	851	183
1998	72.0	70.4	38.9	2,741	4.93	13,494	2,944	2,596	801	348
1999	73.7	72.4	36.6	2,654	4.63	12,205	3,006	2,716	973	290
2000	74.5	72.7	38.1	2,770	4.75	13,073	3,063	2,733	975	330
Hay:			Sh. tons	Mil. sh. tons	$/ton			Mil. sh. tons		
1990	(NA)	61.0	2.40	146	[4][5]80.60	10,462	173	146	(NA)	27
1995	(NA)	59.8	2.58	154	[4][5]82.20	11,042	175	154	(NA)	21
1998	(NA)	60.1	2.53	152	[4][5]84.60	11,607	174	149	(NA)	25
1999	(NA)	63.2	2.53	160	[4][5]76.90	11,014	185	156	(NA)	29
2000	(NA)	59.9	2.54	152	[4][5]80.00	11,180	181	(NA)	(NA)	(NA)
Wheat:			Bu.	Mil. bu.	$/bu.			Mil. bu.		
1990	77.0	69.1	39.5	2,730	2.61	7,184	3,303	2,435	1,069	868
1995	69.0	61.0	35.8	2,183	4.55	9,787	2,757	2,381	1,241	376
1998	65.8	59.0	43.2	2,547	2.65	6,781	3,373	2,427	1,042	946
1999	62.7	53.8	42.7	2,299	2.48	5,594	3,339	2,390	1,090	950
2000	62.5	53.0	41.9	2,223	2.65	5,970	3,263	2,434	1,100	829
Cotton:			Lb.	Mil. bales [6]	cents/lb.			Mil. bales [6]		
1990	12.3	11.7	634	[7]15.5	68.2	5,076	18.5	16.5	7.8	[8]2.3
1995	16.9	16.0	537	[7]17.9	76.5	6,575	21.0	18.3	7.7	[8]2.6
1998	13.4	10.7	625	[7]13.9	61.7	4,120	18.2	14.7	4.3	[8]3.9
1999	14.9	13.4	607	[7]17.0	46.8	3,810	21.0	17.0	6.7	[8]3.9
2000	15.5	13.1	631	[7]17.2	57.8	4,781	21.2	16.2	6.9	[8]5.0
Potatoes:			Cwt.	Mil. cwt.	$/cwt.			Mil. cwt.		
1990	1.4	1.4	293	402	6.08	2,431	347	[9]310	[10]17	20
1995	1.4	1.4	323	445	6.77	2,992	424	[9]365	[10]37	22
1998	1.4	1.4	343	476	5.56	2,635	447	[9]381	[10]43	23
1999	1.4	1.3	359	478	5.77	2,746	464	[9]395	[10]45	24
2000	1.4	1.4	382	516	4.95	2,540	460	[9]394	[10]44	23
Tobacco: [11]			Lb.	Mil. lb.	$/lb.			Mil. lb.		
1990	(NA)	0.7	2,218	1,626	[5]1.74	2,827	3,969	1,796	631	2,149
1995	(NA)	0.7	1,914	1,270	[5]1.82	2,305	3,588	1,362	534	2,225
1998	(NA)	0.7	2,062	1,480	[5]1.83	2,701	3,730	1,442	537	2,298
1999	(NA)	0.6	1,997	1,293	[5]1.83	2,356	3,593	1,192	424	2,388
2000	(NA)	0.5	2,264	1,100	[5]1.87	2,056	3,507	(NA)	(NA)	(NA)
Rice, rough:			Lb.	Mil. cwt.	$/cwt.			Mil. cwt.		
1990	2.9	2.8	5,529	156	6.68	1,047	187	163	71	25
1995	3.1	3.1	5,621	174	9.15	1,587	213	188	82	25
1998	3.3	3.3	5,663	184	8.89	1,654	223	201	87	22
1999	3.5	3.5	5,866	206	5.93	1,230	238	211	89	28
2000	3.1	3.0	6,278	191	5.75	1,073	229	204	83	24
Sorghum for grain:			Bu.	Mil. bu.	$/bu.			Mil. bu.		
1990	10.5	9.1	63.1	573	2.12	1,221	793	651	232	143
1995	9.4	8.3	55.6	459	3.19	1,395	530	512	198	18
1998	9.6	7.7	67.3	520	1.66	905	569	504	197	65
1999	9.3	8.5	69.7	595	1.57	937	660	595	256	65
2000	9.2	7.7	60.9	470	1.75	823	535	490	200	45
Barley:			Bu.	Mil. bu.	$/bu.			Mil. bu.		
1990	8.2	7.5	56.1	422	2.14	912	596	461	81	135
1995	6.7	6.3	57.2	359	2.89	1,029	513	413	62	100
1998	6.3	5.9	60.0	352	1.98	687	501	360	28	142
1999	5.2	4.7	59.2	280	2.13	597	450	338	30	111
2000	5.8	5.2	61.1	318	2.15	632	454	347	55	107

NA Not available. [1] Except as noted, marketing year average price. U.S. prices are computed by weighting U.S. monthly prices by estimated monthly marketings and do not include an allowance for outstanding loans and government purchases and payments. [2] Comprises production, imports, and beginning stocks. [3] Includes feed, residual, and other domestic uses not shown separately. [4] Prices are for hay sold baled. [5] Season average prices received by farmers. U.S. prices are computed by weighting state prices by estimated sales and include an allowance for outstanding loans and government purchases, if any, for crops under government programs. [6] Bales of 480 pounds, net weight. [7] State production figures, which conform with annual ginning enumeration with allowance for cross-state ginnings, rounded to thousands and added for U.S. totals. [8] Stock estimates based on Census Bureau data which results in an unaccounted difference between supply and use estimates and changes in ending stocks. [9] Covers potatoes used for table use, frozen and canned products, chips, and dehydration. [10] Covers fresh potatoes, chips, frozen and dehydrated products. [11] Flue-cured and cigar wrapper, crop year July-June; all other types October-September. Farm-sales-weight basis.

Source: Production—U.S. Dept. of Agriculture, National Agricultural Statistics Service. In *Crop Production*, annual; and *Crop Values*, annual. Supply and disappearance—U.S. Dept. of Agriculture, Economic Research Service, *Feed Situation*, quarterly; *Fats and Oils Situation*, quarterly; *Wheat Situation*, quarterly; *Tobacco Situation*, quarterly; *Cotton and Wool Outlook Statistics*, periodic; and *Agricultural Supply and Demand Estimates*, periodic. Data are also in *Agricultural Statistics*, annual; and *Agricultural Outlook*, monthly.

No. 828. Corn—Acreage, Production, and Value by Leading States: 1998 to 2000

[72,589 represents 72,589,000. One bushel of corn=56 pounds]

State	Acreage harvested (1,000 acres)			Yield per acre (bu.)			Production (mil. bu.)			Price ($/bu.)			Farm value (mil. dol.)		
	1998	1999	2000	1998	1999	2000	1998	1999	2000	1998	1999	2000	1998	1999	2000
U.S. [1]	72,589	70,487	72,732	134	134	137	9,759	9,431	9,968	1.94	1.82	1.85	18,922	17,104	18,621
IA	12,200	11,800	12,000	145	149	145	1,769	1,758	1,740	1.86	1.72	1.75	3,290	3,024	3,045
IL	10,450	10,650	11,050	141	140	151	1,473	1,491	1,669	2.04	1.91	1.90	3,006	2,848	3,170
NE	8,550	8,300	8,050	145	139	126	1,240	1,154	1,014	1.85	1.75	1.95	2,331	2,019	1,978
MN	6,750	6,600	6,600	153	150	145	1,033	990	957	1.71	1.60	1.75	1,766	1,584	1,675
IN	5,550	5,670	5,550	137	132	147	760	748	816	2.11	1.88	1.85	1,604	1,407	1,509
OH	3,340	3,200	3,300	141	126	147	471	403	485	2.03	1.89	2.00	956	762	970
SD	3,550	3,250	3,850	121	113	112	430	367	431	1.61	1.54	1.60	692	566	690
KS	2,850	2,980	3,200	147	141	130	419	420	416	1.96	1.81	2.05	821	761	853
MO	2,500	2,550	2,770	114	97	143	285	247	396	1.92	1.96	1.70	547	485	673
WI	2,950	2,850	2,750	137	143	132	404	408	363	1.84	1.77	1.90	744	721	690
MI	2,050	1,950	1,970	111	130	124	228	254	244	1.90	1.78	1.90	432	451	464
TX	1,850	1,770	1,900	100	129	124	185	228	236	2.26	2.07	2.15	418	473	507
KY	1,180	1,180	1,230	115	105	130	136	124	160	2.17	2.11	2.00	294	261	320
CO	1,070	1,120	1,180	145	142	127	155	159	150	1.96	1.84	2.15	304	293	322
PA	1,050	880	1,080	111	70	127	117	62	137	2.48	2.41	2.00	289	148	274
ND	825	655	930	107	117	112	88	77	104	1.71	1.59	1.60	151	122	167
NC	770	640	650	70	80	116	54	51	75	2.33	2.27	1.90	126	116	143
TN	620	570	590	96	102	114	60	58	67	2.13	1.92	1.85	127	112	124
MD	400	360	405	109	93	155	44	33	63	2.33	2.36	2.00	102	79	126
VA	300	280	330	84	78	146	25	22	48	2.24	2.15	2.00	56	47	96
NY	580	590	480	114	101	98	66	60	47	2.21	2.24	2.20	146	133	103

[1] Includes other states, not shown separately.

Source: U.S. Dept. of Agriculture, National Agricultural Statistics Service, *Crop Production*, annual; and *Crop Values*, annual.

No. 829. Soybeans—Acreage, Production, and Value by Leading States: 1998 to 2000

[70,441 represents 70,441,000. One bushel of soybeans=60 pounds]

State	Acreage harvested (1,000 acres)			Yield per acre (bu.)			Production (mil. bu.)			Price ($/bu.)			Farm value (mil. dol.)		
	1998	1999	2000	1998	1999	2000	1998	1999	2000	1998	1999	2000	1998	1999	2000
U.S. [1]	70,441	72,446	72,718	39	37	38	2,741	2,654	2,770	4.93	4.63	4.75	13,494	12,205	13,073
IL	10,550	10,550	10,450	44	42	44	464	443	460	5.01	4.75	4.85	2,326	2,105	2,230
IA	10,350	10,750	10,680	48	45	43	497	478	459	4.79	4.53	4.75	2,380	2,167	2,181
MN	6,800	6,900	7,150	42	42	41	286	290	293	4.65	4.42	4.60	1,328	1,281	1,348
IN	5,500	5,550	5,630	42	39	46	231	216	259	5.05	4.71	4.75	1,167	1,019	1,230
OH	4,390	4,500	4,440	44	36	42	193	162	186	4.99	4.72	4.80	964	765	895
MO	5,000	5,350	5,000	34	28	35	170	147	175	4.90	4.67	4.75	833	687	831
NE	3,750	4,250	4,575	44	43	38	165	181	174	4.83	4.47	4.70	797	807	817
SD	3,400	4,070	4,370	39	36	35	133	147	153	4.60	4.33	4.45	610	634	681
AR	3,400	3,300	3,200	25	28	26	85	92	83	5.38	4.79	4.90	457	446	408
MI	1,890	1,940	2,080	39	40	36	74	78	75	4.99	4.61	4.75	368	358	356
ND	1,475	1,340	1,850	32	35	33	47	47	61	4.64	4.19	4.20	219	197	256
WI	1,100	1,300	1,450	47	46	40	52	60	58	4.85	4.70	4.70	251	281	273
KS	2,500	2,800	2,500	30	29	20	75	81	50	4.98	4.53	4.75	374	368	238
KY	1,200	1,160	1,180	30	21	39	36	24	46	5.15	4.83	4.85	185	118	223

[1] Includes other states, not shown separately.

Source: U.S. Dept. of Agriculture, National Agricultural Statistics Service, *Crop Production*, annual; and *Crop Values*, annual.

No. 830. Wheat—Acreage, Production, and Value by Leading States: 1998 to 2000

[59,002 represents 59,002,000. One bushel of wheat= 60 pounds]

State	Acreage harvested (1,000 acres)			Yield per acre (bu.)			Production (mil. bu.)			Price ($/bu.)			Farm value (mil. dol.)		
	1998	1999	2000	1998	1999	2000	1998	1999	2000	1998	1999	2000	1998	1999	2000
U.S. [1]	59,002	53,823	53,028	43.2	42.7	41.9	2,547	2,299	2,223	2.65	2.48	2.65	6,781	5,594	5,970
KS	10,100	9,200	9,400	49.0	47.0	37.0	495	432	348	2.53	2.25	2.70	1,252	973	939
ND	9,610	8,657	9,413	32.0	28.0	33.3	308	242	314	3.03	2.77	2.90	931	670	907
WA	2,565	2,290	2,420	61.4	54.2	68.1	157	124	165	2.63	2.77	2.80	414	345	459
OK	5,100	4,300	4,200	39.0	35.0	34.0	199	151	143	2.57	2.24	2.70	511	337	386
MT	5,280	5,320	4,920	32.0	29.0	27.5	169	154	135	3.03	2.93	3.25	513	452	438
SD	3,294	3,024	2,878	36.7	39.9	39.7	121	121	114	2.74	2.55	2.80	327	297	318
ID	1,280	1,350	1,300	80.0	77.4	83.4	102	105	108	2.38	2.59	2.75	242	269	293
MN	1,982	1,990	1,971	40.6	39.8	49.0	80	79	97	3.09	2.87	3.00	248	227	294

[1] Includes other states, not shown separately.

Source: U.S. Dept. of Agriculture, National Agricultural Statistics Service, *Crop Production*, annual; and *Crop Values*, annual.

No. 831. Greenhouse and Nursery Crops—Summary by Type of Product: 1990 to 1999

[In millions of dollars, except per capita (8,677 represents $8,677,000,000). Based on a survey of 36 commercial floriculture states and estimates by source]

Item	Total	Cut flowers	Potted flowering plants	Foliage plants	Bedding plants	Cut cultivated greens	Other [1]
Domestic production: [2]							
1990	8,677	529	701	693	1,032	121	5,601
1995	10,294	479	868	728	1,689	128	6,402
1998	12,041	466	939	733	2,331	133	7,439
1999	12,239	482	975	743	2,423	144	7,472
Imports:							
1990	526	326	18	25	(NA)	14	143
1995	855	512	30	53	(NA)	24	236
1998	1,215	762	52	99	(NA)	36	266
1999	1,238	735	59	119	(NA)	41	283
RETAIL EXPENDITURES [3]							
Total:							
1990	38,624	5,567	2,980	2,764	3,096	779	23,439
1995	46,583	6,662	3,728	3,092	5,067	888	27,147
1998	55,277	8,524	4,039	3,286	6,992	971	31,465
1999	56,077	8,008	4,182	3,443	7,268	1,103	32,073
Per capita (dol.): [4]							
1990	155	22	12	11	12	3	94
1995	177	25	14	12	19	3	103
1998	204	32	15	12	26	4	115
1999	205	29	15	13	27	4	117

NA Not available. [1] Includes turfgrass (sod), bulbs, nursery stock, groundcovers, and other greenhouse and nursery products except the following: seeds, cut Christmas trees, and food crops grown under cover. [2] Equivalent wholesale values. [3] Retail sales values of green goods and associated products and accessories through all marketing channels including delivery, installation, landscaping, and related services. [4] Based on U.S. Census Bureau estimated resident population as of July 1.
Source: U.S. Dept. of Agriculture, Economic Research Service, *Floriculture and Environmental Horticulture Situation and Outlook Report*, annual.

No. 832. Fresh Fruits and Vegetables—Supply and Use: 1990 to 2000

[In millions of pounds, except per capita in pounds (7,327 represents 7,327,000,000)]

Year	Utilized production [1]	Imports [2]	Supply, [1] total	Consumption Total	Consumption Per capita	Exports [2]
FRUITS						
Citrus:						
1990	7,327	184	7,510	5,331	21.4	2,179
1995	8,635	449	9,084	6,333	24.1	2,751
1998	9,308	613	9,922	7,320	27.1	2,602
1999	6,662	756	7,418	5,648	20.7	1,769
2000	8,785	684	9,470	7,029	25.6	2,441
Noncitrus: [3]						
1990	12,122	7,852	19,974	17,978	70.4	1,995
1995	12,983	9,388	22,371	19,521	74.3	2,850
1998	12,348	10,592	22,940	20,407	75.5	2,533
1999	13,610	11,780	25,389	22,360	82.0	3,029
VEGETABLES & MELONS						
1990	34,629	3,265	38,774	34,574	138.5	2,685
1995	38,692	4,698	44,470	39,208	149.3	3,525
1998	40,839	6,478	48,411	42,932	158.6	3,686
1999	43,724	6,470	51,357	45,645	166.7	3,892
POTATOES						
1990	11,335	684	12,019	11,691	46.8	327
1995	13,020	685	13,704	13,121	49.9	584
1998	12,514	1,061	13,575	12,924	47.8	651
1999	12,865	923	13,789	13,190	48.3	599

[1] Crop-year basis for fruits. [2] Fiscal year for fruits; calendar year for vegetables and potatoes. [3] Includes bananas.

No. 833. Nuts—Supply and Use: 1990 to 1999

[In millions of pounds (shelled) (326.2 represents 326,200,000)]

Year	Beginning stocks	Marketable production [1]	Imports	Supply, total	Consumption	Exports	Ending stocks
1990	326.2	961.5	198.4	1,486.1	609.6	522.6	354.0
1995	334.1	770.1	204.0	1,308.2	512.5	543.8	251.9
1998	348.7	851.8	242.0	1,442.5	605.9	612.8	223.9
1999	223.9	1,295.9	283.4	1,803.1	742.2	696.7	364.3

[1] Utilized production minus inedibles and noncommercial usage.
Source of Tables 832 and 833: U.S. Dept. of Agriculture, Economic Research Service, *Fruit and Tree Nuts Situation and Outlook Yearbook* and *Vegetables and Specialties Situation and Outlook Yearbook*.

Agriculture   539

No. 834. Commercial Vegetable and Other Specified Crops—Area, Production, and Value, 1998 to 2000, and Leading Producing States, 2000

[74 represents 74,000. Except as noted, relates to commercial production for fresh market and processing combined. Includes market garden areas but excludes minor producing acreage in minor producing states. Excludes production for home use in farm and nonfarm gardens. Value is for season or crop year and should not be confused with calendar-year income]

Crop	Area [1] (1,000 acres)			Production [2] (1,000 short tons)			Value [3] (mil. dol.)			Leading states in order of production, 2000
	1998	1999	2000	1998	1999	2000	1998	1999	2000	
Asparagus	74	76	77	99	109	114	199	233	221	CA, WA, MI
Beans, snap	287	303	311	975	1,058	1,128	364	396	394	WI, OR, MI [4]
Beans, dry edible. .	1,918	1,877	1,606	1,521	1,654	1,322	567	548	423	ND, MI, NE
Broccoli	134	148	135	868	1,085	981	512	518	597	CA, AZ
Cabbage	83	80	88	1,370	1,268	1,529	312	249	342	NY, CA, TX [5]
Cantaloups	101	107	98	1,075	1,129	1,015	383	389	359	CA, AZ, TX
Carrots	136	130	129	2,346	2,193	2,140	468	583	471	CA, CO, MI [5]
Cauliflower	44	46	47	345	387	388	227	225	260	CA, AZ
Celery	27	28	26	900	936	886	221	225	325	CA, MI, TX
Corn, sweet	704	703	707	4,572	4,586	4,452	691	677	706	(NA)
Fresh market. . .	237	237	247	1,316	1,289	1,296	452	443	474	FL, CA, GA
Processed.	467	466	460	3,256	3,297	3,156	239	234	232	WA, MN, WI
Cucumbers.	160	165	160	1,157	1,224	1,189	367	367	399	MI, NC, FL [4]
Lettuce, head	198	193	198	3,170	3,516	3,601	1,023	936	1,259	CA, AZ, CO
Lettuce, leaf	46	49	48	515	554	565	296	268	312	CA, AZ
Lettuce, Romaine .	37	42	48	533	657	739	236	228	290	CA, AZ, FL
Mushrooms [6]	145	150	151	404	424	427	774	828	829	(NA)
Onions.	171	173	166	3,364	3,678	3,580	838	635	732	CA, OR, WA
Peppers, green . . .	57	57	71	728	778	976	507	484	614	CA, FL, NJ
Potatoes	1,388	1,332	1,352	23,789	23,911	25,798	2,635	2,746	2,540	ID, WA, WI
Strawberries	45	46	48	820	905	924	1,002	1,106	1,014	CA, FL, OR
Sweet potatoes . . .	84	83	94	619	612	681	190	215	209	NC, LA, CA
Tomatoes	422	483	419	11,033	14,673	12,706	1,764	1,864	1,823	(NA)
Fresh market. . .	122	133	129	1,631	1,837	1,848	1,150	951	1,160	FL, CA, GA
Processed.	300	350	290	9,402	12,836	10,858	614	913	663	CA, IN, OH
Watermelons.	169	175	164	1,849	2,058	1,858	285	266	236	FL, CA, TX

NA Not available.   [1] Area of crops for harvest for fresh market, including any partially harvested or not harvested because of low prices or other factors, plus area harvested for processing.   [2] Excludes some quantities not marketed.   [3] Fresh market vegetables valued at f.o.b. shipping point. Processing vegetables are equivalent returns at packinghouse door.   [4] Processed only.   [5] Fresh market only.   [6] Area is shown in million square feet. All data are for marketing year ending June 30.

Source: U.S. Dept. of Agriculture, National Agricultural Statistics Service, *Vegetables*, annual summary. Also in *Agricultural Statistics*, annual.

No. 835. Fruits and Nuts—Utilized Production and Value, 1998 to 2000, and Leading Producing States, 2000

[5,381 represents 5,381,000]

Fruit or nut	Unit	Utilized production [1]			Farm value (mil. dol.)			Leading states in order of production, 2000
		1998	1999	2000	1998	1999	2000	
Apples [2]	1,000 tons .	5,381	5,223	5,192	1,316	1,564	1,336	WA, NY, MI
Apricots	1,000 tons .	108	91	88	35	35	32	CA, WA
Avocados	1,000 tons .	159	183	234	344	379	321	CA, FL
Cherries, sweet	1,000 tons .	194	213	204	213	235	274	WA, OR, CA
Cherries, tart	1,000 tons .	153	127	141	44	56	53	MI, UT, WA
Cranberries	1,000 tons .	272	316	273	199	113	107	WI, MA, NJ
Dates (CA)	1,000 tons .	25	22	15	30	28	18	CA
Grapefruit	1,000 tons .	2,593	2,513	2,758	269	341	423	FL, CA, TX
Grapes (13 states)	1,000 tons .	5,816	6,235	7,657	2,640	2,927	3,104	CA, WA, NY
Lemons	1,000 tons .	897	747	863	241	260	318	CA, AZ
Nectarines (CA)	1,000 tons .	224	274	267	105	112	106	CA
Olives (CA)	1,000 tons .	90	142	53	41	54	32	CA
Oranges	1,000 tons .	13,670	9,824	13,113	1,965	1,701	1,753	FL, CA
Papayas	1,000 tons .	20	21	27	13	16	16	HI
Peaches	1,000 tons .	1,163	1,217	1,254	447	463	489	CA, SC, GA
Pears	1,000 tons .	968	1,013	949	282	298	250	WA, CA, OR
Pineapples	1,000 tons .	332	352	354	93	101	102	HI
Plums (CA)	1,000 tons .	188	196	197	99	82	87	CA
Prunes (dried basis) (CA).	1,000 tons .	103	165	201	79	142	169	CA
Tangerines	1,000 tons .	360	327	451	97	118	113	FL, CA, AZ
Almonds (shelled basis) (CA)	Mil. lb	520	833	703	704	688	682	CA
Hazelnuts (in the shell)	1,000 tons .	16	40	24	15	36	21	OR, WA
Macadamia nuts.	Mil. lb	58	57	50	37	38	30	HI
Pecans (in the shell) (11 states) . . .	Mil. lb	146	406	210	177	330	239	GA, NM, TX
Pistachios	Mil. lb	188	123	243	194	164	238	CA
Walnuts, English (in the shell)	1,000 tons .	227	283	239	238	251	289	CA

[1] Excludes quantities not harvested or not marketed.   [2] Production in commercial orchards with 100 or more bearing age trees.

Source: U.S. Dept. of Agriculture, National Agricultural Statistics Service, *Noncitrus Fruits and Nuts*, annual; and *Citrus Fruits*, annual.

No. 836. Meat Supply and Use: 1980 to 2000

[In millions of pounds (carcass weight equivalent) (53,151 represents 53,151,000,000). Carcass weight equivalent is the weight of the animal minus entrails, head, hide, and internal organs; includes fat and bone. Covers federal and state inspected, and farm slaughter]

Year and type of meat	Production	Imports	Supply, [1] total	Consumption [2]	Exports	Ending stocks
RED MEAT AND POULTRY						
1980	53,151	2,668	57,036	54,695	1,124	1,217
1985	56,271	3,255	60,631	58,651	926	1,054
1990	62,255	3,295	66,673	62,937	2,472	1,263
1995	74,068	2,838	78,636	69,911	6,956	1,768
1999	81,537	3,820	87,372	76,008	9,392	1,972
2000	82,361	4,137	88,470	76,346	10,056	2,068
ALL RED MEATS						
1980	38,978	2,668	42,481	41,170	429	882
1985	39,409	3,255	43,505	42,311	461	733
1990	38,787	3,295	42,742	40,784	1,250	707
1995	43,675	2,832	47,511	43,967	2,614	929
1999	46,284	3,813	51,092	46,477	3,700	914
2000	46,299	4,128	51,341	46,494 ●	3,827	1,020
Beef:						
1980	21,643	2,064	24,166	23,560	173	432
1985	23,728	2,071	26,271	25,523	328	420
1990	22,743	2,356	25,434	24,031	1,006	397
1995	25,222	2,104	27,874	25,534	1,821	519
1999	26,493	2,874	29,760	26,932	2,417	411
2000	26,888	3,032	30,331	27,290	2,516	525
Pork:						
1980	16,617	550	17,521	16,838	252	431
1985	14,807	1,128	16,283	15,865	128	289
1990	15,354	898	16,565	16,031	238	296
1995	17,849	664	18,952	17,768	787	396
1999	19,308	827	20,720	18,952	1,278	489
2000	18,952	967	20,408	18,626	1,305	477
Veal:						
1980	400	21	432	420	2	9
1985	515	20	549	533	4	11
1990	327	(NA)	331	325	(NA)	6
1995	319	(NA)	326	319	(NA)	7
1999	235	(NA)	240	235	(NA)	5
2000	225	(NA)	230	225	(NA)	5
Lamb and mutton:						
1980	318	33	362	351	1	9
1985	359	36	403	389	1	13
1990	363	41	412	397	6	8
1995	287	64	359	346	6	8
1999	248	113	372	358	5	9
2000	234	129	372	353	6	13
POULTRY, TOTAL						
1980	14,173	-	14,555	13,525	695	334
1985	16,862	-	17,126	16,340	465	321
1990	23,468	-	23,931	22,153	1,222	556
1995	30,393	6	31,125	25,944	4,342	839
1999	35,252	7	36,281	29,531	5,692	1,058
2000	36,062	9	37,129	29,852	6,229	1,048
Broilers:						
1980	11,252	-	11,364	10,682	567	115
1985	13,520	-	13,646	13,072	417	158
1990	18,430	-	18,651	17,266	1,143	242
1995	24,827	1	25,287	20,832	3,894	560
1999	29,468	4	30,183	24,468	4,920	796
2000	30,199	6	31,001	24,655	5,548	798
Mature chicken:						
1980	551	-	581	507	53	21
1985	525	-	537	503	21	13
1990	523	-	530	496	25	9
1995	496	3	513	406	99	7
1999	554	2	562	162	393	8
2000	531	2	541	308	223	9
Turkeys:						
1980	2,370	-	2,610	2,337	75	198
1985	2,817	-	2,943	2,765	27	150
1990	4,514	-	4,750	4,390	54	306
1995	5,069	2	5,326	4,706	348	271
1999	5,230	1	5,535	4,902	379	254
2000	5,333	1	5,588	4,889	458	241

- Represents zero. NA Not available. [1] Total supply equals production plus imports plus ending stocks of previous year. [2] Includes shipments to territories.

Source: U.S. Department of Agriculture, Economic Research Service, *Food Consumption, Prices, and Expenditures, 1970-1997;* and *Agricultural Outlook,* monthly.

Agriculture **541**

No. 837. Livestock Inventory and Production: 1980 to 2001

[Production in live weight (111.2 represents 111,200,000). Includes animals for slaughter market, younger animals shipped to other states for feeding or breeding purposes, farm slaughter and custom slaughter consumed on farms where produced, minus livestock shipped into states for feeding or breeding with an adjustment for changes in inventory]

Type of livestock	Unit	1980	1985	1990	1995	1996	1997	1998	1999	2000	2001
ALL CATTLE [1]											
Inventory: [2] Number on farms	Mil.	111.2	109.6	95.8	102.8	103.5	101.7	99.7	99.1	98.2	97.3
Total value	Bil. dol.	55.8	44.0	59.0	63.2	52.1	53.4	60.2	58.8	67.1	70.6
Value per head	Dol	502	402	616	615	503	525	603	594	683	725
Production: Quantity	Bil. lb	40.3	40.1	39.2	42.5	40.9	40.9	41.6	42.5	42.9	(NA)
Beef, price per 100 lb	Dol	62.40	53.70	74.60	61.80	58.70	63.10	59.60	63.40	68.60	(NA)
Calves, price per 100 lb.	Dol	76.80	62.10	95.60	73.10	58.40	78.90	78.80	87.70	104.00	(NA)
Value of production	Bil. dol.	25.5	21.2	29.3	24.7	22.1	24.8	24.2	26.1	28.4	(NA)
HOGS AND PIGS											
Inventory: [3] Number on farms	Mil	67.3	54.1	53.8	59.7	58.2	56.1	61.2	62.2	59.3	59.3
Total value	Bil. dol.	3.8	4.1	4.3	3.2	4.1	5.3	5.0	2.8	4.3	4.5
Value per head	Dol	56.00	75.00	79.10	53.00	71.00	94.00	82.00	44.00	72.00	76.00
Production: Quantity	Bil. lb	23.4	20.2	21.3	24.4	23.1	24.0	25.7	25.8	25.7	(NA)
Price per 100 lb	Dol	38.00	44.00	53.70	40.50	51.90	52.90	34.40	30.30	42.30	(NA)
Value of production	Bil. dol.	8.9	8.9	11.3	9.8	11.9	12.6	8.7	7.8	10.8	(NA)
SHEEP AND LAMBS											
Inventory: [2] Number on farms	Mil	12.7	10.7	11.4	9.0	8.5	8.0	7.8	7.2	7.0	6.9
Total value	Mil. dol	993	654	901	663	732	762	798	638	669	661
Value per head	Dol	78.20	61.10	79.30	74.70	86.50	96.00	102.00	88.00	95.00	96.00
Production: Quantity	Mil. lb	746	704	781	602	572	603	555	534	506	(NA)
Sheep, price per 100 lb.	Dol	21.30	23.90	23.20	28.00	29.90	37.90	30.60	31.10	34.20	(NA)
Lambs, price per 100 lb.	Dol	63.60	67.70	55.50	78.20	88.20	90.30	72.30	-74.50	79.40	(NA)
Value of production	Mil. dol	403	434	374	414	441	490	354	349	357	(NA)

NA Not available. [1] Includes milk cows. [2] As of Jan. 1. [3] As of Dec. 1 of preceding year.
Source: U.S. Dept. of Agriculture, National Agricultural Statistics Service, *Meat Animals—Production, Disposition, and Income,* annual; and annual livestock summaries. Also in *Agricultural Statistics,* annual.

No. 838. Livestock Operations by Size of Herd: 1995 to 2000

[In thousands (1,191 represents 1,191,000). An operation is any place having one or more head on hand at any time during the year]

Size of herd	1995	1999	2000	Size of herd	1995	1999	2000
CATTLE [1]				**MILK COWS** [2]			
Total operations	1,191	1,096	1,076	Total operations	140	111	105
1 to 49 head	746	686	669	1 to 49 head	79	57	53
50 to 99 head	208	186	185	50 to 99 head	39	33	31
100 to 499 head	210	197	193	100 or more head	21	21	21
500 to 999 head	18	18	19	**HOGS AND PIGS**			
1,000 head or more	9	9	10	Total operations	168	99	86
BEEF COWS [2]				1 to 99 head	97	53	48
Total operations	898	844	831	100 to 499 head	44	23	18
1 to 49 head	716	667	654	500 to 999 head	15	9	8
50 to 99 head	105	101	101	1,000 to 1,999 head	7	7	6
100 to 499 head	70	71	71	2,000 to 4,999 head	4	5	5
500 head or more	6	5	6	5,000 head or more	1	2	2

[1] Includes calves. [2] Included in operations with cattle.
Source: U.S. Dept. of Agriculture, National Agricultural Statistics Service, *Cattle Final Estimates, 1994-1998,* January 1999; *Cattle,* January 2001; *Milk Cows and Production Final Estimates 1993-1997,* January 1999; *Hogs and Pigs Final Estimates 1993-1997,* December 1998; *Hogs and Pigs,* December 2000; and *Agricultural Statistics,* annual.

No. 839. Hogs and Pigs—Number, Production, and Value by State: 1998 to 2000

[62,206 represents 62,206,000. See headnote, Table 837]

State	Number on farms [1] (1,000)			Quantity produced (mil. lb.)			Value of production (mil. dol.)			Commercial slaughter [2] (mil. lb.)	
	1998	1999	2000	1998	1999	2000	1998	1999	2000	1999	2000
U.S. [3]	62,206	59,342	59,338	25,715	25,791	25,717	8,674	7,766	10,791	26,256	25,660
IA	15,300	15,400	15,200	6,301	6,495	6,487	1,998	1,891	2,679	7,693	7,294
NC	9,700	9,500	9,300	3,751	3,658	3,705	1,320	1,149	1,624	2,456	2,473
MN	5,700	5,500	5,800	2,403	2,461	2,515	837	735	1,083	2,169	2,086
IL	4,850	4,050	4,150	1,895	1,863	1,776	625	559	762	2,470	2,516
NE	3,400	3,000	3,050	1,451	1,549	1,492	535	488	640	1,643	1,641
IN	4,050	3,250	3,350	1,633	1,535	1,382	531	445	545	1,566	1,621
MO	3,300	3,150	2,900	1,421	1,238	1,215	480	379	507	1,013	981

[1] As of December 1. [2] Includes slaughter in federally inspected and other slaughter plants; excludes animals slaughtered on farms. [3] Includes other states not shown separately.
Source: U.S. Dept. of Agriculture, National Agricultural Statistics Service, *Meat Animals-Production, Disposition and Income,* annual.

No. 840. Cattle and Calves—Number, Production, and Value by State: 1998 to 2001

[99,115 represents 99,115,000. Includes milk cows. See headnote, Table 837]

State	Number on farms [1] (1,000)			Quantity produced (mil. lb.)			Value of production (mil. dol.)			Commercial slaughter [2] (mil. lb.)	
	1999	2000	2001	1998	1999	2000	1998	1999	2000	1999	2000
U.S. [3] ...	99,115	98,198	97,309	41,620	42,468	42,915	24,153	26,051	28,388	44,099	44,558
TX......	14,100	13,900	13,700	7,443	7,417	7,469	4,404	4,638	5,039	7,760	7,623
NE......	6,700	6,650	6,600	4,257	4,326	4,410	2,344	2,519	2,561	9,231	9,558
KS......	6,550	6,600	6,700	3,764	3,973	4,097	2,188	2,442	2,418	9,632	9,858
CO......	3,200	3,150	3,150	1,986	2,072	2,121	1,176	1,293	1,337	3,235	3,265
CA......	5,100	5,100	5,150	1,850	1,972	1,995	852	862	849	1,275	1,309
OK......	5,300	5,200	5,050	1,850	2,050	1,936	1,234	1,449	1,578	38	38
IA	3,700	3,700	3,650	1,749	1,862	1,833	949	1,009	1,078	1,037	846
SD......	3,900	3,900	4,050	1,439	1,546	1,627	914	1,094	1,269	389	402
MO	4,400	4,350	4,250	1,129	1,152	1,188	777	834	1,004	102	99
MN	2,500	2,550	2,550	1,070	1,083	1,144	602	625	706	872	911
WI......	3,400	3,400	3,350	1,055	1,068	1,113	518	581	654	2,254	2,313

[1] As of January 1.   [2] Data cover cattle only. Includes slaughter in federally inspected and other slaughter plants; excludes animals slaughtered on farms.   [3] Includes other states not shown separately.

Source: U.S. Dept. of Agriculture, National Agricultural Statistics Service, *Meat Animals-Production, Disposition and Income*, annual.

No. 841. Milk Cows—Number, Production, and Value by State: 1998 to 2000

[9,154 represents 9,154,000]

State	Number on farms [1] (1,000)			Milk produced on farms (mil. lb.)			Value of production [2] (mil. dol.)		
	1998	1999	2000	1998	1999	2000	1998	1999	2000
United States [3] ..	9,154	9,156	9,210	157,348	162,716	167,658	24,332	23,400	20,786
California	1,420	1,466	1,523	27,654	30,459	32,240	4,151	4,097	3,708
Wisconsin.......	1,369	1,365	1,344	22,842	23,071	23,259	3,541	3,184	2,721
New York	701	701	686	11,750	12,082	11,920	1,810	1,764	1,562
Pennsylvania......	623	616	617	10,847	10,931	11,156	1,736	1,727	1,528
Minnesota.......	551	545	534	9,275	9,478	9,493	1,442	1,327	1,139
Idaho..........	292	318	347	5,765	6,453	7,223	836	839	766
Texas..........	352	345	348	5,605	5,618	5,735	880	843	768
Michigan.........	299	299	300	5,365	5,455	5,705	821	807	736
Washington.......	248	247	247	5,326	5,535	5,593	847	825	716

[1] Average number during year. Represents cows and heifers that have calved, kept for milk; excluding heifers not yet fresh.   [2] Valued at average returns per 100 pounds of milk in combined marketings of milk and cream. Includes value of milk fed to calves.   [3] Includes other states not shown separately.

Source: U.S. Dept. of Agriculture, National Agricultural Statistics Service, *Dairy Products*, annual; and *Milk: Production, Disposition, and Income*, annual.

No. 842. Milk Production and Manufactured Dairy Products: 1980 to 2000

[334 represents 334,000]

Item	Unit	1980	1985	1990	1995	1996	1997	1998	1999	2000
Number of farms with milk cows	1,000	334	269	193	140	131	124	117	111	105
Cows and heifers that have calved, kept for milk..................	Mil. head ..	10.8	11.0	10.0	9.5	9.4	9.3	9.2	9.2	9.2
Milk produced on farms..............	Bil. lb	128	143	148	155	154	156	157	163	168
Production per cow	1,000 lb...	11.9	13.0	14.8	16.4	16.4	16.9	17.2	17.8	18.2
Whole milk sold from farms [1]	Bil. lb	126	141	146	154	153	155	156	161	166
Value of milk produced	Bil. dol. ..	16.9	18.4	20.4	20.1	23.0	21.1	24.3	23.4	20.8
Gross farm income, dairy products.....	Bil. dol.	16.7	18.1	20.2	19.9	22.8	21.0	24.2	23.2	20.6
Cash receipts from marketing of milk and cream [1]	Bil. dol.	16.6	18.1	20.1	19.9	22.8	20.9	24.1	23.2	20.6
Number of dairy manufacturing plants	Number...	2,257	2,061	1,723	1,495	1,422	1,384	1,323	1,192	1,124
Manufactured dairy products:										
Butter (incl. whey butter)	Mil. lb	1,145	1,248	1,302	1,264	1,174	1,151	1,168	1,277	1,274
Cheese, total [2].................	Mil. lb	3,984	5,081	6,059	6,917	7,218	7,330	7,492	7,894	8,255
American (excl. full-skim American)...	Mil. lb	2,376	2,855	2,894	3,131	3,281	3,286	3,315	3,533	3,634
Cream and Neufchatel	Mil. lb	229	294	431	544	575	615	621	639	687
All Italian varieties	Mil. lb	983	1,491	2,207	2,674	2,812	2,881	3,005	3,145	3,311
Cottage cheese: Creamed [3]	Mil. lb	825	716	832	711	690	706	728	720	736
Condensed bulk milk..............	Mil. lb	952	1,232	1,426	1,372	1,270	1,275	1,263	1,365	1,202
Nonfat dry milk [4]...............	Mil. lb	1,168	1,398	902	1,243	1,068	1,223	1,140	1,364	1,457
Dry whey [5]	Mil. lb	690	987	1,143	1,147	1,117	1,137	1,178	1,147	1,188
Yogurt, plain and fruit flavored........	Mil. lb	(NA)	(NA)	(NA)	1,646	1,588	1,574	1,639	1,717	1,835
Ice cream, regular................	Mil. gal ...	830	901	824	862	879	914	935	972	970
Ice cream, lowfat [6]	Mil. gal ...	293	301	352	357	366	386	407	381	382

NA Not available.   [1] Comprises sales to plants and dealers, and retail sales by farmers direct to consumers.   [2] Includes varieties not shown separately.   [3] Includes partially creamed (low fat).   [4] Includes dry skim milk for animal feed.   [5] Includes animal but excludes modified whey production.   [6] Includes freezer-made milkshake in most states.

Source: U.S. Dept. of Agriculture, National Agricultural Statistics Service, *Dairy Products*, annual; and *Milk: Production, Disposition, and Income*, annual.

Agriculture **543**

No. 843. Milk Production and Commercial Use: 1980 to 2000

[In billions of pounds milkfat basis (128.4 represents 128,400,000,000)]

Year	Production	Farm use	Commercial Farm marketings	Beginning stock	Imports	Commercial supply, total	CCC net removals [1]	Commercial Ending stock	Commercial Disappearance	Milk price per 100 lb. [2] (dol.)
1980	128.4	2.3	126.1	5.3	2.1	133.5	8.8	5.6	119.0	13.05
1985	143.0	2.5	140.6	4.8	2.8	148.2	13.2	4.5	130.5	12.76
1990	147.7	2.0	145.7	4.1	2.7	152.5	8.5	5.1	138.8	13.68
1995	155.3	1.6	153.7	4.3	2.9	160.9	2.1	4.1	154.7	12.78
1998	157.3	1.4	155.9	4.9	4.6	165.4	0.4	5.3	159.8	15.46
1999	162.7	1.4	161.3	5.3	4.8	171.4	0.3	6.1	164.9	14.38
2000	167.7	1.3	166.3	6.1	4.4	176.9	0.8	6.9	169.2	12.34

[1] Removals from commercial supply by Commodity Credit Corporation.   [2] Wholesale price received by farmers for all milk delivered to plants and dealers.

Source: U.S. Dept. of Agriculture, Economic Research Service, *Agricultural Outlook*, monthly.

No. 844. Broiler, Turkey, and Egg Production: 1980 to 2000

[For year ending November 30 (392 represents 392,000,000)]

Item	Unit	1980	1985	1990	1994	1995	1996	1997	1998	1999	2000
Chickens:[1]											
Number [2]	Million ..	392	370	353	386	388	393	410	425	436	435
Value per head [2]	Dollars..	1.88	1.90	2.29	2.34	2.41	2.65	2.72	2.69	2.65	2.43
Value, total [2]	Mil. dol.	737	704	808	902	935	1,039	1,113	1,144	1,155	1,058
Number sold [3]	Million ..	238	220	208	197	180	174	191	194	210	218
Price per lb. [3]	Cents ..	11.0	14.8	9.6	7.4	6.5	6.6	7.7	8.1	7.1	5.8
Value of sales [3]	Mil. dol.	129	152	94	73	60	59	71	76	73	65
PRODUCTION											
Broilers:[4]											
Number	Million ..	3,963	4,470	5,864	7,018	7,326	7,597	7,764	7,934	8,146	8,263
Weight	Bil. lb. ..	15.5	18.9	25.6	32.5	34.2	36.5	37.5	38.6	40.8	41.5
Price per lb	Cents ..	27.7	30.1	32.6	35.0	34.4	38.1	37.7	39.3	37.1	33.6
Production value.......	Mil. dol.	4,303	5,668	8,366	11,372	11,762	13,903	14,159	15,145	15,129	13,953
Turkeys:											
Number.............	Million ..	165	185	282	287	292	303	301	285	270	270
Weight	Bil. lb. ..	3.1	3.7	6.0	6.5	6.8	7.2	7.2	7.1	6.9	7.0
Price per lb	Cents ..	41.3	49.1	39.6	40.4	41.0	43.3	39.9	38.0	40.8	40.7
Production value.......	Mil. dol.	1,272	1,820	2,393	2,643	2,769	3,124	2,884	2,679	2,810	2,843
Eggs:											
Number.............	Billion ..	69.7	68.4	68.1	73.9	74.8	76.4	77.5	79.8	82.7	84.4
Price per dozen	Cents ..	56.3	57.2	70.8	61.5	62.5	75.0	70.3	66.8	62.2	61.8
Production value.......	Mil. dol.	3,268	3,262	4,021	3,790	3,893	4,776	4,540	4,439	4,287	4,347

[1] Excludes commercial broilers.   [2] As of December 1.   [3] Data for 1980 represent number produced and production value.
[4] Young chickens of the heavy breeds and other meat-type birds, to be marketed at 2-5 lbs. live weight and from which no pullets are kept for egg production.

Source: U.S. Dept. of Agriculture, National Agricultural Statistics Service, *Poultry—Production and Value*, annual; *Turkeys*, annual; and *Layers and Egg Production*, annual.

No. 845. Broiler and Turkey Production by State: 1998 to 2000

[In millions of pounds, liveweight production (38,554 represents 38,554,000,000)]

State	Broilers 1998	Broilers 1999	Broilers 2000	Turkeys 1998	Turkeys 1999	Turkeys 2000	State	Broilers 1998	Broilers 1999	Broilers 2000	Turkeys 1998	Turkeys 1999	Turkeys 2000
U.S. [1] ..	38,554	40,830	41,516	7,051	6,886	6,988	MS.	3,468	3,676	3,700	(NA)	(NA)	(NA)
AL	4,517	4,953	5,297	(NA)	(NA)	(NA)	MO	1,097	1,124	1,080	598	616	619
AR	5,619	5,861	5,839	496	491	498	NC......	3,592	3,866	4,051	1,270	1,069	1,033
CA......	(NA)	(NA)	(NA)	443	429	439	ND......	(NA)	(NA)	(NA)	42	44	49
DE......	1,429	1,410	1,461	(NA)	(Z)	(Z)	OH......	235	263	224	179	172	165
FL	632	648	648	(NA)	(NA)	(NA)	OK......	994	1,017	1,093	(NA)	(NA)	(NA)
GA......	5,892	6,199	6,149	(NA)	(NA)	(NA)	PA......	691	704	693	233	222	253
IL.......	(NA)	(NA)	(NA)	81	81	82	SC......	848	924	1,004	356	326	335
IN	(NA)	(NA)	(NA)	352	377	383	SD......	(NA)	(NA)	(NA)	123	137	141
IA	(NA)	(NA)	(NA)	(NA)	233	214	TN......	716	724	696	(NA)	(NA)	(NA)
KY	843	982	1,041	(NA)	(NA)	(NA)	TX......	2,160	2,387	2,590	(NA)	(NA)	(NA)
MD......	1,367	1,472	1,360	15	15	15	VA......	1,264	1,317	1,298	533	526	553
MI	3	4	(NA)	(NA)	86	119	WV	358	358	365	88	95	89
MN......	207	217	221	1,028	1,066	1,061	WI	164	159	148	(NA)	(NA)	(NA)

NA Not available.   Z Less than 500,000 pounds.   [1] Includes other states not shown separately.

Source: U.S. Dept. of Agriculture, National Agricultural Statistics Service, *Poultry—Production and Value*, annual; and *Turkeys*, annual.

Natural Resources

This section presents data on the area, ownership, production, trade, reserves, and disposition of natural resources. Natural resources is defined here as including forestry, fisheries, and mining and mineral products.

Forestry—Presents data on the area, ownership, and timber resource of commercial timberland; forestry statistics covering the National Forests and Forest Service cooperative programs; product data for lumber, pulpwood, woodpulp, paper and paperboard, and similar data.

The principal sources of data relating to forests and forest products are *Forest Resources of the United States, 1991; Timber Demand and Technology Assessment, 2001; U.S. Timber Production, Trade, Consumption, and Price Statistics; Land Areas of the National Forest System,* issued annually by the Forest Service of the Department of Agriculture; *Agricultural Statistics* issued by the Department of Agriculture; and reports of the annual survey of manufactures, see Table 851) and the annual *Current Industrial Reports,* issued by the Census Bureau on the Internet and in print in the annual *Manufacturing Profiles.* Additional information is published in the monthly *Survey of Current Business* of the Bureau of Economic Analysis, and the annual *Wood Pulp* and *Fiber Statistics* and *The Statistics of Paper, Paperboard, and Wood Pulp* of the American Forest and Paper Association, Washington, DC.

The completeness and reliability of statistics on forests and forest products vary considerably. The data for forest land area and stand volumes are much more reliable for areas which have been recently surveyed than for those for which only estimates are available. In general, more data are available for lumber and other manufactured products such as particle board and softwood panels, etc., than for the primary forest products such as poles and piling and fuelwood.

Fisheries—The principal source of data relating to fisheries is *Fisheries of the United States,* issued annually by the National Marine Fisheries Service (NMFS), National Oceanic and Atmospheric Administration (NOAA). The NMFS collects and disseminates data on commercial landings of fish and shellfish. Annual reports include quantity and value of commercial landings of fish and shellfish disposition of landings and number and kinds of fishing vessels and fishing gear. Reports for the fish-processing industry include annual output for the wholesaling and fish processing establishments, annual and seasonal employment. The principal source for these data is the annual *Fisheries of the United States.*

Mining and mineral products—Presents data relating to mineral industries and their products, general summary measures of production and employment, and more detailed data on production, prices, imports and exports, consumption, and distribution for specific industries and products. Data on mining and mineral products may also be found in Sections 19, 21, and 28 of this *Abstract;* data on mining employment may be found in Section 12.

Mining comprises the extraction of minerals occurring naturally (coal, ores, crude petroleum, natural gas) and quarrying, well operation, milling, refining and processing, and other preparation customarily done at the mine or well site or as a part of extraction activity. (Mineral preparation plants are usually operated together with mines or quarries.) Exploration for minerals is included as is the development of mineral properties.

The principal governmental sources of these data are the *Minerals Yearbook* and *Mineral Commodity Summaries,* published by the U.S. Geological Survey, Department of the Interior, and various monthly and annual publications of the Energy Information Administration, Department of

Natural Resources 545

Energy. See text, Section 19, for a list of Department of Energy publications. In addition, the Census Bureau conducts a census of mineral industries every 5 years (for 1997 results, see Tables 864 and 865).

Nongovernment sources include the *Annual Statistical Report* of the American Iron and Steel Institute, Washington, DC; *Metals Week* and the monthly *Engineering and Mining Journal*, issued by the McGraw-Hill Publishing Co., New York, NY; *The Iron Age*, issued weekly by the Chilton Co., Philadelphia, PA; and the *Joint Association Survey of the U.S. Oil and Gas Industry*, conducted jointly by the American Petroleum Institute, Independent Petroleum Association of America, and Mid-Continent Oil and Gas Association.

Mineral statistics, with principal emphasis on commodity detail, have been collected by the U.S. Geological Survey and the former Bureau of Mines since 1880. Current data in U.S. Geological Survey publications include quantity and value of nonfuel minerals produced, sold or used by producers, or shipped; quantity of minerals stocked; crude materials treated and prepared minerals recovered; and consumption of mineral raw materials.

Censuses of mineral industries have been conducted by the Census Bureau at various intervals since 1840. Beginning with the 1967 census, legislation provides for a census to be conducted every 5 years for years ending in "2" and "7." The most recent results, published for 1997, are based on the North American Industry Classification System (NAICS). The censuses provide, for the various types of mineral establishments, information on operating costs, capital expenditures, labor, equipment, and energy requirements in relation to their value of shipments and other receipts. Commodity statistics on many manufactured mineral products are also collected by the Census Bureau at monthly, quarterly, or annual intervals and issued in its *Current Industrial Reports* series.

In general, figures shown in the individual commodity tables include data for outlying areas and may therefore not agree with summary tables. Except for crude petroleum and refined products, the export and import figures include foreign trade passing through the customs districts of United States and Puerto Rico but exclude shipments between U.S. territories and the customs districts.

U.S. Census Bureau, Statistical Abstract of the United States: 2001

No. 846. Gross Domestic Product of Natural Resource-Related Industries in Current and Real (1996) Dollars by Industry: 1990 to 1999

[In billions of dollars (5,803.2 represents 5,803,200,000,000). Data are based on the 1987 SIC. Data include nonfactor charges (capital consumption allowances, indirect business taxes, etc.) as well as factor charges against gross product; corporate profits and capital consumption allowances have been shifted from a company to an establishment basis]

Industry	Current dollars				Chained (1996) dollars			
	1990	1995	1998	1999	1990	1995	1998	1999
All industries, total [1]	5,803.2	7,400.5	8,790.2	9,299.2	6,707.9	7,543.8	8,515.7	8,875.8
Industries covered	297	307	329	338	322	330	365	370
Percent of all industries	5.12	4.14	3.75	3.64	4.80	4.37	4.29	4.16
Agriculture, forestry, and fishing	108.3	109.8	127.2	125.4	118.5	123.1	144.0	150.9
Farms	79.6	73.2	80.8	74.2	84.2	85.5	100.2	106.3
Agricultural services	28.7	36.7	46.5	51.2	34.6	37.6	43.2	44.4
Mining	111.9	95.7	105.6	111.8	105.8	113.0	126.2	121.9
Metal mining	5.2	6.5	5.1	5.5	4.4	5.5	7.3	8.6
Coal mining	11.8	10.7	11.3	11.3	7.5	10.1	12.5	13.1
Oil and gas extraction	87.1	69.3	77.4	82.8	87.5	88.6	94.9	89.1
Nonmetallic minerals, except fuels	7.8	9.1	11.8	12.3	8.1	9.1	11.5	11.4
Manufacturing	1,040.6	1,289.1	1,436.0	1,500.8	1,102.3	1,284.7	1,446.4	1,529.4
Timber-related manufacturing	77.2	101.3	96.4	101.1	97.6	93.8	94.9	96.8
Lumber and wood products	32.2	42.3	41.4	44.1	45.1	41.6	39.5	40.8
Paper and allied products	45.0	58.9	55.1	57.0	52.5	52.2	55.3	56.0

[1] Includes private households and statistical discrepancy, not shown separately.

Source: U.S. Bureau of Economic Analysis, *National Income and Product Accounts, 1929-97*, (forthcoming); and *Survey of Current Business*, December 2000.

No. 847. Natural Resource-Related Industries—Employees, Annual Payroll, and Establishments by Industry: 1999

[Excludes government employees, railroad employees, self-employed persons, etc. See "General Explanation" in source for definitions and statement on reliability of data. An *establishment* is a single physical location where business is conducted or where services or industrial operations are performed]

Year and industry	NAICS code [1]	Number of employ-ees[2] (1,000)	Annual payroll (bil. dol.)	Aver-age payroll per em-ployee (dol.)	Establishment by employment size-class (1,000)				
					Total	Under 20 employ-ees	20 to 99 employ-ees	100 to 499 employ-ees	500 and over employ-ees
Natural resource-related industries, total	(X)	1,803.0	42.2	23,397	73,981	58,088	11,828	3,698	367
Percent of all industries	(X)	1.63	1.19	72.87	1.06	0.96	1.47	2.43	2.01
Forestry, fishing, hunting and agriculture support	11	192.2	4.8	25,046	26,926	25,246	1,487	178	15
Forestry and logging	113	83.8	2.3	26,916	13,694	13,019	648	25	2
Timber tract operations	1131	3.3	0.1	37,422	431	392	35	4	-
Forest nurseries & gathering forest products	1132	1.4	-	35,954	252	241	11	-	-
Logging	1133	79.2	2.1	26,326	13,011	12,386	602	21	2
Fishing, hunting & trapping	114	10.0	0.3	33,302	2,541	2,449	78	13	1
Fishing	1141	7.6	0.3	34,645	2,181	2,109	61	11	-
Hunting & trapping	1142	2.4	0.1	28,998	360	340	17	2	1
Agriculture & forestry support activities	115	98.3	2.2	22,613	10,691	9,778	761	140	12
Crop production support activities	1151	67.4	1.6	23,386	5,929	5,276	534	111	8
Animal production support activities	1152	16.7	0.3	19,507	3,269	3,140	113	16	-
Forestry support activities	1153	14.1	0.3	22,603	1,493	1,362	114	13	4
Mining	21	456.6	21.0	45,935	23,699	19,459	3,456	694	90
Oil & gas extraction	211	90.0	5.4	59,742	7,556	6,746	666	128	16
Oil & gas extraction	2111	90.0	5.4	59,742	7,556	6,746	666	128	16
Mining (except oil & gas)	212	215.9	9.6	44,572	7,280	5,104	1,759	377	40
Coal mining	2121	76.4	3.7	48,413	1,336	683	443	196	14
Metal ore mining	2122	39.9	1.8	46,206	529	397	54	57	21
Nonmetallic mineral mining & quarrying	2123	99.6	4.1	40,972	5,415	4,024	1,262	124	5
Mining support activities	213	150.7	6.0	39,641	8,863	7,609	1,031	189	34
Mining support activities	2131	150.7	6.0	39,641	8,863	7,609	1,031	189	34
Timber-related manufacturing	(X)	1,154.2	16.4	14,206	23,356	13,383	6,885	2,826	262
Wood product manufacturing	321	595.2	16.4	27,509	17,473	11,493	4,537	1,364	79
Sawmills & wood preservation	3211	131.9	3.8	28,431	4,839	3,250	1,275	311	3
Veneer, plywood & engineered wood product manufacturing	3212	117.5	3.6	30,846	1,886	770	746	360	10
Other wood product manufacturing	3219	345.7	9.0	26,023	10,748	7,473	2,516	693	66
Paper manufacturing	322	559.0	23.2	41,549	5,883	1,890	2,348	1,462	183
Pulp, paper & paperboard mills	3221	185.2	9.7	52,607	592	72	154	234	132
Converted paper product manufacturing	3222	373.8	13.5	36,071	5,291	1,818	2,194	1,228	51

- Represents zero.   X Not applicable.   [1] North American Industry Classification System, 1977.   [2] Covers full- and part-time employees who are on the payroll in the pay period including March 12.

Source: U.S. Census Bureau, *County Business Patterns*, annual. See also <http://www.census.gov/prod/2001pubs/cbp99/cbp99-1.pdf> (issued April 2001).

No. 848. National Forest System—Summary: 1980 to 1998

[For fiscal years ending in year shown; see text, Section 8, State and Local Government Finances and Employment. Includes Alaska and Puerto Rico, except as noted]

Item	Unit	1980	1990	1993	1994	1995	1996	1997	1998
Timber cut, total value	Mil. dol.	737	1,192	919	787	620	548	502	450
Commercial and cost sales: [1]									
Volume	Mil. bd. ft.	9,178	10,500	5,917	4,815	3,866	3,725	3,285	3,298
Value	Mil. dol.	730	1,188	915	783	616	544	498	446
Livestock grazing: [2]									
Cattle and horses [3]	1,000	1,521	1,236	1,318	1,224	1,311	1,167	1,225	1,208
Sheep and goats	1,000	1,328	958	1,111	925	1,068	859	932	909
Receipts, total	Mil. dol.	703	971	504	515	387	273	285	294
Timber use	Mil. dol.	625	849	425	432	303	195	197	208
Grazing use	Mil. dol.	16	10	11	11	9	7	7	7
Special land use, etc	Mil. dol.	62	112	68	72	75	71	81	79

[1] Includes land exchanges. [2] Covers number actually grazed. Excludes Puerto Rico. [3] Excludes animals under 6 months of age.

Source: U.S. Forest Service, *Timber Demand and Technology Assessment*, RWU-4861. Also in *Agricultural Statistics*, annual.

No. 849. National Forest System Land—State and Other Area: 1999

[In thousands of acres (232,786 represents 232,786,000). As of Sept. 30]

State and other area	Gross area [1]	NFS land [2]	State and other area	Gross area [1]	NFS land [2]	State and other area	Gross area [1]	NFS land [2]
Total	232,786	191,938	IA	-	-	ND	1,106	1,106
			KS	116	108	OH	835	229
U.S.	232,730	191,910	KY	2,102	693	OK	772	397
			LA	1,024	604	OR	17,496	15,656
AL	1,288	665	ME	93	53	PA	743	513
AK	24,355	21,974	MD	-	-	RI	-	-
AZ	11,891	11,255	MA	-	-	SC	1,375	613
AR	3,539	2,579	MI	4,895	2,857	SD	2,367	2,012
CA	24,403	20,653	MN	5,467	2,838	TN	1,212	634
CO	16,052	14,509	MS	2,310	1,159	TX	1,994	755
CT	-	-	MO	3,060	1,495	UT	9,211	8,111
DE	-	-	MT	19,104	16,886	VT	817	368
DC	-	-	NE	442	352	VA	3,224	1,659
FL	1,379	1,147	NV	6,275	5,826	WA	10,088	9,202
GA	1,856	865	NH	1,554	827	WV	1,870	1,033
HI	-	-	NJ	-	-	WI	2,023	1,521
ID	21,655	20,459	NM	10,367	9,327	WY	9,704	9,238
IL	856	292	NY	-	-	PR	56	28
IN	644	196	NC	3,166	1,244	VI	-	-

- Represents zero or rounds to zero. [1] Comprises all publicly and privately owned land within authorized boundaries of national forests, purchase units, national grasslands, land utilization projects, research and experimental areas, and other areas. [2] Federally owned land within the "gross area within unit boundaries."

Source: U.S. Forest Service, *Land Areas of the National Forest System*, annual.

No. 850. Forest and Timberland Area, Sawtimber, and Stock: 1970 to 1996

[754 acres represents 754,000,000 acres. As of Jan. 1]

Year and region	Total forest land (mil. acres)	Timberland, ownership [1]				Sawtimber, net volume [3]		Growing stock, net volume [4]	
		All ownerships (mil. acres)	Federally owned or managed [2] (mil. acres)	State and local (mil. acres)	Private (mil. acres)	Total (bil. bd. ft.)	Softwood (bil. bd. ft.)	Total (bil. cu. ft.)	Softwood (bil. cu. ft.)
United States, 1970	754	504	116	29	360	2,587	2,035	694	458
North	(NA)	154	11	18	126	295	81	146	39
South	(NA)	203	15	3	185	569	302	191	87
Rocky Mountains	(NA)	65	42	2	20	398	384	101	95
Pacific Coast	(NA)	82	47	5	29	1,325	1,268	257	238
United States, 1987	731	485	97	34	354	2,853	2,040	766	453
North	165	154	11	19	124	459	126	190	48
South	203	197	16	4	177	781	388	245	106
Rocky Mountains	142	61	39	3	20	411	394	108	100
Pacific Coast	220	72	31	8	32	1,202	1,132	223	199
United States, 1992	737	490	97	35	358	2,992	2,047	786	450
North	168	158	11	19	127	540	137	207	51
South	212	199	16	4	179	842	389	251	103
Rocky Mountains	140	63	40	3	20	415	397	110	101
Pacific Coast	217	70	30	8	32	1,196	1,124	218	195
United States, 1996	746	518	124	35	357	3,227	2,231	860	503
North	170	180	32	21	127	574	146	213	49
South	214	201	16	5	180	858	393	256	105
Rocky Mountains	143	68	44	2	21	482	457	141	126
Pacific Coast	219	69	32	7	29	1,313	1,235	250	223

NA Not available. [1] Timberland is forest land that is producing or is capable of producing crops of industrial wood and not withdrawn from timber utilization by statute or administrative regulation. Areas qualifying as timberland have the capability of producing in excess of 20 cubic feet per acre per year of industrial wood in natural stands. Currently inaccessible and inoperable areas are included. [2] Includes Indian lands. [3] Sawtimber is timber suitable for sawing into lumber. Live trees of commercial species containing at least one 12-foot sawlog or two noncontiguous 8-foot logs, and meeting regional specifications for freedom from defect. Softwood trees must be at least 9.0-inches diameter, and hardwood trees must be at least 11.0-inches diameter at 4 1/2 feet above ground. International 1/4-inch rule. [4] Live trees of commercial species meeting specified standards of quality or vigor. Cull trees are excluded. Includes only trees 5.0-inches diameter or larger at 4 1/2 feet above ground.

Source: U.S. Forest Service, *Timber Demand and Technology Assessment, 1996*, RWU-4851.

No. 851. Timber-Based Manufacturing Industries—Employees, Payroll, and Shipments: 1999

Selected industries	1987 NAICS code [1]	All employees			Value added by manufactures			
		Number (1,000)	Payroll		Produc-tion workers, total (1,000)		Per produc-tion worker (dol.)	Value of shipments (mil. dol.)
			Total (mil. dol.)	Per employee (dol.)		Total (mil. dol.)		
Manufacturing, all industries . . .	31-33	16,711	600,090	35,910	12,011	1,962,644	163,406	4,038,109
Timber-based manufacturing, total	(X)	1,149	38,743	33,707	925	113,015	122,210	255,074
Percent of total manufacturing	(X)	6.88	6.46	(X)	7.70	5.76	(X)	6.32
Wood product manufacturing	321	589	15,954	27,076	493	38,413	77,932	97,583
Sawmills & wood preservation. .	3211	133	3,644	27,433	113	9,610	84,690	30,209
Sawmills	321113	120	3,311	27,526	103	8,620	83,396	25,249
Wood preservation	321114	13	332	26,540	10	990	97,922	4,960
Veneer, plywood, & engineered wood product	3212	116	3,471	29,953	97	9,553	98,923	21,988
Other wood product.	3219	341	8,839	25,957	283	19,250	68,054	45,386
Millwork	32191	154	4,121	26,838	128	8,619	67,149	21,693
Wood container & pallet . . .	32192	49	1,039	21,009	42	2,128	50,575	4,772
All other wood product	32199	138	3,679	26,753	112	8,503	75,631	18,921
Paper.	322	560	22,789	40,683	432	74,602	172,749	157,491
Pulp, paper, & paperboard mills.	3221	187	9,725	52,137	146	37,526	257,141	73,509
Pulp mills	32211	7	390	53,342	6	1,444	259,688	3,112
Paper mills	32212	128	6,656	51,984	101	25,716	254,761	49,468
Paperboard mills	32213	51	2,678	52,348	39	10,365	262,876	21,229
Converted paper product	3222	374	13,065	34,966	286	37,076	129,675	83,982
Paperboard container	32221	212	7,515	35,493	163	17,526	107,803	44,536
Paper bag & coated & treated paper	32222	73	2,728.	37,402	55	8,763	160,789	19,511
Stationery product	32223	48	1,439	30,041	36	3,626	99,385	7,926
Other converted paper product	32229	41	1,383	33,665	32	7,162	221,302	12,009

X Not applicable. [1] North American Industry Classification System, 1997; see text, Section 15, Business Enterprise.

Source: U.S. Census Bureau, *Annual Survey of Manufactures, 1999,* Series M99(AS)-1.

No. 852. Timber Products—Production, Foreign Trade, and Consumption by Type of Product: 1980 to 1999

[In millions of cubic feet roundwood equivalent (12,081 represents 12,081,000,000)]

Type of product	1980	1990	1991	1992	1993	1994	1995	1996	1997	1998	1999
Industrial roundwood:											
Domestic production [1]	12,081	15,577	14,894	15,280	15,011	15,306	16,681	16,506	16,799	16,918	16,908
Softwoods	8,988	10,968	10,402	10,563	10,090	10,268	10,875	10,812	10,180	10,097	10,389
Hardwoods	3,093	4,609	4,493	4,717	4,921	5,038	5,806	5,694	6,619	6,821	6,519
Imports.	2,395	3,091	2,808	3,090	3,465	3,632	4,174	4,137	4,273	4,388	4,661
Exports.	1,469	2,307	2,393	2,344	2,143	2,139	2,467	2,445	2,475	2,114	2,097
Consumption [2].	13,008	16,361	15,310	16,026	16,334	16,800	18,389	18,197	18,598	19,192	19,471
Softwoods	9,839	11,779	11,011	11,536	11,539	11,906	12,709	12,715	12,114	12,348	12,827
Hardwoods	3,168	4,582	4,299	4,490	4,795	4,894	5,680	5,482	6,483	6,844	6,644
Lumber:											
Domestic production	5,623	7,317	6,746	6,983	6,887	7,052	6,815	6,886	7,103	7,298	7,629
Imports	1,530	1,909	1,714	1,960	2,240	2,395	2,522	2,616	2,619	2,690	2,810
Exports	407	589	619	561	532	512	460	449	452	350	404
Consumption	6,745	8,637	7,841	8,383	8,595	8,935	8,877	9,053	9,270	9,638	10,035
Plywood and veneer:											
Domestic production	1,272	1,423	1,267	1,294	1,293	1,320	1,303	1,281	1,213	1,201	1,208
Imports	81	97	83	100	100	94	107	97	114	131	160
Exports	30	109	95	106	100	86	89	87	103	55	46
Consumption	1,323	1,410	1,255	1,288	1,293	1,328	1,321	1,291	1,224	1,276	1,322
Pulp products:											
Domestic production	4,250	5,313	5,397	5,516	5,423	5,576	7,223	7,001	7,193	7,206	6,838
Imports	765	1,038	969	992	1,065	1,102	1,483	1,352	1,472	1,491	1,597
Exports	510	646	746	801	724	758	1,090	1,072	1,114	981	899
Consumption	4,505	5,704	5,620	5,706	5,764	5,920	7,617	7,281	7,551	7,716	7,536
Logs:											
Imports.	20	4	2	7	15	18	13	18	20	30	47
Exports.	522	674	602	524	460	429	451	422	384	316	326
Pulpwood chips, exports	278	288	332	351	326	354	377	416	422	412	422
Fuelwood consumption	3,105	3,019	3,028	3,044	3,084	3,134	2,937	2,739	2,542	2,523	2,542

[1] Includes log exports. [2] Includes log imports.

Source: U.S. Forest Service, *Timber Demand and Technology Assessment,* RWU-4861. Also in *Agricultural Statistics,* annual.

Product	Unit	1980	1990	1993	1994	1995	1996	1997	1998	1999
IMPORTS [1]										
Lumber, total [2]	Mil. bd. ft	9,866	13,063	15,368	16,534	17,524	18,363	18,237	19,012	19,900
From Canada	Percent	97.5	91.2	98.0	97.4	97.0	97.1	96.2	96	93
Logs, total	Mil. bd. ft.[3]	128	23	94	110	80	115	128	185	294
From Canada	Percent	95	84	95	77	70	82.3	82.9	91	95
Paper and board [4]	1,000 tons	8,013	12,195	12,990	13,651	14,292	13,023	14,525	14,538	16,917
Woodpulp	1,000 tons	4,051	4,893	5,413	5,650	5,969	5,692	6,398	5,984	6,650
Plywood	Mil. sq. ft.[5]	1,235	1,687	1,786	1,693	1,951	1,780	2,111	2,429	2,989
EXPORTS										
Lumber, total [2]	Mil. bd. ft	2,507	4,614	3,280	3,115	2,958	2,898	2,933	2,189	2,549
To: Canada	Percent	25.2	14.3	17.3	19.6	22	22.9	24.3	26.3	25.9
Japan	Percent	26	28	36	34	33	33	27	16	14
Europe	Percent	23.7	14.9	15.7	17.5	17.4	16.7	20.2	25.6	20.8
Logs, total	Mil. bd. ft.[3]	3,261	4,213	2,876	2,684	2,820	2,636	2,398	1,978	2,038
To: Canada	Percent	10	9	14	16	25	20	30	39	39
Japan	Percent	78	62.3	65.4	67.9	61.3	68.6	56.2	50.8	49
China: Mainland	Percent	3	5	5	3	1	1	1	1	-
Paper and board [4]	1,000 tons	4,241	5,163	6,835	7,536	7,621	9,118	10,368	9,103	9,477
Woodpulp	1,000 tons	3,806	5,905	6,499	6,728	8,261	7,170	6,990	6,025	5,438
Plywood	Mil. sq. ft.[5]	413	1,786	1,677	1,455	1,517	1,499	1,802	970	833

- Represents zero. [1] Customs value of imports; see text, Section 28, Foreign Commerce and Aid. [2] Includes railroad ties. [3] Log scale. [4] Includes paper and board products. Excludes hardboard. [5] 3/8 inch basis.

Source: U.S. Forest Service, *Timber Demand and Technology Assessment*, RWU-4851. Also in *Agricultural Statistics*, annual.

No. 854. Lumber Consumption by Species Group and End Use: 1995 to 1999

[In million board feet (59.3 represents 59,300,000), except per capita in board feet. Per capita consumption based on estimated resident population as of July 1]

Item	1995	1996	1997	1998	1999	End-use	1995	1996	1997	1998	1999
Total	59.3	62.2	63.0	65.1	68.3	New housing	15.9	19.0	(NA)	(NA)	(NA)
						Residential upkeep and improvements	12.4	17.7	(NA)	(NA)	(NA)
Per capita	225	234	235	241	250	New nonresidential construction [1]	5.8	4.6	(NA)	(NA)	(NA)
Species group:						Manufacturing	5.5	7.6	(NA)	(NA)	(NA)
Softwoods	47.6	50.2	50.9	52.1	54.5	Shipping	8.5	6.3	(NA)	(NA)	(NA)
Hardwoods	11.7	12.0	12.1	13.0	13.8	Other [2]	8.8	6.8	(NA)	(NA)	(NA)

NA Not available. [1] In addition to new construction, includes railroad ties laid as replacements in existing track and lumber used by railroads for railcar repair. [2] Includes upkeep and improvement of nonresidential buildings and structures; made-at-home projects, such as furniture, boats, and picnic tables; made-on-the-job items such as advertising and display structures; and miscellaneous products and uses.

Source: U.S. Forest Service, *Timber Demand and Technology Assessment*, RWU-4851. Also in *Agricultural Statistics*, annual.

No. 855. Selected Timber Products—Producer Price Indexes: 1990 to 2000

[1982=100. For information about producer prices, see text, Section 14, Prices]

Product	1990	1993	1994	1995	1996	1997	1998	1999	2000, prel.
Lumber and wood products	129.7	174.0	180.0	178.1	176.1	183.8	179.1	183.6	178.2
Lumber	124.6	183.4	188.4	173.4	179.8	194.5	179.5	188.2	178.7
Softwood lumber	123.8	193.0	198.1	178.5	189.5	206.5	182.7	196.0	178.6
Hardwood lumber	131.0	163.3	168.3	167.0	163.9	174.1	178.7	177.3	185.8
Millwork	130.4	156.6	162.4	163.8	166.6	170.9	171.1	174.7	176.4
General millwork	132.0	158.5	163.6	165.4	167.9	171.1	172.4	175.6	178.0
Prefabricated structural members	122.3	159.7	169.3	163.5	167.5	177.8	170.1	178.1	175.0
Plywood	114.2	152.8	158.6	165.3	156.4	159.3	157.3	176.4	157.8
Softwood plywood	119.6	169.7	176.8	188.1	173.7	175.5	174.9	207.0	173.8
Hardwood plywood and related products	102.7	115.4	122.3	122.2	124.9	127.1	126.9	128.6	130.1
Other wood products	114.7	135.3	137.7	143.7	127.5	128.4	135.2	131.1	130.4
Boxes	119.1	138.2	141.3	145.0	147.1	149.2	150.7	152.3	155.2
Pulp, paper, and allied products	141.2	147.3	152.5	172.2	168.7	167.9	171.7	174.1	183.6
Pulp, paper, and prod., ex. bldg. paper	132.9	127.6	133.1	163.4	149.7	144.7	147.0	147.9	161.4
Woodpulp	151.3	104.2	115.9	183.2	133.1	128.6	122.6	119.7	145.4
Wastepaper	138.9	117.4	209.5	371.1	141.6	163.3	145.4	183.6	282.2
Paper	128.8	123.8	126.0	159.0	149.4	143.9	145.4	141.8	149.9
Writing and printing papers	129.1	120.5	121.7	158.4	144.6	140.0	139.9	137.8	146.8
Newsprint	119.6	112.1	116.7	161.8	159.5	133.9	143.4	(NA)	127.3
Paperboard	135.7	130.0	140.5	183.1	155.1	144.4	151.6	153.2	176.6
Converted paper & paperboard products	135.2	133.7	136.7	157.0	153.4	148.4	152.2	153.5	162.6
Office supplies and accessories	121.4	115.3	116.9	134.9	132.9	131.0	131.2	129.5	133.9
Building paper & building board mill prods	112.2	132.7	144.1	144.9	137.2	129.6	132.9	141.6	138.8

Source: U.S. Bureau of Labor Statistics, *Producer Price Indexes*, monthly.

No. 856. Selected Species—Stumpage Prices In Current and Constant (1992) Dollars: 1990 to 1999

[In dollars per 1,000 board feet. Stumpage prices are based on sales of sawtimber from National Forests]

Species	1990	1991	1992	1993	1994	1995	1996	1997	1998	1999
CURRENT DOLLARS										
Softwoods:										
Douglas fir [2]	466	395	477	318	652	454	436	331	254	315
Southern pine [3]	127	166	198	217	266	248	241	307	288	269
Sugar pine [4]	285	241	492	598	625	397	318	234	200	227
Ponderosa pine [4][5]	218	238	292	535	291	150	274	270	205	181
Western hemlock [6]	203	164	165	364	335	297	248	211	161	96
Hardwoods:										
All eastern hardwoods [7]	146	160	167	264	352	309	259	287	241	195
Oak, white, red, and black [7]	188	164	211	195	317	297	237	265	270	317
Maple, sugar [8]	135	121	145	220	313	286	238	357	395	448
CONSTANT (1992) DOLLARS [1]										
Softwoods:										
Douglas fir [2]	470	397	477	313	635	426	400	305	230	262
Southern pine [3]	128	167	198	214	259	233	221	282	261	223
Sugar pine [4]	287	242	492	589	609	373	292	215	181	189
Ponderosa pine [4][5]	220	239	292	527	283	141	251	248	186	151
Western hemlock [6]	205	165	165	359	326	279	227	194	146	80
Hardwoods:										
All eastern hardwoods [7]	293	321	335	530	707	620	520	576	218	162
Oak, white, red, and black [7]	378	329	424	392	637	596	475	531	245	264
Maple, sugar [8]	271	243	291	442	629	574	478	717	358	373

[1] Deflated by the producer price index, all commodities. [2] Western Washington and western Oregon. [3] Southern region. [4] Pacific Southwest region (formerly California region). [5] Includes Jeffrey pine. [6] Pacific Northwest region. [7] Eastern and Southern regions. [8] Eastern region.

Source: U.S. Forest Service, *Timber Demand and Technology Assessment*, RWU-4851. Also in *Agricultural Statistics*, annual.

No. 857. Paper and Paperboard—Production and New Supply: 1990 to 1999

[In thousands of short tons (80,445 represents 80,445,000)]

Item	1990	1992	1993	1994	1995	1996	1997	1998	1999, prel.
Production, total.	**80,445**	**84,701**	**86,693**	**90,897**	**91,325**	**92,199**	**96,846**	**96,343**	**96,902**
Paper, total	39,361	40,973	41,745	43,356	42,868	42,481	44,697	44,777	46,012
Paperboard, total	39,318	41,895	43,113	45,724	46,640	47,901	50,332	49,749	50,890
Unbleached kraft	20,357	21,658	21,447	22,469	22,697	22,178	23,222	23,199	22,958
Semichemical	5,640	5,762	5,672	5,943	5,662	5,619	6,047	5,894	5,954
Bleached kraft.	4,399	4,503	4,583	5,029	5,304	5,236	5,548	5,487	5,712
Recycled	8,921	9,973	11,410	12,283	12,977	14,868	15,514	15,170	16,266
Wet machine board E	96	93	95	96	96	96	96	96	(NA)
Building paper E.	723	795	797	787	787	787	787	787	(NA)
Insulating board E.	946	945	943	934	934	934	934	934	(NA)
New supply, all grades, excluding products	**87,683**	**89,631**	**93,146**	**97,448**	**98,164**	**95,896**	**101,201**	**102,869**	**(NA)**
Paper, total	49,485	49,232	51,246	53,077	52,769	50,687	54,149	55,068	(NA)
Newsprint	13,412	12,658	12,750	12,889	12,762	11,768	12,612	12,721	(NA)
Printing/writing papers	25,456	26,013	27,846	29,444	29,550	28,300	30,751	31,384	(NA)
Packaging and ind. conv. papers . .	4,718	4,783	4,628	4,640	4,241	4,325	4,265	4,285	(NA)
Tissue.	5,899	5,778	6,022	6,105	6,215	6,294	6,521	6,680	(NA)
Paperboard, total	36,301	38,453	39,950	42,435	43,448	43,214	45,061	45,597	(NA)
Construction and other	1,897	1,946	1,949	1,935	1,947	1,994	1,991	2,203	(NA)

NA Not available.

Source: American Forest and Paper Association, Washington, DC, *Monthly Statistical Summary of Paper, Paperboard and Woodpulp.*

U.S. Census Bureau, Statistical Abstract of the United States: 2001

No. 858. Fishery Products—Domestic Catch, Imports, and Disposition: 1990 to 1999

[Live weight, in millions of pounds (16,349 represents 16,349,000,000). For data on commercial catch for selected countries, see Table 1358, Section 30, Comparative International Statistics]

Item	1990	1992	1993	1994	1995	1996	1997	1998	1999
Total	16,349	16,106	20,334	19,309	16,484	16,474	17,131	16,897	17,378
For human food	12,662	13,242	13,821	13,714	13,584	13,625	13,739	14,175	14,462
For industrial use	3,687	2,864	6,513	5,595	2,900	2,848	3,392	2,722	2,916
Domestic catch	9,404	9,637	10,467	10,461	9,788	9,565	9,845	9,194	9,339
For human food	7,041	7,618	8,214	7,936	7,667	7,476	7,248	7,174	6,832
For industrial use	2,363	2,019	2,253	2,525	2,121	2,090	2,597	2,020	2,507
Imports [1]	6,945	6,469	9,867	8,848	6,696	6,909	7,286	7,703	8,039
For human food	5,621	5,624	5,607	5,778	5,917	6,150	6,491	7,001	7,630
For industrial use [2] . . .	1,324	845	4,260	3,070	779	759	795	702	409
Disposition of domestic catch	9,404	9,637	10,467	10,461	9,788	9,565	9,846	9,194	9,339
Fresh and frozen	6,501	7,288	7,744	7,475	7,099	7,054	6,877	6,870	6,416
Canned	751	543	649	622	769	678	648	516	712
Cured.	126	100	115	95	90	93	108	129	133
Reduced to meal, oil, etc.	2,026	1,696	1,959	2,269	1,830	1,740	2,213	1,679	2,078

[1] Excludes imports of edible fishery products consumed in Puerto Rico; includes landings of tuna caught by foreign vessels in American Samoa. [2] Fish meal and sea herring.

No. 859. Fisheries—Quantity and Value of Domestic Catch: 1980 to 1999

Year	Quantity (mil. lb. [1])			Value (mil. dol.)	Average price per lb. (cents)	Year	Quantity (mil. lb. [1])			Value (mil. dol.)	Average price per lb. (cents)
	Total	For human food	For indus-trial prod-ucts [2]				Total	For human food	For indus-trial prod-ucts [2]		
1980 . . .	6,482	3,654	2,828	2,237	34.5	1990	9,404	7,041	2,363	3,522	37.5
1981 . . .	5,977	3,547	2,430	2,388	40.0	1991	9,484	7,031	2,453	3,308	34.9
1982 . . .	6,367	3,285	3,082	2,390	37.5	1992	9,637	7,618	2,019	3,678	38.2
1983 . . .	6,439	3,238	3,201	2,355	36.6	1993	[3]10,467	8,214	2,253	3,471	33.2
1984 . . .	6,438	3,320	3,118	2,350	36.5	1994	10,461	7,936	2,525	3,807	36.8
1985 . . .	6,258	3,294	2,964	2,326	37.2	1995	9,788	7,667	2,121	3,770	38.5
1986 . . .	6,031	3,393	2,638	2,763	45.8	1996	9,565	7,474	2,091	3,487	36.5
1987 . . .	6,896	3,946	2,950	3,115	45.2	1997	9,842	7,244	2,598	3,448	35.0
1988 . . .	7,192	4,588	2,604	3,520	48.9	1998	9,194	7,173	2,021	3,128	34.0
1989 . . .	8,463	6,204	2,259	3,238	38.3	1999	9,339	6,832	2,507	3,467	37.1

[1] Live weight. [2] Meal, oil, fish solubles, homogenized condensed fish, shell products, bait, and animal food. [3] Represents record year.

No. 860. Domestic Fish and Shellfish Catch and Value by Species: 1990 to 1999

Species	Quantity (1,000 lb.)				Value ($1,000)			
	1990	1995	1998	1999	1990	1995	1998	1999
Total.	9,403,571	9,787,554	9,193,970	9,339,034	3,521,995	3,735,615	3,128,469	3,467,084
Fish, total [1].	8,091,068	8,520,086	7,888,020	7,811,868	1,900,097	1,915,642	1,446,942	1,558,292
Cod:								
Atlantic	95,881	29,631	24,514	21,445	61,329	28,184	25,474	23,943
Pacific.	526,396	591,399	555,993	523,987	91,384	109,680	87,717	83,227
Flounder.	254,519	423,443	391,178	331,218	112,921	150,239	96,804	89,946
Halibut	70,454	44,796	73,260	80,330	96,700	66,781	103,974	124,696
Menhaden	1,962,160	1,846,959	1,705,677	1,989,081	93,896	99,131	188,836	113,082
Pollock, Alaska	3,108,031	2,852,618	2,716,458	2,325,889	268,344	259,614	190,152	162,812
Sablefish	89,802	65,904	43,500	48,255	58,865	123,694	91,823	97,148
Salmon.	733,146	1,020,765	644,434	814,896	612,367	486,107	257,456	359,785
Tuna	62,393	63,864	84,999	58,120	105,040	102,638	94,462	86,254
Shellfish, total [1]	1,312,503	1,267,468	1,305,950	1,527,166	1,621,898	1,819,973	1,681,527	1,908,792
Clams	139,198	134,224	.107,959	112,230	130,194	140,414	135,237	135,024
Crabs.	499,416	363,639	552,716	458,307	483,837	511,987	473,378	521,237
Lobsters: American.	61,017	66,406	79,642	87,469	154,677	214,838	253,636	322,957
Oysters	29,193	40,380	33,538	26,983	93,718	101,574	88,627	72,658
Scallops:								
Calico.	(NA)	957	(NA)	4,105	(NA)	1,219	(NA)	3,880
Sea	39,917	18,316	13,061	23,038	153,696	92,826	79,606	125,289
Shrimp	346,494	306,869	277,757	304,173	491,433	570,034	515,616	560,501

NA Not available. [1] Includes other types of fish and shellfish, not shown separately.

Source of Tables 858-860: U.S. National Oceanic and Atmospheric Administration, National Marine Fisheries Service, *Fisheries of the United States,* annual.

U.S. Census Bureau, Statistical Abstract of the United States: 2001

No. 861. U.S. Private Aquaculture—Trout and Catfish Production and Value: 1990 to 2000

[67.8 represents 67,800,000. Periods are from Sept. 1 of the previous year to Aug. 31 of stated year. Data are for foodsize fish, those over 12 inches long]

Item	Unit	1990	1994	1995	1996	1997	1998	1999	2000
TROUT FOODSIZE									
Number sold	Millions .	67.8	58.3	60.2	56.5	59.3	57.6	61.0	58.5
Total weight.	Mil. lb . .	56.8	52.1	55.6	53.6	56.9	57.9	60.2	59.2
Total value of sales.	Mil. dol. .	64.6	52.7	60.8	57.0	60.7	60.3	64.7	63.7
Average price received	Dol./lb .	1.14	1.01	1.09	1.06	1.07	1.04	1.07	1.08
Percent sold to processors.	Percent .	58	68	68	67	63	62	67.7	69.7
CATFISH FOODSIZE									
Number sold	Millions .	272.9	347.6	321.8	375.4	391.8	409.8	424.5	420.1
Total weight.	Mil. lb . .	392.4	479.4	481.5	526.3	569.6	601.4	635.2	633.8
Total value of sales.	Mil. dol. .	305.1	373.6	378.1	403.3	406.8	445.4	464.7	468.8
Average price received	Dol./lb . .	0.78	0.78	0.79	0.77	0.71	0.74	0.73	0.74
Fish sold to processors	Mil. lb . .	360.4	439.3	446.9	472.1	524.9	564.4	596.6	593.6
Avg. price paid by processors.	Cents/lb .	75.8	78.4	78.6	77.3	71.2	74.3	73.7	75.1
Processor sales	Mil. lb . .	183.1	216.5	227.0	237.2	261.8	281.4	292.7	297.2
Avg. price received by processors . . .	Cents/lb .	224.1	238.5	240.3	236.9	226.0	229.0	234.0	236.0
Inventory (Jan. 1).	Mil. lb . .	9.4	11.6	10.9	11.9	11.9	10.8	12.6	13.6

Source: U.S. Dept. of Agriculture, National Agricultural Statistics Service, *Trout Production* released September; *Catfish Production* released February; and *Catfish Processing* released February. Also in *Agricultural Statistics*, annual.

No. 862. Supply of Selected Fishery Items: 1990 to 1999

[In millions of pounds (734 represents 734,000,000). Totals available for U.S. consumption are supply minus exports plus imports. Round weight is the complete or full weight as caught]

Species	Unit	1990	1992	1993	1994	1995	1996	1997	1998	1999
Shrimp.	Heads-off weight. .	734	820	808	847	832	842	923	1,002	1,084
Tuna, canned	Canned weight. . .	856	922	835	850	875	859	829	912	996
Snow crab	Round weight. . .	37	88	66	40	42	46	110	254	216
Clams	Meat weight.	152	155	156	144	144	134	124	119	125
Salmon, canned	Canned weight. . .	148	73	114	117	147	104	82	83	123
American lobster	Round weight. . .	95	95	92	101	94	97	112	110	122
Spiny lobster.	Round weight. . . .	89	81	76	76	89	81	76	100	91
Scallops	Meat weight.	74	69	66	76	62	71	66	58	64
Sardines, canned.	Canned weight. . .	61	41	41	48	44	46	49	50	57
Oysters	Meat weight.	56	50	48	50	63	58	58	61	55
King crab	Round weight. . .	19	15	8	12	21	30	45	62	52
Crab meat, canned	Canned weight. . .	9	9	9	9	12	13	15	22	27

Source: U.S. National Oceanic and Atmospheric Administration, National Marine Fisheries Service, *Fisheries of the United States*, annual.

No. 863. Canned, Fresh, and Frozen Fishery Products: 1990 to 1999

[Fresh fishery products exclude Alaska and Hawaii. Canned fishery products data are for natural pack only]

Product	Production (mil. lb.)					Value (mil. dol.)				
	1990	1995	1997	1998	1999	1990	1995	1997	1998	1999
Canned, total [1]	1,178	1,927	1,565	1,533	1,874	1,562	1,887	1,593	1,775	1,867
Tuna	581	667	627	681	669	902	939	919	983	946
Salmon.	196	244	162	159	234	366	419	253	274	393
Clam products	110	129	125	113	124	76	110	115	105	111
Sardines, Maine	13	14	16	12	12	17	24	29	19	20
Shrimp	1	1	1	2	2	3	7	5	2	2
Crabs	1	(Z)	(Z)	(Z)	1	4	(Z)	(Z)	(Z)	(Z)
Oysters [2]	1	(Z)	(Z)	(Z)	(Z)	1	(Z)	(Z)	(Z)	(Z)
Fish fillets and steaks [3]	441	385	410	422	369	843	841	961	961	835
Cod	65	65	79	67	61	132	152	179	161	109
Flounder.	54	35	27	24	24	154	86	79	70	68
Haddock.	7	3	7	6	5	24	11	24	22	20
Ocean perch, Atlantic	1	(Z)	1	1	1	1	1	2	2	2
Rockfish	33	25	17	16	12	53	38	33	33	25
Pollock, Atlantic	12	4	1	4	2	21	10	2	7	4
Pollock, Alaska	164	135	112	161	144	174	184	129	190	169
Other	105	118	166	143	120	284	359	513	507	438

Z Less than 500,000 pounds or $500,000.   [1] Includes other products, not shown separately.   [2] Includes oyster specialties.   [3] Fresh and frozen.

Source: U.S. National Oceanic and Atmospheric Administration, National Marine Fisheries Service, *Fisheries of the United States*, annual.

Natural Resources   553

No. 864. Mining Industries—Employees, Payroll, and Shipments: 1997

[The mining sector comprises establishments that extract naturally occurring mineral solids, such as coal and ores; liquid minerals and gases, such as natural gas. The term mining is used in the broad sense to include quarrying, well operations, beneficiating (e.g., crushing, screening, washing, and flotation), and other preparation customarily performed at the mine site, or as a part of mining activity]

Selected industries	NAICS code [1]	All employees				Produc-tion workers, total [3] (1,000)	Value added by manufac-tures (mil. dol.)	Value of ship-ments (mil. dol.)
		Establish-ments	Number [2] (1,000)	Payroll				
				Total (mil. dol.)	Per employee (dol.)			
Mining, total	21	25,000	509,006	20,798	40,861	389,232	133,636	173,985
Oil and gas extraction	211	8,312	110,881	5,511	49,698	67,197	82,350	102,834
Oil and gas extraction	2111	8,312	110,881	5,511	49,698	67,197	82,350	102,834
Mining (except oil & gas)	212	7,348	229,319	9,422	41,085	188,988	35,207	51,253
Coal mining	2121	1,511	87,965	3,984	45,289	75,398	15,567	23,427
Metal ore mining	2122	493	45,467	1,993	43,837	39,103	7,387	11,204
Iron ore mining	21221	32	7,920	394	49,738	6,787	992	1,938
Gold ore & silver ore mining . .	21222	316	18,292	810	44,308	16,199	2,865	4,073
Copper, nickel, lead, and zinc mining	21223	80	15,872	640	40,291	13,447	3,050	4,549
Other metal ore mining	21229	65	3,383	149	44,110	2,670	480	644
Nonmetallic mineral mining and quarrying	2123	5,344	95,887	3,445	35,924	74,487	12,253	16,621
Stone mining & quarrying	21231	2,367	44,052	1,551	35,206	35,260	5,549	7,385
Sand, gravel, clay, ceramic and refractory minerals mining and quarrying	21232	2,674	37,052	1,261	34,044	27,646	4,080	5,541
Other nonmetallic mineral mining and quarrying	21239	303	14,783	632	42,777	11,581	2,624	3,695
Support activities for mining	213	9,340	168,806	5,866	34,751	133,047	16,079	19,899

[1] North American Industrial Classification System, 1997; see text, Section 15, Business Enterprise. [2] For pay period including March 12. [3] Covers production, development, and exploration workers. For pay period including March 12.

Source: U.S. Census Bureau, *1997 Economic Census, Mining,* Series EC97N21S-GS, April 2001.

No. 865. Mining Summary by State: 1997

[The mining sector comprises establishments that extract naturally occurring mineral solids, such as coal and ores; liquid minerals and gases, such as natural gas. The term mining is used in the broad sense to include quarrying, well operations, beneficiating (e.g., crushing, screening, washing, and flotation), and other preparation customarily performed at the mine site, or as a part of mining activity]

State	Estab-lish-ments, total	All employees		Produc-tion work-ers [2]	Value added by manu-factures	State	Estab-lish-ments, total	All employees		Produc-tion work-ers [2]	Value added by manu-factures
		Number [1] (1,000)	Payroll (mil. dol.)					Number [1] (1,000)	Payroll (mil. dol.)		
U.S. . . .	25,000	509,006	20,798	389,232	133,636	MT	294	5,328	216	3,864	1,047
						NE	150	1,078	31	858	104
AL	291	9,066	371	7,421	1,775	NV	250	14,035	626	12,451	1,959
AK	141	10,137	672	7,585	9,565	NH	32	396	18	293	44
AZ	206	12,889	510	10,699	2,171	NJ	95	1,864	84	1,350	243
AR	307	3,250	98	2,602	704	NM	606	14,600	574	11,520	5,336
CA	910	22,110	945	16,908	7,497	NY	359	3,879	142	2,819	474
CO	885	12,263	522	7,881	2,872	NC	171	3,231	118	2,644	533
CT [3] . . .	62	626	27	467	105	ND	227	4,098	176	3,361	1,017
DE [3] . . .	11	107	4	90	15	OH	828	11,997	454	8,961	1,746
FL.	225	6,688	249	5,424	1,009	OK	2,271	25,976	967	16,957	5,509
GA	205	6,354	233	4,984	1,024	OR	134	1,739	61	1,216	161
HA	7	120	6	100	22	PA	914	17,522	677	14,262	2,411
ID	118	3,021	118	2,418	291	RI	16	120	5	82	13
IL	650	10,798	437	8,557	1,381	SC	74	1,388	44	1,099	166
IN	347	6,007	241	5,013	795	SD	67	1,837	67	1,635	166
IA	177	1,700	55	1,428	217	TN	221	4,473	137	3,614	479
KS	1,026	7,998	245	5,993	2,178	TX	6,412	105,492	4,334	73,686	32,485
KY	691	22,400	832	19,413	3,297	UT	316	8,134	335	6,593	1,875
LA	1,608	52,816	2,302	38,255	21,889	VT	52	658	22	538	72
ME	21	76	1	50	4	VA	417	11,711	429	9,860	1,449
MD	93	1,771	64	1,429	257	WA	154	2,890	114	2,170	349
MA	72	1,063	42	704	110	WV	766	23,927	1,042	20,450	4,161
MI	445	6,687	271	5,030	1,182	WI	147	2,304	92	1,598	312
MN	145	7,154	348	6,071	954	WY	669	15,436	723	12,367	5,395
MS	368	4,096	115	3,100	531	Offshore areas [3]	41	11,135	455	9,717	5,782
MO	306	4,561	146	3,645	503						

[1] For pay period including March 12. [2] Covers production, development, and exploration workers. For pay period including March 12. [3] District of Columbia is included with Delaware. [3] Not associated with a state.

Source: U.S. Census Bureau, *1997 Economic Census, Mining,* Series EC97N21S-GS, issued April 2001.

No. 866. Mining and Primary Metal Production Indexes: 1990 to 2000

[Index 1992=100]

Industry group	1990	1992	1993	1994	1995	1996	1997	1998	1999	2000
Mining	104.8	100.0	100.0	102.3	102.0	103.5	105.3	103.0	98.0	99.9
Coal	103.7	100.0	94.0	103.0	102.6	105.0	108.2	109.7	107.8	108.9
Oil and gas extraction.	106.4	100.0	101.1	101.6	100.4	101.6	102.6	98.7	92.5	95.0
Crude oil and natural gas. . . .	101.6	100.0	98.0	98.1	96.5	95.9	95.7	93.9	90.5	89.7
Oil and gas drilling	151.1	100.0	122.4	126.2	125.8	137.5	147.8	131.6	103.3	131.8
Metal mining.	93.1	100.0	98.7	100.5	101.8	104.3	108.8	108.1	99.9	96.8
Iron ore	101.4	100.0	100.0	104.3	112.3	111.3	113.6	112.7	103.6	114.0
Nonferrous ores	91.9	100.0	98.5	100.0	100.4	103.4	108.1	107.6	99.4	94.1
Copper ore	89.4	100.0	102.0	104.7	104.7	108.7	109.9	105.4	90.9	83.5
Primary metals, manufacturing . .	104.0	100.0	105.1	113.7	116.2	119.6	125.4	127.8	130.4	133.5
Nonferrous metals	100.9	100.0	104.0	113.1	115.7	120.5	127.4	131.8	135.0	136.4
Copper.	81.6	100.0	116.7	111.7	121.9	103.5	106.3	131.5	115.0	90.9
Aluminum	100.4	100.0	91.7	81.8	83.7	88.5	89.4	92.1	93.7	90.8
Iron and steel	106.4	100.0	105.9	114.3	116.5	118.9	123.8	124.6	126.7	131.0

Source: Board of Governors of the Federal Reserve System, *Federal Reserve Bulletin*, monthly; and *Industrial Production and Capacity Utilization*, Statistical Release G.17, monthly.

No. 867. Mineral Industries—Employment, Hours, and Earnings: 1990 to 1999

[Based on the Current Employment Statistics Program, see Appendix III]

Item	Unit	1990	1995	1999	Item	Unit	1990	1995	1999
All mining:					Avg. weekly hours	Number .	43.9	44.2	42.5
All employees	1,000 . . .	709	581	535	Avg. weekly earnings . .	Dollars . .	568	642	717
Production workers	1,000 . . .	509	424	404	**Metal mining:**				
Avg. weekly hours	Number .	44.1	44.7	43.8	All employees	1,000 . . .	58	51	45
Avg. weekly earnings . .	Dollars . .	603	684	746	Production workers	1,000 . . .	46	41	35
Coal mining:					Avg. weekly hours	Number .	42.8	43.8	44.5
All employees	1,000 . . .	147	104	85	Avg. weekly earnings . .	Dollars . .	601	735	812
Production workers	1,000 . . .	119	84	71	**Nonmetallic minerals,**				
Avg. weekly hours	Number .	44.0	44.9	44.8	**except fuels:**				
Avg. weekly earnings . .	Dollars . .	735	828	866	All employees	1,000 . . .	110	105	112
Oil and gas extraction:					Production workers	1,000 . . .	83	80	82
All employees	1,000 . . .	395	320	293	Avg. weekly hours	Number .	45.3	46.6	46.3
Production workers	1,000 . . .	261	218	212	Avg. weekly earnings . .	Dollars . .	525	624	700

Source: U.S. Bureau of Labor Statistics, *Bulletin 2370* and *Employment and Earnings*, March and June issues.

No. 868. Selected Mineral Products—Average Prices: 1980 to 2000

[Excludes Alaska and Hawaii, except as noted]

Year	Nonfuels								Fuels		
	Copper, electro-lytic (cents per lb.)	Plati-num [1] (dol./ troy oz.)	Gold (dol./ fine oz.)	Silver (dol./ fine oz.)	Lead (cents per lb.)	Tin (New York) (cents per lb.)	Zinc (cents per lb.)	Sulfur, crude [2] (dol./ metric ton)	Bitumi-nous coal [3][4] (dol./ short ton)	Crude petro-leum [3] (dol./ bbl.)	Natural gas [3] (dol./ cu. ft.)
1980	101	677	613	20.63	43	846	37	89.06	29.17	21.59	1.59
1981	84	446	460	10.52	37	733	45	111.48	31.51	31.77	1.98
1982	73	327	376	7.95	26	654	39	108.27	32.15	28.52	2.46
1983	77	424	424	11.44	22	655	41	87.24	31.11	26.19	2.59
1984	67	357	361	8.14	26	624	49	94.31	30.63	25.88	2.66
1985	67	291	318	6.14	19	596	40	106.46	30.78	24.09	2.51
1986	66	461	368	5.47	22	383	38	105.22	28.84	12.51	1.94
1987	83	553	478	7.01	36	419	42	89.78	28.19	15.40	1.67
1988	121	523	438	6.53	37	441	60	85.95	27.66	12.58	1.69
1989	131	507	383	5.50	39	520	82	86.62	27.40	15.86	1.69
1990	123	467	385	4.82	46	386	75	80.14	27.43	20.03	1.71
1991	109	371	363	4.04	34	363	53	71.45	27.49	16.54	1.64
1992	107	360	345	3.94	35	402	58	48.14	26.78	15.99	1.74
1993	92	375	361	4.30	32	350	46	31.86	26.15	14.25	2.04
1994	111	411	385	5.29	37	369	49	28.60	25.68	13.19	1.85
1995	138	425	386	5.15	42	416	56	44.46	25.56	14.62	1.55
1996	109	398	389	5.19	49	412	51	34.11	25.17	18.46	2.17
1997	107	397	332	4.89	47	381	65	36.06	24.64	17.23	2.32
1998	79	375	295	5.54	45	373	51	29.14	24.87	10.87	1.94
1999	76	379	280	5.25	44	366	54	37.81	23.92	15.56	2.17
2000	89	391	280	5.25	44	370	56	32.00	(NA)	26.73	3.60

NA Not available.   [1] Average annual dealer prices.   [2] F.o.b. works.   [3] Average value at the point of production or domestic first purchase price.   [4] Includes lignite.

Source: Nonfuels, through 1994, U.S. Bureau of Mines, thereafter, U.S. Geological Survey, *Minerals Yearbook* and *Mineral Commodities Summaries,* annual; fuels, U.S. Energy Information Administration, *Annual Energy Review* and most recent year from the *Monthly Energy Review.*

No. 869. Mineral Production: 1990 to 2000

[Data represent production as measured by mine shipments, mine sales or marketable production]

Mineral	Unit	1990	1995	1999	2000, est.
FUEL MINERALS					
Coal, total	Mil. sh. tons	1,029.1	1,033.0	1,099.1	1,075.5
Bituminous	Mil. sh. tons	693.2	613.8	621.3	(NA)
Subbituminous	Mil. sh. tons	244.3	328.0	388.3	(NA)
Lignite	Mil. sh. tons	88.1	86.5	84.4	(NA)
Anthracite	Mil. sh. tons	3.5	4.7	5.2	(NA)
Natural gas (marketed production)	Tril. cu. ft.	18.59	19.51	19.67	20.07
Petroleum (crude)	Mil. bbl. [1]	2,686	2,394	2,164	2,125
Uranium (recoverable content)	Mil. lb.	8.9	6.0	4.7	4.0
NONFUEL MINERALS					
Asbestos (sales)	1,000 metric tons . .	(D)	9	7	5
Barite, primary, sold/used by producers	1,000 metric tons . .	430	543	434	600
Boron minerals, sold or used by producers . . .	1,000 metric tons . .	1,090	1,190	1,220	(NA)
Bromine, sold or used by producers	1,000 metric tons . .	177	218	239	229
Cement:					
Portland	Mil. metric tons	67	73	82	(NA)
Masonry	Mil. metric tons	3	4	4	(NA)
Clays	1,000 metric tons . .	42,900	43,100	42,200	40,700
Diatomite	1,000 metric tons . .	631	722	747	808
Feldspar [2]	1,000 metric tons . .	630	880	875	850
Fluorspar, finished shipments	1,000 metric tons . .	64	51	-	-
Garnet (industrial)	1,000 metric tons . .	47	46	61	50
Gypsum, crude	Mil. metric tons . .	15	17	22	25
Helium [3]	Mil. cu. meters	85	101	114	117
Lime, sold or used by producers	Mil. metric tons	16	19	20	20
Mica, scrap & flake, sold/used by producers . .	1,000 metric tons . .	109	108	104	110
Peat, sales by producers	1,000 metric tons . .	721	660	731	727
Perlite, processed, sold or used	1,000 metric tons . .	576	700	711	675
Phosphate rock (marketable)	Mil. metric tons . .	46	44	41	40
Potash (K₂O equivalent) sales	1,000 metric tons . .	1,710	1,480	1,200	1,300
Pumice & pumicite, producer sales	1,000 metric tons . .	443	529	643	749
Salt, common, sold/used by producers	Mil. metric tons . .	37	41	45	45
Sand & gravel, sold/used by producer	Mil. metric tons . .	855	935	1,139	(NA)
Construction	Mil. metric tons . .	829	907	1,110	1,170
Industrial	Mil. metric tons . .	26	28	29	30
Silica [4]	Metric tons	3,710	979	(NA)	(NA)
Sodium carbonate (natural) (soda ash)	1,000 metric tons . .	9,100	10,100	10,200	10,200
Sodium sulfate (natural)	1,000 metric tons . .	349	327	599	525
Stone [5]	Mil. metric tons . .	1,110	2,420	2,600	(NA)
Crushed and broken	Mil. metric tons . .	1,110	1,260	1,540	1,590
Dimension [6]	1,000 metric tons . .	1,120	1,160	1,250	1,250
Sulfur: Total shipments	1,000 metric tons . .	11,500	12,100	11,100	10,600
Sulfur: Frasch mines (shipments)	1,000 metric tons . .	3,680	(D)	(D)	(NA)
Talc, and pyrophyllite, crude	1,000 metric tons . .	1,270	1,060	925	961
Vermiculite concentrate	1,000 metric tons . .	209	171	175	175
METALS					
Antimony ore and concentrate	Metric tons	(D)	262	449	340
Aluminum	1,000 metric tons . .	4,048	3,375	3,779	3,700
Bauxite (dried)	1,000 metric tons . .	(D)	(D)	(NA)	(NA)
Copper (recoverable content)	1,000 metric tons . .	1,590	1,850	1,600	1,450
Gold (recoverable content)	Metric tons	294	317	341	330
Iron ore (gross weight) [7]	Mil. metric tons	57	61	58	61
Lead (recoverable content)	1,000 metric tons . .	484	394	520	480
Magnesium metal	1,000 metric tons . .	139	142	(D)	(D)
Manganiferous ore (gross weight) [8]	1,000 metric ton . .	(D)	(D)	-	-
Mercury [9]	Metric tons	562	(D)	(NA)	(NA)
Molybdenum (concentrate)	1,000 metric tons . .	62	61	43	32
Nickel	1,000 metric tons . .	-	2	-	-
Palladium metal	Kilograms	5,930	5,260	9,800	10,000
Platinum metal	Kilograms	1,810	1,590	2,920	3,050
Silicon (silicon content)	1,000 metric tons . .	418	396	423	374
Silver (recoverable content)	Metric tons	2,120	1,560	1,950	2,060
Titanium concentrate: Ilmenite (gross weight) . .	1,000 metric tons . .	(D)	(D)	(D)	(NA)
Tungsten ore and concentrate [10]	Metric tons	(D)	(D)	-	-
Zinc (recoverable content)	1,000 metric tons . .	515	614	843	860

- Represents zero. D Withheld to avoid disclosing individual company data. NA Not available. [1] 42 gal. bbl.
[2] Beginning 1995, includes aplite. [3] Refined. [4] Includes grindstones, oilstones, whetstones, and deburring media. Excludes grinding pebbles, and tubemill liners. [5] Excludes abrasive stone, bituminous limestone and sandstone, and ground soapstone, all included elsewhere in table. Includes calcareous marl and slate. [6] Includes Puerto Rico. [7] Represents shipments; includes byproduct ores. [8] Five to 35 percent manganiferous ore. [9] Covers mercury recovered as a by products of gold ores only. [10] Content of ore and concentrate.

Source: Nonfuels, through 1995, U.S. Bureau of Mines, thereafter, U.S. Geological Survey, *Minerals Yearbook* and *Mineral Commodities Summaries*, annual; fuels, U.S. Energy Information Administration, *Annual Energy Review* and *Uranium Industry Annual*.

No. 870. Nonfuel Mineral Commodities—Summary: 1999

[Preliminary estimates. Average price in dollars per metric tons except as noted]

Mineral	Unit	Mineral disposition		Net import reliance [1] (percent)	Consumption, apparent	Average price per unit (dollars)	Employment (number)
		Production	Exports				
Aluminum	1,000 metric tons.	3,779	1,640	31	7,740	[2]65.7	18,200
Antimony (contained)	Metric tons	[3]449	3,660	82	36,500	[2]63	75
Asbestos	1,000 metric tons.	7	22	100	(NA)	210	25
Barite	1,000 metric tons.	434	22	66	1,280	[4]25.60	300
Bauxite and alumina	1,000 metric tons.	(NA)	(NA)	100	4,880	[4]22	(NA)
Beryllium (contained)	Metric tons	200	40	48	385	[2][6]327	48
Bismuth (contained)	Metric tons	-	257	95	2,050	[2]3.85	-
Boron (B_2O_3 content)	1,000 metric tons.	618	107	[5]	534	[4][7]376	900
Bromine (contained)	1,000 metric tons.	239	10	[5]	238	[8][9]87.0	1,700
Cadmium (contained)	Metric tons	[3]1,190	20	9	1,300	[2][10]0.14	(NA)
Cement	1,000 metric tons.	85,952	694	21	108,862	[4]78.27	18,000
Chromium	1,000 metric tons.	[11]118	60	79	558	[4][12]145	-
Clays	1,000 metric tons.	42,200	4,800	[5]	37,500	-	9,000
Cobalt (contained)	Metric tons	[11]2,720	1,550	75	10,700	[2]17.02	-
Copper (Mine, contained)	1,000 metric tons.	1,600	(NA)	27	3,130	[14]_	11.6
Diamond (industrial)	Million carats ...	-	98	88	328	[14]_	
Diatomite	1,000 metric tons.	747	123	[5]	625	[4]238	1,000
Feldspar	1,000 metric tons.	875	10	[5]	872	[4]49	400
Fluorspar	1,000 metric tons.	-	55	100	615	-	-
Garnet (industrial)	Metric tons	60,700	10,000	[5]	39,100	[4]50	220
Germanium (contained)	Kilograms	20,000	(NA)	12,400	28,000	(NA)	85
Gold (contained)	Metric tons	341	523	[5]	(NA)	[17]280	10,300
Gypsum (crude)	1,000 metric tons.	(NA)	112	25	36,800	[4]6.99	6,000
Iodine	Metric tons	1,620	1,130	62	4,540	[8][21]16.15	40
Iron ore (usable)	Million metric tons.	58	6	18	70	[4][22]25.52	6,820
Iron and steel slag (metal)	1,000 metric tons.	19,000	12	5	19,900	[4]8.50	2,750
Lead (contained)	1,000 metric tons.	(NA)	94	20	1,760	[2]43.7	(NA)
Lime	1,000 metric tons.	19,600	59	(Z)	19,700	79.70	5,600
Magnesium compounds	1,000 metric tons.	395	52	41	52	(NA)	550
Magnesium metal	1,000 metric tons.	(NA)	29	38	179	(NA)	800
Mercury	Metric tons	[11](NA)	181	(NA)	(NA)	[26]140	(NA)
Mica, scrap and flake	1,000 metric tons.	104	11	17	125	[4]95	(NA)
Molybdenum (contained)	Metric tons	43,000	27,900	[5]	33,100	[8]5.90	475
Nickel (contained)	Metric tons	(NA)	7,430	63	140,000	[2][27]2,732	1
Nitrogen (fixed)-ammonia	1,000 metric tons.	12,900	562	21	16,300	[4][28]109	2,200
Peat	1,000 metric tons.	731	40	54	40	[4]26.48	800
Perlite	1,000 metric tons.	711	47	12	808	[4]33.40	150
Phosphate rock	1,000 metric tons.	40,600	272	7	(NA)	[4]30.56	6,500
Platinum-group metals	Kilograms	(NA)	(NA)	(NA)	(NA)	[17][29](NA)	(NA)
Potash (K_2O equivalent)	1,000 metric tons.	1,200	460	80	5,100	[4][30]145	660
Pumice and pumicite	1,000 metric tons.	643	23	34	23	[4]27.69	85
Salt	1,000 metric tons.	44,900	892	15	52,400	[4][31]112.49	4,100
Silicon (contained)	1,000 metric tons.	423	61	34	61	(NA)	(NA)
Silver (contained)	Metric tons	1,950	481	39	2,660	[17]5.25	1,600
Sodium carbonate (soda ash)	1,000 metric tons.	10,200	3,620	[5]	6,740	[33]105	2,600
Sodium sulfate	1,000 metric tons.	599	137	[5]	549	[34]114	225
Stone (crushed)	Million metric tons.	1,540	4	-	1,548	[4]5.35	79,000
Sulfur (all forms)	1,000 metric tons.	11,300	736	16	13,400	[4][35]37.81	3,000
Talc	1,000 metric tons.	925	147	6	986	[4]116	700
Thallium (contained)	Kilograms	-	(NA)	100	380	[8]1,295	-
Tin (contained)	Metric tons	[11]16,300	6,770	85	59,700	[2]2.55	-
Titanium dioxide	1,000 metric tons.	1,350	383	[5]	1,160	[2][36]1.01	4,600
Tungsten (contained)	Metric tons	(D)	200	81	12,000	[37]47	-
Vermiculite	1,000 metric tons.	(D)	10	(D)	(D)	(D)	230
Zinc (contained)	1,000 metric tons.	775	600	30	1630	[2]0.51	(NA)
Zirconium (ZrO2) content	Metric tons	(D)	46,670	(D)	(NA)	[4][39]300	(D)

- Represents or rounds to zero.   D Withheld to avoid disclosure.   NA Not available.   [1] Calculated as a percent of apparent consumption.   [2] Dollars per pound.   [3] Refinery production.   [4] Dollars per metric ton.   [5] Net exporter.   [6] Metal, vacuum-cast ingot.   [7] Granulated pentahydrate borax in bulk, f.o.b mine.   [8] Dollars per kilogram.   [9] Bulk, purified bromine.   [10] 1- to 5-short ton lots.   [11] Secondary production.   [12] Turkish, chromite price.   [13] Columbite price.   [14] Value of imports, dollars per carat.   [15] Reported consumption.   [16] Zone refined.   [17] Dollars per troy ounce.   [18] Price of flake imports.   [19] Includes employment at calcining plants.   [20] 99.97% indium.   [21] C.i.f. value, crude, per kilogram.   [22] Price of eastern Canadian ore.   [23] Delivered, No. 1 Heavy Melting composite price.   [24] Year-end price.   [25] 46%-48% Mn metallurgical ore, per unit contained Mn, c.i.f. U.S. ports.   [26] Dollars per 76-pound flask.   [27] London Metal Exchange cash price.   [28] F.o.b. gulf coast.   [29] Dealer price of platinum.   [30] Price of K20, muriate.   [31] Vacuum and open pan, bulk, pellets and packaged, f.o.b. mine and plant.   [32] Ferrosilicon, 50% Si.   [33] Quoted year-end price, dense, bulk, f.o.b. Green River, WY, dollars per short ton.   [34] Quoted price, bulk, f.o.b. works, East, dollars per short ton.   [35] Elemental sulfur, f.o.b. mine and/or plant.   [36] Rutile, list, year-end.   [37] Dollars per unit W03 (7.93 kilograms of contained tungsten per unit).   [38] All forms.   [39] Price for imported zircon, f.o.b. U.S. east coast.

Source: U.S. Geological Survey, *Mineral Commodity Summaries,* annual.

Natural Resources   557

No. 871. Value of Domestic Nonfuel Mineral Production by State: 1990 to 2000

[In millions of dollars (33,445 represents 33,445,000,000), except as indicated. For similar data on fuels, see Table 878]

State	1990	1995	1996	1997	1998	1999	2000, prel. Total (mil. dol.)	2000, prel. Rank	2000, prel. Percent of U.S.
United States[1] ..	33,445	38,506	38,800	40,471	39,600	39,100	40,100	(X)	100.00
Alabama	559	706	778	881	1,010	1,080	1,070	13	2.65
Alaska...........	577	538	613	958	999	1,090	1,140	12	2.83
Arizona	3,085	4,190	3,580	3,540	2,770	2,510	2,550	3	6.35
Arkansas........	381	492	435	487	484	518	506	29	1.26
California........	2,771	2,760	2,830	3,040	2,980	3,200	3,350	1	8.34
Colorado	377	570	513	524	650	555	[3]566	27	1.41
Connecticut	122	93	82	80	99	[3]103	[3]100	44	0.25
Delaware [2].......	10	9	7	12	12	[3]10	[3]12	50	0.03
Florida..........	1,574	1,540	1,760	1,830	1,810	1,930	1,920	5	4.78
Georgia..........	1,504	1,690	1,740	1,680	1,720	1,840	1,660	7	4.13
Hawaii..........	106	114	110	94	85	89	91	45	0.23
Idaho	375	510	492	469	453	420	398	34	0.99
Illinois	667	828	846	829	875	913	907	17	2.26
Indiana	428	589	628	670	691	717	729	21	1.82
Iowa	310	456	470	486	518	537	510	28	1.27
Kansas	349	498	530	539	551	566	624	24	1.55
Kentucky	359	432	442	498	498	483	497	30	1.24
Louisiana........	368	434	393	402	347	374	404	33	1.01
Maine	55	68	69	70	92	101	[3]102	43	0.25
Maryland........	368	324	332	371	352	336	357	35	0.89
Massachusetts	128	190	200	193	204	204	210	39	0.52
Michigan	1,440	1,520	1,540	1,660	1,670	1,660	1,670	6	4.17
Minnesota	1,482	1,530	1,540	1,680	1,740	1,580	1,570	8	3.9
Mississippi	111	131	144	175	149	190	157	42	0.39
Missouri.........	1,105	1,140	1,250	1,310	1,320	1,380	1,320	10	3.28
Montana	573	574	491	498	502	491	582	25	1.45
Nebraska........	90	146	148	165	99	163	170	41	0.42
Nevada.........	2,621	3,060	3,230	3,270	3,170	2,780	[3]2,800	2	6.96
New Hampshire	36	50	52	49	68	[3]64	[3]59	46	0.15
New Jersey	229	243	246	267	290	300	286	37	0.71
New Mexico.......	1,103	1,130	992	1,040	888	671	812	18	2.02
New York.........	773	886	891	955	972	935	970	15	2.42
North Carolina	586	735	690	741	750	761	779	19	1.94
North Dakota	25	31	31	34	38	38	42	48	0.1
Ohio	733	891	969	1,040	1,030	1,040	1,060	14	2.63
Oklahoma	259	357	369	386	460	475	[3]453	31	1.13
Oregon	205	239	265	285	301	303	[3]439	32	1.09
Pennsylvania	1,031	1,080	1,170	1,200	1,230	[3]1,270	[3]1,250	11	3.12
Rhode Island	18	31	23	27	25	[3]25	24	49	0.06
South Carolina	450	447	493	567	562	574	560	26	1.4
South Dakota	319	332	357	328	258	226	260	38	0.65
Tennessee........	663	665	662	707	705	710	770	20	1.92
Texas	1,459	1,680	1,730	1,790	1,820	1,780	2,050	4	5.09
Utah	1,335	1,850	1,730	1,680	1,320	1,260	[3]1,420	9	3.53
Vermont	87	60	66	84	74	[3]83	43	47	0.11
Virginia	507	515	549	642	636	667	692	22	1.72
Washington	483	582	535	555	609	631	691	23	1.72
West Virginia	133	181	185	205	170	180	[3]182	40	0.45
Wisconsin	215	416	396	358	323	[3]334	349	36	0.87
Wyoming.........	911	973	1,080	1,120	1,070	956	922	16	2.3

X Not applicable.   [1] Includes undistributed not shown separately.   [2] Includes District of Columbia.   [3] Partial data only; excludes values withheld to avoid disclosing individual company data.

Source: U.S. Bureau of Mines, *Minerals Yearbook,* annual, and *Mineral Commodities Summaries,* annual; thereafter U.S. Geological Survey.

No. 872. Principal Fuels, Nonmetals, and Metals—World Production and the U.S. Share: 1980 to 2000

Mineral	Unit	World production				Percent U.S. of world			
		1980	1990	1995	2000	1980	1990	1995	2000
Fuels: [1]									
Coal	Mil. sh. ton	4,200	5,386	5,161	[2]4,737	19.8	19.1	20.0	[2]23.2
Petroleum (crude)	Bil. bbl	21.8	22.1	22.8	[2]24.0	14.4	12.2	10.5	[2]8.9
Natural gas (dry, marketable).	Tril. cu. ft	53.5	73.6	78.0	[2]84.7	36.3	24.2	23.9	[2]22.0
Natural gas plant liquids	Bil. bbl	1.3	1.7	2.0	[2]2.2	45.7	33.7	32.1	[2]30.9
Nonmetals:									
Asbestos	1,000 metric tons.	4,699	4,003	2,420	1,900	2	(D)	(Z)	(Z)
Barite	1,000 metric tons.	7,495	5,633	4,300	5,700	27	8	13	11
Feldspar	1,000 metric tons.	3,202	5,456	6,780	9,100	20	12	13	9
Fluorspar	1,000 metric tons.	5,006	5,131	4,050	4,480	2	1	1	-
Gypsum.	Mil. metric tons .	78	100	97	110	14	15	17	23
Mica (incl. scrap).	1,000 metric tons.	228	215	253	300	46	51	43	37
Nitrogen, (fixed) - ammonia . .	Mil. metric tons .	74	97	96	104	20	13	14	13
Phosphate rock, gross wt. . . .	Mil. metric tons .	144	162	130	139	38	29	33	29
Potash (k$_2$O equivalent)	Mil. metric tons .	28	28	25	27	8	6	6	5
Sulfur, elemental	Mil. metric tons .	55	58	53	57	22	20	22	19
Metals, mine basis:									
Bauxite	Mil. metric tons .	89	109	107	127	2	(D)	(D)	(NA)
Columbian concentrates									
(Nb content)	1,000 metric tons.	15	15	18	24	-	-	-	-
Copper	1,000 metric tons.	7,405	9,017	10,100	12,900	16	18	18	11
Gold	Metric tons	1,219	2,133	2,220	2,445	2	14	14	14
Iron ore	Mil. metric tons .	891	982	1,027	1,010	8	6	6	6
Lead [3].	1,000 metric tons.	3,470	3,353	2,780	2,980	17	15	14	16
Mercury.	Metric tons	6,806	4,523	3,160	1,800	16	12	(D)	(D)
Molybdenum.	1,000 metric tons.	111	128	141	112	62	48	43	29
Nickel [3]	1,000 metric tons.	779	965	1,030	1,230	2	(Z)	(Z)	(Z)
Silver	1,000 metric tons.	11	16	15	18	9	13	10	12
Tantalum concentrates	Metric tons	544	400	362	513	-	-	-	-
Titanium concentrates:									
Ilmenite	1,000 metric tons.	3,726	4,072	3,970	4,000	14	(D)	(D)	(NA)
Rutile.	1,000 metric tons.	436	481	416	410	(D)	(D)	(D)	(NA)
Tungsten [3].	1,000 metric tons.	52	43	39	32	5	14	-	-
Vanadium [3].	1,000 metric tons.	37	31	35	42	12	(D)	(D)	(D)
Zinc [3].	1,000 metric tons.	5,954	7,184	7,240	8,000	6	8	9	11
Metals, smelter basis:									
Aluminum.	1,000 metric tons.	15,383	19,292	19,900	23,900	30	21	17	16
Cadmium.	1,000 metric tons.	18	20	19	19	9	8	7	6
Copper	1,000 metric tons.	7,649	9,472	10,200	12,900	14	15	16	11
Iron, pig.	Mil. metric tons .	514	532	533	571	12	9	10	9
Lead [4].	1,000 metric tons.	5,430	5,763	5,590	2,980	23	23	25	16
Magnesium [5]	1,000 metric tons.	316	354	389	284	49	39	37	(NA)
Raw Steel	Mil. metric tons .	717	771	755	833	14	12	13	13
Tin [6].	1,000 metric tons.	251	223	201	200	1	-	-	-
Zinc	1,000 metric tons.	6,049	7,060	7,550	8,000	6	5	5	11

- Represents or rounds to zero.   D Withheld to avoid disclosing company data.   NA Not available.   Z Less than half the unit of measure.   [1] Source: Energy Information Administration, *International Energy Annual.*   [2] 1999 production and percent of production.   [3] Content of ore and concentrate.   [4] Refinery production.   [5] Primary production; no smelter processing necessary.   [6] Production from primary sources only.

Source: Nonfuels, through 1990, U.S. Bureau of Mines, thereafter, U.S. Geological Survey, *Minerals Yearbook*, annual, and *Mineral Commodities Summaries*, annual; fuels, U.S. Energy Information Administration, *International Energy Annual.*

No. 873. Federal Strategic and Critical Materials Inventory: 1990 to 1999

[**As of Dec. 31.** Covers strategic and critical materials essential to military and industrial requirements in time of national emergency]

Mineral	Unit	Quantity [1]				Value (mil. dol.) [2]			
		1990	1995	1998	1999	1990	1995	1998	1999
Bauxite [3]	1,000 lg. ton . . .	18,033	16,032	12,288	9,492	888	203	95	71
Chromium [4].	1,000 sh. ton. . .	1,074	1,192	1,070	1,068	917	839	715	628
Cobalt	Mil. lb.	53	44	32	28	443	1,121	504	295
Diamonds: Stones . . .	Carat 1,000	7,777	5,135	3,097	2,497	267	52	31	25
Industrial, bort . . .	Carat 1,000. . . .	17,353	1,967	62	-	16	9	-	-
Lead	1,000 sh. ton . . .	(NA)	(NA)	337	277	(NA)	(NA)	198	140
Manganese [5].	1,000 sh. ton . . .	4,017	2,817	2,251	2,144	962	464	284	270
Palladium	1,000 troy oz. . . .	(NA)	(NA)	1,247	1,099	(NA)	(NA)	183	343
Platinum	1,000 troy oz. . . .	453	453	440	342	186	154	162	120
Silver.	1,000 troy oz. . . .	92,151	46,667	35,121	26,203	374	158	105	86
Tantalum Group	1,000 lb	(NA)	(NA)	82,313	2,689	(NA)	(NA)	127	126
Tin.	1,000 metric ton.	169	130	84	72	962	908	461	391
Titanium	1,000 sh. ton. . .	37	37	35	35	402	221	122	124
Tungsten [6]	Mil. lb.	82	82	82	79	253	253	316	174
Zinc.	1,000 sh. ton. . .	379	301	213	198	483	281	220	203

- Represents or rounds to zero.   NA Not available.   [1] Consists of stockpile and nonstockpile grades and reflects uncommitted balances.   [2] Market values are estimated trade values of similar materials and not necessarily amounts that would be realized at time of sale.   [3] Consists of abrasive grade, metallic grade Jamaica, metallic grade Suriname, and refractory.   [4] Consists of ferro-high carbon, ferro-low carbon, ferro-silicon, and metal.   [5] Consists of chemical grade, dioxide battery natural, dioxide battery synthetic, electrolytic, ferro-high carbon, ferro-med. carbon, ferro-silicon, and metal.   [6] Consists of carbide powder, ferro, metal powder, and ores and concentrates.

Source: U.S. Defense Logistics Agency, *Statistical Supplement, Stockpile Report to the Congress* (AP-3).

U.S. Census Bureau, Statistical Abstract of the United States: 2001

No. 874. Net U.S. Imports of Selected Minerals and Metals as Percent of Apparent Consumption: 1980 to 2000

[In percent. Based on net imports which equal the difference between imports and exports plus or minus government stockpile and industry stock changes]

Mineral	1980	1990	1994	1995	1996	1997	1998	1999	2000
Bauxite [1]	94	98	99	99	100	100	100	100	100
Columbium	100	100	100	100	100	100	100	100	100
Manganese	98	100	100	100	100	100	100	100	100
Mica (sheet) . . .	100	100	100	100	100	100	100	100	100
Strontium	100	100	100	100	100	100	100	100	100
Tin	79	71	83	84	83	86	85	85	86
Tantalum	90	71	75	80	80	75	80	80	80
Chromium	91	84	81	80	79	75	80	80	78
Cobalt	93	86	80	79	76	76	73	73	74
Barite	44	71	64	65	70	76	80	67	71
Potash	65	68	76	75	77	80	80	80	70
Tungsten	53	81	95	90	89	84	77	81	68
Titanium	32	([3])	(D)	64	50	63	49	(NA)	(NA)
Zinc [2]	60	41	35	35	33	35	35	30	60
Nickel	76	64	64	60	59	56	64	63	58
Silver	7	(NA)	(NA)	(NA)	(NA)	([3])	14	14	52
Copper	16	15	12	27	14	13	14	27	37
Aluminum	([3])	36	31	23	22	23	27	30	33
Gypsum	35	46	3	30	29	28	28	29	22
Sulfur	14	21	18	21	13	13	18	17	22
Iron ore	25	3	13	14	14	14	12	17	19
Iron and steel . .	13	13	22	21	20	20	27	22	17
Cadmium	55	([3])	30	23	32	16	20	19	6
Mercury	27	(D)	(D)	(NA)	(NA)	(D)	(NA)	(NA)	(NA)
Platinum group .	87	88	(NA)	(NA)	(NA)	(NA)	(NA)	(NA)	(NA)
Selenium	59	46	31	31	38	(D)	(D)	(D)	(NA)
Vanadium	35	(D)	(D)	84	(D)	(D)	78	80	(NA)

D Withheld to avoid disclosure.   NA Not available.   [1] Includes alumina.   [2] Beginning 1990, effect of sharp rise in exports of concentrates. If calculated on a refined zinc-only basis, reliance would be about the same as pre-1990 level; 1990, 64 percent; 1991, 61 percent; 1992, 61 percent; 1993, 67 percent; 1994, 70 percent; 1995, 71 percent; and 1996 and 1997, 70 percent; 1998, 69 percent; and 1999, 71 percent.   [3] Net exports.

Source: Through 1994, U.S. Bureau of Mines; thereafter, U.S. Geological Survey, *Mineral Commodity Summaries;* import and export data from U.S. Census Bureau.

No. 875. Federal Offshore Leasing, Exploration, Production, and Revenue: 1990 to 2000

[See source for explanation of terms and for reliability statement]

Item	Unit	1990	1994	1995	1996	1997	1998	1999	2000
Tracts offered	Number . .	10,459	10,861	10,995	12,230	9,870	8,205	7,453	7,992
Tracts leased	Number . .	825	560	835	1,537	1,780	1,157	333	553
Acres offered	Millions . .	56.79	58.90	59.70	70.00	26.24	44.10	40.22	42.89
Acres leased	Millions . .	4.30	2.78	4.34	8.15	9.62	6.34	1.77	2.92
Bonus paid for leased tracts	Bil. dol. . .	0.6	0.3	0.4	0.9	(NA)	1.3	0.3	0.3
New wells being drilled:									
Active	Number . .	120	120	124	835	186	173	219	224
Suspended	Number . .	266	222	247	1,323	244	122	110	146
Cumulative wells (since 1953):									
Wells completed	Number . .	13,167	13,342	13,475	13,583	13,546	13,702	13,676	13,718
Wells plugged and abandoned .	Number . .	14,677	17,427	18,008	18,268	18,728	21,050	22,115	22,814
Revenue, total [1]	Bil. dol. . .	3.4	2.9	2.7	4.3	5.3	4.3	3.2	5.2
Bonuses . . . . [1]	Bil. dol. . .	0.8	0.3	0.4	0.8	1.4	1.3	0.2	0.4
Oil and gas royalties [1]	Bil. dol. . .	2.6	2.3	2.1	3.1	3.4	2.7	2.6	4.1
Rentals	Bil. dol. . .	0.09	0.06	0.09	0.16	0.23	0.26	0.21	0.21
Sales value [2]	Bil. dol. . .	17.0	15.0	13.8	19.8	22.3	17.6	17.4	27.4
Oil	Bil. dol. . .	7.0	5.2	6 3	8.0	9.0	6.2	6.5	11.5
Natural gas	Bil. dol. . .	9.5	9.8	7.5	11.8	13.3	11.4	10.9	15.9
Sales volume: [3]									
Oil	Mil. bbls. . .	324	369	409	438	479	477	513	566
Natural gas	Bil. cu. ft .	5,093	4,700	4,692	5,024	5,077	4,836	4,992	4,723

NA Not available.   [1] Includes condensate royalties.   [2] Production value is value at time of production, not current value.   [3] Excludes sales volumes for gas lost, gas plant products or sulfur.

Source: U.S. Dept. of the Interior, Minerals Management Service, *Federal Offshore Statistics,* annual.

No. 876. Petroleum Industry—Summary: 1980 to 2000

[Includes all costs incurred for drilling and equipping wells to point of completion as productive wells or abandonment after drilling becomes unproductive. Based on sample of operators of different size drilling establishments]

Item	Unit	1980	1990	1994	1995	1996	1997	1998	1999	2000
Crude oil producing wells (Dec. 31).	1,000. . .	548	602	582	574	574	573	562	554	(NA)
Daily output per well	Bbl.	15.9	12.2	11.4	11.4	11.3	11.3	11.1	10.7	(NA)
Completed wells drilled, total	1,000. . .	57.73	26.50	17.87	17.75	19.71	24.39	21.39	18.21	17.77
Crude oil.	1,000. . .	30.88	11.54	6.15	7.09	7.83	10.01	6.76	4.72	5.08
Gas	1,000. . .	15.25	10.36	8.81	7.78	8.73	10.79	11.53	10.04	9.75
Dry	1,000. . .	11.60	4.60	2.90	2.88	3.15	3.59	3.10	3.45	2.94
Average depth per well [1]	Feet . . .	4,171	4,653	5,731	5,505	5,506	5,552	6,060	5,632	(NA)
Average cost per well [1]	$1,000. .	368	384	483	513	496	604	769	856	(NA)
Average cost per foot [1]	Dollars. .	77.02	76.07	79.49	87.22	88.92	107.83	128.97	152.02	(NA)
Crude oil production, total	Mil. bbl. .	3,138	2,685	2,432	2,394	2,360	2,355	2,282	2,147	2,125
Value at wells	Bil. dol. .	67.7	53.8	32.1	35.0	43.6	40.6	24.8	33.7	(NA)
Average price per barrel	Dollars. .	21.59	20.03	13.19	14.62	18.46	17.23	10.87	15.56	26.73
Lower 48 states	Mil. bbl. .	2,548	2,037	1,863	1,853	1,851	1,882	1,853	1,763	1,771
Alaska	Mil. bbl. .	590	647	569	542	508	473	429	383	354
Onshore	Mil. bbl. .	2,760	2,290	1,931	1,838	1,789	1,753	1,664	1,650	(NA)
Offshore	Mil. bbl. .	377	395	500	557	570	602	618	513	(NA)
Imports: Crude oil	Mil. bbl. .	1,921	2,151	2,578	2,639	2,740	3,002	3,178	3,187	3,311
Refined petroleum products	Mil. bbl. .	601	775	706	586	719	707	731	775	872
Exports: Crude oil	Mil. bbl. .	104.8	39.8	36.1	34.7	40.2	39.4	40.2	43.1	18.3
Proved reserves	Bil. bbl. .	29.8	26.3	22.5	22.4	22.0	22.5	21.0	21.8	(NA)
Operable refineries.	Number .	319	205	179	175	170	164	163	159	(NA)
Capacity (Jan. 1)	Mil. bbl. .	6,566	5,683	5,486	5,632	5,595	5,639	5,734	5,935	(NA)
Refinery input, total.	Mil. bbl. .	5,117	5,325	5,482	5,555	5,654	5,807	5,891	5,880	(NA)
Crude oil	Mil. bbl. .	4,920	4,895	5,063	5,099	5,179	5,351	5,435	5,406	(NA)
Natural gas plant liquids	Mil. bbl. .	168	172	172	172	164	153	146	135	(NA)
Other liquids	Mil. bbl. .	29	259	252	285	307	303	310	339	(NA)
Refinery output, total.	Mil. bbl. .	5,336	5,574	5,763	5,836	5,957	6,117	6,216	6,209	(NA)
Motor gasoline	Mil. bbl. .	2,369	2,540	2,621	2,723	2,759	2,825	2,880	2,898	(NA)
Jet fuel	Mil. bbl. .	365	544	529	518	555	566	558	573	(NA)
Distillate fuel oil	Mil. bbl. .	971	1,066	1,168	1,153	1,212	1,237	1,248	1,245	(NA)
Residual fuel oil	Mil. bbl. .	577	347	303	288	266	259	277	256	(NA)
Liquefied petroleum gases . . .	Mil. bbl. .	120	183	223	237	241	252	245	252	(NA)
Utilization rate	Percent .	75.4	87.1	92.6	92.0	94.1	95.2	95.6	92.7	(NA)

NA Not available.   [1] Source: American Petroleum Institute, *Joint Association Survey on Drilling Costs*, annual.

Source: Except as noted, U.S. Energy Information Administration, *Annual Energy Review, Petroleum Supply Annual; U.S. Crude Oil, Natural Gas*, and *Natural Gas Liquids Reserves*; and *Monthly Energy Review*.

No. 877. U.S. Petroleum Balance: 1980 to 2000

[In millions of barrels (6,242 represents 6,242,000,000)]

Item	1980	1990	1994	1995	1996	1997	1998	1999	2000
Petroleum products supplied for domestic use	**6,242**	**6,201**	**6,467**	**7,087**	**6,701**	**6,796**	**6,905**	**7,125**	**7,211**
Production of products	5,765	5,934	6,244	6,940	6,511	6,671	6,733	6,774	6,903
Crude input to refineries	4,934	4,894	5,061	5,718	5,195	5,351	5,434	5,403	5,514
Oil, field production	3,138	2,685	2,431	2,406	2,366	2,355	2,282	2,147	2,131
Alaska	592	647	569	542	510	473	429	383	355
Lower 48 states	2,555	2,037	1,863	1,853	1,856	1,882	1,853	1,764	1,776
Net imports	1,821	2,112	2,542	2,604	2,708	2,963	3,137	3,144	3,301
Imports (gross excluding SPR) [1]	1,910	2,142	2,574	2,639	2,748	3,002	3,178	3,184	3,317
SPR [1] imports	16	10	4	-	-	-	-	3	3
Exports	-105	40 .	36	35	40	39	40	43	18
Other sources	33	98	88	102	122	34	15	113	82
Natural gas liquids (NGL), supply	577	574	694	708	716	721	717	757	799
Other liquids	253	465	489	514	599	599	582	614	589
Net imports of refined products	484	326	217	101	181	154	225	252	305
Imports	578	598	518	407	491	469	508	537	648
Exports	94	272	302	307	310	315	283	284	343
Stock withdrawal, refined products	-7	-59	6	46	9	-29	-53	98	2
TYPE OF PRODUCT SUPPLIED									
Total products supplied for domestic use	**6,242**	**6,201**	**6,467**	**6,469**	**6,701**	**6,796**	**6,905**	**7,125**	**7,211**
Finished motor gasoline	2,407	2,641	2,774	2,843	2,888	2,926	3,012	3,077	3,101
Distillate fuel oil.	1,049	1,103	1,154	1,170	1,232	1,254	1,263	1,304	1,362
Residual fuel oil	918	449	373	311	311	291	324	303	333
Liquefied petroleum gases [2]	414	568	686	693	736	744	713	801	816
Other	1,454	1,440	1,480	1,452	1,535	1,582	1,593	1,639	1,598
ENDING STOCKS									
Ending stocks, all oils	**1,392**	**1,621**	**1,653**	**1,563**	**1,052**	**1,560**	**1,647**	**1,493**	**1,468**
Crude oil and lease condensate.	358	323	337	303	284	305	324	284	286
Strategic Petroleum Reserve (SPR) [1]	108	586	592	592	566	563	571	567	541
Other	926	712	724	668	202	692	752	641	641

- Represents zero.   [1] SPR=Strategic petroleum reserve. For more information, see Table 905.   [2] Includes ethane.

Source: U.S. Energy Information Administration, *Petroleum Supply Annual*.

No. 878. Crude Petroleum and Natural Gas—Production and Value by Major Producing States: 1990 to 1999

[2,685 mil. bbl. represents 2,685,000,000 bbl. or 18,594 bil. cu. ft. represents 18,594,000,000,000 cu. ft.]

State	Crude petroleum						Natural gas marketed production [1]					
	Quantity (mil. bbl.)			Value (mil. dol.)			Quantity (bil. cu. ft.)			Value (mil. dol.)		
	1990	1998	1999	1990	1998	1999	1990	1998	1999	1990	1998	1999
Total [2]	2,685	2,282	2,147	53,772	24,804	33,403	18,594	19,646	19,596	31,658	38,206	42,538
AL	18	12	11	387	150	186	135	564	547	373	1,237	1,263
AK	658	429	383	10,086	3,669	4,829	403	467	463	554	614	635
AR	10	8	7	222	89	114	175	188	170	360	738	697
CA	322	284	273	5,732	2,709	3,844	363	315	383	857	621	905
CO	31	22	18	722	281	321	243	696	739	377	1,323	1,436
FL	6	6	5	(NA)	(NA)	(NA)	6	6	6	15	(NA)	(NA)
IL	20	14	12	467	175	210	1	-	-	1	(NA)	(NA)
IN	3	2	2	73	28	34	(Z)	1	1	1	1	2
KS	59	36	29	1,359	433	496	574	604	553	893	1,027	998
KY	5	3	3	:24	34	46	75	82	77	169	196	159
LA	148	134	120	3,409	1,690	2,128	5,242	5,288	5,314	9,587	10,555	11,649
MI	20	9	8	458	111	130	140	278	277	420	491	491
MS	30	22	18	630	228	277	95	108	111	167	153	181
MT	20	16	15	429	186	247	50	58	61	90	88	103
NE	5	3	3	119	37	46	1	2	1	2	2	2
NM	66	72	64	1,472	894	1,124	965	1,501	1,512	1,629	2,649	3,191
NY	(Z)	-	-	9	3	4	25	17	16	55	43	35
ND	39	36	33	849	405	549	52	53	53	93	114	123
OH	8	7	6	196	80	98	155	109	110	393	243	346
OK	117	78	71	2,690	988	1,254	2,258	1,645	1,571	3,548	2,915	3,223
PA	2	2	1	54	27	27	178	68	175	417	-	-
TX	674	505	449	15,060	6,197	7,767	6,343	6,319	6,118	9,939	13,003	14,106
UT	23	19	16	524	240	288	146	277	263	249	479	506
WV	2	1	1	43	18	24	178	178	176	568	-	-
WY	103	65	61	2,169	693	1,007	736	761	823	856	1,352	1,621

- Represents or round to zero. NA Not available. Z Less than 500 million cubic feet or less than $500,000. [1] Excludes nonhydrocarbon gases. [2] Includes other states not shown separately. State production does not include state offshore production.

Source: U.S. Energy Information Administration, *Petroleum Supply Annual,* and *Petroleum Marketing Annual;* and *Natural Gas Annual,* and *Natural Gas Monthly.*

No. 879. Crude Oil, Natural Gas, and Natural Gas Liquids—Reserves by State: 1990 and 1999

[26,254 mil. bbl. represents 26,254,000,000 bbl. As of December 31. Proved reserves are estimated quantities of the mineral, which geological and engineering data demonstrate with reasonable certainty, to be recoverable in future years from known reservoirs under existing economic and operating conditions. Indicated reserves of crude oil are quantities other than proved reserves, which may become economically recoverable from existing productive reservoirs through the application of improved recovery techniques using current technology. Based on a sample of operators of oil and gas wells]

Area	1990				1999			
	Crude oil		Natural gas (bil. cu. ft.)	Natural gas liquids (mil. bbl.)	Crude oil		Natural gas (bil. cu. ft.)	Natural gas liquids (mil. bbl.)
	Proved (mil. bbl.)	Indicated (mil. bbl.)			Proved (mil. bbl.)	Indicated (mil. bbl.)		
United States	26,254	3,483	169,346	7,586	21,765	2,865	167,406	7,906
Lower 48 States	19,730	2,514	160,046	7,246	16,865	2,400	157,672	7,515
Alabama	44	(Z)	4,125	170	49	(NA)	4,287	107
Alaska	6,524	969	9,300	340	4,900	464	9,734	299
Arkansas	60	1	1,731	9	48	-	1,542	5
California	[2]4,658	[2]1,425	[2]3,185	[2]105	3,934	1,400	2,387	98
Colorado	305	8	4,555	169	203	21	8,987	303
Florida	(NA)	(NA)	(NA)	(NA)	J5	-	84	16
Illinois	(NA)	(NA)	(NA)	(NA)	100	-	(NA)	(NA)
Indiana	131	-	(NA)	(NA)	10	-	(NA)	(NA)
Kansas	(NA)	(NA)	(NA)	(NA)	175	-	5,753	358
Kentucky	321	(Z)	9,614	313	24	-	1,435	69
Louisiana	33	-	1,016	25	600	278	9,242	457
Michigan	(NA)	(NA)	(NA)	(NA)	52	-	2,255	48
Mississippi	(NA)	(NA)	(NA)	(NA)	163	-	677	10
Montana	(NA)	(NA)	(NA)	(NA)	207	-	841	8
Nebraska	221	-	899	15	17	-	(NA)	(NA)
New Mexico	(NA)	(NA)	(NA)	(NA)	718	165	15,449	954
New York	687	256	17,260	990	(NA)	(NA)	221	(NA)
North Dakota	285	-	586	60	262	1	416	53
Ohio	65	-	1,214	(NA)	51	-	1,179	(NA)
Oklahoma	734	37	16,151	657	621	58	12,543	749
Pennsylvania	22	-	1,720	(NA)	16	-	1,772	(NA)
Texas	[2]7,106	618	[2]38,192	[2]2,575	5,339	426	40,157	2,584
Utah	249	44	1,510	[3]	268	42	3,213	[3]
Virginia	(NA)	(NA)	138	(NA)	(NA)	(NA)	2,017	(NA)
West Virginia	31	-	2,207	86	21	-	2,936	73
Wyoming	794	42	9,944	[4]812	590	5	14,226	[4]615
Federal offshore	2,805	49	31,433	619	3,297	5	25,987	998

- Represents or rounds to zero. NA Not available. Z Less than 500,000 barrels. [1] Includes state offshore. [2] Excludes federal offshore. [3] Included with Wyoming. [4] Includes Utah.

Source: Energy Information Administration, *U.S. Crude Oil, Natural Gas, and Natural Gas Liquids Reserves, 1999 Annual Report,* September 2000.

No. 880. World Daily Crude Oil Production by Major Producing Country: 1980 to 1999

[In thousands of barrels per day (59,600 barrels represents 59,600,000 barrels)]

Country	1980	1990	1993	1994	1995	1996	1997	1998	1999
World, total [1]	59,600	60,566	60,236	60,991	62,335	63,711	65,690	66,921	65,870
Saudi Arabia	9,900	6,410	8,198	8,120	8,231	8,218	8,362	8,389	7,833
Russia	(X)	(X)	6,730	6,135	5,995	5,850	5,920	5,854	6,079
United States	**8,597**	**7,355**	**6,847**	**6,662**	**6,560**	**6,465**	**6,452**	**6,252**	**5,881**
Iran	1,662	3,088	3,540	3,618	3,643	3,686	3,664	3,634	3,557
China.	2,114	2,774	2,890	2,939	2,990	3,131	3,200	3,198	3,195
Norway.	528	1,704	2,350	2,521	2,768	3,104	3,143	3,017	3,018
Mexico	1,936	2,553	2,673	2,685	2,618	2,855	3,023	3,070	2,906
Venezuela.	2,168	2,137	2,450	2,588	2,750	2,938	3,280	3,167	2,826
United Kingdom	1,622	1,820	1,915	2,375	2,489	2,568	2,518	2,616	2,684
Iraq	2,514	2,040	512	553	560	579	1,155	2,150	2,508
United Arab Emirates	1,709	2,117	2,159	2,193	2,233	2,278	2,316	2,345	2,169
Nigeria	2,055	1,810	1,960	1,931	1,993	2,001	2,132	2,153	2,130
Canada	1,435	1,553	1,679	1,746	1,805	1,837	1,922	1,981	1,907
Kuwait	1,656	1,175	1,852	2,025	2,057	2,062	2,007	2,085	1,898
Indonesia	1,577	1,462	1,511	1,510	1,503	1,547	1,520	1,518	1,472
Libya	1,787	1,375	1,361	1,378	1,390	1,401	1,446	1,390	1,319
Algeria	1,106	1,175	1,162	1,180	1,202	1,242	1,277	1,246	1,202
Brazil.	182	631	643	671	695	795	841	969	1,132
Oman	282	685	776	810	851	883	904	900	887
Egypt.	595	873	890	896	920	922	856	834	852
Colombia	126	440	456	450	585	623	652	733	816
Argentina	491	483	594	650	715	756	834	847	802
Angola	150	475	509	536	646	709	714	735	766
Malaysia.	283	619	640	645	682	695	700	720	693
Qatar.	472	406	413	415	442	510	550	696	665
India	182	660	534	590	703	651	675	661	653
Australia.	380	575	503	536	562	570	588	544	539
Syria	164	388	554	560	575	582	561	553	538
Kazakhstan.	(X)	(X)	408	352	362	403	466	476	530
Yemen	-	193	220	335	345	340	362	388	409

- Represents or rounds to zero.   X Not applicable.   [1] Includes countries not shown separately.

Source: U.S. Energy Information Administration, *International Energy Review, 1999*. See also <http://www.eia.doe.gov/pub/pdf/international/021999.pdf> (issued February 2001).

No. 881. Liquefied Petroleum Gases—Summary: 1980 to 1999

[In millions of 42-gallon barrels (561 barrels represents 561,000,000 barrels). Includes ethane]

Item	1980	1990	1993	1994	1995	1996	1997	1998	1999
Production	**561**	**638**	**850**	**734**	**760**	**789**	**799**	**775**	**814**
At natural gas plants	441	456	634	511	521	547	547	529	564
At refineries	121	182	216	223	234	242	252	246	250
Imports.	79	68	70	67	53	61	62	71	66
Refinery input.	85	107	179	108	105	102	96	92	88
Exports.	9	14	16	14	21	19	18	15	18
Stocks, Dec. 31	116	98	117	99	93	86	89	115	89

Source: U.S. Energy Information Administration, *Petroleum Supply Annual*.

No. 882. Natural Gas Plant Liquids—Production and Value: 1980 to 1999

[Barrels of 42 gallons (576 barrels represents 576,000,000 barrels)]

Item	Unit	1980	1990	1993	1994	1995	1996	1997	1998	1999
Field production [1]	Mil. bbl . . .	576	566	634	630	643	670	663	642	675
Pentanes plus	Mil. bbl . . .	126	112	122	119	122	123	116	113	111
Liquefied petroleum gases .	Mil. bbl . . .	441	454	512	511	521	547	547	529	564
Natural gas processed	Tril. cu. ft. .	15	15	16	16	17	17	17	17	17

[1] Includes other finished petroleum products, not shown separately.

Source: U.S. Energy Information Administration, *Petroleum Supply Annual* and *Natural Gas Annual*.

Natural Resources   563

No. 883. Natural Gas—Supply, Consumption, Reserves, and Marketed Production: 1980 to 1999

[182 represents 182,000 wells]

Item	Unit	1980	1990	1993	1994	1995	1996	1997	1998	1999
Producing wells (year-end)	1,000	182	269	282	292	299	302	311	317	307
Production value at wells	Bil. dol	32.1	31.8	38.7	36.5	30.2	43.0	46.1	38.2	42.5
Avg. per 1,000 cu. ft	Dollars	1.59	1.71	2.04	1.85	1.55	2.17	2.32	1.94	2.17
Proved reserves [1]	Tril. cu. ft	199	169	162	164	165	166	167	164	167
Marketed production [2]	Tril. cu. ft.	20,180	18,594	18,982	19,710	19,506	19,812	19,866	19,809	19,596
Minus: Extraction losses [3]	Tril. cu. ft	777	784	886	889	908	958	964	938	901
Equals: Dry production	Tril. cu. ft	19,403	17,810	18,095	18,821	18,599	18,854	18,902	18,871	18,695
Plus: Withdrawals from storage	Tril. cu. ft	1,972	1,986	2,799	2,579	3,025	2,981	2,894	2,432	2,873
Plus: Imports [4]	Tril. cu. ft	985	1,532	2,350	2,624	2,841	2,937	2,994	3,152	3,586
Plus: Balancing item	Tril. cu. ft	-640	-152	-110	-416	-230	217	61	-180	-683
Equals: Total supply	Tril. cu. ft	21,875	21,299	23,254	23,719	24,345	25,099	24,954	24,377	24,589
Minus: Exports	Tril. cu. ft	49	86	140	162	154	153	157	159	163
Minus: Additions to storage [5]	Tril. cu. ft	1,949	2,499	2,835	2,865	2,610	2,979	2,870	2,961	2,703
Equals: Consumption, total	Tril. cu. ft.	19,877	18,715	20,279	20,708	21,581	21,967	21,959	21,279	21,894
Lease and plant fuel	Tril. cu. ft	1,026	1,236	1,172	1,124	1,220	1,250	1,203	1,174	1,077
Pipeline fuel	Tril. cu. ft	635	680	624	685	700	711	751	635	735
Residential	Tril. cu. ft	4,752	4,391	4,956	4,848	4,850	5,241	4,984	4,520	4,724
Commercial [6]	Tril. cu. ft	2,611	2,623	2,862	2,895	3,031	3,158	3,215	2,999	3,049
Industrial	Tril. cu. ft	7,172	7,018	7,981	8,167	8,580	8,870	8,832	8,686	8,990
Vehicle fuel	Tril. cu. ft	(NA)	-	1	2	3	3	4	5	6
Electric utilities	Tril. cu. ft	3,682	2,786	2,682	2,987	3,197	2,732	2,968	3,258	3,113
World production (dry)	Tril. cu. ft	53.5	73.6	76.4	76.9	78.0	81.7	81.6	82.8	84.7
U.S. production (dry)	Tril. cu. ft	19.4	17.8	18.1	18.8	18.6	18.8	18.9	18.9	18.6
Percent U.S. of world	Percent	36.3	24.2	23.7	24.5	23.9	23.0	23.2	22.8	22.0

- Represents or rounds to zero. NA Not available. [1] Estimated, end of year. Source: U.S. Energy Information Administration, *U.S. Crude Oil, Natural Gas, and Natural Gas Liquids Reserves,* annual. [2] Marketed production includes gross withdrawals from reservoirs less quantities used for reservoir repressuring and quantities vented or flared. For 1980 and thereafter, it excludes the nonhydrocarbon gases subsequently removed. [3] Volumetric reduction in natural gas resulting from the extraction of natural gas constituents at natural gas processing plants. [4] Includes imports of liquefied natural gas. [5] Includes liquefied natural gas (LNG) storage in above ground tanks. [6] Includes deliveries to municipalities and public authorities for institutional heating and other purposes.

Source: Except as noted, U.S. Energy Information Administration, *Annual Energy Review, International Energy Annual, Natural Gas Annual,* Volumes I and II and *Monthly Energy Review.*

No. 884. World Natural Gas Production by Major Producing Country: 1980 to 1999

[In trillion cubic feet (53.35 represents 53,350,000,000,000)]

Country	1980	1990	1993	1994	1995	1996	1997	1998	1999
World, total[1]	53.35	73.57	76.36	76.93	77.96	81.71	81.61	82.79	84.69
Russia	(X)	(X)	21.81	21.45	21.01	21.23	20.17	20.87	20.83
United States	19.40	17.81	18.10	18.82	18.60	18.85	18.90	18.71	18.62
Canada	2.76	3.85	4.91	5.27	5.60	5.78	5.86	6.05	6.26
United Kingdom	1.32	1.75	2.31	2.47	2.67	3.18	3.03	3.14	3.49
Algeria	0.41	1.79	1.90	1.81	2.05	2.19	2.43	2.60	2.90
Netherlands	3.40	2.69	3.11	2.95	2.98	3.37	2.99	2.84	2.65
Indonesia	0.63	1.53	1.97	2.21	2.24	2.35	2.37	2.27	2.34
Uzbekistan	(X)	(X)	1.59	1.67	1.70	1.70	1.74	1.94	1.96
Iran	0.25	0.84	0.96	1.12	1.25	1.42	1.66	1.77	1.87
Norway	0.92	0.98	0.97	1.04	1.08	1.45	1.62	1.63	1.76
Saudi Arabia	0.33	1.08	1.27	1.33	1.34	1.46	1.60	1.65	1.63
Malaysia	0.06	0.65	0.88	0.92	1.02	1.23	1.36	1.37	1.45
United Arab Emirates	0.20	0.78	0.94	0.91	1.11	1.19	1.28	1.31	1.34
Mexico	0.90	0.90	0.95	0.97	0.96	1.06	1.17	1.27	1.29
Argentina	0.28	0.63	0.76	0.79	0.84	0.94	0.97	1.04	1.22
Australia	0.31	0.72	0.86	0.93	1.03	1.06	1.06	1.10	1.10
Venezuela	0.52	0.76	0.81	0.88	0.89	0.96	0.99	1.11	1.09
China	0.51	0.51	0.56	0.59	0.60	0.67	0.75	0.78	0.85
Qatar	0.18	0.28	0.48	0.48	0.48	0.48	0.61	0.69	0.85
Germany	0.93	0.72	0.68	0.70	0.74	0.80	0.79	0.77	0.82
Turkmenistan	(X)	(X)	2.29	1.26	1.14	1.31	0.90	0.47	0.79
Pakistan	0.29	0.48	0.58	0.63	0.65	0.70	0.70	0.71	0.78
India	0.05	0.40	0.53	0.59	0.63	0.70	0.72	0.76	0.75
Thailand	-	0.21	0.31	0.34	0.37	0.43	0.54	0.57	0.63
Ukraine	(X)	(X)	0.68	0.64	0.62	0.64	0.64	0.64	0.63
Italy	0.44	0.61	0.69	0.73	0.72	0.71	0.68	0.67	0.62
Egypt	0.03	0.29	0.40	0.42	0.44	0.47	0.48	0.49	0.55
Romania	1.20	1.00	0.75	0.69	0.68	0.63	0.61	0.52	0.50
Trinidad and Tobago	0.06	0.18	0.22	0.25	0.27	0.30	0.33	0.33	0.41
Brunei	0.32	0.32	0.29	0.30	0.33	0.33	0.32	0.32	0.33

- Represents or rounds to zero. X Not applicable. [1] Includes countries not shown separately.

Source: U.S. Energy Information Administration, *International Energy Review, 1999.* See also <http://www.eia.doe.gov/pub/pdf/international/021999.pdf> (issued February 2001).

No. 885. Coal and Coke—Summary: 1980 to 1999

[830 short tons represents 830,000,000 short tons. Includes coal consumed at mines. Demonstrated coal reserve base for United States on Jan. 1, 1997, was an estimated 508 billion tons. Recoverability varies between 40 and 90 percent for individual deposits; 50 percent or more of overall U.S. coal reserve base is believed to be recoverable]

Item	Unit	1980	1990	1994	1995	1996	1997	1998	1999
COAL									
Coal production, total [1]	Mil. sh. tons . .	830	1,029	1,034	1,033	1,064	1,090	1,118	1,100
Value	Bil. dol.	20.45	22.39	20.06	19.45	19.68	19.77	19.75	19.42
Anthracite production	Mil. sh. tons . . .	6.1	3.5	4.6	4.7	4.8	4.7	5.3	4.8
Bituminous coal and lignite.	Mil. sh. tons . . .	824	1,026	1,029	1,028	1,059	1,085	1,112	1,096
Underground	Mil. sh. tons . . .	337	425	399	396	410	421	417	392
Surface	Mil. sh. tons . . .	487	605	634	637	654	669	700	709
Exports	Mil. sh. tons . . .	92	105.804	71	89	90	84	78	58
Imports.	Mil. sh. tons . . .	1	3	8	9	8	7	9	9
Consumption [2]	Mil. sh. tons . . .	703	896	930	941	1,006	1,030	1,038	1,045
Electric power utilities	Mil. sh. tons . . .	569	774	817	829	875	900	911	894
Industrial.	Mil. sh. tons . . .	126	115	107	106	103	102	96	93
Number of mines	Number.	5,598	3,243	2,354	2,104	1,903	1,828	1,726	1,591
Daily employment.	1,000	225	131	98	90	83	82	85	79
Production, by state:									
Alabama	Mil. sh. tons . . .	26	29	23	25	25	24	23	20
Illinois	Mil. sh. tons . . .	63	60	53	48	47	41	40	40
Indiana	Mil. sh. tons . . .	31	36	31	26	30	35	37	34
Kentucky	Mil. sh. tons . . .	150	173	162	154	152	156	150	140
Montana	Mil. sh. tons . . .	30	38	42	39	38	41	43	41
Ohio	Mil. sh. tons . . .	39	35	30	26	29	29	28	22
Pennsylvania	Mil. sh. tons . . .	93	71	62	62	68	76	81	76
Virginia	Mil. sh. tons . . .	41	47	37	34	36	36	34	32
West Virginia	Mil. sh. tons . . .	122	169	162	163	170	174	171	158
Wyoming.	Mil. sh. tons . . .	95	184	237	264	278	282	314	337
Other states.	Mil. sh. tons . . .	140	187	195	192	192	195	196	200
World production	Mil. sh. tons . . .	4,200	5,386	5,026	5,161	5,165	5,184	5,006	4,737
Percent U.S. of world.	Percent	19.8	19.1	20.6	20.0	20.6	21.0	22.3	23.2
COKE									
Coke production [3]	Mil. sh. tons . . .	46.13	27.62	22.69	23.75	23.08	22.12	20.04	20.02
Imports.	Mil. sh. tons . . .	0.66	0.77	3.34	3.82	2.54	3.14	3.83	3.22
Exports	Mil. sh. tons . . .	2.07	0.57	0.99	1.36	1.62	1.27	1.13	0.90
Consumption	Mil. sh. tons . . .	41.28	27.82	25.56	25.90	23.97	24.02	23.11	22.42

[1] Includes bituminous coal, subbituminous coal, lignite, and anthracite. [2] Includes some categories not shown separately.
[3] Includes beehive coke.

Source: U.S. Energy Information Administration, *Coal Industry,* annual; *Annual Energy Review, International Energy Annual,* and *Quarterly Coal Report.*

No. 886. World Coal Production by Major Producing Country: 1980 to 1999

[In millions of short tons (4,200 represents 4,200,000,000)]

Country	1980	1990	1993	1994	1995	1996	1997	1998	1999
World, total	4,200	5,386	4,952	5,026	5,161	5,165	5,184	5,006	4,737
China	684	1,190	1,304	1,404	1,537	1,515	1,461	1,337	1,118
United States	830	1,029	945	1,034	1,033	1,064	1,090	1,118	1,099
India.	126	233	281	280	298	315	326	322	328
Australia	116	226	248	248	267	272	292	314	321
Russia	(X)	(X)	364	313	296	304	290	257	276
South Africa.	132	193	207	216	227	227	246	248	248
Germany.	532	514	315	292	274	265	252	233	226
Poland	254	237	218	220	220	193	222	197	190
Ukraine.	-	-	128	104	99	83	85	83	91
Korea, North	51	99	109	108	107	106	99	94	85
Canada	40	75	76	80	83	83	87	83	80
Turkey	20	52	54	60	61	62	66	74	74
Indonesia	1	12	30	34	46	55	60	66	71
Greece	26	57	60	62	64	66	65	67	67
Czech Republic	(X)	(X)	94	85	82	84	84	83	65
Kazakhstan	(X)	(X)	123	115	92	85	80	66	64
United Kingdom	144	104	75	54	52	55	54	46	41
Colombia.	5	23	23	25	28	33	36	37	36
Serbia and Montenegro	(X)	(X)	41	42	44	42	45	48	36
Bulgaria	40	39	32	32	34	34	33	34	29
Romania	39	42	44	45	45	46	37	29	28
Spain	41	40	35	33	31	31	29	29	27
Thailand	2	14	17	19	20	24	26	22	20
Hungary	28	20	16	16	16	17	17	16	16
Vietnam	6	5	7	6	9	11	13	12	12

- Represents zero.   X Not applicable.

Source: U.S. Energy Information Administration, *International Energy Review, 1999.* See also <http://www.eia.doe.gov/pub/pdf/international/021999.pdf> (issued February 2001).

Natural Resources 565

No. 887. Demonstrated Coal Reserves by Type of Coal and Major Producing State: 1997

[In millions of short tons. As of January 1. The demonstrated reserve base represents the sum of coal in both measured and indicated resource categories of reliability. Measured resources of coal are estimates that have a high degree of geologic assurance from sample analyses and measurements from closely spaced and geological well known sample sites. Indicated resources are estimates based partly from sample and analyses and measurements and partly from reasonable geologic projections. For more information on the classification of coal resources and related terminology, see report cited below]

State	Total reserves	Type of coal				Method of mining	
		Anthracite	Bituminous	Sub-bituminous	Lignite	Under ground	Surface
United States.....	507,740	7,477	270,910	185,118	44,235	341,775	165,965
Alabama............	4,547	-	3,464	-	1,083	1,290	3,256
Alaska	6,126	-	698	5,414	14	5,423	703
Colorado...........	16,756	26	8,711	3,830	4,190	11,979	4,777
Illinois	105,069	-	105,069	-	-	88,461	16,608
Indiana............	9,917	-	9,917	-	-	8,860	1,057
Iowa	2,190	-	2,190	-	-	1,733	457
Kentucky	32,041	-	32,041	-	-	18,508	13,533
Kentucky, Eastern....	12,086	-	12,086	-	-	2,247	9,839
Kentucky, Western ...	19,954	-	19,954	-	-	16,261	3,694
Missouri	5,994	-	5,994	-	-	1,479	4,515
Montana...........	119,677	-	1,385	102,531	15,760	70,958	48,718
New Mexico	12,483	2	3,706	8,774	-	6,204	6,279
North Dakota........	9,395	-	-	-	9,395	-	9,395
Ohio	23,664	-	23,664	-	-	17,789	5,875
Oklahoma..........	1,575	-	1,575	-	-	1,237	338
Pennsylvania........	28,646	7,220	21,427	-	-	24,232	4,414
Anthracite	7,220	7,220	-	-	-	3,850	3,370
Bituminous	21,427	-	21,427	-	-	20,382	1,044
Texas.............	12,931	-	-	-	12,931	-	12,931
Utah	5,850	-	5,849	1	-	5,583	268
Virginia...........	2,202	126	2,077	-	-	1,528	674
Washington.........	1,390	-	304	1,078	8	1,332	57
West Virginia........	35,397	-	35,397	-	-	30,968	4,429
Wyoming	67,815	-	4,343	63,472	-	42,516	25,299
East of the MS River....	243,156	7,345	234,728	-	1,083	192,939	50,2·7
West of the MS River ...	264,584	132	36,182	185,118	43,152	148,836	115,747

- Represents or rounds to zero.

Source: U.S. Energy Information Administration, *U.S. Coal Reserves: 1997 Update*, February 1999.

No. 888. Uranium Concentrate (U_3O_8) Industry—Summary: 1990 to 2000

[See also Table 914]

Item	Unit	1990	1993	1994	1995	1996	1997	1998	1999	2000
Exploration and development, surface drilling	Mil. ft.	1.7	1.1	0.7	1.3	3.0	4.9	4.6	2.5	1.0
Expenditures...........	Mil. dol.......	17.1	11.3	3.7	6.0	10.1	30.4	21.7	9.0	6.7
Number of mines operated	Number......	39	12	12	12	13	14	15	14	10
Underground............	Number......	27	-	-	-	1	1	4	3	1
Openpit	Number......	2	-	-	-	-	-	-	-	-
In situ leaching	Number......	7	5	5	5	6	7	6	6	4
Other sources	Number......	3	7	7	7	6	6	5	5	5
Mine production	1,000 pounds ..	5,876	2,050	2,526	3,528	4,705	4,710	4,782	4,548	3,123
Underground............	1,000 pounds ..	(D)	-	-	-	-	(D)	(D)	(D)	(D)
Openpit	1,000 pounds ..	1,881	-	-	-	-	-	-	-	-
In situ leaching	1,000 pounds ..	(D)	(D)	2,448	3,372	4,379	4,084	3,721	3,830	2,995
Other sources	1,000 pounds ..	3,995	2,050	78	156	326	626	1,062	718	128
Uranium concentrate production[1]	1,000 pounds ..	8,886	3,063	3,352	6,043	6,321	5,643	4,705	4,611	3,958
Concentrate shipments from mills and plants...........	1,000 pounds ..	12,957	3,374	6,319	5,500	5,982	5,817	4,863	5,527	3,187
Employment.............	Person-years ..	1,335	871	980	1,107	1,118	1,097	1,120	848	627

- Represents or rounds to zero.   D Data withheld to avoid disclosing figures for individual companies.   [1] U_3O_8.

Source: U.S. Department of Energy, *Uranium Industry*, annual.

Energy and Utilities

This section presents statistics on fuel resources, energy production and consumption, electric energy, hydroelectric power, nuclear power, solar energy, wood energy, and the electric and gas utility industries. The principal sources are the U.S. Department of Energy's Energy Information Administration (EIA), the Edison Electric Institute, Washington, DC, and the American Gas Association, Arlington, VA. The Department of Energy was created in October 1977 and assumed and centralized the responsibilities of all or part of several agencies including the Federal Power Commission (FPC), the U.S. Bureau of Mines, the Federal Energy Administration, and the U.S. Energy Research and Development Administration. For additional data on transportation, see Section 23; on fuels, see Section 18; and on energy-related housing characteristics, see Section 20.

The EIA, in its *Annual Energy Review*, provides statistics and trend data on energy supply, demand, and prices. Information is included on petroleum and natural gas, coal, electricity, hydroelectric power, nuclear power, solar, wood, and geothermal energy. Among its annual reports are *Annual Energy Review, Electric Power Annual, Natural Gas Annual, Petroleum Supply Annual, State Energy Data Report, State Energy Price and Expenditure Report, Financial Statistics of Selected Electric Utilities, Performance Profiles of Major Energy Producers, Annual Energy Outlook,* and *International Energy Annual.* These various publications contain state, national, and international data on production of electricity, net summer capability of generating plants, fuels used in energy production, energy sales and consumption, and hydroelectric power. The EIA also issues the *Monthly Energy Review,* which presents current supply, disposition, and price data and monthly publications on petroleum, coal, natural gas, and electric power. Data on residential energy consumption, expenditures, and conservation activities are available from EIA's Residential Energy Consumption Survey and are published triennially in *Residential Energy Consumption Survey: Consumption and Expenditures,* and *Residential Energy Consumption Survey: Housing Characteristics,* and other reports.

The Edison Electric Institute's monthly bulletin and annual *Statistical Year Book of the Electric Utility Industry for the Year* contain data on the distribution of electric energy by public utilities; information on the electric power supply, expansion of electric generating facilities, and the manufacture of heavy electric power equipment is presented in the annual *Year-End Summary of the Electric Power Situation in the United States.* The American Gas Association, in its monthly and quarterly bulletins and its yearbook, *Gas Facts,* presents data on gas utilities and financial and operating statistics.

Btu conversion factors—Various energy sources are converted from original units to the thermal equivalent using British thermal units (Btu). A Btu is the amount of energy required to raise the temperature of 1 pound of water 1 degree Fahrenheit (F) at or near 39.2 degrees F. Factors are calculated annually from the latest final annual data available; some are revised as a result. The following list provides conversion factors used in 2000 for production and consumption, in that order, for various fuels: Petroleum, 5.800 and 5.341 mil. Btu per barrel; total coal, 21.072 and 20.753 mil. Btu per short ton; and natural gas (dry), 1,027 Btu per cubic foot for both. The factors for the production of nuclear power and geothermal power were 10,623 and 21,017 Btu per kilowatt-hour, respectively. The fossil fuel steam-electric power plant generation factor of 10,346 Btu per kilowatt-hour was used for hydroelectric power generation and for wood and waste, wind, photovoltaic, and solar thermal energy consumed at electric utilities.

No. 889. Utilities—Establishments, Revenue, Payroll, and Employees by Kind of Business (NAICS Basis): 1997

Kind of business	NAICS code [1]	Estab-lish-ments (number)	Revenue		Annual payroll		Paid employee for pay period including March 12 (number)
			Total (mil. dol.)	Per paid employee (dol.)	Total (mil. dol.)	Per paid employee (dol.)	
Utilities	22	15,513	411,713	585,899	36,595	52,077	702,703
Electric power generation, transmission, & distribution	2211	7,935	269,095	476,676	30,440	53,921	564,525
Electric power generation	22111	1,745	73,375	493,492	8,369	56,289	148,686
Fossil fuel electric power generation ...	221112	1,009	48,324	515,374	5,049	53,843	93,765
Nuclear electric power generation	221113	67	13,967	406,231	2,202	64,045	34,381
Other electric power generation	221119	316	8,011	608,723	725	55,069	13,160
Electric power transmission, control & distribution	22112	6,190	195,720	470,663	22,070	53,074	415,839
Electric bulk power transmission & control	221121	120	956	395,361	116	47,852	2,418
Electric power distribution	221122	6,070	194,764	471,103	21,955	53,105	413,421
Other combination utilities	2211223	30	428	630,811	52	·76,771	678
Natural gas distribution	2212	2,747	136,995	1,331,629	5,110	49,666	102,878
Natural gas transmission & distribution. .	2212101	713	18,267	629,034	1,534	52,838	29,039
Natural gas distribution	2212102	1,682	87,105	1,387,135	2,955	47,059	62,795
Mixed, manu., or LP gas pro &/or dist...	2212103	86	(D)	(NA)	(D)	(NA)	([2])
Electric & other serv. combined (natural gas distribution)	2212104	145	28,110	4,193,063	413	61,565	6,704
Gas & other serv. combined (natural gas distribution)	2212105	119	2,853	915,151	149	47,705	3,117
Water, sewage, & other systems	2213	4,831	5,623	159,284	1,045	29,614	35,300
Water supply & irrigation systems......	22131	4,052	4,454	159,447	825	29,550	27,933
Sewage treatment facilities	22132	696	596	106,399	139	24,816	5,600
Steam & air-conditioning supply	22133	83	573	324,314	81	45,838	1,767

D Withheld to avoid disclosing data of individual companies; data are included in higher level totals. NA Not available.
[1] North American Industry Classification System, 1997; see text, Section 15, Business Enterprise. [2] 1,000 to 2,499 employees.

Source: U.S. Census Bureau, *1997 Economic Census, Utilities*, Series EC97T22A-US, issued December 1999.

No. 890. Private Utilities—Employees, Annual Payroll, and Establishments by Industry: 1999

[Excludes government employees, railroad employees, self-employed persons, etc. See "General Explanation" in source for definitions and statement on reliability of data. An *establishment* is a single physical location where business is conducted or where services or industrial operations are performed]

Year and industry	NAICS code [1]	Number of employ-ees[2]	Annual payroll (mil. dol.)	Average payroll per em-ployee (dol.)	Establishment by employment size-class				
					Total	Under 20 employ-ees	20 to 99 employ-ees	100 to 499 employ-ees	500 and over employ-ees
Utilities, total	22	667,062	39,355	58,997	16,578	11,510	3,712	1,157	199
Electric power generation, transmission and distribution	2211	533,214	32,443	60,844	8,811	4,859	2,865	912	175
Electric power generation	22111	147,282	9,454	64,187	1,991	1,125	537	275	54
Hydroelectric power generation..	221111	10,573	559	52,912	461	368	73	18	2
Fossil fuel electric power generation...............	221112	87,237	5,343	61,246	1,072	472	363	222	15
Nuclear electric power generation...............	221113	34,901	2,611	74,808	73	17	7	18	31
Other electric power generation .	221119	14,571	940	64,536	385	268	94	17	6
Electric pwr transmsn, control & distribution	22112	385,932	22,989	59,567	6,820	3,734	2,328	637	121
Electric bulk power transmission & control................	221121	5,107	323	63,152	153	101	39	12	1
Electric power distribution	221122	380,825	22,666	59,519	6,667	3,633	2,289	625	120
Natural gas distribution	2212	96,953	5,658	58,354	2,851	2,029	595	205	22
Water, sewage & other systems	2213	36,895	1,255	34,010	4,916	4,622	252	40	2
Water supply & irrigation systems..	22131	29,996	1,016	33,875	4,129	3,918	175	34	2
Sewage treatment facilities	22132	5,270	161	30,583	715	664	46	5	-
Steam & air-conditioning supply ...	22133	1,629	78	47,593	72	40	31	1	-

- Represents zero. [1] North American Industry Classification System, 1977. [2] Covers full- and part-time employees who are on the payroll in the pay period including March 12.

Source: U.S. Census Bureau, *County Business Patterns*, annual. See also <http://www.census.gov/prod/2001pubs/cbp99/cbp99-1.pdf> (issued April 2001).

No. 891. Energy Supply and Disposition by Type of Fuel: 1960 to 1999

[In quadrillion British thermal units (Btu). For Btu conversion factors, see source]

Year	Production — Total[2]	Crude oil[3]	Natural gas	Coal	Nuclear power	Renewable energy — Total[2]	Renewable — Hydro-electric power	Renewable — Biofuel[4]	Renewable — Solar energy	Net trade, total[1]	Consumption — Total[2]	Petro-leum[5]	Natural gas[5]	Coal	Nuclear power	Renewable energy, total
1960	41.49	14.93	12.66	10.82	(Z)	2.93	1.61	1.32	.	−2.75	43.80	19.92	12.39	9.84	0.01	2.98
1965	49.34	16.52	15.78	13.06	0.04	3.40	2.06	1.34	.	−4.07	52.68	23.25	15.77	11.58	0.04	3.40
1970	63.50	20.40	21.67	14.61	0.24	4.07	2.63	1.43	.	−5.73	67.86	29.52	21.80	12.27	0.24	4.09
1971	62.72	20.03	22.28	13.19	0.41	4.27	2.82	1.43	.	−7.40	69.31	30.56	22.47	11.60	0.41	4.30
1972	63.92	20.04	22.21	14.09	0.58	4.40	2.86	1.50	.	−9.32	72.76	32.95	22.70	12.08	0.58	4.48
1973	63.58	19.49	22.19	13.99	0.91	4.43	2.86	1.53	.	−12.68	75.81	34.84	22.51	12.97	0.91	4.58
1974	62.37	18.58	21.21	14.07	1.27	4.77	3.18	1.54	.	−12.19	74.08	33.46	21.73	12.66	1.27	4.90
1975	61.36	17.73	19.64	14.99	1.90	4.72	3.16	1.50	.	−11.75	72.04	32.73	19.95	12.66	1.90	4.79
1976	61.60	17.26	19.48	15.65	2.11	4.77	2.98	1.71	.	−14.65	76.07	35.18	20.35	13.58	2.11	4.86
1977	62.05	17.45	19.57	15.76	2.70	4.25	2.33	1.84	.	−18.02	78.12	37.12	19.93	13.92	2.70	4.43
1978	63.14	18.43	19.49	14.91	3.02	5.04	2.94	2.04	.	−17.32	80.12	37.97	20.00	13.77	3.02	5.24
1979	65.95	18.10	20.08	17.54	2.78	5.16	2.93	2.15	.	−16.75	81.04	37.12	20.67	15.04	2.78	5.38
1980	67.24	18.25	19.91	18.60	2.74	5.49	2.90	2.48	.	−12.25	78.43	34.20	20.39	15.42	2.74	5.71
1981	67.01	18.15	19.70	18.38	3.01	5.47	2.76	2.59	.	−9.64	76.57	31.93	19.93	15.91	3.01	5.82
1982	66.57	18.31	18.32	18.64	3.13	5.98	3.27	2.62	.	−7.46	73.44	30.23	18.51	15.32	3.13	6.29
1983	64.11	18.39	16.59	17.25	3.20	6.48	3.53	2.83	.	−8.31	73.32	30.05	17.36	15.89	3.20	6.86
1984	68.83	18.85	18.01	19.72	3.55	6.43	3.39	2.88	.	−8.96	76.97	31.05	18.51	17.07	3.55	6.85
1985	67.72	18.99	16.98	19.33	4.15	6.03	2.97	2.86	.	−7.87	76.78	30.92	17.83	17.48	4.15	6.46
1986	67.18	18.38	16.54	19.51	4.47	6.13	3.07	2.84	.	−10.38	77.07	32.20	16.71	17.26	4.47	6.51
1987	67.76	17.68	17.14	20.14	4.91	5.69	2.64	2.82	.	−11.91	79.63	32.87	17.74	18.01	4.91	6.17
1988	69.03	17.28	17.60	20.74	5.66	5.49	2.33	2.94	.	−13.15	83.07	34.22	18.55	18.85	5.66	5.82
1989 [7]	69.46	16.12	17.85	21.35	5.68	6.32	2.86	3.05	0.06	−14.19	84.59	34.21	19.38	18.93	5.68	6.47
1990	70.85	15.57	18.36	22.46	6.16	6.16	3.05	2.67	0.06	−14.08	84.19	33.55	19.30	19.10	6.16	6.26
1991	67.51	15.70	18.23	21.59	6.58	6.15	3.02	2.68	0.07	−13.34	84.08	32.85	19.61	18.77	6.58	6.37
1992	70.06	15.22	18.38	21.63	6.61	5.90	2.62	2.83	0.07	−14.62	85.51	33.53	20.13	19.16	6.61	6.17
1993	68.37	14.49	18.58	20.25	6.52	6.15	2.89	2.78	0.07	−17.22	87.31	33.84	20.83	19.78	6.52	6.42
1994	70.83	14.10	19.35	22.11	6.84	6.08	2.69	2.91	0.07	−18.66	89.23	34.67	21.29	19.96	6.84	6.39
1995	71.29	13.89	19.10	22.03	7.18	6.68	3.21	3.04	0.07	−18.00	90.94	34.55	22.16	20.02	7.18	6.96
1996	72.58	13.72	19.38	22.68	7.17	7.15	3.59	3.10	0.08	−19.33	93.91	35.76	22.56	20.94	7.17	7.48
1997	72.53	13.66	19.39	23.21	6.68	7.14	3.72	2.98	0.07	−20.94	94.32	36.27	22.53	21.44	6.68	7.36
1998	72.55	13.24	19.29	23.72	7.16	6.78	3.35	2.99	0.07	−22.51	94.57	36.93	21.92	21.59	7.16	6.98
1999	72.52	12.54	19.30	23.33	7.73	7.18	3.23	3.51	0.08	−23.10	96.60	37.71	22.10	21.70	7.73	7.37

- Represents or rounds to zero. Z Less than 50 trillion. [1] Exports minus imports. [2] Includes types not shown separately. [3] Includes lease condensate. [4] Includes wood, wood waste, peat, wood liquors, railroad ties, pitch, wood sludge, municipal solid waste, agricultural waste, straw, tires, landfill gases, fish oils, and/or other waste. [5] Petroleum products supplied, including natural gas plant liquids and crude oil burned as fuel. [6] Includes supplemental gaseous fuels. [7] There is a discontinuity in this time series between 1989 and 1990 due to the expanded coverage of nonelectric utility use of renewable energy beginning in 1990.

Source: U.S. Energy Information Administration, Annual Energy Review and Internet site <http://www.eia.doe.gov/pub/pdf/multi.fuel/039499.pdf> (released July 2000).

No. 892. Energy Supply and Disposition by Type of Fuel—Estimates, 1998 and 1999, and Projections, 2005 to 2020

[Quadrillion Btu (73.10 represents 73,100,000,000,000,000) per year. Projections are "reference" or mid-level forecasts. See report for methodology and assumptions used in generating projections]

Type of fuel	1998	1999	Projections			
			2005	2010	2015	2020
Production, total.	73.10	73.35	77.16	79.85	83.10	86.30
Crude oil and lease condensate.	13.19	12.45	11.96	10.90	10.76	10.69
Natural gas plant liquids	2.49	2.62	3.03	3.33	3.73	4.10
Natural gas, dry	19.19	19.16	21.35	23.74	26.92	29.79
Coal	23.76	23.09	25.21	26.08	26.42	26.95
Nuclear power	7.19	7.79	7.90	7.69	6.82	6.13
Renewable energy.	6.62	6.58	7.13	7.82	8.12	8.31
Other	0.65	1.65	0.57	0.3	0.32	0.34
Imports, total	26.69	27.35	33.91	38.14	41.44	44.84
Crude oil [1]	18.90	18.96	23.13	25.15	25.94	26.44
Petroleum products [2]	3.99	4.14	4.81	6.49	8.46	10.69
Natural gas	3.22	3.63	4.91	5.61	6.17	6.58
Other imports [3]	0.58	0.62	1.06	0.89	0.88	0.94
Exports, total	4.09	3.62	3.64	3.67	3.72	3.95
Petroleum [4]	1.94	1.96	1.81	1.78	1.83	1.91
Natural gas	0.16	0.17	0.33	0.43	0.53	0.63
Coal	1.99	1.48	1.51	1.46	1.35	1.41
Consumption, total . [5]	94.84	96.14	107.03	114.14	120.75	127.03
Petroleum products [5]	37.16	38.03	41.41	44.41	47.50	50.59
Natural gas	21.96	21.95	25.88	28.75	32.39	35.57
Coal	21.61	21.43	24.15	25.15	25.68	26.20
Nuclear power	7.19	7.79	7.90	7.69	6.82	6.13
Renewable energy/other [6]	6.92	6.93	7.69	8.14	8.36	8.54
Net imports of petroleum.	20.95	21.12	26.13	29.86	32.57	35.22
Prices (1999 dollars per unit):						
World oil price (dol. per brl)	12.02	17.35	20.83	21.37	21.89	22.41
Gas wellhead price (dol. per mcf)	2.02	2.06	2.49	2.69	2.83	3.13
Coal minemouth price (dol. per ton)	18.02	16.98	14.68	13.83	13.38	12.70
Average electric price (cents per kWh)	6.8	6.7	6.2	5.9	5.9	6.0

[1] Includes imports of crude oil for the Strategic Petroleum Reserve.   [2] Includes imports of finished petroleum products, imports of unfinished oils, alcohols, ethers, and blending components.   [3] Includes coal, coal coke (net), and electricity (net).   [4] Includes crude oil and petroleum products.   [5] Includes natural gas plant liquids, crude oil consumed as a fuel, and nonpetroleum based liquids for blending, such as ethanol.   [6] Includes net electricity imports, methanol, and liquid hydrogen.
Source: U.S. Energy Information Administration, *Annual Energy Outlook, 2001*. See also <http://www.eia.doe.gov/olaf/aeo/pdf/0383(2001).pdf> (released December 2000).

No. 893. Energy Consumption by End-Use Sector: 1970 to 1999

[There exits a discontinuity in the series between 1989 and 1990 due to the expanded coverage of nonelectric utility use of renewable energy beginning 1990. Btu=British thermal units. For Btu conversion factors, see text, this section]

Year	Total consumption (quad. Btu)	Residential and commercial (quad. Btu)	Industrial and miscellaneous (quad. Btu)	Transportation (quad. Btu)	Percent of total		
					Residential and commercial	Industrial and miscellaneous	Transportation
1970	67.86	22.11	29.65	16.10	32.6	43.7	23.7
1973	75.81	24.50	32.69	18.61	32.3	43.1	24.5
1975	72.04	24.33	29.46	18.25	33.8	40.9	25.3
1976	76.07	25.51	31.46	19.10	33.5	41.4	25.1
1977	78.12	25.94	32.36	19.82	33.2	41.4	25.4
1978	80.12	26.72	32.79	20.61	33.3	40.9	25.7
1979	81.04	26.55	34.02	20.47	32.8	42.0	25.3
1980	78.43	25.53	32.21	19.69	32.6	41.1	25.1
1981	76.57	26.13	30.93	19.50	34.1	40.4	25.5
1982	73.44	26.59	27.78	19.07	36.2	37.8	26.0
1983	73.32	26.57	27.60	19.14	36.2	37.6	26.1
1984	76.97	27.42	29.75	19.81	35.6	38.7	25.7
1985	76.78	27.62	29.09	20.07	36.0	37.9	26.1
1986	77.06	27.75	28.50	20.82	36.0	37.0	27.0
1987	79.63	28.49	29.68	21.46	35.8	37.3	26.9
1988	83.07	29.83	30.92	22.31	35.9	37.2	26.9
1989	84.59	30.43	31.58	22.57	36.0	37.3	26.7
1990	84.19	29.48	32.15	22.54	35.0	38.2	26.8
1991	84.06	30.14	31.80	22.13	35.9	37.8	26.3
1992	85.51	30.03	33.01	22.47	35.1	38.6	26.3
1993	87.31	31.12	33.30	22.89	35.6	38.1	26.2
1994	89.23	31.37	34.35	23.52	35.2	38.5	26.4
1995	90.94	32.26	34.70	23.97	35.5	38.2	26.4
1996	93.91	33.67	35.71	24.52	35.9	38.0	26.1
1997	94.32	33.64	35.85	24.82	35.7	38.0	26.3
1998	94.57	33.68	35.54	25.36	35.6	37.6	26.8
1999	96.60	34.17	36.50	25.92	35.4	37.8	26.8

Source: U.S. Energy Information Administration, *Annual Energy Review*. See also <http://www.eia.doe.gov/pub/pdf/multi.fuel/038499.pdf> (released July 2000).

No. 894. Energy Consumption—End-Use Sector and Selected Source by State: 1999

[In trillions of Btu (95,682 represents 95,682,000,000,000,000), except as indicated]

State	Total [1]	Per capita[2] (mil. Btu)	End-use sector Resi-dential	End-use sector Com-mercial	End-use sector Indus-trial	End-use sector Trans-portation	Source Petro-leum	Source Natural gas (dry)	Source Coal	Source Hydro-electric power	Source Nuclear electric power
United States..	95,682	351	18,382	15,059	[3]35,917	26,325	37,960	22,295	20,498	3,449	7,736
Alabama	2,005	459	341	226	977	461	551	345	855	80	328
Alaska	695	1,122	48	63	386	198	253	420	11	9	-
Arizona	1,220	255	279	267	222	453	497	163	404	104	323
Arkansas	1,204	472	193	124	589	297	384	266	267	28	137
California	8,375	253	1,416	1,237	2,824	2,899	3,383	2,182	64	425	355
Colorado	1,156	285	261	255	273	366	426	318	355	17	-
Connecticut	839	256	245	197	162	235	440	135	-	14	135
Delaware	279	370	56	45	107	71	141	58	36	-	-
District of Columbia	170	327	34	106	4	27	34	33	-	-	-
Florida.	3,853	255	1,018	810	680	1,346	1,912	542	672	2	335
Georgia.	2,798	359	553	416	957	871	1,044	341	790	28	334
Hawaii.	241	204	23	25	71	122	214	3	3	1	-
Idaho	518	414	96	87	210	126	170	72	8	140	-
Illinois	3,883	320	897	722	1,273	991	1,340	1,058	837	2	868
Indiana	2,736	460	484	301	1,306	645	899	577	1,451	4	-
Iowa	1,122	391	223	159	463	278	419	236	416	10	39
Kansas	1,050	396	201	169	392	288	437	302	329	-	97
Kentucky	1,830	462	316	219	851	444	726	220	885	27	-
Louisiana	3,615	827	325	237	2,249	805	1,452	1,558	228	8	139
Maine	529	422	98	58	260	113	250	6	3	81	-
Maryland	1,378	267	359	337	277	405	584	201	304	15	141
Massachusetts . . .	1,569	254	412	325	391	441	639	356	13	15	48
Michigan	3,240	328	744	568	1,083	845	1,098	930	823	11	155
Minnesota	1,675	351	340	218	618	500	661	346	336	59	142
Mississippi	1,209	437	203	146	451	409	483	346	138	-	90
Missouri.	1,768	323	432	334	380	623	781	270	686	18	91
Montana	412	467	62	48	196	107	174	64	174	143	-
Nebraska	602	361	130	111	166	194	246	121	196	18	107
Nevada	615	340	122	97	198	198	221	157	180	29	-
New Hampshire . .	335	279	82	56	97	101	188	21	35	25	92
New Jersey	2,589	318	540	541	645	863	1,236	641	68	[4]-1	308
New Mexico	635	365	93	106	202	234	257	225	298	3	-
New York.	4,283	235	1,092	1,216	995	980	1,653	1,251	188	265	393
North Carolina . . .	2,447	320	563	440	754	691	937	229	708	40	399
North Dakota	366	577	54	43	186	82	123	59	412	28	-
Ohio	4,323	384	867	632	1,855	969	1,340	878	1,379	4	175
Oklahoma	1,378	410	259	198	518	403	500	543	334	32	-
Oregon	1,109	335	238	191	352	328	392	219	39	475	-
Pennsylvania	3,716	310	859	583	1,290	984	1,385	696	1,143	16	756
Rhode Island	261	264	66	52	77	66	99	86	(Z)	10	-
South Carolina . . .	1,493	384	288	210	618	376	467	163	403	7	540
South Dakota	239	326	53	39	62	84	115	36	46	71	-
Tennessee.	2,071	378	442	328	711	590	713	286	626	74	289
Texas	11,501	574	1,323	1,147	6,482	2,549	5,565	3,982	1,535	13	391
Utah	694	326	128	120	235	211	262	169	382	13	-
Vermont	165	278	43	29	40	53	85	8	2	61	43
Virginia	2,227	324	494	463	614	656	864	275	402	-6	301
Washington	2,241	389	436	332	856	617	878	277	96	988	65
West Virginia	735	407	142	101	311	182	220	147	977	10	-
Wisconsin	1,811	345	376	285	717	432	668	379	472	23	122
Wyoming	422	879	36	42	224	120	156	102	495	12	-

- Represents zero.   Z Less than 0.05 trillion Btu.   [1] Sources of energy includes geothermal, wood and waste, and net interstate sales of electricity, including losses, not shown separately.   [2] Based on estimated resident population as of July 1.   [3] Includes 57.7 trillion Btu of net imports of coal coke not allocated   [4] Minus sign (-) indicates when amount of energy expended exceeds amount of energy consumed.

Source: U.S. Energy Information Administration, *State Energy Data Report, 1999* annual. See also <http://eia.doe.gov/pub/state.data/pdf/sedr.pdf> (released May 2001).

Energy and Utilities   571

No. 895. Renewable Energy Consumption Estimates by Type: 1990 to 1999

[In quadrillion Btu. Renewable energy is obtained from sources that are essentially inexhaustible unlike fossil fuels of which there is a finite supply]

Source and sector	1990	1994	1995	1996	1997	1998	1999
Consumption, total	**6.26**	**6.39**	**6.96**	**7.45**	**7.37**	**6.99**	**7.37**
Conventional hydroelectric power	3.14	2.97	3.47	3.92	3.94	3.55	3.42
Geothermal energy...................	0.36	0.40	0.34	0.35	0.33	0.34	0.33
Biomass.............................	2.67	2.91	3.04	3.10	2.98	2.99	3.51
Solar energy	0.06	0.07	0.07	0.08	0.07	0.07	0.08
Wind energy	0.03	0.04	0.03	0.04	0.03	0.03	0.04
Residential and commercial	0.68	0.66	0.72	0.72	0.56	0.50	0.54
Biomass [1]	0.62	0.58	0.64	0.64	0.48	0.42	0.46
Geothermal energy [2]	0.01	0.01	0.01	0.01	0.01	0.02	0.02
Solar [3]	0.06	0.06	0.07	0.07	0.07	0.07	0.06
Industrial [4]	2.24	2.61	2.69	2.80	2.81	2.84	3.37
Biomass [5]	1.94	2.21	2.28	2.37	2.39	2.44	2.92
Geothermal energy [6]	0.16	0.21	0.21	0.22	0.20	0.21	0.28
Conventional hydroelectric power [7]	0.10	0.14	0.15	0.17	0.19	0.15	0.13
Solar energy	0.01	0.01	0.01	0.01	0.01	0.01	0.01
Wind energy.....................	0.03	0.04	0.03	0.04	0.03	0.03	0.04
Transportation:							
Biomass [8]	0.08	0.10	0.10	0.07	0.10	0.11	0.11
Electric utilities [9]	3.25	3.02	3.46	3.89	3.89	3.53	3.35
Biomass [5]	0.02	0.02	0.02	0.02	0.02	0.02	0.02
Geothermal energy [10]	0.19	0.17	0.12	0.12	0.12	0.11	0.04
Conventional hydroelectric power [7 11] ...	3.04	2.83	3.32	3.74	3.75	3.40	3.29
Solar and wind energy	(Z)	(Z)	(Z)	(Z)	(Z)	(Z)	(Z)

Z Less than 0.005 quadrillion Btu.   [1] Wood.   [2] Geothermal heat pump and direct use energy.   [3] The solar thermal component of 0.06 quadrillion Btu for residential and commercial use is calculated by presuming an overall efficiency of 50 percent for all three categories of solar thermal collectors, a 1,500-Btu per square foot average daily insolation, and the potential thermal energy production from the 219 million square feet of thermal collectors produced between 1980 and 1999.   [4] Generation of electricity by nonutility power producers is included in the industrial sector, not the electric utility sector. Covers facilities of 1 megawatt or greater capacity.   [5] Wood, wood waste, wood liquors, peat, railroad ties, wood sludge, spent sulfite liquors, agricultural waste, straw, tires, fish oils, tall oil, sludge waste, waste alcohol, municipal solid waste, landfill gases, and other waste.   [6] Geothermal electricity generation, heat pump, and direct use energy.   [7] Hydroelectricity generated by pumped storage is not included in renewable energy.   [8] Ethanol blended into motor gasoline.   [9] For Btu conversion rates, see source.   [10] Includes electricity from Mexico that are derived from geothermal energy.   [11] Includes electricity net imports from Canada that are derived from hydroelectric power.

Source: U.S. Energy Information Administration, *Renewable Energy Annual 2000*, Series DOE/EIA-0603 (2000).

No. 896. Energy Expenditures and Average Fuel Prices by Source and Sector: 1970 to 1997

[82,862 represents $82,862,000,000. For definition of Btu, see text, this section. End-use sector and electric utilities exclude expenditures and prices on energy sources such as hydropower, solar, wind, and geothermal. Also excludes expenditures for reported amounts of energy consumed by the energy industry for production, transportation, and processing operations]

Source and sector	1970	1973	1975	1980	1985	1990	1993	1994	1995	1996	1997
EXPENDITURES (mil. dol.)											
Total [1][2]	82,862	111,591	171,828	374,359	437,292	471,786	491,904	505,518	515,321	561,473	567,318
Natural gas...........	10,891	13,933	20,061	51,061	72,938	64,102	75,941	77,716	74,150	85,634	91,769
Petroleum products [2] ...	47,942	65,257	103,372	237,628	223,591	235,224	222,936	229,804	236,937	268,071	266,595
Motor gasoline	31,596	39,667	59,446	124,408	118,043	126,454	126,401	129,897	136,475	148,230	149,549
Coal.................	4,594	6,251	13,047	22,648	29,723	28,372	27,763	27,186	26,861	27,368	27,522
Electricity sales	23,345	33,780	50,680	98,095	149,233	176,737	196,579	200,883	205,932	211,011	213,645
Residential sector.....	20,151	27,078	36,988	69,523	99,009	110,057	125,019	126,963	128,423	137,628	138,691
Commercial sector.....	10,654	15,107	22,839	46,888	70,267	78,828	86,474	89,409	91,587	95,798	100,209
Industrial sector	16,678	23,502	41,068	94,268	106,835	102,336	105,563	109,112	107,732	120,005	119,786
Transportation sector [2] ..	35,379	45,904	70,933	163,680	161,182	180,565	174,847	180,034	187,578	208,041	208,632
Motor gasoline	30,525	38,598	57,992	121,809	115,199	123,742	124,549	127,942	134,471	145,993	147,046
Electric utilities........	-4,316	7,817	-16,396	-37,435	-42,558	-38,276	-36,692	-36,166	-34,810	-36,614	-37,815
AVERAGE FUEL PRICES (dol. per mil. Btu)											
All sectors	1.65	2.02	3.33	6.89	8.36	8.29	8.27	8.31	8.29	8.77	8.82
Residential sector.....	2.11	2.73	3.81	7.44	10.93	11.91	12.29	12.63	12.57	12.68	13.24
Commercial sector.....	1.96	2.56	4.09	7.88	11.71	12.02	12.68	12.87	12.75	12.88	13.15
Industrial sector.......	0.98	1.09	2.12	5.15	6.27	5.25	4.99	4.92	4.74	5.49	5.20
Transportation sector ...	2.31	2.57	4.02	8.61	8.26	8.27	7.87	7.88	8.04	8.72	8.65
Electric utilities........	0.32	0.46	0.96	1.75	1.85	1.46	1.35	1.30	1.23	1.28	1.30

[1] Includes electricity sales; excludes electricity generation.   [2] Includes sources or fuel types not shown separately.

Source: U.S. Energy Information Administration, *State Energy Price and Expenditure Report*, annual. See also <http://tonto.eia.doe.gov/FTPROOT/multifuel/037697.pdf> (released July 2000).

No. 897. Energy Expenditures—End-Use Sector and Selected Source by State: 1997

[In millions of dollars ($567,318 represents $567,318,000,000). End-use sector and electric utilities exclude expenditures on energy sources such as hydropower, solar, wind, and geothermal. Also excludes expenditures for reported amounts of energy consumed by the energy industry for production, transportation, and processing operations]

State		End-use sector				Source			
	Total [1]	Resi-dential	Com-mercial	Industrial	Trans-portation	Petroleum products	Natural gas	Coal	Electricity sales
U.S.	567,318	138,691	100,209	119,786	208,632	266,595	91,769	27,522	213,645
AL.	9,816	2,234	1,342	2,557	3,682	4,312	1,298	1,345	3,884
AK.	2,180	334	344	235	1,266	1,521	252	26	485
AZ.	8,574	2,125	1,712	1,069	3,669	4,005	574	534	4,019
AR.	5,812	1,363	728	1,400	2,322	2,625	981	406	2,216
CA.	55,187	11,970	10,748	8,617	23,854	25,651	8,879	87	21,568
CO	6,881	1,563	1,251	1,013	3,054	3,522	1,097	362	2,244
CT.	7,248	2,387	1,699	797	2,366	3,605	932	54	2,991
DE.	1,692	463	293	351	585	822	232	75	704
DC	1,334	288	763	17	266	306	281	2	747
FL.	25,117	7,515	4,916	2,265	10,421	12,121	1,928	1,206	12,588
GA	15,642	3,906	2,702	3,006	6,028	7,018	1,995	1,234	6,484
HI	2,288	417	415	482	974	1,338	42	6	1,152
ID	2,550	466	338	608	1,139	1,471	226	13	821
IL	25,089	7,065	4,815	5,504	7,706	9,879	5,382	1,492	9,688
IN	14,106	3,178	1,691	4,145	5,092	6,257	2,743	1,782	4,668
IA	6,649	1,650	915	1,701	2,383	3,166	1,220	402	2,157
KS.	5,850	1,344	1,029	1,374	2,104	2,802	1,083	318	2,025
KY.	9,045	1,780	1,074	2,509	3,682	4,755	1,036	1,107	3,067
LA.	15,120	2,237	1,480	6,641	4,762	7,643	3,751	333	4,443
ME	3,158	915	487	654	1,103	1,923	44	12	1,137
MD	9,583	2,851	2,091	1,086	3,554	4,471	1,220	432	3,928
MA	13,087	3,875	3,223	1,790	4,199	5,871	2,622	211	4,993
MI	19,758	5,033	3,726	4,316	6,684	8,499	4,264	1,102	6,806
MN	9,869	2,310	1,252	2,311	3,996	5,176	1,537	392	3,090
MS	5,963	1,334	867	1,276	2,486	3,092	749	205	2,326
MO	11,533	2,996	1,940	1,670	4,927	5,884	1,616	635	4,002
MT.	2,171	403	290	490	989	1,290	258	113	611
NE.	3,814	831	631	717	1,635	1,999	612	120	1,196
NV.	3,637	727	504	792	1,614	1,812	590	232	1,338
NH	2,525	818	512	324	872	1,328	146	73	1,059
NJ	18,764	5,075	4,303	2,925	6,461	8,382	3,532	132	6,925
NM	3,428	658	653	493	1,623	1,824	512	385	1,173
NY.	34,089	11,118	10,342	3,805	8,825	12,117	7,913	463	14,682
NC	15,823	4,277	2,571	3,117	5,858	7,332	1,275	1,067	7,068
ND	1,699	332	226	494	647	894	163	411	466
OH	25,556	6,604	4,407	6,288	8,257	10,321	5,139	1,898	9,831
OK.	7,333	1,661	1,068	1,651	2,954	3,390	1,884	349	2,398
OR.	6,058	1,232	875	1,114	2,838	3,200	610	21	2,197
PA.	25,810	7,598	4,428	5,465	8,318	10,656	4,314	2,113	10,158
RI	2,044	669	443	268	664	941	473	(Z)	716
SC.	8,177	1,993	1,167	2,133	2,885	3,545	741	539	3,771
SD.	1,629	398	231	277	723	981	158	42	483
TN.	11,604	2,621	1,938	2,380	4,664	5,507	1,340	789	4,587
TX.	55,070	9,509	6,834	21,307	17,420	30,027	10,365	1,900	17,386
UT.	3,708	707	550	602	1,849	2,126	529	374	1,042
VT.	1,368	429	239	187	514	794	40	(Z)	525
VA.	13,451	3,710	2,500	1,784	5,457	6,544	1,448	525	5,349
WA	10,330	2,086	1,446	1,647	5,151	5,806	909	136	3,531
WV	4,002	881	520	1,155	1,446	2,062	568	1,119	1,308
WI	10,156	2,553	1,499	2,255	3,849	4,908	2,014	562	3,113
WY	1,873	206	193	656	818	1,076	250	389	499

Z Less than $500,000.   [1] Includes sources not shown separately. Total expenditures are the sum of purchases for each source (including electricity sales) less electric utility purchases of fuel.

Source: U.S. Energy Information Administration, *State Energy Price and Expenditure Report, 1997,* Series DOE/EIA-0376(97). See also <http://www.eia.doe.gov/pub/state.prices/pdf/seper.pdf> (released July 2000).

Energy and Utilities   573

Residential Energy Consumption, Expenditures, and Average Price: 1980 to 1997

[For period April to March for 1980-1985; January to December for 1987 to 1997. Excludes Alaska and Hawaii in 1980. Covers occupied units only. Excludes household usage of gasoline for transportation and the use of wood or coal. Based on Residential Energy Consumption Survey; see source. For composition of regions, see inside front cover. Btu=British thermal unit; see text, this section]

Type of fuel	Unit	1980	1983	1985	1987	1990	1997
CONSUMPTION							
Total	Quad. Btu	9.74	8.62	9.04	9.13	9.22	10.25
Avg. per household	Mil. Btu	126	103	105	101	98	102
Natural gas	Quad. Btu	5.31	4.77	4.98	4.83	4.86	5.28
Electricity	Quad. Btu	2.42	2.42	2.48	2.76	3.03	3.54
Fuel oil, kerosene	Quad. Btu	1.71	1.14	1.26	1.22	1.04	1.07
Liquid petroleum gas	Quad. Btu	0.31	0.29	0.31	0.32	0.28	0.36
EXPENDITURES							
Total	Bil. dol.	63.2	87.8	97.0	97.7	110.2	135.79
Avg. per household	Dollars	(NA)	(NA)	(NA)	1,080	1,172	1,338
Natural gas	Bil. dol.	17.8	27.1	29.8	26.1	27.3	35.8
Electricity	Bil. dol.	32.6	48.4	54.5	61.6	71.5	88.3
Fuel oil, kerosene	Bil. dol.	10.7	9.6	9.6	7.2	8.3	7.6
Liquid petroleum gas	Bil. dol.	2.1	2.7	3.1	2.8	3.1	4.0
AVERAGE PRICE							
Total	Dol./mil. Btu	6.49	10.18	10.73	10.71	12.00	13.25
Natural gas	Dol./mil. Btu	3.36	5.67	5.97	5.41	5.60	6.78
Electricity	Dol./mil. Btu	13.46	19.98	21.94	22.34	23.60	24.97
Fuel oil, kerosene	Dol./mil. Btu	6.29	8.42	7.64	5.89	7.90	15.56
Liquid petroleum gas	Dol./mil. Btu	6.71	9.42	9.91	8.91	11.20	11.23

NA Not available.
Source: U.S. Energy Information Administration, *Residential Energy Consumption Survey: Consumption and Expenditures,* annual through 1983 beginning 1985, triennial. For 1987 to 1997, *Household Energy Consumption and Expenditures,* 1997.

No. 899. Manufacturing Energy Consumption for All Purposes by Type of Fuel and Major Industry Group: 1998

[In trillions of Btu (23,783 represents 23,783,000,000,000). Estimates represented consumption of energy for all purposes (First Use) represents unduplicated demand for energy by manufacturers. "First Use" is all energy produced offsite, all energy produced onsite, either directly from captive minesand wells or as byproducts from nonenergy materials (such as sawdust from furniture production, hydrogen from electrolysis of brine, nut shells from peanut processing). Based on the Manufacturing Energy Consumption Survey and subject to sampling variability]

Industry	NAICS [1] code	Total	Net electricity [2]	Residual fuel oil	Distillate fuel oil [3]	Natural gas [4]	LPG and NGL [5]	Coal	Coke and breeze	Other [6]
All industries, total	(X)	23,783	3,035	406	142	7,426	1,882	1,814	461	8,967
Food and kindred products	311	1,044	213	14	16	568	5	129	2	97
Beverage and tobacco products	312	108	24	2	2	45	1	29	-	4
Textile mills	313	256	102	12	4	103	2	20	-	14
Textile product mills	314	50	18	3	(S)	25	(Z)	3	-	(Z)
Apparel	315	48	18	2	1	23	1	1	-	4
Leather and allied products	316	8	3	(Z)	(Z)	4	(Z)	-	-	(Z)
Wood products	321	509	72	1	13	73	4	2	-	343
Paper	322	2,733	240	151	9	586	5	277	-	1,465
Printing and related support	323	98	51	(Z)	(Z)	44	1	(Z)	-	2
Petroleum and coal products	324	7,320	126	72	28	1,007	39	12	-	6,082
Petroleum refineries	324110	7,130	118	70	4	948	33	(Z)	-	5,957
Chemicals	325	6,064	577	98	10	2,709	1,796	300	7	677
Petrochemicals	325110	723	8	-	(Z)	(D)	222	(D)	-	(D)
Other basic organic chemicals	325199	1,740	73	3	(D)	782	639	(D)	-	201
Plastics materials and resins	325211	1,067	66	2	1	259	675	17	(Z)	60
Nitrogenous fertilizers	325311	592	13	-	(Z)	572	(Z)	-	-	6
Plastics and rubber products	326	328	183	5	1	126	5	3	-	5
Nonmetallic mineral products	327	979	134	4	17	444	3	284	11	82
Primary metals	331	2,560	545	30	9	933	3	715	437	82
Iron and steel mills	331111	1,584	158	29	5	494	(Z)	680	388	22
Alumina and aluminum	3313	490	246	(Z)	1	189	1	2	2	49
Primary aluminum	331312	254	196	(Z)	(Z)	(D)	(Z)	(D)	-	41
Fabricated metal products	332	445	176	2	6	241	5	3	3	10
Machinery	333	217	96	1	3	99	3	6	-	7
Computer and electronic products	334	205	137	1	1	64	(Z)	(Z)	-	1
Electrical equipment, appliances, and component	335	143	55	1	1	53	2	1	(Z)	30
Transportation equipment	336	492	195	5	15	212	4	29	1	31
Furniture and related products	337	88	30	(Z)	1	27	1	2	-	28
Miscellaneous	339	89	40	1	2	40	1	(Z)	-	4

- Represents or rounds to zero.   D Withheld to avoid disclosing data for individual establishments.   S Withheld because Relative Standard Error is greater than 50 percent.   X Not applicable.   Z Less than 0.5 trillion Btu.   [1] North American Industrial Classification System; see text, Section 15, Business Enterprise.   [2] Net electricity is obtained by aggregating purchases, transfers in, and generation from noncombustible renewable resources minus quantities sold and transferred out. Excludes electricity inputs from onsite cogeneration or generation from combustible fuels because that energy has already been included as generating fuel (for example, coal).   [3] Includes Nos.1, 2, and 4 fuel oils and Nos. 1, 2, and 4 diesel fuels.   [4] Includes natural gas obtained from utilities, transmission pipelines, and any other supplier such as brokers and producers.   [5] Liquid petroleum gas and natural gas liquids.   [6] Includes net steam, and other energy that respondents indicated was used to produce heat and power or as feedstock/raw material inputs.
Source: U.S. Energy Information Administration, <http://www.eia.doe.gov/emeu/mecs/mecs98/datatables/contents.html> (accessed 22 January 2001).

No. 900. Commercial Buildings—Energy Consumption and Expenditures: 1995

[Covers buildings using one or more major fuel. Excludes industrial buildings, predominantly residential buildings, and buildings of less than 1,000 sq. ft. Based on a sample survey of building representatives and energy suppliers; therefore, subject to sampling variability. For characteristics of commercial buildings, see tables in Section 20, Construction and Housing. For composition of regions, see inside front cover]

Building characteristic	All buildings using any major fuel		Consumption (tril. Btu)			Expenditures (mil. dol.)		
	Number (1,000)	Square feet (mil.)	Major fuel, total [1]	Electricity	Natural gas	Major fuel, total [1]	Electricity	Natural gas
All buildings	**4,579**	**58,772**	**5,321**	**2,608**	**1,946**	**69,918**	**56,621**	**9,018**
Region:								
Northeast	725	11,883	1,035	436	297	16,479	13,059	1,739
Midwest	1,139	14,322	1,497	558	750	15,076	10,946	2,947
South	1,750	20,830	1,684	1,027	528	22,211	19,009	2,560
West	964	11,736	1,106	587	371	16,152	13,607	1,772
Year constructed:								
1919 or before	353	3,673	292	99	135	3,310	2,290	655
1920 to 1945	562	6,710	508	173	210	5,665	4,012	966
1946 to 1959	867	9,298	826	325	391	9,813	7,395	1,796
1960 to 1969	718	10,858	1,024	472	375	13,135	10,405	1,750
1970 to 1979	813	11,333	1,125	615	393	15,366	13,005	1,695
1980 to 1989	846	12,252	1,059	648	288	15,895	13,844	1,397
1990 to 1992	218	2,590	297	163	100	4,011	3,318	510
1993 to 1995	202	2,059	190	113	54	2,722	2,353	249
Principal activity within building:								
Assembly [2]	682	8,011	677	252	232	7,876	5,688	1,145
Education	309	7,740	614	221	245	7,129	5,168	1,117
Food sales	137	642	137	119	18	2,634	2,532	97
Food service	285	1,353	332	166	158	4,817	3,931	851
Health care	105	2,333	561	211	258	5,261	3,901	838
Lodging	158	3,618	461	187	213	5,114	3,838	966
Mercantile/services	1,289	12,728	973	508	395	14,025	11,655	1,979
Office	705	10,478	1,019	676	239	15,849	14,020	1,150
Warehouse and storage	580	8,481	325	176	106	4,709	3,934	559
Other	67	1,004	173	75	55	1,865	1,473	197
Vacant	261	2,384	51	18	26	638	481	119
Square footage:								
1,001 to 5,000	2,399	6,338	708	380	264	11,577	9,696	1,483
5,001 to 10,000	1,035	7,530	624	238	272	8,063	6,055	1,439
10,001 to 25,000	745	11,617	824	384	356	11,099	8,911	1,775
25,001 to 50,000	213	7,676	630	316	231	8,676	7,005	1,159
50,001 to 100,000	115	7,968	698	363	243	8,824	7,194	1,091
100,001 to 200,000	48	6,776	687	337	244	7,859	6,283	958
200,001 to 500,000	19	5,553	636	307	211	7,291	5,908	729
500,001 and over	6	5,313	514	282	125	6,530	5,568	385

[1] Includes fuel oil, propane, and purchased steam not shown separately.   [2] Includes public assembly, public order and safety, and religious worship.

Source: U.S. Energy Information Administration, *Commercial Buildings Energy Consumption and Expenditures, 1995*. New data for 1999 are scheduled to be available in the fall of 2001.

No. 901. Fossil Fuel Prices in Current and Constant (1996) Dollars: 1980 to 1999

[In cents per million British thermal units (Btu), except as indicated. All fuel prices taken as close to the point of production as possible. See text, this section, for explanation of Btu conversions from mineral fuels]

Fuel	1980	1985	1990	1992	1993	1994	1995	1996	1997	1998	1999
CURRENT DOLLARS											
Composite [1]	2.04	2.51	1.84	1.66	1.67	1.53	1.47	1.82	1.81	1.41	1.63
Crude oil	3.72	4.15	3.45	2.76	2.46	2.27	2.52	3.18	2.97	1.87	2.68
Natural gas . . . . [2]	1.45	2.26	1.55	1.57	1.84	1.67	1.40	1.96	2.10	1.75	1.86
Bituminous coal [2]	1.10	1.15	1.00	0.97	0.93	0.91	0.88	0.87	0.85	0.83	0.83
CONSTANT (1996) DOLLARS											
Composite [1]	3.58	3.41	2.13	1.80	1.78	1.59	1.50	1.82	1.77	1.36	1.55
Crude oil	6.52	5.64	3.99	3.00	2.61	2.37	2.57	3.18	2.92	1.82	2.56
Natural gas	2.54	3.06	1.79	1.71	1.96	1.74	1.43	1.96	2.06	1.70	1.78
Bituminous coal [2]	1.93	1.56	1.15	1.06	0.99	0.94	0.90	0.87	0.84	0.81	0.80

[1] Weighted by relative importance of individual fuels in total fuels production.   [2] Includes subbituminous and lignite.

Source: U.S. Energy Information Administration, *Annual Energy Review*. See also <http://www.eia.doe.gov/pub/pdf/multi.fuel/038499.pdf> (released July 2000).

No. 902. Energy Imports and Exports by Type of Fuel: 1980 to 1999

[In quadrillion of Btu. For definition of Btu, see text, this section]

Type of fuel	1980	1985	1990	1992	1993	1994	1995	1996	1997	1998	1999
Net imports:[1]											
Coal	-4.60	-4.39	-4.42	-4.11	-2.83	-2.58	-3.24	-3.41	-3.13	-2.75	-1.31
Natural gas (dry)	3.98	2.79	2.71	3.47	4.41	4.50	3.86	5.33	6.02	5.82	3.48
Petroleum	10.42	12.57	12.67	7.72	7.59	7.78	6.39	11.01	9.37	7.33	20.57
Other [2]	-0.08	-0.03	0.02	0.10	0.11	0.23	0.27	0.18	0.20	0.25	0.36
Imports:											
Coal	0.03	0.07	0.09	0.13	0.22	0.23	0.25	0.24	0.26	0.28	0.23
Natural gas (dry)	4.21	3.05	2.97	3.96	4.77	4.90	4.23	5.79	6.50	6.33	3.64
Petroleum	12.54	17.47	16.90	11.98	11.74	11.14	9.95	15.27	16.93	13.01	22.53
Other [2]	0.05	0.04	0.07	0.14	0.12	0.13	0.16	0.11	0.12	0.14	0.52
Exports:											
Coal	4.63	4.47	4.51	4.24	3.09	2.85	3.57	3.69	3.39	3.00	1.53
Natural gas (dry)	0.23	0.26	0.27	0.49	0.36	0.40	0.37	0.46	0.47	0.42	0.16
Petroleum	2.12	4.90	4.23	4.27	4.15	3.36	3.56	4.25	7.55	5.67	1.96
Other [2]	0.13	0.08	0.05	0.04	0.06	0.04	0.05	0.06	0.05	0.04	0.17

[1] Net imports equals imports minus exports. Minus sign (-) denotes an excess of exports over imports. [2] Coal coke and small amounts of electricity transmitted across U.S. borders with Canada and Mexico.

Source: U.S. Energy Information Administration, *Annual Energy Review*. See also <http://www.eia.doe.gov/pub/pdf/multi.fuel/038499.pdf> (released July 2000).

No. 903. U.S. Foreign Trade in Selected Mineral Fuels: 1980 to 1998

[Minus sign (-) indicates an excess of imports over exports]

Mineral fuel	Unit	1980	1985	1990	1993	1994	1995	1996	1997	1998
Natural gas:										
Imports	Bil. cu. ft.	985	950	1,532	2,350	2,624	2,841	2,937	2,994	3,152
Exports	Bil. cu. ft.	49	55	86	140	162	154	153	157	159
Net trade	Bil. cu. ft.	-936	-894	-1,446	-2,210	-2,462	-2,687	-2,784	-2,837	-2,993
Crude oil:										
Imports [1]	Mil. bbl.	1,926	1,168	2,151	2,477	2,578	2,639	2,740	3,002	3,178
Exports	Mil. bbl.	105	75	40	36	36	35	40	39	40
Net trade	Mil. bbl.	-1,821	-1,093	-2,112	-2,441	-2,542	-2,604	-2,700	-2,963	-3,138
Petroleum products:										
Imports	Mil. bbl.	603	681	775	669	706	586	719	707	731
Exports	Mil. bbl.	94	211	273	330	308	312	318	318	327
Net trade	Mil. bbl.	-509	-470	-502	-339	-398	-274	-402	-389	-404
Coal:										
Imports	1,000 sh. tons.	1,194	1,952	2,699	7,309	8,870	9,473	8,115	7,487	8,724
Exports	1,000 sh. tons.	91,742	92,680	105,804	74,519	71,359	88,547	90,473	83,545	78,048
Net trade	1,000 sh. tons.	90,548	90,728	103,105	67,210	62,489	79,074	82,358	76,058	69,324

[1] Beginning 1980, includes strategic petroleum reserve imports.

Source: U.S. Energy Information Administration, *Annual Energy Review*.

No. 904. Crude Oil Imports Into the United States by Country of Origin: 1980 to 2000

[In millions of barrels (1,921 represents 1,921,000,000). Barrels contain 42 gallons]

Country of origin	1980	1985	1990	1993	1994	1995	1996	1997	1998	1999	2000
Total imports	**1,921**	**1,168**	**2,151**	**2,477**	**2,578**	**2,639**	**2,748**	**3,002**	**3,178**	**3,187**	**3,320**
OPEC, [1] total	1,410	479	1,283	1,317	1,307	1,303	1,258	1,378	1,522	1,543	1,664
Algeria	166	31	23	9	8	10	3	2	4	9	-
Iraq	10	17	188	-	-	-	-	33	123	265	227
Kuwait [2]	10	1	29	126	112	78	86	92	109	90	96
Qatar	8	-	1	-	-	-	-	-	1	-	-
Saudi Arabia [2]	456	48	436	468	473	460	457	472	512	506	558
United Arab Emirates . .	63	13	3	4	4	2	1	-	1	-	1
Indonesia	115	107	36	24	34	23	16	19	18	25	13
Nigeria	307	102	286	264	228	227	218	252	251	227	320
Venezuela	57	112	243	369	377	420	477	509	503	420	448
Non-OPEC [3], total	511	689	869	1,160	1,271	1,336	1,490	1,624	1,656	1,643	1,657
Canada	73	171	235	329	359	380	394	437	462	430	493
Ecuador [4]	6	20	14	28	33	35	35	42	36	42	46
Gabon [5]	9	19	23	55	71	84	67	84	76	61	52
Malaysia	(NA)	(NA)	(NA)	4	2	2	2	3	9	8	11
Mexico	185	261	251	315	343	375	442	496	482	458	480
Norway	53	11	35	50	69	94	107	105	81	96	111
Trinidad and Tobago . .	42	36	28	20	23	23	21	20	19	15	20
United Kingdom	63	101	57	114	145	124	79	62	59	104	106

- Represents zero.   NA Not available.   [1] OPEC (Organization of Petroleum Exporting Countries) includes the Persian Gulf nations shown below, except Bahrain, which is not a member of OPEC, and also includes nations shown under "Other OPEC."   [2] Imports from the Neutral Zone between Kuwait and Saudi Arabia are included in Saudi Arabia.   [3] Includes petroleum imported into the United States indirectly from member of OPEC, primarily from Caribbean and West European areas, as petroleum products that were refined from crude oil produced by OPEC.   [4] Ecuador withdrew from OPEC on Dec. 31, 1992; therefore, it is included under OPEC for the period 1980 to 1992.   [5] Gabon withdrew from OPEC on Dec. 31, 1994; therefore, it is included under OPEC for the period 1980 to 1994.

Source: U.S. Energy Information Administration, *Petroleum Supply Annual*, Vol. I.

No. 905. Crude Oil and Refined Products—Summary: 1973 to 2000

[Barrels of 42 gallons. Data are averages]

Year	Crude oil (1,000 bbl. per day)					Refined oil products (1,000 bbl. per day)			Total oil imports [2] (1,000 bbl. per day)	Crude oil stocks [3] (mil. bbl.)	
	Input to refineries	Domestic production	Imports			Domestic demand	Imports	Exports		Total	Strategic reserve
			Total [1]	Strategic reserve	Exports						
1973......	12,431	9,208	3,244	(X)	2	17,308	3,012	229	6,256	242	(X)
1975......	12,442	8,375	4,105	(X)	6	16,322	1,951	204	6,056	271	(X)
1976......	13,416	8,132	5,287	(X)	8	17,461	2,026	215	7,313	285	(X)
1980......	13,481	8,597	5,263	44	287	17,056	1,646	258	6,909	466	108
1985......	12,002	8,971	3,201	118	204	15,726	1,866	577	5,067	814	493
1990......	13,409	7,355	5,894	27	109	16,988	2,123	748	8,018	908	586
1991......	13,301	7,417	5,782	-	116	16,714	1,844	885	7,627	893	569
1992......	13,411	7,171	6,083	10	89	17,033	1,805	861	7,888	893	575
1993......	13,613	6,847	6,787	15	98	17,237	1,833	904	8,620	922	587
1994......	13,866	6,662	7,063	12	99	17,718	1,933	843	8,996	929	592
1995......	13,973	6,560	7,230	-	95	17,725	1,605	855	8,835	895	592
1996......	14,195	6,465	7,508	-	110	18,309	1,971	871	9,478	850	566
1997......	14,662	6,452	8,225	-	108	18,620	1,936	896	10,162	868	563
1998......	14,889	6,252	8,706	-	110	18,917	2,002	835	10,708	895	571
1999......	14,804	5,881	8,731	6	118	19,519	2,122	822	10,852	852	567
2000......	15,077	5,839	8,914	8	58	19,484	2,146	974	11,061	829	541

- Represents zero.   X Not applicable.   [1] Includes Strategic Petroleum Reserve.   [2] Crude oil (including Strategic Petroleum Reserve imports) plus refined products.   [3] End of year.
Source: U.S. Energy Information Administration, *Monthly Energy Review*, January 2001 issue.

No. 906. Petroleum and Coal Products Corporations—Sales, Net Profit, and Profit Per Dollar of Sales: 1990 to 2000

[Represents SIC group 29. Profit rates are averages of quarterly figures at annual rates. Beginning 1990, excludes estimates for corporations with less than $250,000 in assets]

Item	Unit	1990	1991	1992	1993	1994	1995	1996	1997	1998	1999	2000
Sales............	Bil. dol..	318.5	282.2	278.0	266.1	268.2	283.1	323.5	320.0	250.4	277.0	416.3
Net profit:												
Before income taxes	Bil. dol..	23.1	12.1	2.0	14.9	17.2	16.5	32.6	36.8	9.7	20.3	57.2
After income taxes	Bil. dol..	17.8	10.8	3.1	13.0	14.9	13.9	26.6	29.4	8.3	17.2	43.0
Depreciation [1]...........	Bil. dol..	18.7	18.0	18.3	17.4	17.1	16.7	15.9	15.6	14.7	13.5	14.5
Profits per dollar of sales:												
Before income taxes	Cents ..	7.3	4.3	0.4	5.6	6.3	5.8	10.1	11.5	3.5	7.1	13.7
After income taxes	Cents ..	5.6	3.8	0.9	4.9	5.5	4.9	8.2	9.2	3.1	6.0	10.3
Profits on stockholders' equity:												
Before income taxes	Percent .	16.4	8.6	1.6	11.8	13.2	12.6	23.2	23.5	6.0	13.0	30.3
After income taxes	Percent .	12.7	7.6	2.5	10.2	11.4	10.6	18.9	18.9	5.2	11.0	22.8

[1] Includes depletion and accelerated amortization of emergency facilities.
Source: U.S. Census Bureau, *Quarterly Financial Report for Manufacturing, Mining and Trade Corporations*.

No. 907. Major Petroleum Companies—Financial Data Summary: 1973 to 1999

[Data represent a composite of approximately 42 major worldwide petroleum companies aggregated on a consolidated total company basis]

Item	1973	1975	1980	1985	1990	1994	1995	1996	1997	1998	1999
FINANCIAL DATA (bil. dol.)											
Net income.............	11.8	11.6	32.9	19.4	26.8	20.3	24.3	39.7	40.0	14.5	35.0
Depreciation, depletion, etc	10.5	11.3	32.5	53.0	38.7	38.9	43.1	44.4	46.0	61.0	45.9
Cash flow [1]	22.3	22.8	65.4	72.4	65.5	59.2	67.4	84.1	86.0	75.5	80.9
Dividends paid.........	4.0	4.7	9.3	12.0	15.9	16.4	17.6	18.9	20.1	20.9	23.2
Net internal funds available for investment or debt repayment [2]	18.3	18.1	56.1	60.4	49.6	42.8	49.8	65.2	65.9	54.6	57.7
Capital and exploratory expenditures.....	16.3	26.9	62.1	58.3	59.6	51.5	59.8	59.3	75.3	83.9	66.2
Long-term capitalization..............	102.9	121.1	211.4	272.1	300.0	299.0	304.3	336.6	372.5	382.0	402.3
Long-term debt..................	22.5	28.9	49.8	93.5	90.4	89.1	85.4	80.8	86.1	103.9	106.8
Preferred stock.................	0.4	0.4	2.0	3.3	5.2	5.4	5.7	5.8	5.1	3.9	3.9
Common stock and retained earnings [3]..	80.0	91.9	159.6	175.3	204.4	204.5	213.2	250.0	281.3	274.2	291.6
Excess of expenditures over cash income [4]...............	-2.0	8.9	6.0	-2.1	10.0	8.7	10.0	-5.9	9.4	29.3	8.5
RATIOS [5] (percent)											
Long-term debt to long-term capitalization	22.0	23.8	23.6	34.4	30.1	29.8	28.1	24.0	23.1	27.2	26.5
Net income to total average capital	12.0	10.0	17.0	7.0	9.1	6.8	8.1	12.4	11.3	3.8	8.9
Net income to average common equity....	15.6	13.1	22.5	10.8	13.5	10.1	11.6	17.1	15.1	5.2	12.4

[1] Generally represents internally-generated funds from operations. Sum of net income and noncash charges such as depreciation, depletion, and amortization.   [2] Cash flow minus dividends paid.   [3] Includes common stock, capital surplus, and earned surplus accounts after adjustments.   [4] Capital and exploratory expenditures plus dividends paid minus cash flow.   [5] Represents approximate year-to-year comparisons because of changes in the makeup of the group due to mergers and other corporate changes.
Source: Carl H. Pforzheimer & Co., New York, NY, *Comparative Oil Company Statements*, annual.

Energy and Utilities   **577**

No. 908. Electric Power Industry—Sales, Prices, Net Generation, Net Summer Capability, and Consumption of Fuels: 1990 to 1999

[Net generation for calendar years; capability as of December 31]

Item	Unit	1990	1995	1996	1997	1998	1999
ELECTRIC POWER INDUSTRY							
Consumption, total	Bil. kWh	2,816.7	3,162.4	3,246.7	3,288.7	3,399.6	(NA)
Net generation, total	Bil. kWh.	3,024.9	3,357.8	3,447.0	3,494.2	3,617.9	3,677.7
Electric utilities	Bil. kWh.	2,808.2	2,994.5	3,077.4	3,122.5	3,212.2	3,182.9
Nonutilities	Bil. kWh.	216.7	363.3	369.6	371.7	405.7	494.8
Electricity imports	Bil. kWh.	18.4	42.9	43.5	43.0	39.5	42.9
Electricity exports	Bil. kWh.	16.1	3.6	3.3	9.0	13.2	14.0
Electricity losses and unaccounted for	Bil. kWh.	210.4	234.6	240.5	239.5	244.5	(NA)
Electric utility retail sales of electricity	Bil. kWh.	2,712.6	3,013.3	3,097.8	3,139.8	3,239.8	3,265.4
Direct use of electricity at nonutilities	Bil. kWh.	84.4	133.6	134.6	130.8	134.0	(NA)
Nonutility sales of electricity to end users	Bil. kWh.	19.8	15.5	14.3	18.1	25.8	(NA)
Electricity retail prices per kWh:							
All sectors, current dollars	Cents	6.57	6.89	6.86	6.85	6.74	6.63
All sectors, real (1996) dollars	Cents	7.59	7.02	6.86	6.72	6.54	6.34
Residential, current dollars	Cents	7.83	8.40	8.36	8.43	8.26	8.17
Residential, real (1996) dollars	Cents	9.05	8.56	8.36	8.27	8.01	7.81
Commercial, current dollars	Cents	7.34	7.69	7.64	7.59	7.41	7.20
Commercial, real (1996) dollars	Cents	8.48	7.84	7.64	7.45	7.19	6.88
Industrial, current dollars	Cents	4.74	4.66	4.60	4.53	4.48	4.42
Industrial, real (1996) dollars	Cents	5.48	4.75	4.60	4.45	4.34	4.23
Other users, current dollars	Cents	6.40	6.88	6.91	6.91	6.63	6.74
Other users, real (1996) dollars	Cents	7.40	7.01	6.91	6.78	6.43	6.44
Net generation, total [1]	Bil. kWh	3,024.9	3,357.8	3,447.0	3,494.2	3,617.9	3,677.7
Coal	Bil. kWh.	1,590.3	1,710.2	1,795.7	1,844.1	1,873.9	1,890.7
Petroleum	Bil. kWh.	124.0	75.3	81.7	93.0	126.9	115.6
Natural gas	Bil. kWh.	378.3	498.5	455.8	485.4	540.6	545.8
Nuclear	Bil. kWh.	577.0	673.4	674.7	628.6	673.7	727.9
Hydroelectric pumped storage plants	Bil. kWh.	-3.5	-2.7	-3.1	-4.0	-4.4	-6.1
Conventional hydroelectric power plants	Bil. kWh.	293.0	311.0	347.4	358.9	323.3	311.7
Geothermal	Bil. kWh.	15.8	14.4	15.1	14.6	14.7	14.2
Wood	Bil. kWh.	30.4	36.4	36.8	34.2	31.8	41.8
Waste	Bil. kWh.	10.8	16.9	16.4	17.6	18.1	19.6
Other waste	Bil. kWh.	2.3	3.4	4.3	3.0	3.2	3.4
Wind	Bil. kWh.	3.0	3.2	3.4	3.2	3.0	3.6
Solar	Bil. kWh.	0.6	0.8	0.9	0.9	0.9	0.3
Net summer capability, total [1]	Mil. kW	734.9	769.5	775.9	778.5	775.9	781.6
Coal-fired plants	Mil. kW	306.7	310.8	313.0	313.1	312.6	312.5
Petroleum-fired plants	Mil. kW	56.7	48.0	47.8	46.3	42.2	42.3
Natural gas-fired plants	Mil. kW	31.0	41.9	48.8	49.9	59.1	57.1
Dual-fired plants	Mil. kW	133.5	152.4	151.6	153.6	148.0	153.1
Nuclear electric power plants	Mil. kW	99.6	99.5	100.8	99.7	97.1	97.2
Hydroelectric pumped storage plants	Mil. kW	19.5	21.4	21.1	19.3	18.9	18.9
Conventional hydroelectric power plants	Mil. kW	74.0	78.6	76.4	79.8	79.6	79.7
Geothermal energy plants	Mil. kW	2.7	3.0	2.9	2.9	2.9	2.9
Wood energy plants	Mil. kW	6.2	6.8	7.1	7.1	6.8	6.8
Waste energy plants	Mil. kW	2.6	3.5	3.5	3.4	3.5	3.5
Wind energy plants	Mil. kW	1.9	1.7	1.7	1.6	1.7	1.7
Solar energy plants	Mil. kW	0.3	0.3	0.3	0.3	0.4	0.4
Fuel consumption:							
Coal	Mil. sh. tons	805.9	879.3	927.9	953.3	967.7	968.5
Residual fuel	Mil. bbl	181.2	86.6	96.4	110.0	156.6	126.1
Distillate fuel and kerosene	Mil. bbl	14.8	15.6	16.9	15.2	22.0	22.8
Petroleum	Mil. bbl	233.6	161.9	177.5	189.6	264.1	217.1
Natural gas	Bil. cu. ft.	4,174.1	5,500.5	5,179.8	5,199.8	5,924.5	5,387.9
ELECTRIC UTILITIES							
Net generation, total [1]	Bil. kWh	2,808.2	2,994.5	3,077.4	3,122.5	3,212.2	3,182.9
Coal	Bil. kWh.	1,559.6	1,652.9	1,737.5	1,787.8	1,807.5	1,773.5
Petroleum	Bil. kWh.	117.0	60.8	67.3	77.8	110.2	89.7
Natural gas	Bil. kWh.	264.1	307.3	262.7	283.6	309.2	297.3
Nuclear	Bil. kWh.	576.9	673.4	674.7	628.6	673.7	725.0
Hydroelectric pumped storage plants	Bil. kWh.	-3.5	-2.7	-3.1	-4.0	-4.4	-6.0
Conventional hydroelectric power plants	Bil. kWh.	283.4	296.4	331.1	341.3	308.8	299.7
Net summer capability, total [1]	Mil. kW	690.5	706.1	709.9	711.9	686.7	641.5
Coal-fired plants	Mil. kW	299.9	300.6	302.4	302.9	299.7	285.8
Petroleum-fired plants	Mil. kW	55.4	46.1	45.7	43.7	39.8	19.9
Natural gas-fired plants	Mil. kW	15.0	17.7	22.7	22.9	26.2	12.4
Dual-fired plants	Mil. kW	127.5	143.2	142.0	144.9	127.2	132.3
Nuclear electric power plants	Mil. kW	99.6	99.5	100.8	99.7	97.1	94.8
Hydroelectric pumped storage plants	Mil. kW	19.5	21.4	21.1	19.3	18.9	18.9
Conventional hydroelectric power plants	Mil. kW	71.4	75.3	73.1	76.2	75.5	74.1
NONUTILITY PLANTS							
Net generation, total [1]	Bil. kWh	21.7	36.3	37.0	37.2	40.6	49.5
Coal	Bil. kWh.	3.1	5.7	5.8	5.6	6.6	11.7
Petroleum	Bil. kWh.	0.7	1.4	1.4	1.5	1.7	2.6
Natural gas	Bil. kWh.	11.4	19.1	19.3	20.2	23.1	24.8
Net summer capability, total [1]	Mil. kW	44.5	63.4	65.9	66.6	89.2	140.1
Coal-fired plants	Mil. kW	6.8	10.2	10.6	10.3	12.8	26.7
Petroleum-fired plants	Mil. kW	1.2	2.0	2.1	2.7	2.4	22.4
Natural gas-fired plants	Mil. kW	16.0	24.2	26.1	26.9	32.9	44.7
Dual-fired plants	Mil. kW	6.0	9.2	9.6	8.8	20.8	20.8

NA Not available.   [1] Includes types not shown separately.
Source: U.S. Energy Information Administration, *Electric Power Annual* and *Annual Energy Review.*

No. 909. Electric Utility Industry—Capability, Peak Load, and Capacity Margin: 1980 to 1999

[Excludes Alaska and Hawaii. Capability represents the maximum kilowatt output with all power sources available and with hydraulic equipment under actual water conditions, allowing for maintenance, emergency outages, and system operating requirements. Capacity margin is the difference between capability and peak load]

Year	Capability at the time of— Summer peak load (1,000 kW)		Winter peak load (1,000 kW)		Noncoincident peak load		Capacity margin Summer		Winter	
	Amount	Change from prior year	Amount	Change from prior year	Summer	Winter	Amount (1,000 kW)	Percent of capability	Amount (1,000 kW)	Percent of capability
1980	558,237	13,731	572,195	17,670	427,058	384,567	131,179	23.5	187,628	32.8
1981	572,219	13,982	586,569	14,374	429,349	397,800	142,870	25.0	188,769	32.2
1982	586,142	13,923	598,066	11,497	415,618	373,985	170,524	29.1	224,081	37.5
1983	596,449	10,307	612,453	14,387	447,526	410,779	148,923	25.0	201,674	32.9
1984	604,240	7,791	622,125	9,672	451,150	436,374	153,090	25.3	185,751	29.9
1985	621,597	17,357	636,475	14,350	460,503	423,660	161,094	25.9	212,815	33.4
1986	633,291	11,694	646,721	10,246	476,320	422,857	156,971	24.8	223,864	34.6
1987	648,118	14,827	662,977	16,256	496,185	448,277	151,933	23.4	214,700	32.4
1988	661,580	13,462	676,940	13,963	529,460	466,533	132,120	20.0	210,407	31.1
1989	673,316	11,736	685,249	8,309	523,432	496,378	149,884	22.3	188,871	27.6
1990	685,091	11,775	696,757	11,508	545,537	484,014	139,554	20.4	212,743	30.5
1991	690,915	5,824	703,212	6,455	551,320	485,435	139,595	20.2	217,777	31.0
1992	695,436	4,521	707,752	4,540	548,707	492,983	146,729	21.1	214,769	30.3
1993	694,250	1,186	711,957	4,205	575,356	521,733	118,894	17.1	190,224	26.7
1994	702,985	8,735	715,090	3,133	585,320	518,253	117,665	16.7	196,837	27.5
1995	714,222	11,237	727,679	12,589	620,249	544,684	93,973	13.2	182,995	25.1
1996	723,571	9,349	740,526	12,847	615,529	545,061	108,042	14.9	195,465	26.4
1997	729,079	5,508	743,774	3,248	631,355	560,228	97,724	13.4	183,546	24.7
1998	824,569	95,490	835,301	91,527	725,745	652,408	98,824	12.0	182,893	21.9
1999	834,035	9,466	848,871	13,570	748,522	656,332	85,513	10.3	192,539	22.7

Source: Edison Electric Institute, Washington, DC, *Statistical Yearbook of the Electric Utility Industry*, annual.

No. 910. Electric Energy Sales by Class of Service and State: 1999

[In billions of kilowatt-hours (3,235.9 represents 3,235,900,000,000)]

State	Total [1]	Residential	Commercial	Industrial	State	Total [1]	Residential	Commercial	Industrial
United States	3,235.9	1,140.8	970.6	1,017.8	Missouri	69.0	27.8	24.0	16.1
					Montana	12.1	3.7	3.0	5.1
Alabama	80.4	27.0	18.1	34.5	Nebraska	22.8	7.9	6.7	6.9
Alaska	5.3	1.9	2.4	0.8	Nevada	26.3	8.4	6.0	10.9
Arizona	57.7	22.5	19.8	12.5	New Hampshire	9.7	3.6	3.5	2.5
Arkansas	39.8	14.0	8.4	16.7					
California	212.0	74.5	78.2	49.6	New Jersey	70.6	24.6	32.4	13.1
					New Mexico	18.0	4.6	5.9	5.9
Colorado	40.6	13.1	17.0	9.5	New York	129.8	42.5	49.4	25.2
Connecticut	29.8	11.6	11.8	5.8	North Carolina	115.0	43.6	35.1	34.2
Delaware	10.5	3.5	3.3	3.6	North Dakota	9.1	3.3	2.4	3.0
District of Columbia	10.4	1.6	8.1	0.2					
Florida	187.3	93.8	69.1	18.6	Ohio	164.3	46.6	39.5	74.3
					Oklahoma	46.7	18.3	12.4	13.3
Georgia	112.7	41.8	34.1	35.3	Oregon	47.0	18.1	14.9	13.6
Hawaii	9.4	2.7	2.9	3.7	Pennsylvania	96.0	41.2	24.8	28.9
Idaho	21.8	6.8	6.5	8.3	Rhode Island	6.7	2.7	2.7	1.1
Illinois	132.2	39.6	41.9	41.6					
Indiana	96.7	28.8	20.2	47.2	South Carolina	73.3	23.7	16.6	32.1
					South Dakota	7.9	3.3	2.3	1.9
Iowa	38.0	11.9	8.3	16.5	Tennessee	93.2	35.4	25.2	31.5
Kansas	33.8	11.3	11.8	10.2	Texas	301.8	108.6	79.4	99.7
Kentucky	79.1	22.5	13.2	40.1	Utah	21.9	6.2	7.3	7.6
Louisiana	78.3	26.4	17.6	31.5					
Maine	11.9	3.7	3.5	4.7	Vermont	5.5	2.0	1.9	1.6
					Virginia	93.0	35.8	27.0	20.3
Maryland	59.1	23.3	25.0	9.9	Washington	94.2	32.8	23.0	34.6
Massachusetts	47.8	17.4	20.5	9.4	West Virginia	27.1	9.5	6.5	11.1
Michigan	103.5	30.7	35.1	36.8	Wisconsin	63.5	19.5	17.6	25.7
Minnesota	57.4	18.0	10.9	27.8	Wyoming	11.8	2.0	2.5	7.1
Mississippi	44.0	16.3	11.2	15.7					

[1] Includes "other service" not shown separately.

Source: U.S. Energy Information Administration, *Electric Power Annual*.

Energy and Utilities 579

No. 911. Electric Utilities—Net Generation and Net Summer Capability by State: 1990 to 1999

[Capability as of Dec. 31 (2,808.2 represents 2,808,200,000,000). Covers utilities for public use]

State	Net generation (bil. kWh) 1990	1995	1998	1999 Total	1999 Percent from coal	Net summer capability (mil. kW) 1990	1995	1998	1999
United States.......	2,808.2	2,994.5	3,212.2	3,173.7	55.7	690.5	706.1	686.7	639.3
Alabama.............	76.2	99.6	113.4	113.9	64.3	20.0	20.5	21.3	21.5
Alaska	4.5	4.8	4.6	4.6	3.4	1.5	1.7	1.7	1.7
Arizona.............	62.3	69.0	81.3	83.1	45.7	14.9	15.2	15.1	15.1
Arkansas	37.1	39.5	43.2	44.1	55.8	9.6	9.6	9.6	9.3
California	114.5	121.9	114.9	87.9	-	43.7	43.3	30.7	24.3
Colorado...........	31.3	32.7	35.5	36.2	90.2	6.6	6.6	6.9	7.3
Connecticut.........	32.2	26.9	15.1	20.5	-	7.1	6.7	5.6	2.9
Delaware	7.1	8.3	6.3	6.2	44.3	2.0	2.2	2.3	2.3
District of Columbia	0.4	0.2	0.2	-	-	0.8	0.8	0.8	0.8
Florida	123.6	147.2	169.4	166.9	37.6	32.7	35.9	36.5	36.5
Georgia	97.6	102.0	108.7	110.5	67.0	20.7	22.3	23.4	23.3
Hawaii	8.0	6.2	6.3	6.5	-	1.5	1.6	1.6	1.6
Idaho..............	8.6	10.1	12.0	12.5	-	2.3	2.6	2.6	2.6
Illinois	127.0	145.2	131.3	149.8	43.3	32.6	33.1	30.4	17.0
Indiana.............	97.7	105.2	112.8	114.2	98.4	20.6	20.7	20.3	20.4
Iowa	29.0	33.5	37.1	37.0	86.3	8.0	8.2	8.4	8.4
Kansas.............	33.9	38.2	41.5	42.0	70.6	9.6	9.7	9.9	10.0
Kentucky	73.8	86.2	86.2	81.7	96.2	15.5	15.4	14.0	14.7
Louisiana	58.2	65.6	66.1	64.8	32.6	16.8	17.0	17.0	16.3
Maine..............	9.1	2.7	3.5	1.2	-	2.4	2.4	1.5	0.1
Maryland	31.5	44.7	48.5	49.3	59.5	9.8	11.0	11.0	11.0
Massachusetts.......	36.5	27.0	26.0	4.4	24.6	9.9	9.3	3.4	2.2
Michigan............	89.1	92.5	85.1	87.9	78.7	22.3	22.0	21.9	22.4
Minnesota...........	41.6	42.5	44.0	44.2	64.2	8.8	8.9	9.1	9.0
Mississippi	22.9	26.4	32.0	32.2	40.5	7.0	7.2	7.2	6.8
Missouri	59.0	65.4	74.9	73.5	83.3	15.2	15.7	16.3	16.8
Montana............	25.7	25.4	27.6	27.6	57.9	4.9	4.9	4.9	3.0
Nebraska	21.6	25.3	28.7	30.0	59.4	5.5	5.5	5.8	5.8
Nevada	19.3	20.0	26.6	26.5	63.8	4.9	5.6	5.6	5.4
New Hampshire........	10.8	13.9	14.2	13.9	24.0	2.6	2.5	2.3	2.3
New Jersey..........	36.5	27.1	35.9	38.9	16.4	13.7	13.8	13.4	12.1
New Mexico	28.5	29.4	31.4	31.7	88.7	5.0	5.1	5.3	5.3
New York	128.7	101.2	115.8	97.0	11.3	31.2	32.1	17.7	17.7
North Carolina	79.8	96.1	113.1	109.9	62.4	20.2	20.6	21.0	21.2
North Dakota.........	26.8	28.8	30.5	31.3	91.5	4.5	4.5	4.7	4.7
Ohio	126.5	137.9	146.4	140.9	87.2	27.0	27.4	26.8	27.1
Oklahoma...........	45.1	48.0	51.5	50.3	60.8	12.8	12.9	12.6	12.9
Oregon.............	49.2	44.0	46.4	51.7	7.2	11.2	10.4	10.4	10.3
Pennsylvania.........	165.7	168.9	173.9	161.6	53.0	33.4	33.7	33.8	25.3
Rhode Island.........	0.6	0.7	2.1	(Z)	-	0.3	0.4	-	-
South Carolina.......	69.3	78.4	84.4	87.3	40.4	14.9	16.7	17.6	17.7
South Dakota	6.4	8.8	9.1	10.6	34.8	2.7	3.0	2.9	2.9
Tennessee	73.9	82.3	94.1	89.7	61.6	17.0	16.1	17.5	17.3
Texas..............	234.0	261.7	293.1	292.5	47.2	62.0	64.4	65.2	65.3
Utah	32.3	32.1	35.2	36.1	94.6	4.8	4.8	5.1	5.1
Vermont	5.0	4.8	4.4	4.7	-	1.1	1.1	0.8	0.8
Virginia.............	47.2	52.7	63.8	65.1	48.8	13.7	14.3	15.3	15.3
Washington..........	100.5	95.7	97.1	112.1	7.7	24.2	24.3	25.2	25.2
West Virginia.........	77.4	77.3	89.6	91.7	99.4	14.4	14.5	14.5	14.5
Wisconsin...........	45.6	51.0	52.5	54.7	72.9	10.6	11.5	11.9	12.1
Wyoming	39.4	39.7	44.7	43.0	97.1	5.8	6.0	6.0	6.0

- Represents zero.   Z Represents less than 50 million kWh.

Source: U.S. Energy Information Administration, *Electric Power Annual, Electric Power Monthly,* December issues, and *Inventory of Power Plants in the United States,* annual.

No. 912. Nuclear Power Plants—Number, Capacity, and Generation: 1980 to 1999

Item	1980	1985	1990	1991	1992	1993	1994	1995	1996	1997	1998	1999
Operable generating units [1]	71	96	112	111	109	`10	109	109	109	107	104	104
Net summer capability [1] [2] (mil. kW) .	51.8	79.4	99.6	99.6	99.0	99.1	99.1	99.5	100.8	99.7	97.1	97.2
Net generation (bil. kWh)	251.1	383.7	577.0	612.6	618.8	610.4	640.5	673.4	674.7	628.6	673.7	727.9
Percent of total electric utility generation	11.0	15.5	19.1	19.9	20.1	19.1	19.7	20.1	19.6	18.0	18.6	19.8
Capacity factor [3]	56.3	58.0	66.0	70.2	70.9	70.5	73.8	77.4	76.2	71.1	78.2	85.5

[1] As of year-end.   [2] Net summer capability is the peak steady hourly output that generating equipment is expected to supply to system load, exclusive of auxiliary and other power plant, as demonstrated by test at the time of summer peak demand. [3] Weighted average of monthly capacity factors. Monthly factors are derived by dividing actual monthly generation by the maximum possible generation for the month (hours in month times net maximum dependable capacity).

Source: U.S. Energy Information Administration, *Annual Energy Review*. See also <http://www.eia.doe.gov/pub/pdf/multi.fuel/ 038499. pdf> (released July 2000).

No. 913. Nuclear Power Plants—Number of Units, Net Generation, and Net Summer Capability by State: 1999

State	Number of units	Net generation Total (mil. kWh)	Percent of total[1]	Net summer capability Total (mil. kW)	Percent of total[1]	State	Number of units	Net generation Total (mil. kWh)	Percent of total[1]	Net summer capability Total (mil. kW)	Percent of total[1]
U.S. . . .	104	725,036	22.8	97.07	15.2	MS.	1	8,428	25.9	1.20	17.7
AL	5	30,892	27.1	4.95	23.1	MO	1	8,587	11.7	1.14	6.8
AZ	3	30,416	36.6	3.73	24.7	NE	2	10,091	33.7	1.25	21.4
AR	2	12,920	29.3	1.69	18.3	NH	1	8,676	62.4	1.16	50.7
CA	4	33,372	37.2	4.31	17.7	NJ	4	28,971	74.5	3.86	32.0
CT	2	12,675	61.6	2.01	68.9	NY	6	37,019	38.2	4.97	28.1
FL	5	31,526	18.9	3.87	10.6	NC	5	37,524	34.2	4.69	22.1
GA	4	31,478	28.6	3.95	16.9	OH	2	16,422	11.6	2.04	7.5
IL	11	81,356	54.4	10.53	62.0	PA	9	70,885	44.0	9.04	35.8
IA	1	3,640	9.8	0.52	6.2	SC	7	50,814	58.2	6.43	36.4
KS	1	9,157	21.8	1.16	11.6	TN	3	27,227	30.4	3.36	19.5
LA	2	13,112	20.3	2.01	12.3	TX	4	36,760	12.7	4.80	7.4
MD	2	13,312	26.9	1.68	15.3	VT	1	4,059	85.3	0.50	63.9
MA	1	1,931	31.3	0.67	30.0	VA	4	28,301	43.5	3.39	22.2
MI	4	14,591	16.6	3.92	17.5	WA	1	6,086	5.4	1.12	4.5
MN.	3	13,316	30.2	1.63	18.1	WI	3	11,495	21.0	1.49	12.4

[1] For total capability and generation, see Table 911.

Source: U.S. Energy Information Administration, *Electric Power Annual* and *Electric Power Monthly*, December issues.

No. 914. Uranium Concentrate—Supply, Inventories, and Average Prices: 1980 to 1999

[Years ending Dec. 31. For additional data on uranium, see Section 18, Natural Resources, on mining]

Item	Unit	1980	1990	1993	1994	1995	1996	1997	1998	1999
Production	Mil. lb. . .	43.70	8.89	3.06	3.35	6.04	6.32	5.64	4.71	4.61
Exports	Mil. lb. . .	5.8	2.0	3.0	17.7	9.8	11.5	17.0	15.1	8.5
Imports	Mil. lb. . .	3.6	23.7	21.0	36.6	41.3	45.4	43.0	43.7	47.6
Utility purchases from domestic suppliers	Mil. lb. . .	(NA)	20.5	15.5	22.7	22.3	22.9	18.7	20.3	19.2
Loaded into U.S. nuclear reactors [1] .	Mil. lb. . .	(NA)	(NA)	45.1	40.4	51.1	46.2	48.2	38.2	58.8
Inventories, total	Mil. lb. . .	(NA)	129.1	105.7	86.9	72.5	80.0	106.2	137.6	127.0
At domestic suppliers	Mil. lb. . .	(NA)	26.4	24.5	21.5	13.7	13.9	40.4	70.7	68.8
At electric utilities	Mil. lb. . .	(NA)	102.7	81.2	65.4	58.7	66.1	65.9	65.8	58.2
Average prices:										
Purchased imports	Dol. per lb.	(NA)	12.55	10.53	8.95	10.20	13.15	11.81	11.19	10.55
Domestic purchases	Dol. per lb.	(NA)	15.70	13.14	10.30	11.11	13.81	12.87	12.31	11.88

NA Not available.   [1] Does not include any fuel rods removed from reactors and later reloaded into the reactor.

Source: U.S. Energy Information Administration, *Annual Energy Review, Uranium Industry Annual*, and unpublished data.

No. 915. Nonutility Electric Power Producers—Summary by Type of Fuel: 1990 to 1999

[A nonutility power producer may be a corporation, person, agency, authority, or other legal entity or instrumentality that owns electric generating capacity and is not an electric utility. Nonutility power producers include qualifying cogenerators, qualifying small power producers, and other nonutility generators (including independent power producers) without a designated franchised service area, and which do not file forms listed in the Code of Federal Regulations, Title 18, Part 141]

Type of fuel	Unit	1990	1992	1993	1994	1995	1996	1997	1998	1999
Installed capacity ...	1,000 kW..	45,271	56,814	60,778	68,461	70,254	73,189	74,004	98,085	167,357
Coal [1] ...	1,000 kW..	6,937	8,503	9,772	10,372	10,877	11,370	11,027	13,712	48,501
Petroleum [2] ...	1,000 kW..	1,038	1,730	2,043	2,262	2,116	2,251	2,924	2,629	3,701
Natural gas ...	1,000 kW..	17,430	21,542	23,463	26,925	27,906	30,166	31,092	37,325	49,353
Other gas [3] ...	1,000 kW..	(4)	(4)	(4)	1,130	1,217	327	35	205	918
Petroleum/natural gas (combined) ...	1,000 kW..	6,468	8,478	8,505	9,820	10,479	10,912	10,029	23,105	40,508
Hydroelectric ...	1,000 kW..	1,968	2,684	2,741	3,364	3,399	3,419	3,770	4,136	5,996
Geothermal ...	1,000 kW..	1,086	1,254	1,318	1,335	1,295	1,346	1,303	1,449	2,698
Solar ...	1,000 kW..	360	360	360	354	354	354	354	385	382
Wind ...	1,000 kW..	1,405	1,822	1,813	1,737	1,723	1,670	1,566	1,689	2,222
Wood [5] ...	1,000 kW..	6,049	6,805	7,046	7,416	6,885	7,263	7,282	6,887	6,647
Waste [6] ...	1,000 kW..	2,323	3,006	3,131	3,150	3,430	3,463	3,394	3,488	4,316
Gross generation ...	Mil. kWh.	220,058	296,001	325,226	354,925	375,901	382,423	384,496	421,364	569,336
Coal [1] ...	Mil. kWh	32,131	47,363	53,367	59,035	60,234	61,375	59,211	70,369	129,502
Petroleum [2] ...	Mil. kWh	7,330	10,963	13,364	15,069	15,049	14,959	15,930	17,533	21,947
Natural gas ...	Mil. kWh	116,969	158,798	174,282	179,735	196,633	198,555	207,527	238,747	295,725
Other gases [3] ...	Mil. kWh	(4)	(4)	(4)	12,480	13,984	14,750	11,687	8,866	8,707
Hydroelectric ...	Mil. kWh	8,153	9,446	11,511	13,227	14,774	16,555	17,902	14,633	21,748
Geothermal ...	Mil. kWh	7,235	8,578	9,749	10,122	9,912	10,198	9,382	9,882	15,581
Solar ...	Mil. kWh	663	746	897	824	824	903	893	887	870
Wind ...	Mil. kWh	2,251	2,916	3,052	3,482	3,185	3,400	3,248	3,015	4,510
Wood [5] ...	Mil. kWh	30,812	36,255	37,421	38,595	37,283	37,525	34,898	32,596	34,999
Waste [6] ...	Mil. kWh	11,688	17,352	18,325	18,797	20,231	20,412	20,246	21,086	22,312
Supply and disposition:										
Gross generation	Mil. kWh ..	220,058	296,001	325,226	354,925	375,901	382,423	384,496	421,364	569,336
Receipts ...	Mil. kWh ..	60,926	83,421	85,323	94,166	89,919	103,219	88,506	90,675	89,688
Sales to utilities ...	Mil. kWh ..	106,224	164,374	187,466	204,688	217,906	224,646	223,532	249,483	369,539
Sales to other end users. ...	Mil. kWh ..	19,824	10,786	15,569	17,626	15,548	14,284	18,147	25,777	42,983
Facility use ...	Mil. kWh ..	154,936	204,261	207,514	226,777	232.367	246,713	231,138	236,770	250,227

[1] Includes coal, anthracite, culm and coal waste. [2] Includes petroleum, petroleum coke, diesel, kerosene, and petroleum sludge and tar. [3] Includes butane, ethane, propane, and other gases. [4] Included in "Natural gas." [5] Includes wood, wood waste, peat, wood liquors, railroad ties, pitch, and wood sludge. [6] Includes municipal solid waste, agricultural waste, straw, tires, landfill gases, and other waste.

Source: Energy Information Administration, *Electric Power Annual*, Vol. II; and *Inventory of Nonutility Electric Power Plants in the United States*, annual.

No. 916. Electric Utilities—Generation, Sales, Revenue, and Customers: 1980 to 1998

[Sales and revenue are to and from ultimate customers]

Class	Unit	1980	1985	1990	1993	1994	1995	1996	1997	1998
Generation [1] ...	Bil. kWh.	2,286	2,470	3,025	3,197	3,254	3,358	3,447	3,494	3,618
Sales [2] ...	Bil. kWh.	2,126	2,306	2,684	2,850	2,935	3,013	3,098	3,140	3,240
Residential or domestic....	Bil. kWh.	734	793	916	994	1,008	1,043	1,082	1,076	1,128
Percent of total ...	Percent .	34.5	34.4	34.1	34.9	34.3	34.6	34.9	34.4	34.8
Commercial [3] ...	Bil. kWh.	524	606	739	803	820	863	887	928	969
Industrial [4] ...	Bil. kWh.	794	820	932	957	1,008	1,013	1,030	1,033	1,040
Revenue [2] ...	Bil. dol.	95.5	149.2	176.5	197.9	202.7	207.7	212.5	215.1	218.3
Residential or domestic....	Bil. dol.	37.6	58.6	71.7	82.4	84.6	87.6	90.5	90.7	93.2
Percent of total ...	Percent .	39.4	39.3	40.7	41.7	41.7	42.2	42.6	42.2	42.7
Commercial [3] ...	Bil. dol.	27.4	44.1	54.2	62.0	63.4	66.4	67.8	70.5	71.8
Industrial [4] ...	Bil. dol.	27.3	41.4	44.9	46.6	48.1	47.2	47.4	46.5	46.5
Ultimate customers, Dec. 31 [2] .	Million..	92.7	101.6	110.1	115.2	116.5	118.3	120.0	122.1	124.0
Residential or domestic....	Million ..	82.2	89.8	97.0	101.3	102.3	103.9	105.3	107.0	108.7
Commercial [3] ...	Million ..	9.7	10.9	12.1	12.5	12.7	13.0	13.2	13.5	13.8
Industrial [4] ...	Million ..	0.5	0.5	0.5	0.5	0.6	0.6	0.6	0.6	0.5
Avg. kWh used per customer .	1,000. ..	23.2	22.9	24.6	24.9	25.2	(NA)	25.8	25.7	(NA)
Residential ...	1,000. ..	9.0	8.9	9.5	9.9	9.9	(NA)	10.3	10.1	(NA)
Commercial [3] ...	1,000. ..	54.5	56.1	61.3	64.4	65.7	(NA)	78.0	68.7	(NA)
Avg. annual bill per customer .	Dollar ..	1,040	1,482	1,614	1,727	1,741	(NA)	1,769	1,761	(NA)
Residential ...	Dollar ..	462	658	744	818	827	(NA)	859	849	(NA)
Commercial [3] ...	Dollar ..	2,848	4,080	4,494	4,977	5,076	(NA)	5,140	5,209	(NA)
Avg. revenue per kWh sold ...	Cents ..	4.49	6.47	6.57	6.94	6.91	6.89	6.86	6.85	6.74
Residential ...	Cents ..	5.12	7.39	7.83	8.29	8.38	8.40	8.36	8.43	8.26
Commercial [3] ...	Cents ..	5.22	7.27	7.33	7.73	7.73	7.69	7.64	7.59	7.41
Industrial [4] ...	Cents ..	3.44	5.04	4.81	4.87	4.77	4.66	4.60	4.53	4.48

NA Not available. [1] Source: U.S. Energy Information Administration, *Monthly Energy Review*, monthly. [2] Includes other types not shown separately. [3] Small light and power. [4] Large light and power.

Source: Except as noted, Edison Electric Institute, Washington, DC, *Statistical Yearbook of the Electric Utility Industry*, annual.

No. 917. Major Investor-Owned Electric Utilities—Balance Sheet and Income Account of Privately Owned Companies: 1994 to 1999

[In millions of dollars (196,282 represents $196,282,000,000). As of Dec. 31. Covers approximately 180 investor-owned electric utilities that during each of the last 3 years met any one or more of the following conditions—1 mil. megawatt-hours of total sales; 100 megawatt-hours of sales for resale, 500 megawatt-hours of gross interchange out, and 500 megawatt-hours of wheeling for other]

Item	1994	1995	1996	1997	1998	1999
COMPOSITE INCOME ACCOUNTS						
Operating revenue	196,282	199,967	207,459	215,083	218,175	214,160
Electric	179,307	183,655	188,901	195,898	201,970	197,578
Gas	16,222	15,580	17,869	18,663	15,735	16,033
Other utility	753	731	689	522	470	550
Operating expenses [1]	164,207	165,321	173,920	182,796	186,498	182,258
Electric [1]	148,663	150,599	156,938	165,443	171,689	167,266
Operation	93,108	91,881	97,207	104,337	110,759	108,461
Maintenance	12,022	11,767	12,050	12,368	12,486	12,276
Depreciation	18,679	19,885	21,194	23,072	24,122	23,968
Taxes other than income taxes	13,275	13,519	13,569	13,612	12,867	12,336
Income taxes	9,626	11,480	11,195	11,862	13,037	14,843
Deferred income tax	1,832	1,474	1,617	25	-476	-2,216
Investment tax credit (net)	-585	-550	-577	-448	-651	-1,695
Gas	14,878	14,073	16,258	16,925	14,396	14,493
Other utility	667	649	725	427	413	499
Operating income	32,074	34,646	33,539	32,286	31,677	31,902
Electric	30,645	33,057	31,963	30,454	30,281	30,311
Gas	1,344	1,507	1,612	1,737	1,339	1,540
Other utility	86	82	-36	95	57	51
Total income before interest charges	33,884	36,457	35,153	34,100	32,788	33,567
Less: Net interest charges	14,162	14,421	13,990	14,086	14,057	13,691
Interest expense	13,915	14,170	13,646	13,768	13,670	13,376
Less allow. for borrowed funds used during constuction	421	435	326	331	328	331
Other charges, net.	667	687	671	649	715	646
Net income before extraordinary charges	19,722	22,036	21,162	20,014	18,732	19,876
Less extraordinary items after taxes.	-165	-25	-66	3,151	1,344	2,793
Equals: Net income.	**19,888**	**22,061**	**21,228**	**16,863**	**17,388**	**17,083**
Dividends declared - preferred stock	1,582	1,519	1,248	1,005	750	687
Earnings available for common stocks	18,306	20,542	19,980	15,857	16,638	16,396
Dividends declared - common stock.	15,876	16,250	16,810	17,756	17,414	18,687
Additions total earnings	2,063	4,282	2,193	-1,960	-199	-2,785
COMPOSITE BALANCE SHEET						
Total assets and other debits	**574,512**	**578,934**	**581,991**	**586,241**	**598,856**	**585,827**
Utility plant, net	397,812	397,383	396,438	385,258	362,388	344,112
Electric utility plant, net.	366,936	366,116	363,854	351,427	327,646	310,317.
Electric utility plant	535,928	553,858	569,969	579,042	575,651	567,825
Construction work in progress	17,148	13,523	11,396	11,164	11,886	12,306
Less accumulated depreciation.	186,140	201,265	217,510	238,779	259,892	269,813
Nuclear fuel, net	5,657	5,286	5,444	5,219	4,731	4,265
Other utility plant, net.	25,219	25,981	27,140	28,613	30,011	29,529
Other property and investments.	23,479	27,988	33,120	43,248	48,853	54,546
Current and accrued assets	41,263	44,140	43,515	47,639	54,901	57,324
Deferred debits	111,957	109,423	108,918	110,096	132,714	129,845
CAPITALIZATION AND LIABILITIES						
Liabilities and other credits.	**574,512**	**578,934**	**581,991**	**586,241**	**598,856**	**585,827**
Capitalization	364,725	365,775	365,783	369,079	367,052	345,786
Common stock equity (end of year)	164,483	170,497	174,325	174,467	172,239	165,341
Preferred stock	24,860	21,569	18,830	16,080	14,447	12,061
Long-term debt	175,382	173,708	172,627	178,532	180,366	168,384
Current liabilities and deferred credits.	209,787	213,159	216,208	217,162	231,803	240,041

[1] Includes items not shown separately.
Source: U.S. Energy Information Administration, *Electric Power Annual*.

No. 918. Water Power—Developed and Undeveloped Capacity by Division: 1980 to 1999

[In millions of kilowatts. (64.4 represents 64,400,000). As of Dec. 31. Excludes all capacity of reversible equipment at pumped storage projects. Also excludes capacity precluded from development due to wild and scenic river legislation. For composition of divisions, see map, inside front cover]

Division	Developed installed capacity						Estimated undeveloped capacity					
	1980	1990	1995	1997	1998	1999	1980	1990	1995	1997	1998	1999
United States	64.4	73.0	74.2	73.5	73.8	73.8	129.9	73.9	71.0	64.1	64.1	64.1
New England	1.5	1.9	1.9	2.0	2.0	2.0	4.7	4.4	4.4	3.9	3.9	3.9
Middle Atlantic	4.3	4.9	4.9	5.6	5.6	5.6	5.1	5.1	4.9	3.6	3.6	3.6
East North Central	0.9	1.1	1.2	1.2	1.2	1.2	2.0	1.7	1.7	1.5	1.5	1.5
West North Central	2.8	3.1	3.1	3.0	3.0	3.0	3.4	3.1	3.1	2.8	2.8	2.8
South Atlantic.	5.9	6.7	6.7	6.8	6.8	6.8	9.6	7.0	7.2	6.8	6.8	6.8
East South Central	5.6	5.9	5.9	5.9	5.9	5.9	3.3	2.4	2.3	2.0	2.0	2.0
West South Central	2.3	2.7	2.7	2.8	2.8	2.8	4.7	4.6	4.6	4.0	4.0	4.0
Mountain.	7.4	9.2	9.5	10.0	10.0	10.0	34.2	19.4	18.8	18.0	18.0	18.0
Pacific	33.7	37.5	38.3	36.2	36.5	36.5	62.9	26.2	24.0	21.5	21.5	21.5

Source: U.S. Federal Energy Regulatory Commission (formerly U.S. Federal Power Commission), *Hydroelectric Power Resources of the United States, Developed and Undeveloped*, January 1, 1988, and unpublished data from the Hydroelectric Power Resources Assessment Database Developed and Undeveloped, March 30, 2001.

Energy and Utilities   **583**

No. 919. Solar Collector Shipments by Type, End Use, and Market Sector: 1980 to 1999

[Shipments in thousands of square feet (19,398 represents 19,398,000). Solar collector is a device for intercepting sunlight, converting the light to heat, and carrying the heat to where it will be either used or stored. 1985 data are not available]

Year	Number of manu-facturers	Total ship-ments [1]	Collector type		End use			Market sector		
			Low tempera-ture	Medium tempera-ture, special, other	Pool heating	Hot water	Space heating	Resi-dential	Com-mercial	Industrial
1980	233	19,398	12,233	7,165	12,029	4,790	1,688	16,077	2,417	488
1981	203	20,133	8,677	11,456	9,781	7,204	2,017	15,773	2,561	1,518
1982	265	18,621	7,476	11,145	7,035	7,444	2,367	13,729	3,789	560
1983	203	16,828	4,853	11,975	4,839	9,323	2,082	11,780	3,039	1,665
1984	225	17,191	4,479	11,939	4,427	8,930	2,370	13,980	2,091	289
1986 [2]	98	9,360	3,751	1,111	3,494	1,181	127	4,131	703	13
1987 [2]	59	7,269	3,157	957	3,111	964	23	3,775	305	11
1988 [2]	51	8,174	3,326	732	3,304	726	7	3,796	255	7
1989 [2]	44	11,482	4,283	1,989	4,688	1,374	205	5,804	424	42
1990	51	11,409	3,645	2,527	5,016	1,091	2	5,835	294	22
1991	48	6,574	5,585	989	5,535	989	24	6,322	225	13
1992	45	7,086	6,187	897	6,210	801	35	6,832	204	27
1993	41	6,968	6,025	931	6,040	880	15	6,694	215	31
1994	41	7,627	6,823	803	6,813	790	19	7,026	583	16
1995	36	7,666	6,813	840	6,763	755	132	6,966	604	82
1996	28	7,616	6,821	785	6,787	765	57	6,873	682	54
1997	29	8,138	7,524	606	7,528	595	10	7,360	768	7
1998	28	7,756	7,292	443	7,201	463	67	7,165	517	62
1999	29	8,583	8,152	427	8,141	373	42	7,774	785	18

[1] Includes high temperature collectors, end uses such process heating, and utility and other market sectors not shown separately.   [2] Declines between 1986 and 1989 are primarily due to the expiration of the federal energy tax credit and industry consolidation.

Source: U.S. Energy Information Administration, 1974-1993, *Solar Collector Manufacturing Activity,* annual reports; thereafter, *Renewable Energy Annual.*

No. 920. Privately Owned Gas Utility Industry—Balance Sheet and Income Account: 1980 to 1999

[In millions of dollars (75,851 represents $75,851,000,000). The gas utility industry consists of pipeline and distribution companies. Excludes operations of companies distributing gas in bottles or tanks]

Item	1980	1990	1993	1994	1995	1996	1997	1998	1999
COMPOSITE BALANCE SHEET									
Assets, total	75,851	121,686	135,813	137,911	141,965	121,328	134,715	119,715	174,272
Total utility plant	67,071	112,863	135,859	139,372	143,636	135,179	140,268	135,092	186,294
Depreciation and amortization. . . .	26,162	49,483	60,152	61,140	62,723	58,815	62,554	61,226	82,781
Utility plant (net).	40,909	63,380	75,707	78,232	80,912	76,364	77,714	73,866	103,513
Investment and fund accounts . . .	15,530	23,872	23,342	22,658	26,489	13,207	22,812	12,337	19,449
Current and accrued assets	17,243	23,268	21,451	20,728	18,564	17,393	19,084	17,348	25,166
Deferred debits [1]	2,169	9,576	13,369	14,234	13,923	11,983	12,844	13,721	23,461
Liabilities, total	75,851	121,686	135,813	137,911	141,965	121,328	134,775	119,715	174,272
Capitalization, total	51,382	74,958	82,755	85,728	90,581	77,440	78,887	71,718	106,802
Capital stock	29,315	43,810	49,051	50,394	54,402	43,555	42,530	37,977	53,241
Long-term debts	22,067	31,148	33,693	35,296	35,548	33,644	35,971	33,386	52,598
Current and accrued liabilities. . . .	18,119	29,550	27,321	25,438	28,272	22,098	33,507	26,953	36,949
Deferred income taxes [2]	4,149	11,360	13,070	13,787	14,393	13,326	13,636	13,239	19,198
Other liabilities and credits.	2,201	5,818	12,667	12,955	8,715	8,464	8,745	7,806	11,323
COMPOSITE INCOME ACCOUNT									
Operating revenues, total . .	85,918	66,027	69,966	63,446	58,390	63,600	62,617	57,117	66,317
Minus: Operating expenses [3]	81,789	60,137	62,977	56,789	50,760	56,695	59,375	50,896	57,054
Operation and maintenance . . .	74,508	51,627	50,468	43,879	37,966	43,742	46,070	41,026	45,366
Federal, state, and local taxes. .	4,847	4,957	6,185	6,613	6,182	6,362	7,182	5,429	6,682
Equals: Operating income	4,129	5,890	6,988	6,657	7,630	6,905	3,242	6,220	9,263
Utility operating income.	4,471	6,077	7,177	6,851	7,848	7,013	3,337	6,361	9,380
Income before interest charges. . .	6,929	8,081	8,754	8,200	9,484	8,030	4,193	7,779	10,882
Net income	4,194	4,410	5,589	5,011	5,139	4,797	48	4,379	6,104
Dividends	2,564	3,191	3,149	3,928	4,037	4,138	6,258	2,263	3,701

[1] Includes capital stock discount and expense and reacquired securities.   [2] Includes reserves for deferred income taxes.
[3] Includes expenses not shown separately.

Source: American Gas Association, Arlington, VA, *Gas Facts,* annual (copyright).

No. 921. Gas Utility Industry—Summary: 1980 to 1999

[Covers natural, manufactured, mixed, and liquid petroleum gas. Based on questionnaire mailed to all privately- and municipally-owned gas utilities in United States, except those with annual revenues less than $25,000]

Item	Unit	1980	1985	1990	1995	1996	1997	1998	1999
End users [1]	1,000	47,223	49,971	54,261	58,728	59,820	59,802	60,437	61,850
Residential	1,000	43,489	45,929	49,802	53,955	54,968	54,998	55,642	56,883
Commercial	1,000	3,498	3,816	4,246	4,530	4,616	4,593	4,595	4,756
Industrial and other	1,000	187	179	166	181	183	173	162	162
Sales [2]	Tril. Btu [3]	15,413	12,616	9,842	9,094	9,532	8,913	8,341	8,747
Residential	Tril. Btu	4,826	4,513	4,468	4,736	5,198	5,021	4,693	4,709
Percent of total	Percent	31.3	35.8	45.4	52.0	54.5	56.3	56.3	53.8
Commercial	Tril. Btu	2,453	2,338	2,192	2,204	2,395	2,244	2,043	2,030
Industrial	Tril. Btu	7,957	5,635	3,010	1,930	1,791	1,524	1,489	1,916
Other	Tril. Btu	177	130	171	224	148	124	116	93
Revenues [2]	Mil. dol	48,303	63,293	45,153	46,381	51,115	51,517	46,924	46,345
Residential	Mil. dol	17,432	26,864	25,000	28,741	32,022	33,068	30,671	30,082
Percent of total	Percent	36.1	42.4	55.4	62.6	62.6	64.2	65.4	64.9
Commercial	Mil. dol	8,183	12,722	10,604	11,410	12,726	12,666	11,189	10,581
Industrial	Mil. dol	22,215	23,086	8,996	5,652	5,821	5,284	4,678	5,319
Other	Mil. dol	473	621	553	579	546	498	387	363
Prices per mil. Btu [3]	Dollars	3.13	5.02	4.59	5.10	5.37	5.78	5.63	5.30
Residential	Dollars	3.61	5.95	5.60	6.06	6.17	6.59	6.54	6.39
Commercial	Dollars	3.34	5.44	4.84	5.18	5.31	5.64	5.48	5.21
Industrial	Dollars	2.79	4.10	2.99	3.00	3.32	3.53	3.28	2.92
Gas mains mileage	1,000	1,052	1,119	1,207	1,262	1,269	1,258	1,280	1,367
Field and gathering	1,000	84	94	90	62	58	46	45	36
Transmission	1,000	266	271	280	265	260	257	254	263
Distribution	1,000	702	754	837	935	952	955	981	1,067
Construction expenditures [4]	Mil. dol	5,350	5,671	7,899	10,829	7,722	7,189	11,941	9,293
Transmission	Mil. dol	1,583	1,562	2,886	3,384	1,316	1,334	2,892	1,994
Distribution	Mil. dol	1,869	2,577	3,714	5,448	4,234	4,404	6,852	4,669
Production and storage	Mil. dol	1,150	790	309	366	651	347	572	180

[1] Annual average.   [2] Excludes sales for resale.   [3] For definition of Btu, see text, this section.   [4] Includes general.

Source: American Gas Association, Arlington, VA, Gas Facts, annual (copyright).

No. 922. Gas Utility Industry—Customers, Sales, and Revenues by State: 1999

[See headnote, Table 921. For definition of Btu, see text, this section]

State	Customers [1] (1,000) Total [2]	Resi-dential	Sales [3] (tril. Btu) Total [2]	Resi-dential	Revenues [3] (mil. dol.) Total [2]	Resi-dential	State	Customers [1] (1,000) Total [2]	Resi-dential	Sales [3] (tril. Btu) Total [2]	Resi-dential	Revenues [3] (mil. dol.) Total [2]	Resi-dential
U.S.	61,869	56,883	8,747	4,709	46,345	29,813	MO	1,455	1,316	181	116	1,055	730
AL	832	765	103	43	612	350	MT	250	219	32	21	155	103
AK	121	90	43	18	97	64	NE	515	456	74	41	350	218
AZ	852	799	81	33	513	300	NV	510	481	46	29	291	198
AR	626	554	73	37	427	255	NH	90	76	19	7	116	46
CA	9,491	9,055	708	507	4,353	3,336	NJ	2,415	2,180	569	201	2,435	1,415
CO	1,345	1,220	224	108	806	553	NM	520	475	58	35	266	181
CT	483	438	97	38	661	385	NY	4,357	4,028	653	375	4,648	3,290
DE	121	111	25	9	141	72	NC	920	805	152	54	863	431
DC	139	125	22	10	177	89	ND	117	102	23	11	100	55
FL	633	580	67	15	433	169	OH	3,133	2,898	406	302	2,389	1,829
GA	1,057	923	202	108	525	287	OK	984	890	123	68	593	382
HI	34	31	3	1	38	10	OR	640	565	92	45	533	300
ID	306	271	66	22	190	111	PA	2,321	2,137	313	207	2,301	1,660
IL	3,809	3,552	527	407	2,628	2,095	RI	229	208	27	17	227	162
IN	1,713	1,564	245	155	1,327	917	SC	511	453	94	26	489	208
IA	888	795	121	73	649	168	SD	156	137	22	12	100	69
KS	1,621	1,471	192	125	1,168	733	TN	1,028	915	170	63	878	403
KY	725	652	96	54	479	287	TX	3,916	3,598	631	183	2,488	1,062
LA	737	686	304	50	763	266	UT	1,255	1,169	177	117	793	576
ME	23	16	5	1	30	6	VT	39	29	8	3	40	19
MD	834	780	86	62	669	512	VA	956	866	128	65	883	546
MA	1,325	1,222	169	102	1,344	912	WA	900	807	155	74	689	392
MI	3,275	3,038	477	348	2,469	1,836	WV	368	336	60	31	331	212
MN	1,297	1,182	245	116	1,097	625	WI	1,411	1,281	256	129	1,298	779
MS	435	396	72	24	319	142	WY	156	139	25	14	107	66

[1] Averages for the year.   [2] Includes other service, not shown separately.   [3] Excludes sales for resale.

Source: American Gas Association, Arlington, VA, Gas Facts, annual (copyright).

No. 923. Public Drinking Water Systems by Size of Community Served and Source of Water: 2000

[As of September. Covers systems that provide water for human consumption through pipes and other constructed conveyances to a least 15 service connection or serve an average of at least 25 persons for at least 60 days a year. Based on reported data in the Safe Drinking Water Information System maintained by the Environmental Protection Agency]

Type of system	Total	Size of community served					Water source	
		500 or fewer persons	501 to 3,300 persons	3,301 to 10,000 persons	10,001 to 100,000	100,000 persons or more	Ground water	Surface water
Total systems	167,833	139,677	19,620	4,684	3,493	359	153,697	14,136
COMMUNITY WATER SYSTEMS [1]								
Number of systems.	54,064	31,688	14,149	4,458	3,416	353	42,661	11,403
Percent of systems	100	59	26	8	6	1	79	21
Population served	263,926	5,149	19,931	25,854	96,709	116,283	85,868	178,058
Percent of population.	100	2	8	10	37	44	33	67
NONTRANSIENT NONCOMMUNITY WATER SYSTEM [2]								
Number of systems.	20,559	17,598	2,839	96	23	3	19,738	821
Percent of systems	100	86	14	-	-	-	96	4
Population served	6,917	2,440	2,796	480	621	580	5,984	932
Percent of population.	100	35	40	7	9	8	87	13
TRANSIENT NONCOMMUNITY WATER SYSTEM [3]								
Number of systems.	93,210	90,391	2,632	130	54	3	91,298	1,912
Percent of systems	100	97	3	-	-	-	98	2
Population served	12,935	7,521	2,618	732	1,329	735	12,017	917
Percent of population.	100	58	20	6	10	6	93	7

- Represents zero. [1] A public water system that supplies water to the same population year-round. [2] A public water system that regularly supplies water to at least 25 of the same people at least 6 months per year, but not year-round. Some examples are schools, factories, and office buildings which have their own water systems. [3] A public water system that provides water in a place such as a gas station or campground where people do not remain for long periods of time.

Source: U.S. Environmental Protection Agency, Internet site <http://www.epa.gov/safewater/data/getdata.html> (accessed 01 February 2001).

No. 924. Wastewater Treatment Facilities: 1988 to 1996

[Covers treatment facilities, which are structures designed to treat wastewater, storm water, or combined sewer overflows prior to discharging to the environment. Treatment is accomplished by subjecting the wastewater to a combination of physical, chemical, and/or biological processes that reduce the concentration of contaminants]

Level of treatment	Number of facilities			1996		
				Present design capacity (mgd [1])	Number of persons served	
	1988	1992	1996		Total	Percent of United States
Total	15,591	15,613	16,024	42,225	189,710,899	71.8
Nondischarge [2]	1,854	1,981	2,032	1,421	7,660,876	2.9
Less than secondary.	1,789	868	176	3,054	17,177,492	6.5
Secondary	8,536	9,086	9,388	17,734	81,944,349	31.0
Greater than secondary.	3,412	3,678	4,428	20,016	82,928,182	31.4

[1] Millions of gallons per day. [2] Facilities that do not discharge effluent to surface waters.

Source: U.S. Environmental Protection Agency, Office of Wastewater Management, *1996 Clean Water Needs Survey Report to Congress.*

Construction and Housing

This section presents data on the construction industry and on various indicators of its activity and costs; on housing units and their characteristics and occupants; and on the characteristics and vacancy rates for commercial buildings. This edition contains data from the 1999 American Housing Survey.

The principal source of these data is the U.S. Census Bureau, which issues a variety of current publications. Construction statistics compiled by the Census Bureau appear in its *New Residential Construction and New Residential Sales* press releases and Web sites <http://census.gov/const/www/>. Statistics on expenditures by owners of residential properties are issued quarterly and annually in *Expenditures for Residential Upkeep and Improvements. Value of New Construction Put in Place* presents data on all types of construction and includes monthly composite cost indexes. Reports of the censuses of construction industries (see below) are also issued on various topics.

Other Census Bureau publications include the *Current Housing Reports* series, which comprises the quarterly *Housing Vacancies,* the quarterly *Market Absorption of Apartments,* the biennial *American Housing Survey* (formerly *Annual Housing Survey),* and reports of the censuses of housing and of construction industries. *Construction Review,* published quarterly by the International Trade Administration, U.S. Department of Commerce, contains many of the census series and other construction statistics series from the federal government and private agencies.

Other sources include the monthly *Dodge Construction Potentials* of F. W. Dodge Division, McGraw-Hill Information Systems Company, New York, NY, which presents national and state data on construction contracts; the National Association of Home Builders with state-level data on housing starts; the NATIONAL ASSOCIATION OF REALTORS®, which presents data

on existing home sales; the Society of Industrial and Office Realtors and Oncor International on commercial office and industrial space; the Bureau of Economic Analysis, which presents data on residential capital and gross housing product; and the U.S. Energy Information Administration, which provides data on commercial buildings through its periodic sample surveys.

Censuses and surveys—Censuses of the construction industry were first conducted by the Census Bureau for 1929, 1935, and 1939; beginning in 1967, a census has been taken every 5 years (through 1997, for years ending in "2" and "7"). The latest complete reports are for 1997. The 1997 census results are part of the 1997 Economic Census. See Table 926. See also text, Section 15, Business Enterprise.

The construction sector of the economic census, covers all employer establishments primarily engaged in (1) building construction by general contractors or operative builders; (2) heavy (nonbuilding) construction by general contractors; and (3) construction by special trade contractors. The 1997 census was conducted in accordance with the 1997 *North American Industry Classification System* (NAICS); the 1992 census was conducted in accordance with the 1987 *Standard Industrial Classification* (SIC). This sector now includes construction management and land subdividers and developers, not included previously. See text, Section 15, Business Enterprise, for general information on the SIC and NAICS.

From 1850 through 1930, the Census Bureau collected some housing data as part of its censuses of population and agriculture. Beginning in 1940, separate censuses of housing have been taken at 10-year intervals. For the 1970 and 1980 censuses, data on year-round housing

U.S. Census Bureau, Statistical Abstract of the United States: 2001

units were collected and issued on occupancy and structural characteristics, plumbing facilities, value, and rent; for 1990 such characteristics were presented for all housing units.

The American Housing Survey (*Current Housing Reports* Series H-150 and H-170), which began in 1973, provided an annual and ongoing series of data on selected housing and demographic characteristics until 1983. In 1984, the name of the survey was changed from the Annual Housing Survey. Currently, national data are collected every other year, and data for selected metropolitan areas are collected on a rotating basis. All samples represent a cross section of the housing stock in their respective areas. Estimates are subject to both sampling and nonsampling errors; caution should therefore be used in making comparisons between years.

Data on residential mortgages were collected continuously from 1890 to 1970, except 1930, as part of the decennial census by the Census Bureau. Since 1973, mortgage status data, limited to single family homes on less than 10 acres with no business on the property, have been presented in the American Housing Survey. Data on mortgage activity are covered in Section 25, Banking and Finance.

Housing units—In general, a housing unit is a house, an apartment, a group of rooms or a single room occupied or intended for occupancy as separate living quarters; that is, the occupants live separately from any other individual in the building, and there is direct access from the outside or through a common hall. Transient accommodations, barracks for workers, and institutional-type quarters are not counted as housing units.

Statistical reliability—For a discussion of statistical collection and estimation, sampling procedures, and measures of statistical reliability applicable to Census Bureau data, see Appendix III.

No. 925. Construction—Establishments, Employees, and Payroll by Kind of Business (NAICS Basis): 1998 and 1999

[For establishments with payroll. (5,798.3 represents 5,798,300). See Appendix III]

Industry	NAICS code [1]	Establishments		Paid employees [2] (1,000)		Annual payroll (mil. dol.)	
		1998	1999	1998	1999	1998	1999
Construction	23	692,296	698,541	5,798.3	6,201.6	198,523.8	219,087.1
Building, developing, & general contracting . .	233	216,691	216,355	1,434.1	1,538.1	50,271.0	55,883.8
Land subdivision & land development	2331	11,359	12,383	56.3	68.0	2,262.5	2,814.5
Residential building construction	2332	161,501	160,178	688.3	741.6	20,340.9	23,225.8
Single-family housing construction	23321	153,422	151,952	626.0	677.1	18,241.2	20,956.6
Multifamily housing construction	23322	8,079	8,226	62.3	64.5	2,099.7	2,269.2
Nonresidential building construction	2333	43,831	43,794	689.5	728.5	27,667.6	29,843.5
Mfg & industrial building construction. . .	23331	6,901	6,998	161.2	166.0	6,145.1	6,461.9
Commercial & institutional building construction	23332	36,930	36,796	528.3	562.5	21,522.5	23,381.6
Heavy construction.	234	40,062	39,556	803.9	848.4	33,345.8	35,807.9
Highway, street, bridge, & tunnel construction	2341	12,186	11,911	267.1	284.4	12,525.5	13,469.4
Highway & street construction	23411	11,261	11,006	232.8	248.8	10,868.0	11,707.0
Bridge & tunnel construction	23412	925	905	34.3	35.6	1,657.5	1,762.5
Other heavy construction	2349	27,876	27,645	536.8	564.0	20,820.3	22,338.5
Water, sewer, & pipeline construction . .	23491	7,818	7,597	156.4	163.8	6,355.6	6,728.8
Power & communication transmission line construction.	23492	3,302	3,436	76.4	85.3	2,786.3	3,187.0
Industrial nonbuilding structure construction	23493	709	696	100.2	98.6	3,784.2	3,844.7
All other heavy construction.	23499	16,047	15,916	203.7	216.4	7,894.2	8,578.0
Special trade contractors	235	435,543	442,630	3,560.2	3,815.2	114,907.0	127,395.4
Plumbing, heating, & air-conditioning contractors.	2351	88,502	89,125	817.3	862.0	28,510.4	31,044.9
Painting & wall covering contractors	2352	39,425	39,767	198.8	212.1	5,226.2	5,684.3
Electrical contractors	2353	65,670	66,220	692.6	742.5	25,344.1	28,361.5
Masonry, drywall, insulation, & tile contractors.	2354	52,501	52,704	497.5	538.9	14,407.0	15,995.3
Masonry & stone contractors	23541	24,453	24,532	169.8	182.7	4,709.5	5,208.9
Drywall, plastering, acoustical, & insulation contractors	23542	21,567	21,515	287.4	312.7	8,535.0	9,454.2
Tile, marble, terrazzo, & mosaic contractors	23543	6,481	6,657	40.3	43.5	1,162.4	1,332.2
Carpentry & floor contractors.	2355	57,265	57,801	303.9	327.8	8,071.8	9,104.4
Carpentry contractors	23551	44,182	44,449	237.2	256.3	6,163.2	6,935.4
Floor laying & other floor contractors . . .	23552	13,083	13,352	66.6	71.5	1,908.6	2,169.1
Roofing, siding, & sheet metal contractors.	2356	30,945	30,767	246.4	257.6	7,085.9	7,614.4
Concrete contractors	2357	29,553	29,870	244.5	269.2	7,719.0	8,718.1
Water well drilling contractors	2358	3,827	3,789	19.9	20.5	594.8	636.8
Other special trade contractors	2359	67,855	72,587	539.3	584.5	17,947.9	20,235.7
Structural steel erection contractors. . . .	23591	4,589	4,945	79.1	86.6	2,846.2	3,199.8
Glass & glazing contractors	23592	5,261	5,450	39.6	42.3	1,247.0	1,409.8
Excavation contractors	23593	23,185	25,060	118.5	133.2	3,977.9	4,625.7
Wrecking & demolition contractors	23594	1,339	1,519	18.3	19.4	638.4	703.0
Building equip & other machinery installation contractors.	23595	4,055	4,374	72.6	73.4	3,198.2	3,472.6
All other special trade contractors	23599	29,426	31,239	211.3	229.6	6,040.2	6,824.9

[1] North American Industry Classification System code; see text, Section 15, Business Enterprise.   [2] Employees on the payroll for the pay period including March 12.

Source: U.S. Census Bureau, *County Business Patterns*, annual.

U.S. Census Bureau, Statistical Abstract of the United States: 2001

No. 926. Construction—Establishments, Employees, and Payroll by Kind of Business (NAICS Basis): 1997

[For establishments with payroll. (174,185 represents $174,185,000,000). Based on the 1997 Economic Census; see Appendix III]

Kind of Business	NAICS code [1]	Number of establishments	Number of employees		Payroll (mil. dol.)		Net value of construction work (mil. dol.)
			All employees	Construction workers	All employees	Construction workers	
Construction.	23	656,448	5,664,853	4,332,737	174,185	119,677	612,209
Building, developing, & general contracting . .	233	199,289	1,342,953	885,939	42,546	23,136	198,827
Land subdivision & land development	2331	8,186	41,827	10,977	1,510	254	10,248
Residential building construction.	2332	146,394	629,887	407,801	16,731	8,762	100,124
Nonresidential building construction	2333	44,710	671,239	467,161	24,305	14,119	88,455
Heavy construction	234	42,557	880,400	710,898	30,292	22,219	105,639
Highway, street, bridge, & tunnel construction	2341	12,448	325,743	265,267	11,375	8,474	46,274
Other heavy construction	2349	30,109	554,657	445,630	18,917	13,745	59,365
Special trade contractors	235	414,602	3,441,500	2,735,901	101,347	74,322	307,743
Plumbing, heating, & air-conditioning contractors	2351	84,876	788,930	599,940	25,720	18,280	78,496
Painting & wall covering contractors	2352	37,480	195,331	160,740	4,543	3,431	12,050
Electrical contractors	2353	61,414	641,985	510,921	21,680	16,261	61,121
Masonry, drywall, insulation, & tile contractors	2354	49,917	470,701	407,700	12,612	10,073	34,843
Carpentry & floor contractors	2355	56,936	290,942	228,273	7,163	5,116	24,049
Roofing, siding, & sheet metal contractors	2356	30,557	253,315	197,294	6,495	4,370	21,976
Concrete contractors	2357	30,417	262,256	222,121	6,858	5,298	23,604
Water well drilling contractors	2358	3,862	21,214	15,360	576	399	2,132
Other special trade contractors	2359	59,143	516,824	393,552	15,699	11,095	19,472

[1] North American Industry Classification System, 1997; see text, Section 15, Business Enterprise.

Source: U.S. Census Bureau, *1997 Economic Census, Construction*, Series EC97C23S-IS, issued January 2000.

No. 927. Construction Materials—Producer Price Indexes: 1990 to 2000

[1982=100, except as noted. Data for 2000 are preliminary. For discussion of producer price indexes, see text, Section 14, Prices. This index, more formally known as the special commodity grouping index for construction materials, covers materials incorporated as integral part of a building or normally installed during construction and not readily removable. Excludes consumer durables such as kitchen ranges, refrigerators, etc. This index is not the same as the stage-of-processing index of intermediate materials and components for construction]

Commodity	1990	1993	1994	1995	1996	1997	1998	1999	2000
Construction materials	119.6	128.6	133.8	138.8	139.6	142.1	141.4	142.8	144.1
Interior solvent based paint	133.0	142.9	148.1	164.5	175.6	180.5	185.7	188.0	191.1
Construction products from plastics	117.2	116.6	122.9	133.8	130.9	128.2	126.2	128.0	135.8
Douglas fir, dressed	138.4	237.6	236.2	198.8	227.1	221.3	186.1	212.1	185.2
Southern pine, dressed	111.2	168.8	182.6	166.9	177.9	201.2	177.3	185.7	160.9
Millwork	130.4	156.6	162.4	163.8	166.8	166.6	170.9	171.1	176.4
Softwood plywood	119.6	169.7	176.8	188.1	173.7	175.5	174.9	207.0	173.8
Hardwood plywood and related products	102.7	115.4	122.3	122.2	124.9	127.1	126.9	128.6	130.1
Softwood plywood veneer, ex. reinforced/backed . . .	142.3	216.0	207.8	203.5	189.3	201.7	180.1	197.4	182.2
Building paper and building board mill products	112.2	132.7	144.1	144.9	137.2	129.6	132.9	141.6	138.8
Steel pipe and tubes [1]	102.6	92.8	96.9	104.4	103.2	106.9	109.4	102.5	106.8
Builders hardware	133.0	144.9	148.0	153.2	156.5	158.4	160.8	161.9	163.9
Plumbing fixtures and brass fittings	144.3	155.9	159.6	166.0	171.1	174.5	175.1	176.7	180.5
Heating equipment	131.6	140.4	142.5	147.5	151.2	152.4	153.3	154.0	155.5
Metal doors, sash, and trim	131.4	136.6	142.0	156.5	159.3	161.0	161.3	162.2	165.0
Siding, aluminum [2]	(NA)	117.2	119.4	132.4	125.5	132.1	134.5	135.4	142.8
Outdoor lighting equipment, including parts [3]	113.0	115.5	*15.4	120.8	122.9	123.2	122.8	122.3	124.7
Commercial fluorescent fixtures [4]	113.0	117.4	116.2	121.0	123.4	122.8	.119.0	118.7	118.3
Architectural and ornamental metalwork [5]	118.7	119.5	123.4	128.0	131.3	133.5	135.4	136.2	139.8
Fabricated ferrous wire products [1]	114.6	119.3	122.6	125.7	126.8	128.0	130.1	130.6	130.0
Elevators, escalators, and other lifts.	110.1	110.7	112.4	113.0	113.7	114.8	116.0	117.5	118.7
Stamped metal switch and receptacle box	158.0	172.9	179.1	183.5	186.3	189.0	191.5	192.8	182.7
Concrete ingredients and related products	115.3	123.4	128.7	134.7	138.8	142.5	147.6	152.1	155.6
Concrete products	113.5	120.2	124.6	129.4	133.2	136.0	140.0	143.7	147.8
Clay construction products exc. refractories.	129.9	135.1	138.3	141.3	142.3	143.5	144.9	148.3	152.8
Prep. asphalt and tar roofing and siding products. . .	95.8	94.9	92.9	97.8	97.4	96.5	95.7	95.2	100.0
Gypsum products	105.2	108.3	136.5	154.0	170.8	177.6	208.0	201.4	
Insulation materials	108.4	105.8	111.9	118.8	118.9	117.7	119.7	131.7	128.4
Paving mixtures and blocks	101.2	102.0	103.2	105.8	107.6	113.2	112.5	112.9	130.3

NA Not available. [1] June 1982=100. [2] December 1982=100. [3] June 1985=100. [4] Recessed nonair. [5] December 1983=100.

Source: U.S. Bureau of Labor Statistics, *Producer Price Indexes*, monthly and annual.

No. 928. Price and Cost Indexes for Construction: 1980 to 2000

[1996=100. Excludes Alaska and Hawaii. Indexes of certain of these sources are published on bases different from those shown here]

Name of index	1980	1985	1990	1995	1996	1997	1998	1999	2000
U.S. Census Bureau Composite:									
Fixed-weighted [1]	59.3	71.8	85.5	97.7	100.0	103.2	106.0	110.3	115.3
Implicit price deflator [2]	59.0	71.1	85.0	97.8	100.0	103.3	106.1	110.4	115.4
U.S. Census Bureau houses under construction: [3]									
Fixed-weighted	58.0	69.8	84.6	98.1	100.0	102.9	105.6	110.4	115.5
Price deflator	57.0	68.3	83.4	98.1	100.0	102.9	105.6	110.4	115.6
Federal Highway Administration, composite [4]	79.7	83.6	88.9	99.8	100.0	107.5	105.2	112.7	119.3
Bureau of Reclamation composite [5]	62	75	85	98	100	103	105	107	111
Turner Construction Co.:									
Building construction [6]	54	74	87	97	100	104	109	113	118
Engineering News-Record: [7]									
Buildings	60.6	75.8	84.4	97.1	100.0	105.0	105.8	107.9	110.5
Construction	57.6	74.6	84.2	97.3	100.0	103.6	105.3	107.8	110.6
Handy-Whitman public utility: [8]									
Buildings	66	76	85	97	100	103	104	107	110
Electric [9]	60	74	86	98	100	102	104	105	109
Gas	60	75	86	99	100	102	104	107	111
Water [10]	64	76	85	98	100	102	104	107	112
C. A. Turner Telephone Plant [11]	79	77	87	96	100	102	102	101	103

[1] Weighted average of the various indexes used to deflate the Construction Put in Place series. In calculating the index, the weights (i.e., the composition of current dollar estimates in 1996 by category) are held constant. [2] Derived ratio of total current to constant dollar Construction Put in Place (multiplied by 100). [3] Excludes value of site. [4] Based on average contract unit bid prices for composite mile (involving specific average amounts of excavation, paving, reinforcing steel, structural steel, and structural concrete). [5] Derived from the four quarterly indexes which are weighted averages of costs of labor, materials, and equipment for the construction of dams and reclamation projects. [6] Based on firm's cost experience with respect to labor rates, materials prices, competitive conditions, efficiency of plant and management, and productivity. [7] Building construction index computed on the basis of a hypothetical unit of construction requiring 6 bbl. of portland cement, 1,088 M bd. ft. of 2" x 4" lumber, 2,500 lb. of structural steel, and 68.38 hours of skilled labor. General construction index based on same materials components combined with 200 hours of common labor. [8] Based on data covering public utility construction costs in six geographic regions. Covers skilled and common labor. [9] As derived by U.S. Census Bureau. Covers steam generation plants only. [10] As derived by U.S. Census Bureau. Reflects costs for structures and improvements at water pumping and treatment plants. [11] Computed by the Census Bureau by averaging the weighted component indexes published for six geographic regions.

Source: U.S. Census Bureau, *Current Construction Reports, Value of Construction Put in Place*, Series C30. Also in U.S. International Trade Administration, *Construction Review*, quarterly.

No. 929. Value of New Construction Put in Place: 1964 to 2000

[In millions of dollars (75,097 represents $75,097,000,000). Represents value of construction put in place during year; differs from building permit and construction contract data in timing and coverage. Includes installed cost of normal building service equipment and selected types of industrial production equipment (largely site fabricated). Excludes cost of shipbuilding, land, and most types of machinery and equipment. For methodology, see Appendix III]

Year	Current dollars					Constant (1996) dollars				
	Total	Private			Public	Total	Private			Public
		Total [1]	Residential buildings	Nonresidential buildings			Total [1]	Residential buildings	Nonresidential buildings	
1964	75,097	54,893	30,526	17,385	20,203	405,864	300,372	169,635	96,497	105,492
1970	105,890	77,982	35,863	28,171	27,908	429,041	321,940	155,113	115,372	107,101
1975	152,635	109,342	51,581	35,409	43,293	404,132	298,555	149,410	96,407	105,577
1980	273,936	210,290	100,381	72,480	63,646	464,144	364,101	175,822	129,275	100,043
1981	289,070	224,378	99,241	85,569	64,691	455,260	361,069	162,706	140,569	94,191
1982	279,332	216,268	84,676	92,690	63,064	423,729	333,894	134,605	145,054	89,835
1983	311,887	248,437	125,833	87,069	63,450	465,073	375,193	195,028	131,289	89,880
1984	370,190	299,952	155,015	107,680	70,238	534,557	437,325	231,396	155,261	97,232
1985	403,416	325,601	160,520	127,466	77,815	567,689	463,854	234,955	178,925	103,835
1986	433,454	348,872	190,677	120,917	84,582	588,804	479,623	266,481	163,740	109,182
1987	446,643	355,994	199,652	123,247	90,648	585,103	470,575	267,063	160,363	114,528
1988	462,012	367,277	204,496	130,854	94,735	583,396	467,599	263,385	164,191	115,797
1989	477,502	379,328	204,255	139,953	98,174	579,583	463,541	252,745	169,173	116,042
1990	476,778	369,300	191,103	143,506	107,478	560,802	436,999	228,943	167,896	123,803
1991	432,592	322,483	166,251	116,570	110,109	503,711	378,245	197,526	135,389	125,467
1992	463,661	347,814	199,393	105,646	115,847	533,322	401,567	232,134	120,921	131,755
1993	491,033	375,073	225,067	107,715	115,960	544,285	415,565	249,763	118,988	128,720
1994	539,193	418,999	258,561	120,284	120,193	574,256	445,414	274,966	127,576	128,842
1995	557,818	427,885	247,351	138,015	129,933	570,148	436,738	251,953	141,218	133,450
1996	615,900	476,638	281,115	155,858	139,263	615,797	476,650	281,207	155,813	139,147
1997	653,429	502,734	289,014	173,875	150,695	632,680	487,197	280,722	167,610	145,483
1998	704,724	551,383	314,607	190,710	153,341	664,244	519,859	297,960	177,644	144,385
1999	763,786	596,280	350,562	193,935	167,507	692,281	540,159	317,232	173,418	152,121
2000	815,414	640,554	374,274	210,140	174,860	706,899	555,089	323,708	179,654	151,810

[1] Includes other types of private construction, not shown separately.

Source: U.S. Census Bureau, *Current Construction Reports*, Series C30, *Value of Construction*, monthly.

Construction and Housing 591

No. 930. Value of New Construction Put in Place by Type: 1990 to 2000

[In millions of dollars (476,778 represents $476,778,000,000). Represents value of construction put in place during year; differs from building permit and construction contract data in timing and coverage. Includes installed cost of normal building service equipment and selected types of industrial production equipment (largely site fabricated). Excludes cost of shipbuilding, land, and most types of machinery and equipment. For methodology, see Appendix III]

Type of construction	Current dollars					Constant (1996) dollars				
	1990	1995	1998	1999	2000	1990	1995	1998	1999	2000
Total new construction	476,778	557,818	704,724	763,786	815,414	560,802	570,188	664,244	692,281	706,899
Private construction	369,300	427,885	551,383	596,280	640,554	436,999	436,738	519,859	540,159	555,089
Residential buildings	191,103	247,351	314,607	350,562	374,274	228,943	251,953	297,960	317,232	323,708
New housing units	132,137	171,404	223,983	251,272	264,864	158,319	174,585	212,068	227,461	229,103
1 unit	112,886	153,515	199,409	223,837	236,788	135,253	156,363	188,785	202,615	204,812
2 or more units	19,250	17,889	24,574	27,434	28,076	23,066	18,222	23,283	24,847	24,292
Improvements	58,966	75,947	90,624	99,290	109,410	70,625	77,368	85,892	89,771	94,605
Nonresidential buildings	143,506	138,015	190,710	193,935	210,140	167,896	141,218	177,644	173,418	179,654
Industrial	33,636	35,498	40,484	32,639	32,073	39,350	36,322	37,720	29,204	27,419
Office	35,055	25,613	42,226	47,582	55,686	41,027	26,218	39,333	42,549	47,594
Hotels, motels	10,679	7,112	14,816	15,951	16,396	12,497	7,274	13,794	·14,273	14,027
Other commercial	40,047	42,654	53,598	56,915	61,453	46,847	43,636	49,915	50,867	52,539
Religious	3,566	4,326	6,594	7,371	8,068	4,169	4,426	6,139	6,590	6,898
Educational	4,616	5,493	9,698	9,645	11,356	5,398	5,621	9,039	8,621	9,707
Hospital and institutional	10,868	11,248	13,793	13,530	14,575	12,710	11,512	12,853	12,101	12,459
Miscellaneous [1]	5,040	6,071	9,501	10,301	10,533	5,897	6,209	8,850	9,214	9,010
Farm nonresidential	2,801	3,014	4,284	5,008	5,158	3,276	3,084	3,989	4,474	4,407
Public utilities	28,933	36,084	39,212	44,066	48,084	33,505	36,965	37,818	42,534	44,749
Telecommunications	9,803	11,093	12,458	18,404	17,994	11,346	11,556	12,188	18,305	17,497
Other public utilities	19,130	24,991	26,754	25,662	30,089	22,159	25,409	25,631	24,229	27,253
Railroads	2,600	3,509	5,736	4,670	4,226	2,969	3,609	5,463	4,311	3,750
Electric light and power	11,299	14,274	12,381	14,585	21,111	13,083	14,535	11,883	13,892	19,251
Gas	4,820	6,279	7,372	4,918	3,750	5,627	6,329	7,072	4,625	3,354
Petroleum pipelines	411	929	1,265	1,489	1,003	480	936	1,213	1,401	897
All other private [2]	2,957	3,420	2,570	2,709	2,899	3,379	3,518	2,447	2,501	2,570
Public construction	107,478	129,933	153,341	167,507	174,860	123,803	133,450	144,385	152,121	151,810
Buildings	43,615	57,754	71,776	76,542	82,275	51,117	59,074	66,920	68,474	70,390
Housing and redevelopment	3,808	4,698	4,922	5,138	5,228	4,560	4,786	4,663	4,653	4,521
Industrial	1,434	1,508	1,010	925	1,159	1,677	1,544	941	827	991
Educational	16,055	25,783	34,828	38,966	43,560	18,772	26,374	32,431	34,821	37,237
Hospital	2,860	4,236	3,906	3,932	4,007	3,348	4,335	3,641	3,516	3,427
Other [3]	19,458	21,528	27,110	27,582	28,321	22,760	22,034	25,245	24,657	24,214
Highways and streets	32,105	37,616	45,565	51,374	52,088	35,879	38,952	43,085	46,858	45,230
Military facilities	2,665	3,011	2,530	2,130	2,337	3,050	3,102	2,377	1,926	2,016
Conservation and development	4,686	6,308	5,452	5,993	6,014	5,482	6,443	5,223	5,594	5,449
Sewer systems	10,276	8,420	9,367	10,343	10,287	12,010	8,600	8,976	9,653	9,324
Water supply facilities	4,909	4,709	6,290	6,844	6,928	5,730	4,809	6,035	6,431	6,160
Miscellaneous public [4]	9,223	12,116	12,361	14,280	14,930	10,535	12,468	11,767	13,185	13,241

[1] Includes amusement and recreational buildings, bus and airline terminals, animal hospitals and shelters, etc. [2] Includes privately owned streets and bridges, parking areas, sewer and water facilities, parks and playgrounds, golf courses, airfields, etc. [3] Includes general administrative buildings, prisons, police and fire stations, courthouses, civic centers, passenger terminals, space facilities, postal facilities, etc. [4] Includes open amusement and recreational facilities, power generating facilities, transit systems, airfields, open parking facilities, etc.

Source: U.S. Census Bureau, *Current Construction Reports*, Series C30, *Value of Construction*, monthly.

No. 931. Value of Private Nonresidential Construction Put in Place: 1993 to 2000

[In millions of dollars (110,996 represents $110,996,000,000). Represents value of construction put in place during year; differs from building permit and construction contract data in timing and coverage. Data are not directly comparable to Tables 929 and 930 due to a new classification system which bases project types on their end usage instead of building/nonbuilding and ownership types. See Appendix III]

Type of construction	1993	1994	1995	1996	1997	1998	1999	2000 [1]
Total construction [2]	**110,996**	**123,174**	**141,435**	**158,663**	**176,267**	**193,280**	**196,644**	**213,039**
Lodging	4,590	4,657	7,131	10,914	12,898	14,818	15,955	16,407
Office	[2]19,999	20,443	22,996	26,530	32,813	40,394	45,052	52,811
General	17,314	18,008	20,569	23,216	29,301	37,615	41,745	49,964
Financial	2,604	2,361	2,339	3,231	3,157	2,636	3,125	2,765
Commercial [2]	31,005	36,389	41,082	45,723	49,273	51,398	54,317	59,050
Automotive [2]	2,077	2,731	4,191	5,251	5,736	5,270	5,904	5,930
Sales	473	659	883	1,250	1,743	1,542	1,573	1,664
Service/parts	1,099	1,613	2,448	2,993	3,213	2,527	3,270	2,894
Parking	421	458	860	1,008	781	1,200	1,062	1,372
Food/beverage [2]	6,201	6,133	7,169	7,478	8,566	9,118	8,277	8,923
Food	2,766	2,627	3,062	3,776	4,658	4,665	4,610	4,933
Dining/drinking	2,108	2,830	3,408	2,958	3,058	3,817	2,874	2,960
Fast food	1,243	670	699	744	850	636	793	1,029
Multiretail [2]	11,483	12,228	11,976	13,331	12,157	13,254	15,234	15,289
General merchandise	3,787	5,421	5,339	5,159	4,083	3,778	4,668	5,226
Shopping center	4,942	4,585	4,086	5,496	5,694	6,045	7,186	6,982
Shopping mall	1,973	1,718	2,175	2,189	1,949	2,917	2,873	2,575
Other commercial [2]	5,934	8,994	8,432	8,202	10,203	11,050	11,179	14,082
Drug store	349	326	536	750	1,007	1,409	1,645	1,692
Building supply store	850	1,194	1,372	1,201	1,323	1,742	1,588	2,692
Other stores	4,264	6,826	5,653	5,327	7,090	7,025	6,849	8,559
Warehouse [2]	5,181	6,298	9,299	11,458	12,563	12,698	13,702	14,781
General commercial	5,079	6,166	8,944	10,849	11,501	11,732	12,756	13,421
Mini-storage	86	126	319	594	993	918	892	1,312
Health care	14,939	15,447	15,259	15,420	17,390	17,737	18,388	19,332
Hospital	9,754	9,891	8,807	8,348	9,968	9,469	9,490	10,309
Medical building	2,840	3,398	4,064	3,728	4,001	4,070	4,911	4,803
Special care	2,345	2,158	2,388	3,344	3,421	4,197	3,987	4,220
Educational [2]	4,814	5,009	5,699	6,985	8,802	9,829	9,756	11,672
Preschool	169	421	326	398	531	619	662	794
Primary/secondary	725	849	1,245	1,560	2,032	2,174	2,421	2,949
Higher education [2]	3,240	2,939	3,055	3,619	4,327	4,945	5,204	6,221
Instructional	1,806	1,937	1,712	2,028	1,991	2,469	2,258	2,949
Dormitory	521	324	483	573	789	955	1,274	1,367
Sports/recreation	220	236	192	260	475	403	515	677
Other educational	549	649	817	1,042	1,714	1,798	1,232	1,372
Gallery/museum	357	387	571	662	1,107	1,127	778	970
Religious [2]	3,894	3,871	4,348	4,537	5,782	6,604	7,372	8,079
House of worship	2,804	2,808	2,951	3,211	3,844	4,549	5,056	5,713
Other religious	1,075	1,051	1,389	1,318	1,935	2,054	2,314	2,339
Auxiliary building	382	507	619	620	874	992	1,252	1,287
Public safety	215	327	185	321	569	586	465	439
Amusement and recreation [2]	4,601	5,108	5,886	7,016	8,537	8,589	9,551	8,995
Theme/amusement park	478	709	563	727	723	866	919	761
Sports	534	716	910	1,193	1,333	1,136	1,495	1,096
Fitness	509	458	637	622	801	889	1,137	1,188
Performance/meeting center	274	369	365	539	628	603	546	796
Social center	1,488	1,293	1,558	1,597	1,979	2,093	2,006	2,361
Movie theater/studio	331	623	848	1,271	2,199	2,441	2,376	1,513
Transportation [2]	1,572	1,364	1,250	1,422	1,285	1,554	1,855	2,555
Air	1,026	914	666	871	901	1,093	1,107	1,736
Land	401	233	499	396	261	376	494	654
Sewage and waste disposal	373	299	576	637	468	339	516	501
Water supply	426	567	670	468	448	543	413	716
Manufacturing	23,371	28,845	35,364	38,101	37,624	40,482	32,631	32,061
Food/beverage/tobacco	2,031	2,809	4,525	4,294	3,957	3,538	3,383	3,357
Textile/apparel/leather & allied	773	651	824	743	584	712	456	347
Wood	279	413	616	689	522	492	427	413
Paper	1,886	1,623	1,448	1,711	1,548	1,232	837	603
Print/publishing	539	739	1,197	993	930	1,104	856	711
Petroleum/coal	2,729	2,593	4,741	2,348	1,186	1,064	927	1,252
Chemical	4,937	6,270	5,531	5,445	6,034	8,264	6,181	3,395
Plastic/rubber	1,808	1,121	1,475	1,632	1,959	2,137	2,222	1,385
Nonmetallic mineral	160	222	856	1,220	1,004	1,481	1,188	1,704
Primary metal	834	2,567	2,533	2,244	2,802	2,603	1,993	1,737
Fabricated metal	442	744	808	1,585	2,162	2,036	1,890	1,880
Machinery	352	1,296	1,275	1,169	1,106	1,257	965	704
Computer/electronic/electrical	2,158	4,118	6,332	8,945	7,537	7,557	4,415	5,379
Transportation equipment	2,289	2,631	2,382	2,948	3,453	3,497	3,418	5,051
Furniture	121	260	213	308	167	296	282	362
Miscellaneous	2,033	788	607	1,827	2,671	3,212	3,190	3,779

[1] Preliminary. [2] Includes other types of construction, not shown separately.

Source: U.S. Census Bureau, Internet site <http://www.census.gov/pub/const/C30/newtc.html> (accessed 7 August 2001).

Construction and Housing 593

[In millions of dollars (101,535 represents $101,535,000,000). See headnote, Table 931]

Type of construction	1993	1994	1995	1996	1997	1998	1999	2000 [1]
Total construction [2]	101,535	105,753	114,181	123,938	136,608	139,023	153,505	161,063
Residential	3,686	3,359	4,043	4,220	4,336	4,090	4,597	4,591
Multifamily	3,441	3,233	3,976	4,144	4,238	3,997	4,578	4,564
Office	3,192	3,559	3,914	4,404	4,619	4,571	4,305	5,268
Commercial [2]	1,119	1,075	1,329	1,724	2,227	1,977	2,408	2,116
Automotive	619	750	965	1,257	1,553	1,590	1,831	1,427
Parking	430	561	794	1,020	1,425	1,536	1,629	1,321
Warehouse	252	135	231	280	295	256	327	396
Health care	2,676	2,856	3,156	3,442	3,501	2,863	3,020	3,295
Hospital	1,431	1,633	1,960	2,108	2,498	1,965	2,118	2,258
Medical building	751	766	801	937	657	512	471	576
Special care	495	458	395	396	345	386	431	461
Educational [2]	19,227	20,541	25,743	28,603	33,758	34,847	39,011	43,607
Primary/secondary [2]	12,781	13,348	17,545	20,009	23,853	25,938	28,923	31,454
Elementary	4,533	4,177	5,242	6,301	8,015	9,447	9,783	11,213
Middle/junior high	2,789	2,637	3,745	3,685	3,988	3,908	5,663	5,395
High	3,170	3,638	4,833	6,130	6,687	7,589	10,485	12,612
Higher education [2]	5,294	6,047	6,883	7,311	8,198	7,681	8,459	9,961
Instructional	3,311	3,977	4,277	4,746	4,459	4,283	5,002	5,933
Parking	91	133	158	169	262	329	350	442
Administration	107	108	128	91	189	178	256	280
Dormitory	346	384	324	396	388	545	761	986
Library	252	212	300	439	695	367	310	271
Student union/cafeteria	104	170	238	231	405	317	283	303
Sports/recreation	474	535	625	538	873	792	728	864
Infrastructure	537	494	788	585	654	777	666	771
Other educational	929	864	1,110	1,121	1,250	1,122	1,301	1,559
Library/archive	475	481	704	853	779	563	896	923
Public safety [2]	5,226	5,371	5,928	6,718	6,868	7,515	7,505	6,854
Correctional	4,459	4,724	4,854	5,586	5,701	6,536	6,284	5,552
Detention	3,964	4,224	4,049	4,749	4,786	5,574	5,102	4,531
Police/sheriff	495	500	804	837	916	962	1,182	1,021
Other public safety	705	634	1,025	1,126	967	979	1,222	1,302
Fire/rescue	496	457	652	831	773	788	1,041	1,175
Amusement and recreation	4,943	5,612	6,142	6,056	6,857	7,605	8,735	8,750
Sports	1,398	1,227	1,637	1,477	2,311	3,147	3,249	2,699
Performance/meeting center	1,517	1,449	1,751	2,127	1,629	1,334	1,497	2,304
Convention center	1,158	1,076	1,224	1,318	938	829	1,047	1,608
Social center	883	1,089	772	911	961	939	1,334	1,367
Neighborhood center	487	670	581	612	673	617	1,010	1,049
Park/camp	916	1,604	1,696	1,430	1,874	2,004	2,462	2,241
Transportation	8,803	8,647	8,967	9,998	9,708	10,115	10,778	12,154
Air [2]	5,088	3,858	3,855	4,666	4,852	5,546	5,690	6,233
Passenger terminal	1,650	996	1,209	1,856	2,086	2,178	2,113	2,718
Runway	2,503	2,085	2,176	2,593	2,260	2,541	2,962	3,011
Land [2]	2,952	3,757	4,009	4,067	3,642	3,794	4,078	4,856
Passenger terminal	526	907	1,147	1,362	1,237	1,212	1,192	1,182
Mass transit	1,273	1,534	1,734	1,787	1,607	1,537	1,288	1,423
Railroad	327	498	462	402	401	559	983	1,364
Water [2]	764	1,033	1,103	1,264	1,214	775	1,011	1,065
Dock/marina	524	579	690	898	729	418	625	810
Dry dock/marine terminal	101	212	204	308	477	349	386	220
Power	3,159	2,763	2,879	2,503	3,101	2,227	2,637	3,502
Electrical	2,654	1,893	2,231	2,225	2,893	2,044	2,440	3,441
Distribution	920	482	733	656	1,650	1,505	1,433	1,378
Highway and street [2]	34,353	37,281	37,616	39,500	43,017	45,722	51,748	52,235
Pavement	26,503	29,402	29,164	30,472	32,416	33,894	38,393	38,271
Lighting	543	570	659	796	812	1,204	956	882
Retaining wall	219	325	187	176	493	723	858	1,116
Tunnel	393	454	346	430	539	877	972	919
Bridge	5,961	5,909	6,615	6,682	7,299	7,371	8,910	9,521
Toll/weigh	170	107	152	138	219	252	291	330
Maintenance building	119	158	53	159	307	369	372	300
Rest facility/streetscape	27	94	167	464	722	857	987	895
Sewage and waste disposal [2]	8,875	8,714	8,419	9,801	10,515	9,366	10,342	10,287
Sewage/dry waste	5,237	5,370	4,825	6,420	6,830	6,208	6,965	6,841
Plant	2,076	1,822	1,641	2,173	1,969	1,813	2,141	1,988
Line/pump station	2,612	3,225	2,960	4,001	4,639	4,165	4,536	4,671
Waste water	3,480	3,215	3,522	3,346	3,664	3,124	3,372	3,447
Plant	2,714	2,367	2,467	2,211	2,680	2,150	2,567	2,385
Line/drain	766	848	1,055	1,135	984	975	805	1,061
Water supply [2]	5,089	4,651	4,713	5,618	6,493	6,290	6,844	6,928
Plant	1,520	1,368	1,204	1,372	1,664	1,804	2,114	2,245
Well	118	170	212	260	179	234	250	272
Line	2,550	2,319	2,516	2,841	3,353	2,923	3,037	3,387
Pump station	193	274	286	437	349	394	559	429
Reservoir	317	260	208	409	514	403	401	194
Tank/tower	262	225	246	298	433	531	483	400
Conservation and development [2]	1,052	1,194	1,265	1,191	1,503	1,433	1,282	1,114
Dam/levee	149	205	329	349	631	593	500	355
Breakwater/jetty	320	431	358	472	360	453	363	316
Dredging	105	176	151	83	161	120	169	171

[1] Preliminary.   [2] Includes other types of construction, not shown separately.
Source: U.S. Census Bureau, Internet site <http://www.census.gov/pub/const/C30/newtc.html> (accessed 7 August 2001).

No. 933. Construction Contracts—Value of Construction and Floor Space of Buildings by Class of Construction: 1980 to 2000

[151.8 represents $151,800,000,000. Building construction includes new structures and additions; nonbuilding construction includes major alterations to existing structures which affect only valuation, since no additional floor area is created by "alteration"]

Year	Total	Residential buildings	Nonresidential buildings Total	Commercial[1]	Manufacturing	Educational[2]	Health	Public buildings	Religious	Social and recreational	Miscellaneous	Nonbuilding construction
VALUE (bil. dol.)												
1980	151.8	60.4	56.9	27.7	9.2	7.4	5.4	1.6	1.2	2.7	1.7	34.5
1985	235.6	102.1	92.1	54.6	8.1	10.0	7.8	3.1	2.0	4.0	2.5	41.4
1990	246.0	100.9	95.4	44.8	8.4	16.6	9.2	5.7	2.2	5.3	3.1	49.7
1991	230.8	94.4	86.2	32.7	8.3	19.0	9.6	6.2	2.4	5.1	3.0	50.2
1992	252.2	110.6	87.0	32.8	8.9	17.6	10.9	5.8	2.5	5.5	3.1	54.6
1993	271.5	123.9	88.8	34.2	9.0	19.3	10.5	3.9	2.4	6.8	2.6	58.9
1994	296.7	133.6	101.5	40.8	11.2	21.0	10.5	6.1	2.5	6.5	3.0	61.6
1995	306.5	127.9	114.2	46.6	13.6	22.9	10.8	6.3	2.8	7.1	3.8	64.4
1996	332.0	146.5	120.5	51.9	13.1	23.0	11.1	6.3	2.9	8.1	4.1	65.1
1997	362.4	153.6	138.9	59.8	14.0	28.4	11.9	7.0	3.8	10.0	4.0	69.8
1998	405.4	179.8	154.3	73.9	12.1	30.1	12.9	6.6	4.3	10.8	3.6	71.3
1999	447.8	195.0	169.2	77.4	11.2	37.2	13.7	8.3	4.6	11.8	5.1	83.6
2000	470.8	207.6	172.5	81.0	8.7	40.8	12.4	7.5	4.7	13.8	3.7	90.6
FLOOR SPACE (mil. sq. ft.)												
1980	3,102	1,839	1,263	738	220	103	55	18	28	49	52	(X)
1985	3,853	2,324	1,529	1,039	165	111	73	28	32	44	38	(X)
1990	3,020	1,817	1,203	694	128	152	69	47	29	51	32	(X)
1991	2,634	1,653	981	476	100	177	72	50	29	45	33	(X)
1992	2,799	1,864	936	462	95	156	77	41	30	42	32	(X)
1993	3,062	2,091	971	481	110	165	75	30	30	51	29	(X)
1994	3,411	2,267	1,144	600	143	172	72	45	30	51	31	(X)
1995	3,454	2,172	1,281	700	163	186	70	40	33	56	33	(X)
1996	3,776	2,479	1,297	723	155	177	77	41	32	60	33	(X)
1997	4,127	2,586	1,540	855	191	204	89	48	42	77	35	(X)
1998	4,811	3,015	1,796	1,106	166	219	96	42	47	85	34	(X)
1999	5,099	3,255	1,844	1,117	141	262	99	50	49	88	39	(X)
2000	4,967	3,105	1,862	1,176	110	273	88	44	50	94	27	(X)

X Not applicable.   [1] Includes nonindustrial warehouses.   [2] Includes science.

Source: F. W. Dodge, a Division of the McGraw-Hill Companies, New York, NY (copyright).

No. 934. Construction Contracts—Value by State: 1990 to 2000

[In millions of dollars (246,022 represents $246,022,000,000). Represents value of construction in states in which work was actually done. See headnote, Table 933]

State	1990	1995	2000 Total[1]	2000 Residential	2000 Nonresidential	State	1990	1995	2000 Total[1]	2000 Residential	2000 Nonresidential
U.S.	246,022	306,527	470,800	207,645	172,505	MO	3,833	6,438	7,485	3,119	2,711
AL	2,939	4,308	7,211	2,546	2,522	MT	332	865	995	386	333
AK	1,919	1,660	1,307	367	472	NE	1,318	1,694	986	986	1,032
AZ	4,553	8,784	13,940	8,171	4,137	NV	3,334	5,555	7,027	3,743	2,337
AR	1,438	2,903	3,705	1,535	1,014	NH	1,021	1,039	2,535	954	808
CA	37,318	29,045	52,918	24,889	18,747	NJ	6,141	6,454	11,153	3,732	5,519
CO	3,235	6,476	12,305	7,122	3,386	NM	1,124	2,108	3,136	859	1,464
CT	3,058	3,124	5,149	1,672	2,862	NY	14,137	13,380	20,455	5,940	9,303
DE	787	871	1,342	510	472	NC	6,614	10,599	17,221	9,497	5,836
DC	795	656	1,879	164	1,600	ND	506	791	863	240	297
FL	16,975	21,453	35,141	18,783	11,598	OH	9,885	12,430	16,260	7,128	6,161
GA	7,120	12,156	20,450	10,553	6,963	OK	2,164	2,968	5,281	1,806	1,686
HI	2,831	2,273	1,392	787	308	OR	3,101	5,451	6,059	2,749	2,098
ID	986	1,864	2,559	1,486	769	PA	10,117	9,348	14,592	4,888	6,385
IL	10,796	11,744	17,175	6,863	6,124	RI	594	465	1,077	354	333
IN	6,350	7,896	10,915	5,234	3,536	SC	3,664	4,580	7,722	3,883	2,273
IA	2,034	2,883	3,777	1,440	1,300	SD	468	706	1,186	415	339
KS	2,193	3,264	4,465	1,724	1,591	TN	4,388	7,167	10,100	4,370	4,136
KY	3,174	4,464	6,650	2,647	2,464	TX	13,197	23,022	39,758	18,035	13,745
LA	3,191	4,354	5,543	1,567	1,994	UT	1,884	4,218	4,406	2,120	1,605
ME	897	1,076	1,712	768	636	VT	515	484	600	259	198
MD	6,056	6,299	7,783	3,744	2,875	VA	7,180	8,794	13,493	6,039	5,112
MA	5,135	7,411	12,024	3,060	5,855	WA	6,185	7,334	10,462	4,564	4,357
MI	7,646	9,947	14,823	6,537	5,494	WV	1,253	1,215	1,675	236	571
MN	4,953	5,607	8,774	4,089	3,025	WI	4,654	5,652	7,958	3,653	2,910
MS	1,769	2,718	2,924	1,129	1,019	WY	462	532	774	305	192

[1] Includes nonbuilding construction, not shown separately.

Source: F. W. Dodge, a Division of the McGraw-Hill Companies, New York, NY (copyright).

Construction and Housing   595

No. 935. New Privately-Owned Housing Units Authorized by State: 1999 and 2000

[1,663.5 represents 1,663,500. Based on about 19,000 places in United States having building permit systems]

State	Housing units (1,000) 1999	Housing units (1,000) 2000 Total	Housing units (1,000) 2000 1 unit	Valuation (mil. dol.) 1999	Valuation (mil. dol.) 2000 Total	Valuation (mil. dol.) 2000 1 unit	State	Housing units (1,000) 1999	Housing units (1,000) 2000 Total	Housing units (1,000) 2000 1 unit	Valuation (mil. dol.) 1999	Valuation (mil. dol.) 2000 Total	Valuation (mil. dol.) 2000 1 unit
U.S.	1,663.5	1,592.3	1,198.1	181,246	185,744	160,623	MO	26.8	24.3	17.9	2,739	2,569	2,234
AL	19.0	17.4	13.7	1,883	1,718	1,499	MT	2.6	2.6	1.6	226	235	182
AK	2.2	2.1	1.6	307	333	274	NE	8.7	9.1	6.5	828	830	716
AZ	65.1	61.5	48.8	7,350	7,158	6,357	NV	32.6	32.3	25.7	2,977	3,312	2,954
AR	11.5	9.2	6.9	966	859	768	NH	6.3	6.7	6.1	782	937	895
CA	138.0	145.6	105.0	21,031	23,344	19,997	NJ	32.0	34.6	25.3	3,162	3,376	2,870
CO	49.3	54.6	38.6	6,036	6,822	5,650	NM	9.7	8.9	8.2	1,080	1,073	1,039
CT	10.6	9.4	8.2	1,466	1,425	1,328	NY	42.6	44.1	23.9	4,411	4,992	3,493
DE	5.3	4.6	3.9	492	414	388	NC	84.8	78.4	59.1	8,617	8,643	7,724
DC	0.7	0.8	0.2	53	54	22	ND	2.6	2.1	1.3	223	190	147
FL	164.7	155.3	106.4	16,102	17,462	13,540	OH	55.9	49.7	38.0	6,401	6,154	5,551
GA	89.6	91.8	68.9	8,749	8,722	7,586	OK	14.2	11.1	9.0	1,430	1,204	1,100
HI	4.2	4.9	4.3	633	823	745	OR	23.2	19.9	15.6	2,653	2,533	2,248
ID	12.2	10.9	9.7	1,357	1,359	1,287	PA	42.7	41.1	34.5	4,635	4,616	4,216
IL	54.0	51.9	37.8	6,538	6,528	5,612	RI	3.4	2.6	2.3	336	296	277
IN	41.5	37.9	30.4	4,748	4,414	4,044	SC	36.2	32.8	24.9	3,615	3,533	3,037
IA	13.4	12.5	8.5	1,400	1,333	1,099	SD	3.7	4.2	3.1	330	369	313
KS	15.7	12.5	9.3	1,667	1,397	1,235	TN	37.0	32.2	24.4	3,835	3,378	2,986
KY	21.6	18.5	14.8	1,909	1,767	1,607	TX	146.6	141.2	108.6	14,041	15,418	13,810
LA	17.8	14.7	13.1	1,767	1,553	1,447	UT	20.5	17.6	14.7	2,287	2,138	1,938
ME	5.7	6.2	5.7	623	723	692	VA	53.2	48.4	39.8	5,142	5,052	4,622
MD	29.8	30.4	25.1	3,102	3,232	2,961	WA	42.8	39.0	25.5	4,578	4,426	3,502
MA	19.0	18.0	14.2	2,666	2,741	2,380	WV	4.2	3.8	3.3	381	360	340
MI	54.3	52.5	43.0	6,205	6,256	5,696	WI	35.6	34.2	24.0	3,863	3,917	3,270
MN	33.3	32.8	25.5	4,053	4,204	3,614	WY	1.9	1.6	1.4	279	314	303
MS	12.9	11.3	7.6	990	918	748							

Source: U.S. Census Bureau, Construction Reports, Series C40, Building Permits, monthly; publication discontinued in 2001. See Internet site <http://www.census.gov/ftp/pub/const/www/newresconstindex.html> and New Residential Construction, monthly.

No. 936. New Privately-Owned Housing Units Started—Selected Characteristics: 1970 to 2000

[In thousands (1,434 represents 1,434,000). For composition of regions, see map, inside front cover]

Year	Total units	Structures with— One unit	Structures with— 2 to 4 units	Structures with— 5 or more units	Region North-east	Region Mid-west	Region South	Region West	Units for sale Total	Units for sale Single-family	Units for sale Multi-family
1970	1,434	813	85	536	218	294	612	311	(NA)	(NA)	(NA)
1975	1,160	892	64	204	149	294	442	275	576	531	45
1976	1,538	1,162	86	289	169	400	569	400	768	705	63
1977	1,987	1,451	122	414	202	465	783	538	994	904	90
1978	2,020	1,433	125	462	200	451	824	545	1,032	901	131
1979	1,745	1,194	122	429	178	349	748	470	915	742	173
1980	1,292	852	110	331	125	218	643	306	689	526	163
1981	1,084	705	91	288	117	165	562	240	584	426	158
1982	1,062	663	80	320	117	149	591	205	549	409	140
1983	1,703	1,068	113	522	168	218	935	382	923	713	210
1984	1,750	1,084	121	544	204	243	866	436	934	728	206
1985	1,742	1,072	93	576	252	240	782	468	867	713	154
1986	1,805	1,179	84	542	294	296	733	483	925	782	143
1987	1,621	1,146	65	409	269	298	634	420	862	732	130
1988	1,488	1,081	59	348	235	274	575	404	808	709	99
1989	1,376	1,003	55	318	179	266	536	396	735	648	87
1990	1,193	895	37	260	131	253	479	329	585	529	56
1991	1,014	840	36	138	113	233	414	254	531	490	41
1992	1,200	1,030	31	139	127	288	497	288	659	618	41
1993	1,288	1,126	29	133	126	298	562	302	760	716	44
1994	1,457	1,198	35	224	138	329	639	351	815	763	52
1995	1,354	1,076	34	244	118	290	615	331	763	712	51
1996	1,477	1,161	45	271	132	322	662	361	833	774	59
1997	1,474	1,134	44	296	137	304	670	363	843	784	59
1998	1,617	1,271	43	303	149	331	743	395	941	832	59
1999	1,641	1,302	32	307	156	347	746	392	981	912	69
2000	1,569	1,231	39	299	155	318	714	383	946	871	75

NA Not available.

Source: U.S. Census Bureau, Current Construction Reports, Series C20, Housing Starts, monthly; publication discontinued in 2001. See Internet site <http://www.census.gov/const/www/newresconstindex.html> and New Residential Construction, monthly.

U.S. Census Bureau. Statistical Abstract of the United States: 2001

No. 937. New Privately-Owned Housing Units Started by State: 1997 to 2000

[In thousands of units (1,476 represents 1,476,000)]

State	1997	1998	1999	2000 Total units	2000 Single-family units	State	1997	1998	1999	2000 Total units	2000 Single-family units
U.S.	1,476	1,623	1,660	1,535	1,223	MO	27.9	29.7	29.6	26.0	22.2
AL	21.7	23.7	23.5	21.2	17.7	MT	2.5	2.4	2.5	2.2	1.4
AK	2.5	2.7	2.4	2.1	1.6	NE	9.8	9.8	9.7	8.4	6.2
AZ	58.2	65.2	66.5	60.0	48.2	NV	35.6	36.4	35.1	34.5	25.3
AR	13.0	12.9	13.7	12.5	9.5	NH	5.3	5.7	6.0	6.0	5.6
CA	109.1	123.0	129.9	128.2	99.9	NJ	26.8	29.7	31.9	31.2	25.4
CO	43.8	50.6	49.9	45.9	36.0	NM	10.5	9.4	9.2	8.1	7.2
CT	9.1	11.0	10.6	10.0	8.7	NY	30.5	34.0	36.3	34.9	22.7
DE	4.9	5.5	5.4	5.2	4.8	NC	74.1	81.5	85.8	74.8	59.2
DC	-	0.4	0.4	0.4	0.3	ND	3.2	3.3	3.2	2.7	1.8
FL	135.2	143.9	152.8	148.1	104.9	OH	44.6	47.0	49.8	45.3	37.7
GA	78.6	87.1	88.4	81.5	68.4	OK	13.2	16.3	16.2	15.5	12.4
HI	3.8	3.4	3.7	3.8	3.2	OR	26.6	25.6	24.5	22.2	15.8
ID	10.5	12.0	12.6	11.5	10.1	PA	38.6	40.1	41.1	37.5	32.4
IL	46.5	49.2	52.4	48.1	38.9	RI	2.6	2.7	2.9	2.7	2.5
IN	36.0	40.8	41.8	37.6	32.3	SC	31.2	33.2	35.8	33.9	27.1
IA	11.2	13.7	13.6	13.0	10.7	SD	3.4	3.8	4.1	3.5	2.8
KS	13.6	15.6	16.4	15.2	11.7	TN	37.8	37.4	37.3	33.9	29.9
KY	20.5	23.2	23.2	21.4	17.5	TX	134.0	159.8	155.2	148.4	108.3
LA	16.7	17.8	18.6	15.8	13.4	UT	19.8	21.1	20.5	19.5	16.1
ME	4.6	5.8	5.8	5.8	5.5	VT	1.8	2.2	2.4	2.4	2.1
MD	26.5	31.2	30.3	27.9	23.0	VA	46.9	50.9	53.0	50.2	42.6
MA	16.9	18.2	18.0	17.7	15.5	WA	40.7	44.0	43.7	40.9	28.4
MI	49.0	54.5	55.4	50.9	44.2	WV	5.1	5.1	5.8	5.3	4.1
MN	25.2	30.8	32.9	30.7	26.8	WI	30.7	34.3	35.4	32.0	24.7
MS	12.2	15.0	15.2	12.8	10.1	WY	1.9	2.1	2.0	1.8	1.5

- Represents or rounds to zero.

Source: National Association of Home Builders, Economics Division, Washington, DC. Data provided by the Econometric Forecasting Service.

No. 938. Characteristics of New Privately-Owned One-Family Houses Completed: 1970 to 1999

[Percent distribution, except as indicated (793 represents 793,000). Data beginning 1980 show percent distribution of characteristics for all houses completed (includes new houses completed, houses built for sale completed, contractor-built and owner-built houses completed, and houses completed for rent). Data for 1970 cover contractor-built, owner-built, and houses for rent for year construction started and houses sold for year of sale. Percents exclude houses for which characteristics specified were not reported]

Characteristic	1970	1980	1990	1995	1999	Characteristic	1970	1980	1990	1995	1999
Total houses (1,000)	793	957	966	1,066	1,307	Bedrooms	100	100	100	100	100
						2 or less	13	17	15	13	12
Financing [1]	100	100	100	100	100	3	63	63	57	57	54
Mortgage	84	82	82	88	91	4 or more	24	20	29	30	34
FHA-insured	30	16	14	8	9	Bathrooms	100	100	100	100	100
VA-guaranteed	7	8	4	5	3	1 1/2 or less	52	27	13	11	7
Conventional	47	55	62	74	79	2	32	48	42	41	38
Rural Housing Service [2]	(3)	3	2	1	1	2 1/2 or more	16	25	45	48	55
Cash or equivalent	16	18	18	12	9	Heating fuel	100	100	100	100	100
Floor area	100	100	100	100	100	Gas	62	41	59	67	70
Under 1,200 sq. ft	36	21	11	10	7	Electricity	28	30	33	28	27
1,200 to 1,599 sq. ft	28	29	22	22	19	Oil	8	3	5	3	3
1,600 to 1,999 sq. ft	16	22	22	23	22	Other	1	5	3	1	1
2,000 to 2,399 sq. ft	21	13	17	17	18	Heating system	100	100	100	100	100
2,400 sq. ft. and over	(4)	15	29	28	34	Warm air furnace	71	57	65	67	72
Average (sq. ft.)	1,500	1,740	2,080	2,095	2,225	Electric heat pump	(NA)	24	23	25	22
Median (sq. ft.)	1,385	1,595	1,905	1,920	2,030	Other	29	19	12	9	6
Number of stories	100	100	100	100	100	Central air-conditioning	100	100	100	100	100
1	74	60	46	49	48	With	34	63	76	80	84
2 or more	17	31	49	48	51	Without	66	37	24	20	16
Split level	10	8	4	3	1	Fireplaces	100	100	100	100	100
Foundation	100	100	100	100	100	No fireplace	65	43	34	37	38
Full or partial basement	37	36	38	39	37	1 or more	35	56	66	63	62
Slab	36	45	40	42	47	Parking facilities	100	100	100	100	100
Crawl space	27	19	21	19	17	Garage	58	69	82	84	87
						Carport	17	7	2	2	1
						No garage or carport	25	24	16	14	12

NA Not available. [1] Excludes homes not yet sold. [2] Prior to 1999, Farmers Home Administration. [3] Included with "Conventional" financing. [4] Included with floor area of 2,000 to 2,399 square feet.

Source: U.S. Census Bureau and U.S. Dept. of Housing and Urban Development, Current Construction Reports, Series C25, New One-Family Houses Sold, monthly, and Characteristics of New Housing, annual; publication discontinued in 2001, see Internet site <http://www.census.gov/const/www/newressalesindex.html>.

No. 939. New Privately Owned One-Family Houses Sold by Region and Type of Financing, 1980 to 2000, and by Sales-Price Group, 2000

[In thousands (545 represents 545,000). Based on a national probability sample of monthly interviews with builders or owners of 1-family houses for which building permits have been issued or, for nonpermit areas, on which construction has started. For details, see source. For composition of regions, see map inside front cover]

Year and sales-price group		Region				Financing type			
	Total sales	North-east	Midwest	South	West	Conven-tional [1]	FHA and VA	Rural Housing Service [2]	Cash
1980	545	50	81	267	145	302	196	14	32
1985	688	112	82	323	170	403	208	11	64
1990	534	71	89	225	149	337	138	10	50
1994	670	61	123	295	191	490	130	9	41
1995	667	55	125	300	187	490	129	9	39
1996	757	74	137	337	209	570	140	9	38
1997	804	78	140	363	223	616	137	6	46
1998	888	81	164	398	243	693	136	9	48
1999	880	76	168	395	242	689	143	6	41
2000	877	71	155	406	244	695	138	4	40
Under $100,000	88	3	13	65	8	(NA)	(NA)	(NA)	(NA)
$100,000 to $149,999	262	12	47	142	62	(NA)	(NA)	(NA)	(NA)
$150,000 to $199,999	200	15	39	89	56	(NA)	(NA)	(NA)	(NA)
$200,000 to $299,999	194	20	35	71	69	(NA)	(NA)	(NA)	(NA)
$300,000 and over	132	22	23	39	49	(NA)	(NA)	(NA)	(NA)

NA Not available.   [1] Includes all other types of financing.   [2] Prior to 1996, the Farmers Home Administration.

Source: U.S. Census Bureau and U.S. Dept. of Housing and Urban Development, *Current Construction Reports*, Series C25, *Characteristics of New Housing*, annual; and *New One-Family Houses Sold*, monthly; publications discontinued in 2001. See Internet site <http://www.census.gov/ftp/pub/const/www/newressalesindex.html> and *New Residential Sales*, monthly.

No. 940. Median Sales Price of New Privately Owned One-Family Houses Sold by Region: 1980 to 2000

[In dollars. For definition of median, see Guide to Tabular Presentation. For composition of regions, see map inside front cover]

Year	U.S.	North-east	Mid-west	South	West	Year	U.S.	North-east	Mid-west	South	West
1980	64,600	69,500	63,400	59,600	72,300	1994	130,000	169,000	132,900	116,900	140,400
1985	84,300	103,300	80,300	75,000	92,600	1995	133,900	180,000	134,000	124,500	141,400
1989	120,000	159,600	108,800	96,400	139,000	1996	140,000	186,000	138,000	126,200	153,900
1990	122,900	159,000	107,900	99,000	147,500	1997	146,000	190,000	149,900	129,600	160,000
1991	120,000	155,900	110,000	100,000	141,100	1998	152,500	200,000	157,500	135,800	163,500
1992	121,500	169,000	115,600	105,500	130,400	1999	161,000	210,500	164,000	145,900	173,700
1993	126,500	162,600	125,000	115,000	135,000	2000	169,000	227,400	169,700	148,000	196,400

Source: U.S. Census Bureau and U.S. Dept. of Housing and Urban Development, *Current Construction Reports*, Series C25, *Characteristics of New Housing*, annual; and *New One-Family Houses Sold*, monthly; publications discontinued in 2001. See Internet site <http://www.census.gov/ftp/pub/const/www/newressalesindex.html> and *New Residential Sales*, monthly.

No. 941. New Manufactured (Mobile) Homes Placed for Residential Use and Average Sales Price by Region: 1980 to 2000

[233.7 represents 233,700. A mobile home is a moveable dwelling, 8 feet or more wide and 40 feet or more long, designed to be towed on its own chassis, with transportation gear integral to the unit when it leaves the factory, and without need of permanent foundation. Excluded are travel trailers, motor homes, and modular housing. Data are based on a probability sample and subject to sampling variability; see source. For composition of regions, see map inside front cover]

Year	Units placed (1,000)					Average sales price (dol.)				
	Total	North-east	Mid-west	South	West	U.S.	North-east	Mid-west	South	West
1980	233.7	12.3	32.3	140.3	48.7	19,800	18,500	18,600	18,200	25,400
1985	283.4	20.2	38.6	187.6	36.9	21,800	22,700	21,500	20,400	28,700
1990	195.4	18.8	37.7	108.4	30.6	27,800	30,000	27,000	24,500	39,300
1992	212.0	15.0	42.2	124.4	30.4	28,400	30,900	28,800	25,400	39,000
1993	242.5	15.4	44.5	146.7	35.9	30,500	32,000	31,400	27,700	40,500
1994	290.9	16.3	53.3	177.7	43.6	32,800	32,900	34,000	30,200	41,900
1995	319.4	15.0	57.5	203.2	43.7	35,300	35,800	35,700	33,300	44,100
1996	337.7	16.2	58.8	218.2	44.4	37,200	37,300	38,000	35,500	45,000
1997	336.3	14.3	55.3	219.4	47.3	39,800	41,300	40,300	38,000	47,300
1998	373.7	14.7	58.3	250.3	50.4	41,600	42,200	42,400	40,100	48,400
1999	338.2	13.7	52.4	229.1	43.1	43,400	44,300	44,400	41,900	49,700
2000	273.0	14.2	46.0	177.7	35.2	46,500	47,200	48,400	44,200	55,400

Source: U.S. Census Bureau, Internet site <http://www.census.gov/ftp/pub/const/www/mhsindex.html>.

No. 942. Existing One-Family Houses Sold and Price by Region: 1970 to 2000

[1,612 represents 1,612,000. Based on data (adjusted and aggregated to regional and national totals) reported by participating real estate multiple listing services. For definition of median, see Guide to Tabular Presentation. For composition of regions, see map inside front cover]

Year	Houses sold (1,000)					Median sales price (dol.)				
	Total	North-east	Mid-west	South	West	Total	North-east	Mid-west	South	West
1970	1,612	251	501	568	292	23,000	25,700	20,100	22,200	24,300
1975	2,476	370	701	862	543	35,300	39,300	30,100	34,800	39,600
1980	2,973	403	806	1,092	672	62,200	60,800	51,900	58,300	89,300
1981	2,419	353	632	917	516	66,400	63,700	54,300	64,400	96,200
1982	1,990	354	490	780	366	67,800	63,500	55,100	67,100	98,900
1983	2,697	477	692	1,004	524	70,300	72,200	56,600	69,200	94,900
1984	2,829	478	720	1,006	624	72,400	78,700	57,100	71,300	95,800
1985	3,134	561	806	1,063	704	75,500	88,900	58,900	75,200	95,400
1986	3,474	635	922	1,145	773	80,300	104,800	63,500	78,200	100,900
1987	3,436	618	892	1,163	763	85,600	133,300	66,000	80,400	113,200
1988	3,513	606	865	1,224	817	89,300	143,000	68,400	82,200	124,900
1989 [1]	3,325	490	832	1,185	818	89,500	127,700	71,800	84,400	127,100
1990	3,219	458	809	1,193	759	92,000	126,400	75,300	85,100	129,600
1991	3,186	463	812	1,173	737	97,100	129,100	79,500	88,500	135,300
1992	3,479	521	913	1,242	802	99,700	128,900	83,000	91,500	131,500
1993	3,786	550	967	1,386	882	103,100	129,100	86,000	94,300	132,500
1994	3,916	552	965	1,436	962	107,200	129,100	89,300	95,700	139,400
1995	3,888	547	945	1,433	964	110,500	126,700	94,800	97,700	141,000
1996	4,196	584	986	1,511	1,116	115,800	127,800	101,000	103,400	147,100
1997	4,382	607	1,005	1,595	1,174	121,800	131,800	107,000	109,600	155,200
1998	4,970	662	1,130	1,868	1,309	128,400	135,900	114,300	116,200	164,800
1999	5,205	656	1,148	2,015	1,386	133,300	139,000	119,600	120,300	173,900
2000	5,113	645	1,115	1,992	1,362	139,000	139,400	123,600	128,300	183,000

[1] Beginning 1989 data not comparable to earlier years due to rebenchmarking.

Source: NATIONAL ASSOCIATION OF REALTORS®, Washington, DC, prior to 1990, *Home Sales*, monthly, and *Home Sales Yearbook: 1990*; (copyright); thereafter, *Real Estate Outlook; Market Trends & Insights*, monthly, (copyright).

No. 943. Median Sales Price of Existing One-Family Homes by Selected Metropolitan Area: 1998 to 2000

[In thousands of dollars (128.4 represents $128,400). For the top 60 areas in sales price in 2000. Areas are metropolitan statistical areas defined by source as of 1992, except as noted]

Metropolitan area	1998	1999	2000	Metropolitan area	1998	1999	2000
United States, all areas.	128.4	133.3	139.0	Miami-Hialeah, FL PMSA	121.5	134.6	144.6
				Milwaukee, WI PMSA	132.9	135.3	140.7
Albuquerque, NM	128.2	130.3	130.4	Minneapolis-St. Paul, MN-WI . . .	128.0	138.7	151.4
Anaheim-Santa Ana, CA PMSA				Nashville, TN	116.7	116.4	(NA)
(Orange Co.) [1]	261.7	280.9	318.0	New Haven-Meriden, CT	137.8	145.7	151.6
Atlanta, GA	115.4	123.7	131.2	NY: Bergen-Passaic, NJ PMSA . .	213.5	221.8	261.2
Aurora-Elgin, IL [2]	146.2	151.9	163.0	NY: Middlesex-Somerset-			
Austin/San Marcos, TX	121.1	128.6	142.8	Hunterdon, NJ PMSA.	184.2	196.8	219.7
Baltimore, MD	120.6	127.4	153.0	NY: Monmouth-Ocean, NJ	152.6	164.4	179.0
Birmingham, AL	122.7	127.1	125.5	NY: Nassau-Suffolk, NY PMSA . .	175.4	190.4	214.0
Boise, ID	109.2	123.9	126.0	NY: New York-North NJ-			
Boston, MA PMSA	258.4	290.0	314.2	Long Island, NY CMSA	188.1	203.2	230.2
Bradenton, FL [2]	107.3	117.2	127.3	NY: Newark, NJ	199.2	212.0	242.4
Charleston, SC.	120.0	131.7	137.9	Philadelphia, PA-NJ PMSA	129.7	124.8	125.2
Charlotte-Gastonia-Rock Hill,				Phoenix, AZ.	120.2	126.4	134.4
NC-SC	134.0	138.2	140.3	Portland, OR PMSA	158.1	165.0	170.1
Chicago, IL PMSA	166.8	171.2	171.8	Providence, RI PMSA	124.4	128.8	137.8
Cincinnati, OH-KY-IN PMSA	116.3	119.9	126.7	Raleigh-Durham, NC	159.8	165.0	158.4
Colorado Springs, CO	138.5	144.9	154.1	Reno, NV	147.2	150.6	157.3
Columbus, OH	121.7	125.0	129.1	Richmond-Petersburg, VA	122.0	128.5	129.8
Dallas, TX PMSA	111.0	115.7	122.5	Riverside-San Bernadino, CA			
Denver, CO PMSA	152.2	171.3	196.8	PMSA [1].	121.5	128.7	138.6
Eugene-Springfield, OR	124.4	129.5	132.8	Sacramento, CA [1]	125.6	131.5	146.5
Ft. Lauderdale-Hollywood-				Salt Lake City-Ogden, UT.	133.5	137.9	141.5
Pompano Bch, FL PMSA	128.6	136.1	148.7	San Diego, CA [1]	207.1	231.6	269.4
Greensboro/Winston Salem/				San Francisco, CA Area [1]	321.7	340.8	454.6
High Point, NC	123.5	124.8	129.3	Sarasota, FL [2]	123.1	134.8	132.0
Hartford, CT PMSA	142.8	150.7	159.9	Seattle, WA	175.3	(NA)	230.1
Honolulu, HI.	297.0	290.0	295.0	Tacoma, WA	(NA)	(NA)	151.1
Kansas City, MO-KS	114.0	120.7	127.4	Trenton, NJ	139.5	144.2	150.9
Lake County, IL	159.4	164.0	169.4	Washington, DC-MD-VA.	172.1	176.5	182.6
Las Vegas, NV.	128.2	130.8	137.4	West Palm Bch-Boca Raton-			
Los Angeles-Long Beach, CA				Delray Bch, FL	126.6	131.0	138.4
PMSA [1]	192.6	199.0	215.9	Wilmington, DE-NJ-MD	123.9	120.6	127.6
Madison, WI	131.8	136.5	153.6	Worcester, MA	110.0	117.0	131.8

NA Not available. [1] California data supplied by the California Association of REALTORS®. [2] In 1992, Bradenton and Sarasota were merg. .d and Aurora/Elgin was incorporated into Chicago. The source still collects price data on the previous jurisdictions.

Source: NATIONAL ASSOCIATION OF REALTORS®, Washington, DC, *Real Estate Outlook: Market Trends & Insights*, monthly, (copyright).

Construction and Housing 599

Existing Home Sales by State: 1990 to 2000

[In thousands (3,599 represents 3,599,000). Includes condos and co-ops as well as single-family homes]

State	1990	1995	1999	2000	State	1990	1995	1999	2000
United States	3,599	4,350	5,929	5,842	Missouri	77.1	100.8	122.9	118.6,
Alabama	52.0	69.0	87.0	75.9	Montana	13.5	14.8	19.1	19.7
Alaska	12.3	10.2	16.0	18.9	Nebraska	23.6	25.0	34.3	31.3
Arizona	71.8	120.3	170.0	180.3	Nevada	26.9	31.0	47.3	56.7
Arkansas	33.7	45.0	63.5	54.7	New Hampshire	13.5	26.2	40.6	43.5
California	413.1	426.7	708.7	733.5	New Jersey	85.7	102.4	141.9	134.4
Colorado	77.7	102.5	136.2	157.3	New Mexico	24.7	27.6	29.8	30.6
Connecticut	37.4	43.3	51.0	53.2	New York	135.9	149.7	179.5	194.7
Delaware	7.9	9.5	8.6	7.7	North Carolina	98.9	157.7	228.6	215.5
District of Columbia	7.2	7.0	13.8	12.7	North Dakota	8.5	8.5	10.3	10.2
Florida	281.1	379.6	509.8	505.4	Ohio	146.9	173.1	194.9	187.9
Georgia	91.2	101.0	149.2	144.5	Oklahoma	62.2	74.5	100.1	91.9
Hawaii	19.0	10.3	17.8	22.8	Oregon	56.6	58.7	62.4	64.0
Idaho	22.3	27.1	28.6	30.4	Pennsylvania	143.2	163.2	177.9	168.3
Illinois	163.3	183.4	243.9	239.0	Rhode Island	9.6	13.6	20.7	21.0
Indiana	83.6	102.6	132.0	126.8	South Carolina	54.3	70.7	104.3	97.0
Iowa	42.8	43.2	57.8	53.1	South Dakota	10.8	11.9	15.4	15.4
Kansas	36.8	50.5	67.9	64.2	Tennessee	66.2	106.6	149.0	140.2
Kentucky	47.9	61.5	77.8	71.3	Texas	311.8	367.9	551.9	518.5
Louisiana	57.1	77.3	88.8	84.2	Utah	29.4	43.5	46.5	50.9
Maine	17.0	25.5	34.7	40.7	Vermont	7.2	7.9	6.9	7.2
Maryland	67.0	63.5	103.1	101.0	Virginia	89.3	94.8	146.9	131.4
Massachusetts	47.9	69.4	97.7	94.1	Washington	85.9	110.9	175.7	189.9
Michigan	137.6	142.2	160.4	150.8	West Virginia	22.6	26.1	26.7	21.5
Minnesota	68.1	81.6	106.5	105.5	Wisconsin	62.1	78.2	100.8	94.2
Mississippi	28.2	41.3	51.1	45.1	Wyoming	8.5	11.4	13.1	13.5

Source: NATIONAL ASSOCIATION OF REALTORS®, Washington, DC, *Real Estate Outlook: Market Trends & Insights*, monthly (copyright).

No. 945. Existing Apartment Condos and Co-Ops—Units Sold and Average Sales Price by Region: 1990 to 2000

[348 represents 348,000. For definition of median, see Guide to Tabular Presentation. For composition of regions, see map inside front cover]

Year	Units sold (1,000)					Median sales price (dol.)				
	Total	North-east	Mid-west	South	West	U.S.	North-east	Mid-west	South	West
1990	348	45	42	151	110	85,200	110,200	70,200	66,800	105,200
1991	333	48	43	145	97	85,800	107,200	73,900	68,300	105,100
1992	361	57	49	153	102	86,000	103,100	79,000	69,400	107,700
1993	400	63	53	175	108	84,400	99,200	78,900	69,300	102,700
1994	439	69	54	196	119	87,200	99,500	86,200	69,500	108,800
1995	428	70	53	188	116	87,400	94,800	90,700	70,600	105,300
1996	476	78	58	206	134	90,900	97,500	95,200	73,500	109,900
1997	524	88	64	220	152	95,500	101,100	99,100	76,300	118,300
1998	607	104	75	252	176	100,600	103,400	106,400	80,000	126,400
1999	681	116	81	295	190	108,000	112,500	114,600	84,100	132,100
2000	711	114	82	315	200	111,800	111,200	121,700	87,700	136,800

Source: NATIONAL ASSOCIATION OF REALTORS®, Washington, DC, *Real Estate Outlook: Market Trends & Insights*, monthly (copyright).

No. 946. New Apartments Completed and Rented in 3 Months by Region: 1980 to 2000

[196.1 represents 196,100. Structures with five or more units, privately financed, nonsubsidized, unfurnished rental apartments. Based on sample and subject to sampling variability; see source for details. For composition of regions, see map, inside front cover]

Year and rent	Number (1,000)					Percent rented in 3 months				
	U.S.	North-east	Mid-west	South	West	U.S.	North-east	Mid-west	South	West
1980	196.1	14.2	43.8	91.5	46.6	75	77	77	74	75
1985	365.2	8.1	54.0	166.1	137.0	65	69	72	59	68
1990 [1]	214.3	12.7	44.3	77.2	80.0	67	66	75	64	65
1995	155.0	7.1	31.7	78.5	37.7	73	74	75	72	73
2000, prel.	226.1	14.9	39.7	125.7	45.8	72	85	77	67	77
Less than $550	19.4	1.4	6.0	10.2	1.8	75	91	83	36	88
$550 to $749	62.6	0.6	16.2	36.0	9.7	72	82	79	70	72
$550 to $649	26.0	0.5	9.8	12.9	2.8	78	97	87	74	66
$650 to $749	36.6	0.1	6.4	23.1	6.9	68	6	68	67	74
$750 to $949	61.1	3.9	10.0	37.0	10.3	70	93	72	67	74
$750 to $849	34.5	1.3	6.8	21.2	5.3	72	100	76	68	76
$850 to $949	26.6	2.6	3.2	15.8	5.0	68	90	63	65	71
$950 or more	82.9	9.0 [2]	7.4	42.5	24.0 [2]	72	81	74	66	79
Median monthly asking rent . .	839	[2]	712	828	[2]	(X)	(X)	(X)	(X)	(X)

X Not applicable.   [1] Due to revised estimation procedures, data beginning 1990 not strictly comparable with prior years.
[2] Over $950.
Source: U.S. Census Bureau, *Current Housing Reports*, Series H130, *Market Absorption of Apartments*, and unpublished data.

No. 947. Total Housing Inventory for the United States: 1980 to 2000

[In thousands, except percent (87,739 represents 87,739,000). Based on the Current Population Survey and the Housing Vacancy Survey and subject to sampling error; see source for details]

Item	1980	1985	1990	1994	1995	1996	1997	1998	1999	2000
All housing units	87,739	97,333	106,283	110,952	112,655	114,139	115,621	117,282	119,044	119,628
Vacant	8,101	9,446	12,059	12,257	12,669	13,155	13,419	13,748	14,116	13,908
Year-round vacant.	5,996	7,400	9,128	9,229	9,570	9,945	10,114	10,516	10,848	10,439
For rent	1,575	2,221	2,662	2,858	2,946	3,008	2,978	3,046	3,119	3,024
For sale only.	734	1,006	1,064	953	1,022	1,082	1,133	1,205	1,184	1,148
Rented or sold	623	664	660	772	810	834	867	927	956	856
Held off market	3,064	3,510	4,742	4,646	4,793	5,022	5,136	5,338	5,589	5,411
Occasional use	814	977	1,485	1,612	1,667	1,709	1,818	1,792	1,948	1,892
Usual residence else where.	568	659	1,068	815	801	852	885	910	965	1,037
Other.	1,683	1,875	2,189	2,219	2,325	2,461	2,433	2,636	2,676	2,482
Seasonal [1]	2,106	2,046	2,931	3,028	3,099	3,209	3,305	3,232	3,268	3,469
Total occupied	79,638	87,887	94,224	98,695	99,985	100,984	102,202	103,534	104,928	105,720
Owner	52,223	56,152	60,248	63,136	64,739	66,041	67,143	68,638	70,097	71,250
Renter	27,415	31,736	33,976	35,558	35,246	34,943	35,059	34,896	34,831	34,470
PERCENT DISTRIBUTION										
All housing units	100.0	100.0	100.0	100.0	100.0	100.0	100.0	100.0	100.0	100.0
Vacant	9.2	9.7	11.3	11.0	11.2	11.5	11.6	11.7	11.9	11.6
Total occupied	90.8	90.3	88.7	89.0	88.8	88.5	88.4	88.3	88.1	88.4
Owner	59.5	57.7	56.7	56.9	57.5	57.9	58.1	58.5	58.9	59.6
Renter	31.2	32.6	32.0	32.0	31.3	30.6	30.3	29.8	29.3	28.8

[1] Beginning 1990 includes vacant seasonal mobile homes. For years shown, seasonal vacant housing units were underreported prior to 1990.

Source: U.S. Census Bureau, Internet site <http://www.census.gov/hhes/www/housing/hvs/historic/index.html>.

No. 948. Occupied Housing Inventory by Age of Householder: 1985 to 2000

[In thousands (87,887 represents 87,887,000). Based on the Current Population Survey/Housing Vacancy Survey; See source for details]

Age of householder	1985	1990	1993 [1]	1994	1995	1996	1997	1998	1999	2000
Total [2]	87,887	94,224	97,717	98,695	99,986	100,983	102,201	103,534	104,929	105,719
Less than 25 years old	5,483	5,143	5,342	5,408	5,502	5,467	5,517	5,750	6,000	6,221
25 to 29 years old	9,543	9,508	8,848	8,628	8,662	8,669	8,755	8,666	8,661	8,482
30 to 34 years old	10,288	11,213	11,406	11,284	11,206	10,936	10,622	10,494	10,400	10,219
35 to 39 years old	9,615	10,914	11,656	11,906	11,993	12,083	12,166	12,026	11,950	11,834
40 to 44 years old	7,919	9,893	10,801	10,931	11,151	11,644	11,869	12,141	12,206	12,377
45 to 49 years old	6,517	8,038	9,191	9,611	10,080	10,523	10,532	10,744	10,973	11,164
50 to 54 years old	6,157	6,532	7,438	7,637	7,882	7,981	8,650	9,040	9,412	9,834
55 to 59 years old	6,558	6,182	6,107	6,284	6,355	6,474	6,731	7,051	7,389	7,602
60 to 64 years old	6,567	6,446	6,091	5,972	5,860	5,836	5,947	6,055	6,183	6,215
65 to 69 years old	5,976	6,407	6,164	6,113	6,088	6,099	5,926	5,852	5,845	5,816
70 to 74 years old	5,003	5,397	5,599	5,681	5,693	5,602	5,574	5,583	5,621	5,567
75 years old and over	7,517	8,546	9,074	9,236	9,514	9,669	9,912	10,131	10,289	10,388

[1] Based on 1990 census. [2] 1985 total includes ages not reported. Thereafter cases allocated by age.

Source: U.S. Census Bureau, Internet site <http://www.census.gov/hhes/www/hvs.html> (accessed 11 July 2001).

No. 949. Vacancy Rates for Housing Units—Characteristics: 1990 to 2000

[In percent. Rate is relationship between vacant housing for rent or for sale and the total rental and homeowner supply, which comprises occupied units, units rented or sold and awaiting occupancy, and vacant units available for rent or sale. For composition of regions, see map inside front cover. Based on the Current Population Survey/Housing Vacancy Survey; see source for details]

Characteristic	Rental units					Homeowner units				
	1990	1995 [1]	1998	1999	2000	1990	1995 [1]	1998	1999	2000
Total units. . . .	7.2	7.6	7.9	8.1	8.0	1.7	1.5	1.7	1.7	1.6
Inside MSAs	7.1	7.6	7.7	7.8	7.7	1.7	1.5	1.6	1.5	1.4
Outside MSAs	7.6	7.9	9.2	9.6	9.5	1.8	1.6	2.0	2.1	2.1
Northeast	6.1	7.2	6.7	6.3	5.6	1.6	1.5	1.5	1.4	1.2
Midwest	6.4	7.2	7.9	8.6	8.8	1.3	1.3	1.4	1.2	1.3
South	8.8	8.3	9.6	10.3	10.5	2.1	1.7	2.0	2.0	1.9
West	6.6	7.5	6.7	6.2	5.8	1.8	1.7	1.7	1.7	1.5
Units in structure:										
1 unit	4.0	5.4	6.3	7.3	7.1	1.4	1.4	1.6	1.5	1.4
2 units or more. . .	9.0	9.0	9.0	8.7	8.6	7.1	4.8	4.4	3.6	4.4
5 units or more. . .	9.6	9.5	9.4	8.9	9.1	8.4	5.1	4.5	3.8	5.5
Units with—										
3 rooms or less . .	10.3	11.4	10.8	10.5	10.1	10.2	9.2	9.7	7.9	9.9
4 rooms	8.0	8.2	8.9	8.3	8.2	3.2	2.8	3.5	2.9	2.8
5 rooms	5.7	5.8	6.5	7.2	7.3	2.0	1.8	1.9	2.0	1.9
6 rooms or more. .	3.0	3.8	4.3	5.2	5.0	1.1	1.1	1.2	1.1	1.0

[1] Beginning 1995, based on 1990 population census controls.

Source: U.S. Census Bureau, Internet site <http://www.census.gov/hhes/www/housing/hvs/historic/index.html>.

[115,905 represents 115,905,000. As of April 1. Based on the 2000 Census of Population and Housing; see text, Section 1, Population, and Appendix III]

State	Housing units				Vacancy rate		Housing tenure			
			Vacant				Owner-occupied units		Renter-occupied units	
	Total (1,000)	Occupied (1,000)	Total	For seasonal use [1]	Homeowner [2]	Renter [3]	Total (1,000)	Average household size	Total (1,000)	Average household size
United States	115,905	105,480	10,425	3,579	1.7	6.8	69,816	2.69	35,664	2.40
Alabama...........	1,964	1,737	227	47	2.0	11.8	1,259	2.57	478	2.30
Alaska	261	222	39	21	1.9	7.8	139	2.89	83	2.49
Arizona............	2,189	1,901	288	142	2.1	9.2	1,294	2.69	608	2.53
Arkansas	1,173	1,043	130	29	2.5	9.6	724	2.54	319	2.40
California	12,215	11,503	712	237	1.4	3.7	6,546	2.93	4,957	2.79
Colorado..........	1,808	1,658	150	72	1.4	5.5	1,116	2.64	542	2.30
Connecticut........	1,386	1,302	84	23	1.1	5.6	870	2.67	432	2.25
Delaware	343	299	44	26	1.5	8.2	216	2.61	83	2.37
District of Columbia	275	248	27	2	2.9	5.9	101	2.31	147	2.06
Florida	7,303	6,338	965	483	2.2	9.3	4,442	2.49	1,896	2.39
Georgia	3,282	3,006	275	50	1.9	8.2	2,029	2.71	977	2.51
Hawaii	461	403	57	26	1.6	8.2	228	3.07	175	2.71
Idaho.............	528	470	58	27	2.2	7.6	340	2.75	130	2.52
Illinois	4,886	4,592	294	30	1.5	6.2	3,089	2.76	1,503	2.37
Indiana............	2,532	2,336	196	34	1.8	8.8	1,669	2.64	667	2.24
Iowa	1,233	1,149	83	16	1.7	6.8	831	2.57	318	2.15
Kansas............	1,131	1,038	93	10	2.0	8.8	719	2.63	319	2.25
Kentucky	1,751	1,591	160	30	1.8	8.7	1,125	2.55	465	2.27
Louisiana	1,847	1,656	191	40	1.6	9.3	1,125	2.70	531	2.44
Maine.............	652	518	134	101	1.7	7.0	371	2.54	147	2.03
Maryland	2,145	1,981	164	39	1.6	6.1	1,342	2.73	639	2.35
Massachusetts......	2,622	2,444	178	94	0.7	3.5	1,508	2.72	936	2.17
Michigan...........	4,234	3,786	449	234	1.6	6.8	2,793	2.67	993	2.24
Minnesota..........	2,066	1,895	171	106	0.9	4.1	1,413	2.69	482	2.03
Mississippi	1,162	1,046	116	22	1.6	9.2	757	2.67	289	2.52
Missouri	2,442	2,195	247	66	2.1	9.0	1,542	2.59	652	2.20
Montana...........	413	359	54	24	2.2	7.6	248	2.55	111	2.22
Nebraska	723	666	56	12	1.8	7.6	449	2.63	217	2.20
Nevada	827	751	76	17	2.6	9.7	457	2.71	294	2.47
New Hampshire......	547	475	72	56	1.0	3.5	331	2.70	144	2.14
New Jersey.........	3,310	3,065	246	109	1.2	4.5	2,011	2.81	1,053	2.43
New Mexico	781	678	103	32	2.2	11.6	474	2.72	204	2.41
New York	7,679	7,057	622	235	1.6	4.6	3,739	2.78	3,318	2.41
North Carolina.......	3,524	3,132	392	135	2.0	8.8	2,172	2.54	960	2.37
North Dakota........	290	257	33	8	2.7	8.2	171	2.60	86	2.02
Ohio	4,783	4,446	337	47	1.6	8.3	3,073	2.62	1,373	2.19
Oklahoma..........	1,514	1,342	172	32	2.5	10.6	918	2.55	424	2.36
Oregon............	1,453	1,334	119	37	2.3	7.3	857	2.59	477	2.36
Pennsylvania........	5,250	4,777	473	148	1.6	7.2	3,406	2.62	1,371	2.12
Rhode Island........	440	408	31	13	1.0	5.0	245	2.66	163	2.19
South Carolina.......	1,754	1,534	220	70	1.9	12.0	1,108	2.59	426	2.37
South Dakota	323	290	33	10	1.8	8.0	198	2.64	92	2.22
Tennessee	2,439	2,233	207	37	2.0	8.8	1,561	2.57	672	2.29
Texas.............	8,158	7,393	764	173	1.8	8.5	4,717	2.87	2,676	2.53
Utah	769	701	67	30	2.1	6.5	502	3.29	200	2.75
Vermont	294	241	54	43	1.4	4.2	170	2.58	71	2.11
Virginia............	2,904	2,699	205	55	1.5	5.2	1,838	2.62	861	2.36
Washington.........	2,451	2,271	180	60	1.8	5.9	1,467	2.65	804	2.32
West Virginia........	845	736	108	33	2.2	9.1	554	2.47	183	2.17
Wisconsin..........	2,321	2,085	237	142	1.2	5.6	1,426	2.66	658	2.15
Wyoming	224	194	30	12	2.1	9.7	136	2.58	58	2.25

[1] For seasonal, recreational or occasional use.   [2] Proportion of the homeowner housing inventory which is vacant for sale.
[3] Porportion of the rental inventory which is vacant for rent.

Source: U.S. Census Bureau, 2000 Census of Population and Housing, Profiles of General Demographic Characteristics.

No. 951. Housing Units and Tenure for Large Cities: 2000

[115,905 represents 115,905,000. As of April 1. For cities with 200,000 or more inhabitants in 2000. Based on the 2000 Census of Population and Housing; see text, Section 1, Population, and Appendix III]

City	Housing units Total (1,000)	Occu-pied (1,000)	Vacant Total	For sea-sonal use [1]	Vacancy rate Home-owner [2]	Renter [3]	Owner-occupied units Total (1,000)	Average house-hold size	Renter-occupied units Total (1,000)	Average house-hold size
United States	**115,905**	**105,480**	**10,425**	**3,579**	**1.7**	**6.8**	**69,816**	**2.69**	**35,664**	**2.40**
Albuquerque, NM	198.5	183.2	15.2	0.8	1.9	11.8	110.6	2.55	72.6	2.16
Anaheim, CA	99.7	97.0	2.8	0.2	0.9	3.2	48.5	3.24	48.5	3.45
Anchorage, AK	100.4	94.8	5.5	1.1	1.4	5.3	57.0	2.81	37.9	2.46
Arlington, TX	130.6	124.7	5.9	0.4	1.4	6.1	68.3	2.87	56.4	2.38
Atlanta, GA	186.9	168.1	18.8	1.1	4.1	7.2	73.5	2.37	94.7	2.25
Aurora, CO	109.3	105.6	3.6	0.2	1.1	3.5	67.5	2.65	38.1	2.50
Austin, TX	276.8	265.6	11.2	1.4	1.0	3.5	119.1	2.65	146.5	2.19
Baltimore, MD	300.5	258.0	42.5	1.4	3.6	7.6	129.9	2.57	128.1	2.27
Boston, MA	251.9	239.5	12.4	1.6	1.0	3.0	77.2	2.51	162.3	2.22
Buffalo, NY	145.6	122.7	22.9	0.3	4.2	11.1	53.3	2.47	69.4	2.16
Charlotte, NC	230.4	215.4	15.0	0.7	2.2	8.4	123.9	2.56	91.6	2.30
Chicago, IL	1,152.9	1,061.9	90.9	4.5	1.7	5.7	464.9	2.90	597.1	2.49
Cincinnati, OH	166.0	148.1	17.9	0.6	2.2	9.9	57.7	2.43	90.4	1.97
Cleveland, OH	215.9	190.6	25.2	0.8	2.1	10.8	92.5	2.56	98.1	2.32
Colorado Springs, CO	148.7	141.5	7.2	0.7	1.2	6.2	86.0	2.65	55.5	2.27
Columbus, OH	327.2	301.5	25.6	1.1	2.0	8.3	148.0	2.48	153.5	2.13
Corpus Christi, TX	107.8	98.8	9.0	1.1	2.0	9.5	58.9	2.89	39.9	2.56
Dallas, TX	484.1	451.8	32.3	1.5	1.4	7.0	195.3	2.78	256.5	2.44
Denver, CO	251.4	239.2	12.2	1.4	1.7	4.5	125.5	2.41	113.7	2.10
Detroit, MI	375.1	336.4	38.7	0.6	1.6	8.3	184.6	2.84	151.8	2.68
El Paso, TX	193.7	182.1	11.6	0.7	1.6	7.9	111.8	3.20	70.3	2.86
Fort Worth, TX	211.0	195.1	16.0	0.6	1.9	9.1	109.1	2.84	86.0	2.44
Fresno, CA	149.0	140.1	8.9	0.4	1.9	6.4	70.9	2.94	69.2	3.05
Honolulu, HI [4]	158.7	140.3	18.3	5.2	1.7	10.2	65.9	2.75	74.5	2.40
Houston, TX	782.0	717.9	64.1	4.2	1.6	8.7	328.7	2.84	389.2	2.54
Indianapolis, IN [5]	352.4	320.1	32.3	1.2	2.0	10.9	187.6	2.53	132.5	2.18
Jacksonville, FL	308.8	284.5	24.3	0.9	1.8	9.0	179.7	2.64	104.8	2.34
Kansas City, MO	202.3	184.0	18.4	0.7	1.9	9.6	106.1	2.52	77.9	2.11
Las Vegas, NV	190.7	176.8	14.0	1.8	2.5	8.4	104.5	2.76	72.3	2.52
Lexington-Fayette, KY	116.2	108.3	7.9	0.9	1.1	8.4	59.9	2.47	48.4	2.07
Long Beach, CA	171.6	163.1	8.5	0.8	2.2	4.2	66.9	2.81	96.2	2.74
Los Angeles, CA	1,337.7	1,275.4	62.3	4.9	1.8	3.5	491.9	2.99	783.5	2.73
Louisville, KY	121.3	111.4	9.9	0.4	1.8	7.5	58.5	2.33	52.9	2.10
Memphis, TN	271.6	250.7	20.8	0.7	2.0	8.4	140.0	2.62	110.7	2.40
Mesa, AZ	175.7	146.6	29.1	18.1	2.4	10.7	97.3	2.74	49.3	2.54
Miami, FL	148.4	134.2	14.2	2.9	2.9	6.6	46.8	2.79	87.4	2.52
Milwaukee, WI	249.2	232.2	17.0	0.5	1.3	6.0	105.2	2.60	127.0	2.42
Minneapolis, MN	168.6	162.4	6.3	0.8	0.7	2.8	83.4	2.43	78.9	2.05
Nashville-Davidson, TN [5]	242.5	227.4	15.0	1.1	2.0	6.5	124.0	2.43	103.4	2.13
New Orleans, LA	215.1	188.3	26.8	2.4	2.2	7.9	87.6	2.60	100.7	2.37
New York, NY	3,200.9	3,021.6	179.3	28.2	1.7	3.2	912.3	2.81	2,109.3	2.50
Newark, NJ	100.1	91.4	8.8	0.1	2.0	5.6	21.7	3.22	69.6	2.74
Oakland, CA	157.5	150.8	6.7	0.4	1.0	2.7	62.5	2.76	88.3	2.49
Oklahoma City, OK	228.1	204.4	23.7	1.1	2.2	12.3	121.5	2.51	82.9	2.27
Omaha, NE	165.7	156.7	9.0	0.5	1.0	7.2	93.4	2.64	63.3	2.10
Philadelphia, PA	662.0	590.1	71.9	1.8	1.9	7.0	349.6	2.65	240.4	2.23
Phoenix, AZ	495.8	465.8	30.0	4.5	1.4	7.9	282.7	2.89	183.2	2.63
Pittsburgh, PA	163.4	143.7	19.6	0.9	2.8	8.8	74.9	2.37	68.8	1.95
Portland, OR	237.3	223.7	13.6	1.0	2.3	6.2	124.8	2.47	99.0	2.08
Raleigh, NC	120.7	112.6	8.1	0.4	2.1	8.3	58.1	2.43	54.5	2.15
Riverside, CA	86.0	82.0	4.0	0.2	1.9	4.8	46.5	3.18	35.6	2.81
Sacramento, CA	164.0	154.6	9.4	0.6	2.0	5.4	77.5	2.65	77.1	2.50
San Antonio, TX	433.1	405.5	27.6	2.3	1.4	6.9	235.7	2.95	169.8	2.51
San Diego, CA	469.7	450.7	19.0	5.1	0.8	3.2	223.3	2.71	227.4	2.52
San Francisco, CA	346.5	329.7	16.8	3.8	0.8	2.5	115.4	2.73	214.3	2.06
San Jose, CA	281.8	276.6	5.2	0.8	0.4	1.8	171.0	3.22	105.6	3.16
Santa Ana, CA	74.6	73.0	1.6	0.1	0.8	1.9	36.0	4.54	37.0	4.57
Seattle, WA	270.5	258.5	12.0	1.8	1.2	3.5	125.2	2.32	133.3	1.84
St. Louis, MO	176.4	147.1	29.3	0.5	3.5	11.8	68.9	2.49	78.1	2.12
St. Paul, MN	115.7	112.1	3.6	0.4	0.7	2.8	61.5	2.72	50.6	2.15
Tampa, FL	135.8	124.8	11.0	0.8	2.1	7.8	68.6	2.49	56.2	2.20
Toledo, OH	139.9	128.9	10.9	0.4	1.5	8.8	77.1	2.50	51.9	2.19
Tucson, AZ	209.6	192.9	16.7	3.5	1.6	8.1	103.1	2.58	89.8	2.24
Tulsa, OK	179.4	165.7	13.7	0.9	1.6	8.7	92.2	2.41	73.5	2.18
Virginia Beach, VA	162.3	154.5	7.8	2.3	1.5	4.0	101.3	2.79	53.1	2.54
Washington, DC	274.8	248.3	26.5	2.2	2.9	5.9	101.2	2.31	147.1	2.06
Wichita, KS	152.1	139.1	13.0	0.4	2.0	12.0	85.7	2.61	53.4	2.17

[1] For seasonal, recreational or occasional use. [2] Porportion of the homeowner housing inventory which is vacant for sale.
[3] Porportion of the rental inventory which is vacant for rent. [4] The population shown in this table is for the census designated place (CDP). [5] Represents the portion of a consolidated city that is not within one or more separately incorporated places.

Source: U.S. Census Bureau, *2000 Census of Population and Housing, Profiles of General Demographic Characteristics.*

Construction and Housing 603

No. 952. Housing Units—Characteristics by Tenure and Region: 1999

[In thousands of units (115,253 represents 115,253,000), except as indicated. As of Oct. 1. Based on the American Housing Survey; see Appendix III. For composition of regions, see map inside front cover]

Characteristic	Total housing units	Sea-sonal	Total	Owner	Renter	North-east	Mid-west	South	West	Vacant
Total units	**115,253**	**2,961**	**102,803**	**68,796**	**34,007**	**19,958**	**24,360**	**36,389**	**22,096**	**9,489**
Percent distribution	100.0	2.6	89.2	59.7	29.5	17.3	21.1	31.6	19.2	8.2
Units in structure:										
Single family detached	70,355	1,754	64,536	56,471	8,065	10,624	17,006	23,431	13,475	4,064
Single family attached	8,027	199	6,963	3,499	3,465	1,948	1,105	2,381	1,530	864
2 to 4 units	9,896	94	8,572	1,466	7,105	2,763	1,988	1,979	1,842	1,230
5 to 9 units	5,578	45	4,847	469	4,378	972	1,010	1,651	1,214	686
10 to 19 units	5,130	46	4,416	357	4,059	739	858	1,721	1,099	668
20 to 49 units	3,919	70	3,343	341	3,002	959	595	849	940	505
50 or more units	3,916	103	3,341	544	2,797	1,390	618	632	700	472
Mobile home or trailer	8,433	649	6,785	5,649	1,136	564	1,179	3,745	1,298	999
Stories in structure: [1]										
One story	37,705	1,248	33,413	24,502	8,911	1,266	4,023	18,071	10,053	3,044
2 stories	37,371	665	33,790	21,304	12,485	6,178	9,719	9,979	7,914	2,917
3 stories	23,865	244	21,894	14,709	7,185	7,937	8,082	3,661	2,214	1,727
4 to 6 stories	5,668	79	5,081	2,258	2,823	3,004	1,027	606	443	508
7 or more stories	2,210	76	1,841	374	1,467	1,009	331	327	174	293
Foundation: [2]										
Full or partial basement	33,750	348	31,903	28,535	3,367	10,593	13,646	4,913	2,750	1,499
Crawlspace	20,864	735	18,421	14,854	3,567	729	2,646	9,547	5,499	1,708
Concrete slab	22,696	597	20,539	16,120	4,419	1,152	1,701	11,083	6,603	1,560
Other	1,070	273	636	459	177	98	119	269	152	161
Year structure built:										
1939 and earlier	22,236	436	19,529	11,547	7,981	7,370	6,250	3,460	2,450	2,271
1940 to 1949	8,334	211	7,426	4,721	2,705	1,695	1,748	2,420	1,564	696
1950 to 1959	13,574	362	12,295	8,919	3,375	2,570	3,225	3,851	2,649	918
1960 to 1969	15,810	455	14,228	9,483	4,746	2,453	3,241	5,120	3,414	1,126
1970 to 1979	23,180	689	20,616	13,271	7,345	2,643	4,466	8,350	5,157	1,875
1980 or later	32,120	807	28,709	20,854	7,856	3,227	5,429	13,189	6,864	2,604
Median year	1,969	1,970	1,969	1,970	1,966	1,954	1,963	1,974	1,972	1,968
Main heating equipment:										
Warm-air furnace	68,268	1,253	62,018	44,901	17,117	8,062	19,224	20,672	14,061	4,997
Electric heat pump	12,620	408	10,992	7,809	3,183	330	628	8,750	1,284	1,221
Steam or hot water system	14,270	129	13,153	7,581	5,572	9,372	2,277	741	764	988
Floor, wall, or pipeless furnace	6,063	192	5,310	2,403	2,907	450	559	1,473	2,828	561
Built-in electric units	5,786	280	4,939	2,285	2,654	1,228	1,135	912	1,664	567
Room heaters with flue	1,908	98	1,624	939	685	182	230	853	359	186
Room heaters without flue	2,064	41	1,790	1,066	723	28	47	1,649	66	234
Stoves	1,433	193	1,113	914	199	187	157	442	327	127
Fireplaces	251	30	211	172	39	10	22	90	89	11
Cooking stoves	151	20	116	47	68	48	9	41	17	15
None	1,131	233	544	206	338	-	10	144	389	355
Portable electric heaters	855	49	705	360	345	30	24	459	192	101
Other	454	38	289	114	176	33	38	164	54	127
Kitchen equipment:										
Lacking complete facilities	5,061	421	1,744	388	1,355	392	359	510	483	2,896
With complete facilities	110,192	2,540	101,059	68,407	32,652	19,566	24,001	35,879	21,613	6,593
Kitchen sink	114,246	2,805	102,439	68,705	33,734	19,853	24,282	36,288	22,016	9,001
Refrigerator	112,393	2,712	102,360	68,633	33,727	19,847	24,260	36,255	21,998	7,321
Cooking stove or range	111,862	2,628	101,955	68,499	33,457	19,774	24,159	36,102	21,921	7,279
Burners only, no stove or range	164	3	141	58	84	35	36	40	30	20
Microwave oven only	407	4	343	129	214	71	78	121	73	60
Dishwasher	62,391	1,040	57,703	44,904	12,799	9,707	12,231	21,659	14,106	3,648
Washing machine	84,889	1,271	80,543	65,140	15,403	14,383	19,633	29,926	16,601	3,075
Clothes dryer	81,426	1,387	76,454	62,738	13,716	13,141	19,278	28,166	15,869	3,585
Disposal in kitchen sink	49,323	737	45,345	31,659	13,685	4,430	10,912	15,130	14,872	3,242
Trash compactor	4,282	118	3,858	3,155	703	576	681	1,433	1,168	306
Air conditioning: Central	63,464	1,006	58,208	43,943	14,265	4,888	14,332	29,768	9,221	4,251
Percent of total units	55.1	34.0	56.6	63.9	41.9	24.5	58.8	81.8	41.7	44.8
One or more room units	29,287	522	26,888	15,842	11,047	9,606	6,941	7,233	3,108	1,878
Source of water:										
Public system or private company	100,115	1,919	89,942	57,390	32,552	16,973	20,493	31,765	20,712	8,254
Percent of total units	86.9	64.8	87.5	83.4	95.7	85.0	84.1	87.3	93.7	100.0
Well serving 1 to 5 units	14,337	861	12,400	11,040	1,360	2,895	3,762	4,410	1,333	1,076
Other	801	181	460	365	95	90	105	214	51	159
Means of sewage disposal:										
Public sewer	88,787	1,458	79,959	48,672	31,287	15,541	19,188	26,012	19,218	7,370
Percent of total units	77.0	49.2	77.8	70.7	92.0	77.9	78.8	71.5	87.0	77.7
Septic tank, cesspool, chemical toilet	26,051	1,293	22,753	20,071	2,683	4,407	5,164	10,317	2,865	2,005
Other	414	210	90	53	37	11	8	59	12	114

- Represents or rounds to zero. [1] Excludes mobile homes. [2] Limited to single-family units.

Source: U.S. Census Bureau, Current Housing Reports, Series H150/99, American Housing Survey for the United States.

No. 953. Housing Inventory for Selected Metropolitan Areas— Summary Characteristics: 1993 to 1999

[**1,684.4 represents 1,684,400.** Based on the American Housing Survey and subject to sampling error; see Appendix III and source for details. For definition of median, see Guide to Tabular Presentation]

Year and metropolitan area	Total units (1,000)	Owner occupied	Renter occupied	Vacant and seasonal	Single-family	Multi-family	Mobile homes	Median monthly housing costs (dol.)	Median value (dol.)	Renter occupied, median monthly housing costs (dol.)
				Percent				**Owner occupied**		
1993										
Boston, MA-NH CMSA........	1,684.4	55.1	36.0	8.8	52.1	46.9	1.0	841	157,089	646
Minneapolis-St. Paul, MN-WI MSA..	1,044.3	67.3	26.7	6.0	68.2	29.6	2.3	733	93,748	523
San Francisco-Oakland, CA Area PMSAs................	1,544.6	50.6	42.6	6.8	56.2	42.5	1.4	1,031	256,258	720
San Jose, CA PMSA..........	556.7	56.8	39.2	4.0	65.2	30.8	4.0	1,155	256,067	828
Tampa-St. Petersburg, FL MSA..	1,076.7	56.7	24.1	19.3	58.6	25.7	15.7	442	69,089	485
Washington, DC-MD-VA MSA.....	1,642.4	57.1	35.4	7.5	64.3	35.0	0.7	1,056	167,103	690
1994										
Anaheim-Santa Ana, CA PMSA....	918.0	56.0	36.8	7.2	56.1	40.2	3.7	1,127	216,962	805
Buffalo, NY CMSA............	503.2	60.9	30.2	8.8	59.9	38.3	1.8	589	85,378	446
Dallas, TX PMSA............	1,152.8	51.3	39.1	9.7	60.7	35.6	3.6	783	87,615	532
Fort Worth-Arlington, TX PMSA....	555.4	57.9	32.4	9.7	69.8	27.3	2.9	668	70,759	509
Milwaukee, WI PMSA..........	593.0	58.5	35.9	5.6	59.6	39.8	0.6	684	101,407	498
Phoenix, AZ MSA............	1,032.8	56.2	30.7	13.2	63.7	26.3	10.0	664	88,269	509
Riverside-San Bernardino-Ontario, CA PMSAs...............	1,121.4	56.5	26.7	16.8	67.4	21.5	11.1	807	123,491	592
San Diego, CA MSA..........	993.3	50.4	39.8	9.7	55.9	39.1	5.0	873	176,277	640
1995										
Charlotte, NC-SC MSA........	539.4	62.7	30.6	6.7	68.4	20.8	10.8	532	86,763	489
Chicago, IL Area PMSAs........	2,987.1	59.6	33.8	6.6	54.7	44.5	0.7	850	136,362	584
Columbus, OH MSA..........	604.9	57.9	34.0	8.1	75.8	21.4	2.8	654	92,664	484
Denver, CO PMSA...........	773.9	61.2	32.5	6.2	68.9	28.8	2.2	763	119,694	539
Detroit, MI PMSA............	1,802.7	66.3	26.9	6.7	75.0	22.9	2.1	551	89,648	508
Kansas City, MO-KS MSA.......	715.5	61.9	30.2	7.9	76.2	21.0	2.8	565	78,542	481
Los Angeles-Long Beach, CA PMSA..	3,276.0	42.0	48.0	10.0	54.7	44.0	1.3	943	192,803	654
Miami-Fort Lauderdale, FL CMSA..	1,483.8	52.1	31.8	16.1	49.9	46.5	3.5	729	97,058	609
New Orleans, LA MSA.........	547.7	54.6	33.9	11.5	65.2	30.2	4.7	404	75,768	441
New York-Nasau-Suffolk-Orange County, NY PMSAs..........	4,577.3	41.0	50.9	8.1	32.3	67.4	0.3	931	172,651	650
Northern New Jersey PMSAs.......	2,442.2	56.0	34.2	9.8	59.2	40.0	0.8	976	176,713	669
Philadelphia, PA-NJ PMSA.......	1,986.6	63.7	28.0	8.4	73.1	25.8	1.0	673	112,769	578
Pittsburgh, PA MSA..........	1,051.7	66.5	25.7	7.8	73.9	21.5	4.7	416	73,383	417
Portland, OR-WA PMSA.........	702.6	60.3	32.9	6.8	70.2	23.9	5.9	704	127,731	566
San Antonio, TX MSA..........	538.7	55.4	34.6	10.0	67.0	27.3	5.6	507	62,577	475
1996										
Atlanta, GA MSA............	1,421.1	58.6	33.4	8.1	66.9	28.6	4.5	803	105,037	651
Cleveland, OH PMSA.........	829.6	62.4	30.7	6.9	67.0	31.5	1.5	552	99,283	492
Hartford, CT MSA............	480.2	60.5	31.1	8.4	63.0	36.5	0.5	888	139,641	616
Indianapolis, IN MSA..........	640.8	62.2	30.2	7.6	73.4	22.5	4.0	603	91,213	507
Memphis, TN-AR-MS MSA.......	442.0	59.3	31.5	9.2	70.0	26.1	3.9	592	76,175	477
Oklahoma City, OK MSA........	446.4	57.8	28.7	13.5	72.0	22.1	6.0	461	65,638	434
Sacramento, CA PMSA.........	625.4	55.1	34.1	10.8	71.2	24.0	4.8	874	140,758	590
St. Louis, MO-IL MSA.........	1,107.0	64.3	26.5	9.2	71.2	23.6	5.2	557	82,111	462
Seattle-Everett, WA PMSA.......	965.3	58.3	35.1	6.5	60.4	33.9	5.7	897	164,554	630
1998										
Baltimore, MD MSA..........	1,028.2	61.7	27.8	10.5	78.8	19.6	1.6	739	127,557	589
Birmingham, AL MSA..........	394.0	64.1	26.9	9.0	75.9	15.6	8.5	385	87,670	480
Boston, MA-NH CMSA.........	1,345.9	56.5	37.4	6.1	59.2	39.8	1.0	933	191,179	748
Cincinnati, OH-KY-IN, PMSA.....	647.5	61.2	30.3	8.5	68.1	28.6	3.3	611	103,553	484
Houston, TX, PMSAs.........	1,547.3	53.0	36.6	10.4	68.7	26.9	4.4	678	82,543	557
Minneapolis-St. Paul, MN-WI MSA..	1,150.3	70.6	26.0	3.3	72.0	25.6	2.4	786	122,624	583
Norfolk-Virginia Beach-Newport News, VA MSA..............	632.1	56.0	33.3	10.8	73.8	22.2	4.0	729	101,935	582
Oakland, CA, PMSA...........	895.0	56.8	38.8	4.4	71.8	26.4	1.9	1,086	226,173	775
Providence-Pawtucket-Warwick, RI-MA PMSAs.............	415.4	57.8	33.6	8.6	62.0	36.6	1.4	768	124,005	540
Rochester, NY, MSA..........	448.5	63.8	27.6	8.6	71.0	24.4	4.6	724	94,468	572
Salt Lake City, UT MSA........	444.0	67.9	24.5	7.5	75.0	21.7	3.3	713	141,888	594
San Francisco, CA, PMSA.......	700.2	46.2	48.5	5.3	57.7	41.4	0.9	1,229	(1)	899
San Jose, CA PMSA..........	591.0	58.2	37.6	4.2	72.7	23.2	4.1	1,186	(1)	1,038
Tampa-St. Petersburg, FL MSA....	1,138.3	58.6	23.6	17.8	62.8	19.6	17.6	541	81,510	565
Washington, DC-MD-VA, MSA.....	1,817.4	59.3	32.7	8.0	72.4	26.7	0.9	1,104	170,022	746
1999										
Chicago, IL, PMSA...........	3,060.7	60.7	32.4	7.0	58.5	40.8	0.7	855	147,742	637
Detroit, MI, PMSA............	1,876.7	68.0	24.8	7.2	77.8	20.1	2.1	583	124,157	557
Los Angeles-Long Beach, CA PMSA.	3,278.5	44.0	49.4	6.6	60.9	37.8	1.3	1,033	199,011	663
New York-Nasau-Suffolk-Orange County, NY PMSAs...........	4,615.9	41.7	52.1	6.2	39.0	60.6	0.4	910	186,164	684
Northern NJ, PMSA...........	2,502.1	59.7	32.9	7.4	65.4	33.8	0.7	983	181,898	732
Philadelphia, PA, PMSA.........	2,025.2	65.9	26.7	7.4	80.6	18.7	0.7	660	116,478	642

[1] More than $300,000.

Source: U.S. Census Bureau, *American Housing Survey for the (name) Metropolitan Area (year)*, Series H-170.

Construction and Housing 605

No. 954. Housing Units—Size of Units and Lot: 1999

[In thousands (115,253 represents 115,253,000), except as indicated. As of Oct. 1. Based on the American Housing Survey; see Appendix III. For composition of regions, see map inside front cover]

Item	Total housing units	Seasonal	Year-round units Occupied Total	Owner	Renter	North-east	Mid-west	South	West	Vacant
Total units	115,253	2,961	102,803	68,796	34,007	19,958	24,360	36,389	22,096	9,489
Rooms:										
1 room	622	74	407	6	401	148	71	54	133	140
2 rooms	1,391	100	1,014	70	943	289	169	221	335	278
3 rooms	11,071	517	8,973	996	7,977	2,305	1,780	2,520	2,368	1,581
4 rooms	23,493	992	19,390	7,322	12,068	3,413	4,281	7,203	4,493	3,110
5 rooms	26,544	706	23,733	16,395	7,338	3,841	5,698	9,443	4,751	2,104
6 rooms	23,268	315	21,662	18,174	3,488	4,290	5,217	7,958	4,198	1,292
7 rooms	14,126	132	13,457	12,314	1,143	2,628	3,411	4,532	2,886	537
8 rooms or more	14,737	125	14,168	13,518	648	3,045	3,732	4,458	2,931	446
Complete bathrooms:										
No bathrooms	2,032	446	676	263	413	188	125	244	119	911
1 bathroom	49,179	1,378	42,838	18,650	24,188	10,358	11,006	13,086	8,386	4,963
1 and one-half bathrooms	17,256	253	16,189	12,743	3,446	3,837	5,189	4,423	2,739	814
2 or more bathrooms	46,786	885	43,100	37,140	5,960	5,575	8,039	18,635	10,851	2,802
Square footage of unit:										
Single detached and mobile homes [1]	78,788	2,404	71,321	62,120	9,201	11,188	18,185	27,176	14,772	5,063
Less than 500	1,380	337	844	580	264	130	113	407	195	199
500 to 749	3,129	461	2,178	1,371	807	287	503	990	399	490
750 to 999	6,490	367	5,314	3,950	1,364	592	1,397	2,282	1,044	808
1,000 to 1,499	19,084	507	17,369	14,581	2,788	1,892	4,193	7,327	3,958	1,208
1,500 to 1,999	17,163	234	16,153	14,542	1,611	2,333	3,845	6,177	3,798	776
2,000 to 2,499	11,351	134	10,782	10,144	638	1,841	2,935	3,791	2,215	435
2,500 to 2,999	5,782	63	5,507	5,253	254	1,083	1,450	1,964	1,011	212
3,000 to 3,999	5,158	54	4,913	4,659	254	1,121	1,310	1,607	876	190
4,000 or more	3,339	31	3,183	3,032	151	747	847	1,121	469	124
Other [2]	5,913	214	5,077	4,007	1,070	1,163	1,594	1,511	809	622
Median square footage	1,685	952	1,730	1,795	1,293	1,953	1,772	1,648	1,683	1,300
Lot size:										
Single detached and attached units and mobile homes [1]	86,815	2,602	78,284	65,619	12,666	13,136	19,290	29,557	16,303	5,927
Less than one-eighth acre	11,993	604	10,296	7,684	2,613	2,035	2,583	2,647	3,031	1,093
One-eighth to one-quarter acre	25,900	659	23,516	18,931	4,585	3,137	5,962	7,927	6,490	1,724
One-quarter to one-half acre	13,123	292	11,939	10,562	1,377	1,909	3,239	4,415	2,376	891
One-half up to one acre	11,442	225	10,668	9,316	1,352	2,130	2,308	4,887	1,344	549
1 to 5 acres	15,013	352	13,851	12,220	1,631	2,666	2,869	6,619	1,697	810
5 to 10 acres	2,694	93	2,509	2,326	183	335	685	1,114	376	92
10 acres or more	4,335	218	3,694	3,151	543	549	1,271	1,429	445	423
Other [3]	2,315	159	1,811	1,429	382	375	373	519	544	345
Median acreage	0.33	0.24	0.34	0.38	0.22	0.41	0.32	0.47	0.22	0.25

[1] Does not include selected vacant units. [2] Represents units not reported or size unknown. [3] Represents condominiums and cooperatives—single detached, single attached, and mobile homes.
Source: U.S. Census Bureau, Current Housing Reports, Series H150/99, American Housing Survey for the United States.

No. 955. Occupied Housing Units—Tenure by Race of Householder: 1991 to 1999

[In thousands (93,147 represents 93,147,000), except percent. As of fall. Based on the American Housing Survey; see Appendix III]

Race of householder and tenure	1991	1993	1995	1997	1999
ALL RACES [1]					
Occupied units, total	93,147	94,724	97,693	99,487	102,803
Owner occupied	59,796	61,252	63,544	65,487	68,796
Percent of occupied	64.2	64.7	65.0	65.8	66.9
Renter occupied	33,351	33,472	34,150	34,000	34,007
WHITE					
Occupied units, total	79,140	80,029	81,611	82,154	83,624
Owner occupied	53,749	54,878	56,507	57,781	60,041
Percent of occupied	67.9	68.6	69.2	70.3	71.8
Renter occupied	25,391	25,151	25,104	24,372	23,583
BLACK					
Occupied units, total	10,832	11,128	11,773	12,085	12,936
Owner occupied	4,635	4,788	5,137	5,457	6,013
Percent of occupied	42.8	43.0	43.6	45.2	46.5
Renter occupied	6,197	6,340	6,637	6,628	6,923
HISPANIC ORIGIN [2]					
Occupied units, total	6,239	6,614	7,757	8,513	9,041
Owner occupied	2,423	2,788	3,245	3,646	4,087
Percent of occupied	38.8	42.2	41.8	42.8	45.2
Renter occupied	3,816	3,826	4,512	4,867	4,955

[1] Includes other races, not shown separately. [2] Persons of Hispanic origin may be of any race.
Source: U.S. Census Bureau, Current Housing Reports, Series H150/91, H150/93, H150/95RV, H150/97, and H150/99, American Housing Survey for the United States.

No. 956. Homeownership Rates by Age of Householder and Family Status: 1985 to 2000

[In percent. Represents the proportion of owner households to the total number of occupied households. Based on the Current Population Survey/Housing Vacancy Survey; see source for details]

Age of householder and family status	1985	1990	1993 [1]	1994	1995	1996	1997	1998	1999	2000
United States	63.9	63.9	64.5	64.0	64.7	65.4	65.7	66.3	66.8	67.4
AGE OF HOUSEHOLDER										
Less than 25 years old.	17.2	15.7	15.0	14.9	15.9	18.0	17.7	18.2	19.9	21.7
25 to 29 years old.	37.7	35.2	34.0	34.1	34.4	34.7	35.0	36.2	36.5	38.1
30 to 34 years old.	54.0	51.8	51.0	50.6	53.1	53.0	52.6	53.6	53.8	54.6
35 to 39 years old.	65.4	63.0	62.1	61.2	62.1	62.1	62.6	63.7	64.4	65.0
40 to 44 years old.	71.4	69.8	69.0	68.2	68.6	69.0	69.7	70.0	69.9	70.6
45 to 49 years old.	74.3	73.9	73.9	73.8	73.7	74.4	74.2	73.9	74.5	74.7
50 to 54 years old.	77.5	76.8	77.1	76.8	77.0	77.2	77.7	77.8	77.8	78.5
55 to 59 years old.	79.2	78.8	78.8	78.4	78.8	79.4	79.7	79.8	80.7	80.4
60 to 64 years old.	79.9	79.8	80.9	80.1	80.3	80.7	80.5	82.1	81.3	80.3
65 to 69 years old.	79.5	80.0	80.6	80.6	81.0	82.4	81.9	81.9	82.9	83.0
70 to 74 years old.	76.8	78.4	79.9	80.1	80.9	81.4	82.0	82.2	82.8	82.6
75 years old and over	69.8	72.3	73.3	73.5	74.6	75.3	75.8	76.2	77.1	77.7
Less than 35 years old.	39.9	38.5	37.9	37.3	38.6	39.1	38.7	39.3	39.7	40.8
35 to 44 years old.	68.1	66.3	65.4	64.5	65.2	65.5	66.1	66.9	67.2	67.9
45 to 54 years old.	75.9	75.2	75.4	75.2	75.2	75.6	75.8	75.7	76.0	76.5
55 to 64 years old.	79.5	79.3	79.8	79.3	79.5	80.0	80.1	80.9	81.0	80.3
65 years and over.	74.8	76.3	77.3	77.4	78.1	78.9	79.1	79.3	80.1	80.4
FAMILY STATUS										
Family households:										
Married-couple families.	78.2	78.1	79.1	78.8	79.6	80.2	80.8	81.5	81.8	82.4
Male householder, no spouse present.	57.8	55.2	54.6	52.8	55.3	55.5	54.0	55.7	56.1	57.5
Female householder, no spouse present.	45.8	44.0	44.5	44.2	45.1	46.1	46.1	47.0	48.2	49.1
Nonfamily households:										
One-person	45.8	49.0	50.0	49.8	50.5	51.4	51.8	52.1	52.7	53.6
Male householder.	38.8	42.4	43.2	43.1	43.8	44.9	45.2	45.7	46.3	47.4
Female householder	51.3	53.6	54.8	54.5	55.4	56.0	56.7	56.9	57.6	58.1
Other:										
Male householder.	30.1	31.7	33.2	33.6	34.2	35.5	35.9	36.7	37.2	38.0
Female householder	30.6	32.5	35.6	34.3	33.0	35.9	39.5	40.3	41.5	40.6

[1] Based on 1990 census controls.

Source: U.S. Census Bureau, Internet site <http://www.census.gov/hhes/www/hvs.html>.

No. 957. Homeownership Rates by State: 1985 to 2000

[In percent. See headnote, Table 956]

State	1985	1990	1995	1996	1999	2000	State	1985	1990	1995	1996	1999	2000
United States. . .	63.9	63.9	64.7	66.3	66.8	67.4	Missouri	69.2	64.0	69.4	70.7	72.9	74.2
Alabama.	70.4	68.4	70.1	72.9	74.8	73.2	Montana	66.5	69.1	68.7	68.6	70.6	70.2
Alaska	61.2	58.4	60.9	66.3	66.4	66.4	Nebraska	68.5	67.3	67.1	68.9	70.9	70.2
Arizona.	64.7	64.5	62.9	64.3	66.3	68.0	Nevada	57.0	55.8	58.6	61.4	63.7	64.0
Arkansas.	66.6	67.8	67.2	66.7	65.6	68.9	New Hampshire . .	65.5	65.0	66.0	69.6	70.2	69.2
California.	54.2	53.8	55.4	56.0	55.7	57.1	New Jersey	62.3	65.0	64.9	63.1	64.5	66.2
Colorado.	63.6	59.0	64.6	65.2	68.1	68.3	New Mexico	68.2	68.6	67.0	71.3	72.6	73.7
Connecticut	69.0	67.9	68.2	69.3	69.1	70.0	New York	50.3	53.3	52.7	52.8	52.8	53.4
Delaware.	70.3	67.7	71.7	71.0	71.6	72.0	North Carolina . . .	68.0	69.0	70.1	71.3	71.7	71.1
Dist of Columbia. . .	37.4	36.4	39.2	40.3	40.0	41.9	North Dakota	69.9	67.2	67.3	68.0	70.1	70.7
Florida	67.2	65.1	66.6	66.9	67.6	68.4	Ohio	67.9	68.7	67.9	70.7	70.7	71.3
Georgia	62.7	64.3	66.6	71.2	71.3	69.8	Oklahoma	70.5	70.3	69.8	69.7	71.5	72.7
Hawaii	51.0	55.5	50.2	52.8	56.6	55.2	Oregon	61.5	64.4	63.2	63.4	64.3	65.3
Idaho	71.0	69.4	72.0	72.6	70.3	70.5	Pennsylvania	71.6	73.8	71.5	73.9	75.2	74.7
Illinois.	60.6	63.0	66.4	68.0	67.1	67.9	Rhode Island	61.4	58.5	57.9	59.8	60.6	61.5
Indiana.	67.6	67.0	71.0	72.6	72.9	74.9	South Carolina . . .	72.0	71.4	71.3	76.6	77.1	76.5
Iowa.	69.9	70.7	71.4	72.1	73.9	75.2	South Dakota. . . .	67.6	66.2	67.5	67.3	70.7	71.2
Kansas.	68.3	69.0	67.5	66.7	67.5	69.3	Tennessee.	67.6	68.3	67.0	71.3	71.9	70.9
Kentucky.	68.5	65.8	71.2	75.1	73.9	73.4	Texas	60.5	59.7	61.4	62.5	62.9	63.8
Louisiana.	70.2	67.8	65.3	66.6	66.8	68.1	Utah.	71.5	70.1	71.5	73.7	74.7	72.7
Maine.	73.7	74.2	76.7	74.6	77.4	76.5	Vermont	69.5	72.6	70.4	69.1	69.1	68.7
Maryland.	65.6	64.9	65.8	68.7	69.6	69.9	Virginia	68.5	69.8	68.1	69.4	71.2	73.9
Massachusetts. . . .	60.5	58.6	60.2	61.3	60.3	59.9	Washington	66.8	61.8	61.6	64.9	64.8	63.6
Michigan.	70.7	72.3	72.2	74.4	76.5	77.2	West Virginia	75.9	72.0	73.1	74.8	74.8	75.9
Minnesota	70.0	68.0	73.3	75.4	76.1	76.1	Wisconsin	63.8	68.3	67.5	70.1	70.9	71.8
Mississippi.	69.6	69.4	71.1	75.1	74.9	75.2	Wyoming.	73.2	68.9	69.0	70.0	69.8	71.0

Source: U.S. Census Bureau, <http://www.census.gov/hhes/www/hvs.html>.

U.S. Census Bureau, Statistical Abstract of the United States: 2001

No. 958. Occupied Housing Units—Costs by Region: 1999

[As of fall (68,796 represents 68,796,000). Specified owner-occupied units are limited to one-unit structures on less than 10 acres and no business on property. Specified renter-occupied units exclude one-unit structures on 10 acres or more. See headnote Table 959 for an explanation of housing costs. For composition of regions, see map inside front cover. Based on the American Housing Survey; see Appendix III]

Category	Number (1,000)					Percent distribution				
	Total units	North-east	Mid-west	South	West	Total units	North-east	Mid-west	South	West
OWNER OCCUPIED UNITS										
Total	68,796	12,644	17,568	25,180	13,403	100.0	100.0	100.0	100.0	100.0
Monthly housing costs:										
Less than $300	18,810	1,929	4,988	8,811	3,082	27.3	15.3	28.4	35.0	23.0
$300 to $399	6,758	1,417	1,965	2,287	1,088	9.8	11.2	11.2	9.1	8.1
$400 to $499	5,096	1,181	1,373	1,790	752	7.4	9.3	7.8	7.1	5.6
$500 to $599	4,593	939	1,370	1,646	638	6.7	7.4	7.8	6.5	4.8
$600 to $699	4,215	778	1,274	1,536	628	6.1	6.2	7.3	6.1	4.7
$700 to $799	4,071	722	1,135	1,632	582	5.9	5.7	6.5	6.5	4.3
$800 to $999	7,205	1,396	1,949	2,565	1,296	10.5	11.0	11.1	10.2	9.7
$1,000 to $1,249	6,166	1,323	1,457	1,828	1,558	9.0	10.5	8.3	7.3	11.6
$1,250 to $1,499	4,240	979	869	1,145	1,246	6.2	7.7	4.9	4.5	9.3
$1,500 or more	7,642	1,979	1,188	1,941	2,534	11.1	15.7	6.8	7.7	18.9
Median (dol.) [1]	581	647	494	439	705	(X)	(X)	(X)	(X)	(X)
RENTER OCCUPIED UNITS										
Total	34,007	7,314	6,791	11,209	8,692	100.0	100.0	100.0	100.0	100.0
Monthly housing costs:										
Less than $300	3,730	853	924	1,347	605	11.0	11.7	13.6	12.0	7.0
$300 to $399	3,340	535	969	1,273	564	9.8	7.3	14.3	11.4	6.5
$400 to $499	4,654	794	1,250	1,655	954	13.7	10.9	18.4	14.8	11.0
$500 to $599	5,289	1,070	1,160	1,746	1,313	15.6	14.6	17.1	15.6	15.1
$600 to $699	4,554	1,031	804	416	1,303	13.4	14.1	11.8	12.6	15.0
$700 to $799	3,414	827	533	1,052	1,002	10.0	11.3	7.8	9.4	11.5
$800 to $999	3,681	904	467	1,023	1,288	10.8	12.4	6.9	9.1	14.8
$1,000 to $1,249	1,779	464	201	419	695	5.2	6.3	3.0	3.7	8.0
$1,250 to $1,499	652	176	36	108	332	1.9	2.4	0.5	1.0	3.8
$1,500 or more	813	256	92	173	293	2.4	3.5	1.4	1.5	3.4
No cash rent	2,100	405	355	996	344	6.2	5.5	5.2	8.9	4.0
Median (dol.) [1]	580	620	506	548	657	(X)	(X)	(X)	(X)	(X)

X Not applicable.   [1] For explanation of median, see Guide to Tabular Presentation.

No. 959. Occupied Housing Units—Financial Summary by Selected Characteristics of the Householder: 1999

[In thousands of units (102,803 represents 102,803,000), except as indicated. As of fall. Housing costs include real estate taxes, property insurance, utilities, fuel, water, garbage collection, and mortgage. Based on the American Housing Survey; see Appendix III]

Characteristic	Total occu-pied units	Tenure		Black		Hispanic origin [1]		Elderly [2]		Households below poverty level	
		Owner	Renter	Owner	Renter	Owner	Renter	Owner	Renter	Owner	Renter
Total units [3]	102,803	68,796	34,007	6,013	6,923	4,087	4,955	17,196	4,227	6,276	7,988
Monthly housing costs:											
Less than $300	22,541	18,810	3,730	1,890	1,161	1,053	481	8,931	980	3,272	2,005
$300-$399	10,098	6,758	3,340	615	751	293	448	2,647	494	725	975
$400-$499	9,749	5,096	4,654	498	1,122	241	709	1,603	526	557	1,197
$500-$599	9,882	4,593	5,289	425	1,064	265	892	1,019	528	361	1,025
$600-$699	8,770	4,215	4,554	393	893	308	776	654	375	298	768
$700-$799	7,485	4,071	3,414	400	594	300	573	468	312	223	487
$800-$999	10,886	7,205	3,681	611	585	418	540	610	279	257	416
$1,000 or more	21,292	18,048	3,244	1,181	350	1,208	333	1,266	309	583	413
Median amount (dol.) [4]	581	581	580	501	521	662	583	292	481	290	459
Monthly housing costs as percent of income: [5]											
Less than 5 percent	5,457	5,163	293	365	68	249	27	1,040	44	33	7
5 to 9 percent	13,195	11,992	1,203	931	212	614	120	3,213	85	103	59
10 to 14 percent	15,070	11,948	3,122	922	518	574	395	3,062	173	233	144
15 to 19 percent	15,333	11,108	4,226	833	708	595	575	2,353	271	280	179
20 to 24 percent	11,996	7,761	4,235	654	811	422	548	1,578	268	266	214
25 to 29 percent	9,066	5,503	3,562	516	718	394	530	1,170	455	380	432
30 to 34 percent	6,281	3,450	2,832	344	589	247	426	769	408	284	438
35 to 39 percent	4,495	2,428	2,067	285	435	198	367	697	281	303	383
40 percent or more	17,539	8,251	9,287	1,016	2,197	724	1,580	2,877	1,720	3,227	4,430
Median amount (percent) . . .	20	17	28	19	31	20	31	17	38	56	64
Median monthly costs (dol.): [4]											
Electricity	60	67	45	72	49	63	42	60	38	59	44
Piped gas	40	43	28	47	33	33	25	43	28	42	29
Fuel oil	56	58	44	58	45	56	32	58	42	49	53

[1] Persons of Hispanic origin may be of any race.   [2] Householders 65 years old and over.   [3] Includes units with mortgage payment not reported and no cash rent not shown separately.   [4] For explanation of median, see Guide to Tabular Presentation.   [5] Money income before taxes.

Source of Tables 958 and 959: U.S. Census Bureau, *Current Housing Reports*, series H150/99, *American Housing Survey for the United States*.

No. 960. Mortgage Characteristics—Owner Occupied Units: 1999

[In thousands (68,796 represents 68,796,000). As of fall. Based on the American Housing Survey; see Appendix III]

Mortgage characteristic	Total occu-pied units	Housing unit characteristics		Household characteristics				
		New construc-tion [1]	Mobile homes	Black	Hispanic	Elderly [2]	Moved in past year	Below poverty level
ALL OWNERS								
Total [3]	**68,796**	**4,825**	**5,649**	**6,013**	**4,087**	**17,196**	**5,636**	**6,276**
Mortgages currently on property:								
None, owned free and clear	25,604	865	2,988	2,086	1,299	13,105	1,187	3,964
Regular and home equity mortgages .	6,279	446	77	372	288	368	246	129
Regular mortgage only	30,102	3,207	2,119	2,846	2,194	2,349	3,763	1,608
Home equity mortgage only	2,784	92	105	208	104	644	74	141
With regular mortgage, home equity not reported	2,503	127	213	269	115	425	238	246
No regular mortgage, home equity not reported	1,525	89	147	232	86	305	128	187
Type of home equity mortgage:								
Units with one or more home equity mortgages	9,062	537	182	580	392	1,013	320	270
Lump sum only.	3,680	229	79	326	212	353	140	129
Credit line only	5,013	280	85	224	159	621	161	118
Both	48	2	2	-	-	7	-	7
OWNERS WITH ONE OR MORE REGULAR MORTGAGES								
Total [3]	**38,883**	**3,779**	**2,409**	**3,487**	**2,598**	**3,142**	**4,247**	**1,963**
Type of primary mortgage:								
FHA.	5,410	452	88	981	647	277	742	237
VA	1,893	144	33	265	129	136	209	62
Farmers Home Administration	330	44	29	52	28	44	55	33
Other types	28,204	2,967	2,026	1,815	1,622	2,116	2,962	1,345
Mortgage origination:								
Placed new mortgage(s)	38,199	3,753	2,328	3,426	2,521	3,084	4,181	1,926
Assumed	585	24	75	44	72	53	52	47
Wrap-around	27	2	5	4	4	5	7	4
Combination of the above	73	-	-	12	1	-	7	5
Payment plan of primary mortgage:								
Fixed payment, self amortizing	31,472	3,164	1,971	2,680	2,099	2,147	3,532	1,369
Adjustable rate mortgage	2,057	171	50	139	147	174	155	79
Adjustable term mortgage	277	30	41	46	16	42	35	41
Graduated payment mortgage.	363	72	24	32	35	21	76	17
Balloon.	302	42	28	22	16	33	34	38
Combination of the above	273	31	14	14	11	20	26	12

- Represents or rounds to zero. [1] Constructed in the past 4 years. [2] 65 years old and over. [3] Includes types not known and not reported.

Source: U.S. Census Bureau, *Current Housing Reports*, Series H150/99, *American Housing Survey for the United States.*

No. 961. Occupied Housing Units—Neighborhood Indicators by Selected Characteristics of the Householder: 1999

[In thousands (102,803 represents 102,803,000). As of fall. Based on the American Housing Survey; see Appendix III]

Characteristic	Total occu-pied units	Tenure		Black		Hispanic origin [1]		Elderly [2]		Households below poverty level	
		Owner	Renter	Owner	Renter	Owner	Renter	Owner	Renter	Owner	Renter
Total units [3]	**102,803**	**68,796**	**34,007**	**6,013**	**6,923**	**4,087**	**4,955**	**17,196**	**4,227**	**6,276**	**7,988**
Street noise or traffic present [3].	28,991	16,561	12,430	1,722	2,759	965	1,601	4,516	1,336	1,794	2,989
Condition not bothersome . .	17,311	9,907	7,404	1,033	1,592	502	861	3,141	909	1,090	1,717
Condition bothersome	11,624	6,632	4,992	686	1,156	464	741	1,370	422	699	1,261
Neighborhood crime present [3]	14,429	7,566	6,863	1,145	1,953	630	1,056	1,578	558	792	1,827
Condition not bothersome . .	6,011	3,123	2,888	443	839	258	330	755	279	308	683
Condition bothersome	8,384	4,435	3,949	697	1,107	372	725	818	277	485	1,129
Other problems:											
Noise	2,659	1,502	1,157	138	215	111	161	341	80	157	275
Litter or housing deteriora-tion.	1,821	1,159	662	195	201	88	124	310	50	121	204
Poor city or county services .	847	532	316	106	102	56	66	101	14	64	99
People	4,494	2,736	1,758	230	385	195	262	547	128	258	468
With public transportation [3] . . .	55,565	31,813	23,752	3,587	5,470	2,490	4,009	7,982	2,977	2,648	5,742
Household uses it at least weekly	10,596	3,564	7,032	847	2,329	430	1,717	785	953	391	2,275
Household uses it less than weekly	19,587	11,914	7,673	1,348	1,587	882	1,096	2,925	1,071	1,095	1,890
Household does not use . . .	25,115	16,254	8,861	1,374	1,508	1,177	1,176	4,250	929	1,154	1,525
No public transportation	43,601	34,755	8,846	2,286	1,272	1,466	800	8,767	1,110	3,416	1,960

[1] Persons of Hispanic origin may be of any race. [2] Householders 65 years old and over. [3] Includes conditions not reported.

Source: U.S. Census Bureau, *Current Housing Reports*, Series H150/99, *American Housing Survey for the United States.*

Construction and Housing 609

No. 962. Heating Equipment and Fuels for Occupied Units: 1991 to 1999

[93,147 represents 93,147,000. As of fall. Based on American Housing Survey. See Appendix III]

Type of equipment or fuel	Number (1,000) 1991	1993	1995	1997	1999	Percent distribution 1991	1999
Occupied units, total	93,147	94,724	97,692	99,487	102,803	100.0	100.0
Heating equipment:							
Warm air furnace	49,423	51,248	53,165	58,603	62,018	53.1	60.3
Heat pumps	7,638	8,422	9,406	11,101	10,992	8.2	10.7
Steam or hot water	13,929	13,657	13,669	12,929	13,153	15.0	12.8
Floor, wall, or pipeless furnace . . .	4,291	4,746	4,963	5,588	5,310	4.6	5.2
Built-in electric units	6,755	6,722	7,035	4,531	4,939	7.3	4.8
Room heaters with flue	2,549	1,766	1,620	1,584	1,624	2.7	1.6
Room heaters without flue	2,111	1,597	1,642	1,754	1,790	2.3	1.7
Fireplaces, stoves, portable heaters or other	5,590	5,654	5,150	2,780	2,434	6.0	2.4
None	861	911	1,044	617	544	0.9	0.5
House main heating fuel:							
Utility gas	47,018	47,669	49,203	51,052	52,366	50.5	50.9
Fuel oil, kerosene, etc.	12,462	12,189	12,029	10,855	10,750	13.4	10.5
Electricity	23,714	25,107	26,771	29,202	31,142	25.5	30.3
Bottled, tank, or LP gas.	3,882	3,922	4,251	5,398	5,905	4.2	5.7
Coal or coke	319	297	210	183	168	0.3	0.2
Wood and other fuel	4,890	4,630	4,186	2,177	1,927	5.2	1.9
None	862	910	1,043	620	545	0.9	0.5
Cooking fuel:							
Electricity	54,232	55,887	57,621	58,818	61,315	58.2	59.6
Gas [1]	38,119	37,996	39,218	40,083	41,051	40.9	39.9
Other fuel	424	479	566	113	69	0.5	0.1
None	372	362	287	473	368	0.4	0.4

[1] Includes utility, bottled, tank, and LP gas.

Source: U.S. Census Bureau, *Current Housing Reports*, Series H150/91, H150/93, H150/95RV, H150/97, and H150/99, *American Housing Survey for the United States.*

No. 963. Occupied Housing Units—Housing Indicators by Selected Characteristics of the Householder: 1999

[In thousands of units (102,803 represents 102,803,000). As of fall. Based on the American Housing Survey; see Appendix III]

Characteristic	Total occu-pied units	Tenure Owner	Renter	Black Owner	Renter	Hispanic origin [1] Owner	Renter	Elderly [2] Owner	Renter	Households below poverty level Owner	Renter
Total units	102,803	68,796	34,007	6,013	6,923	4,087	4,955	17,196	4,227	6,276	7,988
Amenities:											
Porch, deck, balcony, or patio	83,498	61,556	21,942	5,072	4,158	3,493	2,860	15,244	2,468	5,316	4,699
Usable fireplace.	33,269	29,243	4,026	1,772	563	1,218	416	6,044	325	1,552	511
Separate dining room	45,844	36,968	8,875	3,340	1,919	1,950	1,198	8,442	895	2,834	1,679
With two or more living rooms or recreation rooms	30,360	28,203	2,157	2,105	348	1,180	171	6,041	233	1,567	313
Garage or carport with home .	60,553	49,941	10,612	3,254	1,357	2,890	1,540	12,695	1,112	3,570	1,734
Cars and trucks available:											
No cars, trucks, or vans	9,542	2,674	6,867	554	2,369	157	1,212	1,721	1,935	848	3,054
Other households without cars.	10,493	7,328	3,165	345	359	605	555	1,177	189	693	629
One car with or without trucks or vans	51,140	33,510	17,630	2,970	3,292	1,877	2,327	10,277	1,870	3,483	3,553
Two cars	24,628	19,225	5,402	1,622	792	1,100	757	3,449	202	1,026	630
Three or more cars	7,000	6,057	943	523	111	348	103	573	31	226	122
With cars, no trucks or vans. .	49,346	30,843	18,503	3,207	3,595	1,577	2,408	9,891	1,826	3,063	3,580
One truck or van with or without cars	32,168	25,365	6,803	1,782	725	1,584	1,057	4,394	340	1,727	1,042
Two or more trucks or vans . .	11,747	9,913	1,834	471	233	769	278	1,191	126	638	312
Internal deficiencies:											
Signs of rats in last 3 months.	892	415	477	76	163	65	155	74	31	70	180
Holes in floors.	1,183	489	693	76	226	33	146	98	55	125	287
Open cracks or holes	5,675	2,778	2,896	336	837	224	492	448	169	357	936
Broken plaster or peeling paint (interior of unit).	2,834	1,268	1,566	198	428	125	306	246	123	154	495
No electrical wiring	42	30	11	-	-	-	3	7	2	23	9
Exposed wiring	623	343	281	39	53	19	28	88	22	38	89
Rooms without electric outlet .	1,677	870	808	89	196	63	134	211	70	95	238
Water leakage [3]	9,669	5,400	4,269	590	1,027	363	649	875	268	458	1,109

- Represents zero. [1] Persons of Hispanic origin may be of any race. [2] Householders 65 years old and over. [3] During the 12 months prior to the survey.

Source: U.S. Census Bureau, *Current Housing Reports*, Series H150/99, *American Housing Survey for the United States.*

No. 964. Appliances and Office Equipment Used by Households by Region and Household Income: 1997

[101.5 represents 101,500,000. Represents appliances possessed and generally used by the household. Based on Residential Energy Consumption Survey; see source. For composition of regions, see inside front cover]

Type of appliance	House-holds using appli-ance	Region				Household income in 1997			
		North-east	Midwest	South	West	Under $10,000	$10,000 -$24,999	$25,000 -$49,999	$50,000 and over
Total households (mil.)....	**101.5**	**19.7**	**24.1**	**35.9**	**21.8**	**13.3**	**29.1**	**31.1**	**27.9**
PERCENT WITH—									
Air conditioner:									
Central system............	46.8	22.1	51.3	69.4	26.9	27.4	37.3	50.2	62.1
Room...................	24.8	39.6	26.1	23.2	12.8	33.3	28.8	24.0	17.5
Clothes washer.............	77.4	76.0	78.9	82.0	69.5	52.7	69.0	81.5	93.4
Clothes dryer [1]...........	71.2	66.7	75.8	74.2	65.1	36.2	61.0	77.1	91.8
Electric...............	55.1	48.3	50.1	66.4	48.2	31.0	49.0	59.9	67.6
Natural gas...........	15.2	17.7	23.9	7.2	16.5	4.8	11.1	16.3	23.3
Dishwasher...............	50.2	48.5	46.9	51.5	53.1	15.7	35.5	53.6	78.2
Ceiling fan	60.1	51.2	63.6	71.2	46.0	39.3	55.2	64.4	70.3
Freezer.................	33.2	25.7	41.8	36.9	24.2	25.6	30.0	35.1	37.9
One.................	30.2	24.2	38.4	33.1	22.1	23.6	27.5	32.2	34.1
Two or more	2.9	1.5	3.4	3.8	2.2	2.0	2.5	2.9	3.8
Microwave oven............	83.0	78.7	86.9	82.4	83.3	60.3	81.2	86.7	91.5
Oven...................	98.8	99.4	99.1	98.7	98.1	96.6	98.6	99.4	99.3
Electric...............	61.4	49.3	56.6	72.1	60.2	49.1	58.7	63.9	67.4
Natural gas...........	33.3	45.0	38.0	22.1	35.7	42.2	34.9	31.4	29.2
Self cleaning oven	44.1	48.5	45.1	41.8	42.7	18.1	31.1	47.0	66.6
Range	99.2	99.7	99.4	99.1	98.8	97.0	99.1	99.8	99.6
Electric...............	60.2	48.3	55.5	70.9	58.4	49.1	58.3	62.8	64.4
Natural gas...........	34.7	45.7	39.3	23.6	37.8	42.4	35.6	32.9	31.9
Refrigerator..............	99.8	99.9	99.9	99.9	99.7	99.3	99.9	99.9	100.0
Frost free	86.8	85.2	85.1	90.0	84.7	73.0	83.1	88.5	95.2
Water heater [1]...........	100.0	100.0	100.0	100.0	100.0	100.0	100.0	100.0	100.0
Electric...............	39.1	25.9	26.5	58.3	33.0	40.7	43.3	39.9	32.9
Natural gas...........	51.9	46.3	67.6	37.3	63.5	46.9	48.5	51.5	58.2
Stereo equipment...........	68.8	66.7	67.0	67.8	74.4	45.2	60.1	73.7	83.7
Color TV................	98.7	98.9	99.0	98.7	98.2	96.1	98.5	99.2	99.6
One.................	31.8	31.8	32.1	29.1	36.0	55.6	40.5	27.3	16.6
Two.................	37.4	36.1	36.2	38.9	37.3	30.9	37.7	41.6	35.4
Three................	19.1	20.8	20.4	18.4	17.3	7.5	15.6	20.4	26.8
Four.................	7.7	7.5	7.8	8.9	5.5	1.7	3.6	8.2	14.0
Five or more	2.7	2.6	2.5	3.4	2.2	(S)	1.1	1.7	6.8
VCR	87.6	86.1	89.7	86.0	89.0	66.8	84.0	91.6	96.6
Personal computers	35.1	31.9	38.0	31.0	41.3	9.7	16.5	36.9	64.5
One.................	29.2	27.2	32.4	25.9	32.9	8.0	14.5	32.8	50.7
Two or more	5.9	4.7	5.6	5.1	8.5	(S)	2.0	4.1	13.8
With modem	20.4	17.8	21.7	18.2	24.9	5.2	8.6	19.8	40.7
With laser printer	12.5	11.4	12.9	11.7	14.2	2.5	4.5	12.8	25.1
Used 15 hrs. per week or less..	25.2	21.5	27.7	23.0	29.3	6.3	12.2	28.2	44.4
Used 16 hrs. per week or more .	9.9	10.4	10.2	8.0	12.1	3.4	4.2	8.7	20.0
Personal use only	4.7	4.5	5.2	4.2	5.3	2.3	2.3	4.1	9.1
Business use only	2.1	2.3	2.5	1.1	3.1	(S)	(S)	1.4	5.0
Both	3.1	3.6	2.6	2.7	3.7	(S)	1.2	3.3	6.0
Cordless phone	61.4	59.6	63.8	61.5	60.2	35.3	51.5	66.9	77.9
Facsimile machine	6.2	6.5	5.3	5.6	8.1	(S)	2.5	5.3	13.3
Photocopier................	3.7	3.8	3.9	3.5	3.9	(S)	1.5	3.9	7.3
Answering machine	58.4	62.2	61.0	54.2	59.1	30.2	49.1	62.3	77.2

S Figure does not meet publication standards.   [1] Includes other types, not shown separately.
Source: U.S. Energy Information Administration, Internet site <http://www.eia.doe.gov/emeu/recs/contents.html>.

No. 965. Net Stock of Residential Fixed Assets: 1990 to 1999

[In billions of dollars (6,287.4 represents $6,287,400,000,000). End of year estimates]

Item	1990	1992	1993	1994	1995	1996	1997	1998	1999
Total residential fixed assets ..	**6,287.4**	**6,755.5**	**7,161.9**	**7,654.5**	**7,973.1**	**8,391.5**	**8,850.1**	**9,405.3**	**10,061.3**
By type of owner and legal form of organization:									
Private...................	6,137.7	6,595.8	6,991.0	7,472.2	7,784.2	8,195.3	8,646.3	9,191.8	9,835.7
Corporate................	68.0	71.9	73.7	76.0	78.2	81.5	86.5	91.7	96.2
Noncorporate	6,069.6	6,524.0	6,917.2	7,396.3	7,706.0	8,113.8	8,559.8	9,100.1	9,739.5
Government	149.7	159.6	170.9	182.3	188.8	196.2	203.8	213.5	225.6
Federal	52.5	53.5	57.3	60.7	62.4	64.5	66.7	69.5	72.7
State and local	97.2	106.1	113.7	121.6	126.5	131.7	137.2	144.0	152.9
By tenure group: [1]									
Owner-occupied	4,486.9	4,873.5	5,214.1	5,628.7	5,891.6	6,228.8	6,584.7	7,025.0	7,566.1
Farm.................	150.3	155.6	161.1	169.6	174.0	178.9	188.7	198.0	210.6
Nonfarm..............	4,336.6	4,717.9	5,053.0	5,459.1	5,717.7	6,049.9	6,396.0	6,826.9	7,355.5
Tenant-occupied	1,774.5	1,855.7	1,920.3	1,997.3	2,052.5	2,133.1	2,234.9	2,348.5	2,461.4
Farm.................	10.9	11.2	11.7	12.5	12.8	13.2	13.6	14.1	14.8
Nonfarm..............	1,763.6	1,844.5	1,908.6	1,984.8	2,039.7	2,119.9	2,221.4	2,334.4	2,446.6

[1] Excludes stocks of other nonfarm residential assets, which consists primarily of dormitories, and of fraternity and sorority houses.
Source: U.S. Bureau of Economic Analysis, Survey of Current Business, monthly, September 2000 issue.

Construction and Housing 611

No. 966. Expenditures by Residential Property Owners for Improvements and Maintenance and Repairs by Type of Property and Activity: 1980 to 2000

[In millions of dollars (46,338 represents $46,338,000,000)]

Year and type of expenditure	Total	1-unit properties with owner occupant	Other properties	Additions and alterations Total	To structures Additions	To structures Alterations	To property outside of structures	Major replacements	Maintenance and repairs
1980	46,338	31,481	14,857	21,336	4,183	11,193	5,960	9,816	15,187
1985	82,127	48,236	33,891	29,259	4,027	17,922	7,309	16,519	36,349
1987	98,413	56,354	42,059	41,484	9,893	22,503	9,088	16,701	40,227
1988	106,864	63,060	43,804	45,371	11,868	23,789	9,715	17,912	43,580
1989	108,054	62,866	45,188	42,176	7,191	24,593	10,391	19,788	46,089
1990	115,432	63,441	51,991	39,929	9,160	23,510	7,261	19,700	55,800
1991	107,692	62,608	45,084	33,662	8,609	17,486	7,567	18,526	55,505
1992	115,569	72,930	42,639	44,041	7,401	24,870	11,771	20,705	50,821
1993	121,899	77,626	44,273	53,512	16,381	27,657	9,472	22,604	45,785
1994	130,625	85,903	44,722	56,835	12,906	30,395	13,534	26,606	47,185
1995	124,971	79,003	45,968	51,011	11,197	29,288	10,526	26,928	47,032
1996	131,362	84,462	46,900	64,513	17,388	32,889	14,235	26,738	40,108
1997	133,577	90,677	42,900	65,222	14,575	37,126	13,523	27,210	41,145
1998	133,693	96,159	37,534	62,971	11,897	38,787	12,287	28,741	41,980
1999, total [1]	142,900	95,778	47,122	72,056	16,164	42,058	13,833	28,493	42,352
Heating and air conditioning [2]	9,638	6,391	3,247	2,815	(NA)	2,815	(NA)	4,177	2,647
Plumbing	12,254	6,402	5,852	4,377	(NA)	2,730	1,647	3,108	4,767
Roofing	12,480	7,858	4,622	(NA)	(NA)	(NA)	(NA)	8,135	4,345
Painting	11,790	6,398	5,392	(NA)	(NA)	(NA)	(NA)	(NA)	11,790
2000, total [1]	152,975	100,161	52,814	77,979	18,189	40,384	19,407	32,760	42,236
Heating and air conditioning [2]	10,866	7,075	3,791	2,736	(NA)	2,736	(NA)	5,645	2,486
Plumbing	11,518	5,561	5,957	3,359	(NA)	2,186	1,172	3,035	5,123
Roofing	15,834	8,670	7,164	(NA)	(NA)	(NA)	(NA)	11,243	4,591
Painting	13,830	7,592	6,238	(NA)	(NA)	(NA)	(NA)	(NA)	13,830

NA Not available. [1] Includes types of expenditures not separately specified. [2] Central air-conditioning.
Source: U.S. Census Bureau, Current Construction Reports, Series C50, Expenditures for Residential Improvement, quarterly.

No. 967. Home Remodeling—Work Done and Amount Spent: 1999

[In thousands, except percent (1,327 represents 1,327,000). As of spring. For work done in the prior 12 months. Based on survey and subject to sampling error; see source]

Remodeling project	Households with work done [1] Number	Households with work done [1] Percent of households	Work done by— Household member	Work done by— Outside contractor	Amount spent (dol.) Under $1,000	Amount spent (dol.) $1,000 to $2,999	Amount spent (dol.) Over $3,000
Conversion of garage/attic/basement into living space	1,327	1.3	800	282	366	260	478
Remodel bathroom	6,188	6.0	3,998	1,282	3,101	1,138	646
Remodel kitchen	4,695	4.6	2,659	1,253	1,745	780	1,098
Remodel bedroom	3,404	3.3	2,427	320	2,213	247	[2]137
Remodel/convert room to home office	1,106	1.1	844	[2]82	695	[2]92	[2]85
Remodel other rooms	3,228	3.2	2,158	561	1,511	598	368
Add bathroom	611	0.6	270	161	[2]174	[2]81	192
Add/extend garage	599	0.6	336	[2]130	[2]124	[2]56	293
Add other rooms—exterior addition	814	0.8	354	294	[2]154	[2]131	368
Add deck/porch/patio	2,455	2.4	1,246	875	832	650	527
Roofing	5,131	5.0	1,284	2,903	1,294	1,512	1,416
Siding—vinyl/metal	1,512	1.5	449	756	286	299	563
Aluminum windows	1,101	1.1	364	433	452	[2]171	[2]167
Clad-wood/Wood windows	503	0.5	197	254	[2]165	161	[2]106
Vinyl windows	1,780	1.7	811	969	473	486	514
Ceramic tile floors	2,737	2.7	1,235	1,140	1,378	493	344
Hardwood floors	1,553	1.5	579	715	564	391	266
Vinyl flooring	2,801	2.7	1,311	1,076	1,821	225	[2]110
Carpeting	5,633	5.5	1,264	3,524	2,534	1,510	618
Kitchen cabinets	2,255	2.2	837	821	525	451	444
Kitchen counter tops	2,531	2.5	729	1,200	1,276	314	217
Skylights	549	0.5	[2]114	317	226	[2]142	[2]46
Exterior doors	3,069	3.0	1,434	1,149	2,030	308	[2]92
Interior doors	1,603	1.6	816	451	997	[2]93	[2]79
Garage doors	1,792	1.7	509	994	1,095	285	60
Concrete or masonry work	2,418	2.4	975	1,075	1,077	490	393
Swimming pool—in ground	319	0.3	[2]54	223	[2]30	[2]61	168
Wall paneling	728	0.7	433	[2]55	363	[2]2	[2]31
Ceramic wall tile	907	0.9	461	269	598	[2]87	[2]40

[1] Includes no response and amount unknown. [2] Figure does not meet standards of reliability or precision.
Source: Mediamark Research Inc., New York, NY, Top-Line Reports, (copyright) Internet site <http://www.mediamark.com/mri/docs/TopLineReports.html> (accessed 11 June 2001).

612 Construction and Housing

No. 968. Commercial Office Space—Overview for Selected Market Areas: 2000

[As of mid-October (3,095,197 represents 3,095,197,000). For the 76 market areas with the highest vacancy rates in 2000. Data based on responses from individuals knowledgeable in the local markets]

Market area	Inventory (1,000 sq. ft.)	Vacant space (1,000 sq. ft.)	Vacancy rate (percent)	Construction (1,000 sq. ft.)	Net absorption [1] (1,000 sq. ft.)
United States, all market areas [2]	3,095,197	265,516	8.6	118,401	138,230
Albuquerque	11,423	1,056	9.2	57	456
Allentown	8,741	879	10.1	268	339
Atlanta	113,851	12,843	11.3	7,452	5,862
Baton Rouge	3,273	250	7.6	30	55
Birmingham	20,147	1,903	9.4	371	308
Bridgeport/Stratford	6,891	665	9.7	150	653
Buffalo	8,875	1,051	11.8	309	568
Charleston	4,292	474	11.0	106	333
Charlotte	32,763	3,135	9.6	3,190	3,785
Chicago	157,589	21,327	13.5	6,429	7,122
Cincinnati	34,140	2,221	6.5	1,342	398
Cleveland	36,400	3,791	10.4	588	371
Columbia	11,068	912	8.2	255	549
Corpus Christi	2,789	556	19.9	-	18
Dallas	132,755	21,979	16.6	3,061	7,490
Des Moines	10,281	702	6.8	-	1,452
El Paso	7,765	1,239	16.0	-	414
Fargo	3,785	299	7.9	99	214
Fort Lauderdale	18,965	1,695	8.9	1,774	585
Fort Wayne	5,631	392	7.0	180	151
Fort Worth	19,531	3,340	17.1	368	-
Fresno	14,798	1,643	11.1	400	733
Grand Rapids	10,925	1,184	10.8	145	838
Greensboro, High-Point, Winston-Salem . . .	15,277	2,177	14.2	483	567
Greenville	6,117	962	15.7	69	805
Hartford	21,423	3,518	16.4	160	519
Honolulu	11,725	1,598	13.6	-	121
Houston	109,740	11,341	10.3	3,449	2,161
Indianapolis	23,107	3,583	15.5	520	720
Jacksonville	15,286	2,251	14.7	541	1,043
Kansas City	35,772	3,559	9.9	1,296	333
Lansing	8,099	740	9.1	1,035	419
Las Vegas	17,798	1,725	9.7	1,149	2,284
Little Rock	10,996	882	8.0	852	394
Los Angeles-Central	27,761	6,295	22.7	-	-
Los Angeles-East	1,900	152	8.0	-	55
Los Angeles-Inland Empire	6,727	1,191	17.7	-	526
Los Angeles-Orange County	55,276	4,242	7.7	2,001	849
Los Angeles-San Fernando Valley	32,639	2,899	8.9	450	1,130
Los Angeles-South Bay	31,460	3,844	12.2	427	1,384
Madison	7,754	576	7.4	931	475
Medford	6,584	624	9.5	200	29
Memphis	24,005	2,484	10.3	378	788
Miami	29,654	2,531	8.5	3,038	4,824
Milwaukee	26,825	3,270	12.2	600	485
Minneapolis/St. Paul	53,083	4,592	8.7	4,129	3,204
Nashville	22,841	2,376	10.4	893	1,947
New Haven	13,900	1,315	9.5	240	800
New Jersey Central	70,931	5,436	7.7	4,220	6,013
New Jersey Northern	133,894	18,672	13.9	6,049	8,290
New Jersey South	16,174	1,198	7.4	74	342
Norfolk	20,478	1,705	8.3	766	597
NYC-Brooklyn/Queens	68,576	4,800	7.0	-	-
Oklahoma City	14,367	2,483	17.3	86	194
Omaha	8,981	588	6.5	850	123
Philadelphia	73,363	7,168	9.8	2,313	-
Phoenix	27,804	2,907	10.5	2,291	284
Pittsburgh	35,803	5,090	14.2	1,066	475
Richmond	21,083	1,621	7.7	673	1,325
Rochester	14,051	1,298	9.2	-	799
Sacramento	30,605	2,545	8.3	1,497	2,207
San Antonio	17,786	1,806	10.2	297	829
San Diego	36,490	3,082	8.4	2,346	2,888
Santa Rosa/Sonoma Valley	6,226	1,096	17.6	53	754
Shreveport	3,474	601	17.3	-	133
Sioux Falls	2,100	187	8.9	150	173
South Bend	3,184	393	12.3	150	112
Spokane	2,180	185	8.5	-	-
Stamford/Norwalk	25,749	1,689	6.6	-	271
St. Louis	39,887	4,220	10.6	1,479	1,496
Syracuse	7,911	964	12.2	55	411
Toledo	7,588	1,342	17.7	-	45
Tulsa	15,522	1,658	10.7	735	804
Ventura County	7,000	700	10.0	975	550
Wilmington	12,143	957	7.9	-	119
Youngstown	2,650	315	11.9	50	50

- Represents zero.   [1] Net change in occupied stock.   [2] Includes other market areas, not shown separately.

Source: Society of Industrial and Office REALTORS, Washington DC, *2001 Comparative Statistics of Industrial and Office Real Estate Markets* (copyright).

Construction and Housing   613

No. 969. Commercial Buildings—Summary: 1999

[Preliminary. (4,665 represents 4,665,000). Excludes buildings 1,000 square feet or smaller. Building type based on predominant activity in which the occupants were engaged. Based on a sample survey of building representatives conducted in 1999, therefore subject to sampling variability. For composition of regions, see map inside front cover]

Characteristic	All build-ings (1,000)	Floor-space (mil. sq. ft.)	Mean sq. ft. per building (1,000)	Characteristic	All build-ings (1,000)	Floor-space (mil. sq. ft.)	Mean sq. ft. per building (1,000)
All buildings	**4,665**	**67,344**	**14.4**	200,001 to 500,000	23	6,851	296.3
Region and division:				Over 500,000	7	6,627	929.0
Northeast	691	12,384	17.9	Year constructed:			
New England	208	3,735	18.0	1919 or before	418	4,012	9.6
Mid Atlantic	483	8,649	17.9	1920 to 1945	488	6,404	13.1
Midwest	1,188	16,741	14.1	1946 to 1959	760	9,103	12.0
East North Central	782	11,207	14.3	1960 to 1969	678	10,894	16.1
West North Central	406	5,534	13.6	1970 to 1979	762	11,792	15.5
South	1,763	23,499	13.3	1980 to 1989	852	13,931	16.3
South Atlantic	749	11,002	14.7	1990 to 1999	707	11,207	15.9
East South Central	396	5,232	13.2				
West South Central	619	7,265	11.7	Workers (main shift):			
West	1,022	14,720	14.4	Fewer than 5	2,377	14,284	6.0
Mountain	315	4,559	14.5	5 to 9	808	6,329	7.8
Pacific	706	10,161	14.4	10 to 19	689	8,082	11.7
Principal activity within:				20 to 49	488	10,842	22.2
Education	327	8,638	26.4	50 to 99	173	8,870	51.2
Food sales	174	997	5.7	100 to 249	90	8,342	92.4
Food service	350	1,850	5.3	250 or more	39	10,595	270.0
Health care	127	2,918	22.9	Energy sources: [1]			
Inpatient	11	1,865	168.2	Electricity	4,403	65,722	14.9
Outpatient	116	1,053	9.1	Natural gas	2,675	45,525	17.0
Lodging	153	4,528	29.6	Fuel oil	434	13,292	30.6
Mercantile	668	10,372	15.5	District heat	117	5,891	50.2
Retail (other than mall) . . .	534	4,737	8.9	Propane	451	6,276	13.9
Enclosed mall and strip center	134	5,635	42.1	Heating equipment: [1]			
Office	744	12,069	16.2	Heat pumps	492	8,941	18.2
Public assembly	305	4,394	14.4	Furnaces	1,467	14,510	9.9
Public order and safety	72	1,168	16.2	Individual space heaters . . .	894	17,325	19.4
Religious worship	307	3,424	11.1	District heat	96	5,534	57.7
Service	478	3,395	7.1	Boilers	576	19,444	33.7
Warehouse and storage	604	10,462	17.3	Packaged heating units	1,346	25,743	19.1
Other	102	1,222	12.0	Other	189	4,067	21.6
Vacant	253	1,908	7.6	Cooling equipment: [1]			
Building floorspace (sq. ft.):				Residential-type central A/C .	677	8,348	12.3
1,001 to 5,000	2,355	6,806	2.9	Heat pumps	486	9,165	18.9
5,001 to 10,000	1,110	8,234	7.4	Individual A/C	799	14,298	17.9
10,001 to 25,000	708	11,127	15.7	District chilled water	50	2,757	55.5
25,001 to 50,000	257	9,311	36.2	Central chillers	129	12,916	100.1
50,001 to 100,000	145	10,117	70.0	Packaged A/C units	1,959	36,571	18.7
100,001 to 200,000	59	8,271	139.4	Swamp coolers	136	2,210	16.2
				Other	49	1,308	26.6

[1] More than one type may apply.

Source: U.S. Energy Information Administration, Internet site <http://www.eia.doe.gov/emeu/cbecs/contents.html> (accessed 8 August 2001).

No. 970. Office Buildings—Vacancy Rates for Major Markets: 1980 to 2000

[As of end of year. Excludes government owned and occupied, owner-occupied, and medical office buildings]

Market	1980	1985	1990	1993	1994	1995	1996	1997	1998	1999	2000
Atlanta, GA	10.0	21.0	19.1	16.8	13.0	10.4	9.2	10.5	11.2	11.8	11.7
Baltimore, MD	7.2	11.5	20.0	17.3	15.5	17.0	14.3	11.6	10.0	(NA)	9.8
Charlotte, NC	(NA)	16.7	16.5	(NA)	10.0	8.9	8.2	7.1	7.2	9.5	8.6
Chicago, IL	7.0	16.5	18.6	21.4	18.7	15.5	15.5	(NA)	14.4	14.6	11.0
Columbus, OH	(NA)	(NA)	(NA)	(NA)	(NA)	(NA)	(NA)	(NA)	(NA)	(NA)	13.2
Dallas, TX	8.6	23.0	25.8	29.5	21.7	18.7	16.2	14.7	15.0	18.5	15.8
Edmonton, CN	(NA)	(NA)	(NA)	(NA)	(NA)	(NA)	(NA)	(NA)	(NA)	12.0	11.9
Fort Lauderdale, FL	(NA)	(NA)	23.0	(NA)	10.8	(NA)	10.5	10.4	10.0	4.8	10.3
Houston, TX	4.0	27.6	24.9	25.1	24.7	21.9	17.5	12.1	10.7	12.7	11.7
Indianapolis, IN	(NA)	(NA)	21.2	18.8	18.4	14.3	(NA)	14.2	11.2	10.8	14.0
Los Angeles, CA	0.9	15.3	16.8	21.0	19.6	23.2	22.1	13.8	14.2	11.5	9.7
Memphis, TN	(NA)	(NA)	(NA)	(NA)	(NA)	(NA)	13.6	12.0	12.5	11.2	12.6
Milwaukee, WI.	(NA)	(NA)	22.9	21.0	17.6	16.3	(NA)	(NA)	(NA)	16.9	17.4
Minneapolis, MN	(NA)	(NA)	(NA)	(NA)	8.2	(NA)	6.5	6.2	7.0	7.6	9.8
Montreal, CN	(NA)	(NA)	(NA)	(NA)	21.3	(NA)	20.5	19.1	17.5	14.4	11.9
Nashville, TN	(NA)	(NA)	25.1	(NA)	7.5	(NA)	6.9	6.0	7.5	9.7	10.4
New Jersey (North)	(NA)	(NA)	(NA)	(NA)	16.5	(NA)	14.5	11.9	10.0	9.6	10.0
Orlando, FL	(NA)	(NA)	(NA)	(NA)	12.1	(NA)	6.5	6.4	7.1	9.5	9.0
Philadelphia, PA	6.3	14.5	18.2	17.8	16.3	16.2	13.7	10.9	12.4	11.1	9.4
Phoenix, AZ	(NA)	(NA)	27.6	(NA)	11.8	(NA)	11.5	9.3	8.9	13.4	10.8
Pittsburgh, PA	1.2	(NA)	16.3	17.0	15.8	14.5	(NA)	15.4	14.0	13.0	19.4
Sacramento, CA	(NA)	(NA)	(NA)	(NA)	14.1	(NA)	12.4	12.3	11.8	12.4	8.6
St. Louis, MO	(NA)	(NA)	21.0	19.1	18.1	12.7	13.4	12.3	9.6	11.2	13.7
St. Paul, MN	(NA)	(NA)	(NA)	(NA)	15.2	(NA)	12.5	9.9	7.2	9.2	10.7
Tampa/St. Petersburg	(NA)	(NA)	(NA)	(NA)	(NA)	(NA)	13.0	9.1	8.8	10.0	10.5
West Palm Beach, FL.	(NA)	(NA)	(NA)	(NA)	16.8	(NA)	12.0	12.3	13.5	13.0	11.7
Winston-Salem/Greensboro	(NA)	(NA)	(NA)	(NA)	13.2	(NA)	14.1	12.3	14.5	15.7	15.1

NA Not available.

Source: ONCOR International, Houston, TX, 1980 and 1985, National Office Market Report, semiannual; 1989-1990, International Office Market Report, semiannual; thereafter, Year-End (year) Market Data Book, annual (copyright).

Section 21
Manufactures

This section presents summary data for manufacturing as a whole and more detailed information for major industry groups and selected products. The types of measures shown at the different levels include data for establishments, employment and wages, plant and equipment expenditures, value and quantity of production and shipments, value added by manufacture, inventories, and various indicators of financial status.

The principal sources of these data are U.S. Census Bureau reports of the censuses of manufactures conducted every 5 years, the *Annual Survey of Manufactures,* and *Manufacturing Profiles,* an annual compilation of the formerly printed series of *Current Industrial Reports.* Indexes of industrial production are presented monthly in the Federal Reserve Board's *Federal Reserve Bulletin.* These numbers were recently changed to a new index base year (1992 = 100) as of 1997. Reports on current activities of industries or current movements of individual commodities are compiled by such government agencies as the Bureau of Labor Statistics; the Economic Research Service of the Department of Agriculture; the International Trade Administration; and by private research or trade associations such as The Conference Board, Inc., the American Iron and Steel Institute, the Electronic Industries Association, and several others.

Data on financial aspects of manufacturing industries are collected by the Bureau of Economic Analysis (BEA) and the U.S. Census Bureau. Industry aggregates in the form of balance sheets, profit and loss statements, analyses of sales and expenses, lists of subsidiaries, and types and amounts of security issues are published for leading manufacturing corporations registered with the Securities and Exchange Commission. The BEA issues data on capital in manufacturing industries and capacity utilization rates in manufacturing. See also Section 15, Business Enterprise.

Several private trade associations provide industry coverage for certain sections of the economy. They include the Aluminum Association (Table 993), American Iron and Steel Institute (Tables 994-996), Consumer Electronics Association (Tables 1003 and 1004), and the Aerospace Industries Association (Tables 1012-1014). Machine tool consumption data (Table 997) is produced jointly by the Association for Manufacturing Technology and American Machine Tool Distributors Association.

Censuses and annual surveys—The first census of manufactures covered the year 1809. Between 1809 and 1963, a census was conducted at periodic intervals. Since 1967, it has been taken every 5 years (for years ending in "2" and "7"). Results from the 1997 census are presented in this section utilizing the new NAICS (North American Industry Classification System). For additional information see text, Section 15, Business Enterprise, and the Census Bureau Web site at <http://www.census.gov/epcd/www/NAICS.html>. Census data either direct reports or estimates from administrative records, are obtained for every manufacturing plant with one paid employee or more.

The *Annual Survey of Manufactures* (ASM), conducted for the first time in 1949, collects data for the years between censuses for the more general measure of manufacturing activity covered in detail by the censuses. The annual survey data are estimates derived from a scientifically selected sample of establishments. The 1999 annual survey is based on a sample of about 55,000 establishments of an approximate total of 230,000. These establishments represent all manufacturing establishments of multiunit companies and all single-establishment manufacturing companies mailed schedules in the 1997 Census of Manufactures. For the current panel of the ASM sample, all establishments of companies with 1997

Manufactures 615

shipments in manufacturing in excess of $500 million were included in the survey with certainty. For the remaining portion of the mail survey, the establishment was defined as the sampling unit. For this portion, all establishments with 250 employees or more and establishments with a very large value of shipments also were included. Therefore, of the 58,000 establishments included in the ASM panel, approximately 33,000 are selected with certainty. These establishments account for approximately 80 percent of total value of shipments in the 1992 census. Smaller establishments in the remaining portion of the mail survey were selected by sample.

Establishments and classification—
The censuses of manufactures for 1947 through 1992 cover operating manufacturing establishments as defined in the *Standard Industrial Classification Manual* (SIC), issued by the U.S. Office of Management and Budget (see text, Section 12). The Manual is also used for classifying establishments in the annual surveys. The comparability of manufactures data over time is affected by changes in the official definitions of industries as presented in the Manual. It is important to note, therefore, that the 1987 edition of the Manual was used for the 1987 and 1992 censuses; and the 1972 edition of the Manual and the 1977 Supplement were used for the 1972 through 1982 censuses.

The Manual defines an industry as a number of establishments producing a single product or a closely related group of products. In the manual, an establishment is classified in a particular industry if its production of a product or product group exceeds in value added its production of any other product group. While some establishments produce only the products

of the industry in which they are classified, few within an industry specialize to that extent. The statistics on employment, payrolls, value added, inventories, and expenditures, therefore, reflect both the primary and secondary activities of the establishments in that industry. For this reason, care should be exercised in relating such statistics to the total shipments figures of products primary to the industry.

Most tables in this section use the new way of organizing economic statistics called the North American Industry Classification System (NAICS). For more information on this system, see *North American Industry Classification System (NAICS) - United States, 1997.*

Establishment—Establishment signifies a single physical plant site or factory. It is not necessarily identical to the business unit or company, which may consist of one or more establishments. A company operating establishments at more than one location is required to submit a separate report for each location. An establishment engaged in distinctly different lines of activity and maintaining separate payroll and inventory records is also required to submit separate reports.

Durable goods—Items with a normal life expectancy of 3 years or more. Automobiles, furniture, household appliances, and mobile homes are common examples.

Nondurable goods—Items which generally last for only a short time (3 years or less). Food, beverages, clothing, shoes, and gasoline are common examples.

Statistical reliability—For a discussion of statistical collection and estimation, sampling procedures, and measures of statistical reliability applicable to Census Bureau data, see Appendix III.

No. 971. Gross Domestic Product in Manufacturing in Current and Real (1996) Dollars by Industry: 1990 to 1999

[In billions of dollars (5,803.2 represents $5,803,200,000,000). Data are based on the 1987 Standard Industrial Classification (SIC). Data include nonfactor charges (capital consumption allowances, indirect business taxes, etc.) as well as factor charges against gross product; corporate profits and capital consumption allowances have been shifted from a company to an establishment basis]

Industry	1990	1993	1994	1995	1996	1997	1998	1999
CURRENT DOLLARS								
Gross domestic product [1]	5,803.2	6,642.3	7,054.3	7,400.5	7,813.2	8,318.4	8,790.2	9,299.2
Manufacturing	1,040.6	1,131.4	1,223.2	1,289.1	1,316.0	1,379.6	1,436.0	1,500.8
Durable goods	586.6	632.8	694.1	729.8	748.4	791.2	833.4	877.8
Lumber and wood products	32.2	35.7	39.8	42.3	39.9	42.1	41.4	44.1
Furniture and fixtures	15.6	18.1	18.9	19.5	20.7	22.7	24.1	25.9
Stone, clay, and glass products	25.3	26.4	30.4	32.4	33.2	37.2	38.2	41.0
Primary metal industries	43.2	43.0	47.6	53.0	50.8	52.6	54.1	54.9
Fabricated metal products	69.4	73.4	83.2	87.2	93.1	97.6	102.2	105.5
Industrial machinery	118.2	113.7	121.0	132.8	136.3	143.2	150.8	158.2
Electronic & other electric equipment	105.7	121.0	139.3	146.9	153.2	165.9	172.8	186.6
Motor vehicles and equipment	47.3	78.0	95.2	98.2	92.2	96.5	107.2	114.5
Other transportation equipment	60.5	54.2	49.6	47.7	51.4	55.5	59.2	59.6
Instruments and related products	49.3	48.4	46.8	47.2	53.7	53.6	57.7	60.0
Misc. manufacturing industries	19.8	20.9	22.3	22.7	23.8	25.2	25.7	27.6
Nondurable goods	454.0	498.6	529.1	559.2	567.6	588.4	602.6	623.1
Food and kindred products	96.4	107.6	110.2	121.1	118.7	123.1	124.8	131.4
Tobacco manufactures	11.9	12.3	13.2	15.1	14.8	15.4	16.8	19.9
Textile mill products	22.0	25.7	25.6	24.8	25.3	25.7	25.4	25.3
Apparel and other textile products	25.4	27.7	28.5	27.3	27.0	26.5	25.8	25.5
Paper and allied products	45.0	46.9	50.1	58.9	55.9	53.8	55.1	57.0
Printing and publishing	73.1	78.5	83.5	80.8	88.2	91.1	94.0	99.0
Chemicals and allied products	109.9	122.7	138.7	150.8	153.6	164.8	168.4	176.3
Petroleum and coal products	31.7	31.0	29.3	29.0	30.2	31.4	32.9	28.6
Rubber and misc. plastic products	33.9	41.6	44.9	46.1	49.7	52.1	55.1	55.8
Leather and leather products	4.7	4.7	5.0	5.3	4.2	4.3	4.2	4.2
CHAINED (1996) DOLLARS								
Gross domestic product, total [1]	6,707.9	7,062.6	7,347.7	7,543.8	7,813.2	8,159.5	8,515.7	8,875.8
Manufacturing	1,102.3	1,122.9	1,206.0	1,284.7	1,316.0	1,387.3	1,446.4	1,529.4
Durable goods	585.1	600.3	656.5	714.9	748.4	813.0	892.4	970.5
Lumber and wood products	45.1	36.9	38.9	41.6	39.9	39.5	39.5	40.8
Furniture and fixtures	18.1	20.1	20.2	20.7	20.7	22.1	22.7	23.6
Stone, clay, and glass products	29.4	29.1	32.0	32.8	33.2	36.6	35.9	36.9
Primary metal industries	43.7	48.5	50.5	49.6	50.8	52.7	54.7	60.7
Fabricated metal products	76.1	75.8	86.4	90.8	93.1	96.2	96.7	95.9
Industrial machinery	93.5	96.8	106.8	124.7	136.3	158.4	187.0	216.6
Electronic & other electric equipment	68.6	85.0	103.3	128.7	153.2	182.2	225.1	276.8
Motor vehicles and equipment	68.7	85.1	99.1	103.2	92.2	97.1	107.0	110.4
Other transportation equipment	75.7	58.3	52.2	49.4	51.4	54.8	57.5	56.3
Instruments and related products	68.9	57.2	53.8	52.6	53.7	49.8	49.2	48.8
Misc. manufacturing industries	22.8	21.4	22.6	23.3	23.8	24.8	24.6	26.0
Nondurable goods	520.2	525.4	551.2	570.3	567.6	574.7	557.9	566.9
Food and kindred products	109.5	114.6	112.6	133.3	118.7	118.1	115.0	117.1
Tobacco manufactures	14.5	9.3	13.8	15.7	14.8	13.9	11.5	7.0
Textile mill products	22.8	25.9	26.9	26.0	25.3	25.0	23.6	22.9
Apparel and other textile products	27.3	27.6	28.4	28.0	27.0	26.5	25.0	23.6
Paper and allied products	52.5	60.7	61.3	52.2	55.9	58.3	55.3	56.0
Printing and publishing	102.9	90.5	92.6	89.2	88.2	86.4	84.0	84.3
Chemicals and allied products	131.1	132.1	145.5	148.0	153.6	164.2	159.8	168.6
Petroleum and coal products	22.9	21.6	22.0	26.9	30.2	25.6	26.6	34.9
Rubber and misc. plastic products	34.0	41.2	44.9	47.0	49.7	53.2	53.8	54.4
Leather and leather products	5.2	4.9	5.1	5.3	4.2	4.2	4.0	4.0

[1] For additional industry detail, see Table 641.

Source: U.S. Bureau of Economic Analysis, *National Income and Product Accounts, 1929-97*, (forthcoming), and *Survey of Current Business*, December 2000.

Manufactures 617

No. 972. Manufacturing—Establishments, Employees, and Annual Payroll by Industry: 1998 and 1999

[Excludes government employees, railroad employees, self-employed persons, etc. See "General Explanation" in source for definitions and statement on reliability of data. An *establishment* is a single physical location where business is conducted or where services or industrial operations are performed]

Industry	NAICS code [1]	1998 Estab-lish-ments, number	1998 Number of employ-ees [2] (1,000)	1998 Annual payroll (mil. dol.)	1999 Estab-lish-ments, number	1999 Number of employ-ees [2] (1,000)	1999 Annual payroll (mil. dol.)
All industries, total	(X)	**6,941,822**	**108,118**	**3,309,406**	**7,008,444**	**110,706**	**3,554,693**
Manufacturing, total	31-33	**366,249**	**16,946**	**607,333**	**360,244**	**16,660**	**625,536**
Percent of all industries	(X)	5.28	15.67	18.35	5.14	15.05	17.60
Food	311	27,750	1,464	40,209	26,734	1,464	41,858
Beverage & tobacco product	312	2,729	173	6,877	2,789	172	6,992
Textile mills	313	4,692	385	10,222	4,587	362	9,694
Textile product mills	314	7,095	217	5,081	7,152	222	5,313
Apparel manufacturing	315	17,432	671	12,365	16,721	575	11,206
Leather & allied product	316	1,801	79	1,773	1,807	74	1,738
Wood product	321	17,640	580	15,439	17,473	595	16,373
Paper	322	5,927	568	22,686	5,883	559	23,227
Printing & related support activities	323	42,115	845	27,473	40,671	834	27,940
Petroleum & coal products	324	2,221	111	5,997	2,226	109	6,058
Chemical	325	13,595	901	44,124	13,534	886	44,738
Plastics & rubber products	326	16,745	1,030	31,563	16,646	1,047	33,351
Nonmetallic mineral product	327	16,473	508	17,591	16,541	510	18,273
Primary metal	331	5,487	615	24,827	5,900	598	24,766
Fabricated metal product	332	63,438	1,816	60,929	62,242	1,788	61,604
Machinery	333	30,824	1,444	56,533	30,177	1,398	55,874
Computer & electronic product	334	17,625	1,681	79,685	17,279	1,615	83,842
Electrical equip, appliance & component	335	7,147	602	20,229	7,104	586	20,600
Transportation equipment	336	13,196	1,911	84,378	13,042	1,906	90,609
Furniture & related product	337	20,607	604	16,081	20,266	623	17,128
Miscellaneous	339	31,710	737	23,272	31,470	734	24,354

[1] North American Industry Classification System, 1997. [2] Covers full- and part-time employees who are on the payroll in the pay period including March 12.

Source: U.S. Census Bureau, *County Business Patterns,* annual. See also <http://www.census.gov/prod/2001pubs/cbp99/cbp99-1.pdf> (issued April 2001).

No. 973. Manufacturing Establishments, Employees, and Annual Payroll by State: 1999

[Excludes government employees, railroad employees, self-employed persons, etc. See "General Explanation" in source for definitions and statement on reliability of data. An *establishment* is a single physical location where business is conducted or where services or industrial operations are performed]

State	Establish-ments	Number of employ-ees [1] (1,000)	Annual payroll (mil. dol.)	State	Establish-ments	Number of employ-ees [1] (1,000)	Annual payroll (mil. dol.)
United States	**360,244**	**16,659.9**	**625,536**	Missouri	7,465	372.8	12,552
Alabama	5,336	341.9	10,631	Montana	1,207	20.6	634
Alaska	505	11.8	361	Nebraska	1,955	108.8	3,340
Arizona	4,903	192.6	7,581	Nevada	1,701	38.8	1,346
Arkansas	3,294	229.6	6,386	New Hampshire	2,271	97.2	3,625
California	49,330	1,792.2	76,634	New Jersey	11,448	390.4	16,851
Colorado	5,425	164.8	6,628	New Mexico	1,577	38.5	1,218
Connecticut	5,657	238.1	11,112	New York	23,071	728.5	27,063
Delaware	696	41.4	1,777	North Carolina	11,137	754.7	22,754
District of Columbia	186	2.9	93	North Dakota	717	22.9	686
Florida	15,601	420.2	13,796	Ohio	17,930	982.9	39,125
Georgia	8,936	530.7	16,873	Oklahoma	4,017	167.3	5,457
Hawaii	919	14.5	403	Oregon	5,694	210.3	7,774
Idaho	1,649	66.0	2,169	Pennsylvania	17,038	809.8	29,663
Illinois	17,653	861.5	33,839	Rhode Island	2,376	71.6	2,379
Indiana	9,320	637.4	24,712	South Carolina	4,520	336.8	11,193
Iowa	3,828	246.0	8,199	South Dakota	897	47.8	1,452
Kansas	3,295	196.2	6,961	Tennessee	7,248	475.8	15,725
Kentucky	4,291	292.2	10,437	Texas	21,724	955.2	36,486
Louisiana	3,488	165.1	6,311	Utah	2,948	121.9	4,074
Maine	1,917	81.0	2,816	Vermont	1,245	44.7	1,547
Maryland	3,972	159.3	6,386	Virginia	5,949	366.4	12,424
Massachusetts	9,329	404.5	18,833	Washington	7,741	331.2	14,037
Michigan	15,790	816.6	37,206	West Virginia	1,510	73.1	2,591
Minnesota	8,089	379.0	14,368	Wisconsin	10,005	573.4	20,805
Mississippi	2,885	223.3	5,919	Wyoming	559	9.5	308

[1] Covers full- and part-time employees who are on the payroll in the pay period including March 12.

Source: U.S. Census Bureau, *County Business Patterns,* annual. See also <http://www.census.gov/prod/2001pubs/cbp99/cbp99-1.pdf> (issued April 2001).

No. 974. Manufactures—Summary by Selected Industry: 1999

[16,711 represents 16,711,000]

Industry based on shipments	NAICS code [1]	All employees [2]			Produc- tion workers[2] (1,000)	Value added by manufac- tures [3] (mil. dol.)	Value of ship- ments [4] (mil. dol.)
		Number (1,000)	Payroll				
			Total (mil. dol.)	Per employee (dol.)			
Manufacturing, total	31-33	16,711	600,090	35,910	12,011	1,962,644	4,038,109
Food	311	1,488	41,211	27,699	1,139	177,659	429,053
Grain and oilseed milling	3112	59	2,369	40,390	43	16,540	47,094
Fruit and vegetable preserving and specialty food.	3114	180	5,035	27,914	154	25,064	49,373
Dairy product	3115	131	4,303	32,889	87	18,999	62,327
Meat product	3116	477	11,164	23,389	412	34,084	111,970
Bakeries and tortilla.	3118	315	8,606	27,327	194	30,402	47,255
Other food.	3119	150	4,550	30,331	113	28,474	53,189
Beverage and tobacco product	312	167	6,677	39,970	91	68,598	107,437
Beverage	3121	139	5,233	37,724	71	30,539	62,116
Tobacco	3122	28	1,445	50,960	20	38,059	45,321
Textile mills	313	357	9,466	26,535	301	22,954	54,854
Textile product mills	314	240	5,440	22,631	197	14,262	32,642
Apparel	315	576	11,022	19,138	470	30,594	62,798
Cut and sew apparel.	3152	441	8,275	18,777	357	24,753	50,738
Leather and allied product	316	74	1,760	23,791	60	4,551	9,673
Wood product	321	589	15,954	27,076	493	38,413	97,583
Sawmills and wood preservation	3211	133	3,644	27,433	113	9,610	30,209
Other wood product.	3219	341	8,839	25,957	283	19,250	45,386
Paper.	322	560	22,789	40,683	432	74,602	157,491
Pulp, paper, and paperboard mills	3221	187	9,725	52,137	146	37,526	73,509
Converted paper product	3222	374	13,065	34,966	286	37,076	83,982
Printing and related support activities.	323	838	27,369	32,651	609	62,428	102,404
Printing and related support activities	3231	838	27,369	32,651	609	62,428	102,404
Petroleum and coal products	324	104	5,625	54,220	69	42,355	168,096
Petroleum and coal products.	3241	104	5,625	54,220	69	42,355	168,096
Chemical	325	881	42,101	47,765	506	229,284	419,674
Basic chemical	3251	193	10,355	53,516	111	50,239	106,875
Resin, syn rubber, and artif. & syn. fibers	3252	108	5,353	49,382	73	27,308	62,510
Pharmaceutical and medicine	3254	223	11,985	53,764	108	74,108	107,855
Soap, cleaning compound, and toilet preparation .	3256	123	4,626	37,480	75	32,483	53,266
Other chemical product	3259	122	5,071	41,526	74	21,563	39,955
Plastics and rubber products	326	1,069	32,638	30,529	848	91,346	172,397
Plastics product	3261	858	25,368	29,567	680	72,183	136,873
Rubber product	3262	211	7,270	34,439	168	19,163	35,524
Nonmetallic mineral product	327	526	17,948	34,124	411	56,538	97,498
Cement and concrete product	3273	219	7,428	33,967	166	22,714	42,550
Primary metal	331	586	23,726	40,458	466	66,733	158,102
Iron and steel mills and ferroalloy.	3311	141	7,288	51,574	111	21,781	53,054
Alumina and aluminum production and processing	3313	84	3,298	39,411	66	11,423	31,036
Fabricated metal product	332	1,799	59,915	33,309	1,359	142,451	256,899
Architectural and structural metals	3323	412	12,919	31,377	302	30,128	60,138
Machine shops, turned product & screw, nut, bolt .	3327	424	14,512	34,240	328	28,910	44,497
Other fabricated metal product	3329	323	11,346	35,115	234	29,863	51,612
Machinery.	333	1,401	53,802	38,416	922	138,798	277,117
Agriculture, construction, and mining machinery . .	3331	202	7,385	36,545	142	20,733	50,679
Industrial machinery	3332	186	7,553	40,672	107	19,605	36,526
Metalworking machinery.	3335	241	9,858	40,895	173	18,508	30,038
Engine, turbine, and power transmission equipment	3336	117	5,004	42,825	78	16,894	34,834
Other general-purpose machinery	3339	348	13,508	38,842	214	31,689	64,298
Computer and electronic product.	334	1,621	75,130	46,358	830	265,442	458,485
Computer and peripheral equipment.	3341	217	11,433	52,636	81	47,803	112,677
Communications equipment	3342	286	14,553	50,975	124	48,805	90,600
Semiconductor and other electronic component . .	3344	581	23,697	40,776	376	102,003	146,560
Navigational, measuring, medical, control instr. . . .	3345	460	22,756	49,480	195	58,606	90,451
Electrical equipment, appliance, and component . .	335	598	20,253	33,842	438	60,458	119,792
Electrical equipment	3353	207	7,275	35,170	144	19,158	36,720
Other electrical equipment and component	3359	216	7,473	34,665	155	23,482	46,558
Transportation equipment	336	1,876	86,806	46,260	1,371	268,511	675,122
Motor vehicle	3361	233	14,563	62,410	206	80,134	267,476
Motor vehicle parts	3363	795	33,984	42,771	642	86,310	201,470
Aerospace product and parts	3364	490	26,408	53,904	249	73,897	139,662
Furniture and related product	337	628	16,880	26,862	507	40,296	72,752
Miscellaneous	339	732	23,578	32,224	493	66,370	108,238
Medical equipment and supplies	3391	303	11,335	37,440	191	34,868	50,371
Other miscellaneous	3399	429	12,242	28,543	303	31,502	57,868

[1] North American Industrial Classification System, 1997; see text, Section 15, Business Enterprise. [2] Includes employment and payroll at administrative offices and auxiliary units. All employees represents the average of production workers plus all other employees for the payroll period ended nearest the 12th of March. Production workers represents the average of the employment for the payroll periods ended nearest the 12th of March, May, August, and November. [3] Adjusted value added; takes into account (a) value added by merchandising operations (that is, difference between the sales value and cost of merchandise sold without further manufacture, processing, or assembly), plus (b) net change in finished goods and work-in-process inventories between beginning and end of year. [4] Includes extensive and unmeasurable duplication from shipments between establishments in the same industry classification.

Source: U.S. Census Bureau, *Annual Survey of Manufactures, Statistics for Industry Groups and Industries*, Series M99(AS)-1.

No. 975. Manufactures—Summary by State: 1999

[16,711 represents 16,711,000. Sum of state totals may not add to U.S. total because U.S. and state figures were independently derived]

State	All employees [1]			Production workers [1]		Value added by manufactures [2]		Value of shipments [3] (mil. dol.)
		Payroll					Per production worker (dol.)	
	Number (1,000)	Total (mil. dol.)	Per employee (dol.)	Total (1,000)	Wages (mil. dol.)	Total (mil. dol.)		
United States	16,711	600,090	35,910	12,011	355,896	1,962,644	163,406	4,038,109
Alabama............	341	10,421	30,585	269	7,143	30,183	112,011	68,879
Alaska.............	13	370	29,431	10	278	1,111	106,711	3,732
Arizona............	193	7,359	38,059	119	3,329	33,166	279,566	47,337
Arkansas	230	6,238	27,176	189	4,504	20,873	110,275	46,636
California	1,820	69,586	38,228	1,191	33,234	218,179	183,190	407,587
Colorado..........	167	6,483	38,792	111	3,304	19,407	175,490	37,211
Connecticut........	240	10,682	44,561	145	4,962	27,075	187,102	45,833
Delaware	42	1,675	39,621	33	1,129	6,070	185,202	17,134
District of Columbia	3	126	39,788	2	77	142	65,709	233
Florida	425	13,635	32,046	285	7,020	41,963	146,982	80,115
Georgia	524	16,228	30,977	408	10,934	62,640	153,663	133,771
Hawaii............	15	409	26,725	10	220	1,311	129,035	3,142
Idaho.............	65	2,197	33,572	50	1,351	7,309	145,897	15,454
Illinois............	877	33,003	37,626	614	18,877	96,829	157,609	201,214
Indiana...........	633	23,977	37,887	484	16,091	77,906	160,902	159,655
Iowa.............	243	8,053	33,126	184	5,242	28,434	154,697	62,048
Kansas...........	199	7,005	35,119	145	4,460	22,124	152,079	53,371
Kentucky	289	10,116	35,045	224	6,874	40,555	180,717	94,407
Louisiana	164	6,189	37,658	121	4,108	26,607	219,391	75,322
Maine............	82	2,819	34,215	61	1,849	7,592	123,497	14,993
Maryland	164	6,367	38,755	111	3,490	19,144	172,199	37,428
Massachusetts......	394	16,217	41,183	242	7,734	45,753	189,402	81,730
Michigan..........	816	36,046	44,177	622	24,869	101,570	163,183	233,514
Minnesota.........	387	14,294	36,941	261	7,857	40,302	154,585	81,396
Mississippi	227	5,994	26,404	183	4,158	23,790	130,351	46,929
Missouri	369	12,272	33,229	270	7,610	45,556	168,488	96,285
Montana..........	21	627	29,678	16	442	1,792	112,025	4,970
Nebraska	110	3,353	30,404	87	2,320	11,815	136,150	29,117
Nevada	39	1,317	33,352	27	766	3,827	139,307	7,101
New Hampshire......	95	3,449	36,207	67	2,030	9,953	148,975	18,438
New Jersey.........	394	15,797	40,058	266	8,188	51,502	193,682	98,196
New Mexico	36	1,093	30,623	26	740	13,549	513,115	18,859
New York	758	26,961	35,558	524	14,961	80,440	153,420	148,959
North Carolina	760	22,436	29,540	593	14,821	90,442	152,393	175,094
North Dakota	23	622	27,601	16	379	2,264	137,835	5,674
Ohio	984	37,850	38,484	734	24,926	118,178	161,107	252,475
Oklahoma..........	170	5,380	31,627	127	3,466	17,995	141,528	40,833
Oregon...........	211	7,315	34,597	157	4,654	24,593	156,519	48,187
Pennsylvania........	801	28,210	35,235	580	17,420	89,386	154,024	175,450
Rhode Island.......	69	2,249	32,387	48	1,225	5,811	120,932	10,807
South Carolina.......	336	10,789	32,150	261	7,134	35,287	135,449	74,479
South Dakota	48	1,444	29,809	34	810	6,988	204,182	13,941
Tennessee	476	15,120	31,772	368	9,904	47,602	129,500	101,972
Texas............	953	34,908	36,613	659	18,786	131,146	199,018	302,707
Utah	120	3,890	32,403	84	2,268	11,845	140,823	25,465
Vermont...........	43	1,560	35,995	30	821	4,919	161,952	9,008
Virginia...........	361	11,963	33,152	267	7,422	49,194	184,094	91,636
Washington.........	327	13,081	39,955	209	7,047	36,924	176,479	92,277
West Virginia........	71	2,484	35,084	54	1,650	9,190	170,715	17,706
Wisconsin..........	570	20,123	35,311	421	12,795	61,160	145,184	126,271
Wyoming	10	307	31,654	3	218	1,254	165,075	3,127

[1] Includes employment and payroll at administrative offices and auxiliary units. All employees represents the average of production workers plus all other employees for the payroll period ended nearest the 12th of March. Production workers represents the average of the employment for the payroll periods ended nearest the 12th of March, May, August, and November. [2] Adjusted value added; takes into account (a) value added by merchandising operations (that is, difference between the sales value and cost of merchandise sold without further manufacture, processing, or assembly), plus (b) net change in finished goods and work-in-process inventories between beginning and end of year. [3] Includes extensive and unmeasurable duplication from shipments between establishments in the same industry classification.

Source: U.S. Census Bureau, Annual Survey of Manufactures, Geographic Area Statistics, Series M99(AS)-3.

No. 976. Manufacturers' E-Commerce Shipments and Online Purchasing of Materials by Industry: 1999

[In millions of dollars (4,038,109 represents $4,038,109,000,000), except percent. Based on the Annual Survey of Manufactures; subject to sampling variability. E-commerce is the value of goods and services sold over computer-mediated networks (open or proprietary). Online purchases are the cost of materials purchased over computer-mediated networks]

Industry	NAICS code [1]	E-commerce				Online purchases			
		Shipments, total (mil. dol.)	Shipments, total (mil. dol.)	Percent of total shipments	Percent distribution	Costs of materials, total (mil. dol.)	Cost of materials, total (mil. dol.)	Percent of total cost of materials	Percent distribution
Manufacturing, total. . . .	31-33	4,038,109	485,283	12.0	100.0	2,079,523	230,914	11.1	100.0
Food products.	311	429,053	37,548	8.8	7.7	251,736	11,163	4.4	4.8
Beverage and tobacco	312	107,437	8,998	8.4	1.9	38,940	3,365	8.6	1.5
Textile mills.	313	54,854	4,819	8.8	1.0	31,895	1,576	4.9	0.7
Textile product mills	314	32,642	4,896	15.0	1.0	18,548	912	4.9	0.4
Apparel	315	62,798	11,376	18.1	2.3	32,403	1,358	4.2	0.6
Leather and allied products . . .	316	9,673	1,775	18.3	0.4	5,145	105	2.0	(Z)
Wood products	321	97,583	3,373	3.5	0.7	59,516	1,954	3.3	0.8
Paper	322	157,491	13,412	8.5	2.8	82,836	3,596	4.3	1.6
Printing and related support activities.	323	102,404	6,422	6.3	1.3	40,029	1,764	4.4	0.8
Petroleum and coal products . .	324	168,096	6,530	3.9	1.3	127,147	11,595	9.1	5.0
Chemicals	325	419,674	42,891	10.2	8.8	192,190	17,608	9.2	7.6
Plastics and rubber products . .	326	172,397	22,876	13.3	4.7	81,488	4,121	5.1	1.8
Nonmetallic mineral products . .	327	97,498	(S)	(S)	(S)	41,191	1,865	4.5	0.8
Primary metals	331	158,102	12,940	8.2	2.7	91,149	4,683	5.1	2.0
Fabricated metal products	332	256,899	28,109	10.9	5.8	114,654	4,660	4.1	2.0
Machinery	333	277,117	39,942	14.4	8.2	137,903	16,828	12.2	7.3
Computer and electronic products.	334	458,485	46,876	10.2	9.7	193,022	23,182	12.0	10.0
Electrical equipment, appliances, and components .	335	119,792	23,671	19.8	4.9	59,137	6,012	10.2	2.6
Transportation equipment	336	675,122	140,259	20.8	28.9	405,442	111,732	27.6	48.4
Furniture and related products .	337	72,752	6,229	8.6	1.3	32,848	1,265	3.9	0.5
Miscellaneous	339	108,238	10,584	9.8	2.2	42,304	1,569	3.7	0.7

S Does not meet publication standards.   Z Less than 0.05 percent.   [1] North American Industry Classification System, 1997; see text, Section 15, Business Enterprise.

Source: U.S. Census Bureau, Internet site <http://www.census.gov/eos/www/papers/MCDTEXT1.pdf> and <http://www.census.gov/eos/www/papers/MCDtables.pdf> (released 08 June 2001).

No. 977. Manufacturing Employer Costs for Employee Compensation Per Hour Worked: 1990 to 2000

[As of March, for private industry workers. Based on a sample of establishments; see source for details. See also Table 626, Section 12, Labor Force, Employment, and Earnings]

Compensation component	Cost (dol.)					Percent distribution				
	1990	1995	1998	1999	2000	1990	1995	1998	1999	2000
Total compensation . . .	17.33	20.47	22.29	22.77	23.41	100.0	100.0	100.0	100.0	100.0
Wages and salaries	11.86	13.72	15.22	15.66	16.01	68.4	67.0	68.3	68.8	68.4
Total benefits.	5.47	6.74	7.07	7.11	7.40	31.6	32.9	31.7	31.2	31.6
Paid leave	1.31	1.54	1.68	1.73	1.74	7.6	7.5	7.5	7.6	7.4
Vacation.	0.67	0.80	0.86	0.89	0.86	3.9	3.9	3.9	3.9	3.7
Holiday	0.48	0.57	0.62	0.64	0.65	2.8	2.8	2.8	2.8	2.8
Sick	0.12	0.12	0.13	0.13	0.13	0.7	0.6	0.6	0.6	0.6
Other	0.05	0.05	0.07	0.07	0.10	0.3	0.2	0.3	0.3	0.4
Supplemental pay	0.65	0.80	0.91	0.89	1.04	3.8	3.9	4.1	3.9	4.4
Premium pay	0.34	0.40	0.48	0.50	0.58	2.0	2.0	2.2	2.2	2.5
Nonproduction bonuses .	0.22	0.30	0.34	0.29	0.36	1.3	1.5	1.5	1.3	1.5
Shift pay	0.09	0.09	0.09	0.10	0.10	0.5	0.4	0.4	0.4	0.4
Insurance	1.37	1.72	1.70	1.74	1.85	7.9	8.4	7.6	7.6	7.9
Health insurance	(NA)	1.58	1.54	1.58	1.69	(NA)	7.7	6.9	6.9	7.2
Retirement and savings . . .	0.56	0.75	0.76	0.75	0.75	3.2	3.7	3.4	3.3	3.2
Defined benefit	(NA)	(NA)	0.40	0.38	0.34	(NA)	(NA)	1.8	1.7	1.5
Defined contributions . . .	(NA)	(NA)	0.36	0.38	0.41	(NA)	(NA)	1.6	1.7	1.8
Legally required	1.54	1.86	1.93	1.93	1.92	8.9	9.1	8.7	8.5	8.2
Social security.	1.02	1.21	1.30	1.34	1.38	5.9	5.9	5.8	5.9	5.9
Federal unemployment . .	0.03	0.03	0.03	0.03	0.03	0.2	0.1	0.1	0.1	0.1
State unemployment . . .	0.12	0.14	0.12	0.11	0.11	0.7	0.7	0.5	0.5	0.5
Workers compensation . .	0.36	0.48	0.48	0.44	0.40	2.1	2.3	2.2	1.9	1.7
Other benefits [1]	0.04	0.09	0.08	0.08	0.09	0.2	0.4	0.4	0.4	0.4

NA Not available.   [1] Includes severance pay, and supplemental unemployment benefits.

Source: U.S. Bureau of Labor Statistics, News, Employer Costs for Employee Compensation, Bulletin 2526, March 2000, and USDL, 00-186, June 29, 2000.

U.S. Census Bureau, Statistical Abstract of the United States: 2001

No. 978. Average Hourly Earnings of Production Workers in Manufacturing Industries by State: 1980 to 2000

[In dollars]

State	1980	1990	1995	1999	2000	State	1980	1990	1995	1999	2000
United States .	7.27	10.83	12.37	13.91	14.38	Missouri	7.26	10.74	12.17	13.93	14.40
Alabama	6.49	9.39	11.14	12.54	12.94	Montana	8.78	11.51	12.94	14.17	14.34
Alaska	10.22	12.46	11.00	12.16	12.45	Nebraska	7.38	9.66	11.19	12.77	12.93
Arizona	7.29	10.21	11.16	12.70	12.77	Nevada	7.72	11.05	12.62	13.92	13.84
Arkansas	5.71	8.51	10.05	11.55	11.98	New Hampshire . . .	5.87	10.83	11.94	13.17	13.41
California	7.70	11.48	12.55	13.95	14.25	New Jersey	7.31	11.76	13.56	15.11	15.47
Colorado	7.63	10.94	12.51	14.19	14.76	New Mexico	5.79	9.04	10.68	12.53	13.34
Connecticut	7.08	11.53	13.71	15.33	15.69	New York	7.18	11.11	12.50	13.87	14.24
Delaware	7.58	12.39	14.20	15.91	16.54	North Carolina	5.37	8.79	10.56	12.32	12.79
Dist. of Columbia [1] .	8.46	12.51	13.66	15.26	(NA)	North Dakota	6.56	9.27	10.75	11.94	12.66
Florida	5.98	8.98	10.18	11.83	12.28	Ohio	8.57	12.64	14.42	16.26	16.72
Georgia	5.77	9.17	10.71	12.51	13.01	Oklahoma	7.36	10.73	11.52	12.79	13.17
Hawaii	6.83	10.99	12.82	13.49	13.58	Oregon	8.65	11.15	12.75	14.61	15.08
Idaho	7.55	10.60	11.46	13.42	14.17	Pennsylvania	7.59	11.04	12.81	14.19	14.60
Illinois	8.02	11.44	12.64	14.05	14.39	Rhode Island	5.59	9.45	10.62	11.98	12.18
Indiana	8.49	12.03	13.91	15.26	15.83	South Carolina	5.59	8.84	10.16	10.67	10.96
Iowa	8.67	11.27	12.73	14.20	14.66	South Dakota	6.50	8.48	9.36	10.58	10.71
Kansas	7.37	10.94	12.39	14.44	14.98	Tennessee	6.08	9.55	10.78	12.50	12.92
Kentucky	7.34	10.70	12.22	14.27	14.82	Texas	7.15	10.47	11.47	12.25	12.37
Louisiana	7.74	11.61	13.43	15.18	15.57	Utah	7.02	10.32	11.62	13.39	13.69
Maine	6.00	10.59	12.39	13.94	14.28	Vermont	6.14	10.52	12.21	13.65	14.23
Maryland	7.61	11.57	13.49	14.62	14.99	Virginia	6.22	10.07	11.72	13.37	13.82
Massachusetts	6.51	11.39	12.79	14.24	14.65	Washington	(NA)	12.61	14.73	16.14	16.76
Michigan	9.52	13.86	16.31	18.38	19.20	West Virginia	8.08	11.53	12.64	14.09	14.60
Minnesota	7.61	11.23	12.79	14.34	14.99	Wisconsin	8.03	11.11	12.76	14.50	14.85
Mississippi	5.44	8.37	9.76	11.17	11.64	Wyoming	7.01	10.83	11.96	15.40	15.76

NA Not available.   [1] Washington PMSA (primary metropolitan statistical area).

Source: U.S. Bureau of Labor Statistics, *Employment and Earnings*, May 2001 issue and earlier issues.

No. 979. Manufacturing Full-Time Equivalent Employees and Wages by Industry: 1995 to 1999

Industry	SIC code	Full-time equivalent (FTE) employees (1,000)				Wage and salary accruals per FTE worker (dol.)			
		1995	1997	1998	1999	1995	1997	1998	1999
Manufacturing, total	(X)	18,190	18,352	18,501	18,269	35,779	38,941	40,830	42,862
Durable goods	(X)	10,561	10,878	11,089	11,002	37,660	40,770	42,617	44,902
Lumber & wood products	24	772	794	816	843	25,110	27,382	28,278	29,040
Furniture & fixtures	25	502	502	522	540	25,048	27,622	28,860	29,635
Stone, clay, & glass products	32	530	544	558	560	33,283	35,719	36,978	38,621
Primary metal industries	33	697	705	710	692	40,067	42,038	42,855	44,536
Fabricated metal products	34	1,421	1,461	1,491	1,509	32,927	35,152	36,280	37,192
Industrial machinery & equipment . .	35	2,051	2,136	2,177	2,103	40,063	43,987	46,212	49,728
Electronic, other electric equipment .	36	1,607	1,675	1,689	1,646	38,922	42,871	45,729	50,333
Motor vehicles & equipment	371	961	974	989	1,017	46,658	49,662	52,175	53,949
Other transportation equipment . . .	372-9	809	849	891	866	44,611	47,276	48,669	50,329
Instruments & related products	38	827	851	858	836	44,654	48,616	51,403	55,215
Misc. manufacturing industries	39	384	387	388	390	28,219	30,540	31,897	33,118
Nondurable goods	(X)	7,629	7,474	7,412	7,267	33,176	36,278	38,156	39,775
Food & kindred products	20	1,642	1,651	1,648	1,655	30,139	31,895	33,394	34,176
Tobacco products	21	41	40	39	36	53,854	59,375	56,103	60,278
Textile mill products	22	654	611	591	551	23,985	26,354	27,311	28,470
Apparel & other textile products . . .	23	919	804	745	675	18,800	20,838	22,103	23,255
Paper & allied products	26	685	•675	671	661	39,458	42,129	43,185	44,900
Printing & publishing	27	1,450	1,465	1,478	1,465	34,539	37,427	39,256	41,083
Chemicals & allied products	28	1,027	1,020	1,024	1,025	51,054	56,766	60,350	62,859
Petroleum & coal products	29	142	135	134	129	54,739	60,119	63,425	63,651
Rubber & misc. plastics products . .	30	963	984	998	994	29,867	32,237	33,574	34,508
Leather & leather products	31	106	89	84	76	22,321	25,225	25,940	27,882

X Not applicable.

Source: U.S. Bureau of Economics Analysis, *Survey of Current Business*, October 2000.

No. 980. Manufactures' Shipments, Inventories, and New Orders: 1992 to 2000

[In billions of dollars (2,904 represents $2,904,000,000,000), except ratio. Based on a sample survey; for methodology, see publication cited below. These data are now on a NAICS (North American Industry Classification System) basis and not comparable to previous data, which were based on the Standard Industrial Classification system]

Year	Shipments	Inventories (Dec. 31)[1]	Ratio of inventories to shipments[2]	New orders (Dec. 31)	Unfilled orders (Dec. 31)
1992	2,904	370	1.57	(NA)	454
1993	3,020	371	1.51	2,996	430
1994	3,238	391	1.48	3,247	438
1995	3,480	415	1.47	3,496	454
1996	3,597	421	1.44	3,638	495
1997	3,835	433	1.39	3,859	519
1998	3,900	442	1.39	3,885	504
1999	4,043	452	1.37	4,062	523
2000	4,281	472	1.36	4,350	592

NA Not available.   [1] Inventories are stated at current cost.   [2] Ratio based on December seasonally adjusted data.

Source: U.S. Census Bureau, Current Industrial Reports, *Manufacturers' Shipments, Inventories, and Orders: 1992-2000,* Series M3-1(00). See also <http://www.census.gov/prod/2001pubs/m3-00.pdf> (released May 2001).

No. 981. Ratios of Manufacturers' Inventories to Shipments and Unfilled Orders to Shipments by Industry Group: 1992 to 2000

[Based on a sample survey; for methodology; see publication cited below. These data are now on a NAICS (North American Industry Classification System) basis and not comparable to previous data, which were based on the Standard Industrial Classification system]

Industry	1992	1993	1994	1995	1996	1997	1998	1999	2000
INVENTORIES TO SHIPMENTS RATIO									
All manufacturing industries	1.57	1.51	1.48	1.47	1.44	1.39	1.39	1.37	1.36
Durable goods	1.89	1.79	1.73	1.69	1.65	1.57	1.57	1.52	1.53
Wood products	1.32	1.41	1.31	1.34	1.28	1.26	1.26	1.23	1.36
Nonmetallic mineral products	1.55	1.40	1.33	1.35	1.29	1.25	1.19	1.17	1.27
Primary metals	1.75	1.71	1.70	1.61	1.66	1.61	1.62	1.68	1.67
Fabricated metals	1.85	1.78	1.75	1.72	1.69	1.61	1.56	1.55	1.64
Machinery	2.33	2.22	2.18	2.18	2.12	2.04	2.03	2.05	2.06
Computers and electronic products	1.95	1.84	1.76	1.74	1.53	1.51	1.42	1.42	1.31
Electrical equipment, appliances, and components	1.79	1.71	1.73	1.68	1.59	1.51	1.47	1.42	1.44
Transportation equipment	1.85	1.71	1.58	1.50	1.59	1.44	1.57	1.40	1.40
Furniture and related products	1.63	1.63	1.63	1.57	1.49	1.44	1.35	1.37	1.39
Miscellaneous products	2.05	1.96	1.98	2.00	2.02	1.92	1.88	1.88	1.94
Nondurable goods	1.22	1.20	1.20	1.20	1.17	1.16	1.15	1.17	1.13
Food products	0.89	0.86	0.87	0.89	0.88	0.85	0.83	0.85	0.80
Beverages and tobacco products	1.64	1.72	1.58	1.55	1.58	1.71	1.64	1.55	1.47
Textile mills	1.47	1.48	1.47	1.53	1.45	1.41	1.46	1.53	1.55
Textile product mills	1.70	1.70	1.73	1.76	1.72	1.76	1.68	1.67	1.80
Apparel	1.74	1.92	1.94	1.93	1.64	1.70	1.78	1.87	1.93
Leather and allied products	2.04	1.73	1.97	2.03	2.05	1.98	2.07	2.20	1.91
Paper products	1.27	1.27	1.20	1.20	1.20	1.21	1.16	1.17	1.15
Printing	0.98	0.92	0.96	0.97	0.89	0.88	0.82	0.83	0.76
Petroleum and coal products	0.93	0.87	0.95	0.91	0.88	0.82	0.84	0.85	0.69
Basic chemicals	1.41	1.37	1.33	1.34	1.35	1.31	1.32	1.38	1.41
Plastics and rubber products	1.34	1.26	1.28	1.27	1.27	1.22	1.19	1.20	1.22
UNFILLED ORDERS TO SHIPMENTS RATIO									
All manufacturing industries	1.89	1.72	1.64	1.58	1.67	1.64	1.57	1.58	1.68
Durable goods	3.62	3.24	3.01	2.90	3.03	2.93	2.74	2.74	2.96
Primary metals	1.82	1.97	2.04	1.75	1.81	1.94	1.56	1.68	1.45
Fabricated metals	2.09	1.87	1.87	1.83	1.98	2.08	2.00	2.02	2.02
Machinery	2.63	2.55	2.67	2.70	2.63	2.61	2.41	2.51	2.60
Computers and electronic products	4.02	3.73	3.38	3.25	2.98	2.81	2.93	3.54	3.40
Electrical equipment, appliances, and components	1.78	1.75	1.79	1.74	1.61	1.66	1.57	1.80	1.79
Transportation equipment	7.17	6.18	5.47	5.32	6.07	5.58	4.99	4.26	5.14
Furniture and related products	1.11	1.23	1.17	1.02	1.05	1.38	1.19	1.27	1.14
Miscellaneous products	0.25	0.27	0.30	0.31	0.39	0.44	0.54	0.57	0.76

Source: U.S. Census Bureau, Current Industrial Reports, *Manufacturers' Shipments, Inventories, and Orders: 1992-2000,* Series M3-1(00). See also <http://www.census.gov/prod/2001pubs/m3-00.pdf> (released May 2001).

U.S. Census Bureau, Statistical Abstract of the United States: 2001

No. 982. Value of Manufactures' Shipments, Inventories, and New Orders by Industry: 1995 to 2000

[In millions of dollars (3,479,677 represents $3,479,677,000,000). Based on a sample survey; for methodology, see publication cited below. These data are now on a NAICS (North American Industry Classification System) basis and not comparable to previous data, which were based on the Standard Industrial Classification system]

Industry	1995	1996	1997	1998	1999	2000
SHIPMENTS						
All manufacturing industries	3,479,677	3,597,188	3,834,699	3,899,813	4,043,277	4,280,872
Durable goods	1,902,815	1,978,597	2,147,384	2,231,588	2,326,757	2,435,013
Wood products	79,417	81,827	88,470	91,175	97,583	88,692
Nonmetallic mineral products.	74,865	81,308	86,465	92,501	97,498	96,002
Primary metals	160,774	157,638	168,118	166,109	158,102	163,202
Fabricated metals	212,444	222,995	242,812	253,720	256,900	258,960
Machinery	246,277	257,459	270,687	280,651	277,117	299,065
Computers and electronic products.	370,679	399,516	439,380	443,768	463,653	541,887
Electrical equipment, appliances, and components	101,051	105,283	112,116	116,024	119,792	133,893
Transportation equipment	508,271	516,030	575,307	612,882	675,121	662,870
Furniture and related products	58,942	61,156	64,299	69,616	72,752	77,623
Miscellaneous products	90,095	95,385	99,730	105,142	108,239	112,819
Nondurable goods	1,576,862	1,618,591	1,687,315	1,668,225	1,716,520	1,845,859
Food products	393,204	404,173	421,737	428,479	429,054	438,913
Beverages and tobacco products	88,945	94,033	96,971	102,359	107,437	112,366
Textile mills	59,885	59,796	58,707	57,416	54,854	53,282
Textile product mills	27,976	28,515	31,052	31,137	32,642	32,947
Apparel	65,214	64,237	68,018	64,932	62,798	65,097
Leather and allied products	9,922	10,032	10,877	10,186	9,673	9,865
Paper products	166,051	152,860	150,296	154,984	157,491	170,217
Printing	92,155	95,072	97,485	100,297	102,404	105,456
Petroleum and coal products	151,431	174,181	177,394	137,957	168,096	232,581
Basic chemicals	376,995	385,919	415,617	416,742	419,674	442,832
Plastics and rubber products	145,084	149,773	159,161	163,736	172,397	182.303
INVENTORIES (Dec. 31)						
All manufacturing industries	414,969	420,680	433,451	441,740	451,956	472,455
Durable goods	260,148	265,170	273,330	284,374	287,277	301,247
Wood products	9,035	8,879	9,441	9,694	10,165	10,158
Nonmetallic mineral products.	8,248	8,560	8,840	9,012	9,343	10,007
Primary metals	21,598	21,945	22,728	22,542	22,228	22,795
Fabricated metals	29,601	30,611	31,776	32,248	32,626	34,743
Machinery	43,212	43,869	44,490	46,067	46,030	49,931
Computers and electronic products.	51,569	48,997	53,045	50,642	52,712	57,265
Electrical equipment, appliances, and components	13,499	13,342	13,530	13,652	13,657	15,491
Transportation equipment	61,202	65,927	66,414	76,917	75,956	74,409
Furniture and related products	7,530	7,426	7,527	7,648	8,091	8,775
Miscellaneous products	14,654	15,614	15,539	15,952	16,469	17,673
Nondurable goods	154,821	155,510	160,121	157,366	164,679	171,208
Food products	29,440	29,751	30,152	29,690	30,684	29,527
Beverages and tobacco products	11,750	12,731	14,188	14,346	14,221	14,024
Textile mills	7,335	6,972	6,640	6,729	6,720	6,615
Textile product mills	3,914	3,898	4,331	4,161	4,317	4,697
Apparel	10,003	8,397	9,267	9,266	9,477	10,117
Leather and allied products	1,611	1,640	1,718	1,683	1,701	1,505
Paper products	16,404	15,120	15,042	14,785	15,181	16,063
Printing	6,897	6,529	6,621	6,359	6,569	6,247
Petroleum and coal products	10,857	12,087	11,492	9,081	11,160	12,606
Basic chemicals	41,489	42,782	44,691	45,176	47,604	51,449
Plastics and rubber products	15,121	15,603	15,979·	16,090	17,045	18,358
NEW ORDERS						
All manufacturing industries	3,495,515	3,638,149	3,859,016	3,884,868	4,082,133	4,349,672
Durable goods	1,918,653	2,019,558	2,171,701	2,216,643	2,345,613	2,503,813
Wood products	79,417	81,827	88,470	91,175	97,583	88,692
Paper products	74,865	81,308	86,465	92,501	97,498	96,002
Primary metals	159,957	158,066	171,407	160,743	158,580	160,770
Fabricated metals	214,488	227,447	247,839	253,847	257,983	259,406
Machinery	251,307	258,405	272,998	278,100	278,625	305,598
Computers and electronic products.	380,287	398,053	442,816	449,158	490,834	558,875
Electrical equipment, appliances, and components	101,409	104,837	113,411	115,711	122,497	135,889
Transportation equipment	508,133	552,024	581,780	600,205	659,855	706,834
Furniture and related products	58,475	61,499	66,256	69,098	73,489	77,273
Miscellaneous products	90,315	96,092	100,259	106,105	108,669	114,474
Nondurable goods	1,576,862	1,618,591	1,687,315	1,668,225	1,716,520	1,845,859

Source: U.S. Census Bureau, Current Industrial Reports, *Manufacturers' Shipments, Inventories, and Orders: 1992-2000*, Series M3-1(00). See also <http://www.census.gov/prod/2001pubs/m3-00.pdf> (released May 2001).

No. 983. Value of Manufactures' Shipments, Inventories, and New Orders by Market Grouping: 1995 to 2000

[In millions of dollars (3,479,677 represents $3,479,677,000,000). Based on a sample survey; for methodology, see publication cited below. These data are now on a NAICS (North American Industry Classification System) basis and not comparable to previous data, which were based on the Standard Industrial Classification system]

Market grouping	1995	1996	1997	1998	1999	2000
SHIPMENTS						
All manufacturing industries...	**3,479,677**	**3,597,188**	**3,834,699**	**3,899,813**	**4,043,277**	**4,280,872**
Consumer goods	1,273,973	1,309,819	1,375,603	1,372,542	1,457,548	1,558,775
Consumer durable goods.	341,398	345,266	377,280	394,134	438,409	440,113
Consumer nondurable goods	932,575	964,553	998,323	978,408	1,019,139	1,118,662
Aircraft and parts	79,052	80,582	100,126	116,812	120,681	120,498
Defense aircraft and parts	29,984	29,693	27,472	26,938	27,827	26,499
Nondefense aircraft and parts.	49,068	50,889	72,654	89,874	92,854	93,999
Construction materials and supplies. . .	337,569	355,413	385,735	403,682	419,932	419,032
Motor vehicles and parts	379,551	387,394	421,573	439,590	497,577	482,407
Computers and related products	83,855	93,926	110,055	114,482	112,677	135,187
Information technology industries	291,885	311,028	349,846	362,564	370,253	427,631
Nondefense capital goods	590,578	630,932	702,971	747,046	766,473	844,037
Excluding aircraft	565,729	605,295	665,074	695,717	710,288	789,478
Defense capital goods.	75,589	73,703	76,261	74,690	70,437	70,080
Durables excluding capital goods	1,236,648	1,273,962	1,368,152	1,409,852	1,489,847	1,520,896
INVENTORIES (Dec. 31)						
All manufacturing industries...	**414,969**	**420,680**	**433,451**	**441,740**	**451,956**	**472,455**
Consumer goods	115,510	115,489	118,872	117,262	122,971	128,839
Consumer durable goods.	25,533	24,950	25,143	25,338	26,337	28,082
Consumer nondurable goods	89,977	90,539	93,729	91,924	96,634	100,757
Aircraft and parts	31,714	35,905	37,509	47,019	42,754	40,855
Defense aircraft and parts	9,484	8,641	8,380	11,401	11,088	10,653
Nondefense aircraft and parts.	22,230	27,264	29,129	35,618	31,666	30,202
Construction materials and supplies. . .	40,721	41,524	43,502	44,653	45,838	48,708
Motor vehicles and parts	20,359	20,744	20,298	20,527	21,799	22,139
Computers and related products	11,272	8,841	10,289	8,124	7,883	8,517
Information technology industries	44,909	41,784	46,117	44,072	44,489	47,636
Nondefense capital goods	107,315	110,904	117,932	123,328	121,806	127,006
Excluding aircraft	91,080	90,031	95,226	94,902	96,292	103,730
Defense capital goods.	17,929	17,336	14,814	17,869	19,146	18,302
Durables excluding capital goods	134,904	136,930	140,584	143,177	146,325	155,939
NEW ORDERS						
All manufacturing industries...	**3,495,515**	**3,638,149**	**3,859,016**	**3,884,868**	**4,062,133**	**4,349,672**
Consumer goods	1,273,892	1,310,361	1,377,163	1,373,376	1,458,586	1,559,976
Consumer durable goods.	341,317	345,808	378,840	394,968	439,447	441,314
Consumer nondurable goods	932,575	964,553	998,323	978,408	1,019,139	1,118,662
Aircraft and parts	85,190	104,614	109,077	108,004	108,587	152,633
Defense aircraft and parts	27,736	32,520	23,280	23,854	25,973	36,391
Nondefense aircraft and parts.	57,454	72,094	85,797	84,150	82,614	116,242
Construction materials and supplies. . .	339,749	358,254	389,867	405,185	421,215	420,242
Motor vehicles and parts	378,886	385,712	422,427	440,934	498,366	479,432
Computers and related products	84,521	95,070	107,564	115,806	113,887	135,534
Information technology industries	297,605	310,074	352,700	365,723	382,508	438,339
Nondefense capital goods	612,132	648,797	728,362	745,600	769,949	881,415
Excluding aircraft	576,769	607,174	676,119	698,279	724,164	806,465
Defense capital goods.	68,725	88,471	64,497	64,127	66,780	90,873
Durables excluding capital goods	1,237,796	1,282,290	1,378,842	1,406,916	1,508,884	1,531,525

Source: U.S. Census Bureau, Current Industrial Reports, *Manufacturers' Shipments, Inventories, and Orders: 1992-2000*, Series M3-1(00). See also <http://www.census.gov/prod/2001pubs/m3-00.pdf> (released May 2001).

Manufactures 625

No. 984. Finances and Profits of Manufacturing Corporations: 1990 to 2000

[In billions of dollars (2,811 represents $2,811,000,000,000). Data exclude estimates for corporations with less than $250,000 in assets at time of sample selection. See Table 761 for individual industry data]

Item	1990	1992	1993	1994	1995	1996	1997	1998	1999	2000
Net sales.	2 811	2,890	3,014	3,256	3,528	3,758	3,920	3,949	4,149	4,506
Net operating profit	173	151	180	242	268	277	298	298	317	345
Net profit:										
Before taxes	160	33	118	244	274	307	331	315	355	385
After taxes	112	23	83	175	198	225	245	234	258	277
Cash dividends	62	63	67	70	81	96	108	121	104	131
Net income retained in business	49	-40	16	105	117	129	136	114	154	146

Source: U.S. Census Bureau, *Quarterly Financial Report for Manufacturing, Mining, and Trade Corporations.*

No. 985. U.S. Exports of Manufactures—Origin of World Exports of Manufacture: 1991 to 1999

[In billions of dollars (328 represents $328,000,000,000), except percents]

Item	1991	1992	1993	1994	1995	1996	1997	1998	1999
U.S. manufactures export value	328	350	365	409	464	498	566	570	587
Machinery & transport equipment	200	215	225	252	283	308	354	359	371
Chemicals	43	45	46	52	62	63	71	69	72
Other	85	90	94	104	119	128	141	142	144
Origin of world exports of manufactures (percent):									
United States [1]	12.9	12.6	13.1	12.7	12.4	12.8	13.8	13.7	13.7
Machinery & transport equipment	15.9	15.8	16.4	15.7	14.9	15.3	16.6	16.4	16.2
Chemicals	14.4	13.4	13.9	13.5	13.3	13.1	14.2	13.6	13.7
Other	8.5	8.3	8.7	8.5	8.6	9.1	9.7	9.8	9.8
Germany [2]	14.2	13.9	12.0	11.8	12.4	11.8	11.1	11.8	11.0
Japan	11.9	11.8	12.6	11.8	11.4	10.1	9.8	8.9	9.3
Other G-7 countries [3]	21.6	21.0	20.1	19.7	20.3	20.8	20.1	20.5	19.6
East Asian NICs [4]	8.2	8.1	8.8	8.9	9.4	9.2	9.1	9.1	8.6

[1] U.S. exports are domestic exports only. [2] Prior to 1991, data for are for former West Germany only. [3] Other group of seven (G-7) countries: Canada, France, Italy, and United Kingdom. [4] East Asian newly industrialized countries (NICs): Hong Kong, S. Korea, Singapore, and Taiwan.

Source: U.S. Dept. of Commerce, International Trade Administration, Office of Trade and Economic Analysis. Based on United Nations Commodity Trade Statistics, *Statistical Yearbook of the Republic of China (Taiwan),* and unpublished data.

No. 986. Tobacco Products—Summary: 1990 to 2000

[Production data are for calendar years. Excludes cigars produced in customs bonded manufacturing warehouses]

Item	Unit	1990	1993	1994	1995	1996	1997	1998	1999	2000
PRODUCTION										
Cigarettes, total	Billions	710	661	726	747	758	720	680	607	610
Nonfilter tip	Billions	23	15	15	15	14	12	12	8	(NA)
Filter tip	Billions	687	646	710	732	744	708	669	599	(NA)
Cigars	Billions	1.9	1.8	1.9	2.1	2.4	2.3	2.8	7	(NA)
Tobacco [1]	Mil. lb.	142	133	132	131	131	134	131	133	133
Smoking	Mil. lb.	16	14	14	12	12	11	13	15	14
Chewing tobacco	Mil. lb.	73	64	63	63	61	58	53	51	49
Snuff	Mil. lb.	53	59	60	60	62	64	66	67	70
EXPORTS										
Cigarettes	Billions	164.3	195.5	220.2	231.1	243.9	217.0	201.3	151.4	148.3
Cigars	Billions	72	67	74	94	84	86	93	84	113
Smoking tobacco	Billions	0.8	0.4	0.5	0.3	0.7	0.8	1.1	16	0.5
IMPORTS										
Cigarettes	Billions	1.4	11.5	3.5	3.0	2.8	3.2	4.3	8.7	11.8
Cigars	Billions	111	127	146	195	320	576	507	496	480
Smoking tobacco	Billions	2.9	6.8	3.9	4.2	4.2	4.3	4.3	4.3	4.2
CONSUMPTION										
Consumption per person [2]	Lb. [3]	5.6	5.3	4.9	4.7	4.7	4.5	3.9	3.6	3.4
Cigarettes	1,000	3	3	3	3	3	2	2	2	2
Cigars [4]	Number	13	11	12	15	18	18	18	19	19
EXPENDITURES										
Consumer expenditures, total	Bil. dol.	43.8	49.0	47.7	48.7	50.4	52.2	57.3	72.1	(NA)
Cigarettes	Bil. dol.	41.6	46.2	44.5	45.8	47.2	48.7	53.2	68.3	(NA)
Cigars	Bil. dol.	0.7	0.7	0.9	1.0	1.0	1.2	1.6	1.1	(NA)
Other	Bil. dol.	1.5	2.1	2.3	2.5	2.2	2.2	2.4	2.7	(NA)

NA Not available. [1] Smoking and chewing tobaccos and snuff output. [2] Based on estimated population 18 years old and over, as of July 1, including Armed Forces abroad. [3] Unstemmed processing weight equivalent. [4] Weighing over 3 pounds per 1,000.

Source: U.S. Dept. of Agriculture, Economic Research Service, *Tobacco Situation and Outlook,* quarterly.

No. 987. Cotton, Wool, and Manmade Fibers—Consumption by End-Use: 1990 to 1999

[Represents products manufactured by U.S. mills. Excludes glass fiber]

Year	Cotton			Wool		Manufactured fibers					
								Artificial [1]		Synthetic [2]	
	Total (mil. lb.)	Total (mil. lb.)	Percent of end-use	Total (mil. lb.)	Percent of end-use	Total (mil. lb.)	Percent of end-use	Total (mil. lb.)	Percent of end-use	Total (mil. lb.)	Percent of end-use
Total:											
1990	14,011	4,699	33.5	185	1.3	9,127	65.1	599	4.3	8,528	60.9
1995	16,815	5,508	32.8	184	1.1	11,123	66.1	540	3.2	10,583	62.9
1996	17,002	5,520	32.5	189	1.1	11,294	66.4	476	2.8	10,818	63.6
1997	17,520	5,404	30.8	208	1.2	11,908	68.0	438	2.5	11,470	65.5
1998	17,698	5,514	31.2	170	1.0	12,014	67.9	372	2.1	11,643	65.8
1999	17,735	5,328	30.0	135	0.8	12,272	69.2	337	1.9	11,937	67.3
Apparel:											
1990	5,204	2,897	55.7	118	2.3	2,189	42.1	287	5.5	1,902	36.5
1995	6,877	3,640	52.9	132	1.9	3,106	45.2	306	4.4	2,800	40.7
1996	6,771	3,640	53.8	136	2.0	2,994	44.2	278	4.1	2,716	40.1
1997	6,907	3,442	49.8	153	2.2	3,312	47.9	247	3.6	3,064	44.4
1998	6,525	3,329	51.0	113	1.7	3,082	47.2	208	3.2	2,875	44.1
1999	6,404	3,262	50.9	79	1.2	3,063	47.8	170	2.7	2,894	45.2
Home textiles:											
1990	2,235	1,325	59.3	14	0.6	896	40.1	104	4.7	792	35.4
1995	2,530	1,487	58.8	12	0.5	1,030	40.7	93	3.7	937	37.0
1996	2,561	1,503	58.7	12	0.5	1,046	40.8	81	3.2	965	37.7
1997	2,696	1,569	58.2	14	0.5	1,113	41.3	78	2.9	1,035	38.4
1998	2,918	1,779	61.0	15	0.5	1,125	38.6	69	2.4	1,056	36.2
1999	2,809	1,656	59.0	15	0.5	1,139	40.5	71	2.5	1,069	38.1
Floor coverings:											
1990	3,075	18	0.6	21	0.7	3,036	98.7	-	-	3,036	98.7
1995	3,731	25	0.7	25	0.7	3,681	98.7	-	-	3,681	98.7
1996	3,993	25	0.6	25	0.6	3,942	98.7	-	-	3,942	98.7
1997	4,070	32	0.8	26	0.6	4,012	98.6	-	-	4,012	98.6
1998	4,240	36	0.8	29	0.7	4,176	98.5	-	-	4,176	98.5
1999	4,385	39	0.9	29	0.7	4,318	98.5	-	-	4,318	98.5
Industrial: [3]											
1990	2,965	313	10.6	10	0.3	2,642	89.1	179	6.0	2,463	83.1
1995	3,677	355	9.7	15	0.4	3,307	89.9	141	3.8	3,165	86.1
1996	3,678	351	9.5	15	0.4	3,311	90.0	117	3.2	3,195	86.9
1997	3,848	360	9.4	16	0.4	3,472	90.2	113	2.9	3,359	87.3
1998	4,015	371	9.2	13	0.3	3,631	90.4	95	2.4	3,536	88.1
1999	4,136	372	9.0	13	0.3	3,752	90.7	96	2.3	3,656	88.4

- Represents or rounds to zero. [1] Rayon and acetate. [2] Nylon, polyester, acrylic, and olefin. [3] Includes consumer-type products.

Source: Fiber Economics Bureau, Inc., Washington, DC, *Textile Organon*, monthly (copyright).

No. 988. Broadwoven and Knit Fabrics—Shipments, Foreign Trade, and Apparent Consumption: 1999

[3,721,426 represents 3,721,426,000. Fabric blends as shown in the CIR report, MQ22T, are reported based on the chief weight of the fiber; whereas, fabrics blends as shown for imports are based on the chief value of the fiber. Apparent consumption represents new domestic supply and is derived by subtracting exports for the total manufacturers' shipments plus imports]

Product description	Manufac- turers' ship- ments (quantity)	Imports for consumption		Percent imports to manufac- turers' ship- ments	Exports of domestic merchandise		Percent exports to manufac- turers' ship- ments	Apparent consump- tion (quantity)
		Quantity	Value [1] ($1,000)		Quantity	Value ($1,000)		
BROADWOVEN FABRICS (quantity 1,000 sq. meters)								
Cotton fabrics [2]	3,721,426	1,441,820	1,580,363	38.7	409,524	908,138	11.0	4,753,722
Manmade fiber fabrics	9,886,839	1,086,727	1,275,308	11.0	479,941	1,030,537	4.0	10,576,305
Silk fabrics	274	31,483	273,846	11,479.8	2,010	15,647	732.9	29,747
Wool fabrics	64,656	33,879	297,654	52.4	12,907	71,015	20.0	85,628
KNIT FABRICS (quantity in 1,000 kilograms)								
Total	853,621	135,198	1,056,483	16	73,159	620,673	9	915,660
Pile fabrics	93,606	35,325	264,386	38	20,462	179,599	22	108,469
Elastic fabric	39,639	17,841	223,434	45	9,708	126,041	25	47,772
Other warp knit fabrics	105,290	12,763	112,683	12	9,307	87,778	9	108,746
Other narrow knit fabrics	18,185	1,450	16,135	8	3,434	34,362	19	16,201
Other knit fabrics	596,901	67,819	439,845	11	30,248	192,893	5	634,472

[1] Dollar value represents the c.i.f. (cost, insurance, and freight) at the first port of entry in the United States plus calculated import duty. [2] Includes all cotton and chiefly cotton mixed with manmade fiber.

Source: U.S. Census Bureau, *Manufacturing Profiles*, Series MP, annual; and <http://www.census.gov/ftp/pub/industry/1/mq22t995.pdf> (issued June 2000); and <http://www.census.gov/ftp/pub/industry/1/ma22k99.pdf> (issued August 2000).

Manufactures 627

No. 989. Footwear—Production, Foreign Trade, and Apparent Consumption: 1999

[Quantity in thousands of pairs (116,944 represents 116,944,000), value in thousands of dollars (350,372 represents $350,372,000)]

Product description	Manufacturers' shipments (quantity)	Exports of domestic merchandise		Percent exports to domestic production	Imports for consumption		Apparent consumption (quantity)	Percent imports to apparent consumption
		Quantity	Value		Quantity	Value		
Total	116,944	21,012	350,372	18.0	1,592,999	13,817,199	1,688,931	94.3
Rubber or plastic uppers and rubber or plastic soles	13,517	4,687	49,652	34.7	616,693	3,452,228	625,523	98.6
Waterproof	10,833	833	8,280	7.7	7,381	44,476	17,381	42.5
Not waterproof	2,684	3,854	41,372	143.6	609,312	3,407,752	608,142	100.2
Leather uppers	34,680	9,384	225,906	27.1	657,163	8,971,947	682,459	96.3
Athletic	3,925	5,489	108,776	139.8	498,447	6,021,643	496,883	100.3
Leather soles	10,406	2,218	67,628	21.3	43,913	1,013,949	52,101	84.3
Made with steel safety toes	(D)	155	8,663	(D)	9,151	191,191	(D)	(D)
Boots, ex. with steel safety toes	(D)	277	9,273	(D)	5,360	120,503	(D)	(D)
Shoes, ex. with steel safety toes	5,699	1,786	49,692	31.3	29,402	702,255	33,315	88.3
Other soles	20,349	1,677	49,502	8.2	114,803	1,936,355	133,475	86.0
Made with steel safety toes	2,545	-	-	(NA)	-	-	2,545	(NA)
Boots, ex. with steel safety toes	5,511	1,677	49,502	30.4	114,803	1,936,355	118,637	96.8
Shoes, ex. with steel safety toes	12,293	-	-	(NA)	-	-	12,293	(NA)
Fabric uppers	62,743	6,941	74,814	11.1	319,143	1,393,024	374,945	85.1
Rubber or plastic soles	(D)	5,472	61,010	(D)	250,312	989,311	(D)	(D)
Athletic	(D)	4,400	51,757	(D)	36,985	159,177	(D)	(D)
All other	(D)	1,072	9,253	(D)	213,327	830,134	(D)	(D)
With all other soles	(D)	1,469	13,804	(D)	68,831	403,713	(D)	(D)

- Represents zero. D Data withheld to avoid disclosure. NA Not available.

Source: U.S. Census Bureau, *Manufacturing Profiles*, Series MP, annual; and <ftp://ftp.census.gov/pub/industry/1/ma31a99.pdf> (released August 2000).

No. 990. Inorganic Chemicals and Fertilizers—Production: 1995 to 1999

[In thousands of short or metric tons (17,402 represents 17,402,000)]

Product description	Unit	1995	1996	1997	1998	1999
INORGANIC FERTILIZERS						
Ammonia, synthetic anhydrous	1,000 sh. tons	17,402	17,923	17,891	18,475	17,337
Ammonium nitrate, original solution	1,000 sh. tons	8,489	8,498	8,604	9,079	7,971
Ammonium sulfate	1,000 sh. tons	2,647	2,662	2,711	2,787	2,875
Urea (100%)	1,000 sh. tons	8,117	8,548	8,190	8,865	8,907
Nitric acid (100%)	1,000 sh. tons	8,839	9,205	9,433	9,285	8,945
Phosphoric acid (100% P2O5)	1,000 sh. tons	13,134	13,210	13,159	13,891	13,708
Sulfuric acid, gross (100%)	1,000 sh. tons	47,519	47,770	47,929	48,513	44,756
Superphosphates and other fertilizer materials (100% P2O5)	1,000 sh. tons	10,364	10,547	10,473	10,260	9,325
INORGANIC CHEMICALS						
Chlorine gas	1,000 metric tons . .	12,395	12,460	12,922	11,650	12,114
Sodium hydroxide, total liquid	1,000 metric tons . .	11,408	11,563	11,972	11,896	11,954
Potassium hydroxide liquid	1,000 metric tons' . .	(D)	500	533	450	(D)
Finished sodium bicarbonate	1,000 metric tons . .	520	502	522	493	505
Titanium dioxide, composite and pure	1,000 metric tons . .	1,382	1,352	1,477	1,323	1,355
Boric acid	1,000 metric tons . .	(D)	(D)	(D)	(D)	(D)
Hydrochloric acid	1,000 metric tons . .	3,904	4,116	4,411	4,226	4,191
Hydroflouric acid	1,000 metric tons . .	(D)	(D)	(D)	(D)	(D)
Aluminum oxide	1,000 metric tons . .	4,764	4,734	5,072	4,537	4,016
Aluminum sulfate (commercial)	1,000 metric tons . .	1,144	1,197	1,161	1,058	1,085
Sodium metal	1,000 metric tons . .	(D)	(D)	(D)	(D)	(D)
Sodium chlorate	1,000 metric tons . .	617	662	626	707	742
Sodium phosphate tribasic	1,000 metric tons . .	21	20	(D)	19	27
Sodium phosphate tripoly	1,000 metric tons . .	(D)	(D)	(D)	205	178
Sodium silicate [1]	1,000 metric tons . .	1,203	1,105	1,214	1,097	992
Sodium metasilicates	1,000 metric tons . .	93	87	83	70	63
Sodium sulfate	1,000 metric tons . .	(D)	(D)	(D)	571	599
Calcium carbide	1,000 metric tons . .	(D)	(D)	(D)	(D)	(D)
Calcium phosphorpus	1,000 metric tons . .	1,567	1,507	1,486	1,798	1,808
Carbon activated [2]	1,000 metric tons . .	156	170	173	150	151
Hydrogen peroxide	1,000 metric tons . .	355	343	369	324	342
Phosphorous, elemental	1,000 metric tons . .	(D)	(D)	(D)	(D)	(D)
Phosphorous, oxychloride and trichloride . .	1,000 metric tons . .	226	242	298	(D)	163

D Withheld to avoid disclosing data for individual companies. [1] Other than metasilicates. [2] Granular and pulverized.

Source: U.S. Census Bureau, *Manufacturing Profiles*, Series MP, annual; and *Current Industrial Reports*, MAQ325A, and MA325B, annual. See also <ftp://ftp.census.gov/pub/industry/1/mq28a995.pdf> (issued September 2000) and <ftp://ftp.census.gov/puo/industry/1/mq28a995.pdf> (issued September 2000).

628 Manufactures

No. 991. Pharmaceutical Preparations—Value of Shipments: 1990 to 1999

[In millions of dollars (33,954 represents $33,954,000,000)]

Product description	Product code	1990	1995	1996	1997	1998	1999
Pharmaceutical preparations, except biologicals.	(X)	33,954	48,864	5¹,844	57,419	65,712	69,950
Affecting neoplasms, endocrine systems, and metabolic disease	3254121000	2,743	4,076	4,788	5,466	7,633	7,902
Acting on the central nervous system and sense organs	3254124000	7,219	9,228	10,123	11,708	13,605	15,282
Acting on the cardiovascular system.	3254127000	4,815	5,988	6,912	8,799	9,368	9,695
Acting on the respiratory system	325412A000	3,724	5,196	4,994	5,641	6,725	8,136
Acting on the digestive system	325412D000	4,840	8,593	8,494	9,482	9,502	8,719
Acting on the skin	325412G000	1,558	2,171	2,185	1,867	2,245	2,589
Vitamin, nutrient, and hematinic preps.	325412L000	2,588	4,812	5,281	5,088	5,851	6,142
Affecting parasitic and infective disease . . .	325412P000	5,411	7,196	7,304	7,795	8,780	9,176
Pharmaceutical preps. for veterinary use. . .	325412T000	1,057	1,605	1,763	1,572	2,003	2,309

X Not applicable.
Source: U.S. Census Bureau, 1990, *Current Industrial Reports,* MA28G; thereafter, MA325G(99)-1. See also <http://www.census.gov/ftp/pub/industry/1/ma28g99.pdf> (released September 2000).

No. 992. Glass Containers, Clay Construction Products, and Refractories— Quantity and Value of Shipments: 1990 to 1999

[285 represents 285,000,000]

Product description	Unit	1990	1995	1996	1997	1998	1999
Glass container shipments.	Mil. of gross [1].	285	.269	257	254	254	255
Brick shipments: [2]							
Quantity	Mil. of bricks .	(NA)	7,244	7,426	7,838	8,081	8,553
Value	Mil. dol.	1,014	1,092	1,235	1,331	1,453	1,631
Clay floor and wall tile shipments: [3]							
Quantity	Mil. sq. ft. . . .	(NA)	581	576	627	621	625
Value	Mil. dol.	687	728	779	834	837	843
Clay pipe and fittings shipments:							
Quantity		(NA)	138	143	162	165	177
Value	Mil. dol.	60	35	45	47	48	54
Refractory shipments	Mil. dol.	2,003	2,222	2,341	2,566	2,379	2,243
Clay	Mil. dol.	771	941	930	1,084	1,025	965
Nonclay	Mil. dol.	1,232	1,282	1,411	1,482	1,354	1,278

NA Not available. [1] One thousand gross = 144,000. [2] Building or common and face bricks. [3] Floor and wall tile including quarry tile.
Source: U.S. Census Bureau, 1990, *Current Industrial Reports,* M32G, MQ32D, and MA32C, annual; thereafter, M327G, MQ327D, and MA327C. See also *Manufacturing Profiles,* Series MP, annual.

No. 993. Aluminum—Supply, Shipments, and Foreign Trade: 1990 to 2000

[In millions of pounds (17,334 represents 17,334,000,000)]

Item	1990	1993	1994	1995	1996	1997	1998	1999	2000
SUPPLY									
Aluminum supply, total	17,334	19,766	20,989	20,425	20,848	21,945	22,970	24,590	23,586
Primary production	8,925	8,145	7,272	7,441	7,887	7,944	8 185	8,330	8,087
Recovery from scrap	5,276	6,490	6,803	7,028	7,291	7,819	7,589	8,146	7,606
Imports of ingot and mill products.	3,133	5,131	6,913	5,956	5,671	6,183	7,196	8,113	7,893
Aluminum net shipments, total [1]	17,188	18,488	20,596	21,019	21,155	22,513	23,189	24,673	24,486
PRODUCT									
Mill products, total	13,013	13,869	15,605	15,716	15,605	16,609	17,019	17,989	17,666
Sheet, plate, and foil	9,297	9,847	11,096	11,168	10,936	11,536	11,801	12,437	12,116
Rod, bar, and wire	370	393	458	534	582	621	657	670	690
Electrical conductor	542	554	600	566	604	629	631	676	675
Extruded shapes and tube.	2,546	2,799	3,124	3,102	3,139	3,473	3,559	3,817	3,788
Powder and paste	106	105	110	108	108	118	123	130	142
Forgings and impacts	152	171	217	238	236	232	248	259	255
Ingot for castings and other [2]	4,175	4,619	4,991	5,303	5,550	5,904	6,170	6,684	6,820
MARKET									
Domestic, total	14,637	16,082	17,960	18,152	18,313	19,523	20,358	21,707	21,695
Building and construction	2,663	2,728	3,090	2,679	2,921	2,921	3,070	3,237	3,204
Transportation	3,205	4,343	5,104	5,749	5,820	6,592	7,162	7,938	7,963
Consumer durables	1,122	1,246	1,428	1,369	1,443	1,529	1,599	1,675	1,697
Electrical	1,309	1,304	1,456	1,395	1,447	1,532	1,527	1,646	1,698
Machinery and equipment	992	1,053	1,262	1,257	1,254	1,381	1,386	1,458	1,496
Containers and packaging	4,772	4,836	5,012	5,088	4,796	4,895	5,012	5,106	4,992
Other.	574	572	608	615	632	673	602	647	645
Exports	2,551	2,406	2,636	2,867	2,842	2,990	2,831	2,967	2,791
FOREIGN TRADE [3]									
Exports	3,753	2,883	3,319	3,846	3,600	3,763	3,743	3,865	4,097
Imports	3,718	5,819	7,780	6,910	6,580	7,209	8,342	9,506	9,357

[1] Data presented on this report have been adjusted to shipments and inventories plus imports by consumers. [2] Net ingot for foundry castings, export, and destructive uses. [3] U.S. imports and exports of aluminum ingot, mill products, and scrap.
Source: The Aluminum Association, Inc., Washington, DC, *Aluminum Statistical Review,* annual; and *Aluminum Facts at a Glance,* June 2001.

Manufactures 629

No. 994. Iron and Steel Industry—Summary: 1990 to 1999

[95.5 represents 95,500,000 tons. For financial data, the universe in 1992 consists of the companies that produced 68 percent of the total reported raw steel production. The financial data represent the operations of the steel segment of the companies. Minus sign (-) indicates net loss]

Item	Unit	1990	1993	1994	1995	1996	1997	1998	1999
Steel mill products, apparent supply . . .	Mil. tons [1] . .	95.5	99.6	113.4	109.6	117.5	124.6	131.6	127.9
Net shipments.	Mil. tons [1] . .	85.0	89.0	95.1	97.5	100.9	105.9	102.4	106.2
Exports	Mil. tons [1] . .	4.3	4.0	3.8	7.1	5.0	6.0	5.5	5.4
Imports	Mil. tons [1] . .	17.2	19.5	30.1	24.4	29.2	31.2	41.5	31.2
Scrap consumed.	Mil. tons [1] . .	50.1	58.5	60.0	62.0	62.0	64.0	64.0	62.0
Scrap inventory.	Mil. tons [1] . .	3.6	3.6	4.0	4.1	5.3	5.0	4.5	5.3
Iron and steel products: Exports.	Mil. tons [1] . .	5.3	4.7	4.9	8.2	6.2	7.4	6.9	6.7
Imports	Mil. tons [1] . .	21.9	21.8	32.7	27.3	32.1	34.4	45.4	40.2
Capacity by steelmaking process	Mil. net tons.	116.7	109.9	108.2	112.4	116.1	121.4	125.3	128.2
Revenue	Bil. dol.. . . .	30.9	29.5	34.1	35.1	34.9	36.6	38.1	35.3
Net income	Bil. dol.. . . .	0.1	1.9	1.3	1.5	0.4	1.0	1.1	-0.5
Stockholders' equity.	Bil. dol.. . . .	4.3	3.7	7.4	8.6	10.2	9.8	12.5	11.9
Total assets	Bil. dol.. . . .	28.3	30.6	34.3	35.1	35.8	38.3	42.2	43.6
Capital expenditures [2]	Bil. dol.. . . .	2.6	1.5	2.2	2.5	2.3	2.7	3.1	2.8
Working capital ratio [2]	Ratio	1.6	1.3	1.7	1.5	1.7	1.6	1.6	1.7
Inventories.	Bil. dol.. . . .	4.7	4.6	5.0	5.1	5.4	5.8	6.8	6.5
Average employment.	1,000	169	140	127	123	119	112	110	102
Hours worked	Million	350	274	273	269	259	247	240	223
Index of output, all employees [3].	1987=100 . .	109.7	133.6	142.4	142.6	147.5	155.0	151.0	148.9
Producer price indexes: [4]									
Iron and steel, total	1982=100 . .	117.2	116.0	122.0	128.8	125.8	126.5	122.6	(NA)
Steel mill products	1982=100 . .	112.1	108.2	113.4	120.1	115.6	116.4	113.9	(NA)
Electrometallurgical products	1982=100 . .	120.1	115.7	117.0	126.0	157.7	163.0	158.9	(NA)
Iron ore	1982=100 . .	83.3	82.7	82.7	91.8	96.7	96.3	95.5	(NA)
Scrap, iron and steel	1982=100 . .	166.0	172.5	192.9	202.7	191.1	188.9	164.9	(NA)
Foundry and forge shop products . . .	1982=100 . .	117.2	121.3	123.9	129.3	132.6	134.1	135.0	(NA)

NA Not available. [1] In millions of short tons. [2] Current assets to current liabilities. [3] Output per hour. Source: U.S. Bureau of Labor Statistics, Internet site <http://stats.bls.gov/iprhome.htm>. [4] Source: U.S. Bureau of Labor Statistics, Producer Price Indexes, monthly and annual.

Source: Except as noted, American Iron and Steel Institute, Washington, DC, Annual Statistical Report (copyright).

No. 995. Raw Steel, Pig Iron, and Ferroalloys Production: 1990 to 1999

[In millions (849.4 represents 849,400,000), except percent]

Item	1990	1993	1994	1995	1996	1997	1998	1999
Raw steel (net tons):								
World production.	849.4	802.0	799.6	829.4	826.9	874.9	856.8	868.4
U.S. production.	98.9	97.9	100.6	104.9	105.3	108.6	108.8	107.4
Percent of world	11.6	12.2	12.6	12.6	12.7	12.4	12.7	12.4
Furnace:								
Basic oxygen process . .	58.5	59.3	61.0	62.5	60.4	61.1	59.7	57.7
Electric	36.9	38.5	39.6	42.4	44.9	47.5	49.1	49.7
Open hearth	3.5	-	-	-	-	-	-	-
Grade:								
Carbon	86.6	86.9	89.5	92.7	93.6	95.9	97.1	96.5
Alloy and stainless.	12.3	11.0	11.1	12.3	11.7	12.6	11.7	10.9
Pig iron and ferroalloys production (sh. tons)	54.8	53.1	54.4	56.1	54.5	54.7	53.2	51.0

- Represents or rounds to zero.

Source: American Iron and Steel Institute, Washington, DC, Annual Statistical Report (copyright).

No. 996. Steel Products—Net Shipments by Market Classes: 1990 to 1999

[In thousands of short tons (84,981 represents 84,981,000). Comprises carbon, alloy, and stainless steel]

Market class	1990	1993	1994	1995	1996	1997	1998	1999
Total [1]	84,981	89,022	95,084	97,494	100,878	105,858	102,420	106,401
Automotive.	11,100	12,719	14,753	14,622	14,665	15,251	15,842	16,771
Steel service centers, distributors	21,111	23,714	24,153	23,751	27,124	27,800	27,751	28,089
Construction, incl. maintenance [2]	9,245	13,429	10,935	14,892	15,561	15,885	15,289	18,428
Containers, packaging, shipping.	4,474	4,355	4,495	4,139	4,101	4,163	3,829	3,842
Machinery, industrial equipment, tools . .	2,388	2,191	2,427	2,310	2,410	2,355	2,147	1,722
Steel for converting and processing . . .	9,441	9,451	10,502	10,440	10,245	11,263	9,975	11,309
Rail transportation	1,080	1,223	1,248	1,373	1,400	1,410	1,657	1,031
Contractors' products	2,870	2,913	3,348	(2)	(2)	(2)	(2)	(2)
Oil and gas industries	1,892	1,526	1,703	2,643	3,254	3,811	2,649	2,151
Electrical equipment.	2,453	2,213	2,299	2,397	2,401	2,434	2,255	2,267
Appliances, utensils, and cutlery	1,540	1,592	1,736	1,589	1,713	1,635	1,729	1,789

[1] Includes nonclassified shipments and other classes not shown separately. [2] Beginning 1994, contractors' products included with construction.

Source: American Iron and Steel Institute, Washington, DC, Annual Statistical Report (copyright).

No. 997. U.S. Machine Tool Consumption—Gross New Orders and Exports: 1999 and 2000

[Value in millions of dollars (4,459 represents $4,459,000,000)]

Item	1999				2000			
	Total	Metal cutting machines	Metal forming machines	Other manufacturing technology	Total	Metal cutting machines	Metal forming machines	Other manufacturing technology
New order units, total . .	**27,525**	**22,085**	**3,309**	**2,131**	**29,009**	**24,197**	**2,921**	**1,890**
Northeast [1]	5,013	4,135	532	346	5,159	4,286	546	328
South [2]	4,512	3,566	543	403	4,227	3,411	418	399
Midwest [3]	9,301	7,401	1,133	767	8,588	7,171	840	577
Central [4]	4,780	3,683	740	357	5,745	4,750	671	324
West [5]	3,919	3,300	361	258	5,291	4,580	447	263
New order value, total .	**4,459**	**3,396**	**500**	**563**	**4,494**	**3,563**	**459**	**472**
Northeast [1]	722	593	63	66	748	598	75	74
South [2]	665	490	73	103	636	512	56	68
Midwest [3]	1,899	1,440	185	275	1,645	1,268	150	227
Central [4]	712	488	126	98	784	601	100	83
West [5]	460	386	54	20	682	584	78	20
Export order units [6]	1,721	1,329	214	178	2,317	1,837	206	274
Export order value [6]	483	352	49	82	569	416	60	94

[1] Covers Maine, New Hampshire, Vermont, New York, Massachusetts, Connecticut, Rhode Island, New Jersey, and Pennsylvania. [2] Covers Delaware, Maryland, Virginia, West Virginia, Kentucky, North Carolina, South Carolina, Tennessee, Mississippi, Alabama, Georgia, and Florida. [3] Covers Wisconsin, Michigan, Ohio, Illinois, and Indiana. [4] Covers Minnesota, North Dakota, South Dakota, Montana, Wyoming, Idaho, Iowa, Nebraska, Kansas, Missouri, Oklahoma, Arkansas, Louisiana, Texas, New Mexico, Colorado, and Utah. [5] Covers Washington, Oregon, California, Nevada, and Arizona. [6] Represents orders placed with U.S. builders.

Source: The Association for Manufacturing Technology, McLean, VA, (copyright); and American Machine Tool Distributors Association, Rockville, MD, *U.S. Machine Tool Consumption Report*, monthly.

No. 998. Metalworking Machinery—Value of Shipments: 1990 to 2000

[In millions of dollars (3,426.1 represents $3,426,100,000)]

Product	NAICS product code	1990	1995	1996	1997	1998	1999	2000
Metalworking machinery	(X)	**3,426.1**	**4,547.1**	**4,607.8**	**5,010.3**	**4,817.1**	**3,783.3**	**3,632.4**
Metal cutting type [1]	(X)	2,371.3	3,036.6	3,141.1	3,583.3	3,481.8	2,512.6	2,552.4
Boring machines [2]	333512A1	(2)	172.4	88.9	80.2	73.6	53.8	87.2
Drilling machines [2]	333512A1	184.1	78.9	99.5	89.2	102.9	50.6	23.7
Gear cutting machines	33351211	102.7	137.1	164.3	213.5	197.7	132.0	180.6
Grinding and polishing machines	33351220	433.6	549.6	541.3	595.0	535.5	477.1	454.3
Lathes [3]	33351230	355.6	478.0	451.1	480.7	472.9	297.4	287.0
Milling machines [4]	33351240	214.3	194.8	199.7	280.2	281.1	200.5	150.5
Machining centers [5]	33351270	437.0	698.8	779.4	931.6	897.3	597.9	629.7
Station type machines	33351280	502.1	477.0	498.6	551.9	571.0	407.1	401.8
Other metal cutting machine tools [6]	33351290	141.9	246.2	316.0	358.3	344.6	291.7	333.2
Metal forming type	(X)	1,080.2	1,510.5	1,466.6	1,427.0	1,335.3	1,270.7	1,080.0
Punching and shearing machines	33351310 pt.	200.1	326.3	331.4	319.2	254.3	220.0	203.8
Bending and forming machines	33351310 pt.	222.9	256.9	283.0	258.5	262.7	265.8	262.4
Presses, except forging	33351330	308.3	379.2	402.0	422.4	399.5	433.7	303.1
Forging machines [7]	33351350 pt.	73.9	(D)	(D)	(D)	(D)	(D)	(D)
Other metal forming [7]	33351350 pt.	275.0	548.1	450.2	426.9	418.8	351.2	310.7

D Data withheld to avoid disclosure. X Not applicable. [1] Data for "All lathes (turning machines)" and "All milling machines," valued at under $3,025 each are included in total "Metal cutting type" for 1995 through 1999. [2] For 1990, data for "Boring machines" were combined with "Drilling machines" to avoid disclosing individual company data. [3] For 1995 through 2000 product code 33351230, "Lathes," excludes the value for product code 3335123031, All lathes valued under $3,025 each. [4] For 1995 through 2000 product code 33351240, "Milling machines," excludes the value for product code 3335124001, "All milling machines valued under $3,025 each." [5] Multifunction numerically controlled machines. [6] Excludes those designed primarily for home workshops, labs, etc. [7] For 1995 through 2000, data for "Forging machines" have been combined with "Other metal forming machines" to avoid disclosing individual company data.

Source: U.S. Census Bureau, *Manufacturing Profiles*, Series MP, annual; and <http://www.census.gov/ftp/pub/industry/1/mq005.pdf> (released June 2001).

No. 999. Selected Types of Construction Machinery—Value of Shipments: 1990 to 1999

[In millions of dollars (2,235.9 represents $2,235,900,000)]

Product description	Product code	1990	1995	1996	1997	1998	1999
Tractor shovel loaders	33312014	2,235.9	3,041.8	3,340.1	3,912.5	4,235.9	4,144.6
Power cranes, draglines, and shovels	33312011	1,511.8	2,561.4	2,740.3	2,927.4	3,289.2	3,172.2
Mixers, pavers, and related equipment	33312012	609.6	1,168.8	1,145.8	1,283.8	1,480.3	1,624.1
Off-highway trucks, truck-type tractor, chassis trailers, coal haulers, or wagons	33312013	957.7	1,326.9	1,632.6	1,596.3	1,425.6	834.6
Motor graders and light maintainers	33312016	408.0	479.9	588.4	(D)	(D)	(D)
Rough terrain forklifts	33312016	209.3	355.4	412.3	499.5	668.1	641.5
Equipment for mounting on tractors	(X)	258.6	(X)	(X)	(X)	(X)	(X)
Self-propelled continuous ditchers and trenchers	33312016	129.7	193.5	209.1	238.7	266.7	297.6
Construction machinery for mounting on trucks, tractors, and other prime movers	33312017	(X)	(D)	214.5	258.6	278.3	243.6
Aerial work platforms	33392372	814.9	1,131.1	(D)	(D)	2,055.2	2,491.8

D Withheld to avoid disclosing figures for individual companies.   X Not applicable.

Source: U.S. Census Bureau, through 1989, *Current Industrial Reports*, Series MA35D; thereafter, Series, MA333D. See also <http://www.census.gov/ftp/pub/industry/1/ma35d99.pdf> (released September 2000); and *Manufacturing Profiles*, Series MP, annual.

No. 1000. Mining and Mineral Processing Equipment—Shipments: 1998 and 1999

Product	Product code	Number of companies 1999	Quantity (units)		Value (mil. dol.)	
			1998	1999	1998	1999
Mining and mineral processing equipment	(X)	(X)	(X)	(X)	1,639	1,311
Portable crushing, screening, washing, and combination plants	33312081	17	977	956	152	164
Underground mining machinery [1]	33313110	28	16,834	17,486	491	333
Crushing/pulverizing/screening machinery [2] [3]	33313150	34	4,214	4,075	346	316
Drills and other mining machinery, n.e.c. [1] [3]	33313171	26	22,671	17,037	175	132
Portable drilling rigs and parts	3331327	21	1,658	1,620	475	366

X Not applicable.   [1] Excludes parts.   [2] Excludes portables and parts.   [3] N.e.c. = Not elsewhere classified.

Source: U.S. Census Bureau, *Current Industrial Reports*, Series MA333F. See also <http://www.census.gov/ftp/pub/industry/1/ma35f99.pdf> (issued September 2000) and *Manufacturing Profiles*, Series MP, annual.

No. 1001. Engines, Refrigeration and Heating Equipment, and Pumps and Compressors—Shipments: 1995 to 1999

[23,274 represents 23,274,000]

Product	Unit	1995	1996	1997	1998	1999
Internal combustion engines produced	1,000	23,274	23,353	25,077	27,523	27,069
Gasoline (except outboard, aircraft, and auto)	1,000	22,287	22,659	23,989	26,352	25,781
Nonautomotive diesel (except aircraft)	1,000	246	270	300	296	344
Automotive diesel	1,000	732	685	771	851	927
Natural gas and LPG	1,000	9	9	18	24	16
Air-conditioning, heating equipment shipments:						
Heat transfer equipment	Mil. dol	(NA)	4,280	4,246	4,472	4,548
Room air-conditioners and dehumidifiers	Mil. dol	(NA)	1,020	1,020	1,098	1,225
Motor vehicle mechanical air-conditioning systems	Mil. dol	(NA)	2,208	2,221	2,100	2,330
Compressors and compressor units	Mil. dol	(NA)	3,092	2,796	2,814	3,034
Automotive air-conditioning compressors	Mil. dol	(NA)	1,652	1,951	1,977	2,104
Nonelectric warm air furnaces and dehumidifiers	Mil. dol	(NA)	1,562	1,558	1,607	1,564
Unitary air conditioners	Mil. dol	(NA)	4,625	4,615	5,229	5,386
Air source heat pumps	Mil. dol	(NA)	1,046	917	1,054	997
Pumps and compressors [1]	Mil. dol	7,373	8,327	8,879	9,122	8,272
Industrial pumps	Mil. dol	2,700	3,093	2,732	2,924	2,806
Domestic water systems	Mil. dol	329	361	357	409	462
Air and gas compressors	Mil. dol	2,466	2,665	2,635	2,522	2,317

NA Not available.   [1] Includes products not shown separately.

Source: U.S. Census Bureau, *Current Industrial Reports*, Series MA333L, MA333M, and MA333P. See also <http://www.census.gov/ftp/pub/industry/1/ma35199.pdf> (released September 2000); <http://www.census.gov/ftp/pub/industry/1/ma35m99.pdf> (released September 2000); <http://www.census.gov/ftp/pub/industry/1/ma35p99.pdf> (released September 2000); and *Manufacturing Profiles*, Series MP, annual.

No. 1002. Computers and Office and Accounting Machines—Value of Shipments: 1990 to 1999

[In millions of dollars (25,630 represents $25,630,000,000)]

Selected products	1990	1994	1995	1996	1997	1998	1999
Electronic computers [1]	25,630	38,261	49,038	50,682	50,250	56,892	62,712
Host computers (multi-users).	(NA)	(NA)	(NA)	(NA)	12,240	15,010	17,178
Single user computers	(NA)	(NA)	(NA)	(NA)	36,988	41,002	44,541
Other computers.	(NA)	(NA)	(NA)	(NA)	1,022	879	993
Loaded computer processor boards and board subassemblies [2]	2,247	17,515	24,448	24,937	27,040	26,047	30,382
Computer storage devices & equipment	7,488	5,556	7,903	8,909	8,837	9,319	9,720
Parts for computer storage devices & subassemblies	955	1,952	2,236	1,720	2,382	2,310	2,255
Computer terminals.	2,067	1,244	1,086	1,104	781	480	
Computer peripheral equipment, n.e.c.	7,697	11,944	12,331	12,463	13,555	12,145	12,784
Parts for input/output equipment	3,706	2,499	2,391	5,505	2,628	2,630	2,362
Calculating and accounting machines.	(D)	1,262	1,279	1,485	1,622	1,061	940
Magnetic and optical recording media	3,695	4,777	5,106	5,739	5,739	4,736	3,850

D Withheld to avoid disclosing data for individual companies.   NA Not available.   [1] Beginning 1997, computer industry data are not entirely comparable to previous years.   [2] These data are collected on two Current Industrial Report forms, MA35R, "Computers and Office and Accounting Machines (Shipments)" and MA36Q, "Semiconductors, Printed Circuit Boards, and Other Electronic Components."

Source: U.S. Census Bureau, *Current Industrial Reports,* Series MA334R. See also <http://www.census.gov/ftp/pub/industry/1/ma35r99.pdf> (released August 2000); and *Manufacturing Profiles,* series MP, annual.

No. 1003. Computers and Office and Accounting Machines—Shipments: 1998 and 1999

[Quantity in thousands of units (23,064 represents 23,064,000). Value in millions of dollars (56,891 represents $56,891,000,000)]

Product	Number of companies, 1999	Quantity (1,000)		Value (mil. dol.)	
		1998	1999	1998	1999
Electronic computers (automatic data processors)	140	**23,064**	**28,294**	**56,891**	**62,712**
Host computers (multiusers):					
Large scale systems and unix servers.	14	752	1,289	5,201	6,089
Medium-scale systems and unix servers	32	658	966	6,952	8,049
PC servers.	26	(D)	630	(D)	2,499
Other host computers.	11	(D)	27	(D)	542
Single user computers:					
Personal computers.	41	15,585	19,398	24,524	26,308
Workstations.	35	722	745	9,807	10,173
Laptops (AC/DC).	11	190	(D)	538	(D)
Notebooks, subnotebooks (battery operated)	14	2,470	(D)	5,810	(D)
Personal digital assistants.	4	69	(D)	48	(D)
Other portable computers	6	223	(D)	163	(D)
Other single user computers	5	206	207	113	110
Other computers.	38	1,733	1,525	879	993
Computer storage devices and equipment.	79	(X)	(X)	9,319	9,720
Parts for computer storage devices and subassemblies	15	(X)	(X)	2,310	2,255
Computer terminals.	39	(X)	(X)	540	481
Computer peripheral equipment, n.e.c. [1]	237	(X)	(X)	12,145	12,784
Keyboards	25	15,331	10,709	751	737
Computer printers:					
Laser.	27	2,455	1,880	2,158	3,320
Inkjet	15	8,882	11,435	1,232	1,043
Calculating and accounting machines.	37	(X)	(X)	1,060	940
Printed circuit assemblies.	784	(X)	(X)	26,046	30,382
Magnetic and optical recording media	59	(X)	(X)	4,736	3,850

D Withheld to avoid disclosure of individual companies.   X Not applicable.   [1] N.e.c. = Not elsewhere classified.

Source: U.S. Census Bureau, *Current Industrial Reports,* Series MA334R; and *Manufacturing Profiles,* Series MP, annual. See also <http://www.census.gov/ftp/pub/industry/1/ma35r99.pdf> (released August 2000).

No. 1004. Computers and Industrial Electronics—Factory Shipments: 1990 to 1998

[In millions of dollars (50,793 represents $50,793,000,000)]

Item	1990	1993	1994	1995	1996	1997	1998
Computer and peripheral equipment, total .	50,793	54,821	59,254	73,555	78,278	76,287	78,831
Computers	25,973	30,002	38,261	49,038	50,682	50,250	57,347
Peripheral equipment	24,820	24,819	20,993	24,517	27,597	26,037	21,484
Industrial electronics, total	26,183	27,250	29,927	33,732	35,472	38,108	37,640
Controlling, processing equipment	12,728	13,961	15,014	16,450	17,051	18,212	17,860
Testing, measuring equipment	6,859	7,332	8,416	10,109	11,224	11,966	12,312
Nuclear electronic equipment	567	519	477	501	491	516	556
Robots, accessories, and components	275	(NA)	(NA)	(NA)	(NA)	(NA)	(NA)
Other electronic equipment	5,754	5,438	6,020	6,672	6,706	7,414	6,912

NA Not available.

Source: Consumer Electronics Association, Washington, DC, *Electronic Market Data Book,* annual (copyright).

No. 1005. Consumer Electronics and Electronic Components—Factory Sales by Product Category: 1990 to 1999

[In millions of dollars (43,033 represents $43,033,000,000). Factory sales include imports]

Product category	1990	1995	1996	1997	1998	1999
Total [1]	43,033	64,530	68,002	71,814	75,552	80,976
Video products:						
Direct-view color TV	6,197	6,798	6,492	6,026	6,151	6,199
LCD color TV	50	44	39	38	39	36
Projection TV	626	1,417	1,426	1,361	1,577	1,632
TV/VCR combinations	178	723	697	684	831	1,014
Monochrome TV	99	34	29	27	23	20
LCD Monochrome TV	33	31	32	30	28	25
Other video:						
VCR decks	2,439	2,767	2,815	2,618	2,409	2,333
Camcorders	2,260	2,130	2,084	1,894	2,144	2,448
Laserdisc players	72	108	66	25	10	3
Home satellite earth stations	421	1,265	1,201	726	733	957
Videocassette players	65	59	43	39	21	15
Digital versatile disc players (DVD)	(NA)	(NA)	(NA)	171	421	1,099
Home and portable products:						
Compact audio systems	1,270	1,162	1,157	1,419	1,557	1,695
Separate audio components	1,935	1,911	1,808	1,609	1,565	1,530
Home radios	360	284	291	300	300	348
Portable audio equipment	1,645	2,506	2,149	2,033	2,146	1,987
Mobile electronics:						
Aftermarket autosound equipment	1,192	1,931	1,914	1,811	1,859	2,070
Factory installed autosound	3,100	3,100	2,512	2,710	2,540	2,610
Wireless (cellular) telephones	1,133	2,574	2,660	2,750	2,775	2,808
Pagers	118	300	370	460	550	660
Vehicle security	190	142	165	210	213	205
Home office products:						
Cordless telephones	842	1,141	1,176	1,679	1,745	1,808
Corded telephones	638	557	553	528	489	483
Telephone answering devices	827	1,077	1,004	1,020	1,104	1,044
Home computers	4,187	12,600	15,040	15,950	16,640	16,390
Computer printers	(NA)	2,430	2,999	3,900	4,188	4,500
Modems/fax modems	(NA)	770	960	1,170	1,305	1,460
Computer peripherals	1,980	816	975	1,212	1,440	1,950
Computer software (incl. CDROM)	971	2,500	3,000	3,450	3,930	4,480
Home fax machines	920	919	839	1,139	647	455
Digital cameras	(NA)	(NA)	177	483	524	1,207
Electronic gaming:						
Electronic gaming hardware	975	1,500	1,600	1,650	1,980	2,250
Electronic gaming software	2,400	3,000	3,500	3,900	4,480	5,100
Blank media:						
Blank audio cassettes	376	334	314	281	243	208
Blank videocassettes	948	708	725	695	639	590
Blank floppy diskettes	314	373	300	250	232	200
Accessories and batteries:						
Electronic accessories	793	944	982	982	1,178	1,398
Total primary batteries	1,383	2,600	2,676	2,869	2,963	3,620

NA Not available. [1] Includes categories, not shown separately.
Source: Consumer Electronics Association, Washington, DC, *Electronic Market Data Book*, annual (copyright).

No. 1006. Communication Equipment—Value of Shipments: 1990 to 1999

[In millions of dollars (36,990 represents $36,990,000,000]

Product description	Product code	1990	1995	1996	1997	1998	1999
Communication equipment	(X)	36,990	56,362	65,609	73,588	82,198	84,526
Telephone switching and switchboard equipment	3342101	7,537	8,178	9,618	10,302	12,422	13,864
Carrier line equipment and modems	3342104	5,014	5,869	7,545	7,278	9,379	9,065
Other telephone and telegraph equipment and components	3342107	3,181	10,510	14,031	16,488	19,897	20,381
Communication systems and equipment (except broadcast)	3342201	14,768	23,032	25,332	29,416	31,128	31,302
Broadcast, studio, and related electronic equipment	3342203	1,856	2,845	3,000	3,360	3,625	3,947
Intercommunications systems, including inductive paging systems (selective calling)	3342903	346	296	278	256	249	264
Alarm systems	3342901	1,027	1,662	1,803	1,926	2,024	2,118
Vehicular and pedestrian traffic control equipment and electrical railway signals and attachments	3342902	471	711	762	964	912	1,038
Electronic teaching machines, teaching aids, trainers and simulators	3333197	1,209	913	866	872	713	693
Laser sources [1]	3359997	(NA)	788	844	992	(S)	(S)
Ultrasonic equipment	335999A	109	172	184	213	205	203
Other electronic systems and equipment, n.e.c [2]	335999C	1,473	1,387	1,346	1,520	1,645	1,650

NA Not available. S Does not meet publication standards. X Not applicable. [1] Beginning in 1995, data for laser equipment, instrumentation, and components were eliminated from this survey. Only laser sources are being collected. [2] N.e.c. Not elsewhere classified.
Source: U.S. Census Bureau, *Current Industrial Reports*, Series MA334P. See also <http://www.census.gov/ftp/pub/industry/1/ma36p99.pdf> (issued September 2000); and *Manufacturing Profiles*, Series MP, annual.

No. 1007. Semiconductors, Printed Circuit Boards, and Other Electronic Components—Value of Shipments by Class of Product: 1990 to 1999

[In millions of dollars (1,097 represents $1,097,000,000). N.e.c.=not elsewhere classified]

Class of product	Product code	1990	1995	1996	1997	1998	1999
Transmittal, industrial, and special-purpose electron tubes (except x-ray)	3344111	1,097	855	611	656	630	685
Electron tubes, receiving type	(X)	24	[1]	[1]	[1]	[1]	[1]
Receiving type electron tubes and cathode ray picture tubes	3344114	1,344	[1]2,907	[1]3,272	[1]3,434	[1]3,367	3,513
Electron tube parts	3344117	143	120	153	161	147	136
Printed circuit boards	3344120	7,175	8,367	8,217	8,702	8,473	7,977
Integrated microcircuits (semiconductor networks)	3344131	16,623	48,438	52,639	57,019	57,644	62,829
Transistors	3344134	682	943	946	1,500	887	811
Diodes and rectifiers	3344137	668	1,067	861	1,191	908	955
Other semiconductor devices	334413A	5,741	12,639	10,976	10,262	11,056	11,996
Capacitors for electronic applications	3344140	1,392	1,785	1,653	2,099	1,947	1,993
Resistors	3344150	800	953	912	993	945	950
Coils, transformers, reactors, and chokes for electronic applications	3344160	976	1,412	1,436	1,426	1,368	1,391
Coaxial connectors	3344171	420	732	657	581	590	573
Cylindrical connectors	3344174	514	553	643	555	580	504
Rack and panel connectors	3344177	500	541	531	658	746	380
Printed circuit connectors	334417A	805	1,026	1,095	1,277	1,125	1,231
Other connectors including parts	334417D	1,085	1,402	1,617	2,209	1,973	1,990
Filters (except microwave) and piezoelectric devices	3344191	457	729	719	815	798	842
Microwave components and devices	3342207	1,369	1,233	1,251	1,440	1,581	1,467
Transducers, electrical/electronic input or output	3344194	741	1,111	1,105	1,220	1,373	1,499
Switches, mechanical types for electronic circuitry	3344197	579	666	738	791	883	832
Printed circuit assemblies	334418A	8,269	24,448	24,937	27,040	26,047	30,382
All other electronic components n.e.c	334419D	4,898	6,978	7,199	7,485	7,322	7,091

X Not applicable.   [1] Product codes combined to avoid disclosing figures for individual companies.

Source: U.S. Census Bureau, *Current Industrial Reports*, Series MA334P. See also <http://www.census.gov/ftp/pub/industry/1/ma36q99.pdf> (released September 2000); and *Manufacturing Profiles*, Series MP, annual.

No. 1008. Selected Instruments and Related Products—Shipments: 1990 to 1999

[In millions of dollars (1,418 represents $1,418,000,000)]

Product description	Product code	1990	1995	1996	1997	1998	1999
Automatic regulating and control valves	332911F	1,418	1,860	1,893	2,097	2,082	2,213
Solenoid-operated valves (except nuclear and fluid power transfer)	332911H	346	464	522	541	524	468
Aeronautical, nautical, and navigational instruments	3345111	2,518	2,125	2,274	2,531	2,504	2,637
Search & detection, navigation & guidance systems and equipment	3345113	32,420	24,697	26,094	26,584	26,031	23,836
Laboratory apparatus and laboratory furniture	3391110	1,675	1,837	1,799	1,888	1,843	1,823
Controls for monitoring residential and commercial environments and appliance	3345120	1,982	2,533	2,648	2,717	2,860	2,879
Process control instruments	3345130	5,224	6,439	6,745	7,073	6,637	6,546
Integrating and totalizing meters for gas and liquids	3345141	725	915	963	1,079	1,147	1,077
Counting devices	3345143	210	364	367	435	394	408
Motor vehicle instruments	3345145	1,457	2,193	2,219	2,245	2,436	2,799
Integrating instruments, electrical	3345151	396	445	458	457	460	477
Test equipment for testing electrical, radio and communication circuits, and motors	3345153	6,156	9,255	10,390	11,639	10,454	10,762
Instruments to measure electricity	3345155	586	555	500	456	377	360
Analytical, scientific instruments (except optical)	3345160	4,412	5,737	5,478	6,059	6,162	6,222
Sighting, tracking, and fire-control equipment, optical type	3333141	581	655	613	575	510	526
Optical instruments and lenses	3333143	1,252	1,579	1,749	2,005	2,068	2,252
Aircraft engine instruments (except flight)	3345191	579	430	530	521	657	658
Physical properties and kinematic testing equip.	3345193	1,012	1,374	1,369	1,523	1,728	1,693
Nuclear radiation detection and monitoring instruments	3345195	567	501	497	530	567	532
Commercial, geophysical, meteorological, and general purpose instruments	3345197	1,140	1,373	1,452	1,677	1,534	1,111
Surveying and drafting instruments	3345199	274	356	365	360	297	310

Source: U.S. Census Bureau, 1990, *Current Industrial Reports*, Series MA38B; thereafter *MA334B*. See also <http://www.census.gov/ftp/pub/industry/1/ma38b99.pdf> (issued September 2000); and *Manufacturing Profiles*, Series MP, annual.

No. 1009. Motor Vehicle Manufactures—Summary by Selected Industry: 1999

[1,167,167 represents 1,167,167,000. Based on the Annual Survey of Manufactures; see Appendix III]

| Industry | NAICS code [1] | All employees [2] | | | Produc-tion workers[2] (1,000) | Value of ship-ments [3] (mil. dol.) |
| | | Number | Payroll | | | |
			Total (mil. dol.)	Per employee (dol.)		
Motor vehicle manufacturing, total	(X)	**1,167,167**	**52,679**	**45,134**	**962,639**	**497,577**
Motor vehicle, total	3361	233,339	14,563	62,410	205,834	267,476
Automobile & light duty motor vehicle	33611	197,754	12,928	65,372	176,208	245,403
Automobile	336111	104,215	6,253	60,005	90,278	105,210
Light truck & utility vehicle	336112	93,539	6,674	71,353	85,930	140,193
Heavy duty truck	33612	35,585	1,635	45,947	29,625	22,073
Motor vehicle body & trailer	3362	139,265	4,133	29,674	114,313	28,631
Motor vehicle body & trailer	33621	139,265	4,133	29,674	114,313	28,631
Motor vehicle body	336211	43,686	1,392	31,859	34,189	10,461
Truck trailer	336212	35,425	1,005	28,361	30,232	6,839
Motor home	336213	20,005	630	31,514	16,448	5,161
Travel trailer & camper	336214	40,149	1,106	27,540	33,445	6,169
Motor vehicle parts	3363	794,563	33,984	42,771	642,492	201,470
Motor vehicle gasoline engine & engine parts	33631	96,439	4,568	47,369	79,053	30,431
Carburetor, piston, piston ring, & valve	336311	17,727	748	42,204	14,603	3,147
Gasoline engine & engine parts	336312	78,712	3,820	48,532	64,450	27,283
Motor vehicle electrical & electronic equip.	33632	115,022	4,085	35,518	88,031	25,891
Vehicular lighting equipment	336321	17,237	682	39,559	12,952	3,249
Other motor vehicle electrical & electronic equip. .	336322	97,785	3,403	34,806	75,079	22,643
Motor vehicle steering & suspension components, ex. spring	33633	48,697	2,494	51,205	40,480	11,300
Motor vehicle brake system	33634	44,608	1,688	37,834	35,021	12,454
Motor vehicle transmission & power train parts	33635	111,031	5,822	52,437	91,113	35,062
Motor vehicle seating & interior trim.	33636	55,519	1,967	35,424	44,534	14,276
Motor vehicle metal stamping	33637	119,521	5,931	49,627	101,112	24,939
Other motor vehicle parts	33639	203,727	7,429	36,465	163,148	47,118

X Not applicable.   [1] North American Industrial Classification System, 1997; see text, Section 15, Business Enterprise.
[2] Includes employment and payroll at administrative offices and auxiliary units. All employees represents the average of production workers plus all other employees for the payroll period ended nearest the 12th of March. Production workers represents the average of the employment for the payroll periods ended nearest the 12th of March, May, August, and November.   [3] Includes extensive and unmeasurable duplication from shipments between establishments in the same industry classification.
Source: U.S. Census Bureau, Annual Survey of Manufactures, Statistics for Industry Groups and Industries, Series M99(AS)-1.

No. 1010. Motor Vehicle Manufactures—Employees, Payroll, and Shipments by Major State: 1999

[14,563 represents 14,563,000,000. Industry based on the North American Industrial Classification System (NAICS); see text, Section 15, Business Enterprise]

| Major state based on employment | Motor vehicle manufacturing (NAICS 3361) | | | Motor vehicle body and trailer manufacturing (NAICS 3362) | | | Motor vehicle parts manufacturing (NAICS 3363) | | |
	Employ-ees, total	Payroll (mil. dol.)	Ship-ments (mil. dol.)	Employ-ees, total	Payroll (mil. dol.)	Ship-ments (mil. dol.)	Employ-ees, total	Payroll (mil. dol.)	Shipments (mil. dol.)
United States. .	**233,339**	**14,563**	**267,476**	**139,265**	**4,133**	**28,631**	**794,563**	**33,984**	**201,470**
Alabama	(D)	(D)	(D)	4,264	123	932	12,732	651	3,455
Arkansas	(NA)	(NA)	(NA)	2,475	65	526	7,844	181	1,124
California	6,736	349	3,108	11,235	345	4,741	25,420	678	3,613
Florida	(NA)	(NA)	(NA)	4,353	137	763	5,075	147	703
Georgia	8,080	499	11,031	3,612	105	745	9,783	286	2,189
Illinois	9,302	621	9,395	4,611	123	830	30,375	980	5,560
Indiana	7,829	471	9,232	29,254	956	6,895	101,944	4,697	25,758
Iowa	(NA)	(NA)	(NA)	8,804	257	1,464	9,430	306	1,828
Kentucky	18,461	1,381	30,053	(NA)	(NA)	(NA)	25,164	812	6,647
Massachusetts.	(NA)	(NA)	(NA)	(NA)	(NA)	(NA)	6,245	265	1,092
Michigan.	52,783	3,511	65,692	3,807	111	665	197,740	10,390	57,038
Mississippi	(NA)	(NA)	(NA)	1,299	26	183	10,808	289	1,853
Missouri	(D)	(D)	(D)	2,731	63	280	17,751	478	4,300
New York	(NA)	(NA)	(NA)	998	28	179	30,235	1,738	9,403
North Carolina	(D)	(D)	(D)	4,194	150	794	20,283	675	5,318
Ohio	34,797	2,052	38,004	5,165	158	804	108,907	5,607	31,906
Oklahoma	(D)	(D)	(D)	4,682	112	551	6,654	170	1,110
Oregon	3,341	128	2,068	4,235	118	731	2,939	114	622
Pennsylvania	(D)	(D)	(D)	7,771	214	1,431	15,688	615	3,618
South Carolina	4,562	181	3,275	1,455	29	123	15,904	516	4,247
Tennessee	15,278	906	9,559	2,113	69	486	34,266	1,100	8,148
Texas	(D)	(D)	(D)	6,473	186	1,022	16,347	494	3,607
Utah	(NA)	(NA)	(NA)	1,450	35	248	5,287	163	1,721
Virginia	(D)	(D)	(D)	(D)	(D)	(D)	10,651	346	2,364
Wisconsin	(D)	(D)	(D)	5,956	196	1,132	21,793	891	6,413

D Withheld to avoid disclosing data on individual companies.   NA Not available.
Source: U.S. Census Bureau, Annual Survey of Manufactures, Geographic Area Statistics, Series M99(AS)-3.

No. 1011. Aerospace—Sales, New Orders, and Backlog: 1990 to 1999

[In billions of dollars (136.6 represents $136,600,000,000), except as indicated. Reported by establishments in which the principal business is the development and/or production of aerospace products]

Item	1990	1994	1995	1996	1997	1998	1999
Net sales	136.6	104.3	102.8	103.1	114.9	119.2	123.6
Percent U.S. Government	53.8	54.8	49.5	49.8	40.3	39.9	45.6
Complete aircraft and parts [1]	49.9	43.3	42.5	41.8	54.5	63.6	68.3
Aircraft engines and parts	16.4	11.3	12.5	15.7	12.1	12.8	14.4
Missiles and space vehicles, parts	22.0	18.4	18.4	18.5	21.0	16.1	15.7
Other products, services	48.3	31.3	29.4	27.1	27.0	26.7	25.2
Net, new orders	146.0	88.7	109.1	126.3	119.0	109.9	114.2
Backlog, Dec. 31	250.1	192.6	202.6	229.9	219.0	200.2	190.1

[1] Except engines sold separately.

Source: U.S. Census Bureau, 1990-1997, *Current Industrial Reports,* Series M37G; thereafter M336G. See also <http://www.census.gov/ftp/pub/industry/1/m37g9913.pdf> (released September 2000); and *Manufacturing Profiles,* Series MP, annual.

No. 1012. Net Orders for U.S. Civil Jet Transport Aircraft: 1990 to 2000

[1990 data are net new firm orders; beginning 1994, net announced orders. Minus sign (-) indicates net cancellations. In 1997 Boeing acquired McDonnell Douglas]

Type of aircraft and customer	1990	1994	1995	1996	1997	1998	1999	2000
Total number [1]	670	79	421	595	501	601	346	585
U.S. customers	259	12	138	408	258	392	192	412
Foreign customers	411	67	283	187	243	209	70	193
Boeing 737, total	189	49	189	349	280	350	258	378
U.S. customers	38	9	85	284	120	207	155	302
Foreign customers	151	40	104	65	160	143	45	86
Boeing 747, total	153	-5	35	66	37	-4	22	24
U.S. customers	24	-1	2	22	15	1	1	1
Foreign customers	129	-4	33	44	22	-5	19	18
Boeing 757, total	66	5	-7	44	45	47	18	43
U.S. customers	33	-1	-6	35	25	34	7	38
Foreign customers	33	6	-1	9	20	13	2	14
Boeing 767, total	60	27	26	10	96	40	32	6
U.S. customers	23	11	4	11	85	31	21	-2
Foreign customers	37	16	22	-1	11	9	1	14
Boeing 777, total	34	-	83	88	46	65	21	113
U.S. customers	34	-	-	37	24	42	8	60
Foreign customers	-	-	83	51	22	23	8	53
McDonnell Douglas MD-11, total	52	2	-6	9	11	12	-	-
U.S. customers	16	2	3	1	-	3	-	-
Foreign customers	36	-	-9	8	11	9	-	-
McDonnell Douglas MD-80/90, total	116	1	51	29	-14	26	-20	-
U.S. customers	91	-8	-	18	-11	24	-	-
Foreign customers	25	9	51	11	-3	2	-20	-
McDonnell Douglas MD-95, total	-	-	50	-	-	65	15	21
U.S. customers	-	-	50	-	-	50	-	13
Foreign customers	-	-	-	-	-	15	15	8

- Represents zero. [1] Includes types of aircraft not shown separately. Beginning 1999, includes unidentified customers.

Source: Aerospace Industries Association of America, Washington, DC, Research Center, Statistical Series 23, Internet site <http://www.aia-aerospace.org> (released 14 March 2001).

No. 1013. U.S. Aircraft Shipments: 1980 to 2000

Year	Total		Civil						Military	
			Large transports		General aviation [1]		Helicopters			
	Units	Value	Units	Value	Units	Value	Units	Value	Units	Value
1980	14,677	18,929	387	9,895	11,877	2,486	1,366	656	1,047	5,892
1985	3,610	27,269	278	8,448	2,029	1,431	384	506	919	16,884
1990	3,321	38,585	521	22,215	1,144	2,007	603	254	1,053	14,109
1991	3,092	44,657	589	26,856	1,021	1,968	571	211	911	15,622
1992	2,585	47,397	567	28,750	941	1,840	324	142	753	16,665
1993	2,585	41,166	408	24,133	964	2,144	258	113	955	14,776
1994	2,309	36,568	309	18,124	928	2,357	308	185	764	15,902
1995	2,436	33,658	256	15,263	1,077	2,842	292	194	811	15,359
1996	2,235	36,247	269	17,564	1,130	3,127	278	193	558	15,363
1997	2,777	42,614	374	25,810	1,569	4,674	346	231	488	11,899
1998	3,560	55,286	559	36,880	2,220	5,874	363	252	418	12,280
1999	3,823	58,136	620	38,475	2,525	7,935	345	200	333	11,526
2000, est.	3,772	50,481	489	31,171	2,490	8,040	493	270	300	11,500

[1] Excludes off-the-shelf military aircraft.

Source: U.S. Department of Commerce, International Trade Administration, Internet site <http://www.ita.doc.gov/td/aerospace/inform/information.htm>.

No. 1014. Aerospace Industry Sales by Product Group and Customer: 1990 to 2001

[In billions of dollars (134.4 represents $134,400,000,000). Due to reporting practices and tabulating methods, figures may differ from those in Table 1081]

Product group and customer	Current dollars					Constant (1987) dollars [3]				
	1990	1995	1999	2000 [1]	2001 [2]	1990	1995	1999	2000 [1]	2001 [2]
Total sales.	134.4	107.8	151.1	143.7	145.3	123.7	86.6	116.8	109.7	108.8
PRODUCT GROUP										
Aircraft, total	71.4	55.0	86.7	78.1	80.9	65.7	44.2	67.0	59.6	60.6
Civil [4]	31.3	24.0	51.4	45.6	47.6	28.8	19.2	39.8	34.8	35.6
Military	40.1	31.1	35.2	32.5	33.4	36.9	25.0	27.2	24.8	25.0
Missiles	14.2	7.4	8.9	9.7	9.4	13.1	5.9	6.8	7.4	7.0
Space	26.4	27.4	30.4	32.0	30.8	24.4	22.0	23.5	24.4	23.0
Related products and services [5] . .	22.4	18.0	25.2	24.0	24.2	20.6	14.4	19.5	18.3	18.1
CUSTOMER GROUP										
Aerospace, total	112.0	89.8	125.9	119.8	121.1	103.1	71.5	97.3	91.4	90.6
DOD [6]	60.5	42.4	45.1	45.4	47.6	55.7	33.7	34.8	34.6	35.6
NASA [7] and other agencies . . .	11.1	11.4	13.3	12.9	11.4	10.0	9.1	10.3	9.8	8.5
Other customers [8]	40.4	36.0	67.5	61.5	62.1	36.5	28.6	52.2	47.0	46.5
Related products and services [5] . .	22.4	18.0	24.7	24.0	24.2	20.6	14.4	19.5	18.3	18.1

[1] Preliminary. [2] Estimate. [3] Based on AIA's aerospace composite price deflator. [4] All civil sales of aircraft (domestic and export sales of jet transports, commuters, business, and personal aircraft and helicopters). [5] Electronics, software, and ground support equipment, plus sales of nonaerospace products which are produced by aerospace-manufacturing use technology, processes, and materials derived from aerospace products. [6] Department of Defense. [7] National Aeronautics and Space Administration. [8] Includes civil aircraft sales (see footnote 4), commercial space sales, all exports of military aircraft and missiles and related propulsion and parts.
Source: Aerospace Industries Association of America, Inc., Washington, DC, *2000 Year-End Review and Forecast*, Internet site <http://www.aia-aerospace.org>

No. 1015. Firearms Manufacturers—Shipments, Exports, and Imports: 1980 to 1998

[In thousands of units (5,645 represents 5,645,000)]

Year	Shipments				Exports				Imports [1]			
	Total	Hand-guns	Rifles	Shot-guns	Total	Hand-guns	Rifles	Shot-guns	Total	Hand-guns	Rifles	Shot-guns
1980	5,645	2,370	1,936	1,339	517	220	171	127	754	299	182	273
1985	3,460	1,550	1,141	770	183	95	44	45	697	229	271	197
1986	3,040	1,428	971	641	217	121	37	59	701	231	269	201
1987	3,523	1,659	1,006	858	242	159	42	41	1,064	342	414	308
1988	3,818	1,746	1,145	928	254	132	54	69	1,276	622	283	372
1989	4,374	2,031	1,407	936	259	118	73	68	1,008	440	293	274
1990	3,844	1,839	1,156	849	354	178	72	104	844	449	204	192
1991	3,550	1,838	883	828	398	190	91	118	721	293	311	116
1992	4,030	2,010	1,002	1,018	398	189	90	119	2,847	982	1,423	442
1993	5,130	2,825	1,160	1,145	414	149	94	171	3,043	1,205	1,593	246
1994	5,161	2,582	1,324	1,255	401	173	82	147	1,881	915	848	118
1995	4,228	1,723	1,332	1,174	420	230	89	101	1,103	706	261	136
1996	3,835	1,484	1,424	926	326	154	75	97	882	491	263	128
1997	3,574	1,407	1,251	916	271	108	77	86	939	474	359	106
1998	3,645	1,240	1,536	869	200	45	66	90	1,000	532	249	219

[1] 1980-1991, imports are on fiscal year basis; thereafter, calendar year.
Source: U.S. Department of Treasury, Bureau of Alcohol, Tobacco, and Firearms, *Commerce in Firearms in the United States*, February 2000.

No. 1016. Selected Industrial Air Pollution Control Equipment—Shipments: 1998

[Quantity in number of units, value in thousands of dollars (848,174 represents $858,174,000)]

Product	Product code	Number of companies	New orders		Shipments		Backlog (Dec. 31)	
			Quantity	Value	Quantity	Value	Quantity	Value
Total.	(X)	110	(S)	848,174	(S)	844,463	(S)	414,273
Particulate emissions collectors	(X)	86	81,718	511,142	82,013	534,885	11,177	173,440
Electrostatic precipitators	3334111111	14	(D)	(D)	(D)	(D)	(D)	(D)
Fabric filters	3334111114	55	64,888	302,920	65,096	302,850	9,614	72,808
Mechanical collectors	3334111116	34	(D)	(D)	(D)	(D)	(D)	(D)
Wet scrubbers	3334111119	26	1,323	57,706	1,362	42,406	182	32,800
Gaseous emissions control devices . . .	(X)	38	(S)	237,300	(S)	203,048	(S)	217,974
Catalytic oxidation systems	333411111C	11	(D)	(D)	(D)	(D)	(D)	(D)
Nitric oxide (NO) control systems . . .	333411111E	2	(D)	(D)	(D)	(D)	(D)	(D)
Thermal & direct oxidation systems . .	333411111G	17	(S)	61,614	(S)	73,776	(S)	37,719
Scrubbers (gas absorber)	333411111J	11	436	24,494	461	21,678	114	12,473
Wet flue gas desulfurization systems .	333411111N	3	(D)	(D)	(D)	(D)	(D)	(D)
Dry flue gas desulfurization systems .	333411111P	2	(D)	(D)	(D)	(D)	(D)	(D)
Gas absorbers.	333411111R	8	36	14,899	47	14,631	15	9,372
Other	333411111U	16	(S)	99,732	(S)	106,530	(S)	22,859

D Data withheld to avoid disclosure of company data. S Does not meet publication standards. X Not applicable.
Source: U.S. Census Bureau, *Manufacturing Profiles*, Series MP, annual; and <http://www.census.gov/ftp/pub/industry/1/ma35j98.pdf> (released February 2000). Note: 1998 is the last report in the series.

This section presents statistics relating to the distributive trades, specifically wholesale trade and retail trade. Service industries that were formerly included in this section, may now be found in new Section 27, Accommodation, Food Services, and Other Services. Data shown for the trades are classified by kind of business and cover sales or receipts, establishments, employees, payrolls, and other items. The principal sources of these data are from the Census Bureau and include the *1997 Economic Census* reports, annual survey reports, and the *County Business Patterns* program. These data are supplemented by several tables from trade associations such as the National Automobile Dealers Association (Table 1026), and the National Mail Order Association (Table 1041). Several notable research groups are also represented such as Claritas (Table 1024), Simmons Market Research Bureau (Tables 1042 to 1044), National Research Bureau and the International Council of Shopping Centers (Tables 1045 and 1046), Jupiter Communications (Table 1035), and Forrester Research, Inc. (Table 1036).

Data on retail and wholesale trade appear in several other sections. For instance, labor force employment and earnings data (Table 609) appear in Section 12, Labor Force; gross domestic product of the industry (Table 641) appear in the Section 13, Income, Expenditures, and Wealth; financial data (several tables) from the quarterly *Statistics of Income Bulletin,* published by the Internal Revenue Service, appear in Section 15, Business Enterprise.

Censuses—Censuses of retail trade and wholesale trade have been taken at various intervals since 1929. Beginning with the 1967 census, legislation provides for a census of each area to be conducted every 5 years (for years ending in "2" and "7"). For more information on these censuses, see the *History of the 1997 Economic Census* found at <http://www.census.gov/prod/ec97/pol00-hec.pdf>.

The industries covered in the censuses and surveys of business are those classified in 13 sectors defined in the *North American Industry Classification System,* called NAICS (see below). *Retail trade* refers to places of business primarily engaged in retailing merchandise generally in small quantities to the general public; *wholesale trade,* to establishments primarily engaged in selling goods to other businesses and normally operate from a warehouse or office that have little or no display of merchandise; and *services,* to establishments primarily engaged in providing a wide range of services for individuals and for businesses. All Census Bureau tables in this section are utilizing the new NAICS codes, which replaced the Standard Industrial Classification (SIC) system. NAICS makes substantial structural improvements and identifies over 350 new industries. At the same time, it causes breaks in time series far more profound than any prior revision of the previously used SIC system. For information on this system and how it affects the comparability of retail and wholesale statistics historically, see text, Section 15, Business Enterprise, and especially the Census Bureau Web site at <http://www.census.gov/epcd/www/naics.html>. In general, the 1997 Economic Census has two series of publications and documents for these two sectors subject series with reports on such as commodity line sales and establishment and firm sizes and geographic reports with individual reports for each state. For information on these series, see the Census Bureau Web site at <http://www.census.gov/epcd/www/97EC42.htm> and <http://www.census.gov/epcd/www/97EC44.htm>.

Current surveys—Current sample surveys conducted by the Census Bureau cover various aspects of the retail and wholesale trade and selected service industries. Its *Monthly Retail Trade and Food Services* contains monthly estimates of sales, inventories, and inventory/sales ratios, purchases, and accounts receivable

Domestic Trade **639**

for the United States, by kind of business. Annual figures on sales, year-end inventories, and inventory/sales ratios, by kind of business, appear in the *Annual Benchmark Report for Retail Trade and Food Services*. Statistics from the Bureau's monthly wholesale trade survey include national estimates of merchant wholesalers' sales, inventories, and inventory/sales ratios by major summary groups "durable and nondurable," and selected kinds of business. Merchant wholesalers are those wholesalers who take title to the goods they sell (e.g., jobbers, exporters, importers, industrial distributors). These data, based on reports submitted by a sample of firms, appear in the *Monthly Wholesale Trade Report*. Annual figures on sales, inventory/sales ratios, year-end inventories, and purchases appear in the *Annual Benchmark Report for Wholesale Trade*. The reports just mentioned may appear in print in some cases, but principally are available as documents on the Census Bureau Web site at <http://www.census.gov/econ/www/retmenu.html>.

E-commerce—Electronic commerce (or e-commerce) are sales of goods and services over the Internet and extranet,

electronic data interchange (EDI), or other online systems. Payment may or may not be made online. This edition again has several new tables on e-commerce sales such as Tables 1037 to 1039 in this section, 976 in Section 21, Manufactures, and 1265 in the new Section 27, Accomodation, Food Services, and Other Services. Also, there are several private sources for similar data such as Forrester Research Inc., Cambridge MA; BizRate.com, Los Angeles, CA; and Jupiter Communications, New York, NY. These sources show estimated and projected online retail sales by key categories from business to consumers or to other businesses. Their methods of collecting the data vary widely between the sources and consequently these estimates of this activity vary also. Users of these estimates may want to contact the sources for descriptions of their methodology.

Statistical reliability—For a discussion of statistical collection and estimation, sampling procedures, and measures of statistical reliability applicable to Census Bureau data, see Appendix III.

U.S. Census Bureau, Statistical Abstract of the United States: 2001

No. 1017. Retail Trade—Establishments, Employees, and Payroll: 1998 and 1999

[1,113.1 represents 1,113,100 except as indicated. Covers establishments with payroll. Employees are for the week including March 12. Most government employees are excluded. For statement on methodology, see Appendix III]

Kind of business	NAIC code [1]	Establishments (1,000) 1998	Establishments (1,000) 1999	Employees (1,000) 1998	Employees (1,000) 1999	Payroll (bil. dol.) 1998	Payroll (bil. dol.) 1999
Retail trade, total	44-45	1,113.1	1,111.3	14,241	14,477	260.3	281.9
Motor vehicle & parts dealers	441	123.4	123.9	1,757	1,804	55.6	60.2
Automobile dealers	4411	49.9	50.1	1,151	1,175	41.4	45.2
New car dealers	44111	26.2	26.1	1,050	1,070	38.9	42.3
Used car dealers	44112	23.7	24.0	102	105	2.6	2.9
Recreational vehicle dealers	44121	3.0	3.0	31	33	1.0	1.1
Motorcycle & boat & other MV dealers [2]	44122	10.8	11.0	76	82	2.0	2.3
Automotive parts, accessories & tire stores	4413	59.6	59.7	499	514	11.1	11.6
Automotive parts, accessories & tire stores	44131	41.9	41.9	345	354	7.2	7.4
Tire dealers	44132	17.8	17.8	153	160	3.9	4.2
Furniture & home furnishing stores	442	64.4	64.3	510	525	11.3	12.4
Furniture stores	4421	29.7	29.6	267	270	6.4	7.0
Home furnishings stores [2]	4422	34.7	34.7	243	255	4.9	5.4
Electronics & appliance stores	443	45.2	45.2	362	384	8.6	9.6
Appliance, TV & all other electronics stores	44311	28.8	29.0	238	258	5.1	5.9
Computer & software stores	44312	13.2	13.0	103	105	3.1	3.2
Camera & photographic supplies stores	44313	3.2	3.1	20	21	0.4	0.4
Bldg material & garden equip & supp dealers	444	92.8	92.3	1,131	1,184	27.8	30.2
Building material & supplies dealers	4441	71.5	71.2	964	1,012	24.3	26.4
Home centers	44411	3.9	4.4	284	325	5.6	6.8
Paint & wallpaper stores	44412	8.4	8.4	44	43	1.0	1.1
Hardware stores	44413	15.4	15.3	139	145	-2.2	2.3
Other building material dealers	44419	43.8	43.2	496	499	15.4	16.2
Lawn & garden equip & supplies stores	4442	21.3	21.1	168	172	3.5	3.8
Nursery & garden centers	44422	16.5	16.4	141	144	2.9	3.2
Food & beverage stores	445	147.7	151.5	2,944	3,015	43.3	45.9
Grocery stores	4451	96.2	97.4	2,689	2,743	39.7	41.9
Grocery (except convenience) stores	44511	68.5	69.0	2,533	2,584	38.0	39.9
Convenience stores	44512	27.7	28.4	156	159	1.8	1.9
Specialty food stores	4452	23.6	25.9	126	141	1.7	2.1
Meat markets	44521	6.6	6.5	39	40	0.6	0.6
Fish & seafood markets	44522	1.8	1.8	8	8	0.1	0.1
Fruit & vegetable markets	44523	3.2	3.2	18	18	0.3	0.3
Other specialty food stores [2]	44529	12.0	14.4	61	75	0.7	1.1
Beer, wine & liquor stores [3]	4453	27.9	28.1	129	131	1.8	1.9
Health & personal care stores [2]	446	82.7	82.4	940	938	16.1	17.8
Pharmacies & drug stores	44611	42.6	41.8	723	709	12.0	13.4
Cosmetics, beauty supplies & perfume stores	44612	9.5	9.6	58	62	0.7	0.8
Optical goods stores	44613	14.7	14.7	74	76	1.6	1.6
Gasoline stations	447	123.9	121.1	946	930	12.3	12.8
Gasoline stations with convenience stores	44711	82.2	81.5	647	646	8.0	8.4
Clothing & clothing accessories stores	448	152.6	151.7	1,280	1,293	17.8	19.1
Clothing stores	4481	92.8	91.0	929	944	12.1	13.0
Men's clothing stores	44811	11.9	11.4	87	85	1.4	1.5
Women's clothing stores	44812	37.4	36.2	294	284	3.5	3.7
Children's & infants' clothing stores	44813	5.2	5.3	47	51	0.5	0.6
Family clothing stores	44814	20.8	20.9	394	420	5.2	5.7
Clothing accessories stores	44815	5.8	5.5	29	29	0.4	0.4
Shoe stores	4482	29.6	30.0	196	189	2.5	2.6
Jewelry, luggage & leather goods stores	4483	30.2	30.6	156	161	3.2	3.6
Jewelry stores	44831	28.1	28.6	144	149	3.0	3.3
Luggage & leather goods stores	44832	2.1	2.0	12	12	0.2	0.2
Sporting goods, hobby, book & music stores	451	68.1	66.1	580	590	7.9	8.2
Sporting goods, hobby, musical instrument stores	4511	45.8	44.2	378	383	5.4	5.7
Sporting goods stores	45111	24.1	23.1	181	182	2.7	2.8
Hobby, toy & game stores	45112	10.9	10.8	119	125	1.6	1.7
Sewing, needlework & piece goods stores	45113	6.2	5.9	48	45	0.5	0.5
Musical instrument & supplies stores	45114	4.5	4.4	30	32	0.7	0.7
Book, periodical & music stores [2]	4512	22.3	21.8	201	207	2.5	2.6
Book stores & news dealers	45121	14.4	14.1	137	140	1.7	1.8
General merchandise stores	452	36.7	38.1	2,479	2,445	33.7	36.6
Department stores	4521	10.5	10.5	1,784	1,731	23.5	25.3
Other general merchandise stores	4529	26.2	27.6	696	714	10.2	11.2
Miscellaneous store retailers	453	132.4	131.2	796	829	11.9	13.0
Florists	4531	25.6	24.8	123	122	1.5	1.5
Office supplies, stationery & gift stores	4532	44.3	43.6	324	339	4.3	4.8
Office supplies & stationery stores	45321	7.7	8.4	110	124	2.0	2.4
Gift, novelty & souvenir stores	45322	36.6	35.2	214	215	2.3	2.4
Used merchandise stores	4533	18.2	18.0	105	110	1.4	1.5
Other miscellaneous store retailers	4539	44.3	44.8	243	258	4.7	5.1
Pet & pet supplies stores	45391	8.5	8.2	64	66	0.8	0.9
Art dealers	45392	5.9	5.9	22	25	0.5	0.6
Manufactured (mobile) home dealers	45393	5.7	6.0	43	46	1.3	1.4
Nonstore retailers	454	43.3	43.6	515	540	14.2	16.1
Electronic shopping & mail-order houses	4541	9.8	10.6	230	255	7.3	8.9
Vending machine operators	4542	6.4	6.3	66	67	1.4	1.5
Direct selling establishments	4543	27.1	26.7	219	218	5.5	5.8
Fuel dealers	45431	12.5	12.2	106	107	2.9	3.0
Other direct selling establishments	45439	14.6	14.5	113	111	2.6	2.8

[1] Based on North American Industrial Classification System; see text, Section 15, Business Enterprise   [2] Includes kinds of business not shown separately.   [3] Includes government employees.

Source: U.S. Census Bureau, *County Business Patterns*, annual.

U.S. Census Bureau, Statistical Abstract of the United States: 2001

No. 1018. Retail Trade—Establishments, Sales, Payroll, and Employees by Kind of Business: 1997

Kind of business	NAICS code [1]	Establishments (number)	Sales Total (mil. dol.)	Sales Per paid employee (dol.)	Annual payroll Total (mil. dol.)	Annual payroll Per paid employee (dol.)	Paid employee for pay period including March 12 (1,000)
Retail trade	44-45	1,118,447	2,460,886	175,889	237,196	16,953	13,991.1
Motor vehicle & parts dealers	441	122,633	645,368	375,440	50,239	29,226	1,719.0
Automobile dealers	4411	49,237	553,652	486,088	37,400	32,836	1,139.0
New car dealers	44111	25,897	518,972	496,034	35,203	33,647	1,046.2
Used car dealers	44112	23,340	34,680	373,905	2,197	23,691	92.8
Other motor vehicle dealers	4412	13,589	28,891	281,124	2,570	25,007	102.8
Recreational vehicle dealers	44121	3,014	10,070	341,776	814	27,627	29.5
Motorcycle, boat, & other motor vehicle dealers	44122	10,575	18,821	256,746	1,756	23,954	73.3
Automotive parts, accessories, & tire stores	4413	59,807	62,825	131,653	10,269	21,519	477.2
Automotive parts & accessories stores	44131	42,519	43,166	129,024	6,718	20,081	334.6
Tire dealers	44132	17,288	19,659	137,821	3,551	24,892	142.6
Furniture & home furnishings stores	442	64,725	71,691	148,476	9,959	20,627	482.8
Furniture stores	4421	29,461	40,968	163,026	5,620	22,362	251.3
Home furnishings stores	4422	35,264	30,722	132,685	4,340	18,743	231.5
Floor covering stores	44221	16,603	16,472	171,250	2,458	25,557	96.2
Other home furnishings stores	44229	18,661	14,251	105,281	1,882	13,901	135.4
Electronics & appliance stores	443	43,373	68,561	198,704	7,064	20,473	345.0
Appliance, television, & other electronics stores	44311	28,789	42,251	178,249	4,462	18,826	237.0
Computer & software stores	44312	11,741	24,059	265,839	2,278	25,168	90.5
Camera & photographic supplies stores	44313	2,843	2,252	128,609	324	18,504	17.5
Building material & garden equipment & supplies dealers	444	93,117	227,566	203,564	25,609	22,908	1,117.9
Building material & supplies dealers	4441	71,916	195,888	205,701	22,313	23,431	952.3
Home centers	44411	3,997	51,628	181,883	4,996	17,602	283.9
Paint & wallpaper stores	44412	8,429	7,943	182,536	1,011	23,235	43.5
Hardware stores	44413	15,748	13,605	98,710	2,095	15,202	137.8
Other building material dealers	44419	43,742	122,712	251,925	14,210	29,173	487.1
Lawn & garden equipment & supplies stores	4442	21,201	31,678	191,273	3,296	19,900	165.6
Outdoor power equipment stores	44421	4,769	4,069	153,676	535	20,222	26.5
Nursery & garden centers	44422	16,432	27,609	198,428	2,760	19,839	139.1
Food & beverage stores	445	148,528	401,764	138,871	40,581	14,027	2,893.1
Grocery stores	4451	96,542	368,250	139,298	37,426	14,157	2,643.6
Supermarkets & other grocery (except convenience) stores	44511	69,461	351,403	141,141	35,828	14,390	2,489.7
Convenience stores	44512	27,081	16,848	109,481	1,598	10,387	153.9
Specialty food stores	4452	22,373	10,830	91,137	1,456	12,250	118.8
Meat markets	44521	7,214	4,347	109,041	544	13,656	39.9
Fish & seafood markets	44522	1,634	1,038	145,724	102	14,316	7.1
Fruit & vegetable markets	44523	3,179	2,107	122,128	237	13,736	17.3
Other specialty food stores	44529	10,346	3,339	61,152	572	10,483	54.6
Beer, wine, & liquor stores	4453	29,613	22,684	173,645	1,699	13,008	130.6
Health & personal care stores	446	82,941	117,701	130,244	15,191	16,809	903.7
Pharmacies & drug stores	44611	43,615	98,631	140,150	11,588	16,465	703.8
Cosmetics, beauty supplies, & perfume stores	44612	9,014	4,419	94,977	604	12,973	46.5
Optical goods stores	44613	15,192	6,432	88,052	1,401	19,182	73.0
Other health & personal care stores	44619	15,120	8,219	102,269	1,598	19,888	80.4
Gasoline stations	447	126,889	198,166	214,916	11,482	12,453	922.1
Gasoline stations with convenience stores	44711	81,684	127,609	207,847	7,229	11,774	614.0
Other gasoline stations	44719	45,205	70,557	229,002	4,254	13,805	308.1
Clothing & clothing accessories stores	448	156,601	136,398	106,548	16,597	12,965	1,280.2
Clothing stores	4481	94,740	95,918	103,368	11,225	12,097	927.9
Mens clothing stores	44811	12,143	9,865	118,025	1,325	15,855	83.6
Womens clothing stores	44812	39,672	27,258	89,169	3,366	11,011	305.7
Childrens & infants clothing stores	44813	5,115	4,638	99,699	474	10,198	46.5
Family clothing stores	44814	20,450	44,796	114,197	4,797	12,229	392.3
Clothing accessories stores	44815	5,860	2,132	82,794	314	12,184	25.8
Other clothing stores	44819	11,500	7,229	97,535	949	12,799	74.1
Shoe stores	4482	31,399	20,543	110,565	2,349	12,640	185.8
Jewelry, luggage, & leather goods stores	4483	30,462	19,936	119,795	3,024	18,169	166.4
Jewelry stores	44831	28,336	18,511	119,523	2,836	18,311	154.9
Luggage & leather goods stores	44832	2,126	1,425	123,448	188	16,259	11.5
Sporting goods, hobby, book, & music stores	451	69,149	62,011	110,568	7,113	12,683	560.8
Sporting goods, hobby, & musical instrument stores	4511	46,315	41,415	114,100	4,819	13,276	363.0
Sporting goods stores	45111	24,424	20,043	113,760	2,388	13,553	176.2
Hobby, toy, & game stores	45112	10,824	14,388	128,746	1,369	12,247	111.8

See footnotes at end of table.

U.S. Census Bureau, Statistical Abstract of the United States: 2001

No. 1018. Retail Trade—Establishments, Sales, Payroll, and Employees by Kind of Business: 1997—Con.

Kind of business	NAICS code [1]	Estab- lish- ments (number)	Sales		Annual payroll		Paid employee for pay period including March 12 (1,000)
			Total (mil. dol.)	Per paid employee (dol.)	Total (mil. dol.)	Per paid employee (dol.)	
Sewing, needlework, & piece goods stores	45113	6,590	3,183	70,184	495	10,910	45.4
Musical instrument & supplies stores	45114	4,477	3,801	128,078	567	19,119	29.7
Book, periodical, & music stores	4512	22,834	20,596	104,089	2,295	11,597	197.9
Book stores & news dealers	45121	14,676	13,229	100,797	1,567	11,936	131.2
Prerecorded tape, compact disc, & record stores	45122	8,158	7,367	110,575	728	10,927	66.6
General merchandise stores	452	36,171	330,444	131,780	30,871	12,311	2,507.5
Department stores (incl leased depts) [2]	4521	10,366	223,232	(NA)	(NA)	(NA)	(NA)
Department stores (excl leased depts)	4521	10,366	220,108	122,584	22,083	12,299	1,795.6
Other general merchandise stores	4529	25,805	110,336	154,975	8,788	12,343	712.0
Warehouse clubs & superstores	45291	1,530	81,919	191,239	5,863	13,686	428.4
All other general merchandise stores	45299	24,275	28,418	100,201	2,925	10,314	283.6
Miscellaneous store retailers	453	129,838	78,109	103,733	10,165	13,500	753.0
Florists	4531	26,200	6,555	52,359	1,396	11,154	125.2
Office supplies, stationery, & gift stores	4532	44,615	31,573	103,014	3,637	11,868	306.5
Office supplies & stationery stores	45321	7,330	17,076	174,027	1,581	16,110	98.1
Gift, novelty, & souvenir stores	45322	37,285	14,497	69,574	2,057	9,870	208.4
Used merchandise stores	4533	17,990	6,044	61,692	1,204	12,286	98.0
Other miscellaneous store retailers	4539	41,033	33,937	151,958	3,928	17,588	223.3
Pet & pet supplies stores	45391	8,318	5,493	89,763	709	11,588	61.2
Art dealers	45392	5,698	3,001	153,808	401	20,561	19.5
Manufactured (mobile) home dealers	45393	5,485	13,347	330,375	1,123	27,790	40.4
All other miscellaneous store retailers	45399	21,532	12,096	118,324	1,695	16,581	102.2
Nonstore retailers	454	44,482	123,107	243,297	12,323	24,355	506.0
Electronic shopping & mail-order houses	4541	10,013	79,018	361,795	5,743	26,297	218.4
Vending machine operators	4542	7,070	6,884	103,763	1,333	20,097	66.3
Direct selling establishments	4543	27,399	37,204	168,161	5,246	23,714	221.2
Fuel dealers	45431	12,532	22,622	217,987	2,755	26,550	103.8
Other direct selling establishments	45439	14,867	14,582	124,140	2,491	21,209	117.5

NA Not available. [1] North American Industry Classification System, 1997; see text, Section 15 Business Enterprise. [2] Not included in broader kind of business.

Source: U.S. Census Bureau, *1997 Economic Census, Retail Trade,* Series EC97R44A-US(RV), issued March 2000.

No. 1019. Retail Trade and Food Service—Estimated Per Capita Sales by Selected Kinds of Business: 1992 to 2000

[As of Dec. 31. Based on estimated resident as of July 1 population estimates]

Kind of business	NAICS code [1]	1992	1993	1994	1995	1996	1997	1998	1999	2000
Total	44-45	7,304	7,717	8,293	8,640	9,101	9,415	9,791	10,545	11,254
Total (Excluding motor vehicle and parts dealers)	44-45, ex 441	5,617	5,837	6,168	6,391	6,694	6,936	7,191	7,675	8,218
Motor vehicle and parts dealers	441	1,687	1,880	2,125	2,249	2,407	2,479	2,600	2,870	3,036
Furniture, home furnishings	442	217	226	242	251	263	278	292	312	335
Electronics and appliance stores	443	169	190	222	248	260	263	282	301	320
Building material and garden equipment and supply stores	444	632	670	737	761	806	861	905	972	1,012
Food and beverage stores	445	1,466	1,465	1,488	1,497	1,523	1,539	1,567	1,626	1,699
Health and personal care stores	446	358	365	376	392	418	447	484	536	578
Gasoline stations	447	618	634	662	693	737	750	713	766	891
Clothing and clothing accessories stores	448	475	488	499	503	519	527	555	588	615
Sporting goods, hobby, book, and music stores	451	195	204	222	233	243	246	258	271	291
General merchandise stores	452	978	1,038	1,102	1,150	1,195	1,244	1,308	1,404	1,489
Miscellaneous store retailers	453	220	244	273	295	319	344	371	389	397
Nonstore retailers	454	290	312	345	367	413	437	455	509	592
Food services and drinking places	722	803	843	871	894	920	968	1,013	1,054	1,117

[1] North American Industry Classification System, 1997; see text, Section 15, Business Enterprise.

Source: U.S. Census Bureau, *Current Business Reports, Annual Benchmark Report for Retail Trade and Food Services, January 1992 Through December 2000* (BR/00-A) and Population Division, Population Estimates Program.

Domestic Trade   643

No. 1020. Retail Trade and Food Services—Sales by Kind of Business: 1992 to 2000

[In billions of dollars (2,054.6 represents $2,054,600,000)]

Kind of business	NAICS code [1]	1992	1994	1995	1996	1997	1998	1999	2000
Retail and food services, total	44, 45, 72	2,054.6	2,372.8	2,492.4	2,645.2	2,767.4	2,906.7	3,149.2	3,388.8
Retail trade total	44, 45	1,851.2	2,147.2	2,258.8	2,402.3	2,509.3	2,634.1	2,863.0	3,082.8
GAFO, total [2]	(X)	536.9	619.6	653.0	685.3	715.7	762.6	821.3	877.7
Motor vehicle and parts dealers	441	427.6	550.1	588.0	635.3	660.7	699.5	779.2	831.8
Automobile and other motor vehicle dealers	4411, 4412	377.2	492.8	528.7	572.9	596.3	631.9	707.6	758.1
Automobile dealers	4411	359.1	468.9	502.5	544.8	565.5	597.5	669.3	713.3
Auto parts, access., and tire stores	4413	50.4	57.3	59.3	62.3	64.4	67.6	71.6	73.7
Furniture, home furnishings, electronics, and appliance stores	442, 443	97.8	120.2	130.4	137.9	144.3	154.6	166.5	179.3
Furniture and home furnishings stores	442	55.0	62.8	65.5	69.4	74.1	78.6	84.8	91.7
Furniture stores	4421	31.6	35.6	37.0	39.2	41.9	44.1	46.6	49.8
Home furnishings stores	4422	23.4	27.2	28.5	30.2	32.1	34.4	38.3	41.9
Electronics and appliance stores	443	42.8	57.4	64.9	68.5	70.2	76.0	81.7	87.6
Appl., TV., and other elect. stores	44311	29.0	37.9	42.1	43.3	43.1	46.3	51.4	57.7
Computer and software stores	44312	11.5	17.2	20.5	22.9	24.8	27.2	27.6	26.9
Building mat., garden equip., & supply stores	444	160.2	190.8	199.1	212.8	229.5	243.5	264.0	277.2
Building mat. & supply dealers	4441	135.5	165.2	172.3	183.3	197.4	210.0	229.7	240.3
Food and beverage stores	445	371.5	385.3	391.3	402.0	410.3	421.6	441.4	465.3
Grocery stores	4451	337.9	351.1	356.9	366.1	373.1	382.4	400.7	421.9
Beer, wine, and liquor stores	4453	21.8	22.2	22.1	23.3	24.2	25.7	26.9	28.8
Health and personal care stores	446	90.8	97.3	102.5	110.2	119.1	130.2	145.6	158.4
Gasoline stations	447	156.6	171.4	181.3	194.6	199.9	191.7	207.8	244.0
Clothing and clothing access stores	448	120.3	129.3	131.6	136.9	140.6	149.4	159.7	168.5
Clothing stores	4481	85.9	90.8	91.4	94.5	98.5	104.9	112.2	119.3
Shoe stores	4482	18.1	19.4	19.8	20.6	20.8	21.5	21.8	22.1
Sporting goods, hobby, book & music stores	451	49.3	57.5	60.9	64.1	65.6	69.5	73.7	79.6
General merchandise stores	452	248.0	285.3	300.6	315.4	331.5	351.8	381.1	407.8
Department stores (excl. L.D.)	4521	177.1	200.4	207.7	213.9	220.1	221.2	226.3	236.9
Department stores (incl. L.D.)	4521	181.3	205.3	212.8	218.7	225.1	226.0	231.2	242.0
Discount dept. stores	4521102	93.9	113.3	120.5	123.7	128.0	128.5	130.9	140.9
Other general merchandise stores	4529	70.9	84.9	92.9	101.5	111.3	130.6	154.8	170.9
Warehouse clubs and superstores	45291	40.0	56.3	63.3	71.4	81.9	101.2	123.6	136.8
Miscellaneous stores retail	453	55.8	70.6	77.2	84.1	91.7	99.8	105.6	108.6
Nonstore retailers	454	73.4	89.4	95.9	109.1	116.4	122.5	138.3	162.2
Electronic shopping and mail order	4541	35.3	47.1	52.7	61.2	70.1	79.5	92.9	110.0
Fuel dealers	45431	19.3	20.8	21.6	24.1	22.9	19.7	20.7	27.5
Food services and drinking places .	722	203.4	225.6	233.6	242.9	258.0	272.6	286.3	306.1
Full service restaurants	7221	86.5	97.1	99.4	104.5	114.6	119.7	124.5	134.4
Limited service eating places	7222	87.4	98.4	103.1	106.2	109.3	116.8	123.1	127.5
Drinking places	7224	12.4	11.8	12.5	13.0	13.4	14.1	14.8	16.5

X Not applicable.   [1] North American Industry Classification System, 1997; see text, Section 15, Business Enterprise.
[2] GAFO represents store classified in the following NAICS codes: 442,443,448,451,452, and 4532

Source: U.S. Census Bureau, *Current Business Reports, Annual Benchmark Report for Retail Trade and Food Services, January 1992 Through December 2000* (BR/00-A) and Population Division, Population Estimates Program.

No. 1021. Retail Trade—Merchandise Inventories and Inventory/Sales Ratio by Kind of Business: 1992 to 2000

[267.6 represents $267,600,000,000. As of Dec. 31. Includes warehouses. Adjusted for seasonal variations. Sales data also adjusted for holiday and trading-day differences]

Kind of business	NAICS code [1]	Inventories at cost [2] (bil. dol.)				Inventory/sales ratios			
		1992	1995	1999	2000	1992	1995	1999	2000
Total	44, 45	267.6	329.6	391.8	417.9	1.68	1.70	1.56	1.62
Excluding motor vehicle and parts dealers	44, 45 ex 441	196.2	234.5	274.3	285.8	1.61	1.64	1.51	1.51
Motor vehicle and parts dealers	441	71.4	95.1	117.5	132.1	1.92	1.87	1.72	1.92
Furniture, home furnishings, electronics, and appliance stores	442, 443	16.4	22.0	23.8	24.6	1.97	1.95	1.64	1.69
Building material and garden equipment and supplies dealers	444	25.3	31.2	38.9	40.9	1.92	1.81	1.70	1.75
Food and beverage stores	445	27.5	28.8	33.3	33.4	0.88	0.87	0.86	0.84
Clothing and clothing accessories stores . .	448	27.2	29.1	33.0	35.2	2.62	2.59	2.45	2.47
General merchandise stores	452	48.9	59.3	64.4	65.8	2.25	2.32	1.96	1.93
Department stores (ex. L.D.)	4521	37.1	43.0	42.8	43.3	2.41	2.46	2.24	2.20

[1] North American Industry Classification System, 1997; see text, Section 15, Business Enterprise.

Source: U.S. Census Bureau, *Current Business Reports, Annual Benchmark Report for Retail Trade and Food Services; January 1992 Through December 2000* (BR/00-A) and unpublished data.

No. 1022. Retail Trade—Estimated Purchases by Kind of Business: 1992 to 1999

[In billions of dollars (1,345.2 represents $1,345,200,000). As of Dec. 31]

Kind of business	NAICS code [1]	1992	1993	1994	1995	1996	1997	1998	1999
Total.................	44-45	1,345.2	1,442.6	1,570.0	1,643.9	1,747.9	1,828.7	1,916.3	2,092.0
Motor vehicle and parts dealers	441	342.0	387.2	443.2	470.6	509.7	533.9	567.9	634.4
Furniture and home furnishings stores	442	32.2	34.3	36.8	38.4	40.7	43.2	45.4	48.8
Building material, garden equipment and supplies dealers..............	444	115.7	124.9	138.8	145.1	155.0	169.7	177.9	193.1
Food and beverage stores............	445	279.2	281.9	289.0	290.4	298.3	303.7	310.0	323.5
Clothing and clothing accessories stores ..	448	71.7	74.3	76.8	78.3	81.0	83.5	87.3	92.5
General merchandise stores..........	452	181.3	194.8	211.8	222.4	232.1	243.0	257.0	280.3

[1] North American Industry Classification System, 1997; see text, Section 15, Business Enterprise.
Source: U.S. Census Bureau, *Current Business Reports, Annual Benchmark Report for Retail Trade and Food Services, January 1992 Through December 2000* (BR/00-A) and unpublished data.

No. 1023. Retail Trade—Establishments and Sales by Merchandise Lines: 1997

[Covers only establishments with payroll]

Merchandise lines	NAICS code [1] and ML code [2]	Establishments handling merchandise line		Merchandise line sales		
					As a percentage of total sales of—	
		Number	Total sales (mil. dol.)	Amount (mil. dol.)	Establishments handling line	All establishments
Retail trade	**44-45**	**1,118,447**	(X)	**2,460,886**	(X)	**100.0**
Groceries & other foods for human consumption off the premises........................	100	322,867	934,996	367,224	39.3	14.9
Meals, unpackaged snacks, sandwiches, & nonalcoholic beverages................	120	99,363	378,338	10,838	2.9	0.4
Alcoholic drinks (served at this establishment)....	130	1,583	1,352	176	13.0	(Z)
Packaged liquor, wine, & beer	140	148,792	467,821	41,951	9.0	1.7
Cigars, cigarettes, tobacco, & smokers accessories........................	150	234,100	777,117	36,819	4.7	1.5
Drugs, health aids, & beauty aids (including cosmetics).......................	160	231,126	872,109	159,483	18.3	6.5
Soaps, detergents, & household cleaners.......	180	125,320	620,828	19,195	3.1	0.8
Paper & related products..................	190	138,022	603,829	17,066	2.8	0.7
Men's wear........................	200	122,978	478,641	58,249	12.2	2.4
Womens, juniors, & misses wear	220	149,920	497,405	101,860	20.5	4.1
Childrens wear	240	78,123	387,512	27,365	7.1	1.1
Footwear (including accessories)	260	119,579	406,513	39,182	9.6	1.6
Sewing, knitting, & needlework goods	270	24,421	154,306	4,536	2.9	0.2
Curtains, draperies, blinds, slipcovers, & bed & table coverings	280	53,460	359,731	18,437	5.1	0.7
Major household appliances...............	300	40,835	164,558	18,926	11.5	0.8
Small electric appliances.................	310	60,039	395,104	6,992	1.8	0.3
Televisions, video recorders, video cameras, video tapes.........................	320	54,909	274,278	18,334	6.7	0.7
Audio equipment & musical instruments & supplies........................	330	71,151	227,531	27,657	12.2	1.1
Furniture & sleep equipment	340	73,407	302,790	47,541	15.7	1.9
Flooring & floor coverings	360	40,926	165,827	18,408	11.1	0.7
Computer hardware, software, & supplies.......	370	35,312	172,469	56,573	32.8	2.3
Kitchenware & home furnishings............	380	154,091	586,734	32,382	5.5	1.3
Jewelry	400	126,364	440,843	31,358	7.1	1.3
Books	420	64,954	296,122	15,772	5.3	0.6
Photographic equipment & supplies..........	440	43,295	321,637	5,665	1.8	0.2
Toys, hobby goods, & games..............	460	98,308	429,322	24,035	5.6	1.0
Optical goods	490	38,311	120,582	6,931	5.7	0.3
Sporting goods	500	74,961	351,311	35,612	10.1	1.4
Recreational vehicles, parts & accessories	580	4,905	25,643	10,013	39.0	0.4
Hardware, tools, & plumbing & electrical supplies .	600	100,472	507,610	76,821	15.1	3.1
Lawn, garden, & farm equipment & supplies, cut flowers, etc.	620	118,805	541,974	52,123	9.6	2.1
Dimensional lumber & other building/structural materials & supplies..................	640	52,367	164,323	96,583	58.8	3.9
Paint & sundries	670	43,962	165,900	15,005	9.0	0.6
Manufactured (mobile) homes	680	5,643	13,695	12,989	94.8	0.5
Wallpaper & other flexible wallcoverings........	690	11,614	17,126	1,069	6.2	(Z)
Automobiles, vans, trucks, & other powered trans. vehicles	700	55,920	566,370	483,863	85.4	19.7
Automotive fuels	720	137,668	248,978	143,818	57.8	5.8
Automotive lubricants (oil, greases, etc)	730	132,921	601,543	7,060	1.2	0.3
Automotive tires, tubes, batteries, parts, & accessories........................	740	152,701	773,034	82,182	10.6	3.3
Household fuels (oil, LP gas, wood, & coal)	780	36,928	65,038	18,628	28.6	0.8
Pets, pet foods, & pet supplies.............	800	87,399	420,812	12,923	3.1	0.5
All other merchandise..................	850	318,363	804,585	79,496	9.9	3.2

X Not applicable.   Z Less than half the unit shown.   [1] Based on North American Industrial Classification System; see text, Section 15, Business Enterprise.   [2] Merchandise line code.
Source: U.S. Census Bureau, *1997 Economic Census, Merchandise Line Sales*, Series EC97R445-LS(RV), January 2001.

Domestic Trade   645

No. 1024. Retail Trade and Food Services—Sales by Type of Store and State: 2000

[In millions of dollars (3,105,585 represents $3,105,585,000,000) except as indicated. Kind-of-business classification based on North American Industry Classification System (NAICS); see text, Section 15, Business Enterprise. Data are estimates]

State	All stores [1]	Total Retail sales + food and drink	Motor vehicle and parts dealers (NAICS 441)	Furniture and home furnishings (NAICS 442)	Electronics and appliances (NAICS 443)	Building and material supply (NAICS 444)	Food and beverage stores (NAICS 445)	Health and personal care (NAICS 446)
U.S...	3,105,585	3,409,490	927,141	90,503	88,676	298,604	464,288	152,780
AL	42,789	46,650	13,308	1,086	720	4,297	5,978	1,930
AK	7,391	8,248	1,800	117	164	930	1,421	121
AZ	59,816	65,186	18,740	1,906	1,746	5,219	8,791	2,682
AR	26,315	28,448	8,479	552	457	2,756	3,128	911
CA	342,523	384,052	100,228	10,645	15,446	30,644	55,203	17,000
CO	53,066	58,441	15,670	1,965	1,814	5,996	8,323	1,530
CT	43,611	47,287	12,251	1,311	1,318	4,214	7,230	2,485
DE	10,598	11,604	3,080	451	412	1,146	1,497	606
DC	2,911	4,183	146	116	86	234	888	344
FL	202,606	219,334	66,812	6,296	5,777	16,396	31,930	10,934
GA	94,148	102,979	29,741	3,283	2,467	10,900	13,688	3,531
HI.....	11,902	13,915	2,265	192	213	660	2,179	854
ID.....	14,446	15,561	4,509	386	360	1,846	2,121	336
IL.....	131,881	146,588	39,046	3,925	3,872	12,611	19,184	7,747
IN.....	70,788	77,273	22,011	1,696	1,613	7,440	8,640	3,580
IA	33,157	35,830	10,456	832	792	4,522	4,590	1,334
KS	28,707	31,281	8,653	800	858	2,647	4,150	1,065
KY	40,298	44,730	11,546	886	713	4,398	5,865	2,066
LA	43,395	47,947	13,505	961	759	4,199	6,383	2,059
ME	17,225	18,462	4,544	323	224	1,683	3,384	611
MD	56,305	62,221	16,016	1,753	1,908	5,000	10,539	2,989
MA	77,002	86,083	21,034	2,156	1,790	6,374	13,158	4,881
MI	118,280	128,395	38,392	3,277	2,999	10,636	13,851	7,140
MN	67,788	73,262	19,262	2,235	2,320	8,003	8,475	2,806
MS	27,372	29,405	8,479	690	420	3,029	3,994	1,142
MO	64,673	70,565	20,932	1,520	1,435	6,112	8,212	2,589
MT	8,972	9,909	2,571	216	195	1,206	1,587	258
NE	20,031	21,811	5,480	890	428	2,487	2,733	802
NV	24,434	26,949	6,713	692	761	2,363	3,745	968
NH	21,476	22,974	6,840	595	733	1,708	3,189	798
NJ....	74,338	80,398	20,344	2,262	2,333	5,247	14,283	5,107
NM	19,179	20,930	5,371	565	392	1,700	2,626	858
NY	175,762	195,188	43,073	5,325	5,185	14,750	28,985	13,249
NC	91,505	99,946	28,568	3,416	2,059	11,095	12,937	3,973
ND	7,732	8,319	2,210	182	166	1,430	823	339
OH	128,080	140,689	39,254	3,810	3,771	12,408	17,499	7,530
OK	34,054	37,131	11,491	882	907	2,784	4,253	1,419
OR	43,656	47,558	13,090	1,156	1,115	5,034	6,069	1,170
PA	130,198	141,941	39,213	3,086	2,694	11,785	20,735	8,060
RI.....	9,665	10,828	2,615	264	208	674	1,853	864
SC	43,865	48,131	12,942	1,233	771	5,788	6,566	1,860
SD	13,532	14,260	2,693	181	163	1,259	1,252	316
TN	66,237	72,660	20,515	1,828	1,207	6,307	10,622	2,916
TX	240,095	263,431	78,090	6,880	7,465	19,930	31,934	8,283
UT	26,101	28,030	7,713	1,019	834	3,018	4,544	408
VT	7,230	7,795	2,196	144	158	877	1,244	333
VA	74,982	82,071	21,181	2,588	2,509	7,420	11,190	3,266
WA	68,179	76,130	18,087	1,926	1,926	7,550	10,252	2,911
WV	17,252	18,754	5,065	334	235	1,661	2,648	1,196
WI.....	63,950	69,164	19,120	1,556	1,680	7,645	8,971	2,508
WY	6,083	6,565	1,804	114	96	587	947	114

See footnotes at end of table.

U.S. Census Bureau, Statistical Abstract of the United States: 2001

No. 1024. Retail Trade and Food Services—Sales by Type of Store and State: 2000—Con.

[See headnote, page 646]

State	Gasoline service stations (NAICS 447)	Clothing and accessories (NAICS 448)	Sporting goods, hobby, book, & music stores (NAICS 451)	General merchandise (NAICS 452)	Miscellaneous stores (NAICS 453)	Nonstore retailers (NAICS 454)	Food services & drinking establishments (NAICS 722)
U.S...	**199,420**	**169,815**	**74,060**	**417,852**	**93,805**	**128,641**	**303,905**
AL	3,489	2,137	685	7,164	1,245	750	3,862
AK	428	334	191	1,426	211	247	857
AZ	4,348	2,228	1,503	7,776	2,323	2,554	5,370
AR	2,263	990	430	5,123	769	458	2,133
CA	19,750	21,391	9,832	43,581	10,250	8,554	41,529
CO	3,219	2,356	1,820	6,815	1,854	1,704	5,375
CT	2,230	2,970	1,200	3,578	1,290	3,533	3,676
DE	476	600	316	1,337	339	339	1,006
DC	176	415	172	138	151	44	1,273
FL	11,155	11,543	4,311	24,807	5,996	6,648	16,728
GA	7,154	4,865	1,664	12,410	2,695	1,751	8,831
HI	687	1,578	362	2,344	482	86	2,013
ID.....	997	436	374	1,906	475	700	1,115
IL.....	7,524	8,343	3,005	16,309	3,509	6,805	14,707
IN.....	5,218	2,614	1,248	11,010	1,925	3,793	6,485
IA.....	2,952	1,171	567	4,368	712	860	2,673
KS	2,181	1,320	626	5,036	833	538	2,573
KY	3,539	1,556	685	6,976	1,388	680	4,432
LA	3,694	2,042	687	7,352	1,103	649	4,552
ME	1,153	929	358	1,841	472	1,702	1,237
MD	3,098	3,720	1,637	6,598	1,571	1,474	5,916
MA	4,110	6,002	2,396	8,195	2,414	4,492	9,081
MI.....	6,702	5,158	3,426	19,738	4,295	2,667	10,115
MN	4,666	2,710	2,058	8,526	1,988	4,739	5,473
MS	2,404	1,017	333	4,712	749	403	2,033
MO	5,627	2,445	1,226	9,715	1,824	3,037	5,892
MT	642	274	264	1,329	258	171	937
NE	1,449	793	410	2,691	451	1,417	1,781
NV	1,482	1,819	571	2,746	1,100	1,474	2,515
NH	1,107	1,038	619	2,881	600	1,368	1,498
NJ.....	3,397	5,787	2,177	7,580	2,255	3,566	6,060
NM	1,573	787	443	2,945	1,032	887	1,750
NY	8,264	17,571	5,668	19,249	6,663	7,780	19,425
NC	6,264	4,355	1,603	11,367	3,407	2,460	8,441
ND	585	226	188	1,146	188	249	586
OH	8,132	5,739	2,621	18,926	3,183	5,206	12,609
OK	3,016	1,088	641	5,954	981	637	3,077
OR	2,391	1,842	1,154	7,433	1,529	1,674	3,902
PA	7,550	7,333	2,849	14,741	3,196	8,957	11,742
RI.....	600	569	255	899	278	588	1,163
SC	3,484	2,311	668	5,898	1,696	648	4,265
SD	762	281	173	1,134	302	5,015	728
TN	4,853	3,381	1,170	10,409	1,929	1,098	6,422
TX	16,219	11,966	5,007	33,475	6,784	14,062	23,336
UT	1,686	1,095	767	3,567	518	931	1,929
VT	518	317	188	492	204	557	566
VA	5,633	4,228	1,671	10,434	1,892	2,968	7,089
WA	3,711	3,226	2,174	10,961	2,415	3,040	7,951
WV	1,580	670	257	2,878	463	265	1,501
WI.....	4,476	2,067	1,284	9,005	1,423	4,214	5,214
WY	802	180	121	928	189	199	482

[1] Includes other types of stores, not shown separately.

Source: Market Statistics, a division of Claritas Inc., Arlington, VA, *The Survey of Buying Power Data Service*, annual (copyright).

Domestic Trade   647

No. 1025. Retail and Wholesale Trade-Establishments, Employees, and Payroll by State: 1999

[Covers establishments with payroll. Employees are for the week including March 12. Excludes most government employees, railroad employees, and self-employed persons. For statement on methodology, see Appendix III]

State	Wholesale establishments			Retail establishments (44-45)		
	Number of establishments	Number of employees	Annual payroll (1,000)	Number of establishments	Number of employees	Annual payroll (1,000)
United States	450,030	5,972,022	249,997,598	1,111,260	14,476,628	281,946,316
Alabama............	6,226	82,147	2,745,582	19,867	224,493	3,939,356
Alaska.............	765	7,102	281,842	2,762	32,280	772,364
Arizona............	6,724	85,835	3,341,454	16,616	248,866	5,125,832
Arkansas	3,545	42,410	1,292,785	12,236	131,257	2,181,777
California	58,194	773,142	35,451,534	106,864	1,421,434	32,620,675
Colorado...........	7,452	94,637	4,329,944	18,379	240,821	5,155,960
Connecticut.........	5,179	75,745	4,185,453	14,258	194,237	4,277,410
Delaware	1,001	16,326	834,869	3,757	50,116	959,322
District of Columbia	377	5,183	293,541	1,935	18,693	396,477
Florida.............	30,816	302,210	11,223,836	66,928	888,690	16,958,967
Georgia	14,033	197,503	8,581,289	33,375	440,893	8,592,615
Hawaii	1,812	18,219	600,250	4,903	60,266	1,262,964
Idaho..............	2,011	23,998	775,360	5,896	67,227	1,252,387
Illinois	21,764	338,196	16,077,476	44,017	635,558	12,214,416
Indiana............	8,788	118,785	4,384,107	24,431	347,998	6,070,539
Iowa	5,256	64,895	2,111,419	14,494	179,815	3,032,142
Kansas............	4,964	65,292	2,559,720	12,286	149,998	2,645,944
Kentucky	4,986	72,525	2,408,073	17,105	216,211	3,619,769
Louisiana	6,331	79,297	2,635,118	17,655	230,720	3,894,610
Maine.............	1,739	22,332	720,444	6,977	74,881	1,353,044
Maryland	6,197	94,494	4,273,807	19,573	279,135	5,642,129
Massachusetts.......	9,873	148,348	7,605,741	25,924	349,741	7,131,729
Michigan...........	13,689	189,534	8,556,148	39,262	541,841	10,267,842
Minnesota..........	9,344	137,891	6,091,122	20,869	297,066	5,534,859
Mississippi	3,137	39,444	1,186,970	12,744	138,089	2,354,595
Missouri	9,342	134,329	5,057,334	24,023	308,065	5,814,566
Montana...........	1,555	15,009	420,361	5,038	51,148	873,403
Nebraska	3,090	41,276	1,329,863	8,155	104,595	1,743,239
Nevada	2,500	30,257	1,167,604	6,793	101,922	2,279,220
New Hampshire......	2,140	23,739	1,042,636	6,607	90,647	1,791,616
New Jersey.........	17,436	275,609	13,826,891	34,582	422,085	9,238,380
New Mexico	2,163	21,270	683,536	7,359	91,627	1,673,436
New York	36,868	416,351	19,418,436	74,912	813,025	16,643,704
North Carolina.......	12,409	168,881	6,640,454	35,684	435,977	8,111,320
North Dakota........	1,568	17,353	502,408	3,499	41,644	684,909
Ohio	16,944	255,669	9,929,373	43,270	628,586	11,401,943
Oklahoma..........	5,049	60,444	2,001,697	14,296	167,595	2,786,746
Oregon............	5,870	79,849	3,108,247	14,200	186,360	3,894,113
Pennsylvania........	16,909	237,240	9,625,546	48,978	653,260	11,896,641
Rhode Island........	1,534	19,331	702,099	4,182	47,791	931,283
South Carolina.......	5,099	61,329	2,161,692	18,511	217,761	3,769,860
South Dakota	1,425	16,765	475,349	4,183	47,090	825,341
Tennessee	8,125	129,426	4,761,264	24,532	310,229	5,680,134
Texas.............	32,997	442,635	18,333,123	74,023	1,006,271	20,152,923
Utah	3,336	44,125	1,512,741	7,778	119,433	2,174,548
Vermont	930	10,853	368,791	3,968	38,160	700,625
Virginia............	7,935	107,366	4,214,449	28,803	396,336	7,454,836
Washington.........	9,988	122,406	4,951,201	22,582	302,828	6,681,229
West Virginia........	1,893	22,398	685,155	7,883	89,629	1,424,365
Wisconsin	7,941	116,601	4,339,305	21,409	316,102	5,569,946
Wyoming	781	6,021	190,159	2,897	28,136	490,266

Source: U.S. Census Bureau, County Business Patterns, annual.

No. 1026. Franchised New Car Dealerships—Summary: 1980 to 2000

[130.5 represents $130,500,000,000]

Item	Unit	1980	1985	1990	1994	1995	1996	1997	1998	1999	2000
Dealerships [1]	Number .	27,900	24,725	24,825	22,850	22,800	22,750	22,700	22,600	22,400	22,250
Sales	Bil. dol . .	130.5	251.6	316.0	430.6	456.2	490.0	507.5	546.3	606.5	646.8
New cars sold [2]	1,000. . .	8,979	11,042	9,300	8,991	8,635	8,527	8,272	8,137	8,699	8,847
Used vehicles sold	1,000. . .	9.72	13.30	14.18	16,903	18.48	19.17	19.19	19.33	20.07	20.45
Employment	1,000. . .	745	856	924	963	996	1,031	1,046.1	1,047.8	1,081.3	1,110.7
Annual payroll	Bil. dol . .	11.0	20.1	24.0	29.8	33.1	35.4	37.4	39.8	42.5	46.1
Advertising expenses . . .	Bil. dol . .	1.2	2.8	3.7	4.3	4.6	5.0	5.1	5.3	5.6	6.4
Dealer pretax profits as a percentage of sales . . .	Percent .	0.6	2.2	1.0	1.8	1.4	1.5	1.4	1.7	1.8	1.6

[1] At beginning of year. [2] Data provided by Ward's Automotive Reports.

Source: National Automobile Dealers Association, McLean, VA, *NADA Data*, annual.

No. 1027. Motor Vehicle Retail Sales: 1980 to 2000

Type	1980	1985	1990	1993	1994	1995	1996	1997	1998	1999	2000
Retail sales, total	11,466	15,724	14,146	14,199	15,411	15,116	15,455	15,498	15,968	17,414	17,811
Passenger cars (new), total	8,979	11,042	9,300	8,518	8,990	8,635	8,526	8,272	8,142	8,698	8,846
Domestic	6,581	8,205	6,897	6,742	7,255	7,129	7,255	6,917	6,762	6,979	6,830
Imports	2,398	2,838	2,403	1,776	1,735	1,506	1,271	1,355	1,380	1,719	2,016
Trucks (new), total	2,487	4,682	4,846	5,681	6,421	6,481	6,929	7,226	7,826	8,716	8,965
Domestic	2,001	3,902	4,215	5,287	5,995	6,064	6,478	6,632	7,151	7,922	8,092
Imports	486	780	631	394	426	417	452	593	674	795	873
Average expenditure per new car [1]	(NA)	(NA)	(NA)	16,871	17,903	17,959	18,777	19,531	20,364	20,658	20,356
Domestic	(NA)	(NA)	(NA)	15,976	16,930	16,864	17,468	17,907	18,479	18,630	18,685
Import	(NA)	(NA)	(NA)	20,261	21,989	23,202	26,205	27,722	29,614	28,931	25,971

NA Not available. [1] BEA estimate using average base price and adjustment for options, transportation charges, taxes, discounts and rebates for each model, weighted by model's share of sales; not an annual rate.

Source: Wards Communications, Southfield, MI, *Wards Autoinfobank*, (copyright).

No. 1028. Selected Motor Vehicle Indicators by Model Year: 1990 to 1999

[In thousands of units (14,169 represents 14,169,000) except as indicated. A model year begins on Oct.1, and ends on Sept. 30. It covers the fourth quarter of one calendar year and the first three quarters of the next calendar year]

Sales and expenditures	1990	1993	1994	1995	1996	1997	1998	1999
New motor vehicle sales.	14,169	14,199	15,413	15,118	15,456	15,498	15,963	17,414
New-car sales	9,436	8,518	8,990	8,636	8,527	8,273	8,142	8,697
Domestic	6,790	6,734	7,255	7,129	7,254	6,906	6,764	6,982
Import	2,645	1,784	1,735	1,507	1,273	1,366	1,378	1,715
New-truck sales.	4,733	5,681	6,422	6,481	6,929	7,226	7,821	8,717
Light	4,428	5,346	6,034	6,053	6,519	6,797	7,297	8,072
Domestic	3,996	4,981	5,638	5,663	6,088	6,226	6,651	7,310
Import	432	365	396	391	431	571	646	763
Other	306	336	388	428	411	429	524	645
Domestic-car production.	6,231	5,979	6,614	6,350	6,080	5,927	5,547	5,641
Avg. expenditure per new car [1] (dollar) . .	15,926	16,871	17,903	17,959	18,777	19,551	20,849	21,022
Domestic (dollar)	15,470	15,976	16,930	16,864	17,468	17,838	18,579	18,725
Import (dollar)	17,116	20,261	21,989	23,202	26,205	28,193	31,986	30,350

[1] BEA estimate based on the manufacturer's suggested retail price.

Source: U.S. Bureau of Economic Analysis, *Survey of Current Business, November 1997*.

No. 1029. New and Used Car Sales and Leases: 1990 to 1999

[In thousands, except as indicated]

Item	1990	1992	1993	1994	1995	1996	1997	1998	1999
Total car sales	46,830	45,163	46,575	49,132	50,393	49,354	48,542	48,359	(NA)
New passenger car sales [1]	9,300	8,213	8,518	8,991	8,635	8,526	8,272	8,139	(NA)
Used passenger car sales [2]	37,530	36,950	38,057	40,141	41,758	40,828	40,270	40,220	40,890
Value of transactions (bil. dol.).	219	247	279	312	338	337	338	335	361
Average price (dol.).	5,830	6,693	7,335	7,781	8,093	8,257	8,399	8,341	8,828
New passenger car leases [3] . . .	534	882	1,197	1,715	1,795	1,806	2,062	2,174	2,271

NA Not available. [1] Includes leased cars. [2] Used car sales include sales from franchised dealers, independent dealers, and casual sales. [3] Consumer leases only.

Source: Ward's Communications, Southfield, MI, *Motor Vehicle Facts & Figures, 1999*. Used passenger car sales: ADT Automotive, *2000 Used Car Market Report* Nashville, TN; Leased passenger cars: CNW Marketing/Research, Bandon, OR, personal communication, May 31, 2000; and U.S. Bureau of Transportation Statistics, *National Transportation Statistics* 2000.

Domestic Trade 649

Toy Industry—Shipments and Quantity by Type of Product: 1995 to 2000

[Shipments in millions of dollars (15,982 represents $15,982,000,000, quantity in millions of units (2,994 represents 2,994,000,000)]

Products	Shipments (mil. dol.)				Quantity (mil.)			
	1995	1998	1999	2000	1995	1998	1999	2000
Total	15,982	20,414	22,104	21,546	2,994	3,661	3,727	3,555
Video games	2,533	4,855	5,460	5,134	61	157	192	193
Other industry................	13,449	15,559	16,644	16,412	2,933	3,504	3,535	3,362
Infant/preschool.............	1,329	1,408	1,606	1,786	197	219	249	263
Dolls......................	1,896	2,157	2,169	2,255	241	268	269	270
Plush......................	1,004	1,958	2,388	1,553	136	442	515	352
Action figure toys...........	795	907	1,123	823	145	154	195	150
Vehicles....................	1,167	1,665	1,704	1,762	225	414	407	416
Ride-ons	797	728	767	1,140	35	33	34	46
Games/puzzles	1,263	1,475	1,732	1,661	229	250	360	351
Activity toys	1,929	2,096	2,203	2,324	647	686	714	747
All other toys................	3,269	3,165	2,952	3,109	1,078	1,038	792	766

Source: Toy Manufactures of America, Inc., New York, NY, *Toy Industry Fact Book*, annual (copyright).

No. 1031. Retail Foodstores—Number and Sales by Type: 1990 to 1999

[282.6 represents 282,600, except as indicated]

Type of foodstore	Number [1] (1,000)					Sales [2] (bil. dol.)					Percent distribution			
											Number		Sales	
	1990	1995	1997	1999	1998	1990	1995	1997	1998	1999	1990	1999	1990	1999
Total...........	282.6	264.4	256.0	251.9	247.8	368.3	402.5	423.7	435.4	458.3	100.0	100.0	100.0	100.0
Grocery stores	190.3	176.9	171.3	168.5	165.8	348.2	382.2	402.3	412.7	434.7	67.3	66.9	94.5	94.9
Supermarkets [3]	25.0	25.0	23.6	23.8	23.8	260.1	293.2	307.5	312.1	321.1	8.8	9.6	70.6	70.1
Conventional	13.7	12.0	10.6	10.2	9.6	90.7	68.9	59.2	59.4	59.7	4.9	3.9	24.6	13.0
Superstore [4]	5.8	6.8	7.3	7.4	7.6	87.6	116.7	132.9	133.8	138.9	2.1	3.1	23.8	30.3
Warehouse [5]	3.4	2.7	2.2	2.2	2.4	33.1	26.0	22.2	19.3	20.9	1.2	1.0	9.0	4.6
Combination food and drug [6]	1.6	2.7	2.8	3.2	3.4	34.8	59.3	64.7	72.0	75.5	0.6	1.4	9.4	16.5
Superwarehouse [7]...	0.3	0.6	0.5	0.5	0.5	12.6	17.8	11.9	16.7	17.1	0.1	0.2	3.4	3.7
Hypermarket [8]	0.1	0.2	0.2	0.2	0.2	1.3	4.5	16.6	11.0	9.0	-	0.1	0.4	2.0
Convenience stores [9]..	93.0	86.9	84.9	83.9	82.9	37.0	42.4	44.4	45.3	47.6	32.9	33.5	10.0	10.4
Superette [10]	72.3	65.0	62.9	60.9	59.1	51.1	46.6	50.4	55.3	66.0	25.6	23.8	13.9	14.4
Specialized food stores [11].	92.3	87.5	84.7	83.3	82.0	20.1	20.3	21.4	22.7	23.6	32.7	33.1	5.5	5.1

- Represents zero. [1] Estimated. [2] Includes nonfood items. [3] A grocery store, primarily self-service in operation, providing a full range of departments, and having at least $2.5 million in annual sales in 1985 dollars. [4] Contains greater variety of products than conventional supermarkets, including specialty and service departments, and considerable nonfood (general merchandise) products. [5] Contains limited product variety and fewer services provided, incorporating case lot stocking and shelving practices. [6] Contains a pharmacy, a nonprescription drug department, and a greater variety of health and beauty aids than that carried by conventional supermarkets. [7] A larger warehouse store that offers expanded product variety and often service meat, deli, or seafood departments. [8] A very large store offering a greater variety of general merchandise—like clothes, hardware, and seasonal goods—and personal care products than other grocery stores. [9] A small grocery store selling a limited variety of food and nonfood products, typically open extended hours. [10] A grocery store, primarily self-service in operation, selling a wide variety of food and nonfood products with annual sales below $2.5 million (1985 dollars). [11] Primarily engaged in the retail sale of a single food category such as meat and seafood stores and retail bakeries.
Source: U.S. Dept. of Agriculture, Economic Research Service, *Food Marketing Review*, annual.

No. 1032. Food Sales by Nontraditional Retailers: 1997

[308,780,000 represents $308,780,000,000]

Sales outlet	Retail food sales ($1,000)	Share of total retail food sales (percent)	Sales outlet	Retail food sales ($1,000)	Share of total retail food sales (percent)
Traditional foodstores, total	**308,780,000**	**82.6**	Other stores:		
Supermarkets	222,002,648	59.4	Drugstores	5,007,000	1.3
Convenience stores	14,216,118	3.8	Eating and drinking places	923,000	0.2
Other grocery stores...........	50,331,234	13.5	Furniture stores	133,280	(Z)
Specialized food stores	22,230,000	5.9	Gasoline service stations......	10,398,000	2.8
Nontraditional foodstores, total	**64,867,269**	**17.4**	Miscellaneous stores:		
General merchandise stores:			Gift, novelty, and souvenir shops.	198,938	0.1
Department stores	244,000	0.1	Hobby, toy, and game shops ...	266,165	0.1
Discount/mass merchandise stores...............	26,336,000	7.0	Liquor stores	1,234,000	0.3
Variety stores..............	896,000	0.2	Nonstore retailers:		
Warehouse club stores	7,964,000	2.1	Catalog and mail order	1,008,000	0.3
Other general merchandise stores...............	795,000	0.2	Vending machine operators	4,133,700	1.1
			Direct sales (mobile, door to door)	5,052,300	1.4

Z Less than 0.05 percent.
Source: U.S. Dept. of Agriculture, Economic Research Service, *Food Marketing Review*, annual.

No. 1033. Percent of Supermarkets Offering Selected Services and Product Lines: 1990 to 2000

[In percent. Based on a sample survey of chain and independent supermarkets and subject to sampling variability; for details, see source]

Service or product line offered	1990	1992	1993	1996	1997	1998	1999	2000
Service delicatessen	73	78	79	80	81	81	81	81
Service bakery	60	60	62	69	69	69	69	71
Service meat	42	48	47	74	60	59	60	62
Service fish	33	41	37	46	43	43	45	45
Separate cheese department.	33	33	34	31	30	31	32	33
Salad bar.	18	22	19	27	24	24	24	25
Automated teller machines (ATMs)	20	28	38	60	62	62	63	64
Banking in store	(NA)	(NA)	(NA)	14	22	21	22	21
Pharmacy	15	18	20	26	26	32	30	32
Warehouse aisle	(NA)	(NA)	(NA)	10	16	17	17	16

NA Not available.

Source: Progressive Grocer, New York, NY, *Progressive Grocer 66th Annual Report* (copyright). Used by permission of Progressive Grocer magazine.

No. 1034. Food and Alcoholic Beverage Sales by Sales Outlet: 1990 to 1999

[In billions of dollars (565.4 represents $656,400,000,000)]

Sales outlet	1990	1991	1992	1993	1994	1995	1996	1997	1998	1999
Food sales, total [1]	**565.4**	**586.3**	**596.7**	**616.7**	**646.2**	**670.8**	**697.1**	**729.7**	**751.5**	**788.6**
Food at home [2]	316.8	330.0	331.5	335.7	351.1	363.8	376.5	390.5	398.9	413.9
Food stores	267.2	276.4	275.2	275.6	286.7	291.9	299.3	309.4	313.2	327.5
Other stores	30.2	33.9	36.0	39.2	41.9	48.3	52.5	56.1	60.9	61.0
Home-delivered, mail order	5.3	5.8	6.4	7.1	8.4	8.9	10.0	9.9	10.0	10.3
Farmers, manufacturers, wholesalers.	6.3	6.6	6.7	7.0	7.1	7.6	7.8	8.3	8.2	8.4
Food away from home [3]	248.7	256.2	265.1	281.0	295.1	307.0	320.6	339.2	352.6	374.7
Alcoholic beverage sales, total	**73.0**	**74.5**	**74.5**	**75.2**	**77.6**	**80.0**	**83.8**	**88.0**	**90.5**	**96.1**
Packaged alcoholic beverages. . . .	38.2	39.1	38.2	38.2	39.5	40.2	42.2	43.7	44.7	48.7
Liquor stores.	18.6	19.1	18.4	18.3	18.6	18.6	19.5	20.3	21.3	23.4
Food stores	12.9	13.0	12.8	12.6	13.2	13.5	14.0	14.3	13.9	14.4
All other	6.7	7.0	7.0	7.4	7.6	8.2	8.7	9.0	9.6	10.9
Alcoholic drinks.	34.8	35.4	36.3	37.0	38.1	39.7	41.6	44.3	45.8	47.4
Eating and drinking places [4] . . .	26.8	27.3	27.8	28.3	29.0	30.0	31.3	33.4	34.2	35.1
Hotels and motels [4]	3.8	3.7	3.8	3.8	4.0	4.3	4.5	4.8	5.1	5.4
All other	4.2	4.4	4.7	4.9	5.1	5.5	5.8	6.1	6.5	6.9

[1] Includes taxes and tips. Excludes home food production.   [2] Includes home production and donations, not shown separately.   [3] Includes food furnished and donations.   [4] Includes tips.

Source: U.S. Department of Agriculture, Economic Research Service, *Food Consumption, Prices, and Expenditures, 1970-1999*; and *Agricultural Outlook*, monthly. <http://www.ers.usda.gov>.

No. 1035. Online Consumer Spending Forecast by Kind of Business: 1999 to 2001

[As of May 2001. (12.3 represents $12,300,000,000). Note: Figures below reflect a partial revision of the Jupiter Internet Shopping Model]

Category	Online retail spending (bil. dol.)			Percentage of spending online			Number of online buyers (mil.)			Percentage of online buyers that purchase within category		
	1999	2000	2001	1999	2000	2001	1999	2000	2001	1999	2000	2001
Total	12.3	24.1	34.1	(X)	(X)	(X)	(X)	(X)	(X)	(X)	(X)	(X)
PCs	3.6	6.1	7.2	16.2	25.3	29.9	2.4	4.3	5.6	7	9	9
Peripherals	0.9	1.8	2.0	10.1	18.7	20.6	5.0	8.9	10.8	15	18	17
Software	0.7	1.4	2.1	12.7	17.4	26.2	9.8	15.9	20.1	30	32	31
Consumer electronics	0.5	1.1	1.4	1.3	2.4	3.3	2.6	3.8	5.4	8	8	8
Books	1.2	2.2	3.0	4.8	8.9	11.6	14.8	23.2	32.8	45	47	51
Music	0.4	0.7	1.0	2.7	4.6	7.0	12.5	20.7	29.9	38	42	46
Videos	0.3	0.5	0.7	3.0	3.9	5.9	7.8	10.1	13.7	24	21	21
Movie tickets	-	0.1	0.2	0.4	1.4	2.3	0.7	2.7	5.0	2	5	8
Event tickets	0.4	1.0	1.6	2.6	6.2	8.8	4.1	9.9	13.4	12	20	21
Over-the-counter drugs	-	0.1	0.1	0.1	0.3	0.6	0.5	3.2	5.6	2	6	9
Nutraceuticals	-	0.1	0.2	0.2	0.6	1.2	1.3	6.2	8.6	4	13	13
Medical supplies and contact lenses	-	0.1	0.2	0.4	0.9	1.6	1.3	2.7	4.4	4	6	7
Personal care . . . . . . : . . .	0.1	0.1	0.3	0.2	0.3	0.7	1.5	4.5	7.3	4	9	11
Apparel	1.1	2.3	3.5	0.6	1.2	1.8	10.6	17.5	25.9	32	36	40
Footwear	0.2	0.3	0.6	0.4	0.6	1.0	2.7	4.0	6.8	8	8	11
Jewelry	0.3	0.8	1.0	1.1	2.6	3.2	1.9	4.2	5.7	6	9	9
Grocery	0.2	0.6	1.0	-	0.1	0.2	0.5	1.1	1.6	2	2	2
Pets	-	0.1	0.1	0.2	0.3	0.6	1.0	1.6	2.3	3	3	4
Toys	0.4	0.8	1.1	1.4	2.9	3.6	9.2	14.1	18.0	28	29	28
Sporting goods	0.2	0.5	0.7	1.0	2.1	3.0	2.4	4.7	7.5	7	10	12
Flowers	0.2	0.4	0.6	1.6	2.9	3.9	4.7	7.6	10.4	14	16	16
Specialty gifts	0.2	0.4	0.7	0.6	1.2	2.0	4.1	7.8	10.6	13	16	16
Furniture	-	0.1	0.1	0.1	0.1	0.2	0.1	0.3	0.5	-	1	1
Large appliances	-	0.1	0.3	0.1	0.7	1.4	-	0.2	0.5	-	1	1
Housewares/small appliances .	0.1	0.3	0.8	0.2	0.5	1.1	2.0	4.0	6.6	6	8	10
Art and collectibles	0.1	0.2	0.3	0.3	0.8	1.2	0.7	1.0	1.5	2	2	2
Home improvement	-	0.1	0.3	-	0.1	0.2	1.1	2.1	3.7	3	4	6
Garden supplies	-	0.1	0.1	0.1	0.2	0.4	0.7	1.7	2.6	2	3	4
Office products	0.1	0.3	0.8	0.4	1.1	2.4	2.6	5.4	8.5	8	11	13
Auto parts	-	-	0.1	-	-	0.2	0.1	0.1	0.5	-	-	1
Other	0.7	1.4	2.0	(NA)	(NA)	(NA)	(NA)	(NA)	(NA)	(NA)	(NA)	(NA)

- Represents or rounds to zero.   NA Not available.   X Not applicable.

Source: Jupiter Media Metrix, Inc., New York, NY Online Consumer Spending Forecast Summary, May 2001 (copyright).

No. 1036. U.S. Online Retail E-Commerce With Projections: 2000 to 2002

[In millions of dollars (44,784 represents $44,784,000,000). Not all figures add up due to rounding]

Online product or service	Projected online sales			Percent change, 1999-2000	
	2000	2001	2002	2000-2001	2001-2002
U.S. ONLINE RETAIL PROJECTIONS (mil. dol.)					
Retail trade, total [1]	44,784	73,926	110,748	65.1	49.8
Media	6,670	9,807	13,019	47.0	32.8
Event tickets	350	933	1,986	166.6	112.9
Flowers	760	1,266	1,812	66.6	43.1
Recreation	2,626	4,148	5,916	58.0	42.6
Apparel	5,040	8,915	14,461	76.9	62.2
Electronics	6,096	11,856	18,306	94.5	54.4
Leisure travel	12,200	16,700	21,000	36.9	25.7
Automobiles	2,845	5,315	9,360	86.8	76.1
Home products	2,232	4,659	8,256	108.7	77.2
Pet supplies	624	1,523	2,519	144.1	65.4
Health and beauty	1,352	2,656	4,460	96.4	67.9
Food and beverage	1,131	2,455	5,063	117.1	106.2

NA Not available.   [1] Includes items sold to consumers in product categories not listed above.

Source: Forrester Research, Inc., Cambridge, MA Online Retail Ripple Effect (copyright).

No. 1037. Retail E-Commerce Sales, Number of Orders, and Average Purchase Amount in Key Categories: 1999 and 2000

[In billions of dollars (16.20 represents $16,200,000,000). As of fourth quarter. Based on a point-of-sale-survey of online buyers covering approximately 1,000 merchants]

Category	Orders (mil.)			Sales (bil. dol.) [1]			Average purchase amount (dol.) [1]		
	1999	2000	Percent change in prior year	1999	2000	Percent change in prior year	1999	2000	Percent change in prior year
Total	176.19	280.34	59.1	16.20	32.50	100.7	92	116	26.0
Apparel	12.92	18.86	46.0	1.22	1.98	62.2	101	105	3.8
Computer goods . . .	33.18	52.33	57.7	6.69	14.81	121.3	207	283	36.8
Consumer goods . . .	16.47	21.33	29.5	1.82	3.30	81.4	134	155	15.6
Entertainment	59.27	80.89	36.5	3.06	5.02	64.0	55	62	12.8
Food/wine.	10.87	21.49	97.6	0.78	1.45	86.9	71	67	-4.9
Gifts.	31.81	59.11	85.8	1.77	3.59	103.0	58	61	4.6
Home & garden	5.12	14.42	181.9	0.44	1.51	245.4	89	105	18.1
Toys	6.54	11.91	82.1	0.42	0.84	99.0	64	70	9.7

[1] Includes shipping and handling charges.
Source: BizRate.Com, Los Angeles, CA, Consumer Online Report, Fourth Quarter, 2000 (copyright).

No. 1038. Retail Trade Sales—Total and E-Commerce by Kind of Business: 1999

[2,867,810 represents $2,867,810,000,000 sales. Covers retailers with and without payroll. Detail may not add to total due to rounding]

Kind of business	NAICS code [1]	Value of sales		E-commerce as percent of total sales	Percent distribution of E-commerce sales
		Total (mil. dol.)	E-commerce (mil. dol.)		
Retail trade, total	44-45	2,867,810	15,354	0.5	100.0
Motor vehicle and parts dealers.	441	783,156	1,876	0.2	12.2
Furniture and home furnishings stores	442	85,256	(S)	(S)	(S)
Electronics and appliance stores	443	81,802	250	0.3	1.6
Building material and garden equipment supplies stores. .	444	264,385	(S)	(S)	(S)
Food and beverage stores	445	442,185	(S)	(S)	(S)
Health and personal care stores	446	146,202	(S)	(S)	(S)
Gasoline stations	447	207,670	(Z)	(Z)	(Z)
Clothing and clothing acces. stores	448	160,007	120	0.1	0.8
Sporting goods, hobby book and music stores	451	72,555	(S)	(S)	(S)
General merchandise stores	452	379,336	(S)	(S)	(S)
Miscellaneous store retailers	453	106,653	(S)	(S)	(S)
Nonstore retailers	454	138,603	11,783	8.5	76.7
Electronic shopping and mail-order houses.	454110	93,149	11,733	12.6	76.4

S Data do not meet publication standards because of high sampling variability or poor response quality. Unpublished estimates derived from this table by subtraction should be used with caution and not be attributed to the U.S. Census Bureau. For more information on methodology visit www.census.gov/estats. Z Value of sales is less than $500,000; percent is less than 0.05%. [1] North American Industry Classification System; see text, Section 15, Business Enterprise.
Source: U.S. Census Bureau, Internet site <http://www.census.gov/eos/www/papers/estatstables.pdf>.

No. 1039. U.S. Merchant Wholesale Trade Sales—Total and E-Commerce: 1999

[2,541,190 represents $2,541,190,000,000 sales. Covers wholesalers with and without payroll. Detail may not add to total due to rounding]

Kind of business	NAICS code [1]	Value of sales		E-commerce as percent of total revenue	Percent distribution of E-commerce revenue
		Total (mil. dol.)	E-commerce (mil. dol.)		
Merchant wholesale trade, total [2].	42	2,541,190	134,432	5.3	100.0
Durable goods	421	1,354,326	71,104	5.3	52.9
Motor vehicles, parts and supplies.	4211	197,092	33,018	16.8	24.6
Furniture and home furnishings.	4212	42,473	(S)	(S)	(S)
Lumber and other construction materials	4213	71,635	1,402	2.0	1.0
Professional and commercial equipment and supplies. . .	4214	271,783	22,007	8.1	16.4
Computer, peripheral equipment and software	42143	160,790	15,512	9.6	11.5
Metals and minerals, excluding petroleum.	4215	94,099	281	0.3	0.2
Electrical goods	4216	206,767	4,499	2.2	3.3
Hardware, and plumbing and heating equipment and supplies	4217	63,559	4,856	7.6	3.6
Machinery, equipment and supplies	4218	245,404	(S)	(S)	(S)
Miscellaneous durable goods	4219	161,514	3,162	2.0	2.4
Nondurable goods [3].	422	1,186,864	63,328	5.3	47.1
Paper and paper products	4221	76,158	1,500	2.0	1.1
Drugs and druggists' sundries.	4222	145,860	47,063	32.3	35.0

S Data do not meet publication standards because of high sampling variability or poor response quality. Unpublished estimates derived from this table by subtraction should be used with caution and not be attributed to the U.S. Census Bureau. For more information on methodology visit www.census.gov.estats. [1] North American Industry Classification System; see text, Section 15, Business Enterprise. [2] Includes data only for businesses with paid employees. Merchant wholesalers take title to the goods they sell, and include jobbers, industrial distributors, exporters and importers. Excludes manufacturers' sales branches and offices, agents, brokers, commission agents, and electronic marketplaces. [3] Includes kinds of businesses not shown separately.
Source: U.S. Census Bureau, Internet site <http://www.census.gov/eos/www/papers/estatstables.pdf>.

U.S. Census Bureau, Statistical Abstract of the United States: 2001

No. 1040. Electronic Shopping and Mail-Order Houses—Total and E-Commerce Sales by Merchandise Line: 1999

[93,149 represents $93,149,000,000. Represents NAICS code 454110. Covers establishments with payroll. Detail may not add to total due to rounding]

Merchandise line	Value of sales		E-commerce as percent of total sales	Percent distribution of e-commerce sales	Percent distribution of total sales
	Total (mil. dol.)	E-commerce (mil. dol.)			
Electronic shopping and mail-order houses, total [1]	93,149	11,733	12.6	100.0	100.0
Books and magazines	3,611	1,631	45.2	13.9	3.9
Clothing and clothing accessories (includes footwear)	12,362	757	6.1	6.5	13.3
Computer hardware	25,098	4,336	17.3	37.0	26.9
Computer software	2,484	760	30.6	6.5	2.7
Drugs, health aids, beauty aids	10,362	258	2.5	2.2	11.1
Electronics and appliances	2,258	399	17.7	3.4	2.4
Food, beer and wine	1,540	230	14.9	2.0	1.7
Furniture and home furnishings	5,494	240	4.4	2.0	5.9
Music and videos	4,490	809	18.0	6.9	4.8
Office equipment and supplies	7,502	600	8.0	5.1	8.1
Toys, hobby goods, and games	2,052	391	19.1	3.3	2.2
Other merchandise [2]	14,723	966	6.6	8.2	15.8
Nonmerchandise receipts [3]	1,173	356	30.3	3.0	1.3

[1] This industry comprises businesses primarily engaged in retailing all types of merchandise through catalogs, television, and the internet. Data are preliminary and, therefore, subject to revision. [2] Includes other merchandise such as jewelry, sporting foods, collectibles, souvenirs, auto parts and accessories, hardware, and lawn and garden equipment and supplies. [3] Includes nonmerchandise receipts such as auction commissions, shipping and handling, customer training, customer support, and online advertising.

Source: U.S. Census Bureau, Internet site <http://www.census.gov/eos/www/papers/estatstables.pdf>.

No. 1041. U.S. Mail Order Sales by Kind of Business: 1997 and 1998

[In millions of dollars (318,500 represents $318,500,000,000). Mail order sales represent orders placed by mail, phone, or electronically without the person ordering coming to the point of sale to place the order, or the seller coming to the office or home of the orderer to take the order or using an agent to collect the order. Excludes orders placed at catalog desks or elsewhere in stores even in response to a catalog but does include products or services delivered in the store as long as the order was placed by mail, phone, or electronically. Statistics are generated independently each year and are not adjusted for any discontinuity of available data]

Category	1997		1998						
				Percent of—				Percent of —	
	Amount (mil. dol.)	Per capita (dol.)	Amount (mil. dol.)	Total con- sumers	Mail order total	Per capita (dol.)	Retail sales	General mer- chan- dise sales [1]	Con- sumer services
Total mail-order sales	318,500	(X)	357,240	(X)	100	(X)	(X)	(X)	(X)
Total products & services:									
Products	101,690	378	108,910	59	30	403	4.0	11.5	(X)
Specialty	85,350	317	90,810	49	25	336	3.3	9.6	(X)
General merchandise	16,340	61	18,100	10	5	67	0.6	1.9	(X)
Services	67,800	252	76,080	41	21	282	(X)	(X)	2.2
Nonfinancial	37,840	141	39,840	22	11	148	(X)	(X)	1.1
Financial	29,960	111	36,240	20	10	134	(X)	(X)	1.0
Business products & services	85,250	(X)	104,020	(X)	29	(X)	(X)	(X)	(X)
Charitable contributions	63,700	(X)	68,230	(X)	19	(X)	(X)	(X)	(X)

X Not applicable. [1] Includes apparel, drug, liquor, building materials, hardware, garden supply, mobile home, furniture, home furnishings, and equipment.

Source: National Mail Order Association, LLC, Minneapolis, MN *Guide to Mail Order Sales*, annual (copyright).

No. 1042. Catalog Sales—Method Used and Characteristic of Purchaser: 2000

[In thousands (197,772 represents 197,772,000), except percent. Survey conducted fall of 2000. Purchases ordered within 12 months prior to survey. Based on population 18 and over as of July 1. Data are estimates]

Characteristic	Adult population 18 yrs. old and over	Bought from catalog						
		Total	Percent	By fax	By mail	By phone	At catalog store	Via commercial online service
Total adults	197,772	85,267	43.1	1,850	22,548	46,851	4,918	9,099
18-24 years old	25,446	6,897	27.1	147	1,967	3,688	372	723
25-34 years old	38,831	14,917	38.4	289	3,670	7,996	566	2,396
35-44 years old	44,473	21,263	47.8	503	4,635	11,697	1,319	3,109
45-54 years old	34,487	17,644	51.2	531	4,148	10,166	939	1,860
55-64 years old	22,489	11,287	50.2	301	3,123	6,629	603	631
65 years old or older.	32,045	13,258	41.4	80	5,005	6,675	1,119	379
Sex:								
Male.	94,244	29,398	31.2	577	7,538	16,031	1,523	3,730
Female	103,529	55,868	54.0	1,273	15,011	30,821	3,396	5,368
Race:								
White	165,078	76,088	46.1	1,603	19,939	42,306	3,960	8,280
Black	24,029	6,636	27.6	145	1,920	3,449	693	429
Hispanic origin	21,088	6,076	28.8	200	1,696	3,068	499	613

No. 1043. Merchandise or Services Ordered by Mail or Phone by Characteristic of Purchaser: 2000

[In thousands (59,497 represents 59,497,000), except percent. Survey conducted fall of 2000. Purchases ordered within 12 months prior to survey. Based on population 18 and over as of July 1. Data are estimates]

Characteristic	Adult population 18 yrs. old and over	Persons ordering by mail or phone			
		By mail		By phone	
		Persons ordering	Percent	Persons ordering	Percent
Total adults	197,772	59,497	30.1	64,795	32.8
18-24 years old	25,446	6,153	24.2	4,981	19.6
25-34 years old	38,831	10,989	28.3	11,094	28.6
35-44 years old	44,473	13,272	29.8	15,937	35.8
45-54 years old	34,487	10,890	31.6	14,024	40.7
55-64 years old	22,489	7,407	32.9	9,002	40.0
65 years old or older.	32,045	10,785	33.7	9,757	30.4
Sex:					
Males	94,244	21,604	22.9	24,858	26.4
Females	103,529	37,893	36.6	39,937	38.6
Race:					
White	165,078	51,364	31.1	57,790	35.0
Black	24,029	6,178	25.7	5,094	21.2
Hispanic origin	21,088	4,822	22.9	4,723	22.4

No. 1044. Population Ordering by Catalog by Type of Product and Characteristic of Purchaser: 2000

[In thousands (4,740 represents 4,740,000). Survey conducted October 1999-September 2000. Purchases ordered within 12 months prior to survey. See Table 1043 for population 18 and over as of July 1. Data are estimates]

Characteristic	Specific items ordered										
	Food	Clothing	Electronics	Computer products	Gardening	Hardware	Home furnishing (bed & bath)	Housewares	Non-food gifts	Sporting goods	Toys/games
Total adults . . .	4,740	41,316	4,421	4,561	5,979	2,833	11,657	8,032	6,476	6,639	10,936
18-24 years old	238	3,246	347	126	437	191	821	438	309	538	730
25-34 years old	606	6,602	928	821	550	240	2,111	1,463	1,279	1,112	2,627
35-44 years old	1,208	9,996	1,232	1,425	1,292	661	3,132	2,059	1,718	2,018	3,474
45-54 years old	916	8,572	933	1,157	1,482	694	2,335	1,769	1,425	1,619	1,621
55-64 years old	755	5,645	638	691	1,130	457	1,747	1,242	855	827	1,494
65 or older	1,017	7,256	344	342	1,088	590	1,509	1,060	890	526	991
Sex:											
Male.	1,423	11,022	2,541	2,669	2,155	2,052	1,870	1,751	1,295	4,819	2,502
Female	3,317	30,294	1,880	1,892	3,824	781	9,787	6,281	5,181	1,820	8,435
Race:											
White	4,098	36,757	3,641	4,053	5,288	2,421	10,335	6,962	5,964	6,183	9,777
Black	461	3,531	483	230	456	269	1,058	762	362	349	770
Hispanic origin . . .	359	2,607	387	337	542	244	911	772	562	554	1,055

Source of Tables 1042-1044: Simmons Market Research Bureau, New York, NY, *Simmons National Consumer Survey* (copyright).

U.S. Census Bureau, Statistical Abstract of the United States: 2001

No. 1045. Shopping Centers—Number, Gross Leasable Area, and Retail Sales by Gross Leasable Area: 1990 to 2000

[As of December 31. A shopping center is a group of architecturally unified commercial establishments built on a site that is planned, developed, owned, and managed as an operating unit related in its location, size, and type of shops to the trade area that the unit serves. The unit provides on-site parking in definite relationship to the types and total size of the stores. The data base attempts to include all centers with three or more stores. Estimates are based on a sample of data available on shopping center properties; for details, contact source]

Year	Total	Gross leasable area (sq. ft.)					
		Less than 100,001	100,001-200,000	200,001-400,000	400,001-800,000	800,001-1,000,000	More than 1 million
NUMBER							
1990	36,515	23,231	8,756	2,781	1,102	288	357
1995	41,235	26,001	9,974	3,345	1,234	301	380
1998	43,661	27,317	10,581	3,696	1,354	319	395
1999	44,426	27,696	10,770	3,834	1,398	324	404
2000	45,115	28,062	10,958	3,935	1,424	326	410
Percent distribution	100.0	62.2	24.3	8.7	3.2	0.7	0.9
Percent change, 1999-2000	1.6	1.3	1.7	2.6	1.9	0.6	1.5
GROSS LEASABLE AREA							
1990 (mil. sq. ft.)	4,390	1,125	1,197	734	618	259	457
1995 (mil. sq. ft.)	4,967	1,267	1,368	886	689	271	486
1998 (mil. sq. ft.)	5,333	1,340	1,458	988	752	287	507
1999 (mil. sq. ft.)	5,463	1,362	1,486	1,030	776	292	519
2000 (mil. sq. ft.)	5,566	1,383	1,514	1,059	790	294	526
Percent distribution	100.0	25.1	27.3	18.5	14.1	5.4	9.5
Percent change, 1999-2000	1.9	1.6	1.9	2.9	1.8	0.7	1.4
RETAIL SALES							
1990 (bil. dol.)	706.4	205.1	179.5	108.0	91.7	45.1	77.0
1995 (bil. dol.)	893.8	259.6	227.1	136.4	115.8	57.0	97.8
1998 (bil. dol.)	1,032.4	299.7	262.2	157.7	133.7	65.8	113.2
1999 (bil. dol.)	1,105.3	320.8	280.7	168.9	143.0	70.4	121.4
2000 (bil. dol.)	1,181.1	342.8	300.0	180.5	152.8	75.2	129.8
Percent distribution	100.0	29.0	25.4	15.3	12.9	6.4	11.0
Percent change, 1999-2000	6.9	6.8	6.9	6.9	6.8	6.8	7.0

No. 1046. Shopping Centers—Number, Gross Leasable Area, and Retail Sales by State: 2000

[See headnote, Table 1045]

State	Number	Gross leasable area (mil. sq. ft.)	Retail sales (bil. dol.)	Percent change, 1999-2000			State	Number	Gross leasable area (mil. sq. ft.)	Retail sales (bil. dol.)	Percent change, 1999-2000		
				Number	Gross leasable area	Retail sales					Number	Gross leasable area	Retail sales
U.S.	45,115	5,566	1,181.1	1.55	1.87	4.90	MO	903	116	25.8	0.87	1.34	5.09
AL	651	77	17.4	2.77	4.00	1.75	MT	97	10	2.3	3.19	1.42	5.33
AK	68	8	2.4	-	-	8.59	NE	277	36	6.5	3.01	2.90	3.35
AZ	1,062	127	28.2	2.02	1.96	5.01	NV	382	49	7.7	4.23	4.53	2.79
AR	381	37	8.3	1.60	0.72	4.68	NH	229	25	5.2	1.63	1.68	8.14
CA	6,044	705	141.8	1.22	1.53	5.13							
							NJ	1,279	176	32.8	1.96	2.37	5.25
CO	777	104	26.5	2.96	3.98	3.51	NM	311	30	7.2	1.36	1.36	4.67
CT	800	96	21.8	1.16	0.75	7.52	NY	1,800	251	50.8	1.59	1.64	4.91
DE	149	23	5.1	2.05	0.69	7.49	NC	1,649	179	32.9	1.29	1.72	4.70
DC	87	9	2.0	-	-	6.77	ND	87	9	2.4	-	-	6.73
FL	3,452	440	108.3	2.59	2.91	4.63							
							OH	1,741	251	47.1	1.49	1.04	5.26
GA	1,644	183	35.7	1.51	1.48	4.86	OK	577	61	14.6	0.87	0.68	4.44
HI	190	20	5.1	3.17	3.24	6.73	OR	525	59	10.8	1.78	1.05	6.30
ID	168	20	3.7	1.82	1.24	4.43	PA	1,704	248	46.1	1.77	2.50	4.33
IL	2,175	264	48.2	1.34	1.55	5.63	RI	211	20	4.3	2.27	1.86	5.02
IN	926	122	24.2	0.82	0.51	5.71							
							SC	845	84	17.7	2.16	3.12	3.01
IA	326	44	8.5	2.74	2.82	3.51	SD	58	7	1.5	-	-	6.36
KS	493	58	13.2	1.34	1.10	5.21	TN	1,214	137	26.1	0.87	2.18	4.33
KY	625	68	15.7	0.89	0.56	5.58	TX	3,045	376	99.3	0.90	1.97	4.47
LA	710	85	21.2	0.95	0.69	5.67	UT	248	36	7.3	2.56	4.17	1.47
ME	203	17	4.9	1.25	0.79	7.81							
							VT	116	8	2.1	2.21	1.41	6.76
MD	940	130	28.5	1.57	2.86	3.85	VA	1,318	174	36.4	1.62	1.72	5.44
MA	1,008	116	26.9	1.01	1.93	5.45	WA	785	102	20.4	1.26	1.28	5.82
MI	1,056	142	28.8	1.63	2 11	4.44	WV	164	23	4.2	-	-	5.21
MN	483	70	15.9	2.39	2.66	4.12	WI	637	78	16.7	1.18	0.90	6.02
MS	444	44	9.1	1.29	2.27	2.63	WY	53	6	1.5	-	-	5.88

- Represents zero.

Source of Tables 1045 and 1046: National Research Bureau, Chicago, Data for 1993-2000 published by International Council of Shopping Centers in *Shopping Centers Today*, April issues (copyright—Interactive Market Systems, Inc.).

No. 1047. Merchant Wholesalers—Summary: 1992 to 2000

[In billions of dollars (1,731.6 represents $1,731,600,000,000) except ratios. Inventories and stock/sales ratios, as of December, seasonally adjusted. Inventories and stock/sales ratios, as of December, seasonally adjusted. Data reflect latest revision. Based on Current Business Survey; see Appendix III]

Kind of business	NAICS code [1]	1992	1994	1995	1996	1998	1999	2000
SALES (bil. dol.)								
Merchant wholesalers	(X)	1,731.6	1,933.6	2,114.7	2,239.8	2,379.8	2,539.3	2,755.5
Durable goods	(X)	832.8	1,004.2	1,106.8	1,156.6	1,265.8	1,351.8	1,435.1
Motor vehicles, parts, and supplies	4211	149.6	163.4	162.8	165.7	173.2	195.5	195.7
Furniture and home furnishings	4212	28.5	31.3	34.7	36.5	40.4	42.6	46.5
Lumber and construction materials	4213	45.8	56.0	55.2	59.1	63.7	71.3	71.5
Professional and commercial equipment	4214	133.5	165.4	197.9	220.2	254.1	272.3	279.3
Computer,peripheral equipment and software	42143	(NA)	(NA)	(NA)	(NA)	150.8	161.3	164.7
Metals and minerals, except petroleum	4215	76.7	89.1	95.2	94.5	97.1	95.0	103.3
Electrical goods	4216	98.2	141.3	167.9	171.5	186.7	207.7	239.5
Hardware, plumbing, and heating equipment	4217	41.3	49.2	52.0	54.3	60.4	63.4	65.5
Machinery, equipment, and supplies	4218	147.5	174.4	191.3	206.6	242.5	244.7	257.9
Miscellaneous durable goods	4219	111.5	134.0	149.9	148.2	147.7	159.4	175.9
Nondurable goods	(X)	898.8	929.4	1,007.9	1,083.2	1,114.1	1,187.4	1,320.5
Paper and paper products	4221	48.1	55.4	66.1	64.8	69.9	75.0	79.0
Drugs, proprietaries, and sundries	4222	67.1	76.4	83.7	94.3	124.6	146.2	165.3
Apparel, piece goods, and notions	4223	62.7	68.5	67.6	73.1	84.2	85.6	94.2
Groceries and related products	4224	274.8	289.9	309.0	317.8	344.4	361.5	387.9
Farm-product raw materials	4225	106.2	99.1	119.6	137.5	108.0	101.6	106.2
Chemicals and allied products	4226	39.2	43.3	50.3	53.6	55.1	55.4	60.0
Petroleum and petroleum products	4227	137.5	125.4	126.5	143.5	116.4	133.7	171.9
Beer, wine, and distilled beverages	4228	50.4	52.0	52.5	55.9	61.8	67.4	71.7
Miscellaneous nondurable goods	4229	112.8	119.4	132.7	142.5	149.7	161.0	184.3
INVENTORIES (bil. dol.)								
Merchant wholesalers	(X)	193.7	218.9	235.2	237.9	268.1	284.3	303.1
Durable goods	(X)	119.4	137.9	149.7	152.6	173.8	183.8	192.8
Motor vehicles, parts, and supplies	4211	21.6	21.6	22.2	21.7	23.0	25.8	26.7
Furniture and home furnishings	4212	4.2	4.4	4.7	4.7	5.1	5.4	5.9
Lumber and construction materials	4213	4.8	5.4	5.3	5.6	5.9	6.6	6.7
Professional and commercial equipment	4214	16.5	20.5	23.3	24.1	25.9	26.7	26.4
Computer, peripheral equipment and software	42143	0.0	0.0	0.0	0.0	12.1	12.2	11.0
Metals and minerals, except petroleum	4215	10.6	12.8	12.4	13.0	14.6	14.1	14.2
Electrical goods	4216	15.0	18.7	22.3	21.6	23.6	26.5	29.9
Hardware, plumbing, and heating equipment	4217	6.5	8.0	8.2	8.8	9.8	10.0	10.9
Machinery, equipment, and supplies	4218	27.7	31.3	35.4	37.2	47.5	48.5	48.9
Miscellaneous durable goods	4219	12.6	15.2	15.8	15.9	18.5	20.2	23.2
Nondurable goods	(X)	74.3	81.0	85.5	85.2	94.2	100.6	110.2
Paper and paper products	4221	4.4	4.7	5.2	5.1	5.8	6.0	6.9
Drugs, proprietaries, and sundries	4222	9.3	10.7	10.4	11.8	15.4	18.7	22.8
Apparel, piece goods, and notions	4223	10.3	11.8	11.4	11.8	13.3	12.3	12.2
Groceries and related products	4224	18.0	17.9	18.3	18.2	19.2	21.5	22.0
Farm-product raw materials	4225	8.1	10.0	12.0	9.5	10.1	9.9	11.0
Chemicals and allied products	4226	3.7	4.5	5.0	5.3	5.7	5.8	5.7
Petroleum and petroleum products	4227	4.1	4.4	4.2	4.7	3.6	3.9	4.6
Beer, wine, and distilled beverages	4228	4.3	4.5	4.6	5.0	5.7	6.1	6.7
Miscellaneous nondurable goods	4229	12.1	12.4	14.2	13.8	15.3	16.4	18.3
STOCK/SALES RATIO								
Merchant wholesalers	(X)	1.33	1.29	1.28	1.26	1.34	1.28	1.30
Durable goods	4211	1.73	1.58	1.60	1.56	1.56	1.50	1.63
Motor vehicles, parts, and supplies	4212	1.68	1.54	1.60	1.49	1.51	1.46	1.56
Furniture and home furnishings	4213	1.27	1.09	1.17	1.14	1.06	1.07	1.15
Lumber and construction materials	4214	1.41	1.35	1.32	1.30	1.21	1.12	1.19
Professional and commercial equipment	42143	(NA)	(NA)	(NA)	(NA)	0.99	0.85	0.86
Metals and minerals, except petroleum	4215	1.61	1.61	1.58	1.62	1.88	1.68	1.72
Electrical goods	4216	1.74	1.46	1.51	1.59	1.52	1.39	1.48
Hardware, plumbing, and heating equipment	4217	1.89	1.81	1.80	1.88	1.88	1.88	2.01
Machinery, equipment, and supplies	4218	2.21	2.02	2.02	2.07	2.36	2.32	2.24
Miscellaneous durable goods	4219	1.29	1.27	1.23	1.23	1.54	1.40	1.63
Nondurable goods	(X)	1.00	1.00	0.99	0.93	0.99	0.97	0.95
Paper and paper products	4221	1.08	0.91	0.94	0.95	0.95	0.94	1.02
Drugs, proprietaries, and sundries	4222	1.62	1.65	1.40	1.43	1.38	1.42	1.54
Apparel, piece goods, and notions	4223	1.91	2.12	1.97	1.77	1.99	1.65	1.55
Groceries and related products	4224	0.78	0.71	0.69	0.70	0.66	0.69	0.65
Farm-product raw materials	4225	0.95	1.13	1.19	0.87	1.10	1.23	1.17
Chemicals and allied products	4226	1.11	1.14	1.14	1.18	1.27	1.20	1.11
Petroleum and petroleum products	4227	0.37	0.41	0.40	0.36	0.39	0.32	0.30
Beer, wine, and distilled beverages	4228	1.02	1.02	1.03	1.07	1.07	1.06	1.09
Miscellaneous nondurable goods	4229	1.38	1.18	1.22	1.18	1.12	1.13	1.15

NA Not available.   X Not applicable.   [1] North American Industrial Classification System, 1997; see text, Section 15, Business Enterprise.

Source: U.S. Census Bureau, *Current Business Reports, Annual Benchmark Report for Wholesale Trade,*

Domestic Trade   657

No. 1048. Wholesale Trade—Establishments, Sales, Payroll, and Employees by Kind of Business: 1997

Kind of business	NAICS code [1]	Estab-lish-ments (number)	Sales Total (mil. dol.)	Sales Per paid em-ployee (dol.)	Annual payroll Total (mil. dol.)	Annual payroll Per paid em-ployee (dol.)	Paid employee for pay period including March 12 (1,000)
Wholesale trade	42	**453,470**	**4,059,658**	**700,357**	**214,915**	**37,076**	**5,796.6**
Wholesaler distributors and jobbers	(X)	338,872	1,810,730	441,715	139,227	33,963	4,099.3
Importers	(X)	14,417	167,711	849,339	7,825	39,628	197.5
Exporters	(X)	12,236	142,473	1,466,219	3,813	39,243	97.2
Own brand importer-marketers	(X)	3,609	136,820	1,297,697	5,042	47,823	105.4
Terminal grain elevators	(X)	237	8,470	2,833,588	88	29,387	3.0
Country grain elevators	(X)	4,387	39,131	1,078,686	971	26,760	36.3
Assemblers of farm products, except country grain elevators	(X)	2,572	27,797	530,005	1,408	26,839	52.4
Sales branches (with stock)	(X)	16,847	493,597	888,953	25,273	45,516	555.3
Sales offices (without stock)	(X)	12,458	765,278	2,085,499	20,639	56,243	367.0
Auction companies	(X)	1,304	70,174	1,180,068	713	11,997	59.5
Brokers	(X)	8,607	115,265	1,978,349	2,153	36,948	58.3
Commission merchants	(X)	6,784	57,742	1,454,133	1,477	37,199	39.7
Import agents	(X)	609	8,958	2,798,648	189	59,153	3.2
Export agents	(X)	1,282	18,818	3,888,815	171	35,420	4.8
Manufacturers agents	(X)	29,249	196,695	1,670,033	5,926	50,318	117.8
Wholesale trade, durable goods	421	290,629	2,179,717	641,421	133,237	39,207	3,398.3
Motor vehicle & motor vehicle parts & supplies wholesale	4211	29,328	533,352	1,419,505	11,459	30,497	375.7
Furniture & home furnishings wholesale	4212	15,246	75,006	476,337	5,317	33,766	157.5
Lumber & other construction materials wholesale	4213	14,267	89,176	573,349	5,296	34,051	155.5
Professional & commercial equipment & supplies wholesale	4214	45,351	367,384	513,025	33,292	46,490	716.1
Metal & mineral (except petroleum) wholesale	4215	12,583	150,494	864,762	6,898	39,637	174.0
Electrical goods wholesale	4216	38,234	357,692	751,823	22,525	47,344	475.8
Hardware & plumbing & heating equip. & supplies wholesale	4217	21,194	92,190	420,510	7,978	36,390	219.2
Machinery, equipment, & supplies, wholesale	4218	76,643	328,968	425,821	29,402	38,058	772.6
Wholesale trade, nondurable goods	422	162,841	1,879,940	783,865	81,678	34,057	2,398.3
Paper & paper product wholesale	4221	15,848	117,062	546,128	7,730	36,064	214.4
Drugs & druggists' sundries wholesale	4222	8,053	203,148	1,068,485	8,395	44,154	190.1
Apparel, piece goods & notions wholesale	4223	20,707	124,104	597,880	7,760	37,382	207.6
Grocery & related products wholesale	4224	41,760	588,970	688,919	26,778	31,322	854.9
Farm-product raw material wholesale	4225	10,343	166,786	1,710,260	2,306	23,646	97.5
Chemical & allied products wholesale	4226	15,920	128,923	777,735	7,241	43,683	165.8
Petroleum & petroleum products wholesale	4227	11,297	267,624	1,941,710	4,480	32,503	137.8
Beer, wine & distilled alcoholic bev., wholesale	4228	4,850	69,703	459,550	5,667	37,363	151.7
Merchant wholesalers	(X)	376,330	2,333,131	508,187	158,373	34,496	4,591.1
Manufacturers' sales branches & sales offices	(X)	29,305	1,258,875	1,365,066	45,912	49,785	922.2
Agents, brokers and commission merchants	(X)	47,835	467,652	1,650,981	10,630	37,529	283.3

X Not applicable. [1] North American Industry Classification System, 1997; see text, Section 15, Business Enterprise.

Source: U.S. Census Bureau, *1997 Economic Census, Wholesale Trade*, Series EC97W42A-US(RV), issued March 2000.

No. 1049. Wholesale Trade—Establishments, Employees, and Payroll: 1999

Kind of business	NAICS code [1]	Establishments (number)	Employees (number)	Payroll (1,000)
Wholesale trade	42	**450,030**	**5,972,022**	**249,997,598**
Wholesale trade, durable goods	421	290,053	3,527,913	158,783,498
Motor vehicle & motor vehicle parts & supplies wholesale	4211	28,328	391,849	13,568,355
Furniture & home furnishings wholesale	4212	15,008	161,687	6,123,814
Lumber & other construction materials wholesale	4213	14,901	169,013	6,502,996
Professional & commercial equipment & supplies wholesale	4214	45,157	751,200	41,807,488
Metal & mineral (except petroleum) wholesale	4215	12,326	169,728	7,152,802
Electrical goods wholesale	4216	38,512	507,297	29,223,491
Hardware & plumbing & heating equip. & supplies wholesale	4217	21,472	237,954	9,550,548
Machinery, equipment, & supplies, wholesale	4218	75,423	803,332	33,161,822
Misc. durable goods wholesale	4219	38,926	335,853	11,692,182
Wholesale trade, nondurable goods	422	159,977	2,444,109	91,214,100
Paper & paper product wholesale	4221	15,368	228,588	8,331,851
Drugs & druggists' sundries wholesale	4222	7,510	199,759	10,054,870
Apparel, piece goods & notions wholesale	4223	20,284	208,649	8,360,952
Grocery & related products wholesale	4224	40,568	876,175	30,070,803
Farm-product raw material wholesale	4225	9,760	92,219	2,395,925
Chemical & allied products wholesale	4226	15,410	159,824	7,697,921
Petroleum & petroleum products wholesale	4227	11,160	134,052	4,918,105
Beer, wine & distilled alcoholic bev., wholesale	4228	4,720	152,969	6,329,881
Misc. nondurable goods wholesale	4229	35,197	391,874	13,053,792

[1] North American Industry Classification System, 1997; see text, Section 15, Business Enterprise.

Source: U.S. Census Bureau, *1997 Economic Census, Wholesale Trade*, Series EC97W42A-US(RV), issued March 2000.

Section 23
Transportation

This section presents data on civil air transportation, both passenger and cargo, and on water transportation, including inland waterways, oceanborne commerce, the merchant marine, cargo, and vessel tonnages.

This section also presents statistics on revenues, passenger and freight traffic volume, and employment in various revenue-producing modes of the transportation industry, including motor vehicles, trains, and pipelines. Data are also presented on highway mileage and finances, motor vehicle travel, accidents, and registrations; and characteristics of public transit, railroads, and pipelines.

Principal sources of air and water transportation data are the annual *National Transportation Statistics,* issued by the U.S. Bureau of Transportation Statistics; the *Annual Report* issued by the Air Transport Association of America, Washington, DC; and the annual *Waterborne Commerce of the United States* issued by the Corps of Engineers of the Department of the Army. In addition, the U.S. Census Bureau in its commodity transportation survey (part of the census of transportation, taken every 5 years through 1997, for years ending in "2" and "7") provides data on the type, weight, and value of commodities shipped by manufacturing establishments in the United States, by means of transportation, origin, and destination. The latest complete reports for 1997 are part of the 1997 Economic Census. See text, Section 15, Business Enterprise, for a discussion of the 1997 Economic Census.

Additional sources of data on water transportation include *Merchant Fleets of the World,* issued periodically by the U.S. Maritime Administration; *The Bulletin,* issued monthly by the American Bureau of Shipping, New York, NY; and the annual *World Fleet Statistics.*

The principal compiler of data on public roads and on operation of motor vehicles is the U.S. Department of Transportation's (DOT) Federal Highway Administration (FHWA). These data appear in FHWA's annual *Highway Statistics* and other publications.

The U.S. National Highway Traffic Safety Administration issues data on traffic accident deaths and death rates in two annual reports: the *Fact Book* and the *Fatal Accident Reporting System Annual Report.* DOTs Federal Railroad Administration presents data on accidents involving railroads in its annual *Accident/Incident Bulletin,* and the *Rail-Highway Crossing Accident/Incident and Inventory Bulletin.*

The data for the truck transportation component of the 1997 Economic Census are presented in the *Truck Inventory and Use Survey.*

Data are also presented in many nongovernment publications. Among them are the weekly and annual *Cars of Revenue Freight Loaded* and the annual *Yearbook of Railroad Facts,* both published by the Association of American Railroads, Washington, DC; *Transit Fact Book,* containing electric railway and motorbus statistics, published annually by the American Public Transit Association, Washington, DC.; *Accident Facts,* issued by the National Safety Council, Chicago, IL; and *Transportation in America,* issued by the Eno Foundation for Transportation, Westport, Connecticut.

Civil aviation—Federal promotion and regulation of civil aviation have been carried out by the FAA and the Civil Aeronautics Board (CAB). The CAB promoted and regulated the civil air transportation industry within the United States and between the United States and foreign countries. The Board granted licenses to provide air transportation service, approved or disapproved proposed rates and fares, and approved or disapproved proposed agreements and corporate relationships involving air carriers. In December 1984, the CAB ceased to exist as an agency. Some of its functions were transferred to the Department of Transportation (DOT), as outlined below. The responsibility for investigation of aviation accidents resides with the National Transportation Safety Board.

The Office of the Secretary, DOT aviation activities include: negotiation of international air transportation rights, selection of U.S. air carriers to serve capacity controlled international markets, oversight of international rates and fares, maintenance of essential air service to small communities, and consumer affairs. DOT's Bureau of Transportation Statistics (BTS) handles aviation information functions formerly assigned to CAB. Prior to BTS, the Research and Special Programs Administration handled these functions.

The principal activities of the FAA include: the promotion of air safety; controlling the use of navigable airspace; prescribing regulations dealing with the competency of airmen, airworthiness of aircraft and air traffic control; operation of air route traffic control centers, airport traffic control towers, and flight service stations; the design, construction, maintenance, and inspection of navigation, traffic control, and communications equipment; and the development of general aviation.

The CAB published monthly and quarterly financial and traffic statistical data for the certificated route air carriers. BTS continues these publications, including both certificated and noncertificated (commuter) air carriers. The FAA publishes annually data on the use of airway facilities; data related to the location of airmen, aircraft, and airports; the volume of activity in the field of nonair carrier (general aviation) flying; and aircraft production and registration.

General aviation comprises all civil flying (including such commercial operations as small demand air taxis, agriculture application, powerline patrol, etc.) but excludes certificated route air carriers, supplemental operators, large-aircraft commercial operators, and commuter airlines.

Air carriers and service—The CAB previously issued "certificates of public convenience and necessity" under Section 401 of the Federal Aviation Act of 1958 for scheduled and nonscheduled (charter) passenger services and cargo services. It also issued certificates under Section 418 of the Act to cargo air carriers for domestic all-cargo service only. The DOT Office of the Secretary now issues the certificates under a "fit, willing, and able" test of air carrier operations. Carriers operating only a 60-seat-or-less aircraft are given exemption authority to carry passengers, cargo, and mail in scheduled and nonscheduled service under Part 298 of the DOT (formerly CAB) regulations. Exemption authority carriers who offer scheduled passenger service to an essential air service point must meet the "fit, willing, and able" test.

Vessel shipments, entrances, and clearances—Shipments by dry cargo vessels comprise shipments on all types of watercraft, except tanker vessels; shipments by tanker vessels comprise all types of cargo, liquid and dry, carried by tanker vessels.

A vessel is reported as entered only at the first port which it enters in the United States, whether or not cargo is unloaded at that port. A vessel is reported as cleared only at the last port at which clearance is made to a foreign port, whether or not it takes on cargo. Army and Navy vessels entering or clearing without commercial cargo are not included in the figures.

Units of measurement—Cargo (or freight) tonnage and shipping weight both represent the gross weight of the cargo including the weight of containers, wrappings, crates, etc. However, shipping weight excludes lift and cargo vans and similar substantial outer containers. Other tonnage figures generally refer to stowing capacity of vessels, 100 cubic feet being called 1 ton. Gross tonnage comprises the space within the frames and the ceiling of the hull, together with those closed-in spaces above deck available for cargo, stores, passengers, or crew, with certain minor exceptions. Net or registered tonnage is the gross tonnage less the spaces occupied by the propelling machinery, fuel, crew quarters, master's cabin, and navigation spaces. Substantially, it represents space available for cargo and passengers. The net tonnage capacity of a ship may bear little relation to weight of cargo. Deadweight tonnage is the weight in long tons required to depress a vessel from light water line (that is, with only the machinery and equipment on board) to load line. It is, therefore, the weight of the cargo, fuel, etc., which a vessel is designed to carry with safety.

Federal-aid highway systems—The Intermodal Surface Transportation Efficiency Act (ISTEA) of 1991 eliminated the historical Federal-Aid Highway Systems and created the National Highway System (NHS) and other federal-aid highway categories. The final NHS was approved by Congress in December of 1995 under the National Highway System Designation Act.

Functional systems—Roads and streets are assigned to groups according to the character of service intended. The functional systems are (1) arterial highways that generally handle the long trips, (2) collector facilities that collect and disperse traffic between the arterials and the lower systems, and (3) local roads and streets that primarily serve direct access to residential areas, farms, and other local areas.

Regulatory bodies—The ICC, created by the U.S. Congress to regulate transportation in interstate commerce, has jurisdiction over railroads, trucking companies, bus lines, freight forwarders, water carriers, coal slurry pipelines, and transportation brokers. The Federal Energy Regulatory Commission is responsible for setting rates and charges for transportation and sale of natural gas and for establishing rates or charges for transportation.

Motor carriers—For 1960-73, Class I for-hire motor carriers of freight were classified by the ICC as those with $1 million or more of gross annual operating revenue; 1974-79, the class minimum was $3 million. Effective January 1, 1980, Class I carriers are those with $5 million or more in revenue. For 1960-68, Class I motor carriers of passengers were classified by the

ICC as those with $200,000 or more of gross annual operating revenue; for 1969-76, as those with revenues of $1 million or more; and since 1977, as those with $3 million or more. Effective January 1, 1988, Class I motor carriers of passengers are those with $5 million or more in operating revenues; Class II less than $5 million in operating revenues.

Railroads—Railroad companies reporting to the ICC are divided into specific groups as follows: (1) Regular line-haul (interstate) railroads (and their nonoperating subsidiaries), (2) switching and terminal railroads, (3) private railroads prior to 1964 (identified by ICC as "circular" because they reported on brief circulars), and (4) unofficial railroads, so designated when their reports are received too late for tabulation. For the most part, the last three groups are not included in the statistics shown here.

For years prior to 1978, Class I railroads were those with annual revenues of $1 million or more for 1950-55; $3 million or more for 1956-64; $5 million or more for 1965-75; and $10 million or more for 1976-77. In 1978, the classification became Class I, those having more than $50 million gross annual operating revenue; Class II, from $10 million to $50 million+; and Class III, less than $10 million. Effective January 1, 1982, the ICC adopted a procedure to adjust the threshold for inflation by restating current revenues in constant 1978 dollars. In 1988, the criteria for Class I and Class II railroads were $92.0 million and $18.4 million, respectively. Also effective January 1, 1982, the ICC adopted a Carrier Classification Index Survey Form for carriers not filing annual report Form R-1 with the commission. Class II and Class III railroads are currently exempted from filing any financial report with the Commission. The form is used for reclassifying carriers.

The Surface Transportation Board (STB) was established pursuant to the ICC Termination Act of 1995, Pub. L. No. 104-88, 109 Stat. 803 (1995) (ICCTA), to assume certain of the regulatory functions that had been administered by the Interstate Commerce Commission. The Board has broad economic regulatory oversight of railroads, addressing such matters as rate

Transportation 661

reasonableness, car service and interchange, mergers and line acquisitions, line construction, and line abandonments. 49 U.S.C. 10101-11908. Other ICC regulatory functions were either eliminated or transferred to the Federal Highway Administration or the Bureau of Transportation Statistics within DOT.

Class I Railroads are regulated by the STB and subject to the Uniform System of Accounts and required to file annual and periodic reports. Railroads are classified based on their annual operating revenues. The class to which a carrier belongs is determined by comparing its adjusted operating revenues for 3 consecutive years to the following scale: Class I, $250 million or more, Class II $20 million to $250 million, and Class III $0 to 20 million.

Postal Service—The Postal Service provides mail processing and delivery services within the United States. The Postal Reorganization Act of 1970 created the Postal Service, effective July 1971, as an independent establishment of the Federal Executive Branch.

Revenue and cost analysis describes the Postal Service's system of attributing revenues and costs to classes of mail and service. This system draws primarily upon probability sampling techniques to develop estimates of revenues, volumes, and weights, as well as costs by class of mail and special service. The costs attributed to classes of mail and special services are primarily incremental costs which vary in response to changes in volume; they account for roughly 60 percent of the total costs of the Postal Service. The balance represents "institutional costs." Statistics on revenues, volume of mail, and distribution of expenditures are presented in the Postal Service's annual report, *Cost and Revenue Analysis,* and its *Annual Report of the Postmaster General* and its annual *Comprehensive Statement on Postal Operations.*

Statistical reliability—For a discussion of statistical collection and estimation, sampling procedures, and measures of statistical reliability applicable to Census Bureau data, see Appendix III.

No. 1050. Transportation-Related Components of U.S. Gross Domestic Product: 1980 to 1999

[In billions dollars (349.4 represents $349,400,000,000), except percent]

Item	1980	1985	1990	1995	1999
CURRENT DOLLARS					
Total transportation-related final demand	**349.4**	**495.9**	**625.6**	**782.0**	**(NA)**
Total gross domestic product (GDP)	2,795.6	4,213.0	5,803.2	7,400.5	9,256.1
Transportation-related final demand as a percent of GDP	12.5	11.8	10.8	10.6	(NA)
Personal consumption of transportation	238.4	372.9	463.2	560.3	694.9
Motor vehicles and parts	87.0	175.7	210.3	249.3	316.1
Gasoline and oil	86.7	97.2	109.2	113.3	123.8
Transportation services	64.7	100.0	143.7	197.7	255.0
Gross private domestic investment	52.1	74.0	78.5	130.5	197.1
Transportation structures	3.7	4.3	3.0	4.4	(NA)
Transportation equipment	48.4	69.7	75.5	126.1	197.1
Net exports of transportation-related goods and service	-1.1	-34.7	-28.0	-43.3	-82.4
Exports (+)	45.7	57.5	106.7	132.9	176.8
Civilian aircraft, engines, and parts	14.1	13.5	32.2	26.1	53.4
Automotive vehicles, engines, and parts	17.4	24.9	36.5	61.8	74.8
Passenger fares	2.6	4.4	15.3	18.9	21.1
Other transportation	11.6	14.7	22.7	26.1	27.5
Imports (-)	46.8	92.2	134.7	176.2	259.2
Civilian aircraft, engines, and parts	3.1	5.3	10.5	10.7	23.4
Automotive vehicles, engines, and parts	28.3	64.9	88.5	123.8	180.1
Passenger fares	3.6	6.4	10.5	14.7	21.5
Other transportation	11.8	15.6	25.2	27.0	34.2
Government transportation-related purchases	60.0	83.7	111.9	134.5	(NA)
Federal purchases	7.0	10.0	12.9	16.3	(NA)
State and local purchases	48.8	67.5	90.1	109.8	(NA)
Defense-related purchases	4.2	6.2	8.9	8.4	9.0
Total domestic transportation-related final demand	350.5	530.6	653.6	827.4	(NA)
Total gross domestic demand (GDD)	2,810.5	4,327.2	5,874.6	7,484.7	9,510.0
Transportation-related final demand as a percent of GDP	12.5	12.3	11.1	11.1	(NA)
CHAINED 1996 DOLLARS					
Total transportation-related final demand	**543.0**	**592.1**	**719.6**	**797.4**	**(NA)**
Total gross domestic product (GDP)	4,900.9	5,717.1	6,707.9	7,543.8	8,848.2
Transportation-related final demand as a percent of GDP	11.1	10.4	10.7	10.6	(NA)
Personal consumption of transportation	362.3	494.3	532.8	574.6	687.5
Motor vehicles and parts	142.7	236.9	246.1	253.4	318.2
Gasoline and oil	94.9	104.8	113.2	120.2	128.3
Transportation services	124.7	152.6	173.5	201.0	241.0
Gross private domestic investment	77.6	93.9	87.4	128.2	195.7
Transportation structures	(NA)	(NA)	(NA)	(NA)	(NA)
Transportation equipment	77.6	93.9	87.4	128.2	195.7
Net exports of transportation-related goods and service	-5.0	-56.1	-31.3	-43.1	-79.3
Exports (+)	76.2	76.0	123.7	135.4	172.1
Civilian aircraft, engines, and parts	26.9	19.5	40.9	27.2	49.9
Automotive vehicles, engines, and parts	28.3	30.5	39.8	62.5	73.7
Passenger fares	4.5	7.1	19.1	18.9	20.5
Other transportation	16.5	18.9	23.9	26.8	28.0
Imports (-)	81.2	132.1	155.0	178.5	251.4
Civilian aircraft, engines, and parts	6.0	7.7	13.5	11.2	21.7
Automotive vehicles, engines, and parts	52.5	95.8	101.6	124.6	178.3
Passenger fares	5.5	9.3	12.7	14.9	19.5
Other transportation	17.2	19.3	27.2	27.8	31.9
Government transportation-related purchases	108.1	115.8	130.7	137.7	(NA)
Federal purchases	12.5	14.0	15.7	16.6	(NA)
State and local purchases	89.8	93.7	104.6	112.3	(NA)
Defense-related purchases	5.8	8.1	10.4	8.7	8.7
Total domestic transportation-related final demand	554.4	709.7	754.6	845.1	(NA)
Total gross domestic demand (GDD)	4,890.9	5,866.2	6,764.4	7,622.2	9,171.3
Transportation-related final demand as a percent of GDP	11.3	12.1	11.2	11.1	(NA)

NA Not available.

U.S. Bureau or Transportation Statistics, *National Transportation Statistics, 2000.*

U.S. Census Bureau, Statistical Abstract of the United States: 2001

No. 1051. Passenger and Freight Transportation Outlays by Type of Transport: 1990 to 1999

[In billions of dollars (517.2 represents $517,200,000,000). Freight data include outlays for mail and express]

Type of transport	1990	1992	1993	1994	1995	1996	1997	1998	1999
Passenger:									
Private transportation	517.2	523.6	560.2	610.5	642.0	684.0	719.9	738.9	805.0
Automobiles [1][2]	507.3	515.0	551.6	601.2	631.7	672.4	706.1	722.5	787.4
New and used cars	148.1	141.2	153.2	172.2	169.6	174.6	178.0	183.7	200.2
Tires, tubes, accessories	32.9	33.6	35.6	38.7	40.6	42.6	43.6	45.9	49.3
Gasoline and oil	118.0	115.4	117.3	119.9	124.6	136.6	140.9	126.7	141.1
Insurance less claims	19.9	28.3	29.7	30.6	32.7	35.0	39.9	41.8	43.0
Interest on debt	28.2	25.7	28.0	29.3	38.0	39.1	40.3	37.8	40.6
Auto registration fees.	6.1	7.1	7.4	7.4	7.0	7.7	8.2	9.6	9.1
Operators' permit fees.	0.6	0.8	0.7	0.8	0.8	0.9	0.9	0.9	1.0
Repair, greasing, washing, parking, leasing, rentals [3] . . .	93.4	99.3	107.4	121.0	134.4	147.6	160.9	168.4	178.3
Air.	9.9	8.6	8.6	9.3	10.4	11.6	13.8	16.4	17.6
For-hire transportation	124.8	103.2	104.7	107.2	117.2	115.8	126.9	128.6	132.0
Local [2]	31.6	32.8	34.3	35.7	41.0	39.6	41.5	41.6	41.7
Bus and transit [4]	16.7	18.0	18.8	20.1	21.6	21.3	21.9	21.4	21.7
School bus	8.0	8.1	7.6	7.8	9.9	9.1	10.4	10.3	10.3
Taxi	4.0	4.0	4.3	4.7	5.0	5.4	5.7	6.4	6.2
Railroad commutation	2.8	2.7	3.5	3.1	4.5	3.8	3.5	3.5	3.5
Intercity	53.1	53.1	52.8	54.9	57.8	57.6	65.9	68.1	71.1
Air	49.5	49.2	49.3	50.5	54.0	53.9	61.8	64.0	67.0
Rail [5]	1.8	1.9	1.8	1.8	2.2	2.1	2.3	2.2	2.1
Bus	1.8	1.9	1.7	1.4	1.5	1.5	1.6	1.8	1.8
International	14.9	17.3	17.6	17.7	18.4	18.5	19.5	18.9	19.2
Freight, total [2]	350.9	375.1	396.6	420.3	442.4	467.2	494.9	528.8	561.8
Highway [2]	270.8	292.9	311.9	330.7	348.1	368.5	396.7	427.2	456.8
Truck, intercity	162.3	176.8	189.7	204.9	219.6	235.4	257.8	282.8	304.6
Truck, local	108.4	116.0	122.1	125.7	128.4	133.0	138.7	144.3	152.1
Rail.	30.1	30.5	30.8	33.1	34.4	35.1	35.3	35.3	35.9
Water	20.1	19.9	20.8	21.2	22.7	24.6	21.0	22.5	24.5
Oil pipeline	8.5	8.5	8.5	8.7	9.1	8.6	8.6	8.6	9.1
Air carrier.	13.7	15.0	15.8	17.2	18.8	20.4	22.8	24.2	25.3

[1] Includes business-owned vehicles. [2] Includes items not shown separately. [3] Includes storage. [4] Includes federal, state, and local government operating subsidies and capital grants. [5] Includes federal operating subsidies and capital grants for Amtrak.

Source: Eno Transportation Foundation, Inc., Washington, D.C. *Transportation in America*, annual (copyright).

No. 1052. Volume of Domestic Intercity Freight and Passenger Traffic by Type of Transport: 1980 to 1999

[2,487 represents 2,487,000,000,000. Freight traffic in bil. ton-miles; passenger traffic in bil. passenger-miles. A ton-mile is the movement of 1 ton (2,000 pounds) of freight for the distance of 1 mile. A passenger-mile is the movement of one passenger for the distance of 1 mile. Comprises public and private traffic, both revenue and nonrevenue. ICC=Interstate Commerce Commission]

Type of transport	1980	1985	1990	1992	1993	1994	1995	1996	1997	1998	1999
Freight traffic, total . . .	2,487	2,458	2,896	3,023	3,105	3,261	3,407	3,516	3,534	3,591	3,715
Railroads	932	895	1,091	1,138	1,183	1,275	1,375	1,426	1,421	1,442	1,499
Truck:											
ICC truck.	242	250	311	342	365	391	401	428	436	459	499
Non-ICC truck	313	360	424	473	496	517	520	544	560	568	594
Water:											
Rivers/canals	311	306	390	393	373	388	406	408	413	(NA)	(NA)
Great Lakes.	96	76	85	77	83	87	91	93	95	96	95
Oil pipelines	588	564	584	589	593	591	601	619	617	620	623
Domestic airways [1]	5	7	10	11	12	12	13	14	14	14	14
Passenger traffic, total .	1,468	1,636	1,847	1,946	1,985	2,065	2,098	2,182	2,247	2,328	2,400
Private automobiles	1,210	1,310	1,452	1,544	1,575	1,625	1,641	1,693	1,740	1,806	1,850
Domestic airways [2]	15	12	13	11	10	10	11	12	13	13	14
Air, public carrier	204	278	346	354	362	388	404	435	453	(NA)	(NA)
Bus [3]	27	24	23	23	25	28	28	29	31	32	35
Railroads [4]	11	11	13	14	13	14	14	13	13	14	14

NA Not available. [1] Revenue service only for scheduled and nonscheduled carriers, with small Section 418 all-cargo carriers included from 1980. Includes express mail, and excess baggage. [2] Includes general aviation (mostly private business) flying. [3] Excludes school and urban transit buses. [4] Includes intercity (Amtrak) and rail commuter service.

Source: Eno Transportation Foundation, Inc., Washington, DC, *Transportation in America*, annual (copyright).

No. 1053. Transportation and Warehousing—Establishments, Employees, and Payroll by Kind of Business (NAICS Basis): 1998 and 1999

[For establishments with payroll (3,462.5 represents 3,462,500). See Appendix III. County Business Patterns excludes rail transportation (NAICS 482) and the National Postal Service (NAICS 491)]

Industry	NAICS code [1]	Establishments		Paid employees [2] (1,000)		Annual payroll (mil. dol.)	
		1998	1999	1998	1999	1998	1999
Transportation & warehousing.	**48,49**	**186,162**	**187,339**	**3,462.5**	**3,627.1**	**108,592.0**	**116,682.2**
Air transportation	481	5,347	5,285	560.0	582.8	22,591.2	24,414.4
Scheduled air transportation	4811	3,376	3,237	520.8	540.0	20,917.3	22,506.2
Scheduled passenger air transportation	481111	2,827	2,698	490.0	506.1	19,985.5	21,434.4
Scheduled freight air transportation	481112	549	539	30.7	33.9	931.9	1,071.8
Nonscheduled air transportation.	4812	1,971	2,048	39.3	42.8	1,673.9	1,908.2
Water transportation	483	1,908	1,950	72.8	71.8	3,103.7	3,039.5
Deep sea, coastal, & Great Lakes water transportation	4831	1,271	1,307	54.7	52.5	2,383.3	2,312.4
Inland water transportation	4832	637	643	18.1	19.3	720.4	727.1
Inland water freight transportation	483211	386	396	15.1	15.9	622.5	626.4
Inland water passenger transportation	483212	251	247	3.0	3.4	98.0	100.7
Truck transportation	484	107,868	108,749	1,327.1	1,384.2	41,015.5	43,626.2
General freight trucking	4841	49,793	52,724	840.2	897.6	27,247.8	29,343.4
General freight trucking, local.	48411	17,489	18,737	136.0	141.6	3,866.1	4,087.5
General freight trucking, long distance	48412	32,304	33987	704.2	756.0	23,381.8	25,256.0
Specialized freight trucking	4842	58,075	56,025	486.9	486.6	13,767.7	14,282.7
Used household & office goods moving	48421	9,276	9,219	124.0	127.0	3,273.2	3,453.7
Specialized freight (except used goods) trucking, local	48422	34,714	33,459	195.0	197.5	5,181.2	5,457.2
Specialized freight (except used goods) trucking, long-distance	48423	14,085	13,347	167.9	162.1	5,313.3	5,371.9
Transit & ground passenger transportation	485	16,334	16,254	349.3	370.0	6,016.8	6,729.3
Urban transit systems	4851	615	723	32.1	40.1	981.4	1,226.1
Mixed mode systems	485111	45	163	1.2	6.1	32.4	144.7
Commuter rail	485112	18	13	(D)	(D)	(D)	(D)
Bus and other motor vehicle mode systems	485113	526	520	26.4	29.3	740.5	853.7
Other.	485119	26	27	(D)	(D)	(D)	(D)
Interurban & rural bus transportation.	4852	415	440	23.4	21.8	650.8	654.4
Taxi & limousine service	4853	6,619	6,605	60.5	63.4	1,017.9	1,131.2
Taxi service	48531	3,191	3,102	27.6	28.6	412.5	459.3
Limousine service	48532	3,428	3,503	32.9	34.8	605.4	671.9
School & employee bus transportation	4854	4,400	4,341	152.6	161.9	1,950.9	2,178.7
Charter bus industry	4855	1,531	1,480	32.3	33.6	594.4	651.4
Other transit & ground passenger transportation	4859	2,754	2,665	48.4	49.2	821.4	887.5
Special needs transpiration	485991	1,906	1,860	32.0	33.4	536.0	585.8
Pipeline transportation	486	2,495	2,550	49.4	48.1	2,847.8	3,032.7
Pipeline transportation of crude oil	4861	358	327	7.3	7.1	442.0	453.4
Pipeline transportation of natural gas	4862	1,561	1,683	35.1	34.5	1,993.8	2,205.4
Other pipeline transportation	4869	576	540	7.0	6.5	412.0	373.9
Scenic & sightseeing transportation	487	2,353	2,267	23.1	22.9	512.0	540.7
Scenic & sightseeing transportation, land.	4871	472	458	9.0	8.7	187.0	188.3
Scenic & sightseeing transportation, water.	4872	1,718	1,649	12.3	12.3	273.7	295.5
Scenic & sightseeing transportation, other	4879	163	160	1.7	1.9	51.3	56.9
Support activities for transportation	488	31,441	31,392	421.7	440.2	13,840.8	14,915.6
Support activities for air transportation	4881	4,348	4,305	114.7	118.8	3,076.3	3,454.2
Airport operations	48811	1,823	1,834	60.3	62.9	1,215.7	1,431.1
Air traffic control.	488111	127	135	0.7	0.7	24.8	27.3
Other support activities for air transportation	48819	2,525	2,471	54.5	55.9	1,860.6	2,023.1
Support activities for rail transportation	4882	821	837	18.7	21.0	572.5	672.5
Support activities for water transportation	4883	2,683	2,593	72.5	71.4	3,023.6	2,995.3
Port and harbor operations	48831	196	199	7.5	7.4	277.7	264.7
Marine cargo handling	48832	619	601	45.0	43.8	2,029.9	2,016.1
Navigational services to shipping	48833	906	891	11.5	11.4	429.6	430.1
Other.	48839	962	902	8.5	8.8	286.4	284.5
Support activities for road transportation	4884	6,745	6,943	46.7	50.5	1,041.1	1,148.7
Motor vehicle towing.	48841	6,040	6,145	37.3	39.9	808.9	878.7
Freight transportation arrangement.	4885	15,798	15,464	148.4	157.5	5,445.7	5,885.9
Other support activities for transportation.	4889	1,046	1,250	20.7	20.8	681.6	759.1
Couriers & messengers	492	11,704	11,938	539.6	578.4	15,291.6	16,726.0
Couriers	4921	6,085	6,309	469.0	508.6	13,928.0	15,289.5
Local messengers & local delivery	4922	5,619	5,629	70.6	69.8	1,363.5	1,436.5
Warehousing & storage	493	6,712	6,954	119.5	128.6	3,372.5	3,657.9

D Figure withheld to avoid disclosure pertaining to individual companies. [1] North American Industry Classification System, 1997; see text, Section 15, Business Enterprise.

Source: U.S. Census Bureau, *County Business Patterns,* annual.

No. 1054. Transportation and Warehousing—Establishments, Revenue, Payroll, and Employees by Kind of Business (NAICS Basis): 1997

[318,245 represents $318,245,000,000. For establishments with payroll. Based on the 1997 Economic Census; see Appendix III]

Industry	NAICS code [1]	Estab-lish-ments (number)	Revenue Total (mil. dol.)	Revenue Per paid employee (dol.)	Annual payroll Total (mil. dol.)	Annual payroll Per paid employee (dol.)	Paid employee for pay period including March 12 (1,000)
Transportation & warehousing [2] [3]	**48,49**	**178,025**	**318,245**	**108,959**	**82,346**	**28,193**	**2,920.8**
Air transportation [2]	481	3,598	20,249	227,198	2,748	30,834	89.1
Scheduled air transportation [2]	4811	1,798	16,285	246,786	1,921	29,110	66.0
Nonscheduled air transportation	4812	1,800	3,964	171,332	827	35,750	23.1
Water transportation	483	1,921	24,019	329,676	2,834	38,900	72.9
Deep sea, coastal, & Great Lakes water transportation	4831	1,308	20,339	374,565	2,198	40,472	54.3
Inland water transportation	4832	613	3,680	198,323	637	34,300	18.6
Truck transportation	484	103,798	141,225	109,156	38,471	29,735	1,293.8
General freight trucking	4841	44,781	88,426	107,901	25,722	31,387	819.5
Specialized freight trucking	4842	59,017	52,800	111,326	12,749	26,881	474.3
Transit & ground passenger transportation	485	16,013	13,792	40,616	5,549	16,342	339.6
Urban transit systems	4851	618	1,519	46,096	973	29,542	32.9
Interurban & rural bus transportation	4852	407	1,147	57,660	550	27,624	19.9
Taxi & limousine service	4853	6,418	3,155	55,070	881	15,374	57.3
School & employee bus transportation	4854	4,484	4,393	28,964	1,878	12,382	151.7
Charter bus industry	4855	1,531	1,768	56,164	548	17,407	31.5
Other transit & ground passenger transportation	4859	2,555	1,811	39,107	720	15,547	46.3
Pipeline transportation	486	2,311	26,837	544,582	2,661	53,989	49.3
Pipeline transportation of crude oil	4861	382	4,365	548,311	480	60,240	8.0
Pipeline transportation of natural gas	4862	1,450	19,627	548,404	1,871	52,277	35.8
Other pipeline transportation	4869	479	2,846	514,483	310	56,069	5.5
Scenic & sightseeing transportation	487	2,325	1,893	79,200	492	20,600	23.9
Scenic & sightseeing transportation, land	4871	454	558	67,777	170	20,619	8.2
Scenic & sightseeing transportation, water	4872	1,692	1,129	79,565	283	19,940	14.2
Scenic & sightseeing transportation, other	4879	179	207	138,604	40	26,757	1.5
Support activities for transportation	488	30,675	39,758	96,585	12,592	30,591	411.6
Support activities for air transportation	4881	4,231	9,153	79,279	2,820	24,425	115.5
Support activities for rail transportation	4882	816	2,067	109,555	515	27,276	18.9
Support activities for water transportation	4883	2,525	7,515	103,681	2,763	38,125	72.5
Support activities for road transportation	4884	6,424	2,683	60,535	901	20,327	44.3
Freight transportation arrangement	4885	15,782	16,251	114,856	5,015	35,442	141.5
Other support activities for transportation	4889	897	2,090	109,826	579	30,427	19.0
Couriers & messengers	492	10,887	39,812	74,999	14,072	26,508	530.8
Couriers	4921	5,503	36,293	78,315	12,830	27,685	463.4
Local messengers & local delivery	4922	5,384	3,519	52,202	1,242	18,420	67.4
Warehousing & storage	493	6,497	10,658	97,102	2,926	26,659	109.8

[1] North American Industry Classification System, 1997; see text, Section 15, Business Enterprise. [2] Data do not include large certificated passenger carriers that report to the Office of Airline Statistics, U.S. Department of Transportation. [3] Railroad transportation and U.S. Postal Service are out of scope for the 1997 Economic Census.

Source: U.S. Census Bureau, *1997 Economic Census, Transportation & Warehousing*, Series EC97T48A-US, issued January 2000.

No. 1055. Employment and Earnings in Transportation by Industry: 1980 to 2000

[2,960 represents 2,960,000. Annual averages of monthly figures. Based on Current Employment Statistics program; see Appendix III]

Industry	SIC code [1]	1980	1985	1990	1995	1997	1998	1999	2000
NUMBER (1,000)									
Total transportation	(X)	2,960	2,997	3,511	3,904	4,123	4,273	4,409	4,524
Railroads	40	532	359	279	238	227	231	230	220
Local and interurban passengers	41	265	277	338	419	452	469	485	498
Trucking and warehousing	42	(NA)	(NA)	1,395	1,587	1,677	1,744	1,805	1,839
Water transportation	44	211	185	177	175	179	181	187	201
Air transportation	45	(NA)	(NA)	968	1,068	1,134	1,181	1,227	1,282
Pipelines, exc. natural gas	46	21	19	19	15	14	14	13	13
Transportation services	47	(NA)	(NA)	336	401	441	454	463	472
AVG. WEEKLY EARNINGS (dol.)									
Class I railroads	4011	427	595	727	811	892	845	797	799
Local and interurban passengers	41	217	261	310	358	375	387	397	419
Trucking and warehousing	42	(NA)	(NA)	450	504	532	545	561	579
Pipelines, exc. natural gas	46	441	629	711	888	902	918	944	956

NA Not available. X Not applicable. [1] 1987 Standard Industrial Classification, see text, Section 15, Business Enterprise.

Source: U.S. Bureau of Labor Statistics, *Bulletins 2445* and *2481* and *Employment and Earnings*, March and June issues.

No. 1056. Transportation Accidents, Deaths, and Injuries: 1990 to 1999

[6,471 represents 6,471,000]

Year and casualty	Motor vehicle [1] (1,000)	Rail-road [2]	Air-lines [3]	Air		Gen-eral aviation	Recre-ational boat-ing [6]	Pipeline [7]		Water-borne [8]	Rail Rapid Trans-it [9]	Hazard-ous materi-als [10]
				Com-muter air car-riers [4]	On demand air car-riers [5]			Gas	Haz-ardous liquid			
Accidents:												
1990....	6,471	2,879	24	15	106	2,215	6,411	198	180	3,613	12,178	8,880
1995....	6,699	2,459	36	12	75	2,053	8,019	161	188	4,196	14,327	14,743
1998....	6,335	2,575	50	8	77	1,908	8,061	234	154	3,872	13,516	15,349
1999....	6,279	2,768	52	13	76	1,909	7,935	174	167	3,654	(NA)	16,977
Deaths:												
1990....	44.6	599	39	7	50	767	865	6	3	85	117	8
1995....	41.8	567	168	9	52	734	829	18	3	46	79	7
1998....	41.5	577	1	-	45	624	815	17	2	59	54	13
1999....	41.7	530	12	12	38	631	734	17	4	44	(NA)	5
Injuries:												
1990....	3,231	22,736	29	11	36	402	3,822	69	7	175	10,036	423
1995....	3,465	12,546	25	25	14	395	4,141	53	11	145	11,238	400
1998....	3,192	10,156	28	2	10	330	4,612	75	6	83	11,059	198
1999....	3,236	10,509	57	12	14	325	4,315	87	20	113	(NA)	267

- Represents zero. NA Not available. [1] Data on deaths are from U.S. National Highway Traffic Safety Administration and are based on 30 day definition. Includes only police reported crashes. For more detail see Table 1100. [2] Accidents which result in damages to railroad property. Grade crossing accidents are also included when classified as a train accident. Deaths exclude fatalities in railroad-highway grade crossing accidents. [3] Includes scheduled and nonscheduled (charter) air carriers. Represents serious injuries. [4] All scheduled service. Represents serious injuries. [5] All nonscheduled service. Represents serious injuries. [6] Accidents resulting in death; injury or requiring medical treatment beyond first aid; damages exceeding $500; or a person's disappearance. [7] Pipeline accidents/incidents are credited to year of occurrence. [8] Covers accidents involving commercial vessels which must be reported to U.S. Coast Guard if there is property damage exceeding $25,000; material damage affecting the seaworthiness or efficiency of a vessel; stranding or grounding; loss of life; or injury causing a person's incapacity for more than 3 days. [9] Reporting criteria and source of data changed between 1989 and 1990; these data from 1990 to present are not comparable to earlier years. [10] Accidents, deaths, and injuries involving hazardous materials cover all types of transport.

Source: U.S. Bureau of Transportation Statistics, *National Transportation Statistics, annual.*

No. 1057. U.S. Scheduled Airline Industry—Summary: 1990 to 1999

[For calendar years or Dec. 31 (465.6 represents 465,600,000). For domestic and international operations. Covers carriers certificated under Section 401 of the Federal Aviation Act. Minus sign (-) indicates loss]

Item	Unit	1990	1993	1994	1995	1996	1997	1998	1999
SCHEDULED SERVICE									
Revenue passengers enplaned .	Mil.	465.6	488.5	528.8	547.8	581.2	599.1	612.9	635.4
Revenue passenger miles.	Bil.	457.9	489.7	519.4	540.7	578.7	605.6	618.1	651.6
Available seat miles.	Bil.	733.4	771.6	784.3	807.1	835.1	860.8	874.1	917.8
Revenue passenger load factor .	Percent .	62.4	63.5	66.2	67.0	69.3	70.3	70.7	71.0
Mean passenger trip length [1]. . .	Miles . . .	984	1,002	982	987	996	1,011	1,008	1,025
Freight and express ton miles . .	Mil.	10,546	11,944	13,792	14,578	15,301	17,959	18,131	19,346
Aircraft departures.	1,000 . . .	6,924	7,245	7,531	8,062	8,230	8,192	8,292	8,617
FINANCES									
Total operating revenue [2] . .	**Mil. dol. .**	**76,142**	**84,559**	**88,313**	**94,578**	**101,938**	**109,568**	**113,465**	**118,245**
Passenger revenue	Mil. dol. .	58,453	63,945	65,422	69,594	75,286	79,471	80,986	84,167
Freight and express revenue. . .	Mil. dol. .	5,432	6,662	7,284	8,616	9,679	10,477	10,697	11,239
Mail revenue	Mil. dol. .	970	1,212	1,183	1,266	1,279	1,362	1,708	1,734
Charter revenue	Mil. dol. .	2,877	3,082	3,548	3,485	3,447	3,575	3,821	3,706
Total operating expense	Mil. dol. .	78,054	83,121	85,600	88,718	95,729	100,982	104,138	110,342
Operating profit.	Mil. dol. .	-1,912	1,438	2,713	5,860	6,209	8,586	9,327	7,903
Interest expense	Mil. dol. .	1,978	2,027	2,347	2,424	1,981	1,733	1,742	1,825
Net profit	Mil. dol. .	-3,921	-2,136	-344	2,314	2,804	5,170	4,903	5,576
Revenue per passenger mile. . .	Cents . .	12.8	13.1	12.6	12.9	13.0	13.1	13.1	12.9
Rate of return on investment . . .	Percent .	-6.0	-0.4	5.2	11.9	11.5	14.7	12.0	11.5
Operating profit margin.	Percent .	-2.5	1.7	3.1	6.2	6.1	7.8	8.2	6.7
Net profit margin	Percent .	-5.1	-2.5	-0.4	2.4	2.8	4.7	4.3	4.7
EMPLOYEES [3]									
Total	**1,000 . . .**	**545.8**	**537.1**	**539.8**	**547.0**	**564.4**	**586.5**	**621.1**	**646.4**
Pilots and copilots	1,000 . . .	47.1	52.1	52.9	55.4	57.6	60.4	64.1	68.2
Other flight personnel.	1,000 . . .	8.9	8.1	7.7	8.6	8.9	10.7	11.1	14.3
Flight attendants	1,000 . . .	83.4	85.0	86.5	86.7	89.1	96.2	97.6	105.4
Mechanics	1,000 . . .	61.0	57.5	55.8	50.5	50.8	65.5	69.9	73.7
Aircraft and traffic servicing personnel.	1,000 . . .	251.2	242.8	247.2	251.1	266.5	269.6	290.1	294.5
All other.	1,000 . . .	94.2	91.7	89.7	94.8	91.6	84.1	88.3	90.3

[1] For definition of mean, see Guide to Tabular Presentation. [2] Includes other types of revenues, not shown separately. [3] Average number of full time equivalents.

Source: Air Transport Association of America, Washington, DC, *Air Transport*, annual, and *Air Transport, Facts and Figures*, annual.

No. 1058. Airline Cost Indexes: 1980 to 1999

[Covers U.S. major and national service carriers. Major carriers have operating revenues of $1 billion or more; nationals have operating revenues from $75 million to $1 billion]

Index	Index (1982=100)								Percent distribution of total operating expenses [1]			
	1980	1985	1990	1995	1996	1997	1998	1999	1980	1990	1995	1999
Composite index	86.8	102.8	122.6	131.3	136.6	137.4	134.8	137.1	100.0	100.0	100.0	100.0
Labor costs:												
Passenger carriers.	85.8	110.5	121.7	155.7	159.4	163.0	164.5	166.6	35.2	31.6	35.5	35.8
Cargo carriers.	78.3	116.0	148.8	151.7	159.6	156.0	159.1	164.8	27.3	30.0	40.0	30.2
Fuel	89.7	79.6	77.2	55.3	64.6	62.5	49.4	51.4	30.0	17.3	12.0	10.0
Aircraft fleet [2 3].	88.1	123.7	177.0	222.8	230.3	223.4	228.2	229.8	5.2	7.9	9.7	9.4
Interest [2 4]	88.1	98.0	96.0	93.5	86.9	72.1	67.4	68.9	3.2	2.6	3.1	2.0
Insurance	80.4	155.3	68.2	111.6	111.5	96.0	64.5	44.3	0.3	0.3	0.8	0.3
Maintenance material.	104.9	119.9	190.5	153.4	169.4	191.0	201.2	187.0	2.5	3.4	2.8	3.1
Landing fee	87.2	99.9	139.0	176.6	181.5	184.0	177.4	186.8	1.7	1.8	2.2	2.0
Traffic commissions [2].	75.4	112.9	169.2	139.4	130.7	126.9	113.0	97.9	4.9	9.4	8.6	6.0
Communication [2]	65.8	96.6	111.2	116.0	114.8	110.4	119.0	138.1	1.1	1.4	1.6	1.7
Advertising and promotion [2]	67.1	96.2	97.8	63.6	58.4	54.7	59.2	59.7	1.6	2.0	1.5	1.4
Passenger food [2]	90.6	98.9	128.4	110.9	104.0	102.8	105.2	106.8	2.9	3.5	3.4	3.2
All other	86.3	111.3	130.6	147.6	150.4	153.2	155.0	157.3	11.8	19.1	22.7	26.3

[1] Total operating expenses plus interest on long term debt, less depreciation and amortization. [2] Passenger airlines only. [3] Includes lease, aircraft and engine rentals, depreciation and amortization. [4] Interest on debt.

Source: Air Transport Association of America, Washington, DC, *Air Transport,* annual; and unpublished data.

No. 1059. Top 40 Airports in 2000—Passengers Enplaned: 1990 and 2000

[In thousands (438,544 represents 438,544,000), except rank. For calendar year. Airports ranked by total passengers enplaned by large certificated air carriers, 2000]

Airport	1990 Total	1990 Rank	2000 Total	2000 Rank	Airport	1990 Total	1990 Rank	2000 Total	2000 Rank
All airports	438,544	(X)	638,903	(X)	Charlotte (Douglas Muni), NC.	7,077	22	10,378	21
Top 40 airports.	334,833	(X)	496,565	(X)	Cincinnati, OH.	3,908	32	9,963	22
Atlanta (Hartsfield Intl), GA. .	22,666	3	38,256	1	Baltimore, MD	4,420	29	8,979	23
Chicago (O'Hare Intl), IL . .	25,636	1	30,888	2	Salt Lake City, UT	5,388	25	8,701	24
Dallas/Ft. Worth Intl, TX . .	22,899	2	27,841	3	Honolulu, HI	9,002	15	8,685	25
Los Angeles Intl, CA	18,438	4	25,110	4	Pittsburgh, PA.	7,912	17	8,651	26
Denver Intl, CO	11,962	6	17,643	5	San Diego (Intl-Lindbergh), CA.	5,261	26	7,625	27
Phoenix Sky Harbor Intl, AZ . .	10,727	7	17,239	6	Tampa, FL.	4,781	27	7,431	28
Detroit (Wayne County), MI . .	9,903	9	16,930	7	Miami/Ft. Lauderdale, FL. . .	3,875	34	7,141	29
Las Vegas (McCarran Intl) NV . .	7,796	18	16,739	8	Washington (Reagan National), DC.	7,035	23	6,983	30
Minneapolis-St. Paul Intl, MN . .	8,837	16	16,710	9	Chicago, IL (Midway)	3,547	37	6,972	31
San Francisco Intl, CA	13,475	5	16,664	10	Washington (Dulles Intl), DC .	4,449	28	6,649	32
Houston International, TX . . .	7,544	20	15,815	11	Portland, OR.	3,025	42	6,559	33
Newark, NJ.	9,854	10	15,205	12	Cleveland (Hopkins Intl), OH .	3,836	35	6,154	34
St Louis (Lambert-St. Louis Muni), MO.	9,332	13	15,101	13	San Jose Muni, CA.	3,128	41	6,044	35
Orlando Intl, FL	7,678	19	13,466	14	Kansas City, MO	3,358	40	5,749	36
Seattle-Tacoma Intl, WA . . .	7,386	21	13,308	15	Oakland Metro Intl, CA	2,671	44	5,127	37
Miami Intl, FL	9,226	14	12,655	16	Memphis, TN.	3,887	33	4,977	38
Boston (Logan Intl), MA. . . .	9,550	12	11,506	17	Raleigh-Durham, NC.	4,361	30	4,839	39
New York (LaGuardia), NY . . .	10,725	8	11,426	18	San Juan, (Luis Munoz Marin Intl), PR	3,618	36	4,834	40
Philadelphia, PA.	6,971	24	10,973	19					
New York (JFK), NY	9,687	11	10,648	20					

X Not applicable.

Source: U.S. Bureau of Transportation Statistics, Office of Airline Information, *Airport Activity Statistics of Certificated Air Carriers, Calendar Year 2000* and the Federal Aviation Administration, *Airport Activity Statistics of Certificated Air Route Carriers, Calendar Year 1990.*

No. 1060. Domestic Airline Markets: 1999

[In thousands (3,728 represents 3,728,000). For calendar year. Data are for the 30 top markets and include all commercial airports in each metro area. Data do not include connecting passengers]

Market	Passengers	Market	Passengers
New York to—from Los Angeles	3,728	Honolulu to—from Lihue, Kauai.	1,749
New York to—from Chicago	2,982	Chicago to—from Detroit	1,509
New York to—from Boston	2,821	Chicago to—from Atlanta	1,498
New York to—from Miami.	2,800	Los Angeles to—from Oakland	1,493
New York to—from Orlando	2,777	New York to—from Dallas/Ft. Worth	1,475
New York to—from San Francisco	2,743	New York to—from West Palm Beach. . . .	1,468
Honolulu to—from Kahului, Maui	2,691	Honolulu to—from Kona, Hawaii	1,459
New York to—from Washington.	2,551	Boston to—from Washington.	1,425
New York to—from Atlanta	2,546	Atlanta to—from Washington.	1,424
New York to—from Ft. Lauderdale	2,386	Chicago to—from Dallas/Ft. Worth	1,415
Los Angeles to—from Las Vegas.	2,304	Los Angeles to—from Honolulu	1,389
Dallas/Ft. Worth to—from Houston.	2,219	Los Angeles to—from Phoenix	1,383
Los Angeles to—from San Francisco	2,006	New York to—from Houston	1,345
New York to—from San Juan	1,988	New York to—from Las Vegas.	1,320
Chicago to—from Los Angeles . . . . ·	1,772	New York to—from Detroit	1,315

Source: Air Transport Association of America, Washington, DC, *Air Transport 2000.*

No. 1061. Worldwide Airline Fatalities: 1987 to 1999

[For scheduled air transport operations]

Year	Fatal accidents	Passenger deaths	Death rate [1]	Death rate [2]	Year	Fatal accidents	Passenger deaths	Death rate [1]	Death rate [2]
1987	25	900	0.09	0.06	1994	27	1,171	0.09	0.06
1988	29	742	0.07	0.04	1995	25	711	0.05	0.03
1989	29	879	0.08	0.05	1996	24	1,146	0.07	0.05
1990	27	544	0.05	0.03	1997	26	929	0.06	0.04
1991	29	638	0.06	0.03	1998	20	904	0.05	0.03
1992	28	1,076	0.09	0.06	1999	20	489	0.03	0.02
1993	33	864	0.07	0.04					

[1] Rate per 100 million passenger miles flown.   [2] Rate per 100 million passenger kilometers flown.

Source: International Civil Aviation Organization, Montreal, Canada, *Civil Aviation Statistics of the World*, annual.

No. 1062. Airline Passenger Screening Results: 1980 to 1999

[Calendar year data (585 represents 585,000,000)]

Item	1980	1985	1990	1995	1996	1997	1998	1999
Persons screened (mil.)	585	993	1,145	1,263	1,497	1,660	1,903	1,754
WEAPONS DETECTED								
Firearms, total	1,914	2,913	2,549	2,390	2,155	2,067	1,515	1,552
Handguns..................	1,878	2,823	2,490	2,230	1,999	1,905	1,401	1,421
Long guns	36	90	59	160	156	162	114	131
Other/other dangerous articles........	108	74	304	(X)	(X)	(X)	(X)	(X)
Explosive/incendiary devices	8	12	15	(X)	(X)	(X)	(X)	(X)
Persons arrested:								
Carrying firearms/explosives	1,031	1,310	1,336	1,194	999	924	660	633
Giving false information.	32	42	18	68	131	72	86	58
Bomb threats received:								
Against airports	1,179	477	448	346	(X)	(NA)	(NA)	(NA)
Against aircraft	268	153	338	327	(X)	(NA)	(NA)	(NA)

NA Not available.   X Not applicable.

Source: U.S. Bureau of Transportation Statistics, *National Transportation Statistics, 2000*, Internet site <http://www.bts.gov/btsprod/nts/Ch2web/2-16.htm> (accessed 24 August 2001).

No. 1063. Aircraft Accidents: 1982 to 2000

[For years ending December 31]

Item	Unit	1982	1985	1990	1995	1998	1999	2000, prel.
Air carrier accidents, all services [1]	Number...	18	21	24	36	50	52	54
Fatal accidents..................	Number...	5	7	6	3	1	2	3
Fatalities	Number...	235	526	39	168	1	12	92
Aboard...................	Number...	223	525	12	162	–	11	92
Rates per 100,000 flight hours:								
Accidents....................	Rate.....	0.241	0.241	0.198	0.267	0.297	0.299	0.299
Fatal accidents	Rate.....	0.057	0.080	0.049	0.022	0.006	0.012	0.017
Commuter air carrier accidents [2]	Number...	26	18	15	12	8	13	12
Fatal accidents..................	Number...	5	7	4	2	–	5	1
Fatalities	Number...	14	37	7	9	–	12	5
Aboard...................	Number...	14	36	5	9	–	12	5
Rates per 100,000 flight hours:								
Accidents....................	Rate.....	2.000	1.036	0.641	0.457	2.262	2.876	2.182
Fatal accidents	Rate.....	0.385	0.403	0.171	0.076	–	1.106	0.182
On-demand air taxi accidents [3]	Number...	132	157	107	75	77	73	80
Fatal accidents..................	Number...	31	35	29	24	17	12	22
Fatalities	Number...	72	76	51	52	45	38	71
Aboard...................	Number...	72	75	49	52	41	38	68
Rates per 100,000 flight hours:								
Accidents....................	Rate.....	4.39	6.11	4.76	4.39	2.80	3.23	3.29
Fatal accidents	Rate.....	1.03	1.36	1.29	1.41	0.62	0.53	0.91
General aviation accidents [4]	Number...	3,233	2,739	2,215	2,053	1,909	1,913	1,835
Fatal accidents..................	Number...	591	498	443	412	368	342	341
Fatalities	Number...	1,187	956	767	734	631	630	592
Aboard...................	Number...	1,170	945	762	727	625	622	582
Rates per 100,000 flight hours:								
Accidents....................	Rate.....	10.90	9.66	7.77	8.23	7.53	6.49	5.96
Fatal accidents	Rate.....	1.99	1.75	1.55	1.64	1.45	1.16	1.11

- Represents zero.   [1] U.S. air carriers operating under 14 CFR 121. Beginning 1998, includes aircraft with 10 or more seats, previously operating under 14 CFR 135.   [2] All scheduled service of U.S. air carriers operating under 14 CFR 135. Beginning 1998, only aircraft with fewer than 10 seats.   [3] All nonscheduled service of U.S. air carriers operating under 14 CFR 135.   [4] U.S. civil registered aircraft not operated under 14 CFR 121 or 135.

Source: U.S. National Transportation Safety Board, Internet site <http://www.ntsb.gov/aviation/stats.htm> (accessed 17 September 2001).

No. 1064. On-Time Flight Arrivals and Departures at Major U.S. Airports: 2000

[In percent. Quarterly, based on gate arrival and departure times for domestic scheduled operations of U.S. major airlines. All U.S. airlines with 1 percent or more of total U.S. domestic scheduled airline passenger revenues are required to report on-time data. A flight is considered on time if it operated less than 15 minutes after the scheduled time shown in the carrier's computerized reservation system. Cancelled and diverted flights are considered late. See source for data on individual airlines]

Airport	On-time arrivals				On-time departures			
	1st qtr.	2d qtr.	3d qtr.	4th qtr.	1st qtr.	2d qtr.	3d qtr.	4th qtr.
Total, all airports	75.2	72.0	72.7	70.6	79.3	76.4	76.9	74.7
Total major airports	74.6	71.2	71.8	70.1	78.2	74.7	75.0	73.4
Atlanta, Hartsfield International	76.7	77.7	74.6	70.7	79.3	79.1	76.3	71.6
Baltimore/Washington International . . .	74.9	73.0	74.5	77.0	76.7	75.3	76.7	77.2
Boston, Logan International	68.2	62.8	63.2	67.9	76.1	73.1	73.8	75.8
Charlotte Douglas.	79.7	76.9	77.4	78.6	80.8	76.4	78.0	77.8
Chicago, O'Hare	70.1	60.8	57.9	64.4	74.3	65.2	62.4	65.8
Cincinnati International	80.9	81.1	80.6	76.3	83.9	83.3	82.9	77.8
Dallas/Ft. Worth Regional	80.2	75.1	83.1	73.7	79.6	74.5	82.0	76.1
Denver International	78.1	63.8	60.9	70.7	81.7	68.8	62.8	71.9
Detroit, Metro Wayne	82.3	78.5	79.8	75.4	80.5	76.5	77.5	72.4
Houston George Bush.	79.5	79.2	80.8	77.6	83.8	82.3	83.4	82.5
Las Vegas, McCarran International . . .	70.0	70.6	73.5	67.7	70.8	70.6	72.2	68.9
Los Angeles International.	67.6	67.3	68.9	62.4	74.2	72.4	73.0	69.3
Miami International.	78.9	73.6	70.3	72.6	82.1	79.5	75.7	77.9
Minneapolis/St. Paul International	80.0	80.2	81.8	75.7	81.0	81.2	81.3	74.2
Newark International	69.4	63.7	69.0	74.9	77.6	73.1	75.3	79.7
New York, Kennedy International.	75.2	67.5	69.2	75.9	81.0	78.0	78.3	79.9
New York, LaGuardia	67.7	61.8	53.9	46.6	77.8	72.9	70.4	64.3
Orlando International	78.3	73.5	72.6	71.8	83.8	79.0	79.8	78.3
Philadelphia International.	70.0	63.2	62.8	71.0	74.3	68.0	68.6	74.4
Phoenix, Sky Harbor International	71.1	73.5	74.4	66.1	71.0	71.7	71.9	67.5
Pittsburgh, Greater International	79.0	74.7	74.1	78.0	81.4	77.0	76.9	78.6
Portland International	73.4	70.3	75.2	68.6	80.1	78.7	80.4	75.1
Ronald Reagan National	77.5	75.6	75.0	76.7	83.0	81.4	82.7	84.0
St. Louis, Lambert	81.0	76.4	79.5	73.3	81.0	75.3	78.8	73.3
Salt Lake City International	78.8	79.3	79.6	69.8	83.3	83.0	82.3	75.2
San Diego International, Lindbergh . . .	71.8	71.5	74.1	65.8	76.9	75.9	77.1	71.1
San Francisco International	60.6	60.1	59.4	63.2	71.0	69.4	69.8	69.8
Seattle-Tacoma International	70.4	65.5	69.8	65.0	77.2	74.1	74.6	71.6
Tampa International	77.2	73.5	71.8	71.3	83.3	80.5	78.7	79.4

Source: U.S. Department of Transportation, Office of Consumer Affairs, *Air Travel Consumer Report*, monthly.

No. 1065. Consumer Complaints Against U.S. Airlines: 1990 to 2000

[Calendar year data. See source for data on individual airlines]

Complaint category	1990	1993	1994	1995	1996	1997	1998	1999	2000
Total	7,703	4,438	5,179	4,629	5,782	6,394	7,980	17,345	20,564
Flight problems [1]	3,034	1,211	1,586	1,133	1,628	1,699	2,270	6,449	8,698
Customer service [2]	758	599	805	667	999	1,418	1,716	3,657	4,074
Baggage.	1,329	627	761	628	882	826	1,105	2,351	2,753
Ticketing/boarding [3]	624	577	598	666	857	904	805	1,329	1,405
Refunds	701	482	393	576	521	531	601	935	803
Oversales [4]	399	257	301	263	353	414	387	673	759
Fares [5]	312	398	267	185	180	195	276	584	708
Disability [6]	(NA)	(NA)	(NA)	(NA)	(NA)	(NA)	331	520	612
Advertising	96	51	94	66	61	57	39	57	42
Tours	29	16	127	18	16	13	23	28	25
Animals	(NA)	(NA)	(NA)	(NA)	(NA)	(NA)	(NA)	(NA)	1
Smoking.	74	30	20	15	13	5	(7)	(7)	(7)
Credit.	5	4	2	4	3	1	(7)	(7)	(7)
Other	342	186	225	408	269	331	427	759	675

NA Not available. [1] Cancellations, delays, etc. from schedule. [2] Unhelpful employees, inadequate meals or cabin service, treatment of delayed passengers. [3] Errors in reservations and ticketing; problems in making reservations and obtaining tickets. [4] All bumping problems, whether or not airline complied with DOT regulations. [5] Incorrect or incomplete information about fares, discount fare conditions, and availability, etc. [6] Prior to 1998, included in ticketing/boarding. [7] Included in "Other" beginning 1998.

Source: U.S. Dept. of Transportation, Office of Consumer Affairs, *Air Travel Consumer Report*, monthly.

No. 1066. Commuter/Regional Airline Operations—Summary: 1980 to 1999

[Calendar year data (14.8 represents 14,800,000). Commuter/regional airlines operate primarily aircraft of predominately 75 passengers or less and 18,000 pounds of payload capacity serving short haul and small community markets. Represents operations within all North America by U.S. Regional Carriers. Averages are means. For definition of mean, see Guide to Tabular Presentation]

Item	Unit	1980	1985	1990	1995	1996	1997	1998	1999
Passenger carriers operating	Number.	214	179	150	124	109	104	97	97
Passengers enplaned	Millions .	14.8	[1]26.0	42.1	57.2	61.9	66.3	71.1	78.1
Average passengers enplaned per carrier. .	1,000 .	69.2	[1]52.4	277.5	461.4	568.3	637.5	733.0	804.7
Revenue passenger miles (RPM)	Billions .	1.92	[1]4.41	7.61	12.75	14.22	15.30	17.42	20.81
Average RPMs per carrier	Millions .	8.97	[1]24.64	50.75	102.80	130.49	147.09	179.64	214.49
Airports served	Number.	732	854	811	780	782	766	773	734
Average trip length	Miles. . .	129	173	183	223	230	231	245	267
Passenger aircraft operated	Number.	1,339	1,745	1,917	2,138	2,127	2,104	2,150	2,187
Average seating capacity (seats).	Number.	13.9	19.2	22.1	24.6	25.1	25.9	27.7	29.8
Fleet flying hours [2]	1,000 . .	1,740	2,854	3,447	4,659	4,568	4,695	4,631	5,058
Average annual utilization per aircraft. . .	Hours . .	1,299	1,635	1,798	2,179	2,148	2,231	2,154	2,313

[1] Adjusted to exclude a merger in 1986. [2] Prior to 1995, utilization results reflected airborne rather than block hours. Data inclusive of carriers which may have operated during only part of calendar year 1996.

Source: Regional Airline Association and AvStat Associates, Washington, DC, Annual Report of the Regional Airline Industry (copyright).

No. 1067. Civil Flying—Summary: 1970 to 1997

[As of Dec. 31 or for years ending Dec. 31, except as noted (50.5 represents $50,500,000)]

Item	Unit	1970	1980	1985	1990	1995	1996	1997
Airports in operation [1]	Number. . .	11,261	15,161	16,318	17,490	18,224	18,292	18,345
Heliports	Number. . .	790	2,336	3,120	4,085	4,559	4,596	4,626
Private	Number. . .	7,001	·10,347	10,457	12,412	13,092	13,163	13,211
Airports with runway lights	Number. . .	3,554	4,738	4,941	4,822	4,838	4,847	4,832
Airports with paved runways.	Number. . .	3,805	5,833	6,721	7,694	8,195	8,218	8,248
Airport Improvement Program [2]	Mil. dol. . . .	50.5	639.0	842.1	1,244.7	1,418.1	1,379.9	1,475.9
Total civil aircraft	1,000 . .	154.5	259.4	274.9	275.9	(NA)	(NA)	(NA)
Active aircraft [3]	1,000 . .	134.5	214.8	215.4	218.9	195.5	198.6	200.0
Air carriers, total [4]	1,000 . .	2.8	3.8	4.7	6.7	7.4	7.5	7.6
General aviation aircraft [5]	1,000 . .	131.7	211.0	210.7	212.2	188.1	191.1	192.4
Fixed-wing aircraft:								
Multiengine	1,000 . .	18.4	31.7	33.6	32.7	24.6	25.6	26.2
Single-engine.	1,000 . .	109.5	168.4	164.4	165.1	137.7	138.1	140.7
Rotorcraft [6]	1,000 . .	2.2	6.0	6.4	7.4	5.8	6.6	6.8
Balloons, blimps, gliders, etc	1,000 . .	1.6	5.0	6.3	7.0	4.7	4.2	4.1
Airman certificates held [7]	1,000 . .	1,002	1,195	1,105	1,195	1,290	1,157	1,157
Pilot [7]	1,000 . .	733	827	710	703	639	622	616
Held by women	Percent . . .	4.0	6.4	6.1	5.8	6.0	5.9	5.8
Airline transport.	1,000 . .	34	70	83	108	124	127	131
Commercial	1,000 . .	187	183	152	149	134	129	125
Private.	1,000 . .	304	357	311	299	261	254	248
Student	1,000 . .	196	200	147	128	101	95	96
Nonpilot [8]	1,000 . .	269	368	395	492	651	534	541
Ground technicians [9]	1,000 . .	241	321	341	421	574	459	464
FAA employees: Total	Number. . .	53,125	55,340	47,245	51,269	48,324	48,618	49,531
Air traffic control specialists [10]	Number. . .	(NA)	27,190	23,580	24,339	23,208	22,823	22,985
Full performance [11]	Number. . .	(NA)	16,317	11,672	12,985	14,845	15,799	14,630
Developmental [11]	Number. . .	(NA)	4,387	4,304	5,042	2,272	1,999	2,312
Assistants [11]	Number. . .	(X)	(X)	1,465	1,153	355	335	319
Traffic management coordinators [12] . .	Number. . .	(X)	(X)	(X)	370	561	542	584
Electronic technicians/ATSS [13]	Number. . .	(NA)	8,871	6,856	6,458	6,749	6,927	7,021
Aviation safety inspectors	Number. . .	(NA)	2,038	1,897	2,984	2,991	3,265	3,577
Engineers	Number. . .	(NA)	2,436	2,457	2,745	2,810	2,860	2,860
Other	Number. . .	(NA)	14,805	12,455	14,743	12,566	12,743	13,088
General aviation: [5]								
Hours flown	Million	26.0	41.0	34.1	34.8	26.6	26.9	27.7
Fuel consumed: [14]								
Gasoline [15]	Mil. gal. . . .	362	520	420	353	287	289	292
Jet fuel [15].	Mil. gal. . . .	415	766	691	663	560	608	642

NA Not available. X Not applicable. [1] Existing airports, heliports, seaplane bases, etc. recorded with FAA. Includes military airports with joint civil and military use. Includes U.S. outlying areas. Airport-type definitions: Public—publicly owned and under control of a public agency; private—owned by a private individual or corporation. May or may not be open for public use. [2] Fiscal year data. Does not include System Planning Grants. Includes U.S. outlying areas. 1970-1980 data are obligated federal funds for the Airport Development Aid Program. Thereafter, data are appropriated federal funds under the Airport and Airway Improvement Act of 1982. [3] Registered aircraft that flew 1 or more hours during the year. [4] Includes helicopters. [5] See text, this section. Beginning 1995, excludes commuters and includes experimental aircraft, not shown separately. Prior to 1995, experimental. [6] Includes autogyros; excludes air carrier helicopters. [7] Includes all active pilots. An active pilot is one with a pilot certificate and a valid medical certificate. Also includes pilots who hold a recreational certificate or only a helicopter, glider, or lighter than air certificate, not shown separately. [8] Includes dispatchers, flight navigators and engineers, and ground technicians—mechanics, parachute riggers, and ground and ground instructors. Data for 1996 on mechanics, repairmen, parachute riggers, ground instructors, and dispatchers are limited to those ages 70 years and less. [9] No medical examinations are required, therefore, data represent all certificates on record and include retired or otherwise inactive technicians. See footnote 8. [10] Includes all air traffic control specialists (staff positions, managers, supervisors, and for 1970-1985 traffic management coordinators, not shown separately) and air traffic assistants. [11] Serving in-flight service stations, towers, and centers. [12] Prior to 1990, included in total air traffic control specialists. [13] Airway Transportation Systems Specialists [14] Source: 1970, U.S. Bureau of Mines; thereafter, FAA General Aviation Activity and Avionics Survey. Data for 1996 are estimated using new information on survey nonresponse and so are not strictly comparable to earlier years. [15] Includes kerosene-type and naphtha-type jet fuels.

Source: Except as noted, U.S. Federal Aviation Administration, FAA Statistical Handbook of Aviation, annual, last published in 1993. Internet site <http://www.api.faa.gov/handbook96/toc96.htm>; and unpublished data.

Transportation   671

No. 1068. Federal Expenditures for Civil Functions of the Corps of Engineers, United States Army: 1970 to 1999

[In millions of dollars (1,128 represents $1,128,000,000). For fiscal years ending in year shown, see text, Section 8, State and Local Government Finances and Employment. These expenditures represent the work of the Corps of Engineers to plan, design, construct, operate, and maintain civil works projects and activities, particularly in the management and improvement of rivers, harbors, and waterways for navigation, flood control, and multiple purposes. The amounts listed below do not include the expenditure of funds contributed, advanced, or reimbursed by other government agencies or local interests. Includes Puerto Rico and outlying areas]

Fiscal year	Total program [1]	Navigation	Flood control	Multiple purpose	Fiscal year	Total program [1]	Navigation	Flood control	Multiple purpose
1970	1,128	398	379	331	1992	3,675	1,562	1,469	469
1980	3,061	1,225,	1,228	551	1993	3,335	1,461	1,243	464
1985	2,956	1,234	1,187	419	1994	3,727	1,607	1,436	521
1987	2,937	1,135	1,272	411	1995	3,796	1,620	1,399	598
1988	3,086	1,271	1,271	423	1996	3,627	1,566	1,349	557
1989	3,252	1,395	1,253	462	1997	3,745	1,620	1,430	545
1990	3,297	1,391	1,397	375	1998	4,091	1,660	1,523	618
1991	3,511	1,473	1,447	443	1999	4,429	1,709	1,774	592

[1] Includes expenditures which are not associated with a specific purpose (e.g., headquarters staff supervision, management, and administration activities, and some research and development activities).

Source: U.S. Army Corps of Engineers, *Report of Civil Works Expenditures by State and Fiscal Year*, annual.

No. 1069. Freight Carried on Major U.S. Waterways: 1980 to 1999

[In millions of tons (4.0 represents 4,000,000)]

Item	1980	1985	1990	1994	1995	1996	1997	1998	1999
Atlantic intracoastal waterway	4.0	3.1	4.2	3.7	3.5	4.3	3.6	3.8	3.4
Great Lakes.................	183.5	148.1	167.1	175.3	177.7	181.8	188.6	192.2	182.9
Gulf intracoastal waterway	94.5	102.5	115.5	117.6	117.9	118.0	118.1	113.8	109.6
Mississippi River system [1]	584.2	527.8	659.6	693.3	710.1	701.8	707.1	708.3	716.9
Mississippi River mainstream.....	441.5	384.0	475.6	496.8	520.2	505.6	504.7	504.4	512.3
Ohio River system [2]	179.3	203.9	260.0	270.5	267.6	270.9	274.9	278.8	277.9
Columbia River...............	49.2	42.4	51.4	50.9	57.1	51.2	52.7	49.1	50.7
Snake River..................	5.1	3.5	4.8	5.9	6.8	5.7	6.1	5.8	5.8

[1] Main channels and all tributaries of the Mississippi, Illinois, Missouri, and Ohio Rivers. [2] Main channels and all navigable tributaries and embayments of the Ohio, Tennessee, and Cumberland Rivers.

Source: U.S. Army Corps of Engineers, *Waterborne Commerce of the United States*, annual.

No. 1070. Waterborne Commerce by Type of Commodity: 1990 to 1999

[In millions of short tons (2,163.9 represents 2,163,900,000). Domestic trade includes all commercial movements between United States ports and on inland rivers, Great Lakes, canals, and connecting channels of the United States, Puerto Rico, and Virgin Islands]

Commodity	1990	1995	1998	1999 Total	1999 Domestic	1999 Foreign imports	1999 Foreign exports
Total [1]	2,163.9	2,240.4	2,339.5	2,322.6	1,061.8	860.8	400.0
Coal........................	339.9	324.5	316.1	289.2	218.9	11.8	58.5
Petroleum and petroleum products	923.2	907.1	987.5	979.1	361.5	563.9	53.8
Crude petroleum..............	485.7	504.6	539.7	533.4	87.9	439.8	5.7
Petroleum products [1]............	437.5	402.5	447.7	445.7	273.6	124.0	48.1
Gasoline	116.9	114.4	109.0	110.6	88.0	18.4	4.1
Distillate fuel oil...........	77.4	76.7	94.2	93.1	63.2	25.8	4.1
Residual fuel oil............	145.2	111.9	127.2	124.0	78.7	35.2	10.0
Chemicals and related products	123.8	153.7	156.4	155.7	75.3	28.1	52.2
Crude material, inedible [1]	374.7	381.7	394.3	386.6	239.3	92.8	54.5
Forest products, wood and chips	55.7	47.2	39.1	38.9	16.1	5.4	17.5
Pulp and waste paper	11.8	14.9	11.3	12.0	0.2	1.2	10.6
Soil, sand, gravel, rock, and stone	144.2	152.5	173.1	175.5	140.6	28.1	6.8
Primary manufactured goods [1]	76.0	106.3	141.0	147.4	45.0	91.0	11.3
Papers products	10.7	13.1	13.3	12.8	0.6	5.0	7.2
Lime, cement and glass	28.3	33.9	46.1	58.3	21.0	35.8	1.5
Primary iron and steel products	25.1	44.1	63.5	56.2	16.0	39.3	0.9
Food and farm products [1]	267.5	303.2	265.7	287.9	100.0	30.2	157.7
Fish	3.2	3.6	2.0	2.1	0.1	1.2	0.8
Grain [1]	157.3	167.9	132.3	152.7	56.8	1.8	94.1
Corn	96.1	105.0	78.1	95.9	40.9	0.1	54.9
Wheat	44.5	48.5	41.3	44.5	12.5	0.2	31.7
Oilseeds	36.0	46.1	45.6	48.9	24.6	0.5	23.9
Soybeans.................	32.2	42.0	38.6	43.0	19.9		23.1
Vegetables products	6.7	9.0	10.4	9.1	1.7	2.9	4.6
Processed grain and animal feed	28.2	33.0	30.4	29.7	8.2	0.9	20.5

- Represents or rounds to zero. [1] Includes categories not shown separately.

Source: U.S. Army Corps of Engineers, *Waterborne Commerce of the United States*, annual.

No. 1071. Cargo-Carrying U.S.-Flag Fleet by Area of Operation: 2000

[As of July 1. Tons in thousands of metric tons (70,608 represents 70,608,000. One ton equals 100 cubic feet of space. Represents active vessels]

Area of operation	Total fleet Number	Total fleet Tons	Liquid carriers Number	Liquid carriers Tons	Dry bulk carriers Number	Dry bulk carriers Tons	Containerships Number	Containerships Tons	Other freighters[1] Number	Other freighters[1] Tons
Total	**29,446**	**70,608**	**3,544**	**19,734.0**	**21,670**	**39,310.0**	**116**	**3,211**	**4,116**	**8,353.0**
Total commercial fleet	29,263	66,978	3,516	18,850	21,670	39,310	111	3,125	3,966	5,693
Foreign trade	421	8,021	79	2,457	235	2,124	61	2,368	46	1,072
Self-propelled	147	5,849	31	1,952	10	477	61	2,368	45	1,052
Less than 1,000 gross tons	-	-	-	-	-	-	-	-	-	-
Greater than or equal to 1,000 gross tons	147	5,849	31	1,952	10	477	61	2,368	45	1,052
Nonself-propelled	274	2,172	48	505	225	1,647	-	-	1	20
Less than 1,000 gross tons	86	235	6	7	80	228	-	-	-	-
Greater than or equal to 1,000 gross tons	188	1,937	42	498	145	1,419	-	-	1	20
Domestic trade	28,842	58,957	3,437	16,393	21,435	37,186	50	757	3,920	4,621
Coastal (including noncontiguous)	2,532	13,790	599	9,779	448	1,596	50	757	1,435	1,658
Self-propelled	193	6,866	102	6,075	1	33	24	596	66	162
Less than 1,000 gross tons	74	31	18	12	-	-	-	-	56	19
Greater than or equal to 1,000 gross tons	119	6,835	84	6,063	1	33	24	596	10	143
Nonself-propelled	2,339	6,924	497	3,704	447	1,563	26	161	1,369	1,496
Less than 1,000 gross tons	1,596	1,190	87	101	289	411	-	-	1,220	678
Greater than or equal to 1,000 gross tons	743	5,734	410	3,603	158	1,152	26	161	149	818
Internal waterways	26,128	42,833	2,819	6,522	20,912	33,511	-	-	2,397	2,800
Self-propelled	26	18	-	-	-	-	-	-	26	18
Less than 1,000 gross tons	26	18	-	-	-	-	-	-	26	18
Greater than or equal to 1,000 gross tons	-	-	-	-	-	-	-	-	-	-
Nonself-propelled	26,102	42,815	2,819	6,522	20,912	33,511	-	-	2,371	2,782
Less than 1,000 gross tons	24,552	37,833	1,556	2,393	20,697	32,912	-	-	2,299	2,528
Greater than or equal to 1,000 gross tons	1,550	4,982	1,263	4,129	215	599	-	-	72	254
Great Lakes	182	2,334	19	92	75	2,079	-	-	88	163
Self-propelled	61	1,914	4	20	53	1,873	-	-	4	21
Less than 1,000 gross tons	8	3	2	1	3	2	-	-	3	(Z)
Greater than or equal to 1,000 gross tons	53	1,911	2	19	50	1,871	-	-	1	21
Nonself-propelled	121	420	15	72	22	206	-	-	84	142
Less than 1,000 gross tons	96	138	1	2	15	20	-	-	80	116
Greater than or equal to 1,000 gross tons	25	282	14	70	7	186	-	-	4	26
National Defense Reserve Fleet	176	3,393	28	884	-	-	5	86	143	2,423
Ready Reserve Force (RRF)	89	1,857	9	268	-	-	3	50	77	1,539
Other Reserve	87	1,536	19	616	-	-	2	36	66	884
Other government: Sealift vessels	7	237	-	-	-	-	-	-	7	237

- Represents zero. Z Less than 500. [1] Includes general cargo, Ro-Ro, multipurpose, LASH (Lighter Aboard Ship) vessels, and deck barges; excludes offshore supply vessels.

Source: U.S. Maritime Administration, Office of Statistical & Economic Analysis; adapted from U.S. Army Corps of Engineers, U.S. Coast Guard and U.S. Customs Service data.

Transportation   673

No. 1072. Jobs on U.S. Deep Sea Commercial Fleet and Typical Basic Monthly Wage for Able-Bodied Seamen: 1975 to 2000

[Employment in thousands (20.5 represents 20,500)]

Year	Employment [1]	Year	Employment [1]	Year	East coast wage rate [2]	West coast wage rate [2]	Year	East coast wage rate [2]	West coast wage rate [2]
1975......	20.5	1995	7.9	1975	612	900	1995	1,918	2,637
1980......	19.6	1996	7.5	1980	967	1,414	1996	2,014	2,769
1985......	13.1	1997	8.6	1985	1,419	2,029	1997	2,094	2,879
1990......	11.1	1998	7.9	1990	1,505	2,218	1998	2,178	2,994
1993......	9.3	1999	7.3	1993	1,721	2,438	1999	2,265	3,114
1994......	9.1	2000	6.6	1994	1,790	2,536	2000	2,453	3,114

[1] As of June 30, except beginning 1980, as of Sept. 30. Estimates of personnel employed on merchant ships, 1,000 gross tons and over. Excludes vessels on inland waterways, Great Lakes, and those owned by, or operated for, U.S. Army and Navy, and special types such as cable ships, tugs, etc. [2] As of January. Basic monthly wage, over and above subsistence (board and room); excludes overtime and fringe pay benefits. West coast incorporates extra pay for Saturdays and Sundays at sea into base wages but east coast does not.

Source: U.S. Maritime Administration, Office of Maritime Labor, Training and Safety.

No. 1073. Merchant Fleets of the World: 2000

[Vessels of 1,000 gross tons and over. As of Jan. 1. Specified countries have 100 or more ships]

Country of registry, 2000	Total	Tanker	Dry bulk [1]	Container-ship	Roll-on/roll-off	Cruise/passenger	Other [2]
World total, 2000	28,259	7,006	5,684	2,457	1,496	285	11,331
United States	463	154	14	89	58	11	137
Privately-owned	277	126	14	84	26	1	26
Government-owned........	186	28	-	5	32	10	111
Foreign total	27,796	6,852	5,670	2,368	1,438	274	11,194
Panama	4,620	1,057	1,346	493	267	47	1,410
Liberia	1,608	657	420	206	57	39	229
Russia	1,503	275	104	24	8	7	1,085
China	1,449	252	335	94	15	4	749
Malta	1,448	390	416	53	60	3	526
Cyprus	1,365	169	474	129	32	9	552
Bahamas................	1,037	253	157	51	66	60	450
Singapore	883	402	136	162	40	-	143
Saint Vincent	791	96	143	29	35	4	484
Greece .... [3]	696	276	266	42	18	14	80
Norway (NIS) [3]	660	308	95	5	72	11	169
Japan..................	650	268	159	26	118	6	73
Netherlands.............	563	72	5	59	18	8	401
Turkey	540	84	164	22	20	3	247
Indonesia	503	122	25	11	13	-	332
Philippines.............	488	66	178	10	42	1	191
Antigua & Barbuda	483	11	16	132	22	-	302
Korea (South)	442	113	95	46	9	3	176
Germany................	429	18	-	237	16	2	156
Belize	422	61	23	6	4	-	328
Italy	383	206	38	21	70	5	43
Malaysia	357	110	60	49	9	2	127
Denmark (DIS) [3].........	315	69	11	61	10	-	164
India..................	298	98	124	7	-	-	69
Thailand	294	96	36	12	-	1	149
Honduras	248	35	16	4	5	1	187
Ukraine................	244	16	8	5	8	6	201
Hong Kong	242	22	130	47	3	-	40
Cambodia	232	1	22	1	6	-	202
Sweden	179	65	8	-	64	-	42
Taiwan	178	17	53	72	1	-	35
Brazil	160	75	41	6	9	-	29
United Kingdom	155	59	3	33	21	10	29
Isle of Man	145	70	20	19	17	-	19
Portugal (MAR) [3]	139	32	13	4	11	-	79
Marshall Islands	132	57	49	19	1	-	6
Romania	131	6	14	1	6	-	104
Syria..................	130	-	4	-	1	-	125
Norway................	129	45	7	-	11	-	66
Iran	126	26	44	3	2	-	51
Vietnam	121	16	9	1	1	-	94
Spain	119	35	10	17	36	-	21
Bermuda...............	112	37	28	18	11	-	18
Egypt	112	15	22	1	9	1	64
All other	2,535	694	343	130	194	27	1,147

- Represents zero. [1] Includes bulk/oil, ore/oil, and ore/bulk/oil carriers. [2] Breakbulk ships, partial containerships, refrigerated cargo ships, barge and specialized cargo ships. [3] International Shipping Registry which is an open registry under which the ship flies the flag of the specified nation but is exempt from certain taxation and other regulations.

Source: U.S. Maritime Administration, Merchant Fleets of the World, summary report, annual; and unpublished data.

No. 1074. Highway Mileage—Urban and Rural by Ownership: 1980 to 1999

[In thousands (3,955 represents 3,955,000). As of Dec. 31. Includes Puerto Rico beginning 1996]

Type and control	1980	1985	1990	1994	1995	1996	1997	1998	1999
Total mileage [1]	[2]3,955	3,862	3,880	3,906	3,912	3,934	3,959	3,920	3,932
Urban mileage [3]	624	691	757	814	819	834	843	849	853
Under State control	79	111	96	110	112	113	114	111	111
Under local control	543	578	661	702	706	719	728	736	740
Rural mileage	[2]3,331	3,171	3,123	3,093	3,093	3,100	3,116	3,072	3,079
Under state control	702	773	703	690	691	693	695	663	663
Under local control	2,270	2,173	2,242	2,229	2,231	2,238	2,254	2,291	2,299
Under federal control	262	225	178	174	170	169	167	118	117

[1] Beginning 1985, includes only public road mileage as defined 23 USC 402. [2] Includes 98,000 miles of nonpublic road mileage previously contained in other rural categories. [3] Includes a small amount of road owned by the federal government, such as roads in federal parks that are not part of a State or local highway system.

Source: U.S. Federal Highway Administration, *Highway Statistics*, annual.

No. 1075. Highway Mileage—Functional Systems and Urban/Rural: 1999

[As of Dec. 31. Excludes Puerto Rico. For definition of functional systems, see text, this section]

State	Total	Functional systems					Urban	Rural
		Interstate	Other free-ways and express-ways	Arterial	Collector	Local		
U.S.	3,917,240	46,317	9,125	378,924	792,652	2,690,222	846,059	3,071,181
AL.	94,247	905	21	8,758	20,349	64,214	20,658	73,589
AK.	12,667	1,083	-	1,505	2,736	7,343	1,809	10,858
AZ.	54,454	1,168	108	4,745	8,554	39,879	17,277	37,177
AR.	97,562	542	123	6,891	20,146	69,860	10,603	86,959
CA.	166,973	2,456	1,375	26,659	31,839	104,644	83,787	83,186
CO	85,149	953	226	8,182	16,592	59,196	14,248	70,901
CT.	20,788	346	197	2,849	2,994	14,402	11,774	9,014
DE.	5,747	41	11	627	946	4,122	1,969	3,778
DC	1,425	14	18	264	152	977	1,425	-
FL.	115,956	1,472	425	12,047	14,312	87,700	48,320	67,636
GA	113,894	1,244	165	13,133	23,169	76,183	27,459	86,435
HI	4,257	55	34	748	825	2,595	1,895	2,362
ID	45,802	611	-	3,787	9,829	31,575	4,004	41,798
IL	138,246	2,165	84	13,914	21,504	100,579	36,194	102,052
IN	93,605	1,169	137	7,940	22,640	61,719	19,941	73,664
IA . . . . ! .	112,904	782	-	9,495	31,503	71,124	9,519	103,385
KS.	133,963	872	135	9,191	33,282	90,483	10,171	123,792
KY.	74,121	762	91	5,491	17,647	50,130	11,079	63,042
LA.	60,828	894	46	5,300	12,549	42,039	13,942	46,886
ME	22,664	367	18	2,314	5,943	14,022	2,631	20,033
MD	30,322	481	235	3,556	5,021	21,029	14,321	16,001
MA	35,265	566	199	5,638	5,485	23,377	23,063	12,202
MI	121,722	1,241	224	12,220	25,737	82,300	29,932	91,790
MN	131,996	912	146	12,660	29,561	88,717	15,953	116,043
MS	73,318	685	41	7,099	15,529	49,964	7,933	65,385
MO	122,831	1,178	320	9,386	24,978	86,969	16,370	106,461
MT	69,662	1,191	-	6,017	16,406	46,048	2,585	67,077
NE.	92,798	482	17	7,884	20,787	63,628	5,175	87,623
NV.	35,871	560	43	2,864	5,219	27,185	5,789	30,082
NH	15,173	225	40	1,557	2,710	10,641	2,929	12,244
NJ	35,941	420	312	5,340	4,584	25,285	24,165	11,776
NM	59,913	1,000	3	4,513	6,973	47,424	6,074	53,839
NY.	112,659	1,667	792	13,463	20,543	76,194	40,913	71,746
NC	99,302	1,017	272	8,947	17,788	71,278	23,395	75,907
ND	86,615	572	-	5,872	11,538	68,633	1,834	84,781
OH	116,371	1,573	385	10,613	22,102	81,698	33,495	82,876
OK	112,511	930	134	7,846	25,372	78,229	13,286	99,225
OR	66,879	727	55	6,738	17,410	41,949	10,902	55,977
PA	119,384	1,758	485	13,161	19,779	84,201	34,287	85,097
RI	6,052	70	69	845	857	4,211	4,719	1,333
SC.	64,901	828	68	6,809	13,393	43,803	10,619	54,282
SD.	83,410	678	-	6,295	19,271	57,166	1,979	81,431
TN.	87,259	1,074	126	8,711	18,064	59,284	17,722	69,537
TX.	300,507	3,234	1,201	28,345	63,112	204,615	81,969	218,538
UT.	41,456	938	8	3,332	7,811	29,367	7,316	34,140
VT.	14,265	320	19	1,297	3,125	9,504	1,376	12,889
VA.	70,327	1,118	217	8,194	14,181	46,617	19,002	51,325
WA	80,256	764	313	7,304	16,796	55,079	18,194	62,062
WV	36,339	549	9	3,236	8,776	23,769	3,223	33,116
WI	111,906	745	175	11,685	21,530	77,771	16,540	95,366
WY	26,777	913	3	3,657	10,703	11,501	2,294	24,483

- Represents zero.

Source: U.S. Federal Highway Administration, *Highway Statistics*, annual.

U.S. Census Bureau, Statistical Abstract of the United States: 2001

No. 1076. Commodity Shipments—Value, Tons, and Ton-Miles: 1993 and 1997

[Based on the 1997 Economic Census; see Appendix III]

Mode of transportation	Value		Tons		Ton-miles	
	1993	1997	1993	1997	1993	1997
All modes	**5,846,334**	**6,943,988**	**9,688,493**	**11,089,733**	**2,420,915**	**2,661,363**
Single modes	**4,941,452**	**5,719,558**	**8,922,286**	**10,436,538**	**2,136,873**	**2,383,473**
Truck [1]	4,403,494	4,981,531	6,385,915	7,700,675	869,536	1,023,506
For-hire truck	2,625,093	2,901,345	2,808,279	3,402,605	629,000	741,117
Private truck	1,755,837	2,036,528	3,543,513	4,137,294	235,897	268,592
Rail	247,394	319,629	1,544,148	1,549,817	942,561	1,022,547
Water	61,628	75,840	505,440	563,369	271,998	261,747
Shallow draft	40,707	53,897	362,454	414,758	164,371	189,284
Great Lakes	(S)	1,504	33,041	38,421	12,395	13,415
Deep draft	19,749	20,439	109,945	110,191	95,232	59,047
Air (includes truck and air)	139,086	229,062	3,139	4,475	4,009	6,233
Pipeline [2]	89,849	113,497	483,645	618,202	(S)	(S)
Multiple modes	**662,603**	**945,874**	**225,676**	**216,673**	**191,461**	**204,514**
Parcel, U.S. Postal Service or courier	563,277	855,897	18,892	23,689	13,151	17,994
Truck and rail	83,082	75,695	40,624	54,246	37,675	55,561
Truck and water	9,392	8,241	67,995	33,215	40,610	34,767
Rail and water	3,636	1,771	79,222	79,275	70,219	77,590
Other multiple modes	3,216	4,269	18,943	26,248	(S)	18,603
Other and unknown modes	**242,279**	**278,555**	**540,530**	**436,521**	**92,581**	**73,376**

S Data do not meet publication standards due to high sampling variability or other reasons.   [1] Truck as a single mode includes shipments that went by private truck only, for hire truck only, or a combination of private truck and for-hire truck.   [2] Commodity Flow Survey data exclude most shipments of crude oil.

Source: U.S. Bureau of Transportation Statistics and U.S. Census Bureau, *1997 Economic Census, Transportation, 1997 Commodity Flow Survey,* Series EC97TCF-US, issued December 1999.

No. 1077. Hazardous Material Shipment Characteristics: 1997

[Based on the 1997 Economic Census; see Appendix III]

Item	Value		Tons		Ton-miles		Average miles per shipment
	Amount (mil. dol.)	Percent	Number (1,000)	Percent	Number (mil.)	Percent	
MODE OF TRANSPORTATION							
All modes	**466,407**	**100.0**	**1,565,196**	**100.0**	**263,809**	**100.0**	**113**
Single modes	**452,727**	**97.1**	**1,541,716**	**98.5**	**258,912**	**98.1**	**95**
Truck [1]	298,173	63.9	869,796	55.6	74,939	28.4	73
For-hire truck	134,308	28.8	336,363	21.5	45,234	17.1	260
Private truck	160,693	34.5	522,666	33.4	28,847	10.9	35
Rail	33,340	7.1	96,626	6.2	74,711	28.3	853
Water	26,951	5.8	143,152	9.1	68,212	25.9	(S)
Air (includes truck and air)	8,558	1.8	66	(Z)	95	(Z)	1,462
Pipeline [2]	85,706	18.4	432,075	27.6	(S)	(S)	(S)
Multiple modes	**5,735**	**1.2**	**6,022**	**0.4**	**3,061**	**1.2**	**645**
Parcel, U.S. Postal Service or courier	2,874	0.6	143	(Z)	78	(Z)	697
Other multiple modes	2,861	0.6	5,879	0.4	2,982	1.1	(S)
Other and unknown modes	**7,945**	**1.7**	**17,459**	**1.1**	**1,837**	**0.7**	**38**
HAZARDOUS CLASS AND DESCRIPTION							
Total	**466,407**	**100.0**	**1,565,196**	**100.0**	**263,809**	**100.0**	**113**
Class 1, explosives	4,342	0.9	1,517	0.1	(S)	(S)	549
Class 2, gases	40,884	8.8	115,021	7.3	21,842	8.3	66
Class 3, flammable liquids	335,619	72.0	1,264,281	80.8	159,979	60.6	73
Class 4, flammable solids	3,898	0.8	11,804	0.8	9,618	3.6	838
Class 5, oxidizers and organic peroxides	4,485	1.0	9,239	0.6	4,471	1.7	193
Class 6, toxic (poison)	10,086	2.2	6,366	0.4	2,824	1.1	402
Class 7, radioactive materials	2,722	0.6	87	(Z)	48	(Z)	445
Class 8, corrosive materials	40,423	8.7	91,564	5.9	41,161	15.6	201
Class 9, misc. dangerous goods	23,946	5.1	65,317	4.2	22,727	8.6	323

S Data do not meet publication standards because of high sampling variability or other reasons.   Z Represents or rounds to zero.   [1] "Truck" as a single mode includes shipments which went by private truck only, for-hire truck only or a combination of private truck and for-hire truck.   [2] Commodity Flow Survey data exclude most shipments of crude oil.

Source: U.S. Bureau of Transportation Statistics and U.S. Census Bureau, *1997 Economic Census, Transportation, 1997 Commodity Flow Survey, Hazardous Materials,* Series EC97TCF-US(HM)RV, issued April 2000.

No. 1078. Bridge Inventory—Total and Deficient: 1996 to 2000

[As of December, except 2000 as of August. Based on the National Bridge Inventory program]

State and year	Number of bridges	Deficient and obsolete					
		Total number	Percent	Structurally deficient [1]		Functionally obsolete [2]	
				Number	Percent	Number	Percent
1996, total	581,862	182,726	31.4	101,518	17.4	81,208	14.0
1997, total	582,751	175,885	30.2	98,475	16.9	77,410	13.3
1998, total	582,984	172,582	29.6	93,076	16.0	79,506	13.6
1999, total	585,542	170,050	29.0	88,150	15.1	81,900	14.0
U.S. total, 2000	**587,755**	**167,993**	**28.6**	**87,106**	**14.8**	**80,887**	**13.8**
Alabama	15,635	5,053	32.3	2,846	18.2	2,207	14.1
Alaska	1,409	400	28.4	168	11.9	232	16.5
Arizona	6,714	696	10.4	196	2.9	500	7.4
Arkansas	12,451	3,500	28.1	1,482	11.9	2,018	16.2
California	23,672	6,790	28.7	2,458	10.4	4,332	18.3
Colorado	7,977	1,440	18.1	587	7.4	853	10.7
Connecticut	4,178	1,278	30.6	371	8.9	907	21.7
Delaware	824	131	15.9	53	6.4	78	9.5
District of Columbia	250	162	64.8	28	11.2	134	53.6
Florida	11,187	2,227	19.9	311	2.8	1,916	17.1
Georgia	14,382	3,712	25.8	1,774	12.3	1,938	13.5
Hawaii	1,066	550	51.6	201	18.9	349	32.7
Idaho	4,032	752	18.7	317	7.9	435	10.8
Illinois	25,497	4,961	19.5	2,821	11.1	2,140	8.4
Indiana	18,002	4,445	24.7	2,500	13.9	1,945	10.8
Iowa	24,632	7,124	28.9	5,008	20.3	2,116	8.6
Kansas	25,720	6,651	25.9	3,533	13.7	3,118	12.1
Kentucky	13,374	4,072	30.4	1,193	8.9	2,879	21.5
Louisiana	13,485	4,706	34.9	2,542	18.9	2,164	16.0
Maine	2,360	873	37.0	375	15.9	498	21.1
Maryland	4,965	1,445	29.1	440	8.9	1,005	20.2
Massachusetts	4,953	2,480	50.1	705	14.2	1,775	35.8
Michigan	10,581	3,517	33.2	2,181	20.6	1,336	12.6
Minnesota	12,811	1,882	14.7	1,278	10.0	604	4.7
Mississippi	16,672	5,144	30.9	3,851	23.1	1,293	7.8
Missouri	23,388	9,058	38.7	6,361	27.2	2,697	11.5
Montana	4,981	1,194	24.0	625	12.5	569	11.4
Nebraska	15,507	4,477	28.9	2,760	17.8	1,717	11.1
Nevada	1,424	216	15.2	68	4.8	148	10.4
New Hampshire	2,348	799	34.0	389	16.6	410	17.5
New Jersey	6,350	2,367	37.3	965	15.2	1,402	22.1
New Mexico	3,694	673	18.2	314	8.5	359	9.7
New York	17,387	7,038	40.5	3,430	19.7	3,608	20.8
North Carolina	16,822	5,326	31.7	2,606	15.5	2,720	16.2
North Dakota	4,517	1,174	26.0	893	19.8	281	6.2
Ohio	27,902	7,269	26.1	3,472	12.4	3,797	13.6
Oklahoma	22,799	9,497	41.7	8,053	35.3	1,444	6.3
Oregon	7,257	1,642	22.6	322	4.4	1,320	18.2
Pennsylvania	22,052	9,501	43.1	5,405	24.5	4,096	18.6
Rhode Island	747	375	50.2	187	25.0	188	25.2
South Carolina	9,064	1,878	20.7	1,009	11.1	869	9.6
South Dakota	6,032	1,802	29.9	1,430	23.7	372	6.2
Tennessee	19,404	4,954	25.5	1,890	9.7	3,064	15.8
Texas	47,886	10,378	21.7	3,312	6.9	7,066	14.8
Utah	2,750	604	22.0	359	13.1	245	8.9
Vermont	2,703	1,012	37.4	568	21.0	444	16.4
Virginia	12,710	3,524	27.7	1,237	9.7	2,287	18.0
Washington	7,876	2,103	26.7	580	7.4	1,523	19.3
West Virginia	6,730	2,791	41.5	1,205	17.9	1,586	23.6
Wisconsin	13,418	2,677	20.0	1,792	13.4	885	6.6
Wyoming	3,110	662	21.3	399	12.8	263	8.5
Puerto Rico	2,068	1,011	48.9	256	12.4	755	36.5

[1] Bridges are structurally deficient if they have been restricted to light vehicles, require immediate rehabilitation to remain open, or are closed.   [2] Bridges are functionally obsolete if they have deck geometry, load caring capacity, clearance or approach roadway alignment that not longer meet the criteria for the system of which the bridge is a part.

Source: U.S. Federal Highway Administration, Office of Bridge Technology, Internet site <http://www.fhwa.dot.gov/bridge/britab.htm>.

Transportation 677

No. 1079. Funding for Highways and Disposition of Highway-User Revenue: 1990 to 1999

[In millions of dollars (75,444 represents $75,444,000,000). Data compiled from reports of state and local authorities]

Type	1990	1993	1994	1995	1996	1997	1998	1999
Total receipts	75,444	88,380	91,312	96,269	102,771	107,421	109,881	117,878
Current income	69,880	80,610	84,017	87,620	94,972	98,667	100,975	106,602
Highway user revenues	44,346	54,401	55,387	59,331	64,052	66,266	69,227	73,897
Other taxes and fees	19,827	19,375	21,598	21,732	23,830	25,424	24,274	25,989
Investment income, other receipts	5,707	6,834	7,032	6,557	7,090	6,977	7,474	6,715
Bond issue proceeds [1]	5,564	7,770	7,295	8,649	7,799	8,754	8,906	11,276
Funds from (+) or to (-) reserves	-36	-1,955	-1,120	-2,791	-4,689	-5,468	-2,689	-444
Total funds available	75,408	86,425	90,192	93,478	98,082	101,953	107,192	117,434
Total disbursements	75,408	86,425	90,192	93,478	98,082	101,953	107,192	117,434
Current disbursements	72,457	81,233	85,645	88,994	93,492	97,320	101,995	111,963
Capital outlay	35,115	39,528	42,379	44,228	46,810	48,360	51,614	59,499
Maintenance and traffic services	20,365	22,894	23,553	24,319	25,564	26,777	27,235	29,212
Administration and research	6,501	7,921	8,376	8,419	8,445	8,256	8,519	8,722
Law enforcement and safety	7,235	7,157	7,673	8,218	8,897	9,761	10,155	9,946
Interest on debt	3,205	3,733	3,664	3,810	3,776	4,166	4,472	4,584
Bond retirement [1]	2,951	5,192	4,547	4,484	4,590	4,633	5,197	5,471

[1] Excludes issue and redemption of short-term notes or refunding bonds.
Source: U.S. Federal Highway Administration, *Highway Statistics*, annual; and releases.

No. 1080. Federal Aid to State and Local Governments for Highway Trust Fund and Federal Transit Administration (FTA) by State: 2000

[Year ending Sept. 30 (24,149 represents $24,149,000,000)]

State	Highway trust fund Total (mil. dol.)	Per capita (dol.) [1]	FTA Total (mil. dol.)	Per capita (dol.) [1]
U.S.[2]	24,149	84.5	5,087	17.8
AL	473	106.3	14	3.3
AK	336	535.3	7	11.2
AZ	436	85.0	49	9.5
AR	277	103.8	12	4.4
CA	1,967	58.1	871	25.7
CO	297	69.0	83	19.2
CT	399	117.3	60	17.6
DE	120	152.8	8	10.8
DC	131	228.5	171	299.4
FL	1,104	69.1	212	13.3
GA	710	86.7	132	16.1
HI	82	67.3	39	32.1
ID	172	132.9	7	5.7
IL	858	69.1	278	22.4
IN	571	94.0	58	9.5
IA	305	104.1	16	5.4
KS	304	113.2	12	4.3
KY	519	128.4	27	6.6
LA	404	90.4	39	8.7
ME	146	114.9	28	21.8
MD	378	71.5	106	19.9
MA	484	76.3	97	15.3
MI	847	85.2	78	7.9
MN	423	85.9	56	11.4
MS	272	95.6	6	2.1
MO	669	119.6	89	16.0
MT	260	288.4	28	31.5
NE	195	113.8	10	5.7
NV	149	74.7	19	9.3
NH	123	99.4	4	3.3
NJ	588	69.9	459	54.6
NM	263	144.3	10	5.4
NY	1,133	59.7	761	40.1
NC	756	93.9	28	3.5
ND	187	291.8	5	7.2
OH	743	65.4	136	11.9
OK	320	92.8	18	5.3
OR	287	83.9	46	13.3
PA	848	69.1	267	21.8
RI	133	126.9	16	15.5
SC	363	90.6	17	4.1
SD	180	237.9	4	5.8
TN	483	84.8	45	7.9
TX	1,783	85.5	308	14.8
UT	230	103.0	79	35.3
VT	115	189.7	9	14.7
VA	507	71.6	49	7.0
WA	477	81.0	163	27.7
WV	286	158.2	12	6.4
WI	172	32.1	59	11.0
WY	181	366.1	2	4.1

[1] Based on enumerated resident population as of April 1. [2] Includes outlying areas and undistributed funds not shown separately.
Source: U.S. Census Bureau, *Federal Aid to States for Fiscal Year, 2000*.

No. 1081. State Motor Fuel Tax Receipts, 1998 and 1999, and Gasoline Tax Rates, 1999

[555 represents $555,000,000]

State	Net receipts (mil. dol.) 1998	Net receipts (mil. dol.) 1999	Tax rate, [1] 1999
AL	555	571	18.0
AK	23	25	8.0
AZ	508	560	18.0
AR	348	366	19.5
CA	2,775	2,936	18.0
CO	480	512	22.0
CT	524	498	32.0
DE	101	103	23.0
DC	31	33	20.0
FL	1,467	1,525	13.1
GA	421	406	7.5
HI	67	66	16.0
ID	196	209	25.0
IL	1,170	1,212	19.0
IN	716	739	15.0
IA	392	399	20.0
KS	315	338	20.0
KY	454	488	16.4
LA	529	537	20.0
ME	153	155	19.0
MD	633	672	23.5
MA	605	628	21.0
MI	1,005	1,048	19.0
MN	541	580	20.0
MS	363	367	18.4
MO	644	642	17.0
MT	168	173	27.0
NE	270	275	22.8
NV	292	280	24.8
NH	126	130	19.5
NJ	492	501	10.5
NM	244	249	18.5
NY	1,462	1,472	29.3
NC	1,017	1,017	21.2
ND	94	95	21.0
OH	1,421	1,464	22.0
OK	395	401	17.0
OR	383	390	24.0
PA	1,660	1,678	25.9
RI	129	133	29.0
SC	398	424	16.0
SD	109	112	22.0
TN	696	703	20.0
TX	2,518	2,593	20.0
UT	295	311	24.5
VT	84	80	20.0
VA	747	771	17.5
WA	703	716	23.0
WV	297	298	25.4
WI	727	783	25.4
WY	60	90	14.0

[1] Cents per gallon. In effect Dec. 31.
Source: U.S. Federal Highway Administration, *Highway Statistics*, annual.

No. 1082. Public Highway Debt—State and Local Governments: 1980 to 1999

[In millions of dollars (2,381 represents $2,381,000,000). Long-term obligations. Data are for varying calendar and fiscal years. Excludes duplicated and interunit obligations]

Item	1980	1985	1990	1994	1995	1996	1997	1998	1999
Total debt issued.........	2,381	8,194	5,708	10,833	11,305	9,728	12,347	16,412	(NA)
State	1,160	5,397	3,147	5,739	4,718	6,653	8,174	9,789	9,554
Local [1]	1,221	2,797	2,561	5,094	6,587	3,075	4,173	6,623	(NA)
Total debt redeemed	1,987	5,294	3,120	6,178	5,634	6,380	7,043	11,735	(NA)
State	1,114	3,835	1,648	3,698	2,939	4,161	4,228	6,466	3,609
Local [1]	873	1,459	1,472	2,480	2,695	2,219	2,815	5,269	(NA)
Total debt outstanding [2]....	27,616	32,690	46,586	63,062	68,733	72,197	77,501	82,599	(NA)
State	20,210	21,277	28,362	37,449	39,228	41,720	45,666	49,182	55,646
Local [1]	7,406	11,413	18,224	25,613	29,505	30,477	31,835	33,417	(NA)

NA Not available. [1] Local data estimated. [2] End-of-year.

Source: U.S. Federal Highway Administration, *Highway Statistics,* annual.

No. 1083. State Disbursements for Highways by State: 1995 to 1999

[In millions of dollars (67,615 represents $67,615,000,000). Comprises disbursements from current revenues or loans for construction, maintenance, interest and principal payments on highway bonds, transfers to local units, and miscellaneous. Includes transactions by state toll authorities. Excludes amounts allocated for collection expenses and nonhighway purposes, and bonds redeemed by refunding]

State	1995	1996	1997	1998	1999
United States.....................	67,615	71,736	73,994	80,518	83,675
Alabama........................	1,002	1,064	1,019	1,053	1,085
Alaska.........................	438	453	435	404	416
Arizona........................	1,199	1,532	1,359	1,430	1,860
Arkansas	666	755	832	815	736
California	5,966	5,831	6,219	6,574	6,876
Colorado.......................	922	922	887	1,166	1,260
Connecticut.....................	1,153	1,202	1,173	1,427	1,094
Delaware	441	452	449	647	507
District of Columbia	140	163	151	259	242
Florida	3,421	3,472	3,734	4,024	3,992
Georgia	1,437	1,675	1,372	1,613	1,763
Hawaii	360	405	387	326	355
Idaho.........................	350	369	403	414	445
Illinois	3,006	3,097	2,992	3,306	2,957
Indiana........................	1,433	1,444	1,636	1,652	1,522
Iowa	1,078	1,128	1,173	1,177	1,253
Kansas........................	1,019	1,162	1,087	1,306	1,155
Kentucky	1,397	1,372	1,331	1,481	1,578
Louisiana	1,198	1,417	1,189	1,400	1,237
Maine.........................	379	509	474	485	458
Maryland	1,289	1,449	1,489	1,492	1,554
Massachusetts...................	2,501	2,545	3,287	3,351	4,407
Michigan.......................	1,974	1,966	2,100	2,745	2,629
Minnesota......................	1,210	1,374	1,450	1,377	1,534
Mississippi	662	826	809	843	968
Missouri	1,313	1,402	1,492	1,438	1,600
Montana.......................	388	377	379	378	434
Nebraska	578	595	611	589	681
Nevada	484	468	431	446	557
New Hampshire..................	328	346	360	371	416
New Jersey.....................	2,102	2,928	2,247	2,513	2,905
New Mexico	535	532	546	570	753
New York	4,584	4,424	4,778	6,051	5,347
North Carolina...................	1,871	1,939	2,099	2,352	2,441
North Dakota....................	270	266	326	306	413
Ohio	2,637	2,709	2,940	3,327	3,158
Oklahoma......................	828	918	867	944	1,322
Oregon........................	888	995	992	1,051	1,009
Pennsylvania....................	3,153	3,118	3,764	3,902	4,143
Rhode Island....................	290	297	225	339	316
South Carolina...................	668	678	741	766	885
South Dakota	286	289	349	305	371
Tennessee	1,230	1,283	1,351	1,420	1,398
Texas.........................	3,593	4,312	4,253	4,295	4,840
Utah	431	457	802	1,129	1,072
Vermont	194	192	213	222	252
Virginia........................	2,107	2,321	2,358	2,619	2,771
Washington.....................	1,909	1,766	1,851	1,805	1,780
West Virginia....................	781	935	940	893	930
Wisconsin......................	1,252	1,324	1,354	1,398	1,614
Wyoming	272	283	284	321	386

Source: U.S. Federal Highway Administration, *Highway Statistics,* annual.

U.S. Census Bureau, Statistical Abstract of the United States: 2001

No. 1084. State Motor Vehicle Registrations: 1980 to 1999

[In thousands (155,796 represents 155,796,000). Compiled principally from information obtained from state authorities, but it was necessary to draw on other sources and to make numerous estimates in order to complete series. Includes Alaska and Hawaii. See also Table 1087]

Item	1980	1990	1995	1996	1997	1998	1999
All motor vehicles	155,796	188,798	201,530	206,365	207,754	211,617	216,309
Private and commercial	153,265	185,541	197,941	202,714	204,079	207,841	212,474
Publicly owned.	2,531	3,257	3,589	3,651	3,674	3,776	3,834
Automobiles [1]	121,601	133,700	128,387	129,728	129,749	131,839	132,432
Private and commercial	120,743	132,164	126,900	128,439	128,450	130,500	131,077
Publicly owned.	857	1,536	1,487	1,289	1,299	1,339	1,355
Buses	529	627	686	697	698	716	729
Private and commercial	254	275	288	291	294	302	307
Publicly owned.	275	351	398	406	403	413	422
Trucks [1]	33,667	54,470	72,458	75,940	77,307	79,062	83,148
Private and commercial	32,268	53,101	70,754	73,984	75,335	77,039	81,091
Publicly owned.	1,399	1,369	1,704	1,956	1,972	2,024	2,057

[1] Trucks include pickups, panels and delivery vans. Beginning 1990, personal passenger vans, passenger minivans, and utility-type vehicles are no longer included in automobiles but are included in trucks.
Source: U.S. Federal Highway Administration, *Highway Statistics*, annual.

No. 1085. Alternative Fueled Vehicles in Use by Fuel Type: 1999 to 2001

[339,340 represents 339,340,000]

Fuel type	Alternative fueled vehicles			Fuel consumption (1,000 gasoline-equivalent gallons)		
	1999	2000	2001	1999	2000	2001
Fuels	406,841	432,344	456,306	339,340	353,760	366,331
Liquified petroleum gases (LPG) . . .	267,000	268,000	269,000	242,141	242,695	243,196
Compressed natural gas (CNG)	89,556	100,530	109,730	86,286	97,568	107,476
Liquified natural gas (LNG).	1,681	1,900	2,039	5,828	6,847	7,566
M85 (Mixture: 85% methanol + 15% gasoline) . . .	18,964	18,365	16,918	1,073	996	918
Neat methanol (M100).	198	195	184	447	437	406
E85 (Mixture: 85% ethanol + 15% gasoline)	22,464	34,680	48,022	2,075	3,344	4,575
E95 (Mixture: 95% ethanol + 5% gasoline)	14	13	13	59	54	51
Electricity	6,964	8,661	10,400	1,431	1,819	2,143

Source: Energy Information Administration, *Alternatives to Traditional Transportation Fuels: 1992-2001*.

No. 1086. Number of Households, Leasing Vehicles, and Number of Vehicles Leased Per Household: 1989 to 1998

Item	Share of households leasing a vehicle for personal use (percents)				Average number of leased vehicles, among households having such vehicles			
	1989	1992	1995	1998	1989	1992	1995	1998
All households	2.5	2.9	4.5	6.4	1.1	1.1	1.1	1.2
Household income:								
Less than $10,000	(Z)	(Z)	(Z)	(Z)	(Z)	(Z)	(Z)	1.2
$10,000 to $24,999	(Z)	(Z)	1.5	4.0	(Z)	(Z)	1.0	1.1
$25,000 to $49,999	(Z)	3.3	3.4	5.0	(Z)	1.1	1.0	1.1
$50,000 to $99,999	6.1	4.1	9.4	9.5	1.1	1.1	1.2	1.2
$100,000 and over.	5.0	9.6	14.2	14.8	1.2	1.1	1.3	1.3
Age of household head:								
Less than 35 years	4.2	3.2	4.8	8.2	1.1	1.0	1.0	1.1
35 to 44 years	3.0	4.2	5.4	8.3	1.0	1.1	1.1	1.1
45 to 54 years.	3.3	3.2	7.8	7.6	1.1	1.2	1.2	1.3
55 to 64 years.	(Z)	3.2	4.1	4.4	1.6	1.2	1.2	1.1
65 to 74 years.	(Z)	1.0	1.3	2.9	(Z)	1.0	1.1	1.2
75 years and over	(Z)	(Z)	0.5	1.9	(Z)	(Z)	1.0	1.0
Race/ethnicity of respondent:								
White non-Hispanic	2.7	3.1	4.4	6.3	1.1	1.1	1.1	1.1
Non-White and Hispanic	(Z)	2.3	4.9	6.5	(Z)	1.1	1.1	1.3
Work status of household head:								
Work for someone else.	3.5	3.4	6.0	8.1	1.1	1.1	1.1	1.2
Self employed.	3.4	7.2	5.2	9.0	1.0	1.1	1.3	1.1
Retired.	(Z)	0.7	1.3	1.5	(Z)	1.3	1.0	1.2
Other not working	(Z)	(Z)	3.0	(Z)	(Z)	(Z)	1.0	(Z)
Homeownership status:								
Owner.	2.2	3.5	5.8	7.2	1.1	1.1	1.2	1.2
Renter or other	3.0	1.8	2.3	4.8	1.1	1.1	1.1	1.1
Net worth percentile:								
Bottom 25 percent	(Z)	2.1	2.7	4.8	(Z)	1.1	1.1	1.1
25 to 49.9 percent	2.8	(Z)	4.2	5.4	1.1	(Z)	1.0	1.1
50 to 74.9 percent	2.5	3.1	4.2	6.8	1.1	1.1	1.1	1.2
75 to 89.9 percent	2.9	3.5	6.2	7.8	1.0	1.0	1.2	1.2
Top 10 percent	2.5	6.4	8.3	9.5	1.3	1.2	1.3	1.2

Z Ten or fewer observations.
Source: Board of Governors of the Federal Reserve System, *Survey of Consumer Finances*.

680 Transportation

No. 1087. State Motor Vehicle Registrations, 1980 to 1999, and Licensed Drivers and Motorcycle Registrations, 1999 by State

[In thousands (155,796 represents 155,796,000). Motor vehicle registrations cover publicly, privately, and commercially owned vehicles. For uniformity, data have been adjusted to a calendar-year basis as registration years in states differ; figures represent net numbers where possible, excluding re-registrations and nonresident registrations. See also Table 1084]

State	Motor vehicle registrations [1]						1999		1999	
								Automobiles (incl. taxis)	Motorcycle registration (incl. official) [2]	Licensed drivers
	1980	1985	1990	1995	1997	1998	Total			
U.S	155,796	171,689	188,798	201,530	207,754	211,617	216,309	132,432	4,111	187,170
AL......	2,938	3,383	3,744	3,553	3,669	3,859	3,957	1,918	49	3,446
AK......	262	353	477	542	542	546	571	238	15	459
AZ......	1,917	2,235	2,825	2,873	3,143	2,944	3,606	2,037	144	3,297
AR......	1,574	1,384	1,448	1,613	1,634	1,754	1,818	946	22	1,926
CA......	16,873	18,899	21,926	22,432	24,945	25,600	26,362	16,657	406	20,831
CO......	2,342	2,759	3,155	2,812	3,523	3,466	3,858	2,054	95	2,991
CT......	2,147	2,465	2,623	2,622	2,660	2,701	2,766	1,994	53	2,374
DE......	397	465	526	592	614	616	616	402	11	552
DC......	268	306	262	243	234	229	235	197	1	349
FL......	7,614	9,865	10,950	10,369	10,874	11,276	11,390	7,305	230	12,401
GA	3,818	4,580	5,489	6,120	6,242	6,893	6,973	4,012	86	5,471
HI	570	651	771	802	693	704	718	454	19	753
ID	834	854	1,054	1,043	1,081	1,119	1,130	494	41	873
IL	7,477	7,527	7,873	8,973	8,443	9,307	9,355	6,307	217	7,925
IN	3,826	3,824	4,366	5,072	5,346	5,372	5,495	3,224	109	3,856
IA	2,329	2,696	2,632	2,814	2,851	3,053	3,050	1,724	125	1,935
KS......	2,007	2,148	2,012	2,085	2,152	2,121	2,224	1,187	49	1,892
KY......	2,593	2,615	2,909	2,631	2,781	2,845	2,662	1,593	42	2,660
LA......	2,779	3,012	2,995	3,286	3,411	3,431	3,505	1,965	42	2,763
ME	724	840	977	967	1,059	930	915	551	31	912
MD	2,803	3,276	3,607	3,654	3,786	3,750	3,896	2,666	46	3,195
MA	3,749	3,738	3,726	4,502	5,070	5,159	5,333	3,823	103	4,421
MI......	6,488	6,727	7,209	7,674	8,024	8,128	8,290	5,070	167	6,863
MN	3,091	3,385	3,508	3,882	3,927	4,178	4,010	2,265	127	2,907
MS	1,577	1,746	1,875	2,144	2,234	2,256	2,317	1,299	32	1,788
MO	3,271	3,558	3,905	4,255	4,351	4,378	4,404	2,602	57	3,840
MT	680	652	783	968	980	988	998	455	22	660
NE......	1,254	1,258	1,384	1,467	1,507	1,526	1,570	833	19	1,203
NV......	655	709	853	1,047	1,146	1,220	1,162	620	23	1,322
NH	704	974	946	1,122	1,127	1,038	1,051	678	48	919
NJ......	4,761	5,164	5,652	5,906	5,817	5,780	6,103	4,341	105	5,551
NM	1,068	1,226	1,301	1,484	1,514	1,595	1,576	761	30	1,222
NY......	8,002	9,042	10,196	10,274	10,873	10,422	10,756	7,892	142	10,627
NC	4,532	4,501	5,162	5,682	5,786	5,862	5,690	3,424	78	5,491
ND	627	655	630	695	695	672	704	343	16	458
OH	7,771	8,102	8,410	9,810	10,108	10,039	10,236	6,652	240	8,046
OK	2,583	2,911	2,649	2,856	2,884	2,919	2,931	1,524	53	2,313
OR	2,081	2,204	2,445	2,785	2,891	2,980	3,013	1,560	66	2,462
PA......	6,926	7,209	7,971	8,481	8,825	8,979	9,009	6,072	200	8,478
RI	623	610	672	699	710	715	747	535	19	689
SC......	1,996	2,222	2,521	2,833	2,850	2,893	3,026	1,873	47	2,810
SD......	601	657	704	709	718	769	782	379	26	544
TN......	3,271	3,754	4,444	5,400	4,535	4,469	4,427	2,622	63	4,176
TX......	10,475	12,444	12,800	13,682	12,923	13,324	14,069	7,738	164	13,359
UT......	992	1,099	1,206	1,447	1,530	1,532	1,577	857	25	1,440
VT......	347	398	462	492	496	496	518	302	18	496
VA......	3,626	4,253	4,938	5,613	5,709	5,818	5,871	3,769	57	4,729
WA	3,225	3,526	4,257	4,503	4,702	4,824	4,862	2,741	107	4,129
WV	1,320	1,143	1,225	1,425	1,355	1,378	1,379	760	19	1,274
WI......	2,941	3,187	3,815	3,993	4,233	4,203	4,266	2,521	192	3,733
WY	467	500	528	601	553	559	528	196	16	363

[1] Automobiles, trucks, and buses. Excludes vehicles owned by military services.   [2] Private and commercial.

Source: U.S. Federal Highway Administration, *Highway Statistics*, annual; and *Selected Highway Statistics and Charts*, annual.

Transportation   681

No. 1088. Recreational Vehicles—Number and Retail Value of Shipments: 1980 to 1997

[181.4 represents 181,400]

Item	1980	1985	1988	1989	1990	1991	1992	1993	1994	1995	1996	1997
NUMBER (1,000)												
Total................	181.4	351.7	420.0	388.3	347.3	293.7	382.7	420.2	518.8	475.2	466.8	438.8
Motorized homes	99.9	233.5	277.1	261.6	226.5	172.6	226.3	243.8	306.7	281.0	274.6	239.3
Travel trailers	52.0	75.4	89.6	82.9	80.4	77.6	102.5	113.6	128.0	121.2	123.9	131.6
Folding camping trailers	24.5	35.9	42.3	33.9	30.7	33.9	43.3	51.9	61.7	61.1	57.3	57.6
Truck campers	5.0	6.9	11.0	9.9	9.7	9.6	10.6	10.9	11.4	11.9	11.0	10.3
RETAIL VALUE (mil. dol.)												
Total................	1,952	6,904	9,061	9,019	8,101	6,623	8,774	9,518	12,196	12,104	12,365	11,928
Motorized homes	1,381	5,724	7,543	7,420	6,660	5,284	6,963	7,544	9,897	9,768	9,788	9,139
Travel trailers	485	997	1,254	1,252	1,220	1,107	1,523	1,644	1,912	1,927	2,171	2,356
Folding camping trailers	69	137	175	147	134	146	189	(NA)	276	290	284	309
Truck campers	17	46	88	81	86	87	99	(NA)	112	119	122	124

NA Not available.

Source: Recreation Vehicle Industry Association, Reston, VA, *RVIA Industry Profile 1997*. Data also in American Automobile Manufacturers Association of the United States, Inc., Washington, DC, *Motor Vehicle Facts and Figures*, annual.

No. 1089. Roadway Congestion: 1999

[15,960 represents 15,960,000 Various federal, state, and local information sources were used to develop the data base with the primary source being the Federal Highway Administration's Highway Performance Monitoring System. Areas shown are rated the top 40 in annual congestion costs per person]

Urbanized areas	Freeway daily vehicle miles of travel		Annual person hours of delay		Annual congestion cost		
	Total miles (1,000)	Per lane-mile of freeway	Total hours	Per person	Per person (dol.)	Delay and fuel cost (mil. dol.)	Fuel wasted (gal. per person)
Total, average [1]	15,960	15,890	65,930	36	625	1,145	55
Albuquerque NM	3,875	16,850	18,790	33	575	325	50
Atlanta GA	40,630	17,780	152,535	53	915	2,620	84
Austin TX	8,110	14,480	29,450	45	785	510	71
Baltimore MD	21,755	14,800	66,215	31	530	1,150	48
Boston MA	22,500	17,240	126,800	42	715	2,155	63
Charlotte NC..............	7,000	15,555	20,115	32	550	345	51
Chicago IL-Northwestern IN	48,550	18,250	271,420	34	570	4,605	50
Cincinnati OH-KY...........	15,500	15,980	41,285	32	575	735	53
Columbus OH	11,700	14,355	29,500	29	500	515	46
Dallas TX	30,900	14,645	108,785	46	780	1,865	70
Denver CO	16,500	15,940	83,045	45	760	1,415	67
Detroit MI	30,400	16,840	165,035	41	700	2,810	62
Fort Worth TX	16,650	13,590	45,365	33	570	780	51
Ft. Lauderdale-Hollywood-Pompano Beach FL	11,935	16,575	43,015	29	500	735	44
Houston TX...............	37,725	15,400	155,470	50	850	2,665	76
Indianapolis IN.	11,315	15,605	37,470	37	635	645	57
Jacksonville FL	9,355	13,365	25,425	30	520	440	46
Kansas City MO-KS	18,790	10,895	32,665	24	410	570	37
Los Angeles CA	123,200	23,335	711,100	56	1,000	12,570	84
Louisville KY-IN	10,035	14,980	30,970	37	635	530	57
Miami-Hialeah FL...........	12,900	17,225	88,070	42	705	1,485	61
Minneapolis-St. Paul MN	26,165	16,880	89,310	38	670	1,565	61
Nashville TN	10,245	13,570	26,630	42	710	455	64
New York NY-Northeastern NJ ...	100,260	15,215	565,805	34	595	9,745	52
Norfolk VA	7,300	11,230	24,975	24	415	430	38
Orlando FL	8,725	12,375	47,250	42	705	790	61
Philadelphia PA-NJ...........	24,155	14,005	117,105	26	435	1,990	38
Phoenix AZ	16,995	17,705	79,905	31	540	1,385	47
Portland-Vancouver OR-WA	12,350	17,520	51,030	34	610	910	53
Providence-Pawtucket RI-MA	8,255	12,800	25,655	28	490	445	44
Sacramento CA	11,490	16,895	46,055	34	605	830	53
San Antonio TX	15,420	14,345	29,485	24	410	510	37
San Bernardino-Riverside CA....	16,270	18,490	53,285	38	685	965	59
San Diego CA	31,775	17,850	100,180	37	675	1,820	59
San Francisco-Oakland CA	45,710	19,575	168,880	42	760	3,055	65
San Jose CA..............	18,635	16,490	69,605	42	750	1,250	65
Seattle-Everett WA	24,130	18,560	105,165	53	930	1,860	81
St. Louis MO-IL	25,600	14,465	87,405	44	745	1,495	67
Tacoma WA	5,250	17,500	16,195	27	490	295	43
Tampa FL................	6,000	13,795	30,700	35	590	520	50
Washington DC-MD-VA.......	33,875	18,210	160,245	46	780	2,730	69

[1] Includes other areas not shown separately.

Source: Texas Transportation Institute, College Station, Texas; *Roadway Congestion in Major Urban Areas*, annual (copyright). See <http://mobility.tamu.edu/2001/study/finalreport.pdf> (issued May 2001).

No. 1090. Travel in the United States by Selected Trip Characteristics: 1995

[656,462 represents 656,462,000. Trips of 100 miles or more, one way. U.S. destinations only. Data based on a sample and subject to sampling variability. For information and definitions of terms, see source]

Trip characteristic	Household trips Number (1,000)	Per- cent	Person trips Number (1,000)	Per- cent	Person miles Number (1,000)	Per- cent	Personal use vehicle trips Number (1,000)	Per- cent	Personal use vehicle miles Number (1,000)	Per- cent
Total	**656,462**	**100.0**	**1,001,319**	**100.0**	**826,804**	**100.0**	**505,154**	**100.0**	**280,127**	**100.0**
Principal means of transportation:										
Personal use vehicles	505,154	77.0	813,858	81.3	451,590	54.6	505,154	100.0	280,127	100.0
Airplane.	129,164	19.7	161,165	16.1	355,286	43.0	(X)	(X)	(X)	(X)
Commercial airplane.	124,884	19.0	155,936	15.6	347,934	42.1	(X)	(X)	(X)	(X)
Bus [1]	17,340	2.6	20,445	2.0	13,309	1.6	(X)	(X)	(X)	(X)
Intercity bus	2,755	0.4	3,244	0.3	2,723	0.3	(X)	(X)	(X)	(X)
Charter, tour, or school bus .	11,890	1.8	14,247	1.4	9,363	1.1	(X)	(X)	(X)	(X)
Train	4,200	0.6	4,994	0.5	4,356	0.5	(X)	(X)	(X)	(X)
Ship, boat, or ferry.	391	0.1	614	0.1	1,834	0.2	(X)	(X)	(X)	(X)
Other	213	-	243	-	429	0.1	(X)	(X)	(X)	(X)
Round trip distance:										
Less than 300 miles.	194,098	29.6	306,433	30.6	74,658	9.0	185,418	36.7	45,159	16.1
300 to 499 miles	174,389	26.6	274,045	27.4	106,007	12.8	159,743	31.6	61,779	22.1
500 5o 999 miles	140,046	21.3	214,006	21.4	146,631	17.7	106,846	21.2	72,114	25.7
1,000 to 1,999 miles	76,110	11.6	108,331	10.8	153,316	18.5	36,722	7.3	49,953	17.8
2,000 miles or more.	71,819	10.9	98,503	9.8	346,192	41.9	16,425	3.3	51,123	18.3
Mean (miles).	872	(X)	827	(X)	(X)	(X)	555	(X)	(X)	(X)
Median [2] (miles)	438	(X)	425	(X)	(X)	(X)	368	(X)	(X)	(X)
Main purpose of trip:										
Business	192,537	29.3	224,835	22.5	212,189	25.7	125,036	24.8	61,929	22.1
Pleasure	372,586	56.8	630,110	62.9	506,971	61.3	305,571	60.5	177,698	63.4
Visit friends or relatives. . . .	195,468	29.8	330,755	33.0	264,769	32.0	159,981	31.7	92,190	32.9
Leisure [3]	177,119	27.0	299,355	29.9	242,201	29.3	145,590	28.8	85,508	30.5
Rest or relaxation	65,017	9.9	115,154	11.5	100,838	12.2	53,780	10.6	33,598	12.0
Sightseeing	24,272	3.7	42,649	4.3	50,781	6.1	18,069	3.6	14,654	5.2
Outdoor recreation	39,899	6.1	65,418	6.5	41,620	5.0	35,987	7.1	19,407	6.9
Entertainment	37,456	5.7	58,757	5.9	42,929	5.2	27,920	5.5	14,531	5.2
Personal business	91,319	13.9	146,338	14.6	107,621	13.0	74,532	14.8	40,490	14.5
Other	19	-	36	-	23	-	16	-	9	-

- Represents or rounds to zero.   X Not applicable.   [1] Includes other types of buses.   [2] For definition of median, see Guide to Tabular Presentation.   [3] Includes other leisure activities not shown separately.
Source: U.S. Bureau of Transportation Statistics, *1995 American Travel Survey.*

No. 1091. National Personal Transportation Survey (NPTS)—Summary of Travel Trends: 1969 to 1995

[87,284 represents 87,284,000,000. Data obtained by collecting information on all trips taken by the respondent on a specific day (known as travel day), combined with longer trips taken over a 2-week period (known as travel period). For compatibility with previous survey data, all data are based only on trips taken during travel day. Be aware that terminology changes from survey to survey. See source for details. 1995 data not comparable with previous years]

Characteristics	Unit	1969 [1]	1977	1983	1990	1995
Vehicle trips	Millions . . .	87,284	108,826	126,874	158,927	229,745
Vehicle miles of travel (VMT)	Millions . . .	775,940	907,603	1,002,139	1,409,600	2,068,368
Person trips.	Millions . . .	145,146	211,778	224,385	249,562	378,930
Person miles of travel	Millions . . .	1,404,137	1,879,215	1,946,662	2,315,300	3,411,122
Average annual VMT per household [2]	Miles.	12,423	12,036	11,739	15,100	20,895
To or from to work.	Miles.	4,183	3,815	3,538	4,853	6,492
Shopping.	Miles.	929	1,336	1,567	1,743	2,807
Other family or personal business	Miles.	1,270	1,444	1,816	3,014	4,307
Social and recreational.	Miles.	4,094	3,286	3,534	4,060	4,764
Average annual vehicle trips per household [2] . . .	Number. . .	1,396	1,442	1,486	1,702	2,321
To or from to work.	Number. . .	445	423	414	448	553
Shopping.	Number. . .	213	268	297	345	501
Other family or personal business	Number. . .	195	215	272	411	626
Social and recreational.	Number. . .	312	320	335	349	427
Average vehicle trip length [2]	Miles.	8.90	8.35	7.90	8.98	9.06
To or from to work.	Miles.	9.40	9.02	8.55	10.97	11.80
Shopping.	Miles.	4.36	4.99	5.28	5.10	5.64
Other family or personal business	Miles.	6.51	6.72	6.68	7.43	6.93
Social and recreational.	Miles.	13.12	10.27	10.55	11.80	11.24
Average vehicle occupancy [2]	Persons. . .	(NA)	1.9	1.75	1.64	1.59
To or from to work.	Persons. . .	(NA)	1.3	1.29	1.14	1.14
Shopping.	Persons. . .	(NA)	2.1	1.79	1.71	1.74
Other family or personal business	Persons. . .	(NA)	2.0	1.81	1.84	1.78
Social and recreational.	Persons. . .	(NA)	2.4	2.12	2.08	2.04
Workers by usual mode to work	Percent . . .	100.0	100.0	100.0	100.0	100.0
Auto.	Percent . . .	90.8	93.0	92.4	87.8	91.0
Public transit	Percent . . .	8.4	4.7	5.8	5.3	5.1
Other	Percent . . .	0.8	2.3	1.8	6.9	3.9

NA Not available.   [1] Excludes pickups and other light-trucks as household vehicles.   [2] Includes other purposes not shown separately.
Source: U.S. Federal Highway Administration, *Summary of Travel Trends, 1995 National Personal Transportation Survey,* December 1999.

No. 1092. Motor Vehicle Accidents—Number and Deaths: 1980 to 1999

[17.9 represents 17,900,000]

Item	Unit	1980	1985	1990	1994	1995	1996	1997	1998	1999
Motor vehicle accidents [1]	Million .	17.9	19.3	11.5	11.2	10.7	11.2	13.8	12.7	11.4
Vehicles involved:										
Cars	Million .	22.8	25.6	14.3	13.5	12.3	13.3	16.0	13.8	11.6
Trucks	Million .	5.5	6.1	4.4	5.2	4.5	4.8	7.7	7.3	6.2
Motorcycles	1,000 .	560	480	180	178	152	135	138	100	70
Motor vehicle deaths within 1 yr. [2]	1,000 .	53.2	45.9	46.8	42.5	43.4	43.6	43.5	41.8	41.3
Noncollision accidents	1,000 .	14.7	12.6	4.9	4.4	4.4	4.6	4.4	4.2	4.3
Collision accidents:										
With other motor vehicles	1,000 .	23.0	19.9	19.9	18.9	19	19.6	19.9	18.5	18.8
With pedestrians	1,000 .	9.7	8.5	7.3	6.3	6.4	6.1	5.9	5.9	5.8
With fixed objects	1,000 .	3.7	3.2	13.1	11.5	12.1	12.1	12.0	12.0	11.1
Deaths within 30 days [3]	1,000 .	51.1	43.8	44.6	40.7	41.8	42.1	42.0	41.5	41.7
Occupants	1,000 .	41.9	36.0	37.1	34.3	35.3	35.7	35.7	35.4	35.9
Passenger cars	1,000 .	27.4	23.2	24.1	22.0	22.4	22.5	22.2	21.2	20.9
Light trucks	1,000 .	7.5	6.7	8.6	8.9	9.6	9.9	10.2	10.7	11.3
Large trucks	1,000 .	1.3	1.0	0.7	0.7	0.6	0.6	0.7	0.7	0.8
Motorcycles	1,000 .	5.1	4.6	3.2	2.3	2.2	2.2	2.1	2.3	2.5
Buses	1,000 .	(Z)	0.1	(Z)	(Z)	(Z)	(Z)	(Z)	(Z)	0.1
Other/unknown	1,000 .	0.5	0.5	0.5	0.4	0.4	0.5	0.4	0.4	0.4
Nonoccupants	1,000 .	9.2	7.8	7.5	6.4	6.5	6.4	6.3	6.1	5.8
Pedestrians	1,000 .	8.1	6.8	6.5	5.5	5.6	5.4	5.3	5.2	4.9
Pedicyclist	1,000 .	1.0	0.9	0.9	0.8	0.8	0.8	0.8	0.8	0.8
Other/unknown	1,000 .	0.1	0.1	0.1	0.1	0.1	0.1	0.2	0.2	0.1
Traffic death rates: [3][4]										
Per 100,000 resident population	Rate ..	22.5	18.4	17.9	15.6	15.9	15.9	15.7	15.4	15.3
Per 100,000 licensed drivers	Rate ..	35.2	27.9	26.7	23.2	23.7	23.4	23.0	22.4	22.3
Per 100,000 registered vehicles	Rate ..	34.8	26.4	24.2	21.2	21.2	20.9	20.6	20.0	19.6
Per 100 million vehicle miles	Rate ..	3.3	2.5	2.1	1.7	1.7	1.7	1.7	1.6	1.6

Z Fewer than 50. [1] Covers only accidents occurring on the road. [2] Deaths that occur within 1 year of accident. Includes collision categories not shown separately. [3] Within 30 days of accident. Source: U.S. National Highway Traffic Safety Administration, *Traffic Safety Facts, 1999*; and unpublished data. [4] Based on 30-day definition of traffic deaths.

Source: Except as noted, National Safety Council, Itasca, IL, *Injury Facts*, annual (copyright).

No. 1093. Motor Vehicle Deaths by State: 1980 to 1999

[For deaths within 30 days of the accident. Does not reflect revisions to 1999 data. See Tables 1056, 1092, 1094, 1095, 1097, 1098 and 1099]

State	1980	1985	1990	1999	Fatality rate [1] 1980	1999	State	1980	1985	1990	1999	Fatality rate [1] 1980	1999
U.S. [1]	51,091	43,825	44,599	41,611	3.3	1.5	MO	1,175	931	1,097	1,094	3.4	1.6
AL	940	882	1,121	1,138	3.2	2.0	MT	325	223	212	220	4.9	2.2
AK	88	127	98	76	3.3	1.7	NE	396	237	262	295	3.5	1.6
AZ	947	893	869	1,024	5.3	2.2	NV	346	259	343	350	5.7	2.0
AR	588	534	604	604	3.6	2.1	NH	194	191	158	141	3.0	1.2
CA	5,496	4,960	5,192	3,559	3.5	1.2	NJ	1,120	964	886	727	2.2	1.1
CO	709	579	544	626	3.2	1.5	NM	606	535	499	460	5.4	2.1
CT	575	448	385	301	3.0	1.0	NY	2,610	2,006	2,217	1,548	3.4	1.2
DE	153	104	138	100	3.6	1.2	NC	1,503	1,482	1,385	1,505	3.6	1.7
DC	41	60	48	41	1.2	1.2	ND	151	90	112	119	2.9	1.6
FL	2,825	2,832	2,891	2,918	3.6	2.1	OH	2,033	1,646	1,638	1,430	2.8	1.4
GA	1,508	1,361	1,562	1,508	3.5	1.5	OK	959	744	641	739	3.5	1.7
HI	186	126	177	98	3.3	1.2	OR	646	559	579	414	3.4	1.2
ID	331	255	244	278	4.8	2.0	PA	2,089	1,771	1,646	1,549	2.9	1.5
IL	1,975	1,534	1,589	1,456	3.0	1.4	RI	129	109	84	88	2.4	1.1
IN	1,166	974	1,049	1,013	3.0	1.4	SC	852	951	979	1,065	3.8	2.4
IA	626	474	465	490	3.3	1.7	SD	228	130	153	150	3.7	1.8
KS	595	486	444	537	3.4	1.9	TN	1,153	1,101	1,177	1,285	3.4	2.0
KY	820	712	849	814	3.2	1.7	TX	4,366	3,678	3,250	3,518	3.8	1.7
LA	1,219	931	959	924	5.0	2.2	UT	334	303	272	360	3.1	1.6
ME	265	206	213	181	3.5	1.3	VT	137	115	90	90	3.7	1.3
MD	756	729	707	590	2.6	1.2	VA	1,045	976	1,079	877	2.7	1.2
MA	881	742	605	414	2.5	0.8	WA	971	744	825	634	3.4	1.2
MI	1,750	1,545	1,571	1,382	2.8	1.4	WV	523	420	481	395	4.9	2.1
MN	848	608	566	625	3.0	1.2	WI	972	744	769	745	3.1	1.3
MS	695	662	750	927	4.2	2.7	WY	245	152	125	189	4.9	2.4

[1] Deaths per 100 million vehicle miles traveled.

Source: U.S. National Highway Safety Traffic Administration, *Traffic Safety Facts, 1999*.

No. 1094. Fatal Motor Vehicle Accidents—National Summary: 1990 to 1999

[Based on data from the Fatal Accident Reporting System (FARS). FARS gathers data on accidents that result in loss of human life. FARS is operated and maintained by National Highway Traffic Safety Administration's (NHTSA) National Center for Statistics and Analysis (NCSA). FARS data are gathered on motor vehicle accidents that occurred on a roadway customarily open to the public, resulting in the death of a person within 30 days of the accident. Collection of these data depend on the use of police, hospital, medical examiner/coroner, and Emergency Medical Services reports; State vehicle registration, driver licensing, and highway department files; and vital statistics documents and death certificates. See source for further detail]

Item	1990	1993	1994	1995	1996	1997	1998	1999
Fatal crashes, total	**39,836**	**35,780**	**36,254**	**37,241**	**37,494**	**37,324**	**37,107**	**37,140**
One vehicle involved	23,445	20,569	20,526	21,250	21,134	20,807	20,900	20,911
Two or more vehicles involved	16,391	15,211	15,728	15,991	16,360	16,517	16,207	16,229
Persons killed in fatal crashes	**44,599**	**40,150**	**40,716**	**41,817**	**42,065**	**42,013**	**41,501**	**41,717**
Occupants	37,134	33,574	34,318	35,291	35,695	35,725	35,382	35,875
Drivers	25,750	23,142	23,691	24,390	24,534	24,667	24,743	25,257
Passengers	11,276	10,361	10,518	10,782	11,058	10,944	10,530	10,521
Other	108	71	109	119	103	114	109	97
Nonmotorists	7,465	6,576	6,398	6,526	6,370	6,288	6,119	5,842
Pedestrians	6,482	5,649	5,489	5,584	5,449	5,321	5,228	4,939
Pedalcyclists	859	816	802	833	765	814	760	754
Other	124	111	107	109	156	153	131	149
Occupants killed by vehicle type:								
Passenger cars:								
Minicompact (95 inches)	3,556	2,635	2,339	2,207	2,037	1,763	1,480	1,224
Subcompact (95 to 99 inches)	4,753	4,333	4,721	4,584	4,581	4,457	4,034	3,663
Compact (100 to 104 inches)	5,310	5,707	6,322	6,899	7,288	7,195	6,804	6,942
Intermediate (105 to 109) inches	4,849	4,483	4,407	4,666	4,670	4,794	4,617	4,721
Full size (110 to 114) inches	2,386	2,067	2,074	2,116	2,147	2,242	2,014	2,179
Largest (115 inches and over)	2,249	1,608	1,486	1,297	1,270	1,239	1,092	708
Unknown	989	733	648	654	512	509	1,153	1,425
Motorcycles	3,129	2,336	2,190	2,114	2,046	2,028	2,186	2,374
Other motorized cycles	115	113	130	113	115	88	108	109
Light trucks	8,601	8,511	8,904	9,568	9,932	10,249	10,705	11,265
Pickup	5,979	5,538	5,574	5,938	5,904	5,887	5,921	6,127
Utility	1,214	1,521	1,757	1,935	2,147	2,380	2,713	3,026
Van	1,154	1,365	1,508	1,639	1,832	1,914	2,042	2,088
Other	254	87	65	56	49	68	29	24
Medium trucks	134	90	109	96	87	122	99	90
Heavy trucks	571	515	561	552	534	601	643	669
Buses	32	18	18	33	21	18	38	59
Other vehicles	296	306	317	307	340	343	336	355
Unknown	164	119	92	85	115	77	73	92
Persons involved in fatal crashes	**107,777**	**97,589**	**98,945**	**102,102**	**103,347**	**102,197**	**101,100**	**100,666**
Occupants	99,297	90,150	91,644	94,621	96,159	95,050	94,241	93,959
Drivers	58,893	53,401	54,549	56,164	57,001	56,688	56,604	56,502
Passengers	40,229	36,599	36,898	38,252	38,913	38,184	37,448	37,280
Other	175	150	197	205	245	178	189	177
Nonoccupants	8,480	7,439	7,301	7,481	7,188	7,147	6,859	6,707
Vehicle miles traveled (VMT) (100 mil)	21,444	22,964	23,576	24,227	24,858	25,617	26,315	26,913
Licensed drivers (1,000)	167,015	173,149	175,403	176,628	179,539	182,709	184,980	187,170
Registered vehicles (1,000)	184,275	188,350	192,497	197,065	201,631	203,568	208,076	212,685
Fatalities, by road type:								
Interstate	4,993	4,201	4,713	4,835	5,245	5,332	5,388	5,597
Federal-aid primary	14,203	11,317	(NA)	(NA)	(NA)	(NA)	(NA)	(NA)
Federal-aid secondary	6,892	4,907	(NA)	(NA)	(NA)	(NA)	(NA)	(NA)
Federal-aid urban	8,432	6,095	(NA)	(NA)	(NA)	(NA)	(NA)	(NA)
Nonfederal-aid	10,039	8,545	(NA)	(NA)	(NA)	(NA)	(NA)	(NA)
Unknown	40	5,085	(NA)	(NA)	(NA)	(NA)	(NA)	(NA)
Percent distribution of fatal accidents by the highest blood alcohol concentration (BAC) in accident:								
0.00 percent	50.6	56.5	59.1	58.7	59.1	61.5	61.3	61.6
0.01 to 0.09 percent	9.7	8.5	8.4	8.6	8.7	8.1	8.3	8.3
0.10 percent and over	39.7	34.9	32.5	32.6	32.1	30.3	30.4	30.1
Fatalities per 100,000 population:								
Under 5 years old	4.9	4.5	4.8	4.3	4.6	4.1	4.0	3.9
5 years to 15 years old	6.4	5.8	6.0	6.0	5.7	5.6	5.2	5.1
16 years to 24 years old	35.2	30.1	30.6	30.7	30.7	29.3	28.5	28.9
25 years to 44 years old	19.7	16.8	16.3	17.2	16.9	16.6	16.4	16.4
45 years to 64 years old	14.9	13.0	13.3	13.6	13.8	14.2	14.0	13.8
65 years to 79 years old	18.8	17.9	18.7	18.5	18.7	19.2	18.7	18.3
80 years old and over	26.8	27.8	28.0	28.0	27.8	29.2	28.4	27.3
Fatalities per 100 million VMT	2.1	1.7	1.7	1.7	1.7	1.6	1.6	1.6
Fatalities per 100,000 licensed drivers	26.7	23.2	23.2	23.7	23.4	23.0	22.4	22.3
Licensed driver per person	0.7	0.7	0.7	0.7	0.7	0.7	0.7	0.7
Fatal crashes per 100 million VMT	1.9	1.6	1.5	1.5	1.5	1.5	1.4	1.4
Involved vehicles per fatal crash	1.5	1.5	1.5	1.5	1.5	1.5	1.5	1.5
Fatalities per fatal crash	1.1	1.1	1.1	1.1	1.1	1.1	1.1	1.1
Average occupants per fatal crash	2.5	2.5	2.5	2.5	2.6	2.5	2.5	2.5
Fatalities per 100,000 population	17.9	15.6	15.6	15.9	15.9	15.7	15.4	15.3

NA Not available.

Source: National Highway Traffic Safety Administration, *Fatal Accident Reporting System,* annual.

Transportation 685

No. 1095. Motor Vehicle Occupants and Nonoccupants Killed and Injured: 1985 to 1999

[(3,416 represents 3,416,000) For deaths within 30 days of the accident]

Year	Total	Occupants Total	Passenger cars	Light trucks	Large trucks	Motorcycles	Buses	Other/unknown	Nonoccupants Total	Pedestrian	Pedalcyclist	Other/unknown
KILLED												
1985	43,825	36,043	23,212	6,689	977	4,564	57	544	7,782	6,808	890	84
1986	46,087	38,234	24,944	7,317	926	4,566	39	442	7,853	6,779	941	133
1987	46,390	38,565	25,132	8,058	852	4,036	51	436	7,825	6,745	948	132
1988	47,087	39,170	25,808	8,306	911	3,662	54	429	7,917	6,870	911	136
1989	45,582	38,087	25,063	8,551	858	3,141	50	424	7,495	6,556	832	107
1990	44,599	37,134	24,092	8,601	705	3,244	32	460	7,465	6,482	859	124
1991	41,508	34,740	22,385	8,391	661	2,806	31	466	6,768	5,801	843	124
1992	39,250	32,880	21,387	8,098	585	2,395	28	387	6,370	5,549	723	98
1993	40,150	33,574	21,566	8,511	605	2,449	18	425	6,576	5,649	816	111
1994	40,716	34,318	21,997	8,904	670	2,320	18	409	6,398	5,489	802	107
1995	41,817	35,291	22,423	9,568	648	2,227	33	392	6,526	5,584	833	109
1996	42,065	35,695	22,505	9,932	621	2,161	21	455	6,370	5,449	765	156
1997	42,013	35,725	22,199	10,249	723	2,116	18	420	6,288	5,321	814	153
1998	41,501	35,382	21,194	10,705	742	2,294	38	409	6,119	5,228	760	131
1999	41,717	35,875	20,862	11,265	759	2,483	59	447	5,842	4,939	754	149
INJURED (1,000)												
1988	3,416	3,224	2,585	478	37	105	15	4	192	110	75	8
1989	3,284	3,088	2,431	511	43	83	15	5	196	112	73	11
1990	3,231	3,044	2,376	505	42	84	33	4	187	105	75	7
1991	3,097	2,931	2,235	563	28	80	21	4	166	88	67	11
1992	3,070	2,908	2,232	545	34	65	20	12	162	89	63	10
1993	3,149	2,978	2,265	601	32	59	17	4	171	94	68	9
1994	3,266	3,102	2,364	631	30	57	16	4	164	92	62	9
1995	3,465	3,303	2,469	722	30	57	19	4	162	86	67	10
1996	3,483	3,332	2,458	761	33	55	20	4	151	82	58	11
1997	3,348	3,201	2,341	755	31	53	17	6	146	77	58	11
1998	3,192	3,061	2,201	763	29	49	16	4	131	69	53	8
1999	3,236	3,097	2,138	847	33	50	22	7	140	85	51	3

Source: U.S. National Highway Traffic Safety Administration, *Traffic Safety Facts, 1999*; and unpublished data.

No. 1096. Large Truck Involvement in Fatal Crashes by State: 1999

[Medium/heavy trucks represents trucks over 10,000 pounds gross vehicle weight, including single unit trucks]

State	Total vehicles involved in fatal crashes	Large trucks involved in fatal crashes Number	Percent of total vehicles	Percent of U.S. total for large trucks	State	Total vehicles involved in fatal crashes	Large trucks involved in fatal crashes Number	Percent of total vehicles	Percent of U.S. total for large trucks
United States .	56,820	4,920	8.7	100.0	Missouri	1,504	155	10.3	3.2
					Montana	256	15	5.9	0.3
Alabama	1,520	144	9.5	2.9	Nebraska	401	58	14.5	1.2
Alaska	104	5	4.8	0.1	Nevada	461	41	8.9	0.8
Arizona	1,410	108	7.7	2.2	New Hampshire . . .	187	9	4.8	0.2
Arkansas	784	92	11.7	1.9					
California	4,626	319	6.9	6.5	New Jersey	1,000	59	5.9	1.2
Colorado	843	60	7.1	1.2	New Mexico	560	48	8.6	1.0
Connecticut	400	22	5.5	0.4	New York	2,147	159	7.4	3.2
Delaware	153	10	6.5	0.2	North Carolina	2,119	190	9.0	3.9
District of Columbia .	60	2	3.3	(Z)	North Dakota	144	18	12.5	0.4
Florida	4,228	327	7.7	6.6	Ohio	2,022	201	9.9	4.1
Georgia	2,092	220	10.5	4.5	Oklahor..a	970	82	8.5	1.7
Hawaii	141	3	2.1	0.1	Oregon	572	48	8.4	1.0
Idaho	349	25	7.2	0.5	Pennsylvania	2,132	207	9.7	4.2
Illinois	2,034	193	9.5	3.9	Rhode Island	119	9	7.6	0.2
Indiana	1,408	191	13.6	3.9					
Iowa	701	99	14.1	2.0	South Carolina	1,411	124	8.8	2.5
Kansas	711	82	11.5	1.7	South Dakota	197	18	9.1	0.4
Kentucky	1,064	94	8.8	1.9	Tennessee	1,783	168	9.4	3.4
Louisiana	1,243	120	9.7	2.4	Texas	4,819	385	8.0	7.8
Maine	257	25	9.7	0.5	Utah	435	41	9.4	0.8
					Vermont	113	8	7.1	0.2
Maryland	864	57	6.6	1.2	Virginia	1,169	107	9.2	2.2
Massachusetts	574	35	6.1	0.7	Washington	848	59	7.0	1.2
Michigan	2,012	132	6.6	2.7	West Virginia	515	50	9.7	1.0
Minnesota	915	86	9.4	1.7	Wisconsin	1,017	74	7.3	1.5
Mississippi	1,214	111	9.1	2.3	Wyoming	212	25	11.8	0.5

Z Less than 0.05 percent.

Source: U.S. National Highway Traffic Safety Administration, *Traffic Safety Facts*, annual; and unpublished data.

No. 1097. Speeding-Related Traffic Fatalities by Road Type and Speed Limit: 1999

[Speeding consists of exceeding the posted speed limit or driving too fast for the road conditions]

State	Traffic fatalities, total [1]	Speeding-related fatalities by road type and speed limit							
		Interstate		Noninterstate					
		Over 55 mph	At or under 55 mph	55 mph	50 mph	45 mph	40 mph	35 mph	Under 35 mph
United States	41,717	1,340	412	3,778	545	1,485	839	1,347	1,286
Alabama.	1,138	37	4	97	14	154	31	40	19
Alaska	79	3	7	9	4	2	2	6	3
Arizona.	1,024	49	15	51	31	64	51	40	25
Arkansas	604	14	1	83	5	23	4	13	16
California	3,559	191	25	356	60	86	100	153	115
Colorado.	626	27	17	44	19	26	29	37	37
Connecticut.	301	4	9	5	3	24	8	9	49
Delaware	100	-	2	5	10	-	-	2	2
District of Columbia	41	-	-	-	2	2	-	1	6
Florida	2,920	51	20	76	13	90	55	51	59
Georgia	1,508	39	14	118	5	51	13	42	26
Hawaii	98	-	2	1	-	2	-	11	13
Idaho	278	13	-	20	13	8	-	12	4
Illinois	1,456	50	51	203	5	43	19	58	50
Indiana.	1,020	15	10	81	10	28	16	33	37
Iowa	490	7	-	21	-	1	2	2	15
Kansas.	540	15	-	29	5	6	12	8	21
Kentucky	814	10	1	152	4	11	2	24	4
Louisiana	938	5	4	64	8	16	5	20	9
Maine.	181	5	-	5	10	26	8	10	11
Maryland	590	8	3	11	29	5	35	35	35
Massachusetts.	414	15	10	2	6	16	18	20	38
Michigan.	1,382	24	13	154	4	19	10	37	34
Minnesota	626	18	3	88	6	6	7	2	17
Mississippi	927	30	1	72	24	32	9	13	15
Missouri	1,094	57	12	134	5	23	9	35	42
Montana	220	7	-	13	3	5	-	9	9
Nebraska	295	9	-	6	27	6	-	8	4
Nevada	350	30	5	13	5	22	5	9	17
New Hampshire	140	3	-	2	2	-	6	10	24
New Jersey.	726	1	3	4	15	9	5	5	22
New Mexico	460	18	4	28	9	14	11	19	25
New York	1,599	11	13	184	19	21	38	18	88
North Carolina	1,505	36	13	314	12	107	2	70	7
North Dakota	119	4	1	24	2	-	4	1	6
Ohio	1,430	42	9	191	10	29	15	27	19
Oklahoma	741	56	3	40	9	41	21	16	16
Oregon.	414	11	4	75	2	7	9	7	10
Pennsylvania	1,549	35	38	166	11	99	85	104	44
Rhode Island	88	4	1	2	3	1	-	6	8
South Carolina	1,065	55	9	193	11	84	18	52	30
South Dakota	150	4	-	23	2	4	2	5	2
Tennessee	1,302	30	22	105	13	73	38	27	49
Texas.	3,522	165	47	208	38	108	89	103	105
Utah	360	30	3	11	1	5	6	12	10
Vermont	90	4	-	-	20	-	3	8	1
Virginia.	878	16	10	114	4	35	6	30	14
Washington.	637	21	-	22	31	9	17	59	37
West Virginia	395	18	-	43	1	18	11	9	11
Wisconsin.	745	17	2	108	-	22	2	17	24
Wyoming	189	26	1	8	-	2	1	2	2

- Represents zero.   [1] Includes fatalities that occurred on roads for which the speed limit was unknown.

Source: U.S. National Highway Traffic Safety Administration, *Traffic Safety Facts 1995, Speeding. Traffic Safety Facts, Speeding,* annual; and unpublished data.

No. 1098. Traffic Fatalities by State and Highest Blood Alcohol Concentration (BAC) in the Crash: 1998

[BAC means blood alcohol concentration; g/dl means grams per deciliter]

State	Traffic fatalities, total	No alcohol (BAC=0.00 g/dl)		Any alcohol (BAC=0.01 g/dl) or more					
				Total number	Percent	Low alcohol (BAC=0.01-0.09 g/dl)		High alcohol (BAC=0.10 g/dl or more)	
		Number	Percent			Number	Percent	Number	Percent
United States	**41,717**	**25,741**	**62**	**15,976**	**38**	**3,523**	**8**	**12,453**	**30**
Alabama	1,138	708	62	430	38	77	7	353	31
Alaska	79	38	48	41	52	8	10	34	43
Arizona	1,024	618	60	406	40	77	8	329	32
Arkansas	604	414	69	190	31	49	8	140	23
California	3,559	2,208	62	1,351	38	343	10	1,009	28
Colorado	626	405	65	221	35	48	8	173	28
Connecticut	301	166	55	135	45	33	11	102	34
Delaware	100	60	60	40	40	6	6	34	34
District of Columbia	41	19	47	22	53	6	14	16	39
Florida	2,920	1,874	64	1,046	36	215	7	831	28
Georgia	1,508	1,001	66	507	34	136	9	371	25
Hawaii	98	55	56	43	44	11	12	31	32
Idaho	278	179	64	99	36	24	9	75	27
Illinois	1,456	821	56	635	44	131	9	504	35
Indiana	1,020	656	64	364	36	81	8	282	28
Iowa	490	328	67	162	33	43	9	119	24
Kansas	540	357	66	183	34	43	8	139	26
Kentucky	814	530	65	284	35	51	6	233	29
Louisiana	938	504	54	434	46	102	11	332	35
Maine	181	122	68	59	32	8	5	51	28
Maryland	590	388	66	202	34	62	11	140	24
Massachusetts	414	211	51	203	49	63	15	140	34
Michigan	1,382	835	60	547	40	106	8	442	32
Minnesota	626	425	68	201	32	39	6	162	26
Mississippi	927	565	61	362	39	62	7	300	32
Missouri	1,094	655	60	439	40	116	11	323	29
Montana	220	117	53	103	47	16	7	87	40
Nebraska	295	170	58	125	42	38	13	87	30
Nevada	350	194	55	156	45	52	15	105	30
New Hampshire	140	72	51	68	49	25	18	43	31
New Jersey	726	439	60	287	40	76	10	211	29
New Mexico	460	254	55	206	45	37	8	169	37
New York	1,599	1,174	73	425	27	112	7	313	20
North Carolina	1,505	969	64	536	36	123	8	413	27
North Dakota	119	63	53	56	47	11	10	45	38
Ohio	1,430	933	65	497	35	95	7	402	28
Oklahoma	741	494	67	247	33	49	7	197	27
Oregon	414	244	59	170	41	29	7	141	34
Pennsylvania	1,549	953	62	596	38	109	7	488	31
Rhode Island	88	52	59	36	41	12	14	23	27
South Carolina	1,065	732	69	333	31	50	5	283	27
South Dakota	150	85	57	65	43	9	6	56	37
Tennessee	1,302	807	62	495	38	96	7	399	31
Texas	3,522	1,771	50	1,751	50	404	11	1,347	38
Utah	360	286	79	74	21	18	5	56	15
Vermont	90	56	62	34	38	9	10	25	28
Virginia	878	558	64	320	36	74	8	246	28
Washington	637	370	58	267	42	43	7	224	35
West Virginia	395	250	63	145	37	26	6	119	30
Wisconsin	745	436	59	309	41	53	7	256	34
Wyoming	189	119	63	70	37	15	8	56	29

Source: U.S. National Highway Traffic Safety Administration, *Traffic Safety Facts*, annual; and unpublished data.

No. 1099. Fatalities by Highest Blood Alcohol Concentration in the Crash: 1985 to 1999

[BAC means blood alcohol concentration; g/dl means grams per deciliter]

Item	1985	1990	1992	1993	1994	1995	1996	1997	1998	1999
Total fatalities	**43,825**	**44,599**	**39,250**	**40,150**	**40,716**	**41,817**	**42,065**	**42,013**	**41,501**	**41,717**
Fatalities in alcohol-related crashes .	22,716	22,084	17,858	17,473	16,580	17,247	17,218	16,189	16,020	15,976
Percent	51.8	49.5	45.5	43.5	40.7	41.2	40.9	38.5	38.6	38.3
BAC = 0.01-0.09 g/dl:										
Number	4,604	4,434	3,625	3,496	3,480	3,746	3,774	3,480	3,526	3,523
Percent	10.5	9.9	9.2	8.7	8.5	9	9	8.3	8.5	8.4
BAC = 0.10 g/dl or more:										
Number	18,111	17,650	14,234	13,977	13,100	13,501	13,444	12,710	12,494	12,453
Percent	41.3	39.6	36.3	34.8	32.2	32.3	32	30.3	30.1	29.9
Fatalities with BAC = 0.00 g/dl:										
Number	21,109	22,515	21,392	22,677	24,136	24,570	24,847	25,824	25,481	25,741
Percent	48.2	50.5	54.5	56.5	59.3	58.8	59.1	61.5	61.4	61.7

Source: U.S. National Highway Traffic Safety Administration, *Traffic Safety Facts*, annual; and unpublished data.

No. 1100. Crashes by Crash Severity: 1990 to 1999

[**6,471 represents 6,471,000** Does not reflect revisions to 1999 data. See Table 1094. A crash is a police-reported event that produces injury and/or property damage, involves a vehicle in transport and occurs on a traffic way or while the vehicle is in motion after running off the trafficway]

Item	1990	1992	1993	1994	1995	1996	1997	1998	1999
Crashes (1,000)	**6,471**	**6,000**	**6,106**	**6,496**	**6,699**	**6,770**	**6,624**	**6,335**	**6,279**
Fatal	39.8	34.9	35.8	36.3	37.2	37.5	37.3	37.1	37.0
Nonfatal injury	2,122	1,991	2,022	2,123	2,217	2,238	2,149	2,029	2,054
Property damage only	4,309	3,974	4,048	4,336	4,446	4,494	4,438	4,269	4,188
Percent of total crashes:									
Fatal	0.6	0.6	0.6	0.6	0.6	0.6	0.6	0.6	0.6
Nonfatal injury	32.8	33.2	33.1	32.7	33.1	33.1	32.4	32.0	32.7
Property damage only	66.6	66.2	66.3	66.8	66.4	66.4	67.0	67.4	66.7

Source: U.S. National Highway Safety Traffic Administration, *Traffic Safety Facts, 1999.*

No. 1101. Alcohol Involvement for Drivers in Fatal Crashes: 1989 and 1999

[BAC = blood alcohol concentration]

Drivers involved in fatal crashes	1989		1999	
	Number of drivers	Percentage with BAC of .10% or greater	Number of drivers	Percentage with BAC of .10% or greater
Total drivers [1]	**60,435**	**24**	**56,352**	**17**
Drivers by age group:				
16 to 20 years old	9,442	20	7,973	14
21 to 24 years old	7,723	35	5,620	27
25 to 34 years old	15,928	32	11,734	24
35 to 44 years old	10,106	25	11,023	21
45 to 64 years old	10,240	17	12,292	13
65 years old and over	5,431	7	6,559	5
Drivers by sex:				
Male	45,448	27	40,900	20
Female	14,054	14	14,792	10
Drivers by vehicle type:				
Passenger cars	35,204	24	27,806	17
Light trucks	15,579	28	19,801	20
Large trucks	4,903	3	4,847	1
Motorcycles	3,182	40	2,515	28

[1] Includes age, sex, and types of vehicles unknown.

Source: U.S. National Highway Safety Traffic Administration, *Traffic Safety Facts, 1999.*

No. 1102. Licensed Drivers and Number in Accidents by Age: 1999

[**188,167 represents 188,167,000**]

Age group	Licensed drivers		Drivers in accidents				Accidents per number of drivers	
			Fatal		All			
	Number (1,000)	Percent	Number	Percent	Number (1,000)	Percent	Fatal [1]	All [2]
Total	**188,167**	**100.0**	**42,200**	**100.0**	**18,000**	**100.0**	**22**	**10**
Under 16 years old	31	(Z)	300	0.7	130	0.7	([3])	([3])
16 years old	1,707	0.9	1,100	2.6	660	3.7	64	39
17 years old	2,403	1.3	1,200	2.8	730	4.1	50	30
18 years old	2,805	1.5	1,500	3.6	730	4.1	53	26
19 years old	3,040	1.6	1,600	3.8	660	3.7	53	22
19 years old and under	9,986	5.4	5,700	13.5	2,910	16.2	57	29
20 years old	3,106	1.7	1,100	2.6	560	3.1	35	18
21 years old	3,030	1.6	1,100	2.6	530	2.9	36	17
22 years old	3,027	1.6	1,000	2.4	490	2.7	33	16
23 years old	3,141	1.7	900	2.1	450	2.5	29	14
24 years old	3,300	1.8	900	2.1	430	2.4	27	13
20 to 24 years old	15,604	8.4	5,000	11.8	2,460	13.7	32	16
25 to 34 years old	37,781	20.1	8,100	19.2	3,780	21.0	21	10
35 to 44 years old	42,307	22.5	8,100	19.4	3,580	19.9	19	8
45 to 54 years old	34,050	18.1	6,100	14.5	2,490	13.8	18	7
55 to 64 years old	21,651	11.5	3,800	9.0	1,340	7.4	18	6
65 to 74 years old	16,069	8.5	2,500	5.9	840	4.7	16	5
75 years old and over	10,719	5.7	2,900	6.9	600	3.3	27	6

Z Less than 0.05. [1] Per 100,000 licensed drivers. [2] Per 100 licensed drivers. [3] Rates for drivers under age 16 are substantially overstated due to the high proportion of unlicensed drivers involved.

Source: National Safety Council, Itasca, IL, *Injury Facts, 2000,* (copyright).

U.S. Census Bureau, Statistical Abstract of the United States: 2001

No. 1103. Motor Vehicle Distance Traveled by Type of Vehicle: 1970 to 1999

[1,110 represents 1,110,000,000,000. Travel estimates based on automatic traffic recorder data. Speed trend data for 1970 were collected by several state highway agencies, normally during summer months; beginning 1980 all states have monitored speeds at locations on several highway systems Monitoring Program]

Year	Vehicle-miles of travel (bil.)					Avg. miles per vehicle (1,000)				
	Passenger cars					Passenger cars				
	Total	Cars [1]	Buses [2]	Vans, pickups, SUVs	Trucks [3]	Total	Cars [1]	Buses [2]	Vans, pickups, SUVs	Trucks [3]
1970	1,110	920	4.5	123	62	10.0	10.0	12.0	8.7	13.6
1980	1,527	1,122	6.1	291	108	9.5	8.8	11.5	10.4	18.7
1985	1,775	1,256	4.5	391	124	10.0	9.4	7.5	10.5	20.6
1990	2,144	1,418	5.7	575	146	11.1	10.3	9.1	11.9	23.6
1991	2,172	1,367	5.8	649	150	11.3	10.3	9.1	12.2	24.2
1992	2,247	1,381	5.8	707	153	11.6	10.6	9.0	12.4	25.4
1993	2,296	1,385	6.1	746	160	11.6	10.5	9.4	12.4	26.3
1994	2,358	1,416	6.4	765	170	11.7	10.8	9.6	12.2	25.8
1995	2,423	1,438	6.4	790	178	11.8	11.2	9.4	12.0	26.5
1996	2,486	1,470	6.6	817	183	11.8	11.3	9.4	11.8	26.1
1997	2,562	1,503	6.8	851	191	12.1	11.6	9.8	12.1	27.0
1998	2,632	1,550	7.0	868	196	12.2	11.8	9.8	12.2	25.4
1999	2,691	1,569	7.7	901	203	12.2	11.9	10.5	12.0	26.0

[1] Includes motorcycles through 1994; thereafter in total, not shown separately. [2] Includes school buses. [3] Includes combinations.

Source: U.S. Federal Highway Administration, *Highway Statistics,* annual.

No. 1104. Passenger Transit Industry—Summary: 1985 to 1999

[12,195 represents $12,195,000,000. Includes Puerto Rico. Includes aggregate information for all transit systems in the United States. Excludes nontransit services such as taxicab, school bus, unregulated jitney, sightseeing bus, intercity bus, and special application mass transportation systems (e.g., amusement parks, airports, island, and urban park ferries). Includes active vehicles only]

Item	Unit	1985	1990	1995	1997	1998	1999
Operating systems.	Number. . .	4,972	5,078	5,973	5,973	6,000	6,000
Motor bus systems	Number. . .	2,631	2,688	2,250	2,250	2,262	2,262
Passenger vehicles, active [1]	Number. . .	94,368	92,961	115,874	126,360	123,855	128,516
Motor bus	Number. . .	64,258	58,714	67,107	72,770	72,142	74,228
Trolley bus	Number. . .	676	832	885	859	880	859
Heavy rail	Number. . .	9,326	10,419	10,157	10,242	10,301	10,306
Light rail	Number. . .	717	913	999	1,229	1,220	1,297
Commuter rail	Number. . .	4,035	4,415	4,565	4,943	4,963	4,883
Demand response	Number. . .	14,490	16,471	29,352	32,509	29,646	31,884
Operating funding, total	Mil. dol . . .	12,195	16,053	18,241	19,515	21,062	22,220
Passenger funding	Mil. dol . . .	4,575	5,891	6,801	7,546	7,969	8,282
Other operating funding [2]	Mil. dol . . .	702	895	2,812	3,308	3,685	3,648
Operating assistance	Mil. dol . . .	6,918	9,267	8,628	8,661	9,407	10,290
Federal	Mil. dol . . .	940	970	817	647	751	872
Local [3]	Mil. dol . . .	5,979	5,327	3,981	4,095	4,377	4,540
State [3]	Mil. dol . . .	(NA)	2,970	3,830	3,919	4,279	4,878
Total expense	Mil. dol . . .	14,077	17,979	21,540	23,159	24,318	25,538
Operating expense	Mil. dol . . .	12,381	15,742	17,849	18,936	19,739	20,512
Reconciling expense.	Mil. dol . . .	1,696	2,237	3,691	4,223	4,579	5,025
Capital expenditure, federal.	Mil. dol . . .	2,559	2,428	5,534	4,125	4,225	5,395
Capital expenditures	Million	(NA)	(NA)	7,230	7,850	7,893	8,975
Vehicle-miles operated [1]	Million	2,791	3,242	3,550	3,746	3,794	3,972
Motor bus	Million	1,863	2,130	2,184	2,245	2,175	2,276
Trolley bus	Million	16	14	14	14	14	14
Heavy rail	Million	451	537	537	558	566	578
Light rail	Million	17	24	35	41	44	49
Commuter rail	Million	183	213	238	251	260	266
Demand response	Million	247	306	507	585	671	718
Passengers carried [1]	Million	8,636	8,799	7,763	8,374	8,750	9,168
Motor bus	Million	5,675	5,677	4,848	5,013	5,399	5,648
Trolley bus	Million	142	126	119	121	117	120
Heavy rail	Million	2,290	2,346	2,033	2,430	2,393	2,521
Light rail	Million	132	175	251	262	276	292
Commuter rail	Million	275	328	344	357	381	396
Demand response	Million	59	68	88	99	95	100
Avg. funding per passenger.	Cents	53.0	66.9	87.6	88.8	87.1	90.3
Employees, number (avg.) [4]	1,000	270	273	311	334	339	350
Payroll, employee	Mil. dol . . .	5,843	7,226	8,213	8,772	9,211	9,495
Fringe benefits, employee	Mil. dol . . .	2,868	3,986	4,484	4,504	4,844	5,052

NA Not available. [1] Includes other categories not shown separately. [2] Beginning 1995, includes taxes levied directly by transit agency and other dedicated funds, formerly included in Local. [3] Includes other operating revenue, nonoperating revenue, and auxiliary income. Data for 1985 are state and local combined. [4] Through 1990, represents employee equivalents of 2,080 hours = one employee; beginning 1995, equals actual employees.

Source: American Public Transportation Association, Washington, DC, *Public Transportation Fact Book,* annual.

No. 1105. Domestic Motor Fuel Consumption by Type of Vehicle: 1970 to 1999

[92.3 represents 92,300,000,000. Comprises all fuel types used for propulsion of vehicles under state motor fuels laws. Excludes federal purchases for military use. Minus sign (-) indicates decrease]

Year	Annual fuel consumption (bil. gal)					Average miles per gallon				
	All vehicles	Avg. annual percent change [1]	Cars [2]	Vans, pickups, SUVs	Buses [3]	Trucks [4] (bil. gal.)	All vehicles	Cars [2]	Vans, pickups, SUVs	Buses [3]	Trucks [4] (bil. gal.)
1970 ..	92.3	4.8	67.8	12.3	0.8	11.3	12.0	13.5	10.0	5.5	5.5
1975 ..	109.0	2.5	74.3	19.1	1.1	14.6	12.2	14.0	10.5	5.8	5.6
1980 ..	115.0	-5.9	70.2	23.8	1.0	20.0	13.3	16.0	12.2	6.0	5.4
1981 ..	114.5	-0.4	69.3	23.7	1.1	20.4	13.6	16.5	12.5	5.9	5.3
1982 ..	113.4	-1.0	69.3	22.7	1.0	20.4	14.1	16.9	13.5	5.9	5.5
1983 ..	116.1	2.4	70.5	23.9	0.9	20.8	14.2	17.1	13.7	5.9	5.6
1984 ..	118.7	2.2	70.8	25.6	0.8	21.4	14.5	17.4	14.0	5.7	5.7
1985 ..	121.3	2.2	71.7	27.4	0.8	21.4	14.6	17.5	14.3	5.4	5.8
1986 ..	125.2	3.2	73.4	29.1	0.9	21.9	14.7	17.4	14.6	5.3	5.8
1987 ..	127.5	1.8	73.5	30.6	0.9	22.5	15.1	18.0	14.9	5.8	5.9
1988 ..	130.1	2.0	73.5	32.7	0.9	22.9	15.6	18.8	15.4	5.8	6.0
1989 ..	131.9	1.4	74.1	33.3	0.9	23.5	15.9	18.0	16.1	6.0	6.1
1990 ..	130.8	-0.8	69.8	35.6	0.9	24.5	16.4	20.3	16.1	6.4	6.0
1991 ..	128.6	-1.7	64.5	38.2	0.9	25.0	16.9	21.2	17.0	6.7	6.0
1992 ..	132.9	3.3	65.6	40.9	0.9	25.5	16.9	21.0	17.3	6.6	6.0
1993 ..	137.3	3.3	67.2	42.9	0.9	26.2	16.7	20.6	17.4	6.6	6.1
1994 ..	140.8	2.5	68.1	44.1	1.0	27.7	16.7	20.8	17.3	6.6	6.1
1995 ..	143.8	2.1	68.1	45.6	1.0	29.0	16.8	21.1	17.3	6.6	6.1
1996 ..	147.4	2.5	69.2	47.4	1.0	29.6	16.9	21.2	17.2	6.6	6.2
1997 ..	150.4	2.0	69.9	49.4	1.0	29.9	17.0	21.5	17.2	6.7	6.4
1998 ..	155.4	3.3	71.7	50.5	1.1	32.0	16.9	21.6	17.2	6.7	6.1
1999 ..	160.7	3.4	73.2	52.8	1.1	33.4	16.8	21.4	17.1	6.7	6.1

[1] Change from immediate prior year. [2] Includes motorcycles through 1994. Thereafter in total, not shown separately. [3] Includes school buses. [4] Includes combinations.

Source: U.S. Federal Highway Administration, *Highway Statistics*, annual.

No. 1106. Class I Intercity Motor Carriers of Passengers: 1990 to 1999

[943 represents $943,000,000. For carriers whose adjusted annual gross operating revenues are $5 million or more. Intercity carriers have intercity revenues which are 50 percent or more of their total operating revenues. Minus sign (-) indicated deficit]

Item	Unit	1990	1991	1992	1993	1994	1995	1996	1997	1998	1999
Number of intercity carriers [1]	Number.	21	21	21	21	20	20	17	17	15	14
Operating revenue	Mil. dol..	943	980	938	928	870	917	912	1,000	999	1,268
Intercity regular route	Mil. dol..	739	792	755	747	718	767	771	834	860	1,075
Other	Mil. dol..	204	189	182	182	152	150	141	165	139	192
Operating expenses	Mil. dol..	1,026	967	874	880	919	899	878	948	947	1,258
Operating income	Mil. dol..	-83	13	63	48	-48	18	33	52	52	9
Revenue passengers...........	Million..	44	42	41	40	41	43	37	52	47	54
Intercity regular route passengers.	Million..	37	36	36	35	36	38	34	41	37	42
Other passengers	Million..	7	5	5	5	4	5	4	12	10	12
Average fare, intercity regular route .	Dol.	20.22	21.86	21.15	21.32	19.77	20.10	22.85	20.57	23.14	25.56

[1] Excludes carriers preponderantly in local or suburban service and carriers engaged in transportation of both property and passengers.

Source: Bureau of Transportation Statistics, *Selected Earnings Data, Class I Motor Carriers of Passengers. Carriers of Passengers, 1988-1997, 1998,* and *1999.*

U.S. Census Bureau, Statistical Abstract of the United States: 2001

No. 1107. Bus Profile: 1980 to 1999

[3,833 represents $3,833,000,000]

Item	Unit	1980	1990	1995	1998	1999
FINANCIAL						
Expenditures, school bus	Mil. dol. .	3,833	7,605	9,889	10,326	10,340
Operating revenues, intercity bus, Class I [1]	Mil. dol. .	1,397	943	917	999	1,268
Operating expenses, intercity bus, Class I [1]	Mil. dol. .	1,318	1,026	899	947	1,258
INVENTORY						
Operating companies, intercity bus, Class I	Number .	61	31	20	16	14
Vehicles:						
Commercial & federal bus	Number .	110,576	118,726	125,057	133,070	136,748
School & other bus	Number .	418,225	508,261	560,447	582,470	592,029
Employees:						
Intercity & rural bus	Number .	38,000	26,300	23,800	24,400	23,700
School bus	Number .	79,900	111,200	131,100	141,000	146,700
PERFORMANCE						
Vehicle-miles, all buses:						
Rural & urban highway	Millions .	6,059	5,726	6,383	7,007	7,663
Rural highway	Millions .	3,035	3,444	3,817	4,251	4,668
Urban highway	Millions .	3,024	2,283	2,566	2,756	2,995
Revenue:						
Passenger miles, intercity bus	Millions .	(NA)	121,400	136,104	148,558	162,466
Passengers, intercity bus	1,000. . .	370,000	334,000	366,500	357,600	358,900
Avg. miles traveled per vehicle, all buses	Miles . . .	11,458	9,133	9,312	9,793	10,515
Avg. annual fuel consumption, all buses	Gallon . .	1,926	1,428	1,412	1,454	1,573
Avg. miles per gallon, all buses	Mpg . . .	6.0	6.4	6.6	6.7	6.7
Average revenue per passenger mile	Cents . .	7.3	11.6	12.2	12.8	12.8
SAFETY						
Fatalities:						
School bus related	Number .	150	115	123	126	164
School bus occupants	Number .	9	11	13	6	10
Other vehicle occupants	Number .	88	64	72	90	126
Nonoccupants	Number .	53	40	38	30	28
Vehicles involved in fatal accidents, all buses	Number .	390	340	271	289	319
Occupant fatality rate:						
Per 100 million vehicle-miles, all buses	Rate . . .	0.8	0.5	0.5	0.5	0.8
Per 10,000 registered vehicles, all buses	Rate . . .	0.9	0.5	0.5	0.5	0.8

NA Not available.   [1] Intercity regular route carriers only.
Source: U.S. Bureau of Transportation Statistics, *National Transportation Statistics,* annual.

No. 1108. Truck Profile: 1980 to 1999

[5,791 represents 5,791,000]

Item	Unit	1980	1990	1995	1998	1999
INVENTORY						
Truck registrations, total	1,000	5,791	6,196	6,719	7,732	7,792
Single-unit 2-axle 6-tire vehicle	1,000	4,374	4,487	5,024	5,735	5,763
Combination trucks	1,000	1,417	1,709	1,696	1,997	2,029
Employees:						
Trucking & courier services	1,000	1,182	1,274	1,440	1,569	1,611
Truck drivers & deliverymen	1,000	1,931	2,148	2,861	2,685	2,643
PERFORMANCE						
Vehicle miles, total	Millions . . .	108,491	146,242	178,156	196,380	202,697
Rural highway, total	Millions . . .	68,776	89,692	106,031	115,142	117,956
Urban highway, total	Millions . . .	39,715	56,550	72,125	81,238	84,741
Single unit 2-axle 6-tire vehicle	Millions . . .	39,813	51,901	62,705	68,021	70,311
Combination trucks	Millions . . .	68,678	94,341	115,451	128,359	132,386
Passenger miles:						
Single unit 2-axle 6-tire vehicle	Millions . . .	39,813	51,901	62,705	68,021	70,311
Combination trucks	Millions . . .	68,678	94,341	115,451	128,359	132,386
Average miles traveled per vehicle:						
All trucks, total	Avg. mile . .	18,736	23,603	26,514	25,397	26,015
Single unit 2-axle 6-tire vehicle	Avg. mile . .	9,103	11,567	12,482	11,861	12,201
Combination trucks	Avg. mile . .	48,472	55,206	68,083	64,265	65,261
Ton-miles, intercity	Millions . . .	555,000	735,000	921,000	1,027,000	1,093,000
Fuel consumed, all trucks	Mil. gal . . .	19,960	24,490	28,993	31,975	33,363
Single unit 2-axle 6-tire vehicle	Mil. gal . . .	6,923	8,357	9,216	6,817	7,122
Combination trucks	Mil. gal . . .	13,037	16,133	19,777	25,158	26,240
Average fuel consumption per vehicle	Gallons . . .	3,447	3,953	4,315	4,135	4,282
Single unit 2-axle 6-tire vehicle	Gallons . . .	1,583	1,862	1,835	1,189	1,236
Combination trucks	Gallons . . .	9,201	9,441	11,663	12,596	12,935
Highway-user taxes, total	Mil. dol . . .	9,888	19,356	25,116	28,697	(NA)
SAFETY						
Occupant fatalities	Number. . .	8,748	9,306	10,216	11,447	12,001
Light trucks	Number. . .	7,486	8,601	9,568	10,705	11,243
Large trucks	Number. . .	1,262	705	648	742	758
Vehicle involvement, total (per 100 million vehicle-miles)	Rate	4.5	2.9	2.4	2.3	2.2

NA Not available.
Source: U.S. Bureau of Transportation Statistics, *National Transportation Statistics,* annual.

No. 1109. Trucks by Use, Body Type, Miles, and Acquisition: 1992 and 1997

[In thousands (59,200.8 represents 59,200,800), except percent change. Based on the 1997 Economic Census; see Appendix III. Minus sign (-) indicates decrease]

Vehicular and operational characteristics	All trucks 1992	All trucks 1997	Percent change, 1992-97	Trucks, excluding pickups, panels, minivans, sport, utilities, and station wagons 1992	Trucks, excluding pickups, panels, minivans, sport, utilities, and station wagons 1997	Percent change, 1992-97
MAJOR USE						
Total	59,200.8	72,800.3	23.0	5,112.4	5,664.7	10.8
Agriculture	3,554.6	3,377.8	-5.0	898.7	854.7	-4.9
Forestry and lumbering	264.5	276.7	4.6	100.6	112.1	11.4
Mining and quarrying	220.4	250.7	13.7	79.2	82.1	3.7
Construction	4,986.3	6,033.9	21.0	1,015.4	1,161.8	14.4
Manufacturing	786.7	729.4	-7.3	257.6	258.6	0.4
Wholesale trade.........	1,136.1	1,264.6	11.3	438.3	440.4	0.5
Retail trade	1,950.9	2,243.8	15.0	434.9	469.3	7.9
For-hire transportation......	889.2	1,059.4	19.1	769.6	938.2	21.9
Utilities...............	541.2	663.8	22.7	183.4	204.9	11.7
Services	3,123.3	4,233.5	35.5	421.2	591.4	40.4
Daily rental	307.6	508.0	65.1	90.6	171.2	89.0
One-way rental	17.1	31.2	82.5	14.1	28.3	100.7
Personal transportation	40,441.9	50,934.5	25.9	231.0	183.0	-20.8
Not in use.............	981.0	1,193.1	21.6	177.8	168.6	-5.2
BODY TYPE						
Pickup	33,659.6	36,191.8	7.5	(X)	(X)	(X)
Minivan	6,129.6	9,837.9	60.5	(X)	(X)	(X)
Panel or van	5,701.0	5,572.7	-2.3	(X)	(X)	(X)
Utility vehicle	8,598.1	15,533.1	80.7	(X)	(X)	(X)
Sport utility	7,140.2	13,762.5	92.7	(X)	(X)	(X)
Station wagon	1,457.9	1,770.7	21.5	(X)	(X)	(X)
Multistop or stepvan	408.4	560.4	37.2	408.4	560.4	37.2
Platform with added devices..	295.7	308.2	4.2	295.7	308.2	4.2
Low boy or depressed center .	89.8	111.1	23.7	89.8	111.1	23.7
Basic platform	1,183.3	1,176.1	-0.6	1,183.3	1,176.1	-0.6
Livestock truck..........	48.3	39.1	-19.0	48.3	39.1	-19.0
Insulated nonrefrigerated van .	23.3	34.5	48.1	23.3	34.5	48.1
Insulated refrigerated van ...	204.8	234.0	14.3	204.8	234.0	14.3
Drop-frame van	60.1	54.9	-8.7	60.1	54.9	-8.7
Open-top van	20.1	20.8	3.5	20.1	20.8	3.5
Basic enclosed van	785.4	1,009.0	28.5	785.4	1,009.0	28.5
Beverage	73.0	70.2	-3.8	73.0	70.2	-3.8
Utility	157.0	152.0	-3.2	157.0	152.0	-3.2
Winch or crane	58.8	55.0	-6.5	58.8	55.0	-6.5
Wrecker	104.1	111.9	7.5	104.1	111.9	7.5
Pole or logging	53.9	55.7	3.3	53.9	55.7	3.3
Auto transport	22.3	20.1	-9.9	22.3	20.1	-9.9
Service truck	144.1	168.6	17.0	144.1	168.6	17.0
Yard tractor............	8.1	10.8	33.3	8.1	10.8	33.3
Oilfield truck	26.5	26.1	-1.5	26.5	26.1	-1.5
Grain body	310.8	299.1	-3.8	310.8	299.1	-3.8
Garbage hauler	72.4	91.6	26.5	72.4	91.6	26.5
Dump truck............	611.9	670.8	9.6	611.9	670.8	9.6
Tank truck (liquids or gases)..	231.9	249.4	7.5	231.9	249.4	7.5
Tank truck (dry bulk).......	33.8	39.7	17.5	33.8	39.7	17.5
Concrete mixer	61.0	73.1	19.8	61.0	73.1	19.8
Other................	23.7	22.6	-4.6	23.7	22.6	-4.6
ANNUAL MILES						
Less than 5,000.........	12,284.3	13,045.1	6.2	1,663.1	1,554.2	-6.5
5,000 to 9,999.........	12,273.1	13,465.5	9.7	751.9	753.4	0.2
10,000 to 19,999	22,656.5	29,974.6	32.3	978.6	1,128.8	15.3
20,000 to 29,999	7,499.5	10,198.5	36.0	512.6	585.4	14.2
30,000 to 49,999	3,215.3	4,349.9	35.3	458.8	571.1	24.5
50,000 to 74,999	717.0	951.3	32.7	284.9	374.5	31.4
75,000 or more	554.9	815.5	47.0	462.3	697.3	50.8
VEHICLE ACQUISITION						
Purchased new	26,967.2	30,052.9	11.4	2,091.2	2,323.6	11.1
Purchased used.........	30,417.3	37,834.5	24.4	2,601.1	2,762.6	6.2
Leased from someone else ..	1,397.1	4,039.3	189.1	373.6	522.2	39.8
Other and not reported	419.1	873.6	108.4	46.5	56.3	21.1

X Not applicable.

Source: U.S. Census Bureau, *1997 Economic Census, Vehicle Inventory and Use Survey, 1997,* Series EC97TV-US, issued October 1999.

Transportation 693

No. 1110. Truck Transportation, Couriers and Messengers, and Warehousing and Storage—Estimated Revenue

[In millions of dollars (207,535 represents $207,535,000,000), except percent. For taxable and tax-exempt employer firms. Estimates have been adjusted to the results of the 1997 Economic Census. Based on the North American Industry Classification System; see text, Section 15, Business Enterprise]

Kind of business	NAICS code [1]	1998	1999	Percent change, 1998-99
Selected transportation industries	48, 49	**207,535**	**221,729**	**6.8**
Truck transportation	484	150,816	162,083	7.5
General freight trucking	4841	94,419	101,817	7.8
General freight trucking, local.	48411	13,717	14,273	4.1
General freight trucking, long-distance.	48412	80,702	87,544	8.5
General freight trucking, long-distance, truckload	484121	53,085	57,851	9.0
General freight trucking, long-distance, less than truckload	484122	27,617	29,693	7.5
Specialized freight trucking	4842	56,396	60,266	6.9
Used household and office goods moving	48421	13,063	14,931	14.3
Specialized freight (except used goods) trucking, local	48422	22,314	24,088	8.0
Specialized freight (except used goods) trucking, long-distance	48423	21,019	21,247	1.1
Couriers and messengers	492	44,890	47,355	5.5
Couriers	4921	41,002	43,157	5.3
Local messengers and local delivery	4922	3,887	4,198	8.0
Warehousing and storage	493	11,829	12,291	3.9
General warehousing and storage	49311	6,230	6,592	5.8
Refrigerated warehousing and storage	49312	2,344	2,400	2.4
Farm product warehousing and storage	49313	614	642	4.6
Other warehousing and storage	49319	2,641	2,656	0.6

[1] Based in the North American Industry Classification System; see text Section 15, Business Enterprise.
Source: U.S. Census Bureau, 1999 Service Annual Survey, *Truck Transportation, Messenger Services and Warehousing.*

No. 1111. Truck Transportation—Summary

[In millions of dollars (150,816 represents $150,816,000,000), except as indicated. For taxable and tax-exempt employer firms. Covers NAICS 484. Estimates have been adjusted to the results of the 1997 Economic Census. Based on the North American Industry Classification System; see text, Section 15, Business Enterprise. Minus sign (-) indicates decrease]

Item	1998	1999	Percent change, 1998-99
Total operating revenue	**150,816**	**162,083**	**7.5**
Total motor carrier revenue	142,148	152,158	7.0
Local trucking [1]	44,871	49,164	9.6
Long-distance trucking [1]	97,277	102,994	5.9
Size of shipments:			
Less-than-truckload	40,568	44,526	9.8
Truckload.	101,580	107,632	6.0
Commodities handled:			
Agricultural and fish products.	12,101	12,232	1.1
Grains, alcohol, and tobacco products.	5,025	5,441	8.3
Stone, nonmetallic minerals, and metallic ores	9,026	9,502	5.3
Coal and petroleum products.	5,443	5,530	1.6
Pharmaceutical and chemical products	8,434	8,794	4.3
Wood products, textiles, and leathers	14,412	14,804	2.7
Base metal and machinery	11,465	11,674	1.8
Electronic, motorized vehicles, and precision instruments	7,889	9,010	14.2
Used household and office goods	9,098	9,878	8.6
New furniture and miscellaneous manufactured products	13,625	15,189	11.5
Other goods	45,632	50,104	9.8
Hazardous materials	9,688	9,535	-1.6
Origin and destination of shipments:			
U.S. to U.S.	137,191	146,476	6.8
U.S. to Canada.	1,597	1,791	12.1
U.S. to Mexico	827	1,218	47.2
Canada to U.S.	1,137	1,180	3.8
Mexico to U.S.	723	881	21.9
All other destinations	674	612	-9.1
Inventory of revenue generating equipment (1,000):			
Trucks	190	204	7.4
Owned	157	168	7.0
Leased	34	37	8.8
Truck-tractors.	867	900	3.8
Owned	741	763	3.0
Leased	127	137	7.9
Trailers	1,796	1,857	3.4
Owned	1,502	1,550	3.2
Leased	293	307	4.8
Highway miles traveled (mil.):			
Total.	79,148	84,729	7.1
By loaded or partially loaded vehicles	63,117	67,811	7.4
By empty vehicles	16,031	16,917	5.5

[1] Local trucking is the carrying of goods within a single metro area and its adjacent nonurban areas; long-distance trucking is the carrying of goods between metro areas.
Source: U.S. Census Bureau, 1999 Service Annual Survey, *Truck Transportation, Messenger Services and Warehousing.*

No. 1112. Railroads, Class I—Summary: 1990 to 1999

[As of Dec. 31, or calendar year data, except as noted (216 represents 216,000). Compiled from annual reports of class I railroads only except where noted. Minus sign (-) indicates deficit]

Item	Unit	1990	1992	1993	1994	1995	1996	1997	1998	1999
Class I line-hauling companies [1] . . .	Number.	14	13	13	13	11	10	9	9	9
Employees [2]	1,000 . .	216	197	193	190	138	182	178	178	178
Compensation	Mil. dol.	8,654	8,753	8,732	8,874	9,070	9,202	9,235	9,938	9,603
Average per hour	Dollars .	15.83	17.80	17.90	18.50	19.00	20.10	20.30	21.30	21.00
Average per year	Dollars .	39,987	44,336	45,354	46,714	48,188	50,611	51,882	55,764	54,082
Mileage:										
Railroad line owned [3]	1,000 . .	146	141	140	138	137	136	133	132	122
Railroad track owned [4]	1,000 . .	244	238	236	232	228	228	225	224	207
Equipment:										
Locomotives in service	Number.	18,835	18,004	18,161	18,505	18,812	19,269	19,684	20,261	20,256
Average horsepower	1,000 lb.	2,665	2,750	2,777	2,832	2,927	2,985	3,060	3,126	3,200
Cars in service:										
Passenger train	Number.	(NA)	(NA)	(NA)	(NA)	(NA)	(NA)	(NA)	(NA)	(NA)
Freight train [5]	1,000 . .	1,212	1,173	1,173	1,192	1,219	1,241	1,270	1,316	1,369
Freight cars [6]	1,000 . .	659	605	587	591	583	571	568	576	579
Income and expenses:										
Operating revenues	Mil. dol.	28,370	28,349	28,825	30,809	32,279	32,693	33,118	33,151	33,521
Operating expenses	Mil. dol.	24,652	25,325	24,517	25,511	27,897	26,331	27,291	27,916	28,011
Net revenue from operations . . .	Mil. dol.	3,718	3,024	4,308	5,298	4,383	6,361	5,827	5,235	5,510
Income before fixed charges . . .	Mil. dol.	4,627	4,127	4,990	6,184	5,016	7,055	6,168	5,803	6,001
Provision for taxes [7]	Mil. dol.	1,088	1,092	1,810	1,935	1,556	2,056	1,886	1,573	1,664
Ordinary income.	Mil. dol.	1,961	2,055	2,258	3,315	2,439	3,885	3,156	2,807	2,976
Net income	Mil. dol.	1,977	1,800	2,240	3,298	2,324	3,885	3,156	2,807	2,971
Net railway operating income . . .	Mil. dol.	2,648	1,955	2,517	3,392	2,858	4,338	3,984	3,698	4,047
Total taxes [8]	Mil. dol.	3,780	3,732	4,343	4,512	4,075	4,669	4,514	4,411	4,459
Indus. return on net investment. .	Percent.	8.1	6.3	7.1	9.4	7.0	9.4	7.6	7.0	6.9
Gross capital expenditures.	Mil. dol.	3,591	3,680	4,504	5,035	5,720	6,550	6,737	7,357	6,193
Balance sheet:										
Total property investment.	Mil. dol.	70,348	72,677	75,217*	78,384	86,186	90,046	96,058	102,171	103,424
Accrued depreciation and amortization	Mil. dol.	22,222	23,378	23,892	24,200	23,439	23,932	21,862	23,338	23,177
Net investment.	Mil. dol.	48,126	49,299	51,325	54,184	62,746	66,113	74,196	78,832	80,247
Shareholder's equity	Mil. dol.	23,662	23,115	24,658	27,389	31,419	32,255	34,996	32,976	30,478
Net working capital	Mil. dol.	-3,505	-4,372	-3,295	-3,059	-2,634	-2,942	-3,434	-4,443	-4,834
Cash dividends	Mil. dol.	2,074	830	1,054	1,398	1,518	3,937	995	1,521	2,084
AMTRAK passenger traffic:										
Passenger revenue.	Mil. dol.	941.9	933.2	777.6	717.9	734.1	756.2	792.1	821.5	1,067.8
Revenue passengers carried . . .	1,000 . .	22,382	21,678	21,511	21,239	20,349	19,700	20,200	21,248	21,544
Revenue passenger miles	Million. .	6,125	6,181	6,068	5,869	5,401	5,066	5,166	5,325	5,289
Averages:										
Revenue per passenger.	Dollars .	42.1	43.0	36.1	33.8	36.1	38.4	39.2	38.7	49.6
Revenue per passenger mile. .	Cents . .	15.4	15.1	12.8	12.2	13.6	14.9	15.3	15.4	20.2
Freight service:										
Freight revenue	Mil. dol.	24,471	27,508	27,991	29,931	31,356	31,889	32,322	32,247	32,680
Per ton-mile.	Cents . .	2.7	2.6	2.5	2.5	2.4	2.4	2.4	2.3	2.3
Per ton originated.	Dollar . .	19.3	19.7	20.0	20.4	20.2	19.8	20.4	19.6	19.0
Revenue-tons originated	Million. .	1,425	1,399	1,397	1,470	1,550	1,611	1,585	1,649	1,717
Revenue-tons carried	Million. .	2,024	2,022	2,047	2,185	2,322	2,229	2,114	2,158	2,155
Tons carried one mile	Billion . .	1,034	1,067	1,109	1,201	1,306	1,356	1,349	1,377	1,433
Average miles of road operated .	1,000 . .	133	126	124	123	125	127	122	120	121
Revenue ton-miles per mile of road.	1,000 . .	7,763	8,451	8,965	9,735	10,439	10,704	11,087	11,491	11,848
Revenue per ton-mile	Cents . .	3	3	3	2	2	2	2	2	2
Train miles	Million. .	380	390	405	441	458	469	475	475	490
Net ton-miles per train-mile [9] . . .	Number.	2,755	2,759	2,759	2,746	2,870	2,912	2,861	2,923	2,947
Net ton-miles per loaded car-mile [9]	Number.	69.1	70.9	71.6	72.2	73.6	75.0	74.0	73.2	73.8
Train-miles per train-hour.	Miles . .	23.7	23.7	23.1	22.4	21.8	22.0	19.2	19.0	20
Haul per ton, U.S. as a system . .	Miles . .	726	763	794	817	843	842	851	835	835
Accidents/ incidents: [10]										
Persons killed	Number.	1,297	1,170	1,279	1,226	1,146	1,039	1,063	1,008	932
Persons injured	Number.	25,143	21,383	19,121	16,812	14,440	12,558	11,767	11,459	11,700

NA Not available. [1] See text, this section, for definition of Class I. [2] Average mid-month count. [3] Represents the aggregate length of roadway of all line-haul railroads. Excludes yard tracks, sidings, and parallel lines. (Includes estimate for class II and III railroads). [4] Includes multiple main tracks, yard tracks, and sidings owned by both line-haul and switching and terminal. (Includes estimate for class II and III railroads). [5] Includes cars owned by all railroads, private car companies, and shippers. [6] Class I railroads only. [7] Includes state income taxes. [8] Includes payroll, income, and other taxes. [9] Revenue and nonrevenue freight. [10] Source: Federal Railroad Admin., Accident Bulletin, annual. Includes highway grade crossing casualties.

Source: Except as noted, Association of American Railroads, Washington, DC, Railroad Facts, Statistics of Railroads of Class I, annual, and Analysis of Class I Railroads, annual.

Transportation 695

No. 1113. Railroads, Class I-Cars of Revenue Freight Loaded, 1970 to 2000, and by Commodity Group, 1999 and 2000

[In thousands (27,160 represents 27,160,000). Figures are 52-week totals]

Year	Car-loads [1]	Commodity group	Carloads 1999 [2]	Carloads 2000 [3]	Commodity group	Carloads 1999 [2]	Carloads 2000 [3]
1970....	27,160	Coal	6,660	6,620	Metals and products	631	661
1980....	22,598	Metallic ores............	291	301	Stone, clay, and glass products.	489	500
1990....	16,177	Chemicals, allied products....	1,502	1,484	Crushed stone, gravel, sand...	798	840
1992....	15,798	Grain.................	1,183	1,119	Nonmettalic minerals.........	448	419
1993....	15,911	Motor vehicles and equipment .	1,265	1,282	Waste and scrap materials....	459	466
1994....	16,763	Pulp, paper, and allied products.	466	468	Lumber, wood products......	279	275
1995....	16,763	Primary forest products......	264	246	Coke	192	199
1996 [2]..	16,521	Food and kindred products ...	415	428	Petroleum products	284	296
1997 [2]..	16,568	Grain mill products........	449	451	All other carloads..........	331	299
1998 [2]..	16,914						
1999 [2]..	16,407						
2000 [3]..	16,354						

[1] Beginning 1990 excludes intermodal.   [2] Excludes two Class I railroads.   [3] Preliminary. Excludes three Class I railroads.

Source: Association of American Railroads, Washington, DC, *Weekly Railroad Traffic*, annual.

No. 1114. Railroads, Class I Line-Haul-Revenue Freight Originated by Commodity Group: 1990 to 1999

[21,401 represents 21,401,000]

Commodity group	1990	1992	1993	1994	1995	1996	1997	1998	1999
Carloads (1,000) [1]	21,401	21,205	21,683	23,179	23,726	24,159	25,016	25,705	27,096
Coal....................	5,912	5,572	5,310	5,681	6,095	6,746	6,703	7,027	6,965
Transportation equipment	1,091	1,181	1,355	1,448	1,473	1,442	1,485	1,671	1,896
Chemicals, allied products......	1,531	1,568	1,606	1,695	1,642	1,639	1,674	1,653	1,814
Farm products.............	1,689	1,646	1,636	1,459	1,692	1,530	1,408	1,404	1,477
Food and kindred products	1,307	1,352	1,380	1,381	1,377	1,302	1,295	1,282	1,354
Nonmetallic minerals.........	1,202	1,029	1,044	1,138	1,159	1,176	1,160	1,256	1,306
Primary metal products	477	481	528	579	575	597	604	644	682
Lumber and wood products	780	726	710	771	719	682	669	645	673
Waste and scrap materials......	439	487	558	604	623	605	608	581	624
Pulp, paper, and allied products ..	611	618	620	651	628	589	582	547	612
Petroleum and coal products	573	583	584	602	596	567	534	510	543
Stone, clay, and glass products...	539	483	487	512	516	491	485	475	538
Metallic ores	508	489	443	440	463	443	327	311	295
Machinery, exc. electrical.......	39	39	37	40	41	40	43	37	34
Fabricated metal products	31	32	37	37	32	29	29	27	27
Tons (mil.) [1].............	1,425	1,399	1,397	1,470	1,550	1,611	1,585	1,649	1,717
Coal.....................	579	554	534	574	627	705	705	749	751
Chemicals, allied products......	126	130	134	142	138	139	140	139	154
Farm products.............	147	149	147	131	154	142	126	129	139
Nonmetallic minerals..........	109	94	96	106	110	113	109	120	125
Food and kindred products	81	86	88	88	91	87	86	87	92
Primary metal products	38	39	43	47	47	49	50	53	56
Lumber and wood products	53	50	49	54	51	49	48	47	50
Stone, clay, and glass products...	44	40	40	42	43	42	41	41	47
Petroleum and coal products	40	41	41	43	43	42	39	38	40
Transportation equipment	23	25	29	30	30	29	31	36	40
Waste and scrap materials......	28	30	35	37	38	38	37	36	40
Pulp, paper, and allied products ..	33	34	34	37	36	33	32	31	35
Metallic ores	47	45	41	40	44	42	32	31	29
Machinery, exc. electrical.......	1	1	1	1	1	1	1	1	1
Fabricated metal products	1	1	1	1	1	1	1	1	1
Gross revenue (mil. dol.) [1] .	29,775	29,777	30,376	32,424	33,782	34,310	34,964	34,898	35,441
Coal.....................	6,954	6,717	6,481	7,021	7,356	7,706	7,698	7,997	7,739
Chemicals, allied products......	3,933	4,123	4,277	4,520	4,553	4,660	4,764	4,610	4,616
Transportation equipment	3,100	2,753	3,021	3,257	3,269	3,390	3,462	3,339	3,582
Farm products.............	2,422	2,454	2,528	2,407	3,020	2,807	2,645	2,529	2,720
Food and kindred products	2,188	2,308	2,336	2,427	2,464	2,378	2,385	2,378	2,400
Lumber and wood products	1,390	1,342	1,324	1,421	1,385	1,409	1,471	1,487	1,528
Pulp, paper, and allied products ..	1,486	1,508	1,511	1,510	1,543	1,485	1,507	1,472	1,457
Primary metal products	979	970	1,021	1,114	1,199	1,254	1,294	1,304	1,289
Stone, clay, and glass products...	931	911	944	1,009	1,044	1,033	1,063	1,056	1,089
Petroleum and coal products	918	943	929	967	997	1,013	1,028	991	980
Nonmetallic minerals..........	885	812	818	862	875	895	899	920	955
Waste and scrap materials......	504	558	613	655	685	702	711	693	689
Metallic ores	408	409	385	378	394	382	399	373	336
Machinery, exc. electrical.......	67	61	59	65	69	70	73	64	55
Fabricated metal products	42	45	50	50	44	41	41	37	38

[1] Includes commodity groups and small packaged freight shipments, not shown separately.

Source: Association of American Railroads, Washington, DC, *Freight Commodity Statistics*, annual.

696   Transportation

No. 1115. Railroad Freight—Producer Price Indexes: 1990 to 2000

[Dec. 1984=100. Reflects prices for shipping a fixed set of commodities under specified and unchanging conditions]

Commodity	1990	1994	1995	1996	1997	1998	1999	2000, prel.
Railroad line-haul operating.....	**107.5**	**111.8**	**111.7**	**111.5**	**112.1**	**113.4**	**113.0**	**114.5**
Coal.......................	104.2	107.5	107.3	106.7	107.0	108.7	107.3	108.7
Farm products.................	110.4	114.5	115.6	115.7	120.4	123.9	121.7	123.0
Food products.................	105.4	111.0	111.2	108.5	107.6	107.4	99.7	100.4
Metallic ores.................	106.5	104.6	101.9	103.5	103.4	104.4	103.8	105.6
Chemicals and allied products.......	111.7	117.6	120.0	119.2	119.6	120.1	119.1	121.4
Nonmetallic minerals.............	111.7	119.7	119.5	119.2	120.6	121.5	121.7	122.0
Lumber and wood products	107.5	110.0	110.0	112.8	111.0	110.3	109.8	109.0
Transportation equipment...........	107.5	115.3	112.8	114.0	113.2	113.4	113.3	112.8
Pulp, paper, and allied products	108.0	111.1	108.7	(NA)	111.2	113.7	115.5	119.0
Primary metal products	113.1	115.6	115.6	115.4	114.0	116.1	118.4	123.7
Stone, clay, glass, and concrete products	114.1	120.2	121.4	121.1	119.8	121.8	122.6	128.6
Petroleum and coal products	109.2	114.8	114.3	114.1	120.5	122.5	123.0	124.5

NA Not available.

Source: U.S. Bureau of Labor Statistics, *Producer Price Indexes,* monthly and annual.

No. 1116. Petroleum Pipeline Companies—Characteristics: 1980 to 1999

[173 represents 173,000. Covers pipeline companies operating in interstate commerce and subject to jurisdiction of Federal Energy Regulatory Commission]

Item	Unit	1980	1985	1990	1994	1995	1996	1997	1998	1999
Miles of pipeline, total	1,000......	173	171	168	159	177	169	160	157	154
Gathering lines	1,000......	36	35	32	30	35	32	31	21	20
Trunk lines	1,000......	136	136	136	128	142	137	130	136	134
Total deliveries........	Mil. bbl.....	10,600	10,745	11,378	12,159	12,862	12,635	12,481	12,914	13,317
Crude oil..........	Mil. bbl.....	6,405	6,239	6,563	6,785	6,952	6,975	6,795	7,639	7,551
Products	Mil. bbl.....	4,195	4,506	4,816	5,373	5,910	5,660	5,686	5,275	5,766
Total trunk line traffic.....	Bil. bbl-miles..	3,405	3,342	3,500	3,566	3,619	3,734	3,683	3,442	3,738
Crude oil..........	Bil. bbl-miles..	1,948	1,842	1,891	1,823	1,899	1,912	1,901	1,747	1,815
Products	Bil. bbl-miles..	1,458	1,500	1,609	1,743	1,720	1,822	1,782	1,696	1,923
Carrier property value	Mil. dol.....	19,752	21,605	25,828	26,363	27,460	28,043	30,655	30,181	33,780
Operating revenues......	Mil. dol.....	6,356	7,461	7,149	7,281	7,711	7,321	7,215	6,890	7,220
Net income	Mil. dol.....	1,912	2,431	2,340	2,148	2,670	2,372	2,255	2,051	2,929

Source: PennWell Publishing Co., Houston, Texas, *Oil & Gas Journal,* annual (copyright).

No. 1117. U.S. Postal Service Rates for Letters and Postcards: 1958 to 2001

[Domestic airmail letters discontinued in 1973 at 13 cents per ounce; superseded by express mail. Prior to February 3, 1991, international airmail rates were based on international zones which have been discontinued. Rates exclude Canada and Mexico]

Domestic mail date rate of change	Surface mail					International air mail date of change	Letters				
	Letters								Each		
	Each ounce	First ounce	Each added ounce	Post cards	Express mail [1]		First 1/2 ounce	Second 1/2 ounce	added 1/2 ounce	Post cards	Aero-grammes
1958 (Aug. 1) . .	$0.04	(X)	(X)	$0.03	(X)	1961 (July 1) . .	(X)	(X)	(X)	$0.11	$0.11
1963 (Jan. 7). . .	$0.05	(X)	(X)	$0.04	(X)	1967 (May 1) . .	(X)	(X)	(X)	$0.13	$0.13
1968 (Jan. 7). . .	$0.06	(X)	(X)	$0.05	(X)	1971 (July 1) . .	(X)	(X)	(X)	$0.13	$0.13
1971 (May 16)..	$0.08	(X)	(X)	$0.06	(X)	1974 (Mar. 2) . .	(X)	(X)	(X)	$0.18	$0.18
1974 (Mar. 2). .	$0.10	(X)	(X)	$0.08	(X)	1976 (Jan. 3) . .	(X)	(X)	(X)	$0.21	$0.22
1975 (Sept. 14) .	(X)	$0.10	$0.09	$0.07	(X)	1981 (Jan. 1) . .	(X)	(X)	(X)	$0.28	$0.30
1975 (Dec. 31). .	[2](X)	[2]$0.13	[2]$0.11	[2]$0.09	(X)	1985 (Feb. 17) . .	(X)	(X)	(X)	$0.33	$0.36
1978 (May 29). .	(X)	$0.15	$0.13	$0.10	(X)	1988 (Apr. 17) . .	(X)	(X)	(X)	$0.36	$0.39
1981 (Mar. 22)..	(X)	$0.18	$0.17	$0.12	(X)	1991 (Feb. 3) . .	$0.50	$0.45	[3]$0.39	$0.40	$0.45
1981 (Nov. 1) . .	(X)	$0.20	$0.17	$0.13	$9.35	1995 (July 9) . .	$0.60	[3]$0.40	(X)	$0.40	$0.45
1985 (Feb.17) . .	(X)	$0.22	$0.17	$0.14	[4]$10.75	1999 (Jan. 10) . .	$0.60	[3]$0.40	(X)	$0.50	$0.50
1988 (Apr. 3). . .	(X)	$0.25	$0.20	$0.15	[4]$12.00	2001 (Jan. 7) . .	[3][5]$0.80	[3][5]$1.70	(X)	$0.70	$0.70
1991 (Feb. 3) . .	(X)	$0.29	$0.23	$0.19	[4]$13.95						
1995 (Jan. 1). . .	(X)	$0.32	$0.23	$0.20	[4]$15.00						
1999 (Jan. 10). .	(X)	$0.33	$0.22	$0.20	[4]$15.75						
2001 (Jan. 7). . .	(X)	$0.34	$0.21	$0.20	[4]$16.00						

X Not applicable. [1] Post office to addressee rates. Rates shown are for weights up to 2 pounds, all zones. Beginning Feb. 17, 1985, for weights between 2 and 5 lbs, $12.85 is charged. Prior to Nov. 1, 1981, rate varied by weight and distances. Over 5 pounds still varies by distance. [2] As of October 11, 1975, surface mail service upgraded to level of airmail. [3] Up to the limit of 64 ounces. [4] Over 8 ounces and up to 2 pounds. [5] The rate increments changed to 1 oz.

Source: U.S. Postal Service, "United States Domestic Postage Rate: Recent History," and unpublished data.

No. 1118. U.S. Postal Service—Summary: 1980 to 2000

[106,311 represents 106,311,000,000. For fiscal years. Includes Puerto Rico and all outlying areas. See text, this section, and Section 8, State and Local Government Finances and Employment]

Item	1980	1990	1995	1997	1998	1999	2000
Offices, stations, and branches	**39,486**	**40,067**	**39,149**	**38,019**	**38,159**	**38,169**	**38,060**
Number of post offices	30,326	28,959	28,392	28,060	27,952	27,893	27,876
Number of stations and branches	9,160	11,108	10,757	9,959	10,207	10,276	10,184
Pieces of mail handled (mil.)	**106,311**	**166,301**	**180,734**	**190,888**	**196,905**	**201,644**	**207,882**
Domestic [1]	105,348	165,503	179,933	189,881	195,961	200,613	206,782
First class [2]	60,276	89,270	96,296	99,660	100,434	101,937	103,526
Express mail	17	59	57	64	66	69	71
Priority mail	248	518	869	1,068	1,174	1,190	1,223
Periodicals (formerly 2d class)	10,220	10,680	10,194	10,411	10,317	10,274	10,365
Standard A (formerly 3d class)	30,381	63,725	71,112	77,254	82,508	85,662	90,057
Standard B (formerly 4th class)	633	663	936	988	1,023	1,043	1,128
Mailgram	39	14	5	5	4	4	4
U.S. Postal Service	(NA)	538	412	377	380	382	363
Free for the blind	28	35	52	53	53	53	47
International surface	450	166	106	97	96	103	79
International air	513	632	696	910	848	928	1,021
Employees, total (1,000)	**667**	**843**	**875**	**893**	**905**	**906**	**901**
Career	643	761	753	765	792	798	788
Headquarters	3	2	2	2	2	2	2
Headquarters support	(NA)	6	4	4	4	4	6
Inspection service	5	4	4	4	4	4	4
Inspector General	(X)	(X)	(X)	(Z)	(Z)	(Z)	1
Field career	635	747	745	755	781	786	775
Postmasters	29	27	27	26	26	26	26
Supervisors/managers	36	43	35	36	37	39	39
Professional, administrative, and technical	5	10	11	11	12	11	10
Clerks	263	290	274	281	294	292	282
Mail handlers	37	51	57	59	62	62	61
City carriers	187	236	240	234	241	242	241
Motor vehicle operators	6	7	8	9	9	9	9
Rural carriers	33	42	46	50	52	55	57
Special delivery messengers	3	2	2	1	(X)	(X)	(X)
Building and equipment maintenance	27	33	38	40	41	42	42
Vehicle maintenance	5	5	5	6	6	6	6
Other [3]	4	1	2	2	2	2	2
Noncareer	25	83	122	128	113	108	114
Casuals	5	27	26	33	26	25	30
Transitional	(X)	(X)	32	27	17	12	13
Rural substitutes	20	43	50	55	56	57	58
Relief/Leave replacements	(X)	12	13	13	13	12	12
Nonbargaining temporary	(X)	(Z)	1	1	1	1	1
Compensation and employee benefits (mil. dol.)	16,541	34,214	41,931	43,835	45,596	47,333	49,532
Avg. salary per employee (dol.) [4]	24,799	37,570	45,001	48,793	50,117	48,111	50,103
Pieces of mail per employee, (1,000)	159	197	207	214	218	223	231
Total revenue (mil. dol.) [5]	**19,253**	**40,074**	**54,509**	**58,331**	**60,116**	**62,755**	**64,581**
Operating postal revenue	17,143	39,201	54,176	58,331	60,005	62,655	64,476
Mail revenue [6]	16,377	37,892	52,490	56,267	58,033	60,418	62,284
First class mail	10,146	24,023	31,955	33,398	33,861	34,933	35,516
Priority mail [7]	612	1,555	3,075	3,857	4,187	4,533	4,837
Express mail [8]	184	630	711	825	855	942	996
Mailgram	15	8	2	2	2	2	2
Periodicals (formerly 2d class)	863	1,509	1,972	2,068	2,072	2,115	2,171
Standard mail A (formerly 3d class)	2,412	8,082	11,792	12,876	13,702	14,436	15,193
Standard mail B (formerly 4th class)	805	919	1,525	1,628	1,754	1,829	1,912
International surface	154	222	205	192	184	194	180
International air	442	941	1,254	1,423	1,416	1,434	1,477
Service revenue	765	1,310	1,687	1,866	1,972	2,237	2,191
Registry [9]	157	174	118	95	89	95	98
Certified [9]	120	310	560	343	386	377	385
Insurance [9]	55	47	52	61	73	92	109
Collection-on-delivery	21	26	21	22	1	20	22
Special delivery [10]	73	6	3	1	(X)	(X)	(X)
Money orders	95	155	196	212	210	228	235
Other [9]	244	592	737	1,131	1,197	1,425	1,342
Operating expenses (mil. dol.) [11]	19,413	40,490	50,730	54,873	57,786	60,642	62,992

NA Not available.   X Not applicable.   Z Fewer than 500.   [1] Data for 1980 includes penalty and franked mail, not shown separately.   [2] Items mailed at 1st class rates and weighing 11 ounces or less.   [3] Includes discontinued operations, area offices, and nurses.   [4] For career bargaining unit employees. Includes fringe benefits.   [5] Net revenues after refunds of postage. Includes operating reimbursements, stamped envelope purchases, indemnity claims, and miscellaneous revenue and expenditure offsets. Shown in year which gave rise to the earnings.   [6] For 1980, includes penalty and franked mail, not shown separately. Later years have that mail distributed into the appropriate class.   [7] Provides 2 to 3 day delivery service.   [8] Overnight delivery of packages weighing up to 70 pounds.   [9] Beginning 1997, return receipt revenue broken out from registry, certified, and insurance and included in "other."   [10] Special delivery discontinued June 8, 1997.   [11] Shown in year in which obligation was incurred.

Source: U.S. Postal Service, *Annual Report of the Postmaster General* and *Comprehensive Statement on Postal Operations*, annual; and unpublished data.

Section 24
Information and Communications

This section presents statistics on the various information and communications media: publishing, including newspapers, periodicals, books, and software; motion pictures, sound recordings, broadcasting, and telecommunications; and information services, such as libraries. Statistics on computer use and Internet access are also included. Data on the usage, finances, and operations of the Postal Service previously shown in this section are now presented in Section 23, Transportation.

Information industry—The U.S. Census Bureau's *Service Annual Survey, Information Services Sector,* provides estimates of operating revenue of taxable firms and revenues and expenses of firms exempt from federal taxes for industries in the information sector of the economy. Similar estimates were previously issued in the *Annual Survey of Communications Services.* Data for 1998 and 1999 are based on the North American Classification System (NAICS) and the information sector is a newly created economic sector. It comprises establishments engaged in the following processes: (a) producing and distributing information and cultural products, (b) providing the means to transmit or distribute these products as well as data or communications, and (c) processing data. It includes establishments previously classified in the Standard Industrial Classification (SIC) in manufacturing (publishing); transportation, communications, and utilities (telecommunications and broadcasting); and services (software publishing, motion picture production, data processing, online information services, and libraries).

This new sector is comprised of industries which existed previously, were revised from previous industry definitions, or are completely new industries. Among those which existed previously are newspaper publishers, motion picture and video production, and online information services.

Revised industries include book publishers and libraries and archives. Newly created industries include database and directory publishers, record production, music publishers, sound recording studios, cable networks, wired telecommunications carriers, paging, and satellite telecommunications. The following URL contains detailed information about NAICS and provides a comparison of the SIC and NAICS <http://www.census.gov/epcd/www/naics.html>. See also the text in Section 15, Business Enterprise.

The 1997 Economic Census was the first economic census to cover the new information sector of the economy. The census, conducted every 5-years, for the years ending "2" and "7," provides information on the number of establishments, receipts, payroll, and paid employees for the United States and various geographic levels.

The Federal Communications Commission (FCC), established in 1934, regulates wire and radio communications. Only the largest carriers and holding companies file annual financial reports which are publically available. The FCC has jurisdiction over interstate and foreign communication services but not over intrastate or local services. The gross operating revenues of the telephone carriers reporting publically available data annually to the FCC, however, are estimated to cover about 90 percent of the revenues of all U.S. telephone companies. Data are not comparable with Census Bureau *Annual Survey* because of coverage and different accounting practices for those telephone companies which report to the FCC.

Reports filed by the broadcasting industry cover all radio and television stations operating in the United States. The private radio services represent the largest and most diverse group of licensees regulated by the FCC. These services provide voice, data communications, point-to-point, and point-to-multipoint radio communications

U.S. Census Bureau, Statistical Abstract of the United States: 2001

for fixed and mobile communicators. Major users of these services are small businesses, the aviation industry, the maritime trades, the land transportation industry, the manufacturing industry, state and local public safety and governmental authorities, emergency medical service providers, amateur radio operators, and personal radio operations (CB and the General Mobile Radio Service). The FCC also licenses entities as private and common carriers. Private and common carriers provide fixed and land mobile communications service on a for-profit basis. Principal sources of wire, radio, and television data are the FCC's *Annual Report* and its annual *Statistics of Communications Common Carriers.*

Statistics on publishing are available from the Census Bureau, as well as from various private agencies. Editor & Publisher Co., New York, NY, presents annual data on the number and circulation of daily and Sunday newspapers in its *International Year Book.* Data on book production and prices are available from R.R. Bowker, Co., New Providence, NJ. The Book Industry Study Group, New York, NY, collects data on books sold, domestic consumer expenditures, and book purchasing. Data on academic and public libraries are collected by the U.S. National Center for Education Statistics. Public library data are also gathered by R.R. Bowker, New York, NY, and the National Commission on Libraries and Information Science, Washington, DC.

Advertising—Data on advertising previously shown in this section are now presented in Section 27, Accommodation, Food Services, and Other Services.

Statistical reliability—For a discussion of statistical collection and estimation, sampling procedures, and measures of statistical reliability applicable to Census Bureau data, see Appendix III.

U.S. Census Bureau, Statistical Abstract of the United States: 2001

No. 1119. Information Industries—Establishments, Receipts, Payroll, and Employees by Kind of Business (NAICS Basis): 1997

[623,214 represents $623,214,000,000. For establishments with payroll. Based on the 1997 Economic Census; see Appendix III]

Industry	NAICS code [1]	Estab-lish-ments (number)	Receipts Total (mil. dol.)	Receipts Per paid employee (dol.)	Annual payroll Total (mil. dol.)	Annual payroll Per paid employee (dol.)	Paid employee for pay period including March 12 (1,000)
Information industries	51	**114,475**	**623,214**	**203,255**	**129,482**	**42,229**	**3,066.2**
Publishing industries	511	33,896	179,035	177,930	43,358	43,090	1,006.2
Newspaper, periodical, book, & database publishers [2]	5111	21,806	117,336	158,598	24,971	33,753	739.8
Newspaper publishers	51111	8,758	41,601	103,137	11,789	29,228	403.4
Periodical publishers	51112	6,298	29,885	217,265	5,993	43,571	137.6
Book publishers	51113	2,684	22,648	251,933	3,643	40,522	89.9
Database & directory publishers	51114	1,458	12,258	284,312	1,655	38,384	43.1
Software publishers	5112	12,090	61,699	231,622	18,387	69,025	266.4
Motion picture & sound recording industries . .	512	22,204	55,926	202,643	9,392	34,032	276.0
Motion picture & video industries	5121	19,269	44,786	175,998	8,280	32,540	254.5
Sound recording industries	5122	2,935	11,140	517,797	1,112	51,671	21.5
Broadcasting & telecommunications	513	43,480	346,316	241,427	63,480	44,253	1,434.5
Radio & television broadcasting	5131	8,789	40,425	161,885	9,869	39,521	249.7
Radio broadcasting	51311	6,894	10,648	84,060	3,604	28,455	126.7
Television broadcasting	51312	1,895	29,777	242,007	6,264	50,913	123.0
Cable networks & program distribution . . .	5132	4,679	45,390	260,334	6,151	35,280	174.4
Telecommunications [2]	5133	30,012	260,501	257,822	47,460	46,972	1,010.4
Wired telecommunications carriers	51331	20,815	208,791	256,051	39,565	48,520	815.4
Wireless telecommunications carriers (except satellite)	51332	6,386	37,889	258,977	5,839	39,913	146.3
Information services & data processing services	514	14,895	41,937	119,986	13,252	37,915	349.5
Information services [2]	5141	7,307	11,101	127,202	3,478	39,854	87.3
Libraries & archives	51412	2,298	861	39,055	373	16,928	22.0
Other information services	51419	4,482	8,837	158,544	2,639	47,351	55.7
Online information services	514191	4,165	8,043	161,061	2,356	47,181	49.9
Data processing services	5142	7,588	30,837	117,585	9,774	37,269	262.3

[1] North American Industry Classification System, 1997; see text, this section, and Section 15, Business Enterprise.
[2] Includes other industries, not shown separately.

Source: U.S. Census Bureau, *1997 Economic Census, Information*, Series EC97551A-US, issued October 1999.

No. 1120. Information Sector Services—Estimated Revenue: 1998 and 1999

[In millions of dollars (695,153 represents $695,153,000,000), except percent. For taxable and tax-exempt employer and nonemployer firms. Except as indicated, estimates adjusted to the results of the 1997 Economic Census]

Industry	NAICS code [1]	1998	1999	Percent change, 1998-99
Information industries	51	**695,153**	**775,622**	**11.6**
Publishing industries	511	203,773	221,543	8.7
Newspaper, periodical, book, database, and other publishers [2]	5111	131,228	140,064	6.7
Newspaper publishers	51111	45,691	48,594	6.4
Periodical publishers	51112	36,865	39,279	6.5
Book publishers	51113	22,706	24,373	7.3
Database and directory publishers	51114	14,321	15,523	8.4
Software publishers	5112	72,546	81,478	12.3
Motion picture and sound recording industries	512	60,684	65,196	7.4
Motion picture and video	5121	49,558	52,920	6.8
Sound recording [2]	5122	11,126	12,275	10.3
Broadcasting and telecommunications	513	382,293	426,836	11.7
Radio and television broadcasting	5131	44,092	47,630	8.0
Radio broadcasting	51311	11,765	13,236	12.5
Television broadcasting	51312	32,327	34,394	6.4
Cable networks and program distribution [2]	5132	52,320	59,951	14.6
Telecommunications [3]	5133	285,880	319,255	11.7
Wired telecommunications carriers	51331	228,151	247,836	8.6
Wireless telecommunications carriers (except satellite) [2]	51332	42,637	53,822	26.2
Information services and data processing services	514	48,404	62,047	28.2
Information services [3]	5141	15,151	24,136	59.3
Libraries and archives	51412	1,037	1,106	6.6
Other information services	51419	12,476	21,148	69.5
Online information services	514191	11,446	18,932	65.4
Data processing services	5142	33,252	37,911	14.0

[1] Based in the North American Industry Classification System; see text, this section, and Section 15, Business Enterprise.
[2] Estimates not adjusted to the 1997 Economic Census. [3] Includes other industries, not shown separately.

Source: U.S. Census Bureau, *1999 Service Annual Survey, Information Sector Services.*

[3,142.0 represents 3,142,000. For establishments with payroll. Excludes most government employees, railroad employees and self-employed persons]

Industry	NAICS code [1]	Establishments		Paid employees [2] (1,000)		Annual payroll (mil. dol.)	
		1998	1999	1998	1999	1998	1999
Information industries	51	120,552	126,510	3,142.0	3,234.5	146,822	170,282
Publishing industries	511	33,412	32,377	1,011.1	1,004.7	49,764	54,516
Newspaper, periodical, book, & database publishers	5111	21,723	21,245	727.9	700.0	26,148	26,821
Newspaper publishers.	51111	8,686	8,625	401.4	393.5	12,245	12,740
Periodical publishers.	51112	6,244	5,984	131.9	126.8	6,248	6,412
Book publishers.	51113	2,682	2,646	90.5	81.4	3,781	3,767
Database & directory publishers	51114	1,276	970	38.0	31.7	1,643	1,455
Other publishers	51119	2,835	3,020	66.1	66.6	2,232	2,446
Greeting card publishers	511191	107	108	19.8	18.2	669	627
All other publishers	511199	2,728	2,912	46.4	48.5	1,562	1,820
Software publishers	5112	11,689	11,132	283.2	304.7	23,615	27,696
Motion picture & sound recording industries. .	512	23,155	23,102	281.7	293.4	10,137	10,531
Motion picture & video industries	5121	20,049	19,889	255.2	270.2	8,429	9,175
Motion picture & video production	51211	9,691	9,796	63.3	72.5	4,742	5,301
Motion picture & video distribution	51212	711	706	26.9	27.7	889	1,058
Motion picture & video exhibition.	51213	6,279	6,197	132.4	137.1	1,084	1,134
Motion picture theaters (except drive-ins)	512131	5,961	5,885	130.5	135.2	1,061	1,111
Drive-in motion picture theaters	512132	318	312	1.9	1.9	23	22
Post production & other motion picture & video industries	51219	3,368	3,190	32.6	32.9	1,714	1,682
Teleproduction & other postproduction services.	512191	2,990	2,851	28.3	28.5	1,490	1,468
Other motion picture & video industries.	512199	378	339	4.3	4.4	224	214
Sound recording industries	5122	3,106	3,213	26.5	23.2	1,708	1,356
Record production	51221	278	274	1.1	1.0	49	53
Integrated record production/distribution .	51222	289	289	7.0	6.7	676	677
Music publishers	51223	718	701	5.2	5.2	232	252
Sound recording studios	51224	1,419	1,553	10.7	7.3	649	267
Other sound recording industries.	51229	402	396	2.5	3.0	102	108
Broadcasting & telecommunications	513	47,217	50,852	1,462.7	1,504.2	69,681	76,011
Radio & television broadcasting	5131	8,515	8,546	243.0	250.3	10,281	11,364
Radio broadcasting.	51311	6,570	6,537	114.3	123.5	3,627	4,541
Radio networks	513111	320	339	6.4	8.6	255	454
Radio stations	513112	6,250	6,198	107.9	114.8	3,372	4,087
Television broadcasting	51312	1,945	2,009	128.7	126.8	6,654	6,824
Cable networks & program distribution . . .	5132	4,954	5,364	178.7	182.1	7,271	8,060
Cable networks	51321	752	755	32.5	33.2	1,903	2,057
Cable & other program distribution	51322	4,202	4,609	146.2	148.9	5,368	6,002
Telecommunications.	5133	33,748	36,942	1,041.0	1,071.9	52,128	56,586
Wired telecommunications carriers	51331	22,270	23,461	818.2	815.7	42,099	44,614
Wireless telecommunications carriers (except satellite).	51332	7,860	9,263	162.4	186.0	7,101	8,102
Paging	513321	3,943	4,099	70.0	71.2	2,727	3,059
Cellular & other wireless telecommunications	513322	3,917	5,164	92.4	114.8	4,374	5,043
Telecommunications resellers.	51333	2,081	2,208	41.2	43.6	1,698	2,167
Satellite telecommunications	51334	677	791	11.8	17.6	782	1,235
Other telecommunications	51339	860	1,219	7.3	8.9	448	469
Information services & data processing services.	514	16,768	20,179	386.5	432.2	17,241	29,224
Information services.	5141	8,471	11,265	119.0	149.2	6,550	16,473
News syndicates	51411	516	564	9.9	11.4	522	612
Libraries & archives	51412	2,320	2,590	24.1	31.0	416	566
Other information services	51419	5,635	8,111	84.9	106.8	5,612	15,295
Online information services.	514191	5,277	7,714	78.8	98.9	5,005	12,816
All other information services	514199	358	397	6.2	8.0	607	2,479
Data processing services	5142	8,297	8,914	267.5	283.0	10,691	12,751

[1] North American Industry Classification System code; see text, this section, and Section 15, Business Enterprise. [2] For employees on the payroll for the pay period including March 12.

Source: U.S. Census Bureau, County Business Patterns, annual.

No. 1122. Gross Domestic Income in Information Technologies (IT) Industries: 1992 to 2000

[In millions of dollars (371,080 represents $371,080,000,000), except as noted]

Industry	1987 SIC [1] code	1992	1995	1998 est.	1999 est.	2000 est.
Total all IT industries	(X)	371,080	491,292	665,530	746,092	814,727
Percent share of the economy	(X)	5.9	6.7	7.6	8.0	8.3
Hardware	(X)	110,050	155,409	210,914	226,214	243,506
Computers and equipment, calc. machines . .	3571,2,5,7pt, 3578,9pt	24,102	31,036	39,211	42,622	46,330
Computers and equipment wholesale sales . .	5045pt	39,743	51,114	75,084	81,106	88,162
Computers and equipment retail sales	5734pt	1,915	2,861	3,407	3,687	4,008
Electron tubes	3671	1,053	1,206	1,317	1,402	1,493
Printed circuit boards.	3672	3,556	4,406	5,527	5,604	5,683
Semiconductors	3674	18,308	40,836	57,055	60,763	64,713
Passive electronic components	3675,6,7,8,9pt, 3661pt	13,494	15,310	12,072	12,881	13,744
Industrial instruments for measurement.	3823	2,552	2,526	4,874	5,215	5,580
Instruments for measuring electricity.	3825pt	3,493	3,981	8,383	8,953	9,562
Laboratory analytical instruments.	3826	1,835	2,134	3,986	3,982	4,233
Software/services [2]	(X)	75,490	111,350	185,609	213,986	245,644
Computer programming services	7371	18,624	26,120	47,796	55,013	62,715
Prepackaged software	7372	14,555	22,768	34,497	40,016	46,419
Computer integrated systems design	7373	11,814	13,599	24,692	28,420	32,598
Computer processing and data preparation . .	7374	12,554	21,844	28,062	32,300	37,048
Information retrieval services.	7375	2,879	3,910	8,977	10,333	11,852
Computer services management	7376	1,910	2,090	2,942	3,386	3,884
Computer rental leasing.	7377	1,528	1,880	2,944	3,389	3,887
Computer maintenance and repair.	7378	4,989	6,949	10,029	11,544	13,241
Computer related services, n.e.c. [3].	7379	4,406	9,305	21,261	24,472	28,069
Communications hardware [2].	(X)	23,970	30,775	46,710	49,151	51,816
Telephone and telegraph equipment.	3661pt, 3577pt, 3679pt	10,251	12,139	21,807	22,592	23,405
Radio and TV and communications equip . . .	3663, 3679pt, 3699	10,134	14,310	20,642	22,252	23,987
Communications services [2]	(X)	161,570	193,758	222,298	256,740	273,761
Telephone and telegraph communications . . .	481, 2, 9	129,960	145,491	159,712	189,400	199,109
Television broadcasting	4833	11,649	18,442	22,740	23,520	26,551
Cable and other pay TV services	4841	14,992	21,778	29,798	32,266	35,231

X Not applicable.   [1] 1987 Standard Industrial Classification code. See text, Section 15, Business Enterprise.   [2] Includes other industries, not shown separately.   [3] N.e.c. means not elsewhere classified.

No. 1123. Information Technologies (IT)—Employment and Wages: 1992 to 1998

[89,956 represents 89,956,000]

Industry	1987 SIC [1] code	Employment (1,000)			Annual wages per worker (dol.)		
		1992	1995	1998	1992	1995	1998
Total private	(X)	89,956	97,885	106,007	25,400	27,200	31,400
Total IT-producing industries	(X)	3,875	4,240	5,156	41,300	46,400	58,000
Hardware.	(X)	1,436	1,475	1,708	42,400	46,300	58,000
Electronic computers	3571	242	190	200	52,400	59,600	83,900
Computers and equipment wholesalers . .	5045pt	277	285	367	52,500	54,300	69,700
Computers and equipment retailers	5734pt	75	94	126	32,200	33,800	40,400
Computer storage devices & peripheral equipment.	3572,7	91	105	119	41,200	46,500	57,400
Computer terminals, office & accounting, machines, & office machines, n.e.c. [2]. . .	3575,8,9	58	58	61	43,300	46,600	56,900
Electron tubes.	3671	27	24	20	38,400	41,900	46,400
Semiconductors.	3674	217	235	284	44,500	53,800	64,400
Printed circuit boards, electronic capacitors.	3672,5-8	157	187	208	25,700	28,300	32,900
Electronic components, n.e.c. [2].	3679	127	135	148	29,700	32,900	37,500
Industrial instruments for measurement . .	3823	61	64	67	35,100	38,400	46,400
Instruments for measuring electricity	3825	76	71	77	42,500	51,600	62,900
Analytical instruments.	3826	28	28	32	38,700	44,200	54,300
Software/services [3]	(X)	854	1,110	1,625	44,300	50,700	65,300
Computer programming services.	7371	169	245	370	46,200	52,700	64,700
Prepackaged software.	7372	131	181	252	57,000	63,700	94,100
Computer integrated systems design	7373	103	130	178	48,600	54,700	65,400
Computer processing & data preparation .	7374	204	223	254	34,400	39,700	45,800
Information retrieval services	7375	45	57	98	36,700	42,200	63,700
Computer maintenance & repair	7378	43	49	60	36,600	37,800	41,200
Computer services management, rental & leasing, & maintenance & repair.	7376,7,9	141	205	387	46,000	51,800	64,100
Communications equipment [3]	(X)	317	337	353	38,900	43,200	53,700
Telephone and telegraph equipment	3661	110	112	126	42,400	49,900	62,400
Radio and TV communications equipment & communications equipment, n.e.c. [2]. . .	3663,9	129	153	156	39,100	42,700	52,100
Communication services [3].	(X)	1,269	1,318	1,469	38,600	43,700	50,900
Telephone communications	481	885	900	1,007	41,400	46,800	53,700
Telephone & telegraph communications . .	482,489	26	27	35	41,700	48,500	56,200
Television broadcasting	4833	115	123	131	41,400	47,200	54,600
Cable & other pay TV services	4841	131	156	181	29,600	34,600	42,200

X Not applicable.   [1] 1987 Standard Industrial Classification code. See text, Section 15, Business Enterprise.   [2] N.e.c. means not elsewhere classified.   [3] Includes other industries, not shown separately.

Source of Tables 1122 and 1123: U.S. Department of Commerce, Economics and Statistics Administration, *The Digital Economy*, June 2000.

No. 1124. Communications Industry—Finances: 1995 to 1999

[In millions of dollars (161,586 represents $161,586,000,000). Covers publicly reporting media and communications companies with revenues of over $1 million in 13 media and communication industry segments. Minus sign (-) indicates loss]

Industry	Revenue				Operating income			
	1995	1997	1998	1999	1995	1997	1998	1999
Total	161,586	217,697	241,633	271,272	21,218	27,518	30,251	24,872
Television broadcasting	21,517	27,309	29,974	32,345	3,505	5,740	6,030	5,999
Television network companies	16,677	20,550	22,689	24,164	2,275	3,946	4,187	4,254
Television station broadcasters	4,840	6,759	7,285	8,181	1,229	1,794	1,843	1,745
Cable and satellite television	24,640	38,252	39,875	45,524	3,027	3,500	3,321	-643
Cable and satellite providers	18,561	28,504	29,108	33,861	2,320	2,136	1,752	-678
Radio broadcasting	2,254	4,942	6,721	8,093	433	976	1,264	1,409
Radio network companies	167	329	319	434	23	70	47	85
Radio station broadcasters	2,087	4,613	6,402	7,659	411	907	1,217	1,324
Entertainment	29,213	38,682	42,138	43,588	3,509	3,694	4,375	4,048
Newspaper publishing	20,671	24,048	25,954	27,467	2,865	4,827	5,082	5,805
Consumer book publishing	3,490	3,319	3,110	3,098	432	224	83	238
Consumer magazine publishing	6,576	7,395	7,662	7,797	653	831	901	1,020
Business-to-business communications	3,302	3,923	4,290	5,638	321	401	383	796
Professional and educational publishing	9,408	11,632	13,099	14,847	1,340	918	1,377	1,214
Business information services	21,880	28,666	33,105	36,964	3,551	4,924	5,502	5,314
Financial information	9,919	13,178	14,571	15,609	2,041	2,828	2,998	2,979
The Internet	1,296	4,643	5,694	9,641	-78	-1,068	-1,455	-3,875
Internet content providers	87	237	480	1,094	-57	-391	-530	-1,559
Internet search engines	23	165	420	946	-8	-92	-139	-321
Internet service providers	1,150	4,133	4,618	6,937	-8	-507	-651	-1,474
Internet business-to-business	36	109	176	664	-5	-78	-136	-521
Advertising agencies	11,218	15,135	17,476	20,464	1,055	1,538	2,045	2,334
Specialty media	6,120	9,752	12,536	15,806	604	1,012	1,342	1,215
E-marketers	74	329	451	705	5	16	-1	-115

Source: Veronis, Suhler & Associates Inc., New York, NY, *Communications Industry Report,* annual (copyright).

No. 1125. Media Usage and Consumer Spending: 1995 to 2004

[Estimates of time spent were derived using rating data for television, cable and satellite and radio, survey research and consumer purchase data for books, home video, Internet, magazines, movies in theaters, newspapers, recorded music, and video games. Adults 18 and older except for radio, recorded music, movies in theaters, video games and Internet where estimates include persons 12 and older]

Item	1995	1996	1997	1998	1999	2000, proj.	2001, proj.	2002, proj.	2003, proj.	2004, proj.
HOURS PER PERSON PER YEAR										
Total	3,275	3,265	3,249	3,275	3,399	3,491	3,571	3,633	3,700	3,786
Television	1,580	1,559	1,544	1,551	1,588	1,599	1,601	1,590	1,584	1,595
Broadcast TV	1,044	985	923	884	867	873	868	846	828	834
Network stations	865	809	750	710	706	725	718	700	683	688
Independent stations [1]	179	176	173	174	162	148	150	146	145	146
Subscription video services	537	573	620	667	720	725	733	744	756	761
Basic cable and satellite	447	485	519	566	617	622	628	627	640	644
Premium cable and satellite	89	88	101	101	103	104	105	117	116	117
Radio	970	973	964	936	967	980	989	997	1,004	1,012
Recorded music	288	292	270	283	290	309	329	348	368	389
Daily newspapers	166	161	159	156	154	152	150	149	147	147
Consumer books	100	99	95	96	91	91	91	91	92	92
Consumer magazines [2]	83	82	82	81	81	80	79	79	78	77
Home video [2]	49	54	53	55	55	58	64	65	68	71
Movies in theaters	12	12	13	13	13	13	14	14	14	15
Home video games	22	25	36	43	61	76	93	114	136	161
Internet	5	10	34	61	99	135	162	187	208	228
CONSUMER SPENDING PER PERSON PER YEAR (dol.)										
Total	466.32	497.74	525.77	566.24	610.84	655.80	694.24	730.05	760.25	792.41
Television	125.08	138.96	153.62	166.06	180.64	193.63	206.73	219.38	231.76	244.31
Broadcast TV	-	-	-	-	-	-	-	-	-	-
Cable and satellite	125.08	138.96	153.62	166.06	180.64	193.63	206.73	219.38	231.76	244.31
Radio	-	-	-	-	-	-	-	-	-	-
Recorded music	56.87	57.47	55.51	61.67	65.13	71.28	72.56	74.64	70.61	68.38
Daily newspapers	52.03	52.84	52.81	53.30	53.65	53.75	54.56	55.47	56.33	57.04
Consumer books	79.16	80.90	80.51	84.12	85.86	88.99	91.84	94.74	97.69	100.71
Consumer magazines	41.63	42.88	44.70	44.46	45.01	45.95	47.15	48.56	49.76	50.95
Home video [2]	79.94	85.98	85.63	92.38	95.39	105.71	113.10	116.02	119.83	122.54
Box office	25.36	27.11	28.88	31.23	33.11	34.86	36.82	38.90	41.17	43.53
Home video games	10.53	11.47	16.45	18.49	22.99	28.26	34.59	42.01	49.58	58.05
Internet	8.46	13.24	20.87	27.63	41.77	46.29	50.30	53.91	57.58	61.26

- Represents zero.   [1] Includes affiliates UPN and WB.   [2] Playback of prerecorded tapes only.

Source: Veronis, Suhler & Associates Inc., New York, NY, *Communications Industry Forecast* annual (copyright).

704 Information and Communications

No. 1126. Utilization of Selected Media: 1970 to 1999

[62.0 represents 62,000,000]

Item	Unit	1970	1980	1985	1990	1994	1995	1996	1997	1998	1999
Households with—											
Telephone service [1]	Percent .	87.0	93.0	91.8	93.3	93.9	93.9	93.8	93.9	94.1	94.2
Radio [2]	Millions .	62.0	78.6	87.1	94.4	98.0	98.0	98.0	98.0	(NA)	(NA)
Percent of total households ..	Percent .	98.6	99.0	99.0	99.0	99.0	99.0	99.0	99.0	99.0	(NA)
Average number of sets	Number .	5.1	5.5	5.5	5.6	5.6	5.6	5.6	5.6	5.6	(NA)
Television [3]	Millions .	59	76	85	92	94		96	97	98	99
Percent of total households ..	Percent .	95.3	97.9	98.1	98.2	98.3	98.3	98.3	98.4	98.3	98.2
Television sets in homes	Millions .	81	128	155	193	211	217	223	229	235	240
Average number of sets per home.	Number .	1.4	1.7	1.8	2.1	2.2	2.3	2.3	2.4	2.4	2.4
Color set households	Millions .	21	63	78	90	93	94	95	97	98	99
Cable television [4]	Millions .	4	15	36	52	59	60	63	64	66	67
Percent of TV households...	Percent .	6.7	19.9	42.8	56.4	62.4	63.4	65.3	66.5	67.2	67.5
VCRs [4]	Millions .	(NA)	1	18	63	74	77	79	82	83	84
Percent of TV households...	Percent .	(NA)	1.1	20.8	68.6	79.0	81.0	82.2	84.2	84.6	84.6
Commercial radio stations: [2]											
AM................	Number .	4,323	4,589	[5]4,718	4,987	4,913	4,150	4,857	4,762	4,793	4,783
FM................	Number .	2,196	3,282	[5]3,875	4,392	5,109	5,730	5,419	5,542	5,662	5,766
Television stations: [6] Total	Number .	862	1,011	1,197	1,442	1,512	1,532	1,533	1,574	1,572	1,585
Commercial	Number .	677	734	883	1,092	1,145	1,161	1,174	1,205	1,204	1,216
VHF	Number .	501	516	520	547	561	562	554	560	562	561
UHF	Number .	176	218	363	545	584	599	620	645	642	682
Cable television:											
Systems [7]	Number .	2,490	4,225	6,844	9,575	11,214	11,218	11,119	10,950	10,845	10,700
Households served [8]	Millions .	4.5	17.7	39.9	54.9	60.5	63.0	64.6	65.9	67.4	68.0
Daily newspaper circulation [9]	Millions .	62.1	62.2	62.8	62.3	59.3	58.2	57.0	56.7	56.2	56.0

NA Not available.   [1] For occupied housing units. 1970 and 1980 as of April 1; all other years as of March. Source: U.S. Census Bureau, 1970 and 1980 Census of Housing, Vol. 1; thereafter Federal Communications Commission, Trends in Telephone Service, annual.   [2] 1980-1995 as of December 31, except as noted. Source: M Street Corp. as reported by Radio Advertising Bureau New York, NY, through 1990, Radio Facts, annual, (copyright); beginning 1994, Radio Marketing Guide and Fact Book for Advertisers, annual, (copyright). Number of stations on the air compiled from Federal Communications Commission reports. Beginning 1996, Federal Communications Commission, unpublished data as of Sept. 30.   [3] 1970, as of September of prior year; all other years as of January of year shown. Excludes Alaska and Hawaii. Source: Television Bureau of Advertising, Inc., Trends in Television, annual (copyright).   [4] As of February. Excludes Alaska and Hawaii.   [5] As of February 1986.   [6] As of January 1. Source: See footnote 3.   [7] As of January 1. Source: Warren Publishing, Washington DC, Television and Cable Factbook (copyright).   [8] Source: Nielsen Media Research, New Your, NY, Nielsen Station Index, November diary estimates (copyright).   [9] As of September 30. Source: Editor & Publisher, Co., New York, NY, Editor & Publisher International Year Book, annual (copyright).

Source: Compiled from sources mentioned in footnotes.

No. 1127. Multimedia Audiences—Summary: 2000

[In percent, except total (199,438 represents 199,438,000). As of spring. For persons 18 years old and over. Represents the percent of persons participating during the prior week, except as indicated. Based on sample and subject to sampling error; see source for details]

Item	Total population (1,000)	Television viewing	Television prime time viewing	Cable viewing [1]	Radio listening	Newspaper reading	Accessed Internet [2]
Total	199,438	93.5	82.1	71.3	84.0	79.3	45.4
18 to 24 years old	25,691	92.2	73.8	68.6	90.6	73.3	58.7
25 to 34 years old	39,066	92.4	81.3	71.1	90.6	77.0	53.3
35 to 44 years old	44,791	92.4	81.1	71.9	89.7	80.5	53.8
45 to 54 years old	34,774	93.7	83.5	74.7	87.5	83.5	54.8
55 to 64 years old	22,711	94.7	85.6	76.4	80.8	82.4	35.1
65 years old and over	32,404	96.5	86.7	65.4	61.1	78.1	10.7
Male..............	95,691	94.3	82.3	72.0	85.3	79.3	47.1
Female.............	103,747	92.8	81.8	70.6	82.8	79.2	43.8
White	167,002	93.4	82.0	72.6	84.4	80.0	46.8
Black	23,628	95.9	84.9	67.3	84.1	77.3	33.1
Asian	5,507	92.2	77.4	49.8	74.6	68.3	53.5
Other	3,301	88.3	74.4	68.2	78.1	72.0	46.4
Spanish speaking	21,359	93.5	81.6	55.9	84.6	66.3	34.1
Not high school graduate	35,260	94.8	82.7	56.6	73.0	60.0	11.6
High school graduate........	66,360	94.5	84.6	71.8	82.7	78.8	31.0
Attended college	52,878	93.6	80.6	76.2	89.3	83.7	59.5
College graduate.	44,940	91.1	79.4	76.1	88.1	89.7	76.5
Employed:							
Full time.	113,259	92.7	81.0	74.6	91.1	82.0	56.8
Part time	17,176	92.2	78.7	70.9	89.2	82.1	55.1
Not employed	69,003	95.3	84.6	65.9	71.0	74.1	24.2
Household income:							
Less than $10,000	14,292	93.6	81.6	47.7	68.0	58.7	14.6
$10,000 to $19,999	24,406	95.3	84.2	55.8	71.2	68.6	14.2
$20,000 to $29,999	25,327	94.8	84.3	63.8	78.7	73.9	24.5
$30,000 to $39,999	24,055	94.0	82.2	70.4	84.7	77.2	37.5
$40,000 to $49,999	21,816	92.8	82.6	73.9	86.4	79.5	44.1
$50,000 or more	89,542	92.7	80.7	80.9	90.7	87.5	67.1

[1] In the past 7 days.   [2] In the last 30 days.

Source: Mediamark Research Inc., New York, NY, Multimedia Audiences, spring 2000 (copyright).

U.S. Census Bureau, Statistical Abstract of the United States: 2001

No. 1128. Newspapers and Periodicals—Number by Type: 1980 to 2000

[Data refer to year of compilation of the directory cited as the source, i.e., generally to year preceding year shown. Data for 1995 and prior years include Canada and Mexico]

Type	1980	1985	1990	1994	1995	1996	1997	1998	1999	2000
Newspapers [1]	9,620	9,134	11,471	12,513	12,246	10,466	10,042	10,504	10,530	10,696
Semiweekly	537	517	579	661	705	612	558	557	560	558
Weekly	7,159	6,811	8,420	9,067	9,011	7,655	7,191	7,267	7,471	7,594
Daily	1,744	1,701	1,788	1,831	1,710	1,537	1,582	1,461	1,647	1,661
Periodicals [1]	10,236	11,090	11,092	12,136	11,179	9,843	8,530	12,448	11,751	13,019
Weekly	1,716	1,367	553	487	513	442	350	382	366	402
Semimonthly [2]	645	801	435	209	216	307	139	262	123	149
Monthly	3,985	4,088	4,239	4,494	4,067	3,554	3,067	3,378	3,204	3,572
Bimonthly	1,114	1,361	2,087	2,475	2,568	2,216	1,943	2,184	2,034	2,294
Quarterly	1,444	1,759	2,758	3,370	3,621	3,280	2,893	3,386	3,158	3,578

[1] Includes other items not shown separately.   [2] Includes fortnightly (every 2 weeks).

Source: Gale Group, Farmington Hills, MI, *Gale Directory of Publications and Broadcast Media*, annual (copyright).

No. 1129. Newspaper, Periodical, Database, and Directory Publishers—Estimated Revenue, Printing Expenses, and Inventories: 1998 and 1999

[In millions of dollars (45,521 represents $45,521,000,000), except percent. For taxable and tax-exempt employer firms. Estimates have not been adjusted to the results of the 1997 Economic Census. Based on the North American Industry Classification System; see text, Section 15, Business Enterprise. Minus sign (-) indicates decrease]

Item	Newspaper publishers (NAICS 51111)			Periodical publishers (NAICS 51112)			Database and directory publishers (NAICS 51114)		
	1998	1999	Percent change, 1998-99	1998	1999	Percent change, 1998-99	1998	1999	Percent change, 1998-99
Revenue	45,521	48,414	6.4	36,443	38,826	6.5	14,239	15,433	8.4
Single copy and subscription sales, total	8,592	8,818	2.6	14,907	15,670	5.1	1,274	1,409	10.6
Print	8,561	8,760	2.3	14,190	14,700	3.6	631	605	-4.1
Electronic	(S)	(S)	(S)	718	969	35.1	643	804	25.0
Advertising sales, total	32,843	35,513	8.1	16,690	17,989	7.8	9,889	10,679	8.0
Print	32,740	35,376	8.1	16,515	17,766	7.6	9,850	10,590	7.5
Electronic	103	136	32.6	176	223	27.0	39	89	127.6
Contract printing	1,680	1,765	5.1	1,148	1,140	-0.7	127	143	12.7
Other revenue	2,407	2,318	-3.7	3,698	4,028	8.9	2,950	3,202	8.6
Expenses: Purchased printing	3,245	3,427	5.6	4,208	4,287	1.9	1,182	1,198	1.3
Inventories at end of year	740	737	-0.4	1,199	1,258	4.8	227	408	80.1
Finished goods and work-in-process	38	43	14.1	801	877	9.4	206	383	86.1
Materials, supplies, fuel, etc	702	694	-1.1	398	381	-4.4	(S)	(S)	(S)

S Data do not meet publication standards.

Source: U.S. Census Bureau, *1999 Service Annual Survey, Information Sector Services*.

No. 1130. Daily and Sunday Newspapers—Number and Circulation: 1970 to 2000

[62.1 represents 62,100,000. Number of newspapers as of February 1 the following year. Circulation figures as of September 30 of year shown. For English language newspapers only]

Type	1970	1975	1980	1985	1990	1994	1995	1996	1997	1998	1999	2000
NUMBER												
Daily: Total [1]	1,748	1,756	1,745	1,676	1,611	1,548	1,533	1,520	1,509	1,489	1,483	1,480
Morning	334	339	387	482	559	635	656	686	705	721	736	766
Evening	1,429	1,436	1,388	1,220	1,084	935	891	846	816	781	760	727
Sunday	586	639	736	798	863	886	888	890	903	898	905	917
CIRCULATION (mil.)												
Daily: Total [1]	62.1	60.7	62.2	62.8	62.3	59.3	58.2	57.0	56.7	56.2	56.0	55.8
Morning	25.9	25.5	29.4	36.4	41.3	43.4	44.3	44.8	45.4	45.6	46.0	46.8
Evening	36.2	35.2	32.8	26.4	21.0	15.9	13.9	12.2	11.3	10.5	10.0	9.0
Sunday	49.2	51.1	54.7	58.8	62.6	62.3	61.5	60.8	60.5	60.1	59.9	59.4
PER CAPITA CIRCULATION [2]												
Daily: Total [1]	0.30	0.28	0.27	0.26	0.25	0.23	0.22	0.21	0.21	0.21	0.21	0.20
Morning	0.13	0.12	0.13	0.15	0.17	0.17	0.17	0.17	0.17	0.17	0.17	0.17
Evening	0.18	0.16	0.14	0.11	0.08	0.06	0.05	0.05	0.04	0.04	0.04	0.03
Sunday	0.24	0.24	0.24	0.25	0.25	0.24	0.23	0.23	0.23	0.22	0.22	0.22

[1] All-day newspapers are counted in both morning and evening columns but only once in total. Circulation is divided equally between morning and evening.   [2] Based on U.S. Census Bureau estimated resident population as of July 1.

Source: Editor & Publisher Co., New York, NY, *Editor & Publisher International Year Book*, annual (copyright).

No. 1131. Daily Newspapers—Number and Circulation by Size of City: 1980 to 2000

[29,413 represents 29,413,000. Number of newspapers as of February 1 the following year. Circulation as of September 30. For English language newspapers only. See Table 32 for number of cities by population size. All-day newspapers are counted in both morning and evening columns; circulation is divided equally between · iorning and evening]

Type of daily and population-size class	Number					Net paid circulation (1,000)				
	1980	1985	1990	1995	2000	1980	1985	1990	1995	2000
Morning dailies, total ..	**387**	**482**	**559**	**656**	**766**	**29,413**	**36,361**	**41,311**	**44,310**	**46,772**
In cities of—										
1,000,001 or more	20	22	18	25	26	8,795	9,367	6,508	10,173	10,820
500,001 to 1,000,000....	27	24	22	22	25	5,705	6,897	4,804	5,587	5,412
100,001 to 500,000......	99	121	138	153	163	8,996	12,197	20,051	17,214	17,469
50,001 to 100,000.......	75	87	100	138	162	2,973	3,653	4,373	5,602	5,887
25,001 to 50,000	64	83	102	115	141	1,701	2,145	3,209	3,150	3,899
Less than 25,000	102	145	179	203	249	1,243	2,099	2,365	2,584	3,285
Evening dailies, total ..	**1,388**	**1,220**	**1,084**	**891**	**727**	**32,788**	**26,407**	**21,017**	**13,883**	**9,000**
In cities of—										
1,000,001 or more	11	8	7	3	1	2,984	2,169	1,423	390	1
500,001 to 1,000,000....	23	14	12	7	3	4,101	1,626	1,350	1,017	519
100,001 to 500,000......	123	102	71	45	32	8,178	6,987	4,687	2,529	1,603
50,001 to 100,000.......	156	127	94	72	54	4,896	3,942	2,941	2,029	1,332
25,001 to 50,000	246	229	204	158	124	5,106	4,606	4,278	2,819	1,898
Less than 25,000	829	740	696	606	513	7,523	7,075	6,338	5,099	3,648

Source: Editor & Publisher Co., New York, NY, *Editor & Publisher International Year Book,* annual (copyright).

No. 1132. Daily and Sunday Newspapers—Number and Circulation by State: 2000

[55,773 represents 55,773,000. Number of newspapers as of February 1 the following year. Circulation as of September 30. For English language newspapers only. New York, Massachusetts, and Virginia Sunday newspapers include national circulation]

State	Daily			Sunday		State	Daily			Sunday	
		Circulation [1]			Net paid circula- tion [1]			Circulation [1]			Net paid circula- tion [1]
	Number	Net paid (1,000)	Per capita [2]	Number	(1,000)		Number	Net paid (1,000)	Per capita [2]	Number	(1,000)
U.S. ...	1,480	55,773	0.20	917	59,421	MO	43	937	0.17	23	1,209
AL	24	658	0.15	20	739	MT......	11	184	0.20	7	188
AK......	7	107	0.17	5	125	NE......	17	437	0.26	6	410
AZ......	16	778	0.15	11	892	NV......	8	296	0.15	4	320
AR......	30	472	0.18	16	525	NH......	12	234	0.19	8	242
CA......	92	6,175	0.18	61	6,250	NJ......	19	1,367	0.16	16	1,667
CO.....	29	1,267	0.29	16	1,510	NM.....	18	285	0.16	13	288
CT......	17	727	0.21	13	816	NY......	59	6,393	0.34	36	5,455
DE.....	2	140	0.18	2	161	NC......	47	1,334	0.17	39	1,484
DC.....	2	865	1.51	2	1,114	ND......	10	167	0.26	7	171
FL	42	3,067	0.19	38	3,870	OH......	84	2,399	0.21	43	2,705
GA.....	34	1,047	0.13	28	1,336	OK.....	43	639	0.19	36	782
HI	6	221	0.18	5	254	OR.....	19	681	0.20	11	724
ID	12	211	0.16	8	229	PA	84	2,742	0.22	41	3,156
IL......	68	2,342	0.19	30	2,478	RI	6	221	0.21	3	258
IN	68	1,313	0.22	25	1,275	SC.....	15	625	0.16	14	732
IA	37	621	0.21	12	634	SD.....	11	156	0.21	4	135
KS......	45	442	0.16	15	395	TN.....	25	856	0.15	17	1,039
KY.....	23	612	0.15	14	652	TX.....	87	2,926	0.14	83	3,874
LA.....	26	726	0.16	21	802	UT.....	6	330	0.15	6	369
ME.....	7	232	0.18	4	194	VT.....	8	122	0.20	3	98
MD.....	14	612	0.12	8	876	VA	28	2,721	0.38	17	1,165
MA.....	32	1,631	0.26	16	1,595	WA	24	1,107	0.19	18	1,264
MI	49	1,723	0.17	26	1,969	WV	22	363	0.20	12	367
MN.....	25	848	0.17	14	1,149	WI	35	944	0.18	17	1,013
MS.....	23	385	0.14	18	391	WY	9	87	0.18	5	70

[1] Circulation figures based on the principal community served by a newspaper which is not necessarily the same location as the publisher's office. [2] Per capita based on enumerated resident population as of April 1.

Source: Editor & Publisher Co., New York, NY, *Editor & Publisher International Year Book,* annual (copyright).

No. 1133. Periodicals—Average Retail Prices: 1997 to 2001

[In dollars]

Subject	1997	1998	1999	2000	2001
Agriculture	441.87	439.56	465.30	504.55	529.22
Anthropology	204.44	224.95	248.02	261.49	256.68
Art and architecture	100.64	102.15	103.54	106.28	109.53
Astronomy	926.93	963.04	1006.62	1026.76	1,083.91
Biology	791.17	856.22	930.51	1005.77	1,064.33
Botany	627.54	660.61	706.15	760.88	790.28
Business and economics	331.38	366.71	408.48	458.43	500.94
Chemistry	1,428.28	1,534.50	1647.49	1788.09	1,918.09
Education	171.33	185.65	204.54	226.21	249.81
Engineering and technology	798.09	878.66	961.49	1049.59	1,142.84
Food science	473.72	542.13	620.80	675.65	731.26
General science	560.05	620.28	683.25	754.99	830.55
General works	81.21	80.64	82.25	84.70	85.50
Geography	491.30	537.86	566.47	635.13	682.29
Geology	717.98	757.08	793.71	856.10	914.51
Health sciences	524.24	569.73	624.08	675.84	728.14
History	93.87	97.41	106.91	113.18	120.05
Language and literature	85.89	87.24	93.18	96.47	101.34
Law	123.12	131.70	140.32	148.47	159.91
Library and information science	192.27	214.78	232.20	245.75	259.69
Math and computer science	773.66	824.42	881.69	951.70	1,018.57
Military and naval science	177.60	237.30	258.60	281.80	329.00
Music	66.95	69.75	76.40	77.87	79.94
Philosophy and religion	113.45	114.96	123.60	130.78	136.48
Physics	1,541.48	1,631.52	1731.05	1874.46	2,011.13
Political science	164.70	181.59	206.06	225.93	254.19
Psychology	222.17	238.86	271.68	298.80	326.00
Recreation	89.97	96.40	107.25	115.14	127.20
Sociology	197.42	218.88	244.47	268.98	297.18
Technology	712.72	781.48	854.93	932.01	1,013.34
Zoology	622.09	671.59	743.45	818.07	866.03

Source: Library Journal, New York, NY, *Library Journal*, April 15, 2001. (Copyright 2001, used with permission of Library Journal, a publication of Cahner's Business Information, a division of Reed Elsevier.)

No. 1134. Quantity of Books Sold and Value of U.S. Domestic Consumer Expenditures: 1995 to 2000

[2,346 represents 2,346,000,000. Includes all titles released by publishers in the United States and imports which appear under the imprints of American publishers. Multivolume sets, such as encyclopedias, are counted as one unit]

Type of publication and distribution area	Net publishers shipments [1] (mil.)					Domestic consumer expenditures (mil. dol.)				
	1995	1997	1998	1999	2000	1995	1997	1998	1999	2000
Total [1]	2,346	2,325	2,402	2,505	2,493	25,154	27,021	28,786	30,027	32,050
Hardback	879	883	895	929	926	15,011	16,175	17,016	18,438	18,973
Paperback	1,467	1,442	1,507	1,576	1,567	10,143	10,846	11,770	11,589	13,077
Trade	842	819	860	935	904	9,340	9,701	10,350	10,788	11,514
Adult	485	477	497	529	457	7,060	7,339	7,791	8,142	8,691
Juvenile	357	342	364	406	447	2,280	2,362	2,558	2,646	2,874
Mass market paperbacks-rack sized	530	473	484	485	471	2,322	2,220	2,348	2,457	2,622
Bookclubs	126	137	142	146	143	949	1,116	1,176	1,233	1,316
Mail order publications	96	86	78	66	65	578	539	487	553	590
Religious	157	167	171	174	171	1,792	1,958	2,037	2,150	2,295
Professional	165	165	170	178	187	4,153	4,465	4,751	4,959	5,293
University press	28	28	30	32	31	394	427	455	474	506
Elhi text	247	291	302	305	334	2,384	2,911	3,216	3,294	3,516
College text	155	168	176	184	186	2,708	3,110	3,365	3,483	3,718
Subscription reference	1	1	1	1	1	532	579	603	636	679
Domestic distribution	2,196	2,180	2,254	2,348	2,339	25,154	27,021	28,786	30,027	32,050
General retailers	1,145	1,098	1,143	1,199	1,181	11,888	12,332	13,102	13,813	14,557
College stores	284	279	291	299	301	4,311	4,766	5,122	5,280	5,699
Libraries and institutions [2]	97	98	102	105	106	2,111	2,256	2,394	2,496	2,664
Schools [2]	273	313	326	326	343	2,896	3,446	3,780	3,764	4,234
Direct to consumers	289	292	293	312	304	3,544	3,830	3,989	4,239	4,448
Other	108	99	99	108	104	404	391	399	435	449
Exports	149	145	149	157	155	(X)	(X)	(X)	(X)	(X)

X Not applicable.   [1] Net, after returns.   [2] Elhi libraries included in schools.

Source: Book Industry Study Group, Inc., New York, NY, *Book Industry Trends, 2000*, annual (copyright).

No. 1135. American Book Title Production: 1998 and 1999

[1999 data are preliminary. Data compiled from R.R. Bowker's Books in Print database. Includes the output of small presses and self publishers]

Subject	Total		Hardcover		Mass market[1]		Trade[2]	
	1998	1999	1998	1999	1998	1999	1998	1999
Total..............	120,244	100,405	53,922	45,305	6,909	7,323	59,413	47,777
Agriculture	1,201	892	589	438	4	8	608	446
Art.....................	4,934	4,272	2,406	2,016	18	25	2,510	2,231
Biography...............	3,206	2,775	1,649	1,515	55	75	1,502	1,185
Business	3,844	3,154	1,575	1,240	5	10	2,264	1,904
Education...............	3,391	2,492	1,152	855	17	29	2,222	1,608
Fiction	11,016	11,570	3,719	3,854	3,657	4,045	3,640	3,671
General works...........	1,504	1,238	759	630	9	17	736	591
History.................	7,346	6,018	3,627	3,160	34	23	3,685	2,835
Home economics	2,518	2,272	1,103	1,061	51	54	1,364	1,157
Juvenile	9,195	8,320	5,432	5,148	2,267	2,066	1,496	1,106
Language	2,862	1,985	1,103	802	56	46	1,703	1,137
Law....................	3,007	1,996	1,390	983	7	3	1,610	1,010
Literature	3,784	3,262	2,102	1,834	93	119	1,589	1,309
Medicine...............	6,718	5,312	3,122	2,422	100	111	3,496	2,779
Music..................	1,398	1,155	531	452	17	16	850	687
Philosophy, psychology	5,965	4,999	2,312	2,075	93	220	3,560	2,704
Poetry and drama	3,018	2,226	1,126	883	37	46	1,855	1,297
Religion	6,347	4,806	2,624	1,924	137	159	3,586	2,723
Science	8,486	6,410	4,914	3,857	58	64	3,514	2,489
Sociology, economics	14,645	11,895	6,876	5,593	91	88	7,678	6,214
Sports, recreation........	3,718	3,208	1,254	1,189	67	64	2,397	1,955
Technology	9,103	7,359	3,852	2,823	17	20	5,234	4,516
Travel	3,038	2,789	705	551	19	15	2,314	2,223

[1] "Pocket-sized" books sold primarily through magazine and news outlets, supermarkets, variety stores, etc.   [2] All paperbound books, except mass market.

Source: R. R. Bowker Co., New Providence, NJ, The Bowker *Annual Library and Book Trade Almanac, 2000*. (Copyright by R.R. Bowker, A Division of Elsevier, Inc.)

No. 1136. Average Per Volume Book Prices: 1998 and 1999

[In dollars. 1999 data preliminary. Data compiled from R.R. Bowker's Books in Print database. Includes the output of small presses and self publishers]

Subject	Hardcover		Mass market[1]		Trade[2]	
	1998	1999	1998	1999	1998	1999
Total..............	63.53	60.80	5.45	5.58	30.89	30.96
Agriculture	61.99	55.69	5.36	5.91	35.67	38.08
Art.....................	55.43	58.85	7.86	8.33	26.79	26.09
Biography...............	46.40	45.36	6.64	6.43	20.70	19.48
Business	93.43	128.07	5.84	8.32	44.94	46.31
Education...............	60.52	60.96	8.93	7.23	27.27	27.00
Fiction	26.79	27.46	5.43	5.51	16.03	16.09
General works...........	110.66	155.74	6.98	7.92	37.26	43.03
History.................	62.27	53.61	6.80	6.68	26.87	25.32
Home economics	37.97	39.40	6.26	7.43	20.78	18.71
Juvenile	21.10	22.36	4.90	5.02	19.60	19.17
Language	75.98	53.92	6.69	7.02	32.45	29.60
Law....................	94.00	92.19	7.85	6.99	44.72	49.83
Literature	59.00	70.28	6.69	6.59	20.46	19.50
Medicine...............	94.13	85.25	6.01	6.05	38.91	37.89
Music..................	54.60	60.26	7.16	6.55	23.96	22.83
Philosophy, psychology	55.80	57.70	7.05	7.00	21.94	22.20
Poetry and drama	43.07	42.49	6.54	6.55	15.62	15.94
Religion	45.38	41.31	7.42	7.08	19.34	18.38
Science	95.96	94.15	6.72	6.35	40.94	41.19
Sociology, economics	65.97	61.34	6.41	6.43	33.69	37.97
Sports, recreation........	44.15	39.00	6.21	6.05	22.14	22.04
Technology	111.86	104.20	6.68	6.88	60.87	57.74
Travel	38.55	39.73	8.47	8.43	18.94	20.94

[1] "Pocket-sized" books sold primarily through magazine and news outlets, supermarkets, variety stores, etc.   [2] All paperbound books, except mass market.

Source: R. R. Bowker Co., New Providence, NJ, The Bowker *Annual Library and Book Trade Almanac, 2000*. (Copyright by R.R. Bowker, A Division of Elsevier, Inc.)

No. 1137. Book Publishers—Estimated Revenue, Printing Expenses, and Inventories: 1998 and 1999

[In millions of dollars (22,480 represents $22,480,000,000), except percent. For taxable and tax-exempt employer firms. For NAICS 51113. Estimates have not been adjusted to the results of the 1997 Economic Census. Based on the North American Industry Classification System; see text, this section, and Section 15, Business Enterprise. Minus sign (-) indicates decrease]

Item	1998	1999	Percent change, 1998-99
Revenue	22,480	24,129	7.3
Revenue from the sale of printed material............	18,622	19,840	6.5
Revenue from the sale of electronic or nonprinted material (except audio), total....................	2,168	2,434	12.2
Multimedia................................	748	811	8.4
Online...................................	1,420	1,623	14.3
Revenue from the sale of audio books...............	191	198	3.8
Revenue from the sale of publication rights............	235	247	5.2
Contract printing.............................	428	361	-15.7
Other revenues	836	1,048	25.5
Expenses: Purchased printing	3,908	4,104	5.0
Inventories at end of year	2,737	2,984	9.0
Finished goods and work-in-process...............	2,510	2,723	8.5
Materials, supplies, fuel, etc....................	227	261	14.6

Source: U.S. Census Bureau, *1999 Service Annual Survey, Information Sector Services.*

No. 1138. Book Purchasing by Adults: 1991 and 1999

[In percent. Excludes books purchased for or by children under age 13. Based on a survey of 16,000 households conducted over 12 months ending in December of year shown. For details, see source]

Characteristic	Total 1991	Total 1999	Mass market [1] 1991	Mass market [1] 1999	Trade [2] 1991	Trade [2] 1999	Hardcover 1991	Hardcover 1999
Total	100.0	100.0	100.0	100.0	100.0	100.0	100.0	100.0
Age of purchaser:								
Under 25 years old..........	4.3	4.9	3.7	3.7	5.2	6.6	4.4	4.3
25 to 34 years old	18.8	13.9	13.9	10.2	25.4	17.0	19.6	14.6
35 to 44 years old	23.7	22.5	22.8	17.7	25.2	25.7	23.7	24.3
45 to 54 years old	22.4	24.1	26.0	25.2	18.5	22.5	20.5	24.4
55 to 64 years old	15.6	17.3	15.8	20.2	13.9	15.6	17.2	16.0
65 years old and over........	15.2	17.3	17.8	23.0	11.8	12.6	14.6	16.4
Household income:								
Under $30,000	37.1	29.8	41.7	35.6	32.6	27.3	34.1	25.9
$30,000 to 49,999	27.2	20.8	27.3	20.2	27.7	20.6	26.5	21.8
$50,000 to 59,999	11.0	9.8	9.8	10.1	12.3	10.2	11.5	9.1
$60,000 to 69,999	6.9	11.5	7.0	11.9	7.2	11.0	6.3	11.6
$70,000 and over...........	17.8	28.1	14.2	22.2	20.2	30.9	21.6	31.6
Household size:								
Singles	20.8	19.1	17.7	20.7	24.1	18.9	22.8	17.4
Families with no children.......	40.4	44.1	42.3	43.4	38.0	43.4	39.7	45.6
Families with children	38.8	36.8	40.0	35.9	37.9	37.7	37.5	37.0
Age of reader:								
Under 25 years old..........	7.3	7.4	5.2	5.0	10.1	10.2	7.7	6.9
25 to 34 years old	18.7	14.3	14.1	10.1	24.7	17.6	20.2	15.4
35 to 44 years old	22.9	21.7	22.3	17.6	24.0	24.7	22.7	23.6
45 to 54 years old	20.8	23.0	24.9	24.6	16.5	20.8	18.4	22.8
55 to 64 years old	14.9	16.2	15.9	19.9	12.7	14.1	15.6	14.7
65 years old and over........	15.4	17.4	17.6	22.8	12.0	12.7	15.6	16.6
Category of book:								
Popular fiction..............	54.9	53.3	93.0	94.5	14.9	19.7	31.8	43.9
General nonfiction	10.3	7.8	3.6	1.9	15.6	8.9	16.5	13.2
Cooking/crafts..............	10.2	10.0	0.4	0.2	20.6	16.2	18.2	14.4
Other....................	24.6	28.9	3.0	3.4	48.9	55.2	33.5	28.5
Sales outlet:								
Independent	32.5	15.2	26.5	8.9	44.9	22.8	29.0	13.9
Chain book store	22.0	24.6	17.2	21.8	27.4	26.1	25.2	26.0
Book clubs	16.6	17.7	17.8	20.8	9.5	12.9	22.6	19.5
Other [3]	28.9	42.5	38.5	48.5	18.2	38.2	23.2	40.6
Online	(NA)	5.4	(NA)	2.7	(NA)	7.0	(NA)	6.6

NA Not available. [1] "Pocket size" books sold primarily through magazine and news outlets, supermarkets, variety stores, etc. [2] All paperbound books, except mass market. [3] Includes mail order, price clubs, discount stores, food/drug stores, used book stores, and other outlets.

Source: Book Industry Study Group, Inc., New York, NY, *Consumer Research Study on Book Purchasing,* annual (copyright).

710   Information and Communications

No. 1139. Software Publishers—Estimated Revenue, Expenses, and Inventories: 1998 and 1999

[In millions of dollars (72,098 represents $72,098,000,000), except percent. For taxable and tax-exempt employer firms. Covers NAICS 5112. Estimates have been adjusted to the results of the 1997 Economic Census. Based on the North American Industry Classification System; see text, this section, and Section 15, Business Enterprise. Minus sign (-) indicates decrease]

Item	1998	1999	Percent change, 1998-99
Revenue	**72,098**	**80,959**	**12.3**
Personal computer software revenue, total	11,818	12,940	9.5
Enterprise software revenue, total	20,580	22,849	11.0
Systems and systems management software revenue	10,130	12,261	21.0
Electronic commerce enabling technologies and software	(S)	(S)	(S)
Mainframe computer software revenue, total	8,065	8,676	7.6
Other services revenue, total	13,625	16,076	18.0
Implementation and customization	4,597	5,428	18.1
Software upgrades and maintenance	7,224	8,575	18.7
Software user training	1,201	1,313	9.3
Internet access fees	(S)	(S)	(S)
Web hosting and design	(S)	(S)	(S)
Web site advertising	15	35	138.5
Other revenues	7,117	6,883	-3.3
Expenses: Selected purchases, total	**4,751**	**5,460**	**14.9**
Purchased printing	627	693	10.5
Purchased software reproduction	2,136	2,413	13.0
Purchased programming services	1,987	2,354	18.4
Inventories at end of year	**784**	**863**	**10.1**
Finished goods and work-in-process	665	697	4.8
Materials, supplies, fuel, etc.	119	167	39.8

S Data do not meet publication standards.

Source: U.S. Census Bureau, *1999 Service Annual Survey, Information Sector Services.*

No. 1140. Motion Picture and Sound Recording Industries—Estimated Revenue and Inventories: 1998 and 1999

[In millions of dollars (58,850 represents $58,850,000,000), except percent. For taxable and tax-exempt employer firms. For NAICS 512. Except where indicated, estimates have been adjusted to the results of the 1997 Economic Census. Based on the North American Industry Classification System; see text, this section, and Section 15, Business Enterprise. Minus sign (-) indicates decrease]

Item	1998	1999	Percent change, 1998-99
Motion picture and recording industries (NAICS 512):			
Operating revenue	58,850	63,196	7.4
Total inventories	14,370	15,407	7.2
Finished goods and work-in-process	14,208	15,230	7.2
Materials, supplies, fuel, etc.	163	177	8.6
Motion picture and video (NAICS 5121):			
Operating revenue	48,002	51,227	6.7
Total inventories	14,053	15,101	7.5
Finished goods and work-in-process	13,942	14,983	7.5
Materials, supplies, fuel, etc.	112	118	5.7
Sound recording (NAICS 5122): [1]			
Operating revenue	10,848	11,969	10.3
Total inventories	317	306	-3.4
Finished goods and work-in-process	266	248	-6.9
Materials, supplies, fuel, etc.	51	58	15.0

[1] Estimates not adjusted to the results of the 1997 Economic Census.

Source: U.S. Census Bureau, *1999 Service Annual Survey, Information Sector Services.*

No. 1141. Recording Media—Manufacturers' Shipments and Value: 1982 to 2000

[577.4 represents 577,400,000. Domestic shipments based on reports of manufacturers representing more than 85 percent of the market. Domestic value data based on list prices of records and other media]

Medium	1982	1985	1990	1995	1996	1997	1998	1999	2000
UNIT SHIPMENTS [1] (mil.)									
Total [2]	577.4	653.0	865.7	1,112.7	1,137.2	1,063.4	1,124.3	1,160.6	1,079.3
CDs	(X)	22.6	286.5	722.9	778.9	753.1	847.0	938.9	942.5
CD singles	(X)	(X)	1.1	21.5	43.2	66.7	56.0	55.9	34.2
Cassettes	182.3	339.1	442.2	272.6	225.3	172.6	158.5	123.6	76.0
Cassette singles	(X)	(X)	87.4	70.7	59.9	42.2	26.4	14.2	1.3
Albums—LPs and EPs	243.9	167.0	11.7	2.2	2.9	2.7	3.4	2.9	2.2
Vinyl singles	137.2	120.7	27.6	10.2	10.1	7.5	5.4	5.3	4.8
Music video	(X)	(X)	9.2	12.6	16.9	18.6	27.2	19.8	18.2
DVDs [3]	(X)	(X)	(X)	(X)	(X)	(X)	0.5	2.5	3.3
VALUE (mil. dol.)									
Total [2]	3,641.6	4,378.8	7,541.1	12,320.3	12,533.8	12,236.8	13,723.5	14,584.5	14,323.0
CDs	(X)	389.5	3,451.6	9,377.4	9,934.7	9,915.1	11,416.0	12,816.3	13,214.5
CD singles	(X)	(X)	6.0	110.9	184.1	272.7	213.2	222.4	142.7
Cassettes	1,384.5	2,411.5	3,472.4	2,303.6	1,905.3	1,522.7	1,419.9	1,061.6	626.0
Cassette singles	(X)	(X)	257.9	236.3	189.3	133.5	94.4	48.0	4.6
Albums—LPs and EPs	1,925.1	1,280.5	86.5	25.1	36.8	33.3	34.0	31.8	27.7
Vinyl singles	283.0	281.0	94.4	46.7	47.5	35.6	25.7	27.9	26.3
Music video	(X)	(X)	172.3	220.3	236.1	323.9	508.0	376.7	281.9
DVDs [3]	(X)	(X)	(X)	(X)	(X)	(X)	12.2	66.3	80.3

X Not applicable.   [1] Net units, after returns.   [2] Includes discontinued media.   [3] Included in music videos beginning 1999.

Source: Recording Industry Association of America, Washington, DC, Internet site <http://www.riaa.com> (accessed 13 August 2001).

No. 1142. Profile of Consumer Expenditures for Sound Recordings: 1990 to 2000

[In percent, except total value (7,541.1 represents $7,541,100,000). Based on monthly telephone surveys of the population 10 years old and over]

Item	1990	1994	1995	1996	1997	1998	1999	2000
Total value (mil. dol.)	7,541.1	12,068.0	12,320.3	12,533.8	12,236.8	13,723.5	14,584.5	14,323.0
PERCENT DISTRIBUTION [1]								
Age: 10 to 14 years	7.6	7.9	8.0	7.9	8.9	9.1	8.5	8.9
15 to 19 years	18.3	16.8	17.1	17.2	16.8	15.8	12.6	12.9
20 to 24 years	16.5	15.4	15.3	15.0	13.8	12.2	12.6	12.5
25 to 29 years	14.6	12.6	12.3	12.5	11.7	11.4	10.5	10.6
30 to 34 years	13.2	11.8	12.1	11.4	11.0	11.4	10.1	9.8
35 to 39 years	10.2	11.5	10.8	11.1	11.6	12.6	10.4	10.6
40 to 44 years	7.8	7.9	7.5	9.1	8.8	8.3	9.3	9.6
45 years and over	11.1	15.4	16.1	15.1	16.5	18.1	24.7	23.8
Sex: Male	54.4	52.7	53.0	50.9	48.6	48.7	50.3	50.6
Female	45.6	47.3	47.0	49.1	51.4	51.3	49.7	49.4
Sales outlet:								
Record store	69.8	53.3	52.0	49.9	51.8	50.8	44.5	42.2
Other store	18.5	26.7	28.2	31.5	31.9	34.4	38.3	40.8
Music club	8.9	15.1	14.3	14.3	11.6	9.0	7.9	7.6
Internet [2]	(NA)	(NA)	(NA)	(NA)	0.3	1.1	2.4	3.2
Ad or 800 number	2.5	3.4	4.0	2.9	2.7	2.9	2.5	2.4
Music type: [3]								
Rock	36.1	35.1	33.5	32.6	32.5	25.7	25.2	24.8
Rap/Hip Hop	8.5	7.9	6.7	8.9	10.1	9.7	10.8	12.9
Pop	13.7	10.3	10.1	9.3	9.4	10.0	10.3	11.0
Country	9.6	16.3	16.7	14.7	14.4	14.1	10.8	10.7
R&B/Urban	11.6	9.6	11.3	12.1	11.2	12.8	10.5	9.7
Religious	2.5	3.3	3.1	4.3	4.5	6.3	5.1	4.8
Jazz	4.8	3.0	3.0	3.3	2.8	1.9	3.0	2.9
Classical	3.1	3.7	2.9	3.4	2.8	3.3	3.5	2.7
Soundtracks	0.8	1.0	0.9	0.8	1.2	1.7	0.8	0.7
Oldies	0.8	0.8	1.0	0.8	0.8	0.7	0.7	0.9
New age	1.1	1.0	0.7	0.7	0.8	0.6	0.5	0.5
Children	0.5	0.4	0.5	0.7	0.9	0.4	0.4	0.6
Other	5.6	5.3	7.0	5.2	5.7	7.9	9.1	8.3
Media type:								
CDs	31.1	58.4	65.0	68.4	70.2	74.8	83.2	89.3
Cassettes	54.7	32.1	25.1	19.3	18.2	14.8	8.0	4.9
Singles (all types)	8.7	7.4	7.5	9.3	9.3	6.8	5.4	2.5
Music video	(NA)	0.8	0.9	1.0	0.6	1.0	0.9	0.8
Vinyl LPs	4.7	0.8	0.5	0.6	0.7	0.7	0.5	0.5

NA Not available.   [1] Percent distributions exclude nonresponses and responses of don't know.   [2] Excludes record club purchases over the Internet.   [3] As classified by respondent.

Source: Recording Industry Association of America, Inc., Washington, DC, *2000 Consumer Profile.*

No. 1143. Radio and Television Broadcasting—Estimated Revenue and Expenses: 1998 and 1999

[In millions of dollars (43,791 represents $43,791,000,000), except percent. For taxable and tax-exempt employer firms. Covers NAICS 5131. Estimates have been adjusted to the results of the 1997 Economic Census. Based on the North American Industry Classification System; see text, this section, and Section 15, Business Enterprise. Minus sign (-) indicates decrease]

Item	Total (NAICS 5131)			Radio broadcasting (NAICS 51311			TV broadcasting (NAICS 51312)		
	1998	1999	Percent change 1998-99	1998	1999	Percent change 1998-99	1998	1999	Percent change 1998-99
Operating revenue	43,791	47,292	8.0	11,587	13,030	12.4	32,203	34,262	6.4
Station time sales	27,419	29,771	8.6	10,029	11,258	12.3	17,389	18,513	6.5
Network compensation	631	657	4.1	82	97	17.4	549	561	2.1
National/regional advertising	9,769	10,482	7.3	2,483	2,863	15.3	7,286	7,618	4.6
Local advertising revenue	17,018	18,632	9.5	7,464	8,298	11.2	9,554	10,334	8.2
Network time sales	12,603	13,514	7.2	872	996	14.2	11,732	12,518	6.7
Other operating revenue	3,769	4,007	6.3	686	776	13.0	3,082	3,231	4.8
Expenses.	33,760	37,451	10.9	8,939	10,208	14.2	24,821	27,243	9.8
Annual payroll	9,625	10,814	12.4	3,583	4,165	16.2	6,042	6,649	10.0
Employer contributions to social security and other supplemental benefits	1,450	1,427	-1.6	450	503	11.7	1,000	924	-7.6
Broadcast rights and music license fees	10,249	11,337	10.6	563	526	-6.7	9,686	10,811	11.6
Depreciation	2,765	3,411	23.4	1,227	1,579	28.8	1,539	1,832	19.1
Lease and rental.	623	616	-1.2	255	268	4.9	368	349	-5.4
Purchased repairs.	282	266	-5.7	82	86	5.0	200	180	-10.2
Purchased communications and utilities	589	601	1.9	228	258	12.9	361	343	-5.0
Purchased advertising	1,290	1,458	13.1	361	393	8.9	929	1,066	14.7
Other operating expenses (including network compensation fees)	6,886	7,521	9.2	2,190	2,431	11.0	4,696	5,090	8.4

Source: U.S. Census Bureau, *1999 Service Annual Survey, Information Sector Services.*

No. 1144. Cable and Pay TV—Summary: 1975 to 2000

[9,800 represents 9,800,000. Cable TV for calendar year. Pay TV as of Dec. 31 of year shown]

Year	Cable TV				Pay TV					
	Avg. basic subscribers (1,000)	Avg. monthly basic rate (dol.)	Revenue [1] (mil. dol.)		Units [2] (1,000)			Monthly rate (dol.)		
			Total	Basic	Total pay [3]	Pay cable	Non-cable delivered premium	All pay weighted average [3]	Pay cable	Noncable delivered premium
1975	9,800	6.50	804	764	194	194	(NA)	(NA)	7.85	(NA)
1976	11,000	6.45	932	851	611	568	(NA)	7.96	7.87	(NA)
1977	12,200	6.86	1,207	1,004	1,138	1,047	(NA)	8.03	7.92	(NA)
1978	13,400	7.13	1,513	1,147	2,473	2,182	(NA)	8.16	8.01	(NA)
1979	15,000	7.40	1,942	1,332	5,157	4,480	(NA)	8.54	8.24	(NA)
1980	17,500	7.69	2,609	1,615	8,581	7,336	(NA)	8.91	8.62	(NA)
1981	21,100	7.99	3,675	2,023	14,310	12,239	(NA)	9.16	8.92	(NA)
1982	25,250	8.30	5,032	2,515	19,395	17,007	(NA)	9.49	9.30	(NA)
1983	29,430	8.61	6,485	3,041	24,515	22,818	(NA)	9.82	9.70	(NA)
1984	32,800	8.98	7,738	3,534	28,815	27,754	(NA)	10.03	9.96	(NA)
1985	35,440	9.73	8,831	4,138	29,885	29,418	(NA)	10.29	10.25	(NA)
1986	38,170	10.67	9,955	4,887	31,033	30,668	(NA)	10.35	10.31	(NA)
1987	41,160	12.18	11,563	6,016	33,528	33,232	(NA)	10.25	10.23	(NA)
1988	44,160	13.86	13,409	7,345	37,085	36,777	(NA)	10.24	10.17	(NA)
1989	47,500	15.21	15,378	8,670	39,055	38,916	(NA)	10.25	10.20	(NA)
1990	50,520	16.78	17,582	10,174	39,902	39,751	(NA)	10.35	10.30	(NA)
1991	52,570	18.10	19,426	11,418	39,983	36,569	(NA)	10.35	10.27	(NA)
1992	54,300	19.08	21,079	12,433	40,893	36,879	(NA)	10.29	10.17	(NA)
1993	56,200	[4]19.39	22,809	13,528	42,010	37,113	(NA)	9.27	9.11	(NA)
1994	58,450	21.62	23,160	15,164	46,328	41,728	4,600	8.23	8.37	6.99
1995	60,900	23.07	25,556	16,860	53,973	45,598	8,375	8.28	8.54	6.99
1996	62,800	24.41	27,951	18,395	60,372	48,157	12,215	8.04	8.35	6.99
1997	64,410	26.48	30,744	20,383	66,068	49,900	16,160	7.92	8.29	6.99
1998	65,420	27.81	33,003	21,830	72,401	52,703	19,698	7.80	8.20	6.99
1999	66,660	28.92	36,333	23,134	78,097	54,775	23,322	7.66	8.04	6.99
2000, est. . .	67,700	30.08	39,641	24,445	95,570	59,070	36,500	7.57	7.96	6.99

NA Not available. [1] Includes installation revenue, subscriber revenue, and nonsubscriber revenue; excludes telephony and high-speed access. [2] Individual program services sold to subscribers. [3] Includes multipoint distribution service (MDS), satellite TV (STV), multipoint multichannel distribution service (MMDS), satellite master antenna TV (SMATV, C-band satellite, and DBS satellite. [4] Weighted average representing 8 months of unregulated basic rate and 4 months of FCC rolled-back rate.

Source: Paul Kagan Associates Inc., Carmel, CA, a division of MediaCentral, LLC, *The Cable Databook,* annual, 2000 (copyright); and *The Pay TV Newsletter,* May 31, 2000, and various other issues.

No. 1145. Cable Networks and Program Distribution Services—Estimated Revenue and Expenses: 1998 and 1999

[In millions of dollars (52,160 represents $52,160,000,000), except percent. For taxable and tax-exempt employer firms. Covers NAICS 5132. Estimates have not been adjusted to the results of the 1997 Economic Census. Based on the North American Industry Classification System; see text, this section, and Section 15, Business Enterprise]

Item	1998	1999	Percent change, 1998-99
Operating revenue	**52,160**	**59,774**	**14.6**
Advertising revenue (net)	8,034	9,767	21.6
Program revenue	9,454	10,301	9.0
Basic service tier	23,541	26,890	14.2
Pay-per-view service	1,607	1,903	18.5
Other premium service	4,312	4,421	2.5
Installation, startup, and reconnect fees	740	765	3.3
Other cable and pay TV revenue	2,021	2,428	20.1
Internet access fees	138	274	98.8
Local telephone service	144	220	52.6
Long-distance telephone service	(S)	(S)	(S)
Other communication service revenue	228	522	129.0
Other operating revenue	1,915	2,237	16.8
Operating expenses	**45,231**	**52,952**	**17.0**
Annual payroll	7,138	8,388	17.5
Employer contributions to social security and other supplemental benefits	1,443	1,666	15.5
Program and production costs	14,601	16,525	13.2
Depreciation	9,425	11,498	22.0
Lease and rental	760	878	15.5
Purchased repairs	662	721	8.9
Purchased communications and utilities	736	840	14.2
Purchased advertising	1,590	1,836	15.5
Other operating expenses	8,876	10,600	19.4

S Data do not meet publication standards.

Source: U.S. Census Bureau, *1999 Service Annual Survey, Information Sector Services.*

No. 1146. Telecommunications—Estimated Revenue and Expenses: 1998 and 1999

[In millions of dollars (284,916 represents $284,916,000,000), except percent. For taxable and tax-exempt employer firms. Except for NAICS 51332, wireless telecommunications carriers (except satellite), estimates have been adjusted to the results of the 1997 Economic Census. Based on the North American Industry Classification System; see text, this section, and Section 15, Business Enterprise. Minus sign (-) indicates decrease. See Table 1147 for wireless telecommunications carriers, NAICS 51332]

Item	Telecommunications (NAICS 5133)			Wired telecommunications carriers (NAICS 51331)		
	1998	1999	Percent change, 1998-99	1998	1999	Percent change, 1998-99
Operating revenue	**284,916**	**318,097**	**11.6**	**227,868**	**247,532**	**8.6**
Wired telecommunications services	210,866	228,321	8.3	205,223	221,439	7.9
Local service	68,192	76,414	12.1	66,981	74,807	11.7
Basic local service	54,048	60,463	11.9	52,861	58,892	11.4
Value-added services	14,144	15,952	12.8	14,120	15,915	12.7
Long-distance service	96,897	102,251	5.5	92,984	97,670	5.0
Network access	45,778	49,656	8.5	45,257	48,962	8.2
Cellular telephone, PCS, and SMR	34,919	45,061	29.0	400	511	27.8
Basic monthly charges	15,790	19,633	24.3	85	120	40.8
Airtime	11,781	14,966	27.0	82	101	24.2
Long-distance service	1,770	2,156	21.8	(Z)	(Z)	-50.0
Roaming	3,281	5,293	61.3	5	6	24.2
Other	2,296	3,014	31.3	(S)	(S)	(S)
Directory advertising	1,676	1,788	6.6	1,672	1,783	6.6
Other communications services	12,137	13,736	13.2	913	1,586	73.7
Other operating revenue	25,318	29,191	15.3	19,660	22,213	13.0
Operating expenses	**240,055**	**266,420**	**11.0**	**184,779**	**200,461**	**8.5**
Annual payroll	48,612	54,447	12.0	38,941	43,193	10.9
Employer contributions to social security and other supplemental benefits	11,047	12,415	12.4	9,098	10,106	11.1
Access charges	33,665	37,581	11.6	29,412	31,657	7.6
Depreciation	44,291	49,929	12.7	33,462	38,120	13.9
Lease and rental	5,677	6,349	11.8	3,014	3,368	11.8
Purchased repairs	3,033	3,117	2.8	2,186	2,366	8.2
Purchased communications and utilities	15,946	14,330	-10.1	14,449	12,437	-13.9
Purchased advertising	7,327	7,122	-2.8	4,635	4,532	-2.2
Universal service, contributions, and other similar charges	5,297	5,527	4.3	4,900	5,017	2.4
Other operating expenses	65,158	75,602	16.0	44,683	49,665	11.1

S Data do not meet publication standards.   Z Less than $500,000.

Source: U.S. Census Bureau, *1999 Service Annual Survey, Information Sector Services.*

No. 1147. Wireless Telecommunications Carriers (Except Satellite)—Estimated Revenue and Expenses: 1998 and 1999

[In millions of dollars (42,363 represents $42,363,000,000), except percent. For taxable and tax-exempt employer firms. For NAICS 51332. Estimates have not been adjusted to the results of the 1997 Economic Census. Based on the North American Industry Classification System; see text, this section, and Section 15, Business Enterprise . Minus sign (-) indicates decrease. See Table 1146 for telecommunications total and wired carriers (NAICS 5133 and 51331)]

Item	1998	1999	Percent change, 1998-99
Operating revenue	**42,363**	**53,485**	**26.3**
Cellular telephone, PCS, and SMR	32,844	42,654	29.9
Basic monthly charges	15,490	19,269	24.4
Airtime	11,557	14,723	27.4
Long-distance service	1,528	1,919	25.6
Roaming	3,162	5,115	61.8
Other	1,107	1,629	47.1
Other communications services [1]	6,423	6,920	7.7
Other operating revenue	3,096	3,911	26.3
Operating expenses	**39,720**	**50,381**	**26.8**
Annual payroll	6,722	8,259	22.9
Employer contributions to social security and other supplemental benefits	1,490	1,787	20.0
Access charges	2,233	3,371	51.0
Depreciation	8,743	10,376	18.7
Lease and rental	1,923	2,328	21.0
Purchased repairs	719	660	-8.3
Purchased communications and utilities	1,051	1,311	24.7
Purchased advertising	2,467	2,343	-5.0
Universal service, contributions, and other similar charges	325	441	36.0
Other operating expenses	14,047	19,505	38.9

[1] Includes wired telecommunications services revenue.

Source: U.S. Census Bureau, *1999 Service Annual Survey, Information Sector Services.*

No. 1148. Telecommunications Industry—Carriers and Revenue: 1995 to 1999

[Revenue in millions of dollars (190,076 represents $190,076,000,000). Data based on carrier filings to the FCC. Because of reporting changes, data beginning 1997 are not strictly comparable with previous years; see source for details]

Category	Carriers					Telecommunications revenue				
	1995	1996	1997	1998	1999	1995	1996	1997	1998	1999
Total [1]	**3,058**	**3,832**	**3,604**	**4,144**	**4,822**	**190,076**	**211,782**	**231,168**	**246,392**	**268,505**
Local service providers	1,675	2,028	2,066	2,239	2,589	103,792	109,273	108,568	113,369	119,938
Incumbent local exchange carriers (ILECs) [2]	1,347	1,376	1,410	1,348	1,335	102,820	107,905	105,154	108,234	112,216
Pay telephone providers	271	533	509	615	758	349	357	933	1,101	1,213
Competitors of ILECs	57	119	147	276	496	623	1,011	2,481	4,034	6,508
CAPs and CLECs [3]	57	94	129	212	349	623	1,011	1,919	3,348	5,652
Local resellers	(4)	8	11	54	87	(4)	(4)	206	410	511
Other local exchange carriers	(4)	13	3	10	60	(4)	(4)	157	36	171
Private carriers	(4)	(4)	2	(4)	(4)	(4)	(4)	112	147	87
Shared tenant service providers	(4)	4	2	(4)	(4)	(4)	(4)	87	93	87
Wireless service providers [5]	930	1,217	969	1,235	1,495	18,627	25,900	33,030	37,032	50,152
Telephony [6]	792	853	732	808	806	17,208	23,778	29,944	33,139	46,513
Paging service providers	138	200	137	303	427	(4)	(4)	2,861	3,161	3,232
Toll service providers	453	587	569	647	738	76,447	86,896	89,570	95,992	98,414
Interexchange carriers	130	149	151	171	204	70,938	79,057	79,080	83,443	87,570
Operator service providers	25	27	32	24	21	500	461	603	590	337
Prepaid service providers	8	16	18	20	21	16	238	519	888	866
Satellite service carriers	(4)	22	13	13	21	(4)	(4)	1,011	475	280
Toll resellers	260	345	340	388	454	4,220	6,564	8,010	9,885	9,211
Other toll carriers	30	28	15	31	17	773	577	348	710	150

[1] Revenue data include adjustments, not shown separately. Through 1996, revenue data include some nontelecommunications revenue, formerly reported as local exchange wireless revenue. [2] Fewer ILECs filed in 1998 than in 1997 because of consolidation of study areas. [3] Competitive access providers and competitive local exchange carriers. [4] Data not available separately. [5] Includes specialized mobile radio services and other services, not shown separately. [6] Cellular service, personal communications service, and specialized mobile radio.

Source: U.S. Federal Communications Commission, *Trends in Telephone Service,* December 2000.

U.S. Census Bureau, Statistical Abstract of the United States: 2001

No. 1149. Telephone Systems—Summary: 1985 to 1999

[**112 represents 112,000,000.** Covers principal carriers filing annual reports with Federal Communications Commission]

Item	Unit	1985	1990	1993	1994	1995	1996	1997	1998	1999
LOCAL EXCHANGE CARRIERS [1]										
Carriers [2]	Number .	55	51	53	52	53	51	51	52	52
Access lines	Millions..	112	130	149	157	166	178	194	205	228
Business access lines	Millions..	31	36	41	42	46	49	53	57	58
Residential access lines	Millions..	79	89	96	98	101	104	108	110	115
Other access lines (public, mobile, special)	Millions..	2	6	13	17	19	25	33	38	55
Number of local calls (originating)	Billions..	365	402	447	465	484	504	522	544	554
Number of toll calls (originating)	Billions..	(NA)	63	78	83	94	95	101	97	102
Gross book cost of plant	Bil. dol..	191	240	264	272	284	296	309	325	342
Depreciation and amortization reserves..	Bil. dol..	49	89	107	116	127	138	149	163	176
Net plant	Bil. dol..	142	151	156	157	157	158	160	161	166
Total assets	Bil. dol..	162	180	192	196	197	198	198	200	204
Total stockholders equity	Bil. dol..	63	74	73	72	72	74	72	70	67
Operating revenues	Bil. dol..	73	84	90	93	96	101	103	108	113
Local revenues	Bil. dol..	32	37	42	43	46	50	52	55	58
Operating expenses [3]	Bil. dol..	48	62	66	70	72	74	75	78	79
Net operating income [4]	Bil. dol..	13	14	14	13	14	16	16	18	20
Net income	Bil. dol..	9	11	5	9	11	13	12	12	13
Employees	(1,000)..	(NA)	569	507	474	447	437	435	436	436
Compensation of employees	Bil. dol..	(NA)	23	23	22	21	23	22	23	24
Average monthly residential local telephone rate [5]	Dollars ..	(NA)	19.24	19.95	19.81	20.01	19.95	19.88	19.76	19.87
Average monthly single-line business telephone rate [5]	Dollars ..	(NA)	41.21	42.57	41.64	41.80	41.81	41.67	41.29	41.00
LONG DISTANCE CARRIERS										
Number of carriers with presubscribed lines	Number .	(NA)	325	436	511	583	621	(NA)	(NA)	(NA)
Number of presubscribed lines	Millions..	(NA)	132	143	148	153	159	(NA)	(NA)	(NA)
Total toll service revenues	Bil. dol..	43	52	62	67	74	82	89	94	99
Interstate switched access minutes	Bil. min..	167	307	371	401	432	468	497	519	574
INTERNATIONAL TELEPHONE SERVICE [6]										
Number of U.S. billed calls	Millions..	411	984	1,926	2,313	2,821	3,485	4,233	4,439	5,215
Number of U.S. billed minutes	Millions..	3,350	7,215	11,393	11,393	13,393	15,837	19,119	22,611	27,966
U.S. billed revenues	Mil. dol..	3,435	7,626	11,353	12,255	13,990	14,079	15,135	14,154	14,398
U.S. carrier revenue net of settlements with foreign carriers	Mil. dol..	2,305	4,863	7,704	7,966	9,054	8,434	9,691	9,681	9,836
Revenue from private-line service	Mil. dol..	172	201	365	432	432	649	840	902	1,181
Revenue from resale service	Mil. dol..	(NA)	167	593	1,120	1,687	3,457	4,088	4,876	4,254

NA Not available. [1] Gross operating revenues, gross plant, and total assets of reporting carriers estimated at more than 90 percent of total industry. New accounting rules became effective in 1990; prior years may not be directly comparable on a one-to-one basis. Includes Virgin Islands, and prior to 1993, Puerto Rico. [2] The reporting threshold for carriers is $100 million in annual operating revenue. [3] Excludes taxes. [4] After tax deductions. [5] Based on surveys conducted by FCC. [6] Beginning 1993, includes calls to and from Alaska, Hawaii, Puerto Rico, Canada, and Mexico.

Source: U.S. Federal Communications Commission, *Statistics of Communications Common Carriers,* annual.

No. 1150. Cellular Telephone Industry: 1990 to 2000

[**Calendar year data, except as noted (5,283 represents 5,283,000).** Based on a survey mailed to all cellular, personal communications services, and enhanced special mobile radio (ESMR) systems. For 2000 data, the universe was 2,440 systems and the response rate was 86 percent. The number of operational systems in 2000 differs from that reported for previous periods as a result of the consolidated operation of ESMR systems in a broader service area instead of by a city-to-city basis]

Item	Unit	1990	1994	1995	1996	1997	1998	1999	2000
Systems	Number .	751	1,581	1,627	1,740	2,228	3,073	3,518	2,440
Subscribers	1,000 .	5,283	24,134	33,786	44,043	55,312	69,209	86,047	109,478
Cell sites [1]	Number .	5,616	17,920	22,663	30,045	51,600	65,887	81,698	104,288
Employees	Number .	21,382	53,902	68,165	84,161	109,387	134,754	155,817	184,449
Service revenue	Mil. dol..	4,548	14,229	19,081	23,635	27,486	33,133	40,018	52,466
Roamer revenue [2]	Mil. dol..	456	1,830	2,542	2,781	2,974	3,501	4,085	3,883
Capital investment	Mil. dol..	6,282	18,939	24,080	32,574	46,058	60,543	71,265	89,624
Average monthly bill [3]	Dollars..	80.90	56.21	51.00	47.70	42.78	39.43	41.24	45.27
Average length of call [3]	Minutes .	2.20	2.24	2.15	2.32	2.31	2.39	2.38	2.56

[1] The basic geographic unit of a wireless PCS or cellular system. A city or county is divided into smaller "cells," each of which is equipped with a low-powered radio transmitter/receiver. The cells can vary in size depending upon terrain, capacity demands, etc. By controlling the transmission power, the radio frequencies assigned to one cell can be limited to the boundaries of that cell. When a wireless PCS or cellular phone moves from one cell toward another, a computer at the switching office monitors the movement and at the proper time, transfers or hands off the phone call to the new cell and another radio frequency. [2] Service revenue generated by subscribers' calls outside of their system areas. [3] As of December 31.

Source: Cellular Telecommunications & Internet Association, Washington, DC, *Semiannual Wireless Survey* (copyright).

No. 1151. Information Services and Data Processing Services—Estimated Revenue: 1998 and 1999

[In millions of dollars (46,994 represents $46,994,000,000), except percent. For taxable and tax-exempt employer firms. Covers NAICS 514. Except as indicated, estimates adjusted to results of the 1997 Economic Census. Based on the North American Industry Classification System; see text, this section, and Section 15, Business Enterprise. Minus sign (-) indicates decrease]

Item	1998	1999	Percent change, 1998-99
Total (NAICS 514)	**46,994**	**60,130**	**28.0**
News syndicates (NAICS 51411):			
Revenue.................................	1,586	1,823	14.9
Libraries and archives (NAICS 51412):			
Revenue.................................	954	1,018	6.7
Subsidies, contributions, gifts, and grants	631	698	10.6
Other revenue	323	320	-1.0
Online information services (NAICS 514191):			
Revenue.................................	10,882	18,025	65.6
Internet access fees..........................	5,499	8,979	63.3
Advertising..............................	725	1,355	87.0
Web hosting and design.......................	261	520	99.4
Online sales commissions......................	(S)	(S)	(S)
Other revenue	4,322	7,038	62.8
All other information services [1] (NAICS 514199):			
Revenue.................................	985	2,120	115.3
Internet access fees..........................	10	39	294.9
Advertising..............................	658	1,477	124.6
Web hosting and design.......................	3	12	355.6
Online sales commissions......................	1	6	714.3
Other revenue	314	586	87.0
Data processing services (NAICS 5142):			
Revenue.................................	32,588	37,143	14.0
Transaction processing and data exchange	19,511	22,151	13.5
Data capture and imaging......................	1,161	1,308	12.7
Computer timesharing services	748	764	2.1
Web hosting and design.......................	(S)	(S)	(S)
Other data processing services	5,160	5,997	16.2
All other revenue...........................	6,008	6,645	10.6

S Data do not meet publication standards. [1] Estimates not adjusted to the results of the 1997 Economic Census.

Source: U.S. Census Bureau, *1999 Service Annual Survey, Information Sector Services.*

No. 1152. Academic Libraries—Summary: 1998

[For fiscal year. For 2- and 4-year degree granting institutions. Based on survey; see source for details]

Item	Number of libraries	Circulation (1,000) General	Circulation (1,000) Reserve	Paper volumes held (1,000) [1]	Staff [2] Total	Staff [2] Librarians (percent)	Expenditures Total (mil. dol.)	Expenditures Salary [3] (percent)	Percent with access from within library to— Electronic catalog	Percent with access from within library to— Internet
Total	3,658	175,409	40,658	878,906	96,709	25.7	4,593	50.4	84.2	94.6
Control:										
Public.........	1,583	116,158	25,267	521,817	58,314	25.0	2,780	52.4	95.7	97.5
Private	2,075	59,251	15,391	357,090	38,395	26.6	1,813	47.4	75.0	92.3
Level: [4]										
4-year degree and above [5]	2,220	150,575	34,453	821,965	82,533	25.4	4,072	48.5	86.7	95.4
Doctor's......	570	105,614	22,469	569,295	54,478	24.5	2,924	47.1	94.8	97.3
Master's......	944	33,869	8,747	186,922	20,547	27.2	868	52.4	95.7	95.7
Bachelor's	703	11,083	3,236	65,645	7,499	27.0	280	51.0	78.3	93.5
Less than 4-year. .	1,438	24,834	6,205	56,941	14,176	27.4	520	65.4	80.1	93.3
Enrollment: [2]										
Less than 1,500 . .	2,041	24,946	6,173	117,188	14,949	29.3	567	52.0	73.0	91.4
1,500 to 4,999 . .	1,053	33,992	9,259	172,047	22,221	27.2	947	52.8	96.4	98.7
5,000 of more . . .	564	116,472	25,226	589,671	59,539	24.2	3,078	49.3	99.1	98.0

[1] At end-of-year. [2] Full-time equivalent. [3] Salary and wages. [4] Level of highest degree offered. [5] Includes three institutions granting "other" degrees, not shown separately.

Source: U.S. National Center for Education Statistics, *Academic Libraries, 1998,* NCES 2001-341, July 2001.

No. 1153. Libraries—Number by Type: 1980 to 1999

Type	1980	1985	1990	1999	Type	1980	1985	1990	1999
Total [1]	31,564	32,323	34,613	37,263	Junior college . . .	1,191	1,188	1,233	1,274
					Colleges,				
United States . . .	28,638	29,843	30,761	32,852	universities	3,400	3,846	3,360	3,449
Public.	8,717	8,849	9,060	9,837	Departmental .	1,489	1,824	1,454	1,467
Public branches . . .	5,936	6,330	5,833	6,376	Law,				
Special [2]	7,649	7,530	9,051	9,691	medicine,				
Medicine	1,674	1,667	1,861	1,906	religious . . .	269	531	501	493
Religious	913	839	946	1,001	Government.	1,260	1,574	1,735	1,874
Law [3]	417	435	647	1,136	Armed Forces	485	526	489	352
Academic	4,591	5,034	4,593	4,723	Outlying areas . .	113	114	110	(NA)

NA Not available.   [1] Includes Canadian libraries, and libraries in regions administered by the United States, not shown separately. Data are exclusive of elementary and secondary school libraries. Law libraries with fewer than 10,000 volumes are included only if they specialize in a particular field.   [2] Includes other types of special libraries, not shown separately. Increase between 1985 and 1990 is due mainly to revised criteria for identifying special libraries and improved methods of counting.   [3] Increase in 1999 due to increased effort in identifying special libraries.

Source: R.R. Bowker Co., New York, NY, *The Bowker Annual: Library and Book Trade Almanac* and *American Library Directory,* annual. (Copyright by Reed Elsevier Inc.)

No. 1154. Public Libraries by Selected Characteristics: 1998

[6,738 represents $6,738,000,000. Based on survey of public libraries. Data are for public libraries in the 50 states and the District of Columbia. The response rates for these items are between 97 and 100 percent]

Population of service area	Number of—		Operating income—			Paid staff [3]		
				Source (percent)				
	Public libraries	Stationary outlets [1]	Total [2] (mil. dol.)	State govern- ment	Local govern- ment	Total	Librar- ians with ALA- MLS [4]	Libraries with Inter- net access
Total	8,964	16,180	6,738	12.6	77.6	123,443	28,178	7,866
1,000,000 or more	20	875	883	10.4	79.0	14,404	4,258	20
500,000 to 999,000	54	1,167	1,146	16.0	74.0	18,433	4,601	54
250,000 to 499,999	94	1,062	765	12.9	79.8	13,194	3,290	93
100,000 to 249,999	323	1,992	1,116	11.3	80.9	20,422	4,642	320
50,000 to 99,999	513	1,601	843	14.1	76.8	15,961	3,566	505
25,000 to 49,999	860	1,637	806	13.7	77.1	15,493	3,576	845
10,000 to 24,999	1,716	2,228	743	11.3	77.7	14,854	3,063	1,653
5,000 to 9,999	1,475	1,647	254	9.3	75.2	5,769	844	1,383
2,500 to 4,999	1,326	1,369	103	6.9	74.8	2,618	224	1,155
1,000 to 2,499	1,638	1,656	62	6.1	67.1	1,756	94	1,313
Fewer than 1,000	945	946	16	9.9	64.3	538	19	525

[1] The sum of central and branches libraries. The total number of central libraries was 8,887; the total of branch libraries was 7,293.   [2] Includes income from the federal government (0.8%) and other sources (9.0%), not shown separately.   [3] Full-time equivalents.   [4] Librarians with master's degrees from a graduate library education program accredited by the American Library Association (ALA). Total librarians, including those without ALA-MLS, were 40,689.

Source: U.S. National Center for Education Statistics, *Public Libraries in the United States: 1998,* NCES 2001-307, July 2001.

No. 1155. Public Library Use of the Internet: 2000

[In percent, except number of outlets. As of spring. Based on sample survey; see source for details]

Item	Total	Metropolitan status [1]			Poverty status [2]		
		Urban	Sub- urban	Rural	Less than 20 percent	20 to 40 percent	More than 40 percent
All libraries outlets [3]	16,004	2,742	4,764	8,498	12,847	2,832	325
Connected to the Internet	95.7	98.3	98.5	93.3	95.6	96.3	92.8
Connected with public access	94.5	97.7	97.3	91.9	94.3	95.8	93.5
Average number of workstations	8.3	17.3	8.7	4.9	7.3	12.3	7.2
Speed of access:							
Less than 56kpbs	5.8	1.0	2.5	9.4	6.7	2.6	-
56kpbs dial-up	15.5	1.0	7.4	25.3	17.7	5.7	16.2
56kpbs direct connect	25.0	10.0	25.6	29.8	24.4	27.6	26.3
Greater than 56kpbs	53.6	88.2	64.6	35.4	51.3	64.1	57.4
Special software/hardware for persons with disabilities on—							
All workstations	8.5	8.7	7.0	9.3	5.8	20.4	7.5
Some workstations	20.3	26.6	23.9	6.1	18.5	29.6	10.5
No workstations	71.2	64.7	69.1	74.6	75.7	49.9	82.0
On public access workstations—							
No Internet filtering/blocking	75.5	70.8	69.8	80.4	75.9	73.3	77.9
Internet filtering/blocking on some stations	15.0	18.5	21.8	9.7	14.6	16.7	14.5
With acceptable use policies	95.5	96.8	97.1	94.0	94.7	99.4	91.7
With acceptable use policies which differentiate between users (e.g.adults and children).	43.6	31.4	41.1	49.2	43.2	43.9	53.8

- Represents zero.   [1] Urban = inside central city; Suburban = in metro area, outside of a central city; Rural = outside a metro area.   [2] Determined by the 1990 poverty status of the service area of the outlet.   [3] Central libraries and branches; excludes bookmobiles.

Source: National Commission on Libraries and Information Science, Washington, DC, *Public Libraries and the Internet 2000: Summary Findings and Data Tables,* September 2000, by John Carlo Bartot and Charles R. McClure, Florida State University, Tallahassee, FL.

718 Information and Communications

No. 1156. Use of Home Computers: 1997

[In percent, except persons using computers (81,013 represents 81,013,000). As of October. Based on the Current Population Survey and subject to sampling error; see text, Section 1, Population, and Appendix III]

Characteristic	Persons using computers (1,000)	Percent of total	Frequency of use per week				Computer capabilities [1]			
			6 or 7 days	4 or 5 days	2 or 3 days	1 day or less	CD-ROM drive	Printer	Modem	Internet
Total [2]	**81,013**	**30.3**	**23.4**	**20.1**	**32.6**	**24.0**	**71.3**	**85.5**	**71.1**	**52.1**
Sex: Male	41,260	31.6	27.1	20.1	30.6	22.2	72.1	85.5	71.7	52.9
Female	39,753	29.1	19.6	20.0	34.6	25.8	70.6	85.6	70.5	51.2
Age: Under 5 years old	1,675	8.5	12.2	16.3	38.1	33.5	71.9	83.3	74.5	53.8
5 to 9 years old.	7,599	37.1	11.8	17.6	44.2	26.4	74.7	83.8	71.5	50.5
10 to 14 years old	9,500	48.7	21.1	21.8	38.0	19.1	75.5	87.9	70.6	50.3
15 to 19 years old	8,395	43.1	24.7	22.4	32.4	20.5	73.7	88.0	69.9	52.3
20 to 24 years old	4,975	28.5	28.3	20.2	28.9	22.6	69.5	83.4	69.8	53.0
25 to 29 years old	5,963	31.7	26.1	22.3	30.0	21.7	70.1	80.4	75.8	58.4
30 to 39 years old	15,393	35.8	24.2	20.6	32.0	23.2	71.9	84.5	72.8	53.5
40 to 49 years old	15,346	38.3	24.3	18.8	30.3	26.6	73.9	87.4	73.0	54.4
50 to 59 years old	7,679	28.5	26.6	19.8	28.0	25.7	66.5	86.2	67.6	50.7
60 to 69 years old	3,162	16.2	29.7	17.5	24.1	28.6	61.0	86.8	63.5	42.3
70 years old and over.	1,327	5.9	29.4	17.8	25.4	27.5	59.0	86.1	60.4	38.6
Race/ethnicity:										
White, non-Hispanic	68,026	35.5	23.5	20.2	32.1	24.3	72.4	87.1	72.8	53.7
Black, non-Hispanic	4,943	14.7	20.8	20.5	37.6	21.2	58.2	75.2	57.7	40.3
Hispanic.	4,081	13.5	23.3	17.3	36.4	23.1	69.1	78.2	60.8	44.4
Family income: Less than $5,000 . .	1,517	13.3	31.1	16.7	26.8	25.3	63.2	81.9	66.2	44.6
$5,000 to $9,999	1,575	8.1	24.8	19.6	29.4	26.1	59.6	81.0	56.7	40.5
$10,000 to $14,999	2,197	9.7	26.2	17.7	31.4	24.8	55.9	74.5	54.7	38.7
$15,000 to $19,999	2,084	12.0	25.9	20.4	29.9	23.8	60.5	77.8	60.0	42.7
$20,000 to $24,999	3,645	17.1	25.1	18.9	31.4	24.5	59.9	80.9	58.1	38.8
$25,000 to $29,999	4,174	21.0	23.3	19.3	33.3	24.1	62.2	77.6	61.0	42.0
$30,000 to $34,999	5,003	25.7	22.5	20.5	32.9	24.1	66.4	82.6	64.1	43.7
$35,000 to $39,999	5,367	29.1	22.7	18.5	34.1	24.7	65.9	84.3	66.3	46.1
$40,000 to $49,999	9,627	35.4	22.2	19.5	33.3	25.1	68.2	86.0	67.6	46.4
$50,000 to $74,999	21,685	44.6	22.1	20.2	32.5	25.1	73.9	87.2	74.3	53.9
$75,000 and over.	24,138	58.0	24.1	21.1	32.8	22.0	80.9	89.8	81.1	64.5

[1] For the most recently purchased computers for those with more than one. [2] Includes other races, not shown separately.
Source: U.S. National Center for Education Statistics, *Digest of Education Statistics, 1999*.

No. 1157. Internet Access and Usage and Online Service Usage: 2000

[199,438 represents 199,438,000. As of spring. For persons 18 years old and over. Based on sample and subject to sampling error; see source for details]

Item	Total adults	Any online/ Internet usage	Have Internet access			Used the Internet in the last 30 days			Used any online service in the past 30 days
			Home or work	Home only	Work only	Home or work	Home only	Work only	
Total adults (1,000).	**199,438**	**90,458**	**112,949**	**77,621**	**50,476**	**86,289**	**65,471**	**40,449**	**75,409**
PERCENT DISTRIBUTION									
Age:									
18 to 34 years old	32.5	39.7	37.9	35.1	34.9	39.8	36.6	34.6	40.3
35 to 54 years old	39.9	47.7	46.0	49.4	55.4	47.7	49.6	56.3	47.4
55 years old and over	27.6	12.7	16.2	15.5	9.7	12.5	13.8	9.1	12.3
Sex:									
Male	48.0	49.8	48.5	49.3	52.3	49.8	50.1	52.7	49.3
Female	52.0	50.2	51.5	50.7	47.7	50.2	49.9	47.3	50.7
Household size:									
1 to 2 persons	47.9	40.2	41.0	37.9	41.8	40.4	39.0	42.6	39.5
3 to 4 persons	36.9	44.4	43.3	45.9	44.6	44.3	45.6	44.4	44.5
5 or more persons	15.2	15.4	15.7	16.2	13.6	15.3	15.4	13.0	16.1
Any child in household	42.1	47.7	47.0	48.7	48.0	47.3	48.3	46.7	47.9
Marital status:									
Single	23.7	27.5	26.0	23.4	22.6	27.7	24.5	23.3	28.4
Married	57.2	61.6	61.1	66.2	65.3	61.4	65.7	65.1	60.6
Other	19.1	10.9	12.9	10.3	12.0	10.9	9.7	11.6	10.9
Educational attainment:									
Graduated college plus.	22.5	38.0	33.6	38.6	49.2	38.8	41.6	53.1	37.8
Attended college	26.5	34.8	33.7	34.0	30.6	35.0	34.4	30.2	35.0
Did not attend college	51.0	27.2	32.8	27.3	20.3	26.2	24.1	16.7	27.2
Household income:									
Less than $50,000	55.1	33.6	38.3	29.9	23.3	32.9	28.4	20.8	32.9
$50,000 to $74,999	20.7	26.2	25.7	26.9	27.4	26.2	26.5	26.8	26.0
$75,000 to $149,999	20.1	32.6	29.4	34.7	39.6	33.1	36.4	41.8	33.1
$150,000 or more	4.1	7.6	6.7	8.5	9.7	7.8	8.7	10.7	8.0

Source: Mediamark Research Inc., New York, NY, *CyberStats*, spring 2000 (copyright). Internet site <http://www.mediamark.com> (accessed 23 May 2000).

No. 1158. Households With Computers and Internet Access by Selected Characteristic: 2000

[In percent. Based on survey and subject to sampling error; for details, see source]

Characteristic	Households with computers				Households with Internet			
	Total	Rural [1]	Urban [1]	Central city [1]	Total	Rural [1]	Urban [1]	Central city [1]
All households, 2000	**51.0**	**49.6**	**51.5**	**46.3**	**41.5**	**38.9**	**42.3**	**37.7**
Age of householder:								
Under 25 years old	43.8	38.8	44.8	42.8	35.7	29.8	36.9	35.5
25 to 34 years old.	57.0	54.9	57.5	54.2	47.5	42.5	48.7	46.4
35 to 44 years old.	64.1	64.0	64.1	56.7	52.3	50.9	52.7	46.2
45 to 54 years old.	62.7	61.4	63.2	55.8	51.9	49.6	52.7	45.4
55 years old or over	33.7	32.6	34.0	29.4	26.0	24.6	26.5	22.2
Household race/ethnicity:								
White [2]	55.7	51.8	57.3	55.5	46.1	40.9	48.3	47.1
Black [2]	32.6	27.5	33.3	28.7	23.5	19.9	24.0	20.1
Asian, Indian, Eskimo, Aleut [2]	35.5	31.6	38.6	[3]35.1	25.0	[3]19.6	29.3	[3]27.0
Asian or Pacific Islander [2]	65.6	[3]70.3	65.3	61.1	56.8	[3]62.1	56.6	53.0
Hispanic	33.7	28.8	34.2	31.1	23.6	19.9	23.9	21.5
Household type:								
Married couple with children under 18.	73.2	73.3	73.2	65.9	60.6	58.3	61.5	55.1
Male householder with children under 18. . . .	45.6	43.3	46.3	43.1	35.7	30.3	37.4	35.3
Female householder with children under 18. .	42.9	41.6	43.2	34.9	30.0	31.2	29.7	22.8
Family households without children	52.5	48.0	54.4	48.9	43.2	37.7	45.5	41.0
Nonfamily households	34.6	26.2	36.5	37.9	28.1	20.2	29.9	30.8
Education of householder:								
Elementary	12.8	10.5	13.7	15.8	7.2	6.1	7.6	8.4
Some high school	21.9	24.6	20.9	17.4	14.8	16.5	14.2	11.9
High school graduate of GED	39.6	42.6	38.3	33.2	29.9	31.0	29.8	25.7
Some college	60.3	62.9	59.5	53.7	49.0	50.0	48.7	43.6
BA degree or more	75.7	77.8	75.3	72.2	66.0	67.7	65.7	62.3
Household income:								
Under $5,000	21.8	16.0	23.6	23.7	16.0	13.1	16.8	17.0
$5,000 to $9,000	14.6	13.0	15.1	14.7	9.3	9.0	9.4	9.5
$10,000 to $14,999	22.0	20.7	22.4	22.8	14.2	12.5	14.8	15.4
$15,000 to $19,999	28.4	28.3	28.4	29.0	19.2	19.1	19.3	19.2
$20,000 to $24,999	31.4	29.4	32.1	30.6	22.9	21.2	23.5	22.0
$25,000 to $34,999	44.6	43.3	45.1	44.2	34.0	31.5	34.9	34.6
$35,000 to $49,999	58.6	58.1	58.8	57.1	46.1	41.8	47.8	46.0
$50,000 to $74,999	73.2	72.7	73.4	70.7	60.9	59.5	61.4	60.1
$75,000 and over	86.3	86.8	86.2	83.7	77.7	76.6	78.0	76.1

[1] See text, Section 1, Population, and Appendix II.   [2] Non-Hispanic.   [3] Figure does not meet standards of reliability or precision.
Source: U.S. Dept. of Commerce, National Telecommunications and Information Administration, *Falling Through the Net: Defining the Digital Divide,* July 1999 and October 2000.

No. 1159. Households With Computers and Internet Access: 1998 and 2000

[In percent. Based on survey and subject to sampling error; for details, see source]

State	1998		2000		State	1998		2000	
	Computers	Internet access	Computers	Internet access		Computers	Internet access	Computers	Internet access
U.S.	**42.1**	**26.2**	**51.0**	**41.5**	MO	41.8	24.3	52.6	42.5
AL	34.3	21.6	44.2	35.5	MT	40.9	21.5	51.5	40.6
AK	62.4	44.1	64.8	55.6	NE	42.9	22.9	48.5	37.0
AZ	44.3	29.3	53.5	42.5	NV	41.6	26.5	48.8	41.0
AR	29.8	14.7	37.3	26.5	NH	54.2	37.1	63.7	56.0
CA	47.5	30.7	56.6	46.7	NJ	48.1	31.3	54.3	47.8
CO	55.3	34.5	62.6	51.8	NM	42.2	25.8	47.6	35.7
CT	43.8	31.8	60.4	51.2	NY	37.3	23.7	48.7	39.8
DE	40.5	25.1	58.6	50.7	NC	35.0	19.9	45.3	35.3
DC	41.4	24.2	48.8	39.6	ND	40.2	20.6	47.5	37.7
FL	39.5	27.8	50.1	43.2	OH	40.7	24.6	49.5	40.7
GA	35.8	23.9	47.1	38.3	OK	37.8	20.4	41.5	34.3
HI	42.3	27.9	52.4	43.0	OR	51.3	32.7	61.1	50.8
ID	50.0	27.4	54.5	42.3	PA	39.3	24.9	48.4	40.1
IL	42.7	26.5	50.2	40.1	RI	41.0	27.1	47.9	38.8
IN	43.5	26.1	48.8	39.4	SC	35.7	21.4	43.3	32.0
IA	41.4	21.8	53.6	39.0	SD	41.6	23.9	50.4	37.9
KS	43.7	25.7	55.8	43.9	TN	37.5	21.3	45.7	36.3
KY	35.9	21.1	46.2	36.6	TX	40.9	24.5	47.9	38.3
LA	31.1	17.8	41.2	30.2	UT	60.1	35.8	66.1	48.4
ME	43.4	26.0	54.7	42.6	VT	48.7	31.8	53.7	46.7
MD	46.3	31.0	53.7	43.8	VA	46.4	27.9	53.9	44.3
MA	43.4	28.1	53.0	45.5	WA	56.3	36.6	60.7	49.7
MI	44.0	25.4	51.5	42.1	WV	28.3	17.6	42.8	34.3
MN	47.6	29.0	57.0	43.0	WI	43.0	25.1	50.9	40.6
MS	25.7	13.6	37.2	26.3	WY	46.1	22.7	58.2	44.1

Source: U.S. Department of Commerce, National Telecommunications and Information Administration, *Falling through the Net: Defining the Digital Divide,* July 1999 and October 2000.

720   Information and Communications

Section 25
Banking, Finance, and Insurance

This section presents data on the nation's finances, various types of financial institutions, money and credit, securities, insurance, and real estate. The primary sources of these data are publications of several departments of the federal government, especially the Treasury Department, and independent agencies such as the Federal Deposit Insurance Corporation, the Federal Reserve System, and the Securities and Exchange Commission. National data on insurance are available primarily from private organizations, such as the American Council of Life Insurers.

Flow of funds—The flow of funds accounts of the Federal Reserve System bring together statistics on all of the major forms of financial instruments to present an economy-wide view of asset and liability relationships. In flow form, the accounts relate borrowing and lending to one another and to the nonfinancial activities that generate income and production. Each claim outstanding is included simultaneously as an asset of the lender and as a liability of the debtor. The accounts also indicate the balance between asset totals and liability totals over the economy as a whole. Several publications of the Board of Governors of the Federal Reserve System contain information on the flow of funds accounts: Summary data on flows and outstandings, in the *Federal Reserve Bulletin,* and *Flow of Funds Accounts of the United States* (quarterly); and concepts and organization of the accounts, in *Guide to the Flow of Funds Accounts* (2000). Data are also available at the Boards Web site <http://www. federalreserve.gov/ releases>.

Banking system—Banks in this country are organized under the laws of both the states and the federal government and are regulated by several bank supervisory agencies. National banks are supervised by the Comptroller of the Currency. *Reports of Condition* have been collected

from national banks since 1863. Summaries of these reports are published in the Comptroller's *Annual Report,* which also presents data on the structure of the national banking system.

The Federal Reserve System was established in 1913 to exercise central banking functions, some of which are shared with the U.S. Treasury. It includes national banks and such state banks that voluntarily join the system. Statements of state bank members are consolidated by the Board of Governors of the Federal Reserve System with data for national banks collected by the Comptroller of the Currency into totals for all member banks of the system. Balance sheet data for member banks and other commercial banks are published quarterly in the *Federal Reserve Bulletin.* The Federal Deposit Insurance Corporation (FDIC), established in 1933, insures each depositor up to $100,000. Major item balance sheet and income data for all commercial banks are published in the *FDIC Quarterly Banking Profile.* This publication is also available on the Internet at the following address: <http://www.fdic.gov>. Balance sheet and income data for individual institutions are also available at this site in the Institution Directory (ID) system.

The FDIC is the primary federal regulator of state-chartered banks that are not members of the Federal Reserve System and of most savings banks insured by the Bank Insurance Fund (BIF). The agency also has certain backup supervisory authority, for safety and soundness purposes, over state-chartered banks that are members of the Federal Reserve System, national banks, and savings associations.

Savings institutions—Savings institutions are primarily involved in credit extension in the form of mortgage loans. Statistics on savings institutions are collected by the U.S. Office of Thrift Supervision and the FDIC. The Financial Institutions Reform, Recovery, and Enforcement

U.S. Census Bureau, Statistical Abstract of the United States: 2001

Act of 1989 (FIRREA) authorized the establishment of the Resolution Trust Corporation (RTC) which was responsible for the disposal of assets from failed savings institutions. FIRREA gave the FDIC the job of managing the federal deposit insurance fund for savings institutions (SAIF= Savings Association Insurance Fund). Major balance sheet and income data for all insured savings institutions are published in the *FDIC Quarterly Banking Profile.*

Credit unions—Federally chartered credit unions are under the supervision of the National Credit Union Administration. State-chartered credit unions are supervised by the respective state supervisory authorities. The administration publishes comprehensive program and statistical information on all federal and federally insured state credit unions in the *Annual Report of the National Credit Union Administration.* Deposit insurance (up to $100,000 per account) is provided to members of all federal and those state credit unions that are federally-insured by the National Credit Union Share Insurance Fund which was established in 1970. Deposit insurance for state chartered credit unions is also available in some states under private or state-administered insurance programs.

Other credit agencies—Insurance companies, finance companies dealing primarily in installment sales financing, and personal loan companies represent important sources of funds for the credit market. Statistics on loans, investments, cash, etc., of life insurance companies are published principally by the American Council of Life Insurers in its *Life Insurers Fact Book* and in the *Federal Reserve Bulletin.* Consumer credit data are published currently in the *Federal Reserve Bulletin.*

Government corporations and credit agencies make available credit of specified types or to specified groups of private borrowers, either by lending directly or by insuring or guaranteeing loans made by private lending institutions. Data on operations of government credit agencies, along with other government corporations, are available in reports of individual agencies; data on their debt outstanding are published in the *Federal Reserve Bulletin.*

Currency—Currency, including coin and paper money, represents about 46 percent of all media of exchange in the United States, with most payments made by check. All currency is now issued by the Federal Reserve Banks.

Securities—The Securities and Exchange Commission (SEC) was established in 1934 to protect the interests of the public and investors against malpractices in the securities and financial markets and to provide the fullest possible disclosure of information regarding securities to the investing public. Statistical data are published in the *SEC Annual Report.*

Insurance—Insuring companies, which are regulated by the various states or the District of Columbia, are classified as either life or property. Both life and property insurance companies may underwrite health insurance. Insuring companies, other than those classified as life, are permitted to underwrite one or more property lines provided they are so licensed and have the necessary capital or surplus.

There are a number of published sources for statistics on the various classes of insurance—life, health, fire, marine, and casualty. Organizations representing certain classes of insurers publish reports for these classes. The American Council of Life Insurers publishes statistics on life insurance purchases, ownership, benefit payments, and assets in its *Life Insurers Fact Book.*

No. 1160. Gross Domestic Product in Finance, Insurance, and Real Estate in Current and Real (1996) Dollars: 1990 to 1999

[In billions of dollars, except percent (1,010.3 represents $1,010,300,000,000). For definition of gross domestic product, see text, Section 13, Income, Expenditures, and Wealth. Based on 1987 Standard Industrial Classification; see text, Section 15, Business Enterprise]

Industry	Current dollars				Chained (1996) dollars [1]			
	1990	1995	1998	1999	1990	1995	1998	1999
Finance, insurance, real estate, total	**1,010.3**	**1,347.2**	**1,689.5**	**1,792.1**	**1,250.6**	**1,393.0**	**1,605.9**	**1,692.1**
Percent of gross domestic product	17.4	18.2	19.2	19.3	18.6	18.5	18.9	19.1
Depository institutions	171.3	227.4	292.7	305.3	244.0	242.4	249.5	255.0
Nondepository institutions	23.3	34.1	48.4	45.3	26.3	33.4	53.1	52.5
Security and commodity brokers	42.3	77.7	135.3	152.1	42.0	76.5	153.7	207.8
Insurance carriers	64.6	120.2	154.4	165.0	112.2	129.9	139.9	142.6
Insurance agents, brokers, and service	37.7	47.2	52.6	56.9	61.4	49.9	48.5	50.5
Real estate	665.7	832.6	969.2	1,034.0	763.4	852.8	933.5	973.5
Nonfarm housing services	488.3	628.9	714.6	756.8	580.1	648.0	674.2	694.6
Other real estate	177.3	203.7	254.6	277.2	182.9	204.9	260.1	280.7
Holding and other investment offices	5.5	8.0	36.8	33.5	10.2	9.9	25.1	21.5

[1] See text, Section 13, Income, Expenditures, and Wealth.

Source: U.S. Bureau of Economic Analysis, *Survey of Current Business*, December 2000.

No. 1161. Finance and Insurance—Establishments, Revenue, Payroll, and Employees by Kind of Business: 1997

[2,234,737 represents $2,234,737,000,000. Covers taxable firms only]

Kind of business	NAICS code [1]	All firms		Employer firms			
		Establishments (number)	Revenue (mil. dol.)	Establishments (number)	Revenue (mil. dol.)	Annual payroll (mil. dol.)	Paid employees [2] (1,000)
Finance & insurance	**52**	**1,074,360**	**2,234,737**	**395,203**	**2,197,771**	**264,551**	**5,835.2**
Monetary authorities—central bank	521	42	24,582	42	24,582	903	21.7
Credit intermediation & related activities	522	330,563	817,504	166,882	808,811	98,723	2,744.9
Depository credit intermediation	5221	109,389	533,349	102,916	533,134	70,230	2,017.7
Commercial banking	52211	(NA)	(NA)	70,860	421,759	57,247	1,575.4
Savings institutions	52212	(NA)	(NA)	16,264	78,947	8,409	264.8
Credit unions	52213	(NA)	(NA)	15,640	29,694	4,308	172.1
Other depository credit intermediation	52219	(NA)	(NA)	152	2,734	266	5.4
Nondepository credit intermediation	5222	190,287	237,134	47,556	229,214	22,661	556.7
Credit card issuing	52221	(NA)	(NA)	588	24,503	1,783	58.8
Sales financing	52222	(NA)	(NA)	8,143	78,133	6,163	127.8
Other nondepository credit intermediation	52229	(NA)	(NA)	38,825	126,577	14,715	370.1
Activities related to credit intermediation	5223	30,887	47,021	16,410	46,463	5,833	170.5
Mortgage & nonmortgage brokers	52231	(NA)	(NA)	8,967	5,087	1,896	49.3
Financial clearinghouse & reserve activities	52232	(NA)	(NA)	1,239	34,780	2,257	63.7
Other credit intermediation activities	52239	(NA)	(NA)	6,204	6,596	1,680	57.4
Security, commodity contracts & like activity	523	242,901	291,425	54,491	274,987	71,281	706.1
Scrty & comdty contracts intermed & brokerage	5231	55,307	202,576	26,049	196,417	49,983	449.2
Investment banking & securities dealing	52311	7,661	119,338	4,136	118,386	22,330	140.8
Securities brokerage	52312	39,937	77,044	19,869	72,756	26,520	290.7
Commodity contracts dealing	52313	1,800	2,586	630	2,241	341	4.5
Commodity contracts brokerage	52314	5,909	3,608	1,414	3,034	792	13.2
Securities & commodity exchanges	5232	1,193	2,215	30	1,900	442	6.7
Other financial investment activities	5239	186,401	86,634	28,412	76,669	20,857	250.1
Miscellaneous intermediation	52391	(NA)	(NA)	7,190	15,346	1,592	30.4
Portfolio management	52392	(NA)	(NA)	10,888	43,643	13,533	124.0
Investment advice	52393	(NA)	(NA)	7,807	9,398	3,197	42.9
All other financial investment activities	52399	(NA)	(NA)	2,527	8,282	2,534	52.9
Insurance carriers & related activities	524	499,365	1,084,618	172,299	1,072,784	92,230	2,327.3
Insurance carriers	5241	39,640	995,588	38,739	995,512	65,858	1,588.0
Direct life/health/medical insurance carriers	52411	(NA)	(NA)	14,615	666,532	34,474	889.0
Other direct insurance carriers	52412	(NA)	(NA)	23,561	307,695	30,374	683.1
Reinsurance carriers	52413	(NA)	(NA)	563	21,285	1,010	15.9
Agencies & other insurance related activities	5242	459,725	89,030	133,560	77,272	26,372	739.3
Insurance agencies & brokerages	52421	378,410	68,893	120,392	59,174	19,533	557.7
Other insurance related activities	52429	81,315	20,138	13,168	18,098	6,839	181.6
Funds, trusts, & other financial vehicles (part)	525	1,489	16,608	1,489	16,608	1,413	35.3
Other investment pools & funds (part)	5259	1,489	16,608	1,489	16,608	1,413	35.3
Real Estate Investment Trusts (REITs)	52593	1,489	16,608	1,489	16,608	1,413	35.3

NA Not available. [1] North American Industry Classification System, 1997; see text, Section 15, Business Enterprise. [2] For pay period including March 12.

Source: U.S. Census Bureau, *1997 Economic Census, Geographic Area Series* and *Nonemployer Statistics*.

No. 1162. Finance and Insurance—Establishments, Employees, and Payroll: 1998 and 1999

[412.3 represents 412,300. Covers establishments with payroll. Employees are for the week including March 12. Most government employees are excluded. For statement on methodology, see Appendix III]

Kind of business	NAICS code [1]	Establishments (1,000)		Employees (1,000)		Payroll (bil. dol.)	
		1998	1999	1998	1999	1998	1999
Finance & Insurance, total	52	**412.3**	**418.3**	**5,770**	**5,965**	**290.0**	**313.2**
Monetary authorities central bank.	521	(Z)	(Z)	21	22	1.0	1.0
Credit intermediation & related actiivties	522	173.1	173.8	2,688	2,781	105.0	112.6
Depository credit intermediation [2]	5221	105.4	104.0	1,920	1,937	71.2	75.9
Commercial banking	52211	73.0	72.5	1,483	1,494	57.4	61.5
Savings institutions	52212	16.9	15.9	259	254	9.2	9.1
Credit unions	52213	15.5	15.5	176	184	4.5	4.9
Nondepository credit intermediation.	5222	48.0	49.6	566	645	25.6	29.2
Credit card issuing	52221	0.7	0.8	46	59	1.4	1.9
Sales financing	52222	7.6	7.8	140	154	6.9	8.2
Other nondepository credit intermediation [2] . .	52229	39.7	41.0	379	432	17.3	19.1
Real estate credit	522292	16.2	20.5	204	275	10.5	12.5
Activities related to credit intermediation.	5223	19.7	20.2	202	199	8.2	7.5
Security, commodity contracts & like activity	523	63.8	66.4	724	780	83.4	92.9
Scrty & comdty contracts intermed & brokerage [2]	5231	32.9	34.5	457	491	57.4	63.2
Investment banking & securities dealing	52311	7.1	5.9	164	130	26.2	23.7
Securities brokerage	52312	23.6	26.3	274	340	29.8	37.9
Securities & commodity exchanges	5232	0.1	0.1	7	7	0.5	0.5
Other financial investment activities [2]	5239	30.9	31.7	260	282	25.6	29.3
Portfolio management	52392	11.3	11.4	129	140	16.5	18.5
Insurance carriers & related activities	524	173.6	176.1	2,312	2,346	99.3	104.8
Insurance carriers [2]	5241	39.1	42.3	1,533	1,549	69.2	72.6
Direct life/health/medical insurance carriers . .	52411	14.7	14.5	876	859	37.2	38.7
Direct life insurance carriers	524113	11.3	11.2	550	541	24.0	25.3
Direct health & medical insurance carriers .	524114	3.4	3.2	325	317	13.1	13.4
Other direct insurance carriers[2]	52412	24.1	27.2	648	672	31.5	32.5
Direct property & casualty insurance carriers.	524126	21.1	24.0	602	621	29.2	30.2
Agencies & other insurance related activities[2] . .	5242	134.4	133.9	780	797	30.2	32.2
Insurance agencies & brokerages	52421	120.8	120.3	583	593	22.4	23.8
Funds, trusts, & other financial vehicles (part). . . .	525	1.7	2.0	24	36	1.2	1.9

Z Less than 500.   [1] North American Industry Classification System; see text, Section 15, Business Enterprise.   [2] Includes industries not shown separately.
Source: U.S. Census Bureau, *County Business Patterns*, annual.

No. 1163. Flow of Funds Accounts—Financial Assets of Financial and Nonfinancial Institutions by Holder Sector: 1980 to 2000

[In billions of dollars (14,091 represents $14,091,000,000,000). As of Dec. 31]

Sector	1980	1985	1990	1994	1995	1996	1997	1998	1999	2000
All sectors	**14,091**	**24,078**	**36,710**	**47,927**	**54,260**	**60,380**	**68,457**	**76,743**	**87,593**	**89,128**
Households [1]	6,607	10,159	14,989	19,143	21,790	24,176	27,594	30,606	35,398	33,736
Nonfinancial business	1,612	2,935	4,112	5,119	5,682	6,269	6,727	7,238	8,085	8,618
Farm business	24	33	47	59	61	61	62	65	65	65
Nonfarm noncorporate	145	435	486	581	660	748	858	949	1,027	1,093
Nonfinancial corporations	1,443	2,467	3,579	4,479	4,961	5,460	5,807	6,223	6,993	7,461
State and local government	301	645	963	1,026	994	1,008	1,033	1,180	1,268	1,324
U.S. government	229	374	442	440	441	441	438	443	561	512
U.S. govt.-sponsored enterprises	195	324	478	782	897	989	1,099	1,404	1,721	1,969
Federally-related mortgage pools.	114	368	1,020	1,472	1,570	1,711	1,826	2,018	2,292	2,492
Monetary authorities	174	243	342	452	472	495	534	567	697	636
Commercial banking [2]	1,482	2,376	3,337	4,160	4,494	4,710	5,175	5,642	5,989	6,456
U.S.-chartered commercial banks	1,266	1,990	2,644	3,123	3,322	3,445	3,742	4,094	4,433	4,773
Foreign banking offices in U.S.	98	144	367	590	666	715	811	806	756	780
Bank holding companies.	103	219	298	414	467	511	575	686	741	836
Nonbank finance [2]	2,884	5,686	9,028	12,423	14,429	16,380	19,117	22,002	25,228	26,135
Funding corporations	16	135	251	380	394	499	613	734	994	1,127
Savings institutions	792	1,275	1,323	1,009	1,013	1,032	1,029	1,088	1,151	1,219
Credit unions	68	135	217	294	311	330	354	391	415	442
Life insurance	464	796	1,351	1,863	2,064	2,246	2,515	2,770	3,068	3,134
Other insurance	182	299	533	678	740	770	843	894	890	870
Private pension funds.	513	1,226	1,634	2,460	2,923	3,251	3,747	4,205	4,678	4,589
State and local govt. retirement funds . .	197	399	884	1,185	1,465	1,752	2,219	2,620	2,929	3,085
Finance companies	197	338	547	600	672	715	757	828	973	1,101
Real estate investment trusts.	3	10	28	31	33	38	64	71	68	64
Mutual funds	62	246	608	1,477	1,853	2,342	2,989	3,611	4,553	4,433
Closed-end investment funds.	8	8	53	118	134	145	149	.143	167	167
Money market funds	76	242	493	600	741	887	1,043	1,330	1,579	1,812
Security brokers and dealers	45	156	262	455	568	636	779	921	1,001	1,213
Asset-backed securities issuers	-	37	270	568	709	855	1,066	1,385	1,622	1,831
Bank personal trusts, estates.	245	358	522	670	775	841	918	976	1,104	1,012
Rest of the world	493	967	1,998	2,910	3,491	4,200	4,914	5,643	6,353	7,251

- Represents zero.   [1] Includes nonprofit organizations.   [2] Includes other sectors not shown separately.

Source: Board of Governors of the Federal Reserve System, "Federal Reserve Statistical Release, Z.1, Flow of Funds Accounts of the United States"; published: 9 March 2001; <http://www.bog.frb.fed.us/releases/Z1/20010309/data.htm>.

No. 1164. Flow of Funds Accounts—Financial Assets and Liabilities of Foreign Sector: 1980 to 2000

[In billions of dollars (493 represents $493,000,000,000). As of Dec. 31]

Type of instrument	1980	1985	1990	1994	1995	1996	1997	1998	1999	2000
Total financial assets [1]	**493**	**967**	**1,998**	**2,910**	**3,431**	**4,200**	**4,914**	**5,643**	**6,353**	**7,251**
Net interbank assets	-17	-31	53	218	229	177	173	146	139	138
U.S. checkable deposits and currency . .	47	67	107	180	194	214	244	258	298	290
U.S. time deposits.	26	43	49	56	50	61	74	87	102	107
Security RPs [2]	4	8	20	47	68	71	91	72	87	92
Credit market instruments.	186	432	889	1,216	1,531	1,927	2,257	2,540	2,678	2,958
Open market paper	9	8	11	25	43	58	78	115	102	111
U.S. government securities	136	241	488	758	996	1,290	1,499	1,622	1,636	1,725
Official holdings	118	145	291	407	498	610	615	620	629	658
Treasury	111	138	286	397	483	591	590	589	578	567
Agency	7	7	5	10	15	20	25	31	51	91
Private holdings	18	96	197	351	498	679	884	1,002	1,007	1,067
Treasury	16	88	152	236	359	503	662	730	661	608
Agency	1	8	45	115	140	176	222	272	346	459
U.S. corporate bonds [3]	37	126	217	311	369	453	538	660	821	1,002
Loans to U.S. corporate business. . . .	5	56	172	122	122	126	143	142	120	120
U.S. corporate equities	75	137	244	398	528	657	920	1,175	1,523	1,712
Miscellaneous assets.	143	281	591	742	841	1,037	1,096	1,314	1,480	1,909
Foreign direct investment in U.S [4] . . .	126	247	505	618	680	743	825	929	1,125	1,428
Other	17	34	86	124	161	294	271	385	355	481
Total liabilities [1]	**673**	**870**	**1,389**	**1,743**	**2,012**	**2,313**	**2,552**	**2,776**	**3,039**	**3,609**
U.S. private deposits	31	148	298	374	419	522	620	639	726	750
Credit market instruments [1]	197	239	289	375	454	542	608	651	677	739
Commercial paper	7	34	75	43	56	67	65	73	89	121
Bonds	49	72	115	242	299	366	428	462	477	495
Bank loans, n.e.c. [5]	65	28	19	26	35	44	52	59	59	71
U.S. government loans	54	74	63	56	55	55	53	52	48	49
Trade payables	26	16	27	40	45	44	49	46	51	49
Miscellaneous liabilities [1]	406	441	713	901	1,030	1,152	1,227	1,379	1,536	2,025
U.S. direct investment abroad [3][4] . . .	404	409	629	787	886	987	1,059	1,207	1,331	1,491

[1] Includes other items not shown separately. [2] Repurchase agreements. [3] Through 1992, corporate bonds include net issues by Netherlands Antillean financial subsidiaries; U.S. direct investment abroad excludes net inflows from those bond issues. [4] Direct investment is valued on a current-cost basis. [5] Not elsewhere classified.

No. 1165. Flow of Funds Accounts—Credit Market Debt Outstanding: 1980 to 2000

[In billions of dollars (4,733 represents $4,733,000,000,000). As of Dec. 31. N.e.c.=Not elsewhere classified]

Item	1980	1985	1990	1994	1995	1996	1997	1998	1999	2000
Credit market debt.	**4,733**	**8,629**	**13,755**	**17,198**	**18,445**	**19,810**	**21,300**	**23,462**	**25,731**	**27,514**
U.S. government.	735	1,590	2,498	3,492	3,637	3,782	3,805	3,752	3,681	3,385
Nonfederal domestic nonfinancial	3,223	5,542	8,352	9,509	10,076	10,662	11,442	12,539	13,766	14,959
Households [1]	1,404	2,286	3,625	4,535	4,898	5,222	5,560	6,039	6,578	7,169
Corporations	907	1,607	2,516	2,685	2,912	3,095	3,360	3,778	4,294	4,741
Nonfarm noncorporate business	406	798	1,083	1,025	1,049	1,131	1,246	1,358	1,474	1,591
Farm business	161	173	135	142	145	150	156	164	169	179
State and local government	344	678	992	1,122	1,070	1,063	1,119	1,200	1,252	1,279
Rest of the world	197	239	289	375	454	542	608	651	677	739
Financial sectors	578	1,257	2,616	3,822	4,279	4,825	5,445	6,519	7,607	8,431
Commercial banking	91	188	198	228	251	264	309	382	449	509
Thrift institutions [2]	55	111	140	113	115	141	161	214	264	291
Life insurance companies	-	-	-	1	1	2	2	2	3	2
Government-sponsored enterprises [3] .	163	264	399	701	807	897	995	1,274	1,592	1,825
Federally-related mortgage pools. . . .	114	368	1,020	1,472	1,570	1,711	1,826	2,018	2,292	2,492
Asset-backed securities issuers.	-	37	271	570	713	863	1,077	1,398	1,632	1,838
Finance companies.	127	224	374	434	484	530	554	598	660	735
Mortgage companies.	12	17	25	19	17	21	16	18	18	18
Real estate investment trusts	4	8	28	40	45	56	96	159	165	172
Security brokers and dealers	-	1	15	34	29	27	35	43	25	41
Funding corporations	13	39	147	211	249	313	374	414	507	507
CORPORATE CREDIT MARKET DEBT OUTSTANDING, BY TYPE OF INSTRUMENT										
Total	**907**	**1,607**	**2,516**	**2,685**	**2,912**	**3,095**	**3,360**	**3,778**	**4,294**	**4,741**
Commercial paper	28	72	117	139	157	156	169	193	230	278
Municipal securities [4]	46	127	115	132	135	138	142	148	153	154
Corporate bonds	366	578	1,008	1,253	1,344	1,460	1,611	1,830	2,059	2,234
Bank loans, n.e.c.	230	424	545	521	588	627	698	779	852	926
Other loans and advances.	110	248	473	421	454	472	521	568	616	692
Savings institutions.	1	15	17	5	6	8	9	12	15	20
Finance companies.	78	135	241	247	271	279	287.	313	365	424
U.S. Government	8	14	9	8	10	9	8	8	8	7
Acceptance liabilities to banks	17	28	29	15	14	13	11	7	4	4
Rest of the world	5	56	172	122	122	126	143	142	120	120
Asset-backed securities issuers.	-	-	4	24	30	38	62	86	104	116
Mortgages	127	157	257	219	235	241	220	261	383	456

- Represents or rounds to zero. [1] Includes nonprofit organizations. [2] Covers savings institutions and credit unions. [3] U.S. government. [4] Industrial revenue bonds. Issued by state and local governments to finance private investment and secured in interest and principal by the industrial user of the funds.

Source of Tables 1164 and 1165: Board of Governors of the Federal Reserve System, "Federal Reserve Statistical Release, Z.1, Flow of Funds Accounts of the United States"; published: 9 March 2001; <http://www.bog.frb.fed.us/releases/Z1/20010309/data.htm>.

No. 1166. Flow of Funds Accounts—Assets of Households: 1980 to 2000

[As of December 31 (6,607 represents $6,607,000,000,000). Includes nonprofit organizations]

Type of instrument	Total (bil. dol.) 1980	1985	1990	1995	1998	1999	2000	Percent distribution 1980	1990	2000
Total financial assets	**6,607**	**10,159**	**14,989**	**21,790**	**30,606**	**35,398**	**33,736**	**100.0**	**100.0**	**100.0**
Deposits.	1,517	2,484	3,253	3,309	4,030	4,210	4,583	23.0	21.7	13.6
Foreign deposits.	-	8	13	23	38	44	41	-	0.1	0.1
Checkable deposits and currency . .	251	342	409	504	444	389	310	3.8	2.7	0.9
Time and savings deposits	1,203	1,941	2,466	2,337	2,821	2,937	3,238	18.2	16.5	9.6
Money market fund shares	62	193	365	445	726	841	995	0.9	2.4	2.9
Credit market instruments	425	849	1,518	1,946	2,032	2,303	2,171	6.4	10.1	6.4
Open-market paper	38	35	63	48	58	60	63	0.6	0.4	0.2
U.S. Government securities	165	269	555	910	741	925	789	2.5	3.7	2.3
Treasury issues.	160	251	469	734	473	510	306	2.4	3.1	0.9
Savings bonds	73	80	126	185	187	186	185	1.1	0.8	0.5
Other Treasury	88	171	343	549	286	323	122	1.3	2.3	0.4
Agency issues	5	18	86	176	268	415	482	0.1	0.6	1.4
Municipal securities	104	348	575	459	489	533	525	1.6	3.8	1.6
Corporate and foreign bonds.	30	77	181	420	634	674	684	0.5	1.2	2.0
Mortgages	87	120	144	109	110	110	111	1.3	1.0	0.3
Corporate equities [1]	875	1,058	1,795	6,672	8,750	8,750	6,579	13.2	12.0	19.5
Mutual fund shares.	46	198	457	1,159	2,375	3,106	3,026	0.7	3.0	9.0
Security credit	16	35	62	128	277	324	404	0.2	0.4	1.2
Life insurance reserves	221	264	392	566	718	784	824	3.3	2.6	2.4
Pension fund reserves [2]	970	2,085	3,460	5,833	8,760	9,748	9,847	14.7	23.1	29.2
Investment in bank personal trusts . . .	265	384	552	803	1,001	1,130	1,039	4.0	3.7	3.1
Equity in noncorporate business	2,198	2,668	3,275	3,684	4,415	4,705	4,916	33.3	21.9	14.6
Miscellaneous assets	74	133	224	292	327	339	347	1.1	1.5	1.0

- Represents zero. [1] Only those directly held and those in closed-end funds. Other equities are included in mutual funds, life insurance and pension reserves, and bank personal trusts. [2] See also Table 1218.

Source: Board of Governors of the Federal Reserve System, "Federal Reserve Statistical Release, Z.1, Flow of Funds Accounts of the United States"; published: 9 March 2001; <http://www.bog.frb.fed.us/releases/Z1/20010309/data.htm>.

No. 1167. Financial Assets Held by Families by Type of Asset: 1992 to 1998

[Median value in thousands of constant 1998 dollars (13.1 represents $13,100). Constant dollar figures are based on consumer price index data published by U.S. Bureau of Labor Statistics. Families include one-person units; for definition of family, see text, Section 1, Population. Based on Survey of Consumer Finance; see Appendix III. For definition of median, see Guide to Tabular Presentation]

Age of family head and family income	Any financial asset [1]	Trans-action accounts [2]	Certifi-cates of deposit	Savings bonds	Stocks [3]	Mutual funds [4]	Retirement accounts [5]	Life insur-ance [6]	Other man-aged [7]
PERCENT OF FAMILIES OWNING ASSET									
1992, total	90.2	86.9	16.7	22.3	17.0	10.4	39.6	34.9	4.0
1995, total	91.0	87.0	14.3	22.8	15.2	12.3	45.2	32.0	3.9
1998, total	**92.9**	**90.5**	**15.3**	**19.3**	**19.2**	**16.5**	**48.8**	**29.6**	**5.9**
Under 35 years old	88.6	84.6	6.2	17.2	13.1	12.2	39.8	18.0	1.9
35 to 44 years old	93.3	90.5	9.4	24.9	18.9	16.0	59.5	29.0	3.9
45 to 54 years old	94.9	93.5	11.8	21.8	22.6	23.0	59.2	32.9	6.5
55 to 64 years old	95.6	93.9	18.6	18.1	25.0	15.2	58.3	35.8	6.5
65 to 74 years old	95.6	94.1	29.9	16.1	21.0	18.0	46.1	39.1	11.8
75 years old and over . . .	92.1	89.7	35.9	12.0	18.0	15.1	16.7	32.6	11.6
Less than $10,000	70.6	61.9	7.7	3.5	3.8	1.9	6.4	15.7	(B)
$10,000 to $24,999	89.9	86.5	16.8	10.2	7.2	7.6	25.4	20.9	4.9
$25,000 to $49,999	97.3	95.8	15.9	20.4	17.7	14.0	54.2	28.1	3.9
$50,000 to $99,999	99.8	99.3	16.4	30.6	27.7	25.8	73.5	39.8	8.0
$100,000 and more	100.0	100.0	16.8	32.3	56.6	44.8	88.6	50.1	15.8
MEDIAN VALUE [8]									
1992, total	13.1	2.6	12.6	0.7	9.1	18.3	16.0	3.5	22.8
1995, total	16.5	2.3	10.6	1.1	9.6	21.2	18.1	5.3	31.9
1998, total	**22.4**	**3.1**	**15.0**	**1.0**	**17.5**	**25.0**	**24.0**	**7.3**	**31.5**
Under 35 years old	4.5	1.5	2.5	0.5	5.0	7.0	7.0	2.7	19.4
35 to 44 years old	22.9	2.8	8.0	0.7	12.0	14.0	21.0	8.5	25.0
45 to 54 years old	37.8	4.5	11.5	1.0	24.0	30.0	34.0	10.0	39.3
55 to 64 years old	45.6	4.1	17.0	1.5	21.0	58.0	46.8	9.5	65.0
65 to 74 years old	45.8	5.6	20.0	2.0	50.0	60.0	38.0	8.5	41.3
75 years old and over . . .	36.6	6.1	30.0	5.0	50.0	59.0	30.0	5.0	30.0
Less than $10,000	1.1	0.5	7.0	1.8	14.0	6.0	7.5	3.0	(B)
$10,000 to $24,999	4.8	1.3	20.0	1.0	10.0	26.0	8.0	5.0	30.0
$25,000 to $49,999	17.6	2.5	14.5	0.6	8.0	11.0	13.0	5.0	15.0
$50,000 to $99,999	57.2	6.0	13.3	1.0	15.0	25.0	31.0	9.5	32.0
$100,000 and more	244.3	19.0	22.0	1.5	55.0	65.0	93.0	18.0	100.0

B Base figure too small. [1] Includes other types of financial assets, not shown separately. [2] Checking, savings, and money market deposit accounts, money market mutual funds, and call accounts at brokerages. [3] Covers only those stocks that are directly held by families outside mutual funds, retirement accounts and other managed assets. [4] Excludes money market mutual funds and funds held through retirement accounts or other managed assets. [5] Covers IRAs, Keogh accounts, and certain employer-sponsored accounts. [6] Cash value. [7] Includes personal annuities and trusts with an equity interest and managed investment accounts. [8] Median value of financial asset for families holding such assets.

Source: Board of Governors of the Federal Reserve System, *Federal Reserve Bulletin*, January 2000, and unpublished revisions.

No. 1168. Flow of Funds Accounts—Liabilities of Households: 1980 to 2000

[As of December 31 (1,455 represents $1,455,000,000,000). Includes nonprofit organizations]

Type of instrument	Total (bil. dol.)							Percent distribution		
	1980	1985	1990	1995	1998	1999	2000	1980	1990	2000
Total liabilities	1,455	2,377	3,747	5,096	6,335	6,958	7,560	100.0	100.0	100.0
Credit market instruments	1,404	2,286	3,625	4,898	6,039	6,578	7,169	96.5	96.7	94.8
Home mortgages [1]	934	1,458	2,532	3,368	4,204	4,620	5,022	64.2	67.6	66.4
Consumer credit.	355	604	805	1,123	1,332	1,426	1,569	24.4	21.5	20.8
Municipal securities	17	81	87	98	127	137	143	1.1	2.3	1.9
Bank loans, n.e.c. [2]	28	31	18	57	73	66	73	1.9	0.5	1.0
Other loans	55	79	101	160	204	219	247	3.8	2.7	3.3
Commercial mortgages	15	33	83	92	99	110	115	1.0	2.2	1.5
Security credit	25	51	39	79	153	228	233	1.7	1.0	3.1
Trade payables	14	24	67	101	126	133	139	0.9	1.8	1.8
Unpaid life insurance premiums [3]	13	15	16	18	17	19	19	0.9	0.4	0.3

[1] Includes loans made under home equity lines of credit and home equity loans secured by junior liens.   [2] Not elsewhere classified.   [3] Includes deferred premiums.
Source: Board of Governors of the Federal Reserve System, "Federal Reserve Statistical Release, Z.1, Flow of Funds Accounts of the United States"; published: 9 March 2001; <http://www.bog.frb.fed.us/releases/Z1/20010309/data.htm>.

No. 1169. Financial Debt Held by Families by Type of Debt: 1992 to 1998

[Median debt in thousands of constant 1998 dollars (19.9 represents $19,900). See headnote, Table 1167]

Age of family head and family income	Any debt	Home-secured debt [1]	Installment	Other lines of credit	Credit card balances [2]	Other residential property	Other debt [3]
PERCENT OF FAMILIES HOLDING DEBTS							
1992, total	73.2	39.1	46.0	2.3	43.7	5.7	8.4
1995, total	74.5	41.0	45.9	1.9	47.3	4.7	8.5
1998, total	74.1	43.1	43.7	2.3	44.1	5.1	8.8
Under 35 years old	81.2	33.2	60.0	2.4	50.7	2.0	9.6
35 to 44 years old	87.6	58.7	53.3	3.6	51.3	6.7	11.4
45 to 54 years old	87.0	58.8	51.2	3.6	52.5	6.7	11.1
55 to 64 years old	76.4	49.4	37.9	1.6	45.7	7.8	8.3
65 to 74 years old	51.4	26.0	20.2	(B)	29.2	5.1	4.1
75 years old and over	24.6	11.5	4.2	(B)	11.2	1.8	2.0
Less than $10,000.	41.7	8.3	25.7	(B)	20.6	(B)	3.6
$10,000 to $24,999	63.7	21.3	34.4	1.2	37.9	1.8	7.0
$25,000 to $49,999	79.6	43.7	50.0	2.9	49.9	4.1	7.7
$50,000 to $99,999	89.4	71.0	55.0	3.3	56.7	7.7	12.2
$100,000 and more	87.8	73.4	43.2	2.6	40.4	16.4	14.8
MEDIAN DEBT [4]							
1992, total	19.9	50.2	5.3	2.3	1.1	28.5	2.9
1995, total	23.4	54.9	6.4	3.7	1.6	31.9	2.1
1998, total	33.3	62.0	8.7	2.5	1.7	40.0	3.0
Under 35 years old	19.2	71.0	9.1	1.0	1.5	55.0	1.7
35 to 44 years old	55.7	70.0	7.7	1.4	2.0	40.0	3.0
45 to 54 years old	48.4	68.8	10.0	3.0	1.8	40.0	5.0
55 to 64 years old	34.6	49.4	8.3	4.9	2.0	41.0	5.0
65 to 74 years old	11.9	29.0	6.5	(B)	1.1	56.0	4.5
75 years old and over	8.0	21.2	8.9	(B)	0.7	29.8	1.7
Less than $10,000.	4.1	16.0	4.0	(B)	1.1	(B)	0.6
$10,000 to $24,999	8.0	34.2	6.0	1.1	1.0	34.0	1.3
$25,000 to $49,999	27.1	47.0	8.0	3.0	1.9	20.0	2.2
$50,000 to $99,999	75.0	75.0	11.3	2.8	2.4	42.0	3.8
$100,000 and more	135.4	123.8	15.4	5.0	3.2	60.0	10.0

B Base figure too small.   [1] First and second mortgages and home equity loans and lines of credit secured by the primary residence.   [2] Families that had an outstanding balance on any of their credit cards after paying their most recent bills.   [3] Includes loans on insurance policies, loans against pension accounts, borrowing on margin accounts and unclassified loans.   [4] Median amount of financial debt for families holding such debts.

No. 1170. Percent Distribution of Amount of Debt Held by Families: 1995 and 1998

[See headnote, Table 1171]

Type of debt	1995	1998	Purpose of debt	1995	1998	Type of lending institution	1995	1998
Total	100.0	100.0	**Total**	100.0	100.0	**Total**	100.0	100.0
Home-secured debt. . .	73.3	71.9	Home purchase.	70.4	68.1	Commercial bank	35.1	32.6
Installment loans.	11.8	12.8	Home improvement . .	2.0	2.0	Savings and loan	10.8	9.6
Credit card balances . .	3.9	3.8	Investment, excluding			Credit union	4.5	4.2
Other lines of credit. . .	0.6	0.3	real estate	1.0	3.2	Finance or loan company.	3.2	4.2
Other residential			Vehicles.	7.5	7.5	Brokerage	1.9	3.7
property	7.5	7.4	Goods and services . .	5.7	6.0	Real estate lender.	32.7	35.9
Other debt.	2.8	3.7	Investment real estate.	8.2	7.8	Individual lender	5.0	3.4
			Education.	2.7	3.4	Other nonfinancial	0.8	1.3
			Other loans	2.4	1.9	Government	1.3	0.6
						Credit and store cards . .	3.9	3.8
						Other loans	0.9	0.7

Source of Tables 1169 and 1170: Board of Governors of the Federal Reserve System, *Federal Reserve Bulletin*, January 2000, and unpublished data.

No. 1171. Ratios of Debt Payments to Family Income: 1992 to 1998

[In percent. Constant dollar figures are based on consumer price index data published by U.S. Bureau of Labor Statistics. Families include one-person units; for definition of family, see text, Section 1, Population. Based on Survey of Consumer Finance; see Appendix III. For definition of median, see Guide to Tabular Presentation]

Age of family head and family income (constant (1998) dollars)	Ratio of debt payments to family income						Percent of debtors with—					
	Aggregate			Median			Ratios above 40 percent			Any payment 60 days or more past due		
	1992	1995	1998	1992	1995	1998	1992	1995	1998	1992	1995	1998
All families	14.1	13.6	14.5	16.1	16.1	17.6	10.9	10.5	12.7	6.0	7.1	8.1
Under 35 years old	16.5	17.1	16.6	16.6	16.9	17.4	10.5	11.0	11.8	8.3	8.7	11.1
35 to 44 years old	17.8	16.6	17.0	19.0	18.1	19.4	11.6	9.2	11.6	6.8	7.7	8.4
45 to 54 years old	14.6	14.6	16.3	16.1	16.6	17.8	10.2	10.4	11.6	5.4	7.4	7.4
55 to 64 years old	11.4	11.5	12.9	14.5	14.0	16.7	14.3	14.5	13.9	4.7	3.2	7.5
65 to 74 years old	7.8	6.9	8.5	10.6	12.2	13.9	7.8	7.8	17.5	1.0	5.3	3.1
75 years old and over	3.4	2.9	3.9	5.0	3.4	8.9	8.7	8.9	20.9	1.8	5.4	1.1
Less than $10,000	16.8	19.5	19.4	19.5	15.4	20.3	28.4	27.6	32.0	11.6	8.4	15.1
$10,000 to $24,999	14.8	16.1	16.2	15.3	17.7	17.8	15.5	17.3	19.9	9.3	11.3	12.3
$25,000 to $49,999	16.5	16.2	17.4	16.3	16.6	18.1	9.6	8.0	13.8	6.3	8.6	9.2
$50,000 to $99,999	15.3	16.0	17.4	17.0	16.9	18.3	4.4	4.2	5.7	2.2	2.7	4.5
$100,000 and more	10.7	8.7	10.0	13.7	11.1	13.1	2.2	1.7	2.1	0.5	1.3	1.5

Source: Board of Governors of the Federal Reserve System, *Federal Reserve Bulletin*, January 2000, and unpublished data.

No. 1172. Household Debt-Service Payments as a Percentage of Disposable Personal Income: 1980 to 2000

[In percent. As of end of year. Seasonally adjusted. The household debt-service burden is an estimate of the ratio of debt payments to disposable personal income. Debt payments consist of the estimated required payments on outstanding mortgage and consumer debt]

Year	Total	Consumer	Mortgage
1980	12.53	7.96	4.57
1981	12.49	7.60	4.89
1982	12.49	7.45	5.04
1983	12.51	7.46	5.05
1984	12.99	7.81	5.19
1985	13.93	8.29	5.64
1986	14.38	8.48	5.89
1987	13.89	7.91	5.97
1988	13.52	7.58	5.94
1989	13.70	7.58	6.12
1990	13.41	7.10	6.31
1991	12.77	6.51	6.26
1992	11.85	5.97	5.88
1993	11.76	6.09	5.67
1994	12.17	6.48	5.69
1995	12.89	7.04	5.85
1996	13.26	7.43	5.83
1997	13.35	7.44	5.90
1998	13.40	7.51	5.89
1999	13.65	7.56	6.09
2000	14.26	7.82	6.44

Source: Board of Governors of the Federal Reserve System, *"Household Debt Service Burden"*; published: 10 July 2001; <http://www.federalreserve.gov/releases/housedebt/default.htm>.

No. 1173. Banking Offices by Type of Bank: 1980 to 2000

[As of December 31. Includes Puerto Rico and outlying areas. Covers all FDIC-insured commercial banks and savings institutions. Commercial banks include insured branches of foreign banks. Data for 1980 include automatic teller machines which were reported by many banks as branches]

Item	1980	1985	1990	1995	1996	1997	1998	1999	2000
All banking offices . .	(NA)	82,367	84,332	81,273	82,466	84,291	85,190	86,527	87,495
Number of banks	(NA)	18,033	15,192	12,002	11,478	10,923	10,463	10,221	9,908
Number of branches	(NA)	64,334	69,140	69,271	70,988	73,368	74,727	76,306	77,587
Commercial banks	53,172	57,660	62,710	65,827	66,733	69,468	70,731	72,265	72,998
Number of banks	14,434	14,407	12,377	9,972	9,553	9,143	8,774	8,581	8,318
Number of branches	38,738	43,253	50,333	55,855	57,180	60,325	61,957	63,684	64,680
Savings institutions	(NA)	24,707	21,622	15,446	15,733	14,823	14,459	14,262	14,497
Number of banks	(NA)	3,626	2,815	2,030	1,925	1,780	1,689	1,640	1,590
Number of branches	(NA)	21,081	18,807	13,416	13,808	13,043	12,770	12,622	12,907

NA Not available.

Source: U.S. Federal Deposit Insurance Corporation, *Statistics on Banking*, annual; *Historical Statistics on Banking*; and *The FDIC Quarterly Banking Profile Graph Book*.

No. 1174. Selected Financial Institutions—Number and Assets by Asset Size: 2000

[As of December (6,238.7 represents $6,238,700,000,000). FDIC=Federal Deposit Insurance Corporation]

Asset size	Number of institutions			Assets (bil. dol.)		
	F.D.I.C.-insured			F.D.I.C.-insured		
	Commercial banks	Savings institutions	Credit unions [1]	Commercial banks [2]	Savings institutions	Credit unions [1]
Total	**8,315**	**1,590**	**10,316**	**6,238.7**	**1,222.6**	**438.2**
Less than $5.0 million	36	10	4,261	0.1	0.4	8.1
$5.0 million to $9.9 million	126	30	1,603	1.0	0.2	11.4
$10.0 million to $24.9 million	899	97	1,823	16.4	1.8	29.2
$25.0 million to $49.9 million	1,680	187	1,071	62.8	7.0	37.8
$50.0 million to $99.9 million	2,100	299	697	150.9	21.8	49.1
$100.0 million to $499.9 million	2,775	698	729	564.8	160.8	154.2
$500.0 million to $999.9 million	304	122	89	208.3	84.9	60.9
$1.0 billion to $2.9 billion	214	92	37	347.3	150.0	55.2
$3.0 billion or more	181	55	6	4,887.2	796.2	32.3
	Percent distribution					
Total	**100.0**	**100.0**	**100.0**	**100.0**	**100.0**	**100.0**
Less than $5.0 million	0.4	0.6	41.3	(Z)	(Z)	1.8
$5.0 million to $9.9 million	1.5	1.9	15.5	(Z)	(Z)	2.6
$10.0 million to $24.9 million	10.8	6.1	17.7	0.3	0.1	6.7
$25.0 million to $49.9 million	20.2	11.8	10.4	1.0	0.6	8.6
$50.0 million to $99.9 million	25.3	18.8	6.8	2.4	1.8	11.2
$100.0 million to $499.9 million	33.4	43.9	7.1	9.1	13.1	35.2
$500.0 million to $999.9 million	3.7	7.7	0.9	3.3	6.9	13.9
$1.0 billion to $2.9 billion	2.6	5.8	0.4	5.6	12.3	12.6
$3.0 billion or more	2.2	3.5	0.1	78.3	65.1	7.4

Z Less than 0.05 percent. [1] Source: National Credit Union Administration, *National Credit Union Administration Yearend Statistics 2000*. Excludes nonfederally insured state chartered credit unions and federally insured corporate credit unions. [2] Includes foreign branches of U.S. banks.

Source: Except as noted, U.S. Federal Deposit Insurance Corporation, *Statistics on Banking, 2000*.

No. 1175. Insured Commercial Banks—Assets and Liabilities: 1980 to 2000

[In billions of dollars, except as indicated (1,856 represents $1,856,000,000,000). As of Dec. 31. 2000 data preliminary. Includes outlying areas. Except as noted, includes foreign branches of U.S. banks]

Item	1980	1985	1990	1995	1996	1997	1998	1999	2000
Number of banks reporting	14,435	14,417	12,343	9,940	9,528	9,142	8,774	8,580	8,315
Assets, total	**1,856**	**2,731**	**3,389**	**4,313**	**4,578**	**5,015**	**5,443**	**5,735**	**6,239**
Net loans and leases	1,006	1,608	2,055	2,550	2,758	2,916	3,181	3,433	3,752
Real estate loans	269	438	830	1,080	1,139	1,245	1,346	1,510	1,670
Home equity loans [1]	(NA)	(NA)	61	79	85	98	97	102	127
Commercial and industrial loans	391	578	615	661	710	795	899	971	1,048
Loans to individuals	187	309	404	535	562	561	571	558	610
Credit cards and related plans	(NA)	(NA)	134	216	232	231	229	212	249
Farm loans	32	36	33	40	41	45	46	45	48
Other loans and leases	158	288	242	292	364	329	381	410	443
Less: Reserve for losses	10	23	56	53	53	55	57	59	64
Less: Unearned income	21	18	14	6	5	4	4	4	3
Investment securities	325	439	605	811	801	872	980	1,046	1,078
Other	524	684	730	952	1,020	1,227	1,282	1,256	1,409
Domestic office assets	1,533	2,326	2,999	3,728	3,906	4,267	4,719	4,995	5,477
Foreign office assets	323	406	390	585	672	748	723	739	761
Liabilities and capital, total	1,856	2,731	3,369	4,313	4,578	5,015	5,443	5,735	6,239
Noninterest-bearing deposits [2]	432	471	489	612	664	677	720	703	766
Interest-bearing deposits [3]	1,049	1,646	2,162	2,416	2,533	2,745	2,961	3,127	3,411
Subordinated debt	7	15	24	44	51	62	73	76	87
Other liabilities	260	429	496	892	955	1,113	1,226	1,348	1,446
Equity capital	108	169	219	350	375	418	462	480	530
Domestic office deposits	1,187	1,796	2,357	2,573	2,724	2,896	3,109	3,175	3,470
Foreign office deposits	294	322	293	454	474	526	572	656	707

NA Not available. [1] For one- to four-family residential properties. [2] Prior to 1984, demand deposits. [3] Prior to 1984, time and savings deposits.

Source: U.S. Federal Deposit Insurance Corporation, *The FDIC Quarterly Banking Profile, Annual Report*, and *Statistics on Banking*, annual.

No. 1176. Insured Commercial Banks—Income and Selected Measures of Financial Condition: 1980 to 2000

[In billions of dollars, except as indicated (177.4 represents $177,400,000,000). 2000 data preliminary. Includes outlying areas. Includes foreign branches of U.S. banks]

Item	1980	1985	1990	1995	1996	1997	1998	1999	2000
Interest income	177.4	248.2	320.5	302.4	312.7	339.5	362.0	367.3	427.9
Interest expense	120.1	157.3	204.9	148.2	150.0	165.0	179.3	175.1	224.2
Net interest income	57.3	90.9	115.5	154.2	162.8	174.5	182.8	192.2	203.8
Provisions for loan losses	4.5	17.8	32.1	12.6	16.3	19.9	22.2	21.8	29.2
Noninterest income . . . . [1]	13.3	31.1	54.9	82.4	93.6	104.5	123.7	144.4	152.7
Percent of net operating revenue [1]	18.8	25.5	32.2	34.8	36.5	37.5	40.4	42.9	42.8
Noninterest expense	46.7	82.4	115.7	149.7	160.7	170.0	194.1	204.2	215.7
Income taxes	5.0	5.6	7.7	26.1	28.2	31.9	31.9	39.4	38.1
Net income	14.0	18.0	16.0	48.7	52.4	59.2	61.8	71.6	71.2
From domestic operations	11.9	16.3	14.2	43.1	46.0	53.1	56.6	64.8	64.0
From foreign operations	2.0	1.7	1.8	5.7	6.3	6.1	5.2	6.7	7.2
PERFORMANCE RATIOS									
Return on assets [2] (percent)	0.80	0.70	0.48	1.17	1.19	1.23	1.19	1.31	1.19
Return on equity [3] (percent)	13.66	11.31	7.45	14.66	14.45	14.68	13.93	15.31	14.07
Net interest margin [4] (percent)	3.66	4.09	3.94	4.29	4.27	4.21	4.07	4.07	3.95
Net charge-offs [5]	3.6	13.6	29.7	12.2	15.5	18.3	20.7	20.4	23.6
Net charge-offs to loans and leases, total (percent) .	0.36	0.84	1.43	0.49	0.58	0.64	0.67	0.61	0.64
Net charge-off rate, credit card loans (percent) . .	(NA)	2.95	3.86	3.98	4.66	5.34	5.26	4.48	4.32
CONDITION RATIOS									
Equity capital to assets (percent)	5.80	6.20	6.45	8.11	8.20	8.33	8.49	8.37	8.49
Noncurrent assets plus other real estate owned to assets [6] (percent)	(NA)	1.87	2.94	0.85	0.75	0.66	0.65	0.63	0.74
Percentage of banks losing money	3.7	17.1	13.4	3.6	4.3	4.8	6.1	7.5	7.1

NA Not available.   [1] Net operating revenue equals net interest income plus noninterest income.   [2] Net income (including securities transactions and nonrecurring items) as a percentage of average total assets.   [3] Net income as a percentage of average total equity capital.   [4] Interest income less interest expense as a percentage of average earning assets (i.e. the profit margin a bank earns on its loans and investments).   [5] Total loans and leases charged off (removed from balance sheet because of uncollectibility), less amounts recovered on loans and leases previously charged off.   [6] The sum of loans, leases, debt securities and other assets that are 90 days or more past due, or in nonaccrual status plus foreclosed property.

No. 1177. Insured Commercial Banks—Selected Measures of Financial Condition by Asset Size and Region: 2000

[In percent, except as indicated. Preliminary. See headnote, Table 1176]

Asset size and region	Number of banks	Return on assets	Return on equity	Equity capital to assets	Net charge-offs to loans and leases	Percentage of banks losing money
Total	8,315	1.19	14.07	8.49	0.64	7.1
Less than $100 million	4,842	1.01	9.09	11.08	0.40	10.6
$100 million to $1 billion	3,078	1.28	13.56	9.60	0.33	1.8
$1 billion to $10 billion	313	1.29	14.57	8.99	0.68	4.2
$10 billion or more	82	1.16	14.42	8.05	0.71	7.3
Northeast [1]	665	1.31	16.38	8.00	0.79	10.1
Southeast [2]	1,425	1.05	12.37	8.61	0.50	11.8
Central [3]	1,791	1.03	12.89	7.91	0.40	5.7
Midwest [4]	2,144	1.42	15.40	9.50	0.83	3.5
Southwest [5]	1,384	0.98	11.02	8.93	0.43	5.9
West [6]	906	1.38	13.61	9.89	1.01	10.4

[1] CT, DE, DC, ME, MD, MA, NH, NJ, NY, PA, PR, RI, and VT.   [2] AL, FL, GA, MS, NC, SC, TN, VA, and WV.   [3] IL, IN, KY, MI, OH, and WI.   [4] IA, KS, MN, MO, NE, ND, and SD.   [5] AR, LA, NM, OK, and TX.   [6] AK, AZ, CA, CO, HI, ID, MT, NV, OR, Pacific Islands, UT, WA, and WY.

Source of Tables 1176 and 1177: U.S. Federal Deposit Insurance Corporation, *Annual Report; Statistics on Banking*, annual; and *FDIC Quarterly Banking Profile*.

No. 1178. Insured Commercial Banks—Delinquency Rates on Loans: 1990 to 2000

[In percent. Annual averages of quarterly figures, not seasonally adjusted. Delinquent loans are those past due 30 days or more and still accruing interest as well as those in nonaccrual status. They are measured as a percentage of end-of-period loans]

Type of loan	1990	1993	1994	1995	1996	1997	1998	1999	2000
Total loans	5.34	3.97	2.78	2.48	2.41	2.27	2.18	2.13	2.18
Real estate	6.10	4.95	3.52	2.94	2.67	2.37	2.16	1.93	1.89
Residential [1]	(NA)	2.69	2.28	2.20	2.31	2.31	2.16	2.08	2.11
Commercial [2]	(NA)	7.87	5.21	3.94	3.14	2.39	2.05	1.69	1.49
Consumer	3.83	3.25	2.76	3.08	3.53	3.72	3.72	3.61	3.55
Credit cards	(NA)	4.25	3.35	3.73	4.34	4.69	4.70	4.54	4.50
Other	(NA)	2.70	2.42	2.67	2.98	3.08	3.13	3.09	2.98
Leases	1.97	1.41	0.93	0.79	1.07	1.08	1.05	1.28	1.60
Commercial and industrial	5.35	3.59	2.25	1.95	1.88	1.66	1.68	1.91	2.22
Agricultural	3.84	2.98	2.48	2.51	3.01	2.64	2.73	3.00	2.54

NA Not available.   [1] Residential real estate loans include loans secured by one- to four-family properties, including home equity lines of credit.   [2] Commercial real estate loans include construction and land development loans, loans secured by multifamily residences, and loans secured by nonfarm, nonresidential real estate.

Source: Federal Financial Institutions Examination Council (FFIEC), *Consolidated Reports of Condition and Income* (FFIEC 031 through 034).

No. 1179. U.S. Banking Offices of Foreign Banks—Summary: 1980 to 2000

[In billions of dollars, except as indicated (201 represents $201,000,000,000). As of December. Data cover foreign-bank branches and agencies in the 50 states and the District of Columbia, New York investment companies (through 1995) and U.S. commercial banks of which more than 25 percent is owned by foreign banks, and International Banking Facilities]

Item	1980	1985	1990	1995	1997	1998	1999	2000	Share [1] 1980	1990	1995	2000
Assets	201	441	791	984	1,126	1,118	1,228	1,299	11.9	21.4	21.7	19.9
Loans, total	121	247	398	461	495	494	499	531	13.4	18.0	17.3	13.7
Business	60	109	193	249	282	280	279	296	18.2	30.8	35.1	27.1
Deposits	80	237	384	523	603	558	697	709	6.6	14.5	17.6	17.6

[1] Percent of "domestically owned" commercial banks plus U.S. offices of foreign banks.
Source: Board of Governors of the Federal Reserve System, "Selected Assets and Liabilities of U.S. Offices of Foreign Banks"; published July 2001; <http://www.federalreserve.gov/releases/Iba/Share/SHRTBL1.html>.

No. 1180. Claims of U.S. Banking Organizations on Foreign Counterparties by Type of Claim: 2000

[In millions of dollars (836,633 represents $836,633,000,000). As of December. Adjusted cross-border claims are those booked outside the foreign counterparty's home country, usually at a U.S. bank's head office in the United States, and are adjusted for any guarantees. Cross-border claims are usually denominated in U.S. dollars. Local claims on foreign counterparties are those booked in the local offices of the reporting bank, that is, offices located in the country of the counterparty. These claims are usually, but not always, booked in local currency. Revaluation gains stem from the value of foreign exchange and derivatives contracts. U.S. banking organizations continually determine the market value of these contracts - "revaluing" them - to see if a positive or negative value results (based on movements in market factors or other variables)]

Country	Total claims	Adjusted cross-border claims	Local claims	Revalu-ation gains	Country	Total claims	Adjusted cross-border claims	Local claims	Revalu-ation gains
Total [1]	836,633	408,856	329,977	97,800	Italy.	41,328	31,946	4,328	5,054
					Japan	75,390	26,261	37,563	11,566
Argentina	23,817	9,118	14,159	540	Korea, South	18,141	6,588	10,654	899
Australia.	24,616	5,880	14,324	4,412	Mexico.	25,710	13,958	10,065	1,687
Belgium	14,475	10,574	2,586	1,315	Netherlands	28,045	22,460	607	4,978
Brazil.	31,585	14,389	16,107	1,089	Singapore	14,599	2,904	11,126	569
Canada	54,721	16,840	33,722	4,159	Spain	16,486	8,366	5,251	2,869
France.	35,131	23,619	4,173	7,339	Sweden	8,485	5,867	466	2,152
Germany	100,237	70,891	17,086	12,260	Switzerland.	15,645	10,519	1,451	3,675
Greece	9,209	4,864	4,103	242	Taiwan [2].	11,834	2,110	9,479	245
Hong Kong.	23,734	4,095	19,062	577	United Kingdom.	116,703	43,447	59,544	13,712

[1] Includes other countries not shown separately. [2] See footnote 2, Table 1327.
Source: Federal Financial Institutions Examination Council, "Statistical Release E.16, Country Exposure Lending Survey," quarterly, <http://www.ffiec.gov/E16.htm>.

No. 1181. Insured Commercial Banks by State and Other Area: 2000

[In billions of dollars, except number of banks (6,238.7 represents $6,238,700,000,000). As of December 31. Includes foreign branches of U.S. banks]

State	Number	Assets	Deposits	State	Number	Assets	Deposits
Total	8,315	6,238.7	4,176.6	Nevada.	32	37.9	13.3
United States.	8,297	6,185.4	4,146.0	New Hampshire	16	22.4	16.4
Alabama	158	181.5	129.9	New Jersey	81	100.8	80.0
Alaska	6	6.2	4.1	New Mexico.	54	15.4	11.3
Arizona.	45	61.8	30.7	New York	148	1,304.3	790.7
Arkansas.	185	25.7	21.5	North Carolina	75	980.7	645.4
California.	304	320.0	238.5	North Dakota	110	17.6	13.3
Colorado.	181	46.6	37.3	Ohio.	211	361.9	229.8
Connecticut	23	3.4	2.8	Oklahoma	286	43.2	33.4
Delaware.	32	151.6	77.8	Oregon	43	17.3	6.5
District of Columbia.	6	0.8	0.4	Pennsylvania	187	189.6	138.7
Florida	265	58.9	47.7	Rhode Island	7	182.1	114.5
Georgia	337	168.1	109.3	South Carolina	79	23.6	18.4
Hawaii	8	24.4	17.5	South Dakota	97	37.2	13.5
Idaho	18	2.5	2.1	Tennessee.	197	86.9	61.9
Illinois.	711	355.5	249.4	Texas	710	166.4	133.2
Indiana	153	84.6	54.6	Utah.	56	102.9	69.7
Iowa.	431	44.6	34.3	Vermont	18	7.6	6.3
Kansas.	376	37.9	31.0	Virginia	143	59.6	42.9
Kentucky	233	52.5	39.5	Washington	79	14.9	12.3
Louisiana	149	51.7	41.9	West Virginia	70	17.5	13.8
Maine.	15	7.7	5.4	Wisconsin	315	78.8	58.8
Maryland	74	46.9	35.6	Wyoming	46	7.5	5.7
Massachusetts	44	111.4	72.6				
Michigan	168	138.5	97.7	American Samoa.	1	0.1	0.1
Minnesota	492	187.1	122.6	Puerto Rico	12	52.2	29.7
Mississippi	101	34.0	26.4	Guam	2	0.8	0.7
Missouri	362	64.5	52.4	Federated States of			
Montana	84	10.9	8.8	Micronesia	1	(Z)	(Z)
Nebraska	276	30.1	23.7	Virgin Islands	2	0.1	0.1

Z Less than $50 million.
Source: U.S. Federal Deposit Insurance Corporation, Statistics on Banking, annual.

No. 1182. Retail Fees and Services of Banks: 1998 and 1999

[In dollars, except as noted. As of June. For most services, fees are reported in terms of (1) the proportion of those banks offering a service that charge for the service and (2) the average fee charged by the institutions that charge for the service. Based on a random sample of depository institutions belonging to the Bank Insurance Fund, whose members are predominantly commercial banks]

Type of account or service	1998	1999	Type of account or service	1998	1999
NONINTEREST CHECKING ACCOUNT			AUTOMATED TELLER MACHINES (ATMs)		
			Percent offering.	86.5	87.3
Percent offering.	98.5	97.4	Annual fee:		
Single-balance, single-fee account: [1]			Percent charging	15.1	17.4
Percent offering	35.6	40.6	Average	13.11	7.90
Monthly fee (low balance)	6.43	6.15	Fees for customer transactions on us: [4]		
Minimum balance to avoid fee	499	516	Withdrawals:		
Minimum balance to open	115	104	Percent charging.	6.4	6.4
Fee-only account: [2]			Average	0.68	0.54
Percent offering	36.3	38.9	Balance inquiries:		
Monthly fee.	4.73	5.17	Percent charging.	5.7	3.3
Check charge:			Average	0.67	0.70
Percent charging.	45.0	38.0	Fees for customer transactions on others: [4]		
Average	0.40	0.40	Withdrawals:		
Minimum balance to open	76	65	Percent charging.	74.4	72.3
			Average	1.10	1.17
NOW ACCOUNTS [3]			Balance inquiries:		
			Percent charging.	63.2	41.9
Percent offering.	94.3	95.7	Average	1.06	1.12
Single-fee account: [1]			Surcharge: [5]		
Percent offering	50.8	54.2	Percent charging	77.9	82.9
Monthly fee (low balance)	8.07	8.39	Average	1.20	1.26
Minimum balance to avoid fee	1,109	1,060			
Minimum balance to open	616	641			

[1] A monthly fee for balances below the minimum, no monthly fee for balances above the minimum, and no other charges. [2] A monthly fee, no minimum balance to eliminate the fee, and a charge per check in some cases. [3] NOW (negotiable order of withdrawal) accounts are checking accounts that pay interest and often have fee structures that differ from those of noninterest checking accounts. [4] An institution's "customer" is one who has an account at the institution. A customer's ATM transactions in which the machine used is that of the customer's institution are called "on us"; a customer's transactions in which the machine used is that of another institution are called "on others." [5] An ATM surcharge is a fee imposed by the ATM's institution, typically on every transaction by the machine's noncustomer users.
Source: Board of Governors of the Federal Reserve System, *Annual Report to the Congress on Retail Fees and Services of Depository Institutions*, July 2000.

No. 1183. Insured Savings Institutions—Financial Summary: 1985 to 2000

[In billions of dollars, except number of institutions (1,263 represents $1,263,000,000,000). As of December 31. Includes Puerto Rico, Guam, and Virgin Islands. Covers SAIF (Savings Association Insurance Fund) and BIF (Bank Insurance Fund)-insured savings institutions. Excludes institutions in Resolution Trust Corporation conservatorship and, beginning 1993, excludes one self-liquidating institution. Minus sign (-) indicates loss]

Item	1985	1990	1993	1994	1995	1996	1997	1998	1999	2000
Number of institutions	3,626	2,815	2,262	2,152	2,030	1,925	1,780	1,689	1,641	1,590
Assets, total	1,263	1,259	1,001	1,009	1,026	1,028	1,026	1,088	1,149	1,223
Loans and leases, net	821	812	626	635	648	681	692	714	755	824
Liabilities, total.	1,218	1,192	922	929	940	942	937	994	1,054	1,119
Deposits	1,023	987	774	737	742	728	704	705	707	738
Equity capital.	45	68	78	80	86	86	89	95	95	104
Interest and fee income.	119	117	66	63	71	72	69	71	74	84
Interest expense	101	91	35	33	43	42	41	42	43	52
Net interest income.	17	26	32	30	28	30	29	29	31	32
Net income	6	-5	7	6	8	7	9	10	11	11

Source: U.S. Federal Deposit Insurance Corporation, *Statistics on Banking*, annual and *FDIC Quarterly Banking Profile*.

No. 1184. Federal and State-Chartered Credit Unions—Summary: 1980 to 2000

[24,519 represents 24,519,000). As of December 31, except as noted. Federal data include District of Columbia, Puerto Rico, Guam, and Virgin Islands. Excludes state-insured, privately-insured, and noninsured state-chartered credit unions and corporate central credit unions which have mainly other credit unions as members]

Year	Operating credit unions		Number of failed institu- tions [1]	Members (1,000)		Assets (mil. dol.)		Loans outstanding (mil. dol.)		Savings (mil. dol.)	
	Federal	State		Federal	State	Federal	State	Federal	State	Federal	State
1980 . . .	12,440	4,910	239	24,519	12,338	40,092	20,870	26,350	14,582	36,263	18,469
1990 . . .	8,511	4,349	164	36,241	19,454	130,073	68,133	83,029	44,102	117,892	62,082
1995 . . .	7,329	4,358	26	42,163	24,927	193,781	112,860	120,514	71,606	170,300	99,838
1999 . . .	6,566	4,062	23	44,076	31,308	239,316	172,086	155,578	116,366	207,614	149,305
2000 . . .	6,336	3,980	29	43,883	33,705	242,881	195,363	163,851	137,485	210,188	169,053

[1] Through 1990 for year ending September 30; 1995 reflects 15-month period from October 1994 through December 1995; beginning 1999 reflects calendar year. A failed institution is defined as a credit union which has ceased operation because it was involuntarily liquidated or merged with assistance from the National Credit Union Share Insurance Fund. Assisted mergers were not identified until 1981.
Source: National Credit Union Administration, *Annual Report of the National Credit Union Administration*, and unpublished data.

732 Banking, Finance, and Insurance

No. 1185. Characteristics of Conventional First Mortgage Loans for Purchase of Single-Family Homes: 1990 to 2000

[In percent, except as indicated (154.1 represents $154,100). Annual averages. Covers fully amortized conventional mortgage loans used to purchase single-family nonfarm homes. Excludes refinancing loans, nonamortized and balloon loans, loans insured by the Federal Housing Administration, and loans guaranteed by the Veterans Administration. Based on a sample of mortgage lenders, including savings and loans associations, savings banks, commercial banks, and mortgage companies]

Loan characteristics	New homes						Previously occupied homes					
	1990	1995	1997	1998	1999	2000	1990	1995	1997	1998	1999	2000
Contract interest rate,[1]												
all loans	9.7	7.7	7.6	6.9	6.9	7.4	9.8	7.7	7.5	7.0	7.2	7.9
Fixed-rate loans	10.1	8.0	7.7	7.1	7.3	8.0	10.1	8.0	7.7	7.1	7.3	8.2
Adjustable-rate loans[2]	8.9	7.2	6.9	6.4	6.3	6.5	8.9	7.0	6.7	6.3	6.5	7.2
Initial fees, charges[3]	1.98	1.20	1.01	0.88	0.76	0.69	1.74	0.93	0.97	0.84	0.73	0.66
Effective interest rate,[4]												
all loans	10.1	7.9	7.7	7.1	7.0	7.5	10.1	7.8	7.7	7.1	7.3	8.1
Fixed-rate loans	10.4	8.2	7.9	7.2	7.4	8.2	10.4	8.2	7.9	7.2	7.4	8.3
Adjustable-rate loans[2]	9.2	7.4	7.0	6.5	6.3	6.5	9.2	7.1	6.9	6.5	6.6	7.2
Term to maturity (years)	27.3	27.7	28.2	28.4	28.8	29.2	27.0	27.4	27.3	27.7	28.1	28.6
Purchase price ($1,000)	154.1	175.4	181.4	195.0	210.7	234.9	140.3	137.3	161.0	169.5	179.3	191.8
Loan to price ratio	74.9	78.6	80.4	80.1	78.8	77.4	74.9	80.1	79.2	78.7	78.4	77.9
Percent of number of loans with adjustable rates	31	37	21	17	35	40	27	31	22	12	18	21

[1] Initial interest rate paid by the borrower as specified in the loan contract.   [2] Loans with a contractual provision for periodic adjustments in the contract interest rate.   [3] Includes all fees, commissions, discounts and "points" paid by the borrower, or seller, in order to obtain the loan. Excludes those charges for mortgage, credit, life or property insurance; for property transfer; and for title search and insurance.   [4] Contract interest rate plus fees and charges amortized over a 10-year period.

Source: U.S. Federal Housing Finance Board, *Rates & Terms on Conventional Home Mortgages, Annual Summary.*

No. 1186. Mortgage Debt Outstanding by Type of Property and Holder: 1980 to 2000

[In billions of dollars (1,465 represents $1,465,000,000,000). As of Dec. 31. Includes Puerto Rico and Guam]

Type of property and holder	1980	1985	1990	1993	1994	1995	1996	1997	1998	1999	2000
Mortgage debt, total	1,465	2,378	3,808	4,210	4,380	4,581	4,865	5,198	5,698	6,326	6,890
Residential nonfarm	1,110	1,738	2,932	3,412	3,593	3,781	4,004	4,271	4,680	5,147	5,602
One- to four-family homes	969	1,533	2,647	3,146	3,328	3,508	3,716	3,968	4,349	4,774	5,193
Savings institutions	487	554	600	470	478	482	514	521	534	549	595
Mortgage pools or trusts[1]	125	407	1,046	1,519	1,656	1,767	1,935	2,099	2,374	2,690	2,926
Government National Mortgage Association	92	207	392	405	441	461	494	523	522	565	593
Federal Home Loan Mortgage Corp	13	100	308	443	488	512	552	577	643	745	817
Federal National Mortgage Assoc	(X)	54	291	487	521	570	633	688	804	925	1,016
Private mortgage conduits[2]	4	24	55	184	206	224	256	311	405	455	500
Commercial banks	160	211	430	532	590	647	678	746	798	880	967
Individuals and others[3]	117	239	403	387	368	373	363	382	416	441	478
Federal and related agencies	61	110	153	230	228	229	220	213	217	206	222
Federal National Mortgage Assoc	52	92	94	151	159	164	155	150	148	141	144
Life insurance companies	18	12	13	9	9	9	7	7	7	6	5
Five or more units	141	205	286	266	265	273	288	303	331	373	409
Nonfarm, nonresidential	258	534	797	717	705	716	774	837	923	1,077	1,179
Farm	97	106	79	81	83	85	87	90	97	103	109
TYPE OF HOLDER											
Savings institutions	603	760	802	598	596	597	628	632	644	669	724
Commercial banks	264	431	849	948	1,013	1,090	1,145	1,245	1,338	1,497	1,662
Life insurance companies	131	172	268	224	216	213	208	207	214	231	236
Individuals and others[3]	206	408	562	534	515	524	550	595	627	660	694
Mortgage pools or trusts[1]	146	440	1,088	1,580	1,725	1,848	2,038	2,233	2,582	2,948	3,231
Government National Mortgage Assoc	94	212	404	451	472	506	537	537	582	612	
Federal Home Loan Mortgage Corp	17	100	316	447	491	515	554	579	646	749	822
Federal National Mortgage Association	(X)	55	300	496	530	583	651	710	835	961	1,058
Farmers Home Administration[4]	32	48	(Z)	(Z)	(Z)	(Z)	(Z)	(Z)	(Z)	-	-
Private mortgage conduits	4	25	68	224	253	278	326	407	564	656	740
Federal and related agencies	115	167	239	326	316	308	295	286	294	322	344
Federal National Mortgage Association	57	98	105	166	174	179	169	161	158	152	155
Farmers Home Administration[4]	3	1	41	41	42	42	42	41	41	74	73
Federal Land Banks	38	47	29	28	29	28	30	31	33	34	36
Federal Home Loan Mortgage Corp	5	14	22	47	42	44	47	48	57	57	75
Federal Housing and Veterans Admin	6	5	9	12	11	10	6	4	4	4	4
Government National Mortgage Assoc	5	1	(Z)	(Z)	(Z)	(Z)	(Z)	(Z)	(Z)	(Z)	(Z)
Federal Deposit Insurance Corp	(X)	(X)	(X)	14	8	4	2	1	(Z)	(Z)	(Z)
Resolution Trust Corporation	(X)	(X)	33	17	10	2	(X)	(X)	(X)	(X)	(X)

- Represents zero.   X Not applicable.   Z Less than $500 million.   [1] Outstanding principal balances of mortgage pools backing securities insured or guaranteed by the agency indicated. Includes other pools not shown separately.   [2] Includes securitized home equity loans.   [3] Includes mortgage companies, real estate investment trusts, state and local retirement funds, noninsured pension funds, state and local credit agencies, credit unions, and finance companies.   [4] FmHA-guaranteed securities sold to the Federal Financing Bank were reallocated from FmHA mortgage pools to FmHA mortgage holdings in 1986 because of accounting changes by the Farmers Home Administration.

Source: Board of Governors of the Federal Reserve System, *Federal Reserve Bulletin,* monthly.

Banking, Finance, and Insurance   733

No. 1187. Mortgage Delinquency and Foreclosure Rates: 1980 to 2000

[In percent. Covers one- to four-family residential nonfarm mortgage loans]

Item	1980	1985	1990	1995	1996	1997	1998	1999	2000
Delinquency rates: [1]									
Total	5.0	5.8	4.7	4.3	4.3	4.3	4.4	4.1	4.0
Conventional loans	3.1	4.0	3.0	2.8	2.8	2.8	2.9	2.6	2.5
VA loans	5.3	6.6	6.4	6.4	6.7	6.9	7.1	6.8	6.8
FHA loans	6.6	7.5	6.7	7.6	8.1	8.1	8.5	8.6	9.1
Foreclosure rates: [2]									
Total	0.5	1.0	0.9	0.9	1.0	1.1	1.1	1.0	0.9
Conventional loans	0.2	0.7	0.7	0.7	0.7	0.7	0.7	0.6	0.6
VA loans	0.6	1.1	1.2	1.3	1.6	1.8	1.8	1.7	1.2
FHA loans	0.7	1.3	1.3	1.4	1.6	2.0	2.2	2.0	1.7

[1] Number of loans delinquent 30 days or more as percentage of mortgage loans serviced in survey. Annual average of quarterly figures. [2] Percentage of loans in the foreclosure process at yearend, not seasonally adjusted.

Source: Mortgage Bankers Association of America, Washington, DC, *National Delinquency Survey*, quarterly.

No. 1188. Consumer Payment Systems by Method of Payment: 1990 and 1999, and Projections, 2005

[105.5 represents 105,500,000,000]

Method of payment	Transactions				Volume				
	Number (bil.)		Percent distribution		Amount (bil. dol.)			Percent distribution	
	1999	2005, proj.	1999	2005, proj.	1990	1999	2005, proj.	1990	1999	2005, proj.
Total	105.5	135.0	100.0	100.0	2,972	4,863	6,771	100.0	100.0	100.0
Paper	77.8	84.1	73.8	62.3	2,511	3,342	3,380	84.6	68.7	49.9
Checks [1]	29.4	23.8	27.9	17.6	1,821	2,246	1,915	61.3	46.2	28.3
Cash	46.6	58.6	44.2	43.4	582	946	1,289	19.6	19.4	19.0
Money orders	1.2	1.4	1.1	1.1	61	111	136	2.1	2.3	2.0
Travelers cheques	0.2	0.2	0.2	0.1	22	14	12	0.7	0.3	0.2
Official checks [2]	0.1	0.1	0.1	0.1	11	21	27	0.4	0.4	0.4
Food stamps	0.2	-	0.2	-	14	6	-	0.5	0.1	-
Cards [3]	26.1	44.5	24.7	33.0	441	1,355	2,668	14.8	27.9	39.4
Credit cards [3]	18.4	23.2	17.4	17.2	432	1,095	1,864	14.5	22.5	27.5
Debit cards [4]	6.4	18.4	6.1	13.6	9	230	723	0.3	4.7	10.7
Stored value cards [5]	0.9	2.1	0.9	1.5	-	21	57	-	0.4	0.8
EBT cards [6]	0.4	0.8	0.4	0.6	-	9	24	-	0.2	0.4
Electronic	1.6	6.3	1.5	4.7	20	166	723	0.7	3.4	10.7
Preauthorized payments [7]	1.2	3.3	1.2	2.4	18	133	384	0.6	2.7	5.7
Remote payments [8]	0.4	3.0	0.3	2.2	2	33	340	0.1	0.7	5.0

- Represents zero. [1] Excludes repayments and prepayments involving other payment systems. [2] Official checks include cashier's checks, teller checks, and certified checks purchased from financial institutions. Excludes those purchased by businesses. [3] Credit cards include general purpose cards usable at all kinds of merchants and proprietary cards usable only at selected outlets. Includes purchases on commercial cards and business-related spending on personal cards. Cash advances are excluded. [4] Debit cards include general purpose cards carrying the Visa or MasterCard brand, electronic funds transfer (EFT) brands of regional EFT systems, proprietary commercial cards issued by private firms to drivers in the long-haul trucking and business aviation industry, and proprietary consumer cards issued by supermarkets and gasoline marketers. Cash withdrawals at ATMs and cash back over the counter are excluded. [5] Stored value cards are used primarily for gift certificates and telephone calls. [6] Electronic benefits transfer cards are replacements for paper scrip food stamps. [7] Preauthorized payments are handled electronically through an automated clearing house. Mortgages are excluded. [8] Remote payments are made using a telephone, computer service, or the internet. Also included are point-of-service check conversions and utility-bill payments made by clerk-assisted electronic banking machines at supermarkets, ATMs, and self-service kiosks.

Source: HSN Consultants Inc., Oxnard, CA, *The Nilson Report*, twice-monthly. (Copyright used by permission.)

No. 1189. Debit Cards—Number, Transactions, and Volume, 1990 to 1999, and Projections, 2005

[164 represents 164,000,000]

Type of debit card	Number of cards (mil.)				Number of transactions (mil.)				Volume (bil. dol.)			
	1990	1995	1999	2005, proj.	1990	1995	1999	2005, proj.	1990	1995	1999	2005, proj.
Total [1]	164	201	228	270	274	1,558	7,517	20,432	12	61	322	936
Bank [2]	9	40	117	184	127	829	5,147	13,667	8	36	234	689
EFT systems [3]	160	190	217	259	129	672	2,312	6,698	3	23	85	242
Other [4]	4	11	11	12	17	57	59	67	1	2	3	4

[1] Bank cards and EFT cards are the same pieces of plastic that carry multiple brands. The total card figure shown does not include any duplication. [2] Visa Check Card and MasterCard MasterMoney. [3] Cards issued by financial institution members of regional and national switches. EFT=Electronic funds transfer. [4] Commercial fuel cards issued by private-label firms plus retail cards such as those issued by supermarkets and oil companies.

Source: HSN Consultants Inc., Oxnard, CA, *The Nilson Report*, twice-monthly. (Copyright used by permission.)

No. 1190. Consumer Credit Outstanding and Finance Rates: 1980 to 2000

[In billions of dollars, except percent (349.4 represents $349,400,000,000). Covers most short- and intermediate-term credit extended to individuals, excluding loans secured by real estate. Estimated amounts of seasonally adjusted credit outstanding as of end of year; finance rates, annual averages]

Type of credit	1980	1985	1990	1994	1995	1996	1997	1998	1999	2000
Total..................	349.4	593.2	789.3	960.7	1,096.0	1,182.4	1,234.5	1,301.0	1,393.7	1,531.5
Revolving	55.1	124.7	238.6	365.6	443.2	499.4	531.2	560.5	595.6	663.8
Nonrevolving [1]	294.3	468.5	550.7	595.1	652.8	683.1	703.3	740.5	798.0	867.6
FINANCE RATES (percent)										
Commercial banks:										
New automobiles (48 months) [2] ...	14.32	12.91	11.78	8.12	9.57	9.05	9.02	8.72	8.44	9.34
Other consumer goods (24 months) ...	15.48	15.94	15.46	13.19	13.94	13.54	13.90	13.74	13.39	13.90
Credit-card plans............	17.31	18.69	18.17	16.04	15.90	15.63	15.77	15.71	15.21	15.71
Finance companies:										
New automobiles............	14.82	11.98	12.54	9.79	11.19	9.83	7.12	6.30	6.66	6.61
Used automobiles	19.10	17.58	15.99	13.49	14.48	13.53	13.27	12.64	12.60	13.55

[1] Comprises automobile loans and all other loans not included in revolving credit, such as loans for mobile homes, education, boats, trailers, or vacations. These loans may be secured or unsecured. [2] For 1980, maturities were 36 months for new car loans.

Source: Board of Governors of the Federal Reserve System, *Federal Reserve Bulletin*, monthly.

No. 1191. Credit Cards—Holders, Number, Spending, and Debt, 1990 and 1999, and Projections, 2005

[122 represents 122,000,000]

Type of credit card	Cardholders (mil.)			Number of cards (mil.)			Credit card spending (bil. dol.)			Credit card debt outstanding (bil. dol.)		
	1990	1999	2005, proj.	1990	1999	2005, proj.	1990	1999	2005, proj.	1990	1999	2005, proj.
Total [1]...............	122	156	166	1,012	1,395	1,565	466	1,291	2,158	243	614	860
Bank [2]	79	104	120	213	419	502	243	839	1,457	154	430	615
Oil company.............	85	78	77	123	114	112	27	43	70	3	4	7
Phone..................	97	122	132	141	179	190	14	20	24	2	3	3
Store	96	112	120	459	595	657	75	114	121	51	92	99
Travel and entertainment [3] ...	16	23	27	28	32	39	85	198	344	20	45	71
Other [4]	10	7	7	49	57	66	23	78	142	13	40	65

[1] Cardholders may hold more than one type of card. [2] Visa and MasterCard credit cards. Excludes debit cards. [3] Includes American Express and Diners Club. [4] Includes UATP, JCB, automobile rental, other airline including business aviation, hotel, restaurant, and club cards, Discover (except for cardholders), and miscellaneous cards.

Source: HSN Consultants Inc., Oxnard, CA, *The Nilson Report*, twice-monthly. (Copyright used by permission.)

No. 1192. Usage of General Purpose Credit Cards by Families: 1989 to 1998

[General purpose credit cards include MasterCard, Visa, Optima, and Discover cards. Excludes cards used only for business purposes. All dollar figures are given in constant 1998 dollars based on consumer price index data as published by U.S. Bureau of Labor Statistics. Families include one-person units; for definition of family, see text, Section 1, Population. Based on Survey of Consumer Finance; see Appendix III. For definition of median, see Guide to Tabular Presentation]

Age of family head and family income	Percent having a general purpose credit card	Median number of cards	Median new charges on last month's bills	Percent having a balance after last month's bills	Median balance [1]	Percent of cardholding families who—		
						Almost always pay off the balance	Some-times pay off the balance	Hardly ever pay off the balance
1989, total	56.0	2	$100	52.1	$1,300	52.9	21.2	25.8
1992, total	62.4	2	100	52.6	1,100	53.0	19.6	27.4
1995, total	66.4	2	200	56.0	1,600	52.4	20.1	27.5
1998, total	**67.5**	**2**	**200**	**54.7**	**1,900**	**53.8**	**19.3**	**26.9**
Under 35 years old	58.3	2	200	71.6	1,500	39.0	22.5	38.5
35 to 44 years old.......	71.3	2	200	62.5	2,000	46.5	19.1	34.4
45 to 54 years old.......	75.3	2	200	59.2	2,000	48.2	22.7	29.1
55 to 64 years old.......	76.0	2	200	48.8	2,300	61.0	20.1	18.9
65 to 74 years old.......	71.2	2	200	33.9	1,000	74.0	14.9	11.1
75 years old and over	50.8	1	100	16.7	700	86.3	7.8	5.9
Less than $10,000.......	23.2	2	100	64.0	900	46.4	19.9	33.8
$10,000 to $24,999	50.8	2	100	56.9	1,200	52.3	19.3	28.4
$25,000 to $49,999	73.2	2	100	58.2	1,700	48.3	20.5	31.2
$50,000 to $99,999	89.6	2	200	55.9	2,400	53.9	20.2	25.9
$100,000 and more	97.9	2	800	36.4	3,100	72.0	13.8	14.1

[1] Among families having a balance.

Source: Board of Governors of the Federal Reserve System, unpublished data.

Banking, Finance, and Insurance 735

No. 1193. Money Stock: 1980 to 2000

[In billions of dollars (408 represents $408,000,000,000). As of December. Seasonally adjusted averages of daily figures]

Item	1980	1983	1984	1985	1986	1987	1988	1989	1990	1991	1992	1993	1994	1995	1996	1997	1998	1999	2000
M1, total	408	521	551	619	724	749	786	792	824	896	1,024	1,129	1,150	1,126	1,080	1,073	1,097	1,124	1,090
Currency [1],[2]	115	146	156	168	180	197	212	222	247	267	292	322	354	372	394	424	459	517	530
Travelers checks [2]	3	4	4	5	5	6	6	6	7	7	7	7	8	8	8	8	8	8	8
Demand deposits [3]	261	238	243	267	303	287	287	279	277	289	340	385	384	389	402	395	379	356	313
Other checkable deposits [4]	28	132	147	180	236	260	281	285	294	332	384	415	404	357	276	246	250	244	239
M2, total	1,600	2,128	2,312	2,495	2,732	2,831	2,994	3,158	3,277	3,377	3,431	3,484	3,499	3,642	3,814	4,030	4,383	4,650	4,947
M1	408	521	551	619	724	749	786	792	824	896	1,024	1,129	1,150	1,126	1,080	1,073	1,097	1,124	1,090
Non-M1 components in M2	1,192	1,607	1,760	1,876	2,008	2,082	2,208	2,366	2,453	2,481	2,407	2,355	2,349	2,515	2,734	2,957	3,286	3,526	3,857
Money market funds, retail	64	138	167	175	209	223	245	321	357	371	352	354	383	450	516	591	734	833	939
Savings deposits (including MMDAs [5])	400	685	705	815	941	937	926	894	923	1,044	1,187	1,219	1,150	1,134	1,271	1,398	1,600	1,736	1,872
Commercial banks	186	363	389	457	534	535	542	541	581	664	754	785	753	775	904	1,021	1,186	1,287	1,420
Thrift institutions	215	322	315	359	407	403	384	353	342	379	433	434	397	359	367	377	414	449	452
Small time deposits [6]	729	784	889	886	858	921	1,037	1,151	1,173	1,066	868	782	816	931	947	968	952	956	1,046
Commercial banks	286	351	388	386	369	392	451	534	611	602	508	468	503	575	593	626	626	635	700
Thrift institutions	442	433	501	499	489	529	586	618	563	463	360	314	314	357	354	343	326	321	346
M3, total	1,996	2,699	2,993	3,207	3,498	3,685	3,927	4,075	4,150	4,202	4,213	4,275	4,357	4,623	4,968	5,428	6,027	6,527	7,093
M2	1,600	2,128	2,312	2,495	2,732	2,831	2,994	3,158	3,277	3,377	3,431	3,484	3,499	3,642	3,814	4,030	4,383	4,650	4,947
Non-M2 components in M3	396	571	681	712	766	854	933	917	873	826	782	791	859	981	1,154	1,397	1,644	1,877	2,145
Large time deposits [8]	260	316	403	422	419	462	513	528	480	415	350	332	371	430	512	603	664	740	827
Commercial banks	215	220	256	270	269	299	338	367	359	332	283	271	306	355	434	518	575	649	724
Thrift institutions	45	97	147	152	150	163	175	161	121	83	67	62	65	74	78	86	89	91	103
Repurchase agreements [9]	58	97	107	121	146	178	197	169	151	131	142	173	196	198	210	254	298	341	360
Eurodollars [9]	61	117	109	104	116	121	132	109	103	92	80	73	86	94	114	150	152	173	191
Money market funds, institution only	16	41	62	64	85	92	92	110	138	187	211	213	205	259	318	390	530	622	767

[1] Currency outside U.S. Treasury, Federal Reserve Banks and the vaults of depository institutions. [2] Outstanding amount of nonbank issuers. [3] At commercial banks and foreign-related institutions. [4] Consists of negotiable order of withdrawal (NOW) and automatic transfer service (ATS) accounts at all depository institutions, credit union share draft balances, and demand deposits at thrift institutions. [5] Money market deposit accounts (MMDA). [6] Issued in amounts of less than $100,000. Includes retail repurchase agreements. Excludes individual retirement accounts (IRAs) and Keogh accounts. [7] Issued in amounts of $100,000 or more. Excludes those booked at international banking facilities. [8] Excludes those held by money market mutual funds, depository institutions, U.S. government, foreign banks and official institutions. [9] Excludes those held by depository institutions and money market mutual funds.

Source: Board of Governors of the Federal Reserve System, Federal Reserve Bulletin, monthly, and Money Stock, Liquid Assets, and Debt Measures, Federal Reserve Statistical Release H.6, weekly.

No. 1194. Money Market Interest Rates and Mortgage Rates: 1980 to 2000

[Percent per year. Annual averages of monthly data, except as indicated]

Type	1980	1985	1989	1990	1991	1992	1993	1994	1995	1996	1997	1998	1999	2000
Federal funds, effective rate	13.35	8.10	9.21	8.10	5.69	3.52	3.02	4.21	5.83	5.30	5.46	5.35	4.97	6.24
Prime rate charged by banks	15.26	9.93	10.87	10.01	8.46	6.25	6.00	7.15	8.83	8.27	8.44	8.35	8.00	9.23
Eurodollar deposits, 3-month	14.00	8.27	9.16	8.16	5.86	3.70	3.18	4.63	5.93	5.38	5.61	5.45	5.31	6.45
Bankers acceptances, 3-month [1]	12.67	7.91	8.87	7.93	5.70	3.62	3.13	4.56	5.81	5.31	5.54	5.39	5.24	(NA)
Bankers acceptances, 6-month [1]	12.20	7.95	8.67	7.80	5.67	3.67	3.21	4.83	5.80	5.31	5.57	5.30	5.30	(NA)
Large negotiable CDs:														
3-month, secondary market	13.07	8.05	9.09	8.15	5.83	3.68	3.17	4.63	5.92	5.39	5.62	5.47	5.19	6.35
6-month, secondary market	12.94	8.24	9.08	8.17	5.91	3.76	3.28	4.96	5.98	5.47	5.73	5.44	5.33	6.46
Taxable money market funds [2]	12.68	7.71	8.87	7.82	5.71	3.36	2.70	3.75	5.48	4.95	5.10	5.04	4.64	5.89
Tax-exempt money market funds [2]	(NA)	4.90	5.90	5.45	4.13	2.58	1.97	2.38	3.39	2.99	3.14	2.94	2.72	3.54
Certificates of deposit (CDs): [3]														
6-month	(NA)	8.05	8.55	7.79	5.80	3.51	2.88	3.42	4.92	4.68	4.86	4.58	4.27	5.09
1-year	(NA)	8.53	8.65	7.92	6.03	3.78	3.16	4.01	5.39	4.95	5.15	4.81	4.56	5.46
2½-year	(NA)	9.32	8.58	7.96	6.46	4.56	3.80	4.58	5.69	5.14	5.40	4.93	4.74	5.64
5-year	(NA)	9.99	8.56	8.06	7.02	5.76	4.98	5.42	6.00	6.46	5.66	5.08	4.93	5.97
U.S. Government securities:														
Secondary market: [4]														
3-month Treasury bill	11.39	7.47	8.11	7.50	5.38	3.43	3.00	4.25	5.49	5.01	5.06	4.78	4.64	5.82
6-month Treasury bill	11.32	7.65	8.03	7.46	5.44	3.54	3.12	4.64	5.56	5.08	5.18	4.83	4.75	5.90
1-year Treasury bill	10.85	7.81	7.92	7.35	5.52	3.71	3.29	5.02	5.60	5.22	5.36	4.80	4.81	5.78
Auction average: [5]														
3-month Treasury bill	11.51	7.47	8.12	7.51	5.42	3.45	3.02	4.29	5.51	5.02	5.07	4.81	4.66	(NA)
6-month Treasury bill	11.37	7.64	8.04	7.47	5.49	3.57	3.14	4.66	5.59	5.09	5.18	4.85	4.76	(NA)
1-year Treasury bill	10.75	7.76	7.91	7.36	5.54	3.75	3.33	4.98	5.69	5.23	5.36	4.85	4.78	(NA)
Home mortgages:														
HUD series: [6]														
FHA insured, secondary market [7]	13.44	12.24	10.24	10.17	9.25	8.46	7.46	8.68	8.18	8.19	7.89	7.04	7.74	(NA)
Conventional, new-home [8][9]	13.95	12.28	10.21	10.08	9.20	8.43	7.37	8.58	8.05	8.03	7.76	7.00	7.45	(NA)
Conventional, existing-home [8]	13.95	12.29	10.22	10.08	9.20	8.43	7.37	8.59	8.05	8.03	7.76	7.01	7.47	(NA)
Conventional, 15 yr. fixed [3]	(NA)	11.48	10.03	9.73	8.76	7.80	6.65	7.77	7.39	7.28	7.16	6.58	7.09	7.76
Conventional, 30 yr. fixed [3]	(NA)	11.85	10.25	9.97	9.09	8.27	7.17	8.28	7.86	7.76	7.57	6.92	7.46	8.08

NA Not available. [1] Yields are quoted on a bank-discount basis, rather than an investment yield basis (which would give a higher figure). Based on representative closing yields. From Jan. 1, 1981, rates of top-rated banks only. Series ended June 30, 2000. [2] 12 month return for period ending December 31. Source: iMoneyNet, Inc., Westborough, MA, Money Market Insight, monthly, <http://www.imoneynet.com> (copyright). [3] Annual averages. Source: Bankrate, Inc. North Palm Beach, FL, Bank Rate Monitor, weekly (copyright). [4] Averages based on daily closing bid yields in secondary market, bank discount basis. [5] Averages computed on an issue-date basis; bank discount basis. Data for 1999 are auction high. Series ended June 30, 2000. [6] HUD—Housing and Urban Development. Beginning 2000 series have been discontinued. [7] Averages based on quotations for 1 day each month as compiled by FHA. [8] Primary market. [9] Average contract rates on new commitments.

Source: Except as noted, Board of Governors of the Federal Reserve System, Federal Reserve Bulletin, monthly.

No. 1195. Bond Yields: 1980 to 2000

[Percent per year. Annual averages of daily figures, except as indicated]

Type	1980	1985	1990	1993	1994	1995	1996	1997	1998	1999	2000
U.S. Treasury, constant maturities: [1][2]											
1-year	12.00	8.42	7.89	3.43	5.32	5.94	5.52	5.63	5.05	5.08	6.11
2-year	11.73	9.27	8.16	4.05	5.94	6.15	5.84	5.99	5.13	5.43	6.26
3-year	11.51	9.64	8.26	4.44	6.27	6.25	5.99	6.10	5.14	5.49	6.22
5-year	11.45	10.12	8.37	5.14	6.69	6.38	6.18	6.22	5.15	5.55	6.16
7-year	11.40	10.50	8.52	5.54	6.91	6.50	6.34	6.33	5.28	5.79	6.20
10-year	11.43	10.62	8.55	5.87	7.09	6.57	6.44	6.35	5.26	5.65	6.03
20-year	(NA)	(NA)	(NA)	6.29	7.47	6.95	6.83	6.69	5.72	6.20	6.23
30-year	11.27	10.79	8.61	6.59	7.37	6.88	6.71	6.61	5.58	5.87	5.94
U.S. Govt., long-term bonds [2][3]	10.81	10.75	8.74	6.45	7.41	6.93	6.80	6.67	5.69	6.14	6.41
State and local govt. bonds, Aaa	7.86	8.60	6.96	5.38	5.78	5.79	5.52	5.32	4.93	5.29	5.58
State and local govt. bonds, Baa	9.02	9.59	7.30	5.82	6.18	6.05	5.79	5.50	5.14	5.70	6.19
Municipal (Bond Buyer, 20 bonds)	8.55	9.11	7.27	5.59	6.19	5.95	5.76	5.52	5.09	5.43	5.71
Corporate Aaa seasoned [4]	11.94	11.37	9.32	7.22	7.96	7.59	7.37	7.26	6.53	7.04	7.62
Corporate Baa seasoned [4]	13.67	12.71	10.36	7.93	8.62	8.20	8.05	7.86	7.22	7.87	8.36
Corporate (Moody's) [4][5]	12.75	12.05	9.77	7.54	8.25	7.84	7.67	7.53	6.87	7.45	7.98
Industrials (49 bonds) [6]	12.35	11.80	9.77	7.51	8.21	7.76	7.58	7.47	6.79	7.33	7.83
Public utilities (51 bonds) [7]	13.15	12.29	9.76	7.56	8.30	7.90	7.74	7.63	7.00	7.54	8.15

NA Not available. [1] Yields on the more actively traded issues adjusted to constant maturities by the U.S. Treasury. [2] Through September 1996, yields are based on closing bid prices quoted by at least five dealers. Beginning October 1996, yields are based on closing indicative prices quoted by secondary market participants. [3] Averages (to maturity or call) for all outstanding bonds neither due nor callable in less than 10 years, including several very low yielding "flower" bonds. [4] Source: Moody's Investors Service, New York, NY. [5] For 1980 and 1985 includes railroad bonds which were discontinued as part of composite in 1989. [6] Covers 40 bonds for 1980 and 38 bonds for 1985. [7] Covers 40 bonds for 1980 and 1985.
Source: Except as noted, Board of Governors of the Federal Reserve System, *Federal Reserve Bulletin*, monthly.

No. 1196. Volume of Debt Markets by Type of Security: 1990 to 2000

[In billions of dollars (2,780 represents $2,780,000,000,000). Covers debt markets as represented by the source]

Type of security	1990	1995	1996	1997	1998	1999	2000
NEW ISSUE VOLUME							
Total	2,780	6,771	8,180	9,319	10,322	11,016	12,448
U.S. Treasury securities [1]	1,531	2,331	2,485	2,169	1,969	2,028	2,008
Federal agency debt	637	3,531	4,525	5,751	6,348	7,077	8,725
Municipal	163	198	227	267	321	265	240
Mortgage-backed securities [2]	235	269	371	368	727	687	483
Asset-backed securities [3]	42	107	152	185	196	199	230
Corporate debt [4]	173	334	421	579	761	761	761
DAILY TRADING VOLUME							
Total	111.2	246.3	274.0	300.5	352.8	316.5	357.7
U.S. Treasury securities [1][5]	111.2	193.2	203.7	212.1	226.6	186.5	206.6
Federal agency debt [5]	(NA)	23.7	31.1	40.2	47.6	54.6	72.8
Municipal [6]	(NA)	(NA)	1.1	1.1	7.7	8.3	8.8
Mortgage-backed securities [2][5]	(NA)	29.4	38.1	47.1	70.9	67.1	69.5
VOLUME OF SECURITIES OUTSTANDING							
Total	7,434	10,422	11,297	12,225	13,411	14,830	15,801
U.S. Treasury securities [1]	2,196	3,307	3,460	3,457	3,356	3,281	2,967
Federal agency debt [7]	435	845	926	1,023	1,297	1,617	1,907
Municipal	1,184	1,294	1,296	1,368	1,464	1,533	1,555
Mortgage-backed securities [2]	1,024	1,570	1,711	1,826	2,018	2,292	2,491
Asset-backed securities [3][7]	87	292	388	514	633	746	854
Money market instruments [8]	1,157	1,177	1,394	1,693	1,978	2,339	2,656
Corporate debt [4][7]	1,350	1,938	2,122	2,346	2,666	3,023	3,372

NA Not available. [1] Marketable public debt. [2] Includes only Government National Mortgage Association (GNMA), Federal National Mortgage Association (FNMA), and Federal Home Loan Mortgage Corporation (FHLMC) mortgage-backed securities. [3] Excludes mortgage-backed assets. [4] Includes nonconvertible corporate debt, Yankee bonds, and MTNs (Medium-Term Notes), but excludes federal agency debt and all CDs. [5] Primary dealer transactions. [6] Beginning September 1998 includes customer-to-dealer and dealer-to-dealer transactions. [7] The Bond Market Association estimates. [8] Commercial paper, bankers acceptances, and large time deposits.
Source: The Bond Market Association, New York, NY. Copyright. Based on data supplied by Board of Governors of the Federal Reserve System, U.S. Dept. of Treasury, Thompson Financial Securities Data Company, FHLMC, FNMA, GNMA, Federal Home Loan Banks, Student Loan Marketing Association, Federal Farm Credit Banks, Tennessee Valley Authority, and Municipal Securities Rulemaking Board.

No. 1197. Commercial Paper Outstanding by Type of Company: 1980 to 2000

[In billions of dollars (124 represents $124,000,000,000). As of December 31. Seasonally adjusted. Commercial paper is an unsecured promissory note having a fixed maturity of no more than 270 days]

Type of company	1980	1985	1990	1993	1994	1995	1996	1997	1998	1999	2000
All issuers	124	299	563	555	595	675	775	967	1,163	1,403	1,615
Financial companies [1]	87	214	415	399	431	487	591	766	936	1,124	1,272
Dealer-placed paper [2]	20	78	215	219	223	276	361	513	614	787	973
Directly-placed paper [3]	68	135	200	180	208	211	230	253	322	337	299
Nonfinancial companies [4]	37	85	148	156	165	188	185	201	227	279	343

[1] Institutions engaged primarily in commercial, savings, and mortgage banking; sales, personal, and mortgage financing; factoring, finance leasing, and other business lending; insurance underwriting; and other investment activities. [2] Includes all financial company paper sold by dealers in the open market. [3] As reported by financial companies that place their paper directly with investors. [4] Includes public utilities and firms engaged primarily in such activities as communications, construction, manufacturing, mining, wholesale and retail trade, transportation, and services.
Source: Board of Governors of the Federal Reserve System, *Federal Reserve Bulletin*, monthly.

738 Banking, Finance, and Insurance

No. 1198. Total Returns of Stocks, Bonds, and Treasury Bills: 1950 to 2000

[In percent. Average annual percent change. Stock return data are based on the Standard & Poor's 500 index]

Period	Stocks				Treasury bills, total return	Bonds (10-year), total return
	Total return	Capital gains	Dividends and reinvestment	Total return after inflation		
1950 to 1959...............	19.28	13.58	5.02	16.69	2.02	0.73
1960 to 1969...............	7.78	4.39	3.62	5.13	4.06	2.42
1970 to 1979...............	5.82	1.60	4.15	-0.14	6.42	5.84
1980 to 1989...............	17.54	12.59	4.42	11.87	9.21	13.06
1990 to 1999...............	18.17	15.31	2.48	15.09	5.01	7.96
2000	-9.10	-10.14	1.00	-12.08	6.09	17.53

Source: Global Financial Data, Los Angeles, CA, "Stocks, Bills, Bonds And Inflation Sector Total Returns In The United States, 1871-1996"; <http://www.globalfindata.com/trial/trd.html>; and unpublished data. (copyright).

No. 1199. Equities, Corporate Bonds, and Municipal Securities—Holdings and Net Purchases by Type of Investor: 1990 to 2000

[In billions of dollars (3,543 represents $3,543,000,000,000). Holdings as of Dec. 31. Minus sign (-) indicates net sales]

Type of investor	Holdings					Net purchases				
	1990	1995	1998	1999	2000	1990	1995	1998	1999	2000
EQUITIES [1]										
Total [2]............	3,543	8,496	15,428	19,576	17,169	-45.7	-16.0	-174.6	-31.8	-74.5
Household sector [3]..........	1,795	4,071	6,672	8,750	6,579	-44.6	-153.5	-357.2	-340.4	-456.6
State and local governments.....	5	26	102	115	115	1.5	12.1	9.4	3.5	-1.2
Rest of the world [4]..........	244	528	1,175	1,523	1,712	-16.0	16.6	41.9	98.1	172.0
Bank personal trusts and estates ..	190	225	327	378	315	0.5	1.6	-58.9	-18.5	-20.0
Life insurance companies.......	82	315	733	965	938	-5.7	18.6	115.3	111.9	93.4
Other insurance companies......	80	134	201	209	179	-7.0	-0.6	-5.2	-2.1	-9.7
Private pension funds	606	1,289	1,902	2,157	1,999	0.9	-69.5	-113.0	-92.2	-81.4
State and local retirement funds...	271	791	1,681	1,917	1,937	18.5	65.3	68.0	58.4	25.0
Mutual funds	233	1,025	2,509	3,400	3,226	14.4	87.4	143.3	136.9	191.4
CORPORATE & FOREIGN BONDS										
Total [2]............	1,706	2,848	4,145	4,611	5,020	123.4	344.1	550.4	465.9	397.2
Household sector [3]..........	181	420	634	674	684	38.1	94.6	98.5	41.2	-2.5
Rest of the world [4]..........	217	369	660	821	1,002	5.3	58.1	122.2	160.6	181.0
Commercial banking	89	111	181	220	278	4.6	8.4	38.0	38.8	57.8
Life insurance companies.......	567	870	1,130	1,173	1,224	56.5	90.7	84.5	41.5	50.9
Other insurance companies......	89	123	176	187	186	10.4	12.7	16.7	10.4	-0.1
Private pension funds	158	242	296	305	319	19.9	13.4	17.1	9.3	13.8
State and local retirement funds...	180	191	280	315	323	8.5	5.6	35.1	35.4	7.5
Money market mutual funds	2	22	81	124	162	-1.7	6.4	44.8	42.5	38.0
Mutual funds	59	196	339	369	368	4.7	23.3	65.5	29.3	-1.1
MUNICIPAL SECURITIES [5]										
Total [2]............	1,184	1,293	1,464	1,532	1,568	49.3	-48.2	96.8	68.2	35.3
Household sector [3]..........	575	459	489	533	525	27.6	-43.4	15.4	44.5	-8.7
Commercial banking	117	93	105	111	114	-16.4	-4.2	8.2	5.8	3.4
Other insurance companies......	137	161	211	201	200	1.8	7.0	19.2	-9.7	-1.7
Money market mutual funds	84	128	193	210	245	13.9	14.3	26.0	17.5	34.4
Mutual funds	113	210	243	239	231	13.9	3.2	22.8	-3.2	-8.8

[1] Excludes mutual fund shares. [2] Includes other types not shown separately. [3] Includes nonprofit organizations. [4] Holdings of U.S. issues by foreign residents. [5] Includes loans.

Source: Board of Governors of the Federal Reserve System, "Federal Reserve Statistical Release, Z.1, Flow of Funds Accounts of the United States"; published: 9 March 2001; <http://www.bog.frb.fed.us/releases/Z1/20010309/data.htm>.

No. 1200. New Security Issues of Corporations by Type of Offering: 1990 to 2000

[In billions of dollars (339.1 represents $339,100,000,000). Represents gross proceeds of issues maturing in more than one year. Figures are the principal amount or the number of units multiplied by the offering price. Excludes secondary offerings, employee stock plans, investment companies other than closed-end, intracorporate transactions, equities sold abroad, and Yankee bonds. Stock data include equity investments made by limited partnerships]

Type of offering	1990	1992	1993	1994	1995	1996	1997	1998	1999	2000
Total	339.1	559.8	768.3	582.6	672.7	742.3	849.4	1,023.4	996.1	977.6
Bonds, total	298.9	471.5	645.8	498.0	573.0	592.7	695.0	846.8	778.7	686.4
Public, domestic	188.8	378.1	486.2	364.8	408.5	465.6	536.8	731.0	627.6	546.0
Private placement, domestic ...	87.0	65.9	121.2	76.1	87.5	43.7	55.0	37.8	28.5	18.0
Sold abroad	23.1	27.6	38.4	56.8	76.8	83.4	103.2	78.0	122.6	122.4
Stocks, total.............	40.2	88.3	122.5	84.6	99.7	149.6	154.4	176.6	217.4	291.2
Preferred	4.0	21.3	18.9	12.2	11.3	32.2	29.5	38.4	19.3	12.7
Common	19.4	57.1	82.7	47.6	56.3	82.4	81.4	82.9	105.7	129.7
Private placement	16.7	9.9	20.9	24.8	32.1	35.0	43.5	55.3	92.4	148.8

Source: Board of Governors of the Federal Reserve System, Federal Reserve Bulletin, monthly.

Banking, Finance, and Insurance 739

No. 1201. Purchases and Sales by U.S. Investors of Foreign Bonds and Stocks, 1980 to 2000, and by Selected Country, 2000

[In billions of dollars (3.1 represents $3,100,000,000). See headnote, Table 1202. Minus sign (-) indicates net sales by U.S. investors or a net inflow of capital into the United States]

Year and country	Net purchases			Total transactions [1]			Bonds		Stocks	
	Total	Bonds	Stocks	Total	Bonds	Stocks	Purchases	Sales	Purchases	Sales
1980	3.1	1.0	2.1	53	35	18	18	17	10	8
1985	7.9	4.0	3.9	212	166	46	85	81	25	21
1990	31.2	21.9	9.2	907	652	255	337	315	132	123
1992	47.9	15.6	32.3	1,375	1,043	332	529	514	182	150
1993	143.1	80.4	62.7	2,126	1,572	554	826	746	308	245
1994	57.3	9.2	48.1	2,526	1,706	820	858	848	434	386
1995	98.7	48.4	50.3	2,569	1,827	741	938	890	396	346
1996	110.6	51.4	59.3	3,239	2,279	960	1,165	1,114	510	450
1997	89.1	48.1	40.9	4,505	2,952	1,553	1,500	1,452	797	756
1998	11.1	17.3	-6.2	4,527	2,674	1,853	1,346	1,328	923	930
1999	-10.0	5.7	-15.6	3,941	1,602	2,339	804	798	1,162	1,177
2000, total [2]	13.4	3.9	9.5	5,538	1,923	3,616	963	959	1,813	1,803
United Kingdom	29.9	31.9	-1.9	2,381	1,031	1,350	531	499	674	676
Japan	-21.9	-4.5	-17.4	582	81	501	38	43	242	259
British West Indies	3.9	-4.3	8.2	310	93	217	44	48	113	105
Bermuda	0.8	-2.3	3.1	272	167	105	82	85	54	51
Canada	3.9	-4.9	8.8	258	86	172	41	46	90	82
Hong Kong	2.0	-1.0	3.0	181	12	168	6	7	86	83
Germany	-0.7	7.8	-8.6	173	26	148	17	9	70	78
France	-0.4	1.4	-1.9	110	18	92	10	8	45	47
Switzerland	6.9	-0.9	7.8	104	10	95	4	5	51	43
Netherlands	5.2	2.7	2.4	102	22	80	12	10	41	39

[1] Total purchases plus total sales. [2] Includes other countries, not shown separately.

Source: U.S. Dept. of Treasury, *Treasury Bulletin*, quarterly.

No. 1202. Foreign Purchases and Sales of U.S. Securities by Type of Security, 1980 to 2000, and by Selected Country, 2000

[In billions of dollars (15.8 represents $15,800,000,000). Covers transactions in all types of long-term domestic securities by foreigners as reported by banks, brokers, and other entities in the United States (except nonmarketable U.S. Treasury notes, foreign series; and nonmarketable U.S. Treasury bonds and notes, foreign currency series). Data cover new issues of securities, transactions in outstanding issues, and redemptions of securities. Includes transactions executed in the United States for the account of foreigners, and transactions executed abroad for the account of reporting institutions and their domestic customers. Data by country show the country of domicile of the foreign buyers and sellers of the securities; in the case of outstanding issues, this may differ from the country of the original issuer. The term "foreigner" covers all institutions and individuals domiciled outside the United States, including U.S. citizens domiciled abroad, and the foreign branches, subsidiaries and other affiliates abroad of U.S. banks and businesses; the central governments, central banks, and other official institutions of foreign countries; and international and regional organizations. "Foreigner" also includes persons in the United States to the extent that they are known by reporting institutions to be acting on behalf of foreigners. Minus sign (-) indicates net sales by foreigners or a net outflow of capital from the United States]

Year and country	Net purchases					Total transactions [4]				
	Total	Treasury bonds and notes [1]	U.S. Govt. corporations [2] bonds	Corporate bonds [3]	Corporate stocks	Total	Treasury bonds and notes [1]	U.S. Govt. corporations [2] bonds	Corporate bonds [3]	Corporate stocks
1980	15.8	4.9	2.6	2.9	5.4	198	97	17	9	75
1985	78.3	29.2	4.3	39.8	4.9	1,256	968	46	84	159
1990	18.7	17.9	6.3	9.7	-15.1	4,204	3,620	104	117	362
1992	73.2	39.3	18.3	20.8	-5.1	5,282	4,444	204	187	448
1993	111.1	23.6	35.4	30.6	21.6	6,314	5,195	263	239	618
1994	140.4	78.8	21.7	38.0	1.9	6,562	5,343	297	222	699
1995	231.9	134.1	28.7	57.9	11.2	7,243	5,828	222	278	915
1996	370.2	232.2	41.7	83.7	12.5	8,965	7,134	241	422	1,169
1997	388.0	184.2	49.9	84.4	69.6	12,759	9,546	469	617	2,126
1998	277.8	49.0	56.8	121.9	50.0	14,989	10,259	992	641	3,097
1999	350.2	-10.0	92.2	160.4	107.5	14,617	8,586	880	577	4,574
2000, total [5]	456.8	-53.3	152.8	182.4	174.9	16,957	7,843	1,305	773	7,036
United Kingdom	165.2	-33.7	30.2	110.0	58.7	5,331	3,212	312	397	1,410
British West Indies	20.1	-3.4	11.4	13.0	-1.0	2,570	539	310	107	1,615
Bermuda	-0.4	-7.4	6.1	10.9	-10.1	1,558	284	106	52	1,117
Japan	51.5	10.6	23.8	15.0	2.1	1,133	688	185	29	232
Canada	19.4	0.2	10.1	3.2	6.0	894	541	23	23	307
France	3.8	-4.1	0.1	2.2	5.7	733	330	7	12	383
Netherlands Antilles	-0.6	5.4	1.8	0.8	-8.6	477	151	26	10	289
Ireland	9.9	1.0	1.6	2.4	4.9	443	331	28	9	74
Germany	28.5	-7.3	2.5	1.6	31.8	437	198	13	13	213
Switzerland	5.5	-10.3	1.6	2.3	12.0	360	45	15	9	292

[1] Marketable bonds and notes. [2] Includes federally-sponsored agencies. [3] Includes transactions in directly placed issues abroad by U.S. corporations and issues of states and municipalities. [4] Total purchases plus total sales. [5] Includes other countries, not shown separately.

Source: U.S. Dept. of Treasury, *Treasury Bulletin*, quarterly.

No. 1203. Stock Prices and Yields: 1990 to 2000

[Closing values as of end of December, except as noted]

Index	1990	1995	1996	1997	1998	1999	2000
STOCK PRICES							
Standard & Poor's indices: [1]							
S&P 500 composite (1941-43=10)	330.9	614.5	740.5	970.4	1,229.2	1,469.3	1,320.28
Industrials	387.1	719.7	870.0	1,121.4	1,479.2	1,841.9	1,527.86
Utilities	144.8	201.7	198.8	235.8	259.6	227.2	350.61
S&P 400 MidCap Index (1982=100)	100.0	217.8	255.6	333.4	392.3	444.7	516.74
Russell indices: [2]							
Russell 1000 (Dec. 31, 1986=130)...........	171.22	328.89	393.75	513.79	642.87	767.97	700.09
Russell 2000 (Dec. 31, 1986=135)...........	132.16	315.97	362.61	437.02	421.96	504.75	483.53
Russell 3000 (Dec. 31, 1986=140)...........	180.85	351.91	419.44	543.05	664.27	793.31	725.75
N.Y. Stock Exchange common stock index							
Composite (Dec. 31, 1965=50)	180.49	329.51	392.30	511.19	596.05	650.30	656.87
Yearly high	201.55	331.73	401.08	515.24	601.76	663.50	681.20
Yearly low.......................	161.76	249.86	320.90	386.36	462.69	572.40	575.01
Industrial (Dec. 31, 1965=50)............	223.60	413.29	494.38	630.38	743.65	828.21	803.29
Transportation (Dec. 31, 1965=50)	141.49	301.96	352.30	466.25	482.38	466.70	462.76
Utility (Dec. 31, 1965=100)	182.60	252.90	259.91	335.19	445.94	511.15	440.54
Finance (Dec. 31, 1965=50)	122.07	274.25	351.17	495.96	521.42	516.61	646.95
American Stock Exchange Composite Index							
(Dec. 29, 1995=550)	(NA)	550.00	572.34	684.61	688.99	876.97	897.75
NASDAQ composite index (Feb. 5, 1971=100)	373.8	1,052.1	1,291.0	1,570.4	2,192.7	4,069.3	2,470.5
Nasdaq-100 (Jan. 31, 1985=125)...........	200.5	576.2	821.4	990.8	1,836.0	3,708.0	2,341.7
Industrial (Feb. 5, 1971=100)	406.1	964.7	1,109.6	1,221.0	1,304.3	2,239.0	1,483.0
Insurance (Feb. 5, 1971=100)	451.8	1,292.6	1,465.4	1,798.0	1,796.8	1,896.3	2,193.4
Banks (Feb. 5, 1971=100)	254.9	1,009.4	1,273.5	2,083.2	1,838.0	1,691.3	1,939.5
Dow-Jones and Co., Inc.:							
Composite (65 stocks)...................	920.6	1,693.2	2,025.8	2,607.4	2,870.8	3,214.4	3,317.4
Industrial (30 stocks)...................	2,633.7	5,117.1	6,448.3	7,908.3	9,181.4	11,497.1	10,786.9
Transportation (20 stocks)...............	910.2	1,981.0	2,255.7	3,256.5	3,149.3	2,977.2	2,946.6
Utility (15 stocks)....................	209.7	225.4	232.5	273.1	312.3	283.4	412.2
Wilshire 5000 Total Market Index [3]							
(Dec. 31, 1980=1404.596)	3,101.4	6,057.2	7,198.3	9,298.2	11,317.6	13,812.7	12,175.9
COMMON STOCK YIELDS (percent)							
Standard & Poor's composite index (500 stocks): [4]							
Dividend-price ratio [5]..................	3.61	2.56	2.19	1.77	1.49	1.25	1.15
Earnings-price ratio [6].................	6.47	6.09	5.24	4.57	3.46	3.17	3.63

NA Not available. [1] Standard & Poor's Indices are market-value weighted. The S&P 500 index represents the 500 largest publicly traded companies, as determined by Standard & Poor's and represent a broad range of industry segments within the U.S. economy. The S&P MidCap Index tracks midcap companies. [2] The Russell 1000 and 3000 indices show respectively the 1000 and 3000 largest capitalization stocks in the United States. The Russell 2000 index shows the 2000 largest capitalization stocks in the United States after the first 1000. [3] The Wilshire 5000 Total Market Index measures the performance of all U.S. headquartered equity securities with readily available prices. [4] Source: U.S. Council of Economic Advisors, *Economic Report of the President*, annual. [5] Aggregate cash dividends (based on latest known annual rate) divided by aggregate market value based on Wednesday closing prices. Averages of monthly figures. [6] Averages of quarterly ratios which are ratio of earnings (after taxes) for 4 quarters ending with particular quarter to price index for last day of that quarter.

Source: Except as noted, Global Financial Data, Los Angeles, CA, <http://www.globalfindata.com/trial/trd.html>; (copyright).

No. 1204. Dow-Jones U.S. Equity Market Index by Industry: 1992 to 2000

[As of end of year]

Industry	1992	1995	1996	1997	1998	1999	2000
U.S. equity market index, total	**105.78**	**147.49**	**176.38**	**228.67**	**281.61**	**341.57**	**.306.88**
Basic materials	106.62	139.19	153.17	167.34	150.23	187.47	154.49
Consumer, cyclical	118.53	140.43	158.60	210.75	282.04	340.50	277.68
Consumer, noncyclical.	101.28	134.27	165.13	214.90	247.66	246.23	215.56
Energy...........................	100.22	134.70	168.04	201.09	185.82	219.29	272.96
Financial..........................	122.85	176.95	231.31	338.29	356.60	354.82	440.91
Healthcare	84.31	127.76	148.70	200.70	276.30	263.46	360.18
Industrial..........................	107.52	156.26	187.59	224.38	246.65	309.12	276.11
Technology	106.57	229.07	311.14	381.36	647.92	1,186.89	749.01
Telecommunications	111.66	154.78	150.32	205.19	303.78	355.85	210.38
Utilities...........................	101.04	109.20	107.29	130.94	142.14	118.26	177.80

Source: Dow Jones & Company, Inc., New York, NY, *Dow Jones Indexes*, (copyright).

No. 1205. NASDAQ—Securities Listed and Volume of Trading: 1980 to 2000

Item	Unit	1980	1985	1990	1994	1995	1996	1997	1998	1999	2000
Member firms	Number...	2,932	6,307	5,827	5,426	5,451	5,553	5,597	5,592	5,482	5,579
Branch offices	Number...	7,555	15,375	24,457	57,105	58,119	60,151	62,966	70,752	80,035	82,126
Companies listed	Number...	2,894	4,136	4,132	4,902	5,112	5,556	5,487	5,068	4,829	4,734
Issues	Number...	3,050	4,784	4,706	5,761	5,955	6,384	6,208	5,583	5,210	5,053
Shares traded	Billion	6.7	20.7	33.4	74.4	101.2	138.1	163.9	202.0	272.6	442.8
Average daily volume ..	Million	27	82	132	295	401	544	648	802	1,082	1,757
Value of shares traded . . .	Bil. dol.	69	234	452	1,449	2,398	3,302	4,482	5,759	11,013	20,395

Source: National Association of Securities Dealers, Washington, DC, *NASD Annual Report* (copyright).

No. 1206. Sales of Stocks on Registered Exchanges: 1980 to 2000

[522 represents $522,000,000,000. Excludes over-the-counter trading]

Exchange	Unit	1980	1985	1990	1994	1995	1996	1997	1998	1999	2000
Market value of all sales, all exchanges [1][2]	Bil. dol. .	522	1,260	1,752	2,966	3,690	4,735	6,879	8,698	11,220	14,545
New York	Bil. dol . .	398	1,024	1,394	2,483	3,078	4,013	5,848	7,275	9,087	11,213
American.	Bil. dol . .	47	38	65	83	105	131	204	355	543	912
Chicago	Bil. dol . .	21	79	74	98	114	136	213	326	540	1,038
CBOE [3]	Bil. dol . .	28	38	81	87	107	130	179	214	271	330
Pacific	Bil. dol . .	13	40	53	70	94	108	151	182	255	248
Philadelphia	Bil. dol . .	11	23	41	51	59	68	89	97	103	165
STOCKS [4]											
Shares sold, all exchanges [2]. . .	Billion. . .	15.5	37.0	53.3	90.5	106.4	125.7	159.7	206.4	244.1	317.6
New York	Billion. . .	12.4	30.2	43.8	76.7	90.1	108.2	138.8	178.9	207.7	265.6
American	Billion. . .	1.7	2.1	3.1	4.3	4.8	5.3	6.2	7.6	8.7	11.9
Chicago.	Billion. . .	0.6	2.3	2.5	3.5	3.9	4.2	6.0	9.5	14.4	24.1
Pacific.	Billion. . .	0.4	1.4	1.7	2.1	2.7	3.0	3.2	4.0	4.9	4.1
Market value, all exchanges [2] . .	Bil. dol . .	476	1,200	1,612	2,817	3,507	4,511	6,559	8,307	10,680	13,685
New York.	Bil. dol . .	398	1,023	1,390	2,482	3,076	4,011	5,847	7,274	9,087	11,213
American	Bil. dol . .	35	26	36	56	73	86	139	280	446	755
Chicago.	Bil. dol . .	21	79	74	98	114	136	213	326	540	1,038
Pacific.	Bil. dol . .	11	37	45	59	79	92	123	148	206	163

[1] Includes market value of stocks, rights, warrants, and options trading beginning 1990.   [2] Includes other registered exchanges, not shown separately.   [3] Chicago Board Options Exchange, Inc.   [4] Includes voting trust certificates, American Depository Receipts, and certificate of deposit for stocks.

Source: U.S. Securities and Exchange Commission, annual report.

No. 1207. Volume of Trading on New York Stock Exchange: 1980 to 2000

[11,562 represents 11,562,000,000. Round lot: A unit of trading or a multiple thereof. On the NYSE the unit of trading is generally 100 shares in stocks. For some inactive stocks, the unit of trading is 10 shares. Odd lot: An amount of stock less than the established 100-share unit or 10-share unit of trading]

Item	Unit	1980	1985	1990	1995	1996	1997	1998	1999	2000
Shares traded	Million .	11,562	27,774	39,946	87,873	105,477	134,404	171,188	206,299	265,499
Round lots	Million . .	11,352	27,511	39,665	87,218	104,636	133,312	169,745	203,914	262,478
Average daily shares	Million . .	45	109	157	346	412	527	674	809	1,042
High day	Million . .	84	181	292	653	681	1,201	1,216	1,350	1,560
Low day	Million . .	16	62	57	118	130	155	247	312	403
Odd lots	Million . .	209	263	282	656	841	1,091	1,443	2,384	3,021
Value of shares traded .	Bil. dol .	382	981	1,336	3,110	4,102	5,833	7,395	9,073	11,205
Round lots	Bil. dol. .	375	970	1,325	3,083	4,064	5,778	7,318	8,945	11,060
Odd lots	Bil. dol. .	8	10	11	27	38	56	77	128	145
Bond volume [1]	Mil. dol .	5,190	9,047	10,893	6,979	5,529	5,046	3,838	3,221	2,328
Daily average	Mil. dol .	20.5	35.9	43.1	27.7	21.8	19.9	15.2	12.8	9.2

[1] Par value.

Source: New York Stock Exchange, Inc., New York, NY, *Fact Book, 2000* (copyright).

No. 1208. Securities Listed on New York Stock Exchange: 1980 to 2000

[As of December 31, except cash dividends are for calendar year (602 represents $602,000,000,000)]

Item	Unit	1980	1985	1990	1993	1994	1995	1996	1997	1998	1999	2000
BONDS												
Number of issuers	Number .	1,045	1,010	743	574	583	564	563	533	474	416	392
Number of issues.	Number .	3,057	3,856	2,912	2,103	2,141	2,097	2,064	1,965	1,858	1,736	1,627
Face value	Bil. dol . .	602	1,327	1,689	2,342	2,526	2,773	2,845	2,625	2,554	2,402	2,125
STOCKS												
Companies	Number .	1,570	1,541	1,774	2,361	2,570	2,675	2,907	3,047	3,114	3,025	2,862
Number of issues.	Number .	2,228	2,298	2,284	2,904	3,060	3,126	3,285	3,358	3,382	3,286	3,072
Shares listed	Billion. . .	33.7	52.4	90.7	131.1	142.3	154.7	176.9	207.1	239.3	280.9	313.9
Market value	Bil. dol . .	1,243	1,950	2,820	4,541	4,448	6,013	7,300	9,413	10,864	12,296	12,372
Average price	Dollars . .	36.87	37.20	31.08	34.65	31.26	38.86	41.26	45.45	45.40	43.77	42.14
Cash dividends on common stock [1]	Bil. dol .	53.1	74.2	103.2	120.2	130.0	147.0	150.6	159.4	179.0	174.7	165.6

[1] Beginning 1990 estimate based on average annual yield of the NYSE composite index.

Source: New York Stock Exchange, Inc., New York, NY, *Fact Book, 2000* (copyright).

No. 1209. Stock Ownership by Age of Head of Family and Family Income: 1992 to 1998

[Median value in thousands of constant 1998 dollars (12.0 represents $12,000). Constant dollar figures are based on consumer price index data published by U.S. Bureau of Labor Statistics. Families include one-person units; for definition of family, see text, Section 1, Population. Based on Survey of Consumer Finance; see Appendix III For definition of median, see Guide to Tabular Presentation]

Age of family head and family income (constant (1998) dollars)	Families having direct or indirect stock holdings [1] (percent)			Median value among families with holdings			Stock holdings' share of group's financial assets (percent)		
	1992	1995	1998	1992	1995	1998	1992	1995	1998
All families	**36.7**	**40.4**	**48.8**	**12.0**	**15.4**	**25.0**	**33.7**	**40.0**	**53.9**
Under 35 years old	28.3	36.6	40.7	4.0	5.4	7.0	24.8	27.2	44.8
35 to 44 years old	42.4	46.4	56.5	8.6	10.6	20.0	31.0	39.5	54.7
45 to 54 years old	46.4	48.9	58.6	17.1	27.6	38.0	40.6	42.9	55.7
55 to 64 years old	45.3	40.0	55.9	28.5	32.9	47.0	37.3	44.4	58.3
65 to 74 years old	30.2	34.4	42.6	18.3	36.1	56.0	31.6	35.8	51.3
75 years old and over	25.7	27.9	29.4	28.5	21.2	60.0	25.4	39.8	48.7
Less than $10,000	6.8	5.4	7.7	6.2	3.2	4.0	15.9	12.9	24.8
$10,000 to $24,999	17.8	22.2	24.7	4.6	6.4	9.0	15.3	26.7	27.5
$25,000 to $49,999	40.2	45.4	52.7	7.2	8.5	11.5	23.7	30.3	39.1
$50,000 to $99,999	62.5	65.4	74.3	15.4	23.6	35.7	33.5	39.9	48.8
$100,000 and more	78.3	81.6	91.0	71.9	85.5	150.0	40.2	46.4	63.0

[1] Indirect holdings are those in mutual funds, retirement accounts, and other managed assets.
Source: Board of Governors of the Federal Reserve System, *Federal Reserve Bulletin*, January 2000, and unpublished data.

No. 1210. Household Ownership of Equities: 1999

[49.2 represents 49,200,000. Based on a national probability sample of 4,842 household financial decisionmakers. Of these, 2,336 decisionmakers who indicated they owned equities were asked further questions about equity ownership]

Type of holding	Households owning equities		Number of individual investors (mil.)
	Number (mil.)	Percent of all households	
Any type of equity (net) [1].	49.2	48.2	78.7
Any equity inside employer-sponsored retirement plans	32.5	31.8	52.0
Any equity outside employer-sponsored retirement plans	36.3	35.5	61.6
Individual stock (net) [1]	26.7	26.1	40.0
Individual stock inside employer-sponsored retirement plans.	10.7	10.5	14.0
Individual stock outside employer-sponsored retirement plans	21.9	21.4	32.8
Stock mutual funds (net) [1].	41.8	40.9	66.8
Stock mutual funds inside employer-sponsored retirement plans	28.5	27.9	39.9
Stock mutual funds outside employer-sponsored retirement plans . . .	27.8	27.2	44.4

[1] Multiple responses included.

No. 1211. Characteristics of Equity Owners: 1999

[In percent, except as indicated. See headnote, Table 1210. For definition of median, see Guide to Tabular Presentation]

Item	Total	Age				Household income		
		19 to 35 years old	36 to 54 years old	55 to 74 years old	75 years old and over	Less than $50,000	$50,000 to $99,999	$100,000 and over
Median age (years).	47	29	44	61	78	45	44	48
Median household income (dol.)	60,000	47,000	62,500	53,000	30,000	34,000	65,000	125,000
Median household financial assets [1] (dol.).	85,000	25,000	88,000	200,000	200,000	42,500	89,000	300,000
Equity investments owned:								
Individual stock (net) [2]	54	45	52	58	63	44	52	67
Inside employer-sponsored retirement plans . .	20	21	23	17	6	15	20	29
Outside employer-sponsored retirement plans .	44	35	43	51	59	34	44	61
Stock mutual funds (net) [2].	85	83	88	84	80	81	89	88
Inside employer-sponsored retirement plans . .	58	64	67	47	12	49	66	69
Outside employer-sponsored retirement plans .	57	45	57	62	72	51	55	66
Nonequity investments owned: [2]								
Savings accounts, MMDAs, or CDs [3]	83	82	84	82	86	79	84	86
Bond investments (net) [2]	22	14	21	24	44	15	19	31
Individual bonds.	9	4	8	11	25	4	7	15
Bond mutual funds	16	11	16	19	30	12	15	23
Fixed or variable annuities	21	9	20	30	35	17	20	25
Hybrid mutual funds.	39	33	42	41	35	33	42	46
Money market mutual funds	26	17	26	32	30	20	26	38
Investment real estate	26	17	26	34	24	18	26	40
Have employer-sponsored retirement plan coverage.	80	83	86	73	49	73	86	84
Have Individual Retirement Account (IRA).	53	37	53	67	39	41	55	67

[1] Includes assets in employer-sponsored retirement plans but excludes value of primary residence. [2] Multiple responses included. [3] MMDA=money market deposit account; CD=certificate of deposit.
Source of Tables 1210 and 1211: Investment Company Institute, Washington, DC, and Securities Industry Association, New York, NY, *Equity Ownership in America, Fall 1999* (copyright).

No. 1212. Household Ownership of Mutual Funds by Age and Income: 2000

[In percent. Includes money market, stock, bond and hybrid, variable annuity, IRA, Keogh, and employer-sponsored retirement plan fund owners. An estimated 50,600,000 households own mutual funds. Based on a sample survey of 3,000 households; for details, see source]

Age of household head and household income	All house-holds, percent distribution	Households owning mutual funds		Age of household head and household income	All house-holds, percent distribution	Households owning mutual funds	
		Percent distribution	Percent of all house-holds			Percent distribution	Percent of all house-holds
Total	100	100	49	Less than $25,000	26	9	17
Less than 25 years old .	5	2	23	$25,000 to $34,999. . . .	15	11	37
25 to 34 years old.	18	18	49	$35,000 to $49,999. . . .	19	19	49
35 to 44 years old.	23	28	58	$50,000 to $74,999. . . .	20	28	66
45 to 54 years old.	20	25	59	$75,000 to $99,999. . . .	9	14	77
55 to 64 years old.	12	13	54	$100,000 and over	11	19	79
65 years old and over . .	22	14	32				

Source: Investment Company Institute, Washington, DC, *Fundamentals, Investment Company Institute Research in Brief*, Vol. 9, No. 4, August 2000 (copyright).

No. 1213. Characteristics of Mutual Fund Owners: 1998

[In percent, except as indicated. Mutual fund ownership includes holdings of money market, stock, bond, and hybrid mutual funds; and funds owned through variable annuities, Individual Retirement Accounts (IRAs), Keoghs, and employer-sponsored retirement plans. Based on a national probability sample of 1,470 primary financial decisionmakers in households with mutual fund investments. For definition of median, see Guide to Tabular Presentation]

Characteristic	Total	Age			Household income		
		18 to 33 years old	34 to 52 years old	53 years old and over	Less than $50,000	$50,000 to $100,000	Over $100,000
Median age (years)	44	29	43	61	41	43	46
Median household income (dol.).	55,000	44,000	62,000	47,000	35,000	69,000	125,000
Median household financial assets [1] (dol.)	80,000	26,000	90,000	200,000	37,000	100,000	325,000
Own an IRA	57	45	56	73	49	59	71
Household has a defined contribution retirement plan(s), net [2]	77	85	83	59	70	86	89
401(k) plan	60	73	66	39	52	68	77
403(k) plan	12	12	12	13	10	14	19
State, local, or federal government plan	24	21	26	23	24	27	20
Median mutual fund assets (dol.)	25,000	10,000	25,000	62,500	10,000	30,000	70,000
Median number of mutual funds owned	4	3	4	4	2	4	6
Own: [2]							
Equity funds	88	87	88	90	79	91	96
Bond funds	42	34	42	52	34	40	53
Hybrid funds	35	29	36	40	30	33	43
Money market mutual funds.	48	43	47	53	45	40	53
Own mutual funds bought: [2]							
Outside employer-sponsored retirement plan(s) .	54	45	55	59	43	53	65
Inside employer-sponsored retirement plan(s) . .	62	66	70	46	53	73	78

[1] Includes assets in employer-sponsored retirement plans but excludes value of primary residence. [2] Multiple responses included.

Source: Investment Company Institute, Washington, DC, *1998 Profile of Mutual Fund Shareholders*, 1999 (copyright).

No. 1214. Mutual Funds—Summary: 1980 to 2000

[135 represents $135,000,000,000. Number of funds and assets as of December 31. A mutual fund is an open-end investment company that continuously issues and redeems shares that represent an interest in a pool of financial assets. Excludes data for funds that invest in other mutual funds. Minus sign (-) indicates net redemptions]

Type of fund	Unit	1980	1985	1990	1995	1996	1997	1998	1999	2000
Number of funds, total	Number. .	[1]564	1,527	3,081	5,728	6,254	6,684	7,314	7,791	8,171
Equity funds	Number. .	277	579	1,100	2,140	2,572	2,951	3,513	3,952	4,395
Hybrid funds.	Number. .	(NA)	87	194	414	470	501	525	533	525
Bond funds	Number. .	(NA)	404	1,046	2,177	2,224	2,219	2,250	2,261	2,210
Money market funds, taxable [2] . . .	Number. .	96	346	506	674	666	682	685	702	704
Money market funds, tax-exempt [3] . .	Number. .	10	111	235	323	322	331	341	343	337
Assets, total	Bil. dol .	[1]135	495	1,065	2,812	3,526	4,468	5,525	6,846	6,965
Equity funds	Bil. dol . .	44	117	240	1,249	1,726	2,368	2,978	4,042	3,962
Hybrid funds.	Bil. dol . .	(NA)	12	36	211	253	317	365	383	350
Bond funds	Bil. dol . .	(NA)	123	291	599	645	724	831	808	808
Money market funds, taxable [2] . . .	Bil. dol . .	75	208	415	630	762	898	1,163	1,409	1,607
Money market funds, tax-exempt [3] . .	Bil. dol . .	2	36	84	123	140	161	189	204	238
Equity, hybrid and bond funds:										
Sales.	Bil. dol . .	10	114	149	476	681	869	1,058	1,274	1,631
Redemptions.	Bil. dol . .	8	34	98	313	398	541	748	1,021	1,334
Net sales	Bil. dol . .	2	80	51	163	284	328	310	252	297
Money market funds, taxable [2]:										
Sales.	Bil. dol . .	232	730	1,219	2,729	3,524	4,395	5,534	7,083	8,691
Redemptions.	Bil. dol . .	204	732	1,183	2,617	3,415	4,265	5,289	6,866	8,499
Net sales	Bil. dol . .	28	-2	36	112	108	129	244	217	192
Money market funds, tax-exempt [3]:										
Sales.	Bil. dol . .	5	109	197	396	467	536	639	687	788
Redemptions.	Bil. dol . .	4	99	190	385	453	518	612	675	757
Net sales	Bil. dol . .	2	11	7	11	13	18	27	12	31

NA Not available. [1] Includes "income and bond funds," a category subsequently discontinued. [2] Funds invest in short-term, high-grade securities sold in the money market. [3] Funds invest in municipal securities with relatively short maturities.
Source: Investment Company Institute, Washington, DC, *Mutual Fund Fact Book*, annual (copyright).

744 Banking, Finance, and Insurance

No. 1215. Mutual Fund Shares—Holdings and Net Purchases by Type of Investor: 1990 to 2000

[In billions of dollars (608 represents $608,000,000,000). Holdings as of Dec. 31. Minus sign (-) indicates net sales]

Type of investor	Holdings					Net purchases				
	1990	1995	1998	1999	2000	1990	1995	1998	1999	2000
Total	608	1,853	3,611	4,553	4,433	53.7	147.4	274.6	188.3	245.0
Households, nonprofit organizations	457	1,159	2,375	3,106	3,026	22.5	66.0	255.6	164.1	208.6
Nonfinancial corporate business. . .	10	46	91	114	107	-1.0	4.6	7.3	-1.8	-1.8
State and local governments.	5	35	21	26	26	3.3	5.9	-12.3	4.3	0.8
Commercial banking	2	2	9	11	14	-0.3	0.3	-0.4	1.2	2.5
Credit unions	1	3	4	3	2	0.2	0.2	1.2	-1.1	-0.6
Bank personal trusts and estates . .	63	254	378	421	372	9.7	11.9	14.9	-23.9	-8.0
Life insurance companies	31	28	23	43	48	12.6	13.5	-23.4	15.0	11.0
Private pension funds	40	327	709	830	838	6.6	45.0	31.7	30.7	32.5

Source: Board of Governors of the Federal Reserve System, "Federal Reserve Statistical Release, Z.1, Flow of Funds Accounts of the United States"; published 9 March 2001; <http://www.bog.frb.fed.us/releases/Z1/20010309/data.htm>.

No. 1216. Mutual Fund Retirement Assets: 1990 to 2000

[In billions of dollars, except percent (207 represents $207,000,000,000). Based on data from the Institute's Annual Questionnaire for Retirement Statistics. The 2000 survey gathered data from 10,256 mutual fund share classes representing approximately 76 percent of mutual fund industry assets. Assets were estimated for all nonreporting funds. Estimates of retirement assets in street name and omnibus accounts were derived from data reported on the Annual Questionnaire for Retirement Statistics and the Annual Institutional Survey]

Type of account	1990	1994	1995	1996	1997	1998	1999	2000
Mutual fund retirement assets . . .	207	664	915	1,166	1,509	1,899	2,462	2,408
Percent of total retirement assets .	5	11	13	15	17	19	21	21
Individual retirement accounts (IRAs) . . .	140	350	476	598	767	960	1,243	1,232
Employer-sponsored defined contribution retirement plans	67	314	439	568	742	939	1,219	1,176
401(k) plans [1]	35	184	266	346	466	596	780	766
Percent of total 401(k) assets	9	27	31	33	37	41	45	45
403(b) plans [2]	15	90	119	145	183	227	281	259
457 plans [3]	2	6	8	12	16	24	38	38
Other defined contribution plans [4]	15	35	46	65	77	93	119	113
Percent of all mutual funds:								
Mutual fund retirement assets	20	31	33	33	34	34	36	35
Individual retirement accounts (IRAs) . . .	13	16	17	17	17	17	18	18
Employer-sponsored retirement plans . . .	6	15	16	16	17	17	18	17

[1] See headnote, Table 535. May also include some profit-sharing plan assets that do not have a 401(k) feature.   [2] Section 403(b) of the Internal Revenue Code permits employees of certain charitable organizations, nonprofit hospitals, universities, and public schools to establish tax-sheltered retirement programs. These plans may invest in either annuity contracts or mutual fund shares.   [3] These plans are deferred compensation arrangements for government employees and employees of certain tax-exempt organizations.   [4] Includes thrift savings, stock bonus, target benefit, money purchase, and all other defined contribution plans.

Source: Investment Company Institute, Washington, DC, Fundamentals, Investment Company Institute Research in Brief, "Mutual Funds and the Retirement Market in 2000"; Vol. 10, No. 2, June 2001, <http://www.ici.org> (copyright).

No. 1217. Individual Retirement Accounts (IRA) Plans—Value by Institution: 1990 to 2000

[As of December 31 (637 represents $637,000,000,000). Estimated]

Institution	Amount (bil. dol.)									Percent distribution		
	1990	1993	1994	1995	1996	1997	1998	1999	2000	1990	1995	2000
Total IRA assets.	637	993	1,056	1,288	1,467	1,728	2,150	2,663	2,650	100	100	100
Bank and thrift deposits [1] . . .	266	263	255	261	258	254	249	244	250	42	20	9
Life insurance companies [2]. . .	40	61	69	81	92	135	157	202	202	6	6	8
Mutual funds	140	322	350	476	598	767	960	1,243	1,232	22	37	46
Securities held in brokerage accounts	190	346	382	471	519	572	785	975	966	30	37	36

[1] Includes Keogh deposits.   [2] Annuities held by IRAs, excluding variable annuity mutual fund IRA assets.

Source: Investment Company Institute, Washington, DC, Fundamentals, Investment Company Institute Research in Brief, "Mutual Funds and the Retirement Market in 2000"; Vol. 10, No. 2, June 2001, <http://www.ici.org> (copyright).

No. 1218. Assets of Private and Public Pension Funds by Type of Fund: 1980 to 2000

[In billions of dollars (882 represents $882,000,000,000). As of end of year. Except for corporate equities, represents book value. Excludes social security trust funds and U.S. government pension funds; see Tables 526 and 530]

Type of pension fund	1980	1985	1990	1995	1996	1997	1998	1999	2000
Total, all types	882	1,885	3,089	5,269	5,957	7,052	8,035	8,974	9,043
Private funds	685	1,487	2,204	3,804	4,205	4,833	5,415	6,045	5,958
Insured [1]	172	260	570	881	954	1,086	1,210	1,367	1,369
Noninsured [2][3]	513	1,226	1,634	2,923	3,251	3,747	4,205	4,678	4,589
Time and savings deposits	32	77	110	107	112	114	116	108	109
Credit market instruments [3]	151	329	472	631	627	675	731	776	816
U.S. government securities . . .	51	196	263	356	343	355	389	419	446
Treasury	32	129	130	142	139	144	158	168	181
Agency	18	67	133	214	204	211	232	252	265
Corporate and foreign bonds . .	78	97	158	242	245	279	296	305	319
Corporate equities	232	516	606	1,289	1,464	1,696	1,902	2,157	1,999
Mutual fund shares	7	11	40	327	412	570	709	830	838
Unallocated insurance contracts [4] .	(NA)	132	215	332	361	382	423	457	461
State and local pension funds [3]	197	399	884	1,465	1,752	2,219	2,620	2,929	3,085
Credit market instruments [3]	147	252	440	531	568	632	704	753	766
U.S. government securities	40	124	231	291	308	340	360	373	380
Treasury	21	83	144	192	204	217	218	213	195
Agency	19	41	87	99	105	123	142	160	186
Corporate and foreign bonds	92	107	180	191	214	245	280	315	323
Corporate equities	44	120	271	791	1,014	1,383	1,681	1,917	1,937

NA Not available.   [1] Annuity reserves held by life insurance companies, excluding unallocated contracts held by private pension funds.   [2] Private defined benefit plans and defined contribution plans (including 401(k) type plans). Also includes Federal Employees Retirement System (FERS) Thrift Savings Plan.   [3] Includes other types of assets not shown separately.   [4] Assets held at life insurance companies (e.g., guaranteed investment contracts (GICs), variable annuities).

Source: Board of Governors of the Federal Reserve System, "Federal Reserve Statistical Release, Z.1, Flow of Funds Accounts of the United States"; published 9 March 2001; <http://www.bog.frb.fed.us/releases/Z1/20010309/data.htm>.

Figure 25.1
Assets of Private Noninsured Pension Funds: 2000

Billions of dollars

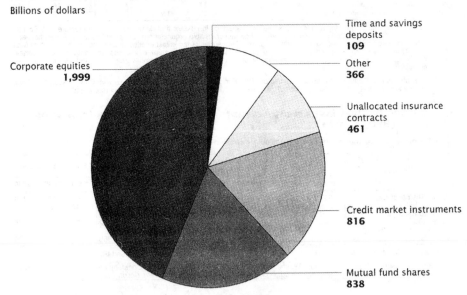

Corporate equities
1,999

Time and savings deposits
109

Other
366

Unallocated insurance contracts
461

Credit market instruments
816

Mutual fund shares
838

Source: Chart prepared by U.S. Census Bureau, for data see Table 1218.

No. 1219. Securities Industry—Revenues and Expenses: 1980 to 1999

[In millions of dollars (19,829 represents $19,829,000,000)]

Type	1980	1985	1990	1993	1994	1995	1996	1997	1998	1999
Revenues, total	**19,829**	**49,844**	**71,356**	**108,844**	**112,758**	**143,414**	**172,411**	**207,245**	**234,964**	**266,809**
Commissions	6,777	10,955	12,032	19,905	19,847	23,215	27,866	32,662	36,696	45,937
Trading/investment gains	5,091	14,549	15,746	25,427	20,219	28,963	30,768	35,958	32,754	55,464
Underwriting profits	1,571	4,987	3,728	11,249	6,844	8,865	12,613	14,611	16,237	17,782
Margin interest	2,151	2,746	3,179	3,235	4,668	6,470	7,386	10,630	12,732	15,247
Mutual fund sales	278	2,754	3,242	8,115	6,887	7,434	10,081	12,422	14,845	16,688
Other	3,960	13,854	33,428	40,913	54,293	68,468	83,697	100,961	121,700	115,692
Expenses, total	**16,668**	**43,342**	**70,566**	**95,805**	**109,266**	**132,089**	**155,433**	**187,281**	**217,780**	**237,693**
Interest expense	3,876	11,470	28,093	26,616	40,250	56,877	64,698	80,659	98,095	87,508
Compensation	7,619	18,112	22,931	39,125	37,595	41,541	51,033	58,558	65,027	81,737
Commissions/clearance paid	1,055	2,314	2,959	5,338	5,360	5,700	7,364	8,864	10,326	13,488
Other	4,119	11,446	16,583	24,726	26,060	27,970	32,338	39,200	44,332	54,959
Net income, pretax	**3,160**	**6,502**	**790**	**13,039**	**3,492**	**11,325**	**16,978**	**19,964**	**17,184**	**29,116**

Source: U.S. Securities and Exchange Commission, *Annual Report*.

No. 1220. Annual Revenues for Selected Securities Industries: 1998 and 1999

[In millions of dollars (245,736 represents $245,736,000,000). Covers taxable employer firms only. Based on the North American Industry Classification System (NAICS); see text, Section 15, Business Enterprise. Estimates have not been adjusted to the results of the 1997 Economic Census]

Kind of business	NAICS code	1998	1999
Total	**523x**	**245,736**	**295,302**
Securities and commodity contracts intermediation and brokerage	5231	168,188	203,744
Investment banking & securities dealing	52311	92,500	113,907
Securities brokerage	52312	71,242	85,282
Commodity contracts dealing	52313	1,632	1,807
Commodity contracts brokerage	52314	2,814	2,748
Other financial investment activities [1]	5239x	77,548	91,558
Portfolio management	52392	66,143	76,275
Investment advice	52393	11,405	15,283

[1] Excludes NAICS 52391 (miscellaneous intermediation) and NAICS 52399 (all other financial investment activities).

Source: U.S. Census Bureau, *Service Annual Survey: 1999*.

No. 1221. Revenues of Selected Securities Industries by Source of Revenues: 1998 and 1999

[In millions of dollars (245,736 represents $245,736,000,000). Covers taxable employer firms only. Based on the North American Industry Classification System (NAICS); see text, Section 15, Business Enterprise. Estimates have not been adjusted to the results of the 1997 Economic Census]

Source of revenue	Total (NAICS 523x)		Security and commodity contracts intermediation and brokerage (NAICS 5231)		Portfolio management and investment advice [1] (NAICS 5239x)	
	1998	1999	1998	1999	1998	1999
Total	**245,736**	**295,302**	**168,188**	**203,744**	**77,548**	**91,558**
Commissions from the sale of securities and commodities	51,997	63,401	47,474	58,198	4,523	5,202
Gains (losses) on trading accounts in securities and commodities (net)	34,102	44,989	31,076	42,839	(S)	(S)
Interest income from trading accounts in securities	14,222	15,463	13,231	14,451	991	1,011
Gains (losses) from trading accounts in securities	16,735	26,127	14,694	24,985	(S)	(S)
Gains (losses) from trading accounts in commodities	3,145	3,400	3,150	3,402	(S)	(S)
Gains from underwriting and selling groups of securities (net)	11,080	15,126	10,882	14,774	198	352
MBS, CMO, and REMIC transactions [2]	2,550	2,995	2,463	2,764	(S)	(S)
All other securities transactions	8,529	12,131	8,419	12,010	111	121
Gains on investment accounts (net)	2,773	4,050	2,153	3,673	(S)	(S)
Dividend income	1,868	2,522	1,031	1,446	(S)	(S)
Margin interest and other interest income	42,364	51,301	34,521	39,901	(S)	(S)
Other investment income	13,434	12,703	9,366	8,135	4,068	4,568
Asset/portfolio management fees	65,665	76,125	21,146	23,112	44,519	53,013
Other revenue	22,454	25,085	10,539	11,666	(S)	(S)

S Data do not meet publication standards because of high sampling variability or poor response quality. [1] Excludes NAICS 52391 (miscellaneous intermediation) and NAICS 52399 (all other financial investment activities). [2] MBS=Mortgage-backed securities; CMO=Collateralized mortgage obligation; REMIC=Real estate mortgage investment conduit.

Source: U.S. Census Bureau, *Service Annual Survey: 1999*.

No. 1222. Property and Casualty Insurance—Summary: 1990 to 1999

[In billions of dollars (217.8 represents $217,800,000,000).] Minus sign (-) indicates loss]

Item	1990	1993	1994	1995	1996	1997	1998	1999
Premiums, net written	217.8	241.7	250.7	259.8	268.6	276.4	281.5	287.0
Automobile, private [1]	78.4	93.4	96.8	102.0	107.7	113.6	117.3	118.6
Automobile, commercial [1]	17.0	16.3	16.7	17.2	17.6	18.0	18.1	18.1
Liability other than auto	22.1	22.1	23.6	23.4	24.5	25.0	24.2	24.1
Fire and allied lines	7.1	7.9	8.7	9.4	9.9	8.4	8.4	8.1
Homeowners' multiple peril	18.6	21.5	22.6	24.0	25.4	26.9	29.0	30.6
Commercial multiple peril	17.7	17.3	17.8	18.8	18.9	19.0	19.0	18.9
Workers' compensation	31.0	30.3	28.9	26.2	25.1	24.1	23.2	22.2
Marine, inland and ocean	5.7	6.1	6.7	7.1	7.5	7.6	7.6	7.7
Accident and health	5.0	6.8	7.2	7.8	7.8	8.3	9.8	11.1
Other lines	15.2	20.0	21.7	23.9	24.2	25.5	24.9	27.6
Losses and expenses	234.7	250.7	263.3	268.4	277.1	272.6	289.7	302.6
Underwriting gain/loss	-20.9	-15.1	-19.0	-14.2	-16.7	-5.8	-16.7	-23.1
Net investment income	32.9	32.6	33.7	36.8	38.0	41.5	39.9	38.9
Operating earnings after taxes	9.0	19.3	10.9	20.6	24.4	36.8	30.8	21.9
Assets	556.3	671.5	704.6	765.2	806.1	870.1	907.4	918.3
Policyholders' surplus	138.4	182.3	193.3	230.0	255.5	308.5	333.2	334.3

[1] Includes premiums for automobile liability and physical damage.

Source: Insurance Information Institute, New York, NY, *The Fact Book, Property/Casualty Insurance Facts*, annual (copyright).

No. 1223. Automobile Insurance—Average Expenditures Per Insured Vehicle by State: 1995 to 1999

[In dollars. The average expenditures for automobile insurance in a state are affected by a number of factors, including the underlying rate structure, the coverages purchased, the deductibles and limits selected, the types of vehicles insured, and the distribution of driver characteristics]

State	1995	1998	1999	State	1995	1998	1999	State	1995	1998	1999
U.S.	667	704	683	KS	474	532	542	ND	381	452	469
				KY	555	617	610	OH	531	581	578
AL	549	632	612	LA	788	830	813	OK	526	575	576
AK	730	771	751	ME	472	492	514	OR	565	630	621
AZ	727	818	789	MD	732	769	757	PA	667	722	693
AR	500	589	597	MA	898	816	889	RI	870	852	834
CA	794	721	659	MI	645	737	706	SC	582	655	575
CO	722	764	744	MN	628	680	688	SD	428	479	484
CT	881	901	824	MS	579	650	655	TN	519	587	582
DE	784	845	863	MO	573	611	605	TX	711	731	696
DC	959	1,031	988	MT	468	510	511	UT	547	619	615
FL	739	771	762	NE	452	518	527	VT	512	534	560
GA	597	672	661	NV	759	843	821	VA	553	564	567
HI	963	797	735	NH	609	622	698	WA	650	710	697
ID	447	494	493	NJ	1,013	1,138	1,034	WV	646	725	684
IL	612	656	646	NM	639	676	664	WI	506	552	545
IN	542	583	582	NY	906	960	943	WY	433	492	491
IA	429	459	466	NC	501	564	547				

Source: National Association of Insurance Commissioners (NAIC), Kansas City, MO, *State Average Expenditures and Premiums for Personal Automobile Insurance,* annual. Permission to reprint given by NAIC (copyright).

No. 1224. Life Insurance in Force in the United States—Summary: 1980 to 1999

[402 represents 402,000,000. As of December 31 or calendar year, as applicable. Covers life insurance with life insurance companies only. Represents all life insurance in force on lives of U.S. residents whether issued by U.S. or foreign companies. For definition of household, see text, Section 1, Population]

Year	Number of policies, total (mil.)	Life insurance in force — Value (bil. dol.)					Average size policy in force (dollars)				Average amount ($1,000)		Disposable personal income per household ($1,000)
		Total	Ordinary [1]	Group	Industrial	Credit [2]	Ordinary [1]	Group	Industrial	Credit [2]	Per household	Per insured household	
1980	402	3,541	1,761	1,579	36	165	11,920	13,410	620	2,110	41.9	51.1	24.4
1985	386	6,053	3,247	2,562	28	216	22,780	19,720	640	3,100	66.6	82.2	34.6
1990	389	9,393	5,367	3,754	24	248	37,910	26,630	670	3,500	98.4	124.5	44.6
1994	390	11,057	6,407	4,442	19	189	45,870	26,338	659	3,609	113.9	146.3	51.7
1995	393	11,638	6,816	4,603	18	201	49,090	27,051	664	3,554	119.1	148.9	54.3
1996	355	12,704	7,408	5,068	18	211	52,912	36,459	695	4,215	128.6	157.3	56.6
1997	351	13,364	7,855	5,279	18	212	57,333	37,176	720	4,516	134.1	167.6	58.1
1998	358	14,471	8,506	5,735	7	213	62,543	37,732	724	4,629	141.1	178.6	58.8
1999	367	15,496	9,172	6,110	(1)	213	56,620	38,429	(1)	4,640	149.2	189.8	63.9

[1] Beginning 1999 industrial policies are included in ordinary. [2] Insures borrower to cover consumer loan in case of death.

Source: American Council of Life Insurers, Washington, DC, *Life Insurers Fact Book,* annual (copyright).

No. 1225. Life Insurance Purchases in the United States—Number and Amount: 1980 to 1999

[29,007 represents 29,007,000. Excludes revivals, increases, dividend additions, and reinsurance acquired. Includes long-term credit insurance (life insurance on loans of more than 10 years' duration). See also headnote, Table 1224]

Year	Number of policies purchased (1,000)				Amount purchased (bil. dol.)			
	Total	Ordinary [1]	Group	Industrial	Total	Ordinary [1]	Group	Industrial
1980	29,007	14,750	11,379	2,878	573	386	183	4
1985	33,880	17,104	16,243	533	[2]1,231	911	[2]320	1
1990	28,791	14,066	14,592	133	1,529	1,070	459	(Z)
1994	32,225	13,675	18,390	160	1,611	1,051	560	(Z)
1995	31,999	12,466	19,404	129	1,543	1,005	538	(Z)
1996	30,783	11,926	18,761	96	1,704	1,089	615	(Z)
1997	31,708	11,667	19,973	68	1,893	1,204	689	(Z)
1998	31,891	11,522	20,332	37	2,065	1,325	740	(Z)
1999	38,584	11,673	26,912	([1])	2,367	1,400	967	([1])

Z Less than $500 million.   [1] Beginning 1999 industrial policies are included in ordinary.   [2] Includes Federal Employees' Group Life Insurance: $11 billion in 1985.

Source: American Council of Life Insurers, Washington, DC, *Life Insurers Fact Book*, annual (copyright).

No. 1226. U.S. Life Insurance Companies—Summary: 1980 to 1999

[130.9 represents $130,900,000,000. As of December 31 or calendar year, as applicable. Covers domestic and foreign business of U.S. companies. Beginning 1994 includes annual statement data for companies that primarily are health insurance companies]

Item	Unit	1980	1985	1990	1993	1994	1995	1996	1997	1998	1999
U.S. companies [1]	Number .	1,958	2,261	2,195	1,844	2,136	2,079	1,679	1,620	1,563	1,470
Income	**Bil. dol.**	**130.9**	**234.0**	**402.2**	**466.4**	**492.6**	**528.1**	**561.1**	**610.6**	**663.4**	**726.9**
Life insurance premiums	Bil. dol .	40.8	60.1	76.7	94.4	98.9	102.8	107.6	115.0	119.9	120.3
Annuity considerations	Bil. dol .	22.4	53.9	129.1	156.4	153.0	158.4	178.4	197.5	229.5	270.2
Health insurance premiums	Bil. dol .	29.4	41.8	58.3	68.7	86.2	90.0	92.2	92.7	94.9	100.0
Investment and other	Bil. dol .	38.3	78.2	138.2	146.8	154.5	176.9	182.9	205.3	219.1	236.4
Payments to life insurance beneficiaries	Bil. dol .	12.9	18.2	24.6	28.8	32.6	34.5	36.3	37.5	40.1	41.4
Payments under life insurance and annuity contracts	Bil. dol .	25.2	48.3	63.8	71.2	168.2	193.1	210.7	239.1	261.8	313.9
Surrender values under life insurance [2]	Bil. dol .	6.7	15.6	18.0	16.9	18.0	19.5	24.5	24.0	26.8	32.8
Surrender values under annuity policies [2]	Bil. dol .	(NA)	(NA)	(NA)	(NA)	92.8	105.4	115.7	140.8	154.5	198.3
Policy dividends	Bil. dol .	6.8	10.1	12.0	12.7	15.9	17.8	18.1	18.0	18.9	19.1
Annuity payments	Bil. dol .	10.2	21.3	32.6	40.3	40.4	48.5	51.1	55.1	60.4	62.5
Matured endowments	Bil. dol .	0.9	0.8	0.7	0.6	0.6	1.0	0.7	0.6	0.6	0.5
Other payments	Bil. dol .	0.6	0.5	0.6	0.6	0.5	0.9	0.6	0.6	0.6	0.6
Health insurance benefit payments .	Bil. dol .	23.0	27.3	40.0	46.0	60.1	64.7	66.7	67.4	70.0	74.5
BALANCE SHEET											
Assets	**Bil. dol.**	**479**	**826**	**1,408**	**1,839**	**1,942**	**2,144**	**2,328**	**2,579**	**2,827**	**3,071**
Government securities	Bil. dol .	33	125	211	384	396	409	411	391	379	362
Corporate securities	Bil. dol .	227	374	711	982	1,072	1,241	1,416	1,658	1,896	2,180
Percent of total assets	Percent .	47.4	45.3	50.5	53.4	55.2	57.9	60.8	64.3	67.1	71.0
Bonds	Bil. dol .	180	297	583	730	791	869	962	1,060	1,140	1,190
Stocks	Bil. dol .	47	77	128	252	282	372	454	598	758	990
Mortgages	Bil. dol .	131	172	270	229	215	212	212	210	216	230
Real estate	Bil. dol .	15	29	43	54	54	52	50	46	41	38
Policy loans	Bil. dol .	41	54	63	78	85	96	102	105	105	99
Other	Bil. dol .	32	72	110	112	120	133	137	169	187	163
Interest earned on assets [3]	Percent .	8.02	9.63	8.89	7.52	7.14	7.34	7.25	7.35	6.95	6.71
Obligations and surplus funds [4]	Bil. dol .	479	826	1,408	1,839	1,942	2,144	2,328	2,579	2,827	3,071
Policy reserves [5]	**Bil. dol.**	**390**	**665**	**1,197**	**1,550**	**1,644**	**1,812**	**1,966**	**2,165**	**2,377**	**2,610**
Annuities [6]	Bil. dol .	172	400	798	1,041	1,095	1,213	1,312	1,455	1,608	1,781
Group	Bil. dol .	140	303	516	602	612	619	690	762	845	907
Individual	Bil. dol .	32	97	282	439	482	594	622	693	763	874
Life insurance	Bil. dol .	198	236	349	436	468	511	556	606	656	705
Health insurance	Bil. dol .	11	19	33	51	58	63	70	75	82	92
Asset valuation reserve	Bil. dol .	6	11	15	25	25	30	33	36	38	40
Capital and surplus	Bil. dol .	34	57	91	128	137	151	147	160	173	181

NA Not available.   [1] Beginning 1994 includes life insurance companies that sell accident and health insurance.   [2] Beginning with 1994, "surrender values" include annuity withdrawals of funds, which were not included in prior years.   [3] Net rate.   [4] Includes other obligations not shown separately.   [5] Includes the business of health insurance departments of life companies. Includes reserves for supplementary contracts with and without life contingencies, not shown separately.   [6] Beginning 1996 data are not comparable with prior years' data due to a change in the treatment of separate account annuities.

Source: American Council of Life Insurers, Washington, DC, *Life Insurers Fact Book*, annual (copyright).

Banking, Finance, and Insurance   749

No. 1227. Real Estate, Rental, and Leasing—Establishments, Revenue, Payroll, and Employees by Kind of Business: 1997

[342,621 represents $342,621,000,000]

Kind of business	NAICS code [1]	All firms		Employer firms			
		Establish-ments (number)	Revenue (mil. dol.)	Establish-ments (number)	Revenue (mil. dol.)	Annual payroll (mil. dol.)	Paid em-ployees [2] (1,000)
Real estate & rental & leasing	**53**	**1,684,976**	**342,621**	**288,273**	**240,918**	**41,591**	**1,702.4**
Real estate	531	1,557,556	252,120	221,650	153,275	27,947	1,117.2
Lessors of real estate..............	5311	681,796	154,509	110,226	85,791	9,484	469.4
Offices of real estate agents & brokers ...	5312	590,388	56,502	60,620	38,945	6,792	219.6
Activities related to real estate	5313	285,372	41,109	50,804	28,538	11,671	428.2
Rental & leasing services..............	532	124,792	79,184	64,472	76,379	12,569	559.4
Automotive equipment rental & leasing ...	5321	25,395	29,513	10,542	28,922	3,871	158.1
Consumer goods rental	5322	49,212	14,917	35,423	14,396	3,097	230.0
General rental centers	5323	7,328	3,963	6,509	3,911	941	40.3
Commercial/industrial equipment rental & leasing.................	5324	42,857	30,791	11,998	29,150	4,660	131.0
Lessors of other nonfinancial intangible assets	533	2,628	11,317	2,151	11,264	1,074	25.8

[1] North American Industry Classification System, 1997; see text, Section 15, Business Enterprise. [2] For pay period including March 12.

Source: U.S. Census Bureau, *1997 Economic Census, Geographic Area Series* and *Nonemployer Statistics.*

No. 1228. Real Estate, Rental, and Leasing—Establishments, Employees, and Payroll: 1998 and 1999

[292.3 represents 292,300. Covers establishments with payroll. Employees are for the week including March 12. Most government employees are excluded. For statement on methodology, see Appendix III]

Kind of business	NAICS code [1]	Establishments (1,000)		Employees (1,000)		Payroll (bil. dol.)	
		1998	1999	1998	1999	1998	1999
Real estate & rental & leasing, total ..	**53**	**292.3**	**298.1**	**1,813**	**1,874**	**49.9**	**54.1**
Real estate	531	227.1	231.3	1,197	1,226	34.4	36.6
Lessors of real estate..............	5311	107.7	107.5	490	484	11.0	11.4
Offices of real estate agents & brokers ...	5312	63.5	64.3	241	260	8.7	9.6
Activities related to real estate	5313	55.9	59.5	466	482	14.7	15.6
Rental & leasing services	532	63.1	64.6	593	622	14.3	16.0
Automotive equipment rental & leasing ...	5321	10.8	11.2	171	179	4.4	4.9
Passenger car rental & leasing	53211	5.1	5.5	120	127	2.8	3.2
Truck, utility trailer & RV rental & leasing	53212	5.8	5.8	51	52	1.6	1.6
Consumer goods rental [2].............	5322	33.9	34.5	242	255	3.4	4.0
Video tape & disc rental...........	53223	21.7	20.9	158	156	1.4	1.5
General rental centers	5323	6.2	6.4	40	42	1.0	1.1
Commercial/industrial equip rental & leasing.....................	5324	12.1	12.5	140	145	5.5	6.1
Lessors of other nonfinancial intangible asset.	533	2.1	2.1	23	26	1.1	1.5

[1] North American Industry Classification System; see text, Section 15, Business Enterprise. [2] Includes other kinds of businesses not shown separately.

Source: U.S. Census Bureau, *County Business Patterns,* annual.

No. 1229. Rental and Leasing Services—Revenue by Kind of Business: 1998 and 1999

[In millions of dollars (90,072 represents $90,072,000,000). Based on the North American Industry Classification System (NAICS); see text, Section 15, Business Enterprise. Estimates have been adjusted to the results of the 1997 Economic Census]

Kind of business	NAICS code	Employer and nonemployer firms		Employer firms	
		1998	1999	1998	1999
Rental & leasing services...........	532	90,072	98,930	85,002	93,156
Automotive equipment rental & leasing.......	5321	31,920	35,244	30,918	34,132
Passenger car rental & leasing	53211	20,663	22,782	20,072	22,137
Truck, utility trailer, & RV rental & leasing ...	53212	11,257	12,463	10,846	11,994
Consumer goods rental [1]...............	5322	16,530	17,739	15,776	16,900
Video tape & disc rental..............	53223	7,944	8,768	7,646	8,434
General rental centers.............	5323	4,493	5,127	4,317	4,914
Commercial/industrial equip rental & leasing ...	5324	37,130	40,820	33,992	37,211

[1] Includes other kinds of businesses not shown separately.

Source: U.S. Census Bureau, *Service Annual Survey: 1999.*

Arts, Entertainment, and Recreation

This section presents data on the arts, entertainment, and recreation economic sector of the economy, and personal recreational activities, the arts and humanities, and domestic and foreign travel.

Arts, Entertainment, and Recreation Industry—The U.S. Census Bureau's *Service Annual Survey, Arts, Entertainment, and Recreation Sector,* provides estimates of operation revenue of taxable firms and revenues and expenses of firms exempt from federal taxes for industries in this sector of the economy. Data for 1998 and 1999 are based on the North American Classification System (NAICS). Most establishments were previously classified in the Standard Industrial Classification (SIC) in services, some in retail trade.

This new sector is comprised of industries which existed previously, were revised from previous industry definitions, or are completely new industries. Among those which existed previously are amusement and theme parks. Revised industries include museums. New industries include theater companies and dinner theaters. The following URL contains detailed information about NAICS and provides a comparison of the SIC and NAICS <http://www.census.gov/epcd/www/naics.html>. See also the text in Section 15, Business Enterprise.

The 1997 Economic Census was the first economic census to cover the new Information Sector of the economy. The Census, conducted every 5-years, for the years ending "2" and "7," provides information on the number of establishments, receipts, payroll and paid employees for the U.S. and various geographic levels.

Recreation and leisure activities—Data on the participation in various recreation and leisure time activities are based on several sample surveys. Data on participation in fishing, hunting, and other forms of wildlife-associated recreation are

published periodically by the U.S. Department of Interior, Fish and Wildlife Service. The most recent data are from the 1996 survey. Data on participation in various sports recreation activities are published by the National Sporting Goods Association. Mediamark, Inc. also conducts periodic surveys on sports and leisure activities, as well as other topics.

Parks and recreation—The Department of the Interior has responsibility for administering the national parks. The National Park Service publishes information on visits to national park areas in its annual report, *National Park Statistical Abstract.* The *National Parks: Index (year)* is a biannual report which contains brief descriptions, with acreages, of each area administered by the service, plus certain "related" areas. The annual *Federal Recreation Fee Report* summarizes the prior year's recreation fee receipts and recreation visitation statistics for seven federal land managing agencies. Statistics for state parks are compiled by the National Association of State Park Directors which issues its *Annual Information Exchange.*

Travel— Statistics on arrivals to the United States are reported by the International Trade Administration (ITA). Statistics on departures from the United States include the Department of Transportation's *International Air Travel Statistics* and other sources. Data on domestic travel, business receipts and employment of the travel industry, and travel expenditures are published by the U.S. Travel Data Center, which is the research department of the Travel Industry Association and the national nonprofit center for travel and tourism research located in Washington, DC. Other data on household transportation characteristics are in Section 23, Transportation.

Statistical reliability—For a discussion of statistical collection and estimation, sampling procedures, and measures of statistical reliability applicable to Census Bureau data, see Appendix III.

Arts, Entertainment, and Recreation 751

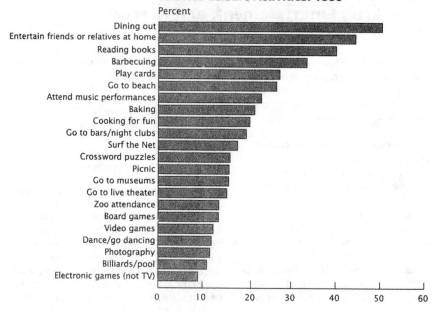

Figure 26.1
Adult Participation During the Last 12 Months in Selected Leisure Activities: 1999

Percent

Dining out
Entertain friends or relatives at home
Reading books
Barbecuing
Play cards
Go to beach
Attend music performances
Baking
Cooking for fun
Go to bars/night clubs
Surf the Net
Crossword puzzles
Picnic
Go to museums
Go to live theater
Zoo attendance
Board games
Video games
Dance/go dancing
Photography
Billiards/pool
Electronic games (not TV)

0   10   20   30   40   50   60

Source: Chart prepared by U.S. Census Bureau. For data, see Table 1243.

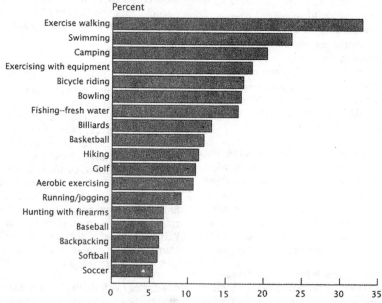

Figure 26.2
Persons Participating in Selected Sports Activities: 1999

Percent

Exercise walking
Swimming
Camping
Exercising with equipment
Bicycle riding
Bowling
Fishing--fresh water
Billiards
Basketball
Hiking
Golf
Aerobic exercising
Running/jogging
Hunting with firearms
Baseball
Backpacking
Softball
Soccer

0   5   10   15   20   25   30   35

Source: Chart prepared by U.S. Census Bureau. For data, see Table 1245.

752   Arts, Entertainment, and Recreation

No. 1230. Arts, Entertainment, and Recreation—Establishments, Receipts, Payroll, and Employees by Kind of Business (NAICS Basis): 1997

[For establishments with payroll. (85,088 represents $85,088,000,000). Based on the 1997 Economic Census; see Appendix III]

Industry	NAICS code [1]	Establishments (number)	Receipts [2] Total (mil. dol.)	Receipts [2] Per paid employee (dol.)	Annual payroll Total (mil. dol.)	Annual payroll Per paid employee (dol.)	Paid employee for pay period including March 12 (1,000)
Taxable establishments	71	79,636	85,088	70,474	26,104	21,620	1,207.4
Performing arts, spectator sports	711	25,942	32,744	138,788	12,834	54,400	235.9
Performing arts companies	7111	5,883	5,272	101,763	1,452	28,033	51.8
Spectator sports	7112	3,881	13,656	147,804	6,151	66,577	92.4
Sports teams & clubs	711211	483	7,809	234,284	4,922	147,686	33.3
Racetracks	711212	807	4,142	92,291	797	17,764	44.9
Other spectator sports	711219	2,591	1,705	120,238	432	30,428	14.2
Promoters of performing arts, sports, & similar events	7113	2,633	5,045	98,133	1,053	20,475	51.4
Agents/managers for artists, athletes, & other public figures	7114	2,532	2,410	182,032	911	68,800	13.2
Independent artists, writers, & performers	7115	11,013	6,361	234,888	3,268	120,657	27.1
Museums, historical sites, & similar	712	787	484	66,431	122	16,811	7.3
Amusement, gambling, & recreation	713	52,907	51,861	53,789	13,147	13,636	964.2
Amusement parks & arcades	7131	3,344	8,418	60,595	1,962	14,121	138.9
Amusement & theme parks	71311	607	7,172	64,733	1,690	15,258	110.8
Amusement arcades	71312	2,737	1,247	44,305	271	9,647	28.1
Gambling industries	7132	2,099	15,542	92,217	3,222	19,117	168.5
Casinos (except casino hotels)	71321	447	10,186	88,413	2,305	20,004	115.2
Other gambling industries	71329	1,652	5,355	100,437	917	17,200	53.3
Other amusement & recreation services	7139	47,464	27,901	42,487	7,963	12,126	656.7
Golf courses & country clubs	71391	8,546	8,637	53,941	2,732	17,062	160.1
Skiing facilities	71392	379	1,341	22,915	431	7,368	58.5
Marinas	71393	4,217	2,541	111,640	517	22,692	22.8
Fitness & recreational sports centers	71394	16,604	7,945	30,987	2,405	9,380	256.4
Bowling centers	71395	5,590	2,821	32,037	821	9,325	88.0
All other amusement & recreation industries	71399	12,128	4,616	65,140	1,058	14,925	70.9
Tax-exempt establishments	71	19,463	19,627	51,610	6,683	17,575	380.3
Performing arts, spectator sports	711	4,624	4,876	53,681	1,622	17,852	90.8
Performing arts companies	7111	3,316	3,299	46,987	1,273	18,135	70.2
Theater companies & dinner theaters	71111	1,647	1,776	54,135	631	19,223	32.8
Dance companies	71112	371	323	47,399	131	19,208	6.8
Musical groups & artists	71113	1,211	1,154	38,767	499	16,756	29.8
Other performing arts companies	71119	87	45	56,119	13	15,726	0.8
Promoters of performing arts, sports, & similar events	7113	1,308	1,577	76,461	348	16,890	20.6
Museums, historical sites, & similar institutions	712	4,793	6,280	74,328	1,715	20,294	84.5
Museums	71211	3,434	4,529	75,334	1,212	20,167	60.1
Historical sites	71212	814	343	50,704	101	15,020	6.8
Zoos & botanical gardens	71213	269	1,279	81,326	364	23,162	15.7
Nature parks & other similar institutions	71219	276	129	68,539	36	19,319	1.9
Other amusement & recreation industries	713	10,046	8,470	41,327	3,347	16,331	205.0
Golf courses & country clubs	71391	3,212	5,583	48,145	2,291	19,761	116.0
Fitness & recreational sports centers	71394	4,679	2,217	29,288	859	11,343	75.7
All other amusement & recreational industries	71399	2,155	670	50,410	197	14,809	13.3

[1] North American Industry Classification System, 1997; see text, this section, and Section 15, Business Enterprise.
[2] Revenue for tax-exempt establishments.
Source: U.S. Census Bureau, *1997 Economic Census, Arts, Entertainment, and Recreation*, Series EC97571A-US(RV), issued April 2000.

No. 1231. Arts, Entertainment, and Recreation Services—Estimated Revenue: 1998 and 1999

[In millions of dollars (108,644 represents $108,644,000,000), except percent. For taxable and tax-exempt employer firms. Except as indicated, estimates adjusted to the results of the 1997 Economic Census. Minus sign (-) indicates decrease]

Industry	NAICS code [1]	Total 1998	Total 1999	Total Percent change, 1998-99	Taxable 1998	Taxable 1999	Taxable Percent change, 1998-99
Arts, entertainment, and recreation	71	108,644	115,366	6.2	88,696	94,119	6.1
Performing arts, spectator sports	711	39,334	41,141	4.6	34,524	36,053	4.4
Performing arts companies [2]	7111	8,618	8,816	2.3	5,415	5,458	0.8
Spectator sports	7112	14,871	15,765	6.0	14,871	15,765	6.0
Sports teams and clubs	711211	8,537	8,973	5.1	8,537	8,973	5.1
Racetracks	711212	4,599	5,106	11.0	4,599	5,106	11.0
Other spectator sports	711219	1,734	1,686	-2.8	1,734	1,686	-2.8
Promoters of performing arts, sports and similar events	7113	6,665	7,168	7.5	5,057	5,438	7.5
Agents and managers for artists, athletes, entertainers and other public figures	7114	2,824	3,054	8.1	2,824	3,054	8.1
Independent artists, writers, and performers	7115	6,356	6,338	-0.3	6,356	6,338	-0.3

See footnotes at end of table.

[See headnote, page 753]

Industry	NAICS code [1]	Total			Taxable		
		1998	1999	Percent change, 1998-99	1998	1999	Percent change, 1998-99
Museums, historical sites, and similar institutions....	712	7,180	7,625	6.2	582	703	20.8
Amusement, gambling, and recreation industries ...	713	62,129	66,601	7.2	53,590	57,363	7.0
Amusement parks and arcades...............	7131	8,525	8,683	1.9	8,525	8,683	1.9
Amusement and theme parks	71311	7,335	7,512	2.4	7,335	7,512	2.4
Amusement arcades	71312	1,191	1,171	-1.7	1,191	1,171	-1.7
Gambling industries	7132	15,597	16,955	8.7	15,597	16,955	8.7
Casinos (except casino hotels)	71321	10,698	11,752	9.9	10,698	11,752	9.9
Other gambling industries	71329	4,899	5,204	6.2	4,899	5,204	6.2
Other amusement and recreation industries	7139	38,007	40,963	7.8	29,468	31,725	7.7
Golf courses and country clubs	71391	14,737	16,116	9.4	9,072	10,099	11.3
Skiing facilities	71392	1,335	1,372	2.8	1,335	1,372	2.8
Marinas [3]	71393	2,832	3,037	7.2	2,832	3,037	7.2
Fitness and recreational sports centers........	71394	10,860	11,836	9.0	8,629	9,292	7.7
Bowling centers	71395	2,819	2,949	4.6	2,819	2,949	4.6
All other amusement and recreation........	71399	5,425	5,654	4.2	4,783	4,977	4.1

[1] Based in the North American Industry Classification System; see text, this section, and Section 15, Business Enterprise. [2] Estimates for NAICS 71113 and 71119 not adjusted to the 1997 Economic Census. [3] Estimates not adjusted to the 1997 Economic Census.

Source: U.S. Census Bureau, *1999 Service Annual Survey, Arts, Entertainment, and Recreation Services.*

No. 1232. Arts, Entertainment, and Recreation—Establishments, Payroll, and Employees by Kind of Business (NAICS Basis): 1998 and 1999

[For establishments with payroll (1,583.8 represents 1,583,800). See Appendix III]

Industry	NAICS code [1]	Establishments		Paid employees [2] (1,000)		Annual payroll (mil. dol.)	
		1998	1999	1998	1999	1998	1999
Arts, entertainment, & recreation, total..	**71**	**102,794**	**102,786**	**1,583.8**	**1,640.0**	**36,045**	**39,416**
Performing arts, spectator sports...........	711	32,731	32,906	312.1	330.4	15,803	17,381
Performing arts companies..............	7111	9,784	9,342	118.1	122.0	2,929	3,053
Theater companies & dinner theaters	71111	3,500	3,322	59.2	61.7	1,289	1,350
Dance companies	71112	581	591	9.6	10.2	178	195
Musical groups & artists	71113	4,732	4,604	40.8	42.6	1,229	1,289
Other performing arts companies	71119	971	825	8.5	7.4	233	219
Spectator sports.....................	7112	4,321	4,372	91.1	91.0	7,060	8,159
Sports teams & clubs...............	711211	633	667	32.7	32.0	5,718	6,708
Racetracks......................	711212	917	888	42.9	42.5	818	880
Other spectator sports	711219	2,771	2,817	15.5	16.5	524	571
Promoters of performing arts, sports, & similar events.....................	7113	4,101	4,224	57.9	65.4	1,365	1,673
Promoters of performing arts, sports, & similar events with facilities	71131	976	1,030	34.5	41.2	570	782
Promoters of performing arts, sports, & similar events without facilities	71132	3,125	3,194	23.4	24.2	795	891
Agents/managers for artists, athletes, & other public figures	7114	2,785	2,837	14.3	15.1	955	1,037
Independent artists, writers, & performers ...	7115	11,740	12,131	30.7	36.9	3,494	3,459
Museums, historical sites, & similar institutions........................	712	5,680	5,714	96.5	104.6	2,086	2,321
Museums.........................	71211	3,901	3,940	66.1	71.4	1,441	1,603
Historical sites	71212	903	891	8.4	8.0	132	131
Zoos & botanical gardens	71213	395	404	17.5	19.6	412	469
Nature parks & other similar institutions	71219	481	479	4.6	5.7	100	118
Amusement, gambling, & recreation industries	713	64,383	64,166	1,175.2	1,205.0	18,156	19,714
Amusement parks & arcades	7131	3,509	3,135	142.6	127.4	2,157	2,266
Amusement & theme parks	71311	930	689	114.8	102.1	1,880	1,963
Amusement arcades	71312	2,579	2,446	27.8	25.3	277	304
Gambling industries.................	7132	2,524	2,238	166.9	178.7	3,473	4,099
Casinos (except casino hotels)	71321	595	546	119.8	128.4	2,611	3,077
Other gambling industries	71329	1,929	1,692	47.1	50.2	862	1,021
Other amusement & recreation services	7139	58,350	58,793	865.7	898.9	12,527	13,349
Golf courses & country clubs	71391	11,751	11,809	270.3	280.1	5,562	5,817
Skiing facilities	71392	400	395	55.7	60.1	421	426
Marinas.........................	71393	4,226	4,170	23.2	24.0	564	599
Fitness & recreational sports centers.....	71394	21,926	22,401	343.5	357.5	3,674	4,035
Bowling centers...................	71395	5,400	5,291	86.5	84.2	822	847
All other amusement & recreation industries......................	71399	14,647	14,727	86.5	93.1	1,483	1,626

[1] North American Industry Classification System code; see text, this section and Section 15, Business Enterprise. [2] For employees on the payroll for the period including March 12.

Source: U.S. Census Bureau, *County Business Patterns,* annual.

No. 1233. Personal Consumption Expenditures for Recreation: 1990 to 1999

[In billions of dollars (284.9 represents $284,900,000,000), except percent. Represents market value of purchases of goods and services by individuals and nonprofit institutions]

Type of product or service	1990	1994	1995	1996	1997	1998	1999
Total recreation expenditures	**284.9**	**368.7**	**401.6**	**429.6**	**456.6**	**489.8**	**534.9**
Percent of total personal consumption [1]	7.4	7.8	8.1	8.2	8.3	8.4	8.5
Books and maps	16.2	20.8	23.1	24.9	26.3	27.8	29.8
Magazines, newspapers, and sheet music	21.6	24.9	26.2	27.6	29.1	32.5	37.0
Nondurable toys and sport supplies	32.8	43.4	47.2	50.6	53.2	57.3	63.1
Wheel goods, sports, and photographic equipment [2]	29.7	35.2	38.5	40.5	42.8	46.4	51.3
Video and audio products, computer equipment, and musical instruments	52.9	71.0	77.0	80.0	83.7	90.7	99.1
Video and audio goods, including and musical instruments	43.9	53.0	55.9	56.4	57.9	62.1	67.3
Computers, peripherals, and software	8.9	18.0	21.0	23.6	25.9	28.6	31.9
Radio and television repair	3.7	3.3	3.6	3.7	4.0	4.0	3.9
Flowers, seeds, and potted plants	10.9	13.2	13.8	14.9	15.3	16.3	17.5
Admissions to specified spectator amusements	14.8	18.2	19.2	20.7	22.1	23.6	25.8
Motion picture theaters	5.1	5.2	5.5	5.8	6.3	6.9	7.4
Legitimate theaters and opera, and entertainments of nonprofit institutions [3]	5.2	7.2	7.6	8.0	8.6	9.1	10.2
Spectator sports [4]	4.5	5.8	6.1	6.9	7.1	7.6	8.2
Clubs and fraternal organizations, except insurance [5]	8.7	11.8	12.7	14.0	14.6	15.0	15.8
Commercial participant amusements [6]	24.6	38.6	43.9	48.3	52.8	56.4	63.1
Parimutuel net receipts	3.5	3.4	3.5	3.5	3.6	3.7	3.8
Other [7]	65.4	84.7	93.1	100.8	109.1	116.0	124.6

[1] See Table 648.   [2] Includes boats and pleasure aircraft.   [3] Except athletic.   [4] Consists of admissions to professional and amateur athletic events and to racetracks, including horse, dog, and auto.   [5] Consists of dues and fees excluding insurance premiums.   [6] Consists of billiard parlors; bowling alleys; dancing, riding, shooting, skating, and swimming places; amusement devices and parks; golf courses; sightseeing buses and guides; private flying operations; casino gambling; and other commercial participant amusements.   [7] Consists of net receipts of lotteries and expenditures for purchases of pets and pet care services, cable TV, film processing, photographic studios, sporting and recreation camps, video cassette rentals, and recreational services, not elsewhere classified.

Source: U.S. Bureau of Economic Analysis, *National Income and Product National Income and Product Accounts of the United States, 1929-97*, (forthcoming); and *Survey of Current Business*, June 2001.

No. 1234. Expenditures Per Consumer Unit for Entertainment and Reading: 1985 to 1999

[Data are annual averages. In dollars, except as indicated. Based on Consumer Expenditure Survey; see text, Section 13, Income, Expenditures, and Wealth, for description of survey. See also headnote, Table 659. For composition of regions, see map, inside front cover]

Year and characteristic	Entertainment and reading		Entertainment				Reading
	Total	Percent of total expenditures	Total	Fees and admissions	Television, radios, and sound equipment	Other equipment and services [1]	
1985	1,311	5.6	1,170	320	371	479	141
1990	1,575	5.6	1,422	371	454	597	153
1991	1,635	5.5	1,472	378	468	627	163
1992	1,662	5.6	1,500	379	492	629	162
1993	1,792	5.8	1,626	414	590	621	166
1994	1,732	5.5	1,567	439	533	595	165
1995	1,775	5.5	1,612	433	542	637	163
1996	1,993	5.9	1,834	459	561	814	159
1997	1,977	5.7	1,813	471	577	766	164
1998	1,907	5.4	1,746	449	535	762	161
1999, total	**2,050**	**5.5**	**1,891**	**459**	**608**	**824**	**159**
Age of reference person:							
Under 25 years old	1,219	5.6	1,149	262	485	402	70
25 to 34 years old	1,892	5.2	1,776	395	636	744	116
35 to 44 years old	2,411	5.6	2,254	528	707	1,019	157
45 to 54 years old	2,578	5.5	2,368	578	741	1,049	210
55 to 64 years old	2,371	6.0	2,176	560	578	1,038	195
65 to 74 years old	1,751	5.9	1,567	438	477	653	184
75 years old and over	1,016	4.4	875	223	341	311	141
Origin of reference person:							
Hispanic	1,316	4.0	1,245	253	554	437	71
Non-Hispanic	2,119	5.7	1,951	478	613	860	168
Race of reference person:							
White and other	2,192	5.7	2,022	498	615	909	170
Black	1,016	3.7	935	175	558	203	81
Region of residence:							
Northeast	2,023	5.3	1,828	505	656	666	195
Midwest	2,233	6.1	2,067	462	596	1,009	166
South	1,684	5.1	1,567	377	570	621	117
West	2,457	5.8	2,268	544	640	1,085	189

[1] Other equipment and services includes pets, toys, and playground equipment; sports, exercise, and photographic equipment; and recreational vehicles.

Source: U.S. Bureau of Labor Statistics, *Consumer Expenditure Survey*, annual.

Arts, Entertainment, and Recreation 755

No. 1235. Performing Arts—Selected Data: 1985 to 1999

[Sales, receipts and expenditures in millions of dollars (209 represents $209,000,000). For season ending in year shown, except as indicated]

Item	1985	1990	1992	1993	1994	1995	1996	1997	1998	1999
Legitimate theater: [1]										
Broadway shows:										
New productions	33	40	37	34	39	33	38	37	33	39
Attendance (mil.)	7.3	8.0	7.4	7.9	8.1	9.0	9.5	10.6	11.5	11.7
Playing weeks [2][3]	1,078	1,070	905	1,019	1,066	1,120	1,146	1,349	1,442	1,441
Gross ticket sales	209	282	293	328	356	406	436	499	558	588
Broadway road tours:										
Attendance (mil.)	8.2	11.1	12.9	14.9	16.0	15.6	18.1	17.6	15.2	14.6
Playing weeks	993	944	1,171	1,296	1,249	1,242	1,345	1,334	1,127	1,082
Gross ticket sales	226	367	503	626	705	701	796	782	721	707
Nonprofit professional theaters: [4]										
Companies reporting	217	185	182	177	231	215	228	197	189	313
Gross income	234.7	307.6	359.1	342.5	455.1	444.4	450.7	565.0	570.0	740.0
Earned income	146.1	188.4	222.5	209.7	277.4	281.2	274.0	349.9	342.0	442.0
Contributed income	88.6	119.2	136.6	132.8	177.7	163.1	176.7	215.1	228.0	298.0
Gross expenses	239.3	306.3	365.6	349.3	460.2	444.9	439.5	526.6	518.5	701.0
Productions	2,710	2,265	2,310	2,319	2,929	2,646	3,074	2,295	2,135	3,921
Performances	52,341	46,131	46,184	44,933	59,542	56,608	56,954	51,453	46,628	64,556
Total attendance (mil.)	14.2	15.2	16.0	16.5	20.7	18.6	17.1	17.2	14.6	18.0
OPERA America professional member companies: [5]										
Number of companies reporting [6] . .	97	98	100	85	86	88	83	91	89	95
Expenses [6]	216.4	321.2	371.8	389.5	404.9	435.0	466.7	534.1	556.3	633.5
Performances [7]	1,909	2,336	2,424	1,945	1,982	2,251	2,019	2,137	2,222	2,200
Total attendance (mil.) [7][8]	6.7	7.5	7.3	5.5	6.0	6.5	6.5	6.9	6.6	6.7
Main season attendance (mil.) [7][9] .	3.3	4.1	4.3	3.6	3.7	3.9	3.9	4.0	3.7	4.1
Symphony orchestras: [10]										
Concerts	19,573	18,931	19,778	18,389	17,795	29,328	28,887	26,906	31,766	31,549
Attendance (mil.)	24.0	24.7	26.3	24.0	24.4	30.9	31.1	31.9	32.2	30.8
Gross revenue	252.4	377.5	414.0	430.5	442.5	536.2	558.9	575.5	627.6	671.8
Operating expenses	426.1	621.7	683.0	689.9	710.0	858.8	892.4	937.1	1,012.0	1,088.0
Support	188.1	257.8	279.6	293.0	293.1	351.0	382.8	401.1	459.7	486.0

[1] Source: The League of American Theaters and Producers, Inc, New York, NY. For season ending in year shown. [2] All shows (new productions and holdovers from previous seasons). [3] Eight performances constitute one playing week. [4] Source: Theatre Communications Group, New York, NY. For years ending on or prior to Aug. 31. [5] Source: OPERA America, Washington, DC. For years ending on or prior to Aug 31. [6] United States companies. [7] Prior to 1993 and for 1999, United States and Canadian companies; 1993 to 1998, U.S. companies only. [8] Includes educational performances, outreach, etc. [9] For paid performances. [10] Source: American Symphony Orchestra League, Inc., Washington, DC. For years ending Aug. 31. Prior to 1995 represents 254 U.S. orchestras; beginning 1995, represents all U.S. orchestras, excluding college/university and youth orchestras. Also, beginning 1995, data based on 1,200 orchestras.

Source: Compiled from sources listed in footnotes.

No. 1236. Attendance Rates for Various Arts Activities: 1997

[In percent. For persons 18 years old and over. Represents attendance at least once in the prior 12 months. Excludes elementary and high school performances. Based on the 1997 household survey Public Participation in the Arts. Data are subject to sampling error; see source. See also Tables 1238 and 1239]

Item	Jazz perfor-mance	Classical music perfor-mance	Opera	Musical play	Non-musical play	Ballet	Art museum	Historic park	Arts/craft fairs
Total	12	16	5	25	16	6	35	47	48
Sex:									
Male	13	14	4	22	15	4	34	48	42
Female	11	17	5	27	17	8	36	46	53
Race:									
Hispanic	7	8	3	16	10	5	29	33	34
White	12	18	5	27	17	7	36	51	52
African American	16	10	2	22	16	4	31	37	34
American Indian	11	9	5	15	5	1	22	42	47
Asian	10	16	7	20	18	4	42	44	39
Age:									
18 to 24 years old	15	16	5	26	20	7	38	46	44
25 to 34 years old	13	11	4	23	13	5	37	49	49
35 to 44 years old	14	14	4	26	15	7	37	52	54
45 to 54 years old	13	20	6	29	20	7	40	54	56
55 to 64 years old	9	16	5	23	14	5	30	45	44
65 to 74 years old	8	18	4	24	15	5	28	37	40
75 years old and over . .	4	14	3	15	13	4	20	25	24
Education:									
Grade school	2	2	-	6	3	2	6	13	13
Some high school	3	4	2	13	7	2	14	27	27
High school graduate . .	7	8	2	16	9	4	25	41	43
Some college	15	18	5	28	19	7	43	56	58
College graduate	21	28	10	44	28	11	58	67	65
Graduate school	28	45	14	50	37	14	70	73	69

- Represents or rounds to zero.

Source: U.S. National Endowment for the Arts, 1997 Survey of Public Participation in the Arts, Research Division Report No. 39, December 1998.

No. 1237. Arts and Humanities—Selected Federal Aid Programs: 1980 to 1999

[In millions of dollars (188.1 represents $188,100,000), except as indicated. For fiscal years ending in year shown, see text, Section 8, State and Local Government Finances and Employment]

Type of fund and program	1980	1985	1990	1994	1995	1996	1997	1998	1999
National Endowment for the Arts:									
Funds available [1]	188.1	171.7	170.8	158.1	132.1	86.9	98.4	85.3	85.0
Program appropriation	97.0	118.7	124.3	116.3	109.0	63.5	65.8	64.3	66.0
Matching funds [2]	42.9	29.5	32.4	29.4	28.5	17.2	16.8	16.8	14.5
Grants awarded (number)	5,505	4,801	4,475	3,843	3,685	1,751	1,098	1,459	1,675
Funds obligated [3][4]	166.4	149.4	157.6	145.2	147.9	75.3	94.4	82.3	82.6
Partnership agreements	22.1	24.4	26.1	40.7	39.2	25.9	30.0	33.4	33.8
Music	13.6	15.3	16.5	10.9	10.9	5.4	(X)	(X)	(X)
Museums	11.2	11.9	12.1	9.4	9.0	3.8	(X)	(X)	(X)
Theater	8.4	10.6	10.6	8.8	7.3	5.2	(X)	(X)	(X)
Dance	8.0	9.0	9.6	7.6	7.1	4.2	(X)	(X)	(X)
Media arts	8.4	9.9	13.9	10.9	8.9	3.0	(X)	(X)	(X)
Challenge [5]	50.8	20.7	19.7	9.6	21.1	4.0	(X)	(X)	(X)
Visual arts	7.3	6.2	5.9	4.8	4.4	1.2	(X)	(X)	(X)
Other	36.6	41.3	43.1	42.5	40.0	22.6	(X)	(X)	(X)
National Endowment for the Humanities:									
Funds available [1]	186.2	125.6	140.6	157.9	151.4	93.1	93.9	93.9	93.9
Program appropriation	100.3	95.2	114.2	131.4	125.7	77.2	80.0	80.0	80.0
Matching funds [2]	38.4	30.4	26.3	26.5	25.7	15.9	13.9	13.9	13.9
Grants awarded (number)	2,917	2,241	2,195	1,881	1,871	815	900	852	874
Funds obligated [3]	185.5	125.7	141.0	159.0	151.8	93.4	94.8	92.7	92.1
Education programs	18.3	17.9	16.3	19.6	19.2	13.5	10.5	10.8	10.3
State programs	26.0	24.4	29.6	32.2	32.0	29.0	29.5	29.1	29.3
Research grants	32.0	24.4	22.5	23.4	22.2	5.1	8.5	7.7	6.6
Fellowship program	18.0	15.3	15.3	17.7	16.5	5.1	5.6	5.7	5.6
Challenge [5]	53.5	19.6	14.6	14.4	13.8	9.9	9.9	9.9	9.9
Public programs	25.1	24.1	25.4	27.5	25.8	12.5	12.6	11.1	12.2
Preservation and access	(X)	(X)	17.5	24.1	22.2	18.3	18.2	18.4	18.2
National Capital Arts and Cultural Affairs Program	(X)	(X)	(X)	(X)	(X)	(X)	(X)	(X)	(X)
Other	12.6	(X)	(X)	(X)	(X)	(X)	(X)	(X)	(X)

X Not applicable.   [1] Includes other funds, shown separately. Excludes administrative funds. Gifts are included in 1980; excluded thereafter.   [2] Represents federal funds obligated only upon receipt or certification by Endowment of matching nonfederal gifts.   [3] Includes obligations for new grants, supplemental awards on previous years' grants, and program contracts.   [4] Beginning with 1997 data, the grantmaking structure changed from discipline-based categories to thematic ones.   [5] Program designed to stimulate new sources and higher levels of giving to institutions for the purpose of guaranteeing long-term stability and financial independence. Program usually requires a match of at least 3 private dollars to each federal dollar. Funds for challenge grants are not allocated by program area because they are awarded on a grant-by-grant basis.

Source: U.S. National Endowment for the Arts, *Annual Report;* and U.S. National Endowment for the Humanities, *Annual Report.*

No. 1238. Participation in Various Leisure Activities: 1997

[In percent, except as indicated (195.6 represents 195,600,000). Covers activities engaged in at least once in the prior 12 months. See headnote, Table 1236. See also Table 1239]

Item	Adult popu- lation (mil.)	Attendance at—			Participation in—				
		Movies	Sports events	Amuse- ment park	Exercise program	Playing sports	Charity work	Home improve- ment/ repair	Computer hobbies
Total	195.6	66	41	57	76	45	43	66	40
Sex: Male	94.2	66	49	58	75	56	40	71	44
Female	101.4	65	34	57	77	35	46	61	37
Race: Hispanic	19.1	59	35	66	69	35	31	61	25
White	146.1	68	44	56	78	48	45	70	43
African American	22.1	60	35	55	74	34	44	51	37
American Indian	3.0	65	34	59	83	49	34	58	37
Asian	5.3	76	29	58	70	48	41	58	62
Age: 18 to 24 years old	23.7	88	51	76	85	67	35	57	68
25 to 34 years old	40.1	79	51	70	82	63	41	63	51
35 to 44 years old	45.3	73	46	68	79	52	50	76	47
45 to 54 years old	33.7	65	42	53	77	40	46	75	40
55 to 64 years old	20.9	46	33	40	69	19	44	71	23
65 to 74 years old	19.6	38	21	29	65	23	40	55	11
75 years old and over	12.3	28	16	18	56	13	40	44	7
Education: Grade school	13.7	14	13	34	46	13	20	40	1
Some high school	26.9	52	25	54	66	30	31	59	19
High school graduate	62.0	62	38	58	74	41	36	65	35
Some college	50.3	78	48	64	81	54	50	71	52
College graduate	25.2	82	59	61	87	61	55	76	63
Graduate school	17.4	81	55	53	88	57	67	73	59
Income: $10,000 or less	15.0	37	15	39	55	19	32	42	19
$10,001 to $20,000	26.5	46	26	51	69	27	34	53	22
$20,001 to $30,000	29.4	56	28	55	72	40	37	61	30
$30,001 to $40,000	32.1	71	42	64	77	46	47	68	40
$40,001 to $50,000	25.9	73	51	67	80	51	42	75	47
$50,001 to $75,000	35.0	82	54	65	86	60	50	80	54
$75,001 to $100,000	16.2	81	66	64	86	61	51	79	64
Over $100,000	15.5	87	65	56	90	66	59	81	69

Source: U.S. National Endowment for the Arts, *1997 Survey of Public Participation in the Arts,* Research Division Report No. 39, December 1998.

No. 1239. Participation in Various Arts Activities: 1997

[In percent. Covers activities engaged in at least once in the prior 12 months. See Table 1238 and headnote, Table 1236]

Item	Playing classical music	Modern dancing [1]	Drawing	Pottery work [2]	Weaving	Photography [3]	Creative writing	Buying art work	Singing in groups
Total	1	13	16	15	28	17	12	35	10
Sex:									
Male	9	13	15	16	5	16	10	36	9
Female	13	12	17	14	49	18	14	34	12
Race:									
Hispanic.	7	14	17	11	17	12	8	33	7
White	12	12	15	16	30	17	12	36	8
African American	8	11	16	11	25	18	14	43	26
American Indian	9	21	18	25	28	28	10	35	7
Asian	12	17	27	13	28	22	21	19	9
Age:									
18 to 24 years old	13	20	39	21	22	28	32	42	14
25 to 34 years old	10	13	18	17	25	18	13	43	9
35 to 44 years old	11	13	15	18	29	18	12	40	9
45 to 54 years old	15	11	13	18	29	18	10	37	13
55 to 64 years old	9	8	9	10	29	10	5	31	11
65 to 74 years old	6	14	7	10	32	10	5	23	10
75 years old and over . .	6	9	4	3	28	5	6	8	7
Education:									
Grade school	2	4	4	7	14	8	2	24	11
Some high school	4	11	13	15	22	12	8	35	9
High school graduate . . .	8	12	15	16	28	13	9	31	9
Some college	14	16	20	18	32	22	17	35	13
College graduate.	18	10	18	13	32	23	14	41	9
Graduate school	20	15	18	13	26	22	19	41	12
Income:									
$10,000 or less	5	9	15	8	28	11	8	29	13
$10,001 to $20,000	7	10	13	12	27	14	8	27	9
$20,001 to $30,000	8	12	17	16	26	14	12	26	11
$30,001 to $40,000	10	14	15	20	29	18	11	44	13
$40,001 to $50,000	11	12	16	17	29	18	13	35	8
$50,001 to $75,000	15	13	17	18	28	18	17	32	10
$70,001 to $100,000 . . .	15	18	18	17	24	23	13	41	11
Over $100,000	18	12	12	14	23	23	11	46	9

[1] Dancing other than ballet (e.g. folk and tap).   [2] Includes ceramics, jewelry, leatherwork, and metalwork.   [3] Includes making movies or video as an artistic activity.

Source: U.S. National Endowment for the Arts, *1997 Survey of Public Participation in the Arts,* Research Division Report No. 39, December 1998.

No. 1240. Retail Sales and Household Participation in Lawn and Garden Activities: 1995 to 1999

[For calendar year (22,242 represents $22,242,000,000). Based on national household sample survey conducted by the Gallup Organization. Subject to sampling variability; see source]

Activity	Retail sales (mil. dol.)					Percent households engaged in activity				
	1995	1996	1997	1998	1999	1995	1996	1997	1998	1999
Total	22,242	22,519	26,639	30,188	33,519	72	64	67	65	64
Lawn care.	7,621	6,925	6,366	8,543	8,986	53	47	45	47	43
Indoor houseplants	864	791	1,107	1,159	1,270	30	31	29	29	32
Flower gardening	2,107	2,987	3,404	3,965	3,976	38	37	38	39	45
Insect control.	1,049	1,734	1,342	1,671	1,214	24	24	21	22	23
Shrub care	774	1,059	1,441	1,635	1,376	25	25	24	25	29
Vegetable gardening	1,359	1,341	1,914	2,006	2,595	28	26	23	24	29
Tree care	1,002	1,362	1,892	1,733	1,732	17	20	18	18	20
Landscaping	5,524	3,964	6,153	6,435	8,585	20	22	23	22	25
Flower bulbs	377	521	573	579	657	21	21	21	21	23
Fruit trees	241	349	455	301	264	11	12	11	10	13
Container gardening	377	387	558	783	1,020	12	10	11	11	15
Raising transplants [1]	187	238	383	160	302	8	8	7	7	12
Herb gardening	140	144	168	146	185	8	9	8	7	11
Growing berries	55	90	60	82	87	5	5	5	5	7
Ornamental gardening.	144	158	251	333	464	5	5	6	5	6
Water gardening	421	469	572	659	806	5	4	5	4	7

[1] Starting plants in advance of planting in ground.

Source: The National Gardening Association, Burlington, VT, *National Gardening Survey,* annual (copyright).

No. 1241. Selected Spectator Sports: 1985 to 1999

[47,742 represents 47,742,000]

Sport	Unit	1985	1987	1990	1995	1996	1997	1998	1999
Baseball, major leagues: [1]									
Attendance	1,000	47,742	53,182	55,512	51,288	61,665	64,921	71,930	71,061
Regular season	1,000	46,824	52,011	54,824	50,469	60,097	63,168	70,372	70,139
National League	1,000	22,292	24,734	24,492	25,110	30,379	31,885	38,424	38,323
American League	1,000	24,532	27,277	30,332	25,359	29,718	31,283	31,948	31,817
Playoffs [2]	1,000	591	784	479	533	1,300	1,349	1,314	706
World Series	1,000	327	387	209	286	268	404	243	216
Players' salaries: [3]									
Average	$1,000	371	412	598	1,111	1,120	1,337	1,399	1,607
Basketball: [4] [5]									
NCAA—Men's college:									
Teams	Number	753	760	767	868	866	865	895	932
Attendance	1,000	26,584	26,798	28,741	28,548	28,225	27,738	28,032	29,025
NCAA—Women's college:									
Teams	Number	746	756	782	864	874	879	911	956
Attendance	1,000	2,072	2,156	2,777	4,962	5,234	6,734	7,387	8,698
Pro: [6]									
Teams	Number	23	23	27	27	29	29	29	(NA)
Attendance, total [7]	1,000	11,534	13,190	18,586	19,883	21,833	21,677	21,801	(NA)
Regular season	1,000	10,506	12,065	17,369	18,516	20,513	20,305	20,373	(NA)
Average per game	Number	11,141	12,795	15,690	16,727	17,252	17,077	17,135	(NA)
Players' salaries:									
Average	$1,000	325	440	750	1,900	2,000	2,200	2,600	(NA)
Football:									
NCAA College: [5]									
Teams	Number	509	507	533	565	566	581	595	601
Attendance	1,000	34,952	35,008	35,330	35,638	36,083	36,858	37,491	39,483
National Football League: [8]									
Teams	Number	28	28	28	30	31	31	31	32
Attendance, total [9]	1,000	14,058	[10]15,180	17,666	19,203	(NA)	19,050	19,742	20,763
Regular season	1,000	13,345	[10]11,406	13,960	15,044	14,612	14,967	15,365	16,207
Average per game	Number	59,567	[10]54,315	62,321	62,682	60,885	62,364	64,020	65,349
Postseason games [11]	1,000	711	656	848	(NA)	(NA)	(NA)	823	794
Players' salaries: [12]									
Average	$1,000	194	203	352	714	791	725	1,138	1,081
Median base salary	$1,000	140	175	236	335	350	340	450	460
National Hockey League: [13]									
Regular season attendance	1,000	11,634	11,856	12,580	9,234	17,042	17,641	17,265	17,995
Playoffs attendance	1,000	1,108	1,384	1,356	1,329	1,540	1,495	1,507	(NA)
Horseracing: [14] [15]									
Racing days	Number	13,745	14,208	13,841	13,243	12,457	11,958	11,380	11,398
Attendance	1,000	73,346	70,105	63,803	38,934	43,367	41,846	37,728	(NA)
Parimutuel turnover	Mil. dol.	12,222	13,122	7,162	14,592	14,902	15,220	15,561	15,828
Revenue to government	Mil. dol.	625	608	624	456	444	422	432	392
Greyhound: [14]									
Total performances	Number	9,590	11,156	14,915	16,110	15,151	14,557	14,943	14,455
Attendance	1,000	23,853	26,215	28,660	(NA)	(NA)	14,306	(NA)	(NA)
Parimutuel turnover	Mil. dol.	2,702	3,193	3,422	2,730	2,433	2,291	2,237	2,130
Revenue to government	Mil. dol.	201	221	235	157	139	114	109	101
Jai alai: [14]									
Total performances	Number	2,736	2,906	3,620	2,748	2,542	2,648	2,600	2,119
Games played	Number	32,260	38,476	(NA)	37,052	34,346	(NA)	37,175	28,706
Attendance	1,000	4,722	6,816	5,329	3,208	(NA)	2,125	(NA)	(NA)
Total handle	Mil. dol.	664.0	707.5	545.5	296.4	273.4	251	153	119
Revenue to government	Mil. dol.	50	51	39	13	12	10	9	5
Professional rodeo: [16]									
Rodeos	Number	617	637	754	739	742	729	703	700
Performances	Number	1,887	1,832	2,159	2,217	2,229	2,213	2,125	2,128
Members	Number	5,239	5,342	5,693	6,894	7,084	7,178	7,301	7,403
Permit-holders (rookies)	Number	2,534	2,746	3,290	3,835	4,141	4,197	4,117	3,511
Total prize money	Mil. dol.	15.1	14.9	18.2	24.5	26.4	28.0	29.9	31.1

NA Not available.   [1] Source: The National League of Professional Baseball Clubs, New York, NY, *National League Green Book;* and The American League of Professional Baseball Clubs, New York, NY, *American League Red Book.* [2] Beginning 1996, two rounds of playoffs were played. Prior years had one round.   [3] Source: Major League Baseball Players Association, New York, NY.   [4] Season ending in year shown.   [5] Source: National Collegiate Athletic Assn., Overland Park, KS. For women's attendance total, excludes double-headers with men's teams.   [6] Source: National Basketball Assn., New York, NY. For season ending in year shown.   [7] Includes All-Star game, not shown separately.   [8] Source: National Football League, New York, NY.   [9] Beginning 1987 includes preseason attendance, not shown separately.   [10] Season was interrupted by a strike. [11] Includes Pro Bowl, a nonchampionship game and Super Bowl.   [12] Source: National Football League Players Association, Washington, DC.   [13] For season ending in year shown. Source: National Hockey League, Montreal, Quebec.   [14] Source: Association of Racing Commissioners International, Inc., Lexington, KY.   [15] Includes thoroughbred, harness, quarter horse, and fairs.   [16] Source: Professional Rodeo Cowboys Association, Colorado Springs, CO., *Official Professional Rodeo Media Guide,* annual (copyright).

Source: Compiled from sources listed in footnotes.

No. 1242. Adult Attendance at Sports Events: 1999

[In thousands (3,595 represents 3,595,000), except percent. For spring 1998. Based on survey and subject to sampling error; see source]

Event	Attend one or more times a month		Attend less than once a month		Event	Attend one or more times a month		Attend less than once a month	
	Number	Percent	Number	Percent		Number	Percent	Number	Percent
Auto racing	3,595	1.8	9,272	4.7	Golf	1,845	0.9	4,711	2.4
Baseball	11,004	5.6	20,022	10.1	High school sports	11,347	5.7	7,414	3.8
Basketball:					Horse racing:				
College games	3,861	2.0	7,314	3.7	Flats, runners	1,296	0.7	3,633	1.8
Professional games	3,350	1.7	8,321	4.2	Trotters/harness	515	0.3	2,834	1.4
Bowling	2,251	1.1	3,026	1.5	Ice hockey	2,752	1.4	7,647	3.9
Boxing	1,203	0.6	2,781	1.4	Motorcycle racing	[1]113	0.6	3,127	1.6
Equestrian events	790	0.4	3,147	1.6	Pro beach volleyball.	[1]210	0.1	2,238	1.1
Figure skating.	652	0.3	3,498	1.8	Rodeo	1,373	0.7	4,539	2.3
Fishing tournaments.	1,253	0.6	2,933	1.5	Soccer.	3,548	1.8	4,323	2.2
Football:					Tennis	870	0.4	3,219	1.6
College games	4,975	2.5	7,861	4.0	Truck and tractor pull/mud				
Monday night prof. games .	2,198	1.1	3,800	1.9	racing	931	0.5	3,723	1.9
Weekend prof. games. . . .	3,782	1.9	7,748	3.9	Wrestling—professional	1,563	0.8	4,122	2.1

[1] Figure does not meet standards of reliability or precision.

Source: Mediamark Research, Inc., New York, NY Top-line Reports (copyright). Internet site <http://www.mediamark.com/mri/docs/TopLineReports.html> (accessed 02 July 2001).

No. 1243. Adult Participation in Selected Leisure Activities by Frequency: 1999

[In thousands (15,430 represents 15,430,000), except percent. For spring 1999. Based on sample and subject to sampling error; see source]

Activity	Participated in the last 12 months		Frequency of participation							
			Two or more times a week		Once a week		Two to three times a month		Once a month or less	
	Number	Percent	Number	Percent	Number	Percent	Number	Percent	Number	Percent
Attend auto shows	15,430	7.8	[1]195	0.1	[1]290	0.1	[1]355	0.2	9,213	4.7
Adult education courses	15,411	7.8	3,137	1.6	3,071	1.6	524	0.3	5,771	2.9
Attend horse races	6,158	3.1	[1]309	0.2	[1]201	0.1	[1]238	0.1	3,915	2.0
Attend music performances . .	45,922	23.3	471	0.2	779	0.4	2,052	1.0	32,766	16.6
Attend dance performances . .	11,406	5.8	[1]136	0.1	[1]325	0.2	508	0.3	7,361	3.7
Backgammon	5,805	2.9	409	0.2	355	0.2	727	0.4	3,054	1.5
Baking	43,111	21.8	9,073	4.6	7,292	3.7	8,676	4.4	12,400	6.2
Barbecuing	66,182	33.5	10,965	5.6	11,375	5.8	15,664	7.9	18,061	9.2
Go to bars/night clubs.	39,314	19.9	3,439	1.7	5,110	2.6	6,388	3.2	17,867	9.0
Go to beach	52,781	26.7	3,292	1.7	2,725	1.4	5,273	2.7	29,757	15.0
Billiards/pool	21,743	11.0	1,730	0.9	1,645	0.8	2,432	1.2	11,376	5.7
Birdwatching	10,419	5.3	4,872	2.5	961	0.5	933	0.5	2,000	1.0
Board games.	26,934	13.6	1,945	1.0	2,275	1.2	4,697	2.4	13,971	7.0
Chess	7,598	3.8	619	0.3	498	0.3	819	0.4	3,822	1.9
Cooking for fun	40,936	20.7	13,933	7.1	6,856	3.5	6,608	3.3	7,320	3.7
Concerts on radio.	11,908	6.0	2,134	1.1	1,420	0.7	1,356	0.7	3,763	1.9
Crossword puzzles	31,949	16.2	14,868	7.5	4,265	2.2	3,297	1.7	5,094	2.6
Dance/go dancing	23,634	12.0	1,458	0.7	2,660	1.3	3,444	1.7	11,382	5.7
Dining out	99,437	50.4	19,324	9.8	23,479	11.9	24,586	12.5	20,930	10.6
Electronic games (not TV) . . .	17,809	9.0	5,265	2.7	2,499	1.3	2,509	1.3	4,374	2.2
Entertain friends or relatives at home	87,636	44.4	7,703	3.9	11,338	5.7	19,905	10.1	36,554	18.5
Fly kites	6,912	3.5	[1]99	-	[1]119	0.1	[1]121	0.1	4,707	2.4
Furniture refinishing	9,304	4.7	[1]386	0.2	[1]235	0.1	383	0.2	6,355	3.2
Go to live theater	30,688	15.5	[1]194	0.1	565	0.3	1,353	0.7	22,686	11.4
Model making	4,055	2.1	[1]329	0.2	[1]160	0.1	[1]360	0.2	2,206	1.1
Go to museums	31,456	15.9	[1]129	0.1	[1]236	0.1	825	0.4	23,808	12.1
Painting, drawing	12,895	6.5	2,498	1.3	1,300	0.7	1,737	0.9	4,738	2.4
Photography	23,161	11.7	1,823	0.9	2,381	1.2	5,060	2.6	10,112	5.1
Picnic.	31,585	16.0	[1]389	0.2	515	0.3	2,410	1.2	20,373	10.3
Play bingo.	11,349	5.7	1,002	0.5	1,551	0.8	1,077	0.5	4,756	2.4
Play cards	54,091	27.4	6,765	3.4	5,318	2.7	7,707	3.9	24,525	12.4
Play musical instrument.	15,003	7.6	5,929	3.0	1,751	0.9	1,403	0.7	3,714	1.9
Reading books	79,218	40.1	43,919	22.2	7,575	3.8	6,861	3.5	11,071	5.6
Surf the net.	35,347	17.9	18,351	9.3	5,038	2.6	3,687	1.9	5,071	2.5
Word games	16,101	8.2	5,502	2.8	1,517	0.8	1,835	0.9	4,376	2.2
Trivia games	13,384	6.8	1,713	0.9	1,113	0.6	1,563	0.8	6,196	3.2
Video games	24,396	12.4	7,802	4.0	2,414	1.2	3,330	1.7	6,196	3.1
Woodworking	10,779	5.5	2,154	1.1	1,012	0.5	1,824	0.9	3,858	2.0
Zoo attendance	26,981	13.7	[1]286	0.1	[1]64	(Z)	553	0.3	19,789	10.0

- Represents zero.   Z Less than 0.05 percent.   [1] Figure does not meet standards of reliability or precision.

Source: Mediamark Research, Inc., New York, NY, Top-line Reports (copyright). Internet site <http://www.mediamark.com/mri/docs/TopLineReports.html> (accessed 02 July 2001).

No. 1244. Selected Recreational Activities: 1975 to 1999

[26 represents 26,000,000]

Activity	Unit	1975	1980	1985	1990	1995	1997	1998	1999
Softball, amateur: [1]									
Total participants [2]	Million ...	26	30	41	41	42	41	40	40
Youth participants	1,000....	450	650	712	1,100	1,350	1,440	1,400	1,400
Adult teams [3]	1,000....	66	110	152	188	187	178	166	163
Youth teams [3]	1,000....	9	18	31	46	74	80	81	83
Golfers (one round or more) [4][5]	1,000....	13,036	15,112	17,520	27,800	25,000	26,474	26,427	26,446
Golf rounds played [4][5]	1,000....	308,562	357,701	414,777	502,000	490,200	547,200	528,500	564,100
Golf facilities [4]	Number ..	11,370	12,005	12,346	12,846	14,074	14,602	14,900	15,195
Classification:									
Private	Number ..	4,770	4,839	4,861	4,810	4,324	4,257	4,251	4,285
Daily fee	Number ..	5,014	5,372	5,573	6,024	7,491	7,984	8,247	8,470
Municipal	Number ..	1,586	1,794	1,912	2,012	2,259	2,361	2,402	2,440
Tennis: [6]									
Players	1,000....	[7]34,000	(NA)	13,000	21,000	17,820	19,500	(NA)	20,800
Courts	1,000....	130	(NA)	220	220	240	245	(NA)	(NA)
Indoor	1,000....	8	(NA)	14	14	15	15	(NA)	(NA)
Tenpin bowling: [8]									
Participants, total	Million ...	62.5	72.0	67.0	71.0	79.0	91.0	91.0	91.0
Male	Million ...	29.9	34.0	32.0	35.4	36.3	41.8	41.8	41.8
Female	Million ...	32.6	38.0	35.0	35.6	42.6	49.2	49.2	49.2
Establishments	Number ..	8,577	8,591	8,275.	7,611	7,049	6,688	6,398	6,398
Lanes	1,000....	141	154	155	148	139	133	128	128
Membership, total [9]	1,000....	8,751	9,664	8,064	6,588	4,925	4,405	3,934	3,934
American Bowling									
Congress	1,000....	4,300	4,688	3,657	3,036	2,370	2,135	1,937	1,937
Women's Bowling									
Congress	1,000....	3,692	4,187	3,714	2,859	2,036	1,798	1,566‾	1,566
Young American Bowling									
Alliance [10]	1,000....	759	789	693	693	519	472	431	431
Motion picture screens [11]	1,000....	15	18	21	24	28	32	34	37
Indoor	1,000....	11	14	18	23	27	31	33	36
Drive-in	1,000....	4	4	3	1	1	1	1	1
Receipts, box office	Mil. dol. .	2,115	2,749	3,749	5,022	5,494	6,366	6,949	7,448
Admission, average price ..	Dollars...	2.05	2.69	3.55	4.23	4.35	4.59	4.69	5.08
Attendance	Million ...	1,033	1,022	1,056	1,189	1,263	1,388	1,481	1,465
Boating: [12]									
Recreational boats owned ...	1,000....	(NA)	11,832	13,778	15,987	15,375	16,230	16,657	16,773
Retail expenditures on									
boating [13]	Mil. dol. ..	4,800	7,370	13,284	13,731	17,226	19,344	19,001	22,215
Retail units purchased:									
Total all boats [14]	1,000....	(NA)	643	675	525	664	610	576	585
Outboard boats	1,000....	(NA)	290	305	227	231	200	214	230
Inboard boats	1,000....	(NA)	8	17	15	12	12	18	19
Sterndrive boats	1,000....	(NA)	56	115	97	94	92	78	80
Jet boats	1,000....	(NA)	(NA)	(NA)	(NA)	15	12	10	8
Personal watercraft	1,000....	(NA)	(NA)	(NA)	(NA)	200	176	130	106
Sailboats	1,000....	(NA)	73	38	21	14	14	19	21
Canoes	1,000....	(NA)	105	79	75	98	104	108	121
Inflatable boats	1,000....	(NA)	16	34	27	(NA)	(NA)	(NA)	(NA)
Sailboard	1,000....	(NA)	21	50	42	(NA)	(NA)	(NA)	(NA)
Boat trailers	1,000....	(NA)	176	192	165	207	181	174	168
Outboard motors	1,000....	(NA)	315	392	352	317	302	314	332
Sterndrive and inboard									
engines	1,000....	(NA)	88	155	134	120	116	105	109

NA Not available.   [1] Source: Amateur Softball Association, Oklahoma City, OK.   [2] Amateur Softball Association teams and other amateur softball teams.   [3] Amateur Softball Association teams only.   [4] Source: National Golf Foundation, Jupiter, FL.   [5] Prior to 1990, for persons 5 years of age and over; thereafter for persons 12 years of age and over.   [6] Source: Tennis Industry Association, Hilton Head, SC. Players for persons 12 years old and over who played at least once.   [7] 1974 data.   [8] For season ending in year shown. Persons 5 years old and over. Source: Bowling Headquarters, Greendale, WI.   [9] Membership totals are for U.S., Canada and for U.S. military personnel worldwide.   [10] Prior to 1985, represents American Jr. Bowling Congress and ABC/WIBC Collegiate Division.   [11] Source: Motion Picture Association of America, Inc., Encino, CA. 1970 figures represent theaters.   [12] Source: National Marine Manufacturers Association, Chicago, IL. (copyright).   [13] Represents estimated expenditures for new and used boats, motors and engines, accessories, safety equipment, fuel, insurance, docking, maintenance, launching, storage, repairs, and other expenses.   [14] 1980 through 1990 includes other boats, not shown separately.

Source: Compiled from sources listed in footnotes.

No. 1245. Participation in Selected Sports Activities: 1999

[In thousands (245,283 represents 245,283,000), except as indicated. For persons 7 years of age or older. Except as indicated, a participant plays a sport more than once in the year]

Activity	All persons Number	All persons Rank	Sex Male	Sex Female	Age 7-11 years	Age 12-17 years	Age 18-24 years	Age 25-34 years	Age 35-44 years	Age 45-54 years	Age 55-64 years	Age 65 years and over	Household income Under 15,000	Household income 15,000-24,999	Household income 25,000-34,999	Household income 35,000-49,000	Household income 50,000-74,999	Household income 75,000 and over
Total	**245,283**	(X)	**119,213**	**126,069**	**20,184**	**23,443**	**25,708**	**37,857**	**44,662**	**35,706**	**23,333**	**34,389**	**34,765**	**30,683**	**35,217**	**45,327**	**50,448**	**48,842**
SERIES I SPORTS [1]																		
Number participated in—																		
Aerobic exercising [2]	26,244	12	6,680	19,564	1,434	2,009	4,370	6,583	5,226	3,390	1,420	1,811	2,145	2,238	4,024	4,620	5,835	7,381
Backpacking [3]	15,293	16	9,296	5,997	1,576	2,396	2,699	3,835	3,136	1,128	335	189	1,850	1,885	2,652	3,152	3,068	2,687
Badminton	4,938	28	2,355	2,583	721	1,240	554	701	1,019	424	182	96	510	427	634	1,295	1,104	969
Baseball	16,326	15	12,798	3,527	4,865	4,068	2,241	1,927	2,003	702	250	269	995	1,473	2,425	3,409	4,268	3,756
Basketball	29,611	9	20,991	8,620	6,021	7,963	5,073	4,833	3,800	1,468	313	141	2,707	3,056	4,463	6,099	6,605	6,681
Bicycle riding [2]	42,406	5	23,556	18,851	10,219	7,870	3,475	6,138	7,398	4,061	1,817	1,427	4,179	4,118	5,605	8,230	10,044	10,231
Billiards	32,148	8	20,169	11,979	1,696	3,120	7,988	8,298	6,293	3,248	917	589	3,835	3,554	4,765	8,317	6,786	6,891
Bowling	41,635	6	21,287	20,348	5,002	6,220	6,859	7,964	8,012	4,175	1,299	2,085	4,043	3,914	5,941	8,195	9,623	9,920
Calisthenics [2]	12,572	20	5,989	6,583	1,792	1,994	1,699	2,045	2,375	1,309	535	825	973	1,282	1,537	2,313	2,843	3,625
Camping [4]	50,094	3	26,815	23,278	6,752	6,355	5,973	9,685	11,075	5,752	2,723	1,778	4,807	5,330	7,553	9,881	12,089	10,434
Exercise walking [2]	80,798	1	30,749	50,049	3,748	4,223	7,467	13,911	16,121	13,780	8,800	12,748	10,067	9,957	11,433	13,601	17,016	18,724
Exercising with equipment [2]	45,207	4	22,123	23,084	1,184	4,040	6,862	9,252	9,929	6,851	3,475	3,612	3,869	4,001	6,221	7,558	10,727	12,831
Fishing—fresh water	40,766	7	27,905	12,861	4,652	4,864	4,122	6,762	8,818	5,333	3,432	2,783	5,347	4,874	6,109	8,642	8,901	6,893
Fishing—salt water	11,910	21	8,416	3,495	849	1,336	1,185	2,049	2,612	1,897	1,019	964	1,231	1,334	1,576	2,237	2,699	2,833
Football—tackle	8,695	25	7,983	712	1,527	3,452	1,807	899	584	232	100	95	1,007	1,135	1,339	1,812	1,867	1,534
Football—touch	11,138	23	9,146	1,992	2,425	2,906	2,371	1,996	1,040	284	46	70	1,170	1,208	1,659	2,262	2,619	2,219
Golf	27,005	11	21,358	5,647	1,055	2,592	3,113	5,280	5,408	4,313	2,520	2,725	1,283	1,771	3,033	4,680	6,902	9,336
Hiking	28,084	10	15,287	12,797	2,788	2,935	3,892	5,895	6,613	3,380	1,498	1,083	2,900	3,121	3,187	5,158	6,140	7,558
Hunting with firearms	16,647	14	14,756	1,891	788	1,890	1,763	3,590	4,038	2,190	1,307	1,082	1,953	2,139	2,671	3,558	3,874	2,452
Martial arts	5,100	27	3,054	2,046	1,318	920	1,001	748	687	263	79	86	480	537	649	800	1,500	1,134
Racquetball	3,187	29	2,242	945	157	236	707	1,058	650	232	84	63	275	335	391	553	703	931
Running/jogging [2]	22,366	13	12,256	10,110	1,933	3,595	4,438	4,694	4,458	2,077	701	467	2,129	2,118	2,593	4,065	5,234	6,227
Soccer	13,218	18	8,375	4,843	5,671	3,299	1,373	1,445	921	386	79	42	802	1,057	1,948	2,365	3,235	3,812
Softball	14,711	17	7,827	6,884	2,485	3,205	2,276	3,163	2,428	834	173	147	1,016	1,781	2,354	2,992	3,425	3,144
Swimming [2]	57,916	2	27,091	30,825	10,269	9,394	6,788	8,299	11,027	5,620	2,752	3,765	4,908	5,276	7,499	10,529	14,244	15,458
Table tennis	8,175	26	5,224	2,950	888	1,822	1,503	1,045	1,500	877	281	259	594	495	1,008	1,663	1,844	2,572
Target shooting	12,972	19	10,649	2,324	1,236	1,602	1,809	2,826	2,668	1,572	746	512	1,399	1,698	1,700	2,722	3,026	2,426
Tennis	10,921	24	5,887	5,034	1,142	2,167	2,021	2,061	1,719	1,082	463	267	859	767	1,226	1,644	2,858	3,567
Volleyball	11,717	22	5,337	6,380	1,074	3,253	2,190	2,444	1,821	665	217	52	987	1,093	1,761	2,395	2,870	2,610

U.S. Census Bureau, Statistical Abstract of the United States: 2001

Activity	All persons Number	Rank	Sex Male	Female	Age 7-11 years	12-17 years	18-24 years	25-34 years	35-44 years	45-54 years	55-64 years	65 years and over	Household income (dol.) Under 15,000	15,000-24,999	25,000-34,999	35,000-49,999	50,000-74,999	75,000 and over
SERIES II SPORTS [5]																		
Total	245,409	(X)	119,265	126,145	20,184	23,443	25,708	37,876	44,662	35,718	23,378	34,441	34,313	31,006	35,622	44,995	50,048	51,426
Number participating in—																		
Archery (target)	4,895	16	3,892	1,003	966	839	651	904	816	423	153	143	478	541	762	1,012	1,050	1,051
Boating, motor/power	24,444	1	13,765	10,679	2,242	2,707	2,792	5,198	5,428	3,306	1,523	1,248	1,819	2,198	3,453	4,752	5,131	7,090
Canoeing	7,339	10	4,243	3,097	908	1,226	882	1,273	1,486	904	405	255	650	697	611	1,355	1,910	2,116
Dart throwing	20,229	4	12,296	7,932	2,071	2,206	3,606	5,819	4,275	1,542	480	230	2,813	2,736	3,300	4,125	3,765	3,490
Hunting with bow arrow	6,024	15	5,448	576	216	473	938	1,555	1,560	845	249	188	887	1,011	954	1,112	1,132	929
Ice hockey	1,880	22	1,415	465	309	367	433	336	322	54	16	42	83	131	134	233	531	767
Ice/figure skating	7,679	8	3,152	4,527	2,293	1,765	703	1,170	1,162	409	125	51	676	417	663	1,122	1,735	3,067
Mountain biking—off road	6,782	12	4,692	2,091	782	1,047	1,082	1,854	1,207	522	184	103	847	511	980	1,329	1,406	1,709
Mountain biking—on road	15,146	5	8,758	6,389	1,941	2,098	2,262	3,777	3,099	1,324	372	273	1,860	1,081	1,777	2,644	3,827	3,956
Roller hockey	2,514	19	2,035	479	794	800	333	251	268	61	7	-	90	177	290	453	746	758
Roller skating/in-line wheels	24,071	3	11,881	12,190	8,924	6,532	2,403	2,967	2,264	579	215	187	2,020	1,822	3,188	4,334	6,076	6,632
Roller skating/traditional 2x2 wheel	8,237	7	3,075	5,162	2,803	2,191	765	1,220	967	202	89	-	1,153	998	1,214	1,712	1,618	1,541
Sailing	2,750	18	1,586	1,164	232	345	115	342	401	663	375	279	149	148	246	293	682	1,231
Scuba (open water)	2,321	20	1,526	795	35	169	339	858	399	347	109	64	146	225	138	395	547	869
Skate boarding	6,957	11	5,715	1,242	2,804	2,821	613	353	195	76	14	81	776	638	982	1,406	1,380	1,775
Skiing—alpine	7,411	9	4,495	2,916	586	1,113	1,344	1,583	1,439	905	266	174	322	376	613	969	1,882	3,249
Skiing—cross country	2,234	21	1,081	1,153	176	142	374	348	425	464	218	86	240	106	208	424	558	699
Snorkeling	6,330	14	3,385	2,945	424	753	786	1,453	1,476	906	378	153	340	335	333	806	1,238	3,277
Snowboarding	3,313	17	2,460	853	703	1,160	636	397	278	78	31	30	185	167	291	546	676	1,447
Step aerobics	8,247	6	924	7,323	178	430	1,358	2,519	1,869	1,014	468	411	904	747	923	1,572	1,958	2,143
Water skiing	6,575	13	3,793	2,782	561	1,342	1,232	1,485	1,313	458	134	50	412	572	569	1,000	1,531	2,491
Wind surfing	491	23	269	223	32	52	16	126	46	121	26	72	69	92	47	79	92	111
Work-out at club	24,071	2	11,175	12,896	292	1,279	4,240	6,451	5,270	3,320	1,496	1,724	1,895	1,939	2,365	3,660	5,272	8,940

- Represents or rounds to zero. X Not applicable. [1] Based on a sampling of 15,000 households. [2] Participant engaged in activity at least six times in the year. [3] Includes wilderness camping. [4] Vacation/overnight. [5] Based on a sampling of 20,000 households.

Source: National Sporting Goods Association, Mt. Prospect, IL, *Sports Participation in 1999: Series I and Series II* (copyright).

No. 1246. High School Students Engaged in Organized Physical Activity: 1999

[In percent. For students in grades 9 to 12. Based on the Youth Risk Behavior Survey, a school-based survey and subject to sampling error; for details see source]

Characteristic	Enrolled in physical education class			Played on a sports team
	Total	Attended daily	Exercised 20 minutes or more per class	
All students	**56.1**	**29.1**	**76.3**	**55.1**
Male	60.7	31.9	82.1	61.7
Grade 9	82.3	44.0	84.4	63.9
Grade 10	65.3	32.8	79.4	62.3
Grade 11	44.6	23.5	82.0	58.8
Grade 12	43.8	23.6	82.3	60.7
Female	51.5	26.3	69.6	48.5
Grade 9	75.6	40.3	72.5	53.4
Grade 10	56.6	27.9	70.2	50.9
Grade 11	36.8	16.6	68.0	45.8
Grade 12	29.4	16.6	60.1	42.3
White, non-Hispanic	56.1	28.3	78.7	56.9
Male	60.2	30.8	83.8	63.0
Female	51.7	25.8	72.4	50.5
Black, non-Hispanic	52.9	29.2	67.8	48.7
Male	59.2	33.1	78.4	62.0
Female	47.1	25.5	55.8	36.3
Hispanic	59.3	40.4	75.5	50.8
Male	65.1	44.6	79.6	57.2
Female	53.6	36.2	70.8	44.5

Source: U.S. Centers for Disease Control and Prevention, Atlanta, GA, *Youth Risk Behavior Surveillance—United States, 1999, Morbidity and Mortality Weekly Report,* Vol. 49, No. SS-5, June 9, 2000.

No. 1247. Participation in High School Athletic Programs: 1971 to 2000

[Data based on number of state associations reporting and may underrepresent the number of schools with and participants in athletic programs]

Year	Participants [1]		Sex and sport	Most popular sports, 1999-2000 [2]	
	Males	Females		Schools	Participants
1971	3,666,917	294,105	MALES		
1972-73	3,770,621	817,073			
1973-74	4,070,125	1,300,169	Football (11-player)	13,313	1,002,734
1975-76	4,109,021	1,645,039	Basketball	16,852	541,130
1977-78	4,367,442	2,083,040	Track & field (outdoor)	14,664	480,791
1978-79	3,709,512	1,854,400	Baseball	14,610	451,701
1979-80	3,517,829	1,750,264	Soccer	9,330	330,044
1980-81	3,503,124	1,853,789	Wrestling	9,046	239,105
1981-82	3,409,081	1,810,671	Cross country	11,891	183,139
1982-83	3,355,558	1,779,972	Golf	12,391	165,857
1983-84	3,303,599	1,747,346	Tennis	9,603	139,507
1984-85	3,354,284	1,757,884	Swimming & diving	5,324	86,640
1985-86	3,344,275	1,807,121	FEMALE		
1986-87	3,364,082	1,836,356			
1987-88	3,425,777	1,849,684	Basketball	16,526	451,600
1988-89	3,416,844	1,839,352	Track & field (outdoor)	14,587	405,305
1989-90	3,398,192	1,858,659	Volleyball	13,426	382,755
1990-91	3,406,355	1,892,316	Softball (fast pitch)	13,009	343,001
1991-92	3,429,853	1,940,801	Soccer	8,218	270,273
1992-93	3,416,389	1,997,489	Tennis	9,468	159,740
1993-94	3,472,967	2,130,315	Cross country	11,277	154,021
1994-95	3,536,359	2,240,461	Swimming & diving	5,536	138,475
1995-96	3,634,052	2,367,936	Competitive spirit squads	3,497	64,319
1996-97	3,706,225	2,474,043	Golf	7,090	54,720
1997-98	3,763,120	2,570,333			
1998-99	3,832,352	2,652,726			
1999-00	3,861,749	2,675,874			

[1] A participant is counted in the number of sports participated in. [2] Ten most popular sports for each sex in terms of number of participants.

Source: National Federation of State High School Associations, Indianapolis, IN, *The 1999-2000 High School Athletics Participation Survey* (copyright).

No. 1248. Participation in NCAA Sports: 1998-99

Sport	Males Teams	Males Athletes	Males Average squad	Females Teams	Females Athletes	Females Average squad
Total [1]	8,004	211,273	(X)	8,374	148,803	(X)
Baseball	844	25,669	30.4	(X)	(X)	(X)
Basketball	980	15,710	16.0	1,001	14,365	14.4
Bowling [2]	10	142	14.2	5	20	4.0
Cross country	827	10,935	13.2	891	12,042	13.5
Equestrian [2]	33	371	11.3	41	633	15.4
Fencing [3]	37	646	17.5	45	594	13.2
Field hockey	(X)	(X)	(X)	240	5,472	22.8
Football	605	56,528	93.4	(X)	(X)	(X)
Golf	716	7,695	10.8	364	2,933	8.1
Gymnastics	26	375	14.4	90	1,490	16.6
Ice hockey [4]	131	3,702	28.3	40	900	22.5
Lacrosse	197	6,193	31.4	213	4,749	22.3
Rifle [3]	41	343	8.4	44	184	4.2
Rowing [5]	70	2,444	34.9	122	5,628	46.1
Sailing [2]	22	288	13.1	(X)	(X)	(X)
Skiing [3]	40	574	14.4	44	535	12.2
Soccer	717	18,238	25.4	790	17,520	22.2
Softball [2]	(X)	(X)	(X)	831	14,943	18.0
Squash [2]	21	347	16.5	27	365	13.5
Swimming/diving	381	7,559	19.8	458	10,012	21.9
Synchronized swimming [4]	(X)	(X)	(X)	7	108	15.4
Tennis	769	7,729	10.1	877	8,492	9.7
Track, indoor	526	16,943	32.2	560	15,460	27.6
Track, outdoor	637	20,401	32.0	671	18,220	27.2
Volleyball	79	1,124	14.2	960	13,194	13.7
Water polo [4]	43	907	21.1	37	746	20.2
Wrestling	242	6,321	26.1	(X)	(X)	(X)

X Not applicable.   [1] Includes other sports, not shown separately.   [2] Sport recognized by the NCAA but does not have an NCAA championship.   [3] Co-ed championship sport.   [4] Sport recognized by the NCAA but does not have an NCAA championship for women.   [5] Sport recognized by the NCAA but does not have an NCAA championship for men.
Source: The National Collegiate Athletic Association (NCAA), Indianapolis, IN, *1998-99 Participation Study.*

No. 1249. Participants in Wildlife Related Recreation Activities: 1996

[In thousands (39,694 represents 39,694,000). For persons 16 years old and over engaging in activity at least once in 1996. Based on survey and subject to sampling error; see source for details]

Participant	Number	Days of participation	Trips	Participant	Number	Days of participation
Total sportsmen [1]	39,694	862,569	729,495	Wildlife watchers [1]	62,868	(X)
Total anglers	35,246	625,893	506,557	Nonresidential [2]	23,652	313,790
Freshwater	29,734	515,115	420,010	Observe wildlife	22,878	278,683
Excluding Great Lakes	28,921	485,474	402,814	Photograph wildlife	12,038	79,342
Great Lakes	2,039	20,095	17,195	Feed wildlife	9,976	89,606
Saltwater	9,438	103,034	86,547			
				Residential [3]	60,751	(X)
Total hunters	13,975	256,676	222,938	Observe wildlife	44,063	(X)
Big game	11,288	153,784	113,971	Photograph wildlife	16,021	(X)
Small game	6,945	75,117	63,744	Feed wild birds [4]	54,122	(X)
Migratory birds	3,073	26,501	22,509	Visit public parks	11,011	(X)
Other animals	1,521	24,522	22,714	Maintain plantings or natural areas	13,401	(X)

X Not applicable.   [1] Detail does not add to total due to multiple responses and nonresponse.   [2] Persons taking a trip of at least 1 mile for activity.   [3] Activity within 1 mile of home.   [4] Or other wildlife.

No. 1250. Expenditures for Wildlife Related Recreation Activities: 1996

[See headnote, Table 1249. (37,797 represents $37,797,000,000)]

Type of expenditure	Fishing Expenditures (mil. dol.)	Fishing Spenders Number (1,000)	Fishing Spenders Percent of anglers	Hunting Expenditures (mil. dol.)	Hunting Spenders Number (1,000)	Hunting Spenders Percent of hunters	Wildlife watching Expenditures (mil. dol.)	Wildlife watching Spenders Number (1,000)	Wildlife watching Spenders Percent of watchers
Total [1]	37,797	34,002	96	20,613	13,769	99	29,228	52,729	84
Food and lodging	5,990	28,452	81	2,512	11,073	79	5,352	17,922	76
Food	4,256	28,267	80	2,078	11,060	79	3,447	17,761	75
Lodging	1,734	8,020	23	434	1,909	14	1,905	6,783	29
Transportation	3,730	28,741	82	1,780	12,022	86	2,943	20,260	86
Public	559	1,780	5	145	479	3	811	2,229	9
Private	3,171	28,382	81	1,634	11,926	85	2,132	19,863	84
Other trip-related costs	5,661	28,398	81	864	4,378	31	1,150	9,340	39
Sport specific equipment [2]	5,309	24,726	70	5,519	11,278	81	8,230	47,355	75
Auxiliary equipment [3]	1,037	6,006	17	1,233	5,730	41	858	4,763	8
Special equipment [4]	12,828	3,599	10	4,521	805	6	7,564	1,094	2
Other expenditures [5]	3,242	24,944	71	4,185	12,471	89	3,132	23,827	40

[1] Total not adjusted for multiple responses or nonresponse.   [2] Items owned primarily for each specific activity, such as rods and reels for fishing and guns and rifles for hunting.   [3] Equipment such as camping gear owned for wildlife-associated recreation.   [4] "Big ticket" equipment such as campers and boats owned for wildlife-associated recreation.   [5] Books, magazines, membership dues and contributions, land leasing and ownership, licenses, and plantings.
Source of Tables 1249 and 1250: U.S. Fish and Wildlife Service, *1996 National Survey of Fishing, Hunting, and Wildlife Associated Recreation.*

No. 1251. Sporting Goods Sales by Product Category: 1990 to 2000

[In millions of dollars (50,725 represents $50,725,000,000), except percent. Based on a sample survey of consumer purchases of 80,000 households, (100,000 beginning 1995), except recreational transport, which was provided by industry associations. Excludes Alaska and Hawaii. Minus sign (-) indicates decrease]

Selected product category	1990	1993	1994	1995	1996	1997	1998	1999	2000, proj.
Sales, all products	50,725	51,900	56,162	59,794	62,818	67,333	69,848	74,359	78,752
Annual percent change [1]	(NA)	4.6	8.2	6.5	5.1	7.2	3.7	6.5	5.9
Percent of retail sales	(NA)	2.6	2.6	2.6	2.6	2.7	2.7	2.6	2.6
Athletic and sport clothing	10,130	9,096	9,521	10,311	11,127	12,035	12,844	13,090	13,704
Athletic and sport footwear [2]	11,654	11,084	11,120	11,415	12,815	13,319	13,068	12,522	13,080
Aerobic shoes	611	500	356	372	401	380	334	275	272
Basketball shoes	918	874	867	999	1,192	1,134	1,000	821	846
Cross training shoes	679	877	1,101	1,191	1,417	1,450	1,402	1,364	1,412
Golf shoes	226	275	238	225	231	239	220	208	219
Gym shoes, sneakers	2,536	2,016	1,869	1,741	1,996	1,980	2,010	1,936	2,013
Jogging and running shoes	1,110	1,231	1,069	1,043	1,132	1,482	1,469	1,502	1,614
Tennis shoes	740	599	556	480	541	545	515	505	520
Walking shoes	2,950	2,673	2,543	2,841	3,079	3,236	3,192	3,099	3,223
Athletic and sport equipment [2]	14,439	16,651	17,966	18,809	18,988	19,033	19,192	19,640	20,474
Archery	265	285	306	287	276	270	255	262	272
Baseball and softball	217	323	295	251	277	290	304	334	344
Billiards and pool	192	313	313	304	271	242	347	354	372
Camping	1,072	906	1,017	1,205	1,127	1,153	1,204	1,264	1,327
Exercise equipment	1,824	2,602	2,781	2,960	3,232	2,968	3,233	3,355	3,657
Fishing tackle	1,910	1,952	1,951	2,010	1,970	1,891	1,903	1,917	1,974
Golf	2,514	2,723	2,747	3,194	3,560	3,703	3,658	3,567	3,674
Hunting and firearms	2,202	2,722	3,523	3,003	2,521·	2,562	2,200	2,437	2,534
In-line skating and wheel sports	·150	377	545	646	590	562	509	468	454
Optics	438	493	503	655	673	690	710	769	800
Skin diving and scuba	294	315	322	328	340	332	345	363	373
Skiing, alpine	475	569	609	562	707	723	718	631	649
Tennis	333	327	313	297	296	319	318	338	345
Recreational transport	14,502	15,069	17,555	19,259	19,888	22,946	24,743	29,108	31,494
Bicycles and supplies	2,423	3,534	3,470	3,390	3,187	4,860	4,957	4,770	4,780
Pleasure boats	7,644	6,246	7,679	9,064	9,399	10,208	10,539	13,098	13,622
Recreational vehicles	4,113	4,775	5,690	5,895	6,327	6,904	8,364	10,413	12,241
Snowmobiles	322	515	715	910	974	975	883	826	851

NA Not available. [1] Represents change from immediate prior year. [2] Includes other products not shown separately.

Source: National Sporting Goods Association, Mt. Prospect, IL, *The Sporting Goods Market in 2000*; and prior issues (copyright).

No. 1252. Consumer Purchases of Sporting Goods by Consumer Characteristics: 1999

[In percent. Based on sample survey of consumer purchases of 100,000 households. Excludes Alaska and Hawaii]

Characteristic	Total house-holds	Footwear				Equipment					
		Aero-bic shoes	Gym shoes/ sneak-ers	Jog-ging/ run-ning shoes	Walk-ing shoes	Fish-ing tackle	Camp-ing equip-ment	Exer-cise equip-ment	Hunt-ing equip-ment	Golf equip-ment	Skate-board-ing
Total	100	100	100	100	100	100	100	100	100	100	100
Age of user:											
Under 14 years old	20	7	47	12	7	6	17	1	3	3	53
14 to 17 years old	6	5	13	14	3	3	9	2	3	5	25
18 to 24 years old	9	12	6	11	4	10	10	3	7	7	11
25 to 34 years old	14	25	10	17	9	20	20	17	20	18	3
35 to 44 years old	16	22	10	22	17	28	18	23	25	23	3
45 to 64 years old	22	23	11	21	39	26	16	41	35	33	2
65 years old and over	13	6	3	3	21	5	3	8	6	11	-
Multiple ages	-	-	-	-	-	2	7	5	1	-	4
Sex of user:											
Male	49	14	51	55	36	86	62	40	92	79	90
Female	51	86	49	45	64	10	31	52	6	21	10
Both sexes	-	-	-	-	-	4	7	8	2	-	-
Education of household head:											
Less than high school	8	7	6	4	5	12	6	2	7	2	4
High school	24	20	23	15	24	21	20	19	26	10	9
Some college	36	32	38	31	35	35	37	34	42	37	42
College graduate	32	41	33	50	36	32	37	45	25	51	46
Annual household income:											
Under $15,000	18	9	10	6	11	9	10	5	8	3·	9
$15,000 to $24,999	14	12	11	7	11	9	9	8	16	7	7
$25,000 to $34,999	14	16	14	12	13	14	13	6	14	7	14
$35,000 to $49,999	16	12	18	16	16	17	19	11	18	16	10
$50,000 to $74,999	19	24	25	26	23	24	24	31	21	25	22
$75,000 and over	10	16	12	16	14	14	14	16	11	19	18
$100,000 and over	9	11	10	17	12	13	11	23	12	23	21

- Represents or rounds to zero.

Source: National Sporting Goods Association, Mt. Prospect, IL, *The Sporting Goods Market in 2000* (copyright).

766 Arts, Entertainment, and Recreation

No. 1253. National Park System—Summary: 1990 to 1999

[986.1 represents $986,100,000. For fiscal years ending in year shown, except as noted; see text, Section 9, Federal Government Finances and Employment. Includes data for five areas in Puerto Rico and Virgin Islands, one area in American Samoa, and one area in Guam]

Item	1990	1993	1994	1995	1996	1997	1998	1999
Finances (mil. dol.): [1]								
Expenditures reported	986.1	1,429.4	1,404.0	1,445.0	1,391.0	1,473.0	1,604.0	1,530.0
Salaries and wages	459.1	596.1	627.2	633.0	650.0	683.0	721.0	733.0
Improvements, maintenance	160.0	224.8	222.9	234.0	234.0	246.0	255.0	289.0
Construction	108.5	226.8	205.6	192.0	168.0	188.0	191.0	62.0
Other	258.5	379.7	348.3	386.0	339.0	356.0	437.0	446.0
Funds available	1,505.5	2,346.5	2,307.7	2,225.0	2,116.0	2,301.0	2,658.0	2,972.0
Appropriations	1,052.5	1,334.0	1,388.8	1,325.0	1,346.0	1,625.0	1,765.0	1,867.0
Other [2]	453.0	1,012.5	918.9	900.0	770.0	676.0	893.0	1,105.0
Revenue from operations	78.6	89.5	97.0	106.3	133.2	174.8	202.8	215.3
Recreation visits (millions): [3]								
All areas	258.7	273.1	268.6	269.6	265.8	275.3	286.7	287.1
National parks [4]	57.7	59.8	63.0	64.8	63.1	65.3	64.5	64.3
National monuments	23.9	26.5	23.6	23.5	23.6	24.1	23.6	24.3
National historical, commemorative, archaeological [5]	57.5	61.9	59.5	56.9	59.0	63.0	74.2	72.6
National parkways	29.1	30.4	29.3	31.3	30.9	31.6	32.8	34.6
National recreation areas [4]	47.2	50.8	52.3	53.7	52.6	51.6	53.0	52.8
National seashores and lakeshores	23.3	24.1	24.0	22.5	20.3	22.4	22.6	22.7
National Capital Parks	7.5	9.1	5.4	5.5	6.1	5.1	4.2	3.9
Recreation overnight stays (millions) [3]	17.6	17.7	18.3	16.8	16.6	15.8	15.6	15.9
In commercial lodgings	3.9	4.0	3.9	3.8	3.7	3.6	3.6	3.7
In Park Service campgrounds	7.9	7.5	7.6	7.1	6.5	6.3	6.1	6.2
In backcountry	1.7	2.4	2.4	2.2	2.1	2.2	2.1	2.0
Other	4.2	3.8	4.4	3.7	3.7	3.8	3.9	4.1
Land (1,000 acres): [6]								
Total	76,362	75,515	74,905	77,355	77,458	77,457	77,654	78,166
Parks	46,089	45,521	48,111	49,307	49,315	49,384	49,416	49,859
Recreation areas	3,344	3,349	3,351	3,353	3,353	3,329	3,361	3,404
Other	26,929	26,645	23,443	24,695	24,790	24,744	24,877	24,903
Acquisition, net	21	39	32	27	98	61	95	44

[1] Financial data are those associated with the National Park System. Certain other functions of the National Park Service (principally the activities absorbed from the former Heritage Conservation and Recreation Service in 1981) are excluded. [2] Includes funds carried over from prior years. [3] For calendar year. Includes other areas, not shown separately. [4] For 1990, combined data for North Cascades National Park and two adjacent National Recreation Areas are included in National Parks total. [5] Includes military areas. [6] Federal land only, as of Dec. 31. Federal land acreages, in addition to National Park Service administered lands, also include lands within national park system area boundaries but under the administration of other agencies. Year-to-year changes in the federal lands figures include changes in the acreages of these other lands and hence often differ from "net acquisition."

Source: U.S. National Park Service, Visits, National Park Statistical Abstract, annual; and unpublished data. Other data are unpublished.

No. 1254. State Parks and Recreation Areas by State: 2000

[For year ending June 30 (12,807 represents 12,807,000). Data are shown as reported by state park directors. In some states, park agency has under its control forests, fish and wildlife areas, and/or other areas. In other states, agency is responsible for state parks only]

State	Acreage (1,000)	Visitors (1,000)[1]	Revenue Total ($1,000)	Revenue Percent of operating expenditures	State	Acreage (1,000)	Visitors (1,000)[1]	Revenue Total ($1,000)	Revenue Percent of operating expenditures
United States...	12,807	786,610	677,911	41.6					
Alabama	50	5,878	25,213	84.4	Missouri	137	18,174	6,947	21.9
Alaska	3,291	3,888	2,012	37.7	Montana	65	1,367	1,652	28.4
Arizona	59	2,371	6,934	44.0	Nebraska	133	9,619	13,706	75.8
Arkansas	51	6,643	13,502	47.7	Nevada	133	3,451	1,903	23.9
California	1,413	98,520	54,926	23.6	New Hampshire	74	5,127	12,319	164.5
Colorado	347	10,284	12,127	57.3	New Jersey	345	15,073	7,283	21.0
Connecticut	183	7,567	3,205	27.8	New Mexico	91	4,639	4,320	27.4
Delaware	21	3,910	6,619	34.4	New York	1,016	59,126	63,254	44.7
Florida	547	16,672	28,577	45.2	North Carolina	159	12,400	3,500	15.5
Georgia	76	16,124	18,172	38.4	North Dakota	20	1,111	1,168	50.4
Hawaii	27	18,171	771	11.4	Ohio	205	55,340	26,467	40.2
Idaho	43	2,573	3,503	42.4	Oklahoma	72	16,148	22,804	52.0
Illinois	305	44,484	5,200	11.7	Oregon	95	38,563	15,254	43.4
Indiana	178	18,475	31,355	76.7	Pennsylvania	288	36,717	12,612	18.8
Iowa	63	15,152	3,234	30.7	Rhode Island	9	6,231	3,237	70.8
Kansas	32	7,202	4,242	58.8	South Carolina	80	9,247	16,057	62.2
Kentucky	44	7,792	50,607	66.8	South Dakota	98	7,038	7,154	71.6
Louisiana	36	1,715	3,484	23.2	Tennessee	141	30,182	28,451	55.3
Maine	95	2,265	1,943	28.9	Texas	631	18,751	21,248	42.2
Maryland	259	10,004	14,202	39.8	Utah	114	6,737	7,849	35.2
Massachusetts	289	12,775	5,725	17.9	Vermont	84	719	5,614	102.2
Michigan	351	27,534	32,347	63.2	Virginia	73	5,717	6,477	41.6
Minnesota	256	8,496	10,939	44.2	Washington	259	46,444	10,574	27.8
Mississippi	24	4,198	7,266	38.8	West Virginia	196	7,990	18,036	61.1
					Wisconsin	129	15,470	12,855	73.9
					Wyoming	121	2,538	1,067	22.3

[1] Includes overnight visitors.
Source: National Association of State Park Directors, Tuscon, AZ, 2001 Annual Information Exchange.

Arts, Entertainment, and Recreation 767

No. 1255. Travel by U.S. Residents—Summary: 1994 to 2000

[In millions (564.8 represents 564,800,000), except party size. See headnote, Table 1256]

Type of trip	1994	1995	1996	1997	1999	1999	2000
All travel:							
Total trips [1]	564.8	577.6	575.7	581.9	594.1	580.8	579.9
Person trips	968.0	994.8	994.2	1,026.6	1,035.6	1,019.6	1,032.7
Party size	1.7	1.7	1.7	1.8	1.7	2.0	2.0
Auto travel:							
Total trips	386.4	396.2	400.7	402.7	410.5	387.7	386.3
Person trips	729.9	751.0	758.6	781.2	784.0	752.5	760.5
Party size	1.9	1.9	1.9	1.9	1.9	2.2	2.2
Air travel:							
Total trips	136.7	138.6	134.1	136.2	140.8	141.2	141.8
Person trips	182.0	185.0	180.9	185.8	192.6	195.5	198.0
Party size	1.3	1.3	1.3	1.4	1.4	1.5	1.5
Business travel:							
Total trips	168.3	173.9	167.5	165.8	171.7	167.4	161.0
Person trips	213.0	219.8	212.8	213.5	219.5	214.1	209.4
Party size	1.3	1.3	1.3	1.3	1.3	1.4	1.4
Pleasure travel:							
Total trips	335.5	338.5	341.4	347.4	348.1	333.7	336.2
Person trips	644.7	653.6	656.2	682.7	681.4	658.3	669.3
Party size	1.9	1.9	1.9	2.0	2.0	2.2	2.2

[1] Includes other trips (e.g. medical, funerals, weddings), not shown separately.

Source: Travel Industry Association of America, Washington, DC, *TravelScope*, annual (copyright).

No. 1256. Characteristics of Pleasure Trips by U.S. Residents: 1995 to 2000

[338.5 represents 338,500,000. Represents trips to destinations 50 miles or more, one-way, away from home or one or more overnight trips. Based on a monthly mail panel survey of 20,000 U.S. households. For details, see source]

Characteristic	Unit	1995	1996	1997	1998	1999	2000
Total trips	Millions...	338.5	341.4	347.4	348.1	333.7	336.2
Average household members on trip	Number...	1.9	1.9	2.0	2.0	2.2	2.2
Average nights per trip [1]	Number...	3.7	3.7	3.6	3.6	3.7	3.6
Traveled primarily by auto/truck/RV rental car	Percent...	77	78	78	77	81	81
Traveled primarily by air	Percent...	17	16	16	16	14	15
Used a rental car while on trip [2]	Percent...	7	7	7	7	5	5
Stayed in a hotel while on trip	Percent...	33	33	33	34	35	35
Household income:							
Less than $40,000	Percent...	51	49	47	44	41	38
$40,000 or more	Percent...	49	51	53	56	59	62

[1] Includes overnight and nonovernight stays. [2] As a secondary mode of transportation.

Source: Travel Industry Association of America, Washington, DC, *TravelScope*, annual (copyright).

No. 1257. Domestic Travel Expenditures by State: 1999

[451,590 represents $451,590,000,000. Represents U.S. spending on domestic overnight trips and day trips of 50 miles or more, one way, away from home. Excludes spending by foreign visitors and by U.S. residents in U.S. territories and abroad]

State	Total (mil. dol.)	Share of total (per-cent)	Rank	State	Total (mil. dol.)	Share of total (per-cent)	Rank	State	Total (mil. dol.)	Share of total (per-cent)	Rank
U.S., total	451,590	100.0	(X)	KS	3,314	0.7	38	ND	1,100	0.2	50
				KY	4,945	1.1	30	OH	12,181	2.7	11
AL	5,002	1.1	28	LA	7,631	1.7	20	OK	3,653	0.8	34
AK	1,292	0.3	48	ME	1,828	0.4	42	OR	5,072	1.1	27
AZ	7,868	1.7	18	MD	7,701	1.7	19	PA	13,733	3.0	8
AR	3,612	0.8	35	MA	10,268	2.3	14	RI	1,312	0.3	46
CA	57,542	12.7	1	MI	10,868	2.4	13	SC	6,602	1.5	23
CO	8,624	1.9	17	MN	6,535	1.4	24	SD	1,149	0.3	49
CT	4,960	1.1	29	MS	4,299	1.0	31	TN	9,414	2.1	15
DE	1,002	0.2	51	MO	9,089	2.0	16	TX	29,889	6.6	3
DC	4,108	0.9	32	MT	1,813	0.4	43	UT	3,566	0.8	36
FL	39,137	8.7	2	NE	2,533	0.6	39	VT	1,312	0.3	47
GA	13,655	3.0	9	NV	18,373	4.1	6	VA	12,415	2.7	10
HI	7,131	1.6	22	NH	2,218	0.5	40	WA	7,568	1.7	21
ID	2,001	0.4	41	NJ	14,164	3.1	7	WV	1,610	0.4	44
IL	20,500	4.5	5	NM	3,418	0.8	37	WI	5,987	1.3	25
IN	5,814	1.3	26	NY	26,868	5.9	4	WY	1,427	0.3	45
IA	4,038	0.9	33	NC	11,452	2.5	12				

X Not applicable.

Source: Travel Industry Association of America, Washington, DC, *Impact of Travel on State Economies, 1999* (copyright).

768 Arts, Entertainment, and Recreation

No. 1258. International Travelers and Expenditures: 1990 to 1999

[47,880 represents $47,880,000,000. For coverage, see Table 1259]

Year	Travel and passenger fare (mil. dol.)				U.S. net travel and passenger payments (mil. dol.)	U.S. travelers to foreign countries (1,000)	International visitors to the U.S. (1,000)
	Payments by U.S. travelers		Receipts from foreign visitors				
	Total [1]	Expenditures abroad	Total [1]	Travel receipts			
1990	47,880	37,349	58,305	43,007	10,425	44,623	39,363
1991	45,334	35,322	64,239	48,385	18,905	41,566	42,674
1992	49,155	38,552	71,360	54,742	22,205	43,898	47,261
1993	52,123	40,713	74,403	57,875	22,280	44,411	45,779
1994	56,844	43,782	75,414	58,417	18,570	46,450	44,753
1995	59,579	44,916	82,304	63,395	22,725	50,763	43,318
1996	63,887	48,078	90,231	69,809	26,344	52,311	46,489
1997	70,189	52,051	94,294	73,426	24,105	52,944	47,752
1998	76,480	56,509	91,384	71,286	14,904	56,287	46,395
1999	80,756	59,351	94,657	74,881	13,901	58,358	48,491

[1] Includes passenger fares not shown separately.

Source: U.S. Dept. of Commerce, International Trade Administration, Tourism Industries, Internet site <http://www.tinet.ita.doc.gov>.

No. 1259. Foreign Travel: 1990 to 1999

[In thousands (44,623 represents 44,623,000). U.S. travelers cover residents of the United States, its territories and possessions. Foreign travelers to the U.S. include travelers for business and pleasure, international travelers in transit through the United States, and students; excludes travel by international personnel and international businessmen employed in the United States]

Item and area	1990	1993	1994	1995	1996	1997	1998	1999
U.S. travelers to foreign countries.	44,623	44,411	46,450	50,763	52,311	52,944	56,287	58,358
Canada	12,252	12,024	12,542	12,933	12,909	13,401	14,880	16,036
Mexico..............	16,381	15,285	15,759	18,771	19,616	17,909	18,338	17,743
Total overseas..........	15,990	17,102	18,149	19,059	19,786	21,634	23,069	24,579
Europe..............	8,043	7,491	8,167	8,596	8,706	9,800	11,143	11,577
Foreign travelers to the U.S......	39,363	45,779	44,753	43,318	46,489	47,752	46,395	48,491
Canada	17,263	17,293	14,974	14,663	15,301	15,127	13,422	14,110
Mexico...............	7,041	9,824	11,321	8,016	8,530	8,431	9,276	9,915
Total overseas..........	15,059	18,662	18,458	20,639	22,658	24,194	23,698	24,466
Europe	6,659	8,630	8,119	8,793	9,727	10,390	10,675	11,243
South America.........	1,328	2,026	2,112	2,449	2,461	2,831	2,957	2,733
Central America	412	545	513	509	524	564	697	731
Caribbean............	1,137	1,098	1,031	1,044	1,133	1,189	1,161	1,258
Far East	4,360	5,165	5,551	6,616	7,500	7,756	6,724	6,935
Middle East...........	365	419	403	454	480	552	587	625
Oceania	662	609	556	588	629	680	639	667
Africa	137	169	173	186	205	234	258	274

Source: U.S. Dept. of Commerce, International Trade Administration, Tourism Industries, Internet site <http://www.tinet.ita.doc.gov>.

No. 1260. Top States and Cities Visited by Overseas Travelers: 1999 and 2000

[24,466 represents 24,466,000. Includes travelers for business and pleasure, international travelers in transit through the United States, and students; excludes travel by international personnel and international businessmen employed in the United States]

State	Overseas visitors (1,000)		Market share (percent)		City	Overseas visitors (1,000)		Market share (percent)	
	1999	2000	1999	2000		1999	2000	1999	2000
Total overseas travelers [1].	24,466	25,975	100.0	100.0	New York City, NY	5,505	5,714	22.5	22.0
California	6,239	6,364	25.5	24.5	Los Angeles, CA	3,572	3,533	14.6	13.6
Florida	5,798	6,026	23.7	23.2	Orlando, FL	2,863	3,013	11.7	11.6
New York	5,798	5,922	23.7	22.8	Miami, FL............	2,863	2,935	11.7	11.3
Hawaiian Islands	2,740	2,727	11.2	10.5	San Francisco, CA......	2,789	2,831	11.4	10.9
Nevada	2,373	2,364	9.7	9.1	Las Vegas, NV	2,251	2,260	9.2	8.7
Massachusetts.........	1,321	1,429	5.4	5.5	Oahu/Honolulu, HI	2,202	2,234	9.0	8.6
Illinois	1,321	1,377	5.4	5.3	Washington, DC	1,297	1,481	5.3	5.7
Guam	1,028	1,325	4.2	5.1	Chicago, IL...........	1,272	1,351	5.2	5.2
Texas................	1,052	1,169	4.3	4.5	Boston, MA	1,199	1,325	4.9	5.1
New Jersey............	905	909	3.7	3.5	San Diego, CA	807	701	3.3	2.7
Arizona...............	881	883	3.6	3.4	Atlanta, GA...........	538	701	2.2	2.7
Georgia	612	805	2.5	3.1	Tampa/St. Petersburg, FL .	489	519	2.0	2.0
Pennsylvania..........	538	649	2.2	2.5	San Jose, CA	514	494	2.1	1.9
Colorado.............	465	519	1.9	2.0	Anaheim, CA	465	494	1.9	1.9
Michigan.............	416	494	1.7	1.9	Dallas/Ft. Worth, TX.....	416	494	1.7	1.9
Washington...........	514	468	2.1	1.8	Ft. Lauderdale, FL.......	465	468	1.9	1.8
Utah	391	416	1.6	1.6	Houston, TX..........	416	442	1.7	1.7
North Carolina	294	416	1.2	1.6	Maui, HI.............	367	442	1.5	1.7
Louisiana	367	390	1.5	1.5	Seattle, WA	465	416	1.9	1.6
Ohio	367	390	1.5	1.5	Philadelphia, PA	343	390	1.4	1.5
Virginia..............	343	364	1.4	1.4	New Orleans, LA.......	294	364	1.2	1.4
Minnesota............	220	364	0.9	1.4	Detroit, MI	294	338	1.2	1.3

[1] Includes other states and cities, not shown separately.

Source: U.S. Dept. of Commerce, International Trade Administration, Internet site <http://www.tinet.ita.doc.gov> (accessed 10 July 2001).

Arts, Entertainment, and Recreation 769

No. 1261. Impact of International Travel on States Economies: 1999

[72,170.6 represents $72,170,600]

State	Travel expenditures (mil. dol.)	Travel generated payroll (mil. dol.)	Travel generated employment (1,000)	Travel generated tax receipts (mil. dol.)	State	Travel expenditures (mil. dol.)	Travel generated payroll (mil. dol.)	Travel generated employment (1,000)	Travel generated tax receipts (mil. dol.)
U.S., total ..	72,170.6	19,690.7	959.4	12,345.7	MO	257.6	71.4	4.0	48.5
AL.........	107.9	24.9	1.7	14.6	MT.......	91.4	22.1	1.9	12.6
AK.........	214.9	86.8	4.1	42.5	NE.......	59.3	16.2	1.1	10.3
AZ.........	1,620.4	479.1	25.9	271.7	NV.......	2,661.2	833.0	40.0	358.0
AR.........	47.4	12.5	0.8	7.1	NH.......	128.7	30.6	2.0	15.6
CA.........	13,828.2	3,732.8	177.5	2,228.7	NJ.......	889.6	240.4	10.6	176.7
CO.........	730.6	240.3	12.8	169.5	NM.......	127.1	31.3	2.2	18.3
CT.........	282.3	69.1	3.4	49.8	NY.......	9,447.6	2,584.6	105.4	1,984.4
DE.........	85.9	20.1	1.2	14.3	NC.......	416.0	130.0	6.8	76.8
DC.........	1,613.2	336.5	13.9	227.7	ND.......	48.3	11.7	1.0	10.8
FL.........	16,648.3	4,337.0	223.3	2,636.7	OH.......	566.9	160.7	9.0	109.1
GA.........	883.3	327.8	14.0	219.8	OK.......	81.3	30.9	1.6	14.5
HI.........	7,092.2	1,723.5	78.5	1,005.9	OR.......	388.6	111.7	6.9	64.3
ID.........	101.0	25.3	1.8	18.8	PA.......	1,030.6	303.4	15.3	187.0
IL.........	1,647.5	449.1	21.4	322.8	RI.......	113.2	24.4	1.5	14.8
IN.........	243.5	78.1	4.3	45.5	SC.......	444.7	111.3	7.2	67.8
IA.........	133.7	33.6	2.4	20.6	SD.......	40.5	10.6	0.9	5.4
KS.........	98.1	23.8	1.7	14.8	TN.......	338.2	151.5	6.1	78.8
KY.........	122.6	50.7	2.6	25.9	TX.......	3,241.6	1,007.7	49.4	604.3
LA.........	458.6	106.5	6.6	65.9	UT.......	358.6	120.7	7.7	72.3
ME.........	245.8	56.7	4.2	33.1	VT.......	130.1	32.2	2.0	18.3
MD.........	342.5	102.9	4.6	71.8	VA.......	447.9	134.2	7.5	75.0
MA.........	1,939.1	506.1	23.9	326.1	WA.......	930.9	252.7	13.3	174.2
MI.........	643.8	176.5	10.1	121.0	WV.......	31.9	7.9	0.5	4.9
MN.........	383.9	144.2	6.9	124.1	WI.......	266.5	75.7	5.2	47.5
MS.........	48.2	21.7	1.2	8.1	WY.......	69.8	18.3	1.6	8.7

Source: Travel Industry Association of America, Washington, DC, *Impact of Travel on State Economies, 1999* (copyright).

No. 1262. Foreign Visitors for Pleasure Admitted by Country of Last Residence: 1985 to 1999

[In thousands (6,609 represents 6,609,000). For years ending September 30. Represents non-U.S. citizens admitted to the country for a temporary period of time (also known as nonimmigrants)]

Country	1985	1990	1995	1999	Country	1985	1990	1995	1999
All countries [1]	6,609	13,418	17,612	24,104	United Arab Emirates ...	6	7	14	25
					Africa [1]	101	105	137	219
Europe [1].............	2,048	5,383	7,012	9,282	South Africa	26	26	59	80
United Kingdom......	598	1,899	2,342	3,610	Other Africa	22	34	35	60
Germany [2].........	373	969	1,550	1,713	Egypt.	16	16	16	31
France............	226	566	738	849	Oceania [1]	282	562	478	552
Italy..............	155	308	427	510	Australia........	195	380	327	376
Netherlands........	82	214	308	395	New Zealand [4]	74	153	115	133
Switzerland.........	110	236	321	328	North America.........	1,664	2,463	2,240	5,088
Spain.............	64	183	248	297	Canada	79	119	127	186
Ireland............	55	81	126	254	Mexico.............	773	1,061	893	3,195
Sweden	71	230	142	224	Caribbean [1].........	584	963	831	1,097
Belgium	39	95	153	184	Bahamas, The	211	332	234	300
Austria............	34	87	146	165	Jamaica...........	74	132	130	184
Norway	41	80	71	109	Dominican Republic ..	57	137	138	169
Denmark	36	75	78	106	Trinidad and Tobago ..	71	81	64	95
Poland............	40	55	36	82	Haiti...............	56	57	43	60
Portugal...........	18	30	40	60	Barbados	17	34	36	47
Finland	24	83	47	60	Cayman Islands	18	31	31	44
Russia	(X)	(X)	33	47	Netherlands Antilles ..	27	31	32	36
Greece	34	43	44	45	Aruba	(Z)	10	19	23
Hungary...........	10	15	29	40	British Virgin Islands ..	4	8	9	21
Czech Republic	(X)	(X)	12	33	Central America [1]......	228	320	387	564
Iceland............	5	10	14	24	Guatemala	53	91	99	130
Asia [1]	1,866	3,830	5,666	6,192	Costa Rica	41	62	91	121
Japan	1,277	2,846	3,986	4,418	El Salvador	38	46	63	121
China [3]	83	187	378	404	Panama	38	43	54	76
Korea	26	120	427	305	Honduras	37	52	37	59
Israel.............	80	128	160	215	Nicaragua	14	13	28	38
India	52	75	75	147	South America [1]	606	1,016	1,978	2,394
Hong Kong.........	64	111	162	143	Brazil.............	148	300	710	643
Philippines.........	59	76	85	113	Venezuela.........	122	199	400	473
Singapore..........	23	32	61	61	Argentina..........	66	136	320	458
Turkey	9	20	27	59	Colombia..........	123	122	174	339
Saudi Arabia........	31	33	45	49	Chile.............	28	54	117	143
Thailand...........	15	25	59	46	Peru	44	97	98	126
Indonesia..........	19	28	44	43	Ecuador...........	42	57	77	100
Malaysia...........	19	27	40	34	Uruguay...........	7	16	37	49
Pakistan...........	17	27	27	31	Bolivia............	10	14	16	29

X Not applicable. Z Fewer than 500. [1] Includes other countries, not shown separately. [2] Data for 1985 and 1990 are for former West Germany. [3] Includes People's Republic of China and Taiwan. [4] Prior to fiscal year 1995, data for Niue are included in New Zealand.

Source: U.S. Immigration and Naturalization Service, *Statistical Yearbook, 1999*, annual.

770 Arts, Entertainment, and Recreation

Accommodation, Food Services, and Other Services

This new section presents statistics relating to services other than those covered in the previous few sections (22 to 26) on domestic trade, transportation, communications, financial services, and recreation services. Many of the tables were previously covered in the former Section 27, Domestic Trade and Services in the 2000 edition of the *Statistical Abstract.* Data shown for the services are classified by kind of business and cover sales or receipts, establishments, employees, payrolls, and other items. The principal sources of these data are from the Census Bureau and include the *1997 Economic Census* reports, annual surveys, and the *County Business Patterns* program. These data are supplemented by data from several sources such as the Economic Research Service of the U.S. Department of Agriculture on food sales (Table 1268), the American Hotel & Motel Association on lodging (Table 1266), and McCann-Erickson, Inc. and Publishers Information Bureau on advertising (Tables 1271 and 1272, respectively).

Data on these services appear in several other sections. For instance, labor force employment and earnings data (Table 609) appear in Section 12, Labor Force; gross domestic product of the industry (Table 641) appear in Section 13, Income, Expenditures, and Wealth; and financial data (several tables) from the quarterly *Statistics of Income Bulletin,* published by the Internal Revenue Service, appear in Section 15, Business Enterprise.

Censuses—Limited coverage of the services industries started in 1933. Beginning with the 1967 census, legislation provides for a census of each area to be conducted every 5 years (for years ending in "2" and "7"). For more information on the most current census, see the *History of the 1997 Economic Census* found at <http://www.census.gov/prod/ec97/pol00-hec.pdf>. The industries covered in the censuses and surveys of business are those classified in 13 sectors defined in the *North American Industry Classification System,* called NAICS (see below). All Census Bureau tables in this section are utilizing the new NAICS codes, which replaced the Standard Industrial Classification (SIC) system. NAICS makes substantial structural improvements and identifies over 350 new industries. At the same time, it causes breaks in time series far more profound than any prior revision of the previously used SIC system. For information on this system and how it affects the comparability of retail and wholesale statistics historically, see text, Section 15, Business Enterprise, and especially the Census Web site at <http://www.census.gov/epcd/www/naics.html>.

The *Accommodation and Food Services sector* (NAICS sector 72) comprises establishments providing customers with lodging and/or prepared meals, snacks, and beverages for immediate consumption. The *Other Services (Except Public Administration) sector* (NAICS sector 81) covers establishments with payroll engaged in providing services not specifically provided for elsewhere in the NAICS. Establishments in this sector are primarily engaged in activities such as repair and maintenance of equipment and machinery, personal and laundry services, and religious, grantmaking, civic, professional, and similar organizations. Establishments providing death care services, pet care services, photofinishing services, temporary parking services, and dating services are also included. Private households that employ workers on or about the premises in activities primarily concerned with the operation of the household are included in this sector but are not included in the scope of the census. In general, the 1997 Economic Census has two series of publications and documents for these two sectors subject series with reports on such as commodity line sales and establishment and firm sizes and geographic reports with individual reports for each state. For information on these series, see the Census Web site at

Accomodation, Food Services, and Other Services **771**

<http://www.census.gov/epcd/www/97EC72.htm> and <http://www.census.gov/epcd/www/97EC81.htm>.

Current surveys—The Service Annual Survey provides annual estimates of nationwide receipts for selected personal, business, leasing and repair, amusement and entertainment, social and health, and other professional service industries in the United States. For selected accommodation, social, health, and other professional service industries, separate estimates are developed for receipts of taxable firms and revenue and expenses for firms and organizations exempt from federal income taxes. Several service sectors from this survey are covered in other sections of this publication. The scope of the current Service Annual Survey has been broadened to encompass the previous Annual Survey of Communication Services and the Transportation Annual Survey. The estimates for tax exempt firms in these industries are derived from a sample of employer firms only. Estimates obtained from annual and monthly surveys are based on sample data and are not expected to agree exactly with results that would be obtained from a complete census of all establishments. Data include estimates for sampling units not reporting.

Statistical reliability—For a discussion of statistical collection and estimation, sampling procedures, and measures of statistical reliability applicable to Census Bureau data, see Appendix III.

Figure 27.1
Advertising Expenditures: 1990 to 2000

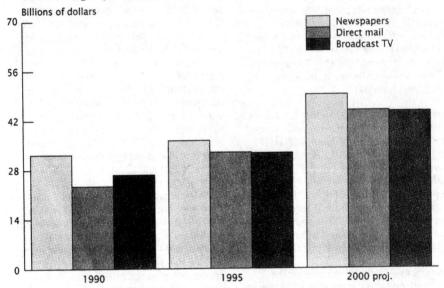

Source: Chart prepared by U.S. Census Bureau. For data, see Table 1271.

U.S. Census Bureau, Statistical Abstract of the United States: 2001

No. 1263. Service-Related Industries—Establishments, Employees, and Payroll by Industry: 1999

[Excludes government employees, railroad employees, self-employed persons, etc. See "General Explanation" in source for definitions and statement on reliability of data. An *establishment* is a single physical location where business is conducted or where services or industrial operations are performed]

Industry	NAICS code [1]	Establish-ments, number	Employ-ees, [2] number	Annual payroll ($1,000)	Average payroll per employee (dol.)
All industries, total	(X)	7,008,444	110,705,661	3,554,692,909	32,109
Service-related industries, total	(X)	3,790,229	59,048,833	1,752,164,813	29,673
Transportation & warehousing	48-49	187,339	3,627,057	116,682,214	32,170
Air transportation	481	5,285	582,838	24,414,357	41,889
Water transportation	483	1,950	71,844	3,039,510	42,307
Truck transportation	484	108,749	1,384,178	43,626,168	31,518
Transit & ground passenger transportation	485	16,254	370,022	6,729,332	18,186
Pipeline transportation	486	2,550	48,149	3,032,689	62,986
Scenic & sightseeing transportation	487	2,267	22,877	540,702	23,635
Transportation support activities	488	31,392	440,175	14,915,625	33,886
Couriers & messengers	492	11,938	578,368	16,725,960	28,919
Warehousing & storage	493	6,954	128,606	3,657,871	28,442
Information	51	126,510	3,234,530	170,282,356	52,645
Publishing industries	511	32,377	1,004,697	54,516,491	54,262
Motion picture & sound recording industries	512	23,102	293,369	10,531,411	35,898
Broadcasting & telecommunications	513	50,852	1,504,242	76,010,594	50,531
Information & data processing services	514	20,179	432,222	29,223,860	67,613
Real estate & rental & leasing	53	298,080	1,873,792	54,095,260	28,869
Real estate	531	231,337	1,225,995	36,593,436	29,848
Rental & leasing services	532	64,644	621,916	16,041,736	25,794
Lessors of other nonfinancial intangible assets except copyrighted works	533	2,099	25,881	1,460,088	56,415
Professional, scientific, & technical services	54	704,779	6,432,422	311,238,501	48,386
Professional, scientific, & technical services	541	704,779	6,432,422	311,238,501	48,386
Legal services	5411	177,037	1,082,253	57,179,550	52,834
Accounting, tax preparation, bookkeeping, and payroll services	5412	99,422	1,093,608	32,697,382	29,899
Architectural, engineering & related services	5413	103,430	1,212,838	59,780,006	49,289
Specialized design services	5414	28,097	131,134	5,362,119	40,890
Computer systems design & related services	5415	93,798	1,013,049	66,314,054	65,460
Management, sci. & tech. consulting services	5416	90,877	658,487	38,585,097	58,597
Scientific R&D services	5417	12,088	338,346	19,917,814	58,868
Advertising & related services	5418	40,052	443,252	19,851,384	44,786
Other professional/scientific/ technical service	5419	59,978	459,455	11,551,095	25,141
Management of companies & enterprises	55	46,528	2,788,276	192,378,035	68,995
Administrative & support & waste management & remediation services	56	350,401	8,366,523	183,100,191	21,885
Administrative & support services	561	334,101	8,079,349	173,116,039	21,427
Waste management & remediation	5613	40,714	3,993,443	81,464,024	20,399
Temporary help services	56132	27,272	2,725,800	51,286,088	18,815
Business support services	5614	34,900	671,035	15,062,208	22,446
Travel arrangement & reservation services	5615	34,569	300,645	8,658,039	28,798
Waste management & remediation services	562	16,300	287,174	9,984,152	34,767
Educational services	61	66,492	2,431,718	56,871,035	23,387
Health care & social assistance	62	649,846	13,865,014	409,223,160	29,515
Ambulatory health care services	621	455,726	4,466,133	169,998,142	38,062
Hospitals	622	6,969	5,000,531	163,440,600	32,685
Nursing & residential care facilities	623	61,557	2,568,012	47,466,468	18,484
Social assistance	624	125,594	1,830,338	28,327,950	15,477
Arts, entertainment, & recreation	71	102,786	1,640,030	39,415,855	24,034
Perform arts, spectator sports, & related industries	711	32,906	330,381	17,380,510	52,607
Performing arts companies	7111	9,342	121,970	3,052,758	25,029
Spectator sports	7112	4,372	91,043	8,159,178	89,619
Museums, historical sites, & like institutions	712	5,714	104,607	2,321,151	22,189
Amusement, gambling, & recreation industries	713	64,166	1,205,042	19,714,194	16,360
Gambling industries	7132	2,238	178,684	4,098,543	22,937
Accommodation & food services	72	539,576	9,638,007	116,924,965	12,132
Accommodation	721	59,278	1,737,734	32,200,402	18,530
Traveler accommodation	7211	48,962	1,685,482	31,220,395	18,523
RV parks & recreational camps	7212	7,123	37,117	796,483	21,459
Rooming & boarding houses	7213	3,193	15,135	183,524	12,126
Food services & drinking places	722	480,298	7,900,273	84,724,563	10,724
Full-service restaurants	7221	190,788	3,788,062	43,410,899	11,460
Limited-service eating places	7222	210,920	3,318,549	31,475,084	9,485
Special food services	7223	27,413	468,838	6,700,510	14,292
Drinking places (alcoholic beverages)	7224	51,177	324,824	3,138,070	9,661
Other services (except public administration)	81	717,892	5,151,464	101,953,241	19,791
Repair & maintenance	811	234,555	1,318,467	34,369,540	26,068
Automotive repair & maintenance	8111	164,898	842,606	19,388,016	23,010
Electronic & precision equipment	8112	16,218	142,210	5,238,955	36,840
Personal and laundry services	812	195,107	1,261,383	21,587,374	17,114
Religious, grantmaking, civic, prof. & like organizations	813	288,230	2,571,614	45,996,327	17,886

X Not applicable. [1] North American Industry Classification System, 1997. [2] Covers full- and part-time employees who are on the payroll in the pay period including March 12.

Source: U.S. Census Bureau, *County Business Patterns*, annual. See also <http://www.census.gov/prod/2001pubs/cbp99/cbp99-1.pdf> (issued April 2001).

Accommodation, Food Services, and Other Services 773

No. 1264. Service-Related Industries—Establishments, Employees, and Payroll by Major Group: 1998 and 1999

[See headnote, Table 1263]

Major group	NAICS code [1]	Establishments (1,000) 1998	Establishments (1,000) 1999	Employees [2] (1,000) 1998	Employees [2] (1,000) 1999	Annual payroll (mil. dol.) 1998	Annual payroll (mil. dol.) 1999
Professional, scientific and technical services.........	54-541	687,230	704,779	6,051,636	6,432,422	277,640	311,239
Management of companies and enterprises..............	55-551	43,678	46,528	2,703,798	2,788,276	175,649	192,378
Admin. & support & waste mngmnt, & remediation services.........	56	350,880	350,401	7,774,610	8,366,523	163,698	183,100
Administrative & support services...	561	333,928	334,101	7,487,211	8,079,349	154,167	173,116
Waste management & remediation services..................	562	16,952	16,300	287,399	287,174	9,531	9,984
Accommodation & food services ...	72	544,250	539,576	9,466,088	9,638,007	109,585	116,925
Accommodation	721	59,315	59,278	1,708,002	1,737,734	30,037	32,200
Food services & drinking places..	722	484,935	480,298	7,758,086	7,900,273	79,548	84,725
Other services (except public administration)	81	718,721	717,892	5,037,866	5,151,464	95,993	101,953
Repair & maintenance..........	811	238,540	234,555	1,302,873	1,318,467	32,811	34,370
Personal & laundry services	812	194,128	195,107	1,247,387	1,261,383	20,522	21,587
Religious, grantmaking, civic, prof., & like organizations	813	286,053	288,230	2,487,606	2,571,614	42,661	45,996

[1] North American Industry Classification System, 1997. [2] Covers full- and part-time employees who are on the payroll in the pay period including March 12.
Source: U.S. Census Bureau, *County Business Patterns*, annual. See also <http://www.census.gov/prod/2001pubs/cbp99/cbp99-1.pdf> (issued April 2001).

No. 1265. Selected Service Industries Revenue—Total and E-Commerce: 1999

[4,276,088 represents $4,276,088,000,000. Includes data only for businesses with paid employees, except for accommodation and food services, which also includes businesses with and without paid employees. Detail may not add to total due to rounding]

Kind of business	NAICS code [1]	Value of revenue Total (mil. dol.)	Value of revenue E-commerce (mil. dol.)	E-commerce as percent of total revenue	Percent distribution of E-commerce revenue
Selected service industries, total	(X)	4,276,088	25,158	0.6	100.0
Selected transportation and warehousing [2]	48-49	221,728	3,019	1.4	12.0
Information	51	768,292	5,221	0.7	20.8
Publishing industries	511	219,804	3,069	1.4	12.2
Online information services..................	51419	20,146	1,027	5.1	4.1
Selected finance [3]	52	295,302	3,996	1.4	15.9
Securities and commodity contracts intermediation and brokerage	5231	203,744	3,831	1.9	15.2
Rental and leasing services	532	93,156	(S)	(S)	(S)
Selected professional, scientific, and technical services [4].	54	732,304	4,127	0.6	16.4
Computer systems design and related services	5415	154,414	2,869	1.9	11.4
Selected administrative and support and waste management and remediation services [5]..........	56	373,956	6,990	1.9	27.8
Health care and social assistance services	62	970,786	(S)	(S)	(S)
Arts, entertainment, and recreation services	71	115,366	(S)	(S)	(S)
Accommodation and food services	72	400,981	(S)	(S)	(S)
Selected other services [6].................	81	304,217	364	0.1	1.4

S Data do not meet publication standards because of high sampling variability or poor response quality. X Not applicable. [1] North American Industry Classification System; see text, Section 15, Business Enterprise. [2] Excludes NAICS 481 (air transportation), 482 (rail transportation), 483 (water transportation), 485 (transit and good passenger transportation), 487 (scenic and sightseeing transportation), 488 (support activities for transportation) and 491 (postal service). [3] Excludes NAICS 521 (monetary authorities-central bank), 522 (credit intermediation and related activities), 5232 (securities and commodity exchanges), NAICS 52391 (miscellaneous intermediation), 52399 (all other financial investment activities), 524 (insurance carriers and related activities) and 525 (funds and trusts). [4] Excludes NAICS 54112 (offices of notaries) and 54132 (landscape architectural services). [5] Excludes NAICS 56173 (landscaping services). [6] Excludes NAICS 81311 (religious organizations), 81393 (labor and similar organizations), 81394 (political organizations) and 814 (private households).
Source: U.S. Census Bureau, Internet site <http://www.census.gov/eos/www/papers/estatstables.pdf>.

No. 1266. Lodging Industry Summary: 1990 to 1999

Year	Average occupancy rate (percent)	Average room rate (dol.)	Room size of property	1998 Establishments	1998 Rooms (mil.)	Item	1998 Business traveler	1998 Leisure traveler
1990	63.3	57.96	Total	52,000	3.9	Typical night:		
1991	60.9	58.08				Made reservations .	91%	83%
1992	61.7	58.91	Percent:			Amount paid	$83.00	$76.00
1993	63.6	60.53	Under 75 rooms...	51.2	22.2			
1994	65.2	62.86	75-149 rooms	33.3	34.6	Length of stay:		
1995	65.5	66.65	150-299 rooms ...	11.4	21.7	One night	36%	43%
1996	65.2	70.93	300-500 rooms ...	2.8	10.0	Two nights	24%	28%
1997	64.5	75.31	Over 500 rooms...	1.3	11.5	Three or more	40%	29%
1998	64.0	78.62						
1999	63.2	81.33						

Source: American Hotel & Motel Association, Washington, DC, *Lodging Industry Profile* (copyright).

774 Accommodation, Food Services, and Other Services

No. 1267. Accommodation and Food Services—Establishments, Employees, and Payroll by Kind of Business: 1998 and 1999

[9,466.1 represents 9,466,100. Covers establishments with payroll. Employees are for the week including March 12. Most government employees are excluded. For statement on methodology, see Appendix III]

Kind of business	NAICS code [1]	Establishments (number) 1998	Establishments (number) 1999	Employees (1,000) 1998	Employees (1,000) 1999	Payroll (mil. dol.) 1998	Payroll (mil. dol.) 1999
Accommodation & food services, total	72	544,250	539,576	9,466.1	9,638.0	109,585	116,925
Accommodation	721	59,315	59,278	1,708.0	1,737.7	30,037	32,200
Traveler accommodation	7211	48,496	48,962	1,655.9	1,685.5	29,108	31,220
Hotels (except casino hotels) & motels	72111	44,279	44,832	1,343.3	1,364.3	21,906	23,290
Casino hotels	72112	295	279	291.5	298.9	6,929	7,635
Other traveler accommodation	72119	3,922	3,851	21.1	22.3	273	295
Bed & breakfast inns	721191	3,066	3,000	17.0	18.2	208	229
All other traveler accommodation	721199	856	851	4.1	4.1	65	67
RV parks & recreational camps	7212	7,428	7,123	36.1	37.1	752	796
RV parks & campgrounds	721211	3,987	3,783	17.2	17.5	315	326
Recreational, vacation camps, exc. campgrounds	721214	3,441	3,340	19.0	19.7	437	471
Rooming & boarding houses	7213	3,391	3,193	16.0	15.1	177	184
Food services & drinking places	722	484,935	480,298	7,758.1	7,900.3	79,548	84,725
Full-service restaurants	7221	193,024	190,788	3,703.2	3,788.1	40,637	43,411
Limited-service eating places	7222	213,543	210,920	3,277.7	3,318.5	29,869	31,475
Limited-service restaurants	722211	172,695	170,421	2,896.8	2,924.6	26,070	27,468
Cafeterias	722212	4,786	4,250	85.9	74.3	992	871
Snack & nonalcoholic beverage bars	722213	36,062	36,249	295.0	319.7	2,807	3,137
Special food services	7223	25,750	27,413	457.0	468.8	6,071	6,701
Food service contractors	72231	15,898	16,455	358.8	356.7	4,793	5,187
Caterers	72232	7,332	8,171	84.7	99.3	1,058	1,293
Mobile food services	72233	2,520	2,787	13.5	12.8	220	221
Drinking places (alcoholic beverages)	7224	52,618	51,177	320.2	324.8	2,971	3,138

[1] North American Industry Classification System, 1997; see text, Section 15, Business Enterprise.

Source: U.S. Census Bureau, *County Business Patterns*, annual. See also <http://www.census.gov/prod/2001pubs/cbp99/cbp99-1.pdf> (issued April 2001).

No. 1268. Commercial and Noncommercial Groups—Food and Drink Establishments and Sales: 1990 to 2001

[Sales in millions of dollars (238,149 represents $238,149,000,000). Excludes military. Data refer to sales to consumers of food and alcoholic beverages. Sales are estimated. For details, see source]

Type of group	Establishments 1990	Establishments 1998	Sales (mil. dol.) 1990	1995	1997	1998	1999	2000	2001 [1]
Total	720,043	842,553	238,149	294,631	322,011	339,842	356,983	377,811	397,591
Commercial restaurant services [2][3]	546,996	659,826	211,606	265,910	291,637	308,816	325,235	345,168	364,183
Eating places [2]	338,724	422,406	155,552	198,293	219,229	232,131	241,083	259,814	274,488
Full-service restaurants	163,514	196,026	77,811	96,396	110,276	117,774	120,994	134,461	143,336
Limited-service restaurants [4]	149,786	176,801	69,798	92,901	103,348	98,120	109,882	107,252	111,972
Bars and taverns [5]	37,227	36,435	9,533	9,948	11,066	11,498	11,515	12,257	12,453
Managed services [2]	15,739	19,117	14,149	18,186	20,621	21,991	23,016	24,844	26,376
Manufacturing and industrial plants	(NA)	(NA)	3,856	4,814	5,437	5,769	5,931	6,221	6,539
Colleges and universities [2]	(NA)	(NA)	2,788	3,989	4,667	5,068	5,449	5,933	6,384
Lodging places [2]	(NA)	12,853	13,568	15,561	16,246	17,153	18,798	19,120	20,127
Retail hosts [2][6]	107,807	130,062	9,513	12,589	12,316	13,135	16,851	14,947	15,863
Department store restaurants	4,980	4,111	876	1,038	798	833	(NA)	(NA)	(NA)
Grocery store restaurants [6]	44,766	60,223	5,432	6,624	6,201	6,495	(NA)	(NA)	(NA)
Gasoline service stations	33,788	49,672	1,718	2,520	3,564	3,928	(NA)	(NA)	(NA)
Recreation and sports	14,447	15,902	2,871	3,866	4,232	4,456	4,760	4,868	5,066
Noncommercial restaurant services [2]	173,047	182,727	26,543	28,722	30,374	31,025	31,749	32,644	33,408
Employee restaurant services	7,717	5,218	1,864	1,364	1,186	1,120	1,044	990	934
Industrial, commercial organizations	3,091	2,008	1,603	1,129	935	864	(NA)	(NA)	(NA)
Educational restaurant services	95,883	100,237	7,671	9,059	9,545	9,737	9,959	10,060	10,169
Elementary and secondary schools	93,104	96,095	3,700	4,533	4,886	4,948	5,099	5,063	5,099
Hospitals	6,613	5,997	8,968	9,219	9,681	9,801	9,895	10,068	10,209
Miscellaneous [2]	29,403	35,591	2,892	3,673	4,060	4,285	4,512	4,934	5,210
Clubs	10,310	10,514	1,993	2,278	2,529	2,691	(NA)	(NA)	(NA)

NA Not available. [1] Projection. [2] Includes other types of groups, not shown separately. [3] Data for establishments with payroll. [4] Fastfood restaurants. [5] For establishments serving food. [6] A portion of delicatessen sales in grocery stores are considered food service.

Source: National Restaurant Association, Washington, DC, *Restaurant Numbers: 25 Year History, 1970-1995*, 1998; *Restaurant Industry in Review*, annual; and *National Restaurant Association Restaurant Industry Forecast*, December 2000 (copyright).

Accommodation, Food Services, and Other Services 775

Kind of business	NAICS code [1]	Estab-lish-ments (number)	Receipts Total (mil. dol.)	Receipts Per paid employee (dol.)	Annual payroll Total (mil. dol.)	Annual payroll Per paid employee (dol.)	Paid employee for pay period including March 12 (1,000)
Professional, scientific, & technical services	54	615,305	579,542	111,178	225,376	43,236	5,212.7
Professional, scientific, & technical services	541	615,305	579,542	111,178	225,376	43,236	5,212.7
Legal services	5411	173,716	127,052	125,534	49,060	48,474	1,012.1
Offices of lawyers	54111	165,757	122,617	128,250	47,410	49,588	956.1
Other legal services	54119	7,959	4,436	79,180	1,650	29,462	56.0
Accounting, tax return prep, bookkeeping, & payroll services	5412	97,512	61,117	63,234	26,104	27,008	966.5
Architectural, engineering, & related services	5413	92,710	116,986	112,669	46,943	45,210	1,038.3
Architectural services	54131	20,602	16,988	115,802	6,469	44,093	146.7
Engineering services	54133	52,526	88,181	120,788	35,338	48,405	730.0
Drafting services	54134	1,872	605	66,160	310	33,917	9.2
Building inspection services	54135	2,771	639	73,673	240	27,678	8.7
Geophysical surveying & mapping services	54136	587	1,088	109,822	446	44,987	9.9
Surveying & mapping (except geophysical services	54137	8,864	3,042	58,708	1,432	27,630	51.8
Testing laboratories	54138	5,488	6,443	78,550	2,709	33,024	82.0
Specialized design services	5414	26,436	14,254	126,103	4,088	36,166	113.0
Interior design services	54141	9,612	4,945	145,816	1,022	30,120	33.9
Industrial design services	54142	1,322	1,363	100,170	583	42,816	13.6
Graphic design services	54143	14,631	7,555	122,601	2,355	38,212	61.6
Other specialized design services	54149	871	391	100,428	129	33,207	3.9
Computer systems design & related services	5415	72,278	108,968	142,505	42,151	55,123	764.7
Management, scientific, & technical consulting services	5416	80,426	63,429	124,066	26,582	51,993	511.3
Management consulting services	54161	60,794	52,225	127,054	22,297	54,244	411.0
Environmental consulting services	54162	6,725	4,781	103,603	1,778	38,522	46.1
Other scientific & technical consulting services	54169	12,907	6,423	118,811	2,507	46,377	54.1
Scientific research & development services	5417	7,830	23,078	130,405	9,322	52,675	177.0
R&D in the physical, engineering, & life sciences	54171	6,855	21,822	135,283	8,821	54,683	161.3
Research & development in the social sciences & humanities	54172	975	1,257	80,188	502	32,000	15.7
Advertising & related services	5418	38,832	49,290	118,141	16,012	38,379	417.2
Advertising agencies	54181	13,390	16,872	120,955	7,557	54,177	139.5
Public relations agencies	54182	6,513	4,772	123,195	1,952	50,384	38.7
Media buying services	54183	882	1,057	123,824	422	49,452	8.5
Media representatives	54184	2,686	3,309	125,153	1,061	40,115	26.4
Display advertising	54185	2,261	4,639	112,169	823	19,901	41.4
Direct mail advertising	54186	3,454	8,672	101,229	2,427	28,325	85.7
Advertising material distribution services	54187	560	830	86,049	175	18,145	9.6
Other services related to advertising	54189	9,086	9,140	135,706	1,596	23,702	67.4
Other professional, scientific, & technical services	5419	25,565	15,368	72,261	5,115	24,049	212.7
Marketing research & public opinion polling	54191	4,030	7,880	73,266	2,963	27,553	107.6
Photographic services	54192	17,573	5,571	66,399	1,540	18,353	83.9
Translation & interpretation services	54193	904	415	85,250	142	29,232	4.9
All other professional, scientific, & technical services	54199	3,058	1,502	91,866	469	28,690	16.3

[1] North American Industry Classification System, 1997; see text, Section 15, Business Enterprise.
Source: U.S. Census Bureau, *1997 Economic Census, Professional, Scientific, and Technical Services*, Series EC97554A-US, issued December 1999.

No. 1270. Professional, Scientific, and Technical Services (Tax-Exempt)— Establishments, Revenue, Payroll, and Employees by Kind of Business: 1997

Kind of business	NAICS code [1]	Estab-lish-ments (number)	Revenue Total (mil. dol.)	Revenue Per paid employee (dol.)	Annual payroll Total (mil. dol.)	Annual payroll Per paid employee (dol.)	Paid employee for pay period including March 12 (1,000)
Professional, scientific, & technical services	54	5,824	15,709	105,806	6,023	40,567	148.5
Professional, scientific, & technical services	541	5,824	15,709	105,806	6,023	40,567	148.5
Legal services	5411	2,532	1,497	64,197	797	34,168	23.3
Offices of lawyers	54111	2,532	1,497	64,197	797	34,168	23.3
Scientific research & development services	5417	3,292	14,212	113,558	5,226	41,759	125.1
R&D in the physical, engineering, & life sciences	54171	2,318	12,324	114,312	4,593	42,606	107.8
Research & development in the social sciences & humanities	54172	974	1,888	108,873	633	36,488	17.3

[1] North American Industry Classification System, 1997; see text, Section 15, Business Enterprise
Source: U.S. Census Bureau, *1997 Economic Census, Professional, Scientific, and Technical Services*, Series EC97554A-US, issued December 1999.

No. 1271. Advertising Estimated Expenditures by Medium: 1990 to 2000

[In millions of dollars (129,590 represents $129,590,000,000). See source, for definitions of types of advertising]

Medium	1990	1992	1994	1995	1996	1997	1998	1999	2000 prel.
Total	129,590	132,650	151,680	162,930	175,230	187,529	201,594	215,301	236,332
National	73,380	76,710	88,250	95,360	103,040	110,232	118,966	127,663	142,742
Local	56,210	55,940	63,430	67,570	72,190	77,297	82,628	87,638	93,590
Newspapers	32,281	30,737	34,356	36,317	38,402	41,670	44,292	46,648	49,246
National	3,867	3,602	3,906	3,996	4,400	5,016	5,402	6,358	7,184
Local	28,414	27,135	30,450	32,321	34,002	36,654	38,890	40,290	42,062
Magazines	6,803	7,000	7,916	8,580	9,010	9,821	10,518	11,433	12,348
Broadcast TV	26,616	27,249	31,133	32,720	36,046	36,893	39,173	40,011	44,438
Four TV networks	9,863	10,249	10,942	11,600	13,081	13,020	13,736	13,961	15,706
(Three TV networks)	9,383	9,549	9,959	10,263	11,423	11,324	12,105	12,195	14,047
Syndication	1,109	1,370	1,734	2,016	2,218	2,438	2,609	2,870	3,128
Spot (National)	7,788	7,551	8,993	9,119	9,803	9,999	10,659	10,500	11,970
Spot (Local)	7,856	8,079	9,464	9,985	10,944	11,436	12,169	12,680	13,631
Cable TV	2,457	3,201	4,302	5,108	6,438	7,237	8,301	10,429	12,364
Cable TV networks	1,860	2,227	3,052	3,535	4,472	5,067	5,827	7,500	9,000
Spot (Local)	597	974	1,250	1,573	1,966	2,170	2,474	2,929	3,364
Radio	8,726	8,654	10,529	11,338	12,269	13,491	15,073	17,215	19,585
Network	482	424	463	480	523	560	622	684	850
Spot (National)	1,635	1,505	1,902	1,959	2,135	2,455	2,823	3,275	3,822
Local (Local)	6,609	6,725	8,164	8,899	9,611	10,476	11,628	13,256	14,913
Yellow Pages	8,926	9,320	9,825	10,236	10,849	11,423	11,990	12,652	13,367
National	1,132	1,188	1,314	1,410	1,555	1,711	1,870	1,986	2,125
Local	7,794	8,132	8,511	8,826	9,294	9,712	10,120	10,666	11,242
Direct mail	23,370	25,392	29,638	32,866	34,509	36,890	39,620	41,403	44,715
Business papers	2,875	3,090	3,358	3,559	3,808	4,109	4,232	4,274	4,700
Billboards	1,084	1,030	1,167	1,263	1,339	1,455	1,576	1,725	1,870
National	640	610	648	701	743	795	845	925	1,010
Local	444	421	519	562	596	660	731	800	860
Internet	(NA)	(NA)	(NA)	(NA)	(NA)	600	1,050	1,940	3,200
Miscellaneous	16,452	16,977	19,456	20,943	22,560	23,940	25,769	27,571	30,502
National	11,956	12,503	14,384	15,539	16,783	17,751	19,153	20,554	22,984
Local	4,496	4,474	5,072	5,404	5,777	6,189	6,616	7,017	7,518

NA Not available.
Source: McCann-Erickson, Inc., New York, NY. Compiled for Crain Communications, Inc. in *Advertising Age* (copyright).

No. 1272. Magazine Advertising Revenue by Category: 1999 and 2000

[15,508.4 represents $15,508,400,000. Represents the volume of advertising in the consumer magazines belonging to the Publishers Information Bureau]

Category	Pages		Volume (mil. dol.)	
	1999	2000	1999	2000
Total [1]	255,146	286,932	15,508.4	17,665.3
Automotive	24,753	22,934	1,843.7	1,751.9
Automotive accessories and equipment .	24,502	22,639	1,833.0	1,732.6
Technology [1]	22,009	35,358	1,384.7	1,945.1
Telecommunications	4,734	5,760	312.2	333.9
Computers and software	13,252	24,020	893.8	1,370.4
Home furnishings and supplies [1]	17,273	17,082	1,185.3	1,230.5
Toiletries and cosmetics [1]	15,857	16,527	1,143.3	1,272.3
Cosmetics and beauty aids [2]	8,484	9,220	578.5	669.7
Personal hygiene and health [2]	3,238	3,031	286.9	286.2
Hair products and accessories [2]	2,589	2,956	185.0	225.0
Direct response companies	22,163	20,342	1,121.4	1,071.3
Apparel and accessories [1]	24,776	26,940	1,119.8	1,314.0
Ready-to-wear	12,771	13,858	499.5	596.1
Footwear	3,349	4,084	158.2	219.7
Jewelry and watches	4,214	5,058	209.9	282.9
Financial, insurance and real estate	16,253	18,776	1,023.0	1,197.8
Financial	12,557	14,986	756.8	932.0
Food and food products [1]	9,894	10,986	1,003.3	1,168.5
Ingredients, mixes and seasonings	1,615	1,695	181.6	195.6
Prepared foods	1,919	2,032	194.2	218.6
Dairy, produce, meat, and bakery goods .	2,809	2,937	287.8	322.0
Beverages	1,854	2,031	165.5	201.6
Drugs and remedies	11,759	12,557	977.3	1,130.0
Medicines and proprietary remedies	10,272	10,812	849.5	983.1
Media and advertising	11,418	17,752	846.0	1,211.4
Retail [1]	15,798	20,014	825.8	1,078.4
Retail [3]	12,786	16,524	670.8	882.3
Department stores	1,852	2,072	90.4	101.5
Public transportation, hotels, and resorts . .	15,231	15,664	705.2	751.4
Cigarettes, tobacco, and accessories	6,034	4,822	481.2	400.6
Beer, wine and liquor	4,565	5,073	299.4	361.2
Liquor	3,600	3,924	235.2	287.6
Local services and amusements	5,424	6,555	276.9	327.3
Sporting goods	10,503	11,851	240.0	245.7
Schools, camps, seminars	2,353	3,049	76.4	118.4

[1] Includes other categories, not shown separately. [2] Women's, men's, and unisex. [3] Includes apparel, business, drugs and toiletries, and food and beverage.
Source: Publishers Information Bureau, Inc., New York, NY, as compiled by Competitive Media Reporting.

Accommodation, Food Services and Other Services 777

No. 1273. Administrative and Support and Waste Management and Remediation Services—Establishments, Receipts, Payroll, and Employees by Kind of Business (NAICS Basis): 1997

Kind of business	NAICS code [1]	Estab-lish-ments (number)	Receipts		Annual payroll		Paid employee for pay period including March 12 (1,000)
			Total (mil. dol.)	Per paid employee (dol.)	Total (mil. dol.)	Per paid employee (dol.)	
Administrative & support & waste management & remediation services	**56**	**276,393**	**295,936**	**40,278**	**137,337**	**18,692**	**7,347.4**
Administrative & support services	561	260,025	256,591	36,310	128,438	18,175	7,066.7
Office administrative services	5611	24,537	28,054	82,906	11,971	35,377	338.4
Facilities support services	5612	2,490	7,576	67,558	3,280	29,251	112.1
Employment services	5613	34,569	86,133	23,780	62,127	17,153	3,622.0
Business support services	5614	32,920	36,026	59,590	11,900	19,683	604.6
Business service centers	56143	10,130	8,504	79,699	2,076	19,459	106.7
Collection agencies	56144	5,250	5,083	60,276	2,128	25,235	84.3
Credit bureaus	56145	1,588	4,699	137,613	1,165	34,128	34.1
Travel arrangement & reservation services	5615	36,578	21,484	71,493	7,699	25,622	300.5
Other travel arrangement & reservation services	56159	3,745	8,725	110,786	2,201	27,949	78.8
Investigation & security services	5616	21,494	20,444	29,938	10,698	15,665	682.9
Investigation, guard, & armored car services	56161	12,539	12,370	22,052	7,759	13,832	561.0
Security systems services	56162	8,955	8,074	66,224	2,938	24,100	121.9
Services to buildings & dwellings	5617	80,807	29,915	28,599	13,317	12,731	1,046.0
Exterminating & pest control services	56171	11,062	4,911	60,466	1,930	23,766	81.2
Janitorial services	56172	55,157	21,128	23,678	10,106	11,326	892.3
Carpet & upholstery cleaning services	56174	9,282	2,156	45,810	729	15,500	47.1
Other support services	5619	26,630	26,958	74,859	7,446	20,677	360.1
Packaging & labeling services	56191	2,331	4,015	70,869	1,073	18,945	56.7
Convention & trade show organizers	56192	3,978	6,260	86,416	1,733	23,925	72.4
Waste management & remediation services	562	16,368	39,346	140,166	8,899	31,702	280.7
Waste collection	5621	8,324	20,145	131,885	4,566	29,893	152.7
Waste treatment & disposal	5622	2,314	10,251	192,225	1,933	36,249	53.3
Remediation & other waste management services	5629	5,730	8,950	119,914	2,400	32,154	74.6
Remediation services	56291	1,677	5,690	138,793	1,500	36,600	41.0

[1] North American Industry Classification System, 1997; see text, Section 15, Business Enterprise.
Source: U.S. Census Bureau, *1997 Economic Census, Administrative & Support and Waste Management & Remediation Services*, Series EC97556A-US, issued January 2000.

No. 1274. Administrative and Support and Waste Management and Remediation Services Landscaping Services (NAICS 56)—Estimated Revenue for Employer Firms: 1998 and 1999

Kind of business	NAICS code [1]	1998	1999	Percent change, 1998-1999
Administrative & support & waste management & remediation services	**56**	**337,806**	**373,956**	**10.7**
Administrative & support services	561	295,279	327,368	10.9
Employment services	5613	102,040	114,361	12.1
Employment placement agencies	56131	5,704	6,894	20.9
Temporary help services	56132	65,656	71,504	8.9
Employee leasing services	56133	30,680	35,964	17.2
Business support services	5614	39,928	43,346	8.6
Document preparation services	56141	1,744	1,955	12.0
Telephone call centers	56142	13,713	14,817	8.0
Business service centers	56143	8,923	9,667	8.3
Collection agencies	56144	5,233	6,100	16.6
Credit bureaus	56145	5,188	5,359	3.3
Other business support services	56149	5,127	5,448	6.3
Travel arrangement & reservation services	5615	23,092	24,996	8.2
Other travel arrangement & reservation services	56159	10,092	11,152	10.5
Investigation, guard, & armored car services [2]	5616	22,013	23,999	
Security systems services	56162	8,962	9,535	6.4
Services to buildings & dwellings	5617	33,712	36,949	9.6
Exterminating & pest control services	56171	5,532	5,955	7.7
Janitorial services	56172	24,181	26,712	10.5
Carpet & upholstery cleaning services	56174	2,271	2,416	6.4
Other services to buildings & dwellings [2]	56179	1,729	1,865	7.9
Other support services	5619	32,056	34,341	7.1
Packaging & labeling services [2]	56191	4,883	5,377	10.1
Convention & trade show organizers	56192	7,303	7,779	6.5
All other support services	56199	19,871	21,185	6.6
Waste management & remediation services	562	42,527	46,588	9.5
Waste collection	5621	22,316	24,832	11.3
Waste treatment & disposal [2]	5622	10,020	11,101	10.8
Remediation & other waste management services	5629	10,191	10,655	4.6
Remediation services	56291	5,376	5,527	2.8
Materials recovery facility	56292	2,365	2,462	4.1
All other waste management services	56299	2,450	2,667	8.8

[1] North American Industry Classification System, 1997; see text, Section 15, Business Enterprise.
Source: U.S. Census Bureau, Current Business Reports; *Service Annual Survey: 1999*, issued July 2001.

No. 1275. Other Services—Establishments, Receipts, Payroll, and Employees by Kind of Business (NAICS Basis): 1997

Kind of business	NAICS code [1]	Estab-lish-ments (number)	Receipts		Annual payroll		Paid employee for pay period including March 12 (1,000)
			Total (mil. dol.)	Per paid employee (dol.)	Total (mil. dol.)	Per paid employee (dol.)	
Other services (except public administration)	81	420,950	163,033	65,381	48,453	19,431	2,493.6
Repair & maintenance	811	235,466	105,154	82,384	29,875	23,406	1,276.4
Automotive repair & maintenance	8111	164,360	62,201	76,306	16,865	20,690	815.1
Automotive mechanical & electrical repair & maintenance	81111	99,444	33,510	86,966	8,634	22,406	385.3
Automotive body, paint, interior, & glass repair	81112	41,168	20,905	89,202	5,926	25,285	234.4
Other automotive repair & maintenance	81119	23,748	7,785	39,829	2,306	11,796	195.5
Electronic & precision equipment repair & maintenance	8112	17,634	14,558	106,087	4,497	32,769	137.2
Commercial & industrial machinery & equip (exc. auto. & electr.) R&M	8113	20,290	17,506	104,851	5,172	30,978	167.0
Personal & household goods repair & maintenance	8114	33,182	10,889	69,335	3,341	21,274	157.1
Home & garden equipment & appliance repair & maintenance	81141	9,790	4,976	77,690	1,536	23,985	64.1
Reupholstery & furniture repair	81142	6,598	1,193	53,480	389	17,416	22.3
Footwear & leather goods repair	81143	2,153	261	47,790	73	13,320	5.5
Other personal & household goods repair & maintenance	81149	14,641	4,458	68,361	1,343	20,599	65.2
Personal & laundry services	812	185,484	57,879	47,552	18,577	15,263	1,217.2
Personal care services	8121	95,708	14,241	30,154	5,972	12,645	472.3
Hair, nail, & skin care services	81211	83,991	12,057	29,335	5,378	13,084	411.0
Other personal care services	81219	11,717	2,184	35,646	594	9,696	61.3
Death care services	8122	23,015	12,621	76,571	3,519	21,349	164.8
Funeral homes & funeral services	81221	16,338	9,633	91,423	2,444	23,192	105.4
Cemeteries & crematories	81222	6,677	2,988	50,252	1,075	18,082	59.5
Drycleaning & laundry services	8123	44,782	17,913	45,303	5,939	15,021	395.4
Coin-operated laundries & drycleaners	81231	13,883	2,873	54,191	606	11,435	53.0
Drycleaning & laundry services (except coin-operated)	81232	27,939	7,092	34,803	2,575	12,637	203.8
Linen & uniform supply	81233	2,960	7,948	57,339	2,758	19,896	138.6
Diaper service	8123312	100	37	41,598	13	15,336	0.9
Other personal services	8129	21,979	13,105	70,959	3,148	17,044	184.7
Photofinishing	81292	7,055	5,520	76,671	1,583	21,986	72.0
Parking lots & garages	81293	10,358	5,175	67,940	968	12,705	76.2
All other personal services	81299	4,566	2,410	65,996	597	16,350	36.5

[1] North American Industry Classification System, 1997; see text, Section 15, Business Enterprise.

Source: U.S. Census Bureau, *1997 Economic Census, Other Services,* Series EC97581A-US, issued December 1999.

U.S. Census Bureau, Statistical Abstract of the United States: 2001

No. 1276. Other Services—Estimated Revenue for Employer and Nonemployer Firms: 1998 and 1999

[In millions of dollars (334,012 represents $334,012,000,000), except percent. Based on the Service Annual Survey; subject to sampling variability. See text, this section]

Kind of business	NAICS code [1]	1998	1999	Percent change, 1998-1999
Other services (except public administration, religious, labor, and political organizations, and private households)...............................	81	334,012	354,667	6.2
Repair & maintenance.................................	811	133,800	139,926	4.6
Automotive repair and maintenance......................	8111	77,969	81,862	5.0
Automotive mechanical and electrical repair and maintenance...	81111	41,416	42,763	3.3
Automotive body, paint, interior, and glass repair............	81112	25,435	26,904	5.8
Other automotive repair and maintenance	811119	11,119	12,196	9.7
Electronic and precision equipment repair and maintenance [2].....	8112	17,598	18,769	6.7
Commercial and industrial machinery and equipment (except automotive electronic) repair and maintenance.............	8113	21,179	21,188	(Z)
Personal and household goods repair and maintenance.........	8114	17,053	18,107	6.2
Home and garden equipment and appliance repair and maintenance.......................................	81141	6,074	6,484	6.7
Reupholstery and furniture repair	81142	2,142	2,363	10.3
Footwear and leather goods repair	81143	383	397	3.7
Other personal and household goods repair and maintenance...	81149	8,456	8,864	4.8
Personal & laundry services............................	812	88,511	95,114	7.5
Personal care services................................	8121	25,050	26,730	6.7
Hair, nail, & skin care services.........................	81211	21,504	22,824	6.1
Other personal care services..........................	81219	3,546	3,905	10.1
Death care services..................................	8122	13,760	13,968	1.5
Funeral homes & funeral services......................	81221	10,857	11,012	1.4
Cemeteries & crematories............................	81222	2,903	2,956	1.8
Drycleaning & laundry services	8123	20,497	21,860	6.6
Coin-operated laundries & drycleaners	81231	3,607	4,028	11.7
Drycleaning and laundry services, except coin-operated	81232	8,353	8,832	5.7
Linen & uniform supply...............................	81233	8,537	8,999	5.4
Other personal services..............................	8129	29,204	32,557	11.5
Photofinishing.....................................	81292	5,822	5,931	1.9
Parking lots & garages	81293	6,431	7,000	8.9
All other personal services	81299	16,951	19,626	15.8
Religious, grantmaking, civic, professional, and similar organizations (except religious, labor, and political organizations) [3]..	813	111,702	119,627	7.1

Z Less than 0.05 percent.   [1] North American Industry Classification System, 1997; see text, Section 15, Business Enterprise.   [2] Estimates for NAICS 811219 (other electronics and precision equipment repair and maintenance) have not been adjusted to the results of the 1997 Economic Census.   [3] Estimates for NAICS 813211 (grantmaking foundations) have not been adjusted to the results of the 1997 Economic Census.

Source: U.S. Census Bureau, *Service Annual Survey: 1999,* Series SAS/99, July 2001. See also <http://www.census.gov/svsd/www/sas99rpt.pdf>.

No. 1277. Other Services (Tax-Exempt)—Establishments, Revenue, Payroll, and Employees by Kind of Business (NAICS Basis): 1997

Kind of business	NAICS code [1]	Estab-lish-ments (number)	Revenue		Annual payroll		Paid employee for pay period including March 12 (1,000)
			Total (mil. dol.)	Per paid employee (dol.)	Total (mil. dol.)	Per paid employee (dol.)	
Other services (except public administration)	81	98,765	102,864	134,886	17,068	22,381	762.6
Grantmaking & giving services	8132	11,906	48,957	467,113	3,080	29,391	104.8
Social advocacy organizations.	8133	10,120	7,525	88,481	2,003	23,554	85.0
Civic & social organizations	8134	28,364	9,916	37,956	2,683	10,269	261.3
Business, professional, labor, political and similar organizations	8139	48,375	36,467	117,071	9,301	29,860	311.5
Business associations	81391	16,928	14,859	128,000	4,180	36,007	116.1
Professional organizations.	81392	7,239	8,292	132,942	2,265	36,306	62.4
Other similar organizations (exc. bus., prof., labor, & political)	81399	24,208	13,316	100,094	2,857	21,474	133.0

[1] North American Industry Classification System, 1997.

Source: U.S. Census Bureau, *1997 Economic Census, Other Services*, Series EC97581A-US.

No. 1278. Religious, Grantmaking, Civic, and Professional Service Firms—Revenue and Expenses for Tax-Exempt Employer Firms: 1998 and 1999

[In millions of dollars (111,702 represents $111,702,000,000) except as indicated. Based on the Service Annual Survey; subject to sampling variability. See text, this section]

Kind of business	NAICS code [1]	Revenue			Expenses		
		1998	1999	Percent change, 1998-1999	1998	1999	Percent change, 1998-1999
Religious, grantmaking, civic, professional, and similar organizations (except religious, labor, and political organizations)	813	111,702	119,627	7.1	81,078	86,057	6.1
Grantmaking and giving services.	8132	52,213	57,667	10.4	27,134	30,181	11.2
Social advocacy organizations	8133	8,877	9,882	11.3	7,716	8,578	11.2
Civic and social organizations.	8134	10,908	11,408	4.6	9,851	10,310	4.7
Business, professional, and other organizations (except labor and political organizations).	8139	39,704	40,670	2.4	36,377	36,989	1.7

[1] North American Industry Classification System, 1997; see text, Section 15, Business Enterprise.

Source: U.S. Census Bureau, *Service Annual Survey: 1999*, Series SAS/99, July 2001. See also <http://www.census.gov/svsd/www/sas99rpt.pdf>.

No. 1279. National Nonprofit Associations—Number by Type: 1980 to 2000

[Data compiled during last few months of year previous to year shown and the beginning months of year shown]

Type	1980	1990	1999	2000	Type	1980	1990	1999	2000
Total	14,726	22,289	22,474	21,840	Fraternal, foreign interest, nationality, ethnic	435	573	552	524
Trade, business, commercial.	3,118	3,918	3,815	3,880	Religious.	797	1,172	1,151	1,122
Agriculture.	677	940	1,113	1,102	Veteran, hereditary, patriotic .	208	462	877	834
Legal, governmental, public admin., military	529	792	778	789	Hobby, avocational	910	1,475	1,463	1,329
Scientific, engineering, tech .	1,039	1,417	1,332	1,301	Athletic sports	504	840	782	716
Educational	[1]2,376	1,291	1,321	1,296	Labor unions	235	253	235	231
Cultural.	([1])	1,886	1,876	1,785	Chambers of Commerce [2] . .	105	168	146	142
Social welfare	994	1,705	1,913	1,828	Greek and non-Greek letter societies	318	340	313	295
Health, medical	1,413	2,227	2,481	2,494	Fan clubs	(NA)	581	449	380
Public affairs	1,068	2,249	1,877	1,775					

NA Not available. [1] Data for cultural associations included with educational associations. [2] National and binational.

Source: Gale Group, Farmington Hills, MI. Compiled from *Encyclopedia of Associations*, annual (copyright).

Accommodation, Food Services, and Other Services 781

No. 1280. Service-Related Industries—Establishments, Employees, and Annual Payroll by State: 1999

[Excludes government employees, railroad employees, self-employed persons, etc. See "General Explanation" in source for definitions and statement on reliability of data. An *establishment* is a single physical location where business is conducted or where services or industrial operations are performed. NAICS=North American Industry Classification System]

State	Professional, scientific, & technical services (NAICS 54)			Accommodation and food services (NAICS 72)			Other services (NAICS 81)		
	Estab-lish-ments	Employ-ees [1]	Annual payroll (mil. dol.)	Estab-lish-ments	Employ-ees [1]	Annual payroll (mil. dol.)	Estab-lish-ments	Employ-ees [1]	Annual payroll (mil. dol.)
United States..	704,779	6,432,422	311,239	539,576	9,638,007	116,925	717,892	5,151,464	101,953
Alabama.........	8,148	69,448	2,834	6,975	133,248	1,253	11,733	81,411	1,283
Alaska	1,592	9,612	466	1,740	20,804	350	1,699	10,298	236
Arizona.	11,758	104,827	4,005	9,120	195,111	2,296	9,935	76,800	1,475
Arkansas	4,700	29,663	953	4,466	74,493	680	6,718	39,922	612
California	90,038	975,340	49,574	62,466	1,079,478	14,296	67,430	538,752	11,412
Colorado.	16,849	132,906	7,155	10,179	198,577	2,372	11,661	85,573	1,789
Connecticut.	10,174	87,130	5,016	6,711	96,985	1,302	9,570	62,132	1,417
Delaware	2,119	18,862	959	1,526	26,260	344	2,111	15,830	288
District of Columbia . .	4,170	74,430	5,327	1,639	41,122	806	3,646	57,805	2,534
Florida	49,243	338,128	14,439	28,333	594,448	7,382	41,576	295,523	5,517
Georgia	21,165	185,219	8,992	14,106	286,264	3,293	19,618	142,470	2,858
Hawaii	2,716	18,137	738	3,082	84,214	1,582	3,136	22,308	462
Idaho.	2,860	22,432	881	2,923	43,725	414	2,979	16,648	273
Illinois	34,856	337,445	18,174	23,579	405,927	4,834	32,305	251,245	5,550
Indiana.	11,223	85,974	3,067	11,673	216,472	2,188	17,258	126,495	2,253
Iowa	5,486	37,151	1,168	6,566	104,419	947	9,737	52,110	822
Kansas.	6,245	52,418	1,914	5,549	93,943	902	8,421	52,772	914
Kentucky	7,097	50,705	1,682	6,507	129,217	1,360	10,026	64,588	1,098
Louisiana	9,928	75,438	2,629	7,284	159,610	1,777	10,280	78,656	1,356
Maine.	3,023	18,677	687	3,680	42,184	540	3,535	17,974	310
Maryland	16,191	182,531	9,134	8,791	160,095	1,943	13,245	107,901	2,421
Massachusetts.	20,614	214,495	13,458	14,586	233,332	3,204	16,807	116,772	2,797
Michigan.	20,991	202,469	9,571	18,541	322,205	3,317	24,967	180,587	3,637
Minnesota.	14,438	115,887	5,497	9,893	187,691	2,061	14,858	116,292	2,058
Mississippi	4,113	26,586	863	4,096	96,429	1,176	6,866	39,703	601
Missouri	12,062	112,157	4,748	10,980	204,696	2,244	16,424	113,618	2,049
Montana	2,532	13,502	397	3,169	37,818	367	3,005	13,652	220
Nebraska	3,561	31,144	1,238	3,954	60,908	570	5,703	35,095	569
Nevada	5,196	36,692	1,610	3,879	257,264	5,861	3,538	26,913	567
New Hampshire	3,794	22,565	995	3,046	46,376	567	3,483	20,667	420
New Jersey.	29,419	251,175	13,910	16,387	250,739	4,091	22,303	143,758	3,127
New Mexico	4,203	36,214	1,565	3,690	66,574	699	4,180	26,668	460
New York	51,237	514,993	29,324	37,036	485,430	7,242	49,689	332,682	7,820
North Carolina.	17,157	137,948	5,607	14,924	270,421	2,889	21,333	137,535	2,479
North Dakota.	1,252	8,681	244	1,772	25,348	215	2,469	13,598	190
Ohio	23,556	217,328	9,170	22,351	409,064	4,055	30,634	230,980	4,105
Oklahoma.	7,801	49,496	1,750	6,277	106,449	1,037	8,998	60,740	967
Oregon.	9,410	64,913	2,577	8,256	124,295	1,447	8,755	57,189	1,076
Pennsylvania.	26,221	284,105	13,915	24,039	364,085	3,915	35,354	243,961	4,359
Rhode Island.	2,636	16,762	695	2,639	35,242	424	2,947	17,580	337
South Carolina.	7,746	58,207	2,308	7,987	149,010	1,618	10,685	70,246	1,153
South Dakota	1,507	7,606	214	2,201	29,609	272	2,627	13,395	194
Tennessee	9,902	94,209	3,661	9,511	194,134	2,127	14,556	110,505	1,943
Texas.	48,058	439,664	21,484	34,398	685,331	7,875	48,042	384,126	7,010
Utah	5,076	47,160	1,843	3,869	77,277	769	3,850	45,068	958
Vermont	1,871	10,027	384	1,843	27,297	318	2,103	9,682	169
Virginia.	20,408	271,952	14,413	12,401	237,305	2,733	19,932	146,758	3,332
Washington	15,628	127,011	5,813	13,051	198,114	2,356	15,223	103,190	2,098
West Virginia.	2,854	19,091	541	3,259	51,441	525	5,117	26,750	407
Wisconsin.	10,512	87,696	3,462	12,934	194,092	1,830	15,080	108,491	1,836
Wyoming	1,443	6,214	183	1,712	23,435	259	1,745	8,050	133

[1] Covers full- and part-time employees who are on the payroll in the pay period including March 12.

Source: U.S. Census Bureau, *County Business Patterns*, annual. See also <http://www.census.gov/prod/2001pubs/cbp99/cbp99-1.pdf> (issued April 2001).

U.S. Census Bureau, Statistical Abstract of the United States: 2001

Section 28
Foreign Commerce and Aid

This section presents data on the flow of goods, services, and capital between the United States and other countries; changes in official reserve assets of the United States; international investments; and foreign assistance programs.

The Bureau of Economic Analysis publishes current figures on U.S. international transactions and the U.S. international investment position in its monthly *Survey of Current Business*. Statistics for the foreign aid programs are presented by the Agency for International Development (AID) in its annual *U.S. Overseas Loans and Grants and Assistance from International Organizations* and by the Department of Agriculture in its *Foreign Agricultural Trade of the United States*.

The principal source of merchandise import and export data is the U.S. Census Bureau. Current data are presented monthly in *U.S. International Trade in Goods and Services* report Series FT 900. The *Guide to Foreign Trade Statistics* found on the Census Bureau Web site at <http://www.census.gov/foreign-trade/guide/index.html> lists the Bureau's monthly and annual products and services in this field. In addition, the International Trade Administration and the Bureau of Economic Analysis present summary as well as selected commodity and country data for U.S. foreign trade in the *U.S. Foreign Trade Highlights* and the *Survey of Current Business*, respectively. The merchandise trade data in the latter source include balance of payments adjustments to the Census Bureau data. The Treasury Department's *Monthly Treasury Statement of Receipts and Outlays of the United States Government* contains information on import duties.

International accounts—The international transactions tables (Nos. 1281 to 1283) show, for given time periods, the transfer of goods, services, grants, and financial assets and liabilities between the United States and the rest of the world.

The international investment position table (No. 1284) presents, for specific dates, the value of U.S. investments abroad and of foreign investments in the United States. The movement of foreign and U.S. capital as presented in the balance of payments is not the only factor affecting the total value of foreign investments. Among the other factors are changes in the valuation of assets or liabilities, including changes in prices of securities, defaults, expropriations, and write-offs.

Direct investment abroad means the ownership or control, directly or indirectly, by one person of 10 percent or more of the voting securities of an incorporated business enterprise or an equivalent interest in an unincorporated business enterprise. Direct investment position is the value of U.S. parents claims on the equity of and receivables due from foreign affiliates, less foreign affiliates receivables due from their U.S. parent's. Income consists of parents shares in the earnings of their affiliates' plus net interest received by parents' on intercompany accounts, less withholding taxes on dividends and interest.

Foreign aid—Foreign assistance is divided into three major categories—grants (military supplies and services and other grants), credits, and other assistance (through net accumulation of foreign currency claims from the sale of agricultural commodities). *Grants* are transfers for which no payment is expected (other than a limited percentage of the foreign currency "counterpart" funds generated by the grant), or which at most involve an obligation on the part of the receiver to extend aid to the United States or other countries to achieve a common objective. *Credits* are loan disbursements or transfers under other agreements which give rise to specific obligations to repay, over a period of years, usually with interest. All known returns to the U.S. government stemming from grants and credits (reverse grants,

Foreign Commerce and Aid 783

returns of grants, and payments of principal) are taken into account in net grants and net credits, but no allowance is made for interest or commissions. *Other assistance* represents the transfer of U.S. farm products in exchange for foreign currencies (plus, since enactment of Public Law 87-128, currency claims from principal and interest collected on credits extended under the farm products program), less the government's disbursements of the currencies as grants, credits, or for purchases. The net acquisition of currencies represents net transfers of resources to foreign countries under the agricultural programs, in addition to those classified as grants or credits.

The basic instrument for extending military aid to friendly nations has been the Mutual Defense Assistance Program authorized by the Congress in 1949. Prior to 1952, economic and technical aid was authorized in the Foreign Assistance Act of 1948, the 1950 Act for International Development, and other legislation which set up programs for specific countries. In 1952, these economic, technical, and military aid programs were combine under the Mutual Security Act, which in turn was followed by the Foreign Assistance Act passed in 1961. Appropriations to provide military assistance were also made in the Department of Defense Appropriation Act (rather than the Foreign Assistance Appropriation Act) beginning in 1966 for certain countries in Southeast Asia and in other legislation concerning program for specific countries (such as Israel). Figures on activity under the Foreign Assistance Act as reported in the *Foreign Grants and Credits* series differ from data published by AID or its immediate predecessors, due largely to differences in reporting, timing, and treatment of particular items.

Exports—The Census Bureau compiles export data primarily from Shipper's Export Declarations required to be filed with customs officials for shipments leaving the United States. They include U.S. exports under mutual security programs and exclude shipments to U.S. Armed Forces for their own use.

The value reported in the export statistics is generally equivalent to a free alongside ship (f.a.s.) value at the U.S. port of export, based on the transaction price, including inland freight, insurance, and other charges incurred in placing the merchandise alongside the carrier at the U.S. port of exportation. This value, as defined, excludes the cost of loading merchandise aboard the exporting carrier and also excludes freight, insurance, and any other charges or transportation and other costs beyond the U.S. port of exportation. The country of destination is defined as the country of ultimate destination or country where the merchandise is to be consumed, further processed, or manufactured, as known to the shipper at the time of exportation. When ultimate destination is not known, the shipment is statistically credited to the last country to which the shipper knows the merchandise will be shipped in the same form as exported.

Effective January 1990, the United States began substituting Canadian import statistics for U.S. exports to Canada. As a result of the data exchange between the United States and Canada, the United States has adopted the Canadian import exemption level for its export statistics based on shipments to Canada.

Data are estimated for shipments valued under $2,501 to all countries, except Canada, using factors based on the ratios of low-valued shipments to individual country totals.

Prior to 1989, exports were based on Schedule B, Statistical Classification of Domestic and Foreign Commodities Exported from the United States. These statistics were retabulated and published using Schedule E, Standard International Trade Classification, Revision 2. Beginning in 1989, Schedule B classifications were based on the Harmonized System and made to coincide with the Standard International Trade Classification, Revision 3. This revision will affect the comparability of most export series beginning with the 1989 data for commodities.

Imports—The Census Bureau compiles import data from various customs forms required to be filed with customs officials. Data on import values are presented on two bases in this section: The c.i.f. (cost, insurance, and freight) and the customs import value (as appraised by the U.S. Customs Service in accordance with legal requirements of the Tariff Act of 1930, as amended). This latter valuation, primarily used for collection of import duties, frequently does not reflect the actual transaction value. Country of origin is defined as country where the merchandise was grown, mined, or manufactured. If country of origin is unknown, country of shipment is reported.

Imports are classified either as "General imports" or "Imports for consumption." *General imports* are a combination of entries for immediate consumption, entries into customs bonded warehouses, and entries into U.S. Foreign Trade Zones, thus generally reflecting total arrivals of merchandise. *Imports for consumption* are a combination of entries for immediate consumption, withdrawals from warehouses for consumption, and entries of merchandise into U.S. customs territory from U.S. Foreign Trade Zones, thus generally reflecting the total of the commodities entered into U.S. consumption channels.

Prior to 1989, imports were based on the Tariff Schedule of the United States Annotated. The statistics were retabulated and published using Schedule A, Standard International Trade Classification, Revision 2. Beginning in 1989, the statistics are based on the Harmonized Tariff Schedule of the United States, which coincides with the Standard International Trade Classification, Revision 3. This revision will affect the comparability of most import series beginning with the 1989 data.

Area coverage—Except as noted, the geographic area covered by the export and import trade statistics is the United States Customs area (includes the 50 states, the District of Columbia, and Puerto Rico), the U.S. Virgin Islands (effective January 1981), and U.S. Foreign Trade Zones (effective July 1982). Data for selected tables and total values for 1980 have been revised to reflect the U.S. Virgin Islands' trade with foreign countries, where possible.

Statistical reliability—For a discussion of statistical collection and estimation, sampling procedures, and measures of statistical reliability applicable to Census Bureau data, see Appendix III.

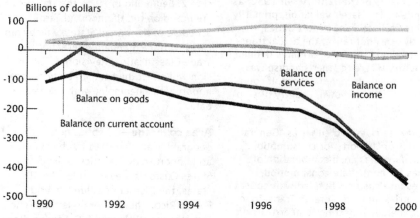

Figure 28.1
U.S. International Transaction Balances: 1990 to 2000

Billions of dollars

Balance on services

Balance on income

Balance on goods

Balance on current account

Source: Chart prepared by U.S. Census Bureau. For data, see Table 1281.

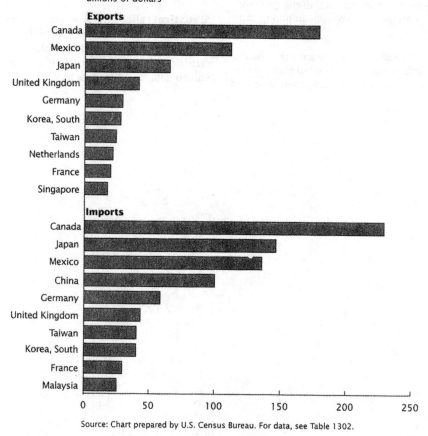

Figure 28.2
Exports and Imports—10 Leading Countries: 2000

Billions of dollars

Exports

Canada
Mexico
Japan
United Kingdom
Germany
Korea, South
Taiwan
Netherlands
France
Singapore

Imports

Canada
Japan
Mexico
China
Germany
United Kingdom
Taiwan
Korea, South
France
Malaysia

Source: Chart prepared by U.S. Census Bureau. For data, see Table 1302.

786   Foreign Commerce and Aid

[In millions of dollars (708,881 represents $708,881,000,000). Minus sign (-) indicates debits]

Type of transaction	1990	1991	1992	1993	1994	1995	1996	1997	1998	1999	2000
Exports of goods and services and income receipts	708,881	730,387	749,324	776,933	868,867	1,006,576	1,075,874	1,194,283	1,191,422	1,232,407	1,414,925
Goods and services	537,139	581,174	617,268	642,773	703,429	795,074	852,064	936,937	932,977	956,242	1,069,531
Goods, balance of payments basis [1]	389,307	416,913	440,352	456,832	502,398	575,845	612,057	679,702	670,324	684,358	773,304
Services	147,832	164,261	176,916	185,941	201,031	219,229	240,007	257,235	262,653	271,884	296,227
Transfers under U.S. military agency sales contracts [3]	9,932	11,135	12,387	13,471	12,787	14,643	16,446	16,836	17,628	16,334	14,604
Travel	43,007	48,385	54,742	57,875	58,417	63,395	69,809	73,426	71,286	74,881	85,153
Passenger fares	15,298	15,854	16,618	16,528	16,997	18,909	20,422	20,868	20,098	19,776	21,313
Other transportation	22,042	22,631	21,531	21,958	23,754	26,081	26,074	27,006	25,604	27,033	29,847
Royalties and license fees [4]	16,634	17,819	20,841	21,695	26,712	30,289	32,470	33,639	36,197	36,467	37,955
Other private services [5]	40,251	47,748	49,956	53,532	61,477	65,094	73,858	84,505	90,914	96,508	106,493
U.S. Government miscellaneous services	668	690	841	883	887	818	928	955	926	885	862
Income receipts	171,742	149,214	132,056	134,159	165,438	211,502	223,810	257,346	258,445	276,165	345,394
Income receipts on U.S.-owned assets abroad	170,570	147,924	130,631	132,725	163,895	209,741	222,054	255,544	256,511	273,957	343,052
Direct investment receipts	65,973	58,718	57,538	67,246	77,344	95,260	102,505	115,536	106,407	118,802	149,459
Other private receipts	94,072	81,186	65,977	60,353	82,423	109,768	114,958	136,449	146,503	151,958	189,765
U.S. Government receipts	10,525	8,019	7,115	5,126	4,128	4,713	4,591	3,559	3,601	3,197	3,828
Compensation of employees	1,172	1,290	1,425	1,434	1,543	1,761	1,756	1,802	1,934	2,208	2,342
Imports of goods and services and income payments	-759,189	-734,524	-762,035	-821,977	-949,212	-1,081,976	-1,159,111	-1,294,029	-1,364,531	-1,515,861	-1,797,061
Goods and services	-615,996	-609,440	-652,934	-711,722	-800,468	-891,021	-954,177	-1,042,869	-1,099,875	-1,221,213	-1,438,011
Goods, balance of payments basis	-498,337	-490,981	-536,458	-589,441	-668,590	-749,574	-803,327	-876,367	-917,178	-1,029,917	-1,222,772
Services	-117,659	-118,459	-116,476	-122,281	-131,878	-141,447	-150,850	-166,502	-182,697	-191,296	-215,239
Direct defense expenditures	-17,531	-16,409	-13,835	-12,086	-10,217	-10,043	-11,061	-11,698	-12,241	-13,650	-13,884
Travel	-37,349	-35,322	-38,552	-40,713	-43,782	-44,916	-48,078	-52,051	-56,509	-59,351	-65,044
Passenger fares	-10,531	-10,012	-10,603	-11,410	-13,062	-14,663	-15,809	-18,138	-19,971	-21,405	-23,902
Other transportation	-24,966	-24,975	-23,767	-24,524	-26,019	-27,034	-27,403	-28,959	-30,363	-34,137	-40,713
Royalties and license fees [5]	-3,135	-4,035	-5,161	-5,032	-5,852	-6,919	-7,837	-9,614	-11,713	-13,275	-16,331
Other private services [5]	-22,229	-25,590	-22,296	-26,261	-30,386	-35,249	-37,975	-43,280	-49,051	-46,657	-52,486
U.S. Government miscellaneous services	-1,919	-2,116	-2,263	-2,255	-2,560	-2,623	-2,687	-2,762	-2,849	-2,821	-2,879
Income payments	-143,192	-125,084	-109,101	-110,255	-148,744	-190,955	-204,934	-251,160	-264,656	-294,648	-359,050
Income payments on foreign-owned assets in the U.S.	-139,728	-121,058	-104,349	-105,123	-142,792	-184,692	-198,634	-244,494	-257,547	-287,059	-351,194
Direct investment payments	-3,450	2,266	-2,189	-7,943	-22,150	-30,318	-33,093	-43,601	-38,679	-56,098	-65,683
Other private payments	-95,508	-82,452	-63,079	-57,804	-76,450	-97,004	-97,901	-112,843	-127,749	-135,830	-177,839
U.S. Government payments	-40,770	-40,872	-39,081	-39,376	-44,192	-57,370	-67,640	-88,050	-91,119	-95,131	-107,672
Compensation of employees	-3,464	-4,026	-4,752	-5,132	-5,952	-6,263	-6,300	-6,666	-7,109	-7,589	-7,856
Unilateral current transfers, net [3]	-26,654	10,752	-35,013	-37,637	-38,260	-34,057	-40,081	-40,794	-44,029	-48,025	-53,241
U.S. Government grants [3]	-10,359	29,193	-16,320	-17,036	-14,978	-11,190	-15,401	-12,472	-13,270	-13,774	-16,448
U.S. Government pensions and other transfers	-3,224	-3,775	-4,043	-4,104	-4,556	-3,451	-4,466	-4,191	-4,305	-4,401	-4,711
Private remittances and other transfers	-13,070	-14,665	-14,650	-16,497	-18,726	-19,416	-20,214	-24,131	-26,454	-29,850	-32,082

See footnotes at end of table.

No. 1281. U.S. International Transactions by Type of Transaction: 1990 to 2000—Con.

[See headnote, page 787]

Type of transaction	1990	1991	1992	1993	1994	1995	1996	1997	1998	1999	2000
Capital account transactions, net	-6,579	-4,479	612	-88	-469	372	693	350	637	-3,500	680
U.S. assets abroad, net (increase/financial outflow (-))	-81,234	-64,388	-74,410	-200,552	-176,056	-352,376	-413,923	-488,940	-335,436	-430,187	-553,349
U.S. official reserve assets, net	-2,158	5,763	3,901	-1,379	5,346	-9,742	6,668	-1,010	-6,783	8,747	-290
Gold [7]											
Special drawing rights	-192	-177	2,316	-537	-441	-808	370	-350	-147	10	-722
Reserve position in the International Monetary Fund	731	-367	-2,692	-44	494	-2,466	-1,280	-3,575	-5,119	5,484	2,308
Foreign currencies	-2,697	6,307	4,277	-797	5,293	-6,468	7,578	2,915	-1,517	3,253	-1,876
U.S. govt. assets, other than official reserve assets, net	2,317	2,924	-1,667	-351	-390	-984	-989	68	-422	2,751	-715
U.S. credits and other long-term assets	-8,410	-12,879	-7,408	-6,311	-5,383	-4,859	-5,025	-5,417	-4,678	-6,175	-4,887
Repayments on U.S. credits and other long-term assets [8]	10,856	16,776	5,807	6,270	5,088	4,125	3,930	5,438	4,111	9,560	4,064
U.S. foreign currency holdings and U.S. short-term assets, net	-130	-974	-66	-310	-95	-250	106	47	145	-634	108
U.S. private assets, net	-81,393	-73,075	-76,644	-198,822	-181,012	-341,160	-419,602	-487,998	-328,231	-441,685	-552,344
Direct investments abroad	-37,183	-37,889	-48,266	-83,950	-80,167	-98,750	-91,885	-105,016	-146,052	-150,901	-161,577
Foreign securities	-28,765	-45,673	-49,166	-146,253	-60,309	-122,506	-149,829	-118,976	-135,995	-128,594	-123,606
U.S. claims on unaffiliated foreigners reported by U.S. nonbanking concerns	-27,824	11,097	-397	766	-36,336	-45,286	-86,333	-122,888	-10,612	-92,328	-156,988
U.S. claims reported by U.S. banks, n.i.e.	12,379	-610	21,175	30,615	-4,200	-75,108	-91,555	-141,118	-35,572	-69,862	-110,173
Foreign assets in the U.S., net (increase/financial inflow (+))	141,571	110,808	170,663	282,040	305,989	465,684	571,706	756,962	482,235	753,564	952,430
Foreign official assets in the U.S., net	33,910	17,389	40,477	71,753	39,583	109,880	126,724	18,876	-20,127	42,864	35,909
Other foreign assets in the U.S., net	107,661	93,420	130,186	210,287	266,406	355,804	444,982	738,086	502,362	710,700	916,521
Direct investments in U.S. [9]	48,494	23,171	19,823	51,362	46,121	57,776	86,502	106,032	186,316	275,533	316,527
U.S. Treasury securities	-2,534	18,826	37,131	24,381	34,274	99,548	154,996	146,433	48,581	-20,464	-52,206
U.S. securities other than U.S. Treasury securities [9]	1,592	35,144	30,043	80,092	56,971	96,367	130,240	197,892	218,075	331,523	465,858
U.S. currency flows	18,800	15,400	13,400	18,900	23,400	12,300	17,362	24,782	16,622	22,407	1,129
U.S. liabilities to unaffiliated foreigners reported by U.S. nonbanking concerns	45,133	-3,115	13,573	10,489	1,302	59,637	39,404	113,921	-7,001	34,298	105,728
U.S. liabilities reported by U.S. banks, n.i.e.	-3,824	3,994	16,216	25,063	104,338	30,176	16,478	149,026	39,769	67,403	79,485
Statistical discrepancy	23,204	-48,557	-49,141	1,281	-10,859	-4,223	-35,158	-127,832	69,702	11,602	35,616
Balance on goods	-109,030	-74,068	-96,106	-132,609	-166,192	-173,729	-191,270	-196,665	-246,854	-345,559	-449,468
Balance on services	30,173	45,802	60,440	63,660	69,153	77,782	89,157	90,733	79,956	80,588	80,988
Balance on income	28,550	24,130	22,954	23,904	16,694	20,547	18,876	6,186	-6,211	-18,483	-13,656
Balance on current account [10]	-76,961	6,616	-47,724	-82,681	-118,605	-109,457	-123,318	-140,540	-217,138	-331,479	-435,377

- Represents or rounds to zero. [1] Excludes exports of goods under U.S. military agency sales contracts identified in Census Bureau export documents, excludes imports of goods under direct defense expenditures identified in Census Bureau import documents, and reflects various other adjustments (for valuation, coverage, and timing) of Census Bureau statistics to balance of payments basis. [2] Includes some goods: Mainly military equipment included in "Transfers under U.S. military agency sales contracts"; major equipment, other materials, supplies, and petroleum products purchased abroad by U.S. military agencies included in "Direct defense expenditures" under "Imports," and fuels purchased by airline and steamship operators included in "Other transportation" under "Exports" and "Imports." [3] Includes transfers of goods and services under U.S. military grant programs. [4] Break in series. See Technical Notes in the June 1989, 1990, 1992, 1993, 1995, and July 1996-99 issues of the Survey. [5] Beginning in 1985, these lines are presented on a gross basis. The definition of exports is revised to exclude U.S. parents' payments to foreign affiliates and to include U.S. affiliates' receipts from foreign parents. The definition of imports is revised to include U.S. parents' payments to foreign affiliates and to exclude U.S. affiliates' receipts from foreign parents. [6] Beginning in 1985, the "other transfers" component includes taxes paid by U.S. private residents to foreign governments and taxes paid by private nonresidents to the U.S. Government. [7] At the present time, all U.S. Treasury-owned gold is held in the United States. [8] Includes sales of foreign obligations to foreigners. [9] For 1960, includes foreign currency-denominated notes sold to private residents abroad. [10] Conceptually, "Balance on current account" is equal to "net foreign investment" in the national income and product accounts (NIPAs). However, the foreign transactions account in the NIPAs (a) includes adjustments to the international transactions accounts for the treatment of gold, (b) includes adjustments for the different geographical treatment of transactions with U.S. territories and Puerto Rico, and (c) includes services furnished without payment by financial pension plans except life insurance carriers and private noninsured pension plans.

Source: U.S. Bureau of Economic Analysis, Survey of Current Business, July 2000 and April 2001.

No. 1282. U.S. Balances on International Transactions by Area and Selected Country: 1999 and 2000

[In millions of dollars (-345,559 represents $-345,559,000,000). Minus sign (-) indicates debits]

Area or country	1999, balance on—				2000, balance on—			
	Goods [1]	Services	Income	Current account	Goods [1]	Services	Income	Current account
All areas	-345,559	80,588	-18,483	-331,479	-449,468	80,988	-13,656	-435,377
Western Europe.	-52,238	18,746	-33,764	-68,333	-65,043	16,451	-28,128	-78,136
European Economic [2]	-45,620	17,679	-32,683	-60,372	-57,585	16,464	-26,989	-68,197
Belgium-Luxembourg . . .	3,750	852	-2,791	1,742	(NA)	(NA)	(NA)	(NA)
France.	-7,213	1,706	-670	-6,411	(NA)	(NA)	(NA)	(NA)
Germany	-28,586	1,049	-2,988	-29,762	(NA)	(NA)	(NA)	(NA)
Italy	-12,447	-196	2,059	-11,183	(NA)	(NA)	(NA)	(NA)
Netherlands	10,876	4,559	4,008	19,396	(NA)	(NA)	(NA)	(NA)
United Kingdom	-1,468	3,156	-36,259	-33,062	-2,288	3,927	-39,686	-36,778
Eastern Europe	-6,253	1,250	965	-8,127	-9,974	1,399	1,706	-10,615
Canada	-34,735	5,812	14,425	-15,141	-53,115	5,970	16,047	-31,784
Latin America, other Western Hemisphere.	-27,759	17,471	7,645	-17,391	-39,549	19,903	5,180	-30,245
Mexico	-23,969	2,580	-360	-27,066	(NA)	(NA)	(NA)	(NA)
Venezuela	-6,006	2,547	-86	-3,674	(NA)	(NA)	(NA)	(NA)
Japan [3]	-74,525	14,569	-27,602	-87,797	-82,467	15,958	-31,871	-98,623
Other Asia and Africa	-156,442	16,982	-4,825	-161,158	-205,150	16,471	-2,745	-212,427
Australia	6,393	1,745	5,471	13,313	5,830	2,029	6,033	13,603
South Africa.	-612	334	1,104	544	-1,136	342	963	-37
International and unallocated .	(NA)	4,013	19,202	13,155	(NA)	2,807	20,122	12,850

NA Not available. [1] Adjusted to balance of payments basis; excludes exports under U.S. military sales contracts and imports under direct defense expenditures. [2] Includes Denmark, Greece, Ireland, Spain, Portugal, European Atomic Energy Community, European Coal and Steel Community, and European Investment Bank, not shown separately. [3] Includes Ryukyu Islands.
Source: U.S. Bureau of Economic Analysis, *Survey of Current Business,* July 2000 and April 2001 issues.

No. 1283. Private International Service Transactions by Type of Service and Country: 1990 to 1999

[In millions of dollars (137,232 represents $137,232,000,000). For all transactions, see Table 1281]

Type of service and country	Exports				Imports			
	1990	1995	1998	1999	1990	1995	1998	1999
Total private services	137,232	203,768	244,099	254,665	98,210	128,781	167,607	174,825
Travel	43,007	63,395	71,286	74,881	37,349	44,916	56,509	59,351
Overseas	30,807	54,331	61,262	64,099	28,929	35,281	44,395	47,142
Canada	7,093	6,207	6,206	6,670	3,541	4,319	5,718	6,135
Mexico	5,107	2,857	3,818	4,112	4,879	5,316	6,396	6,074
Passenger fares	15,298	18,909	20,098	19,776	10,531	14,663	19,971	21,405
Other transportation.	22,042	26,081	25,604	27,033	24,966	27,034	30,363	34,137
Freight.	8,379	11,273	11,048	11,667	15,046	16,455	19,412	22,214
Port services.	13,662	14,809	14,557	15,365	9,920	10,579	10,950	11,925
Royalties and license fees	16,634	30,289	36,197	36,467	3,135	6,919	11,713	13,275
Other private services	40,251	65,094	90,914	96,508	22,229	35,249	49,051	46,657
Affiliated services.	13,622	20,483	28,397	28,943	9,117	13,634	19,756	22,437
Unaffilated services	26,629	44,611	62,517	67,565	13,111	21,615	29,295	24,220
Education	5,126	7,515	9,037	9,572	658	1,125	1,591	1,840
Financial services.	4,417	7,029	11,273	13,925	2,475	2,472	3,561	3,574
Insurance, net	230	1,296	2,189	2,295	1,910	5,360	9,080	4,078
Telecommunications	2,735	3,228	5,538	4,460	5,583	7,305	7,687	6,766
Business, professional, and technical services	7,752	16,078	22,175	24,368	2,093	4,822	6,869	7,430
Advertising.	130	425	488	414	243	833	886	757
Computer and data processing services.	1,031	1,340	1,922	2,291	44	126	399	432
Management, consulting, and public relations services	354	1,489	1,841	1,910	135	465	888	867
Legal services	451	1,667	2,419	2,560	111	469	637	844
Construction, engineering, architectural, & mining services .	867	2,550	3,548	4,071	170	345	544	530
Canada	15,684	17,927	19,156	21,134	9,130	11,160	15,128	15,222
Europe	48,192	73,092	93,864	96,193	39,815	52,708	70,812	72,079
France.	5,542	7,965	9,657	9,821	4,169	5,951	7,598	8,027
Germany	7,364	12,692	14,912	15,326	6,819	7,586	9,810	10,179
Italy.	3,279	4,533	5,499	5,300	3,469	3,743	4,145	4,743
Netherlands	3,269	6,119	7,705	8,396	1,935	3,191	4,462	3,992
Switzerland.	(NA)	3,843	4,915	4,708	(NA)	2,285	3,809	3,670
United Kingdom.	12,989	18,625	26,559	27,224	11,564	16,063	23,206	23,750
Latin America and other Western Hemisphere	21,957	32,872	47,094	49,795	18,643	24,252	32,367	32,346
Brazil.	(NA)	4,997	6,618	5,494	(NA)	1,165	1,803	1,765
Mexico	8,590	8,705	11,706	12,544	6,731	7,930	9,870	9,783
Venezuela	1,273	2,496	3,074	3,260	659	701	709	718
Other countries.	45,321	74,508	77,800	81,547	27,976	38,542	46,763	53,191
Australia.	3,260	4,266	4,724	5,021	2,290	2,142	3,286	3,478
Japan	21,159	33,240	29,887	30,498	10,529	13,463	13,522	15,692
Korea, Republic of	(NA)	5,693	4,770	5,339	(NA)	3,581	4,157	4,458
Taiwan.	(NA)	4,429	4,004	4,860	(NA)	2,856	2,930	3,514
Int'l organizations and unallocated . . .	6,077	5,365	6,187	5,997	2,646	2,119	2,538	1,986

NA Not available.
Source: U.S. Bureau of Economic Analysis, *Survey of Current Business,* October 2000.

Foreign Commerce and Aid   789

No. 1284. International Investment Position by Type of Investment: 1990 to 1999

[In millions of dollars (-245,347 represents $-245,347,000,000). Estimates for end of year; subject to considerable error due to nature of basic data]

Type of investment	1990	1993	1994	1995	1996	1997	1998	1999
U.S. net international investment position:								
Current cost	-245,347	-306,956	-311,872	-514,637	-596,554	-970,503	-1,111,813	-1,082,508
Market value	-164,495	-178,020	-170,505	-418,648	-542,751	-1,065,480	-1,407,670	-1,473,685
U.S.-owned assets abroad:								
Current cost	2,178,978	2,753,648	2,998,633	3,451,983	4,008,872	4,557,945	5,079,056	5,889,028
Market value	2,294,085	3,057,669	3,279,871	3,873,632	4,548,579	5,277,399	6,045,544	7,173,373
U.S. official reserve assets	174,664	164,945	163,394	176,061	160,739	134,836	146,006	136,418
Gold	102,406	102,556	100,110	101,279	96,698	75,929	75,291	75,950
Special drawing rights	10,989	9,039	10,039	11,037	10,312	10,027	10,603	10,336
Reserve position in IMF	9,076	11,818	12,030	14,649	15,435	18,071	24,111	17,950
Foreign currencies	52,193	41,532	41,215	49,096	38,294	30,809	36,001	32,182
U.S. Government assets, other . .	84,344	83,382	83,908	85,064	86,123	86,198	86,768	84,226
U.S. loans and other long-term assets	83,716	81,435	81,884	82,802	83,999	84,130	84,850	81,657
Repayable in dollars.	82,602	80,660	81,389	82,358	83,606	83,780	84,528	81,367
Other	1,114	775	495	444	393	350	322	290
U.S. foreign currency holdings and short-term assets	628	1,947	2,024	2,262	2,124	2,068	1,918	2,569
U.S. private assets:								
Current cost	1,919,970	2,505,321	2,751,331	3,190,858	3,762,010	4,336,911	4,846,282	5,668,384
Market value	2,035,077	2,809,342	3,032,569	3,612,507	4,301,717	5,056,365	5,812,770	6,952,729
Direct investments abroad:								
Current cost	616,655	723,526	786,565	885,506	986,536	1,058,735	1,207,059	1,331,187
Market value	731,762	1,027,547	1,067,803	1,307,155	1,526,243	1,778,189	2,173,547	2,615,532
Foreign securities	342,313	853,528	948,668	1,169,636	1,467,985	1,751,183	2,052,929	2,583,386
Bonds	144,717	309,666	321,208	392,827	465,057	543,396	576,745	556,748
Corporate stocks	197,596	543,862	627,460	776,809	1,002,928	1,207,787	1,476,184	2,026,638
U.S. claims on unaffiliated foreigners [1]	265,315	242,022	322,980	367,567	449,978	544,891	565,466	643,747
U.S. claims reported by U.S. banks [2]	695,687	686,245	693,118	768,149	857,511	982,102	1,020,828	1,110,064
Foreign-owned assets in the United States:								
Current cost	2,424,325	3,060,604	3,310,505	3,966,620	4,605,426	5,528,448	6,190,869	6,971,536
Market value	2,458,580	3,235,689	3,450,376	4,292,280	5,091,330	6,342,879	7,453,214	8,647,058
Foreign official assets in the U.S.	373,293	509,422	535,217	671,710	798,368	835,800	837,701	869,334
U.S. Government securities . . .	291,228	381,687	407,152	497,776	610,469	614,530	620,285	628,907
U.S. Treasury securities . . .	285,911	373,050	396,887	482,773	590,704	589,792	589,023	578,225
Other.	5,317	7,637	10,265	15,003	19,765	24,738	31,262	50,682
Other U.S. Government liabilities	17,243	22,113	23,678	23,573	22,592	21,550	18,000	14,745
U.S. liabilities reported by U.S. banks [2].	39,880	69,721	73,386	107,394	113,098	135,384	125,883	138,575
Other foreign official assets. . . .	24,942	35,901	31,001	42,967	52,209	64,336	73,533	87,107
Other foreign assets in the U.S:								
Current cost	2,051,032	2,551,182	2,775,288	3,294,910	3,807,058	4,692,648	5,353,168	6,102,202
Market value	2,085,287	2,726,267	2,915,159	3,620,570	4,292,962	5,507,079	6,615,513	7,777,724
Direct investments:								
Current cost	505,346	593,313	617,982	680,066	743,214	825,334	928,645	1,125,214
Market value	539,601	768,398	757,853	1,005,726	1,229,118	1,639,765	2,190,990	2,800,736
U.S. Treasury securities	152,452	221,501	235,684	358,537	502,562	662,228	729,738	660,722
U.S. currency	85,933	133,734	157,185	169,484	186,846	211,628	228,250	250,657
U.S. securities other than								
U.S. Treasury securities	460,644	696,449	739,695	971,356	1,199,461	1,578,694	2,012,431	2,509,322
Corporate and other bonds . .	238,903	355,822	368,077	481,214	588,044	715,196	902,155	1,063,730
Corporate stocks	221,741	340,627	371,618	490,142	611,417	863,498	1,110,276	1,445,592
U.S. liabilities to unaffiliated foreigners [1]	213,406	229,038	239,817	300,424	346,727	443,789	437,973	473,825
U.S. liabilities reported by U.S. banks [2].	633,251	677,147	784,925	815,043	828,248	970,975	1,016,131	1,082,462

[1] Reported by U.S. nonbanking concerns. [2] Not included elsewhere.

Source: U.S. Bureau of Economic Analysis, *Survey of Current Business*, July 2000.

No. 1285. U.S. Reserve Assets: 1990 to 2000

[In billions of dollars (83.3 represents $83,300,000,000). As of end of year, except as indicated]

Type	1990	1993	1994	1995	1996	1997	1998	1999	2000
Total	83.3	73.4	74.3	85.8	75.1	70.0	81.8	71.5	67.5
Gold stock.	11.1	11.1	11.1	11.1	11.0	11.0	11.0	11.0	11.0
Special drawing rights	11.0	9.0	10.0	11.0	10.3	10.0	10.6	10.3	10.5
Foreign currencies	52.2	41.5	41.2	49.1	38.3	30.8	36.0	32.2	30.9
Reserve position in IMF [1]. . . .	9.1	11.8	12.0	14.6	15.4	18.1	24.1	18.0	15.1

[1] International Monetary Fund.

Source: Board of Governors of the Federal Reserve System, *Federal Reserve Bulletin*, monthly; and Department of the Treasury, *Treasury Bulletin*, monthly.

No. 1286. Foreign Direct Investment Position in the United States on a Historical-Cost Basis by Industry and Selected Country: 1998 and 1999

[In millions of dollars (793,748 represents $793,748,000,000)]

Country	1998				1999			
	Total [1]	Petro-leum	Manufac-turing, total	Whole-sale	Total [1]	Petro-leum	Manufac-turing, total	Whole-sale
All countries.............	**793,748**	**51,729**	**334,898**	**89,980**	**986,668**	**55,940**	**391,013**	**108,936**
Canada......................	74,143	2,526	26,507	4,216	79,716	2,836	26,270	4,467
Europe.....................	**528,601**	**46,008**	**251,750**	**45,513**	**685,845**	**49,642**	**305,543**	**49,312**
Austin...................	1,969	(D)	360	393	2,483	(D)	674	425
Belgium....................	10,966	(D)	4,068	1,096	11,448	204	3,972	1,516
Denmark	3,312	5	831	1,871	4,959	3	956	3,617
Finland	4,106	(D)	1,262	1,799	4,816	(D)	1,435	(D)
France.....................	58,051	(D)	38,087	2,426	77,622	(D)	39,087	2,191
Germany	94,404	138	54,392	9,226	111,138	173	59,303	10,013
Ireland....................	12,484	739	2,674	3,433	17,969	699	3,868	3,534
Italy......................	4,143	(D)	918	329	4,982	(D)	1,050	292
Luxembourg	26,650	93	(D)	1,326	54,894	(D)	45,305	1,565
Netherlands	98,926	11,400	38,041	5,755	130,703	11,083	42,922	6,659
Norway	3,833	(D)	1,938	161	4,201	1,240	2,044	221
Spain......................	2,285	-3	728	151	2,629	-6	1,014	160
Sweden	15,139	(D)	7,335	4,350	17,904	(D)	6,856	4,856
Switzerland................	48,403	243	24,253	2,307	55,280	572	27,814	2,386
United Kingdom.............	143,165	30,069	54,765	10,692	183,145	33,446	68,242	8,751
Latin America and other								
Western Hemisphere	**27,854**	**917**	**4,351**	**2,109**	**44,591**	**1,836**	**6,028**	**2,402**
South and Central America	9,819	-693	1,159	283	10,606	-370	1,980	328
Mexico	2,432	-8	1,315	451	3,612	-3	2,243	348
Panama	6,504	(D)	165	-104	5,896	13	89	56
Other Western Hemisphere	18,034	1,611	3,192	1,826	33,984	2,206	4,048	2,075
Bahamas	2,077	(D)	147	474	2,163	(D)	136	511
Netherlands Antilles	2,844	(D)	788	(D)	2,695	607	1,268	(D)
United Kingdom Islands, Caribbean .	9009	506	2054	820	13,883	1,247	1,789	1,552
Africa....................	**862**	**3**	**-92**	**98**	**1,545**	**20**	**-172**	**426**
Middle East.................	**6,346**	**925**	**691**	**157**	**7,087**	**868**	**1,150**	**164**
Israel.....................	2,084	-3	867	156	2,680	-	1,144	174
Kuwait.....................	(D)	(D)	1	-	3,391	(D)	1	-
Saudi Arabia...............	(D)	(D)	-6	-	949	(D)	-3	(D)
Asia and Pacific	**155,943**	**1,350**	**51,691**	**37,887**	**167,884**	**737**	**52,195**	**52,165**
Australia..................	12,883	780	2,142	-37	10,818	763	2,574	-1
Hong Kong.................	1,578	(D)	385	413	1,210	(D)	484	362
Japan	134,590	734	47,347	35,462	148,947	165	47,277	49,454
Singapore..................	1,561	-11	243	299	1,049	(Z)	237	234
Taiwan.....................	3,144	-2	1,454	595	2,983	-4	1,257	565

- Represents or rounds to zero.   D Suppressed to avoid disclosure of data of individual companies.   Z Less than $500,000.   [1] Includes other industries not shown separately.
Source: U.S. Bureau of Economic Analysis, *Survey of Current Business*, July 2000.

No. 1287. U.S. Affiliates of Foreign Companies—Assets, Sales, Employment, Land, Exports, and Imports: 1998

[A U.S. affiliate is a U.S. business enterprise in which one foreign owner (individual, branch, partnership, association, trust, corporation, or government) has a direct or indirect voting interest of 10 percent or more. Estimates cover the universe of nonbank affiliates. These data are now on a NAICS (North American Industry Classification System) basis and not comparable to previous data, which were based on the Standard Industrial Classification system]

Industry	Total assets (mil. dol.)	Sales [1] (mil. dol.)	Employ-ment [2] (1,000)	Employee compen-sation (mil. dol.)	P & E [3] (mil. dol.)	Land (mil. dol.)	Merchan-dise exports[4] (mil. dol.)	Merchan-dise imports[4] (mil. dol.)
All industries...........	**3,525,885**	**1,881,865**	**5,633.0**	**260,661**	**927,105**	**57,822**	**150,836**	**289,679**
Manufacturing [5]..............	878,864	834,396	2,539.6	134,886	491,620	14,465	87,581	126,924
Petroleum and coal products...	108,430	95,293	82.8	6,301	120,859	2,208	2,909	9,109
Chemicals	199,557	141,875	380.0	25,798	93,246	2,316	14,930	14,429
Computers and electronic prod..	81,604	97,391	282.9	16,091	33,156	861	14,306	26,771
Transportation equipment.....	143,045	169,701	368.2	21,140	66,567	735	24,609	45,241
Wholesale trade [5].............	283,125	491,520	526.9	27,760	98,578	3,181	56,127	155,164
Motor vehicles, parts, and supp.	87,124	109,545	74.5	4,427	43,664	779	3,732	46,354
Petroleum and petroleum prod..	24,911	60,213	12.7	938	8,673	253	4,940	6,146
Retail trade.................	51,304	97,275	679.2	14,928	29,920	2,914	1,401	4,089
Information	156,163	74,060	266.9	14,877	57,168	939	870	208
Finance (except depository institutions) and insurance	1,789,405	187,956	234.9	22,733	39,816	1,203	4	49
Real estate and rental and leasing	123,474	21,121	39.1	1,772	83,073	16,752	27	224
Professional, scientific, technical services	24,332	20,541	104.5	7,311	5,189	367	283	232
Other industries	219,218	154,995	1,241.9	36,394	121,742	18,000	4,542	2,790

[1] Excludes returns, discounts, allowances, and sales and excise taxes.   [2] Average number of full- and part-time employees.   [3] Plant and equipment (P&E). Includes mineral rights and minor amounts of property other than land.   [4] F.a.s. value at port of exportation.   [5] Includes industries not shown separately.
Source: U.S. Bureau of Economic Analysis, *Survey of Current Business*, August 2000; and *Foreign Direct Investment in the United States, Operations of U.S. Affiliates of Foreign Companies, Preliminary 1998 Estimates.*

Foreign Commerce and Aid   791

No. 1288. Foreign Direct Investment in the United States—Gross Book Value and Employment of U.S. Affiliates of Foreign Companies by State: 1990 to 1998

[578,355 represents $578,355,000,000. A U.S. affiliate is a U.S. business enterprise in which one foreign owner (individual, branch, partnership, association, trust corporation, or government) has a direct or indirect voting interest of 10 percent or more. Estimates cover the universe of nonbank U.S. affiliates]

State and other area	Gross book value of property, plant, and equipment (mil. dol.)				Total employment				
								1998	
	1990	1995	1997	1998	1990 (1,000)	1995 (1,000)	1997 (1,000)	Total (1,000)	Percent of all businesses
Total	578,355	769,491	877,568	984,927	4,734.5	4,941.8	5,201.9	5,633.0	(X)
United States	552,902	733,089	814,054	922,951	4,704.4	4,898.9	5,172.4	5,608.9	5.1
Alabama	7,300	10,598	13,342	15,025	55.7	60.6	66.0	74.8	4.7
Alaska	19,435	25,558	25,885	28,927	13.2	9.8	9.1	10.6	5.1
Arizona	7,234	6,699	9,240	9,734	57.1	51.9	59.7	63.4	3.5
Arkansas	2,344	3,666	3,897	4,188	29.2	32.1	34.0	37.2	3.9
California	75,768	96,576	96,083	103,697	555.9	548.6	569.6	603.2	5.0
Colorado	6,544	8,602	9,884	10,450	56.3	72.2	81.6	79.6	4.4
Connecticut	5,357	8,466	8,930	9,744	75.9	73.3	89.1	98.1	6.6
Delaware	5,818	2,919	3,591	5,095	43.1	15.8	19.1	24.9	7.0
District of Columbia	3,869	4,983	4,595	4,359	11.4	13.4	11.2	13.9	3.4
Florida	18,659	24,865	30,082	33,899	205.7	210.0	242.3	264.0	4.5
Georgia	16,729	22,432	24,940	26,953	161.0	180.1	191.0	200.7	6.2
Hawaii	11,830	15,972	14,805	12,941	53.0	48.9	50.2	45.4	10.4
Idaho	776	1,026	1,420	1,853	11.7	11.3	12.4	14.2	3.2
Illinois	23,420	34,305	33,676	40,764	245.8	237.0	224.9	262.8	5.0
Indiana	13,426	18,782	18,301	28,000	126.9	136.9	128.9	160.8	6.2
Iowa	2,712	4,527	5,174	6,391	32.8	35.8	37.9	35.9	2.9
Kansas	5,134	3,233	5,762	7,717	29.6	34.0	45.8	51.0	4.6
Kentucky	9,229	15,136	17,075	21,083	65.7	83.4	90.0	93.4	6.2
Louisiana	17,432	20,543	25,368	28,422	61.4	51.0	58.3	59.7	3.8
Maine	2,080	3,885	3,988	4,291	26.6	29.1	32.0	32.2	6.6
Maryland	5,713	9,197	10,592	10,577	79.6	95.0	91.8	94.1	4.8
Massachusetts	8,890	12,707	15,358	16,357	131.2	141.5	163.6	178.4	6.2
Michigan	12,012	21,370	21,170	37,438	139.6	170.3	171.6	235.9	6.0
Minnesota	11,972	8,688	14,969	10,343	89.8	79.8	99.0	80.5	3.6
Mississippi	2,989	3,055	3,372	3,694	23.6	22.6	22.9	24.0	2.5
Missouri	5,757	8,327	11,027	13,713	73.7	79.3	85.0	91.6	3.9
Montana	2,181	1,938	2,052	2,474	5.1	4.4	4.5	6.9	2.2
Nebraska	776	1,320	2,007	2,232	14.9	15.7	20.3	21.6	2.9
Nevada	5,450	8,242	8,965	9,365	22.7	25.0	26.5	27.9	3.3
New Hampshire	1,446	2,212	2,470	2,735	25.9	30.0	31.6	36.0	6.9
New Jersey	18,608	26,175	29,766	32,078	227.0	205.2	212.5	235.5	7.1
New Mexico	4,312	4,363	4,414	5,729	17.4	16.2	18.3	18.0	3.2
New York	36,424	52,992	53,642	57,873	347.5	343.8	353.5	386.6	5.5
North Carolina	15,234	21,475	24,507	25,603	181.0	225.3	226.3	238.8	7.3
North Dakota	1,251	915	1,176	1,931	3.1	3.2	3.7	8.6	3.3
Ohio	20,549	29,932	35,019	37,703	219.1	222.1	236.3	260.9	5.4
Oklahoma	6,049	5,448	6,299	8,933	43.6	34.2	34.7	40.6	3.4
Oregon	3,427	5,807	7,524	8,213	39.1	49.7	52.4	54.9	4.1
Pennsylvania	16,587	24,432	25,697	28,122	221.6	231.6	225.2	238.0	4.8
Rhode Island	1,120	2,240	2,610	2,673	13.3	16.2	19.1	20.8	5.1
South Carolina	10,067	13,438	17,488	19,958	104.7	111.6	119.5	125.4	8.2
South Dakota	553	665	879	1,053	4.5	4.6	10.1	10.1	3.3
Tennessee	10,280	14,227	17,340	18,413	116.9	136.3	147.5	155.4	6.7
Texas	57,079	68,142	77,959	92,300	299.5	326.4	351.2	381.2	5.0
Utah	3,918	5,612	7,823	8,921	21.0	28.6	35.3	34.6	3.9
Vermont	631	1,037	1,002	1,364	7.7	10.4	9.4	11.6	4.7
Virginia	10,702	15,129	19,663	19,977	113.3	141.4	147.3	152.2	5.5
Washington	7,985	11,462	13,216	15,453	77.5	83.0	87.6	89.7	4.0
West Virginia	7,975	7,809	7,065	7,460	34.9	31.9	27.6	29.3	5.1
Wisconsin	5,088	7,415	8,118	9,457	81.4	71.5	77.9	86.3	3.6
Wyoming	2,782	4,544	4,827	7,275	5.8	6.9	7.1	7.8	4.4
Puerto Rico	1,499	2,174	1,730	1,803	16.1	27.4	17.4	16.8	(NA)
Other territories and offshore	18,484	17,798	23,076	26,576	9.0	13.1	10.2	7.3	(NA)
Foreign	5,470	16,430	1,596	1,189	5.0	2.4	1.9	(Z)	(NA)
Unspecified [1]	(NA)	(NA)	37,112	32,408	(NA)	(NA)	(NA)	(NA)	(NA)

NA Not available.   X Not applicable.   Z Less than 50.   [1] Covers property, plant, and equipment not located in a particular state, including aircraft, railroad rolling stock, satellites, undersea cable, and trucks engaged in interstate transportation.

Source: U.S. Bureau of Economic Analysis, *Survey of Current Business*, August 2000, and *Foreign Direct Investment in the United States, Operations of U.S. Affiliates of Foreign Companies*, annual.

No. 1289. U.S. Businesses Acquired or Established by Foreign Direct Investors—Investment Outlays by Industry of U.S. Business Enterprise and Country of Ultimate Beneficial Owner: 1990 to 1999

[In millions of dollars (65,932 represents $65,932,000,000). Foreign direct investment is the ownership or control directly or indirectly, by one foreign individual branch, partnership, association, trust, corporation, or government of 10 percent or more of the voting securities of a U.S. business enterprise or an equivalent interest in an unincorporated one. Data represent number and full cost of acquisitions of existing U.S. business enterprises, including business segments or operating units of existing U.S. business enterprises and establishments of new enterprises. Investments may be made by the foreign direct investor itself, or indirectly by an existing U.S. affiliate of the foreign direct investor. Covers investments in U.S. business enterprises with assets of over $1 million, or ownership of 200 acres of U.S. land. These industry data are now on a NAICS (North American Industry Classification System) basis and not comparable to previous data, which were based on the Standard Industrial Classification system]

Industry and country	1990	1993	1994	1995	1996	1997	1998	1999, prel.
Total	65,932	26,229	45,626	57,195	79,929	69,708	215,256	282,946
INDUSTRY								
Manufacturing	(NA)	(NA)	(NA)	(NA)	(NA)	(NA)	149,243	74,195
Wholesale trade	(NA)	(NA)	(NA)	(NA)	(NA)	(NA)	3,321	1,030
Retail trade	(NA)	(NA)	(NA)	(NA)	(NA)	(NA)	1,153	4,564
Information	(NA)	(NA)	(NA)	(NA)	(NA)	(NA)	13,399	93,475
Depository institutions	(NA)	(NA)	(NA)	(NA)	(NA)	(NA)	1,563	11,845
Finance, (except depository institutions) and insurance	(NA)	(NA)	(NA)	(NA)	(NA)	(NA)	21,057	47,023
Real estate and rental and leasing	(NA)	(NA)	(NA)	(NA)	(NA)	(NA)	6,299	5,689
Professional, scientific, and technical services	(NA)	(NA)	(NA)	(NA)	(NA)	(NA)	4,289	11,355
Other industries	(NA)	(NA)	(NA)	(NA)	(NA)	(NA)	14,932	33,771
COUNTRY [1]								
Canada	3,430	3,797	4,128	8,029	9,700	11,755	22,635	11,388
Europe	36,011	16,845	31,920	38,195	49,427	44,014	170,173	205,150
France	10,217	1,249	1,404	1,129	6,021	2,578	14,493	24,579
Germany	2,363	2,841	3,328	13,117	12,858	6,464	39,873	24,393
Netherlands	2,247	2,074	1,537	1,061	6,476	10,244	19,009	26,896
Switzerland	3,905	804	5,044	7,533	4,910	6,745	4,525	7,119
United Kingdom	13,096	8,238	17,261	9,094	14,757	11,834	84,995	110,115
Other Europe	4,183	1,639	3,346	6,261	4,405	6,149	7,278	12,048
Latin America and other Western Hemisphere	796	874	1,352	1,550	1,790	924	11,354	34,013
South and Central America	399	527	(D)	1,283	(D)	166	920	1,377
Other Western Hemisphere	397	347	(D)	267	(D)	758	10,433	32,636
Africa	(D)	(D)	(D)	(D)	(D)	(D)	212	(D)
Middle East	472	1,308	(D)	447	(D)	847	2,810	546
Asia and Pacific	23,170	3,004	5,263	8,688	12,751	11,786	7,329	11,502
Australia	1,412	129	1,522	2,270	2,222	7,600	(D)	(D)
Japan	19,933	2,065	2,715	3,602	8,813	2,326	4,862	8,048
Other Asia and Pacific	1,825	810	1,026	2,816	1,716	1,860	(D)	(D)

D Suppressed to avoid disclosure of data of individual companies.   NA Not available.   [1] For investments in which more than one investor participated, each investor and each investor's outlays are classified by country of each ultimate beneficial owner.

Source: U.S. Bureau of Economic Analysis, *Survey of Current Business,* June 2000, and previous June issues.

No. 1290. U.S. Direct Investment Position Abroad, Capital Outflows, and Income by Industry of Foreign Affiliates: 1997 to 1999

[In millions of dollars (871,316 represents $871,316,000,000)]

Industry	Direct investment position on a historical-cost basis			Capital outflows (inflows (-))			Income		
	1997	1998	1999	1997	1998	1999	1997	1998	1999
All industries, total	871,316	1,014,012	1,132,622	95,769	134,083	138,510	104,794	92,775	105,001
Petroleum	84,116	92,964	99,925	11,555	8,517	8,892	12,508	7,597	10,213
Manufacturing	278,447	294,129	318,121	28,326	22,126	35,524	38,468	29,879	32,472
Food and kindred products	32,773	35,074	36,126	4,080	2,342	1,416	5,030	4,306	3,604
Chemicals and allied products	76,394	79,868	82,794	6,974	5,245	7,100	10,023	9,428	9,431
Primary and fabricated metals	15,898	18,776	18,803	408	2,954	808	1,376	1,281	1,365
Industrial machinery and equipment	30,179	31,348	37,833	4,783	1,888	6,705	5,022	3,986	3,450
Electronic and other electric equipment	31,308	32,398	38,449	2,727	1,866	6,231	4,663	2,147	3,737
Transportation equipment	35,537	33,939	36,013	4,667	-1,190	-4,857	5,478	2,495	4,371
Other manufacturing	56,358	62,726	68,103	4,687	9,021	18,121	6,876	6,236	6,514
Wholesale trade	64,929	70,014	80,148	121	6,434	11,801	9,047	9,909	10,560
Depository institutions	37,932	40,582	39,937	1,508	2,140	-920	3,286	743	1,693
Finance, insurance, and real estate [1]	297,828	375,965	436,024	39,001	62,161	54,475	31,986	34,921	37,867
Services	46,533	60,696	68,763	4,306	12,210	10,778	6,109	5,955	8,193
Other industries	61,532	79,663	89,705	10,953	20,494	17,962	3,391	3,770	4,003

[1] Excludes depository institutions.

Source: U.S. Bureau of Economic Analysis, *Survey of Current Business,* September 2000.

Foreign Commerce and Aid   793

No. 1291. U.S. Direct Investment Position Abroad on a Historical-Cost Basis by Country: 1990 to 1999

[In millions of dollars (430,521 represents $430,521,000,000). U.S. direct investment abroad is the ownership or control by one U.S. person of 10 percent or more of the voting securities of an incorporated foreign business enterprise or an equivalent interest in a unincorporated foreign business enterprise. Negative position can occur when a U.S. parent company's liabilities to the foreign affiliate are greater than its equity in, and loans to the foreign affiliate]

Country	1990	1993	1994	1995	1996	1997	1998	1999
All countries	430,521	564,283	612,893	699,015	795,195	871,316	1,014,012	1,132,622
Canada	69,508	69,922	74,221	83,498	89,592	96,626	101,871	111,707
Europe	214,739	285,735	297,133	344,596	389,378	425,139	528,113	581,791
Austria	1,113	1,312	2,197	2,829	2,854	2,646	3,850	3,696
Belgium	9,464	11,697	14,714	18,706	18,740	17,337	18,637	17,285
Denmark	1,726	1,735	2,030	2,161	2,554	2,385	2,854	3,887
Finland	544	414	761	965	1,070	1,311	1,695	1,355
France	19,164	24,312	27,322	33,358	35,200	36,630	42,067	39,984
Germany	27,609	36,811	38,878	44,242	41,281	40,726	46,405	49,617
Greece	282	410	482	533	566	634	639	602
Ireland	5,894	9,019	7,239	7,996	10,133	11,339	16,991	19,823
Italy	14,063	12,748	14,808	17,096	16,193	15,547	16,008	17,595
Luxembourg.	1,697	5,611	6,310	5,929	7,753	10,258	14,524	15,263
Netherlands	19,120	20,911	29,889	42,113	54,118	68,619	93,592	106,436
Norway	4,209	3,757	5,026	4,741	5,483	6,633	7,015	6,601
Portugal	897	1,264	1,181	1,413	1,423	1,399	1,476	1,478
Spain	7,868	6,689	9,572	10,856	12,252	11,541	13,676	12,456
Sweden	1,787	2,374	1,905	6,816	5,248	3,542	5,339	9,595
Switzerland	25,099	33,056	27,908	31,125	30,744	30,634	40,144	51,227
Turkey	522	995	874	973	1,059	1,033	1,074	1,299
United Kingdom	72,707	109,208	100,817	106,332	134,559	154,462	192,663	213,070
Other	974	3,411	5,219	6,412	8,148	8,464	9,465	10,522
Latin America and other								
Western Hemisphere.	71,413	100,482	116,478	131,377	155,925	180,818	200,477	223,182
South America	22,933	31,210	37,673	49,170	57,372	69,507	74,254	74,839
Argentina	2,531	4,442	5,692	7,660	7,893	10,980	12,834	14,187
Brazil.	14,384	16,772	17,885	25,002	29,105	35,778	38,195	35,003
Chile	1,896	2,749	5,062	6,216	8,156	9,148	9,351	9,886
Colombia	1,677	2,930	3,463	3,506	3,531	4,097	3,732	4,029
Ecuador.	280	555	784	889	922	838	1,017	1,202
Peru	599	622	971	1,335	2,281	2,147	2,088	2,532
Venezuela	1,087	2,362	3,087	3,634	4,474	5,339	5,729	6,750
Other	479	778	728	928	1,010	1,182	1,308	1,250
Central America	20,415	28,092	30,083	33,493	37,667	48,549	57,764	70,774
Costa Rica	251	298	607	921	1,223	1,529	2,080	1,646
Guatemala	130	139	200	233	331	358	405	453
Honduras.	262	159	140	68	129	183	117	56
Mexico	10,313	15,221	16,968	16,873	19,351	24,050	28,396	34,265
Panama	9,289	12.043	11,905	15,123	16,335	22,016	25,982	33,429
Other	169	233	262	273	298	413	785	924
Other Western Hemisphere. . . .	28,065	41,180	48,722	48,714	60,886	62,761	68,459	77,569
Bahamas	4,004	3,138	2,808	1,768	1,876	1,569	160	1,065
Barbados	252	471	391	698	848	787	950	1,131
Bermuda	20,169	28,666	28,355	28,374	37,091	38,071	40,403	45,959
Dominican Republic.	529	1,039	266	330	400	488	653	952
Jamaica.	625	1,049	1,167	1,287	1,583	1,952	2,100	2,469
Netherlands Antilles	-4,501	-62	6,739	6,835	7,597	4,415	4,372	4,377
Trinidad and Tobago	485	691	529	673	786	639	1,005	1,094
U.K. Islands, Caribbean	5,929	5,544	7,858	8,358	10,121	14,044	18,203	19,948
Other	574	645	608	392	583	797	614	573
Africa	3,650	5,469	5,760	6,017	8,162	11,330	14,241	15,062
Egypt	1,231	1,510	1,090	1,093	1,366	1,603	2,036	2,213
Nigeria	-401	478	605	629	1,020	1,396	1,788	1,375
South Africa.	775	900	1,132	1,422	1,495	2,499	2,312	3,258
Other	2,045	2,581	2,933	2,873	4,281	5,833	8,105	8,216
Middle East.	3,959	6,571	6,367	7,198	8,294	8,836	10,632	11,137
Israel	746	1,604	1,483	1,831	2,045	2,071	2,922	3,199
Saudi Arabia	1,899	2,587	2,100	2,741	3,476	3,821	4,276	4,231
United Arab Emirates.	409	524	357	500	598	567	687	543
Other	905	1,856	2,427	2,126	2,174	2,377	2,747	3,163
Asia and Pacific.	64,716	92,671	108,528	122,712	139,548	144,815	155,364	185,912
Australia	15,104	19,047	20,196	24,328	30,006	28,404	31,150	33,662
China	354	916	2,557	2,765	3,848	5,150	6,481	7,766
Hong Kong	6,055	10,063	11,092	11,768	14,391	17,315	18,421	20,848
India	372	599	1,030	1,105	1,344	1,563	1,460	1,189
Indonesia	3,207	4,864	6,355	6,777	8,322	6,729	7,916	10,504
Japan	22,599	31,095	34,117	37,309	34,578	33,854	35,633	47,786
Korea, South	2,695	3,427	4,334	5,557	6,508	6,467	7,395	8,749
Malaysia	1,466	1,975	3,148	4,237	5,663	6,530	5,743	5,989
New Zealand	3,156	3,064	3,893	4,601	5,940	7,160	6,041	6,080
Philippines.	1,355	1,953	2,484	2,719	3,541	3,219	3,930	3,792
Singapore	3,975	8,875	10,940	12,140	14,912	18,026	18,427	24,781
Taiwan	2,226	3,113	3,775	4,293	4,476	5,007	6,262	6,860
Thailand	1,790	2,943	3,585	4,283	5,000	4,332	5,383	6,966
Other	356	737	1,022	830	1,019	1,058	1,123	940
International	2,535	3,433	4,406	3,618	4,295	3,752	3,315	3,832

Source: U.S. Bureau of Economic Analysis, *Survey of Current Business*, September 2000, and earlier issues.

U.S. Government Foreign Grants and Credits by Type and Country: 1966 to 1999

[In millions of dollars (70,381 represents $70,381,000,000). See text, this section. Negative figures (-) occur when the total of grant returns, principal repayments, and/or foreign currencies disbursed by the U.S. government exceeds new grants and new credits utilized and/or acquisitions of foreign currencies through new sales of farm products]

Country	1966-1975, total	1976-1985, total	1986-1995, total	1995	1996	1997	1998	1999
Total, net	**70,381**	**104,191**	**90,677**	**12,666**	**16,701**	**12,833**	**14,029**	**18,656**
Investment in financial institutions	2,719	10,432	13,504	1,517	1,833	1,588	1,580	1,451
Western Europe	**1,004**	**1,618**	**-5,408**	**177**	**197**	**390**	**317**	**428**
Austria	-19	34	-72	-1	-1	-1	(Z)	-
Belgium and Luxembourg	17	-46	-48	-	-	-	-	-
Denmark	64	-58	-13	-	-	-	-	-
Finland	-19	21	-72	-1	-1	-1	(Z)	-
France	-93	-222	-93	1	-	(Z)	-	-
Germany	-117	-117	-6,459	(Z)	(Z)	-	-	-
Iceland	-8	-12	-8	-	-	-	-	-
Ireland	-51	7	5	-	11	39	8	-
Italy	85	133	-233	(Z)	-	-	-	-
Netherlands	116	-180	-2	-	-	-	-	-
Norway	379	-257	-33	-	-	-	-	-
Portugal	34	1,003	796	-16	-3	-	26	4
Spain	607	965	-867	-59	-48	-37	-37	-28
Sweden	17	-1	-15	-	-	-	-	-
United Kingdom	-546	-964	-1,465	-120	-125	-127	-130	-136
Yugoslavia	84	174	-458	(X)	-1	(X)	-1	(X)
Former Yugoslavia [2]:								
Bosnia and Hercegovina	(X)	(X)	268	94	161	311	236	188
Croatia	(X)	(X)	186	9	-10	-7	-11	1
Macedonia	(X)	(X)	73	1	3	18	7	20
Slovenia	(X)	(X)	71	-24	-27	-15	-15	2
Former Yugoslavia - Regional [3]	(X)	(X)	22	(Z)	1	-8	8	21
Other [1] and unspecified [3]	455	1,139	3,007	293	236	220	229	355
Eastern Europe	**226**	**1,029**	**12,368**	**1,979**	**1,957**	**1,410**	**1,790**	**2,152**
Albania	-	-	173	15	58	11	16	4
Bulgaria	-	-	93	6	13	14	14	26
Czechoslovakia	-	-5	17	-2	3	-11	(X)	(X)
Czech Republic	(X)	(X)	7	3	10	5	5	8
Estonia	(X)	(X)	32	2	7	4	6	4
Hungary	-5	6	42	36	15	-16	13	13
Latvia	(X)	(X)	35	2	10	4	8	9
Lithuania	(X)	(X)	96	28	17	23	15	4
Poland	-75	1,017	3,491	6	50	29	38	24
Romania	92	55	44	9	30	5	28	10
Slovakia	(X)	(X)	4	2	12	11	6	8
Soviet Union	214	-44	-267	(X)	(X)	(X)	(X)	(X)
Newly Independent States:								
Armenia	(X)	(X)	352	102	80	26	39	35
Azerbaijan	(X)	(X)	42	19	14	4	6	6
Belarus	(X)	(X)	237	50	31	19	3	6
Georgia	(X)	(X)	285	89	79	38	28	23
Kazakhstan	(X)	(X)	71	17	60	52	70	45
Kyrgyzstan	(X)	(X)	175	33	38	26	30	15
Moldova	(X)	(X)	85	19	15	8	5	32
Russia	(X)	(X)	3,999	465	423	361	444	968
Tajikistan	(X)	(X)	94	34	32	27	30	6
Turkmenistan	(X)	(X)	73	16	19	1	3	3
Ukraine	(X)	(X)	353	171	233	97	172	318
Uzbekistan	(X)	(X)	9	1	5	2	7	19
Former Soviet Union - Regional [3]	(X)	(X)	1,707	613	579	582	603	506
Other [2] and unspecified [3]	(X)	(X)	1,119	241	124	85	200	61
Near East and South Asia	**17,195**	**50,777**	**29,168**	**3,025**	**7,666**	**4,675**	**5,045**	**4,378**
Afghanistan	185	56	403	10	14	17	-	2
Bangladesh	701	1,670	1,590	87	48	42	24	65
Cyprus	20	138	151	6	11	10	14	-
Egypt	271	13,600	26,594	1,639	1,621	1,375	2,018	2,093
Greece	905	362	2,774	261	12	-210	-240	-145
India	3,810	1,021	767	48	55	238	167	-79
Iran	914	-847	-42	-	-21	-	-	-
Iraq [4]	-5	5	892	128	119	11	-	-
Israel	3,760	25,417	25,116	420	5,294	2,896	2,842	2,221
Jordan	618	1,320	754	129	168	279	217	186
Kuwait	-	-	-16,058	-	-	-	-	-
Lebanon	90	233	22	5	11	3	2	9
Nepal	105	177	193	20	21	24	20	19
Oman	(Z)	79	42	4	12	26	20	-6
Pakistan	2,048	1,971	1,222	-187	-164	-62	-82	79
Saudi Arabia	23	-20	-16,855	-	-	-	-	-
Sri Lanka	153	512	596	27	6	7	1	-6
Syria	15	262	3	-	-	-	-	-
Turkey	2,703	3,760	2,957	147	51	-129	-159	-259
United Arab Emirates	-	-	-4,070	-	-	-	-	-
Yemen (Sanaa)	3	(Z)	(X)	(X)	(X)	(X)	(X)	(X)
Yemen	24	216	89	3	5	12	5	10
UNRWA [5]	296	596	622	103	72	59	78	93
West Bank-Gaza	11	13	162	58	33	53	80	88
Other and unspecified [3]	546	236	1,071	118	298	25	39	10

See footnotes at end of table.

Foreign Commerce and Aid   795

[In millions of dollars. See headnote, p. 795]

Country	1966-1975, total	1976-1985, total	1986-1995, total	1995	1996	1997	1998	1999
Africa	3,610	11,067	16,239	2,217	1,957	1,354	1,366	841
Algeria	263	345	413	755	644	93	45	-46
Angola	6	115	120	37	42	41	38	21
Benin	12	44	101	14	13	23	14	23
Botswana	35	169	168	18	9	9	5	3
Burkina	40	287	221	23	11	15	17	9
Burundi	5	62	171	39	2	4	9	6
Cameroon	50	150	247	4	4	(Z)	6	2
Cape Verde	1	68	77	11	10	11	6	1
Chad	20	145	240	14	8	6	3	2
Congo, Democratic Republic of the (former Zaire)	342	939	766	1	(Z)	(Z)	1	2
Cote d'Ivoire	57	57	240	16	22	16	8	11
Eritrea	-	-	41	9	18	17	21	7
Ethiopia	297	310	969	127	104	77	162	44
Ghana	203	152	370	63	34	55	40	38
Guinea	68	74	239	28	29	28	18	22
Kenya	76	549	682	35	6	27	37	31
Lesotho	27	197	166	13	4	5	3	1
Liberia	86	459	438	67	58	28	19	26
Madagascar	13	86	240	33	42	35	44	30
Malawi	30	56	404	64	36	30	23	30
Mali	58	199	367	31	12	11	36	36
Mauritania	20	161	94	2	2	5	4	2
Morocco	413	948	662	-48	-4	-42	-48	-28
Mozambique	1	175	814	115	53	79	81	74
Niger	64	223	342	31	15	11	13	7
Nigeria	284	267	506	1	-4	-10	-4	-38
Rwanda	13	91	513	138	93	88	32	29
Senegal	48	361	458	24	38	36	18	26
Sierra Leone	36	85	111	11	28	18	14	5
Somalia	47	582	1,317	26	10	10	4	12
South Africa	-11	2	376	112	101	113	90	91
Sudan	52	1,358	936	11	16	24	28	16
Swaziland	8	58	125	13	21	12	14	-
Tanzania	123	259	261	19	16	18	27	22
Togo	18	60	109	3	1	1	2	2
Tunisia	376	563	-56	-4	-20	-6	-19	-22
Uganda	33	40	357	56	41	56	19	51
Zambia	35	331	497	27	21	47	14	27
Zimbabwe	(Z)	271	269	29	22	21	47	18
Other and unspecified [3]	361	769	1,868	246	397	343	475	248
Far East and Pacific	34,767	9,651	-8,390	753	783	137	759	1,145
Australia	276	-12	-273	-	-	-	-	-
Burma	43	31	18	-2	-2	-2	-2	-
Cambodia	1,760	87	125	39	36	28	35	16
China	-	49	396	136	113	227	249	294
Hong Kong	41	11	30	73	133	44	17	-17
Indonesia	1,390	1,660	171	25	44	-48	24	483
Japan and Ryukyu Islands	-345	-210	-10,458	(Z)	(Z)	-	-	-
Korea, Republic of	5,426	3,518	-3,569	-49	-62	-51	-52	330
Laos	1,868	8	8	3	4	4	5	4
Malaysia	86	39	-74	(Z)	1	1	2	-
Mongolia	-	-	95	11	7	13	23	14
New Zealand	95	-68	-28	-	-	-	-	-
Pacific Islands, Trust Territory of the [6]	488	1,260	1,962	209	215	140	175	145
Philippines	729	1,466	3,180	56	65	-46	297	-34
Singapore	78	110	-183	1	(Z)	-	-	-
Taiwan	1,523	648	-1,291	-5	-3	-1	-1	-1
Thailand	996	733	681	205	199	-285	-63	-120
Vietnam	19,720	18	7	(Z)	-	49	-9	-6
Other and unspecified [3]	595	302	813	51	34	63	58	36
Western Hemisphere	6,841	9,849	15,425	485	511	663	1,033	5,120
Argentina	34	21	459	-26	-43	-82	-84	-96
Bolivia	270	413	1,371	101	100	122	97	104
Brazil	1,518	399	39	-204	-191	-31	90	38
Canada	272	317	-589	-	-	-	-	-
Chile	724	-565	-176	-24	-3	-2	5	-8
Colombia	846	298	-265	5	27	27	43	173
Costa Rica	103	687	722	-30	-43	-30	-27	-37
Dominican Republic	360	550	614	-15	-19	-29	-14	-13
Ecuador	144	153	352	5	6	6	3	14
El Salvador	93	1,681	2,929	119	79	92	41	38

See footnotes at end of table.

[In millions of dollars. See headnote, p. 795]

Country	1966-1975, total	1976-1985, total	1986-1995, total	1995	1996	1997	1998	1999
Western Hemisphere—Continued:								
Guatemala	160	270	1,013	39	4	37	36	45
Guyana	71	36	116	10	11	12	12	5
Haiti	67	370	835	156	82	93	88	86
Honduras	113	801	1,546	77	31	29	31	82
Jamaica	120	643	915	30	-13	-30	-21	-24
Mexico	305	1,162	-43	-198	-130	-75	-127	-118
Nicaragua	150	197	843	41	37	44	50	53
Panama [8]	210	205	568	8	-4	-15	-20	4,100
Paraguay	86	22	8	1	2	3	2	6
Peru	274	757	1,674	151	76	134	113	101
Trinidad and Tobago	21	151	-95	-14	-15	5	205	-39
Uruguay	116	-9	7	1	3	2	1	2
Venezuela	115	-34	-151	-2	2	3	5	4
Other [7] and unspecified [3]	671	1,325	2,734	251	512	351	505	606
Other international organizations and unspecified areas [3]	4,018	9,768	17,771	2,513	1,798	2,616	2,138	3,141

- Represents zero or rounds to zero.   X Not applicable.   Z Less than $500,000.   [1] Includes European Atomic Energy Community, European Coal and Steel Community, European Payments Union, European Productivity Agency, North Atlantic Treaty Organization, and Organization for European Economic Cooperation.   [2] In 1992, some successor countries assumed portions of outstanding credits of the former Yugoslavia (assignment of the remaining portions is pending). Subsequent negative totals reflect payments to the United States on these assumed credits which were greater than the extension of new credits and grants to these countries.   [3] In recent years, significant amounts of foreign assistance has been reported on a regional, inter-regional, and worldwide basis. Country totals in this table may understate actual assistance to many countries.   [4] Foreign assistance to Iraq in 1991-96 was direct humanitarian assistance to ethnic minorities of Northern Iraq after the conflict in the Persian Gulf.   [5] United Nations Relief and Works Agency for Palestine refugees.   [6] Excludes transactions with Commonwealth of the Northern Mariana Islands after October 1986; includes transactions with Federated States of Micronesia, Republic of the Marshall Islands, and Republic of Palau.   [7] Includes Andean Development Corporation, Caribbean Development Bank, Central American Bank for Economic Integration, Eastern Caribbean Central Bank, Inter-American Institute of Agricultural Science, Organizations of American States, and Pan American Health Organization.   [8] Includes transfer of Panama Canal to the Republic of Panama on December 1999.

Source: U.S. Bureau of Economic Analysis, press releases, and unpublished data.

No. 1293. U.S. Foreign Economic and Military Aid Programs: 1980 to 1999

[In millions of dollars (9,695 represents $9,695,000,000). For years ending September 30. Economic aid shown here represents U.S. economic aid—not just aid under the Foreign Assistance Act. Major components in recent years include AID, Food for Peace, Peace Corps, and paid-in subscriptions to international financial institutions, such as IBRD, and IDB. Annual figures are gross unadjusted program figures]

Year and region	Total economic and military aid	Economic aid			Military aid		
		Total	Loans	Grants	Total	Loans	Grants
1980	9,695	7,573	1,993	5,580	2,122	1,450	672
1981	10,550	7,305	1,460	5,845	3,245	2,546	699
1982	12,324	8,129	1,454	6,675	4,195	3,084	1,111
1983	14,202	8,603	1,619	6,984	5,599	3,932	1,667
1984	15,524	9,038	1,621	7,417	6,486	4,401	2,085
1985	18,128	12,327	1,579	10,748	5,801	2,365	3,436
1986	16,739	10,900	1,330	9,570	5,839	1,980	3,859
1987	14,488	9,386	1,138	8,248	5,102	953	4,149
1988	13,792	8,961	852	8,109	4,831	763	4,068
1989	14,688	9,860	694	9,166	4,828	410	4,418
1990	15,727	10,834	756	10,078	4,893	404	4,489
1991	16,663	11,904	354	11,550	4,760	428	4,332
1992	15,589	11,242	494	10,748	4,347	345	4,002
1993	28,196	24,054	462	23,593	4,143	855	3,288
1994	15,870	11,940	887	11,053	3,931	770	3,161
1995	15,108	11,295	190	11,105	3,813	558	3,255
1996	13,559	9,589	329	9,260	3,970	544	3,426
1997	13,037	9,171	218	8,953	3,866	298	3,568
1998	13,907	10,318	271	10,047	3,589	100	3,489
1999, total	15,987	12,308	408	11,899	3,679	152	3,527
Near East	5,580	2,283	-	2,283	3,296	30	3,267
Sub Saharan Africa	1,360	1,343	5	1,338	16	-	16
Latin America	1,287	1,268	29	1,239	19	5	15
Asia	1,180	1,055	77	978	125	118	7
Eastern Europe	736	654	-	654	82	-	82
Western Europe	61	58	-	58	3	-	3
Eurasia	1,432	1,409	297	1,111	23	-	23
Oceania and other	10	9	-	9	1	-	1
Nonregional	4,343	4,228	-	4,228	114	-	114

- Represents zero.

Source: U.S. Agency for International Development, *U.S. Overseas Loans and Grants and Assistance from International Organizations*, annual.

No. 1294. U.S. Foreign Military Aid by Major Recipient Country: 1997 to 1999

[In millions of dollars (3,864.4 represents $3,864,400,000) except at indicated. For years ending Sept. 30. Military aid data include Military Assistance Program (MAP) grants, foreign military credit sales, International Military Education and Training, and excess defense articles. N.I.S.=New Independent States]

Recipient country	1997	1998	1999 Total (mil. dol.)	1999 Rank	1999 Percent of total assistance
Total [1]...................	3,864.4	3,589.0	3,678.9	(X)	23.0
Albania..........................	0.7	2.3	4.7	20	8.7
Bolivia	0.5	0.6	2.4	26	1.8
Bosnia Hercegovina	0.5	0.6	4.6	21	2.4
Bulgaria	0.9	5.2	9.5	6	25.9
Czech Republic	0.7	17.2	8.3	8	100.0
Egypt...........................	1,301.0	1,301.0	1,301.0	2	60.2
Estonia..........................	0.6	9.0	5.4	16	88.5
Georgia	0.3	5.8	8.3	9	8.2
Honduras	0.4	0.5	3.1	24	2.9
Hungary	1.0	17.1	8.6	7	72.3
Indonesia	0.1	0.5	8.0	11	3.9
Israel	1,800.0	1,800.0	1,860.0	1	63.3
Jordan	31.7	51.6	76.1	4	26.2
Kazakhstan......................	0.4	3.2	2.2	28	4.5
Kyrgyz Republic..................	0.3	2.2	1.9	30	4.4
Latvia...........................	0.5	7.0	5.4	15	72.0
Lithuania	0.5	7.7	5.4	17	54.0
Macedonia	0.5	19.8	6.4	14	14.9
Morocco	0.8	0.9	4.9	19	27.1
Pakistan.........................	-	-	110.8	3	64.2
Philippines	1.3	1.3	2.3	27	3.3
Poland	1.0	125.0	8.2	10	26.7
Romania.........................	0.9	15.0	7.6	13	11.7
Slovakia	0.6	3.8	3.8	22	38.0
Slovenia.........................	0.4	3.2	3.3	23	100.0
Tunisia..........................	0.8	0.9	2.9	25	100.0
Ukraine	1.0	5.1	5.4	18	2.4
Uzberistan	0.3	2.1	2.2	29	6.3

- Represents zero.   X Not applicable.   [1] Includes countries not shown separately.

Source: U.S. Agency for International Development, *U.S. Overseas Loans and Grants and Assistance from International Organizations,* annual.

No. 1295. U.S. Foreign Economic Aid by Major Recipient Country: 1997 to 1999

[In millions of dollars (9,170.3 represents $9,170,300,000), except as indicated. For years ending Sept. 30]

Recipient country	1997	1998	1999 Total (mil. dol.)	1999 Rank	1999 Percent of total assistance
Total [1]...................	9,170.3	10,318.0	12,307.6	(X)	77.0
Armenia	16.8	74.3	74.3	24	100.0
Bangladesh......................	77.8	97.4	190.2	9	99.8
Bolivia	131.2	108.9	133.3	13	98.2
Bosnia Hercegovina	183.6	282.9	185.0	10	97.6
Colombia	35.1	60.9	211.9	6	99.6
Egypt...........................	810.7	828.4	860.3	2	39.8
Ethiopa	79.2	113.8	126.1	14	99.6
Georgia	1.7	75.4	93.0	18	91.8
Ghana	47.3	48.6	74.4	23	99.5
Guatemala	61.4	82.5	101.4	16	99.7
Haiti............................	101.5	102.7	94.1	17	99.5
Honduras	28.5	21.1	102.5	15	97.1
India	125.6	126.7	172.6	11	99.9
Indonesia	34.8	98.7	197.1	7	96.1
Israel	1,200.0	1,200.0	1,080.0	1	36.7
Jordan	152.7	88.0	214.0	5	73.8
Kenya	28.9	66.6	78.3	22	99.4
Korea, South.....................	50.2	-	156.6	12	100.0
Mozambique	55.0	72.2	78.4	21	99.7
Nicaragua	26.8	54.3	65.5	28	99.5
Pakistan.........................	42.3	18.0	61.8	29	35.8
Peru	126.2	168.0	196.3	8	99.7
Philippines	40.4	68.3	66.8	26	96.7
Russia	65.0	135.2	688.9	3	100.0
South Africa	79.5	75.2	57.8	30	98.3
Sudan	27.2	64.1	84.2	19	100.0
Tanzania.........................	12.2	36.2	66.1	27	99.7
Uganda	64.9	84.9	72.8	25	99.6
Ukraine	49.7	159.6	222.5	4	97.6
West Bank/Gaza	67.0	60.7	79.6	20	100.0

- Represents zero.   X Not applicable.   [1] Includes countries not shown separately.

Source: U.S. Agency for International Development, *U.S. Overseas Loans and Grant and Assistance from International Organizations,* annual.

No. 1296. U.S. International Trade in Goods and Services: 1998 to 2000

[In millions of dollars (933,907 represents $933,907,000,000).] Data presented on a balance of payments basis and will not agree with the following merchandise trade Tables 1297 to 1305]

Category	Exports			Imports			Trade balance		
	1998	1999	2000	1998	1999	2000	1998	1999	2000
Total	933,907	956,242	1,068,397	1,098,189	1,221,213	1,438,086	-164,282	-264,971	-369,689
Goods.	670,246	684,358	773,304	917,178	1,029,917	1,222,772	-246,932	-345,559	-449,468
Services	263,661	271,884	295,093	181,011	191,296	215,314	82,650	80,588	79,779
Travel	71,250	74,881	85,149	56,105	59,351	65,774	15,145	15,530	19,375
Passenger fares	19,996	19,776	21,412	19,797	21,405	24,278	199	-1,629	-2,866
Other transportation	25,518	27,033	29,832	30,457	34,137	40,643	-4,939	-7,104	-10,811
Royalties and license fees.	36,808	36,467	37,695	11,292	13,275	15,717	25,516	23,192	21,978
Other private services. . .	92,116	96,508	105,539	47,670	46,657	52,419	44,446	49,851	53,120
Other [1]	17,155	16,334	14,610	12,841	13,650	13,614	4,314	2,684	996
U.S. government miscel. services	818	885	856	2,849	2,821	2,869	-2,031	-1,936	-2,013

[1] Represents transfers under U.S. military sales contracts for exports and direct defense expenditures for imports.

Source: U.S. Census Bureau, *U.S. International Trade in Goods and Services*, Series FT-900 (00-12) and FT-900 (01-02).

No. 1297. U.S. Exports, General Imports, and Trade Balance in Goods: 1970 to 2000

[In billions of dollars (43.8 represents $43,800,000,000).] Domestic and foreign exports are f.a.s. value basis; general imports are on customs value basis]

Year	Total goods [1]			Manufactured goods [2][3]			Agricultural products [4]			Mineral fuels [3][5]		
	Exports	Imports	Balance	Exports	Imports	Balance	Exports	Imports	Balance	Exports	Imports	Balance
1970 . .	43.8	40.4	3.4	31.7	27.3	4.4	7.3	5.8	1.6	1.6	3.1	-1.5
1971 . .	44.7	46.2	-1.5	32.9	32.1	0.8	7.8	5.8	2.0	1.5	3.7	-2.2
1972 . .	50.5	56.4	-5.9	36.5	39.7	-3.2	9.5	6.5	3.0	1.6	4.8	-3.2
1973 . .	72.5	70.5	2.0	48.5	47.1	1.3	17.9	8.5	9.4	1.7	8.2	-6.5
1974 . .	100.0	102.6	-2.6	68.5	57.8	10.7	22.3	10.4	11.9	3.4	25.5	-22.0
1975 . .	109.3	98.5	10.8	76.9	54.0	22.9	22.1	9.5	12.6	4.5	26.5	-22.0
1976 . .	117.0	123.5	-6.5	83.1	67.6	15.5	23.3	11.2	12.1	4.2	34.0	-29.8
1977 . .	123.2	151.0	-27.8	88.9	30.5	8.4	24.2	13.6	10.6	4.2	47.2	-43.0
1978 . .	145.9	174.8	-28.9	103.6	104.3	-0.7	29.8	15.0	14.8	3.9	42.0	-38.1
1979 . .	186.5	209.5	-23.0	132.7	117.1	15.6	35.2	.16.9	18.3	5.7	59.9	-54.2
1980 . .	225.7	245.3	-19.6	160.7	133.0	27.7	41.8	17.4	24.3	8.2	78.9	-70.7
1981 . .	238.7	261.0	-22.3	171.7	149.8	22.0	43.8	17.2	26.6	10.3	81.2	-70.9
1982 . .	216.4	244.0	-27.6	155.3	151.7	3.6	37.0	15.7	21.3	12.8	65.3	-52.5
1983 . .	205.6	258.0	-52.4	148.5	171.2	-22.7	36.5	16.5	19.9	9.8	57.8	-48.0
1983 . .	205.6	258.0	-52.4	148.7	170.9	-22.2	36.1	16.0	20.2	9.8	57.8	-48.0
1984 . .	224.0	330.7	-106.7	164.1	230.9	-66.8	37.9	19.3	18.6	9.7	60.8	-51.1
1985 . .	218.8	336.5	-117.7	168.0	257.5	-89.5	29.3	19.5	9.8	10.3	53.7	-43.4
1986 . .	227.2	365.4	-138.2	179.8	296.7	-116.8	26.3	20.9	5.4	8.4	37.2	-28.8
1987 . .	254.1	406.2	-152.1	199.9	324.4	-124.6	28.7	20.3	8.4	8.0	44.1	-36.1
1988 . .	322.4	441.0	-118.6	255.6	361.4	-105.7	37.1	20.7	16.4	8.5	41.0	-32.5
1989 . .	363.8	473.2	-109.4	287.0	379.4	-92.4	41.6	21.1	20.5	9.9	52.6	-42.7
1990 . .	393.6	495.3	-101.7	315.4	388.8	-73.5	39.6	22.3	17.2	12.4	64.7	-52.3
1991 . .	421.7	488.5	-66.8	345.1	392.4	-47.3	39.4	22.1	17.2	12.3	54.1	-41.8
1992 . .	448.2	532.7	-84.5	368.5	434.3	-65.9	43.1	23.4	19.8	11.3	55.3	-43.9
1993 . .	465.1	580.7	-115.6	388.7	479.9	-91.2	42.8	23.6	19.2	9.9	55.9	-46.0
1994 . .	512.6	663.3	-150.7	431.1	557.3	-126.3	45.9	26.0	20.0	9.0	56.4	-47.4
1995 . .	584.7	743.4	-158.7	486.7	629.7	-143.0	56.0	29.3	26.8	10.5	59.1	-48.6
1996 . .	625.1	795.3	-170.2	524.7	658.8	-134.1	60.6	32.6	28.1	12.4	78.1	-65.7
1997 . .	689.2	870.7	-181.5	592.5	728.9	-136.4	57.1	35.2	21.9	13.0	78.3	-65.3
1998 . .	682.1	911.9	-229.8	596.6	790.8	-194.2	52.0	35.7	16.3	10.4	57.3	-47.0
1999 . .	698.0	1,024.6	-328.8	611.6	882.7	-271.1	48.2	36.7	11.5	9.9	75.2	-65.3
2000 . .	781.9	1,218.0	-436.1	691.5	1,012.7	-321.3	53.0	39.2	13.8	13.4	135.4	-122.0

[1] Includes nonmonetary gold, military grant aid, special category shipments, trade between the U.S. Virgin Islands and foreign countries and undocumented exports to Canada. Adjustments were also made for carryover. Import values are based on transaction prices whenever possible ("f.a.s." for 1974-1979 and Customs value thereafter). Import data before 1974 do not exist on a transaction price valuation basis. [2] Manufactured goods include commodity Sections 5-9 under Schedules A and E for 1970-1982 and SITC Rev. 3 for 1983-forward. Manufactures include undocumented exports to Canada, nonmonetary gold (excluding gold ore, scrap, and base bullion), and special category shipments. [3] Data for 1970-1980 exclude trade between the U.S. Virgin Islands and foreign countries. Census data concordances link the 1980-92 trade figures into time series that are as consistent as possible. Data for 1970-79 are not linked and are from published sources. Import values are "f.a.s." for 1974-1979 and Customs value thereafter; these values are based on transaction prices while maintaining a data series as consistent as possible over time. Import data before 1974 do not exist on a transaction price valuation basis. 1991 Imports include revisions for passenger cars, trucks, petroleum, and petroleum products not included elsewhere. [4] Agricultural products for 1983-forward utilize the latest census definition that excludes manufactured goods that were previously classified as manufactured agricultural products. [5] Mineral fuels include commodity Section 3 under SITC Rev. 1 for 1970-1976, SITC Rev. 2 for 1977-1982 and SITC Rev. 3 for 1983-forward.

Source: U.S. International Trade Administration, through 1996, *U.S. Foreign Trade Highlights*, annual; and thereafter, <http://www.ita.doc.gov/td/industry/otea/usfth/aggregate/HL00T03.txt> (accessed 03 August 2001).

No. 1298. U.S. Exports and Imports for Consumption of Merchandise by Customs District: 1990 to 2000

[In billions of dollars (393.0 represents $393,000,000,000). Exports are f.a.s. (free alongside ship) value all years; imports are on customs value basis]

Customs district	Exports					Imports for consumption				
	1990	1995	1998	1999	2000	1990	1995	1998	1999	2000
Total [1]	393.0	584.7	682.1	695.8	780.0	490.6	738.6	905.7	1,016.9	1,205.6
Anchorage, AK.	3.7	5.9	7.7	8.8	5.9	0.7	5.7	7.3	9.2	13.4
Baltimore, MD	6.7	9.0	6.6	5.9	6.2	11.2	14.4	16.3	17.7	18.6
Boston, ...	5.6	4.6	6.0	6.8	7.0	12.2	13.4	14.7	16.0	18.7
Buffalo, NY . . [2]	15.8	30.5	38.8	37.5	38.2	19.2	29.1	35.4	39.7	38.4
Charleston, SC [2]	6.7	10.1	11.9	11.5	12.6	6.8	10.4	14.0	14.5	16.9
Chicago, IL	10.2	18.4	19.2	19.1	21.7	18.3	31.3	38.5	43.1	51.1
Cleveland, OH	4.0	7.8	15.1	17.5	22.7	11.3	21.7	27.4	29.7	36.5
Dallas/Fort Worth, TX	3.4	4.4	5.9	8.4	11.5	4.8	8.8	12.7	15.2	18.8
Detroit, MI	35.6	56.8	69.8	77.6	79.4	37.8	64.7	76.4	87.9	97.6
Duluth, MN	0.8	1.4	1.5	1.5	1.5	3.9	6.0	5.0	5.5	7.0
El Paso, TX.	3.9	7.9	11.4	13.2	18.0	5.0	12.9	17.4	20.9	24.1
Great Falls, MT	2.4	3.0	4.3	4.3	5.0	4.7	6.9	8.7	11.0	14.3
Honolulu, HI.	0.5	1.1	1.0	1.2	0.7	2.1	2.7	2.2	2.3	2.9
Houston/Galveston, TX . . .	17.6	27.4	27.9	25.7	29.7	21.6	23.4	26.5	27.8	40.9
Laredo, TX	15.2	24.3	41.9	45.2	57.7	10.0	24.7	41.9	51.1	62.7
Los Angeles, CA.	42.1	67.0	63.7	66.4	77.6	64.1	96.3	115.9	128.8	150.1
Miami, FL	11.2	22.7	30.2	28.5	31.0	7.1	11.9	18.5	21.4	23.3
Milwaukee, WI	0.1	0.1	0.2	0.1	0.1	1.1	1.5	1.7	1.5	1.5
Minneapolis, MN.	0.9	1.3	1.1	1.2	1.4	2.0	2.8	4.1	4.0	4.3
Mobile, AL [2]	1.9	3.4	4.0	3.3	4.0	3.4	3.9	4.9	5.5	7.9
New Orleans, LA	18.0	28.4	27.8	28.8	35.9	24.1	34.4	36.3	40.2	54.0
New York, NY	50.9	61.4	67.7	67.2	79.5	68.0	87.6	112.2	122.1	145.6
Nogales, AZ.	2.1	4.0	6.5	5.6	7.3	4.2	7.7	10.5	11.6	14.1
Norfolk, VA [2].	11.7	14.4	15.1	12.9	12.4	7.4	8.6	10.9	12.1	13.6
Ogdensburg, NY.	7.9	9.2	10.6	11.0	12.4	9.8	14.4	18.3	19.8	23.7
Pembina, ND	3.4	5.5	7.4	6.9	8.7	4.1	7.2	8.1	8.8	11.0
Philadelphia, PA	4.0	6.7	7.5	6.9	6.0	18.3	18.3	19.3	21.3	28.3
Port Arthur, TX	0.9	1.3	1.0	0.9	1.2	3.2	4.8	4.6	6.2	10.9
Portland, ME	1.7	2.1	2.1	2.4	2.6	4.3	4.4	5.2	6.9	8.7
Portland, OR	5.8	10.2	7.1	7.5	7.2	5.6	7.9	9.7	10.9	12.5
Providence, RI	(Z)	0.1	-	-	(Z)	1.3	0.9	1.0	1.2	1.3
San Diego, CA	3.4	6.1	9.8	10.7	12.7	4.3	8.9	16.4	19.0	22.2
San Francisco, CA	23.1	43.7	42.7	44.8	58.3	28.0	58.8	55.5	59.1	68.6
San Juan, PR	2.5	2.6	3.4	4.8	4.8	5.4	6.8	8.4	10.8	11.8
Savannah, GA	7.4	10.9	13.5	13.9	15.9	9.8	14.7	19.6	21.8	26.1
Seattle, WA	32.6	31.4	47.2	44.7	40.4	20.9	24.1	32.3	36.8	40.5
St. Albans, VT	4.0	4.4	3.3	4.3	4.5	5.2	7.4	8.3	8.6	9.4
St. Louis, MO.	0.3	0.3	2.0	1.9	1.3	3.0	4.4	6.3	6.6	7.9
Tampa, FL.	4.3	6.7	7.4	5.6	4.8	7.0	9.2	11.6	13.6	14.7
Virgin Islands of the U.S. . .	0.2	0.2	0.2	0.2	0.3	2.1	2.1	2.3	2.9	4.8
Washington, DC	1.1	2.3	2.3	2.7	2.8	0.8	1.2	1.8	2.0	2.6
Wilmington, NC	3.0	4.4	3.9	2.6	2.5	3.3	7.4	8.8	9.9	10.6

- Represents zero.   Z Less than $50 million.   [1] Totals shown for exports reflect the value of estimated parcel post and Special Category shipments, and beginning 1990, adjustments for undocumented exports to Canada which are not distributed by customs district. The value of bituminous coal exported through Norfolk, VA; Charleston, SC; and Mobile, AL is reflected in the total but not distributed by district.   [2] Excludes exports of bituminous coal, which are included in the "Total" line.

Source: U.S. Census Bureau, 1990, *U.S. Merchandise Trade: Selected Highlights*, Series FT 920, monthly; beginning 1995, *U.S. Export History* and *U.S. Import History* on compact disc.

No. 1299. Export and Import Unit Value Indexes—Selected Countries: 1996 to 1999

[Indexes in U.S. dollars, 1995=100. A unit value is an implicit price derived from value and quantity data]

Country	Export unit value				Import unit value			
	1996	1997	1998	1999	1996	1997	1998	1999
United States	100.6	99.0	95.9	94.7	101.0	98.5	92.6	93.4
Australia	101.2	97.7	86.7	82.7	99.9	94.6	86.8	87.2
Belgium	97.8	89.1	87.9	83.7	98.5	90.5	87.4	85.0
Canada	101.3	99.3	93.4	95.2	100.3	99.4	97.2	97.4
Denmark.	98.2	87.8	85.8	83.1	97.3	88.1	86.6	82.8
France	97.4	86.5	86.3	(NA)	98.1	87.3	86.4	(NA)
Ireland	99.2	95.1	91.7	(NA)	98.6	94.0	90.3	(NA)
Italy	110.1	99.4	97.8	(NA)	105.6	95.8	89.6	(NA)
Japan	92.5	86.5	80.5	85.2	100.7	95.1	83.0	83.8
New Zealand.	101.1	94.7	80.3	80.6	101.9	97.1	81.6	82.6
Norway.	106.1	98.7	81.9	88.4	97.8	88.3	84.0	79.5
Singapore	99.6	93.2	81.1	80.2	99.3	92.9	80.9	81.2
Spain	99.5	88.8	87.1	82.7	98.8	88.5	84.8	81.1
Sweden	93.6	87.2	82.7	78.7	95.6	89.2	83.6	82.5
Switzerland	96.6	85.3	84.6	82.7	95.6	85.8	82.4	78.0
United Kingdom	99.9	99.2	95.4	93.2	98.9	97.3	92.5	89.1

NA Not available.

Source: International Monetary Fund, Washington, DC, *International Financial Statistics*, monthly, (copyright).

No. 1300. U.S. Exports by State of Origin: 1990 to 2000

[In millions of dollars (394,045 represents $394,045,000,000). Exports are on a f.a.s. value basis. Exports are based on origin of movement]

State and other area	1990	1999	2000 Total	2000 Rank	State and other area	1990	1999	2000 Total	2000 Rank
Total	394,045	695,009	782,429	(X)	Montana.	229	427	541	48
United States . . .	315,065	624,609	712,055	(X)	Nebraska	693	2,096	2,511	37
					Nevada	394	1,067	1,482	44
Alabama.	2,834	6,192	7,317	25	New Hampshire	973	1,930	2,373	40
Alaska	2,850	2,564	2,464	38					
Arizona.	3,729	11,824	14,334	16	New Jersey.	7,633	15,355	18,638	11
Arkansas	920	2,178	2,599	36	New Mexico	249	2,178	2,391	39
California	44,520	97,920	119,640	1	New York	22,072	37,068	42,846	3
					North Carolina.	8,010	15,007	17,946	12
Colorado.	2,274	5,931	6,593	26	North Dakota.	360	699	626	47
Connecticut.	4,356	7,231	8,047	24					
Delaware	1,344	2,287	2,197	42	Ohio	13,378	24,883	26,322	8
District of Columbia .	320	412	1,003	(X)	Oklahoma.	1,646	2,987	3,072	34
Florida	11,634	24,155	26,543	7	Oregon.	4,065	10,471	11,441	19
					Pennsylvania.	8,491	16,170	18,792	10
Georgia	5,763	13,749	14,925	15	Rhode Island.	595	1,116	1,186	45
Hawaii	179	274	387	50					
Idaho.	898	2,192	3,559	32	South Carolina.	3,116	7,150	8,565	23
Illinois	12,965	29,432	31,438	6	South Dakota	205	495	679	46
Indiana.	5,273	12,910	15,386	14	Tennessee	3,746	9,868	11,592	18
					Texas.	32,931	82,999	103,866	2
Iowa	2,189	4,094	4,466	30	Utah	1,596	3,134	3,221	33
Kansas.	2,113	4,669	5,145	28					
Kentucky	3,175	8,877	9,612	22	Vermont	1,154	4,023	4,097	31
Louisiana	14,199	15,842	16,814	13	Virginia.	9,333	11,483	11,698	17
Maine.	870	2,014	1,779	43	Washington.	24,432	36,731	32,215	5
					West Virginia.	1,550	1,893	2,219	41
Maryland	2,592	4,009	4,593	29	Wisconsin	5,158	9,673	10,508	20
Massachusetts.	9,501	16,805	20,514	9	Wyoming	264	458	503	49
Michigan.	18,474	31,086	33,845	4					
Minnesota.	5,091	9,373	10,303	21	Puerto Rico.	3,600	8,301	9,735	(X)
Mississippi	1,605	2,216	2,726	35	Virgin Islands.	51	155	174	(X)
Missouri	3,130	6,059	6,497	27	Other [1]	75,328	61,944	60,464	(X)

X Not applicable. [1] Includes unreported, not specified, special category, estimated shipments, foreign trade zone, reexports, and any timing adjustments.

Source: U.S. Census Bureau, *U.S. International Trade in Goods and Services,* Series FT-900, December issues.

No. 1301. U.S. Agriculture Exports by State: 1995 to 1999

[In millions of dollars (54,725 represents $54,725,000,000). Fiscal years]

State	1995	1996	1997	1998	1999	State	1995	1996	1997	1998	1999
U.S.	54,725	59,891	57,365	53,730	49,102	MT	470	889	309	330	228
						NE	3,201	3,461	3,333	2,907	2,883
AL	484	489	534	458	366	NV	2	5	6	6	4
AK	(Z)	(Z)	(Z)	(Z)	(Z)	NH	1	1	1	1	1
AZ	436	426	393	377	333						
AR	1,543	1,579	1,799	1,607	1,220	NJ	150	148	172	160	153
CA	6,954	7,188	7,669	7,583	6,932	NM	89	85	79	87	74
						NY	371	408	394	378	368
CO	940	1,087	879	821	828	NC	1,345	1,394	1,529	1,447	1,206
CT	47	43	80	96	93	ND	1,507	1,725	1,037	1,084	918
DE	108	132	148	131	107						
FL	1,203	1,227	1,224	1,087	1,118	OH	1,280	1,546	1,323	1,357	1,200
						OK	444	508	384	424	440
GA	1,130	1,246	1,281	1,121	867	OR	715	744	724	697	681
HI	109	115	125	111	108	PA	529	683	672	600	593
ID	927	930	843	830	789	RI	1	1	1	1	1
IL	3,287	3,764	3,565	3,060	2,751						
IN	1,683	1,959	1,752	1,606	1,430	SC	324	345	358	313	236
						SD	1,114	1,151	1,157	1,058	1,017
IA	3,862	4,461	4,020	3,511	3,152	TN	520	516	555	486	382
KS	3,083	3,102	2,719	2,793	2,824	TX	3,333	3,412	3,009	3,018	2,512
KY	887	1,035	1,110	930	889	UT	169	185	153	139	151
LA	718	690	723	661	481						
ME	36	40	38	42	42	VT	11	8	11	10	10
						VA	426	480	523	447	386
MD	238	286	310	245	200	WA	1,813	1,926	1,859	1,674	1,779
MA	30	29	48	52	44	WV	27	34	31	27	20
MI	905	1,165	877	914	782	WI	1,286	1,394	1,259	1,276	1,261
MN	2,434	3,012	2,612	2,359	2,185	WY	32	51	40	43	31
MS	874	813	852	815	542						
MO	1,237	1,278	1,507	1,341	1,088	Unallocated .	2,415	2,695	3,339	3,210	3,400

Z Less than $500,000.

Source: U.S. Dept. of Agriculture, Economic Research Service, *Foreign Agricultural Trade of the United States (FATUS),* annual.

Foreign Commerce and Aid 801

No. 1302. U.S. Exports, Imports, and Merchandise Trade Balance by Country: 1996 to 2000

[In millions of dollars (625,075.0 represents $625,075,000,000). Includes silver ore and bullion. Country totals include exports of special category commodities, if any. Data include nonmonetary gold and includes trade of Virgin Islands with foreign countries. Minus sign (-) denotes an excess of imports over exports]

Country	Exports, domestic, and foreign					General imports					Merchandise trade balance				
	1996	1997	1998	1999	2000	1996	1997	1998	1999	2000	1996	1997	1998	1999	2000
Total [1]	625,075.0	689,182.4	682,137.7	695,797.2	782,428.8	795,289.3	870,670.7	911,896.1	1,024,618.2	1,216,743.2	-170,214.3	-181,488.2	-229,758.4	-328,821.0	-434,314.4
Afghanistan	16.9	11.5	7.0	18.0	8.2	16.4	10.0	16.7	9.3	0.8	0.5	1.5	-9.7	8.8	7.4
Albania	12.1	3.1	14.9	24.8	21.0	10.3	11.7	12.4	9.0	7.8	1.7	-8.6	2.5	15.8	13.2
Algeria	635.2	691.6	651.4	458.8	867.4	2,125.7	2,439.5	1,638.0	1,824.4	2,724.3	-1,490.5	-1,747.9	-986.6	-1,365.5	-1,856.9
Andorra	24.5	21.7	22.4	7.8	10.2	2.5	0.3	0.1	0.1	0.3	22.0	21.4	22.3	7.7	9.9
Angola	268.3	280.6	354.7	252.0	226.0	2,901.5	2,779.1	2,240.9	2,418.3	3,557.0	-2,633.2	-2,498.6	-1,886.2	-2,166.3	-3,331.0
Anguilla	12.8	18.1	16.7	22.2	29.8	0.8	0.7	2.1	2.3	1.7	12.0	17.4	14.6	19.9	28.1
Antigua	82.4	84.5	96.7	95.2	138.7	8.9	4.8	1.9	1.8	2.3	73.5	79.6	94.8	93.4	136.4
Argentina	4,516.8	5,810.0	5,885.8	4,949.9	4,700.1	2,279.2	2,228.2	2,230.9	2,598.3	3,102.2	2,237.6	3,581.8	3,654.9	2,351.5	1,597.9
Armenia	57.4	62.1	51.4	51.2	57.1	1.5	6.0	16.7	15.3	23.0	56.0	56.1	34.7	35.9	34.1
Aruba	234.6	238.4	351.2	307.2	289.2	558.1	610.2	469.5	674.8	1,510.7	-323.5	-371.8	-118.3	-367.6	-1,221.5
Australia	12,008.4	12,062.9	11,917.6	11,818.4	12,459.7	3,868.9	4,602.3	5,386.8	5,280.1	6,438.6	8,139.6	7,460.6	6,530.8	6,538.2	6,021.1
Austria	2,009.8	2,074.7	2,142.9	2,588.2	2,554.0	2,200.3	2,368.4	2,561.0	2,909.3	3,232.5	-190.5	-293.7	-418.1	-321.1	-678.5
Azerbaijan	54.0	62.3	123.1	54.8	210.3	4.5	5.7	4.9	26.3	20.9	49.5	56.6	118.2	28.6	189.4
Bahamas, The	726.0	809.5	815.6	842.0	1,064.7	164.9	154.9	142.4	195.3	275.0	561.1	654.6	673.2	646.7	789.7
Bahrain	244.2	406.1	294.6	347.8	448.7	116.3	116.4	155.5	225.4	337.6	127.9	289.8	139.1	122.3	111.1
Bangladesh	210.1	258.0	318.4	274.2	239.3	1,343.0	1,679.4	1,845.9	1,918.2	2,418.4	-1,132.9	-1,420.4	-1,527.5	-1,644.0	-2,179.1
Barbados	222.5	280.9	281.4	304.9	305.6	41.2	42.1	34.5	58.9	38.6	181.3	238.7	246.9	246.0	267.0
Byelarus	53.1	40.6	30.4	26.1	31.1	52.2	66.0	105.4	93.6	104.1	0.9	-25.4	-75.0	-67.6	-73.0
Belgium	12,532.2	13,420.3	13,917.8	12,381.4	13,960.1	6,775.7	7,911.9	8,440.0	9,196.1	9,930.8	5,756.6	5,508.4	5,477.8	3,185.4	4,029.3
Belize	106.6	114.8	120.2	135.8	208.5	68.2	77.3	65.9	80.6	93.8	38.5	37.5	54.3	55.2	114.7
Benin	27.4	51.6	43.0	31.4	26.4	13.6	7.7	3.6	17.8	2.4	13.8	43.9	40.0	13.5	24.0
Bermuda	281.9	338.1	400.3	343.8	428.1	11.5	29.8	11.5	24.6	39.0	270.4	308.2	388.8	319.2	389.1
Bolivia	269.5	295.1	416.6	298.3	251.4	275.2	223.3	223.6	223.7	190.7	-5.7	71.9	193.0	74.6	60.7
Bosnia and Herzegovina	58.8	102.5	40.0	43.7	44.1	10.1	8.3	7.4	14.9	17.8	48.6	94.2	32.6	28.8	26.3
Brazil	12,717.5	15,914.7	15,142.0	13,202.6	15,359.6	8,773.4	9,625.5	10,101.9	11,313.8	13,855.0	3,944.2	6,289.2	5,040.1	1,888.8	1,504.6
British Virgin Islands	53.9	64.6	62.6	60.1	64.6	6.6	13.1	7.5	22.3	30.9	47.3	51.5	55.1	37.8	33.7
Brunei	374.7	178.1	122.8	66.7	156.0	48.3	55.8	211.2	388.7	383.3	326.4	122.3	-88.4	-322.0	-227.3
Bulgaria	137.5	109.6	112.4	102.8	112.8	126.5	171.4	219.1	198.8	235.3	11.0	-61.8	-106.7	-96.0	-122.5
Burkina Faso	10.4	18.3	16.1	10.9	15.8	3.9	1.0	0.6	2.8	2.5	6.5	17.3	15.5	8.1	13.3
Burma	32.2	19.9	31.9	8.6	17.1	108.2	114.9	163.7	232.1	470.6	-75.9	-95.0	-131.8	-223.5	-453.5
Cameroon	71.3	121.4	75.1	37.0	59.2	64.5	57.2	53.3	77.4	155.1	6.8	64.3	21.8	-40.4	-95.9
Canada	134,210.3	151,766.7	156,603.4	166,600.0	178,785.6	155,892.6	168,200.9	173,256.1	198,711.1	229,209.1	-21,682.3	-16,434.2	-16,652.7	-32,111.1	-50,423.5
Cayman Islands	208.0	270.3	421.9	368.8	354.0	16.9	19.6	18.1	9.4	6.5	191.2	250.7	403.8	359.4	347.5
Chad	3.4	3.1	3.5	3.7	10.8	7.1	2.9	7.5	6.9	4.8	-3.7	0.2	-4.0	-4.3	6.0
Chile	4,139.5	4,368.4	3,979.3	3,078.3	3,455.1	2,262.2	2,293.1	2,452.5	2,953.1	3,227.9	1,877.3	2,075.3	1,526.8	125.2	227.2
China	11,992.6	12,862.3	14,241.3	13,111.0	16,253.0	51,512.6	62,557.6	71,168.7	81,788.2	100,063.3	-39,520.0	-49,695.3	-56,927.4	-68,677.2	-83,810.0
Colombia	4,714.3	5,197.0	4,816.0	3,559.5	3,688.6	4,423.8	4,737.3	4,656.2	6,259.0	6,968.6	290.5	459.7	159.8	-2,699.4	-3,280.0
Congo (Brazzaville)	62.9	74.7	92.0	47.0	82.1	315.3	471.5	315.4	414.6	509.7	-252.4	-396.8	-223.4	-367.6	-427.6
Congo (Kinshasa)	73.3	37.8	34.1	21.0	26.0	258.7	282.2	171.1	229.0	212.2	-185.3	-244.0	-137.0	-207.9	-186.2
Costa Rica	1,816.4	2,024.4	2,296.5	2,380.6	2,445.4	1,974.2	2,323.2	2,744.9	3,967.8	3,547.2	-157.9	-298.8	-448.4	-1,587.2	-1,101.8
Cote d'Ivoire	141.1	150.9	151.4			397.4	289.0	425.9			-256.3	-138.1	-274.5		
Croatia	106.0	138.7	96.8	107.5	89.8	71.2	82.8	72.6	110.0	140.8	34.8	55.9	24.2	-2.5	-51.0
Cyprus	256.9	244.5	161.9	191.7	191.8	17.4	16.4	31.8	31.4	23.4	239.6	228.1	130.1	160.2	168.4
Czech Republic	412.2	589.8	569.0	609.7	733.5	482.3	609.8	673.4	753.6	1,070.6	-70.1	-20.0	-104.4	-143.9	-337.1

See footnotes at end of table.

Country	Exports, domestic, and foreign					General imports					Merchandise trade balance				
	1996	1997	1998	1999	2000	1996	1997	1998	1999	2000	1996	1997	1998	1999	2000
Denmark	1,731.0	1,756.9	1,874.3	1,725.6	1,512.8	2,141.5	2,137.7	2,395.0	2,818.7	2,974.4	-410.5	-380.8	-520.7	-1,093.1	-1,461.6
Djibouti	8.3	7.3	20.4	26.4	16.8	0.0	0.0	0.5	0.1	0.4	8.3	7.3	19.9	26.3	16.4
Dominica	34.2	37.4	52.1	38.6	37.3	7.7	9.1	6.4	19.1	6.9	26.5	28.3	45.7	19.5	30.4
Dominican Republic	3,190.5	3,924.0	3,943.8	4,100.4	4,443.4	3,574.8	4,326.8	4,441.2	4,286.7	4,384.0	-384.3	-402.8	-497.4	-186.3	59.4
Ecuador	1,258.5	1,525.9	1,683.1	909.9	1,037.3	1,958.1	2,054.8	1,752.1	1,821.3	2,210.5	-699.6	-528.9	-69.0	-911.4	-1,173.2
Egypt	3,153.3	3,835.4	3,058.6	3,000.8	3,329.3	680.5	657.5	660.3	617.6	887.8	2,472.9	3,177.9	2,398.3	2,383.2	2,441.5
El Salvador	1,074.5	1,400.1	1,513.5	1,519.1	1,774.9	975.4	1,346.2	1,437.9	1,605.0	1,933.2	99.1	53.8	75.6	-85.9	-158.3
Estonia	83.6	47.4	87.4	162.9	89.5	55.1	76.8	125.4	237.0	573.1	28.5	-29.3	-38.0	-74.0	-483.6
Ethiopia	148.1	121.2	88.9	163.5	165.2	0.0	0.0	52.3	30.2	28.7	148.1	121.2	36.6	133.3	136.5
Fiji	27.5	32.8	74.2	126.4	23.1	74.7	84.6	101.1	99.8	146.0	-47.2	-51.8	-26.9	26.6	-122.9
Finland	2,438.6	1,741.1	1,914.8	1,668.8	1,570.6	2,388.8	2,391.5	2,595.6	2,907.7	3,249.7	49.8	-650.4	-680.8	-1,238.9	-1,679.1
France	14,455.5	15,964.9	17,728.7	18,877.4	20,252.8	18,645.8	20,636.4	24,015.9	25,708.6	29,782.4	-4,190.3	-4,671.5	-6,287.2	-6,831.2	-9,529.6
French Guiana	300.7	493.7	246.5	194.2	19.0	4.7	2.4	3.2	4.2	2.3	296.0	491.4	243.3	190.0	16.7
French Polynesia	88.1	105.2	99.7	93.5	93.9	17.2	35.4	32.7	42.7	50.0	71.5	69.9	67.0	50.9	43.9
Gabon	56.1	84.5	61.6	45.4	63.4	1,983.7	2,202.3	1,258.8	1,543.2	2,208.9	-1,927.6	-2,117.7	-1,197.2	-1,497.8	-2,145.5
Gambia, The	8.5	9.3	9.3	9.6	10.8	1.9	2.9	2.0	0.2	2.1	6.5	6.8	7.3	9.4	8.7
Georgia	82.5	140.6	136.5	83.5	108.8	7.6	7.0	14.2	18.3	31.9	74.9	133.6	122.3	65.3	76.9
Germany	23,495.0	24,458.3	26,657.4	26,800.2	29,244.0	38,945.1	43,121.5	49,842.0	55,228.4	58,736.6	-15,450.1	-18,663.2	-23,184.6	-28,428.2	-29,492.6
Ghana	295.7	315.0	225.1	232.7	190.8	171.4	155.3	143.2	208.6	204.5	124.3	159.8	81.9	24.1	-13.7
Gibraltar	11.7	8.3	8.8	4.1	15.1	6.5	2.8	6.0	9.5	1.4	5.2	6.0	2.8	-5.5	13.7
Greece	824.5	949.3	1,355.2	995.5	1,217.8	506.0	453.2	466.7	563.1	591.8	318.5	496.2	888.5	432.3	626.0
Greenland	4.7	4.9	6.4	3.1	1.1	6.4	7.9	7.6	13.3	15.8	-2.2	-3.0	-1.2	-10.1	-14.7
Grenada	35.7	40.6	56.4	66.2	79.3	3.6	6.5	12.1	19.8	27.1	32.1	34.1	44.3	46.4	52.2
Guadeloupe	66.0	57.6	64.0	63.2	85.8	1.4	3.5	2.3	2.8	9.6	64.6	54.1	61.7	60.4	76.2
Guatemala	1,566.1	1,729.6	1,937.8	1,811.9	1,895.3	1,678.5	1,990.2	2,071.6	2,265.2	2,605.1	-112.4	-260.6	-133.8	-453.2	-709.8
Guinea	87.1	82.8	65.4	54.6	67.4	116.5	127.7	115.3	116.9	88.4	-29.4	-44.9	-49.9	-62.4	-21.0
Guyana	136.9	142.5	145.6	145.1	159.0	109.5	112.8	137.0	120.5	141.0	27.4	29.7	8.6	24.5	18.0
Haiti	474.8	499.1	548.6	613.8	576.1	143.6	188.2	271.8	301.1	297.0	331.3	310.9	276.8	312.7	279.1
Honduras	1,642.6	2,018.9	2,317.5	2,369.8	2,574.6	1,795.4	2,322.2	2,544.4	2,713.3	3,090.0	-152.8	-303.4	-226.9	-343.5	-515.4
Hong Kong	13,966.3	15,117.1	12,925.3	12,651.8	14,625.2	9,864.5	10,287.8	10,538.2	10,527.9	11,452.2	4,101.8	4,829.3	2,387.1	2,123.9	3,173.0
Hungary	330.7	485.5	482.6	504.1	569.3	676.2	1,078.9	1,566.5	1,892.6	2,715.6	-345.5	-593.5	-1,083.9	-1,388.5	-2,146.3
Iceland	257.1	179.2	236.5	297.6	255.9	236.0	230.8	267.9	303.7	260.1	21.2	-51.6	-31.4	-6.0	-4.2
India	3,328.3	3,607.6	3,564.4	3,687.8	3,662.8	6,169.5	7,322.4	8,237.2	9,070.8	10,686.5	-2,841.2	-3,714.8	-4,672.8	-5,383.0	-7,023.7
Indonesia	3,976.8	4,522.3	2,298.9	2,038.3	2,546.8	8,249.9	9,188.4	9,340.6	9,525.4	10,385.5	-4,273.1	-4,666.1	-7,041.7	-7,487.0	-7,838.7
Iran	0.3	1.1	–	48.1	16.6	(X)	0.1	16.4	2.4	168.7	0.3	1.0	-16.4	45.7	-152.1
Iraq	2.8	82.0	106.4	9.5	10.3	(X)	311.9	1,183.2	4,226.4	6,111.1	2.8	-229.9	-1,076.8	-4,216.9	-6,100.8
Ireland	3,668.7	4,642.2	5,646.8	6,383.6	7,726.5	4,803.9	5,866.6	8,400.9	10,994.3	16,409.1	-1,135.2	-1,224.4	-2,754.1	-4,610.7	-8,683.6
Israel	6,011.9	5,994.9	6,983.3	7,690.8	7,750.3	6,433.6	7,326.0	8,640.4	9,864.3	12,974.6	-421.7	-1,331.0	-1,657.1	-2,173.5	-5,224.3
Italy	8,797.1	8,994.7	8,990.8	10,090.6	10,999.8	18,324.8	19,407.5	20,959.1	22,356.5	25,049.8	-9,527.8	-10,412.8	-11,968.3	-12,265.9	-14,050.0
Jamaica	1,491.0	1,416.5	1,304.2	1,292.9	1,377.6	838.2	738.0	755.0	678.1	647.7	652.9	678.4	549.2	614.8	729.9
Japan	67,606.8	65,548.5	57,831.0	57,465.7	65,254.4	115,187.0	121,663.2	121,845.0	130,863.9	146,576.6	-47,580.2	-56,114.8	-64,014.0	-73,398.2	-81,322.2
Jordan	345.2	402.5	352.9	275.6	312.7	25.2	25.3	16.4	30.9	73.2	320.1	377.1	336.5	244.7	239.5
Kazakhstan	138.3	346.3	103.1	179.5	124.5	121.2	128.9	168.7	229.1	424.8	17.2	217.4	-65.6	-49.6	-300.3
Kenya	104.6	225.3	198.9	189.2	238.0	106.5	114.0	98.5	106.3	109.5	-2.0	111.4	100.4	82.8	128.5

See footnotes at end of table.

U.S. Census Bureau, Statistical Abstract of the United States: 2001

No. 1302. U.S. Exports, Imports, and Merchandise Trade Balance by Country: 1996 to 2000—Con.

[See headnote, page 802]

Country	Exports, domestic, and foreign					General imports					Merchandise trade balance				
	1996	1997	1998	1999	2000	1996	1997	1998	1999	2000	1996	1997	1998	1999	2000
Korea, South	26,621.1	25,046.1	16,485.5	22,958.4	27,901.9	22,655.1	23,173.1	23,941.8	31,178.6	40,300.3	3,966.0	1,873.0	-7,456.3	-8,220.2	-12,398.4
Kuwait	1,983.6	1,390.0	1,524.1	864.4	791.2	1,651.2	1,816.4	1,266.0	1,439.2	2,761.6	332.4	-426.4	258.1	-574.9	-1,970.4
Kyrgyzstan	46.9	28.4	20.6	22.8	24.5	5.0	2.4	0.3	0.5	1.9	41.9	25.9	20.3	22.3	22.6
Latvia	166.6	217.8	186.8	218.2	133.9	102.9	145.1	114.7	228.8	286.5	63.7	72.7	72.1	-10.6	-152.6
Lebanon	627.0	551.9	513.8	356.5	354.1	41.5	77.8	82.5	51.4	76.8	585.6	474.2	431.3	305.1	277.3
Lesotho	2.6	2.4	1.4	0.7	0.9	65.4	86.5	100.0	110.8	140.3	-62.7	-84.2	-98.6	-110.1	-139.4
Liberia	49.8	42.9	50.1	44.7	43.2	26.9	4.8	25.1	30.3	45.4	22.9	38.1	25.0	14.4	-2.2
Liechtenstein	8.9	12.5	7.3	9.1	13.9	91.1	116.5	242.6	276.8	293.6	-82.3	-104.0	-235.3	-267.8	-279.7
Lithuania	62.9	87.4	62.2	66.0	59.3	34.4	79.8	80.9	96.8	135.1	28.6	7.6	-18.7	-30.8	-75.8
Luxembourg	242.2	712.1	605.8	983.4	397.6	203.8	238.8	373.1	313.9	332.5	38.3	473.2	232.7	669.5	65.1
Macau	29.8	65.0	40.7	41.9	69.8	857.6	1,021.0	1,108.6	1,124.4	1,266.4	-827.9	-956.0	-1,067.9	-1,082.5	-1,196.6
Macedonia	14.4	33.8	14.8	56.2	68.5	124.8	147.1	175.4	136.5	137.1	-110.5	-113.3	-160.6	-80.3	-68.6
Madagascar	11.5	11.5	14.9	105.8	15.5	45.5	62.6	71.4	80.3	157.8	-34.0	-51.0	-56.5	25.5	-142.3
Malawi	13.3	17.6	14.5	7.4	13.7	72.5	82.8	60.4	72.5	55.4	-59.2	-65.3	-45.9	-65.1	-41.7
Malaysia	8,546.2	10,780.0	8,957.0	9,060.0	10,995.7	17,828.8	18,026.7	19,000.0	21,424.3	25,568.3	-9,282.6	-7,246.7	-10,043.0	-12,364.3	-14,572.6
Maldives	2.4	5.5	4.8	8.5	6.1	11.6	19.4	32.9	54.9	94.1	-9.2	-13.9	-28.1	-46.4	-88.0
Mali	18.4	26.2	25.3	29.8	32.0	4.9	3.8	3.4	9.0	9.7	13.5	22.3	21.9	20.8	22.3
Malta	125.2	120.9	267.0	190.4	334.6	208.6	223.6	340.3	325.0	484.1	-83.5	-102.7	-73.3	-134.6	-149.5
Marshall Islands	29.4	23.6	25.0	35.8	65.1	3.9	7.3	3.8	9.8	5.0	25.5	16.3	21.2	26.0	60.1
Martinique	35.3	33.9	26.4	34.9	21.6	1.0	2.4	1.0	0.8	1.7	34.3	31.4	25.4	34.1	19.9
Mauritania	15.1	20.9	19.5	25.2	16.2	5.3	0.2	0.4	0.8	0.4	9.8	20.6	19.1	24.4	15.8
Mauritius	25.2	31.4	23.2	39.0	24.3	217.0	238.4	271.6	259.3	286.1	-191.8	-207.0	-248.4	-220.3	-261.8
Mexico	56,791.5	71,388.4	78,772.5	86,908.9	111,720.9	74,297.3	85,937.5	94,629.0	109,720.6	135,910.5	-17,505.8	-14,549.1	-15,856.5	-22,811.6	-24,189.6
Micronesia, Federated States of	24.7	29.0	31.0	25.0	29.2	11.3	11.9	12.6	10.1	13.7	13.5	17.2	18.4	14.9	15.5
Moldova	21.6	19.7	20.6	10.6	27.4	29.7	53.7	109.3	87.1	105.5	-8.1	-34.0	-88.7	-76.6	-78.1
Monaco	3.1	6.9	6.4	12.6	28.2	15.9	19.6	25.7	14.3	22.9	-12.8	-12.7	-19.3	-1.7	5.3
Mongolia	4.2	34.3	20.3	10.1	17.7	30.8	42.4	41.8	60.8	116.6	-26.6	-8.1	-21.5	-50.7	-98.9
Morocco	476.3	434.7	561.4	565.8	524.7	247.1	295.9	343.0	386.4	444.3	229.2	138.9	218.4	179.5	80.4
Mozambique	23.0	45.6	45.7	34.8	58.0	26.6	30.5	25.8	10.3	24.4	-3.5	15.1	19.9	24.5	33.6
Namibia	22.7	25.0	51.2	195.6	80.2	27.1	63.0	51.8	29.7	42.3	-4.5	-38.1	-0.6	165.9	37.9
Netherlands	16,662.6	19,826.7	18,977.1	19,436.6	21,973.7	6,583.1	7,292.8	7,599.3	8,475.0	9,703.6	10,079.4	12,533.8	11,378.4	10,961.6	12,270.1
Netherlands Antilles	529.6	475.2	750.7	597.4	674.1	684.8	579.8	308.2	384.3	718.1	-155.2	-104.6	442.5	213.1	-44.0
New Caledonia	28.7	34.4	19.2	41.7	19.3	54.8	51.9	21.7	8.6	31.4	-26.1	-17.5	-2.5	33.0	-12.1
New Zealand	1,728.5	1,962.1	1,886.5	1,923.4	1,974.0	1,463.2	1,579.2	1,644.6	1,748.2	2,080.5	265.4	382.9	241.9	175.2	-106.5
Nicaragua	262.3	289.8	336.5	373.7	379.1	350.4	439.3	452.7	495.2	590.0	-88.1	-149.5	-116.2	-121.5	-210.9
Niger	27.2	24.8	18.2	18.5	36.2	0.7	29.8	1.7	12.1	7.0	26.5	-5.0	16.5	6.4	29.2
Nigeria	818.4	813.1	816.8	627.8	718.5	5,978.3	6,349.4	4,194.0	4,385.1	10,548.5	-5,159.9	-5,536.4	-3,377.2	-3,757.3	-9,830.0
Norway	1,559.0	1,721.3	1,709.3	1,439.4	1,543.8	3,992.5	3,752.0	2,871.6	4,042.6	5,710.5	-2,433.5	-2,030.7	-1,162.3	-2,603.2	-4,166.7
Oman	216.8	340.8	302.7	188.2	200.3	414.4	424.4	216.8	219.5	257.5	-197.7	-83.6	85.9	-31.3	-57.2
Pakistan	1,271.4	1,240.1	720.4	496.7	462.4	1,265.7	1,442.2	1,691.7	1,740.7	2,167.4	5.7	-202.2	-971.3	-1,244.0	-1,705.0
Panama	1,380.5	1,536.1	1,753.0	1,742.3	1,608.8	346.1	367.2	312.3	364.8	306.9	1,034.4	1,168.9	1,440.7	1,377.5	1,301.9
Papua New Guinea	69.2	116.6	65.3	37.1	21.2	85.6	64.5	129.6	144.5	34.6	-16.4	52.1	-64.3	-107.3	-13.4
Paraguay	897.5	913.4	785.9	514.7	444.0	42.3	40.7	33.5	48.1	40.9	855.2	872.8	752.4	466.6	403.1
Peru	1,773.8	1,953.3	2,062.6	1,696.5	1,661.9	1,260.9	1,772.3	1,975.5	1,928.4	1,995.7	512.9	181.0	87.1	-231.9	-333.8
Philippines	6,142.4	7,417.3	6,736.6	7,222.1	8,790.2	8,161.4	10,445.0	11,947.3	12,352.8	13,936.8	-2,019.0	-3,027.6	-5,210.7	-5,130.6	-5,146.6
Poland	968.3	1,169.9	882.0	826.2	757.2	627.9	695.6	783.7	816.2	1,039.7	340.4	474.4	98.3	10.0	-282.5

See footnotes at end of table.

U.S. Census Bureau, Statistical Abstract of the United States: 2001

Country	Exports, domestic, and foreign					General imports					Merchandise trade balance				
	1996	1997	1998	1999	2000	1996	1997	1998	1999	2000	1996	1997	1998	1999	2000
Portugal	960.7	954.2	888.3	1,091.8	956.6	1,016.5	1,138.0	1,265.3	1,355.8	1,579.4	-55.8	-183.8	-377.0	-264.0	-622.8
Qatar	207.7	379.0	354.4	145.5	192.1	157.1	157.4	220.4	272.2	488.1	50.6	221.7	134.0	-126.7	-296.0
Romania	265.6	258.0	336.6	176.0	232.5	248.5	399.8	393.3	442.4	469.9	17.1	-141.8	-56.7	-266.4	-237.4
Russia	3,345.8	3,364.9	3,552.6	2,059.8	2,318.3	3,576.8	4,319.0	5,747.2	5,920.8	7,796.4	-231.0	-954.0	-2,194.6	-3,861.0	-5,478.1
Saudi Arabia	7,311.3	8,437.8	10,519.8	7,911.9	6,230.3	10,467.2	9,364.8	6,241.3	8,253.5	14,219.1	-3,155.9	-927.0	4,278.5	-341.6	-7,988.8
Senegal	55.8	51.8	59.1	63.4	81.8	5.5	6.8	5.2	9.2	4.2	50.3	44.9	53.9	54.3	77.6
Singapore	16,720.0	17,696.2	15,693.6	16,247.3	17,816.4	20,343.1	20,074.6	18,355.7	18,191.4	19,186.5	-3,623.1	-2,378.4	-2,662.1	-1,944.1	-1,370.1
Slovakia	62.6	82.0	110.6	127.2	110.0	124.6	165.6	165.7	169.3	240.8	-62.0	-83.6	-55.1	-42.1	-130.8
Somalia	4.2	2.8	2.7	2.8	4.9	0.2	0.3	0.6	0.2	0.4	4.1	2.4	2.1	2.6	4.5
South Africa	3,111.9	2,997.2	3,628.0	2,585.5	3,084.7	2,323.3	2,510.1	3,049.1	3,194.4	4,204.2	788.5	487.2	578.9	-609.0	-1,119.5
Spain	5,499.6	5,538.7	5,453.6	6,133.4	6,322.9	4,279.8	4,605.5	4,780.5	5,059.2	5,731.0	1,219.8	933.3	673.4	1,074.2	591.9
Sri Lanka	211.1	154.7	190.4	167.1	203.8	1,393.0	1,620.0	1,766.5	1,742.2	2,001.7	-1,181.9	-1,465.3	-1,576.1	-1,575.1	-1,797.9
St. Lucia	84.5	89.3	92.4	98.1	105.3	22.3	34.2	22.4	28.0	22.3	62.2	55.1	70.0	70.1	83.0
St. Vincent	45.0	54.4	274.2	92.1	37.3	6.8	4.4	4.8	8.2	8.8	38.2	50.0	269.4	83.8	28.5
Sudan	51.3	36.4	6.8	8.8	16.9	18.7	12.1	3.1	0.1	1.8	32.6	24.3	3.7	8.8	15.1
Suriname	222.7	183.0	187.2	143.8	131.0	96.6	91.5	106.1	122.9	135.3	126.0	91.5	81.1	20.9	-4.3
Sweden	3,430.5	3,314.1	3,822.1	4,250.5	4,556.9	7,152.7	7,298.9	7,848.0	8,102.7	9,603.0	-3,722.2	-3,984.8	-4,025.9	-3,852.2	-5,046.1
Switzerland	8,373.4	8,306.9	7,247.4	8,371.3	9,942.5	7,792.6	8,405.1	8,690.3	9,538.6	10,173.9	580.8	-98.2	-1,442.9	-1,167.4	-231.4
Syria	226.3	180.4	161.4	173.1	226.2	15.2	27.9	45.9	94.9	158.3	211.1	152.6	115.5	78.2	67.9
Taiwan	18,460.2	20,365.7	18,164.5	19,131.4	24,380.3	29,907.3	32,628.5	33,124.8	35,204.4	40,514.2	-11,447.1	-12,262.8	-14,960.3	-16,073.1	-16,133.9
Tajikistan	17.2	18.6	12.2	13.8	12.7	32.8	8.5	32.6	22.7	33.7	-15.6	10.0	-20.4	-8.9	-21.0
Tanzania	50.2	64.9	66.9	66.9	44.9	18.9	26.6	31.5	35.4	33.7	31.3	38.3	35.4	33.0	11.2
Thailand	7,197.5	7,349.4	5,238.6	4,984.6	6,642.5	11,336.1	12,601.5	13,436.4	14,329.9	16,389.1	-4,138.6	-5,252.1	-8,197.8	-9,345.3	-9,746.6
Togo	20.0	25.6	25.4	25.7	10.6	4.2	9.4	2.2	3.2	6.0	15.8	16.2	23.2	22.5	4.6
Trinidad and Tobago	665.5	1,105.9	983.1	785.3	1,096.9	1,313.2	1,134.3	976.9	1,286.7	2,228.4	-647.7	-28.3	6.2	-501.4	-1,131.5
Tunisia	189.2	252.3	195.6	280.2	289.0	75.8	63.1	61.5	74.6	94.0	113.4	189.2	134.1	205.6	195.0
Turkey	2,846.6	3,539.5	3,505.5	3,217.1	3,731.3	1,778.2	2,121.1	2,542.7	2,629.4	3,042.0	1,068.4	1,418.5	962.8	587.7	689.3
Turkmenistan	200.8	117.7	28.0	18.4	72.5	0.5	2.1	2.8	8.5	28.0	200.3	115.6	25.2	9.9	44.5
Turks and Caicos Islands	43.5	58.6	63.8	94.8	88.6	5.1	5.3	4.6	6.3	5.9	38.4	53.3	59.2	88.3	82.7
Uganda	17.2	35.2	29.8	25.0	27.4	15.9	37.8	15.1	20.3	29.1	1.3	-2.6	14.7	4.7	-1.7
Ukraine	395.1	402.9	367.5	204.6	186.2	506.9	410.0	531.4	528.9	873.0	-111.9	-7.1	-163.9	-324.3	-686.8
United Arab Emirates	2,533.2	2,607.1	2,365.9	2,707.8	2,291.4	498.8	920.1	659.9	714.3	972.3	2,034.4	1,687.0	1,706.0	1,993.5	1,319.1
United Kingdom	30,962.5	36,425.3	39,058.2	38,407.1	41,579.4	28,978.8	32,659.3	34,838.2	39,237.2	43,458.9	1,983.7	3,766.0	4,220.0	-830.1	-1,879.5
Uruguay	482.9	547.6	591.3	494.5	538.5	260.5	228.9	255.7	198.6	313.0	222.4	318.7	335.6	295.9	225.5
Uzbekistan	351.8	234.1	147.3	339.0	151.4	159.0	39.1	34.1	25.6	34.5	192.8	195.1	113.2	313.4	116.9
Venezuela	4,749.4	6,601.6	6,515.8	5,353.5	5,552.1	13,173.1	13,477.2	9,181.4	11,334.5	18,648.5	-8,423.7	-6,875.6	-2,665.6	-5,981.0	-13,096.4
Vietnam	616.4	286.6	274.1	291.5	367.7	331.8	388.5	554.1	608.3	821.7	284.7	-101.9	-280.0	-316.8	-454.0
Western Samoa	11.9	11.1	10.4	12.4	64.2	1.0	2.5	6.8	5.3	5.5	10.9	8.6	3.6	7.0	58.7
Yemen, Republic of	255.9	153.4	177.7	157.0	189.3	31.2	16.0	37.6	23.6	248.4	224.7	137.4	140.1	133.4	-59.1
Yugoslavia, Fed. Rep. of	46.0	49.1	74.4	58.6	30.1	8.2	10.4	12.6	4.5	2.3	37.8	38.7	61.8	54.1	27.8
Zambia	46.0	29.3	21.7	19.8	19.1	64.2	55.9	47.3	37.7	17.7	-18.3	-26.6	-25.6	-17.8	1.4
Zimbabwe	90.7	81.9	93.1	60.9	53.3	133.0	139.5	127.2	132.8	112.4	-42.3	-57.5	-34.1	-71.9	-59.1

- Represents zero or rounds to zero.   X Not applicable.   [1] Includes timing adjustment and unidentified and unidentified countries, not shown separately.

Source: U.S. Census Bureau, U.S. International Trade in Goods and Services, Series FT-900, December issues.

Foreign Commerce and Aid   805

No. 1303. U.S. Exports and General Imports by Selected SITC Commodity Groups: 1997 to 2000

[In millions of dollars (689,182 represents $689,182,000,000). SITC = Standard International Trade Classification. N.e.s. = Not elsewhere specified]

Commodity group	Exports [1]				General imports [2]			
	1997	1998	1999	2000	1997	1998	1999	2000
Total	689,182	682,138	695,797	782,429	870,671	911,896	1,024,618	1,216,743
Agricultural commodities	55,639	50,654	47,091	50,387	35,164	35,748	36,681	37,755
Animal feeds	4,621	4,054	3,372	3,791	648	607	564	597
Coffee	7	10	9	9	3,575	3,069	2,534	2,350
Corn	5,426	4,618	5,126	4,704	103	142	156	160
Cotton, raw and linters	2,716	2,572	968	1,904	20	19	148	28
Hides and skins	1,503	1,130	1,020	1,484	130	110	100	109
Meat and preparations	6,885	6,427	6,506	7,305	2,656	2,848	3,259	3,840
Soybeans	7,479	4,885	4,569	5,270	86	54	29	34
Sugar	3	3	4	4	956	715	557	462
Tobacco, unmanufactured	1,548	1,459	1,312	1,222	1,129	780	753	568
Vegetables and fruits	7,472	7,324	7,152	7,497	7,752	8,365	9,259	9,283
Wheat	4,196	3,690	3,578	3,379	359	283	273	229
Manufactured goods	550,529	552,778	565,490	623,986	728,928	790,754	882,013	1,013,480
ADP equipment, office machinery . .	43,698	40,735	40,787	46,661	74,993	76,755	84,430	92,165
Airplane parts	13,266	15,035	12,141	15,060	4,917	5,912	5,827	5,550
Airplanes	25,552	35,242	32,665	24,700	4,557	7,052	9,222	12,393
Alcoholic bev, distilled	385	385	432	427	2,186	2,296	2,618	2,946
Aluminum	3,768	3,606	3,564	3,766	5,558	5,970	6,269	6,955
Artwork/antiques	1,120	1,140	1,148	1,388	3,587	3,976	4,890	5,876
Basketware, etc	2,494	2,583	2,872	3,291	3,364	3,834	4,378	4,842
Chemicals, cosmetics	4,873	4,763	4,853	5,316	2,677	2,895	3,148	3,541
Chemicals, dyeing	3,294	3,471	3,620	4,106	2,485	2,472	2,633	2,676
Chemicals, fertilizers	3,123	3,231	2,921	2,301	1,374	1,570	1,501	1,689
Chemicals, inorganic	5,264	4,709	4,632	5,370	5,132	5,126	5,167	6,096
Chemicals, medicinal	8,087	9,341	11,203	12,882	8,748	10,908	13,497	14,694
Chemicals, n.e.s.	11,160	10,838	11,068	12,279	4,821	4,833	5,084	5,731
Chemicals, organic	16,408	14,920	15,376	18,034	16,874	18,327	21,896	28,563
Chemicals, plastics	17,274	16,608	16,832	19,630	8,237	8,565	9,279	10,643
Cigarettes	4,417	4,165	3,226	3,308	75	102	151	258
Clothing	8,396	8,497	7,962	8,173	48,408	53,742	56,412	64,296
Cork, wood, lumber	5,146	4,091	4,253	4,321	8,179	7,616	8,925	8,235
Crude fertilizers	1,621	1,600	1,536	1,717	1,334	1,300	1,268	1,401
Electrical machinery	65,816	65,575	75,249	89,763	80,370	79,365	88,620	108,813
Fish and preparations	2,624	2,172	2,742	2,810	7,687	8,104	8,910	9,906
Footwear	800	720	694	664	14,026	13,881	14,064	14,854
Furniture and parts	3,942	4,411	4,343	4,744	11,144	13,339	16,181	18,927
Gem diamonds	108	124	312	1,289	7,595	8,497	9,885	12,060
General industrial machinery	30,603	30,121	29,882	32,925	26,321	28,811	31,467	34,709
Gold, nonmonetary	5,673	5,464	5,226	5,894	3,035	3,587	3,032	2,659
Iron and steel mill products	5,637	5,481	4,989	5,720	14,285	17,159	13,369	15,808
Lighting, plumbing	1,535	1,405	1,298	1,392	2,944	3,393	4,330	5,106
Metal manufactures, n.e.s.	10,309	10,699	11,185	13,272	12,242	13,506	14,414	16,228
Metal ores; scrap	4,662	3,581	3,484	4,235	4,156	4,099	3,647	3,829
Metalworking machinery	5,702	5,270	5,268	6,169	7,325	7,926	6,782	7,731
Optical goods	1,697	1,907	2,231	3,247	2,493	2,727	3,077	4,021
Paper and paperboard	10,283	9,930	9,863	10,775	11,697	12,793	13,400	15,184
Photographic equipment	3,865	3,481	3,624	4,239	5,759	5,661	6,111	6,915
Plastic articles, n.e.s.	5,092	5,554	6,362	7,613	5,676	6,137	7,013	8,034
Platinum	437	388	503	897	1,973	3,051	3,613	5,688
Power generating machinery	27,221	28,743	30,894	32,542	24,601	28,160	31,551	33,815
Printed materials	4,605	4,671	4,581	4,778	2,871	3,075	3,323	3,698
Pulp and waste paper	3,868	3,443	3,528	4,598	2,639	2,442	2,597	3,381
Records/magnetic media	6,815	6,057	5,802	5,427	4,137	4,383	4,703	5,166
Rubber articles, n.e.s.	1,256	1,301	1,401	1,649	1,553	1,645	1,791	1,963
Rubber tires and tubes	2,394	2,554	2,400	2,405	3,417	4,095	4,638	4,782
Scientific instruments	24,039	24,169	25,644	30,799	13,969	15,500	17,658	22,014
Ships, boats	1,366	1,716	1,632	1,044	875	1,132	1,127	1,178
Silver and bullion	641	629	214	225	472	662	630	775
Spacecraft	994	1,102	641	158	239	91	245	217
Specialized industrial machinery . . .	29,162	27,305	24,941	30,918	21,182	22,986	21,596	22,733
Television, VCR, etc.	24,093	23,417	24,404	27,898	36,771	42,449	50,936	70,487
Textile yarn, fabric	8,975	8,976	9,245	10,540	11,951	12,896	13,578	15,175
Toys/games/sporting goods	3,827	3,342	3,315	3,605	17,374	18,695	18,987	20,017
Travel goods	330	302	329	351	3,841	3,946	4,148	4,432
Vehicles	55,669	53,536	54,299	56,873	112,926	119,726	145,927	161,682
Watches/clocks/parts	310	312	334	348	2,838	3,210	3,258	3,485
Wood manufactures	1,958	1,690	1,739	1,856	4,668	5,647	7,089	7,222
Mineral fuel	12,682	10,251	9,880	13,134	78,277	57,323	75,803	133,590
Coal	3,586	3,176	2,268	2,173	655	724	665	805
Crude oil	1,040	895	772	444	54,226	37,252	50,890	89,786
Petroleum preparations	3,899	2,857	3,414	5,748	13,904	10,947	14,183	25,657
Natural gas	275	243	218	411	5,477	5,273	6,669	10,966
Reexports	44,153	45,683	50,969	68,131	(X)	(X)	(X)	(X)

X Not applicable.   [1] F.a.s. basis.   [2] Customs value basis.

Source: U.S. Census Bureau, *U.S. International Trade in Goods and Services*, Series FT-900, Final Reports.

No. 1304. United States Total and Aerospace Foreign Trade: 1980 to 2000

[In millions of dollars, except percent. Data are reported as exports of domestic merchandise, including Department of Defense shipments and undocumented exports to Canada, f.a.s. (free alongside ship) basis, and general imports, customs value basis. Minus sign (-) indicates deficit]

Year	Merchandise trade			Aerospace trade						
				Trade balance	Imports	Exports				
	Trade balance	General imports	Exports			Total	Percent of U.S. exports	Civil		Military
								Total	Transports	
1980	-19,696	245,262	225,566	11,952	3,554	15,506	6.9	13,248	6,727	2,258
1981	-22,267	260,982	238,715	13,134	4,500	17,634	7.4	13,312	7,180	4,322
1982	-27,510	243,952	216,442	11,035	4,568	15,603	7.2	9,608	3,834	5,995
1983	-52,409	258,048	205,639	12,619	3,446	16,065	7.8	10,595	4,683	5,470
1984	-106,703	330,678	223,976	10,082	4,926	15,008	6.7	9,659	3,195	5,350
1985	-117,712	336,526	218,815	12,593	6,132	18,725	8.6	12,942	5,518	5,783
1986	-138,279	365,438	227,159	11,826	7,902	19,728	8.7	14,851	6,276	4,875
1987	-152,119	406,241	254,122	14,575	7,905	22,480	8.8	15,768	6,377	6,714
1988	-118,526	440,952	322,426	17,860	9,087	26,947	8.4	20,298	8,766	6,651
1989	-109,399	473,211	363,812	22,083	10,028	32,111	8.8	25,619	12,313	6,492
1990	-101,718	495,311	393,592	27,282	11,801	39,083	9.9	31,517	16,691	7,566
1991	-66,723	488,453	421,730	30,785	13,003	43,788	10.4	35,548	20,881	8,239
1992	-84,501	532,665	448,164	31,356	13,662	45,018	10.0	36,906	22,379	8,111
1993	-115,568	580,659	465,091	27,235	12,183	39,418	8.5	31,823	18,146	7,596
1994	-150,630	663,256	512,626	25,010	12,363	37,373	7.3	30,050	15,931	7,322
1995	-158,801	743,543	584,742	21,561	11,509	33,071	5.7	25,079	10,606	7,991
1996	-170,214	795,289	625,075	26,602	13,668	40,270	6.4	29,477	13,624	10,792
1997	-180,522	869,704	689,182	32,239	18,134	50,374	7.3	40,075	21,028	10,299
1998	-229,758	911,896	682,138	40,960	23,110	64,071	9.4	51,999	29,168	12,072
1999	-328,821	1,024,618	695,797	37,381	25,063	62,444	9.0	50,624	25,694	11,820
2000	-434,314	1,216,743	782,429	26,734	27,944	54,679	7.0	45,566	19,615	9,113

Source: Aerospace Industries Association of America, Washington, DC, *Aerospace Facts and Figures,* annual.

No. 1305. U.S. Exporting Companies Profile by Company Type and Employment-Size-Class: 1992 and 1998

Company type and employment-size-class	Number of exporters		Known export value [1] (mil. dol.)		Percent of—			
					Number of exporters		Known export value	
	1992	1998	1992	1998	1992	1998	1992	1998
All companies, total	112,854	205,188	348,960	553,644	100.0	100.0	100.0	100.0
No employees	15,534	49,474	9,178	32,664	13.8	24.1	2.6	5.9
1 to 19 employees	51,186	86,469	29,397	38,252	45.4	42.1	8.4	6.9
20 to 49 employees	18,501	28,573	17,005	23,139	16.4	13.9	4.9	4.2
50 to 99 employees	10,505	15,774	13,840	18,191	9.3	7.7	4.0	3.3
100 to 249 employees	8,679	12,858	18,371	26,911	7.7	6.3	5.3	4.9
250 to 499 employees	3,621	4,953	15,055	22,581	3.2	2.4	4.3	4.1
500 or more employees	4,828	7,087	246,114	391,906	4.3	3.5	70.5	70.8
Manufacturers	42,763	62,523	241,522	376,397	37.9	30.5	69.2	68.0
No employees	1,949	8,445	1,971	11,080	1.7	4.1	0.6	2.0
1 to 19 employees	12,342	17,929	2,534	3,512	10.9	8.7	0.7	0.6
20 to 49 employees	9,949	13,188	4,217	4,955	8.8	6.4	1.2	0.9
50 to 99 employees	6,781	8,906	4,897	6,269	6.0	4.3	1.4	1.1
100 to 249 employees	5,999	7,615	9,809	14,147	5.3	3.7	2.8	2.6
250 to 499 employees	2,594	2,909	8,990	13,202	2.3	1.4	2.6	2.4
500 or more employees	3,149	3,531	209,104	323,231	2.8	1.7	59.9	58.4
Wholesalers	39,713	63,563	50,989	81,678	35.2	31.0	14.6	14.8
No employees	4,503	11,666	1,882	6,277	4.0	5.7	0.5	1.1
1 to 19 employees	25,296	36,962	16,730	19,237	22.4	18.0	4.8	3.5
20 to 49 employees	5,673	8,101	7,128	7,572	5.0	3.9	2.0	1.4
50 to 99 employees	2,182	3,303	5,419	6,807	1.9	1.6	1.6	1.2
100 to 249 employees	1,338	2,177	4,820	7,346	1.2	1.1	1.4	1.3
250 to 499 employees	406	715	1,942	4,234	0.4	0.3	0.6	0.8
500 or more employees	315	639	13,068	30,205	0.3	0.3	3.7	5.5
Other companies	26,910	68,598	53,158	84,788	23.8	33.4	15.2	15.3
No employees	6,030	22,630	2,754	10,407	5.3	11.0	0.8	1.9
1 to 19 employees	13,364	30,299	9,934	14,230	11.8	14.8	2.8	2.6
20 to 49 employees	2,826	6,074	5,625	9,703	2.5	3.0	1.6	1.8
50 to 99 employees	1,488	2,886	3,380	4,408	1.3	1.4	1.0	0.8
100 to 249 employees	1,271	2,630	3,547	4,464	1.1	1.3	1.0	0.8
250 to 499 employees	586	1,274	3,998	4,964	0.5	0.6	1.1	0.9
500 or more employees	1,345	2,805	23,921	36,612	1.2	1.4	6.9	6.6
Unclassified companies	3,468	10,504	3,291	10,781	3.1	5.1	0.9	1.9

[1] Known value is defined as the value of exports by known exporters, i.e., those export transactions that could be matched to specific companies. Export values are on f.a.s. or "free alongside ship basis." Total export value was $251 billion in 1987 and $448 billion in 1992.

Source: U.S. Census Bureau, *A Profile of U.S. Exporting Companies, 1992* and *1996-97,* CB-97-135 and CB-99-76 press releases.

No. 1306. Domestic Exports and Imports for Consumption of Merchandise by Selected Product Category: 1990 to 2000

[In millions of dollars (374,537 represents $374,537,000,000). Includes nonmonetary gold]

Product category	1990	1995	1996	1997	1998	1999	2000
Domestic exports, total [1]	**374,537**	**547,300**	**584,077**	**644,520**	**637,208**	**644,326**	**714,298**
Agricultural, forestry and fishery products	26,225	33,418	36,234	31,224	26,603	25,618	29,153
Agricultural products	22,597	29,391	32,380	27,460	23,336	21,960	23,596
Livestock and livestock products	829	920	989	1,132	1,110	1,029	1,255
Forestry products	281	272	271	279	257	233	1,644
Fish, fresh or chilled; and other marine products [2]	2,518	2,836	2,594	2,352	1,900	2,395	2,658
Mineral commodities	7,335	7,159	7,284	7,598	6,644	5,832	6,186
Metallic ores and concentrates	1,137	1,562	1,091	1,250	981	965	1,021
Bituminous, lignite and anthracite coal	4,513	3,572	3,694	3,406	3,036	2,135	2,041
Crude petroleum and natural gas	638	729	1,197	1,566	1,251	1,445	1,706
Nonmetallic minerals, exc. fuels	1,047	1,296	1,302	1,375	1,377	1,288	1,418
Manufactured commodities	330,403	496,421	530,484	596,539	595,453	601,279	646,798
Food and kindred products	16,160	26,021	27,041	28,488	27,294	25,216	24,966
Tobacco manufactures	5,040	5,222	5,238	4,956	4,827	3,882	5,568
Textile mill products	3,635	5,696	6,177	7,081	7,180	7,541	2,236
Apparel and related products	2,848	7,190	8,104	9,279	9,474	8,541	8,104
Lumber and related products	6,523	7,424	7,401	7,312	5,960	6,236	4,854
Furniture and fixtures	1,589	2,953	3,101	3,643	3,958	2,304	2,882
Paper and allied products	8,631	14,943	14,002	14,512	13,713	13,839	15,539
Printing and publishing	3,150	4,471	4,534	4,791	4,865	4,719	4,869
Chemicals and allied products	37,806	57,897	58,503	65,080	63,896	66,296	77,649
Petroleum and coal products	6,794	6,014	7,158	7,331	5,668	2,892	8,862
Rubber and misc. plastics products	6,398	11,025	12,093	14,187	14,664	15,826	16,970
Leather and leather products	1,388	1,565	1,725	1,907	1,815	2,248	2,322
Stone, clay, and glass products	3,295	4,796	5,097	5,847	5,487	6,427	7,942
Primary metal products	13,116	20,191	21,279	22,694	21,737	19,893	20,126
Fabricated metal products	11,138	15,161	16,612	17,921	19,607	21,644	21,738
Machinery, except electrical	61,229	95,909	104,055	117,531	110,247	108,275	85,038
Electric and electronic machinery	39,807	76,235	79,533	93,767	92,230	97,990	114,700
Transportation equipment	68,113	82,699	92,887	108,465	119,981	119,175	121,701
Instruments and related products	19,524	29,581	32,842	36,978	37,335	38,871	45,963
Misc. manufactured commodities	4,296	7,383	6,763	7,279	6,653	7,047	8,788
Imports for consumption, total [1]	**490,554**	**739,661**	**790,470**	**862,426**	**907,647**	**1,017,435**	**1,205,339**
Agricultural, forestry and fishery products	12,750	19,799	20,661	22,817	22,859	22,968	24,378
Agricultural products	5,925	9,803	10,950	12,231	12,178	12,100	11,771
Livestock and livestock products	1,453	2,450	2,377	2,483	2,472	2,680	3,085
Forestry products	1,015	1,932	1,810	1,625	1,447	1,097	1,409
Fish, fresh or chilled; and other marine products [2]	4,357	5,614	5,525	6,478	6,761	7,090	8,113
Mineral commodities	51,391	51,050	57,144	53,313	38,619	46,043	79,841
Metallic ores and concentrates	1,500	1,413	1,407	1,406	1,509	1,185	1,155
Bituminous, lignite and anthracite coal	93	248	238	257	281	280	377
Crude petroleum and natural gas	48,917	48,495	54,463	50,030	35,323	42,981	76,166
Nonmetallic minerals, exc. fuels	881	894	1,035	1,619	1,506	1,597	2,143
Manufactured commodities	407,043	639,729	680,609	750,206	803,384	906,665	1,040,329
Food and kindred products	16,564	18,326	20,948	22,600	23,811	25,487	18,944
Tobacco manufactures	94	169	245	463	437	413	502
Textile mill products	6,807	6,965	7,169	8,370	8,779	9,044	7,347
Apparel and related products	24,644	41,208	43,075	50,191	55,838	59,156	62,928
Lumber and related products	5,446	10,406	12,194	13,531	14,042	17,480	15,388
Furniture and fixtures	5,235	8,303	9,320	11,008	13,127	11,799	15,607
Paper and allied products	11,669	16,757	14,784	14,839	15,857	16,460	19,080
Printing and publishing	1,849	2,902	2,996	3,210	3,461	3,786	4,197
Chemicals and allied products	21,611	38,079	42,826	48,382	52,355	62,149	76,606
Petroleum and coal products	14,472	8,971	18,768	22,149	18,689	21,972	40,156
Rubber and misc. plastics products	9,731	15,973	16,891	18,320	19,651	18,330	17,326
Leather and leather products	10,944	13,628	14,187	15,459	15,736	19,767	21,463
Stone, clay, and glass products	5,845	8,498	9,088	10,178	11,114	13,289	14,904
Primary metal products	23,232	33,519	34,583	37,727	42,771	39,036	43,833
Fabricated metal products	11,608	16,213	17,492	19,316	21,189	26,074	27,974
Machinery, except electrical	55,021	106,391	112,907	125,777	133,119	126,673	79,366
Electric and electronic machinery	55,736	114,912	114,066	120,879	125,321	163,981	250,694
Transportation equipment	89,599	122,344	129,235	140,684	155,753	182,428	213,110
Instruments and related products	16,846	27,473	28,747	31,545	33,618	35,062	40,537
Misc. manufactured commodities	20,090	28,694	31,088	35,579	38,715	42,492	56,578

[1] Includes scrap and waste, used or secondhand merchandise, manufactured commodities not identified by kind, and timing adjustments. [2] Includes frozen and packaged fish.

Source: U.S. Census Bureau, *U.S. International Trade in Goods and Services*, Series FT-900, December issues; and unpublished data.

Outlying Areas

This section presents summary economic and social statistics for Puerto Rico, Virgin Islands, Guam, American Samoa, and the Northern Mariana Islands. Primary sources are the decennial censuses of population and housing and the censuses of agriculture, business, manufactures, and construction (taken every 5 years) conducted by the U.S. Census Bureau; the annual *Vital Statistics of the United States,* issued by the National Center for Health Statistics; and the annual *Income and Product* of the Puerto Rico Planning Board, San Juan.

Jurisdiction—The United States gained jurisdiction over these areas as follows: The islands of *Puerto Rico and Guam,* surrendered by Spain to the United States in October 1898, were ceded to the United States by the Treaty of Paris, ratified in 1899. Puerto Rico became a commonwealth on July 25, 1952, thereby achieving a high degree of local autonomy under its own constitution. The *Virgin Islands,* comprising 50 islands and cays, was purchased by the United States from Denmark in 1917. *American Samoa,* a group of seven islands, was acquired by the United States in accordance with a convention among the United States, Great Britain, and Germany, ratified in 1900 (Swains Island was annexed in 1925). By an agreement approved by the Security Council and the United States, the Northern Mariana Islands, previously under Japanese mandate, was administered by the United States between 1947 and 1986 under the United Nations trusteeship system. The Northern Mariana Islands became a commonwealth in 1986.

Censuses—Because characteristics of the outlying areas differ, the presentation of census data for them is not uniform. The 1960 Census of Population covered all of the places listed above except the Northern Mariana Islands (their census was conducted in April 1958 by the Office of the High Commissioner), while the 1960 Census of Housing also excluded American Samoa. The 1970, 1980, and 1990 Censuses of Population and Housing covered all five areas. The 1959, 1969, and 1978 Censuses of Agriculture covered Puerto Rico, American Samoa, Guam, and the Virgin Islands; the 1964, 1974, and 1982 censuses covered the same areas except American Samoa; and the 1969, 1978, 1987, 1992, and 1997 censuses included the Northern Mariana Islands. Beginning in 1967, Congress authorized the economic censuses, to be taken at 5-year intervals, for years ending in "2" and "7." Prior economic censuses were conducted in Puerto Rico for 1949, 1954, 1958, and 1963 and in Guam and the Virgin Islands for 1958 and 1963. In 1967, the census of construction industries was added for the first time in Puerto Rico; in 1972, Virgin Islands and Guam were covered. For 1982, 1987, 1992, and 1997 the economic censuses covered the Northern Mariana Islands.

Information in other sections—In addition to the statistics presented in this section, other data are included as integral parts of many tables showing distribution by states in various sections of the *Abstract.* See "Outlying areas of the United States" in the Index. For definition and explanation of terms used, see Section 1, Population; Section 4, Education; Section 17, Agriculture; Section 20, Construction and Housing; Section 21, Manufactures; and Section 22, Domestic Trade.

U.S. Census Bureau, Statistical Abstract of the United States: 2001

Figure 29.1
Selected Outlying Areas of the United States

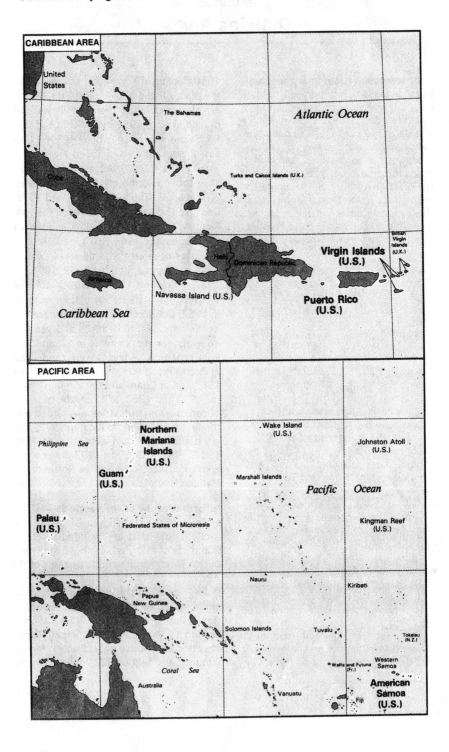

U.S. Census Bureau, Statistical Abstract of the United States: 2001

No. 1307. Estimated Resident Population With Projections: 1970 to 2030

[In thousands (2,722 represents 2,722,000). **Population as of July 1.** Population data generally are de-facto figures for the present territory. Population estimates were derived from information available as of early 1999. See text, Section 30, Comparative International Statistics, for general comments regarding the data. For details of methodology, coverage, and reliability, see source]

Area	1970	1980	1990	1995	1998	1999	2000	2010, proj.	2020, proj.	2030, proj.
Puerto Rico	2,722	3,210	3,537	3,731	3,860	3,890	3,809	4,088	4,196	4,279
American Samoa	27	32	47	57	62	64	57	81	95	109
Guam	86	107	134	144	149	152	155	184	211	236
Virgin Islands	63	98	104	114	118	120	109	133	144	150
Northern Mariana Islands	12	17	44	58	67	69	69	99	123	143

Source: U.S. Census Bureau, International Data Base, see Internet <http://www.census.gov/ipc/www/idbnew.html>.

No. 1308. Vital Statistics—Specified Areas: 1960 to 1999

[Births, deaths, and infant deaths by place of residence. Rates for 1960, 1970, 1980, and 1990 based on population enumerated as of **April 1**; for other years, on population estimated as of **July 1**]

Area and year	Births Number	Births Rate [1]	Deaths Number	Deaths Rate [1]	Infant deaths Number	Infant deaths Rate [2]
Puerto Rico: 1960	76,314	32.5	15,791	6.7	3,307	43.3
1970	67,628	24.8	18,080	6.7	1,930	28.5
1980	72,986	22.8	20,413	6.4	1,351	18.5
1990	66,417	18.8	25,957	7.3	888	13.4
1995	63,425	17.0	30,032	8.1	804	12.7
1997	64,109	16.8	28,963	7.6	724	11.3
1998	60,412	15.7	[3]28,961	7.5	(NA)	(NA)
1999	59,563	15.3	(NA)	(NA)	(NA)	(NA)
Guam: 1965	2,523	32.8	336	4.4	82	32.5
1970	2,842	28.8	355	5.8	62	21.6
1980	2,945	27.8	393	3.7	43	14.6
1990	3,839	28.6	520	3.9	31	8.1
1995	4,180	29.0	592	4.1	38	9.4
1997	4,309	29.5	615	4.2	35	8.1
1998	4,318	29.0	[3]632	4.2	(NA)	(NA)
1999	4,021	26.5	(NA)	(NA)	(NA)	(NA)
Virgin Islands: 1960	1,180	36.8	332	10.3	42	35.6
1970	2,898	46.8	469	7.9	72	24.8
1980	2,504	25.9	504	5.2	61	24.4
1990	2,267	21.8	480	4.6	33	14.6
1995	2,063	18.1	664	5.8	34	16.6
1997	2,017	17.6	620	5.4	26	12.9
1998	1,800	15.2	[3]622	5.3	(NA)	(NA)
1999	1,671	14.0	(NA)	(NA)	(NA)	(NA)

NA Not available.   [1] Per 1,000 population.   [2] Per 1,000 live births.   [3] Preliminary.
Source: U.S. National Center for Health Statistics, *Vital Statistics of the United States,* annual.

No. 1309. Land Area and Population Characteristics by Area: 1990

[As of April 1. For definition of median, see Guide to Tabular Presentation]

Item	United States	Puerto Rico	Virgin Islands	Guam	American Samoa	Northern Mariana Islands
Land area (sq. miles)	3,536,338	3,427	134	210	77	179
Total resident population	248,709,873	3,522,037	101,809	133,152	46,773	43,345
Per square mile	70.3	1,027.9	760.9	634.1	607.4	242.2
Percent increase, 1980-90	9.8	10.2	5.4	25.6	44.8	158.3
Urban	187,053,487	2,508,346	37,885	50,801	15,599	12,151
Rural	61,656,386	1,013,691	63,924	82,351	31,174	31,194
Male	121,239,418	1,705,642	49,210	70,945	24,023	22,802
Female	127,470,455	1,816,395	52,599	62,207	22,750	20,543
Males per 100 females	95.1	93.9	93.6	114.0	105.6	111.0
Median age (years)	32.9	28.4	28.2	25.0	20.9	27.4
Male (years)	31.7	27.2	27.1	25.2	20.6	29.9
Female (years)	34.1	29.6	29.2	24.9	21.2	24.9
Marital status, persons 15 years and over	195,142,002	2,563,818	72,365	93,200	28,952	33,030
Never married	52,559,853	711,470	27,539	30,759	11,412	13,810
Married [1]	111,498,578	1,499,449	35,199	54,717	15,958	17,869
Widowed or divorced	31,083,571	352,899	9,627	7,724	1,582	1,351
Households and families:						
Households	91,947,410	1,054,924	32,020	31,373	6,607	6,873
Persons in households	242,012,129	3,487,667	100,488	124,596	46,267	31,856
Persons per household	2.63	3.31	3.14	3.97	7.00	4.63
Families	64,517,947	886,339	23,012	27,313	6,301	5,312
Husband-wife families	50,708,322	634,872	13,197	21,342	5,153	3,947
Children ever born per 1,000 females 15 to 44 years	1,223	1,512	1,662	1,523	1,757	1,226

[1] For Puerto Rico, includes consensually married couples and for all areas, includes separated couples.
Source: U.S. Census Bureau, *1990 Census of Population,* CP-1 and CP-2 parts 1, (United States), 53 (Puerto Rico), 55 (Virgin Islands); *1990 Census of Population and Housing,* CPH-1, parts 53A and 55; CPH-6, parts G (Guam), AS (American Samoa), and CNMI (Commonwealth of the Northern Mariana Islands); and Summary Tape File, parts 3C, (United States), 3A (Puerto Rico), and 3 (Virgin Islands).

U.S. Census Bureau, Statistical Abstract of the United States: 2001

No. 1310. Puerto Rico—General Demographic Characteristics: 1990 and 2000

[As of April 1]

Characteristic	1990, number	2000 Number	Per-cent	Characteristic	1990, number	2000 Number	Per-cent
Total population	3,522,037	3,808,610	100.0	Not Hispanic or Latino	(NA)	45,864	1.2
Male.	1,705,642	1,833,577	48.1	White alone	(NA)	33,966	0.9
Female	1,816,395	1,975,033	51.9	RELATIONSHIP			
Under 5 years	302,173	295,406	7.8	**Total population**	3,522,037	3,808,610	100.0
5 to 9 years.	316,473	305,162	8.0	In households	3,487,667	3,761,836	98.8
10 to 14 years	339,573	305,800	8.0	Householder.	1,054,924	1,261,325	33.1
15 to 19 years	326,717	313,436	8.2	Spouse	634,872	682,804	17.9
20 to 24 years	287,227	301,191	7.9	Child.	1,475,741	1,431,769	37.6
25 to 34 years	524,849	534,332	14.0	Own child under 18			
35 to 44 years	462,479	515,663	13.5	years	1,013,894	936,719	24.6
45 to 54 years	355,858	463,036	12.2	Other relatives	270,181	305,075	8.0
55 to 59 years	140,952	188,883	5.0	Under 18 years	128,384	139,420	3.7
60 to 64 years	124,852	160,564	4.2	Nonrelatives	51,949	80,863	2.1
65 years and over.	340,884	425,137	11.2	Unmarried partner [2] . . .	22,200	40,238	1.1
65 to 74 years	199,397	240,951	6.3	In group quarters	34,370	46,774	1.2
75 to 84 years	108,822	136,480	3.6	Institutionalized popula-			
85 years and over.	32,665	47,706	1.3	tion	18,734	28,803	0.8
Median age (years).	28.4	32.1	(X)	Noninstitutionalized popu-			
18 years and over.	2,367,510	2,716,509	71.3	lation	15,636	17,971	0.5
Male	1,118,038	1,274,998	33.5	HOUSEHOLD TYPE			
Female	1,249,472	1,441,511	37.8				
21 years and over	2,177,303	2,524,211	66.3	**Total households**	1,054,924	1,261,325	100.0
RACE [1]				Family households (families).	886,339	1,004,080	79.6
				With own children under			
One race.	(NA)	3,650,195	95.8	18 years	487,058	486,409	38.6
White	(NA)	3,064,862	80.5	Married-couple family. . . .	634,872	682,804	54.1
Black or African American .	(NA)	302,933	8.0	With own children under			
American Indian and				18 years	363,989	337,190	26.7
Alaska Native	(NA)	13,336	0.4	Female householder, no			
Asian	(NA)	7,960	0.2	husband present	205,508	268,476	21.3
Asian Indian	(NA)	4,789	0.1	With own children under			
Chinese	(NA)	1,873	-	18 years	105,085	131,584	10.4
Filipino.	(NA)	394	-	Nonfamily households	168,585	257,245	20.4
Japanese	(NA)	251	-	Householder living alone. .	155,151	232,560	18.4
Korean.	(NA)	244	-	Householder 65 years			
Vietnamese.	(NA)	195	-	and over	66,187	92,673	7.3
Other Asian	(NA)	214	-	Average household size. . . .	3.31	2.98	(X)
Native Hawaiian and				HOUSING OCCUPANCY			
Other Pacific Islander . . .	(NA)	1,093	-				
Native Hawaiian.	(NA)	341	-	**Total housing units.** . . .	1,188,985	1,418,476	100.0
Guamanian or				Occupied housing units	1,054,924	1,261,325	88.9
Chamorro	(NA)	149	-	Vacant housing units	134,061	157,151	11.1
Samoan.	(NA)	347	-	For seasonal, recreational,			
Other Pacific Islander . .	(NA)	256	-	or occasional use.	21,413	32,041	2.3
Some other race	(NA)	260,011	6.8	Homeowner vacancy rate			
Two or more races	(NA)	158,415	4.2	(percent)	1.7	1.7	(X)
				Rental vacancy rate			
HISPANIC OR LATINO AND RACE [1]				(percent)	7.3	7.4	(X)
Total population	3,522,037	3,808,610	100.0	HOUSING TENURE			
Hispanic or Latino (of any				**Housing units**	1,054,924	1,261,325	100.0
race).	(NA)	3,762,746	98.8	Owner-occupied housing			
Mexican.	(NA)	11,546	0.3	units	760,233	919,769	72.9
Puerto Rican	(NA)	3,623,392	95.1	Renter-occupied housing			
Cuban.	(NA)	19,973	0.5	units	294,691	341,556	27.1
Other Hispanic or Latino. .	(NA)	107,835	2.8				

- Represents zero.   NA Not available.   X Not applicable.   [1] Data on race and Hispanic origin were not collected in the 1990 census.   [2] Sample data on unmarried partner households.

Source: U.S. Census Bureau, Internet site, <http://www.census.gov/Press-Release/www/2001/tables/redistr.html#demoprofile> (released 03 July 2001).

No. 1311. Selected Social and Economic Characteristics by Area: 1990

[As of April 1]

Characteristic	United States	Puerto Rico	Virgin Islands	Guam	American Samoa	Northern Mariana Islands
EDUCATIONAL ATTAINMENT						
Persons 25 years and over	158,868,436	1,952,297	55,639	66,700	19,570	24,633
Less than 9th grade.	16,502,211	691,835	12,908	9,238	3,664	4,285
9th to 12th grade, no diploma	22,841,507	290,173	11,278	8,602	5,239	4,016
High school graduate.	47,642,763	410,559	14,021	22,220	6,253	8,659
Some college or associate degree	39,571,702	281,248	9,011	14,984	3,062	3,818
Bachelor's degree or higher	32,310,253	278,482	8,421	11,656	1,352	3,855
EMPLOYMENT STATUS						
Total persons, 16 years old and over. .	191,829,271	2,497,078	70,323	90,990	27,991	32,522
In labor force	125,182,378	1,180,162	47,553	66,138	14,198	26,589
Percent of total	65.3	47.3	67.6	72.7	50.7	81.8
Armed forces	1,708,928	5,486	110	11,952	11	8
Civilian labor force	123,473,450	1,174,676	47,443	54,186	14,187	26,581
Employed	115,681,202	934,736	44,267	52,144	13,461	25,965
Unemployed	7,792,248	239,940	3,176	2,042	726	616
Percent of civilian labor force . . .	6.3	20.4	6.7	3.8	5.1	2.3
Not in labor force	66,646,893	1,316,916	22,770	24,852	13,793	5,933
FAMILY INCOME IN 1989						
Families, census year.	65,049,428	889,998	23,012	27,313	6,301	5,312
Percent distribution by income class	100.0	100.0	100.0	100.0	100.0	100.0
Less than $5,000	4.0	25.1	8.8	4.0	11.0	8.2
$5,000 to $9,999	5.6	24.9	9.5	4.7	19.2	13.9
$10,000 to $14,999	7.2	16.5	12.8	8.3	17.0	13.1
$15,000 to $24,999	16.4	17.5	20.6	21.1	23.6	21.6
$25,000 or more	66.9	16.0	48.3	61.9	29.1	43.2
Median income (dollars)	35,225	9,988	24,036	31,178	15,979	21,275
RESIDENCE IN 1985						
Persons 5 years and over	230,445,777	3,219,765	92,579	118,055	39,821	39,206
Same house.	122,796,970	2,190,479	56,098	54,665	30,759	11,479
Different house in this area	102,540,097	879,691	25,003	24,763	2,763	6,870
Outside area	5,108,710	149,595	11,478	38,627	6,299	20,857
LANGUAGE SPOKEN AT HOME						
Persons 5 years and over	230,445,777	3,219,765	92,579	118,055	39,821	39,206
Speak only English at home	198,600,798	(NA)	70,442	44,048	1,203	1,878

NA Not available.

Source: U.S. Census Bureau, *1990 Census of Population and Housing*, Summary Tape File, parts 3C, (United States), 3A, and unpublished data, (Puerto Rico), and 3 (Virgin Islands); *1990 Census of Population*, CP-2 parts 1,(United States), 53 (Puerto Rico), 55 (Virgin Islands); CPH-L-98, *The Foreign Born Population in the United States: 1990*; *1990 Census of Population and Housing*, CPH-6, parts G (Guam), AS (American Samoa), and CNMI (Commonwealth of the Northern Mariana Islands).

No. 1312. Federal Direct Payments for Individuals: 2000

[In thousands of dollars (6,821,003 represents $6,821,003,000). For fiscal years ending September 30]

Selected program payments	Puerto Rico	Guam	Virgin Islands	American Samoa	Northern Mariana Islands	Marshal Islands	Micro- nisia	Palau
Total	**6,821,003**	**218,041**	**202,024**	**34,855**	**16,830**	**776**	**5,160**	**366**
Pell Grants	282,622	2,073	1,290	-	-	-	4,496	-
Medicare: Hospital Insurance [1] .	477,868	681	11,979	-	-	-	-	-
Supplemental medical insurance [1]	712,392	436	7,826	-	-	-	-	-
Social security:								
Disability insurance	1,223,361	9,190	13,509	9,087	1,060	27	-	24
Retirement insurance	1,877,590	47,944	64,741	8,189	3,630	434	83	99
Survivors insurance	845,809	20,799	19,174	8,816	3,510	201	16	28
Federal workers compensation .	14,957	596	151	35	-	-	11	-
Veterans:								
Pension and disability.	377,228	7,825	1,966	4,185	429	30	66	32
Education assistance	6,557	633	121	175	16	-	12	-
Federal retirement and disability [1]	269,078	74,925	18,379	4,351	1,486	85	172	99
Federal payments for unem- ployment compensation	210,459	-	2,550	-	-	-	-	-
Food stamps	(2)	35,880	20,936	-	-	-	-	-
Housing assistance	460,261	16,365	38,063	-	2,327	-	40	84
Other	62,821	692	1,337	18	4,371	-	264	-

- Represents zero. [1] Includes retirement and disability payments to former U.S. Postal Service employees. [2] Food stamp program in Puerto Rico was replaced by the Nutrition Assistance Grant Program in 1982.

Source: U.S. Census Bureau, *Consolidated Federal Funds Report*, annual. See also <http://www.census.gov/govs/www/cffr.html> (accessed 16 August 2001).

Outlying Areas 813

No. 1313. Public Elementary and Secondary Schools by Areas: 1998

[For school year ending in year shown, unless otherwise indicated]

Item	Puerto Rico	Guam	Virgin Islands	American Samoa	Item	Puerto Rico	Guam	Virgin Islands	American Samoa
PUBLIC EL/SEC					School staff	46,911	2,519	2,193	1,079
Enrollment, fall......	613,862	32,222	20,976	15,372	Teachers	39,781	1,052	1,567	764
Elementary (kindergarten-grade 8)........	451,944	23,858	15,198	11,806	Other support services staff.....	17,405	183	314	256
Secondary (grades 9-12 and post graduates)......	161,918	8,364	5,778	3,566	Current expenditures [1] ($1,000)	1,981,603	168,716	131,315	33,088
Staff, fall.........	68,834	3,073	3,055	1,524	HIGHER EDUCATION				
School district staff .	1,967	317	251	130	Enrollment, fall......	(NA)	(NA)	(NA)	(NA)

NA Not available. [1] Public elementary and secondary day schools.

Source: U.S. National Center for Education Statistics, *Digest of Education Statistics,* annual; and unpublished data. See also <http://nces.ed.gov/pubs2001/2001034.pdf> (released January 2001).

No. 1314. Puerto Rico—Summary: 1980 to 2000

Item	Unit	1980	1990	1995	1996	1997	1998	1999	2000
POPULATION									
Total [1]	1,000	3,184	3,527	3,702	3,726	3,770	3,820	3,850	3,873
Persons per family	Number...	4.3	3.7	3.5	3.5	3.5	3.4	3.4	3.4
EDUCATION [2]									
Enrollment, total..........	1,000	1,090.9	(NA)	(NA)	(NA)	(NA)	(NA)	(NA)	(NA)
Public day school	1,000	716.1	651.2	621.4	618.9	618.9	617.2	613.9	612.3
Private schools........	1,000	95.2	145.8	145.9	143.1	143.1	144.1	118.7	131.9
College and university	1,000	130.1	156.0	165.4	172.9	172.9	175.6	174.6	(NA)
Expenses	Mil. dol...	825.0	1,686.4	2,555.8	3,564.2	3,629.1	3,748.7	3,902.0	(NA)
As percent of GNP	Percent ...	7.5	7.8	9.0	7.9	7.5	6.9	6.5	(NA)
P.R. Dept. of Education ..	Mil. dol....	612.2	1,054.2	1,689.4	2,682.9	2,747.8	2,857.9	2,970.0	(NA)
Personal consumption	Mil. dol....	212.8	644.2	866.4	881.3	881.3	890.8	932.0	948.1
LABOR FORCE [3]									
Total [4]	1,000	907	1,124	1,219	1,268	1,298	1,317	1,310	1,303
Employed [5]	1,000	753	963	1,051	1,092	1,128	1,137	1,147	1,159
Agriculture [6]	1,000	38	36	34	32	31	31	27	24
Manufacturing........	1,000	143	168	172	167	162	161	159	159
Trade	1,000	138	185	211	218	228	236	229	239
Government	1,000	184	222	232	246	261	244	246	249
Unemployed	1,000	154	161	168	175	170	179	163	143
Unemployment rate [7] ..	Rate	17	14	14	14	13	14	13	11
Compensation of employees .	Mil. dol....	7,200	13,639	17,773	18,958	20,262	21,139	22,280	23,254
Avg. compensation	Dollar	9,563	14,854	16,911	17,361	17,962	18,592	19,425	20,064
Salary and wages.......	Mil. dol....	6,290	11,681	15,300	16,303	17,472	18,247	19,339	20,299
INCOME [8]									
Personal income:									
Current dollars	Mil. dol....	11,002	21,105	27,378	29,914	32,663	34,395	36,506	38,226
Constant (1954) dollars ...	Mil. dol....	3,985	5,551	6,547	7,074	7,579	7,741	8,050	8,173
Disposable personal income:									
Current dollars	Mil. dol....	10,403	19,914	25,591	27,976	30,607	32,120	33,935	35,456
Constant (1954) dollars ...	Mil. dol....	3,768	5,238	6,119	6,615	7,101	7,229	7,483	7,581
Average family income:									
Current dollars	Dollar	14,858	22,234	25,881	28,097	30,328	30,616	32,240	33,559
Constant (1954) dollars ...	Dollar	5,381	5,848	6,189	6,644	7,037	6,891	7,109	7,175
BANKING [9]									
Assets	Mil. dol....	10,223	27,902	39,859	39,671	42,380	46,088	53,338	(NA)
TOURISM [8]									
Number of visitors	1,000	2,140.0	3,425.8	4,086.6	4,110.2	4,349.7	4,670.8	4,221.3	4,566.0
Visitor expenditures	Mil. dol....	618.7	1,366.4	1,827.6	1,898.3	2,046.3	2,232.9	2,138.5	2,387.9
Average per visitor	Dollar	289	399	447	462	470	478	507	523
Net income from tourism ..	Mil. dol....	202.2	383.3	498.7	526.8	553.5	597.9	577.1	615.4

NA Not available. [1] 1980 and 1990 enumerated as of April 1; all other years estimated as of July 1. [2] Enrollment for the first school month. Expenses for school year ending in year shown. Since 1990, does not include all public schools or enrollment. [3] Annual average of monthly figures. For fiscal years. [4] Beginning 1980, for population 16 years old and over; 1970, for population 14 years and over. [5] Includes other employment not shown separately. [6] Includes forestry and fisheries. [7] Percent unemployed of the labor force. [8] For fiscal years. [9] As of June 30. Does not include federal savings banks and international banking entities.

Source: Puerto Rico Planning Board, San Juan, PR, Income and Product, annual; and Socioeconomics Statistics, annual.

No. 1315. Puerto Rico—Gross Product and Net Income: 1980 to 2000

[In millions of dollars (11,065 represents $11,065,000,000). For fiscal years ending June 30. Data for 2000 are preliminary]

Item	1980	1990	1995	1997	1998	1999	2000
Gross product	**11,065**	**21,619**	**28,452**	**32,343**	**35,161**	**38,297**	**41,366**
Agriculture	380	434	318	466	437	336	450
Manufacturing	5,306	12,126	17,867	19,302	22,976	26,637	27,442
Contract construction and mining [1]	369	720	1,006	1,257	1,483	1,645	1,863
Transportation & other public services [2] . .	1,279	2,468	3,276	3,751	3,979	3,951	4,057
Trade	2,273	4,728	5,989	6,724	7,287	7,896	8,437
Finance, insurance, real estate	1,486	3,896	5,730	6,917	7,672	8,327	8,920
Services	1,279	3,015	4,724	5,314	5,763	6,109	6,679
Government	1,897	3,337	4,440	5,220	5,251	5,526	5,478
Commonwealth	1,574	2,884	3,793	4,457	4,462	4,689	4,601
Municipalities	323	453	647	763	789	836	877
Rest of the world	-3,372	-8,985	-14,195	-15,844	-18,973	-21,743	-21,783
Statistical discrepancy	*166*	*-121*	*-703*	*-765*	*-714*	*-388*	*-176*
Net income	**9,007**	**17,941**	**23,653**	**26,968**	**28,844**	**30,907**	**33,483**
Agriculture	435	486	442	638	594	619	708
Manufacturing	4,756	11,277	16,685	17,969	21,509	24,936	25,557
Mining	9	26	30	34	35	38	41
Contract construction	337	679	903	1,127	1,314	1,458	1,654
Transportation and other public services [2]	1,022	1,778	2,360	2,691	2,784	2,644	2,777
Trade	1,609	3,420	4,108	4,709	5,061	5,364	5,902
Finance, insurance, and real estate	1,200	3,280	4,735	5,773	6,251	6,681	7,340
Services	1,114	2,643	4,146	4,652	5,018	5,385	5,811
Commonwealth government [3]	1,897	3,337	4,440	5,220	5,251	5,526	5,478
Rest of the world	-3,372	-8,985	-14,195	-15,844	-18,973	-21,742	-21,783

[1] Mining includes only quarries. [2] Includes other public utilities, and radio and television broadcasting. [3] Includes public enterprises not elsewhere classified.

No. 1316. Puerto Rico—Transfer Payments: 1985 to 2000

[In millions of dollars (3,531 represents $3,531,000,000). Data represent transfer payments between federal and state governments and other nonresidents. See headnote, Table 1315]

Item	1985	1990	1995	1997	1998	1999	2000
Total receipts	**3,531**	**4,871**	**6,236**	**7,399**	**7,758**	**8,680**	**8,433**
Federal government	3,348	4,649	5,912	7,077	7,364	8,110	7,740
Transfers to individuals [1]	3,283	4,577	5,838	6,943	7,175	7,919	7,573
Veterans benefits	317	349	440	484	495	479	485
Medicare	220	368	661	1,164	1,117	1,112	1,196
Old age, disability, survivors (social security)	1,581	2,055	2,912	3,282	3,472	3,556	3,863
Nutritional assistance	780	880	1,063	1,087	1,109	1,088	1,009
Industry subsidies	65	72	74	134	189	191	167
U.S. state governments	17	18	18	17	18	17	15
Other nonresidents	166	205	307	306	376	553	679
Total payments	**1,180**	**1,801**	**2,301**	**2,394**	**2,551**	**2,683**	**2,826**
Federal government	1,145	1,756	2,132	2,355	2,496	2,617	2,757
Transfers from individuals	508	817	1,052	1,158	1,231	1,296	1,358
Contribution to medicare	44	97	162	165	173	182	191
Employee contribution for social security . .	463	720	888	991	1,056	1,112	1,165
Transfers from industries	13	16	49	48	45	47	51
Unemployment insurance	189	247	184	202	217	216	234
Employer contribution for social security	435	675	847	946	1,003	1,058	1,113
Other nonresidents [2]	35	45	164	39	55	66	69
Net balance	**2,351**	**3,070**	**3,935**	**5,005**	**5,207**	**5,997**	**5,608**
Federal government	2,203	2,893	3,780	4,721	4,868	5,493	4,983
U.S. state governments	14	16	13	13	14	12	11
Other nonresidents	134	162	143	271	325	492	614

[1] Includes other receipts and payments not shown separately. [2] Includes U.S. state governments.

Source of Tables 1315 and 1316: Puerto Rico Planning Board, San Juan, PR, *Economic Report of the Governor*, annual.

No. 1317. Puerto Rico—Merchandise Imports and Exports: 1980 to 1999

[In millions of dollars (9,018 represents $9,018,000,000). Imports are imports for consumption; see text, Section 28, Foreign Commerce and Aid]

Item	1980	1985	1990	1991	1992	1993	1994	1995	1996	1997	1998	1999
Imports	9,018	10,162	16,200	15,079	16,476	16,124	17,152	18,969	19,422	21,928	21,706	26,697
From U.S . . .	5,345	6,130	10,792	10,306	11,463	11,179	11,455	12,213	12,220	13,904	13,318	15,949
From other . . .	3,673	4,032	5,408	4,773	5,013	4,945	5,697	6,756	7,202	8,024	8,388	10,748
Exports	6,576	11,087	20,402	21,128	20,455	20,351	22,711	23,573	22,379	26,653	31,501	37,779
To U.S.	5,643	9,873	17,915	18,729	17,990	17,613	20,098	20,986	19,907	25,045	28,109	33,173
To other	933	1,214	2,487	2,399	2,465	2,738	2,613	2,587	2,472	1,608	3,392	4,606

Source: U.S. Census Bureau, *Foreign Commerce and Navigation of the United States*, annual; *U.S. Trade With Puerto Rico and U.S. Possessions, FT 895*; and, through 1988, *Highlights of U.S. Export and Import Trade, FT990*; thereafter, *FT920* supplement.

No. 1318. Puerto Rico—Farms, Farmland, Farms by Size, Tenure of Operator, Type of Organization, and Farms by Value of Sales: 1993 and 1998

[1 cuerda = .97 acre]

All farms	Unit	1993	1998	All farms	Unit	1993	1998
Farms	Number	22,350	19,951	Average size of farm by operator:			
Farm land	Cuerdas	826,893	865,478	Full owners	Cuerdas	26.6	29.3
Average size of farm	Cuerdas	37.0	43.4	Part owners	Cuerdas	92.3	111.7
				Tenants	Cuerdas	63.4	75.9
Approximate land area	Cuerdas	2,254,365	2,254,365	Farms by type of organization:			
Proportion in farms	Percent	36.7	38.4	Individual or family	Number	19,911	17,887
Farms by size:				Partnership	Number	288	211
Less than 10 cuerdas	Number	10,413	7,759	Corporation	Number	382	437
10 to 19 cuerdas	Number	4,475	4,473	Other	Number	1,769	1,416
20 to 49 cuerdas	Number	3,966	4,023	Farms by value of sales:			
50 to 99 cuerdas	Number	1,723	1,792	Less than $1,200	Number	4,456	3,307
100 to 174 cuerdas	Number	820	809	$1,200 to $2,499	Number	4,591	3,633
175 to 259 cuerdas	Number	366	421	$2,500 to $4,499	Number	4,593	3,900
260 cuerdas or more	Number	587	674	$5,000 to $7,499	Number	2,566	2,408
				$7,500 to $9,999	Number	1,248	1,233
Tenure of operator:				$10,000 to $19,999	Number	2,115	2,366
Operators	Number	22,350	19,951	$20,000 to $39,999	Number	1,071	1,247
Full owners	Number	17,759	15,620	$40,000 to $59,999	Number	348	405
Part owners	Number	2,218	2,207	$60,000 or more	Number	1,362	1,452
Tenants	Number	2,373	2,124				

No. 1319. Puerto Rico—Market Value of Agricultural Products Sold: 1998

Type of product	Number of farms	Market value ($1,000)	Average value per farm (dol.)	Type of product	Number of farms	Market value ($1,000)	Average value per farm (dol.)
Total	**19,951**	**593,082**	**29,727**	Grasses and other crops	288	5,464	18,971
Crops, including horticultural specialties	15,863	225,780	(NA)	Livestock, poultry, and their products	7,580	367,302	48,457
Sugarcane	162	6,973	43,042	Cattle and calves	5,602	53,442	9,540
Coffee	10,441	55,486	5,314	Poultry and poultry products	1,153	99,208	86,043
Pineapples	35	3,275	93,569	Dairy products	447	193,615	433,143
Plantains	6,229	46,021	7,388	Hogs and pigs	1,368	11,365	8,308
Bananas	3,836	11,854	3,090	Sheep and goats	377	380	1,009
Grains	1,256	4,170	3,320	Other livestock and livestock products	858	9,292	10,830
Root crops or tubers	2,517	7,624	3,029				
Fruits and coconuts	4,201	17,343	4,128				
Vegetables or melons	1,639	28,172	17,189				
Horticultural specialties	490	39,399	80,406				

NA Not available.
Source of Tables 1318 and 1319: U.S. Dept. of Agriculture, National Agricultural Statistics Service, *1998 Census of Agriculture-Area Data, Puerto Rico, Volume 1* (AC97-A-52).

No. 1320. Puerto Rico—Economic Census of Manufactures by Industry: 1997

[Covers all establishments in operation at any time during the year. Employees are for the week including March 12. For statement on methodology, see Appendix III]

Manufacturing industries	1987 SIC code [1]	Total establishments (number)	Proprietors and partners (number)	Unpaid family workers (number)	All employees Total (number)	All employees Payroll (mil. dol.)	Value added by manufacture (mil. dol.)	Cost of materials (mil. dol.)	Value of shipments (mil. dol.)
Total	(X)	**2,092**	**601**	**108**	**163,605**	**3,319**	**36,427**	**10,343**	**46,876**
Food and kindred products	20	287	94	14	18,094	352	3,532	1,803	5,333
Tobacco products	21	4	(D)	-	(2)	(D)	(D)	(D)	(D)
Textile mill products	22	20	8	2	2,555	32	89	38	129
Apparel and other textile products	23	223	55	15	21,818	233	678	404	1,080
Lumber and wood products	24	117	(D)	(D)	(2)	(D)	(D)	(D)	(D)
Furniture and fixtures	25	146	65	7	2,472	30	97	69	165
Paper and allied products	26	41	2	1	2,152	43	162	121	283
Printing and publishing	27	208	93	27	6,469	126	430	284	713
Chemicals and allied products	28	186	11	2	37,860	1,149	21,393	3,919	25,418
Petroleum and coal products	29	28	-	3	1,555	49	849	379	1,220
Rubber and miscellaneous plastic products	30	71	5	1	4,924	87	377	236	613
Leather and leather products	31	25	4	-	5,752	80	218	205	426
Stone, clay and glass products	32	159	37	5	5,298	106	565	161	726
Primary metal industries	33	24	7	1	727	13	77	37	111
Fabricated metal products	34	229	87	11	6,048	91	405	214	623
Industrial machinery and equipment	35	78	29	5	4,301	107	2,665	262	2,940
Electronic and other electrical equipment	36	87	6	1	24,931	456	2,897	1,471	4,360
Transportation equipment	37	34	9	2	1,484	27	118	47	166
Instruments and related products	38	64	3	-	12,260	255	1,521	556	2,077
Miscellaneous manufacturing industries	39	61	18	3	2,208	39	164	55	218

- Represents or rounds to zero.   D Withheld to avoid disclosure of information pertaining to a specific organization or individual.   X Not applicable.   [1] 1987 Standard Industrial Classification (SIC) code; see text, Section 12, Labor Force, Employment, and Earnings.   [2] Represents 1,000 to 2,499 employees.
Source: U.S. Census Bureau, *1997 Economic Census of Outlying Areas, Outlying Areas, Series OA97E-4.*

No. 1321. Puerto Rico—Economic Summary by Industry: 1992 and 1997

[Covers establishments with payroll. Employees are for the week including March 12. Most government employees are excluded. For statement on methodology, see Appendix III]

Industry	1987 SIC code [1]	Establish-ments (number)		Sales/receipts shipments (mil. dol.)		Annual payroll (mil. dol.)		Paid employees (number)	
		1992	1997	1992	1997	1992	1997	1992	1997
Construction industries[2].	C	1,529	(NA)	2,587.1	(NA)	506.6	(NA)	47,666	(NA)
General contractors and operative builders	15	574	(NA)	1,241.5	(NA)	234.4	(NA)	22,676	(NA)
Special trade contractors	16	196	(NA)	563.1	(NA)	96.4	(NA)	8,462	(NA)
Special trade contractors	17	732	(NA)	758.8	(NA)	171.9	(NA)	16,134	(NA)
Subdividers and developers, n.e.c. . .	6552	27	(NA)	23.6	(NA)	3.9	(NA)	394	(NA)
Manufactures [2]	D	2,258	2,092	31,325.8	46,876.0	2,706.5	3,318.9	158,181	163,605
Food and kindred products	20	331	287	5,240.0	5,333.0	310.3	351.8	20,193	18,094
Tobacco products	21	6	4	(D)	(D)	(D)	(D)	(D)	(D)
Textile mill products.	22	26	20	180.1	129.4	34.8	31.9	3,324	2,555
Apparel and other textile products . .	23	285	223	1,412.3	1,079.7	312.3	232.5	31,320	21,818
Lumber & wood products	24	106	117	(D)	(D)	(D)	(D)	(D)	(D)
Furniture and Fixtures	25	143	146	179.4	164.7	22.5	29.7	2,310	2,472
Paper and allied products.	26	55	41	321.6	283.3	43.8	42.8	2,732	2,152
Printing and publishing.	27	192	208	448.3	712.8	82.3	126.2	4,121	6,469
Chemicals and allied products.	28	190	186	13,253.4	25,418.3	861.3	1,149.5	31,161	37,860
Petroleum and coal products.	29	24	28	1,707.5	1,219.9	47.2	48.6	1,562	1,555
Rubber and misc. plastic products . .	30	92	71	415.7	612.7	65.8	86.9	4,252	4,924
Leather and leather products	31	31	25	387.5	426.1	65.0	80.3	5,785	5,752
Stone, clay, and glass products	32	174	159	518.6	726.5	81.3	106.0	4,517	5,298
Primary metal industries.	33	27	24	(D)	110.9	(D)	13.2	(D)	727
Fabricated metal products	34	211	229	492.0	622.9	67.4	90.9	4,924	6,048
Industrial machinery and equip	35	74	78	1,292.0	2,940.0	109.5	106.8	5,373	4,301
Electronic & other electrical equipment	36	114	87	2,779.0	4,360.2	277.2	455.8	17,224	24,931
Transportation equipment.	37	34	34	151.5	165.8	20.5	26.9	1,315	1,484
Instruments and related products. . .	38	65	64	1,873.8	2,076.6	220.3	254.9	12,398	12,260
Miscellaneous manufacturing products	39	78	61	264.8	217.6	39.7	38.7	2,754	2,208
Wholesale trade [2].	F	2,651	2,809	10,187.7	12,594.6	673.2	850.9	34,996	39,582
Durable goods	50	1,343	1,468	3,472.9	4,462.3	275.0	375.2	14,688	17,719
Nondurable goods.	51	1,308	1,341	6,714.7	8,132.3	398.2	475.7	20,308	21,863
Merchant wholesalers	(X)	2,408	2,453	8,494.0	9,386.3	487.4	582.2	28,682	31,211
Other operating types	(X)	243	356	1,693.7	3,208.4	185.8	268.7	6,314	8,371
Retail trade [2].	G	13,534	14,582	11,707.0	17,088.0	1,114.0	1,593.2	119,615	153,746
Building materials, garden supplies .	52	991	987	615.8	972.9	60.0	93.4	5,577	7,499
General merchandise stores	53	485	389	1,503.0	2,229.9	162.7	194.6	15,690	19,282
Food stores	54	1,988	2,066	2,959.8	3,620.6	215.9	266.8	26,026	29,088
Automotive dealers & service stations	55, 554	1,118	1,281	1,688.3	3,395.8	95.5	182.5	7,074	11,418
Gasoline service stations	554	1,060	1,115	710.5	1,141.3	32.8	54.7	4,115	5,550
Apparel and accessory stores	56	2,032	1,972	1,205.1	1,413.6	131.1	167.2	16,061	18,208
Furniture and home furnishings	57	1,048	1,096	772.2	1,119.4	77.0	105.6	6,188	8,089
Eating and drinking places	58	2,356	3,021	934.3	1,444.6	185.1	307.9	23,951	36,996
Drug stores & proprietary stores . . .	591	790	756	656.9	896.7	69.6	108.4	6,377	7,949
Miscellaneous retail.	59, 591	1,666	1,899	660.9	853.0	84.3	112.0	8,556	9,667
Service Industries [2]	I	6,356	8,048	3,110.3	5,823.0	893.6	1,546.1	71,378	111,125
Arrangement of passenger transportation	472	384	384	115.2	166.6	15.3	19.9	1,240	1,459
Hotels & other lodging places	70, 702, 704	168	211	(D)	(D)	(D)	(D)	(D)	(D)
Personal services	72	828	983	137.8	208.6	37.2	52.4	3,958	4,944
Business services	73	1,302	1,861	1,030.6	2,251.9	384.5	698.7	36,159	57,109
Auto repair, services, and parking . .	75	972	1,235	329.5	476.9	56.9	79.2	4,851	6,285
Miscellaneous repair services	76	480	564	172.6	239.1	37.1	50.1	2,853	3,919
Motion pictures	78	135	179	107.0	136.4	15.1	22.2	1,414	2,335
Amusement and recreation services.	79	219	345	132.0	268.6	23.2	50.8	2,150	4,498
Dental laboratories	8072	29	39	4.8	(D)	1.4	(D)	144	(D)
Legal services	81	1,153	1,280	288.7	463.0	90.5	122.3	4,169	5,057
Museum, art galleries, botanical, & zoological gardens	84	15	17	(D)	6.3	(D)	1.3	(D)	110
Engineering & management services.	87, 872	671	950	375.8	805.4	100.8	208.6	5,580	10,277

- Represents or rounds to zero.   D Withheld to avoid disclosing individual company data.   NA Not available.   [1] 1987 Standard Industrial Classification (SIC) code; see text, Section 15, Business Enterprise.   [2] Includes other establishments not shown separately.

Source: U.S. Census Bureau Internet site <http://www.census.gov/csd/oat/P_Puerto97.htm>.

[Sales and payroll in millions of dollars (4,640 represents $4,640,000,000)]

Item	Guam	Virgin Islands	N. Mariana Islands	Item	Guam	Virgin Islands	N. Mariana Islands
Total: Establishments	2,707	2,032	1,232	Wholesale trade:			
Sales.	4,640	2,296	2,083	Establishments	270	115	87
Annual payroll	750	382	323	Sales.	941	252	223
Paid employees [1]	42,477	21,216	28,906	Annual payroll	77	27	9
Unpaid family workers [2]	129	107	26	Paid employees [1]	3,393	1,144	745
				Unpaid family workers [2] . . .	-	-	-
Construction: Establishments. .	354	203	85	Retail trade:			
Sales.	506	185	88	Establishments	1,091	973	519
Annual payroll	139	52	21	Sales.	1,840	1,058	570
Paid employees [1]	7,094	2,623	2,302	Annual payroll	221	136	54
Unpaid family workers [2]	9	9	-	Paid employees [1]	15,334	8,966	4,811
Manufacturing:				Unpaid family workers [2] . . .	74	55	14
Establishments	60	74	84	Services: Establishments	932	667	457
Sales.	165	146	762	Sales.	1,188	655	440
Annual payroll	33	28	147	Annual payroll	280	139	91
Paid employees [1]	1,320	1,194	13,715	Paid employees [1]	15,336	7,289	7,333
Unpaid family workers [2] . . .	4	9	-	Unpaid family workers [2] . . .	42	34	12

- Represents zero. [1] For pay period including March 12. [2] Includes those who worked 15 hours or more during the week including March 12.

Source: U.S. Census Bureau, *1997 Economic Census of Outlying Areas*, OA97-E-5 to OA97-E-7.

Area	1990	2000	Population change, 1990 to 2000	
			Number	Percent
PUERTO RICO				
Municipio:				
San Juan	437,745	434,374	-3,371	-0.8
Bayamon.	220,262	224,044	3,782	1.7
Ponce.	187,749	186,475	-1,274	-0.7
Carolina	177,806	186,076	8,270	4.7
Caguas	133,447	140,502	7,055	5.3
Arecibo	93,385	100,131	6,746	7.2
Guaynabo	92,886	100,053	7,167	7.7
Mayaguez	100,371	98,434	-1,937	-1.9
Toa Baja	89,454	94,085	4,631	5.2
Trujillo Alto.	61,120	75,728	14,608	23.9
Aguadilla	59,335	64,685	5,350	9.0
Toa Alta	44,101	63,929	19,828	45.0
Vega Baja	55,997	61,929	5,932	10.6
Humacao	55,203	59,035	3,832	6.9
Rio Grande	45,648	52,362	6,714	14.7
Place:				
San Juan zona urbana.	426,832	421,958	-4,874	-1.1
Bayamon zona urbana.	202,103	203,499	1,396	0.7
Carolina zona urbana	162,404	168,164	5,760	3.5
Ponce zona urbana	159,151	155,038	-4,113	-2.6
Caguas zona urbana	92,429	88,680	-3,749	-4.1
Guaynabo zona urbana	73,385	78,806	5,421	7.4
Mayaguez zona urbana	83,010	78,647	-4,363	-5.3
Trujillo Alto zona urbana.	44,336	50,841	6,505	14.7
Arecibo zona urbana	49,545	49,318	-227	-0.5
Fajardo zona urbana	31,659	33,286	1,627	5.1
Levittown comunidad zona urban.	30,807	30,140	-667	-2.2
Catano zona urbana	34,587	30,071	-4,516	-13.1
GUAM				
Dedido District.	133,152	154,805	21,653	16
Yigo District.	14,213	19,474	5,261	37
Mangilao District	10,483	13,313	2,830	27
U.S. VIRGIN ISLANDS				
St. Croix Island	50,139	53,234	3,095	6
St. Thomas Island	48,166	51,181	3,015	6
Charlotte Amalie subdistrict.	20,589	18,914	-1,675	-8
St. John Island	3,504	4,197	693	20
AMERICAN SAMOA				
Eastern District	21,175	23,441	2,266	11
Ma'oputasi County	10,640	11,695	1,055	10
Western District	23,868	32,435	8,567	36
Tualauta County	14,724	22,025	7,301	50
NORTHERN MARIANA ISLANDS				
Saipan Municipality.	38,896	62,392	23,496	60

Source: U.S. Census Bureau, Internet releases (03 July 2001) <http://www.census.gov/Press-Release/www/2001/tables/redistpr.html#demoprofile>; <http://www.census.gov/Press-Release/www/2001/tables/redistgu.html>; <http://www.census.gov/Press-Release/www/2001/tables/redistvi.html>; <http://www.census.gov/Press-Release/www/2001/tables/redistas.html>; <http://www.census.gov/Press-Release/www/2001/tables/redistnmi.html>.

Comparative International Statistics

This section presents statistics for the world as a whole and for many countries on a comparative basis with the United States. Data are shown for population, births and deaths, social and industrial indicators, finances, agriculture, communication, and military affairs.

Statistics of the individual nations may be found primarily in official national publications, generally in the form of yearbooks, issued by most of the nations at various intervals in their own national languages and expressed in their own or customary units of measure. (For a listing of selected publications, see Guide to Sources.) For handier reference, especially for international comparisons, the United Nations Statistics Division compiles data as submitted by member countries and issues a number of international summary publications, generally in English and French. Among these are the *Statistical Yearbook*; the *Demographic Yearbook*; *International Trade Statistics Yearbook*; *National Accounts Statistics: Main Aggregates and Detailed Tables*; *Population and Vital Statistics Reports* (quarterly); the *Monthly Bulletin of Statistics*; and the *Energy Statistics Yearbook*. Specialized agencies of the United Nations also issue international summary publications on agricultural, labor, health, and education statistics. Among these are the *Production Yearbook* and *Trade Yearbook* issued by the Food and Agriculture Organization, the *Yearbook of Labour Statistics* issued by the International Labour Office, *World Health Statistics* issued by the World Health Organization, and the *Statistical Yearbook* issued by the Educational, Scientific, and Cultural Organization.

The U.S. Census Bureau presents estimates and projections of basic demographic measures for countries and regions of the world in the *World Population Reports* (WP) series. The *International Population Reports* (Series IPC), and *International Briefs* (Series IB) also present population figures for many foreign

countries. Detailed population statistics are also available from the Census Bureau's International Data Base (http://www.census.gov/ipc/www/idb new.html>.

The International Monetary Fund (IMF) and the Organization for Economic Cooperation and Development (OECD) also compile data on international statistics. The IMF publishes a series of reports relating to financial data. These include *International Financial Statistics, Direction of Trade*, and *Balance of Payments Yearbook*, published in English, French, and Spanish. The OECD publishes a vast number of statistical publications in various fields such as economics, health, and education. Among these are *OECD in Figures, Main Economic Indicators, Economic Outlook, National Accounts, Labour Force Statistics, OECD Health Data*, and *Education at a Glance*.

Statistical coverage, country names, and classifications—Problems of space and availability of data limit the number of countries and the extent of statistical coverage shown. The list of countries included and the spelling of country names are based almost entirely on the list of sovereign nations, dependencies, and areas of special sovereignty provided by the U.S. Department of State.

In recent years, several important changes took place in the status of the world's nations. In 1990, a unified Germany was formed from the Federal Republic of Germany (West) and the German Democratic Republic (East). The Republic of Yemen was formed by union of the Yemen Arab Republic and the People's Democratic Republic of Yemen. Also in 1990, Namibia, once a United Nations mandate, realized its independence from South Africa.

In 1991, the Soviet Union broke up into 15 independent countries: Armenia, Azerbaijan, Belarus, Estonia, Georgia, Kazakhstan, Kyrgyzstan, Latvia, Lithuania,

Moldova, Russia, Tajikistan, Turkmenistan, Ukraine, and Uzbekistan.

Following the breakup of the Socialist Federal Republic of Yugoslavia in 1992, the United States recognized Bosnia and Herzegovina, Croatia, Slovenia, and The Former Yugoslav Republic of Macedonia as independent countries.

On January 1, 1993, Czechoslovakia was succeeded by two independent countries: the Czech Republic and Slovakia. Eritrea announced its independence from Ethiopia in April 1993 and was subsequently recognized as an independent nation by the United States.

The population estimates and projections used in Tables 1324, 1325, 1327, 1328 and 1330 were prepared by the Census Bureau. For each country, the data on population, by age and sex, fertility, mortality, and international migration were evaluated and, where necessary, adjusted for inconsistencies and errors in the data. In most instances, comprehensive projections were made by the component method, resulting in distributions of the population by age and sex and requiring an assessment of probable future trends of fertility, mortality, and international migration.

Economic associations—The Organization for European Economic Co-Operation (OEEC), a regional grouping of Western European countries established in 1948 for the purpose of harmonizing national economic policies and conditions, was succeeded on September 30, 1961, by the Organization for Economic Cooperation and Development (OECD). The member nations of the OECD are Australia, Austria, Belgium, Canada, Czech Republic, Denmark, Finland, France, Germany, Greece, Hungary, Iceland, Ireland, Italy, Japan, Luxembourg, Mexico, the Netherlands, New Zealand, Norway, Poland, Portugal, Slovakia, South Korea, Spain, Sweden, Switzerland, Turkey, the United Kingdom, and the United States.

Quality and comparability of the data—The quality and comparability of the data presented here are affected by a number of factors:

(1) The year for which data are presented may not be the same for all subjects for a particular country or for a given subject for different countries, though the data shown are the most recent available. All such variations have been noted. The data shown are for calendar years except as otherwise specified.

(2) The bases, methods of estimating, methods of data collection, extent of coverage, precision of definition, scope of territory, and margins of error may vary for different items within a particular country, and for like items for different countries. Footnotes and headnotes to the tables give a few of the major time-periods and coverage qualifications attached to the figures; considerably more detail is presented in the source publications. Many of the measures shown are, at best, merely rough indicators of magnitude.

(3) Figures shown in this section for the United States may not always agree with figures shown in the preceding sections. Disagreements may be attributable to the use of differing original sources, a difference in the definition of geographic limits (the 50 states, conterminous United States only, or the United States including certain outlying areas and possessions), or to possible adjustments made in the United States figures by other sources in order to make them more comparable with figures from other countries.

International comparisons of national accounts data—In order to compare national accounts data for different countries, it is necessary to convert each country's data into a common unit of currency, usually the U.S. dollar. The market exchange rates which are often used in converting national currencies do not necessarily reflect the relative purchasing power in the various countries. It is necessary that the goods and services produced in different countries be valued consistently if the differences observed are meant to reflect real differences in the volumes of goods and services produced. The use of purchasing power parities (see Table 1340) instead of exchange rates is intended to achieve this objective.

U.S. Census Bureau, Statistical Abstract of the United States: 2001

The method used to present the data shown in Table 1340 is to construct volume measures directly by revaluing the goods and services sold in different countries at a common set of international prices. By dividing the ratio of the gross domestic products of two countries expressed in their own national currencies by the corresponding ratio calculated at constant international prices, it is possible to derive the implied purchasing power parity (PPP) between the two currencies concerned. PPPs show how many units of currency are needed in one country to buy the same amount of goods and services which one unit of currency will buy in the other country. For further information, see *National Accounts, Main Aggregates, Volume I*, issued annually by the Organization for Economic Cooperation and Development, Paris, France.

International Standard Industrial Classification—The original version of the International Standard Industrial Classification of All Economic Activities (ISIC) was adopted in 1948. Wide use has been made both nationally and internationally in classifying data according to kind of economic activity in the fields of production, employment, national income, and other economic statistics. A number of countries have utilized the ISIC as the basis for devising their industrial classification scheme.

Substantial comparability has been attained between the industrial classifications of many other countries, including the United States and the ISIC by ensuring, as far as practicable, that the categories at detailed levels of classification in national schemes fitted into only one category of the ISIC. The United Nations, the International Labour Organization, the Food and Agriculture Organization, and other international bodies have utilized the ISIC in publishing and analyzing statistical data. Revisions of the ISIC were issued in 1958, 1968, and 1989.

International maps—A series of regional world maps is provided on pages 822-828. References are included in Table 1327 for easy location of individual countries on the maps. The Robinson map projection is used for this series of maps. A map projection is used to portray all or part of the round Earth on a flat surface, but this cannot be done without some distortion. For the Robinson projection, distortion is very low along the Equator and within 45 degrees of the center but is greatest near the poles. For additional information on map projections and maps, please contact the Earth Science Information Center, U.S. Geological Survey, 507 National Center, Reston, VA 22092.

U.S. Census Bureau, Statistical Abstract of the United States: 2001

S0

S1

Arctic Ocean

Pacific Ocean

United States

Canada

Greenland

Atlantic Ocean

See Inset

S2

Brazil

S4

Mali

Algeria

Libya

S3

Sudan

Saudi Arabia

Iran

Kazakhstan

Russia

Mongolia

China

Madagascar

Indian Ocean

India

Australia

Philippines

Japan

New Zealand

Arctic Ocean

Pacific Ocean

S5

S6

Inset

Kiribati

Samoa

American Samoa

Tonga

Cook Islands

French Polynesia

U.S. Census Bureau, Statistical Abstract of the United States: 2001

S1

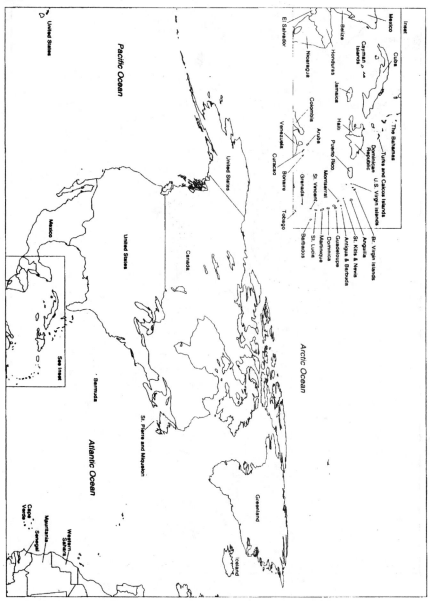

U.S. Census Bureau, Statistical Abstract of the United States: 2001

S5

U.S. Census Bureau, Statistical Abstract of the United States: 2001

No. 1324. Total World Population: 1980 to 2050

[4,457 represents 4,457,000,000. As of midyear]

Year	Population (mil.)	Average annual [1] Growth rate (percent)	Average annual [1] Population change (mil.)	Year	Population (mil.)	Average annual [1] Growth rate (percent)	Average annual [1] Population change (mil.)
1980	4,457	1.70	76.3	2015	7,176	0.97	69.6
1985	4,855	1.70	83.0	2020	7,518	0.88	66.4
1990	5,284	1.56	83.2	2025	7,841	0.78	61.7
1995	5,691	1.36	77.7	2030	8,140	0.70	57.2
2000	6,080	1.26	77.3	2035	8,417	0.62	52.3
2001	6,157	1.24	76.8	2040	8,668	0.55	47.5
2005	6,461	1.14	73.8	2045	8,897	0.48	43.2
2010	6,824	1.03	70.8	2050	9,104	(NA)	(NA)

NA Not available. [1] Represents change from year shown to immediate succeeding year.

Source: U.S. Census Bureau, "Total Midyear Population for the World: 1950-2050," published 10 May 2000; <http://www.census.gov/ipc/www/worldpop.html>.

No. 1325. Population by Continent: 1980 to 2050

[In millions, except percent (4,457 represents 4,457,000,000)]

Year	World	Africa	North America	South America	Asia	Europe	Oceania
1980	4,457	472	373	242	2,654	694	23
1990	5,284	629	424	296	3,186	721	27
2000	6,080	805	481	347	3,688	729	31
2010	6,824	985	534	387	4,155	728	35
2020	7,518	1,173	587	421	4,578	722	38
2030	8,140	1,378	636	449	4,931	705	41
2040	8,668	1,603	682	468	5,194	678	44
2050	9,104	1,846	722	480	5,369	642	45
PERCENT DISTRIBUTION							
1980	100.0	10.6	8.4	5.4	59.5	15.6	0.5
2000	100.0	13.2	7.9	5.7	60.7	12.0	0.5
2050	100.0	20.3	7.9	5.3	59.0	7.1	0.5

Source: U.S. Census Bureau, "International Data Base" (as of 10 May 2000); <http://www.census.gov/ipc/www/idbnew.html>.

No. 1326. World Summary: 1980 to 1999

[4.8 represents 4,800,000. See text of this section for general comments concerning quality of the data]

Item	Unit	1980	1985	1990	1994	1995	1996	1997	1998	1999
Agriculture, forestry, fishing:										
Coffee	Mil. metric tons	4.8	5.8	6.1	5.8	5.5	6.2	6.0	6.5	6.7
Cotton (lint)	Mil. metric tons	13.9	17.3	18.4	18.7	20.3	19.2	19.0	18.1	18.3
Tobacco	Mil. metric tons	5.3	7.1	7.1	6.4	6.3	7.4	9.0	6.9	7.0
Roundwood	Mil. cubic meters	2,920	3,167	3,326	3,162	3,214	3,219	3,298	3,550	3,591
Fish catches	Mil. metric tons	72.3	87.2	99.0	113.5	117.3	120.3	122.4	117.2	(NA)
Textile fiber production, total [1]	Billion pounds	67.4	77.0	87.2	90.9	96.0	96.9	103.6	102.3	105.7
Rayon and acetate	Billion pounds	7.1	6.5	6.1	5.1	5.3	5.0	5.1	4.8	4.7
Noncellulosic fibers	Billion pounds	23.1	27.5	32.8	39.5	40.5	43.6	49.4	51.6	53.9
Cotton	Billion pounds	31.4	38.5	41.8	41.2	44.7	43.2	44.2	41.1	42.3
Wool, clean	Billion pounds	3.7	3.8	4.4	3.4	3.3	3.3	3.2	3.1	3.0
Silk	Billion pounds	0.1	0.2	0.1	0.2	0.2	0.2	0.2	0.2	0.2
Flax [2]	Billion pounds	1.4	1.6	1.6	1.3	1.5	1.4	1.4	1.4	1.4
Hemp [2]	Billion pounds	0.6	0.5	0.4	0.2	0.2	0.1	0.1	0.2	0.2
Industrial production:										
Wine	Mil. hectoliters	352.1	309.5	279.6	238.3	241.9	270.0	265.0	262.0	284.0
Sugar	Mil. metric tons	79.0	90.8	111.2	108.0	118.5	125.8	126.4	129.5	134.3
Wheat flour	Mil. metric tons	229.7	267.9	242.5	247.9	241.7	253.8	254.4	253.3	(NA)
Pig iron and ferroalloys [3]	Mil. metric tons	542	507	522	505	523	515	538	532	(NA)
Crude steel [4]	Mil. metric tons	699	685	773	716	736	731	741	721	(NA)
Sawnwood [5]	Mil. cubic meters	451	468	505	433	426	431	431	421	434
Woodpulp [6]	Mil. metric tons	125.8	141.8	155.1	161.9	161.7	156.4	162.5	160.1	163.2
Newsprint	Mil. metric tons	25.4	28.3	30.2	34.3	35.8	35.3	38.3	37.7	(NA)
Merchant vessels, launched	Mil. gross tons	13.9	17.3	14.8	16.3	23.0	15.5	22.2	23.0	(NA)
External trade:										
Imports, c.i.f	Bil. U.S. dollars	2,045	1,998	3,557	4,279	5,053	5,311	5,533	5,450	5,665
Exports, f.o.b	Bil. U.S. dollars	2,001	1,921	3,438	4,229	5,008	5,206	5,448	5,371	5,546
Civil aviation, kilometers flown [7]	Millions	(NA)	(NA)	(NA)	18,249	19,470	20,601	21,635	22,430	(NA)

NA Not available. [1] Source: U.S. Dept. of Agriculture, Economic Research Service, Cotton and Wool Situation and Outlook Yearbook. Data from International Wool Textile Organization. [2] Beginning 1996 not comparable with earlier years. [3] Pig iron (foundry and steel making) plus other ferro alloys (spiegeleisen and ferro-manganese). [4] Castings and ingots. [5] Broadleaved and coniferous. [6] Mechanical plus dissolving grades plus sulphate and soda plus sulphate and semi-chemical. [7] Scheduled services of members of International Civil Aviation Organization.

Source: Except as noted, Statistical Division of the United Nations, New York, NY, Monthly Bulletin of Statistics, (copyright).

Comparative International Statistics 829

Figure 30.1
Population by Continent: 2000 and 2050

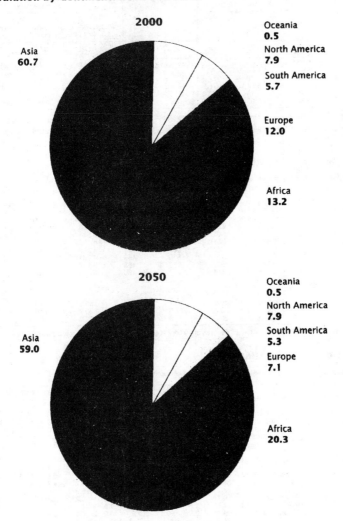

2000

Oceania
0.5

North America
7.9

South America
5.7

Asia
60.7

Europe
12.0

Africa
13.2

2050

Oceania
0.5

North America
7.9

South America
5.3

Asia
59.0

Europe
7.1

Africa
20.3

Source: Chart prepared by U.S. Census Bureau. For data, see Table 1325.

U.S. Census Bureau, Statistical Abstract of the United States: 2001

No. 1327. Population by Country: 1990 to 2010

[5,283,755 represents 5,283,755,000. Population data generally are de facto figures for the present territory. Population estimates were derived from information available as of spring 2000. See text of this section for general comments concerning the data. For details of methodology, coverage, and reliability, see source. Minus sign (-) indicates decrease]

Country or area	Map refer-ence	Midyear population (1,000)				Popu-lation rank, 2001	Annual rate of growth, 2000-2010 (percent)	Popula-tion per sq. mile, 2001	Area (sq. mile)
		1990	2000	2001	2010, proj.				
World..........	S0	5,283,755	6,080,142	6,157,401	6,823,635	(X)	1.2	122	50,580,319
Afghanistan........	S5	14,750	25,889	26,813	33,864	39	2.7	107	250,000
Albania.........	S3	3,258	3,490	3,510	3,827	128	0.9	332	10,579
Algeria.........	S4	25,341	31,194	31,736	36,589	34	1.6	35	919,591
Andorra.........	S3	53	67	68	74	204	1.0	388	174
Angola..........	S4	8,056	10,145	10,366	12,646	71	2.2	22	481,351
Antigua and Barbuda.......	S1	63	66	67	71	206	0.6	394	170
Argentina........	S2	32,634	36,955	37,385	41,082	31	1.1	35	1,056,637
Armenia.........	S5	3,368	3,344	3,336	3,365	130	0.1	290	11,506
Australia........	S6	17,022	19,165	19,358	20,925	53	0.9	7	2,941,285
Austria.........	S3	7,718	8,131	8,151	8,278	86	0.2	255	31,942
Azerbaijan.......	S5	7,200	7,748	7,771	8,221	87	0.6	232	33,436
Bahamas, The	S1	257	295	298	315	176	0.7	77	3,888
Bahrain.........	S4	500	634	645	737	162	1.5	2,700	239
Bangladesh.......	S5	109,897	129,194	131,270	150,392	8	1.5	2,539	51,703
Barbados........	S1	263	274	275	287	178	0.4	1,658	166
Belarus.........	S3	10,215	10,367	10,350	10,294	73	-0.1	129	80,154
Belgium.........	S3	9,969	10,242	10,259	10,340	76	0.1	879	11,672
Belize..........	S1	191	249	256	320	179	2.5	29	8,803
Benin..........	S4	4,656	6,396	6,591	8,411	95	2.7	154	42,710
Bhutan.........	S5	1,598	2,005	2,049	2,476	142	2.1	113	18,147
Bolivia.........	S2	6,574	8,153	8,300	9,499	85	1.5	20	418,683
Bosnia and Herzegovina.....	S3	4,424	3,836	3,922	4,103	121	0.7	199	19,741
Botswana........	S4	1,304	1,576	1,586	1,502	147	-0.5	7	226,012
Brazil..........	S2	151,053	172,860	174,469	186,823	5	0.8	53	3,265,061
Brunei..........	S6	258	336	344	408	174	1.9	169	2,035
Bulgaria.........	S3	8,894	7,797	7,707	7,006	88	-1.1	181	42,683
Burkina Faso.......	S4	9,037	11,946	12,272	15,424	65	2.6	116	105,714
Burma..........	S5	38,519	41,735	41,995	43,674	27	0.5	165	253,954
Burundi.........	S4	5,285	6,055	6,224	7,669	99	2.4	628	9,903
Cambodia........	S5	8,965	12,212	12,492	15,233	64	2.2	183	68,154
Cameroon........	S4	11,761	15,422	15,803	19,202	60	2.2	87	181,251
Canada.........	S1	27,791	31,278	31,593	34,253	35	0.9	9	3,560,219
Cape Verde	S1	349	401	405	431	172	0.7	260	1,556
Central African Republic.....	S4	2,803	3,513	3,577	4,135	127	1.6	15	240,533
Chad..........	S4	6,018	8,425	8,707	11,616	83	3.2	18	486,178
Chile..........	S2	13,128	15,154	15,328	16,727	61	1.0	53	289,112
China [2]	S5	1,138,895	1,261,832	1,273,111	1,359,141	1	0.7	354	3,600,930
Colombia........	S2	32,859	39,686	40,349	46,109	28	1.5	101	401,042
Comoros........	S4	429	578	596	773	163	2.9	712	838
Congo (Brazzaville) [3]......	S4	2,218	2,831	2,894	3,491	132	2.1	22	131,853
Congo (Kinshasa) [3]......	S4	37,991	51,965	53,625	69,846	23	3.0	61	875,521
Costa Rica........	S2	3,027	3,711	3,773	4,306	124	1.5	193	19,560
Cote d'Ivoire.......	S4	11,919	15,981	16,393	20,003	57	2.2	134	122,780
Croatia.........	S3	4,508	4,282	4,334	4,505	117	0.5	199	21,829
Cuba..........	S1	10,545	11,142	11,184	11,526	67	0.3	261	42,803
Cyprus.........	S5	681	758	763	801	158	0.5	214	3,568
Czech Republic.......	S3	10,310	10,272	10,264	10,157	75	-0.1	338	30,365
Denmark........	S3	5,141	5,336	5,353	5,474	105	0.3	327	16,359
Djibouti.........	S4	370	451	461	579	166	2.5	54	8,486
Dominica........	S1	73	72	71	70	202	-0.2	244	290
Dominican Republic......	S1	7,098	8,443	8,581	9,884	84	1.6	459	18,680
Ecuador.........	S2	10,317	12,920	13,184	15,518	62	1.8	123	106,888
Egypt..........	S4	56,106	68,360	69,537	79,811	15	1.5	181	384,344
El Salvador.......	S1	5,100	6,123	6,238	7,293	98	1.7	780	8,000
Equatorial Guinea	S4	368	474	486	604	164	2.4	45	10,830
Eritrea.........	S4	2,945	4,136	4,298	5,709	119	3.2	92	46,842
Estonia.........	S3	1,573	1,431	1,423	1,372	148	-0.4	82	17,413
Ethiopia.........	S4	48,335	64,117	65,892	82,312	18	2.5	152	432,310
Fiji...........	S6	738	832	844	958	156	1.4	120	7,054
Finland.........	S3	4,986	5,167	5,176	5,228	107	0.1	44	117,942
France.........	S3	56,735	59,330	59,551	61,069	21	0.3	283	210,668
Gabon.........	S4	1,069	1,208	1,221	1,309	151	0.8	12	99,486
Gambia, The	S4	962	1,367	1,411	1,833	149	2.9	366	3,861
Georgia.........	S5	5,457	5,020	4,989	4,815	111	-0.4	185	26,911
Germany........	S3	79,380	82,797	83,030	84,616	12	0.2	614	135,236
Ghana..........	S4	15,360	19,534	19,894	22,650	50	1.5	224	88,811
Greece.........	S3	10,158	10,602	10,624	10,758	69	0.1	210	50,502
Grenada........	S2	92	89	89	91	197	0.2	682	131
Guatemala........	S1	9,630	12,640	12,974	16,194	63	2.5	310	41,865
Guinea.........	S4	5,936	7,466	7,614	9,281	89	2.2	80	94,927
Guinea-Bissau......	S4	996	1,286	1,316	1,614	150	2.3	122	10,811
Guyana.........	S2	742	697	697	729	160	0.4	9	76,004
Haiti..........	S1	6,028	6,868	6,965	7,950	94	1.5	655	10,641
Honduras........	S1	4,772	6,250	6,406	7,683	97	2.1	148	43,201
Hungary........	S3	10,372	10,139	10,106	9,831	77	-0.3	283	35,653
Iceland.........	S1	255	276	278	289	177	0.4	7	38,707
India..........	S5	850,558	1,014,004	1,029,991	1,168,205	2	1.4	897	1,147,950
Indonesia........	S6	188,651	224,784	228,438	259,743	4	1.4	324	705,189
Iran..........	S5	55,717	65,620	66,129	73,772	17	1.2	105	631,660

See footnotes at end of table.

U.S. Census Bureau, Statistical Abstract of the United States: 2001

No. 1327. Population by Country: 1990 to 2010—Con.

[See headnote, page 831]

Country or area	Map refer- ence	Midyear population (1,000)				Popu- lation rank, 2001	Annual rate of growth,[1] 2000- 2010 (percent)	Popula- tion per sq. mile, 2001	Area (sq. mile)
		1990	2000	2001	2010, proj.				
Iraq	S5	18,135	22,676	23,332	29,672	44	2.7	139	167,556
Ireland	S3	3,508	3,797	3,841	4,161	123	0.9	144	26,598
Israel	S4	4,512	5,842	5,938	6,645	100	1.3	757	7,849
Italy	S3	56,758	57,634	57,680	57,409	22	-	508	113,521
Jamaica	S1	2,463	2,653	2,666	2,851	135	0.7	638	4,181
Japan	S5	123,537	126,550	126,772	127,252	9	0.1	832	152,411
Jordan	S4	3,262	4,999	5,153	6,486	108	2.6	146	35,344
Kazakhstan	S5	16,708	16,733	16,731	17,276	55	0.3	16	1,049,150
Kenya	S4	23,767	30,340	30,766	33,068	36	0.9	140	219,788
Kiribati	S6	71	92	94	115	195	2.3	340	277
Korea, North	S5	20,019	21,688	21,968	23,753	49	0.9	473	46,490
Korea, South	S5	42,869	47,471	47,904	51,097	25	0.7	1,264	37,911
Kuwait	S5	2,142	1,974	2,042	2,788	144	3.5	297	6,880
Kyrgyzstan	S5	4,390	4,685	4,753	5,444	113	1.5	62	76,641
Laos	S5	4,210	5,497	5,636	6,993	102	2.4	63	89,112
Latvia	S3	2,672	2,405	2,385	2,252	139	-0.7	96	24,903
Lebanon	S4	3,147	3,578	3,628	4,056	125	1.3	918	3,950
Lesotho	S4	1,732	2,143	2,177	2,339	140	0.9	186	11,718
Liberia	S4	2,190	3,164	3,226	4,073	131	2.5	87	37,189
Libya	S4	4,140	5,115	5,241	6,447	106	2.3	8	679,359
Liechtenstein	S3	29	32	33	35	213	0.8	523	62
Lithuania	S5	3,702	3,621	3,611	3,560	126	-0.2	143	25,174
Luxembourg	S3	382	437	443	493	168	1.2	444	998
Macedonia, The Former Yugoslav Republic of	S3	1,893	2,041	2,046	2,115	143	0.4	206	9,928
Madagascar	S4	11,522	15,506	15,983	20,993	58	3.0	71	224,533
Malawi	S4	9,219	10,386	10,548	11,621	70	1.1	290	36,324
Malaysia	S6	17,504	21,793	22,229	26,144	48	1.8	175	126,853
Maldives	S5	216	301	311	400	175	2.8	2,683	116
Mali	S4	8,228	10,686	11,009	14,349	68	2.9	23	471,042
Malta	S4	359	392	395	420	173	0.7	3,184	124
Marshall Islands	S6	46	68	71	100	201	3.9	1,013	70
Mauritania	S4	1,984	2,668	2,747	3,561	134	2.9	7	397,838
Mauritius	S4	1,074	1,179	1,190	1,280	152	0.8	1,667	714
Mexico	S1	84,446	100,350	101,879	114,995	11	1.4	137	742,486
Micronesia, Federated States of	S6	109	133	135	141	191	0.6	497	271
Moldova	S5	4,398	4,431	4,432	4,535	116	0.2	341	13,012
Monaco	S3	30	32	32	33	214	0.4	41,235	1
Mongolia	S5	2,218	2,616	2,655	3,040	136	1.5	4	604,247
Morocco	S4	24,686	30,122	30,645	35,301	37	1.6	178	172,317
Mozambique	S4	14,276	19,105	19,371	20,504	52	0.7	64	302,737
Namibia	S4	1,409	1,771	1,798	1,908	146	0.7	6	317,873
Nauru	S6	9	12	12	14	223	1.9	1,491	8
Nepal	S5	19,325	24,702	25,284	30,758	40	2.2	479	52,819
Netherlands	S3	14,952	15,892	15,981	16,617	59	0.4	1,220	13,104
New Zealand	S6	3,360	3,820	3,864	4,228	122	1.0	37	103,734
Nicaragua	S2	3,643	4,813	4,918	5,839	112	1.9	106	46,430
Niger	S4	7,627	10,076	10,355	13,140	72	2.7	21	489,073
Nigeria	S4	92,483	123,338	126,636	155,588	10	2.3	360	351,649
Norway	S3	4,242	4,481	4,503	4,677	115	0.4	38	118,865
Oman	S5	1,773	2,533	2,622	3,523	137	3.3	32	82,031
Pakistan	S5	113,975	141,554	144,617	171,373	7	1.9	481	300,664
Palau	S6	15	19	19	22	219	1.4	108	177
Panama	S2	2,388	2,808	2,846	3,150	133	1.1	97	29,340
Papua New Guinea	S6	3,825	4,927	5,049	6,171	110	2.3	29	174,405
Paraguay	S2	4,236	5,586	5,734	7,162	101	2.5	37	153,398
Peru	S2	21,989	27,013	27,484	31,471	38	1.5	56	494,208
Philippines	S6	65,037	81,160	82,842	97,898	13	1.9	720	115,124
Poland	S3	38,119	38,646	38,634	38,691	30	-	329	117,571
Portugal	S3	9,923	10,048	10,066	10,183	78	0.1	285	35,382
Qatar	S5	481	744	769	970	157	2.6	181	4,247
Romania	S5	22,866	22,411	22,364	21,920	47	-0.2	251	88,934
Russia	S5	148,082	146,001	145,470	142,328	6	-0.3	22	6,592,817
Rwanda	S4	6,962	7,229	7,313	7,876	91	0.9	759	9,633
Saint Kitts and Nevis	S1	41	39	39	40	211	0.4	279	139
Saint Lucia	S1	140	156	158	177	189	1.3	671	236
Saint Vincent and the Grenadines	S1	107	115	116	119	193	0.3	886	131
Samoa	S0	170	179	179	176	185	-0.2	163	1,100
San Marino	S3	23	27	27	31	216	1.3	1,180	23
Sao Tome and Principe	S4	119	160	165	219	187	3.1	445	371
Saudi Arabia	S4	15,847	22,024	22,757	30,546	45	3.3	27	829,996
Senegal	S4	7,360	9,987	10,285	13,221	74	2.8	139	74,131
Seychelles	S4	73	79	80	83	198	0.4	453	176
Sierra Leone	S4	4,227	5,233	5,427	6,930	103	2.8	196	27,653
Singapore	S6	3,016	4,152	4,300	5,776	118	3.3	17,849	241
Slovakia	S3	5,263	5,408	5,415	5,475	104	0.1	287	18,842
Slovenia	S3	1,896	1,928	1,930	1,947	145	0.1	247	7,819
Solomon Islands	S6	335	466	480	610	165	2.7	45	10,633
Somalia	S4	6,675	7,253	7,489	9,922	90	3.1	31	242,216
South Africa	S4	38,176	43,421	43,586	41,108	26	-0.5	92	471,444
Spain	S3	39,351	39,997	40,038	40,157	29	-	208	192,819
Sri Lanka	S5	17,193	19,239	19,409	20,832	51	0.8	776	24,996

See footnotes at end of table.

U.S. Census Bureau, Statistical Abstract of the United States: 2001

[See headnote, page 831]

Country or area	Map refer-ence	Midyear population (1,000)				Popu-lation rank, 2001	Annual rate of growth, 2000-2010 (percent)	Popula-tion per sq. mile, 2001	Area (sq. mile)
		1990	2000	2001	2010, proj.				
Sudan	S4	26,627	35,080	36,080	45,485	33	2.6	39	917,375
Suriname	S2	395	431	434	450	169	0.4	7	62,344
Swaziland	S4	852	1,083	1,104	1,216	155	1.2	166	6,641
Sweden	S3	8,559	8,873	8,875	8,882	82	-	56	158,927
Switzerland	S3	6,838	7,262	7,283	7,385	92	0.2	474	15,355
Syria	S4	12,436	16,306	16,729	20,606	56	2.3	235	71,062
Tajikistan	S5	5,332	6,441	6,579	8,007	96	2.2	119	55,251
Tanzania	S4	26,224	35,306	36,232	44,957	32	2.4	106	342,100
Thailand	S5	55,052	61,231	61,798	66,291	19	0.8	313	197,595
Togo	S4	3,691	5,019	5,153	6,245	109	2.2	245	21,000
Tonga	S0	92	102	104	123	194	1.8	376	277
Trinidad and Tobago	S2	1,198	1,176	1,170	1,115	154	-0.5	590	1,981
Tunisia	S4	8,207	9,593	9,705	10,661	81	1.1	162	59,985
Turkey	S5	56,085	65,667	66,494	73,322	16	1.1	223	297,591
Turkmenistan	S5	3,668	4,518	4,603	5,431	114	1.8	24	188,456
Tuvalu	S6	9	11	11	13	224	1.5	1,095	10
Uganda	S4	17,186	23,318	23,986	31,395	42	3.0	311	77,108
Ukraine	S5	51,658	49,153	48,760	46,193	24	-0.6	209	233,089
United Arab Emirates	S5	1,951	2,369	2,407	2,763	138	1.5	75	32,278
United Kingdom	S3	57,621	59,508	59,648	60,602	20	0.2	639	93,278
United States	S1	249,948	275,563	278,059	300,118	3	0.9	79	3,539,227
Uruguay	S2	3,106	3,334	3,360	3,600	129	0.8	50	67,035
Uzbekistan	S5	20,624	24,756	25,155	29,280	41	1.7	146	172,741
Vanuatu	S6	154	190	193	221	184	1.5	34	5,699
Venezuela	S2	19,325	23,543	23,917	27,134	43	1.4	70	340,560
Vietnam	S5	66,338	78,774	79,939	90,192	14	1.4	636	125,622
Yemen	S5	12,023	17,479	18,078	24,637	54	3.4	89	203,849
Zambia	S4	7,851	9,582	9,770	11,482	80	1.8	34	285,992
Zimbabwe	S4	10,103	11,343	11,365	11,057	66	-0.3	76	149,293
OTHER									
Montenegro	S3	565	680	674	713	161	0.5	126	5,333
Serbia	S3	9,201	9,982	10,003	9,954	79	-	293	34,116
Taiwan [2]	S5	20,279	22,191	22,370	23,873	46	0.7	1,796	12,456
AREAS OF SPECIAL SOVEREIGNTY AND DEPENDENCIES									
American Samoa	S0	47	65	67	81	205	2.1	873	77
Anguilla	S1	8	12	12	14	222	1.8	345	35
Aruba	S1	67	70	70	73	203	0.5	939	75
Bermuda	S1	58	63	64	67	208	0.6	3,357	19
Cayman Islands	S1	26	35	36	42	212	1.8	354	100
Cook Islands	S0	18	20	21	22	218	0.9	222	93
Faroe Islands	S3	47	45	46	48	210	0.6	84	541
French Guiana	S2	116	173	178	214	186	2.1	5	34,421
French Polynesia	S0	202	249	254	291	180	1.5	179	1,413
Gaza Strip [4]	S4	643	1,132	1,178	1,651	153	3.8	8,009	147
Gibraltar	S3	29	28	28	28	215	0.2	11,935	2
Greenland	S1	56	56	56	56	209	-	(Z)	131,931
Guadeloupe	S1	378	426	431	468	170	0.9	634	680
Guam	S6	134	155	158	184	190	1.7	754	209
Guernsey	S3	63	64	64	66	207	0.3	859	75
Hong Kong	S5	5,688	7,116	7,211	7,981	93	1.1	18,883	382
Jersey	S3	84	89	89	92	196	0.3	1,978	45
Macau	S6	352	446	454	527	167	1.7	73,448	6
Man, Isle of	S3	69	73	73	77	200	0.5	324	227
Martinique	S1	374	415	418	448	171	0.8	1,023	409
Mayotte	S4	90	156	163	231	188	3.9	1,125	145
Montserrat	S1	11	6	8	10	225	4.3	196	39
Netherlands Antilles	S2	189	210	212	228	182	0.8	572	371
New Caledonia	S6	168	202	205	230	183	1.3	28	7,243
Northern Mariana Islands	S6	44	72	75	99	199	3.1	405	184
Puerto Rico	S1	3,537	3,916	3,937	4,088	120	0.4	1,138	3,459
Reunion	S4	597	721	733	829	159	1.4	759	965
Saint Helena	S4	7	7	7	8	226	0.6	46	158
Saint Pierre and Miquelon	S1	6	7	7	7	227	0.2	74	93
Turks and Caicos Islands	S1	12	18	18	24	220	3.0	109	166
Virgin Islands	S1	104	121	122	133	192	1.0	904	135
Virgin Islands, British	S1	16	20	21	25	217	2.0	359	58
Wallis and Futuna	S6	14	15	15	17	221	0.9	146	106
West Bank [4]	S4	1,255	2,020	2,091	2,765	141	3.1	960	2,178
Western Sahara	S4	191	245	251	301	181	2.1	2	102,703

- Represents or rounds to zero. X Not applicable. Z Less than one person per square mile. [1] Computed by the exponential method. For explanation of average annual percent change, see Guide to Tabular Presentation. [2] With the establishment of diplomatic relations with China on January 1, 1979, the U.S. government recognized the People's Republic of China as the sole legal government of China and acknowledged the Chinese position that there is only one China and that Taiwan is part of China. [3] "Congo" is the official short-form name for both the Republic of Congo and the Democratic Republic of the Congo. To distinguish one from the other the U.S. Dept. of State adds the capital in parentheses. This practice is unofficial and provisional. [4] The Gaza Strip and West Bank are Israeli occupied with interim status subject to Israeli/Palestinian negotiations. The final status is to be determined.

Source: U.S. Census Bureau, "International Data Base" (as of 10 May 2000); <http://www.census.gov/ipc/www/idbnew.html>.

Comparative International Statistics   833

No. 1328. Age Distribution by Country: 2001 and 2010

[In percent. Covers countries with 10 million or more population in 2001]

Country or area	2001 Under 15 yrs. old	2001 65 yrs. old and over	2010, proj. Under 15 yrs. old	2010, proj. 65 yrs. old and over	Country or area	2001 Under 15 yrs. old	2001 65 yrs. old and over	2010, proj. Under 15 yrs. old	2010, proj. 65 yrs. old and over
World	29.6	7.0	30.0	8.6	Korea, South	21.6	7.3	21.6	10.6
Afghanistan	42.2	2.8	53.0	3.9	Madagascar	45.0	3.2	60.2	3.9
Algeria	34.2	4.1	33.5	5.2	Malawi	44.4	2.8	45.0	3.4
Angola	43.3	2.7	53.4	3.4	Malaysia	34.5	4.2	37.2	6.1
Argentina	26.5	10.4	27.3	12.3	Mali	47.2	3.1	62.1	3.8
Australia	20.6	12.5	20.4	15.2	Mexico	33.3	4.4	33.2	6.3
Bangladesh	35.0	3.4	34.5	4.5	Morocco	34.4	4.7	34.7	6.1
Belarus	17.9	13.9	15.5	13.5	Mozambique	42.7	2.8	43.1	3.5
Belgium	17.5	16.9	16.1	18.1	Nepal	40.3	3.5	46.5	4.8
Brazil	28.6	5.5	26.4	7.5	Netherlands	18.4	13.7	17.6	16.0
Burkina Faso	47.5	2.9	59.1	3.5	Niger	48.0	2.3	60.0	3.0
Burma	29.1	4.8	26.5	5.5	Nigeria	43.7	2.8	53.5	3.8
Cambodia	41.3	3.5	47.3	4.5	Pakistan	40.5	4.1	41.9	5.3
Cameroon	42.4	3.4	49.5	4.7	Peru	34.4	4.8	34.3	6.7
Canada	18.9	12.8	18.2	15.5	Philippines	36.9	3.7	40.1	5.2
Chile	27.3	7.4	25.1	10.2	Poland	18.4	12.4	15.7	13.1
China [1]	25.0	7.1	22.5	8.9	Portugal	17.0	15.6	16.8	17.1
Colombia	31.9	4.8	33.1	6.6	Romania	17.9	13.5	15.5	14.1
Congo (Kinshasa) [2]	48.2	2.5	63.2	3.2	Russia	17.4	12.8	14.9	12.7
Cote d'Ivoire	46.2	2.2	54.9	3.1	Saudi Arabia	42.5	2.7	58.0	5.1
Cuba	21.0	9.9	18.1	12.5	Senegal	44.1	3.1	53.6	4.0
Czech Republic	16.1	13.9	13.2	15.8	Serbia	19.7	15.1	18.2	15.5
Ecuador	35.8	4.4	37.9	6.0	South Africa	32.0	4.9	26.8	5.8
Egypt	34.6	3.8	34.9	5.2	Spain	14.6	17.2	13.9	18.5
Ethiopia	47.2	2.8	60.3	3.6	Sri Lanka	26.0	6.6	24.4	8.9
France	18.7	16.1	18.0	17.3	Sudan	44.6	2.1	52.8	3.5
Germany	15.6	16.6	14.3	20.1	Syria	39.9	3.2	44.8	4.3
Ghana	41.2	3.5	39.4	4.4	Taiwan [1]	21.2	8.8	21.4	11.1
Greece	15.0	17.7	14.7	19.8	Tanzania	44.8	2.9	54.6	3.9
Guatemala	42.1	3.6	50.4	4.9	Thailand	23.4	6.6	23.7	9.2
Hungary	16.6	14.7	13.9	15.6	Turkey	28.4	6.1	26.2	8.1
India	33.1	4.7	33.6	6.1	Uganda	51.1	2.1	66.0	2.6
Indonesia	30.3	4.6	31.9	6.7	Ukraine	17.3	14.1	14.4	13.9
Iran	33.0	4.6	28.5	5.3	United Kingdom	18.9	15.7	17.1	17.0
Iraq	41.6	3.1	50.3	3.9	United States	21.1	12.6	21.6	14.4
Italy	14.2	18.3	13.1	20.5	Uzbekistan	36.3	4.6	37.5	5.0
Japan	14.6	17.5	14.5	21.9	Venezuela	32.1	4.7	30.7	6.6
Kazakhstan	26.7	7.2	24.9	7.8	Vietnam	32.1	5.4	30.9	6.2
Kenya	41.9	2.8	38.0	3.7	Yemen	47.2	3.0	65.0	3.5
Korea, North	25.5	6.8	24.6	10.7	Zimbabwe	38.7	3.6	32.6	4.4

[1] See footnote 2, Table 1327.   [2] See footnote 3, Table 1327.
Source: U.S. Census Bureau, "International Data Base" (as of 10 May 2000); <http://www.census.gov/ipc/www/idbnew.html>.

No. 1329. Foreign or Foreign-Born Population and Labor Force in Selected OECD Countries: 1988 and 1998

[In Australia, Canada, and the United States the data refer to people present in the country who are foreign born. In the European countries and Japan they generally refer to foreigners and represent the nationalities of residents]

Country	Foreign population [1] Number (1,000) 1988	1998	Percent of total population 1988	1998	Foreign labor force [2] Number (1,000) 1988	1998	Percent of total labor force 1988	1998
United States [3]	[4]19,767	26,300	7.9	9.8	[4]11,565	16,100	9.4	11.7
Australia [3]	[5]3,965	4,394	22.9	23.4	[5]2,182	2,294	25.7	24.8
Austria	344	737	4.5	9.1	161	327	5.4	9.9
Belgium [3]	869	892	8.8	8.7	[6]291	375	7.2	8.8
Canada [3]	[5]4,343	[7]4,971	16.1	17.4	[5]2,681	[7]2,839	18.5	19.2
Denmark	142	256	2.8	4.8	65	[8]94	2.2	3.2
France	[9]3,714	[3]3,597	6.8	6.3	1,557	1,587	6.4	6.1
Germany	4,489	7,320	7.3	8.9	1,911	[8]2,522	7.0	9.1
Italy	645	1,250	1.1	2.1	[5]285	[10]332	1.3	1.7
Japan	941	1,512	0.8	1.2	[11]86	119	0.1	0.2
Luxembourg	106	153	27.4	35.6	[12]69	[12]135	39.9	57.7
Netherlands	624	662	4.2	4.2	176	[8]208	3.0	2.9
Spain	360	720	0.9	1.8	58	191	0.4	1.2
Sweden	421	500	5.0	5.6	220	219	4.9	5.1
Switzerland	1,007	1,348	15.2	19.0	[13]608	[13]691	16.7	17.3
United Kingdom	1,821	2,208	3.2	3.8	871	1,039	3.4	3.9

[1] Data are from population registers except for France (census), Ireland and the United Kingdom (labor force survey), Japan and Switzerland (register of foreigners) and Italy, Portugal, and Spain (residence permits).   [2] Includes unemployed except for Italy, Luxembourg, Netherlands, Norway and United Kingdom. Data for Austria, Germany, and Luxembourg are from social security registers, for Denmark from the register of population, for Norway from the register of employees. Data for Italy, Portugal, Spain, and Switzerland are from residence or work permits. Figures for Japan and Netherlands are estimates. Data for other countries are from labor force surveys.   [3] Census data, except 1998 data for United States from Current Population Survey.   [4] 1990 data.   [5] 1991 data.   [6] 1989 data.   [7] 1996 data.   [8] 1997 data.   [9] 1982 data.   [10] 1995 data.   [11] 1992 data.   [12] Includes cross-border workers.   [13] Foreigners with an annual residence permit or a settlement permit who engage in gainful activity. Seasonal and cross-border workers are excluded.
Source: Organization for Economic Cooperation and Development, Paris, France, Trends in International Migration (2000 Edition) (copyright).

No. 1330. Vital Statistics by Country: 2001 and 2010

[Covers countries with 10 million or more population in 2001]

Country or area	Crude birth rate [1] 2001	2010, proj.	Crude death rate [2] 2001	2010, proj.	Expectation of life at birth (years) 2001	2010, proj.	Infant mortality rate [3] 2001	2010, proj.	Total fertility rate per woman [4] 2001	2010, proj.
United States	14.2	14.3	8.7	8.6	77.3	78.5	6.8	6.2	2.06	2.12
Afghanistan	41.4	37.3	17.7	15.2	46.2	49.6	147.0	126.5	5.79	5.09
Algeria	22.8	19.9	5.2	4.9	70.0	72.5	40.6	28.9	2.72	2.17
Angola	46.5	42.9	24.7	21.6	38.6	41.3	193.7	174.7	6.48	5.94
Argentina	18.4	16.6	7.6	7.5	75.3	77.1	17.8	13.3	2.44	2.19
Australia	12.9	11.7	7.2	7.7	79.9	81.0	5.0	4.4	1.77	1.75
Bangladesh	25.3	22.1	8.6	7.6	60.5	63.9	69.9	54.3	2.78	2.30
Belarus	9.6	12.1	14.0	13.5	68.1	70.6	14.4	11.5	1.28	1.57
Belgium	10.7	9.9	10.1	10.7	78.0	79.4	4.7	4.2	1.61	1.63
Brazil	18.5	15.6	9.3	9.1	63.2	66.3	37.0	27.8	2.09	1.81
Burkina Faso	44.8	40.9	17.1	16.7	46.4	45.3	106.9	92.1	6.35	5.54
Burma	20.1	17.0	12.3	12.0	55.2	57.7	73.7	59.7	2.30	1.86
Cambodia	33.2	30.8	10.7	9.5	56.8	59.8	65.4	53.0	4.74	4.00
Cameroon	36.1	32.0	12.0	12.9	54.6	52.7	69.8	60.4	4.80	4.08
Canada	11.2	10.7	7.5	8.0	79.6	80.7	5.0	4.5	1.60	1.62
Chile	16.8	14.5	5.6	6.0	75.9	77.7	9.4	7.4	2.16	1.90
China [5]	16.0	13.1	6.7	7.1	71.6	73.9	28.1	20.5	1.82	1.82
Colombia	22.4	19.3	5.7	5.6	70.6	73.1	24.0	17.8	2.66	2.44
Congo (Kinshasa) [6]	46.0	42.4	15.2	13.4	48.9	50.7	99.9	83.2	6.84	6.11
Cote d'Ivoire	40.4	36.4	16.7	17.5	44.9	43.4	93.7	80.0	5.70	4.79
Cuba	12.4	11.0	7.3	7.7	76.4	78.1	7.4	6.4	1.60	1.62
Czech Republic	9.1	8.4	10.8	11.2	74.7	76.7	5.6	4.8	1.18	1.23
Ecuador	26.0	21.8	5.4	5.0	71.3	73.8	34.1	25.3	3.12	2.62
Egypt	24.9	20.9	7.7	6.9	63.7	66.9	60.5	44.8	3.07	2.48
Ethiopia	44.7	41.6	17.8	18.7	44.7	42.1	100.0	87.8	7.00	6.36
France	12.1	11.0	9.1	9.8	78.9	80.2	4.5	4.1	1.75	1.74
Germany	9.2	8.7	10.4	11.0	77.6	79.1	4.7	4.2	1.38	1.44
Ghana	29.0	23.3	10.3	11.5	57.2	55.5	56.5	48.9	3.82	2.81
Greece	9.8	9.2	9.7	10.7	78.6	79.9	6.4	5.3	1.33	1.40
Guatemala	34.6	30.4	6.8	5.8	66.5	69.5	45.8	35.2	4.58	3.91
Hungary	9.3	8.9	13.2	12.9	71.6	74.0	9.0	7.4	1.25	1.29
India	24.3	20.7	8.7	7.9	62.9	66.1	63.2	48.5	3.04	2.55
Indonesia	22.3	18.7	6.3	6.3	68.3	71.1	40.9	30.0	2.58	2.28
Iran	17.1	19.7	5.4	5.3	70.0	72.6	29.0	21.0	2.02	1.96
Iraq	34.6	29.4	6.2	4.9	67.0	70.3	60.1	42.2	4.75	3.76
Italy	9.1	7.5	10.1	11.2	79.1	80.2	5.8	5.1	1.18	1.22
Japan	10.0	8.9	8.3	10.2	80.8	81.7	3.9	3.6	1.41	1.47
Kazakhstan	17.3	20.9	10.6	10.4	63.3	65.7	59.2	52.5	2.07	2.38
Kenya	28.5	21.9	14.4	17.9	47.5	44.3	68.0	60.4	3.50	2.40
Korea, North	19.1	13.9	6.9	7.5	71.0	73.5	23.6	17.6	2.26	1.90
Korea, South	14.9	12.2	5.9	6.8	74.7	76.6	7.7	6.6	1.72	1.72
Madagascar	42.7	40.5	12.4	10.1	55.4	58.9	83.6	68.7	5.80	5.47
Malawi	37.8	31.8	22.8	24.1	37.1	35.8	121.1	110.0	5.18	3.94
Malaysia	24.8	22.1	5.2	5.1	71.1	73.6	20.3	15.0	3.24	2.92
Mali	48.8	44.6	18.7	15.3	47.0	50.5	121.4	105.1	6.81	6.06
Mexico	22.8	19.3	5.0	5.0	71.8	74.1	25.4	18.5	2.62	2.27
Morocco	24.2	20.6	5.9	5.4	69.4	72.1	48.1	34.7	3.05	2.46
Mozambique	37.2	31.1	24.2	29.9	36.5	31.4	139.2	131.8	4.82	3.85
Nepal	33.4	28.8	10.2	8.7	58.2	61.7	74.1	58.7	4.58	3.73
Netherlands	11.9	10.1	8.7	8.9	78.4	79.8	4.4	3.9	1.65	1.66
Niger	50.7	45.5	22.7	19.1	41.6	44.6	123.6	111.3	7.08	6.28
Nigeria	39.7	35.3	13.9	15.9	51.1	47.0	73.3	66.1	5.57	4.79
Pakistan	31.2	24.8	9.3	7.5	61.5	64.8	80.5	63.3	4.41	3.16
Peru	23.9	19.8	5.8	5.6	70.3	72.9	39.4	29.3	2.96	2.41
Philippines	27.4	23.3	6.0	5.5	67.8	70.6	28.7	21.8	3.42	2.89
Poland	10.2	10.9	10.0	10.3	73.4	75.6	9.4	7.6	1.37	1.42
Portugal	11.5	10.4	10.2	10.6	75.9	77.7	5.9	5.1	1.48	1.52
Romania	10.8	10.6	12.3	12.4	70.2	72.5	19.4	14.9	1.35	1.42
Russia	9.4	12.1	13.9	14.5	67.3	68.8	20.1	17.7	1.27	1.56
Saudi Arabia	37.3	37.1	5.9	5.4	68.1	70.9	51.3	37.4	6.25	5.74
Senegal	37.5	33.0	8.4	6.7	62.6	65.8	56.8	45.1	5.12	4.29
Serbia	12.5	12.0	10.7	11.3	73.4	75.5	18.0	14.1	1.73	1.69
South Africa	21.1	17.8	16.8	30.3	48.1	35.5	60.3	67.4	2.43	2.09
Spain	9.3	8.5	9.1	10.1	78.9	80.2	4.9	4.4	1.15	1.22
Sri Lanka	16.6	14.8	6.4	6.6	72.1	74.4	16.1	12.5	1.95	1.78
Sudan	37.9	31.8	10.0	8.3	56.9	60.5	68.7	55.2	5.35	4.21
Syria	30.6	25.2	5.2	4.6	68.8	71.5	33.8	25.0	3.95	3.02
Taiwan [5]	14.3	13.0	6.0	6.8	76.5	78.2	6.9	5.9	1.76	1.75
Tanzania	39.7	34.9	13.0	13.4	52.0	50.5	79.4	65.8	5.42	4.62
Thailand	16.6	14.2	7.5	7.8	68.9	71.7	30.5	22.2	1.87	1.80
Turkey	18.3	15.6	6.0	6.1	71.2	73.7	47.3	34.3	2.12	1.82
Uganda	47.5	45.2	18.0	15.1	43.4	46.6	91.3	75.4	6.88	6.12
Ukraine	9.3	11.6	16.4	15.7	66.2	68.5	21.4	17.5	1.29	1.58
United Kingdom . . .	11.5	10.6	10.4	10.2	77.8	79.3	5.5	4.8	1.73	1.72
Uzbekistan	26.1	26.1	8.0	7.4	63.8	66.2	71.9	65.6	3.06	2.80
Venezuela	20.7	17.8	4.9	5.0	73.3	75.5	25.4	18.9	2.46	2.13
Vietnam	21.2	18.3	6.2	5.8	69.6	72.2	30.2	22.7	2.49	2.10
Yemen	43.4	41.8	9.6	7.4	60.2	63.6	68.5	53.4	6.97	6.23
Zimbabwe	24.7	23.0	23.2	31.6	37.1	32.5	62.6	65.9	3.28	2.63

[1] Number of births during 1 year per 1,000 persons (based on midyear population). [2] Number of deaths during 1 year per 1,000 persons (based on midyear population). [3] Number of deaths of children under 1 year of age per 1,000 live births in a calendar year. [4] Average number of children that would be born if all women lived to the end of their childbearing years and, at each year of age, they experienced the birth rates occurring in the specified year. [5] See footnote 2, Table 1327. [6] See footnote 3, Table 1327.

Source: U.S. Census Bureau, "International Data Base" (as of 10 May 2000); <http://www.census.gov/ipc/www/idbnew.html>.

No. 1331. Percent of Births to Unmarried Women for Selected Countries: 1980 and 1998

Country	1980	1998
United States	18	33
Canada	13	[1]28
Denmark	33	45
Finland	13	[1]37
France	11	[1]40
Germany	12	[1]14
Greece	2	4
Iceland	40	64
Ireland	5	28
Italy	4	9
Japan	1	1
Netherlands	4	21
Norway	15	49
Portugal	5	20
Sweden	40	[1]54
United Kingdom	12	38

[1] Data are for 1997.

Source: U.S. National Center for Health Statistics, *Nonmarital Childbearing in the United States, 1940-99, National Vital Statistics Reports*, Vol. 48, No. 16, October 18, 2000.

No. 1332. Medical Doctors and Inpatient Care—Selected Countries: 1990 to 1998

Country	Medical doctors per 1,000 population			Inpatient care					
				Beds per 1,000 population			Average length of stay (days)		
	1990	1997	1998	1990	1997	1998	1990	1997	1998
United States	2.4	2.7	2.7	4.9	3.9	3.7	9	7	7
Australia	(NA)	2.5	(NA)	(NA)	8.3	(NA)	(NA)	15	(NA)
Austria	2.2	2.9	3.0	10.2	9.1	8.9	13	10	9
Belgium	3.2	[1]3.4	(NA)	8.0	[2]7.2	(NA)	14	[2]11	(NA)
Canada	2.1	2.1	2.1	6.3	4.7	(NA)	13	8	(NA)
Czech Republic	2.8	3.0	3.0	11.3	9.0	8.9	15	12	11
Denmark	2.8	[2]2.9	(NA)	5.7	4.6	(NA)	8	7	(NA)
Finland	2.4	3.0	3.0	12.5	7.9	7.8	18	11	11
France	2.6	3.0	3.0	9.7	8.5	8.5	13	11	(NA)
Germany	3.1	3.4	3.5	10.4	9.4	9.3	17	[2]8	12
Greece	3.4	4.1	(NA)	5.1	5.0	(NA)	10	10	(NA)
Hungary	2.9	3.1	(NA)	10.1	8.3	8.3	13	10	9
Iceland	2.8	3.3	(NA)	16.7	[3]15.9	(NA)	18	[3]17	(NA)
Ireland	1.6	2.1	2.2	3.9	3.7	(NA)	8	[2]7	(NA)
Italy	4.7	5.8	5.9	7.2	5.9	(NA)	12	8	(NA)
Japan	1.7	(NA)	1.9	16.0	16.4	16.5	51	43	41
Korea, South	0.8	1.2	1.3	3.1	4.8	5.1	13	13	13
Luxembourg	2.0	3.0	3.0	11.7	8.1	8.0	18	[2]15	(NA)
Mexico	1.1	1.6	1.6	0.8	1.1	1.1	4	4	4
Netherlands	2.5	[4]2.6	(NA)	11.5	11.2	11.3	34	32	34
New Zealand	1.9	2.2	2.2	8.5	6.1	6.2	10	7	7
Norway	3.1	[2]2.4	(NA)	(NA)	14.7	(NA)	(NA)	[2]10	(NA)
Poland	2.1	[2]2.4	(NA)	5.7	5.4	5.3	13	10	10
Portugal	2.8	3.1	3.1	4.6	4.1	4.0	11	9	9
Spain	3.8	4.3	4.4	4.3	[1]3.9	(NA)	12	[2]11	(NA)
Sweden	2.9	[2]3.1	(NA)	12.4	4.0	3.8	18	[2]8	(NA)
Switzerland	1.5	1.8	1.9	(NA)	18.3	18.1	(NA)	15	14
Turkey	0.9	1.2	1.2	2.1	2.5	2.5	7	6	6
United Kingdom	1.4	1.7	1.7	5.9	4.3	4.2	16	[2]10	(NA)

NA Not available. [1] 1995 data. [2] 1996 data. [3] 1992 data. [4] 1991 data.

Source: Organization for Economic Cooperation and Development, Paris, France, *OECD Health Data 2000* (copyright).

No. 1333. Health Expenditures as Percent of GDP by Country: 1980 to 1999

[In percent. G.D.P.=gross domestic product; for explanation, see text, Section 13, Income, Expenditures, and Wealth]

Country	Total health expenditures					Public health expenditures				
	1980	1990	1995	1998	1999	1980	1990	1995	1998	1999
United States	8.9	12.4	13.9	13.6	13.7	3.7	4.9	6.3	6.1	6.1
Australia	7.0	7.9	8.2	8.5	(NA)	4.3	5.3	5.5	5.9	(NA)
Austria	7.7	7.2	8.9	8.2	8.3	5.3	5.3	6.4	5.8	5.9
Belgium	6.4	7.4	8.2	8.8	(NA)	5.4	6.6	7.3	7.9	(NA)
Canada	7.2	9.2	9.5	9.5	9.5	5.4	6.8	6.7	6.6	6.6
Czech Republic	3.8	5.0	7.3	7.2	7.6	3.7	4.8	6.8	6.6	6.9
Denmark	9.2	8.4	8.2	8.3	8.3	8.1	7.0	6.8	6.5	6.8
Finland	6.4	7.9	7.5	6.9	(NA)	5.0	6.4	5.7	5.3	(NA)
France . . , ...	7.4	8.8	9.8	9.6	(NA)	5.8	6.7	7.5	7.3	(NA)
Germany [1]	8.8	8.7	10.2	10.6	10.5	6.9	6.7	8.0	7.9	7.9
Greece	6.6	7.6	8.3	8.3	(NA)	3.7	4.8	4.8	4.7	(NA)
Hungary	(NA)	(NA)	7.6	6.8	(NA)	(NA)	(NA)	5.8	5.2	(NA)
Iceland	6.2	8.0	8.2	8.3	8.4	5.5	6.9	6.9	7.0	7.2
Ireland	8.7	7.0	7.4	6.4	6.1	7.1	5.0	5.4	4.8	4.7
Italy	7.0	8.1	8.0	8.4	8.4	5.6	6.3	5.4	5.7	5.7
Japan	6.5	6.1	7.2	7.6	(NA)	4.6	4.7	5.6	6.0	(NA)
Korea, South	3.4	4.8	4.6	5.0	(NA)	0.7	1.7	1.7	2.3	(NA)
Luxembourg	6.2	6.6	6.3	5.9	(NA)	5.7	6.1	5.8	5.4	(NA)
Mexico	(NA)	3.6	4.9	(NA)	(NA)	(NA)	2.1	2.8	(NA)	(NA)
Netherlands	8.3	8.8	8.9	8.6	(NA)	5.9	6.1	6.5	6.0	(NA)
New Zealand	6.0	7.0	7.3	8.1	(NA)	5.3	5.8	5.6	6.2	(NA)
Norway	7.0	7.8	8.0	8.9	(NA)	5.9	6.5	6.7	7.4	(NA)
Poland	(NA)	5.3	6.0	6.4	6.3	(NA)	4.8	4.6	4.7	4.5
Portugal	5.8	6.4	7.7	7.8	(NA)	3.7	4.2	5.0	5.2	(NA)
Spain	5.6	6.9	7.0	7.1	(NA)	4.5	5.4	5.5	5.4	(NA)
Sweden	9.4	8.8	8.4	8.4	(NA)	8.7	7.9	7.2	7.0	(NA)
Switzerland	6.9	8.3	9.6	10.4	(NA)	4.6	5.7	7.0	7.7	(NA)
Turkey	3.3	3.6	3.3	(NA)	(NA)	0.9	2.2	2.4	(NA)	(NA)
United Kingdom	5.7	6.0	7.0	6.7	7.0	5.1	5.1	5.9	5.6	5.9

NA Not available.   [1] Data prior to 1991 are for former West Germany.

Source: Organization for Economic Cooperation and Development, Paris, France, *OECD Health Data 2000* (copyright).

No. 1334. Average Temperatures and Precipitation—Selected International Cities

[In degrees Fahrenheit, except as noted. Data are generally based on a standard 30-year period; for details, see source. For data on U.S. cities, see Tables 371-374]

City	January					July				
	Average high	Average low	Warm-est	Coldest	Average precipi-tation (inches)	Average high	Average low	Warm-est	Coldest	Average precipita-tion (inches)
Amsterdam, Netherlands .	41	34	57	3	3.1	69	55	90	39	2.9
Athens, Greece	55	44	70	28	1.9	89	73	108	61	0.2
Baghdad, Iraq	58	38	75	25	1.1	110	78	122	61	-
Bangkok, Thailand	89	71	95	54	0.4	90	78	99	72	6.2
Beijing, China	34	17	54	1	0.2	86	72	104	63	8.8
Berlin, Germany	35	26	58	-11	(NA)	73	56	95	41	(NA)
Bogota, Colombia	66	43	84	27	1.9	64	47	82	32	1.8
Brasilia, Brazil	81	64	95	54	(NA)	79	52	97	37	(NA)
Buenos Aires, Argentina .	85	64	104	44	4.2	58	41	88	23	2.3
Cairo, Egypt	65	49	86	32	0.2	93	72	108	63	-
Frankfurt, Germany	38	30	56	-4	1.8	75	57	97	38	2.4
Geneva, Switzerland	39	29	57	-2	2.2	77	56	96	41	2.8
Hong Kong, China	67	58	79	43	1.1	89	81	97	70	14.3
Istanbul, Turkey	46	37	64	18	3.7	82	66	100	50	0.7
Jakarta, Indonesia	83	75	92	72	(NA)	88	74	92	67	(NA)
Kabul, Afghanistan	36	23	64	-4	1.3	88	67	102	49	0.2
Karachi, Pakistan	76	55	93	39	0.3	89	83	109	68	3.5
Lagos, Nigeria	82	79	93	64	(NA)	79	76	88	70	(NA)
London, England	45	36	61	15	2.4	72	56	93	45	1.8
Madrid, Spain	51	32	68	14	1.8	90	61	104	46	0.4
Manila, Philippines	86	71	95	61	0.8	88	76	99	70	15.9
Mexico City, Mexico	70	45	86	26	0.3	74	56	86	37	5.1
Montreal, Canada	21	7	52	-31	2.8	79	61	93	43	3.4
Moscow, Russia	21	11	46	-33	1.4	71	55	95	41	3.2
Nairobi, Kenya	77	58	88	45	1.8	71	54	85	43	0.5
New Delhi, India	68	48	85	32	0.9	93	81	111	70	7.9
Paris, France	43	34	59	1	(NA)	75	58	95	41	(NA)
Rio De Janeiro, Brazil . . .	91	74	109	64	5.3	81	64	102	52	1.8
Rome, Italy	55	39	64	19	3.2	83	66	100	55	0.6
Seoul, Korea	33	21	55	-1	(NA)	82	71	97	55	(NA)
Singapore, Singapore . . .	85	73	100	66	9.4	86	76	99	70	5.9
Sydney, Australia	79	65	109	49	4.0	62	44	80	32	2.5
Tel Aviv, Israel	62	46	84	32	(NA)	87	69	100	55	(NA)
Tokyo, Japan	48	35	66	25	2.0	82	71	95	55	5.3
Toronto, Canada	28	15	59	-24	1.9	79	60	99	45	2.8

- Represents zero.   NA Not available.

Source: U.S. National Oceanic and Atmospheric Administration, *Climates of the World*.

U.S. Census Bureau, Statistical Abstract of the United States: 2001

No. 1335. Selected Environmental Data—OECD Countries

[Figures are for 1998 or the latest available year. Varying definitions and survey methods can limit the comparability across countries]

Country	Air pollutant emissions per capita			Waste generated			
					Nuclear [3]		
	Sulfur oxides (kilograms)	Nitrogen oxides (kilograms)	Carbon dioxide [1] (tons)	Municipal [2] (kilograms per capita)	Amount (tons)	Per unit of energy (tons per Mtoe [4])	Per 1,000 persons (kilograms)
United States	69	80	20	720	2,100	0.9	8.0
Australia	101	118	17	690	-	-	-
Austria	7	21	8	510	-	-	-
Belgium	24	33	12	480	80	2.8	11.9
Canada	90	68	16	500	1,340	6.5	57.1
Czech Republic	68	41	12	310	45	1.0	4.5
Denmark	21	47	11	560	-	-	-
Finland	20	51	12	410	71	2.2	13.3
France	16	29	6	590	1,130	4.6	20.6
Germany	16	22	10	[5]460	450	1.3	5.8
Greece	48	35	8	370	-	-	-
Hungary	65	19	6	490	55	3.2	5.1
Iceland	32	106	8	650	-	-	-
Ireland	49	34	10	560	-	-	-
Italy	23	31	7	460	-	-	-
Japan	7	11	9	400	964	1.8	7.3
Korea, South	33	28	8	400	364	2.3	4.8
Luxembourg	8	40	17	590	-	-	-
Mexico	24	17	4	310	42	0.1	0.2
Netherlands	8	28	11	560	12	0.2	0.9
New Zealand	12	46	8	[6]350	-	-	-
Norway	7	51	8	600	-	-	-
Poland	61	30	8	320	(NA)	(NA)	(NA)
Portugal	38	37	5	440	-	-	-
Spain	49	32	6	390	192	0.9	4.3
Sweden	10	38	6	360	238	4.5	24.1
Switzerland	5	18	6	600	64	2.4	10.9
Turkey	30	15	3	330	-	-	-
United Kingdom	34	35	9	480	820	3.7	29.2

- Represents zero.   NA Not available.   [1] Carbon dioxide from energy use only. Excludes international marine bunkers. [2] Municipal waste is that which is collected and treated by or for municipalities: household waste and bulky waste as well as comparable waste from small communities or industrial enterprises; and market and garden residue.   [3] Wastes from spent fuel arising in nuclear power plants, measured in terms of heavy metal.   [4] Mtoe=million tons of oil equivalent (primary energy supply).   [5] Includes separate collection by private sector.   [6] Household waste only.

Source: Organization for Economic Cooperation and Development, Paris, France, OECD Environmental Data Compendium, 1999 (copyright).

No. 1336. Carbon Dioxide Emissions from Consumption of Fossil Fuels by Country, 1990 to 1999, and Projections, 2005 and 2010

[In million metric tons of carbon (5,873 represents 5,873,000,000). Includes carbon dioxide emissions from the consumption of petroleum, natural gas, and coal, and the flaring of natural gas]

Country	1990	1994	1995	1996	1997	1998	1999, prel.	2005	2010
World, total	5,873	5,913	6,018	6,136	6,231	6,198	6,144	7,015	7,835
Australia	72	77	80	82	89	92	94	(NA)	(NA)
Brazil	63	71	74	76	80	88	89	108	139
Canada	128	135	135	139	145	148	151	158	165
China [1]	617	768	788	794	808	765	669	889	1,131
France	102	97	101	105	104	110	109	116	120
Germany	(X)	230	239	240	238	237	230	246	252
India	156	190	224	224	228	232	243	300	351
Indonesia	41	56	59	65	69	65	64	(NA)	(NA)
Iran	56	68	71	71	81	81	84	(NA)	(NA)
Italy	112	108	118	116	118	122	121	131	137
Japan	269	299	298	301	308	300	307	324	330
Korea, South	61	96	103	107	117	101	107	128	144
Mexico	84	90	88	93	96	105	101	124	145
Netherlands	58	60	61	62	66	66	64	66	67
Poland	89	87	83	78	91	85	85	(NA)	(NA)
Russia	(X)	477	444	444	408	398	400	(NA)	(NA)
Saudi Arabia	59	67	69	71	72	74	74	(NA)	(NA)
South Africa	81	94	94	96	105	102	99	(NA)	(NA)
Spain	62	64	67	63	73	77	82	(NA)	(NA)
Taiwan [1]	32	44	49	53	58	60	63	(NA)	(NA)
Thailand	23	35	43	46	47	44	45	(NA)	(NA)
Turkey	35	38	41	45	50	50	50	57	66
Ukraine	(X)	121	124	108	102	98	104	(NA)	(NA)
United Kingdom	164	155	153	159	154	155	152	168	177
United States	1,355	1,418	1,430	1,481	1,502	1,504	1,520	1,690	1,809

NA Not available.   X Not applicable.   [1] See footnote 2, Table 1327.

Source: U.S. Energy Information Administration, International Energy Annual, 1999, and International Energy Outlook, 2001.

No. 1337. Educational Attainment by Country: 1998

[Percent distribution. Persons 25 to 64 years old]

Country	Total	Preprimary and primary education	Lower secondary education	Upper secondary education	Post-secondary nontertiary education [1]	Non-university tertiary education [2]	University education
United States ...	100	5	9	[3]52	([3])	8	27
Australia	100	[4]44	([4])	[3]31	([3])	9	17
Austria [5]	100	[4]27	([4])	57	6	4	6
Belgium	100	20	23	[3]31	([3])	13	12
Canada	100	[4]20	([4])	28	13	20	19
Czech Republic ..	100	[4]15	([4])	[3]75	([3])	(X)	10
Denmark	100	(Z)	21	[3]54	([3])	20	5
Finland [5]	100	[4]32	([4])	39	(X)	17	13
France	100	21	18	40	(Z)	10	11
Germany	100	2	14	56	4	9	14
Greece [5]	100	45	9	25	4	4	11
Hungary	100	4	32	[3]50	([3])	(NA)	13
Iceland	100	2	36	30	11	5	16
Ireland	100	23	26	[6]30	([6])	[8]10	11
Italy	100	[4]25	31	31	5	([7])	[7]9
Japan	100	[4]20	([4])	50	(NA)	13	18
Korea, South	100	19	[8]16	43	(X)	5	17
Mexico	100	59	[8]20	[8]8	(X)	1	12
Netherlands	100	12	23	40	([7])	([7])	[7]24
New Zealand	100	[4]27	([4])	39	7	[1]4	13
Norway [5]	100	0.2	17	57	1	2	24
Poland	100	[4]22	([4])	64	3	([1])	[7]11
Portugal	100	68	12	[3]11	([3])	3	7
Spain	100	45	22	13	(NA)	3	14
Sweden	100	12	12	48	9	[9]15	13
Switzerland	100	[4]19	([4])	[3]58	([3])	9	14
Turkey	100	74	8	11	(X)	([7])	[7]6
United Kingdom ..	100	[4]19	([4])	57	(NA)	8	15

NA Not available.   X Not applicable.   Z Less than 0.5 percent.   [1] This level straddles the boundary between upper secondary and postsecondary education from an international point of view, even though it might clearly be considered upper secondary or postsecondary in a national context. Although the content may not be significantly more advanced than upper secondary programs, it serves to broaden the knowledge of participants who have already gained an upper secondary qualification.   [2] These programs focus on practical, technical, or occupational skills for direct entry into the labor market, although some theoretical foundations may be covered. They have a minimum duration of 2 years full-time equivalent at the tertiary level.   [3] Postsecondary nontertiary included in upper secondary.   [4] Lower secondary included in preprimary and primary education.   [5] Data for 1997.   [6] Postsecondary nontertiary included in upper secondary and nonuniversity tertiary.   [7] Included in university-level.   [8] Part of upper secondary included in lower secondary.   [9] Postsecondary nontertiary included in nonuniversity tertiary.

Source: Organization for Economic Cooperation and Development, Paris, France, *Education at a Glance*, annual, (copyright).

No. 1338. Participation in Job-Related Continuing Education and Training by Country

[Percentage of the employed population 25 to 64 years old. Data refer to all job-related education and training organized, financed, or sponsored by authorities, provided by employers, or self-financed. Job-related continuing education and training refers to all organized, systematic education and training activities in which people take part in order to obtain knowledge and/or learn new skills for a current or a future job, to increase earnings, improve job and/or career opportunities in current or other fields, and generally to improve their opportunities for advancement and promotion. Data are based on International Adult Literacy Survey 1994-1998 and national household surveys on adult education and training]

Country	Time period	Total	Male	Female
United States.	1999	41	40	42
Australia.	1996-97	47	46	50
Canada .	1997	28	26	30
Czech Republic.	1998-99	27	31	23
Denmark	1998-99	55	52	58
Finland	1995	51	46	56
Germany	1997	42	43	40
Hungary.	1998-99	20	17	23
Ireland.	1995-96	24	21	29
Italy.	1998-99	25	25	25
Netherlands	1994-95	33	35	29
New Zealand	1995-96	47	46	47
Norway	1998-99	51	49	54
Poland.	1994-95	17	16	17
Switzerland.	1998-99	37	39	35
United Kingdom.	1995-96	52	51	53

Source: Organization for Economic Cooperation and Development, Paris, France, *Education at a Glance*, annual (copyright).

[60 represents $60,000,000,000]

Country	Gross national product [1]				GNP on purchasing power parity basis [2]			
	Total (bil. dol.)		Per capita (dol.)		Total (bil. dol.)		Per capita (dol.)	
	1990	1999	1990	1999	1990	1999	1990	1999
Algeria	60	47	2,400	1,550	110	145	4,390	4,840
Argentina	104	276	3,200	7,550	241	437	7,420	11,940
Australia	302	397	17,690	20,950	280	452	16,440	23,850
Austria	152	206	19,610	25,430	145	199	18,780	24,600
Bangladesh	32	47	290	370	113	196	1,020	1,530
Belarus	35	26	3,420	2,620	73	69	7,170	6,880
Belgium	183	252	18,370	24,650	196	263	19,640	25,710
Brazil	394	730	2,670	4,350	802	1,148	5,420	6,840
Bulgaria	20	12	2,260	1,410	47	42	5,360	5,070
Canada	550	614	19,800	20,140	541	776	19,480	25,440
Chile	29	70	2,190	4,630	61	126	4,690	8,410
China [3]	368	980	320	780	1,594	4,452	1,400	3,550
Colombia . . . . . [4] .	41	90	1,180	2,170	159	232	4,560	5,580
Congo (Kinshasa) [4] .	8	[5]5	220	[5]100	46	[5]34	1,240	[5]710
Costa Rica	7	13	2,330	3,570	15	28	5,140	7,880
Cote d'Ivoire	9	10	790	670	16	24	1,330	1,540
Croatia	(NA)	20	(NA)	4,530	34	32	7,050	7,260
Czech Republic	(NA)	52	(NA)	5,020	119	132	11,490	12,840
Denmark	120	171	23,430	32,050	98	136	19,000	25,600
Ecuador	10	17	980	1,360	26	35	2,550	2,820
Egypt	43	87	810	1,380	129	217	2,450	3,460
El Salvador	5	12	930	1,920	15	26	2,910	4,260
Ethiopia	8	7	160	100	25	39	480	620
Finland	124	128	24,890	24,730	87	117	17,380	22,600
France	1,142	1,453	19,660	24,170	1,019	1,349	17,970	23,020
Germany	(NA)	2,104	(NA)	25,620	(NA)	1,930	(NA)	23,510
Greece	80	128	7,910	12,110	118	166	11,620	15,800
Guatemala	8	19	970	1,680	24	40	2,780	3,630
Hong Kong	72	165	12,680	24,570	95	152	16,670	22,570
Hungary	30	47	2,880	4,640	94	111	9,070	11,050
India	330	442	390	440	1,187	2,226	1,400	2,230
Indonesia	111	125	620	600	333	550	1,870	2,660
Iran	141	114	2,590	1,810	213	347	3,910	5,520
Ireland	42	81	11,990	21,470	41	84	11,720	22,460
Israel	51	100	10,860	16,310	61	110	13,190	18,070
Italy	988	1,163	17,420	20,170	978	1,268	17,240	22,000
Japan	3,261	4,055	26,400	32,030	2,477	3,186	20,050	25,170
Kazakhstan	40	19	2,430	1,250	104	71	6,380	4,790
Korea, South	247	398	5,770	8,490	382	728	8,910	15,530
Lebanon	(NA)	16	(NA)	3,700	8	[5]19	2,250	[5]4,410
Luxembourg	13	19	33,590	42,930	10	18	25,000	41,230
Malaysia	43	77	2,370	3,390	83	173	4,560	7,640
Mexico	238	429	2,830	4,440	516	780	6,200	8,070
Morocco	25	34	1,030	1,190	67	94	2,790	3,320
Netherlands	286	397	19,120	25,140	264	386	17,630	24,410
New Zealand	43	53	12,410	13,990	46	67	13,410	17,630
Nigeria	26	32	270	260	66	95	690	770
Norway	108	149	25,470	33,470	81	126	19,020	28,140
Pakistan	46	63	420	470	154	250	1,420	1,860
Peru	17	54	780	2,130	68	113	3,170	4,480
Philippines	45	78	750	1,050	203	296	3,350	3,990
Poland	(NA)	157	(NA)	4,070	205	324	5,380	8,390
Portugal	64	110	6,420	11,030	110	158	11,160	15,860
Romania	40	33	1,720	1,470	146	134	6,270	5,970
Russia	(NA)	329	(NA)	2,250	1,498	1,022	10,100	6,990
Saudi Arabia	106	139	6,700	6,900	161	223	10,170	11,050
Singapore	36	95	11,730	24,150	40	88	13,200	22,310
Slovakia	18	20	3,340	3,770	48	56	9,020	10,430
Slovenia	(NA)	20	(NA)	10,000	24	32	12,130	16,050
South Africa	102	134	2,890	3,170	281	367	7,990	8,710
Spain	458	583	11,790	14,800	500	704	12,880	17,850
Sri Lanka	8	16	470	820	34	61	2,000	3,230
Sweden	214	237	25,050	26,750	151	196	17,610	22,150
Switzerland	225	274	33,520	38,380	170	205	25,290	28,760
Syria	11	15	900	970	28	54	2,320	3,450
Thailand	84	121	1,520	2,010	212	358	3,810	5,950
Turkey	128	186	2,280	2,900	275	415	4,900	6,440
Ukraine	83	42	1,610	840	359	168	6,910	3,360
United Arab Emirates	37	[5]49	19,930	[5]17,870	40	[5]53	21,630	[5]19,340
United Kingdom	934	1,404	16,220	23,590	956	1,322	16,600	22,220
United States	**5,877**	**8,879**	**23,560**	**31,910**	**5,877**	**8,878**	**23,560**	**31,910**
Uruguay	9	21	2,870	6,220	19	29	5,980	8,750
Uzbekistan	(NA)	18	(NA)	720	51	54	2,520	2,230
Venezuela	53	87	2,700	3,680	96	129	4,920	5,420
Vietnam	(NA)	29	(NA)	370	65	144	970	1,860

NA Not available.   [1] Gross national product calculated using the World Bank Atlas method; for details, see source.   [2] See footnote 2, Table 1340.   [3] See footnote 2, Table 1327.   [4] See footnote 3, Table 1327.   [5] 1998 data.

Source: The World Bank, Washington, DC, *World Development Indicators CD-ROM*, annual (copyright).

No. 1340. Gross Domestic Product (GDP) by Country: 1995 to 2000

[23,898 represents $23,898,000,000,000. Except as noted, based on the System of National Accounts, 1993; for details, see source]

Country	Current price levels and exchange rates [1] (bil. dol.)					Constant (1995) price levels and exchange rates [1] (bil. dol.)					GDP per capita, 1999 based on current	
	1995	1997	1998	1999	2000	1995	1997	1998	1999	2000	Exchange rates	PPPs [2]
OECD, total	23,898	23,675	23,865	25,125	25,528	23,898	25,372	25,962	26,713	27,709	22,507	22,658
OECD Europe [3]	9,477	9,120	9,432	9,405	8,720	9,477	9,900	10,181	10,419	10,774	18,119	19,038
European Union [3]	8,605	8,248	8,529	8,523	7,837	8,605	8,957	9,211	9,443	9,758	22,611	22,507
Australia	376	419	374	408	392	376	408	430	449	465	21,492	25,721
Austria	235	206	211	210	190	235	243	251	258	266	25,948	24,668
Belgium	276	244	250	249	227	276	289	296	304	316	24,347	24,868
Canada	579	624	598	635	689	579	614	634	663	694	20,822	26,423
Czech Republic	52	53	57	53	50	52	54	53	52	54	5,156	13,203
Denmark	180	169	175	176	162	180	190	196	200	206	33,124	27,098
Finland	129	122	129	129	122	129	143	151	157	166	25,046	22,743
France [4]	1,553	1,406	1,452	1,438	1,294	1,553	1,600	1,655	1,703	1,756	25,912	22,225
Germany	2,458	2,114	2,151	2,112	1,873	2,458	2,512	2,563	2,603	2,680	25,729	23,840
Greece	118	121	121	125	112	118	125	128	133	138	11,848	15,154
Hungary	45	46	47	48	46	45	47	50	52	54	4,772	11,232
Iceland	7	7	8	9	9	7	8	8	8	9	31,139	26,362
Ireland	66	80	86	93	94	66	79	86	94	105	24,943	25,427
Italy	1,097	1,167	1,197	1,180	1,074	1,097	1,132	1,152	1,171	1,205	20,473	23,261
Japan	5,292	4,313	3,941	4,500	4,750	5,292	5,574	5,513	5,554	5,640	35,517	25,590
Korea, South	489	477	317	406	457	489	549	512	568	618	8,666	16,024
Luxembourg	18	18	18	19	19	18	20	21	23	25	44,688	41,699
Mexico	286	401	421	480	574	286	321	338	350	374	4,921	8,383
Netherlands [5]	415	377	391	394	365	415	444	460	476	495	24,906	25,947
New Zealand [5]	60	65	53	55	50	60	63	63	66	68	14,376	18,532
Norway	147	155	148	155	162	147	161	165	167	171	34,410	28,267
Poland	127	144	159	155	158	127	144	151	157	163	4,011	8,651
Portugal	107	106	112	114	105	107	116	120	124	128	11,424	16,698
Slovakia	18	20	21	20	19	18	21	22	22	23	3,653	10,946
Spain	584	561	586	600	559	584	622	649	675	702	15,220	18,231
Sweden	240	239	240	241	227	240	248	257	267	277	27,256	23,038
Switzerland [3]	307	256	263	259	241	307	314	321	326	337	36,247	28,697
Turkey [3]	169	190	200	185	200	169	195	201	191	205	2,809	6,338
United Kingdom	1,127	1,319	1,410	1,442	1,415	1,127	1,196	1,228	1,256	1,294	24,228	22,882
United States	7,338	8,257	8,729	9,237	9,896	7,338	7,943	8,293	8,645	9,077	33,836	33,836

[1] Based on constant (1995) price data converted to U.S. dollars using 1995 exchange rates. [2] The goods and services produced in different countries should be valued consistently if the differences observed are meant to reflect real differences in the volumes of goods and services produced. The use of purchasing power parities (PPP) instead of exchange rates is intended to achieve this objective. PPPs show how many units of currency are needed in one country to buy the same amount of goods and services which one unit of currency will buy in the other country. See text of this section. [3] European Union: Austria, Belgium, Denmark, Finland, France, Germany, Greece, Ireland, Italy, Luxembourg, Netherlands, Portugal, Spain, Sweden and United Kingdom. [4] Includes overseas departments. [5] Based on System of National Accounts, 1968.

Source: Organization for Economic Cooperation and Development, Paris, France, "OECD Statistics GDP"; published July 2001; <http://www.oecd.org/std/gdp.htm> (copyright) and "GDP per capita based on exchange rates and on PPP"; published July 2001; <http://www.oecd.org/std/gdpperca.htm> (copyright).

U.S. Census Bureau, Statistical Abstract of the United States: 2001

No. 1341. Selected International Economic Indicators by Country: 1980 to 2000

[Data cover gross domestic product (GDP) at market prices. Gross fixed capital formation covers private and government sectors except military. Savings data are calculated by deducting outlays—such as personal consumption expenditures, interest paid, and transfer payments to foreigners—from disposable personal income]

Year	United States	France	Ger-many	Italy	Nether-lands	United Kingdom	Japan	Canada
Ratio of gross fixed capital formation to GDP (current prices):								
1980	19.9	23.8	22.6	25.2	22.9	18.8	31.7	23.1
1985	19.2	20.3	19.5	21.8	21.0	18.1	27.7	19.8
1990	17.0	22.6	20.9	21.5	22.3	20.6	32.2	20.8
1995	17.5	18.8	22.4	18.3	20.3	16.3	27.8	17.0
1998	19.4	18.4	21.3	18.5	21.5	17.4	26.9	19.3
1999	20.0	19.1	21.3	19.0	22.2	17.7	26.2	19.5
2000	20.7	19.7	21.4	19.6	22.3	17.7	26.0	19.3
Ratio of savings to disposable personal income:								
1980	10.2	15.8	14.2	25.1	7.8	11.7	17.9	15.5
1985	9.2	13.8	12.8	21.0	5.6	9.1	19.0	15.7
1990	7.8	13.1	14.7	18.4	11.6	7.4	13.9	12.9
1995	5.6	16.0	11.2	16.6	14.9	10.3	12.3	9.2
1998	4.2	15.6	10.2	12.8	13.4	5.8	11.8	4.4
1999	2.2	15.4	9.9	11.5	10.6	5.2	11.1	4.2
2000	-0.1	15.9	9.8	10.3	9.4	4.5	11.1	3.9

Source: U.S. Dept. of Commerce, International Trade Administration, Office of Trade and Economic Analysis, based on official statistics of listed countries.

No. 1342. International Economic Composite Indexes by Country: 1980 to 2000

[Average annual percent change from previous year; derived from indexes with base 1990=100. The coincident index changes are for calendar years and the leading index changes are for years ending June 30 because they lead the coincident indexes by about 6 months, on average. The G-7 countries are United States, Canada, France, Germany, Italy, United Kingdom, and Japan. Minus sign (-) indicates decrease]

Country	1980	1985	1990	1992	1993	1994	1995	1996	1997	1998	1999	2000
LEADING INDEX												
Total, 13 countries	2.9	2.9	2.7	-1.1	-0.9	3.9	6.9	-0.6	3.0	2.2	-0.4	6.2
12 countries, excluding U.S.	7.7	5.5	4.4	-3.2	-3.3	3.7	6.1	-0.7	1.5	0.5	-1.6	5.3
G-7 countries	2.9	2.0	2.6	-1.6	-1.4	3.5	7.3	-0.6	3.2	2.4	-0.5	6.2
North America	-2.7	-0.4	-0.5	2.3	3.2	4.5	8.3	-0.4	5.1	4.5	1.1	7.4
United States	-3.1	-0.7	-0.4	2.6	3.1	4.2	8.2	-0.4	5.1	4.5	1.1	7.3
Canada	2.0	3.2	-2.6	-1.1	4.5	8.5	10.0	-0.9	5.3	4.6	0.7	9.4
Four European countries	3.1	2.8	1.5	0.3	-1.3	4.1	6.2	-2.3	0.1	5.4	-0.1	1.6
France	3.2	0.8	-1.0	2.7	-0.3	4.7	3.5	-3.4	1.3	3.1	-1.4	-2.0
Germany	2.0	2.1	4.4	-1.1	-4.5	2.0	8.8	-3.5	1.7	7.3	1.3	1.9
Italy	6.1	6.5	1.0	-0.9	-1.0	7.1	9.9	-0.9	-4.4	10.9	-0.6	5.6
United Kingdom	2.5	3.5	0.4	0.8	2.8	4.1	2.3	-	0.1	0.3	-0.5	1.6
Seven Pacific region countries	16.3	9.4	8.0	-6.6	-6.0	2.9	5.5	1.0	2.6	-5.3	-3.7	9.1
Australia	5.7	7.6	0.3	4.9	5.9	7.1	11.3	6.0	3.1	5.9	7.6	7.6
Taiwan [1]	2.6	5.6	6.1	8.4	4.0	8.1	3.1	-1.6	4.2	3.8	-	4.1
Thailand	4.0	7.1	14.4	7.5	9.2	12.0	5.7	2.0	-3.3	-6.0	-1.6	5.9
Japan	19.8	10.3	8.7	-9.7	-9.3	0.6	6.5	1.5	3.5	-6.9	-5.4	10.6
Korea, South	0.4	6.9	7.1	7.0	6.3	13.1	3.1	-0.7	-2.2	-5.3	1.8	8.5
Malaysia	4.9	-1.0	2.0	-1.2	0.7	7.6	1.5	0.2	0.9	-1.0	-1.1	3.8
New Zealand	2.3	6.0	1.8	3.5	4.5	2.7	0.9	-	2.3	1.2	0.1	7.0
COINCIDENT INDEX												
Total, 13 countries	-	3.5	4.0	0.3	-0.9	2.6	5.4	5.5	6.2	4.6	8.1	7.4
12 countries, excluding U.S.	1.9	3.4	6.5	-0.4	-2.6	1.5	4.6	5.3	4.8	2.2	8.8	7.5
G-7 countries	-0.2	3.4	3.9	-	-1.3	2.2	5.2	5.7	6.3	5.2	8.3	7.4
North America	-2.5	3.7	-	1.2	2.1	4.7	8.2	9.5	9.8	7.7	12.0	6.6
United States	-2.9	3.5	-	1.4	2.1	4.7	6.7	6.1	8.4	8.5	7.3	7.4
Canada	2.2	6.3	-0.1	-0.2	1.9	5.1	13.3	20.3	13.9	5.5	24.7	4.9
Four European countries	0.6	2.3	5.4	-1.6	-5.2	1.3	4.2	1.4	4.1	9.1	9.3	13.9
France	-2.3	-1.6	6.0	-2.6	-8.6	1.0	9.0	2.7	7.9	15.8	16.8	21.3
Germany	1.9	3.1	7.3	-0.7	-4.0	1.0	3.9	-1.2	0.5	8.0	7.8	12.3
Italy	6.9	4.1	6.4	-0.9	-8.4	-1.2	-1.5	3.5	5.4	7.1	9.3	16.8
United Kingdom	-2.1	4.1	0.9	-2.7	-	4.3	3.0	2.8	5.0	3.5	0.9	1.9
Seven Pacific region countries	3.5	4.3	8.4	0.7	-0.6	1.3	2.0	2.8	1.3	-5.3	-0.8	2.3
Australia	4.2	7.2	0.6	-2.0	1.3	9.2	8.8	3.8	4.3	6.7	8.0	6.4
Taiwan [1]	8.5	3.2	5.2	8.4	6.9	7.1	2.6	0.2	4.6	3.0	2.6	3.9
Thailand	4.2	3.3	13.0	7.1	11.8	10.2	4.5	1.6	-6.2	-12.3	6.7	3.8
Japan	4.0	4.4	9.1	-0.1	-2.2	-1.0	0.5	2.3	0.7	-5.4	-3.7	-0.1
Korea, South	-7.1	6.7	11.5	5.0	4.5	11.5	7.8	6.4	3.0	-16.9	12.4	14.9
Malaysia	-2.7	-8.2	-0.3	3.1	4.7	4.8	10.7	8.5	6.1	-5.1	5.7	10.8
New Zealand	1.4	1.3	0.6	0.8	3.3	5.4	10.6	10.3	5.5	0.6	8.4	4.6

- Represents or rounds to zero.   [1] See footnote 2, Table 1327.

Source: Foundation for International Business and Economic Research, New York, NY, International Economic Indicators, monthly.

No. 1343. Index of Industrial Production by Country: 1980 to 1999

[Industrial production index measures output in the manufacturing, mining, and electric, gas and water utilities industries. Minus sign (-) indicates decrease]

Country	Index (1995=100)								Annual percent change				
	1980	1985	1990	1994	1996	1997	1998	1999	1994-95	1995-96	1996-97	1997-98	1998-99
OECD, total.....	(NA)	(NA)	(NA)	(NA)	103.0	108.2	110.6	114.3	(NA)	3.0	5.0	2.2	3.3
Australia.........	70.1	77.8	92.9	99.5	103.8	105.5	107.7	111.4	0.5	3.8	1.6	2.1	3.4
Austria.........	70.2	76.6	92.3	95.3	101.0	107.0	116.2	123.2	4.9	1.0	5.9	8.6	6.0
Belgium.........	83.4	86.8	99.3	93.9	100.5	105.2	108.8	109.7	6.5	0.5	4.7	3.4	0.8
Canada [1].......	71.8	83.0	88.4	95.7	101.7	107.3	108.3	113.2	4.5	1.7	5.5	0.9	4.5
Czech Republic....	(X)	(X)	144.9	100.7	102.0	106.5	108.3	104.8	-0.7	2.0	4.4	1.7	-3.2
Denmark........	63.0	77.0	86.0	96.0	102.0	108.0	110.0	113.0	4.2	2.0	5.9	1.9	2.7
Finland.........	66.4	76.7	86.9	94.1	103.7	113.3	122.5	129.1	6.3	3.7	9.3	8.1	5.4
France.........	89.5	89.5	100.4	98.0	100.2	104.1	110.0	112.2	2.0	0.2	3.9	5.7	2.0
Germany........	85.6	88.3	103.2	98.8	100 6	104.1	105.8	110.2	1.2	0.6	3.5	4.2	1.6
Greece.........	92.6	99.2	101.9	98.2	101.2	102.5	109.8	114.1	1.8	1.2	1.3	7.1	3.9
Hungary........	116.7	128.1	113.8	95.5	103.3	114.8	129.1	142.4	4.7	3.3	11.1	12.5	10.3
Ireland.........	34.2	43.9	63.2	84.1	108.0	124.5	142.3	157.2	18.9	8.0	15.3	14.3	10.5
Italy...........	77.2	73.9	93.2	95.2	98.1	101.8	102.9	102.9	5.0	-1.9	3.8	1.1	0.0
Japan.........	69.9	82.8	103.2	96.8	102.3	106.0	99.0	99.8	3.3	2.3	3.6	-6.6	0.8
Korea, South.....	22.0	36.2	66.4	89.3	108.7	114.5	106.2	131.9	12.0	8.7	5.3	-7.2	24.2
Luxembourg	71.0	79.8	97.1	98.0	100.1	105.9	105.8	118.0	2.0	0.1	5.8	-0.1	11.5
Mexico	80.3	85.0	95.7	108.5	110.1	120.3	127.9	132.7	-7.8	10.1	9.3	6.3	3.8
Netherlands	78.7	83.1	90.6	95.4	103.8	106.5	105.1	107.4	4.8	3.8	2.6	-1.3	2.2
New Zealand.....	74.0	85.0	87.0	96.0	103.0	105.0	105.0	105.0	4.2	3.0	1.9	-	-
Norway.........	50.6	61.5	78.6	94.4	105.4	109.0	108.4	108.1	5.9	5.4	3.4	-0.6	-0.3
Poland.........	(X)	107.3	87.7	90.4	109.4	121.7	127.4	133.5	10.6	9.4	11.2	4.7	4.8
Portugal........	62.1	71.7	97.0	89.6	105.3	108.0	114.1	117.6	11.6	5.3	2.6	5.6	3.1
Spain . . ₂	80.1	82.7	96.6	95.4	98.7	105.6	111.4	114.3	4.8	-1.3	7.0	5.5	2.6
Sweden [2].......	73.0	80.5	88.0	91.1	101.0	107.6	112.1	115.5	9.8	1.0	6.5	4.2	3.0
Switzerland......	77.0	80.0	96.0	98.0	100.0	105.0	108.0	112.0	2.0	-	5.0	2.9	3.7
Turkey.........	38.2	57.2	81.3	88.7	107.5	119.0	120.5	116.0	12.7	7.5	10.7	1.3	-3.7
United Kingdom ...	76.8	83.0	94.1	98.2	101.0	102.1	102.8	103.4	1.8	1.0	1.1	0.7	0.6
United States	**69.6**	**76.9**	**86.4**	**95.3**	**104.5**	**110.8**	**117.2**	**122.1**	**4.9**	**4.5**	**6.0**	**5.8**	**4.2**

- Represents or rounds to zero.   NA Not available.   X Not applicable.   [1] Gross domestic product in industry at factor cost and 1986 prices.   [2] Mining and manufacturing.

Source: Organization for Economic Cooperation and Development, Paris, France, *Main Economic Indicators*, monthly (copyright).

No. 1344. Labor Productivity and Hours Worked by Country: 1990 to 2000

[**Annual percent change for period shown.** Data are derived from an annual database supported by the source. The Groningen Growth and Development Centre at the University of Groningen, Netherlands, maintains the database. For OECD countries and Eastern Europe, estimates are based on gross domestic product per hour worked, converted at purchasing power parities for 1996. Hence, estimates expressed in U.S. dollars at the price level of 1996 are corrected for differences in relative price levels. Minus sign (-) indicates decrease]

Country	Labor productivity		Total hours worked	
	1990-1995	1995-2000	1990-1995	1995-2000
OECD, total.................	1.7	2.0	0.2	1.1
OECD, excl. United States...........	1.9	1.6	-0.2	1.0
European Union [1].................	2.4	1.2	-1.0	1.3
Australia........................	2.4	2.2	1.0	1.8
Austria.........................	0.3	2.3	1.7	0.3
Belgium	2.2	1.8	-0.9	0.9
Canada	1.2	1.3	0.3	2.1
Czech Republic	-0.8	1.7	-0.4	-0.7
Denmark........................	3.2	1.8	-0.7	1.0
Finland.........................	2.9	2.3	-3.4	2.5
France	1.4	1.4	-0.4	1.3
Germany	3.2	1.7	-1.6	0.4
Greece.........................	1.0	2.3	0.2	1.0
Hungary........................	3.0	3.0	-5.2	1.1
Ireland.........................	4.4	4.0	1.7	5.5
Italy...........................	2.7	0.6	-1.6	0.9
Japan..........................	1.8	1.8	-0.4	-1.0
Mexico.........................	-1.1	2.3	2.7	3.1
Netherlands	1.0	1.4	1.1	2.4
New Zealand.....................	0.9	0.8	2.1	1.5
Norway.........................	3.4	1.3	0.3	1.7
Poland.........................	4.9	5.0	-2.6	0.4
Portugal	3.1	1.1	-1.3	2.2
South Korea	5.2	2.3	2.2	0.6
Spain..........................	2.5	-0.3	-1.2	3.9
Sweden	1.6	1.8	-1.1	0.9
Switzerland......................	0.8	1.8	-0.8	-0.1
Turkey	1.6	2.1	1.6	1.6
United Kingdom	2.4	1.5	-1.0	1.1
United States...................	**0.8**	**2.6**	**1.3**	**1.6**

[1] For countries, see text of this section.

Source: The Conference Board, New York, NY, *Performance 2000: Productivity, Employment, and Income in the World's Economies*, by Robert H. McGuckin and Bart van Ark, 2001 (copyright).

No. 1345. Annual Percent Change in Consumer Prices by Country: 1995 to 2000

[Change from previous year. See text of this section for general comments concerning the data. For additional qualifications of the data for individual countries, see source. Minus sign (-) indicates decrease]

Country	1995	1997	1998	1999	2000	Country	1995	1997	1998	1999	2000
United States	2.8	2.3	1.6	2.2	3.4	Kenya	0.8	12.0	5.8	2.6	5.9
Argentina	3.4	0.5	0.9	-1.2	-0.9	Korea, South	4.5	4.4	7.5	0.8	2.3
Australia	4.6	0.3	0.9	1.5	4.5	Malaysia	5.3	2.7	5.3	2.7	1.5
Bangladesh	5.8	5.2	8.3	6.2	2.3	Mexico	35.0	20.6	15.9	16.6	9.5
Belgium	1.5	1.6	1.0	1.1	2.5	Netherlands	1.9	2.2	2.0	2.2	2.5
Brazil	66.0	6.9	3.2	4.9	7.0	Nigeria	72.8	8.2	10.3	6.6	6.9
Canada	2.2	1.6	1.0	1.7	2.7	Norway	2.5	2.6	2.3	2.3	3.1
Colombia	21.0	18.9	20.4	11.2	9.5	Pakistan	12.3	11.4	6.2	4.1	4.4
Egypt	15.7	4.6	4.2	3.1	2.7	Philippines	8.0	5.8	9.7	6.7	4.4
France	1.8	1.2	0.7	0.5	1.7	Russia	197.4	14.7	27.7	85.7	20.8
Germany	1.8	1.9	0.9	0.6	1.9	South Africa	8.6	8.6	6.9	5.2	(NA)
Greece	8.9	5.5	4.8	2.6	3.2	Spain	4.7	2.0	1.8	2.3	3.4
India	10.2	7.2	13.2	4.7	4.0	Sweden	2.5	0.5	-0.1	0.5	1.0
Indonesia	9.4	6.7	57.6	20.5	3.7	Switzerland	1.8	0.5	0.1	0.7	1.6
Iran	49.6	17.3	17.9	20.1	14.5	Thailand	5.8	5.6	8.1	0.3	1.5
Israel	10.0	9.0	5.4	5.2	1.1	Turkey	88.1	85.7	84.6	64.9	54.9
Italy	5.2	2.0	2.0	1.7	2.5	United Kingdom	3.4	3.1	3.4	1.6	2.9
Japan	-0.1	1.7	0.6	-0.3	-0.6	Venezuela	59.9	50.0	35.8	23.6	16.2

NA Not available.

Source: International Monetary Fund, Washington, DC, *International Financial Statistics*, monthly (copyright).

No. 1346. Comparative Price Levels—Selected OECD Countries: 2001

[As of May. Example of data: An item that costs $1.00 in the United States would cost $1.38 (U.S. dollars) in Japan]

Country	United States (U.S. dollar)	Canada (Canadian dollar)	Mexico (new peso)	Japan (yen)	France (franc)	Germany (Deutsche mark)	Italy (lire)	United Kingdom (pound)
United States	100	126	124	72	115	111	133	99
Australia [1]	73	92	91	53	84	82	97	73
Austria	89	113	111	65	103	100	119	88
Belgium	84	106	104	61	97	94	112	83
Canada	79	100	98	57	91	88	105	78
Czech Republic	39	49	48	28	44	43	51	38
Denmark	107	135	133	77	123	120	142	106
Finland	102	128	126	73	117	113	135	101
France	87	110	108	63	100	97	116	86
Germany	90	113	111	65	103	100	119	89
Greece	68	86	85	49	78	76	91	67
Hungary	41	52	51	30	47	46	55	41
Iceland	100	126	124	72	115	112	133	99
Ireland	89	112	110	64	102	99	117	88
Italy	75	95	93	54	86	84	100	74
Japan	138	175	172	100	159	154	184	137
Korea, South	55	69	68	40	63	61	73	54
Luxembourg	87	110	108	63	100	97	116	86
Mexico	81	102	100	58	92	90	107	80
Netherlands	84	105	104	60	96	93	111	83
New Zealand [1]	65	82	80	47	74	72	86	64
Norway	116	147	144	84	133	130	154	115
Poland	57	72	71	41	65	63	76	56
Portugal	63	80	79	46	73	71	84	63
Slovakia	32	40	39	23	36	35	42	31
Spain	74	93	91	53	84	82	98	73
Sweden	98	123	121	70	112	109	129	96
Switzerland	115	145	143	83	132	128	153	114
Turkey	43	54	53	31	49	48	57	42
United Kingdom	101	128	125	73	116	113	134	100

[1] Estimates based on quarterly consumer prices.

Source: Organization for Economic Cooperation and Development, Paris, France, *Main Economic Indicators*, August 2001 (copyright).

U.S. Census Bureau, Statistical Abstract of the United States: 2001

No. 1347. Gross Public Debt, Expenditures, and Receipts by Country: 1990 to 2000

[Percent of nominal gross domestic product. 2000 data estimated. Expenditures cover current outlays plus net capital outlays. Receipts cover current receipts but exclude capital receipts. Nontax current receipts include operating surpluses of public enterprises, property income, fees, charges, fines, etc]

Country	Gross debt			Expenditures			Receipts		
	1990	1995	2000	1990	1995	2000	1990	1995	2000
United States [1]	66.6	74.5	59.5	33.6	32.9	29.3	29.3	29.8	31.6
Australia	22.6	42.9	25.4	33.0	35.4	31.4	31.8	31.7	32.3
Austria	56.9	69.1	64.1	48.5	52.4	48.8	46.1	47.3	47.2
Belgium [2]	124.9	129.8	110.7	50.8	50.3	46.7	44.1	46.0	46.6
Canada [2]	93.3	120.6	105.9	46.0	45.3	37.8	40.1	40.0	40.3
Czech Republic	(X)	(NA)	(NA)	(X)	(NA)	47.6	(X)	(NA)	39.9
Denmark	65.8	73.9	50.4	53.6	56.6	51.3	52.5	54.3	54.0
Finland	14.3	57.2	43.5	44.4	54.3	44.8	49.6	50.6	48.8
France [.]	39.5	59.3	64.6	49.6	53.6	51.2	47.4	48.0	49.8
Germany [3]	42.0	57.1	59.6	43.8	46.3	43.0	41.8	43.0	44.4
Greece	89.0	108.7	102.7	47.8	46.6	43.7	31.7	36.4	42.7
Hungary	(NA)	(NA)	(NA)	(NA)	51.2	43.8	(NA)	43.6	39.4
Iceland	36.7	60.1	39.5	39.0	39.2	38.0	35.8	36.2	40.9
Ireland	92.4	80.0	37.3	39.5	37.6	27.7	36.7	35.4	33.2
Italy	103.7	123.1	112.0	53.1	52.3	46.7	42.1	44.7	46.6
Japan [4]	61.5	76.2	112.3	31.3	35.6	38.2	34.2	32.0	32.2
Korea, South	8.2	6.3	10.8	18.3	19.3	23.4	21.8	23.5	27.4
Netherlands	75.6	75.5	57.4	49.4	47.7	41.5	43.7	43.6	43.1
New Zealand	(NA)	(NA)	(NA)	48.8	38.8	40.8	44.0	41.9	41.2
Norway	29.5	35.4	26.1	49.7	47.6	40.6	52.3	51.1	54.7
Portugal	(NA)	64.2	55.9	(NA)	41.2	42.1	(NA)	36.6	40.5
Spain	48.5	71.7	69.7	41.4	44.0	38.5	37.2	37.4	38.2
Sweden	42.7	76.9	56.2	55.8	62.1	53.9	59.8	54.2	57.3
United Kingdom	44.5	61.1	53.5	41.9	44.4	38.4	40.4	38.6	41.2

NA Not available.   X Not applicable.   [1] Includes funded part of central government employee pension liabilities amounting to 8.3 percent of GDP in 1999. Expenditures data includes outlays net of surpluses of public enterprises. Receipts exclude the operating surpluses of public enterprises.   [2] Includes funded government employee pension liabilities amounting to 19 percent of GDP in 1999. This overstates the Canadian debt position relative to countries that have large unfunded liabilities for such pensions which are not counted in those countries' debt figures.   [3] Debt data include accounts of the Inherited Debt Fund from 1995 on. The 1995 outlays are net of the debt taken on this year from the Inherited Debt funds.   [4] Debt data include debt of the Japan Railway Settlement Corporation and the National Forest Special Account from 1998 on. The 1998 expenditures would have risen by 5.4 percentage points of GDP if account were taken of the assumption by the central government of the debt of these two entities.

Source: Organization for Economic Cooperation and Development, Paris, France, *OECD Economic Outlook*, December 2000 (copyright).

No. 1348. Percent Distribution of Tax Receipts by Country: 1980 to 1998

Country	Income and profits taxes [2]				Social security contributions			Taxes on goods and services [5]		
	Total [1]	Total [3]	Individual	Corporate	Total [4]	Employees	Employers	Total [3]	General consumption taxes [6]	Taxes on specific goods, services [7]
United States: 1980	100.0	49.8	39.1	10.8	21.9	9.2	11.9	17.6	7.0	8.3
1990	100.0	45.4	37.7	7.7	25.9	11.0	13.4	17.3	8.0	7.1
1998	100.0	49.5	40.5	9.0	23.7	10.2	12.2	16.2	7.6	6.5
Canada: 1980	100.0	46.6	34.1	11.6	10.5	3.7	6.6	32.6	11.5	13.0
1990	100.0	48.3	40.7	7.0	12.1	4.3	7.5	26.7	14.1	10.5
1998	100.0	48.5	37.8	10.0	13.7	5.3	8.1	24.7	14.0	9.1
France: 1980	100.0	16.8	11.6	5.1	42.7	11.1	28.4	30.4	21.1	8.4
1990	100.0	16.1	10.7	5.3	44.1	13.2	27.2	28.4	18.8	8.7
1998	100.0	23.3	17.4	5.9	36.2	8.7	25.2	26.6	17.5	8.4
Germany: 1980 [8]	100.0	35.1	29.6	5.5	34.3	15.3	18.4	27.1	16.6	9.3
1990	100.0	32.4	27.6	4.8	37.5	16.2	19.1	26.7	16.6	9.2
1998	100.0	29.4	25.0	4.4	40.4	17.9	19.9	27.4	17.9	8.4
Italy: 1980	100.0	31.1	23.1	7.8	38.0	6.9	28.4	26.5	15.6	9.7
1990	100.0	36.5	26.3	10.0	32.9	6.3	23.6	28.0	14.7	10.6
1998	100.0	32.6	25.0	7.0	29.4	6.3	20.5	27.4	14.2	10.2
Japan: 1980	100.0	46.1	24.3	21.8	29.1	10.2	14.8	16.3	-	14.1
1990	100.0	48.5	26.8	21.6	29.0	11.0	15.0	13.2	4.3	7.3
1998	100.0	32.1	18.8	13.3	38.4	15.0	19.6	18.8	8.9	7.7
Netherlands: 1980	100.0	32.8	26.3	6.6	38.1	15.7	17.8	25.2	15.8	7.3
1990	100.0	32.2	24.7	7.5	37.4	23.1	7.5	26.4	16.5	7.5
1998	100.0	25.8	15.2	10.6	39.9	-	12.3	27.7	16.9	8.4
Sweden: 1980	100.0	43.5	41.0	2.5	28.8	0.1	27.6	24.0	13.4	9.2
1990	100.0	41.6	38.5	3.1	27.2	0.1	26.0	25.0	14.9	9.2
1998	100.0	40.7	35.0	5.7	28.7	5.8	22.5	21.6	13.6	7.3
United Kingdom: 1980	100.0	37.8	29.4	8.4	16.7	6.4	10.1	29.1	14.7	13.3
1990	100.0	39.5	27.9	11.6	17.2	6.6	10.0	31.1	17.0	12.7
1998	100.0	38.4	27.5	11.0	17.6	7.3	9.4	32.6	18.1	12.8

- Represents zero.   [1] Includes property taxes, employer payroll taxes other than Social Security contributions, and miscellaneous taxes, not shown separately.   [2] Includes taxes on capital gains.   [3] Includes other taxes not shown separately.   [4] Includes contributions of self-employed not shown separately.   [5] Taxes on the production, sales, transfer, leasing, and delivery of goods and services and rendering of services.   [6] Primary value-added and sales taxes.   [7] For example, excise taxes on alcohol, tobacco, and gasoline.   [8] Data are for former West Germany.

Source: Organization for Economic Cooperation and Development, Paris, France, *Revenue Statistics of OECD Member Countries*, annual (copyright).

Comparative International Statistics   845

No. 1349. Income Tax and Social Security Contributions as Percent of Labor Costs: 1998

[Data are for single individual at the income level of the average production worker]

Country	Labor costs [1] (dol.)	Percent of labor costs			
		Total	Income tax	Social security contributions	
				Employee	Employer [2]
Belgium	40,995	57	22	10	26
Germany	35,863	52	17	17	17
Switzerland	32,535	30	9	10	10
Italy	32,351	47	14	7	26
Netherlands	32,271	44	6	23	14
Denmark	32,214	44	34	10	1
Canada	32,211	32	20	5	6
Norway	31,638	37	19	7	11
United States	31,300	31	17	7	7
Luxembourg	31,102	34	10	11	12
Austria	29,823	46	8	14	24
Sweden	29,768	51	21	5	25
Australia	29,590	25	24	2	-
Finland	29,334	49	22	6	21
United Kingdom	29,277	32	15	8	9
France	28,198	48	10	9	28
Japan	27,664	20	6	7	7
Ireland	24,667	33	18	5	11
Spain	24,454	39	11	5	24
New Zealand	24,332	20	20	-	-
Korea, South	22,962	15	1	4	9
Iceland	22,545	25	20	-	4
Greece	17,880	36	2	12	22
Turkey	15,825	40	21	8	11
Czech Republic	15,781	43	8	9	26
Portugal	13,903	34	6	9	19
Poland	12,696	43	11	-	33
Hungary	9,916	52	12	8	32
Mexico	8,662	22	-	2	20

- Represents or rounds to zero.   [1] Adjusted for purchasing power parities, see text of this section. Labor costs include gross wages plus employers compulsory social security contributions.   [2] Includes reported payroll taxes.

Source: Organization for Economic Cooperation and Development, Paris, France, *Taxing Wages, 1998-1999*, 2000 (copyright).

No. 1350. Patents by Country: 1999

[Includes only U.S. patents granted to residents of areas outside of the United States and its territories]

Country	Total [1]	Inventions	Designs	Country	Total [1]	Inventions	Designs
Total	75,054	69,582	5,078	Sweden	1,542	1,401	136
				Netherlands	1,396	1,247	80
Japan	32,513	31,105	1,310	Switzerland	1,391	1,280	110
Germany	9,896	9,338	485	Australia	832	707	113
Taiwan [2]	4,526	3,693	833	Israel	792	743	42
France	4,097	3,820	253	Belgium	717	648	64
United Kingdom	3,900	3,572	300	Finland	695	649	45
Korea, South	3,679	3,562	109	Denmark	588	487	86
Canada	3,678	3,226	438	Austria	505	479	25
Italy	1,686	1,492	179	Other countries	2,621	2,133	470

[1] Includes patents for botanical plants and reissues, not shown separately.   [2] See footnote 2, Table 1327.

Source: U.S. Patent and Trademark Office, Technology Assessment and Forecast Database.

U.S. Census Bureau, Statistical Abstract of the United States: 2001

No. 1351. Civilian Labor Force, Employment, and Unemployment by Country: 1980 to 2000

[106.9 represents 106,900,000. Data based on U.S. labor force definitions (see source) except that minimum age for population base varies as follows: United States, Canada, France, Sweden, and United Kingdom, 16 years; Australia, Japan, Netherlands, Germany, and Italy (beginning 1995), 15 years; and Italy (1980 and 1990) 14 years]

Year	United States	Canada	Austra- lia	Japan	France	Ger- many[1]	Italy	Nether- lands	Swe- den	United King- dom
Civilian labor force (mil.):										
1980	106.9	11.7	6.7	55.7	22.9	27.3	21.1	5.9	4.3	26.5
1990	[2]125.8	14.0	8.4	63.1	[2]24.3	[2]29.4	[2]22.7	[2]6.6	[2]4.6	28.7
1995	[2]132.3	14.5	9.0	66.0	[2]24.8	[2]39.1	[2]22.5	7.2	4.5	28.5
1998	[2]137.7	15.2	9.3	67.2	25.5	39.5	23.0	7.7	4.4	28.9
1999	[2]139.4	15.5	9.5	67.1	25.9	39.6	23.1	7.8	4.4	[3]29.1
2000	[2]140.9	15.7	9.7	[3]67.0	(NA)	(NA)	(NA)	(NA)	(NA)	(NA)
Labor force participation rate:[4]										
1980	63.8	64.9	62.1	62.6	57.5	54.7	48.2	55.4	66.9	62.5
1990	[2]66.5	67.3	64.6	62.6	55.9	55.3	[2]47.2	[2]56.1	[2]67.4	64.1
1995	[2]66.6	64.9	64.6	62.9	[2]55.3	[2]57.3	[2]47.1	58.9	64.1	62.7
1998	[2]67.1	65.4	64.4	62.8	55.7	57.7	47.6	61.4	62.8	62.7
1999	[2]67.1	65.8	64.2	62.4	56.0	57.9	47.8	61.5	[3]63.2	[3]62.9
2000	[2]67.2	65.9	64.7	[3]62.0	(NA)	(NA)	(NA)	(NA)	(NA)	(NA)
Civilian employment (mil.):										
1980	99.3	10.9	6.3	54.6	21.4	26.5	20.2	5.5	4.2	24.7
1990	[2]118.8	13.0	7.9	61.7	22.1	28.0	[2]21.1	[2]6.2	[2]4.5	26.7
1995	[2]124.9	13.3	8.2	63.9	21.9	[2]35.9	[2]19.8	6.7	4.1	26.0
1998	[2]131.5	14.1	8.6	64.5	22.5	35.8	20.2	7.4	4.0	27.1
1999	[2]133.5	14.5	8.8	63.9	23.0	36.2	20.5	7.5	4.1	[3]27.3
2000	[2]135.2	14.8	9.0	[3]63.8	(NA)	(NA)	(NA)	(NA)	(NA)	(NA)
Employment-population ratio:[5]										
1980	59.2	60.2	58.3	61.3	53.8	53.1	46.1	52.1	65.6	58.1
1990	[2]62.8	62.2	60.1	61.3	50.9	52.6	[2]43.9	[2]52.6	[2]66.1	59.6
1995	[2]62.9	59.4	59.1	60.9	48.8	[2]52.6	[2]41.5	54.9	58.3	57.2
1998	[2]64.1	60.4	59.2	60.2	49.1	52.3	41.9	58.9	57.6	58.7
1999	[2]64.3	61.3	59.6	59.4	49.8	52.8	42.3	59.4	[3]58.7	[3]59.1
2000	[2]64.5	62.1	60.4	[3]59.0	(NA)	(NA)	(NA)	(NA)	(NA)	(NA)
Unemployment rate:										
1980	7.1	7.2	6.1	2.0	6.5	2.8	4.4	6.0	2.0	7.0
1990	[2]5.6	7.7	6.9	2.1	9.1	5.0	[2]7.0	[2]6.2	[2]1.8	6.9
1995	[2]5.6	8.5	8.5	3.2	[2]11.8	[2]8.2	[2]11.8	7.1	9.1	8.7
1998	[2]4.5	7.5	8.0	4.1	11.8	9.3	12.0	4.0	8.4	6.3
1999	[2]4.2	6.8	7.2	4.7	11.2	8.7	11.5	3.4	7.1	[3]6.1
2000	[2]4.0	5.8	6.6	[3]4.8	[3]9.7	[3]8.3	[3]10.7	(NA)	[3]5.9	(NA)
Under 25 years old	9.3	11.2	12.6	[3]9.3	(NA)	(NA)	(NA)	(NA)	(NA)	(NA)
Teenagers[6]	13.1	14.8	17.0	[3]12.3	(NA)	(NA)	(NA)	(NA)	(NA)	(NA)
20 to 24 years old	7.1	9.1	9.5	[3]8.6	(NA)	(NA)	(NA)	(NA)	(NA)	(NA)
25 years old and over	3.0	4.8	5.1	[3]4.2	(NA)	(NA)	(NA)	(NA)	(NA)	(NA)

NA Not available. [1] Data for 1980 and 1990 are for former West Germany (prior to unification); data for other years are for unified Germany. [2] Break in series. Data not comparable with prior years. [3] Preliminary. [4] Civilian labor force as a percent of the civilian working age population. Germany and Japan include the institutionalized population as part of the working age population. [5] Civilian employment as a percent of the civilian working age population. Germany and Japan include the institutionalized population as part of the working age population. [6] 16 to 19 years old in the United States, Canada; 15 to 19 years old in Australia and Japan.

Source: U.S. Bureau of Labor Statistics, *Comparative Civilian Labor Force Statistics, Ten Countries, 1959-2000*, March 2001, and *Monthly Labor Review*.

No. 1352. Percent of Persons 15 to 24 Years Old Not in Education or at Work by Age Group and Sex: 1999

[Represents those person not in education and either unemployed or not in the labor force]

Country	15 to 19 years old			20 to 24 years old		
	Total	Male	Female	Total	Male	Female
Australia	7.4	7.3	7.5	14.5	10.9	18.3
Belgium	7.0	7.5	6.4	15.9	14.7	17.1
Canada	6.9	7.7	6.0	11.7	10.8	12.7
Czech Republic	20.9	21.8	20.0	20.6	12.5	29.0
Denmark	3.4	4.2	2.6	7.6	6.1	8.9
Finland	8.7	12.2	5.2	16.9	17.8	15.9
France	3.3	3.5	3.1	17.5	15.9	19.1
Germany	4.5	4.2	4.9	16.7	14.5	19.0
Greece	10.1	8.0	12.1	25.7	17.1	33.5
Hungary	10.2	9.7	10.8	21.4	16.8	26.1
Italy	14.8	14.1	15.6	29.9	27.4	32.4
Luxembourg	5.0	3.6	6.3	9.6	6.9	12.5
Mexico	17.9	6.2	29.3	26.2	5.1	45.5
Netherlands	3.8	3.6	4.0	8.0	5.7	10.4
Poland	4.6	5.2	3.9	27.2	23.4	30.8
Portugal	8.4	6.9	9.8	12.3	8.8	15.7
Spain	13.8	15.6	12.0	18.8	17.3	20.5
Sweden	4.8	6.3	3.3	11.4	11.7	11.1
Switzerland	[1]6.0	8.0	7.1	8.4	7.4	9.4
United States [2]	7.3	6.5	8.2	14.4	9.7	19.0

[1] Represents only those not in education and not in labor force. [2] Data for 1998.

Source: Organization for Economic Cooperation and Development, Paris, France, *Education at a Glance 2001* (copyright).

Comparative International Statistics 847

No. 1353. Unemployment Rates by Country: 1995 to 2000

[Annual averages. The standardized unemployment rates shown here are calculated as the number of unemployed persons as a percentage of the civilian labor force. The unemployed are persons of working age who, in the reference period, are without work, available for work and have taken specific steps to find work]

Country	1995	1998	1999	2000	Country	1995	1998	1999	2000
OECD, total	7.5	7.1	6.8	6.4	Ireland	12.3	7.5	5.6	4.2
European Union [1] ..	10.7	9.9	9.1	8.2	Italy	11.9	11.8	11.4	10 5
					Japan.........	3.1	4.1	4.7	4.7
United States.....	5.6	4.5	4.2	`4.0	Korea, South	(NA)	(NA)	(NA)	4.3
Australia	8.6	7.7	7.0	6.3	Luxembourg	2.9	2.7	2.4	2.4
Austria	3.9	4.5	4.0	3.7	Netherlands......	6.9	4.0	3.4	2.9
Belgium	9.9	9.5	8.8	7.0	New Zealand	6.3	7.5	6.8	6.0
Canada........	9.5	8.3	7.6	6.8	Norway.........	5.0	3.3	3.2	3.5
Czech Republic ...	(NA)	6.5	8.8	8.9	Poland	(NA)	10.6	(NA)	16.1
Denmark........	7.2	5.2	5.2	4.7	Portugal	7.3	5.2	4.5	4.1
Finland........	16.2	11.4	10.2	9.7	Spain	22.9	18.8	15.9	14.1
France	11.7	11.8	11.2	9.5	Sweden	8.8	8.3	7.2	5.9
Germany........	8.2	9.3	8.6	7.9	Switzerland	3.5	3.5	3.0	(NA)
Hungary	(NA)	8.0	7.1	6.5	United Kingdom ...	8.7	6.3	6.1	5.5

NA Not available.   [1] See footnote 3, Table 1340.

Source: Organization for Economic Cooperation and Development, Paris, France, *Main Economic Indicators*, September 2001 and earlier releases.

No. 1354. Female Labor Force Participation Rates by Country: 1980 to 1999

[In percent. Female labor force of all ages divided by female population 15-64 years old]

Country	1980	1990	1995	1999	Country	1980	1990	1995	1999
Australia	52.7	62.9	64.8	64.4	Korea, South	(NA)	51.3	53.2	53.1
Austria..........	48.7	55.4	62.3	62.2	Luxembourg	39.9	50.7	58.0	64.6
Belgium..........	47.0	52.4	56.1	57.8	Mexico	33.7	23.6	40.1	42.1
Canada..........	57.8	67.8	67.6	69.6	Netherlands...........	35.5	[1]53.1	[1]59.0	64.5
Czech Republic.......	(X)	69.1	[1]65.4	64.9	New Zealand	44.6	[1]62.9	63.3	67.7
Denmark..........	(NA)	78.5	73.6	75.8	Norway	62.3	71.2	72.4	76.3
Finland..........	70.1	72.9	70.3	71.3	Poland..............	(NA)	(NA)	61.1	59.0
France...........	54.4	57.6	59.4	60.8	Portugal............	54.3	62.9	62.4	66.8
Germany [2]........	52.8	57.4	61.7	62.8	Spain	32.2	41.2	45.1	48.9
Greece..........	33.0	43.6	45.9	49.0	Sweden	74.1	[1]80.5	76.1	74.6
Hungary..........	(NA)	(NA)	50.5	52.1	Switzerland	54.1	59.6	[1]67.8	70.3
Iceland	(NA)	65.6	81.9	83.1	Turkey.............	(NA)	36.7	34.2	34.0
Ireland...........	36.3	38.9	47.8	54.9	United Kingdom	58.3	65.5	66.6	67.5
Italy	39.6	45.9	[1]43.3	46.0	United States	59.7	[1]68.8	70.7	71.7
Japan	54.8	60.4	62.2	63.8					

NA Not available.   X Not applicable.   [1] Break in series. Data not comparable with prior years.   [2] Prior to 1991 data are for former West Germany.

Source: Organization for Economic Cooperation and Development, Paris, France, *OECD in Figures*, annual (copyright).

No. 1355. Civilian Employment-Population Ratio by Country: 1980 to 2000

[Civilian employment as a percent of the civilian working age population. See headnote, Table 1351]

Country	Women					Men				
	1980	1990	1995	1999	2000	1980	1990	1995	1999	2000
United States ..	47.7	[1]54.3	55.6	57.4	57.7	72.0	[1]72.0	70.8	71.6	71.8
Canada	46.8	54.1	52.8	55.2	56.1	74.0	70.6	66.2	67.6	68.3
Australia......	41.9	49.3	50.3	51.2	52.4	75.1	71.2	68.1	68.2	68.5
Japan	45.7	48.0	47.7	46.6	[2]46.4	77.9	75.4	75.0	73.0	[2]72.5
France	40.3	41.5	41.2	42.4	(NA)	68.9	61.3	57.2	57.8	(NA)
Germany [3]	38.9	[1]40.9	[1]42.7	[4]43.4	(NA)	69.6	[1]65.6	[1]63.4	[4]62.0	(NA)
Italy	27.9	[1]29.2	[1]28.0	29.7	(NA)	66.0	[1]60.0	[1]56.5	56.1	(NA)
Netherlands ...	31.0	[1]39.1	44.3	50.5	(NA)	74.1	[1]66.7	65.6	68.6	(NA)
Sweden	58.0	[1]61.8	54.7	[2]54.6	(NA)	73.6	[1]70.6	62.1	[2]63.1	(NA)
United Kingdom .	44.8	49.8	49.6	[4]51.0	(NA)	72.8	70.3	65.5	[4]66.9	(NA)

NA Not available.   [1] Break in series. Data not comparable with prior years.   [2] Preliminary.   [3] Data for 1980 and 1990 are for former West Germany (prior to unification); data for other years are for unified Germany.   [4] 1998 data.

Source: U.S. Bureau of Labor Statistics, *Comparative Civilian Labor Force Statistics, Ten Countries, 1959-2000*, March 2001, and *Monthly Labor Review*.

No. 1356. Civilian Employment by Industry and Country: 1990 and 2000

[118,793 represents 118,793,000. Data based on U.S. labor force definitions except that minimum age for population base varies as follows: United States, Canada, France, Sweden, and United Kingdom, 16 years; Australia, Germany, Italy (1999), Japan, 15 years; and Italy (1990), 14 years. Industries based on International Standard Industrial Classification; see text of this section]

Industry	United States	Canada	Australia	Japan	France	Germany[1]	Italy	Sweden	United Kingdom
TOTAL EMPLOYMENT (1,000)									
1990, total	118,793	13,084	7,859	61,710	22,082	27,952	21,080	4,501	26,818
Agriculture, forestry, fishing	3,394	559	440	4,270	1,262	965	1,879	178	573
Industry[2]	29,834	3,063	1,865	20,890	6,403	10,875	6,842	1,268	8,128
Manufacturing	21,346	2,053	1,170	15,010	4,708	8,839	4,755	943	[3]5,971
Services	85,565	9,462	5,554	36,550	14,417	16,112	12,355	3,056	18,117
2000, total	[4]135,208	14,910	9,043	[5]63,790	[6]22,970	[6]36,167	[4][6]20,462	[4]4,105	[7]27,009
Agriculture, forestry, fishing	[4]3,457	492	440	[5]3,120	[6]961	[6]1,025	[4][6]1,127	[6]128	[7]465
Industry[2]	[4]29,894	3,259	1,929	[5]19,710	[6]5,447	[6]12,152	[4][6]6,744	[6]996	[7]7,047
Manufacturing	[4]19,940	2,280	1,145	[5]13,180	(NA)	[6]8,710	[4][6]5,170	[6]759	[7]5,033
Services	[4]101,857	11,158	6,674	[5]40,960	[6]16,562	[6]22,990	[4][6]12,590	[6]2,981	[7]19,497
PERCENT DISTRIBUTION									
1990, total	100	100	100	100	100	100	100	100	100
Agriculture, forestry, fishing	3	4	6	7	6	4	9	4	2
Industry[2]	25	23	24	34	29	39	33	28	30
Manufacturing	18	16	15	24	21	32	23	21	[3]22
Services	72	72	71	59	65	58	59	68	68
2000, total	[4]100	100	100	[5]100	[6]100	[6]100	[4][6]100	[6]100	[7]100
Agriculture, forestry, fishing	[4]3	3	5	[5]5	[6]4	[6]3	[4][6]6	[6]3	[7]2
Industry[2]	[4]22	22	21	[5]31	[6]24	[6]34	[4][6]33	[6]24	[7]26
Manufacturing	[4]15	15	13	[5]21	(NA)	[6]24	[4][6]25	[6]18	[7]19
Services	[4]75	75	75	[5]64	[6]72	[6]64	[4][6]62	[6]73	[7]72

NA Not available. [1] Data for 1990 are for former West Germany (prior to unification); data for 1999 are for unified Germany. [2] Includes mining and construction. [3] Includes mining. [4] Break in series. Data not comparable with prior years. [5] Preliminary. [6] 1999 data. [7] 1998 data.

Source: U.S. Bureau of Labor Statistics, Comparative Civilian Labor Force Statistics, Ten Countries, 1959-2000, March 2001 and unpublished data.

No. 1357. World Food Production by Commodity: 1990 to 2000

[In millions of metric tons (1,768.8 represents 1,768,800,000)]

Commodity	1990	1993	1994	1995	1996	1997	1998	1999	2000
Grains, total	1,768.8	1,714.0	1,760.8	1,712.6	1,871.4	1,879.9	1,872.4	1,871.2	1,837.0
Wheat	588.0	559.0	524.8	538.6	582.8	609.2	588.2	587.9	579.5
Coarse grains	828.7	799.7	871.6	802.7	908.3	883.9	890.0	877.0	859.7
Corn	482.3	476.1	560.2	516.6	592.0	575.2	605.3	605.6	585.6
Rice, milled	352.0	355.4	364.5	371.3	380.4	386.8	394.2	406.3	397.7
Oils	58.1	63.5	70.0	72.8	75.6	76.2	80.6	84.6	86.9
Soybeans	104.2	117.8	137.7	124.9	132.2	158.1	159.7	158.7	168.5
Rapeseed	25.1	26.8	30.4	34.5	31.6	33.2	35.9	42.3	37.6
Pulses[1]	58.4	55.7	56.3	54.8	53.6	55.1	55.9	58.1	55.7
Vegetables and melons[1]	461.4	509.5	532.1	559.6	591.2	607.8	626.0	649.2	670.1
Fruits[1]	352.2	384.7	391.0	406.4	427.3	443.6	432.8	447.2	459.2
Nuts[1]	4.6	5.0	5.3	5.0	5.6	5.9	5.9	6.4	6.2
Red meat	117.2	117.7	119.9	124.2	124.5	130.3	135.3	138.6	139.7
Poultry	37.4	43.6	46.8	50.6	53.0	54.6	55.6	58.5	58.1
Milk	441.3	393.5	383.7	380.8	380.3	381.2	385.7	389.3	391.4

[1] Data from Food and Agriculture Organization of the United Nations, Rome, Italy.

Source: U.S. Dept. of Agriculture, Economic Research Service, Agricultural Outlook, monthly.

No. 1358. Fisheries—Commercial Catch by Country: 1990 to 1998

[In thousands of metric tons, live weight (97,854 represents 97,854,000). Catch of fish, crustaceans, mollusks (including weight of shells). Does not include marine mammals and aquatic plants]

Country	1990	1995	1997	1998	Country	1990	1995	1997	1998
World[1]	97,854	116,042	122,443	117,162	Thailand	2,786	3,573	3,430	3,470
					Norway	1,745	2,803	3,223	3,259
China[2]	12,095	28,418	35,038	38,025	Korea, South	1,745	2,688	2,596	2,354
Japan	10,354	6,787	6,723	6,026	Philippines	2,210	2,222	2,136	2,140
India	3,794	4,906	5,379	5,244	Iceland	1,508	1,616	2,210	1,686
United States	5,868	5,638	5,422	5,154	Vietnam	960	1,394	1,573	1,653
Russia	7,808	4,374	4,715	4,518	Denmark	1,518	2,044	1,866	1,600
Indonesia	3,044	4,139	4,454	4,396	Bangladesh	848	1,173	1,342	1,423
Peru	6,875	8,943	7,877	4,346	Spain	1,380	1,391	1,382	1,420
Chile	5,195	7,591	6,084	3,558	Mexico	1,401	1,355	1,529	1,222

[1] Includes other countries, not shown separately. [2] See footnote 2, Table 1327.

Source: U.S. National Oceanic and Atmospheric Administration, National Marine Fisheries Service, Fisheries of the United States, annual. Data from Food and Agriculture Organization of the United Nations, Rome, Italy.

Comparative International Statistics 849

No. 1359. Meat Production by Type and Country: 1998 to 2000

[In thousand metric tons (48,604 represents 48,604,000). Carcass weight basis for beef, veal, and pork. Excludes offals and rabbit]

Country	Beef and veal		Country	Pork [1]		Country	Poultry meat	
	1998	1999, prel.		1998	1999, prel.		1999	2000, prel.
World [2]	48,604	49,342	World [2]	78,940	81,240	World [2]	56,504	58,010
United States	11,804	12,124	China [3]	38,837	40,056	United States	15,990	16,422
Brazil	6,140	6,270	United States	8,623	8,758	China [3]	11,150	11,350
China [3]	4,799	5,054	Germany	3,833	4,113	Brazil	5,641	5,987
Argentina	2,600	2,840	Spain	2,667	2,892	France	2,228	2,240
Australia	1,989	1,956	France	2,328	2,378	Mexico	1,922	2,036
Russia	2,090	1,900	Brazil	1,690	1,835	United Kingdom	1,516	1,535
Mexico	1,800	1,860	Poland	1,690	1,730	Japan	1,189	1,170
India	1,593	1,660	Netherlands	1,717	1,711	South Africa	1,121	1,150
France	1,593	1,568	Denmark	1,632	1,650	Thailand	1,025	1,117
Germany	1,367	1,374	Canada	1,338	1,562	Italy	1,135	1,098

[1] Includes edible pork fat, but excludes lard and inedible greases (except United States). [2] Includes other countries, not shown separately. [3] See footnote 2, Table 1327.

Source: U.S. Dept. of Agriculture, National Agricultural Statistics Service, *Agricultural Statistics*, annual.

No. 1360. Per Capita Consumption of Meat and Poultry: 2000

[Preliminary. In kilograms per capita. Beef, veal, and pork quantities are as of September and in carcass-weight equivalents; poultry quantities are as of July and are on ready-to-cook basis]

Country	Beef and veal		Country	Pork		Country	Poultry	
	Quantity	Rank		Quantity	Rank		Quantity	Rank
Argentina	68.8	1	Denmark	76.8	1	Hong Kong	57.4	1
Uruguay	61.4	2	Spain	65.0	2	United States	49.3	2
United States	46.4	3	Czech Republic	60.6	3	Canada	34.8	3
Australia	36.1	4	Hong Kong	60.1	4	Saudi Arabia	34.3	4
New Zealand	35.2	5	Austria	57.8	5	Taiwan [1]	34.0	5
Brazil	34.8	6	Germany	56.9	6	United Kingdom	28.4	6
Canada	32.1	7	Belgium-Luxembourg	46.8	7	Brazil	28.2	7
France	25.6	8	Netherlands	43.8	8	South Africa	26.4	8
Italy	24.9	9	Taiwan [1]	42.6	9	Spain	26.4	9
Mexico	23.2	10	Portugal	41.1	10	France	24.9	10
			United States	30.7	19			

[1] See footnote 2, Table 1327.

Source: U.S. Department of Agriculture, Foreign Agricultural Service, *Livestock and Poultry: World Markets and Trade*, annual.

No. 1361. Wheat, Rice, and Corn Production by Country: 1995 to 2000

[In thousands of metric tons (582,774 represents 582,774,000). Rice data cover paddy. Data for each country pertain to the calendar year in which all or most of the crop was harvested. See text of this section for general comments concerning quality of the data]

Country	Wheat			Rice			Corn		
	1995	1999	2000	1995	1999	2000	1995	1999	2000
World	582,774	587,944	579,476	551,036	604,218	591,777	516,637	605,647	585,556
Argentina	8,600	15,500	16,500	877	860	615	11,100	17,200	15,000
Australia	16,504	25,012	20,500	951	1,084	1,600	317	365	400
Bangladesh	1,245	1,900	2,000	26,533	32,298	31,953	-	-	-
Brazil	1,526	2,500	1,600	10,026	11,534	10,882	32,480	31,600	38,500
Burma	150	100	100	17,000	17,000	16,897	270	240	250
Canada	25,037	26,850	26,800	-	-	-	7,271	9,096	6,800
China [1]	102,215	113,880	102,000	185,214	198,480	190,000	112,000	128,086	105,000
Egypt	5,700	6,550	6,600	4,399	5,826	6,000	5,353	5,678	5,800
France	30,862	37,232	37,500	124	103	108	12,394	15,374	16,300
Germany	17,763	19,615	21,600	-	-	-	2,395	3,257	3,250
India	65,470	70,780	75,570	119,442	134,233	132,763	9,530	11,470	12,000
Indonesia	-	-	-	51,100	52,919	53,000	6,000	6,200	6,200
Italy	7,653	7,341	7,100	1,311	1,376	1,360	8,454	10,000	10,800
Mexico	3,468	3,100	3,300	349	450	450	17,780	19,000	18,500
Pakistan	17,002	17,854	21,000	5,951	7,735	6,451	1,283	1,250	1,250
Russia	30,100	31,000	34,400	462	446	577	1,700	1,100	1,500
Thailand	-	-	-	21,800	25,000	25,152	3,700	3,900	4,400
Turkey	15,500	16,500	17,500	346	338	338	1,800	2,400	2,400
United Kingdom	14,310	14,870	16,700	-	-	-	-	-	-
United States	59,404	62,569	60,512	7,887	9,345	8,669	187,970	239,549	253,208

- Represents or rounds to zero. [1] See footnote 2, Table 1327.

Source: U.S. Department of Agriculture, Economic Research Service, unpublished data from the PS&D (Production, supply and distribution) database.

No. 1362. Wheat, Rice, and Corn—Exports and Imports of Leading Countries: 1995 to 2000

[In thousands of metric tons (32,003 represents 32,003,000). Wheat data are for trade year beginning in July of year shown; rice data are for calendar year; corn data are for trade year beginning in October of year shown. Countries listed are the ten leading exporters or importers in 2000]

Leading exporters	Exports 1995	Exports 1999	Exports 2000	Leading importers	Imports 1995	Imports 1999	Imports 2000
WHEAT				**WHEAT**			
European Union [1]	32,003	38,343	35,900	European Union [1]	21,505	25,091	24,775
United States	33,778	29,653	29,937	Brazil	5,600	7,555	7,900
Canada	16,342	19,165	19,000	Iran	3,029	7,000	7,500
Australia	13,311	17,844	15,500	Egypt	5,932	5,973	6,200
Argentina	4,483	11,600	12,000	Japan	6,101	5,960	5,900
Kazakhstan	4,279	6,514	4,500	Korea, South	2,554	3,811	4,000
Hungary	2,239	800	1,500	Algeria	3,782	4,750	5,200
Turkey	1,054	2,163	1,500	Indonesia	3,632	3,900	3,700
India	1,500	200	1,000	Morocco	2,336	3,100	3,100
Czech Republic	596	836	700	Philippines	1,980	3,000	3,000
RICE				**RICE**			
Thailand	5,281	6,549	6,300	European Union [1]	1,680	1,558	1,570
Vietnam	3,040	3,370	3,800	Iran	1,344	1,100	1,400
China [2]	265	2,950	3,200	Indonesia	1,029	1,500	1,300
United States	2,694	2,804	2,553	Iraq	234	1,261	1,300
Pakistan	1,632	1,850	1,800	Nigeria	300	950	1,200
India	3,500	1,400	1,300	Saudi Arabia	638	750	950
European Union [1]	902	1,253	1,219	Bangladesh	1,140	400	900
Australia	475	585	690	Philippines	975	665	800
Uruguay	600	685	685	Japan	451	720	750
Japan	-	200	600	Brazil	770	650	725
CORN				**CORN**			
United States	56,589	49,209	52,072	Japan	15,976	16,117	16,000
European Union [1]	7,480	8,911	8,916	European Union [1]	10,420	10,870	10,605
Argentina	7,494	11,500	8,800	Korea, South	8,963	8,694	8,000
China [2]	168	9,935	6,000	Mexico	6,433	4,911	5,800
South Africa	2,650	1,400	800	Taiwan [2]	5,734	5,023	5,100
Brazil	218	150	750	Egypt	2,257	4,600	4,500
Ukraine	58	57	600	Malaysia	2,309	2,296	2,400
Paraguay	124	196	250	Colombia	1,430	1,900	2,000
Hungary	120	1,786	200	Saudi Arabia	926	1,500	1,600
Former Yugoslavia	228	500	200	Canada	855	691	1,600

- Represents or rounds to zero.   [1] See footnote 3, Table 1340.   [2] See footnote 2, Table 1327.
Source: U.S. Department of Agriculture, Economic Research Service, unpublished data from the PS&D (Production, supply and distribution) database.

No. 1363. Unmanufactured Tobacco and Cigarettes—Selected Countries: 1995 to 2000

[5,546 represents 5,546,000. Tobacco is on dry weight basis]

Country	Unmanufactured tobacco (1,000 metric tons) 1995	1999	2000
PRODUCTION			
World, total	5,546	5,917	5,773
China [1]	2,083	2,075	2,051
India	528	588	599
Brazil	324	498	493
United States	513	528	408
Zimbabwe	179	171	209
EXPORTS			
World, total	1,767	2,054	1,938
Brazil	256	343	350
Zimbabwe	174	216	196
United States	209	192	183
Malawi	99	108	101
Greece	133	100	101
IMPORTS			
World, total	1,781	2,011	2,039
Russia	148	265	275
Germany	210	261	246
United States	199	239	197
United Kingdom	141	137	135
Japan	115	99	104
CONSUMPTION			
World, total	6,305	6,641	6,437
China [1]	2,209	2,696	2,645
India	464	478	470
United States	699	575	436
Russia	142	266	277
Japan	197	184	183

Country	Cigarettes (bil. pieces) 1995	1999	2000
PRODUCTION			
World, total	5,599	5,610	5,625
China [1]	1,735	1,712	1,740
United States	746	635	600
Russia	141	263	273
Japan	263	263	265
Indonesia	186	220	229
United Kingdom	156	155	150
Turkey	100	125	128
EXPORTS			
World, total	987	845	856
United States	231	151	148
United Kingdom	85	115	118
Netherlands	82	105	106
Germany	85	85	85
Singapore	50	59	59
Hong Kong	74	25	26
Bulgaria	61	20	20
Indonesia	21	17	18
IMPORTS			
World, total	668	656	661
Japan	72	83	83
France	51	62	63
Singapore	38	49	49
Italy	39	50	49
United Kingdom	20	44	48
Hong Kong	59	24	25
Russia	78	22	15

[1] See footnote 2, Table 1327.
Source: U.S. Dept. of Agriculture, Foreign Agricultural Service, *Tobacco: World Markets and Trade*, April 2001.

U.S. Census Bureau, Statistical Abstract of the United States: 2001

No. 1364. Wood Products—Production, Exports, and Consumption for Selected Countries: 1990 to 1999

[In thousand cubic meters (5,830 represents 5,830,000)]

Country	Production			Exports			Consumption		
	1990	1995	1999	1990	1995	1999	1990	1995	1999
SOFTWOOD LOGS									
Australia	5,830	8,188	10,760	-	100	785	5,830	8,088	9,976
Canada	122,000	120,000	165,984	800	729	1,908	125,289	124,295	168,536
China [1]	69,080	10,400 ·	33,146	8	22	2	72,835	10,968	37,683
Finland	19,600	24,600	28,000	161	1,000	762	19,734	23,850	31,638
France	14,189	13,550	14,500	477	250	363	13,969	13,419	14,247
Germany [2]	(NA)	20,410	18,897	1,947	3,298	3,044	(NA)	18,234	18,299
Japan	16,775	18,067	15,206	11	4	2	33,446	32,968	27,732
New Zealand	8,361	12,704	13,900	2,931	5,257	5,800	5,435	7,449	8,104
Russia	(NA)	(NA)	58,000	(NA)	(NA)	15,000	(NA)	(NA)	43,000
Sweden	24,700	30,100	30,300	336	500	1,295	24,787	30,200	35,075
SOFTWOOD LUMBER									
Canada	53,777	59,590	68,235	37,008	47,561	48,381	17,767	12,789	20,596
China [1]	17,650	7,200	10,145	15	50	38	17,733	7,400	10,500
Finland	7,400	9,400	11,700	4,152	7,337	8,323	3,261	2,213	3,596
Germany [2]	12,145	13,308	14,736	839	1,618	1,937	15,551	16,455	18,021
Japan	26,551	22,777	18,130	7	-	-	33,854	32,591	26,501
Russia	(NA)	(NA)	13,500	(NA)	(NA)	4,100	(NA)	(NA)	9,400
Sweden	11,785	14,559	14,608	6,500	10,700	10,975	5,431	4,014	3,763
TEMPERATE HARDWOOD LOGS									
China [1]	42,340	3,750	14,519	83	51	4	42,285	5,350	14,957
France	10,157	8,160	7,920	1,655	1,000	1,114	8,621	7,290	7,165
Russia	(NA)	(NA)	19,000	(NA)	(NA)	5,500	(NA)	(NA)	13,500
TEMPERATE HARDWOOD LUMBER									
China [1]	10,819	2,500	5,520	65	177	268	10,755	2,830	7,230
France	3,303	2,908	2,791	646	606	540	2,767	2,793	2,568
Russia	(NA)	(NA)	4,800	(NA)	(NA)	280	(NA)	(NA)	4,520
TROPICAL HARDWOOD LOGS									
Brazil	33,000	25,700	27,300	-	-	570	33,146	25,706	26,735
Indonesia	27,000	25,000	26,000	-	-	-	27,068	25,004	26,000
Malaysia	39,655	31,572	21,741	20,378	7,864	6,998	19,286	23,934	15,382
TROPICAL HARDWOOD LUMBER									
Brazil	8,500	9,220	9,860	525	984	740	8,252	9,719	9,440
Indonesia	9,000	7,500	6,800	561	722	-	8,439	6,778	6,800
Malaysia	8,780	6,950	5,187	5,247	4,151	2,788	3,568	3,896	3,576

- Represents zero.   NA Not available.   [1] See footnote 2, Table 1327.   [2] Data for 1990 do not include East Germany.
Source: U.S. Dept. of Agriculture, Foreign Agricultural Service, *Wood Products: International Trade and Foreign Markets, Biennial Production, Consumption, and Trade Edition,* Circular Series WP-1-01, March 2001.

No. 1365. World Production of Major Mineral Commodities: 1990 to 2000

[5,386 represents 5,386,000,000]

Country	Unit	1990	1995	1999	2000, prel.	Leading producers, 1999
MINERAL FUELS						
Coal	Mil. short tons	5,386	5,161	4,737	(NA)	China, United States, India
Dry natural gas	Tril. cu. ft.	73.6	78.0	84.7	(NA)	Russia, United States, Canada
Natural gas plant liquids [1]	Mil. barrels [2]	1,691	2,002	2,184	(NA)	United States, Saudi Arabia, Canada
Petroleum, crude	Mil. barrels [2]	22,107	22,752	24,043	(NA)	Saudi Arabia, Russia, United States
NONMETALLIC MINERALS						
Cement, hydraulic	Mil. metric tons	1,160	1,444 ·	1,600	1,700	China, India, United States
Diamond, gem and industrial	Mil. carats	111	113	117	(NA)	Australia, Congo (Kinshasa), Russia
Nitrogen in ammonia	Mil. metric tons	97.5	100.0	108.0	104.0	China, United States, India
Phosphate rock	Mil. metric tons	162	130	141	139	United States, China, Morocco
Potash, marketable	Mil. metric tons	27.5	24.6	25.7	26.5	Canada, Russia, Belarus
Salt	Mil. metric tons	183	192	209	210	United States, China, Germany
Sulfur, elemental basis	Mil. metric tons	57.8	53.2	57.1	57.4	United States, Canada, China
METALS						
Aluminum [3]	Mil. metric tons	19.3	19.7	23.1	23.9	United States, Russia, China
Bauxite, gross weight	Mil. metric tons	113.0	112.0	127.0	127.0	Australia, Guinea, Brazil
Chromite, gross weight [1]	1,000 metric tons	13,200	14,300	13,500	13,700	South Africa, Kazakhstan, Turkey
Copper, metal content [4]	1,000 metric tons	8,950	10,100	12,600	12,900	Chile, United States, Indonesia
Gold, metal content	Metric tons	2,180	2,210	2,540	2,445	South Africa, United States, Australia
Iron ore, gross weight [5]	Mil. metric tons	983	1,031	994	1,010	China, Brazil, Australia
Lead, metal content [4]	1,000 metric tons	3,370	2,820	3,020	2,980	Australia, United States, China
Nickel, metal content [4]	1,000 metric tons	974	1,030	1,120	1,230	Russia, Canada, Australia
Tin, metal content [4]	1,000 metric tons	221	193	198	200	China, Indonesia, Peru
Zinc, metal content [4]	1,000 metric tons	7,150	7,280	8,040	8,000	China, Australia, Canada

NA Not available.   [1] Excludes China.   [2] 42-gallon barrels.   [3] Unalloyed ingot metal.   [4] Mine output.   [5] Includes iron ore concentrates and iron ore agglomerates.
Source: Mineral fuels, U.S. Energy Information Administration, *International Energy Annual;* nonmetallic minerals and metals, 1990, U.S. Bureau of Mines, thereafter, U.S. Geological Survey, *Minerals Yearbook; Annual Reports;* and *Mineral Commodity Summaries, 2000.*

No. 1366. World Primary Energy Production by Region and Type: 1980 to 1999

[In quadrillion Btu (286.4 represents 286,400,000,000,000,000). Btu=British thermal units. For Btu conversion factors, see source]

Region and type	1980	1985	1990	1993	1994	1995	1996	1997	1998	1999
World total [1]	286.4	304.2	351.0	350.8	355.8	364.7	373.4	381.1	382.9	380.1
North America	80.9	84.6	92.0	91.9	95.3	96.2	98.6	99.2	99.4	99.0
United States	64.8	64.9	70.9	68.4	70.8	71.3	72.6	72.5	72.6	72.3
Central and South America	12.1	13.6	16.7	18.9	19.9	21.3	22.6	24.3	24.9	24.9
Western Europe	30.7	37.3	38.5	39.5	40.6	41.7	44.0	44.1	43.9	44.2
Eastern Europe and former U.S.S.R.	66.7	75.0	81.9	66.5	61.4	60.1	60.0	58.8	57.8	59.0
Middle East	42.2	25.8	41.0	45.8	46.9	48.0	49.0	51.3	54.5	53.1
Africa	18.1	19.3	21.6	22.8	23.0	24.2	24.7	26.2	26.4	26.8
Far East and Oceania	35.8	48.7	59.3	65.5	68.7	73.4	74.3	77.1	75.9	73.0
Crude oil	128.1	115.4	129.5	128.9	130.5	133.3	136.6	140.5	143.2	140.8
Natural gas	52.7	61.4	75.9	78.4	79.2	80.2	84.1	84.0	85.4	87.3
Natural gas liquids	5.1	5.8	6.9	7.7	7.8	8.1	8.3	8.5	8.7	8.9
Coal	74.5	85.8	91.9	85.2	86.8	89.2	89.2	92.5	89.4	84.9
Hydroelectric power	18.1	20.6	22.6	24.3	24.5	25.7	26.1	26.7	26.7	27.1
Nuclear electric power	7.6	15.4	20.4	22.1	22.5	23.3	24.1	23.9	24.4	25.3
Geothermal, solar, wind wood, and waste	0.4	0.6	1.7	2.1	2.2	2.2	2.4	2.5	2.6	2.8

[1] Includes geothermal, solar, and wood and waste energy produced in the United States and not used for generating electricity, not shown separately by type.

No. 1367. World Primary Energy Consumption by Region and Type: 1980 to 1999

[In quadrillion Btu (282.6 represents 282,600,000,000,000,000). Btu=British thermal units. For Btu conversion factors, see source]

Region and type	1980	1985	1990	1993	1994	1995	1996	1997	1998	1999
World total [1]	282.6	307.5	346.2	352.8	356.4	365.6	374.9	379.8	379.7	381.9
North America	89.3	88.3	100.1	103.9	106.3	108.0	111.7	112.4	112.7	115.7
United States	76.0	74.0	84.2	87.3	89.2	90.9	93.9	94.3	94.6	97.1
Central and South America	11.4	12.3	14.1	15.8	16.5	17.3	18.2	19.0	20.0	20.4
Western Europe	58.6	59.9	63.9	64.6	64.4	66.7	68.5	69.2	70.5	70.5
Eastern Europe and former U.S.S.R.	61.4	70.7	74.2	60.6	54.6	53.2	52.4	50.3	48.9	48.9
Middle East	5.9	8.6	11.1	12.7	13.3	13.9	14.6	15.4	16.1	16.4
Africa	6.8	8.5	9.3	10.2	10.6	10.8	11.1	11.6	11.6	11.8
Far East and Oceania	49.2	59.3	73.4	85.0	90.6	95.8	98.6	101.8	99.9	98.2
Petroleum	130.9	123.1	134.9	136.6	139.1	142.3	145.4	148.3	149.8	152.2
Natural gas	54.2	63.7	74.5	78.4	78.3	80.2	84.0	83.8	84.5	86.9
Coal	71.6	84.2	90.0	87.1	87.4	89.4	90.4	92.1	89.3	84.8
Hydroelectric power	18.3	21.0	22.7	24.6	24.8	26.0	26.4	27.0	26.9	27.3
Nuclear electric power	7.6	15.4	20.4	22.1	22.5	23.3	24.1	23.9	24.4	25.3
Geothermal, solar, wind wood, and waste	0.3	0.5	1.7	2.1	2.2	2.2	2.4	2.5	2.6	2.8

[1] See footnote 1, Table 1366.

Source of Tables 1366 and 1367: U.S. Energy Information Administration, *International Energy Annual.*

No. 1368. World Energy Consumption by Region and Energy Source, 1990 to 1999, and Projections, 2005 to 2020

[In quadrillion Btu (346.0 represents 346,000,000,000,000,000). Btu=British thermal units. For Btu conversion factors, see source]

Region and energy source	1990	1998	1999	Projections			
				2005	2010	2015	2020
World, total	346.0	380.0	381.8	439.3	489.7	547.4	607.1
North America	99.9	113.1	115.7	128.8	138.2	146.9	155.6
United States	84.0	94.7	96.7	107.0	114.1	120.7	127.0
Western Europe	59.8	65.7	65.9	71.5	74.5	77.3	80.7
Industrialized Asia	22.8	27.6	27.9	29.6	30.7	32.7	34.0
Eastern Europe and former Soviet Union	76.3	50.7	50.5	56.0	60.3	67.2	72.3
Developing Asia	51.0	72.9	70.9	92.4	113.4	137.0	162.2
Middle East	13.1	19.1	19.3	22.5	26.9	31.7	37.2
Africa	9.3	11.6	11.8	14.3	16.1	18.6	20.8
Central and South America	13.7	19.4	19.8	24.3	29.6	36.2	44.1
Oil	134.9	149.8	152.2	173.3	193.7	218.1	244.4
Natural gas	74.5	84.5	86.9	106.5	124.2	146.2	168.6
Coal	90.0	89.3	84.8	94.8	102.6	109.6	117.1
Nuclear	20.4	24.4	25.3	26.7	27.4	27.7	27.1
Other	26.3	32.0	32.7	38.1	41.9	45.9	50.0

Source: U.S. Energy Information Administration, *International Energy Outlook 2001.*

U.S. Census Bureau, Statistical Abstract of the United States: 2001

No. 1369. Energy Consumption and Production by Country: 1990 and 1999

[346.2 represents 346,200,000,000,000,000. See text of this section for general comments about the data. For data qualifications for countries, see source]

Country	Primary energy consumed				Dry natural gas production (tril. cu. ft)		Crude petroleum production (1,000 barrels per day)		Coal production (mil. short tons)	
	Total (quad. Btu)		Per capita (mil. Btu)							
	1990	1999, prel.	1990	1999, prel.	1990	1999	1990	1999	1990	1999
World	**346.2**	**381.9**	**66**	**64**	**73.6**	**84.7**	**60,566**	**65,870**	**5,386**	**4,737**
United States	**84.2**	**97.1**	**337**	**356**	**17.8**	**18.6**	**7,355**	**5,881**	**1,029**	**1,099**
Algeria	1.2	1.3	49	43	1.8	2.9	1,175	1,202	(Z)	(Z)
Argentina	1.9	2.7	58	74	0.6	1.2	483	802	(Z)	(Z)
Australia	3.7	4.7	215	250	0.7	1.1	575	539	226	321
Austria	1.2	1.4	151	170	0.1	0.1	22	18	3	1
Bahrain	0.3	0.4	520	552	0.2	0.3	42	37	(NA)	(NA)
Bangladesh	0.3	0.5	2	4	0.2	0.3	1	1	(NA)	(NA)
Belarus	(X)	1.1	(X)	108	(X)	(Z)	(X)	37	(X)	(NA)
Belgium	2.2	2.6	217	256	(Z)	-	(NA)	(NA)	3	(Z)
Brazil	5.7	8.5	39	52	0.1	0.2	631	1,132	5	5
Bulgaria	1.3	0.8	145	102	(Z)	(Z)	4	1	39	29
Burma	(NA)	(NA)	(NA)	(NA)	(Z)	0.1	13	9	(Z)	(Z)
Canada	10.9	12.5	394	411	3.9	6.3	1,553	1,907	75	80
Chile	0.6	1.0	43	65	0.1	0.1	20	8	2	1
China [1]	27.0	31.9	23	25	0.5	0.9	2,774	3,195	1,190	1,118
Colombia	0.9	1.2	25	29	0.2	0.2	440	816	23	36
Congo (Kinshasa) [2]	(NA)	(NA)	(NA)	(NA)	-	(NA)	29	22	(Z)	(Z)
Cuba	0.5	0.4	47	35	(Z)	(Z)	14	38	(NA)	(NA)
Czech Republic	(X)	1.5	(X)	150	(X)	(Z)	(X)	4	(X)	65
Denmark	0.8	0.9	160	167	0.1	0.3	121	300	(NA)	(NA)
Ecuador	(NA)	(NA)	(NA)	(NA)	(Z)	(Z)	285	373	(NA)	(NA)
Egypt	1.4	2.0	27	31	0.3	0.6	873	852	-	(Z)
Finland	1.1	1.3	226	253	(NA)	(NA)	(NA)	(NA)	(NA)	(NA)
France	8.8	10.3	155	174	0.1	0.1	61	30	15	6
Germany	(X)	14.0	(X)	170	(X)	0.8	(X)	55	(X)	226
Greece	1.1	1.3	103	120	(Z)	(Z)	15	(Z)	57	67
Hong Kong	0.5	0.7	84	108	(NA)	(NA)	(NA)	(NA)	(NA)	(NA)
Hungary	1.3	1.1	122	106	0.2	0.1	40	24	20	16
India	7.8	12.2	9	12	0.4	0.8	660	653	233	328
Indonesia	2.3	3.6	13	17	1.5	2.3	1,462	1,472	12	71
Iran	3.1	4.7	57	74	0.8	1.9	3,088	3,557	1	1
Iraq	0.9	1.2	51	52	0.2	0.1	2,040	2,508	(NA)	(NA)
Ireland	0.4	0.6	105	149	0.1	0.1	(NA)	(NA)	(Z)	-
Israel	0.5	0.8	97	128	(Z)	(Z)	(Z)	(Z)	(NA)	(NA)
Italy	7.0	8.0	123	140	0.6	0.6	87	82	1	(Z)
Japan	17.9	21.7	145	172	0.1	0.1	11	8	11	4
Korea, North	1.6	1.5	80	64	(NA)	(NA)	(NA)	(NA)	99	85
Korea, South	3.7	7.4	85	157	(NA)	(NA)	(NA)	(NA)	19	5
Kuwait	0.5	0.7	210	322	0.2	0.3	1,175	1,898	(NA)	(NA)
Libya	0.5	0.6	123	95	0.2	0.2	1,375	1,319	(NA)	(NA)
Malaysia	1.0	1.7	55	75	0.7	1.5	619	693	(Z)	(Z)
Mexico	5.0	6.1	60	63	0.9	1.3	2,553	2,906	9	11
Morocco	0.3	0.4	13	15	(Z)	(Z)	(Z)	(Z)	1	(Z)
Netherlands	3.4	3.9	225	244	2.7	2.7	70	53	(NA)	(NA)
New Zealand	0.7	0.8	217	213	0.2	0.2	40	42	3	4
Nigeria	0.7	0.9	8	8	0.1	0.3	1,810	2,130	(Z)	(Z)
Norway	1.6	1.9	373	425	1.0	1.8	1,704	3,018	(Z)	(Z)
Pakistan	1.2	1.8	10	12	0.5	0.8	62	53	3	4
Peru	(NA)	(NA)	(NA)	(NA)	(Z)	(Z)	129	106	(Z)	(Z)
Philippines	0.7	1.1	12	15	0.0	(Z)	5	1	1	1
Poland	4.0	3.8	104	99	0.2	0.2	2	9	237	190
Portugal	0.8	1.0	76	102	(NA)	(NA)	(NA)	(NA)	(Z)	-
Romania	2.9	1.6	124	73	1.0	0.5	163	125	42	28
Russia	(X)	26.0	(X)	177	(X)	20.8	(X)	6,079	(X)	276
Saudi Arabia	3.2	4.3	212	208	1.1	1.6	6,410	7,833	(NA)	(NA)
Serbia and Montenegro	(X)	0.6	(X)	57	(X)	(Z)	(X)	18	(X)	36
South Africa	3.4	4.4	91	98	0.0	0.1	-	25	193	248
Spain	3.9	5.2	101	133	0.1	(Z)	16	6	40	27
Sweden	2.2	2.2	254	248	(NA)	(NA)	(Z)	-	(Z)	-
Switzerland	1.2	1.2	174	173	(Z)	-	(NA)	(NA)	(NA)	(NA)
Syria	0.6	0.8	49	50	0.1	0.2	388	538	(NA)	(NA)
Taiwan [1]	2.0	3.5	100	159	0.1	(Z)	3	1	1	(Z)
Thailand	1.3	2.5	22	40	0.2	0.6	44	84	14	20
Trinidad and Tobago	(NA)	(NA)	(NA)	(NA)	0.2	0.4	150	125	(NA)	(NA)
Tunisia	(NA)	(NA)	(NA)	(NA)	(Z)	0.1	93	83	(NA)	(NA)
Turkey	2.0	3.0	35	46	(Z)	(Z)	73	59	52	74
Ukraine	(X)	6.4	(X)	127	(X)	0.6	(X)	76	(X)	91
United Arab Emirates	1.2	1.9	641	653	0.8	1.3	2,117	2,169	(NA)	(NA)
United Kingdom	9.3	9.9	161	168	1.8	3.5	1,820	2,684	104	41
Venezuela	2.1	2.8	107	118	0.8	1.1	2,137	2,826	2	8
Vietnam	0.3	0.6	4	7	(Z)	(Z)	50	290	5	12

- Represents zero. NA Not available. X Not applicable. Z Less than 50 billion cubic feet, 500 barrels per day, or 500,000 short tons. [1] See footnote 2, Table 1327. [2] See footnote 3, Table 1327.

Source: U.S. Energy Information Administration, *International Energy Annual.*

No. 1370. Net Electricity Generation by Type and Country: 1998

[13,673.9 represents 13,673,900,000,000]

Country	Total [1] (bil. kWh)	Thermal [2]	Hydro	Nuclear	Country	Total [1] (bil. kWh)	Thermal [2]	Hydro	Nuclear
World, total	13,673.9	62.8	18.8	16.9	Korea, South	222.3	59.8	1.8	38.3
Argentina	80.6	46.5	44.4	8.8	Malaysia	57.3	91.6	8.4	-
Australia	186.6	89.9	8.4	-	Mexico	172.8	77.7	14.1	5.1
Austria	56.0	31.4	65.7	-	Netherlands	89.2	91.0	0.1	4.0
Belgium	78.7	42.4	0.5	55.8	New Zealand	37.0	27.0	65.1	-
Brazil	316.9	4.9	91.0	1.0	Norway	115.2	0.6	99.1	-
Bulgaria	39.0	51.8	8.5	39.7	Pakistan	59.6	62.6	36.6	0.7
Canada	551.1	27.0	59.6	12.3	Paraguay	50.4	0.2	99.8	-
China	1,096.5	80.3	18.5	1.2	Poland	135.0	96.4	3.2	-
Colombia	45.4	30.0	68.7	-	Romania	51.1	53.8	36.6	9.6
Czech Republic	61.5	75.8	2.3	20.3	Russia	786.3	67.4	20.1	12.5
Denmark	40.0	89.8	-	-	Saudi Arabia	116.5	100.0	-	-
Egypt	59.2	79.6	20.4	-	Serbia and Montenegro	38.8	68.8	31.2	-
Finland	76.2	40.9	19.6	27.3	South Africa	191.7	92.1	0.8	7.1
France	485.7	10.9	12.6	75.9	Spain	186.4	50.0	18.1	30.0
Germany	530.2	65.4	3.2	29.0	Sweden	156.1	6.0	47.1	44.8
Greece	43.7	91.3	8.5	-	Switzerland	61.1	3.8	54.2	40.1
Hungary	35.1	61.8	0.6	37.9	Taiwan [3]	137.0	66.9	7.2	25.8
India	424.3	79.5	17.8	2.5	Thailand	85.0	90.4	6.0	-
Indonesia	72.7	80.6	14.4	-	Turkey	106.7	60.5	39.2	-
Iran	97.6	92.8	7.1	-	Ukraine	163.2	47.1	9.7	43.3
Italy	241.7	80.6	16.9	-	United Kingdom	341.9	68.8	1.5	27.8
Japan	1,002.4	57.0	9.1	31.5	United States	3,617.9	70.5	8.8	18.6
Kazakhstan	46.6	86.7	13.1	0.2	Uzbekistan	43.4	86.9	13.1	-
Korea, North	30.1	34.6	65.4	-	Venezuela	74.0	29.2	70.9	-

- Represents zero. [1] Includes geothermal, solar, wind, and wood and waste generation, not shown separately. [2] Electricity generated from coal, oil, and gas. [3] See footnote 2, Table 1327.

Source: U.S. Energy Information Administration, *International Energy Annual 1999.*

No. 1371. Commercial Nuclear Power Generation by Country: 1990 to 1999

[Generation for calendar years; other data as of December (1,743.9 represents 1,743,900,000,000)]

Country	Reactors				Gross electricity generated (bil. kWh)				Gross capacity (1,000 kW)			
	1990	1995	1998	1999	1990	1995	1998	1999	1990	1995	1998	1999
Total	368	423	436	431	1,743.9	2,271.7	2,424.2	2,489.9	301,745	358,414	371,544	367,602
United States	112	109	107	104	606.4	705.7	705.6	760.5	105,998	105,810	106,005	103,095
Argentina	2	2	2	2	7.0	7.0	7.5	7.1	1,005	1,005	1,005	1,005
Armenia	(NA)	1	1	1	(NA)	0.3	1.6	2.2	(NA)	408	408	408
Belgium	7	7	7	7	42.7	41.3	46.1	49.0	5,740	5,911	5,995	5,995
Brazil	1	1	1	1	2.0	2.5	3.3	3.9	657	657	657	657
Bulgaria	(NA)	6	6	6	(NA)	17.1	17.1	15.8	(NA)	3,760	3,760	3,760
Canada	19	22	21	21	74.0	100.2	72.8	74.3	13,855	16,699	15,795	15,795
China	(NA)	(NA)	2	2	(NA)	(NA)	13.0	14.7	(NA)	(NA)	1,968	1,968
Czech Republic	(NA)	(NA)	4	4	(NA)	(NA)	13.2	13.3	(NA)	(NA)	1,760	1,760
Finland	4	4	4	4	18.9	21.8	21.8	22.9	2,400	2,400	2,760	2,760
France	58	56	56	55	314.1	377.2	385.9	378.4	58,862	60,674	60,674	59,888
Germany	22	21	20	19	147.2	154.1	161.7	169.9	23,973	24,035	23,496	22,209
Great Britain	42	34	35	35	68.8	82.7	99.5	93.7	15,274	14,022	15,272	15,272
Hungary	4	4	4	4	13.6	14.0	13.9	14.1	1,760	1,840	1,840	1,840
India	6	10	10	11	6.0	7.6	11.4	13.0	1,330	2,270	2,270	2,505
Italy	2	(NA)	(NA)	(NA)	-	(NA)	(NA)	(NA)	1,132	(NA)	(NA)	(NA)
Japan	40	50	53	52	191.9	286.0	326.9	317.7	31,645	41,356	45,248	45,082
Korea, South	9	10	14	15	52.8	63.9	87.3	94.2	7,616	8,615	12,015	12,768
Lithuania	(NA)	2	2	2	(NA)	9.6	13.5	9.9	(NA)	3,000	3,000	3,000
Mexico	1	2	2	2	2.1	7.9	9.5	10.0	675	1,350	1,350	1,350
Netherlands	2	2	1	1	3.4	4.0	3.8	3.8	540	540	480	480
Pakistan	1	1	1	1	0.4	0.5	0.4	0.8	137	137	137	137
Romania	(NA)	(NA)	1	1	(NA)	(NA)	5.3	5.2	(NA)	(NA)	706	706
Russia	(NA)	29	29	29	(NA)	98.7	103.7	119.8	(NA)	21,266	21,266	21,266
Slovakia	(NA)	(NA)	4	4	(NA)	(NA)	10.3	10.5	(NA)	(NA)	1,760	1,760
Slovenia	1	1	1	1	4.6	4.7	5.0	4.7	664	664	664	664
South Africa	2	2	2	2	8.9	11.9	14.3	13.5	1,930	1,930	1,930	1,930
Spain	10	9	9	9	54.3	55.4	59.1	58.9	7,984	7,400	7,625	7,759
Sweden	12	12	12	11	68.2	69.9	73.5	73.2	10,344	10,442	10,445	10,445
Switzerland	5	5	5	5	23.6	24.8	25.7	24.8	3,079	3,200	3,229	3,314
Taiwan [1]	6	6	6	6	32.9	35.3	36.9	38.4	5,146	5,144	5,144	5,144
Ukraine	(NA)	15	14	14	(NA)	70.5	74.2	72.2	(NA)	13,880	12,880	12,880

- Represents zero. NA Not available. [1] See footnote 2, Table 1327.

Source: McGraw-Hill, Inc., New York, NY, *Nucleonics Week,* March issues (copyright).

U.S. Census Bureau, Statistical Abstract of the United States: 2001

Selected Indexes of Manufacturing Activity by Country: 1980 to 2000

[1992=100. Data relate to employees (wage and salary earners) in Belgium and Italy, and to all employed persons (employees, self-employed workers, and unpaid family workers) in the other countries. Minus sign (-) indicates decrease. For explanation of average annual percent change, see Guide to Tabular Presentation]

Index	United States	Can-ada	Japan	Bel-gium	France	Ger-many	Italy	Neth-erlands	Nor-way	Swe-den	United King-dom
Output per hour:											
1980	70.5	74.4	63.2	65.4	66.6	(NA)	69.6	68.7	76.7	73.1	54.3
1985	86.0	92.2	76.5	87.0	79.1	(NA)	84.1	88.4	90.2	86.2	71.1
1990	96.9	94.7	94.4	96.8	93.6	(NA)	92.2	98.4	96.6	94.6	89.1
1995	113.8	111.3	111.0	113.2	114.7	112.8	109.4	118.0	102.0	121.9	104.8
1999	135.1	114.9	125.8	128.9	132.9	122.4	111.8	127.7	103.1	143.5	110.8
2000	144.7	116.3	132.6	132.8	140.5	129.8	115.7	(NA)	104.2	150.4	118.4
Average annual percent change:											
1979-85	3.5	3.4	3.5	6.0	3.0	(NA)	4.0	4.4	2.4	3.1	4.4
1985-90	2.4	0.5	4.3	2.2	3.4	(NA)	1.9	2.2	1.4	1.9	4.6
1990-2000	4.1	2.1	3.5	3.2	4.1	(NA)	2.3	(NA)	0.8	4.7	2.7
Compensation per hour, national currency basis: [1]											
1980	55.6	47.6	58.5	52.5	40.8	(NA)	28.5	64.4	39.0	37.3	32.3
1985	75.1	71.9	72.4	75.3	72.8	(NA)	60.8	81.8	63.4	58.6	52.3
1990	90.8	88.3	90.5	90.1	90.6	(NA)	84.4	90.8	92.3	87.8	81.6
1995	107.9	106.0	108.3	109.2	108.5	118.2	112.7	110.6	109.2	106.5	107.8
1999	122.1	113.1	115.5	116.8	118.6	129.6	127.5	123.5	133.4	127.5	124.5
2000	130.1	117.0	115.5	119.8	124.9	134.2	131.2	(NA)	140.1	130.7	129.1
Average annual percent change:											
1979-85	7.2	9.1	4.7	8.1	12.8	(NA)	16.5	5.0	10.0	9.8	11.8
1985-90	3.9	4.2	4.6	3.7	4.5	(NA)	6.8	2.1	7.8	8.4	9.3
1990-2000	3.7	2.9	2.5	2.9	3.3	(NA)	4.5	(NA)	4.3	4.1	4.7
Real hourly compensation: [1][2]											
1980	91.6	91.6	75.2	86.5	79.6	(NA)	80.0	87.4	86.0	87.7	67.2
1985	95.5	96.6	81.2	88.3	89.7	(NA)	89.6	90.7	90.8	87.4	76.6
1990	96.6	94.7	95.0	95.2	96.0	(NA)	94.3	96.6	97.7	97.6	89.7
1995	100.4	101.7	106.3	102.3	102.7	108.2	98.6	102.9	102.7	97.6	100.2
1999	104.6	102.4	110.9	103.3	107.6	113.2	101.4	105.7	115.6	109.4	104.2
2000	107.8	103.1	111.7	103.3	111.3	115.0	101.8	(NA)	117.7	115.8	105.0
Average annual percent change:											
1979-85	0.8	1.1	1.1	1.1	2.3	(NA)	1.3	0.4	0.6	-0.5	2.6
1985-90	0.2	-0.4	3.2	1.5	1.4	(NA)	1.0	1.3	1.5	2.2	3.2
1990-2000	1.1	0.9	1.6	0.8	1.5	(NA)	0.8	(NA)	1.9	1.7	1.6
Unit labor costs, national currency:											
1980	78.8	63.9	92.5	80.3	61.3	(NA)	41.0	93.7	50.8	51.0	59.4
1985	87.3	78.0	94.6	86.5	92.0	(NA)	72.2	92.5	70.2	68.0	73.6
1990	93.7	93.3	95.9	93.0	96.8	(NA)	91.5	92.3	95.6	92.9	91.6
1995	94.8	95.2	97.6	96.4	94.6	104.7	103.0	93.7	107.0	87.4	102.9
1999	90.4	98.4	91.8	90.6	89.3	105.9	114.0	96.7	129.5	88.8	112.4
2000	89.9	100.6	87.1	90.2	88.9	103.4	113.4	(NA)	134.5	86.9	110.9
Average annual percent change:											
1979-85	3.6	5.5	1.1	2.0	9.5	(NA)	12.0	0.5	7.4	6.5	7.1
1985-90	1.4	3.7	0.3	1.5	1.0	(NA)	4.8	-0.1	6.4	6.4	4.5
1990-2000	-0.4	0.8	-1.0	-0.3	-0.9	(NA)	2.2	(NA)	3.5	-0.7	1.9
Unit labor costs, U.S. dollar basis: [3]											
1980	78.8	66.1	51.8	88.3	76.7	(NA)	59.0	82.9	63.9	70.2	78.3
1985	87.3	69.0	50.3	46.9	54.2	(NA)	46.6	49.0	50.8	46.1	54.1
1990	93.7	96.6	83.8	89.5	94.0	(NA)	94.1	89.1	95.0	91.3	92.5
1995	94.8	83.8	131.7	105.2	100.4	114.2	77.9	102.7	105.0	71.3	91.9
1999	90.4	80.0	102.4	76.9	76.8	90.1	77.3	82.2	103.1	62.5	102.9
2000	89.9	81.8	102.5	66.4	66.2	76.2	66.6	(NA)	94.8	55.2	95.2
Average annual percent change:											
1979-85	3.6	2.8	-0.3	-9.3	-3.3	(NA)	-2.5	-7.6	-1.7	-5.2	-1.3
1985-90	1.4	7.0	10.8	13.8	11.6	(NA)	15.1	12.7	13.3	14.7	11.3
1990-2000	-0.4	-1.6	2.0	-2.9	-3.5	(NA)	-3.4	(NA)	-	-4.9	0.3
Employment:											
1980	111.6	115.1	88.9	119.3	125.0	(NA)	124.7	107.8	134.5	130.9	151.8
1985	106.0	106.8	93.5	104.0	110.3	(NA)	104.8	95.4	120.7	122.0	120.6
1990	105.4	113.2	97.5	102.5	105.4	(NA)	106.4	101.1	105.4	117.2	115.5
1995	102.5	104.8	90.1	91.9	92.1	86.2	97.2	91.3	107.2	97.9	98.8
1999	102.4	118.5	83.2	88.7	89.7	82.6	98.8	93.4	111.6	98.7	96.8
2000	101.7	123.7	81.7	90.3	90.8	83.2	98.9	(NA)	108.7	100.0	93.2
Average annual percent change:											
1979-85	-1.4	-1.3	1.2	-2.6	-2.3	(NA)	-2.8	-2.2	-1.8	-1.2	-4.6
1985-90	-0.1	1.2	0.8	-0.3	-0.9	(NA)	0.3	1.2	-2.7	-0.8	-0.9
1990-2000	-0.4	0.9	-1.8	-1.3	-1.5	(NA)	-0.7	(NA)	0.3	-1.6	-2.1
Aggregate hours:											
1980	107.5	114.6	95.6	119.7	133.2	(NA)	121.3	111.8	135.0	124.0	160.5
1985	104.6	106.4	100.3	102.4	110.4	(NA)	100.8	96.7	120.2	119.4	125.2
1990	104.8	113.5	102.9	104.3	105.9	(NA)	107.8	101.5	103.7	116.4	118.1
1995	104.0	106.4	89.1	92.0	91.5	84.5	98.0	91.8	106.8	105.3	102.8
1999	104.3	122.6	80.3	91.3	88.3	79.6	98.6	93.0	110.6	107.1	99.4
2000	103.4	128.0	80.6	91.8	86.2	79.4	98.5	(NA)	106.4	108.6	96.1
Average annual percent change:											
1979-85	-1.2	-1.5	1.1	-3.2	-3.3	(NA)	-2.9	-2.5	-1.8	-0.8	-5.3
1985-90	-	1.3	0.5	0.4	-0.8	(NA)	1.3	1.0	-2.9	-0.5	-1.2
1990-2000	-0.1	1.2	-2.4	-1.3	-2.0	(NA)	-0.9	(NA)	0.3	-0.7	-2.0

- Represents or rounds to zero.   NA Not available.   [1] Compensation includes, but real hourly compensation excludes, adjustments for payroll and employment taxes that are not compensation to employees, but are labor costs to employers.   [2] Index of hourly compensation divided by the index of consumer prices to adjust for changes in purchasing power.   [3] Indexes in national currency adjusted for changes in prevailing exchange rates.

Source: U.S. Bureau of Labor Statistics, *International Comparisons of Manufacturing Productivity and Unit Labor Cost Trends*, August 31, 2001.

856   Comparative International Statistics

No. 1373. Indexes of Hourly Compensation Costs for Production Workers in Manufacturing by Country: 1980 to 2000

[United States=100. Compensation costs include pay for time worked, other direct pay (including holiday and vacation pay, bonuses, other direct payments, and the cost of pay in kind), employer expenditures for legally required insurance programs and contractual and private benefit plans, and for some countries, other labor taxes. Data adjusted for exchange rates. Area averages are trade-weighted to account for difference in countries' relative importance to U.S. trade in manufactured goods. The trade weights used are the sum of U.S. imports of manufactured products for consumption (customs value) and U.S. exports of domestic manufactured products (f.a.s. value) in 1992; see source for detail]

Area or country	1980	1985	1990	1995	1999	2000	Area or country	1980	1985	1990	1995	1999	2000
United States	100	100	100	100	100	100	Austria [7]	90	58	119	147	114	98
Total [1]	67	52	83	95	80	76	Belgium.	133	69	129	161	125	106
OECD [2]	74	57	90	103	86	82	Denmark	110	63	121	140	120	103
Europe	100	61	116	128	107	93	Finland [8]	84	63	141	140	112	98
Asian newly industrial-							France	91	58	104	116	94	83
izing economies [3] . . .	12	13	25	37	33	34	Germany [7][9].	124	73	146	184	140	121
Canada	88	84	107	94	82	81	Greece	38	28	45	53	(NA)	(NA)
Mexico	22	12	11	9	11	12	Ireland	61	46	79	80	71	63
Australia [4]	86	63	88	89	82	71	Italy	83	59	117	94	87	74
Hong Kong [5]	15	13	22	28	29	28	Luxembourg.	122	60	112	132	98	84
Israel	38	31	57	61	62	65	Netherlands	122	67	121	140	112	96
Japan	56	49	86	139	109	111	Norway	117	80	144	142	125	111
Korea, South	10	10	25	42	37	41	Portugal	21	12	25	31	28	24
New Zealand	53	34	55	58	48	41	Spain	60	36	76	75	63	55
Singapore	15	19	25	43	37	37	Sweden.	127	74	140	125	113	101
Sri Lanka.	2	2	2	3	2	(NA)	Switzerland	112	74	140	170	123	107
Taiwan [6]	10	12	26	35	29	30	United Kingdom	77	48	85	80	86	80

NA Not available. [1] The 28 foreign economies shown below. [2] Organization for Economic Cooperation and Development; see text of this section. [3] Hong Kong, South Korea, Singapore, and Taiwan. [4] Includes non-production workers, except in managerial, executive, professional, and higher supervisory positions. [5] Average of selected manufacturing industries. [6] See footnote 2, Table 1327. [7] Excludes workers in establishments considered handicraft manufactures (including all printing and publishing and miscellaneous manufacturing in Austria). [8] Includes workers in mining and electrical power plants. [9] Former West Germany.

Source: U.S. Bureau of Labor Statistics, *News Release* USDL 01-311, September 25, 2001.

No. 1374. Motor Vehicle Transportation Indicators for Selected Countries: 1998

[131,839 represents 131,839,000]

Item	United States	Canada	France	Ger-many	Japan	Mexico	Sweden	United Kingdom
NUMBER [1] (1,000)								
Automobiles [2]	131,839	13,487	26,800	41,674	49,896	9,379	3,792	22,115
Motorcycles [2]	3,879	319	(NA)	2,926	14,537	270	252	684
Buses	716	64	82	238	238	109	15	80
Trucks.	79,062	7,237	5,418	4,273	20,813	4,404	338	3,089
Per 1,000 persons:								
Automobiles [2]	487.7	439.7	455.7	507.7	396.2	95.2	426.7	375.0
Motorcycles [2]	14.4	10.4	51.9	35.6	115.4	2.7	28.4	11.6
Buses	2.6	2.1	1.4	1.0	1.9	1.1	1.7	1.4
Trucks	292.5	235.9	92.1	52.1	165.3	44.7	38.1	52.4
ROADS [3]								
Total kilometers (1,000)	6,310	902	893	656	1,152	324	211	372
Kilometers per 1,000 persons	23.34	31.29	15.19	7.99	9.15	3.29	23.73	6.3
Kilometers per square kilometer.	0.69	0.10	1.64	1.88	3.07	0.17	0.51	1.54
VEHICLE KILOMETERS OF TRAVEL [4]								
Automobiles (bil.) [2]	2,488	(NA)	382	525	476	(NA)	57	368
Motorcycles (bil.) [2]	17	(NA)	(NA)	14	(NA)	(NA)	1	4
Buses (bil.)	11	(NA)	2	4	7	(NA)	1	5
Trucks (bil.) [5]	1,710	(NA)	107	55	262	(NA)	9	32
AVERAGE VEHICLE KILOMETERS PER VEHICLE [4]								
Automobiles [2]	18,870	(NA)	14,254	12,593	9,532	(NA)	15,029	16,631
Motorcycles [2]	4,257	(NA)	(NA)	4,922	(NA)	(NA)	2,378	5,848
Buses	15,735	(NA)	28,049	44,426	27,938	(NA)	78,684	61,250
Trucks [5].	22,512	(NA)	21,503	12,777	11,915	(NA)	27,788	14,501

NA Not available. [1] Data for automobiles, motorcycles, and buses for Canada are for 1997. [2] Includes mopeds. [3] Data for Canada are for 1995 and data for Mexico and Japan are for 1997. [4] Data for automobiles, buses, and trucks for Germany, Japan, and United Kingdom are for 1997. [5] Includes two-axle four-tire vehicles that are not cars. These are vans, sport-utility vehicles and pickup trucks. Non-U.S. data excludes travel by combination trucks.

Source: U.S. Federal Highway Administration, *Highway Statistics, 1999.*

U.S. Census Bureau, Statistical Abstract of the United States: 2001

No. 1375. Newspapers, Radio, Television, Telephones, and Computers by Country

[Rates per 1,000 persons. See text of this section for general comments about the data. For data qualifications for countries, see source]

Country	Daily newspaper circulation,[1] 1996	Radio receivers,[2] 1997	Television receivers,[3] 1997	Telephone main lines, 2000	Cellular phone subscribers, 2000	Personal computers,[4] 2000
Algeria	38	242	105	[5]52	[5]2	[5]6
Argentina	123	681	223	215	[5]121	51
Australia	296	1,391	554	524	446	465
Austria	296	751	525	474	786	276
Belgium	161	797	466	499	549	344
Brazil	40	434	223	[5]149	136	44
Bulgaria	254	537	394	[5]354	90	[5]27
Canada	158	1,067	710	[5]654	[5]225	390
Chile	98	354	215	221	224	85
China [6]	(NA)	335	321	[5]86	67	16
Colombia	46	524	115	[5]160	[5]75	[5]34
Cuba	118	352	239	44	1	[5]10
Czech Republic	254	803	531	[5]371	422	122
Denmark	311	1,145	594	705	665	432
Dominican Republic	52	178	95	[5]98	[5]50	(NA)
Ecuador	70	348	130	[5]91	[5]31	[5]20
Egypt	38	317	119	81	20	[5]12
Finland	455	1,498	622	[5]552	726	396
France	218	946	595	580	494	305
Germany	311	948	567	601	586	336
Ghana	14	236	93	12	6	[5]3
Greece	(NA)	475	240	[5]528	559	70
Guatemala	33	79	61	57	[5]30	[5]10
Honduras	55	410	95	46	24	[5]10
Hungary	186	690	435	[5]371	293	85
India	(NA)	120	65	32	4	5
Indonesia	23	155	68	31	17	10
Iran	26	263	71	149	15	[5]56
Iraq	20	229	83	[5]30	[5]-	(NA)
Ireland	149	697	402	[5]478	597	365
Israel	288	524	288	463	702	254
Italy	104	880	528	[5]462	737	[5]209
Jamaica	63	483	183	199	142	[5]43
Japan	578	956	686	[5]558	526	315
Korea, South	(NA)	1,039	348	464	567	190
Kuwait	377	678	505	[5]240	[5]158	[5]121
Lebanon	141	907	375	[5]201	[5]194	[5]46
Malaysia	163	434	172	211	155	105
Mexico	97	329	272	125	142	51
Morocco	27	247	115	50	83	[5]11
Netherlands	306	980	519	[5]607	671	395
New Zealand	216	997	512	[5]496	[5]366	360
Norway	590	917	462	729	703	491
Pakistan	(NA)	94	22	[5]22	[5]2	[5]4
Panama	62	299	187	[5]164	[5]83	[5]32
Peru	84	273	126	64	[5]40	[5]36
Philippines	82	161	52	40	84	20
Poland	113	522	337	[5]263	181	69
Portugal	75	306	336	431	665	105
Puerto Rico	127	714	270	[5]333	[5]209	(NA)
Romania	(NA)	319	233	[5]167	112	[5]27
Russia	105	417	410	217	19	43
Saudi Arabia	59	321	262	[5]129	[5]40	[5]57
Singapore	324	744	388	485	684	483
South Africa	34	355	134	[5]125	[5]120	62
Spain	99	331	409	421	609	143
Sweden	445	932	519	[5]665	703	507
Switzerland	331	979	457	720	645	[5]502
Syria	20	278	70	104	2	[5]14
Taiwan [6]	[7]156	(NA)	(NA)	568	803	225
Thailand	64	234	254	[5]86	44	24
Turkey	110	178	330	280	246	38
United Kingdom	331	1,443	521	[5]567	670	338
United States	212	2,116	806	[5]673	400	585
Uruguay	293	603	239	[5]271	[5]95	[5]100
Venezuela	206	472	180	[5]109	[5]143	46

- Represents zero.   NA Not available.   [1] Publications containing general news and appearing at least 4 times a week; may range in size from a single sheet to 50 or more pages. Circulation data refer to average circulation per issue or number of printed copies per issue and include copies sold outside the country.   [2] Data cover estimated number of receivers in use and apply to all types of receivers for radio broadcasts to the public, including receivers connected to a radio "redistribution system" but excluding television sets.   [3] Estimated number of sets in use.   [4] In many countries mainframe computers are used extensively, and thousands of users can be connected to a single mainframe computer; thus the number of PCs understates the total use of computers.   [5] 1999 data.   [6] See footnote 2, Table 1327.   [7] 1998 data. Source: U.S. Census Bureau. Data from Republic of China publications.

Source: Except as noted, Newspapers, radio, and television—United Nations Educational, Scientific, and Cultural Organization, Montreal, Canada, *Statistical Yearbook*, (copyright); telephones, cellular phones, and personal computers—International Telecommunications Union, Geneva, Switzerland, *World Telecommunication Indicators*, (copyright).

No. 1376. Information and Communication Technology (ICT) Sector—Value Added by Country: 1997

[14,402 represents $14,402,000,000. Dollar values are expressed in terms of purchasing power parities; see footnote 2, Table 1340. The information and communication technology sector is defined as including the following industrial classes from revision 3 of the International Standard Industrial Classification (ISIC): Manufacturing—3000-Office, accounting and computing machinery; 3130-Insulated wire and cable; 3210-Electronic valves and tubes and other electronic components; 3220-Television and radio transmitters and apparatus for line telephony and line telegraphy; 3230-Television and radio receivers, sound or video recording or reproducing apparatus, and associated goods; 3312-Instruments and appliances for measuring, checking, testing, navigating and other purposes, except industrial process equipment; 3313-Industrial process control equipment; Services— 5150-Wholesaling of machinery, equipment and supplies (where possible, member countries were asked to limit this class to include only the wholesaling of ICT goods as shown in the manufacturing component of the definition shown above); 7123-Renting of office machinery and equipment (including computers); 6420-Telecommunications; 72-Computer and related activities]

Country	Total (mil. dol.)	Percent of production in ICT	Per employee in ICT (dol.)	Percent of value added in total business sector
Australia [1]	14,402	31.6	73,636	4.1
Austria [2]	9,379	32.3	56,917	6.8
Belgium	10,029	28.8	76,926	5.8
Canada [2]	34,965	40.7	81,324	6.5
Czech Republic [2]	5,733	43.4	37,716	4.7
Finland	6,139	32.0	69,894	8.3
France	46,033	46.0	67,592	5.3
Germany [3]	89,154	(NA)	91,534	6.1
Hungary [2]	7,048	38.8	44,765	9.2
Italy	53,837	39.5	80,183	5.8
Japan	151,909	35.9	73,743	5.8
Korea, South [3]	62,722	48.1	135,635	10.7
Netherlands [3]	14,131	47.6	71,008	5.1
Norway [4]	3,670	51.0	49,641	6.4
Portugal [2]	6,155	36.4	65,267	5.6
Sweden	11,773	31.4	67,588	9.3
United Kingdom	81,919	35.6	73,692	8.4
United States	581,540	49.5	128,629	8.7

NA Not available.   [1] Data for year 1998-99.   [2] Includes all of Wholesale of machinery, equipment and supplies (ISIC 5150).   [3] Excludes all of Wholesale of machinery, equipment and supplies (ISIC 5150).   [4] Data for year 1995.

Source: Organization for Economic Cooperation and Development, Paris, France, *Measuring the ICT Sector*, 2000

No. 1377. Information and Communication Technology (ICT) Sector— Research and Development (R&D) Expenditures by Country: 1997

[822 represents $822,000,000. Dollar values are expressed in terms of purchasing power parities; see footnote 2, Table 1340. See headnote, Table 1376]

Country	Total (mil. dol.)	Percent of value added for ICT	Percent of R&D in total business sector
Australia	822	[1]4.9	26.8
Belgium	612	6.1	20.1
Canada	3,129	8.9	43.7
Czech Republic	45	0.8	4.6
Denmark	329	(NA)	21.1
Finland	962	15.7	51.0
France	4,366	9.5	26.4
Germany	5,653	6.3	20.1
Greece	76	(NA)	46.9
Hungary	34	0.5	11.3
Iceland	11	(NA)	21.8
Ireland	378	(NA)	47.7
Italy	1,677	3.1	26.5
Japan	26,127	17.2	40.4
Korea, South	5,640	9.0	40.9
Mexico	1	(NA)	0.2
Netherlands	791	5.6	19.6
New Zealand	38	(NA)	17.7
Norway	324	[2]6.3	29.2
Poland	61	(NA)	7.6
Portugal	50	0.8	23.5
Spain	551	(NA)	21.4
Sweden	1,427	12.1	27.9
Turkey	140	(NA)	21.7
United Kingdom	3,227	3.9	21.8
United States	59,916	10.3	38.0

NA Not available.   [1] Data for 1998-99.   [2] Data for 1995.

Source: Organization for Economic Cooperation and Development, Paris, France, *Measuring the ICT Sector*, 2000

U.S. Census Bureau, Statistical Abstract of the United States: 2001

No. 1378. Information and Communication Technology (ICT) Sector— Employment by Country: 1997

[196 represents 196,000. See headnote, Table 1376]

Country	Total ICT employment (1,000)	Percent of employment in total business sector	Country	Total ICT employment (1,000)	Percent of employment in total business sector
Australia [1]	196	2.6	Italy	671	3.5
Austria [2]	165	4.9	Japan [3]	2,060	3.4
Belgium	130	4.3	Korea, South [3]	462	2.5
Canada [2]	430	4.6	Netherlands [3]	199	3.8
Czech Republic [2]	152	3.3	New Zealand	31	2.1
Denmark	96	5.1	Norway [4]	74	5.3
Finland	88	5.6	Portugal [2]	94	2.7
France	681	4.0	Sweden [2]	174	6.3
Germany [3]	974	3.1	Switzerland [5]	172	6.0
Hungary [2]	157	5.7	Turkey [3]	100	0.5
Iceland [4]	4	4.2	United Kingdom	1,112	4.8
Ireland [3]	56	4.6	United States	4,521	3.9

[1] Data for 1998-99. [2] Includes all of Wholesale of machinery, equipment and supplies (ISIC 5150). [3] Excludes all of Wholesale of machinery, equipment and supplies (ISIC 5150). [4] Data for 1996. [5] Data for 1998.

Source: Organization for Economic Cooperation and Development, Paris, France, *Measuring the ICT Sector*, 2000

No. 1379. Information and Communication Technology (ICT) Sector— Foreign Trade by Country: 1998

[In millions of dollars, except as indicated (645,996 represents $645,996,000,000). See headnote, Table 1376]

Country	ICT goods and services			Total imports of goods & services	Total exports of goods & services	Share of ICT in—	
	Imports	Exports	Balance			Total imports (percent)	Total exports (percent)
OECD, total.	645,996	620,358	-25,638	4,880,076	4,978,405	13.2	12.5
European Union [1]	297,578	270,366	-27,212	2,514,582	2,670,379	11.8	10.1
G7 countries [2]	443,055	425,054	-18,001	3,293,874	3,327,553	13.5	12.8
Australia	10,257	3,194	-7,062	78,535	71,993	13.1	4.4
Austria	7,862	4,754	-3,109	95,841	94,711	8.2	5.0
Belgium-Luxembourg	13,331	12,755	-575	179,139	189,208	7.4	6.7
Canada	30,229	18,024	-12,205	242,918	251,563	12.4	7.2
Czech Republic	3,629	1,876	-1,752	34,610	33,817	10.5	5.5
Denmark [3]	5,442	3,910	-1,532	42,951	46,859	12.7	8.3
Finland	6,226	9,829	3,603	38,672	50,121	16.1	19.6
France	37,808	35,426	-2,382	340,042	377,817	11.1	9.4
Germany	64,173	53,580	-10,592	584,683	620,639	11.0	8.6
Greece [3]	2,177	334	-1,843	25,233	7,988	8.6	4.2
Hungary	4,880	5,127	247	24,805	23,815	19.7	21.5
Iceland [3]	264	39	-225	3,242	2,871	8.1	1.3
Ireland [3]	13,563	19,373	5,810	39,988	59,514	33.9	32.6
Italy	23,377	13,742	-9,636	275,361	315,191	8.5	4.4
Japan	47,026	101,358	54,332	348,384	422,608	13.5	24.0
Korea, South	20,590	34,169	13,579	114,400	156,539	18.0	21.8
Mexico [4]	24,513	27,761	3,248	138,135	129,610	17.7	21.4
Netherlands	36,206	34,758	-1,447	216,487	238,410	16.7	14.6
New Zealand	1,759	561	-1,198	15,623	15,928	11.3	3.5
Norway	4,230	1,889	-2,341	53,982	54,623	7.8	3.5
Poland	5,100	1,954	-3,145	53,196	44,851	9.6	4.4
Portugal	3,729	2,149	-1,580	44,341	34,330	8.4	6.3
Spain	13,489	8,409	-5,080	156,038	158,003	8.6	5.3
Sweden	12,700	15,515	2,815	89,222	104,177	14.2	14.9
Switzerland [4]	9,005	5,640	-3,365	95,494	105,469	9.4	5.3
Turkey [3]	3,992	1,309	-2,684	46,269	28,013	8.6	4.7
United Kingdom	57,497	55,831	-1,666	386,585	373,410	14.9	15.0
United States	182,945	147,092	-35,853	1,115,900	966,325	16.4	15.2

[1] For countries, see footnote 3, Table 1340. [2] For countries, see headnote, Table 1341. [3] Trade of ICT goods only. Total imports and total exports of goods and services include goods only. [4] Excludes computer and information services.

Source: Organization for Economic Cooperation and Development, Paris, France, *Measuring the ICT Sector*, 2000

No. 1380. Dow-Jones World Stock Index by Country and Industry: 1995 to 2000

[Index figures shown are as of December 31. Based on share prices denominated in U.S. dollars. Stocks in countries that impose significant restrictions on foreign ownership are included in the world index in the same proportion that shares are available to foreign investors]

Country and Industry	1995	1998	1999	2000	Country and Industry	1995	1998	1999	2000
World, total	132.4	192.1	245.3	210.9	Asia/Pacific	118.5	77.3	133.3	93.0
Americas.	145.3	268.5	330.5	299.1	Australia	132.9	140.9	173.4	156.2
United States	147.5	281.6	341.6	306.9	Hong Kong.	201.9	172.5	288.8	245.6
Canada	112.9	149.3	223.4	225.4	Indonesia.	174.7	40.4	71.7	31.2
Mexico	79.0	89.0	170.1	132.2	Japan	111.1	71.2	128.3	88.3
Europe	131.0	234.0	269.2	241.1	Malaysia	224.3	78.2	111.8	88.5
Austria	103.5	109.2	101.9	86.1	New Zealand	178.8	129.5	141.4	96.7
Belgium	144.0	281.3	228.8	196.7	Singapore	187.8	97.7	177.3	135.3
Denmark	113.0	187.9	199.9	243.9	Thailand	119.5	123.3	175.4	95.9
Finland	267.1	773.3	1,814.0	1,536.0					
France	117.9	210.4	274.5	252.6	Basic materials.	128.1	105.3	134.6	117.7
Germany	133.9	226.1	260.7	218.8	Consumer, cyclical	131.7	186.6	240.0	188.0
Ireland.	155.6	332.8	290.8	312.0	Consumer, noncyclical . .	125.5	198.0	205.2	180.8
Italy	80.3	202.3	203.3	192.0	Energy	132.7	174.2	211.2	230.7
Netherlands	176.0	341.9	365.0	335.3	Financial	134.9	181.9	192.2	207.1
Norway	129.8	123.3	163.6	167.4	Healthcare.	133.3	268.8	254.0	329.8
Spain	111.2	256.4	259.0	193.3	Industrial	124.0	143.2	199.3	167.1
Sweden.	157.0	244.0	409.2	338.9	Technology	188.1	431.8	856.8	552.4
Switzerland	225.7	378.8	357.5	415.5	Telecommunications . . .	146.8	278.8	458.3	273.3
United Kingdom	122.5	202.1	234.0	199.8	Utilities	118.8	156.8	133.6	156.0

Source: Dow Jones & Company, Inc., New York, NY, *Dow Jones Indexes*, (copyright).

No. 1381. Foreign Stock Market Activity—Morgan Stanley Capital International Indexes: 1995 to 2000

[Index figures shown are as of December 31. January 1, 1970=100, except as noted. Based on share prices denominated in U.S. dollars. EM=Emerging Markets]

Index and country	Index 1995	Index 1999	Index 2000	Percent change[1] 1999	Percent change[1] 2000	Index and country	Index 1995	Index 1999	Index 2000	Percent change[1] 1999	Percent change[1] 2000
ALL COUNTRY (AC) INDEXES						Switzerland	1,569	2,570	2,695	-7.8	4.9
						United Kingdom	716	1,326	1,146	9.7	-13.6
AC World index	182.0	341.2	289.8	25.5	-15.1	Hong Kong	4,818	6,595	5,475	54.9	-17.0
AC World index except USA.	153.8	233.4	195.4	29.7	-16.3	Japan	3,348	3,571	2,552	60.6	-28.5
AC Asia Pacific	124.5	130.4	92.7	57.9	-28.9	Singapore	2,735	2,917	2,081	97.1	-28.7
AC Europe	201.9	420.1	376.5	15.2	-10.4						
European Union.	189.2	408.3	361.5	17.0	-11.5	**EMERGING MARKETS**					
						EM Far East index . .	263.7	212.6	123.8	65.7	-41.8
DEVELOPED MARKETS						India [5]	98.8	148.4	114.5	84.7	-22.8
						Indonesia	508.2	211.6	78.2	92.0	-63.0
World index [2]	734	1,421	1,221	23.6	-14.1	Korea, South	173.8	158.4	78.7	90.2	-50.4
EAFE index [3]	1,136	1,760	1,492	25.3	-15.2	Malaysia	347.0	192.9	160.9	107.2	-16.6
Europe index	733	1,526	1,378	14.1	-9.7	Pakistan [5]	91.5	51.4	44.3	42.2	-13.8
Pacific index	2,362	2,490	1,832	56.2	-26.4	Philippines	442.5	247.1	142.2	7.6	-42.5
Far East index	3,384	3,568	2,583	61.1	-27.6	Sri Lanka [5]	105.6	64.7	36.3	-9.7	-43.9
						Taiwan [6]	227.9	350.8	191.7	51.5	-45.4
United States	581	1,446	1,250	20.9	-13.6	Thailand	523.3	121.7	56.9	40.5	-53.2
Canada	403.9	797.2	832.5	51.8	4.4						
						EM Latin America . .	782	1,192	1,002	61.8	-15.9
Australia	304.2	360.8	317.7	15.2	-12.0	Argentina	1,239	1,668	1,233	30.1	-26.1
New Zealand [4]	114.2	88.5	56.4	9.7	-36.3	Brazil	578	952	870	73.0	-8.7
						Chile	903	728	605	36.5	-17.0
Austria	890	818	708	-10.5	-13.4	Colombia [5]	110.2	71.6	42.1	-19.1	-41.2
Belgium	897	1,501	1,222	-15.8	-18.6	Mexico	744	1,525	1,197	80.2	-21.5
Denmark	1,124	2,144	2,201	10.9	2.7	Peru [5]	221.3	170.6	125.0	16.3	-26.7
Finland [4]	129	1,081	922	150.7	-14.7	Venezuela	75.4	105.3	106.1	1.7	0.8
France	672	1,590	1,509	28.0	-5.1						
Germany	818	1,720	1,436	18.7	-16.5	Czech Republic	(NA)	79.4	79.9	4.0	0.7
Ireland [4]	215.7	359.9	308.4	-14.0	-14.3	Greece [4]	238.2	827.7	475.8	47.6	-42.5
Italy	208.6	459.6	447.2	-1.5	-2.7	Hungary	(NA)	322.9	233.6	10.8	-27.7
Luxembourg	(NA)	481.3	491.9	50.5	2.2	Jordan	96.1	73.2	55.1	2.0	-24.7
Netherlands	1,192	2,302	2,177	5.3	-5.4	Poland	(NA)	523.0	499.0	30.5	-4.6
Norway	1,023	1,210	1,181	29.5	-2.4	Russia	(NA)	223.0	155.2	246.2	-30.4
Portugal [4]	68.4	145.5	127.8	-10.9	-12.2	South Africa	(NA)	196.0	157.6	53.4	-19.6
Spain	162.3	417.3	347.1	3.5	-16.8	Turkey	103.1	460.0	247.7	244.4	-46.2
Sweden	1,796	5,432	4,240	77.8	-21.9						

NA Not available. [1] Percent change during calendar year (e.g. December 31, 1998, through December 31, 1999). Adjusted for foreign exchange fluctuations relative to U.S. dollar. [2] Includes South African gold mines quoted in London. [3] Europe, Australia, Far East index. Comprises all European and Far East countries listed under developed markets plus Australia, Malaysia, and New Zealand. [4] January 1, 1988=100. [5] December 1992=100. [6] See footnote 2, Table 1327.

Source: Morgan Stanley Capital International, New York, NY, <http://www.msci.com/equity/index.html> (copyright). This information may not be reproduced or redisseminated in any form without prior written permission from Morgan Stanley Capital International. This information is provided on an "as is" basis. Neither Morgan Stanley or any other party makes any representation or warranty of any kind either express or implied, with respect to this information (or the results to be obtained by the use thereof) and Morgan Stanley expressly disclaims any and all warranties of originality, accuracy, completeness, merchantability, and fitness for any particular purpose. The user of this information assumes the entire risk of any use made of the information. In no event shall Morgan Stanley or any other part be liable to the user for any direct or indirect damages, including without limitation, any lost profits, lost savings, or other incidental or consequential damages arising out of use of this information.

No. 1382. Foreign Stock Market Indices: 1980 to 2000

[As of year end. The DAX index is a total return index which includes dividends, whereas the other foreign indices are price indices which exclude dividends]

Year	London FTSE 100	Tokyo Nikkei 225	Hong Kong Hang Seng	Germany DAX-30	Paris CAC-40
1980	647	7,116	1,477	481	(X)
1985	1,413	13,113	1,752	1,366	(X)
1990	2,144	23,849	3,025	1,398	1,518
1991	2,493	22,984	4,297	1,578	1,766
1992	2,847	16,925	5,512	1,545	1,858
1993	3,418	17,417	11,888	2,267	2,268
1994	3,066	19,723	8,191	2,107	1,881
1995	3,689	19,868	10,073	2,254	1,872
1996	4,119	19,361	13,452	2,889	2,316
1997	5,136	15,259	10,723	4,250	2,999
1998	5,883	13,842	9,507	5,002	3,943
1999	6,930	18,934	16,962	6,958	5,958
2000	6,223	13,786	15,096	6,434	5,926

X Not applicable.

Source: Global Financial Data, Los Angeles, CA, <http://www.globalfindata.com>, unpublished data (copyright).

No. 1383. United States and Foreign Stock Markets—Market Capitalization and Value of Shares Traded: 1990 to 2000

[In billions of U.S. dollars (3,059.4 represents $3,059,400,000,000). Market capitalization is the market value of all domestic listed companies at the end of the year. The market value of a company is the share price times the number of shares outstanding. Value of shares traded is the annual total turnover of listed company shares]

Country	Market capitalization				Value of shares traded			
	1990	1995	1999	2000	1990	1995	1999	2000
United States	3,059.4	6,857.6	(NA)	15,104.0	1,751.3	5,108.6	(NA)	31,862.5
Argentina	3.3	37.8	83.9	166.1	0.9	4.6	7.8	6.0
Australia	107.6	245.2	(NA)	372.8	40.1	98.7	(NA)	226.3
Austria	11.5	32.5	(NA)	29.9	18.6	25.8	(NA)	9.4
Belgium	65.4	105.0	(NA)	182.5	6.4	15.2	(NA)	38.0
Brazil	16.4	147.6	228.0	226.2	5.6	79.2	87.3	101.3
Canada	241.9	366.3	(NA)	841.4	71.3	183.7	(NA)	634.7
Chile	13.6	73.9	68.2	60.4	0.8	11.1	6.9	6.1
China [1]	(NA)	42.1	330.7	581.0	(NA)	49.8	377.1	721.5
Denmark	39.1	56.2	(NA)	107.7	11.1	25.9	(NA)	91.6
Egypt	1.8	8.1	32.8	28.7	0.1	0.7	9.0	11.1
Finland	22.7	44.1	(NA)	293.6	3.9	19.0	(NA)	206.6
France	314.4	522.1	(NA)	1,446.6	116.9	364.6	(NA)	1,083.3
Germany	355.1	577.4	(NA)	1,270.2	501.8	573.5	(NA)	1,069.1
Greece	15.2	17.1	204.2	110.8	3.9	6.1	188.7	95.1
Hong Kong	83.4	303.7	(NA)	623.4	34.6	106.9	(NA)	377.9
India	38.6	127.2	184.6	148.1	21.9	13.7	278.8	509.8
Indonesia	8.1	66.6	64.1	26.8	4.0	14.4	19.9	14.3
Iran	(NA)	6.6	(NA)	34.0	(NA)	0.7	2.3	5.0
Ireland	(NA)	25.8	(NA)	81.9	(NA)	13.2	(NA)	14.4
Israel	3.3	36.4	63.8	64.1	5.5	9.2	15.5	23.4
Italy	148.8	209.5	(NA)	768.4	42.6	86.9	(NA)	778.4
Japan	2,917.7	3,667.3	(NA)	3,157.2	1,602.4	1,231.6	(NA)	2,693.9
Korea, South	110.6	182.0	308.5	171.6	75.9	185.2	825.8	1,067.7
Luxembourg	10.5	30.4	(NA)	34.0	0.1	0.2	(NA)	1.2
Malaysia	48.6	222.7	145.4	116.9	10.9	76.8	48.5	58.5
Mexico	32.7	90.7	154.0	125.2	12.2	34.4	36.0	45.3
Morocco	1.0	6.0	13.7	10.9	0.1	2.4	2.5	1.1
Netherlands	119.8	356.5	(NA)	640.5	40.2	248.6	(NA)	677.2
New Zealand	8.8	32.0	(NA)	18.6	1.9	8.4	(NA)	10.8
Norway	26.1	44.6	(NA)	65.0	14.0	24.4	(NA)	60.1
Philippines	5.9	58.9	48.1	51.6	1.2	14.7	19.7	8.2
Poland	(NA)	4.6	29.6	31.3	(NA)	2.8	11.1	14.6
Portugal	9.2	18.4	(NA)	60.7	1.7	4.2	(NA)	54.4
Russia	(NA)	15.9	72.2	38.9	(NA)	0.5	2.8	20.3
Saudi Arabia	(NA)	40.9	60.4	67.2	(NA)	6.2	14.8	17.3
Singapore	34.3	148.0	(NA)	152.8	20.3	60.5	(NA)	91.5
South Africa	137.5	280.5	262.5	205.0	8.2	17.0	72.9	77.5
Spain	111.4	197.8	(NA)	504.2	41.0	59.8	(NA)	985.9
Sweden	97.9	178.0	(NA)	328.3	17.6	93.2	(NA)	390.0
Switzerland	160.0	433.6	(NA)	792.3	(NA)	310.9	(NA)	609.1
Taiwan [1]	100.7	187.2	376.0	247.6	715.0	383.1	910.0	983.5
Thailand	23.9	141.5	58.4	29.5	22.9	57.0	41.6	23.3
Turkey	19.1	20.8	112.7	69.7	5.8	51.4	81.3	179.2
United Kingdom	848.9	1,407.7	(NA)	2,580.0	278.7	510.1	(NA)	1,835.3

NA Not available. [1] See footnote 2, Table 1327.

Source: Standard and Poor's, New York, NY, Standard & Poor's Emerging Stock Markets Factbook 2001 (copyright).

862 Comparative International Statistics

No. 1384. Foreign Exchange Rates: 2000

[Foreign currency units per U.S. dollar. Rates shown include market, official, principal, and secondary rates, as published by the International Monetary Fund in *International Financial Statistics*]

Country	Currency	2000	Country	Currency	2000
Afghanistan [1]	Afghanis	4,726	Laos	Kip	7,888
Albania	Leks	143.7	Latvia	Lats	0.61
Algeria	Algerian Dinar	75.26	Lebanon	Lebanese Pounds	1,508
Antigua and Barbuda	E. Caribbean Dollar	2.7	Lesotho	Loti	6.94
Argentina	Pesos	1	Liberia	Liberian Dollar	40.85
Armenia	Dram	539.5	Libya	Libyan Dinars	0.5
Aruba	Aruban Florins	1.79	Lithuania	Litai	4
Australia	Australian Dollar	1.72	Luxembourg [2]	Francs	43.77
Austria [2]	Schillings	14.94	Macedonia, The Former		
Bahamas, The	Bahamian Dollar	1	Yugoslav Republic of	Denar	65.9
Bahrain	Dinars	0.38	Madagascar	Malagasy Francs	6,768
Bangladesh	Taka	52.14	Malaysia	Ringgit	3.8
Barbados	Barbados Dollar	2	Mali	Cfa Francs	712.0
Belarus	Rubel	1,180	Malta	Maltese Liri	0.44
Belgium [2]	Francs	43.77	Mauritania	Ouguiyas	238.9
Belize	Belize Dollar	2	Mauritius	Rupees	26.25
Benin	Cfa Francs	712.0	Mexico	New Pesos	9.46
Bolivia	Bolivianos	6.18	Moldova	Lei	12.43
Botswana	Pula	5.1	Mongolia	Tugriks	1,077
Brazil	Reals	1.83	Morocco	Dirhams	10.63
Bulgaria	Leva	2.12	Mozambique	Meticais	15,447
Burkina Faso	Cfa Francs	712.0	Namibia	Namibia Dollar	6.94
Burma	Kyats	6.52	Nepal	Rupees	71.09
Cambodia	Riels	3,841	Netherlands [2]	Guilders	2.39
Cameroon	Cfa Francs	712.0	Netherlands Antilles	Guilders	1.79
Canada	Canadian Dollar	1.49	New Zealand	New Zealand Dollar	2.19
Central African Republic	Cfa Francs	712.0	Nicaragua	Cordobas	12.69
Chad	Cfa Francs	712.0	Niger	Cfa Francs	712.0
Chile	Pesos	535.5	Nigeria	Naira	101.4
China [3]	Yuan	8.28	Norway	Kroner	8.8
Colombia	Pesos	2,088	Oman	Rials Omani	0.38
Comoros	Comorian Francs	534.0	Pakistan	Rupees	52.81
Congo (Brazzaville) [4]	Cfa Francs	712.0	Panama	Balboas	1
Costa Rica	Colones	308.2	Papua New Guinea	Kina	2.76
Cote d'Ivoire	Cfa Francs	712.0	Paraguay	Guaranies	3,486
Croatia	Kuna	8.28	Peru	Nuevos Soles	3.49
Cyprus	Cyprus Pounds	0.62	Philippines	Pesos	44.19
Czech Republic	Koruny	38.6	Poland	Zlotys	4.35
Denmark	Kroner	8.07	Portugal [2]	Escudos	217.5
Djibouti	Djibouti Francs	177.7	Qatar	Riyals	3.64
Dominica	E.Caribbean Dollar	2.7	Romania	Lei	21,709
Dominican Republic	Pesos	16.42	Russia	Rubles	28.13
Ecuador	Sucres	24,988	Rwanda	Rwanda Francs	389.7
Egypt	Egyptian Pounds	3.69	Saint Kitts and Nevis	E.Caribbean Dollar	2.7
El Salvador	Colones	8.76	Saint Lucia	E.Caribbean Dollar	2.7
Equatorial Guinea	Cfa Francs	712.0	Saint Vincent and the		
Estonia	Krooni	16.97	Grenadines	E.Caribbean Dollar	2.7
Ethiopia	Birr	8.22	Saudi Arabia	Riyals	3.75
Euro area (EMU-11) [2]	Euro	1.09	Senegal	Cfa Francs	712.0
Fiji	Fiji Dollar	1.97	Sierra Leone	Leones	2,092
Finland [2]	Markkaa	6.45	Singapore	Singapore Dollar	1.72
France [2]	Francs	7.12	Slovakia	Koruny	46.4
Gabon	Cfa Francs	712.0	Slovenia	Tolars	222.7
Georgia	Lari	1.98	South Africa	Rand	6.94
Germany [2]	Deutsche Mark	2.13	Spain [2]	Pesetas	180.5
Greece	Drachmas	365.4	Sri Lanka	Rupees	77
Guatemala	Quetzales	7.76	Sudan	Sudanese Pounds	257.1
Guyana	Guyana Dollar	181.6	Suriname	Guilders	2,096
Haiti	Gourdes	21.17	Swaziland	Langeni	6.9
Honduras	Lempiras	14.84	Sweden	Kronor	9.16
Hong Kong	Hong Kong Dollar	7.79	Switzerland	Swiss Francs	1.69
Hungary	Forint	282.2	Syria	Syrian Pounds	11.23
Iceland	Kronur	78.62	Tanzania	Tanzania Shilling	800.4
India	Rupees	44.94	Thailand	Baht	40.11
Indonesia	Rupiah	8,422	Togo	Cfa Francs	712.0
Iran	Rials	7,764	Trinidad and Tobago	Tt Dollars	6.3
Iraq	Dinars	0.31	Tunisia	Dinars	1.37
Ireland [2]	Irish Pounds	0.86	Turkey	Liras	625,219
Israel	New Sheqalim	4.08	Uganda	Uganda Shilling	1,645
Italy [2]	Lire	2,111	Ukraine	Hryvnias	5.44
Jamaica	Jamaica Dollars	42.7	United Arab Emirates	Dirhams	3.67
Japan	Yen	107.8	United Kingdom	Pounds Sterling	0.66
Jordan	Dinars	0.71	Uruguay	Pesos	12.1
Kazakhstan	Tenge	142.1	Vanuatu	Vatu	137.6
Kenya	Kenya Shillings	76.18	Venezuela	Venezuela	680.0
Korea, South	Won	1,131	Yemen	Rials	161.7
Kuwait	Dinars	0.31	Zambia	Kwacha	3,111
Kyrgyzstan	Soms	47.7	Zimbabwe	Zimbabwe Dollar	43.29

[1] End-of year values were used if annual averages were unavailable. Some values were estimated using partial year data.
[2] The euro became the official currency of the 11 Euro Area (EMU) nations on January 1, 1999. The values shown in this table are computed values for the former national currencies.   [3] See footnote 2, Table 1327.   [4] See footnote 3, Table 1327.

Source: U.S. Dept. of Commerce, International Trade Administration, "Foreign Exchange Rates, 1994-00"; published 2 August 2001; <http://www.ita.doc.gov/td/industry/otea/usfth/aggregate/HL00T37.txt>.

No. 1385. Reserve Assets and International Transaction Balances by Country: 1995 to 2000

[In millions of U.S. dollars (74,780 represents $74,780,000,000). Assets include holdings of convertible foreign currencies, special drawing rights, and reserve position in International Monetary Fund and exclude gold holdings. Minus sign (-) indicates debits]

Country	Total reserve assets 1995	Total reserve assets 1999	Total reserve assets 2000 Total	Total reserve assets 2000 Currency holdings [1]	Current account balance 1995	Current account balance 1999	Current account balance 2000	Merchandise trade balance 1995	Merchandise trade balance 1999	Merchandise trade balance 2000
United States	74,780	60,500	56,600	31,240	-109,450	-331,480	-435,370	-171,880	-343,260	-447,090
Algeria	2,005	4,526	12,024	11,910	(NA)	(NA)	(NA)	(NA)	(NA)	(NA)
Argentina	14,288	26,252	25,147	24,414	-5,302	-12,446	-9,358	2,358	-770	2,541
Australia	11,896	21,212	18,118	16,782	-19,487	-23,070	(NA)	-4,223	-9,730	(NA)
Austria	18,730	15,120	14,318	13,492	-5,448	-5,747	-5,352	-6,656	-3,649	-2,659
Bangladesh	2,340	1,604	1,486	1,485	-824	-292	(NA)	-2,324	-1,962	(NA)
Belgium	16,177	10,937	9,994	7,988	14,232	13,374	11,650	9,555	6,642	5,346
Brazil	49,708	34,796	32,488	32,488	-18,136	-25,400	-24,632	-3,157	-1,261	-696
Burma	561	266	223	223	-259	-366	-293	-823	-1,035	-843
Cameroon	4	4	212	204	90	(NA)	(NA)	627	(NA)	(NA)
Canada	15,049	28,126	31,924	28,841	-4,328	-2,273	12,666	25,855	22,756	36,609
Chile	14,140	14,407	14,729	14,381	-1,350	-80	(NA)	1,381	1,664	(NA)
China [2]	75,377	157,728	168,278	165,574	1,618	15,667	(NA)	18,050	36,207	(NA)
Colombia . . . . . . [3]	8,452	8,103	9,005	8,498	-4,596	-61	(NA)	-2,545	1,776	(NA)
Congo (Kinshasa) [3] .	59	39	222	221	-650	(NA)	(NA)	516	(NA)	(NA)
Cote d'Ivoire	529	630	668	666	-492	(NA)	(NA)	1,376	(NA)	(NA)
Denmark	11,016	22,287	15,108	14,469	1,855	2,964	2,493	6,528	6,689	6,306
Ecuador	1,628	1,642	947	924	-765	955	(NA)	324	1,665	(NA)
Egypt	16,181	14,484	13,118	12,913	-254	-1,635	(NA)	-7,597	-9,928	(NA)
Finland	10,038	8,207	8,465	7,331	5,231	7,588	9,267	12,437	11,655	13,159
France	26,853	39,701	37,039	32,114	10,840	36,580	24,500	11,000	19,390	3,750
Germany	85,005	61,039	56,890	49,667	-18,930	-19,310	(NA)	65,110	72,000	(NA)
Ghana	698	454	232	232	-145	-766	(NA)	-257	-1,112	(NA)
Greece	14,780	18,122	13,424	13,116	-2,864	(NA)	(NA)	-14,425	(NA)	(NA)
Hungary	11,974	10,954	11,190	10,915	-2,530	-2,106	-1,494	-2,433	-2,189	-2,106
India	17,922	32,667	37,902	37,264	-5,563	-2,784	(NA)	-6,719	-8,029	(NA)
Indonesia	13,708	26,445	22,548	22,326	-6,431	5,785	(NA)	6,533	20,644	(NA)
Ireland	8,630	5,282	5,360	4,983	1,721	595	-792	13,557	24,178	25,523
Israel	8,119	22,605	23,281	23,163	-5,164	-1,881	(NA)	-7,441	-4,408	(NA)
Italy	34,905	22,421	25,566	22,423	25,076	6,304	-5,670	38,729	20,383	10,717
Japan	183,250	286,916	354,902	347,212	111,040	106,870	116,880	131,790	123,320	116,720
Kenya	353	792	898	881	-400	11	(NA)	-750	-829	(NA)
Korea, South	32,678	73,987	96,131	95,855	-8,507	24,477	(NA)	-4,444	28,371	(NA)
Kuwait	3,561	4,824	7,082	6,504	5,016	5,062	(NA)	5,579	5,571	(NA)
Malaysia	23,774	30,588	29,523	28,625	-8,644	12,606	(NA)	-103	22,648	(NA)
Mexico	16,847	31,782	35,509	35,142	-1,576	-14,166	(NA)	7,089	-5,581	(NA)
Morocco	3,601	5,689	4,823	4,612	-1,296	-171	(NA)	-2,482	-2,448	(NA)
Nepal	586	843	947	939	-356	· 11	(NA)	-961	-881	(NA)
Netherlands	33,714	10,098	9,643	7,004	25,751	17,236	14,217	23,808	17,940	18,650
Nigeria	1,443	(NA)	(NA)	(NA)	-2,578	506	(NA)	3,513	4,288	(NA)
Norway	22,518	20,400	20,164	19,274	4,854	6,014	22,986	8,571	10,119	25,500
Pakistan	1,733	1,511	1,513	1,499	-3,349	(NA)	(NA)	-2,891	(NA)	(NA)
Peru	8,222	8,731	8,374	8,373	-4,117	-1,822	-1,648	-2,166	-617	-335
Philippines	6,372	13,230	13,054	12,938	-1,980	7,910	(NA)	-8,944	4,958	(NA)
Poland	14,774	26,355	25,657	25,415	854	-12,487	(NA)	-1,646	-15,072	(NA)
Portugal	15,850	8,848	8,908	8,539	-132	-9,629	-10,632	-8,910	-13,766	-14,143
Romania	1,579	2,687	3,922	3,921	-1,780	-1,297	(NA)	-1,577	-1,092	(NA)
Saudi Arabia	8,622	16,997	19,585	18,036	-5,325	412	15,567	24,390	25,039	51,176
Singapore	68,695	76,843	80,127	79,681	14,436	21,254	(NA)	977	11,303	(NA)
South Africa	2,820	6,353	6,083	5,793	-2,204	-553	-469	2,667	4,150	4,231
Spain	34,485	33,115	30,989	29,516	792	-13,761	-17,257	-18,415	-30,339	-32,755
Sri Lanka	2,088	1,636	1,039	976	-770	-493	(NA)	-985	-707	(NA)
Sudan	163	189	(NA)	(NA)	-500	-465	-557	-510	-476	440
Sweden	24,051	15,019	14,863	13,757	4,940	5,982	(NA)	15,978	15,714	(NA)
Switzerland	36,413	36,321	32,272	30,854	21,804	29,119	(NA)	3,259	723	(NA)
Syria	(NA)	(NA)	(NA)	(NA)	263	201	(NA)	-146	216	(NA)
Thailand	35,982	34,063	32,016	31,933	-13,554	12,428	9,195	-7,968	14,013	11,757
Trinidad and Tobago .	358	945	1,386	1,386	294	(NA)	(NA)	588	(NA)	(NA)
Turkey	12,442	23,340	19,952	19,777	-2,338	-1,360	-9,765	-13,212	-10,443	-22,341
United Kingdom	42,020	35,870	43,890	39,280	-5,970	-15,980	-24,460	-18,530	-42,350	-43,580
Venezuela	6,283	12,277	13,088	12,633	2,014	3,689	13,365	7,013	7,606	17,965

NA Not available.   [1] Holdings of convertible foreign currencies.   [2] See footnote 2, Table 1327.   [3] See footnote 3, Table 1327.

Source: International Monetary Fund, Washington, DC, *International Financial Statistics*, monthly, (copyright).

No. 1386. Foreign Trade—Destination of Exports and Source of Imports for Selected Countries: 1999

[In billions of dollars (56.0 represents $56,000,000,000), except as indicated]

Country	World [1]	Belgium-Luxembourg	Canada	China [2]	France	Germany	Italy	Japan	Netherlands	United Kingdom	United States
EXPORTS											
Australia	56.0	0.7	0.8	2.6	0.6	0.8	0.9	10.8	0.6	2.4	5.4
Austria	62.4	1.0	0.4	0.4	2.7	22.0	5.2	0.8	1.4	2.8	2.8
Belgium	176.2	3.4	0.8	1.0	31.0	31.3	9.9	2.2	22.1	17.8	9.3
Canada	238.8	1.3	(X)	1.8	1.3	1.6	1.0	5.7	1.0	3.2	207.3
Denmark	49.0	0.9	0.3	0.3	2.3	9.1	1.6	1.4	2.1	4.3	2.2
Finland	41.8	1.1	0.3	1.0	2.1	5.3	1.5	0.7	1.7	3.7	3.3
France	302.3	23.2	3.1	3.3	(X)	47.6	27.6	4.6	14.2	31.2	23.5
Germany	535.9	29.1	3.6	7.3	60.4	(X)	39.2	10.8	33.6	44.3	53.9
Ireland	70.5	3.7	0.4	0.1	6.0	8.4	2.6	2.1	4.4	15.4	10.9
Italy	230.2	6.3	2.0	1.9	29.7	37.7	(X)	3.7	6.6	16.3	21.8
Japan	417.1	5.3	6.9	23.3	6.8	18.6	5.1	(X)	12.0	14.2	129.6
Korea, South	143.7	0.9	1.6	13.7	1.7	4.2	1.7	15.9	2.1	4.8	29.6
Netherlands	170.5	18.3	0.6	0.6	17.5	41.7	9.9	1.8	(X)	16.9	7.3
Norway	45.5	1.3	2.2	0.5	3.8	4.6	1.0	1.2	4.8	8.3	3.5
Sweden	84.8	3.7	0.8	1.6	4.5	9.4	3.2	2.0	5.2	8.1	7.8
Switzerland	81.0	1.8	0.7	0.7	7.4	18.3	6.4	3.3	2.5	4.4	10.0
United Kingdom	270.7	14.2	4.1	2.0	26.5	32.1	12.4	5.4	21.3	(X)	39.9
PERCENT DISTRIBUTION											
Australia	100.0	1.3	1.4	4.7	1.0	1.4	1.6	19.2	1.1	4.3	9.7
Austria	100.0	1.6	0.6	0.7	4.4	35.3	8.4	1.2	2.3	4.4	4.5
Belgium	100.0	1.9	0.4	0.6	17.6	17.8	5.6	1.2	12.5	10.1	5.3
Canada	100.0	0.6	(X)	0.7	0.5	0.7	0.4	2.4	0.4	1.4	86.8
Denmark	100.0	1.7	0.5	0.6	4.8	18.6	3.3	2.9	4.3	8.8	4.5
Finland	100.0	2.5	0.8	2.5	5.1	12.7	3.7	1.7	4.2	8.9	7.8
France	100.0	7.7	1.0	1.1	(X)	15.7	9.1	1.5	4.7	10.3	7.8
Germany	100.0	5.4	0.7	1.4	11.3	(X)	7.3	2.0	6.3	8.3	10.1
Ireland	100.0	5.2	0.5	0.2	8.4	11.9	3.7	2.9	6.2	21.8	15.5
Italy	100.0	2.7	0.9	0.8	12.9	16.4	(X)	1.6	2.8	7.1	9.5
Japan	100.0	1.3	1.7	5.6	1.6	4.5	1.2	(X)	2.9	3.4	31.1
Korea, South	100.0	0.6	1.1	9.5	1.2	2.9	1.2	11.0	1.5	3.3	20.6
Netherlands	100.0	10.7	0.4	0.4	10.3	24.4	5.8	1.1	(X)	9.9	4.3
Norway	100.0	2.8	4.8	1.1	8.3	10.0	2.2	2.7	10.5	18.2	7.8
Sweden	100.0	4.4	1.0	1.8	5.4	11.1	3.7	2.4	6.1	9.6	9.2
Switzerland	100.0	2.2	0.8	0.8	9.2	22.6	7.9	4.0	3.1	5.5	12.4
United Kingdom	100.0	5.2	1.5	0.7	9.8	11.9	4.6	2.0	7.9	(X)	14.7
IMPORTS											
Australia	65.5	0.5	1.0	4.3	1.4	3.8	1.9	8.8	0.6	3.5	13.7
Austria	68.7	1.5	0.3	1.0	3.5	29.0	5.3	1.7	2.2	2.2	3.7
Belgium	160.8	0.9	1.2	3.1	21.7	28.4	6.3	4.2	27.0	13.8	12.1
Canada	215.6	0.7	3.7	6.0	3.6	4.7	2.4	10.1	0.8	5.5	145.0
Denmark	44.3	1.6	0.2	1.2	2.5	9.4	2.1	0.8	3.5	3.5	2.0
Finland	31.6	0.8	0.2	0.7	1.3	4.8	1.2	2.0	1.3	2.1	2.5
France	292.8	21.3	1.6	8.2	3.8	50.3	28.2	10.5	14.9	24.5	25.7
Germany	464.8	24.1	2.7	14.4	48.6	(X)	34.3	22.7	35.4	32.0	37.5
Ireland	46.5	0.6	0.4	0.7	1.9	2.9	1.0	2.7	1.4	15.3	7.8
Italy	216.6	9.6	1.5	5.3	26.8	41.2	(X)	5.5	13.3	13.1	10.6
Japan	309.9	1.8	7.9	42.8	6.1	11.5	5.0	(X)	1.9	5.9	67.5
Korea, South	119.8	0.5	1.8	8.9	1.8	3.8	1.3	24.1	1.0	2.1	24.9
Netherlands	167.9	14.9	0.9	3.8	10.3	28.4	4.3	7.6	(X)	15.5	16.7
Norway	34.2	0.8	0.6	0.9	1.5	4.4	1.3	1.4	1.7	3.1	2.7
Sweden	68.5	2.7	0.3	0.8	4.3	12.3	2.4	2.0	5.7	7.2	4.0
Switzerland	80.6	2.4	0.4	1.2	9.7	25.0	7.8	2.3	4.1	4.6	5.7
United Kingdom	323.8	15.2	4.5	10.8	28.7	42.5	15.4	14.7	21.5	(X)	42.3
PERCENT DISTRIBUTION											
Australia	100.0	0.7	1.6	6.5	2.2	5.7	2.9	13.4	0.9	5.3	21.0
Austria	100.0	2.2	0.5	1.4	5.1	42.2	7.7	2.5	3.2	3.1	5.4
Belgium	100.0	0.6	0.8	1.9	13.5	17.7	3.9	2.6	16.8	8.6	7.5
Canada	100.0	0.3	1.7	2.8	1.7	2.2	1.1	4.7	0.4	2.5	67.3
Denmark	100.0	3.6	0.5	2.6	5.7	21.3	4.8	1.9	7.9	7.9	4.5
Finland	100.0	2.5	0.5	2.3	4.2	15.3	3.7	6.2	4.0	6.6	7.9
France	100.0	7.3	0.5	2.8	1.3	17.2	9.6	3.6	5.1	8.4	8.8
Germany	100.0	5.2	0.6	3.1	10.5	(X)	7.4	4.9	7.6	6.9	8.1
Ireland	100.0	1.3	0.9	1.5	4.1	6.2	2.2	5.8	3.0	32.9	16.7
Italy	100.0	4.5	0.7	2.5	12.4	19.0	(X)	2.5	6.2	6.1	4.9
Japan	100.0	0.6	2.6	13.8	2.0	3.7	1.6	(X)	0.6	1.9	21.8
Korea, South	100.0	0.4	1.5	7.4	1.5	3.2	1.1	20.2	0.9	1.8	20.8
Netherlands	100.0	8.9	0.5	2.3	6.1	16.9	2.6	4.5	(X)	9.2	9.9
Norway	100.0	2.3	1.7	2.7	4.3	12.8	3.8	4.2	4.9	9.2	8.0
Sweden	100.0	4.0	0.4	1.1	6.3	18.0	3.5	2.9	8.3	10.5	5.9
Switzerland	100.0	3.0	0.5	1.5	12.0	31.0	9.7	2.9	5.1	5.7	7.1
United Kingdom	100.0	4.7	1.4	3.3	8.9	13.1	4.7	4.5	6.6	(X)	13.1

X Not applicable.   [1] Includes other countries not shown separately.   [2] See footnote 2, Table 1327.

Source: Organization for Economic Cooperation and Development, Paris, France, *OECD International Trade by Commodities Statistics, 2000.*

Comparative International Statistics   865

No. 1387. International Tourism Receipts—Leading Countries: 1990 to 2000

[In millions of dollars, except as indicated (263,357 represents $263,357,000,000). Excludes international transport receipts]

Country	Total receipts						Percent of world total	
	1990	1995	1997	1998	1999	2000	1990	2000
World, total [1]	263,357	405,997	440,858	442,986	455,188	475,761	100.0	100.0
United States	43,007	63,395	73,426	71,286	74,881	85,153	16.3	17.9
Spain	18,593	25,388	26,900	29,839	32,400	(NA)	7.1	(NA)
France	20,184	27,527	28,009	29,931	31,507	(NA)	7.7	(NA)
Italy	16,458	28,729	29,714	29,866	28,359	27,439	6.2	5.8
United Kingdom	13,762	18,554	20,039	20,978	20,223	19,266	5.2	4.0
Germany [2]	14,288	18,135	16,696	16,766	16,730	(NA)	5.4	(NA)
China	2,218	8,733	12,074	12,602	14,098	16,231	0.8	3.4
Austria	13,417	14,586	12,248	12,628	12,533	11,440	5.1	2.4
Canada	6,339	7,882	8,828	9,396	10,171	10,768	2.4	2.3
Greece	2,587	4,136	5,151	6,188	8,783	9,290	1.0	2.0
Australia	4,088	7,873	8,786	7,338	8,017	8,442	1.6	1.8
Switzerland	7,411	9,365	7,915	7,973	7,739	7,303	2.8	1.5
Russia	(NA)	4,312	7,164	6,508	7,510	(NA)	(NA)	(NA)
Mexico	5,467	6,179	7,593	7,493	7,223	8,295	2.1	1.7
Hong Kong	5,032	9,604	9,979	7,496	7,210	7,886	1.9	1.7
Netherlands	4,155	6,563	6,304	6,788	7,092	6,951	1.6	1.5
Belgium	3,721	5,859	5,267	5,443	7,039	(NA)	1.4	(NA)
Korea, South	3,559	5,587	5,116	6,865	6,802	6,609	1.4	1.4
Thailand	4,326	7,664	7,048	5,934	6,695	7,535	1.6	1.6
Poland	358	6,614	8,679	7,946	6,100	(NA)	0.1	(NA)

NA Not available. [1] Includes other countries not shown separately. [2] See footnote 2, Table 1327.

Source: World Tourism Organization, Madrid, Spain, *Yearbook of Tourism Statistics* (copyright)

No. 1388. Net Flow of Financial Resources to Developing Countries and Multilateral Organizations: 1995 to 1999

[165,182 represents $165,182,000,000. Net flow covers loans, grants, and grant-like flows minus amortization on loans. Military flows are excluded. Developing countries cover countries designated by Development Assistance Committee as developing. GNP=gross national product]

Type of aid and country	Amount (mil. dol.)					Percent of GNP	
	1995	1996	1997	1998	1999	1995	1999
Total net flows	165,182	193,561	185,436	182,407	188,943	0.75	0.80
Official Development Assistance [1]	58,926	55,622	48,497	52,084	56,378	(X)	(X)
Other official flows [2]	9,872	5,562	6,125	13,491	15,477	(X)	(X)
Private flows at market terms [3]	90,411	126,809	125,623	111,223	110,404	(X)	(X)
Net grants by nongovernment organizations	5,973	5,568	5,191	5,609	6,684	(X)	(X)
United States	46,984	55,731	74,991	48,421	50,138	0.65	0.54
Australia	2,536	-721	-3,043	1,745	1,749	0.76	0.46
Austria	906	1,878	1,661	889	1,963	0.39	0.96
Belgium	-234	5,614	-10,636	7,725	5,528	-0.09	2.21
Canada	5,724	6,682	10,536	9,227	6,984	1.04	1.13
Denmark	1,799	1,949	1,928	1,806	1,992	1.07	1.16
Finland	604	1,147	449	1,633	875	0.50	0.69
France	12,477	17,486	13,979	8,402	9,125	0.81	0.64
Germany	21,197	20,815	19,785	22,436	20,181	0.87	0.96
Greece	-	184	185	189	195	-	0.16
Ireland	247	371	323	333	251	0.46	0.32
Italy	2,800	4,713	8,116	13,171	11,337	0.26	0.97
Japan	42,295	38,088	29,509	17,902	20,794	0.82	0.47
Luxembourg	72	89	100	118	124	0.40	0.69
Netherlands	6,795	9,514	8,683	12,752	7,985	1.71	2.02
New Zealand	166	147	182	154	163	0.31	0.33
Norway	1,670	1,668	1,647	1,983	2,060	1.16	1.37
Portugal	395	944	1,337	2,015	2,337	0.38	2.17
Spain	2,025	4,259	7,411	11,841	29,029	0.37	4.90
Sweden	2,224	2,003	2,092	2,847	2,892	1.00	1.24
Switzerland	1,118	-1,471	-3,457	4,683	3,226	0.35	1.17
United Kingdom	13,382	22,470	19,659	12,136	10,017	1.19	0.69

- Represents zero. X Not applicable. [1] Grants or loans to countries and territories on Part I of the DAC List of Aid Recipients (developing countries) which are: (a) undertaken by the official sector; (b) with promotion of economic development and welfare as the main objective; (c) at concessional financial terms if a loan, having a grant element of at least 25 percent. Technical cooperation is included in aid. [2] Transactions by the official sector with countries on the List of Aid Recipients which do not meet the conditions for eligibility as Official Development Assistance or Official Aid, either because they are not primarily aimed at development, or because they have a grant element of less than 25 per cent. [3] Consists of flows at market terms financed out of private sector resources (i.e. changes in holdings of private long term assets held by residents of the reporting country) and private grants (i.e. grants by nongovernment organizations, net of subsidies received from the official sector).

Source: Organization for Economic Cooperation and Development, Paris, France, *Annual Reports of the Development Assistance Committee* (copyright).

No. 1389. External Debt by Country: 1990 to 1999

[In millions of dollars (27,877 represents $27,877,000,000). Total external debt is debt owed to nonresidents repayable in foreign currency, goods, or services. It is the sum of public, publicly guaranteed, and private nonguaranteed long-term debt, use of IMF credit, and short-term debt. Short-term debt includes all debt having an origina. maturity of one year or less and interest in arrears on long-term debt. Public debt comprises long-term external obligations of public debtors, including the national government and political subdivisions (or an agency of either) and autonomous public bodies, and external obligations of private debtors that are guaranteed for repayment by a public entity]

Country	1990	1995	1998	1999	Country	1990	1995	1998	1999
Algeria	27,877	32,781	30,665	28,015	Malta	601	962	9,730	10,600
Angola	8,594	11,382	11,223	10,871	Mexico	104,442	166,874	159,778	166,960
Argentina	62,232	98,802	141,549	147,880	Morocco	24,458	22,665	20,491	19,060
Bangladesh	12,768	16,325	16,376	17,534	Mozambique	4,650	7,458	8,315	6,959
Bolivia	4,275	5,272	6,460	6,157	Nicaragua	10,707	10,359	6,442	6,986
Brazil	119,877	159,073	244,833	244,673	Nigeria	33,439	34,093	30,315	29,358
Bulgaria	10,865	10,246	9,801	9,872	Pakistan	20,663	30,229	32,319	34,269
Cameroon	6,676	9,444	9,930	9,443	Panama	6,678	6,275	6,407	6,837
Chile	19,226	25,562	36,321	37,762	Peru	20,064	30,852	32,175	32,284
China [1]	55,301	118,090	154,599	154,223	Philippines	30,580	37,829	47,793	52,022
Colombia	17,222	25,048	33,264	34,538	Poland	49,366	44,263	55,494	54,268
Congo (Kinshasa) [2]	10,274	13,256	13,187	11,906	Romania	1,140	6,666	10,014	9,367
Cote d'Ivoire	17,251	18,898	14,852	13,170	Russia	59,340	121,722	177,710	173,940
Croatia	(X)	3,729	9,159	9,443	Slovakia	2,008	5,821	9,566	9,150
Czech Republic	6,383	16,218	24,007	22,582	South Africa	(NA)	25,358	24,711	24,158
Ecuador	12,108	13,994	15,140	14,506	Sri Lanka	5,863	8,215	8,531	9,472
Egypt	32,949	33,266	31,965	30,404	Sudan	14,762	17,603	16,843	16,132
Ghana	3,881	5,936	6,883	6,928	Syria	17,053	21,318	22,435	22,369
Hungary	21,202	31,590	28,310	29,042	Tanzania	6,451	7,406	7,633	7,967
India	83,717	94,469	97,639	94,393	Thailand	28,165	100,093	104,943	96,335
Indonesia	69,872	124,398	150,884	150,096	Tunisia	7,690	10,820	10,850	11,872
Iran	9,020	21,879	13,999	10,357	Turkey	49,424	73,790	97,212	101,796
Jordan	8,177	8,114	8,451	8,947	Ukraine	(X)	8,429	13,071	14,136
Kenya	7,058	7,412	6,943	6,562	Uruguay	4,415	5,318	7,598	7,447
Korea, South	34,968	85,810	139,097	129,784	Venezuela	33,170	35,848	37,004	35,852
Lebanon	1,779	2,966	6,725	8,441	Vietnam	23,270	25,427	22,502	23,260
Malaysia	15,328	34,343	44,769	45,939	Yugoslavia	17,792	13,839	13,742	12,949

NA Not available.   X Not applicable.   [1] See footnote 2, Table 1327.   [2] See footnote 3, Table 1327.

Source: The World Bank, Washington, DC, 2001 World Development Indicators CD-ROM (copyright).

No. 1390. Foreign Direct Investment Flows in OECD Countries: 1997 to 1999

[In millions of dollars (299,004 represents $299,004,000,000). 1999 data, preliminary. Data are converted to U.S. dollars using the yearly average exchange rate]

Country	Inflows				Outflows			
	1997	1998	1999	Cumulative, 1990-99	1997	1998	1999	Cumulative, 1990-99
OECD, total	299,004	509,313	683,744	2,709,512	414,079	636,480	767,814	3,552,013
Australia	7,510	6,502	4,441	58,910	6,262	2,466	-3,192	26,596
Austria	2,656	4,902	2,952	21,084	1,948	2,948	2,703	18,155
Belgium-Luxembourg	12,093	22,724	15,868	123,206	7,273	28,453	24,937	109,350
Canada	11,470	16,499	24,268	99,000	22,054	26,575	17,362	120,113
Czech Republic	1,300	2,540	4,877	15,233	25	175	197	828
Denmark	2,801	6,722	7,450	32,176	4,210	3,962	8,207	32,958
Finland	2,116	12,141	3,024	22,841	5,292	18,643	4,194	40,760
France	23,174	28,955	37,416	215,804	35,586	41,913	88,324	347,839
Germany	11,092	21,271	52,403	116,467	40,716	91,183	98,853	422,455
Greece [1]	3,586	3,709	539	26,942	(NA)	(NA)	573	573
Hungary	2,173	2,036	1,944	19,618	431	481	249	1,261
Iceland [2]	149	112	90	476	51	99	70	380
Ireland [2]	1,676	3,904	5,422	17,451	(NA)	8,569	18,326	26,895
Italy	3,698	2,611	5,019	37,697	10,619	12,078	3,038	71,148
Japan	3,224	3,193	12,378	26,008	25,991	24,159	20,730	248,729
Korea, South	2,844	5,416	8,798	24,653	4,449	4,799	4,044	29,018
Mexico	12,830	11,311	11,568	81,570	(NA)	(NA)	(NA)	(NA)
Netherlands	14,499	41,977	33,341	159,523	29,247	51,365	45,540	250,860
New Zealand [3]	1,832	2,172	989	20,754	-1,602	376	1,020	5,135
Norway	3,786	3,882	6,579	26,670	5,047	2,418	5,483	28,131
Poland	4,908	6,365	6,471	30,816	45	316	123	639
Portugal	2,278	2,802	570	17,501	1,668	2,901	2,679	10,463
Spain	6,387	11,797	9,357	97,780	12,547	18,935	35,421	93,236
Sweden	10,968	19,569	59,102	127,633	12,648	24,376	18,951	102,114
Switzerland	6,642	7,499	3,412	34,680	17,747	16,631	17,910	119,187
Turkey	805	940	783	8,116	251	367	645	2,087
United Kingdom	33,245	64,388	82,176	319,726	61,620	119,463	199,275	566,400
United States	109,264	193,375	282,507	927,378	109,955	132,829	152,152	876,705

NA Not available.   [1] Includes entrepreneurial capital net and real estate investment flows.   [2] Data shown are for net (inward and outward), direct investment capital flows. For 1999, balance of payments data.   [3] For fiscal year ending March 31.

Source: Organization for Economic Cooperation and Development, Paris, France, Financial Market Trends, No. 76, June 2000.

U.S. Census Bureau, Statistical Abstract of the United States: 2001

No. 1391. Military Expenditures and Armed Forces Personnel by Country: 1990 and 1997

[Military expenditures in millions of dollars, except as indicated (306,000 represents $306,000,000,000). Personnel data as of July. See also Table 495. For most countries, data for expenditures and for gross national product (GNP) were based on local currencies which were deflated to constant 1997 local currency values before conversion to U.S. dollar equivalents. In general, the rates used for conversion are the 1997 average par/market exchange rates as supplied by the World Bank. Armed Forces refer to active-duty military personnel, including paramilitary forces where those forces resemble regular units in their organization, equipment, training, or mission. Reserve forces are not included]

Country	Military expenditures						Armed Forces personnel			
	Current dollars		Constant (1997) dollars				Number (1,000)		Per 1,000 population	
				1997						
	1990	1997	1990	Total	Percent of GNP	Per capita (dollars)	1990	1997	1990	1997
United States......	306,000	276,000	359,000	276,000	3.3	1,030	2,180	1,530	8.7	5.7
Algeria [1]........	726	1,750	850	1,750	3.9	59	126	124	5.0	4.2
Angola [1].........	1,250	1,550	1,470	1,550	20.5	147	115	95	13.6	9.0
Argentina.........	3,350	3,700	3,930	3,700	1.2	103	85	65	2.6	1.8
Australia........	6,090	8,460	7,130	8,460	2.2	459	68	65	4.0	3.5
Bangladesh	301	592	352	592	1.4	5	103	110	0.9	0.9
Belgium	4,450	3,690	5,210	3,690	1.5	363	106	46	10.6	4.5
Brazil..........	9,560	14,100	11,200	14,100	1.8	84	295	296	2.0	1.8
Bulgaria [1].......	3,890	949	4,550	949	3.0	114	129	80	14.4	9.6
Burma [1].........	(NA)	(NA)	(NA)	(NA)	(NA)	(NA)	230	322	5.6	6.9
Canada.........	9,240	7,800	10,800	7,800	1.3	257	87	61	3.3	2.0
Chile [2].........	1,190	2,860	1,390	2,860	3.9	196	95	102	7.2	7.0
China [1][3]......	48,300	74,900	56,600	74,900	2.2	61	3,500	2,600	3.1	2.1
Colombia...... [1][4]	1,300	3,460	1,520	3,460	3.7	91	110	149	3.3	3.9
Congo (Kinshasa) [1][4]	(NA)	252	(NA)	252	5.0	5	55	(NA)	1.5	(NA)
Croatia [1]........	(X)	1,490	(X)	1,490	6.3	319	(X)	58	(X)	12.4
Cuba [1][2]........	1,380	720	1,620	720	2.3	65	297	55	28.1	5.0
Czech Republic [1]....	(X)	1,990	(X)	1,990	1.9	193	(X)	55	(X)	5.3
Egypt..........	1,570	2,180	1,840	2,180	2.8	34	434	430	7.7	6.6
France..........	38,600	41,500	45,200	41,500	3.0	708	550	475	9.7	8.1
Germany	40,900	32,900	47,900	32,900	1.6	401	545	335	6.9	4.1
Greece [1]........	4,230	5,530	4,960	5,530	4.6	521	201	206	19.9	19.4
Hungary [1].......	1,280	1,320	1,500	1,320	1.9	129	94	50	9.1	4.9
India ..... [1]......	6,540	10,900	7,650	10,900	2.8	11	1,260	1,260	1.5	1.3
Indonesia [1][2].....	1,610	4,810	1,880	4,810	2.3	23	283	280	1.5	1.3
Iran [1]..........	6,110	4,730	7,160	4,730	3.0	74	440	575	7.7	9.1
Iraq [1].........	22,500	1,250	26,400	1,250	4.9	59	1,390	400	75.4	19.0
Israel..........	7,360	9,340	8,620	9,340	9.7	1,690	190	185	42.1	33.4
Italy...........	19,400	22,700	22,700	22,700	2.0	395	493	419	8.5	7.3
Japan..........	30,500	40,800	35,700	40,800	1.0	325	250	250	2.0	2.0
Jordan..........	402	626	471	626	9.0	145	100	102	30.5	23.6
Kenya	210	206	246	206	2.1	7	20	24	0.8	0.9
Korea, North [1].....	5,940	6,000	6,960	6,000	27.5	281	1,200	1,100	56.0	51.6
Korea, South	9,720	15,000	11,400	15,000	3.4	327	650	670	15.2	14.6
Kuwait..........	13,000	2,760	15,200	2,760	7.5	1,510	7	28	3.3	15.3
Libya	(NA)	(NA)	(NA)	(NA)	(NA)	(NA)	86	70	19.7	14.7
Malaysia	1,260	2,090	1,480	2,090	2.2	102	130	110	7.4	5.4
Mexico.........	1,330	4,290	1,560	4,290	1.1	44	175	250	2.1	2.6
Netherlands	6,800	6,840	7,960	6,840	1.9	437	104	57	7.0	3.6
New Zealand	884	766	1,040	766	1.3	214	11	10	3.3	2.8
Nigeria [1][2]......	2,200	2,000	2,570	2,000	1.4	19	94	76	1.1	0.7
Pakistan.........	2,810	3,380	3,290	3,380	5.7	26	550	610	4.8	4.6
Peru..........	623	1,350	730	1,350	2.1	53	125	115	5.7	4.5
Philippines	1,230	1,270	1,440	1,270	1.5	17	109	105	1.7	1.4
Poland [1]........	8,750	5,600	10,200	5,600	2.3	145	313	230	8.2	6.0
Romania [1].......	3,870	2,280	4,530	2,280	2.4	102	126	200	5.5	8.9
Russia [1]........	(X)	41,700	(X)	41,700	5.8	283	(X)	1,300	(X)	8.8
Saudi Arabia......	23,200	21,100	27,100	21,100	14.5	1,050	146	180	9.2	9.0
Serbia and Montenegro [1]	(X)	1,200	(X)	1,200	4.9	114	(X)	115	(X)	10.9
Singapore	2,370	5,660	2,780	5,660	5.7	1,650	56	55	18.4	16.0
Slovakia [1].......	(X)	903	(X)	903	2.1	168	(X)	44	(X)	8.2
Slovenia [1].......	(X)	1,220	(X)	1,220	5.2	617	(X)	10	(X)	5.1
South Africa	4,070	2,320	4,770	2,320	1.8	55	85	75	2.3	1.8
Spain	7,410	7,670	8,680	7,670	1.5	196	263	107	6.8	2.7
Sri Lanka	433	762	507	762	5.1	41	22	110	1.3	5.9
Sweden	4,810	5,550	5,630	5,550	2.5	626	65	60	7.6	6.8
Syria [2].........	(NA)	3,400	(NA)	3,400	5.6	211	408	320	32.3	19.8
Taiwan [3]........	8,490	13,100	9,940	13,100	4.6	602	370	400	18.2	18.4
Tanzania	83	87	97	87	1.3	3	40	35	1.6	1.2
Thailand........	2,020	3,380	2,370	3,380	2.3	57	283	288	5.1	4.8
Turkey..........	4,250	7,790	4,980	7,790	4.0	123	769	820	13.7	12.9
Ukraine [1].......	(X)	4,280	(X)	4,280	3.7	85	(X)	450	(X)	8.9
United Kingdom.....	39,300	35,300	46,000	35,300	2.7	600	308	218	5.4	3.7
Vietnam [1].......	4,810	3,390	5,640	3,390	2.8	48	1,050	650	15.9	8.7

NA Not available. X Not applicable. [1] Military expenditures estimated. [2] Data probably omit a major share of total military expenditures, probably including most arms acquisitions. [3] See footnote 2, Table 1327. [4] See footnote 3, Table 1327.

Source: U.S. Dept. of State, Bureau of Verification and Compliance, *World Military Expenditures and Arms Transfers*, annual.

Appendix I
Guide to—Sources of Statistics, State Statistical Abstracts, and Foreign Statistical Abstracts

Alphabetically arranged, this guide contains references to the important primary sources of statistical information for the United States published since 1990. Secondary sources have been included if the information contained in them is presented in a particularly convenient form or if primary sources are not readily available. Nonrecurrent publications presenting compilations or estimates for years later than 1990 or types of data not available in regular series are also included. Much data are also available in press releases.

Much valuable information may also be found in state reports, foreign statistical abstracts, which are included at the end of this appendix and in reports for particular commodities, industries, or similar segments of our economic and social structures, many of which are not included here.

Publications listed under each subject are divided into two main groups: "U.S. Government" and "Nongovernment." The location of the publisher of each report is given except for federal agencies located in Washington, DC. Most federal publications may be purchased from the Superintendent of Documents, U.S. Government Printing Office, Washington, DC 20402, tel. 202-512-1800, (Web site <http.www.access. gpo.gov> or from Government Printing Office bookstores in certain major cities. In some cases, federal publications may be obtained from the issuing agency.

U.S. GOVERNMENT

Administrative Office of the United States Courts
http://www.uscourts.gov
Calendar Year Reports on Authorized Wiretaps. (State and Federal.)
Federal Court Management Statistics. Annual.
Federal Judicial Caseload Statistics. Annual.
Judicial Business of the United States Courts.
Statistical Tables for the Federal Judiciary. Semiannual.

Agency for International Development
http://www.usaid.gov
U.S. Overseas Loans and Grants and Assistance From International Organizations. Annual.

Army, Corps of Engineers
http://www.usace.army.mil
Waterborne Commerce of the United States (in five parts). Annual.

Board of Governors of the Federal Reserve System
http://www.federalreserve.gov
Annual Statistical Digest.
Domestic Offices, Commercial Bank Assets and Liabilities Consolidated Report of Condition. Quarterly.

Board of Governors of the Federal Reserve System —Con.
Federal Reserve Banks. Monthly review published by each Bank with special reference to its own Federal Reserve District.
Federal Reserve Bulletin. Monthly. (Also monthly releases on industrial production indexes.)
Flow of Funds Accounts of the United States: Flows and Outstandings. Z.1(780). Quarterly.
Industrial Production and Capacity Utilization G.17. Monthly.
Money Stock and Debt Measures. H.6. Weekly.

Bureau of Alcohol, Tobacco, and Firearms
http://www.atf.treas.gov
Alcohol and Tobacco Summary Statistics. Annual.

Bureau of Economic Analysis
http://www.bea.doc.gov
National Income and Product Accounts of the United States, 1929-1997: Statistical Tables, early 2001.
Survey of Current Business. Monthly. (March, June, September, and December issues contain data on U.S. international

U.S. Census Bureau, Statistical Abstract of the United States: 2001

Bureau of Economic Analysis —Con.

transactions. Articles on foreign direct investment in the United States, U.S. direct investment abroad, and other topics appear periodically in other issues.)

U.S. Direct Investment Abroad: 1994 Benchmark Survey, 1998.

U.S. Direct Investment Abroad: Operations of U.S. Parent Companies and their Foreign Affiliates. Preliminary, 1997. Estimates, 1999

Bureau of Justice Statistics

http://www.ojp.usdoj.gov

Age Patterns of Victims of Serious Violent Crimes. September 1997.

Alcohol and Crime: An analysis of national data on the prevalence of alcohol involvement in crime. April 1998.

Background Checks for Firearm Transfers, 1999. June 2000.

Campus Law Enforcement Agencies, 1995. December 1996.

Capital Punishment. Annual.

Carjacking in U.S., 1992-96. March 1999.

Census of State and Local Law Enforcement Agencies, 1996. July 1998.

Characteristics of Adults on Probation, 1995, December 1997.

Child Victimizers: Violent offenders and their victims. March 1996.

Civil Rights Complaints in U.S. District Courts, 1990-98. January 2000.

Civil Trial Cases and Verdicts in Large Counties: Civil Justice Survey of State Courts, 1996. September 1999.

Correctional Populations in the United States. Annual.

Crimes Against Persons Age 65 or Older, 1992-97. January 2000.

Criminal Victimization 2000: Changes 1999-00: with trends 1993-00. June 2001.

Federal Criminal Case Processing, 1999: with trends 1982-99. February 2001.

Federal Law Enforcement Officers, 1998. March 2000.

Federal Tort Trials and Verdicts, 1996-97. March 1999.

Felony Defendants in Large Urban Counties. Biennial.

Felony Sentences in State Courts. Biennial.

Firearm Injury From Crime: Firearms, crime, and criminal justice. April 1996.

HIV in Prisons. Annual.

Incarcerated Parents and Their Children. August 2000.

Indicators of School Crime and Safety. Annual.

Indigent Defense Services in Large Counties, 1999. November 2000.

Intimate Partner Violence. May 2000.

Jails in Indian Country, 1998 and 1999. July 2000.

Bureau of Justice Statistics —Con.

Justice Expenditure and Employment in the United States, 1995. November 1999.

Lifetime Likelihood of Going to State or Federal Prison. March 1997.

Local Police Departments. Quadrenniel.

Medical Problems of Inmates, 1997. January 2001.

National Corrections Reporting Program. Annual.

Prior Abuse Reported by Inmates and Probationers. April 1999.

Prison and Jail Inmates. Annual.

Prisoners. Annual.

Profile of State Prisoners Under Age 18, 1985-97. February 2000.

Prosecutors in State Courts. Biennial.

Sex Offenses and Offenders. February 1997.

Sheriffs' Department. Quadrenniel.

Sourcebook of Criminal Justice Statistics. CD-ROM. Annual.

State Court Sentencing of Convicted Felons. Biennial.

Substance Abuse and Treatment, State and Federal Prisoners, 1997. December 1998.

Survey of State Criminal History Information Systems. Annual.

Time Served in Prison by Federal Offenders. 1986-97. June 1999.

Urban, Suburban, and Rural Victimization, 1993-98. October 2000.

Veterans in Prison or Jail. January 2000.

Violence-Related Injuries Treated in Hospital Emergency Departments. August 1997.

Bureau of Labor Statistics

http://www.bls.gov

Comparative Labor Force Statistics, Ten Countries. Annual.

Compensation and Working Conditions. Quarterly.

Consumer Expenditure Survey, Integrated Diary and Interview Survey data.

Consumer Prices: Energy and Food. Monthly.

CPI Detailed Report. Monthly.

Employee Benefits in Medium and Large Firms. Biennial.

Employee Benefits in Small Private Establishments. Biennial.

Employee Benefits in State and Local Governments. Biennial.

Employer Costs for Employee Compensation. Annual.

Employment and Earnings. Monthly.

Employment and Wages. Annual.

Employment Cost Index. Quarterly.

Employment Cost Indexes and Levels. Annual.

Employment, Hours, and Earnings, United States, 1988-96. 1996. (Bulletin 2481.)

Bureau of Labor Statistics —Con.

Employment Outlook: 1994-2005. (Bulletin 2472.)

The Employment Situation. Monthly.

Geographic Profile of Employment and Unemployment. Annual.

International Comparisons of Hourly Compensation Costs for Production Workers in Manufacturing. Annual.

International Comparisons of Manufacturing Productivity and Unit Labor Cost Trends. Annual.

Monthly Labor Review.

Occupational Injuries and Illnesses in the United States by Industry. Annual.

Occupational Projections and Training Data. Biennial.

Producer Price Indexes. Detailed report. Monthly, with annual supplement.

Productivity Measures for Selected Industries and Government Services. Annual.

Real Earnings. Monthly.

Relative Importance of Components in the Consumer Price Indexes. Annual.

State and Metropolitan Area Employment and Unemployment. Monthly.

U.S. Import and Export Price Indexes. Monthly.

Usual Weekly Earnings of Wage and Salary Workers. Quarterly.

Work Experience of the Population. Annual.

Bureau of Land Management

http://www.blm.gov

Public Land Statistics. Annual.

Census Bureau

http://www.census.gov

Major reports, such as the Census of Population, which consist of many volumes, are listed by their general, all-inclusive titles. In most cases, separate reports of the most recent censuses are available for each state, subject, industry, etc.

1997 Economic Census.

Comparative Statistics.

Bridge Between NAICS and SIC.

Business Expenses.

Nonemployer Statistics.

Minority- and Women-Owned Business Enterprises.

Annual Benchmark Report for Retail Trade and Food Services.

Annual Benchmark Report for Wholesale Trade.

Annual Survey of Manufactures. (1996, most recent.)

Census of Governments. Quinquennial.

Compendium of Public Employment. Series GC, Vol. 3.

Employee-Retirement Systems of State and Local Governments. Series GC, Vol. 4.

Employment of Major Local Governments. Series GC, Vol. 3.

Census Bureau —Con.

Finances of County Governments. Series GC, Vol. 4.

Government Organization. Series GC, Vol. 1.

Public Education Finances. Series GC, Vol. 4.

Census of Housing. Decennial. (2000, most recent.)

Census of Population. Decennial. (2000, most recent.)

CFFR Consolidated Federal Funds Report. Annual.

Volume I County Areas

Volume II Subcounty Areas

County Business Patterns. Annual.

Current Construction Reports: New Residential Construction and New Residential Sales: Press Releases and Web Sites. Value of Construction Put in Place, C30 (monthly with occasional historical supplement); Residential Improvements and Repairs, C50 (quarterly and annual).

Current Housing Reports: Housing Vacancies, H111 (quarterly and annual); Who Can Afford to Buy a House, H121 (biennial) Market Absorption of Apartments, H130 (quarterly and annual); Characteristics of Apartments Completed, H131 (annual); American Housing Survey for the United States, H150 (biennial); American Housing Survey for Selected Metropolitan Areas, H170; Survey for Selected Metropolitan Areas, H171.

Current Population Reports. (Series P20.)

Consumer Income and Poverty, P60 and Household Economic Studies, P70.

Economic Census. Quinquennial.

Economic Census of Outlying Areas. Quinquennial.

FAS Federal Aid to States for Fiscal Year. Annual.

International Briefs. (Series IB.)

International Population Reports. (Series IPC.)

Manufacturing Profiles. (Series MP-1.) Annual.

Manufacturers' Shipments, Inventories, and Orders. Monthly.

Manufacturers' Shipments, Inventories, and Orders: 1992-2000.

Population Profile of the United States. (Biennial Series P23.)

Quarterly Financial Report for Manufacturing, Mining, and Trade Corporations.

Service Annual Survey Report.

Summary of U.S. International Trade in Goods and Services: includes cumulative data. (FT 900.)

Survey of Plant Capacity Utilization. (Current Industrial Reports MQ-C1.)

U.S. Trade with Puerto Rico and U.S. Possessions. Monthly and Annual. (FT 895.)

Census Bureau —Con.

Vehicle Inventory and Use Survey. Quinquennial.

World Population Profile: 1998 (Series WP.)

Centers for Disease Control and Prevention, Atlanta, GA

http://www.cdc.gov

Morbidity and Mortality Weekly Report. Annual.

Centers for Medicare and Medicaid Services

http://www.cms.gov

Centers for Medicare and Medicaid Services (CMS)

Health Care Financing Review. Medicare and Medicaid Statistical Supplement. Annual.

Health Care Financing Research Reports. Occasional.

Health Care Financing Review. Quarterly.

Coast Guard

http://www.uscg.mil

Annual Report of the Secretary of Transportation.

Marine Casualty Statistics. Annual.

Polluting Incidents in and Around U.S. Waters. Annual.

Comptroller of the Currency

http://www.occ.treas.gov

Quarterly Journal.

Congressional Clerk of the House

http://clerkweb.house.gov

Statistics of the Presidential and Congressional Election Years. Biennial.

Council of Economic Advisers

http://www.whitehouse.gov

Economic Indicators. Monthly.

Economic Report of the President. Annual.

Council on Environmental Quality

http://www.whitehouse.gov/ceq

Environmental Quality. Annual.

Department of Agriculture

http://www.usda.gov

Agricultural Chemical Usage. Field crops, vegetables (fruits and vegetables alternate years), restricted use pesticides. Chemical application rates and acres treated, selected states and U.S. Annual.

Agricultural Income and Finance. Situation and Outlook Report. Quarterly.

Agricultural Outlook. 11 issues per year.

Agricultural Price Reports. Reports on prices received for farm commodities, prices paid for farm supplies, indexes and parity ratios. Monthly and annual.

Agriculture and Trade Reports (five per year).

Western Europe

China

Developing Economies

Department of Agriculture —Con.

Pacific Rim

USSR

CATFISH. 12 issues of Catfish processing, Catfish and Trout Production. Annual.

Census of Agriculture. Quinquennial. (1997, most recent.)

Cotton Ginnings and Winter Wheat and Rye Seedings.

Crop Production Reports. Acreage, yield, and production of various commodities. Monthly and annual.

Crop Values Report. Price and value of various commodities. Annual.

Dairy Product Prices. U.S. cheddar cheese, butter, nonfat dry milk, and dry whey prices and sales volumes. Regional cheddar cheese prices and sales volumes. Weekly.

Farm Labor. Quarterly.

Farmline. 11 issues per year.

Farm Numbers, Value. Farm numbers and land in farms, agricultural cash rents, agricultural land values, foreign ownership of U.S. Agricultural Land (ERS). Annual.

Financial Characteristics of U.S. (Agriculture Information Bulletin. No. 569.) Annual.

Food Consumption, Prices, and Expenditures, 1970-97. (Statistical Bulletin No. 928.) Revised annually.

Food Marketing Review, (Agricultural Economic Report No. 743). Revised annually.

Food Review. Quarterly.

Food Spending in American Households. (Statistical Bulletin No. 824.) Annual.

Foreign Agricultural Trade of the United States (FATUS). Bimonthly with annual supplements on calendar year and fiscal year trade statistics.

Fruit and Vegetable Reports. Acreage, yield, production, value, and utilization of various fruits and vegetables. Periodic.

Geographic Area Series (Internet, CD-ROM, Print), Volume 1

Journal of Agricultural Economics Research. Quarterly.

Livestock Reports. Cattle, Cattle on Feed, Hogs and Pigs. Sheep, Goats, Wool, and Mohair. Monthly, Quarterly, and Annual.

Milk and Dairy Products Reports. Milk cows, milk production, and dairy products. Monthly and Annual.

National Resource and Conservation Service

http://www.nrcs.usda.gov

National Resources Inventory. Periodic.

Other Reports. Reports on varied items including cold storage, catfish, cherries, cranberries, trout, farm employment and wages, farm production expenditures, mink, mushrooms, and floriculture crops. Monthly and annual.

National Resource and Conservation Service —Con.

Poultry and Egg Reports. Reports covering eggs, chickens, turkeys, hatcheries, egg products, and poultry slaughter. Weekly, monthly, annual.

Rural Conditions and Trends. Quarterly.

Rural Development Perspectives. Three issues per year.

Situation and Outlook Reports. Issued for agricultural exports, cotton and wool, dairy, feed, fruit and tree nuts, agricultural resources, livestock and poultry, oil crops, rice, aquaculture, sugar and sweeteners, tobacco, vegetables, wheat, and world agriculture. Periodic.

Stock Reports. Stocks of grain, hops, peanuts, potatoes, rice, and soybeans. Quarterly, annual, periodic.

Usual planting and harvesting dates. Dates for major field crops. Periodic.

Weekly Weather and Crop Bulletin. Report summarizing weather and its effect on crops the previous week. Weekly.

Department of Agriculture, Food and Nutrition Service

http://www.fns.usda.gov

Annual Historical Review:

Food and Consumer Service Programs.

Department of Defense

http://www.defenselink.mil

Foreign Military Sales and Military Assistance Facts. Annual.

Department of Education

http://www.ed.gov

Rehabilitation Services Administration

http://www.ed.gov

Annual Report.

Department of Health and Human Services

http://www.os.dhhs.gov

Annual Report.

Department of Housing and Urban Development

http://www.hud.gov

Survey of Mortgage Lending Activity. Monthly and quarterly press releases.

Department of Labor

http://www.dol.gov

Annual Report of the Secretary.

Department of State

http://www.state.gov

United States Contribution to International Organizations. Issued in the House Documents series. Annual.

Department of State, Bureau of Consular Affairs

http://travel.state.gov

Report of the Visa Office. Annual. (Dept. of State Pub. 8810.)

Summary of Passport Statistics. Annual.

Department of Transportation

http://www.faa.gov

Airport Activity Statistics of Certified Route Air Carriers. Annual.

Condition and Performance Report. 1999. Biennial.

National Transportation Statistics, 1998.

Report of Passenger Travel Between the United States and Foreign Countries. Annual, semiannual, quarterly. Monthly.

Transportation Safety Information Report. Quarterly.

U.S. International Air Travel Statistics. Annual.

Department of the Treasury

http://www.irs.ustreas.gov

Active Foreign Credits of the United States Government. Quarterly.

Consolidated Financial Statements of the United States Government. (Prototype.)

Daily Treasury Statement.

Monthly Statement of the Public Debt of the United States.

Monthly Treasury Statement of Receipts and Outlays of the United States Government.

Statement of United States Currency and Coin. Monthly.

Treasury Bulletin. Quarterly.

United States Government Annual Report and Appendix.

Department of Veterans Affairs

http://www.va.gov

Annual Report of The Secretary of Veterans Affairs.

Disability Compensation, Pension, and Death Pension Data. Annual.

Government Life Insurance Programs for Veterans and Members of the Service. Annual.

Loan Guaranty Highlights. Quarterly.

Projections of The Veteran Population by State and County to the Year 2010.

Selected Compensation and Pension Data by State of Residence. Annual.

State and County Veteran Population Estimates. Annual.

Summary of Medical Programs. Annual.

Drug Enforcement Administration

http://www.whitehousedrugpolicy.gov

Drug Abuse and Law Enforcement Statistics. Irregular.

Appendix I   873

**Employment and Training
Administration**
http://www.doleta.gov
Employment and Training Report of the
President. Annual.
Unemployment Insurance Claims. Weekly.

Energy Information Administration
http://www.eia.doe.gov
Annual Energy Outlook.
Annual Energy Review.
Coal Industry Annual.
Cost and Quality of Fuels for Electric Utility
Plants. Annual.
Electric Power Annual.
Electric Power Monthly.
Electric Sales and Revenue. Annual.
Financial Statistics of Selected Electric Utili-
ties. Annual
International Energy Annual.
International Energy Outlook.
Inventory of Power Plants in the United
States. Annual.
Monthly Energy Review.
Natural Gas Annual.
Natural Gas Monthly.
Performance Profiles of Major Energy Pro-
ducers. Annual.
Petroleum Marketing Monthly.
Petroleum Supply Annual.
Petroleum Supply Monthly.
Quarterly Coal Report.
Renewable Energy Annual.
Residential Energy Consumption Survey:
Housing Characteristics. Triennial.
Residential Transportation Energy Con-
sumption Survey. Triennial.
Short-Term Energy Outlook. Quarterly. (Web
Only)
State Energy Data Report. Annual.
State Energy Price and Expenditure Report.
Annual.
Uranium Industry Annual.
U.S. Crude Oil, Natural Gas, and Natural Gas
Liquids Reserves. Annual.
Weekly Coal Production. (Electronic Only)

Environmental Protection Agency
http://www.epa.gov
Air Quality Data. Annual.
Cost of Clean Water. Annual.
Drinking Water Infrastructure Needs Survey.
Second Report to Congress (EPA 816-R-
01-004, February 2001).
Federal Certification Test Results for Motor
Vehicles. Annual.
Municipal Water Facilities Inventory. Quin-
quennial.
National Air Quality and Emissions Trends
Report. 1999 Annual
Needs Survey, Conveyance and Treatment
of Municipal Wastewater Summaries of
Technical Data. Biennial.

Environmental Protection Agency —Con.
Pesticides Monitoring Journal. Quarterly.
Radiation Data and Reports. Monthly.
Sewage Facility Construction. Annual.
Summary of Water Enforcement Actions
Pursued by EPA since December 3, 1970.
(Updated continuously)
Toxics Release Inventory (EPA 260-R-01-
001). Annual (Most Recent 1999).
Water Quality Report to Congress, 1998.
Biennial.

Export-Import Bank of the United States
http://www.exim.gov
Annual Report.
Report to the U.S. Congress on Export
Credit Competition and the Export-
Import Bank of the United States.
Annual.

Farm Credit Administration
http://www.fca.gov
Annual Report on the Work of the Coopera-
tive Farm Credit System.
Loans and Discounts of Farm Credit Banks
and Associations. Annual.
Production Credit Association: Summary of
Operations. Annual.
Report to the Federal Land Bank Associa-
tions. Annual.

Federal Bureau of Investigation
http://www.fbi.gov
Bomb Summary. Annual.
Crime in the United States. Annual.
Hate Crime Statistics. Annual.
Law Enforcement Officers Killed and
Assaulted. Annual.

Federal Communications Commission
http://www.fcc.gov
Annual Report.
Statistics of Communications Common
Carriers. Annual.

Federal Deposit Insurance Corporation
http://www.fdic.gov
Annual Report.
Data Book-Operating Banks and Branches.
Annual.
Quarterly Banking Profile.
Quarterly Banking Review.
Statistics on Banking. Annual, and Historical
1934-1996, Volume I.
Trust Assets of Insured Commercial Banks.
Annual.

Federal Highway Administration
http://www.fhwa.dot.gov
Highway Statistics. Annual.

Federal Railroad Administration
http://www.fra.dot.gov
Accident/Incident Bulletin. Summary, statistics, and analysis of accidents on railroads in the United States. Annual.

Federal Railroad Administration —Con.

Rail-Highway Crossing Accident/Incident and Inventory Bulletin. Annual.

Forest Service

http://www.fs.fed.us

An Analysis of the Timber Situation in the United States. 1996-2050.

Land Areas of the National Forest System. Annual.

The 1993 RPA Timber Assessment Update. Forthcoming.

U.S. Timber Production, Trade, Consumption, and Price Statistics. 2001.

Fish and Wildlife Service

http://endangered.fws.gov

Federal Aid in Fish and Wildlife Restoration. Annual.

1996 National Survey of Fishing, Hunting, and Wildlife Associated Recreation.

General Services Administration

http://www.gsa.gov

Inventory Report on Real Property Leased to the United States Throughout the World. Annual.

Inventory Report on Real Property Owned by the United States Throughout the World. Annual.

Geological Survey

http://ask.usgs.gov

A Statistical Summary of Data from the U.S. Geological Survey's National Water Quality Networks. (Open-File Report 83-533.)

Mineral Commodity Summaries. Annual.

Mineral Industry Surveys. (Monthly, quarterly, or annual report.)

Minerals Yearbook. (Monthly, quarterly, or annual report.)

Immigration and Naturalization Service

http://www.ins.gov

I&N Reporter. Quarterly.

Statistical Yearbook of the Immigration and Naturalization Service. Annual.

Wage Statistics of Class I Railroads in the United States. Annual. (Statement No. 300.)

International Trade Administration

http://www.ita.doc.gov

International Construction Review. Quarterly.

Electric Current Abroad. Irregular. (1998, most recent.)

U.S. Foreign Trade Highlights. Annual.

U.S. Global Trade Outlook. Irregular. Discontinued

U.S. Industry and Trade Outlook. Annual. (2000, most recent.)

International Trade Commission

http://www.usitc.gov

Synthetic Organic Chemicals, U.S. Production and Sales. Annual.

Internal Revenue Service

http://www.irs.ustreas.gov

Corporation Income Tax Returns. Annual.

Individual Income Tax Returns. Annual.

IRS Data Book.

Statistics of Income Bulletin. Quarterly.

Statistics of Income Division. (Annual report on Corporation Income Tax Returns. Periodic compendiums on Studies of International Income and Taxes.)

Library of Congress

http://www.loc.gov

Annual Report.

Maritime Administration

http://www.marad.dot.gov

Annual Report.

Cargo-Carrying U.S. Flag Fleet by Area of Operation. (Semi-Annual)

Merchant Fleet Ocean-Going Vessels 1,000 Gross Tons and Over. Quarterly.

Seafaring Wage Rates. Biennial.

Mine Safety and Health Administration

http://www.msha.gov

Informational Reports by Mining Industry: Coal; Metallic Minerals; Nonmetallic Minerals (except stone and coal); Stone, Sand, and Gravel. Annual.

Mine Injuries and Worktime. (Some preliminary data.) Quarterly.

National Aeronautics and Space Administration

http://ifmp.nasa.gov

Annual Procurement Report.

The Civil Service Work Force.

National Center for Education Statistics

http://nces.ed.gov

College and University Library Survey.

The Condition of Education. Annual.

Digest of Education Statistics. Annual.

Earned Degrees Conferred. Annual.

Faculty Salaries, Tenure, and Benefits. Annual.

Fall Enrollment in Colleges and Universities. Annual.

Fall Staff in Postsecondary Institutions. Biennial.

Financial Statistics of Higher Education.

National Assessment of Educational Progress.

Private School Survey. Biennial.

Projections of Education Statistics. Annual.

Revenues and Expenditures for Public Elementary and Secondary Education. Annual.

School and Staffing Survey. Quadrennial.

Statistics of Public Elementary and Secondary School Systems. Fall. Annual.

National Center for Health Statistics

http://www.cdc.gov/nchswww

Ambulatory Care Visits to Physician Offices, Hospital Outpatient Departments and Emergency Departments. Annual.

Health: United States. Annual. (DHHS Pub. No. PHS year-1232.)

National Hospital Discharge Survey: Annual Summary. Annual.

National Vital Statistics Reports (NVRS.) Monthly.

Vital and Health Statistics. (A series of statistical reports covering health-related topics.)

   Series 10: Health Interview Survey Statistics. Irregular.

      Current Estimates from the Health Interview Survey. Annual.

   Series 11: Health and Nutrition Examination Survey Statistics. Irregular.

   Series 13: Health Resources Utilization Statistics. Irregular.

   Series 14: Health Resources: Manpower and Facilities Statistics. Irregular.

   Series 20: Mortality Data. Irregular.

   Series 21: Natality, Marriage, and Divorce Data. Irregular.

   Series 23: National Survey of Family Growth Statistics. Irregular.

Vital Statistics of the United States. Annual.

   Volume I, Natality

   Volume II, Mortality

   Volume III, Marriage and Divorce

National Credit Union Administration

http://www.ncua.gov

Annual Report.

Midyear Statistics.

Yearend Statistics.

National Guard Bureau

http://www.ngb.dtic.mil

Annual Review of the Chief.

The National Library of Medicine
(for clinical medical reports)

http://www.nlm.nih.gov

Annual Report.

National Oceanic and Atmospheric Administration

http://www.lib.noaa.gov

Climates of the World, HCS 6-4. Monthly and annual.

Climatological Data. Issued in sections for states and outlying areas. Monthly with annual summary.

Climatography of the United States, No. 20, Supplement No. 1, Freeze/Frost Data.

Comparative Climatic Data. Annual.

Daily Normals of Temp, Precip, HDD, & CDD/Clim 84. Periodic.

General Summary of Tornadoes. Annual.

National Oceanic and Atmospheric Administration —Con.

Hourly Precipitation Data. Monthly with annual summary; for each state.

Local Climatological Data. Monthly with annual summary; for major cities.

Monthly Climatic Data for the World. Monthly.

Monthly Normals of Temp, Precip, HDD, & CDD/Clim 84. Periodic.

Storm Data. Monthly.

Weekly Weather and Crop Bulletin. National summary.

National Park Service

http://www.nps.gov

Federal Recreation Fee Report. Annual.

National Park Statistical Abstract. Annual.

National Science Foundation

http://www.nsf.gov

Academic Research and Development Expenditures. Detailed Statistical Tables. Annual

Academic Science and Engineering: Graduate Enrollment and Support: Detailed Statistical Tables. Annual

Characteristics of Doctoral Scientists and Engineers in the United States. Detailed Statistical Tables. Biennial.

Characteristics of Recent Science/Engineering Graduates. Detailed Statistical Tables. Biennial.

Federal Funds for Research and Development. Detailed Statistical Tables. Annual.

Federal R&D Funding by Budget Function. Report. Annual.

Federal Science and Engineering Support to Universities, Colleges, and Nonprofit Institutions. Detailed Statistical Tables. Annual.

Federal Support to Universities, Colleges, and Nonprofit Institutions. Detailed Statistical Tables. Annual.

Graduate Students and Post-Doctorates in Science and Engineering. Annual.

Immigrant Scientists, Engineers and Technicians. Detailed Statistical Tables. Annual.

International Science and Technology Data Update. Report. Annual.

National Patterns of R&D Resources. Report. Annual.

Planned R&D Expenditures of Major U.S. Firms. Special Report. (NSF 91-306.)

Research and Development in Industry. Detailed Statistical Tables. Annual.

Science and Engineering Degrees. Annual.

Science and Engineering Degrees, by Race/Ethnicity of Recipients. Detailed Statistical Tables. Annual.

Science and Engineering Doctorates Awards. Detailed Statistical Tables. Annual.

Science and Engineering Indicators. Report. Biennial.

National Science Foundation —Con.

Science and Engineering Personnel: A National Overview. Report. Biennial.

Science and Engineering Profiles. Annual.

Science and Technology Pocket Data Book. Report. Annual.

Science Resources Studies. Data Brief. Frequent.

Scientific and Engineering Research Facilities at Universities and Colleges. Report. Biennial.

Scientists, Engineers, and Technicians in Manufacturing Industries. Detailed Statistical Tables. Triennial.

Scientists, Engineers, and Technicians in Nonmanufacturing Industries. Detailed Statistical Tables. Triennial.

Scientists, Engineers, and Technicians in Trade and Regulated Industries. Detailed Statistical Tables. Triennial.

Survey of Direct U.S. Private Capital Investment in Research and Development Facilities in Japan. Report. (NSH 91-312.)

U.S. Scientists and Engineers. Detailed Statistical Tables. Biennial.

Women, Minorities, and Persons with Disabilities. Report. Biennial

Women, Minorities in Science and Engineering. Report. Biennial.

National Transportation Safety Board
http://www.ntsb.gov

Accidents; Air Carriers. Annual.

Accidents; General Aviation. Annual.

Office of Management and Budget
http://www.whitehouse.gov/omb

The Budget of the United States Government. Annual.

Office of Personnel Management
http://www.opm.gov

Civil Service Retirement and Disability Fund. Report. Annual.

Demographic Profile of the Federal Workforce. Biennial. (Even years.)

Employment and Trends. Bimonthly. (Odd months.)

Employment by Geographic Area. Biennial. (Even years.)

The Fact Book. Annual.

Occupations of Federal White-Collar and Blue-Collar Workers. Biennial. (Odd years.)

Pay Structure of the Federal Civil Service. Annual.

Statistical Abstract for the Federal Employee Benefit Programs. Annual.

Work Years and Personnel Costs. Annual.

Office of Thrift Supervision
http://www.ots.treas.gov

Annual Report.

Patent and Trademark Office
http://www.uspto.gov

Commissioner of Patents and Trademarks Annual Report.

Technology Assessment and Forecast Reports

"All Technologies." Annual.

"Patenting Trends in the United States." Annual.

"State Country." Annual.

Railroad Retirement Board, Chicago, IL
http://www.rrb.gov

Annual Report.

Monthly Benefit Statistics.

Statistical Supplement to the Annual Report.

Rehabilitation Services Administration. Annual Report

Caseload Statistics of State Vocational Rehabilitation Agencies in Fiscal Year. Annual.

Securities and Exchange Commission
http://www.sec.gov

Annual Report.

Small Business Administration
http://www.sbaonline.sba.gov

Annual Report.

Handbook of Small Business Data.

The State of Small Business.

Social Security Administration
http://www.ssa.gov

Income of the Population 55 and over, 1994. 1996. 1998.

Public Social Welfare Expenditures, Fiscal Year 1995. Social Security Bulletin, No. 2, 1999.

Social Security Beneficiaries by State and County Data. Annual.

Social Security Bulletin. Quarterly with annual statistical supplement. (Data on Social Security Benefits, OASDI, Supplemental Security Income, Aid to Families with Dependent Children, Medicare, Medicaid, Low Income Home Energy Assistance, Food Stamps, Black Lung benefits, and other programs.)

Social Security Programs in the United States, 1997.

State Assistance Programs for SSI Recipients. Annual.

Supplemental Security Income, State and County Data. Annual.

AAFRC Trust For Philanthropy, Indianapolis, IN
http://www.aafrc.org
Giving USA. Annual.

Advisory Commission on Intergovernmental Relations, Washington, DC
http://www.library.unt.edu/gpo/ACIR/acir.html
Characteristics of Federal Grant-in-Aid Programs to State and Local Governments: Grants Funded FY 93. (Every 3 years.)
Changing Public Attitudes on Governments and Taxes. Annual.
Significant Features of Fiscal Federalism. Annual.

Aerospace Industries Association, Washington, DC
http://www.aia-aerospace.org
Aerospace Facts and Figures. Annual.
Aerospace Industry Year-End Review and Forecast. Annual.
Commercial Helicopter Shipments. Quarterly.
Employment in the Aerospace Industry. Monthly, Tabulated Quarterly.
Exports of Aerospace Products. Quarterly.
Imports of Aerospace Products. Quarterly.
Manufacturing Production, Capacity, and Utilization in Aerospace and Aircraft and parts. Monthly, Tabulated Quarterly.
Orders, Shipments, Backlog and inventories for Aircraft, Missiles, & Parts. Monthly, Tabulated Quarterly.

Air Transport Association of America Inc., Washington, DC
http://www.air-transport.org
Air Transport Association Annual Report.

The Alan Guttmacher Institute, New York, NY
http://www.agi-usa.org
Family Planning Perspectives. Bimonthly.

American Bureau of Metal Statistics, Inc., Secaucus, NJ
http://www.abms.com
Nonferrous Metal Data.

American Council on Education, Washington, DC
http://www.acenet.edu
A Fact Book on Higher Education. Quarterly.
National Norms for Entering College Freshmen. Annual.

American Council of Life Insurance, Washington, DC
http://www.acli.com
Life Insurance Fact Book. Biennial. (Odd years)

American Dental Association, Chicago, IL
http://www.ada.org
Dental Statistics Handbook. Triennial.
Dental Students' Register. Annual.
Distribution of Dentists in the United States by Region and State. Triennial.
Survey of Dental Practice. Annual.

American Financial Services Association, Washington, DC
http://www.americanfinsvcs.com
AFSA Annual Research Report and Second Mortgage Lending Report on Finance Companies. Annual.
AFSA Annual Research Report and Second Mortgage Lending Report Supplements. Annual.

American Forest & Paper Association, Washington, DC
http://www.afandpa.org
Statistical Roundup.
Statistics of Paper, Paperboard, and Wood Pulp. Annual.
Wood Pulp and Fiber Statistics. Annual.

American Frozen Food Institute, Burlingame, CA
http://www.affi.com
Frozen Food Pack Statistics. Annual.

American Gas Association, Arlington, VA
http://www.aga.org
Gas Facts. Annual.

American Iron and Steel Institute, Washington, DC
http://www.steel.org
Annual Statistical Report.

American Jewish Committee, New York, NY
http://www.ajc.org
American Jewish Year Book.

American Medical Association, Chicago, IL
http://www.ama-assn.org
Physician Characteristics and Distribution in the U.S. Annual.
Physician Marketplace Statistics. Annual.
Physician Socioeconomic Statistics. 1991-2000.
Socioeconomic Characteristics of Medical Practice. 1997/98.
U.S. Medical Licensure Statistics, and License Requirements. Annual.

American Metal Market, New York, NY
http://www.amm.com
Daily Newspapers.
Metal Statistics. Annual.

American Osteopathic Association, Chicago, IL
http://www.aoa-net.org
Yearbook and Directory of Osteopathic Physicians. Annual.

American Petroleum Institute, Washington, DC
http://www.api.org
American Petroleum Institute, Independent Petroleum Association of America, and Mid-Continent Oil and Gas Association
The Basic Petroleum Data Book. Annual.
Petroleum Industry Environmental Report. Annual.
Quarterly Well Completion Report.

American Public Transportation Association, Washington, DC
http://www.apta.com
Public Transportation Fact Book. Annual.

Association of American Railroads, Washington, DC
http://www.aar.org
Analysis of Class I Railroads. Annual.
Cars of Revenue Freight Loaded. Weekly with annual summary.
Freight Commodity Statistics, Class I Railroads in the United States. Annual.
Yearbook of Railroad Facts.

Association of Racing Commissioners International, Inc., Lexington, KY
http://www.arci.com
Statistical Reports on Greyhound Racing in the United States. Annual.
Statistical Reports on Horse Racing in the United States. Annual.
Statistical Reports on Jai Alai in the United States. Annual.

Book Industry Study Group, Inc., New York, NY
http://www.bisg.org
Consumer Research Study on Book Purchasing. Annual.

Bowker (R.R.) Company, New Providence, NJ
http://www.bowker.com
American Library Directory. Annual.
Bowker Annual Library and Book Trade Almanac.

Boy Scouts of America, Irving, TX
http://www.bsa.scouting.org
Annual Report.

Bridge Commodity Research Bureau, a Bridge Information Systems Inc., Chicago, IL
http://www.crbindex.com
The Blue Line. Daily
Bridge News Summaries. Daily
Commodity Year Book Update Disk. (Three editions annually.)

Bridge Commodity Research Bureau, a Bridge Information Systems Inc., Chicago, IL —Con.
CRB Commodity Index Report. Weekly.
CRB Commodity Year Book. Annual.
CRB Futures Perspective. Weekly.
CRB Infotech. CD
Electronic Futures Trend Analyzer. Daily.
Final Markets. End of day.
Futures Market Service. Weekly.
Futures Market Service Fundamental & Technical Commentary. Daily and weekly.
Price Service. Daily

The Bureau of National Affairs, Inc., Washington, DC
http://www.bna.com
Basic Patterns in Union Contracts. Annual.
BNA's Employment Outlook. Quarterly.
BNA's Job Absence and Turnover. Quarterly.
Briefing Sessions on Employee Relations Workbook. Annual.
Calendar of Negotiations. Annual.
Directory of U.S. Labor Organizations. Annual.
National Labor Relations Board Election Statistics. Annual.
NLRB Representation and Decertification Elections Statistics. Quarterly.
PPF Survey (Personnel Policies Forum.) Three times a year.

Carl H. Pforzheimer & Co., New York, NY
(No Web site)
Comparative Oil Company Statistics, 1999. Annual.

Chronicle of Higher Education, Inc., Washington, DC
http://chronicle.com
Almanac. Annual.

College Entrance Examination Board, Princeton, NJ
http://www.collegeboard.com
National Report on College-Bound Seniors. Annual.

The Conference Board, New York, NY
http://www.conference-board.com
The Conference Board Economic Times. Monthly.

Congressional Quarterly Inc., Washington, DC
http://www.cq.com
America Votes. A handbook of contemporary American election statistics, compiled and edited by Richard M. Scammon, Alice V. McGillivray and Rhodes Cook. Biennial.

Corporation for Public Broadcasting, Washington, DC

http://www.cpb.org

Average Revenue Profiles for Public Broadcasting Grantees. Annual.

Frequently asked Questions About Public Broadcasting Periodic.

Public Broadcasting Stations' Income from State Governments and State Colleges & Universities Ranked State-by-State. Annual.

Public Radio and Television Programming Content by Category. Biennial.

The Council of State Governments, Lexington, KY

http://www.statesnews.org

The Book of the States. Biennial.

State Administrative Officials Classified by Function. Biennial.

State Elective Officials and the Legislatures. Biennial.

State Legislative Leadership, Committees, and Staff. Biennial.

Credit Union National Association, Inc., Madison, WI

http://www.cuna.org

The Credit Union Report. Annual.

Credit Union Services Profile. Annual.

Operating Ratios and Spreads. Semiannual.

Dodge, F.W., National Information Services Division, McGraw-Hill Information Systems Co., New York, NY

http://www.fwdodge.com

Dodge Construction Potentials. Monthly.

Dow Jones & Co., New York, NY.

http://www.dj.com

Wall Street Journal.

Daily except Saturdays, Sundays, and holidays.

The Dun & Bradstreet Corporation, Murray Hill, NJ

http://www.dnb.com

The Business Failure Record. Annual.

The Business Starts Record. Annual.

Monthly Business Failure Report.

Monthly Business Starts Report.

Monthly New Business Incorporations Report.

Edison Electric Institute, Washington, DC

http://www.eei.org

Statistical Yearbook of the Electric Utility Industry. Annual.

Editor & Publisher Co., New York, NY

http://209.11.43.220/editorandpublisher/index.jsp

Editor & Publisher. Weekly.

International Year Book. Annual.

Market Guide. Annual.

Electronic Industries Alliance, Arlington, VA

http://www.eia.org

Electronic Market Data Book. Annual.

Electronic Market Trends. Monthly.

Electronics Foreign Trade. Monthly.

ENO Transportation Foundation, Leesburg, VA

http://www.enotrans.com

Transportation in America. Midyear, Annually with Periodic Supplements.

Euromonitor, London, England

http://www.euromonitor.com

Consumer Asia. Annual.

Consumer China. Annual.

Consumer Eastern Europe. Annual.

Consumer Europe. Annual.

Consumer International. Annual.

Consumer Latin America. Annual.

European Marketing Data and Statistics. Annual.

International Marketing Data and Statistics. Annual.

World Economic Factbook. Annual.

Federal National Mortgage Association, Washington, DC

http://www.fanniemae.com

Annual Report.

Food and Agriculture Organization of the United Nations, Rome, Italy

http://www.fao.org

Production Yearbook.

Trade Yearbook.

Yearbook of Fishery Statistics.

Yearbook of Forest Products.

Fortune (Time Warner), New York, NY

http://www.fortunedatastore.com

The Fortune Directory of the 500 Largest Industrial Corporations.

The Fortune Directory of the 500 Global Industrial Corporations.

The Foundation Center, New York, NY

http://www.fdncenter.org

Foundation Giving Trends. Annual.

Foundation Yearbook. Annual.

Gale Research Inc., Farmington Hills, MI

http://www.galegroup.com

Gale Directory of Publications and Broadcast Media. 1999.

General Aviation Manufacturers Association, Washington, DC

http://www.generalaviation.org

Shipment Report. Quarterly and Annual.

Statistical Databook. Annual.

Girl Scouts of the U.S.A., New York, NY
www.gsusa.org
Annual Report.

Health Forum, L.L.C.,an American Hospital Association, Company, Chicago, IL.
http://www.healthforum.com
Annual Report.

Health Insurance Association of America, Washington, DC
http://www.hiaa.org
Source Book of Health Insurance Data. Annual.

Independent Petroleum Association of America, Washington, DC
http://www.ipaa.org
IPAA Weekly Oil Trends.
IPAA Wholesale Oil Prices. Monthly.
The Oil & Natural Gas Producing Industry in Your State. Annual.
U.S. Petroleum Statistics. Semiannual.

Institute for Criminal Justice Ethics, New York, NY
http://www.lib.jjay.cuny.edu/cje/html/institute.html
Criminal Justice Ethics. Semiannual.

Insurance Information Institute, New York, NY
http://www.iii.org
Insurance Facts. Annual.

Inter-American Development Bank, Washington, DC
http://www.iadb.org
Annual Report.
Economic and Social Progress in Latin America. Annual Survey.

International City Management Association, Washington, DC
http://www.icma.org
Baseline Data Reports. Bimonthly.
Compensation: An Annual Report on Local Government Executive Salaries and Fringe Benefits.
Municipal Year Book. Annual.
Special Data Issues. Periodical.

International Labour Office, Geneva, Switzerland
http://www.ilo.org
Yearbook of Labour Statistics.

International Monetary Fund, Washington, DC
http://www.imf.org
Annual Report.
Balance of Payments Statistics. Monthly with annual yearbook.
Direction of Trade Statistics. Monthly with annual yearbook.
Government Finance Statistics Yearbook.
International Financial Statistics. Monthly with annual yearbook.

Investment Company Institute, Washington, DC
http://www.ici.org
Mutual Fund Fact Book. Annual.

Jane's Information Group, Coulsdon, UK and Alexandria, VA
http://www.janes.com
Jane's Air-Launched Weapons. (Binder-4 monthly update.)
Jane's All the World's Aircraft. Annual.
Jane's Armour and Artillery. Annual.
Jane's Avionics. Annual.
Jane's Fighting Ships. Annual.
Jane's Infantry Weapons. Annual.
Jane's Merchant Ships. Annual.
Jane's Military Communications. Annual.
Jane's Military Logistics. Annual.
Jane's Military Training Systems. Annual.
Jane's NATO Handbook. Annual.
Jane's Spaceflight Directory. Annual.

Joint Center for Political and Economic Studies, Washington, DC
http://www.jointcenter.org
Black Elected Officials: A National Roster. Annual.

Laventhol & Horwath, Philadelphia, PA
http://www.legalcasedocs.com
The Executive Conference Center: A Statistical and Financial Profile. Annual.
Gaming Industry Study. Annual.
Lifecare Industry. Annual. (Analysis of facilities by size and section of the country for selected financial data, resident census information, and medical costs.)
National Trends of Business in the Lodging Industry. Monthly. (Analysis of nationwide trends in sales, occupancy, and room rates of hotels, motor hotels, and economy lodging facilities.)
Separate reports on the segments of lodging industries. Annuals. (Reports covering economy, all-suite, and resort.)
U.S. Lodging Industry. Annual. (Report on hotel and motor hotel operations.)
Worldwide Lodging Industry. Annual. (Report on international hotel operations.)

Lebhar-Friedman, Inc., New York, NY
http://www.lf.com
Accounting Today. Biweekly.
Apparel Merchandising. Monthly.

McGraw-Hill Informations Service Co., Washington, DC
http://www.fwdodge.com
Electrical World Directory of Electric Utilities. Annual.
Engineering and Mining Journal. Monthly.
Keystone Coal Industry Manual. Annual.

U.S. Census Bureau, Statistical Abstract of the United States: 2001

Metropolitan Life Insurance Company, New York, NY
http://www.metlife.com
Health and Safety Education.

Moody's Investors Service, New York, NY
http://www.moodys.com

National Academy of Sciences, Washington, DC
http://www.pnas.org
Science, Engineering, and Humanities Doctorates in the United States. Biennial.
Summary Report. Doctorate Recipients from United States Universities. Annual.

National Association of Latino Elected and Appointed Officials, Washington, DC
http://www.naleo.org
National Roster of Hispanic Elected Officials. Annual.

National Association of Realtors. Washington, DC
http://nar.realtor.com
Real Estate Outlook: Market Trends & Insights. Monthly.

National Association of State Budget Officers, Washington, DC
http://www.nasbo.org
"State Expenditure Report". Annual.
Fiscal Survey of the States. Semi-annual.

National Association of State Park Directors, Tuscon, AZ
http://www.indiana.edu/~naspd
Annual Information Exchange.

National Catholic Educational Association, Washington, DC
http://www.ncea.org
Catholic Schools in America. Annual.
United States Catholic Elementary and Secondary Schools. Staffing and Enrollment. Annual.
U.S. Catholic Elementary Schools and their Finances. Biennial.
U.S. Catholic Secondary Schools and their Finances. Biennial.

National Cen͙er for State Courts, Williamsburg, VA
http://www.ncsc.dni.us
State Court Caseload Statistics. Annual.

National Council of the Churches of Christ in the U.S.A., New York, NY
http://www.ncccusa.org
Yearbook of American and Canadian Churches. Annual.

National Council of Savings Institutions, Washington, DC
http://www.bankmag.com
Fact Book of National Council of Savings Institutions. Annual.

National Education Association, Washington, DC
http://www.nea.org
Estimates of School Statistics. Annual.
Rankings of the States. Annual.
Status of the American Public School Teacher, 1995-96. Quinquennial.

National Fire Protection Association, Quincy, MA
http://www.nfpa.org
NFPA Journal. Bimonthly.

National Food Processors Association, Washington, DC
http://www.nfpa-food.org
Canned Fruit and Vegetable Pack and Stock Situation Reports. Quarterly.

National Golf Foundation, Jupiter, FL
http://www.ngf.org
Americans' Attitudes on Golf (in their communities).
Commercial Golf Range Participation and Supply in the U.S.
Commercial Golf Ranges in the U.S.
Directory of Executive and Par-3 Golf Courses in U.S.
Directory of Golf: The People and Businesses in Golf. Annual.
Directory of U.S. Golf Courses.
Directory of U.S. Golf Practice Ranges and Learning Centers.
Directory of Golf Retailers: Off-Course Golf Retail Stores in U.S.
Golf Consumer Potential.
Golf Consumer Spending in the U.S.
Golf Facilities in Canada.
Golf Facilities in the U.S. - 1998.
Golf Facility Employee Compensation Study.
Golf Participation in Canada.
Golf Participation in U.S. - 1998.
Golf Travel Market Report for the U.S.
High-Interest Women Golfers—Target Marketing for Success.
Hot Spots for Golf Course Construction Activity in the USA.
NGF's *Infosearch: Accessing the World's Largest Golf Business Library.*
Operating and Financial Performance Profiles of Golf Facilities in the U.S.
Senior Golfer Profile.
Trends in the Golf Industry. Annually.
Women in Golf—1991-1996

National Marine Manufacturers Association, Chicago, IL
http://www.nmma.org
Boating. (A Statistical Report on America's Top Family Sport.) Annual.
State Boat Registration. Annual.

National Restaurant Association, Washington, DC

http://www.restaurant.org

Compensation for Salaried Personnel in Restaurants. 2001.

Ethnic Cuisines II. 2000.

Holiday Dining. 2001.

Meal Consumption Behavior. 2001.

Quick-Service Restaurant Trends. Annual.

Restaurant Economic Trends. Monthly.

Restaurant Industry Employee Profile. Annual.

Restaurant Industry Forecast. Annual.

Restaurant Industry in Review. Annual.

Restaurant Industry Operations Report. Annual.

Restaurant Industry Pocket Factbook. Annual.

Restaurant Industry 2010. 1999.

Restaurant Numbers: 25-Year History, 1970-95. 1998.

Restaurant Spending. Annual. Restaurants USA. Monthly.

Tableservice Restaurant Trends. Annual

Takeout Foods: A Consumer Study of Carry-out and Delivery. 1998

The Economic Impact of the Nation's Eating and Drinking Places. Annual.

National Sporting Goods Association, Mt. Prospect, IL

http://www.nsga.org

The Sporting Goods Market in 2000. Annual.

Sports Participation in 1999. Annual.

New York Stock Exchange, Inc., New York, NY

http://www.nyse.com

Fact Book. Annual.

Organization for Economic Cooperation and Development, Paris, France

http://www.oecd.org

Annual Oil Market Report.

Coal Information. Annual.

Energy Balances of OECD Countries. Annual.

Energy Prices and Taxes. Quarterly.

Energy Statistics. Annual.

Financial Market Trends. Triennial.

Food Consumption Statistics. Irregular.

Geographical Distribution of Financial Flows to Developing Countries.

Historical Statistics of Foreign Trade Series A. Annual.

Indicators of Industrial Activity. Quarterly.

Industrial Structure Statistics. Annual.

The Iron and Steel Industry. Annual.

Labour Force Statistics. Annual.

Latest Information on National Accounts of Developing Countries. Annual.

Organization for Economic Cooperation and Development, Paris, France —Con.

Main Economic Indicators. Monthly.

Main Science and Technology Indicators. Biennial.

Maritime Transport. Annual.

Meat Balances in OECD Countries. Annual.

Milk and Milk Products Balances in OECD Countries. Annual.

National Accounts of OECD Countries. Annual.

Vol. I: Main Aggregates.

Vol. II: Detailed Tables.

OECD Economic Outlook. Bi-annual. Historical Statistics. Annual.

OECD Economic Studies. Annual for member countries.

OECD Employment Outlook. Annual.

OECD Financial Statistics. Annual (three vols.) and monthly supplements.

OECD Health Data (Diskette)

OECD Health Systems: Facts and Trends.

OECD Microtables on Foreign Trade by Commodities covering Series B (individual reporting countries) and Series C (total reporting countries). Annual from 1977.

Oil and Gas Information. Annual.

The Pulp and Paper Industry. Annual.

Quarterly Labor Force Statistics.

Quarterly National Accounts.

Quarterly Oil Statistics and Energy Balances.

Revenue Statistics of OECD Member Countries. Annual.

Review of Fisheries in OECD Member Countries. Annual.

Statistical Trends in Transport (ECMT.)

Statistics of Area Production and Field of Crop Products in OECD Member Countries.

Statistics of Foreign Trade:

Monthly Statistics of Foreign Trade. (Series A.)

Foreign Trade by Commodities. (Series C.) Annual.

Tourism Policy and International Tourism in OECD Member Countries. Annual.

Uranium Resources Production and Demand. Biennial.

World Energy Statistics and Balances.

Pan American Health Organization, Washington, DC

http://www.paho.org

Health Conditions in the Americas. Quadrennial.

PennWell Publishing Co., Tulsa, OK

http://www.pennwell.com

Offshore. Monthly.

Oil and Gas Journal. Weekly.

Population Association of America, Washington, DC

http://www.popassoc.org

Demography. Quarterly.

Population Index. (Princeton University, Princeton, NJ, Woodrow Wilson School of Public and International Affairs for the Population Association of America, Inc.) Quarterly.

Puerto Rico Planning Board, San Juan, PR

http://http://www.jp.gobierno.pr

Balance of Payments—Puerto Rico. Annual.

Economic Activity Index. Monthly.

Economic Indicators. Monthly.

Economic Projections. Annual.

Economic Report to the Governor. Annual.

External Trade Statistics-Puerto Rico. Annual.

Income and Product. Annual.

Input-Output—Puerto Rico. Every five years.

Statistical Appendix to the Economic Report to the Government. Annual.

Radio Advertising Bureau, New York, NY

http://www.rab.com

Radio Facts. Annual.

Cahners Business Information Unit, New York, NY

http://www.cahners.com

Library Journal. Semimonthly.

Publishers Weekly.

School Library Journal. Monthly.

Reed Elsevier, Inc., Newton, MA

http://www.reed-elsevier.com

Broadcasting & Cable Yearbook.

Regional Airline Association, Washington, DC

http://www.raa.org

Annual Report.

Broadcasting Magazine. Weekly.

Research Associates of Washington, Arlington, VA

http://www.rschassoc.com

Inflation Measures for Schools, Colleges, and Libraries. Annual.

State Rankings: Financing Public Higher Education. Annual.

Prevailing Wages: 1,643 County Indexes. (1994-96, most recent.)

Securities Industry Association, New York, NY

http://www.sia.com

Foreign Activity Report. Quarterly.

Securities Industry Trends. Periodic.

SIA Securities Industry Fact Book. Annual.

Shipbuilders Council of America, Arlington, VA

http://www.shipbuilders.org

Annual Report.

Simmons Market Research Bureau, Chicago, IL

http://www.smrb.com

Study of Media Markets. Annual.

Standard and Poor's Corporation, New York, NY

http://www.standardandpoors.com

Analyst's Handbook. Annual with monthly cumulative supplements.

Corporation Records. Six basic volumes; News Supplements, daily; Dividend Record, daily, and cumulative monthly and annual.

Daily Stock Price Records. Quarterly.

Security Owner's Stock Guide. Monthly.

Statistical Service. (Security Price Index Record; business and financial basic statistics with monthly supplement.)

United Nations Educational, Scientific and Cultural Organization, Paris, France

http://www.unesco.org

Statistical Yearbook.

United Nations Statistics Division, New York, NY

http://www.un.org

Compendium of Human Settlements Statistics. (Series N.)

Demographic Yearbook. (Series R.)

Energy Balances and Electricity Profiles. (Series W.)

Energy Statistics Yearbook. (Series J.)

Industrial Statistics Yearbook: (Series P.)

Commodity Production Statistics.

International Trade Statistics Yearbook. (Series G.)

Monthly Bulletin of Statistics. (Series Q.)

National Accounts Statistics: (Series X, Annually.)

Main Aggregates and Detailed Tables.

Analysis of Main Aggregates.

Population and Vital Statistics Report. (Series A, Quarterly.)

Social Statistics and Indicators: (Series K, Occasional.)

The World's Women: Trends and Statistics.

Women's Indicators and Statistics Database (CD and diskette only.)

Statistical Yearbook. (Series; also available in CD-ROM, Series S/CD)

World Statistics Pocketbook. (Series V, Annually.)

United States League of Savings Institutions, Chicago, IL

http://www.westernleague.org

Savings Institutions Sourcebook. Annual.

United States Telephone Association, Washington, DC

http://www.usta.org

Statistics of the Local Exchange Carriers. Annual.

United Way of America, Alexandria, VA
http://www.unitedway.org
Annual Directory.

University of Michigan, Center for Political Studies, Institute for Social Research, Ann Arbor, MI
http://www.umich.edu
National Election Studies Cumulative Datafile. Biennial.

Warren Publishing, Inc., Washington, DC
http://www.law.emory.edu
Cable Action Update. Weekly.
Cable and Station Coverage Atlas. Annual.
Television Action Update. Weekly.
Television and Cable Factbook. Annual.

Warren Publishing, Inc., Washington, DC —Con.
TV Station & Cable Ownership Directory. Semi-annual.

World Almanac, New York, NY
http://www.worldalmanac.com
The World Almanac and Book of Facts. Annual.

World Health Organization, Geneva, Switzerland
http://www.who.int
Epidemiological and Vital Statistics Report. Monthly.
World Health Statistics. Quarterly and annual.

U.S. Census Bureau, Statistical Abstract of the United States: 2001

Guide to State Statistical Abstracts

This bibliography includes the most recent statistical abstracts for states published since 1995 plus those that will be issued in late 2000. For some states, a near equivalent has been listed in substitution for, or in addition to, a statistical abstract. All sources contain statistical tables on a variety of subjects for the state as a whole, its component parts, or both. The page counts given for publications are approximate. Internet sites also contain statistical data.

Alabama

University of Alabama, Center for Business and Economic Research, Box 870221, Tuscaloosa 35487-0221. 205-348-6191. Internet site <http://cber.cba.ua.edu/>

Economic Abstract of Alabama. 2000. 534 pp.

Alaska

Department of Commerce, Division of Community and Business Development, P.O. Box 110804, Juneau 99811-0804 907-465-2017. Internet site <http://www.dced.state.ak.us/>

The Alaska Economy Performance Report. 1996.

Arizona

University of Arizona, Economic and Business Research, Eller College of Business and Public Administration, McClelland Hall 204, Tucson 85721-0108. 520-621-2155. Fax: 520-621-2150. Internet site <http://www.ebr.bpa.arizona.edu/>

Arizona's Economy. 16-20 pp. Quarterly newsletter. *Arizona Economic Indicators.* 52 pp. Biennial. *Economic Outlook-Annual Forecast.*

Arkansas

University of Arkansas at Little Rock, Institute for Economic Advancement, Economic Research, 2801 South University, Little Rock 72204. 501-569-8551.

Arkansas State and County Economic Data. 2000. 16 pp. (Revised annually.)

University of Arkansas at Little Rock, Institute for Economic Advancement, Census State Data Center, 2801 South University, Little Rock 72204. 501-569-8530. Internet site <http:// www.aiea.ualr.edu/>

Arkansas Statistical Abstract, 2000. 740 pp. (Revised biennially.)

California

Department of Finance, 915 L Street, 8th Floor, Sacramento 95814. 916-445-3878. Internet site <http://www.dof.ca.gov/>

California Statistical Abstract, 1999.

Colorado

University of Colorado, Boulder 80309-0420. 303-492-8227. Internet site <http://www.colorado.edu/libraries/govpubs/online.htm/>

Colorado by the Numbers-online only.

Connecticut

Connecticut Department of Economic & Community Development, 505 Hudson St., Hartford 06106. 1-860-270-8165. Internet site <http://www.state.ct.us/ecd/>

Connecticut Market Data. Fall/winter 1999.

Connecticut Town Profiles, 1998-99. 340 pp.

Delaware

Delaware Economic Development Office, 99 Kings Highway, Dover 19901. 302-739-4271. Internet site <http://www.state.de.us/dedo/>

Delaware Statistical Overview, 2000.

District of Columbia

Office of Planning, Data Management Division, 801 North Capitol St., N.E. Washington 20002. 202-442-7603

Office of Policy and Evaluation, Executive Office of the Mayor, 1 Judiciary Square, Suite 920 So., 441 4th St., NW, Washington 20001. 202-727-6979.

Indices—A Statistical Index to DC Services, Dec. 1997-98. 273 pp.

Florida

University of Florida, Bureau of Economic and Business Research, 221 Matherly Hall, Gainesville 32611-7145 352-392-0171. Internet site <http://www.bebr.ufl.edu/>

Florida Statistical Abstract, 2001. 35th ed. 821 pp. Also available on diskette or CD-ROM.

Florida County Perspectives, 2000. One profile for each county. Annual. Available on CD-ROM.

Florida County Rankings, 2000. 7th edition. Annual. Available on CD-ROM.

Florida and the Nation, 2001. 5th edition. Annual. Available on CD-ROM. Annual. Available on CD-ROM.

Georgia

University of Georgia, Selig Center for Economic Growth, Terry College of Business, Athens 30602-6269. 706-542-4085. Internet site <http://www.selig.uga.edu/>

Georgia Statistical Abstract, 2000-01. 500 pp.

Georgia —Con.

The University of Georgia, Center for Agri-business and Economic Development, Athens 30602-4356. 706-542-8938. Fax 706-542-8934. Internet site <http://www.agecon.uga.edu/countyguide/>

The Georgia County Guide. 2000. 19th ed. Annual. 200 pp.

Hawaii

Hawaii State Department of Business, and Economic Development & Tourism, Research and Economic Analysis Division, Statistics Branch P.O. Box 2359, Honolulu 96804. Inquiries 808-586-2481; Copies 808-586-2423. Internet site <http://www.hawaii.gov/dbedt/>

The State of Hawaii Data Book 1999: A Statistical Abstract. 32nd ed. 700 pp.

Idaho

Department of Commerce, 700 West State St., Boise 83720-0093. 208-334-2470. Internet site <http://www.idoc.state.id.us/>

Idaho Facts, 2000. County Profiles of Idaho, 1999.

University of Idaho, Center for Business Development and Research, Moscow 83844-3227. 208-885-6611. Internet site <http://www.uidaho.edu/cbdr/>

Idaho Statistical Abstract, 4th ed. 1996.

Illinois

University of Illinois, Bureau of Economic and Business Research, 430 Wohlers Hall, 1206 South 6th Street, Champaign 61820. 217-333-2330. Internet site <http://www.cba.uiuc.edu/research/>

Illinois Statistical Abstract. 2000. 15th edition. 759 pp.

Indiana

Indiana University, Indiana Business Research Center, School of Business, 801 W. Michigan St. Indianapolis 46202-5151. 317-274-2979. Internet site <http://www.ibrc.indiana.edu/>

Indiana Factbook, 1998-99. 393 pages.

Kansas

University of Kansas, Policy Research Institute, 607 Blake Hall, Lawrence 66045-2960. 785-864-3701. Internet site <http://www.ukans.edu/cwis/units/IPPBR/>.

Kansas Statistical Abstract, 1999. 34th ed. 2000.

Kentucky

Kentucky Cabinet for Economic Develop-ment, Division of Research, 500 Mero Street, Capital Plaza Tower, Frankfort 40601. 502-564-4886. Internet site <http://www.edc.state.ky.us/>

Kentucky Deskbook of Economic Statistics. 34th ed. 1998.

Louisiana

University of New Orleans, Division of Business and Economic Research, New Orleans 70148. 504-280-6240. Internet site <http://leap.nlu.edu/STAAB.HTM/>.

Statistical Abstract of Louisiana. 10th ed. 1997.

Maine

Maine Department of Economic and Community Development, State House Station 59, Augusta 04333. 207-287-2656. Internet site <http://www.econdevmaine.com/>.

Maine: A Statistical Summary. (Updated periodically.)

Maryland

RESI, 8000 York Road Towson University, Towson 212520001. 410-830-7374. Inter-net site <http://www.resiusa.org/>.

Maryland Statistical Abstract. 2000. 356 pp.

Massachusetts

Massachusetts Institute for Social and Economic Research, Box 37515, University of Massachusetts at Amherst 01003-7515. 413-545-3460. Fax 413-545-3686. Internet site <http://www.umass.edu/miser/>

Minnesota

Department of Trade and Economic Development, Analysis and Evaluation Office, 121 East 7th Place 500 Metro Square Building, St. Paul 55101-2146. 651-297-1291. Internet site <http://www.dted.state.mn.us/>.

Compare Minnesota: An Economic and Statistical Factbook, 2001-02 (forthcoming).

Office of State Demographer, Minnesota Planning, Rm. 300 Centennial Bldg., 658 Cedar Street, St. Paul 55155. 651-296-2557. Internet site <http://www.mnplan.state.mn.us/demography/>.

Mississippi

Mississippi State University, College of Busi-ness and Industry, Division of Research, P.O. Box 5288 Mississippi State 39762. 662-325-3817. Fax 662-325-8686.

Mississippi Statistical Abstract. 1999. 506 pp.

Missouri

University of Missouri, Economic and Policy Analysis Research Center, 10 Professional Bldg., Columbia 65211. 573-882-4805. Internet site <http://econ.missouri.edu/eparc/>.

Statistical Abstract for Missouri, 1999 Biennial.

Montana

Montana Department of Commerce, Census and Economic Information Center, 1424 9th Ave., Helena 59620. 406-444-2896. Internet site <http://commerce.state.mt.us/ceic/>.

Montana County Statistical Reports. (Separate county and state reports; available by subject section as well as complete reports by county and state, updated periodically.)

Nebraska

Department of Economic Development, Box 94666, Lincoln 68509-4666. 402-471-3111. Fax 402-471-3778. Internet site <http://www.ded.state.ne.us/>.

Nebraska Databook, 2000. 300 pp. (Available only on Internet).

Nevada

Department of Administration, Budget and Planning Division, 209 East Musser Street, Suite 200, Carson City 89701. 775-684-0222. Internet site <http://www.state.nv.us/budget/stateab.htm>.

Nevada Statistical Abstract. 1999. Biennial.

New Hampshire

Office of State Planning, 2 1/2 Beacon St., Concord 03301-4497. 603-271-2155. Fax 603-271-1728. Internet site <http://www.state.nh.us/osp/nhresnet/>.

New Hampshire (State Seal) A Brief Look, July 1997. 21 pp. (Contact source for other statistical series).

New Jersey

New Jersey State Data Center, NJ Department of Labor, P.O. Box 388, Trenton 08625-0388. 609-984-2595. Internet site <http://www.wnjpin.state.nj.us/>. OneStopCareerCenter/LaborMarketInformationlist.htm/>

New Mexico

University of New Mexico, Bureau of Business and Economic Research, 1920 Lomas N.E. Albuquerque 87131-6021. 505-277-6626. Fax 505-277-2773. Internet site <http://www.unm.edu/bber/>.

County Profiles. *1997.* 72 pp.

New York

Nelson A. Rockefeller Institute of Government, 411 State Street, Albany 12203-1003. 518-443-5522. Internet site <http:// www.rockinst.org/>

New York State Statistical Yearbook, 1999. 24th ed. 596 pp.

North Carolina

Office of Governor Office of State Budget, Planning, and Management, 20321 Mail Service Center, Raleigh 27699-0321. 919-733-4131. Fax 919-715-3562. Internet site <http://www.osbpm.state.nc.us/#Demographer/>

North Dakota

North Dakota Department of Economic Development & Finance, 1833 E. Bismarck Expressway, Bismarck 58504-6708. 701-328-5300. Internet site <http://www.growingnd.com/>

The Economic Performance and Industrial Structure of the North Dakota Economy, 2000. 118 pp.

Ohio

Department of Development, Office of Strategic Research, P.O. Box 1001, Columbus 43216-1001. 614-466-2116. Internet site <http://www.odod.state.oh.us/osr/data.htm>

Research products and services. (Updated continuously.)

Oklahoma

University of Oklahoma, Center for Economic and Management Research, 307 West Brooks Street, Room 4, Norman 73019. 405-325-2931. Fax 405-325-7688. Internet site <http://origins.ou.edu/>

Statistical Abstract of Oklahoma, 1998. Annual. 409 pp.

Oregon

Secretary of State, Business Services Division, Publication Services Bldg., 255 Capital Street, NE, Suite 180, Salem 97310. 503-986-2234. Internet site <http://www.sos.state.or.us/>

Oregon Blue Book. 1999-2000. Biennial. 431 pp.

Pennsylvania

Pennsylvania State Data Center, Institute of State and Regional Affairs, Penn State Harrisburg, 777 West Harrisburg Pike, Middletown Pennsylvania 17057-4898. 717-948-6336. Internet site <http://pasdc.hbg.psu.edu/pasdc/>

Pennsylvania Statistical Abstract, 2000. 291 pp.

Rhode Island

Rhode Island Economic Development Corporation, 1 West Exchange Street, Providence 02903. 401-222-2601. Fax 401-222-2102. Internet site <http://www.riedc.com/>

Rhode Island Prel. 2000 Census of Population and Housing Summary. Dec. 2000. (updated as available).

The Rhode Island Economy. Aug. 2000.

South Carolina

Budget and Control Board, Office of Research and Statistics, Room 425, 1919 Blanding Str., Columbia 29201. 803-734-3781. Internet site <http://www.ors.state.sc.us/>

South Carolina Statistical Abstract: 1999. 429 pp.

South Dakota

University of South Dakota, State Data Center, Business Research Bureau, Vermillion 57069-2390. 605-677-5287. Internet site <http://www.usd.edu/brbinfo/>

2000 South Dakota Community Abstracts. 400 pp.

Tennessee

University of Tennessee at Knoxville, Center for Business and Economic Research, College of Business Administration 100 Glocker, Knoxville 37996-4170. 865-974-5441. Internet site <http://cber.bus.utk.edu/>

Tennessee Statistical Abstract, 2000. 17th ed. 738 pp. Biennial.

Texas

Dallas Morning News, Communications Center, P.O. Box 655237, Dallas 75265-5237. 214-977-8261. Internet site <http://www.texasalmanac.com/>

Texas Almanac, 2002-2003. 672 pp.

Utah

University of Utah, Bureau of Economic and Business Research, David Eccles School of Business 1645 East Campus Center Drive, Salt Lake City 84112-9302. 801-581-6333. Internet site <http://www.business.utah.edu/BEBR/>

Statistical Abstract of Utah. 1996. (Centennial.)

Utah Foundation, 10 West 100 South, Suite 323, Salt Lake City 84101-1544. 801-364-1837. Internet site <http://www.utah foundation.org/

Statistical Review of Government in Utah. 1999.

Vermont

Labor Market Information, Department of Employment and Training, 5 Green Mountain Drive, P.O. Box 488, Montpelier 05601-0488. 802-828-4202. Internet site <http://www.det.state.vt.us/>

Economic and Demographic Profiles. Annual.

Virginia

University of Virginia, Weldon Cooper Center for Public Service, 918 Emmet Street, North Suite 300, Charlottesville 22903-4832. 804-982-5585. Internet site <http://www.virginia.edu/coopercenter/>

Virginia Statistical Abstract, 2000. Biennial. 1,100 pp.

Washington

Washington State Office of Financial Management, Forecasting Division P.O. Box 43113 Olympia 98504-3113. 360-902-0599. Fax 360-664-8941. Internet site <http://www.ofm.wa.gov/>

Washington State Data Book, 1999. 310 pp.

West Virginia

West Virginia University, College of Business and Economics, Bureau of Business and Economic Research, P.O. Box 6025, Morgantown 26506-6025. 304-293-7831. Internet site <http://www.bber.wvu.edu/>

Regional Economic Outlook. Semiannual. 8 pp.

West Virginia Research League, Inc., P.O. Box 11176, Charleston 25339. 304-766-9495.

The 1999 Statistical Handbook. 94 pp.

Wisconsin

Wisconsin Legislative Reference Bureau, P.O. Box 2037, Madison 53701-2037. 608-266-7098 Internet site <http://www.legis.state.wi.us/lrb/bb/>

1999-2000 State of Wisconsin Blue Book. 950 pp. Biennial.

Wyoming

Department of Administration and Information, Division of Economic Analysis, 2001 Capitol Avenue, 327 E. Emerson Building, Cheyenne 82002-0060. 307-777-7504. Internet site <http://eadiv.state.wy.us/eahome.htm>

The Equality State Almanac 1999. 7th ed. 134 pp.

Guide to Foreign Statistical Abstracts

This bibliography presents recent statistical abstracts for member nations of the Organization for Economic Cooperation and Development, Slovakia, and Russia. All sources contain statistical tables on a variety of subjects for the individual countries. Many of the following publications provide text in English as well as in the national language(s). For further information on these publications, contact the named statistical agency which is responsible for editing the publication.

Australia
Australian Bureau of Statistics, Canberra
Year Book Australia. Annual. 2001. 1,091 pp. (In English.)

Austria
Statistik Austria, A-1033 Wien
Statistisches Jahrbuch Osterreichs. Annual. 2001. 654 pp. (In German.) With English translations of table headings.

Belgium
Institut National de Statistique, Rue de Louvain, 44-1000 Bruxelles
Annuaire statistique de la Belgique. Annual. 1995. 820 pp. (In French.)

Canada
Statistics Canada, Ottawa, Ontario, KIA OT6
Canada Yearbook: A review of economic, social and political developments in Canada. 2001. 564 pp. Irregular. (In English.)

Czech Republic
Czech Statistical Office, Sokolovska 142, 186 04 Praha 8
Statisticka Rocenka Ceske Rpubliky 2000. 759 pp. (In English and Czech.)

Denmark
Danmarks Statistik, Postboks 2550 Sejrogade 11, DK 2100, Copenhagen
Statistical Yearbook. 2000. Annual. 608 pp. (In Danish only.)

Finland
Central Statistical Office of Finland, Box 504 SF-00101 Helsinki
Statistical Yearbook of Finland. Annual. 2000. 685 pp. (In English, Finnish, and Swedish.)

France
Institut National de la Statistique et des Etudes Economiques, Paris 18, Bld. Adolphe Pinard, 75675 Paris (Cedex 14)
Annuaire Statistique de la France. Annual. 2001. 979 pp. (In French.)

Germany
Statistische Bundesamt, Postfach 5528, 6200 Wiesbaden
Statistisches Jahrbuch fur die Bundesrepublic Deutschland. Annual. 2000. 747 pp. (In German.)
Statistisches Jahrbuch fur das Ausland. 2000. 399 pp.

Greece
National Statistical Office, 14-16 Lycourgou St., 101-66 Athens
Concise Statistical Yearbook 2000. 276 pp. (plus13 pages of graphs) (In English.)
Statistical Yearbook of Greece. Annual. 1999. 563 pp. (plus 8 pages of graphs). (In English and Greek.)

Hungary
Hungarian Central Statistical Office, H-1525 Budapest PF.51 H-1024 Budapest
Statistical Yearbook of Hungary, 1999. 587 pp. (In English and Hungarian)

Iceland
Hagstofa Islands/Statistical Bureau, Hverfisgata 8-10, Reykjavik.
Statistical Yearbook of Iceland. 1999. Irregular. 316 pp. (In English and Icelandic.)

Ireland
Central Statistics Office, Skehard Road, Cort
Statistical Abstract. Annual. 1998-99. 419 pp. (In English)

Italy
ISTAT (Istituto Centrale di Statistica), Via Cesare Balbo 16, 00100 Rome
Annuario Statistico Italiano. Annual. 1998. 743 pp. (In Italian.)

Japan
Statistics Bureau, Management & Coordination Agency, 19-1 Wakamatsucho, Shinjuku Tokyo 162
Japan Statistical Yearbook. Annual. 2001. 913 pp. (In English and Japanese.)

Korea, South
National Statistical Office, Government Complex, #920 Dunsan-dong Seo-gu Daejeon 302-701

Korea Statistical Yearbook. Annual. 2000. 777 pp. (In Korean and English)

Luxembourg
STATEC (Service Central de la Statistique et des Etudes), P.O. Box 304, L-2013, Luxembourg

Annuaire Statistique. Annual. 1999. (In French.)

Mexico
Instituto Nacional de Estadistica Geografia e Informatica, Avda. Insurgentes Sur No. 795-PH Col. Napoles, Del. Benito Juarez 03810 Mexico, D.F.

Anuario estadistico de los Estados Unidos Mexicanos. Annual. 1998. 714 pp. Also on disc. (In Spanish.) *Agenda Estadistica 1999.* 149 pp.

Netherlands
Centraal Bureau voor de Statistiek. 428 Prinses Beatrixlaan P.O. Box 959, 2270 AZ Voorburg

Statistical Yearbook 2001 of the Netherlands. 575 pp. (In English.)
Statistisch Jaarboek 2001. 585 pp.

New Zealand
Department of Statistics, Wellington

New Zealand Official Yearbook. Annual. 1998. 606 pp. (In English.)

Norway
Statistics Norway, Kongens gt. 6, P.O.B. 8131 Dep 0033 Oslo

Statistical Yearbook. Annual. 2000. 569 pp. (In English and Norwegian.)

Poland
Central Statistical Office al. Niepodleglosci 208, 00-925 Warsaw

Concise Statistical Yearbook 2000. 700 pp. (In Polish and English) Statistical Yearbook of the Republic of Poland 2000. 800 pp. (In Polish and English)

Portugal
INE (Instituto Nacional de Estatistica), Avenida Antonio Jose de Almeida, P-1078 Lisbon Codex

Anuario Estatistico: de Portugal. 1999. 368 pp. (In Portuguese.)

Russia
State Committee of Statistics of Russia, Moscow

Statistical Yearbook. 2000. 642 pp. (In Russian.)

Slovakia
Statistical Office of the Slovak Republic, Bradacova 7, 852 86 Bratislava

Statisticka Rocenka Slovensak 2000. 719 pp. Plus 16 pages of graphs. (In English and Slovak)

Spain
INE (Instituto Nacional de Estadistica), Paseo de la Castellana, 183, Madrid 16

Espana Anuaria Estadistico Annual. 1996. 848 pp. + 16 pages of graphs (In Spanish.)

Sweden
Statistics Sweden, S-11581 Stockholm

Statistical Yearbook of Sweden. Annual. 2001. 659 pp. (In English and Swedish.)

Switzerland
Bundesamt fur Statistik, Hallwylstrasse 15, CH-3003, Bern

Statistisches Jahrbuch der Schweiz. Annual. 2001. 867 pp. (In French and German.)

Turkey
State Institute of Statistics, Prime Ministry, 114 Necatibey Caddesi, Bakanliklar, Yenisehir, Ankara

Statistical Yearbook of Turkey. 1999. 721 pp. (In English and Turkish.)
Turkey in Statistics 1999. 144 pp. (In English and Turkish.)

United Kingdom
The Stationary Office, P.O. Box 29, Norwich, NR3 1GN

Annual Abstract of Statistics. Annual. 2001. 440 pp. (In English.)

Appendix II

Metropolitan Areas: Concepts, Components, and Population

Statistics for metropolitan areas (MAs) shown in the *Statistical Abstract* represent areas defined by the U.S. Office of Management and Budget (OMB) according to published standards that are applied to Census Bureau data. The general concept of an MA is that of a core area containing a large population nucleus, together with adjacent communities having a high degree of economic and social integration with that core. Currently defined MAs are based on application of 1990 standards (which appeared in the Federal Register on March 30, 1990) to 1990 decennial census data and to subsequent Census Bureau population estimates, special census data and 2000 census results. Current MA definitions were announced by OMB effective June 30, 1999. MAs include metropolitan statistical areas (MSAs), consolidated metropolitan statistical areas (CMSAs), and primary metropolitan statistical areas (PMSAs).

In this appendix, Table E presents geographic components and 2000 census results for each MSA, CMSA, and PMSA. Table D presents definitions and data for New England county metropolitan areas (NECMAs), the county-based alternative metropolitan areas for the city- and town-based MSAs and CMSAs of the six New England states.

Standard definitions of metropolitan areas were first issued in 1949 by the then Bureau of the Budget (predecessor of OMB), under the designation "standard metropolitan area" (SMA). The term was changed to "standard metropolitan statistical area" (SMSA) in 1959 and to "metropolitan statistical area" (MSA) in 1983. The collective term "metropolitan area" (MA) became effective in 1990.

OMB has been responsible for the official metropolitan areas since they were first defined, except for the period 1977 to 1981, when they were the responsibility of the Office of Federal Statistical Policy

and Standards, Department of Commerce. The standards for defining metropolitan areas were modified in 1958, 1971, 1975, 1980, and 1990.

Defining MSAs, CMSAs, and PMSA— The current standards provide that each newly qualifying MSA must include at least: one city with 50,000 or more inhabitants, or a Census Bureau-defined urbanized area (of at least 50,000 inhabitants) and a total metropolitan population of at least 100,000 (75,000 in New England). Under the standards, the county (or counties) that contains the largest city becomes the "central county" (counties), along with any adjacent counties that have at least 50 percent of their population in the urbanized area surrounding the largest city. Additional "outlying counties" are included in the MSA if they meet specified requirements of commuting to the central counties and other selected requirements of metropolitan character (such as population density and percent urban). In New England, the MSAs are defined in terms of cities and towns rather than counties. An area that meets these requirements for recognition as an MSA and also has a population of 1 million or more may be recognized as a CMSA if separate component areas can be identified within the entire area by meeting statistical criteria specified in the standards, and local opinion indicates there is support for the component areas. If recognized, the component areas are designated PMSAs, and the entire area becomes a CMSA. PMSAs, like the CMSAs that contain them, are composed of entire counties, except in New England where they are composed of cities and towns. If no PMSAs are recognized, the entire area is designated as an MSA. As of the June 30, 1999, OMB announcement, there were 258 MSAs, and 18 CMSAs comprising 73 PMSAs in the United States. In addition, there were three MSAs, one CMSA, and three PMSAs in Puerto Rico.

Central cities and MA titles—The largest city in each MSA/CMSA is designated a "central city." Additional cities qualify if specified requirements are met concerning population size and commuting patterns. The title of each MSA consists of the names of up to three of its central cities and the name of each state into which the MSA extends. However, a central city with less than 250,000 population and less than one-third the population of the area's largest city is not included in an MSA title unless local opinion supports its inclusion. Titles of PMSAs also typically are based on central city names but in certain cases consist of county names. Generally, titles of CMSAs are based on the titles of their component PMSAs.

Defining New England County Metropolitan Areas NECMAs—The OMB defines NECMAs as a county-based alternative to the city- and town-based New England MSAs and CMSAs. The NECMA for an MSA or CMSA includes: the county containing the first-named city in that MSA/CMSA title (this county may include the first-named cities of other MSAs/CMSAs as well), and each additional county having at least half its population in the MSAs/CMSAs whose first-named cities are in the previously identified county. NECMAs are not identified for individual PMSAs. There are 12 NECMAs, including 1 for the Boston-Worcester-Lawrence, MA-NH-ME-CT CMSA and 1 for the Connecticut portion of the New York-Northern New Jersey-Long Island, NY-NJ-CT-PA CMSA. Central cities of a NECMA

are those cities in the NECMA that qualify as central cities of an MSA or a CMSA. NECMA titles derive from names of central cities.

Changes in MA definitions over time—Changes in the definitions of MAs since the 1950 census have consisted chiefly of the recognition of new areas as they reached the minimum required city or area population, and the addition of counties (or cities and towns in New England) to existing areas as new decennial census data showed them to qualify. In some instances, formerly separate MAs have been merged, components of an MA have been transferred from one MA to another, or components have been dropped from an MA. The large majority of changes have taken place on the basis of decennial census data. However, Census Bureau population estimates and special censuses serve as the basis for intercensal updates.

Because of these historical changes in geographic definitions, users must be cautious in comparing MA data from different dates. For some purposes, comparisons of data for MAs as defined at given dates may be appropriate; for other purposes, it may be preferable to maintain consistent MA definitions.

In Tables A, B, and C below, data are given for MAs as defined for specific dates, thereby indicating the extent of change in population and land area resulting from revisions in definitions.

U.S. Census Bureau, Statistical Abstract of the United States: 2001

Table A. Number, Population, and Land Area of MAs as Defined at Specified Dates From 1950 to 1999

[The differences in population shown here for each year within each column of the table result entirely from net expansion of metropolitan territory through changes in the MA definitions. The differences in population over time shown for each MA definition (on the successive lines of the table) result entirely from population changes within that territory, unaffected by changes in MA definitions. The changes in 1990 land area result entirely from net change in MA territory. All data include Alaska and Hawaii and exclude Puerto Rico. Subtraction of any line of the table from the line below will show the net effect of change in population and land area undergone by the MAs as the result of changes in definitions between the specified dates. Such changes may have occurred throughout the period, not on any single date, and may have included reductions in, as well as additions to, MA territory. Census population data through 1980 include corrections made since publication. The area data for the 1950, 1960, 1970, and 1980 census definitions of MAs differ from the data published in those censuses because of subsequent remeasurement of land areas and changes in inland water area occurring for the 1990 census]

MA definition as of—	Number of MAs	Population 1960 (April 1)	1970 (April 1)	1980 (April 1)	1990 (April 1)	1998 (July 1)	Land area, 1990 (sq. mi.)
1950 census (Mar. 1952)	169	106,344,548	122,184,836	128,842,628	139,837,153	148,305,142	206,802
1960 census (Nov. 1960)	212	[1]112,885,139	130,982,661	140,793,384	155,090,774	166,591,635	308,742
1970 census (Feb. 28, 1971). .	243	[2]119,593,498	[3]139,479,806	151,660,897	167,899,268	181,502,500	386,241
1980 census (June 30, 1981) [4].	318	131,318,714	153,693,767	169,430,081	188,763,892	205,387,705	565,288
1985 (June 30)..............	[5]280	132,887,134	155,700,823	172,169,761	192,140,319	209,262,496	569,816
1986 (June 30)..............	[5]281	132,977,580	155,805,452	172,304,319	192,318,722	209,460,226	571,745
1987 (June 30) [6]............	[5]281	133,003,445	155,832,688	172,334,850	192,349,750	209,494,587	572,284
1988 (June 30) [7]............	[5]282	133,088,400	155,937,275	172,455,251	192,481,306	209,637,403	573,560
1989 (June 30) [7]............	[5]283	133,233,777	156,084,580	172,602,176	192,623,201	209,775,506	574,622
1990 census (June 30, 1990) [7].	[5]284	133,275,412	156,137,337	172,678,381	192,730,096	209,907,765	580,136
1992 (Dec. 31).............	[5]268	136,171,803	159,395,627	176,662,854	197,470,576	215,395,847	669,927
1993 (June 30) [7][8]...........	[5]268	136,336,055	159,579,651	176,892,735	197,728,901	215,699,322	673,057
1994 (June 30) [7]............	[5]269	136,402,452	159,652,709	176,982,574	197,827,639	215,810,574	674,021
1995 (June 30) [7]............	[5]271	136,497,691	159,757,830	177,143,136	198,022,544	216,043,836	699,960
1996 (June 30) [7]............	[5]273	136,603,905	159,872,025	177,284,523	198,170,345	216,210,902	701,784
1998 (June 30) [7]............	[5]274	136,648,568	159,930,288	177,360,539	198,249,032	216,299,891	704,383
1999 (June 30) [7]............	[5]276	136,737,487	160,045,332	177,505,033	198,406,989	216,478,090	705,668

[1] Corresponds to total MA population for 1960 published in 1960 census (112,885,178), corrected by subtracting population (39) erroneously included in Franklin County, Ohio (Columbus metropolitan area). [2] Corresponds to total 1960 population for 1970 MAs published in 1970 census (119,594,754), corrected by subtracting 1,256 population from Lawrence-Haverhill metropolitan area; this represented an addition to the 1960 population of Andover town made subsequent to the original census tabulations, and therefore not reflected in state or national totals. [3] Corresponds to total MA population for 1970 published in 1970 census (139,418,811), plus net corrections made subsequent to publication. [4] MAs as defined for the 1982 economic censuses. [5] MSAs and CMSAs. [6] MAs as defined for the 1987 economic censuses. [7] Data exclude the portion of Sullivan city in Crawford County, MO (1990 population 1,116) added to the St. Louis, MO-IL MSA by congressional action effective Dec. 22, 1987. [8] MAs as defined for the 1992 economic censuses.

Source: U.S. Census Bureau, 1950-70, U.S. Census of Population, Vol. 1; 1980 Census of Population, Vol. 1, Chapters A and B and Supplementary Report, Metropolitan Statistical Areas (PC80-S1-18); 1990 Census of Population and Housing Data Paper Listing (CPH-L-10 and CPH-L-118); 1990 Census of Population and Housing, Supplementary Reports, Metropolitan Areas as Defined by the Office of Management and Budget, June 30, 1993, (1990 CPH-S-1-1); and Population Paper Listing (PPL-60 and PPL-83).

Table B. Nonmetropolitan Population and Land Area as Defined at Specified Dates From 1950 to 1999

[See headnote for Table A. Nonmetropolitan population and land area are equivalent to that portion of the total national population and land area not included within MAs at the dates specified]

Metropolitan area definition as of—	Population 1960 (April 1)	1970 (April 1)	1980 (April 1)	1990 (April 1)	1998 (July 1)	Land area, 1990 (sq. mi.)
1950 census (Mar. 1952)	72,978,627	81,117,195	97,699,571	108,881,149	121,993,382	3,332,967
1960 census (Nov. 1960)	66,438,036	72,319,370	85,748,815	93,627,518	103,706,889	3,231,027
1970 census (Feb. 28, 1971). .	59,729,677	63,822,225	74,881,302	80,819,024	88,796,024	3,153,527
1980 census (June 30, 1981) . .	48,004,461	49,608,264	57,112,118	59,954,400	64,910,819	2,974,481
1985 (June 30).............	46,436,041	47,601,208	54,372,438	56,577,973	61,036,028	2,969,952
1986 (June 30).............	46,345,595	47,496,579	54,237,880	56,399,570	60,838,298	2,968,023
1987 (June 30).............	46,319,730	47,469,343	54,207,349	56,368,542	60,803,937	2,967,484
1988 (June 30).............	46,234,775	47,364,756	54,086,948	56,236,986	60,661,121	2,966,208
1989 (June 30).............	46,089,398	47,217,451	53,940,023	56,095,091	60,523,018	2,965,146
1990 census (June 30, 1990) ..	46,047,763	47,164,694	53,863,818	55,988,196	60,390,759	2,959,632
1992 (Dec. 31).............	43,151,372	43,906,404	49,879,345	51,247,716	54,902,677	2,866,411
1993 (June 30).............	42,987,120	43,722,380	49,649,464	50,989,391	54,599,202	2,863,281
1994 (June 30).............	42,920,723	43,649,322	49,559,625	50,890,653	54,487,950	2,862,317
1995 (June 30).............	42,825,484	43,544,201	49,399,063	50,695,748	54,254,688	2,836,378
1996 (June 30).............	42,719,270	43,430,006	49,257,676	50,547,947	54,087,622	2,834,554
1998 (June 30).............	42,674,607	43,371,743	49,181,660	50,469,260	53,998,633	2,831,956
1999 (June 30).............	42,585,688	43,256,699	49,037,166	50,311,303	53,820,424	2,830,671

Source: U.S. Census Bureau, 1950-70, U.S. Census of Population, Vol. 1; 1980 Census of Population, Vol. 1, Chapters A and B and Supplementary Report, Metropolitan Statistical Areas (PC80-S1-18); 1990 Census of Population and Housing Data Paper Listing (CPH-L-10 and CPH-L-118); 1990 Census of Population and Housing, Supplementary Reports, Metropolitan Areas as Defined by the Office of Management and Budget, June 30, 1993, (1990 CPH-S-1-1); and Population Paper Listing (PPL-60 and PPL-83).

Table C. Percent of Total U.S. Population and Percent of Land Area Inside MAs as Defined at Specified Dates From 1950 to 1999

[See headnote for Table A]

Metropolitan area definition as of—	Percent of population					Percent of land area, 1990
	1960 (April 1)	1970 (April 1)	1980 (April 1)	1990 (April 1)	1998 (July 1)	
1950 census (Mar. 1952)	59.3	60.1	56.9	56.2	54.9	5.8
1960 census (Nov. 1960)	63.0	64.4	62.1	62.4	61.6	8.7
1970 census (Feb. 28, 1971)	66.7	68.6	66.9	67.5	67.1	10.9
1980 census (June 30, 1981)	73.2	75.6	74.8	75.9	76.0	16.0
1985 (June 30)	74.1	76.6	76.0	77.3	77.4	16.1
1986 (June 30)	74.2	76.6	76.1	77.3	77.5	16.2
1987 (June 30)	74.2	76.7	76.1	77.3	77.5	16.2
1988 (June 30)	74.2	76.7	76.1	77.4	77.6	16.2
1989 (June 30)	74.3	76.8	76.2	77.4	77.6	16.2
1990 census (June 30, 1990)	74.3	76.8	76.2	77.5	77.7	16.4
1992 (Dec. 31)	75.9	78.4	78.0	79.4	79.7	18.9
1993 (June 30)	76.0	78.5	78.1	79.5	79.8	19.0
1994 (June 30)	76.1	78.5	78.1	79.5	79.8	19.1
1995 (June 30)	76.1	78.6	78.2	79.6	79.9	19.8
1996 (June 30)	76.2	78.6	78.3	79.7	80.0	19.8
1998 (June 30)	76.2	78.7	78.3	79.7	80.0	19.9
1999 (June 30)	76.3	78.7	78.4	79.8	80.1	20.0

Source: U.S. Census Bureau, 1950-70, U.S. Census of Population, Vol. 1; 1980 Census of Population, Vol. 1, Chapters A and B and Supplementary Report, Metropolitan Statistical Areas (PC80-S1-18); 1990 Census of Population and Housing Data Paper Listing (CPH-L-10 and CPH-L-118); 1990 Census of Population and Housing, Supplementary Reports, Metropolitan Areas as Defined by the Office of Management and Budget, June 30, 1993, (1990 CPH-S-1-1); and Population Paper Listing (PPL-60 and PPL-83).

Table D. New England County Metropolitan Areas (NECMAs)

[In thousands. As of April]

NECMA	Population, 2000	NECMA	Population, 2000	NECMA	Population, 2000
Bangor, ME	145	Burlington, VT	199	New London-Norwich, CT	259
Penobscot County	145	Chittenden County	147	New London County	259
Barnstable-Yarmouth, MA	222	Franklin County	45	Pittsfield, MA	135
Barnstable County	222	Grand Isle County	7	Berkshire County	135
Boston-Worcester-Lawrence-		Hartford, CT	1,149	Portland, ME	266
Lowell-Brockton, MA-NH	6,058	Hartford County	857	Cumberland County	266
Bristol County, MA	535	Middlesex County	155	Providence-Warwick-	
Essex County, MA	723	Tolland County	136	Pawtucket, RI	963
Middlesex County, MA	1,465	Lewiston-Auburn, ME	104	Bristol County	51
Norfolk County, MA	650	Androscoggin County	104	Kent County	167
Plymouth County, MA	473			Providence County	622
Suffolk County, MA	690	New Haven-Bridgeport-		Washington County	124
Worcester County, MA	751	Stamford-Waterbury-		Springfield, MA	608
Hillsborough County, NH	381	Danbury, CT	1,707	Hampden County	456
Rockingham County, NH	277	Fairfield County	883	Hampshire County	152
Strafford County, NH	112	New Haven County	824		

Source: U.S. Census Bureau, "Census 2000 PHC-T-4. Ranking Tables for Counties: 1990 and 2000; Table 1. Counties in Alphabetic Sort Within State, 1990 and 2000 Population, Numeric and Percent Change: 1990 to 2000"; published 2 April 2001; <http://www.census.gov/population/cen2000/phc-t4/tab01.pdf>.

[Population as of April 2000. All metropolitan areas are arranged alphabetically. PMSAs are included under their respective CMSAs, see CMSA entry]

	Popu-lation, 2000 (1,000)
Abilene, TX MSA	127
Taylor County	127
Albany, GA MSA	121
Dougherty County	96
Lee County	25
Albany-Schenectady-Troy, NY MSA	876
Albany County	295
Montgomery County	50
Rensselaer County	153
Saratoga County	201
Schenectady County	147
Schoharie County	32
Albuquerque, NM MSA	713
Bernalillo County	557
Sandoval County	90
Valencia County	66
Alexandria, LA MSA	126
Rapides Parish	126
Allentown-Bethlehem-Easton, PA MSA	638
Carbon County	59
Lehigh County	312
Northampton County	267
Altoona, PA MSA	129
Blair County	129
Amarillo, TX MSA	218
Potter County	114
Randall County	104
Anchorage, AK MSA	260
Anchorage Borough	260
Anniston, AL MSA	112
Calhoun County	112
Appleton-Oshkosh-Neenah, WI MSA	358
Calumet County	41
Outagamie County	161
Winnebago County	157
Asheville, NC MSA	226
Buncombe County	206
Madison County	20
Athens, GA MSA	153
Clarke County	101
Madison County	26
Oconee County	26
Atlanta, GA MSA	4,112
Barrow County	46
Bartow County	76
Carroll County	87
Cherokee County	142
Clayton County	237
Cobb County	608
Coweta County	89
DeKalb County	666
Douglas County	92
Fayette County	91
Forsyth County	98
Fulton County	816
Gwinnett County	588
Henry County	119
Newton County	62
Paulding County	82
Pickens County	23
Rockdale County	70
Spalding County	58
Walton County	61

	Popu-lation, 2000 (1,000)
Auburn-Opelika, AL	115
Lee County	115
Augusta-Aiken, GA-SC MSA	477
Columbia County, GA	89
McDuffie County, GA	21
Richmond County, GA	200
Aiken County, SC	143
Edgefield County, SC	25
Austin-San Marcos, TX MSA	1,250
Bastrop County	58
Caldwell County	32
Hays County	98
Travis County	812
Williamson County	250
Bakersfield, CA MSA	662
Kern County	662
Bangor, ME MSA	91
Penobscot County (pt.)	87
Waldo County (pt.)	4
Barnstable-Yarmouth, MA MSA	163
Barnstable County (pt.)	163
Baton Rouge, LA MSA	603
Ascension Parish	77
East Baton Rouge Parish	413
Livingston Parish	92
West Baton Rouge Parish	22
Beaumont-Port Arthur, TX MSA	385
Hardin County	48
Jefferson County	252
Orange County	85
Bellingham, WA MSA	167
Whatcom County	167
Benton Harbor, MI MSA	162
Berrien County	162
Billings, MT MSA	129
Yellowstone County	129
Biloxi-Gulfport-Pascagoula, MS MSA	364
Hancock County	43
Harrison County	190
Jackson County	131
Binghamton, NY MSA	252
Broome County	201
Tioga County	52
Birmingham, AL MSA	921
Blount County	51
Jefferson County	662
St. Clair County	65
Shelby County	143
Bismarck, ND MSA	95
Burleigh County	69
Morton County	25
Bloomington, IN MSA	121
Monroe County	121
Bloomington-Normal, IL MSA	150
McLean County	150
Boise City, ID MSA	432
Ada County	301
Canyon County	131

	Popu-lation, 2000 (1,000)
Boston-Worcester-Lawrence, MA-NH-ME-CT CMSA	5,819
Boston, MA-NH PMSA	3,407
Bristol County, MA (pt.)	108
Essex County, MA (pt.)	459
Middlesex County, MA (pt.)	1,172
Norfolk County, MA (pt.)	646
Plymouth County, MA (pt.)	240
Suffolk County, MA	690
Worcester County, MA (pt.)	84
Rockingham County, NH (pt.)	9
Brockton, MA PMSA	255
Bristol County, MA (pt.)	34
Norfolk County, MA (pt.)	4
Plymouth County, MA (pt.)	217
Fitchburg-Leominster, MA PMSA	142
Middlesex County, MA (pt.)	3
Worcester County, MA (pt.)	139
Lawrence, MA-NH PMSA	396
Essex County, MA (pt.)	265
Rockingham County, NH (pt.)	131
Lowell, MA-NH PMSA	302
Middlesex County, MA (pt.)	291
Hillsborough County, NH (pt.)	11
Manchester, NH PMSA	198
Hillsborough County, NH (pt.)	150
Merrimack County, NH (pt.)	17
Rockingham County, NH (pt.)	32
Nashua, NH PMSA	191
Hillsborough County, NH (pt.)	191
New Bedford, MA PMSA	175
Bristol County, MA (pt.)	159
Plymouth County, MA (pt.)	16
Portsmouth-Rochester, NH-ME PMSA	241
York County, ME (pt.)	41
Rockingham County, NH (pt.)	94
Strafford County, NH (pt.)	105
Worcester, MA-CT PMSA	511
Windham County, CT (pt.)	9
Hampden County, MA (pt.)	2
Worcester County, MA (pt.)	500
Brownsville-Harlingen, TX MSA	335
Cameron County	335
Bryan-College Station, TX MSA	152
Brazos County	152
Buffalo-Niagara Falls, NY MSA	1,170
Erie County	950
Niagara County	220

	Popu-lation, 2000 (1,000)
Burlington, VT MSA	169
Chittenden County (pt.)	139
Franklin County (pt.)	27
Grand Isle County (pt.) . . .	4
Canton-Massillon, OH MSA .	407
Carroll County	29
Stark County	378
Casper, WY MSA	67
Natrona County	67
Cedar Rapids, IA MSA	192
Linn County	192
Champaign-Urbana, IL MSA	180
Champaign County	180
Charleston-North Charleston, SC MSA	549
Berkeley County	143
Charleston County	310
Dorchester County	96
Charleston, WV MSA	252
Kanawha County	200
Putnam County	52
Charlotte-Gastonia-Rock Hill, NC-SC MSA	1,499
Cabarrus County, NC	131
Gaston County, NC	190
Lincoln County, NC	64
Mecklenburg County, NC . . .	695
Rowan County, NC	130
Union County, NC	124
York County, SC	165
Charlottesville, VA MSA . . .	160
Albemarle County	79
Fluvanna County	20
Greene County	15
Charlottesville city	45
Chattanooga, TN-GA MSA . .	465
Hamilton County, TN	308
Marion County, TN	28
Catoosa County, GA	53
Dade County, GA	15
Walker County, GA	61
Cheyenne, WY MSA	82
Laramie County	82
Chicago-Gary-Kenosha, IL-IN-WI CMSA	9,158
Chicago, IL PMSA	8,273
Cook County, IL	5,377
DeKalb County, IL	89
DuPage County, IL	904
Grundy County, IL	38
Kane County, IL	404
Kendall County, IL	55
Lake County, IL	644
McHenry County, IL	260
Will County, IL	502
Gary, IN PMSA	631
Lake County, IN	485
Porter County, IN	147
Kankakee, IL PMSA	104
Kankakee County, IL	104
Kenosha, WI PMSA	150
Kenosha County, WI	150
Chico-Paradise, CA MSA . . .	203
Butte County	203
Cincinnati-Hamilton, OH-KY-IN CMSA	1,979
Cincinnati, OH-KY-IN PMSA	1,646
Brown County, OH.	42
Clermont County, OH. . . .	178
Hamilton County, OH . . .	845
Warren County, OH	158

	Popu-lation, 2000 (1,000)
Boone County, KY	86
Campbell County, KY . . .	89
Gallatin County, KY	8
Grant County, KY	22
Kenton County, KY	151
Pendleton County, KY . . .	14
Dearborn County, IN . . .	46
Ohio County, IN.	6
Hamilton-Middletown, OH PMSA	333
Butler County, OH	333
Clarksville-Hopkinsville, TN-KY MSA	207
Montgomery County, TN . .	135
Christian County, KY	72
Cleveland-Akron, OH CMSA	2,946
Akron, OH PMSA	695
Portage County	152
Summit County	543
Cleveland-Lorain-Elyria, OH PMSA	2,251
Ashtabula County	103
Cuyahoga County	1,394
Geauga County	91
Lake County	228
Lorain County	285
Medina County	151
Colorado Springs, CO MSA	517
El Paso County.	517
Columbia, MO MSA	135
Boone County	135
Columbia, SC MSA	537
Lexington County	216
Richland County	321
Columbus, GA-AL MSA	275
Chattahoochee County, GA	15
Harris County, GA	24
Muscogee County, GA. . . .	186
Russell County, AL	50
Columbus, OH MSA	1,540
Delaware County	110
Fairfield County	123
Franklin County	1,069
Licking County	145
Madison County	40
Pickaway County	53
Corpus Christi, TX MSA	381
Nueces County.	314
San Patricio County	67
Corvallis, OR MSA	78
Benton County	78
Cumberland, MD-WV MSA	102
Allegany County, MD.	75
Mineral County, WV.	27
Dallas-Fort Worth, TX CMSA	5,222
Dallas, TX PMSA	3,519
Collin County	492
Dallas County	2,219
Denton County	433
Ellis County	111
Henderson County.	73
Hunt County	77
Kaufman County	71
Rockwall County	43
Fort Worth-Arlington, TX PMSA	1,703
Hood County.	41
Johnson County	127
Parker County.	88
Tarrant County	1,446

	Popu-lation, 2000 (1,000)
Danville, VA MSA	110
Pittsylvania County	62
Danville city	48
Davenport-Moline-Rock Island, IA-IL MSA . . .	359
Scott County, IA	159
Henry County, IL.	51
Rock Island County, IL. . . .	149
Dayton-Springfield, OH MSA	951
Clark County	145
Greene County	148
Miami County	99
Montgomery County	559
Daytona Beach, FL MSA . . .	493
Flagler County	50
Volusia County	443
Decatur, AL MSA	146
Lawrence County	35
Morgan County.	111
Decatur, IL MSA	115
Macon County	115
Denver-Boulder-Greeley, CO CMSA	2,582
Boulder-Longmont, CO PMSA	291
Boulder County	291
Denver, CO PMSA	2,109
Adams County	364
Arapahoe County	488
Denver County	555
Douglas County.	176
Jefferson County	527
Greeley, CO PMSA	181
Weld County	181
Des Moines, IA MSA	456
Dallas County.	41
Polk County	375
Warren County	41
Detroit-Ann Arbor-Flint, MI CMSA	5,456
Ann Arbor, MI PMSA	579
Lenawee County	99
Livingston County	157
Washtenaw County	323
Detroit, MI PMSA	4,442
Lapeer County	88
Macomb County	788
Monroe County	146
Oakland County	1,194
St. Clair County.	164
Wayne County	2,061
Flint, MI PMSA	436
Genesee County	436
Dothan, AL MSA	138
Dale County.	49
Houston County	89
Dover, DE MSA	127
Kent County	127
Dubuque, IA MSA	89
Dubuque County.	89
Duluth, MN-WI MSA	244
St. Louis County, MN. . . .	201
Douglas County, WI.	43
Eau Claire, WI MSA	148
Chippewa County	55
Eau Claire County.	93
El Paso, TX MSA	680
El Paso County.	680
Elkhart-Goshen, IN MSA . . .	183
Elkhart County	183

U.S. Census Bureau, Statistical Abstract of the United States: 2001

Area	Population, 2000 (1,000)
Elmira, NY MSA	91
Chemung County	91
Enid, OK MSA	58
Garfield County	58
Erie, PA MSA	281
Erie County	281
Eugene-Springfield, OR MSA	323
Lane County	323
Evansville-Henderson, IN-KY MSA	296
Posey County, IN	27
Vanderburgh County, IN	172
Warrick County, IN	52
Henderson County, KY	45
Fargo-Moorhead, ND-MN MSA	174
Cass County, ND	123
Clay County, MN	51
Fayetteville, NC MSA	303
Cumberland County	303
Fayetteville-Springdale-Rogers, AR MSA	311
Benton County	153
Washington County	158
Flagstaff, AZ-UT MSA	122
Coconino County, AZ	116
Kane County, UT	6
Florence, AL MSA	143
Colbert County	55
Lauderdale County	88
Florence, SC MSA	126
Florence County	126
Fort Collins-Loveland, CO MSA	251
Larimer County	251
Fort Myers-Cape Coral, FL MSA	441
Lee County	441
Fort Pierce-Port St. Lucie, FL MSA	319
Martin County	127
St. Lucie County	193
Fort Smith, AR-OK MSA	207
Crawford County, AR	53
Sebastian County, AR	115
Sequoyah County, OK	39
Fort Walton Beach, FL MSA	170
Okaloosa County	170
Fort Wayne, IN MSA	502
Adams County	34
Allen County	332
De Kalb County	40
Huntington County	38
Wells County	28
Whitley County	31
Fresno, CA MSA	923
Fresno County	799
Madera County	123
Gadsden, AL MSA	103
Etowah County	103
Gainesville, FL MSA	218
Alachua County	218
Glens Falls, NY MSA	124
Warren County	63
Washington County	61
Goldsboro, NC MSA	113
Wayne County	113
Grand Forks, ND-MN MSA	97
Grand Forks County, ND	66
Polk County, MN	31
Grand Junction, CO MSA	116
Mesa County	116
Grand Rapids-Muskegon-Holland, MI MSA	1,089
Allegan County	106
Kent County	574
Muskegon County	170
Ottawa County	238
Great Falls, MT MSA	80
Cascade County	80
Green Bay, WI MSA	227
Brown County	227
Greensboro—Winston-Salem—High Point, NC MSA	1,252
Alamance County	131
Davidson County	147
Davie County	35
Forsyth County	306
Guilford County	421
Randolph County	130
Stokes County	45
Yadkin County	36
Greenville, NC MSA	134
Pitt County	134
Greenville-Spartanburg-Anderson, SC MSA	962
Anderson County	166
Cherokee County	53
Greenville County	380
Pickens County	111
Spartanburg County	254
Harrisburg-Lebanon-Carlisle, PA MSA	629
Cumberland County	214
Dauphin County	252
Lebanon County	120
Perry County	44
Hartford, CT MSA	1,183
Hartford County (pt.)	855
Litchfield County (pt.)	37
Middlesex County (pt.)	104
New London County (pt.)	21
Tolland County (pt.)	136
Windham County (pt.)	29
Hattiesburg, MS MSA	112
Forrest County	73
Lamar County	39
Hickory-Morganton, NC MSA	342
Alexander County	34
Burke County	89
Caldwell County	77
Catawba County	142
Honolulu, HI MSA	876
Honolulu County	876
Houma, LA MSA	194
Lafourche Parish	90
Terrebonne Parish	105
Houston-Galveston-Brazoria, TX CMSA	4,670
Brazoria, TX PMSA	242
Brazoria County	242
Galveston-Texas City, TX PMSA	250
Galveston County	250
Houston, TX PMSA	4,178
Chambers County	26
Fort Bend County	354
Harris County	3,401
Liberty County	70
Montgomery County	294
Waller County	33
Huntington-Ashland, WV-KY-OH MSA	316
Cabell County, WV	97
Wayne County, WV	43
Boyd County, KY	50
Carter County, KY	27
Greenup County, KY	37
Lawrence County, OH	62
Huntsville, AL MSA	342
Limestone County	66
Madison County	277
Indianapolis, IN MSA	1,607
Boone County	46
Hamilton County	183
Hancock County	55
Hendricks County	104
Johnson County	115
Madison County	133
Marion County	860
Morgan County	67
Shelby County	43
Iowa City, IA MSA	111
Johnson County	111
Jackson, MI MSA	158
Jackson County	158
Jackson, MS MSA	441
Hinds County	251
Madison County	75
Rankin County	115
Jackson, TN MSA	107
Chester County	16
Madison County	92
Jacksonville, FL MSA	1,100
Clay County	141
Duval County	779
Nassau County	58
St. Johns County	123
Jacksonville, NC MSA	150
Onslow County	150
Jamestown, NY MSA	140
Chautauqua County	140
Janesville-Beloit, WI MSA	152
Rock County	152
Johnson City-Kingsport-Bristol, TN-VA MSA	480
Carter County, TN	57
Hawkins County, TN	54
Sullivan County, TN	153
Unicoi County, TN	18
Washington County, TN	107
Scott County, VA	23
Washington County, VA	51
Bristol city, VA	17
Johnstown, PA MSA	233
Cambria County	153
Somerset County	80
Jonesboro, AR MSA	82
Craighead County	82
Joplin, MO MSA	157
Jasper County	105
Newton County	53
Kalamazoo-Battle Creek, MI MSA	453

	Population, 2000 (1,000)
Calhoun County	138
Kalamazoo County	239
Van Buren County	76
Kansas City, MO-KS MSA	**1,776**
Cass County, MO	82
Clay County, MO	184
Clinton County, MO	19
Jackson County, MO	655
Lafayette County, MO	33
Platte County, MO	74
Ray County, MO	23
Johnson County, KS	451
Leavenworth County, KS	69
Miami County, KS	28
Wyandotte County, KS	158
Killeen-Temple, TX MSA	**313**
Bell County	238
Coryell County	75
Knoxville, TN MSA	**687**
Anderson County	71
Blount County	106
Knox County	382
Loudon County	39
Sevier County	71
Union County	18
Kokomo, IN MSA	**102**
Howard County	85
Tipton County	17
La Crosse, WI-MN MSA	**127**
La Crosse County, WI	107
Houston County, MN	20
Lafayette, LA MSA	**386**
Acadia Parish	59
Lafayette Parish	191
St. Landry Parish	88
St. Martin Parish	49
Lafayette, IN MSA	**183**
Clinton County	34
Tippecanoe County	149
Lake Charles, LA MSA	**184**
Calcasieu Parish	184
Lakeland-Winter Haven, FL MSA	**484**
Polk County	484
Lancaster, PA MSA	**471**
Lancaster County	471
Lansing-East Lansing, MI MSA	**448**
Clinton County	65
Eaton County	104
Ingham County	279
Laredo, TX MSA	**193**
Webb County	193
Las Cruces, NM MSA	**175**
Dona Ana County	175
Las Vegas, NV-AZ MSA	**1,563**
Clark County, NV	1,376
Nye County, NV	32
Mohave County, AZ	155
Lawrence, KS MSA	**100**
Douglas County	100
Lawton, OK MSA	**115**
Comanche County	115
Lewiston-Auburn, ME MSA	**91**
Androscoggin County (pt.)	91
Lexington, KY MSA	**479**
Bourbon County	19
Clark County	33

	Population, 2000 (1,000)
Fayette County	261
Jessamine County	39
Madison County	71
Scott County	33
Woodford County	23
Lima, OH MSA	**155**
Allen County	108
Auglaize County	47
Lincoln, NE MSA	**250**
Lancaster County	250
Little Rock-North Little Rock, AR MSA	**584**
Faulkner County	86
Lonoke County	53
Pulaski County	361
Saline County	84
Longview-Marshall, TX MSA	**209**
Gregg County	111
Harrison County	62
Upshur County	35
Los Angeles-Riverside-Orange County, CA CMSA	**16,374**
Los Angeles-Long Beach, CA PMSA	**9,519**
Los Angeles County	9,519
Orange County, CA PMSA	**2,846**
Orange County	2,846
Riverside-San Bernardino, CA PMSA	**3,255**
Riverside County	1,545
San Bernardino County	1,709
Ventura, CA PMSA	**753**
Ventura County	753
Louisville, KY-IN MSA	**1,026**
Bullitt County, KY	61
Jefferson County, KY	694
Oldham County, KY	46
Clark County, IN	96
Floyd County, IN	71
Harrison County, IN	34
Scott County, IN	23
Lubbock, TX MSA	**243**
Lubbock County	243
Lynchburg, VA MSA	**215**
Amherst County	32
Bedford County	60
Campbell County	51
Bedford city	6
Lynchburg city	65
Macon, GA MSA	**323**
Bibb County	154
Houston County	111
Jones County	24
Peach County	24
Twiggs County	11
Madison, WI MSA	**427**
Dane County	427
Mansfield, OH MSA	**176**
Crawford County	47
Richland County	129
McAllen-Edinburg-Mission, TX MSA	**569**
Hidalgo County	569
Medford-Ashland, OR MSA	**181**
Jackson County	181
Melbourne-Titusville-Palm Bay, FL MSA	**476**
Brevard County	476

	Population, 2000 (1,000)
Memphis, TN-AR-MS MSA	**1,136**
Fayette County, TN	29
Shelby County, TN	897
Tipton County, TN	51
Crittenden County, AR	51
DeSoto County, MS	107
Merced, CA MSA	**211**
Merced County	211
Miami-Fort Lauderdale, FL CMSA	**3,876**
Fort Lauderdale, FL PMSA	**1,623**
Broward County	1,623
Miami, FL PMSA	**2,253**
Miami-Dade County	2,253
Milwaukee-Racine, WI CMSA	**1,690**
Milwaukee-Waukesha, WI PMSA	**1,501**
Milwaukee County	940
Ozaukee County	82
Washington County	117
Waukesha County	361
Racine, WI PMSA	**189**
Racine County	189
Minneapolis-St. Paul, MN-WI MSA	**2,969**
Anoka County, MN	298
Carver County, MN	70
Chisago County, MN	41
Dakota County, MN	356
Hennepin County, MN	1,116
Isanti County, MN	31
Ramsey County, MN	511
Scott County, MN	89
Sherburne County, MN	64
Washington County, MN	201
Wright County, MN	90
Pierce County, WI	37
St. Croix County, WI	63
Missoula, MT MSA	**96**
Missoula County	96
Mobile, AL MSA	**540**
Baldwin County	140
Mobile County	400
Modesto, CA MSA	**447**
Stanislaus County	447
Monroe, LA MSA	**147**
Ouachita Parish	147
Montgomery, AL MSA	**333**
Autauga County	44
Elmore County	66
Montgomery County	224
Muncie, IN MSA	**119**
Delaware County	119
Myrtle Beach, SC MSA	**197**
Horry County	197
Naples, FL MSA	**251**
Collier County	251
Nashville, TN MSA	**1,231**
Cheatham County	36
Davidson County	570
Dickson County	43
Robertson County	54
Rutherford County	182
Sumner County	130
Williamson County	127
Wilson County	89
New London-Norwich, CT-RI MSA	**294**
Middlesex County, CT (pt.)	10

U.S. Census Bureau, Statistical Abstract of the United States: 2001

	Population, 2000 (1,000)
New London County, CT (pt.)	233
Windham County, CT (pt.)	19
Washington County, RI (pt.)	31
New Orleans, LA MSA	**1,338**
Jefferson Parish	455
Orleans Parish	485
Plaquemines Parish	27
St. Bernard Parish	67
St. Charles Parish	48
St. James Parish	21
St. John the Baptist Parish	43
St. Tammany Parish	191
New York-Northern New Jersey-Long Island, NY-NJ-CT-PA CMSA	**21,200**
Bergen-Passaic, NJ PMSA	**1,373**
Bergen County, NJ	884
Passaic County, NJ	489
Bridgeport, CT PMSA	**459**
Fairfield County, CT (pt.)	346
New Haven County, CT (pt.)	114
Danbury, CT PMSA	**218**
Fairfield County, CT (pt.)	183
Litchfield County, CT (pt.)	35
Dutchess County, NY PMSA	**280**
Dutchess County, NY	280
Jersey City, NJ PMSA	**609**
Hudson County, NJ	609
Middlesex-Somerset-Hunterdon, NJ PMSA	**1,170**
Hunterdon County, NJ	122
Middlesex County, NJ	750
Somerset County, NJ	297
Monmouth-Ocean, NJ PMSA	**1,126**
Monmouth County, NJ	615
Ocean County, NJ	511
Nassau-Suffolk, NY PMSA	**2,754**
Nassau County, NY	1,335
Suffolk County, NY	1,419
New Haven-Meriden, CT PMSA	**542**
Middlesex County, CT (pt.)	19
New Haven County, CT (pt.)	523
New York, NY PMSA	**9,314**
Bronx County, NY	1,333
Kings County, NY	2,465
New York County, NY	1,537
Putnam County, NY	96
Queens County, NY	2,229
Richmond County, NY	444
Rockland County, NY	287
Westchester County, NY	923
Newark, NJ PMSA	**2,033**
Essex County, NJ	794
Morris County, NJ	470
Sussex County, NJ	144
Union County, NJ	523
Warren County, NJ	102
Newburgh, NY-PA PMSA	**388**
Orange County, NY	341
Pike County, PA	46
Stamford-Norwalk, CT PMSA	**354**
Fairfield County, CT (pt.)	354
Trenton, NJ PMSA	**351**
Mercer County, NJ	351
Waterbury, CT PMSA	**229**
Litchfield County, CT (pt.)	42

	Population, 2000 (1,000)
New Haven County, CT (pt.)	187
Norfolk-Virginia Beach-Newport News, VA-NC MSA	**1,570**
Gloucester County, VA	35
Isle of Wight County, VA	30
James City County, VA	48
Mathews County, VA	9
York County, VA	56
Chesapeake city, VA	199
Hampton city, VA	146
Newport News city, VA	180
Norfolk city, VA	234
Poquoson city, VA	12
Portsmouth city, VA	101
Suffolk city, VA	64
Virginia Beach city, VA	425
Williamsburg city, VA	12
Currituck County, NC	18
Ocala, FL MSA	**259**
Marion County	259
Odessa-Midland, TX MSA	**237**
Ector County	121
Midland County	116
Oklahoma City, OK MSA	**1,083**
Canadian County	88
Cleveland County	208
Logan County	34
McClain County	28
Oklahoma County	660
Pottawatomie County	66
Omaha, NE-IA MSA	**717**
Cass County, NE	24
Douglas County, NE	464
Sarpy County, NE	123
Washington County, NE	19
Pottawattamie County, IA	88
Orlando, FL MSA	**1,645**
Lake County	211
Orange County	896
Osceola County	172
Seminole County	365
Owensboro, KY MSA	**92**
Daviess County	92
Panama City, FL MSA	**148**
Bay County	148
Parkersburg-Marietta, WV-OH MSA	**151**
Wood County, WV	88
Washington County, OH	63
Pensacola, FL MSA	**412**
Escambia County	294
Santa Rosa County	118
Peoria-Pekin, IL MSA	**347**
Peoria County	183
Tazewell County	128
Woodford County	35
Philadelphia-Wilmington-Atlantic City, PA-NJ-DE-MD CMSA	**6,188**
Atlantic-Cape May, NJ PMSA	**355**
Atlantic County, NJ	253
Cape May County, NJ	102
Philadelphia, PA-NJ PMSA	**5,101**
Bucks County, PA	598
Chester County, PA	434
Delaware County, PA	551
Montgomery County, PA	750
Philadelphia County, PA	1,518
Burlington County, NJ	423
Camden County, NJ	509
Gloucester County, NJ	255

	Population, 2000 (1,000)
Salem County, NJ	64
Vineland-Millville-Bridgeton, NJ PMSA	**146**
Cumberland County, NJ	146
Wilmington-Newark, DE-MD PMSA	**586**
New Castle County, DE	500
Cecil County, MD	86
Phoenix-Mesa, AZ MSA	**3,252**
Maricopa County	3,072
Pinal County	180
Pine Bluff, AR MSA	**84**
Jefferson County	84
Pittsburgh, PA MSA	**2,359**
Allegheny County	1,282
Beaver County	181
Butler County	174
Fayette County	149
Washington County	203
Westmoreland County	370
Pittsfield, MA MSA	**85**
Berkshire County (pt.)	85
Pocatello, ID MSA	**76**
Bannock County	76
Portland, ME MSA	**244**
Cumberland County (pt.)	220
York County (pt.)	24
Portland-Salem, OR-WA CMSA	**2,265**
Portland-Vancouver, OR-WA PMSA	**1,918**
Clackamas County, OR	338
Columbia County, OR	44
Multnomah County, OR	660
Washington County, OR	445
Yamhill County, OR	85
Clark County, WA	345
Salem, OR PMSA	**347**
Marion County, OR	285
Polk County, OR	62
Providence-Fall River-Warwick, RI-MA MSA	**1,189**
Bristol County, MA (pt.)	233
Bristol County, RI	51
Kent County, RI	167
Newport County, RI (pt.)	24
Providence County, RI	622
Washington County, RI (pt.)	92
Provo-Orem, UT MSA	**369**
Utah County	369
Pueblo, CO MSA	**141**
Pueblo County	141
Punta Gorda, FL MSA	**142**
Charlotte County	142
Raleigh-Durham-Chapel Hill, NC MSA	**1,188**
Chatham County	49
Durham County	223
Franklin County	47
Johnston County	122
Orange County	118
Wake County	628
Rapid City, SD MSA	**89**
Pennington County	89
Reading, PA MSA	**374**
Berks County	374
Redding, CA MSA	**163**
Shasta County	163

U.S. Census Bureau, Statistical Abstract of the United States: 2001

Area	Population, 2000 (1,000)
Reno, NV MSA	339
Washoe County	339
Richland-Kennewick-Pasco, WA MSA	192
Benton County	142
Franklin County	49
Richmond-Petersburg, VA MSA	997
Charles City County	7
Chesterfield County	260
Dinwiddie County	25
Goochland County	17
Hanover County	86
Henrico County	262
New Kent County	13
Powhatan County	22
Prince George County	33
Colonial Heights city	17
Hopewell city	22
Petersburg city	34
Richmond city	198
Roanoke, VA MSA	235
Botetourt County	30
Roanoke County	86
Roanoke city	95
Salem city	25
Rochester, MN MSA	124
Olmsted County	124
Rochester, NY MSA	1,098
Genesee County	60
Livingston County	64
Monroe County	735
Ontario County	100
Orleans County	44
Wayne County	94
Rockford, IL MSA	371
Boone County	42
Ogle County	51
Winnebago County	278
Rocky Mount, NC MSA	143
Edgecombe County	56
Nash County	87
Sacramento-Yolo, CA CMSA	1,797
Sacramento, CA PMSA	1,628
El Dorado County	156
Placer County	248
Sacramento County	1,223
Yolo, CA PMSA	169
Yolo County	169
Saginaw-Bay City-Midland, MI MSA	403
Bay County	110
Midland County	83
Saginaw County	210
St. Cloud, MN MSA	167
Benton County	34
Stearns County	133
St. Joseph, MO MSA	102
Andrew County	16
Buchanan County	86
St. Louis, MO-IL MSA	2,604
Franklin County, MO	94
Jefferson County, MO	198
Lincoln County, MO	39
St. Charles County, MO	284
St. Louis County, MO	1,016
Warren County, MO	25
St. Louis city, MO	348
Clinton County, IL	36
Jersey County, IL	22
Madison County, IL	259
Monroe County, IL	28
St. Clair County, IL	256
Salinas, CA MSA	402
Monterey County	402
Salt Lake City-Ogden, UT MSA	1,334
Davis County	239
Salt Lake County	898
Weber County	197
San Angelo, TX MSA	104
Tom Green County	104
San Antonio, TX MSA	1,592
Bexar County	1,393
Comal County	78
Guadalupe County	89
Wilson County	32
San Diego, CA MSA	2,814
San Diego County	2,814
San Francisco-Oakland-San Jose, CA CMSA	7,039
Oakland, CA PMSA	2,393
Alameda County	1,444
Contra Costa County	949
San Francisco, CA PMSA	1,731
Marin County	247
San Francisco County	777
San Mateo County	707
San Jose, CA PMSA	1,683
Santa Clara County	1,683
Santa Cruz-Watsonville, CA PMSA	256
Santa Cruz County	256
Santa Rosa, CA PMSA	459
Sonoma County	459
Vallejo-Fairfield-Napa, CA PMSA	519
Napa County	124
Solano County	395
San Luis Obispo-Atascadero-Paso Robles, CA MSA	247
San Luis Obispo County	247
Santa Barbara-Santa Maria-Lompoc, CA MSA	399
Santa Barbara County	399
Santa Fe, NM MSA	148
Los Alamos County	18
Santa Fe County	129
Sarasota-Bradenton, FL MSA	590
Manatee County	264
Sarasota County	326
Savannah, GA MSA	293
Bryan County	23
Chatham County	232
Effingham County	38
Scranton-Wilkes-Barre-Hazleton, PA MSA	625
Columbia County	64
Lackawanna County	213
Luzerne County	319
Wyoming County	28
Seattle-Tacoma-Bremerton, WA CMSA	3,555
Bremerton, WA PMSA	232
Kitsap County	232
Olympia, WA PMSA	207
Thurston County	207
Seattle-Bellevue-Everett, WA PMSA	2,415
Island County	72
King County	1,737
Snohomish County	606
Tacoma, WA PMSA	701
Pierce County	701
Sharon, PA MSA	120
Mercer County	120
Sheboygan, WI MSA	113
Sheboygan County	113
Sherman-Denison, TX MSA	111
Grayson County	111
Shreveport-Bossier City, LA MSA	392
Bossier Parish	98
Caddo Parish	252
Webster Parish	42
Sioux City, IA-NE MSA	124
Woodbury County, IA	104
Dakota County, NE	20
Sioux Falls, SD MSA	172
Lincoln County	24
Minnehaha County	148
South Bend, IN MSA	266
St. Joseph County	266
Spokane, WA MSA	418
Spokane County	418
Springfield, IL MSA	201
Menard County	12
Sangamon County	189
Springfield, MO MSA	326
Christian County	54
Greene County	240
Webster County	31
Springfield, MA MSA	592
Franklin County (pt.)	4
Hampden County (pt.)	444
Hampshire County (pt.)	144
State College, PA MSA	136
Centre County	136
Steubenville-Weirton, OH-WV MSA	132
Jefferson County, OH	74
Brooke County, WV	25
Hancock County, WV	33
Stockton-Lodi, CA MSA	564
San Joaquin County	564
Sumter, SC MSA	105
Sumter County	105
Syracuse, NY MSA	732
Cayuga County	82
Madison County	69
Onondaga County	458
Oswego County	122
Tallahassee, FL MSA	285
Gadsden County	45
Leon County	239
Tampa-St. Petersburg-Clearwater, FL MSA	2,396
Hernando County	131
Hillsborough County	999
Pasco County	345
Pinellas County	921
Terre Haute, IN MSA	149
Clay County	27
Vermillion County	17
Vigo County	106
Texarkana, TX-Texarkana, AR MSA	130
Bowie County, TX	89
Miller County, AR	40

U.S. Census Bureau, Statistical Abstract of the United States: 2001

Area	Population, 2000 (1,000)	Area	Population, 2000 (1,000)	Area	Population, 2000 (1,000)
Toledo, OH MSA	618	Harford County, MD	219	**Wausau, WI MSA**	126
Fulton County	42	Howard County, MD	248	Marathon County	126
Lucas County	455	Queen Anne's County, MD	41	**West Palm Beach-Boca**	
Wood County	121	Baltimore city, MD	651	**Raton, FL MSA**	1,131
Topeka, KS MSA	170	**Hagerstown, MD PMSA**	132	Palm Beach County	1,131
Shawnee County	170	Washington County, MD	132	**Wheeling, WV-OH MSA**	153
Tucson, AZ MSA	844	**Washington, DC-MD-VA-WV PMSA**	4,923	Marshall County, WV	36
Pima County	844	District of Columbia, DC	572	Ohio County, WV	47
Tulsa, OK MSA	803	Calvert County, MD	75	Belmont County, OH	70
Creek County	67	Charles County, MD	121	**Wichita, KS MSA**	545
Osage County	44	Frederick County, MD	195	Butler County	59
Rogers County	71	Montgomery County, MD	873	Harvey County	33
Tulsa County	563	Prince George's County, MD	802	Sedgwick County	453
Wagoner County	57	Arlington County, VA	189	**Wichita Falls, TX MSA**	141
Tuscaloosa, AL MSA	165	Clarke County, VA	13	Archer County	9
Tuscaloosa County	165	Culpeper County, VA	34	Wichita County	132
Tyler, TX MSA	175	Fairfax County, VA	970	**Williamsport, PA MSA**	120
Smith County	175	Fauquier County, VA	55	Lycoming County	120
Utica-Rome, NY MSA	300	King George County, VA	17	**Wilmington, NC MSA**	233
Herkimer County	64	Loudoun County, VA	170	Brunswick County	73
Oneida County	235	Prince William County, VA	281	New Hanover County	160
Victoria, TX MSA	84	Spotsylvania County, VA	90	**Yakima, WA MSA**	223
Victoria County	84	Stafford County, VA	92	Yakima County	223
Visalia-Tulare-Porterville, CA MSA	368	Warren County, VA	32	**York, PA MSA**	382
Tulare County	368	Alexandria city, VA	128	York County	382
		Fairfax city, VA	21	**Youngstown-Warren, OH MSA**	595
Waco, TX MSA	214	Falls Church city, VA	10	Columbiana County	112
McLennan County	214	Fredericksburg city, VA	19	Mahoning County	258
		Manassas city, VA	35	Trumbull County	225
Washington-Baltimore, DC-MD-VA-WV CMSA	7,608	Manassas Park city, VA	10	**Yuba City, CA MSA**	139
Baltimore, MD PMSA	2,553	Berkeley County, WV	76	Sutter County	79
Anne Arundel County, MD	490	Jefferson County, WV	42	Yuba County	60
Baltimore County, MD	754	**Waterloo-Cedar Falls, IA MSA**	128	**Yuma, AZ MSA**	160
Carroll County, MD	151	Black Hawk County	128	Yuma County	160

Source: U.S. Census Bureau, "Ranking Tables for Metropolitan Areas: 1990 and 2000 (PHC-T-3)"; published: 2 April 2001; <http://www.census.gov/population/www/cen2000/phc-t3.html>.

902   Appendix II

Introduction—The data presented in this *Statistical Abstract* came from many sources. The sources include not only federal statistical bureaus and other organizations that collect and issue statistics as their principal activity, but also governmental administrative and regulatory agencies, private research bodies, trade associations, insurance companies, health associations, and private organizations such as the National Education Association and philanthropic foundations. Consequently, the data vary considerably as to reference periods, definitions of terms and, for ongoing series, the number and frequency of time periods for which data are available.

The statistics presented were obtained and tabulated by various means. Some statistics are based on complete enumerations or censuses while others are based on samples. Some information is extracted from records kept for administrative or regulatory purposes (school enrollment, hospital records, securities registration, financial accounts, social security records, income tax returns, etc.), while other information is obtained explicitly for statistical purposes through interviews or by mail. The estimation procedures used vary from highly sophisticated scientific techniques, to crude "informed guesses."

Each set of data relates to a group of individuals or units of interest referred to as the *target universe* or *target population*, or simply as the *universe* or *population*. Prior to data collection the target universe should be clearly defined. For example, if data are to be collected for the universe of households in the United States, it is necessary to define a "household." The target universe may not be completely tractable. Cost and other considerations may restrict data collection to a *survey universe* based on some available list, such list may be it of date. This list is called a *survey frame* or *sampling frame*.

The data in many tables are based on data obtained for all population units, *a census*, or on data obtained for only a portion, or *sample*, of the population units. When the data presented are based on a sample, the sample is usually a scientifically selected *probability sample*. This is a sample selected from a list or sampling frame in such a way that every possible sample has a known chance of selection and usually each unit selected can be assigned a number, greater than zero and less than or equal to one, representing its likelihood or probability of selection.

For large-scale sample surveys, the probability sample of units is often selected as a multistage sample. The first stage of a multistage sample is the selection of a probability sample of large groups of population members, referred to as primary sampling units (PSUs). For example, in a national multistage household sample, PSUs are often counties or groups of counties. The second stage of a multistage sample is the selection, within each PSU selected at the first stage, of smaller groups of population units, referred to as secondary sampling units. In subsequent stages of selection, smaller and smaller nested groups are chosen until the ultimate sample of population units is obtained. To qualify a multistage sample as a probability sample, all stages of sampling must be carried out using probability sampling methods.

Prior to selection at each stage of a multistage (or a single stage) sample, a list of the sampling units or sampling frame for that stage must be obtained. For example, for the first stage of selection of a national household sample, a list of the counties and county groups that form the PSUs must be obtained. For the final stage of selection, lists of households, and sometimes persons within the households, have to be compiled in the field. For surveys of economic entities and for the economic censuses the Bureau generally uses a frame constructed from the Bureau's Business Register. The Business Register contains all establishments with payroll in the United States including small single establishment firms as well as large multi-establishment firms.

Wherever the quantities in a table refer to an entire universe, but are constructed from data collected in a sample survey, the table quantities are referred to as *sample estimates*. In constructing a sample estimate, an attempt is made to come as close as is feasible to the corresponding universe quantity that would be obtained from a complete census of the universe. Estimates based on a sample will, however, generally differ from the hypothetical census figures. Two classifications of errors are associated with estimates based on sample surveys: (1) *sampling error*—the error arising from the use of a sample, rather than a census, to estimate population quantities and (2) *nonsampling error*—those errors arising from nonsampling sources. As discussed below, the magnitude of the sampling error for an estimate can usually be estimated from the sample data. However, the magnitude of the nonsampling error for an estimate can rarely be estimated. Consequently, actual error in an estimate exceeds the error that can be estimated.

The particular sample used in a survey is only one of a large number of possible samples of the same size which could have been selected using the same sampling procedure. Estimates derived from the different samples would, in general, differ from each other. The *standard error* (SE) is a measure of the variation among the estimates derived from all possible samples. The standard error is the most commonly used measure of the sampling error of an estimate. Valid estimates of the standard errors of survey estimates can usually be calculated from the data collected in a probability sample. For convenience, the standard error is sometimes expressed as a percent of the estimate and is called the relative standard error or *coefficient of variation* (CV). For example, an estimate of 200 units with an estimated standard error of 10 units has an estimated CV of 5 percent.

A sample estimate and an estimate of its standard error or CV can be used to construct interval estimates that have a prescribed confidence that the interval includes the average of the estimates derived from all possible samples with a known probability. To illustrate, if all possible samples were selected under essentially the same general conditions, and using the same sample design, and if an estimate and its estimated standard error were calculated from each sample, then: (1) Approximately 68 percent of the intervals from one standard error below the estimate to one standard error above the estimate would include the average estimate derived from all possible samples; (2) approximately 90 percent of the intervals from 1.6 standard errors below the estimate to 1.6 standard errors above the estimate would include the average estimate derived from all possible samples; and (3) approximately 95 percent of the intervals from two standard errors below the estimate to two standard errors above the estimate would include the average estimate derived from all possible samples.

Thus, for a particular sample, one can say with the appropriate level of confidence (e.g., 90 percent or 95 percent) that the average of all possible samples is included in the constructed interval. Example of a confidence interval: An estimate is 200 units with a standard error of 10 units. An approximately 90 percent confidence interval (plus or minus 1.6 standard errors) is from 184 to 216.

All surveys and censuses are subject to nonsampling errors. Nonsampling errors are of two kinds—*random* and *nonrandom*. Random nonsampling errors arise because of the varying interpretation of questions (by respondents or interviewers) and varying actions of coders, keyers, and other processors. Some randomness is also introduced when respondents must estimate. Nonrandom nonsampling errors result from total nonresponse (no usable data obtained for a sampled unit), partial or item nonresponse (only a portion of a response may be usable), inability or unwillingness on the part of respondents to provide correct information, difficulty interpreting questions, mistakes in recording or keying data, errors of collection or processing, and coverage problems (overcoverage and undercoverage of the target universe). Random nonresponse errors usually, but not always, result in an understatement of sampling errors and thus an overstatement of the precision of survey estimates. Estimating the magnitude of nonsampling errors would require special experiments or access to independent data and, consequently, the magnitudes are seldom available.

Nearly all types of nonsampling errors that affect surveys also occur in complete censuses. Since surveys can be conducted on a smaller scale than censuses, nonsampling errors can presumably be controlled more tightly. Relatively more funds and effort can perhaps be expended toward eliciting responses, detecting and correcting response error, and reducing processing errors. As a result, survey results can sometimes be more accurate than census results.

To compensate for suspected nonrandom errors, adjustments of the sample estimates are often made. For example, adjustments are frequently made for nonresponse, both total and partial. Adjustments made for either type of nonresponse are often referred to as *imputations*. Imputation for total nonresponse is usually made by substituting for the questionnaire responses of the nonrespondents the "average" questionnaire responses of the respondents. These imputations usually are made separately within various groups of sample members, formed by attempting to place respondents and nonrespondents together that have "similar" design or ancillary characteristics. Imputation for item nonresponse is usually made by substituting for a missing item the response to that item of a respondent having characteristics that are "similar" to those of the nonrespondent.

For an estimate calculated from a sample survey, the *total error* in the estimate is composed of the sampling error, which can usually be estimated from the sample, and the nonsampling error, which

usually cannot be estimated from the sample. The total error present in a population quantity obtained from a complete census is composed of only nonsampling errors. Ideally, estimates of the total error associated with data given in the *Statistical Abstract* tables should be given. However, due to the unavailability of estimates of nonsampling errors, only estimates of the levels of sampling errors, in terms of estimated standard errors or coefficients of variation, are available. To obtain estimates of the estimated standard errors from the sample of interest, obtain a copy of the referenced report which appears at the end of each table.

Principal data bases.—Beginning below are brief descriptions of 36 of the sample surveys and censuses that provide a substantial portion of the data contained in this *Abstract*.

SECTION 1. POPULATION

Source and Title: U.S. Census Bureau, *Census of Population*

Tables: See Tables citing *Census of Population* in Section 1 and also in Sections 4, 6, 7, 20, and 29.

Universe, Frequency, and Types of Data: Complete count of U.S. population conducted every 10 years since 1790. Data obtained on number and characteristics of people in the U.S.

Type of Data Collection Operation: In 1970, 1980, 1990 and 2000 complete census for some items—age, sex, race, and relationship to householder. In 1970, other items collected from a 5% and a 15% probability (systematic) sample of the population. In 1980, approximately 19% of the housing units were included in the sample; in 1990 and 2000, approximately 17%.

Data Collection and Imputation Procedures: In 1970, extensive use of mail questionnaires in urban areas; personal interviews in most rural areas. In 1980, 1990, and 2000, mail questionnaires were used in even more areas than in 1970, with personal interviews in the remainder. Extensive telephone and personal followup for nonrespondents was done in the censuses. Imputations were made for missing characteristics.

Estimates of Sampling Error: Sampling errors for data are estimated for all items collected by sample and vary by characteristic and geographic area. The CVs for national and state estimates are generally very small.

Other (Nonsampling) Errors: Since 1950, evaluation programs have been conducted to provide information on the magnitude of some sources of nonsampling errors such as response bias and undercoverage in each census. Results from the evaluation program for the 1990 census indicate that the net under coverage amounted to about 1.5 to 2 percent of the total resident population.

Sources of Additional Material: U.S. Census Bureau, *The Coverage of Population in the 1980 Census*, PHC80-E4; *Content Reinterview Study: Accuracy of Data for Selected Population and Housing Characteristics as Measured by Reinterview*, PHC80-E2; *1980 Census of Population*, Vol. 1., (PC80-1), Appendixes B, C, and D.

Source and Title: U.S. Census Bureau, *Current Population Survey (CPS)*

Tables: See Tables citing *Current Population Reports* primarily in Section 1, but also in Sections 2, 3, 4, 7, 11, 12, 13, and 29. Many Bureau of Labor Statistics' (BLS) Tables in Section 13 are CPS based.

Universe, Frequency, and Types of Data: Nationwide monthly sample survey of civilian noninstitutional population, 15 years old or over, to obtain data on employment, unemployment, and a number of other characteristics.

Type of Data Collection Operation: Multistage probability sample of about 50,000 households in 754 PSUs in 1996. Over-sampling in some states and the largest MSAs to improve reliability for those areas of employment data on annual average basis. A continual sample rotation system is used. Households are in sample 4 months, out for 8 months, and in for 4 more. Month-to-month overlap is 75%; year-to-year overlap is 50%.

Data Collection and Imputation Procedures: For first and fifth months that a household is in sample, personal interviews; other months, approximately, 85% of the data collected by phone.

Imputation is done for both item and total nonresponse. Adjustment for total nonresponse is done by a predefined cluster of units, by MSA size and residence; for item nonresponse imputation varies by subject matter.

Estimates of Sampling Error: Estimated CVs on national annual averages for labor force, total employment, and nonagricultural employment, 0.2%; for total unemployment and agricultural employment, 1.0% to 2.5%. The estimated CVs for family income and poverty rate for all persons in 1986 are 0.5% and 1.5%, respectively. CVs for subnational areas, such as states, would be larger and would vary by area.

Other (Nonsampling) Errors: Estimates of response bias on unemployment are not available, but estimates of unemployment are usually 5% to 9% lower than estimates from reinterviews. Six to 7.0% of sample households unavailable for interviews.

Sources of Additional Material: U.S. Census Bureau and Bureau of Labor Statistics, *Current Population Survey; Design and Methodology*, (Tech. Paper 63), available on internet <www.bls.census.gov/cps/tp/tp63.htm and Bureau of Labor Statistics, *Employment and Earnings*, monthly, Explanatory Notes and Estimates of Error, Tables 1-A through 1-D and *BLS Handbook of Methods*, Chapter 1 (Bulletin 2490.)

SECTION 2. VITAL STATISTICS

Source and Title: U.S. National Center for Health Statistics (NCHS), *National Vital Statistics System*

Tables: See Tables citing *Vital Statistics of the United States;* 297 in Section 5; and 1308 in Section 29.

Universe, Frequency, and Types of Data: Annual data on births and deaths in the United States.

Type of Data Collection Operation: Mortality data based on complete file of death records, except 1972, based on 50% sample. Natality statistics 1951-71, based on 50% sample of birth certificates, except a 20% to 50% in 1967, received by NCHS. Beginning 1972, data from some states received through Vital Statistics Cooperative Program (VSCP) and complete file used; data from other states based on 50% sample. Beginning 1986, all reporting areas participated in the VSCP.

Data Collection and Imputation Procedures: Reports based on records from registration offices of all states, District of Columbia, New York City, Puerto Rico, Virgin Islands, and Guam.

Estimates of Sampling Error: For recent years, CVs for births are small due to large portion of total file in sample (except for very small estimated totals).

Other (Nonsampling) Errors: Data on births and deaths believed to be at least 99% complete.

Sources of Additional Material: U.S. National Center for Health Statistics, *Vital Statistics of the United States*, Vol. I and Vol. II, annual, and *National Vital Statistics Report*.

(See Section 1 above for information pertaining to Tables 82-84.)

SECTION 3. HEALTH AND NUTRITION

Source and Title: U.S. National Center for Health Statistics, *National Health Interview Survey (NHIS)*

Tables: 156, 178, 182, 191, 193, and 197.

Universe, Frequency, and Types of Data: Continuous data collection covering the civilian noninstitutional population to obtain information on personal and demographic characteristics, illnesses, injuries, impairments, and other health topics.

Type of Data Collection Operation: Multistage probability sample of 49,000 households (in 198 PSUs)from 1985 to 1994; 43,000 households (358 design PSUs) from 1995 on, selected in groups of about four adjacent households.

Data Collection and Imputation Procedures: Some missing data items (e.g., age) are imputed using an average value. Unit nonresponse is compensated for by an adjustment to the survey weights

Estimates of Sampling Error: Estimated CVs: For physician visits by males, 1.5%; for workdays lost by males, 3.5%; for persons injured at home, 4.7%.

Other (Nonsampling) Errors: Response rate was 93.8% in 1996 for the NHIS.

Sources of Additional Material: U.S. National Center for Health Statistics, "Current Estimates from the National Health Interview Survey, U.S., 1996," *Vital and Health Statistics*, Series 10 #200.

(See Section 1 for information regarding the Current Population Survey, Section 12 for information pertaining to Table 151, Section 14 for Table 129, Section 22 for Table 148, 149, and 150.)

SECTION 4. EDUCATION

Source and Title: U.S. Department of Education, National Center for Education Statistics, *Higher Education General Information Survey (HEGIS), Fall Enrollment in Institutions of Higher Education;* beginning 1986, *Integrated Postsecondary Education Data Survey (IPEDS), Fall Enrollment*

Tables: 205, 207, 263, 264, 265, and 266.

Universe, Frequency, and Types of Data: Annual survey of all institutions and branches listed in the *Directory* to obtain data on total enrollment by sex, level of enrollment, type of program, racial/ethnic characteristics (every other year prior to 1989, then annually) and attendance status of student, and on first-time students.

Type of Data Collection Operation: Complete census.

Data Collection and Imputation Procedures: Survey package is usually mailed in the spring with surveys due at varying dates in the summer and fall; mail and phone followup procedures for nonrespondents. Missing data are imputed by using data of similar institutions.

Estimates of Sampling Error: Not applicable.

Other (Nonsampling) Errors: For degree-granting institutions approximately 92% response rate in fall 1998.

Sources of Additional Material: U.S. Department of Education, National Center for Education Statistics, *Fall Enrollment in Higher Education*, annual.

Source and Title: U.S. Department of Education, National Center for Education

Statistics, *Higher Education General Information Survey (HEGIS), Financial Statistics of Institutions of Higher Education;* beginning 1986, *Integrated Postsecondary Education Data Survey (IPEDS), Finance.*

Tables: 206 and 264.

Universe, Frequency, and Types of Data: Annual survey of all institutions and branches listed in the *Education Directory, Colleges, and Universities* to obtain data on financial status and operations, including current funds revenues, current funds expenditures, and physical plant assets.

Type of Data Collection Operation: Complete census.

Data Collection and Imputation Procedures: Survey package is usually mailed in the spring with surveys due at varying dates in the summer and fall; mail and phone followup procedures for nonrespondents. Missing data are imputed by using data of similar institutions.

Estimates of Sampling Error: Not applicable.

Other (Nonsampling) Errors: For 1997, 95% for degree-granting institutions.

Sources of Additional Material: U.S. Department of Education, National Center for Education Statistics, *Financial Statistics.*

Source and Title: U.S. Department of Education, National Center for Education Statistics, *Higher Education General Information Survey (HEGIS), Degrees and Other Formal Awards Conferred.* Beginning 1986, *Integrated Postsecondary Education Data Survey (IPEDS), Completions.*

Tables: 207, 284, 285, 286, 287, 288, and 289.

Universe, Frequency, and Types of Data: Annual survey of all institutions and branches listed in the *Education Directory, Colleges, and Universities* to obtain data on earned degrees and other formal awards, conferred by field of study, level of degree, sex, and by racial/ethnic characteristics (every other year prior to 1989, then annually).

Type of Data Collection Operation: Complete census.

Data Collection and Imputation Procedures: Survey package is usually mailed in the spring with surveys due at varying dates in the summer and fall; mail and phone followup procedures for nonrespondents. Missing data are imputed by using data of similar institutions.

Estimates of Sampling Error: Not applicable.

Other (Nonsampling) Errors: For 1996-98, approximately 92% response rate for degree-granting institutions.

Sources of Additional Material: U.S. Department of Education, National Center for Education Statistics, *Completions,* annual.

(See Sections 1 and 9 for information pertaining to the Census Bureau and Section 5 for information pertaining to Table 220.)

SECTION 5. LAW ENFORCEMENT, COURTS, AND PRISONS

Source and Title: U.S. Federal Bureau of Investigation, *Uniform Crime Reporting (UCR) Program*

Tables: 291, 292, 293, 294, 295, 296, 298, 299, 300, 301, 308, 309, and 311.

Universe, Frequency, and Types of Data: Monthly reports on the number of criminal offenses that become known to law enforcement agencies. Data are collected on crimes cleared by arrest, by age, sex, and race of offender, and on assaults on law enforcement officers.

Type of Data Collection Operation: Crime statistics are based on reports of crime data submitted either directly to the FBI by contributing law enforcement agencies or through cooperating state UCR programs.

Data Collection and Imputation Procedures: States with UCR programs collect data directly from individual law enforcement agencies and forward reports, prepared in accordance with UCR standards, to FBI. Accuracy and consistency edits are performed by FBI.

Estimates of Sampling Error: Not applicable.

Other (Nonsampling) Errors: Coverage of 95% of the population (96% in MSAs, 92% in "other cities," and 90% in rural areas) by UCR program, though varying number of agencies report. Some error may be present through incorrect reporting.

Sources of Additional Material: U.S. Federal Bureau of Investigation, *Crime in the United States, Hate Crime Statistics,* annual, *Law Enforcement Officers Killed & Assaulted,* annual.

Source and Title: U.S. Bureau of Justice Statistics (BJS), *National Crime Victimization Survey*

Tables: 302, 303, 304, 305, 306, 307, and Table 220 in Section 4.

Universe, Frequency, and Types of Data: Monthly survey of individuals and households in the United States to obtain data on criminal victimization of those units for compilation of annual estimates.

Type of Data Collection Operation: National probability sample survey of about 50,000 interviewed households in 376 PSUs selected from a list of addresses from the 1980 census, supplemented by new construction permits and an area sample where permits are not required.

Data Collection and Imputation Procedures: Interviews are conducted every 6 months for 3 years for each household in the sample; 8,300 households are interviewed monthly. Personal interviews are used in the first interview; the intervening interviews are conducted by telephone whenever possible.

Estimates of Sampling Error: CVs averaged over the period 1996-1999 are: 2.7% for crimes of violence; 8.5% for estimate of rape/sexual assault counts; 5.5% for robbery counts; 2.8% for assault counts; 8.0% for personal theft counts; 1.9% for property crimes; 3.0% for burglary counts; 2.0% for theft; and 4.4% for motor vehicle theft counts.

Other (Nonsampling) Errors: Respondent recall errors which may include reporting incidents for other than the reference period; interviewer coding and processing errors; and possible mistaken reporting or classifying of events. Adjustment is made for a household noninterview rate of about 4% and for a within-household noninterview rate of 7%.

Sources of Additional Material: U.S. Bureau of Justice Statistics, *Criminal Victimization in the United States,* annual.

(See Section 2 for details on Table 297.)

SECTION 7. ELECTIONS

(See Section 1 above for information pertaining to Tables 401 and 402.)

SECTION 8. STATE AND LOCAL GOVERNMENT FINANCES AND EMPLOYMENT

Source and Title: U.S. Census Bureau, *Census of Governments*

Tables: See Tables in Section 8 citing *Census of Governments.*

Universe, Frequency, and Types of Data: Survey of all governmental units in the United States conducted every 5 years to obtain data on government revenue, expenditures, debt, assets, employment and employee retirement systems, property values, public school systems, and number, size, and structure of governments.

Type of Data Collection Operation: Complete census. List of units derived through classification of government units recently authorized in each state and identification, counting, and classification of existing local governments and public school systems.

Data Collection and Imputation Procedures: Data collected through field and office compilation of financial data from official records and reports for states and large local governments; mail canvass of selected data items, like state tax revenue and employee retirement systems; and collection of local government statistics through central collection arrangements with state governments.

Estimates of Sampling Error: Not applicable.

Other (Nonsampling) Errors: Some nonsampling errors may arise due to possible inaccuracies in classification, response, and processing.

Sources of Additional Material: U.S. Census Bureau, *Census of Governments, 1987,* various reports, and *State Government Finances in 1990,* GF 90, No. 3.

Source and Title: U.S. Census Bureau, *Annual Surveys of State and Local Government*

Tables: See Tables citing *Public Employment* and *Government Finances* in Section 8 and Table 241 in Section 4; and Table 531 in Section 11.

Universe, Frequency, and Types of Data: Sample survey conducted annually to obtain data on revenue, expenditure, debt, and employment of state and local governments. Universe is all governmental units in the United States (about 87,000).

Type of Data Collection Operation: Sample of about 22,000 units includes all state governments, county governments with 50,000+ population, municipalities and townships with 25,000+ population, all school districts with 10,000+ enrollment in October 1986, and other governments meeting certain criteria; probability sample for remaining units.

Data Collection and Imputation Procedures: Field and office compilation of data from official records and reports for states and large local governments; central collection of local governmental financial data through cooperative agreements with a number of state governments; mail canvass of other units with mail and telephone followups of nonrespondents. Data for nonresponses are imputed from previous year data or obtained from secondary sources, if available.

Estimates of Sampling Error: CVs for estimates of major employment and financial items are generally less than 2% for most states and less than 1.2% for the majority of states.

Other (Nonsampling) Errors: Nonresponse rate is less than 15% for number of units. Other possible errors may result from undetected inaccuracies in classification, response, and processing.

Sources of Additional Material: U.S. Census Bureau, *Public Employment in 1990*, GE 90, No. 1, *Governmental Finances in 1989-90*, GF 90, No. 5, and *Census of Governments, 1987*, various reports.

SECTION 9. FEDERAL GOVERNMENT

Source and Title: U.S. Internal Revenue Service, *Statistics of Income, Individual Income Tax Returns*

Tables: 473, 474, 475, 476, and 477.

Universe, Frequency, and Types of Data: Annual study of unaudited individual income tax returns, forms 1040, 1040A, and 1040EZ, filed by U.S. citizens and residents. Data provided on various financial characteristics by size of adjusted gross income, marital status, and by taxable and nontaxable returns. Data by state, based on 100% file, also include returns from 1040NR, filed by nonresident aliens plus certain self-employment tax returns.

Type of Data Collection Operation: Annual stratified probability sample of approximately 125,000 returns broken into sample strata based on the larger of total income or total loss amounts as well as the size of business plus farm receipts. Sampling rates for sample strata varied from .025% to 100%.

Data Collection and Imputation Procedures: Computer selection of sample of tax return records. Data adjusted during editing for incorrect, missing, or inconsistent entries to ensure consistency with other entries on return.

Estimates of Sampling Error: Estimated CVs for tax year 1997: Adjusted gross income less deficit .15%; salaries and wages .27%; and tax-exempt interest received 2.15%. (State data not subject to sampling error.)

Other (Nonsampling) Errors: Processing errors and errors arising from the use of tolerance checks for the data.

Sources of Additional Material: U.S. Internal Revenue Service, *Statistics of Income, Individual Income Tax Returns*, annual.

SECTION 11. SOCIAL INSURANCE AND HUMAN SERVICES

Source and Title: U.S. Social Security Administration, *Benefit Data*

Tables: 527 and 528.

Universe, Frequency, and Types of Data: All persons receiving monthly benefits under Title II of Social Security Act. Data on number and amount of benefits paid by type and state.

Type of Data Collection Operation: Data based on administrative records. Data based on 100% files, as well as 10% and 1% sample files.

Data Collection and Imputation Procedures: Records used consist of actions pursuant to applications dated by subsequent post-entitlement actions.

Estimates of Sampling Error: Varies by size of estimate and sample file size.

Other (Nonsampling) Errors: Processing errors, which are believed to be small.

Sources of Additional Material: U.S. Social Security Administration, *Annual Statistical Supplement to the Social Security Bulletin.*

Source and Title: U.S. Social Security Administration, *Supplemental Security Income (SSI) Program*

Tables: 542 and 543.

Universe, Frequency, and Types of Data: All eligible aged, blind, or disabled persons receiving SSI benefit payments under SSI program. Data include number of persons receiving federally administered SSI, amounts paid, and state administered supplementation.

Type of Data Collection Operation: Data based on administrative records.

Data Collection and Imputation Procedures: Data adjusted to reflect returned checks and overpayment refunds. For federally administered payments, actual adjusted amounts are used.

Estimates of Sampling Error: Not applicable.

Other (Nonsampling) Errors: Processing errors, which are believed to be small.

Sources of Additional Material: U.S. Social Security Administration, *Annual Statistical Supplement to the Social Security Bulletin.*

(See Section 1 above for information pertaining to the Current Population Survey, Section 8 for information pertaining to Annual Surveys of State and Local Government, and Section 22 for the 1997 Economic Census and the Service Annual Survey.)

SECTION 12. LABOR FORCE, EMPLOYMENT, AND EARNINGS

Source and Title: U.S. Bureau of Labor Statistics (BLS), *Current Employment Statistics (CES)* Program

Tables: 607, 608, 609, 616, in Section 3, Table 151, and in Section 23, Table 1055.

Universe, Frequency, and Types of Data: Monthly survey covering about 7 million establishments to obtain data on employment, hours, and earnings, by industry.

Type of Data Collection Operation: Sample survey of about 350,000 establishments in June 2001.

Data Collection and Imputation Procedures: Cooperating state agencies mail questionnaires to sample establishments to develop state and local estimates; information is forwarded to BLS where national estimates are prepared.

Estimates of Sampling Error: Not available until survey redesign is completed.

Other (Nonsampling) Errors: Estimates of employment adjusted annually to reflect complete universe. Average adjustment is 0.3% over the last decade.

Sources of Additional Material: U.S. Bureau of Labor Statistics, *Employment and Earnings,* monthly, Explanatory Notes and Estimates of Error, Tables 2-A through 2-H.

(See Section 1 above for information pertaining to the Current Population Survey.)

SECTION 13. INCOME, EXPENDITURES, AND WEALTH

Source and Title: Board of Governors of the Federal Reserve System, *Survey of Consumer Finances*

Tables: 687 and 688, and in Section 25, 1167, 1169, 1170, 1171, 1192, and 1209.

Universe, Frequency, and Types of Data: Periodic sample survey of families. In this survey a given household is divided into a primary economic unit and other economic units. The primary economic unity, which may be a single individual, is generally chosen as the unit that contains the person who either holds the title to the home or is the first person listed on the lease. The primary unit is used as the reference family. The survey collects detailed data on the composition of family balance sheets, the terms of loans, and relationships with financial institutions. It also gathered information on the employment history and pension rights of the survey respondent and the spouse or partner of the respondent.

Type of Data Collection Operation: The survey employs a two-part strategy for sampling families. Some families were selected by standard multistage area-probability sampling methods from the 48 contiguous states. The remaining families in the survey were selected using tax data under the strict rules governing confidentiality and the rights of potential respondents to refuse participation.

Data Collection and Imputation Procedures: The Survey Research Center at the University of Michigan collected the 1989 survey data between August 1989 and March 1990. Adjustments for nonresponse errors are made through systematic imputation of unanswered questions and through weighting adjustments based on data used in the sample design for families that refused participation.

Estimates of Sampling Error: Because of the complex design of the survey, the estimation of potential sampling errors is not straightforward.

Other (Nonsampling) Errors: The achieved sample of 3,143 families represents a response rate of about 69 percent in the area-probability sample and a rate of about 34 percent in the tax-data sample. Proper training of interviewers and careful design of questionnaires were used to control inaccurate survey responses.

Sources of Additional Material: Board of Governors of the Federal Reserve System, "Changes in Family Finances from 1983 to 1989: Evidence from the Survey of Consumer Finances", *Federal Reserve Bulletin,* January 1992.

(See Section 1 above for information pertaining to the Census Bureau.)

SECTION 14. PRICES

Source and Title: U.S. Bureau of Labor Statistics (BLS), *Consumer Price Index (CPI)*

Tables: 691, 692, 693, 694, 706, and in Section 3, Table 129.

Universe, Frequency, and Types of Data: Monthly survey of price changes of all types of consumer goods and services purchased by urban wage earners and clerical workers prior to 1978, and urban consumers thereafter. Both indexes continue to be published.

Type of Data Collection Operation: Prior to 1978, sample of various consumer items in 87 urban areas; thereafter, in 85 PSUs, except from January 1987 through March 1988, when 91 areas were sampled.

Data Collection and Imputation Procedures: Prices of consumer items are obtained from about 50,000 housing units, and 23,000 other reporters in 87 areas. Prices of food, fuel, and a few other items are obtained monthly; prices of most other commodities and services are collected every month in the three largest geographic areas and every other month in others.

Estimates of Sampling Error: Estimates of standard errors are available.

Other (Nonsampling) Errors: Errors result from inaccurate reporting, difficulties in defining concepts and their operational implementation, and introduction of product quality changes and new products.

Sources of Additional Material: U.S. Bureau of Labor Statistics, Internet site and *BLS Handbook of Methods,* Chapter 17, Bulletin 2490.

Source and Title: U.S. Bureau of Labor Statistics, *Producer Price Index (PPI)*

Tables: 691, 697, 698, 699, and in Section 18, Table 855; and in Section 20, Table 927; and in Section 23, Table 1115.

Universe, Frequency, and Types of Data: Monthly survey of producing companies to determine price changes of all commodities produced in the United States for sale in commercial transactions. Data on agriculture, forestry, fishing, manufacturing, mining, gas, electricity, public utilities, and a few services.

Type of Data Collection Operation: Probability sample of approximately 30,000 about 100,000 price quotations per month.

Data Collection and Imputation Procedures: Data are collected by mail. If transaction prices are not supplied, list prices are used. Some prices are obtained from trade publications, organized exchanges, and government agencies. To calculate index, price changes are multiplied by their relative weights taken from 1992 shipment values from the Census of Manufactures.

Estimates of Sampling Error: Not applicable.

Other (Nonsampling) Errors: Not available at present.

Sources of Additional Material: U.S. Bureau of Labor Statistics, *BLS Handbook of Methods,* Chapter 14, Bulletin 2490.

SECTION 15. BUSINESS ENTERPRISE

Source and Title: U.S. Census Bureau, *County Business Patterns*

Tables: 723 and 724, and in Section 18, Table 847; in Section 19, Table 890; in Section 20, Table 925; in Section 21, Tables 972 and 973; in Section 22, Table 1017 and 1049; in Section 23, Table 1053; in Section 24, Table 1121; in Section 25, Table 1162 and 1228; in Section 26, Table 1232; and in Section 27, Tables 1263, 1264, and 1280.

Universe, Frequency, and Types of Data: Annual tabulation of basic data items extracted from the Business Register, a file of all known single and multi-establishment companies maintained and updated by the Census Bureau. Data include number of establishments, number of employees, first-quarter and annual payrolls, and number of establishments by employment size class. Data are excluded for self-employed persons, domestic service workers, railroad employees, agricultural production workers, and most government employees.

Type of Data Collection Operation: The annual Company Organization Survey provides individual establishment data for multiestablishment companies. Data for single establishment companies are obtained from various Census Bureau programs, such as the Annual Survey of Manufactures and Current Business Surveys, as well as from administrative records of the Internal Revenue Service and the Social Security Administration.

Estimates of Sampling Error: Not applicable.

Other (Nonsampling) Error: Response rates of greater than 90% for the 1993 Company Organization Survey.

Sources of Additional Materials: U.S. Census Bureau, *General Explanation of County Business Patterns.*

Source and Title: U.S. Census Bureau, *Surveys of Minority-and Women-Owned Business Enterprises* (SMOBE/SWOBE).

Tables: 728, 729, 730, 731, 732, 733, 734, 735, and 736.

Universe, Frequency, and Types of Data: The surveys provide basic economic data on businesses owned by Blacks, Hispanics, Asians, Pacific Islanders, Alaska Natives, American Indians, and Women. All firms operating during 1997, except those classified as agricultural, are represented. The lists of all firms (or sample frames) are compiled from a combination of business tax returns and data collected on other economic census reports. The published data include the number of firms, gross receipts, number of paid employees, and annual payroll. The data are presented by geographic area, industry, size of firm, and legal form of organization of firm.

Type of Data Collection Operation: The surveys are based on a stratified probability sample of approximately 2.5 million firms from a universe of approximately 20.8 million firms. There were approximately 5.3 million firms with paid employees and 15.5 million firms with no paid employees. The data are based on the entire firm rather than on individual locations of a firm.

Data Collection and Imputation Procedures: Data were collected through a mailout/mailback operation. Compensation for missing data is addressed through reweighting, edit correction, and standard statistical imputation methods.

Estimates of Sampling Error: Variability in the estimates is due to the sample selection and estimation for items collected by SMOBE/SWOBE. CVs are applicable to only published cells in which sample cases are tabulated. The CVs for number of firms and receipts at the national level range from 1 to 4 percent.

Other (Nonsampling) Error: Nonsampling errors are attributed to many sources: inability to obtain information for all cases in the universe, adjustments to the weights of respondents to compensate for nonrespondents, imputation for missing data, data errors and biases, mistakes in recording or keying data, errors in collection or processing, and coverage problems.

Sources of Additional Materials: U.S. Census Bureau, *Guide to the 1997 Economic Census and Related Statistics.*

Source and Title: U.S. Internal Revenue Service, *Statistics of Income, Sole Proprietorship Returns* and *Statistics of Income Bulletin*

Tables: 710, 711, 721, and 713.

Universe, Frequency, and Types of Data: Annual study of unaudited income tax returns of nonfarm sole proprietorships, form 1040 with business schedules. Data provided on various financial characteristics by industry.

Type of Data Collection Operation: Stratified probability sample of approximately 31,000 sole proprietorships for tax year 1990. The sample is classified based on presence or absence of certain business schedules; the larger of total income or loss; and size of business plus farm receipts. Sampling rates vary from .043% to 100%.

Data Collection and Imputation Procedures: Computer selection of sample of tax return records. Data adjusted during editing for incorrect, missing, or inconsistent entries to ensure consistency with other entries on return.

Estimates of Sampling Error: Estimated CVs for tax year 1990 are not available; for 1987 (the latest available): For sole proprietorships, business receipts, 1.66%; net income, (less loss), 1.33%; depreciation 2.17%; interest expense 2.80%; and employee benefit programs 7.55%.

Other (Nonsampling) Errors: Processing errors and errors arising from the use of tolerance checks for the data.

Sources of Additional Material: U.S. Internal Revenue Service, *Statistics of Income, Sole Proprietorship Returns* (for years through 1980) and *Statistics of Income Bulletin*, Vol. 19, No. 1 (summer 1999).

Source and Title: U.S. Internal Revenue Service, *Statistics of Income, Partnership Returns* and *Statistics of Income Bulletin*

Tables: 710, 712, 714, and 715.

Universe, Frequency, and Types of Data: Annual study of unaudited income tax returns of partnerships, Form 1065. Data provided on various financial characteristics by industry.

Type of Data Collection Operation: Stratified probability sample of approximately 28,000 partnership returns from a population of 1,660,000 filed during calendar year 1990. The sample is classified based on combinations of gross receipts, net income or loss, and total assets, and on industry. Sampling rates vary from .04% to 100%.

Data Collection and Imputation Procedures: Computer selection of sample of tax return records. Data are adjusted during editing for incorrect, missing, or inconsistent entries to ensure consistency with other entries on return. Data not available due to regulations are not imputed.

Estimates of Sampling Error: Estimated CVs for tax year 1988 (latest available): For number of partnerships, .51%; business receipts, .78%; net income, 3.03%; net loss, 2.21% and total assets, 1.22%.

Other (Nonsampling) Errors: Processing errors and errors arising from the use of tolerance checks for the data.

Sources of Additional Material: U.S. Internal Revenue Service, *Statistics of Income, Partnership Returns* and *Statistics of Income Bulletin*, Vol. 19, No. 2 (fall 1999).

Source and Title: U.S. Internal Revenue Service, *Corporation Income Tax Returns*

Tables: 710, 711, 712, 718, 719, and 720.

Universe, Frequency, and Types of Data: Annual study of unaudited corporation income tax returns, Forms 1120 and 1120 (A, F, L, PC, REIT, RIC, and S), filed by corporations or businesses legally defined as corporations. Data provided on various financial characteristics by industry and size of total assets, and business receipts.

Type of Data Collection Operation: Stratified probability sample of approximately 85,000 returns for 1987, distributed by sample classes generally based on type of return, size of total assets, size of net income or deficit, and selected business activity. Sampling rates for sample strata varied from .25% to 100%.

Data Collection and Imputation Procedures: Computer selection of sample of tax return records. Data adjusted during editing for incorrect, missing, or inconsistent entries to ensure consistency with other entries on return and to achieve statistical definitions.

Estimates of Sampling Error: Estimated CVs for 1988: Number of returns in subgroups ranged from 1.4% with assets under $100,000, to 0% with assets over $100 mil.; for amount of net income and amount of income tax, .18%

Other (Nonsampling) Errors: Processing errors and errors arising from the use of tolerance checks for the data.

Sources of Additional Material: U.S. Internal Revenue Service, *Statistics of Income, Corporation Income Tax Returns,* annual.

(See Section 15 for Table 721)

SECTION 17. AGRICULTURE

Source and Title: U.S. Department of Agriculture, National Agriculture Statistics Service (NASS),*Census of Agriculture.*

Tables: 796, 797, 798, 799, 800, 801, and 802.

Universe, Frequency, and Types of Data: Complete count of U.S. farms and ranches conducted once every 5 years with data at the national, state, and county level. Data published on farm numbers and related items/ characteristics.

Type of Data Collection Operation: Complete census for—number of farms; land in farms; estimated market value of land and buildings, machinery and equipment, agriculture products sold; total cropland; irrigated land; total farm production expenses; farm operator characteristics; livestock and poultry inventory and sales; and selected crops harvested.

Data Collection and Imputation Procedures: Data collection is by mailing questionnaires to all farmers and ranchers. Nonrespondents are conducted by telephone and correspondence followups. Imputations were made for all nonresponse item/characteristics.

Estimates of Sampling Error: Variability in the estimates is due to the sample selection and estimation for items collected by sample and census nonresponse estimation procedures. The CVs for national and state estimates are generally very small. Approximately 85% response rate.

Other (Nonsampling) Errors: Nonsampling errors are due to incompleteness of the census mailing list, duplications on the list, respondent reporting errors, errors in editing reported data, and in imputation for missing data. Evaluation studies are conducted to measure certain nonsampling errors such as list coverage and classification error. Results from the evaluation program for the 1987 census indicate the net under coverage amounted to about 7.2% of the nations total farms.

Sources of Additional Material: U.S. Department of Agriculture (NASS), *1997 Census of Agriculture,* Volume 2, Subject Series—Part 1, *Agriculture Atlas of the U.S.,* Part 2, *Coverage Evaluation,* Part 3, *Rankings of States and Counties,* Part 4, *History,* Part 5, *ZIP Code Tabulation of Selected Items,* ; and Volume 4 *Farm and Ranch Irrigation Survey.*

Source and Title: U.S. Department of Agriculture, National Agricultural Statistics Service (NASS), *Basic Area Frame Sample*

Tables: See Tables citing NASS in source notes in Section 23, which pertain to this or the following two surveys.

Universe, Frequency, and Types of Data: Two annual area sample surveys of U.S. farm operators: June agricultural survey collects data on planted acreage and livestock inventories; and a February Farm Costs and Returns survey that collects data on total farm production, expenses and specific commodity costs of production.

Type of Data Collection Operation: Stratified probability sample of about 16,000 land area units of about 1 sq. mile (range from 0.1 sq. mile in cities to several sq. miles in open grazing areas). Sample includes 60,000 parcels of agricultural land. About 20% of the sample replaced annually.

Data Collection and Imputation Procedures: Data collection is by personal enumeration. Imputation is based on enumerator observation or data reported by respondents having similar agricultural characteristics.

Estimates of Sampling Error: Estimated CVs range from 1% to 2% for regional estimates to 3% to 6% for state estimates of livestock inventories.

Other (Nonsampling) Errors: Minimized through rigid quality controls on the collection process and careful review of all reported data.

Appendix III   915

Sources of Additional Material: U.S. Department of Agriculture, SRS, *Scope and Methods of the Statistical Reporting Service,* (name changed to National Agricultural Statistics Service), Miscellaneous Publication No. 1308, September 1983 (revised).

Source and Title: U.S. Department of Agriculture National Agricultural Statistics Service (NASS), *Multiple Frame Surveys*

Tables: See Tables citing NASS in source notes in Section 23, which pertain to this or the following survey.

Universe, Frequency, and Types of Data: Surveys of U.S. farm operators to obtain data on major livestock inventories, selected crop acreages and production, grain stocks, and farm labor characteristics; and to obtain farm economic data for price indexing.

Type of Data Collection Operation: Primary frame is obtained from general or special purpose lists, supplemented by a probability sample of land areas used to estimate for list incompleteness.

Data Collection and Imputation Procedures: Mail, telephone, or personal interviews used for initial data collection. Mail nonrespondent followup by phone and personal interviews. Imputation based on average of respondents.

Estimates of Sampling Error: Estimated CV for number of hired farm workers is about 3%. Estimated CVs range from 1% to 2% for regional estimates to 3% to 6% for state estimates of livestock inventories.

Other (Nonsampling) Errors: In addition to above, replicated sampling procedures used to monitor effects of changes in survey procedures.

Sources of Additional Material: U.S. Department of Agriculture, SRS, *Scope and Methods of the Statistical Reporting Service,* (name changed to National Agricultural Statistics Service), Miscellaneous Publication No. 1308, September 1983 (revised).

Source and Title: U.S. Department of Agriculture, National Agricultural Statistics Service (NASS), *Objective Yield Surveys*

Tables: See Tables citing NASS in source notes in Section 23, which pertain to this or the preceding survey.

Universe, Frequency, and Types of Data: Surveys for data on corn, cotton, potatoes, soybeans, wheat, and rice to forecast and estimate yields.

Type of Data Collection Operation: Random location of plots in probability sample s selected in June from Basic Area Frame Sample (see above).

Data Collection and Imputation Procedures: Enumerators count and measure plant characteristics in sample fields. Production measured from plots at harvest. Harvest loss measured from post harvest gleanings.

Estimates of Sampling Error: CVs for national estimates of production are about 2-3%.

Other (Nonsampling) Errors: In addition to above, replicated sampling procedures used to monitor effects of changes in survey procedures.

Sources of Additional Material: U.S. Department of Agriculture, SRS, *Scope and Methods of the Statistical Reporting Service,* (name changed to National Agricultural Statistics Service), Miscellaneous Publication No. 1308, September 1983 (revised).

(See Section 1 above for information pertaining to the Census of Population and Current Population Survey.)

SECTION 18. NATURAL RESOURCES

(See Section 14 for Table 855; Section 15 for Table 847; and Section 22 for Tables 864 and 865.)

SECTION 19. ENERGY AND UTILITIES

Source and Title: U.S. Energy Information Administration, *Residential Energy Consumption Survey*

Tables: 898 and Table 964 in Section 20.

Universe, Frequency, and Types of Data: Quadriennial survey of households and fuel suppliers. Data are obtained on energy-related household characteristics, housing unit characteristics, use of fuels, and energy consumption and expenditures by fuel type.

Type of Data Collection Operation: Probability sample of 5,900 eligible units in 116 PSUs. For responding units, fuel consumption and expenditure data obtained from fuel suppliers to those households.

Data Collection and Imputation Procedures: Personal interviews. Extensive followup of nonrespondents including mail questionnaires for some households. Adjustments for nonrespondents were made in weighting for respondents. Most item nonresponses were imputed.

Estimates of Sampling Error: Estimated CVs for household averages: For consumption, 1.3%; for expenditures, 1.0%; for various fuels, values ranged from 2.0% for electricity to 7.0% for LPG.

Other (Nonsampling) Errors: Household response rate of 81.0%. Nonconsumption data were mostly imputed for mail respondents (2.5% of eligible units). Usable responses from fuel suppliers for various fuels ranged from 80.7% for electricity to 56.6% for fuel oil.

Sources of Additional Material: U.S. Energy Information Administration, A look at Residential Energy Consumption in 1997.

(See Section 15 for Table 890 and Section 22 for Table 889)

SECTION 20. CONSTRUCTION AND HOUSING

Source and Title: U.S. Census Bureau, *Monthly Survey of Construction*

Tables: 936 and 938, 939, 940, and 941

Universe, Frequency, and Types of Data: Survey conducted monthly of newly constructed housing units (excluding mobile homes). Data are collected on the start, completion, and sale of housing. (Annual figures are aggregates of monthly estimates.)

Type of Data Collection Operation: Probability sample of housing units obtained from building permits selected from 17,000 places. For nonpermit places, multistage probability sample of new housing units selected in 169 PSUs. In those areas, all roads are canvassed in selected enumeration districts.

Data Collection and Imputation Procedures: Data are obtained by telephone inquiry and field visit.

Estimates of Sampling Error: Estimated CV of 3% to 4% for estimates of national totals, but are as high as 20% for estimated totals of more detailed characteristics, such as housing units in multiunit structures.

Other (Nonsampling) Errors: Response rate is over 90% for most items. Nonsampling errors are attributed to definitional problems, differences in interpretation of questions, incorrect reporting, inability to obtain information about all cases in the sample, and processing errors.

Sources of Additional Material: U.S. Census Bureau, *Construction Reports*, Series C20, *Housing Starts*; C22, *Housing Completions*; and C25, *New One-Family Houses Sold and For Sale.*

Source and Title: U.S. Census Bureau, *Value of Construction Put in Place*

Tables: 929, 930, 931, and 932.

Universe, Frequency, and Types of Data: Survey conducted monthly on total value of all construction put in place in the current month, both public and private projects. Construction values include costs of materials and labor, contractors' profits, overhead costs, cost of architectural and engineering work, and miscellaneous project costs. (Annual figures are aggregates of monthly estimates.)

Type of Data Collection Operation: Varies by type of activity: Total cost of private one-family houses started each month is distributed into value put in place using fixed patterns of monthly construction progress; using a multistage probability sample, data for private multifamily housing are obtained by mail from owners of multiunit projects. Data for residential additions and alterations are obtained in a quarterly survey measuring expenditures; monthly estimates are interpolated from quarterly data. Estimates of value of private nonresidential construction, and state and local government construction are obtained by mail from owners (or agents) for a probability sample of projects. Estimates of farm nonresidential construction expenditures are based on U.S. Department of Agriculture annual estimates of construction; public utility estimates are obtained from reports submitted to federal regulatory agencies and from private utility companies; estimates of federal construction are based on monthly data supplied by federal agencies.

Data Collection and Imputation Procedures: See "Type of Data Collection Operation." Imputation accounts for approximately 20% of estimated value of construction each month.

U.S. Census Bureau, Statistical Abstract of the United States: 2001

Estimates of Sampling Error: CV estimates for private nonresidential construction range from 3% for estimated value of industrial buildings to 9% for religious buildings. CV is approximately 2% for total new private nonresidential buildings.

Other (Nonsampling) Errors: For directly measured data series based on samples, some nonsampling errors may arise from processing errors, imputations, and misunderstanding of questions. Indirect data series are dependent on the validity of the underlying assumptions and procedures.

Sources of Additional Material: U.S. Census Bureau, *Construction Reports*, Series C30, *Value of Construction Put in Place*.

Source and Title: U.S. Census Bureau, *American Housing Survey*

Tables: See Tables citing *American Housing Survey* in source notes.

Universe, Frequency, and Types of Data: Conducted nationally in the fall in odd numbered years to obtain data on the approximately 112 million occupied or vacant housing units in the United States (group quarters are excluded). Data include characteristics of occupied housing units, vacant units, new housing and mobile home units, financial characteristics, recent mover households, housing and neighborhood quality indicators, and energy characteristics.

Type of Data Collection Operation: The national sample was a multistage probability sample with about 53,000 units eligible for interview in 1997. Sample units, selected within 394 PSUs, were surveyed over a 5-month period.

Data Collection and Imputation Procedures: For 1997, the survey was conducted by personal interviews. The interviewers obtained the information from the occupants or, if the unit was vacant, from informed persons such as landlords, rental agents, or knowledgeable neighbors.

Estimates of Sampling Error: For the national sample, illustrations of the S.E. of the estimates are provided in the Appendix D of the 1997 report. As an example, the estimated CV is about 0.2% for the estimated percentage of owner occupied units with two persons.

Other (Nonsampling) Errors: Response rate was about 97%. Nonsampling errors may result from incorrect or incomplete responses, errors in coding and recording, and processing errors. For the 1997 national sample, approximately 1.7% of the total housing inventory was not adequately represented by the AHS sample.

Sources of Additional Material: U.S. Census Bureau, *Current Housing Reports*, Series H-150 and H-170, *American Housing Survey*.

(See Section 1 above for information pertaining to Tables 950 and 951, Section 14 pertaining to Table 927, Section 15 for Table 925; Section 19 for Table 964; and Section 22 for Table 926.)

SECTION 21. MANUFACTURES

Source and Title: U.S. Census Bureau, *Annual Survey of Manufactures*

Tables: See Tables citing *Annual Survey of Manufactures* in source notes.

Universe, Frequency, and Types of Data: Conducted annually to provide basic measures of manufacturing activity for intercensal years for all manufacturing establishments having one or more paid employees.

Type of Data Collection Operation: Sampling frame is 350,000 establishments in the 1987 Census of Manufactures (see above), supplemented by Social Security Administration lists of new manufacturers and new manufacturing establishments of multi-establishment companies identified annually by the Census Bureau's Company Organization Survey. A probability sample of about 55,000 establishments is selected. All establishments of companies with more than $500 million of manufacturing shipments in 1987 are included with certainty. All establishments with 250+ employees are also included with certainty along with a probability sample of smaller establishments.

Data Collection and Imputation Procedures: Survey is conducted by mail with phone and mail followups of nonrespondents. Imputation (for all nonresponse items) is based on previous year reports, or for new establishments in survey, on industry averages.

Estimates of Sampling Error: Estimated standard errors for number of employees, new expenditure, and for value added totals are given in annual publications. For U.S. level industry statistics, most estimated standard errors are 2% or less, but vary considerably for detailed characteristics.

Other (Nonsampling) Errors: Response rate is about 85%. Nonsampling errors include those due to collection, reporting, and transcription errors, many of which are corrected through computer and clerical checks.

Sources of Additional Material: U.S. Census Bureau, *Annual Survey of Manufactures*, and Technical Paper 24.

(See Section 15 for Tables 972 and 973)

SECTION 22. DOMESTIC TRADE

Source and Title: U.S. Census Bureau, *1997 Economic Census* Geographic Area Series and Subject Series) (for NAICS sectors 22, 42, 44-45, 48-49, and 51-81).

Tables: See tables citing the above census in source notes in Sections 3, 11, 15, 18, 20, 22, 23, 24, 25, 26, 27, and 29.

Universe, Frequency, and Types of Data: Conducted every 5 years to obtain data on number of establishments, number of employees, total payroll size, total sales, and other industry-specific statistics. In 1997, the universe was all employer and nonemployer establishments primarily engaged in wholesale, retail, utilities, finance & insurance, real estate, transportation & warehousing, and other service industries.

Type of Data Collection Operation: All large employer firms were surveyed (i.e. all employer firms above the payroll size cutoff established to separate large from small employers) plus a 5% to 25% sample of the small employer firms. Firms with no employees were not required to file a census return.

Data Collection and Imputation Procedures: Mail questionnaires were used with both mail and telephone followups for nonrespondents. Data for nonrespondents and for small employer firms not mailed a questionnaire were obtained from administrative records of

the IRS and Social Security Administration or imputed. Nonemployer data were obtained exclusively from IRS 1997 income tax returns.

Estimates of Sampling Error: Not applicable for basic data such as sales, revenue, payroll, etc.

Other (Nonsampling) Errors: Trade area level unit response rates in 1997 ranged from 85% to 99%. Item response rates ranged from 60% to 90% with lower rates for the more detailed questions. Nonsampling errors may occur during the collection, reporting, and keying of data, and industry misclassification.

Sources of Additional Material: U.S. Census Bureau, *1997 Economic Census: Geographic Area Series* and *Subject Series* (by NAICS sector), Appendix C and <www.census.gov/epcd/www/econ97.html>

Source and Title: U.S. Census Bureau, *Current Business Surveys*

Tables: 1019, 1020, 1021, 1022, and 1047 and tables citing the *Service Annual Survey* in Sections 3, 11, 23, 24, 25, 26, and 27.

Universe, Frequency, and Types of Data: Provides monthly estimates of retail sales by kind of business and geographic area, and end-of-month inventories of retail stores; wholesale sales and end-of-month inventories; and annual receipts of selected service industries.

Type of Data Collection Operation: Probability sample of all firms from a list frame and, additionally, for retail and service an area frame. The list frame is the Bureau's Standard Statistical Establishment List (SSEL) updated quarterly for recent birth Employer Identification (EI) Numbers issued by the Internal Revenue Service and assigned a kind-of-business code by the Social Security Administration. The largest firms are included monthly; a sample of others is included every three months on a rotating basis. The area frame covers businesses not subjected to sampling on the list frame.

Data Collection and Imputation Procedures: Data are collected by mail questionnaire with telephone followups for nonrespondents. Imputation made for each nonresponse item and each item failing edit checks.

Estimates of Sampling Error: For the 1989 monthly surveys, CVs are about 0.6% for estimated total retail sales, 1.7% for wholesale sales, 1.3% for wholesale inventories. For dollar volume of receipts, CVs from the *Service Annual Survey* vary by kind of business and range between 1.5% to 15.0%. Sampling errors are shown in monthly publications.

Other (Nonsampling) Errors: Imputation rates are about 18% to 23% for monthly retail sales, 20% to 25% for wholesale sales, about 25% to 30% for monthly wholesale inventories and 14% for the *Service Annual Survey*.

Sources of Additional Material: U.S. Census Bureau, *Current Business Reports, Monthly Retail Trade, Monthly Wholesale Trade,* and *Service Annual Survey.*

(See Section 15 for information pertaining to Tables 1017 and 1049.)

SECTION 23. TRANSPORTATION

(See Section 15 for Table 1053; and Section 12 for Table 1055; Section 14 for Table 1115; and Section 22 for Tables 1054 1076, 1077, and 1110.)

SECTION 24. INFORMATION AND COMMUNICATIONS

(See Section 15 for Table 1121 and Section 22 for Tables 1119, 1120, 1129, 1137, 1139, 1140, 1143, 1145, 1146, 1147, and 1151)

SECTION 25. BANKING, FINANCE AND INSURANCE

(See Section 13 for information pertaining to Tables 1167, 1169, 1170, 1171, 1192 and 1209; Section 15 for information pertaining to Table 1162 and 1228; and Section 22 for Tables 1161, 1221, and 1227.)

SECTION 26. ARTS, ENTERTAINMENT, AND RECREATION

(See Section 15 for Table 1232 and Section 22 for Tables 1230 and 1231.)

SECTION 27. ACCOMMODATION, FOOD SERVICES, AND OTHER SERVICES

(See Section 15 for Tables 1263, 1264, 1267, and 1280; and Section 22 for Tables 1265, 1269, 1270, 1273, 1274, 1275, 1276, 1277, and 1278)

SECTION 28. FOREIGN COMMERCE AND AID

Source and Title: U.S. Census Bureau, *Foreign Trade—Export Statistics*

Tables: See Census Bureau citations for export statistics in source notes in Section 28 and also Table 1317 in Section 29.

Universe, Frequency, and Types of Data: The export declarations collected by Customs are processed each month to obtain data on the movement of U.S. merchandise exports to foreign countries. Data obtained include value, quantity, and shipping weight of exports by commodity, country of destination, Customs district of exportation, and mode of transportation.

Type of Data Collection Operation: Shipper's Export Declarations are required to be filed for the exportation of merchandise valued over $1,500. Customs officials collect and transmit the documents to the Census Bureau on a flow basis for data compilation. Value data for shipments valued under $1,501 are estimated, based on established percentages of individual country totals.

Data Collection and Imputation Procedures: Statistical copies of Shipper's Export Declarations are received on a daily basis from Customs ports throughout the country and subjected to a monthly processing cycle. They are fully processed to the extent they reflect items valued over $1,500. Estimates for shipments valued at $1,500 or less are made, based on established percentages of individual country totals.

Estimates of Sampling Error: Not applicable.

Other (Nonsampling) Errors: Clerical and complex computer checks intercept most processing errors and minimize otherwise significant reporting errors; other nonsampling errors are caused by undercounting of exports to Canada due to the nonreceipt of some Shipper's Export Declarations.

Sources of Additional Material: U.S. Census Bureau, *U.S. Merchandise Trade: Exports, General Imports, and Imports for Consumption, SITC, Commodity by Country,* FT 925 (discontinued after 1996).

Source and Title: U.S. Census Bureau, *Foreign Trade—Import Statistics*

Tables: See Census Bureau citations for import statistics in source notes in Section 28 and also Table 1317 in Section 29.

Universe, Frequency, and Types of Data: The import entry documents coll are processed each month to obtain data on the movement of merchandise imported into the United States. Data obtained include value, quantity, and shipping weight by commodity, country of origin, Customs district of entry, and mode of transportation.

Type of Data Collection Operation: Import entry documents are required to be filed for the importation of goods into the United States valued over $1,000 or for articles which must be reported on formal entries. Customs officials collect and transmit statistical copies of the documents to the Census Bureau on a flow basis for data compilation. Estimates for shipments valued under $1,001 and not reported on formal entries are based on established percentages of individual country totals.

Data Collection and Imputation Procedures: Statistical copies of import entry documents, received on a daily basis from Customs ports of entry throughout the country, are subjected to a monthly processing cycle. They are fully processed to the extent they reflect items valued at $1,001 and over or items which must be reported on formal entries.

Estimates of Sampling Error: Not applicable.

Other (Nonsampling) Errors: Verification of statistical data reporting by customs officials prior to transmittal and a subsequent program of clerical and computer checks are utilized to hold nonsampling errors arising from reporting and/or processing errors to a minimum.

Sources of Additional Material: U.S. Census Bureau, *U.S. Merchandise Trade: Exports, General Imports and Imports for Consumption, SITC, Commodity by Country*, FT 925 (discontinued after 1996).

SECTION 29. OUTLYING AREAS

(See Section 1 for information pertaining to Tables 1309, 1311, and 1323; Section 2 for Table 1308; and Section 28 for Table 1317.)

U.S. Census Bureau, Statistical Abstract of the United States: 2001

Appendix IV
Weights and Measures

[For assistance on metric usage, call or write the Office of Metric Programs, U.S. Department of Commerce, Washington, DC 20230 (301-975-3690) Internet site <http://www.nist.gov/>]

Symbol	When you know conventional	Multiply by	To find metric	Symbol
in	inch	2.54	centimeter	cm
ft	foot	30.48	centimeter	cm
yd	yard	0.91	meter	m
mi	mile	1.61	kilometer	km
in^2	square inch	6.45	square centimeter	cm^2
ft^2	square foot	0.09	square meter	m^2
yd^2	square yard	0.84	square meter	m^2
mi^2	square mile	2.59	square kilometer	km^2
	acre	0.41	hectare	ha
oz	ounce [1]	28.35	gram	g
lb	pound [1]	.45	kilograms	kg
oz (troy)	ounce [2]	31.10	gram	g
	short ton (2,000 lb)	0.91	metric ton	t
	long ton (2,240 lb)	1.02	metric ton	t
fl oz	fluid ounce	29.57	milliliter	mL
c	cup	0.24	liter	L
pt	pint	0.47	liter	L
qt	quart	0.95	liter	L
gal	gallon	3.78	liter	L
ft^3	cubic foot	0.03	cubic meter	m^3
yd^3	cubic yard	0.76	cubic meter	m^3
F	degrees Fahrenheit (subtract 32)	0.55	degrees Celsius	C

Symbol	When you know metric	Multiply by	To find conventional	Symbol
cm	centimeter	0.39	inch	in
cm	centimeter	0.03	foot	ft
m	meter	1.09	yard	yd
km	kilometer	0.62	mile	mi
cm^2	square centimeter	0.15	square inch	in^2
m^2	square meter	10.76	square foot	ft^2
m^2	square meter	1.20	square yard	yd^2
km^2	square kilometer	0.39	square mile	mi^2
ha	hectare	2.47	acre	
g	gram	.035	ounce [1]	oz
kg	kilogram	2.21	pounds	lb [1]
g	gram	.032	ounce [2]	oz (troy)
t	metric ton	1.10	short ton (2,000 lb)	
t	metric ton	0.98	long ton (2,240 lb)	
mL	milliliter	0.03	fluid ounce	fl oz
L	liter	4.24	cup	c
L	liter	2.13	pint (liquid)	pt
L	liter	1.05	quart (liquid)	qt
L	liter	0.26	gallon	gal
m^3	cubic meter	35.32	cubic foot	ft^3
m^3	cubic meter	1.32	cubic yard	yd^3
C	degrees Celsius (after multiplying, add 32)	1.80	degrees Fahrenheit	F

[1] For weighing ordinary commodities.   [2] For weighing precious metals, jewels, etc.

U.S. Census Bureau, Statistical Abstract of the United States: 2001

Appendix V

Tables Deleted From the
2000 Edition of the Statistical Abstract

U.S. Census Bureau, Statistical Abstract of the United States: 2001

U.S. Census Bureau, Statistical Abstract of the United States: 2001

U.S. Census Bureau, Statistical Abstract of the United States: 2001

U.S. Census Bureau, Statistical Abstract of the United States: 2001

Appendix VI

New Tables

U.S. Census Bureau, Statistical Abstract of the United States: 2001

U.S. Census Bureau, Statistical Abstract of the United States: 2001

U.S. Census Bureau, Statistical Abstract of the United States: 2001

Index

NOTE: Index citations refer to **table** numbers, not page numbers.

U.S. Census Bureau, Statistical Abstract of the United States: 2001

NOTE: Index citations refer to **table** numbers, not page numbers.

U.S. Census Bureau, Statistical Abstract of the United States: 2001

NOTE: Index citations refer to **table** numbers, not page numbers.

NOTE: Index citations refer to **table** numbers, not page numbers.

U.S. Census Bureau, Statistical Abstract of the United States: 2001

NOTE: Index citations refer to **table** numbers, not page numbers.

NOTE: Index citations refer to **table** numbers, not page numbers.

U.S. Census Bureau, Statistical Abstract of the United States: 2001

NOTE: Index citations refer to **table** numbers, not page numbers.

NOTE: Index citations refer to **table** numbers, not page numbers.

NOTE: Index citations refer to **table** numbers, not page numbers.

U.S. Census Bureau, Statistical Abstract of the United States: 2001

NOTE: Index citations refer to **table** numbers, not page numbers.

Index   943

NOTE: Index citations refer to **table** numbers, not page numbers.

NOTE: Index citations refer to **table** numbers, not page numbers.

U.S. Census Bureau, Statistical Abstract of the United States: 2001

NOTE: Index citations refer to **table** numbers, not page numbers.

946 Index

U.S. Census Bureau, Statistical Abstract of the United States: 2001

NOTE: Index citations refer to **table** numbers, not page numbers.

U.S. Census Bureau, Statistical Abstract of the United States: 2001

NOTE: Index citations refer to **table** numbers, not page numbers.

NOTE: Index citations refer to **table** numbers, not page numbers.

NOTE: Index citations refer to **table** numbers, not page numbers.

U.S. Census Bureau, Statistical Abstract of the United States: 2001

NOTE: Index citations refer to **table** numbers, not page numbers.

NOTE: Index citations refer to **table** numbers, not page numbers.

U.S. Census Bureau, Statistical Abstract of the United States: 2001

NOTE: Index citations refer to **table** numbers, not page numbers.

U.S. Census Bureau, Statistical Abstract of the United States: 2001

NOTE: Index citations refer to **table** numbers, not page numbers.

NOTE: Index citations refer to **table** numbers, not page numbers.

U.S. Census Bureau, Statistical Abstract of the United States: 2001

NOTE: Index citations refer to **table** numbers, not page numbers.

NOTE: Index citations refer to **table** numbers, not page numbers.

U.S. Census Bureau, Statistical Abstract of the United States: 2001

NOTE: Index citations refer to **table** numbers, not page numbers.

U.S. Census Bureau, Statistical Abstract of the United States: 2001

NOTE: Index citations refer to **table** numbers, not page numbers.

U.S. Census Bureau, Statistical Abstract of the United States: 2001

NOTE: Index citations refer to **table** numbers, not page numbers.

U.S. Census Bureau, Statistical Abstract of the United States: 2001

NOTE: Index citations refer to **table** numbers, not page numbers.

NOTE: Index citations refer to **table** numbers, not page numbers.

NOTE: Index citations refer to **table** numbers, not page numbers.

NOTE: Index citations refer to **table** numbers, not page numbers.

NOTE: Index citations refer to **table** numbers, not page numbers.

NOTE: Index citations refer to **table** numbers, not page numbers.

U.S. Census Bureau, Statistical Abstract of the United States: 2001

NOTE: Index citations refer to **table** numbers, not page numbers.

U.S. Census Bureau, Statistical Abstract of the United States: 2001

NOTE: Index citations refer to **table** numbers, not page numbers.

U.S. Census Bureau, Statistical Abstract of the United States: 2001

NOTE: Index citations refer to **table** numbers, not page numbers.

NOTE: Index citations refer to **table** numbers, not page numbers.

NOTE: Index citations refer to **table** numbers, not page numbers.

U.S. Census Bureau, Statistical Abstract of the United States: 2001

NOTE: Index citations refer to **table** numbers, not page numbers.

NOTE: Index citations refer to **table** numbers, not page numbers.

NOTE: Index citations refer to **table** numbers, not page numbers.

974 Index

U.S. Census Bureau, Statistical Abstract of the United States: 2001

NOTE: Index citations refer to **table** numbers, not page numbers.

U.S. Census Bureau, Statistical Abstract of the United States: 2001

NOTE: Index citations refer to **table** numbers, not page numbers.

NOTE: Index citations refer to **table** numbers, not page numbers.

U.S. Census Bureau, Statistical Abstract of the United States: 2001

NOTE: Index citations refer to **table** numbers, not page numbers.

NOTE: Index citations refer to **table** numbers, not page numbers.

U.S. Census Bureau, Statistical Abstract of the United States: 2001

NOTE: Index citations refer to **table** numbers, not page numbers.

NOTE: Index citations refer to **table** numbers, not page numbers.

NOTE: Index citations refer to **table** numbers, not page numbers.

NOTE: Index citations refer to **table** numbers, not page numbers.

U.S. Census Bureau, Statistical Abstract of the United States: 2001

NOTE: Index citations refer to **table** numbers, not page numbers.

NOTE: Index citations refer to **table** numbers, not page numbers.

U.S. Census Bureau, Statistical Abstract of the United States: 2001

NOTE: Index citations refer to **table** numbers, not page numbers.

U.S. Census Bureau, Statistical Abstract of the United States: 2001

NOTE: Index citations refer to **table** numbers, not page numbers.

U.S. Census Bureau, Statistical Abstract of the United States: 2001